World Cars®

1984

ISBN 0-910714-16-9
ISSN 0084-1463
LC 74-643381
Published in the English language
edition throughout the world in 1984
by
HERALD BOOKS
Pelham, New York

WORLD CARS®

1984

Published and edited annually by
L'EDITRICE DELL'AUTOMOBILE LEA
publishing company of the
AUTOMOBILE CLUB D'ITALIA

HERALD BOOKS, PELHAM, NEW YORK

Cover pictures

Ital Design Gabbiano
on Renault mechanicals

Editor

Annamaria Lösch

Cover and layout

Francesco Ricciardi

Contributors and correspondents

Alberto Bellucci
Antonio Lioy

Paolo Appetito
Filippo Crispolti
J.R. Daniels
Flora Di Giovanni
Luigi Falasco
Andrea Lang
Alan Langley (Great Britain)
John McElroy (USA)
Jack K. Yamaguchi (Japan)

Language consultant

Jean Gribble

Editorial offices

L'Editrice dell'Automobile LEA s.r.l.
Viale Regina Margherita 279
00198 Rome, Italy
☎ 06/866156

Composition and printing

Grafica Giorgetti, Rome, Italy

Binding

OGAM, Verona, Italy

Illustrations

Riproduzioni-Lith, Rome, Italy

SUMMARY

Editor's note

The aim of *World Cars* is to present accurate information that is as complete as possible and to present it in a concise form. It is not always easy to reconcile the search for accuracy and completeness, for clarity and uniformity, and one or two preliminary remarks may help readers consulting this reference book.

The technical data is based on questionnaires completed by motor manufacturers throughout the world, and only when this information was incomplete or not made available has it been supplemented from other reliable sources.

Different cultures have always used different formulae to express maximum power and torque. DIN and SAE standards are familiar to most readers, while Japan alone uses the Japanese Industrial Standard (JIS). Expressed in DIN, power or torque is 20% lower than when expressed in SAE gross but about the same as or slightly higher than in SAE net, while JIS ratings roughly correspond to SAE gross ratings. Horsepower in Anglo-Saxon countries expresses slightly higher power than the horsepower used by other countries (1.0139:1).

The innovation that marks recent editions of *World Cars* stems from the new units of measurement established by the Système Internationale d'Unités (SI). These are the kilowatt (kW), which replaces horsepower (hp), and the Newton metre (Nm), which replaces lb/ft. The conversion ratios are:

1 hp = 0.736 kW or 1 kW = 1.360 hp
1 kg m = 7 lb ft = 9.807 Nm or 1 Nm = 0.714 lb ft = 0.012 kg m

Fuel consumption, indicated by figures that are inevitably only a rough calculation, is usually based on a medium load and a cruising speed of about 60% of the car's maximum speed on a varied run; in other cases, the circumstances are stated. By dry weight is meant the fully-equipped car ready for the road but without water, oil and petrol.

Since two valves per cylinder are now the norm and dual braking circuits are prevalent, only exceptions to the two have been indicated. Again, when in V8 engines the cylinders are slanted at 90°, this indication has been omitted. The turning circle should be taken as between walls unless otherwise specified.

Quite often a model is available with engines differing both in size and power: each of these engines is described separately. In this case, whenever they are not given, the measurements and weight are the same as in the standard version. When the power-weight ratio is given, this usually refers to the 4-door sedan version. In certain cases, alternative engines have been listed under "Variations" at the foot of the basic description and — except when otherwise specifically indicated — should be taken as being available for all the models that refer back to the basic description. The "Optionals" also apply to all the models that refer back to the basic description, except when otherwise specified. Some accessories may become "standard" or not be available, and others may be added, but this is always stated.

Editorial problems have prevented us from making certain corrections to the prices in the main body of the volume after the end of 1983 and so the reader is advised to refer to the price index for more recent prices of models, many of which may be raised in the course of the year. When prices are shown in the currency of the country of origin, these should be taken as ex-factory and therefore subject to revision if the car is imported into another country. Prices with a single asterisk include VAT (value added tax) or its equivalent in other European countries, and in Great Britain also SCT (special car tax). Prices with two asterisks are ex-showroom. The prices for American cars refer to models equipped with a standard engine of the lowest power listed (generally a four- or six-cylinder engine). For cars imported into the United States, asterisked figures denote prices ex-showroom. Every attempt is made to quote accurate prices but both variations in what the companies include in the price quoted and frequent price modifications make our task a difficult one.

In view of the requirements of Federal legislation, the specifications of cars imported into the USA (and often those imported into other countries) differ slightly from those in the country of origin. The most common modifications are lower maximum power and compression ratio and therefore different speeds, catalytic silencers, and injection engines instead of carburettor engines. Safety legislation often requires more robust bumpers at required heights, lateral reflectors and so on.

Technical and photographic coverage is given to over 2,500 models at present in production. It has sometimes been necessary to exclude models produced in very small numbers or visually almost identical to others illustrated, and also models that, even if built or assembled under another name outside the country of origin, are to all purposes a repetition of the model presented as part of the maker's standard range.

Motor racing

Formula 1
world championship

Formula 1

A TURBO TAKES THE TITLE

by Filippo Crispolti

The 1983 F.1 season rose from the ashes of a particularly bloody Championship marred by serious accidents. The dangers of Grand Prix racing have always added spice to its spectacular attractions — the crowd is not squeamish and the drivers accept the risks they run. But every now and then there is a revolt. The horror of that puppet-like figure catapulted out of the car when Villeneuve died and the consequences of Pironi's accident could not be forgotten. Finally the constructors, persuaded by Jean-Marie Balestre, agreed to outlaw ground effect. Flat-bottomed cars are the rule for 1983, in the hope of reducing the exceptional speed on bends that had made almost all the circuits inadequate from the point of view of safety.

This is the technical novelty that was to colour the 1983 season which opened — much later than usual to allow the constructors to come into line with the new regulations — on 13 March in the Rio sunshine. The reigning champion, Keke Rosberg, is still driving an aspirated car, but amid a gaggle of roaring turbos he sneaks the pole position. Incredible!

There has been plenty of shifting about in the teams. René Arnoux has moved over from Renault to Ferrari and Eddie Cheever has taken his place in the French team. Mauro Baldi has filled the gap left by Bruno Giacomelli, now with Toleman, at Alfa Romeo. Jacques Laffite is paired with Rosberg at Williams and Marc Surer drives for the Arrows team, while the American newcomer Danny Sullivan is engaged by Tyrrell, and Johnny Cecotto drives for Ensign.

Many of the machines are new from the ground up. During testing in Europe at Le Castellet, designers and engineers have been racking their brains to recover some of the downforce sacrificed with the miniskirts and sidepods which were the key points of the undercar aerodynamics now banned. The big double wings are back on the Toleman but also on the Ligier and others. Some prophets foresee a rapid return to the top and average speeds typical of the "ground effect" era but the drivers are unanimous in their praise of the new rules. And, in the final analysis, they are right.

Nelson Souto Major, better known as Nelson Piquet, three years after his first title made it a double at the final hundle.

It is immediately clear that the new rising star is the Brabham BT 52 designed by Gordon Murray, the brilliant South African engineeer, which inaugurates a new style that is to become very familiar. With its striking arrow-shaped profile, the BT 52 is a lovely, elegant thing. And the front end and front suspension are to show that they are effective, too.

Other teams, such as Renault and Ferrari, have opted for less drastic solutions. For the moment the cars are an adaptation of the ones used the season before, while everyone waits to see what will happen in the early races.

There is a new style, too, in the controls by the race commissioners. All the drivers are carefully weighed, so that their weight can be subtracted when the monocoques are checked at the pit entrance on practice day. For one of the most important changes to the rules is the reduction of the minimum weight from 575 to 540 kg. It wasn't accepted without a lot of heated discussion but, to the powers that be, it seemed necessary to make the British-school teams still using the aspirated Cosworth swallow the bitter pill of the superpowered turbocars allied to the new flat bottoms.

At Rio de Janeiro in practice, the best times, after Rosberg's Williams, are set up by Alain Prost (Renault), Patrick Tambay

(Ferrari) and Nelson Piquet (Brabham). The mid-race refuelling, a dangerous but exciting feature of the whole season, penalizes Rosberg when a flash of petrol vapour catches alight. He is soon pushed away again but is disqualified for this after finishing second behind a magnificent Piquet. Early hopes dashed...

Long Beach (probably the last time the Formula 1 circus will be there) is on 27 March, after only two weeks. It sees the surprise return of Alan Jones, a tight fit in the Arrows cockpit. In the front row of the grid, the two Ferraris. They seem to be the cars to beat, but Gilles Villeneuve and Didier Pironi are sadly missed. Tambay makes a fast start but soon falls victim to Keke Rosberg's eagerness to take the lead. The Finn, undeterred by a frightening 360° spin on the first lap, tried to take Tambay on the slow hairpin. The wheels of the two cars clashed and Tambay was out of the race, to be followed by Rosberg three corners later. Accidents and a rash of retirements due to tyre and engine trouble give John Watson in the aspirated McLaren and his teammate Niki Lauda a chance they snap up. René Arnoux can do no better than third. The Lotus team, sadly deprived of Colin Chapman, is going through a crisis: in fact, Nigel Mansell with the old Cosworth engine is quicker than Elio De Angelis who has the Renault turbo. A black day for Nelson Piquet, too, slow in practice and plagued by engine and throttle trouble.

Two weeks later, the circus comes back to Europe, to the speedy Le Castellet circuit in France where the Renault team throws the opposition into disarray by dominating practice and taking the first row of the grid. In fact, Alain Prost's yellow turbo car has a home win and only Nelson Piquet prevents the Renaults from taking first and second. The French track is hard on the Ferrari's traditional tyres and De Cesari's Alfa Romeo runs into trouble with the commissioners when it is discovered that its extinguishers are empty. But, with the cold wind to help them, it is the turbo's day, with Keke Rosberg's Williams the first nonturbo home, in 5th place.

The home circuit does seem to mean a good deal. At Imola, in the San Marino GP it is the Ferraris (Prost takes second place between the winner, Tambay, and Arnoux) all the way. Piquet had "robbed" Tambay of a place in the front row of the grid but stalled his engine at the start and the two Ferraris were away in the lead until Ricardo Patrese snatched it from them, only to be penalised by a slow refuelling stop. He gave chase again, driving brilliantly, and took the lead only six laps from the flag, only to lose

The protagonists of the final battle for the title in South Africa were Alain Prost (left) and the two Ferrari men – René Arnoux and Patrick Tambay – (right), besides of course Piquet. Below, the Brazilian during practice at Detroit where a flat tyre put his Brabham out of the race.

One of the boasts of the '83 season is that a greater number of constructors were drawn into the Championship. For instance, Porsche, from the Dutch GP on, provided a 6-cylinder 80° V engine for the McLaren team financed by the Arabs of Tag. Watson at the wheel.

The death of Colin Chapman and the arrival of the Renault turbo engine threw the Lotus team into disarray until the arrival of Gerard Ducarouge. The benefits of his intervention were clear from the first time the new car ran at Silverstone.

concentration on a corner. His Brabham nosedived into a protective wall of tyres and the crowd could roar the Ferrari home. Prost's second place gave him the championship lead.

Monaco looked like being another clash at the top between Renaults and Ferraris. Prost in fact takes the pole position with Arnoux alongside him and Cheever and Tambay behind them. But fortunes were decided by the weather. With a wet track at the start, it took courage to start the race with dry-weather slick tyres, but for Keke Rosberg, reigning champion, it meant another win at last after Dijon last year. Laffite, in the other Williams and also on slick tyres, looked ripe for 2nd place but gearbox trouble set in, and so Piquet and Prost took the other places. Rain robbed the two McLarens of qualification but Marc Surer, thrilling the spectators at the wheel of his Cosworth-powered Arrows, and Derek Warwick, (Toleman-Hart) duelling with him for third place until a shunt put them both out, were revelations.

The Belgian Grand Prix is back on the shortened Spa-Franchorchamps circuit after 13 years, the one detested and outlawed by Jackie Stewart who had the worst accident of his brilliant career there. It is a fast, demanding track that seems designed to exalt the power of the turbo cars, and the first four rows of the starting grid are packed with turbos — Brabham and Alfa Romeo seem to have joined Renault and Ferrari in the battle at the top. The start has to be repeated because three cars fail to get away. But both times Andrea De Cesaris flashes through from the second row and leads confidently until his 8-cylinder Alfa Romeo engine lets him down. Prost takes over, worried only by Nelson Piquet who looks dangerous till he loses top gear ten laps from home and Tambay and Cheever go past to take 2nd and 3rd places. Prost, Piquet and Tambay, in that order, are now close together at the top of the table. Another super-Cosworth, Alboreto's Benetton Tyrrell, makes its debut here, but this is no track for an aspirated engine.

Back across the ocean again to Detroit, the capital of the American auto industry. Here the Tyrrell, proudly bearing the Ford logo, comes into its own and Alboreto scores what the Americans interpret as a home win. Maybe Henry Ford II was sorry he went golfing! Before the start, Arnoux and Piquet were thought to have the best chances as Prost's car seems less happy than the Brabham with the Michelin radial tyres. Tambay and Cheever are early out of the race and Arnoux soon takes over the lead from Piquet who, contrary to a pre-race announcement, does not intend to come in for refuelling and new tyres. But Arnoux's Ferrari succumbs to electrical failure and

The frantic mid-race refuelling and tyre changing (on the left Arnoux) meant greater risks for everyone in the pits. Above, the start on the reinstated Spa circuit in Belgium. On the right, one of the many duels between Nelson Piquet and Alain Prost.

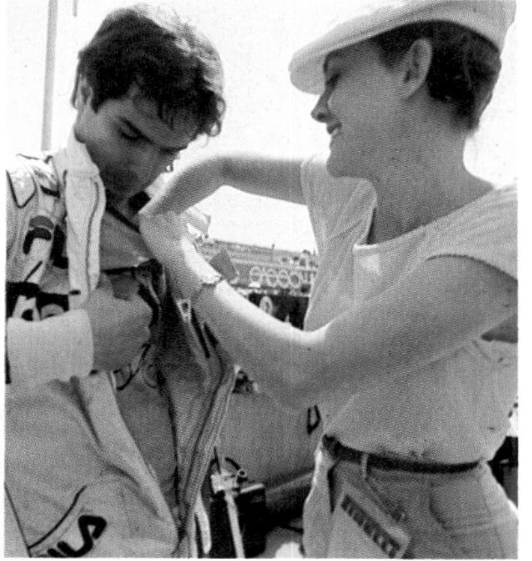

Technology at the service of man and machine. Alongside, Ing. Forghieri of the Ferrari team measures the temperature of the track. Right, a Canadian nurse fixes some electrodes in Nelson Piquet's protective clothing.

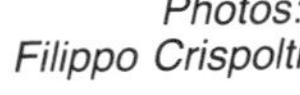

Photos: Filippo Crispolti

From top to bottom. Refuelling stops left their mark on the season but decided no results. Left, the 6-cylinder Honda mounted first on the Spirit and then exclusively on the Williams. In the large photo right, Piquet cuts it fine.

Piquet has a puncture, and so it is aspirated cars first, second and third — Tyrrell, Williams and McLaren, or Alboreto, Rosberg and Watson.

But in Canada, at Montreal on 12 June, it is all turbo cars again. They take the first nine places on the grid, even though the no. 10, Rosberg, does manage to bring his Williams home in fourth place, and Watson's McLaren is an honourable sixth. René Arnoux, in his first win for Ferrari, led all the way except for his pit stops and his victory coincides with the last outing of the Ferrari 126 C/2, decidedly too heavy and hard on tyres. Luck is against the Ferrari's adversaries for gearbox trouble and lack of revs slowed Alain Prost whose Renault could do no better than 4th and Nelson Piquet has to retire with a broken throttle cable. But Prost at the top of the table still has three points more than Piquet who is now joint second with Tambay who finished in third place at Montreal.

For Silverstone, the Ferrari team are fielding the C3 with the Kevlar and carbonium chassis but they have to use the old body. The Ferrari shines in practice but during the race the traditional Goodyear tyres fail to stand up to the high speeds of the fast track. The race, disputed in sweltering conditions, was the fastest ever at Silverstone and Michelin grip allied to turbo power gave Prost the victory ahead of Piquet and Tambay, who saved the honour of the new Ferrari. Novelties abounded in the British GP: the debut of a Honda V6 engine mounted on an adapted F2 chassis for Spirit, a revised BT528 chassis for Brabham which gave Piquet the increased reliability he needed and — last but not least — the all-new John Player Lotus 94T-Renault, designed and built in five weeks flat by Gerard Ducarouge. De Angelis took third place on the grid only to retire with engine trouble, but Nigel Mansell came home 4th.

The Hockenheim GP in Germany is Round 10 of the Championship — the two-thirds stage of the fifteen Grands Prix — and the teams will have only four days between it and the start of practice for the Austrian GP. So things are hotting up. Once again, as in the British GP, Ken Tyrrell enters a formal protest against the water injection used by the Renault and Ferrari teams and this time he is joined by Frank Williams. Most of the teams had a trouble-plagued GP. The BMW engine used by the Brabhams certainly did not cover itself in glory on its home ground, for breakdowns were numerous in practice and, despite the 3rd place which Patrese's fine drive gave him, the engines were never up to par. And so, for problem-free Ferrari, it was roses all the way, taking the front row of the grid and the final flag. René Arnoux came home in front of two Italian drivers, De Cesaris (Alfa Romeo) and Patrese (Brabham). Prost's 4th place confirms his championship lead.

The track at Zeltweg in Austria is ultra-fast and favours outright power. Again the two Ferraris start in front, but after a duel between Arnoux and Piquet, Alain Prost prevails over the former in a fine finish. Prost's intelligent driving and the Renault's reliability (not a single retirement for Prost up to now) give him a clear lead in the championship over Piquet who, but for loss of revs, would almost certainly have won and Tambay whose retirement seems to mean the end of his championship hopes.

And in fact, at Zandvoort, Prost expected to win even though Tambay and Piquet were in front of him on the starting grid. But his luck seemed to turn here. In the early laps, Arnoux showed that his car was was finally right and it looked like being a repetition of the glorious four-way battle we had seen in Austria. But on lap 42 Prost made an uncharacteristic mistake, jamming his brakes as he tried to take the leader, Piquet, on the Tarzan hairpin and putting him out of the race. Before the lap was over, Prost had gone too, his wing taking a bite out of a tyre. So it is Ferraris first and second and suddenly René Arnoux is a contender for the title. John Watson finishes third in the Ford-Cosworth McLaren the day Niki Lauda first drives their new turbo Porsche MP4/1E, which fails to finish. As at Silverstone the Tyrrell and Williams teams protest against the water injection systems used on the Ferraris and Renaults. They believe they are illegal because they boost the octane rating above the regulation 102 RON. This controversy was to drag on, only to peter out in the end, saving this piece of F1 research which reduces pollution and saves energy.

So the championship is wide open and practice at Monza for the Italian GP shows signs of the hopes and tensions of all the teams. Because of threats to his life Prost arrived with two gorillas, lent it is said by François Mitterrand. He can do no better than fifth fastest time in practice and it is Riccardo Patrese who pinches the pole position from Tambay's Ferrari. The Brabhams roar away the start and Nelson Piquet takes over the lead from his team-mate when Patrese blows up — and Arnoux cannot catch him. Once again, Prost is forced to retire and now, with only two races to go, just five points separate the three leaders of the table — Prost, Arnoux and Piquet. The Brabham team seems to be on the up and up, while at Renault they are having trouble in finding more power.

The power unit is worrying other teams, too. Though Derek Warwick and Bruno Giacomelli take 6th and 7th places at Monza, the Hart 4-cylinder turbo has never matched up to the fine British chassis. For Alfa Romeo there is no lack of power but reliability is the problem, while at this stage the Ferrari team is hampered by its tyres. Their traditional Goodyear tyres are less than satisfactory in the heat, especially in long races, though in practice they are just as competitive as the Michelin radial tyres.

Brands Hatch plays host to the second GP in England, now renamed the John Player Grand Prix of Europe. Everybody is here — the weekend is expected to be wet and chilly (it's the end of September) but turns out fine and unusually warm, which favours the teams using Michelin tyres but certainly not the Ferraris. In practice, the John Player-sponsored Lotuses and the two Brabhams make it a very British occasion. Patrese and De Angelis roared away in a private duel, the Brabham in the lead but the Lotus a better car on the day. Soon Piquet in the other Brabham was closing on them and De Angelis had to get past Patrese in a hurry. And that was the downfall of the two Italians, leaving Piquet with a comfortable lead over Prost that he held right through. Arnoux had an ignominious spin early on and could do no better than 9th, while Tambay ran off the track due to faulty brakes.

So, when the teams arrived in Kyalami for the final GP, there are only two points between Alain Prost (57 points) and Nelson Piquet (55) at the top of the table and in theory René Arnoux (49) could also still take the title. For the Constructors' World Championship, Ferrari is leading Renault, followed by Brabham-BMW. None of the top three drivers won the race. What mattered though was that Prost and Arnoux failed to finish the course, no Ferrari took the chequered flag and only one Renault (Eddie Cheever in 6th place), while Piquet and the Brabham team had it all their own way, and Patrese's 1st place and Nelson's confident 3rd allowed them to carry off both Drivers' World Championship and the final honours of the season. Ferrari has the consolation prize of the Constructors' World Championship but it is the Brabham that has dominated the second half of the season.

The race was a fine one to close the season. After some preliminary skirmishing on the question of the fuel to be used, the grid sees Tambay — who already knows that next year Ferrari are replacing him with Alboreto — in pole position, with Piquet alongside him and their two team-mates in the second row. Prost is behind them. Keke Rosberg decides to drive in spite of a liver complaint because Williams are fielding

Cinderella of the season even with its aspirated super-Cosworth engine, the Tyrrell triumphed at Detroit with Michele Alboreto at the wheel. A fine chassis cannot make good a 140 bhp handicap.

their new Honda-powered FW09, and does in fact give it a splendid baptism, finishing fifth. At the start, the two Brabhams tear away. Laffite goes on the first lap in an accident with Cheever, and Arnoux's engine blows soon after. Prost simply has not got the Brabham's speed: his turbo is giving trouble and half-way through he has to retire. In fact, Niki Lauda's McLaren is the only car that has comparable speed and Lauda drives a brilliant race behind the leader till his engine blows close to home. Andrea de Cesaris' 2nd place is the best performance of the season for Alfa Romeo, and Derek Warwick in the Toleman takes points yet again.

And so Nelson Piquet is champion for the second time, a brilliant, modest, relaxed driver whose hobbies, so he says, are "sleeping, watching television and doing nothing". Gordon Murray, the farsighted South African designer, at last sees the reliability of his cars matching up to their speed (speed that had been available from Hockenheim on) and for the first time the title is taken at the wheel of a turbocharged car. The changing of the guard...

Championship Table

Drivers	Team	Country	Pts
Nelson Piquet	Brabham	Brazil	59
Alain Prost	Renault	France	57
René Arnoux	Ferrari	France	49
Patrick Tambay	Ferrari	France	40
Keke Rosberg	Williams	Finland	27
John Watson	McLaren	Great Britain	22
Eddie Cheever	Renault	U.S.A.	22
Andrea de Cesaris	Alfa Romeo	Italy	15
Riccardo Patrese	Brabham	Italy	13
Niki Lauda	McLaren	Austria	12
Jacques Laffite	Williams	France	11
Michele Alboreto	Tyrrell	Italy	10
Nigel Mansel	Lotus	Great Britain	10
Derek Warwick	Toleman	Great Britain	9
Marc Surer	Arrows	Switzerland	4
Mauro Baldi	Alfa Romeo	Italy	3
Elio De Angelis	Lotus	Italy	2
Danny Sullivan	Tyrrell	U.S.A.	2
Bruno Giacomelli	Toleman	Italy	1
Johnny Cecotto	Theodore	Venezuela	1

Drivers failing to take championship points

Drivers	Team	Country	GP drives	Failed to qualify
Kenny Acheson	March	Great Britain	1	6
Raul Boesel	Ligier	Brazil	13	2
Thierry Boutsen	Arrows	Belgium	10	—
Corrado Fabi	Osella	Italy	8	7
Piercarlo Ghinzani	Osella	Italy	6	9
Roberto Guerrero	Theodore	Colombia	13	1
Jean Pierre Jarier	Ligier	France	15	—
Stefan Johannson	Spirit	Sweden	6	—
Alan Jones	Arrows	Australia	1	—
Jonathan Palmer	Williams	Great Britain	1	—
Eliseo Salazar	March	Chile	2	4
Jean-Louis Schlesser	March	France	—	1
Chico Serra	Arrows	Brazil	3	—
Jacques Villeneuve	March	Canada	—	1
Manfred Winkelhock	ATS	Germany	13	1

Teams competing

Team		Cars used	Engines used
Ferrari	(GY)	126/C2, 126/C2B, 126/C3	V6 Turbo
Brabham	(M)	BT52, BT52B	BMW Turbo S4
Renault	(M)	RE30c, RE40	V6 Turbo
McLaren	(M)	MP4/1C, MP4/1E	Porsche TAG Turbo V6, Ford DFY V8
Williams	(GY)	FW08C, FW09	Ford V8, Honda V6 T.
Toleman	(P)	TG183B	Hart S4 Turbo
Alfa Romeo	(M)	183T, 183TB	V8 Turbo
Tyrrell	(GY)	011, 012	Ford Cosworth V8
Arrows	(GY)	A6	Ford Cosworth V8
Lotus	(P)	92, 93T, 94T	Renault V6 Turbo
Theodore	(GY)	N-183	Ford V8
Spirit	(GY)	210C	Honda V6 Turbo
March	(P)	RAM 01	Ford V8
Osella	(M)	FA1D, FA1E	Alfa Romeo V12
Ligier	(M)	JS21	Ford Cosworth V8
ATS	(GY)	S4, D6	BMW Turbo

Tyres used: GY = Goodyear, M = Michelin, P = Pirelli.

Special bodies

Illustrations and technical information

ARAGONA MOTOR VEHICLES — Brasilia — USA

Made in Brazil, this luxury sports car features a full leather interior, electric windows and tilt of steering wheel, tinted glass, air conditioning, power-assisted 4-wheel disc brakes, Pirelli P-6 tyres mounted on light-alloy wheel rims and fully independent suspension. The 2,180 cc engine develops 125 hp SAE.

ASTON MARTIN TICKFORD — Capri — GREAT BRITAIN

Tickford's Capri, originally a styling exercise with Ford, led to its series production. The original 2.8 litre engine is fitted with an IHI turbocharger with Garrett intercooler and the new A.F.T. digital computerized ignition and electronic fuel management system are added. Power output is 205 bhp at 5,000 rpm and top speed 140 mph. Price $ 14,985.

GREAT BRITAIN | **MG Metro Turbo** | **ASTON MARTIN TICKFORD** 

Following up the success of its MG Metro conversion, Tickford have now brought out their Turbo, with similar specifications. It has exterior GRP body panels all round, a glass sunroof, electric windows, a leather dashboard, high power stereo and triple speakers. Cost of the conversion is £ 2,600.

GREAT BRITAIN | **Lagonda** | **ASTON MARTIN TICKFORD** 

The pearlescent white show car launched at London's 1983 Motorfair is to be followed by others costing £ 85,000. The aluminium body panels round the low part of the car improve its aerodynamics. The wide BBS modular alloy wheels have white centres and low profile tyres. Inside a blend of white leather and burr walnut is complemented by TV and stereo front and rear, drinks cabinet and the rest.

AVON COACHWORK **Jaguar/Daimler Estate** **GREAT BRITAIN**

Avon's refined Jaguar estate car is a subtle blend of the comfort and aesthetic criteria of the Jaguar saloon and the sheer practicality of the mass-produced estate cars offered by Ford, Volvo and so on. Based on the Series III Jaguar/Daimler saloon, it offers up to 58 cu ft of luggage space.

AVON COACHWORK **Turbo Acclaim** **GREAT BRITAIN**

Possibly the fastest under-1600 cc 4-door saloon available in the United Kingdom, the Turbo Acclaim rushes from 0 to 60 mph in under 9 seconds, has a top speed of 115 mph and returns 30 mpg. The two-tone paint scheme, luxurious interior and mechanical specifications make it a fine sports saloon.

GREAT BRITAIN **Volvo 760 Limousine** **AVON COACHWORK**

This highly-equipped luxurious limousine is available in three versions – 508.8 cm, 538.8 cm and 568.8 cm, offering either simply additional rear seat legroom or a division and an extra row of seating as well as more back seat accommodation. All three variants are well-equipped and there is a long list of options.

GERMANY FR **Topcabriolet** **BAUR**

The Series 3 is yet another cabriolet in the Baur tradition. Easily recognizable are the robust rollbar, the fixed rear side windows and the side window mountings. The central part of the roof is rigid and the rear part in canvas.

BEAUJARDIN — Stinger — CANADA

Collaboration between designer Beaujardin and the engineering team of Concordia University led by Dr. Clyde Kwok has produced another experimental vehicle. Based on the Nova, it combines luxurious looks with high technology. The front ground clearance can be adjusted from inside the cockpit. Top speed is 124 mph.

BERTONE — Delfino — ITALY

With the Delfino, Bertone takes up again the "gran turismo" theme using the mechanics of the Alfa 6. Sober, modern lines, shorter and lower but wider than the original, this two-seater respects the original layout of the saloon, with front engine and rear-wheel drive.

ITALY Palinuro BERTONE 

The Palinuro is a more exclusive version of the Cabrio, Bertone's convertible based on the Fiat Ritmo. It is available in a choice of two-colour metallic paintwork with the name Palinuro on the doors, and headlamp washers are standard. The 4-cylinder 82 bhp engine ensures a top speed of about 165 mph.

ITALY XI/9 BERTONE 

A centre-mounted engine, 4 disc brakes and a typically racy layout for this 2-seater. The central fuel tank and spare wheel behind the passenger seat contribute to optimum weight distribution. The solid chassis/roll-bar is up to the toughest crash-tilt tests. The removable roof is easily stored in front.

BITTER SC Cabriolet GERMANY FR

The SC, drawn by Eric Bitter himself, both in the cabriolet and coupé versions, is equipped with a Senator floorpan, wheels, facia and a multitude of interior fittings. Customers can have any colour and trim materials they like. The cars are handled by Opel dealers. The 3-litre 6-cylinder Opel Senator engine ensures a top speed of 130 mph.

CLANCY Mirella AUSTRALIA

A private venture by a medical practitioner, Dr. Mike Clancy and the Ford Australia stylist, Clive Potter, this one-off super-compact is a high-performance 2-seater. It has a transverse turbocharged 2.3 6-cylinder engine, steel space frame and foam-filled, box section chassis and FRP panels. The 2 side doors pivot up from the forward edge. Overhang is minimal.

GREAT BRITAIN — Grosvenor Mk VI — COLEMAN-MILNE

A 2.8 litre 6-cylinder engine powers this Ford Granada based six- or seven-seater limousine which has been extended by 33 inches in length. The side-windows and glass division are electrically controlled. Cashmere trim and radio and stereo cassette are features of the opulent interior.

GREAT BRITAIN — Minster — COLEMAN-MILNE

Aimed at the executive who needs to travel in comfort, Coleman's Minster avoids flamboyance and extravagance. A five-seater limousine, it is 10" longer than the Ford Granada on which it is based, with extra room in the rear.

CRAYFORD — Fiesta Fly — GREAT BRITAIN

Based on Ford's best-selling small car, this convertible aims at filling a gap in the small car field. All four side windows can be removed, producing a true open sports car, and rear vision with the hood down is excellent. Two massive 50" chassis members ensure great body strength. The price is £ 6,748.

CRAYFORD — Ford Mk IV — GREAT BRITAIN

Once again a Ford conversion, this time of the Cortina Convertible. It is one of Crayford's most popular conversions and owes its success to the striking styling and its exceptional performance characteristics.

GREAT BRITAIN

Mercedes 350 and 450 G.E.L.

CRAYFORD

Crayford's conversion of the big Mercedes model is aimed at a particular market but one that sadly today is a growing one. These bullet-proof cars are armoured to a specification that will withstand sub-machine gun and hand gun bullets up to .357 magnum carrying a muzzle velocity of up to 1,440 ft/sec at point-blank range.

USA

Martinique

CUMBERFORD

The two-seater convertible body has a cast aluminium exoskeletal structure integrated with the chassis and wrought aluminium panels. It features crushable structures front and rear for crash energy attenuation. A 3,210 cc BMW 3.2 litre engine and ZF automatic transmission are accompanied by ventilated disc brakes all round. Length 189 in (480 cm). The fenders are solid laminated African mahogany.

GATSBY **Cabriolet** **USA**

The Gatsby classic motorcars are designed and built by master coachbuilder Sky Clausen and each is customized to the customer's taste. This Cabriolet version mounts a V8 water-cooled Lincoln-Mercury engine with a 302 cu in displacement. It has rear-wheel drive and a 3-speed fully automatic box.

GATSBY **Griffon** **USA**

The Griffon is a 2-seater roadster that mounts a Ford V8 engine and chassis with full Ford warranty. The length is 188.5 in and the wheelbase 118.4 in, with a curb weight of 3,200 lb. Each car, with leather interior and walnut or burl dash, is handcrafted to the buyer's taste. Price $ 59,500.

ITALY **Barchetta** **GHIA**

The "Little Boat" is a design concept for a small, 2-seater convertible sports car, a joint project of Ford in Europe and Ghia. The wedge-shaped, aerodynamic exterior features flush headlamps, direction indicators and tail lights. The fwd powertrain arrangement uses the Fiesta XR2 platform and mechanicals, plus a 4-cylinder 1.6 ohv engine and 4-speed manual transaxle.

ITALY **Trio** **GHIA**

Economy of operation is the aim of this urban concept car with staggered seating in an arrowhead configuration: 3 adults sit in a width of only 136 cm. The floor is a honeycomb sandwich of glass fibre and kevlar while the seat frames are aluminium and glass fibre. The rear-mounted 250 cc twin-cylinder 2-stroke engine drives the back axle through a continuously-variable belt transmission.

GLENFROME ENGINEERING — Ashton — GREAT BRITAIN

To transform the Range Rover into a luxury 4/5-seater, power-operated 4wd convertible, everything above the waistline except the windscreen is first removed and the vehicle then extended 10" to allow extra legroom and depth of the rear seat. The hood is electro-hydraulically raised and lowered, and there is central door locking.

GLENFROME ENGINEERING — Facet — GREAT BRITAIN

All current Glenfrome models are based on a Middle-East specification air-conditioned Range Rover. The Facet is a luxury all-terrain sports coupé offering all the comforts of a thoroughbred saloon. It features a safety roll-over cage, electric windows with tinted glass and a roof panel that is stored under the power-operated bonnet.

USA **SJJ-1** **GUANCI** 

The fuel-injected GM V8 ohv engine transverse mounted amidships develops 220 bhp at 4,800 rpm and drives the rear wheels of the SJJ-1 through a 3-speed automatic transmission. The seating of this 2-seater offers exceptional comfort including lumbar, thigh and shoulder support adjustment. The wheelbase is 102 in (259 cm).

ITALY **Capsula** **ITAL DESIGN**

Inspired by bus design and based on the engineering of the Alfasud, this is Giugiaro's completely new way of looking at a vehicle consisting of a floor-bearing engine, transmission parts, fuel tank, spare wheel, luggage compartment, brake booster, heater, front and rear lighting clusters. Different body capsules can be fitted to the fully-equipped independent frame, allowing great production economies.

ITAL DESIGN **Gabbiano** ITALY

A Renault inspired research project using a Renault 11 chassis, the Gabbiano is a compact 4-seater coupé with gull-wing doors, allowing direct access to the rear seats. A striking characteristic is the continuous band of glass with windscreen, door and window frames set inside. The bonnet is a single piece with no bumper and retractable headlamps.

ITAL DESIGN **Hyundai Stellar** ITALY

Launched on the overseas market late in 1983, the Korean Hyundai Stellar is a medium-sized family car with aerodynamic styling and luxurious interior powered by a fuel-efficient 1.4 or 1.6 gasoline engine. The flowing wedge-shaped front, slant bonnet, rectangular headlamps and matched wraparound direction indicators are in harmony with the aerofoil radiator grill.

ITALY **Medusa** **ITAL DESIGN** 

With the Medusa, Giugiaro develops the theme of aerodynamics and passenger accommodation in a 4-seater, 4-door saloon with central engine. Its 0.263 drag coefficient makes the Medusa a most efficient car, aerodynamically speaking, vital in these days of high fuel prices. The side windows are fixed, with ventilation by means of cam-operated sliding panels that close flush to the body.

ITALY **Orca** **ITAL DESIGN**

Although an experimental prototype, the Orca mounts the Lancia Delta frame with supercharged engine and 4-wheel drive, with the wheelbase lengthened by 20 cm to 267 cm. It reconciles aerodynamics with roominess. The front door vent wing is lowered below the waistline for increased visibility, and a spoiler runs along the base of the rear window.

JEHLE | Saphier | LIECHTENSTEIN

A 2+2 coupé with an unusual and striking wedge shape, the Saphier uses the chassis of a Volkswagen Beetle dating back to before 1969. The upper part of the glassfibre body hinges forward, carrying the steering wheel up with it, to allow entrance and exit. The front and rear side windows pivot and could be used as an emergency exit.

LOGICAR | Logic | DENMARK

Jakob Jensen, designer of this fiberglass 5-seater, claims that one person can convert it from a passenger car to a pick-up truck in a few minutes. The rear windows slide into the roof, the roof is lowered by a springloaded, telescopic system and becomes the pick-up bed, and the rear window frame rolls forward to lock into a water-tight connection with the cabin.

GREAT BRITAIN | Eventer | LYNX ENGINEERING

First the refined coupé, now the world's fastest estate car based on the XJ-S HE.
The aerodynamic new body panels are specially fabricated in steel, the fuel tank is reshaped and relocated and generous tail-gate and stiffer springs are added. Top speed and external dimensions are those of the Jaguar XJ-S HE.

GREAT BRITAIN | X.J-Spyder | LYNX ENGINEERING

Several years' careful development work have gone into this car which is still the only 4-seater full convertible available in Europe. It has all the lithe sophistication synonymous with Jaguar. The new electric side windows disappear into the rear wings when lowered and the shape of the mohair hood complements the existing lines of the X.J.

MARAUDER | **Di Napoli Coupé** | **USA**

One hundred units are being built of this nostalgic de luxe coupé which has however its full complement of safety equipment. A 350 cu in V8 engine and automatic transmission are standard. It also features automatic air-conditioning, electric windows and a power sunshine roof. Wheelbase 150 in (381 cm).

MICHELOTTI | **CVT 58** | **ITALY**

A concept for a touring car, Michelotti's design stresses simplicity of line, weight reduction and ease of mounting of component parts. The care taken over the smallest details makes a drag coefficient of 0.28 its outstanding feature.

The Meera S, a sports version of the Ferrari 400i, uses its chassis and mechanicals but with a hand-made steel sheet and aluminium alloy body 5 cm shorter than the original. The car looks much more compact thanks to the rounded corners, the shorter roof, and the teardrop-shaped windows.

JAPAN CR-X Pro Pace Car MUGEN

Hirotoshi Honda, son of the founder of the Honda Motor Co., who now heads the independent specialist firm, Mugen, has designed the Honda CR-X. The little sports coupé is ever sportier than the original with larger airdam, side blisters and large rear spoiler. Performance from the mildly tuned 1.5 litre 12-valve four is brisk, exceeding 120 mph.

OGLE — Astra — GREAT BRITAIN

Designed by Ogle Design, the Astra is aimed at the high-mileage executive who wants a compact, luxurious, high performance car with a long range. All four wing panels were flared and front air dam, rear spoiler and twin halogen headlamps added. Acceleration is 0-60 mph in 9 sec and there is an auxiliary 5-gallon fuel tank.

PININFARINA — Coupé — ITALY

Pininfarina's new 4-seater coupé based on the Fiat Ritmo Abarth 125 TC is aimed at the select market for cars with sporting characteristics plus aesthetic beauty and comfort. The new headlamps and rear lamps, designed with Carello, are fitted with shutters the same colour as the car and blend into the body when not in use. Maximum comfort and safety are ensured by padding or recessing.

ITALY — **Spideuropa Volumex** — **PININFARINA**

Volumex is the name given to engines mounted on Lancia Rally cars. The new version of the Spideuropa which features a volumetric compressor is fitted with this 135 bhp engine with 4 cylinders in line. To match its 190 km/h and 0-100 km in 9 sec, the Volumex has new suspension, more powerful brakes, light alloy wheels and Pirelli P7 Rally Type tyres. Price 22,000,000 liras.

USA — **Centurion** — **QUINCY-LYNN**

A Triumph Spitfire chassis and running gear and a 3-cylinder Kabota diesel engine have come together to make this light-weight, 2-passenger sports car that can do 100-plus to the gallon. It has the foam-fiberglass body construction today used on many safety vehicles.

RVIA — Sunrise Roadster — USA

A Ford 302 V8 engine with Ford C-4 automatic transmission is mounted on a square tube steel frame specially designed for maximum strength, safety and longevity. The car features Ford suspension and brakes, plus wire wheels and orthopaedically designed Recaro seats. Length is 180 in (457 cm).

SBARRO — Ford GT 40 — SWITZERLAND

Sbarro's conversion of the Ford GT 40 is being built in three versions – all extra-low 2-seaters but differing in performance, various details and price. The Racing has been rebuilt from top to bottom, while the Street is based on the De Tomaso Pantera. Prices start from 150,000 Swiss francs for the Street, rising to 220,000 francs.

SWITZERLAND — **Mercedes 540 K Spéciale Roadster** — **SBARRO**

An interesting replica of the 1938 Mercedes-Benz 540-K with a fiberglass body has been developed by Sbarro. The mechanical parts, including the 5-litre V8 engine and 4-speed automatic transmission are the ones used in today's Mercedes-Benz 500 SE. It has a rumble seat which, like the top, is electrically operated. It costs 240,000 Swiss francs.

SWITZERLAND — **Mercedes 500 SEC** —

Polyester bodywork has been used for Sbarro's Mercedes 500 which is available with either normal or gullwing doors. The original mechanicals of the 500 SEC are retained or, on request, a 6.9 litre engine. Either leather or other luxury materials are used for the upholstery according to the customer's preference. Price – from 180,000 Swiss francs.

SCARLATTI CARS — Sports Coupé — SOUTH AFRICA

A sleek four-seater built on a Ford chassis with a V6 ohv 3-litre engine, it is handcrafted in South Africa and carries a 12-month warranty. Automatic transmission, air-conditioning and a sunroof are available as optionals. The maximum speed is 180 km/h and fuel consumption at 100 km/h is 25 mpg.

STIMULA — 55 Série 2 — FRANCE

A magnificent polyester body, a chassis drawn directly from racing cars and a BMW 6-cylinder 2 or 2.3 litre injection engine add up to a Bugatti 55 Replica that is worthy of its ancestors. At 195,000 francs for the 2 litre version, you get excellent roadholding and 165 km/h, a hood and doors that stow neatly in the boot and a folding windscreen.

USA — **Vector W2 Twin-Turbo** — **VEHICLE DESIGN FORCE**

The Vector, boasted to be the fastest production car in the world, draws on the technology of the American aerospace industry. The chassis is a semi-monocoque aluminium honeycomb structure and the body a composite of Kevlar, glass and carbon fibers. The powerplant is a 5.7 l CIS fuel-injected V8 developing 600 bhp. It accelerates from 0-60 mph in 4 sec and top speed is 200 plus.

ITALY — **Alfa Zeta 6** — **ZAGATO**

Zagato presented its 2+2 based on the mechanicals of the Alfa Romeo 2,500 cc 6-cylinder GTV at the 1983 Geneva Motor Show. The suspension has been modified and the wheelbase widened. The body is aluminium and the upholstery leather. Many optionals, including air-conditioning, are available. Top speed is 205 km/h.

ALFA ROMEO SVAR/ESVAR ITALY

Presented last year at Kyoto and based on the Alfasud, the SVAR (Synthesis Vehicle Alfa Romeo) has followed the ESVAR or Energy Saving Vehicle Alfa Romeo. The Synthesis Vehicle achieves a higher degree of passive safety. The main aim has been to ensure performance as good or better than that of current cars and to reduce pollution. The 4-cylinder 1,490 cc Alfasud boxer engine with electronic control of fuel injection and of firing by microprocessors has an improved air-petrol ratio and a higher compression ratio.

BL TECHNOLOGY ECV-3 GREAT BRITAIN

BL's Energy Conservation Vehicle (ECV) is a long-term project. The ECV3 is not a production prototype but serves to test and evaluate cost-effective ideas, components, materials and processes. The quantitative targets are a top speed of over 100 mph, acceleration from 0-60 mph in under 12 sec, and consumption figures of 80 mpg at 56 mph. Qualitatively, it must match similar existing cars in ride, handling, noise, safety and accommodation and offer improved resistance to corrosion and accident damage. The targets have been more than achieved using a 1,100 cc 3-cylinder engine, reducing the body weight to 138 kg and the engine weight to 84 kg. Most of the body panels are glass-reinforced reaction injection moulded polyurethane (RRIM PU).

CHEVROLET Citation IV USA

Tipped as a production possibility for the early 1990s, this driveable Chevrolet show car boasts an .18 Cd. thanks to its slippery silhouette. Its 60° transverse-mounted V6 engine is 7 in (17.78 cm) lower than its production counterpart thanks to the single aluminium casting used for the intake manifold and valve covers. The electronic fuel metering and ignition systems used allow the carburettor and distributor to be eliminated. The front suspension features a transverse fiberglass leafspring mounted high on the firewall, just behind the engine. A small cathode ray tube (CRT) on the dashboard reflects the car's speed off the windshield for a "heads up" display.

FORD Electronic Concept 100 USA

Experimental but driveable with all electronic features functional, the Continental Concept 100 has aerodynamic design and a vast array of advanced electronics. The exterior features new low-profile halogen headlamps with aerodynamic covers, bronze-tinted glass with compound curvature, a heated windshield and pearlescent paint. There are no door handles to mar the sleek lines.
There is an aerodynamic antenna for satellite navigation on the multi-display information system called Tripmonitor and sensors for sonar detection. Highmount electroluminescent brake lamps in the rear window contribute to safety.

GENERAL MOTORS Project Saturn USA

GM calls its Saturn project for the later '80s "the American answer to the Japanese challenge". It represents GM's largest single commitment aimed at fully integrating design, engineering and manufacturing and incorporating new technology and assembly techniques. A fwd Chevrolet subcompact that is smaller than the Cavalier and about 600 lb lighter, it will at first be available as 2-door coupé, 4-door sedan and sports utility vehicle but other configurations are being considered. The fuel-injected 4-cylinder transverse engine will be coupled to either a 5-speed manual or 4-speed automatic box. Plans are for 45 mpg/city and 60 mpg highway.

ISUZU CO-A JAPAN

The three letters CO-A stand for Communication Capsule for Open-Air motoring. The open roadster is based on Isuzu's (and General Motors') R-car sub-compact and like it has transverse power unit and front-wheel-drive. The CO-A is equipped with a new electronically-controlled, electrically-shifted 5-speed automatic transmission. It incorporates a number of convenience, comfort and entertainment features for open-air driving, including microphone and headphone built into the head restraints.

MAZDA CLG-323 JAPAN

Although this convertible was developed in Irvine, California by the Mazda American Design Center, it was built for Japan with right-hand drive by Richard Straman, a Newport Beach coachbuilder. It was in fact introduced to the public at the Tokyo Auto Show in 1983. Based on the Familia (GLC in the U.S.) it accommodates four in comfort and has ample luggage space. The soft top is simple to erect.

MAZDA MX-2 JAPAN

Mazda's 4-door running prototype sedan accommodates 5 occupants in a carbon-fiber reinforced plastic body. It has an unusually long wheelbase – 280 cm – made possible by an electronically-controlled 4-wheel steering system which steers the front and rear pairs in opposite directions to describe a tight circle at speeds under 25 mph or steers them in parallel at high speeds for superior lane-changine response and cornering grip. The transversely-mounted 1.3 litre power unit is a high-performance 100 bhp four featuring twin overhead camshafts, 16-valve variable timing and a dual induction system. An 0.25 Cd is claimed.

NISSAN NX-21 JAPAN

With the 21st century in mind, Nissan have built this advance project prototype. The NX-21 is a full four-seater with entry and exit through two large power-operated folding gull-wing doors. The power unit mounted is a two-shaft gas turbine, and for its major component parts, the new ceramic materials have been used. The engine is rated at 100 bhp, and Nissan claim that this diesel with multi-fuel capabilities is as economical as it is advanced. The engine is mounted in the short rear overhang.

OPEL Junior GERMANY FR

The Junior, only 341 cm long, is a realistic study for a 4-seater mini with the emphasis on aerodynamics, progressive engineering and imaginative and versatile use of the interior. The smooth, sharply-slanted front end with flush-fitting headlights and spoiler fashioned into the bumper contribute to the 0.31 Cd as do the flush-fitting and integral glass, doors, hinges and latehes. The higher-than-usual seats save space and have stowage drawers under them. The doors are light-weight and a new system makes conventional window mechanisms superfluous. The rear seat, or half of it, can be folded forward to increase luggage space. The 1.2 engine (40 kW/55 hp) gives a top speed of 150 km/h and consumes about 4 l x 100 km.

PORSCHE 911 "Group B" GERMANY FR

In shape and technical concept, the "Group B" competition car is based on the Porsche 911 Turbo but the modified body has reduced resistance and good downforce at a Cd of 0.32. A 2.85 litre 6-cylinder engine give a 4-litre "sporting" displacement when the turbo factor is considered. It is water-cooled and has 4-valve cylinder heads with hydraulic valve adjustment and dual turbochargers. A 6-speed gearbox and a Porsche-developed, electronically-controlled system for optimum road dynamics perfects 4-wheel drive in everyday driving. The chassis features latest race car technology, including dual wishbones all round and adjustable stabilizers. Homologation is foreseen for the 1985 season.

RENAULT Eve+ FRANCE

The 1981 EVE (Elements for an Economic Vehicle) aimed at reducing consumption by perfecting aerodynamics and electronicaly programming the power group. Taking a Renault 18 TL as a starting point, the EVE+ programme is the perfection of the engine.
The current car has a direct injection diesel engine derived from the F8M series engine, with a KKK type K14 turbocompressor and 5-gear manual JB1 type box featuring a "stop and start" device. The Cd is lower even though the diesel's cooling system means a greater dissipation of energy. Thanks to a new front spoiler, an aerodynamic deflector that is an integral part of the body, a fin under the rear bumper and the lowering of the rear end, the top speed is now 168.8 km/h and consumption 7.7 l x 100 km.

RENAULT **Vesta** **FRANCE**

Renault is going ahead with its VESTA (Véhicule Economique de Sistème et Technologie Avancés) with 50% financial support from the state. It should foreshadow the Renault 5 of the '90s – a 4-seater with the performance, comfort and safety levels of today but consuming under 3 l x 100 km at 90 km/h. To reduce consumption, technical improvements are sought in aerodynamics, weight, rolling resistance, engine and transmission efficiency, and the cooling system. The project is still in its early stages but the car (only 327 cm long) has a 0.28 Cd which should fall to 0.25 when the bodywork is perfected. The 57° windscreen is a compromise between good visibility and aerodynamic needs. The structure is steel with a polyurethane foam roof reinforced with fibreglass, and polypropylene bumpers. The 3-cylinder petrol engine is expected to develop 23.8 kW at 4,250 rpm.

SAAB **900 Turbo Cabriolet** **SWEDEN**

Presented at the 1983 Frankfurt Motor Show, this prototype based on the new 2-door 900 is Saab's concept car for the future. Saab sees it as a barometer for interest in the cabriolet model and a test of the 900's development potential. Powered by a 16-valve turbo engine delivering 175 hp DIN (129 kW) when fitted with an intercooler, it is capable of over 125 mph (200 km/h). It features an electric retracting glass rear window operated from the driver's seat, a rear spoiler mounted on the upper back panel and sculpted into the belt trim mouldings and a sweptback windscreen. The show car was built in cooperation with American Sunroof Company (ASC), designers of special cars.

TOYOTA **FX-1** **JAPAN**

Toyota's 2+2 sporting tourer, introduced at the 1983 Tokyo Motor Show, is designed for the very near future. The FX-1 has a deep section forked steel backbone frame on to which is mounted an aerodynamic body giving a Cd of only 0.25. The body panels are a mixture of steel, composite and plastic materials. The power unit, the Biturbo 24, uses the new FP fibre (aluminium oxyde polycrystalline fibre) piston rods. It is a 2 l twin-cam 24-valve inline six featuring three Vees – variable valve timing, variable displacement and a variable induction system. The engine is mounted at the front and drives the rear wheels.

VOLVO **LCP 200** **SWEDEN**

Two engines – both turbo-charged, direct-injected diesels – are being experimented in Volvo's concept car: a 3-cylinder Volvo-Riccardo 1.3 litre and a 3-cylinder heat-insulated ELKO 1.4 litre with intercooler and multifuel capability. Technical innovations include a greenhouse separate from the bottom plate to facilitate manufacture and assembly, increased use of aluminium and magnesium to save weight, an energy-absorbing sloping radiator giving low air resistance. Increased know-how within the Volvo organization will result from the use of light alloys, powder metallurgy, plastics and adhesives technology. Polyurethane film instead of paint is being experimented on external surfaces.

Electric cars

Illustrations and technical information

USA

BRIGGS & STRATTON Hybrid

An 18 hp Briggs & Stratton i.c. engine coupled by a Borg-Warner duo-cam clutch to a Baldor 8 hp series wound dc electric motor gives this 2+2 sports coupé prototype a range of 30-300 miles (48-480 km) and fuel economy of 30 to 150 mpg. The car can be operated on gasoline or electricity alone, or both at the same time. The separately suspended battery trailer carrier containing 12 6 V lead-acid batteries reduces rolling resistance for improved fuel economy and performance. Top speed is over 70 mph (112 km/h). The overall length is 174 in (442 cm), the wheelbase 86 in and 112 in (218 cm and 284 cm) and the weight 3,200 lb (1,451 kg). The six-wheel design and dual rear axles make this a striking car.

FRANCE

C.E.D.R.E. 1000

To its well-known model 1000, C.E.D.R.E. has added a model 1500 derived from the 1000 and sharing the square tube frame, aluminium and fibre glass platform and plexiglass sliding doors. Both have two series motors and electro-mechanical variable voltage regulation, but the 1500's four 12 V batteries (they both mount 4 in the back but the 1000 also has 2 in the front) develop a maximum power of 7.5 kW at 400 rpm compared with the 1000's 5 kW from its six 6 V batteries. Both have a self-regulated charging system on board. The dimensions are identical except that the 1500 is 2 in (5 cm) longer and 44 lb (20 kg) heavier at 816 lb (370 kg). The 1000 costs 24,500 francs and the 1500 29,650 francs.

JAPAN

DAIHATSU Charade Electric

Daihatsu's Charade is built to order for its Australian distributor. This 4-door hatchback sedan prototype is derived from the Charade 1000 cc sedan. The eight 12 V lead-acid batteries powering the 14 kW dc compound motor are housed in a rear compartment. Recharging takes eight hours from a 240 V source. The maximum speed is 47 mph (75 km/h) and the Charade has a range of 47 miles (75 km) at 32 mph (51 km/h). It has a 3-speed mechanical gearbox and disc brakes at the front and drum at the rear. Overall length is 137 in (348 cm), width 59 in (151 cm), height 51 in (130 cm) and the wheelbase is 90 in (230 cm).

DAIHATSU Charmant Hybrid

Daihatsu's hybrid gasoline-electric car is based on the Charmant 4-door sedan. A central computer is used to alternate the 993 cc 3-cylinder gasoline engine and two dc 10.5 kW electric motors. The latter can be used separately or together. Six 100 Ah/5hr lead-acid batteries are carried in the trunk and control is by thyristor chopper and alternating single or 2-motor mode. The transmission has 2 hydraulic torque converters and 5 forward gears. Maximum speed is claimed to be 62 mph (100 km/h) and fuel consumption on Japan's urban emission test cycle is 70.6 m/imp gal, 58.8 m/US gal (4 l x 100 km). The car carries four adults in comfort or five if squeezed and is 165 in (420 cm) long and 54 in (138 cm) high.

DAIHATSU-MATSUSHITA BCX-M

JAPAN

Another electric derivation of the Charade sedan is the 2-door, 2-seater hatchback prototype jointly developed by Daihatsu and Matsushita Electric. The rear compartment has been converted to accommodate the eight 19 V iron-nickel Matsushita batteries, whose trade name is Panasonic. The 7.4 kW dc compound electric motor, SCR chopper and 5-speed gearbox give a maximum speed of 70 mph (113 km/h) and a range of 94 miles (151 km) at a cruising speed of 25 mph (40 km/h). Overall length is 153 in (389 cm), width 59 in (151 cm), height 51 in (129 cm) and wheelbase 90 in (230 cm). The weight with batteries is 2,380 lb (1,080 kg). There are disc brakes at the front and drum at the rear.

ENFIELD 8000

GREAT BRITAIN

The Electricity Council has been carrying out long-term tests on 66 8000s for over 8 years, and their fleet mileage is over 500,000 miles. The 4-pole 6 kW series-wound motor and transmission have been problem-free. The car is fitted with a solenoid contacter control system substantially modified by the Council to reduce the number of components and greatly increase reliability. Much experimentation has been done on both flat type and tubular plate type lead-acid batteries. 6 V monoblocs have been tested in various arrangements and voltages, showing that battery lives are from 3,000 to over 25,000 miles. Top speed is 40 mph (64 km/h) and range 24-56 miles (39-90 km). It is not in production.

FAIRCLOUGH Telford Mini

Derived from an Austin Mini Clubman, this glass-fibre 2-door hatchback saloon has slightly more legroom as there are no tunnels in the floor. The series-wound traction motor develops 6.5 kW at 1,830 rpm and has thyrister regulation. 12 6 V lead-acid batteries are housed in carriers under the back seat and bonnet. The built-in charger plugs into a normal house socket and recharging takes 10-12 hours. This 4-seater, which costs £ 4,250 plus VAT ex works, is designed to cruise at 40 mph (64 km/h). At this speed, its range is 40-60 miles (64-96 km) but less at its top speed of 60 mph (96 km/h). Braking is by Girling hydraulics with no electric braking. The wheelbase is 80 in (203 cm) and weight with batteries 9.4 tonnes.

GE ETV-1

USA

This experimental 4-passenger 2-door hatchback was developed for the U.S. Department of Energy by the General Electric Research and Development Center and Chrysler Corporation. It is powered by 18 6 V high energy density lead-acid batteries feeding a front-mounted separately excited d.c. motor with a peak rating of 31 kW. The batteries are mounted in a separate tunnel and removable as a unit. There is a transistorized armature chopper. The ETV-1 features low aerodynamic drag, computerized electronic controls, onboard charger and regenerative braking. Its range under certain driving conditions can be over 100 miles (160 km) and top speed is 60 mph (96 km/h). Length is 169 in (430 cm).

USA

GE Hybrid

GE, assisted by an international group of automotive and technology firms, has developed an experimental hybrid car for the U.S. Dept. of Energy. Based on a 1980 Buick Century, the 5-passenger sedan is expected to consume only 30% of the petroleum used over a year by a conventional car of a similar size by functioning electrically in town. A microcomputer controls the electric motor and the i.c. engine operating separately and together. The separately excited motor has automatic field control and voltage switching: max power 33 kW at 2,400 rpm. Ten 12 V 105 Ah batteries are housed under the hood, as are the electric motor and the Audi 1.7 litre fuel-injected engine, modified for on/off operation. Weight is 4,470 lb (2,027 kg).

GLOBE BATTERY Endura

This lightweight fiberglass prototype is designed as a test vehicle for Johnson Controls' technology in batteries. Using a four individual seat configuration, it has the flexibility of a combined sport sedan and station wagon thanks to the easy interchange of a rear quarter panel. The 20 Globe Battery Division high energy density advanced lead-acid 12 V batteries are mounted on an aluminium frame and roller subassembly tray. A Monopanel electronic control board controls ignition, lights, wiper and other accessories. The 20 hp series wound motor allows a top speed of over 60 mph (96 km/h) and a range of 100 miles (161 km). Length is 184 in (467 cm), width 72 in (183 cm), wheelbase 108 in (277 cm).

GLOBE BATTERY Maxima

This prototype developed from the Mercury Zephyr has the safety features of a 1978 model of that car, a steel and fiberglass body with 2 bucket front seats and rear bench seat. Both the 24 hp motor and regulation are by General Electric. The 20 prototype 12 V 70 Ah batteries are housed in 2 packs in the front engine compartment and under the rear cargo area. Recharging is by a current tape with a voltage limit. Top speed is 75 mph (120 km/h) and range is not declared. The car is capable of operating as a 240 or 120 V system for acceleration or economy. The Maxima has a mechanical gearbox, front disc and rear drum brakes and polyester radial tyres. Length is 198 in (503 cm), weight 4,350 lb (1,973 kg).

GREAT BRITAIN

LUCAS Hybrid Electric

As part of Lucas Chloride EV Systems development system, Reliant's engineering expertise has fitted an 848 cc 4-cylinder petrol engine and an electric drive system into a 5-seater GRP hatchback with steel side doors designed by Ogle. The car combines the benefits of electric drive with the total flexibility of a conventional vehicle. For all day-to-day running, the vehicle uses the separately-excited dc motor alone with overnight recharging from a 13 amp plug. For longer journeys range is greatly extended by means of the on-board i.c. engine-generator. 18 Lucas 12 V lead-acid motive power monobloc traction batteries with a 100 Ah capacity are mounted in a detachable underfloor battery pack.

MAZDA Familia EV

Based on the popular Familia/GLC/323 front wheel drive hatchback, Mazda's experimental electric car is powered by a newly developed nickel-zinc battery, which is light, compact and has a very high energy density of 62 Wh/kg. The battery is the 10 V 150 Ah type. The Familia EV, as the car is called, has 3-speed manual transmission and attains a top speed of 50 mph (80 km/h). The range improves to 100 miles (160 km) at a steady 37 mph (60 km/h) at 30° Celsius. The driving motor is a dc separately-excited motor, and control is by thyristor chopper. The car is 156 in (396 cm) long, 64 in (163 cm) wide and 54 in (138 cm) high, scaling 3,009 lb (1,365 kg). It carries four passengers.

MITSUBISHI Econo EV

To supplement research by practical experience, a fleet of Mitsubishi Econo 550 light car-based electric vehicles are in daily use in metropolitan Tokyo as the service vehicles of an electricity company. The Econo EV is a 2-seater electric vehicle with reduced dimensions. It is 126 in (320 cm) long, and 55 in (140 cm) wide. It weighs 2,028 lb (920 kg). It is powered by a dc 14 kW/84 X motor controlled by a thyristor chopper. The battery pack consists of eight 12 V lead-acid batteries. The car attains a top speed of 43 mph (70 km/h) and has a range of 56 miles (90 km) at 25 mph (40 km/h) on a level road at 30° ambient temperature on a single charge. Recharging takes eight hours.

NISSAN March EV

Nissan's latest electric vehicle is based its small mini car, the March hatchback. A 2-seater, it is powered by an induction motor with a 10 kW/85 V output, controlled by a transistor-inverter which drives the front wheels via a 2-speed automatic transmission. 18 iron-nickel-alkali batteries are used with a total voltage of 130 V and amperage rated at 160 Ah/5 hr. Top speed is 56 mph (90 km/h) and range 100 miles (160 km) at a steady 25 mph (40 km/h) on the level at 30° C ambient temperature. The car is 150 in (380 cm) long, 61 in (156 cm) wide and weighs 2,400 lb (1,090 kg). Recharging takes 7 hours. The March EV is an advance research project aiming at improved range, easier operation and maintenance.

PGE 3P

Steel body/chassis units with Fiat suspension are used for the 3P on trial at the British Railway Technical Centre. On both the 3P and the 5P Taxi, fully independent suspension all round is combined with disc brakes at the front and drum at the rear. Transmission is by PGE reduction gear. The thyristor chopper also allows regenerative electric braking. In the 3P, the smaller of the two models, the separately excited 7.8 kW motor has a maximum power of 15 kW and is powered by 72 V 185 Ah Fiamm "Nova" batteries which ensure the same performance as the Taxi attains, but carrying three persons plus 110 lb (50 kg) luggage. Overall length is 106 in (271 cm), height 60 in, (151 cm), and curb weight 2,425 lb (1,100 kg).

ITALY

PGE 5P Taxi

Five doors instead of three and the capacity to carry driver and four passengers plus 154 lb (70 kg) luggage or driver, one passenger and 551 lb (250 kg) luggage in the Mixed version distinguish PGE's Taxi from the 3P model. The 9 kW motor, again with thyrister chopper and regenerative braking, has a maximum power of 18 kW at 5,600 rpm. The 72 V batteries have a capacity of 185 Ah and weigh 1,058 lb (480 kg). Top speed is 37 mph (60 km/h) with a range of 43 miles (70 km) for normal urban driving. The overall length is 143 in (363 cm), width 64 in (163 cm) and height 67 in (170 cm) while curb weight complete with batteries is 2,645 lb (1,200 kg). The brakes are disc at the front and drum at the rear.

USA

QUINCY-LYNN Trimuter E

Quincy-Lynn's unusual little three-wheeler fiberglass sports coupé has a clam-shell canopy for entry to the two side-by-side seats. The series-wound 7 hp motor has a pulse-width modulator and is powered by ten 6 V lead-acid batteries mounted in two packs, 5 down the centre and 5 behind the passenger compartment. There is an on-board charger. Steering is through the single front wheel, with rear-wheel drive. There is direct drive via an HTD timing belt to the differential. At the top speed of 55 mph (88 km/h), the range is 30 miles (50 km) but rises to 65 miles (105 km) at cruising speed. The overall length is 144 in (366 cm), width 66 in (168 cm) and height 46 in (117 cm).

QUINCY-LYNN Urba Electric

Aiming at avoiding unnecessary energy loss, generally caused above all by the speed control system, Quincy-Lynn have patented a continuously variable transmission (CVT). It starts the compound wound Jack & Heinz motor at full voltage, putting the current directly to the 25 hp motor, which runs at constant voltage and speed. Vehicle speed is controlled through the transmission. The CVT shifts in response to a signal from a foot pedal, controlling the speed from 10 to 60 mph (16 to 96 km/h). Transmission efficiency is about 90%. Top speed is 55 mph (88 km/h) or 60 plus with field weakening circuit and range up to 65 miles (104 km). The overall length of this prototype is 126 in (320 cm).

QUINCY-LYNN Hybrid Electric

Hybrid for Quincy-Lynn means an 8 hp at 3,200 rpm series wound electric motor plus an on-board i.c. generator to supply current to the system while driving or to charge the packs of 6 V 244 Ah lead-acid batteries, 5 between the rear seats and 4 at the rear. Top speed is 55 mph (88 km/h) and range about 65 miles (105 km), rising to 125 miles (201 km) if the generator is used. Fuel consumption at a cruising speed of 35 mph (56 km/h) with generator in line is about 80 mpg. The fiberglass-urethane foam body with foam-filled bumpers is mounted on a VW Beetle chassis. Length is 174 in (441 cm), height 50 in (127 cm) and estimated weight with batteries 2,400 lb (1,089 kg). Still in the prototype stage, it seats 2+2.

JAPAN

SUZUKI Alto EV

In this updated electric prototype version of the Suzuki Alto 550 cc, the 2-door hatchback sedan layout has been retained with two seats in the front. A dc electric motor with a maximum power of 10 kW and a thyristor chopper are combined with 8 12 V lead-acid 120 Ah batteries mounted at the rear. Recharging takes 8 hours from a 200-240 V point but a rapid charge is possible in one hour. A 4-speed mechanical gearbox, drum brakes and 5,00-10 tyres are featured. The top speed is 47 mph (75 km/h) and range at a cruising speed of 25 mph (40 km/h) is 56 miles (90 km). Overall length is 126 in (319 cm), width 55 in (139 cm), height 53 in (133 cm), wheelbase 84 in (215 cm) weight 2,035 lb (923 kg).

FRANCE

TEILHOL Citadine/Messagette

Using the same 2-seater polyester body with welded steel tubing frame, Teilhol offers two types of Citadine for urban transport and five versions of the Messagette for leisure use. The beach buggy's top speed is only 15 mph (25 km/h) with a range of 50-62 miles (80-100 km) but this speed is doubled for the Citadine by using 12 V 105 Ah batteries instead of 6 V 220 Ah ones, so that the 96 V motor has 4 kW power as compared with the 2 kW 48 V Messagette. The motor drives the rear wheel through a 2-stage helicoid pinion reduction gear. Length is 91 in (230 cm), width 54 in (138 cm) height 61 in (155 cm), and dry weight with batteries 1,323 lb (600 kg). No driving license is needed in France. Price — 27,500 to 52,919 francs.

TEILHOL Handicar

This 4-wheeler is primarily intended for the disabled or invalids using a wheel-chair. By pressing a button the floor descends to ground level allowing simple access in a wheel-chair by the rear door. The floor is then raised again. The rear door can be opened from the driving seat by pressing a button. The 2-seater stratified polyester body is mounted on a steel frame and has lateral boxes for the eight 12 V Ah batteries. The Handicar has a 4 kW motor, independent wheels and hydraulic drum brakes on all 4 wheels. Length 95.28 in (242 cm), width 53.15 in (135 cm), height 61.02 in (155 cm), dry weight with batteries 1,389 lb (630 kg). Top speed is 30 mph (50 km/h) and range 25-38 miles (40-60 km). Price 58,707 francs.

JAPAN

TOYOTA EV-10

Toyota's new experimental electric car is, as Japanese electric vehicles usually are, based on a small production car, the Corolla II/Tercel front-wheel-drive hatchback. It is intended to be a personal transport vehicle with acceptable on-road performance. The electric system consists of a 15 kW/120 V dc motor driving the front wheels, the battery pack of 12 V lead-acid batteries mounted in the rear compartment and control by a transistorized chopper. The EV-10 is a typical D-segment size car, seating two. It reaches a top speed of 62 mph (100 km/h) and has a range of 70 miles (110 km). The recharger is mounted on the car and recharging takes eight hours.

USA

UNIQUE MOBILITY — ElecTrek Hatchback

The hatchback developed from the ElecTrek sedan (still available at $ 23,585) comes in 2-seater and 2+2-seater versions at $ 22,600 and $ 22,975 respectively. As in the sedan, the fiberglass unitized body and chassis has impact-absorbing front and rear ends. 16 6 V lead-acid batteries housed in a central tray drive a 96 V dc 32 hp motor with separately excited field using transistorized control with field weakening. There is regenerative braking and a 110 V 14 Ah on-board charger. Top speed, as in the sedan, is 75 mph (121 km/h), cruising speed 35-55 mph (56-88 km/h) and range over 75 miles (121 km). A little longer than the sedan at 178 in (452 cm) long and 54 in (137 cm) high, it weighs the same.

SWITZERLAND

VESSA — Carville

Sbarro's elegant little 3-door 2+2 seater features a polyester body. Derived from the Pilcar electric car and the fruit of nine year's research, it has been in production for some time. The 84 V 22 hp dc motor has a maximum power of 8/16 kW. The rear-mounted 12 V batteries are easily accessible and rechargeable from a 220 V electric point. The Carville has 4-speed automatic transmission and hydraulic drum brakes all round. Top speed is 50 mph (80 km/h) and range over 62 miles (100 km). The overall length is 126 in (321 cm), width 57 in (145 cm) and height 59 in (150 cm). The curb weight is 2,535 lb (1,150 kg) and it has a useful load of 661 lb (300 kg). It is available in red, blue, white, black and silver. Price about 30,000 francs.

ITALY

ZAGATO — Golf '83

The Golf '83 is a new version of the electric buggy Zagato has been producing for some years. The open body allowing easy access to the 2 seats has a large, unbreakable windscreen which gives excellent visibility and can be removed. For protection against rain or sun, a canopy can be mounted. 4 golf bags can be stowed on the rear table and there is a ball-holder on the instrument panel. The Golf '83 can cope with 18% gradients and has hydraulic brakes on all 4 wheels. The parking position for the brake pedal blocks the buggy and disconnects the starter. Two models are available, the 1000 with a top speed of 16 km/h and the 2000 doing 18 km/h. Both mount 6 6V 220 Ah batteries, rechargeable in 12 h.

ZAGATO — Minivan

With its new Minivan, Zagato aims at producing, not a rival for the i.c. passenger car, but a vehicle that, since it does not pollute, can be used even in areas from which other vehicles are precluded, such as hospitals and parks. The Minivan has 2+1 doors and an unalterable fiberglass body with thermal and acoustic insulation. The 10 6 V lead-acid batteries are housed in a convenient fiberglass box that slides out. Recharging is by an automatic rectifier. The 60 V 5 kW dc series-wound motor gives a top speed of about 34 mph (55 km/h) and a range of approximately 37 miles (60 km). Drum brakes are mounted all round and the steering is rack-and-pinion. Length is 102 in (260 cm), weight about 1,819 lb (825 kg).

World automobile production

Europe

A CASE OF MIXED FORTUNES

by J.R. Daniels

This year sees a remarkable split in the attitudes and fortunes of Europe's car manufacturers. On the one hand, the "quality" companies can mostly look to increased profits and expanding production. On the other, the mass-manufacturers hope that 1984 will bring about a recovery in the European market and a return from loss to profit; though it is clear that some of them are much better placed than others to take advantage of any upswing in demand.

The split of fortunes is obvious even when one looks at technical trends. The quality manufacturers lead the way in terms of putting high technology into production, not only because they can afford to, but also because their customers expect it and are prepared to pay for it. Thus we have seen a spate of advanced engine designs, electronic control systems, transmissions, sophisticated aerodynamics and weight-saving from the likes of Audi, BMW, Jaguar, Mercedes, Saab and Volvo — who have become the pre-eminent European up-marketeers. The volume manufacturers have sought better financial results, logically enough, by moving their own products up-market in various ways. That is why this year's model lists include so many "three-box" versions of hatchback originals, and why the European motoring public can — after an interval of many years — once again take its pick of several small convertible cars. The same trend can also be seen in the sudden arrival of several models with four-wheel drive.

Where engines are concerned, we can now discern four distinct avenues of advance towards higher efficiency, and therefore better economy. First, there is the movement towards engines with four valves per cylinder, for the sake of easier gas flow through the unit, which in turn makes it possible to achieve higher specific output without sacrificing other important qualities such as flexibility. Second, there is the further development of the turbocharger, which is increasingly seen as a way of improving an engine's overall cycle efficiency rather than merely boosting its power. Third, there is the growth of all-embracing electronic control systems led by the Bosch Motronic, which combines the supervision of fuel injection and ignition within a single

The 105 bhp engine of the 1,397 cc Renault 11 Turbo. Below, the sporting characteristics of the 11 Turbo are very marked.

computer. Finally, after a year or two of hesitation, the diesel engine is once again surging forward.

With the exception of the diesel, all these engine developments are largely the preserve of the six up-market manufacturers already mentioned. For instance, BMW, Jaguar, Saab and Mercedes already have four-valve per cylinder engines in at least limited production, while Volvo have shown experimental units leading towards production soon, and Audi use such engines in competition as well as having access via their colleagues at Volkswagen, who already fit a 16-valve unit to a competition version of the Golf GTi. Of those same six manufacturers, five already offer turbocharged production models (though BMW and Mercedes confine their turbos to diesel engines for the time being). BMW has led the way in the application of Motronic control, but this year should show that their rivals are far from blind to its advantages.

While the makers of expensive cars are leading the technical way, what are the volume manufacturers putting under their bonnets? The trend here is very different. The emphasis is more than anything on

Three views of the Volvo 740 GLE. The choice of engines runs from a 1,986 cc 4-cylinder petrol engine – either aspirated or turbo – to a 2,383 cc 6-cylinder diesel. The power available ranges from 82 to 150 bhp.

Top, the husky Renault 18 Turbo Diesel and above the striking array of instruments and leather steering wheel.

cheap, fully automated production — best seen in the new units recently introduced by Renault and Peugeot-Citroen. At a first glance, these two units are more remarkable for their differences than for their similarity. Considering that each was designed to serve as probably the most important engine in its manufacturer's range until the end of the century, and that they are very close in size and power output, what are we students of design to make of them? Renault uses a "dry" cast-iron block with no water between the cylinder bores, and a completely flat cylinder head face with the combustion chamber formed entirely within the piston; Peugeot runs a classically French wet-linered alloy block and uses "bathtub" combustion chambers formed in the cylinder head! Yet these are mere details compared with the overall context of each operation. The new PSA engine factory at Tremery, and the completely re-equipped Renault complex at Cléon, are both able to produce engines in their thousands with a minimum of human intervention. That is important for two reasons. First because it will ultimately reduce costs, and reducing cost is what the mass-market game in Europe is all about these days. Second because the new machinery can produce engines to very close tolerances, which will become increasingly important as exhaust emission laws begin to tighten and fuel quality gets less reliable. Nor should we lose sight of the way both engines indicate general engineering and marketing trends. They are designed for transverse installation in front-driven cars, they drive through overhung five-speed gearboxes — and they were intended from the outset to serve as diesel as well as spark-ignition power units. In Peugeot's case, the diesel actually came first, by a short head.

The two French engines are evidence that Europe's small and medium-sized cars will soon be universally front-driven (indeed, they very nearly are) and that the diesel will play an increasingly important part in the market. It is not only in France that we see more weight being put behind the compression-ignition engine. This year sees Ford of Europe's major investment in the small diesel — in the shape of the purpose-designed 1.6-litre unit now being built in Dagenham — coming to fruition. The engine will be used in the Fiesta and the Escort, providing Ford with an answer to the General Motors challenge of the diesel Kadett. Meanwhile in Italy, Fiat has launched a diesel version of the Uno and Alfa Romeo continues to work closely with the engineers at VM, the Italian diesel specialists. Volkswagen started the whole European small-diesel trend and continue to work hard to stay ahead of the game, placing particular emphasis on the more efficient (but technically difficult) direct-injection type. Direct injection is also used in the joint project recently announced between Austin-Rover and Perkins in Britain, aimed at producing an ultra-economical version of the BL O-series engine.

Despite some predictions, therefore, it is unlikely that the diesel will go away. On the contrary, this year sees more mid-range diesel models on offer in Europe than ever before. If anything, the main requirement now is for a period of stable fiscal and exhaust emission regulations so that manufacturers and their customers know where they are likely to stand between now and 1990. If the European diesel succeeds, it will be despite the peculiar fiscal measures adopted (for instance) in Italy and Sweden. This year should also see the greater use of turbocharging for diesel engines, since there is more to be gained from a blown diesel than from a spark-ignition engine. Full boost can be used more of the time, since the diesel need observe no knock-limit; and diesel exhausts tend to run cooler, which gives the turbocharger unit an easier time and a longer life.

The engine may be the heart of the car, but it is not what the customer sees and buys. How are the European manufacturers shaping up to 1984 in terms of model ranges? Again, we see the split between the prestige companies and the mass-producers. For those at the top of the tree, 1984 promises well. Audi has added the ultra-fast, but highly efficient 200 to the award-winning 100; the next move will be to replace the 80 with a similarly aerodynamic car. The existing 80 is coming up for five years old, and a lot has happened at Audi in that time. From BMW, 1984 should see the resolution of that argument which seems to have split its board of management (ending with the departure of the much-respected Karl-Heinz Rademacher). BMW's recent approach has been ultra-cautious: as a matter of deliberate policy, its new 3-series and 5-series cars closely resemble their predecessors, gaining efficiency through a painstaking process of fine-tuning. Last year saw no BMW introduction of real significance, save for the turbodiesel and the very expensive 24-valve M 635. This year must see the replacement of the biggest and oldest car in the range, the 7-series: it will be interesting to see if caution remains the watchword at Munich, or if the opportunity will be taken to break more new ground. If these observations imply criticism, it cannot be justified in terms of BMW's output or its profit situation; but can it be that the buyers who opt for the familiar in 1984 will have been educated to expect something altogether different in 1986?

Above, the new Volkswagen Jettas, available with 1,272, 1,595 and 1,781 cc petrol engines and a 1,588 cc diesel, turbo if desired. Top right on this page, the Ford Escort Cabriolet in the XR sports version with 1,597 cc 105 bhp injection engine. Below, the latest version of the BMW Series 7, the 735i or 745i Executive with what the driver sees and the layout of the drive shaft. On the opposite page, the front end and engine of the new 2,260 cc 86 bhp Opel Rekord Turbo Diesel, top speed 169 km/h and 0 to 100 km/h in 15.5 sec.

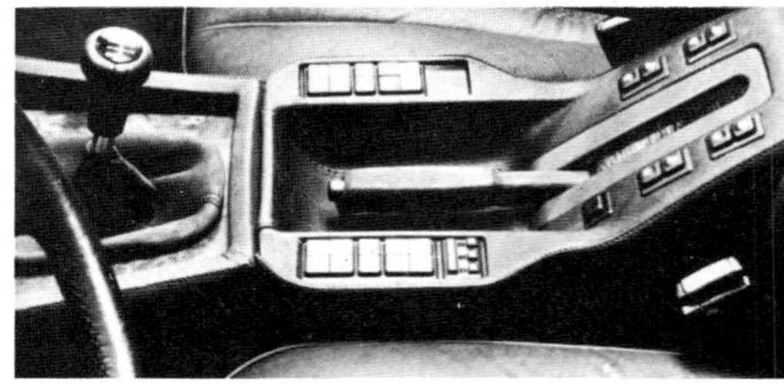

It is interesting to see how Mercedes has reacted to this situation. More than any other manufacturer in the world, Mercedes' reputation and sales rest on a clear family resemblance between all its models. That resemblance has been subtly maintained through the last few years even though the shape of the cars has changed significantly. This year will see the launching of a replacement for what is now the mid-range Mercedes, the W123, and the W124 will take one stage further the deep commitment to aerodynamic efficiency that has become an article of faith in Stuttgart. Like BMW, Mercedes has never been stronger, nor has it ever produced so many cars. The impression remains that it is more adventurous, with the confidence to lead its customers' tastes rather than to reflect them.

There could hardly be a more important year than 1984 where Jaguar is concerned. The Coventry-based prestige offshoot of BL once again operates with complete (rather than merely partial) autonomy: and it has regained its confidence. Recent years have seen quality standards and productivity improve dramatically, and now we shall see the new products to take advantage of that situation. First on the scene was the XJS convertible, powered by the highly significant new AJ6 engine. But the real key to Jaguar's fortunes will be the XJ40 saloon, wich will arrive this year to replace the much admired (but sixteen years old and grossly overweight) XJ6. The XJ40 will also be powered by the AJ6, but Jaguar has already implied that the saloon engine may have a

less exotic cylinder head layout than we have seen in the convertible application.

Like their German counterparts, Saab and Volvo have gone from strength to strength in the last few years. Both companies tend to follow the Mercedes pattern in that they are also very strong in heavy commercial vehicles; but since the European truck business is currently in a very bad way, the Swedes have been glad to find their cars generating large profits. For Saab, 1984 is a highly significant year because it sees the arrival of the first major facelift for the 900 range. For all its technical excellence, the 900 has suffered some consistent criticism, not least of its driver visibility, and the new model can be expected to answer with a significant improvement. Saab is well aware of current engineering trends; it is able to call on the aerodynamic expertise of its aircraft division, and will also lead the way in the use of high-strength steels to achieve weight reduction. Add to this the promise of the 16-valve engine, and the established excellence of the APC turbocharger control system (which takes account of the quality of fuel used and automatically adjusts the boost accordingly) and it is clear that as long as the new car has enough visual appeal, Saab should continue to do well.

Volvo's success in the last few years has been little short of remarkable, but the company plans no major introductions until the very end of the year. The Swedes — with a lot of help from the Dutch — have created a three-series model range tied together by the styling concept that Volvos must look heavy, tough, and safe. It is a concept which has been refined to the point where the current models fulfil it perfectly despite being no heavier (and in many cases are actually lighter) than their main rivals. If Volvo has a problem, it is that two of its model series look almost equally ripe for replacement. The 200-series is ten years old this year, which means it has already lasted considerably longer than its predecessor. The 300-series meanwhile is now eight years old, having fought through a period of initial public disfavour and been developed into a much wider range. The under-powered image of the Renault-powered versions has been firmly squashed by the 2-litre 360 models, a process completed for the 1984 model year by the introduction of the 360GLE with its three-box design to complement the hatchback models. The 300-series is specially noteworthy in that it has given Volvo a useful entry in the medium-car sector. Volvo is the only "prestige" manufacturer genuinely to have achieved such a broadening of interests (by comparison, the Mercedes 190 is no more than half a step in the same direction) and the company will want to make sure this happy position is consolidated as substantially as possible.

So much, then, for those European manufacturers who have properly established themselves up-market. It is noteworthy that no French or Italian company figures in the list. Where the Italians are concerned, both Alfa Romeo and Lancia are striving to re-establish the image they once enjoyed. Alfa Romeo, which had suffered a period in which it seemed quite likely that the state-owned builder would cease to exist as a serious force, finally developed a strategy for survival. The Alfa 33 is not only the first expression of that strategy but the first new Alfa model for many years and we have already seen the beginnings of its development process. The four-wheel-drive version was shown at the Frankfurt Show, followed by an estate car on its heels and the 33Ti will be released later this year. But one new car does not make a model range, which is why observers are looking eagerly to see how Alfa Romeo will replace its mid-range cars, the elderly Giulietta and Alfetta. It is already known that part of Alfa Romeo's strategy is to develop a mid-range car jointly with Fiat Auto — which needs a broadly similar vehicle to replace the equally elderly Argenta and the poorly-received Lancia Trevi. This vehicle, the Type 4, will consist essentially of a common platform and series of mechanical units on which each design team will mount its own body. If the Italian industry is to maintain its credibility as a builder of midrange, up-market cars, the Type 4 must make its appearance this year — and must be good. Alfa Romeo meanwhile has posed Europe a political problem (possibly the first of several we shall see) with the marketing of the Arna. This marriage of a Nissan Cherry body with Alfa Romeo mechanical units certainly extends the Alfa range, and the agreement with Nissan is yet another of the planks in Alfa's survival programme; but is the car really an Alfa? Is it even European? There are those who would argue the point.

Among those inclined to argue is Fiat Auto, which is well advanced with its own recovery programme and is ill-disposed to countenance what it sees as unwarranted outside assistance for one of its main market rivals. Fiat has already established itself powerfully at the bottom end of the market with the Panda and the Uno, and is already busily engaged in broadening the appeal of those two models, as we have seen with the introduction of the ingenious four-wheel-drive Panda. Nor should the contribution of the much-improved Ritmo be overlooked. Again, we can see the manner in which Fiat is edging this model up-market with the addition of versions such as the Abarth 130TC and the Cabriolet. For 1984, however, the real interest in the Fiat range is the Regata, effectively a three-box version of the Ritmo which will replace the woefully outdated Mirafiori. The arrival of the Regata, which Fiat takes care to set apart from the Ritmo through equipment level, marketing techniques and pricing, means that Fiat needs only the addition of the Type 4 to give it a comprehensive modern range of five models. When one takes into account the fact that these cars are assembled in some of the most advanced and ingenious production facilities anywhere in the world, it seems quite possible that Fiat is close to returning to the state of mass-market pre-eminence which it enjoyed after the introduction of the 127 and 128 at the end of the 1960s.

Fiat Auto's remaining problem is the situation of Lancia, which has yet to come anywhere near regaining its former reputation of being to Italy what Mercedes is to Germany, or Rover to Great Britain. Lancia's most recent efforts have been the launch of the three-box Prisma, which is to the hatchback Delta as the Regata is to the Ritmo, and its essay into positive-displacement supercharging (as distinct from turbocharging) as seen in its new range of Volumex versions. But the real answer to Lancia's problems can only be found in new mid-range and up-market designs, and we are not likely to see them this year.

If Fiat's fortunes are improving, the same cannot be said of Renault which has suffered mightily from poor demand in its home market and a slump in sales elsewhere in Europe. The Régie pinned its hopes very largely on two state-of-the-art cars, the 9 and 11, closely related to one another and calculated to respond exactly to that innate conservatism which is wooed by some up-market manufacturers. The trouble is that at this market level, the formula seems not to have worked. To some extent the 9/11 team — the one three-boxed, the other the hatchback — has taken sales more from other Renault models than from the opposition. The 18, highly and deliberately conservative even when it was announced six years ago, has suffered badly. So has the 5, whose declining sales prove that in today's world, twelve years is an over-long life even for a car whose highly individual styling was once much admired. Renault's answer has been to struggle. Its main offering for 1984 is the 25, no doubt a worthy replacement for the 20/30 series but hardly relevant to the real mass-market issue. It is strongly rumoured that the replacement for the 5 is now the subject of a crash programme to bring its launch forward to this year's Paris Salon. Such emergency action is badly needed.

The all-powerful (400 bhp) Ferrari GTO with 2,855 cc biturbo engine. Below, the 4-wheel drive version of the Alfa Romeo 33 and, right, its instrument panel. Bottom photos, the sporting model of the Arna that mounts a 1,350 cc engine providing 86 bhp.

Two of the principal nails in the Renault 5's coffin have been products of the PSA group. The Citroen Visa had done well ever since its inspired facelift three years ago, but the Peugeot 205 is the car which has really made the Régie suffer. The little Peugeot appears to have struck a responsive chord throughout the European market. The problem for some time has been to make enough of them, and this situation is likely to continue. This year should also show more clearly how Peugeot intends to broaden the appeal of the 205 much as it did for the earlier 104. For the time being, the 205 has also had the welcome effect of diverting attention from the troubles of PSA at higher levels. The Peugeot range (305, 505 and 604) has seen some worthwhile developments, and the 305 in particular is now almost a new car, however much its familiar appearance belies the fact. But all three models are well on in their development lives and the masters of Sochaux — when they can divert themselves from their more universal corporate troubles — must be thinking in terms of new cars to interleave with (and ultimately displace) the 305/505 and 505/604. Meanwhile, there remains Talbot: its last "new" car the Samba, the big Tagora already consigned to the scrapheap, and little prospect of a future beyond badge-engineering. Talbot's Matra interest, which might once have led to a promising if specialized future with models like the Rancho and the Murena, has meanwhile had to be sold off to Renault!

Citroen, the remaining arm of PSA, continues to do well with the Visa, the BX and even the big CX — the latter given new interest with the introduction of the higher-performance 25 GTi and Turbo Diesel versions. If a question hangs over Citroen, it concerns the future of the GSA whose advanced concept now blends badly with a body of questionable package efficiency and poor detail. This year may well see Citroen allowing the much improved, and bigger-engined, Visa and the lower end of the BX range to squeeze the GSA gently out of existence. Quite what will become of France's beloved 2CV is another matter. There is a strong body of opinion within Citroen that the only way to replace the car is to return to Monsieur Boulanger's original specification (the umbrella, the basket of eggs, the ploughed field) and to re-interpret it with 1984 materials and technology.

The two American multinational operations in Europe have greatly increased their strength and their competitive position in recent years, and 1984 will show further evidence of their inexorable progress. Ford has secured its position all the way to the mid-market: a substantial facelift for the Fiesta, worthwhile improvements for the Escort, the launch of the Orion (reflecting one of the most popular trends, in that it is the three-box equivalent of the Escort) and the consolidation of the Sierra after a slightly shaky start — some of which amounted to psychological warfare by a worried opposition. Thus there remains only the Granada, whose replacement is the centre-piece of Ford's 1984 programme, plus the possibility that some of the intriguing prototypes from the Ghia studio will eventually lead to a production commitment. Already, Ford has moved (again reflecting a strong current trend) into the convertible saloon market with its soft-top Escort.

General Motors, meanwhile, has itself done proud with the Opel Kadett and Ascona, and their Vauxhall equivalents. GM's European management now looks strong and confident, as though it knows it has made up the ground it lost to Ford through its much later move into truly pan-European operation. The 1984 GM lineup includes the Corsa/Nova at its base, is topped off with the excellent Rekord/Commodore series, and contains a first-class specialized coupé in the Manta. Having seen the impact created by the outstandingly successful launch of the Ascona/Cavalier, GM is aware that it ought to have done better with the Kadett — with the result that when that car's replacement is launched this year, not a trick will be missed on the marketing front.

The Kadett will have strong competition, because Volkswagen's new Golf is already becoming established. There were mixed feelings about the new car at its launch, some observers feeling that Wolfsburg's deliberate conservatism — the conscious effort to make the new car look as comfortingly familiar as possible — might be counter-productive. The first, astonishingly successful, Golf looked very different from the Beetle, after all. Time will tell, and most of all this year: but there is no denying that the new Golf is substantially better in many ways. Its interior space, its economy, are well in line with what 1984 demands. Since the Polo is also a very recent design, Volkswagen's interest now reverts to the top of the range with a hard look at the Passat, and possibly an even harder one at the Santana which has been so completely upstaged by its corporate stablemate the Audi 100.

Of all the European mass-producers, that leaves Austin-Rover. The family-car arm of the former BL is in much better shape than for many years. It has two good products in the form of the Metro and the Maestro; this year sees a further addition to the range in the form of the three-box Montego (LM11). Like its contemporaries the Orion, the Regata, the Prisma and the Volvo 360GLE (not to mention Volkswagen's new Jetta) the LM11 sits in the market almost a full class up from its hatchback equivalent the Maestro. It should perhaps be noted that since the days of the first relatively crude three-box conversions, there has been a tendency to do the job ever more carefully and thoroughly: the Regata and the Orion both show evidence of that. Austin-Rover go further still, insisting that the LM11 is in no sense a mere three-box LM10 Maestro. Before the year is all that old, we shall see.

There has been a ruthless cutting out of old models in the Austin Rover range, and a concentration of production on just two plants which are, by now, among the most modern and best-equipped in Europe. In this corporate blood-letting, not even the big Ambassador has survived. Austin-Rover has in effect become a five-model producer, the cars subsidiary to the Metro/Maestro/LM11 team being the Rover saloon (now eight years old) and the Triumph Acclaim, closely based on a version of the Honda Ballade which has been replaced in its homeland. In addition to LM11, therefore, Austin-Rover's plans for 1984 must include some positive action on the Acclaim — in the form either of updating or of outright replacement. But we shall have to wait a little longer to see an LM11 derivative fill one of the outstanding gaps in the present Austin-Rover armoury: the lack of any estate car. The next stage in the Honda collaboration, the XX executive car, has been much heralded but is still over a year away. When it comes, it will of course replace the existing Rover — giving the British company (at last) a range with which to challenge Europe's best.

One of the charms of Europe is that beneath the churning of the great car factories, one finds the specialist still thriving, in Germany, Italy and Great Britain (though not to anything like the same extent in France). The specialist *par excellence* is Porsche, which maintains a four-model range (911, 924, 944, 928) despite its limited production — and manages to develop each one constantly to new heights of performance and appeal. Much has already been written about the stubborn refusal of the 911 to die: some pundits must despair to realize that the 1984 model-year 3.2-litre Carrera is the best 911 ever, by common consent. Yet Porsche does not simply make cars: it acts as development house to the motor industry world-wide. The great development complex at Weissach has only one serious rival, though on a smaller scale: the Lotus factory at Hethel. Here again we have a specialised company turning out small numbers of high-performance cars (not nearly as many as Porsche, but twice as many as last year all the same) and also carrying out projects for other manufacturers. Alongside such developments, Lotus runs its own research programme, and this has led (among other fascinating developments) to the most promising active ride control system yet seen. The Lotus system ensures that the suspension, instead of acting passively in response to the road surface, is positively controlled to achieve whatever combination of ride and handling is felt most desirable. All those who have ridden Hethel's testbed Esprit have been highly impressed, indeed staggered by the effectiveness of the system, and industry interest is considerable. Could it be that 1984 will be remembered not merely for a most promising crop of new cars, but also for the realization that conventional car design was about to be turned on its head by a combination of electronic speed and human ingenuity?

Jaguar have finally taken the top off the XJ-S coupé to create a pleasing convertible and – much more to the point – have powered it with a brand-new 3.6 litre 24-valve engine of extremely high efficiency and power.

Japan

TECHNOLOGY ON FULL BOOST

by Jack K. Yamaguchi

In the old Japanese calendar, fashioned after the ancient Chinese one to whose twelve-year cycle our ancestors attached the names of twelve animals, 1983 was the year of wild boar. And most appropriately so. Like the proverbial audacious dash of a wild boar, the Japanese automobile industry charged ahead to rewrite its own record book. It was yet another 11 million unit year, falling only slightly behind the all-time record of 1981. So, for four years in row, Japan topped the 10 million mark. Passenger car production accounted for approximately 6.9 million of the aggregate. The industry's charge was fiercer on the domestic front, where last year 5.4 million motor vehicles, including 3.15 million cars, were consumed — an absolute record. Rapid recovery by the Japanese economy in the latter half of the season, a series of deregulatory measures encouraging buyers, the stimulus provided by the biennial Tokyo Motor Show and an almost incessant flow of new and updated models were the major reasons for the buying surge.

The organizers of the annual Japanese Car of the Year award had listed 15 brand new cars, 5 new "one-box" wagons and 22 revamped models with significant changes, including new power units, eligible for the preliminary selection of the top ten and then on to the final ballot for the outright winner. The numbers must stand in the award's history as records that seem unlikely to be challenged for some years to come. Of the fifteen new releases, five failed to make the honourable-mention top ten list, and none of the one-box, updated and upgraded models stood the slightest chance. Such was the frenzied pace of the Japanese season: it boggled many a mind, and drove some intrepid automotive journalists up the deadline wall.

The season may well be described as a year of deregulation for the domestic market. The mandatory biennial roadworthiness inspection, a costly affair entailing thorough maintenance performed by a certified mechanic has now become triennial. The Ministry of Transportation has been easing and lifting those curious rules and regulations that the bureaucrats had been harbouring so long, more like taboos than rational and reasonable measures. New cars may now wear ultra-low-profile tyres of "60" aspect ratio (anything fatter than 60 is not yet recognized as original equipment). Outside rear-view mirrors may now be mounted on doors, freeing Japanese cars of that strange horny look due to tall mirrors sticking up from the fenders. Turbos have now spread from top to bottom of the Japanese product ladder, the former represented by the revamped Nissan-Datsun 300ZX sports car whose boosted V6 puts out 230 hp JIS (handsomely exceeding the once sacred 200 hp limit), and the latter by a number of turbocharged 550 cc micro runabouts. The honourable Minister and his technocrat underlings, who must have felt that wild airdams, spoilers and wings were symbols of "Bosozouku" the "Reckless clan", oriental four-wheeled equivalents of hell's angels, have at long last relented. New cars may now be bedecked with aerodynamic outer panels and pieces.

Toyota offers its exquisite twin-cam 24-valve variable induction six-cylinder engine mounted on a variety of upper-middle and luxury cars.

Fun-to-drive has now progressed to outright excitement on wheels, naturally within the bounds of reasonable fuel economy and clean-air measures (the latter still among the world's most stringent). Statisticians state that 8.2% of new cars sold in Japan last year were turbocharged. Mitsubishi and Nissan are ardent turbo-protagonists, boasting 18% and 14.7% turbo ratios. By contrast, Toyota took a modest 1.7% but then the company powered 14.1% of its new cars with DOHC engines. The industry aggregate of twin-cam models was 7% of the total domestic sales. And 24.7% of new cars were fitted with advanced electronic fuel injection for performance and economy improvement.

In 1982 it was Toyota who married the two most potent power-producing features, a twin-cam engine and a turbocharger in a number of mid-size cars. Last year it was Nissan's turn. It grafted an AiResearch instrument on the type FJ20 2-liter twin-cam 16-valve inline four, hiking up its output to 190 hp JIS, and offered it in the Skyline RS sedan series. Later in the season this power unit combination was used in the new Silvia/Gazelle (Datsun 200SX) sports coupé series, which also adopted independent rear suspension in upper grade models. Many thought it was about the limit in horsepower, however bloated the JIS rating might have been (take Japanese specs with a pinch of salt and reduce by 15 to 20% to reach a comparable SAE net power), half giving up the hope of ever treading on the right pedal of a forthcoming turbocharged big Z. Not so: the new Nissan Fairlady Z (plain Nissan ZX for export) was offered to the domestic clientèle in its most powerful guise, a 300ZX whose turbocharged, fuel-injected overhead cam 60-degree V6 was rated at 230 hp. Apart from its bent six, the like of which will appear from other members of the Japanese industry, the new Z-car is more evolutionary than revolutionary, carefully nurturing its precedessors' successful formula. It has the power unit at the front, driving the rear wheels. All wheels are independently suspended in a familiar front McPherson strut, rear semi-trailing arm configuration. Two body styles, a strict 2-seater and a 2+2, are offered as before. The Z does not have the monopoly on the new VG engine. It debuted in the sedate intermediate-size Cedric/Gloria sedan range, which is again a thoroughly conventional design with sumptuous accommodation and amenities, which include a system that senses how hard it is raining and wipes accordingly. Nissan had deliberated alternative cylinder configurations almost a year before deciding on V6. Major factors in its favour were merchandizing appeal — especially if the company could outdo competitors — performance potential and compact size, particularly a shorter length allowing greater packaging freedom to include transverse mounting. In fact, the replacement for the U.S only, the Nissan Maxima is a stretched transverse-V6 powered version of the new Bluebird fwd. Honda should soon have its own V6, again said to have been developed in two sizes, 2 and 3 liters like

In the large photo, Nissan's lively 300ZX turbocharged sports car, and above, one of the smallest turbo engines, Suzuki's 3-cylinder unit. Alongside, Honda's show-car-for-sale, the City Turbo II and, far left, the Daihatsu Charade Turbo. Below, from right to left, Subaru's mini Rex Combi Turbo, Nissan's updated Silvia/Gazelle range, and Daihatsu's turbo-boosted 1-liter triple.

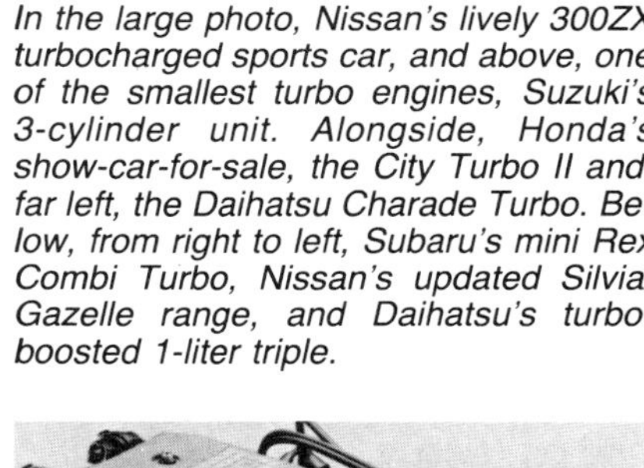

Nissan's VG, which is closely related to its Formula 2 winning engine. Other likely and unlikely V6 converts may include Toyota who has hitherto promoted single and twin cam inline sixes, and Mazda who has so far pinned its performance hopes on the rotary.

We have seen several examples of turbo models fitted with intercoolers further to tweak up their pressure-fed engines. Mitsubishi fitted one on its top Starion coupé models whose 2-liter single cam inline four puts out 175 hp. The company then introduced a Lancer turbo "Intercooler" turbo, an inconspicuous 4-door sedan with blistering performance from its 1.8-liter 160 hp engine. One of the more fervent turbo protagonists in Japan. Mitsubishi, who pioneered the recent micro (550 cc) turbo fad, has turned its attention to 4wd vehicles. It now offers the Pajeros (aka Shogun) with either diesel or gasoline turbo, the latter rated at 145 hp. Honda repeated its Tokyo Show stealing act with the City Turbo II, quickly dubbed "Bulldog" for its wide stance, chubby body and rather fierce appearance. Its 1.2-liter turbocharged fuel-injected engine puts out as much as 110 hp, thanks to the assistance of an air-to-air intercooler. Toyota was the first to adopt an intercooler — on its luxury tourer, the Soarer, powered by the faithful and sturdy type M single cam 2-liter six. Its application was later extended to a 2-liter turbo Celica XX (domestic Supra). The Number One Factory's forte however is a crop of twin cam engines, the latest count being four sizes in 4- and 6-cylinder configurations, that may have been joined by yet another version by the time this report goes to press. The latest type 4A-GEU, powering small and midsize cars including Corolla and Sprinter coupés, is a 1.6 liter inline four with 16 valves operated directly by bucket-type tappets. Like its senior 1G-GEU 2-liter six, it employs a variable induction system with two separate induction ducts for each cylinder, one of which is closed by a butterfly valve under low-load conditions, thus ensuring low- and mid-speed tractability and economy. This engine is produced at a rate of 10,000 a month in a mixed production line at Toyota's ultra-modern and highly automated Shimoyama Plant along with the lesser single cam 4A engines from which it derives.

The forthcoming midship Toyota, codenamed SV-3, will be powered by the 4A-GEU mounted transversely inline with transaxle. A new twin-cam engine, the 2S-GEU base on the 2-liter single cam 2S unit powering the Camry sedan; will most likely be used in the U.S. version of this sporting 2-seater. The SV-3 is something of a GM P-car or Pontiac Fiero, in that it borrows heavily from the corporate parts bins assigned to the new Corolla series cars. Its McPherson strut front suspension and rack-and-pinion steering are straight from the rwd Corolla while the power unit and rear suspension are obviously from the fwd Corolla as are the lower half of the 4A engine, complete transaxle and modified McPherson strut suspension. Creation of the SV-3, too, justified Toyota's rationale of having both front- and rear-wheel-drive Corollas. One of the biggest model changes of the year was indeed that of the Corolla and its Sprinter twin. As the Corolla and Sprinter are more clearly distinguished in appearance than ever, though sharing the same mechanicals, some consider there are actually four different cars. There are two basic lines. The rwd range consists of notchback and hatchback coupé bodies and thoroughly conventional mechanicals, with ubiquitous McPherson front struts and a rigid rear axle on coils. The type 4A-GEU twin cam 16-valve fuel injected four is the top engine offered in this range. Toyota insists that rwd dynamics are more suitable for cars of sporting ambitions. The twin-cam engine soars to seven thou' even in its severely detoxined form, and packs enough punch to bring the tail out smartly, so one has little to argue with in the rationale, specially when it is offered at an equivalent of US $ 6,000. The fwd Corolla is definitely more significant in design, engineering and marketing impact. It, too, comes in two body styles, notchback 4-door and hatchback 5-door sedans. Three gasoline-engine options are offered domestically, all in the A family light compact series featuring cogged belt-driven single overhead camshaft and wedge combustion chambers. Unique in the carbureted version, available in 1.3 and 1.5 liter sizes, is a dual intake port arrangement with a paddle-like swirl control valve in one of the passages. When closed, the port design creates powerful swirl in the charge that stabilizes and improves combustion. The top 1600 cc unit is a digital fuel injection version. Transmission options for the fwd series include an advanced electronically-controlled 4-speed lockup automatic that for performance and economy allows selection of three shift-pattern modes.

Industry observers expected those smart, refined and faster Corollas to take the Japanese small car market by storm. Statistics returned in three consecutive months belied expectations, much to the chagrin, dismay and outright despair of the mighty empire at No. 1, Toyota City. Corolla sales did not fall, but that was not honourable enough, especially when the Corolla was overtaken by offerings from Nos. 2 and 3, such as Nissan's Sunny (Sentra) and Mazda's Familia (GLC). One of the main reasons cited by a senior Toyota engineer for the car's lukewarm performance in the market-place was a lack of a 3-door hatchback model. This body type, as represented by Mazda's extremely popular Familia, had an almost 50% share of the small car class (roughly corresponding to the International C-segment). In fact, the great lil' Mazda was so overwhelmingly popular that a crop of look-alikes were released by rival factories, Nissan even going to the trouble of replacing one body style with another of similar configuration, the new one being deliberately made a "Ginza Familia".

In the small-car class, Mitsubishi carried out the first major change on its Mirage (Colt) series. As before, there are three

Utility vehicles are making a strong showing on the Japanese market this year. The three we are featuring on this page illustrate various interpretations on a theme. From top to bottom. Subaru's Domingo wagon features 3-row seating and has a new little 3-cylinder engine at the rear driving the rear or all four wheels, as the terrain demands. Daihatsu's stylish, powerful four-wheel-drive Rugger is soon to be launched – comfort is its hallmark. And finally, the PTX-1 prototype with its 50 cc engine, a powered shopping cart that is the ultimate in economy runabout proposals.

At the top of the page, Mitsubishi's multi-purpose wagon seats up to 7 passengers. Two centre photos: left, the midship-engined SV-3 sports car using power unit and chassis components from the Corolla series which Toyota is launching this year; right, Suzuki's Cultus 3-cylinder hatchback. Immediately above, Toyota's Corolla series has undergone its biggest model change in its fifth generation, joining the transverse engine, fwd brigade.

body styles, 3 and 5-door hatchbacks and 4-door notchback sedan. Mechanically the new series is an evolution of the predecessor, a transverse-engine, fwd car with fully-independent suspension by front McPherson struts and rear trailing arms. Engine options include 1.3 and 1.5 liter carbureted units, an electronically-controlled carburetor 1.5, a variable displacement 1.5 and a turbocharged fuel-injected 1.6. As in America, even though interest in diesels had somehow waned, major manufacturers continued to add more diesels, as "insurance for contingency", to quote to a senior industry executive. Mitsubishi developed a new 1.8 diesel for the revamped Mirage, while Toyota and Nissan offered compression ignition engine options in the fwd Corolla, Sunny and their twin and quadruple sister models.

Honda surprised them all by introducing four different body types on a common mechanical theme in the new-from-the-ground-up Civic/Ballade series. Honda is undoubtedly the most vocal and candid of an inscrutable race. The original Civic was a success story of the 'seventies, establishing itself as a world car of new dimensions. The Mk II Civic was more of an evolution, the design team endeavoring to improve and refine on it. Although commercially successful in the overall world market, the car had lost some of its original character and appeal, and, in its all-important home market, had been hard pressed by newer competitors, with the Mazda Familia cited as the most potent threat.

Now was the time for the Civic renaissance, declared Nobuhiko Kawamoto, engine-designer-prodigy-turned-senior-executive at Honda. The CR-X coupé heralded its arrival. It is a compact coupé of outstanding dynamic quality and economy ("Economy Fast" is it slogan) making extensive use of new recyclible plastic outer panels of Honda's own concoction. The car was quickly followed by another three distinctive body styles: a 4-door sedan, a 3-door hatchback (which, thank Buddha for once, did not look like a Mazda) whose rear seat could be slid back to create leg space comparable to a good-size intermediate (at a sacrifice of luggage space, or it could be the other way around, massive luggage space with less leg room), and a tall people and cargo hauler, the Shuttle 5-door hatchback. The CR-X and 4-door sedans were also offered as Ballades, the latter serving as the basis for the forthcoming BL Triumph Acclaim revamp. These cars all share common mechanicals, while riding on three different wheelbase lengths, but nothing has been carried over from the precedessor. The engine is a new single overhead cam 12-valve unit, similar in design to the senior Prelude/Accord unit, but having a lightweight aluminum cylinder block. Top domestic models get a 1.5 liter engine fitted with Honda's own electronic fuel injection with digital control and program map. For the economy minded, there are 1.3 liter versions, one of which attained a magic 52 mpg in the U.S. EPA rating. The chassis is also all new: the front McPherson strut suspension is a space-saver design with longitudinal torsion bar springs, and, after having had independent strut suspension for so long, Honda has adopted a lightweight tubular beam axle at the hind end. No, not a twist beam which may hinder providing a supple ride within a narrowish track constraint; Honda engineers have a free-swaying axle with an elaborate torque-tube stabilizer enclosed within the tube. The Civic endeavour was indeed a tour de force for this ambitious newcomer who aspired to greatness.

The mid-size car segment was also very active. Toyota again played a cautious hand by revamping the rwd Corona in the previous season, making sure conservative buyers would be catered for, and then introducing a handsome fwd 5-door hatchback, which was later followed by an equally pleasant 4-door notchback. In essence, the Corona FF is a shortened Camry with style (one thing the senior car lacks), powered by type 3A 1.5 and 1S 1.8 liter gasoline fours. Toyota has developed its own single-point fuel-injection system, and now offers it on certain 1.8 liter models, in addition to the individual port injection 1.8 EFI which is reserved for top models. There is also a diesel model in the range.

Nissan's approach was curious. The series U11 Bluebird is a brand-new transverse engine, a fwd convert, yet outwardly one would be hard put to tell it apart from its conventional predecessor. Perhaps Nissan product planners tried to attain with a single car what it took Toyota two Coronas to do. But so much money spent to achieve so little visible effect! Gasoline engines are from the CA compact lightweight group, in three displacement sizes ranging from the base 1.6 to full 2-liters, including an inevitable 1800 turbo. A 2-liter straight (not turbocharged) diesel is also available. Nissan has developed its own 4-speed lockup automatic that fits inline with the engine for the new series. Suspension is all independent, with McPherson struts fore and aft, a rear pair located by twin parallel transverse links and single trailing link. Shock absorbers that are manually adjustable by a twist of a console-mounted dial are optional on top models, and so is adjustable power-assisted steering. Nissan's latest electronic wonder is SDA (Safety Drive Adviser), an onboard analytic and warning system that memorizes the driver's normal steering habits in the first 10 minutes of a trip. Should it detect any unusual and potentially dangerous behavior when he/she becomes drowsy, it turns on warning light and emits a loud beep. The "Bird" in new feathers is a quantum leap over its staid predecessor in dynamics and comfort. If only the company had had a foresight to hire some designers and stylists... Don't forget that, Nissan also launched a domesticated VW, to be called by its European name of Santana, which in size and performance may crash head-on with top Bluebirds.

Another car of foreign origin, this one by courtesy of General Motors, was introduced to the Japan scene. The Isuzu Aska is a mid-class sedan based on the corporate J-car theme, available in a single body style as a 4-door sedan only. But this didn't stop Isuzu from offering a variety of power unit options of its own design and manufacture. A diesel specialist (63.4% of its sales were thus powered), even its new gasoline engines are derivatives of the diesel block. The most powerful is a 2-liter turbocharger

unit rated at 150 hp JIS, whose turbocharger wastegate is electronically controlled, providing extra boost when required. There are naturally diesel Askas, top versions fitted with turbocharger and intercooler.

Mitsubishi's Galant/Eterna Sigma has joined the rapidly expanding transverse engine, fwd brigade of small and mid-size cars. Aerodynamic drag coefficient numbers are fast diminishing. Anything over 0.4 just isn't respectable enough, the norm for a typical sedan now being of the order of 0.36 to 0.37. The Sigma, something of an ostentatious oriental Audi 100, has gotten down to Cd = 0.36, combined with low lift characteristics. The car is a generous 5-seater with cavernous luggage space. Mitsubishi's familiar MCA-Jet and silent shaft inline four gasoline engines power the Sigma, available in three sizes and four stages of tune, including electronically controlled carburetor and turbocharged fuel injection versions, the latter rated at 145 hp. On the luxury Royal version, the 2-liter engine with electronically controlled feed-back carburetor is located and checked by an electronically-controlled engine mount system, and drives the front wheels via electronically controlled 4-speed lockup automatic. Its suspension, by McPherson struts at the front and a twist beam axle at the rear augmented by adjustable shock absorbers and auxiliary air springs, is electronically controlled for roll, squat, drive and level. One of the electronically-controlled suspension's features is that the car lowers itself by an inch when its speed exceeds 90 km/h, further to reduce aerodynamic drag.

A basic form of "active suspension" had appeared only a year ago in Mazda's Capella/626 whose front shock absorbers are tautened at above certain preset vehicle speeds to add to straightline stability. Now several upper-middle and luxury cars feature more elaborate systems. Toyota's big (an American intermediate size) Crown has such a system, again employing auxiliary air chambers around the shock absorbers. Electronics is generously used in various performance and comfort functions, the top-of-the-range Royal sedan having no less than 68 bits in 11 microprocessors scattered around the sedan body. Its twin-cam fuel-injection engine and 4-speed automatic transmission with three shift modes are collectively managed by a 12-bit CPU (Central Processing Unit). A 4-bit processor regulates the self-levelling suspension. And the car features Japan's second electronically-controlled 4-wheel anti-skid brakes. The electronically-controlled airconditioner has a variable displacement 10-cylinder compressor, of which five are left idle in low-load conditions, thus conserving energy. Other

On the opposite page: above, Honda's tall Civic Shuttle 5-door hatchback and below, their 4-door sedan in Ballade guise. Above, this all-new Honda Ballade CR-X coupé heralded the Civic Renaissance, but all four cars shown here clearly come from the same mould.

electronic devices and features include a superb audio system (4-bit CPU), elaborate power seats with memory (4-bits) rear seats with built-in heater and vibrating massagers (4-bits), and directional and distance navigational aid (4- and 8-bit CPUs). Nissan's Cedric/Gloria twins, (archrivals of the Crown) have also been revamped and are now powered by the new type VG V6 engine. Among many electronic devices, they share with the Fairlady Z sports car the automatic wiper system that senses rain drops and adjusts its intermittent action to rain intensity.

On the lower echelons of the Japanese product scale are the small "One-liter" mini class and the "K" ("kei" is "light weight" in Japanese) 550 cc micro segments, which also saw some heated action in the season. One newcomer in the 1-litre class is Suzuki's Cultus hatchback sedan, powered by a transversely mounted aluminium 3-cylinder engine driving the front wheels that are sprung by the ubiquitous McPherson struts. Simplicity and low cost were clearly the Cultus design criteria, no doubt as specified by its American sponsor, General Motors, who will launch the car as a Chevrolet (GM R-car), as soon as a hopefully-amicable agreement is reached by all concerned on how much of the 1984 quota of 1.85 million cars is to be allocated to the mini runabout. The other new 1-liter mini is Subaru's Domingo, a "one-box" wagon with three rows of seats: it has a new 1-liter triple mounted in the rear overhang, driving either the rear wheels (base models), or the rear/four wheels. The power unit was moved to the front end of a new 3-door hatchback, again to be offered in both 2 and 4wd configurations.

Turbos and 4wd are the latest IN items in the extraordinary "K-class". The four K manufacturers, Mitsubishi, Daihatsu, Suzuki and Honda (Honda commercials only) all offer 4wd variants of micro cars, vans and trucks. The three car specialists have added turbo models, whose 550 cc motors now produce as much as 40 hp, thanks to sake cup sized turbochargers.

The year 1983 was again an extraordinary year for the Japanese industry, which has been growing and growing. Industry speakers, being a cautious lot, forecast a modest 1984. In the case of Toyota, a 3% growth rate is projected for the number of vehicles produced for sale on the home market or for export. If that number is modest, we can still look forward to more interesting features such as more valves per cylinder (one or two of them operating independently of the others), more camshafts, more cylinders, more wheels to be steered, as Mazda foreshadowed in its interesting MX-02 prototype with 4-wheel steering, and of course more CPUs and bits...

Designation used for Japanese models

As so many Japanese models are known by a different name in export markets from the one used in Japan, we feel that a list of nomenclature will be of use to our readers.

Japan	USA	UK
Daihatsu		
Mira and Cuore	—	Domino
Charade	—	Charade
Charmant	—	Charmant
Honda		
Civic/Ballade	Civic	Civic
Quint	—	Quintet
Accord/Vigor	Accord	Accord
Prelude	Prelude	Prelude
Isuzu		
Gemini	I-mark	—
Piazza	Impulse	—
Mazda		
Familia	GLC	323
Capella	626	626
Cosmo/Luce	—	929
Savanna RX7	RX7	RX7
Mitsubishi		
Mirage/ Lancer Fiore	Colt	Mirage
Lancer EX	—	Lancer
Galant/ Eterna Sigma	—	Galant
Galant/ Eterna Lambda	Saporo/ Challenger	Sapporo
Cordia	Cordia	Cordia
Tredia	Tredia	Tredia
Starion	Starion	Starion
Chariot	Dodge Colt Vista	—
Pajero	—	Shogun
Nissan		
March	—	Micra
Sunny	Sentra	Sunny
Pulsar	Pulsar	Cherry
Prairie	—	Prairie
Stanza/Auster	Stanza	Stanza
Bluebird	Maxima (6 cyl)	Bluebird
Laurel	—	Laurel
Skyline	—	—
Silvia/Gazelle	200SX	—
Fairlady Z	300ZX	300ZX
Cedric	—	280C
Safari 4WD	—	Patrol
Subaru		
Leone	Subaru	Subaru
Suzuki		
Alto/Fronte	—	Alto
Jimny 4WD	—	SJ
Toyota		
Starlet	Starlet	Starlet
Corolla/Sprinter	Corolla	Corolla
Sprinter/Carib	Corolla 4WD	Corolla 4WD
Corolla II/ Tercel/Corsa	Tercel	Tercel
Corona	—	—
Camry/Vista	Camry	Camry
Mark II/ Chaser	Cressida	Cressida
Carina	—	Carina
Celica	Celica	Celica
Celica XX	Celica Supra	Celica Supra
Crown	—	Crown
Landcruiser	Landcruiser	Landcruiser

United States of America

THE GIANT AWAKENS

by John McElroy

In many respects 1983 signaled a major turn-around for the American automotive industry. Since the first quarter of 1979, when the fall of the Shah of Iran precipitated an oil shortage and soaring prices, the industry had suffered through the worst downturn in its history. Overnight, market demand shifted to that segment where the American car companies were the least competitive: low cost, fuel-efficient compact cars.

Worse still, the domestic automakers were completely unprepared to compete with the high quality of the imports (mostly Japanese) which flooded the market. This crisis resulted in massive layoffs, plant closings and record losses. At its height, over a quarter of a million autoworkers were without jobs and many "company towns" saw their sole source of employment close permanently. Even General Motors, which never lost money during the Great Depression of the 1930s, posted its first red ink in over 60 years. All told, the automakers lost several billion dollars, to say nothing of the losses of the supplier companies. But for a variety of reasons last year signaled the end of the worst automotive recession on record. And for those who think that the American auto industry can't regain its number one position in the world, beware! The giant awakens.

The best measure of the industry's improved health is its return to profitability. Though 1983 domestic car sales were up about 17% over 1982, only about 7 million units were sold, which is not very good. Nonetheless, GM, Ford and Chrysler posted profits equal to or exceeding their all-time records of 1978. For their own part, the car companies have been able to slash costs drastically, primarily by cutting down the total number of people on the payroll, and also by holding down wages and sup-

Technical innovation is the hallmark of Pontiac's Fiero (above). Its bolt-on plastic body allows faster, more inexpensive styling changes than with steel body stampings. The interior offers ample leg and head room with radio speakers in the headrests. The Roadster (below) is for the future.

pliers' prices. In addition, the U.S. inflation rate (only 4% for the year) and lower interest rates helped to contain costs.

One part of the equation that caught everyone by surprise was the resurgence of large-car sales. These cars are more profitable, but they also caused GM and Ford to miss their federally-mandated Corporate Average Fuel Economy (CAFE) targets. Both companies have used up their carry-forward credits and only the prospect of potential carry-back credits that they might earn in the future prevented them from paying hundreds of millions of dollars in fines to the federal government. In fact, GM has already started a lobbying effort in Washington D.C. to lower the standard from 27.5 mph in 1985 to 26 mpg. However, the return of the full-size car reflected more than just stable gasoline prices. The type of customer that buys big cars and who had been out of the market for the last four years was largely responsible for the overall increase in sales. For these buyers, the large rear-wheel-drive (rwd) autos represent more car for the money than the smaller, more expensive fwd models designed to replace them.

Detroit still suffers from an overwhelming manufacturing cost disadvantage compared to the Japanese automakers. The latest estimates place the difference for a subcompact at over $ 2,000. But the domestic automakers have launched several programs designed to boost their productivity and efficiency. The most dramatic improvement has been their ability to adopt just-in-time inventory controls which has enabled them to cut their inventories by more than $ 3 billion since 1978. Statistical process controls and quality circles (called "Quality of Work Life" at GM and "Employees Involvement" at Ford) are other programs to boost productivity and quality.

Above, the new Oldsmobile Ninety-Eight Regency Brougham, shorter and lighter than the previous version, like all GM's new C-cars. Below, the Olds Tuned Induction Diesel, a high-performance concept car. Its engine power is boosted with a Helmholtz air induction system.

Buick has laid the groundwork for becoming internationally competitive with the new fwd B-cars (GM70) it will build for the 1986 model year. The basic philosophy of the program, which is called Buick City, is that labor/management cooperation will yield productivity benefits that will allow Buick to sell its automobiles and engines and transmission parts competitively on the world market. For an industry that has traditionally thought it could buy its way out of a problem with more automation, this represents a major change. On a broader scale, General Motors has begun its Saturn Project that it hopes will enable it to leapfrog the Japanese automakers on a quality and cost basis by the late 1980s. The Saturn project actually represents the largest single commitment of research and development efforts at GM and is intended to erase the $ 2,000 cost disadvantage in spite of higher American wages.

In the meantime, however, GM is hedging its bets with a number of projects with Japanese automakers. The most important of these is the joint venture with Toyota which will produce 200,000 fwd subcompacts (the Sprinter) annually for Chevrolet, using Japanese components and management systems in a Fremont, California assembly plant. When the plant opens, probably in the summer of 1985, GM will have a unique first-hand opportunity to study Toyota's techniques at close range. Of course, the GM/Toyota tie-up will also force Ford and Chrysler to seek out joint ventures of their own, something neither has been able to accomplish, but not for want of trying. Ford, which owns, 25% of Toyo Kogyo (Mazda), has reportedly approached them with an offer to use TK powertrain and suspension components in a subcompact to be assembled in the USA. Chrysler has approached Peugeot, in which it has a 5% interest, Mitsubishi (it owns 15%) and Volkswagen, with essentially the same type of proposal.

It is likely they will redouble their efforts when and if GM's Fremont operation actually gets under way. However, litigation by the competition may invalidate the agreement with Toyota or seriously delay its implementation. Another major GM gambit, still uncertain, is their plan to import the 300,000 mini cars it wants from Isuzu for Chevrolet.

Whether or not Isuzu and Suzuki will be able to export those cars is still in question because of the continuation of the "voluntary" quotas placed on the Japanese automakers. Though the limits were raised from 1.68 million to 1.82 million units and are slated to expire in April, 1985, some industry observers feel that permanent restrictions might be imposed at that time. Honda is the only Japanese automaker with an

American assembly plant and the additional 150,000 cars it produces here, combined with the cars imported, places its total anticipated American sales very close to Toyota's and Nissan's quota. Because of this, Nissan is reportedly looking to assemble cars in the US in addition to the pickup trucks it makes in Smyrna, Tennessee. And Toyo Kogyo is said to be looking for an assembly facility near Honda's plant in Marysville, Ohio.

All told, 1984 sees the introduction of the largest number new American models in recent memory. Of course, one has to bear in mind that some cars that are classified as 1984 models were actually introduced in the spring of 1983, such as the Chevrolet Chevette and Ford's Tempo and Topaz. But in any case, there are plenty of new models and a host of improvements on carry-over models worth writing about.

The most significant new car is undoubtedly Pontiac's Fiero. In fact, automotive journalists throughout the US and Canada selected the Fiero as the American Car of the Year in a poll organized by the Detroit Auto Writers Group. The Fiero breaks new ground in many aspects of design, engineering and manufacturing and has already sold out its first-year production allotment of 80,000 units. It is an $ 8,000 two-passenger, mid-engine sports car with plastic body panels bolted to a rolling chassis. This set-up will allow future design changes to be made quickly and inexpensively, and somewhere down the road we can expect to see a Fiero roadster. One interesting manufacturing technique used on the car is a mill-and-drill fixture which machines the chassis at various points so the body seams will have no more than a 2 mm tolerance variation. At present, the Fiero is powered by Pontiac's 92 hp 2.5 l 4-in-line engine and while it isn't underpowered it isn't exactly a tire burner, either. But what the car doesn't offer in acceleration it more than makes up with good handling and superb overall balance. In any case, the car is expected to get Chevrolet's 2.8 l V-6 engine for 1985 which will allow it to challenge many other higher-priced sports cars.

Elsewhere at GM the only new cars are the A-car station wagon models, available through every division except Cadillac. Though the new fwd C-cars (Cadillac De Ville, Olds 98 and Buick Electra) were supposed to have debuted at the beginning of the model year, they have been delayed until the spring because of automatic transmission problems. Due to this delay, Cadillac's only new introduction is the convertible Eldorado Biarritz. Oldsmobile has concentrated its 1984 efforts on limiting the emissions of its 4.3 V-6 diesel using microprocessor controls, since the 1985 diesel emission standards will become quite restrictive. But Olds also showed a high performance version of this engine in a concept car called the Tuned Induction Diesel. The engine develops 100 bhp at 3400 rpm with 185 lb/ft at 1600 rpm. In a Cutlass Ciera it delivers 33 mpg/city and 50 mpg/highway on the EPA cycle and runs from 0 to 60 mph in a little over 10 seconds.

Buick has also put its 1984 efforts into its 3.8 V6 engine. The most impressive version is designated SFI for Sequential Fuel Injection. This turbocharged engine develops 200 bhp and 300 lb/ft of torque and will be available on special versions of the Regal and Riviera. One particularly interesting aspect is that it has no distributor: instead, three interconnected coils send high voltage to the sparkplugs. Buick also has a naturally aspirated version of the 3.8 called MFI for Multi-port Fuel Injection, which will be available on all Buick Century and Olds Cutlass Ciera models. Both Buick and Pontiac will offer a 150 hp turbo version of Pontiac's 1.8 4-cylinder engine in their J-cars, the Skyhawk and 2000 Sunbird, respectively.

A fundamental restructuring of GM operations is in prospect according to Chairman Roger B. Smith. The familiar car names will remain but the Cadillac, Oldsmobile and Buick divisions will be consolidated into a single group primarily to market large cars while a second group for small-car sales will consist of Pontiac, Chevrolet and GM of Canada. All engineering will be centralized under a single hat in each of the two groups, as will design and manufacturing and it is expected that distinctive identities will emerge for the various makes which now

GM's new C-cars (Cadillac De Villes, Buick Electra and Oldsmobile Ninety-Eight) are also available in 2-door coupé versions. Above, the Eldorado Biarritz. Below, the Buick Electra T-type accelerates from 0-50 mph in 8.8 sec. Note the different hood, which is hinged from the front.

give evidence of too much inbreeding. Further, GM's streamlining will not only shrink the time lapse between idea and realized product, but will also accomplish economies through enhanced efficiency and elimination of duplication.

Chevrolet's 1984 improvements consist largely of its Celebrity Eurosport which comes with an upgraded suspension and understated trim and provides the car with more of an European flavor. In addition, the Cavalier gets a front-end facelift while the Camaro Berlinetta gets an electronic instrument panel that would makes an astronaut feel at home.

Ford's most important new models for 1984 are the Continental Mark VII and the SVO Mustang. The latter, which was developed by Ford's Special Vehicle Operations (SVO), can honestly be described as a world class GT car. It is powered by a turbocharged 2.3 4-cylinder engine that develops 175 bhp with the help of an intercooler and electronic boost control and is coupled to a 5-speed manual transmission. This propels it from 0 to 60 mph in less than 8 seconds with a top speed of about 134 mph. Better still, the car offers an overall balance that belies its heritage, and though the handling suffers from a solid rear axle, by mid-year it will get the quad rear shock absorbers used on the Mustang GT. The SVO Mustang has been so well received that Ford has been forced to double its planned production run to 16,000 units. As part of the SVO operation, Ford has introduced a turbocharged version of the EXP.

Top two photos, Ford's SVO Mustang and its 2.3 4-cylinder engine developing 175 bhp with turbocharger, intercooler and electronic boost control. Above, the Continental Mark VII featuring electronically-controlled air suspension. Below, the new Pontiac 6000 with backlite opening independently.

The Mark VII represents the most dramatic change in American luxury cars since the introduction of the original Cadillac Seville. The box is gone and in its place is a sleek, 5-passenger luxury touring coupé. Perhaps the most revolutionary aspect of the car is its suspension, called the Electronically Controlled Air Suspension (EAS). The system was developed with Goodyear and consists of four air springs, a compressor, three height sensors and a microprocessor, which work together to maintain a constant ride height. Essentially, the EAS provides the smaller Mark VII with the ride of its larger predecessors but with much better handling. Another first for this car, at least in the US, is its flush headlamps, which were made legal just in time for production. The Mark VII will also get a 2.4 6-cylinder turbo diesel made by BMW which is mated to a ZF automatic 4-speed transmission.

Chrysler's 1984 new model offerings include the Caravan and Voyager mini-vans and the Daytona and Laser sports coupés. The Caravan and Voyager are fwd vans and represent the first time in a long while that Chrysler has led GM or Ford into a new market segment rather than wait to see what they'd do. The vans are powered by a choice of 2.2 or 2.6 4-cylinder engines and offer 5-passenger or 7-passenger accommodation. There is also a windowless, panel version called the Dodge Mini Ram. For 1985 we can expect a turbo option and a stretched version of these vans. Chrysler is so sure that these vehicles will be a success that it is already looking for a second assembly plant to make them, which would raise the company's production capacity to 400,000 vans annually.

The Daytona and Laser are fwd 2+2 sports coupés that are powered by the 2.2 engine in turbocharged and naturally aspirated forms. One interesting aspect of the turbo engine from the standpoint of durability is that it has a water-cooled turbine end shaft bearing — the first on a US production car. A Turbo Z model of the Daytona is also offered with more aerodynamic detailing, including "ground-effect" spoilers that result in a .34 Cd.

American Motors has launched its most important new model line-up in years with its new sport wagons and the Renault Encore (R-11). The sport wagons, called the Cherokee and Wagoneer, are 4wd, 5-passenger vehicles that are powered by AMC's new 2.5 4-cylinder engine or an optional 2.8 V6 from Chevrolet. Unlike its direct competitors (Chevy's S-Blazer or Ford's Bronco II), the Wagoneer can be ordered with 4 doors. Perhaps the most amazing aspect of this launch is that AMC have produced two new sports utility vehicles and a new engine for only $ 250 million. Hopefully, these vehicles will be the ticket AMC needs to return to profitability because it has been losing money for a number of years now. The Encore, which is essentially a hatchback version of the Alliance (R-9), should provide AMC and Renault with a market different from the one for the Alliance. Considering the roaring success of the Alliance, that shouldn't be too difficult to achieve.

Volkswagen of America is struggling to regain its position having lost a serious amount of its market share in a very short time. The company is placing more of an emphasis on the teutonic heritage of the Rabbit (Golf), believing that most of its sales decline can be traced to the Americanization of the car. The Rabbit GTI certainly speaks well of VW's new effort and currently accounts for 25% of all of their American plant's production. Sales of the Rabbit have started to pick up slightly recently, but in the meantime, VW is relying on its German imports to keep its US dealers alive.

Looking to the future, we can expect to see the continued internationalization of the American market. With the federal government having rescinded the 5 mph bumper law and made the headlamp regulations more flexible, it now costs a lot less to convert a foreign-made car to US specifications. This will be particularly true if Germany and other European countries adopt American-style emission controls which require catalytic converters. In fact, Ford will import the Sierra XR4 (to be called the Merkur XR4Ti in the US) from Germany for the 1985 model year and the Granada in 1986. Chrysler is contemplating importing a mid-engined sports car to be made by De Tomaso in Italy. And Cadillac may have a high-priced specialty car designed in Italy, but built in America.

On the other hand, if the American car companies are successful in achieving the productivity and quality standards they have set themselves, and if the dollar should settle to a somewhat more realistic exchange rate, don't be surprised to see the US automakers casting a covetous look at export markets of their own.

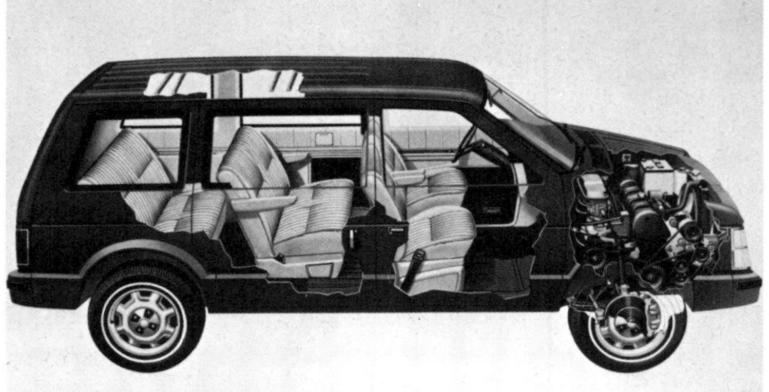

A new market segment is developing in the USA – mini vans and jeeps. Above, the Plymouth Voyager – the cutaway shows the fwd transverse engine layout and seating for seven. Left, the Jeep Wagoneer, AMC's major product innovation with 4wd, available with their new 2.5 litre 4-cylinder engine. Below left, the Dodge Caravan, a 5- or 7-seater on a 112 inch wheelbase. Immediately below, Dodge Truck's mini Ram Van which has great conversion possibilities. Though handling a 1,700 lb payload with ease, it is lightweight, aerodynamic, fuel-efficient, spacious and manoeuvrable.

Europe

Models now in production

Illustrations and technical information

CUSTOCA — AUSTRIA

Hurrycane

PRICE EX WORKS: 170,000 schillings

ENGINE Volkswagen, rear, 4 stroke; 4 cylinders, horizontally opposed; 96.7 cu in, 1,584 cc (3.37 x 2.72 in, 85.5 x 69 mm); max power (DIN): 50 hp (37 kW) at 4,000 rpm; max torque (DIN): 78 lb ft, 10.8 kg m (106 Nm) at 2,800 rpm; 31.6 hp/l (23.2 kW/l).

PERFORMANCE max speeds: (I) 22 mph, 35 km/h; (II) 47 mph, 75 km/h; (III) 68 mph, 110 km/h; (IV) 96 mph, 155 km/h; power-weight ratio: 30.9 lb/hp (41.9 lb/kW), 14 kg/hp (19 kg/kW); acceleration: standing ¼ mile 12.5 sec; consumption: 23.5 m/imp gal, 19.6 m/US gal, 12 l x 100 km.

STEERING turns lock to lock: 2.50.

ELECTRICAL EQUIPMENT 12 V; 4 headlamps.

DIMENSIONS AND WEIGHT wheel base: 94.49 in, 240 cm; tracks: 55.12 in, 140 cm front, 55.91 in, 142 cm rear; length: 171.26 in, 435 cm; width: 67.72 in, 172 cm; height: 44.09 in, 112 cm; ground clearance: 6.30 in, 16 cm; weight: 1,544 lb, 700 kg; weight distribution: 46% front, 54% rear; turning circle: 41 ft, 12.5 m; fuel tank: 9.2 imp gal, 11.1 US gal, 42 l.

BODY coupé, in plastic material; 2 doors; 2+2 seats.

PRACTICAL INSTRUCTIONS tyre pressure: front 19 psi, 1.2 atm, rear 22 psi, 1.5 atm.

CUSTOCA Hurrycane

Strato 80 ES / Taifun

See Hurrycane, except for:

PRICES EX WORKS:	**schillings**
Strato 80 ES 2-dr Coupé	**180,000**
Taifun 2-dr Coupé	**180,000**

PERFORMANCE power-weight ratio: 30 lb/hp (40.7 lb/kW), 13.6 kg/hp (18.5 kg/kW).

DIMENSIONS AND WEIGHT length: 164.57 in, 418 cm; width: 62.99 in, 160 cm; weight: 1,499 lb, 680 kg.

LEDL — AUSTRIA

AS 130

PRICE EX WORKS: 214,634* schillings

ENGINE Ford, centre-rear, transverse, 4 stroke; 4 cylinders, in line; 79.2 cu in, 1,297 cc (3.19 x 2.48 in, 81 x 63 mm); compression ratio: 9.2:1; max power (DIN): 66 hp (49 kW) at 5,600 rpm; max torque (DIN): 70 lb ft, 9.6 kg m (94 Nm) at 3,250 rpm; max engine rpm: 6,000; 50.8 hp/l (37.9 kW/l); cast iron block and head; 3 crankshaft bearings; valves: overhead, in line, push-rods and rockers; camshafts: 1, side, chain-driven; lubrication: gear pump, full flow filter, 5.6 imp pt, 6.8 US pt, 3.2 l; 1 Weber downdraught single barrel carburettor; fuel feed: mechanical pump; semi-sealed circuit cooling, expansion tank, 10.9 imp pt, 13.1 US pt, 6.2 l.

TRANSMISSION driving wheels: rear; clutch: single dry plate (diaphragm); gearbox: mechanical; gears: 4, fully synchronized; ratios: I 3.583, II 2.050, III 1.346, IV 0.959, rev 3.769; lever: central; final drive: spiral bevel; axle ratio: 3.840; width of rims: 6" front, 7" rear; tyres: 185/60 HR x 13 front, 205/60 HR x 13 rear.

PERFORMANCE max speed: 109 mph, 176 km/h; power-weight ratio: 28.4 lb/hp (38.2 lb/kW), 12.9 kg/hp (17.3 kg/kW); carrying capacity: 661 lb, 300 kg; speed in top at 1,000 rpm: 19.9 mph, 32 km/h; consumption: 37.7 m/imp gal, 31.4 m/US gal, 7.5 l x 100 km.

CHASSIS integral; front suspension: independent, by McPherson, coil springs/telescopic damper struts, lower wishbones (trailing links); rear: independent, lower wishbones, trailing radius arms, anti-roll bar, coil springs, telescopic dampers.

STEERING rack-and-pinion.

BRAKES disc, dual circuit, servo.

ELECTRICAL EQUIPMENT 12 V; 43 Ah battery; 540 W alternator; Motorcraft distributor; 4 halogen headlamps, 2 retractable.

DIMENSIONS AND WEIGHT wheel base: 93.90 in, 238 cm; tracks: 56.69 in, 140 cm front, 56.26 in, 143 cm rear; length: 164.17 in, 417 cm; width: 67.32 in, 171 cm; height: 42.91 in, 109 cm; ground clearance: 6.30 in, 16 cm; weight: 1,874 lb, 850 kg; weight distribution: 42% front, 58% rear; turning circle: 34.8 ft, 10.6 m; fuel tank: 12.8 imp gal, 15.3 US gal, 58 l.

BODY coupé, in plastic material; 2 doors; 2 seats, separate front seats.

PRACTICAL INSTRUCTIONS fuel: 98 oct petrol; oil: engine 4.8 imp pt, 5.7 US pt, 2.7 l, SAE 20W-50, change every 6,200 miles, 10,000 km - gearbox and final drive 3.9 imp pt, 4.7 US pt, 2.2 l, SAE 80, change every 18,600 miles, 30,000 km; greasing: none; spark plug: Motorcraft AGR 12; tappet clearances: inlet 0.009 in, 0.25 mm, exhaust 0.022 in, 0.56 mm; tyre pressure: front 20 psi, 1.4 atm, rear 24 psi, 1.7 atm.

OPTIONALS light alloy wheels.

AS 160

See AS 130, except for:

PRICE EX WORKS: 235,647* schillings

ENGINE 95 cu in, 1,597 cc (3.15 x 3.13 in, 80 x 79.5 mm); compression ratio: 9.2:1; max power (DIN): 96 hp (71 kW) at 6,000 rpm; max torque (DIN): 98 lb ft, 13.5 kg m (132 Nm) at 4,000 rpm; max engine rpm: 6,250; 60 hp/l (44.5 kW/l); light alloy head; valves: overhead, transverse, hydraulic tappets, CVH (compound valve hemispherical); camshafts: 1, overhead, cogged belt; 1 Weber DFT downdraught twin barrel carburettor; cooling: 12.1 imp pt, 14.6 US pt, 6.9 l, electric thermostatic fan.

TRANSMISSION gearbox ratios: I 3.150, II 1.910, III 1.270, IV 0.950, rev 3.610.

PERFORMANCE max speed: 129 mph, 207 km/h; power-weight ratio: 19.5 lb/hp (26.4 lb/kW), 8.9 kg/hp (12 kg/kW); consumption: 29.7 m/imp gal, 24.8 m/US gal, 9.5 l x 100 km.

ELECTRICAL EQUIPMENT electronic ignition.

APAL — BELGIUM

Speedster

ENGINE Volkswagen, rear, 4 stroke; 4 cylinders, horizontally opposed; 96.7 cu in, 1,584 cc (3.37 x 2.72 in, 85.5 x 69 mm); compression ratio: 8.5:1; max power (DIN): 50 hp (37 kW) at 3,500 rpm; max torque (DIN): 78 lb ft, 10.8 kg m (106 Nm) at 2,800 rpm; max engine rpm: 4,600; 31.6 hp/l (23.3 kW/l); block with cast iron liners and light alloy fins, light alloy head; 4 crankshaft bearings; valves: overhead, push-rods and rockers; camshafts: 1, central, lower; lubrication: gear pump, filter in sump, oil cooler, 4.4 imp pt, 5.3 US pt, 2.5 l; 1 Solex 1661 downdraught single barrel carburettors; fuel feed: mechanical pump; air-cooled.

TRANSMISSION driving wheels: rear; clutch: single dry plate; gearbox: mechanical; gears: 4, fully synchronized; ratios: I 3.780, II 2.060, III 1.260, IV 0.930, rev 4.010; lever:

LEDL AS 130 - AS 160

APAL Speedster

central; final drive: spiral bevel; axle ratio: 3.875; width of rims: 5.5"; tyres: 175/70 SR x 15.

PERFORMANCE max speed: 96 mph, 155 km/h; power-weight ratio: 34.6 lb/hp (46.7 lb/kW), 15.7 kg/hp (21.2 kg/kW); consumption: 33.6 m/imp gal, 28 m/US gal, 8.4 l x 100 km.

CHASSIS box-section perimeter frame; front suspension: independent, twin swinging longitudinal trailing arms, transverse laminated torsion bars, anti-roll bar, telescopic dampers; rear: independent, swinging semi-axles, swinging longitudinal trailing arms, transverse torsion bars, telescopic dampers.

STEERING worm and roller.

BRAKES drum; lining area: total 111 sq in, 716 sq cm.

ELECTRICAL EQUIPMENT 12 V; 36 Ah battery; alternator; Bosch distributor; 2 headlamps.

DIMENSIONS AND WEIGHT wheel base: 83.86 in, 213 cm; tracks: 51.57 in, 131 cm front, 53.15 in, 135 cm rear; length: 154.72 in, 393 cm; width: 66.14 in, 168 cm; height: 49.61 in, 126 cm; weight: 1,731 lb, 785 kg; weight distribution: 41% front, 59% rear; fuel tank: 5.9 imp gal, 7 US gal, 27 l.

BODY roadster in fiberglass material; 2 doors; 2 seats; tonneau cover.

OPTIONALS leather upholstery; hardtop.

ŠKODA 105 S

ŠKODA — CZECHOSLOVAKIA

105 S

PRICE IN GB: £ 2,378*

ENGINE rear, 4 stroke; 4 cylinders, slanted 30° to right, in line; 63.8 cu in, 1,046 cc (2.68 x 2.83 in, 68 x 72 mm); compression ratio: 8.5:1; max power (DIN): 46 hp (34 kW) at 4,800 rpm; max torque (DIN): 55 lb ft, 7.6 kg m (74 Nm) at 3,000 rpm; max engine rpm: 5,200; 43.2 hp/l (31.8 kW/l); light alloy block, cast iron head, wet liners; 3 crankshaft bearings; valves: overhead, in line, push-rods and rockers; camshafts: 1, side; lubrication: gear pump, full flow filter, 7 imp pt, 8,5 US pt, 4 l; 1 Jikov 32 EDSR downdraught twin barrel carburettor; fuel feed: mechanical pump; water-cooled, front radiator, 20.2 imp pt, 24.3 US pt, 11.5 l.

TRANSMISSION driving wheels: rear; clutch: single dry plate, hydraulically controlled; gearbox: mechanical; gears: 4, fully synchronized; ratios: I 3.800, II 2.120, III 1.410, IV 0.960, rev 3.270; lever: central; final drive: spiral bevel; axle ratio: 4.222; width of rims: 4.5"; tyres: 165 SR x 13.

PERFORMANCE max speeds: (I) 20 mph, 32 km/h; (II) 35 mph, 57 km/h; (III) 54 mph, 87 km/h; (IV) 81 mph, 130 km/h; power-weight ratio: 41 lb/hp (55.6 lb/kW), 18.6 kg/hp (25.2 kg/kW); carrying capacity: 882 lb, 400 kg; speed in top at 1,000 rpm: 16.5 mph, 26.5 km/h; consumption: 44.8 m/imp gal, 37.3 m/US gal, 6.3 l x 100 km at 56 mph, 90 km/h.

CHASSIS integral; front suspension: independent, wishbones, coil springs, anti-roll bar, telescopic dampers; rear: independent, swinging semi-axles, swinging longitudinal leading arms, coil springs, telescopic dampers.

STEERING screw and nut; turns lock to lock: 2.50.

BRAKES front disc (diameter 9.92 in, 25.2 cm), rear drum, vacuum servo; lining area: front 11.8 sq in, 76 sq cm, rear 59.7 sq in, 385 sq cm, total 71.5 sq in, 461 sq cm.

ELECTRICAL EQUIPMENT 12 V; 37 Ah battery; 588 W alternator; Pal distributor; 2 headlamps.

DIMENSIONS AND WEIGHT wheel base: 94.49 in, 240 cm; tracks: 54.72 in, 139 cm front, 53.15 in, 135 cm rear; length: 165.35 in, 420 cm; width: 63.39 in, 161 cm; height: 55.12 in, 140 cm; ground clearance: 5.71 in, 14.5 cm; weight: 1,885 lb, 855 kg; weight distribution: 38.6% front, 61.4% rear; turning circle: 36.1 ft, 11 m; fuel tank: 7.9 imp gal, 9.5 US gal, 36 l.

BODY saloon/sedan; 4 doors; 5 seats, separate front seats.

PRACTICAL INSTRUCTIONS fuel: 90 oct petrol; oil: engine 7 imp pt, 8.5 US pt, 4 l, SAE 10W-50, change every 6,200 miles, 10,000 km - gearbox and final drive 4.4 imp pt, 5.3 US pt, 2.5 l, SAE 90, change every 24,900 miles, 40,000 km; greasing: every 6,200 miles, 10,000 km, 2 points; spark plug: PAL super N7Y; tappet clearances: inlet 0.006 in, 0.15 mm, exhaust 0.08 in, 0.20 mm; valve timing: 14°30' 45°30' 40°10' 13°30'; tyre pressure: front 23 psi, 1.6 atm, rear 30 psi, 2.1 atm.

OPTIONALS radial tyres; laminated windscreen.

105 L

See 105 S, except for:

PERFORMANCE power-weight ratio: 41.9 lb/hp (56.9 lb/kW), 19 kg/hp (25.8 kg/kW).

DIMENSIONS AND WEIGHT weight: 1,929 lb, 875 kg; weight distribution: 38.9% front, 61.1% rear.

OPTIONALS halogen headlamps.

120 L

See 105 S, except for:

PRICE IN GB: £ 2,509*

ENGINE 71.6 cu in, 1,174 cc (2.83 x 2.83 in, 72 x 72 mm); max power (DIN): 52 hp (38 kW) at 5,000 rpm; max torque (DIN): 63 lb ft, 8.7 kg m (85 Nm) at 3,000 rpm; max engine rpm: 5,400; 44.3 hp/l (32.6 kW/l).

PERFORMANCE speeds: (I) 21 mph, 33 km/h; (II) 37 mph, 60 km/h; (III) 56 mph, 90 km/h; (IV) 87 mph, 140 km/h: power-weight ratio: 37.1 lb/hp (50.4 lb/kW), 16.8 kg/hp (22.8 kg/kW); consumption: 44.1 m/imp gal, 36.8 m/US gal, 6.4 l x 100 km at 56 mph, 90 km/h.

STEERING rack-and-pinion; turns lock to lock: 3.80.

BRAKES servo.

DIMENSIONS AND WEIGHT weight: 1,929 lb, 875 kg; weight distribution: 38.9% front, 61.1% rear.

OPTIONALS laminated windscreen; radial tyres; halogen headlamps.

120 LS

See 105 S, except for:

PRICE IN GB: £ 2,889*

ENGINE 71.6 cu in, 1,174 cc (2.83 x 2.83 in, 72 x 72 mm); compression ratio: 9.5:1; max power (DIN): 58 hp (43 kW) at 5,200 rpm; max torque (DIN): 67 lb ft, 9.2 kg m (90 Nm) at 3,500 rpm; max engine rpm: 5,500; 49.4 hp/l (36.2 kW/l); lubrication: oil cooler, 8.1 imp pt, 9.7 US pt, 4.6 l.

PERFORMANCE max speed: 93 mph, 150 km/h; power-weight ratio: 33.7 lb/hp (45.6 lb/kW), 15.3 kg/hp (20.7 kg/kW); consumption: 43.5 m/imp gal, 36.2 m/US gal, 6.5 l x 100 km at 56 mph, 90 km/h.

STEERING rack-and-pinion; turns lock to lock: 3.80.

BRAKES servo.

ELECTRICAL EQUIPMENT 770 W alternator.

DIMENSIONS AND WEIGHT weight: 1,951 lb, 885 kg; weight distribution: 39% front, 61% rear.

PRACTICAL INSTRUCTIONS fuel: 96 oct petrol; oil: engine 8.1 imp pt, 9.7 US pt, 4.6 l; tappet clearances: inlet and exhaust 0.008 in, 0.20 mm.

OPTIONALS laminated windscreen; radial tyres; halogen headlamps; tachometer.

ŠKODA 120 LS

120 GLS

See 105 S, except for:

PRICE IN GB: £ 3,148*

ENGINE 71.6 cu in, 1,174 cc (2.83 x 2.83 in, 72 x 72 mm); compression ratio: 9.5:1; max power (DIN): 58 hp (43 kW) at 5,200 rpm; max torque (DIN): 67 lb ft, 9.2 kg m (90 Nm) at 3,500 rpm; max engine rpm: 5,500; 49.4 hp/l (36.2 kW/l); lubrication: oil cooler, 8.1 imp pt, 9.7 US pt, 4.6 l.

PERFORMANCE max speed: 93 mph, 150 km/h; power-weight ratio: 33.7 lb/hp (45.6 lb/kW), 15.3 kg/hp (20.7 kg/kW); consumption: 43.5 m/imp gal, 36.2 m/US gal, 6.5 l x 100 km at 56 mph, 90 km/h.

STEERING rack-and-pinion; turns lock to lock: 3.80.

BRAKES servo.

ELECTRICAL EQUIPMENT 770 W alternator.

DIMENSIONS AND WEIGHT weight: 1,962 lb, 890 kg; weight distribution: 38.2% front, 61.8% rear.

PRACTICAL INSTRUCTIONS fuel: 96 oct petrol; oil: engine 8.1 imp pt, 9.7 US pt, 4.6 l; tappet clearances: inlet and exhaust 0.008 in, 0.20 mm.

OPTIONALS laminated windscreen; radial tyres; halogen headlamps; tachometer.

ŠKODA Rapid

Rapid

See 105 S, except for:

PRICE IN GB: £ 3,388*

ENGINE 71.6 cu in, 1,174 cc (2.83 x 2.83 in, 72 x 72 mm); compression ratio: 9.5:1; max power (DIN): 58 hp (43 kW) at 5,200 rpm; max torque (DIN): 67 lb ft, 9.2 kg m (90 Nm) at 3,250 rpm; max engine rpm: 5,500; 49.4 hp/l (36.2 kW/l).

PERFORMANCE max speeds: (I) 22 mph, 35 km/h; (II) 39 mph, 62 km/h; (III) 58 mph, 94 km/h; (IV) 95 mph, 153 km/h; power-weight ratio: 34.8 lb/hp (47 lb/kW), 15.8 kg/hp (21.3 kg/kW); carrying capacity: 706 lb, 320 kg; consumption: 47.1 m/imp gal, 39.2 m/US gal, 6 l x 100 km at 56 mph, 90 km/h.

CHASSIS rear suspension; independent, trailing arms, coil springs, telescopic dampers.

STEERING rack-and-pinion; turns lock to lock: 3.80.

BRAKES lining area: front 18 sq in, 116 sq cm, rear 59.7 sq in, 385 sq cm, total 77.7 sq in, 501 sq cm.

ELECTRICAL EQUIPMENT 770 W alternator.

DIMENSIONS AND WEIGHT tracks: 51.97 in, 132 cm front, 50.79 in, 129 cm rear; length: 164.17 in, 417 cm; height: 54.35 in, 138 cm; ground clearance: 6.30 in, 16 cm; weight: 2,018 lb, 915 kg.

BODY coupé; 2 doors; 2+2 seats, separate front seats; heated rear window; (standard) radial tyres and laminated windscreen.

PRACTICAL INSTRUCTIONS fuel: 96 oct petrol; spark plug: PAS super N8Y; tappet clearances: inlet 0.008 in, 0.20 mm, exhaust 0.008 in, 0.20 mm.

TATRA CZECHOSLOVAKIA

T 613-2

ENGINE rear, 4 stroke; 8 cylinders in Vee; 213.3 cu in, 3,495 cc (3.35 x 3.03 in, 85 x 77 mm); compression ratio: 9.2:1; max power (DIN): 165 hp (121 kW) at 5,200 rpm; max torque (DIN): 196 lb ft, 27 kg m (265 Nm) at 2,500 rpm; max engine rpm: 5,600; 47.2 hp/l (34.7 kW/l); light alloy block and head; 5 crankshaft bearings; valves: overhead, Vee-slanted, rockers; camshafts: 2, 1 per bank, overhead; lubrication: gear pump, full flow filter (cartridge), oil cooler, 16.7 imp pt, 20.1 US pt, 9.5 l; 2 Jikov EDSR 32/24 downdraught twin barrel carburettors; fuel feed: mechanical pump; air-cooled.

TRANSMISSION driving wheels: rear; clutch: single dry plate, hydraulically controlled; gearbox: mechanical; gears: 4, fully synchronized; ratios: I 3.394, II 1.889, III 1.165, IV 0.862, rev 3.243; lever: central; final drive: hypoid bevel; axle ratio: 3.909; width of rims: 6"; tyres: 215/70 HR x 14.

PERFORMANCE max speeds: (I) 29 mph, 47 km/h; (II) 53 mph, 85 km/h; (III) 86 mph, 138 km/h; (IV) 118 mph, 190 km/h; power-weight ratio: 21.4 lb/hp (29.1 lb/kW), 9.7 kg/hp (13.2 kg/kW); carrying capacity: 1,036 lb, 470 kg; speed in top at 1,000 rpm: 22.2 mph, 35.8 km/h; consumption: 26.6 m/imp gal, 22.2 m/US gal, 10.6 l x 100 km at 56 mph, 90 km/h.

CHASSIS integral; front suspension: independent, by McPherson, wishbones, coil springs, anti-roll bar, telescopic dampers; rear: independent, swinging semi-axle, swinging longitudinal trailing arms, coil springs, telescopic dampers.

STEERING rack-and-pinion, damper; turns lock to lock: 4.25.

BRAKES disc, servo; lining area: front 30.7 sq in, 198 sq cm, rear 21.1 sq in, 136 sq cm, total 51.8 sq in, 334 sq cm.

ELECTRICAL EQUIPMENT 12 V; 75 Ah or 2 x 6 V batteries; 55 A alternator; PAL Magneton; electronic ignition; 4 headlamps, 2 iodine fog lamps.

DIMENSIONS AND WEIGHT wheel base: 117.72 in, 299 cm; tracks: 59.45 in, 151 cm front, 60 in, 152 cm rear; length: 196.85 in, 500 cm; width: 71 in, 180 cm; height: 56.69 in, 144 cm; ground clearance: 6.30 in, 16 cm; weight: 3,528 lb, 1,600 kg; weight distribution: 43% front, 57% rear; turning circle: 41 ft, 12.5 m; fuel tank: 15.8 imp gal, 19 US gal, 72 l.

BODY saloon/sedan; 4 doors; 5 seats, separate front seats, reclining backrests, built-in headrests.

PRACTICAL INSTRUCTIONS fuel: 96 oct petrol; oil: engine 16.7 imp pt, 20.1 US pt, 9.5 l, SAE 20W-50, change every 6,200 miles, 10,000 km - gearbox 3.5 imp pt, 4.2 US pt, 2 l, SAE 90, change every 18,600 miles, 30,000 km - final drive 1.8 imp pt, 2.1 US pt, 1 l, SAE 90, change every 6,200 miles, 10,000 km; greasing: none; spark plug: 200°; tappet clearances: inlet 0.004 in, 0.10 mm, exhaust 0.004 in, 0.10 mm; valve timing: 10° 32° 32° 10°; tyre pressure: front 24 psi, 1.7 atm, rear 33 psi, 2.3 atm.

T 613-2 Special

See T 613-2, except for:

TRANSMISSION tyres: 205/70 HR x 14.

PERFORMANCE power-weight ratio: 24.7 lb/hp (33.5 lb/kW), 11.2 kg/hp (15.2 kg/kW); carrying capacity: 838 lb, 380 kg; speed in top at 1,000 rpm: 21.7 mph, 34.9 km/h; consumption: 17.9 m/imp gal, 14.9 m/US gal, 15.8 l x 100 km.

STEERING ZF servo; turns lock to lock: 3.80.

ELECTRICAL EQUIPMENT 4 iodine headlamps.

DIMENSIONS AND WEIGHT wheel base: 123.23 in, 313 cm; length: 203.94 in, 518 cm; weight: 4,057 lb, 1,840 kg; weight distribution: 43.7% front, 56.3% rear.

BODY 4 seats; electric windows; heated rear window; telephone; speed control; air-conditioning.

PRACTICAL INSTRUCTIONS tyre pressure: front 18 psi, 1.3 atm, rear 38 psi, 2.7 atm.

ALPINE RENAULT FRANCE

A 310 V6

PRICE EX WORKS: 140,860 francs**

ENGINE Renault, rear, 4 stroke; 6 cylinders, Vee-slanted at 90°; 162.6 cu in, 2,664 cc (3.46 x 2.87 in, 88 x 73 mm); compression ratio: 10.1:1; max power (DIN): 150 hp (108 kW) at 6,000 rpm; max torque (DIN): 151 lb ft, 20.8 kg m (204 Nm) at 3,500 rpm; max engine rpm: 6,200; 56.3 hp/l (40.5 kW/l); light alloy block and head, wet liners, hemispherical combustion chambers; 4 crankshaft bearings; valves: overhead, Vee-slanted, rockers; camshafts: 2, 1 per bank, overhead; lubrication: gear pump, full flow filter, 10 imp pt, 12 US pt, 5.7 l; 1 Solex 34 TBIA downdraught single barrel carburettor and 1 Solex 35 CEEI downdraught twin barrel carburettor; fuel feed: electric pump; sealed circuit cooling, expansion tank, liquid, 21.1 imp pt, 25.4 US pt, 12 l, viscous coupling thermostatic fan.

TRANSMISSION driving wheels: rear; clutch: single dry plate (diaphragm), hydraulically controlled; gearbox: mechanical; gears: 5, fully synchronized; ratios: I 3.364, II 2.059, III 1.318, IV 1.057, V 0.868, rev 3.182; lever: central; final drive: hypoid bevel; axle ratio: 3.444; width of rims: 5" front, 7.5" rear; tyres: 190/55 VR x 13 front, 220/55 VR x 14 rear.

PERFORMANCE max speeds: (I) 39 mph, 62 km/h; (II) 63 mph, 102 km/h; (III) 95 mph, 152 km/h; (IV) 123 mph, 198 km/h; (V) over 140 mph, 225 km/h; power-weight ratio: 15 lb/hp (20.8 lb/kW), 6.8 kg/hp (9.4 kg/kW); carrying capacity: 717 lb, 325 kg; acceleration: standing ¼ mile 15 sec; speed in top at 1,000 rpm: 23 mph, 37.1 km/h; consumption: 32.5 m/imp gal, 27 m/US gal, 8.7 l x 100 km at 75 mph, 120 km/h.

CHASSIS integral, central steel backbone; front suspension: independent, wishbones, rubber elements, coil springs, anti-roll bar, telescopic dampers; rear: independent, wishbones, coil springs, anti-roll bar, telescopic dampers.

STEERING rack-and-pinion; turns lock to lock: 3.60.

BRAKES disc (diameter 10.2 in, 26 cm), front internal radial fins, dual circuit, rear compensator, servo; lining area: front 27.9 in, 180 sq cm, rear 27.9 sq in, 180 sq cm, total 55.8 sq in, 360 sq cm.

ELECTRICAL EQUIPMENT 12 V; 50 Ah battery; 50 A alternator; transistorized ignition; 4 headlamps.

DIMENSIONS AND WEIGHT wheel base: 89.37 in, 227 cm; tracks: 55.51 in, 141 cm front, 56.30 in, 143 cm rear; length: 167.32 in, 425 cm; width: 64.96 in, 165 cm; height: 45.28 in, 115 cm; ground clearance: 6.30 in, 16 cm; weight: 2,245 lb, 1,018 kg; turning circle: 34.8 ft, 10.6 m; fuel tank: 13.6 imp gal, 16.4 US gal, 62 l.

TATRA T 613-2

ALPINE RENAULT A 310 V6

CITROËN 2 CV 6 Charleston Berline

BODY coupé, in plastic material; 2 doors; 2+2 seats, separate front seats, reclining backrests; light alloy wheels; electric windows; heated rear window.

PRACTICAL INSTRUCTIONS fuel: 98-100 oct petrol; oil: engine 10 imp pt, 12 US pt, 5.7 l, SAE 10W-30, change every 4,650 miles, 7,500 km - gearbox 1.8 imp pt, 2.1 US pt, 1 l, SAE 80, change every 9,300 miles, 15,000 km - final drive 6.5 imp pt, 7.8 US pt, 3.7 l, SAE 80, change every 9,300 miles, 15,000 km; tappet clearances: inlet 0.004-0.006 in, 0.10-0.15 mm, exhaust 0.010-0.012 in, 0.25-0.30 mm; valve timing: 9° 45° 45° 9° (left), 7° 43° 43° 7° (right); tyre pressure: front 21 psi, 1.5 atm, rear 28 psi, 2 atm.

OPTIONALS air-conditioning; tinted glass; leather upholstery; metallic spray; Grand Tourisme equipment.

CITROËN FRANCE

2 CV 6

PRICES IN GB AND EX WORKS:	£	francs
Spécial 4-dr Berline	**2,499***	**28,280****
Club 4-dr Berline	**2,798***	**32,000****
Charleston 4-dr Berline	**2,949***	**32,880****

ENGINE front, 4 stroke; 2 cylinders, horizontally opposed; 36.7 cu in, 602 cc (2.91 x 2.76 in, 74 x 70 mm); compression ratio: 8.5:1; max power (DIN): 29 hp (21 kW) at 5,750 rpm; max torque (DIN): 29 lb ft, 4 kg m (39 Nm) at 3,500 rpm; max engine rpm: 5,900; 48.2 hp/l (35.4 kW/l); light alloy block and head, dry liners, light alloy sump, hemispherical combustion chambers; 2 crankshaft bearings; valves: overhead, Vee-slanted at 70°, push-rods and rockers; camshafts: 1, central, lower; lubrication: rotary pump, filter in sump, oil cooler, 4 imp pt, 4.9 US pt, 2.3 l; 1 Solex 26/35 CSIC 225 downdraught twin barrel carburettor; fuel feed: mechanical pump; air-cooled.

TRANSMISSION driving wheels: front (double homokinetic joints); clutch: single dry plate; gearbox: mechanical; gears: 4, II, III and IV synchronized; ratios: I 5.203, II 2.656, III 1.786, IV 1.316, rev 5.203; lever: on facia; final drive: spiral bevel; axle ratio: 4.125; width of rims: 4"; tyres: 125 x 15.

PERFORMANCE max speeds: (I) 19 mph, 30 km/h; (II) 37 mph, 59 km/h; (III) 55 mph, 88 km/h; (IV) 73 mph, 117 km/h; power-weight ratio: 44.5 lb/hp (61.4 lb/kW), 20.2 kg/hp (27.9 kg/kW); carrying capacity: 761 lb, 345 kg; acceleration: standing ¼ mile 22.7 sec; speed in top at 1,000 rpm: 12.7 mph, 20.4 km/h; consumption: 52.3 m/imp gal, 43.6 m/US gal, 5.4 l x 100 km at 56 mph, 90 km/h.

CHASSIS platform; front suspension: independent, swinging leading arms, 2 friction dampers, 2 inertia-type patter dampers; rear: independent, swinging longitudinal trailing arms linked to front suspension by longitudinal coil springs, 2 inertia-type patter dampers, 2 telescopic dampers.

STEERING rack-and-pinion; turns lock to lock: 3.25.

BRAKES front disc (diameter 9.61 in, 24.4 cm), rear drum, dual circuit; lining area: front 13 sq in, 84 sq cm, rear 34.7 sq in, 224 sq cm, total 47.7 sq in, 308 sq cm.

ELECTRICAL EQUIPMENT 12 V; 25 Ah battery; 390 W alternator; 2 headlamps, height adjustable from driving seat.

DIMENSIONS AND WEIGHT wheel base: 94.49 in, 240 cm; tracks: 49.61 in, 126 cm front, 49.61 in, 126 cm rear; length: 150.79 in, 383 cm; width: 58.27 in, 148 cm; height: 62.99 in, 160 cm; ground clearance: 5.91 in, 15 cm; weight: 1,290 lb, 585 kg; weight distribution: 58% front, 42% rear; turning circle: 36.7 ft, 11.2 m; fuel tank: 5.5 imp gal, 6.6 US gal, 25 l.

BODY saloon/sedan; 4 doors; 4 seats, bench front seats; folding rear seat; fully opening canvas sunroof.

PRACTICAL INSTRUCTIONS fuel: 98 oct petrol; oil: engine 4 imp pt, 4.9 US pt, 2.3 l, SAE 20W-50, change every 4,600 miles, 7,500 km - gearbox and final drive 1.6 imp pt, 1.9 US pt, 0.9 l, SAE 80, change every 14,000 miles, 22,500 km; greasing: every 4,700 miles, 7,500 km, 4 points; spark plug: 225°; tappet clearances: inlet 0.008 in, 0.20 mm, exhaust 0.008 in, 0.20 mm; valve timing: 0°5' 49°15' 35°55' 3°30'; tyre pressure: front 20 psi, 1.4 atm, rear 26 psi, 1.8 atm.

OPTIONALS (for Spécial only), separate front seats.

CITROËN Mehari

Mehari

PRICE EX WORKS: 39,200 francs**

ENGINE front, 4 stroke; 2 cylinders, horizontally opposed; 36.7 cu in, 602 cc (2.91 x 2.76 in, 74 x 70 mm); compression ratio: 8.5:1; max power (DIN): 29 hp (21 kW) at 5,750 rpm; max torque (DIN): 29 lb ft, 4 kg m (39 Nm) at 3,500 rpm; max engine rpm: 5,900; 48.2 hp/l (35.4 kW/l); light alloy block and head, dry liners, light alloy sump, hemispherical combustion chambers; 2 crankshaft bearings; valves: overhead, Vee-slanted at 70°, push-rods and rockers; camshafts: 1, central, lower; lubrication: rotary pump, filter in sump, oil cooler, 4 imp pt, 4.9 US pt, 2.3 l; 1 Solex 26/35 CSIC 225 downdraught twin barrel carburettor; fuel feed: mechanical pump; air-cooled.

TRANSMISSION driving wheels: front; clutch: single dry plate; gearbox: mechanical; gears: 4, fully synchronized; ratios: I 6.060, II 3.086, III 1.923, IV 1.421, rev 6.060; lever: on facia; final drive: spiral bevel; axle ratio: 3.875; width of rims: 4"; tyres: 135 x 15.

PERFORMANCE max speeds: (I) 17 mph, 28 km/h; (II) 35 mph, 56 km/h; (III) 55 mph, 88 km/h; (IV) 75 mph, 120 km/h; power-weight ratio: 43.3 lb/hp (59.9 lb/kW), 19.7 kg/hp (27.1 kg/kW); carrying capacity: 849 lb, 385 kg; acceleration: standing ¼ mile 23.6 sec; speed in top at 1,000 rpm: 12.7 mph, 20.4 km/h; consumption: 37.7 m/imp gal, 31.4 m/US gal, 7.5 l x 100 km at 56 mph, 90 km/h.

CHASSIS platform; front suspension: independent, swinging leading arms, telescopic dampers; rear: independent, swinging longitudinal trailing arms linked to front suspension by longitudinal coil springs, patter dampers, telescopic dampers.

STEERING rack-and-pinion; turns lock to lock: 3.25.

BRAKES front disc (diameter 9.61 in, 24.4 cm), rear drum, dual circuit; lining area: front 13 sq in, 84 sq cm, rear 34.7 sq in, 224 sq cm, total 47.7 sq in, 308 sq cm.

ELECTRICAL EQUIPMENT 12 V; 25 Ah battery; 390 W alternator; 2 headlamps, height adjustable from driving seat.

DIMENSIONS AND WEIGHT wheel base: 93.31 in, 237 cm; tracks: 49.61 in, 126 cm front, 49.61 in, 126 cm rear; length: 138.58 in, 352 cm; width: 60.24 in, 153 cm; height: 64.57 in, 164 cm; ground clearance: 9.45 in, 24 cm; weight: 1,257 lb, 570 kg; weight distribution: 63% front, 37% rear; turning circle: 36.1 ft, 11 m; fuel tank: 5.5 imp gal, 6.6 US gal, 25 l.

BODY open, in plastic material; 2 doors; 4 seats, separate front seats.

PRACTICAL INSTRUCTIONS fuel: 98 oct petrol; oil: engine 4 imp pt, 4.9 US pt, 2.3 l, SAE 20W-50, change every 4,600 miles, 7,500 km - gearbox and final drive 1.6 imp pt, 1.9 US pt, 0.9 l, SAE 80, change every 14,000 miles, 22,500 km; greasing: every 4,700 miles, 7,500 km, 8 points; spark plug: 225°; tappet clearances: inlet 0.008 in, 0.20 mm, exhaust 0.008 in, 0.20 mm; valve timing: 2°5' 41°30' 35°55' 3°30'; tyre pressure: front 20 psi, 1.4 atm, rear 26 psi, 1.8 atm.

LNA

PRICE EX WORKS: 34,900 francs**

ENGINE front, 4 stroke; 2 cylinders, horizontally opposed; 39.8 cu in, 652 cc (3.03 x 2.76 in, 77 x 70 mm); compression ratio: 9.5:1; max power (DIN): 35 hp (25 kW) at 5,500 rpm; max torque (DIN): 36 lb ft, 5 kg m (49 Nm) at 3,500 rpm; max engine rpm: 5,850; 53.7 hp/l (38.3 kW/l); light alloy block and head; 3 crankshaft bearings; valves: overhead, Vee-slanted at 90°, push-rods and rockers; camshafts: 1, central, lower; lubrication: rotary pump, filter in sump, oil cooler, 5.3 imp pt, 6.3 US pt, 3 l; 1 Solex 26/35 CSIC 238 downdraught twin barrel carburettor; fuel feed: mechanical pump; air-cooled.

TRANSMISSION driving wheels: front (double homokinetic joints); clutch: single dry plate (diaphragm); gearbox: mechanic-

CITROËN LNA 11 RE Coupé

LNA

al; gears: 4, fully synchronized; ratios: I 4.545, II 2.500, III 1.643, IV 1.147, rev 4.184; lever: central; final drive: spiral bevel; axle ratio: 3.888; width of rims: 4"; tyres: 135 SR x 13.

PERFORMANCE max speeds: (I) 19 mph, 31 km/h; (II) 35 mph, 57 km/h; (III) 53 mph, 86 km/h; (IV) 78 mph, 126 km/h; power-weight ratio: 44.7 lb/hp (62.6 lb/kW), 20.3 kg/hp (28.4 kg/kW); carrying capacity: 728 lb, 320 kg; acceleration: standing ¼ mile 22 sec; speed in top at 1,000 rpm: 13.9 mph, 22.4 km/h; consumption: 55.4 m/imp gal, 46.1 m/US gal, 5.1 l x 100 km at 56 mph, 90 km/h.

CHASSIS platform; front suspension: independent, by McPherson, coil springs/telescopic damper struts, lower wishbones (trailing links), anti-roll bar; rear: independent, swinging longitudinal trailing arms, coil springs, telescopic dampers.

STEERING rack-and-pinion; turns lock to lock: 3.33.

BRAKES front disc (diameter 9.61 in, 24.4 cm), rear drum, dual circuit, rear compensator; lining area: front 23.9 sq in, 154 sq cm, rear 24.5 sq in, 158 sq cm, total 48.4 sq in, 312 sq cm.

ELECTRICAL EQUIPMENT 12 V; 35 Ah battery; 462 W alternator; Thomson fully electronic ignition.

DIMENSIONS AND WEIGHT wheel base: 87.80 in, 223 cm; tracks: 50.79 in, 129 cm front, 50 in, 127 cm rear; length: 133.86 in, 340 cm; width: 59.84 in, 152 cm; height: 54.33 in, 138 cm; ground clearance: 4.72 in, 12 cm; weight: 1,566 lb, 710 kg; weight distribution: 66% front, 34% rear; turning circle: 30.8 ft, 9.4 m; fuel tank: 8.8 imp gal, 10.6 US gal, 40 l.

BODY coupé, luxury equipment; 2+1 doors; 4 seats, separate front and rear seats; reclining driving seat; folding rear seats.

PRACTICAL INSTRUCTIONS fuel: 98 oct petrol; oil: engine 5.3 imp pt, 6.3 US pt, 3 l, SAE 20W-50, change every 4,600 miles, 7,500 km - gearbox and final drive 2.5 imp pt, 3 US pt, 1.4 l, SAE 80, change every 14,000 miles, 22,500 km; greasing: none; spark plug: 225°; tappet clearances: inlet 0.008 in, 0.20 mm, exhaust 0.008 in, 0.20 mm; valve timing: 7° 42° 35° 6°; tyre pressure: front 23 psi, 1.6 atm, rear 27 psi, 1.9 atm.

OPTIONALS rear window wiper-washer; heated rear window; metallic spray; reclining backrests.

LNA 11

See LNA, except for:

PRICES IN GB AND EX WORKS:	£	francs
E 2+1-dr Coupé	3,140*	36,200**
RE 2+1-dr Coupé	3,538*	39,760**

ENGINE transverse, slanted 72° to rear; 4 cylinders, in line; 68.6 cu in, 1,124 cc (2.83 x 2.72 in, 72 x 69 mm); compression ratio: 9.7:1; max power (DIN): 50 hp (36 kW) at 5,500 rpm; max torque (DIN): 62 lb ft, 8.6 kg m (84 Nm) at 2,500 rpm; max engine rpm: 5,750; 44.5 hp/l (32 kW/l); light alloy block and head, wet liners, bihemispherical combustion chambers; 5 crankshaft bearings; valves: overhead, Vee-slanted, rockers; camshafts: 1, overhead; lubrication: gear pump, full flow filter, 7.9 imp pt, 9.5 US pt, 4.5 l; 1 Solex 32 PBISA 12/A230 horizontal single barrel carburettor; sealed circuit cooling, liquid, expansion tank, 13.2 imp pt, 15.9 US pt, 7.5 l, electric thermostatic fan.

TRANSMISSION gearbox ratios: I 3.083, II 1.647, III 1.094, IV 0.750, rev 2.833; axle ratio: 3.176; width of rims: 4.5"; tyres: 145 SR x 13.

PERFORMANCE max speed: 87 mph, 140 km/h; power-weight ratio: 32.6 lb/hp (45.3 lb/kW), 14.8 kg/hp (20.6 kg/kW); carrying capacity: 752 lb, 341 kg; acceleration: standing ¼ mile 19.6 sec; speed in top at 1,000 rpm: 20.7 mph, 33.4 km/h; consumption: 44.8 m/imp gal, 37.3 m/US gal, 6.3 l x 100 km at 75 mph, 120 km/h.

STEERING turns lock to lock: 3.92.

BRAKES servo (for RE only).

ELECTRICAL EQUIPMENT transistorized ignition.

DIMENSIONS AND WEIGHT weight: 1,632 lb, 740 kg.

PRACTICAL INSTRUCTIONS oil: engine, gearbox and final drive 7.9 imp pt, 9.5 US pt, 4.5 l; tappet clearances: inlet 0.006 in, 0.15 mm, exhaust 0.010 in, 025 mm; valve timing: 5°20' 36°50' 36°50' 5°20'; tyre pressure: front 26 psi, 1.8 atm, rear 28 psi, 2 atm.

OPTIONALS tinted glass; light alloy wheels.

Visa

PRICES EX WORKS:	francs
4+1-dr Berline	38,260**
Club 4+1-dr Berline	41,200**

ENGINE front, longitudinal, slanted 7°13' to rear, 4 stroke; 2 cylinders, horizontally opposed; 39.8 cu in, 652 cc (3.03 x 2.76 in, 77 x 70 mm); compression ratio: 9.5:1; max power (DIN): 35 hp (25 kW) at 5,500 rpm; max torque (DIN): 36 lb ft, 5 kg m (49 Nm) at 3,500 rpm; max engine rpm: 5,850; 53.7 hp/l (38.3 kW/l); light alloy block and head; 3 crankshaft bearings; valves: overhead, Vee-slanted at 90°, push-rods and rockers; camshafts: 1, central; lubrication: rotary pump, filter in sump, oil cooler, 5.3 imp pt, 6.3 US pt, 3 l; 1 Solex 26/35 CSIC 238 downdraught twin barrel carburettor; fuel feed: mechanical pump; air-cooled.

TRANSMISSION driving wheels: front (double homokinetic joints); clutch: single dry plate; gearbox: mechanical; gears: 4, fully synchronized; ratios: I 4.545, II 2.500, III 1.643, IV 1.147, rev 4.184; lever: central; final drive: spiral bevel; axle ratio: 3.888; width of rims: 4"; tyres: 135 SR x 13.

PERFORMANCE max speeds: (I) 19 mph, 31 km/h; (II) 35 mph, 57 km/h; (III) 53 mph, 86 km/h; (IV) 78 mph, 125 km/h; power-weight ratio: 46.9 lb/hp (65.7 lb/kW), 21.3 kg/hp (29.8 kg/kW); carrying capacity: 728 lb, 330 kg; acceleration: standing ¼ mile 22.4 sec; speed in top at 1,000 rpm: 13.9 mph, 22.4 km/h; consumption: 54.3 m/imp gal, 45.2 m/US gal, 5.2 l x 100 km at 56 mph, 90 km/h.

CHASSIS integral; front suspension: independent, by McPherson, coil springs/telescopic damper struts, lower wishbones (trailing links), anti-roll bar; rear: independent, swinging longitudinal trailing arms, coil springs, telescopic dampers.

STEERING rack-and-pinion; turns lock to lock: 3.33.

BRAKES front disc (diameter 9.61 in, 24.4 cm), rear drum, dual circuit, rear compensator; lining area: front 23.9 sq in, 154 sq cm, rear 24.5 sq in, 158 sq cm, total 48.4 sq in, 312 sq cm.

ELECTRICAL EQUIPMENT 12 V; 35 Ah battery; 462 W alternator; Thomson fully electronic ignition; 2 headlamps, height adjustable from driving seat.

DIMENSIONS AND WEIGHT wheel base: 95.67 in, 243 cm; tracks: 50.79 in, 129 cm front, 48.82 in, 124 cm rear; length: 145.28 in, 369 cm; width: 60.63 in, 154 cm; height: 55.51 in, 141 cm; ground clearance: 5.16 in, 13.1 cm; weight: 1,643 lb, 745 kg; weight distribution: 59% front, 41% rear; turning circle: 32.1 ft, 9.8 m; fuel tank: 8.8 imp gal, 10.6 US gal, 40 l.

BODY saloon/sedan; 4+1 doors; 4 seats, separate front seats; (for Club only) luxury equipment and reclining backrests.

PRACTICAL INSTRUCTIONS fuel: 98 oct petrol; oil: engine 5.3 imp pt, 6.3 US pt, 3 l, SAE 15W-40 (summer) 10W-30 (winter), change every 4,600 miles, 7,500 km - gearbox and final drive 2.5 imp pt, 3 US pt, 1.4 l, SAE 80 EP, change every 14,000 miles, 22,500 km; greasing: none; tappet clearances: inlet 0.008 in, 0.20 mm, exhaust 0.008 in, 0.20 mm; valve timing: 7° 42° 35° 6°; tyre pressure: front 24 psi, 1.7 atm, rear 28 psi, 2 atm.

OPTIONALS heated rear window; rear window wiper-washer; sunroof; metallic spray; (for Berline only) reclining backrests; (for Club only) headrests on front seats and tinted glass.

Visa 11

See Visa, except for:

PRICES EX WORKS:	francs
E 4+1-dr Berline	41,900**
RE 4+1-dr Berline	44,300**
RE 4-dr Décapotable	58,460**

ENGINE Peugeot, transverse, slanted 72° to rear; 4 cylinders, in line; 68.6 cu in, 1,124 cc (2.83 x 2.72 in, 72 x 69 mm); compression ratio: 9.7:1; max power (DIN): 50 hp (36 kW) at 5,500 rpm; max torque (DIN): 61 lb ft, 8.4 kg m (82 Nm) at 2,500 rpm; max engine rpm: 5,750; 44.5 hp/l (32 kW/l); light alloy block and head, wet liners, bihemispherical combustion chambers; 5 crankshaft bearings; valves: overhead, Vee-slanted, rockers; camshafts: 1, overhead; lubrication: gear pump, full flow filter, 7.9 imp pt, 9.5 US pt, 4.5 l; 1 Solex 32 PBISA 12/A230 horizontal single barrel carburettor; sealed circuit cooling, liquid, expansion tank, 13.2 imp pt, 15.9 US pt, 7.5 l, electric thermostatic fan.

TRANSMISSION gearbox ratios: I 3.083, II 1.647, III 1.094, IV 0.750, rev 2.833; axle ratio: 3.562; width of rims: 4.5"; tyres: 145 SR x 13.

PERFORMANCE max speeds: (I) 25 mph, 41 km/h; (II) 48 mph, 77 km/h; (III) 71 mph, 115 km/h; (IV) 87 mph, 140 km/h; power-weight ratio: 35.7 lb/hp (49.6 lb/kW), 16.2 kg/hp (22.5 kg/kW); carrying capacity: 937 lb, 425 kg; acceleration: standing ¼ mile 19.8 sec; speed in top at 1,000 rpm: 19.1 mph, 30.7 km/h; consumption: 44.8 m/imp gal, 37.3 m/US gal, 6.3 l x 100 km - RE Décapotable 37.7 m/imp gal, 31.4 m/US gal, 7.5 l x 100 km at 75 mph, 120 km/h.

CHASSIS rear suspension: anti-roll bar.

CITROËN Visa Berline

CITROËN Visa 11 RE Décapotable

CITROËN Visa GT

ELECTRICAL EQUIPMENT transistorized ignition.

DIMENSIONS AND WEIGHT wheel base: 95.28 in, 242 cm; ground clearance: 5.91 in, 15 cm; weight: 1,786 lb, 810 kg; weight distribution: 62% front, 38% rear; turning circle: 32.5 ft, 9.9 m.

BODY folding rear seat - RE Décapotable 4 doors and fully opening canvas sunroof.

PRACTICAL INSTRUCTIONS oil: engine, gearbox and final drive 7.9 imp pt, 9.5 US pt, 4.5 l; tappet clearances: inlet 0.006 in, 0.15 mm, exhaust 0.010 in, 0.25 mm; valve timing: 5°20' 36°50' 36°50' 5°20'; tyre pressure: front 26 psi, 1.8 atm, rear 28 psi, 2 atm.

OPTIONALS headrests on front seats; tinted glass; metallic spray; light alloy wheels; (for RE models only) 5-speed mechanical gearbox (I 3.083, II 1.823, III 1.192, IV 0.893, V 0.718, rev 2.833), 3.866 axle ratio.

Visa GT

See Visa, except for:

PRICE IN GB: £ 4,795*
PRICE EX WORKS: 53,700 francs**

ENGINE transverse, slanted 72° to rear; 4 cylinders, in line; 82.9 cu in, 1,360 cc (2.95 x 3.03 in, 75 x 77 mm); compression ratio: 9.3:1; max power (DIN): 80 hp (57 kW) at 5,800 rpm; max torque (DIN): 80 lb ft, 11 kg m (10.9 Nm) at 2,800 rpm; max engine rpm: 6,500; 58.8 hp/l (41.9 kW/l); light alloy block and head, wet liners, bihemispherical combustion chambers; 5 crankshaft bearings; valves: overhead, Vee-slanted, rockers; camshafts: 1, overhead; lubrication: gear pump, full flow filter, 8.8 imp pt, 10.6 US pt, 5 l; 2 Solex 35 BISA 8 downdraught single barrel carburettors; sealed circuit cooling, liquid, expansion tank, 11.4 imp pt, 13.7 US pt, 6.5 l.

TRANSMISSION gears: 5, fully synchronized; ratios: I 3.083, II 1.823, III 1.192, IV 0.893, V 0.718, rev 2.833; axle ratio: 3.866; width of rims: 4.5''; tyres: 160/65 R x 340 TRX.

PERFORMANCE max speeds: (I) 27 mph, 43 km/h; (II) 45 mph, 73 km/h; (III) 70 mph, 112 km/h; (IV) 93 mph, 150 km/h; (V) 104 mph, 168 km/h; power-weight ratio: 22.9 lb/hp (32.1 lb/kW), 10.4 kg/hp (14.6 kg/kW); carrying capacity: 750 lb, 340 kg; acceleration: standing ¼ mile 17.5 sec; speed in top at 1,000 rpm: 17.8 mph, 28.7 km/h; consumption: 38.2 m/imp gal, 31.8 m/US gal, 7.4 l x 100 km at 75 mph, 120 km/h.

CHASSIS rear suspension: anti-roll bar.

STEERING turns lock to lock: 3.75.

BRAKES servo.

ELECTRICAL EQUIPMENT Ducellier transistorized ignition.

DIMENSIONS AND WEIGHT tracks: 51.18 in, 130 cm front, 49.21 in, 125 cm rear; ground clearance: 4.13 in, 10.5 cm; weight: 1,830 lb, 830 kg; turning circle: 32.5 ft, 9.9 m.

BODY folding rear seat; headrests and light alloy wheels (standard).

PRACTICAL INSTRUCTIONS oil: engine, gearbox and final drive 8.8 imp pt, 10.6 US pt, 5 l; tappet clearances: inlet 0.004 in, 0.10 mm, exhaust 0.008 in, 0.20 mm; valve timing: 9°30' 44° 41° 11°; tyre pressure: front 26 psi, 1.8 atm, rear 27 psi, 1.9 atm.

OPTIONALS tinted glass; sunroof.

GSA Berline

PRICES IN GB AND EX WORKS:	£	francs
Spécial 4+1-dr Berline	4,511*	48,000**
Pallas 4+1-dr Berline	5,245*	55,560**
X 1 4+1-dr Berline	5,098*	52,400**
X 3 4+1-dr Berline	—	55,560**

ENGINE front, 4 stroke; 4 cylinders, horizontally opposed; 79.3 cu in, 1,299 cc (3.13 x 2.58 in, 79.4 x 65.6 mm); compression ratio: 8.7:1; max power (DIN): 65 hp (48 kW) at 5,500 rpm; max torque (DIN): 71 lb ft, 9.8 kg m (94 Nm) at 3,500 rpm; max engine rpm: 6,500; 50 hp/l (36.8 kW/l); light alloy block, head with cast iron liners, light alloy fins, hemispherical combustion chambers; 3 crankshaft bearings; valves: overhead, Vee-slanted; camshafts: 2, 1 per bank, overhead, cogged belt; lubrication: rotary pump, full flow filter, oil cooler, 7 imp pt, 8.5 US pt, 4 l; 1 Solex 28 CIC or Weber 30 DGS 16/250 downdraught twin barrel carburettor; fuel feed: mechanical pump; air-cooled.

TRANSMISSION driving wheels: front; clutch: single dry plate (diaphragm); gearbox: mechanical; gears: 4, fully synchronized - X 3 5; ratios: I 3.818, II 2.294, III 1.500, IV 1.031, rev 4.182 - X 3 I 3.818, II 2.294, III 1.500, IV 1.133, V 0.912, rev 4.182; lever: central; final drive: spiral bevel; axle ratio: 4.125 - X 3 4.375; width of rims: 4.5''; tyres: 145 SR x 15.

PERFORMANCE max speeds: (I) 29 mph, 46 km/h; (II) 42 mph, 67 km/h; (III) 73 mph, 118 km/h; (IV) 99 mph, 160 km/h; power-weight ratio: 31.2 lb/hp (42.3 lb/kW), 14.2 kg/hp (19.2 kg/kW); carrying capacity: 882 lb, 400 kg; acceleration: standing ¼ mile 19.2 sec; speed in top at 1,000 rpm: 16.6 mph, 26.7 km/h - X 3 17.6 mph, 28.4 km/h; consumption: 32.1 m/imp gal, 26.7 m/US gl, 8.8 l x 100 km - X 3 34.9 m/imp gal, 29 m/US gal, 8.1 l x 100 km at 75 mph, 120 km/h.

CHASSIS integral; front suspension: independent, wishbones, hydropneumatic suspension, anti-roll bar, automatic levelling control; rear: independent, swinging trailing arms, hydropneumatic suspension, anti-roll bar, automatic levelling control.

STEERING rack-and-pinion; turns lock to lock: 3.80.

BRAKES disc (front diameter 10.63 in, 27 cm, rear diameter 7.01 in, 17.8 cm), servo; lining area: front 22.6 sq in, 146 sq cm, rear 11.2 sq in, 72 sq cm, total 33.8 sq in, 218 sq cm.

ELECTRICAL EQUIPMENT 12 V; 40 Ah battery - X 3 45 Ah; 540 W alternator; transistorized ignition; 2 headlamps.

DIMENSIONS AND WEIGHT wheel base: 100.39 in, 255 cm; tracks: 54.33 in, 138 cm front, 52.36 in, 133 cm rear; length: 164.96 in, 419 cm; width: 63.39 in, 161 cm; constant height: 53.15 in, 135 cm; ground clearance (variable): 6.06 in, 15.4 cm; weight: 2,029 lb, 920 kg; weight distribution: 57% front, 43% rear; turning circle: 34.1 ft, 10.4 m; fuel tank: 9.5 imp gal, 11.4 US gal, 43 l.

BODY saloon/sedan; 4+1 doors; 5 seats, separate front seats, reclining backrests; heated rear window.

PRACTICAL INSTRUCTIONS fuel: 98 oct petrol; oil: engine 7 imp pt, 8.5 US pt, 4 l, SAE 20W-50, change every 4,600 miles, 7,500 km - gearbox 2.5 imp pt, 3 US pt, 1.4 l, SAE 80, change every 14,000 miles, 22,500 km - final drive 7.4 imp pt, 8.9 US pt, 4.2 l, change every 14,000 miles, 22,500 km; greasing: none; spark plug: 200°; tappet clearances: inlet 0.008 in, 0.20 mm, exhaust 0.008 in, 0.20 mm; valve timing: 5°30' 34°30' 32° 4°30'; tyre pressure: front 26 psi, 1.8 atm, rear 27 psi, 1.9 atm.

OPTIONALS (for Spécial, Pallas and X 1 only) 5-speed fully synchronized mechanical gearbox; folding rear seat; sunroof; metallic spray; rear window wiper-washer; Boxline equipment; tinted glass.

CITROËN GSA X 1 Berline

GSA Break

See GSA Berline, except for:

PRICES IN GB AND EX WORKS:	£	francs
Spécial 4+1-dr Break	4,938*	50,000**
Club 4+1-dr Break	—	53,600**

PERFORMANCE max speed: 98 mph, 158 km/h; carrying capacity: 981 lb, 445 kg.

BODY estate car/st. wagon; 4+1 doors; rear window wiper-washer.

OPTIONALS sunroof not available.

CITROËN GSA Club Break

CITROËN BX 16 TRS Berline

BX

PRICE IN GB: £ 4,790*
PRICE EX WORKS: 54,000** francs

ENGINE front, transverse, slanted 72° to rear, 4 stroke; 4 cylinders, in line; 82.9 cu in, 1,360 cc (2.95 x 3.03 in, 75 x 77 mm); compression ratio: 9.3:1; max power (DIN): 62 hp (45 kW) at 5,500 rpm; max torque (DIN): 80 lb ft, 11 kg m (10.9 Nm) at 2,500 rpm; max engine rpm: 6,200; 45.6 hp/l (33.1 kW/l); light alloy block and head, wet liners, bihemispherical combustion chambers; 5 crankshaft bearings; valves: overhead, Vee-slanted, rockers; camshafts: 1, overhead; lubrication: gear pump, full flow filter, 7.9 imp pt, 9.5 US pt, 4.5 l; 1 Solex 30-30 Z2/329 downdraught twin barrel carburettor; fuel feed: mechanical pump; sealed circuit cooling, liquid, 11.4 imp pt, 13.7 US pt, 6.5 l.

TRANSMISSION driving wheels: front; clutch: single dry plate (diaphragm); gearbox: mechanical; gears: 4, fully synchronized; ratios: I 3.882, II 2.074, III 1.377, IV 0.945, rev 3.568; lever: central; final drive: spiral bevel; axle ratio: 3.866; width of rims: 4.5"; tyres: 145 SR x 14.

PERFORMANCE max speeds: (I) 28 mph, 45 km/h; (II) 52 mph, 83 km/h; (III) 78 mph, 126 km/h; (IV) 96 mph, 155 km/h; power-weight ratio: 31.5 lb/hp (43.4 lb/kW), 14.3 kg/hp (19.7 kg/kW); carrying capacity: 1,091 lb, 495 kg; acceleration: standing ¼ mile 19.5 sec; speed in top at 1,000 rpm: 18.4 mph, 29.6 km/h; consumption: 37.7 m/imp gal, 31.4 m/US gal, 7.5 l x 100 km at 75 mph, 120 km/h.

CHASSIS integral; front suspension: independent, wishbones, hydropneumatic suspension combined with coil springs/telescopic damper struts, anti-roll bar, automatic levelling control; rear: independent, swinging trailing arms, hydropneumatic suspension, anti-roll-bar, automatic levelling control.

STEERING rack-and-pinion; turns lock to lock: 3.76

BRAKES disc (front diameter 10.47 in, 26.6 cm, rear diameter 8.82 in, 22.4 cm), dual circuit, servo; lining area: front 21.7 sq in, 140 sq cm, rear 10.5 sq in, 68 sq cm, total 32.2 sq in, 208 sq cm.

ELECTRICAL EQUIPMENT 12 V; 35 Ah battery; 500 W alternator; transistorized ignition; 2 headlamps.

DIMENSIONS AND WEIGHT wheel base: 104.53 in, 266 cm; tracks: 55.51 in, 141 cm front, 53.31 in, 135 cm rear; length: 166.54 in, 423 cm; width: 64.96 in, 165 cm; height: 53.54 in, 136 cm; ground clearance: 6.30 in, 16 cm; weight: 1,951 lb, 885 kg; weight distribution: 61% front, 39% rear; turning circle: 35.7 ft, 10.9 m; fuel tank: 9.7 imp gal, 11.6 US gal, 44 l.

BODY saloon/sedan; 4+1 doors; 5 seats, separate front seats, reclining backrests, headrests; folding rear seats.

PRACTICAL INSTRUCTIONS fuel: 98 oct petrol; oil: engine, gearbox and final drive 8.8 imp pt, 10.6 US pt, 5 l, SAE 15W-40, change every 6,200 miles, 10,000 km; greasing: none; spark plug: Champion BN9Y; tappet clearances: inlet 0.006 in, 0.15 mm, exhaust 0.014 in, 0.35 mm; valve timing: 4° 29° 30° 5°; tyre pressure: front 27 psi, 1.9 atm, rear 28 psi, 2 atm.

OPTIONALS rear window wiper-washer; heated rear window; metallic spray.

BX 14

See BX, except for:

PRICES IN GB AND EX WORKS:	£	francs
E 4-dr Berline	4,990*	57,900**
RE 4+1-dr Berline	5,451*	60,200**

ENGINE max power (DIN): 72 hp (52 kW) at 5,750 rpm; max torque (DIN): 80 lb ft, 11 kg m (10.9 Nm) at 3,000 rpm; 52.9 hp/l (38.2 kW/l); 1 Solex 32-34 Z2/348 downdraught twin barrel carburettor.

TRANSMISSION gears: 5, fully synchronized; ratios: I 3.882, II 2.296, III 1.515, IV 1.124, V 0.904, rev 3.568.

PERFORMANCE max speeds: (I) 28 mph, 45 km/h; (II) 47 mph, 75 km/h; (III) 71 mph, 115 km/h; (IV) 96 mph, 154 km/h; (V) 101 mph, 163 km/h; power-weight ratio: 27.6 lb/hp (38.2 lb/kW), 12.5 kg/hp (17.3 kg/kW); carrying capacity: 1,058 lb, 480 kg; acceleration: standing ¼ mile 18.7 sec; speed in top at 1,000 rpm: 19.2 mph, 30.9 km/h; consumption: 39.8 m/imp gal, 33.1 m/US gal, 7.1 l x 100 km at 75 mph, 120 km/h.

DIMENSIONS AND WEIGHT width: 65.35 in, 166 cm; weight: 1,984 lb, 900 kg.

BX 16

See BX, except for:

PRICES IN GB AND EX WORKS:	£	francs
RS 4+1-dr Berline	5,600*	63,980**
TRS 4+1-dr Berline	6,100*	68,300**

ENGINE transverse, slanted 30° to rear; 96.4 cu in, 1,580 cc (3.27 x 2.87 in, 83 x 73 mm); compression ratio: 9.5:1; max power (DIN): 93 hp (67 kW) at 5,750 rpm; max torque (DIN): 97 lb ft, 13.4 kg m (129 Nm) at 3,500 rpm; 58.9 hp/l (42.4 kW/l); lubrication: 8.8 imp pt, 10.6 US pt, 5 l; 1 Weber 32-34 DRTC 100 W 121-50 downdraught twin barrel carburettor.

TRANSMISSION gears: 5, fully synchronized; ratios: I 3.308, II 1.882, III 1.280, IV 0.969, V 0.757, rev 3.333; axle ratio: 4.187; width of rims: 5"; tyres: 170/65 R x 365 MXL.

PERFORMANCE max speeds: (I) 30 mph, 48 km/h; (II) 53 mph, 85 km/h; (III) 78 mph, 125 km/h; (IV) 102 mph, 165 km/h; (V) 109 mph, 176 km/h; power-weight ratio: 22.5 lb/hp (31.3 lb/kW), 10.2 kg/hp (14.2 kg/kW); carrying capacity: 1,058 lb, 480 kg; acceleration: standing ¼ mile 17.7 sec; speed in top at 1,000 rpm: 21.1 mph, 33.9 km/h; consumption: 38.7 m/imp gal, 32.2 m/US gal, 7.3 l x 100 km at 75 mph, 120 km/h.

ELECTRICAL EQUIPMENT 45 Ah battery.

DIMENSIONS AND WEIGHT width: 65.35 in, 166 cm; weight: 2,095 lb, 950 kg; fuel tank: 11.4 imp gal, 13.7 US gal, 52 l.

PRACTICAL INSTRUCTIONS spark plug: Champion BN7Y; valve timing: 0° 42° 43° 1°; tyre pressure: front and rear 30 psi, 2.1 atm.

OPTIONALS light alloy wheels; tinted glass; sunroof.

BX 19

PRICES EX WORKS:	francs
D 4-dr Berline	65,900**
TRD 4-dr Berline	72,200**

ENGINE diesel, front, transverse, 4 stroke; 4 cylinders, slanted 20° to rear, in line; 116.3 cu in, 1,905 cc (3.27 x 3.46 in, 83 x 88 mm); compression ratio: 23.5:1; max power (DIN): 65 hp (47 kW) at 4,600 rpm; max torque (DIN): 88 lb ft, 12.2 kg m (118 Nm) at 2,000 rpm; max engine rpm: 5,000; 34.1 hp/l (24.7 kW/l); cast iron block, light alloy head; 5 crankshaft bearings; valves: overhead, thimble tappets; camshafts: 1, overhead, cogged belt; lubrication: chain-driven pump, full flow filter (cartridge), 8.8 imp pt, 10.6 US pt, 5 l; Bosch or Rotodiesel injection pump; sealed circuit cooling, liquid, 11.4 imp pt, 13.7 US pt, 6.5 l.

TRANSMISSION driving wheels: front; clutch: single dry plate (diaphragm); gearbox: mechanical; gears: 5, fully synchronized; ratios: I 3.308, II 1.882, III 1.280, IV 0.969, V 0.757, rev 3.333; lever: central; final drive: spiral bevel; axle ratio: 4.187; width of rims: 4.5"; tyres: Michelin 165/70 SR x 14 MXL.

PERFORMANCE max speeds: (I) 24 mph, 38 km/h; (II) 42 mph, 67 km/h; (III) 61 mph, 98 km/h; (IV) 81 mph, 130 km/h, (V) 103 mph, 166 km/h; power-weight ratio: 33.6 lb/hp (46.4 lb/kW), 15.2 kg/hp (21.1 kg/kW); carrying capacity: 1,080 lb, 490 kg; acceleration: standing ¼ mile 19.6 sec; speed in top at 1,000 rpm: 22.5 mph, 36.1 km/h; consumption:

CITROËN BX

45.6 m/imp gal, 37.9 m/US gal, 6.2 l x 100 km at 75 mph, 120 km/h.

CHASSIS integral; front suspension; independent, wishbones, hydropneumatic suspension combined with coil springs/telescopic damper struts, anti-roll bar, automatic levelling control; rear: independent, swinging trailing arms, hydropneumatic suspension, anti-roll bar, automatic levelling control.

STEERING rack-and-pinion; turns lock to lock: 4.38.

BRAKES disc (front diameter 10.47 in, 26.6 cm, rear diameter 8.82 in, 22.4 cm), dual circuit, servo; lining area: front 21.7 sq in, 140 sq cm, rear 10.5 sq in, 68 sq cm, total 32.2 sq in, 208 sq cm.

ELECTRICAL EQUIPMENT 12 V; 50 Ah battery; 500 W alternator; 2 headlamps.

DIMENSIONS AND WEIGHT wheel base: 104.53 in, 266 cm; tracks: 55.91 in, 142 cm front, 53.31 in, 135 cm rear; length: 166.54 in, 423 cm; width: 64.96 in, 165 cm; height: 53.54 in, 136 cm; ground clearance: 6.30 in, 16 cm; weight: 2,183 lb, 990 kg; weight distribution: 61% front, 39% rear; turning circle: 35.7 ft, 10.9 m; fuel tank: 11.4 imp gal, 13.7 US gal, 52 l.

BODY saloon/sedan; 4+1 doors; 5 seats, separate front seats, reclining backrests, headrests; folding rear seats; rear window wiper-washer; heated rear window.

PRACTICAL INSTRUCTIONS fuel: diesel; oil: engine 8.8 imp pt, 10.6 US pt, 5 l, Superdiesel 15W-40, change every 4,600 miles, 7,500 km - gearbox and final drive 2.5 imp pt, 3 US pt, 1.4 l, SAE 80 EP, change every 62,000 miles, 100,000 km; greasing: none; tappet clearance: inlet 0.006 in, 0.15 mm, exhaust 0.009 in, 0.25 mm; valve timing: 8° 40° 56° 12°; tyre pressure: front and rear 30 psi, 2.1 atm.

OPTIONALS power steering; tinted glass; light alloy wheels; metallic spray; sunroof.

CX 20 Berline

PRICES IN GB AND EX WORKS:	£	francs
4-dr Berline	7,590*	75,700**
TRE 4-dr Berline	—	83,300**

ENGINE front, transverse, slanted 15° to front, 4 stroke; 4 cylinders, in line; 121.7 cu in, 1,995 cc (3.46 x 3.23 in, 88 x 82 mm); compression ratio: 9.2:1; max power (DIN): 106 hp (76 kW) at 5,500 rpm; max torque (DIN): 122 lb ft, 16.9 kg m (166 Nm) at 3,250 rpm; max engine rpm: 5,600; 53.1 hp/l (38.1 kW/l); light alloy block and head; 5 crankshaft bearings; valves: overhead, rockers; camshafts: 1, overhead, cogged belt; lubrication: rotary pump, full flow filter, 8.8 imp pt, 10.6 US pt, 5 l; 1 Weber 34 DMTR 46/250 downdraught twin barrel carburettor; fuel feed: mechanical pump; water-cooled, 16.9 imp pt, 20.3 US pt, 9.6 l, electric thermostatic fan.

TRANSMISSION driving wheels: front; clutch: single dry plate (diaphragm); gearbox: mechanical; gears: 4 - TRE 5 (standard), fully synchronized; ratios: I 3.166, II 1.833, III 1.133, IV 0.800, rev 3.153 - TRE I 3.166, II 1.833, III 1.250, IV 0.939, V 0.733, rev 3.153; lever: central; final drive: spiral bevel; axle ratio: 4.538; width of rims: 5.5"; tyres: 185 SR x 14 front, 175 SR x 14 rear.

PERFORMANCE max speeds: (I) 29 mph, 47 km/h; (II) 50 mph, 81 km/h; (III) 81 mph, 131 km/h; (IV) 109 mph, 176 km/h; power-weight ratio: 25.7 lb/hp (35.8 lb/kW), 11.6 kg/hp (16.2 kg/kW); carrying capacity: 1,202 lb, 545 kg; acceleration: standing ¼ mile 17.9 sec; speed in top at 1,000 rpm: 20.2 mph, 32.5 km/h; consumption: 29.1 m/imp gal, 24.2 m/US gal, 9.7 l x 100 km at 56 mph, 90 km/h - TRE 30.7 m/imp gal, 25.6 m/US gal, 9.2 l x 100 km at 75 mph, 120 km/h.

CITROËN BX 16 TRS Berline

CHASSIS integral with front and rear subframes; front suspension: independent, wishbones, hydropneumatic suspension, anti-roll bar, automatic levelling control; rear: independent, swinging trailing arms, hydropneumatic suspension, anti-roll bar, automatic levelling control.

STEERING rack-and-pinion - TRE servo; turns lock to lock: 4.50 - TRE 2.50.

BRAKES disc (front diameter 10.24 in, 26 cm, rear diameter 8.82 in, 22.4 cm), internal radial fins, rear compensator, servo; lining area: front 40.3 sq in, 260 sq cm, rear 34.7 sq in, 224 sq cm, total 75 sq in, 484 sq cm.

ELECTRICAL EQUIPMENT 12 V; 45 Ah battery; 972 W alternator; Ducellier distributor; 2 halogen headlamps.

DIMENSIONS AND WEIGHT wheel base: 112.20 in, 285 cm; tracks: 59.45 in, 151 cm front, 53.94 in, 137 cm rear; length: 183.86 in, 467 cm; width: 69.68 in, 177 cm; height: 53.54 in, 136 cm; ground clearance: 6.10 in, 15.5 cm; weight: 2,723 lb, 1,235 kg; weight distribution: 66% front, 34% rear; turning circle: 38.7 ft, 11.8 m; fuel tank: 15 imp gal, 18 US gal, 68 l.

BODY saloon/sedan; 4 doors; 5 seats, separate front seats, reclining backrests, built-in headrests; heated rear window.

PRACTICAL INSTRUCTIONS fuel: 98 oct petrol; oil: engine 8.8 imp pt, 10.6 US pt, 5 l, SAE 10W-50, change every 4,600 miles, 7,500 km - gearbox and final drive 3 imp pt, 3.6 US pt, 1.7 l, SAE 80, change every 14,000 miles, 22,500 km - hydraulic suspension 7.4 imp pt, 8.9 US pt, 4.2 l, change every 18,900 miles, 30,000 km; greasing: none; spark plug: 225°; tappet clearances: inlet 0.004 in, 0.10 mm, exhaust 0.010 in, 0.25 mm; valve timing: 20° 60° 60° 20°; tyre pressure: front 28 psi, 2 atm, rear 30 psi, 2.1 atm.

OPTIONALS (for Berline only) 5-speed fully synchronized mechanical gearbox and servo brake; tinted glass; electric sunroof; metallic spray.

CX 20 Break / Familiale

See CX 20 Berline, except for:

PRICES IN GB AND EX WORKS:	£	francs
4+1-dr Break	—	86,000**
4+1-dr Familiale	8,311*	90,900**

TRANSMISSION gears: Familiale 5; tyres: 185 SR x 14.

PERFORMANCE max speed: Break 104 mph, 168 km/h - Familiale 102 mph, 165 km/h; power-weight ratio: 28.9 lb/hp (40.3 lb/kW), 13.1 kg/hp (18.3 kg/kW); carrying capacity: 1,521 lb, 690 kg; acceleration: standing ¼ mile 18.6 sec; consumption: Break 26.6 m/imp gal, 22.2 m/US gal, 10.6 l - Familiale 28.8 m/imp gal, 24 m/US gal, 9.8 l x 100 km.

STEERING servo.

DIMENSIONS AND WEIGHT wheel base: 121.85 in, 309 cm; rear track: 54.72 in, 139 cm; length: 195.28 in, 496 cm; height: 57.68 in, 146 cm; weight: Break 3,065 lb, 1,390 kg - Familiale 3,087 lb, 1,400 kg.

BODY estate car/st. wagon; 4+1 doors.

CX 25 Pallas IE

See CX 20 Berline, except for:

PRICE EX WORKS: 104,000 francs**

ENGINE 152.6 cu in, 2,500 cc (3.66 x 3.62 in, 93 x 92 mm); compression ratio: 8.7:1; max power (DIN): 138 hp (100 kW) at 5,000 rpm; max torque (DIN): 156 lb ft, 21.5 kg m (206 Nm) at 4,000 rpm; max engine rpm: 5,500; 55.2 hp/l (40 kW/l); Bosch L-Jetronic injection; fuel feed: electric pump; water-cooled, 21.6 imp pt, 26 US pt, 12.3 l.

TRANSMISSION gears: (standard) 5, fully synchronized; ratios: I 3.166, II 1.833, III 1.250, IV 0.939, V 0.733, rev 3.153; axle ratio: 4.067; tyres: 185 HR x 14 XVS.

PERFORMANCE max speed: 124 mph, 200 km/h; power-weight ratio: 21.9 lb/hp (30.2 lb/kW), 9.9 kg/hp (13.7 kg/kW); acceleration: standing ¼ mile 17 sec; consumption: 30.4 m/imp gal, 25.3 m/US gal, 9.3 l x 100 km at 75 mph, 120 km/h.

STEERING servo, variable ratio; turns lock to lock: 2.50.

CITROËN BX 16

CITROËN CX 20 TRE Berline

CX 25 PALLAS IE

ELECTRICAL EQUIPMENT 60 Ah battery; 1,080 W alternator.

DIMENSIONS AND WEIGHT weight: 3,021 lb, 1,370 kg.

PRACTICAL INSTRUCTIONS tyre pressure: front 30 psi, 2.1 atm, rear 31 psi, 2.2 atm.

OPTIONALS speed control; automatic transmission with 3 ratios (I 2.478, II 1.478, III 1, rev 2.081), 4.769 axle ratio, max speed 121 mph, 194 km/h; consumption 24.8 m/imp gal, 20.6 m/US gal, 11.4 l x 100 km at 75 mph, 120 km/h; 190/65 HR x 390 TRX tyres.

CX 25 GTI

See CX 20 Berline, except for:

PRICE EX WORKS: 106,600 francs**

ENGINE 152.6 cu in, 2,500 cc (3.66 x 3,62 in, 93 x 92 mm); compression ratio: 8.7:1; max power (DIN): 138 hp (100 kW) at 5,000 rpm; max torque (DIN): 156 lb ft, 21.5 kg m (206 Nm) at 4,000 rpm; max engine rpm: 5,500; 55.2 hp/l (40 kW/l); Bosch L-Jetronic injection; fuel feed: electric pump; water-cooled, 21.6 imp pt, 26 US pt, 12.3 l.

TRANSMISSION gears: (standard) 5, fully synchronized; ratios: I 3.166, II 1.833, III 1.250, IV 0.939, V 0.733, rev 3.153; axle ratio: 4.214; width of rims: 6"; tyres: 190/65 HR x 390 TRX.

PERFORMANCE max speed: 125 mph, 201 km/h; power-weight ratio: 21.9 lb/hp (30.2 lb/kW), 9.9 kg/hp (13.7 kg/kW); acceleration: standing ¼ mile 16.6 sec; consumption: 30.4 m/imp gal, 25.3 m/US gal, 9.3 l x 100 km at 75 mph, 120 km/h.

STEERING servo, variable ratio; turns lock to lock: 2.50.

ELECTRICAL EQUIPMENT 60 Ah battery; 1,080 W alternator.

DIMENSIONS AND WEIGHT weight: 3,021 lb, 1,370 kg; weight distribution: 68% front, 32% rear.

BODY metallic spray (standard).

PRACTICAL INSTRUCTIONS tyre pressure: front 31 psi, 2.2 atm, rear 20 psi, 1.4 atm.

OPTIONALS speed control; leather upholstery.

CX 25 Prestige

See CX 20 Berline, except for:

PRICE EX WORKS: 135,000 francs**

ENGINE 152.6 cu in, 2,500 cc (3.66 x 3.62 in, 93 x 92 mm); compression ratio: 8.7:1; max power (DIN): 138 hp (100 kW) at 5,000 rpm; max torque (DIN): 156 lb ft, 21.5 kg m (206 Nm) at 4,000 rpm; max engine rpm: 5,500; 55.2 hp/l (40 kW/l); Bosch L-Jetronic injection; fuel feed: electric pump; water-cooled, 21.6 imp pt, 26 US pt, 12.3 l.

TRANSMISSION gears: (standard) 5, fully synchronized; ratios: I 3.166, II 1.833, III 1.250, IV 0.939, V 0.733, rev 3.153; axle ratio: 4.067; tyres: 190/65 HR x 390 TRX.

PERFORMANCE max speed: 124 mph, 200 km/h; power-weight ratio: 23.2 lb/hp (32 lb/kW), 10.5 kg/hp (14.5 kg/kW); carrying capacity: 1,014 lb, 460 kg; acceleration: standing ¼ mile 17.2 sec; consumption: 29.4 m/imp gal, 24.5 m/US gal, 9.6 l x 100 km at 75 mph, 120 km/h.

STEERING servo, variable ratio; turns lock to lock: 2.50.

CITROËN CX 25 Prestige

ELECTRICAL EQUIPMENT 70 Ah battery; 1,080 W alternator.

DIMENSIONS AND WEIGHT wheel base: 121.65 in, 309 cm; length: 192.91 in, 490 cm; height: 53.94 in, 137 cm; weight: 3,197 lb, 1,450 kg; weight distribution: 67.5% front, 32.5% rear.

BODY luxury equipment; metallic spray (standard); air-conditioning.

PRACTICAL INSTRUCTIONS tyre pressure: front 31 psi, 2.2 atm, rear 20 psi, 1.4 atm.

OPTIONALS automatic transmission with 3 ratios (I 2.478, II 1.478, III 1, rev 2.081), 4.769 axle ratio, max speed 121 mph, 194 km/h, consumption 26.9 m/imp gal, 22.4 m/US gal, 10.5 l x 100 km at 75 mph, 120 km/h; speed control.

CX 25 TRI Break

See CX 20 Berline, except for:

PRICE EX WORKS: 112,500 francs**

ENGINE 152.6 cu in, 2,500 cc (3.66 x 3.62 in, 93 x 92 mm); compression ratio: 8.7:1; max power (DIN): 138 hp (100 kW) at 5,000 rpm; max torque (DIN): 156 lb ft, 21.5 kg m (206 Nm) at 4,000 rpm; max engine rpm: 5,500; 55.2 hp/l (40 kW/l); Bosch L-Jetronic injection; fuel feed: electric pump; water-cooled, 21.6 imp pt, 26 US pt, 12.3 l.

TRANSMISSION gears: (standard) 5, fully synchronized; ratios: I 3.166, II 1.833, III 1.250, IV 0.939, V 0.733, rev 3.153; axle ratio: 4.067; width of rims: 6"; tyres: 195/65 HR x 390 TRX.

PERFORMANCE max speed: 121 mph, 194 km/h; power-weight ratio: 23.4 lb/hp (32.3 lb/kW), 10.6 kg/hp (14.6 kg/kW); carrying capacity: 1,543 lb, 700 kg; acceleration: standing ¼ mile 17.2 sec; consumption: 28.5 m/imp gal, 23.5 m/US gal, 9.9 l x 100 km at 75 mph, 120 km/h.

STEERING servo, variable ratio; turns lock to lock: 2.50.

ELECTRICAL EQUIPMENT 60 Ah battery; 1,080 W alternator.

DIMENSIONS AND WEIGHT wheel base: 121.85 in, 309 cm; rear track: 54.72 in, 139 cm; length: 194.96 in, 495 cm; height: 57.68 in, 147 cm; weight: 3,230 lb, 1,465 kg.

BODY estate car/st. wagon; 4+1 doors.

OPTIONALS automatic transmission with 3 ratios (I 2.478, II 1.478, III 1, rev 2.081), 4.769 axle ratio, max speed 118 mph, 190 km/h, consumption 23.7 m/imp gal, 19.8 m/US gal, 11.9 l x 100 km at 75 mph, 120 km/h; speed control.

CX 25 Diesel

See CX 20 Berline, except for:

PRICES IN GB AND EX WORKS:	£	francs
4-dr Berline	9,116*	87,000**
Pallas 4-dr Berline	9,353*	97,000**
4+1-dr Break	9,188*	98,400**
4+1-dr Familiale	9,452*	103,100**

ENGINE diesel; 152.6 cu in, 2,500 cc (3.66 x 3.62 in, 93 x 92 mm); compression ratio: 22.2:1; max power (DIN): 75 hp (54 kW) at 4,250 rpm; max torque (DIN): 111 lb ft, 15.3 kg m (150 Nm) at 2,000 rpm; max engine rpm: 4,525; 30 hp/l (21.6 kW/l); cast iron block, light alloy head; valves: overhead, push-rods and rockers; camshafts: 1, side, cogged belt; lubrication: 8.1 imp pt, 9.7 US pt, 4.6 l; Roto-Diesel injection pump; cooling: 21.6 imp pt, 26 US pt, 12.3 l.

TRANSMISSION gears: 4 - Pallas and Familiale 5 (standard).

PERFORMANCE max speed: Berline 91 mph, 147 km/h - Pallas 97 mph, 156 km/h - Break 90 mph, 145 km/h - Familiale 94 mph, 151 km/h; power-weight ratio: sedans 40.3 lb/hp (55.9 lb/kW), 18.3 kg/hp (25.4 kg/kW); carrying capacity: sedans 1,147 lb, 520 kg - st. wagons 1,521 lb, 690 kg; acceleration: standing ¼ mile sedans 20.7 sec - st. wagons 21.6 sec; speed in top at 1,000 rpm: 20.3 mph, 32.6 km/h; consumption: sedans 43.5 m/imp gal, 36.2 m/US gal, 6.5 l x 100 km at 56 mph, 90 km/h - st. wagons 32.5 m/imp gal, 27 m/US gal, 8.7 l x 100 km at 75 mph, 120 km/h.

ELECTRICAL EQUIPMENT 88 Ah battery.

DIMENSIONS AND WEIGHT wheel base: st. wagons 121.65 in, 309 cm; length: st. wagons 192.96 in, 490 cm; height: st.

CITROËN CX 25 TRI Break

CITROËN CX 25 Diesel Turbo

CITROËN CX 25 Diesel Turbo RD Berline

wagons 53.94 in, 137 cm; weight: Berline and Pallas 3,021 lb, 1,370 kg - Break and Familiale 3,307 lb, 1,500 kg; weight distribution: sedans 68.4% front, 31.6% rear - st. wagons 64.8% front, 35.2% rear; turning circle: st. wagons 41.7 ft, 12.7 m.

BODY (for estate cars/st. wagons only) 4+1 doors, folding rear seat and heated rear window with wiper-washer; Familiale 8 seats; (for Pallas only) luxury equipment and metallic spray.

PRACTICAL INSTRUCTIONS fuel: diesel; oil: engine 8.1 imp pt, 9.7 US pt, 4.6 l, SAE 15W-40, change every 3,100 miles, 5,000 km; tappet clearances: inlet 0.012 in, 0.30 mm, exhaust 0.008 in, 0.20 mm; valve timing: 2°52' 33°08' 37°48' 4°12'; tyre pressure: sedans front 31 psi, 2.2 atm, rear 30 psi, 2.1 atm - st. wagons front 31 psi, 2.2 atm, rear 31 psi, 2.2 atm.

OPTIONALS (for Berline and Break only) 5-speed fully synchronized mechanical gearbox (I 3.166, II 1.833, III 1.250, IV 0.939, V 0.733, rev 3.153), max speed Berline 97 mph, 156 km/h - Break 94 mph, 151 km/h, acceleration standing ¼ mile 20.4 sec, speed in top at 1,000 rpm 22.1 mph, 35.5 km/h, consumption Berline 46.3 m/imp gal, 38.6 m/US gal, 6.1 l x 100 km at 56 mph, 90 km/h - Break 34.9 m/imp gal, 29 m/US gal, 8.1 l x 100 km at 75 mph, 120 km/h; (for st. wagons only) metallic spray; (for Pallas only) leather upholstery.

CX 25 Diesel Turbo

See CX 20 Berline, except for:

PRICES EX WORKS:	francs
RD 4-dr Berline	**101,700****
TRD 4-dr Berline	**108,200****
4-dr Limousine	**118,200****
TRD 4+1-dr Break	**117,900****

ENGINE diesel, turbocharged; 152.6 cu in, 2,500 cc (3.66 x 3.62 in, 93 x 92 mm); compression ratio: 21:1; max power (DIN): 95 hp (70 kW) at 3,700 rpm; max torque (DIN): 159 lb ft, 22 kg m (216 Nm) at 2,000 rpm; max engine rpm: 4,625; 38 hp/l (28 kW/l); cast iron block, light alloy head; valves: overhead, push-rods and rockers; camshafts: 1, side, cogged belt; lubrication: 8.1 imp pt, 9.7 US pt, 4.6 l; Roto-Diesel injection pump and turbocharger with exhaust gas recirculation; cooling: 22.9 imp pt, 27.5 US pt, 13 l.

TRANSMISSION gears: (standard) 5, fully synchronized; ratios: I 3.167, II 1.833, III 1.207, IV 0.882, V 0.674, rev 3.154; axle ratio: 3.812; width of rims: 6''; tyres: 190/65 HR x 390 TRX.

PERFORMANCE max speed: sedans 108 mph, 174 km/h - Break 106 mph, 170 km/h; power-weight ratio: RD 32.6 lb/hp (44.3 lb/kW), 14.8 kg/hp (20.1 kg/kW); carrying capacity: sedans 1,102 lb, 500 kg - Break 1,499 lb, 680 kg; acceleration: standing ¼ mile 18.7 sec; speed in top at 1,000 rpm: 27.7 mph, 44.7 km/h; consumption: RD and TRD Berline 38.7 m/imp gal, 32.2 m/US gal, 7.3 l x 100 km - Limousine 37.7 m/imp gal, 31.4 m/US gal, 7.5 l x 100 km - Break 34.9 m/imp gal, 29 m/US gal, 8.1 l x 100 km at 75 mph, 120 km/h.

ELECTRICAL EQUIPMENT 88 Ah battery; 1,080 W alternator.

DIMENSIONS AND WEIGHT wheel base: Break 121.65 in, 309 cm; length: Break 194.96 in, 495 cm; height: Break 57.68 in, 146 cm; weight: RD and TRD Berline 3,098 lb, 1,405 kg - Limousine 3,197 lb, 1,450 kg - Break 3,352 lb, 1,520 kg.

BODY (for Break only) 4+1 doors, folding rear seat and heated rear window with wiper-washer; (for TRD Berline only) light alloy wheels.

PRACTICAL INSTRUCTIONS fuel: diesel; oil: engine 8.1 imp pt, 9.7 US pt, 4.6 l, SAE 15W-40, change every 3,100 miles, 5,000 km; tappet clearances: inlet 0.012 in, 0.30 mm, exhaust 0.008 in, 0.20 mm; valve timing: 2°52' 33°08' 37°48' 4°12'; tyre pressure: front 34 psi, 2.4 atm, rear 28 psi, 2 atm.

OPTIONALS light alloy wheels (except for TRD Berline); air-conditioning; speed control.

DANGEL FRANCE

Peugeot 504 4 x 4 Series

PRICES EX WORKS:	francs
1 GR 4+1-dr Break	**109,931***
2 GRD 4+1-dr Break	**117,130***

Power team:	Standard for:	Optional for:
96 hp	1	—
70 hp (diesel)	2	—

96 hp power team

ENGINE Peugeot, front, slanted 45° to right, 4 stroke; 4 cylinders, in line; 120.3 cu in, 1,971 cc (3.46 x 3.19 in, 88 x 81 mm); compression ratio: 8.8:1; max power (DIN): 96 hp (69 kW) at 5,200 rpm; max torque (DIN): 119 lb ft, 16.4 kg m (161 Nm) at 3,000 rpm; max engine rpm: 5,500; 48.7 hp/l (35 kW/l); cast iron block, wet liners, light alloy head, hemispherical combustion chambers; 5 crankshaft bearings; valves: overhead, Vee-slanted, push-rods and rockers; camshafts: 1, side; lubrication: gear pump, metal gauze filter, 7 imp pt, 8.5 US pt, 4 l; 1 Solex 32/35 TMIMA or Zenith 35/40 INAT downdraught twin barrel carburettor; fuel feed: mechanical pump; water-cooled, 13.7 imp pt, 16.5 US pt, 7.8 l, electromagnetic thermostatic fan.

TRANSMISSION driving wheels: front (automatically engaged with transfer box low ratio) and rear; clutch: single dry plate (diaphragm), hydraulically controlled; gearbox: mechanical; gears: 4, fully synchronized; ratios: I 3.592, II 21044, III 1.366, IV 1, rev 3.634; transfer box ratios: low hypoid bevel, limited slip; axle ratio: 4.625; width of rims: 5.5''; tyres: 185 x 13.

PERFORMANCE max speeds: (I) 26 mph, 42 km/h; (II) 45 mph, 72 km/h; (III) 69 mph, 111 km/h; (IV) 91 mph, 146 km/h; power-weight ratio: 35 lb/hp (48.7 lb/kW), 15.9 kg/hp (22.1 kg/kW); carriyng capacity: 981 lb, 445 kg; speed in direct drive at 1,000 rpm: 17.1 mph, 27.6 km/h; consumption: 29.4 m/imp gal, 24.5 m/US gal, 9.6 l x 100 km at 56 mph, 90 km/h.

CHASSIS integral; front suspension: independent, by McPherson, coil springs/telescopic damper struts, lower wishbones; rear: rigid axle, trailing lower radius arms, upper oblique torque arms, 4 coil springs, anti-roll bar, telescopic dampers.

STEERING rack-and-pinion; turns lock to lock: 4.50.

BRAKES front disc (diameter 10.04 in, 25.5 cm), rear drum, dual circuit, rear compensator, servo; swept area: front 217.1 sq in, 1,400 sq cm, rear 144.2 sq in, 930 sq cm, total 361.3 sq in, 2,300 sq cm.

ELECTRICAL EQUIPMENT 12 V; 45 Ah battery; 500 W alternator; Ducellier distributor; 2 headlamps.

DIMENSIONS AND WEIGHT wheel base: 114.57 in, 291 cm; tracks: 59.06 in, 150 cm front, 53.54 in, 136 cm rear; length: 118.98 in, 480 cm; width: 68.11 in, 173 cm; height: 68.50 in, 174 cm; ground clearance: 7.87 in, 20 cm; weight: 3,363 lb, 1,525 kg; weight distribution: 53% front, 47% rear; turning circle: 37.4 ft, 11.4 m; fuel tank: 13.2 imp gal, 15.8 US gal, 60 l.

BODY estate car/st. wagon; 4+1 doors; 5 or 6 seats, separate front seats, reclining backrests; heated rear window; folding rear seat.

PRACTICAL INSTRUCTIONS fuel: 95 oct petrol; oil: engine 7 imp pt, 8.5 US pt, 4 l, SAE 20W-40, change every 3,100 miles, 5,000 km - gearbox 1.9 imp pt, 2.3 US pt, 1.1 l, SAE 20W-40, change every 6,200 miles, 10,000 km - final drive 2.8 imp pt, 3.4 US pt, 1.6 l, GP 90, change every 6,200 miles, 10,000 km; greasing: every 3,100 miles, 5,000 km, 6 points; tyre pressure: front 26 psi, 1.8 atm, rear 28 psi, 2 atm.

70 hp (diesel) power team

See 96 hp power team, except for:

ENGINE diesel; slanted at 20°; 140.6 cu in, 2,304 cc (3.70 x 3.27 in, 94 x 83 mm); compression ratio: 22.2:1; max power (DIN): 70 hp (50 kW) at 4,500 rpm; max torque (DIN): 97 lb ft, 13.4 kg m (131 Nm) at 2,000 rpm; 30.4 hp/l (21.9 kW/l); lubrication: 8.8 imp pt, 10.6 US pt, 5 l; Rotodiesel injection pump; cooling: 17.6 imp pt, 21.1 US pt, 10 l.

TRANSMISSION gearbox ratios: I 3.704, II 2.170, III 1.409, IV 1, rev 3.748.

PERFORMANCE max speed: 77 mph, 124 km/h; power-weight ratio: 50.4 lb/hp (70.6 lb/kW), 22.9 kg/hp (32 kg/kW).

ELECTRICAL EQUIPMENT 60 Ah battery.

DIMENSIONS AND WEIGHT weight: 3,528 lb, 1,600 kg.

PRACTICAL INSTRUCTIONS fuel: diesel; oil: engine 8.8 imp pt, 10.6 US pt, 5 l.

DANGEL Peugeot 504 4x4 GR Break

PEUGEOT 104 GL Berline

PEUGEOT FRANCE

104 Series

PRICES IN GB AND EX WORKS:	£	francs
1 GL 4+1-dr Berline	3,795*	39,750**
2 Z 2+1-dr Coupé	3,845*	35,850**
3 ZS 80 CV 2+1-dr Coupé	—	49,850**

Power team:	Standard for:	Optional for:
50 hp	1,2	—
80 hp	3	—

50 hp power team

ENGINE front, transverse, slanted 72° to rear, 4 stroke; 4 cylinders, in line; 68.6 cu in, 1,124 cc (2.83 x 2.72 in, 72 x 69 mm); compression ratio: 9.7:1; max power (DIN): 50 hp (36 kW) at 4,800 rpm; max torque (DIN): 63 lb ft, 8.7 kg m (85 Nm) at 2,800 rpm; max engine rpm: 5,800; 44.5 hp/l (32 kW/l); light alloy block and head, wet liners, bi-hemispherical combustion chambers; 5 crankshaft bearings; valves: overhead, Vee-slanted, rockers; camshafts: 1, overhead; lubrication: gear pump, full flow filter, 7.9 imp pt, 9.5 US pt, 4.5 l; 1 Solex 32 PBISA 12 downdraught single barrel carburettor; fuel feed: mechanical pump; water-cooled, 9.9 imp pt, 11.8 US pt, 5.6 l, electric thermostatic fan.

TRANSMISSION driving wheels: front; clutch: single dry plate (diaphragm); gearbox: mechanical, in unit with engine and final drive; gears: 4, fully synchronized; ratios: I 3.883, II 2.074, III 1.377, IV 0.944, rev 3.568; lever: central; final drive: spiral bevel; axle ratio: 3.177; width of rims: 4"; tyres: 135 SR x 13.

PERFORMANCE max speeds: (I) 28 mph, 45 km/h; (II) 52 mph, 83 km/h; (III) 78 mph, 126 km/h; (IV) 86 mph, 138 km/h; power-weight ratio: GL 34.8 lb/hp (48.4 lb/kW), 15.8 kg/hp (21.9 kg/kW); carrying capacity: 882 lb, 400 kg; acceleration: GL standing ¼ mile 20.1 sec; speed in top at 1,000 rpm: 20.7 mph, 33.4 km/h; consumption: GL 46.3 m/imp gal, 38.6 m/US gal, 6.1 l x 100 km at 75 mph, 120 km/h.

CHASSIS integral; front suspension: independent, by McPherson, coil springs/telescopic damper struts, lower wishbones (trailing links), anti-roll bar; rear: independent, swinging longitudinal trailing arms, coil springs, telescopic dampers.

STEERING rack-and-pinion; turns lock to lock: 3.90.

BRAKES front disc (diameter 9.49 in, 24.1 cm), rear drum, dual circuit, rear compensator; swept area: front 176.1 sq in, 1,136 sq cm, rear 50.9 in, 328 sq cm, total 227 sq in, 1,464 sq cm.

ELECTRICAL EQUIPMENT 12 V; 25 Ah battery; 500 W alternator; transistorized ignition; 2 headlamps.

DIMENSIONS AND WEIGHT wheel base: GL 95.28 in, 242 cm - Z 87.80 in, 223 cm; tracks: 50.79 in, 129 cm front, 49.96 in, 127 cm rear; length: GL 142.36 in, 362 cm - Z 132.28 in, 337 cm; width: 59.84 in, 152 cm; height: GL 55.28 in, 140 cm - Z 53.42 in, 136 cm; ground clearance: 4.72 in, 12 cm; weight: GL 1,742 lb, 790 kg - Z 1,632 lb, 740 kg; weight distribution: 58.9% front, 41.1% rear; turning circle GL 33.1 ft, 10.1 m - Z 30.8 ft, 9.4 m; fuel tank: 8.8 imp gal, 10.6 US gal, 40 l.

BODY saloon/sedan, 4+1 doors - coupé, 2+1 doors; 5 seats, separate front seats; folding rear seat; rear window wiper-washer.

PRACTICAL INSTRUCTIONS fuel: 97 oct petrol; oil: engine, gearbox and final drive 7.9 imp pt, 9.5 US pt, 4.5 l, SAE 10W-50, change every 3,100 miles, 5,000 km; greasing: every 3,100 miles, 5,000 km, 1 point; valve timing: 2° 36° 23°-11°; tyre pressure: front 28 psi, 2 atm, rear 31 psi, 2.2 atm.

OPTIONALS heated rear window; tinted glass; metallic spray.

VARIATIONS

(for export only)
ENGINE 58.2 cu in, 954 cc (2.76 x 2.44 in, 70 x 62 mm), 8.8 compression ratio, max power (DIN) 45 hp (33 kW) at 6,000 rpm, max torque (DIN) 47 lb ft, 6.5 kgm (62 Nm) at 3,000 rpm, 47.2 hp/l (34.6 kW/l), 1 Solex 32 PBISA 11 carburettor.

PERFORMANCE max speed 80 mph, 128 km/h, power-weight ratio GL 38.2 lb/hp (52.1 lb/kW), 17.3 kg/hp (23.6 kg/kW), consumption GL 47.1 m/imp gal, 39.2 m/US gal, 6 l x 100 km at 56 mph, 90 km/h.
DIMENSIONS AND WEIGHT weight: GL 1,720 lb, 780 kg.

80 hp power team

See 50 hp power team, except for:

ENGINE 83 cu in, 1,360 cc (2.95 x 3.03 in, 75 x 77 mm); compression ratio: 9.3:1; max power (DIN): 80 hp (57 kW) at 5,800 rpm; max torque (DIN): 81 lb ft, 11.2 kg m (109 Nm) at 2,800 rpm; max engine rpm: 6,200; 58.8 hp/l (41.9 kW/l); lubrication: 8.8 imp pt, 10.6 US pt, 5 l; 2 Solex 35 BISA 8 downdraught single barrel carburettors; cooling: 10.6 imp pt, 12.7 US pt, 6 l.

TRANSMISSION gears: 5, fully synchronized; ratios: I 3.883, II 2.296, III 1.501, IV 1.124, V 0.904, rev 3.568; axle ratio: 3.867; width of rims: 5"; tyres: 165/70 SR x 13.

PERFORMANCE max speed: 102 mph, 164 km/h; power-weight ratio: 22.3 lb/hp (31.3 lb/kW), 10.1 kg/hp (14.2 kg/kW); acceleration: standing ¼ mile 17.7 sec; speed in top at 1,000 rpm: 18.5 mph, 29.8 km/h; consumption: 35.8 m/imp gal, 29.8 m/US gal, 7.9 l x 100 km at 75 mph, 120 km/h.

CHASSIS rear suspension: anti-roll bar.

BRAKES servo.

ELECTRICAL EQUIPMENT 29 A battery.

DIMENSIONS AND WEIGHT weight: 1,786 lb, 810 kg.

BODY reclining backrests with headrests; heated rear window; electric windows.

PRACTICAL INSTRUCTIONS oil: engine, gearbox and final drive, 8.8 imp pt, 10.6 US pt, 5 l; valve timing: 9°30' 40°50' 44°10' 11°.

205 Series

PRICES EX WORKS:	francs
1 Standard 4+1-dr Berline	39,800**
2 GL 4+1-dr Berline (954 cc)	42,700**
3 GL 4+1-dr Berline (1,124 cc)	44,600**
4 GR 4+1-dr Berline (1,124 cc)	47,300**
5 GR 4+1-dr Berline (1,360 cc)	49,500**
6 SR 4+1-dr Berline	51,700**
7 GT 4+1-dr Berline	54,800**
8 GTI 2+1-dr Berline	—
9 GTI 4+1-dr Berline	—
10 SRD 4+1-dr Berline	51,500**
11 GLD 4+1-dr Berline	56,360**
12 GRD 4+1-dr Berline	59,800**

For GB prices, see price index.

Power team:	Standard for:	Optional for:
45 hp	1,2	—
50 hp	3,4	—
60 hp	5,6	—
80 hp	7	—
105 hp	8,9	—
60 hp (diesel, 1,768 cc)	10 to 12	—

45 hp power team

ENGINE front, transverse, slanted 72° to rear, 4 stroke; 4 cylinders, in line; 58.2 cu in, 954 cc (2.76 x 2.44 in, 70 x 62 mm); compression ratio: 9.3:1; max power (DIN): 45 hp (33 kW) at 6,000 rpm; max torque (DIN): 51 lb ft, 7 kg m (67 Nm) at 2,750 rpm; max engine rpm: 6,000; 47.2 hp/l (34.6 kW/l); light alloy block and head, wet liners, bi-hemispherical combustion chambers; 5 crankshaft bearings; valves: overhead, Vee-slanted, rockers; camshafts: 1, overhead; lubrication: gear pump, full flow filter, 7 imp pt, 8.5 US pt, 4 l; 1 Solex 32 PBISA 12 downdraught single barrel carburettor; fuel feed: mechanical pump; water-cooled, expansion tank, 10.2 imp pt, 12.3 US pt, 5.8 l, electric thermostatic fan.

TRANSMISSION driving wheels: front; clutch: single dry plate (diaphragm); gearbox: mechanical, in unit with engine and final drive; gears: 4, fully synchronized; ratios: I 3.882, II 2.074, III 1.377, IV 0.944, rev 3.568; lever: central; final drive: spiral bevel; axle ratio: 3.562; width of rims: 4.5"; tyres: 135 SR x 13.

PERFORMANCE max speeds: (I) 27 mph, 43 km/h; (II) 50 mph, 81 km/h; (III) 76 mph, 123 km/h; (IV) 83 mph, 134 km/h; power-weight ratio: 36.3 lb/hp (49.4 lb/kW), 16.4 kg/hp (22.4 kg/kW); carrying capacity: 882 lb, 400 kg; acceleration: standing ¼ mile 20.7 sec; speed in top at 1,000 rpm: 18.5 mph, 29.8 km/h; consumption: 48.7 m/imp gal, 40.6 m/US gal, 5.8 l x 100 km at 75 mph, 120 km/h.

CHASSIS integral; front suspension: independent, by McPherson, coil springs/telescopic damper struts, lower wishbones (trailing links), anti-roll bar; rear: independent, swinging longitudinal trailing arms, transverse torsion bar, telescopic dampers.

STEERING rack-and-pinion; turns lock to lock: 3.80.

BRAKES front disc (diameter 9.72 in, 24.7 cm), rear drum,

PEUGEOT 104 Z Coupé

PEUGEOT 205 GR Berline

dual circuit, rear compensator; swept area: front 176.4 sq in, 1,138 sq cm, rear 52.7 sq in, 340 sq cm, total 229.1 sq in, 1,478 sq cm.

ELECTRICAL EQUIPMENT 12 V; 25 Ah battery; 750 W alternator; transistorized ignition; 2 headlamps.

DIMENSIONS AND WEIGHT wheel base: 95.28 in, 242 cm; tracks: 53.15 in, 135 cm front, 51.18 in, 130 cm rear; length: 145.87 in, 370 cm; width: 61.50 in, 156 cm; height: 54.17 in, 138 cm; ground clearance: 4.72 in, 12 cm; weight: 1,632 lb, 740 kg; weight distribution: 61.5% front, 38.5% rear; turning circle: 34.4 ft, 10.5 m; fuel tank: 8.8 imp gal, 10.6 US gal, 40 l.

BODY saloon/sedan, 4+1 doors; 5 seats, separate front seats, reclining backrests; rear window wiper-washer.

PRACTICAL INSTRUCTIONS fuel: 97 oct petrol; oil: engine, gearbox and final drive 7 imp pt, 8.5 US pt, 4 l, SAE 10W-50, change every 3,100 miles, 5,000 km; valve timing: −4° 30° 29° −5°; tyre pressure: front 28 psi, 2 atm, rear 30 psi, 2.1 atm.

OPTIONALS heated rear window.

50 hp power team

See 45 hp power team, except for:

ENGINE 68.6 cu in, 1,124 cc (2.83 x 2.72 in, 72 x 69 mm); compression ratio: 9.7:1; max power (DIN): 50 hp (36 kW) at 4,800 rpm; max torque (DIN): 63 lb ft, 8.7 kg m (84 Nm) at 2,800 rpm; max engine rpm: 5,800; 44.5 hp/l (32 kW/l); lubrication: 7.9 imp pt, 9.5 US pt, 4.5 l.

TRANSMISSION axle ratio: 3.353; tyres: 145 SR x 13.

PERFORMANCE max speed: 88 mph, 142 km/h; power-weight ratio: GL 32.9 lb/hp (45.6 lb/kW), 14.9 kg/hp (20.7 kg/kW); acceleration: standing ¼ mile 20 sec; speed in top at 1,000 rpm: 20.3 mph, 32.6 km/h; consumption: 48.7 m/imp gal, 40.6 m/US gal, 5.8 l x 100 km at 75 mph, 120 km/h.

BRAKES servo.

DIMENSIONS AND WEIGHT width: GR 61,89 in, 157 cm; height: GR 54.09 in, 137 cm; weight: GL 1,643 lb, 745 kg - GR 1,720 lb, 780 kg; fuel tank: 11 imp gal, 13.2 US gal, 50 l.

BODY heated rear window (standard).

PRACTICAL INSTRUCTIONS oil: engine, gearbox and final drive 7.9 imp pt, 9.5 US pt, 4.5 l; valve timing: 2° 36° 23° −11°.

OPTIONALS tinted glass; metallic spray.

60 hp power team

See 45 hp power team, except for:

ENGINE 83 cu in, 1,360 cc (2.95 x 3.03 in, 75 x 77 mm); max power (DIN): 60 hp (43 kW) at 5,000 rpm; max torque (DIN): 79 lb ft, 10.9 kg m (105 Nm) at 2,500 rpm; 44.1 hp/l (31.6 kW/l); lubrication: 8.8 imp pt, 10.6 US pt, 5 l; 1 Solex 34 PBISA 12 downdraught single barrel carburettor; cooling: 10.6 imp pt, 12.7 US pt, 6 l.

TRANSMISSION gears: 5, fully synchronized; ratios: I 3.882, II 2.296, III 1.502, IV 1.124, V 0.904, rev 3.568; axle ratio: 3.176; width of rims: SR 5"; tyres: GR 145 SR x 13 - SR 165/70 SRX 13.

PERFORMANCE max speed: 96 mph, 154 km/h; power-weight ratio: 28.8 lb/hp (40.3 lb/kW), 13.1 kg/hp (18.3 kg/kW); acceleration: standing ¼ mile 19.2 sec; speed in top at 1,000 rpm: GR 22.3 mph, 35.9 km/h; consumption: 44.1 m/imp gal, 36.8 m/US gal, 6.4 l x 100 km at 75 mph, 120 km/h.

CHASSIS rear suspension: anti-roll bar.

BRAKES servo.

ELECTRICAL EQUIPMENT 29 Ah battery.

DIMENSIONS AND WEIGHT tracks: SR 53.70 in, 136 cm front, 51.73 in, 131 cm rear; width: 61.89 in, 157 cm; height: 54.09 in, 137 cm; weight: GR 1,731 lb, 785 kg - SR 1,764 lb, 800 kg; fuel tank: 11 imp gal, 13.2 US gal, 50 l.

BODY heated rear window (standard).

PRACTICAL INSTRUCTIONS oil: engine, gearbox and final drive 8.8 imp pt, 10.6 US pt, 5 l; valve timing: 2° 36° 23° −11°; tyre pressure: SR front 24 psi, 1.7 atm, rear 27 psi, 1.9 atm.

OPTIONALS tinted glass; metallic spray; (for SR only) electric windows and light alloy wheels.

80 hp power team

See 45 hp power team, except for:

ENGINE 83 cu in, 1,360 cc (2.95 x 3.03 in, 75 x 77 mm); max power (DIN): 80 hp (57 kW) at 5,800 rpm; max torque (DIN): 81 lb ft, 11.2 kg m (109 Nm) at 2,800 rpm; max engine rpm: 6,200; 58.8 hp/l (41.9 kW/l); lubrication: 8.8 imp pt, 10.6 US pt, 5 l; 2 Solex 35 BISA 8 downdraught single barrel carburettors; cooling: 10.6 imp pt, 12.7 US pt, 6 l.

TRANSMISSION gears: 5, fully synchronized; ratios: I 3.883, II 2.296, III 1.502, IV 1.124, V 0.904, rev 3.568; axle ratio: 3.867; width of rims: 5"; tyres: 165/70 SR x 13.

PERFORMANCE max speed: 106 mph, 170 km/h; power-weight ratio: 22.3 lb/hp (31.3 lb/kW), 10.1 kg/hp (14.2 kg/kW); acceleration: standing ¼ mile 17.7 sec; speed in top at 1,000 rpm: 18.5 mph, 29.8 km/h; consumption: 40.4 m/imp gal, 33.6 m/US gal, 7 l x 100 km at 75 mph, 120 km/h.

CHASSIS rear suspension: anti-roller bar.

BRAKES servo.

ELECTRICAL EQUIPMENT 29 Ah battery.

DIMENSIONS AND WEIGHT tracks: 53.70 in, 136 cm front, 51.73 in, 131 cm rear; width: 61.89 in, 157 cm; height: 53.74 in, 136 cm; weight: 1,786 lb, 810 kg; fuel tank: 11 imp gal, 13.2 US gal, 50 l.

BODY heated rear window (standard).

PRACTICAL INSTRUCTIONS oil: engine, gearbox and final drive 8.8 imp pt, 10.6 US pt, 5 l; valve timing: 9°30' 40°50' 44°10' 11°; tyre pressure: front 24 psi, 1.7 atm, rear 27 psi, 1.9 atm.

OPTIONALS tinted glass; metallic spray; electric windows; light alloy wheels.

105 hp power team

See 45 hp power team, except for:

ENGINE front, transverse, slanted 30° to rear; 96.4 cu in, 1,580 cc (3.27 x 2.87 in, 83 x 73 mm); compression ratio: 10.2:1; max power (DIN): 105 hp (76 kW) at 6,250 rpm; max torque (DIN): 99 lb ft, 13.7 kg m (132 Nm) at 4,000 rpm; max engine rpm: 6,750; 66.5 hp/l (48.1 kW/l); valves: overhead, in line, thimble tappets; camshafts: 1, overhead, cogged belt; lubrication: 8.8 imp pt, 10.6 US pt, 5 l; Bosch L-Jetronic injection; cooling: 11.6 imp pt, 13.9 US pt, 6.6 l.

TRANSMISSION gears: 5, fully synchronized; ratios: I 3.202, II 1.882, III 1.360, IV 1.069, V 0.865, rev 3.333; axle ratio: 4.062; width of rims: 5.5"; tyres: 185/60 HR x 14 tubeless.

PERFORMANCE max speed: 118 mph, 190 km/h; power-weight ratio: 17.8 lb/hp (24.7 lb/kW), 8.1 kg/hp (11.2 kg/kW); acceleration: standing ¼ mile 16.7 sec; speed in top at 1,000 rpm: 18.7 mph, 30.1 km/h; consumption: 38.7 m/imp gal, 32.2 m/US gal, 7.3 l x 100 km at 75 mph, 120 km/h.

CHASSIS rear suspension: anti-roll bar.

BRAKES front disc, internal radial fins.

ELECTRICAL EQUIPMENT 29 Ah battery; 2 iodine headlamps and 2 iodine fog lamps.

DIMENSIONS AND WEIGHT tracks: 54.84 in, 139 cm front, 52.28 in, 133 cm rear; width: 61.89 in, 157 cm; height: 53.35 in, 135 cm; weight: 1,874 lb, 850 kg; fuel tank: 11 imp gal, 13.2 US gal, 50 l.

BODY 2+1 or 4+1 doors; tinted glass; light alloy wheels.

PEUGEOT 205 GTI Berline

PEUGEOT 205 GTI Berline

PEUGEOT 205 SRD Berline

105 HP POWER TEAM

PRACTICAL INSTRUCTIONS oil: engine, gearbox and final drive 8.8 imp pt, 10.6 US pt, 5 l; valve timing: 3°30' 38°18' 34°18'-0°30'.

OPTIONALS tinted glass; central door locking.

60 hp (diesel) power team

See 45 hp power team, except for:

ENGINE diesel; 107.9 cu in, 1,768 cc (3.15 x 3.46 in, 80 x 88 mm); compression ratio: 23:1; max power (DIN): 60 hp (43 kW) at 4,600 rpm; max torque (DIN): 80 lb ft, 11 kg m (106 Nm) at 2,000 rpm; max engine rpm: 5,100; 33.9 hp/l (24.3 kW/l); lubrication: 8.8 imp pt, 10.6 US pt, 5 l; Bosch or Rotodiesel injection pump; cooling: 16.7 imp pt, 20.1 US pt, 9.5 l.

TRANSMISSION GLD gearbox ratios: I 3.308, II 1.882, III 1.148, IV 0.800, rev 3.333 - GRD and SRD gears: 5, fully synchronized; ratios: I 3.308, II 1.882, III 1.280, IV 0.969, V 0.757, rev 3.333; axle ratio: 3.588; width of rims: GRD and SRD 5''; tyres: GLD 145 SR x 13 - GRD and SRD 165/70 SR x 13.

PERFORMANCE max speed: 96 mph, 155 km/h; power-weight ratio: GLD 32 lb/hp (44.6 lb/kW), 14.5 kg/hp (20.2 kg/kW); acceleration: standing ¼ mile 19.5 sec; speed in top at 1,000 rpm: GRD and SRD 23.7 mph, 38.1 km/h; consumption: 54.3 m/imp gal, 45.2 m/US gal, 5.2 l x 100 km at 75 mph, 120 km/h.

CHASSIS rear suspension: anti-roll bar.

BRAKES servo.

ELECTRICAL EQUIPMENT 60 Ah battery.

DIMENSIONS AND WEIGHT tracks: GRD and SRD 53.70 in, 136 cm front, 51.73 in, 131 cm rear; width: 61.89 in, 157 cm; height: GRD and SRD 54.09 in, 137 cm; weight: GLD 1,918 lb, 870 kg - GRD 1,973 lb, 895 kg - SRD 1,996 lb, 905 kg.

PRACTICAL INSTRUCTIONS fuel: diesel; oil: engine, gearbox and final drive 8.8 imp pt, 10.6 US pt, 5 l, valve timing: −4° 43° 28° −1°.

OPTIONALS tinted glass; metallic spray; (for GRD and SRD only) electric windows and light alloy wheels.

305 Berline Series

PRICES IN GB AND EX WORKS:	£	francs
1 Standard 4-dr Berline	—	46,600**
2 GL 4-dr Berline	4,945*	52,700**
3 GR 4-dr Berline	5,195*	55,900**
4 SR 4-dr Berline	5,695*	58,200**
5 GT 4-dr Berline	5,895*	63,100**
6 GLD 4-dr Berline	5,795*	61,800**
7 SRD 4-dr Berline	—	68,000**

Power team:	Standard for:	Optional for:
65 hp	1	—
74 hp	2 to 4	—
94 hp	5	—
65 hp (diesel)	6,7	—

65 hp power team

ENGINE front, transverse, slanted 20° to front, 4 stroke; 4 cylinders, in line; 78.7 cu in, 1,290 cc (3.07 x 2.66 in, 78 x 67.5 mm); compression ratio: 8.8:1; max power (DIN): 65 hp (47 kW) at 6,000 rpm; max torque (DIN): 70 lb ft, 9.6 kg m (94 Nm) at 3,750 rpm; max engine rpm: 6,500; 50.4 hp/l (36.4 kW/l); light alloy block and head, wet liners, bi-hemispherical combustion chambers; 5 crankshaft bearings; valves: overhead, Vee-slanted, rockers; camshafts: 1, overhead; lubrication: rotary pump, cartridge on by-pass, 7 imp pt, 8.5 US pt, 4 l; 1 Solex 34 PBISA 14 or Weber IBP 1/100 downdraught single barrel carburettor; fuel feed: mechanical pump; water-cooled, 10.2 imp pt, 12.3 US pt, 5.8 l, electromagnetic fan.

TRANSMISSION driving wheels: front; clutch: single dry plate (diaphragm); gearbox: mechanical; gears: 4, fully synchronized; ratios: I 3.824, II 2.220, III 1.459, IV 0.985, rev 3.942; lever: central; final drive: helical spur gears; axle ratio: 3.733; width of rims: 4.5''; tyres: 145 SR x 14.

PERFORMANCE max speeds: 94 mph, 152 km/h; power-weight ratio: 31 lb/hp (42.9 lb/kW), 14.1 kg/hp (19.5 kg/kW); carrying capacity: 1,003 lb, 455 kg; acceleration: standing ¼ mile 20 sec; speed in top at 1,000 rpm: 18.2 mph, 29.4 km/h; consumption: 34.4 m/imp gal, 28.7 m/US gal, 8.2 l x 100 km at 75 mph, 120 km/h.

CHASSIS integral; front suspension: independent, by McPherson, coil springs/telescopic dampers, lower wishbones, anti-roll bar; rear: independent, coil springs, anti-roll bar, telescopic dampers.

STEERING rack-and-pinion; turns lock to lock: 3.60.

BRAKES front disc (diameter 10.35 in, 26.3 cm), rear drum, dual circuit, rear compensator, servo; swept area: total 283.7 sq in, 1,830 sq cm.

ELECTRICAL EQUIPMENT 12 V; 45 Ah battery; 500 W alternator; Ducellier distributor; 2 headlamps.

DIMENSIONS AND WEIGHT wheel base: 103.15 in, 262 cm; tracks: 55.51 in, 141 cm front, 51.79 in, 132 cm rear; length: 166.93 in, 424 cm; width: 64.17 in, 163 cm; height: 55.12 in, 140 cm; ground clearance: 4.96 in, 12.6 cm; weight: 2,018 lb, 915 kg; turning circle: 35.9 ft, 10.9 m; fuel tank: 12.3 imp gal, 14.8 US gal, 56 l.

BODY saloon/sedan; 4 doors; 5 seats, separate front seats, reclining backrests.

PRACTICAL INSTRUCTIONS fuel: 97 oct petrol; oil: engine, gearbox and final drive 7 imp pt, 8.5 US pt, 4 l, SAE 10W-40, change every 4,750 miles, 7,500 km; valve timing: 6° 38° 45° −1°; tyre pressure: front 26 psi, 1.8 atm, rear 30 psi, 2.1 atm.

OPTIONALS heated rear window; GPL.

74 hp power team

See 65 hp power team, except for:

ENGINE 89.8 cu in, 1,472 cc (3.07 x 3.03 in, 78 x 77 mm); compression ratio: 9.2:1; max power (DIN): 74 hp (53 kW) at 6,000 rpm; max torque (DIN): 86 lb ft, 11.8 kg m (116 Nm) at 3,000 rpm; 50.3 hp/l (36 kW/l).

TRANSMISSION gearbox ratios: I 3.334, II 1.935, III 1.272, IV 0.859, rev 3.436; axle ratio: GL 4.067 - SR 4.200; width of rims: SR 5''; tyres: GR and SR 155 SR x 14.

PERFORMANCE max speed: 97 mph, 156 km/h: power-weight ratio: 28 lb/hp (39.1 lb/kW), 12.7 kg/hp (17.7 kg/kW); acceleration: standing ¼ mile 18.5 sec; speed in top at 1,000 rpm: 19.2 mph, 30.9 km/h; consumption: 35.8 m/imp gal, 29.8 m/US gal, 7.9 l x 100 km at 75 mph, 120 km/h.

DIMENSIONS AND WEIGHT tracks: SR 54.33 in, 138 cm front, 52.36 in, 133 cm rear; ground clearance: 4.72 in, 12 cm; weight: 2,073 lb, 940 kg.

BODY electric windows.

PRACTICAL INSTRUCTIONS valve timing: 3° 41° 42° 2°.

OPTIONALS (for GR and SR only) sunroof; tinted glass; luxury equipment; electric windows.

94 hp power team

See 65 hp power team, except for:

ENGINE 96.4 cu in, 1,580 cc (3.27 x 2.87 in, 83 x 73 mm); compression ratio: 9.5:1; max power (DIN): 94 hp (68 kW) at 6,000 rpm; max torque (DIN): 99 lb ft, 13.7 kg m (132 Nm) at 3,750 rpm; max engine rpm: 6,500; 59.5 hp/l (43 kW/l); valves: overhead, in line, thimble tappets; camshafts: 1, overhead, cogged belt; lubrication: 7.9 imp pt, 9.5 US pt, 4.5 l; 1 Solex 32-34 CISAC downdraught twin barrel carburettor; cooling: 11.8 imp pt, 14.2 US pt, 6.7 l.

TRANSMISSION gears: 5, fully synchronized; ratios: I 3.308, II 1.882, III 1.280, IV 0.969, V 0.757, rev 3.333; axle ratio: 4.063; width of rims: 5''; tyres: 165/70 SR x 14 tubeless.

PERFORMANCE max speed: 106 mph, 170 km/h; power-weight ratio: 22.9 lb/hp (31.6 lb/kW), 10.4 kg/hp (14.3 kg/kW); acceleration: standing ¼ mile 17.8 sec; speed in top at 1,000 rpm: 21.9 mph, 35.2 km/h; consumption: 39.8 m/imp gal, 33.1 m/US gal, 7.1 l x 100 km at 75 mph, 120 km/h.

ELECTRICAL EQUIPMENT 50 A alternator; transistorized ignition; 2 iodine headlamps.

DIMENSIONS AND WEIGHT tracks: 55.91 in, 142 cm front, 52.44 in, 133 cm rear; ground clearance: 4.72 in, 12 cm; weight: 2,150 lb, 975 kg.

BODY electric windows; central door locking.

PRACTICAL INSTRUCTIONS oil: engine, gearbox and final drive 7.9 imp pt, 9.5 US pt, 4.5 l; valve timing: 0°48' 35°36' 37° 2°12'.

OPTIONALS electric sunroof; metallic spray.

65 hp (diesel) power team

See 65 hp power team, except for:

PEUGEOT 305 GR Berline

PEUGEOT 305 SR Break

PEUGEOT 305 SR Berline

ENGINE diesel; 116.2 cu in, 1,905 cc (3.27 x 3.46 in, 83 x 88 mm); compression ratio: 23.5:1; max power (DIN): 65 hp (47 kW) at 4,600 rpm; max torque (DIN): 88 lb ft, 12.2 kg m (118 Nm) at 2,000 rpm; max engine rpm: 5,000; 34.1 hp/l (24.7 kW/l); cast iron block; lubrication: 8.8 imp pt, 10.6 US pt, 5 l; Bosch or Rotodiesel injection pump; cooling: 16.7 imp pt, 20.1 US pt, 9.5 l.

TRANSMISSION GLD gearbox ratios: I 3.308, II 1.882, III 1.148, IV 0.800, rev 3.333 - SRD gears: 5, fully synchronized; ratios: I 3.308, II 1.882, III 1.280, IV 0.969, V 0.757, rev 3.333; axle ratio: GLD 4.063 - SRD 4.188; width of rims: 5"; tyres: 155 SR x 14.

PERFORMANCE max speed: 94 mph, 152 km/h; power-weight ratio: GLD 33.4 lb/hp (46.2 lb/kW), 15.2 kg/hp (20.9 kg/kW); acceleration: standing ¼ mile SRD 19.8 sec; speed in top at 1,000 rpm: SRD 21.7 mph, 35 km/h; consumption: SRD 44.1 m/imp gal, 36.8 m/US gal, 6.4 l x 100 km at 75 mph, 120 km/h.

ELECTRICAL EQUIPMENT 60 Ah battery; 50 A alternator.

DIMENSIONS AND WEIGHT weight: GLD 2,172 lb, 985 kg - SRD 2,227 lb, 1,010 kg.

PRACTICAL INSTRUCTIONS fuel: diesel; oil: engine, gearbox and final drive 8.8 imp pt, 10.6 US pt, 5 l, change every 3,100 miles, 5,000 km; valve timing: -4° 43° 28° -1°.

OPTIONALS (for GLD only) 5-speed mechanical gearbox (I 3.308, II 1.882, III 1.280, IV 0.969, V 0.757, rev 3.333), 4.188 axle ratio; electric sunroof; tinted glass; metallic spray.

305 Break Series

PRICES IN GB AND EX WORKS:	£	francs
1 GL 4+1-dr Break	5,345*	55,800**
2 SR 4+1-dr Break	6,245*	63,800**
3 GLD 4+1-dr Break	6,295*	64,800**
4 SRD 4+1-dr Break	—	73,500**

Power team:	Standard for:	Optional for:
74 hp	1,2	—
65 hp (diesel)	3,4	—

PEUGEOT 305 GR Berline

74 hp power team

ENGINE front, transverse, slanted 20° to front, 4 stroke; 4 cylinders, in line; 89.8 cu in, 1,472 cc (3.07 x 3.03 in, 78 x 77 mm); compression ratio: 9.2:1; max power (DIN): 74 hp (53 kW) at 5,500 rpm; max torque (DIN): 88 lb ft, 12.1 kg m (116 Nm) at 2,500 rpm; 50.3 hp/l (36 kW/l); light alloy block and head, wet liners, bi-hemispherical combustion chambers; 5 crankshaft bearings; valves: overhead, Vee-slanted, rockers; camshafts: 1 overhead; lubrication: rotary pump, cartridge on by-pass, 7 imp pt, 8.5 US pt, 4 l; 1 Solex 34 PBISA 14 or Weber IBP 1/100 downdraught single barrel carburettor; fuel feed: mechanical pump; water-cooled, 10.2 imp pt, 12.3 US pt, 5.8 l, electromagnetic fan.

TRANSMISSION driving wheels: front; clutch: single dry plate (diaphragm), hydraulically controlled; gearbox: mechanical; gears: 4, fully synchronized; ratios: I 3.334, II 1.935, III 1.272, IV 0.859, rev 3.436; lever: central; final drive: helical spur gears; axle ratio: 4.202; width of rims: 5"; tyres: 155 SR x 14.

PERFORMANCE max speed: 98 mph, 158 km/h; power-weight ratio: GL 29.4 lb/hp (41 lb/kW), 13.3 kg/hp (18.6 kg/kW); carrying capacity: 1,125 lb, 510 kg; acceleration: standing ¼ mile 18.7 sec; speed in top at 1,000 rpm: 19.1 mph, 30.8 km/h; consumption: 36.7 m/imp gal, 30.5 m/US gal, 7.7 l x 100 km at 75 mph, 120 km/h.

CHASSIS integral; front suspension: independent, by McPherson, coil springs/telescopic dampers, lower wishbones, anti-roll bar; rear: independent, swinging longitudinal trailing arms, anti-roll bar, coil springs/telescopic dampers.

STEERING rack-and-pinion; turns lock to lock: 4.20.

BRAKES front disc (diameter 10.47 in, 26.6 cm), rear drum, dual circuit, rear compensator, servo; swept area: total 283.7 sq in, 1,830 sq cm.

ELECTRICAL EQUIPMENT 12 V; 45 Ah battery; 500 W alternator; Ducellier distributor; 2 headlamps.

DIMENSIONS AND WEIGHT wheel base: 103.15 in, 262 cm; tracks: 54.41 in, 138 cm front, 53.15 in, 135 cm rear; length: 168.62 in, 428 cm; width: 64.17 in, 163 cm; height: 56.30 in, 143 cm; ground clearance: 4.72 in, 12 cm; weight: GL 2,172 lb, 985 kg - SR 2,205 lb, 1,000 kg; turning circle: 35.8 ft, 10.9 m; fuel tank: 11 imp gal, 13.2 US gal, 50 l.

BODY estate car/st. wagon; 4+1 doors; 5 seats, separate front seats, reclining backrests; heated rear window; folding rear seat.

PRACTICAL INSTRUCTIONS fuel: 95 oct petrol; oil: engine, gearbox and final drive 7 imp pt, 8.5 US pt, 4 l, SAE 20W-40, change every 3,100 miles, 5,000 km; greasing: every 3,100 miles, 5,000 km, 5 points; tyre pressure: front 23 psi, 1.6 atm, rear 36 psi, 2.5 atm.

OPTIONALS rear window wiper-washer; metallic spray; tinted glass.

65 hp (diesel) power team

See 74 hp power team, except for:

ENGINE diesel; 116.2 cu in, 1,905 cc (3.27 x 3.46 in, 83 x 88 mm); compression ratio: 23.5:1; max power (DIN): 65 hp (47 kW) at 4,600 rpm; max torque (DIN): 88 lb ft, 12.2 kg m (118 Nm) at 2,000 rpm; max engine rpm: 5,000; 34.1 hp/l (24.7 kW/l); cast iron block; lubrication: 8.8 imp pt, 10.6 US pt, 5 l; Bosch or Rotodiesel injection pump; cooling: 16.7 imp pt, 20.1 US pt, 9.5 l.

TRANSMISSION GLD gearbox ratios: I 3.308, II 1.882, III 1.148, IV 0.800, rev 3.333 - SRD gears: 5, fully synchronized; ratios: I 3.308, II 1.882, III 1.280, IV 0.969, V 0.757, rev 3.333; axle ratio: GLD 4.063 - SRD 4.188.

PERFORMANCE max speed: 94 mph, 152 km/h; power-weight ratio: GLD 33.4 lb/hp (49 lb/kW), 16.1 kg/hp (22.2 kg/kW); acceleration: standing ¼ mile SRD 20.3 sec; speed in top at 1,000 rpm: SRD 21.7 mph, 35 km/h; consumption: SRD 41.5 m/imp gal, 34.6 m/US gal, 6.8 l x 100 km at 75 mph, 120 km/h.

ELECTRICAL EQUIPMENT 60 Ah battery; 50 A alternator.

DIMENSIONS AND WEIGHT weight: GLD 2,304 lb, 1,045 kg - SRD 2,337 lb, 1,060 kg.

PRACTICAL INSTRUCTIONS fuel: diesel; oil: engine, gearbox and final drive 8.8 imp pt, 12.2 US pt, 5 l, change every 3,100 miles, 5,000 km; valve timing: -4° 43° 28° -1°.

OPTIONALS (for GLD only) 5-speed mechanical gearbox (I 3.308, II 1.882, III 1.280, IV 0.969, V 0.757, rev 3.333), 4.188 axle ratio.

505 Series

PRICES IN GB AND EX WORKS:	£	francs
1 GL 4-dr Berline	—	63,400**
2 GR 4-dr Berline	7,145*	69,400**
3 SR 4-dr Berline	8,095*	77,500**
4 GTI 4-dr Berline	9,195*	86,800**
5 Turbo Injection 4-dr Berline	—	104,100**
6 Turbo Injection 160 hp 4-dr Berline	—	—
7 GLD 4-dr Berline	—	72,700**
8 GRD 4-dr Berline	7,945*	78,700**
9 SRD Turbo 4-dr Berline	9,295*	92,500**
10 GTD Turbo 4-dr Berline	—	97,600**

For USA prices, see price index.

Power team:	Standard for:	Optional for:
100 hp	1 to 3	—
130 hp	4	—
150 hp	5	—
160 hp	6	—
76 hp (diesel)	7,8	—
80 hp (diesel)	9	—
95 hp (diesel)	10	—

100 hp power team

ENGINE front, slanted 45° to right, 4 stroke; 4 cylinders, in line; 120.3 cu in, 1,971 cc (3.46 x 3.19 in, 88 x 81 mm); compression ratio: 8.8:1; max power (DIN): 100 hp (72 kW) at 5,000 rpm; max torque (DIN): 119 lb ft, 16.4 kg m (161 Nm) at 3,000 rpm; max engine rpm: 5,500; 50.7 hp/l (36.5 kW/l); cast iron block, wet liners, light alloy head, hemispherical combustion chambers; 5 crankshaft bearings; valves: overhead, Vee-slanted, push-rods and rockers; camshafts: 1, side; lubrication: gear pump, metal gauze filter, 7 imp pt, 8.5 US pt, 4 l; 1 Zenith 35-40 INAT or Solex 32-35 TMIMAT downdraught twin barrel carburettor; fuel feed: mechanical pump; water-cooled, semi-sealed circuit, expansion tank, 12.5 imp pt, 15 US pt, 7.1 l, electromagnetic thermostatic fan.

TRANSMISSION driving wheels: rear; clutch: single dry plate (diaphragm), hydraulically controlled; gearbox: mechanical; gears: 4, fully synchronized - SR 5, fully synchronized; ratios: I 3.704, II 2.153, III 1.410, IV 1, rev 3.747 - SR I 3.592, II 2.088, III 1.368, V 0.823, rev 3.634; lever: central; final drive: hypoid bevel; axle ratio: 3.584 - SR 3.890; width of rims: 5" - SR 5.5"; tyres: 175 SR x 14 - SR 185/70 T x 14.

PERFORMANCE max speed: 104 mph, 168 km; power-weight ratio: GL 26.5 lb/hp (36.7 lb/kW), 12 kg/hp (16.7 kg/kW); carrying capacity: 1,058 lb, 480 kg; acceleration: standing ¼ mile 18.5 sec; speed in direct drive at 1,000

100 HP POWER TEAM

rpm: 20.1 mph, 32.3 km/h; consumption: GL 31 m/imp gal, 25.8 m/US gal, 9.1 l x 100 km at 75 mph, 120 km/h.

CHASSIS integral; front suspension: independent, by McPherson, coil springs/telescopic damper struts, lower wishbones, anti-roll bar; rear: independent, oblique semi-trailing arms, coil springs/telescopic dampers, anti-roll bar.

STEERING rack-and-pinion, servo (for SR only); turns lock to lock: 4.50.

BRAKES front disc (diameter 10.75 in, 27.3 cm), rear drum, dual circuit, rear compensator, servo; swept area: total 400.5 sq in, 2,583 sq cm.

ELECTRICAL EQUIPMENT 12 V; 45 Ah battery; 500 W alternator; transistorized ignition; 2 halogen headlamps.

DIMENSIONS AND WEIGHT wheel base: 107.87 in, 274 cm; tracks: 57.48 in, 146 cm front, 56.30 in, 143 cm rear; length: 180.31 in, 458 cm; width: 67.72 in, 172 cm; height: 57.09 in, 145 cm; ground clearance: 4.72 in, 12 cm; weight: GL 2,646 lb, 1,200 kg - GR and SR 2,668 lb, 1,210 kg; weight distribution: 53% front, 47% rear; turning circle: 36.7 ft, 11.2 m; fuel tank: 15.4 imp gal, 18.5 US gal, 70 l.

BODY saloon/sedan; 4 doors; 5 seats, separate front seats, reclining backrests; heated rear window; (standard for SR) electric windows, tinted glass and leather upholstery.

PRACTICAL INSTRUCTIONS fuel: 97 oct petrol; oil: engine 7 imp pt, 8.5 US pt, 4 l, SAE 20W-40, change every 3,100 miles, 5,000 km - gearbox 1.9 imp pt, 2.3 US pt, 1.1 l, SAE 20W-40, change every 6,200 miles, 10,000 km - final drive 2.8 imp pt, 3.4 US pt, 1.6 l, GP 90, change every 6,200 miles, 10,000 km; greasing: every 3,100 miles, 5,000 km, 6 points; tappet clearances: inlet 0.004 in, 0.10 mm, exhaust 0.010 in, 0.25 mm; valve timing: 2° 34° 35° 4°30'; tyre pressure: front 23 psi, 1.6 atm, rear 27 psi, 1.9 atm.

OPTIONALS (for SR only) ZF 3 HP 22 automatic transmission, hydraulic torque converter and planetary gears with 3 ratios (I 2.480, II 1.480, III 1, rev 2.090), max ratio of converter at stall 2.3, max speed 99 mph, 160 km/h; (for GR only) 5-speed fully synchronized mechanical gearbox (I 3.592, II 2.088, III 1.368, IV 1, V 0.823, rev 3.634), 3.890 axle ratio, consumption 32.5 m/imp gal, 27 m/US gal, 8.7 l x 100 km at 75 mph, 120 km/h; leather upholstery; sunroof; tinted glass; electric windows; metallic spray; (for GR only) power steering; (for GL only) GPL.

VARIATIONS

(for USA only)
ENGINE compression ratio 8.3:1, max power (SAE net) 97 hp at 5,000 rpm, max torque (SAE net) 116 lb ft, 16 kg m at 3,500 rpm, 49.2 hp/l, K-Jetronic injection.

130 hp power team

See 100 hp power team, except for:

ENGINE slanted 12° to right; 132.1 cu in, 2,165 cc (3.46 x 3.50 in, 88 x 89 mm); compression ratio: 9.8:1; max power (DIN): 130 hp (94 kW) at 5,750 rpm; max torque (DIN): 139 lb ft, 19.2 kmg (185 Nm) at 4,250 rpm; max engine rpm: 6,000; 60 hp/l (43.4 kW/l); light alloy block; bi-hemispherical combustion chambers; valves: overhead, in line, rockers; camshafts: 1, overhead, cogged belt; lubrication: 8.8 imp pt, 10.6 US pt, 5 l; fuel feed: electric pump; Bosch L-Jetronic injection; cooling: 13.2 imp pt, 15.9 US pt, 7.5 l.

TRANSMISSION gears: 5, fully synchronized; ratios: I 3.592, II 2.088, III 1.368, IV 1, V 0.823, rev 3.634; axle ratio: 3.890; width of rims: 5.5''; tyres: 185/70 T x 14.

PERFORMANCE max speed: 115 mph, 185 km/h; power-weight ratio: 20.9 lb/hp (29 lb/kW), 9.5 kg/hp (13.1 kg/kW); acceleration: standing ¼ mile 17 sec; speed in top at 1,000 rpm: 22.1 mph, 35.5 km/h; consumption: 33.6 m/imp gal, 28 m/US gal, 8.4 l x 100 km at 75 mph, 120 km/h.

STEERING servo.

BRAKES disc.

ELECTRICAL EQUIPMENT 750 W alternator.

DIMENSIONS AND WEIGHT tracks: 58.31 in, 148 cm front, 57.01 in, 145 cm rear; height: 56.38 in, 143 cm; weight: 2,723 lb, 1,235 kg.

BODY electric windows, tinted glass and leather upholstery (standard).

PRACTICAL INSTRUCTIONS oil: engine 8.8 imp pt, 10.6 US pt, 5 l; valve timing: 9° 54° 50° 5°.

OPTIONALS ZF 3HP 22 automatic transmission, hydraulic torque converter and planetary gears with 3 ratios (I 2.560, II 1.520, III 1, rev 2), max ratio of converter at stall 2.3, max speed 112 mph, 180 km/h, consumption 30.1 m/imp gal, 25 m/US gal, 9.4 l x 100 km at 75 mph, 120 km/h.

VARIATIONS

(for USA only)
ENGINE compression ratio 8.3:1, max power (SAE net) 97 hp at 5,000 rpm, max torque (SAE net) 116 lb ft, 16 kg m at 3,500 rpm, 49.2 hp/l, K-Jetronic injection.

PEUGEOT 505 GL Berline

150 hp power team

See 100 hp power team, except for:

ENGINE turbocharged; slanted 15° to right; 131.5 cu in, 2,155 cc (3.61 x 3.21 in, 91.7 x 81.6 mm); compression ratio: 7.5:1; max power (DIN): 150 hp (108 kW) at 5,200 rpm; max torque (DIN): 174 lb ft, 24 kg m (232 Nm) at 3,000 rpm; 69.6 hp/l (50.1 kW/l); valves: overhead, in line, rockers; camshafts: 1, overhead; lubrication: 8.8 imp pt, 10.6 US pt, 5 l; fuel feed: electric pump; Bosch L-Jetronic injection; 1 Garrett AiResearch T3 turbocharger; cooling: 16.7 imp pt, 20.1 US pt, 9.5 l, 2 electric thermostatic fans.

TRANSMISSION gears: 5, fully synchronized; ratios: I 3.457, II 2.061, III 1.407, IV 1, V 0.823, rev 3.493; width of rims: 6''; tyres: Pirelli 195/60 HR x 15 P6.

PERFORMANCE max speed: 124 mph, 200 km/h; power-weight ratio: 19.6 lb/hp (27.2 lb/kW), 8.9 kg/hp (12.3 kg/kW); acceleration: standing ¼ mile 16.3 sec; speed in top at 1,000 rpm: 22 mph, 35.4 km/h; consumption: 24.6 m/imp gal, 20.5 m/US gal, 11.5 l x 100 km at 75 mph, 120 km/h.

STEERING servo.

BRAKES disc, front internal radial fins.

ELECTRICAL EQUIPMENT 1,200 W alternator.

DIMENSIONS AND WEIGHT tracks: 58.74 in, 149 cm front, 57,40 in, 146 cm rear; height: 56.06 in, 142 cm; weight: 2,933 lb, 1,330 kg.

BODY electric windows, tinted glass (standard).

PRACTICAL INSTRUCTIONS oil: engine 8.8 imp pt, 10.6 US pt, 5 l; valve timing: 19°34' 55°10' 56°26' 12°50'.

OPTIONALS leather upholstery.

160 hp power team

See 100 hp power team, except for:

ENGINE turbocharged; slanted 15° to right; 131.5 cu in, 2,155 cc (3.61 x 3.21 in, 91.7 x 81.6 mm); compression ratio: 8:1; max power (DIN): 160 hp (115 kW) at 5,200 rpm; max torque (DIN): 181 lb ft, 25 kg m (240 Nm) at 3,000 rpm; 74.2 hp/l (53.4 kW/l); valves: overhead, rockers; camshafts: 1, overhead; lubrication: 8.8 imp pt, 10.6 US pt, 5 l; fuel feed: electric pump; Bosch L-Jetronic injection; 1 Garrett AiResearch T3 turbocharger; air-to-air exchanger; cooling: 16.7 imp pt, 20.1 US pt, 9.5 l, 2 electric thermostatic fans.

TRANSMISSION gears: 5, fully synchronized; ratios: I 3.457, II 2.061, III 1.407, IV 1, V 0.823, rev 3.493; axle ratio: 3.700; width of rims: 6''; tyres: Pirelli 195/60 HR x 15 P6.

PERFORMANCE max speed: 127 mph, 205 km/h; power-weight ratio: 18.3 lb/hp (25.5 lb/kW), 8.3 kg/hp (11.6 kg/kW); acceleration: standing ¼ mile 16.2 sec; speed in top at 1,000 rpm: 22.9 mph, 36.9 km/h; consumption: 28.8 m/imp gal, 24 m/US gal, 9.8 l x 100 km at 75 mph, 120 km/h.

STEERING servo.

BRAKES disc, front internal radial fins.

ELECTRICAL EQUIPMENT 1,200 W alternator.

DIMENSIONS AND WEIGHT tracks: 58.74 in, 149 cm front, 57,40 in, 146 cm rear; height: 56.06 in, 142 cm; weight: 2,933 lb, 1,330 kg.

BODY electric windows, tinted glass (standard).

PRACTICAL INSTRUCTIONS oil: engine 8.8 imp pt, 10.6 US pt, 5 l; valve timing: 19°34' 55°10' 56°26' 12°50'.

OPTIONALS leather upholstery.

76 hp (diesel) power team

See 100 hp power team, except for:

ENGINE diesel; slanted at 20°; 152.4 cu in, 2,498 cc (3.70 x 3.54 in, 94 x 90 mm); compression ratio: 23:1; max power (DIN): 76 hp (55 kW) at 4,500 rpm; max torque (DIN): 111 lb ft, 15.3 kg m (150 Nm) at 2,000 rpm; max engine rpm: 4,750; 30.4 hp/l (22 kW/l); turbulence chambers; valves: overhead, in line; lubrication: 8.8 imp pt, 10.6 US pt, 5 l; Rotodiesel injection pump; cooling: 17.6 imp pt, 21.1 US pt, 10 l.

PEUGEOT 505 Turbo Injection 160 hp Berline

PEUGEOT 505 GTD Turbo Berline

PEUGEOT 505 GTD Turbo Berline

TRANSMISSION gears: 4, fully synchronized; ratios: I 3.817, II 2.219, III 1.453, IV 1, rev 3.861; axle ratio: 3.461.

PERFORMANCE max speed: 93 mph, 150 km/h; power-weight ratio: GRD 37.9 lb/hp (52.3 lb/kW), 17.2 kg/hp (23.7 kg/kW); acceleration: standing ¼ mile 20.7 sec; speed in direct drive at 1,000 rpm: 20.8 mph, 33.4 km/h; consumption: 32.8 m/imp gal, 27.3 m/US gal, 8.6 l x 100 km at 75 mph, 120 km/h.

ELECTRICAL EQUIPMENT 60 Ah battery.

DIMENSIONS AND WEIGHT weight: GLD 2,855 lb, 1,295 kg - GRD 2,878 lb, 1,305 kg.

PRACTICAL INSTRUCTIONS fuel: diesel; oil: engine 8.8 imp pt, 10.6 US pt, 5 l.

OPTIONALS 5-speed mechanical gearbox, consumption 34.4 m/imp gal, 28.7 m/US gal, 8.2 l x 100 km at 75 mph, 120 km/h; (for GRD only) power steering.

80 hp (diesel) power team

See 100 hp power team, except for:

ENGINE diesel, turbocharged; slanted at 20°; 140.6 cu in, 2,304 cc (3.70 x 3.27 in, 94 x 83 mm); compression ratio: 21:1; max power (DIN): 80 hp (59 kW) at 4,150 rpm; max torque (DIN): 133 lb ft, 18.4 kg m (181 Nm) at 2,000 rpm; max engine rpm: 4,800; 34.7 hp/l (25.6 kW/l); 5 crankshaft bearings; turbulence chambers; valves: overhead, in line; lubrication: 8.8 imp pt, 10.6 US pt, 5 l; Bosch VE injection pump; 1 Garrett AiResearch TO3 turbocharger; cooling: 17.6 imp pt, 21.1 US pt, 10 l.

TRANSMISSION gears: 5, fully synchronized; ratios: I 3.862, II 2.183, III 1.445, IV 1, V 0.844, rev 3.587; axle ratio: 3.460; width of rims: 5.5"; tyres: 185/70 T x 14.

PERFORMANCE max speed: 99 mph, 160 km/h; power-weight ratio: 36.7 lb/hp (49.7 lb/kW), 16.6 kg/hp (22.5 kg/kW); acceleration: standing ¼ mile 20 sec; speed in direct drive at 1,000 rpm: 24.6 mph, 39.6 km/h; consumption: 32.8 m/imp gal, 27.3 m/US gal, 8.6 l x 100 km at 75 mph, 120 km/h.

STEERING servo.

ELECTRICAL EQUIPMENT 60 Ah battery.

DIMENSIONS AND WEIGHT weight: 2,933 lb, 1,330 kg.

BODY electric windows, tinted glass and leather upholstery (standard).

PRACTICAL INSTRUCTIONS fuel: diesel; oil: engine 8.8 imp pt, 10.6 US pt, 5 l.

OPTIONALS ZF 3HP 22 automatic transmission, 3.077 axle ratio, max speed 94 mph, 152 km/h, consumption 30.4 m/imp gal, 25.3 m/US gal, 9.3 l x 100 km at 75 mph, 120 km/h.

95 hp (diesel) power team

See 100 hp power team, except for:

ENGINE diesel, turbocharged; slanted at 20°; 152.4 cu in, 2,498 cc (3.70 x 3.54 in, 94 x 90 mm); compression ratio: 21:1; max power (DIN): 95 hp (70 kW) at 4,150 rpm; max torque (DIN): 152 lb ft, 21 kg m (206 Nm) at 2,000 rpm; max engine rpm: 4,800; 38 hp/l (28 kW/l); 5 crankshaft bearings; turbulence chambers; valves: overhead, in line; lubrication: 8.8 imp pt, 10.6 US pt, 5 l; Bosch or Rotodiesel injection pump; 1 Garrett AiResearch TO3 turbocharger; cooling: 17.6 imp pt, 21.1 US pt, 10 l.

TRANSMISSION gears: 5, fully synchronized; ratios: I 3.862, II 2.183, III 1.445, IV 1, V 0.844, rev 3.587; axle ratio: 3.308; width of rims: 5.5"; tyres: 185/70 T x 14.

PERFORMANCE max speed: 106 mph, 170 km/h; power-weight ratio: 31.1 lb/hp (42.2 lb/kW), 14.1 kg/hp (19.1 kg/kW); acceleration: standing ¼ mile 19 sec; speed in top at 1,000 rpm: 25.3 mph, 40.7 km/h; consumption: 33.2 m/imp gal, 27.7 m/US gal, 8.5 l x 100 km at 75 mph, 120 km/h.

STEERING servo.

ELECTRICAL EQUIPMENT 60 Ah battery.

DIMENSIONS AND WEIGHT weight: 2,955 lb, 1,340 kg.

BODY electric windows, tinted glass and leather upholstery (standard).

PEUGEOT 505 Turbo Injection 160 hp Berline

PRACTICAL INSTRUCTIONS fuel: diesel; oil: engine 8.8 imp pt, 10.6 US pt, 5 l.

OPTIONALS ZF 3HP 22 automatic transmission, 2.867 axle ratio, max speed 101 mph, 162 km/h, consumption 31 m/imp gal, 25.8 m/US gal, 9.1 l x 100 km at 75 mph, 120 km/h.

505 Break Familial Series

PRICES IN GB AND EX WORKS:	£	francs
1 GL 4+1-dr Break	7,665*	68,200**
2 GR 4+1-dr Break	8,385*	74,100**
3 SR 4+1-dr Break	—	83,600**
4 GR 4+1-dr Familial	8,835*	82,500**
5 SR 4+1-dr Familial	—	91,400**
6 GLD 4+1-dr Break	—	77,500**
7 GRD 4+1-dr Break	9,335*	84,800**
8 SRD 4+1-dr Break	—	92,900**
9 GRD 4+1-dr Familial	9,635*	93,200**
10 SRD 4+1-dr Familial	—	100,700**

For USA prices, see price index.

Power team:	Standard for:	Optional for:
96 hp	1 to 5	—
76 hp (diesel)	6 to 10	—

96 hp power team

ENGINE front, slanted 45° to right, 4 stroke; 4 cylinders, in line; 120.3 cu in, 1,971 cc (3.46 x 3.19 in, 88 x 81 mm); compression ratio: 8.8:1; max power (DIN): 96 hp (69 kW) at 5,200 rpm; max torque (DIN): 119 lb ft, 16.4 kg m (158 Nm) at 3,000 rpm; max engine rpm: 5,600; 48.7 hp/l (35 kW/l); cast iron block, wet liners, light alloy head, hemispherical combustion chambers; 5 crankshaft bearings; valves: overhead, Vee-slanted, push-rods and rockers; camshafts: 1, side; lubrication: gear pump, metal gauze filter, 7 imp pt, 8.5 US pt, 4 l; 1 Solex 32/35 TMIMAT or Zenith 35/40 INAT downdraught twin barrel carburettor; fuel feed: mechanical pump; water-cooled, semi-sealed circuit, expansion tank, 14.8 imp pt, 17.8 US pt, 8.4 l, electromagnetic thermostatic fan.

TRANSMISSION driving wheels: rear; clutch: single dry plate (diaphragm), hydraulically controlled; gearbox: mechanical; gears: 4, fully synchronized - SR models 5, fully synchronized; ratios: I 3.817, II 2.219, III 1.453, IV 1, rev 3.861 - SR models I 3.592, II 2.088, III 1.368, IV 1, V 0.823, rev 3.634; lever: central; final drive: hypoid bevel; axle ratio: 3.889 - SR models 4.222; width of rims: 5"; tyres: 185 SR x 14.

PERFORMANCE max speed: 101 mph, 162 km/h; power-weight ratio: GL 29.2 lb/hp (40.6 lb/kW), 13.2 kg/hp (18.4 kg/kW); carrying capacity: 1,555 lb, 705 kg; acceleration: standing ¼ mile 18.9 sec; speed in direct drive at 1,000 rpm: 18.9 mph, 30.4 km/h; consumption: GL 28.5 m/imp gal, 23.5 m/US gal, 9.9 l x 100 km at 75 mph, 120 km/h.

CHASSIS integral; front suspension: independent, by McPherson, coil springs/telescopic damper struts, lower wishbones, anti roll-bar; rear: independent, oblique semi-trailing arms, coil springs/telescopic dampers, anti-roll bar.

STEERING rack-and-pinion, servo (for SR models only); turns lock to lock: 4.50.

BRAKES front disc (diameter 10.75 in, 27.3 cm), rear drum, dual circuit, rear compensator, servo; swept area: total 361.2 sq in, 2,330 sq cm.

ELECTRICAL EQUIPMENT 12 V; 45 Ah battery; 500 W alternator; transistorized ignition; 2 halogen headlamps.

DIMENSIONS AND WEIGHT wheel base: 114.17 in, 290 cm; tracks: 57.87 in, 147 cm front, 56.69 in, 144 cm rear;

96 HP POWER TEAM

length: 192.83 in, 490 cm; width: 68.11 in, 173 cm; height: 60.63 in, 154 cm; weight: GL and GR Break models 2,800 lb, 1,270 kg - SR Break 2,855 lb, 1,295 kg - GR Familial 2,889 lb, 1,310 kg - SR Familial 2,911 lb, 1,320 kg; turning circle: 38 ft, 11.6 m; fuel tank: 15.4 imp gal, 18.5 US gal, 70 l.

BODY estate car/st. wagon; 4+1 doors; 5 seats, separate front seats, reclining backrests; heated rear window.

PRACTICAL INSTRUCTIONS fuel: 97 oct petrol; oil: engine 7 imp pt, 8.5 US pt, 4 l, SAE 20W-40, change every 3,100 miles, 5,000 km - gearbox 1.9 imp pt, 2.3 US pt, 1.1 l, SAE 20W-40, change every 6,200 miles, 10,000 km - final drive 2.8 imp pt, 3.4 US pt, 1.6 l, GP 90, change every 6,200 miles, 10,000 km; greasing: every 3,100 miles, 5,000 km, 6 points; valve timing: 2° 34° 35° 4°30'; tyre pressure: front 23 psi, 1.6 atm, rear 36 psi, 2.5 atm.

OPTIONALS (for GR models only) 5-speed mechanical gearbox, consumption 29.4 m/imp gal, 24.5 m/US gal, 9.6 l x 100 km at 75 mph, 120 km/h; (for SR models and USA version only) ZF HP 22 automatic transmission with 3 ratios (I 2.479, II 1.479, III 1, rev 2.086), max speed 97 mph, 156 km/h, consumption 26.9 m/imp gal, 22.4 m/US gal, 10.5 l x 100 km at 75 mph, 120 km/h; (for GR models only) power steering; headrests; rear window wiper-washer; metallic spray.

VARIATIONS

(for USA only)
ENGINE compression ratio 8.3:1, max power (SAE net) 97 hp at 5,000 rpm, max torque (SAE net) 116 lb ft, 16 kg m at 3,500 rpm, 49.2 hp/l, K-JEtronic injection.

76 hp (diesel) power team

See 96 hp power team, except for:

ENGINE diesel; slanted 20° to right; 152.4 cu in, 2,498 cc (3.70 x 3.54 in, 94 x 90 mm); compression ratio: 23:1; max power (DIN): 76 hp (55 kW) at 4,500 rpm; max torque (DIN): 111 lb ft, 15.3 kg m (147 Nm) at 2,000 rpm; max engine rpm: 5,000; 30.4 hp/l (22 kW/l); turbulence chambers; valves: overhead, in line; lubrication: 8.8 imp pt, 10.6 US pt, 5 l; Rotodiesel injection pump; cooling: 17.6 imp pt, 21.1 US pt, 10 l.

TRANSMISSION gears: GLD 4, fully synchronized - GRD and SRD models 5, fully synchronized; axle ratio: GLD 3.778 - GRD and SRD models 4.222.

PERFORMANCE max speed: GRD and SRD models 91 mph, 146 km/h; power-weight ratio: GRD models 40.2 lb/hp (55.5 lb/kW), 18.2 kg/hp (25.2 kg/kW); acceleration: GRD and SRD models standing ¼ mile 20.5 sec; consumption: GRD and SRD models 31.4 m/imp gal, 26.1 m/US gal, 9 l x 100 km at 75 mph, 120 km/h.

ELECTRICAL EQUIPMENT 60 Ah battery.

DIMENSIONS AND WEIGHT weight: GLD 2,811 lb, 1,375 kg - GRD and SRD Break models 3,054 lb, 1,385 kg - GRD and SRD Familial models 3,120 lb, 1,415 kg.

PRACTICAL INSTRUCTIONS fuel: diesel; oil: engine 8.8 imp pt, 10.6 US pt, 5 l.

VARIATIONS

(for USA only)
ENGINE diesel turbocharged, 140.6 cu in, 2,304 cc (3.70 x 3.27 in, 94 x 83 mm), compression ratio 21:1, max power (SAE net) 80 hp at 4,150 rpm, max torque (SAE net) 133 lb ft, 18.4 kg m at 2,000 rpm, 34.7 hp/l, Bosch VE injection pump, 1 Garrett AiResearch T03 turbocharger.

604 Series

PRICES IN GB AND IN USA:

	£	$
1 GTI 4-dr Berline	12,395*	—
2 GTD Turbo 4-dr Berline	11,395*	21,285*

Power team:	Standard for:	Optional for:
155 hp	1	—
95 hp (diesel)	2	—

155 hp power team

ENGINE PRV, front, 4 stroke; 6 cylinders, Vee-slanted at 90°; 173.8 cu in, 2,849 cc (3.58 x 2.87 in, 91 x 73 mm); compression ratio: 9.5:1; max power (DIN): 155 hp (112 kW) at 5,750 rpm; max torque (DIN): 176 lb ft, 24.2 kg m (234 Nm) at 3,000 rpm; 54.4 hp/l (39.3 kW/l); light alloy block and head, wet liners, bi-hemispherical combustion chambers; 4 crankshaft bearings; valves: overhead, Vee-slanted, rockers; camshafts: 2, 1 per bank, overhead; lubrication: gear pump, full flow filter, 10.6 imp pt, 12.7 US pt, 6 l; Bosch K-Jetronic injection; fuel feed: electric pump; water-cooled, expansion tank, 18.1 imp pt, 21.8 US pt, 10.3 l, viscous coupling thermostatic fan.

PEUGEOT 505 SR Break

TRANSMISSION driving wheels: rear; clutch: single dry plate (diaphragm), hydraulically controlled; gearbox: mechanical; gears: 5, fully synchronized; ratios: I 3.498, II 2.183, III 1.445, IV 1, V 0.844, rev 3.587; lever: central; final drive: hypoid bevel; axle ratio: 3.699; width of rims: 6"; tyres: Pirelli 195/60 HR x 15 P6.

PERFORMANCE max speeds: (I) 28 mph, 45 km/h; (II) 50 mph, 80 km/h; (III) 75 mph, 121 km/h; (IV) 109 mph, 175 km/h; (V) 118 mph, 190 km/h; power-weight ratio: 20.2 lb/hp (27.9 lb/kW), 9.2 kg/hp (12.7 kg/kW); carrying capacity: 1,235 lb, 560 kg; acceleration: standing ¼ mile 16.8 sec; speed in direct drive at 1,000 rpm: 22.3 mph, 35.9 km/h; consumption: 25.9 m/imp gal, 21.6 m/US gal, 10.9 l x 100 km at 75 mph, 120 km/h.

CHASSIS integral; front suspension: independent, by McPherson, coil springs/telescopic damper struts, lower wishbones, anti-roll bar; rear: independent, oblique semi-trailing arms, coil springs, anti-roll bar, telescopic dampers.

STEERING rack-and-pinion, servo; turns lock to lock: 3.50.

BRAKES disc (diameter 10.75 in, 27.3 cm), front internal radial fins, dual circuit, rear compensator, servo; swept area: front 223 sq in, 1,438 sq cm, rear 192 sq in, 1,239 sq cm, total 415 sq in, 2,677 sq cm.

ELECTRICAL EQUIPMENT 12 V; 45 Ah battery; 750 W alternator; electronic ignition; 4 halogen headlamps.

DIMENSIONS AND WEIGHT wheel base: 110.24 in, 280 cm; tracks: 58.66 in, 149 cm front, 56.30 in, 143 cm rear; length: 185.83 in, 472 cm; width: 70.24 in, 178 cm; height: 56.30 in, 143 cm; ground clearance: 5.91 in, 15 cm; weight: 3,131 lb, 1,420 kg; turning circle: 37.7 ft, 11.5 m; fuel tank: 15.4 imp gal, 18.5 US gal, 70 l.

BODY saloon/sedan; 4 doors; 5 seats, separate front seats, reclining backrests with built-in headrests; electric windows; heated rear window; sunroof with tinted glass.

PRACTICAL INSTRUCTIONS fuel: 95 oct petrol; oil: engine 10.6 imp pt, 12.7 US pt, 6 l, SAE 10W-50, change every 3,100 miles, 5,000 km - gearbox 2.3 imp pt, 2.7 US pt, 1.3 l, SAE 20W-40, change every 6,200 miles, 10,000 km - final drive 2.6 imp pt, 3.2 US pt, 1.5 l, SAE 80, change every 6,200 miles, 10,000 km; greasing: every 3,100 miles, 5,000 km; tappet clearances: inlet 0.006 in, 0.15 mm, exhaust 0.012 in, 0.30 mm; valve timing: 8° 42° 42° 8°.

OPTIONALS automatic transmission with 3 ratios (I 2.400, II 1.480, III 1, rev 1.920), max ratio of converter at stall 2.3, possible manual selection, 3.077 axle ratio, max speed 115 mph, 185 km/h, acceleration standing ¼ mile 18.2 sec, consumption 24.1 m/imp gal, 20.1 m/US gal, 11.7 l x 100 km at 75 mph, 120 km/h; air-conditioning; electric sunroof; leather upholstery; metallic spray.

95 hp (diesel) power team

See 155 hp power team, except for:

ENGINE diesel, turbocharged; 4 cylinders, in line, slanted at 20°; 152.4 cu in, 2,498 cc (3.70 x 3.54 in, 94 x 90 mm); compression ratio: 21:1; max power (DIN): 95 hp (70 kW) at 4,150 rpm; max torque (DIN): 152 lb ft, 21 kg m (206 Nm) at 2,000 rpm; max engine rpm: 4,800; 38 hp/l (28 kW/l); cast iron block; 5 crankshaft bearings; turbulence chambers; valves: overhead, in line; camshafts: 1, side, chain-driven; lubrication: 8.8 imp pt, 10.6 US pt, 5 l; Bosch VE injection pump; 1 Garrett AiResearch TO3 turbocharger; cooling: 17.6 imp pt, 21.1 US pt, 10 l.

TRANSMISSION axle ratio: 3.308.

PERFORMANCE max speed: 102 mph, 165 km/h; power-weight ratio: 34 lb/hp (46.1 lb/kW), 15.4 kg/hp (20.9 kg/kW); acceleration: standing ¼ mile 19.6 sec; speed in direct drive at 1,000 rpm: 25 mph, 40.2 km/h; consumption: 32.1 m/imp gal, 26.7 m/US gal, 8.8 l x 100 km at 75 mph, 120 km/h.

ELECTRICAL EQUIPMENT 60 Ah battery.

DIMENSIONS AND WEIGHT weight: 3,230 lb, 1,465 kg; weight distribution: 53% front, 47% rear.

BODY sunroof with tinted glass.

PRACTICAL INSTRUCTIONS fuel: diesel; oil: engine 8.8 imp pt, 10.6 US pt, 5 l.

OPTIONALS ZF 3HP 22 automatic transmission (standard for USA version only), 2.867 axle ratio, max speed 98 mph, 158 km/h, consumption 28.2 m/imp gal, 23.5 m/US gal, 10 l x 100 km at 75 mph, 120 km/h.

PEUGEOT 604 GTI Berline

RENAULT 4 GTL Break

RENAULT FRANCE

4 Series

PRICES IN GB AND EX WORKS:	£	francs
1 4+1-dr Break	—	30,088**
2 TL 4+1-dr Break	—	33,188**
3 GTL 4+1-dr Break	3,424*	36,288**

Power team:	Standard for:	Optional for:
29 hp	1,2	—
34 hp	3	—

29 hp power team

ENGINE front, 4 stroke; 4 cylinders, vertical, in line; 51.6 cu in, 845 cc (2.28 x 3.15 in, 58 x 80 mm); compression ratio: 8:1; max power (DIN): 29 hp (21 kW) at 4,500 rpm; max torque (DIN): 33 lb ft, 5.8 kg m (59 Nm) at 2,250 rpm; max engine rpm: 5,000; 34.3 hp/l (24.9 kW/l); cast iron block, wet liners, light alloy head; 3 crankshaft bearings; valves: overhead, in line, push-rods and rockers; camshafts: 1, side; lubrication: gear pump, filter in sump, 4.8 imp pt, 5.8 US pt, 2.7 l; 1 Zenith 28 IF downdraught single barrel carburettor; fuel feed: mechanical pump; sealed circuit cooling, expansion tank, 9.7 imp pt, 11.6 US pt, 5.5 l.

TRANSMISSION driving wheels: front; clutch: single dry plate (diaphragm); gearbox: mechanical; gears: 4, fully synchronized; ratios: I 3.833, II 2.235, III 1.458, IV 1.026, rev 3.545; lever: on facia; final drive: spiral bevel; axle ratio: 3.777; width of rims: 4"; tyres: 135 SR x 13.

PERFORMANCE max speed: 75 mph, 120 km/h; power-weight ratio: Break 50.6 lb/hp (69.8 lb/kW), 22.9 kg/hp (31.7 kg/kW); carrying capacity: 728 lb, 330 kg; acceleration: standing ¼ mile 22.5 sec; speed in top at 1,000 rpm: 16 mph, 25.8 km/h; consumption: 50.4 m/imp gal, 42 m/US gal, 5.6 l x 100 km at 56 mph, 90 km/h.

CHASSIS platform; front suspension: independent, wishbones, longitudinal torsion bars, anti-roll bar, telescopic dampers; rear: independent, swinging longitudinal trailing arms, transverse torsion bars, telescopic dampers.

STEERING rack-and-pinion; turns lock to lock: 3.75.

BRAKES drum (front diameter 7.87 in, 20 cm, rear 6.30 in, 16 cm), dual circuit, rear compensator; lining area: front 36.4 sq in, 235 sq cm, rear 18 sq in, 116 sq cm, total 54.4 sq in, 351 sq cm.

ELECTRICAL EQUIPMENT 12 V; 28 Ah battery; 40 A alternator; Ducellier distributor; 2 headlamps.

DIMENSIONS AND WEIGHT wheel base: 96.46 in, 245 cm (right), 94.49 in, 240 cm (left); tracks: 50.39 in, 128 cm front, 48.82 in, 124 cm rear; length: 144.49 in, 367 cm; width: 58.27 in, 148 cm; height: 61.02 in, 155 cm; ground clearance: 6.89 in, 17.5 cm; weight: Break 1,466 lb, 665 kg - TL Break 1,532 lb, 695 kg; weight distribution: 56.1% front, 43.9% rear; turning circle: 33.1 ft, 10.1 m; fuel tank: 7.5 imp gal, 9 US gal, 34 l.

BODY estate car/st. wagon; 4+1 doors; 4 seats, bench front seats - TL Break separate front seats; folding rear seat; heated rear window.

PRACTICAL INSTRUCTIONS fuel: 88 oct petrol; oil: engine 4.8 imp pt, 5.8 US pt, 2.7 l, SAE 10W-40, change every 4,650 miles, 7,500 km - gearbox and final drive 3.2 imp pt, 3.8 US pt, 1.8 l, SAE 80 EP, change every 9,300 miles, 15,000 km; greasing: none; tappet clearances: inlet 0.006-0.007 in, 0.15-0.18 mm, exhaust 0.007-0.009 in, 0.18-0.22 mm; valve timing: 16° 52° 52° 22°; tyre pressure: front 20 psi, 1.4 atm, rear 24 psi, 1.7 atm.

OPTIONALS luxury interior; (for TL Break only) metallic spray and reclining backrests.

34 hp power team

See 29 hp power team, except for:

ENGINE 67.6 cu in, 1,108 cc (2.76 x 2.83 in, 70 x 72 mm); compression ratio: 9.5:1; max power (DIN): 34 hp (25 kW) at 4,000 rpm; max torque (DIN): 54 lb ft, 7.5 kg m (74 Nm) at 2,500 rpm; 42.4 hp/l (22.6 kW/l); 5 crankshaft bearings; lubrication: 5.6 imp pt, 6.8 US pt, 3.2 l; water-cooled, 10.4 imp pt, 18.1 US pt, 5.9 l, electric thermostatic fan.

TRANSMISSION axle ratio: 3.100.

PERFORMANCE max speed: over 75 mph, 120 km/h; power-weight ratio: 46.7 lb/hp (63.5 lb/kW), 21.2 kg/hp (28.8 kg/kW); acceleration: standing ¼ mile 22.4 sec; speed in top at 1,000 rpm: 19.6 mph, 31.5 km/h; consumption: 52.3 m/imp gal, 43.6 m/US gal, 5.4 l x 100 km at 56 mph, 90 km/h.

BRAKES front disc (diameter 9.06 in, 23 cm).

DIMENSIONS AND WEIGHT weight: 1,588 lb, 720 kg.

BODY separate front seats.

PRACTICAL INSTRUCTIONS fuel: 98-100 oct petrol; oil: engine 5.3 imp pt, 6.3 US pt, 3 l; tappet clearances: inlet 0.012 in, 0.30 mm, exhaust 0.012 in, 0.30 mm; valve timing: 12° 48° 52° 8°; tyre pressure: rear 21 psi, 1.5 atm.

OPTIONALS GPL; sunroof; metallic spray; reclining backrests.

5 Series

PRICES IN GB AND EX WORKS:	£	francs
1 2+1-dr Berline	3,290*	35,088**
2 4+1-dr Berline	—	36,988**
3 TL 2+1-dr Berline	3,995*	40,188**
4 TL 4+1-dr Berline	—	42,088**
5 GTL 2+1-dr Berline	4,350*	45,188**
6 GTL 4+1-dr Berline	4,510*	47,088**
7 Automatic 2+1-dr Berline	4,950*	48,860**
8 Automatic 4+1-dr Berline	—	50,760**
9 TS 2+1-dr Berline	—	47,892**
10 TX 2+1-dr Berline	5,250*	55,092**
11 TX Automatic 2+1-dr Berline	—	57,060**
12 Alpine Turbo 2+1-dr Berline	5,950*	64,524**

Power team:	Standard for:	Optional for:
37 hp	1,2	—
45 hp	3 to 6	—
58 hp	7,8,11	—
63 hp	9,10	—
110 hp	12	—

37 hp power team

ENGINE front, 4 stroke; 4 cylinders, vertical, in line; 51.6 cu in, 845 cc (2.28 x 3.15 in, 58 x 80 mm); compression ratio: 8:1; max power (DIN): 37 hp (27 kW) at 5,500 rpm; max torque (DIN): 43 lb ft, 5.9 kg m (57 Nm) at 2,500 rpm; max engine rpm: 6,000; 43.8 hp/l (31.4 kW/l); cast iron block, wet liners, light alloy head; 3 crankshaft bearings; valves: overhead, in line, push-rods and rockers; camshafts: 1, side; lubrication: gear pump, filter in sump (cartridge), 4.8 imp pt, 5.8 US pt, 2.7 l; 1 Solex 32 DIS downdraught single barrel carburettor; fuel feed: mechanical pump; sealed circuit cooling, expansion tank, liquid, 11.3 imp pt, 13.5 US pt, 6.4 l.

TRANSMISSION driving wheels: front; clutch: single dry plate (diaphragm); gearbox: mechanical; gears: 4, fully synchronized; ratios: I 3.833, II 2.235, III 1.458, IV 1.026, rev 3.545; lever: central; final drive: spiral bevel; axle ratio: 3.777; width of rims: 4"; tyres: 135 SR x 13.

PERFORMANCE max speeds: (I) 24 mph, 38 km/h; (II) 39 mph, 63 km/h; (III) 60 mph, 97 km/h; (IV) 78 mph, 126 km/h; power-weight ratio: 42.9 lb/hp (52.8 lb/kW), 19.5 kg/hp (26.7 kg/kW); carrying capacity: 728 lb, 330 kg; acceleration: standing ¼ mile 22 sec; speed in top at 1,000 rpm: 16 mph, 25.8 km/h; consumption: 52.3 m/imp gal, 43.6 m/US gal, 5.4 l x 100 km at 56 mph, 90 km/h.

CHASSIS integral; front suspension: independent, wishbones, longitudinal torsion bars, anti-roll bar, telescopic

RENAULT 4 GTL Break

RENAULT 5 TX Berline

37 HP POWER TEAM

dampers; rear: independent, swinging longitudinal trailing arms, transverse torsion bars, telescopic dampers.

STEERING rack-and-pinion; turns lock to lock: 3.75.

BRAKES drum (diameter 9.06 in, 23 cm front, 6.30 in, 16 cm rear), dual circuit, rear compensator; lining area: front 79.9 sq in, 503 sq cm, rear 38.9 sq in, 251 sq cm, total 118.8 sq in, 754 sq cm.

ELECTRICAL EQUIPMENT 12 V; 28 Ah battery; 50 A alternator; R 220 distributor; 2 headlamps.

DIMENSIONS AND WEIGHT wheel base: 94.49 in, 240 cm (right), 95.67 in, 243 cm (left); tracks: 50.39 in, 128 cm front, 48.82 in, 124 cm rear; length: 138.19 in, 351 cm; width: 59.84 in, 152 cm; height: 55.12 in, 140 cm; ground clearance: 7.87 in, 20 cm; weight: 1,588 lb, 720 kg; weight distribution: 58.2% front, 41.8% rear; turning circle: 33.1 ft, 10.1 m; fuel tank: 8.4 imp gal, 10 US gal, 38 l.

BODY saloon/sedan; 2+1 or 4+1 doors; 5 seats, separate front seats; heated rear window; folding rear seat.

PRACTICAL INSTRUCTIONS fuel: 92 oct petrol; oil: engine 4.8 imp pt, 5.8 US pt, 2.7 l, SAE 20W-40, change every 4,650 miles, 7,500 km - gearbox and final drive 3.2 imp pt, 3.8 US pt, 1.8 l, SAE 80 EP, change every 9,300 miles, 15,000 km; greasing: none; tappet clearances: inlet 0.006-0.007 in, 0.15-0.18 mm, exhaust 0.007-0.009 in, 0.18-0.22 mm; valve timing: 20° 56° 53° 23°; tyre pressure: front 24 psi, 1.7 atm, rear 28 psi, 1.9 atm.

OPTIONALS luxury interior; metallic spray.

45 hp power team

See 37 hp power team, except for:

ENGINE 68.2 cu in, 1,118 cc (2.76 x 2.83 in, 70 x 72 mm); compression ratio: 9.5:1; max power (DIN): 45 hp (32 kW) at 4,400 rpm; max torque (DIN): 63 lb ft, 8.7 kg m (84 Nm) at 2,000 rpm; max engine rpm: 5,000; 40.2 hp/l (28.6 kW/l); 5 crankshaft bearings; lubrication: 5.6 imp pt, 6.8 US pt, 3.2 l; 1 Zenith 32 IF7 downdraught carburettor; cooling: 11.1 imp pt, 13.3 US pt, 6.3 l, electric thermostatic fan.

TRANSMISSION gears: GTL 5, fully synchronized; ratios: I 3.833, II 2.235, III 1.458, IV 1.171, V 0.948, rev 3.545; axle ratio: 3.100; width of rims: GTL 4.5".

PERFORMANCE max speeds: (I) 26 mph, 42 km/h; (II) 45 mph, 72 km/h; (III) 68 mph, 110 km/h; (IV) 85 mph, 137 km/h; power-weight ratio: TL 38 lb/hp (53.4 lb/kW), 17.2 kg/hp (24.2 kg/kW); acceleration: standing ¼ mile 21 sec; speed in top at 1,000 rpm: 19.6 mph, 31.5 km/h; consumption: TL 45.6 m/imp gal, 37.9 m/US gal, 6.2 l x 100 km - GTL 46.3 m/imp gal, 38.6 m/US ga, 6.1 l x 100 km at 75 mph, 120 km/h.

BRAKES front disc (diameter 8.98 in, 22.8 cm).

DIMENSIONS AND WEIGHT width: GTL 61.02 in, 155 cm; weight: TL 1,709 lb, 755 kg - GTL 1,731 lb, 785 kg.

PRACTICAL INSTRUCTIONS fuel: 98 oct petrol; valve timing: 12° 48° 52° 8°.

VARIATIONS

(for Italy only)
ENGINE 58.3 cu in, 956 cc (2.56 x 2.83 in, 65 x 72 mm), 9.25:1 compression ratio, max power (DIN) 44 hp (32 kW) at 5,500 rpm, max torque (DIN) 48 lb ft, 6.5 kg m (64 Nm) at 3,500 rpm, 46 hp/l (33.2 kW/l), 1 Solex 32 DIS carburettor.

RENAULT 5 Alpine Turbo Berline

TRANSMISSION 4.125 axle ratio, 145 SR x 13 tyres (standard).
PERFORMANCE power-weight ratio 38.8 lb/hp (53.9 lb/kW), 17.6 kg/hp (24.4 kg/kW), consumption 34.4 m/imp gal, 28.7 m/US gal, 8.2 l x 100 km at 75 mph, 120 km/h.
DIMENSIONS AND WEIGHT weight 1,709 lb, 775 kg.

OPTIONALS 145 SR x 13 tyres; tinted glass; sunroof; rear window wiper-washer; metallic spray.

58 hp power team

See 37 hp power team, except for:

ENGINE 85.2 cu in, 1,397 cc (2.99 x 3.03 in, 76 x 77 mm); compression ratio: 9.25:1; max power (DIN): 58 hp (42 kW) at 5,000 rpm; max torque (DIN): 75 lb ft, 10.3 kg m (99 Nm) at 3,000 rpm; max engine rpm: 5,500; 41.9 hp/l (30.1 kW/l); 5 crankshaft bearings; lubrication: 5.6 imp pt, 6.8 US pt, 3.2 l; 1 Weber 32 DIR downdraught twin barrel carburettor; cooling: 11.1 imp pt, 13.3 US pt, 6.3 l, electric thermostatic fan.

TRANSMISSION gearbox: automatic transmission, hydraulic torque converter and planetary gears with 3 ratios, max ratio of converter at stall 2, possible manual selection; ratios: I 2.266, II 1.403, III 1, rev 1.943; axle ratio: 3.555; width of rims: 4.5"; tyres: TX Automatic 145 SR x 13 (standard).

PERFORMANCE max speeds: (I) 32 mph, 52 km/h; (II) 62 mph, 100 km/h; (III) 88 mph, 142 km/h; power-weight ratio: 31.1 lb/hp (43.3 lb/kW), 14.1 kg/hp (19.6 kg/kW); acceleration: standing ¼ mile 21.2 sec; speed in direct drive at 1,000 rpm: 22.1 mph, 35.5 km/h; consumption: 34.9 m/imp gal, 29 m/US gal, 8.1 l x 100 km at 75 mph, 120 km/h.

BRAKES front disc (diameter 8.98 in, 22.8 cm), servo.

ELECTRICAL EQUIPMENT 36 Ah battery.

DIMENSIONS AND WEIGHT width: 61.02 in, 155 cm; weight: 1,819 lb, 825 kg.

PRACTICAL INSTRUCTIONS fuel: 98 oct petrol; valve timing: 12° 48° 52° 8°.

OPTIONALS 145 SR x 13 tyres; power steering; tinted glass; rear window wiper-washer; sunroof; metallic spray.

RENAULT Rodeo 5

63 hp power team

See 37 hp power team, except for:

ENGINE 85.2 cu in, 1,397 cc (2.99 x 3.03 in, 76 x 77 mm); compression ratio: 9.25:1; max power (DIN): 63 hp (45 kW) at 5,250 rpm; max torque (DIN): 76 lb ft, 10.5 kg m (101 Nm) at 3,000 rpm; max engine rpm: 5,750; 45.1 hp/l (32.2 kW/l); 5 crankshaft bearings; lubrication: 5.6 imp pt, 6.8 US pt, 3.2 l; 1 Weber 32 DIR 100 downdraught twin barrel carburettor; cooling: 11.1 imp pt, 13.3 US pt, 6.3 l, electric thermostatic fan.

TRANSMISSION gears: 5, fully synchronized; ratios: I 3.833, II 2.235, III 1.458, IV 1.171, V 0.948, rev 3.545; axle ratio: 3.444; width of rims: 4.5"; tyres: 145 SR x 13.

PERFORMANCE max speeds: (I) 28 mph, 45 km/h; (II) 48 mph, 77 km/h; (III) 73 mph, 118 km/h; (IV) 91 mph, 147 km/h; (V) 96 mph, 154 km/h; power-weight ratio: TS 28.3 lb/hp (39.7 lb/kW), 12.9 kg/hp (18 kg/kW); acceleration: standing ¼ mile 19.2 sec; speed in top at 1,000 rpm: 19.7 mph, 31.7 km/h; consumption: 42.2 m/imp gal, 35.1 m/US gal, 6.7 l x 100 km at 75 mph, 120 km/h.

BRAKES front disc (diameter 8.98 in, 22.8 cm), servo.

ELECTRICAL EQUIPMENT 36 Ah battery.

DIMENSIONS AND WEIGHT weight: TS 1,786 lb, 810 kg - TX 1,830 lb, 830 kg.

BODY 2+1 doors.

PRACTICAL INSTRUCTIONS fuel: 98 oct petrol; valve timing: 12° 56° 56° 12°.

OPTIONALS tinted glass; sunroof; metallic spray.

110 hp power team

See 37 hp power team, except for:

ENGINE 85.2 cu in, 1,397 cc (2.99 x 3.03 in, 76 x 77 mm); compression ratio: 8.6:1; max power (DIN): 110 hp (81 kW) at 6,000 rpm; max torque (DIN): 109 lb ft, 15 kg m (147 Nm) at 4,000 rpm; max engine rpm: 6,000; 78.7 hp/l (58 kW/l); hemispherical combustion chambers; 5 crankshaft bearings; lubrication: 4.6 imp pt, 5.5 US pt, 2.6 l; 1 Weber 32 DIR 75 downdraught twin barrel carburettor; 1 Garrett AiResearch T3 turbocharger; cooling: 8.6 imp pt, 10.4 US pt, 4.9 l, electric thermostatic fan.

TRANSMISSION gears: 5, fully synchronized; ratios: I 3.818, II 2.176, III 1.409, IV 1.030, V 0.861, rev 3.777; axle ratio: 3.777; width of rims: 5.5"; tyres: 175/60 HR x 13 P6.

PERFORMANCE max speeds: (I) 26 mph, 42 km/h; (II) 46 mph, 74 km/h; (III) 71 mph, 114 km/h; (IV) 97 mph, 155 km/h; (V) 116 mph, 186 km/h; power-weight ratio: 17.4 lb/hp (23.7 lb/kW), 7.9 kg/hp (10.7 kg/kW); carrying capacity: 882 lb, 400 kg; acceleration: standing ¼ mile 16.5 sec; speed in top at 1,000 rpm: 19.3 mph, 31 km/h; consumption: 33.2 m/imp gal, 27.7 m/US gal, 8.5 l x 100 km at 75 mph, 120 km/h.

CHASSIS rear suspension: anti-roll bar.

BRAKES disc (diameter 8.98 in, 22.8 cm), front internal radial fins, servo; lining area: front 22.2 sq in, 143 sq cm, rear 22.2 sq in, 143 sq cm, total 44.4 sq in, 286 sq cm.

ELECTRICAL EQUIPMENT 36 Ah battery; Renix electronic ignition; iodine headlamps.

DIMENSIONS AND WEIGHT wheel base: 94.96 in, 241 cm (right), 96.14 in, 244 cm (left); tracks: 50.94 in, 129 cm front, 50 in, 127 cm rear; length: 140.08 in, 356 cm; height: 54.17 in, 138 cm; ground clearance: 4.72 in, 12 cm; weight: 1,918 lb, 870 kg; fuel tank: 11.7 imp gal, 14 US gal, 53 l.

BODY 2+1 doors.

PRACTICAL INSTRUCTIONS fuel: 98 oct petrol; valve timing: 10° 50° 50° 10°; tyre pressure: front 24 psi, 1.7 atm, rear 29 psi, 2.1 atm.

OPTIONALS sunroof; metallic spray.

Rodeo 5

PRICE EX WORKS: 39,197 francs**

ENGINE front, 4 stroke; 4 cylinders, vertical, in line; 67.6 cu in, 1,108 cc (2.76 x 2.83 in, 70 x 72 mm); compression ratio: 9.5:1; max power (DIN): 34 hp (25 kW) at 4,000 rpm; max torque (DIN): 54 lb ft, 7.5 kg m (74 Nm) at 2,500 rpm; max engine rpm: 4,500; 42.4 hp/l (22.6 kW/l); cast iron block, wet liners, light alloy head; 3 crankshaft bearings; valves: overhead, in line, push-rods and rockers; camshafts: 1, side; lubrication: gear pump, filter in sump, 5.6 imp pt, 6.8 US pt, 3.2 l; 1 Zenith 28 IF downdraught single barrel carburettor; fuel feed: mechanical pump; water-cooled, sealed circuit, 10.4 imp pt, 18.1 US pt, 5.9 l.

TRANSMISSION driving wheels: front; clutch: single dry plate (diaphragm); gearbox: mechanical; gears: 4, fully synchronized; ratios: I 3.833, II 2.235, III 1.458, IV 1.026, rev 3.545; lever: on facia; final drive: spiral bevel; axle ratio: 3.100; width of rims: 4"; tyres: 145 SR x 13.

PERFORMANCE max speeds: (I) 21 mph, 34 km/h; (II) 35 mph, 56 km/h; (III) 53 mph, 86 km/h; (IV) 68 mph, 109 km/h; power-weight ratio: 46.7 lb/hp (63.5 lb/kW), 21.2 kg/hp (28.8 kg/kW); carrying capacity: 882 lb, 400 kg; acceleration: standing ¼ mile 22.9 sec; speed in top at 1,000 rpm: 20.2 mph, 32.4 km/h; consumption: 42.8 m/imp gal, 35.6 m/US gal, 6.6 l x 100 km at 56 mph, 90 km/h.

CHASSIS reinforced platform; front suspension: independent, wishbones, longitudinal torsion bars, anti-roll bar, telescopic dampers; rear: independent, swinging longitudinal trailing arms, transverse torsion bars, telescopic dampers.

STEERING rack-and-pinion; turns lock to lock: 3.75.

BRAKES front disc (diameter 9.06 in, 23 cm), rear drum, dual circuit, rear compensator.

ELECTRICAL EQUIPMENT 12 V; 28 Ah battery; 40 A alternator; 2 headlamps.

DIMENSIONS AND WEIGHT wheel base: 94.49 in, 240 cm (right), 95.67 in, 243 cm (left); tracks: 50.36 in, 128 cm front, 49.13 in, 125 cm rear; length: 140.31 in, 356 cm; width: 58.66 in, 149 cm; height: 57.51 in, 151 cm; ground clearance: 5.51 in, 14 cm; weight: 1,588 lb, 720 kg; turning circle: 33.1 ft, 10.1 m; fuel tank: 7.5 imp gal, 9 US gal, 34 l.

BODY open, in plastic material; 2+1 doors; 2 or 4 seats, folding rear seat.

PRACTICAL INSTRUCTIONS fuel: 98 oct petrol; oil: engine 5.3 imp pt, 6.3 US pt, 3 l, SAE 10W-50, change every 4,600 miles, 7,500 km - gearbox and final drive 3.2 imp pt, 3.8 US pt, 1.8 l, SAE 80 EP, change every 9,300 miles, 15,000 km; greasing: none; tappet clearances: inlet 0.012 in, 0.30 mm, exhaust 0.012 in, 0.30 mm; valve timing: 12° 48° 52° 8°; tyre pressure: front 21 psi, 1.5 atm, rear 24 psi, 1.7 atm.

OPTIONALS Quatre Saisons version.

5 Turbo 2

PRICE EX WORKS: 102,492 francs**

ENGINE turbocharged; central, rear, longitudinal, 4 stroke; 4 cylinders, vertical, in line; 85.2 cu in, 1,397 cc (2.99 x 3.03 in, 76 x 77 mm); compression ratio: 7:1; max power (DIN): 160 hp (116 kW) at 6,000 rpm; max torque (DIN): 163 lb ft, 22.5 kg m (221 Nm) at 3,250 rpm; max engine rpm: 6,400; 114.5 hp/l (83 kW/l); cast iron block, wet liners, light alloy head, hemispherical combustion chambers; 5 crankshaft bearings; valves: Vee-slanted, overhead, push-rods and rockers; camshafts: 1, side; lubrication: gear pump, full flow filter (cartridge), 6.5 imp pt, 7.8 US pt, 3.7 l; Bosch K-Jetronic injection with Garrett AiResearch T3 turbocharger; fuel feed: electric pump; sealed circuit cooling, expansion tank, liquid, 18.5 imp pt, 22.2 US pt, 10.5 l, electric thermostatic fan.

RENAULT 5 Turbo 2

TRANSMISSION driving wheels: rear; clutch: dual dry plate, hydraulically controlled; gearbox: mechanical; gears: 5, fully synchronized; ratios: I 3.364, II 2.059, III 1.381, IV 1.057, V 0.868, rev 3.182; lever: central; final drive: hypoid bevel, ZF limited slip; axle ratio: 3.889; width of rims: 5" front, 7.5" rear; tyres: 190/55 HR x 13 front, 220/55 HR x 14 rear.

PERFORMANCE max speeds: (I) 34 mph, 54 km/h; (II) 55 mph, 89 km/h; (III) 82 mph, 132 km/h; (IV) 107 mph, 173 km/h; (V) 130 mph, 210 km/h; power-weight ratio: 13.4 lb/hp (18.4 lb/kW), 6 kg/hp (8.4 kg/kW); carrying capacity: 595 lb, 270 kg; acceleration: standing ¼ mile 15 sec; speed in top at 1,000 rpm: 20.4 mph, 32.9 km/h; consumption: 28.2 m/imp gal, 23.5 m/US gal, 10 l x 100 km at 75 mph, 120 km/h.

CHASSIS integral, central steel backbone; front suspension: independent, wishbones, longitudinal torsion bars, anti-roll bar, telescopic dampers; rear: independent, wishbones, anti-roll bar, telescopic dampers.

STEERING rack-and-pinion; turns lock to lock: 3.25.

BRAKES disc (diameter 10.20 in, 26 cm), internal radial fins, dual circuit, rear compensator, servo; lining area: front 27.9 sq in, 180 sq cm, rear 27.9 sq in, 180 sq cm, total 55.8 sq in, 360 sq cm.

ELECTRICAL EQUIPMENT 12 V; 50 Ah battery; 50 A alternator; electronic ignition; 4 iodine headlamps.

DIMENSIONS AND WEIGHT wheel base: 95.67 in, 243 cm; tracks: 52.99 in, 135 cm front, 57.95 in, 147 cm rear; length: 144.25 in, 366 cm; width: 68.98 in, 175 cm; height: 52.09 in, 132 cm; ground clearance: 5.71 in, 14.5 cm; weight: 2,139 lb, 970 kg; weight distribution: 40% front, 60% rear; turning circle: 34.1 ft, 10.4 m; fuel tank: 11.2 imp gal, 13.5 US gal, 51 l.

BODY saloon/sedan, in steel-light alloy and plastic material; 2+1 doors; 2 seats.

PRACTICAL INSTRUCTIONS fuel: 98 oct petrol; oil: engine 6.5 imp pt, 7.8 US pt, 3.7 l, SAE 20W-50, change every 4,650 miles, 7,500 km - gearbox and final drive 4.9 imp pt, 5.9 US pt, 2.8 l, SAE 80, change every 18,600 miles, 30,000 km; greasing: none; valve timing: 28° 52° 66° 14°; tyre pressure: front 21 psi, 1.5 atm, rear 28 psi, 2 atm.

OPTIONALS leather upholstery; heated rear window; tinted glass; electric windows.

9 Series

PRICES IN GB AND EX WORKS:	£	francs
1 C 4-dr Berline	—	45,460**
2 TC 4-dr Berline	4,495*	48,060**
3 TL 4-dr Berline	—	49,524**
4 GTL 4-dr Berline	4,995*	52,924**
5 Automatic 4-dr Berline	5,595*	57,692**
6 GTS 4-dr Berline	—	57,524**
7 TSE 4-dr Berline	5,860*	59,624**
8 TD 4-dr Berline	5,195*	54,860**
9 GTD 4-dr Berline	—	59,060*
10 TDE 4-dr Berline	—	64,760*

Power team:	Standard for:	Optional for:
48 hp	1,2	—
60 hp	3,4	—
68 hp	5	—
72 hp	6,7	—
55 hp (diesel)	8 to 10	—

48 hp power team

ENGINE front, transverse, 4 stroke; 4 cylinders, vertical, in line; 67.6 cu in, 1,108 cc (2.76 x 2.83 in, 70 x 72 mm); compression ratio: 9.2:1; max power (DIN): 48 hp (35 kW) at 5,250 rpm; max torque (DIN): 59 lb ft, 8.1 kg m (78 Nm) at 2,500 rpm; max engine rpm: 6,000; 43.3 hp/l (31.9 kW/l); cast iron block, wet liners, light alloy head; 5 crankshaft bearings; valves: overhead, push-rods and rockers; camshafts: 1, side; lubrication: gear pump, full flow filter, 5.7 imp pt, 6.9 US pt, 3.2 l; 1 Zenith 32 IF2 downdraught single barrel carburettor; fuel feed: mechanical pump; sealed circuit cooling, liquid, expansion tank, 10.7 imp pt, 12.9 US pt, 6.1 l, electric thermostatic fan.

RENAULT 9 Automatic Berline

RENAULT 9 Automatic Berline

RENAULT 9 TDE Berline

48 HP POWER TEAM

TRANSMISSION driving wheels: front; clutch: single dry plate (diaphragm); gearbox: mechanical; gears: 4, fully synchronized; ratios: I 3.545, II 2.062, III 1.320, IV 0.903, rev 3.545; lever: central; final drive: helical spur gear; axle ratio: 3.867; width of rims: 4.5''; tyres: 145 SR x 13.

PERFORMANCE max speed: 86 mph, 138 km/h; power-weight ratio: 37.7 lb/hp, (51.7 lb/kW), 17.1 kg/hp (23.4 kg/kW); carrying capacity: 926 lb, 420 kg; acceleration: standing ¼ mile 21 sec; speed in top at 1,000 rpm: 18.4 mph, 29.6 km/h; consumption: 38.2 m/imp gal, 31.8 m/US gal, 7.4 l x 100 km at 75 mph, 120 km/h.

CHASSIS integral; front suspension: independent, by McPherson, coil springs/telescopic damper struts, lower wishbones, anti-roll bar; rear: independent, swinging longitudinal trailing arms, transverse semi-torsion bars, telescopic dampers.

STEERING rack-and-pinion; turns lock to lock: 4.

BRAKES front disc (diameter 9.37 in, 23.8 cm), rear drum, dual circuit, servo.

ELECTRICAL EQUIPMENT 12 V; 30 Ah battery; 50 A alternator; 2 headlamps.

DIMENSIONS AND WEIGHT wheel base: 97.52 in, 248 cm; tracks: 54.53 in, 138 cm front, 53.03 in, 135 cm rear; length: 159.96 in, 406 cm; width: 64.33 in, 163 cm; height: 55.31 in, 140 cm; ground clearance: 4.72 in, 12 cm; weight: 1,808 lb, 820 kg; turning circle: 34.1 ft, 10.4 m; fuel tank: 10.3 imp gal, 12.4 US gal, 47 l.

BODY saloon/sedan; 4 doors; 5 seats, separate front seats, reclining backrests; heated rear window.

PRACTICAL INSTRUCTIONS fuel: 98 oct petrol; oil: engine 5.3 imp pt, 6.3 US pt, 3 l, SAE 10W-50, change every 4,600 miles, 7,500 km - gearbox and final drive 4.9 imp pt, 5.9 US pt, 2.8 l, SAE 80 EP, change every 9,300 miles, 15,000 km; greasing: none; valve timing: 12° 48° 52° 8°; tyre pressure: front 24 psi, 1.7 atm, rear 27 psi, 1.9 atm.

OPTIONALS tinted glass and metallic spray (except for C).

60 hp power team

See 48 hp power team, except for:

ENGINE 85.2 cu in, 1,397 cc (2.99 x 3.03 in, 76 x 77 mm); max power (DIN): 60 hp (43 kW) at 5,250 rpm; max torque (DIN): 75 lb ft, 10.4 kg m (100 Nm) at 3,000 rpm; 42.9 hp/l (30.8 kW/l); 1 Solex 32 BIS downdraught single barrel carburettor.

TRANSMISSION width of rims: GTL 5.5''; tyres: GTL 155 SR x 13.

PERFORMANCE max speed: 95 mph, 153 km/h; power-weight ratio: TL 31.2 lb/hp (43.6 lb/kW), 14.2 kg/hp (19.8 kg/kW); acceleration: standing ¼ mile 19.2 sec; consumption: 39.8 m/imp gal, 33.1 m/US gal, 7.1 l x 100 km at 75 mph, 120 km/h.

BRAKES rear compensator.

ELECTRICAL EQUIPMENT electronic ignition.

DIMENSIONS AND WEIGHT tracks: GTL 54.92 in, 139 cm front, 53.43 in, 136 cm rear; width: GTL 64.96 in, 165 cm; weight: TL 1,874 lb, 850 kg - GTL 1,885 lb, 855 kg.

PRACTICAL INSTRUCTIONS valve timing: 12° 56° 56° 12°.

OPTIONALS 5-speed mechanical gearbox (I 3.545, II 2.062, III 1.320, IV 0.903, V 0.758, rev 3.545), 4.214 axle ratio; 155 SR x 13 tyres with 5.5'' wide rims.

68 hp power team

See 48 hp power team, except for:

ENGINE 85.2 cu in, 1,397 cc (2.99 x 3.03 in, 76 x 77 mm); max power (DIN): 68 hp (49 kW) at 5,250 rpm; max torque (DIN): 78 lb ft, 10.8 kg m (104 Nm) at 3,000 rpm; 48.7 hp/l (35.1 kW/l); 1 Weber 32 DRT downdraught twin barrel carburettor.

TRANSMISSION gearbox: automatic transmission, hydraulic torque converter and planetary gears with 3 ratios, max ratio of converter at stall 2.3, possible manual selection; ratios: I 2.500, II 1.500, III 1, rev 2; axle ratio: 3.563; width of rims: 5.5''; tyres: 155 SR x 13.

PERFORMANCE max speed: 95 mph, 153 km/h; power-weight ratio: 28.7 lb/hp (39.8 lb/kW), 13 kg/hp (18.1 kg/kW); speed in direct drive at 1,000 rpm: 20 mph, 32.2 km/h; consumption: 34.4 m/imp gal, 28.7 m/US gal, 8.2 l x 100 km at 75 mph, 120 km/h.

BRAKES rear compensator.

ELECTRICAL EQUIPMENT electronic ignition.

DIMENSIONS AND WEIGHT tracks: 54.92 in, 139 cm front, 53.43 in, 136 cm rear; width: 64.96 in, 165 cm; weight: 1,951 lb, 885 kg.

PRACTICAL INSTRUCTIONS valve timing: 12° 56° 56° 12°.

72 hp power team

See 48 hp power team, except for:

ENGINE 85.2 cu in, 1,397 cc (2.99 x 3.03 in, 76 x 77 mm); max power (DIN): 72 hp (52 kW) at 5,750 rpm; max torque (DIN): 78 lb ft, 10.8 kg m (104 Nm) at 3,500 rpm; 51.5 hp/l (37.2 kW/l); 1 Weber 32 DRT downdraught twin barrel carburettor.

TRANSMISSION gears: 5, fully synchronized; ratios: I 3.545, II 2.062, III 1.320, IV 0.903, V 0.758, rev 3.545; axle ratio: 4.214; width of rims: 5.5''; tyres: 155 SR x 13.

PERFORMANCE max speed: 101 mph, 162 km/h; power-weight ratio: GTS 26.5 lb/hp (36.7 lb/kW), 12 kg/hp (16.6 kg/kW); acceleration: standing ¼ mile 18.6 sec; speed in top at 1,000 rpm: 20.6 mph, 33.1 km/h; consumption: 39.2 m/imp gal, 32.7 m/US gal, 7.2 l x 100 km at 75 mph, 120 km/h.

BRAKES rear compensator.

ELECTRICAL EQUIPMENT electronic ignition.

DIMENSIONS AND WEIGHT tracks: 54.92 in, 139 cm front, 53.43 in, 136 cm rear; width: 64.96 in, 165 cm; weight: GTS 1,907 lb, 865 kg - TSE 1,940 lb, 880 kg.

PRACTICAL INSTRUCTIONS valve timing: 22° 62° 65° 25°.

55 hp (diesel) power team

See 48 hp power team, except for:

ENGINE diesel; 98.9 cu in, 1,595 cc (3.07 x 3.29 in, 78 x 83.5 mm); compression ratio: 22.5:1; max power (DIN): 55 hp (40 kW) at 4,800 rpm; max torque (DIN): 75 lb ft, 10.4 kg m (100 Nm) at 2,250 rpm; max engine rpm: 5,000; 34.5 hp/l (25.1 kW/l); valves: overhead, thimble tappets; camshafts: 1, overhead, cogged belt; lubrication: 9 imp pt, 10.8 US pt, 5.1 l; Bosch injection pump; cooling: 14.1 imp pt, 17 US pt, 8 l.

TRANSMISSION gears: 5, fully synchronized; ratios: I 3.545, II 2.062, III 1.320, IV 0.903, V 0.730, rev 3.545; width of rims: 5.5''; tyres: 155 SR x 13.

PERFORMANCE max speed: 91 mph, 146 km/h; power-weight ratio: 36.7 lb/hp (50.4 lb/kW), 16.6 kg/hp (22.9 kg/kW); acceleration: standing ¼ mile 20.3 sec; speed in top at 1,000 rpm: 23.2 mph, 37.4 km/h; consumption: 44.8 m/imp gal, 37.3 m/US gal, 6.3 l x 100 km at 75 mph, 120 km/h.

BRAKES rear compensator.

ELECTRICAL EQUIPMENT 50 Ah battery.

DIMENSIONS AND WEIGHT tracks: 54.92 in, 139 cm front, 53.43 in, 136 cm rear; weight: T and GTD 2,018 lb, 915 kg - TDE 2,029 lb, 920 kg.

PRACTICAL INSTRUCTIONS fuel: diesel; oil: engine 9 imp pt, 10.8 US pt, 5.1 l, change every 3,100 miles, 5,000 km.

RENAULT 9 TDE Berline

11 Series

PRICES IN GB AND EX WORKS:	£	francs
1 TC 2+1-dr Berline	4,350*	47,060**
2 GTC 4+1-dr Berline	—	52,660**
3 TL 4+1-dr Berline	—	51,024**
4 GTL 2+1-dr Berline	5,070*	55,024**
5 GTL 4+1-dr Berline	—	—
6 Automatic 4+1-dr Berline	5,870*	60,392**
7 Automatic Electronic 4+1-dr Berline	—	71,292**
8 GTS 4+1-dr Berline	—	56,824**
9 TSE 4+1-dr Berline	5,975*	63,024**
10 TSE Electronic 4+1-dr Berline	—	68,924**
11 GTX 2+1-dr Berline	—	—
12 TXE 2+1-dr Berline	—	—
13 TXE Electronic 2+1-dr Berline	—	—

Power team:	Standard for:	Optional for:
48 hp	1,2	—
60 hp	3 to 5	—
68 hp	6,7	—
72 hp	8 to 10	—
80 hp	11 to 13	—

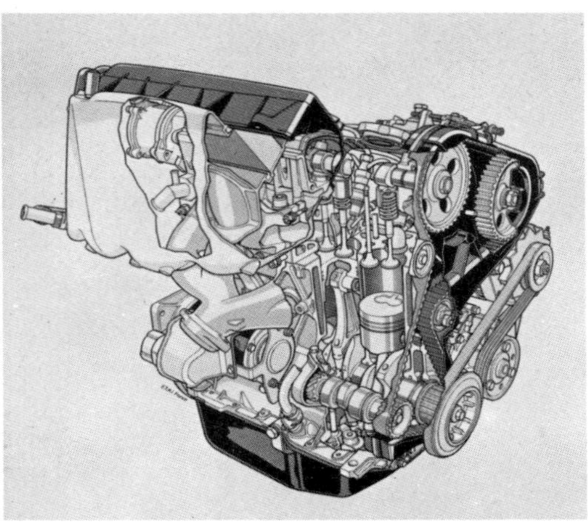

RENAULT 9 TDE Berline

RENAULT 11 TSE Electronic Berline

48 hp power team

ENGINE front, transverse, 4 stroke; 4 cylinders, vertical, in line; 67.6 cu in, 1,108 cc (2.76 x 2.83 in, 70 x 72 mm); compression ratio: 9.2:1; max power (DIN): 48 hp (35 kW) at 5,250 rpm; max torque (DIN): 59 lb ft, 8.1 kg m (78 Nm) at 2,500 rpm; max engine rpm: 6,000; 43.3 hp/l (31.9 kW/l); cast iron block, wet liners, light alloy head; 5 crankshaft bearings; valves: overhead, push-rods and rockers; camshafts: 1, side; lubrication: gear pump, full flow filter, 5.7 imp pt, 6.9 US pt, 3.2 l; 1 Zenith 32 IF2 downdraught single barrel carburettor; fuel feed: mechanical pump; sealed circuit cooling, liquid, expansion tank, 10.7 imp pt, 12.9 US pt, 6.1 l, electric thermostatic fan.

TRANSMISSION driving wheels: front; clutch: single dry plate (diaphragm); gearbox: mechanical; gears: 4, fully synchronized; ratios: I 3.545, II 2.062, III 1.320, IV 0.903, rev 3.545; lever: central; final drive: helical spur gear; axle ratio: 3.867; width of rims: 4.5"; tyres: 145 SR x 13.

PERFORMANCE max speed: 86 mph, 138 km/h; power-weight ratio: 38.1 lb/hp (52.3 lb/kW), 17.3 kg/hp (23.7 kg/kW); carrying capacity: 882 lb, 400 kg; acceleration slanding ¼ mile 21 sec; speed in top at 1,000 rpm: 18.4 mph, 29.6 km/h; consumption: 38.2 m/imp gal, 31.8 m/US gal, 7.4 l x 100 km at 75 mph, 120 km/h.

CHASSIS integral; front suspension: independent, by McPherson, coil springs/telescopic damper struts, lower wishbones, anti-roll bar; rear: independent, swinging longitudinal trailing arms, transverse torsion bars, telescopic dampers.

STEERING rack-and-pinion; turns lock to lock: 4.

BRAKES front disc (diameter 9.37 in, 23.8 cm), rear drum, dual circuit, servo.

ELECTRICAL EQUIPMENT 12 V; 32 Ah battery; 50 A alternator; 2 headlamps.

DIMENSIONS AND WEIGHT wheel base: 97.52 in, 248 cm; tracks: 54.53 in, 138 cm front, 53.03 in, 135 cm rear; length: 156.42 in, 397 cm; width: TC 64.33 in, 163 cm - GTC 65.35 in, 166 cm; height: 55.31 in, 140 cm; ground clearance: 4.72 in, 12 cm; weight: TC 1,830 lb, 830 kg - GTC 1,885 lb, 855 kg; turning circle: 34.1 ft, 10.4 m; fuel tank: 10.3 imp gal, 12.4 US gal, 47 l.

RENAULT 11 TSE Electronic Berline

BODY saloon/sedan; 2+1 doors or 4+1 doors; 5 seats, separate front seats, reclining backrests; heated rear window.

PRACTICAL INSTRUCTIONS fuel: 98 oct petrol; oil: engine 5.3 imp pt, 6.3 US pt, 3 l, SAE 10W-50, change every 4,600 miles, 7,500 km - gearbox and final drive 4.9 imp pt, 5.9 US pt, 2.8 l, SAE 80 EP, change every 9,300 miles, 15,000 km; greasing: none; valve timing: 12° 48° 52° 8°; tyre pressure: front 24 psi, 1.7 atm, rear 27 psi, 1.9 atm.

OPTIONALS (for GTL only) tinted glass and metallic spray.

60 hp power team

See 48 hp power team, except for:

ENGINE 85.2 cu in, 1,397 cc (2.99 x 3.03 in, 76 x 77 mm); max power (DIN): 60 hp (43 kW) at 5,250 rpm; max torque (DIN): 75 lb ft, 10.4 kg m (100 Nm) at 3,000 rpm; 42.9 hp/l (30.8 kW/l); 1 Solex 32 BIS downdraught single barrel carburettor.

TRANSMISSION gears: GTL 5, fully synchronized; ratios: I 3.545, II 2.062, III 1.320, IV 0.903, V 0.758, rev 3.545; axle ratio: 4.214; width of tims: GTL 5.5"; tyres: GTL 155 SR x 13.

PERFORMANCE max speed: TL 94 mph, 151 km/h - GTL 97 mph, 156 km/h; power-weight ratio: TL 32 lb/hp (44.6 lb/kW), 14.5 kg/hp (20.2 kg/kW); acceleration: standing ¼ mile 19.2 sec; consumption: TL 39.8 m/imp gal, 33.1 m/US gal, 7.1 l x 100 km at 75 mph, 120 km/h - GTL 40.9 m/imp gal, 34.1 m/US gal, 6.9 l x 100 km at 75 mph, 120 km/h.

BRAKES rear compensator.

ELECTRICAL EQUIPMENT electronic ingition.

DIMENSIONS AND WEIGHT tracks: GTL 54.92 in, 139 cm front, 53.43 in, 136 cm rear; width: GTL 64.17 in, 163 cm; weight: TL 1,918 lb, 870 kg - GTL 2+1-dr 1,896 lb, 860 kg - GTL 4+1-dr 1,940 lb, 880 kg.

PRACTICAL INSTRUCTIONS valve timing: 12° 56° 56° 12°.

68 hp power team

See 48 hp power team, except for:

ENGINE 85.2 cu in, 1,397 cc (2.99 x 3.03 in, 76 x 77 mm); max power (DIN): 68 hp (49 kW) at 5,250 rpm; max torque (DIN): 78 lb ft, 10.8 kg m (104 Nm) at 3,000 rpm; 48.7 hp/l (35.1 kW/l); 1 Weber 32 DRT downdraught twin barrel carburettor.

TRANSMISSION gearbox: automatic transmission, hydraulic torque converter and planetary gears with 3 ratios, max ratio of converter at stall 2,30, possible manual selection; ratios: I 2.500, II 1.500, III 1, rev 2; axle ratio: 3.563; width of rims: 5.5"; tyres: 155 SR x 13.

PERFORMANCE max speed: 97 mph, 156 km/h; power-weight ratio: 29.3 lb/hp (40.7 lb/kW), 13.3 kg/hp (18.5 kg/kW); speed in direct drive at 1,000 rpm: 20 mph, 32.2 km/h; consumption: 36.2 m/imp gal, 30.2 m/US gal, 7.8 l x 100 km at 75 mph, 120 km/h.

BRAKES rear compensator.

ELECTRICAL EQUIPMENT electronic ignition.

DIMENSIONS AND WEIGHT tracks: 54.92 in, 139 cm front, 53.43 in, 136 cm rear; length: 156.89 in, 398 cm; weight: 1,996 lb, 905 kg.

BODY 4+1 doors; (for Automatic Electronic only) Automatic Electronic panel, trip computer, voice syntonizer and Philips HI-FI system.

PRACTICAL INSTRUCTIONS valve timing: 12° 56° 56° 12°.

OPTIONALS sunroof; air-conditioning.

72 hp power team

See 48 hp power team, except for:

ENGINE 85.2 cu in, 1,397 cc (2.99 x 3.03 in, 76 x 77 mm); max power (DIN): 72 hp (52 kW) at 5,750 rpm; max torque (DIN): 78 lb ft, 10.8 kg m (104 Nm) at 3,500 rpm; 51.5 hp/l (37.2 kW/l); 1 Weber 32 DRT downdraught twin barrel carburettor.

TRANSMISSION gears: 5, fully synchronized; ratios: I 3.545, II 2.062, III 1.320, IV 0.903, V 0.758, rev 3.545; axle ratio: 4.214; width of rims: 5.5"; tyres: 155 SR x 13.

PERFORMANCE max speed: 102 mph, 165 km/h; power-weight ratio: GTS 27.1 lb/hp (37.5 lb/kW), 12.3 kg/hp (17 kg/kW); acceleration: standing ¼ mile 18.6 sec; speed in top at 1,000 rpm: 20.6 mph, 33.1 km/h; consumption: 39.8 m/imp gal, 33.1 m/US gal, 7.1 l x 100 km at 75 mph, 120 km/h.

BRAKES rear compensator.

ELECTRICAL EQUIPMENT electronic ignition; 4 headlamps.

DIMENSIONS AND WEIGHT tracks: 54.92 in, 139 cm front, 53.43 in, 136 cm rear; length: 156.89 in, 398 cm; weight: GTS 1,951 lb, 885 kg - TSE and TSE Electronic 1,984 lb, 900 kg.

BODY 4+1 doors; (for TSE Electronic only) Automatic Electronic panel, trip computer, voice syntonizer and Philips HI-FI system.

PRACTICAL INSTRUCTIONS valve timing: 22° 62° 65° 25°.

OPTIONALS sunroof; air-conditioning.

80 hp power team

See 48 hp power team, except for:

ENGINE 105 cu in, 1,721 cc (3.19 x 3.29 in, 81 x 83.5 mm); compression ratio: 10:1; max power (DIN): 80 hp (59 kW) at 5,000 rpm; max torque (DIN): 99 lb ft, 13.7 kg m (133 Nm) at 3,250 rpm; 46.5 hp/l (34.3 kW/l); valves: overhead, rockers; camshafts: 1, overhead; lubrication: 9.7 imp pt, 11.6 US pt, 5.5 l; 1 Weber 32 DRT downdraught twin barrel carburettor; cooling: 11.1 imp pt, 13.3 US pt, 6.3 l.

TRANSMISSION gears: 5, fully synchronized; ratios : I 3.727, II 2.053, III 1.320, IV 0.967, V 0.794, rev 3.545; axle ratio: 3.562; width of rims: 5.5"; tyres: 175/70 SR x 13.

PERFORMANCE max speed: 106 mph, 170 km/h; power-weight ratio: GTX 24.7 lb/hp (33.4 lb/kW), 11.2 kg/hp (15.2 kg/kW); acceleration: standing ¼ mile 18.1 sec; speed in top at 1,000 rpm: 23.2 mph, 37.3 km/h; consumption: 42.2 m/imp gal, 35.1 m/US gal, 6.7 l x 100 km at 75 mph, 120 km/h.

BRAKES rear compensator.

ELECTRICAL EQUIPMENT electronic ignition.

DIMENSIONS AND WEIGHT tracks: 54.92 in, 139 cm front, 53.43 in, 136 cm rear; length: 156.89 in, 398 cm; weight: GTX 1,973 lb, 895 kg - TXE and TXE Electronic 1,984 lb, 900 kg.

BODY 2+1 doors; (for TXE Electronic only) Automatic Electronic panel, trip computer, voice syntonizer and Philips HI-FI system.

PRACTICAL INSTRUCTIONS oil: engine 9.7 imp pt, 11.6 US pt, 5.5 l.

OPTIONALS sunroof; air-conditioning.

RENAULT 18 GTX Berline

RENAULT 18 Turbo Berline

18 Series

PRICES IN GB AND EX WORKS:		£	francs
1	4-dr Berline	—	**47,024****
2	4+1-dr Break	—	**51,492****
3	TL 4-dr Berline	**4,870***	**52,892****
4	TL 4+1-dr Break	**5,550***	**57,392****
5	GTL 4-dr Berline	**5,700***	**57,024****
6	GTL 4+1-dr Break	**6,100***	**61,524****
7	GTL 4x4 4+1-dr Break	—	**76,000****
8	GTX 4-dr Berline	**6,890***	**66,500****
9	GTX 4+1-dr Break	**7,390***	**71,200****
10	Automatic 4-dr Berline	**6,010***	**67,620****
11	TD 4-dr Berline	**5,575***	**62,424****
12	TD 4+1-dr Break	**6,470***	**66,924****
13	GTD 4-dr Berline	—	**68,392****
14	GTD 4+1-dr Break	—	**72,892****
15	GTD 4x4 4+1-dr Break	—	**87,400****

Power team:	Standard for:	Optional for:
64 hp	1 to 4	—
73 hp	5 to 7	—
104 hp	8,9	—
110 hp	10	—
66 hp (diesel)	11 to 15	—

64 hp power team

ENGINE front, 4 stroke; 4 cylinders, vertical, in line; 85.2 cu in, 1,397 cc (2.99 x 3.03 in, 76 x 77 mm); compression ratio: 9.2:1; max power (DIN): 64 hp (46 kW) at 5,500 rpm; max torque (DIN): 76 lb ft, 10.5 kg m (103 Nm) at 3,000 rpm; max engine rpm: 5,700; 45.8 hp/l (32.9 kW/l); light alloy head, cast iron block, wet liners; 5 crankshaft bearings; valves: overhead, in line, push-rods and rockers; camshafts: 1, side; lubrication: gear pump, filter in sump, 5.6 imp pt, 6.8 US pt, 3.2 l; 1 Solex 32 SEIA or Zenith 32 IF downdraught single barrel carburettor; fuel feed: mechanical pump; sealed circuit cooling, expansion tank, liquid, 10.5 imp pt, 12.7 US pt, 6 l, electric thermostatic fan.

TRANSMISSION driving wheels: front; clutch: single dry plate (diaphragm); gearbox: mechanical; gears: 4, fully synchronized; ratios: I 4.091, II 2.176, III 1.409, IV 0.971, rev 3.545; lever: central; final drive: hypoid bevel; axle ratio: 3.556; width of rims: 5''; tyres: 155 SR x 13.

PERFORMANCE max speeds: (I) 25 mph, 40 km/h; (II) 42 mph, 68 km/h; (III) 64 mph, 103 km/h; (IV) 97 mph, 156 km/h; power-weight ratio: sedans 32.4 lb/hp (45.1 lb/kW), 14.7 kg/hp (20.4 kg/kW); carrying capacity: sedans 882 lb, 400 kg - st. wagons 992 lb, 450 kg; acceleration: standing ¼ mile 19.2 sec; speed in top at 1,000 rpm: 19 mph, 30.6 km/h; consumption: 38.2 m/imp gal, 31.8 m/US gal, 7.4 l x 100 km at 75 mph, 120 km/h.

CHASSIS integral; front suspension: independent, wishbones, anti-roll bar, coil springs/telescopic dampers; rear: rigid axle, trailing arms, A-bracket, anti-roll bar, coil springs/telescopic dampers.

STEERING rack-and-pinion; turns lock to lock: 3.55.

BRAKES front disc, rear drum, dual circuit, rear compensator, servo; lining area: front 22.2 sq in, 143 sq cm, rear 66.4-70.4 sq in, 428-454 sq cm, total 86.8-92.6 sq in, 571-597 sq cm.

ELECTRICAL EQUIPMENT 12 V; 36 Ah battery; 50 A alternator; electronic ignition; 2 headlamps.

DIMENSIONS AND WEIGHT wheel base: 96.10 in, 244 cm; tracks: 55.70 in, 142 cm front, 53.40 in, 136 cm rear; length: sedans 173 in, 439 cm - st. wagons 176.65 in, 449 cm; width 66.50 in, 169 cm; height: 55.30 in, 140 cm; weight: sedans 2,073 lb, 940 kg - st. wagons 2,194 lb, 995 kg; weight distribution: 60.3% front, 39.7% rear; turning circle: 36.1 ft, 11 m; fuel tank: sedans 11.7 imp gal, 14 US gal, 53 l - st. wagons 12.5 imp gal, 15 US gal, 57 l.

BODY saloon/sedan, 4 doors - estate car/st. wagon, 4+1 doors; 5 seats, separate front seats, reclining backrests; heated rear window; luxury interior; electric windows; headrests; rear window wiper-washer and folding rear seat (for st. wagons only).

PRACTICAL INSTRUCTIONS fuel: 98-100 oct petrol; oil: engine 5.6 imp pt, 6.8 US pt, 3.2 l, SAE 15W-40, change every 4,650 miles, 7,500 km - gearbox and final drive 3.5 imp pt, 4.2 US pt, 2 l, SAE 80 EP, change every 18,600 miles, 30,000 km; greasing: none; tappet clearances: inlet 0.006 in, 0.15 mm, exhaust 0.008 in, 0.20 mm; valve timing: 22° 62° 65° 25°; tyre pressure: front 26 psi, 1.8 atm, rear 28 psi, 2 atm.

OPTIONALS (for TL models only) 5-speed fully synchronized mechanical gearbox (I 4.091, II 2.176, III 1.409, IV 0.970, V 0.730, rev 3.545), consumption 40.9 m/imp gal, 34.1 m/US gal, 6.9 l x 100 km at 75 mph, 120 km/h; tinted glass; metallic spray.

RENAULT 18 GTD 4x4 Break

73 hp power team

See 64 hp power team, except for:

ENGINE 100.5 cu in, 1,647 cc (3.11 x 3.31 in, 79 x 84 mm); compression ratio: 9.3:1; max power (DIN): 73 hp (53 kW) at 5,000 rpm; max torque (DIN): 96 lb ft, 13.3 kg m (127 Nm) at 3,000 rpm; max engine rpm: 5,500; 44.3 hp/l (32.2 kW/l); light alloy block; lubrication: 7.4 imp pt, 8.9 US pt, 4.2 l; 1 Weber 32 DIR downdraught twin barrel carburettor; cooling: 11.1 imp pt, 13.3 US pt, 6.3 l.

TRANSMISSION driving wheels: GTL 4x4 Break front and rear; (standard) gears: 5, fully synchronized; ratios: I 4.091, II 2.176, III 1.409, IV 0.970, V 0.784, rev 3.545; axle ratio: 3.444 - GTL 4x4 Break front and rear 3.778; width of rims: 5''; tyres: 155 SR x 13.

PERFORMANCE max speed: 96 mph, 155 km/h; power-weight ratio: GTL Berline 29.3 lb/hp (40.4 lb/kW), 13.3 kg/hp (18.3 kg/kW); speed in top at 1,000 rpm: 24.3 mph, 39.1 km/h; consumption: 42.2 m/imp gal, 35.1 m/US gal, 6.7 l x 100 km at 75 mph, 120 km/h.

ELECTRICAL EQUIPMENT iodine headlamps.

DIMENSIONS AND WEIGHT weight: GTL Berline 2,139 lb, 970 kg - GTL Break 2,260 lb, 1,025 kg - GTL 4x4 Break 2,359 lb, 1,070 kg.

PRACTICAL INSTRUCTIONS oil: engine 7.4 imp pt, 8.9 US pt, 4.2 l; valve timing: 10° 54° 54° 10°.

OPTIONALS power steering; air-conditioning; sunroof; tinted glass; metallic spray.

104 hp power team

See 64 hp power team, except for:

ENGINE 121.7 cu in, 1,995 cc (3.46 x 3.23 in, 88 x 82 mm); compression ratio: 9.2:1; max power (DIN): 104 hp (75 kW) at 5,500 rpm; max torque (DIN): 118 lb ft, 16.3 kg m (157 Nm) at 3,250 rpm; max engine rpm: 5,700; 52.1 hp/l (37.6 kW/l); hemispherical combustion chambers; valves: Vee-slanted, rockers; camshafts: 1, overhead, cogged belt; lubrication: 9.2 imp pt, 11 US pt, 5.2 l; 1 Weber 32 DARA downdraught twin barrel carburettor; cooling: 14.1 imp pt, 16.9 US pt, 8 l.

TRANSMISSION (standard) gears: 5, fully synchronized; ratios: I 4.091, II 2.176, III 0.409, IV 0.970, V 0.784, rev 3.545; axle ratio: 3.444; tyres: 165 HR x 13.

PERFORMANCE max speed: GTX Berline 115 mph, 185 km/h - GTX Break 112 mph, 181 km/h; power-weight ratio: GTX Berline 21.5 lb/hp (29.8 lb/kW), 9.8 kg/hp (13.5 kg/kW); acceleration: standing ¼ mile 17.7 sec; speed in top at 1,000 rpm: 22.8 mph, 36.7 km/h; consumption: GTX Berline 37.2 m/imp gal, 30.9 m/US gal, 7.6 l x 100 km at 75 mph, 120 km/h - GTX Break 32.8 m/imp gal, 27.3 m/US gal, 8.6 l x 100 km at 75 mph, 120 km/h.

BRAKES disc, front internal radial fins.

ELECTRICAL EQUIPMENT iodine headlamps.

DIMENSIONS AND WEIGHT weight: GTX Berline 2,238 lb, 1,015 kg - GTX Break 2,525 lb, 1,145 kg.

PRACTICAL INSTRUCTIONS oil: engine 9.2 imp pt, 11 US pt, 5.2 l.

RENAULT 18 Turbo Berline

OPTIONALS power steering; air-conditioning; sunroof; tinted glass; light alloy wheels.

110 hp power team

See 64 hp power team, except for:

ENGINE 121.7 cu in, 1,995 cc (3.46 x 3.23 in, 88 x 82 mm); compression ratio: 9.2:1; max power (DIN): 110 hp (79 kW) at 5,500 rpm; max torque (DIN): 120 lb ft, 16.6 kg m (160 Nm) at 3,000 rpm; max engine rpm: 5,700; 55.1 hp/l (39.6 kW/l); hemispherical combustion chambers; valves: Vee-slanted, rockers; camshafts: 1, overhead, cogged belt; lubrication: 9.2 imp pt, 11 US pt, 5.2 l; 1 Weber 32 DARA downdraught twin barrel carburettor; cooling: 14.1 imp pt, 16.9 US pt, 8 l.

TRANSMISSION gearbox: automatic transmission, hydraulic torque converter and planetary gears with 3 ratios, max ratio of converter at stall 2.30, possible manual selection; ratios: I 2.500, II 1.500, III 1, rev 2; tyres: 165 HR x 13.

PERFORMANCE max speed: 114 mph, 184 km/h; power-weight ratio: 20.8 lb/hp (29 lb/kW), 9.5 kg/hp (13.2 kg/kW); acceleration: standing ¼ mile 18.5 sec; speed in direct drive at 1,000 rpm: 19.8 mph, 31.8 km/h; consumption: 31.7 m/imp gal, 26.4 m/US gal, 8.9 l x 100 km at 75 mph, 120 km/h.

BRAKES disc, front internal radial fins.

ELECTRICAL EQUIPMENT iodine headlamps.

DIMENSIONS AND WEIGHT weight: 2,293 lb, 1,040 kg.

BODY saloon/sedan; 4 doors.

PRACTICAL INSTRUCTIONS oil: engine 9.2 imp pt, 11 US pt, 5.2 l.

OPTIONALS power steering; air-conditioning; sunroof; tinted glass; light alloy wheels.

66 hp (diesel) power team

See 64 hp power team, except for:

ENGINE diesel; 126.2 cu in, 2,068 cc (3.39 x 3.50 in, 86 x 89 mm); compression ratio: 21.5:1; max power (DIN): 66 hp (48 kW) at 4,500 rpm; max torque (DIN): 94 lb ft, 13 kg m (128 Nm) at 2,250 rpm; max engine rpm: 4,500; 31.9 hp/l (23.2 kW/l); light alloy block; valves: overhead, thimble tappets; camshafts: 1, overhead, cogged belt; lubrication: 8.8 imp pt, 10.6 US pt, 5 l; Bosch injection pump; cooling: 15 imp pt, 18 US pt, 8.5 l.

TRANSMISSION driving wheels: GTD 4x4 Break front and rear; (standard for GTD models) gears: 5, fully synchronized; ratios: I 4.091, II 2.176, III 1.409, IV 0.970, V 0.730, rev 3.545; axle ratio: 3.444 - GTD Break front and rear 3.778; width of rims: 5.5"; tyres: 165 SR x 13.

PERFORMANCE max speed: GTD Berline 99 mph, 160 km/h - GTD Break 97 mph, 156 km/h - GTD 4x4 Break 92 mph, 148 km/h; power-weight ratio: sedans 35.1 lb/hp (48.2 lb/kW), 15.9 kg/hp (21.9 kg/kW); acceleration: standing ¼ mile 20.1 sec; speed in top at 1,000 rpm: GTD models 25 mph, 40.3 km/h; consumption: GTD Berline 42.2 m/imp gal, 35.1 m/US gal, 6.7 l x 100 km at 75 mph, 120 km/h.

ELECTRICAL EQUIPMENT 65 Ah battery.

DIMENSIONS AND WEIGHT weight: sedans 2,315 lb, 1,050 kg - st. wagons 2,481 lb, 1,125 kg - GTD 4x4 Break 2,580 lb, 1,170 kg.

PRACTICAL INSTRUCTIONS fuel: diesel; oil: engine 8.8 imp pt, 10.6 US pt, 5 l, change every 3,100 miles, 5,000 km; valve timing: 14° 46° 50° 10°; tyre pressure: front 27 psi, 1.9 atm, rear 27 psi, 1.9 atm.

OPTIONALS (for TD models only) 5-speed mechanical gearbox; automatic transmission with 3 ratios (I 2.500, II 1.500, III 1, rev 2), 3.556 axle ratio; tinted glass; metallic spray; (for GTD Berline only) sunroof; (for GTD models only) power steering and light alloy wheels.

18 Turbo

PRICES IN GB AND EX WORKS:	£	francs
4-dr Berline	7,464*	78,324**
4+1-dr Break	—	83,024**

ENGINE turbocharged; front, 4 stroke; 4 cylinders, vertical, in line; 95.5 cu in, 1,565 cc (3.03 x 3.30 in, 77 x 84 mm); compression ratio: 8.6:1; max power (DIN): 125 hp (92 kW) at 5,500 rpm; max torque (DIN): 134 lb ft, 18.5 kg m (181 Nm) at 2,500 rpm; max engine rpm: 6,000; 79.9 hp/l (58.8 kW/l); light alloy block and head, wet liners, hemispherical combustion chambers; 5 crankshaft bearings; valves: Vee-slanted, overhead, push-rods and rockers; camshafts: 1, side; lubrication: gear pump, full flow filter (cartridge), 7.6 imp pt, 9.1 US pt, 4.3 l; 1 Solex 32 DIS downdraught single barrel carburettor; Garrett AiResearch T3 turbocharger; fuel feed: electric pump; sealed circuit cooling, expansion tank, liquid, 11.1 imp pt, 13.3 US pt, 6.3 l, electric thermostatic fan.

TRANSMISSION driving wheels: front; clutch: single dry plate (diaphragm); gearbox: mechanical; gears: 5, fully synchronized; ratios: I 4.091, II 2.176, III 1.409, IV 0.970, V 0.784, rev 3.545; lever: central; final drive: hypoid bevel; axle ratio: 3.778; width of rims: 5.5"; tyres: Pirelli 185/65 HR x 14 P6.

PERFORMANCE max speeds: (I) 26 mph, 42 km/h; (II) 46 mph, 74 km/h; (III) 71 mph, 114 km/h; (IV) 97 mph, 156 km/h; (V) Berline 121 mph, 195 km/h - Break 118 mph, 190 km/h; power-weight ratio: Berline 18.3 lb/hp (24.9 lb/kW), 8.3 kg/hp (11.3 kg/kW); carrying capacity: 882 lb, 400 kg; acceleration: standing ¼ mile 16.9 sec; speed in top at 1,000 rpm: 22.9 mph, 36.8 km/h; consumption: Berline 36.7 m/imp gal, 30.5 m/US gal, 7.7 l x 100 km at 75 mph, 120 km/h - Break 34 m/imp gal, 28.3 m/US gal, 8.3 l x 100 km at 75 mph, 120 km/h.

CHASSIS integral; front suspension: independent, by McPherson, coil springs/telescopic damper struts, anti-roll bar; rear: rigid axle, longitudinal trailing arms, A-bracket, anti-roll bar, coil springs/telescopic dampers.

STEERING rack-and-pinion; turns lock to lock: 3.72.

BRAKES disc (front diameter 10.2 in, 25.9 cm), front internal radial fins, dual circuit, rear compensator, servo.

ELECTRICAL EQUIPMENT 12 V; 36 Ah battery; 50 A alternator; AEI Renix electronic ignition; 2 iodine headlamps.

DIMENSIONS AND WEIGHT wheel base: 96.10 in, 244 cm; tracks: 55.70 in, 142 cm front, 52.99 in, 135 cm rear; length: 172.99 in, 439 cm; width: 66.77 in, 170 cm; height: 55.30 in, 140 cm; weight: Berline 2,293 lb, 1,040 kg - Break 2,459 lb, 1,115 kg; weight distribution: 60.3% front, 39.7% rear; turning circle: 36.7 ft, 11.2 m; fuel tank: 11.7 imp gal, 14 US gal, 53 l.

BODY saloon/sedan, 4 doors - estate car/st. wagon, 4+1 doors; 5 seats; electric windows; light alloy wheels; tinted glass; (for Break only) rear window wiper-washer and folding rear seat.

PRACTICAL INSTRUCTIONS fuel: 98 oct petrol; oil: engine 7.6 imp pt, 9.1 US pt, 4.3 l, SAE 20W-40, change every 4,650 miles, 7,500 km - gearbox 3.5 imp pt, 4.2 US pt, 2 l, SAE 80, change every 18,600 miles, 30,000 km; greasing: none; valve timing: 10° 50° 50° 10°; tyre pressure: front 28 psi, 2 atm, rear 31 psi, 2.2 atm.

OPTIONALS leather upholstery; power steering.

Fuego Series

PRICES IN GB AND EX WORKS:	£	francs
1 TL 2+1-dr Coupé	5,350*	56,892*
2 GTL 2+1-dr Coupé	—	66,924*
3 GTS 2+1-dr Coupé	5,990*	69,756*
4 Turbo 2+1-dr Coupé	—	—
5 Turbo D 2+1-dr Coupé	—	93,992*

Power team:	Standard for:	Optional for:
64 hp	1	—
73 hp	2	—
96 hp	3	—
132 hp	4	—
88 hp (diesel)	5	—

64 hp power team

ENGINE front, 4 stroke; 4 cylinders, vertical, in line; 85.2 cu in, 1,397 cc (2.99 x 3.03 in, 76 x 77 mm); compression ratio: 9.2:1; max power (DIN): 64 hp (46 kW) at 5,500 rpm; max torque (DIN): 76 lb ft, 10.5 kg m (103 Nm) at 3,000 rpm; max engine rpm: 5,700; 45.8 hp/l (32.9 kW/l); light alloy head, cast iron block, wet liners; 5 crankshaft bearings; valves: overhead, in line, push-rods and rockers; camshafts: 1, side; lubrication: gear pump, full flow filter, 5.6 imp pt, 6.8 US pt, 3.2 l; 1 Solex 32 SEIA or Zenith 32 IF7 downdraught single barrel carburettor; fuel feed: mechanical pump; sealed circuit cooling, expansion tank, liquid, 10.5 imp pt, 12.7 US pt, 6 l.

TRANSMISSION driving wheels: front; clutch: single dry plate (diaphragm); gearbox: mechanical; gears: 4, fully synchronized; ratios: I 4.091, II 2.176, III 1.409, IV 0.971, rev 3.545; lever: central; final drive: hypoid bevel; axle ratio: 3.555; width of rims: 5.5"; tyres: 155 SR x 13.

PERFORMANCE max speeds: (I) 26 mph, 42 km/h; (II) 45 mph, 73 km/h; (III) 70 mph, 113 km/h; (IV) 99 mph, 160 km/h; power-weight ratio: 32.4 lb/hp (45.1 lb/kW), 14.7 kg/hp (20.4 kg/kW); carrying capacity: 706 lb, 320 kg; acceleration: standing ¼ mile 19.2 sec; speed in top at

RENAULT Fuego Turbo Coupé

64 HP POWER TEAM

1,000 rpm: 19 mph, 30.6 km/h; consumption: 40.4 m/imp gal, 33.6 m/US gal, 7 l x 100 km at 75 mph, 120 km/h.

CHASSIS integral; front suspension: independent, by McPherson, coil springs/telescopic damper struts, anti-roll bar; rear: rigid axle, longitudinal trailing arms, A-bracket, anti-roll bar, coil springs/telescopic dampers.

STEERING rack-and-pinion; turns lock to lock: 3.72.

BRAKES front disc (diameter 9.40 in, 23.8 cm), rear drum, dual circuit, rear compensator, servo; lining area: front 21.7 sq in, 140 sq cm, rear 89 sq in, 574 sq cm, total 110.7 sq in, 714 sq cm.

ELECTRICAL EQUIPMENT 12 V; 36 Ah battery; 60 A alternator; electronic ignition; 2 headlamps.

DIMENSIONS AND WEIGHT wheel base: 96.22 in, 244 cm; tracks: 56.30 in, 143 cm front, 53.15 in, 135 cm rear; length: 171.65 in, 436 cm; width: 66.54 in, 169 cm; height: 51.97 in, 132 cm; weight: 2,073 lb, 940 kg; weight distribution: 57% front, 43% rear; turning circle: 34.8 ft, 10.6 m; fuel tank: 12.5 imp gal, 15 US gal, 57 l.

BODY coupé; 2+1 doors; 4 seats, separate front seats, reclining backrests, built-in headrests; electric windows.

PRACTICAL INSTRUCTIONS fuel: 98 oct petrol; oil: engine 5.6 imp pt, 6.8 US pt, 3.2 l, SAE 20W-40, change every 4,650 miles, 7,500 km - gearbox and final drive 3.5 imp pt, 4.2 US pt, 2 l, SAE 80, change every 18,600 miles, 30,000 km; greasing: none; valve timing: 22° 62° 65° 25°; tyre pressure: front 27 psi, 1.9 atm, rear 30 psi, 2.1 atm.

OPTIONALS 5-speed fully synchronized mechanical gearbox (I 4.091, II 2.176, III 1.409, IV 1.030, V 0.861, rev 3.545), consumption 42.8 m/imp gal, 35.6 m/US gal, 6.6 l x 100 km at 75 mph, 120 km/h; sunroof; metallic spray; tinted glass.

73 hp power team

See 64 hp power team, except for:

ENGINE 100.5 cu in, 1,647 cc (3.11 x 3.31 in, 79 x 84 mm); compression ratio: 9.3:1; max power (DIN): 73 hp (53 kW) at 5,000 rpm; max torque (DIN): 96 lb ft, 13.3 kg m (127 Nm) at 3,000 rpm; max engine rpm: 5,500; 44.3 hp/l (32.2 kW/l); light alloy block; lubrication: 7.4 imp pt, 8.9 US pt, 4.2 l; 1 Weber 32 DIR downdraught twin barrel carburettor; cooling: 11.1 imp pt, 13.3 US pt, 6.3 l.

TRANSMISSION gears: 5, fully synchronized; ratios: I 4.091, II 2.176, III 1.409, IV 0.970, V 0.730, rev 3.545; axle ratio: 3.444; tyres: 175/70 SR x 13.

PERFORMANCE max speed: 101 mph, 163 km/h; power-weight ratio: 30.5 lb/hp (42 lb/kW), 13.8 kg/hp (19.1 kg/kW); aceleration: standing ¼ mile 19.1 sec; speed in top at 1,000 rpm: 24.3 mph, 39.1 km/h; consumption: 42.8 m/imp gal, 35.6 m/US gal, 6.6 l x 100 km at 75 mph, 120 km/h.

DIMENSIONS AND WEIGHT weight: 2,227 lb, 1,010 kg.

PRACTICAL INSTRUCTIONS oil: engine 7.4 imp pt, 8.9 US pt, 4.2 l; valve timing: 10° 54° 54° 10°.

OPTIONALS power steering; air-conditioning; sunroof; tinted glass; metallic spray.

96 hp power team

See 64 hp power team, except for:

ENGINE 100.5 cu in, 1,647 cc (3.11 x 3.31 in, 79 x 84 mm); compression ratio: 9.3:1; max power (DIN): 96 hp (69 kW) at 5,750 rpm; max torque (DIN): 99 lb ft, 13.6 kg m (130 Nm) at 3,500 rpm; max engine rpm: 5,950; 58.3 hp/l (41.9 kW/l); hemispherical combustion chambers; valves: Vee-slanted; lubrication: 7.4 imp pt, 8.9 US pt, 4.2 l; 1 Weber 32 DARA downdraught twin barrel carburettor; cooling: 11.1 imp pt, 13.3 US pt, 6.3 l, electric thermostatic fan.

TRANSMISSION gears: 5, fully synchronized; ratios: I 4.091, II 2.176, III 1.409, IV 1.030, V 0.861, rev 3.545; axle ratio: 3.777; tyres: 175/70 SR x 13.

PERFORMANCE max speed: 112 mph, 180 km/h; power-weight ratio: 23.4 lb/hp (32.6 lb/kW), 10.6 kg/hp (14.8 kg/kW); acceleration: standing ¼ mile 17.9 sec; speed in top at 1,000 rpm: 20.2 mph, 32.5 km/h; consumption: 34.9 m/imp gal, 29 m/US gal, 8.1 l x 100 km at 75 mph, 120 km/h.

BRAKES front disc, internal radial fins.

DIMENSIONS AND WEIGHT weight: 2,249 lb, 1,020 kg.

PRACTICAL INSTRUCTIONS oil: engine 7.4 imp pt, 8.9 US pt, 4.2 l.

OPTIONALS automatic transmission, hydraulic torque converter and planetary gears with 3 ratios (I 2.500, II 1.500, III 1, rev 2), max speed 107 mph, 173 km/h, consumption 33.6 m/imp gal, 28 m/US gal, 8.4 l x 100 km at 75 mph, 120 km/h; power steering; air-conditioning; 185/65 HR x 14 tyres.

132 hp power team

See 64 hp power team, except for:

RENAULT Fuego Turbo Coupé

ENGINE 95.5 cu in, 1,565 cc (3.03 x 3.30 in, 77 x 84 mm); compression ratio: 8:1; max power (DIN): 132 hp (97 kW) at 5,500 rpm; max torque (DIN): 148 lb ft, 20.4 kg m (200 Nm) at 3,000 rpm; max engine rpm: 6,000; light alloy block and head, wet liners, hemispherical combustion chambers; valves: Vee-slanted, overhead, push-rods and rockers; lubrication: 7.6 imp pt, 9.1 US pt, 4.3 l; 1 Solex 32 DIS downdraught single barrel carburettor; Garrett AiResearch T3 turbocharger; fuel feed: electric pump; cooling: 11.1 imp pt, 13.3 US pt, 6.3 l, electric thermostatic fan.

TRANSMISSION gears: 5, fully synchronized; ratios: I 4.091, II 2.176, III 1.409, IV 0.970, V 0.784, rev 3.545; axle ratio: 3.778; tyres: Pirelli 185/65 HR x 14 P6.

PERFORMANCE max speed: over 124 mph, 200 km/h; power-weight ratio: 17.5 lb/hp (23.9 lb/kW), 7.9 kg/hp (10.8 kg/kW); acceleration: standing ¼ mile 16.5 sec; speed in top at 1,000 rpm: 22.8 mph, 36.8 km/h; consumption: 36.7 m/imp gal, 30.5 m/US gal, 7.7 l x 100 km at 75 mph, 120 km/h.

STEERING servo.

BRAKES disc (front diameter 10.2 in, 25.9 cm), front internal radial fins.

ELECTRICAL EQUIPMENT iodine headlamps.

DIMENSIONS AND WEIGHT weight: 2,315 lb, 1,050 kg.

BODY light alloy wheels; tinted glass (standard).

PRACTICAL INSTRUCTIONS oil: engine 7.6 imp pt, 9.1 US pt, 4.3 l.

OPTIONALS leather upholstery; sunroof.

88 hp (diesel) power team

See 64 hp power team, except for:

ENGINE diesel, turbocharged; 126.2 cu in, 2,068 cc (3.39 x 3.50 in, 86 x 89 mm); compression ratio: 21.5:1; max power (DIN): 88 hp (65 kW) at 4,250 rpm; max torque (DIN): 134 lb ft, 18.5 kg m (181 Nm) at 2,000 rpm; max engine rpm: 4,500; 42.6 hp/l (31.4 kW/l); turbulence chambers; camshafts: 1, overhead, cogged belt; lubrication: 11.1 imp pt, 13.3 US pt, 6.3 l; Bosch injection pump; 1 Garrett AiResearch turbocharger; cooling: 15 imp pt, 18 US pt, 8.5 l.

TRANSMISSION gears: 5, fully synchronized; ratios: I 4.091, II 2.176, III 1.409, IV 0.970, V 0.784, rev 3.545; axle ratio: 3.444; tyres: 185/65 HR x 14.

PERFORMANCE max speed: 109 mph, 175 km/h; power-weight ratio: 28.8 lb/hp (39 lb/kW), 13.1 kg/hp (17.7 kg/kW); acceleration: standing ¼ mile 18.6 sec; speed in top at 1,000 rpm: 25 mph, 40.3 km/h; consumption: 42.2 m/imp gal, 35.1 m/US gal, 6.7 l x 100 km at 75 mph, 120 km/h.

STEERING servo.

BRAKES front disc (diameter 10.2 in, 25.9 cm), internal radial fins.

ELECTRICAL EQUIPMENT 65 Ah battery; iodine headlamps.

DIMENSIONS AND WEIGHT weight: 2,536 lb, 1,150 kg.

BODY light alloy wheels; tinted glass (standard).

PRACTICAL INSTRUCTIONS fuel: diesel; oil: engine 11.1 imp pt, 13.3 US pt, 6.3 l, change every 3,100 miles, 5,000 km.

OPTIONALS leather upholstery; sunroof.

25 Series

1 TS 4+1-dr Berline
2 GTS 4+1-dr Berline
3 GTX 4+1-dr Berline
4 V6 Injection 4+1-dr Berline
5 TD 4+1-dr Berline
6 GTD 4+1-dr Berline
7 Turbo D 4+1-dr Berline
8 Turbo DX 4+1-dr Berline

Power team:	Standard for:	Optional for:
103 hp	1,2	—
123 hp	3	—
144 hp	4	—
64 hp (diesel)	5,6	—
85 hp (diesel)	7,8	—

RENAULT Fuego Turbo Coupé

RENAULT 25 TS Berline

RENAULT 25 TS Berline

103 hp power team

ENGINE front, 4 stroke; 4 cylinders, vertical, in line; 121.7 cu in, 1,995 cc (3.46 x 3.23 in, 88 x 82 mm); compression ratio: 9.2:1; max power (DIN): 103 hp (74 kW) at 5,500 rpm; max torque (DIN): 120 lb ft, 16.5 kg m (158 Nm) at 3,000 rpm; max engine rpm: 5,700; 51.6 hp/l (37.1 kW/l); light alloy block and head, wet liners, hemispherical combustion chambers; 5 crankshaft bearings; valves: overhead, Vee-slanted, rockers; camshafts: 1, overhead, cogged belt; lubrication: gear pump, full flow filter (cartridge), 9.3 imp pt, 11.2 US pt, 5.3 l; 1 Weber 28-36 DARA downdraught twin barrel carburettor; fuel feed: mechanical pump; sealed circuit cooling, liquid, expansion tank, 12.8 imp pt, 15.4 US pt, 7.3 l, electric thermostatic fan.

TRANSMISSION driving wheels: front; clutch: single dry plate (diaphragm); gearbox: mechanical, in unit with engine and final drive; gears: 5, fully synchronized; ratios: TS I 4.091, II 2.176, III 1.409, IV 0.971, V 0.784, rev 3.545 - GTS I 4.091, II 2.176, III 1.409, IV 1.030, V 0.861, rev 3.545; lever: central; final drive: hypoid bevel; axle ratio: TS 3.222 - GTS 3.555; width of rims: 5.5"; tyres: TS 165/80 R x 14 T tubeless - GTS 185/70 R x 14 T tubeless.

PERFORMANCE max speed: 113 mph, 182 km/h; power-weight ratio: TS 26.8 lb/hp (37.4 lb/kW), 10.9 kg/hp (15.1 kg/kW); carrying capacity: 1,036 lb, 470 kg; acceleration: standing ¼ mile 17.5 sec; speed in top at 1,000 rpm: TS 28 mph, 45 km/h; consumption: TS 40.4 m/imp gal, 33.6 m/US gal, 7 l x 100 km at 75 mph, 120 km/h.

CHASSIS integral; front suspension: independent, by McPherson, coil springs/telescopic damper struts, lower wishbones, anti-roll bar; rear: independent, lower wishbones, coil springs, anti-roll bar, telescopic dampers.

STEERING rack-and-pinion, adjustable height of steering wheel, GTS servo; turns lock to lock: TS 4.50 - GTS 3.

BRAKES front disc (diameter 10.20 in, 25.9 cm), internal radial fins, rear drum, dual circuit, rear compensator, servo; lining area: front 22.08 sq in, 142 sq cm, rear 42.17 sq in, 272 sq cm, total 64.25 sq in, 414 sq cm.

ELECTRICAL EQUIPMENT 12 V; 50 Ah battery; 60 A alternator; electronic ignition; 2 iodine headlamps.

DIMENSIONS AND WEIGHT wheel base: 107.01 in, 272 cm; tracks: 58.74 in, 149 cm front, 58.11 in, 148 cm rear; length: 182.01 in, 462 cm; width: 69.76 in, 177 cm; height: 55.31 in, 140 cm; weight: TS Berline 2,766 lb, 1,120 kg - GTS Berline 2,547 lb, 1,155 kg; turning circle: 38 ft, 11.6 m; fuel tank: 14.7 imp gal, 17.7 US gal, 67 l.

BODY saloon/sedan; 4+1 doors; 5 seats, separate front seats, reclining backrests; headrests, heated rear window.

PRACTICAL INSTRUCTIONS fuel: 98 oct petrol; oil: engine 9.3 imp pt, 11.2 US pt, 5.3 l, SAE 10W-50, change every 4,600 miles, 7,500 km - gearbox and final drive 6 imp pt, 7.2 US pt, 3.4 l, SAE 20W-40, change every 9,300 miles, 15,000 km; greasing: none; valve timing: 12° 52° 52° 12°; tyre pressure: front 31 psi, 2.2 atm, rear 28 psi, 2 atm.

OPTIONALS (for GTS only) tinted glass, electric sunroof and light alloy wheels.

123 hp power team

See 103 hp power team, except for:

ENGINE 132.1 cu in, 2,165 cc (3.46 x 3.50 in, 88 x 89 mm); compression ratio: 9.9:1; max power (DIN): 123 hp (89 kW) at 5,250 rpm; max torque (DIN): 134 lb ft, 18.5 kg m (178 Nm) at 2,750 rpm; 56.8 hp/l (41.1 kW/l); Renault electronic injection.

TRANSMISSION clutch: single dry plate, hydraulically controlled; gearbox ratios: I 3.364, II 2.059, III 1.381, IV 1.037, V 0.821, rev 3.545; axle ratio: 3.888; width of rims: 6"; tyres: 195/60 R x 15 H.

PERFORMANCE max speed: 121 mph, 195 km/h; power-weight ratio: 21.5 lb/hp (29.7 lb/kW), 9.8 kg/hp (13.5 kg/kW); carrying capacity: 1,014 lb, 460 kg; acceleration: standing ¼ mile 17.2 sec; speed in top at 1,000 rpm: 22.1 mph, 35.6 km/h; consumption: 35.8 m/imp gal, 29.8 m/US gal, 7.9 l x 100 km at 75 mph, 120 km/h.

STEERING servo; turns lock to lock: 3.

DIMENSIONS AND WEIGHT weight: 2,646 lb, 1,200 kg.

BODY light alloy wheels (standard).

PRACTICAL INSTRUCTIONS valve timing: 17° 63° 63° 17°.

OPTIONALS automatic transmission, hydraulic torque converter and planetary gears with 3 ratios (I 2.500, II 1.515, III 1, rev 2), 3.555 axle ratio, max speed 119 mph, 192 km/h, consumption 34.4 m/imp gal, 28.7 m/US gal, 8.2 l x 100 km at 75 mph, 120 km/h; air-conditioning; leather upholstery; electric sunroof.

144 hp power team

See 103 hp power team, except for:

ENGINE 6 cylinders, Vee-slanted at 90°; 162.6 cu in, 2,664 cc (3.46 x 2.87 in, 88 x 73 mm); max power (DIN): 144 hp (104 kW) at 5,500 rpm; max torque (DIN): 162 lb ft, 22.4 kg m (215 Nm) at 3,000 rpm; max engine rpm: 6,000; 54.1 hp/l (39 kW/l); 4 crankshaft bearings; camshafts: 2, 1 per bank, overhead; Bosch KA-Jetronic injection; fuel feed: electric pump; liquid-cooled, 16.4 imp pt, 20.6 US pt, 9.3 l, viscous coupling thermostatic fan.

TRANSMISSION clutch: single dry plate, hydraulically controlled; gearbox ratios: I 3.364, II 2.059, III 1.381, IV 0.964, V 0.756, rev 3.545; axle ratio: 3.888; width of rims: 6"; tyres: 195/60 R x 15 H.

PERFORMANCE max speed: 125 mph, 201 km/h; power-weight ratio: 19.6 lb/hp (27.1 lb/kW), 8.9 kg/hp (12.3 kg/kW); carrying capacity: 1,058 lb, 480 kg; acceleration: standing ¼ mile 16.8 sec; speed in top at 1,000 rpm: 23.8 mph, 38.6 km/h; consumption: 31.7 m/imp gal, 26.4 m/US gal, 8.9 l x 100 km at 75 mph, 120 km/h.

STEERING servo; turns lock to lock: 3.

BRAKES disc (front diameter 11.02 in, 28 cm, rear 10 in, 25.4 cm), front internal radial fins; lining area: front 30.1 sq in, 194 sq cm, rear 22.2 sq in, 143 sq cm, total 52.3 sq in, 337 sq cm.

ELECTRICAL EQUIPMENT 90 A alternator; 4 iodine headlamps.

DIMENSIONS AND WEIGHT weight: 2,822 lb, 1,280 kg; fuel tank: 15.8 imp gal, 19 US gal, 72 l.

BODY electric front windows; tinted glass (standard); light alloy wheels (standard).

RENAULT 25 GTX Berline

RENAULT 25 V6 Injection Berline

RENAULT 25 V6 Injection Berline

RENAULT 25 V6 Injection Berline

144 HP POWER TEAM

PRACTICAL INSTRUCTIONS valve timing: 21° 57° 57° 21° (left), 19° 55° 55° 19° (right).

OPTIONALS automatic transmission, hydraulic torque converter and planetary gears with 3 ratios (I 2.439, II 1.471, III 1, rev 1.923), 3.444 axle ratio, max speed 122 mph, 196 km/h, consumption 28.8 m/imp gal, 24 m/US gal, 9.8 l x 100 km at 75 mph, 120 km/h; air-conditioning; leather upholstery; electric sunroof.

64 hp (diesel) power team

See 103 hp power team, except for:

ENGINE diesel; 126.2 cu in, 2,068 cc (3.39 x 3.50 in, 86 x 89 mm); compression ratio: 21.5:1; max power (DIN): 64 hp (46 kW) at 4,500 rpm; max torque (DIN): 93 lb ft, 12.9 kg m (124 Nm) at 2,250 rpm; max engine rpm: 4,500; 30.9 hp/l (22.2 kW/l); turbulence chambers; valves: in line; lubrication: 10.6 imp pt, 12.7 US pt, 6 l; Bosch VE or Roto Diesel DPC injection pump; liquid-cooled, 12.7 imp pt, 15.2 US pt, 7.2 l.

TRANSMISSION gearbox ratios: I 4.091, II 2.176, III 1.409, IV 1.030, V 0.861, rev 3.545; axle ratio: 3.777; tyres: GTD 185/70 R x 14 T.

PERFORMANCE max speed: 96 mph, 155 km/h; power-weight ratio: TD 40.7 lb/hp (56.6 lb/kW), 18.4 kg/hp (25.7 kg/kW); acceleration: standing ¼ mile 20.8 sec; speed in top at 1,000 rpm: 21.7 mph, 34.9 km/h; consumption: 39.8 m/imp gal, 33.1 m/US gal, 7.1 l x 100 km at 75 mph, 120 km/h.

STEERING GTD servo; turns lock to lock: 3.

ELECTRICAL EQUIPMENT 65 Ah battery.

DIMENSIONS AND WEIGHT weight: TD Berline 2,602 lb, 1,180 kg - GTD Berline 2,679 lb, 1,215 kg.

PRACTICAL INSTRUCTIONS fuel: diesel; oil: engine 10.6 imp pt, 12.7 US pt, 6 l; valve timing: 14° 46° 50° 10°.

OPTIONALS (for GTD only) tinted glass, electric sunroof and light alloy wheels.

85 hp (diesel) power team

See 103 hp power team, except for:

ENGINE diesel, turbocharged; 126.2 cu in, 2,068 cc (3.39 x 3.50 in, 86 x 89 mm); compression ratio: 21.5:1; max power (DIN): 85 hp (63 kW) at 4,250 rpm; max torque (DIN): 134 lb ft, 18.5 kg m (181 Nm) at 2,000 rpm; max engine rpm: 4,500; 41.1 hp/l (30.5 kW/l); turbulence chambers; valves: in line; lubrication: 10.6 imp pt, 12.7 US pt, 6 l; Bosch VE injection pump; 1 Garrett AiResearch turbocharger; liquid-cooled, 13 imp pt, 15.6 US pt, 7.4 l.

TRANSMISSION gearbox ratios: I 4.091, II 2.176, III 1.409, IV 0.971, V 0.784, rev 3.545; axle ratio: 3.555; width of rims: 6"; tyres: 195/60 R x 15 H.

PERFORMANCE max speed: 107 mph, 172 km/h; power-weight ratio: Turbo D 31.9 lb/hp (43 lb/kW), 14.5 kg/hp (19.5 kg/kW); acceleration: standing ¼ mile 18.5 sec; speed in top at 1,000 rpm: 25.3 mph, 40.8 km/h; consumption: 40.9 m/imp gal, 34.1 m/US gal, 6.9 l x 100 km at 75 mph, 120 km/h.

STEERING servo; turns lock to lock: 3.

ELECTRICAL EQUIPMENT 65 Ah battery; 70 A alternator.

DIMENSIONS AND WEIGHT weight: Turbo D Berline 2,712 lb, 1,230 kg - Turbo DX Berline 2,745 lb, 1,245 kg.

BODY light alloy wheels (standard).

PRACTICAL INSTRUCTIONS fuel: diesel; oil: engine 10.6 imp pt, 12.7 US pt, 6 l; valve timing: 14° 46° 50° 10".

OPTIONALS air-conditioning; leather upholstery; electric sunroof.

STIMULA — FRANCE

Bugatti 55 Série II

PRICE EX WORKS: 186,000* francs

ENGINE BMW, front, 4 stroke; 6 cylinders, in line; 141 cu in, 2,315 cc (3.15 x 3.02 in, 80 x 76.8 mm); compression ratio: 9.5:1; max power (DIN): 143 hp (105 kW) at 5,800 rpm; max torque (DIN): 141 lb ft, 19.4 kg m (190 Nm) at 4,500 rpm; max engine rpm: 6,400; 61.8 hp/l (45.4 kW/l); cast iron block, light alloy head; 7 crankshaft bearings; valves: overhead, Vee-slanted, rockers; camshafts: 1, overhead; lubrication: gear pump, full flow filter, 10 imp pt, 12 US pt, 5.7 l; Bosch L-Jetronic injection; fuel feed: mechanical pump; water-cooled, 21.1 imp pt, 25.4 US pt, 12 l.

TRANSMISSION driving wheels: rear; clutch: single dry plate (diaphragm), hydraulically controlled; gearbox: mechanical; gears: 5, fully synchronized; ratios: I 3.764, II 2.325, III 1.612, IV 1.229, V 1, rev 4.096; lever: central; final drive: hypoid bevel; axle ratio: 3.640; width of rims: 5.5"; tyres: Michelin XWX 205 x 15 or Pirelli P6.

PERFORMANCE max speed: 112 mph, 180 km/h; power-weight ratio: 14.5 lb/hp (19.8 lb/kW), 6.6 kg/hp (9 kg/kW); carrying capacity: 397 lb, 180 kg.

CHASSIS tubular and box-type; front suspension: independent, wishbones, lower trailing links, coil springs, anti-roll bar, telescopic dampers; rear: rigid axle, twin trailing radius arms, upper torque arms, transverse linkage bar, coil springs, anti-roll bar, telescopic dampers.

STEERING rack-and-pinion; turns lock to lock: 4.

BRAKES front disc, rear drum, dual circuit, rear compensator, servo.

ELECTRICAL EQUIPMENT 12 V; 44 Ah battery; 910 W alternator; transistorized ignition; 2 halogen headlamps.

DIMENSIONS AND WEIGHT wheel base: 110.24 in, 280 cm; front and rear track: 57.09 in, 145 cm; length: 161.42 in, 410 cm; width: 68.90 in, 175 cm; weight: 2,095 lb, 950 kg; weight

STIMULA Bugatti 55 Série II

STIMULA Bugatti 55 Série II

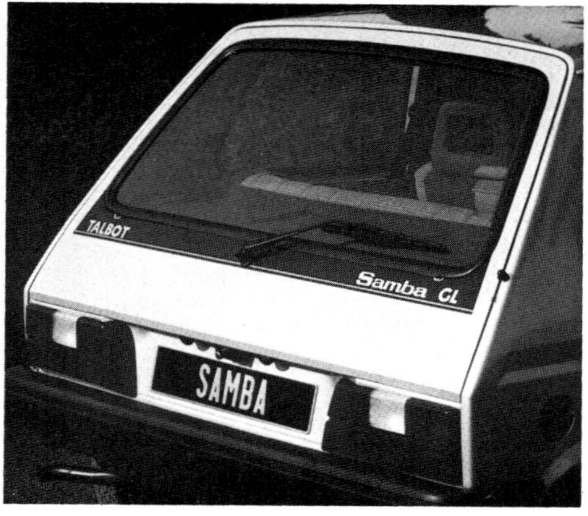

TALBOT Samba GL Berline

TALBOT Samba LS Berline

distribution: 50% front axle, 50% rear axle; turning circle: 34.4 ft, 10.5 m; fuel tank: 12.1 imp gal, 14.5 US gal, 55 l.

BODY roadster, in plastic material; no doors; 2 seats; soft canvas top; trip computer; light alloy wheels; laminated windscreen.

PRACTICAL INSTRUCTIONS fuel: 98 oct petrol; oil: engine 10 imp pt, 12 US pt, 5.7 l, SAE 20W-50, change every 3,200 miles, 6,000 km - gearbox 1.8 imp pt, 2.1 US pt, 1 l, SAE 80, change every 14,800 miles, 24,000 km - final drive 1.6 imp pt, 1.9 US pt, 0.9 l, SAE 90, no change recommended; greasing: none; tyre pressure: front 26 psi, 1.8 atm, rear 26 psi, 1.8 atm.

OPTIONALS ZF 3 HP 22 automatic transmission with 3 ratios (I 2.478, II 1.478, III 1, rev 2.090); 185 x 15 tyres; tonneau cover; air-conditioning; hardtop; leather upholstery; 2 doors.

TALBOT FRANCE

Samba Series

PRICES IN GB AND EX WORKS:	£	francs
1 LS 2+1-dr Berline	—	38,950**
2 GL 2+1-dr Berline	4,345*	42,950**
3 72 CV 2-dr Cabriolet	6,595*	62,850**
4 GLS 2+1-dr Berline	4,990**	50,950**
5 80 CV 2-dr Cabriolet	—	69,200**
6 Rallye 2+1-dr Berline	—	49,900**

Power team:	Standard for:	Optional for:
50 hp	1,2	—
72 hp	3	—
80 hp	4,5	—
90 hp	6	—

50 hp power team

ENGINE front, transverse, slanted 72° to rear, 4 stroke; 4 cylinders, in line; 68.6 cu in, 1,124 cc (2.83 x 2.72 in, 72 x 69 mm); compression ratio: 9.7:1; max power (DIN): 50 hp (36 kW) at 4,800 rpm; max torque (DIN): 63 lb ft, 8.7 kg m (83 Nm) at 2,800 rpm; max engine rpm: 5,500; 44.5 hp/l (32 kW/l); light alloy block and head, wet liners, bi-hemispherical combustion chambers; 5 crankshaft bearings; valves: overhead, Vee-slanted, rockers; camshafts: 1, overhead; lubrication: gear pump, full flow filter, 7.9 imp pt, 9.5 US pt, 4.5 l; 1 Solex 32 PBISA 12 downdraught single barrel carburettor; fuel feed: mechanical pump; water-cooled, expansion tank, 9.9 imp pt, 11.8 US pt, 5.6 l, electric thermostatic fan.

TRANSMISSION driving wheels: front; clutch: single dry plate (diaphragm); gearbox: mechanical, in unit with engine and final drive; gears: 4, fully synchronized; ratios: I 3.883, II 2.074, III 1.377, IV 0.944, rev 3.568; lever: central; final drive: spiral bevel; axle ratio: LS 3.177 - GL 3.353; width of rims: 4.5"; tyres: LS 135 SR x 13 - GL 145 SR x 13.

PERFORMANCE max speed: 89 mph, 143 km/h; power-weight ratio: 32.6 lb/hp (45.3 lb/kW), 14.8 kg/hp (20.6 kg/kW); carrying capacity: 706 lb, 320 kg; acceleration: standing ¼ mile 20.1 sec; speed in top at 1,000 rpm: 20.7 mph, 33.4 km/h; consumption: 44.8 m/imp gal, 37.3 m/US gal, 6.3 l x 100 km at 75 mph, 120 km/h.

CHASSIS integral; front suspension: independent, by McPherson, coil springs/telescopic damper struts, lower wishbones (trailing links), anti-roll bar; rear: independent, swinging longitudinal trailing arms, coil springs, telescopic dampers.

STEERING rack-and-pinion; turns lock to lock: 3.92.

BRAKES front disc (diameter 9.49 in, 24.1 cm), rear drum, dual circuit, rear compensator.

ELECTRICAL EQUIPMENT 12 V; 28 Ah battery; 500 W alternator; electronic ignition; 2 headlamps.

DIMENSIONS AND WEIGHT wheel base: 92.13 in, 234 cm; tracks: 50.87 in, 129 cm front, 50.08 in, 127 cm rear; length: 138.03 in, 351 cm; width: 60.16 in, 153 cm; height: 53.62 in, 136 cm; ground clearance: 5.12 in, 13 cm; weight: 1,632 lb, 740 kg; turning circle: 32.5 ft, 9.9 m; fuel tank: 8.8 imp gal, 10.6 US gal, 40 l.

BODY saloon/sedan; 2+1 doors; 4 seats, separate front seats; folding rear seat; (for GL only) heated rear window and rear window wiper-washer.

PRACTICAL INSTRUCTIONS fuel: 98 oct petrol; oil: engine, gearbox and final drive 7 imp pt, 8.5 US pt, 4 l, SAE 10W-50, change every 3,100 miles, 5,000 km; greasing: every 3,100 miles, 5,000 km; valve timing: 2° 36° 23°-11°; tyre pressure: front 26 psi, 1.8 atm, rear 28 psi, 2 atm.

VARIATIONS

(for export only)
ENGINE 58.2 cu in, 954 cc (2.76 x 2.44 in, 70 x 62 mm), 8.8:1 compression ratio, max power (DIN) 45 hp (33 kW) at 6,000 rpm, max torque (DIN) 47 lb ft, 6.5 kg m (62 Nm) at 3,000 rpm, 47.2 hp/l (34.6 kW/l), 1 Solex 32 PBISA 11.
PERFORMANCE max speed 84 mph, 135 km/h, power-weight ratio 36.3 lb/hp (49.5 lb/kW), 16.4 kg/hp (22.4 kg/kW), consumption 37.2 m/imp gal, 30.9 m/US gal, 7.6 l x 100 km at 75 mph, 120 km/h.

OPTIONALS (for LS only) heated rear window and rear window wiper-washer; (for GL only) 5-speed mechanical gearbox (I 3.883, II 2.297, III 1.501, IV 1.124, V 0.904, rev 3.568) and tinted glass; metallic spray.

72 hp power team

See 50 hp power team, except for:

ENGINE 83 cu in, 1,360 cc (3.95 x 3.03 in, 75 x 77 mm); compression ratio: 9.3:1; max power (DIN): 72 hp (53 kW) at 6,000 rpm; max torque (DIN): 79 lb ft, 10.9 kg m (107 Nm) at 3,000 rpm; max engine rpm: 6,500; 53 hp/l (39 kW/l); 1 Solex 32/35 TACIC A 314 downdraught twin barrel carburettor.

TRANSMISSION gears: 5, fully synchronized; ratios: I 3.883, II 2.297, III 1.501, IV 1.124, V 0.904, rev 3.568; axle ratio: 3.562; width of rims: 5"; tyres: 165/70 SR x 13.

PERFORMANCE max speed: 99 mph, 159 km/h; power-weight ratio: 26 lb/hp (35.4 lb/kW), 11.8 kg/hp (16 kg/kW); acceleration: standing ¼ mile 18.2 sec; speed in top at 1,000 rpm: 20.3 mph, 32.3 km/h; consumption: 40.4 m/imp gal, 33.6 m/US gal, 7 l x 100 km at 75 mph, 120 km/h.

CHASSIS rear suspension: anti-roll bar.

BRAKES servo.

DIMENSIONS AND WEIGHT tracks: 51.34 in, 130 cm front, 49.45 in, 126 cm rear; weight: 1,874 lb, 850 kg.

BODY convertible; 2 doors.

OPTIONALS light alloy wheels; tinted glass.

80 hp power team

See 50 hp power team, except for:

ENGINE 83 cu in, 1,360 cc (2.95 x 3.03 in, 75 x 77 mm); compression ratio: 9.3:1; max power (DIN): 80 hp (57 kW) at 5,800 rpm; max torque (DIN): 81 lb ft, 11.2 kg m (109 Nm) at 2,800 rpm; max engine rpm: 6,200; 58.8 hp/l (41.9 kW/l); 2 Solex 45 BISA 8 downdraught single barrel carburettors.

TRANSMISSION gears: 5, fully synchronized; ratios: I 3.883, II 2.296, III 1.501, IV 1.124, V 0.904, rev 3.568; axle ratio: 3.867; width of rims: 5"; tyres: 165/70 SR x 13.

PERFORMANCE max speed: 104 mph, 168 km/h; power-weight ratio: Berline 22 lb/hp (30.9 lb/kW), 10 kg/hp (14 kg/kW); acceleration: standing ¼ mile 17.9 sec; speed in top at 1,000

TALBOT Samba GLS Berline

80 HP POWER TEAM

rpm: 18.5 mph, 29.8 km/h; consumption: 37.7 m/imp gal, 31.4 m/US gal, 7.5 l x 100 km at 75 mph, 120 km/h.

CHASSIS rear suspension: anti-roll bar.

BRAKES servo.

DIMENSIONS AND WEIGHT weight: Berline 1,764 lb, 800 kg - Cabriolet 1,874 lb, 850 kg.

BODY saloon/sedan, 2+1 doors - convertible, 2 doors; reclining backrests with headrests; electric windows.

OPTIONALS light alloy wheels.

90 hp power team

See 50 hp power team, except for:

ENGINE 74.4 cu in, 1,219 cc (2.95 x 2.72 in, 75 x 69 mm); compression ratio: 9.7:1; max power (DIN): 90 hp (65 kW) at 6,700 rpm; max torque (DIN): 76 lb ft, 10.5 kg m (102 Nm) at 5,400 rpm; max engine rpm: 7,000; 73.8 hp/l (53.3 kW/l); 2 Weber 40 DCOE horizontal twin barrel carburettors.

TRANSMISSION gears: 5, fully synchronized; ratios: I 3.883, II 2.296, III 1.501, IV 1.124, V 0.904, rev 3.568; axle ratio: 4.066; width of rims: 5"; tyres: 165/70 SR x 13.

PERFORMANCE max speed: 109 mph, 176 km/h; power-weight ratio: 19.1 lb/hp (26.5 lb/kW), 8.7 kg/hp (12 kg/kW); acceleration: standing ¼ mile 17.6 sec; speed in top at 1,000 rpm: 17.4 mph, 28.1 km/h; consumption: 32.5 m/imp gal, 27 m/US gal, 8.7 l x 100 km at 75 mph, 120 km/h.

CHASSIS rear suspension: anti-roll bar.

BRAKES servo.

DIMENSIONS AND WEIGHT weight: 1,720 lb, 780 kg.

OPTIONALS rear window wiper-washer.

Horizon Series

PRICES EX WORKS:	francs
1 LS 4+1-dr Berline	**44,400****
2 GL 4+1-dr Berline	**51,400****
3 EX 4+1-dr Berline	**54,600****
4 GLS 4+1-dr Berline	**55,900****
5 Premium 4+1-dr Berline	**60,600****
6 LD 4+1-dr Berline	**53,600****
7 EXD 4+1-dr Berline	**63,700****

Power team:	Standard for:	Optional for:
59 hp	1	—
65 hp	2,3	—
83 hp	4	2,3
90 hp	5	—
65 hp (diesel)	6,7	—

59 hp power team

ENGINE front, transverse, slanted 41° to rear, 4 stroke; 4 cylinders, in line; 68.2 cu in, 1,118 cc (2.91 x 2.56 in, 74 x 65 mm); compression ratio: 9.6:1; max power (DIN): 59 hp (43 kW) at 5,600 rpm; max torque (DIN): 67 lb ft, 9.3 kg m (91 Nm) at 3,000 rpm; max engine rpm: 6,300; 52.8 hp/l (38.8 kW/l); cast iron block, light alloy head; 5 crankshaft bearings; valves: overhead, push-rods and rockers; camshafts: 1, side; lubrication: gear pump, full flow filter, 5.3 imp pt, 6.3 US pt, 3 l; 1 Solex 32 BISA 7 or Weber 32 IBSA single barrel carburettor; fuel feed: mechanical pump; sealed circuit cooling, expansion tank, liquid, 10.6 imp pt, 12.7 US pt, 6 l, electric thermostatic fan.

TRANSMISSION driving wheels: front; clutch: single dry plate (diaphragm), hydraulically controlled; gearbox: mechanical; gears: 4, fully synchronized; ratios: I 3.900, II 2.313, III 1.524, IV 1.080, rev 3.769; lever: central; final drive: cylindrical gears; axle ratio: 3.705; width of rims: 4.5"; tyres: 145 SR x 13.

PERFORMANCE max speed: 91 mph, 147 km/h; power-weight ratio: 35.3 lb/hp (48 lb/kW), 16 kg/hp (21.8 kg/kW); carrying capacity: 981 lb, 445 kg; acceleration: standing ¼ mile 20 sec; consumption: 32.5 m/imp gal, 27 m/US gal, 8.7 l x 100 km at 75 mph, 120 km/h.

CHASSIS integral; front suspension: independent, longitudinal torsion bars, wishbones, anti-roll bar, telescopic dampers; rear: independent, swinging longitudinal trailing arms, coil springs, anti-roll bar, telescopic dampers.

STEERING rack-and-pinion; turns lock to lock: 4.35.

BRAKES front disc (diameter 9.37 in, 23.8 cm), rear drum, rear compensator, servo; swept area: front 155 sq in, 1,000 sq cm, rear 89 sq in, 574 sq cm, total 244 sq in, 1,574 sq cm.

ELECTRICAL EQUIPMENT 12 V; 35 Ah battery; 50 A alternator; transistorized ignition; 2 headlamps.

DIMENSIONS AND WEIGHT wheel base: 99.21 in, 252 cm; tracks: 55.91 in, 142 cm front, 53.94 in, 137 cm rear; length: 155.91 in, 396 cm; width: 66.14 in, 168 cm; height: 55.51 in, 141 cm; ground clearance: 7.09 in, 18 cm; weight: 2,084 lb, 945 kg; weight distribution: 59.4% front, 40.6% rear; turning circle: 33.5 ft, 10.2 m; fuel tank: 9.9 imp gal, 11.9 US gal, 45 l.

BODY saloon/sedan; 4+1 doors; 5 seats, separate front seats, reclining backrests; heated rear window; folding rear seat.

PRACTICAL INSTRUCTIONS fuel: 98-100 oct petrol; oil: engine 5.3 imp pt, 6.3 US pt, 3 l, SAE 20W-40, change every 4,650 miles, 7,500 km - gearbox and final drive 1.9 imp pt, 2.3 US pt, 1.1 l, SAE 90 EP, change every 9,300 miles, 15,000 km; greasing: none; tyre pressure: front and rear 26 psi, 1.8 atm.

OPTIONALS metallic spray; iodine headlamps; rear window wiper-washer; tinted glass; adjustable headrests on front seats; vinyl roof.

TALBOT Samba 72 CV Cabriolet

65 hp power team

See 59 hp power team, except for:

ENGINE 88 cu in, 1,442 cc (3.02 x 3.07 in, 76.7 x 78 mm); compression ratio: 9.5:1; max power (DIN): 65 hp (47 kW) at 5,200 rpm; max torque (DIN): 87 lb ft, 12 kg m (118 Nm) at 2,400 rpm; 45.1 hp/l (32.6 kW/l); 1 Solex 32 BISA 8 single barrel carburettor.

TRANSMISSION GL gearbox ratios: I 3.754, II 2.177, III 1.409, IV 1.040, rev 3.769 - EX gears: 5, fully synchronized; ratios: I 3.308, II 1.882, III 1.280, IV 0.969, V 0.757, rev 3.333; axle ratio: GL 3.471 - EX 3.846.

PERFORMANCE max speed: 95 mph, 153 km/h; power-weight ratio: 33.6 lb/hp (46.4 lb/kW), 15.2 kg/hp (21 kg/kW); carrying capacity: 882 lb, 400 kg; acceleration: standing ¼ mile 19.5 sec; consumption: 37.2 m/imp gal, 30.9 m/US gal, 7.6 l x 100 km at 75 mph, 120 km/h.

ELECTRICAL EQUIPMENT 40 Ah battery.

DIMENSIONS AND WEIGHT weight: 2,183 lb, 990 kg.

OPTIONALS (for GL only) 5 - speed mechanical gearbox.

83 hp power team

See 59 hp power team, except for:

ENGINE 88 cu in, 1,442 cc (3.02 x 3.07 in, 76.7 x 78 mm); compression ratio: 9.5:1; max power (DIN): 83 hp (61 kW) at 5,600 rpm; max torque (DIN): 89 lb ft, 12.3 kg m (121 Nm) at 3,000 rpm; 57.6 hp/l (42.4 kW/l); 1 Weber 36 DCA 2 downdraught twin barrel carburettor.

TRANSMISSION gears: 5, fully synchronized; ratios: I 3.308, II 1.882, III 1.280, IV 0.969, V 0.757, rev 3.333; axle ratio: 4.429; width of rims: 5"; tyres: 155 SR x 13.

PERFORMANCE max speed: 102 mph, 164 km/h; power-weight ratio: 26.3 lb/hp (35.8 lb/kW), 11.9 kg/hp (16.2 kg/kW); acceleration: standing ¼ mile 18.8 sec; consumption: 35.8 m/imp gal, 29.8 m/US gal, 7.9 l x 100 km at 75 mph, 120 km/h.

ELECTRICAL EQUIPMENT 40 Ah battery; 2 iodine headlamps (standard).

DIMENSIONS AND WEIGHT tracks: 56.46 in, 143 cm front, 54.61 in, 139 cm rear; weight: 2,183 lb, 990 kg.

BODY (standard) adjustable backrests on front seats, rear window wiper-washer, automatic speed control, trip computer.

OPTIONALS (for GL and EX only) automatic transmission with 3 ratios (2.690, II 1.550, III 1, rev 2.100), 2.842 axle ratio, max speed 98 mph, 157 km/h, consumption 31 m/imp gal, 25.8 m/US gal, 9.1 l x 100 km at 75 mph, 120 km/h; light alloy wheels; headlamps with wiper-washers; speed control.

90 hp power team

See 59 hp power team, except for:

ENGINE 97.2 cu in, 1,592 cc (3.17 x 3.07 in, 80.6 x 78 mm); compression ratio: 9.3:1; max power (DIN): 90 hp (64 kW) at 5,400 rpm; max torque (DIN): 98 lb ft, 13.5 kg m (132 Nm) at 4,000 rpm; max engine rpm: 6,000; 56.5 hp/l (40.2 kW/l); valves: overhead, rochers; camshafts: 1, overhead; 1 Weber 36 DCNVH-12 downdraught twin barrel carburettor; liquid-cooled, 11.3 imp pt, 13.5 US pt, 6.4 l.

TRANSMISSION gears: 5, fully synchronized; ratios: I 3.308, II 1.882, III 1.280, IV 0.969, V 0.757, rev 3.333; axle ratio: 4.429; width of rims: 5"; tyres: 175/70 SR x 13.

PERFORMANCE max speed: 109 mph, 175 km/h; power-weight ratio: 24.3 lb/hp (34.1 lb/kW), 11 kg/hp (15.5 kg/kW); accelera-

TALBOT Samba Rallye Berline

TALBOT Horizon Premium Berline

TALBOT Matra Rancho Break

tion: standing ¼ mile 17.6 sec; consumption: 35.3 m/imp gal, 29.4 m/US gal, 8 l x 100 km at 75 mph, 120 km/h.

STEERING servo.

ELECTRICAL EQUIPMENT 40 Ah battery; 2 iodine headlamps (standard).

DIMENSIONS AND WEIGHT tracks: 56.46 in, 143 cm front, 54.61 in, 139 cm rear; weight: 2,183 lb, 990 kg.

BODY (standard) adjustable backrests on front seats, rear window wiper-washer, automatic speed control, trip computer, light alloy wheels, central door locking.

65 hp (diesel) power team

See 59 hp power team, except for:

ENGINE diesel; front, transverse, slanted 20° to rear; 116.3 cu in, 1,905 cc (3.27 x 3.46 in, 83 x 88 mm); compression ratio: 23.5:1; max power (DIN): 65 hp (47 kW) at 4,600 rpm; max torque (DIN): 88 lb ft, 12.2 kg m (118 Nm) at 2,000 rpm; max engine rpm: 5,000; 34.1 hp/l (24.7 kW/l); valves: overhead, rockers; camshafts: 1, overhead; lubrication: 8.8 imp pt, 10.6 US pt, 5 l; Rotodiesel injection pump.

TRANSMISSION LD gearbox ratios: I 3.308, II 1.882, III 1.148, IV 0.799, rev 3.333 - EXD gears: 5, fully synchronized; ratios: I 3.308, II 1.882, III 1.280, IV 0.969, V 0.757, rev 3.333; axle ratio: LD 3.814 - EXD 3.939.

PERFORMANCE max speed: LD 93 mph, 149 km/h - EXD 97 mph, 156 km/h; power-weight ratio: 34.6 lb/hp (47.9 lb/kW), 15.7 kg/hp (21.7 kg/kW); acceleration: standing ¼ mile 20.5 sec; consumption: 43.5 m/imp gal, 36.2 m/US gal, 6.5 l x 100 km at 75 mph, 120 km/h.

ELECTRICAL EQUIPMENT 60 Ah battery.

DIMENSIONS AND WEIGHT tracks: EXD 56.46 in, 143 cm front, 54.61 in, 139 cm rear; weight: 2,249 lb, 1,020 kg.

OPTIONALS (for LD only) 5-speed mechanical gearbox; (for EXD only) tinted glass and central door locking; power steering.

Solara Series

PRICES EX WORKS:	francs
1 LS 4-dr Berline	52,500**
2 GL 4-dr Berline	59,300**
3 GLS 4-dr Berline	62,400**
4 SX 4-dr Berline	68,100**

Power team:	Standard for:	Optional for:
70 hp	1,2	—
90 hp	3,4	—

70 hp power team

ENGINE front, transverse, slanted 41° to rear, 4 stroke; 4 cylinders, in line; LS 88 cu in, 1,442 cc (3.02 x 3.07 in, 76.7 x 78 mm) - GL 97.1 cu in, 1,592 cc (3.17 x 3.07 in, 80.6 x 78 mm); compression ratio: LS 9.5:1 - GL 9.3:1; max power (DIN): LS 70 hp (50 kW) at 5,200 rpm - GL at 5,000 rpm; max torque (DIN): LS 86 lb ft, 11.9 kg m (117 Nm) at 3,000 rpm - GL 99 lb ft, 13.7 kg m (133 Nm) at 2,600 rpm; max engine rpm: 6,000; LS 48.5 hp/l (34.7 kW/l) - GL 43.9 hp/l (31.4 kW/l); cast iron block, light alloy head; 5 crankshaft bearings; valves: overhead, in line, push-rods and rockers; camshafts: 1, side; lubrication: gear pump, full flow filter, 5.3 imp pt, 6.3 US pt, 3 l; LS 1 Solex 32 BISA 7 downdraught single barrel carburettor - GL Solex 32 BISA 8; fuel feed: mechanical pump; sealed circuit cooling, expansion tank, liquid, 11.3 imp pt, 13.5 US pt, 6.4 l, electric thermostatic fan.

TRANSMISSION driving wheels: front; clutch: single dry plate (diaphragm), hydraulically controlled; gearbox: mechanical; LS gears: 4, fully synchronized; ratios: I 3.900, II 2.312, III 1.524, IV 1.040, rev 3.769 - GL gears: 5, fully synchronized; ratios; I 3.308, II 1.882, III 1.280, IV 0.969, V 0.757, rev 3.333; lever: central; final drive: cylindrical gears; axle ratio: LS 3.588 - GL 3.814; width of rims: 5"; tyres: LS 155 SR x 13 - GL 165 SR x 13.

PERFORMANCE max speeds: (I) 28 mph, 45 km/h; (II) 47 mph, 76 km/h; (III) 72 mph, 116 km/h; (IV) 98 mph, 157 km/h; power-weight ratio: 32.8 lb/hp (45.9 lb/kW), 14.9 kg/hp (20.8 kg/kW); carrying capacity: 970 lb, 440 kg; acceleration: standing ¼ mile 19.5 sec; speed in top at 1,000 rpm: 17.6 mph, 28.3 km/h; consumption: LS 34 m/imp gal, 28.3 m/US gal, 8.3 l - GL 35.3 m/imp gal, 29.4 m/US gal, 8 l x 100 km at 75 mph, 120 km/h.

CHASSIS integral; front suspension: independent, wishbones, longitudinal torsion bars, anti-roll bar, telescopic dampers; rear: independent, swinging longitudinal trailing arms, coil springs, anti-roll bar, telescopic dampers.

STEERING rack-and-pinion; turns lock to lock: 4.15.

BRAKES front disc (diameter 9.45 in, 24 cm), rear drum, dual circuit, rear compensator, servo; swept area: front 172.1 sq in, 1,110 sq cm, rear 89 sq in, 574 sq cm, total 261.1 sq in, 1,684 sq cm.

ELECTRICAL EQUIPMENT 12 V; 40 Ah battery; 50 A alternator; electronic ignition; 2 headlamps.

DIMENSIONS AND WEIGHT wheel base: 102.36 in, 260 cm; tracks: 56.10 in, 142 cm front, 55.12 in, 140 cm rear; length: 172.91 in, 439 cm; width: 66.14 in, 168 cm; height: 54.72 in, 139 cm; ground clearance: 5.12 in, 13 cm; weight: 2,293 lb, 1,040 kg; weight distribution: 48% front, 52% rear; turning circle: 34.8 ft, 10.6 m; fuel tank: 12.8 imp gal, 15.3 US gal, 58 l.

BODY saloon/sedan; 4 doors; 5 seats, separate front seats, reclining backrests; heated rear window.

PRACTICAL INSTRUCTIONS fuel: 98-100 oct petrol; oil: engine 5.3 imp pt, 6.3 US pt, 3 l, SAE 20W-40, change every 4,650 miles, 7,500 km - gearbox and final drive 1.9 imp pt, 2.3 US pt, 1.1 l, SAE 90 EP, change every 9,300 miles, 15,000 km; greasing: none.

OPTIONALS metallic spray; iodine headlamps; headrests; (for GL only) tinted glass.

90 hp power team

See 70 hp power team, except for:

ENGINE 97.1 cu in, 1,592 cc (3.17 x 3.07 in, 80.6 x 78 mm); compression ratio: 9.3:1; max power (DIN): 90 hp (66 kW) at 5,400 rpm; max torque (DIN): 96 lb ft, 13.3 kg m (131 Nm) at 3,800 rpm; 56.5 hp/l (41.5 kW/l); valves: overhead, rockers; camshafts: 1, overhead; 1 Weber 36 DCNVH 12 downdraught twin barrel carburettor.

TRANSMISSION gears: 5, fully synchronized; ratios: I 3.308, II 1.882, III 1.280, IV 0.969, V 0.757, rev 3.333; axle ratio: 4.216; tyres: 165 SR x 13.

PERFORMANCE max speed: 104 mph, 167 km/h; power-weight ratio: 26.5 lb/hp (36.2 lb/kW), 12 kg/hp (16.4 kg/kW); carrying capacity: 882 lb, 400 kg; speed in top at 1,000 rpm: 20.9 mph, 33.6 km/h; consumption: 37.2 m/imp gal, 30.9 m/US gal, 7.6 l x 100 km at 75 mph, 120 km/h.

ELECTRICAL EQUIPMENT iodine headlamps (standard).

DIMENSIONS AND WEIGHT weight: 2,381 lb, 1,080 kg.

OPTIONALS automatic transmission with 3 ratios (I 2.475, II 1.475, III 1, rev 2.103), 3.056 axle ratio, max speed 101 mph, 163 km/h, consumption 29.1 m/imp gal, 24.2 m/US gal, 9.7 l x 100 km at 75 mph, 120 km/h; sunroof; light alloy wheels; metallic spray; tinted glass; (for GLS only) power steering.

Matra Rancho

PRICES IN GB AND EX WORKS:	£	francs
2+1-dr Break	6,995*	72,100**
X 2+1-dr Break	—	78,800**

ENGINE front, transverse, slanted 41° to rear, 4 stroke; 4 cylinders, in line; 88 cu in, 1,442 cc (3.02 x 3.07 in, 76.7 x 78 mm); compression ratio: 9.5:1; max power (DIN): 80 hp

TALBOT Solara SX Berline

MATRA RANCHO

(57 kW) at 5,600 rpm; max torque (DIN): 87 lb ft, 12 kg m (118 Nm) at 3,000 rpm: max engine rpm: 6,000; 55.5 hp/l (39.5 kW/l); cast iron block, light alloy head; 5 crankshaft bearings; valves: overhead, in line, push-rods and rockers; camshafts: 1, side; lubrication: gear pump, full flow filter, 5.3 imp pt, 6.3 US pt, 3 l; 1 Weber 36 DCNVH5 downdraught twin barrel carburettor; fuel feed: mechanical pump; sealed circuit cooling, expansion tank, liquid, 10.6 imp pt, 12.7 US pt, 6 l, electric thermostatic fan.

TRANSMISSION driving wheels: front; clutch: single dry plate (diaphragm), hydraulically controlled; gearbox: mechanical; gears: 4, fully synchronized; ratios: I 3.900, II 2.312, III 1.524, IV 1.080, rev 3.769; lever: central; final drive: cylindrical gears; axle ratio: 3.938; width of rims: 5.5"; tyres: 185/70 HR x 14.

PERFORMANCE max speed: 90 mph, 145 km/h; power-weight ratio: 31.1 lb/hp (43.7 lb/kW), 14.1 kg/hp (19.8 kg/kW); carrying capacity: 1,147 lb, 520 kg; speed in top at 1,000 rpm: 16.7 mph, 26.9 km/h; acceleration: standing ¼ mile 20 sec; consumption: 24.6 m/imp gal, 20.5 m/US gal, 11.5 l x 100 km at 75 mph, 120 km/h.

CHASSIS integral, box-type reinforced platform; front suspension: independent, wishbones, longitudinal torsion bars, anti-roll bar, telescopic dampers; rear: independent, swinging longitudinal trailing arms, transverse torsion bars, anti-roll bar, telescopic dampers.

STEERING rack-and-pinion; turns lock to lock: 3.75.

BRAKES front disc (diameter 9.37 in, 23.8 cm), rear drum, rear compensator, servo; swept area: front 158.8 sq in, 1,024 sq cm, rear 90.2 sq in, 582 sq cm, total 249 sq in, 1,606 sq cm.

ELECTRICAL EQUIPMENT 12 V; 48 Ah battery; 40 A alternator; transistorized ignition; 4 iodine headlamps.

DIMENSIONS AND WEIGHT wheel base: 99.21 in, 252 cm; tracks: 55.51 in, 141 cm front, 53.15 in, 135 cm rear; length: 169.68 in, 431 cm; width: 65.35 in, 166 cm; height: 68.11 in, 173 cm; ground clearance: 6.57 in, 16.7 cm front, 6.69 in, 17 cm rear; weight: 2,492 lb, 1,130 kg; turning circle: 34.7 ft, 10.6 m; fuel tank: 13.2 imp gal, 15.8 US gal, 60 l.

BODY estate car/st. wagon, roof in plastic material; 2+1 doors; 5+1 seats, separate front seats, reclining backrests with built-in headrests; folding rear seat; heated rear window wiper-washer.

PRACTICAL INSTRUCTIONS fuel: 98-100 oct petrol; oil: engine 5.3 imp pt, 6.3 US pt, 3 l, SAE 20W-40, change every 3,100 miles, 5,000 km - gearbox and final drive 1.9 imp pt, 2.3 US pt, 1.1 l, SAE 90 EP, change every 6,200 miles, 10,000 km; greasing: none; valve timing: 19° 59° 61° 21°; tyre pressure: front 26 psi 1.8 atm, rear 36 psi, 2.5 atm.

OPTIONALS limited slip differential; air-conditioning; tinted glass; metallic spray.

VARIATIONS

ENGINE 8.8:1 compression ratio, max power (DIN) 78 hp (56 kW) at 5,600 rpm, max torque (DIN) 88 lb ft, 12.1 kg m (119 Nm) at 3,200 rpm, 54.1 hp/l (38.8 kW/l), 1 Weber 36 DCNVH 10 downdraught twin barrel carburettor.
PERFORMANCE power-weight ratio: 31.4 lb/hp (43.8 lb/kW), 14.3 kg/hp (19.9 kg/kW), consumption 25.2 m/imp gal, 21 m/US gal, 11.2 l x 100 km at 75 mph, 120 km/h.
DIMENSIONS AND WEIGHT weight 2,452 lb, 1,112 kg.
PRACTICAL INSTRUCTIONS fuel 85 oct petrol.

TALBOT Matra Murena S

Matra Murena S

PRICE EX WORKS: 103,900 francs**

ENGINE central, transverse, 4 stroke; 4 cylinders, in line; 131.6 cu in, 2,155 cc (3.61 x 3.21 in, 91.7 x 81.6 mm); compression ratio: 9.4:1; max power (DIN): 142 hp (102 kW) at 6,000 rpm; max torque (DIN): 138 lb ft, 19.1 kg m (187 Nm) at 3,800 rpm; max engine rpm: 6,500; 65.9 hp/l (47.3 kW/l); cast iron block, light alloy head; 5 crankshaft bearings; valves: overhead, thimble tappets; camshafts: 1, overhead, chain-driven; lubrication: gear pump, full flow filter (cartridge), 7.9 imp pt, 9.5 US pt, 4.5 l; 2 Weber 40 ADDHE downdraught twin barrel carburettors; fuel feed: mechanical pump; sealed circuit cooling, expansion tank, liquid, front radiator, 22.9 imp pt, 27.5 US pt, 13 l, electric thermostatic fan.

TRANSMISSION driving wheels: rear; clutch: single dry plate (diaphragm), hydraulically controlled; gearbox: mechanical; gears: 5, fully synchronized; ratios: I 3.167, II 1.833, III 1.250, IV 0.939, V 0.733, rev 3.154; lever: central; final drive: cylindrical gears; axle ratio: 4.357; width of rims: 6"; tyres: 185/60 VR x 14 front, 195/60 VR x 14 rear.

PERFORMANCE max speeds: (I) 29 mph, 47 km/h; (II) 50 mph, 81 km/h; (III) 74 mph, 119 km/h; (IV) 99 mph, 159 km/h; (V) 130 mph, 210 km/h; power-weight ratio: 16.3 lb/hp (22.7 lb/kW), 7.4 kg/hp (10.3 kg/kW); carrying capacity: 573 lb, 260 kg; consumption: 31.7 m/imp gal, 25.4 m/US gal, 8.9 l x 100 km at 75 mph, 120 km/h.

CHASSIS integral, box-type reinforced platform; front suspension: independent, wishbones, longitudinal torsion bars, anti-roll bar, telescopic dampers; rear: independent, lower wishbones, anti-roll bar, coil springs/telescopic damper struts.

STEERING rack-and-pinion; turns lock to lock: 3.18.

BRAKES disc (front diameter 9.45 in, 24 cm, rear 9.17 in, 23.3 cm), dual circuit, rear compensator, servo; swept area: front 169.3 sq in, 1,092 sq cm, rear 161.6 sq in, 1,042 sq cm, total 330.9 sq in, 2,134 sq cm.

ELECTRICAL EQUIPMENT 12 V; 48 Ah battery; 55 A alternator; electronic ignition; 2 retractable headlamps.

DIMENSIONS AND WEIGHT wheel base: 95.87 in, 243 cm; tracks: 55.51 in, 141 cm front, 60.08 in, 153 cm rear; length: 160.24 in, 407 cm; width: 68.98 in, 175 cm; height: 48.03 in, 122 cm; ground clearance: 6.22 in, 15.8 cm; weight: 2,315 lb, 1,050 kg; weight distribution: 41% front, 59% rear; turning circle: 37.4 ft, 11.4 m; fuel tank: 12.3 imp gal, 14.8 US gal, 56 l.

BODY coupé, in plastic material; 2+1 doors; 3 front seats, separate driving seat, built-in headrests; heated rear window; electric windows.

PRACTICAL INSTRUCTIONS fuel: 98 oct petrol; oil: engine 7.9 imp pt, 9.5 US pt, 4.5 l, SAE 20W-40, change every 3,100 miles, 5,000 km - gearbox and final drive: 2.3 imp pt, 2.7 US pt, 1.3 l, SAE 90 EP, change every 12,400 miles, 20,000 km; valve timing: 27° 72° 69°50' 29°50'; tyre pressure: front 26 psi, 1.8 atm, rear 34 psi, 2.4 atm.

OPTIONALS light alloy wheels; metallic spray; tinted glass.

TRABANT GERMANY DR

601 Limousine

Standard 2-dr Limousine
S 2-dr Limousine

ENGINE front, transverse, 2 stroke; 2 cylinders, in line; 36.2 cu in, 594.5 cc (2.83 x 2.87 in, 72 x 73 mm); compression ratio: 7.6:1; max power (DIN): 26 hp (19 kW) at 4,200 rpm; max torque (DIN): 40 lb ft, 5.5 kg m (54 Nm) at 3,000 rpm; max engine rpm: 4,500; 43.7 hp/l (32.1 kW/l); light alloy block and head, dry liners; 3 crankshaft bearings; valves: 1 per cylinder, rotary; lubrication: mixture; 1 BVF type 28 HB 2-8 horizontal single barrel carburettor; fuel feed: gravity; air-cooled.

TALBOT Matra Murena S

TRABANT 601 Universal

TRANSMISSION driving wheels: front; clutch: single dry plate; gearbox: mechanical; gears: 4, fully synchronized; ratios: I 4.080, II 2.320, III 1.520, IV 1.103, rev 3.940; lever: on facia; final drive: helical spur gears; axle ratio: 3.950; width of rims: 4"; tyres: 5.20 or 145 SR x 13.

PERFORMANCE max speeds: (I) 16 mph, 25 km/h; (II) 28 mph, 45 km/h; (III) 43 mph, 70 km/h; (IV) 62 mph, 100 km/h; power-weight ratio: 52.1 lb/hp (71 lb/kW), 23.6 kg/hp (32.2 kg/kW); carrying capacity: 849 lb, 385 kg; acceleration: 0-50 mph (0-80 km/h) 22.5 sec; speed in top at 1,000 rpm: 14.6 mph, 23.5 km/h; consumption: 40.4 m/imp gal, 33.6 m/US gal, 7 l x 100 km.

CHASSIS integral; front suspension: independent, wishbones, transverse leafspring upper arms, telescopic dampers; rear: independent, swinging semi-axle, transverse semi-elliptic leafspring, telescopic dampers.

STEERING rack-and-pinion; turns lock to lock: 2.60.

BRAKES drum, double circuit; swept area: front 38.9 sq in, 251 sq cm, rear 34.1 sq in, 220 sq cm, total 73 sq in, 471 sq cm.

ELECTRICAL EQUIPMENT 6 V; 56 Ah battery - S Limousine 84 Ah battery; 220 W dynamo; AKA distributor; 2 headlamps.

DIMENSIONS AND WEIGHT wheel base: 79.53 in, 202 cm; tracks: 47.64 in, 121 cm front, 49.21 in, 125 cm rear; length: 138.19 in, 351 cm; width: 59.06 in, 150 cm; height: 56.69 in, 144 cm; ground clearance: 6.10 in, 15.5 cm; weight: 1,356 lb, 615 kg; weight distribution: 45% front, 55% rear; turning circle: 32.8 ft, 10 m; fuel tank: 5.7 imp gal, 6.9 US gal, 26 l.

BODY saloon/sedan; 2 doors; 4 seats, separate front seats, reclining backrests; (for S Limousine only) rear fog lamps and chromium bumpers.

PRACTICAL INSTRUCTIONS fuel: mixture 1:50, 88 oct petrol, SAE 20; oil: gearbox and final drive 2.6 imp pt, 3.2 US pt, 1.5 l, SAE 10W-30, change every 9,300 miles, 15,000 km; greasing: every 3,100 miles, 5,000 km, 9 points; spark plug: 14 x 225°; valve timing: 45° 45° 72°5' 72°5'; tyre pressure: front 20 psi, 1.4 atm, rear 20 psi, 1.4 atm.

OPTIONALS Hycomat automatic clutch.

601 Universal / S De Luxe

See 601 Limousine, except for:

PERFORMANCE power-weight ratio: 55.1 lb/hp (75 lb/kW), 25 kg/hp (34 kg/kW); carrying capacity: 860 lb, 390 kg.

DIMENSIONS AND WEIGHT length: 140.16 in, 356 cm; width: 59.45 in, 151 cm; height: 57.87 in, 147 cm; weight: 1,433 lb, 650 kg; weight distribution: 44% front, 56% rear.

BODY estate car/st. wagon; 2+1 doors; folding rear seat.

WARTBURG GERMANY DR

353 W

ENGINE front, 2 stroke; 3 cylinders, vertical, in line; 60.5 cu in, 992 cc (2.89 x 3.07 in, 73.5 x 78 mm); compression ratio: 7.5:1; max power (DIN): 50 hp (37 kW) at 4,250 rpm; max torque (DIN): 72 lb ft, 10 kg m (98 Nm) at 3,000 rpm; max engine rpm: 5,000; 50.4 hp/l (37.1 kW/l); cast iron block, light alloy head; 4 crankshaft bearings; lubrication: mixture 1:50; 1 Jikov 32 SEDR carburettor; fuel feed: mechanical pump; sealed circuit cooling, liquid, 11.8 imp pt, 14.2 US pt, 6.7 l.

WARTBURG 353 W

TRANSMISSION driving wheels: front; clutch: single dry plate; gearbox: mechanical; gears: 4, fully synchronized; ratios: I 3.769, II 2.160, III 1.347, IV 0.906, rev 3.385; lever: steering column or central; final drive: spiral bevel; axle ratio: 4.222; width of rims: 4.5"; tyres: 6.00 x 13 or 165 SR x 13.

PERFORMANCE max speeds: (I) 20 mph, 32 km/h; (II) 35 mph, 57 km/h; (III) 56 mph, 90 km/h; (IV) 81 mph, 130 km/h; power-weight ratio: 40.6 lb/hp (55.1 lb/kW), 18.4 kg/hp (25 kg/kW); carrying capacity: 882 lb, 400 kg; acceleration: 0-50 mph (0-80 km/h) 14.5 sec; speed in top at 1,000 rpm: 17.4 mph, 28 km/h; consumption: 30.1 m/imp gal, 25 m/US gal, 9.4 l x 100 km.

CHASSIS box-type ladder frame; front suspension: independent, wishbones, coil springs, rubber elements, telescopic dampers; rear: independent, semi-trailing arms, coil springs, rubber elements, anti-roll bar, telescopic dampers.

STEERING rack-and-pinion; turns lock to lock: 3.50.

BRAKES front disc, rear drum, rear compensator; lining area: front 20 sq in, 129 sq cm, rear 61.4 sq in, 396 sq cm, total 81.4 sq in, 525 sq cm.

ELECTRICAL EQUIPMENT 12 V; 38 Ah battery; 588 W alternator; FEK distributor; 2 headlamps.

DIMENSIONS AND WEIGHT wheel base: 96.46 in, 245 cm; tracks: 50.39 in, 128 cm front, 51.18 in, 130 cm rear; length: 166.14 in, 422 cm; width: 64.57 in, 164 cm; height: 58.66 in, 149 cm; ground clearance: 6.10 in, 15.5 cm; weight: 2,029 lb, 920 kg; weight distribution: 51.5% front, 48.5% rear; turning circle: 33.5 ft, 10.2 m; fuel tank: 8.8 imp gal, 10.6 US gal, 40 l.

BODY saloon/sedan; 4 doors; 5 seats, separate front seats, reclining backrests.

PRACTICAL INSTRUCTIONS fuel: mixture 1:50, SAE 20-40; oil: gearbox and final drive 3.2 imp pt, 3.8 US pt, 1.8 l, SAE 80 EP, change every 31,100 miles, 50,000 km; greasing: every 6,200 miles, 10,000 km, 3 points; spark plug: 175°; opening timing: 62°17' 62°17' 78°2' 78°2'; tyre pressure: front 23 psi, 1.6 atm, rear 24 psi, 1.7 atm.

OPTIONALS central lever; halogen headlamps; sunroof; luxury version.

353 W Tourist / De Luxe

See 353 W, except for:

PERFORMANCE max speed: 78 mph, 125 km/h; power-weight ratio: 42.8 lb/hp (58.1 lb/kW), 19.4 kg/hp (26.4 kg/kW); carrying capacity: 970 lb, 440 kg; consumption: 29.4 m/imp gal, 24.5 m/US gal, 9.6 l x 100 km.

DIMENSIONS AND WEIGHT length: 172.44 in, 438 cm; weight: 2,139 lb, 970 kg.

BODY estate car/st. wagon; 4+1 doors; folding rear seat; (for De Luxe only) luxury equipment and sunroof.

PRACTICAL INSTRUCTIONS rear tyre pressure: 27 psi, 1.9 atm.

AUDI GERMANY FR

Audi 80 Series

PRICES EX WORKS:		DM
1	C 1.3 2-dr Limousine	16,345*
2	C 1.3 4-dr Limousine	17,075*
3	CL 1.3 2-dr Limousine	17,475*
4	CL 1.3 4-dr Limousine	18,205*
5	CL 1.6 2-dr Limousine	18,175*
6	CL 1.6 4-dr Limousine	18,905*
7	GL 1.6 2-dr Limousine	19,515*
8	GL 1.6 4-dr Limousine	20,245*
9	CL 1.8 2-dr Limousine	18,815*
10	CL 1.8 4-dr Limousine	19,545*
11	GL 1.8 2-dr Limousine	20,155*
12	GL 1.8 4-dr Limousine	20,885*
13	GTE 1.8 2-dr Limousine	22,265*
14	GTE 1.8 4-dr Limousine	22,995*
15	CD 2.0 4-dr Limousine	25,455*

For GB and USA prices, see price index.

Power team:	Standard for:	Optional for:
60 hp	1 to 4	—
75 hp	5 to 8	—
90 hp	9 to 12	—
112 hp	13,14	—
115 hp	15	—

60 hp power team

ENGINE front, 4 stroke; 4 cylinders, in line; 79.1 cu in, 1,296 cc (2.95 x 2.89 in, 75 x 73.4 mm); compression ratio: 9:1; max power (DIN): 60 hp (44 kW) at 5,600 rpm; max torque (DIN): 74 lb ft, 10.2 kg m (100 Nm) at 3,500 rpm; max engine rpm: 6,000; 46.3 hp/l (33.9 kW/l); cast iron block, light alloy head; 5 crankshaft bearings; valves: overhead, in line, thimble tappets; camshafts: 1, overhead, cogged belt; lubrication: gear pump, full flow filter, 6.2 imp pt, 7.4 US pt, 3.5 l; 1 Solex 32-35 TDID downdraught twin barrel carburettor; fuel feed: mechanical pump; water-cooled, 11.4 imp pt, 13.7 US pt, 6.5 l, electric thermostatic fan.

TRANSMISSION driving wheels: front; clutch: single dry plate (diaphragm); gearbox: 3+E mechanical; gears: 4, fully synchronized; ratios: I 3.455, II 1.789, III 1.065, IV 0.703,

AUDI 80 GTE 1.8 Limousine

AUDI 80 CD 2.0 Limousine

AUDI 80 Quattro Limousine

60 HP POWER TEAM

rev 3.167; lever: central; final drive: spiral bevel; axle ratio: 4.111; width of rims: 5"; tyres: 155 SR x 13.

PERFORMANCE max speeds: (I) 25 mph, 41 km/h; (II) 42 mph, 68 km/h; (III) 68 mph, 110 km/h; (IV) 93 mph, 150 km/h; power-weight ratio: 34.9 lb/hp (47.6 lb/kW), 15.8 kg/hp (21.6 kg/kW); carrying capacity: 1,014 lb, 460 kg; acceleration: 0-50 mph (0-80 km/h) 9.9 sec; speed in top at 1,000 rpm: 22.4 mph, 36 km/h; consumption: 40.9 m/imp gal, 34.1 m/US gal, 6.9 l x 100 km at 75 mph, 120 km/h.

CHASSIS integral, front auxiliary subframe; front suspension: independent, by McPherson, lower wishbones, coil springs/telescopic damper struts; rear: rigid axle, trailing radius arms, Panhard rod, coil springs/telescopic damper struts.

STEERING rack-and-pinion; turns lock to lock: 3.94.

BRAKES front disc (diameter 9.43 in, 23.9 cm), dual circuit, rear drum, servo.

ELECTRICAL EQUIPMENT 12 V; 36 Ah battery; 55 A alternator; electronic ignition; 2 headlamps.

DIMENSIONS AND WEIGHT wheel base: 100 in, 254 cm; tracks: 55.10 in, 140 cm front, 55.90 in, 142 cm rear; length: 172.60 in, 438 cm; width: 66.20 in, 168 cm; height: 53.54 in, 136 cm; ground clearance: 4.21 in, 10.7 cm; weight: 2,095 lb, 950 kg; turning circle: 34.1 ft, 10.4 m; fuel tank: 15 imp gal, 18 US gal, 68 l.

BODY saloon/sedan; 2 or 4 doors; 5 seats, separate front seats, headrests; heated rear window.

PRACTICAL INSTRUCTIONS fuel: 91 oct petrol; oil: engine 5.3 imp pt, 6.3 US pt, 3 l, SAE 20W-30, change every 4,700 miles, 7,500 km - gearbox and final drive 3.2 imp pt, 3.8 US pt, 1.8 l, SAE 80 or 90; greasing: none; spark plug: 175°; tappet clearances: inlet 0.008-0.012 in, 0.20-0.30 mm, exhaust 0.016-0.020 in, 0.40-0.50 mm; tyre pressure: front 26 psi, 1.8 atm, rear 26 psi, 1.8 atm.

OPTIONALS 175/70 SR x 13 tyres; halogen headlamps; sunroof; vinyl roof; metallic spray.

75 hp power team

See 60 hp power team, except for:

ENGINE 97.3 cu in, 1,595 cc (3.19 x 3.05 in, 81 x 77.4 mm); max power (DIN): 75 hp (55 kW) at 5,000 rpm; max torque (DIN): 92 lb ft, 12.7 kg m (125 Nm) at 2,500 rpm; max engine rpm: 5,600; 47 hp/l (34.5 kW/l); 1 Solex 32-35TDID downdraught twin barrel carburettor.

TRANSMISSION gearbox ratios: I 3.455, II 1.944, III 1.286, IV 0.882, rev 3.167; tyres: 165 SR x 13.

PERFORMANCE max speed: (I) 28 mph, 46 km/h; (II) 51 mph, 82 km/h; (III) 77 mph, 124 km/h; (IV) 99 mph, 160 km/h; power-weight ratio: 27.9 lb/hp (37.9 lb/kW), 12.7 kg/hp (17.2 kg/kW); acceleration: 0-50 mph (0-80 km/h) 8.5 sec.; speed in top at 1,000 rpm: 18.3 mph, 29.5 km/h; consumption: 32.1 m/imp gal, 26.7 m/US gal, 8.8 l x 100 km at 75 mph, 120 km/h.

CHASSIS front suspension: anti-roll-bar.

OPTIONALS 4+E 5-speed mechanical gearbox (I 3.455, II 1.944, III 1.286, IV 0.882, V 0.730, rev 3.167), consumption 35.3 m/imp gal, 29.4 m/US gal, 8 l x 100 km at 75 mph, 120 km/h; automatic transmission, hydraulic torque converter and planetary gears with 3 ratios (I 2.714, II 1.500, III 1, rev 2.429), max ratio of converter at stall 2.20, possible manual selection, 3.727 axle ratio, max speed 97 mph, 156 km/h, consumption 31 m/imp gal, 25.8 m/US gal, 9.1 l x 100 km at 75 mph, 120 km/h; power steering; air-conditioning.

90 hp power team

See 60 hp power team, except for:

ENGINE 108.7 cu in, 1,781 cc (3.19 x 3.40 in, 81 x 86.4 mm); compression ratio: 10:1; max power (DIN): 90 hp (66 kW) at 5,200 rpm; max torque (DIN): 107 lb ft, 14.8 kg m (145 Nm) at 3,300 rpm; max engine rpm: 5,800; 50.5 hp/l (37.1 kW/l); valves: overhead, thimble tappets; 1 Solex downdraught twin barrel carburettor.

TRANSMISSION gearbox ratios: I 3.455, II 1.789, III 1.333, IV 0.829, rev 3.167; tyres: 175/70 SR x 13.

PERFORMANCE max speeds: (I) 30 mph, 49 km/h; (II) 58 mph, 94 km/h; (III) 78 mph, 126 km/h; (IV) 104 mph, 168 km/h; power-weight ratio: 23.3 lb/hp (31.7 lb/kW), 10.6 kg/hp (14.4 kg/kW); acceleration: 0-50 mph (0-80 km/h) 7.2 sec.; speed in top at 1,000 rpm: 19.1 mph, 30.7 km/h; consumption: 34.4 m/imp gal, 28.7 m/US gal, 8.2 l x 100 km at 75 mph, 120 km/h.

CHASSIS front suspension: anti-roll-bar.

ELECTRICAL EQUIPMENT 40 Ah battery; halogen headlamps.

PRACTICAL INSTRUCTIONS fuel: 98 oct petrol.

OPTIONALS 4+E 5-speed mechanical gearbox (I 3.455, II 1.789, III 1.333, IV 0.829, V 0.684, rev 3.167), consumption 37.7 m/imp gal, 31.4 m/US gal, 7.5 l x 100 km at 75 mhp, 120 km/h; automatic transmission, hydraulic torque converter and planetary gears with 3 ratios (I 2.714, II 1.500, III 1, rev 2.429), 3.250 axle ratio, max speed 102 mph, 164 km/h, consumption 34 m/imp gal, 28.3 m/US gal, 8.3 l x 100 km at 75 mph, 120 km/h; power steering; air-conditioning.

112 hp power team

See 60 hp power team, except for:

ENGINE 108.7 cu in, 1,781 cc (3.19 x 3.40 in, 81 x 86 mm); compression ratio: 10:1; max power (DIN): 112 hp (82 kW) at 5,800 rpm; max torque (DIN): 118 lb ft, 16.3 kg m (160 Nm) at 3,500 rpm; max engine rpm: 6,700; 62.9 hp/l (46 kW/l); valves: overhead, thimble tappets; Bosch K-Jetronic injection; fuel feed: electric pump.

TRANSMISSION gears: 5, fully synchronized; ratios: I 3.455, II 1.944, III 1.286, IV 0.969, V 0.800, rev 3.167; tyres: 175/70 HR x 13.

PERFORMANCE max speeds: (I) 33 mph, 53 km/h; (II) 59 mph, 95 km/h; (III) 89 mph, 143 km/h; (IV) 114 mph, 184 km/h; (V) 112 mph, 180 km/h; power-weight ratio: 19.3 lb/hp (26.4 lb/kW), 8.7 kg/hp (11.9 kg/kW); acceleration: 0-50 mph (0-80 km/h) 6.3 sec.; speed in top at 1,000 rpm: 19.7 mph, 31.7 km/h; consumption: 34.9 m/imp gal, 29 m/US gal, 8.1 l x 100 km at 75 mph, 120 km/h.

CHASSIS front and rear suspension: anti-roll bar.

ELECTRICAL EQUIPMENT 50 Ah battery; halogen headlamps.

PRACTICAL INSTRUCTIONS fuel: 98 oct petrol.

OPTIONALS 185/60 HR x 14 tyres with 6" wide rims and light alloy wheels; power steering; air-conditioning.

115 hp power team

See 60 hp power team, except for:

ENGINE slanted 20° to right; 5 cylinders, in line; 121.7 cu in, 1,994 cc (3.19 x 3.05 in, 81 x 77.4 mm); compression ratio: 10:1; max power (DIN): 115 hp (85 kW) at 5,400 rpm; max torque (DIN): 122 lb ft, 16.8 kg m (165 Nm) at 3,200 rpm; max engine rpm: 6,200; 59.2 hp/l (43.7 kW/l); 6 crankshaft bearings; Bosch K-Jetronic injection; fuel feed: electric pump; water-cooled; 14 imp pt, 16.9 US pt, 8 l.

TRANSMISSION gearbox: 4+E mechanical; gears: 5, fully synchronized; ratios: I 2.846, II 1.524, III 0.939, IV 0.658, V 0.537, rev 3.167; axle ratio: 4.900; width of rims: 5.5"; tyres: 175/70 HR x 13.

PERFORMANCE max speed: 114 mph, 184 km/h; power-weight ratio: 20.1 lb/hp (27.2 lb/kW), 9.1 kg/hp (12.4 kg/kW); acceleration: 0-50 mph (0-80 km/h) 6.5 sec; speed in top at 1,000 rpm: 24.7 mph, 39.8 km/h; consumption: 35.3 m/imp gal, 29.4 m/US gal, 8 l x 100 km at 75 mph, 120 km/h.

CHASSIS front and rear suspension: anti-roll bar.

AUDI GT 2.0 Coupé

ELECTRICAL EQUIPMENT 63 Ah battery; 65 A alternator; 4 halogen headlamps.

DIMENSIONS AND WEIGHT weight: 2,315 lb, 1,050 kg.

OPTIONALS automatic transmission with 3 ratios (I 2.714, II 1.500, III 1, rev 2.429), 3.250 axle ratio, max speed 111 mph, 178 km/h, consumption 30.7 m/imp gal, 25.6 m/US gal, 9.2 l x 100 km at 75 mph, 120 km/h; 185/60 HR x 14 tyres with 6" wide rims and light alloy wheels; power steering; electric windows; sunroof; air-conditioning.

Audi 80 Diesel Series

PRICES EX WORKS:		DM
1	C 2-dr Limousine	**18,250***
2	C 4-dr Limousine	**18,980***
3	CL 2-dr Limousine	**19,380***
4	CL 4-dr Limousine	**20,110***
5	GL 2-dr Limousine	**20,720***
6	GL 4-dr Limousine	**21,450***
7	C Turbo 4-dr Limousine	**21,175***
8	CL Turbo 4-dr Limousine	**22,305***
9	GL Turbo 4-dr Limousine	**23,645***
10	CD Turbo 4-dr Limousine	**25,545***

Power team:	Standard for:	Optional for:
54 hp	1 to 6	—
70 hp	7 to 10	—

54 hp power team

ENGINE diesel, front, 4 stroke; 4 cylinders, vertical, in line; 96.9 cu in, 1,588 cc (3.01 x 3.40 in, 76.5 x 86.4 mm); compression ratio: 23:1; max power (DIN): 54 hp (40 kW) at 4,800 rpm; max torque (DIN): 77 lb ft, 10.6 kg m (104 Nm) at 2,500 rpm; max engine rpm: 5,000; 34 hp/l (25.2 kW/l); cast iron block, light alloy head; 5 crankshaft bearings; valves: overhead, in line, thimble tappets; camshafts: 1, overhead, cogged belt; lubrication: gear pump, full flow filter, 6.2 imp pt, 7.4 US pt, 3.5 l; Bosch injection pump; liquid-cooled, expansion tank, 11.4 imp pt, 13.7 US pt, 6.5 l, electric thermostatic fan.

TRANSMISSION driving wheels: front; clutch: single dry plate (diaphragm); gearbox: mechanical; gears: 4, fully synchronized; ratios: I 3.455, II 1.944, III 1.286, IV 0.882, rev 3.167; lever: central; final drive: spiral bevel; axle ratio: 4.111; width of rims: 5"; tyres: 165 SR x 13.

PERFORMANCE max speed: 89 mph, 144 km/h; power-weight ratio: 40 lb/hp (54 lb/kW), 18.1 kg/hp (24.5 kg/kW); carrying capacity: 1,014 lb, 460 kg; acceleration: 0-50 mph (0-80 km/h) 12 sec; speed in top at 1,000 rpm: 17.4 mph, 28 km/h; consumption: 38.7 m/imp gal, 32.2 m/US gal, 7.3 l x 100 km.

CHASSIS integral, front auxiliary subframe; front suspension: independent, by McPherson, lower wishbones, coil springs/telescopic damper struts; rear: rigid axle, trailing radius arms, Panhard rod, coil springs/telescopic damper struts.

STEERING rack-and-pinion; turns lock to lock: 3.94.

BRAKES front disc (diameter 9.43 in, 23.9 cm), dual circuit, rear drum, servo.

ELECTRICAL EQUIPMENT 12 V; 63 Ah battery; 45 A alternator; 2 headlamps.

DIMENSIONS AND WEIGHT wheel base: 100 in, 254 cm; tracks: 55.10 in, 140 cm front, 55.90 in, 142 cm rear; length: 172.60 in, 438 cm; width: 66.20 in, 168 cm; height: 53.54 in, 136 cm; ground clearance: 4.21 in, 10.7 cm; weight: 2,161 lb, 980 kg; turning circle: 34.1 ft, 10.4 m; fuel tank: 15 imp gal, 18 US gal, 68 l.

AUDI Quattro 2.2 Coupé

BODY saloon/sedan; 2 or 4 doors; 5 seats, separate front seats, headrests; heated rear window.

PRACTICAL INSTRUCTIONS fuel: diesel oil: engine 6.2 imp pt, 7.4 US pt, 3.5 l - gearbox and final drive 3.2 imp pt, 3.8 US pt, 1.8 l, SAE 80 or 90; greasing: none; tyre pressure: front 26 psi, 1.8 atm, rear 26 psi, 1.8 atm.

OPTIONALS 4+E 5-speed fully synchronized mechanical gearbox (I 3.455, II 1.944, III 1.286, IV 0.909, V 0.730, rev 3.167), consumption 43.5 m/imp gal, 36.2 m/US gal, 6.5 l x 100 km at 75 mph, 120 km/h; automatic transmission with 3 ratios (I 2.714, II 1.500, III 1, rev 2.429), 3.727 axle ratio, max speed 87 mph, 140 km/h, consumption 34.4 m/imp gal, 28.7 m/US gal, 8.2 l x 100 km at 75 mph, 120 km/h; halogen headlamps; sunroof; vinyl roof; metallic spray.

70 hp power team

See 54 hp power team, except for:

ENGINE turbocharged; max power (DIN): 70 hp (51 kW) at 4,500 rpm; max torque (DIN): 99 lb ft, 13.6 kg m (133 Nm) at 2,600 rpm; max engine rpm: 5,100; 44.1 hp/l (32.1 kW/l); 1 Garrett AiResearch turbocharger.

TRANSMISSION gearbox: 4 + E mechanical; gears: 5, fully synchronized; ratios: I 3.455, II 1.944, III 1.286, IV 0.909, V 0.730, rev 3.167.

PERFORMANCE max speed: 98 mph, 158 km/h; power-weight ratio: 32.1 lb/hp (44.1 lb/kW), 14.6 kg/hp (20 kg/kW); acceleration: 0-50 mph (0-80 km/h) 9.1 sec; consumption: 41.5 m/imp gal, 34.6 m/US gal, 6.8 l x 100 km at 75 mph, 120 km/h.

DIMENSIONS AND WEIGHT weight: 2,249 lb, 1,020 kg.

BODY 4 doors.

Audi 80 Quattro Series

PRICES EX WORKS:		DM
1	2-dr Limousine	**27,890***
2	4-dr Limousine (115 hp)	**28,620***
3	4-dr Limousine (136 hp)	**33,785***

AUDI GT 2.0 Coupé

For GB and USA prices, see price index.

Power team:	Standard for:	Optional for:
115 hp	1,2	—
136 hp	3	—

115 hp power team

ENGINE front, 4 stroke; 5 cylinders, in line; 121.7 cu in, 1,994 cc (3.19 x 3.05 in, 81 x 77.4 mm); compression ratio: 10:1; max power (DIN): 115 hp (85 kW) at 5,400 rpm; max torque (DIN): 122 lb ft, 16.8 kg m (165 Nm) at 3,200 rpm; max engine rpm: 6,000; 59.2 hp/l (43.7 kW/l); cast iron block, light alloy head; 6 crankshaft bearings; valves: overhead, in line, rockers; camshafts: 1, overhead, cogged belt; lubrication: gear pump, full flow filter, 6.2 imp pt, 7.4 US pt, 3.5 l; Bosch K-Jetronic injection; fuel feed: electric pump; water-cooled, 14 imp pt, 16.9 US pt, 8 l, electric thermostatic fan.

TRANSMISSION driving wheels: front and rear; clutch: single dry plate (diaphragm); gearbox: mechanical; gears: 5, fully synchronized; integral front differential, additional lockable inter - axle differential, lockable rear axle differential, ratios: I 3.600, II 2.125, III 1.458, IV 1.071, V 0.829, rev 3.500; lever: central; final drive: spiral bevel; front and rear axle ratio: 4.111; width of rims: 5.5"; tyres: 175/70 HR x 14.

PERFORMANCE max speed: 114 mph, 184 km/h; power-weight ratio: 22.8 lb/hp (30.9 lb/kW), 10.3 kg/hp (14 kg/kW); carrying capacity: 1,014 lb, 460 kg; acceleration: 0-50 mph (0-80 km/h) 6.8 sec; speed in top at 1,000 rpm: 20 mph, 32.2 km/h; consumption: 31.7 m/imp gal, 26.4 m/US gal, 8.9 l x 100 km at 75 mph, 120 km/h.

CHASSIS integral, front auxiliary subframe; front suspension: independent, by McPherson, lower wishbones, coil springs/telescopic damper struts, anti-roll bar; rear: independent, by McPherson, lower wishbones, coil springs/telescopic damper struts, anti-roll bar.

STEERING rack-and-pinion; servo.

BRAKES disc, front internal radial fins, dual circuit, rear compensator, servo.

ELECTRICAL EQUIPMENT 12 V; 63 Ah battery; 65 A alternator; electronic ignition; 4 halogen headlamps.

DIMENSIONS AND WEIGHT wheel base: 99.41 in, 252 cm; tracks: 55.24 in, 140 cm front, 55.39 in, 141 cm rear; length: 172.56 in, 438 cm; width: 66.22 in, 168 cm; height: 54.17 in, 138 cm; weight: 2,624 lb, 1,190 kg; turning circle: 34.4 ft, 10.5 m; fuel tank: 15.4 imp gal, 18.5 US gal, 70 l.

BODY saloon/sedan; 2 or 4 doors; 5 seats, separate front seats, reclining backrests, headrests; heated rear window.

PRACTICAL INSTRUCTIONS fuel: 98 oct petrol; oil: engine 6.2 imp pt, 7.4 US pt, 3.5 l, SAE 10W - 50, change every 4,700 miles, 7,500 km - gearbox and front final drive 3.2 imp pt, 3.8 US pt, 1.8 l, SAE 90 or 80, change every 18,600 miles, 30,000 km - rear final drive 2.3 imp pt, 2.7 US pt, 1.3 l, SAE 90 or 80, change every 18,600 miles, 30,000 km; greasing: none; tyre pressure: front 28 psi, 2 atm, rear 28 psi, 2 atm.

OPTIONALS light alloy wheels; max speed 112 mph, 180 km/h with 175/70 R x 14 M+S tyres.

136 hp power team

See 115 hp power team, except for:

ENGINE 130.8 cu in, 2,144 cc (3.13 x 3.40 in, 79.5 x 86.4 mm); compression ratio: 9.3:1; max power (DIN): 136 hp

136 HP POWER TEAM

(100 kW) at 5,900 rpm; max torque (DIN): 130 lb ft, 18 kg m (176 Nm) at 4,500 rpm; max engine rpm: 6,500; 63.4 hp/l (46.6 kW/l).

PERFORMANCE max speed: 120 mph, 193 km/h; power-weight ratio: 19.3 lb/hp (26.2 lb/kW), 8.7 kg/hp (11.9 kg/kW); carrying capacity: 1,014 lb, 460 kg; acceleration: 0-50 mph (0-80 km/h) 6.2 sec; speed in top at 1,000 rpm: 20 mph, 32.2 km/h; consumption: 31 m/imp gal, 25.8 m/US gal, 9.1 l x 100 km at 75 mph, 120 km/h.

BODY 4 doors.

OPTIONALS max speed 118 mph, 190 km/h with 175/70 R x 14 M+S tyres.

Audi Coupé Series

PRICES IN GB AND EX WORKS:	£	DM
1 GL 1.8 2-dr Coupé	—	22,440*
2 GT 2.0 2-dr Coupé	9,172*	27,085*
3 GT 2.2 2-dr Coupé	—	29,190*
4 Quattro 2.2 2-dr Coupé	17,722*	66,685*
5 Quattro Sport 2.2 2-dr Coupé	—	200,000*

For USA prices, see price index.

Power team:	Standard for:	Optional for:
90 hp	1	—
115 hp	2	—
130 hp	3	—
200 hp	4	—
300 hp	5	—

90 hp power team

ENGINE front, 4 stroke; 4 cylinders, in line; 108.7 cu in, 1,781 cc (3.19 x 3.40 in, 81 x 86.4 mm); compression ratio: 10:1; max power (DIN): 90 hp (66 kW) at 5,200 rpm; max torque (DIN): 107 lb ft, 14.8 kg m (145 Nm) at 3,300 rpm; max engine rpm: 6,000; 50.5 hp/l (37.1 kW/l); cast iron block, light alloy head; 5 crankshaft bearings; valves: overhead, in line, thimble tappets; camshafts: 1, overhead, cogged belt; lubrication: gear pump, full flow filter, 6.2 imp pt, 7.4 US pt, 3.5 l; 1 Solex downdraught twin barrel carburettor; fuel feed: mechanical pump; water-cooled, 11.4 imp pt, 13.7 US pt, 6.5 l, electric thermostatic fan.

TRANSMISSION driving wheels: front; clutch: single dry plate (diaphragm); gearbox: mechanical; gears: 4, fully synchronized; ratios: I 3.455, II 1.789, III 1.133, IV 0.829, rev 3.167; lever: central; final drive: spiral bevel; axle ratio: 4.111; width of rims: 5''; tyres: 175/70 SR x 13.

PERFORMANCE max speed: 106 mph, 170 km/h; power-weight ratio: 23.3 lb/hp (31.7 lb/kW), 10.6 kg/hp (14.4 kg/kW); carrying capacity: 1,014 lb, 460 kg; acceleration: 0-50 mph (0-80 km/h) 7.2 sec; speed in top at 1,000 rpm: 19.1 mph, 30.7 km/h; consumption: 34.4 m/imp gal, 28.7 m/US gal, 8.2 l x 100 km at 75 mph, 120 km/h.

CHASSIS integral, front auxiliary subframe; front suspension: independent, by McPherson, lower wishbones, coil springs/telescopic damper struts, anti-roll bar; rear: rigid axle, trailing radius arms, Panhard rod, anti-roll bar, coil springs/telescopic damper struts.

STEERING rack-and-pinion.

BRAKES front disc (diameter 9.41 in, 23.9 cm), 2 X circuits, rear drum, servo.

AUDI Quattro 2.2 Coupé

ELECTRICAL EQUIPMENT 12 V; 40 Ah battery; 65 A alternator; electronic ignition; 4 halogen headlamps.

DIMENSIONS AND WEIGHT wheel base: 100 in, 254 cm; tracks: 55.10 in, 140 cm front, 55.90 in, 142 cm rear; length: 171.20 in, 435 cm; width: 66.20 in, 168 cm; height: 53.10 in, 135 cm; weight: 2,095 lb, 950 kg; turning circle: 34.1 ft, 10.4 m; fuel tank: 15 imp gal, 16 US gal, 68 l.

BODY coupé; 2 doors; 5 seats, separate front seats, headrests; heated rear window; rear window wiper-washer.

PRACTICAL INSTRUCTIONS fuel: 98 oct petrol; oil: engine 6.2 imp pt, 7.4 US pt, 3.5 l, SAE 20W-30, change every 4,700 miles, 7,500 km - gearbox and final drive 3.2 imp pt, 3.8 US pt, 1.8 l, SAE 80 or 90, change every 18,600 miles, 30,000 km; greasing: none; tyre pressure: front 26 psi, 1.8 atm, rear 26 psi, 1.8 atm.

OPTIONALS 4+E 5-speed fully synchronized mechanical gearbox (I 3.455, II 1.789, III 1.133, IV 0.829, V 0.684, rev 3.167), consumption 37.7 m/imp gal, 31.4 m/US gal, 7.5 l x 100 km at 75 mph, 120 km/h; automatic transmission with 3 ratios (I 2.714, II 1.500, III 1, rev 2.429), 3.250 axle ratio, max speed 103 mph, 166 km/h, consumption 34 m/imp gal, 28.3 m/US gal, 8.3 l x 100 km at 75 mph, 120 km/h; 185/60 HR x 14 tyres; light alloy wheels; electric windows; sunroof; power steering; metallic spray; tinted glass.

115 hp power team

See 90 hp power team, except for:

ENGINE slanted 20° to right; 5 cylinders, in line; 121.7 cu in, 1,994 cc (3.19 x 3.05 in, 81 x 77.4 mm); compression ratio: 10:1; max power (DIN): 115 hp (85 kW) at 5,400 rpm; max torque (DIN): 122 lb ft, 16.8 kg m (165 Nm) at 3,200 rpm; max engine rpm: 6,200; 59.2 hp/l (43.7 kW/l); 6 crankshaft bearings; lubrication: 7.9 imp pt, 9.5 US pt, 4.5 l; Bosch K-Jetronic injection; fuel feed: electric pump; water-cooled, 14 imp pt, 16.9 US pt, 8 l.

TRANSMISSION gearbox: 4+E mechanical; gears: 5, fully synchronized; ratios: I 2.846, II 1.524, III 0.939, IV 0.658, V 0.537, rev 3.167; axle ratio: 4.900; width of rims: 5.5''; tyres: 175/70 HR x 13.

PERFORMANCE max speed: 116 mph, 186 km/h; power-weight ratio: 20.1 lb/hp (27.2 lb/kW), 9.1 kg/hp (12,4 kg/kW); acceleration: 0-50 mph (0-80 km/h) 6.5 sec; speed in top at 1,000 rpm: 24.7 mph, 39.8 km/h; consumption: 35.3 m/imp gal, 29.4 m/US gal, 8 l x 100 km at 75 mph, 120 km/h.

ELECTRICAL EQUIPMENT 63 Ah battery.

DIMENSIONS AND WEIGHT weight: 2,315 lb, 1,050 kg.

OPTIONALS automatic transmission with 3 ratios (I 2.714, II 1.500, III 1, rev 2.429), 3.250 axle ratio, max speed 112 mph, 180 km/h, consumption 30.7 m/imp gal, 25.6 m/US gal, 9.2 l x 100 km at 75 mph, 120 km/h; 185/60 HR x 14 tyres with 6'' wide rims and light alloy wheels.

130 hp power team

See 90 hp power team, except for:

ENGINE 5 cylinders, in line; 130.8 cu in, 2,144 cc (3.13 x 3.40 in, 79.5 x 86.4 mm); compression ratio: 9.3:1; max power (DIN): 130 hp (96 kW) at 5,900 rpm; max torque (DIN): 126 lb ft, 17.4 kg m (171 Nm) at 4,800 rpm; max engine rpm: 6,500; 60.6 hp/l (44.8 kW/l); 6 crankshaft bearings; Bosch K-Jetronic injection; water-cooled, 14 imp pt, 16.9 US pt, 8 l.

TRANSMISSION gears: 5, fully synchronized; ratios: I 2.846, II 1.524, III 1.065, IV 0.778, V 0.641, rev 3.167; axle ratio: 4.900; width of rims: 6''; tyres: 185/60 HR x 14.

PERFORMANCE max speeds: (I) 30 mph, 49 km/h; (II) 57 mph, 91 km/h; (III) 81 mph, 130 km/h; (IV) 111 mph, 178 km/h; (V) 122 mph, 196 km/h; power-weight ratio: 17.8 lb/hp (24.1 lb/kW), 8.1 kg/hp (10.9 kg/kW); acceleration: 0-50 mph (0-80 km/h) 6 sec; consumption: 34 m/imp gal, 28.3 m/US gal, 8.3 l x 100 km at 75 mph, 120 km/h.

STEERING servo (standard).

ELECTRICAL EQUIPMENT 63 Ah battery; 65 A alternator.

DIMENSIONS AND WEIGHT weight: 2,315 lb, 1,050 kg.

BODY light alloy wheels (standard).

OPTIONALS sunroof; electric windows; tinted glass; metallic spray.

AUDI Quattro Sport 2.2 Coupé

AUDI Quattro Sport 2.2 Coupé

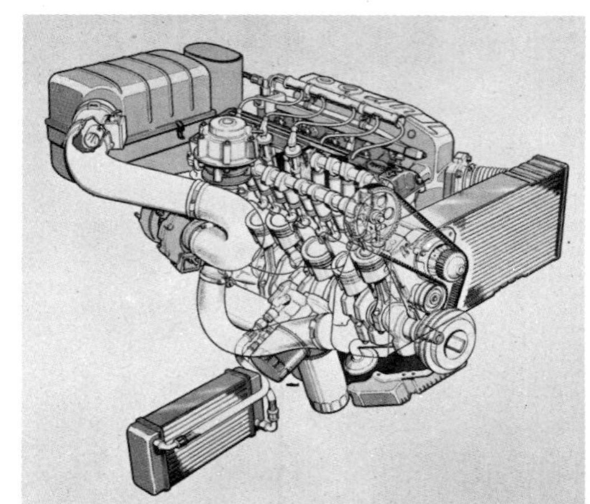

AUDI 100 CC Limousine

AUDI 100 CC Limousine

200 hp power team

See 90 hp power team, except for:

ENGINE turbocharged; 5 cylinders, in line; 130.8 cu in, 2,144 cc (3.13 x 3.40 in, 79.5 x 86.4 mm); compression ratio: 7:1; max power (DIN): 200 hp (147 kW) at 5,500 rpm; max torque (DIN): 211 lb ft, 29.1 kg m (285 Nm) at 3,500 rpm; 93.3 hp/l (68.6 kW/l); 6 crankshaft bearings; lubrication: 7.9 imp pt, 9.5 US pt, 4.5 l; Bosch K-Jetronic injection; 1 KKK turbocharger, air charge cooling and fuel injection; fuel feed: electric pump; water-cooled, 16.4 imp pt, 19.7 US pt, 9.3 l.

TRANSMISSION driving wheels: front and rear; gears: 5, fully synchronized; integral front differential, additional lockable inter-axle differential, lockable rear axle differential; ratios: I 3.600, II 2.125, III 1.458, IV 1.071, V 0.778, rev 3.500; front and rear axle ratio: 3.889; width of rims: 6"; tyres: 205/60 VR x 15.

PERFORMANCE max speed: over 138 mph, 222 km/h; power-weight ratio: 14.3 lb/hp (19.5 lb/kW), 6.5 kg/hp (8.8 kg/kW); acceleration: 0-50 mph (0-80 km/h) 4.7 sec; speed in top at 1,000 rpm: 23.3 mph, 37.5 km/h; consumption: 28.5 m/imp gal, 23.5 m/US gal, 9.9 l x 100 km at 75 mph, 120 km/h.

CHASSIS rear suspension: independent, by McPherson, lower wishbones, coil springs/telescopic damper struts, anti-roll bar.

STEERING servo (standard).

BRAKES disc, front internal radial fins, rear compensator.

ELECTRICAL EQUIPMENT 63 Ah battery; 90 A alternator; all electronic transistorized ignition responding to air charge temperature and engine load condition.

DIMENSIONS AND WEIGHT wheel base: 99.37 in, 252 cm; tracks: 55.94 in, 142 cm front, 57.13 in, 145 cm rear; length: 173.39 in, 440 cm; width: 67.83 in, 172 cm; height: 52.91 in, 134 cm; weight: 2,866 lb, 1,300 kg; turning circle: 37.1 ft, 11.3 m; fuel tank: 15.4 imp gal, 18.5 US gal, 70 l.

OPTIONALS light alloy wheels with 7" wide rims; central locking; air-conditioning.

300 hp power team

See 90 hp power team, except for:

ENGINE turbocharged; 5 cylinders, in line; 130.2 cu in, 2,133 cc (3.12 x 3.40 in, 79.3 x 86.4 mm); compression ratio: 8:1; max power (DIN): 300 hp (220 kW) at 6,500 rpm; max torque (DIN): 244 lb ft, 33.6 kg m (330 Nm) at 4,500; max engine rpm: 7,500; 140.6 hp/l (103.1 kW/l); light alloy block and head, wet liners; 6 crankshaft bearings; valves: 4 per cylinder, overhead, wee-slanted, thimble tappets: camshaft: 2, overhead, cogged belt; lubrication: gear pump, full flow filter, oil cooler; Bosch all-electronic data program HI-Jetronic injection with air mass sensor; Längerer & Reich intercooler; KKK - K 27 exhaust turbocharger; full feed; electric pump; water-cooled, 16.4 imp pt, 19.7 US pt, 9.3 l.

TRANSMISSION driving wheels: front and rear; gears: 5, fully synchronized; integral front differential, additional lockable inter-axle differential, lockable rear axle differential; ratios: I 3.500, II 2.083, III 1.368, IV 0.962, V 0.759, rev 3.455; front and rear axle ratio: 3.875; width of rims: 9"; tyres: 225/50 VR x 15.

PERFORMANCE max speed: 155 mph, 250 km/h; power-weight ratio: 7.3 lb/hp (10 lb/kW), 3.3 kg/hp (4.5 kg/kW); speed in top at 1,000 rpm: 23.1 mph, 37.3 km/h; consumption: not declared.

CHASSIS rear suspension: independent, by McPherson, lower wishbones, coil springs/telescopic damper struts, anti-roll bar.

STEERING servo (standard).

BRAKES disc, front and rear internal radial fins, rear compensator, anti-brake-locking system (ABS).

ELECTRICAL EQUIPMENT 63 Ah battery; 90 A alternator; all electronic transistorized ignition responding to air charge temperature and engine load condition.

DIMENSIONS AND WEIGHT wheel base: 86.77 in, 220 cm; tracks: 59.68 in, 152 cm front, 58.74 in, 149 cm rear; length: 163.94 in, 416 cm; width: 70.98 in, 180 cm; height: 52.95 in, 134 cm; weight: 2,205 lb, 1,000 kg; fuel tank: 19.8 imp gal, 23.8 US gal, 90 l.

Audi 100 Series

PRICES EX WORKS:		DM
1	1.8 (75 hp) 4-dr Limousine	22,915*
2	CC 1.8 (75 hp) 4-dr Limousine	24,295*
3	1.8 (90 hp) 4-dr Limousine	23,825*
4	CC 1.8 (90 hp) 4-dr Limousine	25,205*
5	CS 1.8 4-dr Limousine	28,255*
6	CD 1.8 4-dr Limousine	30,285*
7	1.9 4-dr Limousine	25,045*
8	CC 1.9 4-dr Limousine	26,425*
9	CS 1.9 4-dr Limousine	29,475*
10	CD 1.9 4-dr Limousine	31,505*
11	2.2 4-dr Limousine	27,865*
12	CC 2.2 4-dr Limousine	29,245*
13	CS 2.2 4-dr Limousine	32,295*
14	CD 2.2 4-dr Limousine	33,635*
15	Diesel 4-dr Limousine	27,725*
16	CC Diesel 4-dr Limousine	29,105*
17	Turbo-Diesel 4-dr Limousine	30,945*
18	CC Turbo-Diesel 4-dr Limousine	32,325*
19	CS Turbo-Diesel 4-dr Limousine	35,375*
20	CD Turbo-Diesel 4-dr Limousine	36,715*

For GB and USA prices, see price index.

Power team:	Standard for:	Optional for:
75 hp	1,2	—
90 hp	3 to 8	—
100 hp	7 to 10	—
136 hp	11 to 14	—
70 hp (diesel)	15,16	—
87 hp (diesel)	17 to 20	—

75 hp power team

ENGINE front, 4 stroke; 4 cylinders, in line; 108.7 cu in, 1,781 cc (3.19 x 3.40 in, 81 x 86.4 mm); compression ratio: 8.7:1; max power (DIN): 75 hp (55 kW) at 4,600 rpm; max torque (DIN): 102 lb ft, 14.1 kg m (138 Nm) at 2,500 rpm; max engine rpm: 5,500; 42.1 hp/l (30.9 kW/l); cast iron block, light alloy head; 5 crankshaft bearings; valves: overhead, in line, thimble tappets; camshafts: 1, overhead, cogged belt; lubrication: gear pump, full flow filter, 5.3 imp pt, 6.3 US pt, 3 l; 1 Solex downdraught single barrel carburettor; fuel feed: mechanical pump; water-cooled, 12.3 imp pt, 14.8 US pt, 7 l, electric thermostatic fan.

TRANSMISSION driving wheels: front; clutch: single dry plate (diaphgram); gearbox: mechanical; gears: 4, fully synchronized; ratios: I 3.455, II 1.789, III 1.065, IV 0.703, rev 3.167; lever: central; final drive: spiral bevel; axle ratio: 4.111; width of rims: 5.5"; tyres: 165 SR x 14.

PERFORMANCE max speed: 102 mph, 165 km/h; power-weight ratio: 31.8 lb/hp (43.3 lb/kW), 14.4 kg/hp (19.6 kg/kW); carrying capacity: 1,102 lb, 500 kg; acceleration: 0-50 mph (0-80 km/h) 9.6 sec; speed in top at 1,000 rpm: 24.1 mph, 38.8 km/h; consumption: 39.8 m/imp gal, 33.1 m/US gal, 7.1 l x 100 km at 75 mph, 120 km/h.

CHASSIS integral, front auxiliary subframe; front suspension: independent, by McPherson, lower wishbones, anti-roll bar, coil springs/telescopic damper struts; rear: rigid axle, swinging longitudinal trailing radius arms, Panhard rod, anti-roll bar, coil springs, telescopic dampers.

STEERING rack-and-pinion.

BRAKES front disc, rear drum, dual circuit, rear compensator, servo.

ELECTRICAL EQUIPMENT 12 V; 40 Ah battery; 65 A alternator; electronic ignition; 2 halogen headlamps.

DIMENSIONS AND WEIGHT wheel base: 105.79 in, 269 cm; front and rear track: 57.76 in, 147 cm; length: 188.70 in, 479 cm; width: 71.42 in, 181 cm; height: 55.98 in, 142 cm; weight: 2,381 lb, 1,080 kg; turning circle: 38 ft, 11.6 m; fuel tank: 17.6 imp gal, 21.1 US gal, 80 l.

BODY saloon/sedan; 4 doors; 5 seats, separate front seats, reclining backrests; heated rear window.

PRACTICAL INSTRUCTIONS fuel: 91 oct petrol; oil: engine 5.3 imp pt, 6.3 US pt, 3 l, SAE 20W-30, change every 4,700 miles, 7,500 km - gearbox and final drive 3.2 imp pt, 3.8 US pt, 1.8 l, SAE 80 or 90, change every 18,600 miles, 30,000 km; greasing: none; tyre pressure: front 28 psi, 2 atm, rear 28 psi, 2 atm.

OPTIONALS 4+E 5-speed fully synchronized mechanical gearbox (I 3.455, II 1.789, III 1.065, IV 0.778, V 0.600, rev 3.167), consumption 42.2 m/imp gal, 35.1 m/US gal, 6.7 l x 100 km at 75 mph, 120 km/h; automatic transmission with 3 ratios (I 2.714, II 1.500, III 1, rev 2.429), 3.417 axle ratio, max speed 101 mph, 162 km/h, consumption 33.2 m/imp gal, 27.7 m/US gal, 8.5 l x 100 km at 75 mph, 120 km/h; 185/70 SR x 14 tyres; light alloy wheels; electric windows; sunroof; central door locking; metallic spray; tinted glass; power steering.

90 hp power team

See 75 hp power team, except for:

ENGINE compression ratio: 10:1, max power (DIN): 90 hp (66 kW) at 5,200 rpm; max torque (DIN): 107 lb ft, 14.8 kg m

AUDI 100 CS 1.9 Limousine

AUDI 100 CD Turbo-Diesel Limousine

AUDI 100 CS 1.9 Limousine

90 HP POWER TEAM

(145 Nm) at 3,300 rpm; max engine rpm: 5,800; 50.5 hp/l (37.1 kW/l); 1 Solex downdraught twin barrel carburettor.

TRANSMISSION tyres: 185/70 SR x 14.

PERFORMANCE max speed: 109 mph, 176 km/h; power-weight ratio: 26.7 lb/hp (36.4 lb/kW), 12.1 kg/hp (16.5 kg/kW); acceleration: 0-50 mph (0-80 km/h) 7.8 sec; consumption: 40.9 m/imp gal, 34.1 m/US gal, 6.9 l x 100 km at 75 mph, 120 km/h.

DIMENSIONS AND WEIGHT weight: 2,403 lb, 1,090 kg.

PRACTICAL INSTRUCTIONS fuel: 98 oct petrol.

OPTIONALS 4+E 5-speed mechanical gearbox (I 3.455, II 1.789, III 1.133, IV 0.829, V 0.694, rev 3.167), consumption 41.5 m/imp gal, 34.6 m/US gal, 6.8 l x 100 km at 75 mph, 120 km/h; automatic trasmission with 3 ratios (I 2.714, II 1.500, III 1, rev 2.429), 3.417 axle ratio, consumption 35.3 m/imp gal, 29.4 m/US gal, 8 l x 100 km at 75 mph, 120 km/h.

100 hp power team

See 75 hp power team, except for:

ENGINE 5 cylinders, in line; 117.2 cu in, 1,921 cc (3.13 x 3.05 in, 79.5 x 77.4 mm); compression ratio: 10:1; max power (DIN): 100 hp (74 kW) at 5,600 rpm; max torque (DIN): 111 lb ft, 15.3 kg m (150 Nm) at 3,200 rpm; max engine rpm: 6,200; 52.1 hp/l (38.5 kW/l); 6 crankshaft bearings; lubrication: 7.9 imp pt, 9.5 US pt, 4.5 l; 1 Solex 2 B2 downdraught twin barrel carburettor; water-cooled, 14.3 imp pt, 17.1 US pt, 8.1 l.

TRANSMISSION gearbox: 4+E mechanical (standard); gears: 5, fully synchronized; ratios: I 2.846, II 1.524, III 0.909, IV 0.641, V 0.488, rev 3.167; axle ratio: 5.222; tyres: 185/70 SR x 14.

PERFORMANCE max speed: 109 mph, 176 km/h; power-weight ratio: 25.2 lb/hp (34.1 lb/kW), 11.4 kg/hp (15.5 kg/kW); acceleration: 0-50 mph (0-80 km/h) 8 sec; speed in top at 1,000 rpm: 27,3 mph, 43.9 km/h; consumption: 40.9 m/imp gal, 34.1 m/US gal, 6.9 l x 100 km at 75 mph, 120 km/h.

ELECTRICAL EQUIPMENT 63 Ah battery.

DIMENSIONS AND WEIGHT weight: 2,525 lb, 1,145 kg.

PRACTICAL INSTRUCTIONS fuel: 98 oct petrol; oil: engine 7.9 imp pt, 9.5 US pt, 4.5 l.

OPTIONALS with automatic transmission 3.455 axle ratio, max speed 107 mph, 173 km/h and consumption 34 m/imp gal, 28.3 m/US gal, 8.3 l x 100 km at 75 mph, 120 km/h; power steering; air-conditioning.

136 hp power team

See 75 hp power team, except for:

ENGINE 5 cylinders, in line; 130.8 cu in, 2,144 cc (3.13 x 3.40 in, 79.5 x 86.4 mm); compression ratio: 9.3:1; max power (DIN): 136 hp (100 kW) at 5,700 rpm; max torque (DIN): 133 lb ft, 18.4 kg m (180 Nm) at 4,800 rpm; max engine rpm: 6,200; 63.4 hp/l (46.7 kW/l); 6 crankshaft bearings; lubrication: 7.9 imp pt, 9.5 US pt, 4.5 l; Bosch K-Jetronic injection; water-cooled, 14.3 imp pt, 17.1 US pt, 8.1 l.

TRANSMISSION gearbox: 4+E mechanical (standard) - 5-speed mechanical; gears: 5, fully synchronized; ratios: I 3.600, II 1.882, III 1.185, IV 0.844, V 0.641, rev 3.500 - I 3.600, II 2.125, III 1.458, IV 1.071, V 0.829, rev 3.500; axle ratio: 3.889; tyres: 185/70 HR x 14.

PERFORMANCE max speed: 124 mph, 200 km/h; power-weight ratio: 19.6 lb/hp (26.7 lb/kW), 8.9 kg/hp (12.1 kg/kW); acceleration: 0-50 mph (0-80 km/h) 6.8 sec, speed in top at 1,000 rpm: 28 mph, 45 km/h; consumption: 39.2 m/imp gal, 32.7 m/US gal, 7.2 l x 100 km at 75 mph, 120 km/h.

STEERING servo (standard).

BRAKES disc, front internal radial fins.

ELECTRICAL EQUIPMENT 63 Ah battery; 90 A alternator.

DIMENSIONS AND WEIGHT weight: 2,268 lb, 1,210 kg.

AUDI 100 Avant CC Limousine

PRACTICAL INSTRUCTIONS fuel: 98 oct petrol; oil: engine 7.9 imp pt, 9.5 US pt. 4.5 l.

OPTIONALS with automatic transmission 3.250 axle ratio, max speed 121 mph, 195 km/h and consumption 33.2 m/imp gal, 27.7 m/US gal, 8.5 l x 100 km at 75 mph, 120 km/h; air-conditioning; anti-brake-locking system (ABS).

70 hp (diesel) power team

See 75 hp power team, except for:

ENGINE diesel; 5 cylinders, in line; 121.2 cu in, 1,986 cc (3.01 x 3.40 in, 76.5 x 86.4 mm); compression ratio: 23:1; max power (DIN): 70 hp (51 kW) at 4,800 rpm; max torque (DIN): 91 lb ft, 12.5 kg m (123 Nm) at 2,800 rpm; max engine rpm: 5,000; 35.2 hp/l (25.9 kW/l); 6 crankshaft bearings; lubrication: 8.8 imp pt, 10.6 US pt, 5 l; Bosch injection pump; water-cooled, 16.5 imp pt, 19.9 US pt, 9.4 l.

TRANSMISSION gearbox: 4+E mechanical (standard); gears: 5, fully synchronized; ratios: I 3.600, II 1.882, III 1.185, IV 0.844, V 0.641, rev 3.500; axle ratio: 4.556; tyres: 185/70 SR x 14.

PERFORMANCE max speed: 96 mph, 155 km/h; power-weight ratio: 38.1 lb/hp (51.8 lb/kW), 17.3 kg/hp (23.5 kg/kW); acceleration: 0-50 mph (0-80 km/h) 11.6 sec; consumption: 44.8 m/imp gal, 37.3 m/US gal, 6.3 l x 100 km at 75 mph, 120 km/h.

STEERING servo (standard).

ELECTRICAL EQUIPMENT 88 Ah battery; 55 A alternator.

DIMENSIONS AND WEIGHT weight: 2,668 lb, 1,210 kg.

PRACTICAL INSTRUCTIONS fuel: diesel; oil: engine 8.8 imp pt, 10.6 US pt, 5 l.

OPTIONALS with automatic transmission 3.455 axle ratio, max speed 95 mph, 153 km/h and consumption 35.8 m/imp gal, 28.9 m/US gal, 7.9 l x 100 km at 75 mph, 120 km/h.

87 hp (diesel) power team

See 75 power team, except for:

ENGINE diesel; turbocharged; 5 cylinders, in line; 121.2 cu in, 1,986 cc (30.1 x 3.40 in, 76.5 x 86.4 mm); compression ratio: 23:1; max power (DIN): 87 hp (64 kW) at 4,500 rpm; max torque (DIN): 127 lb ft, 17.5 kg m (172 Nm) at 2,750 rpm; max engine rpm: 5,000; 43.8 hp/l (32.2 kW/l); 6 crankshaft bearings; lubrication: 8.8 imp pt, 10.6 US pt, 5 l; Bosch injection pump; 1 Garrett AiResearch turbocharger; water-cooled, 16.5 imp pt, 19.9 US pt, 9.4 l.

TRANSMISSION gearbox: 4+E mechanical (standard); gears: 5, fully synchronized; ratios: I 3.600, II 1.882, III 1.185, IV 0.844, V 0.641, rev 3.500; tyres: 185/70 SR x 14.

PERFORMANCE max speed: 107 mph, 172 km/h; power-weight ratio: 31.7 lb/hp (43.1 lb/kW), 14.4 kg/hp (19.5 kg/kW); acceleration: 0-50 mph (0-80 km/h) 8.4 sec; speed in top at 1,000 rpm: 26.5 mph, 42.6 km/h; consumption: 40.9 m/imp gal, 34.1 m/US gal, 6.9 l x 100 km at 75 mph, 120 km/h.

STEERING servo (standard).

ELECTRICAL EQUIPMENT 88 Ah battery; 55 A alternator.

DIMENSIONS AND WEIGHT 2,756 lb, 1,250 kg.

PRACTICAL INSTRUCTIONS fuel: diesel; oil: engine 8.8 imp pt, 10.6 US pt, 5 l.

OPTIONALS with automatic trasmission 3.083 axle ratio, max speed 102 mph, 164 km/h and consumption 34 m/imp gal, 28.3 m/US gal, 8.3 l x 100 km at 75 mph, 120 km/h.

Audi 100 Avant Series

PRICES EX WORKS: DM

		DM
1	1.8 (75 hp) 4+1-dr Limousine	25,365*
2	CC 1.8 (75 hp) 4+1-dr Limousine	26,745*
3	1.8 (90 hp) 4+1-dr Limousine	26,275*
4	CC 1.8 (90 hp) 4+1-dr Limousine	27,655*
5	CS 1.8 4+1-dr Limousine	30,705*
6	CD 1.8 4+1-dr Limousine	32,735*
7	2.2 4+1-dr Limousine	30,315*
8	CC 2.2 4+1-dr Limousine	31,695*
9	CS 2.2 4+1-dr Limousine	34,745*
10	CD 2.2 4+1-dr Limousine	36,085*
11	Diesel 4+1-dr Limousine	30,175*
12	CC Diesel 4+1-dr Limousine	31,555*
13	Turbo-Diesel 4+1-dr Limousine	33,395*
14	CC Turbo-Diesel 4+1-dr Limousine	34,775*
15	CS Turbo-Diesel 4+1-dr Limousine	37,825*
16	CD Turbo-Diesel 4+1-dr Limousine	39,165*

For GB and USA prices, see price index.

Power team:	Standard for:	Optional for:
75 hp	1,2	—
90 hp	3 to 6	—
136 hp	7 to 10	—
70 hp (diesel)	11,12	—
87 hp (diesel)	13 to 16	—

AUDI 100 Avant CC Limousine

75 hp power team

ENGINE front, 4 stroke; 4 cylinders, in line; 108.7 cu in, 1,781 cc (3.19 x 3.40 in, 81 x 86.4 mm); compression ratio: 8.7:1; max power (DIN): 75 hp (55 kW) at 4,600 rpm; max torque (DIN): 102 lb ft, 14.1 kg m (138 Nm) at 2,500 rpm; max engine rpm: 5,500; 42.1 hp/l (30.9 kW/l); cast iron block, light alloy head; 5 crankshaft bearings; valves: overhead, in line, thimble tappets; camshafts: 1, overhead, cogged belt; lubrication: gear pump, full flow filter, 5.3 imp pt, 6.3 US pt, 3 l; 1 Solex downdraught single barrel carburettor; fuel feed: mechanical pump; water-cooled, 12.3 imp pt, 14.8 US pt, 7 l, electric thermostatic fan.

TRANSMISSION driving wheels: front; clutch: single dry plate (diaphgram); gearbox: mechanical; gears: 4, fully synchronized; ratios: I 3.455, II 1.789, III 1.065, IV 0.703, rev 3.167; lever: central; final drive: spiral bevel; axle ratio: 4.111; width of rims: 5.5"; tyres: 185/70 SR x 14.

PERFORMANCE max speed: 101 mph, 163 km/h; power-weight ratio: 33.2 lb/hp (45.3 lb/kW), 15.1 kg/hp (20.5 kg/kW); carrying capacity: 1,102 lb, 500 kg; acceleration: 0-50 mph (0-80 km/h) 10.2 sec; speed in top at 1,000 rpm: 24.2 mph, 38.9 km/h; consumption: 36.7 m/imp gal, 30.5 m/US gal, 7.7 l x 100 km at 75 mph, 120 km/h.

CHASSIS integral, front auxiliary subframe; front suspension: independent, by McPherson, lower wishbones, anti-roll bar, coil springs/telescopic damper struts; rear: rigid axle, swinging longitudinal trailing radius arms, Panhard rod, anti-roll bar, coil springs, telescopic dampers.

STEERING rack-and-pinion.

BRAKES front disc, internal radial fins, rear drum, dual circuit, rear compensator, servo.

ELECTRICAL EQUIPMENT 12 V; 40 Ah battery; 90 A alternator; 2 halogen headlamps.

DIMENSIONS AND WEIGHT wheel base: 105.79 in, 269 cm; tracks: 57.80 in, 147 cm front, 57.76 in, 147 cm rear; length: 188.70 in, 479 cm; width: 71.42 in, 181 cm; height: 55.98 in, 142 cm; weight: 2,492 lb, 1,130 kg; turning circle: 38 ft, 11.6 m; fuel tank: 17.6 imp gal, 21.1 US gal, 80 l.

BODY saloon/sedan; 4+1 doors; 5 seats, separate front seats, reclining backrests; heated rear window.

PRACTICAL INSTRUCTIONS fuel: 91 oct petrol; oil: engine 5.3 imp pt, 6.3 US pt, 3 l, SAE 20W-30, change every 4,700 miles, 7,500 km - gearbox and final drive 3.2 imp pt, 3.8 US pt, 1.8 l, SAE 80 or 90, change every 18,600 miles, 30,000 km; greasing: none; tyre pressure: front 28 psi, 2 atm, rear 28 psi, 2 atm.

OPTIONALS 4+E 5-speed fully synchronized mechanical gearbox (I 3.455, II 1.789, III 1.065, IV 0.778, V 0.600, rev. 3.167), consumption 39.2 m/imp gal, 32.7 m/US gal, 7.2 l x 100 km at 75 mph, 120 km/h; automatic transmission with 3 ratios (I 2.714, II 1.500, III 1, rev 2.429), 3.417 axle ratio, max speed 99 mph, 160 km/h, consumption 30.7 m/imp gal, 25.6 m/US gal, 9.2 l x 100 km at 75 mph, 120 km/h; light alloy wheels; electric windows; sunroof; central door locking; metallic spray; tinted glass; power steering.

90 hp power team

See 75 hp power team, except for:

ENGINE compression ratio: 10:1, max power (DIN): 90 hp (66 kW) at 5,200 rpm; max torque (DIN): 107 lb ft, 14.8 kg m (145 Nm) at 3,300 rpm; max engine rpm: 5,800; 50.5 hp/l (37.1 kW/l); 1 Solex downdraught twin barrel carburettor.

PERFORMANCE max speed: 108 mph, 174 km/h; power-weight ratio: 27.9 lb/hp (38.1 lb/kW), 12.7 kg/hp (17.3 kg/kW); acceleration: 0-50 mph (0-80 km/h) 8.4 sec; consumption: 37.7 m/imp gal, 31.4 m/US gal, 7.5 l x 100 km at 75 mph, 120 km/h.

DIMENSIONS AND WEIGHT weight: 2,514 lb, 1,140 kg.

PRACTICAL INSTRUCTIONS fuel: 98 oct petrol.

OPTIONALS 4+E 5-speed mechanical gearbox (I 3.455, II 1.789, III 1.133, IV 0.829, V 0.694, rev 3.167), consumption 38.7 m/imp gal, 32.2 m/US gal, 7.3 l x 100 km at 75 mph, 120 km/h; automatic transmission with 3 ratios (I 2.714, II 1.500, III 1, rev 2.429), 3.417 axle ratio, consumption 32.8 m/imp gal, 27.3 m/US gal, 8.6 l x 100 km at 75 mph, 120 km/h.

136 hp power team

See 75 hp power team, except for:

ENGINE 5 cylinders, in line; 130.8 cu in, 2,144 cc (3.13 x 3.40 in, 79.5 x 86.4 mm); compression ratio: 9.3:1; max power (DIN): 136 hp (100 kW) at 5,700 rpm; max torque (DIN): 133 lb ft, 18.4 kg m (180 Nm) at 4,800 rpm; max engine rpm: 6,200; 62.4 hp/l (46.7 kW/l); 6 crankshaft bearings; lubrication: 7.9 imp pt, 9.5 US pt, 4.5 l; Bosch K-Jetronic injection; water-cooled, 14.3 imp pt, 17.1 US pt, 8.1 l.

TRANSMISSION gearbox: 4+E mechanical (standard) - 5-speed mechanical; gears: 5, fully synchronized; ratios: I 3.600, II 1.882, III 1.185, IV 0.844, V 0.641, rev 3.500 - I 3.600, II 2.125, III 1.458, IV 1.071, V 0.829, rev 3.500; axle ratio: 3.889; tyres: 185/70 HR x 14.

PERFORMANCE max speed: 122 mph, 196 km/h; power-weight ratio: 20.4 lb/hp (27.8 lb/kW), 9.3 kg/hp (12.6 kg/kW); acceleration: 0-50 mph (0-80 km/h) 7.2 sec; speed in top at 1,000 rpm: 28 mph, 45 km/h; consumption: (5-speed mechanical gearbox) 33.6 m/imp gal, 28 m/US gal, 8.4 l x 100 km at 75 mph, 120 km/h.

STEERING servo (standard).

BRAKES disc.

ELECTRICAL EQUIPMENT 63 Ah battery; 90 A alternator.

DIMENSIONS AND WEIGHT weight: 2,778 lb, 1,260 kg.

PRACTICAL INSTRUCTIONS fuel: 98 oct petrol; oil: engine 7.9 imp pt, 9.5 US pt, 4.5 l.

OPTIONALS with automatic transmission 3.250 axle ratio, max speed 119 mph, 191 km/h and consumption 31 m/imp gal, 25.8 m/US gal, 9.1 l x 100 km at 75 mph, 120 km/h; air-conditioning; anti-brake-locking system (ABS).

70 hp (diesel) power team

See 75 hp power team, except for:

ENGINE diesel; 5 cylinders, in line; 121.2 cu in, 1,986 cc (3.01 x 3.40 in, 76.5 x 86.4 mm); compression ratio: 23:1; max power (DIN): 70 hp (51 kW) at 4,800 rpm; max torque (DIN): 91 lb ft, 12.5 kg m (123 Nm) at 2,800 rpm; max engine rpm: 5,000; 35.2 hp/l (25.9 kW/l); 6 crankshaft bearings; lubrication: 8.8 imp pt, 10.6 US pt, 5 l; Bosch injection pump; water-cooled, 16.5 imp pt, 19.9 US pt, 9.4 l.

TRANSMISSION gearbox: 4+E mechanical (standard); gears: 5, fully synchronized; ratios: I 3.600, II 1.882, III 1.185, IV 0.844, V 0.641, rev 3.500; axle ratio: 4.556.

PERFORMANCE max speed: 96 mph, 154 km/h; power-weight ratio: 39.7 lb/hp (54.5 lb/kW), 18 kg/hp (24.7 kg/kW); acceleration: 0-50 mph (0-80 km/h) 12 sec; speed in top at 1,000 rpm: 23.9 mph, 38.5 km/h; consumption: 42.8 m/imp gal, 35.6 m/US gal, 6.6 l x 100 km at 75 mph, 120 km/h.

STEERING servo (standard).

ELECTRICAL EQUIPMENT 88 Ah battery; 55 A alternator.

DIMENSIONS AND WEIGHT weight: 2,778 lb, 1,260 kg.

PRACTICAL INSTRUCTIONS fuel: diesel; oil: engine 8.8 imp pt, 10.6 US pt, 5 l.

OPTIONALS with automatic transmission 3.455 axle ratio max speed 94 mph, 151 km/h and consumption 34 m/imp gal, 28.3 m/US gal, 8.3 l x 100 km at 75 mph, 120 km/h.

87 hp (diesel) power team

See 75 hp power team, except for:

AUDI 100 Avant CC Limousine

AUDI 100 Avant CC Limousine

AUDI 200 Turbo Limousine

AUDI 200 Turbo Limousine

87 HP (DIESEL) POWER TEAM

ENGINE diesel, turbocharged; 5 cylinders, in line; 121.2 cu in, 1,986 cc (3.01 x 3.40 in, 76.5 x 86.4 mm); compression ratio: 23:1; max power (DIN): 87 hp (64 kW) at 4,500 rpm; max torque (DIN): 127 lb ft, 17.5 kg m (172 Nm) at 2,750 rpm; max engine rpm: 5,000; 43.8 hp/l (32.2 kW/l); 6 crankshaft bearings; lubrication: 8.8 imp pt, 10.6 US pt, 5 l; Bosch injection pump; 1 Garrett AiResearch turbocharger; water-cooled, 16.5 imp pt, 19.9 US pt, 9.4 l.

TRANSMISSION gearbox: 4+E mechanical (standard); gears: 5, fully synchronized; ratios: I 3.600, II 1.882, III 1.185, IV 0.844, V 0.641, rev 3.500.

PERFORMANCE max speed: 106 mph, 170 km/h; power-weight ratio: 32.9 lb/hp (44.8 lb/kW), 14.9 kg/hp (20.3 kg/kW); acceleration: 0-50 mph (0-80 km/h) 8.8 sec; speed in top at 1,000 rpm: 26.5 mph, 42.6 km/h; consumption: 38.7 m/imp gal, 32.2 m/US gal, 7.3 l x 100 km at 75 mph, 120 km/h.

STEERING servo (standard).

ELECTRICAL EQUIPMENT 88 Ah battery; 55 A alternator.

DIMENSIONS AND WEIGHT weight: 2,866 lb, 1,300 kg.

PRACTICAL INSTRUCTIONS fuel: diesel; oil: engine 8.8 imp pt, 10.6 US pt, 5 l.

OPTIONALS with automatic transmission 3.083 axle ratio, max speed 101 mph, 162 km/h and consumption 32.1 m/imp gal, 26.7 m/US gal, 8.8 l x 100 km at 75 mph, 120 km/h.

Audi 200 Series

PRICES IN USA AND EX WORKS:	$	DM
1 4-dr Limousine	—	39,950*
2 Turbo 4-dr Limousine	22,250*	44,950*

Power team:	Standard for:	Optional for:
136 hp	1	—
182 hp	2	—

136 hp power team

ENGINE front, 4 stroke; 5 cylinders, in line; 130.8 cu in, 2,144 cc (3.13 x 3.40 in, 79.5 x 86.4 mm); compression ratio: 9.3:1; max power (DIN): 136 hp (100 kW) at 5,700 rpm; max torque (DIN): 133 lb ft, 18.4 kg m (180 Nm) at 4,800 rpm; max engine rpm: 6,200; 62.4 hp/l (46.7 kW/l); cast iron block, light alloy head; 6 crankshaft bearings; valves: overhead, in line, thimble tappets; camshafts: 1, overhead, cogged belt; lubrication: gear pump, full flow filter, 7.9 imp pt, 9.5 US pt, 4.5 l; Bosch K-Jetronic injection; fuel feed: electric pump; water-cooled, 14.3 imp pt, 17.1 US pt, 8.1 l, electric thermostatic fan.

TRANSMISSION driving wheels: front; clutch: single dry plate (diaphragm); gearbox: 4+E mechanical - 5-speed mechanical; gears: 5, fully synchronized; ratios: I 3.600, II 1.882, III 1.185, IV 0.844, V 0.641, rev 3.500 - I 3.600, II 2.125, III 1.458, IV 1.071, V 0.829, rev 3.500; lever: central; final drive: spiral bevel; axle ratio: 3.889; width of rims: 6"; tyres: 205/60 HR x 15.

PERFORMANCE max speed: 124 mph, 200 km/h; power-weight ratio: 20.4 lb/hp (27.8 lb/kW), 9.3 kg/hp (12.6 kg/kW); carrying capacity: 1,102 lb, 500 kg; acceleration: 0-50 mph (0-80 km/h) 7.4 sec; speed in top at 1,000 rpm: 28 mph, 45 km/h; consumption: (4+E mechanical) 38.7 m/imp gal, 32.2 m/US gal, 7.3 l x 100 km at 75 mph, 120 km/h.

CHASSIS integral, front auxiliary frame; front suspension: independent, by McPherson, lower wishbones, anti-roll bar, coil springs/telescopic damper struts; rear: rigid axle, swinging longitudinal trailing radius arms, Panhard rod, anti-roll bar, telescopic dampers.

STEERING rack-and-pinion servo.

BRAKES disc, front internal radial fins, dual circuit rear compensator, servo.

ELECTRICAL EQUIPMENT 12 V; 63 Ah battery; 90 A alternator; 4 halogen headlamps.

DIMENSIONS AND WEIGHT wheel base: 105.79 in, 269 cm; tracks: 57.80 in, 147 cm front, 57.76 in, 147 cm rear; length: 189.25 in, 481 cm; width: 71.42 in, 181 cm; height: 55.98 in, 142 cm; weight: 2,778 lb, 1,260 kg; turning circle: 38 ft, 11.6 m; fuel tank: 17.6 imp gal, 21.1 US gal, 80 l.

BODY saloon/sedan; 4 doors; 5 seats, separate front seats, reclining backrests; heated rear window; electric windows; light alloy wheels; central door locking; tinted glass.

PRACTICAL INSTRUCTIONS fuel: 98 oct petrol; oil: engine 7.9 imp pt, 9.5 US pt, 4.5 l, SAE 10W-50, change every 4,700 miles, 7,500 km - gearbox and final drive 3.2 imp pt, 3.8 US pt, 1.8 l, SAE 80 or 90, change every 18,600 miles, 30,000 km; tyre pressure: front 28 psi, 2 atm, rear 28 psi, 2 atm.

OPTIONALS automatic transmission with 3 ratios (I 2.714, II 1.500, III 1, rev 2.429), 3.250 axle ratio, max speed 121 mph, 195 km/h, consumption 32.6 m/imp gal, 27.3 m/US gal, 8.6 l x 100 km at 75 mph, 120 km/h; anti-brake-locking system (ABS); air-conditioning; sunroof; metallic spray.

182 hp power team

See 136 hp power team, except for:

ENGINE turbocharged; compression ratio: 8.8:1; max power (DIN): 182 hp (134 kW) at 5,700 rpm; max torque (DIN): 186 lb ft, 25.7 kg m (252 Nm) at 3,600 rpm; 84.9 hp/l (62.5 kW/l); Bosch K-Jetronic injection with KKK exhaust turbocharger.

TRANSMISSION gearbox ratios: I 3.600, II 2.125, III 1.360, IV 0.967, V 0.778, rev 3.500; tyres: 205/60 VR x 15.

PERFORMANCE max speed: 143 mph, 230 km/h; power-weight ratio: 15.6 lb/hp (21.2 lb/kW), 7.1 kg/hp (9.6 kg/kW); acceleration: 0-50 mph (0-80 km/h) 5.8 sec; speed in top at 1,000 rpm: 23.3 mph, 37.5 km/h; consumption: 31.7 m/imp gal, 26.4 m/US gal, 8.9 l x 100 km at 75 mph, 120 km/h.

BRAKES anti-brake-locking system (ABS) (standard).

DIMENSIONS AND WEIGHT weight: 2,844 lb, 1,290 kg.

OPTIONALS with automatic transmission 3.083 axle ratio, max speed 139 mph, 223 km/h and consumption 28.8 m/imp gal, 24 m/US gal, 9.8 l x 100 km at 75 mph, 120 km/h.

BITTER AUTOMOBILE GERMANY FR

SC Coupé

PRICE EX WORKS: DM 70,200*

ENGINE Opel, front, 4 stroke; 6 cylinders, in line; 181.1 cu in, 2,968 cc (3.74 x 2.75 in, 95 x 69.8 mm); compression ratio: 9.4:1; max power (DIN): 170 hp (125 kW) at 5,800 rpm; max torque (DIN): 173 lb ft, 23.9 kg m (234 Nm) at 4,500 rpm; max engine rpm: 6,300; 57.3 hp/l (42.1 kW/l); cast iron block and head; 7 crankshaft bearings; valves: overhead, in line, hydraulic tappets; camshafts: 1, overhead, chain-driven; lubrication: gear pump, full flow filter 10.8 imp pt, 12.7 US pt, 6 l; Bosch L-Jetronic injection; fuel feed: mechanical pump; anti-freeze liquid cooled, 18 imp pt, 21.6 US pt, 10.2 l.

TRANSMISSION driving wheels: rear; clutch: single dry plate (diaphragm); gearbox: Opel automatic transmission, hydraulic torque converter and planetary gears, with 3 ratios, max ratio of converter at stall 2.50, possible manual selection; ratios: I 2.400, II 1.480, III 1, rev 1.920; lever: central; final drive:

BITTER AUTOMOBILE SC Coupé

BMW 316

hypoid bevel, limited slip; axle ratio: 3.450; width of rims: 7" front, 8" rear; tyres: Pirelli 215/60 VR x 15 front, 235/55 VR x 15 rear.

PERFORMANCE max speed: 125 mph, 201 km/h; power-weight ratio: 19.8 lb/hp (27.3 lb/kW), 9 kg/hp (12.4 kg/kW); carrying capacity: 882 lb, 400 kg; speed in direct drive at 1,000 rpm: 21.7 mph, 34.9 km/h; consumption: 26.2 m/imp gal, 21.8 m/US gal, 10.8 l x 100 km.

CHASSIS integral; front suspension: independent, by McPherson, wishbones, lower trailing arms, coil springs, telescopic damper struts, anti-roll bar; rear: independent, semi-trailing arms, progressively acting coil springs, anti-roll bar, telescopic dampers.

STEERING recirculating ball, adjustable height, servo; turns lock to lock: 4.

BRAKES disc, internal radial fins (diameter 10.71 in, 27.2 cm front, 10.98 in, 27.9 cm rear), dual circuit, rear compensator, servo; lining area: total 40.9 sq in, 264 sq cm.

ELECTRICAL EQUIPMENT 12 V; 55 Ah battery; 960 W alternator; electronic ignition; 4 halogen headlamps.

DIMENSIONS AND WEIGHT wheel base: 105.59 in, 268 cm; tracks: 57.76 in, 147 cm front, 59.61 in, 151 cm rear; length: 193.31 in, 491 cm; width: 71.65 in, 182 cm; height: 53.15 in, 135 cm; ground clearance: 5.12 in, 13 cm; weight: 3,418 lb, 1,550 kg; turning circle: 35.4 ft, 10.8 m; fuel tank: 16.1 imp gal, 19.3 US gal, 73 l.

BODY coupé; 2 doors; 5 seats, separate front seats, reclining backrests, headrests; leather upholstery; leather steering wheel spokes; heated rear window; rear fog lamp; air-conditioning; electric windows; light alloy wheels; cruise control.

PRACTICAL INSTRUCTIONS fuel: 98 oct petrol; oil: engine 10.8 imp pt, 12.7 US pt, 6 l, SAE 20W-50, change every 3,100 miles, 5,000 km - gearbox 1.9 imp pt, 2.3 US pt, 1.1 l, SAE 80, no change recommended - final drive 2.5 imp pt, 3 US pt, 1.4 l, SAE 90, no change recommended; greasing: none; sparking plug: AC 42-6 FS; valve timing: 32° 90° 72° 50°; tyre pressure: front 28 psi, 2 atm, rear 30 psi, 2.2 atm.

OPTIONALS 3.9-litre engine; 5-speed fully synchronized mechanical gearbox (I 3.822, II 2.223, III 1.398, IV 1, V 0.872, rev 3.705), max speed 130 mph, 210 km/h; Ferguson 4-wheel-drive; electric sunroof.

BMW GERMANY FR

315

PRICE EX WORKS: DM 17,900*

ENGINE front, 4 stroke; 4 cylinders, slanted at 30°, in line; 96 cu in, 1,573 cc (3.31 x 2.80 in, 84 x 71 mm); compression ratio: 9.5:1; max power (DIN): 75 hp (55 kW) at 5,800 rpm; max torque (DIN): 81 lb ft, 11.2 kg m (110 Nm) at 3,200 rpm; max engine rpm: 6,300; 47.7 hp/l (35 kW/l); cast iron block, light alloy head, hemispherical combustion chambers; 5 crankshaft bearings; valves: overhead, Vee-slanted at 52°, rockers; camshafts: 1, overhead; lubrication: gear pump, full flow filter, 7.4 imp pt, 8.9 US pt, 4.2 l; 1 Solex 1B2 downdraught single barrel carburettor; fuel feed: mechanical pump; water-cooled, 12.3 imp pt, 14.8 US pt, 7 l.

TRANSMISSION driving wheels: rear; clutch: single dry plate (diaphragm), hydraulically controlled; gearbox: mechanical; gears: 4, fully synchronized; ratios: I 3.764, II 2.043, III 1.320, IV 1, rev 4.096; lever: central; final drive: hypoid bevel; axle ratio: 4.100; width of rims: 5"; tyres: 165 SR x 13.

PERFORMANCE max speeds: (I) 25 mph, 41 km/h; (II) 47 mph, 75 km/h; (III) 73 mph, 117 km/h; (IV) 96 mph, 154 km/h; power-weight ratio: 29.7 lb/hp (40.5 lb/kW), 13.5 kg/hp (18.4 kg/kW); carrying capacity: 948 lb, 430 kg; speed in direct drive at 1,000 rpm: 15.9 mph, 25.7 km/h; consumption: 31.4 m/imp gal, 26.1 m/US gal, 9 l x 100 km at 75 mph, 120 km/h.

CHASSIS integral; front suspension: independent, by McPherson, coil springs/telescopic damper struts, auxiliary rubber springs, lower wishbones, lower trailings links, anti-roll bar; rear: independent, oblique semi-trailing arms, auxiliary rubber springs, coil springs, telescopic dampers.

STEERING ZF, rack-and-pinion; turns lock to lock: 4.05.

BRAKES front disc (diameter 10.04 in, 25.5 cm), rear drum, dual circuit, servo; lining area: front 23.9 sq in, 154 sq cm, rear 51.5 sq in, 332 sq cm, total 75.4 sq in, 486 sq cm.

ELECTRICAL EQUIPMENT 12 V; 44 Ah battery; 45 A alternator; 2 halogen headlamps.

DIMENSIONS AND WEIGHT wheel base: 100.79 in, 256 cm; tracks: 53.80 in, 137 cm front, 54.10 in, 137 cm rear; length: 171.26 in, 435 cm; width: 63.39 in, 161 cm; height: 54.33 in, 138 cm; ground clearance: 5.51 in, 14 cm; weight: 2,227 lb, 1,010 kg; turning circle: 33.8 ft, 10.3 m; fuel tank: 12.8 imp gal, 15.3 US gal, 58 l.

BODY saloon/sedan; 2 doors; 5 seats, separate front seats, reclining backrests, built-in headrests; heated rear window.

PRACTICAL INSTRUCTIONS fuel: 97 oct petrol; oil: engine 7.4 imp pt, 8.9 US pt, 4.2 l, SAE 10W-50, change every 3,700 miles, 6,000 km - gearbox 1.8 imp pt, 2.1 US pt, 1 l, SAE 80, change every 14,800 miles, 24,000 km - final drive 1.6 imp pt, 1.9 US pt, 0.9 l, SAE 90, no change recommended; greasing: none; tyre pressure: front 26 psi, 1.8 atm, rear 26 psi, 1.8 atm.

OPTIONALS 5-speed mechanical gearbox (I 3.681, II 2.002, III 1.329, IV 1, V 0.805, rev 3.681), consumption 34.4 m/imp gal, 28.7 m/US gal, 8.2 l x 100 km at 75 mph, 120 km/h; limited slip differential; 185/70 SR x 13 tyres; light alloy wheels; power steering; anti-roll bar on rear suspension; fog lamps; 55 Ah battery; sunroof; metallic spray; tinted glass.

316

PRICES IN GB AND EX WORKS:	£	DM
2-dr Limousine	6,995*	20,700*
4-dr Limusine	7,345*	21,560*

ENGINE front, 4 stroke; 4 cylinders, slanted at 30°, in line; 107.8 cu in, 1,766 cc (3.50 x 2.80 in, 89 x 71 mm); compression ratio: 9.5:1; max power (DIN): 90 hp (66 kW) at 5,500 rpm; max torque (DIN): 103 lb ft, 14.3 kg m (140 Nm) at 4,000 rpm; max engine rpm: 6,000; 50.9 hp/l (37.4 kW/l); cast iron block, light alloy head, hemispherical combustion chambers; 5 crankshaft bearings; valves: overhead, Vee-slanted at 52°, rockers; camshafts: 1, overhead; lubrication: gear pump, full flow filter, 7 imp gal, 8.5 US gal, 4 l; 1 Solex 2B4 downdraught twin barrel electronic carburettor; fuel feed: mechanical pump; water-cooled, 12.3 imp pt, 14.8 US pt, 7 l.

TRANSMISSION driving wheels: rear; clutch: single dry plate (diaphragm), hydraulically controlled; gearbox: mechanical; gears: 4, fully synchronized; ratios: I 3.760, II 2.040, III 1.320, IV 1, rev 4.100; lever: central; final drive: hypoid bevel; axle ratio: 3.640; width of rims: 5"; tyres: 175/70 HR x 14.

PERFORMANCE max speed: 109 mph, 175 km/h; power-weight ratio: 24.3 lb/hp (33.1 lb/kW), 11 kg/hp (15 kg/kW); carrying capacity: 1,014 lb, 460 kg; acceleration: standing ¼ mile 18.2 sec; consumption: 33.6 m/imp gal, 28 m/US gal, 8.4 l x 100 km at 75 mph, 120 km/h.

CHASSIS integral; front suspension: independent, by McPherson, coil springs/telescopic damper struts, auxiliary rubber springs, lower wishbones, lower trailings links, anti-roll bar; rear: independent, oblique semi-trailing arms, auxiliary rubber springs, coil springs, telescopic dampers.

STEERING ZF, rack-and-pinion; turns lock to lock: 4.05.

BRAKES front disc (diameter 10.04 in, 25.5 cm), rear drum, dual circuit, servo; lining area: front 23.9 sq in, 154 sq cm, rear 51.5 sq in, 332 sq cm, total 75.4 sq in, 486 sq cm.

ELECTRICAL EQUIPMENT 12 V; 44 Ah battery; 65 A alternator; 4 halogen headlamps with automatically adjustable height.

DIMENSIONS AND WEIGHT wheel base: 101.18 in, 257 cm; tracks: 55.39 in, 141 cm front, 55.71 in, 142 cm rear; length: 170.28 in, 432 cm; width: 64.76 in, 164 cm; height: 54.33 in, 138 cm; ground clearance: 5.51 in, 14 cm; weight: 2,183 lb, 990 kg; turning circle: 34.4 ft, 10.5 m; fuel tank: 12.1 imp gal, 14.5 US gal, 55 l.

BODY saloon/sedan; 2 or 4 doors; 5 seats, separate front seats, reclining backrests, built-in headrests; heated rear window; energy control; check control.

PRACTICAL INSTRUCTIONS fuel: 97 oct petrol; oil: engine 7 imp pt, 8.5 US pt, 4 l, SAE 10W-50, change every 3,700 miles,

BITTER AUTOMOBILE SC Coupé

BMW 320i

316

6,000 km - gearbox 1.8 imp pt, 2.1 US pt, 1 l, SAE 80, change every 14,800 miles, 24,000 km - final drive 1.6 imp pt, 1.9 US pt, 0.9 l, SAE 90, no change recommended; greasing: none; spark plug: Bosch W7C; tyre pressure: front 28 psi, 2 atm, rear 28 psi, 2 atm.

OPTIONALS 5-speed mechanical gearbox (I 3.681, II 2.002, III 1.329, IV 1, V 0.805, rev 3.681), consumption 37.2 m/imp gal, 30.9 m/US gal, 7.6 l x 100 km at 75 mph, 120 km/h; ZF 3HP 22 automatic transmission, hydraulic torque converter and planetary gears with 3 ratios (I 2.478, II 1.478, III 1, rev 2.090), max speed 106 mph, 170 km/h, consumption 30.7 m/imp gal, 25.6 m/US gal, 9.2 l x 100 km at 75 mph, 120 km/h; limited slip differential; power steering; headlamps with wiper-washer; anti-roll bar on rear suspension; 55 Ah battery; 195/60 HR x 14 tyres; light alloy wheels; sunroof; metallic spray; tinted glass; air-conditioning; trip computer.

318i

See 316, except for:

PRICES IN USA AND EX WORKS:	$	DM
2-dr Limousine	16,430*	22,800*
4-dr Limousine	—	23,660*

ENGINE compression ratio: 10:1; max power (DIN): 105 hp (77 kW) at 5,800 rpm; max torque (DIN): 107 lb ft, 14.8 kg m (145 Nm) at 4,500 rpm; 59.4 hp/l (43.6 kW/l); Bosch L-Jetronic injection.

PERFORMANCE max speed: 114 mph, 184 km/h; power-weight ratio: 21 lb/hp (28.6 lb/kW), 9.5 kg/hp (13 kg/kW); acceleration: standing ¼ mile 17.6 sec; consumption: 34 m/imp gal, 28.3 m/US gal, 8.3 l x 100 km at 75 mph, 120 km/h.

DIMENSIONS AND WEIGHT weight: 2,205 lb, 1,000 kg.

OPTIONALS 5-speed mechanical gearbox (I 3.681, II 2.002, III 1.329, IV 1, V 0.805, rev 3.681), consumption 37.2 m/imp gal, 30.9 m/US gal, 7.6 l x 100 km at 75 mph, 120 km/h; ZF 3HP 22 automatic transmission, hydraulic torque converter and planetary gears with 3 ratios (I 2.478, II 1.478, III 1, rev 2.090), max speed 111 mph, 179 km/h, consumption 30.7 m/imp gal, 25.6 m/US gal, 9.2 l x 100 km at 75 mph, 120 km/h.

320i

See 316, except for:

PRICES IN GB AND EX WORKS:	£	DM
2-dr Limousine	8,845*	26,050*
4-dr Limousine	9,195*	26,710*

ENGINE 6 cylinders, in line; 121.4 cu in, 1,990 cc (3.15 x 2.60 in, 80 x 66 mm); compression ratio: 9.8:1; max power (DIN): 125 hp (92 kW) at 5,800 rpm; max torque (DIN): 126 lb ft, 17.3 kg m (170 Nm) at 4,000 rpm; max engine rpm: 6,400; 62.8 hp/l (46.2 kW/l); 7 crankshaft bearings; valves: overhead, Vee-slanted, rockers; lubrication: 7.6 imp pt, 9.1 US pt, 4.3 l; Bosch L-Jetronic injection; cooling: 21.1 imp pt, 25.4 US pt, 12 l.

TRANSMISSION gears: 5, fully synchronized; ratios: I 3.720, II 2.020, III 1.320, IV 1, V 0.810, rev 3.460; axle ratio: 3.450; width of rims: 5.5"; tyres: 195/60 HR x 14 (standard).

PERFORMANCE max speed: 122 mph, 196 km/h; power-weight ratio: 18.5 lb/hp (25.2 lb/kW), 8.4 kg/hp (11.4 kg/kW); acceleration: standing ¼ mile 17.2 sec; consumption: 34.9 m/imp gal, 29 m/US gal, 8.1 l x 100 km at 75 mph, 120 km/h.

BRAKES front disc, internal radial fins, rear drum, servo.

BMW 525e

BMW 323i

DIMENSIONS AND WEIGHT weight: 2,315 lb, 1,050 kg.

PRACTICAL INSTRUCTIONS oil: engine 7.6 imp pt, 9.1 US pt, 4.3 l.

OPTIONALS ZF 3HP 22 automatic transmission, hydraulic torque converter and planetary gears with 3 ratios (I 2.478, II 1.478, III 1, rev 2.090), max speed 119 mph, 191 km/h, consumption 34.4 m/imp gal, 28.7 m/US gal, 8.2 l x 100 km at 75 mph, 120 km/h; anti-brake-locking system (ABS).

323i

See 316, except for:

PRICES IN GB AND EX WORKS:	£	DM
2-dr Limousine	9,935*	29,050*
4-dr Limousine	10,285*	29,910*

ENGINE 6 cylinders, in line; 141.3 cu in, 2,316 cc (3.15 x 3.02 in, 80 x 76.8 mm); compression ratio: 9.8:1; max power (DIN): 150 hp (110 kW) at 6,000 rpm; max torque (DIN): 151 lb ft, 20.9 kg m (205 Nm) at 4,000 rpm; max engine rpm: 6,600; 64.8 hp/l (47.7 kW/l); 7 crankshaft bearings; valves: overhead, Vee-slanted, rockers; lubrication: 7.6 imp pt, 9.1 US pt, 4.3 l; Bosch L-Jetronic injection; cooling: 21.1 imp pt, 25.4 US pt, 12 l.

TRANSMISSION gears: 5, fully synchronized; ratios: I 3.830, II 2.200, III 1.400, IV 1, V 0.810, rev 3.460; axle ratio: 3.450; width of rims: 5.5"; tyres: 195/60 HR x 14 (standard).

PERFORMANCE max speed: 127 mph, 204 km/h; power-weight ratio: 16 lb/hp (21.8 lb/kW), 7.3 kg/hp (9.9 kg/kW); acceleration: standing ¼ mile 16.5 sec; consumption: 33.6 m/imp gal, 28 m/US gal, 8.4 l x 100 km at 75 mph, 120 km/h.

CHASSIS rear suspension: anti-roll bar.

BRAKES disc, front internal radial fins.

DIMENSIONS AND WEIGHT weight: 2,403 lb, 1,090 kg.

PRACTICAL INSTRUCTIONS oil: engine 7.6 imp pt, 9.1 US pt, 4.3 l.

OPTIONALS ZF 3HP 22 automatic transmission, hydraulic torque converter and planetary gears with 3 ratios (I 2.478, II 1.478, III 1, rev 2.090), max speed 124 mph, 200 km/h; anti-brake-locking system (ABS).

BMW 524td

518

PRICE IN GB: £ 8,455*
PRICE EX WORKS: DM 24,300

ENGINE front, 4 stroke; 4 cylinders, in line; 107.8 cu in, 1,766 cc (3.50 x 2.80 in, 89 x 71 mm); compression ratio: 9.5:1; max power (DIN): 90 hp (66 kW) at 5,500 rpm; max torque (DIN): 104 lb ft, 14.3 kg m (140 Nm) at 4,000 rpm; max engine rpm: 6,300; 51 hp/l (37.5 kW/l); cast iron block, light alloy head, hemispherical combustion chambers; 5 crankshaft bearings; valves: overhead, Vee-slanted at 52°, rockers; camshafts: 1, overhead; lubrication: rotary pump, full flow filter, 7.4 imp pt, 8.9 US pt, 4.2 l; 1 Solex 2B4 downdraught twin barrel electronic carburettor; fuel feed: mechanical pump; water-cooled, 12.3 imp pt, 14.8 US pt, 7 l.

TRANSMISSION driving wheels: rear; clutch: single dry plate, hydraulically controlled; gearbox: mechanical; gears: 4, fully synchronized; ratios: I 3.764, II 2.043, III 1.320, IV 1, rev 4.096; lever: central; final drive: hypoid bevel; axle ratio: 4.270; width of rims: 5.5"; tyres: 175 SR x 14.

PERFORMANCE max speeds: (I) 27 mph, 43 km/h; (II) 49 mph, 79 km/h; (III) 76 mph, 122 km/h; (IV) 102 mph, 164 km/h; power-weight ratio: 27.9 lb/hp (38.1 lb/kW), 12.7 kg/hp (17.3 kg/kW); carrying capacity: 1,125 lb, 510 kg; acceleration: standing ¼ mile 18.9 sec; speed in direct drive at 1,000 rpm: 16.2 mph, 26 km/h; consumption: 31.4 m/imp gal, 26.1 m/US gal, 9 l x 100 km at 75 mph, 120 km/h.

CHASSIS integral; front suspension: independent, by McPherson, coil springs/telescopic damper struts, auxiliary rubber springs, lower wishbones, lower trailing links, anti-roll bar; rear: independent, oblique semi-trailing arms, auxiliary rubber springs, coil springs, telescopic dampers.

STEERING ZF, worm and roller.

BRAKES front disc (diameter 11 in, 28 cm), internal radial fins, rear drum, dual circuit, rear compensator, servo.

ELECTRICAL EQUIPMENT 12 V; 44 Ah battery; 65 A alternator; electronic ignition; 4 halogen headlamps.

DIMENSIONS AND WEIGHT wheel base: 103.35 in, 262 cm; tracks: 56.30 in, 143 cm front, 57.90 in, 147 cm rear; length: 181.89 in, 462 cm; width: 66.93 in, 170 cm; height: 55.91 in, 142 cm; ground clearance: 5.51 in, 14 cm; weight: 2,514 lb, 1,140 kg; turning circle: 35.8 ft, 10.9 m; fuel tank: 15.4 imp gal, 18.5 US gal, 70 l.

BODY saloon/sedan; 4 doors; 5 seats, separate front seats, reclining backrests; heated rear window.

PRACTICAL INSTRUCTIONS fuel: 98 oct petrol; oil: engine 7.4 imp pt, 8.9 US pt, 4.2 l, SAE 20W-50, change every 3,700 miles, 6,000 km - gearbox 1.8 imp pt, 2.1 US pt, 1 l, SAE 80, change every 14,900 miles, 24,000 km - final drive 1.6 imp pt, 1.9 US pt, 0.9 l, SAE 90, no change recommended; greasing: none; tyre pressure: front and rear 27 psi, 1.9 atm.

OPTIONALS 5-speed mechanical gearbox (I 3.682, II 2.002, III 1.330, IV 1, V 0.805, rev 3.682), consumption 34.4 m/imp gal, 28.7 m/US gal, 8.2 l x 100 km at 75 mph, 120 km/h; limited slip differential; 195/70 HR x 14 tyres; light alloy wheels; power steering; manual or electric sunroof; fog lamps; metallic spray; 55 Ah battery; 770 W alternator; air-conditioning.

520i

See 518, except for:

PRICE IN GB: £ 10,195*
PRICE EX WORKS: DM 28,650*

ENGINE 6 cylinders, in line; 121.4 cu in, 1,990 cc (3.15 x 2.60 in, 80 x 66 mm); compression ratio: 9.8:1; max power (DIN): 125 hp (92 kW) at 5,800 rpm; max torque (DIN): 125 lb ft, 17.3 kg m (170 Nm) at 4,000 rpm; max engine rpm: 6,300; 62.8 hp/l

BMW 524td

46.2 kW/l); 7 crankshaft bearings; lubrication: 10 imp pt, 12 US t, 5.7 l; Bosch L-Jetronic injection; cooling: 21.1 imp pt, 25.4 JS pt, 12 l.

TRANSMISSION gears: 5, fully synchronized; ratios: I 3.720, II .020, III 1.320, IV 1, V 0.800, rev 3.456; axle ratio: 3.910; yres: 175 HR x 14.

PERFORMANCE max speed: 115 mph, 185 km/h; power-weight atio: 21.5 lb/hp (29.2 lb/kW), 9.8 kg/hp (13.3 kg/kW); acceleraion: standing ¼ mile 17.6 sec; speed in direct drive at 1,000 pm: 18.3 mph, 29.4 km/h; consumption: 33.2 m/imp gal, 27.7 n/US gal, 8.5 l x 100 km at 75 mph, 120 km/h.

STEERING servo (standard).

ELECTRICAL EQUIPMENT 55 Ah battery (standard); 80 A alternator.

DIMENSIONS AND WEIGHT weight: 2,690 lb, 1,220 kg.

PRACTICAL INSTRUCTIONS oil: engine 10 imp pt, 12 US pt, .7 l.

OPTIONALS ZF automatic transmission with 4 ratios (I 2.478, II .478, III 1, IV 0.730, rev 2.090), max speed 111 mph, 179 m/h; anti-brake-locking system (ABS).

525e

See 518, except for:

PRICE EX WORKS: DM 30,600*

ENGINE 6 cylinders, in line; 164.3 cu in, 2,693 cc (3.31 x 3.19 n, 84 x 81 mm); compression ratio: 11:1; max power (DIN): 125 p (92 kW) at 4,250 rpm; max torque (DIN): 178 lb ft, 24.5 kg m 240 Nm) at 3,250 rpm; max engine rpm: 5,000; 46.4 hp/l (34.2 W/l); 7 crankshaft bearings; Bosch Motronic II injection; cooling: 21.1 imp pt, 25.4 US pt, 12 l.

TRANSMISSION gears: 5, fully synchronized; ratios: I 3.830, II .200, III 1.400, IV 1, V 0.810, rev 3.460; axle ratio: 2.930; yres: 175 HR x 14.

PERFORMANCE max speed: 115 mph, 185 km/h; power-weight atio: 22 lb/hp (30 lb/kW), 10 kg/hp (13.6 kg/kW); acceleration: standing ¼ mile 17.4 sec; consumption: 37.2 m/imp gal, 30.9 n/US gal, 7.6 l x 100 km at 75 mph, 120 km/h.

STEERING servo (standard).

BRAKES front disc, internal radial fins.

ELECTRICAL EQUIPMENT 66 Ah battery; 80 A alternator.

DIMENSIONS AND WEIGHT weight: 2,756 lb, 1,250 kg..

OPTIONALS ZF automatic transmission with 4 ratios (I 2.478, II 1.478, III 1, IV 0.730, rev 2.090), max speed 112 mph, 180 km/h, consumption 37.7 m/imp gal, 31.4 m/US gal, 7.5 l x 100 km at 75 mph, 120 km/h; anti-brake-locking system (ABS).

524td

See 518, except for:

PRICE EX WORKS: DM 32,300*

ENGINE diesel, turbocharged; 6 cylinders, in line; 149.1 cu in, 2,443 cc (3.15 x 3.19 in, 80 x 81 mm); compression ratio: 22:1; max power (DIN): 115 hp (85 kW) at 4,800 rpm; max torque (DIN): 155 lb ft, 21.4 kg m (210 Nm) at 2,400 rpm; 7 crankshaft bearings; valves: overhead, in line, rockers; camshafts: 1, overhead, cogged belt; Bosch injection pump; 1 turbocharger; cooling: 21.1 imp pt, 25.4 US pt, 12 l.

TRANSMISSION gears: 5, fully synchronized; ratios: I 4.350, II 2.330, III 1.390, IV 1, V 0.810, rev 3.730; axle ratio: 3.150; tyres: 175 HR x 14.

PERFORMANCE max speed: 112 mph, 180 km/h; power-weight ratio: 24.9 lb/hp (33.7 lb/kW), 11.3 kg/hp (15.3 kg/kW); consumption: 40.4 m/imp gal, 33.6 m/US gal, 7 l x 100 km at 75 mph, 120 km/h.

STEERING servo (standard).

ELECTRICAL EQUIPMENT 90 Ah battery.

DIMENSIONS AND WEIGHT weight: 2,866 lb, 1,300 kg.

PRACTICAL INSTRUCTIONS fuel: diesel.

OPTIONALS ZF automatic transmission with 4 ratios (I 2.730, II 1.560, III 1, IV 0.730, rev 2.090), max speed 109 mph, 175 km/h; anti-brake-locking system (ABS).

BMW 745i Automatic

525i

See 518, except for:

PRICE IN GB: £ 12,135*
PRICE EX WORKS: DM 33,650*

ENGINE 6 cylinders, in line; 152.2 cu in, 2,494 cc (3.39 x 2.82 in, 86 x 71 mm); compression ratio: 9.6:1; max power (DIN): 150 hp (110 kW) at 5,500 rpm; max torque (DIN): 159 lb ft, 21.9 kg m (215 Nm) at 4,000 rpm; max engine rpm: 6,000; 60.1 hp/l (44.1 kW/l); 7 crankshaft bearings; lubrication: 10 imp pt, 12 US pt, 5.7 l; Bosch L-Jetronic injection; cooling: 21.1 imp pt, 25.4 US pt, 12 l.

TRANSMISSION gears: 5, fully synchronized; ratios: I 3.822, II 2.202, III 1.398, IV 1, V 0.813, rev 3.460; axle ratio: 3.450; tyres: 175 HR x 14.

PERFORMANCE max speed: 122 mph, 197 km/h; power-weight ratio: 18.8 lb/hp (25.7 lb/kW), 8.5 kg/hp (11.6 kg/kW); acceleration: standing ¼ mile 16.9 sec; speed in direct drive at 1,000 rpm: 20.4 mph, 32.8 km/h; consumption: 32.8 m/imp gal, 27.3 m/US gal, 8.6 l x 100 km at 75 mph, 120 km/h.

STEERING servo (standard).

BRAKES rear disc.

ELECTRICAL EQUIPMENT 55 Ah battery (standard); 80 A alternator.

DIMENSIONS AND WEIGHT weight: 2,822 lb, 1,280 kg.

PRACTICAL INSTRUCTIONS oil: engine 10 imp pt, 12 US pt, 5.7 l.

OPTIONALS ZF automatic transmission with 4 ratios (I 2.478, II 1.478, III 1, IV 0.730, rev 2.090), max speed 118 mph, 190 km/h; anti-brake-locking system (ABS); 200/60 HR x 390 tyres.

528i

See 518, except for:

PRICE IN GB: £ 13,575*
PRICE IN USA: $ 24,565*

ENGINE 6 cylinders, in line; 170.1 cu in, 2,788 cc (3.39 x 3.15 in, 86 x 80 mm); compression ratio: 9.3:1; max power (DIN): 184 hp (135 kW) at 5,800 rpm; max torque (DIN): 177 lb ft, 24.5 kg m (240 Nm) at 4,200 rpm; max engine rpm: 6,300; 65.9 hp/l (48.4 kW/l); 7 crankshaft bearings; lubrication: 10 imp pt, 12 US pt, 5.7 l; Bosch L-Jetronic injection; cooling: 21.1 imp pt, 25.4 US pt, 12 l.

TRANSMISSION gears: 5, fully synchronized; ratios: I 3.822, II 2.202, III 1.398, IV 1, V 0.813, rev 3.460; axle ratio: 3.250; width of rims: 6"; tyres: 195/70 VR x 14.

PERFORMANCE max speed: 132 mph, 212 km/h; power-weight ratio: 15.6 lb/hp (21.2 lb/kW), 7.1 kg/hp (9.6 kg/kW); acceleration: standing ¼ mile 16.2 sec; speed in top at 1,000 rpm: 20.6 mph, 33.2 km/h; consumption: 32.8 m/imp gal, 27.3 m/US gal, 8.6 l x 100 km at 75 mph, 120 km/h.

STEERING servo (standard).

BRAKES rear disc.

ELECTRICAL EQUIPMENT 55 Ah battery (standard); 80 A alternator.

DIMENSIONS AND WEIGHT rear track: 57.48 in, 146 cm; weight: 2,866 lb, 1,300 kg.

PRACTICAL INSTRUCTIONS oil: engine 10 imp pt, 12 US pt, 5.7 l.

OPTIONALS ZF automatic transmission with 4 ratios (I 2.478, II 1.478, III 1, IV 0.730, rev 2.090), max speed 128 mph, 206 km/h; anti-brake-locking system (ABS); 200/60 HR x 390 tyres.

728i

PRICE IN GB: £ 14,545*
PRICE EX WORKS: DM 41,150

ENGINE front, 4 stroke; 6 cylinders, in line; 170.1 cu in, 2,788 cc (3.39 x 3.15 in, 86 x 80 mm); compression ratio: 9.3:1; max power (DIN): 184 hp (135 kW) at 5,800 rpm; max torque (DIN): 177 lb ft, 24.5 kg m (240 Nm) at 4,200 rpm; max engine rpm: 6,500; 65.9 hp/l (48.4 kW/l); cast iron block, light alloy head, polispherical combustion chambers; 7 crankshaft bearings; valves: overhead, Vee-slanted, rockers; camshafts: 1, overhead; lubrication: rotary pump, full flow filter, 10 imp pt, 12 US pt, 5.7 l; Bosch L-Jetronic injection; fuel feed: electric pump; water-cooled, 21.1 imp pt, 25.4 US pt, 12 l.

TRANSMISSION driving wheels: rear; clutch: single dry plate (diaphragm), hydraulically controlled; gearbox: mechanical; gears: 5, fully synchronized; ratios: I 3.830, II 2.202, III 1.398, IV 1, V 0.813, rev 3.460; lever: central; final drive: hypoid bevel; axle ratio: 3.640; width of rims: 6.5"; tyres: 195/70 VR x 14.

PERFORMANCE max speed: 125 mph, 201 km/h; power-weight ratio: 17.6 lb/hp (24 lb/kW), 8 kg/hp (10.9 kg/kW); carrying capacity: 1,125 lb, 510 kg; acceleration: standing ¼ mile 16.6 sec; consumption: 27.7 m/imp gal, 23.1 m/US gal, 10.2 l x 100 km at 75 mph, 120 km/h.

CHASSIS integral; front suspension: independent, by McPherson, coil springs/telescopic damper struts, auxiliary rubber

BMW M 635 CSi

728i

springs, lower wishbones (trailing links), anti-roll bar; rear: independent, semi-trailing arms, auxiliary rubber springs, coil springs, telescopic dampers.

STEERING ZF, recirculating ball, variable ratio servo; turns lock to lock: 3.80.

BRAKES disc (diameter 11 in, 28 cm), front internal radial fins, 2 X circuits, servo.

ELECTRICAL EQUIPMENT 12 V; 55 Ah battery; 80 A alternator; contactless fully electronic distributor; 4 halogen headlamps.

DIMENSIONS AND WEIGHT wheel base: 110 in, 279 cm; tracks: 59.13 in, 150 cm front, 59.84 in, 152 cm rear; length: 191.30 in, 486 cm; width: 70.90 in, 180 cm; height: 56.30 in, 143 cm; weight: 3,241 lb, 1,470 kg; turning circle: 38 ft, 11.6 m; fuel tank: 22 imp gal, 26.4 US gal, 100 l.

BODY saloon/sedan; 4 doors; 5 seats, separate front seats, reclining backrests, adjustable built-in headrests; heated rear window.

PRACTICAL INSTRUCTIONS fuel: 98 oct petrol; oil: engine 10 imp pt, 12 US pt, 5.7 l, SAE 20W-50, change every 3,700 miles, 6,000 km - gearbox 2.1 imp pt, 2.5 US pt, 1.2 l, SAE 20W-50, change every 14,800 miles, 24,000 km - final drive 2.6 imp pt, 3.2 US pt, 1.5 l, SAE 90, no change recommended; greasing: none; tyre pressure: front and rear 29 psi, 2.1 atm.

OPTIONALS ZF automatic transmission, hydraulic torque converter and planetary gears with 4 ratios (I 2.478, II 1.478, III 1, IV 0.730, rev 2.090), max ratio of converter at stall 2, possible manual selection, max speed 121 mph, 195 km, consumption 28.5 m/imp gal, 23.5 m/US gal, 9.9 l x 100 km at 75 mph, 120 km/h; limited slip differential; anti-brake-locking system (ABS); light alloy wheels; sunroof; air-conditioning.

732i

See 728 i, except for:

PRICE IN GB: £ 16,360*
PRICE EX WORKS: DM 46,250*

ENGINE 195.81 cu in, 3,210 cc (3.50 x 3.39 in, 89 x 86 mm); compression ratio: 10:1; max power (DIN): 197 hp (145 kW) at 5,500 rpm; max torque (DIN): 210 lb ft, 29.1 kg m (285 Nm) at 4,300 rpm; 61.4 hp/l (45.2 kW/l); Bosch Motronic II injection.

TRANSMISSION gearbox ratios: I 3.820, II 2.200, III 1.400, IV 1, V 0.810, rev 3.710; axle ratio: 3.450; tyres: 205/70 VR x 14.

PERFORMANCE max speed: 129 mph, 208 km/h; power-weight ratio: 16.8 lb/hp (22.8 lb/kW), 7.6 kg/hp (10.3 kg/kW); acceleration: standing ¼ mile 16.1 sec; speed in direct drive at 1,000 rpm: 19.6 mph, 31.5 km/h; consumption: 27.7 m/imp gal, 23.1 m/US gal, 10.2 l x 100 km at 75 mph, 120 km/h.

ELECTRICAL EQUIPMENT 66 Ah battery; digital engine and electronic ignition (Bosch Motronic).

DIMENSIONS AND WEIGHT weight: 3,307 lb, 1,500 kg.

OPTIONALS ZF automatic transmission, max speed 125 mph, 202 km/h, consumption 28.8 m/imp gal, 24 m/US gal, 9.8 l x 100 km at 75 mph, 120 km/h.

735i

See 728i, except for:

PRICE IN GB: £ 18,830*
PRICE EX WORKS: DM 52,600*

ENGINE 209.3 cu in, 3,430 cc (3.62 x 3.39 in, 92 x 86 mm); compression ratio: 10:1; max power (DIN): 218 hp (160 kW) at 5,200 rpm; max torque (DIN): 229 lb ft, 31.6 kg m (310 Nm) at 4,000 rpm; max engine rpm: 5,600; 63.1 hp/l (46.3 kW/l); lubrication: thermostatic oil cooler; Bosch Motronic II injection.

TRANSMISSION gearbox ratios: I 3.820, II 2.200, III 1.400, IV 1, V 0.810, rev 3.710; axle ratio: 3.250; tyres: 205/70 VR x 14.

PERFORMANCE max speed: 135 mph, 217 km/h; power-weight ratio: 15.2 lb/hp (20.7 lb/kW), 6.9 kg/hp (9.4 kg/kW); acceleration: standing ¼ mile 15.6 sec; consumption: 28.2 m/imp gal, 23.5 m/US gal, 10 l x 100 km at 75 mph, 120 km/h.

ELECTRICAL EQUIPMENT 66 Ah battery; digital engine and electronic ignition (Bosch Motronic).

DIMENSIONS AND WEIGHT weight: 3,307 lb, 1,500 kg.

BODY light alloy wheels (standard).

OPTIONALS ZF automatic transmission, max speed 128 mph, 206 km/h, consumption 28.8 m/imp gal, 24 m/US gal, 9.8 l x 100 km at 75 mph, 120 km/h.

745i Automatic

See 728i, except for:

PRICE EX WORKS: DM 64,150*

ENGINE turbocharged; 209.3 cu in, 3,430 cc (3.62 x 3.39 in, 92 x 86 mm); compression ratio: 8:1; max power (DIN): 252 hp (185 kW) at 5,200 rpm; max torque (DIN): 280 lb ft, 38.7 kg m (380 Nm) at 2,200 rpm; 73.5 hp/l (53.9 kW/l); lubrication: thermostatic oil cooler; Bosch Motronic II injection; 1 turbocharger.

TRANSMISSION gearbox: ZF automatic transmission, hydraulic torque converter and planetary gears with 4 ratios, max ratio of converter at stall 2, possible manual selection; ratios: I 2.478, II 1.478, III 1, IV 0.730, rev 2.090; lever: central; axle ratio: 2.930; tyres: 205/70 VR x 14.

PERFORMANCE max speed: above 141 mph, 227 km/h; power-weight ratio: 13.9 lb/hp (18.9 lb/kW), 6.3 kg/hp (8.6 kg/kW); acceleration: standing ¼ mile 15.8 sec, 0-50 mph (0-80 km/h) 5.6 sec; consumption: 27.2 m/imp gal, 22.6 m/US gal, 10.4 l x 100 km at 75 mph, 120 km/h.

CHASSIS rear suspension: hydropneumatic autolevelling system.

BRAKES anti-brake-locking system (ABS) (standard).

ELECTRICAL EQUIPMENT 66 Ah battery; 1,120 W alternator.

DIMENSIONS AND WEIGHT weight: 3,506 lb, 1,590 kg.

BODY light alloy wheels (standard).

628 CSi

PRICE IN GB: £ 18,710*
PRICE EX WORKS: DM 55,900*

ENGINE front, 4 stroke; 6 cylinders, in line; 170.1 cu in, 2,788 cc (3.39 x 3.15 in, 86 x 80 mm); compression ratio: 9.3:1; max power (DIN): 184 hp (135 kW) at 5,800 rpm; max torque (DIN): 177 lb ft, 24.5 kg m (240 Nm) at 4,200 rpm; max engine rpm: 6,500; 65.9 hp/l (48.4 kW/l); cast iron block, light alloy head, polispherical combustion chambers; 7 crankshaft bearings; valves: overhead, Vee-slanted at 52°, rockers; camshafts: 1, overhead, chain-driven; lubrication: rotary pump, full flow filter, 10 imp pt, 12 US pt, 5.7 l; Bosch L-Jetronic injection; fuel feed: electric pump; water-cooled, 21.1 imp pt, 25.4 US pt, 12 l.

TRANSMISSION driving wheels: rear; clutch: single dry plate (diaphragm), hydraulically controlled; gearbox: mechanical; gears: 5, fully synchronized; ratios: I 3.830, II 2.202, III 1.398, IV 1, V 0.813, rev 3.460; lever: central; final drive: hypoid bevel; axle ratio: 3.450; width of rims: 6.5"; tyres: 205/70 VR x 14.

PERFORMANCE max speed: 132 mph, 212 km/h; power-weight ratio: 16.9 lb/hp (23 lb/kW), 7.7 kg/hp (10.4 kg/kW); carrying capacity: 926 lb, 420 kg; acceleration: standing ¼ mile 16.4 sec; consumption: 32.1 m/imp gal, 26.7 m/US gal, 8.8 l x 100 km at 75 mph, 120 km/h.

CHASSIS integral; front suspension: independent, by McPherson, coil springs/telescopic damper struts, auxiliary rubber springs, anti-roll bar, lower wishbones; rear: independent, semi-trailing arms, auxiliary rubber springs, coil springs, telescopic dampers.

STEERING ZF, recirculating ball, variable ratio servo; turns lock to lock: 3.50.

BRAKES disc (diameter 11 in, 28 cm), internal radial fins, dual circuit, rear compensator, servo.

ELECTRICAL EQUIPMENT 12 V; 66 Ah battery; 80 A alternator; contactless fully electronic ignition; 4 halogen headlamps.

DIMENSIONS AND WEIGHT wheel base: 103.54 in, 263 cm; tracks: 56.30 in, 143 cm front, 57.48 in, 146 cm rear; length: 187.01 in, 475 cm; width: 67.72 in, 172 cm; height: 53.54 in, 136 cm; ground clearance: 5.51 in, 14 cm; weight: 3,109 lb, 1,410 kg; turning circle: 36.7 ft, 11.2 m; fuel tank: 15.4 imp gal, 18.5 US gal, 70 l.

BODY coupé; 2 doors; 4 seats, separate front seats, reclining backrests; tinted glass; heated rear window; light alloy wheels.

PRACTICAL INSTRUCTIONS fuel: 98 oct petrol; oil: engine 10 imp pt, 12 US pt, 5.7 l, change every 3,700 miles, 6,000 km - gearbox 2.1 imp pt, 2.5 US pt, 1.2 l, SAE 20W-50, change every 14,800 miles, 24,000 km - final drive 2.6 imp pt, 3.2 US pt, 1.5 l, SAE 90, no change recommended; greasing: none; spark plug: 175° T30; tappet clearances: inlet 0.010 in, 0.25 mm, exhaust 0.012 in, 0.30 mm; valve timing: 6° 50° 50° 6°; tyre pressure: front 28 psi, 2 atm, rear 27 psi, 1.9 atm.

OPTIONALS ZF automatic transmission, hydraulic torque converter and planetary gears with 4 ratios (I 2.478, II 1.478, III 1, IV 0.730, rev 2.090), max ratio of converter at stall 2, possible manual selection, max speed 127 mph, 204 km/h; limited slip differential; Michelin TRX 220/55 VR x 390 tyres.

BMW 745i Automatic

BMW M 635 CSi

635 CSi

See 628 CSi, except for:

PRICE IN GB: £ 23,995*
PRICE EX WORKS: DM 66,150*

ENGINE 209.3 cu in, 3,430 cc (3.62 x 3.39 in, 92 x 86 mm); compression ratio: 10:1; max power (DIN): 218 hp (160 kW) at 5,200 rpm; max torque (DIN): 229 lb ft, 31.6 kg m (310 Nm) at 4,000 rpm; max engine rpm: 5,600; 63.6 hp/l (46.6 kW/l); Bosch Motronic II injection.

TRANSMISSION gearbox ratios: I 3.820, II 2.200, III 1.400, IV 1, V 0.810, rev 3.710; axle ratio: 3.070.

PERFORMANCE max speed: 142 mph, 229 km/h; power-weight ratio: 14.5 lb/hp (19.7 lb/kW), 6.6 kg/hp (8.9 kg/kW); acceleration: standing ¼ mile 15.3 sec.

ELECTRICAL EQUIPMENT digital engine and electronic ignition (Bosch Motronic).

DIMENSIONS AND WEIGHT weight: 3.153 lb, 1,430 kg.

OPTIONALS ZF automatic transmission, hydraulic torque converter and planetary gears with 4 ratios (I 2.478, II 1.478, III 1, IV 0.730, rev 2.090), max speed 137 mph, 221 km/h, consumption 32.5 m/imp gal, 27 m/US gal, 8.7 l x 100 km at 75 mph, 120 km/h.

M 635 CSi

See 628 CSi, except for:

PRICE EX WORKS: DM 89,500*

ENGINE 210.7 cu in, 3,453 cc (3.68 x 3.31 in, 93.4 x 84 mm); compression ratio: 10.5:1; max power (DIN): 286 hp (210 kW) at 6,500 rpm; max torque (DIN): 251 lb ft, 34.7 kg m (340 Nm) at 4,000-4,500 rpm; max engine rpm: 7,000; 82.8 hp/l (60.8 kW/l); valves: 4 per cylinder; camshafts: 2, overhead; Bosch Motronic II injection.

TRANSMISSION gearbox ratios: I 3.510, II 2.080, III 1.350, IV 1, V 0.810, rev 3.710; axle ratio: 3.730; tyres: Michelin TRX 220/55 VR x 390 (standard).

PERFORMANCE max speed: 158 mph, 255 km/h; power-weight ratio: 11.6 lb/hp (15.7 lb/kW), 5.2 kg/hp (7.1 kg/kW); carrying capacity: 772 lb, 350 kg; consumption: 27.7 m/imp gal, 23.1 m/US gal, 10.2 l x 100 km at 75 mph, 120 km/h.

ELECTRICAL EQUIPMENT 90 Ah battery; digital engine and electronic ignition (Bosch Motronic).

DIMENSIONS AND WEIGHT wheel base: 103.34 in, 262 cm; rear track:57.64 in, 146 cm; height: 53.31 in, 135 cm; weight: 3,307 lb, 1,500 kg.

CLASSIC-CAR JANSSEN
GERMANY FR

Gepard SS 100

PRICE EX WORKS: DM 43,000*

ENGINE Volkswagen, rear, 4 stroke; 4 cylinders, horizontally opposed; 96.7 cu in, 1,584 cc (3.37 x 2.72 in, 85.5 x 69 mm); compression ratio: 7.5:1; max power (DIN): 50 hp (37 kW) at 4,000 rpm; max torque (DIN): 78 lb ft, 10.8 kg m (106 Nm) at 2,800 rpm; max engine rpm: 4,500; 31.6 hp/l (23.2 kW/l); block with cast iron liners and light alloy fins, light alloy head; 4 crankshaft bearings; valves: overhead, push-rods and rockers; camshafts: 1, central, lower; lubrication: gear pump, filter in sump, oil cooler, 5.3 imp pt, 6.3 US pt, 3 l; 1 Solex 34 PICT 2 downdraught carburettor; fuel feed: mechanical pump; air-cooled.

TRANSMISSION driving wheels: rear; clutch: single dry plate; gearbox: mechanical; gears: 4, fully synchronized; ratios: I 3.780, II 2.060, III 1.260, IV 0.930, rev 4.010; lever: central; final drive: spiral bevel; axle ratio: 4.375; width of rims: 4.5"; tyres: 155 x 15.

PERFORMANCE max speed: 82 mph, 132 km/h; power-weight ratio: 37.9 lb/hp (51.2 lb/kW), 17.2 kg/hp (23.2 kg/kW); carrying capacity: 442 lb, 200 kg; speed in top at 1,000 rpm: 21.7 mph, 35 km/h; consumption: 30.7 m/imp gal, 25.6 m/US gal, 9.2 l x 100 km.

CHASSIS backbone platform; front suspension: independent, twin swinging longitudinal trailing arms, transverse laminated torsion bars, anti roll bar, telescopic dampers; rear: independent, semi-trailing arms, transverse compensating torsion bar, telescopic dampers.

STEERING worm and roller, telescopic damper; turns lock to lock: 2.60.

BRAKES front disc (diameter 10.91 in, 27.7 cm), rear drum; lining area: front 12.4 sq in, 80 sq cm, rear 55.5 sq in, 358 sq cm, total 67.9 sq in, 438 sq cm.

CLASSIC-CAR JANSSEN Gepard SS 100

ELECTRICAL EQUIPMENT 12 V; 36 Ah battery; 50 A alternator; Bosch distributor; 2 headlamps.

DIMENSIONS AND WEIGHT wheel base: 108.66 in, 276 cm; tracks: 56 in, 142 cm front, 57 in, 144 cm rear; length: 159.45 in, 405 cm; width: 62.99 in, 160 cm; height: 48.82 in, 124 cm; ground clearance: 9 in, 22.9 cm; weight: 1,896 lb, 860 kg; fuel tank: 8.8 imp gal, 10.6 US gal, 40 l.

BODY sports, in plastic material; 2 doors; 2 seats.

PRACTICAL INSTRUCTIONS fuel: 91 oct petrol; oil: engine 4.4 imp pt, 5.3 US pt, 2.5 l, SAE 10W-20 (winter), 20W-30 (summer), change every 3,100 miles, 5,000 km - gearbox and final drive 5.3 imp pt, 6.3 US pt, 3 l, SAE 90, change every 31,000 miles, 50,000 km; greasing: every 6,200 miles, 10,000 km, 4 points; spark plug: 175°; tappet clearances: inlet 0.004 in, 0.10 mm, exhaust 0.004 in, 0.10 mm; valve timing: 7°30' 37° 44°30' 4°.

OPTIONALS 3-speed automatic transmission; 185/70 x 15 or F 78 x 15 tyres; tonneau cover; wire wheels.

CLASSIC-CAR-OLDTIMERBAU
GERMANY FR

Bugatti 35 B / 55

PRICES EX WORKS:	DM
Bugatti 35 B	17,000*
Bugatti 55	17,900*

ENGINE Volkswagen, rear, 4 stroke; 4 cylinders, horizontally opposed; 96.7 cu in, 1,584 cc (3.37 x 2.72 in, 85.5 x 69 mm); compression ratio: 7.5:1; max power (DIN): 50 hp (37 kW) at 4,000 rpm; max torque (DIN): 78 lb ft, 10.8 kg m (106 Nm) at 2,800 rpm; max engine rpm: 4,500; 31.6 hp/l (23.2 kW/l); block with cast iron liners and light alloy fins, light alloy head; 4 crankshaft bearings; valves: overhead, push-rods and rockers; camshafts: 1, central, lower; lubrication: gear pump, filter in sump, oil cooler, 5.3 imp pt, 6.3 US pt, 3 l; 1 Solex 34 PICT 2 downdraught carburettor; fuel feed: mechanical pump; air-cooled.

TRANSMISSION driving wheels: rear; clutch: single dry plate; gearbox: mechanical; gears: 4, fully synchronized; ratios: I 3.780, II 2.060, III 1.260, IV 0.930, rev 4.010; lever: central; final drive: spiral bevel; axle ratio: 4.375; width of rims: 4.5"; tyres: 155 x 15.

PERFORMANCE max speed: about 84 mph, 135 km/h; power-weight ratio: 33.5 lb/hp (45.2 lb/kW), 15.2 kg/hp (20.5 kg/kW); carrying capacity: 442 lb, 200 kg; speed in top at 1,000 rpm: 21.7 mph, 35 km/h; consumption: 30.7 m/imp gal, 25.6 m/US gal, 9.2 l x 100 km.

CHASSIS backbone platform; front suspension: independent, twin swinging longitudinal trailing arms, transverse laminated torsion bars, anti-roll bar, telescopic dampers; rear: independent, semi-trailing arms, transverse compensating torsion bar, telescopic dampers.

STEERING worm and roller, telescopic damper; turns lock to lock: 2.60.

BRAKES front disc (diameter 10.91 in, 27.7 cm), rear drum; lining area: front 12.4 sq in, 80 sq cm, rear 55.5 sq in, 358 sq cm, total 67.9 sq in, 438 sq cm.

ELECTRICAL EQUIPMENT 12 V; 36 Ah battery; 50 A alternator; Bosch distributor; 2 headlamps.

DIMENSIONS AND WEIGHT wheel base: 94.50 in, 240 cm; tracks: 56 in, 142 cm front, 57 in, 144 cm rear; length: 153.54 in, 390 cm; width: 64.96 in, 165 cm; height: 50.39 in, 128 cm; ground clearance: 9 in, 22.9 cm; weight: 1,676 lb, 760 kg; fuel tank: 8.8 imp gal, 10.6 US gal, 40 l.

BODY sports, in plastic material; no doors; 2 seats.

PRACTICAL INSTRUCTIONS fuel: 91 oct petrol; oil: engine 4.4 imp pt, 5.3 US pt, 2.5 l, SAE 10W-20 (winter) 20W-30 (summer), change every 3,100 miles, 5,000 km - gearbox and final drive 5.3 imp pt, 6.3 US pt, 3 l, SAE 90, change every 31,000 miles, 50,000 km; greasing: every 6,200 miles, 10,000 km, 4 points; spark plug: 175°; tappet clearances: inlet 0.004 in, 0.10 mm, exhaust 0.004 in, 0.10 mm; valve timing: 7°30' 37° 44°30' 4°.

OPTIONALS 3-speed automatic transmission; 185/70 x 15 or F 78 x 15 tyres; tonneau cover; wire wheels.

CLASSIC-CAR OLDTIMERBAU Bugatti 35 B

FORD Fiesta Ghia Limousine

FORD — GERMANY FR

Fiesta Series

PRICES EX WORKS:	DM
1 2+1-dr Limousine	11,985*
2 L 2+1-dr Limousine	12,995*
3 S 2+1-dr Limousine	13,285*
4 Ghia 2+1-dr Limousine	14,517*
5 XR2 2+1-dr Limousine	—

Power team:	Standard for:	Optional for:
45 hp	1,2,4	—
50 hp	3	1,2,4
69 hp	—	2 to 4
96 hp	5	—
54 hp (diesel)	—	1,2,4

45 hp power team

ENGINE front, transverse, 4 stroke; 4 cylinders, vertical, in line; 58.4 cu in, 957 cc (2.91 x 2.19 in, 74 x 55.7 mm); compression ratio: 8.5:1; max power (DIN): 45 hp (33 kW) at 5,750 rpm; max torque (DIN): 50 lb ft, 6.9 kg m (68 Nm) at 3,700 rpm; max engine rpm: 6,000; 47 hp/l (34.5 kW/l); cast iron block and head; 3 crankshaft bearings; valves: overhead, in line, push-rods and rockers; camshafts: 1, side, chain-driven; lubrication: gear pump, full flow filter (cartridge), 5.6 imp pt, 6.8 US pt, 3.2 l; 1 Ford downdraught single barrel carburettor; fuel feed: mechanical pump; liquid-cooled, expansion tank, 9.5 imp pt, 11.4 US pt, 5.4 l, electric thermostatic fan.

TRANSMISSION driving wheels: front; clutch: single dry plate (diaphragm); gearbox: mechanical, in unit with final drive; gears: 4, fully synchronized; ratios: I 3.583, II 2.043, III 1.346, IV 0.951, rev 3.769; lever: central; final drive: spiral bevel; axle ratio: 4.056; width of rims: 4.5" - Ghia 5"; tyres: 135 SR x 13 - Ghia 155/70 SR x 13..

PERFORMANCE max speed: 84 mph, 136 km/h; power-weight ratio: 36.7 lb/hp (50.1 lb/kW), 16.7 kg/hp (22.7 kg/kW); carrying capacity: 937 lb, 425 kg; consumption: 39.8 m/imp gal, 33.1 m/US gal, 7.1 l x 100 km at 75 mph, 120 km/h.

CHASSIS integral; front suspension: independent, by McPherson, coil springs/telescopic damper struts, lower wishbones (trailing links); rear: rigid axle, swinging longitudinal trailing arms, upper oblique torque arms, Panhard rod, coil springs, telescopic dampers.

STEERING rack-and-pinion; turns lock to lock: 3.40.

BRAKES front disc (diameter 8.71 in, 22.1 cm), rear drum, dual circuit, rear compensator, servo; lining area: front 18.6 sq in, 120 sq cm, rear 26.4 sq in, 169.9 sq cm, total 45 sq in, 289.9 sq cm.

ELECTRICAL EQUIPMENT 12 V; 35 Ah battery; 45 A alternator; 2 headlamps - 2 halogen fog lamps (standard for Ghia only).

DIMENSIONS AND WEIGHT wheel base: 90.16 in, 229 cm; tracks: 53.82 in, 137 cm front, 51.97 in, 132 cm rear; length: 143.62 in, 365 cm - Ghia 146.14 in, 371 cm; width: 62.40 in, 158 cm; height: 52.52 in, 133 cm; ground clearance: 5.51 in, 14 cm; weight: 1,654 lb, 750 kg; turning circle: 33.8 ft, 10.3 m; fuel tank: 7.5 imp gal, 9 US gal, 34 l.

BODY saloon/sedan; 2+1 doors; 5 seats, separate front seats; folding rear seat; light alloy wheels (standard for Ghia only).

PRACTICAL INSTRUCTIONS fuel: 90 oct petrol; oil: engine 5.6 imp pt, 6.8 US pt, 3.2 l, SAE 10W-50, change every 6,200 miles, 10,000 km - gearbox and final drive 3.9 imp pt, 4.7 US pt, 2.2 l, SAE 90, change every 18,600 miles, 30,000 km; greasing: none; tyre pressure: front 23 psi, 1.6 atm, rear 26 psi, 1.8 atm

OPTIONALS 155/70 SR x 13 tyres; light alloy wheels (except for Ghia); headrests on front seats; tinted glass; sunroof; rear window wiper-washer; headlamps with wiper-washer; halogen fog lamps (except for Ghia); metallic spray.

50 hp power team

See 45 hp power team, except for:

ENGINE 68.2 cu in, 1,117 cc (2.91 x 2.56 in, 74 x 65 mm); compression ratio: 9.5:1; max power (DIN): 50 hp (37 kW) at 5,000 rpm; max torque (DIN): 62 lb ft, 8.5 kg m (83 Nm) at 2,700 rpm; max engine rpm: 5,500; 44.8 hp/l (33.1 kW/l); 1 Ford VV downdraught single barrel carburettor.

TRANSMISSION gearbox ratios: I 3.583, II 2.043, III 1.296, IV 0.878, rev 3.769; axle ratio: 3.583.

PERFORMANCE max speed: 88 mph, 142 km/h; power-weight ratio: 33.3 lb/hp (45 lb/kW), 15.1 kg/hp (20.4 kg/kW); consumption: 41.5 m/imp gal, 34.6 m/US gal, 6.8 l x 100 km at 75 mph, 120 km/h.

CHASSIS rear suspension: (for S only) anti-roll bar.

ELECTRICAL EQUIPMENT (standard for S only) halogen fog lamps.

DIMENSIONS AND WEIGHT weight: 1,665 lb, 755 kg.

BODY (standard for S only) rear window wiper-washer.

PRACTICAL INSTRUCTIONS fuel: 97 oct petrol.

OPTIONALS 5-speed mechanical gearbox (I 3.583, II 2.043, III 1.346, IV 0.951, V 0.756, rev 3.615), 3.842 axle ratio.

69 hp power team

See 45 hp power team, except for:

ENGINE 79.1 cu in, 1,296 cc (3.15 x 2.54 in, 80 x 64.5 mm); compression ratio: 9.5:1; max power (DIN): 69 hp (51 kW) at 6,000 rpm; max torque (DIN): 74 lb ft, 10.2 kg m (100 Nm) at 4,000 rpm; max engine rpm: 6,500; 53.2 hp/l (39.3 kW/l); 5 crankshaft bearings; valves: overhead, hydraulic tappets, CVH (compound valve hemispherical); camshafts: 1, overhead, cogged belt; lubrication: 6.2 imp pt, 7.4 US pt, 3.5 l; 1 Ford VV downdraught single barrel carburettor; liquid-cooled, 13.2 imp pt, 15.9 US pt, 7.5 l.

TRANSMISSION gears: 5, fully synchronized; ratios: I 3.583, II 2.043, III 1.346, IV 0.951, V 0.756, rev 3.615; axle ratio: 3.842 width of rims: 5"; tyres: 155/70 SR x 13 (standard).

PERFORMANCE max speed: 100 mph, 161 km/h; power-weight ratio: 24.8 lb/hp (33.5 lb/kW), 11.2 kg/hp (15.2 kg/kW); consumption: 40.4 m/imp gal, 33.6 m/US gal, 7 l x 100 km at 75 mph, 120 km/h.

CHASSIS rear suspension: anti-roll bar.

ELECTRICAL EQUIPMENT electronic ignition.

DIMENSIONS AND WEIGHT weight: 1,709 lb, 775 kg.

PRACTICAL INSTRUCTIONS fuel: 97 oct petrol, oil: engine 6.2 imp pt, 7.4 US pt, 3.5 l.

96 hp power team

See 45 hp power team, except for:

ENGINE 97.4 cu in, 1,597 cc (3.15 x 3.13 in, 80 x 79.5 mm); compression ratio: 9.5:1; max power (DIN): 96 hp (71 kW) at 6,000 rpm; max torque (DIN): 98 lb ft, 13.5 kg m (132 Nm) at 4,000 rpm; max engine rpm: 6,500; 60.1 hp/l (44.5 kW/l); 5 crankshaft bearings; valves: overhead, hydraulic tappets, CVH (compound valve hemispherical); camshafts: 1, overhead, cogged belt; lubrication: 6.2 imp pt, 7.4 US pt, 3.5 l; 1 Weber downdraught single barrel carburettor; liquid-cooled, 14.1 imp pt, 16.9 US pt, 8 l.

TRANSMISSION gears: 5, fully synchronized; ratios: I 3.154, II 1.913, III 1.275, IV 0.951, V 0.756, rev 3.615; axle ratio: 3.583; width of rims: 6"; tyres: 185/60 HR x 13.

PERFORMANCE max speed: 111 mph, 178 km/h; power-weight ratio: 19.3 lb/hp (26.1 lb/kW), 8.7 kg/hp (11.8 kg/kW); consumption: 37.7 m/imp gal, 31.4 m/US gal, 7.5 l x 100 km at 75 mph, 120 km/h.

CHASSIS rear suspension: anti-roll bar.

BRAKES front disc (diameter 9.41 in, 23.9 cm).

ELECTRICAL EQUIPMENT 43 Ah battery; electronic ignition.

DIMENSIONS AND WEIGHT tracks: 54.53 in, 138 cm front, 52.72 in, 134 cm rear; width: 63.78 in, 162 cm; weight: 1,852 lb, 840 kg; fuel tank: 8.8 imp gal, 10.6 US gal, 40 l.

PRACTICAL INSTRUCTIONS fuel: 97 oct petrol; oil: engine 6.2 imp pt, 7.4 US pt, 3.5 l.

54 hp (diesel) power team

See 45 hp power team, except for:

ENGINE diesel; 98.1 cu in, 1,608 cc (3.15 x 3.15 in, 80 x 80 mm); compression ratio: 21.5:1; max power (DIN): 54 hp (40 kW) at 4,800 rpm; max torque (DIN): 70 lb ft, 9.7 kg m (95 Nm) at 3,000 rpm; max engine rpm: 5,000; 33.6 hp/l (24.9 kW/l); 5 crankshaft bearings; valves: overhead, thimble tappets; camshafts: 1, overhead, cogged belt; lubrication: 8.8 imp pt, 10.6 US pt, 5 l; Bosch injection pump; liquid-cooled, 15 imp pt, 18 US pt, 8.5 l.

TRANSMISSION gears: 5, fully synchronized; ratios: I 3.583, II 1.913, III 1.275, IV 0.951, V 0.756, rev 3.615; axle ratio: 3.333; tyres: 155/70 SR x 13 (standard).

PERFORMANCE max speed: 91 mph, 147 km/h; power-weight ratio: 34.1 lb/hp (46 lb/kW), 15.5 kg/hp (20.9 kg/kW); consumption: 50.4 m/imp gal, 42 m/US gal, 5.6 l x 100 km at 75 mph, 120 km/h.

FORD Fiesta Ghia Limousine

FORD Escort L Limousine

ELECTRICAL EQUIPMENT 54 Ah battery.

DIMENSIONS AND WEIGHT weight: 1,841 lb, 835 kg.

PRACTICAL INSTRUCTIONS fuel: diesel; oil: engine 8.8 imp pt, 10.6 US pt, 5 l.

Escort Series

PRICES EX WORKS:	DM
1 2+1-dr Limousine	13,110*
2 4+1-dr Limousine	13,811*
3 2+1-dr Turnier	14,285*
4 4+1-dr Turnier	14,986*
5 L 2+1-dr Limousine	14,114*
6 L 4+1-dr Limousine	14,815*
7 L 2+1-dr Turnier	15,108*
8 L 4+1-dr Turnier	15,809*
9 GL 2+1-dr Limousine	15,960*
10 GL 4+1-dr Limousine	16,061*
11 GL 2+1-dr Turnier	17,703*
12 GL 4+1-dr Turnier	17,655*
13 Ghia 4+1-dr Limousine	17,761*
14 2-dr Cabriolet	—
15 XR 3 i 2+1-dr Limousine	20,328*

For GB prices, see price index.

Power team:	Standard for:	Optional for:
50 hp	1 to 8, 10	—
69 hp	9,12 to 14	1 to 8,10
79 hp	11,14	2,4,5,6,9,10,12,13
105 hp	14,15	—
54 hp (diesel)	—	1,2,3,5,6,8,9,10,12

50 hp power team

ENGINE front, transverse, 4 stroke; 4 cylinders, vertical, in line; 68.2 cu in, 1,117 cc (2.91 x 2.56 in, 74 x 65 mm); compression ratio: 9.5:1; max power (DIN): 50 hp (37 kW) at 5,000 rpm; max torque (DIN): 62 lb ft, 8.5 kg m (83 Nm) at 2,700 rpm; max engine rpm: 5,500; 44.8 hp/l (33.1 kW/l); cast iron block and head; 3 crankshaft bearings; valves: overhead, in line, push-rods and rockers; camshafts: 1, side, chain-driven; lubrication: gear pump, full flow filter (cartridge), 5.6 imp pt, 6.8 US pt, 3.2 l; 1 Ford VV downdraught single barrel carburettor; fuel feed: mechanical pump; semi-sealed circuit cooling, expansion tank, 11.8 imp pt, 14.2 US pt, 6.7 l, electric thermostatic fan.

TRANSMISSION driving wheels: front; clutch: single dry plate (diaphragm); gearbox: mechanical, in unit with final drive; gears: 4, fully synchronized; ratios: I 3.580, II 2.040, III 1.350, IV 0.950, rev 3.770; lever: central; final drive: spiral bevel; axle ratio: 3.840; width of rims: 4.5" - 5" (standard for GL Limousine and Turnier models only); tyres: 145 SR x 13 - 155 SR x 13 (standard for GL Limousine and Turnier models only).

PERFORMANCE max speed: 89 mph, 144 km/h - Turnier models 88 mph, 142 km/h; power-weight ratio: 4+1-dr Limousine 35,7 lb/hp (48.3 lb/kW), 16.2 kg/hp (21.9 kg/kW); carrying capacity: 1,025 lb, 465 kg; consumption: 39.8 m/imp gal, 33.1 m/US gal, 7.1 l x 100 km at 75 mph, 120 km/h.

CHASSIS integral; front suspension: independent, by McPherson, lower wishbones, coil springs/telescopic damper struts, anti-roll bar; rear: independent, lower wishbones, trailing radius arms, coil springs, telescopic dampers.

STEERING rack-and-pinion.

BRAKES front disc (diameter 9.45 in, 24 cm), rear drum, dual circuit, rear compensator, servo; lining area: front 23.4 sq in, 151 sq cm, rear 28.8 sq in, 186 sq cm, total 52.2 sq in, 337 sq cm.

ELECTRICAL EQUIPMENT 12 V; 35 Ah battery 45 A alternator; Motorcraft distributor; 2 headlamps.

DIMENSIONS AND WEIGHT wheel base: 94.57 in, 240 cm; tracks: 55.10 in, 140 cm front, 56.02 in, 142 cm rear; length: 156.30 in, 397 cm - Turnier models 158.78 in, 403 cm; width: 64.57 in, 164 cm; height: 54.33 in, 138 cm; ground clearance: 4.72 in, 12 cm; weight: 2+1-dr Limousine 1,742 lb, 790 kg - 4+1-dr Limousine 1,786 lb, 810 kg -2+1-dr Turnier 1,830 lb, 830 kg - 4+1-dr Turnier 1,874 lb, 850 kg - L 2+1-dr Limousine 1,786 lb, 810 kg - L 4+1-dr Limousine 1,830 lb, 830 kg - L 2+1-dr Turnier 1,830 lb, 830 kg - 4+1-dr Turnier 1,896 lb, 860 kg - GL 4+1-dr Limousine 1,874 lb, 850 kg; turning circle: 34.4 ft, 10.5 m; fuel tank: 10.6 imp gal, 12.7 US gal, 48 l.

BODY saloon/sedan - estate car/st. wagon; 2+1 or 4+1 doors; 5 seats, separate front seats.

PRACTICAL INSTRUCTIONS fuel: 97 oct petrol; oil: engine 5.6 imp pt, 6.8 US pt, 3.2 l, SAE 10W-30, change every 6,200 miles, 10,000 km - gearbox and final drive 4.9 imp pt, 5.9 US pt, 2.8 l, SAE 80W-90, change every 18,600 miles, 30,000 km; tyre pressure: front 23 psi, 1.6 atm, rear 26 psi, 1.8 atm.

OPTIONALS 5-speed mechanical gearbox (I 3.580, II 2.040, III 1.350, IV 0.950, V 0.760, rev 3.260), 4.060 axle ratio, consumption 40.9 m/imp gal, 34.1 m/US gal, 6.9 l x 100 km at 75 mph, 120 km/h; 155 SR x 13 tyres with 5" wide rims; halogen headlamps; tinted glass; light alloy wheels; sunroof; rear window wiper-washer; fog lamps; metallic spray.

69 hp power team

See 50 hp power team, except for:

ENGINE 79.08 cu in, 1,296 cc (3.15 x 2.54 in, 80 x 64.5 mm); compression ratio: 9.5:1; max power (DIN): 69 hp (51 kW) at 6,000 rpm; max torque (DIN): 74 lb ft, 10.2 kg m (100 Nm) at 3,500 rpm; 53.2 hp/l (39.4 kW/l); light alloy head; 5 crankshaft bearings; valves: overhead, hydraulic tappets, CVH (compound valve hemispherical); camshafts: 1, overhead, cogged belt; lubrication: 6.2 imp pt, 7.4 US pt, 3.5 l; 1 Ford VV downdraught single barrel carburettor; cooling: 13.4 imp pt, 16.1 US pt, 7.6 l.

TRANSMISSION axle ratio: 3.840; width of rims: 5" (standard); tyres: 155 SR x 13 (standard).

PERFORMANCE max speed: 98 mph, 157 km/h - Turnier models 96 mph, 155 km/h; power-weight ratio: GL 2+1-dr Limousine 27.2 lb/hp (36.7 lb/kW), 12.3 kg/hp (16.7 kg/kW);

FORD Escort L Turnier

carrying capacity: 992 lb, 450 kg; consumption: 36.7 m/imp gal, 30.5 m/US gal, 7.7 l x 100 km at 75 mph, 120 km/h.

ELECTRICAL EQUIPMENT contactless fully electronic distributor.

DIMENSIONS AND WEIGHT weight: GL 2+1-dr Limousine 1,874 lb, 850 kg - GL 4+1-dr Turnier 1,984 lb, 900 kg - Ghia 4+1-dr Limousine 1,940 lb, 880 kg - 2-dr Cabriolet 1,996 lb, 905 kg.

BODY saloon/sedan - estate car/st. wagon - cabriolet; 2, 2+1 or 4+1 doors.

PRACTICAL INSTRUCTIONS oil: engine 6.2 imp pt, 7.4 US pt, 3.5 l.

OPTIONALS 5-speed mechanical gearbox (I 3.580, II 2.040, III 1.350, IV 0.950, V 0.760, rev 3.620), consumption 37.7 m/imp gal, 31.4 m/US gal, 7.5 l x 100 km at 75 mph, 120 km/h.

79 hp power team

See 50 hp power team, except for:

ENGINE 97.45 cu in, 1,597 cc (3.15 x 3.13 in, 80 x 79.5 mm); compression ratio: 9.5:1; max power (DIN): 79 hp (58 kW) at 5,800 rpm; max torque (DIN): 92 lb ft, 12.7 kg m (125 Nm) at 3,000 rpm; 49.5 hp/l (36.3 kW/l); light alloy head; 5 crankshaft bearings; valves: overhead, hydraulic tappets, CVH (compound valve hemispherical); camshafts: 1, overhead, cogged belt; lubrication: 6.2 imp pt, 7.4 US pt, 3.5 l; 1 Weber downdraught single barrel carburettor; cooling: 13.7 imp pt, 16.5 US pt, 7.8 l.

TRANSMISSION gears: 5, fully synchronized; ratios: I 3.150, II 1.910, III 1.280, IV 0.950, V 0.760, rev 3.620; axle ratio: 3.580; width of rims: 5" (standard); tyres: 155 SR x 13 (standard).

PERFORMANCE max speed: 104 mph, 167 km/h - Turnier models 103 mph, 165 km/h; power-weight ratio: GL 2+1-dr Turnier 25 lb/hp (34 lb/kW), 11.3 kg/hp (15.4 kg/kW); carrying capacity: 1,003 lb, 455 kg; consumption: 36.7 m/imp gal, 30.5 m/US gal, 7.7 l x 100 km at 75 mph, 120 km/h.

ELECTRICAL EQUIPMENT 43 Ah battery; contactless fully electronic distributor.

DIMENSIONS AND WEIGHT weight: GL 2+1-dr Turnier 1,973 lb, 895 kg - 2+1-dr Cabriolet 2,018 lb, 915 kg.

BODY saloon/sedan - estate car/st. wagon - cabriolet; 2, 2+1 or 4+1 doors.

PRACTICAL INSTRUCTIONS oil: engine 6.2 imp pt, 7.4 US pt, 3.5 l.

OPTIONALS Ford ATX automatic transmission with 3 ratios (I 2.790, II 1.610, III 1, rev 1.970), 3.310 axle ratio, max speed 101 mph, 163 km/h, consumption 32.8 m/imp gal, 27.3 m/US gal, 8.6 l x 100 km at 75 mph, 120 km/h.

105 hp power team

See 50 hp power team, except for:

ENGINE 97.45 cu in, 1,597 cc (3.15 x 3.13 in, 80 x 79.5 mm); compression ratio: 9.5:1; max power (DIN): 105 hp (77 kW) at 6,000 rpm; max torque (DIN): 102 lb ft, 14.1 kg m (138 Nm) at 4,800 rpm; max engine rpm: 6,250; 65.7 hp/l (48.2 kW/l); light alloy head; 5 crankshaft bearings; valves: overhead, hydraulic tappets, CVH (compound valve hemispherical); camshafts: 1, overhead, cogged belt; lubrication: 6.8 imp pt, 8.1 US pt, 3.8 l, oil cooler; Bosch K-Jetronic injection; cooling: 13.7 imp pt, 16.5 US pt, 7.8.

TRANSMISSION gears: 5, fully synchronized; ratios: I 3.150, II 1.910, III 1.280, IV 0.950, V 0.760, rev 3.620; axle ratio: 4.290; width of rims: 6"; tyres: 185/60 HR x 14.

PERFORMANCE max speed: 116 mph, 186 km/h; power-weight ratio: XR 3 i 2+1-dr Limousine 19.3 lb/hp (26.3 lb/kW), 8.8 kg/hp (11.9 kg/kW); carrying capacity: 893 lb, 405 kg; consumption: 34.9 m/imp gal, 29 m/US gal, 8.1 l x 100 km at 75 mph, 120 km/h.

CHASSIS front suspension: reinforced anti-roll bar.

ELECTRICAL EQUIPMENT 43 Ah battery; 55 A alternator; contactless fully electronic distributor.

DIMENSIONS AND WEIGHT height: 54.05 in, 137 cm; weight: XR3 i 2+1-dr Limousine 2,029 lb, 920 kg - 2-dr Cabriolet 2,139 lb, 970 kg.

BODY saloon/sedan - cabriolet; 2 or 2+1 doors.

PRACTICAL INSTRUCTIONS oil: engine 6.8 imp pt, 8.1 US pt, 3.8 l.

OPTIONALS light alloy wheels; 52 Ah battery; halogen headlamps; sunroof; electric windows.

54 hp (diesel) power team

See 50 hp power team, except for:

ENGINE diesel; 98.1 cu in, 1,608 cc (3.15 x 3.15 in, 80 x 80 mm); compression ratio:21.5:1; max power (DIN): 54 hp (40 kW) at 4,800 rpm; max torque (DIN): 70 lb ft, 9.7 kg m (95 Nm) at 3,000 rpm; max engine rpm: 5,000; 33.6 hp/l (24.9 kW/l); 5 crankshaft bearings; valves: overhead, thimble tappets; cam-

54 HP (DIESEL) POWER TEAM

shafts: 1, overhead, cogged belt; lubrication: 8.8 imp pt, 10.6 US pt, 5 l, Bosch injection pump; liquid-cooled, 15 imp pt, 18 US pt, 8.5 l.

TRANSMISSION gears: 5, fully synchronized; ratios: I 3.580, II 1.910, III 1.280, IV 0.950, V 0.760, rev 3.620; axle ratio: 3.580; width of rims: 5" (standard); tyres: 155 SR x 13 (standard).

PERFORMANCE max speed: 91 mph, 146 km/h; power-weight ratio: 4+1-dr Limousine 36.3 lb/hp (39 lb/kW), 16.5 kg/hp (22.2 kg/kW); consumption: 48.7 m/imp gal, 40.6 m/US gal, 5.8 l x 100 km at 75 mph, 120 km/h.

ELECTRICAL EQUIPMENT 66 Ah battery.

DIMENSIONS AND WEIGHT weight: 2+1-dr Limousine 1,918 lb, 870 kg - 4+1-dr Limousine 1,962 lb, 890 kg - 2+1-dr Turnier 2,007 lb, 910 kg - L 2+1-dr Limousine 1,962 lb, 890 kg - L 4+1-dr Limousine 2,007 lb, 910 kg - L 4+1-dr Turnier 2,073 lb, 940 kg - GL 2+1-dr Limousine 2,007 lb, 910 kg - GL 4+1-dr Limousine 2,051 lb, 930 kg - GL 4+1-dr Turnier 2,117 lb, 960 kg.

PRACTICAL INSTRUCTIONS fuel: diesel; oil: engine 8.8 imp pt, 10.6 US pt, 5 l.

FORD Escort Cabriolet

Orion Series

PRICES EX WORKS:	DM
1 1.3 GL 4-dr Limousine	**17,085***
2 1.6 GL 4-dr Limousine	**17,835***
3 1.6 Injection 4-dr Limousine	**21,125***
4 1.6 Diesel 4-dr Limousine	**19,015***

Power team:	Standard for:	Optional for:
69 hp	1	—
79 hp	2	—
105 hp	3	—
54 hp (diesel)	4	—

69 hp power team

ENGINE front, transverse, 4 stroke; 4 cylinders, vertical, in line; 79.08 cu in, 1,296 cc (3.15 x 2.54 in, 80 x 64.5 mm); compression ratio: 9.5:1; max power (DIN): 69 hp (51 kW) at 6,000 rpm; max torque (DIN): 74 lb ft, 10.2 kg m (100 Nm) at 3,500 rpm; max engine rpm: 6,500; 53.2 hp/l (39.4 kW/l); cast iron block, light alloy head; 5 crankshaft bearings; valves: overhead, hydraulic tappets, CVH (compound valve hemispherical); camshafts: 1, overhead, cogged belt; lubrication: gear pump, full flow filter (cartridge), 6.2 imp pt, 7.4 US pt, 3.5 l; 1 Ford VV downdraught single barrel carburettor; fuel feed: mechanical pump; liquid-cooled, expansion tank, 13.4 imp pt, 16.1 US pt, 7.6 l, electric thermostatic fan.

TRANSMISSION driving wheels: front; clutch: single dry plate (diaphragm); gearbox: mechanical; in unit with final drive; gears: 4, fully synchronized; ratios: I 3.580, II 2.040, III 1.350, IV 0.950, rev 3.770; lever: central; final drive: spiral bevel; axle ratio: 3.840; width of rims: 5"; tyres: 155 SR x 13.

PERFORMANCE max speed: 98 mph, 157 km/h; power-weight ratio: 28 lb/hp (37.8 lb/kW), 12.7 kg/hp (17.2 kg/kW); carrying capacity: 937 lb, 425 kg; speed in top at 1,000 rpm: 16.3 mph, 26.2 km/h; consumption: 36.7 m/imp gal, 30.5 m/US gal, 7.7 l x 100 km at 75 mph, 120 km/h.

CHASSIS integral; front suspension: independent, by McPherson, lower wishbones, coil springs/telescopic damper struts; rear: independent, lower wishbones, trailing radius arms, coil springs, telescopic dampers.

STEERING rack-and-pinion.

BRAKES front disc, (diameter 9.45 in, 24 cm), rear drum, dual circuit, rear compensator, servo; lining area: front 23.4 sq in 151 sq cm, rear 28.8 sq in, 186 sq cm, total 52.2 sq in, 337 sq cm.

ELECTRICAL EQUIPMENT 12 V; 35 Ah battery; 45 A alternator; contactless fully electronic distributor; 2 halogen headlamps.

DIMENSIONS AND WEIGHT wheel base: 94.57 in, 240 cm; tracks: 55.12 in, 140 cm front, 56.02 in, 142 cm rear; lenght: 165.08 in, 419 cm; width: 64.57 in, 164 cm; height: 54.92 in, 139 cm; weight: 1,929 lb, 875 kg; turning circle: 34.8 ft, 10.6 m; fuel tank: 10.6 imp gal, 12.7 US gal, 48 l.

BODY saloon/sedan; 4 doors; 5 seats, separate front seats; reclining backrests, headrests; heated rear window.

PRACTICAL INSTRUCTIONS fuel: 97 oct petrol; oil: engine 6.2 imp pt, 7.4 US pt, 3.5 l, SAE 10W-50, change every 6,200 miles, 10,000 km - gearbox and final drive 4.9 imp pt, 5.9 US pt, 2.8 l, SAE 80W-90, change every 18,600 miles, 30,000 km; greasing: none; tyre pressure: front 23 psi, 1.6 atm, rear 26 psi, 1.8 atm.

OPTIONALS 5-speed mechanical gearbox (I 3.580, II 2.040, III 1.350, IV 0.950, V 0.760, rev 3.770), consumption 40.4 m/imp gal, 33.6 m/US gal, 7 l x 100 km at 75 mph, 120 km/h; electric windows; sunroof; metallic spray.

79 hp power team

See 69 hp power team, except for:

ENGINE 97.45 cu in, 1,597 cc (3.15 x 3.13 in, 80 x 79,5 mm); max power (DIN): 79 hp (58 kW) at 5,800 rpm; max torque (DIN): 92 lb ft, 12.7 kg m (125 Nm) at 3,000 rpm; 49.5 hp/l (36.3 kW/l); liquid-cooled, 13.7 imp pt, 16.5 US pt, 7.8 l.

TRANSMISSION gears: 5, fully synchronized; ratios: 3.150, II 1.910, III 1.280, IV 0.950, V 0.760, rev 3.620; axle ratio: 3.580.

PERFORMANCE max speed: 104 mph, 167 km/h; power-weight ratio: 24.8 lb/hp (33.8 lb/kW), 11.3 kg/hp (15.3 kg/kW); speed in top at 1,000 rpm: 17.3 mph, 27.8 km/h; consumption: 40.4 m/imp gal, 33.6 m/US gal, 7 l x 100 km at 75 mph, 120 km/h.

ELECTRICAL EQUIPMENT 43 Ah battery.

DIMENSIONS AND WEIGHT weight: 1,962 lb, 890 kg.

OPTIONALS Ford ATX automatic transmission with 3 ratios (I 2.790, II 1.610, III 1, rev 1.970), 3.310 axle ratio, max speed 101 mph, 163 km/h, consumption 34 m/imp gal, 28.3 m/US gal, 8.3 l x 100 km at 75 mph, 120 km/h.

105 hp power team

See 69 hp power team, except for:

ENGINE 97.5 cu in, 1,597 cc (3.15 x 3.13 in, 80 x 79.5 mm); max power (DIN): 105 hp (77 kW) at 6,000 rpm; max torque (DIN): 102 lb ft, 14.1 kg m (138 Nm) at 4,800 rpm; max engine rpm: 6,250; 65.7 hp/l (48.2 kW/l); lubrication: 6.8 imp pt, 8.1 US pt, 3.8 l, oil cooler; Bosch K-Jetronic injection; liquid-cooled, 13.7 imp pt, 16.5 US pt, 7.8 l.

TRANSMISSION gears: 5, fully synchronized; ratios: I 3.150, II 1.910, III 1.280, IV 0.950, V 0.760, rev 3.620; width of rims: 5.5"; tyres: 175/70 HR x 13.

PERFORMANCE max speed: 116 mph, 186 km/h; power-weight ratio: 19.3 lb/hp (26.3 lb/kW), 8.8 kg/hp (11.9 kg/kW).

CHASSIS front suspension: reinforced anti-roll bar; rear: anti-roll bar.

ELECTRICAL EQUIPMENT 43 Ah battery; 55 A alternator.

DIMENSIONS AND WEIGHT weight: 2,029 lb, 920 kg.

PRACTICAL INSTRUCTIONS oil: engine 6.8 imp pt, 8.1 US pt, 3.8 l.

54 hp (diesel) power team

See 69 hp power team, except for:

ENGINE diesel; 98.1 cu in, 1,608 cc (3.15 x 3.15 in, 80 x 80 mm); compression ratio: 21.5:1; max power (DIN): 54 hp (40 kW) at 4,800 rpm; max torque (DIN): 70 lb ft, 9.7 kg m (95 Nm) at 3,000 rpm; max engine rpm: 5,000; 33.6 hp/l (24.9 kW/l); valves: overhead, thimble tappets; lubrication: 8.8 imp pt, 10.6 US pt, 5 l; Bosch injection pump; liquid-cooled, 15 imp pt, 18 US pt, 8.5 l.

TRANSMISSION gears: 5, fully synchronized (standard); ratios: I 3.580, II 2.040, III 1.350, IV 0.950, V 0.760, rev 3.770; axle ratio: 3.580.

PERFORMANCE max speed: 93 mph, 150 km/h; power-weight ratio: 38.2 lb/hp (51.6 lb/kW), 17.3 kg/hp (23.4 kg/kW); consumption: 52.3 m/imp gal, 43.6 m/US gal, 5.4 l x 100 km at 75 mph, 120 km/h.

ELECTRICAL EQUIPMENT 66 Ah battery.

DIMENSIONS AND WEIGHT weight: 2,062 lb, 935 kg.

PRACTICAL INSTRUCTIONS fuel: diesel; oil: engine 8.8 imp pt, 10.6 US pt, 5 l.

Sierra Series

PRICES EX WORKS:	DM
1 2+1-dr Limousine	**15,995***
2 4+1-dr Limousine	**17,350***
3 4+1-dr Turnier	**18,250***
4 L 2+1-dr Limousine	**17,275***
5 L 4+1-dr Limousine	**18,630***
6 L 4+1-dr Turnier	**19,530***
7 GL 4+1-dr Limousine	**19,965***
8 GL 4+1-dr Turnier	**20,865***
9 Ghia 4+1-dr Limousine	**22,600***
10 Ghia 4+1-dr Turnier	**24,130***
11 XR 4 i 2+1-dr Limousine	**28,601***

Power team:	Standard for:	Optional for:
75 hp	1 to 9	—
90 hp	—	4 to 10
105 hp	10	4 to 9
114 hp	—	7 to 10
150 hp	11	—
67 hp (diesel)	—	1 to 8

75 hp power team

ENGINE front, 4 stroke; 4 cylinders, vertical, in line; 97.2 cu in, 1,593 cc (3.45 x 2.60 in, 87.7 x 66 mm); compression ratio: 9.2:1; max power (DIN): 75 hp (55 kW) at 5,300 rpm; max torque (DIN): 88 lb ft, 12.2 kg m (120 Nm) at 2,900 rpm; max engine rpm: 5,800; 47.1 hp/l (34.5 kW/l); cast iron block and head; 5 crankshaft bearings; valves: overhead, Vee-slanted, rockers; camshafts: 1, overhead, cogged belt; lubrication: gear pump, full flow filter (cartridge), 6.6 imp pt, 7.9 US pt, 3.7 l; 1 Ford downdraught single barrel carburettor; fuel feed: mechanical pump; semi-sealed circuit cooling, expansion tank, 14.1 imp pt, 16.9 US pt, 8 l, electric thermostatic fan.

TRANSMISSION driving wheels: rear; clutch: single dry plate (diaphragm); gearbox: mechanical; gears: 4, fully synchronized; ratios: I 3.340, II 1.990, III 1.420, IV 1, rev 3.870; lever: central; final drive: hypoid bevel; axle ratio: 3.620; width of rims: 5.5"; tyres: 165 SR x 13 - Turnier models 175 SR x 13 - Ghia Limousine 185/70 SR x 13.

PERFORMANCE max speed: 102 mph, 165 km/h; power-weight ratio: L limousine 29.7 lb/hp (40.5 lb/kW), 13.5 kg/hp (18.4 kg/kW); carrying capacity: 1,080 lb, 490 kg; consumption: 34.9 m/imp gal, 29 m/US gal, 8.1 l x 100 km at 75 mph, 120 km/h.

CHASSIS integral; front suspension: independent, by McPherson, lower wishbones, coil springs/telescopic damper struts, anti-roll bar; rear: independent, lower wishbones, trailing radius arms, coil springs, telescopic dampers, anti-roll bar.

STEERING rack-and-pinion.

BRAKES front disc (diameter 9.43 in, 23.9 cm), rear drum, dual circuit, rear compensator, servo.

ELECTRICAL EQUIPMENT 12 V; 35 Ah battery; 55 A alternator; transistorized ignition; 2 headlamps - Ghia Limousine 4 halogen headlamps.

DIMENSIONS AND WEIGHT wheel base: limousines 102.68 in, 261 cm; tracks: 57.17 in, 145 cm front, 57.80 in, 147 cm - Turnier models 57.44 in, 146 cm rear; length: Limousines and L limousines 172.99 in, 439 cm - GL Limousine 173.54 in, 441 cm - Ghia Limousine 174.21 in, 442 cm - Turnier 176.81 in, 449 cm - GL Turnier 177.36 in, 450 cm; width: limousines and L limousines 67.05 in, 170 cm - GL Limousine 67.72 in, 172 cm - Ghia Limousine 67.91 in, 172 cm - Turnier 67.40 in, 171 cm - GL Turnier 68.07 in, 173 cm; height: limousines 55.43 in, 141 cm - Turnier models 56.61 in, 144 cm; weight: limousines 2,183 lb, 990 kg - L limousines 2,227 lb, 1,010 kg - GL Limousine 2,271 lb, 1,030 kg - Ghia Limousine 2,337 lb, 1,060 kg - Turnier 2,293 lb, 1,040 kg - L Turnier 2,348 lb, 1,065 kg - GL Turnier

FORD Orion 1.6 Injection Limousine

2,381 lb, 1,080 kg; turning circle: 34.8 ft, 10.6 m; fuel tank: 13.2 imp gal, 15.8 US gal, 60 l.

BODY saloon/sedan, 2+1 or 4+1 doors - estate car/st. wagon, 4+1 doors; 5 seats, separate front seats; heated rear window.

PRACTICAL INSTRUCTIONS fuel: 98 oct petrol; oil: engine 6.6 imp pt, 7.9 US pt, 3.7 l, SAE 15W-50, change every 6,200 miles, 10,000 km - gearbox 1.4 imp pt, 1.7 US pt, 0.8 l, SAE 80 EP, change every 12,400 miles, 20,000 km - final drive 1.8 imp pt, 2.1 US pt, 1 l, change every 12,400 miles, 20,000 km; greasing: none; tyre pressure: front 26 psi, 1.8 atm, rear 26 psi, 1.8 atm.

VARIATIONS

(only for export)
ENGINE 78.9 cu in, 1,294 cc (3.11 x 2.60 in, 79 x 66 mm), 9:1 compression ratio.
TRANSMISSION gearbox ratios I 3.660, II 2.180, III 1.420, IV 1, rev 3.870, 3.770 axle ratio.
PERFORMANCE max speed 94 mph, 152 km/h.

OPTIONALS E 4-speed mechanical gearbox (I 3.580, II 2.010, III 1.400, IV 1, rev 3.320), 3.380 axle ratio, consumption 38.2 m/imp gal, 31.8 m/US gal, 7.4 l x 100 km at 75 mph, 120 km/h; E 5-speed mechanical gearbox (I 3.650, II 1.970, III 1.370, IV 1, V 0.820, rev 3.660), 3.380 axle ratio, consumption 40.4 m/imp gal, 33.6 m/US gal, 7 l x 100 km at 75 mph, 120 km/h; 5-speed mechanical gearbox (I 3.650, II 1.970, III 1.370, IV 1, V 0.820, rev 3.660), consumption 36.7 m/imp gal, 30.3 m/US gal, 7.7 l x 100 km at 75 mph, 120 km/h; Ford C3 automatic transmission with 3 ratios (I 2.474, II 1.474, III 1, rev 2.111), max speed 98 mph, 157 km/h, consumption 33.2 m/imp gal, 27.7 m/US gal, 8.5 l x 100 km at 75 mph, 120 km/h; 185/70 or 195/70 R x 13 tyres; limited slip differential; electric windows; sunroof; 55 Ah battery.

90 hp power team

See 75 hp power team, except for:

ENGINE 6 cylinders, Vee-slanted at 60°; 121.9 cu in, 1,998 cc (3.31 x 2.37 in, 84 x 60.1 mm); compression ratio: 9:1; max power (DIN): 90 hp (66 kW) at 5,000 rpm; max torque (DIN): 111 lb ft, 15.3 kg m (150 Nm) at 3,000 rpm; 45 hp/l (33 kW/l); 4 crankshaft bearings; camshafts: 1, at centre of Vee; lubrication: 7.4 imp pt, 8.9 US pt, 4.2 l; 1 Weber downdraught twin barrel carburettor; cooling: 15 imp pt, 18 US pt, 8.5 l.

TRANSMISSION gearbox ratios: I 3.650, II 1.970, III 1.370, IV 1, rev 3.660; axle ratio: 3.380 - Turnier models 3.620; width of rims: 5.5"; tyres: 165 HR x 13 - Turnier models 175 HR x 13 - Ghia models 185/70 HR x 13.

PERFORMANCE max speed: 109 mph, 176 km/h; power-weight ratio: L limousines 26.7 lb/hp (36.4 lb/kW), 12.1 kg/hp (16.5 kg/kW); consumption: 33.6 m/imp gal, 28 m/US gal, 8.4 l x 100 km at 75 mph, 120 km/h.

ELECTRICAL EQUIPMENT 44 Ah battery.

DIMENSIONS AND WEIGHT weight: L limousines 2,403 lb, 1,090 kg - GL Limousine 2,448 lb, 1,110 kg - Ghia Limousine 2,514 lb, 1,140 kg - L Turnier 2,503 lb, 1,135 kg - GL Turnier 2,536 lb, 1,150 kg - Ghia Turnier 2,613 lb, 1,185 kg.

PRACTICAL INSTRUCTIONS oil: engine 7.4 imp pt, 8.9 US pt, 4.2 l.

OPTIONALS 5-speed mechanical gearbox (I 3.650, II 1.970, III 1.370, IV 1, V 0.820, rev 3.660), consumption 35.8 m/imp gal, 29.8 m/US gal, 7.9 l x 100 km at 75 mph, 120 km/h; Ford C3 automatic transmission with 3 ratios (I 2.474, II 1.474, III 1, rev 2.111), max speed 104 mph, 168 km/h, consumption 29.1 m/imp gal, 24.2 m/US gal, 9.7 l x 100 km at 75 mph, 120 km/h, power steering.

105 hp power team

See 75 hp power team, except for:

ENGINE 121.6 cu in, 1,993 cc (3.89 x 3.03 in, 90.8 x 76.9 mm); max power (DIN): 105 hp (77 kW) at 5,200 rpm; max torque (DIN): 116 lb ft, 16 kg m (157 Nm) at 4,000 rpm; 52.7 hp/l (38.6 kW/l); 1 Weber downdraught single barrel carburettor.

TRANSMISSION gearbox ratios: I 3.650, II 1.970, III 1.370, IV 1, rev 3.600; axle ratio: 3.380; width of rims: 5.5"; tyres: 195/70 HR x 13 - limousines 165 HR x 13 - Ghia Limousine 185/70 HR x 13.

PERFORMANCE max speed: 115 mph, 185 km/h; power-weight ratio: Ghia Turnier 23.9 lb/hp (32.6 lb/kW), 10.9 kg/hp (14.8 kg/kW); consumption: Ghia Turnier 34 m/imp gal, 28.3 m/US gal, 8.3 l x 100 km at 75 mph, 120 km/h.

ELECTRICAL EQUIPMENT 44 Ah battery.

DIMENSIONS AND WEIGHT weight: L limousines 2,304 lb, 1,045 kg - GL Limousine 2,348 lb, 1,065 kg - Ghia Limousine 2,414 lb, 1,095 kg - L Turnier 2,403 lb, 1,090 kg - GL Turnier 2,437 lb, 1,105 kg - Ghia Turnier 2,514 lb, 1,140 kg.

OPTIONALS 5-speed mechanical gearbox (I 3.650, II 1.970, III 1.370, IV 1, V 0.820, rev 3.660), consumption Ghia Turnier 36.7 m/imp gal, 30.5 m/US gal, 7.7 l x 100 km at 75 mph, 120 km/h; Ford C3 automatic transmission with 3 ratios (I 2.474, II 1.474, III 1, rev 2.111), max speed 110 mph, 177 km/h, consumption Ghia Turnier 29.4 m/imp gal, 24.5 m/US gal, 9.6 l x 100 km at 75 mph, 120 km/h; power steering.

114 hp power team

See 75 hp power team, except for:

ENGINE 6 cylinders, Vee-slanted at 60°; 139.9 cu in, 2,294 cc (3.54 x 2.37 in, 90 x 60.1 mm); compression ratio: 9:1; max power (DIN): 114 hp (84 kW) at 5,300 rpm; max torque (DIN): 130 lb ft, 18 kg m (176 Nm) at 3,000 rpm; 49.6 hp/l (37 kW/l); 4 crankshaft bearings; camshafts: 1, at centre of Vee; lubrication: 7.4 imp pt, 8.9 US pt, 4.2 l; 1 Solex 35/35 EEIT downdraught twin barrel carburettor; cooling: 15 imp pt, 18 US pt, 8.5 l.

TRANSMISSION gearbox ratios: I 3.650, II 1.970, III 1.370, IV 1, rev 3.660; axle ratio: 3.380; width of rims: 5.5"; tyres: 185/70 SR x 13 - Turnier models 175 HR x 13.

PERFORMANCE max speed: 118 mph, 190 km/h; power-weight ratio: GL Limousine 21.6 lb/hp (29.3 lb/kW), 9.8 kg/hp (13.3 kg/kW); consumption: 32.5 m/imp gal, 27 m/US gal, 8.7 l x 100 km at 75 mph, 120 km/h.

ELECTRICAL EQUIPMENT 44 Ah battery.

DIMENSIONS AND WEIGHT weight: GL Limousine 2,459 lb, 1,115 kg - Ghia Limousine 2,525 lb, 1,145 kg - GL Turnier 2,547 lb, 1,155 kg - Ghia Turnier 2,624 lb, 1,190 kg.

BODY saloon/sedan, estate car/st. wagon; 4+1 doors.

PRACTICAL INSTRUCTIONS oil: engine 7.4 imp pt, 8.9 US pt, 4.2 l.

OPTIONALS 5-speed mechanical gearbox (I 3.650, II 1.970, III 1.370, IV 1, V 0.820, rev 3.660), consumption 35.3 m/imp gal, 29.4 m/US gal, 8 l x 100 km at 75 mph, 120 km/h; Ford C3 automatic transmission with 3 ratios (I 2.474, II 1.474, III 1, rev 2.111), max speed 113 mph, 182 km/h, consumption 29.1 m/imp gal, 24.2 m/US gal, 9.7 l x 100 km at 75 mph, 120 km/h; power steering.

150 hp power team

See 75 hp power team, except for:

ENGINE 6 cylinders, Vee-slanted at 60°; 170.4 cu in, 2,792 cc (3.66 x 2.70 in, 93 x 68.5 mm); max power (DIN): 150 hp (110 kW) at 5,700 rpm; max torque (DIN): 159 lb ft, 22 kg m (216 Nm) at 3,800 rpm; max engine rpm: 6,200; 53.7 hp/l (39.4 kW/l); 4 crankshaft bearings; camshafts: 1, at centre of Vee; valves: overhead, push-rods and rockers; lubrication: 7.4 imp pt, 8.9 US pt, 4.2 l; Bosch K-Jetronic injection; cooling: 15 imp pt, 18 US pt, 8.5 l.

TRANSMISSION gears: 5, fully synchronized; ratios: I 3.360, II 1.810, III 1.260, IV 1, V 0.820, rev 3.360; axle ratio: 3.620; tyres: 195/60 VR x 14.

PERFORMANCE max speed: 130 mph, 210 km/h; power-weight ratio: 17.3 lb/hp (23.6 lb/kW), 7.8 kg/hp (10.7 kg/kW); consump-

FORD Orion 1.6 Injection Limousine

FORD Sierra L Limousine

FORD Sierra L Turnier

150 HP POWER TEAM

tion: 29.4 m/imp gal, 24.5 m/US gal, 9.6 l x 100 km at 75 mph, 120 km/h.

ELECTRICAL EQUIPMENT 44 Ah battery; 70 A alternator; 4 halogen headlamps.

DIMENSIONS AND WEIGHT weight: 2,591 lb, 1,175 kg.

BODY saloon/sedan; 2+1 doors; electric windows (standard); light alloy wheels.

PRACTICAL INSTRUCTIONS oil: engine 7.4 imp pt, 8.9 US pt, 4.2 l.

67 hp (diesel) power team

See 75 hp power team, except for:

ENGINE Peugeot, diesel; 140.6 cu in, 2,304 cc (3.70 x 3.27 in, 94 x 83 mm); compression ratio: 22.2:1; max power (DIN): 67 hp (49 kW) at 4,200 rpm; max torque (DIN): 103 lb ft, 14.2 kg m (139 Nm) at 2,000 rpm; 29.1 hp/l (21.3 kW/l); light alloy head; valves: overhead, in line, push-rods and rockers; camshafts: 1, side; lubrication: 9.9 imp pt, 11.8 US pt, 5.6 l; Rotodiesel injection pump; cooling: 16.7 imp pt, 20.1 US pt, 9.5 l.

TRANSMISSION gears: 5, fully synchronized; ratios: I 3.910, II 2.320, III 1.400, IV 1, V 0.820, rev 3.660; axle ratio: 3.140; tyres: 165 SR x 13 - Turnier models 175 SR x 13.

PERFORMANCE max speed: 96 mph, 155 km/h; power-weight ratio: L limousines 38.7 lb/hp (52.9 lb/kW), 17.5 kg/hp (24 kg/kW); consumption: 42.2 m/imp gal, 35.1 m/US gal, 6.7 l x 100 km at 75 mph, 120 km/h.

ELECTRICAL EQUIPMENT 88 Ah battery.

PRACTICAL INSTRUCTIONS fuel: diesel; oil: engine 9.9 imp pt, 11.8 US pt, 5.6 l.

OPTIONALS power steering.

Capri Series

PRICES EX WORKS:		DM
1	GT 2+1-dr Coupé	16,732*
2	S 2+1-dr Coupé	19,637*
3	2.8 Injection 2+1-dr Coupé	28,601*

Power team:	Standard for:	Optional for:
101 hp	1	—
114 hp	2	1
160 hp	3	—

101 hp power team

ENGINE front, 4 stroke; 4 cylinders, vertical, in line; 121.6 cu in, 1,993 cc (3.89 x 3.03 in, 90.8 x 76.9 mm); compression ratio: 9.2:1; max power (DIN): 101 hp (74 kW) at 5,200 rpm; max torque (DIN): 113 lb ft, 15.6 kg m (153 Nm) at 4,000 rpm; max engine rpm: 6,000; 50.7 hp/l (37.8 kW/l); cast iron block and head; 5 crankshaft bearings; valves: overhead, Vee-slanted, rockers; camshafts: 1, overhead, cogged belt; lubrication: rotary pump, full flow filter (cartridge), 6.5 imp pt, 7.8 US pt, 3.7 l; 1 Weber 32/36 DGAV downdraught single barrel carburettor; fuel feed: mechanical pump; liquid-cooled, 10.7 imp pt, 12.9 US pt, 6.1 l, electric thermostatic fan.

TRANSMISSION driving wheels: rear; clutch: single dry plate (diaphragm); gearbox: mechanical; gears: 5, fully synchronized; ratios: I 3.650, II 1.970, III 1.370, IV 1, V 0.825, rev 3.370; lever: central; final drive: hypoid bevel; axle ratio: 3.440; width of rims: 5.5"; tyres: 185/70 HR x 13.

PERFORMANCE max speed: 111 mph, 179 km/h; power-weight ratio: 22.5 lb/hp (30.7 lb/kW), 10.2 kg/hp (13.9 kg/kW); carrying capacity: 838 lb, 380 kg; speed in top at 1,000 rpm: 21.4 mph, 34.4 km/h; consumption: 34.4 m/imp gal, 28.7 m/US gal, 8.2 l x 100 km at 75 mph, 120 km/h.

CHASSIS integral; front suspension: independent, by McPherson, coil springs/telescopic damper struts, lower transverse arm, anti-roll bar; rear: rigid axle, semi-elliptic leafsprings, rubber springs, anti-roll bar, telescopic dampers.

STEERING rack-and-pinion.

BRAKES front disc (diameter 9.61 in, 24.4 cm), rear drum, servo; lining area: front 17.4 sq in, 151 sq cm, rear 45.4 sq in, 293 sq cm, total 62.8 sq in, 444 sq cm.

ELECTRICAL EQUIPMENT 44 Ah battery; 55 A alternator; Motorcraft distributor; 2 halogen headlamps.

DIMENSIONS AND WEIGHT wheel base: 100.79 in, 256 cm; tracks: 53.15 in, 135 cm front, 54.33 in, 138 cm rear; length: 174.80 in, 444 cm; width: 66.93 in, 170 cm; height: 51.97 in, 132 cm; ground clearance: 4.92 in, 12.5 cm; weight: 2,271 lb, 1,030 kg; turning circle: 35.4 ft, 10.8 m; fuel tank: 12.8 imp gal, 15.3 US gal, 58 l.

BODY coupé; 2+1 doors; 5 seats, separate front seats, reclining backrests; headrests; folding rear seat; heated rear window; rear window wiper-washer.

PRACTICAL INSTRUCTIONS fuel: 97 oct petrol; oil: engine 6.5 imp pt, 7.8 US pt, 3.7 l, SAE 10W-50, change every 6,200 miles, 10,000 km - gearbox 2.3 imp pt, 2.7 US pt, 1.3 l, SAE 80, change every 12,400 miles, 20,000 km - final drive 1.9 imp pt, 2.3 US pt, 1.1 l, SAE 90, change every 12,400 miles, 20,000 km; greasing: none; tyre pressure: front 23 psi, 1.6 atm, rear 26 psi, 1.8 atm.

OPTIONALS sunroof; metallic spray; sport wheels; fog lamps.

114 hp power team

See 101 hp power team, except for:

ENGINE 6 cylinders, Vee-slanted at 60°; 139.9 cu in, 2,294 cc (3.54 x 2.37 in, 90 x 60.1 mm); compression ratio: 9:1; max power (DIN): 114 hp (84 kW) at 5,300 rpm; max torque (DIN): 130 lb ft, 18 kg m (176 Nm) at 3,000 rpm; max engine rpm: 5,600; 49.6 hp/l (37 kW/l); 4 crankshaft bearings; valves: overhead, push-rods and rockers; camshafts: 1, at centre of Vee; lubrication: 7.4 imp pt, 8.9 US pt, 4.2 l; 1 Solex 35/35 EEIT downdraught twin barrel carburettor; cooling: 13.7 imp pt, 16.5 US pt, 7.8 l.

TRANSMISSION axle ratio: 3.220; width of rims: 6"; tyres: 185/70 HR x 13.

PERFORMANCE max speed: 116 mph, 186 km/h; power-weight ratio: 21.5 lb/hp (29.1 lb/kW), 9.7 kg/hp (13.2 kg/kW); speed in top at 1,000 rpm: 20.8 mph, 33.4 km/h; consumption: 31.4 m/imp gal, 26.1 m/US gal, 9 l x 100 km at 75 mph, 120 km/h.

ELECTRICAL EQUIPMENT halogen headlamps and fog lamps.

DIMENSIONS AND WEIGHT weight: 2,447 lb, 1,110 kg.

BODY light alloy wheels; headrests on front seats; heated rear window.

OPTIONALS Ford C3 automatic transmission with 3 ratios (I 2.474, II 1.474, III 1, rev 2.111), max speed 112 mph, 181 km/h, consumption 26.2 m/imp gal, 21.8 m/US gal, 10.8 l x 100 km at 75 mph, 120 km/h; power steering; 52 Ah battery.

160 hp power team

See 101 hp power team, except for:

ENGINE 6 cylinders, Vee-slanted at 60°; 170.4 cu in, 2,792 cc (3.66 x 2.70 in, 93 x 68.5 mm); compression ratio: 9.2:1; max power (DIN): 160 hp (118 kW) at 5,700 rpm; max torque (DIN): 163 lb ft, 22.5 kg m (221 Nm) at 4,300 rpm; 57.3 hp/l (42.3 kW/l); 4 crankshaft bearings; valves: overhead, push-rods and rockers; camshafts: 1, at centre of Vee; lubrication: 7.4 imp pt, 8.9 US pt, 4.2 l; Bosch K-Jetronic injection; cooling: 15.3 imp pt, 18.4 US pt, 8.7 l.

TRANSMISSION gearbox ratios: I 3.360, II 1.810, III 1.260, IV 1, V 0.825, rev 3.370; axle ratio: 3.090; width of rims: 7"; tyres: 205/60 VR x 13.

PERFORMANCE max speed: 130 mph, 210 km/h; power-weight ratio: 16.9 lb/hp (23 lb/kW), 7.7 kg/hp (10.4 kg/kW); speed in top at 1,000 rpm: 21.1 mph, 33.9 km/h; consumption: 30.1 m/imp gal, 25 m/US gal, 9.4 l x 100 km at 75 mph, 120 km/h.

CHASSIS front and rear suspension: reinforced anti-roll bar.

STEERING servo.

BRAKES front disc (diameter 9.72 in, 24.7 cm), internal radial fins, rear drum, rear compensator.

ELECTRICAL EQUIPMENT 52 Ah battery; 70 A alternator; electronic ignition; 4 halogen headlamps, fog lamps (standard).

DIMENSIONS AND WEIGHT tracks: 55.12 in, 140 cm front, 56.34 in, 143 cm rear; weight: 2,712 lb, 1,230 kg.

BODY light alloy wheels; tinted glass.

PRACTICAL INSTRUCTIONS oil: engine 7.4 imp pt, 8.9 US pt, 4.2 l.

Granada Series

PRICES EX WORKS:		DM
1	L 4-dr Limousine	20,995*
2	L 4+1-dr Turnier	22,245*
3	GL 4-dr Limousine	23,970*
4	GL 4+1-dr Turnier	25,525*
5	Ghia 4-dr Limousine	30,055*

FORD Sierra XR 4 i Limousine

FORD Capri 2.8 Injection Coupé

6	Ghia 4+1-dr Turnier	**31,855***
7	2.8 Injection 4-dr Limousine	**31,380***
8	2.8 Injection 4+1-dr Turnier	**33,721***

Power team:	Standard for:	Optional for:
105 hp	1,2	3,4
90 hp	—	1,2
114 hp	3 to 6	1,2
135 hp	—	3 to 6
150 hp	7,8	5,6
69 hp (diesel)	—	1 to 4

105 hp power team

ENGINE front, 4 stroke; 4 cylinders, in line; 121.6 cu in, 1,993 cc (3.89 x 3.03 in, 90.8 x 76.9 mm); compression ratio: 9.2:1; max power (DIN): 105 hp (77 kW) at 5,200 rpm; max torque (DIN): 116 lb/ft, 16 kg m (157 Nm) at 4,000 rpm; max engine rpm: 5,600; 52.7 hp/l (38.6 kW/l); cast iron block and head; 5 crankshaft bearings; valves: overhead, Vee-slanted, rockers; camshafts: 1, overhead, cogged belt; lubrication: rotary pump, full flow filter (cartridge), 6.5 imp pt, 7.8 US pt, 3.7 l; 1 Weber downdraught single barrel carburettor; fuel feed: mechanical pump; semi-sealed circuit cooling, expansion tank, 13 imp pt, 15.6 US pt, 7.4 l, electric thermostatic fan.

TRANSMISSION driving wheels: rear; clutch: single dry plate (diaphragm); gearbox: mechanical; gears: 5 fully synchronized; ratios: I 3.650, II 1.970, III 1.370, IV 1, V 0.816, rev 3.660; lever: central; final drive: hypoid bevel; axle ratio: 3.890; width of rims: 6"; tyres: 185 SR x 14.

PERFORMANCE max speed: 104 mph, 168 km/h; power-weight ratio: limousines 25.9 lb/hp (35.4 lb/kW), 11.8 kg/hp (16 kg/kW); carrying capacity: 1,136 lb, 515 kg; consumption: 29.7 m/imp gal, 24.8 m/US gal, 9.5 l x 100 km at 75 mph, 120 km/h.

CHASSIS integral, front and rear auxiliary frames; front suspension: independent, wishbones, lower trailing links, coil springs, anti-roll bar, telescopic dampers; rear: independent, semi-trailing arms, coil springs, telescopic dampers.

STEERING rack-and-pinion, servo.

BRAKES front disc (diameter 10.31 in, 26.2 cm), rear drum, dual circuit, servo; lining area: front 40.6 sq in, 262 sq cm, rear 35.4 sq in, 228.6 sq cm - Turnier models 39.4 sq in, 254 sq cm, total 76 sq in, 490.6 sq cm - Turnier models 80 sq in, 516 sq cm.

ELECTRICAL EQUIPMENT 12 V; 43 Ah battery; 55 A alternator; transistorized ignition; 2 headlamps.

DIMENSIONS AND WEIGHT wheel base: 109.05 in, 277 cm; tracks: 59.45 in, 151 cm front, 60.24 in, 153 cm rear; length: 187.68 in, 477 cm; width: 70.87 in, 180 cm; height: 55.91 in, 142 cm; weight: limousines 2,723 lb, 1,235 kg - Turnier models 2,866 lb, 1,300 kg; turning circle: 36.7 ft, 11.2 m; fuel tank: 14.3 imp gal, 17.2 US gal, 65 l.

BODY saloon/sedan, 4 doors - estate car/st. wagon, 4+1 doors; 5 seats, separate front seats; heated rear window.

PRACTICAL INSTRUCTIONS fuel: 98 oct petrol; oil: engine 6.5 imp pt, 7.8 US pt, 3.7 l, SAE 10W-40, change every 6,200 miles, 10,000 km - gearbox 3 imp pt, 3.6 US pt, 1.8 l, SAE 80, no change recommended - final drive 3 imp pt, 3.6 US pt, 1.8 l, no change recommended; greasing: none; tyre pressure: front 26 psi, 1.8 atm, rear 26 psi, 1.8 atm.

OPTIONALS Ford C3 automatic transmission with 3 ratios (I 2.470, II 1.470, III 1, rev 2.110), max speed 99 mph, 160 km/h, consumption 25.9 m/imp gal, 21.6 m/US gal, 10.9 l x 100 km at 75 mph, 120 km/h; sunroof; metallic spray; 52 Ah battery; S equipment.

90 hp power team

See 105 hp power team, except for:

ENGINE 6 cylinders, Vee-slanted at 60°; 121.9 cu in, 1,999 cc (3.31 x 2.37 in, 84 x 60.1 mm); compression ratio: 9:1; max power (DIN): 90 hp (66 kW) at 5,000 rpm; max torque (DIN): 112 lb ft, 15.4 kg m (151 Nm) at 3,000 rpm; 45 hp/l (33 kW/l); 4 crankshaft bearings; lubrication: 7.4 imp pt, 8.9 US pt, 4.2 l; 1 Weber 32/32 DGAV downdraught twin barrel carburettor; cooling: 15.8 imp pt, 19 US pt, 9 l.

TRANSMISSION axle ratio: Limousine 3.890 - Turnier 4.110.

PERFORMANCE max speed: 99 mph, 160 km/h; power-weight ratio: L Limousines 31.1 lb/hp (42.4 lb/kW), 14.1 kg/hp (19.2 kg/kW); speed in top at 1,000 rpm: 17.3 mph, 27.9 km/h; consumption: Limousine 27.7 m/imp gal, 23.1 m/US gal, 10.2 l x 100 km at 75 mph, 120 km/h.

DIMENSIONS AND WEIGHT weight: L Limousine 2,800 lb, 1,270 kg - L Turnier 2,944 lb, 1,335 kg.

PRACTICAL INSTRUCTIONS oil: engine 7 imp pt, 8.5 US pt, 4 l.

114 hp power team

See 105 hp power team, except for:

ENGINE 6 cylinders, Vee-slanted at 60°; 139.9 cu in, 2,294 cc (3.54 x 2.37 in, 90 x 60.1 mm); compression ratio: 9:1; max power (DIN): 114 hp (85 kW) at 5,300 rpm; max torque (DIN): 130 lb ft, 18 kg m (176 Nm) at 3,000 rpm; 49.6 hp/l (37 kW/l); 4 crankshaft bearings; camshafts: 1, at centre of Vee; valves: overhead, push-rods and rockers; lubrication: 7.4 imp pt, 8.9 US pt, 4.2 l; 1 Solex 35/35 EEIT downdraught twin barrel carburettor; cooling: 15.5 imp pt, 18.6 US pt, 8.8 l.

TRANSMISSION axle ratio: 3.640.

PERFORMANCE max speed: 106 mph, 170 km/h; power-weight ratio: limousines 24.7 lb/hp (33.1 lb/kW), 11.2 kg/hp (15 kg/kW); speed in top at 1,000 rpm: 18.5 mph, 29.8 km/h; consumption: limousines 28.2 m/imp gal, 23.5 m/US gal, 10 l x 100 km at 75 mph, 120 km/h.

STEERING servo.

BRAKES lining area (except for Turnier models): front 23.4 sq in, 151 sq cm, rear 75.3 sq in, 486 sq cm, total 98.7 sq in, 637 sq cm.

DIMENSIONS AND WEIGHT weight: limousines 2,811 lb, 1,275 kg - Turnier models 2,955 lb, 1,340 kg.

PRACTICAL INSTRUCTIONS oil: engine 7 imp pt, 8.5 US pt, 4 l.

OPTIONALS Ford C3 automatic transmission, hydraulic torque converter and planetary gears with 3 ratios (I 2.474, II 1.474, III 1, rev 2.111), max ratio of converter at stall 2, possible manual selection, oil cooler, max speed 103 mph, 166 km/h, consumption limousines 24.1 m/imp gal, 20.1 m/US gal, 11.7 l x 100 km at 75 mph, 120 km/h; 55 Ah battery; light alloy wheels (for GL models only); air-conditioning.

135 hp power team

See 105 hp power team, except for:

ENGINE 6 cylinders, Vee-slanted at 60°; 170.4 cu in, 2,792 cc (3.66 x 2.70 in, 93 x 68.5 mm); max power (DIN): 135 hp (99 kW) at 5,200 rpm; max torque (DIN): 159 lb ft, 22 kg m (216 Nm) at 3,000 rpm; 48.4 hp/l (35.6 kW/l); 4 crankshaft bearings; camshafts: 1, at centre of Vee; valves: overhead, push-rods and rockers; lubrication: 7.4 imp pt, 8.9 US pt, 4.2 l; 1 Solex downdraught twin barrel carburettor; cooling: 15.8 imp pt, 19 US pt, 9 l.

TRANSMISSION gearbox ratios: I 3.360, II 1.810, III 1.260, IV 1, V 0.825, rev 3.370; axle ratio: 3.450; tyres: 185 HR x 14.

PERFORMANCE max speed: 112 mph, 181 km/h; power-weight ratio: limousines 22.1 lb/hp (30.1 lb/kW), 10 kg/hp (13.6 kg/kW); speed in top at 1,000 rpm: 20.7 mph, 33.3 km/h; consumption: limousines 27.4 m/imp gal, 22.8 m/US gal, 10.3 l x 100 km at 75 mph, 120 km/h.

BRAKES front disc with internal radial fins; lining area (except Turnier models): front 29.3 sq in, 189 sq cm, rear 75.3 sq in, 486 sq cm, total 104.6 sq in, 675 sq cm.

DIMENSIONS AND WEIGHT weight: limousines 2,977 lb, 1,350 kg - Turnier models 3,098 lb, 1,405 kg.

PRACTICAL INSTRUCTIONS oil: engine 7.4 imp pt, 8.9 US pt, 4.2 l.

OPTIONALS Ford C3 automatic transmission, hydraulic torque converter and planetary gears with 3 ratios (I 2.474, II 1.474, III 1, rev 2.111), max ratio of converter at stall 2, possible manual selection, oil cooler, max speed 109 mph, 175 km/h, consumption limousines 23.9 m/imp gal, 19.9 m/US gal, 11.8 l x 100 km at 75 mph, 120 km/h; 55 Ah battery; air-conditioning; S equipment with 190/65 HR x 390 TRX tyres.

150 hp power team

See 105 hp power team, except for:

ENGINE 6 cylinders, Vee-slanted at 60°; 170.4 cu in, 2,792 cc (3.66 x 2.70 in, 93 x 68.5 mm); max power (DIN): 150 hp (110 kW) at 5,700 rpm; max torque (DIN): 159 lb ft, 22 kg m (216 Nm) at 4,000 rpm; max engine rpm: 6,200; 53.7 hp/l (39.4 kW/l); 4 crankshaft bearings; camshafts: 1, at centre of Vee; valves: overhead, push-rods and rockers; lubrication: 7.4 imp pt, 8.9 US pt, 4.2 l; Bosch K-Jetronic injection; cooling: 16.7 imp pt, 20.1 US pt, 9.5 l.

FORD Granada L Limousine

150 HP POWER TEAM

TRANSMISSION gearbox ratios: I 3.360, II 1.810, III 1.260, IV 1, V 0.825, rev 3.370; axle ratio: 3.450; tyres: 190/65 HR x 390 TRX.

PERFORMANCE max speed: 118 mph, 190 km/h; power-weight ratio: limousines 20.3 lb/hp (27.7 lb/kW), 9.2 kg/hp (12.5 kg/kW); speed in top at 1,000 rpm: 21.2 mph, 33.9 km/h; consumption: limousines 28 m/imp gal, 23.3 m/US gal, 10.1 l x 100 km at 75 mph, 120 km/h.

BRAKES front disc with internal radial fins; lining area (except Turnier models): front 29.3 sq in, 189 sq cm, rear 75.3 sq in, 486 sq cm, total 104.6 sq in, 675 sq cm.

ELECTRICAL EQUIPMENT 70 A alternator.

DIMENSIONS AND WEIGHT weight: limousines 3,043 lb, 1,380 kg - Turnier models 3,153 lb, 1,430 kg.

PRACTICAL INSTRUCTIONS oil: engine 7.4 imp pt, 8.9 US pt, 4.2 l.

OPTIONALS Ford C3 automatic transmission, hydraulic torque converter and planetary gears with 3 ratios (I 2.474, II 1.474, III 1, rev 2.111), max ratio converter at stall 2, possible manual selection, oil cooler, max speed 114 mph, 184 km/h, consumption limousines 24.4 m/imp gal, 20.3 m/US gal, 11.6 l x 100 km at 75 mph, 120 km/h.

69 hp (diesel) power team

See 105 hp power team, except for:

ENGINE Peugeot, diesel; 152.4 cu in, 2,499 cc (3.70 x 3.54 in, 94 x 90 mm); compression ratio: 23:1; max power (DIN): 69 hp (51 kW) at 4,200 rpm; max torque (DIN): 109 lb ft, 15.1 kg m (148 Nm) at 2,000 rpm; max engine rpm: 4,600; 27.6 hp/l (20.4 kW/l); light alloy head; valves: overhead, in line, push-rods and rockers; camshafts: 1, side, chain-driven; lubrication: 9.9 imp pt, 11.8 US pt, 5.6 l; Rotodiesel injection pump; cooling: 18 imp pt, 21.6 US pt, 10.2 l.

TRANSMISSION gearbox ratios: I 3.910, II 2.320, III 1.400, IV 1, V 0.816, rev 3.660; axle ratio: limousines 3.640 - Turnier models 3.890.

PERFORMANCE max speed: 90 mph, 145 km/h; power-weight ratio: limousines 43.9 lb/hp (59.3 lb/kW), 19.9 kg/hp (26.9 kg/kW); consumption: 32.1 m/imp gal, 26.7 m/US gal, 8.8 l x 100 km at 75 mph, 120 km/h.

ELECTRICAL EQUIPMENT 88 Ah battery.

DIMENSIONS AND WEIGHT weight: limousines 3,021 lb, 1,370 kg - Turnier models 3,164 lb, 1,435 kg.

PRACTICAL INSTRUCTIONS fuel: diesel; oil: engine 9.9 imp pt, 11.8 US pt, 5.6 l.

MERCEDES-BENZ GERMANY FR

190 Series

PRICES IN GB AND EX WORKS:	£	DM
1 4-dr Limousine	9,685*	26,026*
2 E 4-dr Limousine	10,640*	28,785*
3 E 2.3-16 4-dr Limousine	—	—
4 D 4-dr Limousine	—	—

For USA prices, see price index.

Power team:	Standard for:	Optional for:
90 hp	1	—
122 hp	2	—
185 hp	3	—
72 hp (diesel)	4	—

90 hp power team

ENGINE front, slanted at 15° to right, 4 stroke; 4 cylinders, in line; 121.9 cu in, 1,997 cc (3.50 x 3.16 in, 89 x 80.2 mm); compression ratio: 9:1; max power (DIN): 90 hp (66 kW) at 5,000 rpm; max torque (DIN): 122 lb ft, 16.8 kg m (165 Nm) at 2,500 rpm; max engine rpm: 6,000; 45.1 hp/l (33 kW/l); cast iron block, light alloy head, hemispherical combustion chambers; 5 crankshaft bearings; valves: overhead, Vee-slanted, finger levers; camshafts: 1, overhead; lubrication: gear pump, full flow filter (cartridge); 7.9 imp pt, 9.5 US pt, 4.5 l; 1 Stromberg 175 CDT horizontal carburettor; air cleaner: dry, thimble type thermostatic intake; fuel feed: mechanical pump; water-cooled, 14.9 imp pt, 17.9 US pt, 8.5 l, electromagnetic fan.

TRANSMISSION driving wheels: rear; clutch: single dry plate, hydraulically controlled; gearbox: mechanical; gears: 4, fully synchronized; ratios: I 3.910, II 2.170, III 1.370, IV 1, rev 3.780; lever: central; final drive: hypoid bevel; axle ratio: 3.230; width of rims: 5''; tyres: 175/70 R x 14 82S.

PERFORMANCE max speed: 109 mph, 175 km/h; power-weight ratio: 26.5 lb/hp (36.1 lb/kW), 12 kg/hp (16.4 kg/kW); carrying capacity: 1,102 lb, 500 kg; speed in direct drive at 1,000 rpm: 18.1 mph, 29.2 km/h; consumption: 33.6 m/imp gal, 28 m/US gal, 8.4 l x 100 km at 75 mph, 120 km/h.

CHASSIS integral; front suspension: independent, wishbones, coil springs, anti-roll bar, telescopic dampers; rear: independent, semi-trailing arms, coil springs, anti-roll bar, telescopic dampers.

STEERING recirculating ball; turns lock to lock: 5.

BRAKES disc, dual circuit, servo.

ELECTRICAL EQUIPMENT 12 V; 55 Ah battery; 770 W alternator; electronic ignition; 4 headlamps.

DIMENSIONS AND WEIGHT wheel base: 104.92 in, 266 cm; tracks: 56.22 in, 143 cm front, 55.71 in, 141 cm rear; length: 174.02 in, 442 cm; width: 66.06 in, 168 cm; height: 54.45 in, 138 cm; weight: 2,381 lb, 1,080 kg; turning circle: 34.8 ft, 10.6 m; fuel tank: 12.1 imp gal, 14.5 US gal, 55 l.

BODY saloon/sedan; 4 doors; 5 seats, separate front seats, reclining backrests, headrests; heated rear window.

PRACTICAL INSTRUCTIONS fuel: 98 oct petrol; oil: engine 7.9 imp pt, 9.5 US pt, 4.5 l, SAE 10W-50, change every 6,200 miles, 10,000 km - gearbox 2.8 imp pt, 3.4 US pt, 1.6 l, ATF, change every 12,400 miles, 20,000 km - final drive 1.9 imp pt, 2.3 US pt, 1.1 l, SAE 90, change every 12,400 miles, 20,000 km; greasing: none; tyre pressure: front 21 psi, 1.5 atm, rear 26 psi, 1.8 atm.

OPTIONALS 5-speed mechanical gearbox (I 4.230, II 2.410, III 1.490, IV 1, V 0.840, rev 4.630), consumption 36.2 m/imp gal, 30.2 m/US gal, 7.8 l x 100 km at 75 mph, 120 km/h; MB automatic transmission, hydraulic torque converter and planetary gears with 4 ratios (I 4.250, II 2.410, III 1.490, IV 1, rev 5.670), possible manual selection, max speed 106 mph, 170 km/h, consumption 31.7 m/imp gal, 26.4 m/US gal, 8.9 l x 100 km at 75 mph, 120 km/h; anti-brake-locking system (ABS); power steering; electric or manual sunroof; electric windows; tinted glass; air-conditioning; light alloy wheels; metallic spray.

MERCEDES-BENZ 190 E 2.3-16 Limousine

122 hp power team

See 90 hp power team, except for:

ENGINE compression ratio: 9.1:1; max power (DIN): 122 hp (90 kW) at 5,100 rpm; max torque (DIN): 132 lb ft, 18.2 kg m (178 Nm) at 3,500 rpm; max engine rpm: 6,000; 61.1 hp/l (45.1 kW/l); Bosch injection (mechanical system with electronic control).

TRANSMISSION axle ratio: 3.250; tyres: 175/70 R x 14 82H.

PERFORMANCE max speed: 121 mph, 195 km/h; power-weight ratio: 19.9 lb/hp (26.9 lb/kW), 9 kg/hp (12.2 kg/kW); speed in direct drive at 1,000 rpm: 20.2 mph, 32.5 km/h; consumption: 34 m/imp gal, 28.3 m/US gal, 8.3 l x 100 km at 75 mph, 120 km/h.

DIMENSIONS AND WEIGHT weight: 2,425 lb, 1,100 kg.

OPTIONALS 5-speed mechanical gearbox (I 3.910, II 2.170, III 1.370, IV 1, V 0.780, rev 4.270), consumption 36.2 m/imp gal, 30.2 m/US gal, 7.8 l x 100 km at 75 mph, 120 km/h; MB automatic transmission with 4 ratios (I 4.250, II 2.410, III 1.490, IV 1, rev 5.670), max speed 118 mph, 190 km/h, consumption 32.5 m/imp gal, 27 m/US gal, 8.7 l x 100 km at 75 mph, 120 km/h.

185 hp power team

See 90 hp power team, except for:

ENGINE 140.3 cu in, 2,299 cc (3.76 x 3.16 in, 95.5 x 80.2 mm); compression ratio: 10.5:1; max power (DIN): 185 hp (136 kW) at 6,000 rpm; max torque (DIN): 177 lb ft, 24.5 kg m (240 Nm) at 4,500 rpm; max engine rpm: 6,500; 80.5 hp/l (59.2 kW/l); valves: 4 per cylinder, overhead, Vee-slanted, finger levers; camshafts: 2, overhead, cogged belt; lubrication: 8.8 imp pt, 10.6 US pt, 5 l, oil cooler; Bosch KE-Jetronic injection; fuel feed: electric pump.

TRANSMISSION gears: 5, fully synchronized; ratios: I 4.080, II 2.520, III 1.770, IV 1.260, V 1, rev 4.400; final drive: limited slip; axle ratio: 3.070 or 2.880; width of rims: 6''; tyres: Pirelli 205/55 VR x 15 P7.

MERCEDES-BENZ 190 E Limousine

MERCEDES-BENZ 190 E 2.3-16 Limousine

MERCEDED-BENZ 190 D Limousine

PERFORMANCE max speed: 143 mph, 230 km/h; power-weight ratio: 14.3 lb/hp (19.5 lb/kW), 6.5 kg/hp (8.8 kg/kW); speed in top at 1,000 rpm: 22.5 mph, 36.2 km/h; consumption: 31.4 m/imp gal, 26.1 m/US gal, 9 l x 100 km at 75 mph, 120 km/h.

CHASSIS rear suspension: automatic levelling control.

BRAKES disc, internal radial fins.

DIMENSIONS AND WEIGHT length: 174.41 in, 443 cm; width: 66.53 in, 169 cm; height: 53.94 in, 137 cm; weight: 2,646 lb, 1,200 kg.

BODY front and rear spoiler; light alloy wheels (standard).

PRACTICAL INSTRUCTIONS oil: engine 8.8 imp pt, 10.6 US pt, 5 l.

72 hp (diesel) power team

See 90 hp power team, except for:

ENGINE diesel; 121.9 cu in, 1,997 cc (3.43 x 3.31 in, 87 x 84 mm); compression ratio: 22:1; max power (DIN): 72 hp (53 kW) at 4,600 rpm; max torque (DIN): 91 lb ft, 12.5 kg m (123 Nm) at 2,800 rpm; max engine rpm: 5,150; 36.1 hp/l (26.5 kW/l); valves: overhead, hydraulic tappets; lubrication: gear pump, full flow (cartridge) and by-pass filters, 10.6 imp pt, 12.7 US pt, 6 l; Bosch injection pump.

TRANSMISSION gearbox ratios: I 4.230, II 2.360, III 1.490, IV 1, rev 4.100.

PERFORMANCE max speed: 99 mph, 160 km/h; power-weight ratio: 34 lb/hp (46.2 lb/kW), 15.4 kg/hp (20.9 kg/kW); consumption: 40.9 m/imp gal, 34.1 m/US gal, 6.9 l x 100 km at 75 mph, 120 km/h.

ELECTRICAL EQUIPMENT 72 Ah battery.

DIMENSIONS AND WEIGHT weight: 2,448 lb, 1,110 kg.

PRACTICAL INSTRUCTIONS fuel: diesel; oil: engine 10.6 imp pt, 12.7 US pt, 6 l.

OPTIONALS with 5-speed mechanical gearbox, consumption 42.8 m/imp gal, 35.6 m/US gal, 6.6 l x 100 km at 75 mph, 120 km/h; with MB automatic transmission, max speed 97 mph, 156 km/h, consumption 38.7 m/imp gal, 32.2 m/US gal, 7.3 l x 100 km at 75 mph, 120 km/h.

200 Series

PRICES IN GB AND EX WORKS:	£	DM
1 4-dr Limousine	9,965*	26,881*
2 T 4+1-dr Limousine	10,750*	31,019*
3 D 4-dr Limousine	—	27,417*

Power team:	Standard for:	Optional for:
109 hp	1,2	—
60 hp (diesel)	3	—

109 hp power team

ENGINE front, 4 stroke; 4 cylinders, vertical, in line; 121.9 cu in, 1,997 cc (3.50 x 3.16 in, 89 x 80.2 mm); compression ratio: 9:1; max power (DIN): 109 hp (80 kW) at 5,200 rpm; max torque (DIN): 126 lb ft, 17.3 kg m (170 Nm) at 3,000 rpm; max engine rpm: 6,000; 54.6 hp/l (40.1 kW/l); cast iron block, light alloy head, hemispherical combustion chambers; 5 crankshaft bearings; valves: overhead, Vee-slanted, finger levers; camshafts: 1, overhead; lubrication: gear pump, oil-water heat exchanger, full flow filter (cartridge), 7.9 imp pt, 9.5 US pt, 4.5 l; 1 Stromberg 175 CDT horizontal carburettor; air cleaner: dry, thimble type thermostatic intake; fuel feed: mechanical pump; water-cooled, 14.9 imp pt, 17.9 US pt, 8.5 l.

TRANSMISSION driving wheels: rear; clutch: single dry plate, hydraulically controlled; gearbox: mechanical; gears: 4, fully synchronized; ratios: I 3.910, II 2.170, III 1.370, IV 1, rev 3.780; lever: central; final drive: hypoid bevel; axle ratio: 3.690; width of rims: 5.5''; tyres: Limousine 175 SR x 14 - T Limousine 190/70 SR x 14.

PERFORMANCE max speed: 104 mph, 168 km/h; power-weight ratio: Limousine 27.5 lb/hp (37.5 lb/kW), 12.5 kg/hp (17 kg/kW); carrying capacity: Limousine 1,147 lb, 520 kg - T Limousine 1,367 lb, 620 kg; speed in direct drive at 1,000 rpm: 17.4 mph, 28 km/h; consumption: 27.7 m/imp gal, 23.1 m/US gal, 10.2 l x 100 km at 75 mph, 120 km/h.

MERCEDES-BENZ 200 Limousine

CHASSIS integral, front auxiliary frame; front suspension: independent, wishbones, coil springs, auxiliary rubber springs, anti-roll bar, telescopic dampers; rear: independent, oblique semi-trailing arms, coil springs, auxiliary rubber springs, anti-roll bar.

STEERING recirculating ball.

BRAKES disc (front diameter 10.75 in, 27.3 cm, rear 10.98 in, 27.9 cm), dual circuit, servo; swept area: front 225.4 sq in, 1,454 sq cm, rear 195.8 sq in, 1,263 sq cm, total 421.2 sq in, 2,717 sq cm.

ELECTRICAL EQUIPMENT 12 V; 55 Ah battery; 770 W alternator; electronic ignition; 4 headlamps.

DIMENSIONS AND WEIGHT wheel base: 110.04 in, 279 cm; tracks: 58.58 in, 149 cm front, 56.93 in, 145 cm rear; length: 186.02 in, 472 cm; width: 70.31 in, 179 cm; height: 56.69 in, 144 cm; ground clearance: 6.50 in, 16.5 cm; weight: Limousine 2,999 lb, 1,360 kg - T Limousine 3,263 lb, 1,480 kg; turning circle: 37.1 ft, 11.3 m; fuel tank: Limousine 14.3 imp gal, 17.2 US gal, 65 l - T Limousine 15.4 imp gal, 18.5 US gal, 70 l.

BODY saloon/sedan, 4 doors - estate car/st. wagon, 4+1 doors; 5 seats, separate front seats, reclining backrests.

PRACTICAL INSTRUCTIONS fuel: 98 oct petrol; oil: engine 7.9 imp pt, 9.5 US pt, 4.5 l, SAE 20W-30, change every 6,200 miles, 10,000 km - gearbox 2.8 imp pt, 3.4 US pt, 1.6 l, ATF, change every 12,400 miles, 20,000 km - final drive 1.9 imp pt, 2.3 US pt, 1.1 l, SAE 90, change every 12,400 miles, 20,000 km; greasing: none; tyre pressure: front 21 psi, 1.5 atm, rear 26 psi, 1.8 atm.

OPTIONALS MB automatic transmission, hydraulic torque converter and planetary gears with 4 ratios (I 4.250, II 2.410, III 1.490, IV 1, rev 5.670), possible manual selection, max speed 101 mph, 163 km/h, consumption 25.7 m/imp gal, 21.4 m/US gal, 11 l x 100 km at 75 mph, 120 km/h; 5-speed mechanical gearbox (I 3.820, II 2.200, III 1.400, IV 1, V 0.810, rev 3.710), consumption 29.4 m/imp gal, 24.5 m/US gal, 9.6 l x 100 km at 75 mph, 120 km/h; anti-brake-locking system (ABS); automatic levelling control on rear suspension; power steering; halogen fog lamps; electric or manual sunroof; heated rear window; electric windows; tinted glass; air-conditioning; light alloy wheels; metallic spray.

60 hp (diesel) power team

See 109 hp power team, except for:

ENGINE diesel; 121.3 cu in, 1,988 cc (3.43 x 3.29 in, 87 x 83.6 mm); compression ratio: 21:1; max power (DIN): 60 hp (44 kW) at 4,400 rpm; max torque (DIN): 83 lb ft, 11.5 kg m (113 Nm) at 2,400 rpm; max engine rpm: 5,300; 30.2 hp/l (22.1 kW/l); cast iron block and head; lubrication: gear pump, full flow (cartridge) and by-pass filters, 11.4 imp pt, 13.7 US pt, 6.5 l; 4-cylinder Bosch injection pump.

TRANSMISSION axle ratio: 3.920.

PERFORMANCE max speeds: (I) 21 mph, 33 km/h; (II) 35 mph, 56 km/h; (III) 57 mph, 92 km/h; (IV) 84 mph, 135 km/h; power-weight ratio: 51.4 lb/hp (70.2 lb/kW), 23.3 kg/hp (31.8 kg/kW); consumption: 27.7 m/imp gal, 23.1 m/US gal, 10.2 l x 100 at 75 mph, 120 km/h.

ELECTRICAL EQUIPMENT 88 Ah battery.

DIMENSIONS AND WEIGHT weight: 3,087 lb, 1,400 kg.

BODY saloon/sedan, 4 doors.

PRACTICAL INSTRUCTIONS fuel: diesel; oil: engine 11.4 imp pt, 13.7 US pt, 6.5 l, change every 3,100 miles, 5,000 km; tappet clearances: inlet 0.008 in, 0.10 mm, exhaust 0.016 in, 0.40 mm; valve timing: 12°30' 42°30' 45° 9°.

OPTIONALS with MB automatic transmission, max speeds (I) 20 mph, 32 km/h, (II) 35 mph, 56 km/h, (III) 57 mph, 92 km/h, (IV) 81 mph, 130 km/h, consumption 26.2 m/imp gal, 21.8 m/US gal, 10.8 l x 100 km at 75 mph, 120 km/h; with 5-speed mechanical gearbox, consumption 30.4 m/imp gal, 25.3 m/US gal, 9.3 l x 100 km at 75 mph, 120 km/h.

230 E

PRICES IN GB AND EX WORKS:	£	DM
E 4-dr Limousine	10,957*	30,153*
CE 2-dr Coupé	12,900*	35,967*
TE 4+1-dr Limousine	12,775*	34,291*

ENGINE front, 4 stroke; 4 cylinders, vertical, in line; 140.3 cu in, 2,299 cc (3.76 x 3.16 in, 95.5 x 80.2 mm); compression ratio: 9:1; max power (DIN): 136 hp (100 kW) at 5,100 rpm; max torque (DIN): 152 lb ft, 20.9 kg m (205 Nm) at 3,500 rpm; max engine rpm: 6,000; 59.2 hp/l (43.5 kW/l); cast iron block, light alloy head, hemispherical combustion chambers; 5 crankshaft bearings; valves: overhead, Vee-slanted, finger levers; camshafts: 1, overhead; lubrication: gear pump, oil-water heat exchanger, full flow filter (cartridge), 7.9 imp pt, 9.5 US pt, 4.5 l; Bosch injection with air flow metering device; fuel feed: mechanical pump; water-cooled, 14.9 imp pt, 17.9 US pt, 8.5 l.

TRANSMISSION driving wheels: rear; clutch: single dry plate, hydraulically controlled; gearbox: mechanical; gears: 4, fully synchronized; ratios: I 3.910, II 2.170, III 1.370, IV

230 E

MERCEDES-BENZ 230 CE Coupé

1, rev 3.780; lever: central; final drive: hypoid bevel; axle ratio: 3.580; width of rims: 5.5" - CE Coupé and TE Limousine 6"; tyres: 175 HR x 14 - CE Coupé and TE Limousine 195/70 HR x 14.

PERFORMANCE max speed: 112 mph, 180 km/h; power-weight ratio: E Limousine 22.2 lb/hp (30.2 lb/kW), 10.1 kg/hp (13.7 kg/kW); carrying capacity: 1,147 lb, 520 kg - TE Limousine 1,367 lb, 620 kg; speed in direct drive at 1,000 rpm: 18.6 mph, 30 km/h; consumption: 27.4 m/imp gal, 22.8 m/US gal, 10.3 l x 100 km at 75 mph, 120 km/h.

CHASSIS integral, front auxiliary frame; front suspension: independent, wishbones, coil springs, auxiliary rubber springs, anti-roll bar, telescopic dampers; rear: independent, oblique semi-trailing arms, coil springs, auxiliary rubber springs, anti-roll bar.

STEERING recirculating ball, CE Coupé servo (standard).

BRAKES disc (front diameter 10.75 in, 27.3 cm, rear 10.98 in, 27.9 cm), dual circuit, servo; swept area: front 225.4 sq in, 1,454 sq cm, rear 195.8 sq in, 1,263 sq cm, total 421.2 sq in, 2,717 sq cm.

ELECTRICAL EQUIPMENT 12 V; 55 Ah battery; 770 W alternator; electronic ignition; 4 headlamps.

DIMENSIONS AND WEIGHT wheel base: 110.04 in, 279 cm - CE Coupé 106.69 in, 271 cm; tracks: 58.58 in, 149 cm front, 56.93 in, 145 cm rear; length: 186.02 in, 472 cm - CE Coupé 182.68 in, 464 cm; width: 70.31 in, 179 cm; height: 56.69 in, 144 cm; ground clearance: 6.50 in, 16.5 cm; weight: E Limousine 3,021 lb, 1,370 kg - CE Coupé 3,043 lb, 1,380 kg - TE Limousine 3,285 lb, 1,490 kg; turning circle: 37.1 ft, 11.3 m; fuel tank: 14.3 imp gal, 17.2 US gal, 65 l - TE Limousine 15.4 imp gal, 18.5 US gal, 70 l.

BODY saloon/sedan, 4 doors - coupé, 2 doors - estate car/st. wagon, 4+1 doors; 5 seats, separate front seats, reclining backrests.

PRACTICAL INSTRUCTIONS fuel: 98 oct petrol; oil: engine 7.9 imp pt, 9.5 US pt, 4.5 l, SAE 20W-30, change every 6,200 miles, 10,000 km - gearbox 2.8 imp pt, 3.4 US pt, 1.6 l, ATF, change every 12,400 miles, 20,000 km - final drive 1.9 imp pt, 2.3 US pt, 1.1 l, SAE 90, change every 12,400 miles, 20,000 km; greasing: none; tyre pressure: front 29 psi, 2 atm, rear 33 psi, 2.3 atm.

OPTIONALS MB automatic transmission, hydraulic torque converter and planetary gears with 4 ratios (I 4.250, II 2.410, III 1.490, IV 1, rev 5.670), possible manual selection, max speed 109 mph, 175 km/h, consumption 25.9 m/imp gal, 21.6 m/US gal, 10.9 l x 100 km at 75 mph, 120 km/h; 5-speed mechanical gearbox (I 3.820, II 2.200, III 1.400, IV 1, V 0.810, rev 3.710), consumption 29.4 m/imp gal, 24.5 m/US gal, 9.6 l x 100 km at 75 mph, 120 km/h; anti-brake-locking system (ABS); automatic levelling control on rear suspension; power steering; halogen fog lamps; electric or manual sunroof; heated rear window; electric windows; tinted glass; air-conditioning; light alloy wheels; metallic spray.

250

PRICES IN GB AND EX WORKS:	£	DM
4-dr Limousine	**12,320***	**31,578***
Long Wheelbase 4-dr Limousine	**18,500***	**46,968***

ENGINE front, 4 stroke; 6 cylinders, vertical, in line; 154.1 cu in, 2,525 cc (3.39 x 2.85 in, 86 x 72.4 mm); compression ratio: 9:1; max power (DIN): 140 hp (103 kW) at 5,500 rpm; max torque (DIN): 177 lb ft, 24.4 kg m (239 Nm) at 3,500 rpm; max engine rpm: 6,000; 55.4 hp/l (40.8 kW/l); cast iron block, light alloy head; 4 crankshaft bearings; valves: overhead, in line, finger levers; camshafts: 1, overhead; lubrication: gear pump, oil-water heat exchanger, full flow filter (cartridge), 10.6 imp pt, 12.7 US pt, 6 l; 1 Solex 4 A 1 downdraught twin barrel carburettor; fuel feed: mechanical pump; water-cooled, 18.8 imp pt, 22.6 US pt, 10.7 l.

TRANSMISSION driving wheels: rear; clutch: single dry plate, hydraulically controlled; gearbox: mechanical; gears: 4, fully synchronized; ratios: I 3.980, II 2.290, III 1.450, IV 1, rev 3.740; lever: steering column or central; final drive: hypoid bevel; axle ratio: 3.580 - Long Wheelbase 3.690; width of rims: 6" - Long Wheelbase 5.5"; tyres: 195/70 HR x 14 - Long Wheelbase 185 SR x 15.

PERFORMANCE max speeds: (I) 30 mph, 48 km/h; (II) 50 mph, 80 km/h; (III) 83 mph, 134 km/h; (IV) 115 mph, 185 km/h; power weight ratio: Limousine 22.2 lb/hp (28.2 lb/kW), 10.1 kg/hp (13.7 kg/kW); carrying capacity: Limousine 1,145 lb, 520 kg - Long Wheelbase 1,466 lb, 665 kg; consumption: 24.8 m/imp gal, 20.6 m/US gal, 11.4 l x 100 km at 75 mph, 120 km/h.

CHASSIS integral, front auxliary frame; front suspension: independent, wishbones, coil springs, auxiliary rubber springs, anti-roll bar, telescopic dampers; rear: independent, oblique semi-trailing arms, coil springs, auxiliary rubber springs, anti-roll bar, telescopic dampers.

STEERING recirculating ball, servo.

BRAKES disc (front diameter 10.75 in, 27.3 cm, rear 10.98 in, 27.9 cm), dual circuit, servo; swept area: front 225.4 sq in, 1,454 sq cm, rear 195.8 sq in, 1,263 sq cm, total 421.2 sq in, 2,717 sq cm.

ELECTRICAL EQUIPMENT 12 V; 55 Ah battery; 770 W alternator; electronic ignition; 4 headlamps.

DIMENSIONS AND WEIGHT wheel base: 110.04 in, 279 cm - Long Wheelbase 134.65 in, 342 cm; tracks: 58.58 in, 149 cm - Long Wheelbase 58.27 in, 148 cm front, 56.93 in, 145 cm - Long Wheelbase 56.30 in, 143 cm rear; length: 186.02 in, 472 cm - Long Wheelbase 210.36 in, 535 cm; width: 70.31 in, 179 cm; height: 56.69 in, 144 cm - Long Wheelbase 58.27 in, 148 cm; ground clearance: 6.50 in, 16.5 cm; weight: 3,109 lb, 1,410 kg - Long Wheelbase 3,462 lb, 1,570 kg; turning circle: 37.1 ft, 11.3 m - Long Wheelbase 43.6 ft, 13.3 m; fuel tank: 17.6 imp gal, 21.1 US gal, 80 l.

MERCEDES-BENZ 300 TD Turbodiesel Limousine

BODY saloon/sedan, 5 seats - Long Wheelbase, saloon/sedan, 7-8 seats; 4 doors; separate front seats, reclining backrests.

PRACTICAL INSTRUCTIONS fuel: 98 oct petrol; oil: engine 10.6 imp pt, 12.7 US pt, 6 l, SAE 20W-30, change every 4,600 miles, 7,500 km - gearbox 2.8 imp pt, 3.4 US pt, 1.6 l, ATF, change every 12,400 miles, 20,000 km - final drive 1.9 imp pt, 2.3 US pt, 1.1 l, SAE 90; change every 12,400 miles, 20,000 km; greasing: none; tappet clearances: inlet 0.003 in, 0.08 mm, exhaust 0.008 in, 0.20 mm; valve timing: 11° 47° 48° 16°; tyre pressure: front 21 psi, 1.5 atm, rear 26 psi, 1.8 atm.

OPTIONALS MB automatic transmission, hydraulic torque converter and planetary gears with 4 ratios (I 3.680, II 2.410, III 1.440, IV 1, rev 5.140), possible manual selection, max speeds (I) 25 mph, 40 km/h, (II) 50 mph, 80 km/h, (III) 83 mph, 134 km/h, (IV) 112 mph, 180 km/h, consumption 23.7 m/imp gal, 19.8 m/US gal, 11.9 l x 100 km at 75 mph, 120 km/h; 5-speed mechanical gearbox (I 3.820, II 2.200, III 1.400, IV 1, V 0.810, rev 3.710), consumption 27.2 m/imp gal, 22.6 m/US gal, 10.4 l x 100 km at 75 mph, 120 km/h; anti-brake-locking system (ABS); automatic levelling control on rear suspension; halogen headlamps; fog lamps; electric or manual sunroof; heated seats; electric windows; tinted glass; air-conditioning; light alloy wheels; metallic spray.

240 D

PRICES IN GB AND EX WORKS:	£	DM
D 4-dr Limousine	**10,660***	**29,241***
D Long Wheelbase 4-dr Limousine	—	**44,688***
TD 4+1-dr Limousine	**12,025***	**33,379***

ENGINE diesel; front, 4 stroke; 4 cylinders, vertical, in line; 146.4 cu in, 2,399 cc (3.58 x 3.64 in, 91 x 92.4 mm); compression ratio: 21:1; max power (DIN): 72 hp (53 kW) at 4,400 rpm; max torque (DIN): 101 lb ft, 14 kg m (137 Nm) at 2,400 rpm; max engine rpm: 5,300; 30 hp/l (22.1 kW/l); cast iron block and head; 5 crankshaft bearings; valves: overhead, in line, finger levers; camshafts: 1, overhead; lubrication: gear pump, oil cooler, full flow (cartridge) and by-pass filters, 11.4 imp pt, 13.7 US pt, 6.5 l; Bosch injection pump; fuel feed: mechanical pump; cooling: 17.6 pt, 21.1 US pt, 10 l.

TRANSMISSION driving wheels: rear; clutch: single dry plate, hydraulically controlled; gearbox: mechanical; gears: 4, fully synchronized; ratios: I 4.230, II 2.360, III 1.490, IV 1, rev 4.100; lever: steering column or central; final drive: hypoid bevel; axle ratio: 3.690 - D Long Wheelbase 3.920; width of rims: 5.5" - TD 6"; tyres: 175 SR x 14 - D Long Wheelbase 185 SR x 15 - TD 195/70 SR x 14.

PERFORMANCE max speeds: (I) 22 mph, 35 km/h; (II) 37 mph, 60 km/h; (III) 61 mph, 98 km/h; (IV) 89 mph, 143 km/h; power-weight ratio: D 43 lb/hp (58.5 lb/kW), 19.5 kg/hp (26.5 kg/kW); carrying capacity: D 1,145 lb, 520 kg - D Long Wheelbase 1,466 lb, 665 kg - TD 1,367 lb, 620 kg; consumption: 28.5 m/imp gal, 23.5 m/US gal, 9.9 l x 100 km at 75 mph, 120 km/h.

CHASSIS integral, front auxiliary frame; front suspension: independent, wishbones, coil springs, auxiliary rubber springs, anti-roll bar, telescopic dampers; rear: independent, oblique semi-trailing arms, coil springs, auxiliary rubber springs, anti-roll bar, telescopic dampers, automatic levelling control (standard for TD only).

STEERING recirculating ball, servo (standard for D Long Wheelbase only).

BRAKES disc (front diameter 10.75 in, 27.3 cm, rear 10.98 in, 27.9 cm), dual circuit, servo; swept area: front 225.4 sq in, 1,454 sq cm, rear 195.8 sq in, 1,263 sq cm, total 421.2 sq in, 2,717 sq cm.

MERCEDES-BENZ 300 TD Turbodiesel Limousine

ELECTRICAL EQUIPMENT 12 V; 88 Ah battery; 770 W alternator; 4 headlamps.

DIMENSIONS AND WEIGHT wheel base: 110.04 in, 279 cm - D Long Wheelbase 134.65 in, 342 cm; tracks: 58.58 in, 149 cm - D Long Wheelbase 58.27 in, 148 cm front, 56.93 in, 145 cm - D Long Wheelbase 56.30 in, 143 cm rear; length: 186.02 in, 472 cm - D Long Wheelbase 210.36 in, 535 cm; width: 70.31 in, 179 cm; height: D 56.69 in, 144 cm - D Long Wheelbase 58.27 in, 148 cm - TD 56.10 in, 142 cm; ground clearance: 6.50 in, 16.5 cm; weight: D 3,098 lb, 1,405 kg - D Long Wheelbase 3,495 lb, 1,585 kg - TD 3,363 lb, 1,525 kg; turning circle: 37.1 ft, 11.3 m - D Long Wheelbase 43.6 ft, 13.3 m; fuel tank: 14.3 imp gal, 17.2 US gal, 65 l - TD 15.4 imp gal, 18.5 US gal, 70 l.

BODY saloon/sedan, 4 doors, 5 seats - D Long Wheelbase, saloon/sedan, 7-8 seats - TD, estate car/st. wagon, 4+1 doors, 5-7 seats, folding rear seats, rear window wiper-washer; separate front seats, reclining backrests; heated rear window.

PRACTICAL INSTRUCTIONS fuel: diesel; oil: engine 11.4 imp pt, 13.7 US pt, 6.5 l, SAE 20W-30, change every 4,600 miles, 7,500 km - gearbox 2.8 imp pt, 3.4 US pt, 1.6 l, ATF, change every 12,400 miles, 20,000 km - final drive 1.9 imp pt, 2.3 US pt, 1.1 l, SAE 90, change every 12,400 miles, 20,000 km; greasing: none; tappet clearances: inlet 0.003 in, 0.08 mm, exhaust 0.008 in, 0.20 mm; valve timing: 11° 47° 48° 16°; tyre pressure: front 21 psi, 1.5 atm, rear 26 psi, 1.8 atm.

OPTIONALS MB automatic transmission, hydraulic torque converter and planetary gears with 4 ratios (I 4.250, II 2.410, III 1.490, IV 1, rev 5.670), possible manual selection, max speeds (I) 21 mph, 34 km/h, (II) 37 mph, 60 km/h, (III) 61 mph, 98 km/h, (IV) 86 mph, 138 km/h, consumption 26.6 m/imp gal, 22.2 m/US gal, 10.6 l x 100 km at 75 mph, 120 km/h; 5-speed mechanical gearbox (I 3.820, II 2.200, III 1.400, IV 1, V 0.810, rev 3.710), consumption 32.5 m/imp gal, 27 m/US gal, 8.7 l x 100 km at 75 mph, 120 km/h; anti-brake-locking system (ABS); (for D and D Long Wheelbase only) automatic levelling control on rear suspension; halogen headlamps; fog lamps; electric or manual sunroof; heated seats; electric windows; tinted glass; air-conditioning; light alloy wheels; metallic spray.

300 D Series

PRICES IN GB AND EX WORKS:	£	DM
1 D 4-dr Limousine	12,280*	31,692*
2 D Long Wheelbase 4-dr Limousine	18,500*	47,139*
3 TD 4+1-dr Limousine	13,055*	35,830*
4 TD Turbodiesel 4+1-dr Limousine	—	42,579*

For USA prices, see price index.

Power team:	Standard for:	Optional for:
88 hp (diesel)	1 to 3	—
125 hp (diesel)	4	—

88 hp power team

ENGINE diesel; front, 4 stroke; 5 cylinders, vertical, in line; 182.9 cu in, 2,998 cc (3.58 x 3.64 in, 90.9 x 92.4 mm); compression ratio: 21:1; max power (DIN): 88 hp (65 kW) at 4,400 rpm; max torque (DIN): 127 lb ft, 17.5 kg m (172 Nm) at 2,400 rpm; max engine rpm: 5,300; 29.3 hp/l (21.7 kW/l); cast iron block and head; 6 crankshaft bearings; valves: overhead, in line, finger levers; camshafts: 1, overhead; lubrication: gear pump, oil cooler, full flow (cartridge) and by-pass filters, 11.4 imp pt, 13.7 US pt, 6.5 l; Bosch injection pump; fuel feed: mechanical pump; cooling: 19 imp pt, 22.8 US pt, 10.8 l.

TRANSMISSION driving wheels: rear; clutch: single dry plate, hydraulically controlled; gearbox: mechanical; gears: 4, fully synchronized; ratios: I 3.900, II 2.300, III 1.410, IV 1, rev 3.660; lever: steering column or central; final drive: hypoid bevel; axle ratio: 3.460 - D Long Wheelbase 3.690; width of rims: 5.5" - TD 6"; tyres: 175 SR x 14 - D Long Wheelbase 185 SR x 15 - TD 195/70 SR x 14.

PERFORMANCE max speeds: (I) 24 mph, 38 km/h; (II) 40 mph, 64 km/h; (III) 65 mph, 104 km/h; (IV) 96 mph, 155 km/h; power-weight ratio: D 36.3 lb/hp (49.2 lb/kW), 16.5 kg/hp (22.3 kg/kW); carrying capacity: 1,445 lb, 520 kg - D Long Wheelbase 1,466 lb, 665 kg - TD 1,367 lb, 620 kg; consumption: 27.2 m/imp gal, 22.6 m/US gal, 10.4 l x 100 km at 75 mph, 120 km/h.

CHASSIS integral, front auxiliary frame; front suspension: independent, wishbones, coil springs, auxiliary rubber springs, anti-roll bar, telescopic dampers; rear: independent, oblique semi-trailing arms, coil springs, auxiliary rubber springs, anti-roll bar, telescopic dampers, (for TD only) automatic levelling control.

STEERING recirculating ball, servo.

BRAKES disc (front diameter 10.75 in, 27.3 cm, rear 10.98 in, 27.9 cm), dual circuit, servo; swept area: front 225.4 sq in, 1,454 sq cm, rear 195.8 sq in, 1,263 sq cm, total 421.2 sq in, 2,717 sq cm.

ELECTRICAL EQUIPMENT 12 V; 88 Ah battery; 770 W alternator; 4 headlamps.

DIMENSIONS AND WEIGHT wheel base: 110.04 in, 279 cm - D Long Wheelbase 134.65 in, 342 cm; tracks: 58.58 in, 149 cm - D Long Wheelbase 58.27 in, 148 cm front, 56.93 in, 145 cm - D Long Wheelbase 56.30 in, 143 cm rear; length: 186.02 in, 472 cm - D Long Wheelbase 210.36 in, 535 cm; width: 70.31 in, 179 cm; height: D 56.69 in, 144 cm - D Long Wheelbase 58.27 in, 148 cm - TD 56.10 in, 142 cm; ground clearance: 6.50 in, 16.5 cm; weight: D 3,197 lb, 1,450 kg - D Long Wheelbase 3,594 lb, 1,630 kg - TD 3,462 lb, 1,570 kg; turning circle: 37.1 ft, 11.3 m - D Long Wheelbase 43.6 ft, 13.3 m; fuel tank: 14.3 imp gal, 17.2 US gal, 65 l - TD 15.4 imp gal, 18.5 US gal, 70 l.

BODY saloon/sedan, 5 seats - D Long Wheelbase, saloon/sedan, 7-8 seats - TD, estate car/st. wagon, 5-7 seats, folding rear seat, rear window wiper-washer; separate front seats, reclining backrests; heated rear window.

PRACTICAL INSTRUCTIONS fuel: diesel; oil: engine 11.4 imp pt, 13.7 US pt, 6.5 l, SAE 20W-30, change every 4,600 miles, 7,500 km - gearbox 2.8 imp pt, 3.4 US pt, 1.6 l, ATF, change every 12,400 miles, 20,000 km - final drive 1.9 imp pt, 2.3 US pt, 1.1 l, SAE 90, change every 12,400 miles, 20,000 km; greasing: none; tappet clearances: inlet 0.003 in, 0.08 mm, exhaust 0.008 in, 0.20 mm; valve timing: 11° 47° 48° 16°; tyre pressure: front 21 psi, 1.5 atm, rear 26 psi, 1.8 atm.

OPTIONALS MB automatic transmission, hydraulic torque converter and planetary gears with 4 ratios (I 4.250, II 2.410, III 1.490, IV 1, rev 5.670), possible manual selection, max speeds (I) 22 mph, 36 km/h, (II) 40 mph, 64 km/h, (III) 65 mph, 104 km/h, (IV) 93 mph, 150 km/h, consumption 25.7 m/imp gal, 21.4 m/US gal, 11 l x 100 km at 75 mph, 120 km/h; 5-speed mechanical gearbox (I 3.820, II 2.200, III 1.400, IV 1, V 0.810, rev 3.710), consumption 29.7 m/imp gal, 24.8 m/US gal, 9.5 l x 100 km at 75 mph, 120 km/h; anti-brake-locking system (ABS); (for D and D Long Wheelbase only) automatic levelling control on rear suspension; halogen headlamps; fog lamps; electric or manual sunroof; heated seats; electric windows; tinted glass; air-conditioning; light alloy wheels; metallic spray.

125 hp power team

See 88 hp power team, except for:

ENGINE diesel, turbocharged; compression ratio: 21.5:1; max power (DIN): 125 hp (92 kW) at 4,350 rpm; max torque (DIN): 185 lb ft, 25.5 kg m (250 Nm) at 2,400 rpm; max engine rpm: 5,100; 41.7 hp/l (30.7 kW/l); lubrication: full flow filter, 13.2 imp pt, 15.8 US pt, 7.5 l; Bosch injection pump; 1 Garrett AiResearch turbocharger.

TRANSMISSION gearbox: MB automatic transmission, hydraulic torque converter and planetary gears with 4 ratios, possible manual selection; ratios: I 3.680, II 2.410, III 1.440, IV 1, rev 5.140; axle ratio: 3.070; width of rims: 6"; tyres: 195/70 SR x 14.

PERFORMANCE max speed: 103 mph, 165 km/h; power-weight ratio: 28.6 lb/hp (38.8 lb/kW), 13 kg/hp (17.6 kg/kW); carrying capacity: 1,345 lb, 610 kg; speed in direct drive at 1,000 rpm: 20.1 mph, 32.4 km/h; consumption: 25.9 m/imp gal, 21.6 m/US gal, 10.9 l x 100 km at 75 mph, 120 km/h.

CHASSIS front suspension: upper wishbones with single transverse rod, longitudinal leading arm in unit with anti-roll bar.

STEERING damper, servo.

BRAKES (front diameter 10.94 in, 27.8 cm); swept area: front 255.5 sq in, 1,648 sq cm, rear 195.8 sq in, 1,263 sq cm, total 451.3 sq in, 2,911 sq cm.

DIMENSIONS AND WEIGHT height: 57.87 in, 147 cm; weight: 3,572 lb, 1,620 kg.

PRACTICAL INSTRUCTIONS oil: engine 13.2 imp pt, 15.8 US pt, 7.5 l.

280 E

PRICES IN GB AND EX WORKS:	£	DM
E 4-dr Limousine	14,280*	37,882*
CE 2-dr Coupé	16,200*	42,636*
TE 4+1-dr Limousine	15,810*	41,952*

ENGINE front, 4 stroke; 6 cylinders, vertical, in line; 167.6 cu in, 2,746 cc (3.39 x 3.10 in, 86 x 78.8 mm); compression ratio: 9:1; max power (DIN): 185 hp (136 kW) at 5,800 rpm; max torque (DIN): 177 lb ft, 24.5 kg m (240 Nm) at 4,500

MERCEDES-BENZ 280 CE Coupé

280 E

rpm; max engine rpm: 6,500; 67.4 hp/l (49.6 kW/l); cast iron block, light alloy head; 7 crankshaft bearings; valves: overhead, Vee-slanted at 54°, finger levers; camshafts: 2, overhead; lubrication: gear pump, oil-water heat exchanger, filter (cartridge) on by-pass, oil cooler, 10.6 imp pt, 12.7 US pt, 6 l; Bosch K-Jetronic injection; fuel feed: electric pump; water-cooled, 17.1 imp pt, 20.5 US pt, 9.7 l, electric thermostatic fan.

TRANSMISSION driving wheels: rear; clutch: single dry plate, hydraulically controlled; gearbox: mechanical; gears: 4, fully synchronized; ratios: I 3.980, II 2.290, III 1.450, IV 1, rev 3.740; lever: central; final drive: hypoid bevel; axle ratio: 3.580; width of rims: 6"; tyres: 195/70 HR x 14.

PERFORMANCE max speeds: (I) 34 mph, 55 km/h; (II) 55 mph, 88 km/h; (III) 90 mph, 145 km/h; (IV) 124 mph, 200 km/h; power-weight ratio: E 17.6 lb/hp (23.9 lb/kW), 8 kg/hp (10.8 kg/kW); carrying capacity: 1,147 lb, 520 kg - TE 1,367 lb, 620 kg; consumption: 24.1 m/imp gal, 20.1 m/US gal, 11.7 l x 100 km at 75 mph, 120 km/h.

CHASSIS integral; front suspension: independent, upper wishbones with single transverse rod, longitudinal leading arm in unit with anti-roll bar, coil springs, telescopic dampers; rear: independent, oblique semi-trailing arms, coil springs, auxiliary rubber springs, anti-roll bar, telescopic dampers.

STEERING recirculating ball, damper, servo.

BRAKES disc (front diameter 10.94 in, 27.8 cm, rear 10.98 in, 27.9 cm), rear compensator, dual circuit, servo; swept area: front 255.5 sq in, 1,648 sq cm, rear 195 sq in, 1,263 sq cm, total 451.3 sq in, 2,911 sq cm.

ELECTRICAL EQUIPMENT 12 V; 55 Ah battery; 770 W alternator; electronic ignition; 4 halogen headlamps.

DIMENSIONS AND WEIGHT wheel base: 110.04 in, 279 cm - CE 106.69 in, 271 cm; tracks: 58.58 in, 149 cm front, 56.93 in, 145 cm rear; length: 186.02 in, 472 cm - CE 182.68 in, 464 cm; width: 70.31 in, 179 cm; height: 56.69 in, 144 cm; ground clearance: 6.50 in, 16.5 cm; weight: E 3,253 lb, 1,475 kg - CE 3,219 lb, 1,460 kg - TE 3,440 lb, 1,560 kg; turning circle: 37.1 ft, 11.3 m; fuel tank: 17.6 imp gal, 21.1 US gal, 80 l - TE 15.4 imp gal, 18.5 US gal, 70 l.

BODY saloon/sedan, 4 doors - coupé, 2 doors - TE, estate car/st. wagon, 4+1 doors; 5 seats, separate front seats, reclining backrests.

PRACTICAL INSTRUCTIONS fuel: 98 oct petrol; oil: engine 10.6 imp pt, 12.7 US pt, 6 l, SAE 20W-30, change every 4,600 miles, 7,500 km - gearbox 3.2 imp pt, 3.8 US pt, 1.8 l, ATF, change every 12,400 miles, 20,000 km - final drive 4.4 imp pt, 5.3 US pt, 2.5 l, SAE 90, change every 12,400 miles, 20,000 km; greasing: every 3,100 miles, 5,000 km, 20 points; tyre pressure: front 29 psi, 2 atm, rear 33 psi, 2.3 atm.

OPTIONALS MB automatic transmission, hydraulic torque converter and planetary gears with 4 ratios (I 3.680, II 2.410, III 1.440, IV 1, rev 5.140), max ratio of converter at stall 2.20, possible manual selection, max speed 121 mph, 195 km/h, consumption 23.3 m/imp gal, 19.4 m/US gal, 12.1 l x 100 km at 75 mph, 120 km/h; 5-speed mechanical gearbox (I 3.820, II 2.200, III 1.400, IV 1, V 0.810, rev 3.710), consumption 26.4 m/imp gal, 22 m/US gal, 10.7 l x 100 km at 75 mph, 120 km/h; anti-brake-locking system (ABS); automatic levelling control on rear suspension; fog lamps; electric or manual sunroof; heated rear window; heated seats; electric windows; tinted glass; air-conditioning; light alloy wheels; metallic spray.

280 / 380 / 500 S Series

PRICES IN GB AND EX WORKS:	£	DM
1 280 S 4-dr Limousine	—	43,890*
2 280 SE 4-dr Limousine	16,990*	47,618*
3 280 SEL 4-dr Limousine	—	50,445*
4 380 SE 4-dr Limousine	20,435*	57,513*
5 380 SEL 4-dr Limousine	22,855*	60,340*
6 500 SE 4-dr Limousine	24,675*	62,463*
7 500 SEL 4-dr Limousine	27,770*	68,742*

For USA prices, see price index.

Power team:	Standard for:	Optional for:
156 hp	1	—
185 hp	2,3	—
204 hp	4,5	—
231 hp	6,7	—

156 hp power team

ENGINE front, 4 stroke; 6 cylinders, vertical, in line; 167.6 cu in, 2,746 cc (3.39 x 3.10 in, 86 x 78.8 mm); compression ratio: 9:1; max power (DIN): 156 hp (115 kW) at 5,500 rpm; max torque (DIN): 164 lb ft, 22.7 kg m (223 Nm) at 4,000 rpm; max engine rpm: 6,500; 56.8 hp/l (41.8 kW/l); cast iron block, light alloy head; 7 crankshaft bearings; valves: overhead, Vee-slanted at 54°, finger levers; camshafts: 2, overhead; lubrication: gear pump, oil-water heat exchanger, filter (cartridge) on by-pass, oil cooler, 10.6 imp pt, 12.7 US pt, 6 l; 1 Solex 4 A 1 downdraught twin barrel carburettor; fuel feed: mechanical pump; water-cooled, 19.4 imp pt, 23.3 US pt, 11 l, electric thermostatic fan.

TRANSMISSION driving wheels: rear; clutch: single dry plate, hydraulically controlled; gearbox: mechanical; gears: 4, fully synchronized; ratios: I 3.980, II 2.290, III 1.450, IV 1, rev 3.740; lever: central; final drive: hypoid bevel; axle ratio: 3.460; width of rims: 6"; tyres: 195/70 HR x 14.

PERFORMANCE max speeds: (I) 34 mph, 55 km/h; (II) 55 mph, 88 km/h; (III) 90 mph, 145 km/h; (IV) 124 mph, 200 km/h; power-weight ratio: 22.1 lb/hp (29.9 lb/kW), 10 kg/hp (13.6 kg/kW); carrying capacity: 1,147 lb, 520 kg; consumption: 25.9 m/imp gal, 21.6 m/US gal, 10.9 l x 100 km at 75 mph, 120 km/h.

CHASSIS integral; front suspension: independent, upper wishbones with single transverse rod, longitudinal leading arm in unit with anti-roll bar, coil springs, telescopic dampers; rear: independent, oblique semi-trailing arms, coil springs, auxiliary rubber springs, automatic levelling control, anti-roll bar, telescopic dampers.

STEERING recirculating ball, damper, servo.

BRAKES disc (front diameter 10.94 in, 27.8 cm, rear 10.98 in, 27.9 cm), rear compensator, dual circuit, servo; swept area: front 255.5 sq in, 1,648 sq cm, rear 195 sq in, 1,263 sq cm, total 451.3 sq in, 2,911 sq cm.

ELECTRICAL EQUIPMENT 12 V; 55 Ah battery; 910 W alternator; Bosch distributor; 4 halogen headlamps.

DIMENSIONS AND WEIGHT wheel base: 115.55 in, 293 cm; tracks: 60.83 in, 154 cm front, 59.72 in, 152 cm rear; length: 196.65 in, 499 cm; width: 71.65 in, 182 cm; height: 56.30 in, 143 cm; ground clearance: 5.91 in, 15 cm; weight: 3,440 lb, 1,560 kg; turning circle: 38.7 ft, 11.8 m; fuel tank: 19.8 imp gal, 23.8 US gal, 90 l.

BODY saloon/sedan; 4 doors; 5 seats, separate front seats, reclining backrests with built-in headrests.

PRACTICAL INSTRUCTIONS fuel: 98 oct petrol; oil: engine 10.6 imp pt, 12.7 US pt, 6 l, SAE 20W-30, change every 4,600 miles, 7,500 km - gearbox 3.2 imp pt, 3.8 US pt, 1.8 l, ATF, change every 12,400 miles, 20,000 km - final drive 4.4 imp pt, 5.3 US pt, 2.5 l, SAE 90, change every 12,400 miles, 20,000 km; greasing: every 3,100 miles, 5,000 km, 20 points; tyre pressure: front 30 psi, 2.1 atm, rear 33 psi, 2.3 atm.

OPTIONALS MB automatic transmission, hydraulic torque converter and planetary gears with 4 ratios (I 3.680, II 2.410, III 1.440, IV 1, rev 5.140), max ratio of converter at stall 2.20, possible manual selection, max speeds (I) 26 mph, 42 km/h, (II) 55 mph, 88 km/h, (III) 90 mph, 145 km/h, (IV) 121 mph, 195 km/h, consumption 24.6 m/imp gal, 20.5 m/US gal, 11.5 l x 100 km at 75 mph, 120 km/h; 5-speed mechanical gearbox (I 3.820, II 2.200, III 1.400, IV 1, V 0.810, rev 3.710), consumption 28.5 m/imp gal, 23.5 m/US gal, 9.9 l x 100 km at 75 mph, 120 km/h; anti-brake-locking system (ABS); fog lamps; electric or manual sunroof; heated rear window; heated seats; electric windows; tinted glass; air-conditioning; light alloy wheels; metallic spray.

185 hp power team

See 156 hp power team, except for:

ENGINE max power (DIN): 185 hp (136 kW) at 5,800 rpm; max torque (DIN): 177 lb ft, 24.5 kg m (240 Nm) at 4,500 rpm; 67.4 hp/l (49.6 kW/l); Bosch K-Jetronic injection; fuel feed: electric pump.

TRANSMISSION tyres: 195/70 VR x 14.

PERFORMANCE max speeds: (I) 34 mph, 55 km/h; (II) 55 mph, 88 km/h; (III) 90 mph, 145 km/h; (IV) 130 mph, 210 km/h; power-weight ratio: SEL 19 lb/hp (25.8 lb/kW), 8.6 kg/hp (11.7 kg/kW); consumption: 25.2 m/imp gal, 21 m/US gal, 11.2 l x 100 km at 75 mph, 120 km/h.

ELECTRICAL EQUIPMENT electronic ignition.

DIMENSIONS AND WEIGHT wheel base: SEL 120.87 in, 307 cm; length: SEL 202.16 in, 513 cm; weight: SEL 3,506 lb, 1,590 kg; turning circle: SEL 40.3 ft, 12.3 m.

OPTIONALS with MB automatic transmission, max speed 127 mph, 205 km/h, consumption 24.4 m/imp gal, 20.3 m/US gal, 11.6 l x 100 km at 75 mph, 120 km/h; with 5-speed

MERCEDES-BENZ 380 SE Limousine

MERCEDES-BENZ 380 SEC Coupé

MERCEDES-BENZ 500 SEC Coupé

mechanical gearbox, consumption 27.4 m/imp gal, 22.8 m/US gal, 10.3 l x 100 km at 75 mph, 120 km/h; (for SEL only) hydropneumatic suspension.

204 hp power team

See 156 hp power team, except for:

ENGINE 8 cylinders in Vee; 234.3 cu in, 3,839 cc (3.46 x 3.11 in, 88 x 78.9 mm); compression ratio: 9.4:1; max power (DIN): 204 hp (150 kW) at 5,250 rpm; max torque (DIN): 233 lb ft, 32.1 kg m (315 Nm) at 3,250 rpm; max engine rpm: 5,950; 53.1 hp/l (39.1 kW/l); light alloy block and head; 5 crankshaft bearings; camshafts: 2, 1 per bank, overhead; lubrication: 14.1 imp pt, 16.9 US pt, 8 l; Bosch K-Jetronic injection; fuel feed: electric pump; water-cooled, 26.4 imp pt, 31.7 US pt, 15 l.

TRANSMISSION gearbox: MB automatic transmission, hydraulic torque converter and planetary gears with 4 ratios, max ratio of converter at stall 2.20, possible manual selection; ratios: I 3.680, II 2.410, III 1.440, IV 1, rev 5.140; lever: steering column or central; final drive: hypoid bevel; axle ratio: 2.470; width of rims: 6.5''; tyres: 205/70 VR x 14.

PERFORMANCE max speeds: (I) 39 mph, 62 km/h; (II) 76 mph, 122 km/h; (III) 127 mph, 204 km/h; (IV) 130 mph, 210 km/h; power-weight ratio: SE 17.2 lb/hp (23.4 lb/kW), 7.8 kg/hp (10.6 kg/kW); consumption: 26.2 m/imp gal, 21.8 m/US gal, 10.8 l x 100 km at 75 mph, 120 km/h.

ELECTRICAL EQUIPMENT 66 Ah battery; 980 W alternator; electronic ignition.

DIMENSIONS AND WEIGHT wheel base: SEL 120.87 in, 307 cm; length: SEL 202.16 in, 513 cm; weight: SE 3,517 lb, 1,595 kg - SEL 3,561 lb, 1,615 kg; turning circle: SEL 40.3 ft, 12.3 m.

OPTIONALS (for SEL only) hydropneumatic suspension.

231 hp power team

See 156 hp power team, except for:

ENGINE 8 cylinders in Vee; 303.5 cu in, 4,973 cc (3.80 x 3.35 in, 96.5 x 85 mm); compression ratio: 9.2:1; max power (DIN): 231 hp (170 kW) at 4,750 rpm; max torque (DIN): 299 lb ft, 41.3 kg m (405 Nm) at 3,000 rpm; max engine rpm: 5,950; 46.5 hp/l (34.2 kW/l); light alloy block and head; 5 crankshaft bearings; camshafts: 2, 1 per bank, overhead; lubrication: 14.1 imp pt, 16.9 US pt, 8 l; Bosch K-Jetronic injection; fuel feed: electric pump; water-cooled, 24.4 imp pt, 31.7 US pt, 15 l.

TRANSMISSION gearbox: MB automatic transmission, hydraulic torque converter and planetary gears with 4 ratios, max ratio of converter at stall 2.20, possible manual selection; ratios: I 3.680, II 2.410, III 1.440, IV 1, rev 5.140; lever: steering column or central; final drive: hypoid bevel; axle ratio: 2.240; width of rims: 6.5''; tyres: 205/70 VR x 14.

PERFORMANCE max speeds: (I) 37 mph, 60 km/h; (II) 83 mph, 133 km/h; (III) 137 mph, 220 km/h; (IV) 140 mph, 225 km/h; power-weight ratio: SE 15.5 lb/hp (21 lb/kW), 7 kg/hp (9.5 kg/kW); consumption: 24.8 m/imp gal, 20.6 m/US gal, 11.4 l x 100 km at 75 mph, 120 km/h.

ELECTRICAL EQUIPMENT 66 Ah battery; 980 W alternator; electronic ignition.

DIMENSIONS AND WEIGHT wheel base: SEL 120.87 in, 307 cm; length: SEL 202.16 in, 513 cm; weight: SE 3,572 lb, 1,620 kg - SEL 3,649 lb, 1,655 kg; turning circle: SEL 40.3 ft, 12.3 m.

OPTIONALS (for SEL only) hydropneumatic suspension.

380 / 500 SEC Series

PRICES IN GB AND EX WORKS:	£	DM
1 380 SEC 2-dr Coupé	**28,560***	**77,292***
2 500 SEC 2-dr Coupé	**31,890***	**82,422***

For USA prices, see price index.

Power team:	Standard for:	Optional for:
204 hp	1	—
231 hp	2	—

204 hp power team

ENGINE front, 4 stroke; 8 cylinders in Vee; 243.3 cu in, 3,839 cc (3.46 x 3.11 in, 88 x 78.9 mm); compression ratio: 9.4:1; max power (DIN): 204 hp (150 kW) at 5,250 rpm; max torque (DIN): 233 lb ft, 32.1 kg m (315 Nm) at 3,250 rpm; max engine rpm: 5,950; 53.1 hp/l (39.1 kW/l); light alloy block and head; 5 crankshaft bearings; valves: overhead, Vee-slanted at 54°, finger levers; camshafts: 2, 1 per bank, overhead; lubrication: gear pump, oil-water heat exchanger, filter (cartridge) on by-pass, oil cooler, 14.1 imp pt, 16.9 US pt, 8 l; Bosch K-Jetronic ignition; fuel feed: electric pump; water-cooled, 26.4 imp pt, 31.7 US pt, 15 l, electric thermostatic fan.

TRANSMISSION driving wheels: rear; gearbox: MB automatic transmission, hydraulic torque converter and planetary gears with 4 ratios, max ratio of converter at stall 2.20, possible manual selection; ratios: I 3.680, II 2.410, III 1.440, IV 1, rev 5.140; lever: steering column or central; final drive: hypoid bevel; axle ratio: 2.470; width of rims: 6.5''; tyres: 205/70 VR x 14.

PERFORMANCE max speeds: (I) 39 mph, 62 km/h; (II) 76 mph, 122 km/h; (III) 127 mph, 204 km/h; (IV) 130 mph, 210 km/h; power-weight ratio: 17.1 lb/hp (23.3 lb/kW), 7.8 kg/hp (10.6 kg/kW); carrying capacity: 1,147 lb, 520 kg; consumption: 26.2 m/imp gal, 21.8 m/US gal, 10.8 l x 100 km at 75 mph, 120 km/h.

CHASSIS integral; front suspension: independent, upper wishbones with single transverse rod, longitudinal leading arm in unit with anti-roll bar, coil springs, telescopic dampers; rear: independent, oblique semi-trailing arms, coil springs, auxiliary rubber springs, anti-roll bar, telescopic dampers.

STEERING recirculating ball, damper, servo; turns lock to lock: 2.90.

BRAKES disc (front diameter 10.94 in, 27.8 cm, rear 10.98 in, 27.9 cm), front internal radial fins, rear compensator, dual circuit, servo; swept area: front 255.5 sq in, 1,648 sq cm, rear 195.8 sq in, 1,263 sq cm, total 451.3 sq in, 2,911 sq cm.

ELECTRICAL EQUIPMENT 12 V; 66 Ah battery; 980 W alternator; electronic ignition; 2 halogen headlamps.

DIMENSIONS AND WEIGHT wheel base: 112.20 in, 285 cm; tracks: 60.83 in, 154 cm front, 59.72 in, 152 cm rear; length: 193.31 in, 491 cm; width: 71.97 in, 183 cm; height: 55.35 in, 141 cm; ground clearance: 6.30 in, 16 cm; weight: 3,495 lb, 1,585 kg; turning circle: 37.8 ft, 11.5 m; fuel tank: 19.8 imp gal, 23.8 US gal, 90 l.

BODY coupé; 2 doors; 5 seats, separate front seats, reclining backrests.

PRACTICAL INSTRUCTIONS fuel: 98 oct petrol; oil: engine 14.1 imp pt, 16.9 US pt, 8 l, SAE 20W-30, change every 4,600 miles, 7,500 km; greasing: every 3,100 miles, 5,000 km, 20 points; spark plug: 215°; tyre pressure: front 30 psi, 2.1 atm, rear 34 psi, 2.4 atm.

OPTIONALS anti-brake-locking system (ABS); limited slip differential; fog lamps; electric sunroof; heated seats; electric windows; tinted glass; air-conditioning; light alloy wheels; metallic spray.

231 hp power team

See 204 hp power team, except for:

ENGINE 303.5 cu in, 4,973 cc (3.80 x 3.35 in, 96.5 x 85 mm); compression ratio: 9.2:1; max power (DIN): 231 hp (170 kW) at 4,750 rpm; max torque (DIN): 299 lb ft, 41.3 kg m (405 Nm) at 3,000 rpm; 46.5 hp/l (34.2 kW/l).

TRANSMISSION axle ratio: 2.240.

PERFORMANCE max speeds: (I) 37 mph, 60 km/h; (II) 83 mph, 133 km/h; (III) 137 mph, 220 km/h; (IV) 140 mph, 225 km/h; power-weight ratio: 15.4 lb/hp (20.9 lb/kW), 6.9 kg/hp (9.5 kg/kW); consumption: 24.8 m/imp gal, 20.6 m/US gal, 11.4 l x 100 km at 75 mph, 120 km/h.

DIMENSIONS AND WEIGHT weight: 3,550 lb, 1,610 kg.

280 / 380 / 500 SL Series

PRICES IN GB AND EX WORKS:	£	DM
1 280 SL 2-dr Roadster	**18,480***	**54,002***
2 380 SL 2-dr Roadster	**21,760***	**64,353***
3 500 SL 2-dr Roadster	**23,990***	**73,530***

For USA prices, see price index.

Power team:	Standard for:	Optional for:
185 hp	1	—
204 hp	2	—
231 hp	3	—

185 hp power team

ENGINE front, 4 stroke; 6 cylinders, vertical, in line; 167.6 cu in, 2,746 cc (3.39 x 3.10 in, 86 x 78.8 mm); compression ratio: 9:1; max power (DIN): 185 hp (136 kW) at 5,800 rpm; max torque (DIN): 177 lb ft, 24.5 kg m (240 Nm) at 4,500

MERCEDES-BENZ 500 SL Roadster

185 HP POWER TEAM

rpm; max engine rpm: 6,500; 67.4 hp/l (49.6 kW/l); cast iron block, light alloy head; 7 crankshaft bearings; valves: overhead, Vee-slanted at 54°, finger levers; camshafts: 2, overhead; lubrication: gear pump, oil-water heat exchanger, filter (cartridge) on by-pass, oil cooler, 10.6 imp pt, 12.7 US pt, 6 l; Bosch K-Jetronic injection; fuel feed: electric pump; water-cooled, 19.4 imp pt, 23.3 US pt, 11 l, electric thermostatic fan.

TRANSMISSION driving wheels: rear; clutch: single dry plate, hydraulically controlled; gearbox: mechanical; gears: 5, fully synchronized; ratios: I 3.820, II 2.200, III 1.400, IV 1, V 0.810, rev 3.710; lever: central; final drive: hypoid bevel; axle ratio: 3.580; width of rims: 6"; tyres: 195/70 HR x 14.

PERFORMANCE max speed: 124 mph, 200 km/h; power-weight ratio: 17.9 lb/hp (24.3 lb/kW), 8.1 kg/hp (11 kg/kW); carrying capacity: 926 lb, 420 kg; speed in top at 1,000 rpm: 19.1 mph, 30.8 km/h; consumption: 26.9 m/imp gal, 22.4 m/US gal, 10.5 l x 100 km at 75 mph, 120 km/h.

CHASSIS integral; front suspension: independent, upper wishbones with single transverse rod, longitudinal leading arm in unit with anti-roll bar, coil springs, telescopic dampers; rear: independent, oblique semi-trailing arms, coil springs, auxiliary rubber springs, anti-roll bar, telescopic dampers.

STEERING recirculating ball, damper, servo.

BRAKES disc (front diameter 10.94 in, 27.8 cm, rear 10.98 in, 27.9 cm), rear compensator, dual circuit, servo; swept area: front 255.5 sq in, 1,648 sq cm, rear 195.8 sq in, 1,263 sq cm, total 451.3 sq in, 2,911 sq cm.

ELECTRICAL EQUIPMENT 12 V; 55 Ah battery; 770 W alternator; electronic ignition; 2 halogen headlamps.

DIMENSIONS AND WEIGHT wheel base: 96.85 in, 246 cm; tracks: 57.17 in, 145 cm front, 56.69 in, 144 cm rear; length: 172.83 in, 439 cm; width: 70.47 in, 179 cm; height: 51.18 in, 130 cm; ground clearance: 5.51 in, 14 cm; weight: 3,307 lb, 1,500 kg; turning circle: 33.8 ft, 10.3 m; fuel tank: 18.7 imp gal, 22.4 US gal, 85 l.

BODY roadster; 2 doors; 2+2 seats.

PRACTICAL INSTRUCTIONS fuel: 98 oct petrol; oil: engine 10.6 imp pt, 12.7 US pt, 6 l, SAE 20W-30, change every 4,600 miles, 7,500 km - gearbox 3.2 imp pt, 3.8 US pt, 1.8 l, ATF, change every 12,400 miles, 20,000 km - final drive 4.4 imp pt, 5.3 US pt, 2.5 l, SAE 90, change every 12,400 miles, 20,000 km; greasing: every 3,100 miles, 5,000 km, 20 points; tyre pressure: front 31 psi, 2.2 atm, rear 36 psi, 2.5 atm.

OPTIONALS MB automatic transmission, hydraulic torque converter and planetary gears with 4 ratios (I 3.980, II 2.390, III 1.460, IV 1, rev 5.470), max ratio of converter at stall 2.20, possible manual selection, max speed 121 mph, 195 km/h, consumption 23.5 m/imp gal, 19.6 m/US gal, 12 l x 100 km at 75 mph, 120 km/h; anti-brake-locking system (ABS); air-conditioning; fog lamps; electric windows; light alloy wheels; hardtop.

204 hp power team

See 185 hp power team, except for:

ENGINE 8 cylinders in Vee; 234.3 cu in, 3,839 cc (3.46 x 3.11 in, 88 x 78.9 mm); compression ratio: 9.4:1; max power (DIN): 204 hp (150 kW) at 5,250 rpm; max torque (DIN): 233 lb ft, 32.1 kg m (315 Nm) at 3,250 rpm; max engine rpm: 5,950; 53.1 hp/l (39.1 kW/l); light alloy block and head; 5 crankshaft bearings; camshafts: 2, 1 per bank, overhead; lubrication: 14.1 imp pt, 16.9 US pt, 8 l; water-cooled, 26.4 imp pt, 31.7 US pt, 15 l.

TRANSMISSION gearbox: MB automatic transmission, hydraulic torque converter and planetary gears with 4 ratios, max ratio of converter at stall 2.20, possible manual selection; ratios: I 3.680, II 2.410, III 1.440, IV 1, rev 5.140; lever: steering column or central; final drive: hypoid bevel; axle ratio: 2.470; width of rims: 6.5"; tyres: 205/70 VR x 14.

PERFORMANCE max speed: 127 mph, 205 km/h; power-weight ratio: 16.6 lb/hp (22.6 lb/kW), 7.5 kg/hp (10.3 kg/kW); consumption: 25 m/imp gal, 20.8 m/US gal, 11.3 l x 100 km at 75 mph, 120 km/h.

ELECTRICAL EQUIPMENT 66 Ah battery; 980 W alternator.

DIMENSIONS AND WEIGHT wheel base: 96.65 in, 245 cm; weight: 3,396 lb, 1,540 kg.

MERCEDES-BENZ 280 GE

231 hp power team

See 185 hp power team, except for:

ENGINE 8 cylinders in Vee; 303.5 cu in, 4,973 cc (3.80 x 3.35 in, 96.5 x 85 mm); compression ratio: 9.2:1; max power (DIN): 231 hp (170 kW) at 4,750 rpm; max torque (DIN): 299 lb ft, 41.3 kg m (405 Nm) at 3,000 rpm; max engine rpm: 5,950; 46.5 hp/l (34.2 kW/l); light alloy block and head; 5 crankshaft bearings; camshafts: 2, 1 per bank, overhead; lubrication: 14.1 imp pt, 16.9 US pt, 8 l; water-cooled, 24.4 imp pt, 31.7 US pt, 15 l.

TRANSMISSION gearbox: MB automatic transmission, hydraulic torque converter and planetary gears with 4 ratios, max ratio of converter at stall 2.20, possible manual selection; ratios: I 3.680, II 2.410, III 1.440, IV 1, rev 5.140; lever: steering column or central; final drive: hypoid bevel; axle ratio 2.240; width of rims: 6.5"; tyres: 205/70 VR x 14.

PERFORMANCE max speed: 137 mph, 220 km/h; power-weight ratio: 14.7 lb/hp (20 lb/kW), 6.7 kg/hp (9.1 kg/kW); consumption: 24.6 m/imp gal, 20.5 m/US gal, 11.5 l x 100 km at 75 mph, 120 km/h.

ELECTRICAL EQUIPMENT 66 Ah battery; 980 W alternator.

DIMENSIONS AND WEIGHT wheel base: 96.65 in, 245 cm; weight: 3,396 lb, 1,540 kg.

230 G

2-dr Open
2+1-dr St. Wagon
4+1-dr Long Wheelbase St. Wagon

ENGINE front, 4 stroke; 4 cylinders, vertical, in line; 140.8 cu in, 2,307 cc (3.69 x 3.29 in, 93.7 x 83.6 mm); compression ratio: 9:1; max power (DIN): 102 hp (75 kW) at 5,200 rpm; max torque (DIN): 127 lb ft, 17.5 kg m (172 Nm) at 3,000 rpm; max engine rpm: 6,000; 22.6 hp/l (30.8 kW/l); cast iron block, light alloy head; 5 crankshaft bearings; valves: overhead, in line, finger levers; camshafts: 1, overhead; lubrication: gear pump, oil-water heat exchanger, full flow filter (cartridge), 9.7 imp pt, 11.6 US pt, 5.5 l; 1 Stromberg 175 CD horizontal carburettor; fuel feed: mechanical pump; water-cooled, 18.8 imp pt, 22.6 US pt, 10.7 l, thermostatic fan.

TRANSMISSION driving wheels: front (automatically engaged with transfer box low ratio) and rear; clutch: single dry plate, hydraulically controlled; gearbox: mechanical; gears: 4, fully synchronized and 2-ratio transfer box (high 1, low 2.140); ratios: I 4.628, II 2.462, III 1.473, IV 1, rev 4.348; gear and transfer levers: central; front and rear final drive: hypoid bevel; front and rear axle ratio: 5.330; width of rims: 5.5"; tyres: 205 R x 16.

PERFORMANCE max speeds: (I) 20 mph, 33 km/h; (II) 39 mph, 62 km/h; (III) 64 mph, 103 km/h; (IV) 85 mph, 137 km/h; power-weight ratio: 39.3 lb/hp (53.5 lb/kW), 17.8 kg/hp (24.3 kg/kW); carrying capacity: Open 1,499 lb, 680 kg - St. Wagon 1,389 lb, 630 kg - Long Wheelbase 1,786 lb, 810 kg; consumption: 14.6 m/imp gal, 12.2 m/US gal, 19.3 l x 100 km at 75 mph, 120 km/h.

CHASSIS welded frame with box sections and tubular members; front suspension: rigid axle, longitudinal control arms, transverse control arm (Panhard rod), coil springs, helper springs, torsion anti-roll bar, telescopic dampers; rear: rigid axle, longitudinal control arms, transverse control arm (progressively acting Panhard rod), coil springs, helper springs, telescopic dampers.

STEERING recirculating ball, worm and nut.

BRAKES front disc, rear drum, dual circuit, servo.

ELECTRICAL EQUIPMENT 12 V; 55 Ah battery; 55 A alternator; Bosch distributor; 2 headlamps.

DIMENSIONS AND WEIGHT wheel base: 94.49 in, 240 cm - Long Wheelbase 112.20 in, 285 cm; front and rear track: 56.30 in, 143 cm; length: 155.51 in, 395 cm - Long Wheelbase 173.03 in, 439 cm; width: 66.93 in, 170 cm; height: 77.76 in, 197 cm - st. wagons 77.17 in, 196 cm; ground clearance: 8.46 in, 21.5 cm; weight: Open 4,013 lb, 1,820 kg - St. Wagon 4,123 lb, 1,870 kg - Long Wheelbase 4,388 lb, 1,990 kg; turning circle: 37.4 ft, 11.4 m - Long Wheelbase 42.6 ft, 13 m; fuel tank: 16.5 imp gal, 19.8 US gal, 75 l.

BODY open, 2 doors - estate car/st. wagon, 2+1 or 4+1 doors; 5 seats, separate front seats.

PRACTICAL INSTRUCTIONS fuel: 98 oct petrol; oil: engine 9.7 imp pt, 11.6 US pt, 5.5 l, SAE 20W-30, change every 4,600 miles, 7,500 km - gearbox 2.8 imp pt, 3.4 US pt, 1.6 l, ATF, change every 12,400 miles, 20,000 km - final drive 1.9 imp pt, 2.3 US pt, 1.1 l, SAE 90, change every 12,400 miles, 20,000 km; tappet clearances: inlet 0.003 in, 0.08 mm, exhaust 0.008 in, 0.20 mm; valve timing: 11° 47° 48° 16°.

VARIATIONS

ENGINE 8:1 compression ratio, max power (DIN) 90 hp (66 kW) at 5,000 rpm, max torque (DIN) 123 lb ft, 17 kg m (167 Nm) at 2,500 rpm, 39 hp/l (28.6 kW/l).

OPTIONALS limited slip differential; power steering; hardtop.

MERCEDES-BENZ 230 GE Station Wagon

MERCEDES-BENZ 230 GE Station Wagon

MERCEDES-BENZ 280 GE Long Wheelbase Station Wagon

230 GE

See 230 G, except for:

PRICES IN GB AND EX WORKS	£	DM
2-dr Open	—	42,180*
2+1-dr St. Wagon	14,195*	46,455*
4+1-dr Long Wheelbase St. Wagon	—	51,927*

ENGINE 140.3 cu in, 2,299 cc (3.76 x 3.16 in, 95.5 x 80.2 mm); max power (DIN): 125 hp (92 kW) at 5,000 rpm; max torque (DIN): 142 lb ft, 19.6 kg m (192 Nm) at 4,000 rpm; 54.4 hp/l (40 kW/l); lubrication: 11.4 imp pt, 13.7 US pt, 6.5 l; Bosch injection with air flow metering device.

TRANSMISSION axle ratio: 4.900.

PERFORMANCE max speeds: (I) 22 mph, 35 km/h; (II) 42 mph, 67 km/h; (III) 70 mph, 112 km/h; (IV) 88 mph, 142 km/h; power-weight ratio: 32.3 lb/hp (43.9 lb/kW), 14.6 kg/hp (19.9 kg/kW); carrying capacity: Open 1,477 lb, 670 kg - St. Wagon 1,367 lb, 620 kg - Long Wheelbase 1,764 lb, 800 kg.

ELECTRICAL EQUIPMENT 66 Ah battery.

DIMENSIONS AND WEIGHT weight: Open 4,035 lb, 1,830 kg - St. Wagon 4,145 lb, 1,880 kg - Long Wheelbase 4,410 lb, 2,000 kg.

280 GE

See 230 G, except for:

PRICES IN GB AND EX WORKS:	£	DM
2-dr Open	—	47,994*
2+1-dr St. Wagon	14,675*	52,269*
4+1-dr Long Wheelbase St. Wagon	15,460*	57,741*

ENGINE 6 cylinders; 167.6 cu in, 2,746 cc (3.39 x 3.10 in, 86 x 78.8 mm); compression ratio: 8:1; max power (DIN): 156 hp (115 kW) at 5,250 rpm; max torque (DIN): 167 lb ft, 23 kg m (226 Nm) at 4,250 rpm; max engine rpm: 6,000; 56.8 hp/l (41.9 kW/l); 7 crankshaft bearings; valves: overhead, Vee-slanted at 54°; camshafts: 2, overhead; lubrication: 11.4 imp pt, 13.7 US pt, 6.5 l; Bosch injection with air flow metering device; air-cooled: 17.1 imp pt, 20.5 US pt, 9.7 l.

TRANSMISSION gearbox ratios: I 4.043, II 2.206, III 1.381, IV 1, rev 3.787; axle ratio: 4.900.

PERFORMANCE max speeds: (I) 25 mph, 41 km/h; (II) 46 mph, 74 km/h; (III) 70 mph, 113 km/h; (IV) 96 mph, 155 km/h; power-weight ratio: 26.4 lb/hp (35.8 lb/kW), 12.1 kg/hp (16.5 kg/kW); carrying capacity: Open 1,334 lb, 605 kg - St. Wagon 1,224 lb, 555 kg - Long Wheelbase 1,620 lb, 735 kg; consumption: 15 m/imp gal, 12.5 m/US gal, 18.8 l x 100 km at 75 mph, 120 km/h.

STEERING servo (standard).

DIMENSIONS AND WEIGHT weight: Open 4,112 lb, 1,895 kg - St. Wagon 4,289 lb, 1,945 kg - Long Wheelbase 4,553 lb, 2,065 kg.

PRACTICAL INSTRUCTIONS fuel: 98 oct petrol; oil: engine 11.4 imp pt, 13.7 US pt, 6.5 l, SAE 20W-30, change every 4,600 miles, 7,500 km - gearbox 3.2 imp pt, 3.8 US pt, 1.8 l, ATF, change every 12,400 miles, 20,000 km - final drive 4.4 imp pt, 5.3 US pt, 2.5 l, SAE 90, change every 12,400 miles, 20,000 km.

OPTIONALS MB automatic transmission (I 4.007, II 2.392, III 1.463, IV 1, rev 5.495).

240 GD

PRICES EX WORKS:	DM
2-dr Open	39,843*
2+1-dr St. Wagon	44,118*
4+1-dr Long Wheelbase St. Wagon	49,590*

ENGINE diesel; front, 4 stroke; 4 cylinders, vertical, in line; 146.4 cu in, 2,399 cc (3.58 x 3.64 in, 91 x 92.4 mm); compression ratio: 21:1; max power (DIN): 72 hp (53 kW) at 4,400 rpm; max torque (DIN): 101 lb ft, 14 kg m (137 Nm) at 2,400 rpm; max engine rpm: 5,300; 30 hp/l (22.1 kW/l); cast iron block and head; 5 crankshaft bearings; valves: overhead, in line, finger levers; camshafts: 1, overhead; lubrication: gear pump, oil cooler, full flow (cartridge) and by-pass filters, 11.4 imp pt, 13.7 US pt, 6.5 l; Bosch injection pump; fuel feed: mechanical pump; cooling: 17.6 imp pt, 21.1 US pt, 10 l, thermostatic fan.

TRANSMISSION driving wheels: front (automatically engaged with transfer box low ratio) and rear; clutch: single dry plate, hydraulically controlled; gearbox: mechanical; gears: 4, fully synchronized and 2-ratio transfer box (high 1, low 2.140); ratios: I 4.628, II 2.462, III 1.473, IV 1, rev 4.348; gear and transfer levers: central; front and rear final drive: hypoid bevel; front and rear axle ratio: 5.330; width of rims: 5.5"; tyres: 205 R x 16.

PERFORMANCE max speeds: (I) 16 mph, 25 km/h; (II) 30 mph, 48 km/h; (III) 49 mph, 79 km/h; (IV) 71 mph, 115 km/h; power-weight ratio: 56.7 lb/hp (76.9 lb/kW), 25.7 kg/hp (34.9 kg/kW); carrying capacity: Open 1,433 lb, 650 kg - St. Wagon 1,323 lb, 600 kg - Long Wheelbase 1,720 lb, 780 kg; consumption: 23.5 m/imp gal, 19.6 m/US gal, 12 l x 100 km at 56 mph, 90 km/h.

CHASSIS welded frame with box sections and tubular members; front suspension: rigid axle, longitudinal control arms, transverse control arm (Panhard rod), coil springs, helper springs, torsion anti-roll bar, telescopic dampers; rear: rigid axle, longitudinal control arms, transverse control arm (progressively acting Panhard rod), coil springs, helper springs, telescopic dampers.

STEERING recirculating ball, worm and nut.

BRAKES front disc, rear drum, dual circuit, servo.

ELECTRICAL EQUIPMENT 12 V; 88 Ah battery; 55 A alternator; 2 headlamps.

DIMENSIONS AND WEIGHT wheel base: 94.49 in, 240 cm - Long Wheelbase 112.20 in, 285 cm; front and rear track: 56.30 in, 143 cm; length: 155.51 in, 395 cm - Long Wheelbase 173.03 in, 439 cm; width: 66.93 in, 170 cm; height: 77.76 in, 197 cm - st. wagons 77.17 in, 196 cm; ground clearance: 8.46 in, 21.5 cm; weight: Open 4,079 lb, 1,850 kg - St. Wagon 4,189 lb, 1,900 kg - Long Wheelbase 4,454 lb, 2,020 kg; turning circle: 37.4 ft, 11.4 m - Long Wheelbase 42.6 ft, 13 m; fuel tank: 16.5 imp gal, 19.8 US gal, 75 l.

BODY open, 2 doors - estate car/st. wagon, 2+1 or 4+1 doors; 5 seats, separate front seats.

PRACTICAL INSTRUCTIONS fuel: diesel; oil: engine 11.4 imp pt, 13.7 US pt, 6.5 l, SAE 20W-30, change every 4,600 miles, 7,500 km.

OPTIONALS limited slip differential; power steering; hardtop.

300 GD

See 240 GD, except for:

PRICES IN GB AND EX WORKS:	£	DM
2-dr Open	—	44,004*
2+1-dr St. Wagon	14,035*	48,279*
4+1-dr Long Wheelbase St. Wagon	14,800*	53,751*

ENGINE 5 cylinders, vertical, in line; 128.9 cu, 2,998 cc (3.58 x 3.64 in, 91 x 92.4 mm); max power (DIN): 88 hp (65 kW) at 4,400 rpm; max torque (DIN): 127 lb ft, 17.5 kg m (172 Nm) at 2,400 rpm; max engine rpm: 5,300; 29.4 hp/l (21.7 kW/l); 6 crankshaft bearings; lubrication: 12.3 imp pt, 14.8 US pt, 7 l; Bosch injection pump; cooling: 19 imp pt, 22.8 US pt, 10.8 l.

TRANSMISSION axle ratio: 4.900.

PERFORMANCE max speeds: (I) 17 mph, 28 km/h; (II) 32 mph, 52 km/h; (III) 54 mph, 87 km/h; (IV) 81 mph, 130 km/h; power-weight ratio: 47.2 lb/hp (63.9 lb/kW), 21.4 kg/hp (29 kg/kW); carrying capacity: Open 1,356 lb, 615 kg - St. Wagon 1,246 lb, 565 kg - Long Wheelbase 1.643 lb, 745 kg; consumption: 23.7 m/imp gal, 19.8 m/US gal, 11.9 l x 100 km at 75 mph, 120 km/h.

STEERING servo (standard).

DIMENSIONS AND WEIGHT weight: Open 4,156 lb, 1,885 kg - St. Wagon 4,267 lb, 1,935 kg - Long Wheelbase 4,531 lb, 2,055 kg.

OPTIONALS MB automatic transmission (I 4.007, II 2.392, III 1.463, IV 1, rev 5.495).

OPEL Corsa Luxus Limousine

OPEL GERMANY FR

Corsa Series

PRICES EX WORKS:	DM
1 2+1-dr Limousine	11,753*
2 TR 2-dr Limousine	12,358*
3 Luxus 2+1-dr Limousine	12,898*
4 TR Luxus 2-dr Limousine	13,503*
5 Berlina 2+1-dr Limousine	13,872*
6 TR Berlina 2-dr Limousine	14,321*
7 SR 2+1-dr Limousine	15,006*

Power team:	Standard for:	Optional for:
45 hp	1 to 6	—
55 hp	—	1 to 6
70 hp	7	1 to 6

OPEL Corsa TR Berlina Limousine

45 hp power team

ENGINE front, transverse, 4 stroke; 4 cylinders, in line; 60.59 cu in, 993 cc (2.83 x 2.40 in, 72 x 61 mm); compression ratio: 9.2:1; max power (DIN): 45 hp (33 kW) at 5,400 rpm; max torque (DIN): 50 lb ft, 6.9 kg m (68 Nm) at 2,600 rpm; max engine rpm: 6,000; 45.3 hp/l (33.2 kW/l); cast iron block and head; 3 crankshaft bearings; valves: overhead, push-rods and rockers; camshafts: 1, side, chain-driven; lubrication: gear pump, full flow filter, 4.4 imp pt, 5.3 US pt, 2.5 l; 1 Weber 32 TL downdraught single barrel carburettor; fuel feed: mechanical pump; anti-freeze liquid cooled, 9.7 imp pt, 11.6 US pt, 5.5 l, electric thermostatic fan.

TRANSMISSION driving wheels: front; clutch: single dry plate (diaphragm); gearbox: mechanical; gears: 4, fully synchronized; ratios: I 3.550, II 1.960, III 1.300, IV 0.890, rev 3.180; lever: central; final drive: helical spur gears; axle ratio: 3.940; width of rims: 4.5"; tyres: 135 SR x 13.

PERFORMANCE max speed: 87 mph, 140 km/h; power-weight ratio: 36 lb/hp (49.1 lb/kW), 16.3 kg/hp (22.3 kg/kW); carrying capacity: 1,058 lb, 480 kg; consumption: 42.8 m/imp gal, 35.6 m/US gal, 6.6 l x 100 km at 75 mph, 120 km/h.

CHASSIS integral; front suspension: independent, by McPherson, coil springs/telescopic damper struts, heavy-duty rubber bearings, direction stabilizing radius arms; rear: crank compound, progressively acting coil springs, auxiliary rubber springs, telescopic dampers.

STEERING rack-and-pinion; turns lock to lock: 3.90.

BRAKES front disc, rear drum, dual circuit, servo; lining area: total 55.81 sq in, 360 sq cm.

ELECTRICAL EQUIPMENT 12 V; 36 Ah battery; 45 A alternator; 2 headlamps.

DIMENSIONS AND WEIGHT wheel base: 92.24 in, 234 cm; tracks: 51.97 in, 132 cm front, 51.18 in, 130 cm rear; length: 142.60 in, 362 cm - TR models 154.41 in, 395 cm; width: 60.31 in, 153 cm - TR models 60.63 in, 154 cm; height: 53.74 in, 136 cm; weight: 1,621 lb, 735 kg - TR models 1,632 lb, 740 kg; turning circle: 30.5 ft, 9.3 m; fuel tank: 9.2 imp gal, 11.1 US gal, 42 l.

BODY saloon/sedan; 2+1 or 2 doors; 5 seats, separate front seats, headrests; heated rear window.

PRACTICAL INSTRUCTIONS fuel: 98 oct petrol; oil: engine 4.4 imp pt, 5.3 US pt, 2.5 l, SAE 20W-50, change every 6,200 miles, 10,000 km - gearbox and final drive 3.2 imp pt, 3.8 US pt, 1.8 l, SAE 90 EP, no change recommended; greasing: none; spark plug: ACR42-6FS; tappet clearances: inlet 0.006 in, 0.15 mm, exhaust 0.009 in, 0.25 mm; valve timing: 27°30' 68°30' 46°30' 29°30'; tyre pressure: front 25 psi, 1.8 atm, rear 25 psi, 1.8 atm.

OPTIONALS 5-speed mechanical gearbox (I 3.550, II 1.960, III 1.300, IV 0.890, V 0.710, rev 3.180), 4.180 axle ratio, consumption 44.1 m/imp gal, 36.8 m/US gal, 6.4 l x 100 km at 75 mph, 120 km/h; 145 SR x 13 or 155/70 SR x 13 tyres; light alloy wheels; sunroof.

55 hp power team

See 45 hp power team, except for:

ENGINE 73 cu in, 1,196 cc (3.06 x 2.48 in, 78 x 63 mm); max power (DIN): 55 hp (40 kW) at 5,600 rpm; max torque (DIN): 67 lb ft, 9.2 kg m (90 Nm) at 2,200 rpm; max engine rpm: 6,200; 46 hp/l (33.4 kW/l); light alloy head; 5 crankshaft bearings; valves: overhead, in line, rockers, hydraulic tappets; camshafts: 1, overhead, cogged belt; lubrication: 5.3 imp pt, 6.3 US pt, 3 l; 1 Pierburg 1B1 downdraught single barrel carburettor; cooling: 10.7 imp pt, 12.9 US pt, 6.1 l.

TRANSMISSION axle ratio: 3.740; tyres: 145 SR x 13.

PERFORMANCE max speed: 94 mph, 152 km/h; power-weight ratio: 29.7 lb/hp (40.8 lb/kW), 13.4 kg/hp (18.5 kg/kW); carrying capacity: 1,047 lb, 475 kg; consumption: 43.5 m/imp gal, 36.2 m/US gal, 6.5 l x 100 km at 75 mph, 120 km/h.

CHASSIS front and rear suspension: anti-roll bar (for TR models only).

BRAKES rear compensator.

ELECTRICAL EQUIPMENT transistorized ignition.

DIMENSIONS AND WEIGHT weight: 1,632 lb, 740 kg.

PRACTICAL INSTRUCTIONS oil: engine 5.3 imp pt, 6.3 US pt, 3 l; spark plug: AC R42 XLS; valve timing: 19° 51° 59° 22°.

OPTIONALS with 5-speed mechanical gearbox 3.940 axle ratio and consumption 44.8 m/imp gal, 37.3 m/US gal, 6.3 l x 100 km at 75 mph, 120 km/h; anti-roll bar on front and rear suspension (for 2+1-dr models only).

70 hp power team

See 45 hp power team, except for:

ENGINE 79.1 cu in, 1,297 cc (2.95 x 2.89 in, 75 x 73.4 mm); max power (DIN): 70 hp (51 kW) at 5,800 rpm; max torque (DIN): 75 lb ft, 10.3 kg m (101 Nm) at 3,800 rpm; max engine rpm: 6,400; 53.9 hp/l (39.3 kW/l); light alloy head; 5 crankshaft bearings; valves: overhead, in line, rockers, hydraulic tappets; camshafts: 1, overhead, cogged belt; lubrication: 5.3 imp pt, 6.3 US pt, 3 l; 1 Pierburg 1B1 downdraught single barrel carburettor; cooling: 10.7 imp pt, 12.9 US pt, 6.1 l.

TRANSMISSION (standard) gears: 5, fully synchronized; ratios: I 3.550, II 1.960, III 1.300, IV 0.890, V 0.710, rev 3.180; axle ratio: SR 4.180 - other models 3.940; tyres: SR 155/70 SR x 13 (standard) - other models 145 SR x 13.

PERFORMANCE max speed: SR 103 mph, 166 km/h - other models 101 mph, 162 km/h; power-weight ratio: SR 25.8 lb/hp (33.5 lb/kW), 11.7 kg/hp (15.2 kg/kW); consumption: SR 42.8 m/imp gal, 35.6 m/US gal, 6.6 l x 100 km - other models 44.8 m/imp gal, 37.3 m/US gal, 6.3 l x 100 km at 75 mph, 120 km/h.

CHASSIS front and rear suspension: anti-roll bar.

BRAKES rear compensator.

ELECTRICAL EQUIPMENT transistorized ignition.

DIMENSIONS AND WEIGHT weight: SR 1,709 lb, 775 kg - other models 1,654 lb, 750 kg.

PRACTICAL INSTRUCTIONS oil: engine 5.3 imp pt, 6.3 US pt, 3 l; spark plug: AC R42 XLS; valve timing: 24° 78° 68° 36°.

OPTIONALS (for SR only) light alloy wheels and 165/65 SR x 14 tyres.

Kadett Series

PRICES EX WORKS:		DM
1	2+1-dr Limousine	**13,297***
2	4+1-dr Limousine	**13,993***
3	Luxus 2+1-dr Limousine	**14,356***
4	Luxus 4+1-dr Limousine	**15,052***
5	Berlina 2+1-dr Limousine	**15,592***
6	Berlina 4+1-dr Limousine	**16,288***
7	2+1-dr Caravan	**14,472***
8	4+1-dr Caravan	**15,168***
9	Luxus 2+1-dr Caravan	**15,410***
10	Luxus 4+1-dr Caravan	**16,106***
11	Voyage 2+1-dr Caravan	**16,520***
12	Voyage 4+1-dr Caravan	**17,216***
13	Voyage Berlina 4+1-dr Caravan	**18,200***

Power team:	Standard for:	Optional for:
60 hp (1,196 cc)	1 to 10	—
60 hp (1,297 cc)	11 to 13	1 to 10
75 hp	—	all
90 hp	—	all
54 hp (diesel)	—	all

60 hp (1,196 cc) power team

ENGINE front, transverse, 4 stroke; 4 cylinders, in line; 73 cu in, 1,196 cc (3.11 x 2.40 in, 79 x 61 mm); compression ratio: 9:1; max power (DIN): 60 hp (44 kW) at 5,800 rpm; max torque (DIN): 65 lb ft, 9 kg m (88 Nm) at 3,000 rpm; max engine rpm: 6,000; 50.2 hp/l (36.8 kW/l); cast iron block and head; 3 crankshaft bearings; valves: overhead, push-rods and rockers; camshafts: 1, side, chain-driven; lubrication: gear pump, full flow filter, 4.8 imp pt, 5.7 US pt, 2.7 l; 1 Solex 35 PDSI downdraught single barrel carburettor; fuel feed: mechanical pump; anti-freeze liquid cooled, 10 imp pt, 12 US pt, 5.7 l, electric thermostatic fan.

TRANSMISSION driving wheels: front; clutch: single dry plate (diaphragm); gearbox: mechanical; gears: 4, fully synchronized; ratios: I 3.550, II 1.960, III 1.300, IV 0.890, rev 3.330; lever: central; final drive: helical spur gears; axle ratio: 3.940 - Caravan models 4.180; width of rims: 4.5" - Luxus and Caravan models 5" - Berlina models 5.5"; tyres: 145 SR x 13 - Luxus, Caravan and Berlina models 155 SR x 13.

PERFORMANCE max speed: 93 mph, 150 km/h; power-weight ratio: 4+1-dr limousine models 31.6 lb/hp (43.1 lb/kW), 14.3 kg/hp (19.5 kg/kW); carrying capacity: 1,102 lb, 500 kg; consumption: limousine models 38.2 m/imp gal, 31.8 m/US gal, 7.4 l x 100 km - Caravan models 36.7 m/imp gal, 30.5 m/US gal, 7.7 l x 100 km at 75 mph, 120 km/h.

CHASSIS integral; front suspension: independent, by McPherson, coil springs/telescopic damper struts, heavy-duty rubber bearings, direction stabilizing radius arm; rear: crank compound, progressively acting coil springs, auxiliary rubber springs, telescopic dampers.

STEERING rack-and-pinion; turns lock to lock: 3.90.

OPEL Corsa SR Limousine

OPEL Kadett Berlina Limousine

BRAKES front disc, rear drum, dual circuit, servo; lining area: total 57.05 sq in, 368 sq cm.

ELECTRICAL EQUIPMENT 12 V; 36 Ah battery; 45 A alternator; Bosch distributor; 2 headlamps.

DIMENSIONS AND WEIGHT wheel base: 98.98 in, 251 cm; tracks: 55.12 in, 140 cm front, 55.35 in, 141 cm rear; length: 157.40 in, 399 cm - Caravan models 165.63 in, 421 cm; width: 64.41 in, 164 cm; height: 54.33 in, 138 cm - Caravan models 55.12 in, 140 cm; ground clearance: 5.12 in, 13 cm; weight: 2+1-dr limousine models 1,852 lb, 840 kg - 4+1-dr limousine models 1,896 lb, 860 kg - Caravan models 1,973 lb, 895 kg; turning circle: 34.4 ft, 10.5 m; fuel tank: limousine models 9.2 imp gal 11.1 US gal, 42 l - Caravan models 11 imp gal, 13.2 US gal, 50 l.

BODY saloon/sedan - estate car/st. wagon; 2+1 or 4+1 doors; 5 seats, separate front seats.

PRACTICAL INSTRUCTIONS fuel: 98 oct petrol; oil: engine 4.8 imp pt, 5.7 US pt, 2.7 l, SAE 20W-30, change every 6,200 miles, 10,000 km - gearbox and final drive 3.2 imp pt, 3.8 US pt, 1.8 l, SAE 90 EP, no change recommended; greasing: none; spark plug: ACR42-6FS; tappet clearances: inlet 0.006 in, 0.15 mm, exhaust 0.009 in, 0.25 mm; valve timing: 27°30' 68°30' 46°30' 29°30'; tyre pressure: front 25 psi, 1.8 atm, rear 25 psi, 1.8 atm.

OPTIONALS 5-speed mechanical gearbox (I 3.550, II 1.960, III 1.300, IV 0.890, V 0.710, rev 3.330), consumption 37.7 m/imp gal, 31.4 m/US gal, 7.5 l x 100 km at 75 mph, 120 km/h; 175/70 SR x 13 tyres with 5.5" wide rims; anti-roll bar on front and rear suspension (for limousine models only); 44 or 55 Ah battery; sunroof; metallic spray; rear window wiper-washer.

60 hp (1,297 cc) power team

See 60 hp (1,196 cc) power team, except for:

ENGINE 79.1 cu in, 1,297 cc (2.95 x 2.89 in, 75 x 73.4 mm); compression ratio: 8.2:1; max power (DIN): 60 hp (44 kW) at 5,800 rpm; max torque (DIN): 69 lb ft, 9.6 kg m (94 Nm) at 3,400-3,800 rpm; 46.3 hp/l (33.9 kW/l); light alloy head; 5 crankshaft bearings; valves: overhead, in line, rockers, hydraulic tappets; camshafts: 1, overhead, cogged belt; lubrication: 5.3 imp pt, 6.3 US pt, 3 l; anti- freeze liquid cooled, 12.3 imp pt, 14.8 US pt, 7 l.

OPEL Kadett 60 hp (1,297 cc engine)

TRANSMISSION (standard) width of rims: Voyage models 5.5"; tyres: Voyage models 175/70 SR x 13.

PERFORMANCE max speed: 93 mph, 150 km/h; power-weight ratio: 4+1-dr limousine models 31.6 lb/hp (43.1 lb/kW), 14.3 kg/hp (19.5 kg/kW); consumption: limousine models 35.8 m/imp gal, 29.8 m/US gal, 7.9 l x 100 km at 75 mph, 120 km/h.

DIMENSIONS AND WEIGHT weight: 2+1-dr sedans 1,852 lb, 840 kg - 4+1-dr sedans 1,896 lb, 860 kg - Voyage 2+1-dr Caravan 2,084 lb, 945 kg - Voyage 4+1-dr Caravan 2,128 lb, 965 kg.

PRACTICAL INSTRUCTIONS fuel: 91 oct petrol; oil: engine 5.3 imp pt, 6.3 US pt, 3 l; spark plug: ACR42XLS; valve timing: 24° 73° 66° 30°.

OPTIONALS 5-speed mechanical gearbox (I 3.550, II 1.960, III 1.300, IV 0.890, V 0.710, rev 3.330), consumption 36.7 m/imp gal, 30.5 m/US gal, 7.7 l x 100 km at 75 mph, 120 km/h; Opel automatic transmission with 3 ratios (I 2.840, II 1.600, III 1, rev 2.070), 3.740 axle ratio, max speed 90 mph, 145 km/h, consumption sedans 30.7 m/imp gal, 25.6 m/US gal, 9.2 l x 100 km at 75 mph, 120 km/h; (except Voyage models) 175/70 SR x 13 tyres with 5.5" wide rims; anti-roll bar on front and rear suspension (for limousine models only); 44 or 55 Ah battery; sunroof; metallic spray; rear window wiper-washer.

75 hp power team

See 60 hp (1,196 cc) power team, except for:

ENGINE 79.1 cu in, 1,297 cc (2.95 x 2.89 in, 75 x 73.4 mm); compression ratio: 9.2:1; max power (DIN): 75 hp (55 kW) at 5,800 rpm; max torque (DIN): 75 lb ft, 10.3 kg m (101 Nm) at 3,800-4,600 rpm; 57.8 hp/l (42.4 kW/l); light alloy head; 5 crankshaft bearings; valves: overhead, in line, rockers, hydraulic tappets; camshafts: 1, overhead, cogged belt; lubrication: 5.3 imp pt, 6.3 US pt, 3 l; 1 GMF Varajet II downdraught single barrel carburettor; anti-freeze liquid cooled, 12.3 imp pt, 14.8 US pt, 7 l.

TRANSMISSION axle ratio: sedans 3.940 - Caravan models 4.180.

PERFORMANCE max speed: 101 mph, 162 km/h; power-weight ratio: 4+1-dr limousine models 25.3 lb/hp (34.5 lb/kW), 11.5 kg/hp (15.6 kg/kW); consumption: limousine models 38.2 m/imp gal, 31.8 m/US gal, 7.4 l x 100 km at 75 mph, 120 km/h.

CHASSIS front and rear suspension: anti-roll bar (standard).

BRAKES rear compensator.

ELECTRICAL EQUIPMENT transistorized ignition.

DIMENSIONS AND WEIGHT weight: 2+1-dr sedans 1,852 lb, 840 kg - 4+1-dr limousine models 1,896 lb, 860 kg - Voyage 2+1-dr Caravan 2,084 lb, 945 kg - Voyage 4+1-dr Caravan 2,128 lb, 965 kg.

PRACTICAL INSTRUCTIONS oil: engine 5.3 imp pt, 6.3 US pt, 3 l; spark plug: ACR42X LS; valve timing: 24° 78° 68° 36°.

OPTIONALS 5-speed mechanical gearbox (I 3.550, II 1.960, III 1.300, IV 0.890, V 0.710, rev 3.330), consumption 39.8 m/imp gal, 33.1 m/US gal, 7.1 l x 100 km at 75 mph, 120 km/h; Opel automatic transmission with 3 ratios (I 2.840, II 1.600, III 1, rev 2.070), 3.740 axle ratio, max speed 96 mph, 155 km/h, consumption sedans 33.2 m/imp gal, 27.7 m/US gal, 8.5 l x 100 km at 75 mph, 120 km/h; 175/70 SR x 13 tyres with 5.5" wide rims; 44 or 55 Ah battery; sunroof; metallic spray; rear window wiper-washer.

90 hp power team

See 60 hp (1,196 cc) power team, except for:

ENGINE 97.5 cu in, 1,598 cc (3.15 x 3.13 in, 80 x 79.5 mm); compression ratio: 9.2:1; max power (DIN): 90 hp (66 kW) at 5,800 rpm; max torque (DIN): 93 lb ft, 12.8 kg m (126 Nm) at 3,800 - 4,200 rpm; 56.3 hp/l (41.3 kW/l); light alloy head; 5 crankshaft bearings; valves: overhead, in line, rockers, hydraulic tappets; camshafts: 1, overhead, cogged belt; lubrication: 5.6 imp pt, 6.8 US pt, 3.2 l; 1 GMF Varajet II downdraught single barrel carburettor; anti-freeze liquid cooled, 13.6 imp pt, 16.3 US pt, 7.7 l.

TRANSMISSION gearbox ratios: I 3.420, II 1.950, III 1.280, IV 0.890, rev 3.333; axle ratio: 3.740.

PERFORMANCE max speed: 106 mph, 170 km/h; power-weight ratio: 4+1-dr limousine models 23 lb/hp (31.4 lb/kW), 10.4 kg/hp (14.2 kg/kW); consumption: limousine models 36.2 m/imp gal, 30.2 m/US gal, 7.8 l x 100 km at 75 mph, 120 km/h.

CHASSIS front and rear suspension: anti-roll bar (standard).

BRAKES rear compensator.

ELECTRICAL EQUIPMENT 44 Ah battery (standard); transistorized ignition.

DIMENSIONS AND WEIGHT weight: 2+1-dr sedans 2,029 lb, 920 kg - 4+1-dr limousine models 2,073 lb, 940 kg - 2+1-dr Caravan models 2,084 lb, 945 kg - 4+1-dr Caravan models 2,128 lb, 965 kg - Voyage 2+1-dr Caravan 2,194 lb, 995 kg - Voyage 4+1-dr Caravan 2,238 lb, 1,015 kg.

PRACTICAL INSTRUCTIONS oil: engine 5.6 imp pt, 6.8 Us pt, 3.2 l; valve timing: 29° 80° 68° 42°.

OPTIONALS 5-speed mechanical gearbox (I 3.420, II 1.950, III 1.280, IV 0.890, V 0.710, rev 3.330), 3.940 axle ratio, consumption 37.2 m/imp gal, 30.9 m/US gal, 7.6 l x 100 km at 75 mph, 120 km/h; Opel automatic transmission with 3 ratios (I 2.840, II 1.600, III 1, rev 2.070), 3.330 axle ratio, max speed 102 mph, 165 km/h, consumption limousine models 32.5 m/imp gal, 27 m/US gal, 8.7 l x 100 km at 75 mph, 120 km/h; 175/70 SR x 13 tyres with 5.5" wide rims; 55 Ah battery; sunroof; metallic spray; rear window wiper-washer.

54 hp (diesel) power team

See 60 hp (1,196 cc) power team, except for:

ENGINE diesel; 97.5 cu in, 1,598 cc (3.15 x 3.13 in, 80 x 79.5 mm); compression ratio: 23:1, max power (DIN): 54 hp (40 kW) at 4,600 rpm; max torque (DIN): 71 lb ft, 9.8 kg m (96 Nm) at 2,400 rpm; max engine rpm: 5,000; 33.8 hp/l (25 kW/l); light alloy head; 5 crankshaft bearings; valves: overhead, in line, rockers, hydraulic tappets; camshafts: 1, overhead, cogged belt; lubrication: 6.5 imp pt, 7.8 US pt, 3.7 l; Bosch VER 82 injection pump; cooling: 13.2 imp pt, 15.9 US pt, 7.5 l.

TRANSMISSION gearbox ratios: I 3.420, II 1.950, III 1.280, IV 0.890, rev 3.333; axle ratio: 3.740; width of rims: 5"; tyres: 155 SR x 13.

PERFORMANCE max speed: 89 mph, 143 km/h; power-weight ratio: 4+1-dr limousine models 39.6 lb/hp (53.5 lb/kW), 17.9 kg/hp (24.2 kg/kW); consumption: 38.7 m/imp gal, 32.2 m/US gal, 7.3 l x 100 km at 75 mph, 120 km/h.

ELECTRICAL EQUIPMENT 66 Ah battery.

DIMENSIONS AND WEIGHT weight: 2+1-dr limousine models 2,095 lb, 950 kg - 4+1-dr limousine models 2,139 lb, 970 kg - 2+1-dr Caravan models 2,172 lb, 985 kg - 4+1-dr Caravan model 2,216 lb, 1,005 kg.

PRACTICAL INSTRUCTIONS fuel: diesel; oil: engine 6.5 imp pt, 7.8 US pt, 3.7 l; valve timing: 16° 66° 54° 28°.

OPTIONALS 5-speed mechanical gearbox (I 3.420, II 1.950, III 1.280, IV 0.890, V 0.710, rev 3.330), consumption 41.5 m/imp gal, 34.6 m/US gal, 6.8 l x 100 km at 75 mph, 120 km/h; Opel automatic transmission with 3 ratios (I 2.840, II 1.600, III 1, rev 2.070), 3.330 axle ratio, max speed 86 mph, 138 km/h, consumption 33.6 m/imp gal, 28 m/US gal, 8.4 l x 100 km at 75 mph, 120 km/h.

Kadett 1.3 SR

PRICES EX WORKS:	DM
2+1-dr Limousine	**16,964***
4+1-dr Limousine	**17,660***

ENGINE front, transverse, 4 stroke; 4 cylinders, in line; 79.1 cu in, 1,297 cc (2.95 x 2.89 in, 75 x 73.4 mm); compression ratio: 9.2:1; max power (DIN): 75 hp (55 kW) at 5,800 rpm; max torque (DIN): 75 lb ft, 10.3 kg m (101 Nm) at 3,800-4,600 rpm; max engine rpm: 6,200; 57.8 hp/l (42.4 kW/l); cast iron block, light alloy head; 5 crankshaft bearings; valves: overhead, in line, rockers, hydraulic tappets; camshafts: 1, overhead, cogged belt; lubrication: gear pump, full flow filter, 4.3 imp pt, 6.3 US pt, 3 l; 1 GMF Varajet II downdraught single barrel carburettor; fuel feed: mechanical pump; anti-freeze liquid cooled, 11.1 imp pt, 13.3 US pt, 6.3 l, electric thermostatic fan.

OPEL Kadett GTE Limousine

KADETT 1.3 SR

TRANSMISSION driving wheels: front; clutch: single dry plate (diaphragm); gearbox: mechanical; gears: 5, fully synchronized; ratios: I 3.550, II 1.960, III 1.300, IV 0.890, V 0.710, rev 3.330; lever: central; final drive: helical spur gears; axle ratio: 4.180; width of rims: 5.5"; tyres: 175/65 SR x 14.

PERFORMANCE max speed: 101 mph, 162 km/h; power-weight ratio: 2+1-dr 26.5 lb/hp (36.1 lb/kW), 12 kg/hp (16.4 kg/kW); carrying capacity: 1,014 lb, 460 kg; consumption: 39.8 m/imp gal, 33.1 m/US gal, 7.1 l x 100 km at 75 mph, 120 km/h.

CHASSIS integral; front suspension: independent, by McPherson, coil springs/telescopic damper struts, anti-roll bar, heavy-duty rubber bearings, direction stabilizing radius arm; rear: crank compound, progressively acting coil springs, anti-roll bar, auxiliary rubber springs, telescopic dampers.

STEERING rack-and-pinion; turns lock to lock: 3.90.

BRAKES front disc, rear drum, dual circuit, rear compensator, servo; lining area: total 57.05 sq in, 368 sq cm.

ELECTRICAL EQUIPMENT 12 V; 36 Ah battery; 45 A alternator; transistorized ignition; 2 headlamps.

DIMENSIONS AND WEIGHT wheel base: 98.98 in, 251 cm; tracks: 55.12 in, 140 cm front, 55.35 in, 141 cm rear; length: 157.40 in, 399 cm; width: 65.19 in, 166 cm; height: 54.33 in, 138 cm; ground clearance: 5.12 in, 13 cm; weight: 2+1-dr 1,984 lb, 900 kg - 4+1-dr 2,029 lb, 920 kg; turning circle: 34.4 ft, 10.5 m; fuel tank: 9.2 imp gal, 11.1 US gal, 42 l.

BODY saloon/sedan; 2+1 or 4+1 doors; 5 seats; heated rear window; rear window wiper-washer; light alloy wheels.

PRACTICAL INSTRUCTIONS fuel: 98 oct petrol; oil: engine 4.8 imp pt, 5.7 US pt, 2.7 l, SAE 20W-30, change every 6,200 miles, 10,000 km - gearbox and final drive 3.5 imp pt, 4.2 US pt, 2 l, SAE 90 EP, no change recommended; greasing: none; spark plug: ACR42XLS; valve timing: 24° 78° 68° 36°; tyre pressure: front 25 psi, 1.8 atm, rear 25 psi, 1.8 atm.

OPTIONALS 185/60 HR x 14 tyres; limited slip differential; metallic spray; 55 A alternator; 44 or 55 Ah battery; sunroof.

OPEL Kadett GTE Limousine

Kadett 1.6 SR

See Kadett 1.3 SR, except for:

PRICES EX WORKS:	**DM**
2+1-dr Limousine	**17,677***
4+1-dr Limousine	**18,373***

ENGINE 97.5 cu in, 1,598 cc (3.15 x 3.13 in, 80 x 79.5 mm); max power (DIN): 90 hp (66 kW) at 5,800 rpm; max torque (DIN): 93 lb ft, 12.8 kg m (126 Nm) at 3,800-4,200 rpm; 56.3 hp/l (41.3 kW/l); lubrication: 5.6 imp pt, 6.8 US pt, 3.2 l; cooling: 13.7 imp pt, 16.5 US pt, 7.8 l.

TRANSMISSION gearbox ratios: I 3.420, II 1.950, III 1.280, IV 0.890, V 0.710, rev 3.330; axle ratio: 3.940.

PERFORMANCE max speed: 106 mph, 170 km/h; power-weight ratio: 2+1-dr 23.3 lb/hp (31.7 lb/kW), 10.6 kg/hp (14.4 kg/kW); consumption: 37.2 m/imp gal, 30.9 m/US gal, 7.6 l x 100 km at 75 mph, 120 km/h.

ELECTRICAL EQUIPMENT 44 Ah battery (standard).

DIMENSIONS AND WEIGHT weight: 2+1-dr 2,095 lb, 950 kg - 4+1-dr 2,139 lb, 970 kg.

PRACTICAL INSTRUCTIONS valve timing: 29° 80° 68° 42°.

Kadett GTE

PRICES EX WORKS:	**DM**
2+1-dr Limousine	**20,434***
4+1-dr Limousine	**21,130***

ENGINE front, transverse, 4 stroke; 4 cylinders, in line; 109.6 cu in, 1,796 cc (3.34 x 3.13 in, 84.8 x 79.5 mm); compression ratio: 9.5:1; max power (DIN): 115 hp (85 kW) at 5,800 rpm; max torque (DIN): 112 lb ft, 15.4 kg m (151 Nm) at 4,800 rpm; max engine rpm: 6,300; 64 hp/l (47.3 kW/l); cast iron block, light alloy head; 5 crankshaft bearings; valves: overhead, in line, rockers; camshafts: 1, overhead, cogged belt; lubrication: gear pump, full flow filter, 5.6 imp pt, 6.8 US pt, 3.2 l; Bosch LE-Jetronic injection; fuel feed: mechanical pump; anti-freeze liquid cooled, 13.2 imp pt, 15.9 US pt, 7.5 l, electric thermostatic fan.

TRANSMISSION driving wheels: front; clutch: single dry plate (diaphragm); gearbox: mechanical; gears: 5, fully synchronized; ratios: I 3.420, II 1.950, III 1.280, IV 0.890, V 0.710, rev 3.330; lever: central; final drive: helical spur gears; axle ratio: 3.940; width of rims: 5.5"; tyres: 185/60 HR x 14.

PERFORMANCE max speed: 116 mph, 187 km/h; power-weight ratio: 2+1-dr 18.8 lb/hp (25.4 lb/kW), 8.5 kg/hp (11.5 kg/kW); carrying capacity: 1,014 lb, 460 kg; consumption: 37.2 m/imp gal, 30.9 m/US gal, 7.6 l x 100 km at 75 mph, 120 km/h.

CHASSIS integral; front suspension: independent, by McPherson, coil springs/telescopic damper struts, anti-roll bar, heavy-duty rubber bearings, direction stabilizing radius arm; rear: crank compound, progressively acting coil springs, anti-roll bar, auxiliary rubber springs, telescopic dampers.

STEERING rack-and-pinion; turns lock to lock: 4.10.

BRAKES front disc, rear drum, dual circuit, rear compensator; lining area: total 70.08 sq in, 452 sq cm.

ELECTRICAL EQUIPMENT 12 V; 44 Ah battery; 45 A alternator; transistorized ignition; 2 headlamps.

DIMENSIONS AND WEIGHT wheel base: 99.21 in, 252 cm; front and rear track: 55.35 in, 141 cm; length: 157.40 in, 399 cm; width: 65.19 in, 166 cm; height: 54.33 in, 138 cm; ground clearance: 5.12 in, 13 cm; weight: 2+1-dr 2,161 lb, 980 kg - 4+1-dr 2,205 lb, 1,000 kg; turning circle: 35.1 ft, 10.7 m; fuel tank: 9.2 imp gal, 11.1 US gal, 42 l.

BODY saloon/sedan; 2+1 or 4+1 doors; 5 seats, separate front seats; heated rear window; rear window wiper-washer; light alloy wheels.

PRACTICAL INSTRUCTIONS fuel: 98 oct petrol; oil: engine 5.6 imp pt, 6.8 US pt, 3.2 l, SAE 15W-50, change every 6,200 miles, 10,000 km - gearbox and final drive 3.5 imp pt, 4.2 US pt, 2 l, SAE 90 EP, no change recommended; greasing: none; spark plug: ACR42XLS; valve timing: 28° 89° 72° 45°; tyre pressure: front 28 psi, 2 atm, rear 28 psi, 2 atm.

OPTIONALS 55 A alternator; trip computer; metallic spray; sunroof.

Ascona Series

	PRICES EX WORKS:	**DM**
1	2-dr Limousine	**15,430***
2	4-dr Limousine	**16,126***
3	4+1-dr Limousine	**16,671***
4	Luxus 2-dr Limousine	**16,399***
5	Luxus 4-dr Limousine	**17,085***
6	Luxus 4+1-dr Limousine	**17,630***
7	Berlina 2-dr Limousine	**17,725***
8	Berlina 4-dr Limousine	**18,240***
9	Berlina 4+1-dr Limousine	**19,289***
10	SR 2-dr Limousine	**19,884***
11	SR 4-dr Limousine	**20,580***
12	SR 4+1-dr Limousine	**21,317***
13	SR/E 2-dr Limousine	**21,272***
14	SR/E 4-dr Limousine	**21,968***
15	SR/E 4+1-dr Limousine	**22,704***
16	CD 4-dr Limousine	**23,274***
17	CD 4+1-dr Limousine	**24,303***

Power team:	**Standard for:**	**Optional for:**
60 hp	—	1 to 9
75 hp (1,297 cc)	1 to 9	—
75 hp (1,598 cc)	—	1 to 9
90 hp	10 to 12	1 to 9
115 hp	13 to 17	4 to 9
54 hp (diesel)	—	1 to 9

60 hp power team

ENGINE front, transverse, 4 stroke; 4 cylinders, in line; 79.1 cu in, 1,297 cc (2.95 x 2.89 in, 75 x 73.4 mm); compression ratio: 8.2:1; max power (DIN): 60 hp (44 kW) at 5,800 rpm; max torque (DIN): 69 lb ft, 9.5 kg m (94 Nm) at 3,400-3,800 rpm; max engine rpm: 6,300; 46.3 hp/l (33.9 kW/l); cast iron block, light alloy head; 5 crankshaft bearings; valves: overhead, in line, rockers, hydraulic tappets; camshafts: 1, overhead, cogged belt; lubrication: gear pump, full flow filter, 5.3 imp pt, 6.3 US pt, 3 l; 1 Solex 35 PDSI downdraught single barrel carburettor; fuel feed: mechanical pump; anti-freeze liquid cooled, 11.1 imp pt, 13.3 US pt, 6.3 l, electric thermostatic fan.

TRANSMISSION driving wheels: front; clutch: single dry plate (diaphragm); gearbox: mechanical; gears: 4, fully synchronized; ratios: I 3.636, II 2.211, III 1.429, IV 0.969, rev 3.182; lever: central; final drive: helical spur gears; axle ratio: 4.180; width of rims: 5" - Berlina models 5.5"; tyres: 155 R x 13 - Luxus models 165 R x 13 - Berlina models 185/70 R x 13.

PERFORMANCE max speed: 93 mph, 150 km/h; power-weight ratio: 4-dr 34.6 lb/hp (47.1 lb/kW), 15.7 kg/hp (21.4 kg/kW); carrying capacity: 1,102 lb, 500 kg; speed in top at 1,000 rpm: 14.8 mph, 23.8 km/h; consumption: 31.4 m/imp gal, 26.1 m/US gal, 9 l x 100 km at 75 mph, 120 km/h.

CHASSIS integral; front suspension: independent, by McPherson, coil springs/telescopic damper struts, anti-roll bar, heavy-duty rubber bearings, direction stabilizing radius arm; rear: crank compound, progressively acting coil springs, auxiliary rubber springs, telescopic dampers.

STEERING rack-and-pinion, damper.

BRAKES front disc, rear drum, dual circuit, servo; lining area: total 70.08 sq in, 452 sq cm.

ELECTRICAL EQUIPMENT 12 V; 36 Ah battery; 45 A alternator; transistorized ignition; 2 headlamps.

DIMENSIONS AND WEIGHT wheel base: 101.34 in, 257 cm; tracks: 55.12 in, 140 cm front, 55.35 in, 141 cm rear; length: 171.89 in, 437 cm - 4+1-dr models 167.80 in, 426 cm; width: 65.67 in, 167 cm; height: 54.92 in, 139 cm; ground clearance: 5.12 in, 13 cm; weight: 2-dr 2,029 lb, 920 kg - 4-dr 2,073 lb, 940 kg - 4+1-dr 2,128 lb, 965 kg - 2-dr Luxus and Berlina models 2,073 lb, 940 kg - 4-dr Luxus and

Berlina models 2,117 lb, 960 kg - 4+1-dr Luxus and Berlina models 2,172 lb, 985 kg; turning circle: 33.1 ft, 10.1 m; fuel tank: 13.4 imp gal, 16.1 US gal, 61 l.

BODY saloon/sedan; 2, 4 or 4+1 doors; 5 seats.

PRACTICAL INSTRUCTIONS fuel: 91 oct petrol; oil: engine 5.3 imp pt, 6.3 US pt, 3 l, SAE 20W-50, change every 6,200 miles, 10,000 km - gearbox and final drive 3.5 imp pt, 4.2 US pt, 2 l, SAE 90 EP, no change recommended; greasing: none; spark plug: ACR42XLS; valve timing: 24° 73° 66° 30°; tyre pressure: front 25 psi, 1.8 atm, rear 25 psi, 1.8 atm.

OPTIONALS metallic spray; 55 A alternator; 44 or 55 Ah battery; sunroof; light alloy wheels; tinted glass.

75 hp (1,297 cc) power team

See 60 hp power team, except for:

ENGINE compression ratio: 9.2:1; max power (DIN): 75 hp (55 kW) at 5,800 rpm; max torque (DIN): 75 lb ft, 10.3 kg m (101 Nm) at 3,800-4,600 rpm; 57.8 hp/l (42.4 kW/l); 1 GMF Varajet II downdraught single barrel carburettor.

PERFORMANCE max speed: 99 mph, 160 km/h; power-weight ratio: 4-dr 27.6 lb/hp (20.7 lb/kW), 12.5 kg/hp (17.1 kg/kW); consumption: 33.6 m/imp gal, 28 m/US gal, 8.4 l x 100 km at 75 mph, 120 km/h.

PRACTICAL INSTRUCTIONS fuel: 98 oct petrol; valve timing: 24° 78° 68° 36°.

OPTIONALS Opel automatic transmission with 3 ratios (I 2.840, II 1.600, III 1, rev 2.070), 3.740 axle ratio, max speed 96 mph, 155 km/h, consumption 31.7 m/imp gal, 26.4 m/US gal, 8.9 l x 100 km at 75 mph, 120 km/h; anti-roll bar on rear suspension; 55 A alternator; 44 or 55 Ah battery; sunroof; metallic spray; light alloy wheels; tinted glass.

75 hp (1,598 cc) power team

See 60 hp power team, except for:

ENGINE 97.5 cu in, 1,598 cc (3.15 x 3.13 in, 80 x 79.5 mm); max power (DIN): 75 hp (55 kW) at 5,600 rpm; max torque (DIN): 91 lb ft, 12.5 kg m (123 Nm) at 3,000-3,400 rpm; 46.9 hp/l (34.4 kW/l); 1 Solex 1B1 downdraught single barrel carburettor; cooling: 13.9 imp pt, 16.7 US pt, 7.9 l.

TRANSMISSION gearbox ratios: I 3.545, II 2.158, III 1.370, IV 0.971, rev 3.333; axle ratio: 3.940.

PERFORMANCE max speed: 99 mph, 160 km/h; power-weight ratio: 4-dr models 28.8 lb/hp (39.3 lb/kW), 13.1 kg/hp (17.8 kg/kW); consumption: 31.7 m/imp gal, 26.4 m/US gal; 8.9 l x 100 km at 75 mph, 120 km/h.

ELECTRICAL EQUIPMENT 44 Ah battery (standard).

DIMENSIONS AND WEIGHT weight: 2-dr models 2,117 lb, 960 kg - 4-dr models 2,161 lb, 980 kg - 4+1-dr models 2,216 lb, 1,005 kg - 2-dr Luxus and Berlina models 2,172 lb, 985 kg - 4-dr Luxus and Berlina models 2,216 lb, 1,005 kg - 4+1-dr Luxus and Berlina models 2,271 lb, 1,030 kg.

PRACTICAL INSTRUCTIONS valve timing: 29° 80° 68° 42°.

OPTIONALS Opel automatic transmission with 3 ratios (I 2.840, II 1.600, III 1, rev 2.070), 3.740 axle ratio, max speed 96 mph, 155 km/h, consumption 29.7 m/imp gal, 24.8 m/US gal, 9.5 l x 100 km at 75 mph, 120 km/h; anti-roll bar on rear suspension; 55 A alternator; 55 Ah battery; sunroof; metallic spray; light alloy wheels; tinted glass.

OPEL Ascona SR/E Limousine

90 hp power team

See 60 hp power team, except for:

ENGINE 97.5 cu in, 1,598 cc (3.15 x 3.13 in, 80 x 79.5 mm); compression ratio: 9.2:1; max power (DIN): 90 hp (66 kW) at 5,800 rpm; max torque (DIN): 93 lb ft, 12.8 kg m (126 Nm) at 3,800-4,200 rpm; 56.3 hp/l (41.3 kW/l); 1 GMF Varajet II downdraught single barrel carburettor; cooling: 13.9 imp pt, 16.7 US pt, 7.9 l.

TRANSMISSION gearbox ratios: I 3.545, II 2.158, III 1.370, IV 0.971, rev 3.333; axle ratio: 3.740; width of rims: SR limousines 5.5"; tyres: 165 R x 13 - SR models 195/60 R x 14.

PERFORMANCE max speed: 106 mph, 170 km/h; power-weight ratio: SR 4-dr 25.1 lb/hp (34.4 lb/kW), 11.4 kg/hp (15.6 kg/kW); consumption: 34 m/imp gal, 28.3 m/US gal, 8.3 l x 100 km at 75 mph, 120 km/h.

CHASSIS rear suspension: anti-roll bar.

ELECTRICAL EQUIPMENT 44 Ah battery (standard).

DIMENSIONS AND WEIGHT weight: 2-dr 2,139 lb, 970 kg - 4-dr, 2-dr Luxus and Berlina models 2,183 lb, 990 kg - 4+1-dr Luxus, Berlina and SR 2-dr models 2,227 lb, 1,010 kg - SR 4-dr 2,271 lb, 1,030 kg - SR 4+1-dr 2,337 lb, 1,060 kg.

PRACTICAL INSTRUCTIONS fuel: 98 oct petrol; valve timing: 29° 80° 68° 42°.

OPTIONALS 5-speed mechanical gearbox (I 3.420, II 1.950, III 1.280, IV 0.890, V 0.710, rev 3.333), consumption 38.7 m/imp gal, 32.2 m/US gal, 7.3 l x 100 km at 75 mph, 120 km/h; Opel automatic transmission with 3 ratios (I 2.840, II 1.600, III 1, rev 2.070), 3.330 axle ratio, max speed 102 mph, 165 km/h, consumption 32.5 m/imp gal, 27 m/US gal, 8.7 l x 100 km at 75 mph, 120 km/h; 55 A alternator; 55 Ah battery; sunroof; metallic spray; light alloy wheels; tinted glass.

115 hp power team

See 60 hp power team, except for:

ENGINE 109.6 cu in, 1,796 cc (3.34 x 3.13 in, 84.8 x 79.5 mm); compression ratio: 9.5:1; max power (DIN): 115 hp (85 kW) at 5,800 rpm; max torque (DIN): 112 lb ft, 15.4 kg m (151 Nm) at 4,800 rpm; 64 hp/l (47.3 kW/l); lubrication: 5.6 imp pt, 6.8 US pt, 3.2 l; Bosch LE-Jetronic injection; cooling: 13.4 imp pt, 16.1 US pt, 7.6 l.

TRANSMISSION gears: 5, fully synchronized; ratios: I 3.420, II 1.950, III 1.280, IV 0.890, V 0.710, rev 3.333; axle ratio: 3.940; width of rims: 5.5"; tyres: Luxus models 165 HR x 13 - Berlina and CD models 185/70 HR x 13 - SR/E models 195/60 HR x 14.

PERFORMANCE max speed: 116 mph, 187 km/h; power-weight ratio: 4+1-dr 20.3 lb/hp (27.5 lb/kW), 9.2 kg/hp (12.5 kg/kW); carrying capacity: 1,047 lb, 475 kg; consumption: 36.7 m/imp gal, 30.5 m/US gal, 7.7 l x 100 km at 75 mph, 120 km/h.

CHASSIS rear suspension: anti-roll bar.

ELECTRICAL EQUIPMENT 44 Ah battery (standard).

DIMENSIONS AND WEIGHT weight: Luxus and Berlina 2-dr models 2,227 lb, 1,010 kg - Luxus and Berlina 4-dr models 2,271 lb, 1,030 kg - Luxus and Berlina 4+1-dr models 2,337 lb, 1,060 kg - SR and SR/E 2-dr models 2,293 lb, 1,040 kg - SR and SR/E 4-dr models 2,337 lb, 1,060 kg - SR and SR/E 4+1-dr models 2,403 lb, 1,090 kg - CD 4-dr 2,348 lb, 1,065 kg - CD 4+1-dr 2,414 lb, 1,095 kg.

PRACTICAL INSTRUCTIONS fuel: 98 oct petrol; oil: engine 5.6 imp pt, 6.8 US pt, 3.2 l; valve timing: 28° 89° 72° 45°.

OPTIONALS Opel automatic transmission with 3 ratios (I 2.840, II 1.600, III 1, rev 2.070), 3.330 axle ratio, max speed 112 mph, 180 km/h, consumption 31.7 m/imp gal, 26.4 m/US gal, 8.9 l x 100 km at 75 mph, 120 km/h; 55 Ah battery; 55 A alternator; sunroof; metallic spray; light alloy wheels; tinted glass.

OPEL Ascona CD Limousine

54 hp (diesel) power team

See 60 hp power team, except for:

ENGINE diesel; 97.5 cu in, 1,598 cc (3.15 x 3.13 in, 80 x 79.5 mm); compression ratio: 23:1; max power (DIN): 54 hp (40 kW) at 4,600 rpm; max torque (DIN): 71 lb ft, 9.8 kg m (96 Nm) at 2,400 rpm; max engine rpm: 5,000; 33.8 hp/l (25 kW/l); light alloy head; lubrication: 6.5 imp pt, 7.8 US pt, 3.7 l; Bosch VER 82 injection pump; cooling: 13.6 imp pt, 16.3 US pt, 7.7 l.

TRANSMISSION gearbox ratios: I 3.420, II 1.950, III 1.280, IV 0.890, rev 3.333; axle ratio: 3.940; width of rims: 5"; tyres: 165 SR x 13.

PERFORMANCE max speed: 89 mph, 143 km/h; power-weight ratio: 4-dr 42.3 lb/hp (57.1 lb/kW), 19.2 kg/hp (25.9 kg/kW); consumption: 36.7 m/imp gal, 30.5 m/US gal, 7.7 l x 100 km at 75 mph, 120 km/h.

ELECTRICAL EQUIPMENT 66 Ah battery.

DIMENSIONS AND WEIGHT weight: 2-dr 2,239 lb, 1,015 kg - 4-dr 2,282 lb, 1,035 kg - 4+1-dr 2,337 lb, 1,060 kg - Luxus and Berlina 2-dr models 2,249 lb, 1,020 kg - Luxus and Berlina 4-dr models 2,293 lb, 1,040 kg - Luxus and Berlina 4+1-dr models 2,359 lb, 1,070 kg.

PRACTICAL INSTRUCTIONS fuel: diesel; oil: engine 6.5 imp pt, 7.8 US pt, 3.7 l; valve timing: 16° 66° 54° 28°.

OPTIONALS 5-speed mechanical gearbox (I 3.420, II 1.950, III 1.280, IV 0.890, V 0.710, rev 3.330), consumption 39.8 m/imp gal, 33.1 m/US gal, 7.1 l x 100 km at 75 mph, 120 km/h; Opel automatic transmission with 3 ratios (I 2.840, II 1.600, III 1, rev 2.070), 3.740 axle ratio, max speed 86 mph, 138 km/h, consumption 32.8 m/imp gal, 27.3 m/US gal, 8.6 l x 100 km at 75 mph, 120 km/h.

Manta Series

PRICES IN GB AND EX WORKS:	£	DM
1 GT 2-dr Coupé	—	17,433*
2 CC GT 2+1-dr Hatchback Coupé	—	17,885*
3 GT/E 2-dr Coupé	6,794*	20,970*
4 CC GT/E 2+1-dr Hatchback Coupé	7,005*	21,574*

Power team:	Standard for:	Optional for:
75 hp	1,2	—
90 hp	—	1,2
110 hp	3,4	—

75 hp power team

ENGINE front, 4 stroke; 4 cylinders, in line; 79.1 cu in, 1,297 cc (2.95 x 2.89 in, 75 x 73.4 mm); compression ratio: 9.2:1; max power (DIN): 75 hp (55 kW) at 5,800 rpm; max torque (DIN): 72 lb ft, 10 kg m (98 Nm) at 3,800-4,600 rpm; max engine rpm: 6,200; 57.8 hp/l (42.4 kW/l); cast iron block, light alloy head; 5 crankshaft bearings; valves: overhead, rockers, hydraulic tappets; camshafts: 1, overhead, cogged belt; lubrication: gear pump, full flow filter, 4.4 imp pt, 5.3 US pt, 2.5 l; 1 GMF Varajet II downdraught single barrel carburettor; fuel feed: mechanical pump; anti-freeze liquid cooled, 10.2 imp, 12.3 US pt, 5.8 l.

TRANSMISSION driving wheels: rear; clutch: single dry plate (diaphragm); gearbox: mechanical; gears: 4, fully synchronized; ratios: I 3.640, II 2.120, III 1.336, IV 1, rev 3.522; lever: central; final drive: hypoid bevel; axle ratio: 3.890; width of rims: 5.5"; tyres: 185/70 SR x 13.

PERFORMANCE max speed: 102 mph, 165 km/h; power-weight ratio: GT 28.4 lb/hp (38.7 lb/kW), 12.9 kg/hp (17.5 kg/kW); carrying capacity: 838 lb, 380 kg; acceleration: standing ¼ mile 21 sec, 0-50 mph (0-80 km/h) 12 sec; speed in direct drive at 1,000 rpm: 23.7 mph, 38.1 km/h; consumption: GT 36.2 m/imp gal, 30.2 m/US gal, 7.8 l x 100 km at 75 mph, 120 km/h.

CHASSIS integral; front suspension: independent, wishbones (lower trailing links), coil springs, anti-roll bar, telescopic dampers; rear: rigid axle (torque tube), trailing radius arms, transverse linkage bar, coil springs, anti-roll bar, telescopic dampers.

STEERING rack-and-pinion; turns lock to lock: 4.

BRAKES front disc, rear drum, dual circuit, rear compensator, servo; lining area: total 85.7 sq in, 553 sq cm.

ELECTRICAL EQUIPMENT 12 V; 36 Ah battery; 45 A alternator; transistorized ignition; 2 headlamps.

DIMENSIONS AND WEIGHT wheel base: 99.13 in, 252 cm; tracks: 54.33 in, 138 cm front, 54.13 in, 137 cm rear; length: 175.39 in, 444 cm - CC GT 172.28 in, 438 cm; width: 65.75 in, 167 cm; height: 52.36 in, 133 cm; ground clearance: 5.12 in, 13 cm; weight: GT 2,128 lb, 965 kg - CC GT 2,183 lb, 990 kg; turning circle: 33.8 ft, 10.3 m; fuel tank: 11 imp gal, 13.2 US gal, 50 l.

BODY coupé; 2 or 2+1 doors; 5 seats, separate front seats, adjustable backrests.

PRACTICAL INSTRUCTIONS fuel: 98 oct petrol; oil: engine 4.4 imp pt, 5.3 US pt, 2.5 l, SAE 20W-30, change every 6,200 miles, 10,000 km - gearbox 1.1 imp pt, 1.3 US pt, 0.6 l, SAE 80, no change recommended - final drive 1.1 imp pt, 1.3 US pt, 0.6 l, SAE 90, no change recommended; greasing: none; spark plug: ACR42XLS; valve timing: 24° 78° 68° 36°; tyre pressure: front 24 psi, 1.7 atm, rear 24 psi, 1.7 atm.

OPTIONALS light alloy wheels with 185/70 HR x 13 tyres and 6" wide rims; limited slip differential; 44 or 55 Ah battery; heated rear window; sunroof; headrests; metallic spray; halogen headlamps; vinyl roof; headlamps with wiper-washers.

90 hp power team

See 75 hp power team, except for:

ENGINE 109.6 cu in, 1,796 cc (3.34 x 3.13 in, 84.8 x 79.5 mm); max power (DIN): 90 hp (66 kW) at 5,400 rpm; max torque (DIN): 106 lb ft, 14.6 kg m (143 Nm) at 3,000-3,400 rpm; max engine rpm: 6,000; 50.1 hp/l (36.7 kW/l); lubrication: 6.5 imp pt, 7.8 US pt, 3.7 l; cooling: 11.9 imp pt, 14.4 US pt, 6.8 l.

TRANSMISSION axle ratio: 3.670.

PERFORMANCE max speed: 109 mph, 175 km/h; power-weight ratio: GT 24.5 lb/hp (33.4 lb/kW), 11.1 kg/hp (15.2 kg/kW); consumption: 35.3 m/imp gal, 29.4 m/US gal, 8 l x 100 km at 75 mph, 120 km/h.

ELECTRICAL EQUIPMENT 44 Ah battery (standard).

DIMENSIONS AND WEIGHT weight: GT 2,205 lb, 1,000 kg - CC GT 2,260 lb, 1,025 kg.

PRACTICAL INSTRUCTIONS oil: engine 6.5 imp pt, 7.8 US pt, 3.7 l; valve timing: 36° 69° 70° 35°.

OPTIONALS 5-speed mechanical gearbox (I 3.720, II 2.020, III 1.320, IV 1, V 0.800, rev 3.450), consumption 38.2 m/imp gal, 31.8 m/US gal, 7.4 l x 100 km at 75 mph, 120 km/h; Opel automatic transmission with 3 ratios (I 2.400, II 1.480, III 1, rev 1.920), max speed 106 mph, 170 km/h, consumption 32.1 m/imp gal, 26.7 m/US gal, 8.8 l x 100 km at 75 mph, 120 km/h; air-conditioning; 55 Ah battery; sunroof.

OPEL Manta CC GT/E Hatchback Coupé

110 hp power team

See 75 hp power team, except for:

ENGINE 120.8 cu in, 1,979 cc (3.74 x 2.75 in, 95 x 69.8 mm); compression ratio: 9.4:1; max power (DIN): 110 hp (81 kW) at 5,400 rpm; max torque (DIN): 120 lb ft, 16.5 kg m (162 Nm) at 3,400 rpm; max engine rpm: 6,000; 55.6 hp/l (40.9 kW/l); valves: hydraulic tappets; lubrication: 6.7 imp pt, 8 US pt, 3.8 l; Bosch L-Jetronic injection; cooling: 10.9 imp pt, 13.1 US pt, 6.2 l.

TRANSMISSION gears: 5, fully synchronized; ratios: I 3.720, II 2.020, III 1.320, IV 1, V 0.800, rev 3.450; axle ratio: 3.440; width of rims: 6"; tyres: 195/60 HR x 14.

PERFORMANCE max speed: 119 mph, 192 km/h; power-weight ratio: 21.3 lb/hp (29 lb/kW), 9.7 kg/hp (13.1 kg/kW); acceleration: standing ¼ mile 20 sec, 0-50 mph (0-80 km/h) 11 sec; speed in direct drive at 1,000 rpm: 19.6 mph, 31.5 km/h; consumption: 37.2 m/imp gal, 30.9 m/US gal, 7.6 l x 100 km at 75 mph, 120 km/h.

ELECTRICAL EQUIPMENT 44 Ah battery (standard).

DIMENSIONS AND WEIGHT weight: GT/E 2,348 lb, 1,065 kg - CC GT/E 2,403 lb, 1,090 kg.

PRACTICAL INSTRUCTIONS oil: engine 6.7 imp pt, 8 US pt, 3.8 l, SAE 20W-30, change every 6,200 miles, 10,000 km - gearbox 1.9 imp pt, 2.3 US pt, 1.1 l, SAE 90, no change recommended; tappet clearances (hot): inlet 0.012 in, 0.30 mm, exhaust 0.012 in, 0.30 mm; valve timing: 34° 88° 74° 48°.

OPTIONALS Opel automatic transmission with 3 ratios (I 2.400, II 1.480, III 1, rev 1.920), max ratio of converter at stall 2.5, max speed 116 mph, 187 km/h, consumption 31.4 m/imp gal, 26.1 m/US gal, 9 l x 100 km at 75 mph, 120 km/h; air-conditioning; 55 Ah battery; heated rear window; headrests; metallic spray; halogen headlamps; vinyl roof; sunroof; headlamps with wiper-washers.

Rekord Series

PRICES EX WORKS:	DM
1 4-dr Limousine	19,314*
2 Luxus 4-dr Limousine	20,152*
3 Berlina 4-dr Limousine	21,256*
4 CD 4-dr Limousine	25,574*
5 2+1-dr Caravan	19,617*
6 4+1-dr Caravan	20,364*
7 Luxus 4+1-dr Caravan	21,201*
8 Berlina 4+1-dr Caravan	23,026*
9 CD 4+1-dr Caravan	27,006*

Power team:	Standard for:	Optional for:
75 hp	—	1 to 3,5 to 8
90 hp	1 to 3,5 to 8	—
100 hp	—	1 to 3,5 to 8
110 hp	4,9	1 to 3,5 to 8
70 hp (diesel)	—	1 to 3,5 to 8

75 hp power team

ENGINE front, 4 stroke; 4 cylinders, in line; 109.6 cu in, 1,796 cc (3.34 x 3.13 in, 84.8 x 79.5 mm); compression ratio: 8.2:1; max power (DIN): 75 hp (55 kW) at 5,400 rpm; max torque (DIN): 100 lb ft, 13.8 kg m (135 Nm) at 3,000 rpm; max engine rpm: 6,000; 41.8 hp/l (30.6 kW/l); cast iron block and head; 5 crankshaft bearings; valves: overhead, in line, rockers; camshafts: 1, overhead, cogged belt; lubrication: gear pump, full flow filter, 6.7 imp pt, 8 US pt, 3.8 l; 1 Pierburg 1B1 downdraught single barrel carburettor; fuel feed: mechanical pump; anti-freeze liquid cooled, 12 imp pt, 14.4 US pt, 6.8 l.

TRANSMISSION driving wheels: rear; clutch: single dry plate (diaphragm); gearbox: mechanical; gears: 4, fully synchronized; ratios: I 4.016, II 2.147, III 1.318, IV 1, rev 3.765; lever: central; final drive: hypoid bevel; axle ratio: 3.700; width of rims: 5.5"; tyres: 175 SR x 14.

PERFORMANCE max speed: limousine models 99 mph, 160 km/h - st. wagons 96 mph, 154 km/h; power-weight ratio: limousine models 32.8 lb/hp (44.7 lb/kW), 14.9 kg/hp (20.3

OPEL Rekord Berlina Limousine

OPEL Rekord Luxus Caravan

kg/kW); carrying capacity: 1,191 lb, 540 kg; speed in direct drive at 1,000 rpm: 16.6 mph, 26.7 km/h; consumption: limousine models 30.4 m/imp gal, 25.3 m/US gal, 9.3 l x 100 km - st. wagons 28 m/imp gal, 23.3 m/US gal, 10.1 l x 100 km at 75 mph, 120 km/h.

CHASSIS integral; front suspension: independent, by McPherson, lower wishbones, anti-roll bar, coil springs/telescopic damper struts; rear: rigid axle, trailing lower radius arms, upper torque arms, transverse linkage bar, coil springs, telescopic dampers.

STEERING recirculating ball; turns lock to lock: 4.

BRAKES front disc (diameter 9.37 in, 23.8 cm), rear drum, dual circuit, rear compensator, servo; lining area: total 85.7 sq in, 553 sq cm.

ELECTRICAL EQUIPMENT 12 V; Opel Freedom 44 Ah battery; 45 A alternator; transistorized ignition; 2 headlamps.

DIMENSIONS AND WEIGHT wheel base: 105.04 in, 267 cm; tracks: 56.34 in, 143 cm front, limousine models 55.59 in, 141 cm - st. wagons 56.38 in, 143 cm rear; length: 183.15 in, 465 cm; width: 68.03 in, 173 cm; height: limousine models 55.91 in, 142 cm - st. wagons 57.87 in, 147 cm; ground clearance: 5.12 in, 13 cm; weight: limousine models 2,459 lb, 1,115 kg - 2+1-dr Caravan 2,481 lb, 1,125 kg - 4+1-dr st. wagons 2,536 lb, 1,150 kg; turning circle: 35.4 ft, 10.8 m; fuel tank: 14.3 imp gal, 17.2 US gal, 65 l.

BODY saloon/sedan, 4 doors - estate car/st. wagon, 2+1 or 4+1 doors; 5 seats, separate front seats, reclining backrests; heated rear window.

PRACTICAL INSTRUCTIONS fuel: 91 oct petrol; oil: engine 6.7 imp pt, 8 US pt, 3.8 l, SAE 20W-50, change every 6,200 miles, 10,000 km - gearbox 1.9 imp pt, 2.3 US pt, 1.1 l, SAE 80, no change recommended - final drive 1.9 imp pt, 2.3 US pt, 1.1 l, SAE 90, no change recommended; greasing: none; spark plug: ACR42XLS; valve timing: 36° 69° 70° 35°; tyre pressure: front 24 psi, 1.7 atm, rear 25 psi, 1.8 atm.

OPTIONALS 185/70 SR x 14 tyres; light alloy wheels; power steering; sunroof; headrests; 55 Ah battery; 55 A alternator; halogen headlamps; headlamps with wiper-washer; rear window wiper-washer (for st. wagons only); air-conditioning; metallic spray.

90 hp power team

See 75 hp power team, except for:

ENGINE compression ratio: 9.2:1; max power (DIN): 90 hp (66 kW) at 5,400 rpm; max torque (DIN): 106 lb ft, 14.6 kg m (143 Nm) at 3,000-3,400 rpm; 50.1 hp/l (36.7 kW/l); 1 GMF Varajet II downdraught carburettor; cooling: thermostatic fan.

PERFORMANCE max speed: limousine models 107 mph, 173 km/h - st. wagons 104 mph, 167 km/h; power-weight ratio: limousine models 27.3 lb/hp (37.3 lb/kW), 12.4 kg/hp (16.9 kg/kW); speed in direct drive at 1,000 rpm: 17.9 mph, 28.8 km/h; consumption: limousine models 33.6 m/imp gal, 28 m/US gal, 8.4 l x 100 km - st. wagons 31.7 m/imp gal, 26.4 m/US gal, 8.9 l x 100 km at 75 mph, 120 km/h.

PRACTICAL INSTRUCTIONS fuel: 98 oct petrol.

OPTIONALS 5-speed mechanical gearbox (I 3.717, II 2.019, III 1.316, IV 1, V 0.805, rev 3.445), consumption limousine models 35.8 m/imp gal, 29.8 m/US gal, 7.9 l x 100 km - st. wagons 33.6 m/imp gal, 28 m/US gal, 8.4 l x 100 km at 75 mph, 120 km/h; Opel automatic transmission with 3 ratios (I 2.400, II 1.480, III 1, rev 1.920), 3.450 axle ratio, max speed limousine models 104 mph, 167 km/h - st. wagons 100 mph, 161 km/h, consumption limousine models 31.4 m/imp gal, 26.1 m/US gal, 9 l x 100 km - st. wagons 29.7 m/imp gal, 24.8 m/US gal, 9.5 l x 100 km at 75 mph, 120 km/h; limited slip differential.

100 hp power team

See 75 hp power team, except for:

ENGINE 120.8 cu in, 1,979 cc (3.74 x 2.75 in, 95 x 69.8 mm); compression ratio: 9:1; max power (DIN): 100 hp (74 kW) at 5,200 rpm; max torque (DIN): 115 lb ft, 15.9 kg m (156 Nm) at 3,800 rpm; max engine rpm: 5,500; 50.5 hp/l (37.2 kW/l); valves: hydraulic tappets; 1 GMF Varajet II downdraught carburettor; cooling: 11.1 imp pt, 13.3 US pt, 6.3 l, thermostatic fan.

TRANSMISSION axle ratio: 3.450; tyres: (for limousine models only) 175 HR x 14.

PERFORMANCE max speed: limousine models 112 mph, 181 km/h - st. wagons 109 mph, 175 km/h; power-weight ratio: limousine models 25 lb/hp (33.8 lb/kW), 11.3 kg/hp (15.3 kg/kW); speed in direct drive at 1,000 rpm: 20.4 mph, 32.9 km/h; consumption: limousine models 33.2 m/imp gal, 27.7 m/US gal, 8.5 l x 100 km - st. wagons 31 m/imp gal, 25.8 m/US gal, 9.1 l x 100 km at 75 mph, 120 km/h.

DIMENSIONS AND WEIGHT weight: limousine models 2,503 lb, 1,135 kg - 2+1-dr Caravan 2,536 lb, 1,150 kg - 4+1-dr st. wagons 2,591 lb, 1,175 kg.

PRACTICAL INSTRUCTIONS fuel: 98 oct petrol; spark plug: ACR426FS; valve timing: 32° 90° 72° 50°.

OPTIONALS 5-speed mechanical gearbox (I 3.717, II 2.019, III 1.316, IV 1, V 0.805, rev 3.445), consumption limousine models 34 m/imp gal, 28.3 m/US gal, 8.3 l x 100 km - st. wagons 31.7 m/imp gal, 26.4 m/US gal, 8.9 l x 100 km at 75 mph, 120 km/h; Opel automatic transmission with 3 ratios (I 2.400, II 1.480, III 1, rev 1.920), max speed limousine models 109 mph, 175 km/h - st. wagons 105 mph, 169 km/h, consumption limousine models 30.7 m/imp gal, 25.6 m/US gal, 9.2 l x 100 km - st. wagons 28.8 m/imp gal, 24 m/US gal, 9.8 l x 100 km at 75 mph, 120 km/h; limited slip differential.

110 hp power team

See 75 hp power team, except for:

ENGINE 120.8 cu in, 1,979 cc (3.74 x 2.75 in, 95 x 69.8 mm); compression ratio: 9.4:1; max power (DIN): 110 hp (81 kW) at 5,400 rpm; max torque (DIN): 120 lb ft, 16.5 kg m (162 Nm) at 3,000 rpm; 55.6 hp/l (40.9 kW/l); valves: hydraulic tappets; Bosch LE-Jetronic injection; cooling: 16 imp pt, 19.2 US pt, 9.1 l; thermostatic fan.

TRANSMISSION gears: (standard) CD models 5, fully synchronized; ratios: I 3.717, II 2.019, III 1.316, IV 1, V 0.805, rev 3.445; axle ratio: 3.450; tyres: CD models 185/70 HR x 14 - other models 175 HR x 14.

PERFORMANCE max speed: limousine models 116 mph, 187 km/h - st. wagons 112 mph, 181 km/h; power-weight ratio: limousine models 22.9 lb/hp (31.2 lb/kW), 10.4 kg/hp (14.1 kg/kW); speed in direct drive at 1,000 rpm: 19.4 mph, 31.2 km/h; consumption: limousine models 33.2 m/imp gal, 27.7 m/US gal, 8.5 l x 100 km - st. wagons 31 m/imp gal, 25.8 m/US gal, 9.1 l x 100 km at 75 mph, 120 km/h.

DIMENSIONS AND WEIGHT weight: limousine models 2,525 lb, 1,145 kg - 2+1-dr Caravan 2,536 lb, 1,150 kg - 4+1-dr st. wagons 2,591 lb, 1,175 kg.

PRACTICAL INSTRUCTIONS fuel: 98 oct petrol; spark plug: ACR426FS; valve timing: 34° 88° 74° 48°.

OPTIONALS (except CD models) 5-speed mechanical gearbox (I 3.717, II 2.019, III 1.316, IV 1, V 0.805, rev 3.445), consumption limousine models 34 m/imp gal, 28.3 m/US gal, 8.3 l x 100 km - st. wagons 31.7 m/imp gal, 26.4 m/US gal, 8.9 l x 100 km at 75 mph, 120 km/h; Opel automatic transmission with 3 ratios (I 2.400, II 1.480, III 1, rev 1.920), max speed limousine models 112 mph, 181 km/h - st. wagons 109 mph, 175 km/h, consumption limousine models 30.7 m/imp gal, 25.6 m/US gal, 9.2 l x 100 km - st. wagons 28.8 m/imp gal, 24 m/US gal, 9.8 l x 100 km at 75 mph, 120 km/h; limited slip differential.

70 hp (diesel) power team

See 75 hp power team, except for:

ENGINE diesel; 137.9 cu in, 2,260 cc (3.62 x 3.35 in, 92 x 85 mm); compression ratio: 22:1; max power (DIN): 70 hp (52 kW) at 4,400 rpm; max torque (DIN): 99 lb ft, 13.7 kg m (135 Nm) at 2,400 rpm; max engine rpm: 4,600; 31 hp/l (23 kW/l); lubrication: 9.7 imp pt, 11.6 US pt, 5.5 l; Bosch injection pump; cooling: 20.6 imp pt, 24.7 US pt, 11.7 l.

TRANSMISSION axle ratio: 3.450.

PERFORMANCE max speed: limousine models 99 mph, 160 km/h - st. wagons 95 mph, 153 km/h; power-weight ratio: limousine models 39.4 lb/hp (53 lb/kW), 17.9 kg/hp (24 kg/kW); speed in direct drive at 1,000 rpm: 20.9 mph, 33.7 km/h; consumption: limousine models 37.7 m/imp gal, 31.4 m/US gal, 7.5 l x 100 km - st. wagons 35.3 m/imp gal, 29.4 m/US gal, 8 l x 100 km at 75 mph, 120 km/h.

ELECTRICAL EQUIPMENT 2 x 44 Ah batteries; 55 A alternator (standard).

DIMENSIONS AND WEIGHT height: 56.50 in, 143 cm; weight: limousine models 2,756 lb, 1,250 kg - 2+1-dr Caravan 2,811 lb, 1,275 kg - 4+1-dr st. wagons 2,866 lb, 1,300 kg.

PRACTICAL INSTRUCTIONS fuel: diesel; oil: engine 9.7 imp pt, 11.6 US pt, 5.5 l; tappet clearances (hot): inlet 0.008 in, 0.20 mm, exhaust 0.012 in, 0.30 mm; valve timing: 32° 58° 54° 18°; tyre pressure: front 28 psi, 2 atm, rear 28 psi, 2 atm.

OPTIONALS 5-speed mechanical gearbox (I 3.717, II 2.019, III 1.316, IV 1, V 0.805, rev 3.445), 3.700 axle ratio, consumption limousine models 38.7 m/imp gal, 32.2 m/US gal, 7.3 l x 100 km - st. wagons 36.2 m/imp gal, 30.2 m/US gal, 7.8 l x 100 km at 75 mph, 120 km/h; Opel automatic transmission with 3 ratios (I 2.400, II 1.480, III 1, rev 1.920), max speed limousine models 96 mph, 155 km/h - st. wagons 92 mph, 148 km/h, consumption limousine models 34 m/imp gal, 28.3 m/US gal, 8.3 l x 100 km - st. wagons 32.1 m/imp gal, 26.7 m/US gal, 8.8 l x 100 km at 75 mph, 120 km/h.

OPEL Rekord CD Limousine

Senator Series

PRICES IN GB AND EX WORKS	£	DM
1 4-dr Limousine	—	27,642*
2 C 4-dr Limousine	—	30,356*
3 CD Automatic 4-dr Limousine	13,994*	48,051*

Power team:	Standard for:	Optional for:
115 hp	1,2	—
136 hp	—	1,2
180 hp	3	1,2

115 hp power team

ENGINE front, 4 stroke; 4 cylinders, in line; 120.8 cu in, 1,979 cc (3.74 x 2.75 in, 95 x 69.8 mm); compression ratio: 9.4:1; max power (DIN): 115 hp (85 kW) at 5,600 rpm; max torque (DIN): 118 lb ft, 16.3 kg m (160 Nm) at 4,200 rpm; max engine rpm: 6,000; 58.1 hp/l (43 kW/l); cast iron block and head; 5 crankshaft bearings; valves: overhead, in line, hydraulic tappets; camshafts: 1, overhead; lubrication: gear pump, full flow filter, 6.7 imp pt, 8 US pt, 3.8 l; Bosch LE-Jetronic injection; fuel feed: mechanical pump; anti-freeze liquid cooled, 16 imp pt, 19.2 US pt, 9.1 l.

TRANSMISSION driving wheels: rear; clutch: single dry plate (diaphragm); gearbox: mechanical; gears: 4, fully synchronized; ratios: I 4.016, II 1.147, III 1.318, IV 1, rev 3.765; lever: central; final drive: hypoid bevel; axle ratio: 3.700; width of rims: 6"; tyres: 175 HR x 14.

PERFORMANCE max speed: 112 mph, 180 km/h; power-weight ratio: 25.6 lb/hp (34.6 lb/kW), 11.6 kg/hp (15.7 kg/kW); carrying capacity: 1,213 lb, 550 kg; speed in direct drive at 1,000 rpm: 20 mph, 32.1 km/h; consumption: 28.8 m/imp gal, 24 m/US gal, 9.8 l x 100 km at 75 mph, 120 km/h.

CHASSIS integral; front suspension: independent, by McPherson, wishbones, lower trailing links, anti-roll bar, coil springs/telescopic damper struts; rear: independent, semi-trailing arms, coil springs, anti-roll bar, telescopic dampers.

STEERING recirculating ball, servo; turns lock to lock: 4.

BRAKES disc, front internal radial fins, dual circuit, rear compensator, servo; lining area: total 40.9 sq in, 264 sq cm.

ELECTRICAL EQUIPMENT 12 V; 44 Ah battery; 45 A alternator; electronic ignition; 2 headlamps.

DIMENSIONS AND WEIGHT wheel base: 105.63 in, 268 cm; tracks: 56.97 in, 145 cm front, 57.95 in, 147 cm rear; length: 190.51 in, 484 cm; width: 67.80 in, 172 cm; height: 55.71 in, 141 cm; ground clearance: 5.57 in, 14 cm; weight: 2,944 lb, 1,335 kg - C 2,968 lb, 1,346 kg; turning circle: 35.4 ft, 10.8 m; fuel tank: 16.5 imp gal, 19.8 US gal, 75 l.

BODY saloon/sedan; 4 doors; 5 seats, separate front seats, reclining backrests, headrests; heated rear window.

PRACTICAL INSTRUCTIONS fuel: 98 oct petrol; oil: engine 6.7 imp pt, 8 US pt, 3.8 l, SAE 10W-50, change every 3,100 miles, 5,000 km - gearbox 1.9 imp pt, 2.3 US pt, 1.1 l, SAE 80, no change recommended - final drive 2.5 imp pt, 3 US pt, 1.4 l, SAE 90, no change recommended; greasing: none; spark plug: ACR426FS; valve timing: 34° 88° 74° 48°; tyre pressure: front 28 psi, 2 atm, rear 30 psi, 2.2 atm.

OPTIONALS 5-speed mechanical gearbox (I 3.717, II 2.019, III 1.316, IV 1, V 0.805, rev 3.445), 3.450 axle ratio, consumption 31.4 m/imp gal, 26.1 m/US gal, 9 l x 100 km at 75 mph, 120 km/h; Opel automatic transmission with 3 ratios (I 2.400, II 1.480, III 1, rev 1.920), max speed 109 mph, 175 km/h, consumption 28 m/imp gal, 23.3 m/US gal, 10.1 l x 100 km at 75 mph, 120 km/h; limited slip differential; 195/70 HR x 14 or 205/60 VR x 15 tyres; light alloy wheels; electric windows; air-conditioning; automatic levelling control; sunroof.

136 hp power team

See 115 hp power team, except for:

ENGINE 6 cylinders, in line; 151.9 cu in, 2,490 cc (3.43 x 2.75 in, 87 x 69.8 mm); compression ratio: 9.2:1; max power (DIN): 136 hp (100 kW) at 5,600 rpm; max torque (DIN): 137 lb ft, 18.9 kg m (186 Nm) at 4,600 rpm; max engine rpm: 6,100; 54.6 hp/l (40.2 kW/l); 7 crankshaft bearings; lubrication: 9.7 imp pt, 11.6 US pt, 5.5 l; Bosch L-Jetronic injection; cooling: 18 imp pt, 21.6 US pt, 10.2 l.

TRANSMISSION gears: (standard) 5, fully synchronized; ratios: I 3.717, II 2.019, III 1.316, IV 1, V 0.805, rev 3.445; axle ratio: 3.450.

PERFORMANCE max speed: 121 mph, 195 km/h; power-weight ratio: 22.2 lb/hp (30.2 lb/kW), 10.1 kg/hp (13.7 kg/kW); carrying capacity: 1,169 lb, 530 kg; speed in direct drive at 1,000 rpm: 19.3 mph, 31.1 km/h; consumption: 29.1 m/imp gal, 24.2 m/US gal, 9.7 l x 100 km at 75 mph, 120 km/h.

ELECTRICAL EQUIPMENT 65 A alternator.

DIMENSIONS AND WEIGHT weight: 3,021 lb, 1,370 kg - C 3,045 lb, 1,381 kg.

PRACTICAL INSTRUCTIONS oil: engine 9.7 imp pt, 11.6 US pt, 5.5 l.

OPTIONALS Opel automatic transmission with 3 ratios (I 2.400, II 1.480, III 1, rev 1.920), max speed 118 mph, 190 km/h, consumption 24.6 m/imp gal, 20.5 m/US gal, 11.5 l x 100 km at 75 mph, 120 km/h.

OPEL Senator CD Automatic Limousine

180 hp power team

See 115 hp power team, except for:

ENGINE 6 cylinders, in line; 181.1 cu in, 2,968 cc (3.74 x 2.75 in, 95 x 69.8 mm); max power (DIN): 180 hp (132 kW) at 5,800 rmp; max torque (DIN): 183 lb ft, 25.2 kg m (248 Nm) at 4,200-4,800 rpm; 60.6 hp/l (44.4 kW/l); 7 crankshaft bearings; lubrication: 9.7 imp pt, 11.6 US pt, 5.5 l; Bosch LE-Jetronic injection; cooling: 18 imp pt, 21.6 US pt, 10.2 l.

TRANSMISSION gears: 5, fully synchronized; ratios: I 3.822, II 2.199, III 1.398, IV 1, V 0.813, rev 3.705 - CD (standard) Opel automatic transmission I 2.400, II 1.480, III 1, rev 1.920; axle ratio: 3.450 - CD 3.150; tyres: 195/70 VR x 14.

PERFORMANCE max speed: CD 127 mph, 205 km/h - other models 130 mph, 210 km/h; power-weight ratio: CD 18.2 lb/hp (24.8 lb/kW), 8.2 kg/hp (11.2 kg/kW); consumption: CD 24.6 m/imp gal, 20.5 m/US gal, 11.5 l x 100 km - other models 28.5 m/imp gal, 23.5 m/US gal, 9.9 l x 100 km at 75 mph, 120 km/h.

ELECTRICAL EQUIPMENT 65 A alternator.

DIMENSIONS AND WEIGHT weight: CD 3,274 lb, 1,485 kg.

PRACTICAL INSTRUCTIONS oil: engine 9.7 imp pt, 11.6 US pt, 5.5 l; valve timing: 32° 90° 72° 50°.

OPTIONALS (except CD) Opel automatic transmission.

Monza Series

PRICES IN GB AND EX WORKS:	£	DM
1 2+1-dr Hatchback Coupé	—	29,125*
2 C 2+1-dr Hatchback Coupé	—	32,218*
3 GSE 2+1-dr Hatchback Coupé	13,501*	42,000*

Power team:	Standard for:	Optional for:
115 hp	1,2	—
136 hp	—	1,2
180 hp	3	1,2

115 hp power team

ENGINE front, 4 stroke; 4 cylinders, in line; 120.8 cu in, 1,979 cc (3.74 x 2.75 in, 95 x 69.8 mm); compression ratio: 9.4:1; max power (DIN): 115 hp (85 kW) at 5,600 rpm; max torque (DIN): 118 lb ft, 16.3 kg m (160 Nm) at 4,200 rpm; max engine rpm: 6,000; 58.1 hp/l (43 kW/l); cast iron block and head; 5 crankshaft bearings; valves: overhead, in line, hydraulic tappets; camshafts: 1, overhead; lubrication: gear pump, full flow filter, 6.7 imp pt, 8 US pt, 3.8 l; Bosch LE-Jetronic injection; fuel feed: mechanical pump; anti-freeze liquid cooled, 16 imp pt, 19.2 US pt, 9.1 l.

TRANSMISSION driving wheels: rear; clutch: single dry plate (diaphragm); gearbox: mechanical; gears: 4, fully synchronized; ratios: I 4.016, II 2.147, III 1.318, IV 1, rev 3.765; lever: central; final drive: hypoid bevel; axle ratio: 3.700; width of rims: 6"; tyres: 175 HR x 14.

PERFORMANCE max speed: 115 mph, 185 km/h; power-weight ratio: 25.6 lb/hp (34.6 lb/kW), 11.6 kg/hp (15.7 kg/kW); carrying capacity: 1,213 lb, 550 kg; speed in direct drive at 1,000 rpm: 20.5 mph, 33 km/h; consumption: 30.4 m/imp gal, 25.3 m/US gal, 9.3 l x 100 km at 75 mph, 120 km/h.

CHASSIS integral; front suspension: independent, by McPherson, wishbones, lower trailing links, anti-roll bar, coil springs/telescopic damper struts; rear: independent, semi-trailing arms, coil springs, anti-roll bar, telescopic dampers.

STEERING recirculating ball, servo; turns lock to lock: 4.

BRAKES disc, front internal radial fins, dual circuit, rear compensator, servo; lining area: total 40.9 sq in, 264 sq cm.

ELECTRICAL EQUIPMENT 12 V; 44 Ah battery; 45 A alternator; electronic ignition; 2 headlamps.

DIMENSIONS AND WEIGHT wheel base: 105.12 in, 267 cm; tracks: 56.97 in, 145 cm front, 57.95 in, 147 cm rear; length: 185.83 in, 472 cm; width: 67.80 in, 172 cm; height: 45.33 in, 138 cm; ground clearance: 5.51 in, 14 cm; weight: 2,944 lb, 1,335 kg - C 2,970 lb, 1,335 kg; turning circle: 35.4 ft, 10.8 m; fuel tank: 15.4 imp gal, 18.5 US gal, 70 l.

BODY coupé; 2+1 doors; 4 seats, separate front seats, reclining backrests, headrests; heated rear window; rear window wiper-washer.

OPEL Monza GSE Hatchback Coupé

PRACTICAL INSTRUCTIONS fuel: 98 oct petrol; oil: engine 6.7 imp pt, 8 US pt, 3.8 l, SAE 10W-50, change every 3,100 miles, 5,000 km - gearbox 1.9 imp pt, 2.3 US pt, 1.1 l, SAE 80, no change recommended - final drive 2.5 imp pt, 3 US pt, 1.4 l, SAE 90, no change recommended; greasing: none; spark plug: ACR426FS; valve timing: 34° 88° 74° 48°; tyre pressure: front 28 psi, 2 atm, rear 30 psi, 2.2 atm.

OPTIONALS 5-speed mechanical gearbox (I 3.717, II 2.019, III 1.316, IV 1, V 0.805, rev 3.445), 3.450 axle ratio, consumption 33.2 m/imp gal, 27.7 m/US gal, 8.5 l x 100 km at 75 mph, 120 km/h; Opel automatic transmission with 3 ratios (I 2.400, II 1.480, III 1, rev 1.920), max speed 112 mph, 180 km/h, consumption 29.4 m/imp gal, 24.5 m/US gal, 9.6 l x 100 km at 75 mph, 120 km/h; limited slip differential; 195/70 HR x 14 or 205/60 VR x 15 tyres; light alloy wheels; electric windows; air-conditioning; automatic levelling control; sunroof.

136 hp power team

See 115 hp power team, except for:

ENGINE 6 cylinders, in line; 151.9 cu in, 2,490 cc (3.43 x 2.75 in, 87 x 69.8 mm); compression ratio: 9.2:1; max power (DIN): 136 hp (100 kW) at 5,600 rpm; max torque (DIN): 137 lb ft, 18.9 kg m (186 Nm) at 4,600 rpm; max engine rpm: 6,100; 54.6 hp/l (40.2 kW/l); 7 crankshaft bearings; lubrication: 9.7 imp pt, 11.6 US pt, 5.5 l; Bosch L-Jetronic injection; cooling: 18 imp pt, 21.6 US pt, 10.2 l.

TRANSMISSION gears: (standard) 5, fully synchronized; ratios: I 3.717, II 2.019, III 1.316, IV 1, V 0.805, rev 3.445; axle ratio: 3.450; tyres: 195/70 VR x 14 (standard).

PERFORMANCE max speed: 124 mph, 200 km/h; power-weight ratio: 22.2 lb/hp (30.2 lb/kW), 10.1 kg/hp (13.7 kg/kW); carrying capacity: 1,246 lb, 565 kg; speed in top at 1,000 rpm: 22.2 mph, 35.7 km/h; consumption: 30.7 m/imp gal, 25.6 m/US gal, 9.2 l x 100 km at 75 mph, 120 km/h.

ELECTRICAL EQUIPMENT 65 A alternator.

DIMENSIONS AND WEIGHT weight: 3,021 lb, 1,370 kg - C 3,047 lb, 1,382 kg.

PRACTICAL INSTRUCTIONS oil: engine 9.7 imp pt, 11.6 US pt, 5.5 l.

OPTIONALS Opel automatic transmission with 3 ratios (I 2.400, II 1.480, III 1, rev 1.920), max speed 121 mph, 195 km/h, consumption 25.7 m/imp gal, 21.4 m/US gal, 11 l x 100 km at 75 mph, 120 km/h.

180 hp power team

See 115 hp power team, except for:

ENGINE 6 cylinders, in line; 181.1 cu in, 2,968 cc (3.74 x 2.75 in, 95 x 69.8 mm); max power (DIN): 180 hp (132 kW) at 5,800 rpm; max torque (DIN): 183 lb ft, 25.2 kg m (248 Nm) at 4,200-4,800 rpm; 60.6 hp/l (44.4 kW/l); 7 crankshaft bearings; lubrication: 9.7 imp pt, 11.6 US pt, 5.5 l; Bosch LE-Jetronic injection; cooling: 18 imp pt, 21.6 Us pt, 10.2 l.

TRANSMISSION gearbox: GSE (standard) Opel automatic transmission with 3 ratios - other models mechanical; gears: 5 fully synchronized; ratios: GSE I 2.400, II 1.380, III 1, rev 1.920 - other models I 3.822, II 2.199, III 1.398, IV 1, V 0.813, rev 3.705; axle ratio: GSE 3.150 - other models 3.450; tyres: 195/70 VR x 14 (standard).

PERFORMANCE max speed: GSE 130 mph, 210 km/h - other models 134 mph, 215 km/h; power-weight ratio: GSE 17.1 lb/hp (23.3 lb/kW), 7.8 kg/hp (10.6 kg/kW); consumption: GSE 25.7 m/imp gal, 21.4 m/US gal, 11 l x 100 km - other models 30.1 m/imp gal, 25 m/US gal, 9.4 l x 100 km at 75 mph, 120 km/h.

PORSCHE 924

ELECTRICAL EQUIPMENT 65 A alternator.

DIMENSIONS AND WEIGHT weight: GSE 3,080 lb, 1,397 kg.

PRACTICAL INSTRUCTIONS oil: engine 9.7 imp pt, 11.6 US pt, 5.5 l; valve timing: 32° 90° 72° 50°.

OPTIONALS (except GSE) Opel automatic transmission.

PORSCHE GERMANY FR

924

PRICE IN GB: £ 10,880*
PRICE EX WORKS: DM 32,950*

ENGINE Audi, front, 4 stroke; 4 cylinders, vertical, in line; 121.1 cu in, 1,984 cc (3.41 x 3.32 in, 86.5 x 84.4 mm); compression ratio: 9.3:1; max power (DIN): 125 hp (92 kW) at 5,800 rpm; max torque (DIN): 122 lb ft, 16.8 kg m (165 Nm) at 3,500 rpm; max engine rpm: 6,500; 63 hp/l (46.3 kW/l); cast iron block, light alloy head; 5 crankshaft bearings; valves: overhead, in line, thimble tappets; camshsfts: 1, overhead, cogged belt; lubrication: gear pump, full flow filter, 8.8 imp pt, 10.6 US pt, 5 l; Bosch K-Jetronic injection; fuel feed: electric pump; water-cooled, 12.3 imp pt, 14.8 US pt, 7 l, electric thermostatic fan.

TRANSMISSION driving wheels: rear; clutch: single dry plate; gearbox: rear, mechanical, in unit with final drive; gears: 5, fully synchronized; ratios: I 3.600, II 2.125, III 1.458, IV 1.107, V 0.857, rev 3.500; lever: central; final drive: hypoid bevel; axle ratio: 3.889; width of rims: 6"; tyres: 185/70 HR x 14.

PERFORMANCE max speeds: (I) 35 mph, 56 km/h; (II) 60 mph, 96 km/h; (III) 93 mph, 150 km/h; (IV) 127 mph, 204 km/h; power-weight ratio: 19.9 lb/hp (27.1 lb/kW), 9 kg/hp (12.3 kg/kW); carrying capacity: 706 lb, 320 kg; speed in top at 1,000 rpm: 19.5 mph, 31.4 km/h; consumption: 34.9 m/imp gal, 29 m/US gal, 8.1 l x 100 km at 75 mph, 120 km/h.

CHASSIS integral; front suspension: independent, by McPherson, lower wishbones, coil springs/telescopic damper struts; rear: independent, semi-trailing arms, transverse torsion bars, coil springs/telescopic damper struts.

STEERING rack-and-pinion; turns lock to lock: 4.02.

BRAKES front disc, rear drum, 2 X circuits, servo; lining area: total 72.9 sq in, 470 sq cm.

ELECTRICAL EQUIPMENT 12 V; 45 Ah battery; 1,050 W alternator; Bosch electronic ignition; 4 headlamps, 2 retractable.

DIMENSIONS AND WEIGHT wheel base: 94.49 in, 240 cm; tracks: 55.83 in, 142 cm front, 54.02 in, 137 cm rear; length: 165.83 in, 421 cm; width: 66.34 in, 168 cm; height: 50 in, 127 cm; weight: 2,492 lb, 1,130 kg; fuel tank: 14.5 imp gal, 17.4 US gal, 66 l.

BODY coupé; 2 doors; 2 + 2 seats, separate front seats, reclining backrests with built-in headrests; heated rear window; light alloy wheels.

PRACTICAL INSTRUCTIONS fuel: 98 oct petrol; oil: engine 8.8 imp pt, 10.6 US pt, 5 l, SAE 30W (summer), 20W (winter), change every 6,100 miles, 10,000 km - gearbox and final drive 4.6 imp pt, 5.5 US pt, 2.6 l, SAE 80; greasing: none; spark plug: 225°; valve timing: 6° 42° 47° 2°; tyre pressure: front and rear 28 psi, 2 atm.

OPTIONALS automatic transmission, hydraulic torque converter and planetary gears with 3 ratios (I 2.714, II 1.500, III 1, rev 2.429), max ratio of converter at stall 2.50, possible manual selection, 3.455 axle ratio, max speed 121 mph, 195 km/h, consumption 30.7 m/imp gal, 25.6 m/US gal, 9.2 l x 100 km at 75 mph, 120 km/h; limited slip differential; 205/60 HR x 15 tyres; anti-roll bar on front and rear suspension; headlamps with wiper-washer; metallic spray; air-conditioning; sunroof; fog lamps; 63 Ah battery.

PORSCHE 944

944

PRICE IN GB: £ 15,309*
PRICE EX WORKS: DM 42,950*

ENGINE front, 4 stroke; 4 cylinders, in line; 151.3 cu in, 2,479 cc (3.94 x 3.11 in, 100 x 78.9 mm); compression ratio: 10.6:1; max power (DIN): 163 hp (120 kW) at 5,800 rpm; max torque (DIN): 151 lb ft, 20.9 kg m (205 Nm) at 3,000 rpm; max engine rpm: 6,500; 65.8 hp/l (48.4 kW/l); light alloy block and head; 5 crankshaft bearings; valves: overhead, in line, hydraulic tappets; camshafts: 1, overhead, cogged belt; lubrication: gear pump, full flow filter, 9.7 imp pt, 11.6 US pt, 5.5 l; Bosch L-Jetronic injection with digital engine electronic unit (DEE), coasting cut-off system; ; fuel feed: electric pump; water-cooled, 15 imp pt, 18 US pt, 8.5 l.

TRANSMISSION driving wheels: rear; clutch: single dry plate; gearbox: mechanical; gears: 5, fully synchronized; ratios: I 3.600, II 2.125, III 1.458, IV 1.071, V 0.828, rev 3.500; lever: central; final drive: hypoid bevel; axle ratio: 3.888; width of rims: 7"; tyres: 185/70 VR x 15.

PERFORMANCE max speeds: (I) 30 mph, 49 km/h; (II) 51 mph, 82 km/h; (III) 76 mph, 123 km/h; (IV) 102 mph, 165 km/h; (V) 137 mph, 220 km/h; power-weight ratio: 15.9 lb/hp (21.7 lb/kW), 7.2 kg/hp (9.8 kg/kW); carrying capacity: 706 lb, 320 kg; speed in top at 1,000 rpm: 22.8 mph, 36.7 km/h; consumption: 32.5 m/imp gal, 27 m/US gal, 8.7 l x 100 km at 75 mph, 120 km/h.

CHASSIS integral; front suspension: independent, by McPherson, coil springs/telescopic damper struts, wishbones, anti-roll bar; rear: independent, Weissach axle, wishbones, semi-trailing arms, transverse torsion bars, coil springs, telescopic damper struts.

STEERING rack-and-pinion; turns lock to lock: 4.02.

BRAKES disc, (front diameter 11.12 in, 28.2 cm, rear 11.38 in, 28.9 cm), internal radial fins, dual circuit, servo; lining area: total 48.1 sq in, 310 sq cm.

PORSCHE 911 Carrera Cabriolet

944

ELECTRICAL EQUIPMENT 12 V; 50 Ah battery; 1,260 W alternator; electronic ignition; 2 retractable headlamps.

DIMENSIONS AND WEIGHT wheel base: 94.49 in, 240 cm; tracks: 58.15 in, 148 cm front, 57.13 in, 145 cm rear; length: 165.35 in, 420 cm; width: 68.31 in, 173 cm; height: 50.20 in, 127 cm; weight: 2,602 lb, 1,180 kg; fuel tank: 14.5 imp gal, 17.4 US gal, 66 l.

BODY coupé; 2 doors; 2+2 seats, separate front seats, reclining backrests, built-in headrests; heated rear window; light alloy wheels.

PRACTICAL INSTRUCTIONS fuel: 98 oct petrol; oil: engine 9.7 imp pt, 11.6 US pt, 5.5 l, SAE 20W-50, change every 6,200 miles, 10,000 km - gearbox and final drive 4.6 imp pt, 5.5 US pt, 2.6 l, SAE 80, change every 18,600 miles, 30,000 km; greasing: none; spark plug: Bosch WR 7 D; valve timing: 1° 49° 43° 3°; tyre pressure: front 28 psi, 2 atm, rear 35 psi, 2.5 atm.

OPTIONALS automatic transmission, hydraulic torque converter and planetary gears with 3 ratios (I 2.714, II 1.500, III 1, rev 2.429), max ratio of converter at stall 2.10, possible manual selection, 3.083 axle ratio, consumption 30.1 m/imp gal, 25 m/US gal, 9.4 l x 100 km at 75 mph, 120 km/h; anti-roll bar on front and rear suspension; 205/55 VR x 16 tyres; limited slip differential; power steering; air-conditioning; metallic spray; sunroof.

944 (USA)

See 944, except for:

PRICE IN USA: $ 21,440*

ENGINE compression ratio: 9.5:1; max power (DIN): 150 hp (110 kW) at 5,500 rpm; max torque (DIn): 142 lb ft, 19.6 kg m (192 Nm) at 3,000 rpm; 60.5 hp/l (44.4 kW/l).

PERFORMANCE max speed: 130 mph, 210 km/h; power-weight ratio: 18.5 lb/hp (25.3 lb/kW), 8.4 kg/hp (11.5 kg/kW).

ELECTRICAL EQUIPMENT 63 Ah battery.

DIMENSIONS AND WEIGHT length: 168.90 in, 429 cm; weight: 2,778 lb, 1,260 kg.

PRACTICAL INSTRUCTIONS fuel: 91 oct petrol; spark plug: Bosch WR 8-DS.

911 Carrera Coupé

PRICE IN GB: £ 21,464*
PRICE EX WORKS: DM 61,950*

ENGINE rear, 4 stroke; 6 cylinders, horizontally opposed; 193.1 cu in, 3,164 cc (3.74 x 2.93 in, 95 x 74.4 mm); compression ratio: 10.3:1; max power (DIN): 231 hp (170 kW) at 5,900 rpm; max torque (DIN): 207 lb ft, 28.6 kg m (284 Nm) at 4,800 rpm; max engine rpm: 6,520; 73 hp/l (53.7 kW/l); light alloy block with cast iron liners, light alloy head; 8 crankshaft bearings; valves: overhead, Vee-slanted, rockers; camshafts: 2, 1 per bank, overhead, double cogged belt; lubrication: gear pump, full flow filter, dry sump, thermostatic oil cooler, 22.9 imp pt, 27.5 US pt, 13 l; Bosch L-Jetronic injection with digital motor electronics (DME); fuel feed: electric pump; air-cooled.

TRANSMISSION driving wheels: rear; clutch: single dry plate; gearbox: mechanical; gears: 5, fully synchronized; ratios: I 3.182, II 1.833, III 1.261, IV 0.966, V 0.763, rev 3.325; lever: central; final drive: spiral bevel; axle ratio: 3.875; width of rims: 6" front, 7" rear; tyres: 185/70 VR x 15 front, 215/60 VR x 15 rear.

PERFORMANCE max speeds at 6,500 rpm: (I) 39 mph, 63 km/h; (II) 67 mph, 108 km/h; (III) 96 mph, 155 km/h; (IV) 126 mph, 203 km/h; (V) 152 mph, 245 km/h; power-weight ratio: 11.1 lb/hp (15 lb/kW), 5 kg/hp (6.8 kg/kW); carrying capacity: 750 lb, 340 kg; acceleration: 0-50 mph (0-80 km/h) 4.9 sec; consumption 31.4 m/imp gal, 26.1 m/US gal, 9 l x 100 km at 75 mph, 120 km/h.

CHASSIS integral; front suspension: independent, by McPherson, coil springs/telescopic damper struts, longitudinal torsion bars, lower wishbones, anti-roll bar; rear: independent, semi-trailing arms, transverse torsion bars, anti-roll bar, telescopic dampers.

STEERING ZF rack-and-pinion; turns lock to lock: 3.

BRAKES disc (front diameter 9.25 in, 23.5 cm, rear 9.61 in, 24.4 cm), internal radial fins, dual circuit, servo; lining area: total 39.8 sq in, 257 sq cm.

ELECTRICAL EQUIPMENT 12 V; 66 Ah battery; 1,260 W alternator; Bosch electronic ignition; 2 iodine headlamps.

DIMENSIONS AND WEIGHT wheel base: 89.41 in, 227 cm; tracks: 54.02 in, 137 cm front, 54.33 in, 138 cm rear; length: 168.90 in, 429 cm; width: 64.96 in, 165 cm; height: 51.97 in, 132 cm; ground clearance: 4.72 in, 12 cm; weight: 2,558 lb, 1,160 kg; turning circle: 35.8 ft, 10.9 m; fuel tank: 17.6 imp gal, 21.1 US gal, 80 l.

BODY coupé; 2 doors; 2 + 2 seats, separate front seats, adjustable backrests, built-in headrests; electric windows; heated rear window; light alloy wheels; automatic heating.

PRACTICAL INSTRUCTIONS fuel: 98 oct petrol; oil: engine 17.6 imp pt, 21.1 US pt, 10 l, SAE 30 (summer) 20 (winter), change every 6,200 miles, 10,000 km - gearbox and final drive 5.3 imp pt, 6.3 US pt, 3 l, SAE 90, change every 6,200 miles, 10,000 km; greasing: none; spark plug: Bosch W4 CC; tappet clearances: inlet 0.004 in, 0.10 mm, exhaust 0.004 in, 0.10 mm; valve timing: 4° 50° 46° 6°; tyre pressure: front 29 psi, 2 atm, rear 35 psi, 2.5 atm.

OPTIONALS ZF limited slip differential; air-conditioning; electric sunroof; rear window wiper-washer; tinted glass; 88 Ah battery; 205/55 VR x 16 front tyres, 225/50 VR x 16 rear tyres; metallic spray; fog lamps; turbo look.

911 SC Coupé (USA)

See 911 Carrera Coupé, except for:

PRICE IN USA: $ 31,950*

ENGINE compression ratio: 9.5:1; max power (DIN): 207 hp (152 kW) at 5,900 rpm; max torque (DIN): 192 lb ft, 26.5 kg m (260 Nm) at 4,800 rpm; 65.4 hp/l (48 kW/l).

TRANSMISSION gearbox ratios: I 3.182, II 1.778, III 1.261, IV 0.966, V 0.790, rev 3.325.

PERFORMANCE max speed: 146 mph, 235 km/h; power-weight ratio: 13.3 lb/hp (18.1 lb/kW), 6 kg/hp (8.2 kg/kW); acceleration: standing ¼ mile 14.7 sec.

DIMENSIONS AND WEIGHT weight: 2,756 lb, 1,250 kg.

PRACTICAL INSTRUCTIONS fuel: 91 oct petrol.

911 Carrera Targa

See 911 Carrera Coupé, except for:

PRICE IN GB: £ 21,464*
PRICE IN USA: $ 33,450*

BODY convertible; roll bar, detachable roof.

911 Carrera Cabriolet

See 911 Carrera Coupé, except for:

PRICE IN GB: £ 24,340*
PRICE IN USA: $ 36,450*

BODY sports; soft top.

911 Turbo

See 911 Carrera Coupé, except for:

PRICE IN GB: £ 33,878*
PRICE EX WORKS: DM 102,000*

ENGINE turbocharged; 201.3 cu in, 3,299 cc (3.82 x 2.93 in, 97 x 74.4 mm); compression ratio: 7:1; max power (DIN): 300 hp (221 kW) at 5,500 rpm; max torque (DIN): 319 lb ft, 44 kg m (430 Nm) at 4,000 rpm; max engine rpm: 7,000; 90.9 hp/l (67 kW/l); Bosch K-Jetronic injection; 1 KKK turbocharger; fuel feed: 2 electric pumps.

TRANSMISSION gears: 4, fully synchronized; ratios: I 2.250, II 1.304, III 0.892, IV 0.625, rev 2.437; axle ratio: 4.222; width of rims: 7" front, 8" rear; tyres: 205/55 VR x 16 front, 225/50 VR x 16 rear (standard).

PERFORMANCE max speeds: (i) 52 mph, 84 km/h; (II) 33 mph, 150 km/h; (III) 137 mph, 220 km/h; (IV) 162 mph, 260 km/h; power-weight ratio: 9.6 lb/hp (13 lb/kW), 4.3 kg/hp (5.9 kg/kW); carrying capacity: 838 lb, 380 kg; acceleration: 0-50 mph (0-80 km/h) 3 sec; speed in top at 1,000 rpm: 29.3 mph, 47.2 km/h; consumption: 23.9 m/imp gal, 19.9 m/US gal, 11.8 l x 100 km at 75 mph, 120 km/h.

BRAKES lining area: total 53.3 sq in, 344 sq cm.

DIMENSIONS AND WEIGHT tracks: 56.30 in, 143 cm front, 59.06 in, 150 cm rear; width: 69.68 in, 177 cm; height: 51.57 in, 131 cm; weight: 2,867 lb, 1,300 kg; turning circle: 35.1 ft, 10.7 m.

BODY roll bar; rear window wiper-washer (standard).

OPTIONALS only ZF limited slip differential, electric sunroof and air-conditioning.

PORSCHE 911 Turbo

PORSCHE 928 S

928 S

PRICE IN GB: £ 30,679*
PRICE EX WORKS: DM 84,950*

ENGINE front, 4 stroke; 8 cylinders in Vee; 284.6 cu in, 4,664 cc (3.82 x 3.11 in, 97 x 78.9 mm); compression ratio: 10.4:1; max power (DIN): 310 hp (228 kW) at 5,900 rpm; max torque (DIN): 295 lb ft, 40.7 kg m (400 Nm) at 4,100 rpm; max engine rpm: 6,390; 66.5 hp/l (48.9 kW/l); light alloy block and head; 5 crankshaft bearings; valves: overhead, in line, hydraulic tappets; camshafts: 2, 1 per bank, overhead, cogged belt; lubrication: gear pump, full flow filter, 13.2 imp pt, 15.9 US pt, 7.5 l; Bosch LH-Jetronic injection; fuel feed: electric pump; water-cooled, 28.2 imp pt, 33.8 US pt, 16 l.

TRANSMISSION driving wheels: rear; clutch: single dry plate; gearbox: mechanical, in unit with final drive; gears: 5, fully synchronized; ratios: I 3.765, II 2.512, III 1.790, IV 1.354, V 1, rev 3.306; lever: central; final drive: hypoid bevel; axle ratio: 2.727; width of rims: 7"; tyres: 225/50 VR x 16.

PERFORMANCE max speeds at 6,390 rpm: (i) 43 mph, 70 km/h; (II) 68 mph, 110 km/h; (III) 88 mph, 142 km/h; (IV) 126 mph, 203 km/h; (V) 158 mph, 255 km/h; power-weight ratio: 10.7 lb/hp (14.5 lb/kW), 4.8 kg/hp (6.6 kg/kW); carrying capacity: 816 lb, 370 kg; acceleration: 0-50 mph (0-80 km/h) 4.5 sec; consumption: 27.7 m/imp gal, 23.1 m/US gal, 10.2 l x 100 km at 75 mph, 120 km/h.

CHASSIS integral; front suspension: independent, by McPherson, wishbones, coil springs/telescopic damper struts, anti-roll bar; rear: independent, Weissach axle, wishbones, semi-trailing arms, transverse torsion bars, coil springs/telescopic damper struts.

STEERING rack-and-pinion, servo; turns lock to lock: 3.13.

BRAKES disc (front diameter 11.10 in, 28.2 cm, rear 11.38 in, 28.9 cm), 2 X circuits, internal radial fins, servo; lining area: total 50.5 sq in, 326 sq cm.

ELECTRICAL EQUIPMENT 12 V; 88 Ah battery; 1,260 W alternator; electronic ignition; 4 headlamps; 2 retractable.

DIMENSIONS AND WEIGHT wheel base: 98.43 in, 250 cm; tracks: 60.98 in, 155 cm front, 59.88 in, 152 cm rear; length: 175.20 in, 445 cm; width: 72.44 in, 184 cm; height: 50.47 in, 128 cm; weight: 3,307 lb, 1,500 kg; turning circle: 37.7 ft, 11.5 m; fuel tank: 18.9 imp gal, 22.7 US gal, 86 l.

BODY coupé; 2 doors; 2 + 2 seats, separate front seats, reclining backrests, built-in headrests; heated rear window with wiper-washer.

PRACTICAL INSTRUCTIONS fuel: 98 oct petrol; oil: engine 13.2 imp pt, 15.9 US pt, 7.5 l, SAE 15W-50/20W-50 - gearbox and final drive 6.7 imp pt, 8 US pt, 3.8 l, SAE 80; spark plug: Bosch W 7D or WR 7D; valve timing: 6° 54° 43° 4°; tyre pressure: front 35 psi, 2,5 atm, rear 43 psi, 3 atm.

OPTIONALS automatic transmission with 4 ratios (I 3.676, II 2.412, III 1.436, IV 1, rev 5.139), 2.357 axle ratio, max ratio of converter at stall 2, possible manual selection, max speed 155 mph, 250 km/h, consumption 26.9 m/imp gal, 22.4 m/US gal, 10.5 l x 100 km at 75 mph, 120 km/h; 225/50 VR x 16 tyres; limited slip differential; air-conditioning; metallic spray; sunroof.

928 S (USA)

See 928 S, except for:

PRICE IN USA: $ 44,000*

ENGINE compression ratio: 9.3:1; max power (DIN): 242 hp (178 kW) at 5,250 rpm; max torque (DIN): 270 lb ft, 37.2 kg m (365 Nm) at 4,000 rpm; max engine rpm: 6,300; 51.9 hp/h (38.2 kW/l); Bosch L-Jetronic injection.

TRANSMISSION gearbox ratios: I 4.271, II 2.850, III 2.031, IV 1.536, V 1, rev 3.750; axle ratio: 2.266.

PERFORMANCE max speed: 146 mph, 235 km/h; power-weight ratio: 13.8 lb/hp (18.8 lb/kW), 6.3 kg/hp (8.5 kg/kW); carrying capacity: 772 lb, 350 kg; consumption: 32.5 m/imp gal, 27 m/US gal, 8.7 l x 100 km.

DIMENSIONS AND WEIGHT length: 175.67 in, 446 cm; weight: 3,352 lb, 1,520 kg.

PRACTICAL INSTRUCTIONS fuel: 91 oct petrol; spark plug: Bosch WR 8 DS; valve timing: 11° 46° 25° 2°.

OPTIONALS with automatic transmission, max ratio of converter at stall 2.12, 2.200 axle ratio, max speed 143 mph, 230 km/h and consumption 30.1 m/imp gal, 25 m/US gal, 9.4 l x 100 km.

VOLKSWAGEN GERMANY FR

Polo Limousine Series

PRICES EX WORKS:	DM
1 C 1.0 2+1-dr Limousine	12,230*
2 CL 1.0 2+1-dr Limousine	13,145*
3 GL 1.0 2+1-dr Limousine	14,125*
4 C 1.3 2+1-dr Limousine	12,870*
5 CL 1.3 2+1-dr Limousine	13,785*
6 GL 1.3 2+1-dr Limousine	14,765*

For GB and USA prices, see price index.

Power team:	Standard for:	Optional for:
40 hp	1 to 3	—
55 hp	4 to 6	—

40 hp power team

ENGINE front, transverse, slanted 15° to front, 4 stroke; 4 cylinders, in line; 63.6 cu in, 1,043 cc (2.95 x 2.32 in, 75 x 59 mm); compression ratio: 9.5:1; max power (DIN): 40 hp (29 kW) at 5,300 rpm; max torque (DIN): 55 lb ft, 7.5 kg m (74 Nm) at 2,700 rpm; max engine rpm: 5,800; 38.3 hp/l (27.8 kW/l); cast iron block, light alloy head; 5 crankshaft bearings; valves: overhead, in line, rockers; camshafts: 1, overhead, cogged belt; lubrication: gear pump, full flow filter, 6.2 imp pt, 7.4 US pt, 3.5 l; 1 Solex 35 PICT-5 downdraught single barrel carburettor; fuel feed: mechanical pump; water-cooled, 11.4 imp pt, 13.7 US pt, 6.5 l, electric thermostatic fan.

TRANSMISSION driving wheels: front; clutch: single dry plate; gearbox: mechanical; gears: 4, fully synchronized; ratios: I 3.450, II 1.950, III 1.250, IV 0.890, rev 3.380; lever: central; final drive: spiral bevel; axle ratio: 4.270; width of rims: 4.5"; tyres: 135 SR x 13.

PERFORMANCE max speeds: (I) 27 mph, 43 km/h; (II) 46 mph, 74 km/h; (III) 62 mph, 110 km/h; (IV) 84 mph, 135 km/h; power-weight ratio: 38.6 lb/hp (53.2 lb/kW), 17.5 kg/hp (24.1 kg/kW); carrying capacity: 948 lb, 430 kg; acceleration: 0-50 mph (0-80 km/h) 12.7 sec; speed in top at 1,000 rpm: 14.2 mph, 22.8 km/h; consumption: 37.2 m/imp gal, 30.9 m/US gal, 7.6 l x 100 km at 75 mph, 120 km/h.

CHASSIS integral; front suspension: independent, by McPherson, lower wishbones, anti-roll bar, coil springs/telescopic damper struts; rear: independent, torsion beam trailing arm axle, longitudinal trailing radius arms, coil springs/telescopic damper struts.

STEERING rack-and-pinion; turns lock to lock: 3.25.

BRAKES front disc, rear drum, dual circuit.

ELECTRICAL EQUIPMENT 12 V; 36 Ah battery; 55 A alternator; Bosch distributor; 2 headlamps.

DIMENSIONS AND WEIGHT wheel base: 91.93 in, 233 cm; tracks: 51.42 in, 131 cm front, 52.44 in, 133 cm rear; length: 143.90 in, 365 cm; width: 62.20 in, 158 cm; height: 53.35 in, 135 cm; ground clearance: 4.72 in, 12 cm; weight: 1,544 lb, 700 kg; turning circle: 32.8 ft, 10 m; fuel tank: 7.9 imp gal, 9.5 US gal, 36 l.

BODY saloon/sedan; 2+1 doors; 5 seats, separate front seats, reclining backrests with built-in headrests; heated rear window; folding rear seat.

PRACTICAL INSTRUCTIONS fuel: 97 oct petrol; oil: engine 5.3 imp pt, 6.3 US pt, 3 l, SAE 20W-50, change every 4,700 miles, 7,500 km - gearbox and final drive 4 imp pt, 4.9 US pt, 2.3 l, SAE 90, change every 18,600 miles, 30,000 km; greasing: none; tyre pressure: front 26 psi, 1.8 atm, rear 28 psi, 2 atm.

OPTIONALS 155/70 SR x 13 tyres; light alloy wheels; sunroof; halogen headlamps; metallic spray.

55 hp power team

See 40 hp power team, except for:

ENGINE 77.6 cu in, 1,272 cc (2.95 x 2.83 in, 75 x 72 mm); max power (DIN): 55 hp (40 kW) at 5,400 rpm; max torque (DIN): 71 lb ft, 9.8 kg m (96 Nm) at 3,300 rpm; 43.2 hp/l (31.4 kW/l); 1 Solex 31 PC 7 downdraught single barrel carburettor.

TRANSMISSION axle ratio: 4.060; tyres: 145 SR x 13.

PERFORMANCE max speed: 95 mph, 153 km/h: power-weight ratio: 29.1 lb/hp (40 lb/kW), 13.2 kg/hp (18.1 kg/kW); acceleration: 0-50 mph (0-80 km/h) 8.8 sec; consumption: 39.2 m/imp gal, 32.7 m/US gal, 7.2 l x 100 km at 75 mph, 120 km/h.

BRAKES rear compensator, servo.

DIMENSIONS AND WEIGHT weight: 1,599 lb, 725 kg.

VOLKSWAGEN Polo GL Limousine

Polo Classic Series

PRICES IN GB AND EX WORKS:	£	DM
1 C 1.0 2-dr Limousine	4,195*	12,690*
2 CL 1.0 2-dr Limousine	4,646*	13,660*
3 GL 1.0 2-dr Limousine	—	14,255*
4 C 1.3 2-dr Limousine	—	13,330*
5 CL 1.3 2-dr Limousine	—	14,300*
6 GL 1.3 2-dr Limousine	5,047*	14,895*

Power team:	Standard for:	Optional for:
40 hp	1 to 3	—
55 hp	4 to 6	—

40 hp power team

ENGINE front, transverse, slanted 15° to front, 4 stroke; 4 cylinders, in line; 63.6 cu in, 1,043 cc (2.95 x 2.32 in, 75 x 59 mm); compression ratio: 9.5:1; max power (DIN): 40 hp (29 kW) at 5,300 rpm; max torque (DIN): 55 lb ft, 7.5 kg m (74 Nm) at 2,700 rpm; max engine rpm: 5,800; 38.3 hp/l (27.8 kW/l); cast iron block, light alloy head; 5 crankshaft bearings; valves: overhead, in line, thimble tappets; camshafts: 1, overhead, cogged belt; lubrication: gear pump, full flow filter, 6.2 imp pt, 7.4 US pt, 3.5 l; 1 Solex 35 PICT-5 downdraught single barrel carburettor; fuel feed: mechanical pump; water-cooled, 7.9 imp pt, 9.5 US pt, 4.5 l, electric thermostatic fan.

TRANSMISSION driving wheels: front; clutch: single dry plate; gearbox: mechanical; gears: 4, fully synchronized; ratios: I 3.454, II 1.950, III 1.250, IV 0.890, rev 3.380; lever: central; final drive: spiral bevel; axle ratio: 4.270; width of rims: 4.5''; tyres: 145 SR x 13.

PERFORMANCE max speeds: (I) 27 mph, 43 km/h; (II) 46 mph, 74 km/h; (III) 62 mph, 110 km/h; (IV) 84 mph, 135 km/h; power-weight ratio: 39.4 lb/hp (53.4 lb/kW), 17.9 kg/hp (24.7 kg/kW); carrying capacity: 948 lb, 430 kg; acceleration: 0-50 mph (0-80 km/h) 12.7 sec; speed in top at 1,000 rpm: 14.2 mph, 22.8 km/h; consumption: 37.2 m/imp gal, 30.9 m/US gal, 7.6 l x 100 km at 75 mph, 120 km/h.

CHASSIS integral; front suspension: independent, by McPherson, lower wishbones, anti-roll bar, coil springs/telescopic damper struts; rear: independent, torsion beam trailing arm axle, longitudinal trailing radius arms, coil springs/telescopic damper struts.

STEERING rack-and-pinion; turns lock to lock: 3.25.

BRAKES front disc, rear drum, dual circuit.

ELECTRICAL EQUIPMENT 12 V; 36 Ah battery; 55 A alternator; Bosch distributor; 2 headlamps.

DIMENSIONS AND WEIGHT wheel base: 91.93 in, 233 cm; tracks: 51.42 in, 131 cm front, 52.44 in, 133 cm rear; length: 156.50 in, 397 cm; width: 62.20 in, 158 cm; height: 53.35 in, 135 cm; ground clearance: 4.72 in, 12 cm; weight: 1,577 lb, 715 kg; turning circle: 32.8 ft, 10 m; fuel tank: 7.9 imp gal, 9.5 US gal, 36 l.

BODY saloon/sedan; 2 doors; 5 seats, separate front seats, reclining backrests with built-in headrests; heated rear window; folding rear seat.

PRACTICAL INSTRUCTIONS fuel: 97 oct petrol; oil: engine 5.3 imp pt, 6.3 US pt, 3 l, SAE 20W-50, change every 4,700 miles, 7,500 km - gearbox and final drive 4 imp pt, 4.9 US pt, 2.3 l, SAE 90, change every 18,600 miles, 30,000 km; greasing: none; tyre pressure: front 26 psi, 1.8 atm, rear 28 psi, 2 atm.

OPTIONALS 155/70 SR x 13 tyres; light alloy wheels; sunroof; halogen headlamps; metallic spray.

VOLKSWAGEN Polo Classic GL Limousine

55 hp power team

See 40 hp power team, except for:

ENGINE 77.6 cu in, 1,272 cc (2.95 x 2.83 in, 75 x 72 mm); max power (DIN): 55 hp (40 kW) at 5,400 rpm; max torque (DIN): 71 lb ft, 9.8 kg m (96 Nm) at 3,300 rpm; 43.2 hp/l (31.4 kW/l); 1 Solex 31 PC 7 downdraught single barrel carburettor.

TRANSMISSION axle ratio: 4.060.

PERFORMANCE max speed: 95 mph, 153 km/h; power-weight ratio: 29.7 lb/hp (40.8 lb/kW), 13.5 kg/hp (18.5 kg/kW); acceleration: 0-50 mph (0-80 km/h) 8.8 sec; consumption: 39.2 m/imp gal, 32.7 m/US gal, 7.2 l x 100 km at 75 mph, 120 km/h.

BRAKES rear compensator, servo.

DIMENSIONS AND WEIGHT weight: 1,632 lb, 740 kg.

PRACTICAL INSTRUCTIONS fuel: 90 oct petrol.

Polo Coupé Series

PRICES EX WORKS:	DM
1 1.3 2+1-dr Coupé	14,750*
2 GT 1.3 2+1-dr Coupé	16,045*

Power team:	Standard for:	Optional for:
55 hp	1	—
75 hp	2	—

55 hp power team

ENGINE front, transverse, slanted 15° to front, 4 stroke; 4 cylinders, in line; 77.6 cu in, 1,272 cc (2.95 x 2.83 in, 75 x 72 mm); compression ratio: 9.5:1; max power (DIN): 55 hp (40 kW) at 5,400 rpm; max torque (DIN): 71 lb ft, 9.8 kg m (96 Nm) at 3,300 rpm; max engine rpm: 6,000; 43.2 hp/l (31.4 kW/l); cast iron block, light alloy head; 5 crankshaft bearings; valves: overhead, in line, rockers; camshafts: 1, overhead, cogged belt; lubrication: gear pump, full flow filter, 6.2 imp pt, 7.4 US pt, 3.5 l; 1 Solex 31 PC 7 downdraught single barrel carburettor; fuel feed: mechanical pump; water-cooled, 11.4 imp pt, 13.7 US pt, 6.5 l, electric thermostatic fan.

TRANSMISSION driving wheels: front; clutch: single dry plate; gearbox: mechanical; gears: 4, fully synchronized; ratios: I 3.454, II 1.950, III 1.250, IV 0.890, rev 3.380; lever: central; final drive: spiral bevel; axle ratio: 4.060; width of rims: 5.5''; tyres: 165/65 SR x 13.

PERFORMANCE max speed: 95 mph, 153 km/h; power-weight ratio: 29.1 lb/hp (40 lb/kW), 13.2 kg/hp (18.1 kg/kW); carrying capacity: 893 lb, 405 kg; acceleration: 0-50 mph (0-80 km/h) 8.8 sec; consumption: 39.2 m/imp gal, 32.7 m/US gal, 7.2 l x 100 km at 75 mph, 120 km/h.

CHASSIS integral; front suspension: independent, by McPherson, lower wishbones, anti-roll bar, coil springs/telescopic damper struts; rear: independent, torsion beam trailing arm axle, longitudinal trailing radius arms, coil springs/telescopic damper struts.

STEERING rack-and-pinion; turns lock to lock: 3.25.

BRAKES front disc, rear drum, dual circuit, servo.

ELECTRICAL EQUIPMENT 12 V; 36 Ah battery; 55 A alternator; Bosch distributor; 2 headlamps.

DIMENSIONS AND WEIGHT wheel base: 91.93 in, 233 cm; tracks: 51.97 in, 132 cm front, 52.99 in, 135 cm rear; length: 143.90 in, 365 cm; width: 62.60 in, 159 cm; height: 53.35 in, 135 cm; weight: 1,599 lb, 725 kg; turning circle: 32.8 ft, 10 m; fuel tank: 7.9 imp gal, 9.5 US gal, 36 l.

BODY coupé; 2+1 doors; 5 seats, separate front seats, reclining backrests with built-in headrests; heated rear window; folding rear seat.

PRACTICAL INSTRUCTIONS fuel: 97 oct petrol; oil: engine 5.3 imp pt, 6.3 US pt, 3 l, SAE 20W-50, change every 4,700 miles, 7,500 km - gearbox and final drive 4 imp pt, 4.9 US pt, 2.3 l, SAE 90, change every 18,600 miles, 30,000 km; greasing: none; tyre pressure: front 26 psi, 1.8 atm, rear 28 psi, 2 atm.

OPTIONALS light alloy wheels; sunroof; tinted glass; halogen headlamps; metallic spray.

VOLKSWAGEN Polo GT 1.3 Coupé

75 hp power team

See 55 hp power team, except for:

ENGINE compression ratio: 11:1; max power (DIN): 75 hp (55 kW) at 5,800 rpm; max torque (DIN): 77 lb ft, 10.6 kg m (104 Nm) at 3,600 rpm; 59 hp/l (43.2 kW/l); 1 Solex 34 PC 5 downdraught twin barrel carburettor.

PERFORMANCE max speed: 106 mph, 170 km/h; power-weight ratio: 21.5 lb/hp (29.3 lb/kW), 9.7 kg/hp (13.3 kg/kW); acceleration: 0-50 mph (0-80 km/h) 7.2 sec; consumption: 39.8 m/imp gal, 33.1 m/US gal, 7.1 l x 100 km at 75 mph, 120 km/h.

CHASSIS rear suspension: anti-roll bar.

STEERING damper.

BRAKES rear compensator.

ELECTRICAL EQUIPMENT 65 A alternator; transistorized ignition; 4 halogen headlamps (standard).

DIMENSIONS AND WEIGHT weight: 1,610 lb, 730 kg.

1200 L

PRICE EX WORKS: DM 9,480*

(For technical data, see Volkswagen Mexico)

VOLKSWAGEN Jetta GL Limousine

Jetta Series

PRICES EX WORKS:	DM
1 C 1.3 2-dr Limousine	**14,050***
2 C 1.3 4-dr Limousine	**14,750***
3 CL 1.3 2-dr Limousine	**15,095***
4 CL 1.3 4-dr Limousine	**15,795***
5 GL 1.3 2-dr Limousine	**16,405***
6 GL 1.3 4-dr Limousine	**17,105***
7 C 1.5 2-dr Limousine	**14,910***
8 C 1.5 4-dr Limousine	**15,610***
9 CL 1.5 2-dr Limousine	**15,955***
10 CL 1.5 4-dr Limousine	**16,655***
11 GL 1.5 2-dr Limousine	**17,265***
12 GL 1.5 4-dr Limousine	**17,965***
13 CL 1.6 2-dr Limousine	**16,300***
14 CL 1.6 4-dr Limousine	**17,000***
15 GL 1.6 2-dr Limousine	**17,610***
16 GL 1.6 4-dr Limousine	**18,310***

For GB and USA prices, see price index.

Power team:	Standard for:	Optional for:
60 hp	1 to 6	—
70 hp	7 to 12	—
85 hp	13 to 16	—

60 hp power team

ENGINE front, transverse, slanted 15° to front, 4 stroke; 4 cylinders, vertical, in line; 77.6 cu in, 1,272 cc (2.95 x 2.83 in, 75 x 72 mm); compression ratio: 8.2:1; max power (DIN): 60 hp (44 kW) at 5,600 rpm; max torque (DIN): 70 lb ft, 9.7 kg m (95 Nm) at 3,500 rpm; max engine rpm: 6,000; 47.2 hp/l (34.7 kW/l); cast iron block, light alloy head; 5 crankshaft bearings; valves: overhead, in line, rockers; camshafts: 1, overhead, cogged belt; lubrication: gear pump, full flow filter, 6.2 imp pt, 7.4 US pt, 3.5 l; 1 Solex 35 PICT-5 downdraught single barrel carburettor; fuel feed: mechanical pump; liquid-cooled, expansion tank, 7.9 imp pt, 9.5 US pt, 4.5 l, electric thermostatic fan.

TRANSMISSION driving wheels: front; clutch: single dry plate, hydraulically controlled; gearbox: mechanical; gears: 4, fully synchronized; ratios: I 3.450, II 1.950, III 1.250, IV 0.890, rev 3.380; lever: central; final drive: spiral bevel; axle ratio: 4.270; width of rims: 5"; tyres: 155 SR x 13.

PERFORMANCE max speeds: (I) 26 mph, 42 kmh; (II) 43 mph, 70 km/h; (III) 66 mph, 107 km/h; (IV) 91 mph, 147 km/h; power-weight ratio: 4-dr 31.2 lb/hp (42.6 lb/kW), 14.2 kg/hp (19.3 kg/kW); carrying capacity: 948 lb, 430 kg; acceleration: 0-50 mph (0-80 km/h) 9.6 sec; speed in top at 1,000 rpm: 14.9 mph, 24 km/h; consumption: 32.5 m/imp gal, 27 m/US gal, 8.7 l x 100 km at 75 mph, 120 km/h.

CHASSIS integral; front suspension: independent, by McPherson, lower wishbones, coil springs/telescopic damper struts; rear: semi-independent, torsion beam trailing arm, anti-roll bar, coil springs/telescopic damper struts.

STEERING rack-and-pinion.

BRAKES front disc (diameter 9.41 in, 23.9 cm), rear drum, 2 X circuits, servo.

ELECTRICAL EQUIPMENT 12 V; 36 Ah battery; 45 A alternator; Bosch distributor; 2 headlamps.

DIMENSIONS AND WEIGHT wheel base: 94.49 in, 240 cm; tracks: 54.72 in, 139 cm front, 53.46 in, 136 cm rear; length: 164.98 in, 419 cm; width: 63.39 in, 161 cm; height: 55.51 in, 141 cm; ground clearance: 4.92 in, 12.5 cm; weight: 2-dr 1,819 lb, 825 kg - 4-dr 1,874 lb, 850 kg; turning circle: 33.8 ft, 10.3 m; fuel tank: 8.8 imp gal, 10.6 US gal, 40 l.

BODY saloon/sedan; 2 or 4 doors; 5 seats, separate front seats, reclining backrests with built-in headrests; heated rear window.

PRACTICAL INSTRUCTIONS fuel: 91 oct petrol; oil: engine 5.3 imp pt, 6.3 US pt, 3 l, SAE 20W-30, change every 4,700 miles, 7,500 km - gearbox and final drive 3.2 imp pt, 3.8 US pt, 1.8 l, SAE 80 or 90, change every 18,600 miles, 30,000 km; greasing: none; spark plug: Bosch 200 T 30; tyre pressure: front 26 psi, 1.8 atm, rear 26 psi, 1.8 atm.

OPTIONALS light alloy wheels with 5.5" wide rims; 175/70 SR x 13 tyres; halogen headlamps; metallic spray; sunroof.

VOLKSWAGEN Jetta Turbo-Diesel

70 hp power team

See 60 hp power team, except for:

ENGINE front, transverse, slanted 20° to rear; 88.9 cu in, 1,457 cc (3.13 x 2.89 in, 79.5 x 73.4 mm); max power (DIN): 70 hp (51 kW) at 5,600 rpm; max torque (DIN): 81 lb ft, 11.2 kg m (110 Nm) at 2,500 rpm; 48 hp/l (35.3 kW/l); valves: overhead, thimble tappets; 1 Solex 34 PICT-5 downdraught single barrel carburettor.

TRANSMISSION gearbox ratios: I 3.450, II 1.940, III 1.290, IV 0.910, rev 3.170; axle ratio: 3.890; width of rims: 5.5"; tyres: 175/70 SR x 13 (standard).

PERFORMANCE max speed: 97 mph, 156 km/h; power-weight ratio: 4-dr 27.4 lb/hp (37.6 lb/kW), 12.4 kg/hp (17.1 kg/kW); acceleration: 0-50 mph (0-80 km/h) 8.8 sec; speed in top at 1,000 rpm: 18.2 mph, 29.3 km/h; consumption: 30.1 m/imp gal, 25 m/US gal, 9.4 l x 100 km at 75 mph, 120 km/h.

BRAKES rear compensator.

DIMENSIONS AND WEIGHT tracks: 55.27 in, 140 cm front, 54.02 in, 137 cm rear; width: 64.17 in, 163 cm; weight: 2-dr 1,863 lb, 845 kg - 4-dr 1,918 lb, 870 kg.

OPTIONALS 4+E 5-speed fully synchronized mechanical gearbox (I 3.450, II 1.940, III 1.290, IV 0.910, V 0.710, rev 3.170), consumption 34.4 m/imp gal, 28.7 m/US gal, 8.2 l x 100 km at 75 mph, 120 km/h; automatic transmission, hydraulic torque converter and planetary gears with 3 ratios (I 2.710, II 1.500, III 1, rev 2.430), 3.570 axle ratio, max speed 94 mph, 151 km/h, acceleration 0-50 mph (0-80 km/h) 10.4 sec, consumption 27.4 m/imp gal, 22.8 m/US gal, 10.3 l x 100 km at 75 mph, 120 km/h.

85 hp power team

See 60 hp power team, except for:

ENGINE front, transverse, slanted 20° to rear; 96.9 cu in, 1,588 cc (3.13 x 3.15 in, 79.5 x 80 mm); max power (DIN): 85 hp (63 kW) at 5,600 rpm; max torque (DIN): 92 lb ft, 12.8 kg m (125 Nm) at 3,800 rpm; 53.5 hp/l (39.4 kW/l); valves: overhead, thimble tappets; 1 Solex 2 B 5 downdraught twin barrel carburettor.

TRANSMISSION gearbox ratios: I 3.450, II 1.940, III 1.290, IV 0.910, rev 3.170; axle ratio: 3.890; width of rims: 5.5"; tyres: 175/70 SR x 13 (standard).

PERFORMANCE max speed: 103 mph, 166 km/h; power-weight ratio: 4-dr 22.6 lb/hp (30.4 lb/kW), 10.2 kg/hp (13.8 kg/kW); acceleration: 0-50 mph (0-80 km/h) 7.4 sec; consumption: 30.7 m/imp gal, 25.6 m/US gal, 9.2 l x 100 km at 75 mph, 120 km/h.

BRAKES rear compensator.

DIMENSIONS AND WEIGHT tracks: 55.27 in, 140 cm front, 54.02 in, 137 cm rear; width: 64.17 in, 163 cm; weight: 2-dr 1,863 lb, 845 kg - 4-dr 1,918 lb, 870 kg.

OPTIONALS 4+E 5-speed fully synchronized mechanical gearbox (I 3.450, II 1.940, III 1.290, IV 0.910, V 0.710, rev 3.170), consumption 35.3 m/imp gal, 29.4 m/US gal, 8 l x 100 km at 75 mph, 120 km/h.

Jetta Diesel

PRICES EX WORKS:	DM
C 1.6 2-dr Limousine	**15,825***
C 1.6 4-dr Limousine	**16,525***
CL 1.6 2-dr Limousine	**16,870***
CL 1.6 4-dr Limousine	**17,570***
GL 1.6 2-dr Limousine	**18,180***
GL 1.6 4-dr Limousine	**18,880***

For GB and USA prices, see price index.

ENGINE diesel, front, transverse, 4 stroke; 4 cylinders, vertical, in line; 96.9 cu in, 1,588 cc (3.01 x 3.40 in, 76.5 x 86.4 mm); compression ratio: 23:1; max power (DIN): 54 hp (40 kW) at 4,800 rpm; max torque (DIN): 74 lb ft, 10.2 kg m (100 Nm) at 2,300 rpm; max engine rpm: 5,000; 34 hp/l (25.2 kW/l); cast iron block, light alloy head; 5 crankshaft bearings; valves: overhead, in line, thimble tappets; camshafts: 1, overhead, cogged belt; lubrication: gear pump, full flow filter, 6.2 imp pt, 7.4 US pt, 3.5 l; Bosch injection pump; liquid-cooled, expansion tank, 11.4 imp pt, 13.7 US pt, 6.5 l, electric thermostatic fan.

TRANSMISSION driving wheels: front; clutch: single dry plate, hydraulically controlled; gearbox: mechanical; gears: 4, fully synchronized; ratios: I 3.450, II 1.940, III 1.290, IV 0.910, rev 3.170; lever: central; final drive: spiral bevel; axle ratio: 3.890; width of rims: 5"; tyres: 155 SR x 13.

PERFORMANCE max speed: 88 mph, 141 km/h; power-weight ratio: 2-dr 35.3 lb/hp (47.7 lb/kW), 16 kg/hp (21.6 kg/kW); carrying capacity: 1,069 lb, 485 kg; acceleration: 0-50 mph (0-80 km/h) 11.2 sec; speed in top at 1,000 rpm: 17.5 mph, 28.2 km/h; consumption: 36.7 m/imp gal, 30.5 m/US gal, 7.7 l x 100 km at 75 mph, 120 km/h.

CHASSIS integral; front suspension: independent, by McPherson, lower wishbones, coil springs/telescopic damper struts; rear: semi-independent, torsion beam trailing arm, anti-roll bar, coil springs/telescopic damper struts.

STEERING rack-and-pinion.

BRAKES front disc, rear drum, 2 X circuits, rear compensator, servo.

ELECTRICAL EQUIPMENT 12 V; 63 Ah battery; 45 A alternator; 2 headlamps.

DIMENSIONS AND WEIGHT wheel base: 94.49 in, 240 cm; tracks: 55.27 in, 140 cm front, 54.02 in, 137 cm rear; length: 164.98 in, 419 cm; width: 64.17 in, 163 cm; height: 55.51 in, 141 cm; ground clearance: 4.92 in, 12.5 cm; weight: 2-dr 1,907 lb, 865 kg - 4-dr 1,962 lb, 890 kg; turning circle: 34.4 ft, 10.5 m; fuel tank: 8.8 imp gal, 10.6 US gal, 40 l.

BODY saloon/sedan; 2 or 4 doors; 5 seats, separate front seats, reclining backrests with built-in headrests; heated rear window.

PRACTICAL INSTRUCTIONS fuel: diesel; oil: engine 5.3 imp pt, 6.3 US pt, 3 l - gearbox and final drive 3.2 imp pt, 3.8 US pt, 1.8 l, SAE 80; greasing: none; tyre pressure: front 26 psi, 1.8 atm, rear 26 psi, 1.8 atm.

OPTIONALS 4+E 5-speed fully synchronized mechanical gearbox (I 3.450, II 1.940, III 1.290, IV 0.910, V 0.710, rev 3.170), consumption 39.2 m/imp gal, 32.7 m/US gal, 6.9 l x 100 km at 75 mph, 120 km/h; automatic transmission with 3 ratios (I 2.710, II 1.500, III 1, rev 2.430), 3.570 axle ratio, max speed 84 mph, 136 km/h, consumption 33.2 m/imp gal, 27.7 m/US gal, 8.5 l x 100 km at 75 mph, 120 km/h; 175/70 SR x 13 tyres; halogen headlamps; sunroof; metallic spray; tinted glass.

Jetta Turbo-Diesel

See Jetta Diesel, except for:

PRICES EX WORKS:	DM
C 1.6 2-dr Limousine	**18,055***
C 1.6 4-dr Limousine	**18,755***
CL 1.6 2-dr Limousine	**19,100***
CL 1.6 4-dr Limousine	**19,800***
GL 1.6 2-dr Limousine	**20,410***
GL 1.6 4-dr Limousine	**21,110***

For USA prices, see price index.

ENGINE diesel, turbocharged; max power (DIN): 70 hp (51 kW) at 4,500 rpm; max torque (DIN): 98 lb ft, 13.6 kg m (133 Nm) at 2,600 rpm; 44.1 hp/l (32.1 kW/l); Bosch injection pump; 1 Garrett AiResearch turbocharger.

TRANSMISSION (standard) gearbox: 4+E mechanical; gears: 5, fully synchronized; ratios: I 3.450, II 1.940, III 1.290, IV 0.910, V 0.710, rev 3.170; width of rims: 5.5"; tyres: 175/70 SR x 13.

PERFORMANCE max speed: 95 mph, 153 km/h; power-weight ratio: 2-dr 28 lb/hp (38.5 lb/kW), 12.7 kg/hp (17.5 kg/kW); carrying capacity: 2-dr 1,014 lb, 460 kg - 4-dr 959 lb, 435 kg; acceleration: 0-50 mph (0-80 km/h) 9.1 sec; consumption: 40.9 m/imp gal, 34.1 m/US gal, 6.9 l x 100 km at 75 mph, 120 km/h.

BRAKES rear compensator.

DIMENSIONS AND WEIGHT weight: 2-dr 1,962 lb, 890 kg - 4-dr 2,018 lb, 915 kg.

Golf Limousine Series

PRICES EX WORKS:		DM
1	C 1.3 2+1-dr Limousine	**13,490***
2	C 1.3 4+1-dr Limousine	**14,190***
3	CL 1.3 2+1-dr Limousine	**14,485***
4	CL 1.3 4+1-dr Limousine	**15,185***
5	GL 1.3 2+1-dr Limousine	**16,015***
6	GL 1.3 4+1-dr Limousine	**16,715***
7	C 1.6 2+1-dr Limousine	**14,620***
8	C 1.6 4+1-dr Limousine	**15,320***
9	CL 1.6 2+1-dr Limousine	**15,615***
10	CL 1.6 4+1-dr Limousine	**16,315***
11	GL 1.6 2+1-dr Limousine	**17,145***
12	GL 1.6 4+1-dr Limousine	**17,845***
13	Carat 1.8 (90 hp) 4+1-dr Limousine	**22,165***
14	GTI 1.8 (112 hp) 2+1-dr Limousine	**21,115***
15	GTI 1.8 (112 hp) 4+1-dr Limousine	**21,815***

For GB and USA prices, see price index.

Power team:	Standard for:	Optional for:
55 hp	1 to 6	—
75 hp	7 to 12	—
90 hp	13	—
112 hp	14,15	—

55 hp power team

ENGINE front, transverse, slanted 15° to front, 4 stroke; 4 cylinders, vertical, in line; 77.6 cu in, 1,272 cc (2.95 x 2.83 in, 75 x 72 mm); compression ratio: 9.5:1; max power (DIN): 55 hp (40 kW) at 5,400 rpm; max torque (DIN): 71 lb ft, 9.8 kg m (96 Nm) at 3,300 rpm; max engine rpm: 6,000; 43.2 hp/l (31.4 kW/l); cast iron block, light alloy head; 5 crankshaft bearings; valves: overhead, in line, rockers; camshafts: 1, overhead, cogged belt; lubrication: gear pump, full flow filter, 6.2 imp pt, 7.4 US pt, 3.5 l; 1 Solex 31 PC 7 downdraught single barrel carburettor; fuel feed: mechanical pump; liquid-cooled, expansion tank, 11.4 imp pt, 13.7 US pt, 6.5 l, electric thermostatic fan.

VOLKSWAGEN Golf GL Limousine

TRANSMISSION driving wheels: front; clutch: single dry plate, hydraulically controlled; gearbox: mechanical; gears: 4, fully synchronized; ratios: I 3.450, II 1.950, III 1.250, IV 0.890, rev 3.380; lever: central; final drive: spiral bevel; axle ratio: 4.060; width of rims: 5"; tyres: 155 SR x 13.

PERFORMANCE max speeds: (I) 30 mph, 48 km/h; (II) 53 mph, 85 km/h; (III) 75 mph, 120 km/h; (IV) 94 mph, 151 km/h; power-weight ratio: 2+1-dr 33.9 lb/hp (46.6 lb/kW), 15.4 kg/hp (21.1 kg/kW); carrying capacity: 1,047 lb, 475 kg; acceleration: 0-50 mph (0-80 km/h) 10.3 sec; speed in top at 1,000 rpm: 17.3 mph, 27.9 km/h; consumption: 38.7 m/imp gal, 32.2 m/US gal, 7.3 l x 100 km at 75 mph, 120 km/h.

CHASSIS integral; front suspension: independent, by McPherson, lower wishbones, coil springs/telescopic damper struts; rear: semi-independent, torsion beam trailing arm, coil springs/telescopic damper struts.

STEERING rack-and-pinion.

BRAKES front disc, rear drum, 2 X circuits, servo.

ELECTRICAL EQUIPMENT 12 V; 36 Ah battery; 65 A alternator; Bosch distributor; 2 headlamps.

DIMENSIONS AND WEIGHT wheel base: 97.44 in, 247 cm; tracks: 55.63 in, 141 cm front, 55.43 in, 141 cm rear; length: 156.89 in, 398 cm; width: 65.55 in, 166 cm; height: 55.71 in, 141 cm; ground clearance: 4.92 in, 12.5 cm; weight: 2+1-dr 1,863 lb, 845 kg - 4+1-dr 1,907 lb, 865 kg; turning circle: 34.4 ft, 10.5 m; fuel tank: 12.1 imp gal, 14.5 US gal, 55 l.

BODY saloon/sedan; 2+1 or 4+1 doors; 5 seats, separate front seats; folding rear seat; heated rear window.

PRACTICAL INSTRUCTIONS fuel: 97 oct petrol; oil: engine 6.2 imp pt, 7.4 US pt, 3.5 l, SAE 10W-50, change every 4,700 miles, 7,500 km - gearbox and final drive 3.2 imp pt, 3.8 US pt, 1.8 l, SAE 80 or 90, change every 18,600 miles, 30,000 km; greasing: none; spark plug: Bosch WG 175 T 30; tyre pressure: front 26 psi, 1.8 atm, rear 26 psi, 1.8 atm.

VOLKSWAGEN Golf GL Limousine

OPTIONALS 3+E 4-speed fully synchronized mechanical gearbox (I 3.450, II 1.950, III 1.250, IV 0.890, rev 3.380), 3.880 axle ratio, consumption 39.8 m/imp gal, 33.1 m/US gal, 7.1 l x 100 km at 75 mph, 120 km/h; light alloy wheels; 175/70 SR x 13 tyres; halogen headlamps; sunroof; power steering; tinted glass; metallic spray; air-conditioning.

75 hp power team

See 55 hp power team, except for:

ENGINE 97.3 cu in, 1,595 cc (3.19 x 3.05 in, 81 x 77.4 mm); compression ratio: 9:1; max power (DIN): 75 hp (55 kW) at 5,000 rpm; max torque (DIN): 92 lb ft, 12.7 kg m (125 Nm) at 2,500 rpm; max engine rpm: 6,000; 47 hp/l (35.4 kW/l); valves: overhead, thimble tappets; 1 Solex 34 PC 5 downdraught twin barrel carburettor with fully automatic choke and fuel cut-off system.

TRANSMISSION gearbox ratios: I 3.450, II 1.940, III 1.290, IV 0.910, rev 3.170; axle ratio: 3.670; width of rims: 5.5"; tyres: 175/70 SR x 13 (standard).

PERFORMANCE max speeds: (I) 31 mph, 50 km/h; (II) 54 mph, 87 km/h; (III) 79 mph, 128 km/h; (IV) 104 mph, 167 km/h; power-weight ratio: 2-dr 25.6 lb/hp (34.9 lb/kW), 11.6 kg/hp (15.8 kg/kW); acceleration: 0-50 mph (0-80 km/h) 8.4 sec; speed in top at 1,000 rpm: 20.7 mph, 33.4 km/h; consumption: 36.2 m/imp gal, 30.2 m/US gal, 7.8 l x 100 km at 75 mph, 120 km/h.

DIMENSIONS AND WEIGHT tracks: 56.18 in, 143 cm front, 55.98 in, 142 cm rear; weight: 2+1-dr 1,918 lb, 870 kg - 4+1-dr 1,962 lb, 890 kg.

OPTIONALS 4+E 5-speed fully synchronized mechanical gearbox (I 3.450, II 1.940, III 1.290, IV 0.910, V 0.750, rev 3.170), consumption 39.8 m/imp gal, 33.1 m/US gal, 7.1 l x 100 km at 75 mph, 120 km/h; automatic transmission, hydraulic torque converter and planetary gears with 3 ratios (I 2.710, II 1.500, III 1, rev 2.430), 3.410 axle ratio, max speed 101 mph, 162 km/h, acceleration 0-50 mph (0-80 km/h) 10 sec, consumption 34.9 m/imp gal, 29 m/US gal, 8.1 l x 100 km at 75 mph, 120 km/h; 185/60 SR x 13 tyres.

90 hp power team

See 55 hp power team, except for:

ENGINE 108.7 cu in, 1,781 cc (3.19 x 3.40 in, 81 x 86.4 mm); compression ratio: 10:1; max power (DIN): 90 hp (66 kW) at 5,200 rpm; max torque (DIN): 107 lb ft, 14.8 kg m (145 Nm) at 3,300 rpm; max engine rpm: 6,000; 50.5 hp/l (37.1 kW/l); valves: overhead, thimble tappets; 1 Weber 2 BC downdraught twin barrel carburettor with fully automatic choke and fuel cut-off system.

TRANSMISSION gearbox: 4+E mechanical; gears: 5, fully synchronized; ratios: I 3.450, II 1.940, III 1.290, IV 0.910, V 0.750, rev 3.170; axle ratio: 3.670; width of rims: 5.5"; tyres: 175/70 HR x 13.

PERFORMANCE max speeds: (I) 32 mph, 51 km/h; (II) 55 mph, 89 km/h; (III) 82 mph, 132 km/h; (IV) 93 mph, 150 km/h; (V) 111 mph, 178 km/h; power-weight ratio: 22 lb/hp (30.1 lb/kW), 10 kg/hp (13.6 kg/kW); acceleration: 0-50 mph (0-80 km/h) 7 sec; speed in top at 1,000 rpm: 21.3 mph, 34.2 km/h; consumption: 38.7 m/imp gal, 32.2 m/US gal, 7.3 l x 100 km at 75 mph, 120 km/h.

BRAKES rear compensator.

DIMENSIONS AND WEIGHT tracks: 56.18 in, 143 cm front, 55.98 in, 142 cm rear; weight: 1,984 lb, 900 kg.

BODY 4+1 doors.

OPTIONALS automatic transmission, hydraulic torque converter and planetary gearx with 3 ratios (I 2.710, II 1.500, III

VOLKSWAGEN Golf GL Limousine

VOLKSWAGEN Golf GTI 1.8 Limousine

1, rev 2.430), 3.120 axle ratio, max speed 107 mph, 173 km/h, acceleration 0-50 mph (0-80 km/h) 8.6 sec, consumption 34 m/imp gal, 28.3 m/US gal, 8.3 l x 100 km at 75 mph, 120 km/h; 185/60 HR x 13 tyres.

112 hp power team

See 55 hp power team, except for:

ENGINE 108.7 cu in, 1,781 cc (3.19 x 3.40 in, 81 x 86.4 mm); compression ratio: 10:1; max power (DIN): 112 hp (82 kW) at 5,500 rpm; max torque (DIN): 115 lb ft, 15.8 kg m (155 Nm) at 3,100 rpm; max engine rpm: 6,700; 62.9 hp/l (46 kW/l); valves: overhead, thimble tappets; Bosch K-Jetronic injection; fuel feed: electric pump.

TRANSMISSION gears: 5, fully synchronized; ratios: I 3.450, II 2.120, III 1.440, IV 1.130, V 0.890, rev 3.170; axle ratio: 3.670; width of rims: 5.5"; tyres: 175/70 HR x 13.

PERFORMANCE max speeds: (I) 32 mph, 52 km/h; (II) 53 mph, 85 km/h; (III) 79 mph, 127 km/h; (IV) 98 mph, 158 km/h; (V) 119 mph, 191 km/h; power-weight ratio: 2+1-dr 18.1 lb/hp (24.7 lb/kW), 8.2 kg/hp (11.2 kg/kW); acceleration: 0-50 mph (0-80 km/h) 6.5 sec; speed in top at 1,000 rpm; 21.6 mph, 34.7 km/h; consumption: 37.7 m/imp gal, 31.4 m/US gal, 7.5 l x 100 km at 75 mph, 120 km/h.

CHASSIS front and rear suspension: anti-roll bar.

BRAKES disc, front internal radial fins, rear compensator.

ELECTRICAL EQUIPMENT 45 Ah battery; 55 A alternator; transistorized ignition; speed limiter at 6,700 rpm.

DIMENSIONS AND WEIGHT tracks: 56.18 in, 143 cm front, 55.98 in, 142 cm rear; width: 66.14 in, 168 cm; height: 55.31 in, 140 cm; weight: 2+1-dr 2,029 lb, 920 kg - 4+1-dr 2,073 lb, 940 kg.

OPTIONALS light alloy wheels with 185/60 HR x 13 tyres.

Golf Diesel

PRICES EX WORKS:	DM
C 1.6 2+1-dr Limousine	**15,265***
C 1.6 4+1-dr Limousine	**15,965***
CL 1.6 2+1-dr Limousine	**16,260***
CL 1.6 4+1-dr Limousine	**16,960***
GL 1.6 2+1-dr Limousine	**17,790***
GL 1.6 4+1-dr Limousine	**18,490***

For USA prices, see price index.

ENGINE diesel, front, transverse, 4 stroke; 4 cylinders, vertical, in line; 96.9 cu in, 1,588 cc (3.01 x 3.40 in, 76.5 x 86.4 mm); compression ratio: 23:1; max power (DIN): 54 hp (40 kW) at 4,800 rpm; max torque (DIN): 74 lb ft, 10.2 kg m (100 Nm) at 2,300 rpm; max engine rpm: 5,000; 34 hp/l (25.2 kW/l); cast iron block, light alloy head; 5 crankshaft bearings; valves: overhead, in line, thimble tappets; camshafts: 1, overhead, cogged belt; lubrication: gear pump, full flow filter, 6.2 imp pt, 7.4 US pt, 3.5 l; Bosch injection pump; liquid-cooled, expansion tank, 11.4 imp pt, 13.7 US pt, 6.5 l, electric thermostatic fan.

TRANSMISSION driving wheels: front; clutch: single dry plate, hydraulically controlled; gearbox: mechanical; gears: 4, fully synchronized; ratios: I 3.450, II 1.940, III 1.290, IV 0.880, rev 3.170; lever: central; final drive: spiral bevel; axle ratio: 3.940; width of rims: 5"; tyres: 155 SR x 13.

PERFORMANCE max speeds: (I) 22 mph, 36 km/h; (II) 40 mph, 65 km/h; (III) 64 mph, 103 km/h; (IV) 92 mph, 148 km/h; power-weight ratio: 2+1-dr 37.6 lb/hp (50.7 lb/kW), 16.7 kg/hp (22.5 kg/kW); carrying capacity: 2+1-dr 1,169 lb, 530 kg - 4+1-dr 1,125 lb, 510 kg; acceleration: 0-50 mph (0-80 km/h) 11.7 sec; speed in top at 1,000 rpm: 19.2 mph, 30.8 km/h; consumption: 41.5 m/imp gal, 34.6 m/US gal, 6.8 l x 100 km at 75 mph, 120 km/h.

CHASSIS integral; front suspension: independent, by McPherson, lower wishbones, coil springs/telescopic damper struts; rear: semi-independent, torsion beam trailing arm, coil springs/telescopic damper struts.

STEERING rack-and-pinion.

BRAKES front disc, rear drum, 2 X circuits, servo.

ELECTRICAL EQUIPMENT 12 V; 63 Ah battery; 45 A alternator; 2 headlamps.

DIMENSIONS AND WEIGHT wheel base: 97.44 in, 247 cm; tracks: 55.63 in, 141 cm front, 55.43 in, 141 cm rear; length: 156.89 in, 398 cm; width: 65.55 in, 166 cm; height: 55.71 in, 141 cm; ground clearance: 4.92 in, 12.5 cm; weight: 2+1-dr 1,984 lb, 900 kg - 4+1-dr 2,029 lb, 920 kg; turning circle: 34.4 ft, 10.5 m; fuel tank: 10.5 imp gal, 12.1 US gal, 55 l.

BODY saloon/sedan; 2+1 or 4+1 doors; 5 seats, separate front seats, built-in headrests; folding rear seat; heated rear window.

PRACTICAL INSTRUCTIONS fuel: diesel; oil: engine 5.3 imp pt, 6.3 US pt, 3 l - gearbox and final drive 3.2 imp pt, 3.8 US pt, 1.8 l, SAE 80; tyre pressure: front 26 psi, 1.8 atm, rear 26 psi, 1.8 atm.

OPTIONALS 4+E 5-speed fully synchronized mechanical gearbox (I 3.450, II 1.940, III 1.290, IV 0.910, V 0.750, rev 3.170), consumption 45.6 m/imp gal, 37.9 m/US gal, 6.2 l x 100 km at 75 mph, 120 km/h; automatic transmission with 3 ratios (I 2.710, II 1.500, III 1, rev 2.430), 3.410 axle ratio, max speed 89 mph, 143 km/h, consumption 37.7 m/imp gal, 31.4 m/US gal, 7.5 l x 100 km at 75 mph, 120 km/h; 175/70 SR x 13 tyres; power steering; halogen headlamps; sunroof; metallic spray; rear window wiper-washer; tinted glass; air-conditioning.

Golf Turbo-Diesel

See Golf Diesel, except for:

PRICES EX WORKS:	DM
C 1.6 2+1-dr Limousine	**17,495***
C 1.6 4+1-dr Limousine	**18,195***
CL 1.6 2+1-dr Limousine	**18,490***
CL 1.6 4+1-dr Limousine	**19,190***
GL 1.6 2+1-dr Limousine	**20,020***
GL 1.6 4+1-dr Limousine	**20,720***
GTD 1.6 2+1-dr Limousine	**19,405***
GTD 1.6 4+1-dr Limousine	**20,105***

ENGINE diesel, turbocharged; max power (DIN): 70 hp (51 kW) at 4,500 rpm; max torque (DIN): 98 lb ft, 13.6 kg m (133 Nm) at 2,600 rpm; 44.1 hp/l (32.1 kW/l); Bosch injection pump; 1 Garrett AiResearch turbocharger.

TRANSMISSION (standard) gearbox: 4+E mechanical; gears: 5 fully synchronized; ratios: I 3.450, II 1.940, III 1.290, IV 0.910, V 0.750, rev 3.170; axle ratio: 3.670; width of rims: 5.5"; tyres: 175/70 SR x 13.

PERFORMANCE max speed: 99 mph, 160 km/h; power-weight ratio: 2+1-dr 29 lb/hp, (39.8 lb/kW), 13.1 kg/hp (18 kg/kW); carrying capacity: 2+1-dr 1,125 lb, 510 kg - 4+1-dr 1,080 lb, 490 kg; acceleration: 0-50 mph (0-80 km/h) 9.4 sec; consumption: 46.3 m/imp gal, 38.6 m/US gal, 6.1 l x 100 km at 75 mph, 120 km/h.

BRAKES rear compensator.

DIMENSIONS AND WEIGHT tracks: 56.18 in, 143 cm front, 55.98 in, 142 cm rear; width: GTD 66.14 in, 168 cm; weight: 2+1-dr 2,029 lb, 920 kg - 4+1-dr 2,073 lb, 940 kg.

Golf Cabriolet Series

PRICES IN GB AND EX WORKS:	£	DM
1 GL 1.6 2-dr Cabriolet	**7,415***	**22,250***
2 GLI 1.8 2-dr Cabriolet	**8,361***	**25,815***

For USA prices, see price index.

Power team:	Standard for:	Optional for:
75 hp	1	—
112 hp	2	—

75 hp power team

ENGINE front, transverse, 4 stroke; 4 cylinders, vertical, in line; 97.3 cu in, 1,595 cc (3.19 x 3.05 in, 81 x 77.4 mm); compression ratio: 9:1; max power (DIN): 75 hp (55 kW) at 5,000 rpm; max torque (DIN): 92 lb ft, 12.7 kg m (125 Nm) at 2,500 rpm; max engine rpm: 6,000; 47 hp/l (34.5 kW/l); cast iron block, light alloy head; 5 crankshaft bearings; valves: overhead, in line, thimble tappets; camshafts: 1, overhead, cogged belt; lubrication: gear pump, full flow filter, 6.2 imp pt, 7.4 US pt, 3.5 l; 1 Solex 34 PC 5 downdraught twin barrel carburettor with fully automatic choke and fuel cut-off system; fuel feed: mechanical pump; liquid-cooled, expansion tank, 11.4 imp pt, 13.7 US pt, 6.5 l, electric thermostatic fan.

TRANSMISSION driving wheels: front; clutch: single dry plate, hydraulically controlled; gearbox: mechanical; gears: 4, fully synchronized; ratios: I 3.450, II 1.940, III 1.290, IV 0.910, rev 3.170; lever: central; final drive: spiral bevel; axle ratio: 3.670; width of rims: 5"; tyres: 155 SR x 13.

PERFORMANCE max speed: 96 mph, 154 km/h; power-weight ratio: 26.8 lb/hp (36.5 lb/kW), 12.1 kg/hp (16.5 kg/kW); carrying capacity: 794 lb, 360 kg; acceleration: 0-50 mph (0-80 km/h) 8.2 sec; speed in top at 1,000 rpm: 19.1 mph, 30.8 km/h; consumption: 33.2 m/imp gal, 27.7 m/US gal, 8.5 l x 100 km at 75 mph, 120 km/h.

CHASSIS integral; front suspension: independent, by McPherson, lower wishbones, coil springs/telescopic damper struts; rear: semi-independent, torsion beam trailing arm, coil springs/telescopic damper struts.

VOLKSWAGEN Golf Limousine Series

VOLKSWAGEN Golf GL 1.6 Cabriolet

75 HP POWER TEAM

STEERING rack-and-pinion.

BRAKES front disc, rear drum, 2 X circuits, servo.

ELECTRICAL EQUIPMENT 12 V; 36 Ah battery; 65 A alternator; transistorized ignition; 2 halogen headlamps.

DIMENSIONS AND WEIGHT wheel base: 94.49 in, 240 cm; tracks: 54.72 in, 139 cm front, 53.46 in, 136 cm rear; length: 150.20 in, 381 cm; width: 63.39 in, 161 cm; height: 55.51 in, 141 cm; ground clearance: 4.92 in, 12.5 cm; weight: 2,007 lb, 910 kg; turning circle: 33.8 ft, 10.3 m; fuel tank: 8.8 imp gal, 10 US gal, 40 l.

BODY convertible; 2 doors; 5 seats, separate front seats; reclining backrests.

PRACTICAL INSTRUCTIONS fuel: 91 oct petrol; oil: engine 6.2 imp pt, 7.4 US pt, 3.5 l, SAE 10W-50, change every 4,700 miles, 7,500 km - gearbox and final drive 3.2 imp pt, 3.8 US pt, 1.8 l, SAE 80 or 90, change every 18,600 miles, 30,000 km; greasing: none; tyre pressure: front 26 psi, 1.8 atm, rear 26 psi, 1.8 atm.

OPTIONALS 4+E 5-speed fully synchronized mechanical gearbox (I 3.450, II 1.940, III 1.290, IV 0.910, V 0.750, rev 3.170), consumption 36.2 m/imp gal, 30.2 m/US gal, 7.8 l x 100 km at 75 mph, 120 km/h; automatic transmission, hydraulic torque converter and planetary gears with 3 ratios (I 2.710, II 1.500, III 1, rev 2.430), 3.410 axle ratio, max speed 93 mph, 149 km/h, acceleration 0-50 mph (0-80 km/h) 9.8 sec, consumption 32.1 m/imp gal, 26.7 m/US gal, 8.8 l x 100 km at 75 mph, 120 km/h; light alloy wheels with 175/70 SR x 13 tyres; tinted glass; metallic spray; air-conditioning.

112 hp power team

See 75 hp power team, except for:

ENGINE 108.7 cu in, 1,781 cc (3.19 x 3.40 in, 81 x 86.4 mm); compression ratio: 10:1; max power (DIN): 112 hp (82 kW) at 5,800 rpm; max torque (DIN): 113 lb ft, 15.6 kg m (153 Nm) at 3,500 rpm; max engine rpm: 6,700; 62.9 hp/l (46 kW/l); Bosch K-Jetronic injection; fuel feed: electric pump.

TRANSMISSION gears: 5, fully synchronized; ratios: I 3.450, II 2.120, III 1.440, IV 1.130, V 0.890, rev 3.170; width of rims: 5.5"; tyres: 175/70 HR x 13.

PERFORMANCE max speed: 107 mph, 173 km/h; power-weight ratio: 18.5 lb/hp (25.3 lb/kW), 8.4 kg/hp (11.5 kg/kW); acceleration: 0-50 mph (0-80 km/h) 6.3 sec; speed in top at 1,000 rpm: 18.5 mph, 29.8 km/h; consumption: 32.8 m/imp gal, 27.3 m/US gal, 8.6 l x 100 km at 75 mph, 120 km/h.

CHASSIS front and rear suspension: anti-roll bar.

BRAKES front disc, internal radial fins, rear compensator.

ELECTRICAL EQUIPMENT 45 Ah battery; 55 A alternator; transistorized ignition; speed limiter at 6,700 rpm.

DIMENSIONS AND WEIGHT tracks: 55.28 in, 140 cm front, 54.02 in, 137 cm rear; width: 64.17 in, 163 cm; height: 54.92 in, 139 cm; weight: 2,073 lb, 940 kg.

Passat Series

PRICES EX WORKS:		DM
1	C 1.3 2+1-dr Limousine	**16,145***
2	C 1.3 4+1-dr Limousine	**16,855***
3	C 1.3 4+1-dr Variant	**17,390***
4	CL 1.3 2+1-dr Limousine	**17,190***
5	CL 1.3 4+1-dr Limousine	**17,900***
6	CL 1.3 4+1-dr Variant	**18,470***
7	C 1.6 2+1-dr Limousine	**16,830***
8	C 1.6 4+1-dr Limousine	**17,540***
9	C 1.6 4+1-dr Variant	**18,075***
10	CL 1.6 2+1-dr Limousine	**17,875***
11	CL 1.6 4+1-dr Limousine	**18,585***
12	CL 1.6 4+1-dr Variant	**19,155***
13	GL 1.6 2+1-dr Limousine	**19,530***
14	GL 1.6 4+1-dr Limousine	**20,240***
15	GL 1.6 4+1-dr Variant	**21,015***
16	C 1.8 2+1-dr Limousine	**17,455***
17	C 1.8 4+1-dr Limousine	**18,165***
18	C 1.8 4+1-dr Variant	**18,700***
19	CL 1.8 2+1-dr Limousine	**18,500***
20	CL 1.8 4+1-dr Limousine	**19,210***
21	CL 1.8 4+1-dr Variant	**19,780***
22	GL 1.8 2+1-dr Limousine	**20,155***
23	GL 1.8 4+1-dr Limousine	**20,865***
24	GL 1.8 4+1-dr Variant	**21,640***
25	CL 2.0 4+1-dr Limousine	**22,135***
26	CL 2.0 4+1-dr Variant	**22,705***
27	GL 2.0 4+1-dr Limousine	**23,790***
28	GL 2.0 4+1-dr Variant	**24,565***

VOLKSWAGEN Passat GL Limousine

For GB and USA prices, see price index.

Power team:	Standard for:	Optional for:
60 hp	1 to 6	—
75 hp	7 to 15	—
90 hp	16 to 24	—
115 hp	25 to 28	—

60 hp power team

ENGINE front, slanted 20° to right, 4 stroke; 4 cylinders, in line; 79.1 cu in, 1,296 cc (2.95 x 2.83 in, 75 x 73.4 mm); compression ratio: 9:1; max power (DIN): 60 hp (44 kW) at 5,600 rpm; max torque (DIN): 74 lb ft, 10.2 kg m (100 Nm) at 3,500 rpm; max engine rpm: 6,000; 46.3 hp/l (33.9 kW/l); cast iron block, light alloy head; 5 crankshaft bearings; valves: overhead, in line, thimble tappets; camshafts: 1, overhead, cogged belt; lubrication: gear pump, full flow filter, 6.2 imp pt, 7.4 US pt, 3.5 l; 1 Solex downdraught single barrel carburettor; fuel feed: mechanical pump; liquid-cooled, expansion tank, 7 imp pt, 8.5 US pt, 4 l, electric thermostatic fan.

TRANSMISSION driving wheels: front; clutch: single dry plate (diaphragm); gearbox: mechanical; gears: 4, fully synchronized; ratios: I 3.450, II 1.940, III 1.290, IV 0.910, rev 3.170; lever: central; final drive: spiral bevel; axle ratio: 4.110; width of rims: 5.5"; tyres: 165 SR x 13.

PERFORMANCE max speeds: (I) 25 mph, 41 km/h; (II) 42 mph, 68 km/h; (III) 68 mph, 100 km/h; (IV) 94 mph, 152 km/h - Variant models 92 mph, 148 km/h; power-weight ratio: 2+1-dr sedans 34.5 lb/hp (47.1 lb/kW), 15.7 kg/hp (21.4 kg/kW); carrying capacity: 1,058 lb, 480 kg; acceleration: 0-50 mph (0-80 km/h) 10.4 sec - Variant models 10.8 sec; speed in top at 1,000 rpm: 16.9 mph, 27.1 km/h; consumption: 36.7 m/imp gal, 30.5 m/US gal, 7.7 l x 100 km - Variant models 35.8 m/imp gal, 29.8 m/US gal, 7.9 l x 100 km at 75 mph, 120 km/h.

CHASSIS integral, front auxiliary subframe; front suspension: independent, by McPherson, lower wishbones, coil springs/telescopic damper struts; rear: semi-independent, torsion beam trailing arm, toe-correcting mountings.

STEERING rack-and-pinion.

BRAKES front disc (diameter 9.41 in, 23.9 cm), rear drum, 2 X circuits, rear compensator (for Variant models only), servo.

ELECTRICAL EQUIPMENT 12 V; 36 Ah battery; 65 A alternator; transistorized ignition; 4 headlamps.

DIMENSIONS AND WEIGHT wheel base: 100.39 in, 255 cm; tracks: 55.67 in, 141 cm front, 55.98 in, 142 cm rear; length: 174.61 in, 443 cm - Variant models 178.74 in, 454 cm; width: 66.34 in, 168 cm; height: 54.53 in, 138 cm; weight: 2+1-dr sedans 2,073 lb, 940 kg - 4+1-dr sedans 2,128 lb, 965 kg - Variant models 2,172 lb, 985 kg; turning circle: 35.1 ft, 10.7 m; fuel tank: 13.2 imp gal, 15.8 US gal, 60 l.

BODY saloon/sedan, 2+1 or 4+1 doors - estate car/st. wagon, 4+1 doors; 5 seats, separate front seats, reclining backrests with headrests; heated rear window; folding rear seat (for Variant models only).

PRACTICAL INSTRUCTIONS fuel: 91 oct petrol; oil: engine 6.2 imp pt, 7.4 US pt, 3.5 l, SAE 10W-50, change every 9,000 miles, 15,000 km - gearbox and final drive 3.2 imp pt, 3.8 US pt, 1.8 l, SAE 80, no change recommended; greasing: none; tyre pressure: front 26 psi, 1.8 atm, rear 26 psi, 1.8 atm.

OPTIONALS sport wheels; power steering; electric windows; sunroof; halogen headlamps; metallic spray; tinted glass; rear window wiper-washer (for Variant models only).

75 hp power team

See 60 hp power team, except for:

ENGINE 97.3 cu in, 1,595 cc (3.19 x 3.05 in, 81 x 77.4 mm); max power (DIN): 75 hp (55 kW) at 5,000 rpm; max torque (DIN): 92 lb ft, 12.7 kg m (125 Nm) at 2,500 rpm; 47 hp/l (34.5 kW/l); 1 Solex 34 PC 5 downdraught twin barrel carburettor; cooling: 7.9 imp pt, 9.5 US pt, 4.5 l.

TRANSMISSION gearbox ratios: I 3.450, II 1.940, III 1.290, IV 0.880, rev 3.170.

PERFORMANCE max speed: 102 mph, 164 km/h - Variant moels 99 mph, 160 km/h; power-weight ratio: 2+1-dr sedans 28.2 lb/hp (38.5 lb/kW), 12.8 kg/hp (17.5 kg/kW); acceleration: 0-50 mph (0-80 km/h) 8.7 sec - Variant models 9.1 sec; speed in top at 1,000 rpm: 20.4 mph, 32.8 km/h; consumption: 32.1 m/imp gal, 26.7 m/US gal, 8.8 l x 100 km - Variant models 31.4 m/imp gal, 26.1 m/US gal, 9 l x 100 km at 75 mph, 120 km/h.

VOLKSWAGEN Passat Series (90 hp engine)

CHASSIS front suspension: anti-roll-bar.

STEERING damper.

ELECTRICAL EQUIPMENT 4 halogen headlamps (standard for GL models only).

DIMENSIONS AND WEIGHT weight: 2+1-dr sedans 2,117 lb, 960 kg - 4+1-dr sedans 2,172 lb, 985 kg - Variant models 2,216 lb, 1,005 kg.

OPTIONALS 4+E 5-speed fully synchronized mechanical gearbox (I 3.450, II 1.940, III 1.290, IV 0.910, V 0.730, rev 3.170), consumption 35.3 m/imp gal, 29.4 m/US gal, 8 l x 100 km at 75 mph, 120 km/h; automatic transmission, hydraulic torque converter and planetary gears with 3 ratios (I 2.710, II 1.500, III 1, rev 2.430), 3.420 axle ratio, max speed 99 mph, 159 km/h - Variant models 96 mph, 155 km/h, acceleration 0-50 mph (0-80 km/h) 10.3 sec, consumption 31 m/imp gal, 25.8 m/US gal, 9.1 l x 100 km at 75 mph, 120 km/h; light alloy wheels; air-conditioning.

90 hp power team

See 60 hp power team, except for:

ENGINE 108.7 cu in, 1,781 cc (3.19 x 3.40 in, 81 x 86.4 mm); compression ratio: 10:1; max power (DIN): 90 hp (66 kW) at 5,200 rpm; max torque (DIN): 107 lb ft, 14.8 kg m (145 Nm) at 3,300 rpm; 50.5 hp/l (37.1 kW/l); 1 Weber 2 BC downdraught twin barrel carburettor with fully automatic choke and fuel cut-off system; cooling: 7.9 imp pt, 9.5 US pt, 4.5 l.

TRANSMISSION gearbox ratios: I 3.450, II 1.790, III 1.130, IV 0.830, rev 3.170; tyres: 185/70 HR x 13.

PERFORMANCE max speed: 109 mph, 176 km/h - Variant models 105 mph, 169 km/h; power-weight ratio: 2+1-dr sedans 23.5 lb/hp (32.1 lb/kW), 10.7 kg/hp (14.5 kg/kW); acceleration: 0-50 mph (0-80 km/h) 7.4 sec - Variant models 7.7 sec; speed in top at 1,000 rpm: 21 mph, 33.8 km/h; consumption: 34.4 m/imp gal, 28.7 m/US gal, 8.2 l x 100 km - Variant models 33.6 m/imp gal, 28 m/US gal, 8.4 l x 100 km at 75 mph, 120 km/h.

CHASSIS front suspension: anti-roll bar.

STEERING damper.

ELECTRICAL EQUIPMENT 45 Ah battery; 4 halogen headlamps (standard for GL models only).

DIMENSIONS AND WEIGHT weight: 2+1-dr sedans 2,117 lb, 960 kg - 4+1-dr sedans 2,172 lb, 985 kg - Variant models 2,216 lb, 1,005 kg.

PRACTICAL INSTRUCTIONS fuel: 97 oct petrol.

OPTIONALS 4+E 5-speed fully synchronized mechanical gearbox (I 3.450, II 1.790, III 1.130, IV 0.830, V 0.680, rev 3.170), consumption 37.7 m/imp gal, 31.4 m/US gal, 7.5 l x 100 km at 75 mph, 120 km/h; automatic transmission, hydraulic torque converter and planetary gears with 3 ratios (I 2.710, II 1.500, III 1, rev 2.430), 3.250 axle ratio, max speed 106 mph, 171 km/h - Variant models 102 mph, 164 km/h, acceleration 0-50 mph (0-80 km/h) 9.1 sec, consumption 33.2 m/imp gal, 27.7 m/US gal, 8.5 l x 100 km at 75 mph, 120 km/h; light alloy wheels; air-conditioning.

115 hp power team

See 60 hp power team, except for:

ENGINE 5 cylinders, in line; 121.7 cu in, 1,994 cc (3.19 x 3.05 in, 81 x 77.4 mm); compression ratio: 10:1; max power (DIN): 115 hp (85 kW) at 5,400 rpm; max torque (DIN): 122 lb ft, 16.8 kg m (165 Nm) at 3,200 rpm; 57.7 hp/l (42.6 kW/l); 6 crankshaft bearings; lubrication: 7.9 imp pt, 9.5 US pt, 4.5 l; Bosch K-Jetronic injection; cooling: 10.6 imp pt, 12.7 US pt, 6 l.

TRANSMISSION gearbox: 4+E mechanical; gears: 5, fully synchronized; ratios: I 2.850, II 1.520, III 0.940, IV 0.660, V 0.540, rev 3.170; axle ratio: 4.900; tyres: 185/70 HR x 13.

PERFORMANCE max speed: 117 mph, 188 km/h - Variant models 113 mph, 182 km/h; power-weight ratio: 20.8 lb/hp (28.1 lb/kW), 9.4 kg/hp (12.8 kg/kW); acceleration: 0-50 mph (0-80 km/h) 7.1 sec - Variant models 7.3 sec; speed in top at 1,000 rpm: 21.6 mph, 34.8 km/h; consumption: 36.2 m/imp gal, 30.2 m/US gal, 7.8 l x 100 km - Variant models 34.4 m/imp gal, 28.7 m/US gal, 8.2 l x 100 km at 75 mph, 120 km/h.

CHASSIS front suspension: anti-roll bar.

STEERING damper.

BRAKES front disc, internal radial fins.

ELECTRICAL EQUIPMENT 63 Ah battery; 4 halogen headlamps (standard).

DIMENSIONS AND WEIGHT weight: 2,392 lb, 1,085 kg - Variant models 2,437 lb, 1,105 kg.

BODY saloon/sedan - estate car/st. wagon; 4+1 doors.

PRACTICAL INSTRUCTIONS fuel: 97 oct petrol; oil: engine 7.9 imp pt, 9.5 US pt, 4.5 l.

OPTIONALS automatic transmission, hydraulic torque converter and planetary gears with 3 ratios (I 2.710, II 1.500, III 1, rev 2.430), 3.250 axle ratio, max speed 112 mph, 180 km/h - Variant models 108 mph, 174 km/h, acceleration 0-50 mph (0-80 km/h) 8.6 sec, consumption 30.7 m/imp gal, 25.6 m/US gal, 9.2 l x 100 km at 75 mph, 120 km/h; light alloy wheels with 6" wide rims and 195/60 HR x 14 tyres; air-conditioning.

Passat Diesel

PRICES EX WORKS:	DM
C 1.6 2+1-dr Limousine	18,010*
C 1.6 4+1-dr Limousine	18,720*
C 1.6 4+1-dr Variant	19,255*
CL 1.6 2+1-dr Limousine	19,055*
CL 1.6 4+1-dr Limousine	19,765*
CL 1.6 4+1-dr Variant	20,335*
GL 1.6 2+1-dr Limousine	20,710*
GL 1.6 4+1-dr Limousine	21,420*
GL 1.6 4+1-dr Variant	22,195*

VOLKSWAGEN Passat CL Variant

ENGINE diesel, front, 4 stroke; 4 cylinders, vertical, in line; 96.9 cu in, 1,588 cc (3.01 x 3.40 in, 76.5 x 86.4 mm); compression ratio: 23:1; max power (DIN): 54 hp (40 kW) at 4,800 rpm; max torque (DIN): 74 lb ft, 10.2 kg m (100 Nm) at 2,300 rpm; max engine rpm: 5,000; 34 hp/l (25.2 kW/l); cast iron block, light alloy head; 5 crankshaft bearings; valves: overhead, in line, thimble tappets; camshafts: 1, overhead, cogged belt; lubrication: gear pump, full flow filter, 6.2 imp pt, 7.4 US pt, 3.5 l; Bosch injection pump; liquid-cooled, expansion tank, 9.8 imp pt, 11.8 US pt, 5.6 l, electric thermostatic fan.

TRANSMISSION driving wheels: front; clutch: single dry plate (diaphragm); gearbox: mechanical; gears: 4, fully synchronized; ratios: I 3.450, II 1.940, III 1.290, IV 0.880, rev 3.170; lever: central; final drive: spiral bevel; axle ratio: 4.111; width of rims: 5.5"; tyres: 165 SR x 13.

PERFORMANCE max speed: 89 mph, 143 km/h - Variant models 87 mph, 140 km/h; power-weight ratio: 2+1-dr 40.8 lb/hp (55.1 lb/kW), 18.5 kg/hp (25 kg/kW); carrying capacity: 1,114 lb, 505 kg; acceleration: 0-50 mph (0-80 km/h) 12.6 sec; speed in top at 1,000 rpm: 17.8 mph, 28.6 km/h; consumption: 38.7 m/imp gal, 32.2 m/US gal, 7.3 l x 100 km at 75 mph, 120 km/h.

CHASSIS integral, front auxiliary subframe; front suspension: independent, by McPherson, lower wishbones, anti-roll bar, coil springs/telescopic damper struts; rear: semi-independent, torsion beam trailing arm, toe-correcting mounting.

STEERING rack-and-pinion.

BRAKES front disc (diameter 9.41 in, 23.9 cm), rear drum, 2 X circuits, rear compensator (for Variant models only), servo.

ELECTRICAL EQUIPMENT 12 V; 63 Ah battery; 45 A alternator; 4 headlamps.

DIMENSIONS AND WEIGHT wheel base: 100.39 in, 255 cm; tracks: 55.67 in, 141 cm front, 55.98 in, 142 cm rear; length: 174.61 in, 443 cm - Variant models 178.74 in, 454 cm; width: 66.34 in, 168 cm; height: 54.53 in, 138 cm; weight: 2+1-dr 2,205 lb, 1,000 kg - 4+1-dr 2,260 lb, 1,025 kg - Variant models 2,304 lb, 1,045 kg; turning circle: 35.1 ft, 10.7 m; fuel tank: 13.2 imp gal, 15.8 US gal, 60 l.

BODY saloon/sedan, 2+1 or 4+1 doors - estate car/st. wagon, 4+1 doors; 5 seats, separate front seats, reclining backrests with headrests; heated rear window; front electric windows; folding rear seat (for Variant models only).

PRACTICAL INSTRUCTIONS fuel: diesel; oil: engine 5.3 imp pt, 6.3 US pt, 3 l - gearbox and final drive 3.2 imp pt, 3.8 US pt, 1.8 l, SAE 80; greasing: none; tyre pressure: front 26 psi, 1.8 atm, rear 26 psi, 1.8 atm.

OPTIONALS 4+E 5-speed fully synchronized mechanical gearbox (I 3.450, II 1.940, III 1.290, IV 0.910, V 0.730, rev 3.170), consumption 42.8 m/imp gal, 35.6 m/US gal, 6.6 l x 100 km at 75 mph, 120 km/h; automatic transmission with 3 ratios (I 2.710, II 1.500, III 1, rev 2.430), 3.730 axle ratio, max speed 86 mph, 138 km/h, consumption 34.4 m/imp gal, 28.7 m/US gal, 8.2 l x 100 km at 75 mph, 120 km/h; 185/70 SR x 13 tyres; sport wheels; power steering; sunroof; halogen headlamps; metallic spray; tinted glass; tailgate with folding rear seat (for sedans only); rear window wiper-washer (for Variant models only).

Passat Turbo-Diesel

See Passat Diesel, except for:

PRICES EX WORKS:	DM
C 1.6 4+1-dr Limousine	20,870*
C 1.6 4+1-dr Variant	21,405*
CL 1.6 4+1-dr Limousine	21,915*
CL 1.6 4+1-dr Variant	22,485*
GL 1.6 4+1-dr Limousine	23,570*
GL 1.6 4+1-dr Variant	24,345*

For USA prices, see price index.

ENGINE diesel, turbocharged; max power (DIN): 70 hp (51 kW) at 4,500 rpm; max torque (DIN): 98 lb ft, 13.6 kg m (133 Nm) at 2,600 rpm; 44.1 hp/l (32.1 kW/l); Bosch injection pump; 1 Garrett AiResearch turbocharger.

TRANSMISSION (standard) gearbox: 4+E mechanical; gears: 5, fully synchronized; ratios: I 3.450, II 1.940, III 1.290, IV 0.910, V 0.730, rev 3.170; tyres: 185/70 SR x 13.

PERFORMANCE max speed: 97 mph, 157 km/h - Variant models 94 mph, 152 km/h; power-weight ratio: sedans 33.2 lb/hp (45.6 lb/kW), 15.1 kg/hp (20.7 kg/kW); acceleration: 0-50 mph (0-80 km/h) 9.9 sec; consumption: 40.9 m/imp gal, 34.1 m/US gal, 6.9 l x 100 km at 75 mph, 120 km/h.

BRAKES rear compensator.

DIMENSIONS AND WEIGHT weight: sedans 2,326 lb, 1,055 kg - Variant models 2,370 lb, 1,075 kg.

BODY saloon/sedan - estate car/st. wagon; 4+1 doors.

Passat Variant Tetra

ENGINE front, 4 stroke; 5 cylinders, vertical, in line; 121.7 cu in, 1,994 cc (3.19 x 3.05 in, 81 x 77.4 mm); compression ratio: 10:1; max power (DIN): 115 hp (85 kW) at 5,400 rpm; max torque (DIN): 122 lb ft, 16.8 kg m (165 Nm) at 3,200 rpm; max engine rpm: 6,000; 57.7 hp/l (42.6 kW/l); cast iron block, light alloy head; 6 crankshaft bearings; valves: overhead, in line, thimble tappets; camshafts: 1, overhead, cogged belt; lubrication: gear pump, full flow filter, 7.9 imp pt, 9.5 US pt, 4.5 l; Bosch K-Jetronic injection; fuel feed: mechanical pump; liquid-cooled, expansion tank, 10.6 imp pt, 12.7 US pt, 6 l, electric thermostatic fan.

TRANSMISSION driving wheels: front and rear; clutch: single dry plate (diaphragm); gearbox: mechanical; gears: 5, fully synchronized, integral front differential, additional lockable inter-axle differential, lockable rear axle differential; ratios: I 2.850, II 1.520, III 0.940, IV 0.660, V 0.540, rev 3.170; lever: central; final drive: spiral bevel; front and rear axle ratio: 4.900; width of rims: 6"; tyres: 195/60 HR x 14.

PERFORMANCE max speed: 113 mph, 182 km/h; power-weight ratio: 25.1 lb/hp (34 lb/kW), 11.4 kg/hp (15.4 kg/kW); carrying capacity: 1,125 lb, 510 kg; speed in top at 1,000 rpm: 20.9 mph, 33.7 km/h; consumption: 32.5 m/imp gal, 27 m/US gal, 8.7 l x 100 km at 75 mph, 120 km/h.

CHASSIS integral, front auxiliary subframe; front suspension: independent, by McPherson, lower wishbones, anti-roll bar, coil springs/telescopic damper struts; rear: independent, wishbones, anti-roll bar, coil springs/telescopic damper struts.

STEERING rack-and-pinion, servo.

BRAKES disc front internal radial fins, 2 X circuits, rear compensator, servo.

ELECTRICAL EQUIPMENT 12 V; 63 Ah battery; 65 A alternator; transistorized ignition; 4 halogen headlamps.

DIMENSIONS AND WEIGHT wheel base: 100.39 in, 255 cm; tracks: 55.67 in, 141 cm front, 55.98 in, 142 cm rear; length: 178.74 in, 454 cm; width: 66.34 in, 168 cm; height: 54.53 in, 138 cm; weight: 2,889 lb, 1,310 kg; turning circle: 35.1 ft, 10.7 m; fuel tank: 15.4 imp gal, 18.5 US gal, 70 l.

BODY estate car/st. wagon; 4+1 doors; 5 seats, separate front seats, reclining backrests, headrests; heated rear window; folding rear seat; rear window wiper-washer; tinted glass; metallic spray.

PRACTICAL INSTRUCTIONS fuel: 97 oct petrol; oil: engine 7.9 imp pt, 9.5 US pt, 4.5 l, SAE 10W-50, change every 9,000 miles, 15,000 km - gearbox and front final drive 3.2 imp pt, 3.8 US pt, 1.8 l, SAE 80, no change recommended - rear final drive 2.3 imp pt, 2.7 US pt, 1.3 l, SAE 80, no change recommended; tyre pressure: front 28 psi, 2 atm, rear 28 psi, 2 atm.

OPTIONALS light alloy wheels.

VOLKSWAGEN Passat Variant Tetra

Santana Series

PRICES EX WORKS:		DM
1	CX 1.3 4-dr Limousine	—
2	CX 1.6 4-dr Limousine	—
3	LX 1.6 4-dr Limousine	**19,310***
4	GX 1.6 4-dr Limousine	**22,185***
5	CX 1.8 4-dr Limousine	—
6	LX 1.8 4-dr Limousine	**19,935***
7	GX 1.8 4-dr Limousine	**22,810***
8	LX5 2.0 4-dr Limousine	**22,860***
9	GX5 2.0 4-dr Limousine	**25,735***
10	LX 1.6 Diesel 4-dr Limousine	**20,490***
11	GX 1.6 Diesel 4-dr Limousine	**23,365***
12	LX 1.6 Turbo-Diesel 4-dr Limousine	**22,640***
13	GX 1.6 Turbo-Diesel 4-dr Limousine	**25,515***

For GB prices, see price index.

Power team:	Standard for:	Optional for:
60 hp	1	—
75 hp	2 to 4	—
90 hp	5 to 7	—
115 hp	8,9	—
54 hp (diesel)	10,11	—
70 hp (diesel)	12,13	—

60 hp power team

ENGINE front, slanted 20° to right, 4 stroke; 4 cylinders, in line; 79.1 cu in, 1,296 cc (2.95 x 2.89 in, 75 x 73.4 mm); compression ratio: 9:1; max power (DIN): 60 hp (44 kW) at 5,600 rpm; max torque (DIN): 74 lb ft, 10.2 kg m (100 Nm) at 3,500 rpm; max engine rpm: 6,000; 46.3 hp/l (33.9 kW/l); cast iron block, light alloy head; 5 crankshaft bearings; valves: overhead, in line, thimble tappets; camshafts: 1, overhead, cogged belt; lubrication: gear pump, full flow filter, 6.2 imp pt, 7.4 US pt, 3.5 l; 1 Solex downdraught single barrel carburettor; fuel feed: mechanical pump; liquid-cooled, expansion tank, 7 imp pt, 8.5 US pt, 4 l, electric thermostatic fan.

TRANSMISSION driving wheels: front; clutch: single dry plate, (diaphragm); gearbox: mechanical; gears: 4, fully synchronized; ratios: I 3.450, II 1.940, III 1.290, IV 0.910, rev 3.170; lever: central; final drive: spiral bevel; axle ratio: 4.110; width of rims: 5.5"; tyres: 185/70 SR x 13.

PERFORMANCE max speeds: (I) 25 mph, 41 km/h; (II) 42 mph, 68 km/h; (III) 68 mph, 100 km/h; (IV) 92 mph, 148 km/h; power-weight ratio: 35.5 lb/hp (48.4 lb/kW), 16.1 kg/hp (21.9 kg/kW); carrying capacity: 1,003 lb, 455 kg; acceleration: 0-50 mph (0-80 km/h) 10.4 sec; speed in top at 1,000 rpm: 16.9 mph, 27.1 km/h; consumption: 36.2 m/imp gal, 30.2 m/US gal, 7.8 l x 100 km at 75 mph, 120 km/h.

CHASSIS integral; front auxiliary subframe; front suspension: independent, by McPherson, lower wishbones, anti-roll bar, coil spring/telescopic damper struts; rear: semi-independent, torsion beam trailing arm, toe-correcting mountings.

STEERING rack-and-pinion, damper.

BRAKES front disc (diameter 9.41 in, 23.9 cm), rear drum, 2 X circuits, servo.

ELECTRICAL EQUIPMENT 12 V; 36 Ah battery; 65 A alternator; transistorized ignition; 2 headlamps.

DIMENSIONS AND WEIGHT wheel base: 100.39 in, 255 cm; tracks: 55.7 in, 141 cm front, 55.98 in, 142 cm rear; length: 178.74 in, 454 cm; width: 66.73 in, 169 cm; height: 55.12 in, 140 cm; weight: 2,128 lb, 965 kg; turning circle: 35.4 ft, 10.8 m; fuel tank: 13.2 imp gal, 15.8 US gal, 60 l.

BODY saloon/sedan; 4 doors; 5 seats, separate front seats, reclining backrests with headrests; heated rear window; folding rear seat.

PRACTICAL INSTRUCTIONS fuel: 91 oct petrol; oil: engine 6.2 imp pt, 7.4 US pt, 3.5 l, SAE 10W-50, change every 9,000 miles, 15,000 km - gearbox and final drive 3.2 imp pt, 3.8 US pt, 1.8 l, SAE 80, no change recommended; greasing: none; tyre pressure: front 26 psi, 1.8 atm, rear 26 psi, 1.8 atm.

OPTIONALS power steering; electric windows; sunroof; halogen headlamps; metallic spray; tinted glass; light alloy wheels; central door locking.

75 hp power team

See 60 hp power team, except for:

ENGINE 97.3 cu in, 1,595 cc (3.19 x 3.05 in, 81 x 77.4 mm); max power (DIN): 75 hp (55 kW) at 5,000 rpm; max torque (DIN): 92 lb ft, 12.7 kg m (125 Nm) at 2,500 rpm; 47 hp/l (34.5 kW/l); 1 Solex 34 PC 5 downdraught twin barrel carburettor; cooling: 8.1 imp pt, 9.7 Us pt, 4.6 l.

TRANSMISSION gearbox ratios: I 3.450, II 1.940, III 1.290, IV 0.880, rev 3.170.

PERFORMANCE max speed: 99 mph, 160 km/h; power-weight ratio: 29 lb/hp (39.5 lb/kW), 13.1 kg/hp (17.9 kg/kW); acceleration: 0-50 mph (0-80 km/h) 8.7 sec; speed in top at 1,000 rpm: 16.6 mph, 26.7 km/h; consumption: 31.7 m/imp gal, 26.4 m/US gal, 8.9 l x 100 km at 75 mph, 120 km/h.

DIMENSIONS AND WEIGHT weight: 2,172 lb, 985 kg.

BODY light alloy wheels (standard for GX only).

OPTIONALS 4+E 5-speed fully synchronized mechanical gearbox (I 3.450, II 1.940, III 1.290, IV 0.910, V 0.730, rev 3.170), consumption 34.9 m/imp gal, 29 m/US gal, 8.1 l x 100 km at 75 mph, 120 km/h; automatic transmission, hydraulic torque converter and planetary gears with 3 ratios (I 2.710, II 1.500, III 1, rev 2.430), 3.420 axle ratio, max speed 96 mph, 155 km/h, acceleration 0-50 mph (0-80 km/h) 10.3 sec, consumption 30.7 m/imp gal, 25.6 m/US gal, 9.2 l x 100 km at 75 mph, 120 km/h; air-conditioning.

90 hp power team

See 60 hp power team, except for:

ENGINE 108.7 cu in, 1,781 cc (3.19 x 3.40 in, 81 x 86.4 mm); compression ratio: 10:1; max power (DIN): 90 hp (66 kW) at 5,200 rpm; max torque (DIN): 107 lb ft, 14.8 kg m (145 Nm) at 3,300 rpm; 50.5 hp/l (37.1 kW/l); 1 Weber 2BC downdraught twin barrel carburettor with fully automatic choke and fuel cut-off system; cooling: 8.1 imp pt, 9.7 US pt, 4.6 l.

TRANSMISSION gearbox ratios: I 3.450, II 1.790, III 1.130, IV 0.830, rev 3.170.

VOLKSWAGEN Santana GX Limousine

VOLKSWAGEN Scirocco GT Coupé

PERFORMANCE max speed: 105 mph, 169 km/h; power-weight ratio: 24.1 lb/hp (32.9 lb/kW), 10.9 kg/hp (14.9 kg/kW); acceleration: 0-50 mph (0-80 km/h) 7.4 sec; speed in top at 1,000 rpm: 20.2 mph, 32.5 km/h; consumption: 34 m/imp gal, 28.3 m/US gal, 8.3 l x 100 km at 75 mph, 120 km/h.

ELECTRICAL EQUIPMENT 45 Ah battery.

DIMENSIONS AND WEIGHT weight: 2,172 lb, 985 kg.

BODY light alloy wheels (standard for GX only).

PRACTICAL INSTRUCTIONS fuel: 97 oct petrol.

OPTIONALS 4+E 5-speed fully synchronized mechanical gearbox (I 3.450, II 1.790, III 1.130, IV 0.830, V 0.680, rev 3.170), consumption 37.2 m/imp gal, 30.9 m/US gal, 7.6 l x 100 km at 75 mph, 120 km/h; automatic transmission, hydraulic torque converter and planetary gears with 3 ratios (I 2.710, II 1.500, III 1, rev 2.430), 3.250 axle ratio, max speed 102 mph, 164 km/h, acceleration 0-50 mph (0-80 km/h) 9.1 sec, consumption 32.8 m/imp gal, 27.3 m/US gal, 8.6 l x 100 km at 75 mph, 120 km/h; air-conditioning.

115 hp power team

See 60 hp power team, except for:

ENGINE 5 cylinders, in line; 121.7 cu in, 1,994 cc (3.19 x 3.05 in, 81 x 77.4 mm); compression ratio: 10:1; max power (DIN): 115 hp (85 kW) at 5,400 rpm; max torque (DIN): 122 lb ft, 16.8 kg m (165 Nm) at 3,200 rpm; 57.7 hp/l (42.6 kW/l); 6 crankshaft bearings; lubrication: 7.9 imp pt, 9.5 US pt, 4.5 l; Bosch K-Jetronic injection; cooling: 11.3 imp pt, 13.5 US pt, 6.4 l.

TRANSMISSION gearbox: 4+E mechanical; gears: 5, fully synchronized; ratios: I 2.850, II 1.520, III 0.940, IV 0.660, V 0.540, rev 3.170; axle ratio: 4.900; tyres: 185/70 HR x 13.

PERFORMANCE max speed: 114 mph, 184 km/h; power-weight ratio: 20.8 lb/hp (28.1 lb/kW), 9.4 kg/hp (12.8 kg/kW); acceleration: 0-50 mph (0-80 km/h) 7.1 sec; speed in top at 1,000 rpm: 21.2 mph, 34.1 km/h; consumption: 35.8 m/imp gal, 29.8 m/US gal, 7.9 l x 100 km at 75 mph, 120 km/h.

BRAKES front disc, internal radial fins, rear compensator.

ELECTRICAL EQUIPMENT 63 Ah battery.

DIMENSIONS AND WEIGHT weight: 2,392 lb, 1,085 kg.

BODY light alloy wheels (standard for GX5 only).

PRACTICAL INSTRUCTIONS fuel: 97 oct petrol; oil: engine 7.9 imp pt, 9.5 US pt, 4.5 l.

OPTIONALS automatic transmission, hydraulic torque converter and planetary gears with 3 ratios (I 2.710, II 1.500, III 1, rev 2.430), 3.250 axle ratio, max speed 109 mph, 176 km/h, acceleration 0-50 mph (0-80 km/h) 8.6 sec, consumption 30.4 m/imp gal, 25.3 m/US gal, 9.3 l x 100 km at 75 mph, 120 km/h; light alloy wheels with 6" wide rims and 195/60 HR x 14 tyres; air-conditioning.

54 hp (diesel) power team

See 60 hp power team, except for:

ENGINE diesel; 96.9 cu in, 1,588 cc (3.01 x 3.40 in, 76.5 x 86.4 mm); compression ratio: 23:1; max power (DIN): 54 hp (40 kW) at 4,800 rpm; max torque (DIN): 74 lb ft, 10.2 kg m (100 Nm) at 2,300 rpm; Bosch injection pump; cooling: 9.8 imp pt, 11.8 US pt, 5.6 l.

TRANSMISSION gearbox ratios: I 3.450, II 1.940, III 1.290, IV 0.880, rev 3.170.

PERFORMANCE max speed: 87 mph, 140 km/h; power-weight ratio: 41.9 lb/hp (56.5 lb/kW), 19 kg/hp (25.6 kg/kW); carrying capacity: 1,058 lb, 480 kg; acceleration: 0-50 mph (0-80 km/h) 12.6 sec; speed in top at 1,000 rpm: 17.8 mph, 28.6 km/h; consumption: 38.7 m/imp gal, 32.2 m/US gal, 7.3 l x 100 km at 75 mph, 120 km/h.

ELECTRICAL EQUIPMENT 63 Ah battery.

DIMENSIONS AND WEIGHT weight: 2,260 lb, 1,025 kg.

PRACTICAL INSTRUCTIONS fuel: diesel.

OPTIONALS 4+E 5-speed fully synchronized mechanical gearbox (I 3.450, II 1.940, III 1.290, IV 0.910, V 0.730, rev 3.170), consumption 42.8 m/imp gal, 35.6 m/US gal, 6.6 l x 100 km at 75 mph, 120 km/h; automatic transmission with 3 ratios (I 2.710, II 1.500, III 1, rev 2.430), 3.730 axle ratio, max speed 84 mph, 135 km/h, acceleration 0-50 mph (0-80 km/h) 14.9 sec, consumption 34.4 m/imp gal, 28.7 m/US gal, 8.2 l x 100 km at 75 mph, 120 km/h.

70 hp (diesel) power team

See 60 hp power team, except for:

ENGINE diesel, turbocharged; 96.9 cu in, 1,588 cc (3.01 x 3.40 in, 76.5 x 86.4 mm); compression ratio: 23:1; max power (DIN): 70 hp (51 kW) at 4,500 rpm; max torque (DIN): 98 lb ft, 13.6 kg m (133 Nm) at 2,600 rpm; 44.1 hp/l (32.1 kW/l); Bosch injection pump; 1 Garrett AiResearch turbocharger; cooling: 9.8 imp pt, 11.8 US pt, 5.6 l.

TRANSMISSION gearbox: 4+E mechanical; gears: 5, fully synchronized; ratios: I 3.450, II 1.940, III 1.290, IV 0.910, V 0.730, rev 3.170.

PERFORMANCE max speed: 96 mph, 154 km/h; power-weight ratio: 33.2 lb/hp (45.6 lb/kW), 15.1 kg/hp (20.7 kg/kW); acceleration: 0-50 mph (0-80 km/h) 9.9 sec; consumption: 40.9 m/imp gal, 34.1 m/US gal, 6.9 l x 100 km at 75 mph, 120 km/h.

ELECTRICAL EQUIPMENT 63 Ah battery.

DIMENSIONS AND WEIGHT weight: 2,326 lb, 1,055 kg.

PRACTICAL INSTRUCTIONS fuel: diesel.

Scirocco Series

PRICES EX WORKS:		DM
1	CL 1.6 2+1-dr Coupé	**18,890***
2	GL 1.6 2+1-dr Coupé	**20,980***
3	GT 1.6 2+1-dr Coupé	**21,275***
4	CL 1.8 (90 hp) 2+1-dr Coupé	**19,945***
5	GL 1.8 (90 hp) 2+1-dr Coupé	**22,035***
6	GT 1.8 (90 hp) 2+1-dr Coupé	**22,330***
7	GTS 1.8 (90 hp) 2+1-dr Coupé	**20,660***
8	GTX 1.8 (90 hp) 2+1-dr Coupé	**22,020***
9	GLI 1.8 (112 hp) 2+1-dr Coupé	**24,460***
10	GTI 1.8 (112 hp) 2+1-dr Coupé	**24,755***
11	GTS 1.8 (112 hp) 2+1-dr Coupé	**23,035***
12	GTX 1.8 (112 hp) 2+1-dr Coupé	**24,445***

For USA prices, see price index.

Power team:	Standard for:	Optional for:
75 hp	1 to 3	—
90 hp	4 to 8	—
112 hp	9 to 12	—

75 hp power team

ENGINE front, transverse, 4 stroke; 4 cylinders, vertical, in line; 97.3 cu in, 1,595 cc (3.19 x 3.05 in, 81 x 77.4 mm); compression ratio: 9:1; max power (DIN): 75 hp (55 kW) at 5,000 rpm; max torque (DIN): 92 lb ft, 12.7 kg m (125 Nm) at 2,500 rpm; max engine rpm: 6,000; 47 hp/l (34.5 kW/l); cast iron block, light alloy head; 5 crankshaft bearings; valves: overhead, in line, thimble tappets; camshafts: 1, overhead, cogged belt; lubrication: gear pump, full flow filter, 6.2 imp pt, 7.4 US pt, 3.5 l; 1 Solex 34 PC 5 downdraught twin barrel carburettor with fully automatic choke and fuel cut-off system; fuel feed: mechanical pump; liquid-cooled, expansion tank, 7.9 imp pt, 9.5 US pt, 4.5 l, electric thermostatic fan.

TRANSMISSION driving wheels: front; clutch: single dry plate, hydraulically controlled; gearbox: mechanical; gears: 4, fully synchronized; ratios: I 3.450, II 1.940, III 1.290, IV 0.910, rev 3.170; lever: central; final drive: spiral bevel; axle ratio: 3.670; width of rims: 5"; tyres: 155 SR x 13.

PERFORMANCE max speed: 104 mph, 167 km/h; power-weight ratio: 25.1 lb/hp (34.3 lb/kW), 11.4 kg/hp (15.5 kg/kW); carrying capacity: 893 lb, 405 kg; acceleration: 0-50 mph (0-80 km/h) 7.6 sec; speed in top at 1,000 rpm: 20.7 mph, 33.4 km/h; consumption: 36.7 m/imp gal, 30.5 m/US gal, 7.7 l x 100 km at 75 mph, 120 km/h.

CHASSIS integral; front suspension: independent, by McPherson, lower wishbones, coil springs/telescopic damper struts; rear: semi-independent, torsion beam trailing arm, coil springs/telescopic damper struts.

STEERING rack-and-pinion.

BRAKES front disc, rear drum, 2 X circuits, rear compensator, servo.

ELECTRICAL EQUIPMENT 12 V; 36 Ah battery; 65 A alternator; electronic ignition; 4 halogen headlamps.

DIMENSIONS AND WEIGHT wheel base: 94.49 in, 240 cm; tracks: 54.72 in, 139 cm front, 53.46 in, 136 cm rear; length: 159.45 in, 405 cm; width: 63.78 in, 162 cm; height: 50.39 in, 128 cm; ground clearance: 4.92 in, 12.5 cm; weight: 1,885 lb, 855 kg; turning circle: 34.4 ft, 10.5 m; fuel tank: 8.8 imp gal, 10.6 US gal, 40 l.

BODY coupé; 2+1 doors; 4 seats, separate front seats, built-in headrests; heated rear window; folding rear seat.

PRACTICAL INSTRUCTIONS fuel: 91 oct petrol; oil: engine 6.2 imp pt, 7.4 US pt, 3.5 l, SAE 10W-50, change every 4,700 miles, 7,500 km - gearbox and final drive 3.2 imp pt, 3.8 US pt, 1.8 l, SAE 80 or 90, change every 18,600 miles, 30,000 km; greasing: none; tyre pressure: front 26 psi, 1.8 atm, rear 26 psi, 1.8 atm.

OPTIONALS 4+E 5-speed fully synchronized mechanical gearbox (I 3.450, II 1.940, III 1.290, IV 0.910, V 0.750, rev 3.170), consumption 40.4 m/imp gal, 33.6 m/US gal, 7 l x 100 km at 75 mph, 120 km/h; automatic transmission with 3 ratios (I 2.710, II 1.500, III 1, rev 2.430), 3.410 axle ratio, max speed 101 mph, 162 km/h, acceleration 0-50 mph (0-80 km/h) 9.2 sec, consumption 35.3 m/imp gal, 29.4 m/US gal, 8 l x 100 km at 75 mph, 120 km/h; light alloy wheels; 175/70 SR x 13 tyres; electric windows; rear window wiper-washer; tinted glass; metallic spray; air-conditioning.

90 hp power team

See 75 hp power team, except for:

ENGINE 108.7 cu in, 1,781 cc (3.19 x 3.40 in, 81 x 86.4 mm); compression ratio: 10:1; max power (DIN): 90 hp (66 kW) at 5,200 rpm; max torque (DIN): 107 lb ft, 14.8 kg m (145 Nm) at 3,300 rpm; 50.5 hp/l (37.1 kW/l); valves: overhead, thimble tappets; 1 Weber 2 BC downdraught twin barrel carburettor with fully automatic choke and fuel cut-off system.

TRANSMISSION (standard) gearbox: 4+E mechanical; gears: 5, fully synchronized; ratios: I 3.450, II 1.940, III 1.290, IV 0.910, V 0.750, rev 3.170; width of rims: 5.5"; tyres: 175/70 HR x 13.

PERFORMANCE max speeds: (I) 32 mph, 51 km/h; (II) 55 mph, 89 km/h; (III) 82 mph, 132 km/h; (IV) 93 mph, 150 km/h; (V) 111 mph, 178 km/h; power-weight ratio: 20.9 lb/hp (28.6 lb/kW), 9.5 kg/hp (13 kg/kW); acceleration: 0-50 mph (0-80 km/h) 6.6 sec; speed in top at 1,000 rpm: 21.3 mph, 34.2 km/h; consumption: 39.2 m/imp gal, 32.7 m/US gal, 7.2 l x 100 km at 75 mph, 120 km/h.

CHASSIS front and rear suspension: anti-roll bar.

DIMENSIONS AND WEIGHT tracks: 55.28 in, 140 cm front, 54.02 in, 137 cm rear.

BODY metallic spray (standard for GTS and GTX only).

PRACTICAL INSTRUCTIONS fuel: 97 oct petrol.

OPTIONALS automatic transmission, hydraulic torque converter and planetary gears with 3 ratios (I 2.710, II 1.500, III 1, rev 2.430), 3.120 axle ratio, max speed 107 mph, 173 km/h, acceleration 0-50 mph (0-80 km/h) 8.2 sec, consumption 34.4 m/imp gal, 28.7 m/US gal, 8.2 l x 100 km at 75 mph, 120 km/h.

VOLKSWAGEN Scirocco 16 V Coupé

112 hp power team

See 75 hp power team, except for:

ENGINE 108.7 cu in, 1,781 cc (3.19 x 3.40 in, 81 x 86.4 mm); compression ratio: 10:1; max power (DIN): 112 hp (82 kW) at 5,800 rpm; max torque (DIN): 113 lb ft, 15.6 kg m (153 Nm) at 3,500 rpm; max engine rpm: 6,700; 62.9 hp/l (46 kW/l); Bosch K-Jetronic injection; fuel feed: electric pump.

TRANSMISSION gears: 5, fully synchronized; ratios: I 3.450, II 2.120, III 1.440, IV 1.130, V 0.890, rev 3.170; width of rims: 5.5''; tyres: 175/70 HR x 13.

PERFORMANCE max speed: 119 mph, 191 km/h; power-weight ratio: 17.6 lb/hp (24.1 lb/kW), 8 kg/hp (10.9 kg/kW); acceleration: 0-50 mph (0-80 km/h) 6.1 sec; speed in top at 1,000 rpm: 20.5 mph, 32.9 km/h; consumption: 38.2 m/imp gal, 31.8 m/US gal, 7.4 l x 100 km at 75 mph, 120 km/h.

CHASSIS front and rear suspension: anti-roll bar.

BRAKES front disc, internal radial fins, rear compensator.

ELECTRICAL EQUIPMENT 45 Ah battery; 55 A alternator; speed limiter at 6,700 rpm.

DIMENSIONS AND WEIGHT tracks: 55.28 in, 140 cm front, 54.02 in, 137 cm rear; weight: 1,973 lb, 895 kg.

BODY metallic spray (standard for GTS and GTX only).

PRACTICAL INSTRUCTIONS fuel: 97 oct petrol.

Scirocco 16 V Coupé

ENGINE front, transverse, 4 stroke; 4 cylinders, vertical, in line; 108.7 cu in, 1,781 cc (3.19 x 3.40 in, 81 x 86.4 mm); compression ratio: 10:1; max power (DIN): 139 hp (102 kW) at 6,300 rpm; max torque (DIN): 118 lb ft, 16.3 kg m (160 Nm) at 4,500 rpm; max engine rpm: 6,700; 78 hp/l (57.3 kW/l); cast iron block, light alloy head; 5 crankshaft bearings; valves: 4 per cylinder, overhead, Vee-slanted, thimble tappets; camshafts: 2, overhead, cogged belt; lubrication: gear pump, full flow filter, 6.5 imp pt, 7.8 US pt, 3.7 l, oil cooler; Bosch K-Jetronic injection; fuel feed: electric pump; liquid-cooled, expansion tank, 7.9 imp pt, 9.5 US pt, 4.5 l, electric thermostatic fan.

TRANSMISSION driving wheels: front; clutch: single dry plate, hydraulically controlled; gearbox: mechanical; gears: 5, fully synchronized; ratios: I 3.450, II 2.120, III 1.440, IV 1, V 0.890, rev 3.170; lever: central; final drive: spiral bevel; axle ratio: 3.650; width of rims: 6''; tyres: 185/60 VR x 14.

PERFORMANCE max speed: 130 mph, 210 km/h; power-weight ratio: 15.1 lb/hp (20.5 lb/kW), 6.8 kg/hp (9.3 kg/kW); carrying capacity: 805 lb, 365 kg; speed in top at 1,000 rpm: 20.3 mph, 32.6 km/h; consumption: 38.2 m/imp gal, 31.8 m/US gal, 7.4 l x 100 km at 75 mph, 120 km/h.

CHASSIS integral; front suspension: independent, by McPherson, lower wishbones, anti-roll bar, coil springs/telescopic damper struts; rear: semi-independent, torsion beam trailing arm, anti-roll bar, coil springs/telescopic damper struts.

STEERING rack-and-pinion.

BRAKES disc, front internal radial fins, 2 X circuits, rear compensator, servo.

ELECTRICAL EQUIPMENT 12 V; 45 Ah battery; 55 A alternator; electronic ignition; 4 halogen headlamps; speed limiter at 6,700 rpm.

DIMENSIONS AND WEIGHT wheel base: 94.49 in, 240 cm; tracks: 55.28 in, 140 cm front, 54.02 in, 137 cm rear; length: 159.45 in, 405 cm; width: 63.78 in, 162 cm; height: 50.39 in, 128 cm; ground clearance: 4.13 in, 10.5 cm; weight: 2,095 lb, 950 kg; turning circle: 34.4 ft, 10.5 m; fuel tank: 12.1 imp gal, 14.5 US gal, 55 l.

BODY coupé; 2+1 doors; 4 seats, separate front seats, built-in headrests; heated rear window; folding rear seat; light alloy wheels; front and rear spoiler.

PRACTICAL INSTRUCTIONS fuel: 97 oct petrol; oil: engine 6.5 imp pt, 7.8 US pt, 3.7 l, SAE 10W-50, change every 4,700 miles, 7,500 km - gearbox and final drive 3.2 imp pt, 3.8 US pt, 1.8 l, SAE 80 or 90, change every 18,600 miles, 30,000 km; greasing: none; tyre pressure: front 31 psi, 2.2 atm, rear 31 psi, 2.2 atm.

AC 3000 ME

AC — GREAT BRITAIN

3000 ME

PRICE EX WORKS: £ 12,658*

ENGINE Ford, centre-rear, transverse, 4 stroke; 6 cylinders, Vee-slanted at 60°; 182.7 cu in, 2,994 cc (3.69 x 2.85 in, 93.7 x 72.4 mm); compression ratio: 8.9:1; max power (DIN): 138 hp (102 kW) at 5,000 rpm; max torque (DIN): 174 lb ft, 24 kg m (235 Nm) at 3,000 rpm; max engine rpm: 5,500; 46.1 hp/l (33.9 kW/l); cast iron block and head; 4 crankshaft bearings; valves: overhead, push-rods and rockers; camshafts: 1, at centre of Vee; lubrication: rotary pump, full flow filter, oil cooler, 10 imp pt, 12 US pt, 5.7 l; 1 Weber 38/38 EGAS downdraught twin barrel carburettor; fuel feed: mechanical pump; water-cooled, 12.8 imp pt, 15.4 US pt, 7.3 l, electric thermostatic fan.

TRANSMISSION driving wheels: rear; clutch: single dry plate; gearbox: mechanical; gears: 5, fully synchronized; ratios: I 3.242, II 1.947, III 1.403, IV 1, V 0.835, rev 2.901; lever: central; final drive: hypoid bevel; axle ratio: 3.167; width of rims: 7''; tyres: 195/60 VR x 14.

PERFORMANCE max speeds: (I) 40 mph, 64 km/h; (II) 80 mph, 128 km/h; (III) 100 mph, 161 km/h; (IV) 120 mph, 193 km/h; (V) 125 mph, 201 km/h; power-weight ratio: 17 lb/hp (23.1 lb/kW), 7.7 kg/hp (10.5 kg/kW); speed in top at 1,000 rpm: 25 mph, 40.2 km/h; consumption: 25 m/imp gal, 20.8 m/US gal, 11.3 l x 100 km.

CHASSIS monocoque frame; front suspension: independent, wishbones, vertical links, coil springs, telescopic dampers; rear: independent, wishbones, vertical links, coil springs, telescopic dampers.

STEERING rack-and-pinion, adjustable steering wheel; turns lock to lock: 3.

BRAKES disc (front diameter 10 in, 25.4 cm, rear 9.41 in, 23.9 cm), dual circuit; swept area: front 116.40 sq in, 751 sq cm, rear 78.30 sq in, 505 sq cm, total 194.70 sq in, 1,256 sq cm.

ELECTRICAL EQUIPMENT 12 V; 44 A alternator; Lucas distributor; 2 retractable headlamps, rear fog lamps.

DIMENSIONS AND WEIGHT wheel base: 90.50 in, 230 cm; tracks: 55 in, 140 cm front, 56 in, 142 cm rear; length: 157 in, 399 cm; width: 65 in, 165 cm; height: 45 in, 114 cm; ground clearance: 5.25 in, 13.3 cm; weight: 2,352 lb, 1,066 kg; weight distribution: 46% front, 54% rear; turning circle: 31 ft, 9.4 m; fuel tank: 14 imp gal, 16.8 US gal, 64 l.

BODY coupé, in plastic material; 2 doors; 2 seats with built-in headrests; detachable roof; electric windows; light alloy wheels; leather upholstery.

PRACTICAL INSTRUCTIONS fuel: 90 oct petrol; oil: engine 10 imp pt, 12 US pt, 5.7 l, SAE 20W-50, change every 6,200 miles, 10,000 km - gearbox 7 imp pt, 8.5 US pt, 4 l; greasing: every 6,200 miles, 10,000 km, 6 points; tappet clearances (cold): inlet 0.013 in, 0.33 mm, exhaust 0.022 in, 0.55 mm; valve timing: 29° 67° 70° 14°; tyre pressure: front 20 psi, 1.4 atm, rear 30 psi, 2.1 atm.

ARGYLL — GREAT BRITAIN

Turbo GT

PRICE EX WORKS: £ 23,750*

ENGINE Rover, turbocharged, central, transverse, 4 stroke; 8 cylinders in Vee; 215 cu in, 3,528 cc (3.50 x 2.80 in, 88.9 x 71.1 mm); compression ratio: 8.5:1; max power (DIN): 250 hp (184 kW) at 5,200-6,200 rpm; max torque (DIN): 310 lb ft, 42.8 kg m (420 Nm) at 3,500-4,500 rpm; max engine rpm: 6,200; 70.9 hp/l (52.2 kW/l); light alloy block and head, dry liners; 5 crankshaft bearings; valves: overhead, in line, push-rods and rockers, hydraulic tappets; camshafts: 1, at centre of Vee; lubrication: gear pump, full flow filter, oil cooler, 15 imp pt, 18 US pt, 8.5 l; 1 Minnow Fish TM7 carburettor; turbocharger; fuel feed: electric pump; water-cooled, 30 imp pt, 35.9 US pt, 17 l.

TRANSMISSION driving wheels: rear; clutch: single dry plate; gearbox: ZF mechanical; gears: 5, fully synchronized; ratios: I 2.580, II 1.520, III 1.040, IV 0.850, V 0.740, rev 2.860; lever: central; final drive: hypoid bevel, limited slip; width of rims: 8''; tyres: 205 x 15.

PERFORMANCE max speed: over 150 mph, 241 km/h; power-weight ratio: 9.3 lb/hp (12.6 lb/kW), 4.2 kg/hp (5.7 kg/kW); carrying capacity: 353 lb, 160 kg; consumption: not declared.

CHASSIS box-section with integral roll cage; front suspension: independent, coil springs, double wishbone, anti-roll bar, telescopic dampers; rear: independent, double wishbone, coil springs, telescopic dampers.

STEERING rack-and-pinion; turns lock to lock: 2.50.

BRAKES disc (diameter 10.30 in, 26 cm), servo.

ELECTRICAL EQUIPMENT 12 V; 60 Ah battery; alternator; Lucas distributor; 4 headlamps.

DIMENSIONS AND WEIGHT wheel base: 118 in, 300 cm; front and rear track: 59.50 in, 151 cm; length: 183 in, 465 cm; width: 72 in, 183 cm; height: 48 in, 122 cm; ground clearance: 6 in, 15 cm; weight: 2,300 lb, 1,043 kg; weight distribution: 48% front, 52% rear; fuel tank: 20 imp gal, 24 US gal, 91 l.

BODY coupé, in plastic material; 2 doors; 2 seats.

PRACTICAL INSTRUCTIONS fuel: 97 oct petrol; oil: engine 15 imp pt, 18 US pt, 8.5 l, SAE 20W-30, change every 3,100 miles, 5,000 km - gearbox and final drive 5.8 imp pt, 7 US pt, 3.3 l, SAE 90, change every 12,400 miles, 20,000 km; tyre pressure: front 22 psi, 1.5 atm, rear 24 psi, 1.7 atm.

VARIATIONS

ENGINE 6 cylinders, Vee-slanted at 90°, 162.6 cu in, 2,664 cc (3.46 x 2.87 in, 88 x 73 mm), max engine rpm 6,500, 93.8 hp/l (69.1 kW/l), 2 overhead camshafts, 1 per bank, 1 Minnow Fish TB7 carburettor.
TRANSMISSION 185 x 15 tyres.
PERFORMANCE max speed 140 mph, 225 km/h, carrying capacity 706 lb, 320 kg.
ELECTRICAL EQUIPMENT Bosch distributor.
BODY 2+2 seats.

OPTIONALS power steering; luxury equipment.

ARGYLL Turbo GT

ARKLEY GREAT BRITAIN

SS

PRICE EX WORKS: £ 8,750*

ENGINE Triumph, front, 4 stroke; 4 cylinders, vertical, in line; 91.1 cu in, 1,493 cc (2.90 x 3.44 in, 73.7 x 87.5 mm); compression ratio: 9:1; max power (DIN): 65 hp (48 kW) at 5,500 rpm; max torque (DIN): 84 lb ft, 11.6 kg m (114 Nm) at 3,000 rpm; max engine rpm: 6,000; 43.5 hp/l (32 kW/l); cast iron block and head; 3 crankshaft bearings; valves: overhead, in line, push-rods and rockers; camshafts: 1, side; lubrication: eccentric pump, full flow filter, 7 imp pt, 8.5 US pt, 4 l; 2 SU type HS4 horizontal carburettors; fuel feed: electric pump; sealed circuit cooling, water, 6 imp pt, 7.2 US pt, 3.4 l.

TRANSMISSION driving wheels: rear; clutch: single dry plate (diaphragm); gearbox: mechanical; gears: 4, fully synchronized; ratios: I 3.412, II 2.112, III 1.433, IV 1, rev 3.753; lever: central; final drive: hypoid bevel; axle ratio: 3.900; width of rims: 7"; tyres: 195/70 x 13.

PERFORMANCE max speeds: (I) 35 mph, 57 km/h; (II) 59 mph, 96 km/h; (III) 85 mph, 137 km/h; (IV) 110 mph, 177 km/h; power-weight ratio: 19.8 lb/hp (26.9 lb/kW), 9 kg/hp (12.2 kg/kW); carrying capacity: 353 lb, 160 kg; acceleration: standing ¼ mile 17.5 sec, 0-50 mph (0-80 km/h) 8.2 sec; speed in direct drive at 1,000 rpm: 19.8 mph, 31.8 km/h; consumption: 38 m/imp gal, 31.8 m/US gal, 7.4 l x 100 km.

CHASSIS integral; front suspension: independent, wishbones, coil springs, anti-roll bar, telescopic dampers; rear: rigid axle, semi-elliptic leafsprings, telescopic dampers.

STEERING rack-and-pinion; turns lock to lock: 2.25.

BRAKES front disc (diameter 8.25 in, 21 cm), rear drum.

ELECTRICAL EQUIPMENT 12 V; 40 Ah battery; 34 A alternator; Lucas distributor; 2 headlamps.

DIMENSIONS AND WEIGHT wheel base: 79.92 in, 203 cm; tracks: 46.46 in, 118 cm front, 44.88 in, 114 cm rear; length: 123 in, 312 cm; width: 60 in, 152 cm; height: 47.50 in, 121 cm; ground clearance: 4.50 in, 10.3 cm; weight: 1,288 lb, 584 kg; weight distribution: 52.4% front, 47.6% rear; turning circle: 32 ft, 9.8 m; fuel tank: 7 imp gal, 8.4 US gal, 32 l.

BODY convertible; 2 doors; 2 seats, reclining backrests with built-in headrests.

PRACTICAL INSTRUCTIONS fuel: 98 oct petrol; oil: engine 6.5 imp pt, 7.8 US pt, 3.7 l, SAE 10W-30 (winter) 20W-50 (summer), change every 6,000 miles, 9,700 km - gearbox 2.3 imp pt, 2.7 US pt, 1.3 l, SAE 10W-30 (winter) 20W-50 (summer) - final drive 1.4 imp pt, 1.7 US pt, 0.8 l, SAE 90, change every 6,000 miles, 9,700 km; greasing: every 3,000 miles, 4,800 km, 8 points; tappet clearances: inlet 0.010 in, 0.25 mm, exhaust 0.010 in, 0.25 mm; valve timing: 18° 58° 58° 18°; tyre pressure: front 18 psi, 1.3 atm, rear 20 psi, 1.4 atm.

ASTON MARTIN GREAT BRITAIN

V8

PRICE IN USA: $ 96,000*
PRICE EX WORKS: £ 42,498*

ENGINE front, 4 stroke; 8 cylinders in Vee; 325.8 cu in, 5,340 cc (3.94 x 3.35 in, 100 x 85 mm); compression ratio: 9.3:1; max engine rpm: 6,000; light alloy block and head, wet liners, hemispherical combustion chambers; 5 crankshaft bearings; valves: overhead, Vee-slanted at 64°, thimble tappets; camshafts: 4, 2 per bank, overhead; lubrication: rotary pump, full flow filter, 2 oil coolers, 19.9 imp pt, 23.9 US pt, 11.3 l; 4 Weber 42 DCNF downdraught twin barrel carburettors; fuel feed: 2 electric pumps; water-cooled, 32 imp pt, 38.5 US pt, 18.2 l, viscous coupling fan.

TRANSMISSION driving wheels: rear; clutch: single dry plate (diaphragm), hydraulically controlled; gearbox: mechanical or Chrysler-Torqueflite automatic transmission hydraulic torque converter and planetary gears with 3 ratios, max ratio of converter at stall 2.10, possible manual selection; gears: 5, fully synchronized; ratios: I 2.900, II 1.780, III 1.220, IV 1, V 0.845, rev 2.630 - automatic transmission I 2.450, II 1.450, III 1, rev 2.200; lever: central; final drive: hypoid bevel, limited slip; axle ratio: 3.540 - automatic transmission 3.070; width of rims: 7"; tyres: GR 70 VR x 15.

PERFORMANCE max speeds: (I) 47 mph, 75 km/h; (II) 77 mph, 124 km/h; (III) 112 mph, 180 km/h; (IV) 136 mph, 219 km/h; (V) 160 mph, 257 km/h; acceleration: standing ¼ mile 14 sec, 0-50 mph (0-80 km/h) 4.5 sec; speed in top at 1,000 rpm: 27 mph, 43.5 km/h; consumption: 17 m/imp gal, 14.2 m/US gal, 16.6 l x 100 km.

CHASSIS box-type platform; front suspension: independent, wishbones, coil springs, anti-roll bar, telescopic dampers; rear: de Dion axle, parallel trailing arms, transverse Watt linkage, coil springs, telescopic dampers.

STEERING rack-and-pinion, adjustable height of steering wheel, servo; turns lock to lock: 2.80.

BRAKES disc (front diameter 11.50 in, 29.2 cm, rear 10.80 in, 27.4 cm), internal radial fins, rear compensator, dual circuit, dual servo; swept area: front 259 sq in, 1,670 sq cm, rear 209 sq in, 1,348 sq cm, total 468 sq in, 3,018 sq cm.

ELECTRICAL EQUIPMENT 12 V; 68 Ah battery; 75 A alternator; Lucas transistorized ignition; 4 halogen headlamps.

DIMENSIONS AND WEIGHT wheel base: 102.75 in, 261 cm; front and rear track: 59 in, 150 cm; length: 182 in, 462 cm; width: 72 in, 183 cm; height: 52.25 in, 133 cm; ground clearance: 5.50 in, 14 cm; weight: 4,000 lb, 1,815 kg; weight distribution: 51% front, 49% rear; turning circle: 43 ft, 13.1 m; fuel tank: 23 imp gal, 27.5 US gal, 104 l.

BODY coupé; 2 doors; 4 seats, separate front seats, reclining backrests; adjustable 2-position clutch, brake and accelerator

ARGYLL Turbo GT

ARKLEY SS

ASTON MARTIN V8 Vantage

ASTON MARTIN V8 Volante

V8

pedals; leather upholstery; heated rear window; electric windows; air-conditioning.

PRACTICAL INSTRUCTIONS fuel: 98 oct petrol; oil: engine 19.9 imp pt, 23.9 US pt, 11.3 l, SAE 10W-50, change every 5,000 miles, 8,000 km; greasing: every 5,000 miles, 8,000 km, 6 points; tappet clearances: inlet 0.017 in, 0.42 mm, exhaust 0.018 in, 0.45 mm; valve timing: 27° 63° 52° 17°; tyre pressure: front 35 psi, 2.4 atm, rear 35 psi, 2.4 atm.

OPTIONALS sunroof; headlamps with wiper-washers.

V8 Vantage

See V8, except for:

PRICE IN USA: $ 120,000*
PRICE EX WORKS: £ 47,499*

ENGINE max engine rpm: 6,500; 4 Weber 48IDF downdraught twin barrel carburettors.

TRANSMISSION tyres: 275/55 VR x 15.

PERFORMANCE max speeds: (I) 46 mph, 74 km/h; (II) 75 mph, 120 km/h; (III) 109 mph, 175 km/h; (IV) 133 mph, 214 km/h; (V) 170 mph, 273 km/h; acceleration: 0-50 mph (0-80 km/h) 3.8 sec.

ELECTRICAL EQUIPMENT 4 headlamps.

PRACTICAL INSTRUCTIONS valve timing: 37°5' 74°5' 70° 32°; tyre pressure: front 50 psi, 3.5 atm, rear 50 psi, 3.5 atm.

V8 Volante

See V8, except for:

PRICE IN USA: $ 115,000*
PRICE EX WORKS: £ 52,498*

TRANSMISSION tyres: 235/70 VR x 15.

PERFORMANCE max speeds: (I) 45 mph, 72 km/h; (II) 73 mph, 116 km/h; (III) 104 mph, 166 km/h; (IV) 120 mph, 192 km/h; (V) 130 mph, 209 km/h; acceleration: 0-50 mph (0-80 km/h) 4.8 sec.

DIMENSIONS AND WEIGHT fuel tank: 21.6 imp gal, 26 US gal, 98 l.

BODY convertible; electric hood.

Lagonda

PRICE IN USA: 150,000*
PRICE EX WORKS: £ 65,999*

ENGINE front, 4 stroke; 8 cylinders in Vee; 325.8 cu in, 5,340 cc (3.94 x 3.35 in, 100 x 85 mm); compression ratio: 9.3:1; max engine rpm: 6,000; light alloy block and head; 5 crankshaft bearings; valves: overhead, Vee-slanted at 64°, thimble tappets; camshafts: 4, 2 per bank, overhead; lubrication: rotary pump, full flow filter, 2 oil coolers, 24 imp pt, 28.8 US pt, 13.6 l; 4 Weber 42 DCNF downdraught twin barrel carburettors; fuel feed: electric pump; water-cooled, 32 imp pt, 38.5 US pt, 18.2 l, 2 electric fans.

TRANSMISSION driving wheels: rear; gearbox: Chrysler-Torqueflite automatic transmission, hydraulic torque converter and planetary gears with 3 ratios, max ratio of converter at stall 2.10, possible manual selection; ratios: I 2.450, II 1.450, III 1, rev 2.200; lever: central; final drive: hypoid bevel, limited slip; axle ratio: 3.058; width of rims: 6"; tyres: 235/70 VR x 15.

PERFORMANCE max speed: 140 mph, 225 km/h; speed in direct drive at 1,000 rpm: 25.8 mph, 41.5 km/h; consumption: 15 m/imp gal, 12.5 m/US gal, 18.8 l x 100 km.

CHASSIS box-type platform; front suspension: independent, wishbones, coil springs, anti-roll bar, telescopic dampers; rear: de Dion axle, parallel trailing arms, transverse Watt linkage, coil springs, telescopic dampers, self-levelling system.

STEERING rack-and-pinion, variable ratio servo; turns lock to lock: 2.30.

BRAKES disc, internal radial fins, rear compensator, dual circuit, dual servo.

ELECTRICAL EQUIPMENT 12 V; 75 Ah battery; 100 A alternator; Lucas transistorized ignition; 4 halogen headlamps.

DIMENSIONS AND WEIGHT wheel base: 114.02 in, 290 cm; tracks: 58.27 in, 148 cm front, 59.06 in, 150 cm rear; length: 207.99 in, 528 cm; width: 72 in, 183 cm; height: 51.50 in, 131 cm; ground clearance: 9.84 in, 25 cm; weight: 4,551 lb, 2,063 kg; weight distribution: 52% front, 48% rear; turning circle: 38 ft, 11.6 m; fuel tank: 25.1 imp gal, 30.1 US gal, 114 l.

BODY saloon/sedan; 4 doors; 4 seats, separate front seats, reclining backrests, headrests; adjustable 2-position clutch brake and accelerator pedals; leather upholstery; heated rear window; electric windows; air-conditioning; cruise control; laminated windscreen; glass panel in roof above rear compartment; tinted glass.

PRACTICAL INSTRUCTIONS fuel: 98 oct petrol; oil: engine 19.9 imp pt, 23.9 US pt, 11.3 l, SAE 10W-50, change every 5,000 miles, 8,000 km; greasing: every 5,000 miles, 8,000 km, 6 points; tappet clearances: inlet 0.017 in, 0.42 mm, exhaust 0.018 in, 0.45 mm; valve timing: 27° 63° 52° 17°; tyre pressure: front 35 psi, 2.4 atm, rear 35 psi, 2.4 atm.

ASTON MARTIN V8

ATLANTIS GREAT BRITAIN

A.1.

PRICE EX WORKS: £ 33,150*

ENGINE Jaguar, front, 4 stroke; 6 cylinders, vertical, in line; 259.6 cu in, 4,235 cc (3.63 x 4.17 in, 92.1 x 106 mm); compression ratio: 8.7:1; max power (DIN): 205 hp (151 kW) at 5,000 rpm; max torque (DIN): 232 lb ft, 32 kg m (314 Nm) at 3,750 rpm; max engine rpm: 5,500; 48.4 hp/l (35.7 kW/l); cast iron block, light alloy head; 7 crankshaft bearings; valves: overhead, Vee-slanted at 45°, thimble tappets; camshafts: 2, overhead; lubrication: rotary pump, full flow filter, 14.5 imp pt, 17.3 US pt, 8.2 l; Lucas-Bosch L-Jetronic electronic injection; fuel feed: electric pump; water-cooled, 32 imp pt, 38.5 US pt, 18.2 l.

TRANSMISSION driving wheels: rear; gearbox: automatic transmission, hydraulic torque converter and planetary gears with 3 ratios, possible manual selection; ratios: I 2.390, II 1.450, III 1, rev 2.090; lever: central; axle ratio 3.540; width of rims: 6.5"; tyres: 235/70 x 15.

PERFORMANCE max speeds: (I) 49 mph, 79 km/h; (II) 81 mph, 130 km/h; (III) 115 mph, 185 km/h; power-weight ratio 16.1 lb/hp (22 lb/kW), 7.3 kg/hp (10 kg/kW); carrying capacity: 992 lb, 450 kg; acceleration: standing ¼ mile 17.5 sec, 0-50 mph (0-80 km/h) 6.6 sec; speed in direct drive at 1,000 rpm: 23.5 mph, 37.8 km/h; consumption: 18 m/imp gal, 15 m/US gal, 15.7 l x 100 km.

CHASSIS integral, front and rear auxiliary frames; front suspension: independent, wishbones, coil springs, anti-roll bar, telescopic dampers; rear: independent, lower wishbones, semi-axle as upper arms, trailing lower radius arms, 4 coil springs, anti-roll bar, 4 telescopic dampers.

STEERING rack-and-pinion, servo; turns lock to lock: 2.75.

BRAKES disc servo; swept area: front 234.5 sq in, 1,512 sq cm, 213.7 sq in, 1,378 sq cm, total 448.2 sq in, 2,890 sq cm.

ELECTRICAL EQUIPMENT 12 V; 66 Ah battery; 800 W alternator; Lucas contactless distributor; 4 headlamps.

DIMENSIONS AND WEIGHT wheel base: 125.98 in, 320 cm; tracks: 58.27 in, 148 cm front, 58.66 in, 149 cm rear; length: 198.03 in, 503 cm; width: 68.90 in, 175 cm; height

ASTON MARTIN Lagonda

55.51 in, 141 cm; ground clearance: 5.91 in, 15 cm; weight: 3,314 lb, 1,503 kg; weight distribution: 52% front, 48% rear; turning circle: 36.4 ft, 11.1 m; fuel tank: 16.9 imp gal, 20.3 US gal, 77 l.

BODY coupé; 2 doors; 4 seats, separate front seats; air-conditioning; Connoly leather upholstery.

PRACTICAL INSTRUCTIONS fuel: 97 oct petrol; oil: engine 14.5 imp pt, 17.3 US pt, 8.2 l, SAE 20W-50, change every 6,000 miles, 9,700 km - gearbox 14.5 imp pt, 17.3 Us pt, 8.2 l - final drive 2.7 imp pt, 3.4 US pt, 1.6 l, SAE 90, change every 12,000 miles, 19,300 km; greasing: every 6,000 miles, 9,700 km; spark plug: Champion N11Y; tappet clearances: inlet 0.012-0.014 in, 0.30-0.35 mm, exhaust 0.012-0.014 in, 0.30-0.35 mm; valve timing: 17° 59° 59° 17°; tyre pressure: front 24 psi, 1.7 atm, rear 26 psi, 1.8 atm.

OPTIONALS light alloy body; detachable roof.

AUSTIN — GREAT BRITAIN

Metro Series

PRICES EX WORKS:

		£
1	City 2+1-dr Saloon	**3,548***
2	Standard 2+1-dr Saloon	**3,899***
3	L 2+1-dr Saloon	**4,269***
4	HLE 2+1-dr Saloon	**4,600***
5	1.3 L 2+1-dr Saloon	**4,499***
6	1.3 HLE 2+1-dr Saloon	**4,829***
7	1.3 Automatic 2+1-dr Saloon	**5,275***
8	Vanden Plas 2+1-dr Saloon	**5,249***

Power team:	Standard for:	Optional for:
44 hp	1 to 3	—
46 hp	4	—
63 hp	5 to 7	—
73 hp	8	—

44 hp power team

ENGINE front, transverse, in unit with gearbox and final drive, 4 stroke; 4 cylinders, vertical, in line; 60.9 cu in, 998 cc (2.54 x 3 in, 64.6 x 76.2 mm); compression ratio: 9.6:1; max power (DIN): 44 hp (32 kW) at 5,250 rpm; max torque (DIN): 52 lb ft, 7.2 kg m (71 Nm) at 3,000 rpm; max engine rpm: 5,500; 44.1 hp/l (32.1 kW/l); cast iron block and head; 3 crankshaft bearings; valves: overhead, in line, push-rods and rockers; camshafts: 1, side; lubrication: rotary pump, full flow filter by cartridge, 8.4 imp pt, 10.1 US pt, 4.8 l; 1 SU type HIF semi-downdraught carburettor; fuel feed: electric pump; water-cooled, 8.6 imp pt, 10.4 US pt, 4.9 l, electric thermostatic fan.

TRANSMISSION driving wheels: front; clutch: single dry plate (diaphragm), hydraulically controlled; gearbox: mechanical; gears: 4, fully synchronized; ratios: I 3.525, II 2.217, III 1.433, IV 1, rev 3.544; lever: central; final drive: helical spur gears; axle ratio: 3.647; width of rims: 4.5"; tyres: 135 SR x 12.

PERFORMANCE max speed: 87 mph, 140 km/h; power-weight ratio: 37.2 lb/hp (51.2 lb/kW), 16.9 kg/hp (23.2 kg/kW); carrying capacity: 706 lb, 320 kg; speed in direct drive at 1,000 rpm: 16.3 mph, 21.2 km/h; consumption: 38.7 m/imp gal, 32.2 m/US gal, 7.3 l x 100 km at 75 mph, 120 km/h.

CHASSIS integral, front and rear auxiliary frames; front suspension: independent, wishbones, hydragas springs, anti-roll bar, telescopic dampers; rear: independent, swinging longitudinal trailing arms, hydragas springs with internal damping, pre-load springs.

STEERING rack-and-pinion; turns lock to lock: 3.30.

BRAKES front disc (diameter 8.40 in, 21.3 cm), rear drum, dual circuit, rear compensator; swept area: front 139 sq in, 897 sq cm, rear 55 sq in, 355 sq cm, total 194 sq in, 1,252 sq cm.

ELECTRICAL EQUIPMENT 12 V; 30 Ah battery; 45 A alternator; Lucas distributor; 2 headlamps.

DIMENSIONS AND WEIGHT wheel base: 88.62 in, 225 cm; tracks: 50.39 in, 128 cm front, 50.07 in, 127 cm rear; length: 134.05 in, 340 cm; width: 60.86 in, 155 cm; height: 53.60 in, 136 cm; weight: 1,638 lb, 743 kg; turning circle: 34.4 ft, 10.5 m; fuel tank: 7 imp gal, 8.4 US gal, 32 l.

BODY saloon/sedan; 2+1 doors; 5 seats, separate front seats; heated rear window.

PRACTICAL INSTRUCTIONS fuel: 98 oct petrol; oil: engine, gearbox and final drive 8.4 imp pt, 10.1 US pt, 4.8 l, SAE 20W-50, change every 12,000 miles, 19,300 km; greasing: every 12,000 miles, 19,300 km; tyre pressure: front 31 psi, 2.2 atm, rear 28 psi, 2 atm.

OPTIONALS low compression engine, 8.3:1 compression ratio, max power (DIN) 41 hp (30 kW), max speed 84 mph, 135 km/h (for Standard only); rear window wiper-washer (for Standard only).

46 hp power team

See 44 hp power team, except for:

ENGINE compression ratio: 10.3:1; max power (DIN): 46 hp (33 kW) at 5,500 rpm; max torque (DIN): 54 lb ft, 7.4 kg m (73 Nm) at 3,300 rpm; max engine rpm: 6,000; 46.1 hp/l (33.1 kW/l).

TRANSMISSION axle ratio: 3.444.

PERFORMANCE max speed: 88 mph, 142 km/h; power-weight ratio: 35.8 lb/hp (49.9 lb/kW), 16.2 kg/hp (22.6 kg/kW); speed in direct drive at 1,000 rpm: 17.2 mph, 27.7 km/h; consumption: 41.5 m/imp gal, 34.6 m/US gal, 6.8 l x 100 km at 75 mph, 120 km/h.

ELECTRICAL EQUIPMENT 2 halogen headlamps.

DIMENSIONS AND WEIGHT weight: 1,646 lb, 747 kg.

63 hp power team

See 44 hp power team, except for:

ENGINE 77.8 cu in, 1,275 cc (2.78 x 3.20 in, 70.6 x 81.3 mm); compression ratio: 9.4:1; max power (DIN): 63 hp (46 kW) at 5,650 rpm; max torque (DIN): 72 lb ft, 9.9 kg m (97 Nm) at 3,100 rpm; 49.4 hp/l (36.1 kW/l).

TRANSMISSION 1.3 Automatic gearbox: AP automatic transmission, hydraulic torque converter and planetary gears with 4 ratios, max ratio of converter at stall 2, possible manual selection; ratios: I 2.690, II 1.845, III 1.460, IV 1, rev 2.690; axle ratio: 3.444 - 1.3 Automatic 2.760; tyres: 155/70 SR x 12.

PERFORMANCE max speed: 97 mph, 156 km/h - 1.3 Automatic 92 mph, 148 km/h; power-weight ratio: 1.3 L 26.4 lb/hp (36.1 lb/kW), 11.9 kg/hp (16.4 kg/kW); speed in direct drive at 1,000 rpm: 17.2 mph, 27.7 km/h - 1.3 Automatic 18.7 mph, 30.1 km/h; consumption: 37.7 m/imp gal, 31.4 m/US gal, 7.5 l - 1.3 Automatic 34.9 m/imp gal, 29 m/US gal, 8.1 l x 100 km at 75 mph, 120 km/h.

BRAKES servo.

ELECTRICAL EQUIPMENT 40 Ah battery; 2 halogen headlamps.

DIMENSIONS AND WEIGHT weight: 1.3 L Saloon 1,662 lb, 754 kg - 1.3 Automatic Saloon 1,733 lb, 786 kg - 1.3 HLE Saloon 1,695 lb, 769 kg.

PRACTICAL INSTRUCTIONS tyre pressure: front 28 psi, 2 atm, rear 26 psi, 1.8 atm.

73 hp power team

See 44 hp power team, except for:

ENGINE 77.8 cu in, 1,275 cc (2.78 x 3.20 in, 70.6 x 81.3 mm); compression ratio: 10.5:1; max power (DIN): 73 hp (54

ATLANTIS A.1.

AUSTIN Metro City Saloon

73 HP POWER TEAM

kW) at 6,000 rpm; max torque (DIN): 73 lb ft, 10.1 kg m (99 Nm) at 4,000 rpm; max engine rpm: 6,000; 57.3 hp/l (42.4 kW/l); 1 SU type HIF-44 semi-downdraught carburettor.

TRANSMISSION gearbox ratios: I 3.647, II 2.185, III 1.425, IV 1, rev 3.666; width of rims: 5''; tyres: 155/70 SR x 12.

PERFORMANCE max speed: 101 mph, 163 km/h; power-weight ratio: 23.4 lb/hp (31.6 lb/kW), 10.6 kg/hp (14.4 kg/kW); speed in direct drive at 1,000 rpm: 17.2 mph, 27.7 km/h; consumption: 39.2 m/imp gal, 32.7 m/US gal, 7.2 l x 100 km at 75 mph, 120 km/h.

ELECTRICAL EQUIPMENT 40 Ah battery; 2 halogen headlamps.

DIMENSIONS AND WEIGHT weight: 1,709 lb, 775 kg.

OPTIONALS AP automatic transmission, hydraulic torque converter and planetary gears with 4 ratios (I 2.690, II 1.845, III 1.460, IV 1, rev 2.690), max ratio of converter at stall 2, possible manual selection.

AUSTIN Maestro 1.3 HLE Saloon

Maestro Series

PRICES EX WORKS:

		£
1	1.3 4+1-dr Saloon	**4,749***
2	1.3 L 4+1-dr Saloon	**5,199***
3	1.3 HLE 4+1-dr Saloon	**5,599***
4	1.6 L 4+1-dr Saloon	**5,499***
5	1.6 HLS 4+1-dr Saloon	**5,870***
6	1.6 Automatic 4+1-dr Saloon	**6,290***
7	1.6 Vanden Plas 4+1-dr Saloon	**6,775***

Power team:	Standard for:	Optional for:
68 hp	1,2	—
64 hp (economy)	3	—
81 hp	4 to 7	—

68 hp power team

ENGINE front, transverse, in unit with gearbox and final drive, 4 stroke; 4 cylinders, vertical, in line; 77.8 cu in, 1,275 cc (2.78 x 3.20 in, 70.6 x 81.3 mm); compression ratio: 9.7:1; max power (DIN): 68 hp (51 kW) at 5,800 rpm; max torque (DIN): 75 lb ft, 10.4 kg m (102 Nm) at 3,500 rpm; max engine rpm: 6,300: 53.3 hp/l (40 kW/l); cast iron block and head; 3 crankshaft bearings; valves: overhead, in line, push-rods and rockers; camshafts: 1, side; lubrication: rotary pump, full flow filter (cartridge), 8.4 imp pt, 10.1 US pt, 4.8 l; 1 ARG variable carburettor with electronic control; fuel feed: electric pump; water-cooled, 8.6 imp pt, 10.4 US pt, 4.9 l, electric thermostatic fan.

TRANSMISSION driving wheels: front; clutch: single dry plate (diaphragm), hydraulically controlled; gearbox: mechanical; gears: 4, fully synchronized; ratios: I 3.450, II 1.940, III 1.290, IV 0.910, rev 3.170; lever: central; final drive: helical spur gears; axle ratio: 4.170; width of rims: 4.5''; tyres: 155 SR x 13.

PERFORMANCE max speed: 97 mph, 156 km/h; power-weight ratio: 1.3 28.4 lb/hp (37.8 lb/kW), 12.9 kg/hp (17.2 kg/kW); carrying capacity: 1,091 lb, 495 kg; acceleration: 0-50 mph (0-80 km/h) 8.6 sec; speed in top at 1,000 rpm: 17.3 mph, 27.8 km/h; consumption: 36.1 m/imp gal, 30.2 m/US gal, 7.8 l x 100 km at 75 mph, 120 km/h.

CHASSIS integral; front suspension: independent, by McPherson, lower wishbones, coil springs/telescopic damper struts, anti-roll bar; rear: semi-independent, trailing arms, H-beam, coil springs, telescopic dampers.

STEERING rack-and-pinion; turns lock to lock: 4.18.

BRAKES front disc (diameter 9.50 in, 24.1 cm), rear drum, dual circuit, rear compensator; swept area: front 221.9 sq in, 1,431 sq cm, rear 95.8 sq in, 618 sq cm, total 317.7 sq in, 2,049 sq cm.

ELECTRICAL EQUIPMENT 12 V; 40 Ah battery; 45 A alternator; transistorized ignition; 2 headlamps.

DIMENSIONS AND WEIGHT wheel base: 98.70 in, 251 cm; tracks: 57.70 in, 146 cm front, 56.70 in, 144 cm rear; length: 157.50 in, 400 cm; width: 66.40 in, 169 cm; height: 55.80 in, 142 cm; ground clearance: 5.50 in, 14 cm; weight: 1.3 Saloon 1,929 lb, 875 kg - 1.3 L Saloon 1,995 lb, 905 kg; turning circle: 33.1 ft, 10.3 m; fuel tank: 11.9 imp gal, 14.3 US gal, 54 l.

BODY saloon/sedan; 4+1 doors; 5 seats, separate front seats; heated rear window; (for 1.3 L only) rear window wiper-washer; folding rear seat.

PRACTICAL INSTRUCTIONS fuel: 97 oct petrol; oil: engine, gearbox and final drive 8.4 imp pt, 10.1 US pt, 4.8 l, SAE 20W-50, change every 12,000 miles, 19,300 km; greasing: none; tyre pressure: front 31 psi, 2.2 atm, rear 28 psi, 2 atm.

OPTIONALS rear window wiper-washer (for 1.3 only); metallic spray; tinted glass; headrests; sunroof (for 1.3 L only).

64 hp (economy) power team

See 68 hp power team, except for:

ENGINE max power (DIN): 64 hp (48 kW) at 5,500 rpm; max engine rpm: 6,000; 50.2 hp/l (37.6 kW/l).

TRANSMISSION gears: 3+E, fully synchronized; ratios: I 3.450, II 1.750, III 1.060, IV 0.700, rev 3.170; axle ratio: 3.890.

PERFORMANCE max speed: 95 mph, 153 km/h; power-weight ratio: 31.5 lb/hp (42 lb/kW), 14.3 kg/hp (19.1 kg/kW); acceleration: 0-50 mph (0-80 km/h) 9.8 sec; speed in top at 1,000 rpm: 24.1 mph, 38.8 km/h; consumption: 41.5 m/imp gal, 34.6 m/US gal, 6.8 l x 100 km at 75 mph, 120 km/h.

DIMENSIONS AND WEIGHT weight: 2,017 lb, 915 kg.

BODY rear window wiper-washer and headrests (standard).

81 hp power team

See 68 hp power team, except for:

ENGINE 97.5 cu in, 1,598 cc (3 x 3.45 in, 76.2 x 87.6 mm); max power (DIN): 81 hp (60 kW) at 5,500 rpm; max torque (DIN): 91 lb ft, 12.6 kg m (124 Nm) at 3,500 rpm; 50.7 hp/l (37.5 kW/l); cast iron block, light alloy head; 5 crankshaft bearings; valves: overhead, thimble tappets; camshafts: 1, overhead, chain-driven.

TRANSMISSION 1.6 Automatic gearbox: VW automatic transmission, hydraulic torque converter and planetary gears with 3 ratios, possible manual selection; ratios: I 2.714, II 1.500, III 1, rev 2.429 - 1.6 HLS and Vanden Plas gears: 5, fully synchronized; ratios: I 3.450, II 1.940, III 1.290, IV 0.910, V 0.710, rev 3.170; axle ratio: 1.6 HLS and Vanden Plas 3.890 - 1.6 Automatic 3.409; width of rims: 5''; tyres: 165 SR x 13.

PERFORMANCE max speed: 1.6 HLS and Vanden Plas 101 mph, 162 km/h - 1.6 Automatic 98 mph, 157 km/h; power-weight ratio: 1.6 L 25.7 lb/hp (34.7 lb/kW), 11.7 kg/hp (15.7 kg/kW); acceleration: 0-50 mph (0-80 km/h) 7.7 sec; speed in IV at 1,000 rpm: 19.2 mph, 30.9 km/h; consumption: 1.6 HLS 37.1 m/imp gal, 30.9 m/US gal, 7.6 l - 1.6 Automatic 32.7 m/imp gal, 27.3 m/US gal, 8.6 l x 100 km at 75 mph, 120 km/h.

CHASSIS front suspension: anti-roll bar.

BRAKES servo.

DIMENSIONS AND WEIGHT length: 159.50 in, 405 cm; height: 56.30 in, 143 cm; weight: 1.6 L Saloon 2,083 lb, 945 kg - 1.6 HLS Saloon 2,116 lb, 960 kg - 1.6 Vanden Plas Saloon 2,172 lb, 985 kg.

BODY (for 1.6 Vanden Plas only) tinted glass, sunroof, electric window and central door locking; rear window wiper-washer and headrests (standard).

OPTIONALS (for 1.6 Vanden Plas only VW automatic transmission, hydraulic torque converter and planetary gears with 3 ratios (I 2.714, II 1.500, III 1, rev 2.429), possible manual selection, 3.409 axle ratio; (for 1.6 L and 1.6 HLS only) tinted glass, sunroof, electric windows and central door locking; light alloy wheels.

AUSTIN Maestro 1.6 Vanden Plas Saloon

AUTOKRAFT GREAT BRITAIN

AC Mark IV

PRICE EX WORKS: £ 25,000

ENGINE Ford, front, 4 stroke; 8 cylinders in Vee; 302 cu in, 4,949 cc (4 x 3 in, 101.5 x 76.1 mm); compression ratio: 9:1; max power (DIN): 280 hp (206 kW) at 5,500 rpm; max torque (DIN): 320 lb ft, 44.1 kg m (432 Nm) at 4,200 rpm; max engine rpm: 6,000; 56.6 hp/l (41.6 kW/l); cast iron block and head; 5 crankshaft bearings; valves: overhead, push-rods and rockers; camshafts: 1, at centre of Vee; lubrication: gear pump, filter in sump, 9 imp pt, 10.8 US pt, 5.1 l; 1 Holley downdraught 4-barrel carburettor; fuel feed: mechanical pump; water-cooled, 28 imp pt, 33.6 US pt, 15.9 l.

TRANSMISSION driving wheels: rear; clutch: single dry plate; gearbox: mechanical; gears: 5, fully synchronized; lever: central; final drive: limited slip; axle ratio: 3.540; width of rims: front 7.5'', rear 9.5''; tyres: front 215 x 60, rear 255 x 60.

AUTOKRAFT AC Mark IV

BENTLEY Mulsanne

PERFORMANCE max speeds: (I) 45 mph, 72 km/h; (II) 84 mph, 135 km/h; (III) 106 mph, 170 km/h; (IV) 128 mph, 206 km/h, (V) 142 mph, 228 km/h; power-weight ratio: 9.5 lb/hp (12.8 lb/kW), 4.3 kg/hp (5.8 kg/kW); carrying capacity: 353 lb, 160 kg; acceleration: standing ¼ mile 12.5 sec, 0-50 mph (0-80 km/h) 4.2 sec; speed in top at 1,000 rpm: 24 mph, 38.6 km/h; consumption: 18 m/imp gal, 15 m/US gal, 15.7 l x 100 km.

CHASSIS tubular space-frame; front suspension: independent, unequal wishbones, coil springs, telescopic dampers; rear: independent, unequal wishbones, coil springs, telescopic dampers.

STEERING rack-and-pinion; turns lock to lock: 3.25.

BRAKES disc, internal radial fins, servo.

ELECTRICAL EQUIPMENT 12 V; 65 Ah battery; 72 A alternator; Ford distributor; 2 headlamps.

DIMENSIONS AND WEIGHT wheel base: 90 in, 229 cm; tracks: 54 in, 137 cm front, 55 in, 142 cm rear; length: 130 in, 330 cm; width: 59 in, 150 cm; height: 40 in, 102 cm; ground clearance: 5 in, 12.7 cm; weight: 2,650 lb, 1,202 kg; weight distribution: 52% front, 48% rear; turning circle: 24 ft, 7.3 m; fuel tank: 16 imp gal, 19.3 US gal, 73 l.

BODY open, in light alloy material; 2 doors; 2 separate seats.

PRACTICAL INSTRUCTIONS fuel: 98 oct petrol; oil: engine 9 imp pt, 10.8 US pt, 5.1 l - gearbox 5 imp pt, 5.9 US pt, 2.8 l, SAE 80 - final drive 2.5 imp pt, 3 US pt, 1.4 l, EP 90 LS; greasing: none; valve timing: 48° 84° 94° 36°; tyre pressure: front 26 psi, 1.8 atm, rear 26 psi, 1.8 atm.

OPTIONALS anti-roll bar on front and rear suspension.

BENTLEY GREAT BRITAIN

Mulsanne

PRICE IN USA: $ 97,950*
PRICE EX WORKS: £ 55,240*

ENGINE front, 4 stroke; 8 cylinders in Vee; 411.9 cu in, 6,750 cc (4.10 x 3.90 in, 104.1 x 99.1 mm); compression ratio: 9:1; aluminium alloy block and head, cast iron wet liners; 5 crankshaft bearings; valves: overhead, in line, slanted, push-rods and rockers, hydraulic tappets; camshafts: 1, at centre of Vee; lubrication: gear pump, full flow filter (cartridge), 16.5 imp pt, 19.9 US pt, 9.4 l; 2 SU type HIF7 horizontal carburettors; dual exhaust system; fuel feed: Pierburg electric pump; sealed circuit cooling, expansion tank, 28.5 imp pt, 34.2 US pt, 16.2 l, viscous coupling electric thermostatic fan.

TRANSMISSION driving wheels: rear; gearbox: Turbo-Hydramatic 400 automatic transmission, hydraulic torque converter and planetary gears with 3 ratios, max ratio of converter at stall 2, possible manual selection; ratios: I 2.500, II 1.500, III 1, rev 2; lever: steering column; final drive: hypoid bevel; axle ratio: 3.080; width of rims: 6"; tyres: 235/70 HR x 15.

PERFORMANCE max speeds: (I) 47 mph, 76 km/h; (II) 79 mph, 126 km/h; (III) 118 mph, 190 km/h; carrying capacity: 1,014 lb, 460 kg; speed in direct drive at 1,000 rpm: 26.2 mph, 42.2 km/h; consumption: 16.1 m/imp gal, 13.4 m/US gal, 17.5 l x 100 km at 75 mph, 120 km/h.

CHASSIS integral, front and rear auxiliary frames; front suspension: independent, lower wishbones, coil springs, anti-roll bar, telescopic dampers; rear: independent, trailing arms, coil springs, auxiliary gas springs, anti-roll bar, automatic levelling control, telescopic dampers.

STEERING rack-and-pinion, servo, right- or left-hand drive; turns lock to lock: 3.20.

BRAKES disc (diameter 11 in, 27.9 cm), front internal radial fins, dual circuit, servo; swept area: front 227 sq in, 1,464 sq cm, rear 286 sq in, 1,845 sq cm, total 513 sq in, 3,309 sq cm.

ELECTRICAL EQUIPMENT 12 V; 68 Ah battery; 75 A alternator; Lucas transistorized distributor; 4 headlamps, 2 front and 2 rear fog lamps.

DIMENSIONS AND WEIGHT wheel base: 120.47 in, 306 cm; front and rear track: 60.63 in, 154 cm; length: 209.05 in, 531 cm; width: 74.41 in, 189 cm; height: 58.66 in, 149 cm; ground clearance: 6.50 in, 16.5 cm; weight: 4,950 lb, 2,245 kg; turning circle: 39.7 ft, 12.1 m; fuel tank: 23.5 imp gal, 28.2 US gal, 107 l.

BODY saloon/sedan; 4 doors; 5 seats, separate front seats, adjustable and reclining backrests; automatic air-conditioning; heated rear window; electric windows; seat adjustment; gear range selector; exterior mirrors; central door locking.

PRACTICAL INSTRUCTIONS fuel: 98 oct petrol; oil: engine 16.5 imp pt, 19.9 US pt, 9.4 l, SAE 20W-50, change every 6,000 miles, 9,700 km - automatic transmission 18.6 imp pt, 22.4 US pt, 10.6 l, Dexron, change every 24,000 miles, 38,600 km - final drive 4.5 imp pt, 5.3 US pt, 2.5 l, SAE 90 EP, change every 24,000 miles, 38,600 km - power steering and automatic levelling control change every 20,000 miles, 32,000 km; greasing: every 12,000 miles, 19,300 km, 5 points; spark plug: Champion RN14Y; valve timing: 26° 60° 68° 18°; tyre pressure: front 24 psi, 1.7 atm, rear 28 psi, 2 atm.

OPTIONALS fire extinguisher; initials on doors; white side-wall tyres; hide trim to facia roll.

VARIATIONS

(for USA only)
ENGINE 8:1 compression ratio, exhaust emission control, exhaust gas recirculation, catalytic converter, Bosch K-Jetronic injection.

(for Australia only)
ENGINE 8:1 compression ratio, exhaust emission control, exhaust gas recirculation.

Mulsanne Turbo

See Mulsanne, except for:

PRICE EX WORKS: £ 61,744*

ENGINE turbocharged; compression ratio: 8:1; 1 Solex A1 downdraught 4-barrel carburettor with Garrett AiResearch TO4B turbocharger; fuel feed: Bosch electric pump.

TRANSMISSION axle ratio: 2.690; tyres: 235/70 VR x 15.

PERFORMANCE max speeds: (I) 52 mph, 83 km/h; (II) 82 mph, 132 km/h; (III) 135 mph, 217 km/h; speed in direct drive at 1,000 rpm: 29.9 mph, 48.1 km/h; consumption: 16.3 m/imp gal, 13.6 m/US gal, 17.3 l x 100 km at 75 mph, 120 km/h.

DIMENSIONS AND WEIGHT weight: 5,052 lb, 2,291 kg.

PRACTICAL INSTRUCTIONS spark plug: NGK BPR 5ES; tyre pressure: front 27 psi, 1.9 atm, rear 35 psi, 2.5 atm.

Corniche

See Mulsanne, except for:

PRICE IN USA: $ 155,470*
PRICE EX WORKS: £ 73,168*

ENGINE 1 Solex 4A1 4-barrel carburettor.

PERFORMANCE consumption: 14.6 m/imp gal, 12.2 m/US gal, 19.3 l x 100 km at 75 mph, 120 km/h.

DIMENSIONS AND WEIGHT wheel base: 120.10 in, 305 cm; tracks: 60 in, 152 cm front, 60.63 in, 154 cm rear; length: 204.55 in, 520 cm; width: 71.65 in, 182 cm; height: 60 in, 152 cm; ground clearance: 6 in, 15.2 cm; weight: 5,204 lb 2,360 kg.

ELECTRICAL EQUIPMENT 55 A alternator.

BODY convertible; 2 doors; 4 seats.

BENTLEY Corniche

BRISTOL Beaufighter - Brigand

CORNICHE

VARIATIONS

(for USA and Japan only)
ENGINE 8:1 compression ratio, exhaust emission control, exhaust gas recirculation, catalytic converter, Bosch K-Jetronic injection.

(for Australia only)
ENGINE 8:1 compression ratio, exhaust emission contro, exhaust gas recirculation, 2 SU type HIF7 horizontal carburettors.

BRISTOL GREAT BRITAIN

Britannia

PRICE EX WORKS: £ 47,778*

ENGINE Chrysler, front, 4 stroke; 8 cylinders, in Vee; 360 cu in, 5,900 cc (4 x 3.58 in, 101.6 x 90.9 mm); compression ratio: 8:1; cast iron block and head; 5 crankshaft bearings; valves: overhead, hydraulic tappets, push-rods and rockers; camshafts: 1, at centre of Vee, chain-driven; lubrication: rotary pump, full flow filter, 8.4 imp pt, 10.1 US pt, 4.8 l; 1 Carter downdraught 4-barrel carburettor; air cleaner; fuel feed: mechanical pump; water-cooled, 29 imp pt, 34.9 US pt, 16.5 l, 2 electric thermostatic fans.

TRANSMISSION driving wheels: rear; gearbox: Torqueflite automatic transmission, hydraulic torque converter and planetary gears with 3 ratios, max ratio of converter at stall 2.20, possible manual selection; ratios: I 2.450, II 1.450, III 1, rev 2.200; lever: central; final drive: hypoid bevel, limited slip; axle ratio: 2.880; width of rims: 6"; tyres: 215 VR x 15.

PERFORMANCE max speeds: (I) 54 mph, 87 km/h; (II) 92 mph, 148 km/h; (III) 140 mph, 230 km/h; speed in direct drive at 1,000 rpm: 28.4 mph, 45.7 km/h; consumption: 21 m/imp gal, 17.6 m/US gal, 13.4 l x 100 km at 56 mph, 90 km/h.

CHASSIS box-type ladder frame with cross members; front suspension: independent, wishbones, coil springs, anti-roll bar, adjustable telescopic dampers; rear: rigid axle, longitudinal torsion bars, trailing lower radius arms, upper torque link, transverse Watts linkage, automatic levelling control, adjustable telescopic dampers.

STEERING ZF recirculating ball, servo; turns lock to lock: 4.

BRAKES disc (front diameter 10.91 in, 27.7 cm, rear 10.60 in, 26.9 cm), dual circuit, servo; swept area: front 224 sq in, 1,445 sq cm, rear 196 sq in, 1,264 sq cm, total 420 sq in, 2,709 sq cm.

ELECTRICAL EQUIPMENT 12 V; 71 Ah battery; 62 A alternator; Chrysler electronic ignition; 2 halogen headlamps.

DIMENSIONS AND WEIGHT wheel base: 114 in, 290 cm; tracks: 54.50 in, 138 cm front, 55.50 in, 141 cm rear; length: 197 in, 500 cm; width: 69.50 in, 177 cm; height: 56.50 in, 144 cm; ground clearance: 5 in, 13 cm; weight: 3,850 lb, 1,746 kg; weight distribution: 53% front, 47% rear; turning circle: 39.4 ft, 12 m; fuel tank: 18 imp gal, 21.6 US gal, 82 l.

BODY saloon/sedan; 2 doors; 4 seats, reclining backrests, front and rear detachable headrests; leather upholstery; electric windows; heated rear window; air-conditioning; electric seats; aluminium panels.

OPTIONALS light alloy wheels with 6" or 7" wide rims.

Brigand

See Britannia, except for:

PRICE EX WORKS: £ 49,827*

ENGINE turbocharged.

TRANSMISSION width of rims: 7" (standard).

PERFORMANCE max speeds: (I) 54 mph, 87 km/h; (II) 100 mph, 161 km/h; (III) 150 mph, 241 km/h; consumption: 17-20 m/imp gal, 14-17 m/US gal, 14-17 l x 100 km.

BODY light alloy wheels (standard).

Beaufighter

See Britannia, except for:

PRICE EX WORKS: £ 45,847*.

ENGINE turbocharged.

TRANSMISSION width of rims: 7" (standard).

PERFORMANCE max speeds: (I) 54 mph, 87 km/h; (II) 100 mph, 161 km/h; (III) 150 mph, 241 km/h; consumption: 17-20 m/imp gal, 14-17 m/US gal, 14-17 l x 100 km.

ELECTRICAL EQUIPMENT 4 halogen headlamps.

BODY convertible; removable glass roof; light alloy wheels (standard).

CATERHAM CARS GREAT BRITAIN

Super 7

PRICE EX WORKS: £ 7,476*

ENGINE Lotus, front, 4 stroke; 4 cylinders, vertical, in line; 97.6 cu in, 1,599 cc (3.19 x 3.06 in, 81 x 77.6 mm); compression ratio: 9.5:1; max power (DIN): 120 hp (88 kW) at 6,200 rpm; max torque (DIN): 106 lb ft, 14.6 kg m (143 Nm) at 5,500 rpm; max engine rpm: 6,500; 75 hp/l (55.2 kW/l); cast iron block, light alloy head; 5 crankshaft bearings; valves: overhead, Vee-slanted, thimble tappets; camshafts: 2, overhead; lubrication: rotary pump, full flow filter by cartridge, 7.5 imp pt, 8.9 US pt, 4.2 l; 2 Dell'Orto 40 DHLA twin barrel carburettors; fuel feed: mechanical pump; water-cooled, 12 imp pt, 14.4 US pt, 6.8 l.

TRANSMISSION driving wheels: rear; clutch: single dry plate (diaphragm); gearbox: mechanical; gears: 4, fully synchronized; ratios: I 3.300, II 2, III 1.400, IV 1, rev 3.325; lever: central; final drive: hypoid bevel; axle ratio: 3.640; width of rims: 5.5"; tyres: 165 SR x 13.

PERFORMANCE max speeds: (I) 42 mph, 68 km/h; (II) 62 mph, 100 km/h; (III) 89 mph, 143 km/h; (IV) 112 mph, 180 km/h; power-weight ratio: 9.3 lb/hp (12.8 lb/kW), 4.2 kg/hp (5.8 kg/kW); carrying capacity: 450 lb, 204 kg; acceleration: standing ¼ mile 14.6 sec, 0-50 mph (0-80 km/h) 4.4 sec; speed in direct drive at 1,000 rpm: 18.5 mph, 29.7 km/h; consumption: 25 m/imp gal, 20.8 m/US gal, 11.3 l x 100 km.

CHASSIS tubular space-frame with aluminium panels; front suspension: independent, lower wishbones, anti-roll bar, coil springs/telescopic damper units; rear: rigid axle, twin trailing radius arms, A-bracket, coil springs/telescopic damper units.

STEERING rack-and-pinion; turns lock to lock: 2.75.

BRAKES front disc, rear drum; swept area: front 150 sq in, 967 sq cm, rear 73.2 sq in, 472 sq cm, total 223.2 sq in, 1,439 sq cm.

ELECTRICAL EQUIPMENT 12 V; 39 Ah battery; 420 W alternator; Lucas distributor; 2 headlamps.

DIMENSIONS AND WEIGHT wheel base: 88 in, 223 cm; tracks: 49 in, 124 cm front, 51.97 in, 132 cm rear; length: 133 in, 338 cm; width: 65.50 in, 159 cm; height: 43.50 in, 110 cm; ground clearance: 4 in, 10 cm; weight: 1,125 lb, 510 kg; turning circle: 29.6 ft, 9 m; fuel tank: 8 imp gal, 9.5 US gal, 36 l.

BODY sports; no doors; 2 seats.

Super 7 1600

See Super 7, except for:

PRICES EX WORKS:	£
GT Roadster	**5,996***
L-C Roadster	**6,181***

ENGINE Ford, front, 4 stroke; compression ratio: 9:1; max power (DIN): 84 hp (62 kW) at 5,500 rpm; max torque (DIN): 91 lb ft, 12.5 kg m (123 Nm) at 4,000 rpm; 52.5 hp/l (38.8 kW/l); cast iron block and head; valves: overhead, push-rods and rockers; camshafts: 1, in block; lubrication: 6.5 imp pt, 7.8 US pt, 3.7 l; 1 Weber 32 DGAV carburettor.

PERFORMANCE max speed: 100 mph, 161 km/h; power-weight ratio: 13.4 lb/hp (18.1 lb/kW), 6.1 kg/hp (8.2 kg/kW); carrying capacity: 441 lb, 200 kg; acceleration: standing ¼ mile 15.7 sec, 0-50 mph (0-80 km/h) 5.3 sec; consumption: 29 m/imp gal, 24.2 m/US gal, 9.7 l x 100 km.

ELECTRICAL EQUIPMENT Ford distributor.

DIMENSIONS AND WEIGHT weight distribution: 55% front axle, 45% rear axle.

OPTIONALS light alloy wheels with 6" wide rims and 185 HR x 13 tyres; long wheel base.

Super 7 1600 GT Sprint

See Super 7, except for:

PRICE EX WORKS: £ 6,471*

ENGINE Ford, front, 4 stroke; compression ratio: 9:1; max power (DIN): 110 hp (81 kW) at 6,000 rpm; max torque (DIN): 97 lb ft, 13.4 kg m (131 Nm) at 5,000 rpm; 68.8 hp/l (50.7 kW/l); cast iron block and head; valves: overhead, push-rods and rockers; camshafts: 1, in block; lubrication: 6.5 imp pt, 7.8 US pt, 3.7 l; 2 Weber 40 DCOE carburettor.

PERFORMANCE max speed: 106 mph, 170 km/h; power-weight ratio: 10.1 lb/hp (13.9 lb/kW), 4.6 kg/hp (6.3 kg/kW); carrying capacity: 441 lb, 200 kg; acceleration: standing ¼ mile 15.2 sec, 0-50 mph (0-80 km/h) 5 sec; consumption: 26 m/imp gal, 21.6 m/US gal, 10.9 l x 100 km.

ELECTRICAL EQUIPMENT Ford distributor.

DIMENSIONS AND WEIGHT weight distribution: 55% front axle, 45% rear axle.

OPTIONALS light alloy wheels with 6" wide rims and 185 HR x 13 tyres.

CATERHAM CARS Super 7

DAIMLER 4.2

DAIMLER — GREAT BRITAIN

4.2

PRICE EX WORKS: £ 21,952*

ENGINE front, 4 stroke; 6 cylinders, vertical, in line; 258.4 cu in, 4,235 cc (3.63 x 4.17 in, 92 x 106 mm); compression ratio: 8.7:1; max power (DIN): 205 hp (151 kW) at 5,000 rpm; max torque (DIN): 232 lb ft, 32 kg m (314 Nm) at 4,500 rpm; max engine rpm: 5,500; 48.4 hp/l (35.6 kW/l); cast iron block, light alloy head, hemispherical combustion chambers; 7 crankshaft bearings; valves: overhead, Vee-slanted, thimble tappets; camshafts: 2, overhead; lubrication: rotary pump, full flow filter, oil cooler, 14.5 imp pt, 17.3 US pt, 8.2 l; Lucas-Bosch L-Jetronic injection; fuel feed: electric pump; water-cooled, 32.5 imp pt, 38.9 US pt, 18.4 l, viscous coupling thermostatic fan.

TRANSMISSION driving wheels: rear; gearbox: Borg-Warner 66 automatic transmission, hydraulic torque converter and planetary gears with 3 ratios, max ratio of converter at stall 2, possible manual selection; ratios: I 2.400, II 1.460, III 1, rev 2.090; lever: central; final drive: hypoid bevel; axle ratio: 3.058; width of rims: 6"; tyres: 205/70 VR x 15.

PERFORMANCE max speeds: (I) 49 mph, 79 km/h; (II) 81 mph, 130 km/h; (III) 127 mph, 204 km/h; power-weight ratio: 19.7 lb/hp (26.7 lb/kW), 8.9 kg/hp (12.1 kg/kW); carrying capacity: 926 lb, 420 kg; acceleration: standing ¼ mile 17.5 sec; consumption: 23.7 m/imp gal, 19.8 m/US gal, 11.9 l x 100 km at 75 mph, 120 km/h.

CHASSIS integral, front and rear auxiliary frames; front suspension: independent, wishbones, coil springs, anti-roll bar, telescopic dampers; rear: independent, lower wishbones, semi-axles as upper arms, trailing lower radius arms, 4 coil springs, 4 telescopic dampers.

STEERING rack-and-pinion, adjustable steering wheel, servo; turns lock to lock: 3.30.

BRAKES disc (front diameter 11.18 in, 28.4 cm, rear 10.38 in, 26.4 cm), front internal radial fins, servo; swept area: front 234.5 sq in, 1,512 sq cm, rear 213.7 sq in, 1,378 sq cm, total 448.2 sq in, 2,890 sq cm.

ELECTRICAL EQUIPMENT 12 V; 75 Ah no-maintenance battery; 65 A alternator; Lucas distributor; 4 halogen headlamps.

DIMENSIONS AND WEIGHT wheel base: 112.80 in, 286 cm; tracks: 57.99 in, 147 cm front, 58.58 in, 149 cm rear; length: 195.20 in, 496 cm; width: 69.68 in, 177 cm; height: 54 in, 137 cm; ground clearance: 7.09 in, 18 cm; weight: 4,035 lb, 1,830 kg; turning circle: 40 ft, 12.2 m; fuel tank: 20 imp gal, 24 US gal, 91 l (2 separate tanks).

BODY saloon/sedan; 4 doors; 5 seats, electrically adjusted, separate front seats, reclining backrests, front and rear headrests; heated rear window; electric windows; tinted glass; cruise control; air-conditioning; front fog lamps; electric sunroof; light alloy wheels; headlamps with wiper-washer; leather upholstery.

PRACTICAL INSTRUCTIONS fuel: 97 oct petrol; oil: engine 14.5 imp pt, 17.3 US pt, 8.2 l, SAE 20W-50, change every 7,500 miles, 12,000 km; tappet clearances: inlet 0.012-0.014 in, 0.30-0.35 mm, exhaust 0.012-0.014 in, 0.30-0.35 mm; tyre pressure: front 33 psi, 2.2 atm, rear 36 psi, 2.4 atm.

OPTIONALS limited slip differential; trip computer.

Double-Six

PRICE EX WORKS: £ 24,991*

ENGINE front, 4 stroke; 12 cylinders, Vee-slanted at 60°; 326 cu in, 5,343 cc (3.54 x 2.76 in, 90 x 70 mm); compression ratio: 12.5:1; max power (DIN): 295 hp (217 kW) at 5,500 rpm; max torque (DIN): 320 lb ft, 44.2 kg m (434 Nm) at 3,250 rpm; max engine rpm: 6,500; 56 hp/l (41.2 kW/l); light alloy block and head, wet liners; 7 crankshaft bearings; valves: overhead, in line, thimble tappets; camshafts: 2, 1 per bank, overhead; lubrication: rotary pump, full flow filter, oil cooler, 19 imp pt, 22.8 US pt, 10.8 l; Lucas-Bosch digital injection; fuel feed: electric pump; water-cooled, 36 imp pt, 43.3 US pt, 20.5 l, 1 viscous coupling thermostatic and 1 electric thermostatic fan.

TRANSMISSION driving wheels: rear; gearbox: GM 400 automatic transmission, hydraulic torque converter and planetary gears with 3 ratios, max ratio of converter at stall 2, possible manual selection; ratios: I 2.500, II 1.500, III 1, rev 2; lever: central; final drive: hypoid bevel, limited slip; axle ratio: 2.880; width of rims: 6"; tyres: 215/70 VR x 15.

PERFORMANCE max speeds: (I) 70 mph, 112 km/h; (II) 118 mph, 189 km/h; (III) 150 mph, 241 km/h; power-weight ratio: 14.4 lb/hp (19.6 lb/kW), 6.5 kg/hp (8.9 kg/kW); carrying capacity: 926 lb, 420 kg; acceleration: standing ¼ mile 16.2 sec, 0-50 mph (0-80 km/h) 6.4 sec; speed in direct drive at 1,000 rpm: 26.9 mph, 43.3 km/h; consumption: 21.6 m/imp gal, 18 m/US gal, 13.1 l x 100 km at 75 mph, 120 km/h.

CHASSIS integral, front and rear auxiliary frames; front suspension: independent, wishbones, coil springs, anti-roll bar, telescopic dampers; rear: independent, wishbones, semi-axle as upper arms, trailing lower radius arms, 4 coil springs, 4 telescopic dampers.

STEERING rack-and-pinion, adjustable steering wheel, servo; turns lock to lock: 3.30.

BRAKES disc (front diameter 11.18 in, 28.4 cm, rear 10.38 in, 26.4 cm), front internal radial fins, servo; swept area: front 234.5 sq in, 1,512 sq cm, rear 213.7 sq in, 1,378 sq cm, total 448.2 sq in, 2,890 sq cm.

ELECTRICAL EQUIPMENT 12 V; 75 Ah no maintenance battery; 60 A alternator; Lucas electronic distributor; 4 halogen headlamps.

DIMENSIONS AND WEIGHT wheel base: 112.80 in, 286 cm; tracks: 57.99 in, 147 cm front, 58.58 in, 149 cm rear; length: 194.68 in, 494 cm; width: 69.68 in, 177 cm; height: 54.13 in, 137 cm; ground clearance: 7.09 in, 18 cm; weight: 4,256 lb, 1,930 kg; turning circle: 40 ft, 12.2 m; fuel tank: 20 imp gal, 24 US gal, 91 l (2 separate tanks).

BODY saloon/sedan; 4 doors; 5 seats, electrically adjusted separate front seats, reclining backrests, built-in headrests; heated rear window; electric windows; air-conditioning; fog lamps; light alloy wheels; cruise control; leather upholstery; electric sunroof; tinted glass; headlamps with wiper-washer.

PRACTICAL INSTRUCTIONS fuel: 97 oct petrol; oil: engine 19 imp pt, 22.8 US pt, 10.8 l, SAE 20W-50, change every 7,500 miles, 12,000 km; tyre pressure: front 36 psi, 2.4 atm, rear 36 psi, 2.4 atm.

DAIMLER 4.2

DAIMLER Double-Six

Limousine

PRICE EX WORKS: £ 25,994*

ENGINE front, 4 stroke; 6 cylinders, vertical, in line; 258.4 cu in, 4,235 cc (3.63 x 4.17 in, 92.1 x 106 mm); compression ratio: 7.5:1; max power (DIN): 165 hp (121 kW) at 4,500 rpm; max torque (DIN): 222 lb ft, 30.6 kg m (300 Nm) at 2,500 rpm; max engine rpm: 5,500; 39 hp/l (28.7 kW/l); cast iron block, light alloy head, hemispherical combustion chambers; 7 crankshaft bearings; valves: overhead, Vee-slanted at 70°, thimble tappets; camshafts: 2, overhead; lubrication: mechanical pump, full flow filter, 12 imp pt, 14.4 US pt, 6.8 l; 2 SU type HIF 7 horizontal carburettors; fuel feed: 2 electric pumps; water-cooled, 25.5 imp pt, 30.7 US pt, 14.5 l, viscous coupling thermostatic fan.

TRANSMISSION driving wheels: rear; gearbox: GM 400 automatic transmission, hydraulic torque converter and planetary gears with 3 ratios, max ratio of converter at stall 2, possible manual selection; ratios: I 2.500, II 1.500, III 1, rev 2; lever: central; final drive: hypoid bevel; axle ratio: 3.540; tyres: 205/70 HR x 15.

PERFORMANCE max speeds: (I) 48 mph, 78 km/h; (II) 79 mph, 127 km/h; (III) 115 mph, 185 km/h; power-weight ratio: 28.5 lb/hp (38.9 lb/kW), 12.9 kg/hp (17.6 kg/kW); carrying capacity: 1,213 lb, 550 kg; acceleration: standing ¼ mile 19.5 sec; speed in direct drive at 1,000 rpm: 20.9 mph, 33.6 km/h; consumption: 18.2 m/imp gal, 15.2 m/US gal, 15.5 l x 100 km at 75 mph, 120 km/h.

CHASSIS integral, front and rear auxiliary frames; front suspension: independent, wishbones, coil springs, anti-roll bar, telescopic dampers; rear: independent, wishbones, semi-axle as upper arm, trailing lower radius arms, 4 coil springs, 4 telescopic dampers.

STEERING recirculating ball, adjustable steering wheel, variable ratio gearing, servo; turns lock to lock: 2.75.

BRAKES disc (front diameter 11.18 in, 28.4 cm, rear 10.38 in, 26.4 cm), internal radial fins, servo; swept area: front 234 sq in, 1,509 sq cm, rear 212 sq in, 1,367 sq cm, total 446 sq in, 2,876 sq cm.

ELECTRICAL EQUIPMENT 12 V; 68 Ah no maintenance battery; 45 A alternator; Lucas distributor; 4 halogen headlamps.

DIMENSIONS AND WEIGHT wheel base: 141 in, 358 cm; front and rear track: 58 in, 147 cm; length: 226 in, 574 cm; width: 77.56 in, 197 cm; height: 63.39 in, 161 cm; ground clearance: 7.09 in, 18 cm; weight: 4,702 lb, 2,133 kg; turning circle: 46 ft, 14 m; fuel tank: 20 imp gal, 24 US gal, 91 l (2 separate tanks).

BODY limousine; 4 doors; 8 seats, bench front seats; glass partition.

PRACTICAL INSTRUCTIONS fuel: 97 oct petrol; oil: engine 12 imp pt, 14.4 US pt, 6.8 l, multigrade, change every 3,000 miles, 5,000 km; tappet clearances: inlet 0.012-0.014 in, 0.31-0.36 mm, exhaust 0.012-0.014 in, 0.31-0.36 mm.

OPTIONALS air-conditioning; electric glass partition; electric windows; tinted glass; heated rear window; central door locking; front fog lamps.

DAIMLER Limousine

DESANDE — GREAT BRITAIN

Roadster

PRICE EX WORKS: £ 47,800

ENGINE GM, front, 4 stroke; 8 cylinders in Vee; 305.2 cu in, 5,001 cc (3.74 x 3.48 in, 94.9 x 88.4 mm); compression ratio: 8.6:1; max power (SAE): 157 hp (115 kW) at 4,000 rpm; max torque (SAE): 241 lb ft, 33.2 kg m (326 Nm) at 1,600 rpm; max engine rpm: 4,400; 31.4 hp/l (23.1 kW/l); cast iron block and head; 5 crankshaft bearings; valves: overhead, in line, push-rods and rockers, hydraulic tappets; camshafts: 1, at centre of Vee; lubrication: gear pump, full flow filter, 6.5 imp pt, 7.8 US pt, 3.7 l; 1 Rochester downdraught 4-barrel carburettor; thermostatic air cleaner; fuel feed: mechanical pump; water-cooled, 26 imp pt, 31.3 US pt, 14.8 l.

TRANSMISSION driving wheels: rear; gearbox: Turbo-Hydramatic 350 automatic transmission, hydraulic torque converter and planetary gears with 3 ratios, max ratio of converter at stall 2, possible manual selection; ratios: I 2.520, II 1.520, III 1, rev 1.940; lever: steering column; final drive: hypoid bevel, limited slip; axle ratio: 2.560; width of rims: 7"; tyres: 225/75 R x 15.

PERFORMANCE max speed: 109 mph, 175 km/h; power-weight ratio: 22.3 lb/hp (30.3 lb/kW), 10.1 kg/hp (13.8 kg/kW); speed in direct drive at 1,000 rpm: 31.8 mph, 51 km/h; consumption: 14.1 m/imp gal, 11.8 m/US gal, 20 l x 100 km.

CHASSIS box-type ladder frame; front suspension: independent, lower wishbones, rubber elements, coil springs, anti-roll bar; rear: rigid axle, trailing lower radius arms, coil springs, telescopic dampers.

STEERING recirculating ball, servo.

BRAKES front disc (diameter 11.85 in, 30.1 cm), rear drum.

ELECTRICAL EQUIPMENT 12 V; 61 Ah battery; 63 A alternator; 2 headlamps.

DIMENSIONS AND WEIGHT wheel base: 115.75 in, 294 cm; front and rear track: 61.81 in, 157 cm; length: 195.28 in, 496 cm; width: 77.17 in, 196 cm; height: 57.09 in, 145 cm; ground clearance: 5.91 in, 15 cm; weight: 3,517 lb, 1,595 kg; weight distribution: 50% front, 50% rear; turning circle: 42.6 ft, 13 m; fuel tank: 22 imp gal, 26.4 US gal, 100 l.

BODY roadster; 2 doors; 2 seats, reclining backrests.

PRACTICAL INSTRUCTIONS fuel: 99 oct petrol; oil: engine 6.5 imp pt, 7.8 US pt, 3.7 l, SAE 20W-50, change every 6,000 miles, 9,700 km - gearbox Dexron II D-20 577, change every 15,000 miles, 24,100 km - final drive change every 6,000 miles, 9,700 km; greasing: every 6,000 miles, 9,700 km, 9 points; tyre pressure: front 28 psi, 2 atm, rear 28 psi, 2 atm.

OPTIONALS hardtop.

DUTTON — GREAT BRITAIN

Moke Californian

PRICE EX WORKS: £ 4,100

ENGINE Mini, front, transverse, in unit with gearbox and final drive; 4 stroke, 4 cylinders, vertical, in line; 60.9 cu in, 998 cc (2.54 x 2.86 in, 64.5 x 72.6 mm); compression ratio: 8.3:1; max power (DIN): 40 hp (29 kW) at 5,200 rpm; max torque (DIN): 50 lb ft, 6.9 kg m (68 Nm) at 2,500 rpm; max engine rpm: 5,500; 40.1 hp/l (29.1 kW/l); cast iron block and head; 3 crankshaft bearings; valves: overhead, in line, push-rods and rockers; camshafts: 1, side; lubrication: rotary pump, full flow filter by cartridge, 8.4 imp pt, 10.1 US pt, 4.8 l; 1 SU type HS4 semi-downdraught carburettor; fuel feed: electric pump; water-cooled, 6.2 imp pt, 7.4 US pt, 3.5 l.

TRANSMISSION driving wheels: front; clutch: single dry plate (diaphragm), hydraulically controlled; gearbox: mechanical; gears: 4, fully synchronized; ratios: I 3.647, II 2.185, III 1.425, IV 1, rev 3.667; lever: central; final drive: helical spur gears; axle ratio: 2.950; width of rims: 5"; tyres: 5.60 x 13.

PERFORMANCE max speed: 81 mph, 130 km/h; power-weight ratio: 31.8 lb/hp (43.9 lb/kW), 14.4 kg/hp (19.9 kg/kW); carrying capacity: 706 lb, 320 kg; consumption: 40.7 m/imp gal, 34.1 m/US gal, 6.9 l x 100 km.

CHASSIS integral; front suspension: independent, unequal transverse arms, rubber springs, telescopic dampers; rear: independent, trailing arms, rubber springs, telescopic dampers.

STEERING rack-and-pinion; turns lock to lock: 2.72.

BRAKES drum.

ELECTRICAL EQUIPMENT 12 V; 36 Ah battery; 34 A alternator; 2 headlamps.

DIMENSIONS AND WEIGHT wheel base: 80 in, 203 cm; length: 120 in, 305 cm; width: 51 in, 129 cm; height: 56 in, 142 cm; ground clearance: 8 in, 20.3 cm; weight: 1,275 lb, 578 kg; turning circle: 29 ft, 8.8 m; fuel tank: 7.5 imp gal, 9 US gal, 34 l.

BODY open; no doors; 4 seats, front separate seats; roll-bar; soft top.

PRACTICAL INSTRUCTIONS fuel: 94 oct petrol; oil: engine, gearbox and final drive 8.4 imp pt, 10.1 US pt, 4.8 l, SAE 20W-50, change every 12,000 miles, 19,300 km; tyre pressure: front 28 psi, 2 atm, rear 22 psi, 1.5 atm.

FORD — GREAT BRITAIN

Fiesta Series

PRICES EX WORKS:		£
1	950 Popular 2+1-dr Saloon	3,560*
2	950 Popular Plus 2+1-dr Saloon	3,950*
3	950 L 2+1-dr Saloon	4,320*
4	1100 Popular Plus 2+1-dr Saloon	4,155*
5	1100 L 2+1-dr Saloon	4,525*
6	1100 Ghia 2+1-dr Saloon	5,100*

DESANDE Roadster

DUTTON Moke Californian

FORD Escort 1600 Ghia Saloon

Power team:	Standard for:	Optional for:
45 hp	1 to 3	—
50 hp	4 to 6	—

45 hp power team

ENGINE front, transverse, 4 stroke; 4 cylinders, vertical, in line; 58.4 cu in, 957 cc (2.91 x 2.19 in, 74 x 55.7 mm); compression ratio: 8.3:1; max power (DIN): 45 hp (33 kW) at 5,750 rpm; max torque (DIN): 50 lb ft, 6.9 kg m (68 Nm) at 3,700 rpm; max engine rpm: 6,000; 47 hp/l (34.5 kW/l); cast iron block and head; 3 crankshaft bearings; valves: overhead, in line, push-rods and rockers; camshafts: 1, side, chain-driven; lubrication: gear pump, full flow filter (cartridge), 5.6 imp pt, 6.8 US pt, 3.2 l; 1 Ford single barrel carburettor; fuel feed: mechanical pump; liquid-cooled, expansion tank, 9.5 imp pt, 11.4 US pt, 5.4 l, electric thermostatic fan.

TRANSMISSION driving wheels: front; clutch: single dry plate (diaphragm); gearbox: mechanical, in unit with final drive; gears: 4, fully synchronized; ratios: I 3.583, II 2.043, III 1.346, IV 0.951, rev 3.769; lever: central; final drive: spiral bevel; axle ratio: 4.056; width of rims: 4.5", tyres: 135 SR x 13.

PERFORMANCE max speed: 84 mph, 136 km/h; power-weight ratio: 36.7 lb/hp (50.1 lb/kW), 16.7 kg/hp (22.7 kg/kW); carrying capacity: 937 lb, 425 kg; consumption: 39.8 m/imp gal, 33.1 m/US gal, 7.1 l x 100 km at 75 mph, 120 km/h.

CHASSIS integral; front suspension: independent, by McPherson, coil springs/telescopic damper struts, lower wishbones (trailing links); rear: rigid axle, swinging longitudinal trailing arms, upper oblique torque arms, Panhard rod, coil springs, telescopic dampers.

STEERING rack-and-pinion; turns lock to lock: 3.40.

BRAKES front disc (diameter 8.71 in, 22.1 cm), rear drum, dual circuit, rear compensator, servo; lining area: front 18.6 sq in, 120 sq cm, rear 26.4 sq in, 169.9 sq cm, total 45 sq in, 289.9 sq cm.

ELECTRICAL EQUIPMENT 12 V; 35 Ah battery; 45 A alternator; 2 halogen headlamps.

DIMENSIONS AND WEIGHT wheel base: 90.16 in, 229 cm; tracks: 53.82 in, 137 cm front, 51.97 in, 132 cm rear; length: 143.62 in, 365 cm; width: 62.40 in, 158 cm; height: 52.20 in, 133 cm; ground clearance: 5.51 in, 14 cm; weight: 1,654 lb, 750 kg; turning circle: 33.8 ft, 10.3 m; fuel tank: 7.5 imp gal, 9 US gal, 34 l.

BODY saloon/sedan; 2+1 doors; 5 seats, separate front seats; headrests; folding rear seat; (for L only) heated rear window and rear window wiper-washer.

PRACTICAL INSTRUCTIONS fuel: 90 oct petrol; oil: engine 5.6 imp pt, 6.8 US pt, 3.2 l, SAE 10W-50, change every 6,200 miles, 10,000 km - gearbox and final drive 3.9 imp pt, 4.7 US pt, 2.2 l, SAE 90, change every 18,600 miles, 30,000 km; greasing: none; tyre pressure: front 23 psi, 1.6 atm, rear 26 psi, 1.8 atm.

OPTIONALS (for Popular sedans only) heated rear window and rear window wiper-washer; (for L only) sunroof and tinted glass; (for Popular Plus and L sedans only) metallic spray.

50 hp power team

See 45 hp power team, except for:

ENGINE 68.2 cu in, 1,117 cc (2.91 x 2.56 in, 74 x 65 mm); compression ratio: 9.5:1; max power (DIN): 50 hp (37 kW) at 5,000 rpm; max torque (DIN): 62 lb ft, 8.5 kg m (83 Nm) at 2,700 rpm; max engine rpm: 5,500; 44.8 hp/l (33.1 kW/l); 1 Ford VV downdraught single barrel carburettor.

TRANSMISSION gearbox ratios: I 3.583, II 2.043, III 1.296, IV 0.878, rev 3.769; axle ratio: 3.583; tyres: (for Ghia only) 155/70 SR x 13.

PERFORMANCE max speed: 88 mph, 142 km/h; power-weight ratio: 33.3 lb/hp (45 lb/kW), 15.1 kg/hp (20.4 kg/kW); consumption: 41.5 m/imp gal, 34.6 m/US gal, 6.8 l x 100 km at 75 mph, 120 km/h.

DIMENSIONS AND WEIGHT weight: 1,665 lb, 755 kg.

PRACTICAL INSTRUCTIONS fuel: 97 oct petrol.

OPTIONALS 5-speed fully synchronized mechanical gearbox (I 3.583, II 2.043, III 1.346, IV 0.951, V 0.756, rev 3.615), 3.842 axle ratio, max speed 90 mph, 145 km/h.

FORD Fiesta 1100 L Saloon

Escort Series

PRICES EX WORKS:

		£
1	1100 2+1-dr Saloon	4,188*
2	1100 4+1-dr Saloon	4,370*
3	1100 2+1-dr Estate	4,638*
4	1100 2+1-dr Estate	4,820*
5	1100 L 2+1-dr Saloon	4,652*
6	1100 L 4+1-dr Saloon	4,835*
7	1300 2+1-dr Saloon	4,568*
8	1300 4+1-dr Saloon	4,750*
9	1300 2+1-dr Estate	4,943*
10	1300 4+1-dr Estate	5,126*
11	1300 L 2+1-dr Saloon	5,032*
12	1300 L 4+1-dr Saloon	5,215*
13	1300 L 2+1-dr Estate	5,408*
14	1300 L 4+1-dr Estate	5,590*
15	1300 GL 2+1-dr Saloon	5,307*
16	1300 GL 4+1-dr Saloon	5,490*
17	1300 GL 2+1-dr Estate	5,682*
18	1300 GL 4+1-dr Estate	5,865*
19	1300 Ghia 4+1-dr Saloon	6,017*
20	1600 L 2+1-dr Saloon	5,325*
21	1600 L 4+1-dr Saloon	5,507*
22	1600 L 2+1-dr Estate	5,700*
23	1600 L 4+1-dr Estate	5,883*
24	1600 GL 2+1-dr Saloon	5,599*
25	1600 GL 4+1-dr Saloon	5,782*
26	1600 GL 4+1-dr Estate	6,157*
27	1600 Ghia 4+1-dr Saloon	6,309*
28	1600 XR3i 2+1-dr Saloon	6,520*

Power team:	Standard for:	Optional for:
50 hp	1 to 6	—
69 hp	7 to 19	—
79 hp	20 to 27	—
105 hp	28	—

50 hp power team

ENGINE front, transverse, 4 stroke; 4 cylinders, vertical, in line; 68.2 cu in, 1,117 cc (2.91 x 2.56 in, 74 x 65 mm); compression ratio: 9.5:1; max power (DIN): 50 hp (37 kW) at 5,000 rpm; max torque (DIN): 62 lb ft, 8.5 kg m (83 Nm) at 2,700 rpm; max engine rpm: 5,800; 44.8 hp/l (33.1 kW/l); cast iron block and head; 3 crankshaft bearings; valves: overhead, in line, push-rods and rockers; camshafts: 1, side, chain-driven; lubrication: gear pump, full flow filter (cartridge), 5.6 im pt, 6.8 US pt, 3.2 l; 1 Ford VV downdraught single barrel carburettor; fuel feed: mechanical pump; semi-sealed circuit cooling, expansion tank, 11.8 imp pt, 14.2 US pt, 6.7 l, electric thermostatic fan.

TRANSMISSION driving wheels: front; clutch: single dry plate (diaphragm); gearbox: mechanical, in unit with final drive; gears: 4, fully synchronized; ratios: I 3.580, II 2.040, III 1.350, IV 0.950, rev 3.770; lever: central; final drive: spiral bevel; axle ratio: 3.840; width of rims: 4.5" - saloons 5"; tyres: 145 SR x 13 - saloons 155 SR x 13.

PERFORMANCE max speed: 88 mph, 142 km/h - st. wagons 89 mph, 144 km/h; power-weight ratio: 4+1-dr saloons 35.7 lb/hp (48.3 lb/kW), 16.2 kg/hp (21.9 kg/kW); carriyng capacity: 1,025 lb, 465 kg; speed in top at 1,000 rpm: 15.1 mph, 24.3 km/h; consumption: 39.8 m/imp gal, 33.1 m/US gal, 7.1 l x 100 km at 75 mph, 120 km/h.

CHASSIS integral; front suspension: independent, by McPherson, lower wishbones, coil springs/telescopic damper struts, anti-roll bar; rear: independent, lower wishbones, trailing radius arms, coil springs, telescopic dampers.

STEERING rack-and-pinion.

BRAKES front disc (diameter 9.45 in, 24 cm), rear drum, dual circuit, rear compensator, servo; lining area: front 23.4

50 HP POWER TEAM

sq in, 151 sq cm, rear 28.8 sq in, 186 sq cm, total 52.2 sq in, 337 sq cm.

ELECTRICAL EQUIPMENT 12 V; 35 Ah; 45 A alternator; Motorcraft distributor; 2 headlamps.

DIMENSIONS AND WEIGHT wheel base: 94.57 in, 240 cm; tracks: 55.10 in, 140 cm front, 56.02 in, 142 cm rear; length: 156.30 in, 397 cm - st. wagons 158.78 in, 403 cm; width: 64.57 in, 164 cm; height: 54.33 in, 138 cm; ground clearance: 4.72 in, 12 cm; weight: 2+1-dr saloons 1,742 lb, 790 kg - 4+1-dr saloons 1,786 lb, 810 kg - 2+1-dr st. wagons 1,830 lb, 830 kg - 4+1-dr st. wagons 1,874 lb, 850 kg; turning circle: 34.4 ft, 10.5 m; fuel tank: 10.6 imp gal, 12.7 US gal, 48 l.

BODY saloon/sedan - estate car/st. wagon, 2+1 or 4+1 doors; 5 seats, separate front seats.

PRACTICAL INSTRUCTIONS fuel: 97 oct petrol; oil: engine 5.6 imp pt, 6.8 US pt, 3.2 l, SAE 10W-30, change every 6,200 miles, 10,000 km - gearbox and final drive 4.9 imp pt, 5.9 US pt, 2.8 l, SAE 80W-90, change every 18,600 miles, 30,000 km; valve timing: 21° 55° 70° 22°; tyre pressure: front 23 psi, 1.6 atm, rear 26 psi, 1.8 atm.

OPTIONALS 5-speed fully synchronized mechanical gearbox (I 3.580, II 2.040, III 1.350, IV 0.950, V 0.760, rev 3.620), 4.060 axle ratio, consumption 40.9 m/imp gal, 34.1 m/US gal, 6.9 l x 100 km at 75 mph, 120 km/h; 155 SR x 13 tyres with 5'' wide rims; halogen headlamps; tinted glass; light alloy wheels; sunroof; rear window wiper-washer; fog lamps; metallic spray.

69 hp power team

See 50 hp power team, except for:

ENGINE 79.1 cu in, 1,296 cc (3.15 x 2.54 in, 80 x 64.5 mm); max power (DIN): 69 hp (51 kW) at 6,000 rpm; max torque (DIN): 74 lb ft, 10.2 kg m (100 Nm) at 3,500 rpm; max engine rpm: 6,300; 53.2 hp/l (39.4 kW/l); light alloy head; 5 crankshaft bearings; valves: overhead, hydraulic tappets, CVH (compound valve hemispherical); camshafts: 1, overhead, cogged belt; lubrication: 6.2 imp pt, 7.4 US pt, 3.5 l; cooling: 13.4 imp pt, 16.1 US pt, 7.6 l.

TRANSMISSION width of rims: 5'' (standard); tyres: 155 SR x 13 (standard).

PERFORMANCE max speed: 98 mph, 157 km/h - st. wagons 96 mph, 155 km/h; power-weight ratio: 4+1-dr saloons 27.2 lb/hp (36.7 lb/kW), 12.3 kg/hp (16.7 kg/kW); carrying capacity: 992 lb, 450 kg; speed in top at 1,000 rpm: 16.3 mph, 26.2 km/h; consumption: 36.7 m/imp gal, 30.5 m/US gal, 7.7 l x 100 km at 75 mph, 120 km/h.

ELECTRICAL EQUIPMENT contactless fully electronic ignition.

DIMENSIONS AND WEIGHT weight: 2+1-dr saloons 1,830 lb, 830 kg - 4+1-dr saloons 1,874 lb, 850 kg - 2+1-dr st. wagons 1,940 lb, 880 kg - 4+1-dr st. wagons 1,984 lb, 900 kg.

PRACTICAL INSTRUCTIONS oil: engine 6.2 imp pt, 7.4 US pt, 3.5 l; valve timing: 13° 28° 30° 15°.

79 hp power team

See 50 hp power team, except for:

ENGINE 97.4 cu in, 1,597 cc (3.15 x 3.13 in, 80 x 79.5 mm); max power (DIN): 79 hp (58 kW) at 5,800 rpm; max torque (DIN): 92 lb ft, 12.7 kg m (125 Nm) at 3,000 rpm; 49.5 hp/l (36.3 kW/l); light alloy head; 5 crankshaft bearings; valves: overhead, hydraulic tappets, CVH (compound valve hemispherical); camshafts: 1, overhead, cogged belt; lubrication: 6.2 imp pt, 7.4 US pt, 3.5 l; 1 Weber downdraught single barrel carburettor; cooling: 13.7 imp pt, 16.5 US pt, 7.8 l.

FORD Orion 1600 GL Saloon

TRANSMISSION gears: 5, fully synchronized; ratios: I 3.150, II 1.910, III 1.280, IV 0.950, V 0.760, rev 3.620; axle ratio: 3.580; width of rims: 5'' (standard); tyres: 155 SR x 13 (standard).

PERFORMANCE max speed: 104 mph, 167 km/h - st. wagons 102 mph, 165 km/h; power-weight ratio: 4+1-dr saloons 23.7 lb/hp (32.3 lb/kW), 10.8 kg/hp (14.7 kg/kW); carrying capacity: 992 lb, 450 kg; speed in top at 1,000 rpm: 17.3 mph, 27.8 km/h; consumption: 36.7 m/imp gal, 30.5 m/US gal, 7.7 l x 100 km at 75 mph, 120 km/h.

ELECTRICAL EQUIPMENT 43 Ah battery; contactless fully electronic ignition.

DIMENSIONS AND WEIGHT weight: 2+1-dr saloons 1,830 lb, 830 kg - 4+1-dr saloons 1,874 lb, 850 kg - 2+1-dr st. wagons 1,940 lb, 880 kg - 4+1-dr st. wagons 1,984 lb, 900 kg.

PRACTICAL INSTRUCTIONS oil: engine 6.2 imp pt, 7.4 US pt, 3.5 l.

OPTIONALS Ford ATX automatic transmission with 3 ratios (I 2.790, II 1.610, III 1, rev 1.970), 3.310 axle ratio, max speed 101 mph, 163 km/h, consumption 32.8 m/imp gal, 27.3 m/US gal, 8.6 l x 100 km at 75 mph, 120 km/h.

105 hp power team

See 50 hp power team, except for:

ENGINE 97.4 cu in, 1,597 cc (3.15 x 3.13 in, 80 x 79.5 mm); max power (DIN): 105 hp (77 kW) at 6,000 rpm; max torque (DIN): 102 lb ft, 14.1 kg m (138 Nm) at 4,800 rpm; max engine rpm: 6,250; 65.7 hp/l (48.2 kW/l); light alloy head; 5 crankshaft bearings; valves: overhead, hydraulic tappets, CVH (compound valve hemispherical); camshafts: 1, overhead, cogged belt; lubrication: 6.8 imp pt, 8.1 US pt, 3.8 l, oil cooler; Bosch K-Jetronic injection; cooling: 13.7 imp pt, 16.5 US pt, 7.8 l.

FORD Orion 1600 Injection Ghia Saloon

TRANSMISSION gears: 5, fully synchronized; ratios: I 3.150, II 1.910, III 1.280, IV 0.950, V 0.760, rev 3.620; axle ratio: 4.290; width of rims: 6''; tyres: 185/60 HR x 14.

PERFORMANCE max speed: 116 mph, 186 km/h; power-weight ratio: 19.3 lb/hp (26.3 lb/kW), 8.8 kg/hp (11.9 kg/kW); carrying capacity: 893 lb, 405 kg; consumption: 34.9 m/imp gal, 29 m/US gal, 8.1 l x 100 km at 75 mph, 120 km/h.

CHASSIS front suspension: reinforced anti-roll bar.

BRAKES front disc, internal radial fins.

ELECTRICAL EQUIPMENT 43 Ah battery; 55 A alternator; contactless fully electronic ignition.

BODY saloon/sedan; 2+1 doors.

DIMENSIONS AND WEIGHT height: 54.05 in, 137 cm; weight: 2,029 lb, 920 kg.

PRACTICAL INSTRUCTIONS oil: engine 6.8 imp pt, 8.1 US pt, 3.8 l.

OPTIONALS light alloy wheels; 52 Ah battery; halogen headlamps; sunroof; electric windows.

Orion Series

PRICES EX WORKS:

		£
1	1300 GL 4-dr Saloon	**5,905***
2	1600 GL 4-dr Saloon	**6,200***
3	1600 Ghia 4-dr Saloon	**7,235***
4	1600 Injection Ghia 4-dr Saloon	**7,435***

Power team:	Standard for:	Optional for:
69 hp	1	—
79 hp	2,3	—
105 hp	4	—

69 hp power team

ENGINE front, transverse, 4 stroke; 4 cylinders, vertical, in line; 79.1 cu in, 1,296 cc (3.15 x 2.54 in, 80 x 64.5 mm); compression ratio: 9.5:1; max power (DIN): 69 hp (51 kW) at 6,000 rpm; max torque (DIN): 74 lb ft, 10.2 kg m (100 Nm) at 3,500 rpm; max engine rpm: 6,500; 53.2 hp/l (39.4 kW/l); cast iron block, light alloy head; 5 crankshaft bearings; valves: overhead, hydraulic tappets, CVH (compounds valve hemispherical); camshafts: 1, overhead, cogged belt; lubrication: gear pump, full flow filter (cartridge), 6.2 im pt, 7.4 US pt, 3.5 l; 1 Ford VV downdraught single barrel carburettor; fuel feed: mechanical pump; liquid-cooled, expansion tank, 13.4 imp pt, 16.1 US pt, 7.6 l, electric thermostatic fan.

TRANSMISSION driving wheels: front; clutch: single dry plate (diaphragm); gearbox: mechanical, in unit with final drive; gears: 4, fully synchronized; ratios: I 3.580, II 2.040, III 1.350, IV 0.950, rev 3.770; lever: central; final drive: spiral bevel; axle ratio: 3.840; width of rims: 5''; tyres: 155 SR x 13.

PERFORMANCE max speed: 98 mph, 157 km/h; power-weight ratio: 28 lb/hp (37.8 lb/kW), 12.7 kg/hp (17.2 kg/kW); carrying capacity: 937 lb, 425 kg; speed in top at 1,000 rpm: 16.3 mph, 26.2 km/h; consumption: 36.7 m/imp gal, 30.5 m/US gal, 7.7 l x 100 km at 75 mph, 120 km/h.

CHASSIS integral; front suspension: independent, by McPherson, lower wishbones, coil springs/telescopic damper struts, anti-roll bar; rear: independent, lower wishbones, trailing radius arms, coil springs, telescopic dampers.

STEERING rack-and-pinion.

BRAKES front disc (diameter 9.45 in, 24 cm), rear drum, dual circuit, rear compensator, servo; lining area: front 23.4 sq in, 151 sq cm, rear 28.8 sq in, 186 sq cm, total 52.2 sq in, 337 sq cm.

STEERING rack-and-pinion; turns lock to lock: 4.15.

BRAKES front disc, rear drum, rear compensator, servo; swept area: front 160.8 sq in, 1,037 sq cm, rear 71.2 sq in, 459 sq cm, total 232 sq in, 1,496 sq cm.

ELECTRICAL EQUIPMENT 12 V; 50 Ah battery; 45 A alternator; Bosch transistorized ignition; 2 headlamps.

DIMENSIONS AND WEIGHT wheel base: 102.68 in, 261 cm; tracks: 57.17 in, 145 cm front, 57.80 in, 147 cm rear; length: 172.99 in, 439 cm; width: 67.05 in, 170 cm; height: 55.43 in, 141 cm; weight: 2+1-dr Saloon 2,139 lb, 970 kg - 4+1-dr saloons 2,183 lb, 990 kg; weight distribution: 51.5% front, 48.5% rear; turning circle: 34.8 ft, 10.6 m; fuel tank: 13.2 imp gal, 15.8 US gal, 60 l.

BODY saloon/sedan; 2+1 or 4+1 doors; 5 seats, separate front seats; heated rear window; folding rear seat.

PRACTICAL INSTRUCTIONS fuel: 98 oct petrol; oil: engine 6.5 imp pt, 7.8 US pt, 3.7 l, SAE 15W-50, change every 6,200 miles, 10,000 km - gearbox 1.4 imp pt, 1.7 US pt, 0.8 l, SAE 80 EP, change every 12,400 miles, 20,000 km - final drive 1.8 imp pt, 2.1 US pt, 1 l, SAE 90, change every 12,400 miles, 20,000 km; greasing: none; tyre pressure: front 26 psi, 1.8 atm, rear 26 psi, 1.8 atm.

OPTIONALS sunroof; central door locking; metallic spray.

FORD Sierra 1600 L Saloon

ELECTRICAL EQUIPMENT 12 V; 35 Ah battery; 45 A alternator; contactless fully electronic ignition; 2 halogen headlamps.

DIMENSIONS AND WEIGHT wheel base: 94.57 in, 240 cm; tracks: 55.12 in, 140 cm front, 56.02 in, 142 cm rear; length: 165.08 in, 419 cm; width: 64.57 in, 164 cm; height: 54.92 in, 139 cm; weight: 1,929 lb, 875 kg; turning circle: 34.8 ft, 10.6 m; fuel tank: 10.6 imp gal, 12.7 US gal, 48 l.

BODY saloon/sedan; 4 doors; 5 seats, separate front seats, reclining backrests, headrests; heated rear window.

PRACTICAL INSTRUCTIONS fuel: 97 oct petrol; oil: engine 6.2 imp pt, 7.4 US pt, 3.5 l, SAE 10W-50, change every 6,200 miles, 10,000 km - gearbox and final drive 4.9 imp pt, 5.9 US pt, 2.8 l, SAE 80W-90, change every 18,600 miles, 30,000 km; greasing: none; tyre pressure: front 23 psi, 1.6 atm, rear 26 psi, 1.8 atm.

OPTIONALS 5-speed fully synchronized mechanical gearbox (I 3.580, II 2.040, III 1.350, IV 0.950, V 0.760, rev 3.770), consumption 40.4 m/imp gal, 33.6 m/US gal, 7 l x 100 km at 75 mph, 120 km/h; electric windows; sunroof; tinted glass; metallic spray.

79 hp power team

See 69 hp power team, except for:

ENGINE 97.4 cu in, 1,597 cc (3.15 x 3.13 in, 80 x 79.5 mm); max power (DIN): 79 hp (58 kW) at 5,800 rpm; max torque (DIN): 92 lb ft, 12.7 kg m (125 Nm) at 3,000 rpm; 49.5 hp/l (36.3 kW/l); cooling: 13.7 imp pt, 16.5 US pt, 7.8 l.

TRANSMISSION gears: 5, fully synchronized; ratios: I 3.150, II 1.910, III 1.280, IV 0.950, V 0.760, rev 3.620; axle ratio: 3.580.

PERFORMANCE max speed: 104 mph, 167 km/h; power-weight ratio: 24.8 lb/hp (33.8 lb/kW), 11.3 kg/hp (15.3 kg/kW); speed in top at 1,000 rpm: 17.3 mph, 27.8 km/h; consumption: 40.4 m/imp gal, 33.6 m/US gal, 7 l x 100 km at 75 mph, 120 km/h.

ELECTRICAL EQUIPMENT 43 Ah battery.

DIMENSIONS AND WEIGHT weight: 1,962 lb, 890 kg.

OPTIONALS Ford ATX automatic transmission with 3 ratios (I 2.790, II 1.610, III 1, rev 1.970), 3.310 axle ratio, max speed 101 mph, 163 km/h, consumption 34 m/imp gal, 28.3 m/US gal, 8.3 l x 100 km at 75 mph, 120 km/h.

105 hp power team

See 69 hp power team, except for:

ENGINE 97.4 cu in, 1,597 cc (3.15 x 3.13 in, 80 x 79.5 mm); max power (DIN): 105 hp (77 kW) at 6,000 rpm; max torque (DIN): 102 lb ft, 14.1 kg m (138 Nm) at 4,800 rpm; max engine rpm: 6,250; 65.7 hp/l (48.2 kW/l); lubrication: 6.8 imp pt, 8.1 US pt, 3.8 l, oil cooler; Bosch K-Jetronic injection; cooling: 13.7 imp pt, 16.5 US pt, 7.8 l.

TRANSMISSION gears: 5, fully synchronized; ratios: I 3.150, II 1.910, III 1.280, IV 0.950, V 0.760, rev 3.620; width of rims: 5.5"; tyres: 175/70 HR x 13.

PERFORMANCE max speed: 116 mph, 186 km/h; power-weight ratio: 19.3 lb/hp (26.3 lb/kW), 8.8 kg/hp (11.9 kg/kW).

CHASSIS front suspension: reinforced anti-roll bar; rear: anti-roll bar.

ELECTRICAL EQUIPMENT 43 Ah battery; 55 A alternator.

DIMENSIONS AND WEIGHT weight: 2,029 lb, 920 kg.

PRACTICAL INSTRUCTIONS oil: engine 6.8 imp pt, 8.1 US pt, 3.8 l.

Sierra Series

PRICES EX WORKS:

		£
1	1300 2+1-dr Saloon	**5,000***
2	1300 4+1-dr Saloon	**5,183***
3	1300 L 4+1-dr Saloon	**5,672***
4	1600 2+1-dr Saloon	**5,312***
5	1600 4+1-dr Saloon	**5,495***
6	1600 4+1-dr Estate	**6,012***
7	1600 L 2+1-dr Saloon	**5,802***
8	1600 L 4+1-dr Saloon	**5,984***
9	1600 L 4+1-dr Estate	**6,510***
10	1600 GL 4+1-dr Saloon	**6,748***
11	1600 GL 4+1-dr Estate	**7,274***
12	1600 Ghia 4+1-dr Saloon	**8,042***
13	2000 GL 4+1-dr Saloon	**7,168***
14	2000 GL 4+1-dr Estate	**7,694***
15	2000 Ghia 4+1-dr Saloon	**8,462***
16	2000 Ghia 4+1-dr Estate	**8,972***
17	2300 GL V6 Automatic 4+1-dr Saloon	**8,061***
18	2300 GL V6 Automatic 4+1-dr Estate	**8,587***
19	2300 Ghia V6 Automatic 4+1-dr Saloon	**9,355***
20	2300 Ghia V6 Automatic 4+1-dr Estate	**9,865***
21	2800 XR4i 2+1-dr Saloon	**9,656***
22	2300 Diesel 2+1-dr Saloon	**5,749***
23	2300 Diesel 4+1-dr Saloon	**5,932***
24	2300 Diesel 4+1-dr Estate	**6,449***
25	2300 L Diesel 2+1-dr Saloon	**6,238***
26	2300 L Diesel 4+1-dr Saloon	**6,421***
27	2300 L Diesel 4+1-dr Estate	**6,947***
28	2300 GL 4+1-dr Saloon	**7,185***
29	2300 GL 4+1-dr Estate	**7,711***

Power team:	Standard for:	Optional for:
60 hp	1 to 3	—
75 hp	4 to 12	—
105 hp	13 to 16	—
114 hp	17 to 20	—
150 hp	21	—
67 hp (diesel)	22 to 29	—

60 hp power team

ENGINE front, 4 stroke; 4 cylinders, vertical, in line; 78.9 cu in, 1,294 cc (3.11 x 2.60 in, 79 x 66 mm); compression ratio: 9:1; max power (DIN): 60 hp (44 kW) at 5,700 rpm; max torque (DIN): 72 lb ft, 10 kg m (98 Nm) at 3,100 rpm; max engine rpm: 6,200; 46.4 hp/l (34 kW/l); cast iron block and head; 5 crankshaft bearings; valves: overhead, Vee-slanted, rockers; camshafts: 1, overhead, cogged belt; lubrication: gear pump, full flow filter (cartridge), 6.5 imp pt, 7.8 US pt, 3.7 l; 1 Ford downdraught single barrel carburettor; fuel feed: mechanical pump; semi-sealed circuit cooling, expansion tank, 14.1 imp pt, 16.9 US pt, 8 l, electric thermostatic fan.

TRANSMISSION driving wheels: rear; clutch: single dry plate (diaphragm); gearbox: mechanical; gears: 4, fully synchronized; ratios: I 3.660, II 2.180, III 1.420, IV 1, rev 4.230; lever: central; final drive: hypoid bevel; axle ratio: 3.770; width of rims: 4.5"; tyres: 165 SR x 13.

PERFORMANCE max speeds: (I) 29 mph, 46 km/h; (II) 51 mph, 82 km/h; (III) 74 mph, 119 km/h; (IV) 94 mph, 152 km/h; power-weight ratio: 4+1-dr saloons 36.4 lb/hp (49.6 lb/kW), 16.5 kg/hp (22.5 kg/kW); carrying capacity: 1,058 lb, 480 kg; speed in direct drive at 1,000 rpm: 17.8 mph, 28.7 km/h; consumption: 35.8 m/imp gal, 29.8 m/US gal, 7.9 l x 100 km at 75 mph, 120 km/h.

CHASSIS integral; front suspension: independent, by McPherson, lower wishbones, coil springs/telescopic damper struts, anti-roll bar; rear: independent, lower wishbones, trailing radius arms, coil springs, telescopic dampers, anti-roll bar.

75 hp power team

See 60 hp power team, except for:

ENGINE 97.2 cu in, 1,593 cc (3.45 x 2.60 in, 87.7 x 66 mm); compression ratio: 9.2:1; max power (DIN): 75 hp (55 kW) at 5,300 rpm; max torque (DIN): 88 lb ft, 12.2 kg m (120 Nm) at 2,900 rpm; max engine rpm: 5,800; 47.1 hp/l (34.5 kW/l).

TRANSMISSION gearbox ratios: I 3.340, II 1.990, III 1.420, IV 1, rev 3.870; axle ratio: 3.620 - st. wagons 3.920; tyres: st. wagons 175 SR x 13.

PERFORMANCE max speed: 102 mph, 165 km/h; power-weight ratio: GL Saloon 30.2 lb/hp (41.2 lb/kW), 13.7 kg/hp (18.7 kg/kW); carrying capacity: 1,014 lb, 460 kg; consumption: 34.9 m/imp gal, 29 m/US gal, 8.1 l x 100 km at 75 mph, 120 km/h.

ELECTRICAL EQUIPMENT (for GL and Ghia models only) 55 A alternator.

DIMENSIONS AND WEIGHT length: GL Saloon 173.54 in, 441 cm - Ghia Saloon 174.21 in, 442 cm - Estate 176.81 in, 449 cm - GL Estate 177.36 in, 450 cm; width: GL Saloon 67.72 in, 172 cm - Ghia Saloon 67.91 in, 172 cm - Estate 67.40 in, 171 cm - GL Estate 68.07 in, 173 cm; height: st. wagons 56.61 in, 144 cm; weight: GL Saloon 2,271 lb, 1,030 kg - Ghia Saloon 2,337 lb, 1,060 kg - Estate 2,293 lb, 1,040 kg - L Estate 2,348 lb, 1,065 kg - GL Estate 2,381 lb, 1,080 kg.

BODY saloon/sedan, 2+1 or 4+1 doors - estate car/st. wagon, 4+1 doors.

OPTIONALS Economy version 4-speed mechanical gearbox (I 3.580, II 2.010, III 1.400, IV 1, rev 3.320), 3.140 axle ratio, max speed 101 mph, 162 km/h, consumption 38.2 m/imp gal, 31.8 m/US gal, 7.4 l x 100 km at 75 mph, 120 km/h; 5-speed mechanical gearbox (I 3.650, II 1.970, III 1.370, IV 1, V 0.820, rev 3.660), 3.380 axle ratio; consumption 36.7 m/imp gal, 30.3 m/US gal, 7.7 l x 100 km at 75 mph, 120 km/h; Ford C3 automatic transmission with 3 ratios (I 2.474, II 1.474, III 1, rev 2.111), consumption 33.2 m/imp gal, 27.7 m/US gal, 8.5 l x 100 km at 75 mph, 120 km/h; 185/70 or 195/70 R x 13 tyres; central door locking; electric windows; metallic spray.

FORD Sierra 1600 L Saloon

FORD Sierra 1600 L Estate

FORD Sierra 2000 Ghia Saloon

105 hp power team

See 60 hp power team, except for:

ENGINE 121.6 cu in, 1,993 cc (3.89 x 3.03 in, 90.8 x 76.9 mm); max power (DIN): 105 hp (77 kW) at 5,200 rpm; max torque (DIN): 116 lb ft, 16 kg m (157 Nm) at 4,000 rpm; 52.7 hp/l (38.6 kW/l); 1 Weber downdraught single barrel carburettor.

TRANSMISSION gearbox ratios: I 3.650, II 1.970, III 1.370, IV 1, rev 3.660; axle ratio: 3.380; width of rims: 5.5"; 165 HR x 13 - st. wagons 195/70 HR x 13.

PERFORMANCE max speed: 115 mph, 185 km/h; power-weight ratio: Ghia Estate 23.9 lb/hp (32.6 lb/kW), 10.9 kg/hp (14.8 kg/kW); consumption: Ghia Estate 34 m/imp gal, 28.3 m/US gal, 8.3 l x 100 km at 75 mph, 120 km/h.

BRAKES front internal radial fins.

ELECTRICAL EQUIPMENT 55 A alternator.

DIMENSIONS AND WEIGHT length: GL Saloon 173.54 in, 441 cm - Ghia Saloon 174.21 in, 442 cm - GL Estate 177.36 in, 450 cm - Ghia Estate 178.03 in, 452 cm; width: GL Saloon 67.72 in, 172 cm - Ghia Saloon 67.91 in, 172 cm - st. wagons 68.07 in, 173 cm; height: st. wagons 56.61 in, 144 cm; weight: GL Saloon 2,348 lb, 1,065 kg - Ghia Saloon 2,414 lb, 1,095 kg - GL Estate 2,437 lb, 1,105 kg - Ghia Estate 2,514 lb, 1,140 kg.

BODY saloon/sedan - estate car/st. wagon; 4+1 doors.

OPTIONALS 5-speed mechanical gearbox (I 3.650, II 1.970, III 1.370, IV 1, V 0.820, rev 3.660), consumption Ghia Estate 36.7 m/imp gal, 30.5 m/US gal, 7.7 l x 100 km at 75 mph, 120 km/h; Ford C3 automatic transmission with 3 ratios (I 2.474, II 1.474, III 1, rev 2.111), max speed 110 mph, 177 km/h, consumption Ghia Estate 29.4 m/imp gal, 24.5 m/US gal, 9.6 l x 100 km at 75 mph, 120 km/h; power steering; central door locking; electric windows; metallic spray.

114 hp power team

See 60 hp power team, except for:

ENGINE 6 cylinders, Vee-slanted at 60°; 139.9 cu in, 2,294 cc (3.54 x 2.37 in, 90 x 60.1 mm); max power (DIN): 114 hp (84 kW) at 5,300 rpm; max torque (DIN): 130 lb ft, 18 kg m (176 Nm) at 3,000 rpm; 49.6 hp/l (37 kW/l); 4 crankshaft bearings; valves: overhead, push-rods and rockers; camshafts: 1, at centre of Vee; lubrication: 7.4 imp pt, 8.9 US pt, 4.2 l; 1 Solex 35/35 EEIT downdraught twin barrel carburettor; cooling: 15 imp pt, 18 US pt, 8.5 l.

TRANSMISSION gearbox: Ford C3 automatic transmission, hydraulic torque converter and planetary gears with 3 ratios, possible manual selection; ratios: I 2.474, II 1.474, III 1, rev 2.111; axle ratio: 3.140 - st. wagons 3.380; width of rims: 5.5"; tyres: 185/70 HR x 13 - st. wagons 175 HR x 13.

PERFORMANCE max speed: 113 mph, 182 km/h; power-weight ratio: GL V6 Saloon 21.6 lb/hp (29.3 lb/kW), 9.8 kg/hp (13.3 kg/kW); consumption: 29.1 m/imp gal, 24.2 m/US gal, 9.7 l x 100 km at 75 mph, 120 km/h.

BRAKES front internal radial fins.

ELECTRICAL EQUIPMENT 55 A alternator.

DIMENSIONS AND WEIGHT length: GL V6 Saloon 173.54 in, 441 cm - Ghia V6 Saloon 174.21 in, 442 cm - GL V6 Estate 177.36 in, 450 cm - Ghia V6 Estate 178.03 in, 452 cm; width: GL V6 Saloon 67.72 in, 172 cm - Ghia V6 Saloon 67.91 in, 172 cm - st. wagons 68.07 in, 173 cm; height: st. wagons 56.61 in, 144 cm; weight: GL V6 Saloon 2,459 lb, 1,115 kg - Ghia V6 Saloon 2,525 lb, 1,145 kg - GL V6 Estate 2,547 lb, 1,155 kg - Ghia V6 Estate 2,624 lb, 1,190 kg.

BODY saloon/sedan - estate car/st. wagon; 4+1 doors.

PRACTICAL INSTRUCTIONS oil: engine 7.4 imp pt, 8.9 US pt, 4.2 l - gearbox 11.1 imp pt, 13.3 US pt, 6.3 l.

OPTIONALS (for st. wagons only) 4-speed mechanical gearbox (I 3.650, II 1.970, III 1.370, IV 1, rev 3.660); power steering; central door locking; electric windows; metallic spray.

150 hp power team

See 60 hp power team, except for:

ENGINE 6 cylinders, Vee-slanted at 60°; 170.4 cu in, 2,792 cc (3.66 x 2.70 in, 93 x 68.5 mm); max power (DIN): 150 hp (110 kW) at 5,700 rpm; max torque (DIN): 159 lb ft, 22 kg m (216 Nm) at 3,800 rpm; 53.7 hp/l (39.4 kW/l); 4 crankshaft bearings; camshafts: 1, at centre of Vee; valves: overhead, push-rods and rockers; lubrication: 7.4 imp pt, 8.9 US pt, 4.2 l; Bosch K-Jetronic injection; cooling: 15 imp pt, 18 US pt, 8.5 l.

TRANSMISSION gears: 5, fully synchronized; ratios: I 3.360, II 1.810, III 1.260, IV 1, V 0.820, rev 3.360; axle ratio: 3.620; tyres: 195/60 VR x 14.

PERFORMANCE max speed: 130 mph, 210 km/h; power-weight ratio: 17.3 lb/hp (23.6 lb/kW), 7.8 kg/hp (10.7 kg/kW); speed in top at 1,000 rpm: 24.2 mph, 38.9 km/h; consumption: 29.4 m/imp gal, 24.5 m/US gal, 9.6 l x 100 km at 75 mph, 120 km/h.

BRAKES front internal radial fins.

ELECTRICAL EQUIPMENT 44 Ah battery; 70 A alternator; 4 halogen headlamps.

DIMENSIONS AND WEIGHT weight: 2,591 lb, 1,175 kg.

BODY 2+1 doors; electric windows; light alloy wheels.

PRACTICAL INSTRUCTIONS oil: engine 7.4 imp pt, 8.9 US pt, 4.2 l.

67 hp (diesel) power team

See 60 hp power team, except for:

ENGINE Peugeot, diesel; 140.6 cu in, 2,304 cc (3.70 x 3.27 in, 94 x 83 mm); compression ratio: 22.2:1; max power (DIN): 67 hp (49 kW) at 4,200 rpm; max torque (DIN): 103 lb ft, 14.2 kg m (139 Nm) at 2,000 rpm; 29.1 hp/l (21.3 kW/l); light alloy head; valves: overhead, push-rods and rockers; camshafts: 1, side; lubrication: 9.9 imp pt, 11.8 US pt, 5.6 l; Rotodiesel injection pump; cooling: 16.7 imp pt, 20.1 US pt, 9.5 l.

TRANSMISSION gears: 5, fully synchronized; ratios: I 3.910, II 2.320, III 1.300, IV 1, V 0.820, rev. 3.660; axle ratio: 3.140; tyres: st. wagons 175 SR x 13.

PERFORMANCE max speed: 96 mph, 155 km/h; power-weight ratio: L saloons 38.7 lb/hp (52.9 lb/kW), 17.5 kg/hp (24 kg/kW); consumption: 42.2 m/imp gal, 35.1 m/US gal, 6.7 l x 100 km at 75 mph, 120 km/h.

ELECTRICAL EQUIPMENT 88 Ah battery; (for GL models only) 55 A alternator.

DIMENSIONS AND WEIGHT length: GL Saloon 173.54 in, 441 cm - Estate 176.81 in, 449 cm - GL Estate 177.36 in, 450 cm; width: GL Saloon 67.72 in, 172 cm - Estate 67.40 in, 171 cm - GL Estate 68.07 in, 173 cm; height: st. wagons 56.61 in, 144 cm; weight: saloons 2,547 lb, 1,155 kg - L saloons 2,591 lb, 1,175 kg - GL Saloon 2,635 lb, 1,195 kg - Estate 2,635 lb, 1,195 kg - L Estate 2,690 lb, 1,220 kg - GL Estate 2,723 lb, 1,235 kg.

BODY saloon/sedan, 2+1 or 4+1 doors - estate car/st. wagon, 4+1 doors.

PRACTICAL INSTRUCTIONS fuel: diesel; oil: engine 9.9 imp pt, 11.8 US pt,5.6 l.

OPTIONALS power steering; central door locking; electric windows; metallic spray.

Capri Series

PRICES EX WORKS: £

		£
1	1600 LS 2+1-dr Coupé	**5,320***
2	2000 S 2+1-dr Coupé	**6,385***
3	2.8 Injection 2+1-dr Coupé	**8,653***

Power team:	Standard for:	Optional for:
73 hp	1	—
101 hp	2	—
160 hp	3	—

73 hp power team

ENGINE front, 4 stroke; 4 cylinders, vertical, in line; 97.2 cu in, 1,593 cc (3.45 x 2.60 in, 87.7 x 66 mm); compression ratio: 9.2:1; max power (DIN): 73 hp (54 kW) at 5,300 rpm; max torque (DIN): 86 lb ft, 11.9 kg m (117 Nm) at 2,700 rpm; max engine rpm: 6,000; 45.8 hp/l (33.9 kW/l); cast iron block and head; 5 crankshaft bearings; valves: overhead, Vee-slanted, rockers; camshafts: 1, overhead, cogged belt; lubrication: rotary pump, full flow filter (cartridge), 6.5 im pt, 7.8 US pt, 3.7 l; 1 Ford VV downdraught carburettor; fuel feed: mechanical pump; water-cooled, 10.2 imp pt, 12.3 US pt, 5.8 l, electric thermostatic fan.

TRANSMISSION driving wheels: rear; clutch: single dry plate (diaphragm); gearbox: mechanical; gears: 4, fully synchronized; ratios: I 3.650, II 1.970, III 1.370, IV 1, rev 3.660; lever: central; final drive: hypoid bevel; axle ratio: 3.770; width of rims: 5.5"; tyres: 165 SR x 13.

PERFORMANCE max speed: 102 mph, 164 km/h; power-weight ratio: 30.5 lb/hp (41.2 lb/kW), 13.8 kg/hp (18.7 kg/kW); carrying capacity: 882 lb, 400 kg; speed in direct drive at 1,000 rpm: 16.6 mph, 26.7 km/h; consumption: 32.5 m/imp gal, 27 m/US gal, 8.7 l x 100 km at 75 mph, 120 km/h.

CHASSIS integral; front suspension: independent, by McPherson, coil springs/telescopic damper struts, lower transverse arm, anti-roll bar; rear: rigid axle, semi-elliptic leafsprings, rubber springs, anti-roll bar, telescopic dampers.

STEERING rack-and-pinion.

BRAKES front disc (diameter 9.61 in, 24.4 cm), rear drum, servo; lining area: front 17.4 sq in, 151 sq cm, rear 45.4 sq in, 293 sq cm, total 62.8 sq in, 444 sq cm.

ELECTRICAL EQUIPMENT 35 Ah battery; 55 A alternator.

DIMENSIONS AND WEIGHT wheel base: 100.79 in, 256 cm; tracks: 53.15 in, 135 cm front, 54.33 in, 138 cm rear; length: 174.80 in, 444 cm; width: 66.93 in, 170 cm; height: 51.97 in, 132 cm; ground clearance: 4.92 in, 12.5 cm; weight : 2,227 lb, 1,010 kg; turning circle: 35.4 ft, 10.8 m; fuel tank: 12.8 imp gal, 15.3 US gal, 58 l.

BODY coupé; 2+1 doors; 5 seats, separate front seats, reclining backrests; folding rear seat.

PRACTICAL INSTRUCTIONS fuel: 97 oct petrol; oil: engine 5.6 imp pt, 6.8 US pt, 3.2 l, SAE 20W-40, change every 6,200 miles, 10,000 km - gearbox 2.3 imp pt, 2.7 US pt, 1.3 l, SAE 80, change every 12,400 miles, 20,000 km - final drive 1.9 imp pt, 2.3 US pt, 1.1 l, SAE 90, change every 12,400 miles, 20,000 km; greasing: none; tyre pressure: front 21 psi, 1.5 atm, rear 26 psi, 1.8 atm.

OPTIONALS 5-speed mechanical gearbox (I 3.650, II 1.970, III 1.370, IV 1, V 0.825, rev 3.370), consumption 34.4 m/imp gal, 28.7 m/US gal, 8.2 l x 100 km at 75 mph, 120 km/h; heatd rear window; rear window wiper-washer; headrests on front seats; sunroof; vinyl roof; halogen headlamps; metallic spray; 185/70 SR x 13 tyres.

FORD Capri 2.8 Injection Coupé

FORD Granada 2300 L Saloon

101 hp power team

See 73 hp power team, except for:

ENGINE 121.68 cu in, 1,993 cc (3.89 x 3.03 in, 90.8 x 76.9 mm); max power (DIN): 101 hp (74 kW) at 5,200 rpm; max torque (DIN): 113 lb ft, 15.6 kg m (153 Nm) at 4,000 rpm; max engine rpm: 6,500; 50.7 hp/l (37.8 kW/l); 1 Weber 32 36 DGAV downdraught single barrel carburettor; cooling: 10.7 imp pt, 12.9 US pt, 6.1 l.

TRANSMISSION gears: 5, fully synchronized (standard); ratios: I 3.650, II 1.970, III 1.370, IV 1, V 0.825, rev 3.370; axle ratio: 3.440; width of rims: 6"; tyres: 185/70 HR x 13 (standard).

PERFORMANCE max speed: 113 mph, 182 km/h; power-weight ratio: 22.5 lb/hp (30.7 lb/kW), 10.2 kg/hp (13.9 kg/kW); speed in direct drive at 1,000 rpm: 18.5 mph, 29.8 km/h.

ELECTRICAL EQUIPMENT 44 Ah battery; 4 headlamps.

DIMENSIONS AND WEIGHT weight: 2,271 lb, 1,030 kg.

OPTIONALS Ford C3 automatic transmission, hydraulic torque converter and planetary gears with 3 ratios (I 2.474, II 1.474, III 1, rev 2.111), max ratio of converter at stall 2, possible manual selection, max speed 108 mph, 174 km/h, consumption 29.7 m/imp gal, 24.8 m/US gal, 9.5 l x 100 km at 75 mph, 120 km/h; power steering.

160 hp power team

See 73 hp power team, except for:

ENGINE 6 cylinders, Vee-slanted at 60°; 170.4 cu in, 2,792 cc (3.66 x 2.70 in, 93 x 68.5 mm); max power (DIN): 160 hp (118 kW) at 5,700 rpm; max torque (DIN): 163 lb ft, 22.5 kg m (221 Nm) at 4,300 rpm; 57.3 hp/l (42.3 kW/l); 4 crankshaft bearings; valves: overhead, push-rods and rockers; camshafts: 1, at centre of Vee; lubrication: 7.4 imp pt, 8.9 US pt, 4.2 l, oil cooler; Bosch K-Jetronic injection; cooling: 15.3 imp pt, 18.4 US pt, 8.7 l.

TRANSMISSION gearbox ratios: I 3.360, II 1.810, III 1.260, IV 1, V 0.825, rev 3.370; axle ratio: 3.090; width of rims: 7"; tyres: 205/60 VR x 13.

PERFORMANCE max speed: 130 mph, 210 km/h; power-weight ratio: 16.9 lb/hp (23 lb/kW), 7.7 kg/hp (10.4 kg/kW); speed in top at 1,000 rpm: 21.1 mph, 33.9 km/h; consumption: 30.1 m/imp gal, 25 m/US gal, 9.4 l x 100 km at 75 mph, 120 km/h.

CHASSIS front and rear suspension: reinforced anti-roll bar.

STEERING servo.

BRAKES front disc (diameter 9.72 in, 24.7 cm), internal radial fins, rear drum, rear compensator.

ELECTRICAL EQUIPMENT 52 Ah battery; 70 A alternator; electronic ignition; 4 halogen headlamps, fog lamps (standard).

DIMENSIONS AND WEIGHT tracks: 55.12 in, 140 cm front, 56.34 in, 143 cm rear; weight: 2,712 lb, 1,230 kg.

BODY light alloy wheels; tinted glass.

PRACTICAL INSTRUCTIONS oil: engine 7.4 imp pt, 8.9 US pt, 4.2 l.

FORD Granada 2300 L Saloon

Granada Series

PRICES EX WORKS:

		£
1	2000 L 4-dr Saloon	7,545*
2	2000 L 4+1-dr Estate	7,826*
3	2000 GL 4-dr Saloon	9,226*
4	2000 GL 4+1-dr Estate	9,453*
5	2300 L 4-dr Saloon	8,362*
6	2300 L 4+1-dr Estate	8,643*
7	2300 GL 4-dr Saloon	9,834*
8	2300 GL 4+1-dr Estate	10,061*
9	2300 Ghia X 4-dr Saloon	11,854*
10	2800 GL Automatic 4-dr Saloon	10,527*
11	2800 GL Automatic 4+1-dr Estate	10,754*
12	2800 Ghia Automatic 4+1-dr Saloon	10,919*
13	2800 Ghia Automatic 4+1-dr Estate	11,097*
14	2800 Ghia X Automatic 4-dr Saloon	12,547*
15	2800 Ghia X Automatic 4+1-dr Estate	12,710*
16	2800 Injection 4-dr Saloon	11,734*
17	2800 Injection 4+1-dr Estate	11,960*
18	2800i Ghia X Automatic 4-dr Saloon	13,099*
19	2800i Ghia X Automatic 4+1-dr Estate	13,262*
20	2500 Diesel L 4-dr Saloon	8,579*
21	2500 Diesel L 4+1-dr Estate	8,860*

Power team:	Standard for:	Optional for:
105 hp	1 to 4	—
114 hp	5 to 9	—
135 hp	10 to 15	—
150 hp	16 to 19	—
69 hp (diesel)	20,21	—

105 hp power team

ENGINE front, 4 stroke; 4 cylinders, in line; 121.6 cu in, 1,993 cc (3.89 x 3.03 in, 90.8 x 76.9 mm); compression ratio: 9.2:1; max power (DIN): 105 hp (77 kW) at 5,200 rpm; max torque (DIN): 116 lb ft, 16 kg m (157 Nm) at 4,000 rpm; max engine rpm: 5,800; 52.7 hp/l (38.6 kW/l); cast iron block and head; 5 crankshaft bearings; valves: overhead, Vee-slanted, rockers; camshafts: 1, overhead, cogged belt; lubrication: rotary pump, full flow filter (cartridge), 6.5 im pt, 7.8 US pt, 3.7 l; 1 Weber downdraught single barrel carburettor; fuel feed: mechanical pump; semi-sealed circuit cooling, expansion tank, 13 imp pt, 15.6 US pt, 7.4 l, electric thermostatic fan.

TRANSMISSION driving wheels: rear; clutch: single dry plate (diaphragm); gearbox: mechanical; gears: 5, fully synchronized; ratios: I 3.650, II 1.970, III 1.370, IV 1, V 0.816, rev 3.660; lever: central; final drive: hypoid bevel; axle ratio: 3.890; width of rims: 6"; tyres: 185 SR x 14.

PERFORMANCE max speed: 104 mph, 168 km/h - st. wagons 100 mph, 161 km/h; power-weight ratio: saloons 25.9 lb/hp (35.4 lb/kW), 11.8 kg/hp (16 kg/kW); carrying capacity: 1,136 lb, 515 kg; consumption: 29.7 m/imp gal, 24.8 m/US gal, 9.5 l x 100 km at 75 mph, 120 km/h.

CHASSIS integral, front and rear auxiliary frames; front suspension: independent, wishbones, lower trailing links, coil springs, anti-roll bar, telescopic dampers; rear: independent, semi-trailing arms, coil springs, telescopic dampers.

STEERING rack-and-pinion, servo.

BRAKES front disc (diameter 10.31 in, 26.2 cm), rear drum, dual circuit, servo; lining area: front 40.6 sq in, 262 sq cm, rear 35.4 sq in, 228.6 sq cm - st. wagons 39.4 sq in, 254 sq cm, total 76 sq in, 490.6 sq cm - st. wagons 80 sq in, 516 sq cm.

ELECTRICAL EQUIPMENT 12 V; 43 Ah battery; 55 A alternator; transistorized ignition; 2 headlamps.

DIMENSIONS AND WEIGHT wheel base: 109.05 in, 277 cm; tracks: 59.45 in, 151 cm front, 60.24 in, 153 cm rear; length: 187.68 in, 477 cm; width: 70.87 in, 180 cm; height: 55.91 in, 142 cm; weight: saloons 2.723 lb, 1,235 kg - st. wagons 2,866 lb, 1,300 kg; turning circle: 36.7 ft, 11.2 m; fuel tank: 14.3 imp gal, 17.2 US gal, 65 l.

BODY saloon/sedan, 4 doors - estate car/st. wagon, 4+1 doors; 5 seats, separate front seats; heated rear window.

PRACTICAL INSTRUCTIONS fuel: 98 oct petrol; oil: engine 6.5 imp pt, 7.8 US pt, 3.7 l, SAE 10W-40, change every 6,200 miles, 10,000 km - gearbox 3 imp pt, 3.6 US pt, 1.8 l, SAE 80, no change recommended - final drive 3 imp pt, 3.6 US pt, 1.8 l, no change recommended; greasing: none; tyre pressure: front 26 psi, 1.8 atm, rear 26 psi, 1.8 atm.

OPTIONALS Ford C3 automatic transmission with 3 ratios (I 2.470, II 1.470, III 1, rev 2.110), max speed 99 mph, 160 km/h, consumption 25.9 m/imp gal, 21.6 m/US gal, 10.9 l x 100 km at 75 mph, 120 km/h; 52 Ah battery; sunroof; metallic spray.

114 hp power team

See 105 hp power team, except for:

ENGINE 6 cylinders, Vee-slanted at 60°; 139.9 cu in, 2,294 cc (3.54 x 2.37 in, 90 x 60.1 mm); compression ratio: 9:1; max power (DIN): 114 hp (85 kW) at 5,300 rpm; max torque (DIN): 130 lb ft, 18 kg m (176 Nm) at 3,000 rpm; max engine rpm: 5,700; 49.6 hp/l (37 kW/l); 4 crankshaft bearings; valves: overhead, push-rods and rockers; camshafts: 1, at centre of Vee; lubrication: 7.4 imp pt, 8.9 US pt, 4.2 l; 1 Solex 35/35 EEII downdraught twin barrel carburettor; cooling: 15.5 imp pt, 18.6 US pt, 8.8 l.

TRANSMISSION axle ratio: 3.640.

PERFORMANCE max speed: 106 mph, 171 km/h - st. wagon 103 mph, 166 km/h; power-weight ratio: saloons 24.7 lb/hp (33.1 lb/kW), 11.2 kg/hp (15 kg/kW); speed in top at 1,000 rpm: 18.5 mph, 29.8 km/h; consumption: saloons 28.2 m/imp gal, 23.5 m/US gal, 10 l x 100 km at 75 mph, 120 km/h.

BRAKES lining area (for saloons only): front 23.4 sq in, 151 sq cm, rear 75.3 sq in, 486 sq cm, total 98.7 sq in, 637 sq cm.

DIMENSIONS AND WEIGHT weight: saloons 2,811 lb, 1,275 kg - st. wagons 2,955 lb, 1,340 kg.

PRACTICAL INSTRUCTIONS oil: engine 7 imp pt, 8.5 US pt, 4 l.

OPTIONALS Ford C3 automatic transmission, hydraulic torque converter and planetary gears with 3 ratios (I 2.474, II

114 HP POWER TEAM

1.474, III 1, rev 2.111), max ratio of converter at stall 2, possible manual selection, oil cooler, max speed 101 mph, 163 km/h, consumption sedans 24.1 m/imp gal, 20.1 m/US gal, 11.7 l x 100 km at 75 mph, 120 km/h; 55 Ah battery; light alloy wheels (for GL models only); air-conditioning.

135 hp power team

See 105 hp power team, except for:

ENGINE 6 cylinders, Vee-slanted at 60°; 170.4 cu in, 2,792 cc (3.66 x 2.70 in, 93 x 68.5 mm); max power (DIN): 135 hp (99 kW) at 5,200 rpm; max torque (DIN): 159 lb ft, 22 kg m (216 Nm) at 3,000 rpm; max engine rpm: 5,700; 48.4 hp/l (35.6 kW/l); 4 crankshaft bearings; valves: overhead, push-rods and rockers; camshafts: 1, at centre of Vee; lubrication: 7.4 imp pt, 8.9 US pt, 4.2 l; 1 Solex downdraught twin barrel carburettor; cooling: 15.8 imp pt, 19 US pt, 9 l.

TRANSMISSION ratios: I 3.360, II 1.810, III 1.260, IV 1, V 0.825, rev 3.370; axle ratio: 3.450; tyres: 185 HR x 14.

PERFORMANCE max speed: 112 mph, 181 km/h - st. wagons 109 mph, 175 km/h; power-weight ratio: saloons 21.3 lb/hp (29.1 lb/kW), 9.7 kg/hp (13.2 kg/kW); speed in top at 1,000 rpm: 20.7 mph, 33.3 km/h; consumption: saloons 27.4 m/imp gal, 22.8 m/US gal, 10.3 l x 100 km at 75 mph, 120 km/h.

BRAKES front: internal radial fins; lining area: (for sedans only) front: 29.3 sq in, 189 sq cm, rear 75.3 sq in, 486 sq cm, total 104.6 sq in, 675 sq cm.

DIMENSIONS AND WEIGHT weight: saloons 2,977 lb, 1,350 kg - st. wagons 3,098 lb, 1,405 kg.

PRACTICAL INSTRUCTIONS oil: engine 7.4 imp pt, 8.9 US pt, 4.2 l.

OPTIONALS Ford C3 automatic transmission, hydraulic torque converter and planetary gears with 3 ratios (I 2.474, II 1.474, III 1, rev 2.111), max ratio of converter at stall 2, possible manual selection, oil cooler, max speed 109 mph, 175 km/h, consumption saloons 23.9 m/imp gal, 19.9 m/US gal, 11.8 l x 100 km at 75 mph, 120 km/h; 55 Ah battery; air-conditioning.

150 hp power team

See 105 hp power team, except for:

ENGINE 6 cylinders, Vee-slanted at 60°; 170.4 cu in, 2,792 cc (3.66 x 2.70 in, 93 x 68.5 mm); max power (DIN): 150 hp (110 kW) at 5,700 rpm; max torque (DIN): 159 lb ft, 22 kg m (216 Nm) at 4,000 rpm; max engine rpm: 6,200; 53.7 hp/l (39.4 kW/l); 4 crankshaft bearings; valves: overhead, push-rods and rockers; camshafts: 1, at centre of Vee; lubrication: 7.4 imp pt, 8.9 US pt, 4.2 l; Bosch K-Jetronic injection; cooling: 16.7 imp pt, 20.1 US pt, 9.5 l.

TRANSMISSION gearbox ratios: I 3.360, II 1.810, III 1.260, IV 1, V 0.825, rev 3.370; axle ratio: 3.450; tyres: 190/65 HR x 390 TRX.

PERFORMANCE max speed: 118 mph, 190 km/h - st. wagons 114 mph, 184 km/h; power-weight ratio: saloons 20.3 lb/hp (27.7 lb/kW), 9.2 kg/hp (12.5 kg/kW); speed in top at 1,000 rpm: 21.2 mph, 33.9 km/h; consumption: saloons 28 m/imp gal, 23.3 m/US gal, 10.1 l x 100 km at 75 mph, 120 km/h.

BRAKES front internal radial fins; lining area (for sedans only): front 29.3 sq in, 189 sq cm, rear 75.3 sq in, 486 sq cm, total 104.6 sq in, 675 sq cm.

ELECTRICAL EQUIPMENT 70 A alternator.

DIMENSIONS AND WEIGHT weight: saloons 3,043 lb, 1,380 kg - st. wagons 3,153 lb, 1,430 kg.

PRACTICAL INSTRUCTIONS oil: engine 7 imp pt, 8.5 US pt, 4.2 l.

OPTIONALS Ford C3 automatic transmission, hydraulic torque converter and planetary gears with 3 ratios (I 2.474, II 1.474, III 1, rev 2.111), max ratio of converter at stall 2, possible manual selection, oil cooler, max speed 114 mph, 184 km/h, consumption saloons 24.4 m/imp gal, 20.3 m/US gal, 11.6 l x 100 km at 75 mph, 120 km/h.

69 hp (diesel) power team

See 105 hp power team, except for:

ENGINE Peugeot, diesel; 152.4 cu in, 2,499 cc (3.70 x 3.54 in, 94 x 90 mm); compression ratio: 23:1; max power (DIN): 69 hp (51 kW) at 4,200 rpm; max torque (DIN): 109 lb ft, 15.1 kg m (148 Nm) at 2,000 rpm; max engine rpm: 4,600; 27.6 hp/l (20.4 kW/l); light alloy head; valves: overhead, in line, push-rods and rockers; camshafts: 1, side; lubrication: 9.9 imp pt, 11.8 US pt, 5.6 l; Rotodiesel injection pump; cooling: 18 imp pt, 21.6 US pt, 10.2 l.

TRANSMISSION gearbox ratios: I 3.910, II 2.320, III 1.400, IV 1, V 0.816, rev 3.660; axle ratio: Saloon 3.640 - Estate 3.890.

GINETTA G 25

PERFORMANCE max speed: 90 mph, 145 km/h - Estate 86 mph, 138 km/h; power-weight ratio: Saloon 43.9 lb/hp (59.3 lb/kW), 19.9 kg/hp (26.9 kg/kW); consumption: Saloon 32.1 m/imp gal, 26.7 m/US gal, 8.8 l x 100 km at 75 mph, 120 km/h.

ELECTRICAL EQUIPMENT 88 Ah battery.

DIMENSIONS AND WEIGHT weight: Saloon 3,021 lb, 1,370 kg - Estate 3,164 lb, 1,435 kg.

PRACTICAL INSTRUCTIONS fuel: diesel; oil: engine 9.9 imp pt, 11.8 US pt, 5.6 l.

GINETTA — GREAT BRITAIN

G 25

PRICE EX WORKS: £ 7,500

ENGINE Ford, central, 4 stroke; 4 cylinders, in line; 97.4 cu in, 1,597 cc (3.15 x 3.13 in, 80 x 79.5 mm); compression ratio: 9.5:1; max power (DIN): 96 hp (71 kW) at 6,000 rpm; max torque (DIN): 98 lb ft, 13.5 kg m (132 Nm) at 4,000 rpm; max engine rpm: 6,250; 60.1 hp/l (44.5 kW/l); cast iron block, light alloy head; 5 crankshaft bearings; valves: overhead, hydraulic tappets; camshafts: 1, overhead; lubrication: gear pump, full flow filter (cartridge), 7 imp pt, 8.5 US pt, 4 l; 1 Weber DFT downdraught twin barrel carburettor; fuel feed: mechanical pump; water-cooled, 16 imp pt, 19.2 US pt, 9.1 l.

TRANSMISSION driving wheels: rear; clutch: single dry plate (diaphragm); gearbox: mechanical, in unit with final drive; gears: 4, fully synchronized; ratios: I 3.150, II 1.910, III 1.270, IV 0.950, rev 3.610; lever: central; final drive: spiral bevel; axle ratio: 3.840; width of rims: 6''; tyres: 185/60 x 14.

PERFORMANCE max speed: 120 mph, 193 km/h; power-weight ratio: 14.6 lb/hp (19.6 lb/kW), 6.6 kg/hp (8.9 kg/kW); carrying capacity: 353 lb, 160 kg; acceleration: 0-50 mph (0-80 km/h) 5 sec; speed in top at 1,000 rpm: 18.1 mph, 29.1 km/h; consumption: 36 m/imp gal, 30.2 m/US gal, 7.8 l x 100 km.

CHASSIS box-type platform; front suspension: independent, wishbones, coil springs, anti-roll bar, telescopic dampers; rear: independent, lower wishbones, coil springs.

STEERING rack-and-pinion.

BRAKES disc, dual circuit; lining area: front 18.6 sq in, 120 sq cm, rear 18.6 sq in, 120 sq cm, total 37.2 sq in, 240 sq cm.

ELECTRICAL EQUIPMENT 12 V; 43 Ah battery; 45 A alternator; Motorcraft contactless electronic ignition; 2 headlamps.

DIMENSIONS AND WEIGHT wheel base: 83 in, 211 cm; front and rear track: 54.25 in, 138 cm; length: 146 in, 371 cm; width: 61 in, 155 cm; height: 47.75 in, 119 cm; ground clearance: 5 in, 12.7 cm; weight: 1,400 lb, 635 kg; weight distribution: 45% front, 55% rear; fuel tank: 7.5 imp gal, 9 US gal, 34 l.

BODY coupé, in reinforced plastic material; 2 doors; 2 separate seats; laminated windscreen; heated rear window.

PRACTICAL INSTRUCTIONS fuel: 97 oct petrol; tyre pressure: front 20 psi, 1.4 atm, rear 22 psi, 1.5 atm.

GP — GREAT BRITAIN

Talon

PRICE EX WORKS: £ 6,500*

ENGINE Volkswagen, rear, 4 stroke; 4 cylinders, horizontally opposed; 96.7 cu in, 1,584 cc (3.37 x 2.72 in, 85.5 x 69 mm); compression ratio: 7.5:1; max power (DIN): 50 hp (37 kW) at 4,000 rpm; max torque (DIN): 78 lb ft, 10.7 kg m (105 Nm) at 2,800 rpm; max engine rpm: 4,600; 31.6 hp/l (23.3

GP Spyder

GP Talon

GP Madison Coupé

kW/l); block with cast iron liners and light alloy fins, light alloy head; 4 crankshaft bearings; valves: overhead, push-rods and rockers; lubrication: gear pump, 4.4 imp pt, 5.3 US pt, 2.5 l; camshafts: 1 Solex 34 PICT downdraught carburettor; fuel feed: mechanical pump; air-cooled.

TRANSMISSION driving wheels: rear; clutch: single dry plate; gearbox: mechanical; gears: 4, fully synchronized; ratios: I 3.760, II 2.060, III 1.260, IV 0.930, rev 4.010; lever: central; final drive: spiral bevel; axle ratio: 3.875; width of rims: 7''; tyres: 195 VR x 14.

PERFORMANCE max speed: 85 mph, 136 km/h; power-weight ratio: 24 lb/hp (32.4 lb/kW), 10.9 kg/hp (14.7 kg/kW); carrying capacity: 1,200 lb, 545 kg; consumption: 30-35 m/imp gal, 25-29 m/US gal, 9.4-8.1 l x 100 km.

CHASSIS backbone platform; front suspension: independent, twin swinging longitudinal trailing arms, transverse laminated torsion bars, anti-roll bar, telescopic dampers; rear: independent, swinging semi-axles, swinging longitudinal trailing arms, transverse torsion bars, telescopic dampers.

STEERING worm and roller; turns lock to lock: 2.60.

BRAKES drum; lining area: total 111 sq in, 716 sq cm.

ELECTRICAL EQUIPMENT 12 V; 50 Ah battery; 270 W dynamo; Bosch distributor; 2 headlamps.

DIMENSIONS AND WEIGHT wheel base: 94.49 in, 240 cm; tracks: 51.57 in, 131 cm front, 53.15 in, 135 cm rear; length: 78.74 in, 200 cm; width: 57 in, 145 cm; height: 47.24 in, 120 cm; ground clearance: 11.81 in, 30 cm; weight: 1,200 lb, 544 kg; turning circle: 36 ft, 11 m; fuel tank: 9 imp gal, 10.8 US gal, 41 l.

BODY sports, in fiberglass material; 2 gullwing doors; 2+2 seats, separate front seats, reclining backrests.

PRACTICAL INSTRUCTIONS fuel: 87 oct petrol.

Spyder

PRICE EX WORKS: £ 6,300*

ENGINE Volkswagen, rear, 4 stroke; 4 cylinders, horizontally opposed; 96.7 cu in, 1,584 cc (3.37 x 2.72 in, 85.5 x 69 mm); compression ratio: 7.5:1; max power (DIN): 50 hp (37 kW) at 4,000 rpm; max torque (DIN): 78 lb ft, 10.7 kg m (105 Nm) at 2,800 rpm; max engine rpm: 4,600; 31.6 hp/l (23.3 kW/l); block with cast iron liners and light alloy fins, light alloy head; 4 crankshaft bearings; valves: overhead, push-rods and rockers; camshafts: 1, overhead; lubrication: gear pump, full flow filter, 4.4 imp pt, 5.3 US pt, 2.5 l; 1 Solex 34 PICT downdraught carburettor; fuel feed: mechanical pump; air-cooled.

TRANSMISSION driving wheels: rear; clutch: single dry plate (diaphragm); gearbox: mechanical; gears: 4, fully synchronized; ratios: I 3.760, II 2.060, III 1.260, IV 0.930, rev 4.010; lever: central; final drive: spiral bevel; axle ratio: 3.875; width of rims: 4.5''; tyres: 165 x 15.

PERFORMANCE max speed: 98 mph, 160 km/h; power-weight ratio: 20 lb/hp (27.2 lb/kW), 9.1 kg/hp (12.3 kg/kW); carrying capacity: 600 lb, 270 kg; acceleration: 0-50 mph (0-80 km/h) 9 sec; consumption: 45 m/imp gal, 37.3 m/US gal, 6.3 l x 100 km.

CHASSIS backbone platform; front suspension: independent, swinging longitudinal trailing arms, transverse torsion bar, anti-roll bar, telescopic dampers; rear: independent, swinging semi-axles, swinging longitudinal trailing arms, transverse torsion bar, telescopic dampers.

STEERING worm and roller; turns lock to lock: 2.60.

BRAKES drum; lining area: total 111 sq in, 716 sq cm.

ELECTRICAL EQUIPMENT 12 V; 50 Ah battery; 270 W alternator; Bosch distributor; 2 headlamps.

DIMENSIONS AND WEIGHT wheel base: 83.20 in, 211 cm; tracks: 51.57 in, 131 cm front, 51 in, 130 cm rear; length: 149.61 in, 380 cm; width: 59.06 in, 150 cm; height: 35.43 in, 90 cm; ground clearance: 6 in, 15 cm; weight: 1,000 lb, 454 kg; weight distribution: 40% front, 60% rear; turning circle: 36 ft, 11 m; fuel tank: 4.5 imp gal, 5.4 US gal, 21 l.

BODY sport; 2 doors; 2 separate seats.

PRACTICAL INSTRUCTIONS fuel: 91 oct petrol.

Madison Roadster

PRICE EX WORKS: £ 5,500*

ENGINE Volkswagen, rear, 4 stroke; 4 cylinders, horizontally opposed; 96.7 cu in, 1,584 cc (3.37 x 2.72 in, 85.5 x 69 mm); compression ratio: 7.5:1; max power (DIN): 50 hp (37 kW) at 4,000 rpm; max torque (DIN): 78 lb ft, 10.7 kg m (105 Nm) at 2,800 rpm; max engine rpm: 4,600; 31.6 hp/l (23.3 kW/l); block with cast iron liners and light alloy fins, light alloy head; 4 crankshaft bearings; valves: overhead, push-rods and rockers; camshafts: 1, overhead; lubrication: gear pump, 4.4 imp pt, 5.3 US pt, 2.5 l; 1 Solex 34 PICT downdraught carburettor; fuel feed: mechanical pump; air-cooled.

TRANSMISSION driving wheels: rear; clutch: single dry plate; gearbox: mechanical; gears: 4, fully synchronized; ratios: I 3.760, II 2.060, III 1.260, IV 0.930, rev 4.010; lever: central; final drive: spiral bevel; axle ratio: 3.875; width of rims: 6''; tyres: 185/70 x 14.

PERFORMANCE max speed: 85 mph, 136 km/h; power-weight ratio: 26 lb/hp (35.4 lb/kW), 11.8 kg/hp (16 kg/kW); carrying capacity: 600 lb, 270 kg; consumption: 35 m/imp gal, 29 m/US gal, 8.1 l x 100 km.

CHASSIS backbone platform; front suspension: independent, swinging longitudinal trailing arms, transverse torsion bar, anti-roll bar, telescopic dampers; rear: independent, swinging semi-axles, swinging longitudinal trailing arms, transverse torsion bar, telescopic dampers.

STEERING worm and roller; turns lock to lock: 2.60.

BRAKES drum; lining area: total 111 sq in, 716 sq cm.

ELECTRICAL EQUIPMENT 12 V; 50 Ah battery; 270 W alternator; Bosch distributor; 2 headlamps.

DIMENSIONS AND WEIGHT wheel base: 95.67 in, 243 cm; tracks: 51.57 in, 131 cm front, 53.15 in, 135 cm rear; length: 147.64 in, 375 cm; width: 62.99 in, 160 cm; height: 66.93 in, 170 cm; ground clearance: 5.50 in, 14 cm; weight: 1,300 lb, 590 kg; weight distribution: 40% front, 60% rear; turning circle: 36 ft, 11 m; fuel tank: 9 imp gal, 10.8 US gal, 41 l.

BODY roadster, in plastic material; 2 seats.

PRACTICAL INSTRUCTIONS fuel: 87 oct petrol.

OPTIONALS wire wheels; light alloy wheels.

Madison Coupé

PRICE EX WORKS: £ 6,000*

ENGINE Ford, front, 4 stroke; 4 cylinders, in line; 97.2 cu in, 1,593 cc (3.45 x 2.60 in, 87.7 x 66 mm); compression ratio: 9.2:1; max power (DIN): 75 hp (55 kW) at 5,300 rpm; max torque (DIN): 88 lb ft, 12.2 kg m (120 Nm) at 2,900 rpm; max engine rpm: 5,800; 47.1 hp/l (34.5 kW/l); cast iron block and head; 5 crankshaft bearings; valves: overhead; camshafts: 1, overhead; lubrication: gear pump, 6.5 imp pt, 7.8 US pt, 3.7 l; 1 Ford downdraught carburettor; fuel feed: mechanical pump; water-cooled, 14.1 imp pt, 16.9 US pt, 8 l.

TRANSMISSION driving wheels: rear; clutch: single dry plate; gearbox: mechanical; gears: 4, fully synchronized; ratios: I 3.580, II 2.010, III 1.400, IV 1, rev 3.320; lever: central; final drive: hypoid bevel; axle ratio: 3.770; width of rims: 6''; tyres: 185/70 x 14.

PERFORMANCE carrying capacity: 353 lb, 160 kg.

CHASSIS space-frame; front suspension: independent, wishbones, coil springs, anti-roll bar, telescopic dampers; rear: rigid axle, lower longitudinal trailing arms, upper oblique torque arms, coil springs, telescopic dampers.

STEERING rack-and-pinion; turns lock to lock: 3.70.

BRAKES front disc, rear drum.

GP Madison Roadster

MADISON COUPÉ

ELECTRICAL EQUIPMENT 12 V; 38 Ah battery; 35 A alternator; 2 headlamps.

DIMENSIONS AND WEIGHT wheel base: 97 in, 246 cm; tracks: 56.90 in, 144 cm front, 56 in, 142 cm rear; length: 148 in, 376 cm; width: 62 in, 160 cm; height: 36 in, 91 cm; ground clearance: 6 in, 15.2 cm; weight distribution: 60% front, 40% rear; turning circle: 32 ft, 9.8 m; fuel tank: 10 imp gal, 11.9 US gal, 45 l.

BODY coupé; 2 doors; 2 separate seats.

JAGUAR GREAT BRITAIN

XJ6 3.4

PRICE EX WORKS: £ 13,991*

ENGINE front, 4 stroke; 6 cylinders, vertical, in line; 210 cu in, 3,442 cc (3.28 x 4.17 in, 83 x 106 mm); compression ratio: 8.4:1; max power (DIN): 162 hp (119 kW) at 5,250 rpm; max torque (DIN): 188 lb ft, 26 kg m (255 Nm) at 3,500 rpm; max engine rpm: 5,500; 47.1 hp/l (34.6 kW/l); cast iron block, light alloy head, hemispherical combustion chambers; 7 crankshaft bearings; valves: overhead, Vee-slanted, thimble tappets; camshafts: 2, overhead; lubrication: rotary pump, full flow filter, 14.5 imp pt, 17.3 US pt, 8.2 l; 2 SU type HIF7 horizontal carburettors; fuel feed: 2 electric pumps; water-cooled, 32.5 imp pt, 38.9 US pt, 18.4 l, viscous coupling thermostatic fan.

TRANSMISSION driving wheels: rear; clutch: single dry plate, hydraulically controlled; gearbox: mechanical; gears: 5, fully synchronized; ratios: I 3.321, II 2.087, III 1.396, IV 1, V 0.792, rev 3.428; lever: central; final drive: hypoid bevel; axle ratio: 3.540; width of rims: 6"; tyres: 205/70 VR x 15.

PERFORMANCE max speeds: (I) 36 mph, 58 km/h; (II) 58 mph, 93 km/h; (III) 86 mph, 138 km/h; (IV) 117 mph, 187 km/h; (V) 117 mph, 187 km/h; power-weight ratio: 24 lb/hp (32.7 lb/kW), 10.9 kg/hp (14.8 kg/kW); carrying capacity: 926 lb, 420 kg; acceleration: standing ¼ mile 18.1 sec; consumption: 25.7 m/imp gal, 21.4 m/US gal, 11 l x 100 km at 75 mph, 120 km/h.

CHASSIS integral, front and rear auxiliary frames; front suspension: independent, wishbones, coil springs, anti-roll bar, telescopic dampers; rear: independent, lower wishbones, semi-axles as upper arms, trailing lower radius arms, 4 coil springs, 4 telescopic dampers.

STEERING rack-and-pinion, adjustable steering wheel, servo; turns lock to lock: 3.30.

BRAKES disc (front diameter 11.18 in, 28.4 cm, rear 10.36 in, 26.4 cm), front internal radial fins, servo; swept area: front 234.5 sq in, 1,512 sq cm, rear 213.7 sq in, 1,378 sq cm, total 448.2 sq in, 2,890 sq cm.

ELECTRICAL EQUIPMENT 12 V; 75 Ah no maintenance battery; 45 A alternator; Lucas distributor; 4 halogen headlamps.

DIMENSIONS AND WEIGHT wheel base: 112.83 in, 287 cm; tracks: 57.99 in, 147 cm front, 58.58 in, 149 cm rear; length: 195.20 in, 496 cm; width: 69.68 in, 177 cm; height: 54 in, 138 cm; ground clearance: 7.09 in, 18 cm; weight: 3,894 lb, 1,766 kg; turning circle: 40 ft, 12.2 m; fuel tank: 20 imp gal, 24 US gal, 91 l (2 separate tanks).

BODY saloon/sedan; 4 doors; 5 seats, separate front seats, reclining backrests, headrests; heated rear window; electric windows; central door locking.

JAGUAR XJ6 3.4

PRACTICAL INSTRUCTIONS fuel: 97 oct petrol; oil: engine 14.5 imp pt, 17.3 US pt, 8.2 l, SAE 20W-50, change every 7,500 miles, 12,000 km; tappet clearances: inlet 0.012-0.014 in, 0.30-0.35 mm, exhaust 0.012-0.014 in, 0.30-0.35 mm; tyre pressure: front 33 psi, 2.2 atm, rear 36 psi, 2.4 atm.

OPTIONALS automatic transmission, hydraulic torque converter and planetary gears with 3 ratios (I 2.400, II 1.460, III 1, rev 2.090), consumption 21.1 m/imp gal, 17.6 m/US gal, 13.4 l x 100 km at 75 mph, 120 km/h; fog lamps; tinted glass; limited slip differential; light alloy wheels; air-conditioning; leather upholstery; electric sunroof; rear headrests; electric windows; cruise control; headlamps with wiper-washer; electrically adjustable driving seat; metallic spray.

XJS 3.6 / XJSC 3.6

PRICES EX WORKS:	£
XJS 3.6 2-dr Coupé	**19,248***
XJSC 3.6 5-dr Convertible	**20,756***

ENGINE front, 4 stroke; 6 cylinders, vertical, in line; 219.1 cu in, 3,590 cc (3.58 x 3.62 in, 91 x 92 mm); compression ratio: 9.6:1; max power (DIN): 225 hp (168 kW) at 5,300 rpm; max torque (DIN): 240 lb ft, 33.2 kg m (325 Nm) at 4,000 rpm; max engine rpm: 5,800; 62.7 hp/l (46.8 kW/l); light alloy block and head, pent roof combustion chambers, wet liners; 7 crankshaft bearings; valves: 4 per cylinder, overhead, Vee-slanted, thimble tappets; camshafts: 2, overhead, duplex chain-driven; lubrication: rotary pump, full flow filter, oil cooler, 15 imp pt, 18 US pt, 8.5 l; Lucas-Bosch digital injection with overrun fuel cut-off; fuel feed: electric pump, water-cooled, 20.5 imp pt, 24.6 US pt, 11.6 l, viscous coupling thermostatic fan.

TRANSMISSION driving wheels: rear; clutch: single dry plate, hydraulically controlled; gearbox: mechanical; gears: 5, fully synchronized; ratios: I 3.573, II 2.056, III 1.390, IV 1, V 0.760, rev 3.463; lever: central; final drive: hypoid bevel; axle ratio: 3.540; width of rims: 6" - XJSC 6.5"; tyres: 215/70 VR x 15.

PERFORMANCE max speeds: (I) 36 mph, 58 km/h; (II) 62 mph, 100 km/h; (III) 92 mph, 148 km/h; (IV) 128 mph, 206 km/h; (V) 145 mph, 233 km/h - XJSC 142 mph, 229 km/h; power-weight ratio: 16.3 lb/hp (21.8 lb/kW), 7.4 kg/hp (9.9 kg/kW); carrying capacity: 772 lb, 350 kg; speed in top at 1,000 rpm: 28.9 mph, 46.5 km/h; consumption: 29.4 m/imp gal, 24.5 m/US gal, 9.6 l x 100 km at 75 mph, 120 km/h.

CHASSIS integral, front and rear auxiliary frames; front suspension: independent, wishbones, coil springs, anti-roll bar, telescopic dampers; rear: independent, lower wishbones, semi-axles as upper arms, trailing lower radius arms, 4 coil springs, anti-roll bar, 4 telescopic dampers.

STEERING rack-and-pinion, servo; turns lock to lock: 2.70.

BRAKES disc (front diameter 11.18 in, 28.4 cm, rear 10.38 in, 26.4 cm), front internal radial fins, servo; swept area: front 252 sq in, 1,624 sq cm, rear 192 sq in, 1,240 sq cm, total 444 sq in, 2,864 sq cm.

ELECTRICAL EQUIPMENT 12 V; 75 Ah no-maintenance battery; 75 A alternator; Lucas contactless electronic ignition; 2 halogen headlamps.

DIMENSIONS AND WEIGHT wheel base: 102 in, 259 cm; tracks: 58.30 in, 148 cm front - XJSC 58.60 in, 149 cm, 58.90 in, 149 cm rear - XJSC 59.20 in, 150 cm; length: 187.60 in, 476 cm; width: 70.60 in, 179 cm; height: 49.65 in, 126 cm; ground clearance: 5.50 in, 14 cm; weight: 3,660 lb, 1,660 kg; turning circle: 39.3 ft, 12 m; fuel tank: 20 imp gal, 24 US gal, 91 l.

BODY coupé, 4 seats - convertible, 2 seats; 2 doors; headrests; heated rear window; leather upholstery; tinted glass; air-conditioning; electric windows; light alloy wheels; cruise control.

PRACTICAL INSTRUCTIONS fuel: 98 oct petrol; oil: engine 15 imp pt, 18 US pt, 8.5 l, SAE 10W-50, change every 7,500 miles, 12,000 km; spark plug: Champion RC 12 YC; valve timing: 13° 55° 55° 13°; tyre pressure: front 32 psi, 2.2 atm, rear 32 psi, 2.2 atm.

OPTIONALS headlamps with wiper-washer; trip computer.

JAGUAR XJSC 3.6 Convertible

XJ6 4.2

PRICE IN USA: $ 31,100*
PRICE EX WORKS: £ 15,996*

ENGINE front, 4 stroke; 6 cylinders, vertical, in line; 258.4 cu in, 4,235 cc (3.63 x 4.17 in, 92 x 106 mm); compression ratio: 8.7:1; max power (DIN): 205 hp (151 kW) at 5,000 rpm; max torque (DIN): 231 lb ft, 31.9 kg m (313 Nm) at 4,500 rpm; max engine rpm: 5,500; 48.4 hp/l (35.6 kW/l); cast iron block, light alloy head, hemispherical combustion chambers; 7 crankshaft bearings; valves: overhead, Vee-slanted, thimble tappets; camshafts: 2, overhead; lubrication: rotary pump, full flow filter, oil cooler, 14.5 imp pt, 17.3 US pt, 8.2 l; Lucas-Bosch L-Jetronic injection; fuel feed: electric pump, water-cooled, 32.5 imp pt, 38.9 US pt, 18.4 l, viscous coupling thermostatic fan.

TRANSMISSION driving wheels: rear; clutch: single dry plate, hydraulically controlled; gearbox: mechanical; gears: 5, fully synchronized; ratios: I 3.321, II 2.087, III 1.396, IV 1, V 0.792, rev 3.428; lever: central; final drive: hypoid bevel; axle ratio: 3.058; width of rims: 6"; tyres: 205/70 VR x 15.

PERFORMANCE max speeds: (I) 38 mph, 61 km/h; (II) 61 mph, 98 km/h; (III) 91 mph, 147 km/h; (IV) 126 mph, 203 km/h; (V) 130 mph, 209 km/h; power-weight ratio: 19.7 lb/hp (26.7 lb/kW), 8.9 kg/hp (12.1 kg/kW); carrying capacity: 926 lb, 420 kg; acceleration: standing ¼ mile 17.1 sec; consumption: 25.9 m/imp gal, 21.6 m/US gal, 10.9 l x 100 km at 75 mph, 120 km/h.

CHASSIS integral, front and rear auxiliary frames; front suspension: independent, wishbones, coil springs, anti-roll bar, telescopic dampers; rear: independent, lower wishbones, semi-axle as upper arms, trailing lower radius arms, 4 coil springs, anti-roll bar, 4 telescopic dampers.

STEERING rack-and-pinion, adjustable steering wheel, servo; turns lock to lock: 3.30.

BRAKES disc (front diameter 11.18 in, 28.4 cm, rear 10.38 in, 26.4 cm), front internal radial fins, vacuum servo; swept area:

front 234.5 sq in, 1,512 sq cm, rear 213.7 sq in, 1,378 sq cm, total 448.2 sq in, 2,890 sq cm.

ELECTRICAL EQUIPMENT 12 V; 75 Ah no-maintenance battery; 65 A alternator; Lucas distributor; 4 halogen headlamps.

DIMENSIONS AND WEIGHT wheel base: 112.80 in, 286 cm; tracks: 57.99 in, 147 cm front, 58.58 in, 149 cm rear; length: 195.20 in, 496 cm; width: 69.68 in, 177 cm; height: 54 in, 138 cm; ground clearance: 7.09 in, 18 cm; weight: 4,035 lb, 1,830 kg; turning circle: 40 ft, 12.2 m; fuel tank: 20 imp gal, 24 US gal, 91 l (2 separate tanks).

BODY saloon/sedan; 4 doors; 5 seats, separate front seats, reclining backrests, headrests; heated rear window; electric windows; leather upholstery; tinted glass; central door locking.

PRACTICAL INSTRUCTIONS fuel: 97 oct petrol; oil: engine 14.5 imp pt, 17.3 US pt, 8.2 l, SAE 20W-50, change every 7,500 miles, 12,000 km; tappet clearances: inlet 0.012-0.014 in, 0.30-0.35 mm, exhaust 0.012-0.014 in, 0.30-0.35 mm; tyre pressure: front 33 psi, 2.2 atm, rear 36 psi, 2.4 atm.

OPTIONALS automatic transmission, hydraulic torque converter and planetary gears with 3 ratios (I 2.400, II 1.460, III 1, rev 2.090), max speed 127 mph, 204 km/h, consumption 23.7 m/imp gal, 19.8 m/US gal, 11.9 l x 100 km at 75 mph, 120 km/h; limited slip differential; air-conditioning; light alloy wheels; cruise control with automatic transmission; electric sunroof; fog lamps; electrically adjustable driving seat; rear headrests; headlamps with wiper-washer; trip computer; metallic spray.

Sovereign 4.2

PRICE EX WORKS: £ 18,494*

ENGINE front, 4 stroke; 6 cylinders, vertical, in line; 258.4 cu in, 4,235 cc (3.63 x 4.17 in, 92 x 106 mm); compression ratio: 8.7:1; max power (DIN): 205 hp (151 kW) at 5,000 rpm; max torque (DIN): 232 lb ft, 32 kg m (314 Nm) at 4,500 rpm; max engine rpm: 5,500; 48.4 hp/l (35.6 kW/l); cast iron block, light alloy head, hemispherical combustion chambers; 7 crankshaft bearings; valves: overhead, Vee-slanted, thimble tappets; camshafts: 2, overhead; lubrication: rotary pump, full flow filter, oil cooler, 14.5 imp pt, 17.3 US pt, 8.2 l; Lucas-Bosch L-Jetronic injection; fuel feed: electric pump; water-cooled, 32.5 imp pt, 38.9 US pt, 18.4 l, viscous coupling thermostatic fan.

TRANSMISSION driving wheels: rear; gearbox: Borg-Warner 66 automatic transmission, hydraulic torque converter and planetary gears with 3 ratios, max ratio of converter at stall 2, possible manual selection; ratios: I 2.400, II 1.460, III 1, rev 2.090; lever: central; final drive: hypoid bevel; axle ratio: 3.058; width of rims: 6"; tyres: 205/70 VR x 15.

PERFORMANCE max speeds: (I) 49 mph, 79 km/h; (II) 81 mph, 130 km/h; (III) 127 mph, 204 km/h; power-weight ratio: 19.7 lb/hp (26.7 lb/kW), 8.9 kg/hp (12.1 kg/kW); carrying capacity: 926 lb, 420 kg; acceleration: standing ¼ mile 17.5 sec; consumption: 23.7 imp gal, 19.8 Us gal, 11.9 l x 100 km at 75 mph, 120 km/h.

CHASSIS integral, front and rear auxiliary frames; front suspension: independent, wishbones, coil springs, anti-roll bar, telescopic dampers; rear: independent, lower wishbones, semi-axles as upper arms, trailing lower radius arms, 4 coil springs, 4 telescopic dampers.

STEERING rack-and-pinion, adjustable steering wheel, servo; turns lock to lock: 3.30.

BRAKES disc (front diameter 11.18 in, 28.4 cm, rear 10.38 in, 26.4 cm), front internal radial fins, servo; swept area: front 234.5 sq in, 1,512 sq cm, rear 213.7 sq in, 1,378 sq cm, total 448.2 sq in, 2,890 sq cm.

ELECTRICAL EQUIPMENT 12 V; 75 Ah no-maintenance battery; 65 A alternator; Lucas distributor; 4 halogen headlamps.

DIMENSIONS AND WEIGHT wheel base: 112.80 in, 286 cm; tracks: 57.99 in, 147 cm front, 58.58 in, 149 cm rear; length:

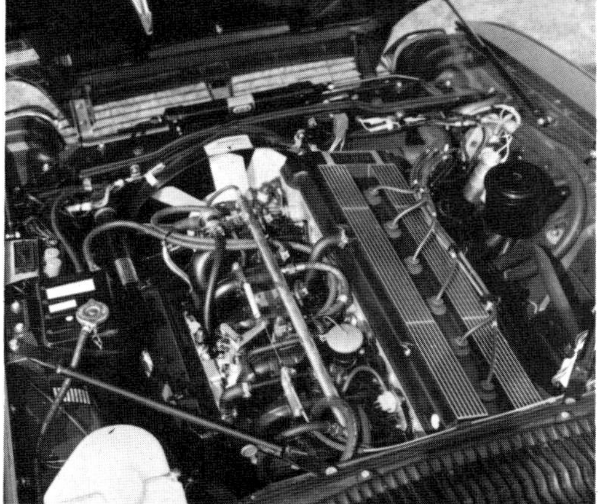

JAGUAR XJSC 3.6 Convertible

195.20 in, 496 cm; width: 69.68 in, 177 cm; height: 54 in, 137 cm; ground clearance: 7.09 in, 18 cm; weight: 4,035 lb, 1,830 kg; turning circle: 40 ft, 12.2 m; fuel tank: 20 imp gal, 24 US gal, 91 l (2 separate tanks).

BODY saloon/sedan; 4 doors; 5 seats, electrically adjusted, separate front seats, reclining backrests, front and rear headrests; heated rear window; electric windows; tinted glass; trip computer; air-conditioning; light alloy wheels; leather upholstery.

PRACTICAL INSTRUCTIONS fuel: 97 oct petrol; oil: engine 14.5 imp pt, 17.3 US pt, 8.2 l, SAE 20W-50, change every 7,500 miles, 12,000 km; tappet clearances: inlet 0.012-0.014 in, 0.30-0.35 mm, exhaust 0.012-0.014 in, 0.30-0.35 mm; tyre pressure: front 33 psi, 2.2 atm, rear 36 psi, 2.4 atm.

OPTIONALS limited slip differential; electric sunroof; fog lamps; headlamps with wiper-washer.

Sovereign HE

PRICE EX WORKS: £ 20,955*

ENGINE front, 4 stroke; 12 cylinders, Vee-slanted at 60°; 326 cu in, 5,343 cc (3.54 x 2.76 in, 90 x 70 mm); compression ratio: 12.5:1; max power (DIN): 295 hp (217 kW) at 5,500 rpm; max torque (DIN): 320 lb ft, 44.2 kg m (434 Nm) at 3,250 rpm; max engine rpm: 6,500; 56 hp/l (41.2 kW/l); light alloy block and head, wet liners; 7 crankshaft bearings; valves: overhead, in line, thimble tappets; camshafts: 2, 1 per bank, overhead; lubrication: rotary pump, full flow filter, oil cooler, 19 imp pt, 22.8 US pt, 10.8 l; Lucas-Bosch digital injection; fuel feed: electric pump; water-cooled, 36 imp pt, 43.3 US pt, 20.5 l, 1 viscous coupling thermostatic and 1 electric thermostatic fan.

TRANSMISSION driving wheels: rear; gearbox: GM 400 automatic transmission, hydraulic torque converter and planetary gears with 3 ratios, max ratio of converter at stall 2, possible manual selection; ratios: I 2.500, II 1.500, III 1, rev 2; lever: central; final drive: hypoid bevel, limited slip; axle ratio: 2.880; width of rims: 6"; tyres: 215/70 VR x 15.

PERFORMANCE max speeds: (I) 70 mph, 112 km/h; (II) 118 mph, 189 km/h; (III) 150 mph, 241 km/h; power-weight ratio: 14.4 lb/hp (19.6 lb/kW), 6.5 kg/hp (8.9 kg/kW); carrying capacity: 926 lb, 420 kg; acceleration: standing ¼ mile 16.2 sec, 0-50 mph (0-80 km/h) 6.4 sec; speed in direct drive at 1,000 rpm: 26.9 mph, 43.3 km/h; consumption: 21.6 m/imp gal, 18 m/US gal, 13.1 l x 100 km at 75 mph, 120 km/h.

CHASSIS integral, front and rear auxiliary frames; front suspension: independent, wishbones, coil springs, anti-roll bar, telescopic dampers; rear: independent, wishbones, semi-axle as upper arms, trailing lower radius arms, 4 coil springs, 4 telescopic dampers.

STEERING rack-and-pinion, adjustable steering wheel, servo; turns lock to lock: 3.30.

BRAKES disc (front diameter 11.18 in, 28.4 cm, rear 10.38 in, 26.4 cm), front internal radial fins, servo; swept area: front 234.5 sq in, 1,512 sq cm, rear 213.7 sq in, 1,378 sq cm, total 448.2 sq in, 2,890 sq cm.

ELECTRICAL EQUIPMENT 12 V; 75 Ah no-maintenance battery; 60 A alternator; Lucas electronic distributor; 4 halogen headlamps.

DIMENSIONS AND WEIGHT wheel base: 112.80 in, 286 cm; tracks: 57.99 in, 147 cm front, 58.58 in, 149 cm rear; length: 194.68 in, 494 cm; width: 69.68 in, 177 cm; height: 54.13 in, 137 cm; ground clearance: 7.09 in, 18 cm; weight: 4,256 lb, 1,930 kg; turning circle: 40 ft, 12.2 m; fuel tank: 20 imp gal, 24 US gal, 91 l (2 separate tanks).

BODY saloon/sedan; 4 doors; 5 seats, electrically adjustable separate front seats, reclining backrests, built-in headrests; heated rear window; electric windows; cruise control; air-conditioning; light alloy wheels; trip computer; metallic spray; leather upholstery; tinted glass; headlamps with wiper-washer.

PRACTICAL INSTRUCTIONS fuel: 97 oct petrol; oil: engine 19 imp pt, 22.8 US pt, 10.8 l, SAE 20W-50, change every 7,500 miles, 12,000 km; tyre pressure: front 36 psi, 2.4 atm, rear 36 psi, 2.4 atm.

OPTIONALS electric sunroof; fog lamps.

XJS HE

PRICE IN USA: $ 34,700*
PRICE EX WORKS: £ 21,752*

ENGINE front, 4 stroke; 12 cylinders, Vee-slanted at 60°; 326 cu in, 5,343 cc (3.54 x 2.76 in, 90 x 70 mm); compression ratio: 12.5:1; max power (DIN): 295 hp (217 kW) at 5,500 rpm; max torque (DIN): 320 lb ft, 44.2 kg m (434 Nm) at 3,250 rpm; max engine rpm: 6,500; 55.2 hp/l (40.6 kW/l); light alloy block and head, wet liners; 7 crankshaft bearings; valves: overhead, in line, thimble tappets; camshafts: 2, 1 per bank, overhead; lubrication: rotary pump, full flow filter, oil cooler, 19 imp pt, 22.8 US pt, 10.8 l; Lucas-Bosch digital injection; fuel feed: electric pump; water-cooled, 37.5 imp pt, 47.2 US pt, 21.3 l, 1 viscous coupling thermostatic and 1 electric thermostatic fans.

TRANSMISSION driving wheels: rear; gearbox: GM 400 automatic transmission, hydraulic torque converter and planetary gears with 3 ratios, max ratio of converter at stall 2, possible manual selection; ratios: I 2.500, II 1.500, III 1, rev 2; lever: central; final drive: hypoid bevel, limited slip; axle ratio: 2.880; width of rims: 6.5"; tyres: 215/70 VR x 15.

PERFORMANCE max speeds: (I) 70 mph, 113 km/h; (II) 116 mph, 187 km/h; (III) 150 mph, 241 km/h; power-weight ratio: 13.1 lb/hp (17.8 lb/kW), 5.9 kg/hp (8.1 kg/kW); carrying capacity: 783 lb, 355 kg; speed in direct drive at 1,000 rpm: 26.9 mph, 43.3 km/h; consumption: 22.5 m/imp gal, 18.7 m/US gal, 12.6 l x 100 km at 75 mph, 120 km/h.

CHASSIS integral, front and rear auxiliary frames; front suspension: independent, wishbones, coil springs, anti-roll bar, telescopic dampers; rear: independent, lower wishbones, semi-axles as upper arms, trailing lower radius arms, 4 coil springs, anti-roll bar, 4 telescopic dampers.

STEERING rack-and-pinion, servo; turns lock to lock: 2.70.

BRAKES disc (front diameter 11.18 in, 28.4 cm, rear 10.38 in,

JAGUAR Sovereign HE

JAGUAR XJS HE

XJS HE

26.4 cm), front internal radial fins, servo; swept area: front 252 sq in, 1,624 sq cm, rear 148 sq in, 956 sq cm, total 400 sq in, 2,580 sq cm.

ELECTRICAL EQUIPMENT 12 V; 75 Ah no-maintenance battery; 75 A alternator; Lucas contactless electronic ignition; 2 halogen headlamps.

DIMENSIONS AND WEIGHT wheel base: 102 in, 259 cm; tracks: 58.60 in, 149 cm front, 59.20 in, 150 cm rear; length: 187.60 in, 476 cm; width: 70.60 in, 179 cm; height: 49.65 in, 126 cm; ground clearance: 5.50 in, 14 cm; weight: 3,870 lb, 1,755 kg; turning circle: 39.4 ft, 12 m; fuel tank: 20 imp gal, 24 US gal, 91 l.

BODY coupé; 2 doors; 4 seats, separate front seats, reclining backrests, built-in headrests; heated rear window; leather upholstery; tinted glass; air-conditioning; electric windows; light alloy wheels; metallic spray; trip computer; headlamps with wiper-washer; cruise control.

PRACTICAL INSTRUCTIONS fuel: 98 oct petrol; oil: engine 16 imp pt, 19.2 US pt, 9.1 l, SAE 20W-50, change every 7,500 miles, 12,000 km; tyre pressure: front 32 psi, 2.2 atm, rear 32 psi, 2.2 atm.

OPTIONALS rear seat belts.

KOUGAR GREAT BRITAIN

Monza

PRICE EX WORKS: £ 10,000*

ENGINE front, 4 stroke; 6 cylinders, Vee-slanted; 182.7 cu in, 2,994 cc (3.70 x 2.85 in, 93.9 x 72.4 mm); compression ratio: 9.1:1; max power (DIN): 138 hp (102 kW) at 5,200 rpm; max torque (DIN): 174 lb ft, 24 kg m (235 Nm) at 3,000 rpm; max engine rpm: 6,000; 46.1 hp/l (34.1 kW/l); cast iron block and head; 4 crankshaft bearings; valves: overhead, push-rods and rockers; camshafts: 1, at centre of Vee; lubrication: full flow filter, 8.5 imp pt, 10.1 US pt, 4.8 l; 1 Weber downdraught twin barrel carburettor; fuel feed: mechanical pump; water-cooled, 12 imp pt, 14.4 US pt, 6.8 l.

TRANSMISSION driving wheels: rear; clutch: single dry plate; gearbox: mechanical; gears: 4, fully synchronized; ratios: I 2.961, II 2.072, III 1.322, IV 1, rev 3.132; lever: central; final drive: hypoid bevel; axle ratio: 3.440; width of rims: 6"; tyres: 186 x 15.

PERFORMANCE max speeds: (I) 42 mph, 67 km/h; (II) 74 mph, 119 km/h; (III) 99 mph, 159 km/h; (IV) 130 mph, 209 km/h; power-weight ratio: 13.2 lb/hp (17.9 lb/kW), 6 kg/hp (8.1 kg/kW); carrying capacity: 353 lb, 160 kg; acceleration: 0-50 mph (0-80 km/h) 5 sec; speed in direct drive at 1,000 rpm: 23.5 mph, 37.8 km/h; consumption: 24 m/imp gal, 19.9 m/US gal, 11.8 l x 100 km.

CHASSIS front suspension: independent, double wishbones, coil springs, telescopic dampers; rear: rigid axle, 4 links, coaxial coil springs, telescopic dampers.

STEERING rack-and-pinion; turns lock to lock: 3.50.

BRAKES front disc, rear drum, servo.

ELECTRICAL EQUIPMENT 12 V; 38 Ah battery; alternator; Motorcraft Autolite ignition; 2 headlamps.

DIMENSIONS AND WEIGHT wheel base: 96.50 in, 245 cm; tracks: 56.50 in, 143 cm front, 52 in, 132 cm rear; length: 170 in, 432 cm; width: 72 in, 183 cm; height: 40 in, 102 cm; ground clearance: 6 in, 15.2 cm; weight: 1,826 lb, 828 kg; weight distribution: 50% front, 50% rear; turning circle: 34 ft, 10.4 m; fuel tank: 13 imp gal, 15.6 US gal, 59 l.

BODY sports; 2 doors; 2 separate seats.

PRACTICAL INSTRUCTIONS fuel: 94 oct petrol; oil: engine 8.5 imp pt, 10.1 US pt, 4.8 l, SAE 20/50, change every 6,000 miles, 9,700 km - gearbox 3.5 imp pt, 4.2 US pt, 2 l, SAE 90, change every 12,000 miles, 19,300 km - final drive 1.7 imp pt, 2.1 US pt, 1 l, SAE 90, no change recommended; greasing: none; spark plug: Autolite AGR 22; tappet clearances: inlet 0.013 in, 0.32 mm, exhaust 0.022 in, 0.55 mm; tyre pressure: front 22 psi, 1.5 atm, rear 22 psi, 1.5 atm.

OPTIONALS 121.9 cu in, 1,998 cc engine.

Sports

PRICE EX WORKS: £ 12,500*

ENGINE front, 4 stroke; 6 cylinders, in line; 210 cu in, 3,442 cc (3.27 x 4.17 in, 83 x 106 mm); compression ratio: 8:1; max power (DIN): 205 hp (151 kW) at 5,200 rpm; max torque (DIN): 270 lb ft, 37.2 kg m (365 Nm) at 3,000 rpm; max engine rpm: 6,000; 59.6 hp/l (43.9 kW/l); cast iron block, light alloy head; 7 crankshaft bearings; valves: overhead; camshafts: 2, overhead; lubrication: gear pump, full flow filter, 12.5 imp pt, 15 US pt, 7.1 l; 2 SU type HD8 downdraught carburettors; fuel feed: electric pump; water-cooled, 16 imp pt, 19.2 US pt, 9.1 l.

TRANSMISSION driving wheels: rear; clutch: single dry plate; gearbox: mechanical; gears: 4, fully synchronized, and overdrive; ratios: I 3.041, II 2.328, III 1.973, IV 1, overdrive 0.780, rev 3.490; lever: central; final drive: hypoid bevel; axle ratio: 3.770; width of rims: 7"; tyres: 205 x 15.

PERFORMANCE max speeds: (I) 38 mph, 61 km/h; (II) 68 mph, 109 km/h; (III) 91 mph, 146 km/h; (IV) 110 mph, 177 km/h; overdrive 125 mph, 201 km/h; power-weight ratio: 9 lb/hp (12.4 lb/kW), 4.1 kg/hp (5.6 kg/kW); carrying capacity: 265 lb, 120 kg; acceleration: standing ¼ mile 14 sec, 0-50 mph (0-80 km/h) 4.9 sec; speed in overdrive/top at 1,000 rpm: 22 mph, 35.4 km/h; consumption: 22-24 m/imp gal, 18.2-19.9 m/US gal, 12.9-11.8 l x 100 km.

CHASSIS tubular frame; front suspension: independent, double wishbones, coaxial coil springs, telescopic dampers; rear: independent, lower wishbone, coaxial coil springs, telescopic dampers.

STEERING rack-and-pinion; turns lock to lock: 3.30.

BRAKES disc, servo.

ELECTRICAL EQUIPMENT 12 V; 40 Ah battery; dynamo; Lucas distributor; 2 headlamps.

DIMENSIONS AND WEIGHT wheel base: 100 in, 254 cm; tracks: 55 in, 140 cm front, 56 in, 142 cm rear; length: 159 in, 404 cm; width: 68 in, 173 cm; height: 40 in, 102 cm; ground clearance: 5.25 in, 13.3 cm; weight: 1,874 lb, 850 kg; weight distribution: 50% front, 50% rear; turning circle: 33 ft, 10.1 m; fuel tank: 14 imp gal, 16.6 US gal, 63 l.

BODY sports, in fiberglass material; no doors; 2 separate seats.

PRACTICAL INSTRUCTIONS fuel: 97 oct petrol; oil: engine 12 imp pt, 14.4 US pt, 6.8 l, SAE 20/50, change every 6,000 miles, 9,700 km - gearbox 4 imp pt, 4.9 US pt, 2.3 l, SAE 20/50, change every 12,000 miles, 19,300 km - final drive 2.7 imp pt, 3.4 US pt, 1.6 l, SAE 90, change every 12,000 miles, 19,300 km; greasing: every 3,000 miles, 4,800 km, 12 points; spark plug: Champion N11Y; tappet clearances: inlet 0.004 in, 0.10 mm, exhaust 0.006 in, 0.14 mm; tyre pressure: front 22 psi, 1.5 atm, rear 22 psi, 1.5 atm.

OPTIONALS 258.4 cu in, 4,234 cc engine; 3.540 or 3.310 axle ratios; leather upholstery; wire wheels.

LAND ROVER GREAT BRITAIN

88" Short Wheelbase

PRICES EX WORKS:	£
2-dr Soft Top	**6,729***
2+1-dr St. Wagon	**8,534***
County 2+1-dr St. Wagon	**8,979***

ENGINE front, 4 stroke; 4 cylinders, vertical, in line; 139.5 cu in, 2,286 cc (3.56 x 3.50 in, 90.5 x 88.9 mm); compression ratio: 8:1; max power (DIN): 70 hp (52 kW) at 4,000 rpm; max torque (DIN): 117 lb ft, 16.2 kg m (159 Nm) at 2,000 rpm; max engine rpm: 5,000; 30.6 hp/l (22.7 kW/l); cast iron block and head; 5 crankshaft bearings; valves: overhead, in line, roller tappets, push-rods and rockers; camshafts: 1, side, chain-driven; lubrication: gear pump, full flow filter, 10.9 imp pt, 13.1 US pt, 6.2 l; 1 Zenith 36 IV downdraught single barrel carburettor; fuel feed: mechanical pump; water-cooled, 14.2 imp pt, 17.1 US pt, 8.1 l, thermostatic fan.

TRANSMISSION driving wheels: front (automatically engaged with transfer box low ratio) and rear; clutch: single dry plate (diaphragm), hydraulically controlled; gearbox: mechanical; gears: 4, fully synchronized and 2-ratio transfer box (high 1.148, low 2.350); ratios: I 3.680, II 2.220, III 1.500, IV 1, rev 4.020; gear and transfer levers: central; front and rear final drive: spiral bevel; front and rear axle ratio: 4.700; width of rims: 5"; tyres: 6.00 x 16.

PERFORMANCE max speeds: (I) 21 mph, 33 km/h; (II) 34 mph, 54 km/h; (III) 50 mph, 80 km/h; (IV) 66 mph, 106 km/h; power-weight ratio: 42.8 lb/hp (58 lb/kW), 19.4 kg/hp (26.3 kg/kW); carrying capacity: 1,499 lb, 680 kg; acceleration: 0-50 mph (0-80 km/h) 16.3 sec; speed in direct drive at 1,000 rpm: 15 mph, 24.1 km/h; consumption: 19.1 m/imp gal, 15.9 m/US gal, 14.8 l x 100 km.

CHASSIS box type ladder frame; front suspension: rigid axle, semi-elliptic leafsprings, telescopic dampers; rear: rigid axle, semi-elliptic leafsprings, telescopic dampers.

STEERING recirculating ball; turns lock to lock: 3.50.

BRAKES drum; lining area: total 105 sq in, 677 sq cm.

ELECTRICAL EQUIPMENT 12 V; 58 Ah battery; 34 A alternator; Lucas distributor; 2 headlamps.

DIMENSIONS AND WEIGHT wheel base: 88 in, 223 cm; front and rear track: 51.50 in, 131 cm; length: 142.35 in, 362 cm; width: 66.54 in, 169 cm; height: 77.56 in, 197 cm; ground clearance: 6.89 in, 17.5 cm; weight: 2,953 lb, 1,339 kg; weight distribution: 52.5% front, 47.5% rear; turning circle: 38 ft, 11.6 m; fuel tank: 10 imp gal, 12 US gal, 45 l.

BODY open or estate car/st. wagon; 2 or 2+1 doors; 7 seats, separate front seats.

PRACTICAL INSTRUCTIONS fuel: 90 oct petrol; oil: engine 10.9 imp pt, 13.1 US pt, 6.2 l, SAE 20W, change every 6,200 miles, 10,000 km - gearbox 2.5 imp pt, 3 US pt, 1.4 l, SAE 90 EP, change every 24,000 miles, 39,000 km - transfer box 4.4 imp pt, 5.3 US pt, 2.5 l, SAE 90 EP, change every 24,000 miles, 39,000 km - final drive 3 imp pt, 3.6 US pt, 1.7 l, SAE 90 EP, change every 24,000 miles, 39,000 km; greasing: every 6,200 miles, 10,000 km, 1 point; tappet clearances: inlet 0.010 in, 0.25 mm, exhaust 0.010 in, 0.25 mm; valve timing: 6° 52° 34° 24°; tyre pressure: front 25 psi, 1.7 atm, rear 25 psi, 1.7 atm.

VARIATIONS

ENGINE 7:1 compression ratio, max power (DIN) 65 hp (48 kW) at 4,000 rpm, max torque (DIN) 114 lb ft, 15.7 kg m (154 Nm) at 2,000 rpm, 28.4 hp/l (21 kW/l).

ENGINE diesel, 23:1 compression ratio, max power (DIN) 60 hp (45 kW) at 4,000 rpm, max torque (DIN) 103 lb ft, 14.2 kg m

KOUGAR Monza

KOUGAR Sports

LAND ROVER 88" Short Wheelbase County Station Wagon

LAND ROVER One Ten 2¼ P Station Wagon

(140 Nm) at 1,800 rpm, max engine rpm 4,000, 26.2 hp/l (19.7 kW), cast iron head with precombustion chambers, CAV injection pump, cooling: 13.7 imp pt, 16.5 US pt, 7.8 l.
PERFORMANCE power-weight ratio 50.7 lb/hp (69 lb/kW), 23 kg/hp (31.3 kg/kW), consumption 26.9 m/imp gal, 22.4 m/US gal, 10.5 l x 100 km.
ELECTRICAL EQUIPMENT 95 Ah battery.
DIMENSIONS AND WEIGHT weight 3,041 lb, 1,379 kg.

OPTIONALS overdrive, 0.790 ratio; oil cooler; front and rear power take-off; 7.50 x 16 tyres; servo brake; 45 A alternator; steering damper.

109" Long Wheelbase

See 88" Short Wheelbase, except for:

PRICES EX WORKS:	£
2-dr Soft Top	7,936*
4+1-dr St. Wagon	9,121*
County 4+1-dr St. Wagon	9,537*

TRANSMISSION width of rims: 5.5"; tyres: 7.50 x 16.

PERFORMANCE power-weight ratio: 54.5 lb/hp (73.6 lb/kW), 24.7 kg/hp (33.4 kg/kW); carrying capacity: 2,220 lb, 1,005 kg.

BRAKES servo (standard); swept area: total 171.9 sq in, 1,109 sq cm.

DIMENSIONS AND WEIGHT wheel base: 109 in, 277 cm; front and rear track: 52.36 in, 133 cm; length: 175.20 in, 445 cm; height: 79.13 in, 201 cm; ground clearance: 8.25 in, 21 cm; weight: 3,752 lb, 1,702 kg; weight distribution: 46.5% front, 53.5% rear; turning circle: 46.9 ft, 14.3 m; fuel tank: 15 imp gal, 18 US gal, 68 l.

BODY 2 or 4+1 doors; 10-12 seats, separate front seats.

109" V8 Long Wheelbase

See 88" Short Wheelbase, except for:

PRICES EX WORKS:	£
2-dr Soft Top	8,707*
4+1-dr St. Wagon	9,824*
County 4+1-dr St. Wagon	10,241*

ENGINE 8 cylinders, in Vee; 215.3 cu in, 3,528 cc (3.50 x 2.80 in, 88.9 x 71.1 mm); compression ratio: 8.1:1; max power (DIN): 91 hp (67 kW) at 3,500 rpm; max torque (DIN): 167 lb ft, 23 kg m (226 Nm) at 2,000 rpm; 25.8 hp/l (19 kW/l); light alloy block and head, dry liners; camshafts: 1, central, chain-driven; lubrication: 10 imp pt, 12 US pt, 5.7 l; 2 Zenith-Stromberg CDSE semi-downdraught carburettors; cooling: 17 imp pt, 20.3 US pt, 9.7 l.

TRANSMISSION gearbox ratios: I 4.070, II 2.450, III 1.505, IV 1, rev 3.660; transfer box ratios: high 1.336, low 3.320; width of rims: 5.5"; tyres: 7.50 V x 16.

PERFORMANCE max speed: about 73 mph, 118 km/h; power-weight ratio: 43.7 lb/hp (59.5 lb/kW), 19.8 kg/hp (27 kg/kW); carrying capacity: 2,220 lb, 1,005 kg; consumption: 17.1 m/imp gal, 14.3 m/US gal, 16.5 l x 100 km.

STEERING damper (standard).

BRAKES servo (standard); swept area: total 171.9 sq in, 1,109 sq cm.

ELECTRICAL EQUIPMENT 45 A alternator (standard).

DIMENSIONS AND WEIGHT wheel base: 109 in, 277 cm; front and rear track: 52.36 in, 133 cm; length: 175.20 in, 445 cm; height: 79.13 in, 201 cm; ground clearance: 8.25 in, 21 cm; weight: 3,980 lb, 1,805 kg; turning circle: 46.9 ft, 14.3 m; fuel tank: 15 imp gal, 18 US gal, 68 l.

BODY 2 or 4+1 doors; 10-12 seats, separate front seats.

One Ten 2¼ P

PRICES EX WORKS:	£
2-dr Soft Top	8,009*
4+1-dr St. Wagon	9,300*
County 4+1-dr St. Wagon	9,730*

ENGINE front, 4 stroke; 4 cylinders, vertical, in line; 139.5 cu in, 2,286 cc (3.56 x 3.50 in, 90.5 x 88.9 mm); compression ratio: 8:1; max power (DIN): 74 hp (55 kW) at 4,000 rpm; max torque (DIN): 120 lb ft, 16.5 kg m (162 Nm) at 2,000 rpm; max engine rpm: 5,000; 32.4 hp/l (23.6 kW/l); cast iron block and head; 5 crankshaft bearings; valves: overhead, in line, roller tappets, push-rods and rockers; camshafts: 1, side, chain-driven; lubrication: gear pump, full flow filter, 10.9 imp pt, 13.1 US pt, 6.2 l; 1 Weber 32/34 DMTL downdraught twin barrel carburettor; fuel feed: mechanical pump; water-cooled, 14.2 imp pt, 17.1 US pt, 8.1 l, thermostatic fan.

TRANSMISSION driving wheels: front (automatically engaged with transfer box low ratio) and rear; clutch: single dry plate (diaphragm), hydraulically controlled; gearbox: mechanical; gears: 5, fully synchronized and 2-ratio transfer box; ratios: I 3.585, II 2.301, III 1.507, IV 1, V 0.830, rev 3.701; transfer box ratios: high 1.667, low 3.320; gear and transfer levers: central; final drive: spiral bevel; axle ratio: 3.540; width of rims: 5.5"; tyres: 7.50 x 16.

PERFORMANCE max speed: 68 mph, 110 km/h; power-weight ratio: Soft Top 51.3 lb/hp (69.1 lb/kW), 23.3 kg/hp (31.3 kg/kW); carrying capacity: 2,977 lb, 1,350 kg; speed in direct drive at 1,000 rpm: 15 mph, 24.1 km/h; consumption: not declared.

CHASSIS box-type ladder frame; front suspension: rigid axle, twin radices arms, Panhard rod, coil springs, telescopic dampers; rear: rigid axle, twin tubular trailing links, control A bracket, coil springs, telescopic dampers, (for County only) Boge automatic levelling control.

STEERING recirculating ball; turns lock to lock: 4.40.

BRAKES front disc (diameter 11.81 in, 30 cm), rear drum, dual circuit, servo.

ELECTRICAL EQUIPMENT 12 V; 55 Ah battery; 34 A alternator; Lucas distributor; 2 headlamps.

DIMENSIONS AND WEIGHT wheel base: 110 in, 279 cm; front and rear track: 58.50 in, 149 cm; length: 175 in, 444 cm; width: 70.50 in, 179 cm; height: 80.10 in, 203 cm; weight: Soft Top 3,799 lb, 1,723 kg - st. wagon 3,253 lb, 1,887 kg; turning circle: 42 ft, 12.8 m; fuel tank: 17.5 imp gal, 21 US gal, 79 l.

BODY open, 2 doors - estate car/st. wagon, 4+1 doors; 3 or 12 seats.

PRACTICAL INSTRUCTIONS fuel: 90 oct petrol; oil: engine 10.9 imp pt, 13.1 US pt, 6.2 l, SAE 20W, change every 6,200 miles, 10,000 km - gearbox 2.5 imp pt, 3 US pt, 1.4 l, SAE 90 EP, change every 24,000 miles, 39,000 km - transfer box 4.4 imp pt, 5.3 US pt, 2.5 l, SAE 90 EP, change every 24,000 miles, 39,000 km - final drive 3 imp pt, 3.6 US pt, 1.7 l, SAE 90 EP, change every 24,000 miles, 39,000 km; greasing: none; tappet clearances: inlet 0.010 in, 0.25 mm, exhaust 0.010 in, 0.25 mm; tyre pressure: front 25 psi, 1.7 atm, rear 25 psi, 1.7 atm.

OPTIONALS (for Soft Top only) hardtop; power steering; (except County) Boge automatic levelling control.

VARIATIONS

ENGINE diesel, 23:1 compression ratio, max power (DIN) 60 hp (45 kW) at 4,000 rpm, max torque (DIN) 103 lb ft, 14.2 kg m (140 Nm) at 1,800 rpm, max engine rpm 4,000, 26.2 hp/l (19.7 kW/l), cast iron head with precombustion chambers, CAV injection pump, cooling 13.7 imp pt, 16.5 US pt, 7.8 l.
PERFORMANCE power-weight ratio Soft Top 64 lb/hp (85.4 lb/kW), 29 kg/hp (38.7 kg/kW).
ELECTRICAL EQUIPMENT 96 Ah battery.
DIMENSIONS AND WEIGHT weight Soft Top 3,841 lb, 1,742 kg - st. wagons 4,203 lb, 1,906 kg.

One Ten 3½ P

See One Ten 2¼P, except for:

PRICES EX WORKS:	£
2-dr Soft Top	8,939*
4+1-dr St. Wagon	10,251*
County 4+1-dr St. Wagon	10,680*

LAND ROVER 109" Long Wheelbase County Station Wagon

LAND ROVER Range Rover

LENHAM Austin-Healey 3000

ONE TEN 3½ P

ENGINE 8 cylinders in Vee; 215.3 cu in, 3,528 cc (3.50 x 2.80 in, 88.9 x 71.1 mm); compression ratio: 8.1:1; max power (DIN): 114 hp (85 kW) at 4,000 rpm; max torque (DIN): 185 lb ft, 25.6 kg m (251 Nm) at 2,500 rpm; 32.3 hp/l (24.1 kW/l); light alloy block and head, dry liners; camshafts: 1, central, chain-driven; lubrication: 9 imp pt, 10.8 US pt, 5.1 l; 2 Zenith-Stromberg CDSE semi-downdraught carburettors; cooling: 17 imp pt, 20.3 US pt, 9.7 l.

TRANSMISSION driwing wheels: front and rear with lockable differential in transfer box; gears: 4, fully synchronized and 2-ratio transfer box; ratios: I 4.060, II 2.044, III 1.500, IV 1, rev 3.660; transfer box ratios: high 1.340, low 3.320.

PERFORMANCE max speed: about 87 mph, 140 km/h; power-weight ratio: Soft Top 32.8 lb/hp (44 lb/kW), 14.9 kg/hp (20 kg/kW); consumption: not declared.

ELECTRICAL EQUIPMENT 45 A alternator.

DIMENSIONS AND WEIGHT weight: Soft Top 3,744 lb, 1,698 kg - st. wagons 4,106 lb, 1,862 kg.

Range Rover

PRICES EX WORKS:	£
2+1-dr Fleet Line 2	**13,530***
2+1-dr St. Wagon	**14,483***
4+1-dr St. Wagon	**15,374***

ENGINE front, 4 stroke; 8 cylinders, in Vee; 215 cu in, 3,528 cc (3.50 x 2.80 in, 88.9 x 71.1 mm); compression ratio: 9.3:1; max power (DIN): 125 hp (92 kW) at 4,000 rpm; max torque (DIN): 190 lb ft, 26.2 kg m (258 Nm) at 2,500 rpm; max engine rpm: 5,200; 35.4 hp/l (26.1 kW/l); light alloy block and head, dry liners; 5 crankshaft bearings; valves: overhead, in line, push-rods and rockers, hydraulic tappets; camshafts: 1, at centre of Vee; lubrication: gear pump, full flow filter, 10 imp pt, 12 US pt, 5.7 l; 2 Zenith-Stromberg CD2 semi-downdraught carburettors; fuel feed: electric pump; water-cooled, expansion tank, 17 imp pt, 20.5 US pt, 9.7 l, thermostatic fan.

TRANSMISSION driving wheels: front and rear with lockable differential in transfer box; clutch: single dry plate (diaphragm), hydraulically controlled; gearbox: mechanical; gears: 5, fully synchronized and 2-ratio transfer box; ratios: I 3.320, II 2.130, III 1.400, IV 1, V 0.770, rev 3.430; transfer box ratios: high 1.192, low 3.320; gear and transfer levers: central; front and rear final drive: spiral bevel; front and rear axle ratio: 3.540; width of rims: 6"; tyres: 205 x 16.

PERFORMANCE max speeds: (I) 24 mph, 39 km/h; (II) 41 mph, 66 km/h; (III) 68 mph, 109 km/h; (IV) 98 mph, 158 km/h; power-weight ratio: 31.1 lb/hp (41.7 lb/kW), 14.1 kg/hp (18.9 kg/kW); carrying capacity: 1,649 lb, 748 kg; acceleration: standing ¼ mile 19.3 sec, 0-50 mph (0-80 km/h) 9.9 sec; speed in direct drive at 1,000 rpm: 23.7 mph, 38.1 km/h; consumption: 18.2 m/imp gal, 15.1 m/US gal, 15.5 l x 100 km.

CHASSIS box-type ladder frame; front suspension: rigid axle, longitudinal radius arms, transverse linkage bar, coil springs/telescopic damper units; rear: rigid axle, longitudinal radius arms, upper A-bracket, Boge Hydromat self-energizing levelling device, coil springs, telescopic dampers.

STEERING recirculating ball, worm and nut, servo (except Fleet Line); turns lock to lock: 3.50.

BRAKES disc, dual circuit, servo.

ELECTRICAL EQUIPMENT 12 V; 60 Ah battery; 65 A alternator; Lucas distributor; 2 halogen headlamps.

DIMENSIONS AND WEIGHT wheel base: 100 in, 254 cm; front and rear track: 58.50 in, 149 cm; length: 176 in, 447 cm; width: 70 in, 178 cm; height: 70 in, 178 cm; ground clearance: 7.50 in, 19 cm; weight: 3,883 lb, 1,762 kg; weight distribution: 51% front, 49% rear; turning circle: 37 ft, 11.3 m; fuel tank: 18 imp gal, 21.6 US gal, 82 l.

BODY estate car/st. wagon; 2+1 or 4+1 doors; 5 seats, separate front seats, headrests; tinted glass; heated rear window with wiper-washer; laminated windscreen; folding rear seat; (for 4+1-dr St. Wagon only) central door locking and luxury equipment.

PRACTICAL INSTRUCTIONS fuel: 97 oct petrol; oil: engine 10 imp pt, 12 US pt, 5.7 l, SAE 20W, change every 6,200 miles, 10,000 km - gearbox 4.5 imp pt, 5.5 US pt, 2.6 l, SAE 80 EP, change every 24,000 miles, 39,000 km - transfer box 5.5 imp pt, 6.6 US pt, 3.1 l, SAE 80 EP, change every 6,200 miles, 10,000 km - final drive rear 2.7 imp pt, 3.2 US pt, 1.5 l, SAE 80 EP, change every 24,000 miles, 39,000 km, front 3 imp pt, 3.6 US pt, 1.7 l, SAE 80 EP, change every 24,000 miles, 39,000 km; greasing: every 6,200 miles, 10,000 km, 6 points; valve timing: 30° 75° 68° 37°; tyre pressure: front 25 psi, 1.7 atm, rear 35 psi, 2.4 atm.

OPTIONALS Chrysler A727 automatic transmission with 3 ratios (I 2.450, II 1.450, III 1, rev 2.200), transfer box ratios (high 1.003, low 3.320); light alloy wheels with 7" wide rims; metallic spray; special equipment; air-conditioning.

VARIATIONS

ENGINE 8.1:1 compression ratio, max power (DIN) 130 hp (97 kW) at 5,000 rpm, max torque (DIN) 190 lb ft, 25.4 kg m (258 Nm) at 2,500 rpm, 36.8 hp/l (27.5 kW/l).

LENHAM — GREAT BRITAIN

Austin-Healey 3000

PRICE EX WORKS: £ 11,000*

ENGINE Austin-Healey, front, 4 stroke; 6 cylinders, in line; 178.1 cu in, 2,912 cc (3.28 x 3.50 in, 83.3 x 88.9 mm); compression ratio: 8.5:1; max power (DIN): 120 hp (88 kW) at 4,600 rpm; max torque (DIN): 167 lb ft, 23 kg m (226 Nm) at 2,700 rpm; max engine rpm: 5,000; 41.2 hp/l (30.3 kW/l); cast iron block and head; 4 crankshaft bearings; valves: overhead, push-rods and rockers; camshafts: 1, side; lubrication: rotary pump, full flow filter, 12 imp pt, 14.4 US pt, 6.8 l; 2 SU type HD6 or HS6 semi-downdraught carburettor; fuel feed: electric pump; water-cooled, 30 imp pt, 35.9 US pt, 17 l.

TRANSMISSION driving wheels: rear; clutch: single dry plate; gearbox: mechanical; gears: 4 + overdrive; ratios: I 2.930, II 2.053, III 1.309, IV 1; lever: central; final drive: hypoid bevel; axle ratio: 3.900; width of rims: 6"; tyres: 185 x 15.

PERFORMANCE max speeds: (I) 28 mph, 45 km/h; (II) 45 mph, 72 km/h; (III) 80 mph, 128 km/h; (IV) 100 mph, 161 km/h; (overdrive-top) 120 mph, 193 km/h; power-weight ratio: 16.1 lb/hp (22 lb/kW), 7.3 kg/hp (10 kg/kW); carrying capacity: 353 lb, 160 kg; acceleration: 0-50 mph (0-80 km/h) 6 sec; speed in direct drive at 1,000 rpm: 20 mph, 32.2 km/h; consumption: 25 m/imp gal, 20.8 m/US gal, 11.3 l x 100 km.

CHASSIS box section frame; front suspension: independent, unequal length wishbones, oil springs, anti-roll bar, lever dampers; rear: rigid axle, two longitudinal leafsprings, lever dampers.

STEERING cam and peg; turns lock to lock: 2.75.

BRAKES front disc (diameter 11.25 in, 28.6 cm), rear drum.

ELECTRICAL EQUIPMENT 12 V; 50 Ah battery; dynamo; Lucas distributor; 2 headlamps.

DIMENSIONS AND WEIGHT wheel base: 92.13 in, 234 cm; tracks: 50.50 in, 128 cm front, 52.50 in, 133 cm rear; length: 151 in, 383 cm; width: 63 in, 160 cm; height: 47 in, 119 cm; ground clearance: 6 in, 15 cm; weight: 1,940 lb, 880 kg; weight distribution: 60% front, 40% rear; turning circle: 36 ft, 11 m; fuel tank: 12 imp gal, 14.3 US gal, 54 l.

BODY open, in composite aluminium and fiberglass material; no doors; 2 seats; folding windscreen; outside handbrake; Connelly hide trim; stainless steel exhaust system; screen washers and wipers; tonneau cover; wood rim steering wheel; centre-hinged bonnet.

PRACTICAL INSTRUCTIONS fuel: 98 oct petrol; oil: engine 12 imp pt, 14.4 US pt, 6.8 l, SAE 20/50, change every 3,000 miles, 4,800 km - gearbox 6 imp pt, 7.2 US pt, 3.4 l, SAE 20/50 - final drive 3 imp pt, 3.6 US pt, 1.7 l; greasing: every 2,000 miles, 3,200 km, 10 points; tappet clearances (hot): inlet and exhaust 0.012 in, 0.30 mm; valve timing: 5° 45° 40° 10°; tyre pressure: front 24 psi, 1.7 atm, rear 20 psi, 1.4 atm.

OPTIONALS 3.540 axle ratio without overdrive; side-mounted spare wheel; hood; heater.

LOTUS — GREAT BRITAIN

Excel

PRICE EX WORKS: £ 14,735*

ENGINE front, 4 stroke; 4 cylinders, in line, slanted 45° to left; 132.7 cu in, 2,174 cc (3.70 x 3 in, 95.3 x 76.2 mm); compression ratio: 9.4:1; max power (DIN): 160 hp (115 kW) at 6,500 rpm; max torque (DIN): 160 lb ft, 22.1 kg m (217 Nm) at 5,000 rpm; max engine rpm: 7,000; 73.6 hp/l (52.9 kW/l); light alloy block and head, wet liners; 5 crankshaft

LOTUS Turbo Esprit

bearings; valves: 4 per cylinder, overhead, slanted at 38°, thimble tappets; camshafts: 2, overhead, cogged belt; lubrication: rotary pump, full flow filter (cartridge), 16.6 imp pt, 12.7 US pt, 6 l; 2 Dell'Orto DHLA 45E horizontal twin barrel carburettors; fuel feed: electric pump; water-cooled, 15 imp pt, 18 US pt, 8.5 l, electric thermostatic fan.

TRANSMISSION driving wheels: rear; clutch: single dry plate (diaphragm); gearbox: mechanical; gears: 5, fully synchronized; ratios: I 3.240, II 1.890, III 1.230, IV 1, V 0.780, rev 3.705; lever: central; final drive: hypoid bevel; axle ratio: 4.100; width of rims: 7"; tyres: 205/60 VR x 14.

PERFORMANCE max speeds: (I) 46 mph, 74 km/h; (II) 61 mph, 98 km/h; (III) 85 mph, 135 km/h; (IV) 116 mph, 186 km/h; (V) 134 mph, 216 km/h; power-weight ratio: 15.4 lb/hp (21 lb/kW), 7 kg/hp (9.5 kg/kW); carrying capacity: 706 lb, 320 kg; acceleration: standing ¼ mile 14.9 sec, 0-50 mph (0-80 km/h) 5 sec; speed in direct drive at 1,000 rpm: 16.6 mph, 26.7 km/h; consumption: 29.4 m/imp gal, 24.5 m/US gal, 9.6 l x 100 km at 75 mph, 120 km/h.

CHASSIS box-type backbone; front suspension: independent, upper and lower wishbones, coil springs/telescopic damper struts, anti-roll bar; rear: independent, trailing arms, lower links, coil springs, telescopic damper struts.

STEERING rack-and-pinion; turns lock to lock: 3.50.

BRAKES disc, internal radial fins, servo; swept area: front 108 sq in, 697 sq cm, rear 79.6 sq in, 514 sq cm, total 187.6 sq in, 1,211 sq cm.

ELECTRICAL EQUIPMENT 12 V; 55 Ah battery; 70 A alternator; Lucas electronic ignition; 2 retractable halogen headlamps, 2 rear fog lamps.

DIMENSIONS AND WEIGHT wheel base: 97.65 in, 248 cm; front and rear track: 57.50 in, 146 cm; length: 172.30 in, 437 cm; width: 71.50 in, 182 cm; height: 47.65 in, 121 cm; ground clearance: 4.80 in, 12.2 cm; weight: 2,503 lb, 1,135 kg; weight distribution: 53% front, 47% rear; turning circle: 34.5 ft, 10.5 m; fuel tank: 14.7 imp gal, 17.7 US gal, 67 l.

BODY coupé, in reinforced plastic material; 2 doors; 2+2 seats, separate front seats, headrests; impact absorbing bumpers; rear spoiler; electric windows; heated rear window; tinted glass.

PRACTICAL INSTRUCTIONS fuel: 97 oct petrol; oil: engine 8.8 imp pt, 10.6 US pt, 5 l, SAE 20W-50, change every 5,000 miles, 8,000 km - gearbox 2.8 imp pt, 3.4 US pt, 1.6 l, SAE 90 EP, change every 10,000 miles, 16,100 km - final drive 2 imp pt, 2.3 US pt, 1.1 l, SAE 90 EP, change every 10,000 miles, 16,100 km; greasing: every 5,000 miles, 8,000 km, 6 points; spark plug: NGK BPR6ES; tappet clearances: inlet 0.005 in, 0.13 mm, exhaust 0.010 in, 0.25 mm; tyre pressure: front 22 psi, 1.6 atm, rear 22 psi, 1.6 atm.

OPTIONALS power steering; air-conditioning; metallic spray; light alloy wheels.

LOTUS Excel

Esprit Series 3

PRICE EX WORKS: £ 15,985*

ENGINE central, rear, longitudinal, 4 stroke; 4 cylinders, in line, slanted 45° to left; 132.7 cu in, 2,174 cc (3.70 x 3 in, 95.3 x 76.2 mm); compression ratio: 9.5:1; max power (DIN): 160 hp (115 kW) at 6,500 rpm; max torque (DIN): 160 lb ft, 22.1 kg m (217 Nm) at 5,000 rpm; max engine rpm: 7,000; 73.6 hp/l (52.9 kW/l); light alloy block and head, wet liners; 5 crankshaft bearings; valves: 4 per cylinder, overhead, slanted at 38°, thimble tappets; camshafts: 2, overhead, cogged belt; lubrication: rotary pump, full flow filter (cartridge), 10.6 imp pt, 12.7 US pt, 6 l; 2 Dell'Orto DHLA 45 horizontal twin barrel carburettors; fuel feed: electric pump; water-cooled, 19 imp pt, 22.8 US pt, 10.8 l, front radiator, electric thermostatic fan.

TRANSMISSION driving wheels: rear; clutch: single dry plate (diaphragm), hydraulically controlled; gearbox: mechanical; gears: 5, fully synchronized; ratios: I 3.460, II 2.920, III 1.320, IV 0.970, V 0.760, rev 3.150; lever: central; final drive: hypoid bevel; axle ratio: 4.375; width of rims: 7" front, 7.5" rear; tyres: 205/60 VR x 14 front, 205/70 VR x 14 rear.

PERFORMANCE max speeds: (I) 40 mph, 64 km/h; (II) 60 mph, 97 km/h; (III) 88 mph, 142 km/h; (IV) 120 mph, 193 km/h; (V) 138 mph, 222 km/h; power-weight ratio: 14 lb/hp (19.6 lb/kW), 6.4 kg/hp (8.9 kg/kW); carrying capacity: 500 lb, 227 kg; acceleration: standing ¼ mile 15 sec, 0-50 mph (0-80 km/h) 5 sec; speed in top at 1,000 rpm: 21.4 mph, 34.4 km/h; consumption: 33.3 m/imp gal, 27.7 m/US gal, 8.5 l x 100 km at 75 mph, 120 km/h.

CHASSIS box-type backbone with space-frame section; front suspension: independent, upper wishbones, lower link, coil springs, anti-roll bar, telescopic dampers; rear: independent, trailing radius arms, lower links and drive shafts, coil springs, telescopic dampers.

STEERING rack-and-pinion; turns lock to lock: 3.50.

BRAKES disc, dual circuit, servo; total swept area: 404.6 sq in, 2,610 sq cm.

ELECTRICAL EQUIPMENT 12 V; 44 Ah battery; 70 A alternator; Lucas electronic ignition; 4 retractable halogen headlamps, 2 rear fog lamps.

DIMENSIONS AND WEIGHT wheel base: 96 in, 244 cm; front and rear track: 59.50 in, 151 cm; length: 164 in, 416 cm; width: 73 in, 185 cm; height: 44 in, 112 cm; ground clearance: 5 in, 12.7 cm; weight: 2,249 lb, 1,020 kg; weight distribution: 43% front, 57% rear; turning circle: 34.8 ft, 10.6 m; fuel tank: 15 imp gal, 18 US gal, 67 l.

BODY coupé, in reinforced plastic material; 2 doors; 2 seats, built-in headrests; electric windows; heated rear window; light alloy wheels; rear window wiper-washer; tinted glass; heater.

PRACTICAL INSTRUCTIONS fuel: 97 oct petrol; oil: engine 8.8 imp pt, 10.6 US pt, 5 l, SAE 20W-50, change every 5,000 miles, 8,000 km - gearbox 2.8 imp pt, 3.4 US pt, 1.6 l, SAE 80 EP, change every 10,000 miles, 16,100 km - final drive 2 imp pt, 2.3 US pt, 1.1 l, SAE 90 EP, change every 10,000 miles, 16,100 km; greasing: every 5,000 miles, 8,000 km, 4 points; spark plug: NGK BPR6ES; tappet clearances: inlet 0.005 in, 0.13 mm, exhaust 0.010 in, 0.25 mm; tyre pressure: front 21 psi, 1.5 atm, rear 25 psi, 1.8 atm.

OPTIONALS air-conditioning; metallic spray.

Turbo Esprit

See Esprit Series 3, except for:

PRICE EX WORKS: £ 19,490*

ENGINE turbocharged; compression ratio: 7.5:1; max power (DIN): 210 hp (151 kW) at 6,000-6,500 rpm; max torque (DIN): 200 lb ft, 27.6 kg m (271 Nm) at 4,000-4,500 rpm; 96.6 hp/l (69.5 kW/l); lubrication: dry sump, 11.4 imp pt, 13.7 US pt, 6.5 l; 2 Dell'Orto DHLA H 40 horizontal twin barrel carburettors; 1 Garrett AiResearch T 3 turbocharger; fuel feed: Lucas 4 FP electric pump.

TRANSMISSION width of rims: 7" front, 8" rear; tyres: 195/60 VR x 15 front, 235/60 VR x 15 rear.

PERFORMANCE max speeds: (I) 41 mph, 66 km/h; (II) 62 mph, 100 km/h; (III) 91 mph, 147 km/h; (IV) 124 mph, 200 km/h; (V) 152 mph, 245 km/h; power-weight ratio: 12.8 lb/hp (17.8 lb/kW), 5.8 kg/hp (8.1 kg/kW); acceleration: standing ¼ mile 14.4 sec, 0-50 mph (0-80 km/h) 4.2 sec; speed in top at 1,000 rpm: 22.6 mph, 36.4 km/h; consumption: 24.1 m/imp gal, 20.1 m/US gal, 11.7 l x 100 km at 75 mph, 120 km/h.

DIMENSIONS AND WEIGHT tracks: 60.50 in, 154 cm front, 61.20 in, 155 cm rear; length: 165 in, 419 cm; weight: 2,690 lb, 1,220 kg; weight distribution: 42% front, 58% rear; fuel tank: 19 imp gal, 23 US gal, 86 l (2 separate tanks).

BODY air-conditioning (standard).

PRACTICAL INSTRUCTIONS oil: engine 11.4 imp pt, 13.7 US pt, 6.5 l; tyre pressure: front 21 psi, 1.5 atm, rear 25 psi, 1.7 atm.

OPTIONALS Triplex glass sunroof.

LOTUS Esprit Series 3

LYNX — GREAT BRITAIN

D Type

PRICE EX WORKS: £ 24,800*

ENGINE Jaguar XKE, front, 4 stroke; 6 cylinders, in line; 258.4 cu in, 4,235 cc (3.63 x 4.17 in, 92.1 x 106 mm); compression ratio: 9:1; max power (DIN): 171 hp (126 kW) at 4,500 rpm; max torque (DIN): 230 lb ft, 31.8 kg m (312 Nm) at 2,500 rpm; max engine rpm: 5,500; 40.4 hp/l (29.7 kW/l); block with chrome iron dry liners, head with aluminium alloy hemispherical combustion chambers; 7 crankshaft bearings; valves: overhead, Vee-slanted at 70°, thimble tappets; camshafts: 2, overhead; lubrication: rotary pump, full flow filter, 15 imp pt, 18 US pt, 8.5 l; 3 Weber semi-downdraught carburettors; fuel feed: electric pump; water-cooled, 32.9 imp pt, 39.5 US pt, 18.7 l, automatic thermostatic fan.

TRANSMISSION driving wheels: rear; clutch: single dry plate (diaphragm), hydraulically controlled; gearbox: mechanical; gears: 4, fully synchronized; ratios: I 2.933, II 1.905, III 1.389, IV 1, rev 3.378; lever: central; final drive: hypoid bevel, limited slip; axle ratio: 3.070; width of rims: 6"; tyres: E70 VR x 15.

LYNX D Type

MARCOS 3-litre Coupé

D TYPE

PERFORMANCE max speeds: (I) 48 mph, 77 km/h; (II) 73 mph, 117 km/h; (III) 108 mph, 174 km/h; (IV) 150 mph, 241 km/h; power-weight ratio: 12.8 lb/hp (17.4 lb/kW), 5.8 kg/hp (7.9 kg/kW); carrying capacity: 408 lb, 185 kg; acceleration: standing ¼ mile 16 sec, 0-50 mph (0-80 km/h) 5.4 sec; consumption: 18.8 m/imp gal, 15.7 m/US gal, 15 l x 100 km.

CHASSIS integral, front and rear tubular auxiliary frames; front suspension: independent, wishbones, swinging longitudinal torsion bars, anti-roll bar, telescopic dampers; rear: independent, wide-based wishbones, semi-axles as upper arms, trailing lower radius arms, 4 coil springs, 4 telescopic dampers.

STEERING rack-and-pinion.

BRAKES disc (front diameter 11.18 in, 28.4 cm, rear 10.38 in, 26.4 cm), twin master cylinder; swept area: front 234.5 sq in, 1,512 sq cm, rear 213.7 sq in, 1,378 sq cm, total 448.2 sq in, 2,890 sq cm.

ELECTRICAL EQUIPMENT 12 V; 68 Ah battery; 60 A alternator; Lucas distributor; 2 headlamps.

DIMENSIONS AND WEIGHT wheel base: 90.50 in, 230 cm; tracks: 50.75 in, 129 cm front, 51.50 in, 131 cm rear; length: 159 in, 404 cm; width: 63 in, 160 cm; height: 45.50 in, 116 cm; ground clearance: 5 in, 12.7 cm; weight: 2,184 lb, 990 kg; weight distribution: 51% front, 49% rear; turning circle: 32 ft, 9.8 m; fuel tank: 20 imp gal, 24 US gal, 91 l.

BODY sports; 2 doors; 2 seats.

PRACTICAL INSTRUCTIONS fuel: 97 oct petrol; oil: engine 15 imp pt, 18 US pt, 8.5 l, SAE 20W-50, change every 6,000 miles, 9,700 km - gearbox 2.5 imp pt, 3 US pt, 1.4 l, SAE 90 EP, change every 12,000 miles, 19,300 km - final drive 2.7 imp pt, 3.2 US pt, 1.5 l, SAE 90 EP, change every 12,000 miles,19,300 km; greasing: every 6,000-12,000 miles, 9,700-19,300 km; tappet clearances: inlet 0.012-0.014 in, 0.30-0.35 mm, exhaust 0.012-0.014 in, 0.30-0.35 mm; valve timing: 17° 59° 59° 17°; tyre pressure: front 24 psi, 1.7 atm, rear 28 psi, 2 atm.

VARIATIONS

ENGINE Jaguar, tuned, max power (DIN) 285 hp (210 kW).
ENGINE Jaguar, tuned, max power (DIN) 320 hp (235 kW).

OPTIONALS 8:1 compression ratio; XKSS model; short nose bodywork; dry sump lubrication with oil tank; oil cooler; light alloy peg-drive wheels; 6.50L x 15 tyres; side exit exhaust.

MARCOS GREAT BRITAIN

3-litre Coupé

PRICE EX WORKS: £ 8,500*

ENGINE Ford, front, 4 stroke; 6 cylinders in Vee; 170.4 cu in, 2,792 cc (3.66 x 2.70 in, 93 x 68.5 mm); compression ratio: 9:1; max power (DIN): 136 hp (100 kW) at 5,200 rpm; max torque (DIN): 159 lb ft, 22 kg m (216 Nm) at 3,000 rpm; max engine rpm: 6,000; 48.7 hp/l (35.8 kW/l); cast iron block and head; 5 crankshaft bearings; valves: overhead, push-rods and rockers; camshafts: 1, overhead; lubrication: rotary pump, full flow filter (cartridge), 8.3 imp pt, 9.9 US pt, 4.7 l; 1 Solex downdraught twin barrel carburettor; fuel feed: electric pump; water-cooled, 18 imp pt, 21.6 US pt, 10.2 l.

TRANSMISSION driving wheels: rear; clutch: single dry plate (diaphragm); gearbox: mechanical; gears: 5, fully synchronized; ratios: I 3.650, II 1.970, III 1.370, IV 1, V 0.820, rev 3.660; lever: central; final drive: hypoid bevel; axle ratio: 3.090; width of rims: 6"; tyres: 185/70 HR x 13.

PERFORMANCE max speeds: (I) 30 mph, 48 km/h; (II) 56 mph, 90 km/h; (III) 85 mph, 137 km/h; (IV) 110 mph, 177 km/h; (V) 130 mph, 210 km/h; power-weight ratio: 14.6 lb/hp (19.8 lb/kW), 6.6 kg/hp (9 kg/kW); carrying capacity: 617 lb, 280 kg; acceleration: 0-50 mph (0-80 km/h) 5.5 sec; speed in top at 1,000 rpm: 26.5 mph, 42.6 km/h; consumption: 26 m/imp gal, 21.6 m/US gal, 10.9 l x 100 km.

CHASSIS integral; front suspension: independent, wishbones, coil springs, telescopic dampers; rear: rigid axle, leading links, Panhard rod, coil springs, telescopic dampers.

STEERING rack-and-pinion; turns lock to lock: 2.20.

BRAKES front disc, rear drum.

ELECTRICAL EQUIPMENT 12 V; 48 Ah battery; 35 A alternator; Ford distributor; 4 headlamps.

DIMENSIONS AND WEIGHT wheel base: 89.50 in, 227 cm; tracks: 48.73 in, 128 cm front, 51.18 in, 130 cm rear; length: 160.50 in, 407 cm; width: 62.50 in, 158 cm; height: 42.50 in, 108 cm; ground clearance: 5.58 in, 12.5 cm; weight: 1,985 lb, 900 kg; weight distribution: 55% front, 45% rear; turning circle: 32 ft, 9.8 m; fuel tank: 10.6 imp gal, 12.7 US gal, 48 l.

BODY coupé; 2 doors; 2 separate seats.

PRACTICAL INSTRUCTIONS fuel: 98 oct petrol; oil: engine 8.3 imp pt, 9.9 US pt, 4.7 l, SAE 20W-50, change every 6,200 miles, 10,000 km - gearbox 3 imp pt, 3.6 US pt, 1.7 l, no change recommended - final drive 3.2 imp pt, 3.8 US pt, 1.8 l, no change recommended; greasing: none; spark plug: Champion; tappet clearances: inlet 0.008 in, 0.20 mm, exhaust 0.010 in, 0.25 mm; valve timing: 18° 70° 64° 24°; tyre pressure: front 24 psi, 1.7 atm, rear 24 psi, 1.7 atm.

OPTIONALS fuel injection; limited slip differential; leather upholstery; air-conditioning.

Mantula

PRICE EX WORKS: £ 11,200*

ENGINE Rover, front, 4 stroke; 8 cylinders in Vee; 215 cu in, 3,528 cc (3.50 x 2.80 in, 88.8 x 71.1 mm); compression ratio: 9.3:1; max power (DIN): 155 hp (114 kW) at 5,200 rpm; max torque (DIN): 198 lb ft, 27.3 kg m (268 Nm) at 2,500 rpm; max engine rpm: 5,500; 43.9 hp/l (32.3 kW/l); light alloy block and head; 5 crankshaft bearings; valves: overhead, in line, push-rods and rockers; camshafts: 1, at centre of Vee; lubrication: gear pump, full flow filter by cartridge, 8 imp pt, 9.6 US pt, 4.5 l; 2 Solex 175 CDEF horizontal carburettors; fuel feed: electric pump; water-cooled, 15.2 imp pt, 18.3 US pt, 8.7 l.

TRANSMISSION driving wheels: rear; clutch: single dry plate (diaphragm); gearbox: mechanical; gears: 5, fully synchronized; ratios: I 3.321, II 2.087, III 1.396, IV 1, V 0.833, rev 3.428; lever: central; final drive: hypoid bevel; axle ratio: 3.090; width of rims: front 6", rear 7"; tyres: front 195/60 x 14, rear 215/60 x 14.

PERFORMANCE max speeds: (I) 35 mph, 56 km/h; (II) 62 mph, 100 km/h; (III) 80 mph, 129 km/h; (IV) 120 mph, 193 km/h; (V) over 155 mph, 249 km/h; power-weight ratio: 11.5 lb/hp (15.7 lb/kW), 5.2 kg/hp (7.1 kg/kW); carrying capacity: 661 lb, 300 kg; acceleration: standing ¼ mile 11.5 sec, 0-50 mph (0-80 km/h) 5 sec; speed in direct drive at 1,000 rpm: 28.4 mph, 45.7 km/h.

CHASSIS tubular space-frame; front suspension: independent, wishbones, coil springs, adjustable telescopic dampers; rear: rigid axle, leading links, Panhard rod, coil springs, telescopic dampers.

STEERING rack-and-pinion; turns lock to lock: 2.20.

BRAKES front disc, front internal radial fins, rear drum.

ELECTRICAL EQUIPMENT 12 V; 40 Ah battery; 45 A alternator; Lucas distributor; 4 headlamps.

DIMENSIONS AND WEIGHT wheel base: 89.50 in, 227 cm; tracks: 48.73 in, 128 cm front, 51.18 in, 130 cm rear; length: 162.50 in, 413 cm; width: 62.50 in, 158 cm; height: 42.50 in, 108 cm; ground clearance: 4.95 in, 12.6 cm; weight: 1,786 lb, 810 kg; weight distribution: 52% front, 48% rear; turning circle: 32 ft, 9.8 m; fuel tank: 10.7 imp gal, 12.9 US gal, 49 l.

MARCOS Mantula

BODY coupé; 2 doors; 2 separate seats.

PRACTICAL INSTRUCTIONS fuel: 98 oct petrol; oil: engine 8 imp pt, 9.6 US pt, 4.5 l, no change recommended - gearbox 4.5 imp pt, 5.4 US pt, 2.6 l, change every 7,500 miles, 12,000 km - final drive 2 imp pt, 2.4 US pt, 1.1 l, no change recommended; greasing: (front suspension) every 18,600 miles, 30,000 km; spark plug: Champion; valve timing: 31° 73° 80° 34°; tyre pressure: front 22 psi, 1.5 atm, rear 26 psi, 1.8 atm.

OPTIONALS limited slip differential; leather upholstery.

MG — GREAT BRITAIN

Metro 1300

PRICE EX WORKS: £ 5,249*

ENGINE Austin, front, transverse, in unit with gearbox and final drive, 4 stroke; 4 cylinders, vertical, in line; 77.8 cu in, 1,275 cc (2.78 x 3.20 in, 70.6 x 81.3 mm); compression ratio: 10.5:1; max power (DIN): 73 hp (54 kW) at 6,000 rpm; max torque (DIN): 73 lb ft, 10.1 kg m (99 Nm) at 4,000 rpm; max engine rpm: 6,000; 57.3 hp/l (42.4 kW/l); cast iron block and head; 3 crankshaft bearings; valves: overhead, push-rods and rockers; camshafts: 1, side; lubrication: gear pump, full flow filter (cartridge), oil cooler, 8.4 imp pt, 10.1 US pt, 4.8 l; 1 SU type HIF-44 semi-downdraught carburettor; fuel feed: electric pump; water-cooled, 8.6 imp pt, 10.4 US pt, 4.9 l, electric thermostatic fan.

TRANSMISSION driving wheels: front; clutch: single dry plate (diaphragm), hydraulically controlled; gearbox: mechanical; gears: 4, fully synchronized; ratios: I 3.647, II 2.185, III 1.425, IV 1, rev 3.666; lever: central; final drive: helical spur gears; axle ratio: 3.444; width of rims: 5"; tyres: 155/70 SR x 12.

PERFORMANCE max speed: 101 mph, 163 km/h; power-weight ratio: 23.4 lb/hp (31.6 lb/kW), 10.6 kg/hp (14.4 kg/kW); carrying capacity: 717 lb, 325 kg; speed in direct drive at 1,000 rpm: 17.2 mph, 27.7 km/h; consumption: 39.2 m/imp gal, 32.7 m/US gal, 7.2 l x 100 km at 75 mph, 120 km/h.

CHASSIS integral, front and rear auxiliary frames; front suspension: independent, wishbones, hydragas springs, anti-roll bar, telescopic dampers; rear: independent, swinging longitudinal trailing arms, hydragas springs with internal damping, coil pre-load springs.

STEERING rack-and-pinion; turns lock to lock: 3.30.

BRAKES front disc (diameter 8.40 in, 21.3 cm), rear drum, dual circuit, rear compensator, servo.

ELECTRICAL EQUIPMENT 12 V; 40 Ah battery; 45 A alternator; Lucas distributor; 2 halogen headlamps.

DIMENSIONS AND WEIGHT wheel base: 88.62 in, 225 cm; tracks: 50.39 in, 128 cm front, 50.07 in, 127 cm rear; length: 134.05 in, 340 cm; width: 60.86 in, 155 cm; height: 53.60 in, 136 cm; weight: 1,709 lb, 775 kg; turning circle: 34.4 ft, 10.5 m; fuel tank: 7 imp gal, 8.4 US gal, 32 l.

BODY saloon/sedan; 2+1 doors; 5 seats, separate front seats, headrests; heated rear window; light alloy wheels.

PRACTICAL INSTRUCTIONS fuel: 97 oct petrol; oil: engine, gearbox and final drive 8.4 imp pt, 10.1 US pt, 4.8 l, SAE 20W-50, change every 12,000 miles, 19,300 km; tyre pressure: front 31 psi, 2.2 atm, rear 28 psi, 2 atm.

OPTIONALS rear window wiper-washer; laminated windscreen; sunroof.

MG Metro Turbo

Metro Turbo

See Metro 1300, except for:

PRICE EX WORKS: £ 5,899*

ENGINE turbocharged; compression ratio: 9.4:1; max power (DIN): 94 hp (69 kW) at 6,130 rpm; max torque (DIN): 86 lb ft, 11.8 kg m (115 Nm) at 2,650 rpm; 73.7 hp/l (54.1 kW/l); Garrett AiResearch T3 turbocharger.

TRANSMISSION axle ratio: 3.210; width of rims: 5.5"; tyres: 165/60 VR x 13.

PERFORMANCE max speed: 112 mph, 180 km/h; power-weight ratio: 19.7 lb/hp (26.8 lb/kW), 8.9 kg/hp (12.2 kg/kW); speed in direct drive at 1,000 rpm: 18.6 mph, 29.9 km/h; consumption: 35.3 m/imp gal, 29.4 m/US gal, 8 l x 100 km at 75 mph, 120 km/h.

DIMENSIONS AND WEIGHT tracks: 51.57 in, 131 cm front, 50.59 in, 128 cm rear; weight: 1,852 lb, 840 kg.

Maestro 1600

PRICE EX WORKS: £ 6,554*

ENGINE front, transverse, in unit with gearbox and final drive, 4 stroke; 4 cylinders, vertical, in line; 97.5 cu in, 1,598 cc (3 x 3.45 in, 76.2 x 87.6 mm); compression ratio: 9.7:1; max power (DIN): 102 hp (76 kW) at 6,000 rpm; max torque (DIN): 100 lb ft, 13.8 kg m (135 Nm) at 4,000 rpm; max engine rpm: 6,500; 63.8 hp/l (47.6 kW/l); cast iron block, light alloy head; 5 crankshaft bearings; valves: overhead, in line, thimble tappets; camshafts: 1, overhead; lubrication: rotary pump, full flow filter (cartridge), 8.4 imp pt, 10.1 US pt, 4.8 l; 2 Weber 40 DCNF downdraught twin barrel carburettors; fuel feed: electric pump; water-cooled, 8.6 imp pt, 10.4 US pt, 4.9 l, electric thermostatic fan.

TRANSMISSION driving wheels: front; clutch: single dry plate (diaphragm), hydraulically controlled; gearbox: mechanical; gears: 5, fully synchronized; ratios: I 3.450, II 2.120, III 1.440, IV 1.130, V 0.910, rev 3.170; lever: central; final drive: helical spur gears; axle ratio: 3.650; width of rims: 5.5"; tyres: 175/65 SR x 14.

PERFORMANCE max speed: 109 mph, 175 km/h; power-weight ratio: 20.9 lb/hp (28 lb/kW), 9.5 kg/hp (12.7 kg/kW); carrying capacity: 1,047 lb, 475 kg; speed in top at 1,000 rpm: 19.8 mph, 31.9 km/h; consumption: not declared.

CHASSIS integral; front suspension: independent, by McPherson, lower wishbones, coil springs/telescopic damper struts, anti-roll bar; rear: semi-independent, trailing arms, H-beam, coil springs, telescopic dampers.

STEERING rack-and-pinion; turns lock to lock: 4.18.

BRAKES front disc (diameter 9.50 in, 24.1 cm), rear drum, dual circuit, rear compensator; swept area: front 221.9 sq in, 1,431 sq cm, rear 95.8 sq in, 618 sq cm, total 317.7 sq in, 2,049 sq cm.

ELECTRICAL EQUIPMENT 12 V; 40 Ah battery; 45 A alternator; transistorized ignition; 2 halogen headlamps.

DIMENSIONS AND WEIGHT wheel base: 98.70 in, 251 cm; tracks: 57.70 in, 146 cm front, 56.70 in, 144 cm rear; length: 157.50 in, 400 cm; width: 66.40 in, 169 cm; height: 55.80 in, 142 cm; ground clearance: 6 in, 15 cm; weight: 2,127 lb, 965 kg; turning circle: 33.1 ft, 10.3 m; fuel tank: 10.3 imp gal, 11.9 US gal, 54 l.

BODY saloon/sedan; 4+1 doors; 5 seats, separate front seats, headrests; heated rear window; rear window wiper-washer; light alloy wheels.

PRACTICAL INSTRUCTIONS fuel: 97 oct petrol; oil: engine, gearbox and final drive 8.4 imp pt, 10.1 US pt, 4.8 l, SAE 20W-50, change every 12,000 miles, 19,300 km; greasing: none; tyre pressure: front 31 psi, 2.2 atm, rear 28 psi, 2 atm.

OPTIONALS metallic spray; tinted glass; sunroof; electric windows; central door locking.

MG Maestro 1600

MIDAS — GREAT BRITAIN

Gold 1.3 S Coupé

PRICE EX WORKS: £ 5,150*

ENGINE MG Metro, front, transverse, in unit with gearbox and final drive, 4 stroke; 4 cylinders, vertical, in line; 77.8 cu in, 1,275 cc (2.78 x 3.20 in, 70.6 x 81.3 mm); compression ratio: 10.5:1; max power (DIN): 73 hp (54 kW) at 6,000 rpm; max torque (DIN): 73 lb ft, 10.1 kg m (99 Nm) at 4,000 rpm; max engine rpm: 6,000; 57.3 hp/l (42.4 kW/l); cast iron block and head; 3 crankshaft bearings; valves: overhead, push-rods and rockers; camshafts: 1, side; lubrication: gear pump, full flow filter (cartridge), oil cooler, 8.4 imp pt, 10.1 US pt, 4.8 l; 1 SU type HIF-44 semi-downdraught carburettor; fuel feed: electric pump; water-cooled, 8.6 imp pt, 10.4 US pt, 4.9 l, electric thermostatic fan.

TRANSMISSION driving wheels: front; clutch: single dry plate (diaphragm), hydraulically controlled; gearbox: mechanical; gears: 4, fully synchronized; ratios: I 3.647, II 2.185, III 1.425, IV 1, rev 3.666; lever: central; final drive: helical spur gears; axle ratio: 2.950; width of rims: 5"; tyres: 155/70 SR x 12.

PERFORMANCE max speeds: (I) 33 mph, 53 km/h; (II) 55 mph, 89 km/h; (III) 85 mph, 137 km/h; (IV) 110 mph, 177 km/h; power-weight ratio: 18.6 lb/hp (25.2 lb/kW), 8.5 kg/hp (11.4 kg/kW); carrying capacity: 750 lb, 340 kg; acceleration: standing ¼ mile 17 sec, 0-50 mph (0-80 km/h) 6.8 sec; speed in direct drive at 1,000 rpm: 20.2 mph, 32.5 km/h; consumption: 40.4 m/imp gal, 33.6 m/US gal, 7 l x 100 km.

MIDAS Gold 1.3 S Coupé

MINI Mayfair Saloon

GOLD 1.3 S COUPÉ

CHASSIS integral; front suspension: independent, unequal wishbones, rubber springs, telescopic dampers; rear: independent, trailing radius arms, variable rate coil springs, adjustable telescopic dampers.

STEERING rack-and-pinion; turns lock to lock: 2.75.

BRAKES front disc, rear drum, dual circuit; lining area: front 134.5 sq in, 867 sq cm, rear 40.5 sq in, 261 sq cm, total 175 sq in, 1,128 sq cm.

ELECTRICAL EQUIPMENT 12 V; 30 Ah battery; 45 A alternator; Lucas distributor; 2 halogen headlamps.

DIMENSIONS AND WEIGHT wheel base: 84 in, 213 cm; tracks: 51 in, 130 cm front, 48 in, 122 cm rear; length: 134 in, 340 cm; width: 62 in, 157 cm; height: 45 in, 114 cm; ground clearance: 5.50 in, 14 cm; weight: 1,360 lb, 617 kg; fuel tank: 6 imp gal, 7.1 US gal, 27 l.

BODY coupé, in g.r.p.; 2 doors; 2+2 seats, separate front seats; light alloy wheels; sunroof.

PRACTICAL INSTRUCTIONS fuel: 97 oct petrol; oil: engine, gearbox and final drive, 8.4 imp pt, 10.1 US pt, 4.8 l, SAE 20W-50, change every 12,000 miles, 19,300 km; tyre pressure: front 28 psi, 2 atm, rear 22 psi, 1.5 atm.

MINI GREAT BRITAIN

City E / Mayfair

PRICES EX WORKS:	£
City E 2-dr Saloon	**3,098***
Mayfair 2-dr Saloon	**3,630***

ENGINE front, transverse, in unit with gearbox and final drive, 4 stroke; 4 cylinders, vertical, in line; 60.9 cu in, 998 cc (2.54 x 3 in, 64.6 x 76.2 mm); compression ratio: 10.3:1; max power (DIN): 40 hp (29 kW) at 5,000 rpm; max torque (DIN): 50 lb ft, 6.9 kg m (68 Nm) at 2,500 rpm; max engine rpm: 5,500; 40.1 hp/l (29.1 kW/l); cast iron block and head; 3 crankshaft bearings; valves: overhead, in line, push-rods and rockers; camshafts: 1, side; lubrication: rotary pump, full flow filter by cartridge, 8.4 imp pt, 10.1 US pt, 4.8 l; 1 SU type HS4 semi-downdraught carburettor; fuel feed: electric pump; water-cooled, 6.2 imp pt, 7.4 US pt, 3.5 l.

TRANSMISSION driving wheels: front; clutch: single dry plate (diaphragm), hydraulically controlled; gearbox: mechanical; gears: 4, fully synchronized; ratios: I 3.647, II 2.185, III 1.425, IV 1, rev 3.667; lever: central; final drive: helical spur gears; axle ratio: 2.950; width of rims: 3.5"; tyres: 145 SR x 10.

PERFORMANCE max speed: 81 mph, 131 km/h; power-weight ratio: 32.9 lb/hp (45.4 lb/kW), 14.9 kg/hp (20.6 kg/kW); carrying capacity: 706 lb, 320 kg; consumption: 40.7 m/imp gal, 33.6 m/US gal, 7 l x 100 km.

CHASSIS integral, front and rear auxiliary frames; front suspension: independent, wishbones, rubber cone springs, telescopic dampers; rear: independent, swinging longitudinal trailing arms, rubber cone springs, telescopic dampers.

STEERING rack-and-pinion; turns lock to lock: 2.72.

BRAKES drum, dual circuit; lining area: front 66 sq in, 425 sq cm, rear 55 sq in, 355 sq cm, total 121 sq in, 780 sq cm.

ELECTRICAL EQUIPMENT 12 V; 36 Ah battery; 34 A alternator; 2 headlamps.

DIMENSIONS AND WEIGHT wheel base: 80.16 in, 204 cm; tracks: 47.75 in, 122 cm front, 46.50 in, 118 cm rear; length: City 120.25 in, 305 cm - Mayfair 121 in, 307 cm; width: 55.50 in, 141 cm; height: 52.50 in, 133 cm; ground clearance: 5.75 in, 14.7 cm; weight: 1,318 lb, 598 kg; weight distribution: 61% front, 39% rear; turning circle: 29 ft, 8.8 m; fuel tank: 7.5 imp gal, 9 US gal, 34 l.

BODY saloon/sedan; 2 doors; 4 seats, separate front seats.

PRACTICAL INSTRUCTIONS fuel: 94 oct petrol; oil: engine, gearbox and final drive 9 imp pt, 10.8 US pt, 5.1 l, SAE 20W-50, change every 12,000 miles, 19,300 km; greasing: every 6,000 miles, 9,700 km, 8 points; tappet clearances: inlet 0.012 in, 0.30 mm, exhaust 0.012 in, 0.30 mm; valve timing: 5° 45° 40° 10°; tyre pressure: front 24 psi, 1.7 atm, rear 21 psi, 1.5 atm.

OPTIONALS AP automatic transmission, hydraulic torque converter with 2 conic bevel gears (twin concentric differential-like gear clusters) with 4 ratios (I 2.690, II 1.845, III 1.460, IV 1.269, rev 2.690), operated by 3 brake bands and 2 multi-disc clutches, max ratio of converter at stall 2, possible manual selection; light alloy wheels and metallic spray (for Mayfair only).

MORGAN GREAT BRITAIN

4/4 1600

PRICES EX WORKS:	£
2-seater	**8,569***
4-seater	**9,431***

ENGINE Ford, front, 4 stroke; 4 cylinders, vertical, in line; 97.4 cu in, 1,597 cc (3.14 x 3.12 in, 80 x 79.5 mm); compression ratio: 9.5:1; max power (DIN): 96 hp (71 kW) at 6,000 rpm; max torque (DIN): 98 lb ft, 13.5 kg m (132 Nm) at 4,000 rpm; max engine rpm: 6,500; 60 hp/l (44 kW/l); cast iron block, light alloy head; 5 crankshaft bearings; valves: overhead; camshafts: 1, side; lubrication: rotary pump, full flow filter, 7.5 imp pt, 8.9 US pt, 4.2 l; 1 Weber 32/34 downdraught twin barrel carburettor; fuel feed: mechanical pump; water-cooled, 13.2 imp pt, 15.8 US pt, 7.5 l.

TRANSMISSION driving wheels: rear; clutch: single dry plate; gearbox: mechanical; gears: 5, fully synchronized; ratios: I 3.650, II 1.970, III 1.370, IV 1, V 0.830, rev 3.650; lever: central; final drive: hypoid bevel; axle ratio: 4.100; tyres: 165 x 15.

PERFORMANCE max speeds: (I) 33 mph, 53 km/h; (II) 60 mph, 96 km/h; (III) 87 mph, 140 km/h; (IV) and (V) 115 mph, 185 km/h; power-weight ratio: 2-seater 15.7 lb/hp (21.4 lb/kW), 7.1 kg/hp (9.6 kg/kW); carrying capacity: 353 lb, 160 kg; speed in direct drive at 1,000 rpm: 18.5 mph, 29.7 km/h; consumption: 35.3 m/imp gal, 29.4 m/US gal, 8 l x 100 km.

CHASSIS ladder frame, Z-section long members, tubular and box-type cross members; front suspension: independent, vertical sliding pillars, coil springs, telescopic dampers; rear: rigid axle, semi-elliptic leafsprings, lever dampers.

STEERING cam and peg; turns lock to lock: 2.25.

BRAKES front disc (diameter 11 in, 27.9 cm), rear drum, dual circuit; swept area: total 325.1 sq in, 2,097 sq cm.

ELECTRICAL EQUIPMENT 12 V; 38 Ah battery; alternator; 2 headlamps.

DIMENSIONS AND WEIGHT wheel base: 96 in, 244 cm; tracks: 47 in, 119 cm front, 49 in, 124 cm rear; length: 144 in, 366 cm; width: 56 in, 142 cm; height: 51 in, 129 cm; ground clearance: 7 in, 17.8 cm; weight: 2-seater 1,624 lb, 736 kg; weight distribution: 48% front, 52% rear; turning circle: 32 ft, 9.8 m; fuel tank: 2-seater 8.5 imp gal, 10.3 US gal, 39 l - 4-seater 10 imp gal, 12.1 US gal, 46 l.

BODY roadster; 2 doors; 2 or 4 seats.

PRACTICAL INSTRUCTIONS fuel: 97 oct petrol; oil: engine 7 imp pt, 8.5 US pt, 4 l, SAE 10W-30, change every 6,000 miles, 9,700 km - gearbox 1.8 imp pt, 2.1 US pt, 1 l, SAE 80 - final drive 1.9 imp pt, 2.3 US pt, 1.1 l, SAE 90; greasing: every 3,000 and 9,000 miles, 4,800 and 14,500 km, 10

MINI Mayfair Saloon

MORGAN 4/4 1600 4-seater

MORGAN Plus 8

points; tyre pressure: front 17 psi, 1.2 atm, rear 17 psi, 1.2 atm.

OPTIONALS wire wheels; tonneau cover; reclining backrests; leather upholstery; headrests; light alloy body.

4/4 1600 TC

See 4/4 1600, except for:

PRICES EX WORKS:	£
2-seater	8,766*
4-seater	9,628*

ENGINE Fiat, front, 4 stroke; 4 cylinders, vertical, in line; 96.7 cu in, 1,585 cc (3.31 x 2.81 in, 84 x 71.5 mm); max power (DIN): 97 hp (71 kW) at 6,000 rpm; max torque (DIN): 94 lb ft, 13 kg m (127 Nm) at 3,800 rpm; 61.2 hp/l (44.8 kW/l); valves: overhead, Vee-slanted, thimble tappets; camshafts: 2, overhead, cogged belt; lubrication: 8.3 imp pt, 9.9 US pt, 4.7 l; 1 Weber 32 ADF 53/250 or Solex C 32 TEE/10 downdraught twin barrel carburettor; cooling: 13.5 imp pt, 16.1 US pt, 7.7 l.

TRANSMISSION gearbox: mechanical; gears: 5, fully synchronized; ratios: I 3.612, II 2.045, III 1.357, IV 1, V 0.834, rev 3.244.

PERFORMANCE max speeds: (I) 35 mph, 56 km/h; (II) 62 mph, 100 km/h; (III) 88 mph, 141 km/h; (IV) 115 mph, 185 km/h; (V) 117 mph, 188 km/h; power-weight ratio: 15.7 lb/hp (21.4 lb/kW), 7.1 kg/hp (9.6 kg/kW); consumption: 34 m/imp gal, 28.3 m/US gal, 8.3 l x 100 km.

PRACTICAL INSTRUCTIONS fuel: 98 oct petrol; oil: engine 8.3 imp pt, 9.9 US pt, 4.7 l, SAE 10W-30, change every 6,000 miles, 9,700 km - gearbox 3.2 imp pt, 3.8 US pt, 1.8 l, SAE 90 EP - final drive 1.9 imp pt, 2.3 US pt, 1.1 l, SAE 90 EP; greasing: every 3,000 and 9,000 miles, 4,800 and 14,500 km, 10 points.

Plus 8

See 4/4 1600, except for:

PRICE EX WORKS: £ 11,651*

ENGINE Rover; 8 cylinders, in Vee; 215.3 cu in, 3,528 cc (3.50 x 2.80 in, 89 x 71 mm); compression ratio: 9.3: 1; max power (DIN): 155 hp (114 kW) at 5,250 rpm; max torque (DIN): 199 lb, 27.5 kg m (270 Nm) at 2,500 rpm; max engine rpm: 5,800; 43.9 hp/l (32.3 kW/l); light alloy block and head; valves: hydraulic tappets; camshafts: 1, at centre of Vee; lubrication: gear pump, full flow filter, 9.5 imp pt, 11.4 US pt, 5.4 l; 2 Zenith-Stromberg 175 CDEF carburettors; water-cooled, 15 imp pt, 18 US pt, 8.5 l, electric thermostatic fan.

TRANSMISSION clutch: single dry plate (diaphragm), hydraulically controlled; gears: 5, fully synchronized; ratios: I 3.320, II 2.080, III 1.390, IV 1, V 0.792, rev 3.110; final drive: hypoid bevel, limited slip; axle ratio: 3.310; width of rims: 6.5"; tyres: 205 x 15.

PERFORMANCE max speeds: (I) 40 mph, 64 km/h; (II) 64 mph, 103 km/h; (III) 95 mph, 153 km/h; (IV) 125 mph, 201 km/h; (V) 130 mph, 209 km/h; power-weight ratio: 11.8 lb/hp (16 lb/kW), 5.3 kg/hp (7.3 kg/kW); acceleration: standing ¼ mile 14.5 sec, 0-50 mph (0-80 km/h) 5.1 sec; speed in direct drive at 1,000 rpm: 27.4 mph, 44.1 km/h; consumption: 24 m/imp gal, 20.1 m/US gal, 11.7 l x 100 km.

ELECTRICAL EQUIPMENT 58 Ah battery; 4 headlamps.

DIMENSIONS AND WEIGHT wheel base: 98 in, 249 cm; tracks: 52 in, 132 cm front, 53 in, 135 cm rear; length: 147 in, 373 cm; width: 62 in, 158 cm; height: 52 in, 132 cm; weight: 1,826 lb, 828 kg; turning circle: 38 ft, 11.5 m; fuel tank: 13.5 imp gal, 16.1 US gal, 61 l.

OPTIONALS leather upholstery; reclining backrests; rack-and-pinion steering; headrests; light alloy body.

MORRIS GREAT BRITAIN

Ital Series

	PRICES EX WORKS:	£
1	1.3 SL 4-dr Saloon	4,354*
2	1.3 SL 4+1-dr Estate	5,168*
3	1.3 SLX 4-dr Saloon	4,897*
4	1.7 SL 4+1-dr Estate	5,388*
5	1.7 SLX 4-dr Saloon	5,115*
6	1.7 SLX 4+1-dr Estate	5,651*

Power team:	Standard for:	Optional for:
61 hp	1 to 3	—
77 hp	4 to 6	—

61 hp power team

ENGINE front, 4 stroke; 4 cylinders, in line; 77.8 cu in, 1,275 cc (2.78 x 3.20 in, 70.6 x 81.3 mm); compression ratio: 9.4:1; max power (DIN): 61 hp (44 kW) at 5,300 rpm; max torque (DIN): 69 lb ft, 9.5 kg m (93 Nm) at 2,950 rpm; max engine rpm: 6,000; 47.8 hp/l (34.5 kW/l); cast iron block and head; 3 crankshaft bearings; valves: overhead, in line, push-rods and rockers; camshafts: 1, side; lubrication: rotary pump, full flow filter, 6.5 imp pt, 7.8 US pt, 3.7 l; 1 SU type HIF 44 semi-downdraught carburettor; fuel feed: mechanical pump; water-cooled, 7.4 imp pt, 8.9 US pt, 4.2 l.

TRANSMISSION driving wheels: rear; clutch: single dry plate (diaphragm), hydraulically controlled; gearbox: mechanical; gears: 4, fully synchronized; ratios: I 3.410, II 2.110, III 1.430, IV 1, rev 3.750; lever: central; final drive: hypoid bevel; axle ratio: 3.890; width of rims: 4.5"; tyres: 155 SR x 13.

PERFORMANCE max speeds: (I) 30 mph, 48 km/h; (II) 49 mph, 79 km/h; (III) 72 mph, 116 km/h; (IV) 86 mph, 138 km/h; power-weight ratio: saloons 33.9 lb/hp (47 lb/kW), 15.4 kg/hp (21.3 kg/kW); carrying capacity: 882 lb, 400 kg; speed in direct drive at 1,000 rpm: 16.8 mph, 27 km/h; consumption: 40.4 m/imp gal, 33.6 m/US gal, 7 l x 100 km.

CHASSIS integral; front suspension: independent, wishbones, lower trailing links, longitudinal torsion bars, lever dampers as upper arms, anti-roll bar (except Estate), telescopic dampers; rear: rigid axle, semi-elliptic leafsprings, anti-roll bar (except Estate), telescopic dampers.

STEERING rack-and-pinion; turns lock to lock: 3.70.

BRAKES front disc (diameter 9.78 in, 24.8 cm), rear drum, dual circuit, servo; swept area: front 182.2 sq in, 1,175 sq cm, rear 76 sq in, 490 sq cm, total 258.2 sq in, 1,665 sq cm.

ELECTRICAL EQUIPMENT 12 V; 40 Ah battery; 34 A alternator; Lucas distributor; 2 halogen headlamps.

DIMENSIONS AND WEIGHT 96 in, 244 cm; front and rear track: 52 in, 132 cm; length: 170.98 in, 434 cm - Estate 172.36 in, 438 cm; width: 64.41 in, 164 cm; height: 55.83 in, 142 cm; ground clearance: 6.10-6.30 in, 15.5-16 cm; weight: SL and SLX saloons 2,070 lb, 939 kg - SL Estate 2,181 lb, 989 kg; turning circle: 33 ft, 10.1 m; fuel tank: 11.5 imp gal, 13.7 US gal, 52 l.

BODY saloon/sedan, 4 doors - estate car/st. wagon, 4+1 doors; 5 seats, separate front seats, reclining backrests; heated rear window; (for SLX Saloon only) headrests and tinted glass; (for SL Estate only) rear window wiper-washer.

PRACTICAL INSTRUCTIONS fuel: 97 oct petrol; oil: engine 6.5 imp pt, 7.8 US pt, 3.7 l, SAE 20W-50, change every 12,000 miles, 19,300 km - gearbox 2.2 imp pt, 2.5 US pt, 1.2 l, SAE 90 EP, change every 18,600 miles, 30,000 km - final drive 1.2 imp pt, 1.5 US pt, 0.7 l, change every 18,600 miles, 30,000 km; greasing: every 6,000 miles, 9,700 km; tyre pressure: front 26 psi, 1.8 atm, rear 28 psi, 2 atm.

MORRIS Ital 1.7 SLX Estate

77 hp power team

See 61 hp power team, except for:

ENGINE 103.4 cu in, 1,695 cc (3.33 x 2.98 in, 84.5 x 75.8 mm); compression ratio: 9:1; max power (DIN): 77 hp (57 kW) at 5,150 rpm; max torque (DIN): 93 lb ft, 12.9 kg m (127 Nm) at 3,400 rpm; max engine rpm: 5,600; 45.9 hp/l (32.9 kW/l); cast iron block, light alloy head; 5 crankshaft bearings; camshafts: 1, overhead, cogged belt; 1 SU type HIF 6 semi-downdraught carburettor; cooling: 10 imp pt, 12 US pt, 5.7 l.

TRANSMISSION gearbox ratios: I 3.110, II 1.930, III 1.310, IV 1, rev 3.420; axle ratio: 3.640.

PERFORMANCE max speeds: (I) 33 mph, 53 km/h; (II) 53 mph, 85 km/h; (III) 78 mph, 125 km/h; (IV) 95 mph, 153 km/h; power-weight ratio: SLX Saloon 27.8 lb/hp (37.5 lb/kW), 12.6 kg/hp (17 kg/kW); speed in direct drive at 1,000 rpm: 18.1 mph, 29.2 km/h; consumption: 29.8 m/imp gal, 24 m/US gal, 9.8 l x 100 km at 75 mph, 120 km/h.

ELECTRICAL EQUIPMENT 55 Ah battery.

DIMENSIONS AND WEIGHT weight: SLX Saloon 2,139 lb, 970 kg - SL and SLX estate cars 2,260 lb, 1,025 kg.

NOVA Sports

NOVA GREAT BRITAIN

Sports

PRICE EX WORKS: £ 4,300*

ENGINE Volkswagen, rear, 4 stroke; 4 cylinders, horizontally opposed; 96.7 cu in, 1,584 cc (3.37 x 2.72 in, 85.5 x 69 mm); compression ratio: 7.5:1; max power (DIN): 50 hp (37 kW) at 4,000 rpm; max torque (DIN): 78 lb ft, 10.8 kg m (106 Nm) at 2,800 rpm; max engine rpm: 4,500; 31.6 hp/l (23.2 kW/l); block with cast iron liners and light alloy fins, light alloy head; 4 crankshaft bearings; valves: overhead, push-rods and rockers; camshafts: 1, central, lower; lubrication: gear pump, filter in sump, oil cooler, 4.4 imp pt, 5.3 US pt, 2.5 l; 1 Nikki downdraught carburettor; fuel feed: mechanical pump; air-cooled.

TRANSMISSION driving wheels: rear; clutch: single dry plate, heavy-duty; gearbox: mechanical; gears: 4, fully synchronized; ratios: I 3.800, II 2.060, III 1.260, IV 0.890, rev 3.610; lever: central; final drive: spiral bevel; axle ratio: 4.125; width of rims: 7''; tyres: 205 x 14.

PERFORMANCE max speed: 110 mph, 177 km/h; power-weight ratio: 31.3 lb/hp (42.6 lb/kW), 14.2 kg/hp (19.3 kg/kW); carrying capacity: 353 lb, 160 kg; consumption: 35 m/imp gal, 29 m/US gal, 8.1 l x 100 km.

CHASSIS backbone platform; front suspension: independent, twin swinging longitudinal trailing arms, transverse laminated torsion bars, anti-roll bar, lowered and uprated telescopic dampers; rear: independent, semi-trailing arms, transverse compensating torsion bar, lowered telescopic dampers.

STEERING worm and roller, telescopic damper.

BRAKES front disc, rear drum.

ELECTRICAL EQUIPMENT 12 V; 12 V heavy-duty battery; dynamo; Bosch distributor; 2 headlamps.

DIMENSIONS AND WEIGHT length: 174 in, 442 cm; width: 67 in, 170 cm; height: 42 in, 107 cm; ground clearance: 5 in, 13 cm; weight: 1,568 lb, 711 kg; weight distribution: 40% front, 60% rear; fuel tank: 9 imp gal, 10.8 US gal, 41 l.

BODY sports, in plastic material with lift-up roof section; 1 door; 2 seats.

PRACTICAL INSTRUCTIONS fuel: 87 oct petrol; oil: engine 4.4 imp pt, 5.3 US pt, 2.5 l, SAE 10W-20 (winter) 20W-30 (summer), change every 3,100 miles, 5,000 km - gearbox and final drive 5.3 imp pt, 6.3 US pt, 3 l, SAE 90, change every 31,000 miles, 50,000 km; greasing: every 6,200 miles, 10,000 km, 4 points; spark plug: 175°; tappet clearances: inlet 0.004 in, 0.10 mm, exhaust 0.004 in, 0.10 mm; valve timing: 7°30' 37° 43°30' 4°.

OPTIONALS servo brake; electric roof; air-conditioning; tinted glass; Bermuda sunroof; spare wheel; halogen head-lamps; BL suspension.

OB & D GREAT BRITAIN

Madison Special

PRICE EX WORKS: £ 8,951*

ENGINE VW-Porsche, rear, 4 stroke; 4 cylinders, horizontally opposed; 112 cu in, 1,835 cc (3.62 x 2.72 in, 92 x 69 mm); compression ratio: 8.5:1; max power (DIN): 94 hp (69 kW) at 5,200 rpm; max engine rpm: 6,000; 51.2 hp/l (37.6 kW/l); light alloy block and head; 4 crankshaft bearings; valves: overhead, slanted at 160°, push-rods and rockers; camshafts: 1, central; lubrication: gear pump, full flow filter, 7.5 imp pt, 8.9 US pt, 4.2 l; 1 Weber 40 DCNF downdraught twin barrel carburettor; fuel feed: mechanical pump; air-cooled.

TRANSMISSION driving wheels: rear; clutch: single dry plate (diaphragm), hydraulically controlled; gearbox: mechanical; gears: 4, fully synchronized; ratios: I 3.810, II 2.110, III 1.400, IV 1, rev 4.300; lever: central; final drive: hypoid bevel; axle ratio: 3.910; width of rims: 6''; tyres: Michelin XZX 185/70 HR x 15.

PERFORMANCE max speed: 110 mph, 177 km/h; power-weight ratio: 21.4 lb/hp (29.1 lb/kW), 9.7 kg/hp (13.2 kg/kW); carrying capacity: 353 lb, 160 kg; consumption: 30 m/imp gal, 25 m/US gal, 9.4 l x 100 km.

CHASSIS box type frame; front suspension: independent, twin transverse laminated torsion bars, trailing arms, coil springs, anti-roll bar, telescopic dampers; rear: independent, coil springs, anti roll bar, telescopic dampers.

STEERING recirculating ball.

BRAKES front disc, rear drum, dual circuit, servo; swept area: front 108.8 sq in, 702 sq cm, rear 111 sq in, 716 sq cm, total 219.8 sq in, 1,418 sq cm.

ELECTRICAL EQUIPMENT 12 V; 36 Ah battery; 30 A alternator; Bosch transistorized ignition; 2 halogen headlamps.

DIMENSIONS AND WEIGHT wheel base: 95 in, 241 cm; tracks: 51.50 in, 131 cm front, 53 in, 135 cm rear; length: 147 in, 373 cm; width: 69 in, 175 cm; height: 45.75 in, 116 cm; ground clearance: 6 in, 15.2 cm; weight: 2,015 lb, 914 kg; weight distribution: 35% front, 65% rear; fuel tank: 12.5 imp gal, 15 US gal, 57 l.

BODY sports, in fiberglass material; 2 doors; 2 separate seats.

PRACTICAL INSTRUCTIONS oil: engine 7.5 imp pt, 8.9 US pt, 4.2 l, SAE 30, change every 3,000 miles, 4,800 km; spark plug: Bosch 175 T1; tappet clearances: inlet 0.006 in, 0.15 mm, exhaust 0.006 in, 0.15 mm; valve timing: 7°30' 37° 44°30' 4°; tyre pressure: front 24 psi, 1.7 atm, rear 28 psi, 2 atm.

OPTIONALS turbocharger; air-conditioning.

OB & D Madison Special

PANTHER GREAT BRITAIN

Kallista 1.6

PRICE EX WORKS: £ 6,945*

ENGINE Ford, front, 4 stroke; 4 cylinders, in line; 97.4 cu in, 1,597 cc (3.15 x 3.13 in, 80 x 79.5 mm); compression ratio: 9.5:1; max power (DIN): 96 hp (71 kW) at 6,000 rpm; max torque (DIN): 98 lb ft, 13.5 kg m (132 Nm) at 4,000 rpm; max engine rpm: 6,250; 60.1 hp/l (44.2 kW/l); cast iron block, light alloy head, hemispherical combustion chambers; 5 crankshaft bearings; valves: overhead, transverse, hydraulic tappets, CVH (compound valve hemispherical); camshafts: 1, overhead, cogged belt; lubrication: gear pump, full flow filter (cartridge), 6.5 imp pt, 7.8 US pt, 3.7 l; 1 Weber-Venturi DFT downdraught twin barrel carburettor; fuel feed: mechanical pump; water-cooled, 15 imp pt, 18 US pt, 8.5 l, electric thermostatic fan.

TRANSMISSION driving wheels: rear; clutch: single dry plate (diaphragm); gearbox: mechanical; gears: 5, fully synchronized; ratios: I 3.650, II 1.950, III 1.370, IV 1, V 0.820, rev 3.660; lever: central; final drive: spiral bevel; axle ratio: 3.750; width of rims: 4.5''; tyres: 165 SR x 13.

PERFORMANCE max speed: 100 mph, 161 km/h; power-weight ratio: 20.1 lb/hp (27.3 lb/kW), 9.1 kg/hp (12.9 kg/kW); carrying capacity: 221 lb, 100 kg; speed in top at 1,000 rpm: 21.9 mph, 35.2 km/h; consumption: 34 m/imp gal, 28.3 m/US gal, 8.3 l x 100 km.

CHASSIS box-type ladder frame; front suspension: independent, upper and lower wishbones, coil springs, telescopic dampers; rear: rigid axle, Panhard rod, upper and lower trailing radius arms, coil springs, telescopic dampers.

STEERING rack-and-pinion; turns lock to lock: 3.71.

BRAKES front disc, rear drum, dual circuit, servo.

ELECTRICAL EQUIPMENT 12 V; 40 Ah battery; 500 W alternator; Motorcraft or Bosch electronic ignition; 2 headlamps.

DIMENSIONS AND WEIGHT wheel base: 100.35 in, 255 cm; tracks: 57.48 in, 146 cm front, 54.33 in, 138 cm rear; length: 153.74 in, 390 cm; width: 67.32 in, 171 cm; height: 49.02 in, 124 cm; ground clearance: 3.94 in, 10 cm; weight: 1,918 lb, 870 kg; weight distribution: 50% front, 50% rear; turning circle: 33.1 ft, 10.1 m; fuel tank: 11.4 imp gal, 13.7 US gal, 52 l.

BODY roadster; 2 doors; 2 seats, separate front seats.

PRACTICAL INSTRUCTIONS fuel: 97 oct petrol; oil: engine 6.5 imp pt, 7.8 US pt, 3.7 l, SAE W30, change every 6,000 miles, 9,700 km - gearbox 3.5 imp pt, 4.2 US pt, 2 l, SAE 80, no change recommended - final drive 1.9 imp pt, 2.3 US pt, 1.1 l, no change recommended; greasing: none; spark plug: AGR22C; tyre pressure: front 23 psi, 1.6 atm, rear 24 psi, 1.7 atm.

OPTIONALS 185/70 HR x 13 tyres with 5.5" wide rims; light alloy wheels; halogen headlamps; electric windows; headrests; tinted glass; metallic spray; Connolly leather upholstery.

PANTHER Kallista 2.8 Injection

Kallista 2.8

See Kallista 1.6, except for:

PRICE EX WORKS: £ 7,485*

ENGINE 6 cylinders, Vee-slanted at 60°; 170.4 cu in, 2,792 cc (3.66 x 2.70 in, 93 x 68.5 mm); compression ratio: 9.2:1; max power (DIN): 135 hp (99 kW) at 5,200 rpm; max torque (DIN): 162 lb ft, 22.3 kg m (217 Nm) at 3,000 rpm; 48.4 hp/l (35.6 kW/l); cast iron block and head; 4 crankshaft bearings; valves: overhead, push-rods and rockers; lubrication: 9.3 imp pt, 11.2 US pt, 5.3 l; 1 Solex-Venturi downdraught twin barrel carburettor; cooling: 18.3 imp pt, 21.8 US pt, 10.5 l.

TRANSMISSION gearbox ratios: I 3.360, II 1.810, III 1.260, IV 1, V 0.830, rev 3.370; axle ratio: 3.090; width of rims: 5"; tyres: 185/70 HR x 13 (standard).

PERFORMANCE max speed: 110 mph, 177 km/h; power-weight ratio: 15.4 lb/hp (20.9 lb/kW), 7 kg/hp (9.5 kg/kW); speed in top at 1,000 rpm: 26.6 mph, 42.8 km/h.

DIMENSIONS AND WEIGHT weight: 2,073 lb, 940 kg; weight distribution: 52% front, 48% rear.

PRACTICAL INSTRUCTIONS oil: engine 9.3 imp pt, 11.2 US pt, 5.3 l, SAE W30, change every 6,000 miles, 9,700 km - final drive 2.5 imp pt, 3 US pt, 1.4 l, SAE 90, no change recommended.

OPTIONALS automatic transmission with 3 ratios, possible manual selection (I 2.470, II 1.470, III 1, rev 2.110), speed in top at 1,000 rpm 22.1 mph, 35.5 km/h; 205/60 HR x 14 tyres with 6" wide rims; light alloy wheels; halogen headlamps; electric windows; headrests; tinted glass; metallic spray; Connolly leather upholstery.

Kallista 2.8 Injection

See Kallista 1.6, except for:

PRICE EX WORKS: £ 8,985*

ENGINE 6 cylinders, Vee-slanted at 60°; 170.4 cu in, 2,792 cc (3.66 x 2.70 in, 93 x 68.5 mm); compression ratio: 9.2:1; max power (DIN): 150 hp (110 kW) at 5,700 rpm; max torque (DIN): 159 lb ft, 22 kg m (216 Nm) at 4,000 rpm; max engine rpm: 6,300; 53.7 hp/l (39.4 kW/l); cast iron block and head; 4 crankshaft bearings; valves: overhead, push-rods and rockers; lubrication: 7.5 imp pt, 9.1 US pt, 4.3 l; Bosch K-Jetronic injection; fuel feed: electric pump; cooling: 7.7 imp pt, 9.3 US pt, 4.4 l.

TRANSMISSION gearbox ratios: I 3.360, II 1.810, III 1.260, IV 1, V 0.830, rev 3.370; axle ratio: 3.090; width of rims: 6"; tyres: 195/60 HR x 14.

PERFORMANCE max speed: 123 mph, 198 km/h; power-weight ratio: 14.1 lb/hp (19.4 lb/kW), 6.4 kg/hp (8.8 kg/kW);carrying capacity: 441 lb, 200 kg; speed in top at 1,000 rpm: 26.6 mph, 42.8 km/h.

ELECTRICAL EQUIPMENT 50 Ah battery; Bosch electronic ignition.

DIMENSIONS AND WEIGHT tracks: 57.10 in, 145 cm front, 53.95 in, 137 cm rear; length: 151.55 in, 385 cm; width: 66.55 in, 169 cm; height: 50 in, 127 cm; ground clearance: 4.35 in, 11 cm; weight: 2,128 lb, 965 kg; weight distribution: 52% front axle, 48% rear axle; fuel tank: 11 imp gal, 13.2 Us gal, 50 l.

BODY headrests (standard).

PRACTICAL INSTRUCTIONS oil: engine 7.5 imp pt, 9.1 US pt, 4.3 l, SAE 20W-50, change every 6,000 miles, 9,700 km - final drive 2.5 imp pt, 3 US pt, 1.4 l, SAE 90, no change recommended; spark plug: Motorcraft Super AGP 22C; tappet clearances: inlet 0.014 in, 0.35 mm, exhaust 0.016 in, 0.40 mm; valve timing: 24° 70° 73° 25°; tyre pressure: front 20 psi, 1.4 atm, rear 22 psi, 1.5 atm.

OPTIONALS light alloy wheels; halogen headlamps; electric windows; tinted glass; metallic spray; Connolly leather upholstery.

RELIANT GREAT BRITAIN

Rialto

PRICES EX WORKS:

	£
2-dr Saloon	3,335*
2+1-dr Saloon	3,535*
GLS 2-dr Saloon	3,635*
GLS 2+1-dr Saloon	3,835*

ENGINE front, 4 stroke; 4 cylinders, in line; 51.7 cu in, 848 cc (2.46 x 2.72 in, 62.5 x 69.1 mm); compression ratio: 9.5:1; max power (DIN): 40 hp (29 kW) at 5,500 rpm; max torque (DIN): 46 lb ft, 6.3 kg m (62 Nm) at 3,500 rpm; max engine rpm: 5,500; 47.2 hp/l (34.7 kW/l); light alloy block and head; 3 crankshaft bearings; valves: overhead, push-rods and rockers; camshafts: 1, side; lubrication: rotary pump, full flow filter, 5.5 imp pt, 6.6 US pt, 3.1 l; 1 SU type HS2 1¼ semi-downdraught carburettor; fuel feed: mechanical pump; water-cooled, 5 imp pt, 5.9 US pt, 2.8 l.

TRANSMISSION driving wheels: rear; clutch: single dry plate; gearbox: mechanical; gears: 4, fully synchronized; ratios: I 3.880, II 2.050, III 1.320, IV 1, rev 3.250; lever: central; final drive: spiral bevel; axle ratio: 3.230; width of rims: 3.5"; tyres: 5.20 x 10.

PERFORMANCE max speeds: (I) 25 mph, 40 km/h; (II) 47 mph, 75 km/h; (III) 73 mph, 117 km/h; (IV) 80 mph, 128 km/h; power-weight ratio: 24 lb/hp (32.7 lb/kW), 10.9 kg/hp (14.8 kg/kW); carrying capacity: 788 lb, 357 kg; acceleration: standing ¼ mile 20.9 sec, 0-50 mph (0-80 km/h) 11.4 sec; speed in direct drive at 1,000 rpm: 17 mph, 27.3 km/h; consumption: 60 m/imp gal, 50 m/US gal, 4.7 l x 100 km.

CHASSIS box-section ladder frame, tubular cross members; front suspension: single wheel, swinging leading arm, coil springs, telescopic dampers; rear: rigid axle, semi-elliptic leafsprings, anti-roll bar, telescopic dampers.

STEERING worm and peg; turns lock to lock: 2.25.

BRAKES drum, single circuit; swept area: front 33 sq in, 213 sq cm, rear 55 sq in, 355 sq cm, total 88 sq in, 568 sq cm.

ELECTRICAL EQUIPMENT 12 V; 30 Ah battery; 28 A alternator; Lucas distributor; 2 headlamps.

DIMENSIONS AND WEIGHT wheel base: 85 in, 216 cm; front and rear track: 49 in, 124 cm; length: 133 in, 338 cm - GLS saloons 134 in, 340 cm; width: 57 in, 145 cm; height: 55 in, 140 cm; ground clearance: 5 in, 12.7 cm; weight: 962 lb, 436 kg; weight distribution: 35% front, 65% rear; turning circle: 27 ft, 8.2 m; fuel tank: 6 imp gal, 7.1 US gal, 27 l.

BODY saloon/sedan, in g.r.p. material; 2 or 2+1 doors; 4 seats, separate front seats.

PRACTICAL INSTRUCTIONS fuel: 97 oct petrol; oil: engine 5.5 imp pt, 6.6 US pt, 3.1 l, SAE 20W-50, change every 6,000 miles, 9,700 km - gearbox 1.1 imp pt, 1.3 US pt, 0.6 l, SAE 80 EP, change every 12,000 miles, 19,300 km - final drive 2.2 imp pt, 2.5 US pt, 1.2 l, SAE 90 EP; greasing: every 6,000 miles, 9,700 km, 4 points; spark plug: Motorcraft AGR 32; tappet clearances: inlet 0.010 in, 0.25 mm, exhaust 0.010 in, 0.25 mm; valve timing: 13° 72° 54° 29°; tyre pressure: front 30 psi, 2.1 atm, rear 24 psi, 1.7 atm.

OPTIONALS 145 x 10 tyres.

Fox

PRICE EX WORKS: £ 3,250*

ENGINE front, 4 stroke; 4 cylinders, in line; 51.7 cu in, 848 cc (2.46 x 2.72 in, 62.5 x 69.1 mm); compression ratio: 9.5:1; max power (DIN): 40 hp (29 kW) at 5,500 rpm; max torque (DIN): 46 lb ft, 6.4 kg m (63 Nm) at 3,500 rpm; max engine rpm: 6,000; 47.2 hp/l (34.7 kW/l); light alloy block and head; 3 crankshaft bearings; valves: overhead, push-

RELIANT Rialto Saloon

FOX

rods and rockers; camshafts: 1, side; lubrication: gear pump, full flow filter, 5.5 imp pt, 6.6 US pt, 3.1 l; 1 SU type H52 downdraught carburettor; fuel feed: mechanical pump; water-cooled, 6.5 imp pt, 7.8 US pt, 3.7 l.

TRANSMISSION driving wheels: rear; clutch: single dry plate (diaphragm); gearbox: mechanical; gears: 4, fully synchronized; ratios: I 3.880, II 2.050, III 1.320, IV 1, rev 3.250; lever: central; final drive: hypoid bevel; axle ratio: 4.100; width of rims: 4.5"; tyres: 155 SR x 12.

PERFORMANCE carrying capacity: 840 lb, 380 kg.

CHASSIS integral; front suspension: independent, coil springs, anti-roll bar, telescopic dampers; rear: independent, semi-elliptic leafsprings, telescopic dampers.

STEERING rack-and-pinion; turns lock to lock: 3.66.

BRAKES drum.

ELECTRICAL EQUIPMENT 12 V; 30 Ah battery; 30 A alternator; Lucas distributor; 2 headlamps.

DIMENSIONS AND WEIGHT wheel base: 84.50 in, 214 cm; tracks: 48.30 in, 122 cm front, 49.61 in, 126 cm rear; length: 133.15 in, 338 cm; width: 60.75 in, 154 cm; height: 59.97 in, 152 cm; ground clearance: 6.51 in, 16.5 cm; fuel tank: 5.9 imp gal, 7.1 US gal, 27 l.

BODY hardtop, in g.r.p. material; 2 doors; 2+2 seats, separate front seats.

PRACTICAL INSTRUCTIONS fuel: 97 oct petrol; oil: engine 5.5 imp pt, 6.6 US pt, 3.1 l, SAE 20W-40, change every 6,200 miles, 10,000 km - gearbox 1.7 imp pt, 1.3 US pt, 0.6 l, SAE 80 EP - final drive 2.3 imp pt, 2.7 US pt, 1.3 l; greasing: every 6,200 miles, 10,000 km, 7 points; spark plug: AGR 32; tappet clearances: inlet 0.010 in, 0.25 mm, exhaust 0.010 in, 0.25 mm; valve timing: 20° 20° 20° 20°; tyre pressure: front 26 psi, 1.8 atm, rear 26 psi, 1.8 atm.

Scimitar

PRICES EX WORKS:	£
GTC 2-dr Convertible	**11,990***
GTE 2+1-dr Estate Car	**11,990***

ENGINE Ford, front, 4 stroke; 6 cylinders, Vee-slanted at 60°; 170.4 cu in, 2,792 cc (3.66 x 2.70 in, 93 x 68.5 mm); compression ratio: 9.2:1, max power (DIN): 135 hp (99 kW) at 5,200 rpm; max torque (DIN): 152 lb ft, 21 kg m (206 Nm) at 3,000 rpm; max engine rpm: 6,000; 48.4 hp/l (35.6 kW/l); cast iron block and head; 4 crankshaft bearings; valves: overhead, push-rods and rockers; camshafts: 1, at centre of Vee; lubrication: rotary pump, full flow filter, 7.5 imp pt, 8.9 US pt, 4.2 l; 1 Solex 78TF 9510 CA/DA downdraught twin barrel carburettor; fuel feed: mechanical pump; water-cooled, 21.5 imp pt, 26 US pt, 12.2 l, electric thermostatic fan.

TRANSMISSION driving wheels: rear; clutch: single dry plate (diaphragm); gearbox: mechanical; gears: 4 and overdrive on III and IV, fully synchronized; ratios: I 3.163, II 1.950, III 1.412 (overdrive 1.160), IV 1 (overdrive 0.780), rev 3.350; lever: central; final drive: hypoid bevel; axle ratio: 3.540; width of rims: 6"; tyres: 185 HR x 14.

PERFORMANCE max speed: 120 mph, 193 km/h; power-weight ratio: 20.7 lb/hp (28.1 lb/kW), 9.4 kg/hp (12.8 kg/kW); carrying capacity: 990 lb, 449 kg; speed in direct drive at 1,000 rpm: 20.9 mph, 33.6 km/h; consumption: 35.6 m/imp gal, 29.8 m/US gal, 7.9 l x 100 km at 56 mph, 90 km/h.

CHASSIS box-type ladder frame, tubular cross members; front suspension: independent, wishbones, anti-roll bar, coil springs/telescopic damper units; rear: rigid axle, twin trailing arms, transverse Watts linkage, coil springs/telescopic damper units.

STEERING rack-and-pinion, servo; turns lock to lock: 2.50.

BRAKES front disc (diameter 10.51 in, 26.6 cm), rear drum, rear compensator, servo; swept area: front 237 sq in, 1,529 sq cm, rear 110 sq in, 710 sq cm, total 347 sq in, 2,239 sq cm.

ELECTRICAL EQUIPMENT 12 V; 55 Ah battery; 770 W alternator; Motorcraft distributor; 4 headlamps.

DIMENSIONS AND WEIGHT wheel base: 103.80 in, 264 cm; tracks: 58.10 in, 148 cm front, 56.10 in, 142 cm rear; length: 174.50 in, 443 cm; width: 67.80 in, 172 cm; height: 52 in, 132 cm; ground clearance: 5.50 in, 14 cm; weight: 2,790 lb, 1,265 kg; weight distribution: 52% front, 48% rear; turning circle: 38.5 ft, 11.7 m; fuel tank: 20 imp gal, 24 US gal, 91 l.

BODY convertible, 2 doors - estate car/st. wagon, 2+1 doors, in g.r.p. material; 4 seats, separate front seats, reclining backrests; folding rear seats; heated rear window; (for GTE only) rear window wiper-washer.

PRACTICAL INSTRUCTIONS fuel: 97 oct petrol; oil: engine 7.5 imp pt, 8.9 US pt, 4.2 l, SAE 10W-40, change every 6,000 miles, 9,700 km - gearbox 5 imp pt, 6 US pt, 2.8 l, SAE 80, change every 6,000 miles, 9,700 km - final drive 3.5 imp pt, 4.2 US pt, 2 l, SAE 90, change every 6,000 miles, 9,700 km; greasing: every 6,000 miles, 9,700 km, 4 points; tappet clearances: inlet 0.014 in, 0.35 mm, exhaust 0.016 in, 0.40 mm; valve timing: 20° 56° 62° 14°; tyre pressure: front 24 psi, 1.6 atm, rear 24 psi, 1.6 atm.

OPTIONALS Ford C3 automatic transmission, hydraulic torque converter and planetary gears with 3 ratios (I 2.474, II 1.474, III 1, rev 2.111), max ratio of converter at stall 2, possible manual selection; electric windows; fog lamps; leather upholstery; light alloy wheels; (for GTC only) hardtop.

RELIANT Scimitar GTC Convertible

ROLLS-ROYCE GREAT BRITAIN

Silver Spirit

PRICE IN USA: $ 98,500*
PRICE EX WORKS: £ 55,240*

ENGINE front, 4 stroke; 8 cylinders, in Vee; 411.9 cu in, 6,750 cc (4.10 x 3.90 in, 104.1 x 99.1 mm); compression ratio: 9:1; aluminium alloy block and head, cast iron wet liners; 5 crankshaft bearings; valves: overhead, in line, slanted, push-rods and rockers, hydraulic tappets; camshafts: 1, at centre of Vee; lubrication: gear pump, full flow filter (cartridge), 16.5 imp pt, 19.9 US pt, 9.4 l; 2 SU type HIF7 horizontal carburettors; dual exhaust system; fuel feed: Pierburg electric pump; sealed circuit cooling, expansion tank, 28.5 imp pt, 34.2 US pt, 16.2 l, viscous coupling thermostatic fan, electric fan.

TRANSMISSION driving wheels: rear; gearbox: Turbo-Hydramatic 400 automatic transmission, hydraulic torque converter and planetary gears with 3 ratios, max ratio of converter at stall 2, possible manual selection; ratios: I 2.500, II 1.500, III 1, rev 2; lever: steering column; final drive: hypoid bevel; axle ratio: 3.080; width of rims: 6"; tyres: 235/70 HR x 15.

PERFORMANCE max speeds: (I) 47 mph, 76 km/h; (II) 79 mph, 126 km/h; (III) 118 mph, 190 km/h; carrying capacity: 1,014 lb, 460 kg; speed in direct drive at 1,000 rpm: 26.2 mph, 42.2 km/h; consumption: 16.1 m/imp gal, 13.4 m/US gal, 17.5 l x 100 km at 75 mph, 120 km/h.

CHASSIS integral, front and rear auxiliary frames; front suspension: independent, lower wishbones, coil springs, anti-roll bar, telescopic dampers; rear: independent, semi-trailing arms, coil springs, anti-roll bar, automatic levelling control, telescopic dampers.

STEERING rack-and-pinion, servo, right- or left-hand drive; turns lock to lock: 3.20.

BRAKES disc (diameter 11 in, 27.9 cm), front internal radial fins, dual circuit, servo; swept area: front 227 sq in, 1,464 sq cm, rear 286 sq in, 1,845 sq cm, total 513 sq in, 3,309 sq cm.

ELECTRICAL EQUIPMENT 12 V; 68 Ah battery; 75 A alterna-

RELIANT Fox

ROLLS-ROYCE Silver Spirit

ROLLS-ROYCE Silver Spur with division

ROLLS-ROYCE Silver Spur

tor; Lucas transistorized distributor; 4 headlamps, 2 front and 2 rear fog lamps.

DIMENSIONS AND WEIGHT wheel base: 120.47 in, 306 cm; front and rear track: 60.63 in, 154 cm; length: 207.48 in, 527 cm; width: 74.41 in, 189 cm; height: 58.66 in, 149 cm; ground clearance: 6.50 in, 16.5 cm; weight: 4,950 lb, 2,245 kg; turning circle: 39 ft, 11.9 m; fuel tank: 23.5 imp gal, 28.2 US gal, 107 l.

BODY saloon/sedan; 4 doors; 5 seats, separate front seats, adjustable and reclining backrests; automatic air-conditioning; heated rear window; electric windows; seat adjustment; gear range selector; exterior mirrors; central door locking.

PRACTICAL INSTRUCTIONS fuel: 98 oct petrol; oil: engine 16.5 imp pt, 19.9 US pt, 9.4 l, SAE 20W-50, change every 6,000 miles, 9,700 km - automatic transmission 18.6 imp pt, 22.4 US pt, 10.6 l, Dexron, change every 24,000 miles, 38,600 km - final drive 4.5 imp pt, 5.3 US pt, 2.5 l, SAE 90 EP, change every 24,000 miles, 38,600 km - power steering and automatic levelling control change every 20,000 miles, 32,000 km; greasing: every 12,000 miles 19,300 km, 5 points; spark plug: Champion RN 14Y; valve timing: 26° 60° 68° 18°; tyre pressure: front 24 psi, 1.7 atm, rear 28 psi, 2 atm.

VARIATIONS

(for USA and Japan only)
ENGINE 8:1 compression ratio, exhaust emission control, exhaust gas recirculation, catalytic converter, Bosch K-Jetronic injection.

(for Australia only)
ENGINE 8:1 compression ratio, exhaust emission control, exhaust gas recirculation.

OPTIONALS fire extinguisher; initials on doors; white sidewall tyres; hide trim to facia roll.

Silver Spur

See Silver Spirit, except for:

PRICE IN USA: $ 109,000*
PRICE EX WORKS: £ 62,778*

DIMENSIONS AND WEIGHT wheel base: 124.41 in, 316 cm; length: 211.42 in, 537 cm; weight: 5,012 lb, 2,273 kg; turning circle: 40.3 ft, 12.3 m.

Silver Spur with division

See Silver Spirit, except for:

PRICE EX WORKS: £ 68,278**

DIMENSIONS AND WEIGHT wheel base: 124.41 in, 316 cm; length: 211.42 in, 537 cm; weight: 5,180 lb, 2,349 kg; turning circle: 40.3 ft, 12.3 m.

BODY electric glass partition; air-conditioning.

Corniche

See Silver Spirit, except for:

PRICE IN USA: $ 156,000*
PRICE EX WORKS: £ 73,168*

ENGINE 1 Solex 4A1 4-barrel carburettor.

PERFORMANCE consumption: 14.6 m/imp gal, 12.2 m/US gal, 19.3 l x 100 km at 75 mph, 120 km/h.

DIMENSIONS AND WEIGHT wheel base: 120.10 in, 305 cm; tracks: 60 in, 152 cm front, 60.63 in, 154 cm rear; length: 204.55 in, 520 cm; width: 71.65 in, 182 cm; height: 60 in, 152 cm; ground clearance: 6 in, 15.2 cm; weight: 5,204 lb, 2,360 kg.

ELECTRICAL EQUIPMENT 55 A alternator.

BODY convertible; 2 doors; 4 seats.

VARIATIONS

(for USA and Japan only)
ENGINE 8:1 compression ratio, exhaust emission control, exhaust gas recirculation, catalytic converter, Bosch K-Jetronic injection.

(for Australia only)
ENGINE 8:1 compression ratio, exhaust emission control, exhaust gas recirculation, 2 SU type HIF7 horizontal carburettors.

ROLLS-ROYCE Camargue

Camargue

PRICE IN USA: $ 150,600*
PRICE EX WORKS: £ 83,122*

ENGINE front, 4 stroke; 8 cylinders in Vee; 411.9 cu in, 6,750 cc (4.10 x 3.90 in, 104.1 x 99.1 mm); compression ratio: 9:1; aluminium alloy block and head, cast iron wet liners; 5 crankshaft bearings; valves: overhead, in line, push-rods and rockers, hydraulic tappets; camshafts: 1, at centre of Vee; lubrication: gear pump, full flow filter (cartridge), 16.5 imp pt, 19.9 US pt, 9.4 l; 1 Solex 4A1 horizontal 4-barrel carburettor; dual exhaust system; fuel feed: Pierburg electric pump; sealed circuit cooling, expansion tank, 28.5 imp pt, 34.2 US pt, 16.2 l, viscous coupling thermostatic fan, electric fan.

TRANSMISSION driving wheels: rear; gearbox: Turbo-Hydramatic 400 automatic transmission, hydraulic torque converter and planetary gears with 3 ratios, max ratio of converter at stall 2, possible manual selection; ratios: I 2.500, II 1.500, III 1, rev 2; lever: steering column; final drive: hypoid bevel; axle ratio: 3.080; width of rims: 6''; tyres: HR70 x 15 or 235/70 HR x 15.

PERFORMANCE max speeds: (I) 47 mph, 76 km/h; (II) 79 mph, 127 km/h; (III) 118 mph, 190 km/h; carrying capacity: 882 lb, 400 kg; speed in direct drive at 1,000 rpm: 26.2 mph, 42.2 km/h; consumption: 14.6 m/imp gal, 12.2 m/US gal, 19.3 l x 100 km at 75 mph, 120 km/h.

CHASSIS integral, front and rear auxiliary frames; front suspension: independent, lower wishbones, coil springs, anti-roll bar, telescopic dampers; rear: independent, semi-trailing arms, coil springs, auxiliary gas spring, anti-roll bar, automatic levelling control, telescopic dampers.

STEERING rack-and-pinion, servo; turns lock to lock: 3.20.

BRAKES disc [diameter (twin calipers) 11 in, 27.9 cm], front internal radial fins, dual circuit, servo; swept area: front 227 sq in, 1,464 sq cm, rear 286 sq in, 1,845 sq cm, total 513 sq in, 3,309 sq cm.

ELECTRICAL EQUIPMENT 12 V; 68 Ah battery; 75 A alternator; Lucas Opus electronic ignition; 4 headlamps, 2 front and 2 rear fog lamps.

DIMENSIONS AND WEIGHT wheel base: 120.10 in, 305 cm; tracks: 60 in, 152 cm front, 59.60 in, 151 cm rear; length: 203.50 in, 517 cm; width: 75.59 in, 192 cm; height: 57.87 in, 147 cm; ground clearance: 6.50 in, 16.5 cm; weight: 5,138 lb, 2,330 kg; turning circle: 38.5 ft, 11.7 m; fuel tank: 23.5 imp gal, 28.2 US gal, 107 l.

BODY saloon/sedan; 2 doors; 5 seats, separate front seats, adjustable and reclining backrests, built-in headrests; leather upholstery; automatic air-conditioning; electric windows; seat adjustment; gear range selector; heated rear window; central door locking.

PRACTICAL INSTRUCTIONS fuel: 98 oct petrol; oil: engine 16.5 imp pt, 19.9 US pt, 9.4 l, SAE 20W-50, change every 6,000 miles, 9,700 km - automatic transmission 18.6 imp pt, 22.4 US pt, 10.6 l, Dexron, change every 24,000 miles, 38,600 km - final drive 4.5 imp pt, 5.3 US pt, 2.5 l, SAE 90 EP, change every 24,000 miles, 38,600 km - automatic levelling control 4.5 imp pt, 5.3 US pt, 2.5 l - power steering 3 imp pt, 3.6 US pt, 1.7 l; greasing: every 12,000 miles, 19,300 km; spark plug: Champion RN 14Y; tyre pressure: front 24 psi, 1.7 atm, rear 28 psi, 2 atm.

ROLLS-ROYCE Phantom VI

ROVER 2300 S Saloon

CAMARGUE

VARIATIONS

(for USA and Japan only)
ENGINE 8:1 compression ratio, exhaust emission control, exhaust gas recirculation, Bosch K-Jetronic injection.

(for Australia only)
ENGINE 8:1 compression ratio, exhaust emission control, exhaust gas recirculation, 2 SU type HIF7 horizontal carburettors.

Phantom VI

PRICE EX WORKS: quotation on request

ENGINE front, 4 stroke; 8 cylinders, in Vee; 411.9 cu in, 6,750 cc (4.10 x 3.90 in, 104.1 x 99.1 mm); compression ratio: 9:1; aluminium alloy block and head, cast iron wet liners; 5 crankshaft bearings; valves: overhead, in line, slanted, push-rods and rockers, hydraulic tappets; camshafts: 1, at centre of Vee; lubrication: gear pump, full flow filter (cartridge), 16.5 imp pt, 19.9 US pt, 9.4 l; 2 SU type HIF7 horizontal carburettors; fuel feed: 2 electric pumps; sealed circuit cooling, expansion tank, 28.5 imp pt, 34.2 US pt, 16.2 l, viscous coupling thermostatic fan.

TRANSMISSION driving wheels: rear; gearbox: Turbo-Hydramatic 400 automatic transmission, hydraulic torque converter and planetary gears with 3 ratios, max ratio of converter at stall 2, possible manual selection; ratios: I 2.500, II 1.500, III 1, rev 2; lever: steering column; final drive: hypoid bevel; axle ratio: 3.890; width of rims: 6"; tyres: 8.90 S x 15.

PERFORMANCE max speeds: (I) 38 mph, 61 km/h; (II) 66 mph, 106 km/h; (III) 112 mph, 180 km/h; carrying capacity: 1,235 lb, 560 kg; acceleration: standing ¼ mile 19.4 sec, 0-50 mph (0-80 km/h) 9.7 sec; speed in direct drive at 1,000 rpm: 22.5 mph, 36.2 km/h; consumption: 12.6 m/imp gal, 10.5 m/US gal, 22.5 l x 100 km at 75 mph, 120 km/h.

CHASSIS box-type ladder frame; front suspension: independent, wishbones, coil springs, anti-roll bar, lever dampers; rear: rigid axle, asymmetrical semi-elliptic leafsprings, Z-type transverse linkage bar, electrically adjustable lever dampers.

STEERING worm and roller, progressive servo (50%-80%); turns lock to lock: 4.25.

BRAKES drum, dual circuit, servo; swept area: front 211.9 sq in, 1,361 sq cm, rear 211.9 sq in, 1,361 sq cm, total 423.8 sq in, 2,722 sq cm.

ELECTRICAL EQUIPMENT 12 V; 68 Ah battery; 75 A alternator; Lucas Opus Mark II distributor; 4 headlamps.

DIMENSIONS AND WEIGHT wheel base: 145 in, 368 cm; tracks: 60.87 in, 155 cm front, 64 in, 162 cm rear; length: 238 in, 604 cm; width: 79 in, 201 cm; height: 69 in, 175 cm; ground clearance: 7.25 in, 18.4 cm; weight: 6,045 lb, 2,742 kg; weight distribution: 48% front, 52% rear; turning circle: 52 ft, 15.9 m; fuel tank: 23 imp gal, 27.7 US gal, 105 l.

BODY limousine; 4 doors; 7 seats, separate front seats; glass partition; air-conditioning; electric windows; heated rear window; central door locking.

PRACTICAL INSTRUCTIONS fuel: 98 oct petrol; oil: engine 16.5 imp pt, 19.9 US pt, 9.4 l, SAE 20W-50, change every 6,000 miles, 9,700 km - automatic transmission 18.6 imp pt, 22.4 US pt, 10.6 l, change every 24,000 miles, 38,600 km - final drive 1.8 imp pt, 2.1 US pt, 1 l, SAE 90 EP, change every 24,000 miles, 38,600 km; greasing: every 12,000 miles, 19,300 km, 21 points; spark plug: Champion RN 14Y; valve timing: 20° 61° 62° 19°; tyre pressure: front 24 psi, 1.7 atm, rear 30 psi, 2.1 atm.

OPTIONALS Landaulette version.

ROVER GREAT BRITAIN

3500 SE / Vanden Plas

PRICES EX WORKS:	£
3500 SE 4+1-dr Saloon	**12,747***
Vanden Plas 4+1-dr Saloon	**14,179***

ENGINE front, 4 stroke; 8 cylinders in Vee; 215 cu in, 3,528 cc (3.50 x 2.80 in, 88.9 x 71.1 mm); compression ratio: 9.3:1; max power (DIN): 155 hp (114 kW) at 5,200 rpm; max torque (DIN): 198 lb ft, 27.3 kg m (268 Nm) at 2,500 rpm; max engine rpm: 5,500; 43.9 hp/l (32.3 kW/l); light alloy block and head, dry liners; 5 crankshaft bearings; valves: overhead, in line, push-rods and rockers, hydraulic tappets; camshafts: 1, at centre of Vee; lubrication: gear pump, full flow filter, 9.7 imp pt, 11.6 US pt, 5.5 l; 2 Solex 175 CDEF horizontal carburettors; fuel feed: electric pump; water-cooled, 19.5 imp pt, 23.5 US pt, 11.1 l, viscous-coupling thermostatic fan.

TRANSMISSION driving wheels: rear; clutch: single dry plate (diaphragm), hydraulically controlled; gearbox: mechanical; gears: 5, fully synchronized; ratios: I 3.321, II 2.087, III 1.396, IV 1, V 0.792, rev 3.428; lever: central; final drive: hypoid bevel; axle ratio: 3.080; width of rims: 6"; tyres: 195 HR x 14.

PERFORMANCE max speed: 126 mph, 203 km/h; power-weight ratio: 3500 SE 19.9 lb/hp (27 lb/kW), 9 kg/hp (12.3 kg/kW); carrying capacity: 1,105 lb, 501 kg; acceleration: 0-50 mph (0-80 km/h) 6.4 sec; speed in top at 1,000 rpm: 29.7 mph, 47.8 km/h; consumption: 28 m/imp gal, 23.3 m/US gal, 10.1 l x 100 km at 75 mph, 120 km/h.

CHASSIS integral, front cross members; front suspension: independent, by McPherson, wishbones (lower trailing links), coil springs/telescopic damper struts, anti-roll bar; rear: rigid axle (torque tube), coil springs with combined telescopic dampers and self-levelling struts, Watts linkage.

STEERING rack-and-pinion, adjustable steering column, servo; turns lock to lock: 2.75.

BRAKES front disc (diameter 10.15 in, 25.8 cm), rear drum, dual circuit, rear compensator, servo.

ELECTRICAL EQUIPMENT 12 V; 68 Ah battery; 65 A alternator; Lucas electronic ignition; 4 halogen headlamps, 2 fog lamps.

DIMENSIONS AND WEIGHT wheel base: 111 in, 282 cm; front and rear track: 59 in, 150 cm; length: 185 in, 469 cm; width: 69.60 in, 177 cm; height: 54.33 in, 138 cm; weight: 3500 SE Saloon 3,080 lb, 1,397 kg - Vanden Plas Saloon 3,097 lb, 1,404 kg; weight distribution: 55% front, 45% rear; turning circle: 34.3 ft, 10.5 m; fuel tank: 14.5 imp gal, 17.4 US gal, 66 l.

BODY saloon/sedan; 4+1 doors; 5 seats, separate front seats, reclining backrests, adjustable built-in headrests; electric windows; laminated windscreen with tinted glass; heated rear window; metallic spray; folding rear seat; sunroof; leather upholstery, air-conditioning and cruise control (for Vanden Plas only).

PRACTICAL INSTRUCTIONS fuel: 97 oct petrol; oil: engine 9.7 imp pt, 11.6 US pt, 5.5 l, SAE 20W-30, change every 12,000 miles, 19,300 km - gearbox 2.7 imp pt, 3.2 US pt, 1.5 l, SAE 90 EP - final drive 1.6 imp pt, 1.9 US pt, 0.9 l, SAE 90 EP; valve timing: 30° 75° 68° 37°; tyre pressure: front 26 psi, 1.8 atm, rear 26 psi, 1.8 atm.

OPTIONALS automatic transmission, hydraulic torque converter and planetary gears with 3 ratios (I 2.390, II 1.450, III 1, rev 2.090), max ratio of converter at stall 2.08, possible manual selection, max speed 123 mph, 198 km/h, speed in direct drive at 1,000 rpm 23.5 mph, 37.9 km/h, consumption 23.5 m/imp gal, 19.6 m/US gal, 12 l x 100 km; leather upholstery; air-conditioning and cruise control (for 3500 SE only); central door locking.

2000

See 3500 SE/Vanden Plas, except for:

PRICE EX WORKS: £ 8,098*

ENGINE 4 cylinders, in line; 121.7 cu in, 1,994 cc (3.33 x 3.50 in, 84.5 x 89 mm); max power (DIN): 100 hp (74 kW) at 5,250 rpm; max torque (DIN): 120 lb ft, 16.6 kg m (163 Nm) at 3,250 rpm; max engine rpm: 6,000; 50.2 hp/l (37.1 kW/l); cast iron block, light alloy head; valves: overhead, thimble tappets; cam-

ROVER Vitesse

ROVER Vitesse

shafts: 1, overhead; lubrication: rotary pump, full flow filter, 8.1 imp pt, 9.7 US pt, 4.6 l; 2 Solex HIF 44 horizontal carburettors; cooling: 13 imp pt, 15.6 US pt, 7.4 l.

TRANSMISSION axle ratio: 3.900; width of rims: 5.5"; tyres: 175 HR x 14.

PERFORMANCE max speed: 104 mph, 167 km/h; power-weight ratio: 27.8 lb/hp (37.6 lb/kW), 12.6 kg/hp (17.1 kg/kW); acceleration: standing ¼ mile 19 sec, 0-50 mph (0-80 km/h) 8.8 sec; speed in top at 1,000 rpm: 23.3 mph, 37.5 km/h; consumption: 32.8 m/imp gal, 27.3 m/US gal, 8.6 l x 100 km at 75 mph, 120 km/h.

STEERING rack-and-pinion; turns lock to lock: 4.50.

ELECTRICAL EQUIPMENT Lucas 48 D4 distributor; 4 headlamps.

DIMENSIONS AND WEIGHT height: 54.53 in, 138 cm; weight: 2,785 lb, 1,263 kg.

PRACTICAL INSTRUCTIONS oil: engine 8.1 imp pt, 9.7 US pt, 4.6 l; valve timing: 12° 48° 54° 22°; tyre pressure: front 28 psi, 1.9 atm, rear 30 psi, 2.1 atm.

OPTIONALS 3-speed automatic transmission; power steering; central door locking; electric windows; fog lamps; light alloy wheels; sunroof.

2300

See 3500 SE/Vanden Plas, except for:

PRICES EX WORKS:	£
4+1-dr Saloon	8,697*
S 4+1-dr Saloon	9,965*

ENGINE 6 cylinders, in line; 143.5 cu in, 2,351 cc (3.19 x 2.99 in, 81 x 76 mm); max power (DIN): 118 hp (88 kW) at 5,250 rpm; max torque (DIN): 134 lb ft, 18.5 kg m (181 Nm) at 4,000 rpm; 50.2 hp/l (37.4 kW/l); cast iron block, light alloy head; 4 crankshaft bearings; valves: overhead, Vee-slanted, thimble tappets; camshafts: 1, overhead, cogged belt; lubrication: rotary pump, full flow filter, 10.8 imp pt, 12.9 US pt, 6.1 l; 2 Solex HIF 44 horizontal carburettors; cooling: 18.2 imp pt, 21.8 US pt, 10.3 l.

TRANSMISSION axle ratio: 3.450; width of rims: 5.5" - 2300 S 6"; tyres: 175 HR x 14.

PERFORMANCE max speed: 112 mph, 180 km/h; power-weight ratio: 25.6 lb/hp (34.3 lb/kW), 11.6 kg/hp (15.6 kg/kW); speed in top at 1,000 rpm: 26.3 mph, 42.3 km/h; consumption: 30.8 m/imp gal, 25.6 m/US gal, 9.2 l x 100 km at 75 mph, 120 km/h.

ELECTRICAL EQUIPMENT 55 A alternator.

DIMENSIONS AND WEIGHT weight: 3,020 lb, 1,370 kg.

PRACTICAL INSTRUCTIONS oil: engine 10.8 imp pt, 12.9 US pt, 6.1 l; tappet clearances: inlet 0.018 in, 0.46 mm, exhaust 0.018 in, 0.46 mm; valve timing: 16° 56° 56° 16°; tyre pressure: front 28 psi, 1.9 atm, rear 30 psi, 2.1 atm.

OPTIONALS 3-speed automatic transmission; fog lamps; tinted glass; metallic spray; light alloy wheels; electric windows; sunroof (for 2300 only).

2600

See 3500 SE/Vanden Plas, except for:

PRICES EX WORKS:	£
S 4+1-dr Saloon	10,520*
SE 4+1-dr Saloon	11,449*

ENGINE 6 cylinders, in line; 158.5 cu in, 2,597 cc (3.19 x 3.31 in, 81 x 84 mm); max power (DIN): 130 hp (97 kW) at 5,000 rpm; max torque (DIN): 152 lb ft, 21 kg m (206 Nm) at 3,750 rpm; 50.1 hp/l (37.4 kW/l); cast iron block, light alloy head; 4 crankshaft bearings; valves: overhead, Vee-slanted, thimble tappets; camshafts: 1, overhead, cogged belt; lubrication: rotary pump, full flow filter, 10.8 imp pt, 12.9 US pt, 6.1 l; 2 Solex HIF 44 horizontal carburettors; cooling: 18.2 imp pt, 21.8 US pt, 10.3 l.

TRANSMISSION axle ratio: 3.450; width of rims: 5.5"; tyres: 175 HR x 14.

PERFORMANCE max speed: 116 mph, 187 km/h; power-weight ratio: 23.6 lb/hp (31.6 lb/kW), 10.7 kg/hp (14.3 kg/kW); speed in top at 1,000 rpm: 26.3 mph, 42.3 km/h; consumption: 31.4 m/imp gal, 26.1 m/US gal, 9 l x 100 km at 75 mph, 120 km/h.

ELECTRICAL EQUIPMENT 55 A alternator.

DIMENSIONS AND WEIGHT weight: 3,063 lb, 1,389 kg.

PRACTICAL INSTRUCTIONS oil: engine 10.8 imp pt, 12.9 US pt, 6.1 l; tyre pressure: front 28 psi, 1.9 atm, rear 30 psi, 2.1 atm.

OPTIONALS 3-speed automatic transmission; fog lamps; tinted glass; metallic spray; light alloy wheels; air-conditioning.

Vitesse

See 3500 SE/Vanden Plas, except for:

PRICE EX WORKS: £ 15,249*

ENGINE compression ratio: 9.7:1; max power (DIN): 190 hp (140 kW) at 5,280 rpm; max torque (DIN): 220 lb ft, 30.4 kg m (298 Nm) at 4,000 rpm; 53.9 hp/l (39.7 kW/l); Lucas L electronic ignition.

TRANSMISSION width of rims: 6.5"; tyres: 205/60 VR x 15.

PERFORMANCE max speed: 135 mph, 217 km/h; power-weight ratio: 16.8 lb/hp (22.7 lb/kW), 7.6 kg/hp (10.3 kg/kW); consumption: 30.1 m/imp gal, 25 m/US gal, 9.4 l x 100 km at 75 mph, 120 km/h.

BRAKES front disc, internal radial fins.

ELECTRICAL EQUIPMENT 75 A alternator.

DIMENSIONS AND WEIGHT wheel base: 110.80 in, 281 cm; front and rear track: 59.30 in, 151 cm; length: 186.25 in, 473 cm; height: 53.40 in, 136 cm;, weight: 3,175 lb, 1,440 kg.

OPTIONALS GM automatic transmission, hydraulic torque converter and planetary gears with 3 ratios (I 2.400, II 1.480, III 1, rev 1.920), possible manual selection, 2.850 axle ratio; max speed 132 mph, 212 km/h, consumption 26.7 m/imp gal, 22.2 m/US gal, 10.6 l x 100 km at 75 mph, 120 km/h.

2400 SD Turbo

See 3500 SE/Vanden Plas, except for:

PRICE EX WORKS: £ 10,899*

ENGINE VM, diesel, turbocharged; 4 cylinders, vertical, in line; 146 cu in, 2,393 cc (3.62 x 3.54 in, 92 x 90 mm); compression ratio: 22:1; max power (DIN): 93 hp (68 kW) at 4,000 rpm; max torque (DIN): 139 lb ft, 19.2 kg m (188 Nm) at 2,450 rpm; 38.9 hp/l (28.4 kW/l); cast iron block, light alloy head; valves: overhead, in line, push-rods and rockers; camshafts: 1, side; lubrication: rotary pump, full flow filter, oil cooler, 12.7 imp pt, 15.2 US pt, 7.2 l; Bosch VE 4/10 injection pump; 1 KKK K24 turbocharger; cooling: 17.6 imp pt, 21.1 US pt, 10 l.

TRANSMISSION gearbox ratios: I 3.321, II 2.087, III 1.396, IV 1, V 0.770, rev 3.428; axle ratio: 3.900.

PERFORMANCE max speed: 102 mph, 165 km/h; power-weight ratio: 35.6 lb/hp (48.6 lb/kW), 16.1 kg/hp (22.1 kg/kW); consumption: 32.8 m/imp gal, 27.3 m/US gal, 8.6 l x 100 km at 75 mph, 120 km/h.

ELECTRICAL EQUIPMENT 66 Ah battery.

DIMENSIONS AND WEIGHT weight: 3,307 lb, 1,500 kg.

PRACTICAL INSTRUCTIONS fuel: diesel; oil: engine 12.7 imp pt, 15.2 US pt, 7.2 l, change every 3,100 miles, 5,000 km.

OPTIONALS 3-speed automatic transmission; sunroof; central door locking; metallic spray.

TALBOT GREAT BRITAIN

Horizon Series

PRICES EX WORKS:	£
1 1.1 LE 4+1-dr Saloon	4,145*
2 1.1 LS 4+1-dr Saloon	4,645*
3 1.3 LS 4+1-dr Saloon	4,845*
4 1.5 GL 4+1-dr Saloon	5,445*
5 1.5 GLS 4+1-dr Saloon	5,850*
6 1.9 LD 4+1-dr Saloon	5,420*

Power team:	Standard for:	Optional for:
58 hp	1,2	—
64 hp (1,294 cc)	3	2
64 hp (1,442 cc)	4	—
82 hp	5	—
64 hp (diesel)	6	—

58 hp power team

ENGINE front, transverse, slanted 41° to rear, 4 stroke; 4 cylinders, in line; 68.2 cu in, 1,118 cc (2.91 x 2.56 in, 74 x 65 mm); compression ratio: 9.6:1; max power (DIN): 58 hp (43 kW) at 5,600 rpm; max torque (DIN): 67 lb ft, 9.3 kg m (91 Nm) at 3,000 rpm; max engine rpm: 6,300; 51.9 hp/l (38.8 kW/l); cast iron block, light alloy head; 5 crankshaft bearings; valves: overhead, push-rods and rockers, thimble tappets; camshafts: 1, side; lubrication: gear pump, full flow filter, 5.3 imp pt, 6.3 US pt, 3 l; 1 Solex 32 BISA 7 or Weber 32 IBSA single barrel carburettor; fuel feed: mechanical pump; sealed circuit cooling, expansion tank, liquid, 10.6 imp pt, 12.7 US pt, 6 l, electric thermostatic fan.

TRANSMISSION driving wheels: front; clutch: single dry plate (diaphragm); gearbox: mechanical; gears: 4, fully synchronized; ratios: I 3.900, II 2.312, III 1.524, IV 1.080, rev 3.769; lever: central; final drive: cylindrical gears; axle ratio: 3.706; width of rims: 4.5"; tyres: 145 SR x 13.

PERFORMANCE max speed: 91 mph, 147 km/h; power-weight ratio: 35.9 lb/hp (48 lb/kW), 16.3 kg/hp (21.8 kg/kW); carrying capacity: 981 lb, 445 kg; acceleration: standing ¼ mile 20 sec; speed in top at 1,000 rpm: 16 mph, 25.8 km/h; consumption: 33.2 m/imp gal, 27.7 m/US gal, 8.5 l x 100 km at 75 mph, 120 km/h.

CHASSIS integral; front suspension: independent, longitudinal torsion bars, wishbones, anti-roll bar, telescopic dampers; rear: independent, swinging longitudinal trailing arms, coil springs, anti-roll bar, telescopic dampers.

STEERING rack-and-pinion; turns lock to lock: 4.35.

BRAKES front disc (diameter 9.37 in, 23.8 cm), rear drum, rear compensator, servo; swept area: front 155 sq in, 1,000 sq cm, rear 89 sq in, 574 sq cm, total 244 sq in, 1,574 sq cm.

ELECTRICAL EQUIPMENT 12 V; 35 Ah battery; 50 A alternator; electronic ignition; 2 headlamps.

DIMENSIONS AND WEIGHT wheel base: 99.21 in, 252 cm;

TALBOT Horizon 1.5 GL Saloon

TALBOT Horizon 1.9 LD Saloon

58 HP POWER TEAM

tracks: 55.91 in, 142 cm front, 53.94 in, 137 cm rear; length: 155.91 in, 396 cm; width: 66.14 in, 168 cm; height: 55.51 in, 141 cm; ground clearance: 7.09 in, 18 cm; weight: 2,084 lb, 945 kg; weight distribution: 59.4% front, 40.6% rear; turning circle: 33.5 ft, 10.2 m; fuel tank: 10.3 imp gal, 12.4 US gal, 47 l.

BODY saloon/sedan; 4+1 doors; 5 seats, separate front seats, reclining backrests; heated rear window; folding rear seat.

PRACTICAL INSTRUCTIONS fuel: 98-100 oct petrol; oil: engine 5.3 imp pt, 6.3 US pt, 3 l, SAE 20W-40, change every 4,600 miles, 7,500 km - gearbox and final drive 1.9 imp pt, 2.3 US pt, 1.1 l, SAE 90 EP, change every 9,300 miles, 15,000 km; greasing: none; tyre pressure: front and rear 26 psi, 1.8 atm.

OPTIONALS (for LS only) metallic spray and laminated windscreen; iodine headlamps; rear window wiper-washer; tinted glass; adjustable headrests on front seats; vinyl roof.

64 hp (1,294 cc) power team

See 58 hp power team, except for:

ENGINE 79 cu in, 1,294 cc (3.02 x 2.76 in, 76.7 x 70 mm); compression ratio: 9.5:1; max power (DIN): 64 hp (47 kW) at 5,600 rpm; max torque (DIN): 80 lb ft, 11 kg m (108 Nm) at 2,800 rpm; 49.5 hp/l (37 kW/l).

TRANSMISSION axle ratio: 3.471.

PERFORMANCE max speed: 97 mph, 156 km/h; power-weight ratio: 32.6 lb/hp (44.3 lb/kW), 14.8 kg/hp (20.1 kg/kW); carrying capacity: 948 lb, 430 kg; acceleration: standing ¼ mile 19.5 sec; consumption: 37.2 m/imp gal, 30.9 m/US gal, 7.6 l x 100 km at 75 mph, 120 km/h.

OPTIONALS 3-speed automatic transmission with 82 hp engine.

64 hp (1,442 cc) power team

See 58 hp power team, except for:

ENGINE 88 cu in, 1,442 cc (3.02 x 3.07 in, 76.7 x 78 mm); compression ratio: 9.5:1; max power (DIN): 64 hp (47 kW) at 5,200 rpm; max torque (DIN): 89 lb ft, 12.3 kg m (121 Nm) at 2,400 rpm; 44.4 hp/l (32.6 kW/l).

TRANSMISSION gears: 5, fully synchronized; ratios: I 3.308, II 1.882, III 1.280, IV 0.969, V 0.757, rev 3.333; axle ratio: 4.428.

PERFORMANCE max speed: 95 mph, 153 km/h; power-weight ratio: 33.1 lb/hp (45 lb/kW), 15 kg/hp (20.4 kg/kW); carrying capacity: 882 lb, 400 kg; acceleration: standing ¼ mile 19.5 sec; consumption: 39.2 m/imp gal, 32.7 m/US gal, 7.2 l x 100 km at 75 mph, 120 km/h.

ELECTRICAL EQUIPMENT 40 Ah battery; 2 halogen headlamps.

DIMENSIONS AND WEIGHT weight: 2,117 lb, 960 kg.

OPTIONALS 3-speed automatic transmission with 82 hp engine.

82 hp power team

See 58 hp power team, except for:

ENGINE 88 cu in, 1,442 cc (3.02 x 3.07 in, 76.7 x 78 mm); compression ratio: 9.5:1; max power (DIN): 82 hp (60 kW) at 5,600 rpm; max torque (DIN): 91 lb ft, 12.5 kg m (123 Nm) at 3,000 rpm; 56.9 hp/l (41.6 kW/l); 1 Weber 36 DCA 2 downdraught twin barrel carburettor; liquid-cooled, 11.3 imp pt, 13.5 US pt, 6.4 l.

TRANSMISSION gears: 5, fully synchronized; ratios: I 3.308, II 1.882, III 1.280, IV 0.969, V 0.757, rev 3.333; axle ratio: 4.428; width of rims: 5"; tyres: 155 SR x 13.

PERFORMANCE max speed: 102 mph, 164 km/h; power-weight ratio: 26.2 lb/hp (35.7 lb/kW), 11.9 kg/hp (16.2 kg/kW); acceleration: standing ¼ mile 18.8 sec; consumption: 35.8 m/imp gal, 29.8 m/US gal, 7.9 l x 100 km at 75 mph, 120 km/h.

ELECTRICAL EQUIPMENT 40 Ah battery; 2 iodine headlamps (standard).

DIMENSIONS AND WEIGHT tracks: 56.46 in, 143 cm front, 54.61 in, 139 cm rear; weight: 2,150 lb, 975 kg.

BODY (standard) adjustable backrests on front seats and rear window wiper-washer; automatic speed control; trip computer.

OPTIONALS light alloy wheels; headlamps with wiper-washer; central door locks.

64 hp (diesel) power team

See 58 hp power team, except for:

ENGINE diesel; front, transverse, slanted 20° to rear; 116.3 cu in, 1,905 cc (3.27 x 3.46 in, 83 x 88 mm); compression ratio: 23.5:1; max power (DIN): 64 hp (47 kW) at 4,600 rpm; max torque (DIN): 88 lb ft, 12.2 kg m (118 Nm) at 2,000 rpm; max engine rpm: 5,000; 33.6 hp/l (24.7 kW/l); valves: overhead, rockers; camshafts: 1, overhead; lubrication: 8.8 imp pt, 10.6 US pt, 5 l; Rotodiesel injection pump.

TRANSMISSION gearbox ratios: I 3.308, II 1.882, III 1.148, IV 0.799, rev 2.584; axle ratio: 3.813.

PERFORMANCE max speed: 93 mph, 149 km/h; power-weight ratio: 35.3 lb/hp (47.9 lb/kW), 16 kg/hp (21.7 kg/kW); acceleration: standing ¼ mile 20.5 sec; consumption: 43.5 m/imp gal, 36.2 m/US gal, 6.5 l x 100 km at 75 mph, 120 km/h.

ELECTRICAL EQUIPMENT 60 ah battery.

DIMENSIONS AND WEIGHT tracks: 56.46 in, 143 cm front, 54.61 in, 139 cm rear; weight: 2,249 lb, 1,020 kg.

PRACTICAL INSTRUCTIONS fuel: diesel; oil: engine 8.8 imp pt, 10.6 US pt, 5 l.

OPTIONALS 5-speed mechanical gearbox (I 3.308, II 1.882, III 1.280, IV 0.969, V 0.757, rev 3.333), 3.937 axle ratio, max speed 97 mph, 156 km/h, consumption 44.1 m/imp gal, 36.8 m/US gal, 6.4 l x 100 km at 75 mph, 120 km/h; power steering.

Alpine Series

PRICES EX WORKS:		£
1	1.3 LE 4+1-dr Saloon	4,895*
2	1.3 LS 4+1-dr Saloon	5,345*
3	1.3 GL 4+1-dr Saloon	5,995*
4	1.6 LE 4+1-dr Saloon	5,145*
5	1.6 LS 4+1-dr Saloon	5,595*
6	1.6 GL 4+1-dr Saloon	6,245*
7	1.6 GLS 4+1-dr Saloon	7,095*

Power team:	Standard for:	Optional for:
67 hp	1 to 3	—
89 hp	4 to 7	—

67 hp power team

ENGINE front, transverse, slanted 41° to rear, 4 stroke; 4 cylinders, in line; 79 cu in, 1,294 cc (3.02 x 2.76 in, 76.7 x 70 mm); compression ratio: 9.5:1; max power (DIN): 67 hp (49 kW) at 5,600 rpm; max torque (DIN): 78 lb ft, 10.7 kg m (105 Nm) at 2,800 rpm; max engine rpm: 6,300; 51.8 hp/l (37.9 kW/l); cast iron block, light alloy head; 5 crankshaft bearings; valves: overhead, in line, push-rods and rockers; camshafts: 1, side; lubrication: gear pump, full flow filter, 5.3 imp pt, 6.3 US pt, 3 l; 1 Solex 32 BISA 7 downdraught single barrel carburettor; fuel feed: mechanical pump; sealed circuit cooling, expansion tank, liquid, 10.7 imp pt, 12.9 US pt, 6.1 l, electric thermostatic fan.

TRANSMISSION driving wheels: front; clutch: single dry plate (diaphragm); gearbox: mechanical; gears: 4, fully synchronized; ratios: I 3.308, II 1.882, III 1.148, IV 1.086, rev 3.333; lever: central; final drive: cylindrical gears; axle ratio: 4.786; width of rims: 5"; tyres: 155 SR x 13.

PERFORMANCE max speed: 95 mph, 153 km/h; power-weight ratio: 34.6 lb/hp (47.2 lb/kW), 15.7 kg/hp (21.4 kg/kW); carrying capacity: 882 lb, 400 kg; acceleration: standing ¼ mile 20.1 sec, 0-50 mph (0-80 km/h) 10.7 sec; speed in top at 1,000 rpm: 16.4 mph, 26.4 km/h; consumption: 32.8 m/imp gal, 27.3 m/US gal, 8.6 l x 100 km at 75 mph, 120 km/h.

CHASSIS integral; front suspension: independent, wishbones, longitudinal torsion bars, anti-roll bar, telescopic dampers; rear: independent, swinging longitudinal trailing arms, coil springs, anti-roll bar, telescopic dampers.

STEERING rack-and-pinion; turns lock to lock: 4.15.

BRAKES front disc (diameter 9.45 in, 24 cm), rear drum, dual circuit, rear compensator, servo; swept area: front 169.3 sq in, 1,092 sq cm, rear 90.2 sq in, 582 sq cm, total 259.5 sq in, 1,674 sq cm.

ELECTRICAL EQUIPMENT 12 V; 40 Ah battery; 50 A alternator; electronic ignition; 2 headlamps.

DIMENSIONS AND WEIGHT wheel base: 102.36 in, 260 cm; tracks: 56.10 in, 142 cm front, 55.12 in, 140 cm rear; length: 169.68 in, 431 cm; width: 66.14 in, 168 cm; height: 54.72 in, 139 cm; ground clearance: 5.12 in, 13 cm; weight: 2,315 lb, 1,050 kg; turning circle: 36.1 ft, 11 m; fuel tank: 12.8 imp gal, 15.3 US gal, 58 l.

BODY saloon/sedan; 4+1 doors; 5 seats, separate front seats, reclining backrests; heated rear window; folding rear seat.

PRACTICAL INSTRUCTIONS fuel: 98-100 oct petrol; oil: engine 5.3 imp pt, 6.3 US pt, 3 l, SAE 20W-40, change every 4,600 miles, 7,500 km - gearbox and final drive 1.9 imp pt, 2.3 US pt, 1.1 l, SAE 90 EP, change every 9,300 miles, 15,000 km, greasing: none; tyre pressure: front and rear 26 psi, 1.8 atm.

OPTIONALS (for LS and GL only) metallic spray; iodine head-

TALBOT Alpine 1.6 GLS Saloon

lamps; adjustable headrests on front seats; tinted glass; vinyl roof; (for GL only) sliding sunroof; rear window wiper-washer.

89 hp power team

See 67 hp power team, except for:

ENGINE 97.1 cu in, 1,592 cc (3.17 x 3.07 in, 80.6 x 78 mm); compression ratio: 9.3:1; max power (DIN): 89 hp (66 kW) at 5,400 rpm; max torque (DIN): 101 lb ft, 14 kg m (137 Nm) at 3,800 rpm; 55.9 hp/l (41.5 kW/l); 1 Weber 36 DCNVH 12 downdraught twin barrel carburettor; cooling: 11.1 imp pt, 13.3 US pt, 6.3 l.

TRANSMISSION (for GL and GLS only) gears: 5, fully synchronized; ratios: I 3.308, II 1.882, III 1.280, IV 0.969, V 0.757, rev 3.333; axle ratio: LS 4.428 - GL and GLS 4.187; tyres: 165 SR x 13.

PERFORMANCE max speed: 104 mph, 167 km/h; power-weight ratio: 26.2 lb/hp (35.5 lb/kW), 11.9 kg/hp (16.1 kg/kW); speed in top at 1,000 rpm: 20.9 mph, 33.6 km/h; consumption: 34.9 m/imp gal, 29 m/US gal, 8.1 l x 100 km at 75 mph, 120 km/h.

STEERING servo; turns lock to lock: 2.80.

ELECTRICAL EQUIPMENT iodine headlamps with wiper-washers (standard)

DIMENSIONS AND WEIGHT weight: 2,343 lb, 1,063 kg.

BODY (standard) adjustable headrests on front seats and rear window wiper-washer; speed control; (for GLS only) light alloy wheels.

OPTIONALS (for LS only) 5-speed mechanical gearbox; (for GL and GLS only) automatic transmission with 3 ratios (I 2.475, II 1.475, III 1, rev 2.103), 3.030 axle ratio, max speed 101 mph, 163 km/h, consumption 28.5 m/imp gal, 23.5 m/US gal, 9.9 l x 100 km at 75 mph, 120 km/h; (for GL and GLS only) sliding sunroof; (for LS and GL only) light alloy wheels and metallic spray; leather upholstery.

Solara Series

PRICES EX WORKS:	£
1 1.3 LE 4-dr Saloon	**4,795***
2 1.3 LS 4-dr Saloon	**5,195***
3 1.3 GL 4-dr Saloon	**5,845***
4 1.6 LE 4-dr Saloon	**5,045***
5 1.6 LS 4-dr Saloon	**5,445***
6 1.6 GL 4-dr Saloon	**6,095***
7 1.6 GLS 4-dr Saloon	**6,945***

Power team:	Standard for:	Optional for:
67 hp	1 to 3	—
89 hp	4 to 7	—

67 hp power team

ENGINE front, transverse, slanted 41° to rear, 4 stroke; 4 cylinders, in line; 79 cu in, 1,294 cc (3.02 x 2.76 in, 76.7 x 70 mm); compression ratio: 9.5:1; max power (DIN): 67 hp (49 kW) at 5,600 rpm; max torque (DIN): 78 lb ft, 10.7 kg m (105 Nm) at 2,800 rpm; max engine rpm: 6,300; 51.8 hp/l (37.9 kW/l); cast iron block, light alloy head; 5 crankshaft bearings; valves: overhead, in line, push-rods and rockers; camshafts: 1, side; lubrication: gear pump, full flow filter, 5.3 imp pt, 6.3 US pt, 3 l; 1 Solex 32 BISA 7 downdraught single barrel carburettor; fuel feed: mechanical pump; sealed circuit cooling, expansion tank, liquid, 10.7 imp pt, 12.9 US pt, 6.1 l, electric thermostatic fan.

TRANSMISSION driving wheels: front; clutch: single dry plate (diaphragm); gearbox: mechanical; gears: 4, fully synchronized; ratios: I 3.308, II 1.882, III 1.148, IV 1.086, rev 3.333; lever: central; final drive: cylindrical gears; axle ratio: 4.786; width of rims: 5"; tyres: 155 SR x 13.

PERFORMANCE max speed: 95 mph, 153 km/h; power-weight ratio: LE 32.9 lb/hp (45 lb/kW), 14.9 kg/hp (20.4 kg/kW); carrying capacity: 882 lb, 400 kg; acceleration: standing ¼ mile 20.1 sec, 0-50 mph (0-80 km/h) 10.7 sec; speed in top at 1,000 rpm: 16.4 mph, 26.4 km/h; consumption: 32.8 m/imp gal, 27.3 m/US gal, 8.6 l x 100 km at 75 mph, 120 km/h.

CHASSIS integral; front suspension: independent, wishbones, longitudinal torsion bars, anti-roll bar, telescopic dampers; rear: independent, swinging longitudinal trailing arms, coil springs, anti-roll bar, telescopic dampers.

STEERING rack-and-pinion; turns lock to lock: 4.15.

BRAKES front disc (diameter 9.45 in, 24 cm), rear drum, dual circuit, rear compensator, servo; swept area: front 169.3 sq in, 1,092 sq cm, rear 90.2 sq in, 582 sq cm, total 259.5 sq in, 1,674 sq cm.

ELECTRICAL EQUIPMENT 12 V; 40 Ah battery; 50 A alternator; electronic ignition; 2 headlamps.

DIMENSIONS AND WEIGHT wheel base: 102.36 in, 260 cm; tracks: 56.10 in, 142 cm front, 55.12 in, 140 cm rear; length: 173 in, 439 cm; width: 66.14 in, 168 cm; height: 54.72 in, 139 cm; ground clearance: 5.12 in, 13 cm; weight: LE 2,202 lb, 999 kg - LS 2,254 lb, 1,022 kg - GL 2,297 lb, 1,042 kg; turning circle: 36.1 ft, 11 m; fuel tank: 12.8 imp gal, 15.3 US gal, 58 l.

BODY saloon/sedan; 4 doors; 5 seats, separate front seats, reclining backrests; heated rear window.

PRACTICAL INSTRUCTIONS fuel: 98-100 oct petrol; oil: engine 5.3 imp pt, 6.3 US pt, 3 l, SAE 20W-40, change every 4,600 miles, 7,500 km - gearbox and final drive 1.9 imp pt, 2.3 US pt, 1.1 l, SAE 90 EP, change every 9,300 miles, 15,000 km, greasing: none; tyre pressure: front and rear 26 psi, 1.8 atm.

OPTIONALS (for LS and GL only) metallic spray; iodine headlamps; adjustable headrests on front seats; tinted glass; vinyl roof; (for GL only) sliding sunroof; rear window wiper-washer.

TALBOT Solara 1.6 LS Saloon

89 hp power team

See 67 hp power team, except for:

ENGINE 97.1 cu in, 1,592 cc (3.17 x 3.07 in, 80.6 x 78 mm); compression ratio: 9.3:1; max power (DIN): 89 hp (66 kW) at 5,400 rpm; max torque (DIN): 101 lb ft, 14 kg m (137 Nm) at 3,800 rpm; 55.9 hp/l (41.5 kW/l); 1 Weber 36 DCNVH 12 downdraught twin barrel carburettor; cooling: 11.1 imp pt, 13.3 US pt, 6.3 l.

TRANSMISSION (for GL and GLS only) gears: 5, fully synchronized; ratios: I 3.308, II 1.882, III 1.280, IV 0.969, V 0.757, rev 3.333; axle ratio: LE 4.428 - LS, GL and GLS 4.187; tyres: 165 SR x 13.

PERFORMANCE max speed: 104 mph, 167 km/h; power-weight ratio: GLS 26.2 lb/hp (35.2 lb/kW), 11.9 kg/hp (16 kg/kW); speed in top at 1,000 rpm: 20.9 mph, 33.6 km/h; consumption: 34.4 m/imp gal, 28.7 m/US gal, 8.2 l x 100 km at 75 mph, 120 km/h.

STEERING (for LS, GL and GLS only) servo; turns lock to lock: 2.80.

ELECTRICAL EQUIPMENT iodine headlamps with wiper-washers (standard)

DIMENSIONS AND WEIGHT weight: GLS 2,326 lb, 1,055 kg.

BODY (for LS, GL and GLS only) adjustable headrests on front seats and speed control (standard); (for GLS only) light alloy wheels.

OPTIONALS (for LS only) 5-speed mechanical gearbox; (for LS, GL and GLS only) automatic transmission with 3 ratios (I 2.475, II 1.475, III 1, rev 2.103), 3.030 axle ratio, max speed 101 mph, 163 km/h, consumption 28.5 m/imp gal, 23.5 m/US gal, 9.9 l x 100 km at 75 mph, 120 km/h; (for GL and GLS only) sliding sunroof; (for LS and GL only) light alloy wheels and metallic spray; leather upholstery.

TRIUMPH GREAT BRITAIN

Acclaim

PRICES EX WORKS:	£
L 4-dr Saloon	**4,998***
HL 4-dr Saloon	**5,249***
HLS 4-dr Saloon	**5,620***
CD 4-dr Saloon	**5,999***

ENGINE Honda, front, 4 stroke, stratified charge; 4 cylinders, vertical, in line; 81.5 cu in, 1,335 cc (2.83 x 3.23 in, 72 x 82 mm); compression ratio: 8.4:1; max power (DIN): 70 hp (51 kW) at 5,750 rpm; max torque (DIN): 74 lb ft, 10.2 kg m (100 Nm) at 3,500 rpm; max engine rpm: 6,000; 52.4 hp/l (38.6 kW/l); light alloy block with cast iron liners, light alloy head; 5 crankshaft bearings; valves: 3 per cylinder (one intake and one exhaust in main combustion chamber, one intake in auxiliary chamber), overhead, Vee-slanted, rockers; camshafts: 1, overhead, cogged belt; lubrication: rotary pump, full flow filter, 6.3 imp pt, 7.6 US pt, 3.6 l; 2 Keihin Seiki downdraught twin barrel carburettors; fuel feed: electric pump; emission control by CVCC controlled combustion, catalytic converter and exhaust gas recirculation; water-cooled, 8.8 imp pt, 10.6 US pt, 5 l.

TRANSMISSION driving wheels: front; clutch: single dry plate (diaphragm); gearbox: mechanical; gears: 5, fully synchronized; ratios: I 2.916, II 1.764, III 1.181, IV 0.846, V 0.712, rev 2.916; lever: central; final drive: helical spur gears; axle ratio: 4.642; width of rims: 4.5"; tyres: 155 x 13 - CD 165/70 x 13.

PERFORMANCE max speeds: (I) 30 mph, 48 km/h; (II) 48 mph, 78 km/h; (III) 73 mph, 118 km/h; (IV) 93 mph, 150 km/h; (V) 96 mph, 154 km/h; power-weight ratio: HL 25.5 lb/hp (34.6 lb/kW), 11.5 kg/hp (15.7 kg/kW); carrying capacity: 882 lb, 400 kg; speed in top at 1,000 rpm: 19.4 mph, 31.3 km/h; consumption: 34 m/imp gal, 28.3 m/US gal, 8.3 l x 100 km at 75 mph, 120 km/h.

CHASSIS integral, front auxiliary frame; front suspension: independent, by McPherson, coil springs/telescopic damper struts, lower wishbones (trailing links), anti-roll bar; rear: independent, by McPherson, coil springs/telescopic damper struts, lower wishbones (torque arms).

TRIUMPH Acclaim CD Saloon

ACCLAIM

STEERING rack-and-pinion; turns lock to lock: 3.30.

BRAKES front disc (diameter 8.50 in, 21.5 cm), rear drum, servo; swept area: front 127 sq in, 820 sq cm, rear 43.7 sq in, 282 sq cm, total 170.7 sq in, 1,102 sq cm.

ELECTRICAL EQUIPMENT 12 V; 45 Ah battery; 60 A alternator; contactless fully electronic ignition; 2 headlamps - HLS and CD 2 halogen headlamps.

DIMENSIONS AND WEIGHT wheel base: 91.34 in, 232 cm; tracks: 53.54 in, 136 cm front, 54.33 in, 138 cm rear; length: 161.22 in, 409 cm; width: 62.99 in, 160 cm; height: 52.95 in, 134 cm; ground clearance: 6.49 in, 16 cm; weight: HL Saloon 1,784 lb, 809 kg - HLS Saloon 1,797 lb, 815 kg - CD Saloon 1,819 lb, 825 kg; weight distribution: 60% front, 40% rear; turning circle: 32.1 ft, 9.8 m; fuel tank: 10.1 imp gal, 12.1 US gal, 46 l.

BODY saloon/sedan; 4 doors; 5 seats, separate front seats; laminated windscreen; heated rear window; (for HLS and CD saloons only) tinted glass; (for CD Saloon only) electric windows.

PRACTICAL INSTRUCTIONS fuel: 91 oct petrol; oil: engine 6.3 imp pt, 7.6 US pt, 3.6 l, SAE 20W-50, change every 7,800 miles, 12,500 km - gearbox and final drive 4.4 imp pt, 5.3 US pt, 2.5 l, SAE 80 EP, change every 31,100 miles, 50,000 km; tyre pressure: front 24 psi, 1.7 atm, rear 24 psi, 1.7 atm.

OPTIONALS Trio-matic semi-automatic transmission with 3 ratios (I 2.047, II 1.370, III 1.032, rev 1.954), hydraulic torque converter, 3.105 axle ratio, consumption 30.4 m/imp gal, 25.3 m/US gal, 9.3 l x 100 km at 75 mph, 120 km/h; air-conditioning.

TVR — GREAT BRITAIN

Tasmin 200

PRICES EX WORKS:

	£
2-dr Coupé	**10,384***
2-dr Convertible	**10,280***

ENGINE Ford, front, 4 stroke; 4 cylinders, vertical, in line; 121.6 cu in, 1,993 cc (3.89 x 3.03 in, 90.8 x 76.9 mm); compression ratio: 9.2:1; max power (DIN): 98 hp (72 kW) at 5,200 rpm; max torque (DIN): 112 lb ft, 15.4 kg m (110 Nm) at 3,500 rpm; max engine rpm: 6,000; 49.2 hp/l (36.1 kW/l); cast iron block and head; 5 crankshaft bearings; valves: overhead, push-rods and rockers; camshafts: 1, overhead, chain-driven; lubrication: rotary pump, full flow filter, 6.5 imp pt, 7.8 US pt, 3.7 l; 1 Weber 32/36 DGAV downdraught twin barrel carburettor; fuel feed: mechanical pump; water-cooled, 13.7 imp pt, 16.5 US pt, 7.8 l.

TRANSMISSION driving wheels: rear; clutch: single dry plate (diaphragm); gearbox: mechanical; gears: 4, fully synchronized; ratios: I 3.651, II 1.968, III 1.368, IV 1, rev 3.660; lever: central; final drive: hypoid bevel; axle ratio: 3.540; width of rims: 6"; tyres: 195/60 HR x 14.

PERFORMANCE max speed: 115 mph, 185 km/h; power-weight ratio: Coupé 24 lb/hp (32.6 lb/kW), 10.9 kg/hp (14.8 kg/kW); carrying capacity: 330 lb, 150 kg; acceleration: 0-50 mph (0-80 km/h) 9 sec; consumption: 30 m/imp gal, 25 m/US gal, 9.4 l x 100 km.

CHASSIS tubular backbone with perimeter tubes; front suspension: independent, wishbones, lower transverse link, anti-roll bar, coil springs, telescopic dampers; rear: independent, lower transverse link, radius arms, coil springs, telescopic dampers.

STEERING rack-and-pinion; turns lock to lock: 3.70.

BRAKES disc, servo; swept area: front 209.9 sq in, 1,354 sq cm, rear 189.1 sq in, 1,220 sq cm, total 399 sq in, 2,574 sq cm.

ELECTRICAL EQUIPMENT 12 V; 60 Ah battery; 55 A alternator; electronic Motorcraft ignition; 2 halogen retractable headlamps.

DIMENSIONS AND WEIGHT wheel base: 94 in, 239 cm; tracks: 56.50 in, 143 cm front, 56.70 in, 144 cm rear; length: 158 in, 401 cm; width: 68 in, 173 cm; height: 47 in, 119 cm; ground clearance: 5.50 in, 14 cm; weight: Coupé 2,348 lb, 1,065 kg - Convertible 2,335 lb, 1,050 kg; weight distribution: 50.8% front, 49.2% rear; turning circle: 31.5 ft, 9.6 m; fuel tank: 14 imp gal, 16.6 US gal, 63 l.

BODY coupé, 2+1 doors - convertible, 2 doors, in g.r.p.; 2 separate seats, adjustable headrests.

PRACTICAL INSTRUCTIONS fuel: 97 oct petrol; oil: engine 6.5 imp pt, 7.8 US pt, 3.7 l, SAE 10W-30, change every 6,000 miles, 9,700 km - gearbox 1.3 imp pt, 1.5 US pt, 0.7 l, SAE 80 EP, change every 24,000 miles, 38,600 km - final drive 1.8 imp pt, 2.1 US pt, 1 l, SAE 90 EP, change every 24,000 miles, 38,600 km; greasing: every 6,000 miles, 9,700 km, 7 points; spark plug: Motorcraft BF 32; tappet clearances (cold): inlet 0.008 in, 0.20 mm, exhaust 0.010 in, 0.25 mm; valve timing: 18° 70° 64° 24°; tyre pressure: front 22 psi, 1.5 atm, rear 22 psi, 1.5 atm.

OPTIONALS Borg-Warner 35 automatic transmission, hydraulic torque converter and planetary gears with 3 ratios (I 2.474, II 1.474, III 1, rev 2.111); power-steering; air-conditioning; leather upholstery; metallic spray; electric windows; laminated windscreen.

Tasmin 280i

See Tasmin 200, except for:

PRICES EX WORKS:

	£
2-dr Coupé	**14,377***
+2 2-dr Coupé	**15,500***
2-dr Convertible	**13,254***

ENGINE Ford, front, 4 stroke; 6 cylinders, Vee-slanted at 60°; 170.4 cu in, 2,792 cc (3.66 x 2.07 in, 93 x 68.5 mm); max power (DIN): 160 hp (118 kW) at 5,700 rpm; max torque (DIN): 162 lb ft, 22.3 kg m (219 Nm) at 4,300 rpm; 57.3 hp/l (42.2 kW/l); 4 crankshaft bearings; camshafts: 1, at centre of Vee; lubrication: eccentric pump, full flow filter, 8.3 imp pt, 9.9 US pt, 4.7 l; 2 Bosch K-Jetronic injection; fuel feed: electric pump; water-cooled, 18 imp pt, 21.6 US pt, 10.2 l.

TRANSMISSION gearbox ratios: I 3.160, II 1.940, III 1.410, IV 1, rev 3.350; axle ratio: 3.070; width of rims: 6"; tyres: 205/60 VR x 14.

PERFORMANCE max speeds: (I) 42 mph, 67 km/h; (II) 68 mph, 109 km/h; (III) 94 mph, 151 km/h; (IV) 133 mph, 214 km/h; power-weight ratio: Coupé 14.8 lb/hp (19.8 lb/kW), 6.7 kg/hp (9 kg/kW); acceleration: standing ¼ mile 16 sec, 0-50 mph (0-80 km/h) 5.6 sec; speed in direct drive at 1,000 rpm: 22.2 mph, 35.7 km/h; consumption: 24-30 m/imp gal, 20.3-25 m/US gal, 11.6-9.4 l x 100 km.

DIMENSIONS AND WEIGHT weight: +2 Coupé 2,536 lb, 1,150 kg.

BODY 2+2 seats (for +2 Coupé only); electric windows, metallic spray and laminated windscreen (standard).

PRACTICAL INSTRUCTIONS oil: engine 8.3 imp pt, 9.9 US pt, 4.7 l, SAE 20W-50, change every 6,000 miles, 9,700 km - gearbox 3.6 imp pt, 4.2 US pt, 2 l, SAE 80, no change recommended - final drive 2 imp pt, 2.3 US pt, 1.1 l, SAE 90; greasing: every 6,000 miles, 9,700 km, 5 points; spark plug: AGR 22 Motorcraft; tappet clearances: inlet 0.014 in, 0.35 mm, exhaust 0.016 in, 0.40 mm; valve timing: 24° 72° 73° 25°.

TVR Tasmin 350i Convertible

OPTIONALS Borg-Warner 35 automatic transmission, hydraulic torque converter and planetary gears with 3 ratios (I 2.474, II 1.474, III 1, rev 2.111); 5-speed mechanical gearbox; power steering; air-conditioning; leather upholstery.

Tasmin 350i Convertible

PRICE EX WORKS: £ 14,800**

ENGINE Rover, front, 4 stroke; 8 cylinders in Vee; 215 cu in, 3,528 cc (3.50 x 2.80 in, 88.8 x 71 mm); compression ratio: 9.8:1; max power (DIN): 190 hp (140 kW) at 5,280 rpm; max torque (DIN): 220 lb ft, 30.4 kg m (298 Nm) at 4,000 rpm; max engine rpm: 6,000; 53.9 hp/l (39.7 kW/l); light alloy block and head; 5 crankshaft bearings; valves: overhead, hydraulic tappets; camshafts: 1, at centre of Vee; digital electronic injection; fuel feed: electric pump; water-cooled.

TRANSMISSION driving wheels: rear; clutch: single dry plate (diaphragm); gearbox: mechanical; gears: 5, fully synchronized; ratios: I 3.320, II 2.090, III 1.400, IV 1, V 0.792, rev 3.430; lever: central; final drive: hypoid bevel; axle ratio: 3.540; tyres: Goodyear 205/60 VR x 15.

PERFORMANCE max speeds: (I) 36 mph, 58 km/h; (II) 57 mph, 91 km/h; (III) 86 mph, 138 km/h; (IV) 120 mph, 193 km/h; (V) 153 mph, 246 km/h; carrying capacity: 353 lb, 160 kg; acceleration: standing ¼ mile 14.8 sec, 0-50 mph (0-80 km/h) 5.1 sec; speed in top at 1,000 rpm: 25.4 mph, 40.5 km/h; consumption: 22-24 m/imp gal, 18.2-19.9 m/US gal, 12.9-11.8 l x 100 km.

CHASSIS multi-tubular frame; front suspension: independent, upper wishbones, coil springs, anti-roll bar, telescopic dampers; rear: rigid axle, side links, trailing arms, coil springs, telescopic dampers.

STEERING rack-and-pinion; turns lock to lock: 3.70.

BRAKES disc (front diameter 10.60 in, 26.9 cm, rear 10.90 in, 27.7 cm), servo.

ELECTRICAL EQUIPMENT 12 V; 60 Ah battery; 55 A alternator; Lucas ignition; 2 headlamps.

DIMENSIONS AND WEIGHT wheel base: 94 in, 239 cm; tracks: 56.50 in, 143 cm front, 56.70 in, 144 cm rear; length: 158 in, 401 cm; width: 68 in, 173 cm; height: 47.50 in, 121 cm; ground clearance: 6 in, 15.2 cm; weight distribution: 50% front, 50%

TVR Tasmin 280i Coupé

TVR Tasmin 350i Convertible

rear; turning circle: 31.5 ft, 9.6 m; fuel tank: 14 imp gal, 16.6 US gal, 63 l.

BODY convertible; 2 doors; 2 separate seats, electric windows; laminated windscreen; metallic spray.

PRACTICAL INSTRUCTIONS oil: engine SAE 20/50, change every 6,000 miles, 9,700 km - gearbox change every 6,000 miles, 9,700 km - final drive no change recommended; greasing: every 12,000 miles, 19,300 km, 6 points.

OPTIONALS Borg-Warner 35 automatic transmission, hydraulic torque converter and planetary gears with 3 ratios (I 2.474, II 1.474, III 1, rev 2.111); power-steering; air-conditioning; leather upholstery.

VAUXHALL — GREAT BRITAIN

Nova Series

PRICES EX WORKS:		£
1	1.0 2-dr Saloon	3,653*
2	1.0 2+1-dr Hatchback Saloon	3,799*
3	1.0 L 2-dr Saloon	4,175*
4	1.0 L 2+1-dr Hatchback Saloon	4,372*
5	1.2 2-dr Saloon	3,789*
6	1.2 2+1-dr Hatchback Saloon	3,935*
7	1.2 L 2-dr Saloon	4,311*
8	1.2 L 2+1-dr Hatchback Saloon	4,507*
9	1.3 SR 2+1-dr Hatchback Saloon	5,199*

Power team:	Standard for:	Optional for:
45 hp	1 to 4	—
55 hp	5 to 8	—
70 hp	9	—

45 hp power team

ENGINE front, transverse, 4 stroke; 4 cylinders, in line; 60.6 cu in, 933 cc (2.83 x 2.40 in, 72 x 61 mm); compression ratio: 9.2:1; max power (DIN): 45 hp (33 kW) at 5,400 rpm; max torque (DIN): 50 lb ft, 6.9 kg m (68 Nm) at 2,600 rpm; max engine rpm: 6,000; 45.3 hp/l (33.2 kW/l); cast iron block and head; 3 crankshaft bearings; valves: overhead, push-rods and rockers; camshafts: 1, side, chain-driven; lubrication: gear pump, full flow filter, 4.4 imp pt, 5.3 US pt, 2.5 l; 1 Weber 32 TL downdraught single barrel carburettor; fuel feed: mechanical pump; anti-freeze liquid-cooled, 9.7 imp pt, 11.6 US pt, 5.5 l, electric thermostatic fan.

TRANSMISSION driving wheels: front; clutch: single dry plate (diaphragm); gearbox: mechanical; gears: 4, fully synchronized; ratios: I 3.550, II 1.960, III 1.300, IV 0.890, rev 3.180; lever: central; final drive: helical spur gears; axle ratio: 3.940; width of rims: 4.5"; tyres: 135 SR x 13.

PERFORMANCE max speed: 87 mph, 140 km/h; power-weight ratio: sedans 36.2 lb/hp (49.4 lb/kW), 16.4 kg/hp (22.4 kg/kW); carrying capacity: 1,058 lb, 480 kg; consumption: 42.8 m/imp gal, 35.6 m/US gal, 6.6 l x 100 km at 75 mph, 120 km/h.

CHASSIS integral; front suspension: independent, by McPherson, coil springs/telescopic damper struts, heavy-duty rubber bearings, direction stabilizing radius arms; rear: crank compound, progressively acting coil springs, auxiliary rubber springs, telescopic dampers.

STEERING rack-and-pinion; turns lock to lock: 3.90.

BRAKES front disc, rear drum, dual circuit, servo; lining area: total 55.81 sq in, 360 sq cm.

ELECTRICAL EQUIPMENT 12 V; 36 Ah battery; 45 A alternator; 2 headlamps.

DIMENSIONS AND WEIGHT wheel base: 92.24 in, 234 cm; tracks: 51.97 in, 132 cm front, 51.18 in, 130 cm rear; length: 142.60 in, 362 cm - sedans 155.70 in, 395 cm; width: 60.31 in, 153 cm - sedans 60.63 in, 154 cm; height: 53.74 in, 136 cm; weight: 1,621 lb, 735 kg - sedans 1,632 lb, 740 kg; turning circle: 30.5 ft, 9.3 m; fuel tank: 9.2 imp gal, 11.1 US gal, 42 l.

BODY saloon/sedan; 2 or 2+1 doors; 5 seats, separate front seats, headrests; heated rear window.

PRACTICAL INSTRUCTIONS fuel: 98 oct petrol; oil: engine 4.4 imp pt, 5.3 US pt, 2.5 l, SAE 20W-50, change every 6,200 miles, 10,000 km - gearbox and final drive 3.2 imp pt, 3.8 US pt, 1.8 l, SAE 90 EP, no change recommended; greasing: none; spark plug: AC R42 6FS; tappet clearances: inlet 0.006 in, 0.15 mm, exhaust 0.009 in, 0.25 mm; valve timing: 27°30' 68°30' 46°30' 29°30'; tyre pressure: front 25 psi, 1.8 atm, rear 25 psi, 1.8 atm.

OPTIONALS 5-speed mechanical gearbox (I 3.550, II 1.960, III 1.300, IV 0.890, V 0.710, rev 3.180), 4.180 axle ratio, consumption 44.1 m/imp gal, 36.8 US gal, 6.4 l x 100 km at 75 mph, 120 km/h; 145 SR x 13 or 155/70 SR x 13 tyres; light alloy wheels; sunroof.

VAUXHALL Nova 1.0 Saloon

55 hp power team

See 45 hp power team, except for:

ENGINE 73 cu in, 1,196 cc (3.06 x 2.48 in, 78 x 63 mm); max power (DIN): 55 hp (40 kW) at 5,600 rpm; max torque (DIN): 67 lb ft, 9.2 kg m (90 Nm) at 2,200 rpm; max engine rpm: 6,200; 46 hp/l (33.4 kW/l); light alloy head; 5 crankshaft bearings; valves: overhead, in line, rockers, hydraulic tappets; camshafts: 1, overhead, cogged belt; lubrication: 5.3 imp pt, 6.3 US pt, 3 l; 1 Pierburg 1B1 downdraught single barrel carburettor; cooling: 10.7 imp pt, 12.9 US pt, 6.1 l.

TRANSMISSION axle ratio: 3.740; tyres: 145 SR x 13 (standard).

PERFORMANCE max speed: 94 mph, 152 km/h; power-weight ratio: 29.7 lb/hp (40.8 lb/kW), 13.4 kg/hp (18.5 kg/kW); carrying capacity: 1,047 lb, 475 kg; consumption: 43.5 m/imp gal, 36.2 m/US gal, 6.5 l x 100 km at 75 mph, 120 km/h.

CHASSIS front and rear suspension: anti-roll bar (standard for sedans only).

BRAKES rear compensator.

ELECTRICAL EQUIPMENT transistorized ignition.

DIMENSIONS AND WEIGHT weight: 1,632 lb, 740 kg.

PRACTICAL INSTRUCTIONS oil: engine 5.3 imp pt, 6.3 US pt, 3 l; spark plug: AC R42 XLS; valve timing: 19° 51° 59° 22°.

OPTIONALS with 5-speed mechanical gearbox 3.940 axle ratio and consumption 44.8 m/imp gal, 37.3 m/US gal, 6.3 l x 100 km at 75 mph, 120 km/h; anti-roll bar on front and rear suspension (for hatchback sedans only).

70 hp power team

See 45 hp power team, except for:

ENGINE 79.1 cu in, 1,297 cc (2.95 x 2.89 in, 75 x 73.4 mm); max power (DIN): 70 hp (51 kW) at 5,800 rpm; max torque (DIN): 75 lb ft, 10.3 kg m (101 Nm) at 3,800 rpm; max engine rpm: 6,400; 53.9 hp/l (39.3 kW/l); light alloy head; 5 crankshaft bearings; valves: overhead, in line, rockers, hydraulic tappets; camshafts: 1, overhead, cogged belt; lubrication: 5.3 imp pt, 6.3 US pt, 3 l; 1 Pierburg 1B1 downdraught single barrel carburettor; cooling: 10.7 imp pt, 12.9 US pt, 6.1 l.

TRANSMISSION (standard) gears: 5, fully synchronized; ratios: I 3.550, II 1.960, III 1.300, IV 0.890, V 0.710, rev 3.180; axle ratio: 4.180; tyres: 155 SR x 13.

PERFORMANCE max speed: 101 mph, 162 km/h; power-weight ratio: 23.6 lb/hp (32.4 lb/kW), 10.7 kg/hp (14.7 kg/kW); consumption: 44.8 m/imp gal, 37.3 m/US gal, 6.3 l x 100 km at 75 mph, 120 km/h.

CHASSIS front and rear suspension: anti-roll bar.

BRAKES rear compensator.

ELECTRICAL EQUIPMENT transistorized ignition.

DIMENSIONS AND WEIGHT weight: 1,654 lb, 750 kg.

BODY 2+1 doors.

PRACTICAL INSTRUCTIONS oil: engine 5.3 imp pt, 6.3 US pt, 3 l; spark plug: AC R42 XLS; valve timing: 29° 80° 68° 42°.

OPTIONALS light alloy wheels with 165/65 SR x 14 tyres.

Astra Series

PRICES EX WORKS:		£
1	1200S 2+1-dr Hatchback Saloon	4,494*
2	1200S 4+1-dr Hatchback Saloon	4,669*
3	1200S L 2+1-dr Hatchback Saloon	4,932*
4	1200S L 4+1-dr Hatchback Saloon	5,108*
5	1300S 2+1-dr Estate Car	5,026*
6	1300S L 2+1-dr Hatchback Saloon	5,110*
7	1300S L 4+1-dr Hatchback Saloon	5,286*
8	1300S L 2+1-dr Estate Car	5,520*
9	1300S L 4+1-dr Estate Car	5,697*
10	1300S GL 4+1-dr Hatchback Saloon	5,697*
11	1600S L 4+1-dr Hatchback Saloon	5,499*
12	1600S L 4+1-dr Estate Car	5,910*
13	1600S GL 4+1-dr Hatchback Saloon	5,910*

VAUXHALL Nova 1.3 SR Hatchback Saloon

ASTRA SERIES

14	1600S GL 4+1-dr Estate Car	**6,321***
15	1600S SR 2+1-dr Hatchback Saloon	**6,029***
16	1600D L 2+1-dr Hatchback Saloon	**5,910***
17	1600D L 4+1-dr Estate Car	**6,320***

Power team:	Standard for:	Optional for:
60 hp	1 to 4	—
75 hp	5 to 10	—
90 hp	11 to 15	—
54 hp (diesel)	16,17	—

60 hp power team

ENGINE front, transverse, 4 stroke; 4 cylinders, in line; 73 cu in, 1,196 cc (3.11 x 2.40 in, 79 x 61 mm); compression ratio: 9:1; max power (DIN): 60 hp (44 kW) at 5,800 rpm; max torque (DIN): 65 lb ft, 9 kg m (88 Nm) at 3,000 rpm; max engine rpm: 6,000; 50.2 hp/l (36.8 kW/l); cast iron block and head; 3 crankshaft bearings; valves: overhead, push-rods and rockers; camshafts: 1, side, chain-driven; lubrication: gear pump, full flow filter, 4.8 imp pt, 5.7 US pt, 2.7 l; 1 Solex 35 PDSI downdraught single barrel carburettor; fuel feed: mechanical pump; anti-freeze liquid-cooled, 10.4 imp pt, 12.5 US pt, 5.9 l, electric thermostatic fan.

TRANSMISSION driving wheels: front; clutch: single dry plate (diaphragm); gearbox: mechanical; gears: 4, fully synchronized; ratios: I 3.550, II 1.960, III 1.300, IV 0.890, rev 3.182; lever: central; final drive: helical spur gears; axle ratio: 3.940; width of rims: 5''; tyres: 155 SR x 13.

PERFORMANCE max speed: 93 mph, 150 km/h; power-weight ratio: 4+1-dr Hatchback Saloon 31.6 lb/hp (43.1 lb/kW), 14.3 kg/hp (19.5 kg/kW); carrying capacity: 1,102 lb, 500 kg; consumption: 38.2 m/imp gal, 31.8 m/US gal, 7.4 l x 100 km at 75 mph, 120 km/h.

CHASSIS integral; front suspension: independent, by McPherson, coil springs/telescopic damper struts, heavy-duty rubber bearings, direction stabilizing radius arm; rear: crank compound, coil springs with progressively acting, auxiliary rubber springs, telescopic dampers.

STEERING rack-and-pinion; turns lock to lock: 3.90.

BRAKES front disc, rear drum, dual circuit, servo; lining area: total 57.05 sq in, 368 sq cm.

ELECTRICAL EQUIPMENT 12 V; 36 Ah battery; 45 A alternator; Bosch distributor; 2 headlamps.

DIMENSIONS AND WEIGHT wheel base: 99 in, 251 cm; tracks: 55.12 in, 140 cm front, 55.35 in, 141 cm rear; length: 157.40 in, 400 cm; width: 64.41 in, 164 cm; height: 53 in, 135 cm; weight: 2+1-dr Hatchback Saloon 1,852 lb, 840 kg - 4+1-dr Hatchback Saloon 1,896 lb, 860 kg - 2+1-dr L Hatchback Saloon 1,907 lb, 865 kg - 4+1-dr L Hatchback Saloon 1,951 lb, 885 kg; turning circle: 34.4 ft, 10.5 m; fuel tank: 9.2 imp gal, 11.1 US gal, 42 l.

BODY saloon/sedan; 2+1 or 4+1 doors; 5 seats; separate front seats.

PRACTICAL INSTRUCTIONS fuel: 98 oct petrol; oil: engine 4.8 imp pt, 5.7 US pt, 2.7 l, SAE 20W-30, change every 6,200 miles, 10,000 km - gearbox and final drive 3.2 imp pt, 3.8 US pt, 1.8 l, SAE 90 EP, no change recommended; greasing: none; spark plug: AC R42-6FS; tappet clearances: inlet 0.006 in, 0.15 mm, exhaust 0.009 in, 0.25 mm; valve timing: 27°30' 68°30' 46°30' 29°30'; tyre pressure: front 25 psi, 1.8 atm, rear 25 psi, 1.8 atm.

OPTIONALS 5-speed mechanical gearbox (I 3.550, II 1.960, III 1.300, IV 0.890, V 0.710, rev 3.330); (for L Hatchback saloons only) light alloy wheels, rear window wiper-washer, tinted glass and sunroof; metallic spray.

75 hp power team

See 60 hp power team, except for:

ENGINE 79.1 cu in, 1,297 cc (2.95 x 2.89 in, 75 x 73.4 mm); compression ratio: 9.2:1; max power (DIN): 75 hp (55 kW) at 5,800 rpm; max torque (DIN): 75 lb ft, 10.3 kg m (101 Nm) at 3,800-4,600 rpm; 57.8 hp/l (42.4 kW/l); light alloy head; 5 crankshaft bearings; valves: overhead, in line, rockers, hydraulic tappets; camshafts: 1, overhead, cogged belt; lubrication: 5.3 imp pt, 6.3 US pt, 3 l; 1 GMF Varajet II downdraught carburettor; cooling: 11.1 imp pt, 13.3 US pt, 6.3 l.

TRANSMISSION axle ratio: sedans 3.940 - st. wagons 4.180; width of rims: GL 5.5''.

PERFORMANCE max speed: 101 mph, 162 km/h; power-weight ratio: L 4+1-dr Hatchback Saloon 26.3 lb/hp (35.9 lb/kW), 11.9 kg/hp (16.3 kg/kW); consumption: Estate Car 36.7 m/imp gal, 30.5 m/US gal, 7.7 l x 100 km at 75 mph, 120 km/h.

CHASSIS front and rear suspension: anti-roll bar.

BRAKES rear compensator.

ELECTRICAL EQUIPMENT transistorized ignition.

DIMENSIONS AND WEIGHT length: st. wagons 165.63 in, 421 cm; height: st. wagons 55.12 in, 140 cm; weight: L and GL 4+1-dr Hatchback saloons and 2+1-dr Estate Car 1,973 lb, 895 kg - L 2+1-dr Hatchback Saloon 1,929 lb, 875 kg - L 2+1-dr Estate Car 2,083 lb, 945 kg - L 4+1-dr Estate Car 2,127 lb, 965 kg.

BODY saloon/sedan - estate car/st. wagon; 2+1 or 4+1 doors; rear folding seats (for st. wagons only).

PRACTICAL INSTRUCTIONS oil: engine 5.3 imp pt, 6.3 US pt, 3 l; spark plug: AC R42 XLS; valve timing: 24° 78° 68° 36°.

OPTIONALS 5-speed mechanical gearbox (I 3.550, II 1.960, III 1.300, IV 0.890, V 0.710, rev 3.330); automatic transmission with 3 ratios (I 2.840, II 1.600, III 1, rev 2.070), 3.740 axle ratio, max speed 96 mph, 155 km/h, consumption sedans 32.8 m/imp gal, 27.3 m/US gal, 8.6 l x 100 km at 75 mph, 120 km/h.

90 hp power team

See 60 hp power team, except for:

ENGINE 97.5 cu in, 1,598 cc (3.15 x 3.13 in, 80 x 79.5 mm); compression ratio: 9.2:1; max power (DIN): 90 hp (66 kW) at 5,800 rpm; max torque (DIN): 93 lb ft, 12.8 kg m (126 Nm) at 3,800-4,200 rpm; 56.3 hp/l (41.3 kW/l); light alloy head; 5 crankshaft bearings; valves: overhead, in line, rockers, hydraulic tappets; camshafts: 1, overhead, cogged belt; lubrication: 5.6 imp pt, 6.8 US pt, 3.2 l; 1 GMF Varajet II downdraught carburettor; cooling: 13.7 imp pt, 16.5 US pt, 7.8 l.

TRANSMISSION gearbox ratios: I 3.420, II 1.950, III 1.280, IV 0.890, rev 3.333; axle ratio: 3.740; width of rims: GL and SR models 5.5''; tyres: SR Hatchback Saloon 185/60 HR x 14.

PERFORMANCE max speed: 106 mph, 170 km/h; power-weight ratio: L Hatchback Saloon 23 lb/hp (31.4 lb/kW), 10.4 kg/hp (14.2 kg/kW); consumption: 36.2 m/imp gal, 30.2 m/US gal, 7.8 l x 100 km at 75 mph, 120 km/h.

CHASSIS front and rear suspension: anti-roll bar.

BRAKES rear compensator.

ELECTRICAL EQUIPMENT 44 Ah battery; 55 A alternator (for SR Hatchback Saloon only); transistorized ignition.

DIMENSIONS AND WEIGHT length: st. wagons 165.63 in, 421 cm; height: st. wagons 55.12 in, 140 cm; weight: L and GL Hatchback saloons 2,072 lb, 940 kg - L and GL st. wagons 2,238 lb, 1,015 kg - SR Hatchback Saloon 2,094 lb, 950 kg.

BODY saloon/sedan, 2+1 or 4+1 doors - estate car/st. wagon, 4+1 doors; rear folding seats (for st. wagons only).

PRACTICAL INSTRUCTIONS oil: engine 5.6 imp pt, 6.8 US pt, 3.2 l; valve timing: 29° 80° 68° 42°.

OPTIONALS 5-speed mechanical gearbox (I 3.420, II 1.950, III 1.280, IV 0.890, V 0.710, rev 3.330), consumption 38.2 m/imp gal, 31.8 m/US gal, 7.4 l x 100 km at 75 mph, 120 km/h; automatic transmission with 3 ratios (I 2.840, II 1.600, III 1, rev 2.070), 3.330 axle ratio, max speed 102 mph, 165 km/h, consumption 31.4 m/imp gal, 26.1 m/US gal, 9 l x 100 km at 75 mph, 120 km/h.

54 hp (diesel) power team

See 60 hp power team, except for:

ENGINE diesel; 97.5 cu in, 1,598 cc (3.15 x 3.13 in, 80 x 79.5 mm); compression ratio: 23:1; max power (DIN): 54 hp (40 kW) at 4,600 rpm; max torque (DIN): 71 lb ft, 9.8 kg m (96 Nm) at 2,400 rpm; max engine rpm: 5,000; 33.8 hp/l (25 kW/l); light alloy head; 5 crankshaft bearings; valves: overhead, in line, rockers, hydraulic tappets; camshafts: 1, overhead, cogged belt; lubrication: 6.5 imp pt, 7.8 US pt, 3.7 l; Bosch VER 82 injection pump; cooling: 13.6 imp pt, 16.3 US pt, 7.7 l.

TRANSMISSION gears: 5, fully synchronized; ratios: I 3.420, II 1.950, III 1.280, IV 0.890, V 0.710, rev 3.333; axle ratio: 3.740 - Estate Car 3.940.

PERFORMANCE max speed: 89 mph, 143 km/h; power-weight ratio: Saloon 39 lb/hp (52.6 lb/kW), 17.7 kg/hp (23.9 kg/kW); consumption: Saloon 41.5 m/imp gal, 34.6 m/US gal, 6.8 l x 100 km at 75 mph, 120 km/h.

CHASSIS front and rear suspension: anti-roll bar.

BRAKES rear compensator.

ELECTRICAL EQUIPMENT 66 Ah battery.

DIMENSIONS AND WEIGHT length: Estate Car 165.63 in, 421 cm; height: Estate Car 55.12 in, 140 cm; weight: L Hatchback Saloon 2,105 lb, 955 kg - L Estate Car 2,282 lb, 1,035 kg.

BODY saloon/sedan, 2+1 doors - estate car/st. wagon, 4+1 doors; rear folding seats (for Estate Car only).

PRACTICAL INSTRUCTIONS fuel: diesel; oil: engine 6.5 imp pt, 7.8 US pt, 3.7 l; valve timing: 16° 66° 54° 28°.

Astra 1800i GTE

PRICE EX WORKS: £ 6,739*

ENGINE front, transverse, 4 stroke; 4 cylinders, in line; 109.6 cu in, 1,796 cc (3.34 x 3.13 in, 84.8 x 79.5 mm); compression ratio: 9.5:1; max power (DIN): 115 hp (85 kW) at 5,800 rpm; max torque (DIN): 112 lb ft, 15.4 kg m (151 Nm) at 4,800 rpm; max engine rpm: 6,300; 64 hp/l (47.3 kW/l); cast iron block, light alloy head; 5 crankshaft bearings; valves: overhead, in line, rockers; camshafts: 1, overhead, cogged belt; lubrication: gear pump, full flow filter, 5.6 imp pt, 6.8 US pt, 3.2 l; Bosch LE-Jetronic injection; fuel feed: mechanical pump; anti-freeze liquid-cooled, 13.4 imp pt, 16.1 US pt, 7.6 l, electric thermostatic fan.

TRANSMISSION driving wheels: front; clutch: single dry plate (diaphragm); gearbox: mechanical; gears: 5, fully synchronized; ratios: I 3.420, II 1.950, III 1.280, IV 0.890, V 0.710, rev 3.330; lever: central; final drive: helical spur gears; axle ratio: 3.940; width of rims: 5.5''; tyres: 185/60 HR x 14.

PERFORMANCE max speeds: (I) 31 mph, 50 km/h; (II) 54

VAUXHALL Astra 1200S Hatchback Saloon

VAUXHALL Astra 1800i GTE

mph, 87 km/h; (III) 82 mph, 132 km/h; (IV) 116 mph, 187 km/h; (V) 116 mph, 187 km/h; power-weight ratio: 18.7 lb/hp (25.4 lb/kW), 8.5 kg/hp (11.5 kg/kW); carrying capacity: 882 lb, 400 kg; speed in top at 1,000 rpm: 23.5 mph, 37.9 km/h; consumption: 37.1 m/imp gal, 30.9 m/US gal, 7.6 l x 100 km at 75 mph, 120 km/h.

CHASSIS integral; front suspension: independent, by McPherson, coil springs/telescopic damper struts, anti-roll bar, heavy-duty rubber bearings, stabilizing radius arm; rear: crank compound, progressively acting coil springs, anti-roll bar, auxiliary rubber springs, telescopic dampers.

STEERING rack-and-pinion; turns lock to lock: 4.10.

BRAKES front disc, rear drum, dual circuit, rear compensator, servo; lining area: total 70.08 sq in, 452 sq cm.

ELECTRICAL EQUIPMENT 12 V; 44 Ah battery; 55 A alternator; transistorized breakerless ignition; 2 halogen headlamps.

DIMENSIONS AND WEIGHT wheel base: 99.21 in, 252 cm; front and rear track: 55.35 in, 141 cm; length: 157.40 in, 399 cm; width: 65.19 in, 166 cm; height: 54.33 in, 138 cm; ground clearance: 5.12 in, 13 cm; weight: 2,160 lb, 980 kg; turning circle: 35.1 ft, 10.7 m; fuel tank: 9.2 imp gal, 11.1 US gal, 42 l.

BODY saloon/sedan; 2+1 doors; 5 seats, separate front seats; heated rear window; rear window wiper-washer; light alloy wheels.

PRACTICAL INSTRUCTIONS fuel: 98 oct petrol; oil: engine 5.6 imp pt, 6.8 US pt, 3.2 l, SAE 15W-50, change every 6,200 miles, 10,000 km - gearbox and final drive 3.5 imp pt, 4.2 US pt, 2 l, SAE 90 EP, no change recommended; greasing: none; spark plug: AC R42 XLS; valve timing: 28° 89° 72° 45°; tyre pressure: front 28 psi, 2 atm, rear 28 psi, 2 atm.

OPTIONALS trip computer; metallic spray; sunroof.

VAUXHALL Chevette L Hatchback Saloon

Chevette

PRICES EX WORKS:	£
L 4-dr Saloon	**4,024***
L 2+1-dr Hatchback Saloon	**3,939***
L 2+1-dr Estate Car	**4,451***

ENGINE front, 4 stroke; 4 cylinders, vertical, in line; 76.6 cu in, 1,256 cc (3.19 x 2.40 in, 81 x 61 mm); compression ratio: 8.7:1 (7.3:1 for export only); max power (DIN): 57 hp (42 kW) at 5,400 rpm; max torque (DIN): 66 lb ft, 9.2 kg m (90 Nm) at 2,600 rpm; max engine rpm: 6,000; 45.4 hp/l (33.4 kW/l); chromium cast iron block and head; 3 crankshaft bearings; valves: overhead, in line, push-rods and rockers; camshafts: 1, side; lubrication: gear pump, full flow filter, 5 imp pt, 6.1 US pt, 2.9 l; 1 Zenith-Stromberg 150 CDSEV downdraught single barrel carburettor; fuel feed: mechanical pump; water-cooled, 10.2 imp pt, 12.3 US pt, 5.8 l, viscous coupling fan.

TRANSMISSION driving wheels: rear; clutch: single dry plate (diaphragm); gearbox: mechanical; gears: 4, fully synchronized; ratios: I 3.760, II 2.213, III 1.404, IV 1, rev 3.707; lever: central; final drive: hypoid bevel; axle ratio: 4.111; width of rims: 5"; tyres: 155 SR x 13.

PERFORMANCE max speeds: (I) 31 mph, 50 km/h; (II) 49 mph, 79 km/h; (III) 77 mph, 124 km/h; (IV) 91 mph, 146 km/h; power-weight ratio: Hatchback Saloon 33.1 lb/hp (44.9 lb/kW), 15 kg/hp (20.4 kg/kW); carrying capacity: 1,076 lb, 488 kg; acceleration: standing ¼ mile 19.6 sec, 0-50 mph (0-80 km/h) 9.6 sec; speed in direct drive at 1,000 rpm: 15.9 mph, 25.6 km/h; consumption: Hatchback Saloon 30.1 m/imp gal, 25 m/US gal, 9.4 l x 100 km at 75 mph, 120 km/h.

CHASSIS integral; front suspension: independent, wishbones, coil springs, anti-roll bar, telescopic dampers; rear: rigid axle (torque tube), longitudinal trailing radius arms, coil springs, Panhard rod, anti-roll bar, (for Estate Car only) telescopic dampers.

STEERING rack-and-pinion; turns lock to lock: 3.50.

BRAKES front disc (diameter 9.37 in, 23.8 cm), self-adjusting rear drum, rear compensator, dual circuit, servo; swept area: front 157.5 sq in, 1,016 sq cm, rear 73.8 sq in, 476 sq cm, total 231.3 sq in, 1,492 sq cm.

ELECTRICAL EQUIPMENT 12 V; 36 Ah battery; 45 A alternator; AC Delco distributor; 2 headlamps.

DIMENSIONS AND WEIGHT wheel base: 94.30 in, 239 cm; front and rear track: 51.20 in, 130 cm; length: 164.40 in, 417 cm - Hatchback Saloon 155.20 in, 394 cm - Estate Car 164.90 in, 419 cm; width: 61.80 in, 157 cm; height: Hatchback Saloon 51.50 in, 131 cm - Saloon 51.30 in, 130 cm - Estate Car 52.10 in, 132 cm; ground clearance: 4.70 in, 11.9 cm; weight: Saloon 1,918 lb, 870 kg - Hatchback Saloon 1,885 lb, 855 kg - Estate Car 1,951 lb, 885 kg; turning circle: 32.8 ft, 10 m; fuel tank: Saloon and Estate Car 9.8 imp gal, 11.9 US gal, 45 l - Hatchback Saloon 8.4 imp gal, 10 US gal, 38 l.

BODY saloon/sedan, 4 or 2+1 doors - estate car/st. wagon, 2+1 doors; 5 seats, separate front seats.

PRACTICAL INSTRUCTIONS fuel: 98 oct petrol; oil: engine 5 imp pt, 6.1 US pt, 2.9 l, SAE 10W-30, change every 6,000 miles, 9,700 km - gearbox 1.1 imp pt, 1.3 US pt, 0.6 l, SAE 90, change every 6 months - final drive 1.2 imp pt, 1.5 US pt, 0.7 l, SAE 90, no change recommended; greasing: every 6 months, 4 points; tappet clearances: inlet 0.008 in, 0.20 mm, exhaust 0.008 in, 0.20 mm; valve timing: 37° 71° 69° 39°; tyre pressure: front 21 psi, 1.5 atm, rear 25 psi, 1.7 atm.

OPTIONALS automatic transmission with 3 ratios (I 2.400, II 1.480, III 1, rev 1.920), consumption 28.8 m/imp gal, 24 m/US gal, 9.8 l x 100 km at 75 mph, 120 km/h; metallic spray.

Cavalier Series

	PRICES EX WORKS:	£
1	1300S 4-dr Saloon	**5,239***
2	1300S 4+1-dr Hatchback Saloon	**5,371***
3	1300S L 4-dr Saloon	**5,570***
4	1300S L 4+1-dr Hatchback Saloon	**5,702***
5	1300S GL 4-dr Saloon	**6,324***
6	1300S GL 4+1-dr Hatchback Saloon	**6,559***
7	1600S 4-dr Saloon	**5,550***
8	1600S 4+1-dr Hatchback Saloon	**5,682***
9	1600S 4+1-dr Estate Car	**6,143***
10	1600S L 4-dr Saloon	**5,882***
11	1600S L 4+1-dr Hatchback Saloon	**6,014***
12	1600S L 4+1-dr Estate Car	**6,562***
13	1600S GL 4-dr Saloon	**6,634***
14	1600S GL 4+1-dr Hatchback Saloon	**6,871***
15	1600S GL 4+1-dr Estate Car	**7,475***
16	1600S GLS 4-dr Saloon	**7,301***
17	1600S GLS 4+1-dr Hatchback Saloon	**7,537***
18	1800i SRi 4-dr Saloon	**7,127***
19	1800i SRi 4+1-dr Hatchback Saloon	**7,364***
20	1800i CD 4-dr Saloon	**8,459***
21	1800i CD 4+1-dr Hatchback Saloon	**8,696***
22	1600D L 4-dr Saloon	**6,314***
23	1600D L 4+1-dr Hatchback Saloon	**6,446***

Power team:	Standard for:	Optional for:
75 hp	1 to 6	—
90 hp	7 to 17	—
115 hp	18 to 21	—
54 hp (diesel)	22,23	—

75 hp power team

ENGINE front, transverse, 4 stroke; 4 cylinders, in line; 79.1 cu in, 1,297 cc (2.95 x 2.89 in, 75 x 73.4 mm); compression ratio: 9.2:1; max power (DIN): 75 hp (55 kW) at 5,800 rpm; max torque (DIN): 75 lb ft, 10.3 kg m (101 Nm) at 3,800-4,600 rpm; max engine rpm: 6,300; 57.8 hp/l (42.4 kW/l); cast iron block, light alloy head; 5 crankshaft bearings; valves: overhead, in line, rockers, hydraulic tappets; camshafts: 1, overhead, cogged belt; lubrication: gear pump, full flow filter, 5.3 imp pt, 6.3 US pt, 3 l; 1 GMF Varajet II downdraught single barrel carburettor; fuel feed: mechanical pump; anti-freeze liquid-cooled, 11.1 imp pt, 13.3 US pt, 6.3 l, electric thermostatic fan.

TRANSMISSION driving wheels: front; clutch: single dry plate (diaphragm); gearbox: mechanical; gears: 4, fully synchronized; ratios: I 3.550, II 1.960, III 1.300, IV 0.890, rev 3.180; lever: central; final drive: helical spur gears; axle ratio: 4.180; width of rims: 5" - GL 5.5"; tyres: 155 SR x 13 - L and GL 165 SR x 13.

PERFORMANCE max speed: 99 mph, 160 km/h; power-weight ratio: Saloon 28.2 lb/hp (38.5 lb/kW), 12.8 kg/hp (17.5 kg/kW); carrying capacity: 1,070 lb, 485 kg; speed in top at 1,000 rpm: 17.7 mph, 28.5 km/h; consumption: 36.2 m/imp gal, 30.2 m/US gal, 7.8 l x 100 km at 75 mph, 120 km/h.

CHASSIS integral; front suspension: independent, by McPherson, coil springs/telescopic damper struts, anti-roll bar, heavy-duty rubber bearings, direction stabilizing radius arm; rear: crank compound, progressively acting coil springs, auxiliary rubber springs, telescopic dampers.

STEERING rack-and-pinion, damper.

BRAKES front disc, rear drum, dual circuit, servo; lining area: total 70.08 sq in, 452 sq cm.

ELECTRICAL EQUIPMENT 12 V; 36 Ah battery; 45 A alternator; transistorized ignition; 2 headlamps.

DIMENSIONS AND WEIGHT wheel base: 101.34 in, 257 cm; tracks: 55.12 in, 140 cm front, 55.35 in, 141 cm rear; length: 171.89 in, 437 cm - hatchback saloons 167.80 in, 426 cm; width: 65.67 in, 167 cm; height: 54.92 in, 139 cm; ground clearance: 5.12 in, 13 cm; weight: Saloon 2,072 lb,

VAUXHALL Cavalier 1300S L Saloon

75 HP POWER TEAM

940 kg - L and GL saloons 2,127 lb, 965 kg - L and GL hatchback saloons 2,194 lb, 995 kg; turning circle: 33.1 ft, 10.1 m; fuel tank: 13.4 imp gal, 16.1 US gal, 61 l.

BODY saloon/sedan; 4 or 4+1 doors; 5 seats.

PRACTICAL INSTRUCTIONS fuel: 98 oct petrol; oil: engine 5.3 imp pt, 6.3 US pt, 3 l, SAE 20W-50, change every 6,200 miles, 10,000 km - gearbox and final drive 3.5 imp pt, 4.2 US pt, 2 l, SAE 90 EP, no change recommended; greasing: none; spark plug: AC R42 XLS; valve timing: 24° 78° 68° 36°; tyre pressure: front 25 psi, 1.8 atm, rear 25 psi, 1.8 atm.

OPTIONALS 5-speed mechanical gearbox (I 3.550, II 1.960, III 1.300, IV 0.890, V 0.710, rev 3.180), consumption 39.2 m/imp gal, 32.7 m/US gal, 7.2 l x 100 km at 75 mph, 120 km/h; automatic transmission with 3 ratios (I 2.840, II 1.600, III 1, rev 2.070), 3.740 axle ratio, max speed 96 mph, 155 km/h, consumption 31.4 m/imp gal, 26.1 m/US gal, 9 l x 100 km at 75 mph, 120 km/h; light alloy wheels; sunroof; tinted glass.

90 hp power team

See 75 hp power team, except for:

ENGINE 97.5 cu in, 1,598 cc (3.15 x 3.13 in, 80 x 79.5 mm); max power (DIN): 90 hp (66 kW) at 5,800 rpm; max torque (DIN): 93 lb ft, 12.8 kg m (126 Nm) at 3,800-4,200 rpm; 56.3 hp/l (41.3 kW/l); cooling: 13.9 imp pt, 16.7 US pt, 7.9 l.

TRANSMISSION gearbox ratios: I 3.420, II 1.950, III 1.280, IV 0.890, rev 3.333; axle ratio: 3.740 - st. wagons 3.940; width of rims: GL and GLS saloons 5.5"; tyres: 165 SR x 13.

PERFORMANCE max speed: 106 mph, 170 km/h; power-weight ratio: L Saloon 24.9 lb/hp (33.9 lb/kW), 11.3 kg/hp (15.4 kg/kW); consumption: 36.2 m/imp gal, 30.2 m/US gal, 7.8 l x 100 km at 75 mph, 120 km/h.

DIMENSIONS AND WEIGHT wheel base: st. wagons 101.50 in, 258 cm; length: st. wagons 170.30 in, 433 cm; width: st. wagons 66.40 in, 169 cm; height: st. wagons 53.90 in, 137 cm; weight: Saloon 2,205 lb, 1,000 kg - Hatchback Saloon 2,227 lb, 1,010 kg - L, GL and GLS saloons 2,238 lb, 1,015 kg - L, GL and GLS hatchback saloons 2,304 lb, 1,045 kg - Estate Car 2,297 lb, 1,042 kg - L Estate Car 2,341 lb, 1,062 kg - GL Estate Car 2,401 lb, 1,089 kg.

BODY saloon/sedan, 4 or 4+1 doors - estate car/st. wagon, 4+1 doors.

PRACTICAL INSTRUCTIONS valve timing: 29° 80° 68° 42°.

OPTIONALS 5-speed mechanical gearbox (I 3.420, II 1.950, III 1.280, IV 0.890, V 0.710, rev 3.333), 3.940 axle ratio, consumption 37.2 m/imp gal, 30.9 m/US gal, 7.6 l x 100 km at 75 mph, 120 km/h; with 3-speed automatic transmission, 3.330 axle ratio, max speed 102 mph, 165 km/h and consumption 32.5 m/imp gal, 27 m/US gal, 8.7 l x 100 km at 75 mph, 120 km/h; light alloy wheels; power steering; sunroof; tinted glass.

115 hp power team

See 75 hp power team, except for:

ENGINE 109.6 cu in, 1,796 cc (3.34 x 3.13 in, 84.8 x 79.5 mm); compression ratio: 9.5:1; max power (DIN): 115 hp (85 kW) at 5,800 rpm; max torque (DIN): 112 lb ft, 15.4 kg m (151 Nm) at 4,800 rpm; 64 hp/l (47.3 kW/l); lubrication: 5.6 imp pt, 6.8 US pt, 3.2 l; Bosch LE-Jetronic injection; cooling: 13.4 imp pt, 16.1 US pt, 7.6 l.

TRANSMISSION gears: 5, fully synchronized; ratios: I 3.420, II 1.950, III 1.280, IV 0.890, V 0.710, rev 3.333; axle ratio: 3.940; width of rims: 5.5"; tyres: SRi sedans 195/60 HR x 14 - CD sedans 185/70 HR x 13.

PERFORMANCE max speed: 116 mph, 187 km/h; power-weight ratio: CD Saloon 19.7 lb/hp (26.7 lb/kW), 9 kg/hp (12.1 kg/kW); consumption: 36.7 m/imp gal, 30.5 m/US gal, 7.7 l x 100 km at 75 mph, 120 km/h.

CHASSIS rear suspension: anti-roll bar.

STEERING (standard for CD sedans only) servo.

DIMENSIONS AND WEIGHT weight: SRi Saloon 2,359 lb, 1,070 kg - SRi Hatchback Saloon 2,425 lb, 1,100 kg - CD Saloon 2,271 lb, 1,030 kg - CD Hatchback Saloon 2,337 lb, 1,060 kg.

PRACTICAL INSTRUCTIONS oil: engine 5.6 imp pt, 6.8 US pt, 3.2 l; valve timing: 28° 89° 72° 45°.

OPTIONALS Opel automatic transmission with 3 ratios (I 2.840, II 1.600, III 1, rev 2.070), 3.330 axle ratio, max speed 112 mph, 180 km/h, consumption 31.7 m/imp gal, 26.4 m/US gal, 8.9 l x 100 km at 75 mph, 120 km/h; 55 Ah battery; 55 A alternator; sunroof; metallic spray; light alloy wheels; power steering; tinted glass.

54 hp (diesel) power team

See 75 hp power team, except for:

ENGINE diesel; 97.5 cu in, 1,598 cc (3.15 x 3.13 in, 80 x 79.5 mm); compression ratio: 23:1; max power (DIN): 54 hp (40 kW) at 4,600 rpm; max torque (DIN): 71 lb ft, 9.8 kg m (96 Nm) at 2,400 rpm; max engine rpm: 5,000; 33.8 hp/l (25 kW/l); light alloy head; lubrication: 6.5 imp pt, 7.8 US pt, 3.7 l; Bosch VER 82 injection pump; cooling: 13.6 imp pt, 16.3 US pt, 7.7 l.

TRANSMISSION gears: 5, fully synchronized; ratios: I 3.420, II 1.950, III 1.280, IV 0.890, V 0.710, rev 3.330; axle ratio: 3.940; width of rims: 5"; tyres: 165 SR x 13.

PERFORMANCE max speed: 89 mph, 143 km/h; power-weight ratio: L Saloon 42.6 lb/hp (57.3 lb/kW), 19.3 kg/hp (26 kg/kW); consumption: 39.8 m/imp gal, 33.1 m/US gal, 7.1 l x 100 km at 75 mph, 120 km/h.

ELECTRICAL EQUIPMENT 66 Ah battery.

DIMENSIONS AND WEIGHT weight: L Saloon 2,293 lb, 1,040 kg - L Hatchback Saloon 2,359 lb, 1,070 kg.

PRACTICAL INSTRUCTIONS fuel: diesel; oil: engine 6.5 imp pt, 7.8 Us pt, 3.7 l; valve timing: 16° 66° 54° 28°.

OPTIONALS Opel automatic transmission with 3 ratios (I 2.840, II 1.600, III 1, rev 2.070), 3.740 axle ratio, max speed 86 mph, 138 km/h, consumption 32.8 m/imp gal, 27.3 m/US gal, 8.6 l x 100 km at 75 mph, 120 km/h; power steering.

Carlton Series

PRICES EX WORKS:		£
1	1800 L 4-dr Saloon	**7,094***
2	1800 L 4+1-dr Estate Car	**7,784***
3	1800 GL 4-dr Saloon	**7,553***
4	1800 GL 4+1-dr Estate Car	**8,383***
5	2000 L 4-dr Saloon	**7,429***
6	2000 L 4+1-dr Estate Car	**8,119***
7	2000 GL 4-dr Saloon	**7,889***
8	2000 GL 4+1-dr Estate Car	**8,718***
9	2000i CD 4-dr Saloon	**9,039***
10	2300D L 4-dr Saloon	**7,707***
11	2300D L 4+1-dr Estate Car	**8,397***

VAUXHALL Cavalier L Series

Power team:	Standard for:	Optional for:
90 hp	1 to 4	—
100 hp	5 to 8	—
110 hp	9	—
71 hp (diesel)	10,11	—

90 hp power team

ENGINE front, 4 stroke; 4 cylinders, in line; 190.6 cu in, 1,796 cc (3.34 x 3.13 in, 84.8 x 79.5 mm); compression ratio: 9.2:1; max power (DIN): 90 hp (66 kW) at 5,400 rpm; max torque (DIN): 106 lb ft, 14.6 kg m (143 Nm) at 3,000-3,400 rpm; max engine rpm: 6,000; 50.1 hp/l (36.7 kW/l); cast iron block and head; 5 crankshaft bearings; valves: overhead, in line, rockers; camshafts: 1, overhead, cogged belt; lubrication: gear pump, full flow filter, 6.7 imp pt, 8 US pt, 3.8 l; 1 GMF Varajet II downdraught carburettor; fuel feed: mechanical pump; anti-freeze liquid-cooled, 12 imp pt, 14.4 US pt, 6.8 l, electric thermostatic fan.

TRANSMISSION driving wheels: rear; clutch: single dry plate (diaphragm); gearbox: mechanical; gears: 5, fully synchronized; ratios: I 3.717, II 2.019, III 1.316, IV 1, V 0.805, rev 3.445; lever: central; final drive: hypoid bevel; axle ratio: 3.700; width of rims: 5.5"; tyres: 175 SR x 14.

PERFORMANCE max speed: 107 mph, 173 km/h - st. wagons 104 mph, 167 km/h; power-weight ratio: saloons 27.3 lb/hp (37.3 lb/kW), 12.4 kg/hp (16.9 kg/kW); carrying capacity: 1,191 lb, 540 kg; consumption: 35.8 m/imp gal, 29.8 m/US gal, 7.9 l x 100 km at 75 mph, 120 km/h.

CHASSIS integral; front suspension: independent, by McPherson, lower wishbones, anti-roll bar, coil springs/telescopic damper struts; rear: rigid axle, trailing lower radius arms, upper torque arms, transverse linkage bar, coil springs, telescopic dampers.

STEERING recirculating ball, servo.

BRAKES front disc (diameter 9.37 in, 23.8 cm), rear drum, dual circuit, rear compensator, servo; lining area: total 85.7 sq in, 553 sq cm.

ELECTRICAL EQUIPMENT 12 V; Freedom 44 Ah battery; 45 A alternator; transistorized ignition; 2 headlamps.

VAUXHALL Cavalier 1600S L Estate Car

VAUXHALL Carlton 2000i CD Saloon

DIMENSIONS AND WEIGHT wheel base: 105.04 in, 267 cm; tracks: 56.34 in, 143 cm front, 55.59 in, 141 cm rear - st. wagons 56.38 in, 143 cm; length: 183.15 in, 465 cm - st. wagons 184.20 in, 468 cm; width: 68.03 in, 173 cm; height: 55.91 in, 142 cm - st. wagons 57.87 in, 147 cm; ground clearance: 5.12 in, 13 cm; weight: saloons 2,459 lb, 1,115 kg - st. wagons 2,536 lb, 1,150 kg; turning circle: 35.4 ft, 10.8 m; fuel tank: 14.3 imp gal, 17.2 US gal, 65 l.

BODY saloon/sedan, 4 doors - estate car/st. wagon, 4+1 doors; 5 seats, separate front seats, reclining backrests; heated rear window.

PRACTICAL INSTRUCTIONS fuel: 98 oct petrol; oil: engine 6.7 imp pt, 8 US pt, 3.8 l, SAE 20W-50, change every 6,200 miles, 10,000 km - gearbox 1.9 imp pt, 2.3 US pt, 1.1 l, SAE 80, no change recommended - final drive 1.9 imp pt, 2.3 US pt, 1.1 l, SAE 90, no change recommended; greasing: none; spark plug: AC R42 XLS; valve timing: 36° 69° 70° 35°; tyre pressure: front 24 psi, 1.7 atm, rear 25 psi, 1.8 atm.

OPTIONALS automatic transmission with 3 ratios (I 2.400, II 1.480, III 1, rev 1.920), 3.450 axle ratio, max speed 104 mph, 167 km/h - st. wagons 100 mph, 161 km/h, consumption 31.4 m/imp gal, 26.1 m/US gal, 9 l x 100 km at 75 mph, 120 km/h; 185/70 SR x 14 tyres; light alloy wheels; central door locking; sunroof; headrests; 55 Ah battery; 55 A alternator; halogen headlamps; headlamps with wiper-washer; rear window wiper-washer (for st. wagons only); air-conditioning; limited slip differential; metallic spray.

100 hp power team

See 90 hp power team, except for:

ENGINE 120.8 cu in, 1,979 cc (3.74 x 2.75 in, 95 x 69.8 mm); compression ratio: 9:1; max power (DIN): 100 hp (74 kW) at 5,200 rpm; max torque (DIN): 115 lb ft, 15.9 kg m (156 Nm) at 3,800 rpm; max engine rpm: 5,500; 50.5 hp/l (37.2 kW/l); valves: hydraulic tappets; 1 GMF Varajet II downdraught carburettor; cooling: 11.1 imp pt, 13.3 US pt, 6.3 l, thermostatic fan.

TRANSMISSION tyres: 175 HR x 14.

PERFORMANCE max speed: 112 mph, 181 km/h - st. wagons 109 mph, 175 km/h; power-weight ratio: saloons 25 lb/hp (33.8 lb/kW), 11.3 kg/hp (15.3 kg/kW); consumption: saloons 34 m/imp gal, 28.3 m/US gal, 8.3 l x 100 km at 75 mph, 120 km/h - st. wagons 31.7 m/imp gal, 26.4 m/US gal, 8.9 l x 100 km at 75 mph, 120 km/h.

DIMENSIONS AND WEIGHT weight: saloons 2,503 lb, 1,135 kg - st. wagons 2,591 lb, 1,175 kg.

PRACTICAL INSTRUCTIONS spark plug: AC R42 6FS; valve timing: 32° 90° 72° 50°.

OPTIONALS automatic transmission with 3 ratios (I 2.400, II 1.480, III 1, rev 1.920), max speed 109 mph, 175 km/h - st. wagons 105 mph, 169 km/h, consumption sedans 30.7 m/imp gal, 25.6 m/US gal, 9.2 l x 100 km at 75 mph, 120 km/h - st. wagons 28.8 m/imp gal, 24 m/US gal, 9.8 l x 100 km at 75 mph, 120 km/h.

110 hp power team

See 90 hp power team, except for:

ENGINE 120.8 cu in, 1,979 cc (3.74 x 2.75 in, 95 x 69.8 mm); compression ratio: 9.4:1; max power (DIN): 110 hp (81 kW) at 5,400 rpm; max torque (DIN): 120 lb ft, 16.5 kg m (162 Nm) at 3,400 rpm; 55.6 hp/l (40.9 kW/l); valves: hydraulic tappets; Bosch LE-Jetronic injection; cooling: 16 imp pt, 19.2 US pt, 9.1 l.

TRANSMISSION width of rims: 6"; tyres: 185/70 HR x 14.

PERFORMANCE max speed: 116 mph, 187 km/h; power-weight ratio: 22.9 lb/hp (31.2 lb/kW), 10.4 kg/hp (14.1 kg/kW); speed in top at 1,000 rpm: 24 mph, 38.6 km/h; consumption: 32.2 m/imp gal, 26.7 m/US gal, 8.8 l x 100 km at 75 mph, 120 km/h.

DIMENSIONS AND WEIGHT weight: 2,525 lb, 1,145 kg.

BODY saloon/sedan; 4 doors.

PRACTICAL INSTRUCTIONS spark plug: AC R42 6FS; valve timing: 34° 88° 74° 48°.

OPTIONALS automatic transmission with 3 ratios (I 2.400, II 1.480, III 1, rev 1.920), 3.450 axle ratio, max speed 112 mph, 181 km/h, consumption 29.7 m/imp gal, 24.8 m/US gal, 9.5 l x 100 km at 75 mph, 120 km/h; limited slip differential; electric levelling system; electric sunroof; trip computer; light alloy wheels.

71 hp (diesel) power team

See 90 hp power team, except for:

ENGINE diesel; 137.9 cu in, 2,260 cc (3.62 x 3.35 in, 92 x 85 mm); compression ratio: 22:1; max power (DIN): 71 hp (52 kW) at 4,400 rpm; max torque (DIN): 99 lb ft, 13.7 kg m (135 Nm) at 2,400 rpm; max engine rpm: 4,600; 31 hp/l (23 kW/l); lubrication: 9.7 imp pt, 11.6 US pt, 5.5 l; Bosch injection pump; cooling: 20.6 imp pt, 24.7 US pt, 11.7 l.

TRANSMISSION gears: 4, fully synchronized; ratios: I 4.016, II 2.147, III 1.318, IV 1, rev 3.765; axle ratio: 3.450.

PERFORMANCE max speed: Saloon 99 mph, 160 km/h - Estate Car 95 mph, 153 km/h; power-weight ratio: Saloon 39.4 lb/hp (53 lb/kW), 17.9 kg/hp (24 kg/kW); speed in direct drive at 1,000 rpm: 20.9 mph, 33.7 km/h; consumption: Saloon 37.7 m/imp gal, 31.4 m/US gal, 7.5 l x 100 km at 75 mph, 120 km/h - Estate Car 35.3 m/imp gal, 29.4 m/US gal, 8 l x 100 km at 75 mph, 120 km/h.

ELECTRICAL EQUIPMENT 2 x 44 Ah batteries; 55 A alternator (standard).

DIMENSIONS AND WEIGHT weight: Saloon 2,756 lb, 1,250 kg - Estate Car 2,866 lb, 1,300 kg.

PRACTICAL INSTRUCTIONS fuel: diesel; oil: engine 9.7 imp pt, 11.6 US pt, 5.5 l; valve timing: 32° 58° 54° 18°; tyre pressure: front 28 psi, 2 atm, rear 28 psi, 2 atm.

OPTIONALS 5-speed mechanical gearbox (I 3.717, II 2.019, III 1.316, IV 1, V 0.805, rev 3.445), 3.700 axle ratio, consumption Saloon 38.7 m/imp gal, 32.2 m/US gal, 7.3 l x 100 km at 75 mph, 120 km/h - Estate Car 36.2 m/imp gal, 30.2 m/US gal, 7.8 l x 100 km at 75 mph, 120 km/h; automatic transmission with 3 ratios (I 2.400, II 1.480, III 1, rev 1.920), max speed Saloon 96 mph, 155 km/h - Estate Car 92 mph, 148 km/h, consumption Saloon 34 m/imp gal, 28.3 m/US gal, 8.3 l x 100 km at 75 mph, 120 km/h - Estate Car 32.1 m/imp gal, 26.7 m/US gal, 8.8 l x 100 km at 75 mph, 120 km/h.

DONKERVOORT HOLLAND

Super Eight

PRICE EX WORKS: 34,500 florins

ENGINE Ford, front, 4 stroke; 4 cylinders, in line; 121.6 cu in, 1,993 cc (3.89 x 3.03 in, 90.8 x 76.9 mm); compression ratio: 9.2:1; max power (DIN): 105 hp (77 kW) at 5,400 rpm; max torque (DIN): 116 lb ft, 16 kg m (157 Nm) at 4,000 rpm; max engine rpm: 6,000; 52.7 hp/l (38.8 kW/l); cast iron block and head; 5 crankshaft bearings; valves: overhead, Vee-slanted; camshafts: 1, overhead; lubrication: rotary pump, full flow filter (cartridge), 6.5 imp pt, 7.8 US pt, 3.7 l; 1 Weber 77IF downdraught twin barrel carburettor; fuel feed: mechanical pump; water-cooled, 10.9 imp pt, 13.1 US pt, 6.2 l.

TRANSMISSION driving wheels: rear; clutch: single dry plate (diaphragm); gearbox: mechanical; gears: 4, fully synchronized; ratios: I 3.651, II 1.968, III 1.368, IV 1, rev 3.660; lever: central; final drive: hypoid bevel; axle ratio: 3.540; width of rims: 7"; tyres: 195/60 HR x 14.

PERFORMANCE max speeds: (I) 37 mph, 60 km/h; (II) 62 mph, 100 km/h; (III) 93 mph, 150 km/h; (IV) 121 mph, 195 km/h; power-weight ratio: 11.5 lb/hp (15.7 lb/kW), 5.2 kg/hp (7.1 kg/kW); carrying capacity: 463 lb, 210 kg; acceleration: 0-50 mph (0-80 km/h) 4 sec; speed in direct drive at 1,000 rpm: 20 mph, 32 km/h; consumption: 35.3 m/imp gal, 29.4 m/US gal, 8 l x 100 km.

CHASSIS tubular space frame; front suspension: independent, wishbones, coil springs, anti-roll bar, telescopic damper struts; rear: independent, swinging longitudinal trailing arms, Panhard rod, coil springs, anti-roll bar, telescopic dampers.

STEERING rack-and-pinion; turns lock to lock: 2.70.

BRAKES front disc, rear drum.

ELECTRICAL EQUIPMENT 12 V; 50 Ah battery; 55 A alternator; Bosch distributor; 2 headlamps.

DIMENSIONS AND WEIGHT wheel base: 90.55 in, 230 cm; tracks: 51.97 in, 132 cm front, 53.15 in, 135 cm rear; length: 140.16 in, 356 cm; width: 62.99 in, 160 cm; height: 42.13 in, 107 cm; ground clearance: 4.72 in, 12 cm; weight: 1,213 lb, 550 kg; weight distribution: 45% front, 55% rear; turning circle: 26.2 ft, 8 m; fuel tank: 8.8 imp gal, 10.6 US gal, 40 l.

BODY sports; no doors; 2 separate seats.

PRACTICAL INSTRUCTIONS fuel: 98 oct petrol; oil: engine 6.5 imp pt, 7.8 US pt, 3.7 l, SAE 20W-50, change every 3,100 miles, 5,000 km - gearbox and final drive 3.5 imp pt, 4.2 US pt, 2 l, SAE 80 EP, change every 31,100 miles, 50,000 km; greasing: every 6,200 miles, 10,000 km; spark plug: N7Y; tappet clearances: inlet 0.008 in, 0.20 mm, exhaust 0.010 in, 0.25 mm; valve timing: 24° 64° 70° 18°; tyre pressure: front 14 psi, 1 atm, rear 14 psi, 1 atm.

RUSKA HOLLAND

Regina

PRICE EX WORKS: 18,000 florins

ENGINE Volkswagen, rear, 4 stroke; 4 cylinders, horizontally opposed; 78.4 cu in, 1,285 cc (3.03 x 2.72 in, 77 x 69 mm); compression ratio: 7.5:1; max power (DIN): 44 hp (32 kW) at 4,100 rpm; max torque (DIN): 64 lb ft, 8.8 kg m (86 Nm) at 3,000 rpm; max engine rpm: 4,600; 34.2 hp/l (24.9 kW/l); cast iron block, light alloy head; 4 crankshaft bearings; valves: overhead, push-rods and rockers; camshafts: 1, central, lower; lubrication: gear pump, filter in sump, oil cooler, 4.4 imp pt, 5.3 US pt, 2.5 l; 1 Solex 30 PITC-2 downdraught carburettor; fuel feed: mechanical pump; air-cooled.

DONKERVOORT Super Eight

RUSKA Regina

REGINA

TRANSMISSION driving wheels: rear; clutch: single dry plate; gearbox: mechanical; gears: 4, fully synchronized; ratios: I 3.800, II 2.060, III 1.260, IV 0.890, rev 3.610; lever: central; final drive: spiral bevel; axle ratio: 4.375; width of rims: 5.5"; tyres: 195 VR x 14.

PERFORMANCE max speed: 78 mph, 125 km/h; power-weight ratio: 38.1 lb/hp (51.8 lb/kW), 17.3 kg/hp (23.5 kg/kW); carrying capacity: 882 lb, 400 kg; speed in top at 1,000 rpm; 16.8 mph, 27.1 km/h; consumption: 33.2 m/imp gal, 27.7 m/US gal, 8.5 l x 100 km.

CHASSIS backbone platform; front suspension: independent, by McPherson, coil springs/telescopic damper struts, anti-roll bar, lower swinging trailing arms; rear: independent, swinging semi-axles, swinging longitudinal trailing arms, transverse compensating torsion bar, telescopic dampers.

STEERING worm and roller; turns lock to lock: 2.60.

BRAKES drum, dual circuit; lining area: front 55.8 sq in, 3.60 sq cm, rear 40.3 sq in, 260 sq cm, total 96.1 sq in, 620 sq cm.

ELECTRICAL EQUIPMENT 12 V; 36 Ah battery; 280 W alternator; Bosch distributor; 4 headlamps.

DIMENSIONS AND WEIGHT wheel base: 94.49 in, 240 cm; tracks: 53.15 in, 135 cm front, 55.12 in, 140 cm rear; length: 165.35 in, 420 cm; width: 64.96 in, 165 cm; height: 59.06 in, 150 cm; ground clearance: 5.91 in, 15 cm; weight: 1,676 lb, 760 kg; turning circle: 26.2 ft, 8 m; fuel tank: 9.9 imp gal, 11.9 US gal, 45 l.

BODY roadster; no doors; 2 separate seats.

Regina Royal / Sagitta

PRICES EX WORKS:	florins
Regina Royal 2-dr Roadster	**19,500**
Sagitta 2-dr Roadster	**19,500**

ENGINE Volkswagen, rear, 4 stroke; 4 cylinders, horizontally opposed; 91.1 cu in, 1,496 cc (3.30 x 2.72 in, 83.5 x 69 mm); compression ratio: 8:1; max power (DIN): 48 hp (35 kW) at 4,000 rpm; max torque (DIN): 22.7 lb ft, 10.3 kg m (101 Nm) at 2,900 rpm; max engine rpm: 4,500; 32.1 hp/l (23.6 kW/l); light alloy block and head; 4 crankshaft bearings; valves: overhead, push-rods and rockers; camshafts: 1, central, lower; lubrication: gear pump, filter in sump, 5.3 imp pt, 6.1 US pt, 3 l; 1 Solex 34 PICT downdraught single barrel carburettor; fuel feed: mechanical pump; air-cooled.

TRANSMISSION driving wheels: rear; clutch: single dry plate (diaphragm); gearbox: mechanical; gears: 4, fully synchronized; ratios: I 3.800, II 2.080, III 1.260, IV 0.890, rev 3.880; lever: central; final drive: spiral bevel; axle ratio: 4.125; width of rims: 5.5"; tyres: 195 VR x 14.

PERFORMANCE max speed: 83 mph, 135 km/h; power-weight ratio: 36.3 lb/hp (49.3 lb/kW), 16.4 kg/hp (22.4 kg/kW); carrying capacity: 882 lb, 400 kg; acceleration: standing ¼ mile 21.4 sec, 0-50 mph (0-80 km/h) 15 sec; speed in top at 1,000 rpm: 19.6 mph, 31.5 km/h; consumption: 33.6 m/imp gal, 28 m/US gal, 8.4 l x 100 km.

CHASSIS backbone platform, rear auxiliary frame; front suspension: independent, twin swinging longitudinal trailing arms, transverse torsion bars, anti-roll bar, telescopic dampers; rear: independent, semi-trailing arms, transverse torsion bars, telescopic dampers.

STEERING worm and roller; turns lock to lock: 2.80.

RUSKA Regina

BRAKES front disc (diameter 10.91 in 27.7 cm), rear drum, dual circuit.

ELECTRICAL EQUIPMENT 12 V; 36 Ah battery; 420 W alternator; Bosch distributor; 2 headlamps.

DIMENSIONS AND WEIGHT wheel base: 94.49 in, 240 cm; tracks: 53.15 in, 135 cm front, 55.12 in, 140 cm rear; length: 177.17 in, 450 cm; width: 64.96 in, 165 cm; height: 59.06 in, 150 cm; ground clearance: 5.91 in, 15 cm; weight: 1,742 lb, 790 kg; weight distribution: 39.6% front, 60.4% rear; turning circle: 36.7 ft, 11.2 m; fuel tank: 9.9 imp gal, 11.9 US gal, 45 l.

BODY roadster; 2 doors; 2 separate seats.

VOLVO HOLLAND

340 Series

	PRICES IN GB AND EX WORKS:	£	florins
1	Winner 2+1-dr Hatchback Sedan	—	**17,490***
2	Luxe 2+1-dr Hatchback Sedan	—	**18,390***
3	DL 2+1-dr Hatchback Sedan	**4,892***	**19,990***
4	DL 4+1-dr Hatchback Sedan	**5,246***	**21,550***
5	GL 2+1-dr Hatchback Sedan	**5,165***	**21,990***
6	GL 4+1-dr Hatchback Sedan	**5,517***	**23,350***
7	GL 4-dr Sedan	—	—

Power team:	Standard for:	Optional for:
64 hp	1 to 3	—
72 hp	4 to 7	—

64 hp power team

ENGINE Renault, front, 4 stroke; 4 cylinders, vertical, in line; 85.2 cu in, 1,397 cc (2.99 x 3.03 in, 76 x 77 mm); compression ratio: 9.2:1; max power (DIN): 64 hp (47 kW) at 5,500 rpm; max torque (DIN): 78 lb ft, 10.7 kg m (105 Nm) at 2,500 rpm; max engine rpm: 6,000; 45.8 hp/l (33.7 kW/l); cast iron block, wet liners, light alloy head; 5 crankshaft bearings; valves: overhead, in line, slanted, push-rods and rockers; camshafts: 1, side; lubrication: gear pump, full flow filter, 6.5 imp pt, 7.8 US pt, 3.7 l; 1 Solex 32 SEIA carburettor; fuel feed: mechanical pump; sealed circuit cooling, 9.3 imp pt, 11.2 US pt, 5.3 l, electric fan.

TRANSMISSION driving wheels: rear; clutch: single dry plate (diaphragm); gearbox: mechanical; gears: 4, fully synchronized; ratios: I 3.705, II 2.159, III 1.369, IV 1, rev 3.683; lever: central; final drive: hypoid bevel; axle ratio: 3.636; width of rims: 5"; tyres: 155 SR x 13.

PERFORMANCE max speed: 93 mph, 150 km/h; power-weight ratio: 33.3 lb/hp (45.4 lb/kW), 15.1 kg/hp (20.6 kg/kW); carrying capacity: 1,041 lb, 472 kg; acceleration: 0-50 mph (0-80 km/h) 11 sec; consumption: 36.2 m/imp gal, 30.2 m/US gal, 7.8 l x 100 km at 75 mph, 120 km/h.

CHASSIS integral; front suspension: independent, by McPherson, lower wishbones, coil springs/telescopic damper struts, anti-roll bar; rear: de Dion axle, single leaf semi-elliptic springs, swinging longitudinal trailing arm, telescopic dampers.

STEERING rack-and-pinion; turns lock to lock: 4.13.

BRAKES front disc, rear drum, servo; swept area: front 167.8 sq in, 1,082 sq cm, rear 72.2 sq in, 466 sq cm, total 240 sq in, 1,548 sq cm.

ELECTRICAL EQUIPMENT 12 V; 36 Ah battery; 700 W alternator; Ducellier distributor; 2 halogen headlamps.

DIMENSIONS AND WEIGHT wheel base: 94.09 in, 239 cm; tracks: 53.94 in, 137 cm front, 55.12 in, 140 cm rear; length: 169.29 in, 430 cm; width: 65.35 in, 166 cm; height: 54.80 in, 139 cm; ground clearance: 5.55 in, 14.1 cm; weight: 2,134 lb, 968 kg; weight distribution: 53% front, 47% rear; turning circle: 30.2 ft, 9.2 m; fuel tank: 9.9 imp gal, 11.9 US gal, 45 l.

BODY saloon/sedan; 2+1 doors; 4-5 seats, separate front seats, reclining backrests with built-in headrests; heated rear window; laminated windscreen.

PRACTICAL INSTRUCTIONS fuel: 97 oct petrol; oil: engine 6.5 imp pt, 7.8 US pt, 3.7 l, SAE 10W-30 (summer) - SAE

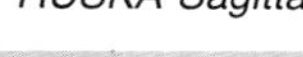

RUSKA Sagitta

VOLVO 360 GLT Hatchback Sedan

20W-40 (winter), change every 6,200 miles, 10,000 km - gearbox 3.7 imp pt, 4.4 US pt, 2.1 l, ATF - final drive 2.4 imp pt, 2.8 US pt, 1.3 l, SAE 80 EP, change every 24,000 miles, 40,000 km; greasing: none; tappet clearances: inlet 0.006 in, 0.15 mm, exhaust 0.008 in, 0.20 mm; tyre pressure: front 27 psi, 1.9 atm, rear 30 psi, 2.1 atm.

OPTIONALS 5-speed fully synchronized mechanical gearbox (I 3.705, II 2.159, III 1.369, IV 1, V 0.826, rev 3.683), 3.818 axle ratio, consumption 37.7 m/imp gal, 31.4 m/US gal, 7.5 l x 100 km at 75 mph, 120 km/h; C.V.T. automatic transmission with gearbox ratios continuously variable between 14.22 and 3.86, max speed 90 mph, 145 km/h, consumption 33.6 m/imp gal, 28 m/US gal, 8.4 l x 100 km at 75 mph, 120 km/h; sunroof; tinted glass; metallic spray; headlamps with wiper-washer; vinyl upholstery; light alloy wheels with 5.5" wide rims; air-conditioning.

72 hp power team

See 64 hp power team, except for:

ENGINE max power (DIN): 72 hp (53 kW) at 5,500 rpm; max torque (DIN): 78 lb ft, 10.7 kg m (105 Nm) at 2,500 rpm; 51.5 hp/l (37.9 kW/l); 1 Weber 32 DIR downdraught carburettor.

TRANSMISSION gears: 5, fully synchronized (standard); ratios: I 3.705, II 2.159, III 1.369, IV 1, V 0.826, rev 3.185; axle ratio: 3.818; tyres: 175/70 SR x 13.

PERFORMANCE max speed: 99 mph, 160 km/h; power-weight ratio: 2+1-dr hatchback sedans 29.6 lb/hp (40.3 lb/kW), 13.4 kg/hp (18.3 kg/kW); acceleration: 0-50 mph (0-80 km/h) 10.1 sec; consumption: 36.7 m/imp gal, 30.5 m/US gal, 7.7 l x 100 km at 75 mph, 120 km/h.

ELECTRICAL EQUIPMENT electronic mapping system.

DIMENSIONS AND WEIGHT length: 4-dr sedans 173.82 in, 441 cm; weight: 4+1-dr hatchback sedans 2,183 lb, 990 kg - 4-dr sedans 2,139 lb, 970 kg.

BODY saloon/sedan, 4 doors - hatchback, 2+1 or 4+1 doors; tinted glass and metallic spray (standard).

OPTIONALS C.V.T. automatic transmission with gearbox ratios continuously variable between 14.22 and 3.86, max speed 96 mph, 155 km/h, consumption 32.8 m/imp gal, 27.3 m/US gal, 8.6 l x 100 km at 75 mph, 120 km/h; 185/60 SR x 14 tyres with 5.5" wide rims and light alloy wheels; headlamps with wiper-washers; vinyl upholstery; sunroof; air-conditioning.

360 Series

PRICES IN GB AND EX WORKS:	£	florins
1 2+1-dr Hatchback Sedan	—	22,990*
2 4+1-dr Hatchback Sedan	—	24,350*
3 GLS 2+1-dr Hatchback Sedan	5,814*	24,990*
4 GLS 4+1-dr Hatchback Sedan	6,174*	26,350*
5 GLS 4-dr Sedan	—	—
6 GLT 2+1-dr Hatchback Sedan	6,446*	29,790*
7 GLT 4+1-dr Hatchback Sedan	6,810*	—
8 GLE 4-dr Sedan	6,699*	31,750*

Power team:	Standard for:	Optional for:
92 hp	1 to 5	—
115 hp	6 to 8	—

92 hp power team

ENGINE front, 4 stroke; 4 cylinders, vertical, in line; 121 cu in, 1,986 cc (3.50 x 3.15 in, 88.9 x 80 mm); compression ratio: 10:1; max power (DIN): 92 hp (68 kW) at 5,400 rpm; max torque (DIN): 116 lb ft, 16 kg m (150 Nm) at 3,600 rpm; max engine rpm: 6,000; 46.3 hp/l (34 kW/l); cast iron block, wet liners, light alloy head; 5 crankshaft bearings; valves: overhead, thimble tappets; camshafts: 1, overhead, cogged belt; lubrication: gear pump, full flow filter, 7.9 imp pt, 9.4 US pt, 4.5 l; 1 Zenith CD-54-HIF6 carburettor; fuel feed: mechanical pump; water-cooled, 14.1 imp pt, 15.9 US pt, 8 l, electric fan.

TRANSMISSION driving wheels: rear; clutch: single dry plate (diaphragm); gearbox: mechanical; gears: 5, fully synchronized; ratios: I 3.705, II 2.159, III 1.369, IV 1, V 0.826, rev 3.683; lever: central; final drive: hypoid bevel; axle ratio: 3.363; width of rims: 5"; tyres: 175/70 SR x 13.

PERFORMANCE max speeds: (I) 30 mph, 49 km/h; (II) 52 mph, 83 km/h; (III) 81 mph, 130 km/h; (IV) 106 mph, 170 km/h; (V) 103 mph, 165 km/h; power-weight ratio: 2+1-dr hatchback sedans 26.6 lb/hp (36 lb/kW), 12.1 kg/hp (16.3 kg/kW); acceleration: standing ¼ mile 18.6 sec, 0-50 mph (0-80 km/h) 8.7 sec; speed in direct drive at 1,000 rpm: 19.1 mph, 30.8 km/h; consumption: 35.3 m/imp gal, 29.4 m/US gal, 8 l x 100 km at 75 mph, 120 km/h.

CHASSIS integral; front suspension: independent, by McPherson, lower wishbones, coil springs/telescopic damper struts, anti-roll bar; rear: de Dion axle, single leaf semi-elliptic springs, swinging longitudinal trailing arm, telescopic dampers.

STEERING rack-and-pinion; turns lock to lock: 4.40.

VOLVO 360 GLE Sedan

BRAKES front disc, rear drum, servo; swept area: front 167.8 sq in, 1,082 sq cm, rear 89 sq in, 574 sq cm, total 256.7 sq in, 1,656 sq cm.

ELECTRICAL EQUIPMENT 12 V; 55 Ah battery; 700 W alternator; transistorized ignition; 2 halogen headlamps.

DIMENSIONS AND WEIGHT wheel base: 94.50 in, 240 cm; tracks: 53.94 in, 137 cm front, 55.12 in, 140 cm rear; length: 169.29 in, 430 cm - 4-dr sedans 173.82 in, 441 cm; width: 65.35 in, 166 cm; height: 54.80 in, 139 cm; ground clearance: 5.37 in, 13.7 cm; weight: 2+1-dr hatchback sedans 2,448 lb, 1,110 kg - 4+1-dr hatchback sedans 2,494 lb, 1,131 kg - 4-dr sedans 2,410 lb, 1,039 kg; weight distribution: 55% front, 45% rear; turning circle: 30.7 ft, 9.3 m; fuel tank: 9.9 imp gal, 11.9 US gal, 45 l.

BODY saloon/sedan, 4 doors - hatchback, 2+1 or 4+1 doors; 4-5 seats, separate front seats, reclining backrests with built-in headrests; heated rear window; tinted glass; metallic spray; laminated windscreen.

PRACTICAL INSTRUCTIONS fuel: 97 oct petrol; oil: engine 7.9 imp pt, 9.4 US pt, 4.5 l, SAE 15W-40, change every 6,200 miles, 10,000 km - gearbox 3.7 imp pt, 4.4 US pt, 2.1 l - final drive 2.3 imp pt, 2.7 US pt, 1.3 l; greasing: none; spark plug: Bosch W7DC; tappet clearances: inlet 0.014 in, 0.35 mm, exhaust 0.014 in, 0.35 mm; tyre pressure: front 27 psi, 1.9 atm, rear 30 psi, 2.1 atm.

OPTIONALS light alloy wheels with 5.5" wide rims; sunroof.

115 hp power team

See 92 hp power team, except for:

ENGINE max power (DIN): 115 hp (85 kW) at 5,700 rpm; max torque (DIN): 123 lb ft, 17 kg m (160 Nm) at 3,600 rpm; 57.9 hp/l (42.6 kW/l); Bosch LE-Jetronic injection; fuel feed: electric pump.

TRANSMISSION axle ratio: 3.636 - GLE 3.363; tyres 185/60 HR x 14.

PERFORMANCE max speed: 112 mph, 180 km/h; power-weight ratio: GLE Sedan 20.9 lb/hp (28.4 lb/kW), 9.5 kg/hp (12.9 kg/kW); acceleration: standing ¼ mile 18 sec, 0-50 mph (0-80 km/h) 7.5 sec; speed in direct drive at 1,000 rpm: 17.8 mph, 28.7 km/h; consumption: GLT hatchback sedans 32.1 m/imp gal, 26.7 m/US gal, 8.8 l x 100 km - GLE Sedan 34.9 m/imp gal, 29 m/US gal, 8.1 l x 100 km at 75 mph, 120 km/h.

BODY light alloy wheels (standard).

OPTIONALS none.

TMC — IRELAND

Costin 1600

PRICE EX WORKS: £ 7,417*

ENGINE Ford, front, 4 stroke; 4 cylinders, vertical, in line; 97.5 cu in, 1,598 cc (3.19 x 3.06 in, 81 x 77.6 mm); compression ratio: 9:1; max power (DIN): 84 hp (62 kW) at 5,500 rpm; max torque (DIN): 92 lb ft, 12.7 kg m (124 Nm) at 2,800 rpm; max engine rpm: 6,000; 52.6 hp/l (38.8 kW/l); cast iron block and head; 5 crankshaft bearings; valves: overhead, in line, push-rods and rockers; camshafts: 1, side, chain-driven; lubrication: gear pump, full flow filter (cartridge), 6.2 imp pt, 7.4 US pt, 3.5 l; 1 Weber DATR downdraught twin barrel carburettor; fuel feed: mechanical pump; water-cooled, expansion tank, 8.8 imp pt, 10.6 US pt, 5 l, electric fan.

TRANSMISSION driving wheels: rear; clutch: single dry plate (diaphragm); gearbox: mechanical; gears: 4, fully synchronized; ratios: I 3.540, II 1.905, III 1.276, IV 0.951, rev 3.617; lever: central; final drive: hypoid bevel; axle ratio: 3.890; width of rims: 5.5"; tyres: 185/50 HR x 13.

PERFORMANCE max speed: about 112 mph, 180 km/h; power-weight ratio: 18.4 lb/hp (24.9 lb/kW), 8.3 kg/hp (11.3 kg/kW); carrying capacity: 397 lb, 180 kg; consumption: 35.3 m/imp gal, 29.4 m/US gal, 8 l x 100 km.

CHASSIS 3-cell space-frame; front suspension: independent, unequal top and bottom wishbones, coil springs/telescopic

TMC Costin 1600

COSTIN 1600

damper struts; rear: rigid axle, long parallel leading radius arms controlled by Pahnard rod.

STEERING rack-and-pinion.

BRAKES front disc, rear drum (front diameter 7.87 in, 20 cm).

ELECTRICAL EQUIPMENT 12 V; 50 Ah battery; 630 W alternator; 2 headlamps.

DIMENSIONS AND WEIGHT length: 150 in, 381 cm; width: 65 in, 165 cm; height: 48 in, 122 cm; weight: 1,543 lb, 700 kg; weight distribution: 50% front axle, 50% rear axle.

BODY sports in plastic material and light alloy; no doors; 2 separate seats; light alloy wheels.

PRACTICAL INSTRUCTIONS fuel: 97 oct petrol; oil: engine 6.2 imp pt, 7.4 US pt, 3.5 l, SAE 10W-50, change every 6,000 miles, 9,700 km - gearbox 1.1 imp pt, 1.3 US pt, 0.6 l, SAE 90 - final drive 1.2 imp pt, 1.5 US pt, 0.7 l, SAE 90; tyre pressure: front 24 psi, 1.7 atm, rear 28 psi, 2 atm.

OPTIONALS soft top; tonneau cover; hardtop; automatic levelling control on rear suspension.

ALFA ROMEO Arna 1.2 SL Berlina

ALFA ROMEO ITALY

Arna

PRICES IN GB AND EX WORKS:	£	liras
1.2 L 2+1-dr Berlina	—	7,917,000
1.2 SL 4+1-dr Berlina	4,185*	8,542,000

ENGINE front, 4 stroke; 4 cylinders, horizontally opposed; 72.4 cu in, 1,186 cc (3.15 x 2.32 in, 80 x 59 mm); compression ratio: 8.8:1; max power (DIN): 63 hp (46 kW) at 6,000 rpm; max torque (DIN): 65 lb ft, 9 kg m (88 Nm) at 3,200 rpm; max engine rpm: 6,000; 53.1 hp/l (38.8 kW/l); cast iron block, light alloy head; 3 crankshaft bearings; valves: overhead, in line, thimble tappets, new Alfa Romeo patent valve adjustment; camshafts: 2, 1 per bank, overhead, cogged belt; lubrication: gear pump, full flow filter (cartridge), 7 imp pt, 8.5 US pt, 4 l; 1 Solex C32 DIS 40 or Dell'Orto SRDA 32 F downdraught single barrel carburettor; air cleaner: dry, thimble type thermostatic intake; fuel feed: mechanical pump; water-cooled, expansion tank, 12.8 imp pt, 15.4 US pt, 7.3 l, electric thermostatic fan.

TRANSMISSION driving wheels: front; clutch: single dry plate (diaphragm), hydraulically controlled; gearbox: mechanical; gears: 5, fully synchronized; ratios: I 3.750, II 2.050, III 1.387, IV 1.027, V 0.825, rev 3.091; lever: central; final drive: hypoid bevel; axle ratio: 3.889; width of rims: 5"; tyres: 165/70 SR x 13.

PERFORMANCE max speeds: (I) 25 mph, 41 km/h; (II) 43 mph, 70 km/h; (III) 63 mph, 101 km/h; (IV) 81 mph, 130 km/h; (V) over 93 mph, 150 km/h; power-weight ratio: 32.2 lb/hp (44.1 lb/kW), 14.6 kg/hp (20 kg/kW); carrying capacity: 783 lb, 355 kg; acceleration: standing ¼ mile 19.5 sec; speed in top at 1,000 rpm: 20 mph, 32.2 km/h; consumption: 32.5 m/imp gal, 27 m/US gal, 8.7 l x 100 km at 75 mph, 120 km/h.

CHASSIS integral; front suspension: independent, by McPherson, coil springs/telescopic damper struts, lower trailing links, anti-roll bar; rear: independent, lower wishbones, coil springs, telescopic dampers.

STEERING rack-and-pinion, adjustable height of steering wheel; turns lock to lock: 3.70.

BRAKES front disc (diameter 9.41 in, 23.9 cm) rear drum, front compensator, dual circuit, servo; swept area: front 193 sq in, 1,245 sq cm, rear 35.7 sq in, 230 sq cm, total 228.7 sq in, 1,475 sq cm.

ELECTRICAL EQUIPMENT 12 V; 45 Ah battery; 600 W alternator; Bosch or Marelli distributor; 2 headlamps.

DIMENSIONS AND WEIGHT wheel base: 95.12 in, 242 cm; tracks: 54.80 in, 139 cm front, 55.20 in, 140 cm rear; length: 157.48 in, 400 cm; width: 63.78 in, 162 cm; height: 52.76 in, 134 cm; weight: 2,029 lb, 920 kg; turning circle: 35.6 ft, 10.8 m; fuel tank: 11 imp gal, 13.2 US gal, 50 l.

BODY saloon/sedan; 2+1 or 4+1 doors; 5 seats, separate front seats; headrests; heated rear window; folding rear seats.

PRACTICAL INSTRUCTIONS fuel: 97 oct petrol; oil: engine 7 imp pt, 8.5 US pt, 4 l, SAE 20W-50, change every 6,200 miles, 10,000 km - gearbox and final drive 4.6 imp pt, 5.5 US pt, 2.6 l, SAE 90, change every 24,900 miles, 40,000 km; greasing: none; spark plug: Lodge 25 HL; tappet clearances: inlet 0.014-0.016 in, 0.35-0.40 mm, exhaust 0.018-0.020 in, 0.45-0.50 mm; valve timing: 44° 80° 63° 25°; tyre pressure: front 26 psi, 1.8 atm, rear 23 psi, 1.6 atm.

OPTIONALS metallic spray; (for SL only) sunroof.

Alfasud TI 1.3

PRICE IN GB: £ 5,995*
PRICE EX WORKS: 9,510,000 liras

ENGINE front, 4 stroke; 4 cylinders, horizontally opposed; 82.4 cu in, 1,350 cc (3.15 x 2.65 in, 80 x 67.2 mm); compression ratio: 9.7:1; max power (DIN): 86 hp (63 kW) at 5,800 rpm; max torque (DIN): 88 lb ft, 12.1 kg m (119 Nm) at 4,000 rpm; max engine rpm: 5,800; 63.7 hp/l (46.7 kW/l); cast iron block, light alloy head; 3 crankshaft bearings; valves: overhead, in line, thimble tappets, new Alfa Romeo patent valve adjustment; camshafts: 2, 1 per bank, overhead, cogged belt; lubrication: gear pump, full flow filter (cartridge), 7 imp pt, 8.5 US pt, 4 l; 2 Weber 36 IDF 44 AIE downdraught twin barrel carburettors; air cleaner: dry, thimble type thermostatic intake; fuel feed: mechanical pump; water-cooled, expansion tank, 12.8 imp pt, 15.4 US pt, 7.3 l, electric thermostatic fan.

TRANSMISSION driving wheels: front; clutch: single dry plate (diaphragm), hydraulically controlled; gearbox: mechanical; gears: 5, fully synchronized; ratios: I 3.750, II 2.050, III 1.387, IV 1.027, V 0.825, rev 3.091; lever: central; final drive: hypoid bevel; axle ratio: 3.545; width of rims: 5"; tyres: 165/70 SR x 13.

PERFORMANCE max speeds: (I) 29 mph, 46 km/h; (II) 52 mph, 84 km/h; (III) 78 mph, 125 km/h; (IV) 105 mph, 170 km/h; (V) over 102 mph, 165 km/h; power-weight ratio: 21.7 lb/hp (29.6 lb/kW), 9.8 kg/hp (13.4 kg/kW); carrying capacity: 992 lb, 450 kg; speed in top at 1,000 rpm: 21.9 mph, 35.2 km/h; consumption: 35.8 m/imp gal, 29.8 m/US gal, 7.9 l x 100 km at 75 mph, 120 km/h.

CHASSIS integral; front suspension: independent, by McPherson, coil springs/telescopic damper struts, lower trailing links, anti-roll bar; rear: rigid axle, longitudinal Watt linkage, Panhard transverse linkage bar, coil springs, telescopic dampers.

STEERING rack-and-pinion, adjustable height of steering wheel; turns lock to lock: 3.40.

BRAKES disc (front diameter 10.16 in, 25.8 cm, rear 9.17 in, 23.3 cm), dual circuit, rear compensator, servo; swept area: front 193 sq in, 1,245 sq cm, rear 155.5 sq in, 1,003 sq cm, total 348.5 sq in, 2,248 sq cm.

ELECTRICAL EQUIPMENT 12 V; 43 Ah battery; 630 W alternator; contactless transistorized ignition; 4 iodine headlamps.

DIMENSIONS AND WEIGHT wheel base: 96.65 in, 245 cm; tracks: 54.80 in, 139 cm front, 53.70 in, 136 cm rear; length: 156.61 in, 398 cm; width: 63.78 in, 162 cm; height: 53.94 in, 137 cm; ground clearance: 5.91 in, 15 cm; weight: 1,863 lb, 845 kg; turning circle: 34.1 ft, 10.4 m; fuel tank: 11 imp gal, 13.2 US gal, 50 l.

BODY saloon/sedan; 2+1 doors; 5 seats, separate front seats, headrests; heated rear window.

PRACTICAL INSTRUCTIONS fuel: 97 oct petrol; oil: engine 7 imp pt, 8.5 US pt, 4 l, SAE 20W-50, change every 6,200 miles, 10,000 km - gearbox and final drive 6 imp pt, 7.2 US pt, 3.4 l, SAE 90, change every 24,900 miles, 40,000 km; greasing: none; spark plug: Lodge 25 HL; tappet clearances: inlet 0.014-0.016 in, 0.35-0.40 mm, exhaust 0.018-0.020 in, 0.45-0.50 mm; valve timing: 18° 48° 45° 15°; tyre pressure: front 26 psi, 1.8 atm, rear 23 psi, 1.6 atm.

OPTIONALS light alloy wheels; metallic spray.

ALFA ROMEO Alfasud TI Quadrifoglio Verde

Alfasud TI Quadrifoglio Verde

See Alfasud TI 1.3, except for:

PRICE IN GB: £ 6,395*
PRICE EX WORKS: 10,415,000 liras

ENGINE 90.9 cu in, 1,490 cc (3.31 x 2.65 in, 84 x 67.2 mm); compression ratio: 9.5:1; max power (DIN): 105 hp (77 kW) at 6,000 rpm; max torque (DIN): 99 lb ft, 13.6 kg m (133 Nm) at 4,000 rpm; 70.5 hp/l (51.7 kW/l); 2 Weber 36 IDF 53 and 36 IDF 52 downdraught twin barrel carburettors.

TRANSMISSION axle ratio: 4.111; tyres: Michelin TRX 190/55 HR x 340 or Pirelli P6 185/60 HR x 14.

PERFORMANCE max speeds: (I) 25 mph, 41 km/h; (II) 47 mph, 75 km/h; (III) 69 mph, 111 km/h; (IV) 93 mph, 150 km/h; (V) over 112 mph, 180 km/h; power-weight ratio: 17.7 lb/hp (24.2 lb/kW), 8 km/hp (11 kg/kW); speed in top at 1,000 rpm: 18.9 mph, 30.5 km/h.

BODY light alloy wheels (standard).

Sprint 1.3

PRICE IN GB: £ 6,495*
PRICE EX WORKS: 10,995,000 liras

ALFA ROMEO Sprint Quadrifoglio Verde

ALFA ROMEO Alfa 33 Quadrifoglio Oro

ENGINE front, 4 stroke; 4 cylinders, horizontally opposed; 82.4 cu in, 1,350 cc (3.15 x 2.65 in, 80 x 67.2 mm); compression ratio: 9.7:1; max power (DIN): 86 hp (63 kW) at 5,800 rpm; max torque (DIN): 88 lb ft, 12.1 kg m (119 Nm) at 4,000 rpm; max engine rpm: 5,800; 63.7 hp/l (46.7 kW/l); cast iron block, light alloy head; 3 crankshaft bearings; valves: overhead, in line, thimble tappets, new Alfa Romeo patent valve adjustment; camshafts: 2, 1 per bank, overhead, cogged belt; lubrication: gear pump, full flow filter (cartridge), 7 imp pt, 8.5 US pt, 4 l; 2 Weber 36 IDF 44 AIE downdraught twin barrel carburettors; air cleaner: dry, thimble type thermostatic intake; fuel feed: mechanical pump; water-cooled, expansion tank, 12.8 imp pt, 15.4 US pt, 7.3 l, electric thermostatic fan.

TRANSMISSION driving wheels: front; clutch: single dry plate (diaphragm), hydraulically controlled; gearbox: mechanical; gears: 5, fully synchronized; ratios: I 3.750, II 2.050, III 1.387, IV 1.027, V 0.825, rev 3.091; lever: central; final drive: hypoid bevel; axle ratio: 3.545; width of rims: 5''; tyres: 165/70 SR x 13.

PERFORMANCE max speeds: (I) 29 mph, 46 km/h; (II) 52 mph, 84 km/h; (III) 78 mph, 125 km/h; (IV) 105 mph, 170 km/h; (V) 102 mph, 165 km/h; power-weight ratio: 23.5 lb/hp (32 lb/kW), 10.6 kg/hp (14.5 kg/kW); carrying capacity: 882 lb, 400 kg; speed in top at 1,000 rpm: 21.9 mph, 35.3 km/h; consumption: 35.8 m/imp gal, 29.8 m/US gal, 7.9 l x 100 km at 75 mph, 120 km/h.

CHASSIS integral; front suspension: independent, by McPherson, coil springs/telescopic damper struts, lower trailing links, anti-roll bar; rear: rigid axle, longitudinal Watt linkage, Panhard transverse linkage bar, coil springs, telescopic dampers.

STEERING rack-and-pinion, adjustable height of steering wheel; turns lock to lock: 3.40.

BRAKES disc (front diameter 10.16 in, 25.8 cm, rear 9.17 in, 23.3 cm), dual circuit, rear compensator, servo; swept area: front 193 sq in, 1,245 sq cm, rear 155.5 sq in, 1,003 sq cm, total 348.5 sq in, 2,248 sq cm.

ELECTRICAL EQUIPMENT 12 V; 43 Ah battery; 630 W alternator; contactless transistorized ignition; 4 iodine headlamps.

DIMENSIONS AND WEIGHT wheel base: 96.65 in, 245 cm; tracks: 55 in, 140 cm front, 53.70 in, 136 cm rear; length: 158.27 in, 402 cm; width: 63.78 in, 162 cm; height: 51.38 in, 130 cm; ground clearance: 5.51 in, 14 cm; weight: 2,018 lb, 915 kg; turning circle: 34.1 ft, 10.4 m; fuel tank: 11 imp gal, 13.2 US gal, 50 l.

ALFA ROMEO Alfa 33 Quadrifoglio Oro

BODY coupé; 2+1 doors; 5 seats, separate front seats, headrests; heated rear window.

PRACTICAL INSTRUCTIONS fuel: 97 oct petrol; oil: engine 7 imp pt, 8.5 US pt, 4 l, SAE 20W-50, change every 6,200 miles, 10,000 km - gearbox and final drive 6 imp pt, 7.2 US pt, 3.4 l, SAE 90, change every 24,900 miles, 40,000 km; greasing: none; spark plug: Lodge 2 HL; tappet clearances: inlet 0.014-0.016 in, 0.35-0.40 mm, exhaust 0.018-0.020 in, 0.45-0.50 mm; valve timing: 49° 79° 64° 34°; tyre pressure: front 26 psi, 1.8 atm, rear 23 psi, 1.6 atm.

OPTIONALS light alloy wheels; metallic spray.

Sprint Quadrifoglio Verde

See Sprint 1.3, except for:

PRICE IN GB: £ 7,145*
PRICE EX WORKS: 12,590,000 liras

ENGINE 90.9 cu in, 1,490 cc (3.31 x 2.65 in, 84 x 67.2 mm); compression ratio: 9.5:1; max power (DIN): 105 hp (77 kW) at 6,000 rpm; max torque (DIN): 99 lb ft, 13.6 kg m (133 Nm) at 4,000 rpm; 70.5 hp/l (51.7 kW/l); 2 Weber 36 IDF 53 and 36 IDF 52 downdraught twin barrel carburettors.

TRANSMISSION tyres: Michelin TRX 190/55 HR x 340 or Pirelli P6 185/60 HR x 14.

PERFORMANCE max speeds: (I) 25 mph, 41 km/h; (II) 47 mph, 75 km/h; (III) 69 mph, 111 km/h; (IV) 93 mph, 150 km/h; (V) over 112 mph, 180 km/h; power-weight ratio: 19.2 lb/hp (26.2 lb/kW), 8.7 km/hp (11.9 kg/kW); speed in top at 1,000 rpm: 21.9 mph, 35.3 km/h; consumption: 37.7 m/imp gal, 31.4 m/US gal, 7.5 l x 100 km at 75 mph, 120 km/h.

BODY light alloy wheels (standard).

PRACTICAL INSTRUCTIONS valve timing: 19° 53° 45° 11°.

Alfa 33 1.3

PRICE IN GB: £ 5,690*
PRICE EX WORKS: 10,170,000 liras

ENGINE front, 4 stroke; 4 cylinders, horizontally opposed; 82.4 cu in, 1,350 cc (3.15 x 2.65 in, 80 x 67.2 mm); compression ratio: 9:1; max power (DIN): 79 hp (58 kW) at 6,000 rpm; max torque (DIN): 81 lb ft, 11.3 kg m (111 Nm) at 3,500 rpm; max engine rpm: 6,000; 58.5 hp/l (43 kW/l); cast iron block, light alloy head; 3 crankshaft bearings; valves: overhead, in line, thimble tappets, new Alfa Romeo patent valve adjustment; camshafts: 2, 1 per bank, overhead, cogged belt; lubrication: gear pump, full flow filter (cartridge), 7 imp pt, 8.5 US pt, 4 l; 1 Weber 32 DIR 81/250 or Solex C 32 EIF 44 downdraught twin barrel carburettor; air cleaner: dry, thimble type thermostatic intake; fuel feed: mechanical pump; water-cooled, expansion tank, 12.8 imp pt, 15.4 US pt, 7.3 l, electric thermostatic fan.

TRANSMISSION driving wheels: front; clutch: single dry plate (diaphragm), hydraulically controlled; gearbox: mechanical; gears: 5, fully synchronized; ratios: I 3.750, II 2.050, III 1.387, IV 1.027, V 0.825, rev 3.091; lever: central; final drive: hypoid bevel; axle ratio: 3.889; width of rims: 5''; tyres: 165/70 SR x 13.

PERFORMANCE max speeds: (I) 26 mph, 42 km/h; (II) 48 mph, 77 km/h; (III) 71 mph, 115 km/h; (IV) 96 mph, 155 km/h; (V) over 102 mph, 165 km/h; power-weight ratio: 24.8 lb/hp (33.8 lb/kW), 11.3 kg/hp (15.3 kg/kW); carrying capacity: 937 lb, 425 kg; acceleration: standing ¼ mile 18.1 sec; speed in top at 1,000 rpm: 20 mph, 32.2 km/h; consumption: 35.8 m/imp gal, 29.8 m/US gal, 7.9 l x 100 km at 75 mph, 120 km/h.

CHASSIS integral; front suspension: independent, by McPherson, coil springs/telescopic damper struts, lower trailing links, anti-roll bar; rear: rigid axle, longitudinal Watt linkage, Panhard transverse linkage bar, coil springs/telescopic damper struts.

STEERING rack-and-pinion, adjustable height of steering wheel; turns lock to lock: 3.40.

BRAKES front disc (diameter 9.41 in, 23.9 cm), rear drum, rear compensator, dual circuit, servo; swept area: front 193 sq in, 1,245 sq cm, rear 46.8 sq in, 302 sq cm, total 239.8 sq in, 1,547 sq cm.

ELECTRICAL EQUIPMENT 12 V; 45 Ah battery; 540 W alternator; contactless transistorized ignition; 4 halogen headlamps.

DIMENSIONS AND WEIGHT wheel base: 106.10 in, 245 cm; tracks: 54.80 in, 139 cm front, 53.50 in, 136 cm rear; length: 158.07 in, 401 cm; width: 63.46 in, 161 cm; height: 51.38 in, 130 cm; weight: 1,962 lb, 890 kg; turning circle: 34.1 ft, 10.4 m; fuel tank: 11 imp gal, 13.2 US gal, 50 l.

BODY saloon/sedan; 4+1 doors; 5 seats, separate front seats, headrests; heated rear window; electric windows; folding rear seats; tinted glass.

PRACTICAL INSTRUCTIONS fuel: 97 oct petrol; oil: engine 7 imp pt, 8.5 US pt, 4 l, SAE 15W-50, change every 6,200 miles, 10,000 km - gearbox and final drive 4.6 imp pt, 5.5 US pt, 2.6 l, SAE 90, change every 24,900 miles, 40,000 km; greasing: none; spark plug: Lodge 25 HL; tappet clearances: inlet 0.014-0.016 in, 0.35-0.40 mm, exhaust 0.018-0.020 in, 0.45-0.50 mm; valve timing: 44° 80° 63° 25°; tyre pressure: front 26 psi, 1.8 atm, rear 23 psi, 1.6 atm.

OPTIONALS metallic spray.

Alfa 33 Quadrifoglio Oro

See Alfa 33 1.3, except for:

PRICE EX WORKS: 11,220,000 liras

ENGINE 90.9 cu in, 1,490 cc (3.31 x 2.65 in, 84 x 67.2 mm); max power (DIN): 84 hp (62 kW) at 5,800 rpm; max torque (DIN): 89 lb ft, 12.3 kg m (121 Nm) at 3,500 rpm; max engine rpm: 6,200; 56.4 hp/l (41.6 kW/l); 1 Weber 32 DIR 71/250 downdraught twin barrel carburettor.

TRANSMISSION axle ratio: 3.545.

PERFORMANCE max speeds: (I) 28 mph, 45 km/h; (II) 51 mph, 82 km/h; (III 76 mph, 122 km/h; (IV) 102 mph, 164 km/h; (V) over 106 mph, 170 km/h; power-weight ratio: 23.4 lb/hp (31.6 lb/kW), 10.6 kg/hp (14.4 kg/kW); acceleration: standing ¼ mile 17.5 sec; speed in top at 1,000 rpm: 21.9 mph, 35.3 km/h; consumption: 37.7 m/imp gal, 31.4 m/US gal, 7.5 l x 100 km at 75 mph, 120 km/h.

BODY headlamps with wiper-washer; central door locking; trip computer; check control; metallic spray (standard).

OPTIONALS light alloy wheels.

Alfa 33 1.5 4 x 4

ENGINE front, 4 stroke; 4 cylinders, horizontally opposed; 90.9 cu in, 1,490 cc (3.31 x 2.65 in, 84 x 67.2 mm); compression ratio: 9:1; max power (DIN): 84 hp (62 kW) at 5,750 rpm; max torque (DIN): 89 lb ft, 12.3 kg m (121 Nm) at 3,500 rpm; max engine rpm: 6,200; 56.4 hp/l (41.6 kW/l); cast iron block, light alloy head; 3 crankshaft bearings; valves: overhead, in line, thimble tappets, new Alfa Romeo patent valve adjustment; camshafts: 2, 1 per bank, overhead, cogged belt; lubrication: gear pump, full flow filter (cartridge), 7 imp pt, 8.5 US pt, 4 l; 1 Weber 32 DIR 71/250 downdraught twin barrel carburettor; fuel feed: mechanical pump; water-cooled, expansion tank, 12.8 imp pt, 15.4 US pt, 7.3 l, electric thermostatic fan.

TRANSMISSION driving wheels: front or front and rear, possible manual selection; clutch: single dry plate (diaphragm), hydraulically controlled; gearbox: mechanical; gears: 5, fully synchronized; ratios: I 3.750, II 2.050, III 1.387, IV 1.027, V 0.825, rev 3.091; lever: central plus central rear traction engagement lever; final drive: hypoid bevel; axle ratio: front and rear 4.111; width of rims: 5.5''; tyres: 175/70 R x 13 82 T.

ALFA ROMEO Alfa 33 1.5 4 x 4

ALFA 33 1.5 4 x 4

PERFORMANCE max speeds: (I) 24 mph, 38 km/h; (II) 43 mph, 69 km/h; (III) 65 mph, 105 km/h; (IV) 85 mph, 137 km/h; (V) over 102 mph, 165 km/h; power-weight ratio: 25.5 lb/hp (34.5 lb/kW), 11.5 kg/hp (15.6 kg/kW); carrying capacity: 937 lb, 425 kg; acceleration: standing ¼ mile 18.4 sec; speed in top at 1,000 rpm: 19.3 mph, 31.1 km/h; consumption: 35.3 m/imp gal, 29.4 m/US gal, 8 l x 100 km at 75 mph, 120 km/h.

CHASSIS integral; front suspension: independent, by McPherson, coil springs/telescopic damper struts, lower trailing links, anti-roll bar; rear: rigid axle, longitudinal Watt linkage, Panhard transverse linkage bar, coil springs/telescopic damper struts.

STEERING rack-and-pinion, adjustable height of steering wheel; turns lock to lock: 3.40.

BRAKES front disc (diameter 9.41 in, 23.9 cm), rear drum, rear compensator, dual circuit, servo; swept area: front 193 sq in, 1,245 sq cm, rear 46.8 sq in, 302 sq cm, total 239.8 sq in, 1,547 sq cm.

ELECTRICAL EQUIPMENT 12 V; 60 Ah battery; 540 W alternator; contactless transistorized ignition; 2 halogen headlamps.

DIMENSIONS AND WEIGHT wheel base: 106.10 in, 245 cm; tracks: 54.80 in, 139 cm front, 54.13 in, 137 cm rear; length: 158.07 in, 401 cm; width: 63.46 in, 161 cm; height: 52.17 in, 132 cm; weight: 2,139 lb, 970 kg; turning circle: 34.1 ft, 10.4 m; fuel tank: 11.7 imp gal, 14 US gal, 53 l.

BODY saloon/sedan; 4+1 doors; 5 seats, separate front seats, headrests; heated rear window; electric windows; folding rear seats; tinted glass; metallic spray.

PRACTICAL INSTRUCTIONS fuel: 97 oct petrol; oil: engine 7 imp pt, 8.5 US pt, 4 l, SAE 10W-50, change every 6,200 miles, 10,000 km - gearbox and final drive 4.6 imp pt, 5.5 US pt, 2.6 l, SAE 90, change every 24,900 miles, 40,000 km - rear final drive 1.8 imp pt, 2.1 US pt, 1 l, SAE 90, change every 24,900 miles, 40,000 km; greasing: none; spark plug: Lodge 25 HL; tappet clearances: inlet 0.014-0.016 in, 0.35-0.40 mm, exhaust 0.018-0.020 in, 0.45-0.50 mm; valve timing: 44° 80° 63° 25°; tyre pressure: front 26 psi, 1.8 atm, rear 26 psi, 1.8 atm.

OPTIONALS light alloy wheels.

Nuova Giulietta 1.6 L

PRICE IN GB: £ 6,695*
PRICE EX WORKS: 12,500,000 liras

ENGINE front, 4 stroke; 4 cylinders, vertical, in line; 95.8 cu in, 1,570 cc (3.07 x 3.23 in, 78 x 82 mm); compression ratio: 9:1; max power (DIN): 109 hp (80 kW) at 5,600 rpm; max torque (DIN): 105 lb ft, 14.5 kg m (142 Nm) at 4,300 rpm; max engine rpm: 6,000; 69.4 hp/l (51.1 kW/l); light alloy block and head, wet liners, hemispherical combustion chambers; 5 crankshaft bearings; valves: overhead, Vee-slanted at 80°, thimble tappets; camshafts: 2, overhead, chain-driven; lubrication: gear pump, full flow filter (cartridge), 11.4 imp pt, 13.7 US pt, 6.5 l; 2 Solex CHO ADDHE downdraught twin barrel carburettors; fuel feed: mechanical pump; water-cooled, expansion tank, 14.1 imp pt, 16.9 US pt, 8 l, electric thermostatic fan.

TRANSMISSION driving wheels: rear; clutch: single dry plate (diaphragm), hydraulically controlled; gearbox: mechanical, in unit with differential; gears: 5, fully synchronized; ratios: I 3.500, II 1.956, III 1.258, IV 0.946, V 0.780, rev 3; lever: central; final drive: hypoid bevel; axle ratio: 3.818; width of rims: 5.5"; tyres: 165 SR x 13 tubeless.

PERFORMANCE max speeds: (I) 28 mph, 45 km/h; (II) 51 mph, 82 km/h; (III) 78 mph, 126 km/h; (IV) 109 mph, 175 km/h; (V) 105 mph, 169 km/h; power-weight ratio: 21.6 lb/hp (29.3 lb/kW), 9.8 kg/hp (13.3 kg/kW); carrying capacity: 882 lb, 400 kg; acceleration: standing ¼ mile 17.6 sec; speed in top at 1,000 rpm: 18.8 mph, 30.2 km/h; consumption: 31 m/imp gal, 25.8 m/US gal, 9.1 l x 100 km at 75 mph, 120 km/h.

CHASSIS integral; front suspension: independent, wishbones (upper trailing links), torsion bars, anti-roll bar, telescopic dampers; rear: de Dion axle, oblique trailing arms, transverse Watt linkage, coil springs, anti-roll bar, telescopic dampers.

STEERING rack-and-pinion, adjustable height of steering wheel; turns lock to lock: 3.50.

BRAKES disc (diameter 9.84 in, 25 cm), dual circuit, rear compensator, servo; swept area: front 173.3 sq in, 1,118 sq cm, rear 156.6 sq in, 1,010 sq cm, total 329.9 sq in, 2,128 sq cm.

ELECTRICAL EQUIPMENT 12 V; 50 Ah battery; 540 W alternator; Bosch or Marelli contactless transistorized ignition; 2 iodine headlamps.

ALFA ROMEO Nuova Giulietta 1.8 L

DIMENSIONS AND WEIGHT wheel base: 98.82 in, 251 cm; front and rear track: 53.54 in, 136 cm; length: 165.75 in, 421 cm; width: 64.96 in, 165 cm; height: 55.12 in, 140 cm; ground clearance: 5.51 in, 14 cm; weight: 2,359 lb, 1,070 kg; weight distribution: 50% front, 50% rear; turning circle: 35.8 ft, 10.9 m; fuel tank: 11 imp gal, 13.2 US gal, 50 l.

BODY saloon/sedan; 4 doors; 5 seats, separate front seats, reclining backrests, adjustable headrests; heated rear window; tinted glass.

PRACTICAL INSTRUCTIONS fuel: 98 oct petrol; oil: engine 11.4 imp pt, 13.7 US pt, 6.5 l, SAE 10W-50, change every 6,200 miles, 10,000 km - gearbox and final drive 4.9 imp pt, 5.9 US pt, 2.8 l, SAE 90, change every 24,900 miles, 40,000 km; spark plug: Lodge 2 HL; tappet clearances: inlet 0.019-0.020 in, 0.47-0.50 mm, exhaust 0.020-0.022 in, 0.52-0.55 mm; valve timing: 33°54' 57°54' 57°14' 21°14'; tyre pressure: front 26 psi, 1.8 atm, rear 28 psi, 2 atm.

OPTIONALS 185/70 SR x 13 tyres; light alloy wheels; front electric windows; sunroof; air-conditioning; metallic spray.

Nuova Giulietta 1.8 L

See Nuova Giulietta 1.6 L, except for:

PRICE IN GB: £ 7,550*
PRICE EX WORKS: 13,675,000 liras

ENGINE 108.6 cu in, 1,779 cc (3.15 x 3.48 in, 80 x 88.5 mm); compression ratio: 9.5:1; max power (DIN): 122 hp (90 kW) at 5,300 rpm; max torque (DIN): 123 lb ft, 17 kg m (167 Nm) at 4,000 rpm; max engine rpm: 5,300; 68.6 hp/l (50.6 kW/l); 2 Dell'Orto DHLA 40 A or Solex C 40 ADDHE downdraught twin barrel carburettors with thermostatic filter.

TRANSMISSION tyres: 185/70 SR x 13 tubeless (standard).

PERFORMANCE max speeds: (I) 27 mph, 43 km/h; (II) 47 mph, 76 km/h; (III) 75 mph, 120 km/h; (IV) 112 mph, 180 km/h; (V) 111 mph, 178 km/h; power-weight ratio: 19.9 lb/hp (26.9 lb/kW), 9 kg/hp (12.2 kg/kW); acceleration: standing ¼ mile 17.1 sec; speed in top at 1,000 rpm: 19.8 mph, 31.8 km/h; consumption: 31.4 m/imp gal, 26.1 m/US gal, 9 l x 100 km at 75 mph, 120 km/h.

DIMENSIONS AND WEIGHT weight: 2,425 lb, 1,100 kg.

BODY front electric windows (standard).

OPTIONALS 4.300 axle ratio; light alloy wheels; central door locking; rear electric windows.

Nuova Giulietta 2.0 L

See Nuova Giulietta 1.6 L, except for:

PRICE IN GB: £ 7,250*

ENGINE 119.7 cu in, 1,962 cc (3.31 x 3.48 in, 84 x 88.5 mm); max power (DIN): 130 hp (96 kW) at 5,400 rpm; max torque (DIN): 131 lb ft, 18.1 kg m (177 Nm) at 4,000 rpm; max engine rpm: 5,600; 66.2 hp/l (48.7 kW/l); 2 Dell'Orto DHLA 40 horizontal twin barrel carburettors.

TRANSMISSION axle ratio: 4.300; tyres: Pirelli P6 185/65 HR x 14.

PERFORMANCE max speeds: (I) 24 mph, 39 km/h; (II) 43 mph, 70 km/h; (III) 67 mph, 108 km/h; (IV) 89 mph, 144 km/h; (V) 115 mph, 185 km/h; power-weight ratio: 18.6 lb/hp (25.3 lb/kW), 8.5 kg/hp (11.5 kg/kW); acceleration: standing ¼ mile 16.5 sec; speed in top at 1,000 rpm: 20.1 mph, 32.4 km/h; consumption: 29.1 m/imp gal, 24.2 m/US gal, 9.7 l x 100 km.

DIMENSIONS AND WEIGHT 2,425 lb, 1,100 kg.

BODY metallic spray, central door locking and electric windows (standard).

PRACTICAL INSTRUCTIONS valve timing: 41°20' 60°20' 53°40' 34°40'.

Nuova Giulietta 2.0 Turbodelta

PRICE EX WORKS: 22,000,000 liras

ENGINE turbocharged, front, 4 stroke; 4 cylinders, vertical, in line; 119.7 cu in, 1,962 cc (3.31 x 3.48 in, 84 x 88.5 mm); compression ratio: 7:1; max power (DIN): 170 hp (125 kW) at 5,000 rpm; max torque (DIN): 209 lb ft, 28.8 kg m (283 Nm) at 3,500 rpm; max engine rpm: 6,000; 86.6 hp/l (63.7 kW/l); light alloy block and head, wet liners, hemispherical combustion chambers; 5 crankshaft bearings; valves: overhead, Vee-slanted at 80°, thimble tappets; camshafts: 2, overhead, chain-driven; lubrication: gear pump, full flow filter (cartridge), 13.7 imp pt, 16.5 US pt, 7.8 l, oil cooler; 2 Weber downdraught twin barrel carburettors; 1 KKK exhaust turbocharger; fuel feed: electric pump; water-cooled, expansion tank, 14.1 imp pt, 16.9 US pt, 8 l, electric thermostatic fan.

TRANSMISSION driving wheels: rear; clutch: single dry plate (diaphragm), hydraulically controlled; gearbox: mechanical, in unit with differential; gears: 5, fully synchronized; ratios: I 3.500, II 1.956, III 1.258, IV 0.946, V 0.780, rev 3; lever: central; final drive: hypoid bevel; axle ratio: 4.100; width of rims: 150 TR 365 FH 40; tyres: Michelin TRX 200/60 HR x 365 tubeless.

PERFORMANCE max speeds: (I) 25 mph, 40 km/h; (II) 43 mph, 70 km/h; (III) 67 mph, 108 km/h; (IV) 89 mph, 143 km/h; (V) 128 mph, 206 km/h; power-weight ratio: 14.8 lb/hp (20.1 lb/kW), 6.7 kg/hp (9.1 kg/kW); carrying capacity: 937 lb, 425 kg; acceleration: standing ¼ mile 15.2 sec; speed in top at 1,000 rpm: 21.6 mph, 34.7 km/h; consumption: 23.5 m/imp gal, 19.6 m/US gal, 12 l x 100 km at 75 mph, 120 km/h.

CHASSIS integral; front suspension: independent, wishbones (upper trailing links), torsion bars, anti-roll bar, telescopic dampers; rear: de Dion axle, oblique trailing arms, transverse Watt linkage, coil springs, anti-roll bar, telescopic dampers.

STEERING rack-and-pinion, adjustable height of steering wheel; turns lock to lock: 3.50.

BRAKES disc (diameter 10.43 in, 26.5 cm front, 9.80 in, 25 cm rear), internal radial fins, dual circuit, rear compensator, servo; swept area: front 197.2 sq in, 1,272 sq cm, rear 156.6 sq in, 1,010 sq cm, total 353.8 sq in, 2,282 sq cm.

ELECTRICAL EQUIPMENT 12 V; 50 Ah battery; 540 W alternator; Bosch or Marelli contactless transistorized ignition; 2 iodine headlamps, 2 iodine fog lamps.

DIMENSIONS AND WEIGHT wheel base: 98.82 in, 251 cm; tracks: 54.02 in, 137 cm front, 53.70 in, 136 cm rear; length: 165.75 in, 421 cm; width: 64.96 in, 165 cm; height: 55.12 in, 140 cm; weight: 2,514 lb, 1,140 kg; weight distribution: 50% front, 50% rear; turning circle: 35.8 ft, 10.9 m; fuel tank: 11 imp gal, 13.2 US gal, 50 l.

BODY saloon/sedan; 4 doors; 5 seats, separate front seats, headrests; heated rear window; tinted glass; front electric windows; check control; light alloy wheels; metallic spray.

PRACTICAL INSTRUCTIONS fuel: 98 oct petrol; oil: engine 13.7 imp pt, 16.5 US pt, 7.8 l, SAE 10W-50, change every 3,100 miles, 5,000 km - gearbox and final drive 4.9 imp pt, 5.9 US pt, 2.8 l, SAE 90, change every 24,900 miles, 40,000 km; greasing: none; valve timing: 40°34' 64°34' 63°54' 27°54'; tyre pressure: front 26 psi, 1.8 atm, rear 28 psi, 2 atm.

Nuova Giulietta 2.0 TD L

PRICE EX WORKS: 14,375,000* liras

ENGINE VM diesel, turbocharged, front, 4 stroke; 4 cylinders, vertical, in line; 121.7 cu in, 1,995 cc (3.46 x 3.23 in, 88 x 82 mm); compression ratio: 22:1; max power (DIN): 82 hp (60 kW) at 4,300 rpm; max torque (DIN): 120 lb ft, 16.5 kg m (162 Nm) at 2,300 rpm; max engine rpm: 4,300; 41.1 hp/l (30.1 kW/l); cast iron block, 4 separate light alloy heads; 5 crankshaft bearings; valves: overhead, in line, push-rods and rockers; camshafts: 1, side; lubrication: gear pump, full flow filter, 10.7 imp pt, 12.9 US pt, 6.1 l; Bosch or Spica injection pump with KKK exhaust turbocharger; water-cooled, expansion tank, 17.6 imp pt, 21.1 US pt, 10 l, 2 electric thermostatic fans.

TRANSMISSION driving wheels: rear; clutch: single dry plate (diaphragm), hydraulically controlled; gearbox: mechanical, in unit with differential; gears: 5, fully synchronized; ratios: I 3.500, II 1.956, III 1.258, IV 0.946, V 0.780, rev 3; lever: central; final drive: hypoid bevel; axle ratio: 3.910; width of rims: 5.5"; tyres: 165 SR x 14.

PERFORMANCE max speeds: (I) 21 mph, 34 km/h; (II) 38 mph, 61 km/h; (III) 59 mph, 95 km/h; (IV) 78 mph, 126 km/h; (V) over 96 mph, 155 km/h; power-weight ratio: 33.1 lb/hp (45.2 lb/kW), 15 kg/hp (20.5 kg/kW); carrying capacity: 937 lb, 425 kg; acceleration: standing ¼ mile 19.4 sec; consumption: 34.9 m/imp gal, 29 m/US gal, 8.1 l x 100 km at 75 mph, 120 km/h.

CHASSIS integral; front suspension: independent, wishbones (upper trailing links), torsion bars, anti-roll bar, telescopic dampers; rear: de Dion axle, oblique trailing arms, transverse Watt linkage, coil springs, anti-roll bar, telescopic dampers.

STEERING rack-and-pinion, adjustable height of steering wheel; turns lock to lock: 3.80.

BRAKES disc, dual circuit, rear compensator, servo; swept area: front 192.3 sq in, 1,176 sq cm, rear 156.6 sq in, 1,010 sq cm, total 338.9 sq in, 2,186 sq cm.

ELECTRICAL EQUIPMENT 12 V; 77 Ah battery; 770 W alternator; 2 iodine headlamps.

DIMENSIONS AND WEIGHT wheel base: 98.82 in, 251 cm; tracks: 53.54 in, 136 cm front, 53.46 in, 136 cm rear; length: 165.75 in, 421 cm; width: 64.96 in, 165 cm; height: 55.12 in, 140 cm; ground clearance: 5.51 in, 14 cm; weight: 2,712 lb, 1,230 kg; weight distribution: 50% front, 50% rear; turning circle: 33.1 ft, 10.1 m; fuel tank: 11 imp gal, 13.2 US gal, 50 l.

BODY saloon/sedan; 4 doors; 5 seats, separate front seats, reclining backrests, headrests; heated rear window; tinted glass; front electric windows; check control.

PRACTICAL INSTRUCTIONS fuel: diesel; oil: engine 10.7 imp pt, 12.9 US pt, 6.1 l, change every 3,100 miles, 5,000 km - gearbox and final drive 4.9 imp pt, 5.9 US pt, 2.8 l, SAE 90, change every 24,800 miles, 40,000 km; greasing: none; tappet clearances: inlet 0.012 in, 0.30 mm, exhaust 0.018 in, 0.45 mm; valve timing: 30° 62° 76° 32°; tyre pressure: front 29 psi, 2.1 atm, rear 29 psi, 2.1 atm.

ALFA ROMEO Nuova Giulietta 2.0 Turbodelta

OPTIONALS 185/70 SR x 14 tyres; light alloy wheels; metallic spray; air-conditioning; sunroof; rear electric windows.

Alfetta 1.6

PRICE EX WORKS: 13,660,000 liras

ENGINE front, 4 stroke; 4 cylinders, vertical, in line; 95.8 cu in, 1,570 cc (3.07 x 3.23 in, 78 x 82 mm); compression ratio: 9:1; max power (DIN): 109 hp (80 kW) at 5,600 rpm; max torque (DIN): 105 lb ft, 14.5 kg m (142 Nm) at 4,300 rpm; max engine rpm: 5,600; 69.4 hp/l (51.6 kW/l); light alloy block and head, wet liners, hemispherical combustion chambers; 5 crankshaft bearings; valves: overhead, Vee-slanted at 80°, thimble tappets; camshafts: 2, overhead; lubrication: gear pump, full flow filter (cartridge), 9.9 imp pt, 11.8 US pt, 5.6 l; 2 Dell'Orto DHLA 40F horizontal twin barrel carburettors; fuel feed: mechanical pump; water-cooled, expansion tank, 14.1 imp pt, 16.9 US pt, 8 l, electric thermostatic fan.

TRANSMISSION driving wheels: rear; clutch: single dry plate (diaphragm), hydraulically controlled; gearbox: mechanical, in unit with differential; gears: 5, fully synchronized; ratios: I 3.500, II 1.956, III 1.258, IV 0.946, V 0.780, rev 3; lever: central; final drive: hypoid bevel; axle ratio: 3.909; width of rims: 5.5"; tyres: 165 SR x 14.

PERFORMANCE max speeds: (I) 29 mph, 46 km/h; (II) 52 mph, 83 km/h; (III) 80 mph, 129 km/h; (IV) 108 mph, 174 km/h; (V) 106 mph, 171 km/h; power-weight ratio: 22.7 lb/hp (30.9 lb/kW), 10.3 kg/hp (14 kg/kW); carrying capacity: 937 lb, 425 kg; acceleration: standing ¼ mile 18 sec; speed in top at 1,000 rpm: 19.4 mph, 31.2 km/h; consumption: 31.4 m/imp gal, 26.1 m/US gal, 9 l x 100 km at 75 mph, 120 km/h.

CHASSIS integral; front suspension: independent, wishbones (upper trailing links), longitudinal torsion bars, anti-roll bar, telescopic dampers; rear: de Dion axle, oblique trailing arms, transverse Watt linkage, coil springs, anti-roll bar, telescopic dampers.

STEERING rack-and-pinion, adjustable height of steering wheel; turns lock to lock: 3.50.

BRAKES disc (diameter 10.28 in, 26.1 cm front, 9.80 in, 25 cm rear), dual circuit, rear compensator, servo; swept area: front 182.3 sq in, 1,176 sq cm, rear 156.6 sq in, 1,010 sq cm, total 338.9 sq in, 2,186 sq cm.

ELECTRICAL EQUIPMENT 12 V; 50 Ah battery; 540 W alternator; Bosch or Marelli contactless transistorized ignition; 2 iodine headlamps.

DIMENSIONS AND WEIGHT wheel base: 98.82 in, 251 cm; tracks: 53.78 in, 137 cm front, 53.46 in, 136 cm rear; length: 172.64 in, 438 cm; width: 64.57 in, 164 cm; ground clearance: 5.51 in, 14 cm; weight: 2,470 lb, 1,120 kg; weight distribution: 50% front, 50% rear; turning circle: 33.1 ft, 10.1 m; fuel tank: 10.8 imp gal, 12.9 US gal, 49 l.

BODY saloon/sedan; 4 doors; 5 seats, separate front seats, reclining backrests; heated rear window; tinted glass.

PRACTICAL INSTRUCTIONS fuel: 98 oct petrol; oil: engine 9.9 imp pt, 11.8 US pt, 5.6 l, SAE 20W-50, change every 6,200 miles, 10,000 km - gearbox and final drive 4.9 imp pt, 5.9 US pt, 2.8 l, SAE 90, change every 18,600 miles, 30,000 km; greasing: none; spark plug: Lodge 2 HL; tappet clearances: inlet 0.019-0.020 in, 0.47-0.50 mm, exhaust 0.020-0.022 in, 0.52-0.55 mm; valve timing: 57° 58° 60°20' 41°20'; tyre pressure: front 22 psi, 1.6 atm, rear 26 psi, 1.8 atm.

OPTIONALS 3.818 axle ratio; 185/70 SR x 14 tyres; light alloy wheels; metallic spray; central door locking; front electric windows; sunroof.

Alfetta 1.8

See Alfetta 1.6, except for:

PRICE EX WORKS: 14,275,000 liras

ENGINE 108.6 cu in, 1,779 cc (3.15 x 3.48 in, 80 x 88.5 mm); compression ratio: 9.5:1; max power (DIN): 122 hp (90 kW) at 5,800 rpm; max torque (DIN): 123 lb ft, 17 kg m (167 Nm) at 4,000 rpm; max engine rpm: 5,800; 68.6 hp/l (50.6 kW/l); 2 Dell'Orto DHLA 40 or Solex C40 DDHE or Weber 40 DCOE 32 horizontal twin barrel carburettors.

TRANSMISSION axle ratio: 3.818 (standard).

PERFORMANCE max speeds: (I) 28 mph, 45 km/h; (II) 50 mph, 80 km/h; (III) 78 mph, 125 km/h; (IV) 111 mph, 178 km/h; (V) 109 mph, 176 km/h; power-weight ratio: 20.2 lb/hp (27.4 lb/kW), 9.2 kg/hp (12.4 kg/kW); acceleration: standing ¼ mile 17.3 sec; speed in top at 1,000 rpm: 20.8 mph, 33.5 km/h; consumption: 31.7 m/imp gal, 26.4 m/US gal, 8.9 l x 100 km at 75 mph, 120 km/h.

OPTIONALS air-conditioning.

Alfetta 2.0

See Alfetta 1.6, except for:

PRICE IN GB: £ 8,750*
PRICE EX WORKS: 15,355,000 liras

ENGINE 119.7 cu in, 1,962 cc (3.31 x 3.48 in, 84 x 88.5 mm); max power (DIN): 130 hp (96 kW) at 5,400 rpm; max torque (DIN): 131 lb ft, 18.1 kg m (177 Nm) at 4,000 rpm; 66.2 hp/l (48.7 kW/l); 2 Dell'Orto DHLA 40 horizontal twin barrel carburettors.

TRANSMISSION final drive: limited slip; axle ratio: 3.818 (standard); tyres: 185/70 HR x 14.

PERFORMANCE max speeds: (I) 29 mph, 46 km/h; (II) 51 mph, 82 km/h; (III) 79 mph, 127 km/h; (IV) over 115 mph, 185 km/h; (V) 114 mph, 184 km/h; power-weight ratio: 18.5 lb/hp (24.1 lb/kW), 8.4 kg/hp (11.4 kg/kW); acceleration: standing ¼ mile 16.4 sec; speed in top at 1,000 rpm: 20.6 mph, 33.2 km/h; consumption: 31.7 m/imp gal, 26.4 m/US gal, 8.9 l x 100 km at 75 mph, 120 km/h.

ELECTRICAL EQUIPMENT 60 Ah battery.

DIMENSIONS AND WEIGHT weight: 2,514 lb, 1,140 kg.

BODY front electric windows (standard); check control.

PRACTICAL INSTRUCTIONS valve timing: 57° 58° 60°20' 41°20'; tyre pressure: front 26 psi, 1.8 atm, rear 26 psi, 1.8 atm.

OPTIONALS air-conditioning; rear electric windows.

Alfetta Quadrifoglio Injection

See Alfetta 1.6, except for:

PRICE EX WORKS: 17,280,000 liras

ENGINE 119.7 cu in, 1,962 cc (3.31 x 3.48 in, 84 x 88.5 mm); compression ratio: 10:1; max power (DIN): 130 hp (96 kW) at 5,400 rpm; max torque (DIN): 134 lb ft, 18.5 kg m (182 Nm) at 4,000 rpm; max engine rpm: 6,000; 66.3 hp/l (48.9 kW/l); Bosch Motronic injection; air cleaner: dry, thimble type thermostatic intake; fuel feed: electric pump.

TRANSMISSION axle ratio: 3.818 (standard); tyres: 185/70 HR x 14.

PERFORMANCE max speeds: (I) 29 mph, 46 km/h; (II) 51 mph, 82 km/h; (III) 79 mph, 127 km/h; (IV) over 115 mph,

ALFETTA QUADRIFOGLIO INJECTION

185 km/h; (V) 114 mph, 184 km/h; power-weight ratio: 19.3 lb/hp (26.2 lb/kW), 8.8 kg/hp (11.9 kg/kW); consumption: 32.8 m/imp gal, 27.3 m/US gal, 8.6 l x 100 km at 75 mph, 120 km/h.

ELECTRICAL EQUIPMENT 66 Ah battery; digital engine and electronic ignition (Bosch Motronic); Alfa Romeo patent variable stroke; 4 iodine headlamps.

DIMENSIONS AND WEIGHT weight: 2,514 lb, 1,140 kg.

BODY check control; trip computer; front and rear electric windows; light alloy wheels (standard).

PRACTICAL INSTRUCTIONS valve timing: 32° 37° 40° 16°.

OPTIONALS air-conditioning; sunroof.

Alfetta 2.0 TD

PRICE EX WORKS: 15,600,000 liras

ENGINE diesel VM, turbocharged, front, 4 stroke; 4 cylinders, vertical, in line; 121.7 cu in, 1,995 cc (3.46 x 3.23 in, 88 x 82 mm); compression ratio: 22:1; max power (DIN): 82 hp (60 kW) at 4,300 rpm; max torque (DIN): 120 lb ft, 16.5 kg m (162 Nm) at 2,300 rpm; max engine rpm: 4,300; 41.1 hp/l (30.1 kW/l); cast iron block, 4 separate light alloy heads; 5 crankshaft bearings; valves: overhead, in line, push-rods and rockers; camshafts: 1, side; lubrication: gear pump, full flow filter, 10.7 imp pt, 12.9 US pt, 6.1 l, oil cooler; Bosch or Spica injection pump; 1 KKK turbocharger; water-cooled, expansion tank, 17.6 imp pt, 21.1 US pt, 10 l, 2 electric thermostatic fans.

TRANSMISSION driving wheels: rear; clutch: single dry plate (diaphragm), hydraulically controlled; gearbox: mechanical, in unit with differential; gears: 5, fully synchronized; ratios: I 3.500, II 1.956, III 1.258, IV 0.946, V 0.780, rev 3; lever: central; final drive: hypoid bevel; axle ratio: 4.100; width of rims: 5.5"; tyres: 165 SR x 14.

PERFORMANCE max speeds: (I) 21 mph, 34 km/h; (II) 38 mph, 61 km/h; (III) 55 mph, 88 km/h; (IV) 72 mph, 116 km/h; (V) over 96 mph, 155 km/h; power-weight ratio: 34.2 lb/hp (46.7 lb/kW), 15.5 kg/hp (21.2 kg/kW); carrying capacity: 882 lb, 400 kg; acceleration: standing ¼ mile 19.7 sec; speed in top at 1,000 rpm: 21.9 mph, 35.3 km/h; consumption: 35.3 m/imp gal, 29.4 m/US gal, 8 l x 100 km at 75 mph, 120 km/h.

CHASSIS integral; front suspension: independent, wishbones (upper trailing links), torsion bars, anti-roll bar, telescopic dampers; rear: de Dion axle, oblique trailing arms, transverse Watt linkage, coil springs, anti-roll bar, telescopic dampers.

STEERING rack-and-pinion, adjustable height of steering wheel; turns lock to lock: 3.80.

BRAKES disc, dual circuit, rear compensator, servo; swept area: front 192.3 sq in, 1,176 sq cm, rear 156.6 sq in, 1,010 sq cm, total 338.9 sq in, 2,186 sq cm.

ELECTRICAL EQUIPMENT 12 V; 77 Ah battery; 770 W alternator; 2 iodine headlamps.

DIMENSIONS AND WEIGHT wheel base: 98.82 in, 251 cm; tracks: 53.78 in, 137 cm front, 53.46 in, 136 cm rear; length: 172.64 in, 438 cm; width: 64.57 in, 164 cm; height: 56.30 in, 143 cm; ground clearance: 5.51 in, 14 cm; weight: 2,800 lb, 1,270 kg; weight distribution: 50% front, 50% rear; turning circle: 33.1 ft, 10.1 m; fuel tank: 10.8 imp gal, 12.9 US gal, 49 l.

BODY saloon/sedan; 4 doors; 5 seats, separate front seats, reclining backrests; heated rear window; central door locking.

PRACTICAL INSTRUCTIONS fuel: diesel; oil: engine 10.7 imp pt, 12.9 US pt, 6.1 l, change every 3,100 miles, 5,000 km - gearbox and final drive 4.9 imp pt, 5.9 US pt, 2.8 l, SAE 90, change every 24,800 miles, 40,000 km; greasing: none; tappet clearances: inlet 0.012 in, 0.30 mm, exhaust 0.018 in, 0.45 mm; valve timing: 10° 42° 56° 12°; tyre pressure: front 22 psi, 1.6 atm, rear 26 psi, 1.8 atm.

OPTIONALS 185/70 SR x 14 tyres; light alloy wheels; metallic spray; air-conditioning; sunroof.

Alfetta 2.4 TD

See Alfetta 2.0 TD, except for:

PRICE EX WORKS: 16,730,000 liras

ENGINE 146 cu in, 2,393 cc (3.62 x 3.54 in, 92 x 90 mm); compression ratio: 23:1; max power (DIN): 95 hp (70 kW) at 4,200 rpm; max torque (DIN): 138 lb ft, 19 kg m (186 Nm) at 2,400 rpm; max engine rpm: 4,200; 39.7 hp/l (29.3 kW/l).

TRANSMISSION axle ratio: 3.818.

PERFORMANCE max speeds: (I) 22 mph, 36 km/h; (II) 40 mph, 64 km/h; (III) 61 mph, 99 km/h; (IV) 82 mph, 132 km/h; (V) over 102 mph, 165 km/h; power-weight ratio: 29.5 lb/hp (40 lb/kW), 13.4 kg/hp (18.1 kg/kW); carrying capacity: 937 lb, 425 kg; consumption: 34 m/imp gal, 28.3 m/US gal, 8.3 l x 100 km at 75 mph, 120 km/h.

ALFA ROMEO Alfetta Quadrifoglio Injection

GTV 2.0

PRICE IN GB: £ 8,800*
PRICE EX WORKS: 15,865,000 liras

ENGINE front, 4 stroke; 4 cylinders, vertical, in line; 119.7 cu in, 1,962 cc (3.31 x 3.48 in, 84 x 88.5 mm); compression ratio: 9:1; max power (DIN): 130 hp (96 kW) at 5,400 rpm; max torque (DIN): 133 lb ft, 18.3 kg m (180 Nm) at 4,000 rpm; max engine rpm: 5,600; 66.2 hp/l (48.7 kW/l); light alloy block and head, wet liners, hemispherical combustion chambers; 5 crankshaft bearings; valves: overhead, Vee-slanted at 80°, thimble tappets; camshafts: 2, overhead; lubrication: gear pump, full flow filter (cartridge), 11.4 imp pt, 13.7 US pt, 6.5 l; 2 Dell'Orto DHLA 40 or Solex C 40 ADDHE/27 horizontal twin barrel carburettors; fuel feed: mechanical pump; water-cooled, 14.1 imp pt, 16.9 US pt, 8 l, electric thermostatic fan.

TRANSMISSION driving wheels: rear; clutch: single dry plate (diaphragm), hydraulically controlled; gearbox: mechanical, in unit with differential; gears: 5, fully synchronized; ratios: I 3.500, II 1.956, III 1.258, IV 0.943, V 0.780, rev 3; lever: central; final drive: hypoid bevel; axle ratio: 4.300; width of rims: 5.5"; tyres: 185/70 HR x 14.

PERFORMANCE max speeds: (I) 25 mph, 41 km/h; (II) 45 mph, 73 km/h; (III) 70 mph, 113 km/h; (IV) 94 mph, 151 km/h; (V) over 118 mph, 190 km/h; power-weight ratio: 18.8 lb/hp (25.5 lb/kW), 8.5 kg/hp (11.6 kg/kW); carrying capacity: 750 lb, 340 kg; acceleration: standing ¼ mile 16.4 sec; speed in top at 1,000 rpm: 21 mph, 33.8 km/h; consumption: 30.4 m/imp gal, 25.3 m/US gal, 9.3 l x 100 km at 75 mph, 120 km/h.

CHASSIS integral; front suspension: independent, wishbones (upper trailing links), longitudinal torsion bars, anti-roll bar, telescopic dampers; rear: de Dion axle, oblique trailing arms, transverse Watt linkage, coil springs, anti-roll bar, telescopic dampers.

STEERING rack-and-pinion; turns lock to lock: 3.50.

BRAKES disc, dual circuit, rear compensator, servo; swept area: front 182.3 sq in, 1,176 sq cm, rear 156.6 sq in, 1,010 sq cm, total 338.9 sq in, 2,186 sq cm.

ELECTRICAL EQUIPMENT 12 V; 50 Ah battery; 540 W alternator; Bosch or Marelli contactless transistorized ignition; 4 iodine headlamps.

DIMENSIONS AND WEIGHT wheel base: 94.49 in, 240 cm; tracks: 53.54 in, 136 cm front, 53.46 in, 136 cm rear; length: 167.72 in, 426 cm; width: 65.51 in, 166 cm; height: 51.18 in, 130 cm; ground clearance: 4.80 in, 12 cm; weight: 2,448 lb, 1,110 kg; weight distribution: 52% front, 48% rear; turning circle: 33.1 ft, 10.1 m; fuel tank: 11.9 imp gal, 14.3 US gal, 54 l.

BODY coupé; 2+1 doors; 4 seats, separate front seats, reclining backrests, headrests.

PRACTICAL INSTRUCTIONS fuel: 98 oct petrol; oil: engine 10.4 imp pt, 12.5 US pt, 5.9 l, SAE 20W-50, change every 6,200 miles, 10,000 km - gearbox and final drive 4.9 imp pt, 5.9 US pt, 2.8 l, SAE 90, change every 18,600 miles, 30,000 km; greasing: none; spark plug: Lodge 2 HL; tappet clearances: inlet 0.018-0.019 in, 0.45-0.47 mm, exhaust 0.019-0.021 in, 0.50-0.52 mm; valve timing: 48° 67° 60°20' 41°20'; tyre pressure: front 26 psi, 1.8 atm, rear 28 psi, 2 atm.

OPTIONALS 195/60 HR x 15 P6 tyres; light alloy wheels; air-conditioning; metallic spray; leather upholstery; sunroof; electric windows.

GTV 6 2.5

See GTV 2.0, except for:

PRICE IN GB: £ 10,950*
PRICE IN USA: $ 18,995*

ENGINE 6 cylinders, Vee-slanted at 60°; 152.1 cu in, 2,492 cc (3.46 x 2.69 in, 88 x 68.3 mm); max power (DIN): 160 hp (118 kW) at 5,800 rpm; max torque (DIN): 157 lb ft, 21.7 kg m (213 Nm) at 4,000 rpm; max engine rpm: 6,000; 64.2 hp/l (47.4 kW/l); 4 crankshaft bearings; valves: overhead, Vee-slanted at 46°45', thimble tappets, push-rods and rockers; camshafts: 2, 1 per bank, overhead, cogged belt; Bosch L-Jetronic injection; fuel feed: electric pump; liquid-cooled, 21.1 imp pt, 25.4 US pt, 12 l.

TRANSMISSION final drive: limited slip; axle ratio: 4.100; width of rims: 6"; tyres: Pirelli P6 195/60 HR x 15 tubeless.

PERFORMANCE max speeds: (I) 27 mph, 44 km/h; (II) 48 mph, 78 km/h; (III) 76 mph, 122 km/h; (IV) 101 mph, 162 km/h; (V) 127 mph, 205 km/h; power-weight ratio: 16.7 lb/hp (22.6 lb/kW), 7.6 kg/hp (10.3 kg/kW); acceleration: standing ¼ mile 16 sec; speed in top at 1,000 rpm: 21.7 mph, 35 km/h; consumption: 28.5 m/imp gal, 23.5 m/US gal, 9.9 l x 100 km at 75 mph, 120 km/h.

BRAKES disc, front internal radial fins; swept area: front 222.8 sq in, 1,437 sq cm, rear 156.6 sq in, 1,010 sq cm, total 379.4 sq in, 2,447 sq cm.

ELECTRICAL EQUIPMENT 66 Ah battery; 840 W alternator; Bosch contactless electronic ignition; speed limiter at 6,300 rpm.

DIMENSIONS AND WEIGHT tracks: 54.06 in, 137 cm front, 53.23 in, 135 cm rear; weight: 2,668 lb, 1,210 kg; fuel tank: 16.5 imp gal, 19.8 US gal, 75 l.

BODY light alloy wheels, electric windows and metallic spray (standard).

PRACTICAL INSTRUCTIONS valve timing: 36°50' 60°50' 59°55' 23°55.

VARIATIONS

(for USA only)
ENGINE max power (SAE net) 154 hp (113 kW) at 5,500 rpm, max torque (SAE net) 152 lb ft, 20.9 kg m (205 Nm) at 3,200 rpm, 61.8 hp/l (45.3 kW/l).

Spider 1.6

PRICE EX WORKS: 14,450,000 liras

ENGINE front, 4 stroke; 4 cylinders, vertical, in line; 95.8 cu in, 1,570 cc (3.07 x 3.28 in, 78 x 82 mm); compression ratio: 9:1; max power (DIN): 104 hp (76 kW) at 5,500 rpm; max torque (DIN): 105 lb ft, 14.5 kg m (142 Nm) at 4,000 rpm; max engine rpm: 6,000; 64.9 hp/l (47.8 kW/l); light alloy block and head, wet liners, hemispherical combustion chambers; 5 crankshaft bearings; valves: overhead, Vee-slanted at 80°, thimble tappets; camshafts: 2, overhead; lubrication: gear pump, full flow filter (cartridge), 11.4 imp pt, 13.7 US pt, 6.5 l; 2 Weber 40 DCOE 33 horizontal twin barrel carburettors; fuel feed: mechanical pump; water-cooled, 17.1 imp pt, 20.5 US pt, 9.7 l.

TRANSMISSION driving wheels: rear; clutch: single dry plate, hydraulically controlled; gearbox: mechanical; gears: 5, fully synchronized; ratios: I 3.300, II 1.990, III 1.350, IV 1, V 0.790, rev 3.010; lever: central; final drive: hypoid bevel; axle ratio: 4.555; width of rims: 5.5"; tyres: 165 HR x 14.

PERFORMANCE max speeds: (I) 27 mph, 44 km/h; (II) 46 mph, 74 km/h; (III) 66 mph, 106 km/h; (IV) 91 mph, 146 km/h; (V) over 112 mph, 180 km/h; power-weight ratio: 21.6 lb/hp (29.6 lb/kW), 9.8 kg/hp (13.4 kg/kW); carrying capacity: 772 lb, 350 kg; acceleration: standing ¼ mile 17.9 sec; speed in top at 1,000 rpm: 19.8 mph, 31.8 km/h; consumption: 29.1 m/imp gal, 24.2 m/US gal, 9.7 l x 100 km at 75 mph, 120 km/h.

CHASSIS integral; front suspension: independent, wishbones (lower trailing links), coil springs, anti-roll bar, tele-

ALFA ROMEO GTV 6 2.5

ALFA ROMEO Spider 1.6

scopic dampers; rear: rigid axle, trailing lower radius arms, upper transverse Vee radius arm, coil springs, anti-roll bar, telescopic dampers.

STEERING recirculating ball or worm and roller; turns lock to lock: 3.70.

BRAKES disc, rear compensator, servo; swept area: front 184.5 sq in, 1,190 sq cm, rear 167.1 sq in, 1,078 sq cm, total 351.6 sq in, 2,268 sq cm.

ELECTRICAL EQUIPMENT 12 V; 50 Ah battery; 420 W alternator; Bosch or Marelli distributor; 2 iodine headlamps.

DIMENSIONS AND WEIGHT wheel base: 88.58 in, 225 cm; tracks: 52.13 in, 132 cm front, 50.16 in, 127 cm rear; length: 167.32 in, 425 cm; width: 64.17 in, 163 cm; height: 50.79 in, 129 cm; ground clearance: 4.72 in, 12 cm; weight: 2,249 lb, 1,020 kg; turning circle: 34.4 ft, 10.5 m; fuel tank: 10.1 imp gal, 12.1 US gal, 46 l.

BODY convertible; 2 doors; 2+2 seats, separate front seats, reclining backrests; headrests; heated rear window.

PRACTICAL INSTRUCTIONS fuel: 98-100 oct petrol; oil: engine 10.4 imp pt, 12.5 US pt, 5.9 l, SAE 20W-50, change every 6,200 miles, 10,000 km - gearbox 3.2 imp pt, 3.8 US pt, 1.8 l, SAE 90 EP, change every 11,200 miles, 18,000 km - final drive 2.5 imp pt, 3 US pt, 1.4 l, SAE 90 EP, change every 11,200 miles, 18,000 km; greasing: every 18,600 miles, 30,000 km, 1 point; spark plug: Lodge 2 HL; tappet clearances: inlet 0.017-0.018 in, 0.42-0.45 mm, exhaust 0.019-0.020 in, 0.47-0.50 mm; valve timing: 40°34' 64°34' 63°54' 27°54; tyre pressure: front 24 psi, 1.7 atm, rear 26 psi, 1.8 atm.

OPTIONALS hardtop; light alloy wheels; metallic spray.

Spider 2.0

See Spider 1.6, except for:

PRICE IN USA: $ 16,000*
PRICE EX WORKS: 15,325,000 liras

ENGINE 119.7 cu in, 1,962 cc (3.31 x 3.48 in, 84 x 88.5 mm); max power (DIN): 128 hp (94 kW) at 5,400 rpm; max torque (DIN): 131 lb ft, 18.1 kg m (178 Nm) at 4,000 rpm; max engine rpm: 5,600; 65.2 hp/l (47.9 kW/l); 2 Solex C 40 DDH5 or Dell'Orto DHLA 40 horizontal twin barrel carburettors.

TRANSMISSION final drive: limited slip; axle ratio: 4.300; tyres: 185/70 HR x 14.

PERFORMANCE max speeds: (I) 27 mph, 43 km/h; (II) 44 mph, 71 km/h; (III) 65 mph, 105 km/h; (IV) 88 mph, 141 km/h; (V) over 118 mph, 190 km/h; power-weight ratio: 17.9 lb/hp (24.4 lb/kW), 8.1 kg/hp (11.1 kg/kW); acceleration: standing ¼ mile 16.8 sec; speed in top at 1,000 rpm: 20.9 mph, 33.6 km/h; consumption: 25.7 m/imp gal, 21.4 m/US gal, 11 l x 100 km at 75 mph, 120 km/h.

DIMENSIONS AND WEIGHT weight: 2,293 lb, 1,040 kg.

VARIATIONS

(for USA only)
ENGINE max power (SAE net) 115 hp (85 kW) at 5,500 rpm, max torque (SAE net) 119 lb ft, 16.5 kg m (162 Nm) at 2,750 rpm, 58.6 hp/l (43.3 kW/l), Bosch L-Jetronic injection.

Alfa 6 2.0

PRICE IN GB: £ 12,500*
PRICE EX WORKS: 20,890,000 liras

ENGINE front, 4 stroke; 6 cylinders, Vee-slanted at 60°; 121.9 cu in, 1,997 cc (3.15 x 2.61 in, 80 x 66.2 mm); compression ratio: 9:1; max power (DIN): 135 hp (99 kW) at 5,600 rpm; max torque (DIN): 131 lb ft, 18.1 kg m (178 Nm) at 4,500 rpm; max engine rpm: 5,600; 67.6 hp/l (49.6 kW/l); light alloy block and head, wet liners, hemispherical combustion chambers; 4 crankshaft bearings; valves: overhead, Vee-slanted at 46°45', thimble tappets, push-rods and rockers; camshafts: 2, 1 per bank, overhead, cogged belt; lubrication: gear pump, full flow filter, 11.4 imp pt, 13.7 US pt, 6.5 l; 6 Dell'Orto FRPA 40 downdraught single barrel carburettors with thermostatic filter; fuel feed: electric pump; liquid-cooled, 21.1 imp pt, 25.4 US pt, 12 l, electric thermostatic fan.

TRANSMISSION driving wheels: rear; clutch: single dry plate (diaphragm), hydraulically controlled; gearbox: mechanical; gears: 5, fully synchronized; ratios: I 3.420, II 1.940, III 1.390, IV 1, V 0.790, rev 3.670; lever: central; final drive: hypoid bevel, limited slip (25%); axle ratio: 4.545; width of rims: 6"; tyres: 195/70 HR x 14 tubeless.

PERFORMANCE max speeds: (I) 28 mph, 45 km/h; (II) 49 mph, 79 km/h; (III) 68 mph, 110 km/h; (IV) 95 mph, 153 km/h; (V) over 112 mph, 180 km/h; power-weight ratio: 24 lb/hp (32.7 lb/kW), 10.9 kg/hp (14.8 kg/kW); carrying capacity: 937 lb, 425 kg; speed in top at 1,000 rpm: 19.9 mph, 32 km/h; consumption: 24.6 m/imp gal, 20.5 m/US gal, 11.5 l x 100 km at 75 mph, 120 km/h.

CHASSIS integral; front suspension: independent, wishbones (upper trailing links), torsion bars, anti-roll bar, telescopic dampers; rear: de Dion axle, oblique trailing arms, transverse Watt linkage, coil springs, anti-roll bar, telescopic dampers.

STEERING rack-and-pinion, adjustable height of steering wheel, servo; turns lock to lock: 3.70.

BRAKES disc (diameter 10.47 in, 26.6 cm front, 10.24 in, 26 cm rear), front internal radial fins, dual circuit, rear compensator, servo; swept area: front 222.8 sq in, 1,437 sq cm, rear 180.2 sq in, 1,162 sq cm, total 403 sq in, 2,599 sq cm.

ELECTRICAL EQUIPMENT 12 V; 77 Ah battery; 770 W alternator; Marelli or Bosch contactless transistorized ignition; 4 iodine headlamps; speed limiter at 6,100 rpm.

DIMENSIONS AND WEIGHT wheel base: 102.36 in, 260 cm; tracks: 55.43 in, 141 cm front, 53.74 in, 136 cm rear; length: 184.21 in, 468 cm; width: 66.30 in, 168 cm; height: 54.88 in, 139 cm; ground clearance: 5.51 in, 14 cm; weight: 3,241 lb, 1,470 kg; turning circle: 36.7 ft, 11.2 m; fuel tank: 16.9 imp gal, 20.3 US gal, 77 l.

BODY saloon/sedan; 4 doors; 5 seats, separate front seats, reclining backrests, built-in headrests; electric windows; heated rear window; tinted glass.

PRACTICAL INSTRUCTIONS fuel: 98 oct petrol; oil: engine 10.6 imp pt, 12.7 US pt, 6 l, SAE 10W-50, change every 6,200 miles, 10,000 km - gearbox 2.8 imp pt, 3.4 US pt, 1.6 l, SAE 30W, change every 24,800 miles, 40,000 km - final drive 2.1 imp pt, 2.5 US pt, 1.2 l, SAE 80W-90, change every 24,800 miles, 40,000 km; greasing: none; spark plug: Lodge 2 HL; tappet clearances: inlet 0.018 in, 0.47 mm, exhaust 0.009 in, 0.25 mm (adjustable); valve timing: 36°50' 60°50' 59°55' 23°55'; tyre pressure: front 27 psi, 1.9 atm, rear 28 psi, 2 atm.

OPTIONALS light alloy wheels; metallic spray; air-conditioning.

ALFA ROMEO GTV 6 2.5

Alfa 6 2.5 Quadrifoglio Oro

See Alfa 6 2.0, except for:

PRICE EX WORKS: 22,500,000 liras

ENGINE 152.1 cu in, 2,492 cc (3.46 x 2.69 in, 88 x 68.3 mm); max power (DIN): 158 hp (116 kW) at 5,600 rpm; max torque (DIN): 156 lb ft, 21.5 kg m (211 Nm) at 4,000 rpm; 63.4 hp/l (46.5 kW/l); Bosch L-Jetronic injection.

TRANSMISSION axle ratio: 4.272.

PERFORMANCE max speeds: (I) 27 mph, 44 km/h; (II) 48 mph, 78 km/h; (III) 68 mph, 109 km/h; (IV) 94 mph, 152 km/h; (V) over 121 mph, 195 km/h; power-weight ratio: 20.5 lb/hp (27.9 lb/kW), 9.3 kg/hp (12.7 kg/kW); speed in top at 1,000 rpm: 21.2 mph, 34.1 km/h; consumption: 26.4 m/imp gal, 22 m/US gal, 10.7 l x 100 km at 75 mph, 120 km/h.

OPTIONALS ZF automatic transmission with 3 ratios (I 2.480, II 1.480, III 1, rev 2.090), 3.610 axle ratio, max speed 108 mph, 174 km/h, consumption 24.4 m/imp gal, 20.3 m/US gal, 11.6 l x 100 km at 75 mph, 120 km/h; leather upholstery.

Alfa 6 2.5 TD

See Alfa 6 2.0, except for:

PRICE EX WORKS: 20,500,000 liras

ENGINE VM diesel, turbocharged; 5 cylinedrs, in line; 152.2 cu in, 2,494 cc (3.46 x 3.23 in, 88 x 82 mm); compression ratio: 22:1; max power (DIN): 105 hp (77 kW) at 4,300 rpm; max torque (DIN): 152 lb ft, 21 kg m (206 Nm) at 2,400 rpm; max engine rpm: 4,300; 42.1 hp/l (30.9 kW/l); cast iron block, 5 separate light alloy heads; 6 crankshaft bearings; valves: overhead, in line, push-rods and rockers; camshafts: 1, side; lubrication: oil cooler; Bosch or Spica injection pump with KKK exhaust turbocharger; water-cooled, 18.5 imp pt, 22.2 US pt, 10.5 l, 2 electric thermostatic fans.

TRANSMISSION axle ratio: 4.830.

PERFORMANCE max speeds: (I) 24 mph, 38 km/h; (II) 42 mph, 67 km/h; (III) 58 mph, 94 km/h; (IV) 81 mph, 130 km/h; (V) over 106 mph, 170 km/h; power-weight ratio: 33.2 lb/hp (45.2 lb/kW), 15 kg/hp (20.5 kg/kW); speed in top at 1,000 rpm: 23.6 mph, 38 km/h; consumption: 30.1 m/imp gal, 25 m/US gal, 9.4 l x 100 km at 75 mph, 120 km/h.

DIMENSIONS AND WEIGHT weight: 3,484 lb, 1,580 kg.

PRACTICAL INSTRUCTIONS fuel: diesel; valve timing: 30° 62° 76° 32°.

ALFA ROMEO Alfa 6 2.5 Quadrifoglio Oro

AUTOBIANCHI ITALY

A 112 Junior

PRICE EX WORKS: 7,452,000 liras**

ENGINE front, transverse, 4 stroke; 4 cylinders, in line; 55.1 cu in, 903 cc (2.56 x 2.68 in, 65 x 68 mm); compression ratio: 9:1; max power (DIN): 42 hp (31 kW) at 5,500 rpm; max torque (DIN): 49 lb ft, 6.8 kg m (67 Nm) at 3,000 rpm; max engine rpm: 6,400; 46.5 hp/l (34.2 kW/l); cast iron block, light alloy head; 3 crankshaft bearings; valves: overhead, push-rods and rockers; camshafts: 1, side; lubrication: gear pump, cartridge filter, 6.2 imp pt, 7.4 US pt, 3.5 l; 1 Weber 30 IBA 28/250 downdraught single barrel carburettor; fuel feed: mechanical pump; water-cooled, 8.8 imp pt, 10.6 US pt, 5 l, electric thermostatic fan.

TRANSMISSION driving wheels: front; clutch: single dry plate; gearbox: mechanical; gears: 4, fully synchronized; ratios: I 3.909, II 2.055, III 1.342, IV 0.963, rev 3.615; lever: central; final drive: cylindrical gears; axle ratio: 4.071; width of rims: 4"; tyres: 135 SR x 13.

PERFORMANCE max speeds: (I) 23 mph, 37 km/h; (II) 43 mph, 70 km/h; (III) 66 mph, 107 km/h; (IV) 81 mph, 130 km/h; power-weight ratio: 34.4 lb/hp (46.7 lb/kW), 15.6 kg/hp (21.2 kg/kW); carrying capacity: 882 lb, 400 kg; acceleration: standing ¼ mile 20.8 sec; speed in top at 1,000 rpm: 15.8 mph, 25.4 km/h; consumption: 50.4 m/imp gal, 42 m/US gal, 5.6 l x 100 km at 56 mph, 90 km/h.

CHASSIS integral; front suspension: independent, by McPherson, coil springs/telescopic damper struts, lower wishbones (trailing links), anti-roll bar; rear: independent, wishbones, transverse anti-roll leafspring, lower arms, telescopic dampers.

STEERING rack-and-pinion; turns lock to lock: 3.40.

BRAKES front disc, rear drum, dual circuit, rear compensator; lining area: front 19.2 sq in, 124 sq cm, rear 33.5 sq in, 216 sq cm, total 52.7 sq in, 340 sq cm.

ELECTRICAL EQUIPMENT 12 V; 34 Ah battery; 45 A alternator; Marelli distributor; 2 headlamps.

DIMENSIONS AND WEIGHT wheel base: 80.24 in, 204 cm; tracks: 49.21 in, 125 cm front, 48.19 in, 122 cm rear; length: 128.66 in, 327 cm; width: 58.27 in, 148 cm; height: 53.54 in, 136 cm; ground clearance: 5.59 in, 14.2 cm; weight: 1,444 lb, 655 kg; weight distribution: 62% front, 38% rear; turning circle: 29.2 ft, 8.9 m; fuel tank: 6.6 imp gal, 7.9 US gal, 30 l.

BODY saloon/sedan; 2+1 doors; 5 seats, separate front seats, reclining backrests; folding rear seat; special luxury interior; sunroof.

PRACTICAL INSTRUCTIONS fuel: 98 oct petrol; oil: engine 6.2 imp pt, 7.4 US pt, 3.5 l, SAE 10W-20 (winter) 30W-40 (summer), change every 6,200 miles, 10,000 km - gearbox and final drive 3.8 imp pt, 4.5 US pt, 2.1 l, ZC 90, change every 18,600 miles, 30,000 km; greasing: none; spark plug: Champion RN 7Y; tappet clearances: inlet 0.006 in, 0.15 mm, exhaust 0.006 in, 0.15 mm; valve timing: 7° 36° 38° 5°; tyre pressure: front 24 psi, 1.7 atm, rear 27 psi, 1.9 atm.

OPTIONALS light alloy wheels with 4.5" wide rims; heated rear window; headrests; iodine headlamps; rear window wiper-washer; rev counter; metallic spray.

A 112 Elite

See A 112 Junior, except for:

PRICE EX WORKS: 8,298,000 liras**

ENGINE 58.9 cu in, 965 cc (2.65 x 2.68 in, 67.2 x 68 mm); compression ratio: 9.2:1; max power (DIN): 48 hp (35 kW) at 5,600 rpm; max torque (DIN): 53 lb ft, 7.3 kg m (72 Nm) at 3,300 rpm; 49.7 hp/l (36.5 kW/l); 1 Weber 30 IBA 27/350 or Solex C30 DI 41 downdraught single barrel carburettor.

TRANSMISSION gears: 5, fully synchronized; ratios: I 3.909, II 2.055, III 1.342, IV 0.963, V 0.828, rev 3.615; axle ratio: 4.461.

PERFORMANCE max speed: 85 mph, 137 km/h; power-weight ratio: 31 lb/hp (42.2 lb/kW), 14 kg/hp (19.1 kg/kW); acceleration: standing ¼ mile 20.3 sec; speed in top at 1,000 rpm: 16.8 mph, 27 km/h; consumption: 37.2 m/imp gal, 30.9 m/US gal, 7.6 l x 100 km at 75 mph, 120 km/h.

ELECTRICAL EQUIPMENT transistorized ignition with impulser unit.

DIMENSIONS AND WEIGHT weight: 1,488 lb, 675 kg.

BODY luxury interior; heated rear window, rear window wiper-washer, reclining backrests, headrests, tinted glass, iodine headlamps and rev counter (standard).

PRACTICAL INSTRUCTIONS tappet clearances: inlet 0.006 in, 0.15 mm, exhaust 0.008 in, 0.20 mm; valve timing: 17° 43° 57° 3°.

A 112 LX

See A 112 Junior, except for:

PRICE EX WORKS: 9,114,000 liras**

ENGINE 58.9 cu in, 965 cc (2.65 x 2.68 in, 67.2 x 68 mm); compression ratio: 9.2:1; max power (DIN): 48 hp (35 kW) at 5,600 rpm; max torque (DIN): 53 lb ft, 7.3 kg m (72 Nm) at 3,300 rpm; 49.7 hp/l (36.5 kW/l); 1 Weber 30 IBA 27/350 or Solex C30 DI 41 downdraught single barrel carburettor.

TRANSMISSION gears: 5, fully synchronized; ratios: I 3.909, II 2.055, III 1.342, IV 0.963, V 0.828, rev 3.615; axle ratio: 4.461.

PERFORMANCE max speed: 85 mph, 137 km/h; power-weight ratio: 31 lb/hp (42.2 lb/kW), 14 kg/hp (19.1 kg/kW); acceleration: standing ¼ mile 20.3 sec; consumption: 37.2 m/imp gal, 30.9 m/US gal, 7.6 l x 100 km at 75 mph, 120 km/h.

ELECTRICAL EQUIPMENT transistorized ignition with impulser unit.

DIMENSIONS AND WEIGHT weight: 1,488 lb, 675 kg.

BODY special luxury interior; heated rear window, rear window wiper-washer, reclining backrests, headrests, tinted glass, iodine headlamps and rev counter (standard); electric windows.

PRACTICAL INSTRUCTIONS tappet clearances: inlet 0.006 in, 0.15 mm, exhaust 0.008 in, 0.20 mm; valve timing: 17° 43° 57° 3°.

A 112 Abarth

See A 112 Junior, except for:

PRICE EX WORKS: 9,270,000 liras**

ENGINE 64.1 cu in, 1,050 cc (2.65 x 2.91 in, 67.2 x 74 mm); compression ratio: 10.4:1; max power (DIN): 70 hp (51 kW) at 6,600 rpm; max torque (DIN): 64 lb ft, 8.8 kg m (87 Nm) at 4,200 rpm; max engine rpm: 7,000; 66.7 hp/l (49.1 kW/l); lubrication: 6.6 imp pt, 7.9 US pt, 3.7 l; 1 Weber 32 DMTR 38/250 vertical twin barrel carburettor.

TRANSMISSION gears: 5, fully synchronized; ratios: I 3.909, II 2.055, III 1.342, IV 0.963, V 0.828, rev 3.615; axle ratio: 4.461.

PERFORMANCE max speed: over 96 mph, 155 km/h; power-weight ratio: 22.1 lb/hp (30 lb/kW), 10 kg/hp (13.6 kg/kW); acceleration: standing ¼ mile 18.6 sec; speed in top at 1,000 rpm: 16.8 mph, 27 km/h; consumption: 36.7 m/imp gal, 30.5 m/US gal, 7.7 l x 100 km at 75 mph, 120 km/h.

BRAKES servo.

ELECTRICAL EQUIPMENT transistorized ignition with impulser unit; 2 iodine headlamps (standard).

DIMENSIONS AND WEIGHT weight: 1,544 lb, 700 kg; weight distribution: 61.4% front, 38.6% rear.

BODY heated rear window, rear window wiper-washer, reclining backrests, headrests, tinted glass, iodine headlamps and rev counter (standard).

PRACTICAL INSTRUCTIONS oil: engine 6.6 imp pt, 7.9 US pt, 3.7 l - gearbox and final drive 3.9 imp pt, 4.7 US pt, 2.2 l; tappet clearances: inlet 0.010 in, 0.25 mm, exhaust 0.012 in, 0.30 mm; valve timing: 16° 56° 56° 16°.

AUTOBIANCHI A 112 Elite

BERTONE Palinuro

BERTONE Cabrio

BERTONE ITALY

Cabrio / Palinuro

PRICES IN GB AND EX WORKS:	£	liras
2-dr Cabrio	7,198*	15,600,000**
2-dr Palinuro	—	16,200,000**

ENGINE Fiat, front, transverse, 4 stroke; 4 cylinders, in line; 91.4 cu in, 1,498 cc (3.40 x 2.52 in, 86.4 x 63.9 mm); compression ratio: 9.2:1; max power (DIN): 82 hp (60 kW) at 5,800 rpm; max torque (DIN): 88 lb ft, 12.2 kg m (120 Nm) at 3,000 rpm; max engine rpm: 6,300; 54.7 hp/l (40.1 kW/l); cast iron block, light alloy head; 5 crankshaft bearings; valves: overhead, thimble tappets; camshafts: 1, overhead, cogged belt; lubrication: gear pump, full flow filter (cartridge), 7.2 imp pt, 8.7 US pt, 4.1 l; 1 Weber 32/34 DMTR 81/250 or Solex 32/34 CIC-1 downdraught twin barrel carburettor; fuel feed: mechanical pump; water-cooled, expansion tank, 12.3 imp pt, 14.8 US pt, 7 l, electric thermostatic fan.

TRANSMISSION driving wheels: front; clutch: single dry plate; gearbox: mechanical; gears: 5, fully synchronized; ratios: I 4.090, II 2.235, III 1.461, IV 1.034, V 0.827, rev 3.714; lever: central; final drive: helical cylindrical; axle ratio: 3.588; width of rims: 5.5"; tyres: 165/65 SR x 14.

PERFORMANCE max speed: 99 mph, 160 km/h; power-weight ratio: 23.4 lb/hp (32 lb/kW), 10.6 kg/hp (14.5 kg/kW); carrying capacity: 838 lb, 380 kg; speed in top at 1,000 rpm: 21.6 mph, 34.7 km/h; consumption: 38.2 m/imp gal, 31.8 m/US gal, 7.4 l x 100 km at 75 mph, 120 km/h.

CHASSIS integral; front suspension: independent, by McPherson, lower wishbones, trailing links, coil springs/telescopic damper struts; rear: independent, lower wishbones, transverse anti-roll leafspring, telescopic dampers.

STEERING rack-and-pinion, adjustable height of steering wheel; turns lock to lock: 3.50.

BRAKES front disc (diameter 8.94 in, 22.7 cm), rear drum, dual circuit, rear compensator, servo; lining area: front 21.7 sq in, 140 sq cm, rear 33.3 sq in, 215 sq cm, total 55 sq in, 355 sq cm.

ELECTRICAL EQUIPMENT 12 V; 40 Ah battery; 55 A alternator; Marelli distributor; 4 headlamps.

DIMENSIONS AND WEIGHT wheel base: 96.38 in, 245 cm; tracks: 55.83 in, 142 cm front, 55.67 in, 141 cm rear; length: 158.03 in, 401 cm; width: 64.96 in, 165 cm; height: 55.67 in, 141 cm; weight: 1,918 lb, 870 kg; weight distribution: 50% front, 50% rear; turning circle: 33.8 ft, 10.3 m; fuel tank: 12.1 imp gal, 14.5 US gal, 55 l.

BODY convertible; 2 doors; 5 seats, separate front seats; electric windows; central door locking; (for Palinuro only) two-tone metallic spray and headlamps with wiper-washers.

PRACTICAL INSTRUCTIONS fuel: 98 oct petrol; oil: engine 7.2 imp pt, 8.7 US pt, 4.1 l, SAE 10W-40, change every 6,200 miles, 10,000 km - gearbox and final drive 5.7 imp pt, 6.9 US pt, 3.3 l, SAE 80W-90, change every 18,600 miles, 30,000 km; greasing: none; spark plug: Magneti Marelli CW 7 LPR or CW 78 LPR; valve timing: 6° 46° 47° 7°; tyre pressure: front 27 psi, 1.9 atm, rear 31 psi, 2.2 atm.

OPTIONALS light alloy wheels; metallic spray.

X1/9

PRICE IN GB: £ 6,590*
PRICE IN USA: $ 12,990*

ENGINE Fiat, centre-rear, transverse, 4 stroke; 4 cylinders, vertical, in line; 91.4 cu in, 1,498 cc (3.40 x 2.52 in, 86.4 x 63.9 mm); compression ratio: 9.2:1; max power (DIN): 85 hp (62 kW) at 6,000 rpm; max torque (DIN): 87 lb ft, 12 kg m (118 Nm) at 3,200 rpm; max engine rpm: 6,500; 56.7 hp/l (41.7 kW/l); cast iron block, light alloy head; 5 crankshaft bearings; valves: overhead, in line, thimble tappets; camshafts: 1, overhead, cogged belt; lubrication: 7.9 imp pt, 9.5 US pt, 4.5 l; 1 Weber 34 DATR 7/250 downdraught twin barrel carburettor; fuel feed: mechanical pump; water-cooled, 20.4 imp pt, 24.5 US pt, 11.6 l, electric thermostatic fan.

TRANSMISSION driving wheels: rear; clutch: single dry plate (diaphragm), hydraulically controlled; gearbox: mechanical; gears: 5, fully synchronized; ratios: I 3.583, II 2.235, III 1.454, IV 1.042, V 0.863, rev 3.714; lever: central; final drive: helical cylindrical; axle ratio: 4.076; width of rims: 5"; tyres: 165/70 SR x 13.

PERFORMANCE max speeds: (I) 47 mph, 80 km/h; (II) 47 mph, 80 km/h; (III) 77 mph, 124 km/h; (IV) 102 mph, 165 km/h; (V) 112 mph, 180 km/h; power-weight ratio: 23.9 lb/hp (32.5 lb/kW), 10.8 kg/hp (14.7 kg/kW); carrying capacity: 441 lb, 200 kg; acceleration: standing ¼ mile 17.8 sec; speed in top at 1,000 rpm: 17.2 mph, 27.7 km/h; consumption: 36.7 m/imp gal, 30.5 m/US gal, 7.7 l x 100 km at 75 mph, 120 km/h.

CHASSIS integral; front suspension: independent, by McPherson (lower trailing links), coil springs/telescopic damper struts, lower wishbones; rear: independent, lower wishbones, each with articulated transverse control bar, coil springs/telescopic damper struts.

STEERING rack-and-pinion; turns lock to lock: 3.05.

BRAKES disc (diameter 8.94 in, 22.7 cm), dual circuit, servo; lining area: front 19.2 sq in, 124 sq cm, rear 19.2 sq in, 124 sq cm, total 38.4 sq in, 248 sq cm.

ELECTRICAL EQUIPMENT 12 V; 45 Ah battery; 45 A alternator; 2 retractable headlamps.

DIMENSIONS AND WEIGHT wheel base: 86.69 in, 220 cm; front and rear track: 53.35 in, 133 cm; length: 156.26 in, 397 cm; width: 61.81 in, 157 cm; height: 46.46 in, 118 cm; ground clearance: 4.92 in, 12.5 cm; weight: 2,029 lb, 920 kg; weight distribution: 40.2% front, 59.8% rear; turning circle: 32.8 ft, 10 m; fuel tank: 10.8 imp gal, 12.9 US gal, 49 l.

BODY sports; 2 doors; 2 seats, built-in headrests; roll bar; detachable roof; heated rear window; light alloy wheels; tinted glass.

PRACTICAL INSTRUCTIONS fuel: 98-100 oct petrol; oil: engine 7.9 imp pt, 9.5 US pt, 4.5 l, SAE 10W-50, change every 6,200 miles, 10,000 km - gearbox and final drive 4.9 imp pt, 5.9 US pt, 2.8 l, change every 18,600 miles, 30,000 km; greasing: none; valve timing: 24° 68° 64° 28°; tyre pressure: front 26 psi, 1.8 atm, rear 28 psi, 2 atm.

BERTONE X1/9

DE TOMASO ITALY

Pantera L

PRICE EX WORKS: 49,800,000 liras**

ENGINE Ford, centre-rear, 4 stroke; 8 cylinders, in Vee; 351.7 cu in, 5,763 cc (4 x 3.50 in, 101.6 x 89 mm); compression ratio: 8.5:1; max power (SAE): 330 hp (243 kW) at 5,400 rpm; max torque (SAE): 326 lb ft, 45 kg m (441 Nm) at 3,400 rpm; max engine rpm: 6,000; 53.8 hp/l (42.2 kW/l); cast iron block and head; 5 crankshaft bearings; valves: overhead, slanted, push-rods and rockers, hydraulic tappets; camshafts: 1, at centre of Vee; lubrication: rotary pump, full flow filter, 9.7 imp pt, 11.6 US pt, 5.5 l; 1 Motorcraft downdraught 4-barrel carburettor; fuel feed: mechanical pump; water-cooled, 42.2 imp pt, 50.7 US pt, 24 l, electric fan.

TRANSMISSION driving wheels: rear; clutch: single dry plate, hydraulically controlled; gearbox: ZF mechanical; gears: 5, fully synchronized; ratios: I 2.230, II 1.475, III 1.040, IV 0.846, V 0.705, rev 2.865; lever: central; final drive: spiral bevel, limited slip; axle ratio: 4.220; width of rims: 7" front, 8" rear; tyres: 185/70 VR x 15 front, 215/70 VR x 15 rear.

PERFORMANCE max speed: 158 mph, 254 km/h; power-weight ratio: 9.5 lb/hp (12.9 lb/kW), 4.3 kg/hp (5.8 kg/kW); speed in top at 1,000 rpm: 27 mph, 43.5 km/h; consumption: 14.1 m/imp gal, 11.8 m/US gal, 20 l x 100 km.

CHASSIS integral; front and rear suspension: independent, wishbones, coil springs, anti-roll bar, telescopic dampers.

DE TOMASO Pantera GTS

PANTERA L

STEERING rack-and-pinion; turns lock to lock: 3.40.

BRAKES disc (front diameter 11.18 in, 28.4 cm, rear 11.10 in, 28.2 cm), dual circuit, internal radial fins, servo.

ELECTRICAL EQUIPMENT 12 V; 72 Ah battery; 60 A alternator; 4 retractable headlamps.

DIMENSIONS AND WEIGHT wheel base: 98.82 in, 251 cm; tracks: 57.09 in, 145 cm front, 57.48 in, 146 cm rear; length: 168.11 in, 427 cm; width: 72.05 in, 183 cm; height: 43.31 in, 110 cm; ground clearance: 4.72 in, 12 cm; weight: 3,131 lb, 1,420 kg; turning circle: 39.4 ft, 12 m; fuel tank: 17.6 imp gal, 21.1 US gal, 80 l.

BODY coupé; 2 doors; 2 seats, built-in headrests; electric windows; tinted glass; heated rear window; air-conditioning; light alloy wheels.

PRACTICAL INSTRUCTIONS fuel: 98-100 oct petrol; oil: engine 9.2 imp pt, 11 US pt, 5.2 l, SAE 10W-40 (winter) 20W-50 (summer), change every 3,100 miles, 5,000 km - gearbox and final drive 6 imp pt, 7.2 US pt, 3.4 l, SAE 90, change every 3,700 miles, 6,000 km; valve timing: 14° 72° 70° 20°.

OPTIONALS 225/50 VR x 15 P7 front and 285/50 VR x 15 P7 rear tyres with 10" wide rims; right hand drive; metallic spray; leather interior.

Pantera GTS

See Pantera L, except for:

PRICE IN GB: £ 22,730*
PRICE EX WORKS: 55,500,000 liras**

ENGINE max power (SAE): 350 hp (258 kW) at 6,000 rpm; max torque (SAE): 333 lb ft, 46 kg m (451 Nm) at 3,800 rpm; 60.7 hp/l (44.7 kW/l).

PERFORMANCE max speed: about 174 mph, 280 km/h; power-weight ratio: 9 lb/hp (12.2 lb/kW), 4.1 kg/hp (5.5 kg/kW).

BODY front and rear spoiler.

Pantera GT5

See Pantera L, except for:

PRICE IN GB: £ 28,528*
PRICE EX WORKS: 62,900,000 liras**

ENGINE max power (SAE): 350 hp (258 kW) at 6,000 rpm; max torque (SAE): 333 lb ft, 45.9 kg m (450 Nm) at 3,800 rpm; 60.7 hp/l (44.7 kW/l).

TRANSMISSION width of rims: 10" front, 13" rear; tyres: 285/40 VR x 15 front, 345/35 VR x 15 rear.

PERFORMANCE max speed: 162 mph, 260 km/h; power-weight ratio: 9 lb/hp (12.1 lb/kW), 4.1 kg/hp (5.5 kg/kW).

DIMENSIONS AND WEIGHT tracks: 59.45 in, 151 cm front, 62.20 in, 158 cm rear; width: 77.56 in, 197 cm.

BODY front and rear spoiler.

Deauville

See Pantera L, except for:

PRICE IN GB: £ 31,800*
PRICE EX WORKS: 64,000,000 liras**

ENGINE Ford, front, 4 stroke; cooling: 31.7 imp pt, 38.1 US pt, 18 l.

TRANSMISSION gearbox: Select-Shift Cruise-o-Matic automatic transmission, hydraulic torque converter and planetary gears with 3 ratios, max ratio of converter at stall 2.05, possible manual selection; ratios: I 2.460, II 1.460, III 1, rev 2.100; axle ratio: 3.070; width of rims: 7"; tyres: 215/70 VR x 15.

PERFORMANCE max speed: over 143 mph, 230 km/h; power-weight ratio: 13 lb/hp (17.6 lb/kW), 5.9 kg/hp (8 kg/kW); carrying capacity: 1,169 lb, 530 kg; acceleration: standing ¼ mile 16 sec; speed in direct drive at 1,000 rpm: 23.9 mph, 38.4 km/h; consumption: 16 m/imp gal, 13.4 m/US gal, 17.6 l x 100 km.

CHASSIS rear suspension: trailing radius arms, 4 coil springs, 4 telescopic dampers.

STEERING servo.

ELECTRICAL EQUIPMENT 4 headlamps.

DIMENSIONS AND WEIGHT wheel base: 109.05 in, 277 cm; front and rear track: 59.84 in, 152 cm; length: 195.52 in, 489 cm; width: 73.94 in, 188 cm; height: 53.86 in, 137 cm; ground clearance: 5.12 in, 13 cm; weight: 4,278 lb, 1,940 kg; turning circle: 42.6 ft, 13 m; fuel tank: 26.4 imp gal, 31.7 US gal, 120 l.

BODY saloon/sedan; 4 doors; 5 seats, separate front seats, reclining backrests; air-conditioning; electric windows; tinted glass; electric rear view mirror; roll safety belts; adjustable steering wheel; halogen headlamps; light alloy wheels; headrests; leather upholstery; heated rear window; front spoiler.

PRACTICAL INSTRUCTIONS oil: engine 7 imp pt, 8.5 US pt, 4 l - automatic transmission 17.6 imp pt, 21.1 US pt, 10 l - final drive 3.2 imp pt, 3.8 US pt, 1.8 l.

OPTIONALS oil cooler; right hand drive; metallic spray.

Longchamp 2+2

See Pantera L, except for:

PRICES IN GB AND EX WORKS:	**£**	**liras**
2-dr Coupé	29,058*	60,850,000**
2-dr Spyder	—	89,600,000**

ENGINE Ford, front, 4 stroke; cooling: 31.7 imp pt, 38.1 US pt, 18 l.

TRANSMISSION gearbox: Select-Shift Cruise-o-Matic automatic transmission, hydraulic torque converter and planetary gears with 3 ratios, max ratio of converter at stall 2.05, possible manual selection; ratios: I 2.460, II 1.460, III 1, rev 2.100; axle ratio: 3.070; width of rims: 7"; tyres: 215/70 VR x 15.

PERFORMANCE max speed: 149 mph, 240 km/h; power-weight ratio: 11.6 lb/hp (16.3 lb/kW), 5.3 kg/hp (7.2 kg/kW); speed in direct drive at 1,000 rpm: 24.9 mph, 40 km/h; consumption: 16.6 m/imp gal, 13.8 m/US gal, 17 l x 100 km.

CHASSIS rear suspension: trailing radius arms, 4 coil springs, 4 telescopic dampers.

STEERING servo.

ELECTRICAL EQUIPMENT 61 A alternator; 2 headlamps.

DIMENSIONS AND WEIGHT wheel base: 102.36 in, 260 cm; front and rear track: 59.84 in, 152 cm; length: 177.95 in, 452 cm; width: 72.44 in, 184 cm; height: 50.79 in, 129 cm; ground clearance: 5.91 in, 15 cm; weight: 3,858 lb, 1,750 kg; turning circle: 37.7 ft, 11.5 m; fuel tank: 22 imp gal, 26.4 US gal, 100 l.

BODY coupé - convertible; 2 doors; 2 + 2 seats, separate front seats, reclining backrests; air-conditioning; electric windows; tinted glass; electric rear view mirror; roll safety belts; adjustable steering wheel; halogen headlamps; light alloy wheels; headrests; leather upholstery; heated rear window; front spoiler.

PRACTICAL INSTRUCTIONS oil: engine 7 imp pt, 8.5 US pt, 4 l - automatic transmission 17.6 imp pt, 21.1 US pt, 10 l - final drive 3.2 imp pt, 3.8 US pt, 1.8 l.

OPTIONALS oil cooler; right hand drive; metallic spray.

Longchamp GTS

See Pantera L, except for:

PRICE EX WORKS: 64,800,000 liras**

ENGINE Ford, front, 4 stroke; cooling: 31.7 imp pt, 38.1 US pt, 18 l.

DE TOMASO Deauville

DE TOMASO Longchamp 2+2 Spyder

FERRARI 208 Turbo GTB Coupé

TRANSMISSION gearbox: Select-Shift Cruise-o-Matic automatic transmission, hydraulic torque converter and planetary gears with 3 ratios, max ratio of converter at stall 2.05, possible manual selection; ratios: I 2.460, II 1.460, III 1, rev 2.100; axle ratio: 3.070; width of rims: 8" front, 10" rear; tyres: 225/50 VR x 15 front, 285/50 VR x 15 rear.

PERFORMANCE max speed: 149 mph, 240 km/h; power-weight ratio: 11.6 lb/hp (16.3 lb/kW), 5.3 kg/hp (7.2 kg/kW); speed in direct drive at 1,000 rpm: 24.9 mph, 40 km/h; consumption: 16.6 m/imp gal, 13.8 m/US gal, 17 l x 100 km.

CHASSIS rear suspension: trailing radius arms, 4 coil springs, 4 telescopic dampers.

STEERING servo.

ELECTRICAL EQUIPMENT 61 A alternator; 2 headlamps.

DIMENSIONS AND WEIGHT wheel base: 102.36 in, 260 cm; tracks: 61.81 in, 157 cm front, 63.78 in, 162 cm rear; length: 181.10 in, 460 cm; width: 76.77 in, 195 cm; height: 50.79 in, 129 cm; ground clearance: 5.91 in, 15 cm; weight: 3,858 lb, 1,750 kg; turning circle: 37.7 ft, 11.5 m; fuel tank: 22 imp gal, 26.4 US gal, 100 l.

BODY coupé; 2 doors; 2+2 seats, separate front seats, reclining backrests; headrests; air-conditioning; electric windows; tinted glass; electric rear view mirror; roll safety belts; adjustable upholstery; heated rear window; front spoiler.

PRACTICAL INSTRUCTIONS oil: engine 7 imp pt, 8.5 US pt, 4 l - automatic transmission 17.6 imp pt, 21.1 US pt, 10 l - final drive 3.2 imp pt, 3.8 US pt, 1.8 l.

OPTIONALS oil cooler; right hand drive; metallic spray.

FERRARI ITALY

208 Turbo

PRICES EX WORKS:	liras
GTB 2-dr Coupé	**57,600,000***
GTS 2-dr Spider	**59,160,000***

ENGINE turbocharged, centre, rear, transverse, 4 stroke; 8 cylinders in Vee; 121.5 cu in, 1,991 cc (2.63 x 2.79 in, 66.8 x 71 mm); compression ratio: 7:1; max power (DIN): 220 hp (162 kW) at 7,000 rpm; max torque (DIN): 177 lb ft, 24.5 kg m (240 Nm) at 4,800 rpm; max engine rpm: 7,800; 110.5 hp/l (81.3 kW/l); light alloy block and head, wet liners; 5 crankshaft bearings; valves: overhead, Vee-slanted, thimble tappets; camshafts: 4, 2 per bank, overhead, cogged belts; lubrication: gear pump, full flow filter, 15.8 imp pt, 19 US pt, 9 l, oil cooler, crankcase emission control system; Bosch K-Jetronic injection; 1 KKK turbocharger; fuel feed: electric pump; anti-freeze liquid-cooled, expansion tank, 31.7 imp pt, 38.1 US pt, 18 l, front radiator, 2 electric thermostatic fans.

TRANSMISSION driving wheels: rear; clutch: single dry plate (diaphragm); gearbox: mechanical; gears: 5, fully synchronized; ratios: I 3.590, II 2.353, III 1.693, IV 1.244, V 0.881, rev 3.248; lever: central; final drive: helical spur gear, limited slip; axle ratio: 4.312; width of rims: 6.5"; tyres: Michelin TRX 220/55 VR x 390.

PERFORMANCE max speed: 150 mph, 242 km/h; max speeds at 7,000 rpm: (I) 33 mph, 53 km/h; (II) 50 mph, 81 km/h; (III) 70 mph, 113 km/h; (IV) 95 mph, 153 km/h; (V) 134 mph, 216 km/h; power-weight ratio: GTB Coupé 12.3 lb/hp (16.8 lb/kW), 5.6 kg/hp (7.6 kg/kW); carrying capacity: 397 lb, 180 kg; acceleration: standing ¼ mile 15.2 sec; speed in top at 1,000 rpm: 19.2 mph, 30.9 km/h; consumption: 21.7 m/imp gal, 18.1 m/US gal, 13 l x 100 km at 87 mph, 140 km/h.

CHASSIS tubular; front suspension: independent, wishbones, anti-roll bar, coil springs, telescopic dampers; rear: independent, wishbones, anti-roll bar, coil springs, telescopic dampers.

STEERING rack-and-pinion; turns lock to lock: 3.28.

BRAKES disc, internal radial fins, dual circuit, servo; swept area: front 230.8 sq in, 1,489 sq cm, rear 192.5 sq in, 1,242 sq cm, total 423.3 sq in, 2,731 sq cm.

ELECTRICAL EQUIPMENT 12 V; 66 Ah battery; 65 A alternator; Marelli Digiplex electronic ignition; 2 retractable iodine headlamps.

DIMENSIONS AND WEIGHT wheel base: 92.13 in, 234 cm; front and rear track: 57.48 in, 146 cm; length: 166.54 in, 423 cm; width: 67.72 in, 172 cm; height: 44.09 in, 112 cm; ground clearance: 4.72 in, 12 cm; weight: GTB Coupé 2,717 lb, 1,232 kg - GTS Spider 2,741 lb, 1,243 kg; turning circle: 39.4 ft, 12 m; fuel tank: 16.3 imp gal, 19.5 US gal, 74 l.

BODY coupé; 2 doors; 2 seats, separate front seats, built-in headrests; leather upholstery; electric windows; heated rear window; tinted glass; light alloy wheels; check control; central door locking.

PRACTICAL INSTRUCTIONS fuel: 97 oct petrol; oil: engine 15.8 imp pt, 19 US pt, 9 l, SAE 10W-50, change every 6,200 miles, 10,000 km - gearbox and final drive 7 imp pt, 8.5 US pt, 4 l, SAE 80W-90, change every 12,400 miles, 20,000 km; greasing: none; spark plug: Champion N 2 G; valve timing: 20° 44° 54° 10°; tyre pressure: front 33 psi, 2.3 atm, rear 33 psi, 2.3 atm.

OPTIONALS Pirelli P7 205/55 VR x 16 front tyres with 7" wide rims and Pirelli P7 225/50 VR x 16 rear tyres with 8" wide rims; air-conditioning; front spoiler; metallic spray.

308 quattrovalvole

PRICES IN GB AND USA:	£	$
GTB 2-dr Coupé	**26,181***	**52,900***
GTS 2-dr Spider	**27,303***	**61,175***

ENGINE centre, rear, transverse, 4 stroke; 8 cylinders in Vee; 178.6 cu in, 2,927 cc (3.19 x 2.79 in, 81 x 71 mm); compression ratio: 9.2:1; max power (DIN): 240 hp (176 kW) at 7,000 rpm; max torque (DIN): 192 lb ft, 26.5 kg m (260 Nm) at 5,000 rpm; max engine rpm: 7,700; 82 hp/l (60.3 kW/l); light alloy block and head, wet liners; 5 crankshaft bearings; valves: 4 per cylinder, overhead, Vee-slanted, thimble tappets; camshafts: 4, 2 per bank, overhead, cogged belts; lubrication: gear pump, full flow filter, 17.6 imp pt, 21.1 US pt, 10 l, oil cooler, crankcase emission control system; Bosch K-Jetronic injection; fuel feed: electric pump; anti-freeze liquid-cooled, expansion tank, 31.7 imp pt, 38.1 US pt, 18 l, front radiator, 2 electric fans.

TRANSMISSION driving wheels: rear; clutch: single dry plate (diaphragm); gearbox: mechanical; gears: 5, fully synchronized; ratios: I 3.390, II 2.353, III 1.693, IV 1.244, V 0.919, rev 3.248; lever: central; final drive: helical spur gear, limited slip; axle ratio: 3.824; width of rims: 6.5"; tyres: Michelin TRX 240/55 VR x 415.

PERFORMANCE max speeds: (I) 43 mph, 70 km/h; (II) 62 mph, 100 km/h; (III) 87 mph, 139 km/h; (IV) 118 mph, 190 km/h; (V) 158 mph, 255 km/h; power-weight ratio: GTB Coupé 11.7 lb/hp (16 lb/kW), 5.3 kg/hp (7.2 kg/kW); carrying capacity: 297 lb, 180 kg; acceleration: standing ¼ mile 14.5 sec; speed in top at 1,000 rpm: 21 mph, 33.7 km/h; consumption: 26 m/imp gal, 21.6 m/US gal, 10.9 l x 100 km at 75 mph, 120 km/h.

CHASSIS tubular; front suspension: independent, wishbones, anti-roll bar, coil springs, telescopic dampers; rear: independent, wishbones, anti-roll bar, coil springs, telescopic dampers.

STEERING rack-and-pinion; turns lock to lock: 3.28.

BRAKES disc, internal radial fins, dual circuit, servo; swept area: front 230.8 sq in, 1.489 sq cm, rear 192.5 sq in, 1,242 sq cm, total 423.3 sq in, 2,731 sq cm.

ELECTRICAL EQUIPMENT 12 V; 66 Ah battery; 960 W alternator; Marelli Digiplex electronic ignition; 2 retractable iodine headlamps.

DIMENSIONS AND WEIGHT wheel base: 92.13 in, 234 cm; front and rear track: 57.48 in, 146 cm; length: 166.50 in, 423 cm; width: 67.72 in, 172 cm; height: 44.09 in, 112 cm; ground clearance: 4.72 in, 12 cm; weight: GTB Coupé 2,811 lb, 1,275 kg - GTS Spider 2,836 lb, 1,286 kg; weight distribution: 43.4% front, 56.6% rear; turning circle: 39.4 ft, 12 m; fuel tank: 16.3 imp gal, 19.5 US gal, 74 l.

BODY coupé - spider; 2 doors; 2 seats, separate front seats, built-in headrests; leather upholstery; electric windows; heated rear window; tinted glass; light alloy wheels; (for GTS Spider only) detachable roof; central door locking.

PRACTICAL INSTRUCTIONS fuel: 97 oct petrol; oil: engine 17.6 imp pt, 21.1 US pt, 10 l, SAE 10W-50, change every 6,200 miles, 10,000 km - gearbox and final drive 7 imp pt, 8.5 US pt, 4 l, SAE 80W-90, change every 12,400 miles, 20,000 km; greasing: none; spark plug: Champion N 6 GY; tappet clearances: inlet 0.008-0.010 in, 0.20-0.25 mm, exhaust 0.014-0.016 in, 0.35-0.40 mm; valve timing: 16° 48° 54° 10°; tyre pressure: front 33 psi, 2.3 atm, rear 33 psi, 2.3 atm.

VARIATIONS

(for USA only)
ENGINE 8.6:1 compression ratio, max power (SAE net) 230

FERRARI 308 quattrovalvole GTS Spider

308 QUATTROVALVOLE

hp (169 kW) at 6,800 rpm, max torque (SAE net) 188 lb ft, 26 kg m (255 Nm) at 5,500 rpm, 78.6 hp/l (57.7 kW/l).

OPTIONALS Pirelli P7 205/55 VR x 16 front tyres with 7" wide rims and Pirelli P7 225/50 VR x 16 rear tyres with 8" wide rims; air-conditioning; front spoiler; metallic spray.

Mondial quattrovalvole

PRICES IN GB AND USA:	£	$
2-dr Coupé	29,732*	59,500*
2-dr Cabriolet	—	66,675*

ENGINE centre, rear, transverse, 4 stroke; 8 cylinders in Vee; 178.6 cu in, 2,927 cc (3.19 x 2.79 in, 81 x 71 mm); compression ratio: 9.2:1; max power (DIN): 240 hp (176 kW) at 7,000 rpm; max torque (DIN): 192 lb ft, 26.5 kg m (260 Nm) at 5,000 rpm; max engine rpm: 7,700; 82 hp/l (60.3 kW/l); light alloy block and head, wet liners; 5 crankshaft bearings; valves: 4 per cylinder, overhead, Vee-slanted, thimble tappets; camshafts: 4, 2 per bank, overhead, cogged belts; lubrication: gear pump, full flow filter, 17.6 imp pt, 21.1 US pt, 10 l, oil cooler, crankcase emission control system; Bosch K-Jetronic injection; fuel feed: electric pump; anti-freeze liquid-cooled, expansion tank, 26.4 imp pt, 31.7 US pt, 15 l, front radiator, 2 electric thermostatic fans.

TRANSMISSION driving wheels: rear; clutch: single dry plate (diaphragm); gearbox: mechanical; gears: 5, fully synchronized; ratios: I 3.419, II 2.353, III 1.693, IV 1.244, V 0.919, rev 3.248; lever: central; final drive: helical spur gear, limited slip; axle ratio: 4.062; width of rims: 180 TR 390; tyres: Michelin TRX 240/55 VR x 390 tubeless.

PERFORMANCE max speed: 149 mph, 240 km/h; max speeds at 7,000 rpm: (I) 38 mph, 60 km/h; (II) 55 mph, 88 km/h; (III) 76 mph, 122 km/h; (IV) 103 mph, 166 km/h; (V) 139 mph, 224 km/h; power-weight ratio: Coupé 13.7 lb/hp (18.7 lb/kW), 6.2 kg/hp (8.5 kg/kW); carrying capacity: 706 lb, 320 kg; acceleration: standing ¼ mile 14.8 sec; speed in top at 1,000 rpm: 19.9 mph, 32 km/h; consumption: 25.3 m/imp gal, 21.2 m/US gal, 11.1 l x 100 km at 75 mph, 120 km/h.

CHASSIS tubular; front suspension: independent, wishbones, anti-roll bar, coil springs, telescopic dampers; rear: independent, wishbones, anti-roll bar, coil springs, telescopic dampers.

STEERING rack-and-pinion; turns lock to lock: 3.45.

BRAKES disc (diameter 11.10 in, 28.2 cm front, 11.69 in, 29.7 cm rear), internal radial fins, dual circuit, servo.

ELECTRICAL EQUIPMENT 12 V; 66 Ah battery; 85 A alternator; Marelli Digiplex electronic ignition; 4 retractable iodine headlamps.

DIMENSIONS AND WEIGHT wheel base: 104.33 in, 265 cm; tracks: 58.86 in, 149 cm front, 59.72 in, 152 cm rear; length: 180.31 in, 458 cm; width: 70.47 in, 179 cm; height: 49.61 in, 126 cm; ground clearance: 4.92 in, 12.5 cm; weight: Coupé 3,285 lb, 1,490 kg - Cabriolet 3,440 lb, 1,560 kg; turning circle: 41 ft, 12.5 m; fuel tank: 19.1 imp gal, 22.9 US gal, 87 l.

BODY coupé - cabriolet; 2 doors; 2+2 seats, separate front seats, reclining backrests, headrests; leather upholstery; electric windows; heated rear window; tinted glass; light alloy wheels; metallic spray; cheek control; central door locking; air-conditioning.

PRACTICAL INSTRUCTIONS fuel: 97 oct petrol; oil: engine 17.6 imp pt, 21.1 US pt, 10 l, SAE 10W-50, change every 6,200 miles, 10,000 km - gearbox and final drive 7 imp pt, 8.5 US pt, 4 l, SAE 80W-90, change every 12,400 miles, 20,000 km; greasing: none; spark plug: Champion N 6 GY; valve timing: 16° 48° 54° 10°; tyre pressure: front 33 psi, 2.3 atm, rear 35 psi, 2.4 atm.

OPTIONALS electric sunroof.

FERRARI Mondial quattrovalvole Cabriolet

VARIATIONS

(for USA only)
ENGINE 8.6:1 compression ratio, max power (SAE net) 230 hp (169 kW) at 6,800 rpm, max torque (SAE net) 188 lb ft, 26 kg m (255 Nm) at 5,500 rpm, 78.6 hp/l (57.7 kW/l).

400 Automatic i

PRICE IN GB: £ 43,561*
PRICE EX WORKS: 106,950,000* liras

ENGINE front, 4 stroke; 12 cylinders, Vee-slanted at 60°; 294.3 cu in, 4,823 cc (3.19 x 3.07 in, 81 x 78 mm); compression ratio: 8.8:1; max power (DIN): 315 hp (232 kW) at 6,400 rpm; max torque (DIN): 304 lb ft, 42 kg m (412 Nm) at 4,200 rpm; max engine rpm: 6,500; 65.3 hp/l (48.1 kW/l); light alloy block and head, wet liners; 7 crankshaft bearings; valves: overhead, Vee-slanted at 46°, thimble tappets; camshafts: 4, 2 per bank, overhead; lubrication: gear pump, 31.7 imp pt, 38.1 US pt, 18 l, oil cooler; Bosch K-Jetronic injection; fuel feed: 2 electric pumps; water-cooled, 22.9 imp pt, 27.5 US pt, 13 l, 3 electric thermostatic fans.

TRANSMISSION driving wheels: rear; gearbox: GM automatic transmission, hydraulic torque converter and planetary gears with 3 ratios, max ratio of converter at stall 2.20, possible manual selection; ratios: I 2.481, II 1.481, III 1, rev 2.077; lever: central; final drive: spiral bevel, limited slip; axle ratio: 3.417; width of rims: 180 TR 415; tyres: Michelin 240/55 VR x 415 TRX.

PERFORMANCE max speeds: (I) 60 mph, 97 km/h; (II) 99 mph, 159 km/h; (III) 146 mph, 235 km/h; power-weight ratio: 12.7 lb/hp (17.3 lb/kW), 5.8 kg/hp (7.8 kg/kW); acceleration: standing ¼ mile 15.6 sec; speed in direct drive at 1,000 rpm: 22.1 mph, 35.6 km/h; consumption: 15.7 m/imp gal, 13.1 m/US gal, 18 l x 100 km at 75 mph, 120 km/h.

CHASSIS tubular; front suspension: independent, wishbones, anti-roll bar, coil springs, telescopic dampers; rear: independent, wishbones, anti-roll bar, coil springs, telescopic dampers, automatic levelling control.

STEERING recirculating ball, ZF servo; turns lock to lock: 3.80.

BRAKES disc (front diameter 11.89 in, 30.2 cm, rear 11.69 in, 29.7 cm), internal radial fins, dual circuit, servo; lining area: front 28.8 sq in, 186 sq cm, rear 19.5 sq in, 126 sq cm, total 48.3 sq in, 312 sq cm.

ELECTRICAL EQUIPMENT 12 V; 84 Ah battery; 2 x 55 A alternators; Marelli electronic ignition; 4 retractable iodine headlamps.

DIMENSIONS AND WEIGHT wheel base: 106.30 in, 270 cm; tracks: 57.87 in, 147 cm front, 59.06 in, 150 cm rear; length: 189.37 in, 481 cm; width: 70.87 in, 180 cm; height: 51.57 in, 131 cm; ground clearance: 5.12 in, 13 cm; weight: 4,009 lb, 1,818 kg; turning circle: 40 ft, 12.2 m; fuel tank: 26.4 imp gal, 31.7 US gal, 120 l.

BODY coupé; 2 doors; 2+2 seats, separate front seats, reclining backrests, built-in headrests; folding rear seat; air-conditioning; electric windows; heated rear window.

PRACTICAL INSTRUCTIONS fuel: 97 oct petrol; oil: engine 31.7 imp pt, 38.1 US pt, 18 l, SAE 10W-50, change every 6,200 miles, 10,000 km - gearbox 7.9 imp pt, 9.5 US pt, 4.5 l, ATF Dexron, change every 12,400 miles, 20,000 km - final drive 4.4 imp pt, 5.3 US pt, 2.5 l, SAE 80W-90, change every 12,400 miles, 20,000 km; spark plug: Champion N 6 GY; tappet clearances: inlet 0.008-0.010 in, 0.20-0.25 mm, exhaust 0.012-0.044 in, 0.30-0.35 mm; valve timing: 20° 44° 54° 10°; tyre pressure: front 35 psi, 2.5 atm, rear 35 psi, 2.5 atm.

OPTIONALS 5-speed fully synchronized mechanical-gearbox (I 2.837, II 1.706, III 1.254, IV 1, V 0.795, rev 2.314), 4.300 axle ratio, max speed 152 mph, 245 km/h, acceleration standing ¼ mile 14.8 sec; 3.250 axle ratio; dual air-conditioning.

BB 512i

PRICE IN GB: £ 47,298*
PRICE EX WORKS: 116,610,000* liras

ENGINE centre, rear, 4 stroke; 12 cylinders, horizontally opposed; 301.6 cu in, 4,942 cc (3.23 x 3.07 in, 82 x 78 mm); compression ratio: 9.2:1; max power (DIN): 340 hp (250 kW) at

FERRARI 400 Automatic i

FERRARI 400 Automatic i

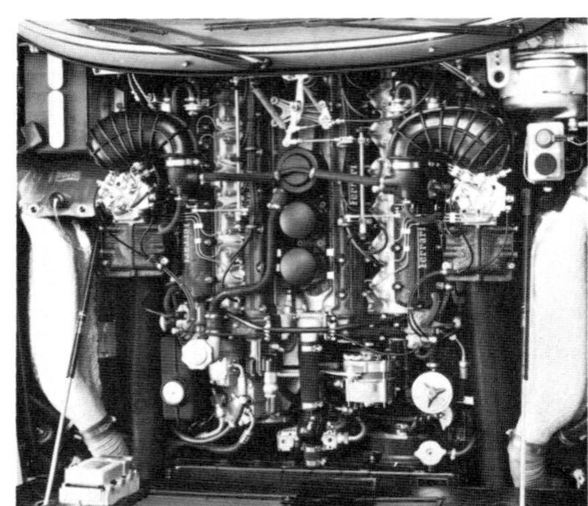

6,000 rpm; max torque (DIN): 333 lb ft, 46 kg m (451 Nm) at 4,200 rpm; max engine rpm: 6,600; 68.8 hp/l (50.6 kW/l); light alloy block and head, cast iron liners; 7 crankshaft bearings; valves: overhead, Vee-slanted, thimble tappets; camshafts: 4, 2 per bank, cogged belt; lubrication: gear pump, full flow filter, dry sump, oil tank, 22.9 imp pt, 27.5 US pt, 13 l; Bosch K-Jetronic injection; fuel feed: 2 electric pumps; water-cooled, 38.7 imp pt, 46.5 US pt, 22 l, 3 electric thermostatic fans.

TRANSMISSION driving wheels: rear; clutch: double dry plate, hydraulically controlled; gearbox: mechanical, in unit with differential; gears: 5, fully synchronized; ratios: I 2.937, II 2.099, III 1.587, IV 1.200, V 0.913, rev 2.620; lever: central; final drive: hypoid bevel, limited slip; axle ratio: 3.214; width of rims: 7.5" front, 9" rear; tyres: 180/TR x 415 front, 210 TR x 415 rear.

PERFORMANCE max speed: 176 mph, 283 km/h; max speeds at 6,200 rpm: (I) 53 mph, 85 km/h; (II) 73 mph, 118 km/h; (III) 97 mph, 156 km/h; (IV) 129 mph, 207 km/h; (V) 174 mph, 280 km/h; power-weight ratio: 9.7 lb/hp (13.2 lb/kW), 4.4 kg/hp (6 kg/kW); acceleration: standing ¼ mile 14.2 sec; speed in top at 1,000 rpm: 27.4 mph, 44 km/h; consumption: 19.5 m/imp gal, 16.2 m/US gal, 14.5 l x 100 km at 75 mph, 120 km/h.

CHASSIS tubular; front suspension: independent, wishbones, anti-roll bar, coil springs, telescopic dampers; rear: independent, wishbones, coil springs, anti-roll bar, 4 telescopic dampers.

STEERING rack-and-pinion; turns lock to lock: 3.50.

BRAKES disc, internal radial fins, dual circuit, servo.

ELECTRICAL EQUIPMENT 12 V; 77 Ah battery: 2 x 55 A alternators; Marelli electronic ignition; 2 retractable headlamps.

DIMENSIONS AND WEIGHT wheel base: 98.43 in, 250 cm; tracks: 59.06 in, 150 cm front, 61.89 in, 157 cm rear; length: 173.23 in, 440 cm; width: 72.05 in, 183 cm; height: 44.09 in, 112 cm; ground clearance: 4.92 in, 12.5 cm; weight: 3,305 lb, 1,499 kg; turning circle: 40 ft, 12.2 m; fuel tank: 26.4 imp gal, 31.7 US gal, 120 l (2 separate tanks).

BODY coupé; 2 doors; 2 seats; light alloy wheels; electric windows; central door locking; air-conditioning.

PRACTICAL INSTRUCTIONS fuel: 98-100 oct petrol; oil: engine 22.9 imp pt, 27.5 US pt, 13 l, SAE 10W-50, change every 6,200 miles, 10,000 km - gearbox and final drive 15.8 imp pt, 19 US pt, 9 l, SAE 80 or 90, change every 12,400 miles, 20,000 km; greasing: none; spark plug: Champion N 63 Y; valve timing: 12° 52° 54° 10°; tyre pressure: front 43 psi, 3 atm, rear 43 psi, 3 atm.

FERRARI BB 512i

FIAT — ITALY

126

PRICE IN GB: £ 2,098*
PRICE EX WORKS: 5,059,000 liras**

ENGINE rear, 4 stroke; 2 cylinders, vertical, in line; 39.8 cu in, 652 cc (3.03 x 2.76 in, 77 x 70 mm); compression ratio: 7.5:1; max power (DIN): 24 hp (18 kW) at 4,500 rpm; max torque (DIN): 30 lb ft, 4.2 kg m (41 Nm) at 3,000 rpm; max engine rpm: 5,200; 36.8 hp/l (27.1 kW/l); light alloy block and head; 2 crankshaft bearings; valves: overhead, in line, push-rods and rockers; camshafts: 1, side; lubrication: gear pump, centrifugal filter, 4.4 imp pt, 5.3 US pt, 2.5 l; 1 Weber 28 IMB downdraught carburettor; fuel feed: mechanical pump; air-cooled.

TRANSMISSION driving wheels: rear; clutch: single dry plate; gearbox: mechanical; gears: 4, II, III and IV silent claw coupling; ratios: I 3.250, II 2.067, III 1.300, IV 0.872, rev 4.024; lever: central; final drive: spiral bevel; axle ratio: 4.875; width of rims: 4"; tyres: 135 SR x 12.

PERFORMANCE max speeds: (I) 19 mph, 30 km/h; (II) 31 mph, 50 km/h; (III) 50 mph, 80 km/h; (IV) over 65 mph, 105 km/h; power-weight ratio: 55.1 lb/hp (73.5 lb/kW), 25 kg/hp (33.3 kg/kW); carrying capacity: 706 lb, 320 kg; acceleration: standing ¼ mile 21 sec; speed in top at 1,000 rpm: 14 mph, 22.6 km/h; consumption: 46.3 m/imp gal, 38.6 m/US gal, 6.1 l x 100 km at 56 mph, 90 km/h.

CHASSIS integral; front suspension: independent, wishbones, transverse leafspring lower arms, telescopic dampers; rear: independent, oblique semi-trailing arms, coil springs, telescopic dampers.

STEERING screw and sector; turns lock to lock: 2.90.

BRAKES drum; lining area: front 33.3 sq in, 215 sq cm, rear 33.3 sq in, 215 sq cm, total 66.6 sq in, 430 sq cm.

ELECTRICAL EQUIPMENT 12 V; 34 Ah battery; 33 A alternator; Marelli distributor; 2 headlamps.

DIMENSIONS AND WEIGHT wheel base: 72.44 in, 184 cm; tracks: 44.96 in, 114 cm front, 47.36 in, 120 cm rear; length: 120.24 in, 305 cm; width: 54.21 in, 138 cm; height: 52.56 in, 133 cm; ground clearance: 4.92 in, 12.5 cm; weight: 1,323 lb, 600 kg; weight distribution: 40% front, 60% rear; turning circle: 28.2 ft, 8.6 m; fuel tank: 4.6 imp gal, 5.5 US gal, 21 l.

BODY saloon/sedan; 2 doors; 4 seats, separate front seats.

PRACTICAL INSTRUCTIONS fuel: 80-85 oct petrol; oil: engine 4.4 imp pt, 5.3 US pt, 2.5 l, SAE 30W (summer) 20W (winter), change every 6,200 miles, 10,000 km - gearbox and final drive 1.9 imp pt, 2.3 US pt, 1.1 l, FIAT ZC 90, change every 18,600 miles, 30,000 km; greasing: every 3,100 miles, 5,000 km, 2 points; tappet clearances: inlet 0.008 in, 0.20 mm, exhaust 0.010 in, 0.25 mm; valve timing: 26° 57° 66° 17°; tyre pressure: front 22 psi, 1.4 atm, rear 28 psi, 2 atm.

OPTIONALS reclining backrests; headrests; heated rear window.

Panda 30

PRICE EX WORKS: 6,661,000 liras**

ENGINE front, 4 stroke; 2 cylinders, vertical, in line; 39.8 cu in, 652 cc (3.03 x 2.76 in, 77 x 70 mm); compression ratio: 8:1; max power (DIN): 30 hp (22 kW) at 5,500 rpm; max torque (DIN): 30 lb ft, 4.2 kg m (41 Nm) at 3,000 rpm; max engine rpm: 6,000; 46 hp/l (33.7 kW/l); light alloy block and head; 2 crankshaft bearings; valves: overhead, in line, push-rods and rockers; camshafts: 1, side; lubrication: gear pump, centrifugal filter, 4.9 imp pt, 5.9 US pt, 2.8 l; 1 Weber 30 DGF 1/250 or Solex C 30 DID/1 downdraught twin barrel carburettor; fuel feed: mechanical pump; air-cooled.

TRANSMISSION driving wheels: front; clutch: single dry plate (diaphragm); gearbox: mechanical; gears: 4, II, III and IV synchronized; ratios: I 3.500, II 2.067, III 1.300, IV 0.872, rev 4.237; lever: central; final drive: hypoid bevel; axle ratio: 5.125; width of rims: 4"; tyres: 135 SR x 13.

PERFORMANCE max speeds: (I) 20 mph, 33 km/h; (II) 35 mph, 57 km/h; (III) 56 mph, 90 km/h; (IV) 71 mph, 115 km/h; power-weight ratio: 47.8 lb/hp (65.1 lb/kW), 21.7 kg/hp (29.5 kg/kW); carrying capacity: 882 lb, 400 kg; acceleration: standing ¼ mile 23.8 sec; speed in top at 1,000 rpm: 13.9 mph, 22.4 km/h; consumption: 52.3 m/imp gal, 43.6 m/US gal, 5.4 l x 100 km at 56 mph, 90 km/h.

CHASSIS integral; front suspension: independent, by McPherson, coil springs/telescopic damper struts, lower wishbones; rear: rigid axle, semi-elliptic leafsprings, telescopic dampers.

STEERING rack-and-pinion; turns lock to lock: 3.40.

BRAKES front disc (diameter 8.94 in, 22.7 cm), rear drum, dual circuit, rear compensator; lining area: front 21.7 sq in, 140 sq cm, rear 33.3 sq in, 215 sq cm, total 55 sq in, 355 sq cm.

ELECTRICAL EQUIPMENT 12 V; 32 Ah battery; 45 A alternator; Marelli distributor; 2 headlamps.

DIMENSIONS AND WEIGHT wheel base: 85.04 in, 216 cm; tracks: 49.37 in, 125 cm front, 49.17 in, 125 cm rear; length: 133.07 in, 338 cm; width: 57.48 in, 146 cm; height: 56.89 in, 144 cm; weight: 1,433 lb, 650 kg; weight distribution: 61% front, 39% rear; turning circle: 30.2 ft, 9.2 m; fuel tank: 7.7 imp gal, 9.2 US gal, 35 l.

FIAT 126

FIAT Panda 30 Super

PANDA 30

BODY saloon/sedan; 2+1 doors; 5 seats, separate front seats; folding rear seat.

PRACTICAL INSTRUCTIONS fuel: 97 oct petrol; oil: engine 4.9 imp pt, 5.9 US pt, 2.8 l, SAE 20W (winter) 30W (summer), change every 6,200 miles, 10,000 km - gearbox and final drive 2.6 imp pt, 3.2 US pt, 1.5 l, SAE 90, change every 18,600 miles, 30,000 km; greasing: every 18,600 miles, 30,000 km, homokinetic joints; spark plug: Marelli CW 7 NP or Champion L 82 Y; tappet clearances: inlet 0.008 in, 0.20 mm, exhaust 0.010 in, 0.25 mm; valve timing: 21° 62° 61° 22°; tyre pressure: front 26 psi, 1.8 atm, rear 28 psi, 2 atm.

OPTIONALS headrests; reclining backrests; heated rear window; rear window wiper-washer; sunroof.

Panda 30 Super

See Panda 30, except for:

PRICE EX WORKS: 7,111,000 liras**

BODY luxury interior; headrests and reclining backrests (standard).

OPTIONALS metallic spray.

Panda 45

See Panda 30, except for:

PRICE IN GB: £ 3,030*
PRICE EX WORKS: 7,501,000 liras**

ENGINE front, transverse, 4 stroke; 4 cylinders, vertical, in line; 55.1 cu in, 903 cc (2.56 x 2.68 in, 65 x 68 mm); compression ratio: 9:1; max power (DIN): 45 hp (33 kW) at 5,600 rpm; max torque (DIN): 49 lb ft, 6.8 kg m (67 Nm) at 3,000 rpm; max engine rpm: 6,400; 49.8 hp/l (36.7 kW/l); cast iron block, light alloy head; 3 crankshaft bearings; lubrication: gear pump, full flow filter (cartridge), 6.9 imp pt, 8.2 US pt, 3.9 l; 1 Weber 32 ICEV 50/250 or Solex C32 DISA/11 downdraught single barrel carburettor; water-cooled, expansion tank, 9.2 imp pt, 11 US pt, 5.2 l, electric thermostatic fan.

TRANSMISSION gears: 4, fully synchronized; ratios: I 3.909, II 2.055, III 1.432, IV 0.964, rev 3.615; final drive: helical cylindrical; axle ratio: 4.071.

PERFORMANCE max speed: about 87 mph, 140 km/h; power-weight ratio: 33.3 lb/hp (45.4 lb/kW), 15.1 kg/hp (20.6 kg/kW); acceleration: standing ¼ mile 20.2 sec; speed in top at 1,000 rpm: 15.8 mph, 25.4 km/h; consumption: 40.4 m/imp gal, 33.6 m/US gal, 7 l x 100 km at 75 mph, 120 km/h.

ELECTRICAL EQUIPMENT Marelli S 146 A distributor.

DIMENSIONS AND WEIGHT weight: 1,499 lb, 680 kg; weight distribution: 49% front, 51% rear.

BODY headrests and reclining backrests (standard).

PRACTICAL INSTRUCTIONS oil: engine 6.9 imp pt, 8.2 US pt, 3.9 l, SAE 20W (winter) 30W (summer), change every 6,200 miles, 10,000 km - gearbox and final drive 4.2 imp pt, 5.1 US pt, 2.4 l, SAE 90, change every 18,600 miles, 30,000 km; spark plug: Marelli CW 7 LPR or Champion RN 9 Y; valve timing: 7° 36° 38° 5°.

OPTIONALS 145 SR x 13 tyres; tinted glass; heated rear window; rear window wiper-washer; sunroof.

Panda 45 Super

See Panda 30, except for:

PRICE IN GB: £ 3,260*
PRICE EX WORKS: 8,113,000 liras**

ENGINE front, transverse, 4 stroke; 4 cylinders, vertical, in line; 55.1 cu in, 903 cc (2.56 x 2.68 in, 65 x 68 mm); compression ratio: 9:1; max power (DIN): 45 hp (33 kW) at 5,600 rpm; max torque (DIN): 49 lb ft, 6.8 kg m (67 Nm) at 3,000 rpm; max engine rpm: 6,400; 49.8 hp/l (36.7 kW/l); cast iron block, light alloy head; 3 crankshaft bearings; lubrication: gear pump, full flow filter (cartridge), 6.9 imp pt, 8.2 US pt, 3.9 l; 1 Weber 32 ICEV 50/250 or Solex C32 DISA/11 downdraught single barrel carburettor; water-cooled, expansion tank, 9.2 imp pt, 11 US pt, 5.2 l, electric thermostatic fan.

TRANSMISSION gears: 4, fully synchronized; ratios: I 3.909, II 2.055, III 1.342, IV 0.964, rev 3.615; final drive: helical cylindrical; axle ratio: 4.071.

PERFORMANCE max speed: about 87 mph, 140 km/h; power-weight ratio: 33.3 lb/hp (45.4 lb/kW), 15.1 kg/hp (20.6 kg/kW); acceleration: standing ¼ mile 20.2 sec; speed in top at 1,000 rpm: 15.8 mph, 25.4 km/h; consumption: 40.4 m/imp gal, 33.6 m/US gal, 7 l x 100 km at 75 mph, 120 km/h.

ELECTRICAL EQUIPMENT Marelli S 146 A distributor.

DIMENSIONS AND WEIGHT weight: 1,499 lb, 680 kg; weight distribution: 49% front, 51% rear.

BODY luxuty interior; headrests, heated rear window wiper-washer and reclining backrests (standard).

FIAT Panda 4 x 4

PRACTICAL INSTRUCTIONS oil: engine 6.9 imp pt, 8.2 US pt, 3.9 l, SAE 20W (winter) 30W (summer), change every 6,200 miles, 10,000 km - gearbox and final drive 4.2 imp pt, 5.1 US pt, 2.4 l, SAE 90, change every 18,600 miles, 30,000 km; spark plug: Marelli CW 7 LPR or Champion RN 9 Y; valve timing: 7° 36° 38° 5°.

OPTIONALS 5-speed fully synchronized mecanical gearbox (I 3.909, II 2.055, III 1.342, IV 0.964, V 0.831, rev 3.615), consumption 42.2 m/imp gal, 35.1 m/US gal, 6.7 l x 100 km at 75 mph, 120 km/h; light alloy wheels; 145 SR x 13 tyres; tinted glass; metallic spray; sunroof.

Panda 4 x 4

See Panda 30, except for:

PRICE EX WORKS: 10,591,000 liras**

ENGINE front, transverse, 4 stroke; 4 cylinders, vertical, in line; 58.9 cu in, 965 cc (2.65 x 2.68 in, 67.2 x 68 mm); compression ratio: 9.2:1; max power (DIN): 48 hp (35 kW) at 5,600 rpm; max torque (DIN): 51 lb ft, 7.1 kg m (70 Nm) at 3,500 rpm; max engine rpm: 6,400; 49.7 hp/l (36.5 kW/l); cast iron block, light alloy head; 3 crankshaft bearings; valves: overhead, push-rods and rockers; camshafts: 1, side; lubrication: gear pump, cartridge filter, 6.7 imp pt, 8 US pt, 3.8 l; 1 Weber 32 DAT R 10/100 downdraught twin barrel carburettor; water-cooled, 9.2 imp pt, 11 US pt, 5.2 l, electric thermostatic fan.

TRANSMISSION driving wheels: front and rear (possible manual selection); gears: 5, fully synchronized; ratios: I 3.909, II 2.055, III 1.342, IV 0.964, V 0.723, rev 3.615; final drive: front helical cylindrical, rear hypoid bevel; axle ratio: front 5.455, rear 2.929; tyres: 145 SR x 13 winter.

PERFORMANCE max speed: 84 mph, 135 km/h; power-weight ratio: 34 lb/hp (46.6 lb/kW), 15.4 kg/hp (21.1 kg/kW); acceleration: standing ¼ mile 19.9 sec; speed in top at 1,000 rpm: 16.3 mph, 26.2 km/h; consumption: 35.8 m/imp gal, 29.8 m/US gal, 7.9 l x 100 km at 75 mph, 120 km/h.

ELECTRICAL EQUIPMENT Marelli S 146 A distributor.

DIMENSIONS AND WEIGHT wheel base: 85.43 in, 217 cm; rear track: 49.53 in, 126 cm; length: 133.46 in, 339 cm; width: 58.46 in, 148 cm; height: 57.52 in, 146 cm; weight: 1,632 lb, 740 kg.

BODY tinted glass.

PRACTICAL INSTRUCTIONS oil: engine 6.7 imp pt, 8 US pt, 3.8 l, SAE 10W-50 - gearbox and front final drive 4.2 imp pt, 5.1 US pt, 2.4 l - rear final drive 2.1 imp pt, 2.5 US pt, 1.2 l; greasing: none; spark plug: Marelli CW 7 LPR; valve timing: 17° 43° 57° 3°; tyre pressure: front 28 psi, 2 atm, rear 28 psi, 2 atm.

OPTIONALS metallic spray.

Uno Series

PRICES IN GB AND EX WORKS:		£	liras
1	45 2+1-dr Berlina	3,377*	8,329,000**
2	45 Super 2+1-dr Berlina	—	9,073,000**
3	ES 2+1-dr Berlina	4,070*	9,655,000**
4	55 4+1-dr Berlina	3,776*	9,307,000**
5	55 Super 2+1-dr Berlina	3,980*	9,787,000**
6	55 Super 4+1-dr Berlina	4,160*	10,093,000**
7	70 Super 2+1-dr Berlina	4,420*	10,171,000**
8	DS 2+1-dr Berlina	—	10,177,000**
9	DS Super 4+1-dr Berlina	—	10,903,000**

Power team:	Standard for:	Optional for:
45 hp	1,2	—
45 hp (Energy Saving)	3	—
55 hp	4 to 6	—
70 hp	7	—
45 hp (diesel)	8,9	—

45 hp power team

ENGINE front, transverse, 4 stroke; 4 cylinders, vertical, in line; 55.1 cu in, 903 cc (2.56 x 2.68 in, 65 x 68 mm); compression ratio: 9:1; max power (DIN): 45 hp (33 kW) at 5,600 rpm; max torque (DIN): 49 lb ft, 6.8 kg m (67 Nm) at 3,000 rpm; max engine rpm: 6,000; 49.8 hp/l (36.7 kW/l); cast iron block, light alloy head; 3 crankshaft bearings; valves: overhead, in line, push-rods and rockers; camshafts: 1, side; lubrication: gear pump, full flow filter (cartridge), 6 imp pt, 7.2 US pt, 3.4 l; 1 Weber 32 ICEV 50/250 or Solex C32 DISA/11 downdraught single barrel carburettor; fuel feed: mechanical pump; water-

FIAT Uno ES Berlina

FIAT Uno 55 Super Berlina

cooled, expansion tank, 8.1 imp pt, 9.7 US pt, 4.6 l, electric thermostatic fan.

TRANSMISSION driving wheels: front; clutch: single dry plate; gearbox: mechanical; gears: 4, fully synchronized; ratios: I 3.909, II 2.055, III 1.342, IV 0.964, rev 3.615; lever: central; final drive: helical cylindrical; axle ratio: 4.071; width of rims: 4.5"; tyres: 135 SR x 13.

PERFORMANCE max speeds: (I) 22 mph, 35 km/h; (II) 43 mph, 70 km/h; (III) 65 mph, 105 km/h; (IV) 87 mph, 140 km/h; power-weight ratio: 34.3 lb/hp (46.8 lb/kW), 15.6 kg/hp (21.2 kg/kW); carrying capacity: 882 lb, 400 kg; acceleration: standing ¼ mile 19.8 sec; speed in top at 1,000 rpm: 15.8 mph, 25.4 km/h; consumption: 42.8 m/imp gal, 35.6 m/US gal, 6.6 l x 100 km at 75 mph, 120 km/h.

CHASSIS integral; front suspension: independent, by McPherson, coil springs/telescopic damper struts, lower wishbones; rear: independent, torsion axle beam and tension arms, gas operated telescopic dampers.

STEERING rack-and-pinion; turns lock to lock: 4.

BRAKES front disc (diameter 8.94 in, 22.7 cm), rear drum, dual circuit, rear compensator; lining area: front 21.7 sq in, 140 sq cm, rear 33.3 sq in, 215 sq cm, total 55 sq in, 355 sq cm.

ELECTRICAL EQUIPMENT 12 V; 30 Ah battery (sealed energy); 45 A alternator; Marelli distributor; 2 headlamps.

DIMENSIONS AND WEIGHT wheel base: 92.99 in, 236 cm; tracks: 52.76 in, 134 cm front, 51.18 in, 130 cm rear; length: 143.46 in, 364 cm; width: 60.94 in, 155 cm; height: 56.30 in, 143 cm; weight: 1,543 lb, 700 kg; weight distribution: 48.4% front, 51.6% rear; turning circle: 30.8 ft, 9.4 m; fuel tank: 9.2 imp gal, 11.1 US gal, 42 l.

BODY saloon/sedan; 2+1 doors; 5 seats, separate front seats; folding rear seat; (for Super only) headrests, reclining backrests, heated rear window and rear window wiper-washer (standard).

PRACTICAL INSTRUCTIONS fuel: 97 oct petrol; oil: engine 6 imp pt, 7.2 US pt, 3.4 l, SAE 10W-50, change every 6,200 miles, 10,000 km - gearbox and final drive 4.2 imp pt, 5.1 US pt, 2.4 l, SAE 90, change every 18,600 miles, 30,000 km; greasing: none; spark plug: Champion RN 9Y; valve timing: 7° 36° 38° 5°; tyre pressure: front 27 psi, 1.9 atm, rear 27 psi, 1.9 atm.

OPTIONALS (for Super only) 5-speed mechanical gearbox (I 3.909, II 2.055, III 1.348, IV 0.964, V 0.831, rev 3.615), consumption 45.6 m/imp gal, 37.9 m/US gal, 6.2 l x 100 km at 75 mph, 120 km/h; vacuometer; (except Super) headrests, reclining backrests and heated rear window wiper-washer; (for Super only) electric windows.

45 hp (Energy Saving) power team

See 45 hp power team, except for:

ENGINE compression ratio: 9.7:1; max torque (DIN): 50 lb ft, 6.9 kg m (68 Nm) at 3,000 rpm; 1 Weber 32 ICEE/250 or Solex C32 DISA/14 downdraught single barrel carburettor; recirculation system with fuel flow cut-off when the accelerator is released.

TRANSMISSION gears: 5, fully synchronized; ratios: I 3.909, II 2.055, III 1.342, IV 0.964, V 0.780, rev 3.615; axle ratio: 3.867.

PERFORMANCE speed in top at 1,000 rpm: 20.6 mph, 33.2 km/h; consumption: 48.7 m/imp gal, 34.6 m/US gal, 5.8 l x 100 km at 75 mph, 120 km/h.

ELECTRICAL EQUIPMENT Marelli Digiplex electronic ignition.

55 hp power team

See 45 hp power team, except for:

ENGINE 68.1 cu in, 1,116 cc (3.15 x 2.19 in, 80 x 55.5 mm); compression ratio: 9.2:1; max power (DIN): 55 hp (41 kW) at 5,600 rpm; max torque (DIN): 64 lb ft, 8.8 kg m (86 Nm) at 2,900 rpm; 49.3 hp/l (36.7 kW/l); 5 cranckshaft bearings; valves: overhead, thimble tappets; camshafts: 1, overhead, cogged belt; lubrication: 7 imp pt, 8.5 US pt, 4 l; 1 Weber 32 ICEV 51/250 or Solex C 32 DISA 12 downdraught single barrel carburettor; air cleaner: dry, thimble type thermostatic intake; cooling: 10.6 imp pt, 12.7 US pt, 6 l.

TRANSMISSION gears: Super saloons 5, fully synchronized; ratios: I 3.909, II 2.055, III 1.342, IV 0.964, V 0.780, rev 3.615; axle ratio: 3.733; tyres: Super saloons 155/70 SR x 13.

PERFORMANCE max speeds Super saloons: (I) 25 mph, 40 km/h; (II) 47 mph, 75 km/h; (III) 71 mph, 115 km/h; (IV) 93 mph, 150 km/h; (V) 90 mph, 145 km/h; power-weight ratio: 4+1-dr saloon 29.7 lb/hp (39.8 lb/kW), 13.5 kg/hp (18 kg/kW); acceleration: standing ¼ mile 19.2 sec; speed in top at 1,000 rpm: Super saloons 21.2 mph, 34.2 km/h; consumption: Berlina 41.5 m/imp gal, 34.6 m/US gal, 6.8 l x 100 km at 75 mph, 120 km/h - Super saloons 44.1 m/imp gal, 36.8 m/US gal, 6.4 l x 100 km at 75 mph, 120 km/h.

BRAKES servo.

DIMENSIONS AND WEIGHT width: 61.22 in, 156 cm; weight: Super 2+1-dr Berlina 1,607 lb, 730 kg - 4+1-dr saloons 1,632 lb, 740 kg.

BODY 2+1 or 4+1 doors; 5 seats, separate front seats, headrests, reclining backrests (standard); heated rear window and rear window wiper-washer (standard); folding rear seat.

PRACTICAL INSTRUCTIONS oil: engine 7 imp pt, 8.5 US pt, 4 l; valve timing: 7° 35° 37° 5°.

OPTIONALS vacuometer; (for Super saloons only) sunroof, metallic spray and electric windows.

70 hp power team

See 45 hp power team, except for:

ENGINE 79.4 cu in, 1,301 cc (3.40 x 2.18 in, 86.4 x 55.5 mm); compression ratio: 9.1:1; max power (DIN): 70 hp (52 kW) at 5,700 rpm; max torque (DIN): 74 lb ft, 10.2 kg m (100 Nm) at 2,900 rpm; 53.8 hp/l (40 kW/l); 5 crankshaft bearings; valves: overhead, thimble tappets; camshafts: 1, overhead, cogged belt; lubrication: 7 imp pt, 8.5 US pt, 4 l; 1 Weber 30/32 DMTR 90/250 or Solex C 30/32 CIC-1 downdraught twin barrel carburettor; air cleaner: dry, thimble type thermostatic intake; water-cooled, 10.9 imp pt, 13.1 US pt, 6.2 l.

TRANSMISSION gears: 5, fully synchronized; ratios: I 3.909, II 2.055, III 1.342, IV 0.964, V 0.780, rev 3.615; axle ratio: 3.733; tyres: 155/70 SR x 13.

PERFORMANCE max speeds: (I) 25 mph, 40 km/h; (II) 47 mph, 75 km/h; (III) 75 mph, 120 km/h; (IV) 102 mph, 165 km/h; (V) 99 mph, 160 km/h; power-weight ratio: 23.6 lb/hp (31.8 lb/kW), 10.7 kg/hp (14.4 kg/kW); acceleration: standing ¼ mile 17.9 sec; speed in top at 1,000 rpm: 21.3 mph, 34.3 km/h; consumption: 43.5 m/imp gal, 36.2 m/US gal, 6.5 l x 100 km at 75 mph, 120 km/h.

BRAKES servo.

DIMENSIONS AND WEIGHT weight: 1,654 lb, 750 kg.

BODY headrests, reclining backrests, heated rear window and rear window wiper-washer (standard).

PRACTICAL INSTRUCTIONS oil: engine 7 imp pt, 8.5 US pt, 4 l; valve timing: 7° 35° 37° 5°.

OPTIONALS Van Dorne automatic transmission with gearbox ratios continuously variable between 1:13.370 and 1:2.409, max speed 99 mph, 160 km/h, consumption 42.2 m/imp gal, 35.1 m/US gal, 6.7 l x 100 km at 75 mph, 120 km/h; vacuometer; sunroof; metallic spray; electric windows.

45 hp (diesel) power team

See 45 hp power team, except for:

ENGINE diesel; 79.4 cu in, 1,301 cc (2.99 x 2.81 in, 76.1 x 71.5 mm); compression ratio: 20:1; max power (DIN): 45 hp (33 kW) at 5,000 rpm; max torque (DIN): 55 lb ft, 7.6 kg m (74 Nm) at 3,000 rpm; 34.6 hp/l (25.4 kW/l); 5 crankshaft bearings; valves: overhead, thimble tappets; camshafts: 1, overhead, cogged belt; lubrication: 7 imp pt, 8.5 US pt, 4 l; Bosch VE 4/8F 2500 R 61 injection pump; water-cooled, 14.1 imp pt, 16.9 US pt, 8 l.

TRANSMISSION gears: 5, fully synchronized; ratios: I 3.909, II 2.055, III 1.342, IV 0.942, V 0.831, rev 3.615; tyres: 155/70 SR x 13.

PERFORMANCE max speed: 87 mph, 140 km/h; power-weight ratio: 2+1-dr Berlina 39.2 lb/hp (53.5 lb/kW), 17.8 kg/hp (24.2 kg/kW); acceleration: standing ¼ mile 20.5 sec; speed in top at 1,000 rpm: 18.3 mph, 29.5 km/h; consumption: 43.5 m/imp gal, 36.2 m/US gal, 6.5 l x 100 km at 75 mph, 120 km/h.

ELECTRICAL EQUIPMENT 55 Ah battery; 55 A alternator.

DIMENSIONS AND WEIGHT weight: 2+1-dr Berlina 1,764 lb, 800 kg - 4+1-dr Berlina 1,786 lb, 810 kg.

BODY 2+1 or 4+1 doors.

PRACTICAL INSTRUCTIONS fuel: diesel; oil: engine 7 imp pt, 8.5 US pt, 4 l; valve timing: 3° 29° 29° 3°.

127 Series

PRICES EX WORKS:

		liras
1	1050 2+1-dr Berlina	**7,441,000****
2	1050 2+1-dr Panorama	**8,629,000****
3	Diesel 2+1-dr Berlina	**9,595,000****
4	Diesel 2+1-dr Panorama	**10,195,000****

Power team:	Standard for:	Optional for:
50 hp	1,2	—
45 hp (diesel)	3,4	—

FIAT 127 1050 Berlina

50 hp power team

ENGINE front, transverse, 4 stroke; 4 cylinders, vertical, in line; 64 cu in, 1,049 cc (2.99 x 2.27 in, 76 x 57.8 mm); compression ratio: 9.3:1; max power (DIN): 50 hp (37 kW) at 5,600 rpm; max torque (DIN): 57 lb ft, 7.9 kg m (77 Nm) at 3,000 rpm; max engine rpm: 6,000; 55.4 hp/l (40.7 kW/l); cast iron block, light alloy head; 5 crankshaft bearings; valves: overhead, thimble tappets; camshafts: 1, overhead, cogged belt; lubrication: gear pump, full flow filter (cartridge), 6.3 imp pt, 7.6 US pt, 3.6 l; 1 Weber 32 ICEV 34/150 or Solex C 32 TDI/2 downdraught single barrel carburettor; fuel feed: mechanical pump; water-cooled, expansion tank, 10.2 imp pt, 12.3 US pt, 5.8 l, electric thermostatic fan.

TRANSMISSION driving wheels: front; clutch: single dry plate (diaphragm); gearbox: mechanical; gears: 5, fully synchronized; ratios: I 4.091, II 2.235, III 1.461, IV 1.034, V 0.863, rev 3.714; lever: central; final drive: helical cylindrical; axle ratio: 4.077; width of rims: 4"; tyres: 145 SR x 13.

PERFORMANCE max speed: 84 mph, 135 km/h; power-weight ratio: Berlina 35.1 lb/hp (47.4 lb/kW), 15.9 kg/hp (21.5 kg/kW); carrying capacity: Berlina 882 lb, 400 kg - Panorama 992 lb, 450 kg; acceleration: standing ¼ mile Berlina 19.8 sec - Panorama 20.3 sec; speed in top at 1,000 rpm: 18.2 mph, 29.4 km/h; consumption: 33.2 m/imp gal, 27.7 m/US gal, 8.5 l x 100 km at 75 mph, 120 km/h.

CHASSIS integral; front suspension: independent, by McPherson, coil springs/telescopic damper struts, lower wishbones, anti-roll bar; rear: independent, single wide-based wishbones, transverse anti-roll leafspring, telescopic dampers.

STEERING rack-and-pinion; turns lock to lock: 3.80.

BRAKES front disc (diameter 8.94 in, 22.7 cm), rear drum, dual circuit, rear compensator, servo; lining area: front 22.5 sq in, 145 sq cm, rear 34.9 sq in, 225 sq cm, total 57.4 sq in, 370 sq cm.

ELECTRICAL EQUIPMENT 12 V; 34 Ah battery; 32 A alternator; Marelli S 146 A distributor; 2 headlamps.

DIMENSIONS AND WEIGHT wheel base: 89.90 in, 223 cm; tracks: Berlina 50.24 in, 128 cm front, 51.30 in, 130 cm rear - Panorama 50.55 in, 128 cm front, 50.63 in, 129 cm rear; length: Berlina 147.36 in, 374 cm - Panorama 154.53 in, 392 cm; width: 60.47 in, 154 cm; height: Berlina 55.31 in, 140 cm - Panorama 56.10 in, 142 cm; ground clearance: 5.12 in, 13 cm; weight: Berlina 1,753 lb, 795 kg - Panorama 1,830 lb, 830 kg; weight distribution: Berlina 62% front, 38% rear - Panorama 58% front, 42% rear; turning circle: 29.8 ft, 9.1 m; fuel tank: Berlina 9.2 imp gal, 11.1 US gal, 42 l - Panorama 11.4 imp gal, 13.7 US gal, 52 l.

BODY saloon/sedan - estate car/st. wagon; 2+1 doors; 5 seats, separate front seats, reclining backrests; folding rear seat.

PRACTICAL INSTRUCTIONS fuel: 97 oct petrol; oil: engine 6.3 imp pt, 7.6 US pt, 3.6 l, SAE 10W-50, change every 6,200 miles, 10,000 km - gearbox and final drive 6 imp pt, 7.2 US pt, 3.4 l, SAE 90, change every 18,600 miles, 30,000 km; greasing: none; spark plug: Marelli CW 7 LPR; valve timing: 2° 42° 42° 2°; tyre pressure: front 27 psi, 1.9 atm, rear 27 psi, 1.9 atm.

OPTIONALS heated rear window; rear window wiper-washer; headrests; metallic spray.

45 hp (diesel) power team

See 50 hp power team, except for:

ENGINE diesel; 79.4 cu in, 1,301 cc (2.99 x 2.81 in, 76.1 x 71.5 mm); compression ratio: 20:1; max power (DIN): 45 hp (33 kW) at 5,000 rpm; max torque (DIN): 55 lb ft, 7.6 kg m (74 Nm) at 3,000 rpm; 34.6 hp/l (25.4 kW/l); lubrication: 6.7 imp pt, 8 US pt, 3.8 l; Bosch VE 4/8 F 2500 injection pump; cooling: 12.3 imp pt, 14.8 US pt, 7 l.

FIAT 127 Diesel Panorama

PERFORMANCE max speed: 81 mph, 130 km/h; power-weight ratio: Berlina 40.9 lb/hp (55.8 lb/kW), 18.6 kg/hp (25.3 kg/kW); acceleration: standing ¼ mile Berlina 21 sec - Panorama 21.5 sec; speed in top at 1,000 rpm: 18.2 mph, 29.3 km/h; consumption: 38.2 m/imp gal, 31.8 m/US gal, 7.4 l x 100 km at 75 mph, 120 km/h.

ELECTRICAL EQUIPMENT 55 Ah battery; 45 A alternator.

DIMENSIONS AND WEIGHT weight: Berlina 1,841 lb, 835 kg - Panorama 1,918 lb, 870 kg.

PRACTICAL INSTRUCTIONS fuel: diesel; oil: engine 6.7 imp pt, 8 US pt, 3.8 l; valve timing: 3° 29° 29° 3°.

Ritmo Series

PRICES IN GB AND EX WORKS:		£	liras
1	60 2+1-dr Berlina	4,061*	9,319,000**
2	60 4+1-dr Berlina	—	10,375,000**
3	ES 4+1-dr Berlina	4,476*	11,149,000**
4	70 Automatica 4+1-dr Berlina	—	11,401,000**
5	Super 70 4+1-dr Berlina	—	11,791,000**
6	Super 85 4+1-dr Berlina	5,272*	12,865,000**
7	Diesel 4+1-dr Berlina	—	10,848,000**
8	Diesel L 4+1-dr Berlina	—	12,613,000**

Power team:	Standard for:	Optional for:
55 hp	1,2	—
55 hp (energy saving)	3	—
68 hp (1,299 cc)	4	—
68 hp (1,301 cc)	5	—
82 hp	6	—
58 hp (diesel)	7,8	—

55 hp power team

ENGINE front, transverse, 4 stroke; 4 cylinders, in line; 68.1 cu in, 1,116 cc (3.15 x 2.19 in, 80 x 55.5 mm); compression ratio: 9.2:1; max power (DIN): 55 hp (40 kW) at 5,600 rpm; max torque (DIN): 63 lb ft, 8.7 kg m (85 Nm) at 2,900 rpm; max engine rpm: 6,000; 49.3 hp/l (35.8 kW/l); cast iron block, light alloy head; 5 crankshaft bearings; valves: overhead, in line, slanted at 18°, thimble tappets; camshafts: 1, overhead, cogged belt; lubrication: gear pump, full flow filter (cartridge), 7.7 imp pt, 9.3 US pt, 4.4 l; 1 Weber 32 ICEV 51/250 or Solex C32 DISA 12 downdraught single barrel carburettor; fuel feed: mechanical pump; water-cooled, expansion tank, 11.8 imp pt, 14.2 US pt, 6.7 l, electric thermostatic fan.

TRANSMISSION driving wheels: front; clutch: single dry plate; gearbox: mechanical; gears: 4, fully synchronized; ratios: I 4.090, II 2.235, III 1.461, IV 1.034, rev 3.714; lever: central; final drive: helical cylindrical; axle ratio: 3.765; width of rims: 4.5"; tyres: 145 SR x 13.

PERFORMANCE max speed: 90 mph, 145 km/h; power-weight ratio: 60 4+1-dr Berlina 33.7 lb/hp (46.3 lb/kW), 15.3 kg/hp (21 kg/kW); carrying capacity: 882 lb, 400 kg; speed in top at 1,000 rpm: 16.5 mph, 26.5 km/h; consumption: 34.4 m/imp gal, 28.7 m/US gal, 8.2 l x 100 km at 75 mph, 120 km/h.

CHASSIS integral; front suspension: independent, by McPherson, lower wishbones, trailing links, coil springs/telescopic damper struts; rear: independent, lower wishbones, transverse anti-roll leafspring, telescopic dampers.

STEERING rack-and-pinion; turns lock to lock: 4.

BRAKES front disc (diameter 8.94 in, 22.7 cm), rear drum, dual circuit, rear compensator, servo; lining area: front 21.7 sq in, 140 sq cm, rear 33.3 sq in, 215 sq cm, total 55 sq in, 355 sq cm.

ELECTRICAL EQUIPMENT 12 V; 32 Ah battery; 55 A alternator; Marelli distributor; 4 headlamps.

DIMENSIONS AND WEIGHT wheel base: 96.22 in, 244 cm; tracks: 55.47 in, 141 cm front, 55.67 in, 141 cm rear; length: 158.03 in, 401 cm; width: 65 in, 165 cm; height: 55.12 in, 140 cm; weight: 60 2+1-dr Berlina 1,797 lb, 815 kg - 60 4+1-dr Berlina 1,852 lb, 840 kg; weight distribution: 62% front, 38% rear; turning circle: 33.8 ft, 10.3 m; fuel tank: 12.1 imp gal, 14.5 US gal, 55 l.

BODY saloon/sedan; 2+1 or 4+1 doors; 5 seats, separate front seats; folding rear seat.

PRACTICAL INSTRUCTIONS fuel: 97 oct petrol; oil: engine 7.7 imp pt, 9.3 US pt, 4.4 l, SAE 10W-40, change every 6,200 miles, 10,000 km - gearbox and final drive 5.3 imp pt, 6.3 US pt, 3 l, SAE 80W-90, change every 18,600 miles, 30,000 km; greasing: none; spark plug: Marelli CW 7 LPR or Champion RN 9 Y; valve timing: 7° 35° 37° 5°; tyre pressure: front 27 psi, 1.9 atm, rear 26 psi, 1.8 atm.

OPTIONALS 5-speed fully synchronized mechanical gearbox (I 4.090, II 2.235, III 1.461, IV 1.034, V 0.863, rev 3.714), consumption 37.2 m/imp gal, 30.9 m/US gal, 7.6 l x 100 km at 75 mph, 120 km/h; 165/70 SR x 13 or 165/65 SR x 14 tyres; heated rear window; rear window wiper-washer; headrests; metallic spray; tinted glass.

FIAT Ritmo ES Berlina

55 hp (energy saving) power team

See 55 hp power team, except for:

ENGINE compression ratio: 9.6:1; max torque (DIN): 65 lb ft, 9 kg m (88 Nm) at 2,900 rpm; 1 Weber 30 DMTE/250 or Solex C30 CIC-1 downdraught single barrel carburettor with fuel cut-off system.

TRANSMISSION (standard) gears: 5, fully synchronized; ratios: I 4.090, II 2.235, III 1.461, IV 1.034, V 0.863, rev 3.714.

PERFORMANCE max speed: 93 mph, 150 km/h; speed in top at 1,000 rpm: 19.7 mph, 31.7 km/h; consumption: 42.8 m/imp gal, 35.6 m/US gal, 6.6 l x 100 km at 75 mph, 120 km/h.

ELECTRICAL EQUIPMENT Marelli Digiplex electronic ignition.

BODY 4+1 doors; rear spoiler.

PRACTICAL INSTRUCTIONS valve timing: 9° 31° 39° 1°.

FIAT 127 Diesel Panorama

FIAT Ritmo Abarth 130 TC

68 hp (1,299 cc) power team

See 55 hp power team, except for:

ENGINE 79.3 cu in, 1,299 cc (3.40 x 2.18 in, 86.4 x 55.4 mm); compression ratio: 9.1:1; max power (DIN): 68 hp (50 kW) at 5,700 rpm; max torque (DIN): 74 lb ft, 10.2 kg m (100 Nm) at 2,900 rpm; 52.3 hp/l (38.5 kW/l); 1 Weber 30/32 DMTR 80/250 or 90/450 or Solex C 30/32 CIC-1 downdraught twin barrel carburettor; air cleaner: dry, thimble type thermostatic intake; cooling: 12.1 imp pt, 14.6 US pt, 6.9 l.

TRANSMISSION gearbox: VW automatic transmission, hydraulic torque converter and planetary gears with 3 ratios, possible manual selection; ratios: I 2.550, II 1.450, III 1, rev 2.460; axle ratio: 3.565; tyres: 165/70 SR x 13 (standard).

PERFORMANCE max speed: 93 mph, 150 km/h; power-weight ratio: 28.5 lb/hp (38.8 lb/kW), 12.9 kg/hp (17.6 kg/kW); consumption: not declared.

CHASSIS front suspension: anti-roll bar.

STEERING adjustable height.

ELECTRICAL EQUIPMENT 45 Ah battery.

DIMENSIONS AND WEIGHT weight: 1,940 lb, 880 kg.

BODY 4+1 doors.

68 hp (1,301 cc) power team

See 55 hp power team, except for:

ENGINE 79.4 cu in, 1,301 cc (3.40 x 2.19 in, 86.4 x 55.5 mm); compression ratio: 9.1:1; max power (DIN): 68 hp (50 kW) at 5,700 rpm; max torque (DIN): 74 lb ft, 10.2 kg m (100 Nm) at 2,900 rpm; 52.3 hp/l (38.5 kW/l); 1 Weber 30/32 DMTR 80/250 or 90/450 or Solex C 30/32 CIC-1 downdraught twin barrel carburettor; air cleaner: dry, thimble type thermostatic intake; cooling: 12.1 imp pt, 14.6 US pt, 6.9 l.

TRANSMISSION (standard) gears: 5, fully synchronized; ratios: I 4.090, II 2.235, III 1.461, IV 1.034, V 0.827, rev 3.714; width of rims: 5.5"; tyres: 165/65 SR x 14 (standard).

PERFORMANCE max speed: 96 mph, 155 km/h; power-weight ratio: 27.2 lb/hp (37 lb/kW), 12.4 kg/hp (16.8 kg/kW); speed in top at 1,000 rpm: 20.6 mph, 33.1 km/h; consumption: 34 m/imp gal, 32.2 m/US gal, 7.3 l x 100 km at 75 mph, 120 km/h.

STEERING adjustable height.

ELECTRICAL EQUIPMENT 40 Ah battery; 4 iodine headlamps.

BODY 4+1 doors; heated rear window, rear window wiper-washer and headrests (standard); laminated windscreen; check control.

OPTIONALS electric windows; central door locking; tinted glass; metallic spray.

82 hp power team

See 55 hp power team, except for:

ENGINE 91.4 cu in, 1,498 cc (3.40 x 2.52 in, 86.4 x 63.9 mm); max power (DIN): 82 hp (60 kW) at 5,800 rpm; max torque (DIN): 88 lb ft, 12.2 kg m (120 Nm) at 3,000 rpm; 54.7 hp/l (40.1 kW/l); 1 Weber 32/34 DMTR 81/250 or Solex 32/34 CIC-1 downdraught twin barrel carburettor; air cleaner: dry, thimble type thermostatic intake; cooling: 12.3 imp pt, 14.8 US pt, 7 l.

TRANSMISSION (standard) gears: 5, fully synchronized; ratios: I 4.090, II 2.235, III 1.461, IV 1.034, V 0.827, rev 3.714; axle ratio: 3.588; width of rims: 5.5"; tyres: 165/65 SR x 14 (standard).

PERFORMANCE max speed: 102 mph, 165 km/h; power-weight ratio: 22.9 lb/hp (31.2 lb/kW), 10.4 kg/hp (14.2 kg/kW); speed in top at 1,000 rpm: 21.6 mph, 34.7 km/h; consumption: 38.2 m/imp gal, 31.8 m/US gal, 7.4 l x 100 km at 75 mph, 120 km/h.

STEERING adjustable height.

ELECTRICAL EQUIPMENT 40 Ah battery; 4 iodine headlamps.

BODY 4+1 doors; heated rear window, rear window wiper-washer and headrests (standard); laminated windscreen; check control.

PRACTICAL INSTRUCTIONS valve timing: 6° 46° 47° 7°.

OPTIONALS VW automatic transmission with 3 ratios (I 2.550, II 1.450, III 1, rev 2.460); air-conditioning; sunroof; electric windows; central door locking; tinted glass; metallic spray.

58 hp (diesel) power team

See 55 hp power team, except for:

ENGINE diesel; 104.6 cu in, 1,714 cc (3.27 x 3.12 in, 83 x 79.2 mm); compression ratio: 20.5:1; max power (DIN): 58 hp (43 kW) at 4,500 rpm; max torque (DIN): 76 lb ft, 10.5 kg m (103 Nm) at 3,000 rpm; 33.8 hp/l (25.1 kW/l); Bosch VE 4/9F 2300/R 54 injection pump; cooling: 13.2 imp pt, 15.9 US pt, 7.5 l, 2 electric thermostatic fans.

TRANSMISSION (standard) gears: Diesel Berlina 5, fully synchronized; ratios: I 4.090, II 2.235, III 1.461, IV 1.034, V 0.863, rev 3.714; tyres: 155 SR x 13.

PERFORMANCE max speed: 91 mph, 147 km/h; power-weight ratio: 35 lb/hp (47.2 lb/kW), 15.9 kg/hp (21.4 kg/kW); speed in top at 1,000 rpm: 20.1 mph, 32.4 km/h; consumption: Diesel Berlina 38.7 m/imp gal, 32.2 m/US gal, 7.3 l x 100 km at 75 mph, 120 km/h.

CHASSIS front suspension: anti-roll bar.

ELECTRICAL EQUIPMENT 65 Ah battery; Diesel L Berlina 2 headlamps.

DIMENSIONS AND WEIGHT weight: 2,029 lb, 920 kg.

BODY 4+1 doors.

PRACTICAL INSTRUCTIONS fuel: diesel; valve timing: 4° 40° 45° 5°.

OPTIONALS (for Diesel L Berlina only) 5-speed fully synchronized mechanical gearbox.

Ritmo 105 TC

PRICE IN GB: £ 5,930*
PRICE EX WORKS: 13,123,000 liras**

ENGINE front, transverse, 4 stroke; 4 cylinders, in line; 96.7 cu in, 1,585 cc (3.31 x 2.81 in, 84 x 71.5 mm); compression ratio: 9.3:1; max power (DIN): 105 hp (77 kW) at 6,100 rpm; max torque (DIN): 99 lb ft, 13.6 kg m (133 Nm) at 4,000 rpm; max engine rpm: 6,500; 66.2 hp/l (48.6 kW/l); cast iron block, light alloy head; 5 crankshaft bearings; valves: overhead, Vee-slanted, thimble tappets; camshafts: 2, overhead, cogged belt; lubrication: gear pump, full flow filter (cartridge), 8.1 imp pt, 9.7 US pt, 4.6 l; 1 Weber 32/34 DMTR 82/250 downdraught twin barrel carburettor; air cleaner: dry, thimble type thermostatic intake; fuel feed: mechanical pump; water-cooled, expansion tank, 13.2 imp pt, 15.8 US pt, 7.5 l, electric thermostatic fan.

TRANSMISSION driving wheels: front; clutch: single dry plate; gearbox: mechanical; gears: 5, fully synchronized; ratios: I 3.583, II 2.235, III 1.553, IV 1.163, V 0.960, rev 3.714; lever: central; final drive: helical cylindrical; axle ratio: 3.588; width of rims: 5.5"; tyres: 165/65 SR x 14.

PERFORMANCE max speed: 112 mph, 180 km/h; power-weight ratio: 19 lb/hp (25.9 lb/kW), 8.6 kg/hp (11.8 kg/kW); carrying capacity: 882 lb, 400 kg; acceleration: standing ¼ mile 17 sec; speed in top at 1,000 rpm: 18.7 mph, 30.1 km/h; consumption: 33.6 m/imp gal, 28 m/US gal, 8.4 l x 100 km at 75 mph, 120 km/h.

CHASSIS integral; front suspension: independent, by McPherson, lower wishbones, trailing links, coil springs/telescopic damper struts, anti-roll bar; rear: independent, lower wishbones, transverse anti-roll leafspring, telescopic dampers.

STEERING rack-and-pinion; turns lock to lock: 3.50.

BRAKES front disc (diameter 10.12 in, 25.7 cm), rear drum, dual circuit, rear compensator, servo; lining area: front 22.3 sq in, 144 sq cm, rear 33.3 sq in, 215 sq cm, total 55.6 sq in, 359 sq cm.

ELECTRICAL EQUIPMENT 12 V; 45 Ah battery; 55 A alternator; Marelli Digiplex electronic ignition; 4 headlamps, 2 halogen.

DIMENSIONS AND WEIGHT wheel base: 110.35 in, 244 cm; tracks: 55.87 in, 142 cm front, 55.79 in, 142 cm rear; length: 158.03 in, 401 cm; width: 65.47 in, 166 cm; height: 54.72 in, 139 cm; ground clearance: 5.12 in, 13 cm; weight: 1,996 lb, 905 kg; turning circle: 33.8 ft, 10.3 m; fuel tank: 12.1 imp gal, 14.5 US gal, 55 l.

BODY saloon/sedan; 2+1 doors; 5 seats, separate front seats, headrests; folding rear seat; heated rear window; rear window wiper-washer; tinted glass.

PRACTICAL INSTRUCTIONS fuel: 97 oct petrol; oil: engine 8.1 imp pt, 9.7 US pt, 4.6 l, SAE 20W-40, change every 6,200 miles, 10,000 km - gearbox and final drive 5.1 imp pt, 6.1 US pt, 3 l, SAE 80W-40, change every 18,600 miles, 30,000 km; greasing: none; spark plug: Marelli CW 7 LPR or Champion RN 9 Y; valve timing: 10° 48° 53° 5°; tyre pressure: front 32 psi, 2.2 atm, rear 34 psi, 2.4 atm.

OPTIONALS 185/60 HR x 14 tyres and light alloy wheels; electric windows; central door locking; metallic spray.

Ritmo Abarth 130 TC

See Ritmo 105 TC, except for:

PRICE EX WORKS: 15,793,000 liras**

ENGINE 121.7 cu in, 1,995 cc (3.31 x 3.54 in, 84 x 90 mm); compression ratio: 9.4:1; max power (DIN): 130 hp (96 kW) at 5,900 rpm; max torque (DIN): 130 lb ft, 18 kg m (176 Nm) at

FIAT Ritmo Abarth 130 TC

RITMO ABARTH 130 TC

3,600 rpm; max engine rpm: 6,300; 65.2 hp/l (48.1 kW/l); lubrication: oil cooler, 10 imp pt, 12 US pt, 5.7 l; 2 Weber 40 DCOE 145/146 or Solex C 40 ADDHE horizontal twin barrel carburettors.

TRANSMISSION gearbox: ZF mechanical; ratios: I 3.583, II 2.235, III 1.542, IV 1.154, V 0.967, rev 3.667; axle ratio: 3.400; tyres: (standard) Pirelli P6 185/60 HR x 14.

PERFORMANCE max speed: over 118 mph, 190 km/h; power-weight ratio: 16.1 lb/hp (21.8 lb/kW), 7.3 kg/hp (9.9 kg/kW); carrying capacity: 728 lb, 330 kg; acceleration: standing ¼ mile 15.8 sec; speed in top at 1,000 rpm: 19.8 mph, 31.8 km/h; consumption: 32.1 m/imp gal, 26.7 m/US gal, 8.8 l x 100 km at 75 mph, 120 km/h.

BRAKES front disc (diameter 9.57 in, 24.3 cm), internal radial fins; lining area: front 22 sq in, 142 sq cm, rear 33.3 sq in, 215 sq cm, total 55.3 sq in, 357 sq cm.

DIMENSIONS AND WEIGHT wheel base: 95.75 in, 243 cm; tracks: 57.28 in, 145 cm front, 55.91 in, 142 cm rear; height: 54.09 in, 137 cm; weight: 2,095 lb, 950 kg; weight distribution: 64.2% front, 35.8% rear; turning circle: 34.8 ft, 10.6 m.

PRACTICAL INSTRUCTIONS oil: engine 10 imp pt, 12 US pt, 5.7 l - gearbox and final drive 5.8 imp pt, 7 US pt, 3.3 l; spark plug: Marelli CW 78 LPR or Champion RN 7 Y; valve timing: 7° 52° 51° 8°; tyre pressure: front 28 psi, 2 atm, rear 29 psi, 2.1 atm.

Regata Series

PRICES EX WORKS:	liras
1 70 4-dr Berlina	**11,383,000****
2 70 Super 4-dr Berlina	**12,853,000****
3 ES 4-dr Berlina	**11,983,000****
4 85 Super 4-dr Berlina	**13,171,000****
5 100 Super 4-dr Berlina	**14,059,000****
6 DS 4-dr Berlina	**13,255,000****

Power team:	Standard for:	Optional for:
68 hp	1,2	—
65 hp (energy saving)	3	—
82 hp	4	—
100 hp	5	—
58 hp (diesel)	6	—

68 hp power team

ENGINE front, transverse, 4 stroke; 4 cylinders, in line; 79.4 cu in, 1,301 cc (3.40 x 2.19 in, 86.4 x 55.5 mm); compression ratio: 9.1:1; max power (DIN): 68 hp (50 kW) at 5,700 rpm; max torque (DIN): 74 lb ft, 10.2 kg m (100 Nm) at 2,900 rpm; max engine rpm: 6,100; 52.3 hp/l (38.5 kW/l); cast iron block, light alloy head; 5 crankshaft bearings; valves: overhead, in line, slanted at 18°, thimble tappets; camshafts: 1, overhead, cogged belt; lubrication: gear pump, full flow filter (cartridge), 7.7 imp pt, 9.3 US pt, 4.4 l; 1 Weber 30/32 DMTR 80/250 or Solex C 30/32 CIC-1 downdraught twin barrel carburettor; air cleaner: dry, thimble type thermostatic intake; fuel feed: mechanical pump; water-cooled, expansion tank, 12.1 imp pt, 14.6 US pt, 6.9 l, electric thermostatic fan.

TRANSMISSION driving wheels: front; clutch: single dry plate (diaphragm); gearbox: mechanical; gears: 5, fully synchronized; ratios: I 4.090, II 2.235, III 1.461, IV 1.034, V 0.827, rev 3.714; lever: central; final drive: helical cylindrical; axle ratio: 3.765; width of rims: 4.5" - Super 5.5"; tyres: 155 SR x 13 - Super 165/65 SR x 14.

PERFORMANCE max speed: over 96 mph, 155 km/h; power-weight ratio: 28.9 lb/hp (39.2 lb/kW), 12.7 kg/hp (17.8 kg/kW); carrying capacity: 882 lb, 400 kg; acceleration: standing ¼ mile 18.6 sec, 0-50 mph (0-80 km/h) 8.3 sec; speed in top at 1,000 rpm: 21 mph, 33.8 km/h; consumption: 39.8 m/imp gal, 33.1 m/US gal, 7.1 l x 100 km at 75 mph, 120 km/h.

CHASSIS integral; front suspension: independent, by McPherson, lower wishbones, trailing links, coil springs/telescopic damper struts; rear: independent, lower wishbones, transverse anti-roll leafsprings, telescopic dampers.

STEERING rack-and-pinion, adjustable height; turns lock to lock: 4.

BRAKES front disc (diameter 8.94 in, 22.7 cm), rear drum, dual circuit, rear compensator, servo; lining area: front 21.7 sq in, 140 sq cm, rear 33.3 sq in, 215 sq cm, total 55 sq in, 355 sq cm.

ELECTRICAL EQUIPMENT 12 V; 40 Ah battery; 55 A alternator; Marelli distributor; 2 headlamps.

DIMENSIONS AND WEIGHT wheel base: 96.38 in, 245 cm; tracks: 55.31 in, 140 cm front - Super 55.67 in, 141 cm, 55.59 in, 141 cm rear; length: 167.72 in, 426 cm; width: 64.96 in, 165 cm; height: 55.59 in, 141 cm; weight: 1,962 lb, 890 kg; weight distribution: 59.5% front, 40.5% rear; turning circle: 33.8 ft, 10.3 m; fuel tank: 12.1 imp gal, 14.5 US gal, 55 l.

BODY saloon/sedan; 4 doors; 5 seats, separate front seats; (for Super only) check control, electric windows and central door locking.

PRACTICAL INSTRUCTIONS fuel: 97 oct petrol; oil: engine 7.7 imp pt, 9.3 US pt, 4.4 l, SAE 10W-50, change every 6,200 miles, 10,000 km - gearbox and final drive 5.8 imp pt, 7 US pt, 3.3 l, SAE 80, change every 18,600 miles, 30,000 km; greasing: none; spark plug: Marelli CW 7 LPR or Champion RN 9 Y; valve timing: 7° 35° 37° 5°; tyre pressure: front 27 psi, 1.9 atm, rear 26 psi, 1.8 atm.

OPTIONALS (for Berlina only) headrests; tinted glass; metallic spray.

65 hp (energy saving) power team

See 68 hp power team, except for:

ENGINE compression ratio: 9.6:1; max power (DIN): 65 hp (48 kW) at 5,800 rpm; 50 hp/l (36.9 kW/l); 1 Weber 30/32 DMTE 1/250 downdraught twin barrel carburettor with fuel cut-off system.

PERFORMANCE power-weight ratio: 30.2 lb/hp (40.9 lb/kW), 13.7 kg/hp (18.5 kg/kW); consumption: 40.4 m/imp gal, 33.6 m/US gal, 7 l x 100 km at 75 mph, 120 km/h.

ELECTRICAL EQUIPMENT 55 Ah battery; 65 A alternator; Marelli Digiplex electronic ignition.

BODY rear spoiler.

PRACTICAL INSTRUCTIONS valve timing: 9° 31° 39° 1°.

82 hp power team

See 68 hp power team, except for:

ENGINE 91.4 cu in, 1,498 cc (3.40 x 2.52 in, 86.4 x 63.9 mm); compression ratio: 9.2:1; max power (DIN): 82 hp (60 kW) at 5,600 rpm; max torque (DIN): 88 lb ft, 12.2 kg m (120 Nm) at 3,000 rpm; 54.7 hp/l (40.1 kW/l); 1 Weber 32/34 DMTR 81/250 or Solex 32/34 CIC-1 downdraught twin barrel carburettor; cooling: 12.3 imp pt, 14.8 US pt, 7 l.

TRANSMISSION axle ratio: 3.588; width of rims: 5.5"; tyres: 165/65 SR x 14.

PERFORMANCE max speed: over 102 mph, 165 km/h; power-weight ratio: 24.3 lb/hp (33.3 lb/kW), 11 kg/hp (15.1 kg/kW); speed in top at 1,000 rpm: 21.7 mph, 34.9 km/h; consumption: 38.2 m/imp gal, 31.8 m/US gal, 7.4 l x 100 km at 75 mph, 120 km/h.

CHASSIS front suspension: anti-roll bar.

DIMENSIONS AND WEIGHT weight: 1,996 lb, 905 kg.

PRACTICAL INSTRUCTIONS spark plug: Marelli CW 78 LPR or Champion RN 7 Y; valve timing: 6° 46° 47° 7°.

OPTIONALS VW automatic transmission with 3 ratios (I 2.550, II 1.450, III 1, rev 2.460), 3.565 axle ratio, max speed 99 mph, 160 km/h, consumption 31.7 m/imp gal, 26.4 m/US gal, 8.9 l x 100 km at 75 mph, 120 km/h; air conditioning.

100 hp power team

See 68 hp power team, except for:

ENGINE 96.7 cu in, 1,585 cc (3.31 x 2.81 in, 84 x 71.5 mm); compression ratio: 9.3:1; max power (DIN): 100 hp (73 kW) at 5,900 rpm; max torque (DIN): 99 lb ft, 13.6 kg m (133 Nm) at 3,800 rpm; max engine rpm: 6,500; 63.1 hp/l (46.1 kW/l); valves: overhead, Vee-slanted, thimble tappets; camshafts: 2, overhead, cogged belt; lubrication: 8.1 imp pt, 9.7 US pt, 4.6 l; 1 Weber 32/34 DMTR 92/250 downdraught twin barrel carburettor; cooling: 13.2 imp pt, 15.8 US pt, 7.5 l.

TRANSMISSION gearbox ratios: I 4.090, II 2.235, III 1.553, IV 1.163, V 0.960, rev 3.920; axle ratio: 3.210; width of rims: 5.5"; tyres: 165/65 SR x 14.

PERFORMANCE max speed: 112 mph, 180 km/h; power-weight ratio: 21.4 lb/hp (29.3 lb/kW), 9.7 kg/hp (13.3 kg/kW); acceleration: standing ¼ mile 17.4 sec, 0-50 mph (0-80 km/h) 7.1 sec; speed in top at 1,000 rpm: 20.9 mph, 33.7 km/h; consumption: 35.8 m/imp gal, 29.8 m/US gal, 7.9 l x 100 km at 75 mph, 120 km/h.

CHASSIS front suspension: anti-roll bar.

STEERING damper.

BRAKES front disc (diameter 10.12 in, 25.7 cm); lining area: front 22.3 sq in, 144 sq cm, rear 33.3 sq in, 215 sq cm, total 55.6 sq in, 359 sq cm.

ELECTRICAL EQUIPMENT Marelli Digiplex electronic ignition.

BODY check control.

DIMENSIONS AND WEIGHT weight: 2,139 lb, 970 kg; weight distribution: 61.8% front, 38.2% rear.

FIAT Regata ES Berlina

FIAT Regata 100 Super Berlina

FIAT Regata 100 Super Berlina

FIAT 131 Diesel Super 2500 Panorama

PRACTICAL INSTRUCTIONS oil: engine 8.1 imp pt, 9.7 US pt, 4.6 l - gearbox and final drive 5.1 imp pt, 6.1 US pt, 2.9 l; valve timing: 10° 48° 53° 5°; tyre pressure: front 32 psi, 2.2 atm, rear 32 psi, 2.2 atm.

OPTIONALS power steering; air-conditioning; headlamps with wiper-washer; sunroof; trip computer; folding rear seat.

58 hp (diesel) power team

See 68 hp power team, except for:

ENGINE diesel; 104.6 cu in, 1,714 cc (3.27 x 3.12 in, 83 x 79.2 mm); compression ratio: 20.5:1; max power (DIN): 58 hp (43 kW) at 4,500 rpm; max torque (DIN): 76 lb ft, 10.5 kg (103 Nm) at 3,000 rpm; 33.8 hp/l (25.1 kW/l); Bosch VE 4/9F 2300/R 54 injection pump; cooling: 13.2 imp pt, 15.9 US pt, 7.5 l, 2 electric thermostatic fans.

TRANSMISSION gearbox ratios: I 4.090, II 2.235, III 1.461, IV 1.034, V 0.863, rev 3.714.

PERFORMANCE max speed: 93 mph, 150 km/h; power-weight ratio: 37.3 lb/hp (50.3 lb/kW), 16.9 kg/hp (22.8 kg/kW); speed in top at 1,000 rpm: 20.1 mph, 32.4 km/h; consumption: 38.7 m/imp gal, 32.2 m/US gal, 7.3 l x 100 km at 75 mph, 120 km/h.

CHASSIS front suspension: anti-roll bar.

ELECTRICAL EQUIPMENT 66 Ah battery.

DIMENSIONS AND WEIGHT weight: 2,161 lb, 980 kg; weight distribution: front 62.7%, rear 37.3%.

PRACTICAL INSTRUCTIONS fuel: diesel; valve timing: 4° 40° 45° 5°.

131 Series

PRICES EX WORKS:	liras
1 CL 1300 4+1-dr Panorama	12,085,000**
2 Super 2000 4+1-dr Panorama	14,725,000**
3 Diesel CL 2000 4+1-dr Panorama	14,179,000**
4 Diesel Super 2500 4+1-dr Panorama	16,099,000**

Power team:	Standard for:	Optional for:
70 hp	1	—
113 hp	2	—
60 hp (diesel)	3	—
72 hp (diesel)	4	—

70 hp power team

ENGINE front, 4 stroke; 4 cylinders, vertical, in line; 83.4 cu in, 1,367 cc (3.07 x 2.81 in, 78 x 71.5 mm); compression ratio: 9:1; max power (DIN): 70 hp (51 kW) at 5,500 rpm; max torque (DIN): 80 lb ft, 11 kg m (108 Nm) at 3,000 rpm; 51.2 hp/l (37.3 kW/l); cast iron block, light alloy head; 5 crankshaft bearings; valves: overhead, in line, slanted at 6°, rockers; camshafts: 1, overhead, cogged belt; lubrication: gear pump, full flow filter (cartridge), 7.6 imp pt, 9.1 US pt, 4.3 l; 1 Weber 32 ADF 51/250 or Solex C32 TEIE/7 downdraught twin barrel carburettor; fuel feed: mechanical pump; water-cooled, expansion tank, 13.4 imp pt, 16.1 US pt, 7.6 l, electric thermostatic fan.

TRANSMISSION driving wheels: rear; clutch: single dry plate (diaphragm); gearbox: mechanical; gears: 4, fully synchronized; ratios: I 3.612, II 2.045, III 1.357, IV 1, rev 3.244; lever: central; final drive: hypoid bevel; axle ratio: 4.100; width of rims: 5"; tyres: 165 SR x 13.

PERFORMANCE max speed: 93 mph, 150 km/h; power-weight ratio: 33.1 lb/hp (45.4 lb/kW), 15 kg/hp (20.6 kg/kW); carrying capacity: 948 lb, 430 kg; acceleration: standing ¼ mile 19.1 sec; speed in direct drive at 1,000 rpm: 16.4 mph, 26.4 km/h; consumption: 31.7 m/imp gal, 26.4 m/US gal, 8.9 l x 100 km at 75 mph, 120 km/h.

CHASSIS integral; front suspension: independent, by McPherson, coil springs/telescopic damper struts, lower wishbones, anti-roll bar; rear: rigid axle, twin trailing lower radius arms, transverse linkage bar, coil springs, telescopic dampers.

STEERING rack-and-pinion, adjustable height; turns lock to lock: 3.50.

BRAKES front disc (diameter 8.94 in, 22.7 cm), rear drum, dual circuit, rear compensator, servo; lining area: 19.2 sq in, 124 sq cm, rear 41.9 sq in, 270 sq cm, total 61.1 sq in, 394 sq cm.

ELECTRICAL EQUIPMENT 12 V; 45 Ah battery; 45 A alternator; Marelli distributor; 2 headlamps.

DIMENSIONS AND WEIGHT wheel base: 98.03 in, 249 cm; tracks: 54.57 in, 139 cm front, 52.24 in, 133 cm rear; length: 167.72 in, 426 cm; width: 64.96 in, 165 cm; height: 56.14 in, 143 cm; weight: 2,315 lb, 1,050 kg; turning circle: 34 ft, 10.3 m; fuel tank: 11.7 imp gal, 14 US gal, 53 l.

BODY estate car/st. wagon; 4+1 doors; 5 seats, separate front seats, reclining backrests; folding rear seat.

PRACTICAL INSTRUCTIONS fuel: 98-100 oct petrol; oil: engine 7 imp pt, 8.5 US pt, 4 l, SAE 10W-30 (winter) 20W-40 (summer), change every 6,200 miles, 10,000 km - gearbox 3.2 imp pt, 3.8 US pt, 1.8 l, SAE 90 EP, change every 18,600 miles, 30,000 km - final drive 1.8 imp pt, 2.1 US pt, 1 l, SAE 90 EP, change every 18,600 miles, 30,000 km; spark plug: Marelli CW 7 LP or Champion N 9 Y; valve timing: 2° 42° 42° 2°; tyre pressure: front 26 psi, 1.8 atm, rear 31 psi, 2.2 atm.

OPTIONALS 5-speed fully synchronized mechanical gearbox (I 3.612, II 2.045, III 1.357, IV 1, V 0.834, rev 3.244), consumption 31.7 m/imp gal, 26.4 m/US gal, 8.9 l x 100 km at 75 mph, 120 km/h; light alloy wheels; heated rear window; tinted glass with heated rear window; reclining backrests with built-in headrests; metallic spray; rear window wiper-washer.

113 hp power team

See 70 hp power team, except for:

ENGINE 121.7 cu in, 1,995 cc (3.31 x 3.54 in, 84 x 90 mm); max power (DIN): 113 hp (83 kW) at 5,600 rpm; max torque (DIN): 123 lb ft, 17 kg m (167 Nm) at 3,600 rpm; valves: overhead, Vee-slanted, thimble tappets; camshafts: 2, overhead, cogged belt; lubrication: 8.8 imp pt, 10.6 US pt, 5 l; 1 Weber 34 ADF 54/250 downdraught twin barrel carburettor; cooling: 14.4 imp pt, 17.3 US pt, 8.2 l.

TRANSMISSION (standard) gears: 5, fully synchronized; ratios: I 3.612, II 2.045, III 1.357, IV 1, V 0.834, rev 3.244; axle ratio: 3.583; tyres: 185/70 SR x 13 or 185/65 SR x 13.

PERFORMANCE max speed: 109 mph, 175 km/h; power-weight ratio: 21.6 lb/hp (29.3 lb/kW), 9.8 kg/hp (13.3 kg/kW); acceleration: standing ¼ mile 17 sec; speed in top at 1,000 rpm: 22.7 mph, 36.5 km/h; consumption: 28.8 m/imp gal, 24 m/US gal, 9.8 l x 100 km at 75 mph, 120 km/h.

STEERING servo.

ELECTRICAL EQUIPMENT 2 halogen headlamps.

DIMENSIONS AND WEIGHT length: 166.54 in, 423 cm; weight: 2,437 lb, 1,105 kg.

BODY built-in headrests on front and rear seats.

PRACTICAL INSTRUCTIONS valve timing: 5° 53° 53° 5°.

OPTIONALS sunroof; air-conditioning; metallic spray.

60 hp (diesel) power team

See 70 hp power team, except for:

ENGINE diesel; 121.7 cu in, 1,995 cc (3.46 x 3.23 in, 88 x 82 mm); compression ratio: 22:1; max power (DIN): 60 hp (44 kW) at 4,400 rpm; max torque (DIN): 83 lb ft, 11.5 kg m (113 Nm) at 2,400 rpm; 30.1 hp/l (22.1 kW/l); valves: overhead, rockers; lubrication: 11.6 imp pt, 13.9 US pt, 6.6 l; Bosch injection pump; sealed circuit cooling, liquid, expansion tank, 19.4 imp pt, 23.3 US pt, 11 l, electromagnetic thermostatic fan.

TRANSMISSION (standard) gears: 5, fully synchronized; ratios: I 3.612, II 2.045, III 1.357, IV 1, V 0.834, rev 3.244.

PERFORMANCE max speed: 87 mph, 140 km/h; power-weight ratio: 43.9 lb/hp (60 lb/kW), 19.9 kg/hp (27.2 kg/kW); acceleration: standing ¼ mile 21.5 sec; speed in top at 1,000 rpm: 19.8 mph, 31.9 km/h; consumption: 30.7 m/imp gal, 25.6 m/US gal, 9.2 l x 100 km at 75 mph, 120 km/h.

STEERING damper; turns lock to lock: 4.08.

ELECTRICAL EQUIPMENT 88 Ah battery; 55 A alternator; 4 iodine headlamps.

DIMENSIONS AND WEIGHT weight: 2,635 lb, 1,195 kg.

PRACTICAL INSTRUCTIONS fuel: diesel; oil: engine 9.7 imp pt, 11.6 US pt, 5.5 l; valve timing: 8° 48° 48° 8°; tyre pressure: front 30 psi, 2.1 atm, rear 28 psi, 2 atm.

72 hp (diesel) power team

See 70 hp power team, except for:

ENGINE diesel; 149.2 cu in, 2,445 cc (3.66 x 3.54 in, 93 x 90 mm); compression ratio: 22:1; max power (DIN): 72 hp (53 kW) at 4,200 rpm; max torque (DIN): 109 lb ft, 15 kg m (147 Nm) at 2,400 rpm; 29.4 hp/l (21.7 kW/l); valves: overhead, rockers; lubrication: 11.6 imp pt, 13.9 US pt, 6.6 l; Bosch injection pump; sealed circuit cooling, liquid, expansion tank, 19.4 imp pt, 23.3 US pt, 11 l, electromagnetic thermostatic fan.

TRANSMISSION (standard) gears: 5, fully synchronized; ratios: I 3.612, II 2.045, III 1.357, IV 1, V 0.834, rev 3.244; axle ratio: 3.583.

PERFORMANCE max speed: over 93 mph, 150 km/h; power-weight ratio: 37.3 lb/hp (50.7 lb/kW), 16.9 kg/hp (23 kg/kW); acceleration: standing ¼ mile 20.8 sec; consumption: 33.6 m/imp gal, 28 m/US gal, 8.4 l x 100 km at 75 mph, 120 km/h.

STEERING servo; turns lock to lock: 4.08.

ELECTRICAL EQUIPMENT 88 Ah battery; 55 A alternator; 4 iodine headlamps.

DIMENSIONS AND WEIGHT length: 166.54 in, 423 cm; weight: 2,690 lb, 1,220 kg.

BODY built-in headrests on front and rear seats.

PRACTICAL INSTRUCTIONS fuel: diesel; oil: engine 9.7 imp pt, 11.6 US pt, 5.5 l; valve timing: 8° 48° 48° 8°; tyre pressure: front 30 psi, 2.1 atm, rear 28 psi, 2 atm.

Argenta 100

PRICE EX WORKS: 13,921,000**

ENGINE front, 4 stroke; 4 cylinders, vertical, in line; 96.7 cu in, 1,585 cc (3.31 x 2.81 in, 84 x 71.5 mm); compression ratio: 9:1; max power (DIN): 98 hp (72 kW) at 6,000 rpm; max torque (DIN): 99 lb ft, 13.6 kg m (133 Nm) at 3,800 rpm; max engine rpm: 6,000; 61.8 hp/l (45.5 kW/l); cast iron block, light alloy head; 5 crankshaft bearings; valves: overhead, Vee-slanted, thimble tappets; camshafts: 2, overhead, cogged belt; lubrication: gear pump, full flow filter (cartridge), 8.3 imp pt, 9.9 US pt, 4.7 l; 1 Weber 32 ADF 64/250 or Solex C 32 TEIE 46(5) downdraught twin barrel carburettor; fuel feed: mechanical pump; water-cooled, expansion tank, 14.1 imp pt, 16.9 US pt, 8 l, electric thermostatic fan.

TRANSMISSION driving wheels: rear; clutch: single dry plate; gearbox: mechanical; gears: 5, fully synchronized; ratios: I 3.615, II 2.043, III 1.363, IV 1, V 0.838, rev 3.437; lever:

ARGENTA 100

central; final drive: hypoid bevel; axle ratio: 4.100; width of rims: 5.5"; tyres: 185/65 SR x 14.

PERFORMANCE max speeds: (I) 28 mph, 45 km/h; (II) 50 mph, 80 km/h; (III) 78 mph, 125 km/h; (IV) 103 mph, 165 km/h; (V) about 96 mph, 155 km/h; power-weight ratio: 25.7 lb/hp (34.9 lb/kW), 10.6 kg/hp (14.4 kg/kW); carrying capacity: 882 lb, 400 kg; acceleration: standing ¼ mile 18.2 sec; speed in direct drive at 1,000 rpm: 16.7 mph, 26.9 km/h; consumption: 30.1 m/imp gal, 25 m/US gal, 9.4 l x 100 km at 75 mph, 120 km/h.

CHASSIS integral; front suspension: independent, wishbones (lower trailing links), coil springs, anti-roll bar, telescopic dampers; rear: rigid axle, lower longitudinal trailing radius arms, upper oblique torque arms, coil springs, telescopic dampers.

STEERING recirculation ball, servo; turns lock to lock: 3.05.

BRAKES front disc (diameter 10.12 in, 25.7 cm), rear drum, rear compensator, dual circuit, servo; lining area: front 21.7 sq in, 140 sq cm, rear 41.9 sq in, 270 sq cm, total 63.6 sq in, 410 sq cm.

ELECTRICAL EQUIPMENT 12 V; 45 Ah battery; 45 A alternator; Marelli distributor; 2 headlamps.

DIMENSIONS AND WEIGHT wheel base: 100.67 in, 256 cm; tracks: 54.37 in, 138 cm front, 53.27 in, 135 cm rear; length: 174.57 in, 443 cm; width: 64.96 in, 165 cm; height: 56.50 in, 143 cm; ground clearance: 4.92 in, 12.5 cm; weight: 2,514 lb, 1,040 kg; weight distribution: 53% front, 47% rear; turning circle: 35.4 ft, 10.8 m; fuel tank: 13.2 imp gal, 15.8 US gal, 60 l.

BODY saloon/sedan; 4 doors; 5 seats, separate front seats, reclining backrests; check panel.

PRACTICAL INSTRUCTIONS fuel: 98-100 oct petrol; oil: engine 7.2 imp pt, 8.7 US pt, 4.1 l, SAE 30W (summer) 20W (winter), change every 6,200 miles, 10,000 km - gearbox 3.2 imp pt, 3.8 US pt, 1.8 l, FIAT ZC 90, change every 18,600 miles, 30,000 km - final drive 2.3 imp pt, 2.7 US pt, 1.3 l, FIAT W90/M, change every 18,600 miles, 30,000 km; greasing: every 18,600 miles, 30,000 km, 4 points; spark plug: Marelli CW 7 LP or Champion N 9 Y; tappet clearances: inlet 0.018 in, 0.45 mm, exhaust 0.024 in, 0.60 mm; valve timing: 5° 53° 53° 5°; tyre pressure: front 27 psi, 1.9 atm, rear 28 psi, 2 atm.

OPTIONALS GM automatic transmission, hydraulic torque converter and planetary gears with 3 ratios (I 2.400, II 1.480, III 1, rev 1.920), 3.727 axle ratio, max speed 99 mph, 160 km/h, consumption 25.4 m/imp gal, 21.2 m/US gal, 11.1 l x 100 km at 75 mph, 120 km/h; electric windows; tinted glass; central door locking; metallic spray.

Argenta 120 IE

See Argenta 100, except for:

PRICE IN GB: £ 6,810*
PRICE EX WORKS: 17,053,000 liras**

ENGINE 121.7 cu in, 1,995 cc (3.31 x 3.54 in, 84 x 90 mm); max power (DIN): 122 hp (90 kW) at 5,300 rpm; max torque (DIN): 127 lb ft, 17.5 kg m (172 Nm) at 3,500 rpm; max engine rpm: 5,800; 61.2 hp/l (45.1 kW/l); Bosch LE-Jetronic injection with fuel cut-off system; fuel feed: electric pump.

TRANSMISSION axle ratio: 3.727.

PERFORMANCE max speed: 109 mph, 175 km/h; power-weight ratio: 21.5 lb/hp (29.2 lb/kW), 9.8 kg/hp (13.2 kg/kW); acceleration: standing ¼ mile 17.2 sec; consumption: 31.4 m/imp gal, 26.1 m/US gal, 9 l x 100 km at 75 mph, 120 km/h.

ELECTRICAL EQUIPMENT electronic ignition.

DIMENSIONS AND WEIGHT weight: 2,624 lb, 1,190 kg.

BODY electric windows, check panel and central door locking (standard).

PRACTICAL INSTRUCTIONS valve timing: 15° 55° 57° 13°.

VARIATIONS

(for export only)
ENGINE max power (DIN) 113 hp (83 kW) at 5,600 rpm, max torque (DIN) 123 lb ft, 17 kg m (167 Nm) at 3,700 rpm, 56.6 hp/l (41.6 kW/l), 1 Weber 34 ADF 54/250 downdraught twin barrel carburettor.
PERFORMANCE max speed 106 mph, 170 km/h.

OPTIONALS GM automatic transmission, hydraulic torque converter and planetary gears with 3 ratios (I 2.400, II 1.480, III 1, rev 1.920), 3.417 axle ratio, max speed 106 mph, 170 km/h, acceleration standing ¼ mile 18.8 sec, consumption 27.4 m/imp gal, 22.8 m/US gal, 10.3 l x 100 km at 75 mph, 120 km/h; light alloy wheels with 185/65 HR x 14 P6 tyres; tinted glass; air-conditioning; sunroof; metallic spray.

Argenta Diesel

See Argenta 100, except for:

PRICE EX WORKS: 15,366,000 liras**

ENGINE diesel; 149.2 cu in, 2,445 cc (3.66 x 3.54 in, 93 x 90 mm); compression ratio: 22:1; max power (DIN): 72 hp (53 kW) at 4,200 rpm; max torque (DIN): 109 lb ft, 15 kg m (147 Nm) at 2,400 rpm; 29.4 hp/l (21.7 kW/l); valves: overhead, in line; camshafts: 1, overhead, cogged belt; lubrication: 11.6 imp pt, 13.9 US pt, 6.6 l; Bosch VER 87 or CAV DPA 3342 F 890 injection pump; sealed circuit cooling, liquid, 19.4 imp pt, 23.3 US pt, 11 l, electromagnetic thermostatic fan.

TRANSMISSION axle ratio: 3.727.

PERFORMANCE max speed: 93 mph, 150 km/h; power-weight ratio: 40.6 lb/hp (53.5 lb/kW), 17.8 kg/hp (24.2 kg/kW); acceleration: standing ¼ mile 20.5 sec; speed in direct drive at 1,000 rpm: 18.4 mph, 29.6 km/h; consumption: 31 m/imp gal, 25.8 m/US gal, 9.1 l x 100 km at 75 mph, 120 km/h.

ELECTRICAL EQUIPMENT 88 Ah battery; 55 A alternator.

DIMENSIONS AND WEIGHT weight: 2,833 lb, 1,285 kg; weight distribution: 58.8% front, 41.2% rear.

PRACTICAL INSTRUCTIONS fuel: diesel; oil: engine 9.7 imp pt, 11.6 US pt, 5.5 l; valve timing: 8° 37° 48° 8°; tyre pressure: front 31 psi, 2.2 atm, rear 30 psi, 2.1 atm.

OPTIONALS air-conditioning; check control; central door locking.

Argenta Turbo Diesel

See Argenta 100, except for:

PRICE EX WORKS: 18,823,000 liras**

ENGINE diesel, turbocharged; 149.2 cu in, 2,445 cc (3.66 x 3.54 in, 93 x 90 mm); compression ratio: 22:1; max power (DIN): 90 hp (66 kW) at 4,100 rpm; max torque (DIN): 145 lb ft, 20 kg m (196 Nm) at 2,400 rpm; 36.8 hp/l (27 kW/l); valves: overhead, in line; camshafts: 1, overhead, cogged belt; lubrication: 11.6 imp pt, 13.9 US pt, 6.6 l; water-oil heater exchanger; Bosch VER 124 injection pump and 1 KKK turbocharger with exhaust gas recirculation; sealed circuit cooling, liquid, 19.4 imp pt, 23.3 US pt, 11 l, electromagnetic thermostatic fan.

TRANSMISSION axle ratio: 3.154.

PERFORMANCE max speed: 99 mph, 160 km/h; power-weight ratio: 32 lb/hp (43.6 lb/kW), 14.5 kg/hp (19.8 kg/kW); acceleration: standing ¼ mile 18 sec; speed in direct drive at 1,000 rpm: 21.5 mph, 34.6 km/h; consumption: 33.2 m/imp gal, 27.7 m/US gal, 8.5 l x 100 km at 75 mph, 120 km/h.

CHASSIS rear suspension: anti-roll bar.

BRAKES disc.

ELECTRICAL EQUIPMENT 88 Ah battery; 55 A alternator.

DIMENSIONS AND WEIGHT weight: 2,878 lb, 1,305 kg; weight distribution: 58.8% front, 41.2% rear.

PRACTICAL INSTRUCTIONS fuel: diesel; oil: engine 9.7 imp pt, 11.6 US pt, 5.5 l; valve timing: 8° 37° 48° 8°.

OPTIONALS light alloy wheels with 185/65 HR x 14 P6 tyres.

Campagnola

PRICE EX WORKS: 21,325,000 liras**

ENGINE front, 4 stroke; 4 cylinders, vertical, in line; 121.7 cu in, 1,995 cc (3.31 x 3.54 in, 84 x 90 mm); compression ratio: 8.6:1; max power (DIN): 80 hp (59 kW) at 4,600 rpm; max torque (DIN): 112 lb ft, 15.4 kg m (151 Nm) at 2,800 rpm; 40.1 hp/l (29.5 kW/l); cast iron block, light alloy head; 5 crankshaft bearings; valves: overhead, slanted at 10°, push-rods and rockers; camshafts: 1, side, cogged belt; lubrication: gear pump, full flow filter (cartridge), 8.4 imp pt, 10.1 US pt, 4.8 l; 1 Solex C 32 PHHE 1 RM horizontal twin barrel carburettor; fuel feed: mechanical pump; water-cooled, 15.7 imp pt, 18.8 US pt, 8.9 l.

TRANSMISSION driving wheels: front and rear; clutch: single dry plate; gearbox: mechanical, in unit with engine; gears: 5, fully synchronized; high ratios: I 3.612, II 2.045, III 1.357, IV 1, V 0.870, rev 3.244; low ratios: 1.100 and 3.870; gear and transfer levers: central; final drive: hypoid bevel, rear limited slip; front and rear axle ratio: 5.375; width of rims: 4.5" K; tyres: 7.00 x 16 C 6PR.

PERFORMANCE max speeds (high ratios): (I) 20 mph, 33 km/h; (II) 35 mph, 57 km/h; (III) 55 mph, 88 km/h; (IV) 71 mph, 115 km/h; (V) over 75 mph, 120 km/h - max speeds (low ratios): (I) 7 mph, 11 km/h; (II) 12 mph, 19 km/h; (III) 18 mph, 29 km/h; (IV) 25 mph, 40 km/h; (V) 31 mph, 50 km/h; power-weight ratio: 44.3 lb/hp (60.2 lb/kW), 20.1 kg/hp (27.3 kg/kW); carrying

FIAT Argenta 120 IE

FIAT Argenta Diesel

FIAT Campagnola Diesel Lunga

capacity: 1,103 lb, 500 kg; speed in direct drive at 1,000 rpm: 14 mph, 22.5 km/h; consumption: 20.8 m/imp gal, 17.3 m/US gal, 13.6 l x 100 km (DIN).

CHASSIS integral; front suspension: independent, by McPherson, coil springs/telescopic damper struts, lower wishbones, torsion bars, anti-roll bar; rear: independent, by McPherson, coil springs, 4 telescopic dampers, lower wishbones, torsion bars, anti-roll bar.

STEERING worm and roller; turns lock to lock: 4.60.

BRAKES drum, dual circuit; swept area: front 91.5 sq in, 590 sq cm, rear 91.5 sq in, 590 sq cm, total 183 sq in, 1,180 sq cm.

ELECTRICAL EQUIPMENT 12 V; 55 Ah battery; 55 A alternator; Marelli distributor; 2 headlamps.

DIMENSIONS AND WEIGHT wheel base: 90.55 in, 230 cm; tracks: 53.54 in, 136 cm front, 55.91 in, 142 cm rear; length: 148.42 in, 377 cm; width: 62.20 in, 158 cm; height: 76.77 in, 195 cm; ground clearance: 10.16 in, 25.8 cm; weight: 3,550 lb, 1,610 kg; turning circle: 35.4 ft, 10.8 m; fuel tank: 12.5 imp gal, 15 US gal, 57 l.

BODY open; 2 doors; 7 seats, separate front seats.

PRACTICAL INSTRUCTIONS fuel: 99 oct petrol; oil: engine 7.4 imp pt, 8.9 US pt, 4.2 l, SAE 10W-40, change every 3,100 miles, 5,000 km - gearbox 2.5 imp pt, 3 US pt, 1.4 l, SAE 90 EP, change every 12,400 miles, 20,000 km - transfer box 3.9 imp pt, 4.7 US pt, 2.2 l, SAE 90 EP, change every 12,400 miles, 20,000 km - final drive 3.2 imp pt, 3.8 US pt, 1.8 l front, 3.2 imp pt, 3.8 US pt, 1.8 l rear, SAE 90 EP, change every 12,400 miles, 20,000 km; valve timing: 10° 49° 50° 9°; tyre pressure: front 26 psi, 1.8 atm, rear 36 psi, 2.5 atm.

OPTIONALS hardtop; front limited slip final drive; 7.50 x 16 C 6 PR tyres; power steering.

Campagnola Lunga

See Campagnola, except for:

PRICE EX WORKS: 21,877,000 liras**

TRANSMISSION front and rear axle ratio: 5.625; width of rims: 5" K or 5" F.

PERFORMANCE max speeds (high ratios): (I) 19 mph, 31 km/h; (II) 34 mph, 54 km/h; (III) 52 mph, 84 km/h; (IV) 68 mph, 110 km/h; (V) 71 mph, 115 km/h - max speeds (low ratios): (I) 6 mph, 10 km/h; (II) 11 mph, 18 km/h; (III) 17 mph, 28 km/h; (IV) 24 mph, 38 km/h; (V) 28 mph, 45 km/h; power-weight ratio: 46.8 lb/hp (63.6 lb/kW), 21.3 kg/hp (28.9 kg/kW); carrying capacity: 1,433 lb, 650 kg.

DIMENSIONS AND WEIGHT length: 158.46 in, 403 cm; weight: 3,748 lb, 1,700 kg.

Campagnola Diesel

See Campagnola, except for:

PRICE EX WORKS: 25,165,000 liras**

ENGINE diesel; 149.2 cu in, 2,445 cc (3.66 x 3.54 in, 93 x 90 mm); compression ratio: 22:1; max power (DIN): 72 hp (53 kW) at 4,200 rpm; max torque (DIN): 109 lb ft, 15 kg m (147 Nm) at 2,400 rpm; 29.4 hp/l (21.7 kW/l); valves: overhead, in line; camshafts: 1, overhead, cogged belt; lubrication: 11.6 imp pt, 13.9 US pt, 6.6 l; Bosch or CAV injection pump; sealed circuit cooling, liquid, expansion tank, 16.9 imp pt, 20.3 US pt, 9.6 l, electromagnetic thermostatic fan.

PERFORMANCE max speed: 71 mph, 115 km/h; power-weight ratio: 53.9 lb/hp (73.2 lb/kW), 24.4 kg/hp (33.2 kg/kW); carrying capacity: 1,654 lb, 750 kg; consumption: 22.4 m/imp gal, 18.7 m/US gal, 12.6 l x 100 km (DIN).

STEERING recirculating ball, servo (standard).

ELECTRICAL EQUIPMENT 88 Ah battery.

DIMENSIONS AND WEIGHT weight: 3,881 lb, 1,760 kg.

Campagnola Diesel Lunga

See Campagnola, except for:

PRICE EX WORKS: 25,777,000 liras**

ENGINE diesel; 149.2 cu in, 2,445 cc (3.66 x 3.54 in, 93 x 90 mm); compression ratio: 22:1; max power (DIN): 72 hp (53 kW) at 4,200 rpm; max torque (DIN): 109 lb ft, 15 kg m (147 Nm) at 2,400 rpm; 29.4 hp/l (21.7 kW/l); valves: overhead, in line; camshafts: 1, overhead, cogged belt; lubrication: 11.6 imp pt, 13.9 US pt, 6.6 l; Bosch or CAV injection pump; sealed circuit cooling, liquid, expansion tank, 16.9 imp pt, 20.3 US pt, 9.6 l, electromagnetic thermostatic fan.

TRANSMISSION front and rear axle ratio: 5.625; width of rims: 5" K or 5" F.

PERFORMANCE max speed: 68 mph, 110 km/h; power-weight ratio: 56 lb/hp (76.1 lb/kW), 25.4 kg/hp (34.5 kg/kW).

STEERING recirculating ball, servo (standard).

ELECTRICAL EQUIPMENT 88 Ah battery.

DIMENSIONS AND WEIGHT height: 158.46 in, 403 cm; weight: 4,035 lb, 1,830 kg.

GIANNINI ITALY

Fiat Giannini 126 Series

PRICES EX WORKS:	liras
1 GP Base 2-dr Berlina	**5,280,000***
2 GP Personal 2-dr Berlina	**5,680,000***
3 GPS Base 2-dr Berlina	**5,670,000***
4 GPS Personal 2-dr Berlina	**6,010,000***

Power team:	Standard for:	Optional for:
30 hp	1,2	—
34 hp	3,4	—
37 hp	3,4	—

30 hp power team

ENGINE rear, 4 stroke; 2 cylinders, vertical, in line; 39.8 cu in, 652 cc (3.03 x 2.76 in, 77 x 70 mm); compression ratio: 8.7:1; max power (DIN): 30 hp (22 kW) at 5,000 rpm; max torque (DIN): 35 lb ft, 4.8 kg m at 3,500 rpm; max engine rpm: 5,300; 46 hp/l (33.7 kW/l); light alloy block and head; 2 crankshaft bearings; valves: overhead, in line, push-rods and rockers; camshafts: 1, side; lubrication: gear pump, centrifugal filter, 6.2 imp pt, 7.4 US pt, 3.5 l; 1 Weber 28 IMB downdraught carburettor; fuel feed: mechanical pump; air-cooled.

TRANSMISSION driving wheels: rear; clutch: single dry plate; gearbox: mechanical; gears: 4, II, III and IV silent claw coupling; ratios: I 3.250, II 2.067, III 1.300, IV 0.872, rev 4.024; lever: central; final drive: spiral bevel; axle ratio: 4.875; width of rims: 4"; tyres: 135 SR x 12.

PERFORMANCE max speed: 75 mph, 120 km/h; power-weight ratio: 43 lb/hp (58.6 lb/kW), 19.5 kg/hp (26.6 kg/kW); carrying capacity: 706 lb, 320 kg; speed in top at 1,000 rpm: 14.3 mph, 23 km/h; consumption: 56.5 m/imp gal, 47 m/US gal, 5 l x 100 km.

CHASSIS integral; front suspension: independent, wishbones, transverse leafspring lower arms, telescopic dampers; rear: independent, oblique semi-trailing arms, coil springs, telescopic dampers.

STEERING screw and sector; turns lock to lock: 2.90.

BRAKES drum; lining area: front 33.5 sq in, 216 sq cm, rear 33.5 sq in, 216 sq cm, total 67 sq in, 432 sq cm.

ELECTRICAL EQUIPMENT 12 V; 34 Ah battery; 230 W alternator; Marelli distributor; 2 headlamps.

DIMENSIONS AND WEIGHT wheel base: 72.44 in, 184 cm; tracks: 44.96 in, 114 cm front, 47.36 in, 120 cm rear; length: 120.24 in, 305 cm; width: 54.21 in, 138 cm; height: 52.56 in, 133 cm; ground clearance: 5.51 in, 14 cm; weight: 1,290 lb, 585 kg; weight distribution: 40% front, 60% rear; turning circle: 28.2 ft, 8.6 m; fuel tank: 4.6 imp gal, 5.5 US gal, 21 l.

BODY saloon/sedan; 2 doors; 4 seats, separate front seats.

PRACTICAL INSTRUCTIONS fuel: 98-100 oct petrol; oil: engine 6.2 imp pt, 7.4 US pt, 3.5 l, SAE 20W-50, change every 3,700 miles, 6,000 km - gearbox and final drive 1.9 imp pt, 2.3 US pt, 1.1 l, Fiat ZC 90, change every 18,600 miles, 30,000 km; greasing: every 3,100 miles, 5,000 km, 2 points; spark plug: 240°; tappet clearances: inlet 0.008 in, 0.20 mm, exhaust 0.010 in, 0.25 mm; valve timing: 28° 72° 66° 32°; tyre pressure: front 22 psi, 1.4 atm, rear 28 psi, 2 atm.

OPTIONALS headrests; light alloy wheels; electronic injection; sunroof; roll-bar; horizontal twin barrel carburettor; front spoiler; special versions.

GIANNINI 126 GP Personal Berlina

34 hp power team

See 30 hp power team, except for:

ENGINE 42.3 cu in, 694 cc (3.13 x 2.76 in, 79.5 x 70 mm); compression ratio: 8.5:1; max power (DIN): 34 hp (25 kW) at 5,400 rpm; max torque (DIN): 37 lb ft, 5.1 kg m (50 Nm) at 3,500 rpm; max engine rpm: 5,800; 49 hp/l (36.1 kW/l).

PERFORMANCE max speed: about 81 mph, 130 km/h; power-weight ratio: 42.8 lb/hp (58.2 lb/kW), 19.4 kg/hp (26.4 kg/kW); consumption: 52.3 m/imp gal, 43.6 m/US gal, 5.4 l x 100 km.

DIMENSIONS AND WEIGHT weight: 1,455 lb, 660 kg.

37 hp power team

See 30 hp power team, except for:

ENGINE 42.3 cu in, 694 cc (3.13 x 2.76 in, 79.5 x 70 mm); compression ratio: 8.8:1; max power (DIN): 37 hp (27 kW) at 5,700 rpm; max torque (DIN): 41 lb ft, 5.7 kg m (56 Nm) at 3,500 rpm; max engine rpm: 6,000; 53.3 hp/l (39.2 kW/l); 1 Weber DMIS 32 horizontal twin barrel carburettor.

PERFORMANCE max speed: 87 mph, 140 km/h; power-weight ratio: 35.7 lb/hp (48.9 lb/kW), 16.2 kg/hp (22.2 kg/kW); consumption: 51.4 m/imp gal, 42.8 m/US gal, 5.5 l x 100 km.

DIMENSIONS AND WEIGHT weight: 1,323 lb, 600 kg.

Fiat Giannini Panda Series

PRICES EX WORKS:		liras
1	GT 30 2+1-dr Berlina	**6,990,000****
2	GT Super 2+1-dr Berlina	**7,470,000****
3	GTS 30 2+1-dr Berlina	**7,430,000****
4	GTS Super 2+1-dr Berlina	**7,890,000****
5	GT 45 2+1-dr Berlina	**7,890,000****

Power team:	Standard for:	Optional for:
36 hp	1,2	—
40 hp	3,4	—
58 hp	5	—

36 hp power team

ENGINE front, 4 stroke; 2 cylinders, vertical, in line; 39.8 cu in, 652 cc (3.03 x 2.76 in, 77 x 70 mm); compression ratio: 8.9:1; max power (DIN): 36 hp (26 kW) at 5,500 rpm; max torque (DIN): 36 lb ft, 4.9 kg m (48 Nm) at 4,800 rpm; max engine rpm: 6,000; 55.2 hp/l (39.9 kW/l); light alloy block and head; 2 crankshaft bearings; valves: overhead, in line, push-rods and rockers; camshafts: 1, side; lubrication: gear pump, centrifugal filter, 6.7 imp pt, 8 US pt, 3.5 l; 1 Weber 30 DG F1 downdraught twin barrel carburettor; fuel feed: mechanical pump; air-cooled.

TRANSMISSION driving wheels: front; clutch: single dry plate (diaphragm); gearbox: mechanical; gears: 4, II, III and IV synchronized; ratios: I 3.500, II 2.067, III 1.300, IV 0.872, rev 4.237; lever: central; final drive: hypoid bevel; axle ratio: 5.125; width of rims: 4"; tyres: 135 SR x 13.

PERFORMANCE max speed: 81 mph, 130 km/h; power-weight ratio: 39.9 lb/hp (55.1 lb/kW), 18.1 kg/hp (25 kg/kW); carrying capacity: 882 lb, 400 kg; consumption: 56.5 m/imp gal, 47 m/US gal, 5 l x 100 km.

CHASSIS integral; front suspension: independent, by McPherson, coil springs/telescopic damper struts, lower wishbones; rear: rigid axle, semi-elliptic leafsprings, telescopic dampers.

GIANNINI Panda GT 30 Berlina

STEERING rack-and-pinion; turns lock to lock: 3.40.

BRAKES front disc (diameter 8.94 in, 22.7 cm), rear drum, dual circuit, rear compensator; lining area: front 19.2 sq in, 124 sq cm, rear 32.4 sq in, 209 sq cm, total 51.6 sq in, 333 sq cm.

ELECTRICAL EQUIPMENT 12 V; 34 Ah battery; 45 A alternator; contactless Marelli distributor; 2 headlamps.

DIMENSIONS AND WEIGHT wheel base: 85.04 in, 216 cm; tracks: 49.37 in, 125 cm front, 49.17 in, 125 cm rear; length: 133.07 in, 338 cm; width: 57.48 in, 146 cm; height: 56.89 in, 144 cm; weight: 1,433 lb, 650 kg; weight distribution: 61% front, 39% rear; turning circle: 30.2 ft, 9.2 m; fuel tank: 7.7 imp gal, 9.2 US gal, 35 l.

BODY saloon/sedan; 2+1 doors; 5 seats, separate front seats; folding rear seat.

PRACTICAL INSTRUCTIONS fuel: 98 oct petrol; oil: engine 4.9 imp pt, 5.9 US pt, 2.8 l, SAE 20W (winter) 30W (summer), change every 6,200 miles, 10,000 km - gearbox and final drive 2.6 imp pt, 3.2 US pt, 1.5 l, SAE 90, change every 18,600 miles, 30,000 km; greasing: every 18,600 miles, 30,000 km, homokinetic joints; spark plug: Champion L 81 Y; tappet clearances: inlet 0.008 in, 0.20 mm, exhaust 0.010 in, 0.25 mm; valve timing: 21° 62° 61° 22°; tyre pressure: front 24 psi, 1.7 atm, rear 27 psi, 1.9 atm.

OPTIONALS sunroof; light alloy wheels; electric windows; electronic injection.

40 hp power team

See 36 hp power team, except for:

ENGINE 46.2 cu in, 757 cc (3.27 x 2.75 in, 83 x 70 mm); compression ratio: 8.7:1; max power (DIN): 40 hp (29 kW) at 5,500 rpm; max torque (DIN): 40 lb ft, 5.5 kg m (54 Nm) at 3,500 rpm; 52.8 hp/l (38.3 kW/l).

PERFORMANCE max speed: 87 mph, 140 km/h; power-weight ratio: 35.7 lb/hp (49.4 lb/kW), 16.2 kg/hp (22.4 kg/kW); consumption: 56.5 m/imp gal, 47 m/US gal, 5 l x 100 km.

GIANNINI Ritmo Turbo Diesel R

58 hp power team

See 36 hp power team, except for:

ENGINE front, transverse, 4 stroke; 4 cylinders, vertical, in line; 55.1 cu in, 903 cc (2.56 x 2.68 in, 65 x 68 mm); compression ratio: 9.6:1; max power (DIN): 58 hp (43 kW) at 6,500 rpm; max torque (DIN): 50 lb ft, 6.9 kg m (68 Nm) at 4,600 rpm; max engine rpm: 7,000; 64.2 hp/l (47.6 kW/l); cast iron block, light alloy head; 3 crankshaft bearings; lubrication: 6.9 imp pt, 8.2 US pt, 3.9 l; 1 Weber 30 DIC downdraught twin barrel carburettor; water-cooled, 9.2 imp pt, 11 US pt, 5.2 l.

TRANSMISSION gears: 4, fully synchronized; ratios: I 3.910, II 2.055, III 1.348, IV 0.963, rev 3.615; final drive: helical cylindrical; axle ratio: 4.462.

PERFORMANCE max speed: 96 mph, 155 km/h; power-weight ratio: 25.8 lb/hp (34.8 lb/kW), 11.7 kg/hp (15.8 kg/kW); consumption: 40.9 m/imp gal, 34.1 m/US gal, 6.9 l x 100 km.

DIMENSIONS AND WEIGHT weight: 1,499 lb, 680 kg; weight distribution: 49% front, 51% rear.

PRACTICAL INSTRUCTIONS oil: engine 6.9 imp pt, 8.2 US pt, 3.9 l, SAE 20W (winter) 30W (summer), change every 6,200 miles, 10,000 km - gearbox and final drive 4.2 imp pt, 5.1 US pt, 2.4 l, SAE 90, change every 18,600 miles, 30,000 km; spark plug: Champion L 9 Y; valve timing: 17° 43° 57° 3°.

Fiat Giannini Ritmo Veloce 60 R

PRICES EX WORKS:	liras
2+1-dr Berlina	**9,730,000***
4+1-dr Berlina	**10,690,000***

ENGINE front, transverse, 4 stroke; 4 cylinders, vertical, in line; 68.1 cu in, 1,116 cc (3.15 x 2.19 in, 80 x 55.5 mm); compression ratio: 9.6:1; max power (DIN): 73 hp (54 kW) at 6,600 rpm; max torque (DIN): 62 lb ft, 8.6 kg m (84 Nm) at 4,200 rpm; max engine rpm: 6,500; 65.4 hp/l (48.4 kW/l); cast iron block, light alloy head; 5 crankshaft bearings; valves: overhead, thimble tappets; camshafts: 1, overhead, cogged belt; lubrication: gear pump, full flow filter (cartridge), 5.8 imp pt, 7 US pt, 3.3 l; 1 Weber 32 ICEV downdraught single barrel carburettor; fuel feed: mechanical pump; water-cooled, 11.4 imp pt, 13.7 US pt, 6.5 l, electric thermostatic fan.

TRANSMISSION driving wheels: front; clutch: single dry plate; gearbox: mechanical; gears: 4, fully synchronized; ratios: I 3.583, II 2.235, III 1.454, IV 1.047, rev 3.714; lever: central; final drive: cylindrical gears; axle ratio: 4.077; width of rims: 4.5"; tyres: 145 SR x 13.

PERFORMANCE max speed: 99 mph, 160 km/h; power-weight ratio: 27.8 lb/hp (36.6 lb/kW), 12.3 kg/hp (16.6 kg/kW); carrying capacity: 882 lb, 400 kg; speed in top at 1,000 rpm: 15.1 mph, 24.3 km/h; consumption: 40.4 m/imp gal, 33.6 m/US gal, 7 l x 100 km.

CHASSIS integral; front suspension: independent, by McPherson, coil springs/telescopic damper struts, lower wishbones, anti-roll bar; rear: independent, single wide-based wishbones, transverse anti-roll leafsprings, telescopic dampers.

STEERING rack-and-pinion; turns lock to lock: 3.50.

BRAKES front disc (diameter 8.94 in, 22.7 cm), rear drum, dual circuit, rear compensator, servo; lining area: front 19.2 sq in, 124 sq cm, rear 33.5 sq in, 216 sq cm, total 52.7 sq in, 340 sq cm.

ELECTRICAL EQUIPMENT 12 V; 34 Ah battery; 230 W dynamo; Marelli distributor; 2 headlamps.

LAMBORGHINI Jalpa P 350

DIMENSIONS AND WEIGHT wheel base: 96.22 in, 244 cm; tracks: 55.47 in, 141 cm front, 55.67 in, 141 cm rear; length: 158.03 in, 401 cm; width: 65 in, 165 cm; height: 55.12 in, 140 cm; weight: 1,973 lb, 895 kg; weight distribution: 61.5% front, 38.5% rear; turning circle: 33.8 ft, 10.3 m; fuel tank: 12.1 imp gal, 14.5 US gal, 55 l.

BODY saloon/sedan; 4 doors; 5 seats, separate front seats, reclining backrests.

PRACTICAL INSTRUCTIONS fuel: 98 oct petrol; oil: engine 5.8 imp pt, 7 US pt, 3.3 l, SAE 20W (winter) 30 (summer), change every 6,200 miles, 10,000 km - gearbox and final drive 5.5 imp pt, 6.6 US pt, 3.1 l, SAE 90, change every 18,600 miles, 30,000 km; greasing: every 18,600 miles, 30,000 km; spark plug: 240°; tappet clearances: inlet 0.012 in, 0.30 mm, exhaust 0.016 in, 0.40 mm; valve timing: 12° 52° 52° 12°; tyre pressure: front 26 psi, 1.8 atm, rear 24 psi, 1.7 atm.

OPTIONALS 5-speed fully synchronized mechanical gearbox (V 0.863 ratio); light alloy wheels; iodine fog lamps; electronic injection; special instrument panel with electronic rev counter; front and rear spoiler; headrests; front electric windows; sunroof.

Fiat Giannini Ritmo Turbo Diesel R

PRICE EX WORKS: 14,850,000* liras

ENGINE diesel, turbocharged; front, transverse, 4 stroke; 4 cylinders, in line; 104.6 cu in, 1,714 cc (3.27 x 3.12 in, 83 x 79.2 mm); compression ratio: 20:1; max power (DIN): 77 hp (57 kW) at 4,500 rpm; max torque (DIN): 99 lb ft, 13.6 kg m (133 Nm) at 3,000 rpm; max engine rpm: 4,500; 44.9 hp/l (33.3 kW/l); cast iron block, light alloy head; 5 crankshaft bearings; valves: overhead, thimble tappets; camshafts: 1, overhead, cogged belt; lubrication: gear pump, cartridge filter, 8.3 imp pt, 9.9 US pt, 4.7 l; 1 IHI turbocharger; Bosch injection pump; fuel feed: mechanical pump; water-cooled, expansion tank, 15.7 imp pt, 18.8 US pt, 8.9 l, 2 electric thermostatic fans.

TRANSMISSION driving wheels: front; clutch: single dry plate; gearbox: mechanical; gears: 5, fully synchronized; ratios: I 4.091, II 2.235, III 1.461, IV 1.033, V 0.863, rev 3.714; lever: central; final drive: helical cylindrical; axle ratio: 3.400; width of rims: 4.5"; tyres: 155 SR x 13.

PERFORMANCE max speeds: (I) 25 mph, 40 km/h; (II) 40 mph, 65 km/h; (III) 59 mph, 95 km/h; (IV) 78 mph, 125 km/h; (V) 103 mph, 165 km/h; power-weight ratio: 28 lb/hp (37.9 lb/kW), 12.7 kg/hp (17.2 kg/kW); carrying capacity: 882 lb, 400 kg; consumption: 40.4 m/imp gal, 33.6 m/US gal, 7 l x 100 km.

CHASSIS integral; front suspension: independent, coil springs, anti-roll bar, telescopic dampers; rear: independent, anti-roll bar, telescopic dampers.

STEERING rack-and-pinion; turns lock to lock: 4.

BRAKES front disc, rear drum, servo.

ELECTRICAL EQUIPMENT 12 V; 65 Ah battery; 660 W dynamo; 4 headlamps.

DIMENSIONS AND WEIGHT wheel base: 96.22 in, 244 cm; tracks: 55.47 in, 141 cm front, 55.67 in, 141 cm rear; length: 158.03 in, 401 cm; width: 65 in, 165 cm; height: 55.12 in, 140 cm; weight: 2,161 lb, 980 kg; weight distribution: 62.5% front, 37.5% rear; turning circle: 33.8 ft, 10.3 m; fuel tank: 12.1 imp gal, 14.5 US gal, 55 l.

BODY saloon/sedan; 4+1 doors; 5 seats, separate front seats; folding rear seat.

PRACTICAL INSTRUCTIONS fuel: diesel; oil: engine 7.7 imp pt, 9.3 US pt, 4.4 l, SAE 10W-40, change every 6,200 miles, 10,000 km - gearbox and final drive 5.3 imp pt, 6.3 US pt, 3 l, SAE 80W-90, change every 18,600 miles, 30,000 km; valve timing: 4° 40° 45° 5°; tyre pressure: front 27 psi, 1.9 atm, rear 26 psi, 1.8 atm.

OPTIONALS light alloy wheels; iodine fog lamps; electronic injection; special instrument panel with electronic rev counter; front and rear spoilers; headrests; front electric windows; sunroof.

LAMBORGHINI ITALY

Jalpa P 350

PRICE IN GB: £ 26,000*
PRICE EX WORKS: 65,000,000* liras

ENGINE centre-rear, transverse, 4 stroke; 8 cylinders in Vee; 212.7 cu in, 3,485 cc (3.39 x 2.95 in, 86 x 75 mm); compression ratio: 9.2:1; max power (DIN): 255 hp (188 kW) at 7,000 rpm; max torque (DIN): 232 lb ft, 32 kg m (314 Nm) at 3,500 rpm; max engine rpm: 7,400; 73.2 hp/l (53.9 kW/l); light alloy block and head, wet liners; 5 crankshaft bearings; valves: overhead, in line, thimble tappets; camshafts: 2, 1 per bank, cogged belt; lubrication: gear pump, full flow filter (cartridge), 15.8 imp pt, 19 US pt, 9 l; 4 Weber 42 DCNF downdraught twin barrel carburettors; fuel feed: electric pump; water-cooled, 26.4 imp pt, 31.7 US pt, 15 l, 2 front fans, 1 electric and 1 thermostatic.

TRANSMISSION driving wheels: rear; clutch: single dry plate (diaphragm), hydraulically controlled; gearbox: mechanical; gears: 5, fully synchronized; ratios: I 2.800, II 2.105, III 1.478, IV 1.185, V 0.871, rev 2.190; lever: central; final drive: hypoid bevel; axle ratio: 4; width of rims: 7.5": tyres: Pirelli 205/55 VR x 16 P7 front, 225/50 VR x 16 P7 rear.

PERFORMANCE max speed: 154 mph, 248 km/h; max speeds at 7,000 rpm: (I) 45 mph, 73 km/h; (II) 60 mph, 97 km/h; (III) 86 mph, 138 km/h; (IV) 107 mph, 172 km/h; (V) 145 mph, 234 km/h; power-weight ratio: 13.1 lb/hp (17.7 lb/kW), 5.9 kg/hp (8 kg/kW); carrying capacity: 496 lb, 225 kg; speed in top at 1,000 rpm: 20.8 mph, 33.5 km/h; consumption: 20.2 m/imp gal, 16.8 m/US gal, 14 l x 100 km at 75 mph, 120 km/h.

CHASSIS integral, rear auxiliary frame; front suspension: independent, by McPherson, coil springs/telescopic damper struts, lower wishbones (trailing links), anti-roll bar; rear: independent, by McPherson, coil springs/telescopic damper struts, lower wishbones, anti-roll bar.

STEERING rack-and-pinion; turns lock to lock: 4.

BRAKES disc, internal radial fins, dual circuit, servo; lining area: front 38.9 sq in, 251 sq cm, rear 28.2 sq in, 182 sq cm, total 67.1 sq in, 433 sq cm.

ELECTRICAL EQUIPMENT 12 V; 55 Ah battery; 770 W alternator; electronic ignition; 4 headlamps, 2 retractable.

DIMENSIONS AND WEIGHT wheel base: 96.46 in, 245 cm; tracks: 59.06 in, 150 cm front, 61.18 in, 155 cm rear; length: 170.47 in, 433 cm; width: 74.02 in, 188 cm; height: 44.88 in, 114 cm; ground clearance: 5.51 in, 14 cm; weight: 3,330 lb, 1,510 kg; weight distribution: 41% front, 59% rear; turning circle: 36.1 ft, 11 m; fuel tank: 17.6 imp gal, 21.1 US gal, 80 l.

BODY spider; 2 doors; 2 seats; detachable roof.

PRACTICAL INSTRUCTIONS fuel: 97 oct petrol; oil: engine 15.8 imp pt, 19 US pt, 9 l, SAE 10W-50, change every 4,300 miles, 7,000 km - gearbox and final drive 6.2 imp pt, 7.4 US pt, 3.5 l, SAE 85W-90, change every 37,300 miles, 60,000 km; greasing: none; spark plug: Bosch W 235 P21; tappet clearances: inlet 0.012 in, 0.30 mm, exhaust 0.016 in, 0.40 mm; valve timing: 32° 60° 60° 32°; tyre pressure: front 36 psi, 2.5 atm, rear 36 psi, 2.5 atm.

OPTIONALS air-conditioning.

Countach LP 500 S

PRICE IN GB: £ 54,000*
PRICE EX WORKS: 125,000,000* liras

ENGINE centre-rear, longitudinal, 4 stroke; 12 cylinders, Vee-slanted at 60°; 290.1 cu in, 4,754 cc (3.37 x 2.72 in, 85.5 x 69 mm); compression ratio: 9.2:1; max power (DIN): 375 hp (276 kW) at 7,000 rpm; max torque (DIN): 303 lb ft, 41.8 kg m (410 Nm) at 4,500 rpm; max engine rpm: 7,000; 78.9 hp/l (58.1 kW/l); light alloy block and head, wet liners; 7 crankshaft bearings; valves: overhead, Vee-slanted at 70°, thimble tappets; camshafts: 4, 2 per bank, overhead, chain-driven; lubrication: gear pump, full flow filter, oil cooler, 30.8 imp pt, 37 US pt, 17.5 l; 6 Weber 45 DCOE horizontal twin barrel carburettors; fuel feed: 2 electric pumps; water-cooled, 29.9 imp pt, 35.9 US pt, 17 l, 2 radiators, 2 electric fans (1 thermostatic).

TRANSMISSION driving wheels: rear; clutch: single dry plate (diaphragm), hydraulically controlled; gearbox: mounted ahead of engine, mechanical; gears: 5, fully synchronized; ratios: I 2.232, II 1.625, III 1.086, IV 0.858, V 0.707, rev 1.960; lever: central; final drive: hypoid bevel, limited slip; axle ratio: 4.090; width of rims: 8.5" front, 12" rear; tyres: Pirelli P7 205/50 VR x 15 front, 345/35 VR x 15 rear.

PERFORMANCE max speeds: (I) 55 mph, 88 km/h; (II) 75 mph, 121 km/h; (III) 112 mph, 180 km/h; (IV) 143 mph, 230 km/h; (V) over 180 mph, 290 km/h; power-weight ratio: 8.7 lb/hp (11.8 lb/kW), 3.9 kg/hp (5.4 kg/kW); carrying capacity: 397 lb, 180 kg; speed in top at 1,000 rpm: 25.7 mph, 41.4 km/h; consumption: 11.8 m/imp gal, 9.8 m/US gal, 24 l x 100 km.

CHASSIS tubular; front suspension: independent, wishbones, coil springs, anti-roll bar, telescopic dampers; rear: independent, wishbones (trailing links), coil springs, anti-roll bar, 4 telescopic dampers.

STEERING rack-and-pinion; turns lock to lock: 3.

BRAKES disc (diameter 11.81 in, 30 cm front, 11.02 in, 28 cm rear), internal radial fins, dual circuit, rear compensator, servo;

LAMBORGHINI Countach LP 500 S

LAMBORGHINI LM-002

LM-004 / 7000

See LM-002, except for:

ENGINE 427.1 cu in, 7,000 cc; max power (DIN): 420 hp (309 kW) at 5,400 rpm; max torque (DIN): 435 lb ft, 60 kg m (589 Nm) at 3,500 rpm; max engine rpm: 6,400; 60 hp/l (44.1 kW/l).

TRANSMISSION gearbox: ZF S5-24/3 PKW mechanical; ratios: I 2.422, II 1.792, III 1.304, IV 1, V 0.746, rev 2.867; width of rims: 11''; tyres: 325/65 VR x17.

PERFORMANCE max speeds: (I) 40 mph, 64 km/h; (II) 53 mph, 86 km/h; (III) 73 mph, 118 km/h; (IV) 96 mph, 154 km/h; (V) 128 mph, 206 km/h; power-weight ratio: 14.2 lb/hp (19.3 lb/kW), 6.4 kg/hp (8.7 kg/kW).

BRAKES front disc, internal radial fins, rear drum.

ELECTRICAL EQUIPMENT 80 A alternator.

DIMENSIONS AND WEIGHT weight: 5,953 lb, 2,700 kg; fuel tank: 70 imp gal, 84 US gal, 320 l.

COUNTACH LP 500 S

lining area: front 27.9 sq in, 180 sq cm, rear 26.5 sq in, 171 sq cm, total 54.4 sq in, 351 sq cm.

ELECTRICAL EQUIPMENT 12 V; 72 Ah battery; 70 A alternator; electronic ignition; 4 iodine retractable headlamps.

DIMENSIONS AND WEIGHT wheel base: 96.46 in, 245 cm; tracks: 58.66 in, 149 cm front, 63.39 in, 161 cm rear; length: 162.99 in, 414 cm; width: 78.74 in, 200 cm; height: 42.13 in, 107 cm; ground clearance: 4.92 in, 12.5 cm; weight: 3,263 lb, 1,480 kg; weight distribution: 42% front axle, 58% rear axle; turning circle: 42.6 ft, 13 m; fuel tank: 26.4 imp gal, 31.7 US gal, 120 l (2 separate tanks).

BODY coupé; 2 doors; 2 seats; leather upholstery; tinted glass; heated rear window; light alloy wheels.

PRACTICAL INSTRUCTIONS fuel: 98-100 oct petrol; oil: engine 30.8 imp pt, 37 US pt, 17.5 l, SAE 20W-50, change every 3,100 miles, 5,000 km - gearbox 5.6 imp pt, 6.8 US pt, 3.2 l, SAE 90, change every 9,300 miles, 15,000 km - final drive 11.3 imp pt, 13.5 US pt, 6.4 l, SAE 90, change every 9,300 miles, 15,000 km; greasing: none; spark plug: 235°; tappet clearances: inlet 0.010 in, 0.25 mm, exhaust 0.010 in, 0.25 mm; valve timing: 42° 70° 64° 40°; tyre pressure: front 34 psi, 2.4 atm, rear 34 psi, 2.4 atm.

OPTIONALS right hand drive; air-conditioning.

LM-002

ENGINE front, 4 stroke; 12 cylinders, Vee-slanted at 60°; 290.1 cu in, 4,754 cc (3.37 x 2.72 in, 85.5 x 69 mm); compression ratio: 9:1; max power (DIN): 332 hp (244 kW) at 6,000 rpm; max torque (DIN): 315 lb ft, 43.5 kg m (427 Nm) at 4,500 rpm; max engine rpm: 7,000; 69.8 hp/l (51.3 kW/l); light alloy block and head, wet liners; 7 crankshaft bearings; valves: overhead, Vee-slanted, thimble tappets; camshafts: 4, 2 per bank, chain-driven; lubrication: gear pump, full flow filter, 30.8 imp pt, 37 US pt, 17.5 l; 6 Weber 45 DCOE horizontal twin barrel carburettors; fuel feed: electric pump; water-cooled, 29.9 imp pt, 35.9 US pt, 17 l, 2 electric thermostatic fans.

TRANSMISSION driving wheels: rear (automatically engaged with transfer box low ratio) and front; clutch: single dry plate (diaphragm), hydraulically controlled; gearbox: ZF S5-24/3 mechanical; gears: 5, fully synchronized and 2-ratio transfer box; ratios: I 2.990, II 1.900, III 1.330, IV 1, V 0.890, rev 2.700; gear and transfer levers: central; rear and front final drive: spiral bevel, limited slip; rear and front axle ratio: 4.125; width of rims: 9''; tyres: 14x16 LT.

PERFORMANCE max speeds: (I) 35 mph, 56 km/h; (II) 55 mph, 88 km/h; (III) 78 mph, 126 km/h; (IV) 104 mph, 167 km/h; (V) 117 mph, 188 km/h; power-weight ratio: 17.3 lb/hp (23.5 lb/kW), 7.8 kg/hp (10.7 kg/kW); carrying capacity: 2,205 lb, 1,000 kg; speed in direct drive at 1,000 rpm: 19.3 mph, 31 km/h; consumption: 14.1 m/imp gal, 11.8 m/US gal, 20 l x 100 km.

CHASSIS tubular; front suspension: independent, lower wishbones, coil springs, anti-roll bar, telescopic dampers; rear: independent, lower wishbones, coil springs, anti-roll bar, telescopic dampers.

STEERING rack-and-pinion, servo; turns lock to lock: 4.50.

BRAKES disc, internal radial fins, dual circuit, servo; lining area: front 38.8 sq in, 250 sq cm, rear 38.8 sq in, 250 sq cm, total 77.6 sq in, 500 sq cm.

ELECTRICAL EQUIPMENT 12 V; 90 Ah battery; 90 A alternator; electronic ignition; 2 headlamps.

DIMENSIONS AND WEIGHT wheel base: 118.11 in, 300 cm; front and rear track: 63.58 in, 161 cm; length: 192.91 in, 490 cm; width: 78.74 in, 200 cm; height: 72.83 in, 185 cm; ground clearance: 11.61 in, 29.5 cm; weight: 5,733 lb, 2,600 kg; weight distribution: 50% front, 50% rear; turning circle: 40 ft, 12.2 m; fuel tank: 61.6 imp gal, 73.9 US gal, 280 l.

BODY convertible, in plastic material; 4 doors; 4+4 seats, separate front seats; sunroof.

PRACTICAL INSTRUCTIONS fuel: 94 oct petrol; oil: engine 30.8 imp pt, 37 US pt, 17.5 l, SAE 10W-50, change every 4,300 miles, 7,000 km - gearbox 3.5 imp pt, 4.2 US pt, 2 l, SAE 90, change every 15,500 miles, 25,000 km - front and rear final drive 6.7 imp pt, 8 US pt, 3.8 l, SAE 90, change every 15,500 miles, 25,000 km; greasing: none; spark plug: Bosch W 235 P21; tappet clearances: inlet 0.010 in, 0.25 mm, exhaust 0.016 in, 0.40 mm; valve timing: 42° 70° 64° 40°; tyre pressure: front 23 psi, 1.6 atm, rear 26 psi, 1.8 atm.

LANCIA ITALY

Delta Berlina 1300

PRICE IN GB: £ 4,950*
PRICE EX WORKS: 12,276,000 liras**

ENGINE front, transverse, 4 stroke; 4 cylinders, in line; 79.4 cu in, 1,301 cc (3.40 x 2.18 in, 86.4 x 55.5 mm); compression ratio: 9.5:1; max power (DIN): 78 hp (57 kW) at 5,800 rpm; max torque (DIN): 78 lb ft, 10.7 kg m (105 Nm) at 3,400 rpm; max engine rpm: 6,200; 60 hp/l (43.8 kW/l); cast iron block, light alloy head; 5 crankshaft bearings; valves: overhead, thimble tappets; camshafts: 1, overhead, cogged belt; lubrication: gear pump, full flow filter (cartridge), 7.6 imp pt, 9.1 US pt, 4.3 l; 1 Weber 32 DAT 12/250 downdraught twin barrel carburettor; air cleaner: dry, thimble type thermostatic intake; fuel feed: mechanical pump; liquid-cooled, expansion tank, 10.6 imp pt, 12.7 US pt, 6 l, electric thermostatic fan.

TRANSMISSION driving wheels: front; clutch: single dry plate; gearbox: mechanical; gears: 5, fully synchronized; ratios: I 4.090, II 2.235, III 1.462, IV 1.034, V 0.863, rev 3.714; lever: central; final drive: helical spur gears; axle ratio: 3.765; width of rims: 5''; tyres: 165/70 SR x 13.

PERFORMANCE max speed: 99 mph, 160 km/h; power-weight ratio: 26.4 lb/hp (36.2 lb/kW), 12 kg/hp (16.4 kg/kW); carrying capacity: 992 lb, 450 kg; acceleration: standing ¼ mile 18.7 sec; speed in top at 1,000 rpm: 20 mph, 32.2 km/h; consumption: 35.8 m/imp gal, 29.8 m/US gal, 7.9 l x 100 km at 75 mph, 120 km/h.

CHASSIS integral; front suspension: independent, by McPherson, coil springs/telescopic damper struts, lower wishbones, anti-roll bar; rear: independent, by McPherson, transverse links, longitudinal reaction rods, coil springs/telescopic damper struts, anti-roll bar.

STEERING rack-and-pinion; turns lock to lock: 3.80.

BRAKES front disc (diameter 8.94 in, 22.7 cm), rear drum, 2 X circuits, rear compensator, servo; lining area: front 21.4 sq in, 138 sq cm, rear 32.4 sq in, 209 sq cm, total 53.8 sq in, 347 sq cm.

ELECTRICAL EQUIPMENT 12 V; 40 Ah battery (sealed energy); 55 A alternator; transistorized ignition; 2 iodine headlamps.

LAMBORGHINI LM-002

LANCIA Delta Berlina 1300

LANCIA Delta Berlina 1600 HF Turbo

DIMENSIONS AND WEIGHT wheel base: 97.40 in, 247 cm; front and rear track: 55.10 in, 140 cm; length: 153.35 in, 389 cm; width: 63.80 in, 162 cm; height: 54.30 in, 138 cm; weight: 2,062 lb, 935 kg; weight distribution: 58.8% front, 41.2% rear; turning circle: 34.8 ft, 10.6 m; fuel tank: 9.9 imp gal, 11.9 US gal, 45 l.

BODY saloon/sedan; 4+1 doors; 5 seats, separate front seats; headrests; heated rear window.

PRACTICAL INSTRUCTIONS fuel: 97 oct petrol; oil: engine 7.6 imp pt, 9.1 US pt, 4.3 l, SAE 10W-50, change every 6,200 miles, 10,000 km - gearbox and final drive 5.4 imp pt, 6.5 US pt, 3.1 l, SAE 90, change every 18,600 miles, 30,000 km; greasing: none; spark plug: Champion RN 7Y or Marelli CW 78 LPR; valve timing: 11° 41° 52° 2°; tyre pressure: front 28 psi, 2 atm, rear 28 psi, 2 atm.

OPTIONALS light alloy wheels; electric windows; tinted glass; sunroof; central door locking; metallic spray.

Delta Berlina 1500 Automatica

See Delta Berlina 1300, except for:

PRICE IN GB: £ 5,868*
PRICE EX WORKS: 14,412,000 liras**

ENGINE 91.4 cu in, 1,498 cc (3.40 x 2.51 in, 86.4 x 63.9 mm); compression ratio: 9.2:1; max power (DIN): 85 hp (63 kW) at 5,800 rpm; max torque (DIN): 90 lb ft, 12.5 kg m (126 Nm) at 3,500 rpm; 56.7 hp/l (42.1 kW/l); 1 Weber 34 DAT 8/252 downdraught twin barrel carburettor.

TRANSMISSION gearbox: automatic transmission, hydraulic torque converter and planetary gears with 3 ratios, possible manual selection; ratios: I 2.346, II 1.402, III 1, rev 2.346; axle ratio: 3.635.

PERFORMANCE power-weight ratio: 24.9 lb/hp (33.6 lb/kW), 11.3 kg/hp (15.2 kg/kW); acceleration: standing ¼ mile 18.9 sec; speed in direct drive at 1,000 rpm: 17.6 mph, 28.4 km/h; consumption: 29.4 m/imp gal, 24.5 m/US gal, 9.6 l x 100 km at 75 mph, 120 km/h.

DIMENSIONS AND WEIGHT weight: 2,117 lb, 960 kg; weight distribution: 60% front, 40% rear.

PRACTICAL INSTRUCTIONS oil: automatic transmission and final drive 11.4 imp pt, 13.7 US pt, 6.5 l; valve timing: 12° 52° 52° 12°.

OPTIONALS trip computer.

Delta Berlina 1600 GT

See Delta Berlina 1300, except for:

PRICE IN GB: £ 5,990*
PRICE EX WORKS: 13,854,000 liras**

ENGINE 96.7 cu in, 1,585 cc (3.31 x 2.81 in, 84 x 71.5 mm); compression ratio: 9.3:1; max power (DIN): 105 hp (77 kW) at 5,800 rpm; max torque (DIN): 100 lb ft, 13.8 kg m (135 Nm) at 3,300 rpm; 66.2 hp/l (48.6 kW/l); hemispherical combustion chambers; valves: overhead, Vee-slanted at 65°, thimble tappets; camshafts: 2, overhead, cogged belt; lubrication: 8.4 imp pt, 10.1 US pt, 4.8 l; 1 Weber 34 DAT 13/250 downdraught twin barrel carburettor.

TRANSMISSION gearbox ratios: I 3.583, II 2.235, III 1.550, IV 1.163, V 0.959, rev 3.714; final drive: cylindrical gears, in unit with gearbox; axle ratio: 3.588; width of rims: 5.5"; tyres: 165/65 SR x 14.

PERFORMANCE max speed: about 112 mph, 180 km/h; power-weight ratio: 20.5 lb/hp (27.9 lb/kW), 9.3 kg/hp (12.7 kg/kW); acceleration: standing ¼ mile 16.8 sec; speed in top at 1,000 rpm: 18 mph, 29 km/h; consumption: 34 m/imp gal, 28.3 m/US gal, 8.3 l x 100 km at 75 mph, 120 km/h.

BRAKES disc (front diameter 10.12 in, 25.7 cm, rear 8.94 in, 22.7 cm); lining area: front 22.2 sq in, 143 sq cm, rear 21.7 sq in, 140 sq cm, total 43.9 sq in, 283 sq cm.

ELECTRICAL EQUIPMENT Marelli Digiplex electronic ignition.

DIMENSIONS AND WEIGHT weight: 2,150 lb, 975 kg; weight distribution: 60.5% front, 39.5% rear.

PRACTICAL INSTRUCTIONS oil: engine 8.4 imp pt, 10.1 US pt, 4.8 l; valve timing: 10° 48° 53° 5°; tyre pressure: front 31 psi, 2.2 atm, rear 31 psi, 2.2 atm.

OPTIONALS air-conditioning; light alloy wheels; trip computer.

Delta Berlina 1600 HF Turbo

PRICE EX WORKS: 16,788,000 liras**

ENGINE turbocharged; front, transverse, slanted 20° to rear, 4 stroke; 4 cylinders, in line; 96.7 cu in, 1,585 cc (3.31 x 2.81 in, 84 x 71.5 mm); compression ratio: 8:1; max power (DIN): 130 hp (96 kW) at 5,600 rpm; max torque (DIN): 141 lb ft, 19.5 kg m (191 Nm) at 3,700 rpm; max engine rpm: 6,400; 82 hp/l (60.6 kW/l); cast iron block, light alloy head; 5 crankshaft bearings; valves: overhead, Vee-slanted at 65°, thimble tappets; camshafts: 2, overhead, cogged belt; lubrication: gear pump, full flow filter, oil cooler, 10.6 imp pt, 12.7 US pt, 6 l; 1 Weber 32 DAT 18/250 downdraught twin barrel carburettor; 1 Garrett T3 AiResearch turbocharger with exhaust gas recirculation; air-to-air heat exchanger; fuel feed: electric pump; liquid-cooled, expansion tank, 10.6 imp pt, 12.7 US pt, 6 l, electric thermostatic fan.

TRANSMISSION driving wheels: front; clutch: single dry plate; gearbox: mechanical; gears: 5, fully synchronized; ratios: I 3.583, II 2.235, III 1.542, IV 1.154, V 0.903, rev 3.667; lever: central; final drive: cylindrical gears in unit with gearbox; axle ratio: 3.400; width of rims: 5.5"; tyres: Michelin TRX AS 170/65 R 340.

PERFORMANCE max speeds: (I) 37 mph, 60 km/h; (II) 60 mph, 96 km/h; (III) 86 mph, 139 km/h; (IV) 105 mph, 169 km/h; (V) 121 mph, 195 km/h; power-weight ratio: 17 lb/hp (23 lb/kW), 7.7 kg/hp (10.4 kg/kW); carrying capacity: 992 lb, 450 kg; acceleration: standing ¼ mile 16.1 sec; speed in top at 1,000 rpm: 20.9 mph, 33.7 km/h; consumption: 30.4 m/imp gal, 25.3 m/US gal, 9.3 l x 100 km at 75 mph, 120 km/h.

LANCIA Delta Berlina 1600 HF Turbo

CHASSIS integral; front suspension: independent, by McPherson, coil springs/telescopic damper struts, lower wishbones, anti-roll bar; rear: independent, by McPherson, transverse links, longitudinal reaction rods, coil springs/telescopic damper struts, anti-roll bar.

STEERING rack-and-pinion; turns lock to lock: 3.80.

BRAKES disc (front diameter 10.12 in, 25.7 cm, rear diameter 8.94 in, 22.7 cm), 2 X circuits, rear compensator, servo; lining area: front 22.2 sq in, 143 sq cm, rear 21.7 sq in, 140 sq cm, total 43.9 sq in, 283 sq cm.

ELECTRICAL EQUIPMENT 12 V; 40 Ah battery (sealed energy); 55 A alternator; Marelli Microplex electronic ignition with knocking sensor; 2 halogen headlamps.

DIMENSIONS AND WEIGHT wheel base: 97.44 in, 247 cm; front and rear track: 55.10 in, 140 cm; length: 153.35 in, 389 cm; width: 63.80 in, 162 cm; height: 54.30 in, 138 cm; weight: 2,205 lb, 1,000 kg; weight distribution: 61.5% front, 38.5% rear; turning circle: 34.8 ft, 10.6 m; fuel tank: 9.9 imp gal, 11.9 US gal, 45 l.

BODY saloon/sedan; 4+1 doors; 5 seats, separate front seats, reclining backrests, headrests; heated rear window; rear window wiper-washer; tinted glass; light alloy wheels.

PRACTICAL INSTRUCTIONS fuel: 97 oct petrol; oil: engine 10.6 imp pt, 12.7 US pt, 6 l, SAE 10W-50, change every 6,200 miles, 10,000 km - gearbox and final drive 3.2 imp pt, 3.8 US pt, 1.8 l, SAE 90, change every 18,600 miles, 30,000 km; greasing: none; spark plug: Champion RN6Y; valve timing: 0° 40° 40° 0°; tyre pressure: front 28 psi, 2 atm, rear 28 psi, 2 atm.

OPTIONALS electric windows; sunroof; central door locking; metallic spray; Recaro anatomical seats.

Prisma Berlina 1300

PRICE EX WORKS: 13,320,000 liras**

ENGINE front, transverse, 4 stroke; 4 cylinders, in line; 79.4 cu in, 1,301 cc (3.40 x 2.18 in, 86.4 x 55.5 mm); compression ratio: 9.5:1; max power (DIN): 78 hp (57 kW) at 5,800 rpm; max torque (DIN): 78 lb ft, 10.7 kg m (105 Nm) at 3,400 rpm; max engine rpm: 6,200; 60 hp/l (43.8 kW/l); cast iron block, light alloy head; 5 crankshaft bearings; valves: overhead, thimble tappets; camshafts: 1, overhead, cogged belt; lubrication: gear pump, full flow filter (cartridge), 7.6 imp pt, 9.1 US pt, 4.3 l; 1 Weber 32 DAT 12/250 downdraught twin barrel carburettor; air cleaner: dry, thimble type thermostatic intake; fuel feed: mechanical pump; liquid-cooled, expansion tank, 10.6 imp pt, 12.7 US pt, 6 l, electric thermostatic fan.

TRANSMISSION driving wheels: front; clutch: single dry plate; gearbox: mechanical; gears: 5, fully synchronized; ratios: I 4.090, II 2.235, III 1.462, IV 1.034, V 0.863, rev 3.714; lever: central; final drive: helical spur gears; axle ratio: 3.765; width of rims: 5"; tyres: 165/70 SR x 13.

PERFORMANCE max speed: 99 mph, 160 km/h; power-weight ratio: 26.4 lb/hp (36.2 lb/kW), 12 kg/hp (16.4 kg/kW); carrying capacity: 992 lb, 450 kg; acceleration: standing ¼ mile 18.7 sec; speed in top at 1,000 rpm: 19.8 mph, 31.8 km/h; consumption: 35.3 m/imp gal, 29.4 m/US gal, 8 l x 100 km at 75 mph, 120 km/h.

CHASSIS integral; front suspension: independent, by McPherson, coil springs/telescopic damper struts, lower wishbones, anti-roll bar; rear: independent, by McPherson, transverse links, longitudinal reaction rods, coil springs/telescopic damper struts, anti-roll bar.

STEERING rack-and-pinion; turns lock to lock: 3.80.

BRAKES front disc (diameter 8.94 in, 22.7 cm), rear drum, 2 X circuits, rear compensator, servo; lining area: front 21.4 sq in, 138 sq cm, rear 32.4 sq in, 209 sq cm, total 53.8 sq in, 347 sq cm.

ELECTRICAL EQUIPMENT 12 V; 40 Ah battery (sealed energy); 55 A alternator; transistorized ignition; 2 iodine headlamps.

DIMENSIONS AND WEIGHT wheel base: 97.44 in, 247 cm; front and rear track: 55.10 in, 140 cm; length: 164.57 in, 418 cm; width: 63.80 in, 162 cm; height: 54.33 in, 138 cm; weight: 2,062 lb, 935 kg; weight distribution: 58.8% front, 41.2% rear; turning circle: 34.8 ft, 10.6 m; fuel tank: 9.9 imp gal, 11.9 US gal, 45 l.

BODY saloon/sedan; 4 doors; 5 seats, separate front seats; headrests; heated rear window.

PRACTICAL INSTRUCTIONS fuel: 97 oct petrol; oil: engine 7.6 imp pt, 9.1 US pt, 4.3 l, SAE 10W-50, change every 6,200 miles, 10,000 km - gearbox and final drive 5.4 imp pt, 6.5 US pt, 3.1 l, SAE 90, change every 18,600 miles, 30,000 km; greasing: none; spark plug: Champion RN 7Y or Marelli CW 78 LPR; valve timing: 11° 41° 52° 2°; tyre pressure: front 28 psi, 2 atm, rear 28 psi, 2 atm.

OPTIONALS light alloy wheels; electric windows; tinted glass; sunroof; central door locking; metallic spray; trip computer; folding rear seats; check control.

Prisma Berlina 1500

See Prisma Berlina 1300, except for:

PRICE IN GB: £ 5,550*
PRICE EX WORKS: 13,626,000 liras**

ENGINE 91.4 cu in, 1,498 cc (3.40 x 2.51 in, 86.4 x 63.9 mm); compression ratio: 9.2:1; max power (DIN): 85 hp (63 kW) at 5,800 rpm; 56.7 hp/l (42.1 kW/l); 1 Weber 34 DAT 8/252 downdraught twin barrel carburettor.

PERFORMANCE max speed: 102 mph, 165 km/h; power-weight ratio: 24.4 lb/hp (32.9 lb/kW), 11.1 kg/hp (14.9 kg/kW); acceleration: standing ¼ mile 17.9 sec; speed in top at 1,000 rpm: 20.7 mph, 33.4 km/h; consumption: 35.8 m/imp gal, 29.8 m/US gal, 7.9 l x 100 km at 75 mph, 120 km/h.

DIMENSIONS AND WEIGHT weight: 2,073 lb, 940 kg.

PRACTICAL INSTRUCTIONS valve timing: 12° 52° 52° 12°.

Prisma Berlina 1500 Automatica

See Prisma Berlina 1300, except for:

PRICE IN GB: £ 5,989*
PRICE EX WORKS: 14,862,000 liras**

ENGINE 91.4 cu in, 1,498 cc (3.40 x 2.51 in, 86.4 x 63.9 mm); compression ratio: 9.2:1; max power (DIN): 85 hp (63 kW) at 5,800 rpm; max torque (DIN): 90 lb ft, 12.5 kg m (126 Nm) at 3,500 rpm; 56.7 hp/l (42.1 kW/l); 1 Weber 34 DAT 8/252 downdraught twin barrel carburettor.

TRANSMISSION gearbox: automatic transmission, hydraulic torque converter and planetary gears with 3 ratios, possible manual selection; ratios: I 2.346, II 1.402, III 1, rev 2.346; axle ratio: 3.635.

PERFORMANCE power-weight ratio: 24.9 lb/hp (33.6 lb/kW), 11.3 kg/hp (15.2 kg/kW); acceleration: standing ¼ mile 18.9 sec; speed in direct drive at 1,000 rpm: 17.6 mph, 28.4 km/h; consumption: 29.4 m/imp gal, 24.5 m/US gal, 9.6 l x 100 km at 75 mph, 120 km/h.

DIMENSIONS AND WEIGHT weight: 2,117 lb, 960 kg; weight distribution: 60% front, 40% rear.

PRACTICAL INSTRUCTIONS oil: automatic transmission and final drive 11.4 imp pt, 13.7 US pt, 6.5 l; valve timing: 12° 52° 52° 12°.

Prisma Berlina 1600

See Prisma Berlina 1300, except for:

PRICE IN GB: £ 6,150*
PRICE EX WORKS: 15,060,000 liras**

ENGINE 96.7 cu in, 1,585 cc (3.31 x 2.81 in, 84 x 71.5 mm); compression ratio: 9.3:1; max power (DIN): 105 hp (77 kW) at 5,800 rpm; max torque (DIN): 100 lb ft, 13.8 kg m (135 Nm) at 3,300 rpm; 66.2 hp/l (48.6 kW/l); hemispherical combustion chambers; valves: overhead, Vee-slanted at 65°, thimble tappets; camshafts: 2, overhead, cogged belt; lubrication: 8.4 imp pt, 10.1 US pt, 4.8 l; 1 Weber 34 DAT 13/250 downdraught twin barrel carburettor.

TRANSMISSION gearbox ratios: I 3.583, II 2.235, III 1.550, IV 1.163, V 0.959, rev 3.714; final drive: cylindrical gears, in unit with gearbox; axle ratio: 3.588; width of rims: 5.5"; tyres: 165/65 SR x 14.

PERFORMANCE max speed: 111 mph, 178 km/h; power-weight ratio: 20.5 lb/hp (27.9 lb/kW), 9.3 kg/hp (12.7 kg/kW); acceleration: standing ¼ mile 16.8 sec; speed in top at 1,000 rpm: 18.6 mph, 30 km/h; consumption: 33.6 m/imp gal, 28 m/US gal, 8.4 l x 100 km at 75 mph, 120 km/h.

BRAKES disc (front diameter 10.12 in, 25.7 cm, rear 8.94 in, 22.7 cm); lining area: front 22.2 sq in, 143 sq cm, rear 21.7 sq in, 140 sq cm, total 43.9 sq in, 283 sq cm.

ELECTRICAL EQUIPMENT Marelli Digiplex electronic ignition.

DIMENSIONS AND WEIGHT weight: 2,150 lb, 975 kg; weight distribution: 60.5% front, 39.5% rear.

BODY check control and central door locking (standard).

PRACTICAL INSTRUCTIONS oil: engine 8.4 imp pt, 10.1 US pt, 4.8 l; valve timing: 10° 48° 53° 5°; tyre pressure: front 31 psi, 2.2 atm, rear 31 psi, 2.2 atm.

OPTIONALS air-conditioning; light alloy wheels; trip computer.

Beta Coupé 1300

PRICE EX WORKS: 14,208,000* liras

ENGINE front, transverse, slanted 20° to rear, 4 stroke; 4 cylinders, in line; 83.4 cu in, 1,366 cc (3.07 x 2.81 in, 78 x 71.5 mm); compression ratio: 8.9:1; max power (DIN): 84 hp (62 kW) at 5,800 rpm; max torque (DIN): 82 lb ft, 11.3 kg m (110 Nm) at 3,200 rpm; max engine rpm: 6,000; 61.5 hp/l (45.4 kW/l); cast iron block, light alloy head, hemispherical combustion chambers; 5 crankshaft bearings; valves: overhead, Vee-slanted at 65°, thimble tappets; camshafts: 2, overhead, cogged belt; lubrication: gear pump, full flow filter, 6.7 imp pt, 8 US pt, 3.8 l; 1 Weber 32 DAT 3 downdraught twin barrel carburettor with power-valve; air cleaner: dry, thimble type thermostatic intake; fuel feed: mechanical pump; liquid-cooled, expansion tank, 13.4 imp pt, 16.1 US pt, 7.6 l, electric thermostatic fan.

TRANSMISSION driving wheels: front; clutch: single dry plate; gearbox: mechanical; gears: 5, fully synchronized; ratios: I 3.500, II 2.235, III 1.522, IV 1.152, V 0.925, rev 3.071; lever: central; final drive: cylindrical gears, in unit with gearbox; axle ratio: 4.214; width of rims: 5"; tyres: 155 SR x 14.

PERFORMANCE max speeds: (I) 28 mph, 45 km/h; (II) 43 mph, 70 km/h; (III) 64 mph, 103 km/h; (IV) 85 mph, 137 km/h; (V) 104 mph, 168 km/h; power-weight ratio: 26.2 lb/hp (35.6 lb/kW), 11.9 kg/hp (16.1 kg/kW); carrying capacity: 882 lb, 400 kg; acceleration: standing ¼ mile 18.6 sec; speed in top at 1,000 rpm: 17.7 mph, 28.5 km/h; consumption: 32.8 m/imp gal, 27.3 m/US gal, 8.6 l x 100 km at 75 mph, 120 km/h.

CHASSIS integral; front suspension: independent, by McPherson, lower wide-based wishbones, coil springs/telescopic damper struts, anti-roll bar; rear: independent, by McPherson, wishbones, coil springs/telescopic damper struts, anti-roll bar acting as longitudinal torque arm.

STEERING rack-and-pinion, damper; turns lock to lock: 4.

BRAKES disc (diameter 9.88 in, 25.1 cm), rear compensator, Superduplex circuit, servo; lining area: front 24.8 sq in, 160 sq cm, rear 22 sq in, 142 sq cm, total 46.8 sq in, 302 sq cm.

ELECTRICAL EQUIPMENT 12 V; 45 Ah battery; 45 A alternator; Bosch or Marelli electronic ignition; 4 iodine headlamps.

DIMENSIONS AND WEIGHT wheel base: 92.52 in, 235 cm; tracks: 55.35 in, 141 cm front, 54.80 in, 139 cm rear; length: 157.28 in, 399 cm; width: 64.96 in, 165 cm; height: 50.59 in, 128 cm; ground clearance: 5.12 in, 13 cm; weight: 2,205 lb, 1,000 kg; turning circle: 33.5 ft, 10.2 m; fuel tank: 11.4 imp gal, 13.7 US gal, 52 l.

BODY coupé; 2 doors; 4 seats, separate front seats, front and rear headrests.

PRACTICAL INSTRUCTIONS fuel: 97 oct petrol; oil: engine 6.7 imp pt, 8 US pt, 3.8 l, SAE 10W-50, change every 6,200 miles, 10,000 km - gearbox and final drive 3.2 imp pt, 3.8 US pt, 1.8 l, SAE 90, change every 18,600 miles, 30,000 km; greasing: none; spark plug: Champion N 7 Y; tappet clearances: inlet 0.018-0.020 in, 0.39-0.45 mm, exhaust 0.016-0.019 in, 0.42-0.48 mm; valve timing: 17° 37° 48° 6°; tyre pressure: front 27 psi, 1.9 atm, rear 27 psi, 1.9 atm.

OPTIONALS 185/70 HR x 14 tyres; tinted glass; sunroof; metallic spray.

Beta Coupé 1600

See Beta Coupé 1300, except for:

PRICE EX WORKS: 15,690,000 liras**

ENGINE 96.7 cu in, 1,585 cc (3.31 x 2.81 in, 84 x 71.5 mm); compression ratio: 9.4:1; max power (DIN): 100 hp (74 kW) at 5,800 rpm; max torque (DIN): 99 lb ft, 13.7 kg m (134 Nm) at 3,000 rpm; max engine rpm: 6,400; 63.1 hp/l (46.4 kW/l); 1 Weber 34 DAT 1 or Solex C34 TCI C5 downdraught twin barrel carburettor with power-valve and automatic starter.

TRANSMISSION axle ratio: 3.929; width of rims: 5.5"; tyres: 175/70 SR x 14 tubeless.

PERFORMANCE max speeds: (I) 31 mph, 50 km/h; (II) 48 mph, 78 km/h; (III) 71 mph, 114 km/h; (IV) 94 mph, 151 km/h; (V) 109 mph, 176 km/h; power-weight ratio: 22 lb/hp (29.8 lb/kW), 10 kg/hp (13.5 kg/kW); acceleration: standing ¼ mile 18 sec; speed in top at 1,000 rpm: 18.9 mph, 30.5 km/h; consumption: 34.4 m/imp gal, 28.7 m/US gal, 8.2 l x 100 km at 75 mph, 120 km/h.

ELECTRICAL EQUIPMENT 55 A alternator.

OPTIONALS Lancia/AP automatic transmission, hydraulic torque converter and planetary gears with 3 ratios (I 2.346, II 1.402, III 1, rev 2.346), max ratio of converter at stall 2.05, possible manual selection, 3.740 axle ratio, max speed 107 mph, 172 km/h, consumption 27.7 m/imp gal, 23.1 m/US gal, 10.2 l x 100 km at 75 mph, 120 km/h; air-conditioning; ZF progressive power steering; light alloy wheels; 185/65 HR x 14 tyres; sunroof; electric windows; metallic spray.

LANCIA Prisma Berlina 1600

LANCIA Beta Coupé Volumex VX

LANCIA Trevi Berlina Volumex VX

Beta Coupé 2000 IE

See Beta Coupé 1300, except for:

PRICE IN GB: £ 7,276*
PRICE EX WORKS: 17,370,000 liras**

ENGINE 121.7 cu in, 1,995 cc (3.31 x 3.54 in, 84 x 90 mm); max power (DIN): 122 hp (90 kW) at 5,500 rpm; max torque (DIN): 130 lb ft, 17.9 kg m (175 Nm) at 2,800 rpm; max engine rpm: 6,200; 61.2 hp/l (45.1 kW/l); lubrication: 7.9 imp pt, 9.5 US pt, 4.5 l; Bosch LE-Jetronic injection with fuel cut-off system.

TRANSMISSION axle ratio: 3.611; width of rims: 5.5"; tyres: 175/70 HR x 14 tubeless.

PERFORMANCE max speeds: (I) 34 mph, 54 km/h; (II) 52 mph, 84 km/h; (III) 76 mph, 123 km/h; (IV) 101 mph, 163 km/h; (V) 115 mph, 185 km/h; power-weight ratio: 18.1 lb/hp (24.5 lb/kW), 8.2 kg/hp (11.1 kg/kW); acceleration: standing ¼ mile 17.3 sec; speed in top at 1,000 rpm: 20.6 mph, 33.2 km/h; consumption: 32.1 m/imp gal, 26.7 m/US gal, 8.8 l x 100 km at 75 mph, 120 km/h.

STEERING ZF progressive servo.

ELECTRICAL EQUIPMENT 65 A alternator; Marelli Digiplex electronic ignition.

PRACTICAL INSTRUCTIONS oil: engine 7.9 imp pt, 9.5 US pt, 4.5 l; spark plug: Champion N9Y valve timing: 13° 45° 49° 9°.

OPTIONALS Lancia/AP automatic transmission, hydraulic torque converter and planetary gears with 3 ratios (I 2.346, II 1.402, III 1, rev 2.346), max ratio of converter at stall 2.05, possible manual selection, max speed 112 mph, 180 km/h, consumption 27.4 m/imp gal, 22.8 m/US gal, 10.3 l x 100 km at 75 mph, 120 km/h; light alloy wheels; 185/65 HR x 14 tyres; sunroof; electric windows; metallic spray.

Beta Coupé Volumex VX

See Beta Coupé 1300, except for:

PRICE IN GB: £ 7,995*
PRICE EX WORKS: 19,080,000 liras**

ENGINE charged; 121.7 cu in, 1,995 cc (3.31 x 3.54 in, 84 x 90 mm); compression ratio: 7.5:1; max power (DIN): 135 hp (99 kW) at 5,500 rpm; max torque (DIN): 152 lb ft, 21 kg m (206 Nm) at 3,000 rpm; 67.7 hp/l (49.6 kW/l); lubrication: oil cooler, 7.9 imp pt, 9.5 US pt, 4.5 l; 1 Weber 36 DCA 5/250 downdraught twin barrel carburettor; Roots volumetric supercharger; fuel feed: electric pump.

TRANSMISSION axle ratio: 3.263; width of rims: 5.5"; tyres: Pirelli P6 185/65 HR x 14.

PERFORMANCE max speed: 124 mph, 200 km/h; power-weight ratio: 17.9 lb/hp (24.4 lb/kW), 8.1 kg/hp (11.1 kg/kW); acceleration: standing ¼ mile 16.1 sec; speed in top at 1,000 rpm: 22.4 mph, 36.1 km/h; consumption: 31 m/imp gal, 25.8 m/US gal, 9.1 l x 100 km at 75 mph, 120 km/h.

STEERING ZF progressive servo.

ELECTRICAL EQUIPMENT 65 A alternator.

DIMENSIONS AND WEIGHT weight: 2,414 lb, 1,095 kg.

PRACTICAL INSTRUCTIONS oil: engine 7.9 imp pt, 9.5 US pt, 4.5 l; valve timing: 13° 39° 37° 3°; tyre pressure: front 31 psi, 2.2 atm, rear 31 psi, 2.2 atm.

Trevi Berlina 1600

PRICE IN GB: £ 6,620*
PRICE EX WORKS: 15,420,000 liras**

ENGINE front, transverse, slanted 20° to rear, 4 stroke; 4 cylinders, in line; 96.7 cu in, 1,585 cc (3.31 x 2.81 in, 84 x 71.5 mm); compression ratio: 9.4:1; max power (DIN): 100 hp (74 kW) at 5,800 rpm; max torque (DIN): 99 lb ft, 13.7 kg m (134 Nm) at 3,000 rpm; max engine rpm: 6,400; 63.1 hp/l (46.4 kW/l); cast iron block, light alloy head, hemispherical combustion chambers; 5 crankshaft bearings; valves: overhead, Vee-slanted at 65°, thimble tappets; camshafts: 2, overhead, cogged belt; lubrication: gear pump, full flow filter, 6.7 imp pt, 8 US pt, 3.8 l; 1 Weber 34 DAT 1 or Solex C34 TCI C5 downdraught twin barrel carburettor with power-valve and automatic starter; air cleaner: dry, thimble type thermostatic intake; fuel feed: mechanical pump; liquid-cooled, expansion tank, 13.4 imp pt, 16.1 US pt, 7.6 l, electric thermostatic fan.

TRANSMISSION driving wheels: front; clutch: single dry plate; gearbox: mechanical; gears: 5, fully synchronized; ratios: I 3.500, II 2.235, III 1.522, IV 1.152, V 0.925, rev 3.071; lever: central; final drive: cylindrical gears, in unit with gearbox; axle ratio: 3.929; width of rims: 5.5"; tyres: 175/70 SR x 14 tubeless.

PERFORMANCE max speeds: (I) 31 mph, 50 km/h; (II) 48 mph, 78 km/h; (III) 71 mph, 114 km/h; (IV) 94 mph, 151 km/h; (V) about 106 mph, 170 km/h; power-weight ratio: 25.2 lb/hp (34.1 lb/kW), 11.4 kg/hp (15.5 kg/kW); carrying capacity: 1,102 lb, 500 kg; acceleration: standing ¼ mile 18.4 sec, 0-50 mph (0-80 km/h) 7.3 sec; speed in top at 1,000 rpm: 18.2 mph, 29.3 km/h; consumption: 32.5 m/imp gal, 27 m/US gal, 8.7 l x 100 km at 75 mph, 120 km/h.

CHASSIS integral; front suspension: independent, by McPherson, lower wide-based wishbones, coil springs/telescopic damper struts, anti-roll bar; rear: independent, by McPherson, wishbones, coil springs/telescopic damper struts, anti-roll bar acting as longitudinal torque arm.

STEERING rack-and-pinion, damper; turns lock to lock: 4.

BRAKES disc (diameter 9.88 in, 25.1 cm), rear compensator, Superduplex circuits, servo; lining area: front 24.8 sq in, 160 sq cm, rear 22 sq in, 142 sq cm, total 46.8 sq in, 302 sq cm.

ELECTRICAL EQUIPMENT 12 V; 45 Ah battery; 55 A alternator; Bosch or Marelli electronic ignition; 4 iodine headlamps with automatically adjustable height.

DIMENSIONS AND WEIGHT wheel base: 100 in, 254 cm; tracks: 55.35 in, 141 cm front, 54.80 in, 139 cm rear; length: 171.46 in, 435 cm; width: 66.93 in, 171 cm; height: 55.12 in, 140 cm; ground clearance: 5.12 in, 13 cm; weight: 2,525 lb, 1,145 kg; turning circle: 35.7 ft, 10.9 m; fuel tank: 11.4 imp gal, 13.7 US gal, 52 l.

BODY saloon/sedan; 4 doors; 5 seats, separate front seats, reclining backrests; heated rear window.

PRACTICAL INSTRUCTIONS fuel: 97 oct petrol; oil: engine 6.7 imp pt, 8 US pt, 3.8 l, SAE 10W-50, change every 6,200 miles, 10,000 km - gearbox and final drive 3.2 imp pt, 3.8 US pt, 1.8 l, SAE 90, change every 18,600 miles, 30,000 km; greasing: none; spark plug: Champion N 7 Y; tappet clearances: inlet 0.018-0.020 in, 0.39-0.45 mm, exhaust 0.016-0.019 in, 0.42-0.48 mm; valve timing: 17° 37° 48° 6°; tyre pressure: front 27 psi, 1.9 atm, rear 27 psi, 1.9 atm.

OPTIONALS Lancia/AP automatic transmission, hydraulic torque converter and planetary gears with 3 ratios (I 2.346, II 1.402, III 1, rev 2.346), max ratio of converter at stall 2.05, possible manual selection, 3.740 axle ratio, max speed 102 mph, 165 km/h, consumption 28.8 m/imp gal, 24 m/US gal, 9.8 l x 100 km at 75 mph, 120 km/h; air-conditioning; tinted glass; ZF progressive power steering; light alloy wheels; 185/65 HR x 14 tyres; sunroof; rear window wiper-washer; electric windows; tail-tale warning light; metallic spray.

Trevi Berlina 2000 IE

See Trevi Berlina 1600, except for:

PRICE IN GB: £ 7,192*
PRICE EX WORKS: 17,748,000 liras**

ENGINE 121.7 cu in, 1,995 cc (3.31 x 3.54 in, 84 x 90 mm); compression ratio: 8.9:1; max power (DIN): 122 hp (90 kW) at 5,500 rpm; max torque (DIN): 130 lb ft, 17.9 kg m (176 Nm) at 2,800 rpm; 61.2 hp/l (45.1 kW/l); lubrication: 7.9 imp pt, 9.5 US pt, 4.5 l; Bosch LE-Jetronic injection with fuel cut-off system; fuel feed: electric pump.

TRANSMISSION axle ratio: 3.611.

PERFORMANCE max speed: 112 mph, 180 km/h; power-weight ratio: 21.1 lb/hp (28.5 lb/kW), 9.5 kg/hp (12.9 kg/kW); acceleration: standing ¼ mile 17.5 sec; consumption: 30.7 m/imp gal, 25.6 m/US gal, 9.2 l x 100 km at 75 mph, 120 km/h.

STEERING ZF progressive servo (standard).

ELECTRICAL EQUIPMENT 65 A alternator; Marelli Digiplex electronic ignition.

DIMENSIONS AND WEIGHT weight: 2,569 lb, 1,165 kg.

BODY electric windows and control system (standard).

PRACTICAL INSTRUCTIONS oil: engine 7.9 imp pt, 9.5 US pt, 4.5 l; spark plug: Champion N9Y; valve timing: 13° 45° 49° 9°.

OPTIONALS Lancia/AP automatic transmission, hydraulic torque converter and planetary gears with 3 ratios (I 2.346, II 1.402, III 1, rev 2.346), max ratio of converter at stall 2.05, possible manual selection, 3.534 axle ratio, max speed 109 mph, 175 km/h, consumption 26.9 m/imp gal, 22.4 m/US gal, 10.5 l x 100 km at 75 mph, 120 km/h.

Trevi Berlina Volumex VX

See Trevi Berlina 1600, except for:

PRICE EX WORKS: 18,984,000 liras**

ENGINE charged; 121.7 cu in, 1,995 cc (3.31 x 3.54 in, 84 x 90 mm); compression ratio: 7.5:1; max power (DIN): 135 hp

LANCIA H.P. Executive Volumex VX

LANCIA Montecarlo

LANCIA Rally

TREVI BERLINA VOLUMEX VX

(99 kW) at 5,500 rpm; max torque (DIN): 152 lb ft, 21 kg m (206 Nm) at 3,000 rpm; 67.7 hp/l (49.6 kW/l); lubrication: oil cooler, 7.9 imp pt, 9.5 US pt, 4.5 l; 1 Weber 36 DCA 5/250 downdraught twin barrel carburettor; Roots volumetric supercharger; fuel feed: electric pump.

TRANSMISSION gearbox ratios: I 3.500, II 2.235, III 1.522, IV 1.152, V 0.925, rev 3.071; axle ratio: 3.263; tyres: Pirelli P6 185/65 HR x 14.

PERFORMANCE max speed: 118 mph, 190 km/h; power-weight ratio: 19.5 lb/hp (26.6 lb/kW), 8.9 kg/hp (12.1 kg/kW); acceleration: standing ¼ mile 16.7 sec; speed in top at 1,000 rpm: 22.4 mph, 36.1 km/h; consumption: 29.4 m/imp gal, 24.5 m/US gal, 9.6 l x 100 km at 75 mph, 120 km/h.

STEERING ZF progressive servo (standard).

ELECTRICAL EQUIPMENT 65 A alternator.

DIMENSIONS AND WEIGHT weight: 2,635 lb, 1,195 kg.

BODY light alloy wheels and electric windows (standard).

PRACTICAL INSTRUCTIONS oil: engine 7.9 imp pt, 9.5 US pt, 4.5 l; spark plug: Champion N7Y; valve timing: 13° 39° 37° 3°; tyre pressure: front 31 psi, 2.2 atm, rear 31 psi, 2.2 atm.

H.P. Executive 1600

PRICE IN GB: £ 6,990*
PRICE EX WORKS: 15,486,000 liras**

ENGINE front, transverse, slanted 20° to rear, 4 stroke; 4 cylinders, in line; 96.7 cu in, 1,585 cc (3.31 x 2.81 in, 84 x 71.5 mm); compression ratio: 9.4:1; max power (DIN): 100 hp (74 kW) at 5,800 rpm; max torque (DIN): 99 lb ft, 13.7 kg m (134 Nm) at 3,000 rpm; max engine rpm: 6,400; 63.1 hp/l (46.4 kW/l); cast iron block, light alloy head, hemispherical combustion chambers; 5 crankshaft bearings; valves: overhead, Vee-slanted at 65°, thimble tappets; camshafts: 2, overhead, cogged belt; lubrication: gear pump, full flow filter, 6.7 imp pt, 8 US pt, 3.8 l; 1 Weber 34 DAT 1 or Solex C34 TCI C5 downdraught twin barrel carburettor with power-valve and automatic starter; air cleaner: dry, thimble type thermostatic intake; fuel feed: mechanical pump; liquid-cooled, expansion tank, 13.4 imp pt, 16.1 US pt, 7.6 l, electric thermostatic fan.

TRANSMISSION driving wheels: front; clutch: single dry plate; gearbox: mechanical; gears: 5, fully synchronized; ratios: I 3.500, II 2.235, III 1.522, IV 1.152, V 0.925, rev 3.071; lever: central; final drive: cylindrical gears, in unit with gearbox; axle ratio: 3.929; width of rims: 5.5"; tyres: 175/70 SR x 14 tubeless.

PERFORMANCE max speeds: (I) 31 mph, 50 km/h; (II) 48 mph, 78 km/h; (III) 71 mph, 114 km/h; (IV) 94 mph, 151 km/h; (V) 107 mph, 172 km/h; power-weight ratio: 23.4 lb/hp (31.6 lb/kW), 10.6 kg/hp (14.3 kg/kW); carrying capacity: 1,102 lb, 500 kg; acceleration: standing ¼ mile 18.3 sec; speed in top at 1,000 rpm: 18.9 mph, 30.5 km/h; consumption: 34.4 m/imp gal, 28.7 m/US gal, 8.2 l x 100 km at 75 mph, 120 km/h.

CHASSIS integral; front suspension: independent, by McPherson, lower wide-based wishbones, coil springs/telescopic damper struts, anti-roll bar; rear: independent, by McPherson, wishbones, coil springs/telescopic damper struts, anti-roll bar acting as longitudinal torque arm.

STEERING rack-and-pinion, damper; turns lock to lock: 4.

BRAKES disc (diameter 9.88 in, 25.1 cm), rear compensator, Superduplex circuit, servo; lining area: front 24.8 sq in, 160 sq cm, rear 22 sq in, 142 sq cm, total 46.8 sq in, 302 sq cm.

ELECTRICAL EQUIPMENT 12 V; 45 Ah battery; 55 A alternator; Bosch or Marelli electronic ignition; 4 iodine headlamps.

DIMENSIONS AND WEIGHT wheel base: 100 in, 254 cm; tracks: 55.35 in, 141 cm front, 54.80 in, 139 cm rear; length: 168.70 in, 428 cm; width: 64.96 in, 165 cm; height: 51.57 in, 131 cm; ground clearance: 5.12 in, 13 cm; weight: 2,337 lb, 1,060 kg; turning circle: 34.8 ft, 10.6 m; fuel tank: 11.4 imp gal, 13.7 US gal, 52 l.

BODY coupé; 2+1 doors; 5 seats, headrests; rear window wiper-washer; heated rear window.

PRACTICAL INSTRUCTIONS fuel: 97 oct petrol; oil: engine 6.7 imp pt, 8 US pt, 3.8 l, SAE 10W-50, change every 6,200 miles, 10,000 km - gearbox and final drive 3.2 imp pt, 3.8 US pt, 1.8 l, SAE 90, change every 18,600 miles, 30,000 km; greasing: none; spark plug: Champion N 7Y; tappet clearances: inlet 0.018-0.020 in, 0.39-0.45 mm, exhaust 0.016-0.019 in, 0.42-0.48 mm; valve timing: 17° 37° 48° 6°; tyre pressure: front 27 psi, 1.9 atm, rear 27 psi, 1.9 atm.

OPTIONALS Lancia/AP automatic transmission, hydraulic torque converter and planetary gears with 3 ratios (I 2.346, II 1.402, III 1, rev 2.346), max ratio of converter at stall 2.05, possible manual selection, 3.740 axle ratio, max speed 104 mph, 167 km/h, consumption 27.7 m/imp gal, 23.1 m/US gal, 10.2 l x 100 km at 75 mph, 120 km/h; air-conditioning; tinted glass; ZF progressive power steering; light alloy wheels; 185/65 HR x 14 tyres; sunroof; electric windows; metallic spray.

H.P. Executive 2000 IE

See H.P. Executive 1600, except for:

PRICE IN GB: £ 7,975*
PRICE EX WORKS: 17,172,000 liras**

ENGINE 121.7 cu in, 1,995 cc (3.31 x 3.54 in, 84 x 90 mm); compression ratio: 8.9:1; max power (DIN): 122 hp (90 kW) at 5,500 rpm; max torque (DIN): 130 lb ft, 17.9 kg m (175 Nm) at 2,800 rpm; max engine rpm: 6,200; 61.2 hp/l (45.1 kW/l); lubrication: 7.9 imp pt, 9.5 US pt, 4.5 l; Bosch LE-Jetronic injection with fuel cut-off system.

TRANSMISSION axle ratio: 3.611.

PERFORMANCE max speeds: (I) 33 mph, 53 km/h; (II) 52 mph, 83 km/h; (III) 76 mph, 123 km/h; (IV) 101 mph, 162 km/h; (V) 115 mph, 185 km/h; power-weight ratio: 19.2 lb/hp (26 lb/kW), 8.7 kg/hp (11.8 kg/kW); acceleration: standing ¼ mile 17.5 sec; consumption: 31.7 m/imp gal, 26.4 m/US gal, 8.9 l x 100 km at 75 mph, 120 km/h.

STEERING ZF progressive servo (standard).

ELECTRICAL EQUIPMENT 65 A alternator; Marelli Digiplex electronic ignition.

PRACTICAL INSTRUCTIONS oil: engine 7.9 imp pt, 9.5 US pt, 4.5 l; spark plug: Champion N9Y; valve timing: 13° 45° 49° 9°.

OPTIONALS with Lancia/AP automatic transmission, 3.534 axle ratio, max speed 112 mph, 180 km/h and consumption 27.4 m/imp gal, 22.8 m/US gal, 10.3 l x 100 km at 75 mph, 120 km/h.

H.P. Executive Volumex VX

See H.P. Executive 1600, except for:

PRICE IN GB: £ 8,500*
PRICE EX WORKS: 18,690,000 liras**

ENGINE charged; 121.7 cu in, 1,995 cc (3.31 x 3.54 in, 84 x 90 mm); compression ratio: 7.5:1; max power (DIN): 135 hp (99 kW) at 5,500 rpm; max torque (DIN): 152 lb ft, 21 kg m (206 Nm) at 3,000 rpm; 67.7 hp/l (49.6 kW/l); lubrication: oil cooler, 7.9 imp pt, 9.5 US pt, 4.5 l; 1 Weber 36 DCA 5/250 downdraught twin barrel carburettor; Roots volumetric supercharger; fuel feed: electric pump.

TRANSMISSION gearbox ratios: I 3.500, II 2.235, III 1.522, IV 1.152, V 0.925, rev 3.071; axle ratio: 3.263; tyres: Pirelli P6 185/65 HR x 14.

PERFORMANCE max speed: 124 mph, 200 km/h; power-weight ratio: 18.5 lb/hp (25.3 lb/kW), 8.4 kg/hp (11.5 kg/kW); acceleration: standing ¼ mile 16.5 sec; speed in top at 1,000 rpm: 22.4 mph, 36.1 km/h; consumption: 31 m/imp gal, 25.8 m/US gal, 9.1 l x 100 km at 75 mph, 120 km/h.

STEERING ZF progressive servo (standard).

ELECTRICAL EQUIPMENT 65 A alternator.

DIMENSIONS AND WEIGHT weight: 2,503 lb, 1,135 kg.

PRACTICAL INSTRUCTIONS oil: engine 7.9 imp pt, 9.5 US pt, 4.5 l; spark plug: Champion N7Y; valve timing: 13° 39° 37° 3°; tyre pressure: front 31 psi, 2.2 atm, rear 31 psi, 2.2 atm.

Montecarlo

PRICE IN GB: £ 8,990*
PRICE EX WORKS: 19,710,000 liras**

ENGINE central, rear, transverse, in unit with gearbox and final drive, 4 stroke; 4 cylinders, in line; 121.7 cu in, 1,995 cc (3.31 x 3.54 in, 84 x 90 mm); compression ratio: 9.3:1; max power (DIN): 120 hp (88 kW) at 6,000 rpm; max torque (DIN): 126 lb ft, 17.4 kg m (171 Nm) at 3,400 rpm; max engine rpm: 6,200; 60.1 hp/l (44.3 kW/l); cast iron block, light alloy head, hemispherical combustion chambers; 5 crankshaft bearings; valves: overhead, Vee-slanted at 65°, thimble tappets; camshafts: 2, overhead, cogged belt; lubrication: gear pump, full flow filter (cartridge), 10.9 imp pt, 13.1 US pt, 6.2 l; 1 Weber 34 DATR 4/250 downdraught twin barrel carburettor; fuel feed: mechanical pump; liquid-cooled, 24.6 imp pt, 29.6 US pt, 14 l, electric thermostatic fan.

TRANSMISSION driving wheels: rear; clutch: single dry plate (diaphragm), hydraulically controlled; gearbox: mechanical; gears: 5, fully synchronized; ratios: I 3.750, II 2.235, III 1.522, IV 1.152, V 0.925, rev 3.071; lever: cen-

LANCIA Montecarlo

tral; final drive: helical spur gears; axle ratio: 3.714; width of rims: 5.5"; tyres: 185/65 HR x 14 P6.

PERFORMANCE max speeds: (I) 30 mph, 48 km/h; (II) 50 mph, 81 km/h; (III) 75 mph, 120 km/h; (IV) 98 mph, 157 km/h; (V) about 121 mph, 195 km/h; power-weight ratio: 17.8 lb/hp (24.3 lb/kW), 8.1 kg/hp (11 kg/kW); carrying capacity: 463 lb, 210 kg; acceleration: standing ¼ mile 16.5 sec; speed in top at 1,000 rpm: 19.6 mph, 31.6 km/h; consumption: 30.7 m/imp gal, 25.6 m/US gal, 9.2 l x 100 km at 75 mph, 120 km/h.

CHASSIS integral; front suspension: independent, by McPherson, coil springs/telescopic damper struts, lower wishbones; rear: independent, by McPherson, coil springs/telescopic damper struts, lower wishbones.

STEERING rack-and-pinion.

BRAKES disc (diameter 8.94 in, 22.7 cm), dual circuit, servo.

ELECTRICAL EQUIPMENT 12 V; 45 Ah battery; 55 A alternator; Marelli electronic ignition; 2 iodine headlamps.

DIMENSIONS AND WEIGHT wheel base: 90.55 in, 230 cm; tracks: 55.90 in, 142 cm front, 57.87 in, 147 cm rear; length: 150.12 in, 381 cm; width: 66.77 in, 170 cm; height: 46.85 in, 119 cm; ground clearance: 5.20 in, 13.2 cm; weight: 2,139 lb, 970 kg; turning circle: 31.1 ft, 9.5 m; fuel tank: 13 imp gal, 15.6 US gal, 59 l.

BODY coupé; 2 doors; separate seats, built-in headrests; detachable roof; headrests; heated rear window; light alloy wheels.

PRACTICAL INSTRUCTIONS fuel: 98 oct petrol; oil: engine 10.9 imp pt, 13.1 US pt, 6.2 l, SAE 10W-50, change every 3,100 miles, 5,000 km - gearbox and final drive 3 imp pt, 3.6 US pt, 1.7 l, SAE 90, change every 18,600 miles, 30,000 km; greasing: none; spark plug: 200°; tappet clearances: inlet 0.016-0.020 in, 0.40-0.50 mm, exhaust 0.022-0.026 in, 0.55-0.65 mm; valve timing: 15° 55° 57° 13°; tyre pressure: front 27 psi, 1.9 atm, rear 28 psi, 2 atm.

OPTIONALS tinted glass; metallic spray; leather upholstery; electric windows.

Rally

PRICE EX WORKS: 47,508,000 liras**

ENGINE charged, central, rear, longitudinal, 4 stroke; 4 cylinders, in line; 121.7 cu in, 1,995 cc (3.31 x 3.54 in, 84 x 90 mm); compression ratio: 7.5:1; max power (DIN): 205 hp (151 kW) at 7,000 rpm; max torque (DIN): 167 lb ft, 23 kg m (233 Nm) at 5,000 rpm; max engine rpm: 7,600; 102.8 hp/l (75.7 kW/l); cast iron block, light alloy head, hemispherical combustion chambers; 5 crankshaft bearings; valves: 4 per cylinder, overhead, Vee-slanted, thimble tappets; camshafts: 2, overhead, cogged belt; lubrication: gear pump, full flow filter (cartridge), dry sump, oil cooler, 14.1 imp pt, 16.9 US pt, 8 l; 1 Weber 40 DCNVH 15/250 twin barrel carburettor; Roots volumetric supercharger; fuel feed: electric pump; cooling: water, expansion tank, 15.8 imp pt, 19 US pt, 9 l, electric thermostatic fan.

TRANSMISSION driving wheels: rear; clutch: single dry plate (diaphragm), hydraulically controlled; gearbox: mechanical; gears: 5, fully synchronized; ratios: I 2.417, II 1.611, III 1.136, IV 0.846, V 0.704, rev 2.867; lever: central; final drive: helical spur gears, limited slip; axle ratio: 5.250; width of rims: front 8", rear 9"; tyres: front Pirelli 205/55 VR x 16 P7, rear Pirelli 225/50 VR x 16 P7.

PERFORMANCE max speed: 137 mph, 220 km/h; power-weight ratio: 12.6 lb/hp (17.1 lb/kW), 5.7 kg/hp (7.7 kg/kW); carrying capacity: 353 lb, 160 kg; acceleration: standing ¼ mile 15 sec; speed in top at 1,000 rpm: 19.4 mph, 31.3 km/h; consumption: 25.9 m/imp gal, 21.6 m/US gal, 10.9 l x 100 km at 75 mph, 120 km/h.

CHASSIS tubular type; front suspension: independent, wishbones, progressively acting coil springs, coaxial telescopic dampers, anti-roll bar; rear: independent, wishbones, progressively acting coil springs, 4 telescopic dampers.

STEERING rack-and-pinion; turns lock to lock: 2.80.

BRAKES disc (diameter 11.81 in, 30 cm), dual circuit, rear compensator, dual servo; lining area: front 22.9 sq in, 148 sq cm, rear 22.9 sq in, 148 sq cm, total 45.8 sq in, 296 sq cm.

ELECTRICAL EQUIPMENT 12 V; 48 Ah battery; 55 A alternator; electronic ignition; 4 iodine headlamps.

DIMENSIONS AND WEIGHT wheel base: 96.06 in, 244 cm; tracks: 59.37 in, 151 cm front, 58.66 in, 149 cm rear; length: 154.13 in, 391 cm; width: 72.83 in, 185 cm; height: 49.02 in, 124 cm; weight: 2,580 lb, 1,170 kg; weight distribution: 45% front, 55% rear; turning circle: 34.8 ft, 10.6 m; fuel tank: 15.4 imp gal, 18.5 US gal, 70 l (2 separate tanks).

BODY coupé, in plastic material; 2 doors; 2 seats, separate front seats, headrests; fog lamps.

PRACTICAL INSTRUCTIONS fuel: 97 oct petrol; oil: engine 14.1 imp pt, 16.9 US pt, 8 l, SAE 10W-50, change every 6,200 miles, 10,000 km - gearbox and final drive 5.3 imp pt, 6.3 US pt, 3 l, SAE 90, change every 18,600 miles, 30,000 km; greasing: none; spark plug: Champion N2G; tyre pressure: front 28 psi, 2 atm, rear 36 psi, 2.5 atm.

LANCIA Gamma Coupé 2500 IE

Gamma Berlina 2000

PRICE EX WORKS: 21,882,000 liras**

ENGINE front, 4 stroke; 4 cylinders, horizontally opposed; 122 cu in, 1,999 cc (3.60 x 2.99 in, 91.5 x 76 mm); compression ratio: 9:1; max power (DIN): 115 hp (85 kW) at 5,500 rpm; max torque (DIN): 127 lb ft, 17.5 kg m (172 Nm) at 3,500 rpm; max engine rpm: 6,200; 57.5 hp/l (42.5 kW/l); 3 crankshaft bearings; valves: overhead; camshafts: 2, 1 per bank, overhead; lubrication: rotary pump, full flow filter (cartridge), 10.7 imp pt, 12.9 US pt, 6.1 l; 1 Weber 36 ADL 1/250 twin barrel carburettor with power-valve and automatic starter; air cleaner: dry, thimble type thermostatic intake; fuel feed: mechanical pump; liquid-cooled 15.8 imp pt, 19 US pt, 9 l.

TRANSMISSION driving wheels: front; clutch: single dry plate (diaphragm); gearbox: mechanical; gears: 5, fully synchronized; ratios: I 3.462, II 2.105, III 1.458, IV 1.129, V 0.897, rev 3.214; lever: central; final drive: hypoid bevel, in unit with gearbox; axle ratio: 4.100; width of rims: 6"; tyres: 185/70 HR x 14 tubeless.

PERFORMANCE max speeds: (I) 31 mph, 50 mph; (II) 51 mph, 82 km/h; (III) 73 mph, 118 km/h; (IV) 94 mph, 152 km/h; (V) over 112 mph, 180 km/h; power-weight ratio: 25.3 lb/hp (34.2 lb/kW), 11.5 kg/hp (15.5 kg/kW); carrying capacity: 1,102 lb, 500 kg; acceleration: standing ¼ mile 18 sec; consumption: 25.7 m/imp gal, 21.4 m/US gal, 11 l x 100 km at 75 mph, 120 km/h.

CHASSIS integral; front and rear suspension: independent, wishbones, coil springs, telescopic damper struts, anti-roll bar.

STEERING rack-and-pinion, ZF progressive servo, adjustable height and tilt; turns lock to lock: 3.

BRAKES disc, internal radial fins, Superduplex circuit, servo.

ELECTRICAL EQUIPMENT 12 V; 60 Ah battery; 770 W alternator; Bosch or Marelli electronic ignition with impulser unit; 4 iodine headlamps with automatically adjustable height.

DIMENSIONS AND WEIGHT wheel base: 105.12 in, 267 cm; tracks: 57.09 in, 145 cm front, 56.69 in, 144 cm rear; length: 180.31 in, 458 cm; width: 68.11 in, 173 cm; height: 55.51 in, 141 cm; weight: 2,911 lb, 1,320 kg; fuel tank: 13.9 imp gal, 16.6 US gal, 63 l.

BODY saloon/sedan; 4 doors; 5 seats, separate front seats, 4 built-in headrests, reclining backrests; front electric windows; tinted glass; light alloy wheels.

PRACTICAL INSTRUCTIONS fuel: 98 oct petrol; oil: engine 10.7 imp pt, 12.9 US pt, 6.1 l, SAE 15W-50, change every 6,200 miles, 10,000 km - gearbox and final drive 6.2 imp pt, 7.4 US pt, 3.5 l, SAE 85W-90, change evey 18,600 miles, 30,000 km; greasing: none; spark plug: Bosch W200 T 30 OV or Champion N6Y; tappet clearances: inlet 0.012 in, 0.30 mm, exhaust 0.014 in, 0.35 mm; valve timing: 14°30' 38°30' 47°30' 5°30'; tyre pressure: front and rear 26 psi, 1.8 atm.

OPTIONALS Lancia/AP automatic transmission, hydraulic torque converter and planetary gears with 4 ratios (I 2.612, II 1.806, III 1.446, IV 1, rev 2.612), max speed over 109 mph, 175 km/h, consumption 25 m/imp gal, 20.8 m/US gal, 11.3 l x 100 km at 75 mph, 120 km/h; air-conditioning; metallic spray; rear electric windows; leather upholstery; front and rear (wrap-round) belts; fog lamps and rear red fog lamp; central door locking.

Gamma Coupé 2000

See Gamma Berlina 2000, except for:

PRICE EX WORKS: 28,170,000 liras**

PERFORMANCE power-weight ratio: 23.3 lb/hp (31.7 lb/kW), 10.6 kg/hp (14.4 kg/kW); consumption: 25.9 m/imp gal, 21.6 m/US gal, 10.9 l x 100 km at 75 mph, 120 km/h.

DIMENSIONS AND WEIGHT wheel base: 100.59 in, 255 cm; length: 176.57 in, 448 cm; height: 52.36 in, 133 cm; weight: 2,800 lb, 1,270 kg.

BODY coupé; 2 doors.

OPTIONALS with Lancia/AP automatic transmission consumption 25.4 m/imp gal, 21.2 m/US gal, 11.1 l x 100 km at 75 mph, 120 km/h.

Gamma Berlina 2500 IE

See Gamma Berlina 2000, except for:

PRICE IN GB: £ 9,650*
PRICE EX WORKS: 28,186,500 liras**

ENGINE 151.6 cu in, 2,484 cc (4.02 x 2.99 in, 102 x 76 mm); max power (DIN): 140 hp (103 kW) at 5,400 rpm; max torque (DIN): 154 lb ft, 21.2 kg m (208 Nm) at 3,000 rpm; max engine rpm: 6,000; 56.4 hp/l (41.5 kW/l); Bosch L-Jetronic injection; fuel feed: electric pump.

TRANSMISSION axle ratio: 3.700; width of rims: 6"; tyres: 195/60 HR x 15 P6.

PERFORMANCE max speed: 121 mph, 195 km/h; power-weight ratio: 21.1 lb/hp (28.7 lb/kW), 9.6 kg/hp (13 kg/kW); consumption: 27.7 m/imp gal, 23.1 m/US gal, 10.2 l x 100 km at 75 mph, 120 km/h.

DIMENSIONS AND WEIGHT weight: 2,955 lb, 1,340 kg.

OPTIONALS with Lancia/AP automatic transmission max speed over 115 mph, 185 km/h and consumption 24.6 m/imp gal, 20.5 m/US gal, 11.5 l x 100 km at 75 mph, 120 km/h.

LANCIA Gamma Coupé 2500 IE

Gamma Coupé 2500 IE

See Gamma Berlina 2000, except for:

PRICE IN GB: £ 12,200*
PRICE EX WORKS: 34,141,000 liras**

ENGINE 151.6 cu in, 2,484 cc (4.02 x 2.99 in, 102 x 76 mm); max power (DIN): 140 hp (103 kW) at 5,400 rpm; max torque (DIN): 154 lb ft, 21.2 kg m (208 Nm) at 3,000 rpm; max engine rpm: 6,000; 56.4 hp/l (41.5 kW/l); Bosch L-Jetronic injection; fuel feed: electric pump.

TRANSMISSION axle ratio: 3.700; width of rims: 6"; tyres: 195/60 HR x 15 P6.

PERFORMANCE max speed: over 121 mph, 195 km/h; power-weight ratio: 20.3 lb/hp (27.6 lb/kW), 9.2 kg/hp (12.5 kg/kW); consumption: 27.7 m/imp gal, 23.1 m/US gal, 10.2 l x 100 km at 75 mph, 120 km/h.

DIMENSIONS AND WEIGHT weight: 2,844 lb, 1,290 kg.

OPTIONALS with Lancia/AP automatic transmission max speed over 115 mph, 185 km/h and consumption 24.8 m/imp gal, 20.6 m/US gal, 11.4 l x 100 km at 75 mph, 120 km/h.

LAWIL — ITALY

S3 Varzina Spider

PRICE EX WORKS: 5,004,000 liras**

ENGINE front, 2 stroke; 2 cylinders, in line; 15 cu in, 246 cc (2.05 x 2.28 in, 52 x 58 mm); compression ratio: 7.5:1; max power (SAE): 14 hp (10 kW) at 4,400 rpm; max torque (SAE): 14 lb ft, 1.9 kg m (19 Nm) at 3,000 rpm; max engine rpm: 4,500; 56.9 hp/l (41.8 kW/l); cast iron block, light alloy head; 3 crankshaft bearings; lubrication: mixture; 1 Dell'Orto WHB horizontal carburettor; fuel feed: gravity; air-cooled.

TRANSMISSION driving wheels: rear; clutch: single dry plate; gearbox: mechanical; gears: 4, silent claw coupling; ratios: I 2.449, II 1.492, III 0.986, IV 0.674, rev 2.760; lever: central; final drive: spiral bevel; axle ratio: 3.083; width of rims: 3"; tyres: 4.00 x 10.

PERFORMANCE max speeds: (I) 12 mph, 20 km/h; (II) 19 mph, 30 km/h; (III) 29 mph, 47 km/h; (IV) 39 mph, 63 km/h; power-weight ratio: 50.5 lb/hp (68.6 lb/kW), 22.9 kg/hp (31.1 kg/kW); carrying capacity: 353 lb, 160 kg; consumption: 70.6 m/imp gal, 58.8 m/US gal, 4 l x 100 km.

CHASSIS tubular; front suspension: independent, wishbones, transverse semi-elliptic leafsprings, telescopic dampers; rear: rigid axle, semi-elliptic leafsprings, telescopic dampers.

STEERING rack-and-pinion; turns lock to lock: 3.50.

BRAKES drum, single circuit.

ELECTRICAL EQUIPMENT 12 V; 35 Ah battery; 160 W alternator; Ducati (electronic) distributor; 2 headlamps.

DIMENSIONS AND WEIGHT wheel base: 46.06 in, 117 cm; tracks: 40.94 in, 104 cm front, 42.32 in, 107 cm rear; length: 81.50 in, 207 cm; width: 50 in, 127 cm; height: 53.54 in, 136 cm; ground clearance: 4.72 in, 12 cm; weight: 706 lb, 320 kg; weight distribution: 55% front, 45% rear; turning circle: 19.7 ft, 6 m; fuel tank: 2.4 imp gal, 2.9 US gal, 11 l.

BODY open; no doors; 2 seats, bench front seats.

LAWIL S3 Varzina Spider

PRACTICAL INSTRUCTIONS fuel: mixture 1:50; oil: gearbox 1.8 imp pt, 2.1 US pt, 1 l, SAE 90 EP, change every 3,100 miles, 5,000 km - final drive 1.1 imp pt, 1.3 US pt, 0.6 l, SAE 90 EP, change every 6,200 miles, 10,000 km; greasing: every 3,100 miles, 5,000 km, 3 points; spark plug: 240°; tyre pressure: front 18 psi, 1.3 atm, rear 20 psi, 1.4 atm.

OPTIONALS tonneau cover; roll-bar.

A4 City Berlina

See S3 Varzina Spider, except for:

PRICE EX WORKS: 5,079,0000 liras**

PERFORMANCE power-weight ratio: 55.1 lb/hp (75 lb/kW), 25 kg/hp (34 kg/kW).

DIMENSIONS AND WEIGHT length: 80.71 in, 205 cm; width: 50.39 in, 128 cm; height: 56.69 in, 144 cm; weight: 772 lb, 350 kg.

BODY saloon/sedan.

OPTIONALS none.

MASERATI — ITALY

2000 Biturbo

PRICE IN USA: $ 25,945*
PRICE EX WORKS: 25,710,000* liras

ENGINE turbocharged; front, 4 stroke; 6 cylinders, Vee-slanted at 90°; 121.8 cu in, 1,996 cc (3.23 x 3.50 in, 82 x 63.5 mm); compression ratio: 7.8:1; max power (DIN): 180 hp (132 kW) at 6,000 rpm; max torque (DIN): 188 lb ft, 26 kg m (255 Nm) at 3,500 rpm; max engine rpm: 6,400; 90.2 hp/l (66.1 kW/l); light alloy block and head, wet liners, hemispherical combustion chambers; 4 crankshaft bearings; valves: 3 per cylinder (two intake and one exhaust in main combustion chamber), overhead, thimble tappets; camshafts: 2, 1 per bank, overhead, cogged belt; lubrication: gear pump, full flow filter, 10.6 imp pt, 12.7 Us pt, 6 l; 1 Weber 36 DCNVH 16/100 downdraught twin barrel carburettor with 2 IHI exhaust turbochargers, 1 per bank; fuel feed: electric pump; water-cooled, 15 imp pt, 18 US pt, 8.5 l, electric thermostatic fan.

TRANSMISSION driving wheels: rear; clutch: single dry plate (diaphragm), hydraulically controlled; gearbox: ZF S. 5. 18/3 mechanical; gears: 5, fully synchronized; ratios: I 3.420, II 2.080, III 1.390, IV 1, V 0.870, rev 3.660; lever: central; final drive: hypoid bevel; axle ratio: 3.730; width of rims: 5.5"; tyres: Pirelli P6 195/60 HR x 14.

PERFORMANCE max speeds: (I) 34 mph, 55 km/h; (II) 56 mph, 90 km/h; (III) 84 mph, 135 km/h; (IV) 116 mph, 187 km/h; (V) 134 mph, 215 km/h; power-weight ratio: 13.3 lb/hp (18.1 lb/kW), 6 kg/hp (8.2 kg/kW); carrying capacity: 882 lb, 400 kg; speed in top at 1,000 rpm: 20.9 mph, 33.6 km/h; consumption: 24.1 m/imp gal, 20.1 m/US gal, 11.7 l x 100 km at 75 mph, 120 km/h.

CHASSIS integral; front suspension: independent, by McPherson, coil springs/telescopic damper struts, wishbones, anti-roll bar; rear: independent, by McPherson, coil springs/telescopic damper struts, wishbones.

STEERING rack-and-pinion, adjustable tilt and height.

BRAKES disc, dual circuit, servo.

ELECTRICAL EQUIPMENT 12 V; 60 Ah battery; 65 A alternator; electronic ignition; 4 iodine headlamps.

DIMENSIONS AND WEIGHT wheel base: 98.98 in, 251 cm; tracks: 55.91 in, 142 cm front, 56.34 in, 143 cm rear; length: 163.50 in, 415 cm; width: 67.48 in, 171 cm; height: 51.38 in, 130 cm; ground clearance: 4.92 in, 12.5 cm; weight: 2,395 lb, 1,086 kg; turning circle: 38.4 ft, 11.7 m.

BODY coupé; 2 doors; 5 seats, separate front seats, reclining backrests, headrests; central door locking; electric windows; tinted glass; light alloy wheels; air-conditioning.

PRACTICAL INSTRUCTIONS fuel: 97 oct petrol; oil: engine 10.6 imp pt, 12.7 US pt, 6 l, SAE 10W-50, change every 3,100 miles, 5,000 km - gearbox 3 imp pt, 3.6 US pt, 1.7 l, SAE 90, change every 12,400 miles, 20,000 km - final drive 1.6 imp pt, 1.9 US pt, 0.9 l, change every 12,400 miles, 20,000 km; tyre pressure: front 33 psi, 2.3 atm, rear 33 psi, 2.3 atm.

VARIATIONS

ENGINE max power (DIN) 210 hp (156 kW) at 6,000 rpm, 105.2 hp/l (78.2 kW/l), intercooler.

OPTIONALS ZF 3HP 22 automatic transmission with 3 ratios (I 2.480, II 1.480, III 1, rev 2.090), 3.310 axle ratio; power steering; leather upholstery; metallic spray.

Biturbo 425

ENGINE turbocharged; front, 4 stroke; 6 cylinders, Vee-slanted at 90°; 152 cu in, 2,491 cc (3.61 x 2.48 in, 91.6 x 63 mm); compression ratio: 7.8:1; max power (DIN): 200 hp (147 kW) at 5,500 rpm; max torque (DIN): 223 lb ft, 30.8 kg m (302 Nm) at 3,000 rpm; max engine rpm: 6,200; 80.3 hp/l (59 kW/l); light alloy block and head, wet liners, hemispherical combustion chambers; 4 crankshaft bearings; valves: 3 per cylinder (two intake and one exhaust in main combustion chamber), overhead, thimble tappets; camshafts: 2, 1 per bank, overhead, cogged belt; lubrication: gear pump, full flow filter, 10.6 imp pt, 12.7 US pt, 6 l; 1 Weber downdraught twin barrel carburettor, with 2 IHI exhaust turbochargers, 1 per bank; MABC (Maserati Automatic Boost Control) electronic system; fuel feed: electric pump; water-cooled, 15 imp pt, 18 US pt, 8.5 l, electric thermostatic fan.

TRANSMISSION driving wheels: rear; clutch: single dry plate (diaphragm), hydraulically controlled; gearbox: ZF S.5.18/3 mechanical; gears: 5, fully synchronized; ratios: I 3.420, II 1.940, III 1.390, IV 1, V 0.870, rev 3.660; lever: central; final drive: hypoid bevel; axle ratio: 3.310; tyres: Pirelli P6 205/60 VR x 14.

PERFORMANCE max speed: over 134 mph, 215 km/h; power-weight ratio: 13 lb/hp (17.7 lb/kW), 5.9 kg/hp (8 kg/kW); carrying capacity: 882 lb, 400 kg; speed in top at 1,000 rpm: 21.5 mph, 34.7 km/h; consumption: not declared.

CHASSIS integral; front suspension: independent, by McPherson, coil springs/telescopic damper struts, wishbones, anti-roll bar; rear: independent, by McPherson, coil springs/telescopic damper struts, wishbones.

STEERING rack-and-pinion, adjustable tilt and height.

BRAKES disc, dual circuit, servo.

ELECTRICAL EQUIPMENT 12 V; 60 Ah battery; 65 A alternator; electronic ignition; 4 iodine headlamps.

DIMENSIONS AND WEIGHT wheel base: 102.36 in, 260 cm; tracks: 56.77 in, 144 cm front, 57.09 in, 145 cm rear; length: 173.23 in, 440 cm; width: 68.11 in, 173 cm; height: 53.54 in, 136 cm; ground clearance: 4.92 in, 12.5 cm; weight: 2,602 lb, 1,180 kg.

BODY saloon/sedan; 4 doors; 5 seats, separate front seats, reclining backrests; heated rear window; central door locking; light alloy wheels; tinted glass; electric windows; air-conditioning.

MASERATI 2000 Biturbo

MASERATI 2000 Biturbo

MASERATI Biturbo 425

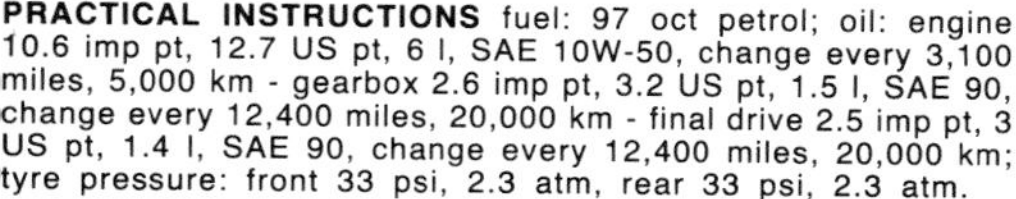

PRACTICAL INSTRUCTIONS fuel: 97 oct petrol; oil: engine 10.6 imp pt, 12.7 US pt, 6 l, SAE 10W-50, change every 3,100 miles, 5,000 km - gearbox 2.6 imp pt, 3.2 US pt, 1.5 l, SAE 90, change every 12,400 miles, 20,000 km - final drive 2.5 imp pt, 3 US pt, 1.4 l, SAE 90, change every 12,400 miles, 20,000 km; tyre pressure: front 33 psi, 2.3 atm, rear 33 psi, 2.3 atm.

OPTIONALS ZF 3HP 22 automatic transmission with 3 ratios (I 2.480, II 1.480, III 1, rev 2.090); power steering; headrests; leather upholstery.

Quattroporte

PRICE IN USA: $ 66,210*
PRICE EX WORKS: 72,698,000* liras

ENGINE front, 4 stroke; 8 cylinders in Vee; 300.8 cu in, 4,930 cc (3.70 x 3.50 in, 93.9 x 89 mm); compression ratio: 8.5:1; max power (DIN): 280 hp (206 kW) at 5,600 rpm; max torque (DIN): 289 lb ft, 40 kg m (392 Nm) at 3,000 rpm; max engine rpm: 6,000; 56.8 hp/l (41.8 kW/l); light alloy block and head, wet liners, hemispherical combustion chambers; 5 crankshaft bearings; valves: overhead; camshafts: 4, 2 per bank, overhead, chain-driven; lubrication: gear pump, full flow filter, 17 imp pt, 21 US pt, 9 l; 4 Weber 42 DCNF downdraught twin barrel carburettors; fuel feed: electric pump; water-cooled, 28 imp pt, 33.5 US pt, 16 l, 2 electric fans.

TRANSMISSION driving wheels: rear; gearbox: automatic transmission, hydraulic torque converter and planetary gears with 3 ratios, max ratio of converter at stall 2.75, possible manual selection; ratios: I 2.400, II 1.470, III 1, rev 2.700; lever: central; final drive: hypoid bevel; axle ratio: 3.540; width of rims: 7"; tyres: 225/70 VR x 15 XDX tubeless.

PERFORMANCE max speed: 143 mph, 230 km/h; power-weight ratio: 15 lb/hp (20.3 lb/kW), 6.8 kg/hp (9.2 kg/kW); carrying capacity: 1,103 lb, 500 kg; speed in direct drive at 1,000 rpm: 24.2 mph, 39.5 km/h; consumption: 14.9 m/imp gal, 12.4 m/US gal, 19 l x 100 km.

CHASSIS integral; front suspension: independent, by McPherson, coil springs/telescopic damper struts, wishbones, anti-roll bar; rear: independent, 4 coil springs with 4 coaxial telescopic dampers, wishbones, anti-roll bar.

STEERING rack-and-pinion, adjustable height and distance, servo; turns lock to lock: 2.50.

BRAKES disc, internal radial fins, dual circuit, servo; swept area: front 245.4 sq in, 1,583 sq cm, rear 188.5 sq in, 1,216 sq cm, total 433.9 sq in, 2,799 sq cm.

ELECTRICAL EQUIPMENT 12 V; 72 Ah battery; 650 W alternator; Bosch electronic ignition; 4 iodine headlamps.

DIMENSIONS AND WEIGHT wheel base: 110.20 in, 280 cm; front and rear track: 60.03 in, 152 cm; length: 196 in, 498 cm; width: 70.47 in, 179 cm; height: 53.14 in, 135 cm; ground clearance: 5.55 in, 14 cm; weight: 4,190 lb, 1,900 kg; turning circle: 35 ft, 11.5 m; fuel tank: 22 imp gal, 26.4 US gal, 100 l.

BODY saloon/sedan; 4 doors; 5 seats, separate and reclining front seats; tinted glass; electric windows; heated rear window.

PRACTICAL INSTRUCTIONS fuel: 98-100 oct petrol; oil: engine 17 imp pt, 21 US pt, 9 l, SAE 10W-50, change every 3,000 miles, 5,000 km - gearbox 2.5 imp pt, 3 US pt, 1.4 l - final drive 2.5 imp pt, 3 US pt, 1.4 l, SAE 90, change every 12,400 miles, 20,000 km; greasing: every 3,100 miles, 5,000 km; spark plug: Bosch 200 T 30; tappet clearances: inlet 0.011 in, 0.25 mm, exhaust 0.024 in, 0.50 mm; valve timing: 40° 80° 55° 25°; tyre pressure: front 36 psi, 2.5 atm, rear 37 psi, 2.6 atm.

VARIATIONS

ENGINE 252.3 cu in, 4,136 cc (3.46 x 3.35 in, 88 x 85 mm), max power (DIN) 255 hp (188 kW) at 6,000 rpm, max torque (DIN) 261 lb ft, 36 kg m (353 Nm) at 3,200 rpm, 61.7 hp/l (45.4 kW/l).
PERFORMANCE power-weight ratio 16.5 lb/hp (22.3 lb/kW), 7.5 kg/hp (10.1 kg/kW).

OPTIONALS ZF 5-speed fully synchronized mechanical gearbox (I 2.990, II 1.900, III 1.320, IV 1, V 0.890, rev 2.700); limited slip differential; air-conditioning; central door locking; leather upholstery; metallic spray.

NUOVA INNOCENTI ITALY

3 Cilindri

PRICES EX WORKS:	liras
S 2+1-dr Berlina	7,063,000**
SL 2+1-dr Berlina	7,629,000**
SE 2+1-dr Berlina	8,261,000**

ENGINE Daihatsu, front, transverse, 4 stroke; 3 cylinders, vertical, in line; 60.6 cu in, 993 cc (2.99 x 2.87 in, 76 x 73 mm); compression ratio: 9.1:1; max power (DIN): 52 hp (38 kW) at 5,600 rpm; max torque (DIN): 55 lb ft, 7.6 kg m (74 Nm) at 3,200 rpm; max engine rpm: 6,000; 52.4 hp/l (38.3 kW/l); cast iron block, light alloy head; 4 crankshaft bearings; valves: overhead, Vee-slanted, rockers; camshafts: 1, overhead, cogged belt; lubrication: trochoid pump, driven by balance shaft, full flow filter (cartridge), 5.1 imp pt, 6.1 US pt, 2.9 l; 1 Aisan downdraught twin barrel carburettor; fuel feed: mechanical pump; liquid-cooled, sealed circuit, 7.6 imp pt, 9.1 US pt, 4.3 l, electric thermostatic fan.

TRANSMISSION driving wheels: front; clutch: single dry plate (diaphragm); gearbox: mechanical, in line with engine, in unit with differential; gears: 5, fully synchronized; ratios: I 3.667, II 2.100, III 1.464, IV 0.971, V 0.795, rev 3.529; lever: central; final drive: helical spur gears; axle ratio: 4.278; width of rims: 4"; tyres: 135 SR x 12.

PERFORMANCE max speeds: (I) 22 mph, 36 km/h; (II) 39 mph, 63 km/h; (III) 57 mph, 91 km/h; (IV) 85 mph, 137 km/h; (V) 88 mph, 142 km/h; power-weight ratio: 27.1 lb/hp (37 lb/kW), 12.3 kg/hp (16.8 kg/kW); carrying capacity: 882 lb, 400 kg; acceleration: standing ¼ mile 20.2 sec, 0-50 mph (0-80 km/h) 13.9 sec; speed in top at 1,000 rpm: 17.4 mph, 28 km/h; consumption: 54.3 m/imp gal, 45.2 m/US gal, 5.2 l x 100 km at 56 mph, 90 km/h.

CHASSIS integral; front suspension: independent, by McPherson, lower wishbones, coil springs/telescopic damper struts; rear: independent, transverse leafspring, lower wishbones, telescopic dampers.

STEERING rack-and-pinion; turns lock to lock: 3.13.

MASERATI Quattroporte

NUOVA INNOCENTI 3 Cilindri

NUOVA INNOCENTI Turbo De Tomaso

3 CILINDRI

BRAKES front disc, dual circuit, servo; lining area: front 15.8 sq in, 102 sq cm, rear 32.6 sq in, 210 sq cm, total 48.4 sq in, 312 sq cm.

ELECTRICAL EQUIPMENT 12 V; 43 Ah battery; 540 W alternator; Nippon-Denso distributor; 2 headlamps.

DIMENSIONS AND WEIGHT wheel base: 80.16 in, 204 cm; tracks: 49.09 in, 125 cm front, 51.10 in, 130 cm rear; length: 124.41 in, 316 cm; width: 59.84 in, 152 cm; height: 54.33 in, 138 cm; ground clearance: 4.92 in, 12.5 cm; weight: 1,407 lb, 638 kg; weight distribution: 63% front, 37% rear; turning circle: 28.5 ft, 8.7 m; fuel tank: 8.8 imp gal, 10.6 US gal, 40 l.

BODY saloon/sedan; 2+1 doors; 5 seats, separate front seats; folding rear seat; (for SL and SE only) luxury interior.

PRACTICAL INSTRUCTIONS fuel: 97 oct petrol; oil: engine 5.1 imp pt, 6.1 US pt, 2.9 l, SAE 10W-50, change every 6,200 miles, 10,000 km - gearbox and final drive 2.8 imp pt, 3.4 US pt, 1.6 l, SAE 80W-90, change every 24,800 miles, 40,000 km; spark plug: Champion RN-12Y; tappet clearances: inlet 0.008 in, 0.20 mm, exhaust 0.008 in, 0.20 mm; valve timing: 19° 51° 51° 19°; tyre pressure: front 26 psi, 1.8 atm, rear 26 psi, 1.8 atm.

OPTIONALS heated rear window; rear window wiper-washer; (for SL only) headrests, tinted glass, halogen headlamps and metallic spray; (for SE only) electric windows.

Turbo De Tomaso

See 3 Cilindri, except for:

PRICE EX WORKS: 10,200,000 liras**

ENGINE turbocharged; max power (DIN): 72 hp (53 kW) at 6,200 rpm; max torque (DIN): 70 lb ft, 9.7 kg m (95 Nm) at 4,400 rpm; max engine rpm: 6,200; 72.5 hp/l (53.4 kW/l); lubrication: 6.2 imp pt, 7.4 US pt, 3.5 l; Aisan IHI RHB5 turbocharger.

TRANSMISSION gearbox ratios: I 3.091, II 1.842, III 1.231, IV 0.865, V 0.707, rev 3.143; axle ratio: 4.500; width of rims: 4.5"; tyres: 165/70 HR x 13.

PERFORMANCE max speed: 103 mph, 165 km/h; power-weight ratio: 20.5 lb/hp (27.9 lb/kW), 9.3 kg/hp (12.6 kg/kW); acceleration: standing ¼ mile 17.6 sec, 0-50 mph (0-80 km/h) 10.8 sec; speed in top at 1,000 rpm: 18.6 mph, 30 km/h; consumption: 39.8 m/imp gal, 33.1 m/US gal, 7.1 l x 100 km at 75 mph, 120 km/h.

CHASSIS front suspension: anti-roll bar.

ELECTRICAL EQUIPMENT 40 Ah battery; 45 A alternator.

DIMENSIONS AND WEIGHT weight: 1,477 lb, 670 kg; weight distribution: 64% front, 36% rear.

BODY laminated windscreen; heated rear window (standard).

PRACTICAL INSTRUCTIONS oil: engine 6.2 imp pt, 7.4 US pt, 3.5 l, SAE 10W-50, change every 6,200 miles, 10,000 km; tyre pressure: front 28 psi, 2 atm, rear 31 psi, 2.2 atm.

OPTIONALS rear window wiper-washer; headrests; tinted glass; halogen headlamps; metallic spray; electric windows.

PININFARINA ITALY

Spidereuropa

PRICE IN USA: $ 16,000*
PRICE EX WORKS: 16,300,000 liras**

ENGINE Fiat, front, 4 stroke; 4 cylinders, vertical, in line; 121.7 cu in, 1,995 cc (3.31 x 3.54 in, 84 x 90 mm); compression ratio: 8.2:1; max power (DIN): 105 hp (77 kW) at 5,500 rpm; max torque (DIN): 111 lb ft, 15.3 kg m (150 Nm) at 3,300 rpm; max engine rpm: 6,000; 52.6 hp/l (38.6 kW/l); cast iron block, light alloy head; 5 crankshaft bearings; valves: overhead, Vee-slanted at 65°, thimble tappets; camshafts: 2, overhead, cogged belt; lubrication: gear pump, full flow filter (cartridge), 8.3 imp pt, 9.9 US pt, 4.7 l; Bosch L-Jetronic injection; fuel feed: electric pump; water-cooled, expansion tank, 14.1 imp pt, 16.9 US pt, 8 l, electric thermostatic fan.

TRANSMISSION driving wheels: rear; clutch: single dry plate; gearbox: mechanical; gears: 5, fully synchronized; ratios: I 3.667, II 2.100, III 1.361, IV 1, V 0.881, rev 3.526; lever: central; final drive: hypoid bevel; axle ratio: 3.900; width of rims: 5.5"; tyres: Pirelli 185/60 HR x 14 P6 or 165 SR x 13.

PERFORMANCE max speeds: (I) 31 mph, 50 km/h; (II) 53 mph, 85 km/h; (III) 81 mph, 130 km/h; (IV) 102 mph, 165 km/h; (V) over 112 mph, 180 km/h; power-weight ratio: 22.3 lb/hp (30.4 lb/kW), 10.1 kg/hp (13.8 kg/kW); carrying capacity: 706 lb, 320 kg; acceleration: 0-50 mph (0-80 km/h) 8.4 sec; speed in top at 1,000 rpm: 16.6 mph, 26.8 km/h; consumption: 31.4 m/imp gal, 26.1 m/US gal, 9 l x 100 km at 75 mph, 120 km/h.

CHASSIS integral; front suspension: independent, wishbones, coil springs, anti-roll bar, telescopic dampers; rear: rigid axle, twin trailing radius arms, transverse linkage bar, coil springs, telescopic dampers.

PININFARINA Spidereuropa Volumex

STEERING worm and roller; turns lock to lock: 2.75.

BRAKES disc (diameter 8.94 in, 22.7 cm), dual circuit, servo; lining area: front 19.2 sq in, 124 sq cm, rear 19.2 sq in, 124 sq cm, total 38.4 sq in, 248 sq cm.

ELECTRICAL EQUIPMENT 12 V; 55 Ah battery; 65 A alternator; Marelli electronic ignition; 2 iodine headlamps.

DIMENSIONS AND WEIGHT wheel base: 89.76 in, 228 cm; front and rear track: 52.99 in, 135 cm; length: 161.69 in, 411 cm; width: 63.50 in, 161 cm; height: 50 in, 127 cm; ground clearance: 4.80 in, 12 cm; weight: 2,337 lb, 1,060 kg; weight distribution: 53% front, 47% rear; turning circle: 33.8 ft, 10.3 m; fuel tank: 9.9 imp gal, 11.9 US gal, 45 l.

BODY sports; 2 doors; 2+2 seats, separate front seats, reclining backrests, headrests; tinted glass; light alloy wheels; electric windows.

PRACTICAL INSTRUCTIONS fuel: 97 oct petrol; oil: engine 7.2 imp pt, 8.7 US pt, 4.1 l, SAE 10W-50, change every 6,200 miles, 10,000 km - gearbox 2.8 imp pt, 3.5 US pt, 1.6 l, SAE 80W-90, change every 18,600 miles, 30,000 km - final drive 2.3 imp pt, 2.7 US pt, 1.3 l, change every 18,600 miles 30,000 km; greasing: none; spark plug: Champion RN9Y; tappet clearances: inlet 0.018 in, 0.45 mm, exhaust 0.020 in, 0.50 mm; valve timing: 5° 53° 53° 5°; tyre pressure: front 28 psi, 2 atm, rear 28 psi, 2 atm.

VARIATIONS

(for USA, Canada and Japan only)
ENGINE max power (SAE net) 102 hp (75 kW) at 5,500 rpm, max torque (DIN) 110 lb ft, 15.2 kg m (149 Nm) at 3,000 rpm, 51.1 hp/h (37.6 kW/l).
TRANSMISSION GM automatic transmission, hydraulic torque converter and planetary gears with 3 ratios (I 2.400, II 1.480, III 1, rev 1.920), max ratio of converter at stall 2.40, possible manual selection, 3.583 axle ratio.
PERFORMANCE max speed 104 mph, 167 km/h.

OPTIONALS metallic spray.

Spidereuropa Volumex

See Spidereuropa, except for:

PRICE EX WORKS: 22,000,000 liras**

ENGINE charged; compression ratio: 7.5:1; max power (DIN): 135 hp (99 kW) at 5,600 rpm; max torque (DIN): 152 lb ft, 21 kg m (206 Nm) at 3,000 rpm; 67.7 hp/l (49.6 kW/l); lubrication: oil cooler, 7.7 imp pt, 9.3 US pt, 4.4 l; 1 Weber 36 DCA 7/250 downdraught twin barrel carburettor; Roots volumetric supercharger.

TRANSMISSION axle ratio: 3.727; tyres: 195/50 VR x 15.

PERFORMANCE max speed: over 118 mph, 190 km/h; power-weight ratio: 17.3 lb/hp (23.6 lb/kW), 7.9 kg/hp (10.7 kg/kW); acceleration: standing ¼ mile 16 sec; consumption: 28.2 m/imp gal, 23.5 m/US gal, 10 l x 100 km at 75 mph, 120 km/h.

BRAKES front disc, internal radial fins.

ELECTRICAL EQUIPMENT 55 A alternator.

DIMENSIONS AND WEIGHT tracks: 54.53 in, 138 cm front, 54.09 in, 137 cm rear; width: 63.98 in, 162 cm; turning circle: 34.3 ft, 10.4 m.

PRACTICAL INSTRUCTIONS oil: engine 7.7 imp pt, 9.3 US pt, 4.4 l; spark plug: Champion N6Y.

FSO POLAND

126 P / 650

ENGINE rear, 4 stroke; 2 cylinders, vertical, in line; 39.8 cu in, 652 cc (3 x 2.70 in, 77 x 70 mm); compression ratio: 7.5:1; max power (DIN): 24 hp (18 kW) at 4,500 rpm; max torque (DIN): 30 lb ft, 4.2 kg m (41 Nm) at 3,000 rpm; max engine rpm: 5,400; 36.8 hp/l (27 kW/l); light alloy block and head; 2 crankshaft bearings; valves: overhead, in line, push-rods and rockers; camshafts: 1, side, chain-driven; lubrication: gear pump, centrifugal filter, 4.8 imp pt, 5.7 US pt, 2.7 l; 1 Fos 28 IMB 5/250 downdraught carburettor; fuel feed: mechanical pump; air-cooled.

TRANSMISSION driving wheels: rear; clutch: single dry plate (diaphragm); gearbox: mechanical; gears: 4, II, III and IV silent claw coupling; ratios: I 3.250, II 2.067, III 1.300, IV 0.872, rev 4.024; lever: central; final drive: spiral bevel; axle ratio: 4.875; width of rims: 4"; tyres: 135 SR x 12.

PERFORMANCE max speeds: (I) 19 mph, 30 km/h; (II) 31 mph, 50 km/h; (III) 50 mph, 80 km/h; (IV) 65 mph, 105 km/h; power-weight ratio: 55.6 lb/hp (75.7 lb/kW), 25.2 kg/hp (34.3 kg/kW); carrying capacity: 706 lb, 320 kg; acceleration: 0-50 mph (0-80 km/h) 24 sec; speed in top at 1,000 rpm: 14.7 mph, 23.6 km/h; consumption: 49.5 m/imp gal, 41.3 m/US gal, 5.7 l x 100 km.

FSO 126 P / 650

CHASSIS integral; front suspension: independent, wishbones, transverse leafspring lower arms, telescopic dampers; rear: independent, semi-trailing arms, coil springs, telescopic dampers.

STEERING screw and sector; turns lock to lock: 2.90.

BRAKES drum; swept area: front 32.4 sq in, 209 sq cm, rear 32.4 sq in, 209 sq cm, total 64.8 sq in, 418 sq cm.

ELECTRICAL EQUIPMENT 12 V; 34 Ah battery; 400 W alternator; Zelmot distributor; 2 headlamps.

DIMENSIONS AND WEIGHT wheel base: 72.44 in, 184 cm; tracks: 44.88 in, 114 cm front, 47.24 in, 120 cm rear; length: 120.08 in, 305 cm; width: 54.33 in, 138 cm; height: 52.36 in, 133 cm; ground clearance: 5.51 in, 14 cm; weight: 1,323 lb, 600 kg; weight distribution: 40.5% front, 59.5% rear; turning circle: 28.2 ft, 8.6 m; fuel tank: 4.6 imp gal, 5.5 US gal, 21 l.

BODY saloon/sedan; 2 doors; 4 seats, separate front seats; heated rear window.

PRACTICAL INSTRUCTIONS fuel: 94 oct petrol; oil: engine 4.4 imp pt, 5.3 US pt, 2.5 l, SAE 10W-30 or 20W-40, change every 6,200 miles, 10,000 km - gearbox and final drive 1.9 imp pt, 2.3 US pt, 1.1 l, SAE 90, change every 18,600 miles, 30,000 km; greasing: every 6,200 miles, 10,000 km, 2 points; tappet clearances: inlet 0.008 in, 0.20 mm, exhaust 0.010 in, 0.25 mm; valve timing: 26° 56° 66° 16°; tyre pressure: front 22 psi, 1.4 atm, rear 29 psi, 2 atm.

OPTIONALS S version, reclining backrests, tinted windscreen and heated rear window; K version, retractable seat belts, rear side windows opening half way down and heavy-duty brakes.

125 P / 1300

PRICE IN GB: £ 2,599*

ENGINE front, 4 stroke; 4 cylinders, overhead, in line; 79.3 cu in, 1,299 cc (2.83 x 3.13 in, 72 x 79.5 mm); compression ratio: 9:1; max power (DIN): 64 hp (47 kW) at 5,200 rpm; max torque (DIN): 69 lb ft, 9.5 kg m (93 Nm) at 4,000 rpm; max engine rpm: 6,000; 49.3 hp/l (36.2 kW/l); cast iron block, light alloy head, polispherical combustion chambers; 3 crankshaft bearings; valves: overhead, push-rods and rockers; camshafts: 1, side, in crankcase; lubrication: gear pump, centrifugal filter (cartridge), 6.9 imp pt, 8.2 US pt, 3.9 l; 1 Weber 34 DCHD downdraught twin barrel carburettor; air cleaner; fuel feed: mechanical pump; water-cooled, 11.8 imp pt, 14.2 US pt, 6.7 l, thermostatic fan.

TRANSMISSION driving wheels: rear; clutch: single dry plate, hydraulically controlled; gearbox: mechanical; gears: 4, fully synchronized; ratios: I 3.753, II 2.303, III 1.493, IV 1, rev 3.867; lever: central; final drive: hypoid bevel; axle ratio: 4.100; width of rims: 4.5''; tyres: 165 SR x 13.

PERFORMANCE max speeds: (I) 25 mph, 40 km/h; (II) 40 mph, 65 km/h; (III) 62 mph, 100 km/h; (IV) over 90 mph, 145 km/h; power-weight ratio: 35.1 lb/hp (47.8 lb/kW), 15.9 kg/hp (21.7 kg/kW); carrying capacity: 882 lb, 400 kg; acceleration: 0-50 mph (0-80 km/h) 11.8 sec; speed in direct drive at 1,000 rpm: 16.4 mph, 26.4 km/h; consumption: 35.8 m/imp gal, 29.8 m/US gal, 7.9 l x 100 km at 56 mph, 90 km/h.

CHASSIS integral; front suspension: independent, wishbones, coil springs, anti-roll bar acting as lower trailing arms, telescopic dampers; rear: rigid axle, semi-elliptic leafsprings, telescopic dampers.

STEERING worm and roller; turns lock to lock: 3.

BRAKES disc (diameter 8.94 in, 22.7 mm), vacuum servo; lining area: front 19.2 sq in, 124 sq cm, rear 19.2 sq in, 124 sq cm, total 38.4 sq in, 248 sq cm.

ELECTRICAL EQUIPMENT 12 V; 48 Ah battery; 53 A alternator; Zelmot-Marelli distributor; 4 headlamps.

DIMENSIONS AND WEIGHT wheel base: 98.82 in, 251 cm; tracks: 51.18 in, 130 cm front, 50 in, 127 cm rear; length: 166.65 in, 423 cm; width: 64.17 in, 163 cm; height: 56.69 in, 144 cm; ground clearance: 5.51 in, 14 cm; weight: 2,249 lb, 1,020 kg; weight distribution: 41% front, 59% rear; turning circle: 35.4 ft, 10.8 m; fuel tank: 9.9 imp gal, 11.9 US gal, 45 l.

BODY saloon/sedan; 4 doors; 5 seats, separate front seats, reclining backrests, built-in headrests; laminated windscreen.

PRACTICAL INSTRUCTIONS fuel: 94 oct petrol; oil: engine 6.2 imp pt, 7.4 US pt, 3.5 l, SAE 10W-30/20W-40, change every 6,200 miles, 10,000 km - gearbox 2.3 imp pt, 2.7 US pt, 1.3 l, SAE 90 EP, change every 18,600 miles, 30,000 km - final drive 2.1 imp pt, 2.5 US pt, 1.2 l, SAE 90 EP, change every 18,600 miles, 30,000 km; greasing: none; spark plug: Champion N 9 Y; tappet clearances: inlet 0.008 in, 0.20 mm, exhaust 0.010 in, 0.25 mm; valve timing: 5° 44° 47° 2°; tyre pressure: front 24 psi, 1.7 atm, rear 27 psi, 1.9 atm.

FSO 125 P 1300 - 1500 Sedan

VARIATIONS

(high performance engine)
ENGINE max power (DIN) 82 hp (60 kW) at 5,200 rpm, max torque (DIN) 88 lb ft, 12.2 kg m (120 Nm) at 4,000 rpm, 9.5:1 compression ratio, 63.1 hp/l (46.2 kW/l).

OPTIONALS luxury interior; sunroof; heated rear window.

125 P / 1500 Sedan

See 125 P / 1300, except for:

PRICES IN GB:	£
Populare II 4-dr Sedan	—
4-dr Sedan	**2,899***

ENGINE 90.4 cu in, 1,481 cc (3.03 x 3.13 in, 77 x 79.5 mm); max power (DIN): 75 hp (55 kW) at 5,400 rpm; max torque (DIN): 83 lb ft, 11.5 kg m (113 Nm) at 3,200 rpm; 50.6 hp/l (37.2 kW/l); 1 Weber 34 DCHD-16 carburettor; electric thermostatic fan.

PERFORMANCE max speed: 96 mph, 155 km/h; power-weight ratio: 30 lb/hp (40.8 lb/kW), 13.6 kg/hp (18.5 kg/kW); consumption: 35.3 m/imp gal, 29.4 m/US gal, 8 l x 100 km at 56 mph, 90 km/h.

BODY (for GLS only) luxury equipment.

125 P / 1500 Estate

See 125 P / 1300, except for:

PRICE IN GB: £ 3,299*

ENGINE 90.4 cu in, 1,481 cc (3.03 x 3.13 in, 77 x 79.5 mm); max power (DIN): 75 hp (55 kW) at 5,400 rpm; max torque (DIN): 83 lb ft, 11.5 kg m (113 Nm) at 3,800 rpm; 50.6 hp/l (37.2 kW/l); 1 Weber 34 DCHD-16 carburettor; electric thermostatic fan.

TRANSMISSION width of rims: 5''; tyres: 175 SR x 13.

PERFORMANCE max speed: 93 mph, 150 km/h; power-weight ratio: 31.3 lb/hp (42.6 lb/kW), 14.2 kg/hp (19.3 kg/kW); carrying capacity: 992 lb, 450 kg; consumption: 32.1 m/imp gal, 26.7 m/US gal, 8.8 l x 100 km at 56 mph, 90 km/h.

DIMENSIONS AND WEIGHT tracks: 51.57 in, 131 cm front, 50.79 in, 129 cm rear; width: 63.39 in, 161 cm; height: 57.87 in, 147 cm; ground clearance: 6.06 in, 15.4 cm; weight: 2,348 lb, 1,065 kg.

BODY estate car/st. wagon; 4+1 doors; folding rear seat.

Polonez LE

PRICES IN GB:	£
Populare II 4+1-dr Hatchback Sedan	—
X 4+1-dr Hatchback Sedan	**3,899***

ENGINE front, 4 stroke; 4 cylinders, overhead, in line; 90.4 cu in, 1,481 cc (3.03 x 3.13 in, 77 x 79.5 mm); compression ratio: 9.2:1; max power (DIN): 82 hp (60 kW) at 5,250 rpm; max torque (DIN): 84 lb ft, 11.6 kg m (114 Nm) at 3,400 rpm; max engine rpm; 6,000; 55.4 hp/l (40.5 kW/l); cast iron block, light alloy head; 3 crankshaft bearings; valves: overhead, push-rods and rockers; camshafts: 1, side, chain-driven; lubrication: gear pump, full flow filter, 7 imp pt, 8.5 US pt, 4 l; 1 Weber 34 DCMPI downdraught twin barrel carburettor; air cleaner; fuel feed: mechanical pump; water-cooled, 13.2 imp pt, 15.8 US pt, 7.5 l, electric thermostatic fan.

TRANSMISSION driving wheels: rear; clutch: single dry plate (diaphragm), hydraulically controlled; gearbox: mechanical; gears: 5, fully synchronized; ratios: I 3.753, II 2.132, III 1.378, IV 1, V 0.880, rev 3.867; lever: central; final drive: hypoid bevel; axle ratio: 4.100; width of rims: 5''; tyres: 170/175 SR x 13.

PERFORMANCE max speeds: (I) 26 mph, 42 km/h; (II) 47 mph, 75 km/h; (III) 71 mph, 115 km/h; (IV) 93 mph, 150 km/h; power-weight ratio: 30.6 lb/hp (41.9 lb/kW), 13.9 kg/hp (19 kg/kW); carrying capacity: 882 lb, 400 kg; acceleration: standing ¼ mile 11 sec; speed in direct drive at 1,000 rpm: 16.8 mph, 27 km/h; consumption: 36.2 m/imp gal, 30.2 m/US gal, 7.8 l x 100 km at 56 mph, 90 km/h.

CHASSIS integral; front suspension: independent, wishbones, coil springs, anti-roll bar acting as lower trailing arms, telescopic dampers; rear: rigid axle, 2 semi-elliptic leafsprings, telescopic dampers.

STEERING worm and roller; turns lock to lock: 3.05.

BRAKES disc (diameter 8.94 in, 22.7 cm), dual circuit, vacuum servo; lining area: front 19.2 sq in, 124 sq cm, rear 19.2 sq in, 124 sq cm, total 38.4 sq in, 248 sq cm.

POLONEZ LE

ELECTRICAL EQUIPMENT 12 V; 48 Ah battery; 553 W alternator; Zelmot-Marelli distributor; 4 headlamps, 2 halogen fog lamps.

DIMENSIONS AND WEIGHT wheel base: 98.78 in, 251 cm; tracks: 50.79 in, 129 cm front, 50 in, 127 cm rear; length: 168.20 in, 427 cm; width: 64.96 in, 165 cm; height: 54.33 in, 138 cm; ground clearance: 5.12 in, 13 cm; weight: 2,514 lb, 1,140 kg; weight distribution: 45% front, 55% rear; turning circle: 35.4 ft, 10.8 m; fuel tank: 9.9 imp gal, 11.9 US gal, 45 l.

BODY saloon/sedan; 4+1 doors; 5 seats, separate front seats, reclining backrests, adjustable headrests; heated rear window; rear window wiper-washer; laminated windscreen.

PRACTICAL INSTRUCTIONS fuel: 94 oct petrol; oil: engine 6.2 imp pt, 7.4 US pt, 3.5 l, SAE 10W-30/20W-40, change every 6,200 miles, 10,000 km - gearbox 2.3 imp pt, 2.7 US pt, 1.3 l, SAE 90 EP, change every 18,600 miles, 30,000 km - final drive 2.5 imp pt, 3 US pt, 1.4 l, SAE 90 EP, change every 18,600 miles, 30,000 km; spark plug: Champion N 9 Y; tappet clearances: inlet 0.008 in, 0.20 mm, exhaust 0.010 in, 0.25 mm; valve timing: 25° 51° 64° 12°; tyre pressure: front 26 psi, 1.8 atm, rear 28 psi, 2 atm.

OPTIONALS folding rear seat.

FSO Polonez LE X Hatchback Sedan

SYRENA POLAND

105

ENGINE front, 2 stroke; 3 cylinders, vertical, in line; 51.4 cu in, 842 cc (2.76 x 2.87 in, 70 x 73 mm); compression ratio: 7-7.2:1; max power (DIN): 40 hp (29 kW) at 4,300 rpm; max torque (DIN): 58 lb ft, 8 kg m (78 Nm) at 2,750 rpm; max engine rpm: 5,200; 47.5 hp/l (34.9 kW/l); cast iron block, dry liners, light alloy head; 4 crankshaft bearings on ball bearings; lubrication: mixture; 1 Jikov 35POH/048 horizontal carburettor; fuel feed: mechanical pump; water-cooled, 12.3 imp pt, 14.8 US pt, 7 l.

TRANSMISSION driving wheels: front; clutch: single dry plate; gearbox: mechanical; gears: 4, free wheel, fully synchronized; ratios: I 3.900, II 2.357, III 1.474, IV 0.958, rev 3.273; lever: steering column; final drive: spiral bevel; axle ratio: 4.875; width of rims: 4''; tyres: 5.60 x 15.

PERFORMANCE max speeds: (I) 19 mph, 31 km/h; (II) 32 mph, 51 km/h; (III) 50 mph, 81 km/h; (IV) 75 mph, 120 km/h; power-weight ratio: 47.8 lb/hp (65 lb/kW), 21.7 kg/hp (29.5 kg/kW); carrying capacity: 706 lb, 320 kg; acceleration: 0-50 mph (0-80 km/h) 21 sec; speed in top at 1,000 rpm: 14.9 mph, 24 km/h; consumption: 32.1 m/imp gal, 26.7 m/US gal, 8.8 l x 100 km.

CHASSIS box-type ladder frame; front suspension: independent, wishbones, transverse leafspring lower arms, telescopic dampers; rear: rigid axle, transverse upper leafspring, trailing radius arms, telescopic dampers.

STEERING worm and roller; turns lock to lock: 2.80.

BRAKES drum; swept area: front 76.3 sq in, 492 sq cm, rear 45 sq in, 290 sq cm, total 121.3 sq in, 782 sq cm.

ELECTRICAL EQUIPMENT 12 V; 42 Ah battery; 300 W dynamo; 2 headlamps.

DIMENSIONS AND WEIGHT wheel base: 90.55 in, 230 cm; tracks: 47.24 in, 120 cm front, 48.82 in, 124 cm rear; length: 159.05 in, 404 cm; width: 61.42 in, 156 cm; height: 59.65 in, 151 cm; ground clearance: 7.87 in, 20 cm; weight: 1,912 lb, 867 kg; weight distribution: 48% front, 52% rear; turning circle: 34.1 ft, 10.4 m; fuel tank: 7 imp gal, 9.2 US gal, 35 l.

BODY saloon/sedan; 2 doors; 5 seats, separate front seats.

PRACTICAL INSTRUCTIONS fuel: mixture 1:30; oil: gearbox and final drive 4 imp pt, 4.9 US pt, 2.3 l, SAE 90, change every 7,500 miles, 12,000 km; greasing: every 7,500 miles, 12,000 km, 29 points; spark plug: 175° or 225°; tyre pressure: front 23 psi, 1.6 atm, rear 23 psi, 1.6 atm.

CITROËN PORTUGAL

FAF

ENGINE front, 4 stroke; 2 cylinders, horizontally opposed; 36.7 cu in, 602 cc (2.91 x 2.76 in, 74 x 70 mm); compression ratio: 8.5:1; max power (DIN): 29 hp (21 kW) at 5,750 rpm; max torque (DIN): 29 lb ft, 4 kg m (39 Nm) at 3,500 rpm; max engine rpm: 5,900; 48.2 hp/l (35.4 kW/l); light alloy block and head, dry liners, hemispherical combustion chambers; 2 crankshaft bearings; valves: overhead, Vee-slanted at 70°, push-rods and rockers; camshafts: 1, central, lower; lubrication: rotary pump, filter in sump, oil cooler, 4 imp pt, 4.9 US pt, 2.3 l; 1 Solex 26/35 CSIC 225 downdraught twin barrel carburettor; fuel feed: mechanical pump; air-cooled.

TRANSMISSION driving wheels: front; clutch: single dry plate; gearbox: mechanical; gears: 4, fully synchronized; ratios: I 6.060, II 3.125, III 1.923, IV 1.421, rev 6.060; lever: on facia; final drive: spiral bevel; axle ratio: 3.875; width of rims: 4''; tyres: 135 x 15.

PERFORMANCE max speeds: (I) 17 mph, 27 km/h; (II) 34 mph, 54 km/h; (III) 53 mph, 86 km/h; (IV) 73 mph, 117 km/h; power-weight ratio: 54.8 lb/hp (74.5 lb/kW), 24.8 kg/hp (33.8 kg/kW); carrying capacity: 882 lb, 400 kg; acceleration: standing ¼ mile 24.9 sec; speed in top at 1,000 rpm: 12.7 mph, 20.4 km/h; consumption: 37.7 m/imp gal, 31.4 m/US gal, 7.5 l x 100 km at 56 mph, 90 km/h.

CHASSIS platform; front suspension: independent, swinging leading arms, anti-roll bar, telescopic dampers; rear: independent, swinging longitudinal trailing arms linked to front suspension, telescopic dampers.

STEERING rack-and-pinion; turns lock to lock: 3.25.

BRAKES front disc (diameter 9.61 in, 24.4 cm), rear drum, dual circuit; lining area: front 13 sq in, 84 sq cm, rear 34.7 sq in, 224 sq cm, total 47.7 sq in, 308 sq cm.

ELECTRICAL EQUIPMENT 12 V; 25 Ah battery; 290 W alternator; 2 headlamps.

DIMENSIONS AND WEIGHT wheel base: 94.49 in, 240 cm; front and rear track: 49.61 in, 126 cm; length: 141.94 in, 359 cm; width: 61.42 in, 156 cm; height: 62.44 in, 159 cm; ground clearance: 7.09 in, 18 cm; weight: 1,588 lb, 720 kg; weight distribution: 63% front, 37% rear; turning circle: 36.7 ft, 11.2 m; fuel tank: 7 imp gal, 8.4 US gal, 32 l.

BODY estate car/st. wagon; 2+1 doors; 5 seats, separate front seats.

PRACTICAL INSTRUCTIONS fuel: 98 oct petrol; oil: engine 4 imp pt, 4.9 US pt, 2.3 l, SAE 20W-50, change every 4,600 miles, 7,500 km - gearbox and final drive 1.6 imp pt, 1.9 US pt, 0.9 l, SAE 80, change every 14,000 miles, 22,500 km; greasing: every 1,900 miles, 3,000 km, 8 points; spark plug: 225°; tappet clearances: inlet 0.008 in, 0.20 mm, exhaust 0.008 in, 0.20 mm; valve timing: 2°50' 41°30' 35°55' 3°30'; tyre pressure: front 20 psi, 1.4 atm, rear 26 psi, 1.8 atm.

VARIATIONS

TRANSMISSION front or front and rear driving wheels, low ratios I 16, II 8.167, III 5.086, rev 16, central transfer lever.
BRAKES disc.
ELECTRICAL EQUIPMENT 24 V, 2 x 25 Ah batteries.

SYRENA 105

CITROËN FAF

PORTARO PORTUGAL

260

PRICES EX WORKS: **escudos**

DCM 2+1-dr St. Wagon **827,900**
Celta 2+1-dr St. Wagon **969,600**

ENGINE DG Daihatsu, front, diesel; 4 cylinders, in line; 154.4 cu in, 2,530 cc (3.46 x 4.09 in, 88 x 104 mm); compression ratio: 21:1; max power (JIS): 72 hp (53 kW) at 3,600 rpm; max torque (JIS): 127 lb ft, 17.5 kg m (172 Nm) at 2,200 rpm; max engine rpm: 4,200; 28.5 hp/l (20.9 kW/l); cast iron block and head; 4 crankshaft bearings; valves: overhead; camshafts: 1, overhead; lubrication: rotary pump, full flow filter, 11.4 imp pt, 13.7 US pt, 6.5 l; 1 Nippon Denso injection pump; fuel feed: mechanical pump; water-cooled, 17.6 imp pt, 21.1 US pt, 10 l.

TRANSMISSION driving wheels: rear, or front and rear; clutch: single dry plate (diaphragm), hydraulically controlled; gearbox: mechanical; gears: 4, fully synchronized, with 2 ratio transfer box; ratios: I 3.717, II 2.177, III 1.513, IV 1, rev 4.434; transfer box ratios: high 1.300, low 2.407; lever: central; final drive: spiral bevel; axle ratio: 3.700; tyres: 6.50 x 16.

PERFORMANCE max speeds: (I) 19 mph, 30 km/h; (II) 30 mph, 48 km/h; (III) 45 mph, 72 km/h; (IV) 70 mph, 112 km/h; power-weight ratio: 260 DMC 50.5 lb/hp (68.6 lb/kW), 22.9 kg/hp (31.1 kg/kW); carrying capacity: 3,638 lb, 1,650 kg; speed in direct drive at 1,000 rpm: 17.4 mph, 28 km/h; consumption: 25.7 m/imp gal, 21.4 m/US gal, 11 l x 100 km.

CHASSIS ladder frame; front suspension: independent, swinging arms, coil springs, telescopic dampers; rear: rigid axle, semi-elliptic leafsprings with rubber elements, telescopic dampers.

STEERING recirculating ball, servo; turns lock to lock: 2.25.

BRAKES drum, servo; lining area: front 19.4 sq in, 125 sq cm, rear 19.4 sq in, 125 sq cm, total 38.8 sq in, 250 sq cm.

ELECTRICAL EQUIPMENT 12 V; 120 Ah battery; 35 A alternator; 2 headlamps.

DIMENSIONS AND WEIGHT wheel base: 92.51 in, 235 cm; front and rear track: 56.89 in, 144 cm; length: 157.48 in, 400 cm; width: 70.24 in, 178 cm; height: 77.95 in, 198 cm; ground clearance: 8.66 in, 22 cm; weight: 260 DCM 3,638 lb, 1,650 kg - 260 Celta 3,748 lb, 1,700 kg; weight distribution; 52% front, 48% rear; turning circle: 39.4 ft, 12 m; fuel tank: 19.8 imp gal, 23.8 US gal, 90 l.

BODY estate car/st. wagon; 2+1 doors; 9 seats, separate front seats; hardtop.

PRACTICAL INSTRUCTIONS fuel: diesel; oil: engine 11.4 imp pt, 13.7 US pt, 6.5 l, SAE 20W/40, change every 3,100 miles, 5,000 km - gearbox 3.5 imp pt, 4.2 US pt, 2 l, SAE 90 EP, change every 6,200 miles, 10,000 km - final drive 2.1 imp pt, 2.5 US pt, 1.2 l, SAE 90 EP, change every 6,200 miles, 10,000 km; greasing: every 3,100 miles, 5,000 km, 6 points; tappet clearances: inlet 0.010 in, 0.25 mm, exhaust 0.010 in, 0.25 mm; valve timing: 25° 55° 60° 20°; tyre pressure: front 28 psi, 2 atm, rear 30 psi, 2.1 atm.

OPTIONALS front and rear bumpers; folding rear seats; air-conditioning; 4.5'' wide rims.

260 Celta Turbo

See 260, except for:

PRICE EX WORKS: 1,050,900 escudos

PORTARO 260 Celta Turbo

ENGINE turbocharged; max power (JIS): 95 hp (70 kW) at 4,000 rpm; max torque (JIS): 152 lb ft, 21 kg m (206 Nm) at 2,200 rpm; 37.5 hp/l (27.7 kW/l); turbocharger.

TRANSMISSION gearbox ratios: I 5.141, II 3.013, III 2.086, IV 1.382, rev 6.122.

PERFORMANCE max speed: 81 mph, 130 km/h; power-weight ratio: 39.5 lb/hp (53.6 lb/kW), 17.9 kg/hp (24.3 kg/kW); carrying capacity: 2,977 lb, 1,350 kg; consumption: 23.5 m/imp gal, 19.6 m/US gal, 12 l x 100 km.

CHASSIS front and rear suspension: heavy-duty dampers.

BODY hardtop, in fiberglass material.

PRACTICAL INSTRUCTIONS tyre pressure: front and rear 54 psi, 3.8 atm.

OPTIONALS front and rear bumpers; sliding roof; H 78 x 15 tyres.

PORTARO 260 Celta Station Wagon

ARO ROMANIA

10.0 / 10.1 / 10.3 / 10.4 54 hp power team

(standard)

ENGINE front, 4 stroke; 4 cylinders, vertical, in line; 78.7 cu in, 1,289 cc (2.87 x 3.03 in, 73 x 77 mm); compression ratio: 8.5:1; max power (DIN): 54 hp (40 kW) at 5,250 rpm; max torque (DIN): 65 lb ft, 9 kg m (88 Nm) at 3,000 rpm; max engine rpm: 5,250; 41.8 hp/l (30.8 kW/l); cast iron block, light alloy head; 5 crankshaft bearings; valves: overhead, push-rods and rockers; camshafts: 1, side; lubrication: mechanical pump, 5.3 imp pt, 6.3 US pt, 3 l; 1 Solex 32 IRM downdraught carburettor; fuel feed: mechanical pump; water-cooled, 11.4 imp pt, 13.7 US pt, 6.5 l.

TRANSMISSION driving wheels: front and rear; clutch: single dry plate (diaphragm); gearbox: mechanical; gears: 4, fully synchronized with 2 ratio transfer box; ratios: I 4.376, II 2.455, III 1.514, IV 1, rev 3.660; transfer box ratios: high 1.047, low 2.249; lever: central; final drive: spiral bevel; axle ratio: 4.571; width of rims: 5''; tyres: 175 SR x 14 M+S.

PERFORMANCE max speeds: (I) 17 mph, 27 km/h; (II) 30 mph, 49 km/h; (III) 47 mph, 76 km/h; (IV) 71 mph, 115 km/h; power-weight ratio: 10.0 model 45.6 lb/hp (61.7 lb/kW), 20.7 kg/hp (28 kg/kW); carrying capacity: 10.0 model 1,103 lb, 500 kg - 10.1 model 1,058 lb, 480 kg - 10.3 model 992 lb, 450 kg - 10.4 model 948 lb, 430 kg; acceleration: standing ¼ mile 30 sec; speed in direct drive at 1,000 rpm: 13.8 mph, 22.2 km/h; consumption: 22.6 m/imp gal, 18.8 m/US gal, 12.5 l x 100 km.

CHASSIS box-type ladder frame; front suspension: independent, swinging semi-axles, coil springs, telescopic dampers; rear: rigid axle, leafsprings with rubber elements, telescopic dampers.

STEERING worm and double roller; turns lock to lock: 3.50.

BRAKES front disc, rear drum, double circuit; swept area: front 80 sq in, 516 sq cm, rear 80 sq in, 516 sq cm, total 160 sq in, 1,032 sq cm.

ELECTRICAL EQUIPMENT 12 V; 45 Ah battery; 500 W alternator; 2 headlamps.

DIMENSIONS AND WEIGHT wheel base: 94.49 in, 240 cm; front and rear track: 51.18 in, 130 cm; length: 150.79 in, 383 cm; width: 62.99 in, 160 cm; height: 64.96 in, 165 cm; ground clearance: 7.48 in, 19 cm; weight: 10.0 model 2,470 lb, 1,120 kg - 10.1 model 2,492 lb, 1,130 kg - 10.3 model 2,558 lb, 1,160 kg - 10.4 model 2,602 lb, 1,180 kg; weight distribution: 45% front, 55% rear; turning circle: 37.7 ft, 11.5 m; fuel tank: 10.1 imp gal, 12.1 US gal, 46 l.

BODY 10.0 and 10.1 models open with canvas top - 10.3 and 10.4 models hardtop; 2 doors; 10.0 and 10.3 models 2 seats - 10.1 and 10.4 models 5 seats, separate front seats, folding rear seats.

PRACTICAL INSTRUCTIONS fuel: 98 oct petrol; oil: engine 5.3 imp pt, 6.3 US pt, 3 l, SAE 10W-40, change every 3,100 miles, 5,000 km - gearbox 2.6 imp pt, 3.2 US pt, 1.5 l, SAE 90, change every 9,300 miles, 15,000 km - final drive 1.2 imp pt, 1.5 US pt, 0.7 l (front), 1.6 imp pt, 1.9 US pt, 0.9 l (rear), SAE 90, change every 9,300 miles, 15,000 km; spark plug: Sinter-on M14 x 225; tappet clearances: inlet 0.006 in, 0.15 mm, exhaust 0.008 in, 0.20 mm; valve timing: 22° 62° 60° 20°; tyre pressure: front 24 psi, 1.7 atm, rear 27 psi, 1.9 atm.

OPTIONALS 7.00 x 14 8PR tyres; rear suspension with independent wheels, swinging semi-axles, coil springs and telescopic dampers; servo brake.

62 hp power team

(optional)

See 54 hp power team, except for:

ENGINE 85.2 cu in, 1,397 cc (2.99 x 3.03 in, 76 x 77 mm); compression ratio: 9.5:1; max power (DIN): 62 hp (46 kW) at 5,500 rpm; max torque (DIN): 74 lb ft, 10.2 kg m (100 Nm) at 3,300 rpm; max engine rpm: 5,500; 44.4 hp/l (32.9 kW/l).

PERFORMANCE max speed: 75 mph, 120 km/h; power-weight ratio: 10.0 model 39.9 lb/hp (53.6 lb/kW), 18.1 kg/hp (24.3 kg/kW).

240 / 241 / 243 / 244 83 hp power team

(standard)

ENGINE front, 4 stroke; 4 cylinders, vertical, in line; 152.2 cu in, 2,495 cc (3.82 x 3.32 in, 97 x 84.4 mm); compression ratio: 8:1; max power (DIN): 83 hp (61 kW) at 4,200 rpm; max torque (DIN): 118 lb ft, 16.3 kg m (160 Nm) at 3,000 rpm; max engine rpm: 4,200; 33.3 hp/l (24.5 kW/l); cast iron block and head; 5 crankshaft bearings; valves: overhead, Vee-slanted, push-rods and rockers; camshafts: 1, side; lubrication: mechanical pump, full flow filter, 10.8 imp pt, 12.7 US pt, 6 l; 1 Weber DCD twin barrel carburettor; fuel feed: mechanical pump; water-cooled, 22 imp pt, 26.4 US pt, 12.5 l.

TRANSMISSION driving wheels: front and rear; clutch: single dry plate, hydraulically controlled; gearbox: mechanical; gears: 4, fully synchronized and 2 ratios transfer box; ratios: I 4.644, II 2.532, III 1.561, IV 1, rev 4.795; transfer box ratios: high 1, low 2.127; lever: central; final drive: spiral bevel; axle ratio: 4.125; width of rims: 4.5''; tyres: 6.50 x 16.

PERFORMANCE max speeds: (I) 16 mph, 25 km/h; (II) 28 mph, 45 km/h; (III) 46 mph, 74 km/h; (IV) 240 and 243 models 76 mph, 122 km/h - 241 and 244 models 78 mph, 125 km/h; power-weight ratio: 240 model 41.2 lb/hp (56 lb/kW), 18.7 kg/hp (25.4 kg/kW); carrying capacity: 240 and 243 models 1,764 lb, 800 kg - 242 model 662 lb, 300 kg - 241 and 244 models 992 lb, 450 kg; acceleration: standing ¼ mile 23 sec; speed in direct drive at 1,000 rpm: 18.1 mph, 29.2 km/h; consumption: 18.2 m/imp gal, 15.2 m/US gal, 15.5 l x 100 km.

ARO 10.1

ARO 244

83 HP POWER TEAM

CHASSIS box-type ladder frame; front suspension: independent, swinging semi-axles, coil springs, telescopic dampers; rear: rigid axle, leafsprings with rubber elements, telescopic dampers.

STEERING worm and double roller; turns lock to lock: 3.40.

BRAKES drum, servo; swept area: front 101.4 sq in, 654 sq cm, rear 77.7 sq in, 501 sq cm, total 179.1 sq in, 1,155 sq cm.

ELECTRICAL EQUIPMENT 12 V; 66 Ah battery; 500 W alternator; 2 headlamps.

DIMENSIONS AND WEIGHT wheel base: 92.52 in, 235 cm; front and rear track: 56.69 in, 144 cm; length: 161.42 in, 410 cm - 243 model 159.84 in, 406 cm; width: 69.68 in, 177 cm; height: 240 and 241 models 78.27 in, 199 cm - 241 model 74.41 in, 189 cm - 243 model 79.13 in, 201 cm - 244 model 74.02 in, 188 cm; ground clearance: 8.66 in, 22 cm; weight: 240 model 3,418 lb, 1,550 kg - 241 model 3,506 lb, 1,590 kg - 243 model 3,572 lb, 1,620 kg - 244 model 3,660 lb, 1,660 kg; weight distribution: 39% front, 61% rear; turning circle: 39.4 ft, 12 m; fuel tank: 20.9 imp gal, 25.1 US gal, 95 l.

BODY 240 and 241 models open with canvas top - 243 and 244 models hardtop; 240 and 243 models 2 doors - 241 and 244 models 4 doors; 240 and 243 models 8 seats - 241 and 244 models 5 seats, separate front seats.

PRACTICAL INSTRUCTIONS fuel: 90 oct petrol; oil: engine 10.6 imp pt, 12.7 US pt, 6 l, SAE 10W-40, change every 3,100 miles, 5,000 km - gearbox 3.5 imp pt, 4.2 US pt, 2 l, SAE 90, change every 9,300 miles, 15,000 km - final drive 1.8 imp pt, 2.1 US pt, 1 l (front), 3 imp pt, 3.6 US pt, 1.7 l (rear), SAE 90, change every 9,300 miles, 15,000 km; spark plug: Sinteron M14 x 225S; tappet clearances: inlet 0.018 in, 0.45 mm, exhaust 0.018 in, 0.45 mm; valve timing: 12° 57° 58° 8°; tyre pressure: front 28 psi, 2 atm, rear 46 psi, 3.2 atm - 242 model 50 psi, 3.5 atm.

OPTIONALS electric fuel pump; JR 78 x 15 tyres; fog lamps; power take-off; headrests; collapsible windscreen; air-conditioning.

70 hp (diesel) power team

(optional)

See 83 hp power team, except for:

ENGINE diesel; 152.3 cu in, 2,660 cc (3.82 x 3.54 in, 97 x 90 mm); compression ratio: 20.8:1; max power (DIN): 70 hp (52 kW) at 3,200 rpm; max torque (DIN): 105 lb ft, 14.5 kg m (142 Nm) at 1,600 rpm; max engine rpm: 3,200; 26.3 hp/l (19.5 kW/l); lubrication: 13.2 imp pt, 15.9 US pt, 7.5 l; cooling: 24.6 imp pt, 29.8 US pt, 14 l.

TRANSMISSION axle ratio: 3.720.

PERFORMANCE max speeds: 240 and 243 models 71 mph, 115 km/h - 241 and 244 models 73 mph, 118 km/h; power-weight ratio: 240 model 48.7 lb/hp (65.7 lb/kW), 22.1 kg/hp (29.8 kg/kW); speed in direct drive at 1,000 rpm: 23 mph, 37 km/h; consumption: 25.7 m/imp gal, 21.4 m/US gal, 11 l x 100 km.

PRACTICAL INSTRUCTIONS fuel: diesel; oil: engine 13.2 imp pt, 15.9 US pt, 7.5 l; tappet clearances: inlet 0.010 in, 0.25 mm, exhaust 0.014 in, 0.35 mm; valve timing: 3° 43° 48°30' 6°.

DACIA — ROMANIA

1310

PRICES IN GB:	£
Standard 4-dr Sedan	**3,190***
L 4-dr Sedan	**3,490***
L 4+1-dr Break	**3,900***
GL 4-dr Sedan	**3,900***
GL 4+1-dr Break	**4,295***
GLX 4-dr Sedan	**4,295***

DACIA 1310 L Sedan

ENGINE Renault, front, 4 stroke; 4 cylinders, vertical, in line; 78.7 cu in, 1,289 cc (2.87 x 3.03 in, 73 x 77 mm); compression ratio: 9.5:1; max power (DIN): 56 hp (41 kW) at 5,300 rpm; max torque (DIN): 65 lb ft, 9 kg m (88 Nm) at 3,000 rpm; max engine rpm: 5,500; 43.1 hp/l (31.7 kW/l); cast iron block, light alloy head; 5 crankshaft bearings; valves: overhead, slanted, push-rods and rockers; camshafts: 1, side; lubrication: gear pump, filter in sump, 5.3 imp pt, 6.3 US pt, 3 l; 1 type 32 IRMA-Careil downdraught carburettor; fuel feed: mechanical pump; water-cooled.

TRANSMISSION driving wheels: front; clutch: single dry plate (diaphragm); gearbox: mechanical; gears: 4, fully synchronized; ratios: I 3.830, II 2.240, III 1.480, IV 1.040, rev 3.080; lever: central; final drive: hypoid bevel; axle ratio: 3.770; width of rims: 4.5"; tyres: 155 SR x 13.

PERFORMANCE max speed: 87 mph, 140 km/h; power-weight ratio: sedans 34.9 lb/hp (47.4 lb/kW), 15.8 kg/hp (21.5 kg/kW); carrying capacity: 882 lb, 400 kg; acceleration: 0-50 mph (0-80 km/h) 11 sec.

CHASSIS integral; front suspension: independent, wishbones, anti-roll bar, coil springs, telescopic dampers; rear: rigid axle, trailing arms, A-bracket, anti-roll bar, coil springs, telescopic dampers.

STEERING rack-and-pinion; turns lock to lock: 3.30.

BRAKES front disc, rear drum, rear compensator, servo.

ELECTRICAL EQUIPMENT 12 V; 45 Ah battery; 50 A alternator; 4 headlamps.

DIMENSIONS AND WEIGHT wheel base: 96.06 in, 244 cm; front and rear track: 51.57 in, 131 cm; length: sedans 170.87 in, 434 cm - st. wagons 173.23 in, 440 cm; width: 64.57 in, 164 cm; height: sedans 56.30 in, 143 cm - st. wagons 57.28 in, 145 cm; ground clearance: 6.68 in, 17 cm; weight: sedans 1,949 lb, 884 kg - st. wagons 2,037 lb, 924 kg; turning circle: 33.5 ft, 10.2 m; fuel tank: 10.2 imp gal, 12.1 US gal, 46 l.

BODY saloon/sedan, 4 doors - estate car/st. wagon, 4+1 doors; 4 or 5 seats, separate front seats.

PRACTICAL INSTRUCTIONS fuel: 98 oct petrol; oil: engine 5.3 imp pt, 6.3 US pt, 3 l, SAE 20W-50, change every 3,700 miles, 6,000 km - gearbox 3.5 imp pt, 4.1 US pt, 2.1 l, SAE 80, change every 9,300 miles, 15,000 km; tappet clearances: inlet 0.006 in, 0.15 mm, exhaust 0.008 in, 0.20 mm; valve timing: 22° 62° 60° 20°; tyre pressure: front 23 psi, 1.6 atm, rear 26 psi, 1.8 atm.

OPTIONALS heated rear window (except Standard 4-dr Sedan); headrests (for GL models only).

OLTCIT — ROMANIA

Special

ENGINE Citroën, front, longitudinal, slanted 7°13' to rear, 4 stroke; 2 cylinders, horizontally opposed; 39.8 cu in, 652 cc (3.03 x 2.76 in, 77 x 70 mm); compression ratio: 9:1; max power (DIN): 34 hp (25 kW) at 5,250 rpm; max torque (DIN): 37 lb ft, 5.1 kg m (50 Nm) at 3,500 rpm; max engine rpm: 5,850; 52.1 hp/l (38.3 kW/l); light alloy block and head; 3 crankshaft bearings; valves: overhead, Vee-slanted at 33°, push-rods and rockers; camshafts: 1, central; lubrication: rotary pump, filter in sump, oil cooler, 5.8 imp pt, 7 US pt, 3.3 l; 1 Solex 26/35 CSIC 238 downdraught twin barrel carburettor; fuel feed: mechanical pump; air-cooled.

TRANSMISSION driving wheels: front (double homokinetic joints); clutch: single dry plate (diaphragm); gearbox: mechanical; gears: 4, fully synchronized; ratios: I 4.545, II 2.500, III 2.643, IV 1.147, rev 4.182; lever: central; final drive: spiral bevel; axle ratio: 4.125; width of rims: 4"; tyres: 145 x 13.

PERFORMANCE max speeds: (I) 19 mph, 30 km/h; (II) 34 mph, 55 km/h; (III) 52 mph, 84 km/h; (IV) 75 mph, 120 km/h; power-weight ratio: 54.1 lb/hp (73.6 lb/kW), 24.5 kg/hp (33.3 kg/kW); acceleration: standing ¼ mile 23 sec, 0-50 mph (0-80 km/h) 22.4 sec; speed in top at 1,000 rpm: 12.7 mph, 20.5 km/h; consumption: 47.1 m/imp gal, 39.2 m/US gal, 6 l x 100 km at 56 mph, 90 km/h.

CHASSIS integral; front suspension: independent, wishbones, coil springs, swinging longitudinal trailing arms, telescopic damper struts; rear: independent, trailing links, torsion bar, coil springs, telescopic damper struts.

STEERING rack-and-pinion; turns lock to lock: 3.50.

BRAKES front disc, rear drum, dual circuit.

ELECTRICAL EQUIPMENT 12 V; 35 Ah battery; 462 W alternator; electronic ignition; 2 headlamps.

DIMENSIONS AND WEIGHT wheel base: 93.31 in, 237 cm; tracks: 52.36 in, 133 cm front, 48.82 in, 124 cm rear; length: 146.85 in, 373 cm; width: 60.63 in, 154 cm; height: 56.30 in, 143 cm; ground clearance: 5.91 in, 15 cm; weight: 1,863 lb, 835 kg; weight distribution: 61% front, 39% rear; turning circle: 32.1 ft, 9.8 m; fuel tank: 9.2 imp gal, 11.1 US gal, 42 l.

BODY saloon/sedan; 2+1 doors; 5 seats, separate front seats, reclining backrests; detachable rear seat; laminated windscreen.

PRACTICAL INSTRUCTIONS fuel: 98 oct petrol; oil: engine 5.3 imp pt, 6.3 US pt, 3 l, SAE 15W-40 (summer) 10W-30 (winter), change every 4,600 miles, 7,500 km - gearbox and final drive 2.5 imp pt, 3 US pt, 1.4 l, SAE 80 EP, change every 14,000 miles, 22,500 km; greasing: none; tyre pressure: front 27 psi, 1.9 atm, rear 28 psi, 2 atm.

Club

See Special, except for:

ENGINE Citroën, front, 4 stroke; 4 cylinders, horizontally opposed; 68.9 cu in, 1,129 cc (2.91 x 2.58 in, 74 x 65.6 mm); max power (DIN): 56 hp (41 kW) at 5,750 rpm; max torque (DIN): 59 lb ft, 8.2 kg m (80 Nm) at 3,500 rpm; max engine rpm: 6,000; 49.6 hp/l (36.5 kW/l); light alloy block, head with cast iron liners, light alloy fins and hemispherical combustion chambers; camshafts: 2, 1 per bank, overhead, cogged belt; lubrication: gear pump, full flow filter, oil cooler, 7 imp pt, 8.5 US pt, 4 l; 1 Solex CIC 229 downdraught twin barrel carburettor.

TRANSMISSION gearbox ratios: I 3.818, II 2.294, III 1.500, IV 1.031, rev 4.182.

PERFORMANCE max speeds: (I) 24 mph, 39 km/h; (II) 40 mph, 65 km/h; (III) 62 mph, 100 km/h; (IV) 93 mph, 149 km/h; power-weight ratio: 34.4 lb/hp (46.8 lb/kW), 15.6 kg/hp (21.2 kg/kW); acceleration: standing ¼ mile 19.6 sec; speed in direct drive at 1,000 rpm: 15 mph, 24.2 km/h; consumption: 39.2 m/imp gal, 32.7 m/US gal, 7.2 l x 100 km at 56 mph, 90 km/h.

ELECTRICAL EQUIPMENT 40 Ah battery; 540 W alternator; Sev distributor.

DIMENSIONS AND WEIGHT weight: 1,929 lb, 875 kg; weight distribution: 63% front, 37% rear.

PRACTICAL INSTRUCTIONS oil: engine 7 imp pt, 8.5 US pt, 4 l, SAE 20W-50, change every 4,600 miles, 7,500 km; spark plug: 200°; tappet clearances: inlet 0.008 in, 0.20 mm, exhaust 0.008 in, 0.20 mm; valve timing: 4°10' 31°50' 36°10' 0°20'.

OLTCIT Club

FASA-RENAULT SPAIN

4 TL

PRICE EX WORKS: 519,100 pesetas**

ENGINE front, 4 stroke; 4 cylinders, vertical, in line; 67.6 cu in, 1,108 cc (2.76 x 2.83 in, 70 x 72 mm); compression ratio: 8.3:1; max power (DIN): 38 hp (28 kW) at 4,500 rpm; max torque (DIN): 53 lb ft, 7.3 kg m (72 Nm) at 2,000 rpm; max engine rpm: 5,100; 34.3 hp/l (25.2 kW/l); 5 crankshaft bearings; valves: overhead, in line, push-rods and rockers; camshafts: 1, side; lubrication: gear pump, filter in sump, 5.3 imp pt, 6.3 US pt, 3 l; 1 Zenith 28 IF downdraught single barrel carburettor; fuel feed: mechanical pump; sealed circuit cooling, expansion tank, 10.2 imp pt, 12.2 US pt, 5.8 l.

TRANSMISSION driving wheels: front; clutch: single dry plate (diaphragm); gearbox: mechanical; gears: 4, fully synchronized; ratios: I 3.833, II 2.235, III 1.458, IV 1.026, rev 3.545; lever: on facia; final drive: spiral bevel; axle ratio: 4.125; width of rims: 4"; tyres: 135 SR x 13.

PERFORMANCE max speed: 73 mph, 118 km/h; power-weight ratio: 40.3 lb/hp (54.8 lb/kW), 18.3 kg/hp (24.8 kg/kW); carrying capacity: 860 lb, 390 kg; acceleration: standing ¼ mile 22 sec; speed in top at 1,000 rpm: 19.6 mph, 31.5 km/h; consumption: 52.3 m/imp gal, 43.6 m/US gal, 5.4 l x 100 km at 56 mph, 90 km/h.

CHASSIS platform; front suspension: independent, wishbones, longitudinal torsion bars, anti-roll bar, telescopic dampers; rear: independent, swinging longitudinal trailing arms, transverse torsion bars, telescopic dampers.

STEERING rack-and-pinion; turns lock to lock: 3.75.

BRAKES front disc, rear drum, rear compensator.

ELECTRICAL EQUIPMENT 12 V; 28 Ah battery; alternator; 2 headlamps.

DIMENSIONS AND WEIGHT wheel base: 96.46 in, 245 cm (right), 94.49 in, 240 cm (left); tracks: 50.39 in, 128 cm front, 48.82 in, 124 cm rear; length: 144.49 in, 367 cm; width: 58.27 in, 148 cm; height: 61.02 in, 155 cm; weight: 1,544 lb, 700 kg; turning circle: 31.8 ft, 9.7 m; fuel tank: 7.5 imp gal, 9 US gal, 34 l.

BODY estate car/st. wagon; 4+1 doors; 4 seats, separate front seats, reclining backrests; folding rear seat; luxury interior.

PRACTICAL INSTRUCTIONS fuel: 98-100 oct petrol; oil: engine 5.3 imp pt, 6.3 US pt, 3 l, SAE 10W-40, change every 4,700 miles, 7,500 km - gearbox and final drive 3.2 imp pt, 3.8 US pt, 1.8 l, SAE 80 EP, change every 9,300 miles, 15,000 km; tappet clearances: inlet 0.012 in, 0.30 mm, exhaust 0.012 in, 0.30 mm; valve timing: 12° 48° 52° 8°; tyre pressure: front 20 psi, 1.4 atm, rear 24 psi, 1.7 atm.

OPTIONALS metallic spray; heated rear window; sunroof.

FASA-RENAULT 4 TL

FASA-RENAULT 5 TX Berlina

5 Series

PRICES EX WORKS:		pesetas
1	TL 2+1-dr Berlina	622,600**
2	TL 4+1-dr Berlina	649,600**
3	GTL 2+1-dr Berlina	693,400**
4	GTL 4+1-dr Berlina	720,700**
5	TX 2+1-dr Berlina	827,500**
6	Copa Turbo 2+1-dr Berlina	1,114,300**

Power team:	Standard for:	Optional for:
45 hp	1 to 4	—
63 hp	5	—
110 hp	6	—

45 hp power team

ENGINE front, 4 stroke; 4 cylinders, vertical, in line; 67.6 cu in, 1,108 cc (2.75 x 2.83 in, 70 x 72 mm); compression ratio: 8.3:1; max power (DIN): 45 hp (33 kW) at 5,000 rpm; max torque (DIN): 58 lb ft, 9 kg m (88 Nm) at 2,500 rpm; max engine rpm: 6,000; 40.6 hp/l (29.9 kW/l); cast iron block, light alloy head; 5 crankshaft bearings; 1 Solex or Zenith 32 downdraught single barrel carburettor.

TRANSMISSION driving wheels: front; clutch: single dry plate; gearbox: mechanical; gears: 4, fully synchronized; ratios: I 3.830, II 2.230, III 1.450, IV 1.020, rev 3.540; lever: central; final drive: spiral bevel; axle ratio: 3.625; width of rims: 4"; tyres: 135 x 330.

PERFORMANCE max speed: 84 mph, 135 km/h; power-weight ratio: 38 lb/hp (51.7 lb/kW), 17.2 kg/hp (23.4 kg/kW); speed in top at 1,000 rpm: 16.7 mph, 26.9 km/h; consumption: 54.3 m/imp gal, 45.2 m/US gal, 5.2 l x 100 km at 56 mph, 90 km/h.

CHASSIS integral; front suspension: independent, wishbones, longitudinal torsion bar, anti-roll bar, telescopic dampers; rear: independent, swinging longitudinal trailing arms, transverse torsion bars, anti-roll bar, telescopic dampers.

STEERING rack-and-pinion.

BRAKES front disc, rear drum, rear compensator; lining area: front 78.6 sq in, 507 sq cm, rear 26.2 sq in, 169 sq cm, total 104.8 sq in, 676 sq cm.

ELECTRICAL EQUIPMENT 12 V; 28 Ah battery; 30 A alternator; 2 headlamps.

DIMENSIONS AND WEIGHT wheel base: 94.49 in, 240 cm (right), 95.83 in, 243 cm (left); tracks: 50.71 in, 129 cm front, 49.22 in, 125 cm rear; length: 138.19 in, 352 cm; width: 59.84 in, 152 cm; height: 55.12 in, 140 cm; ground clearance: 5.12 in, 13 cm; weight: 1,711 lb, 775 kg; turning circle: 31.3 ft, 9.5 m; fuel tank: 8.4 imp gal, 10 US gal, 38 l.

BODY saloon/sedan; 2+1 or 4+1 doors; 4 seats, separate front seats, reclining backrests, built-in headrests.

45 HP POWER TEAM

VARIATIONS

(for GTL models only)
ENGINE 9.5:1 compression ratio, max power (DIN) 45 hp (33 kW) at 4,400 rpm, max torque (DIN) 58 lb ft, 8 kg m (78 Nm) at 2,000 rpm, max engine rpm 6,000, 1 Zenith 32 downdraught single barrel carburettor.
TRANSMISSION 4.5" wide rims, 155/70 SR x 13 tyres.
PERFORMANCE max speed 86 mph, 138 km/h; power-weight ratio 38.4 lb/hp (52.5 lb/kW), 17.4 kg/hp (23.8 kg/kW); speed in top at 1,000 rpm, 17 mph, 27.3 km/h.
BRAKES front disc, rear drum, rear compensator, servo.
ELECTRICAL EQUIPMENT 32 A alternator.
DIMENSIONS AND WEIGHT weight 1,730 lb, 785 kg.

OPTIONALS 5-speed mechanical gearbox; metallic spray.

63 hp power team

See 45 hp power team, except for:

ENGINE 85.2 cu in, 1,397 cc (2.99 x 3.03 in, 76 x 77 mm); compression ratio: 9.2:1; max power (DIN): 63 hp (46 kW) at 5,250 rpm; max torque (DIN): 76 lb ft, 10.5 kg m (101 Nm) at 3,000 rpm; max engine rpm: 5,750; 45.1 hp/l (33.2 kW/l); 1 Weber 32 DIR 11 downdraught twin barrel carburettor.

TRANSMISSION gears: 5, fully synchronized (standard); ratios: I 3.833, II 2.235, III 1.458, IV 1.171, V 0.948, rev 3.545; axle ratio: 3.445; width of rims: 4.5"; tyres: 155 x 330.

PERFORMANCE max speed: 93 mph, 150 km/h; power-weight ratio: 13.1 lb/hp (17.8 lb/kW), 6.1 kg/hp (8.3 kg/kW); speed in top at 1,000 rpm: 19.3 mph, 31.1 km/h; consumption: 54.3 m/imp gal, 45.2 m/US gal, 5.2 l x 100 km at 56 mph, 90 km/h.

ELECTRICAL EQUIPMENT 36 Ah battery; 50 A alternator.

110 hp power team

See 45 hp power team, except for:

ENGINE turbocharged; 85.2 cu in, 1,397 cc (2.99 x 3.03 in, 76 x 77 mm); compression ratio: 8.6:1; max power (DIN): 110 hp (81 kW) at 6,000 rpm; max torque (DIN): 109 lb ft, 15 kg m (147 Nm) at 4,000 rpm; max engine rpm: 6,000; 78.7 hp/l (58 kW/l); hemispherical combustion chambers; 5 crankshaft bearings; lubrication: 5.3 imp pt, 6.3 US pt, 3 l; 1 Weber 32 DIR 107 downdraught twin barrel carburettor; Garrett AiResearch T3 turbocharger; cooling: 11.1 imp pt, 13.3 US pt, 6.3 l, electric thermostatic fan.

TRANSMISSION gears: 5, fully synchronized (standard); ratios: I 3.818, II 2.176, III 1.409, IV 1.030, V 0.861, rev 3.540; axle ratio: 3.777; width of rims: 5.5"; tyres: 175/60 HR x 13 P6.

PERFORMANCE max speeds: (I) 26 mph, 42 km/h; (II) 46 mph, 74 km/h; (III) 71 mph, 114 km/h; (IV) 97 mph, 155 km/h; (V) 116 mph, 186 km/h; power-weight ratio: 17.4 lb/hp (23.7 lb/kW), 7.9 kg/hp (10.7 kg/kW); carrying capacity: 882 lb, 400 kg; acceleration: standing 1/4 mile 16.5 sec; speed in top at 1,000 rpm: 19.3 mph, 31 km/h; consumption: 9.7 m/imp gal, 11.6 m/US gal, 5.5 l x 100 km at 56 mph, 90 km/h.

BRAKES disc, servo; lining area: front 22.2 sq in, 143 sq cm, rear 22.2 sq in, 143 sq cm, total 44.4 sq in, 286 sq cm.

ELECTRICAL EQUIPMENT 36 Ah battery; 50 A alternator; fog lamps.

DIMENSIONS AND WEIGHT wheel base: 94.96 in, 241 cm (right), 96.14 in, 244 cm (left); tracks: 50.94 in, 129 cm front, 50 in, 127 cm rear; length: 140.08 in, 356 cm; height: 54.17 in, 138 cm; ground clearance: 4.72 in, 12 cm; weight: 1,918 lb, 870 kg.

BODY 2+1 doors; heated rear window; rear window wiper-washer.

OPTIONALS metallic spray.

6 GTL

PRICE EX WORKS: 659,300 pesetas**

ENGINE front, 4 stroke; 4 cylinders, vertical, in line; 67.6 cu in, 1,108 cc (2.83 x 2.83 in, 72 x 72 mm); compression ratio: 8.3:1; max power (DIN): 45 hp (33 kW) at 5,000 rpm; max torque (DIN): 58 lb ft, 8 kg m (78 Nm) at 2,500 rpm; max engine rpm: 6,000; 40.6 hp/l (29.9 kW/l); cast iron block, light alloy head; 5 crankshaft bearings; 1 Solex or Zenith 32 IF downdraught single barrel carburettor.

TRANSMISSION driving wheels: front; clutch: single dry plate; gearbox: mechanical; gears: 4, fully synchronized; ratios: I 3.830, II 2.230, III 1.450, IV 1.020, rev 3.540; lever: on facia; final drive: spiral bevel; axle ratio: 3.875; width of rims: 4.5"; tyres: 145 SR x 13.

PERFORMANCE max speed: 83 mph, 133 km/h; power-weight ratio: 40.6 lb/hp (55.3 lb/kW), 18.4 kg/hp (25.1 kg/kW); carrying capacity: 860 lb, 390 kg; speed in top at 1,000 rpm: 16.2 mph, 26.1 km/h; consumption: 46.8 m/imp gal, 37.9 m/US gal, 6.2 l x 100 km at 56 mph, 90 km/h.

CHASSIS integral; front suspension: independent, swinging arms, longitudinal torsion bars, anti-roll bar, telescopic dampers; rear: independent, swinging longitudinal leading arms, transverse torsion bars, anti-roll bar, telescopic dampers.

STEERING rack-and-pinion.

BRAKES front disc, rear drum, rear compensator; lining area: front 78.6 sq in, 507 sq cm, rear 26.3 sq in, 169 sq cm, total 104.9 sq in, 676 sq cm.

ELECTRICAL EQUIPMENT 12 V; 28 Ah battery; 35 A alternator; 2 headlamps.

DIMENSIONS AND WEIGHT wheel base: 96.46 in, 245 cm (right), 94.49 in, 240 cm (left); tracks: 50.39 in, 128 cm front, 48.82 in, 124 cm rear; length: 151.97 in, 386 cm; width: 59.06 in, 150 cm; height: 56.69 in, 144 cm; ground clearance: 4.88 in, 12.4 cm; weight: 1,830 lb, 830 kg; turning circle: 32.5 ft, 9.9 m; fuel tank: 8.8 imp gal, 10.5 US gal, 40 l.

BODY saloon/sedan; 4+1 doors; 4 seats, separate front seats; folding rear seat.

OPTIONALS metallic spray; luxury interior.

7 GTL

See 6 GTL, except for:

PRICE EX WORKS: 674,700 pesetas**

ENGINE compression ratio: 9.5:1; max power (DIN): 45 hp (33 kW) at 4,400 rpm; max torque (DIN): 58 lb ft, 8 kg m (78 Nm) at 2,000 rpm; max engine rpm: 5,400; 48.7 hp/l (35.8 kW/l).

TRANSMISSION gearbox ratios: I 3.830, II 2.370, III 1.520, IV 1.020, rev 3.540; lever: central; axle ratio: 3.525.

PERFORMANCE power-weight ratio: 39.9 lb/hp (54.2 lb/kW), 18.1 kg/hp (24.6 kg/kW); carrying capacity: 882 lb, 400 kg; speed in top at 1,000 rpm: 17 mph, 27.7 km/h; consumption: 53.3 m/imp gal, 44.4 m/US gal, 5.3 l x 100 km at 56 mph, 90 km/h.

ELECTRICAL EQUIPMENT 30 A alternator.

DIMENSIONS AND WEIGHT ground clearance: 5.12 in, 13 cm.

FASA-RENAULT 9 GTD Berlina

9 Series

PRICES EX WORKS:	pesetas
1 GTL 4-dr Berlina	845,300**
2 TSE 4-dr Berlina	941,800**
3 GTD 4-dr Berlina	980,500**

Power team:	Standard for:	Optional for:
60 hp	1	—
72 hp	2	—
55 hp (diesel)	3	—

(For technical data, see Renault France)

11 Series

PRICES EX WORKS:	pesetas
1 GTL 4+1-dr Berlina	886,000**
2 TSE 4+1-dr Berlina	968,800**

Power team:	Standard for:	Optional for:
60 hp	1	—
72 hp	2	—

(For technical data, see Renault France)

12 GTL Familiar

PRICE EX WORKS: 908,900 pesetas**

ENGINE front, 4 stroke; 4 cylinders, vertical, in line; 85.2 cu in, 1,397 cc (2.99 x 3.03 in, 76 x 77 mm); compression ratio: 9.2:1; max power (DIN): 70 hp (55 kW) at 5,500 rpm; max torque (DIN): 80 lb ft, 11 kg m (108 Nm) at 3,500 rpm; max engine rpm: 6,500; 50.1 hp/l (36.9 kW/l); 5 crankshaft bearings; valves: overhead, slanted, push-rods and rockers; camshafts: 1, side; lubrication: gear pump, filter in sump, 5.3 imp pt, 6.3 US pt, 3 l; 1 Solex 32 downdraught single barrel carburettor; fuel feed: mechanical pump; sealed circuit cooling, liquid, 9.7 imp pt, 11.6 US pt, 5.5 l.

FASA-RENAULT 6 GTL

FASA-RENAULT 7 GTL

FASA-RENAULT 11 TSE Berlina

TRANSMISSION driving wheels: front; clutch: single dry plate; gearbox: mechanical; gears: 4, fully synchronized; ratios: I 3.818, II 2.170, III 1.400, IV 1.036, rev 3.083; lever: central; final drive: hypoid bevel; axle ratio: 3.778; width of rims: 5"; tyres: 155 x 330.

PERFORMANCE max speed: 87 mph, 140 km/h; power-weight ratio: 30.7 lb/hp (41.8 lb/kW), 13.9 kg/hp (18.9 kg/kW); carrying capacity: 882 lb, 400 kg; speed in top at 1,000 rpm: 16.8 mph, 27.1 km/h; consumption: 40.9 m/imp gal, 34.1 m/US gal, 6.9 l x 100 km at 56 mph, 95 km/h.

CHASSIS integral; front suspension: independent, wishbones, anti-roll bar, coil springs, telescopic dampers; rear: rigid axle, trailing arms, A-bracket, anti-roll bar, coil springs, telescopic dampers.

STEERING rack-and-pinion.

BRAKES front disc, rear drum, rear compensator, servo; swept area: front 78.6 sq in, 507 sq cm, rear 35 sq in, 226 sq cm, total 113.6 sq in, 733 sq cm.

ELECTRICAL EQUIPMENT 12 V; alternator; 36 Ah battery; 4 iodine headlamps.

DIMENSIONS AND WEIGHT wheel base: 96.06 in, 244 cm; front and rear track: 51.96 in, 132 cm; length: 173.22 in, 440 cm; width: 63.78 in, 162 cm; height: 57.08 in, 145 cm; ground clearance: 5.12 in, 13 cm; weight: 2,150 lb, 975 kg; turning circle: 33 ft, 10.1 m; fuel tank: 11 imp gal, 13.2 US gal, 50 l.

BODY estate car/st. wagon; 4+1 doors; 5-7 seats, separate front seats, built-in headrests; heated rear window.

OPTIONALS metallic spray.

14 Series

PRICES EX WORKS:	pesetas
1 GTL 4+1-dr Berlina	812,600**
2 GTS 4+1-dr Berlina	922,600**

Power team:	Standard for:	Optional for:
59 hp	1	—
70 hp	2	—

59 hp power team

ENGINE front, transverse, slanted at 72° to rear, 4 stroke; 4 cylinders, vertical, in line; 74.3 cu in, 1,218 cc (2.95 x 2.72 in, 75 x 69 mm); compression ratio: 9.3:1; max power (DIN): 59 hp (43 kW) at 5,500 rpm; max torque (DIN): 68 lb ft, 9.4 kg m (92 Nm) at 3,000 rpm; max engine rpm: 6,000; 48.4 hp/l (35.6 kW/l); light alloy block and head, wet liners, hemispherical combustion chambers; 5 crankshaft bearings; valves: overhead, Vee-slanted, rockers; camshafts: 1, overhead; lubrication: gear pump, full flow filter, 7 imp pt, 8.3 US pt, 4 l; 1 Solex 32 PBISA 11 single barrel carburettor; sealed circuit cooling, liquid, expansion tank, 10.6 imp pt, 12.7 US pt, 6 l.

TRANSMISSION driving wheels: front; clutch: single dry plate; gearbox: mechanical; gears: 4, fully synchronized; ratios: I 3.080, II 1.820, III 1.190, IV 0.820, rev 2.830; lever: central; final drive: spiral bevel; axle ratio: 3.860; width of rims: 4.5"; tyres: 165/70 x 330.

PERFORMANCE max speed: 90 mph, 145 km/h; power-weight ratio: 32.3 lb/hp (43.9 lb/kW), 14.7 kg/hp (19.9 kg/kW); speed in top at 1,000 rpm: 15.9 mph, 25.6 km/h; consumption: 45.6 m/imp gal, 37.9 m/US gal, 6.2 l x 100 km.

CHASSIS integral; front suspension: independent, by McPherson, coil springs/telescopic damper struts, lower wishbones, anti-roll bar; rear: independent, swinging longitudinal trailing arms, transverse torsion bars, telescopic dampers.

STEERING rack-and-pinion.

BRAKES front disc, rear drum, dual circuit, rear compensator, servo; lining area: front 86.1 sq in, 555 sq cm, rear 35.2 sq in, 227 sq cm, total 59.3 sq in, 533 sq cm.

ELECTRICAL EQUIPMENT 12 V; 50 A alternator; 32 Ah battery; 2 headlamps.

DIMENSIONS AND WEIGHT wheel base: 98.42 in, 250 cm (right), 99.60 in, 253 cm (left); tracks: 53.23 in, 135 cm front, 54.25 in, 138 cm rear; length: 158.46 in, 402 cm; width: 63.94 in, 162 cm; height: 55.31 in, 140 cm; ground clearance: 5.91 in, 15 cm; weight: 1,907 lb, 865 kg; turning circle: 32.8 ft, 10 m; fuel tank: 10.5 imp gal, 12.7 US gal, 48 l.

BODY saloon/sedan; 4+1 doors; 5 seats, separate front seats; folding rear seat; heated rear window.

OPTIONALS metallic spray.

FASA-RENAULT 12 GTL Familiar

70 hp power team

See 59 hp power team, except for:

ENGINE 83 cu in, 1,360 cc (2.95 x 3.03 in, 75 x 77 mm); max power (DIN): 70 hp (51 kW) at 6,000 rpm; max torque (DIN): 80 lb ft, 11 kg m (108 Nm) at 3,000 rpm; max engine rpm: 6,500; 51.5 hp/l (37.9 kW/l); 1 Solex 32 CICSA downdraught twin barrel carburettor.

PERFORMANCE max speed: 97 mph, 156 km/h; power-weight ratio: 28 lb/hp (38.1 lb/kW), 12.7 kg/hp (17.3 kg/kW); speed in top at 1,000 rpm: 17.3 mph, 27.8 km/h; consumption: 47.8 m/imp gal, 39.9 m/US gal, 5.9 l x 100 km at 56 mph, 90 km/h.

DIMENSIONS AND WEIGHT weight: 1,962 lb, 890 kg.

18 Series

PRICES EX WORKS:	pesetas
1 GTS 4-dr Berlina	1,092,500**
2 GTS 4+1-dr Familiar	1,148,200**
3 Turbo 4-dr Berlina	1,303,200**
4 GTD 4-dr Berlina	1,257,200**
5 GTD 4+1-dr Familiar	1,314,400**

Power team:	Standard for:	Optional for:
79 hp	2	—
83 hp	1	—
125 hp	3	—
66 hp (diesel)	4,5	—

79 hp power team

ENGINE front, 4 stroke; 4 cylinders, vertical, in line; 100.5 cu in, 1,647 cc (3.11 x 3.31 in, 79 x 84 mm); compression ratio: 9.3:1; max power (DIN): 79 hp (58 kW) at 5,500 rpm; max torque (DIN): 91 lb ft, 12.5 kg m (123 Nm) at 3,000 rpm; max engine rpm: 6,000; 48 hp/l (35.3 kW/l); light alloy block and head, wet liners; 5 crankshaft bearings; valves: overhead, in line, push-rods and rockers; camshafts: 1, in side; lubrication: gear pump, filter in sump, 7 imp pt, 8.5 US pt, 4 l; 1 Solex downdraught single barrel carburettor; fuel feed: mechanical pump.

TRANSMISSION driving wheels: front; clutch: single dry plate; gearbox: mechanical; gears: 5, fully synchronized; ratios: I 4.090, II 2.170, III 1.400, IV 1.030, V 0.860, rev 3.540; lever: central; final drive: hypoid bevel; axle ratio: 3.777; width of rims: 5"; tyres: 155 x 330.

PERFORMANCE max speed: 101 mph, 163 km/h; power-weight ratio: 28.6 lb/hp (38.9 lb/kW), 13 kg/hp (17.6 kg/kW); carrying capacity: 992 lb, 450 kg; speed in top at 1,000 rpm: 20 mph, 32.3 km/h; consumption: 44.1 m/imp gal, 36.7 m/US gal, 6.4 l x 100 km at 56 mph, 90 km/h.

CHASSIS integral; front suspension: independent, wishbones, anti-roll bar, coil springs/telescopic dampers; rear: rigid axle, trailing arms, A-bracket, anti-roll bar, coil springs/telescopic dampers.

STEERING rack-and-pinion.

BRAKES front disc, rear drum, dual circuit, rear compensator, servo; lining area: front 78.6 sq in, 507 sq cm, rear 44.5 sq in, 287 sq cm, total 123.1 sq in, 794 sq cm.

ELECTRICAL EQUIPMENT 12 V; 36 Ah battery; 50 A alternator; 2 headlamps.

DIMENSIONS AND WEIGHT wheel base: 96.10 in, 244 cm; tracks: 55.70 in, 142 cm front, 52.76 in, 134 cm rear; length: 175.59 in, 446 cm; width: 66.20 in, 168 cm; height: 55.30 in, 140 cm; weight: 2,260 lb, 1,025 kg; turning circle: 33.8 ft, 10.3 m; fuel tank: 12.5 imp gal, 15 US gal, 57 l.

BODY estate car/st. wagon; 4+1 doors; 5 seats, separate front seats, reclining backrests.

OPTIONALS metallic spray; air-conditioning.

83 hp power team

See 79 hp power team, except for:

ENGINE max power (DIN): 83 hp (61 kW) at 5,500 rpm; max torque (DIN): 96 lb ft, 13.3 kg m (130 Nm) at 3,000 rpm; 50.4 hp/l (37.1 kW/l); 1 Weber 32 DIR downdraught twin barrel carburettor.

TRANSMISSION width of rims: 5.5"; tyres: 175/70 x 330.

PERFORMANCE power-weight ratio: 27.3 lb/hp (37 lb/kW); 12.4 kg/hp (16.8 kg/kW); speed in top at 1,000 rpm: 20.2 mph, 32.6 km/h; consumption: 47.1 m/imp gal, 39.2 m/US gal, 6 l x 100 km at 56 mph, 90 km/h.

BRAKES lining area: front 78.6 sq in, 507 sq cm, rear 35 sq in, 226 sq cm, total 113.6 sq in, 733 sq cm.

DIMENSIONS AND WEIGHT length: 172.83 in, 439 cm; fuel tank: 117 mp gal, 14 US gal, 53 l.

BODY saloon/sedan; 4 doors.

125 hp power team

See 79 hp power team, except for:

125 HP POWER TEAM

ENGINE turbocharged; 95.5 cu in, 1,565 cc (3.03 x 3.30 in, 77 x 84 mm); compression ratio: 8.6:1; max power (DIN): 125 hp (92 kW) at 5,500 rpm; max torque (DIN): 134 lb ft, 18.5 kg m (181 Nm) at 2,500 rpm; 79.8 hp/l (58.7 kW/l); valves: overhead, Vee-slanted; 1 Solex 32 DIS downdraught single barrel carburettor; Garrett AiResearch turbocharger.

TRANSMISSION gearbox ratios: I 4.090, II 2.171, III 1.400, IV 0.970, V 0.780, rev 3.540; tyres: 185/65 x 355.

PERFORMANCE max speed: 115 mph, 185 km/h; power-weight ratio: 18.3 lb/hp (24.9 lb/kW), 8.3 kg/hp (11.3 kg/kW); speed in top at 1,000 rpm: 22.9 mph, 36.8 km/h; consumption: 36.7 m/imp gal, 30.5 m/US gal, 7.5 l x 100 km at 75 mph, 120 km/h.

STEERING servo.

DIMENSIONS AND WEIGHT weight: 2,293 lb, 1,040 kg; turning circle: 34.1 ft, 10.4 m.

BODY saloon/sedan; 4 doors; 5 seats.

66 hp (diesel) power team

See 79 hp power team, except for:

ENGINE diesel; 126.2 cu in, 2,068 cc (3.39 x 3.50 in, 86 x 89 mm); compression ratio: 21.5:1; max power (DIN): 66 hp (49 kW) at 4,500 rpm; max torque (DIN): 94 lb ft, 13 kg m (128 Nm) at 2,250 rpm; max engine rpm: 4,500; 31.9 hp/l (23.2 kW/l); camshafts: 1, overhead, cogged belt; lubrication: 8.8 imp pt, 10.6 US pt, 5 l; injection pump; cooling: 15 imp pt, 18 US pt, 8.5 l.

TRANSMISSION axle ratio: 3.444.

PERFORMANCE max speed: Berlina 97 mph, 156 km/h - Familiar 95 mph, 153 km/h; power-weight ratio: Berlina 31.5 lb/hp (48.2 lb/kW), 15.9 kg/hp (21.9 kg/kW) - Familiar 37.6 lb/hp (51.1 lb/kW), 17 kg/hp (23.2 kg/kW); speed in top at 1,000 rpm: 22.2 mph, 35.8 km/h; consumption: Berlina 54.3 m/imp gal, 45.2 m/US gal, 5.2 l x 100 km - Familiar 50.4 m/imp gal, 42 m/US gal, 5.6 l x 100 km at 56 mph, 90 km/h.

BRAKES swept area: front 166.2 sq in, 1,072 sq cm, rear Berlina 70.1 sq in, 452 sq cm - Familiar 89 sq in, 574 sq cm, total Berlina 236.3 sq in, 1,524 sq cm - Familiar 255.2 sq in, 1,646 sq cm.

ELECTRICAL EQUIPMENT 65 Ah battery.

DIMENSIONS AND WEIGHT rear track: Familiar 56.70 in, 144 cm; length: Familiar 176 in, 447 cm; weight: Berlina 2,315 lb, 1,050 kg - Familiar 2,481 lb, 1,125 kg; turning circle: 33.5 ft, 10.2 m; fuel tank: Familiar 12.5 imp gal, 15 US gal, 57 l.

BODY saloon/sedan, 4 doors - estate car/st. wagon, 4+1 doors.

OPTIONALS tinted glass; power steering.

SEAT — SPAIN

Panda Series

PRICES EX WORKS:	pesetas
1 40 2+1-dr Berlina	385,000
2 40 Terra 2+1-dr Familiar	430,000
3 Marbella 2+1-dr Berlina	469,000

FASA-RENAULT 18 Turbo Berlina

Power team:	Standard for:	Optional for:
42 hp	1,2	—
45 hp	3	—

42 hp power team

ENGINE front, transverse, 4 stroke; 4 cylinders, vertical, in line; 55.1 cu in, 903 cc (2.56 x 2.68 in, 65 x 68 mm); compression ratio: 7.8:1; max power (DIN): 42 hp (31 kW) at 5,800 rpm; max torque (DIN): 49 lb ft, 6.7 kg m (65 Nm) at 3,000 rpm; max engine rpm: 6,000; 46.5 hp/l (34.2 kW/l); cast iron block, light alloy head; 3 crankshaft bearings; valves: overhead, in line, push-rods and rockers; camshafts: 1, side; lubrication: gear pump, full flow filter, 7.7 imp pt, 9.3 US pt, 4.4 l; 1 Weber or Solex downdraught single barrel carburettor; fuel feed: mechanical pump; water-cooled, 9.2 imp pt, 12 US pt, 5.2 l, electric fan.

TRANSMISSION driving wheels: front; clutch: single dry plate; gearbox: mechanical; gears: 4, fully synchronized; ratios: I 3.909, II 2.055, II 1.342, IV 0.963, rev 3.615; lever: central; final drive: hypoid bevel; axle ratio: 4.071; width of rims: 4''; tyres: 135 SR x 13.

PERFORMANCE max speeds: (I) 25 mph, 40 km/h; (II) 43 mph, 70 km/h; (III) 68 mph, 110 km/h; (IV) 81 mph, 130 km/h; power-weight ratio: 40 Berlina 34.1 lb/hp (46.3 lb/kW), 15.4 kg/hp (21 kg/kW); carrying capacity: 827 lb, 375 kg; consumption: 54.3 m/imp gal, 45.2 m/US gal, 5.2 l x 100 km at 56 mph, 90 km/h.

CHASSIS integral; front suspension: independent, by McPherson, lower wishbones, coil springs/telescopic damper struts; rear: rigid axle, semi-elliptic leafsprings, telescopic dampers.

STEERING rack-and-pinion; turns lock to lock: 3.40.

BRAKES front disc, rear drum, dual circuit; lining area: front 19.2 sq in, 124 sq cm, rear 32.4 sq in, 209 sq cm, total 51.6 sq in, 333 sq cm.

ELECTRICAL EQUIPMENT 12 V; 34 Ah battery; 45 A alternator; 2 headlamps.

DIMENSIONS AND WEIGHT wheel base: 85.04 in, 216 cm; front and rear track: 49.21 in, 125 cm; length: 133.07 in, 338 cm; width: 57.48 in, 146 cm; height: 56.69 in, 144 cm; weight: 40 Berlina 1,431 lb, 649 kg; weight distribution: 63.2% front, 36.8% rear; turning circle: 30.2 ft, 9.2 m; fuel tank: 7.7 imp gal, 9.2 US gal, 35 l.

BODY saloon/sedan - estate car/st. wagon; 2+1 doors; 4-5 seats, separate front seats.

PRACTICAL INSTRUCTIONS fuel: 90 oct petrol; oil: engine 6.9 imp pt, 8.2 US pt, 3.9 l, SAE 20W-30, change every 6,200 miles, 10,000 km - gearbox 4.2 imp pt, 5.1 US pt, 2.4 l, SAE 90 EP, change every 18,600 miles, 30,000 km - final drive 4.2 imp pt, 5.1 US pt, 2.4 l, change every 18,600 miles, 30,000 km; tappet clearances: inlet 0.006 in, 0.15 mm, exhaust 0.008 in, 0.20 mm; tyre pressure: front 26 psi, 1.8 atm, rear 28 psi, 2 atm.

OPTIONALS sunroof.

45 hp power team

See 42 hp power team, except for:

ENGINE 55.1 cu in, 903 cc (2.56 x 2.63 in, 65 x 68 mm); compression ratio: 9:1; max power (DIN): 45 hp (33 kW) at 5,600 rpm; max torque (DIN): 49 lb ft, 6.8 kg m (67 Nm) at 3,000 rpm; 49.8 hp/l (36.5 kW/l); 1 Weber 32 ICEV 50/250 downdraught single barrel carburettor.

TRANSMISSION axle ratio: 4.071.

PERFORMANCE max speed: 87 mph, 140 km/h; power-weight ratio: 33.3 lb/hp (45.4 lb/kW), 15.1 kg/hp (20.6 kg/kW); consumption: 57.6 m/imp gal, 48 m/US gal, 4.9 l x 100 km at 56 mph, 90 km/h.

BODY saloon/sedan; 2+1 doors; 4-5 seats, separate front seats, reclining front seats; laminated windscreen; heated rear window; rear window wiper-washer; tinted glass.

PRACTICAL INSTRUCTIONS fuel: 96 oct petrol.

OPTIONALS 5 speed fully synchronized mechanical gearbox.

SEAT Panda 40 Terra Familiar

SEAT Fura Series

Fura

PRICES EX WORKS:	pesetas
L 2+1-dr Berlina	451,000
CL 2+1-dr Berlina	500,600
CL 4+1-dr Berlina	526,600

ENGINE front, transverse, 4 stroke; 4 cylinders, vertical, in line; 55.1 cu in, 903 cc (2.56 x 2.68 in, 65 x 68 mm); compression ratio: 8.7:1; max power (DIN): 43 hp (32 kW) at 5,600 rpm; max torque (DIN): 44 lb ft, 6.1 kg m (60 Nm) at 3,000 rpm; max engine rpm: 6,200; 47.6 hp/l (35 kW/l); cast iron block, light alloy head; 3 crankshaft bearings; valves: overhead, in line, push-rods and rockers; camshafts: 1, side; lubrication: gear pump, full flow filter (cartridge), 5.8 imp pt, 7 US pt, 3.3 l; 1 Bressel 30 IBA-22/450 downdraught single barrel carburettor; fuel feed: mechanical pump; water-cooled, 8.8 imp pt, 10.6 US pt, 5 l, electric fan.

TRANSMISSION driving wheels: front; clutch: single dry plate; gearbox: mechanical; gears: 5, fully synchronized; ratios: I 3.583, II 2.235, III 1.454, IV 1.042, V 0.863, rev 3.714; lever: central; final drive: cylindrical gears; axle ratio: 4.077; width of rims: 4.5"; tyres: 135 SR x 13.

PERFORMANCE max speeds: (I) 21 mph, 35 km/h; (II) 40 mph, 65 km/h; (III) 62 mph, 100 km/h; (IV) and (V) 82 mph, 132 km/h; power-weight ratio: 36.6 lb/hp (48.5 lb/kW), 16.6 kg/hp (22 kg/kW); carrying capacity: 882 lb, 400 kg; acceleration: standing ¼ mile 20.9 sec; consumption: 52.3 m/imp gal, 43.6 m/US gal, 5.4 l x 100 km.

CHASSIS integral; front suspension: independent, by McPherson, coil springs/telescopic damper struts, lower swinging arms, anti-roll bar; rear: independent, lower swinging arms, transverse anti-roll leafsprings, coil springs, telescopic dampers.

STEERING rack-and-pinion; turns lock to lock: 3.40.

BRAKES front disc (diameter 8.94 in, 22.7 cm), rear drum, rear compensator, dual circuit; lining area: front 19.2 sq in, 124 sq cm, rear 33.5 sq in, 216 sq cm, total 52.7 sq in, 340 sq cm.

ELECTRICAL EQUIPMENT 12 V; 45 Ah battery; 462 W alternator; Femsa distributor; 2 headlamps.

DIMENSIONS AND WEIGHT wheel base: 87.40 in, 222 cm; tracks: 50.39 in, 128 cm front, 50.79 in, 129 cm rear; length: 146.06 in, 371 cm; width: 60.24 in, 153 cm; height: 53.94 in, 137 cm; ground clearance: 5.12 in, 13 cm; weight: 1,577 lb, 715 kg; weight distribution: 48% front, 52% rear; turning circle: 31.5 ft, 9.6 m; fuel tank: 6.6 imp gal, 7.9 US gal, 30 l.

BODY saloon/sedan; 2+1 or 4+1 doors; 5 seats, separate front seats.

PRACTICAL INSTRUCTIONS fuel: 90 oct petrol; oil: engine 5.8 imp pt, 7 US pt, 3.3 l, SAE 30W-40, change every 6,200 miles, 10,000 km - gearbox and final drive 4.2 imp pt, 5.1 US pt, 2.4 l, SAE 50, change every 18,600 miles, 30,000 km; greasing: none; tappet clearances: inlet 0.006 in, 0.15 mm, exhaust 0.008 in, 0.20 mm; valve timing: 17° 43° 57° 3°; tyre pressure: front 24 psi, 1.7 atm, rear 27 psi, 1.9 atm.

OPTIONALS metallic spray.

Ronda Series

PRICES EX WORKS:		pesetas
1	65 CL 4+1-dr Berlina	629,100
2	75 CL 4+1-dr Berlina	650,000
3	75 CLX star 4+1-dr Berlina	720,000
4	Crono 4+1-dr Berlina	780,000
5	Diesel L 4+1-dr Berlina	725,000
6	Diesel CL 4+1-dr Berlina	750,000
7	Diesel CLX 4+1-dr Berlina	805,000

SEAT Ronda 65 CL Berlina

SEAT Fura CL Berlina

Power team:	Standard for:	Optional for:
65 hp	1	—
75 hp	2,3	—
95 hp	4	—
55 hp (diesel)	5 to 7	—

65 hp power team

ENGINE front, transverse, 4 stroke; 4 cylinders, in line; 73 cu in, 1,197 cc (2.87 x 2.81 in, 73 x 71.5 mm); compression ratio: 8.4:1; max power (DIN): 65 hp (47 kW) at 5,800 rpm; max torque (DIN): 67 lb ft, 9.2 kg m (90 Nm) at 3,000 rpm; max engine rpm: 6,000; 54.3 hp/l (40 kW/l); cast iron block, light alloy head; 5 crankshaft bearings; valves: overhead, thimble tappets; camshafts: 1, side, in crankcase, cogged belt; lubrication: gear pump, full flow filter (cartridge), 6.9 imp pt, 8.2 US pt, 3.9 l; 1 Bressel 32 DMTR 59/250 semi-downdraught twin barrel carburettor; fuel feed: mechanical pump; water-cooled, expansion tank, 13.2 imp pt, 15.9 US pt, 7.5 l, electric thermostatic fan.

TRANSMISSION driving wheels: front; clutch: single dry plate (diaphragm); gearbox: mechanical; gears: 5, fully synchronized; ratios: I 3.583, II 2.235, III 1.454, IV 1.042, V 0.863, rev 3.714; lever: central; final drive: spiral bevel; axle ratio: 3.760; width of rims: 5"; tyres: 155 SR x 13.

PERFORMANCE max speed: 93 mph, 150 km/h; power-weight ratio: 30.3 lb/hp (41.2 lb/kW), 13.7 kg/hp (18.7 kg/kW); carrying capacity: 1,091 lb, 495 kg; acceleration: standing ¼ mile 19.9 sec; speed in top at 1,000 rpm: 16.3 mph, 26.2 km/h; consumption: 52.3 m/imp gal, 42.6 m/US gal, 5.4 l x 100 km at 56 mph, 90 km/h.

CHASSIS integral; front suspension: independent, by McPherson, lower wishbones, trailing links, coil springs, telescopic dampers; rear: independent, by McPherson, lower wishbones, transverse anti-roll leafspring, telescopic dampers.

STEERING rack-and-pinion; turns lock to lock: 3.50.

BRAKES front disc (diameter 8.94 in, 22.7 cm), rear drum, dual circuit, rear compensator, servo; lining area: front 19.2 sq in, 124 sq cm, rear 33.5 sq in, 216 sq cm, total 52.7 sq in, 340 sq cm.

SEAT Ronda (diesel engine)

ELECTRICAL EQUIPMENT 12 V; 45 Ah battery; 45 A alternator; 2 headlamps.

DIMENSIONS AND WEIGHT wheel base: 96.38 in, 245 cm; tracks: 55.12 in, 140 cm front, 55.51 in, 141 cm rear; length: 161.42 in, 401 cm; width: 65 in, 165 cm; height: 55.12 in, 140 cm; ground clearance: 5.71 in, 14.5 cm; weight: 1,940 lb, 880 kg; weight distribution: 63% front, 37% rear; turning circle: 33.8 ft, 10.3 m; fuel tank: 11.2 imp gal, 13.5 US gal, 51 l.

BODY saloon/sedan; 4+1 doors; 5 seats, separate front seats; folding rear seat.

PRACTICAL INSTRUCTIONS fuel: 90 oct petrol; oil: engine 6.9 imp pt, 8.2 US pt, 3.9 l, SAE 30W-40, change every 6,200 miles, 10,000 km - gearbox and final drive 5.3 imp pt, 6.3 US pt, 3 l, SAE 90 EP, change every 18,600 miles, 30,000 km; greasing: none; spark plug: Champion N9Y-Marelli CW7LP-Bosch W 7 D; tappet clearances: inlet 0.008 in, 0.20 mm, exhaust 0.010 in, 0.25 mm; valve timing: 10° 49° 50° 9°; tyre pressure: front 28 psi, 2 atm, rear 31 psi, 2.2 atm.

75 hp power team

See 65 hp power team, except for:

ENGINE 87.7 cu in, 1,438 cc (3.15 x 2.81 in, 80 x 71.5 mm); compression ratio: 9:1; max power (DIN): 75 hp (55 kW) at 5,600 rpm; max torque (DIN): 83 lb ft, 11.5 kg m (112 Nm) at 3,000 rpm; 52.1 hp/l (38.4 kW/l).

TRANSMISSION axle ratio: 3.714; tyres: 165/65 HR x 14.

PERFORMANCE max speed: 99 mph, 160 km/h; power-weight ratio: 29.8 lb/hp (41.2 lb/kW), 13.5 kg/hp (18.7 kg/kW); consumption: 50.4 m/imp gal, 42 m/US gal, 5.6 l x 100 km at 56 mph, 90 km/h.

STEERING adjustable height of steering wheel.

PRACTICAL INSTRUCTIONS fuel: 96 oct petrol; valve timing: 10° 49° 50° 9°.

95 hp power team

See 65 hp power team, except for:

ENGINE 97.1 cu in, 1,592 cc (3.15 x 3.12 in, 80 x 79.2 mm); compression ratio: 8.9:1; max power (DIN): 95 hp (70 kW) at 6,000 rpm; max torque (DIN): 91 lb ft, 12.5 kg m (124 Nm) at 3,800 rpm; 59.7 hp/l (43.9 kW/l); valves: overhead, Vee-slanted at 65°15', thimble tappets; camshafts: 2, overhead, cogged belt; 1 Weber 34 DAT twin barrel downdraught carburettor.

PERFORMANCE max speed: 109 mph, 175 km/h; power-weight ratio: 21.6 lb/hp (29.3 lb/kW), 9.8 kg/hp (13.3 kg/kW); consumption: 46.3 m/imp gal, 38.6 m/US gal, 6.2 l x 100 km at 56 mph, 90 km/h.

DIMENSIONS AND WEIGHT weight: 2,051 lb, 930 kg.

55 hp (diesel) power team

See 65 hp power team, except for:

ENGINE diesel; 104.6 cu in, 1,714 cc (3.27 x 3.12 in, 83 x 79.2 mm); compression ratio: 20:1; max power (DIN): 55 hp (40 kW) at 4,500 rpm; max torque (DIN): 72 lb ft, 10 kg m (98 Nm) at 3,000 rpm; 32.1 hp/l (23.3 kW/l); Bosch injection pump; cooling: 15.7 imp pt, 18.8 US pt, 8.9 l, 2 electric thermostatic fans.

TRANSMISSION tyres: 155 SR x 13.

PERFORMANCE max speed: over 87 mph, 140 km/h; power-weight ratio: 38.8 lb/hp (53.4 lb/kW), 17.6 kg/hp (24.2 kg/kW); consumption: 50.4 m/imp gal, 42 m/US gal, 5.6 l x 100 km at 56 mph, 90 km/h.

PRACTICAL INSTRUCTIONS fuel: diesel.

131 Series

PRICES EX WORKS:		pesetas
1	Mirafiori 1600 CL 4-dr Berlina	719,300
2	Supermirafiori 1600 4-dr Berlina	765,600
3	Panorama Super 1600 4+1-dr Familiar	833,900
4	Supermirafiori 2000 4-dr Berlina	832,000
5	Diplomatic 4-dr Berlina	975,200
6	Mirafiori Diesel CL 2500 4-dr Berlina	919,600
7	Supermirafiori Diesel 2500 4-dr Berlina	991,700
8	Panorama Super Diesel 2500 4+1-dr Familiar	1,030,200

Power team:	Standard for:	Optional for:
95 hp	1 to 3	—
113 hp	4,5	—
72 hp (diesel)	6 to 8	—

95 hp power team

ENGINE front, 4 stroke; 4 cylinders, vertical, in line; 97.1 cu in, 1,592 cc (3.15 x 3.12 in, 80 x 79.2 mm); compression ratio: 8.9:1; max power (DIN): 95 hp (70 kW) at 6,000 rpm; max torque (DIN): 93 lb ft, 12.8 kg m (125 Nm) at 4,000 rpm; max

95 HP POWER TEAM

engine rpm: 6,700; 59.7 hp/l (43.9 kW/l); cast iron block, light alloy head; 5 crankshaft bearings; valves: overhead, push-rods and rockers, thimble tappets; camshafts: 2, overhead; lubrication: gear pump, full flow filter (cartridge), 6.5 imp pt, 7.8 US pt, 3.7 l; 1 Bressel 34 DMS-1 downdraught twin barrel carburettor; fuel feed: mechanical pump; water-cooled, 14.1 imp pt, 16.9 US pt, 8 l, electric thermostatic fan.

TRANSMISSION driving wheels: rear; clutch: single dry plate; gearbox: mechanical; gears: 5, fully synchronized; ratios: I 3.667, II 2.100, III 1.361, IV 1, V 0.881, rev 3.526; lever: central; final drive: helical spur gears; axle ratio: 3.900; width of rims: 5"; tyres: 165 SR x 13.

PERFORMANCE max speeds: (I) 28 mph, 45 km/h; (II) 47 mph, 75 km/h; (III) 71 mph, 115 km/h; (IV) 99 mph, 160 km/h; (V) 103 mph, 165 km/h; power-weight ratio: 24.5 lb/hp (33.2 lb/kW), 11.1 kg/hp (15.1 kg/kW); carrying capacity: 1,239 lb, 562 kg; acceleration: standing ¼ mile 18.4 sec; consumption: 44.8 m/imp gal, 37.3 m/US gal, 6.3 l x 100 km at 56 mph, 90 km/h.

CHASSIS integral; front suspension: independent, by McPherson, lower wishbones, anti-roll bar, coil springs/telescopic damper struts; rear: rigid axle, twin trailing lower radius arms, transverse linkage bar, coil springs, telescopic dampers.

STEERING rack-and-pinion; turns lock to lock: 3.50.

BRAKES front disc, rear drum, rear compensator, dual circuit, vacuum servo; lining area: front 19.2 sq in, 124 sq cm, rear 41.7 sq in, 269 sq cm, total 60.9 sq in, 393 sq cm.

ELECTRICAL EQUIPMENT 12 V; 45 Ah battery; 45 A alternator; Femsa distributor; 2 halogen headlamps.

DIMENSIONS AND WEIGHT wheel base: 98.03 in, 249 cm; tracks: 54.33 in, 138 cm front, 51.97 in, 132 cm rear; length: 166.54 in, 423 cm; width: 64.57 in, 164 cm; height: 55.12 in, 140 cm; weight: 2,238 lb, 1,015 kg; weight distribution: 53.9% front, 46.1% rear; turning circle: 33.8 ft, 10.3 m; fuel tank: 12.1 imp gal, 14.5 US gal, 55 l.

BODY saloon/sedan, 4 doors - estate car/st. wagon, 4+1 doors; 5 seats, separate front seats, reclining backrests, headrests; tinted glass; heated rear window.

PRACTICAL INSTRUCTIONS fuel: 96 oct petrol; oil: engine 6.5 imp pt, 7.8 US pt, 3.7 l, SAE 30W (winter) - 40 (summer), change every 6,200 miles, 10,000 km - gearbox 2.8 imp pt, 3.4 US pt, 1.6 l, SAE 50 Mizard H.D., change every 18,600 miles, 30,000 km - final drive 1.3 imp pt, 2.1 US pt, 1 l, change every 18,600 miles, 30,000 km; greasing: none; spark plug: 175°; tappet clearances: inlet 0.018 in, 0.45 mm, exhaust 0.024 in, 0.60 mm; valve timing: 12° 53° 54° 11°; tyre pressure: front 26 psi, 1.8 atm, rear 28 psi, 2 atm.

113 hp power team

See 95 hp power team, except for:

ENGINE 121.7 cu in, 1,995 cc (3.31 x 3.54 in, 84 x 90 mm); max power (DIN): 113 hp (83 kW) at 5,600 rpm; max torque (DIN): 123 lb ft, 17 kg m (167 Nm) at 3,600 rpm; 56.6 hp/l (41.7 kW/l); camshafts: 2, overhead; lubrication: 8.4 imp pt, 10.1 US pt, 4.8 l; 1 Weber 34 ADF 54/250 downdraught twin barrel carburettor; cooling: 14.4 imp pt, 17.3 US pt, 8.2 l.

TRANSMISSION axle ratio: 4.100; width of rims: 5.5"; tyres: 185/70 SR x 13.

PERFORMANCE max speeds: (I) 28 mph, 45 km/h; (II) 47 mph, 75 km/h; (III) 75 mph, 120 km/h; (IV) 99 mph, 160 km/h; (V) 112 mph, 180 km/h; power-weight ratio: 18.8 lb/hp (25.5 lb/kW), 8.5 kg/hp (11.5 kg/kW); acceleration: standing ¼ mile 17.3 sec; consumption: 42.8 m/imp gal, 36.6 m/US gal, 6.6 l x 100 km at 56 mph, 90 km/h.

SEAT 131 Supermirafiori 2000 Berlina

SEAT 131 Panorama Super 1600 Familiar

STEERING adjustable height of steering wheel, servo.

ELECTRICAL EQUIPMENT electronic ignition; 4 headlamps.

DIMENSIONS AND WEIGHT weight: 2,239 lb, 1,040 kg.

72 hp (diesel) power team

See 95 hp power team, except for:

ENGINE diesel; 149.2 cu in, 2,445 cc (3.66 x 3.54 in, 93 x 90 mm); compression ratio: 22:1; max power (DIN): 72 hp (53 kW) at 4,200 rpm; max torque (DIN): 109 lb ft, 15 kg m (147 Nm) at 2,400 rpm; 29.4 hp/l (21.7 kW/l); lubrication: 9.7 imp pt, 11.6 US pt, 5.5 l; Bosch injection pump; sealed circuit cooling, liquid, expansion tank, 19.4 imp pt, 23.3 US pt, 11 l, electromagnetic thermostatic fan.

TRANSMISSION tyres: 165/60 SR x 13.

PERFORMANCE max speed: over 93 mph, 150 km/h; power-weight ratio: 36.6 lb/hp (49.7 lb/kW), 16.6 kg/hp (22.5 kg/kW); acceleration: standing ¼ mile 20.8 sec; consumption: 51.4 m/imp gal, 42.8 m/US gal, 5.5 l x 100 km at 56 mph, 90 km/h.

STEERING servo; turns lock to lock: 4.08.

ELECTRICAL EQUIPMENT 88 Ah battery; 55 A alternator; 4 iodine headlamps.

DIMENSIONS AND WEIGHT length: 166.54 in, 423 cm; weight: Supermirafiori 2,525 lb, 1,145 kg - Panorama 2,569 lb, 1,165 kg.

BODY built-in headrests on front and rear seats.

PRACTICAL INSTRUCTIONS fuel: diesel; oil: engine 9.7 imp pt, 11.6 US pt, 5.5 l; valve timing: 8° 48° 48° 8°; tyre pressure: front 30 psi, 2.1 atm, rear 28 psi, 2 atm.

TALBOT SPAIN

Samba Series

PRICES EX WORKS:		pesetas
1	LE 2+1-dr Berlina	581,900*
2	LS 2+1-dr Berlina	619,500*
3	GL 2+1-dr Berlina	681,400*
4	GL Confort 2+1-dr Berlina	722,700*
5	S 2+1-dr Berlina	806,800*
6	S 2-dr Cabriolet	1,707,100*
7	Rallye 2+1-dr Berlina	800,600*

Power team:	Standard for:	Optional for:
55 hp	1,2	—
58 hp	3,4	—
80 hp	5,6	—
90 hp	7	—

55 hp power team

ENGINE front, transverse, slanted 72° to rear, 4 stroke; 4 cylinders, in line; 68.6 cu in, 1,124 cc (2.83 x 2.72 in, 72 x 69 mm); compression ratio: 8.2:1; max power (DIN): 55 hp (40 kW) at 5,800 rpm; max torque (DIN): 58 lb ft, 8 kg m (78 Nm) at 3,000 rpm; max engine rpm: 6,200; 48.9 hp/l (36 kW/l); light alloy block and head, wet liners, bi-hemispherical combustion chambers; 5 crankshaft bearings; valves: overhead, Vee-slanted, rockers; camshafts: 1, overhead; lubrication: gear pump, full flow filter, 7.9 imp pt, 9.5 US pt, 4.5 l; 1 Solex downdraught single barrel carburettor; fuel feed: mechanical pump; water-cooled, expansion tank, 9.9 imp pt, 11.8 US pt, 5.6 l, electric thermostatic fan.

TRANSMISSION driving wheels: front; clutch: single dry plate (diaphragm); gearbox: mechanical, in unit with engine and final drive; gears: 4, fully synchronized; ratios: I 3.883, II 2.074, III 1.377, IV 0.944, rev 3.568; lever: central; final drive: spiral bevel; axle ratio: 3.177; width of rims: 4.5"; tyres: 135 SR x 13.

PERFORMANCE max speed: 94 mph, 151 km/h; power-weight ratio: 29.7 lb/hp (40.3 lb/kW), 13.4 kg/hp (18.3 kg/kW); speed in top at 1,000 rpm: 20.7 mph, 33.4 km/h; consumption: 36.2 m/imp gal, 30.2 m/US gal, 7.8 l x 100 km at 75 mph, 120 km/h.

CHASSIS integral; front suspension: independent, by McPherson, coil springs/telescopic damper struts, lower wishbones (trailing links), anti-roll bar; rear: independent, swinging longitudinal trailing arms, coil springs, telescopic dampers.

STEERING rack-and-pinion; turns lock to lock: 3.92.

BRAKES front disc (diameter 9.49 in, 24.1 cm), rear drum, dual circuit, rear compensator.

ELECTRICAL EQUIPMENT 12 V; 28 Ah battery; 500 W alternator; electronic ignition; 2 headlamps.

DIMENSIONS AND WEIGHT wheel base: 92.13 in, 234 cm; tracks: 50.87 in, 129 cm front, 50.08 in, 127 cm rear; length: 138.03 in, 351 cm; width: 60.16 in, 153 cm; height: 53.62 in, 136 cm; ground clearance: 5.12 in, 13 cm; weight: 1,632 lb, 740 kg; turning circle: 32.5 ft, 9.9 m; fuel tank: 8.8 imp gal, 10.6 US gal, 40 l.

BODY saloon/sedan; 2+1 doors; 5 seats, separate front seats; folding rear seat; heated rear window.

OPTIONALS rear window wiper-washer.

58 hp power team

See 55 hp power team, except for:

ENGINE max power (DIN): 58 hp (43 kW) at 6,000 rpm; max torque (DIN): 60 lb ft, 8.3 kg m (81 Nm) at 3,000 rpm; max engine rpm: 6,500; 51.6 hp/l (38 kW/l).

TALBOT Samba GL Berlina

TRANSMISSION axle ratio: 3.353; tyres: 145 SR x 13.

PERFORMANCE max speed: 96 mph, 155 km/h; power-weight ratio: 28.1 lb/hp (38.2 lb/kW), 12.7 kg/hp (17.3 kg/kW); consumption: 36.7 m/imp gal, 30.5 m/US gal, 7.7 l x 100 km at 75 mph, 120 km/h.

80 hp power team

See 55 hp power team, except for:

ENGINE 83 cu in, 1,360 cc (2.95 x 3.03 in, 75 x 77 mm); compression ratio: 9.3:1; max power (DIN): 80 hp (57 kW) at 5,800 rpm; max torque (DIN): 81 lb ft, 11.2 kg m (109 Nm) at 2,800 rpm; max engine rpm: 6,200; 58.8 hp/l (41.9 kW/l); 2 Solex downdraught single barrel carburettors.

TRANSMISSION gears: 5, fully synchronized; ratios: I 3.883, II 2.296, III 1.501, IV 1.124, V 0.904, rev 3.568; axle ratio: 3.867; width of rims: 5"; tyres: 165/70 SR x 13.

PERFORMANCE max speed: 104 mph, 168 km/h; power-weight ratio: 21.8 lb/hp (29.6 lb/kW), 9.9 kg/hp (13.4 kg/kW); speed in top at 1,000 rpm: 18.5 mph, 29.8 km/h; consumption: 32.5 m/imp gal, 27 m/US gal, 8.7 l x 100 km at 75 mph, 120 km/h.

BRAKES servo.

ELECTRICAL EQUIPMENT 36 Ah battery.

DIMENSIONS AND WEIGHT weight: 1,741 lb, 790 kg.

BODY saloon/sedan, 2+1 doors - convertible, 2 doors; reclining backrests with headrests; electric windows.

90 hp power team

See 55 hp power team, except for:

ENGINE 74.4 cu in, 1,219 cc (2.95 x 2.72 in, 75 x 69 mm); compression ratio: 9.7:1; max power (DIN): 90 hp (65 kW) at 6,700 rpm; max torque (DIN): 76 lb ft, 10.5 kg m (102 Nm) at 5,400 rpm; max engine rpm: 7,000; 73.8 hp/l (53.3 kW/l); 2 Weber 40 DCOE horizontal twin barrel carburettors.

TRANSMISSION gears: 5, fully synchronized; ratios: I 3.883, II 2.296, III 1.501, IV 1.124, V 0.904, rev 3.568; axle ratio: 4.066; width of rims: 5"; tyres: 165/70 SR x 13.

PERFORMANCE max speed: 109 mph, 176 km/h; power-weight ratio: 19.1 lb/hp (26.5 lb/kW), 8.7 kg/hp (12 kg/kW); acceleration: standing ¼ mile 17.6 sec; speed in top at 1,000 rpm: 17.4 mph, 28.1 km/h; consumption: 32.5 m/imp gal, 27 m/US gal, 8.7 l x 100 km at 75 mph, 120 km/h.

CHASSIS rear suspension: anti-roll bar.

BRAKES servo.

DIMENSIONS AND WEIGHT weight: 1,720 lb, 780 kg.

Horizon Series

PRICES EX WORKS:	pesetas
1 LS 4+1-dr Berlina	811,400*
2 GL 4+1-dr Berlina	854,900*
3 GL Automatic 4+1-dr Berlina	966,300*
4 GLS 4+1-dr Berlina	956,300*
5 S-2 4+1-dr Berlina	950,100*
6 GT 4+1-dr Berlina	1,043,400*
7 LD 4+1-dr Berlina	997,600*
8 GLD 4+1-dr Berlina	1,047,400*
9 EXD 4+1-dr Berlina	1,127,300*

Power team:	Standard for:	Optional for:
59 hp	1	—
65 hp	2	—
83 hp	3,4	—
90 hp	5,6	—
65 hp (diesel)	7 to 9	—

59 hp power team

ENGINE front, transverse, slanted 41° to rear, 4 stroke; 4 cylinders, in line; 79 cu in, 1,294 cc (3.02 x 2.76 in, 76.7 x 70 mm); compression ratio: 8.8:1; max power (DIN): 59 hp (43 kW) at 5,500 rpm; max torque (DIN): 75 lb ft, 10.3 kg m (101 Nm) at 2,800 rpm; max engine rpm: 6,000; 45.6 hp/l (33.6 kW/l); 5 crankshaft bearings; valves: overhead, in line, push-rods and rockers; camshafts: 1, side; lubrication: gear pump, full flow filter, 5.3 imp pt, 6.3 US pt, 3 l; 1 single barrel downdraught carburettor; fuel feed: mechanical pump; sealed circuit cooling, liquid, expansion tank, 10.6 imp pt, 12.7 US pt, 6 l, electric thermostatic fan.

TRANSMISSION driving wheels: front; clutch: single dry plate (diaphragm), hydraulically controlled; gearbox: mechanical; gears: 4, fully synchronized; ratios: I 3.900, II 2.312, III 1.524, IV 1.080, rev 3.769; lever: central; final drive: cylindrical gears; axle ratio: 3.706; width of rims: 4.5"; tyres: 145 SR x 13.

PERFORMANCE max speed: 94 mph, 152 km/h; power-weight ratio: 35.3 lb/hp (48 lb/kW), 16 kg/hp (21.8 kg/kW); carrying capacity: 981 lb, 445 kg; consumption: 32.5 m/imp gal, 27 m/US gal, 8.7 l x 100 km at 75 mph, 120 km/h.

TALBOT Samba LS Berlina

CHASSIS integral; front suspension: independent, wishbones, longitudinal torsion bars, anti-roll bar, telescopic dampers; rear: independent, linkage trailing arms, coil springs, anti-roll bar, telescopic dampers.

STEERING rack-and-pinion; turns lock to lock: 4.48.

BRAKES front disc (diameter 9.40 in, 24 cm), rear drum, dual circuit, rear compensator, servo; swept area: front 155 sq in, 1,000 sq cm, rear 89 sq in, 574 sq cm, total 244 sq in, 1,574 sq cm.

ELECTRICAL EQUIPMENT 12 V; 40 Ah battery; 50 A alternator; transistorized ignition; 2 headlamps.

DIMENSIONS AND WEIGHT wheel base: 99 in, 252 cm; tracks: 55.91 in, 142 cm front, 53.94 in, 137 cm rear; length: 155.91 in, 396 cm; width: 66 in, 168 cm; height: 56 in, 141 cm; weight: 2,084 lb, 945 kg; turning circle: 33 ft, 10.2 m; fuel tank: 10.5 imp gal, 12.5 US gal, 47 l.

BODY saloon/sedan; 4+1 doors; 5 seats, separate front seats, reclining backrests; folding rear seat.

OPTIONALS heated rear window; rear window wiper-washer; tinted glass; metallic spray; headrests on front seats; vinyl roof.

65 hp power team

See 59 hp power team, except for:

ENGINE 88 cu in, 1,442 cc (3.02 x 3.07 in, 76.7 x 78 mm); compression ratio: 9.5:1; max power (DIN): 65 hp (48 kW) at 5,200 rpm; max torque (DIN): 89 lb ft, 12.3 kg m (121 Nm) at 2,400 rpm; 45.1 hp/l (33.2 kW/l); 1 single barrel downdraught carburettor.

TRANSMISSION axle ratio: 3.588; width of rims: 5"; tyres: 155 SR x 13.

PERFORMANCE max speed: 95 mph, 153 km/h; power-weight ratio: 32.1 lb/hp (43.6 lb/kW), 14.5 kg/hp (19.8 kg/kW).

DIMENSIONS AND WEIGHT weight: 2,084 lb, 945 kg.

BODY heated rear window (standard).

OPTIONALS trip computer.

83 hp power team

See 59 hp power team, except for:

ENGINE 88 cu in, 1,442 cc (3.02 x 3.07 in, 76.7 x 78 mm); compression ratio: 9.5:1; max power (DIN): 83 hp (61 kW) at 5,600 rpm; max torque (DIN): 90 lb ft, 12.5 kg m (122 Nm) at 3,000 rpm; 57.6 hp/l (42.4 kW/l); 1 twin barrel downdraught carburettor.

TRANSMISSION gearbox: (for GL Automatic only) automatic transmission - (for GLS) mechanical; gears: 5, fully synchronized; ratios: I 3.308, II 1.882, III 1.280, IV 0.969, V 0.757, rev 3.333; axle ratio: GL Automatic 3.588 - GLS 4.336; width of rims: 5"; tyres: 155 SR x 13.

PERFORMANCE max speed: GL Automatic 97 mph, 157 km/h - GLS 102 mph, 164 km/h; power-weight ratio: GLS 25.1 lb/hp (34.1 lb/kW), 11.4 kg/hp (15.5 kg/kW).

DIMENSIONS AND WEIGHT weight: GLS 2,083 lb, 945 kg - GL Automatic 2,193 lb, 995 kg.

BODY (standard) heated rear window, tinted glass, headrests on front seats and rear window wiper-washer.

OPTIONALS trip computer.

90 hp power team

See 59 hp power team, except for:

ENGINE 97.2 cu in, 1,592 cc (3.17 x 3.07 in, 80.6 x 78 mm); compression ratio: 9.3:1; max power (DIN): 90 hp (64 kW) at 5,400 rpm; max torque (DIN): 93 lb ft, 12.9 kg m (127 Nm) at 4,000 rpm; max engine rpm: 6,000; 56.5 hp/l (40.2 kW/l); 1 Weber 36 DCNVH-12 downdraught twin barrel carburettor; liquid-cooled, 11.3 imp pt, 13.5 US pt, 6.4 l.

TRANSMISSION gears: 5, fully synchronized; ratios: I 3.308, II 1.882, III 1.280, IV 0.969, V 0.757, rev 3.333; axle ratio: 4.429; width of rims: 5"; tyres: 175/70 SR x 13.

PERFORMANCE max speed: 109 mph, 175 km/h; power-weight ratio: 24.3 lb/hp (13.5 lb/kW), 11 kg/hp (15.5 kg/kW); acceleration: standing ¼ mile 17.6 sec; consumption: 35.3 m/imp gal, 29.4 m/US gal, 8 l x 100 km at 75 mph, 120 km/h.

TALBOT Horizon EXD Berlina

TALBOT 150 GT-2 Berlina

90 HP POWER TEAM

STEERING servo.

ELECTRICAL EQUIPMENT 2 iodine headlamps.

DIMENSIONS AND WEIGHT tracks: 56.46 in, 143 cm front, 54.61 in, 139 cm rear; weight: 2,183 lb, 990 kg.

BODY adjustable backrests on front seats (standard); rear window wiper-washer; trip computer; light alloy wheels; central door locking.

65 hp (diesel) power team

See 59 hp power team, except for:

ENGINE diesel; front, transverse, slanted 20° to rear; 116.3 cu in, 1,905 cc (3.27 x 3.46 in, 83 x 88 mm); compression ratio: 23.5:1; max power (DIN): 65 hp (47 KW) at 4,600 rpm; max torque (DIN): 88 lb ft, 12.2 kg m (118 Nm) at 2,000 rpm; max engine rpm: 5,000; 34.1 hp/l (24.7 kW/l); valves: overhead, rockers; camshafts: 1, overhead; Rotodiesel injection pump.

TRANSMISSION gears: GLD and EXD 5, fully synchronized; ratios: LD I 3.308, II 1.882, III 1.148, IV 0.799, rev 3.333 - GLD and EXD: I 3.308, II 1.882, III 1.280, IV 0.969, V 0.757, rev 3.333; axle ratio: LD 3.814 - GLD and EXD 3.939.

PERFORMANCE max speed: LD 93 mph, 149 km/h - GLD and EXD 97 mph, 156 km/h; power-weight ratio: 34.6 lb/hp (47 lb/kW), 15.7 kg/hp (21.3 kg/kW); consumption: 43.5 m/imp gal, 36.2 m/US gal, 6.5 l x 100 km at 75 mph, 120 km/h.

STEERING (for EXD only) servo.

ELECTRICAL EQUIPMENT 60 Ah battery.

DIMENSIONS AND WEIGHT tracks: GLD and EXD 56.46 in, 143 cm front, 54.61 in, 139 cm rear; weight: 2,249 lb, 1,020 kg.

OPTIONALS (for LD only) 5-speed fully synchronized mechanical gearbox; (for GLD and EXD only) tinted glass and central door locking; (for LD and GLD only) power steering.

150 Series

PRICES EX WORKS:	pesetas
1 GL 4+1-dr Berlina	**1,038,900***
2 LS 4+1-dr Berlina	**999,700***
3 LS Confort 4+1-dr Berlina	**1,030,800***
4 GT-2 4+1-dr Berlina	**1,114,000***

Power team:	Standard for:	Optional for:
73 hp	1	—
75 hp	2,3	—
90 hp	4	—

73 hp power team

ENGINE front, transverse, slanted 41° to rear, 4 stroke; 4 cylinders, in line; 97.2 cu in, 1,592 cc (3.17 x 3.07 in, 80.6 x 78 mm); compression ratio: 9.35:1; max power (DIN): 73 hp (54 kW) at 5,200 rpm; max torque (DIN): 96 lb ft, 13.3 kg m (131 Nm) at 3,000 rpm; max engine rpm: 5,700; 45.8 hp/l (33.7 kW/l); cast iron block, light alloy head; 5 crankshaft bearings; valves: overhead, in line, push-rods and rockers; camshafts: 1, side; lubrication: gear pump, full flow filter, 5.3 imp pt, 6.3 US pt, 3 l; 1 Solex downdraught single barrel carburettor; fuel feed: mechanical pump; sealed circuit cooling, liquid, expansion tank, 11.4 imp pt, 13.7 US pt, 6.5 l, electric thermostatic fan.

TRANSMISSION driving wheels: front; clutch: single dry plate (diaphragm); gearbox: mechanical; gears: 4, fully synchronized; ratios: I 3.900, II 2.312, III 1.524, IV 1.080, rev 3.769; lever: central; final drive: cylindrical gears; axle ratio: 3.588; width of rims: 5.5"; tyres: 165 SR x 13.

PERFORMANCE max speed: 97 mph, 157 km/h; power-weight ratio: 31.4 lb/hp (42.7 lb/kW), 14.2 kg/hp (19.3 kg/kW); acceleration: standing ¼ mile 19 sec, 0-50 mph (0-80 km/h) 8.9 sec; consumption: 32.1 m/imp gal, 26.7 m/US gal, 8.8 l x 100 km.

CHASSIS integral; front suspension: independent, wishbones, longitudinal torsion bars, anti-roll bar, telescopic dampers; rear: independent, swinging longitudinal trailing arms, coil springs, anti-roll bar, telescopic dampers.

TALBOT Solara Pullman Berlina

STEERING rack-and-pinion; turns lock to lock: 4.15.

BRAKES front disc, rear drum, rear compensator, servo.

ELECTRICAL EQUIPMENT 12 V; 40 Ah battery; 50 A alternator; electronic ignition; 2 headlamps.

DIMENSIONS AND WEIGHT wheel base: 102.36 in, 260 cm; tracks: 55.51 in, 141 cm front, 54.72 in, 139 cm rear; length: 169.68 in, 431 cm; width: 66.14 in, 168 cm; height: 54.72 in, 139 cm; ground clearance: 5.12 in, 13 cm; weight: 2,293 lb, 1,040 kg; turning circle: 36.1 ft, 11 m; fuel tank: 12.8 imp gal, 15.3 US gal, 58 l.

BODY saloon/sedan; 4+1 doors; 5 seats, separate front seats, reclining backrests; heated rear window; folding rear seat.

OPTIONALS iodine long-distance lights; headrests on front seats; tinted glass; headlamps with wiper-washers; rear window wiper-washer; electric windows; vinyl roof; sunroof; power steering; tinted glass; metallic spray; light alloy wheels.

75 hp power team

See 73 hp power team, except for:

ENGINE 88 cu in, 1,442 cc (3.02 x 3.07 in, 76.7 x 78 mm); compression ratio: 8.5:1; max power (DIN): 75 hp (55 kW) at 5,500 rpm; max torque (DIN): 80 lb ft, 11.1 kg m (109 Nm) at 3,500 rpm; max engine rpm: 6,000; 52 hp/l (38 kW/l); 1 Weber 36 DCNVA downdraught twin barrel carburettor.

TRANSMISSION tyres: 155 SR x 13.

PERFORMANCE power-weight ratio: 30.6 lb/hp (41.6 lb/kW), 13.8 kg/hp (18.8 kg/kW); consumption: 30.4 m/imp gal, 23.3 m/US gal, 9.3 l x 100 km at 75 mph, 120 km/h.

90 hp power team

See 73 hp power team, except for:

ENGINE max power (DIN): 90 hp (66 kW) at 5,400 rpm; max torque (DIN): 93 lb ft, 12.9 kg m (126 Nm) at 4,000 rpm; max engine rpm: 5,900; 56.5 hp/l (41.6 kW/l); 1 Weber 36 DCA 100 downdraught twin barrel carburettor.

TRANSMISSION gears: 5, fully synchronized; ratios: I 3.167, II 1.680, III 1.250, IV 0.939, V 0.767, rev 3.155; axle ratio: 4.216.

PERFORMANCE max speed: 102 mph, 165 km/h; power-weight ratio: 26.4 lb/hp (36 lb/kW), 12 kg/hp (16.3 kg/kW); consumption: 34.9 m/imp gal, 29 m/US gal, 8.1 l x 100 km at 75 mph, 120 km/h.

DIMENSIONS AND WEIGHT weight: 2,381 lb, 1,080 kg.

Solara Series

PRICES EX WORKS:	pesetas
1 GL 4-dr Berlina	**1,045,500***
2 LS 4-dr Berlina	**1,006,300***
3 Pullman 4-dr Berlina	**1,028,100***
4 GLS 4-dr Berlina	**1,095,400***
5 SX 4-dr Berlina	**1,178,500***
6 SX Automatico 4-dr Berlina	**1,265,000***

Power team:	Standard for:	Optional for:
73 hp	1	—
75 hp	2,3	—
90 hp	4 to 6	—

73 hp power team

ENGINE front, transverse, slanted 41° to rear, 4 stroke; 4 cylinders, in line; 97.2 cu in, 1,592 cc (3.17 x 3.07 in, 80.6 x 78 mm); compression ratio: 9.35:1; max power (DIN): 73 hp (54 kW) at 5,200 rpm; max torque (DIN): 96 lb ft, 13.3 kg m (131 Nm) at 3,000 rpm; max engine rpm: 5,700; 45.8 hp/l (33.7 kW/l); cast iron block, light alloy head; 5 crankshaft bearings; valves: overhead, in line, push-rods and rockers; camshafts: 1, side; lubrication: gear pump, full flow filter, 5.3 imp pt, 6.3 US pt, 3 l; 1 Solex downdraught single barrel carburettor; fuel feed: mechanical pump; sealed circuit cooling, liquid, expansion tank, 10.7 imp pt, 11.9 US pt, 6.1 l, electric thermostatic fan.

TRANSMISSION driving wheels: front; clutch: single dry plate (diaphragm); gearbox: mechanical; gears: 4, fully synchronized; ratios: I 3.900, II 2.312, III 1.524, IV 1.080, rev 3.769; lever: central; final drive: cylindrical gears; axle ratio: 3.588; width of rims: 5"; tyres: 165 SR x 13.

PERFORMANCE max speed: 97 mph, 157 km/h; power-weight ratio: 32 lb/hp (43.5 lb/kW), 14.5 kg/hp (19.7 kg/kW); carrying capacity: 970 lb, 440 kg; acceleration: standing ¼ mile 19.5 sec; speed in top at 1,000 rpm: 17.6 mph, 28.3 km/h; consumption: 31.7 m/imp gal, 26.4 m/US gal, 8.9 l x 100 km at 75 mph, 120 km/h.

CHASSIS integral; front suspension: independent, wishbones, longitudinal torsion bars, anti-roll bar, telescopic dampers; rear: independent, swinging longitudinal trailing arms, coil springs, anti-roll bar, telescopic dampers.

STEERING rack-and-pinion; turns lock to lock: 4.15.

BRAKES front disc (diameter 9.45 in, 24 cm), rear drum, dual circuit, rear compensator, servo; swept area: front 172.1 sq in, 1,110 sq cm, rear 89 sq in, 574 sq cm, total 261.1 sq in, 1,684 sq cm.

ELECTRICAL EQUIPMENT 12 V; 40 Ah battery; 560 W alternator; electronic ignition; 2 halogen headlamps.

DIMENSIONS AND WEIGHT wheel base: 102.36 in, 260 cm; tracks: 56.10 in, 142 cm front, 55.12 in, 140 cm rear; length: 172.91 in, 439 cm; width: 66.14 in, 168 cm; height: 54.72 in, 139 cm; ground clearance: 5.12 in, 13 cm; weight: 2,293 lb, 1,040 kg; weight distribution: 48% front, 52% rear; turning circle: 34.8 ft, 10.6 m; fuel tank: 12.8 imp gal, 15.3 US gal, 58 l.

BODY saloon/sedan; 4 doors; 5 seats, separate front seats, reclining backrests; heated rear window.

OPTIONALS metallic spray; iodine headlamps; headrests; vinyl roof; power steering.

75 hp power team

See 73 hp power team, except for:

ENGINE 88 cu in, 1,442 cc (3.02 x 3.07 in, 76.7 x 78 mm); compression ratio: 8.5:1; max power (DIN): 75 hp (55 kW) at 5,500 rpm; max torque (DIN): 80 lb ft, 11.1 kg m (109 Nm) at 3,500 rpm; max engine rpm: 6,000; 52 hp/l (38 kW/l); 1 Weber downdraught twin barrel carburettor.

PERFORMANCE power-weight ratio: 30.6 lb/hp (41.6 lb/kW), 13.8 kg/hp (18.8 kg/kW); consumption: 30.4 m/imp gal, 25.3 m/US gal, 9.3 l x 100 km at 75 mph, 120 km/h.

ELECTRICAL EQUIPMENT (for Pullman only) electronic ignition.

BODY (for Pullman only) light alloy wheels.

90 hp power team

See 73 hp power team, except for:

ENGINE max power (DIN): 90 hp (66 kW) at 5,400 rpm; max torque (DIN): 93 lb ft, 12.9 kg m (126 Nm) at 4,000 rpm; max engine rpm: 5,900; 56.5 hp/l (41.6 kW/l); 1 Weber downdraught twin barrel carburettor.

TRANSMISSION gears: 5, fully synchronized - SX Automatico automatic transmission with 3 ratios; ratios: I 3.307, II 1.882, III 1.280, IV 0.968, V 0.756, rev 3.333 - SX Automatico I 2.465, II 1.477, III 1, rev 2.103; axle ratio: 4.216 - SX Automatico 3.056.

PERFORMANCE max speed: 104 mph, 167 km/h - SX Automatico 94 mph, 152 km/h; power-weight ratio: GLS 26.2 lb/hp (35.6 lb/kW), 11.8 kg/hp (16.2 kg/kW); carrying capacity: 882 lb, 400 kg; speed in top at 1,000 rpm: 20.9 mph, 33.6 km/h; consumption: 34.4 m/imp gal, 28.7 m/US gal, 8.2 l x 100 km - SX Automatico 29.1 m/imp gal, 24.2 m/US gal, 9.7 l x 100 km at 75 mph, 120 km/h.

STEERING (standard) servo; turns lock to lock: 2.80.

DIMENSIONS AND WEIGHT weight: GLS 2,359 lb, 1,070 kg - SX 2,403 lb, 1,090 kg.

OPTIONALS sunroof; light alloy wheels; metallic spray; tinted glass.

SAAB SWEDEN

99

PRICES IN GB: £

	£
GL 4 gear 2-dr Sedan	—
GL 5 gear 2-dr Sedan	6,110*
GL 5 gear 4-dr Sedan	6,435*

ENGINE front, 4 stroke; 4 cylinders, slanted at 45°, in line; 121.1 cu in, 1,985 cc (3.54 x 3.07 in, 90 x 78 mm); compression ratio: 9.5:1; max power (DIN): 100 hp (74 kW) at 5,200 rpm; max torque (DIN): 120 lb ft, 16.5 kg m (162 Nm) at 3,500 rpm; max engine rpm: 6,000; 50.4 hp/l (37.1 kW/l); cast iron block, light alloy head; 5 crankshaft bearings; valves: overhead, thimble tappets; camshafts: 1, overhead, driven by double chain; lubrication: gear pump, full flow filter, 6.2 imp pt, 7.4 US pt, 3.5 l; 1 Zenith-Stromberg 175 CDSEVX horizontal carburettor; fuel feed: mechanical pump; liquid-cooled, expansion tank, 14.1 imp pt, 16.9 US pt, 8 l, thermostatic fan.

TRANSMISSION driving wheels: front; clutch: single dry plate, hydraulically controlled; gearbox: mechanical, in unit with differential and engine (transfer chain in front of engine, ratio GL 4 gear 0.968 - GL 5 gear 0.781); gears: GL 4 gear 4, fully synchronized (ratios: I 3.882, II 2.194, III 1.473, IV 1, rev 4.271) - GL 5 gear 5, fully synchronized (ratios I 4.533, II 2.562, III 1.716, IV 1.236, V 1, rev 4.987); lever: central; final drive: spiral bevel; axle ratio: 3.667; width of rims: GL 4 gear 5" - GL 5 gear 5.5"; tyres: GL 4 gear 165 SR x 15 - GL 5 gear 185/65 SR x 15.

SAAB 99 GL 5 gear Sedan

PERFORMANCE max speed: 99 mph, 160 km/h; power-weight ratio: 2-dr models 25.1 lb/hp (34.1 lb/kW), 11.4 kg/hp (15.5 kg/kW); carrying capacity: 970 lb, 440 kg; speed in top at 1,000 rpm: 24.6 mph, 39.6 km/h; consumption: 5 gears 30.1 m/imp gal, 25 m/US gal, 9.4 l x 100 km at 75 mph, 120 km/h.

CHASSIS integral; front suspension: independent, double wishbones, progressively-acting coil springs, telescopic dampers; rear: rigid axle, twin longitudinal leading arms, twin swinging trailing radius arms, transverse linkage bar, coil springs, telescopic dampers.

STEERING rack-and-pinion; turns lock to lock: 4.10.

BRAKES disc (front diameter 10.9 in, 27.6 cm, rear 10.5 in, 26.8 cm), 2 separate X hydraulic circuits, servo; swept area: total 388.2 sq in, 2,504 sq cm.

ELECTRICAL EQUIPMENT 12 V; 60 Ah battery; 930 W alternator; Bosch distributor; 2 halogen headlamps with wiper-washers.

DIMENSIONS AND WEIGHT wheel base: 97.05 in, 246 cm; tracks: 55.51 in, 141 cm front, 56.69 in, 144 cm rear; length: 176.38 in, 448 cm; width: 66.54 in, 169 cm; height: 56 in, 143 cm; ground clearance: 5.51 in, 14 cm; weight: 2-dr models 2,459 lb, 1,115 kg - 4-dr Sedan 2,510 lb, 1,140 kg; weight distribution: 61% front, 39% rear; turning circle: 36.7 ft, 11.2 m; fuel tank: 12.8 imp gal, 15.3 US gal, 58 l.

BODY saloon/sedan; 2 or 4 doors; 5 seats, separate front seats, adjustable backrests; heated driving seat; folding rear seat; impact-absorbing bumpers; hazard lights; heated rear window.

PRACTICAL INSTRUCTIONS fuel: 97 oct petrol; oil: engine 6.2 imp pt, 7.4 US pt, 3.5 l, SAE 10W-40, change every 9,300 miles, 15,000 km - gearbox 4.4 imp pt, 5.3 US pt, 2.5 l, SAE 10W-30/40, change every 18,600 miles, 30,000 km; greasing: every 6,200 miles, 10,000 km; tappet clearances: inlet 0.006-0.012 in, 0.15-0.30 mm, exhaust 0.014-0.20 in, 0.35-0.50 mm; valve timing: 10° 54° 54° 10°; tyre pressure: front 31 psi, 2.2 atm, rear 34 psi, 2.4 atm.

OPTIONALS (for GL 5 gear only) sunroof.

900 Series

PRICES IN GB:

		£
1	GL 2+1-dr Hatchback Sedan	—
2	GL 4-dr Sedan	7,320*
3	GL 4+1-dr Hatchback Sedan	—
4	GLS 2+1-dr Hatchback Sedan	7,740*
5	GLS 4-dr Sedan	7,990*
6	GLS 4+1-dr Hatchback Sedan	8,390*
7	I 2-dr Sedan	—
8	GLI 2+1-dr Hatchback Sedan	—
9	GLI 4-dr Sedan	8,690*
10	GLI 4+1-dr Hatchback Sedan	9,090*
11	GLE 4-dr Sedan	9,990*
12	Turbo 2+1-dr Hatchback Sedan	11,550*
13	Turbo 4-dr Sedan	11,890*
14	Turbo 4+1-dr Hatchback Sedan	12,450*
15	Turbo De Luxe 2+1-dr Hatchback Sedan	13,390*
16	Turbo De Luxe 4-dr Sedan	—
17	Turbo De Luxe 4+1-dr Sedan	—
18	CD 4-dr Sedan	15,750*
19	Turbo 16 2+1-dr Hatchback Sedan	—
20	Turbo 16 4-dr Sedan	—
21	Turbo 16 4+1-dr Hatchback Sedan	—
22	Turbo 16 S 2+1-dr Hatchback Sedan	—

For USA prices, see price index.

Power team:	Standard for:	Optional for:
100 hp	1 to 3	—
108 hp	4 to 6	—
118 hp	7 to 11	—
145 hp	12 to 18	—
175 hp	19 to 22	—

100 hp power team

ENGINE front, 4 stroke; 4 cylinders, slanted at 45°, in line; 121.1 cu in, 1,985 cc (3.54 x 3.07 in, 90 x 78 mm); compression ratio: 9.5:1; max power (DIN): 100 hp (74 kW) at 5,200 rpm; max torque (DIN): 120 lb ft, 16.5 kg m (162 Nm) at 3,500 rpm; max engine rpm: 5,500; 50.4 hp/l (37.1 kW/l); cast iron block, light alloy head; 5 crankshaft bearings;

SAAB 900 GLI Hatchback Sedan

SAAB 900 Turbo Hatchback Sedan

SAAB 900 Turbo 16 (16-valve engine)

100 HP POWER TEAM

valves: overhead, thimble tappets; camshafts: 1, overhead, driven by double chain; lubrication: rotary pump, full flow filter, 6.2 imp pt, 7.4 US pt, 3.5 l; 1 Zenith-Stromberg 175 CDSEVX horizontal carburettor; fuel feed: mechanical pump; liquid-cooled, expansion tank, 17.6 imp pt, 21.1 US pt, 10 l, thermostatic fan.

TRANSMISSION driving wheels: front; clutch: single dry plate, hydraulically controlled; gearbox: mechanical, in unit with differential and engine, transfer chain in front of engine, ratio 0.900; gears: 4, fully synchronized; ratios: I 3.882, II 2.194, III 1.473, IV 1, rev 4.271; lever: central; final drive: spiral bevel; axle ratio: 3.667; width of rims: 5''; tyres: 165 SR x 15.

PERFORMANCE max speed: 99 mph, 160 km/h; power weight ratio: 25.2 lb/hp (34.3 lb/kW), 11.4 kg/hp (15.6 kg/kW); carrying capacity: 1,047 lb, 475 kg; speed in direct drive at 1,000 rpm: 22.1 mph, 35.6 km/h; consumption: 28.2 m/imp gal, 23.5 m/US gal, 10 l x 100 km at 75 mph, 120 km/h.

CHASSIS integral; front suspension: independent, double wishbones, progressively-acting coil springs, telescopic dampers; rear: rigid axle, twin longitudinal leading arms, twin swinging trailing radius arms, transverse linkage bar, coil springs, telescopic dampers.

STEERING rack-and-pinion; turns lock to lock: 4.20.

BRAKES disc (front diameter 10.87 in, 27.6 cm, rear 10.55 in, 26.8 cm), 2 separate X hydraulic circuits, servo; swept area: total 388.2 sq in, 2,504 sq cm.

ELECTRICAL EQUIPMENT 12 V; 60 Ah battery; 930 W alternator; Bosch electronic ignition; 2 halogen headlamps with wiper-washers.

DIMENSIONS AND WEIGHT wheel base: 99.09 in, 252 cm; tracks: 55.91 in, 142 cm front, 56.30 in, 143 cm rear; length: 186.57 in, 474 cm; width: 66.54 in, 169 cm; height: 55.91 in, 142 cm; ground clearance: 5.91 in, 15 cm; weight: 2,530 lb, 1,145 kg; turning circle: 36.7 ft, 11.2 m; fuel tank: 13.9 imp gal, 16.6 US gal, 63 l.

BODY saloon/sedan; 2+1, 4 or 4+1 doors; 5 seats, separate front seats, adjustable backrests; folding rear seat; impact-absorbing bumpers; hazard lights; heated rear window.

PRACTICAL INSTRUCTIONS fuel: 97 oct petrol; oil: engine 6.2 imp pt, 7.4 US pt, 3.5 l, SAE 10W-40, change every 9,300 miles, 15,000 km - gearbox 4.4 imp pt, 5.3 US pt, 2.5 l, SAE 10W-30/40, change every 18,600 miles, 30,000 km; greasing: every 6,200 miles, 10,000 km; tappet clearances: inlet 0.006-0.012 in, 0.15-0.30 mm, exhaust 0.014-0.020 in, 0.35-0.50 mm; valve timing: 10° 54° 54° 10°; tyre pressure: front 27 psi, 1.9 atm, rear 34 psi, 2.4 atm.

108 hp power team

See 100 hp power team, except for:

ENGINE max power (DIN): 108 hp (79 kW) at 5,200 rpm; max torque (DIN): 121 lb ft, 16.7 kg m (164 Nm) at 3,300 rpm; 54.4 hp/l (39.8 kW/l); 2 Zenith-Stromberg 150 CDSEVX horizontal carburettors.

TRANSMISSION transfer chain ratio 0.781; gears: 5, fully synchronized; ratios: I 4.533, II 2.562, III 1.720, IV 1.236, V 1, rev 4.987; width of rims: 5.5''; tyres: 185/65 SR x 15.

PERFORMANCE max speed: 105 mph, 170 km/h; power-weight ratio: Sedan 23.5 lb/hp (32.1 lb/kW), 10.7 kg/hp (14.6 kg/kW); carrying capacity: 1,058 lb, 480 kg; speed in direct drive at 1,000 rpm: 23.8 mph, 38.3 km/h; consumption: 28.8 m/imp gal, 24 m/US gal, 9.8 l x 100 km at 75 mph, 120 km/h.

STEERING servo; turns lock to lock: 3.70.

DIMENSIONS AND WEIGHT weight: Sedan 2,590 lb, 1,171 kg - Hatchback Sedan 2,610 lb, 1,181 kg.

BODY saloon/sedan; 4 or 4+1 doors.

OPTIONALS Borg-Warner 37 automatic transmission, hydraulic torque converter and planetary gears with 3 ratios (I 2.390, II 1.450, III 1, rev 2.090), 0.925 transfer chain ratio, max speed 99 mph, 160 km/h; sunroof.

118 hp power team

See 100 hp power team, except for:

ENGINE max power (DIN): 118 hp (87 kW) at 5,500 rpm; max torque (DIN): 123 lb ft, 17 kg m (167 Nm) at 3,700 rpm; 59.4 hp/l (43.8 kW/l); Bosch CI injection; fuel feed: electric pump.

TRANSMISSION transfer chain ratio: 0.781; gears; 5, fully synchronized; ratios I 4.533, II 2.562, III 1,720, IV 1.236, V 1, rev 4.987; width of rims: 5.5; tyres: 185/65 SR x 15.

PERFORMANCE max speeds: (I) 30 mph, 48 km/h; (II) 53 mph, 85 km/h; (III) 79 mph, 126 km/h; (IV) and (V) 109 mph, 175 km/h - GLE 103 mph, 165 km/h; power-weight ratio: GLI 4+1-dr Hatchback Sedan 22.2 lb/hp (30.2 lb/kW), 10.1 kg/hp (13.7 kg/kW); speed in direct drive at 1,000 rpm: GLI 24.6 mph, 39.6 km/h; consumption: GLI 29.4 m/imp gal, 24.5 m/US gal, 9.6 l x 100 km at 75 mph, 120 km/h.

STEERING servo; turns lock to lock: 3.70.

DIMENSIONS AND WEIGHT tracks: 56.30 in, 143 cm front, 56.69 in, 144 cm rear; weight: GLI 4-dr Sedan 2,610 lb, 1,181 kg - GLI 4+1-dr Hatchback Sedan 2,624 lb, 1,190 kg - GLE 4-dr Sedan 2,670 lb, 1,211 kg.

VARIATIONS

(for USA only)
ENGINE 9.2:1 compression ratio, max power (SAE net) 110 hp (81 kW) at 5,500 rpm, max torque (SAE net) 119 lb ft, 16.5 kg/m (161 Nm) at 3,500 rpm, 55.4 hp/l (40.8 kW/l).

OPTIONALS (for GLI sedans only) Borg-Warner 37 automatic transmission, hydraulic torque converter and planetary gears with 3 ratios (I 2.390, II 1.450, III 1, rev 2.090), 3.667 axle ratio, max speed 103 mph, 165 km/h, speed in direct drive at 1,000 rpm 20.8 mph, 33.5 km/h; sunroof; (for GLI sedans only) central door locking; metallic spray.

145 hp power team

See 100 hp power team, except for:

ENGINE turbocharged; compression ratio: 8.5:1; max power (DIN): 145 hp (107 kW) at 5,000 rpm; max torque (DIN): 174 lb ft, 24 kg m (235 Nm) at 3,000 rpm; max engine rpm: 6,000; 73 hp/l (53.9 kW/l); lubrication: oil cooler, 7 imp pt, 8.5 US pt, 4 l; Bosch CI injection; 1 Garrett AiResearch turbocharger; APC (automatic performance control) optimizing engine operation in relation to petrol quality; fuel feed: electric pump.

TRANSMISSION transfer chain ratio: 0.878; gears: 5, fully synchronized; ratios: I 4.533, II 2.562, III 1.720, IV 1.236, V 1, rev 4.987; axle ratio: 3.667; width of rims: 5.5''; tyres: 195/60 HR x 15.

PERFORMANCE max speeds at 6,000 rpm: (I) 30 mph, 48 km/h; (II) 53 mph, 85 km/h; (III) 79 mph, 127 km/h; (IV) 110 mph, 177 km/h; (V) 122 mph, 195 km/h; power-weight ratio: Turbo 2+1-dr Hatchback Sedan 18.2 lb/hp (24.6 lb/kW), 8.2 kg/hp (11.2 kg/kW); speed in direct drive at 1,000 rpm: 22.6 mph, 36.4 km/h; consumption: 26.4/imp gal, 22 m/US gal, 10.7 l x 100 km at 75 mph, 120 km/h.

STEERING servo; turns lock to lock: 3.70.

ELECTRICAL EQUIPMENT 60 Ah battery (maintenance-free).

DIMENSIONS AND WEIGHT wheel base: CD 106.97 in, 272 cm; tracks: 56.30 in, 143 cm front, 56.69 in, 144 cm rear; length: CD 194.45 in, 474 cm; weight: 2+1-dr hatchback sedans 2,635 lb, 1,195 kg - 4+1-dr hatchback sedans 2,723 lb, 1,235 kg - 4-dr sedans 2,679 lb, 1,215 kg - CD 2,847 lb, 1,291 kg.

BODY light alloy wheels; central door locking; front and rear spoiler; tinted glass; electric windows.

PRACTICAL INSTRUCTIONS fuel: 92 or 97 oct petrol; oil: engine 7 imp pt, 8.5 US pt, 4 l.

SAAB 900 Turbo 16 S Hatchback Sedan

VOLVO 240 GLT Sedan

VARIATIONS

(for USA only)
ENGINE max power (SAE net) 135 hp (100 kW) at 4,800 rpm, max torque (SAE net) 172 lb ft, 23.8 kg m (233 Nm) at 3,500 rpm, 68 hp/l (50.4 kW/l).

OPTIONALS Borg-Warner 37 automatic transmission, hydraulic torque converter and planetary gears with 3 ratios (I 2.390, II 1.450, III 1, rev 2.090), 3.667 axle ratio; air-conditioning; de luxe version with leather upholstery; special equipment.

175 hp power team

See 100 hp power team, except for:

ENGINE turbocharged; compression ratio: 9:1; max power (DIN): 175 hp (129 kW) at 5,300 rpm; max torque (DIN): 199 lb ft, 27.5 kg m (270 Nm) at 3,000 rpm; max engine rpm: 5,500; 88.2 hp/l (64.9 kW/l); valves: 4 per cylinder; camshafts: 2, overhead; Bosch LH Jetronic electronic injection with turbocharger; APC (automatic performance control) optimizing engine operation in relation to petrol quality; intercooler; fuel feed: electric pump; oil cooler.

TRANSMISSION transfer chain ratio: 0.839; gears: 5, fully synchronized; ratios: I 4.533, II 2.562, III 1.720, IV 1.236, V 1, rev 4.987; width of rims: 5.5"; tyres: 195/60 VR x 15.

PERFORMANCE max speed: 130 mph, 210 km/h; power-weight ratio: 2+1-dr sedans 16.9 lb/hp (23 lb/kW), 7.7 kg/hp (10.4 kg/kW); speed in direct drive at 1,000 rpm: 24.4 mph, 39.3 km/h; consumption: 30.4 m/imp gal, 25.3 m/US gal, 9.3 l x 100 km at 75 mph, 120 km/h.

CHASSIS front and rear suspension: anti-roll bar.

STEERING servo; turns lock to lock: 3.65.

ELECTRICAL EQUIPMENT 60 Ah battery (maintenance-free); Bosch electronic ignition.

DIMENSIONS AND WEIGHT wheel base: 107 in, 272 cm; tracks: 56.30 in, 143 cm front, 56.70 in, 144 cm rear; length: 194.51 in, 494 cm; weight: 2+1-dr sedans 2,955 lb, 1,340 kg.

BODY sunroof; central door locking system; electric windows; air-conditioning; front and rear spoilers; leather upholstery; light alloy wheels.

VOLVO — SWEDEN

---

240 Series

PRICES IN GB AND EX WORKS:	£	crowns
1 4-dr Sedan	7,720*	67,600*
2 4+1-dr St. Wagon	8,250*	71,400*
3 GL 4-dr Sedan	8,351*	73,300*
4 GL 4+1-dr St. Wagon	8,880*	76,900*
5 GLE 4-dr Sedan	9,831*	83,800*
6 GLE 4+1-dr St. Wagon	9,780*	88,900*
7 GLT 4-dr Sedan	11,070*	90,400*
8 GLT 4+1-dr St. Wagon	10,560*	90,800*
9 Turbo 4-dr Sedan	—	95,900*
10 Turbo 4+1- dr St. Wagon	—	98,600*

For USA prices, see price index.

Power team:	Standard for:	Optional for:
106 hp	1 to 4	—
112 hp	—	1 to 4
129 hp	5 to 8	—
155 hp	9,10	—

106 hp power team

ENGINE B21A, front, 4 stroke; 4 cylinders, in line; 130 cu in, 2,127 cc (3.62 x 3.15 in, 92 x 80 mm); compression ratio: 9.3:1; max power (DIN): 106 hp (78 kW) at 5,250 rpm; max torque (DIN): 127 lb ft, 17.5 kg m (172 Nm) at 2,500 rpm; max engine rpm: 6,500; 49.8 hp/l (36.7 kW/l); cast iron block, light alloy head; 5 crankshaft bearings; valves: overhead, thimble tappets; camshafts: 1, overhead, cogged belt; lubrication: gear pump, full flow filter, 6.8 imp pt, 8.1 US pt, 3.8 l; 1 Zenith Stromberg 175 CD-2SE carburettor; fuel feed: mechanical pump; water-cooled, 16.7 imp pt, 20.1 US pt, 9.5 l.

TRANSMISSION driving wheels: rear; clutch: single dry plate (diaphragm); gearbox: mechanical; gears: 4, fully synchronized; ratios: I 4.032, II 2.160, III 1.370, IV 1, rev 3.680; lever: central; final drive: hypoid bevel; axle ratio: 3.730; width of rims: sedans 5" - st. wagon 5.5"; tyres: sedans 175 SR x 14 - st. wagons 185 SR x 14.

PERFORMANCE max speed: 103 mph, 165 km/h; power-weight ratio: sedans 27.5 lb/hp (37.3 lb/kW), 12.5 kg/hp (16.9 kg/kW); carrying capacity: sedans 1,000 lb, 450 kg - st. wagons 1,240 lb, 560 kg; speed in direct drive at 1,000 rpm: 19.2 mph, 30.8 km/h; consumption: GL models 29.1 m/imp gal, 24.2 m/US gal, 9.7 l x 100 km at 75 mph, 120 km/h.

CHASSIS integral; front suspension: independent, by McPherson, lower wishbones, coil springs/telescopic damper struts, anti-roll bar; rear: rigid axle, twin trailing radius arms, transverse linkage bar, coil springs, anti-roll bar, telescopic dampers.

STEERING rack-and-pinion; turns lock to lock: 4.30.

BRAKES disc (front diameter 10.71 in, 27.2 cm, rear 11.61 in, 29.5 cm), dual circuit, rear compensator, servo.

ELECTRICAL EQUIPMENT 12 V; 60 Ah battery; 55 A alternator; Bosch distributor; 2 halogen headlamps.

DIMENSIONS AND WEIGHT wheel base: 104 in, 264 cm; tracks: 56.30 in, 143 cm front, 53.50 in, 136 cm rear; length: 189 in, 479 cm; width: 67.30 in, 171 cm; height: sedans 56.30 in, 143 cm - st. wagons 57.40 in, 146 cm; ground clearance: 4.30 in, 11 cm; weight: sedans 2,911 lb, 1,320 kg - st. wagons 3,043 lb, 1,380 kg; turning circle: 32.1 ft, 9.8 m; fuel tank: 13.2 imp gal, 15.8 US gal, 60 l.

BODY saloon/sedan, 4 doors - estate car/st. wagon, 4+1 doors; 5 seats, separate front seats, reclining backrests, built-in adjustable headrests; heated rear window.

PRACTICAL INSTRUCTIONS fuel: 98 oct petrol; oil: engine 5.6 imp pt, 6.8 US pt, 3.2 l, SAE 10W-40, change every 6,200 miles, 10,000 km - gearbox 1.2 imp pt, 1.5 US pt, 0.7 l, SAE 80-90, change every 24,900 miles, 40,000 km - final drive 2.3 imp pt, 2.7 US pt, 1.3 l, SAE 90; greasing: none; spark plug: 175°; tappet clearances: inlet and exhaust 0.016-0.018 in, 0.40-0.45 mm; tyre pressure: front 26 psi, 1.8 atm, rear 28 psi, 1.9 atm.

VARIATIONS

(for Europe only)
ENGINE max power (DIN) 107 hp (79 kW) at 5,500 rpm, max torque (DIN) 125 lb ft, 17.3 kg m (170 Nm) at 2,500 rpm, 50.3 hp/l (37.1 kW/l).

OPTIONALS limited slip differential; Borg-Warner 55 automatic transmission, hydraulic torque converter and planetary gears with 3 ratios (I 2.450, II 1.450, III 1, rev 2.090), max ratio of converter at stall 2; power steering (standard in GB); air-conditioning; sunroof; electric windows; electric rear mirrors; light alloy wheels; headlamps with wiper-washers.

112 hp power team

See 106 hp power team, except for:

ENGINE B23A; 141.3 cu in, 2,316 cc (3.78 x 3.15 in, 96 x 80 mm); compression ratio: 10.3:1; max power (DIN): 112 hp (82 kW) at 5,000 rpm; max torque (DIN): 137 lb ft, 18.9 kg m (185 Nm) at 2,500 rpm; 48.3 hp/l (35.3 kW/l); 1 DVG 175 CDUS carburettor.

TRANSMISSION gears: 5, fully synchronized; ratios: I 4.030, II 2.160, III 1.370, IV 1, V 0.800, rev 3.680; axle ratio: 3.540.

PERFORMANCE max speed: 106 mph, 170 km/h; power-weight ratio: sedans 26 lb/hp (35.5 lb/kW), 11.8 kg/hp (16.1 kg/kW); carrying capacity: 915 lb, 415 kg; consumption: 28.5 m/imp gal, 23.5 m/US gal, 9.9 l x 100 km at 75 mph, 120 km/h.

129 hp power team

See 106 hp power team, except for:

ENGINE B23E; 141.3 cu in, 2,316 cc (3.78 x 3.15 in, 96 x 80 mm); compression ratio: 10.3:1; max power (DIN): 129 hp (95 kW) at 5,250 rpm; max torque (DIN): 141 lb ft, 19.4 kg m (190 Nm) at 3,000 rpm; 55.7 hp/l (41 kW/l); Bosch injection.

TRANSMISSION gears: 4 and overdrive; ratios: I 4.030, II 2.160, III 1.370, IV 1, overdrive 0.800, rev 3.680; width of rims: 5.5"; tyres: 185/70 HR x 14.

PERFORMANCE max speed: 112 mph, 180 km/h; power-weight ratio: sedans 22.6 lb/hp (30.6 lb/kW), 10.2 kg/hp (13.9 kg/kW); consumption: 25.9 m/imp gal, 21.6 m/US gal, 10.9 l x 100 km at 75 mph, 120 km/h.

ELECTRICAL EQUIPMENT Bosch contactless transistorized ignition.

VARIATIONS

(for Europe only)
ENGINE max power (DIN) 131 hp (96 kW) at 5,400 rpm, max torque (DIN) 141 lb ft, 19.4 kg m (190 Nm) at 3,600 rpm, 56.6 hp (41.5 kW/l).

VOLVO 240 GL Station Wagon

155 hp power team

See 106 hp power team, except for:

ENGINE B21ET turbocharged; compression ratio: 7.5:1; max power (DIN): 155 hp (114 kW) at 5,500 rpm; max torque (DIN): 178 lb ft, 24.5 kg m (240 Nm) at 3,750 rpm; 72.9 hp/l (53.7 kW/l); Bosch K-Jetronic injection with Garrett AiResearch exhaust turbocharger.

TRANSMISSION gears: 4 and overdrive; ratios: I 4.030, II 2.160, III 1.370, IV 1, overdrive 0.800, rev 3.680; width of rims: 6"; tyres: 195/60 HR x 15.

PERFORMANCE max speed: 118 mph, 190 km/h; power-weight ratio: Turbo Sedan 20.8 lb/hp (28 lb/kW), 9.4 kg/hp (12.7 kg/kW); consumption: 31 m/imp gal, 25.8 m/US gal, 9.1 l x 100 km at 75 mph, 120 km/h.

BRAKES disc, front internal radial fins.

ELECTRICAL EQUIPMENT Bosch contactless transistorized ignition.

DIMENSIONS AND WEIGHT weight: Turbo Sedan 3,197 lb, 1,450 kg - Turbo St. Wagon 3,219 lb, 1,460 kg.

240 Diesel

PRICES IN USA AND EX WORKS:	$	crowns
4-dr Sedan	15,480*	90,500*
4+1-dr St. Wagon	16,035*	94,800*

ENGINE D24, Volkswagen, diesel, front, 4 stroke; 6 cylinders, in line; 145.4 cu in, 2,383 cc (3.01 x 3.40 in, 76.5 x 86.4 mm); compression ratio: 23:1; max power (DIN): 82 hp (60 kW) at 4,800 rpm; max torque (DIN): 104 lb ft, 14.3 kg m (140 Nm) at 2,800 rpm; 34.4 hp/l (25.4 kW/l); cast iron block, light alloy head; 7 crankshaft bearings; valves: overhead, thimble tappets; camshafts: 1, overhead, cogged belt; lubrication: gear pump, full flow filter, 12.3 imp pt, 14.8 US pt, 7 l; Bosch VE injection pump; water-cooled, 16.4 imp pt, 19.7 US pt, 9.3 l.

TRANSMISSION driving wheels: rear; clutch: single dry plate (diaphragm); gearbox: mechanical; gears: 4, fully synchronized and overdrive; ratios: I 4.030, II 2.160, III 1.370, IV 1, overdrive 0.798, rev 3.680; lever: central; final drive: hypoid bevel; axle ratio: 3.730; width of rims: 5.5"; tyres: Sedan 175 SR x 14 - St. Wagon 185 SR x 14.

PERFORMANCE max speed: 93 mph, 150 km/h; power-weight ratio: Sedan 36.6 lb/hp (50 lb/kW), 16.6 kg/hp (22.7 kg/kW); speed in overdrive/top at 1,000 rpm: 24 mph, 38.7 km/h; consumption: 28.8 m/imp gal, 24 m/US gal, 9.8 l x 100 km at 75 mph, 120 km/h.

CHASSIS integral; front suspension: independent, by McPherson, lower wishbones, coil springs/telescopic damper struts, anti-roll bar; rear: rigid axle, twin trailing radius arms, transverse linkage bar, coil springs, anti-roll bar, telescopic dampers.

STEERING rack-and-pinion, servo; turns lock to lock: 3.50.

BRAKES disc, dual circuit, rear compensator, servo.

ELECTRICAL EQUIPMENT 12 V; 90 Ah battery; 55 A alternator; 2 halogen headlamps.

DIMENSIONS AND WEIGHT wheel base: 104.33 in, 265 cm; tracks: Sedan 55.91 in, 142 cm front, 53.15 in, 135 cm rear - St. Wagon 56.30 in, 143 cm front, 53.54 in, 136 cm rear; length: 189 in, 479 cm; width: 67.32 in, 171 cm; height: Sedan 56.30 in, 143 cm - St. Wagon 57.40 in, 146 cm; ground clearance: 5.51 in, 14 cm; weight: Sedan 2,999 lb, 1,360 kg - St. Wagon 3,131 lb, 1,420 kg; turning circle: 32.1 ft, 9.8 m; fuel tank: 13.2 imp gal, 15.8 US gal, 60 l.

BODY saloon/sedan, 4 doors - estate car/st. wagon, 4+1 doors; 5 seats, separate front seats, reclining backrests, built-in adjustable headrests; heated rear window; heated driving seat; (for St. Wagon only) folding rear seat.

PRACTICAL INSTRUCTIONS fuel: diesel; oil: engine 12.3 imp pt, 14.8 US pt, 7 l.

OPTIONALS Borg-Warner automatic transmission, hydraulic torque converter and planetary gears with 3 ratios (I 2.450, II 1.450, III 1, rev 2.210), 3.540 axle ratio, max speed 90 mph, 145 km/h.

760 GLE

PRICE IN GB: £ 13,250*
PRICE IN USA: $ 21,225*

ENGINE B28E, PRV, front, 4 stroke; 6 cylinders, Vee-slanted at 90°; 174 cu in, 2,849 cc (3.58 x 2.87 in, 91 x 73 mm); compression ratio: 9.5:1; max power (DIN): 156 hp (115 kW) at 5,700 rpm; max torque (DIN): 174 lb ft, 24 kg m (235 Nm) at 3,000 rpm; max engine rpm: 6,200; 54.8 hp/l (40.4 kW/l); light alloy block and head; 7 crankshaft bearings; valves: overhead, Vee-slanted, rockers; camshafts: 2, 1 per bank, overhead; lubrication: gear pump, full flow filter, 11.4 imp pt, 13.7 US pt, 6.5 l; K-Jetronic injection; fuel feed: electric pump; water-cooled, sealed circuit, 19.2 imp pt, 23 US pt, 10.9 l.

TRANSMISSION driving wheels: rear; gearbox: Borg-Warner AW 71 automatic transmission, hydraulic torque converter and planetary gears with 3 ratios and overdrive, possible manual selection; ratios: I 2.450, II 1.450, III 1, overdrive 0.690, rev 2.210; lever: central; final drive: hypoid bevel; axle ratio: 3.540; width of rims: 6"; tyres: 195/60 HR x 15.

PERFORMANCE max speed: 118 mph, 190 km/h; power-weight ratio: 18.8 lb/hp (25.5 lb/kW), 8.5 kg/hp (11.6 kg/kW); carrying capacity: 1,102 lb, 500 kg; consumption: 25 m/imp gal, 20.8 m/US gal, 11.3 l x 100 km at 75 mph, 120 km/h.

CHASSIS integral; front suspension: independent, by McPherson, lower wishbones, coil springs/telescopic damper struts, anti-roll bar; rear: rigid axle, with sub-frame, trailing arms, Panhard rod, coil springs, telescopic dampers.

STEERING rack-and-pinion, servo; turns lock to lock: 3.50.

BRAKES disc, front internal radial fins, dual circuit, servo; lining area: front 26.4 sq in, 170 sq cm, rear 15.5 sq in, 100 sq cm, total 41.9 sq in, 270 sq cm.

ELECTRICAL EQUIPMENT 12 V; 66 Ah battery; 90 A alternator; transistorized ignition; 2 halogen headlamps.

DIMENSIONS AND WEIGHT wheel base: 109.05 in, 277 cm; front and rear track: 57.48 in, 146 cm; length: 188.39 in, 478 cm; width: 69.29 in, 176 cm; height: 56.30 in, 143 cm; ground clearance: 4.13 in, 10.5 cm; weight: 2,933 lb, 1,330 kg; turning circle: 32.1 ft, 9.8 m; fuel tank: 18 imp gal, 21.6 US gal, 82 l.

BODY saloon/sedan; 4 doors; 5 seats, separate front seats, reclining backrests, built-in headrests; heated rear window; heated driving and passenger seat; electric windows; air-conditioning; light alloy wheels; central door locking; tinted glass.

PRACTICAL INSTRUCTIONS fuel: 98 oct petrol; oil: engine 10.6 imp pt, 12.7 US pt, 6 l, SAE 10W-40, change every 3,700 miles, 6,000 km - gearbox 1.9 imp pt, 2.3 US pt, 1.1 l, SAE 90, change every 24,900 miles, 40,000 km - final drive 2.8 imp pt, 3.4 US pt, 1.6 l, SAE 90 EP, change every 24,900 miles, 40,000 km; greasing: none; spark plug: Champion BN 9Y; tyre pressure: front 26 psi, 1.8 atm, rear 27 psi, 1.9 atm.

760 Turbo

See 760 GLE, except for:

PRICE IN GB: £ 13,250*
PRICE EX WORKS: 131,800* crowns

VOLVO 760 Turbo

ENGINE B23ET, turbocharged; 4 cylinders, in line; 141.3 cu in, 2,316 cc (3.78 x 3.15 in, 96 x 80 mm); compression ratio: 9:1; max power (DIN): 173 hp (127 kW) at 5,700 rpm; max torque (DIN): 185 lb ft, 25.5 kg m (250 Nm) at 3,400 rpm; 74.7 hp/l (54.8 kW/l); cast iron block; 5 crankshaft bearings; valves: overhead, in line; camshafts: 1, overhead, cogged belt; lubrication: 7.9 imp pt, 9.5 US pt, 4.5 l; Bosch Motronic DME-L injection with Garrett AiResearch T3 exhaust turbocharger; intercooler; cooling: 16.7 imp pt, 20.1 US pt, 9.5 l.

TRANSMISSION clutch: single dry plate (diaphragm); gearbox: mechanical; gears: 4, fully synchronized and overdrive; ratios: I 4.032, II 2.160, III 1.370, IV 1, overdrive 0.790, rev 3.680.

PERFORMANCE max speed: over 124 mph, 200 km/h; power-weight ratio: 16.3 lb/hp (22.2 lb/kW), 7.4 kg/hp (10.1 kg/kW); speed in overdrive/top at 1,000 rpm: 25 mph, 40.2 km/h; consumption: 26.2 m/imp gal, 21.8 m/US gal, 10.8 l x 100 km at 75 mph, 120 km/h.

ELECTRICAL EQUIPMENT 55 Ah battery; 70 A alternator; electronic ignition (Bosch Motronic).

DIMENSIONS AND WEIGHT weight: 2,822 lb, 1,280 kg.

PRACTICAL INSTRUCTIONS oil: engine 7.9 imp pt, 9.5 US pt, 4.5 l.

760 Turbo Diesel

See 760 GLE, except for:

PRICE IN GB: £ 13,649*
PRICE IN USA: $ 22,035*

ENGINE TD 24, Volkswagen, diesel, turbocharged; 6 cylinders, in line; 145.4 cu in, 2,383 cc (3.01 x 3.40 in, 76.5 x 86.4 mm); compression ratio: 23:1; max power (DIN): 109 hp (80 kW) at 4,800 rpm; max torque (DIN): 151 lb ft, 20.9 kg m (205 Nm) at 2,400 rpm; 45.7 hp/l (33.6 kW/l); cast iron block; valves: overhead, in line; camshafts: 1, overhead, cogged belt; lubrication: 12.3 imp pt, 14.8 US pt, 7 l; Bosch injection pump with Garrett AiResearch turbocharger; cooling: 16.4 imp pt, 19.7 US pt, 9.3 l.

TRANSMISSION clutch: single dry plate (diaphragm); gearbox: mechanical; gears: 4, fully synchronized and overdrive; ratios: I

VOLVO 760 Turbo

VOLVO 760 GLE (injection engine)

4.030, II 2.160, III 1.370, IV 1, overdrive 0.790, rev 3.680; tyres: 185/65 SR x 15.

PERFORMANCE max speed: 106 mph, 170 km/h; power-weight ratio: 26.9 lb/hp (36.7 lb/kW), 12.2 kg/hp (16.6 kg/kW); speed in overdrive/top at 1,000 rpm: 21.1 mph, 34 km/h; consumption: 32.1 m/imp gal, 26.7 m/US gal, 8.8 l x 100 km at 75 mph, 120 km/h.

ELECTRICAL EQUIPMENT 88 Ah battery; 55 A alternator.

PRACTICAL INSTRUCTIONS fuel: diesel; oil: engine 12.3 imp pt, 14.8 US pt, 7 l.

MONTEVERDI SWITZERLAND

Tiara 3.8 / 5.0

PRICES EX WORKS:	francs
3.8 Luxus 4-dr Limousine	187,000*
5.0 Luxus 4-dr Limousine	—

Power team:	Standard for:	Optional for:
204 hp	1	—
231 hp	2	—

204 hp power team

ENGINE Mercedes-Benz, front, 4 stroke; 8 cylinders in Vee; 243.3 cu in, 3,839 cc (3.46 x 3.11 in, 88 x 78.9 mm); compression ratio: 9.4:1; max power (DIN): 204 hp (150 kW) at 5,250 rpm; max torque (DIN): 233 lb ft, 32.1 kg m (315 Nm) at 3,250 rpm; max engine rpm: 5,950; 53.1 hp/l (39.1 kW/l); light alloy block and head; 5 crankshaft bearings; valves: overhead, Vee-slanted at 54°, finger levers; camshafts: 2, 1 per bank, overhead; lubrication: gear pump, oil-water heat exchanger, filter (cartridge) on by-pass, oil-cooler, 13.2 imp pt, 15.9 US pt, 7.5 l; Bosch K-Jetronic electronic ignition; fuel feed: electric pump; water-cooled, 22 imp pt, 26.4 US pt, 12.5 l, electric thermostatic fan.

TRANSMISSION driving wheels: rear; gearbox: MB automatic transmission, hydraulic torque converter and planetary gears with 4 ratios, max ratio of converter at stall 2.20, possible manual selection; ratios: I 3.680, II 2.410, III 1.440, IV 1, rev 5.140; lever: steering column or central; final drive: hypoid bevel, limited slip; axle ratio: 2.470; width of rims: 6.5"; tyres: 205/70 VR x 14.

PERFORMANCE max speed: about 134 mph, 215 km/h; power-weight ratio: 17.8 lb/hp (24.3 lb/kW), 8.1 kg/hp (11 kg/kW); carrying capacity: 1,069 lb, 485 kg; consumption: 26.2 m/imp gal, 21.8 m/US gal, 10.8 l x 100 km at 75 mph, 120 km/h.

CHASSIS integral; front suspension: independent, upper wishbones with single transverse rod, longitudinal leading arm in unit with anti-roll bar, coil springs, telescopic dampers; rear: independent, oblique semi-trailing arms, coil springs, auxiliary rubber springs, automatic levelling control, anti-roll bar, telescopic dampers.

STEERING recirculating ball, damper, servo; turns lock to lock: 2.90.

BRAKES disc (front diameter 10.94 in, 27.8 cm, rear 10.98 in, 27.9 cm), rear compensator, dual circuit, servo, anti-brake locking system (ABS); swept area: front 255.5 sq in, 1,648 sq cm, rear 195.8 sq in, 1,263 sq cm, total 451.3 sq in, 2,911 sq cm.

ELECTRICAL EQUIPMENT 12 V; 66 Ah battery; 980 W alternator; electronic ignition; 2 halogen headlamps.

DIMENSIONS AND WEIGHT wheel base: 120.87 in, 307 cm; tracks: 60.83 in, 154 cm front, 59.72 in, 152 cm rear; length: 207.48 in, 527 cm; width: 71.65 in, 182 cm; height: 56.69 in, 144 cm; ground clearance: 6.30 in, 16 cm; weight: 3,638 lb, 1,650 kg; turning circle: 40.3 ft, 12.3 m; fuel tank: 19.8 imp gal, 23.8 US gal, 90 l.

BODY saloon/sedan; 4 doors; 5 seats, separate front seats, heated seats, reclining backrests, headrests; electric windows; heated rear window; electric sunroof; tinted glass; air-conditioning; central door locking.

PRACTICAL INSTRUCTIONS fuel: 98 oct petrol; oil: engine 13.2 imp pt, 15.9 US pt, 7.5 l, SAE 20W-30, change every 4,600 miles, 7,500 km; greasing: every 3,100 miles, 5,000 km, 20 points; spark plug: 215°; tyre pressure: front 30 psi, 2.1 atm, rear 34 psi, 2.4 atm.

231 hp power team

See 204 hp power team, except for:

ENGINE 303.5 cu in, 4,973 cc (3.80 x 3.35 in, 96.5 x 85 mm); compression ratio: 9.2:1; max power (DIN): 231 hp (170 kW) at 4,750 rpm; max torque (DIN): 299 lb ft, 41.2 kg m (404 Nm) at 3,000 rpm; 46.5 hp/l (34.2 kW/l); cooling: 22.9 imp pt, 27.5 US pt, 13 l.

TRANSMISSION axle ratio: 2.240.

MONTEVERDI Tiara 3.8 - 5.0 Luxus Limousine

PERFORMANCE max speed: about 146 mph, 235 km/h; power-weight ratio: 16.1 lb/hp (21.9 lb/kW), 7.3 kg/hp (9.9 kg/kW); consumption: 24.8 m/imp gal, 20.6 m/US gal, 11.4 l x 100 km at 75 mph, 120 km/h.

DIMENSIONS AND WEIGHT weight: 3,726 lb, 1,690 kg.

SBARRO SWITZERLAND

Replica BMW 328 Standard / Spéciale

PRICES EX WORKS:	francs
Standard 2-dr Roadster	50,000
Spéciale 2-dr Roadster	60,000

(Also available with BMW engines from 1,990 cc to 3,205 cc)

ENGINE BMW, front, 4 stroke; 4 cylinders, slanted at 30°, in line; 96 cu in, 1,573 cc (3.31 x 2.80 in, 84 x 71 mm); compression ratio: 8.3:1; max power (DIN): 90 hp (66 kW) at 6,000 rpm; max torque (DIN): 91 lb ft, 12.5 kg m (123 Nm) at 4,000 rpm; max engine rpm: 6,200; 57.2 hp/l (42.1 kW/l); cast iron block, light alloy head, hemispherical combustion chambers; 5 crankshaft bearings; valves: overhead, Vee-slanted at 52°, rockers; camshafts: 1, overhead; lubrication: gear pump, full flow filter, 7.4 imp pt, 8.9 US pt, 4.2 l; 1 Solex DIDTA 32/32 downdraught twin barrel carburettor; fuel feed: mechanical pump; water-cooled, 12.3 imp pt, 14.8 US pt, 7 l.

TRANSMISSION driving wheels: rear; clutch: single dry plate (diaphragm), hydraulically controlled; gearbox: mechanical; gears: 4, fully synchronized; ratios: I 3.764, II 2.022, III 1.320, IV 1, rev 4.096; lever: central; final drive: hypoid bevel; axle ratio: 4.100; width of rims: 6".

SBARRO Replica BMW 328 Spéciale Roadster

PERFORMANCE max speeds: (I) 30 mph, 48 km/h; (II) 55 mph, 89 km/h; (III) 85 mph, 136 km/h; (IV) 112 mph, 180 km/h; power-weight ratio: 18.3 lb/hp (24.9 lb/kW), 8.3 kg/hp (11.3 kg/kW); carrying capacity: 353 lb, 160 kg; speed in direct drive at 1,000 rpm: 18 mph, 29 km/h; consumption: 29.4 m/imp gal, 24.5 m/US gal, 9.6 l x 100 km.

CHASSIS integral, box-type reinforced platform; front suspension: independent, coil springs/telescopic damper struts, auxiliary rubber springs, lower wishbones, lower links; rear: independent, oblique semi-trailing arms, auxiliary rubber springs, coil springs, telescopic dampers.

STEERING rack-and-pinion.

BRAKES front disc (diameter 10.71 in, 27.2 cm), dual circuit, rear drum, servo.

ELECTRICAL EQUIPMENT 12 V; 36 Ah battery; 630 W alternator; Bosch distributor; 2 headlamps.

DIMENSIONS AND WEIGHT wheel base: 94.49 in, 240 cm; front and rear track: 57.09 in, 145 cm; length: 145.67 in, 370 cm; width: 61.42 in, 156 cm; ground clearance: 7.90 in, 18 cm; weight: 1,654 lb, 750 kg; turning circle: 29.5 ft, 9 m; fuel tank: 8.8 imp gal, 10.6 US gal, 40 l.

BODY roadster, in plastic material; 2 doors; 2 seats.

PRACTICAL INSTRUCTIONS fuel: 92 oct petrol; oil: engine 7.4 imp pt, 8.9 US pt, 4.2 l, SAE 20W-50, change every 3,700 miles, 6,000 km - gearbox 1.8 imp pt, 2.1 US pt, 1 l, SAE 80, change every 14,800 miles, 24,000 km - final drive 1.6 imp pt, 1.9 US pt, 0.9 l, SAE 90, no change recommended; greasing: none; spark plug: 145°.

OPTIONALS 5-speed fully synchronized mechanical gearbox (I 3.368, II 2.160, III 1.579, IV 1.241, V 1, rev 4); 3.640 or 3.450 axle ratio; 7" or 8" wide rims; disc brakes; leather upholstery; wire wheels; metallic spray.

Replica BMW 328 America

See Replica BMW 328 Standard/Spéciale, except for:

PRICE EX WORKS: 60,000 francs

(Also available with BMW engines from 2,788 cc to 3,205 cc)

ENGINE 6 cylinders, in line; 152.2 cu in, 2,494 cc (3.39 x 2.82 in, 86 x 71.6 mm); compression ratio: 9:1; max power (DIN): 150 hp (110 kW) at 6,000 rpm; max torque (DIN): 154 lb ft, 21.2 kg m (208 Nm) at 4,000 rpm; 60.1 hp/l (44.2 kW/l); polispherical combustion chambers; 7 crankshaft bearings; lubrication: 10 imp pt, 12 US pt, 5.7 l; 1 Solex 4A1 downdraught twin barrel carburettor; cooling: 21.1 imp pt, 25.4 US pt, 12 l.

PERFORMANCE max speed: 132 mph, 212 km/h; power-weight ratio: 13.3 lb/hp (18 lb/kW), 6 kg/hp (8.2 kg/kW); speed in direct drive at 1,000 rpm: 21.3 mph, 34.2 km/h; consumption: 25.9 m/imp gal, 21.6 m/US gal, 10.9 l x 100 km.

BRAKES disc.

ELECTRICAL EQUIPMENT 55 Ah battery; 770 W alternator.

DIMENSIONS AND WEIGHT wheel base: 100.39 in, 255 cm; front and rear track: 64.17 in, 163 cm; length: 149.61 in, 380 cm; width: 67.32 in, 171 cm; weight: 1,989 lb, 902 kg.

BODY 2+1 seats, separate reclining front seats.

PRACTICAL INSTRUCTIONS oil: engine 10 imp pt, 12 US pt, 5.7 l; tappet clearances: inlet 0.010 in, 0.25 mm, exhaust 0.012 in, 0.30 mm; valve timing: 6° 50° 50° 6°.

Stash

PRICES EX WORKS:	francs
2-dr Coupé	120,000
2-dr Cabriolet	120,000
HS 2-dr Cabriolet	140,000

(Also available with 3-litre BMW and Mercedes-Benz engines)

ENGINE Mercedes-Benz, centre-rear, 4 stroke; 8 cylinders in Vee; 417 cu in, 6,834 cc (4.21 x 3.74 in, 107 x 95 mm); compression ratio: 8.8:1; max power (DIN): 286 hp (210 kW) at 4,250 rpm; max torque (DIN): 406 lb ft, 56 kg m (549 Nm) at 3,000 rpm; max engine rpm: 5,300; 41.8 hp/l (30.8 kW/l); cast iron block, light alloy head; 5 crankshaft bearings; valves: overhead, finger levers; camshafts: 2, 1 per bank, overhead; lubrication: gear pump, full flow filter, dry sump, oil cooler, 21.1 imp pt, 25.4 US pt, 12 l; Bosch K-Jetronic injection; air cleaner; fuel feed: electric pump; water-cooled, viscous coupling thermostatic fan, 26.4 imp pt, 31.7 US pt, 15 l.

TRANSMISSION driving wheels: rear; gearbox: MB automatic transmission, hydraulic torque converter and planetary gears with 3 ratios, max ratio of converter at stall 2.50, possible manual selection; ratios: I 2.310, II 1.460, III 1, rev 1.840; lever: central or steering column; final drive: hypoid bevel; axle ratio: 2.650; width of rims: 7" front, 9" rear.

PERFORMANCE max speed: about 149 mph, 240 km/h; power-weight ratio: 10.8 lb/hp (14.7 lb/kW), 4.9 kg/hp (6.6 kg/kW)); carrying capacity: 926 lb, 420 kg; speed in direct drive at 1,000 rpm: 28.3 mph, 45.5 km/h; consumption: 17.7 m/imp gal, 14.7 m/US gal, 16 l x 100 km.

CHASSIS integral, box-type reinforced platform; front suspension: independent, wishbones, coil springs/telescopic damper struts; rear: independent, wishbones, coil springs, anti-roll bar, telescopic dampers.

STEERING recirculating ball.

BRAKES disc, dual circuit, rear compensator, servo.

ELECTRICAL EQUIPMENT 12 V; 88 Ah battery; 1,050 W alternator; Bosch transistorized ignition; 2 iodine headlamps.

DIMENSIONS AND WEIGHT wheel base: 104.33 in, 265 cm; tracks: 55.90 in, 142 cm front, 62.99 in, 160 cm rear; length: 181.10 in, 460 cm; width: 74.80 in, 190 cm; height: 45.67 in, 116 cm; ground clearance: 5.91 in, 15 cm; weight: 3,087 lb, 1,400 kg; turning circle: 35.4 ft, 10.8 m; fuel tank: 11 imp gal, 13.2 US gal, 50 l.

BODY coupé - convertible, in plastic material; 2 doors; 2+2 seats; detachable roof.

PRACTICAL INSTRUCTIONS fuel: 98 oct petrol.

OPTIONALS limited slip differential.

Royale

PRICE EX WORKS: 250,000 francs

ENGINE 2 Rover 3.5-litre engines, one behind the other, front, 4 stroke; 8 cylinders in Vee; 215.3 cu in, 3,528 cc (3.50 x 2.80 in, 88.9 x 73.1 mm); compression ratio: 9.3:1; max power (DIN): 157 hp (115 kW) at 5,250 rpm; max torque (DIN): 191 lb ft, 26.4 kg m (259 Nm) at 2,500 rpm; 44.5 hp/l (32.7 kW/l); valves: overhead, push-rods and rockers; camshafts: 1, central, chain-driven; lubrication: gear pump, full flow filter, 11.1 imp pt, 13.3 US pt, 6.3 l; 2 SU type HIF6 semi-downdraught carburettors; fuel feed: mechanical pump; water-cooled, 19.3 imp pt, 23.5 US pt, 11.1 l.

TRANSMISSION driving wheels: rear; gearbox: automatic transmission, hydraulic torque converter and planetary gears with 3 ratios; ratios: I 2.390, II 1.450, III 1, rev 2.090; lever: central; final drive: hypoid bevel; axle ratio: 3.080; width of rims: 7".

PERFORMANCE max speed: 112 mph, 180 km/h; power-weight ratio: 35.3 lb/hp (48 lb/kW), 16 kg/hp (21.6 kg/kW).

CHASSIS ladder frame; front suspension: independent, wishbones, anti-roll bar, telescopic dampers; rear: independent, oblique longitudinal trailing arms, telescopic dampers.

STEERING rack-and-pinion, servo.

BRAKES front disc, rear drum, dual circuit, servo.

ELECTRICAL EQUIPMENT 12 V; 68 Ah battery; 55 A alternator; 4 headlamps.

DIMENSIONS AND WEIGHT wheel base: 151.57 in, 358 cm; front and rear track: 63.78 in, 162 cm; length: 236.22 in, 600 cm; width: 74.80 in, 190 cm; height: 80.71 in, 205 cm; ground clearance: 9.84 in, 25 cm; weight: 5,513 lb, 2,500 kg; turning circle: 47.6 ft, 14.5 m.

BODY saloon/sedan; 4 doors; 5-6 seats, separate front seats.

Windhound 4 x 4

PRICE EX WORKS: 85,000 francs

ENGINE BMW, front, 4 stroke; 6 cylinders, in line; 182 cu in, 2,982 cc (3.58 x 3.15 in, 89 x 80 mm); compression ratio: 8:1; max power (DIN): 175 hp (129 kW) at 5,500 rpm; max torque (DIN): 185 lb ft, 25.5 kg m (250 Nm) at 4,500 rpm; max engine rpm: 6,500; 58.7 hp/l (43.2 kW/l); cast iron block, light alloy head, polispherical combustion chambers; 7 crankshaft bearings; valves: overhead, Vee-slanted, rockers; camshafts: 1, overhead; lubrication: rotary pump, full flow filter, 10 imp pt, 12 US pt, 5.7 l; Bosch electronic injection, exhaust thermal reactor; fuel feed: mechanical pump; water-cooled, 21.1 imp pt, 25.4 US pt, 12 l.

SBARRO Stash Cabriolet

SBARRO Windhound 4 x 4

TRANSMISSION driving wheels: front and rear; clutch: single dry plate; gearbox: mechanical; gears: 4, fully synchronized; ratios: I 3.855, II 2.203, III 1.402, IV 1, rev 4.030; gear and transfer levers: central; final drive: hypoid bevel; axle ratio (front and rear): 3.640; tyres: 12 x 15.

PERFORMANCE max speed: 112 mph, 180 km/h; power-weight ratio: 23.3 lb/hp (31.7 lb/kW), 10.6 kg/hp (14.4 kg/kW); consumption: 15.4 m/imp gal, 18.5 m/US gal, 14.4 l x 100 km.

CHASSIS integral, box-type reinforced platform; front suspension: independent, by McPherson, coil springs/telescopic damper struts, lower wishbones, torsion bar, automatic levelling control; rear: independent, oblique semi-trailing arms, coil springs, torsion bar, automatic levelling control.

STEERING rack-and-pinion.

BRAKES front disc, rear drum, dual circuit, servo.

ELECTRICAL EQUIPMENT 12 V; 65 Ah battery; 55 A alternator; 4 headlamps.

DIMENSIONS AND WEIGHT wheel base: 111.02 in, 282 cm; tracks: 61.02 in, 155 cm front, 62.99 in, 160 cm rear; length: 177.16 in, 450 cm; width: 71.26 in, 181 cm; height: 66.93 in, 170 cm; ground clearance: 10.6-19.3 in, 27-49 cm; weight: 4,079 lb, 1,850 kg; fuel tank: 15.4 imp gal, 18.5 US gal, 70 l.

BODY estate car/st. wagon, in plastic material; 4+1 doors; 4-6 seats.

PRACTICAL INSTRUCTIONS fuel: 98 oct petrol; oil: engine 10 imp pt, 12 US pt, 5.7 l, SAE 20W-50, change every 3,700 miles, 6,000 km - gearbox 1.8 imp pt, 2.1 US pt, 1 l, SAE 80, change every 14,900 miles, 24,000 km - final drive (front and rear) 1.6 imp pt, 1.9 US pt, 0.9 l, SAE 90, no change recommended; greasing: none; tyre pressure: front 36 psi, 2.5 atm, rear 36 psi, 2.5 atm.

VARIATIONS

ENGINE 4 cylinders - 6 cylinders - 8 cylinders - 12 cylinders.

OPTIONALS 5-speed mechanical gearbox; ZF automatic transmission.

AZLK USSR

Moskvich 2138

ENGINE front, 4 stroke; 4 cylinders, in line; 82.8 cu in, 1,357 cc (2.99 x 2.95 in, 76 x 75 mm); compression ratio: 7:1; max power (DIN): 50 hp (37 kW) at 4,750 rpm; max torque (DIN): 67 lb ft, 9.3 kg m (91 Nm) at 2,750 rpm; max engine rpm: 4,750; 36.8 hp/l (27.1 kW/l); cast iron block, light alloy head; 3 crankshaft bearings; valves: overhead; camshafts: 1, side; lubrication: gear pump, filter on by-pass, 7.9 imp pt, 9.5 US pt, 4.5 l; 1 downdraught twin barrel carburettor; fuel feed: mechanical pump; water-cooled, 12.3 imp pt, 14.8 US pt, 7 l.

TRANSMISSION driving wheels: rear; clutch: single dry plate, hydraulically controlled; gearbox: mechanical; gears: 4, II, III and IV synchronized; ratios: I 3.810, II 2.242, III 1.450, IV 1, rev 4.710; lever: central; final drive: hypoid bevel; axle ratio: 4.220; width of rims: 4"; tyres: 6.95 or 175 SR x 13.

PERFORMANCE max speed: 75 mph, 120 km/h; power-weight ratio: 47.6 lb/hp (64.4 lb/kW), 21.6 kg/hp (29.2 kg/kW); carrying capacity: 882 lb, 400 kg; speed in direct drive at 1,000 rpm: 16.2 mph, 26 km/h; consumption: 26.9 m/imp gal, 22.4 m/US gal, 10.5 l x 100 km.

CHASSIS integral; front suspension: independent, wishbones, coil springs, anti-roll bar, telescopic dampers; rear: rigid axle, semi-elliptic leafsprings, telescopic dampers.

STEERING worm and roller.

BRAKES drum; lining area: front 59.5 sq in, 384 sq cm, rear 59.5 sq in, 384 sq cm, total 119 sq in, 768 sq cm.

ELECTRICAL EQUIPMENT 12 V; 42 or 55 Ah battery; 250 W dynamo; R 107 distributor; 2 headlamps.

DIMENSIONS AND WEIGHT wheel base: 94.49 in, 240 cm; front and rear track: 50 in, 127 cm; length: 167.32 in, 425 cm; width: 61.02 in, 155 cm; height: 58.27 in, 148 cm; ground clearance: 7.09 in, 18 cm; weight: 2,381 lb, 1,080 kg; turning circle: 37.7 ft, 11.5 m; fuel tank: 10.1 imp gal, 12.1 US gal, 46 l.

BODY saloon/sedan; 4 doors; 5 seats.

PRACTICAL INSTRUCTIONS fuel: 85 oct petrol; spark plug: 175°.

SBARRO Royale

AZLK Moskvich 2140

VARIATIONS

(for export only)
ENGINE Perkins, diesel, 4 cylinders, in line with pre-combustion chamber, 107.4 cu in, 1,760 cc (3.13 x 3.50 in, 79.4 x 88.9 mm), 22:1 compression ratio, max power (DIN) 50 hp (37 kW) at 4,000 rpm, max torque (DIN) 80 lb ft, 11 kg m (108 Nm) at 2,200 rpm, 28.4 hp/l (20.9 kW/l), 1 camshaft in crankcase, lubrication 10.6 imp pt, 12.7 US pt, 6 l, sealed circuit cooling, water, 17.6 imp pt, 21.1 US pt, 10 l.
TRANSMISSION gearbox ratios I 3.490, II 2.040, III 1.330, IV 1, rev 3.390, 4.5" wide rims, 165/175 SR x 13 tyres.
PERFORMANCE max speed 75 mph, 120 km/h, power-weight ratio 46.7 lb/hp (63.5 lb/kW), 21.2 kg/hp (28.8 kg/kW), consumption 33.6 m/imp gal, 28 m/US gal, 8.4 l x 100 km.
BRAKES front disc, rear drum, servo.
ELECTRICAL EQUIPMENT 66 Ah battery, 480 W alternator.

OPTIONALS 4.550 axle ratio; 4.5" or 5" wide rims; front disc brakes with servo.

Moskvich 2136

See Moskvich 2138, except for:

TRANSMISSION tyres: 175 x 13.

PERFORMANCE power-weight ratio: 52 lb/hp (70.3 lb/kW), 23.6 kg/hp (31.9 kg/kW).

DIMENSIONS AND WEIGHT height: 59.84 in, 152 cm; weight: 2,602 lb, 1,180 kg.

BODY estate car/st. wagon; 4+1 doors.

Moskvich 2140 / 2140 IZh

ENGINE front, slanted at 20°, 4 stroke; 4 cylinders, in line; 90.2 cu in, 1,478 cc (3.23 x 2.76 in, 82 x 70 mm); compression ratio: 8.8:1; max power (DIN): 75 hp (55 kW) at 5,800 rpm; max torque (DIN): 83 lb ft, 11.4 kg m (118 Nm) at 3,400 rpm; max engine rpm: 6,500; 50.7 hp/l (37.2 kW/l); cast iron block, light alloy head, wet liners; 5 crankshaft bearings; valves: overhead, Vee-slanted at 52°, rockers; camshafts: 1, overhead, chain-driven; lubrication: gear pump, full flow filter, 8.8 imp pt, 10.6 US pt, 5 l; 1 K-126 H vertical twin barrel carburettor; fuel feed: mechanical pump; sealed circuit cooling, water, 17.6 imp pt, 21.1 US pt, 10 l.

TRANSMISSION driving wheels: rear; clutch: single dry plate (diaphragm), hydraulically controlled; gearbox: mechanical; gears: 4, fully synchronized; ratios: I 3.490, II 2.040, III 1.330, IV 1, rev 3.390; lever: central; final drive: hypoid bevel; axle ratio: 4.220; width of rims: 4.5" or 5"; tyres: 6.45 or 6.95 x 13.

PERFORMANCE max speeds: (I) 27 mph, 43 km/h; (II) 45 mph, 73 km/h; (III) 70 mph, 113 km/h; (IV) 87 mph, 140 km/h; power-weight ratio: 31.7 lb/hp (43.2 lb/kW), 14.4 kg/hp (19.6 kg/kW); carrying capacity: 882 lb, 400 kg; speed in direct drive at 1,000 rpm: 16.9 mph, 27.2 km/h; consumption: 32.1 m/imp gal, 26.7 m/US gal, 8.8 l x 100 km.

CHASSIS integral; front suspension: independent, wishbones, coil springs, anti-roll bar, telescopic dampers; rear: rigid axle, semi-elliptic leafsprings, telescopic dampers.

STEERING rack-and-pinion; turns lock to lock: 3.50.

BRAKES front disc, rear drum, dual circuit, vacuum servo; lining area: front 31.6 sq in, 204 sq cm, rear 59.5 sq in, 384 sq cm, total 91.1 sq in, 588 sq cm.

ELECTRICAL EQUIPMENT 12 V; 55 Ah battery; 40 A alternator; R 107 distributor; 2 headlamps.

DIMENSIONS AND WEIGHT wheel base: 94.88 in, 241 cm; front and rear track: 50 in, 127 cm; length: 94.88 in, 421 cm; width: 61.02 in, 155 cm; height: 57.48 in, 146 cm; ground clearance: 7.87 in, 20 cm; weight: 2,381 lb, 1,080 kg; turning circle: 33.5 ft, 10.2 m; fuel tank: 10.1 imp gal, 12.1 US gal, 46 l.

BODY saloon/sedan; 4 doors; 5 seats, separate front seats, reclining backrests, adjustable headrests; headlamps with wiper-washers; heated rear window.

OPTIONALS 3.890 axle ratio; 165 SR or 175 SR x 13.

Moskvich 2137 / 2140 Combi IZh

See Moskvich 2140 / 2140 IZh, except for:

TRANSMISSION axle ratio: 4.550.

PERFORMANCE power-weight ratio: 34.6 lb/hp (47.4 lb/kW), 15.7 kg/hp (21.5 kg/kW).

DIMENSIONS AND WEIGHT height: 59.84 in, 152 cm; weight: 2,602 lb, 1,180 kg.

BODY estate car/st. wagon; 4+1 doors.

GAZ USSR

Volga 3102 Sedan

ENGINE front, 4 stroke; 4 cylinders, in line; 149.3 cu in, 2,446 cc (3.62 x 3.62 in, 92 x 92 mm); compression ratio: 8:1; max power (DIN): 105 hp (77 kW) at 4,500 rpm; max torque (DIN): 134 lb ft, 18.5 kg m (181 Nm) at 2,500 rpm; max engine rpm: 4,500; 42.9 hp/l (31.5 kW/l); light alloy block and head, wet liners; 5 crankshaft bearings; valves: overhead, in line, push-rods and rockers; camshafts: 1, side; lubrication: gear pump, filter on by-pass, 10.4 imp pt, 12.5 US pt, 5.9 l; 1 K-126 G downdraught twin barrel carburettor; air cleaner; fuel feed: mechanical pump; water-cooled, 20.2 imp pt, 24.3 US pt, 11.5 l.

TRANSMISSION driving wheels: rear; clutch: single dry plate, hydraulically controlled; gearbox: mechanical; gears: 4, fully synchronized; ratios: I 3.500, II 2.260, III 1.450, IV 1, rev 3.540; lever: central; final drive: hypoid bevel; axle ratio: 3.900; width of rims: 5"; tyres: 205/70 SR x 14.

PERFORMANCE max speeds: (I) 25 mph, 41 km/h; (II) 40 mph, 64 km/h; (III) 62 mph, 100 km/h; (IV) 93 mph, 150 km/h; power-weight ratio: 30.9 lb/hp (42.1 lb/kW), 14 kg/hp (19.1 kg/kW); carrying capacity: 1,058 lb, 480 kg; speed in direct drive at 1,000 rpm: 19.1 mph, 30.7 km/h; consumption: 24.4 m/imp gal, 20.3 m/US gal, 11.6 l x 100 km.

CHASSIS integral; front suspension: independent, wishbones, coil springs, anti-roll bar, telescopic dampers; rear: rigid axle, semi-elliptic leafsprings, telescopic dampers.

STEERING worm and roller; turns lock to lock: 3.50.

BRAKES front disc, rear drum, servo; swept area: front 87.6 sq in, 565 sq cm, rear 87.6 sq in, 565 sq cm, total 175.2 sq in, 1,130 sq cm.

ELECTRICAL EQUIPMENT 12 V; 54 Ah battery; 40 A alternator; R 119-B distributor; 2 headlamps.

DIMENSIONS AND WEIGHT wheel base: 110.24 in, 280 cm; tracks: 57.87 in, 147 cm front, 55.91 in, 142 cm rear; length: 195.28 in, 496 cm; width: 71.65 in, 182 cm; height: 57.87 in, 147 cm; ground clearance: 7.09 in, 18 cm; weight: 3,241 lb, 1,470 kg; turning circle: 40.7 ft, 12.4 m; fuel tank: 12.1 imp gal, 14.5 US gal, 55 l.

BODY saloon/sedan; 4 doors; 5-6 seats, separate front seats, reclining backrests.

PRACTICAL INSTRUCTIONS fuel: 94 oct petrol; oil: engine 10.4 imp pt, 12.5 US pt, 5.9 l - gearbox 1.6 imp pt, 1.9 US pt, 0.9 l - final drive 0.2 imp pt, 0.2 US pt, 0.1 l; greasing: 9 points; spark plug: 175°; tappet clearances: inlet 0.014 in, 0.35 mm, exhaust 0.014 in, 0.35 mm; tyre pressure: front 24 psi, 1.7 atm, rear 24 psi, 1.7 atm.

VARIATIONS

ENGINE 6.7:1 compression ratio, max power (DIN) 85 hp (63 kW) at 4,500 rpm, max torque (DIN) 127 lb ft, 17.5 kg m (172 Nm) at 2,300 rpm, 34.8 hp/l (25.8 kW/l).
TRANSMISSION 4.100 axle ratio, 5" or 6" wide rims, 7.35/185 or 195 x 14 tyres.
PERFORMANCE max speed 96 mph, 155 km/h, power-weight ratio 38.4 lb/hp (51.8 lb/kW), 17.4 kg/hp (23.5 kg/kW), consumption 21.4 m/imp gal, 17.8 m/US gal, 13.2 l x 100 km.
BRAKES drum, servo.
DIMENSIONS AND WEIGHT length 187.40 in, 476 cm, height 58.66 in, 149 cm, weight 3,263 lb, 1,480 kg.

ENGINE 8.2:1 compression ratio, max power (DIN) 95 hp (70 kW) at 4,500 rpm, max torque (DIN) 138 lb ft, 19 kg m (186 Nm) at 2,400 rpm, 38.8 hp/l (28.6 kW/l).
PERFORMANCE power-weight ratio 34.2 lb/hp (46.3 lb/kW), 15.5 kg/hp (21 kg/kW).

Volga 3102 Station Wagon

See Volga 3102 Sedan, except for:

PERFORMANCE power-weight ratio: 33.3 lb/hp (45.4 lb/kW), 15.1 kg/hp (20.6 kg/kW).

DIMENSIONS AND WEIGHT length 186.22 in, 473 cm; height 60.63 in, 154 cm; weight 3,506 lb, 1,590 kg.

BODY estate car/st. wagon; 4+1 doors.

GAZ Chaika

GAZ Volga 3102 Sedan

UAZ 469 B

Volga Indenor Diesel

(for export only)

See Volga 3102 Sedan, except for:

ENGINE Peugeot, diesel; 4 cylinders, in line, slanted at 20° to right; 140.6 cu in, 2,304 cc (3.70 x 3.27 in, 94 x 83 mm); compression ratio: 22.2:1; max power (DIN): 70 hp (51 kW) at 4,500 rpm; max torque (DIN): 97 lb ft, 13.4 kg m (131 Nm) at 2,200 rpm; 30.4 hp/l (22.1 kW/l); Roto-Diesel injection pump.

PERFORMANCE max speed: 84 mph, 135 km/h; power-weight ratio: 46.3 lb/hp (63.5 lb/kW), 21 kg/hp (28.8 kg/kW); consumption: 35.3 m/imp gal, 29.4 m/US gal, 8 l x 100 km.

ELECTRICAL EQUIPMENT 88 Ah battery; 50 A alternator.

PRACTICAL INSTRUCTIONS fuel: diesel oil.

VARIATIONS

ENGINE 118.9 cu in, 1,948 cc (3.46 x 3.15 in, 88 x 80 mm); 21.8:1 compression ratio, max power (DIN) 50 hp (37 kW) at 4,500 rpm, max torque (DIN) 79 lb ft, 10.9 kg m (107 Nm) at 2,250 rpm, 25.7 hp/l (18.9 kW/l).
PERFORMANCE power-weight ratio 64.8 lb/hp (87.5 lb/kW), 29.4 kg/hp (39.7 kg/kW).

Chaika

ENGINE front, 4 stroke; 8 cylinders in Vee; 337 cu in, 5,522 cc (3.94 x 3.46 in, 100 x 88 mm); compression ratio: 8.5:1; max power (DIN): 220 hp (162 kW) at 4,200 rpm; max torque (DIN): 333 lb ft, 46 kg m (451 Nm) at 2,750 rpm; max engine rpm: 4,400; 39.8 hp/l (29.3 kW/l); cast iron block, light alloy head; 5 crankshaft bearings; valves: overhead, in line; camshafts: 1, central; lubrication: gear pump, full flow filter, 15 imp pt, 18 US pt, 8.5 l; 2 LK3 type K113 downdraught 4-barrel carburettors; fuel feed: electric pump; water-cooled, 37.8 imp pt, 45.5 US pt, 21.5 l, thermostatic fan.

TRANSMISSION driving wheels: rear; gearbox: automatic transmission, hydraulic torque converter and planetary gears with 3 ratios, possible manual selection, max ratio of converter at stall 2.35; ratios: I 2.640, II 1.550, III 1, rev 2; lever: push button control; final drive: hypoid bevel; axle ratio: 3.380; tyres: 9.35 x 15 or 235 x 380.

PERFORMANCE max speed: about 112 mph, 180 km/h; power-weight ratio: 26 lb/hp (35.5 lb/kW), 11.8 kg/hp (16.1 kg/kW); carrying capacity: 1,235 lb, 560 kg; consumption: about 14.1 m/imp gal, 11.8 m/US gal, 20 l x 100 km.

CHASSIS integral; front suspension: independent, wishbones, coil springs, anti-roll bar, telescopic dampers; rear: rigid axle, semi-elliptic springs, telescopic dampers.

STEERING roller and sector, servo.

BRAKES front disc, rear drum, servo.

ELECTRICAL EQUIPMENT 12 V; 2 x 54 Ah batteries; 500 W alternator; P13 distributor; 4 headlamps.

DIMENSIONS AND WEIGHT wheel base: 135.80 in, 345 cm; front and rear track: 62.20 in, 158 cm; length: 240.70 in, 611 cm; width: 79.50 in, 202 cm; height: 62.20 in, 158 cm; ground clearance: 7.10 in, 18 cm; weight: 5,744 lb, 2,605 kg; turning circle: 53.8 ft, 16.4 m; fuel tank: 26.4 imp gal, 31.7 US gal, 120 l.

BODY saloon/sedan; 4 doors; 7 seats; folding rear seat; headlamps with wiper-washers.

UAZ USSR

469 B

ENGINE front, 4 stroke; 4 cylinders, vertical, in line; 149.3 cu in, 2,446 cc (3.62 x 3.62 in, 92 x 92 mm); compression ratio: 6.7:1; max power (DIN): 75 hp (55 kW) at 4,000 rpm; max torque (DIN): 123 lb ft, 17 kg m (167 Nm) at 2,000-2,500 rpm; max engine rpm: 4,500; 30.7 hp/l (22.5 kW/l); light alloy block and head, wet liners; 5 crankshaft bearings; valves: overhead, in line, push-rods and rockers; camshafts: 1, side; lubrication: gear pump, full flow filter, oil cooler, 10.4 imp pt, 12.5 US pt, 5.9 l; 1 K-126 B downdraught twin barrel carburettor; fuel feed: mechanical pump; water-cooled, 22.9 imp pt, 27.5 US pt, 13 l.

TRANSMISSION driving wheels: front (automatically engaged with transfer box low ratio) and rear; clutch: single dry plate; gearbox: mechanical; gears: 4, III and IV synchronized; ratios: I 4.124, II 2.641, III 1.580, IV 1, rev 5.224; low ratios: I 1, II 1.940; lever: central; final drive: spiral bevel; width of rims: 6''; axle ratio: 5.125 or 5.380; tyres: 8.40 x 15 or 215 x 380.

PERFORMANCE max speed: about 71 mph, 115 km/h; power-weight ratio: 48.5 lb/hp (66.1 lb/kW), 22 kg/hp (30 kg/kW); carrying capacity: 1,654 lb, 750 kg; speed in direct drive at 1,000 rpm: 15.9 mph, 25.6 km/h; consumption: 18.5 m/imp gal, 15.4 m/US gal, 15.3 l x 100 km.

CHASSIS box-type ladder frame; front and rear suspension: rigid axle, semi-elliptic leafsprings, telescopic dampers.

STEERING worm and double roller.

BRAKES drum; lining area: total 153.5 sq in, 990 sq cm.

ELECTRICAL EQUIPMENT 12 V; 54 Ah battery; 350 W alternator; 2 headlamps.

DIMENSIONS AND WEIGHT wheel base: 93.70 in, 238 cm; front and rear track: 57.09 in, 145 cm; length: 158.27 in, 402 cm; width: 70.08 in, 178 cm; height: 80.71 in, 205 cm; ground clearance: 8.66 in, 22 cm; weight: 3,638 lb, 1,650 kg; turning circle: 44.6 ft, 13.6 m; fuel tank: 8.6 imp gal, 10.3 US gal, 39 l (2 separate tanks).

BODY open; 4 doors; 7 seats, separate front seats.

PRACTICAL INSTRUCTIONS fuel: 72 oct petrol.

VARIATIONS

ENGINE Peugeot, diesel, 128.9 cu in, 2,112 cc (3.54 x 3.27 in, 90 x 83 mm), 22.8:1 compression ratio, max power (DIN) 65 hp (48 kW) at 4,500 rpm, max torque (DIN) 89 lb ft, 12.3 kg m (121 Nm) at 2,200 rpm, max engine rpm 4,750, 30.8 hp/l (22.6 kW/l).
PERFORMANCE max speed 62 mph, 100 km/h, power-weight ratio 56 lb/hp (75.8 lb/kW), 25.4 kg/hp (34.4 kg/kW), consumption 31.7 m/imp gal, 26.4 m/US gal, 8.9 l x 100 km.

OPTIONALS independent heating; hardtop; fabric top.

VAZ USSR

Lada Series

PRICES IN GB:		£
1	1200 4-dr Sedan	2,740*
2	1200 4+1-dr St. Wagon	3,034*
3	1300 4-dr Sedan	—
4	1300 4+1-dr St. Wagon	—
5	1500 4-dr Sedan	3,482*
6	1500 DL 4+1-dr St. Wagon	3,520*
7	1600 2107 4-dr Sedan	3,681*

Power team:	Standard for:	Optional for:
62 hp	1,2	—
70 hp	3,4	—
77 hp	5,6	—
78 hp	7	—

62 hp power team

ENGINE front, 4 stroke; 4 cylinders, in line; 73.1 cu in, 1,198 cc (2.99 x 2.60 in, 76 x 66 mm); compression ratio: 8.8:1; max power (DIN): 62 hp (46 kW) at 5,600 rpm; max torque (DIN): 64 lb ft, 8.9 kg m (87 Nm) at 3,400 rpm; max engine rpm: 6,000; 51.7 hp/l (38 kW/l); cast iron block, light alloy head; 5 crankshaft bearings; valves: overhead, in line, rockers; camshafts: 1, overhead, chain-driven; lubrication: gear pump, full flow filter, 6.5 imp pt, 7.8 pt, 3.7 l; 1 Weber 32 DCR downdraught twin barrel carburettor; fuel feed: mechanical pump; sealed circuit cooling, liquid, 15 imp pt, 18 US pt, 8.5 l.

TRANSMISSION driving wheels: rear; clutch: single dry plate (diaphragm), hydraulically controlled; gearbox: mechanical; gears: 4, fully synchronized; ratios: I 3.753, II 2.303, III 1.493, IV 1, rev 3.867; lever: central; final drive: hypoid bevel; axle ratio: 4.300 - St. Wagon 4.440; width of rims: 4.5'' or 5''; tyres: 6.15/155 SR/165 SR x 13 - St. Wagon 6.45/165 SR x 13.

PERFORMANCE max speeds: (I) 25 mph, 40 km/h; (II) 40 mph, 65 km/h; (III) 62 mph, 100 km/h; (IV) 87 mph, 140 km/h; power-weight ratio: Sedan 34 lb/hp (45.9 lb/kW), 15.4 kg/hp (20.8 kg/kW); carrying capacity: 882 lb, 400 kg; acceleration: 0-50 mph (0-80 km/h) 12 sec; speed in direct drive at 1,000 rpm: 14.9 mph, 24 km/h; consumption: 31.4 m/imp gal, 26.1 m/US gal, 9 l x 100 km - St. Wagon 29.1 m/imp gal, 24.2 m/US gal, 9.7 l x 100 km.

CHASSIS integral; front suspension: independent, wishbones, coil springs, anti-roll bar, telescopic dampers; rear: rigid axle, twin trailing radius arms, transverse linkage bar, coil springs, Panhard rod, telescopic dampers.

STEERING worm and roller; turns lock to lock: 3.

BRAKES front disc (diameter 9.96 in, 25.3 cm), dual circuit, rear drum, rear compensator; lining area: front 20.9 sq in, 135 sq cm, rear 76.9 sq in, 496 sq cm, total 97.8 sq in, 631 sq cm.

ELECTRICAL EQUIPMENT 12 V; 55 Ah heavy-duty battery; 40 A alternator; R 125 distributor; 2 headlamps.

DIMENSIONS AND WEIGHT wheel base: 95.47 in, 242 cm; tracks: 53.15 in, 135 cm front, 51.38 in, 130 cm rear; length: 162.60 in, 413 cm - St. Wagon 159.84 in, 406 cm; width: 63.43 in, 161 cm; height: 56.69 in, 144 cm - St. Wagon 57.48 in, 146 cm; ground clearance: 6.69 in, 17 cm; weight: Sedan 2,106 lb, 955 kg - St. Wagon 2,161 lb, 980 kg; turning circle: 37.4 ft, 11.4 m; fuel tank: 8.6 imp gal, 10.3 US gal, 39 l - St. Wagon 9.9 imp gal, 11.9 US gal, 45 l.

VAZ Lada 1300 Sedan

BODY saloon/sedan, 4 doors - estate car/st. wagon, 4+1 doors; 5 seats, separate front seats, reclining backrests, adjustable headrests; laminated windscreen; radial tyres.

OPTIONALS servo brake.

70 hp power team

See 62 hp power team, except for:

ENGINE 79 cu in, 1,294 cc (3.11 x 2.60 in, 79 x 66 mm); compression ratio: 8.5:1; max power (DIN): 70 hp (51 kW) at 5,600 rpm; max torque (DIN): 69 lb ft, 9.5 kg m (93 Nm) at 3,400 rpm; 54.1 hp/l (39.4 kW/l).

TRANSMISSION gearbox ratios: I 3.667, II 2.100, III 1.361, IV 1, rev 3.526; axle ratio: 4.100 or 4.300.

PERFORMANCE max speed: 92 mph, 148 km/h; power-weight ratio: Sedan 30 lb/hp (41.2 lb/kW), 13.6 kg/hp (18.7 kg/kW).

CHASSIS rear suspension: anti-roll bar.

77 hp power team

See 62 hp power team, except for:

ENGINE 88.6 cu in, 1,452 cc (2.99 x 3.15 in, 76 x 80 mm); compression ratio: 8.5:1; max power (DIN): 77 hp (57 kW) at 5,600 rpm; max torque (DIN): 78 lb ft, 10.8 kg m (106 Nm) at 3,500 rpm; max engine rpm: 6,500; 53 hp/l (39.3 kW/l).

TRANSMISSION axle ratio: 4.100; width of rims: 5"; tyres: 165 SR x 13.

PERFORMANCE max speed: 93 mph, 150 km/h; power-weight ratio: Sedan 28.4 lb/hp (38.6 lb/kW), 12.9 kg/hp (17.5 kg/kW).

BRAKES servo (standard).

ELECTRICAL EQUIPMENT 53 A alternator.

DIMENSIONS AND WEIGHT wheel base: 94.88 in, 241 cm; tracks: 52.95 in, 135 cm front, 50.79 in, 129 cm rear; length: 159.84 in, 406 cm; height: 55.12 in, 140 cm; ground clearance: 6.89 in, 17.5 cm; weight: Sedan 2,194 lb, 995 kg - St. Wagon 2,271 lb, 1,030 kg.

BODY heated rear window with wiper-washer; vinyl roof; hazard lights.

78 hp power team

See 62 hp power team, except for:

ENGINE 95.7 cu in, 1,569 cc (3.11 x 3.15 in, 79 x 80 mm); compression ratio: 8.5:1; max power (DIN): 78 hp (57 kW) at 5,400 rpm; max torque (DIN): 91 lb ft, 12.5 kg m (123 Nm) at 3,400 rpm; max engine rpm: 6,500; 49.7 hp/l (36.3 kW/l).

TRANSMISSION axle ratio: 4.100; width of rims: 5"; tyres: 165 SR x 13.

PERFORMANCE max speed: 96 mph, 155 km/h; power-weight ratio: 28.7 lb/hp (39.2 lb/kW), 13 kg/hp (17.8 kg/kW).

CHASSIS rear suspension: anti-roll bar.

BRAKES servo (standard).

ELECTRICAL EQUIPMENT 53 A alternator; 4 headlamps.

DIMENSIONS AND WEIGHT tracks: 53.54 in, 136 cm front, 51.97 in, 132 cm rear; length: 161.81 in, 411 cm; ground clearance: 6.88 in, 17.5 cm; weight: 2,238 lb, 1,015 kg.

BODY saloon/sedan; 4 doors.

Lada Niva 2121 4 x 4

PRICE IN GB: £ 5,395*

ENGINE front, 4 stroke; 4 cylinders, in line; 95.7 cu in, 1,569 cc (3.11 x 3.15 in, 79 x 80 mm); compression ratio: 8.5:1; max power (DIN): 80 hp (59 kW) at 5,400 rpm; max torque (DIN): 90 lb ft, 12.4 kg m (122 Nm) at 3,200 rpm; max engine rpm: 6,000; 51 hp/l (37.6 kW/l); cast iron block, light alloy head; 5 crankshaft bearings; valves: overhead, in line, rockers; camshafts: 1, overhead, chain-driven; lubrication: gear pump, full flow filter, 6.5 imp pt, 7.8 US pt, 3.7 l; 1 Weber 32 DCR downdraught carburettor: fuel feed: mechanical pump; sealed circuit cooling, water, 18.8 imp pt, 22.6 US pt, 10.7 l.

TRANSMISSION driving wheels: front and rear; clutch: single dry plate (diaphragm), hydraulically controlled; gearbox: mechanical; gears: 4, fully synchronized and 2-ratio transfer box; ratios: I 3.242, II 1.989, III 1.289, IV 1, rev 3.340; transfer box ratios: I 1.190, II 2.120; lever: central; final drive: hypoid bevel; axle ratio: 4.300; width of rims: 5" or 5.5"; tyres: 6.95/175 SR x 16.

PERFORMANCE max speeds: (I) 25 mph, 40 km/h; (II) 41 mph, 66 km/h; (III) 63 mph, 101 km/h; (IV) 82 mph, 132 km/h; power-weight ratio: 31.8 lb/hp (43 lb/kW), 14.4 kg/hp (19.5 kg/kW); carrying capacity: 882 lb, 400 kg; acceleration: standing ¼ mile 22.2 sec; consumption: 24.4 m/imp gal, 20.3 m/US gal, 11.6 l x 100 km.

CHASSIS integral; front suspension: independent, wishbones, coil springs, anti-roll bar, telescopic double action dampers; rear: rigid axle, coil springs, transverse (Panhard) arm, 4 longitudinal arms, telescopic double action dampers.

STEERING worm and roller; turns lock to lock: 3.

BRAKES front disc (diameter 10.75 in, 27.3 cm), dual circuit, rear drum, vacuum servo.

ELECTRICAL EQUIPMENT 12 V; 55 Ah heavy-duty battery; 42 A alternator; 2 headlamps.

DIMENSIONS AND WEIGHT wheel base: 86.61 in, 220 cm; tracks: 56.30 in, 143 cm front, 55.12 in, 140 cm rear; length: 146.46 in, 372 cm; width: 66.14 in, 168 cm; height: 64.57 in, 164 cm; ground clearance: 8.66 in, 22 cm; weight: 2,536 lb, 1,150 kg; weight distribution: 60% front, 40% rear; turning circle: 38 ft, 11.6 m; fuel tank: 9.9 imp gal, 11.9 US gal, 45 l.

BODY estate car/st. wagon; 2+1 doors; 4-5 seats, separate front seats, reclining backrests, adjustable headrests; folding rear seat; heated rear window with wiper-washer; impact-absorbing bumpers; laminated windscreen.

PRACTICAL INSTRUCTIONS fuel: 93 oct petrol; oil: engine 6.5 imp pt, 7.8 US pt, 3.7 l, change every 6,000 miles, 9,700 km - gearbox 2.3 imp pt, 2.7 US pt, 1.3 l, change every 6,000 miles, 9,700 km - final drive 2.3 imp pt, 2.7 US pt, 1.3 l; spark plug: KLG 707 LS; tyre pressure: front 24 psi, 1.7 atm, rear 24 psi, 1.7 atm.

ZAZ USSR

968 M

ENGINE rear, 4 stroke; 4 cylinders, Vee-slanted at 90°; 73 cu in, 1,196 cc (2.99 x 2.60 in, 76 x 66 mm); compression ratio: 7.2:1; max power (DIN): 41 hp (30 kW) at 4,400 rpm; max torque (DIN): 55 lb ft, 7.6 kg m (54 Nm) at 2,800 rpm; max engine rpm: 4,600; 34.3 hp/l (25.1 kW/l); light alloy block and head; 3 crankshaft bearings; valves: overhead, push-rods and rockers; camshafts: 1, at centre of Vee; lubrication: gear pump, full flow filter, 6.5 imp pt, 7.8 US pt, 3.7 l; 1 Dell'Orto FRDC32 single barrel downdraught carburettor; fuel feed: mechanical pump; air-cooled.

TRANSMISSION driving wheels: rear; clutch: single dry plate, hydraulically controlled; gearbox: mechanical; gears: 4, II, III and IV synchronized; ratios: I 3.800, II 2.120, III 1.409, IV 0.964, rev 4.165; lever: central; final drive: hypoid bevel; axle ratio: 4.125; width of rims: 4"; tyres: 6.15/5.20/5.60/145 SR x 13.

VAZ Lada 1500 DL Station Wagon

VAZ Lada Niva 2121 4 x 4

968 M

PERFORMANCE max speed: 76 mph, 122 km/h; power-weight ratio: 45.2 lb/hp (61.7 lb/kW), 20.5 kg/hp (28 kg/kW); carrying capacity: 706 lb, 320 kg; speed in top at 1,000 rpm: 16.5 mph, 26.5 km/h; consumption: 25.7 m/imp gal, 21.4 m/US gal, 11 l x 100 km.

CHASSIS integral; front suspension: independent, swinging longitudinal trailing arms, transverse torsion bars, telescopic dampers; rear: independent, semi-trailing arms, coil springs, telescopic dampers.

STEERING worm and double roller.

BRAKES drum, dual circuit; lining area: total 43.4 sq in, 280 sq cm.

ELECTRICAL EQUIPMENT 12 V; 42/55 Ah battery; 30 A alternator; 2 headlamps.

DIMENSIONS AND WEIGHT wheel base: 85.04 in, 216 cm; tracks: 48.03 in, 122 cm front, 47.24 in, 120 cm rear; length: 148.42 in, 377 cm; width: 61.81 in, 157 cm; height: 55.12 in, 140 cm; ground clearance: 7.48 in, 19 cm; weight: 1,852 lb, 840 kg; turning circle: 38.7 ft, 11.8 m; fuel tank: 8.8 imp gal, 10.6 US gal, 40 l.

BODY saloon/sedan; 2 doors; 4 seats, separate front seats, front and rear reclining backrests; independent heating; antitheft; hazard lights; front spoiler.

VARIATIONS

ENGINE 8.4:1 compression ratio, max power (DIN) 45 hp (33 kW) at 4,600 rpm, 37.6 hp/l (27.6 kW/l).
PERFORMANCE power-weight ratio 41.2 lb/hp (56.2 lb/kW), 18.7 kg/hp (25.5 kg/kW).

OPTIONALS 155 SR x 13 tyres; front disc brakes; front track 48.82 in, 124 cm, rear track 48.23 in, 122 cm.

969-A 4 x 4

See 968 M, except for:

ENGINE front, 4 stroke; max power (DIN): 40 hp (29 kW) at 4,200 rpm; 33.4 hp/l (24.2 kW/l).

TRANSMISSION driving wheels: front and rear; gears: 4, fully synchronized and low ratio; low ratios: I 1.294, II 4.125; axle ratio: 5.338; tyres: 5.90 x 13.

PERFORMANCE max speed: 56 mph, 90 km/h; power-weight ratio: 54 lb/hp (74.5 lb/kW), 24.5 kg/hp (33.8 kg/kW); consumption: 20.9 m/imp gal, 17.4 m/US gal, 13.5 l x 100 km.

DIMENSIONS AND WEIGHT wheel base: 70.87 in, 180 cm; front and rear track: 51.97 in, 132 cm; length: 133.46 in, 339 cm; width: 64.57 in, 164 cm; height: 70.47 in, 179 cm; weight: 2,161 lb, 980 kg; turning circle: 36.1 ft, 11 m; fuel tank: 7.5 imp gal, 9 US gal, 34 l.

BODY open.

ZIL — USSR

114 Limousine

ENGINE front, 4 stroke; 8 cylinders in Vee; 424.8 cu in, 6,962 cc (4.25 x 3.74 in, 108 x 95 mm); compression ratio: 9.5:1; max power (DIN): 300 hp (221 kW) at 4,400 rpm; max torque (DIN): 420 lb ft, 58 kg m (569 Nm) at 2,900 rpm; max engine rpm: 4,500; 43.1 hp/l (31.7 kW/l); cast iron block, light alloy head; 5 crankshaft bearings; valves: overhead, push-rods and rockers; camshafts: 1, at centre of Vee; lubrication: gear pump, full flow filter, 15.8 imp pt, 19 US pt, 9 l; 1 K 85 downdraught 4-barrel carburettor; fuel feed: electric pump; water-cooled, 26.4 imp pt, 31.7 US pt, 15 l.

TRANSMISSION driving wheels: rear; gearbox: automatic transmission, hydraulic torque converter and planetary gears with 3 ratios, max ratio of converter at stall 2.50; ratios: I 2.020, II 1.420, III 1, rev 1.420; lever: push button control; final drive: hypoid bevel; axle ratio: 3.540; width of rims: 6.5"; tyres: 9.35 x 15 or 235 HR x 380.

PERFORMANCE max speed: 124 mph, 200 km/h; power-weight ratio: 22.7 lb/hp (30.9 lb/kW), 10.3 kg/hp (14 kg/kW); carrying capacity: 1,411 lb, 640 kg; consumption: 12.8 m/imp gal, 10.7 m/US gal, 22 l x 100 km.

CHASSIS box-type ladder frame and X cross members; front suspension: independent, wishbones, coil springs, anti-roll bar, lever dampers; rear: rigid axle, semi-elliptic leafsprings, telescopic dampers.

STEERING recirculating ball, servo; turns lock to lock: 4.30.

BRAKES disc, servo.

ELECTRICAL EQUIPMENT 12 V; 2 x 54 Ah batteries; 500 W dynamo; R-4 distributor; 4 headlamps, 2 fog lamps.

ZAZ 968 M

DIMENSIONS AND WEIGHT wheel base: 152.76 in, 388 cm; tracks: 62.99 in, 160 cm front, 63.35 in, 166 cm rear; length: 248.03 in, 630 cm; width: 81.50 in, 207 cm; height: 60.63 in, 154 cm; ground clearance: 6.69 in, 17 cm; weight: 6,802 lb, 3,085 kg; turning circle: 53.8 ft, 16.4 m; fuel tank: 26.4 imp gal, 31.7 US gal, 120 l.

BODY limousine; 4 doors; 7 seats, separate front seats; air-conditioning; electric windows.

117 Limousine

See 114 Limousine, except for:

PERFORMANCE power-weight ratio: 21.2 lb/hp (28.7 lb/kW), 9.6 kg/hp (13 kg/kW).

DIMENSIONS AND WEIGHT wheel base: 129.92 in, 330 cm; length: 225.20 in, 572 cm; height: 59.84 in, 152 cm; weight: 6,350 lb, 2,880 kg; turning circle: 51.8 ft, 15.8 m.

BODY 5 seats.

4104 Limousine

See 114 Limousine, except for:

ENGINE 469.3 cu in, 7,691 cc (4.25 x 4.13 in, 108 x 105 mm); compression ratio: 9.3:1; max power (DIN): 315 hp (232 kW) at 4,600 rpm; max torque (DIN): 449 lb ft, 62 kg m (608 Nm) at 4,000 rpm; 40.9 hp/l (30.1 kW/l); lubrication: 21.1 imp pt, 25.4 US pt, 12 l; cooling: 37.8 imp pt, 45.5 US pt, 21.5 l.

TRANSMISSION axle ratio: 3.620.

PERFORMANCE power-weight ratio: 23.4 lb/hp (31.8 lb/kW), 10.6 kg/hp (14.4 kg/kW).

ELECTRICAL EQUIPMENT 2 x 60 Ah batteries.

DIMENSIONS AND WEIGHT tracks: 64.57 in, 164 cm front, 65.35 in, 166 cm rear; length: 249.61 in, 634 cm; width: 82.28 in, 209 cm; height: 61.02 in, 155 cm; ground clearance: 6.89 in, 17.5 cm; turning circle: 54.1 ft, 16.5 m; weight: 7,354 lb, 3,335 kg.

ZCZ — YUGOSLAVIA

Zastava 750 LE

PRICE EX WORKS: 129,000 dinars

ENGINE rear, longitudinal, 4 stroke; 4 cylinders, vertical, in line; 46.8 cu in, 767 cc (2.44 x 2.50 in, 62 x 63.5 mm); compression ratio: 7.5:1; max power (DIN): 25 hp (18 kW) at 4,600 rpm; max torque (DIN): 37 lb ft, 5.1 kg m (50 Nm) at 2,500 rpm; max engine rpm: 4,800; 32.6 hp/l (23.9 kW/l); cast iron block, light alloy head; 3 crankshaft bearings; valves: overhead, in line, push-rods and rockers; camshafts: 1, side; lubrication: gear pump, 6.5 imp pt, 7.8 US pt, 3.7 l; 1 IPM 28 MGV-10 downdraught single barrel carburettor; fuel feed: mechanical pump; water-cooled, 7.9 imp pt, 9.5 US pt, 4.5 l.

TRANSMISSION driving wheels: rear; clutch: single dry plate; gearbox: mechanical; gears: 4, II, III and IV synchronized; ratios: I 3.384, II 2.055, III 1.333, IV 0.869, rev 4.275; lever: central; final drive: spiral bevel; axle ratio: 4.875; width of rims: 3.5"; tyres: 145 SR x 12.

PERFORMANCE max speeds: (I) 19 mph, 30 km/h; (II) 28 mph, 45 km/h; (III) 43 mph, 70 km/h; (IV) 68 mph, 110 km/h; power-weight ratio: 53.4 lb/hp (74.1 lb/kW), 24.2 kg/hp (36.6 kg/kW); carrying capacity: 706 lb, 320 kg; acceleration: 0-50 mph (0-80 km/h) 24 sec; speed in top at 1,000 rpm: 14.1 mph, 22.7 km/h; consumption: 38.2 m/imp gal, 31.8 m/US gal, 7.4 l x 100 km.

CHASSIS integral; front suspension: independent, wishbones, transverse leafspring lower arms, telescopic dampers; rear: independent, oblique semi-trailing arms, coil springs, telescopic dampers.

STEERING screw and sector; turns lock to lock: 2.12.

BRAKES drum, single circuit; lining area: front 33.5 sq in, 216 sq cm, rear 33.5 sq in, 216 sq cm, total 67 sq in, 432 sq cm.

ELECTRICAL EQUIPMENT 12 V; 34 Ah battery; 340 W alternator; Marelli distributor; 2 headlamps.

ZIL 114 Limousine

ZCZ Zastava 750 LE

ZCZ Zastava 750 LE

DIMENSIONS AND WEIGHT wheel base: 78.74 in, 200 cm; front and rear track: 45.43 in, 115 cm; length: 127.48 in, 324 cm; width: 54.25 in, 138 cm; height: 52.36 in, 133 cm; ground clearance: 5.90 in, 15 cm; weight: 1,334 lb, 605 kg; weight distribution: 43% front, 57% rear; turning circle: 28.5 ft, 8.7 m; fuel tank: 6.6 imp gal, 7.9 US gal, 30 l.

BODY saloon/sedan; 2 doors; 4 seats, separate front seats, reclining backrests; folding rear seat; luxury interior.

PRACTICAL INSTRUCTIONS fuel: 86 oct petrol; oil: engine 5.3 imp pt, 6.3 US pt, 3 l, SAE 20W-40/10W-30, change every 3,100 miles, 5,000 km - gearbox and final drive 2.6 imp pt, 3.2 US pt, 1.5 l, SAE 90, change every 12,400 miles, 20,000 km; spark plug: Bosna FE 70; tappet clearances: inlet 0.006 in, 0.15 mm, exhaust 0.006 in, 0.15 mm; valve timing 4° 34° 29° 1°; tyre pressure: front 14 psi, 1 atm, rear 22 psi, 1.6 atm.

Zastava 850

See Zastava 750 LE, except for:

PRICE EX WORKS: 131,400 dinars

ENGINE 51.7 cu in, 848 cc (2.48 x 2.68 in, 63 x 68 mm); compression ratio: 9:1; max power (DIN): 32 hp (24 kW) at 4,600 rpm; max torque (DIN): 41 lb ft, 5.6 kg m (55 Nm) at 2,500 rpm; max engine rpm: 5,400; 37.7 hp/l (27.7 kW/l).

PERFORMANCE max speeds: (I) 20 mph, 33 km/h; (II) 34 mph, 55 km/h; (III) 53 mph, 86 km/h; (IV) 78 mph, 125 km/h; power-weight ratio: 44.1 lb/hp (60 lb/kW), 20 kg/hp (27.2 kg/kW); speed in top at 1,000 rpm: 18.6 mph, 30 km/h; consumption: 44.1 m/imp gal, 36.8 m/US gal, 6.4 l x 100 km.

DIMENSIONS AND WEIGHT length: 128.58 in, 327 cm; ground clearance: 5.71 in, 14.5 cm; weight: 1,411 lb, 640 kg.

PRACTICAL INSTRUCTIONS spark plug: Bosna FE 80.

Zastava Jugo 45

PRICE IN GB: £ 2,749*
PRICE EX WORKS: 197,500 dinars

ENGINE front, trasverse, 4 stroke; 4 cylinders, in line; 55.1 cu in, 903 cc (2.56 x 2.72 in, 65 x 68 mm); compression ratio: 9:1; max power (DIN): 45 hp (33 kW) at 6,100 rpm; max torque (DIN): 46 lb ft, 6.3 kg m (62 Nm) at 3,400 rpm; max engine rpm: 6,300; 49.8 hp/l (36.7 kW/l); cast iron block, light alloy head; 3 crankshaft bearings; valves: overhead; camshafts: 1, in crankcase; lubrication: gear pump, 7 imp pt, 8.5 US pt, 4 l; 1 Weber 32 ICEV 31 or Solex C 30 DI-40 single barrel carburettor; fuel feed: mechanical pump; water-cooled, 9.7 imp pt, 11.6 US pt, 5.5 l.

TRANSMISSION driving wheels: front; clutch: single dry plate; gearbox: mechanical; gears: 4, fully synchronized; ratios: I 3.583, II 2.235, III 1.454, IV 1.042, rev 3.714; lever: central; final drive: cylindrical gears; axle ratio: 4.077; width of rims: 4"; tyres: 135 SR x 13.

PERFORMANCE max speeds: (I) 26 mph, 42 km/h; (II) 42 mph, 68 km/h; (III) 65 mph, 105 km/h; (IV) 84 mph, 135 km/h; power-weight ratio: 35.9 lb/hp (49.2 lb/kW), 16.3 kg/hp (22.3 kg/kW); carrying capacity: 882 lb, 400 kg; consumption: 37.2 m/imp gal, 30.9 m/US gal, 7.6 l x 100 km.

CHASSIS integral; front suspension: independent, by McPherson, swinging arms, coil springs/telescopic damper struts; rear: independent, swinging arms, transverse leafsprings, telescopic dampers.

STEERING rack-and-pinion.

BRAKES front disc, rear drum.

ELECTRICAL EQUIPMENT 12 V; 34 Ah battery; 400 W alternator; RPS-15 distributor; 2 headlamps.

DIMENSIONS AND WEIGHT wheel base: 84.64 in, 215 cm; tracks: 51.49 in, 131 cm front, 50.98 in, 129 cm rear; length: 137.40 in, 349 cm; width: 60.71 in, 154 cm; height: 54.72 in, 139 cm; ground clearance: 5.31 in, 13.5 cm; weight: 1,621 lb, 735 kg; weight distribution: 48% front, 52% rear; turning circle: 31.2 ft, 9.5 m; fuel tank: 7 imp gal, 8.4 US gal, 32 l.

BODY saloon/sedan; 2+1 doors; 5 seats, separate front seats.

PRACTICAL INSTRUCTIONS fuel: 98 oct petrol; oil: engine 7 imp pt, 8.5 US pt, 4 l, SAE 10W-30/20W-40, change every 3,100 miles, 5,000 km - gearbox and final drive 5.5 imp pt, 6.6 US pt, 3.1 l; spark plug: Bosna FE 65-P or Marelli CW7LP; tappet clearances: inlet 0.006 in, 0.15 mm, exhaust 0.006 in, 0.15 mm; tyre pressure: front 27 psi, 1.9 atm, rear 28 psi, 2 atm.

Zastava Jugo 55

See Zastava Jugo 45, except for:

ENGINE 68.1 cu in, 1,116 cc (3.15 x 2.19 in, 80 x 55.5 mm); compression ratio: 9.2:1; max power (DIN): 55 hp (40 kW) at 6,000 rpm; max torque (DIN): 57 lb ft, 7.9 kg m (77 Nm) at 3,000 rpm; 49.3 hp/l (36.2 kW/l).

TRANSMISSION width of rims: 4.5"; tyres: 145 SR x 13.

PERFORMANCE max speed: 90 mph, 145 km/h; power-weight ratio: 29.5 lb/hp (40.6 lb/kW), 13.4 kg/hp (18.4 kg/kW); consumption: 36.2 m/imp gal, 30.2 m/US gal, 7.8 l x 100 km.

PRACTICAL INSTRUCTIONS tyre pressure: front 23 psi, 1.6 atm, rear 26 psi, 1.8 atm.

Zastava 128 CL 1100

PRICE EX WORKS: 260,000 dinars

ENGINE front, transverse, 4 stroke; 4 cylinders, in line; 68.1 cu in, 1,116 cc (3.15 x 2.19 in, 80 x 55.5 mm); compression ratio: 9.2:1; max power (DIN): 55 hp (40 kW) at 6,000 rpm; max torque (DIN): 60 lb ft, 8.3 kg m (81 Nm) at 2,800 rpm; max engine rpm: 6,600; 49.3 hp/l (36.2 kW/l); cast iron block, light alloy head; 5 crankshaft bearings; valves: overhead; camshafts: 1, overhead; lubrication: gear pump, 7.4 imp pt, 8.9 US pt, 4.2 l; 1 Weber Holley 32 ICEV-10 or Weber Holley 32 ICEV 18/250 downdraught carburettor; fuel feed: mechanical pump; water-cooled, 11.4 imp pt, 13.7 US pt, 6.5 l.

TRANSMISSION driving wheels: front; clutch: single dry plate; gearbox: mechanical; gears: 4, fully synchronized; ratios: I 3.583, II 2.235, III 1.454, IV 1.042, rev 3.714; lever: central; final drive: cylindrical gears; width of rims: 4.5"; tyres: 145 SR x 13.

PERFORMANCE max speeds: (I) 31 mph, 50 km/h; (II) 50

ZCZ Zastava Jugo 45

ZCZ Zastava Jugo 55

ZASTAVA 128 CL 1100

mph, 80 km/h; (III) 74 mph, 120 km/h; (IV) 84 mph, 135 km/h; power-weight ratio: 32.3 lb/hp (44.4 lb/kW), 14.6 kg/hp (20.1 kg/kW); carrying capacity: 882 lb, 400 kg; acceleration: 0-50 mph (0-80 km/h) 19.6 sec; speed in top at 1,000 rpm: 16.4 mph, 26.4 km/h; consumption: 34 m/imp gal, 28.3 m/US gal, 8.3 l x 100 km.

CHASSIS integral; front suspension: independent, by McPherson, coil springs/telescopic damper struts; rear: independent, wishbones, telescopic dampers.

STEERING rack-and-pinion; turns lock to lock: 3.50.

BRAKES front disc, rear drum, servo.

ELECTRICAL EQUIPMENT 12 V; 45 Ah battery; 480 W alternator; Marelli TR 12A 17 - S 135 BX 4/70 distributor; 2 headlamps.

DIMENSIONS AND WEIGHT wheel base: 96.38 in, 245 cm; front and rear track: 51.57 in, 131 cm; length: 151.18 in, 384 cm; width: 62.60 in, 159 cm; height: 55.90 in, 142 cm; ground clearance: 5.71 in, 14.5 cm; weight: 1,775 lb, 805 kg; weight distribution: 50% front, 50% rear; turning circle: 33.8 ft, 10.3 m; fuel tank: 8.4 imp gal, 10 US gal, 38 l.

BODY saloon/sedan; 4 doors; 5 seats, separate front seats.

PRACTICAL INSTRUCTIONS fuel: 98 oct petrol; oil: engine 7.4 imp pt, 8.9 US pt, 4.2 l, SAE 10W-30/20W-40, change every 3,100 miles, 5,000 km - gearbox and final drive 6.2 imp pt, 7.4 US pt, 3.5 l; spark plug: Marelli CV 7 LP or Champion N9Y; tappet clearances: inlet 0.016 in, 0.40 mm, exhaust 0.019 in, 0.50 mm; valve timing: 12° 52° 52° 12°; tyre pressure: front 25 psi, 1.8 atm, rear 24 psi, 1.7 atm.

Zastava 128 CL 1300

See Zastava 128 CL 1100, except for:

PRICE EX WORKS: 286,000 dinars

ENGINE 79.1 cu in, 1,297 cc (3.39 x 2.19 in, 86 x 55.5 mm); max power (DIN): 60 hp (44 kW) at 6,000 rpm; max torque (DIN): 72 lb ft, 10 kg m (98 Nm) at 2,800 rpm; 46.3 hp/l (33.9 kW/l).

PERFORMANCE max speed: 90 mph, 145 km/h; power-weight ratio: 29.5 lb/hp (40.3 lb/kW), 13.4 kg/hp (18.3 kg/kW); acceleration: 0-50 mph (0-80 km/h) 15.1 sec; consumption: 31 m/imp gal, 25.8 m/US gal, 9.1 l x 100 km at 56 mph, 90 km/h.

Zastava 101 Series

PRICES IN GB AND EX WORKS:	£	dinars
1 GT 55 2+1-dr Sedan	2,699*	215,000
2 GT 55 4+1-dr Sedan	2,849*	225,000
3 GTL 55 2+1-dr Sedan	3,199*	235,000
4 GTL 55 4+1-dr Sedan	—	245,000
5 GT 65 2+1-dr Sedan	—	220,000
6 GT 65 4+1-dr Sedan	2,999*	230,000
7 GTL 65 2+1-dr Sedan	—	240,000
8 GTL 65 4+1-dr Sedan	3,549*	250,000

Power team:	Standard for:	Optional for:
55 hp	1 to 4	—
65 hp	5 to 8	—

ZCZ Zastava 128 CL 1100 - 1300

55 hp power team

ENGINE front, transverse, slanted 20° to front, 4 stroke; 4 cylinders, in line; 68.1 cu in, 1,116 cc (3.15 x 2.19 in, 80 x 55.5 mm); compression ratio: 9.2:1; max power (DIN): 55 hp (40 kW) at 6,000 rpm; max torque (DIN): 60 lb ft, 8.3 kg m (81 Nm) at 2,800 rpm; max engine rpm: 6,600; 49.3 hp/l (36.2 kW/l); cast iron block, light alloy head; 5 crankshaft bearings; valves: overhead, thimble tappets; camshafts: 1, overhead; lubrication: gear pump (cartridge), 7.4 imp pt, 8.9 US pt, 4.2 l; 1 Weber Holley 32 ICEV 10 or Solex C2 DISA-20 downdraught carburettor; fuel feed: mechanical pump; water-cooled, 11.4 imp pt, 13.7 US pt, 6.5 l, electric thermostatic fan.

TRANSMISSION driving wheels: front; clutch: single dry plate; gearbox: mechanical; gears: 4, fully synchronized; ratios: I 3.583, II 2.235, III 1.454, IV 1.042, rev 3.714; lever: central; final drive: cylindrical gears; axle ratio: 4.077; width of rims: 4.5"; tyres: 145 SR x 13.

PERFORMANCE max speeds: (I) 29 mph, 47 km/h; (II) 47 mph, 75 km/h; (III) 71 mph, 115 km/h; (IV) 84 mph, 135 km/h; power-weight ratio: 33.5 lb/hp (45.5 lb/kW), 15.2 kg/hp (20.7 kg/kW); carrying capacity: 882 lb, 400 kg; acceleration: 0-50 mph (0-80 km/h) 12.7 sec; speed in top at 1,000 rpm: 16.4 mph, 26.4 km/h; consumption: 33.6 m/imp gal, 28 m/US gal, 8.4 l x 100 km.

CHASSIS integral; front suspension: independent, by McPherson, coil springs/telescopic damper struts, lower wishbones, anti-roll bar; rear: independent, single wide-based wishbones, transverse leafspring, telescopic dampers.

STEERING rack-and-pinion; turns lock to lock: 3.40.

BRAKES front disc (diameter 8.94 in, 22.7 cm), rear drum, rear compensator, servo; lining area: front 19.2 sq in, 124 sq cm, rear 33.5 sq in, 216 sq cm, total 52.7 sq in, 340 sq cm.

ELECTRICAL EQUIPMENT 12 V; 34 Ah battery; 480 W alternator; Marelli TK 12 A17 or RPS 12 distributor; 2 headlamps.

DIMENSIONS AND WEIGHT wheel base: 96.42 in, 245 cm; tracks: 51.18 in, 130 cm front, 51.97 in, 132 cm rear; length: 150.39 in, 382 cm; width: 62.60 in, 159 cm; height: 53.94 in, 137 cm; ground clearance: 5.71 in, 14.5 cm; weight: 1,841 lb, 835 kg; weight distribution: 50% front, 50% rear; turning circle: 33.8 ft, 10.3 m; fuel tank: 8.4 imp gal, 10 US gal, 38 l.

BODY saloon/sedan; 2+1 or 4+1 doors; 5 seats, separate front seats.

PRACTICAL INSTRUCTIONS fuel: 98 oct petrol; oil: engine 7.4 imp pt, 8.9 US pt, 4.2 l, SAE 10W-30/20W-40, change every 3,100 miles, 5,000 km - gearbox and final drive 5.5 imp pt, 6.6 US pt, 3.1 l, SAE 80W-90 CZ, change every 12,400 miles, 20,000 km; spark plug: Marelli CW 7 LP or Champion N9Y; tappet clearances: inlet 0.015 in, 0.40 mm, exhaust 0.020 in, 0.50 mm; valve timing: 12° 52° 52° 12°; tyre pressure: front 26 psi, 1.8 atm, rear 24 psi, 1.7 atm.

65 hp power team

See 55 hp power team, except for:

ENGINE 79.1 cu in, 1,297 cc (3.39 x 2.19 in, 86 x 55.5 mm); compression ratio: 9.1:1; max power (DIN): 65 hp (48 kW) at 6,000 rpm; max torque (DIN): 72 lb ft, 10 kg m (98 Nm) at 3,500 rpm; 50.1 hp/l (36.9 kW/l).

PERFORMANCE max speeds: (I) 31 mph, 50 km/h; (II) 50 mph, 80 km/h; (III) 75 mph, 120 km/h; (IV) 87 mph, 140 km/h; power-weight ratio: 28.8 lb/hp (39 lb/kW), 13.1 kg/hp (17.7 kg/kW); consumption: 31.7 m/imp gal, 26.4 m/US gal, 8.9 l x 100 km.

ELECTRICAL EQUIPMENT 45 Ah battery.

DIMENSIONS AND WEIGHT weight: 1,874 lb, 850 kg.

PRACTICAL INSTRUCTIONS valve timing: 20° 44° 60° 4°.

ZCZ Zastava 101 GTL 55 Sedan

ZCZ Zastava 101 GTL 55 Sedan

The Americas

Models now in production

Illustrations and technical information

FORD ARGENTINA

Taunus L 2000

PRICE EX WORKS: 97,465 pesos

ENGINE front, 4 stroke; 4 cylinders, in line; 121.4 cu in, 1,990 cc (3.52 x 3.13 in, 89.3 x 79.4 mm); compression ratio: 8:1; max power (SAE): 92 hp (68 kW) at 5,500 rpm; max torque (SAE): 109 lb ft, 15.1 kg m (148 Nm) at 3,000 rpm; max engine rpm: 6,000; 46.2 hp/l (34 kW/l); cast iron block and head; 5 crankshaft bearings; valves: overhead, push-rods and rockers; camshafts: 1, overhead, cogged belt; lubrication: gear pump, full flow filter, 7.9 imp pt, 9.5 US pt, 4.5 l; 1 Galileo Argentina downdraught single barrel carburettor; fuel feed: mechanical pump; water-cooled, 13.9 imp pt, 16.7 US pt, 7.9 l.

TRANSMISSION driving wheels: rear; clutch: single dry plate; gearbox: mechanical; gears: 4, fully synchronized; ratios: I 3.360, II 1.810, III 1.260, IV 1, rev 3.360; lever: central; final drive: hypoid bevel; axle ratio: 3.540; width of rims: 5.5"; tyres: 6.95 S x 13.

PERFORMANCE max speed: 95 mph, 153 km/h; power-weight ratio: 27.1 lb/hp (36.8 lb/kW), 12.3 kg/hp (16.7 kg/kW); speed in direct drive at 1,000 rpm: 18.5 mph, 29.7 km/h; consumption: 26.6 m/imp gal, 22.2 m/US gal, 10.6 l x 100 km.

CHASSIS integral; front suspension: independent, wishbones, coil springs/telescopic dampers, anti-roll bar; rear: rigid axle, lower trailing arms, upper oblique trailing arms, coil springs, telescopic dampers.

STEERING rack-and-pinion.

BRAKES front disc (diameter 9.75 in, 24.8 cm), rear drum; lining area: front 28.5 sq in, 184 sq cm, rear 59.8 sq in, 386 sq cm, total 88.3 sq in, 570 sq cm.

ELECTRICAL EQUIPMENT 12 V; 45 Ah battery; 540 W alternator; 2 headlamps.

DIMENSIONS AND WEIGHT wheel base: 101.57 in, 258 cm; front and rear track: 55.91 in, 142 cm; length: 171.26 in, 435 cm; width: 66.93 in, 170 cm; height: 52.76 in, 134 cm; ground clearance: 4.61 in, 11.7 cm; weight: 2,496 lb, 1,132 kg; turning circle: 35.1 ft, 10.7 m; fuel tank: 11.9 imp gal, 14.3 US gal, 54 l.

BODY saloon/sedan; 4 doors; 5 seats.

OPTIONALS servo brake; 175 SR x 13 tyres; anti-roll bar on rear suspension.

Taunus Ghia 2300

See Taunus L 2000, except for:

PRICES EX WORKS:	**pesos**
4-dr Sedan	**112,157**
S 4-dr Sedan	**144,269**

ENGINE 140.3 cu in, 2,299 cc (3.78 x 3.13 in, 96 x 79.4 mm); compression ratio: 9:1; max power (SAE): 122 hp (90 kW) at 5,000 rpm; max torque (SAE): 142 lb ft, 19.6 kg m (192 Nm) at 3,500 rpm; max engine rpm: 5,500; 53 hp/l (39 kW/l); 1 Argelite downdraught twin barrel carburettor; cooling: 13.7 imp pt, 16.5 US pt, 7.8 l.

PERFORMANCE max speed: 106 mph, 170 km/h; power-weight ratio: 20.5 lb/hp (27.8 lb/kW), 9.3 kg/hp (12.6 kg/kW); consumption: 28.5 m/imp gal, 23.8 m/US gal, 9.9 l x 100 km.

ELECTRICAL EQUIPMENT 60 A alternator.

BODY luxury equipment.

OPTIONALS 5-speed fully synchronized mechanical gearbox (I 3.360, II 1.810, III 1.260, IV 1, V 0.820, rev 3.360); automatic transmission with 3 ratios (I 2.470, II 1.470, III 1), 3.310 axle ratio; air-conditioning.

Taunus GT / SP

See Taunus L 2000, except for:

PRICES EX WORKS:	**pesos**
GT 2-dr Coupé	**118,099**
SP 2-dr Coupé	**138,534**

ENGINE 140.3 cu in, 2,299 cc (3.78 x 3.13 in, 96 x 79.4 mm); compression ratio: 9:1; max power (SAE): 132 hp (97 kW) at 5,500 rpm; max torque (SAE): 147 lb ft, 20.3 kg m (199 Nm) at 3,500 rpm; max engine rpm: 6,000; 44 hp/l (32.3 kW/l); 1 Argelite downdraught twin barrel carburettor; cooling: 13.7 imp pt, 16.5 US pt, 7.8 l.

PERFORMANCE max speed: 106 mph, 170 km/h; power-weight ratio: 18.9 lb/hp (25.7 lb/kW), 8.6 kg/hp (11.7 kg/kW); consumption: 28.5 m/imp gal, 23.8 m/US gal, 9.9 l x 100 km.

ELECTRICAL EQUIPMENT 60 A alternator.

DIMENSIONS AND WEIGHT height: 51.97 in, 132 cm.

FORD Taunus SP Coupé

BODY coupé; 2 doors.

OPTIONALS 5-speed fully synchronized mechanical gearbox (I 3.360, II 1.810, III 1.260, IV 1, V 0.820, rev 3.360); automatic transmission with 3 ratios (I 2.470, II 1.470, III 1), 3.310 axle ratio; air-conditioning.

Fairlane 3600 LTD

PRICE EX WORKS: 107,469 pesos

ENGINE front, 4 stroke; 6 cylinders, in line; 221 cu in, 3,620 cc (3.68 x 3.46 in, 93.5 x 87.9 mm); compression ratio: 8.2:1; max power (SAE): 132 hp (97 kW) at 4,000 rpm; max torque (SAE): 201 lb ft, 27.8 kg m (273 Nm) at 1,800 rpm; 36.6 hp/l (26.9 kW/l); cast iron block and head; 7 crankshaft bearings; valves: overhead, push-rods and rockers; camshafts: 1, side, timing chain; lubrication: gear pump, full flow filter, 7.9 imp pt, 9.5 US pt, 4.5 l; 1 Argelite downdraught twin barrel carburettor; fuel feed: mechanical pump; water-cooled, 14.7 imp pt, 17.6 US pt, 8.3 l.

TRANSMISSION driving wheels: rear; clutch: single dry plate; gearbox: mechanical; gears: 3, fully synchronized; ratios: I 2.990, II 1.750, III 1, rev 3.170; lever: steering column; axle ratio: 3.310; tyres: 7.35 x 14.

PERFORMANCE max speed: 96 mph, 154 km/h; power-weight ratio: 25.9 lb/hp (35.2 lb/kW), 11.7 kg/hp (15.9 kg/kW); acceleration: standing ¼ mile 20 sec, 0-50 mph (0-80 km/h) 10.5 sec; consumption: 19.4 m/imp gal, 16.2 m/US gal, 14.5 l x 100 km.

CHASSIS integral; front suspension: independent, coil springs, anti-roll bar, telescopic dampers; rear: rigid axle, long leafsprings, telescopic dampers.

STEERING recirculating ball, servo.

BRAKES front disc (diameter 10.90 in, 27.7 cm), rear drum, servo; lining area: front 28 sq in, 181 sq cm, rear 85 sq in, 548 sq cm, total 113 sq in, 729 sq cm.

ELECTRICAL EQUIPMENT 12 V; 55 Ah battery; 725 W alternator; 4 headlamps.

DIMENSIONS AND WEIGHT wheel base: 116 in, 295 cm; front and rear track: 58.50 in, 149 cm; length: 205 in, 520 cm; width: 74.80 in, 190 cm; height: 55 in, 140 cm; ground clearance: 6.70 in, 17 cm; weight: 3,418 lb, 1,550 kg; fuel tank: 16.5 imp gal, 19.8 US gal, 75 l.

BODY saloon/sedan; 4 doors; 5 seats.

OPTIONALS air-conditioning; twin drive rear axle.

Fairlane V8 Elite

See Fairlane 3600 LTD, except for:

PRICE EX WORKS: 114,350 pesos

ENGINE 8 cylinders in Vee; 292 cu in, 4,785 cc (3.75 x 3.30 in, 95.2 x 83.8 mm); compression ratio: 8:1; max power (SAE): 180 hp (132 kW) at 4,500 rpm; max torque (SAE): 270 lb ft, 37.3 kg m (367 Nm) at 2,500 rpm; 37.6 hp/l (27.7 kW/l); cast iron block and head; 5 crankshaft bearings; valves: overhead, push-rods and rockers; camshafts: 1; lubrication: full flow filter, 9.7 imp pt, 11.6 US pt, 5.5 l; water-cooled, 28.2 imp pt, 33.8 US pt, 16 l.

TRANSMISSION tyres: 7.75 x 14.

PERFORMANCE max speed: 109 mph, 175 km/h; power-weight ratio: 20.4 lb/hp (27.7 lb/kW), 9.6 kg/hp (12.6 kg/kW); acceleration: standing ¼ mile 19.5 sec, 0-50 mph (0-80 km/h) 9.8 sec; consumption: 18.4 m/imp gal, 15.4 m/US gal, 15.3 l x 100 km.

BRAKES front disc (diameter 11.30 in, 28.7 cm), rear drum; lining area: front 38.5 sq in, 248 sq cm, rear 84.8 sq in, 547 sq cm, total 123.3 sq in, 795 sq cm.

DIMENSIONS AND WEIGHT weight: 3,667 lb, 1,663 kg.

Falcon 2.3 Sedan

PRICES EX WORKS:	**pesos**
Standard 4-dr Sedan	**91,032**
De Luxe 4-dr Sedan	**97,022**

ENGINE front, 4 stroke; 4 cylinders, in line; 140.3 cu in, 2,299 cc (3.78 x 3.13 in, 96 x 79.4 mm); compression ratio: 7.5:1; max power (SAE): 90 hp (66 kW) at 5,000 rpm; max

FORD Fairlane V8 Elite

FORD Falcon Ghia SP

RENAULT 4

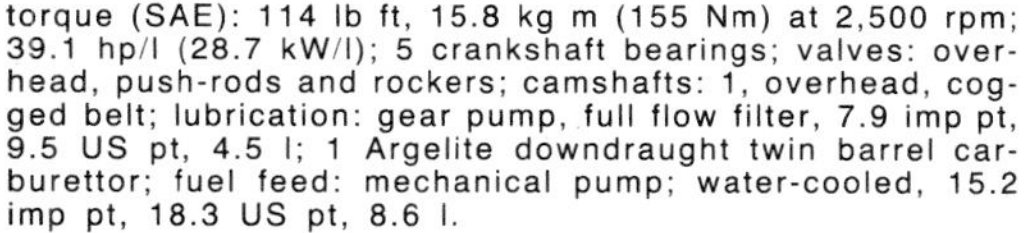

torque (SAE): 114 lb ft, 15.8 kg m (155 Nm) at 2,500 rpm; 39.1 hp/l (28.7 kW/l); 5 crankshaft bearings; valves: overhead, push-rods and rockers; camshafts: 1, overhead, cogged belt; lubrication: gear pump, full flow filter, 7.9 imp pt, 9.5 US pt, 4.5 l; 1 Argelite downdraught twin barrel carburettor; fuel feed: mechanical pump; water-cooled, 15.2 imp pt, 18.3 US pt, 8.6 l.

TRANSMISSION driving wheels: rear; clutch: single dry plate; gearbox: mechanical; gears: 4, fully synchronized; ratios: I 3.650, II 2.135, III 1.370, IV 1, rev 3.660; lever: central; axle ratio: 3.540; tyres: 6.95 x 14.

PERFORMANCE max speed: 95 mph, 153 km/h; power-weight ratio: 30.4 lb/hp (41.5 lb/kW), 13.8 kg/hp (18.8 kg/kW); acceleration: standing ¼ mile 20.9 sec, 0-50 mph (0-80 km/h) 11.5 sec; consumption: 23.7 m/imp gal, 19.7 m/US gal, 11.9 l x 100 km.

CHASSIS integral; front suspension: independent, coil springs, suspension arms mounted on silent blocks, anti-roll bar, telescopic dampers; rear: rigid axle, leafsprings, telescopic dampers.

STEERING recirculating ball.

BRAKES front disc (diameter 10.96 in, 27.7 cm), rear drum; lining area: front 28 sq in, 180 sq cm, rear 67.3 sq in, 434 sq cm, total 95.3 sq in, 614 sq cm.

ELECTRICAL EQUIPMENT 12 V; 45 Ah battery; 540 W alternator; 2 headlamps.

DIMENSIONS AND WEIGHT wheel base: 109.50 in, 278 cm; tracks: 55.60 in, 141 cm front, 54.50 in, 138 cm rear; length: 186.30 in, 473 cm; width: 70.60 in, 179 cm; height: 55.20 in, 140 cm; ground clearance: 7.04 in, 18 cm; weight: 2,740 lb, 1,243 kg; fuel tank: 11.6 imp gal, 14 US gal, 53 l.

BODY saloon/sedan; 4 doors; 5 seats; (for De Luxe only) luxury equipment.

Falcon 3.0 Sedan

See Falcon 2.3 Sedan, except for:

PRICES EX WORKS:	**pesos**
Standard 4-dr Sedan	**95,483**
De Luxe 4-dr Sedan	**103,429**

ENGINE 6 cylinders, in line; 188 cu in, 3,080 cc (3.68 x 2.94 in, 93.5 x 74.7 mm); compression ratio: 7.4:1; max power (SAE): 116 hp (85 kW) at 4,000 rpm; max torque (SAE): 176 lb ft, 24.3 kg m (238 Nm) at 2,300 rpm; 37.7 hp/l (27.7 kW/l); 7 crankshaft bearings; camshafts: 1, side, timing chain; 1 Galileo or Argelite downdraught single barrel carburettor.

TRANSMISSION gears: 3, fully synchronized; ratios: I 2.990, II 1.750, III 1, rev 3.170; lever: steering column; axle ratio: 3.310.

PERFORMANCE power-weight ratio: 23.6 lb/hp (32 lb/kW), 10.7 kg/hp (14.5 kg/kW).

OPTIONALS 4-speed fully synchronized mechanical gearbox; power steering; twin drive rear axle; air-conditioning; halogen headlamps.

Falcon 3.0 St.Wagon

See Falcon 2.3 Sedan, except for:

PRICES EX WORKS:	**pesos**
Standard 4+1-dr St. Wagon	**102,185**
De Luxe 4+1-dr St. Wagon	—

ENGINE 6 cylinders, in line; 188 cu in, 3,080 cc (3.68 x 2.94 in, 93.5 x 74.7 mm); compression ratio: 7.4:1; max power (SAE): 116 hp (85 kW) at 4,000 rpm; max torque (SAE): 176 lb ft, 24.3 km m (238 Nm) at 2,300 rpm; 37.7 hp/l (27.7 kW/l); 7 crankshaft bearings; camshafts: 1, side, timing chain; 1 Galileo or Argelite downdraught single barrel carburettor.

TRANSMISSION gears: 3, fully synchronized; ratios: I 2.990, II 1.750, III 1, rev 3.170; lever steering column.

PERFORMANCE power-weight ratio: 26 lb/hp (35.3 kg/kW), 11.8 kg/hp (16 kg/kW).

DIMENSIONS AND WEIGHT weight: 3,013 lb, 1,367 kg; fuel tank: 14.4 imp gal, 17.3 US gal, 65 l.

BODY estate car/st. wagon; 4+1 doors.

Falcon 3.6 Ghia Sedan

See Falcon 2.3 Sedan, except for:

PRICE EX WORKS: 120,340 pesos

ENGINE 6 cylinders, in line; 221 cu in, 3,621 cc (3.68 x 3.46 in, 93.5 x 87.9 mm); compression ratio: 8.2:1; max power (SAE): 132 hp (97 kW) at 4,000 rpm; max torque (SAE): 201 lb ft, 27.8 kg m (273 Nm) at 1,800 rpm; 36.6 hp/l (26.9 kW/l); 7 crankshaft bearings; camshafts: 1, side, timing chain; 1 Galileo or Argelite downdraught single barrel carburettor.

TRANSMISSION gearbox ratios: I 2.850, II 2.020, III 1.260, IV 1, rev 2.850; axle ratio: 2.870.

PERFORMANCE max speed: 97 mph, 156 km/h; power-weight ratio: 21.3 lb/hp (28.9 lb/kW), 9.7 kg/hp (13.2 kg/kW); acceleration: standing ¼ mile 19 sec, 0-50 mph (0-80 km/h) 13.8 sec; consumption: 21.5 m/imp gal, 17.9 m/US gal, 13.1 l x 100 km.

DIMENSIONS AND WEIGHT weight: 2,811 lb, 1,275 kg.

BODY bucket seats; vinyl roof.

Falcon Ghia SP

See Falcon 2.3 Sedan, except for:

PRICE EX WORKS: 122,218 pesos

ENGINE 6 cylinders, in line; 221 cu in, 3,621 cc (3.68 x 3.46 in, 93.5 x 87.9 mm); compression ratio: 8.1:1; max power (SAE): 166 hp (122 kW) at 4,500 rpm; max torque (SAE): 225 lb ft, 31 kg m (304 Nm) at 3,000 rpm; 46.1 hp/l (33.9 kW/l); 7 crankshaft bearings; camshafts: 1, side, timing chain.

TRANSMISSION gearbox ratios: I 2.850, II 2.020, III 1.260, IV 1, rev 2.850; axle ratio: 3.070; tyres: 175 R x 14.

PERFORMANCE max speed: 112 mph, 180 km/h; power-weight ratio: 17.3 lb/hp (23.5 lb/kW), 7.8 kg/hp (10.6 kg/kW); acceleration: standing ¼ mile 16.6 sec, 0-50 mph (0-80 km/h) 6.5 sec; consumption: 21.4 m/imp gal, 17.8 m/US gal, 13.2 l x 100 km.

BODY bucket seats; vinyl roof.

RENAULT ARGENTINA

4

ENGINE front, 4 stroke; 4 cylinders, vertical, in line; 62.2 cu in, 1,020 cc (2.56 x 2.64 in, 65 x 77 mm); compression ratio: 7.8:1; max power (DIN): 34 hp (25 kW) at 5,500 rpm; max torque (DIN): 47 lb ft, 6.5 kg m (64 Nm) at 2,500 rpm; 33 hp/l (24.5 kW/l); cast iron block, wet liners, light alloy head; 5 crankshaft bearings; valves: overhead, in line, push-rods and rockers; camshafts: 1, side; 1 Weber 28 ICP downdraught single barrel carburettor; fuel feed: mechanical pump; water-cooled.

TRANSMISSION driving wheels: front; clutch: single dry plate (diaphragm); gearbox: mechanical; gears: 4, fully synchronized; lever: on facia; final drive: hypoid bevel; axle ratio: 3.875; width of rims: 4"; tyres: 145 x 13.

PERFORMANCE max speed: over 75 mph, 120 km/h; power-weight ratio: 48.1 lb/hp (65.4 lb/kW), 21.8 kg/hp (29.7 kg/kW); consumption: 40.9 m/imp gal, 34.1 m/US gal, 6.9 l x 100 km.

CHASSIS platform; front suspension: independent, wishbones, longitudinal torsion bars, anti-roll bar, telescopic dampers; rear: independent, swinging longitudinal trailing arms, transverse torsion bars, telescopic dampers.

STEERING rack-and-pinion; turns lock to lock: 3.10.

BRAKES drum.

ELECTRICAL EQUIPMENT 12 V; 40 Ah battery; 28 A alternator; 2 headlamps.

DIMENSIONS AND WEIGHT wheel base: 96.06 in, 244 cm (right), 94.09 in, 239 cm (left); tracks: 50.39 in, 128 cm front, 49.21 in, 125 cm rear; length: 147.64 in, 375 cm; width: 59.45 in, 151 cm; height: 60.63 in, 154 cm; ground clearance: 8.07 in, 20.5 cm; weight: 1,636 lb, 742 kg; turning circle: 33 ft, 10 m; fuel tank: 5.7 imp gal, 6.9 US gal, 26 l.

BODY estate car/st. wagon; 4+1 doors; 4-5 seats, separate front seats; folding rear seat.

PRACTICAL INSTRUCTIONS fuel: 85 oct petrol.

6 GTL

ENGINE front, 4 stroke; 4 cylinders, vertical, in line; 85.4 cu in, 1,397 cc (2.99 x 3.03 in, 76 x 77 mm); compression ratio: 9:1; max power (DIN): 46 hp (34 kW) at 4,500 rpm; max torque (DIN): 75 lb ft, 10.4 kg m (102 Nm) at 2,000 rpm; 32.9 hp/l (24.2 kW/l); cast iron block, wet liners, light alloy head; 5 crankshaft bearings; valves: overhead, in line, push-rods and rockers; camshafts: 1, side; 1 Weber 30 ICF downdraught single barrel carburettor; fuel feed: mechanical pump; water-cooled, electric fan.

TRANSMISSION driving wheels: front; clutch: single dry plate (diaphragm); gearbox: mechanical; gears: 4, fully synchronized; lever: on facia; final drive: hypoid bevel; axle ratio: 3.180; width of rims: 4"; tyres: 145 x 13.

PERFORMANCE max speed: 78 mph, 125 km/h; power-weight ratio: 40.1 lb/hp (54.2 lb/kW), 18.2 kg/hp (24.6 kg/kW); consumption: 45.6 m/imp gal, 37.9 m/US gal, 6.2 l x 100 km.

CHASSIS platform; front suspension: independent, wishbones, longitudinal torsion bars, anti-roll bar, telescopic dampers; rear: independent, swinging longitudinal trailing arms, transverse torsion bars, anti-roll bar, telescopic dampers.

STEERING rack-and-pinion; turns lock to lock: 3.10.

BRAKES drum, rear compensator.

ELECTRICAL EQUIPMENT 12 V; 40 Ah battery; 28 A alternator; 2 headlamps.

DIMENSIONS AND WEIGHT wheel base: 96.06 in, 244 cm (right), 94.09 in, 239 cm (left); tracks: 50.39 in, 128 cm front, 49.21 in, 125 cm rear; length: 154.72 in, 393 cm; width: 59.05 in, 150 cm; height: 59.05 in, 150 cm; ground clearance: 8.27 in, 21 cm; weight: 1,841 lb, 835 kg; fuel tank: 7.9 imp gal, 9.5 US gal, 36 l.

RENAULT 18 GTX Sedan

6 GTL

BODY saloon/sedan; 4+1 doors; 4-5 seats, separate front seats; folding rear seat.

PRACTICAL INSTRUCTIONS fuel: 92 oct petrol.

12 TL

ENGINE front, 4 stroke; 4 cylinders, vertical, in line; 85.4 cu in, 1,397 cc (2.99 x 3.03 in, 76 x 77 mm); compression ratio: 8:1; max power (DIN): 57 hp (42 kW) at 5,000 rpm; max torque (DIN): 74 lb ft, 10.2 kg m (100 Nm) at 3,000 rpm; 40.8 hp/l (30 kW/l); cast iron block, wet liners, light alloy head; 5 crankshaft bearings; valves: overhead; 1 Carter CS 32-2067-S downdraught carburettor; fuel feed: mechanical pump; water-cooled.

TRANSMISSION driving wheels: front; clutch: single dry plate (diaphragm); gearbox: mechanical; gears: 4, fully synchronized; lever: central; final drive: hypoid bevel; axle ratio: 3.770; width of rims: 4.5"; tyres: 5.60 S x 13.

PERFORMANCE max speed: 87 mph, 140 km/h; power-weight ratio: 35.7 lb/hp (48.5 lb/kW), 16.2 kg/hp (22 kg/kW); consumption: 37.2 m/imp gal, 30.9 m/US gal, 7.6 l x 100 km.

CHASSIS integral; front suspension: independent, wishbones, anti-roll bar, coil springs, telescopic dampers; rear: rigid axle, trailing arms, A-bracket, anti-roll bar, coil springs, telescopic dampers.

STEERING rack-and-pinion.

BRAKES front disc, rear drum, dual circuit, servo.

ELECTRICAL EQUIPMENT 12 V; 40 Ah battery; 38 A alternator; 2 headlamps.

DIMENSIONS AND WEIGHT wheel base: 96.06 in, 244 cm; front and rear track: 51.57 in, 131 cm; length: 172.05 in, 437 cm; width: 64.56 in, 164 cm; height: 56.69 in, 144 cm; ground clearance: 6.70 in, 17 cm; weight: 2,033 lb, 922 kg; turning circle: 33 ft, 10 m; fuel tank: 9.9 imp gal, 11.9 US gal, 45 l.

BODY saloon/sedan; 4 doors; 5 seats, separate front seats.

PRACTICAL INSTRUCTIONS fuel: 85 oct petrol.

12 TS Break

See 12 TL, except for:

ENGINE compression ratio: 9.5:1; max power (DIN): 74 hp (54 kW) at 5,500 rpm; max torque (DIN): 81 lb ft, 11.2 kg m (110 Nm) at 3,500 rpm; 53 hp/l (39 kW/l); 1 Solex C 34 EIES2 downdraught twin barrel carburettor.

TRANSMISSION tyres: 165 SR x 13.

PERFORMANCE max speed: 96 mph, 155 km/h; power-weight ratio: 29.2 lb/hp (39.7 lb/kW), 13.2 kg/hp (18 kg/kW).

BRAKES dual circuit, servo.

DIMENSIONS AND WEIGHT length: 164.54 in, 418 cm; height: 63.39 in, 161 cm; ground clearance: 7.50 in, 19 cm; weight: 2,158 lb, 979 kg.

BODY estate car/st. wagon; 4+1 doors; folding rear seat.

OPTIONALS air-conditioning.

18 GTL Sedan

ENGINE front, 4 stroke; 4 cylinders, vertical, in line; 85.2 cu in, 1,397 cc (2.99 x 3.03 in, 76 x 77 mm); compression ratio: 9.5:1; max power (DIN): 77 hp (57 kW) at 5,500 rpm; max torque (DIN): 83 lb ft, 11.5 kg m (113 Nm) at 3,500 rpm; max engine rpm: 5,500; 55.1 hp/l (40.5 kW/l); cast iron block, light alloy head; 5 crankshaft bearings; valves: overhead, in line, push-rods and rockers; camshafts: 1, side; lubrication: gear pump, filter in sump, 5.6 imp pt, 6.8 US pt, 3.2 l; 1 Solex 32 EIS 2 downdraught twin barrel carburettor; fuel feed: mechanical pump; water-cooled, 11.4 imp pt, 13.7 US pt, 6.5 l.

TRANSMISSION driving wheels: front; clutch: single dry plate (diaphragm); gearbox: mechanical; gears: 4, fully synchronized; ratios: I 3.818, II 2.176, III 1.409, IV 0.971, rev 3.545; lever: central; final drive: hypoid bevel; axle ratio: 3.778; width of rims: 5.5"; tyres: 175 S x 13.

PERFORMANCE max speed: 98 mph, 157 km/h; power-weight ratio: 28.6 lb/hp (38.9 lb/kW), 13 kg/hp (17.7 kg/kW); carrying capacity: 1,014 lb, 460 kg; consumption: 38.2 m/imp gal, 31.8 m/US gal, 7.4 l x 100 km.

CHASSIS integral; front suspension: independent, wishbones, anti-roll bar, coil springs, telescopic dampers; rear: rigid axle, trailing arms, anti-roll bar, coil springs, telescopic dampers.

STEERING rack-and-pinion; turns lock to lock: 4.

BRAKES front disc, rear drum, dual circuit, rear compensator, servo; lining area: front 22.2 sq in, 143 sq cm, rear 66.4 sq in, 228 sq cm, total 86.8 sq in, 571 sq cm.

ELECTRICAL EQUIPMENT 12 V; 45 Ah battery; 55 A alternator; 2 headlamps.

DIMENSIONS AND WEIGHT wheel base: 96.10 in, 244 cm; tracks: 56.30 in, 143 cm front, 53.15 in, 134 cm rear; length: 175.98 in, 447 cm; width: 66.14 in, 168 cm; height: 55.91 in, 142 cm; weight: 2,205 lb, 1,000 kg; turning circle: 34.1 ft, 10.4 m; fuel tank: 11.7 imp gal, 14 US gal, 53 l.

BODY saloon/sedan; 4 doors; 5 seats, separate front seats.

PRACTICAL INSTRUCTIONS fuel: 98 oct petrol; oil: engine 5.6 imp pt, 6.8 US pt, 3.2 l, SAE W30, change every 4,600 miles, 7,500 km - gearbox and final drive 3.3 imp pt, 4 US pt, 1.9 l, SAE 80 EP, change every 9,300 miles, 15,000 km; greasing: none; tyre pressure: front 24 psi, 1.7 atm, rear 24 psi, 1.7 atm.

OPTIONALS 5-speed fully synchronized mechanical gearbox; air-conditioning; tinted glass.

18 GTX Sedan / Break

See 18 GTL Sedan, except for:

ENGINE 121.7 cu in, 1,995 cc (3.46 x 3.23 in, 88 x 82 mm); compression ratio: 8.7:1; max power (DIN): 103 hp (76 kW) at 5,700 rpm; max torque (DIN): 117 lb ft, 16.2 kg m (159 Nm) at 3,000 rpm; max engine rpm: 5,700; 51.6 hp/l (38.1 kW/l); light alloy block and head, wet liners, hemispherical combustion chambers; lubrication: gear pump, full flow filter, 9.2 imp pt, 11 US pt, 5.2 l; 1 Weber 32 DARA downdraught twin barrel carburettor; sealed circuit cooling, liquid, expansion tank, 17.6 imp pt, 21.1 US pt, 10 l.

TRANSMISSION (standard) gears: 5, fully synchronized; ratios: I 3.818, II 2.176, III 1.409, IV 1.030, V 0.861, rev 3.545; tyres: 185/70 x 13.

PERFORMANCE max speed: 106 mph, 170 km/h; power-weight ratio: 23.4 lb/hp (31.7 lb/kW), 10.6 kg/hp (14.4 kg/kW).

STEERING turns lock to lock: 2.80.

ELECTRICAL EQUIPMENT 70 A alternator.

DIMENSIONS AND WEIGHT weight: 2,408 lb, 1,092 kg.

BODY saloon/sedan, 4 doors - estate car/st. wagon, 4+1 doors; light alloy wheels; air-conditioning (standard); adjustable height of steering wheel.

PRACTICAL INSTRUCTIONS oil: engine 9.2 imp pt, 11 US pt, 5.2 l - gearbox and final drive 3.5 imp pt, 4.2 US pt, 2 l, change every 18,600 miles, 30,000 km; tyre pressure: front 27 psi, 1.9 atm, rear 30 psi, 2.1 atm.

Fuego GTX

See 18 GTL Sedan, except for:

ENGINE 121.7 cu in, 1,995 cc (3.46 x 3.23 in, 88 x 82 mm); compression ratio: 8.7:1; max power (DIN): 103 hp (76 kW) at 5,700 rpm; max torque (DIN): 117 lb ft, 16.2 kg m (159 Nm) at 3,000 rpm; max engine rpm: 5,700; 51.6 hp/l (38.1

RENAULT 6 GTL

RENAULT 12 TS Break

kW/l); light alloy block and head, wet liners, hemispherical combustion chambers; lubrication: gear pump, full flow filter, 9.2 imp pt, 11 US pt, 5.2 l; 1 Weber 32 DARA downdraught twin barrel carburettor; sealed circuit cooling, liquid, expansion tank, 17.6 imp pt, 21.1 US pt, 10 l.

TRANSMISSION (standard) gears: 5, fully synchronized; ratios: I 3.818, II 2.176, III 1.409, IV 1.030, V 0.861, rev 3.545; tyres: 185/70 x 13.

PERFORMANCE max speed: 115 mph, 185 km/h; power-weight ratio: 23.6 lb/hp (32 lb/kW), 10.7 kg/hp (14.5 kg/kW).

ELECTRICAL EQUIPMENT 70 A alternator.

DIMENSIONS AND WEIGHT length: 171.26 in, 435 cm; width: 66.54 in, 169 cm; height: 52.36 in, 133 cm; weight: 2,426 lb, 1,100 kg; turning circle: 33.5 ft, 10.2 m; fuel tank: 12.5 imp gal, 15 US gal, 57 l.

BODY coupé; 2 doors.

PRACTICAL INSTRUCTIONS oil: engine 9.2 imp pt, 11 US pt, 5.2 l - gearbox and final drive 3.5 imp pt, 4.2 US pt, 2 l, change every 18,600 miles, 30,000 km; tyre pressure: front 28 psi, 2 atm, rear 28 psi, 2 atm.

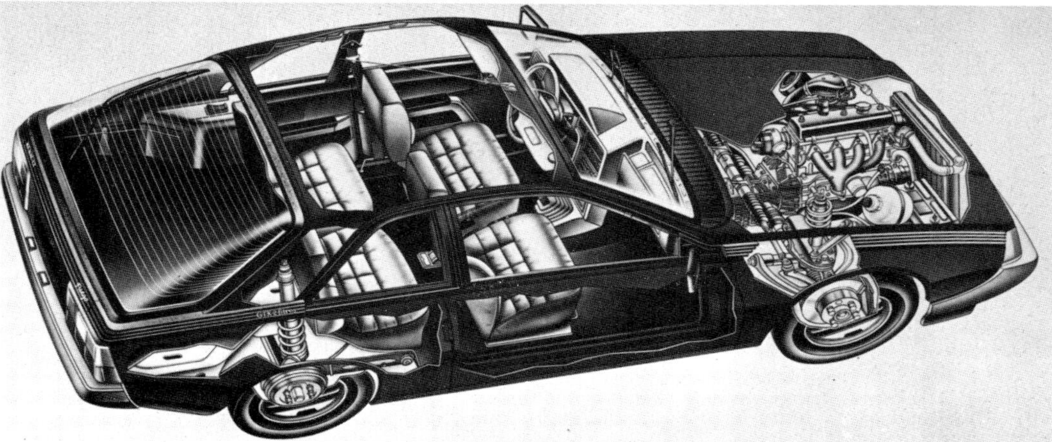

RENAULT Fuego GTX

SEVEL ARGENTINA

Fiat 147 Series

1 1100 CL5 2+1-dr Sedan
2 1300 TR5 2+1-dr Sedan

Power team:	Standard for:	Optional for:
53 hp	1	—
61 hp	2	—

53 hp power team

ENGINE Fiat, front, transverse, 4 stroke; 4 cylinders, in line; 68.1 cu in, 1,116 cc (3.15 x 2.19 in, 80 x 55.5 mm); compression ratio: 9.2:1; max power (DIN): 53 hp (39 kW) at 6,150 rpm; max torque (DIN): 59 lb ft, 8.1 kg m (79 Nm) at 3,200 rpm; max engine rpm: 6,500; 47.5 hp/l (34.9 kW/l); cast iron block, light alloy head; 5 crankshaft bearings; valves: overhead, thimble tappets; camshafts: 1, overhead, cogged belt; lubrication: gear pump, cartridge filter, 8.3 imp pt, 9.9 US pt, 4.7 l; 1 Weber 32 ICEV 21 or Solex C 32 DISA/1 downdraught single barrel carburettor; fuel feed: mechanical pump; water-cooled, expansion tank, 12.5 imp pt, 15 US pt, 7.1 l, electric thermostatic fan.

TRANSMISSION driving wheels: front; clutch: single dry plate (diaphragm); gearbox: mechanical; gears: 5, fully synchronized; ratios: I 3.583, II 2.235, III 1.454, IV 1.042, V 0.863, rev 3.714; lever: central; final drive: helical cylindrical; axle ratio: 4.417; width of rims: 4.5"; tyres: 145 SR x 13.

PERFORMANCE max speeds: (I) 25 mph, 40 km/h; (II) 43 mph, 70 km/h; (III) 65 mph, 105 km/h; (IV) and (V) 84 mph, 135 km/h; power-weight ratio: 34.1 lb/hp (46.4 lb/kW), 15.5 kg/hp (21 kg/kW); carrying capacity: 1,213 lb, 550 kg; acceleration: standing ¼ mile 20.4 sec; speed in top at 1,000 rpm: 15.8 mph, 25.4 km/h; consumption: 35.8 m/imp gal, 29.8 m/US gal, 7.9 l x 100 km at 75 mph, 120 km/h.

CHASSIS integral; front suspension: independent, by McPherson, coil spring/telescopic damper struts, lower wishbones, anti-roll bar; rear: independent, wishbones, transverse anti-roll leafspring, telescopic dampers.

STEERING rack-and-pinion; turns lock to lock: 3.50.

BRAKES front disc (diameter 8.94 in, 22.7 cm), rear drum, dual circuit, rear compensator; lining area: front 19.2 sq in, 124 sq cm, rear 33.3 sq in, 215 sq cm, total 52.6 sq in, 339 sq cm.

ELECTRICAL EQUIPMENT 12 V; 34 Ah battery; 33 A alternator; Marelli S146A distributor; 2 headlamps.

DIMENSIONS AND WEIGHT wheel base: 87.60 in, 222 cm; tracks: 50.71 in, 129 cm front, 51.30 in, 130 cm rear; length: 147.44 in, 374 cm; width: 60.83 in, 154 cm; height: 53.15 in, 135 cm; ground clearance: 5.10 in, 14 cm; weight: 1,808 lb, 820 kg; weight distribution: 50% front, 50% rear; turning circle: 39 ft, 9.1 m; fuel tank: 11.7 imp gal, 14 US gal, 53 l.

BODY saloon/sedan; 2+1 doors; 5 seats, separate front seats, reclining backrests.

OPTIONALS metallic spray; rear window wiper-washer; heated rear window; servo brake.

61 hp power team

See 53 hp power team, except for:

ENGINE 79.4 cu in, 1,301 cc (3.40 x 2.19 in, 86.4 x 55.5 mm); compression ratio: 9.1:1; max power (DIN): 61 hp (44 kW) at 5,800 rpm; max torque (DIN): 60 lb ft, 8.3 kg m (81 Nm) at 3,500 rpm; max engine rpm: 6,000; 46.9 hp/l (33.8 kW/l); lubrication: four-lobe rotary pump, 7.4 imp pt, 8.9 US pt, 4.2 l; 1 Weber 32 ICEV 26 downdraught single barrel carburettor.

PERFORMANCE max speed: 90 mph, 145 km/h; power-weight ratio: 29.6 lb/hp (41 lb/kW), 13.4 kg/hp (18.6 kg/kW); consumption: 36.7 m/imp gal, 30.5 m/US gal, 7.7 l x 100 km at 75 mph, 120 km/h.

BRAKES servo (standard).

BODY (standard) metallic spray, rear window wiper-washer and heated rear window; tinted glass.

Fiat Super Europa Series

1 1300 4-dr Sedan
2 1500 4-dr Sedan
3 1500 4+1-dr Familiar

Power team:	Standard for:	Optional for:
60 hp	1	—
82 hp	2,3	—

60 hp power team

ENGINE Fiat, front, transverse, 4 stroke; 4 cylinders, in line; 79.4 cu in, 1,301 cc (3.40 x 2.19 in, 86.4 x 55.5 mm); compression ratio: 9.1:1; max power (DIN): 60 hp (44 kW) at 6,000 rpm; max torque (DIN): 60 lb ft, 8.3 kg m (81 Nm) at 3,500 rpm; max engine rpm: 6,000; 46.9 hp/l (33.8 kW/l); cast iron block, light alloy head; 5 crankshaft bearings; valves: overhead, thimble tappets; camshafts: 1, overhead, cogged belt; lubrication: gear pump, full flow filter (cartridge), 7.9 imp pt, 9.5 US pt, 5 l; 1 Weber 32 ICEV 26 downdraught single barrel carburettor; fuel feed: mechanical pump; water-cooled, 11.4 imp pt, 13.7 US pt, 6.5 l, electric thermostatic fan.

TRANSMISSION driving wheels: front; clutch: single dry plate; gearbox: mechanical; gears: 5, fully synchronized; ratios: I 3.583, II 2.235, III 1.454, IV 1.042, V 0.863, rev 3.714; lever: central; final drive: cylindrical gears; axle ratio: 3.764; width of rims: 4.5"; tyres: 145 SR x 13.

PERFORMANCE max speed: over 90 mph, 145 km/h; power-weight ratio: 30.4 lb/hp (41.7 lb/kW), 13.8 kg/hp (18.9 kg/kW); consumption: 35.3 m/imp gal, 29.4 m/US gal, 8 l x 100 km.

CHASSIS integral; front suspension: independent, by McPherson, coil springs/telescopic damper struts, lower wishbones, anti-roll bar; rear: independent, single wide-based wishbones, transverse anti-roll leafsprings, telescopic dampers.

STEERING rack-and-pinion; turns lock to lock: 3.50.

BRAKES front disc (diameter 8.94 in, 22.7 cm), rear drum, rear compensator, servo; lining area: front 19.2 sq in, 124 sq cm, rear 33.5 sq in, 216 sq cm, total 52.7 sq in, 340 sq cm.

ELECTRICAL EQUIPMENT 12 V; 34 Ah battery; 38 A alternator; Garef-Marelli distributor; 2 headlamps.

DIMENSIONS AND WEIGHT wheel base: 96.46 in, 245 cm; front and rear track: 51.57 in, 131 cm; length: 154.33 in, 392 cm; width: 62.60 in, 159 cm; height: 55.91 in, 142 cm; ground clearance: 7.60 in, 19.3 cm; weight: 1,830 lb, 830 kg; weight distribution: 61.5% front, 38.5% rear; turning circle: 33.8 ft, 10.3 m; fuel tank: 8.4 imp gal, 10 US gal, 38 l.

BODY saloon/sedan; 4 doors; 5 seats, separate front seats.

PRACTICAL INSTRUCTIONS fuel: 97 oct petrol; oil: engine 7 imp pt, 8.4 US pt, 4 l, SAE 20W-40, change every 3,100 miles, 5,000 km - gearbox and final drive 5.6 imp pt, 6.7 US pt, 3.2 l, SAE 90 EP, change every 18,600 miles, 30,000 km; tyre pressure: front 25 psi, 1.8 atm, rear 24 psi, 1.7 atm.

OPTIONALS 165/70 SR x 13 tyres; air-conditioning; tinted glass; metallic spray.

82 hp power team

See 60 hp power team, except for:

ENGINE 91.4 cu in, 1,498 cc (3.40 x 2.52 in, 86.4 x 63.9 mm); compression ratio: 9.2:1; max power (DIN): 82 hp (60 kW) at 5,500 rpm; max torque (DIN): 87 lb ft, 12 kg m (118 Nm) at 3,000 rpm; 54.7 hp/l (40.1 kW/l); 1 Weber 32/34

SEVEL Fiat 147 1100 GL5 Sedan

82 HP POWER TEAM

DMTR 81/250 or Solex 32/34 CIC-1 downdraught twin barrel carburettor.

TRANSMISSION width of rims: 5.5"; tyres: 165 SR x 13.

PERFORMANCE max speed: 102 mph, 165 km/h; power-weight ratio: 22.3 lb/hp (30.5 lb/kW), 10.1 kg/hp (13.8 kg/kW); consumption: 33.2 m/imp gal, 27.7 m/US gal, 8.5 l x 100 km.

BODY saloon/sedan, 4 doors - estate car/st. wagon, 4+1 doors; luxury equipment; reclining front seats.

Peugeot 504 GR II

ENGINE Peugeot, front, slanted 45° to right, 4 stroke; 4 cylinders, in line; 120.3 cu in, 1,971 cc (3.46 x 3.19 in, 88 x 81 mm); compression ratio: 8.8:1; max power (DIN): 100 hp (72 kW) at 5,000 rpm; max torque (DIN): 119 lb ft, 16.4 kg m (161 Nm) at 3,000 rpm; max engine rpm: 5,500; 50.7 hp/l (36.5 kW/l); cast iron block with wet liners, light alloy head with hemispherical combustion chambers; 5 crankshaft bearings; valves: overhead, Vee-slanted, push-rods and rockers; camshafts: 1, side; lubrication: gear pump, metal gauze filter, 7 imp pt, 8.5 US pt, 4 l; 1 Zenith 35-40 INAT or Solex 32-35 TMIMAT downdraught twin barrel carburettor; fuel feed: mechanical pump; water-cooled, 13.7 imp pt, 16.5 US pt, 7.8 l, electromagnetic thermostatic fan.

TRANSMISSION driving wheels: rear; clutch: single dry plate (diaphragm); gearbox: mechanical; gears: 5, fully synchronized; ratios: I 3.592, II 2.088, III 1.368, IV 1, V 0.823, rev 3.634; lever: central; final drive: hypoid bevel; axle ratio: 3.890; width of rims: 5.5"; tyres: 185/70 SR x 14.

PERFORMANCE max speed: 104 mph, 168 km/h; power-weight ratio: 24.9 lb/hp (34.6 lb/kW), 11.3 kg/hp (15.7 kg/kW); carrying capacity: 1,169 lb, 530 kg; consumption: 30.1 m/imp gal, 25 m/US gal, 9.4 l x 100 km.

CHASSIS integral; front suspension: independent, by McPherson, coil springs/telescopic damper struts, lower wishbones, anti-roll bar; rear: rigid axle, trailing lower radius arms, upper oblique torque arms, coil springs, anti-roll bar, telescopic dampers.

STEERING rack-and-pinion, servo; turns lock to lock: 4.50.

BRAKES front disc (diameter 10.75 in, 27.3 cm), rear drum, dual circuit, rear compensator, servo; swept area: total 400.5 sq in, 2,583 sq cm.

ELECTRICAL EQUIPMENT 12 V; 45 Ah battery; 500 W alternator; transistorized ignition; 2 headlamps.

DIMENSIONS AND WEIGHT wheel base: 107.87 in, 274 cm; tracks: 55.91 in, 142 cm front, 52.36 in, 133 cm rear; length: 176.77 in, 449 cm; width: 66.54 in, 169 cm; height: 57.48 in, 146 cm; ground clearance: 6.30 in, 16 cm; weight: 2,492 lb, 1,130 kg; turning circle: 35.8 ft, 10.9 m; fuel tank: 11 imp gal, 13.2 US gal, 50 l.

BODY saloon/sedan; 4 doors; 5 seats, separate front seats, reclining backrests; tinted glass; heated rear window.

PRACTICAL INSTRUCTIONS fuel: 95 oct petrol; oil: engine 7 imp pt, 8.5 US pt, 4 l, SAE 20W-40, change every 3,100 miles, 5,000 km - gearbox 1.9 imp pt, 2.3 US pt, 1.1 l, SAE 20W-40, change every 6,200 miles, 10,000 km - final drive 1.5 imp pt, 2.1 US pt, 1.2 l, change every 6,200 miles, 10,000 km; greasing: every 3,100 miles, 5,000 km, 6 points; tappet clearances: inlet 0.004 in, 0.10 mm, exhaust 0.010 in, 0.25 mm; tyre pressure: front 21 psi, 1.5 atm, rear 26 psi, 1.8 atm.

OPTIONALS leather upholstery; metallic spray; air-conditioning; laminated windscreen.

SEVEL Fiat Super Europa 1300 Sedan

Peugeot 505 SR II

ENGINE Peugeot, front, slanted 45° to right, 4 stroke; 4 cylinders, in line; 120.3 cu in, 1,971 cc (3.46 x 3.19 in, 88 x 81 mm); compression ratio: 8.8:1; max power (DIN): 100 hp (72 kW) at 5,000 rpm; max torque (DIN): 119 lb ft, 16.4 kg m (161 Nm) at 3,000 rpm; max engine rpm: 5,500; 50.7 hp/l (36.5 kW/l); cast iron block with wet liners, light alloy head with hemispherical combustion chambers; 5 crankshaft bearings; valves: overhead, Vee-slanted, push-rods and rockers; camshafts: 1, side; lubrication: gear pump, metal gauze filter, 7 imp pt, 8.5 US pt, 4 l; 1 Zenith 35-40 INAT or Solex 32-35 TMIMAT downdraught twin barrel carburettor; fuel feed: mechanical pump; water-cooled, 12.5 imp pt, 15 US pt, 7.1 l, electromagnetic thermostatic fan.

TRANSMISSION driving wheels: rear; clutch: single dry plate (diaphragm); gearbox: mechanical; gears: 5, fully synchronized; ratios: I 3.592, II 2.088, III 1.368, IV 1, V 0.823, rev 3.634; lever: central; final drive: hypoid bevel; axle ratio: 3.890; width of rims: 5.5"; tyres: 185/70 SR x 14.

PERFORMANCE max speed: 104 mph, 168 km/h; power-weight ratio: 26.5 lb/hp (36.7 lb/kW), 12 kg/hp (16.7 kg/kW); carrying capacity: 1,058 lb, 480 kg; acceleration: standing ¼ mile 18.5 sec; speed in direct drive at 1,000 rpm: 20.1 mph, 32.3 km/h; consumption: 31 m/imp gal, 25.8 m/US gal, 9.1 l x 100 km at 75 mph, 120 km/h.

CHASSIS integral; front suspension: independent, by McPherson, coil springs/telescopic damper struts, lower wishbones, anti-roll bar; rear: rigid axle, trailing lower radius arms, upper oblique torque arms, coil springs, anti-roll bar, telescopic dampers.

STEERING rack-and-pinion, servo; turns lock to lock: 4.50.

BRAKES front disc (diameter 10.75 in, 27.3 cm), rear drum, dual circuit, rear compensator, servo; swept area: total 400.5 sq in, 2,583 sq cm.

ELECTRICAL EQUIPMENT 12 V; 45 Ah battery; 500 W alternator; transistorized ignition; 2 halogen headlamps.

DIMENSIONS AND WEIGHT wheel base: 107.87 in, 274 cm; tracks: 57.48 in, 146 cm front, 56.30 in, 143 cm rear; length: 180.31 in, 458 cm; width: 67.72 in, 172 cm; height: 57.09 in, 145 cm; ground clearance: 4.72 in, 12 cm; weight: 2,646 lb, 1,200 kg; weight distribution: 53% front, 47% rear, turning circle: 36.7 ft, 11.2 m; fuel tank: 11 imp gal, 13.2 US gal, 50 l.

BODY saloon/sedan; 4 doors; 5 seats, separate front seats, reclining backrests, headrests; tinted glass; air-conditioning; heated rear window.

PRACTICAL INSTRUCTIONS fuel: 95 oct petrol; oil: engine 7 imp pt, 8.5 US pt, 4 l, SAE 20W-40, change every 3,100 miles, 5,000 km - gearbox 1.9 imp pt, 2.3 US pt, 1.1 l, SAE 20W-40, change every 6,200 miles, 10,000 km - final drive 1.5 imp pt, 2.1 US pt, 1.2 l, change every 6,200 miles, 10,000 km; greasing: every 3,100 miles, 5,000 km, 6 points; tappet clearances: inlet 0.004 in, 0.10 mm, exhaust 0.010 in, 0.25 mm; tyre pressure: front 23 psi, 1.6 atm, rear 27 psi, 1.9 atm.

OPTIONALS metallic spray; leather upholstery.

SEVEL Peugeot 505 SR II

VOLKSWAGEN ARGENTINA

1500 W

PRICE EX WORKS: 99,000* pesos

ENGINE front, 4 stroke; 4 cylinders, vertical, in line; 91.4 cu in, 1,498 cc (3.39 x 2.53 in, 86.1 x 64.3 mm); compression ratio: 8:1; max power (DIN): 61 hp (45 kW) at 5,000 rpm; max torque (DIN): 78 lb ft, 10.8 kg m (106 Nm) at 2,800 rpm; max engine rpm: 5,400; 40.7 hp/l (30 kW/l); cast iron block and head; 5 crankshaft bearings; valves: overhead, in line, push-rods and rockers; camshafts: 1, side; lubrication: rotary pump, full flow filter, 7 imp pt, 8.5 US pt, 4 l; 1 Holley A-RX-7034A single barrel carburettor; fuel feed: mechanical pump; water-cooled, 13 imp pt, 15.6 US pt, 7.4 l.

TRANSMISSION driving wheels: rear; clutch: single dry plate (diaphragm); gearbox: mechanical; gears: 4, fully synchronized; ratios: I 3.317, II 2.029, III 1.366, IV 1, rev 3.450; lever: central; final drive: hypoid bevel; axle ratio: 3.540; width of rims: 4.5"; tyres: 5.60 S x 13.

PERFORMANCE max speeds: (I) 29 mph, 46 km/h; (II) 48 mph, 77 km/h; (III) 71 mph, 114 km/h; (IV) 90 mph, 145 km/h; power-weight ratio: 34.4 lb/hp (46.5 lb/kW), 15.6 kg/hp (21.1 kg/kW); carrying capacity: 882 lb, 400 kg; acceleration: 0-50 mph (0-80 km/h) 9.5 sec; speed in direct drive at 1,000 rpm: 18.6 mph, 30 km/h; consumption: 25.7 m/imp gal, 21.4 m/US gal, 11 l x 100 km.

CHASSIS integral; front suspension: independent, by McPherson, lower trailing links, coil springs, anti-roll bar, telescopic dampers; rear: rigid axle, lower trailing radius arms, upper oblique torque arms, coil springs, telescopic dampers.

STEERING rack-and-pinion; turns lock to lock: 3.66.

BRAKES front disc, rear drum, servo, dual circuit; lining area: front 15.7 sq in, 101 sq cm, rear 53.5 sq in, 345 sq cm, total 69.2 sq in, 446 sq cm.

ELECTRICAL EQUIPMENT 12 V; 48 Ah battery; 38 A alternator; Chrysler-TRIA distributor; 2 headlamps.

DIMENSIONS AND WEIGHT wheel base: 97.99 in, 249 cm; tracks: 50.98 in, 129 cm front, 51.26 in, 130 cm rear; length: 166.54 in, 423 cm; width: 62.52 in, 159 cm; height: 57.48 in, 146 cm; ground clearance: 6.10 in, 15.5 cm; weight: 2,095 lb, 950 kg; weight distribution: 54.2% front, 45.8% rear; turning circle: 31.8 ft, 9.7 m; fuel tank: 9.9 imp gal, 11.9 US gal, 45 l.

VOLKSWAGEN Gacel GL

BODY saloon/sedan; 4 doors, 5 seats, separate front seats, reclining backrests.

PRACTICAL INSTRUCTIONS fuel: 89-100 oct petrol; oil: engine 7 imp pt, 8.5 US pt, 4 l, change every 3,700 miles, 6,000 km - gearbox 3 imp pt, 3.6 US pt, 1.7 l - final drive 2.3 imp pt, 2.7 US pt, 1.3 l; greasing: 2 points; tyre pressure: front 24 psi, 1.7 atm, rear 26 psi, 1.8 atm.

OPTIONALS 155 SR x 13 tyres.

Gacel GL

PRICE EX WORKS: 125,400* pesos

ENGINE front, 4 stroke; 4 cylinders, in line; 96.9 cu in, 1,588 cc (3.13 x 3.15 in, 79.5 x 80 mm); compression ratio: 8.3:1; max power (DIN): 74 hp (54 kW) at 5,200 rpm; max torque (DIN): 88 lb ft, 12.1 kg m (119 Nm) at 2,600 rpm; max engine rpm: 6,300; 47.3 hp/l (34 kW/l); cast iron block, light alloy head; 5 crankshaft bearings; valves: overhead; camshafts: 1, overhead; lubrication: gear pump, 6.2 imp pt, 7.4 US pt, 3.5 l; fuel feed: mechanical pump; water-cooled, 9.9 imp pt, 11.8 US pt, 5.6 l, electric thermostatic fan.

TRANSMISSION driving wheels: front; clutch: single dry plate (diaphragm); gearbox: mechanical; gears: 4, fully synchronized; ratios: I 3.450, II 1.940, III 1.290, IV 0.910, rev 3.170; lever: central; final drive: spiral bevel; axle ratio: 4.110; width of rims: 5"; tyres: 155 SR x 13.

PERFORMANCE max speeds: (I) 28 mph, 45 km/h; (II) 50 mph, 80 km/h; (III) 75 mph, 121 km/h; (IV) 97 mph, 156 km/h; power-weight ratio: 25.4 lb/hp (34.6 lb/kW), 11.5 kg/hp (15.7 kg/kW); carrying capacity: 772 lb, 350 kg; acceleration: standing ¼ mile 18.6 sec, 0-50 mph (0-80 km/h) 8 sec; speed in top at 1,000 rpm: 17.5 mph, 28.1 km/h; consumption: 40.9 m/imp gal, 34.1 m/US gal, 6.9 l x 100 km at 50 mph, 80 km/h.

CHASSIS front suspension: independent, by McPherson, wishbones, double action coil springs/telescopic damper struts, anti-roll bar; rear: rigid axle, longitudinal tubular arms, progressively acting coil springs, double action telescopic dampers.

STEERING rack-and-pinion; turns lock to lock: 3.40.

BRAKES front disc, rear drum, servo; lining area: front 22.9 sq in, 148 sq cm, rear 21.2 sq in, 137 sq cm, total 44.1 sq in, 285 sq cm.

ELECTRICAL EQUIPMENT 12 V; 36 Ah battery; 420 W alternator; Chrysler-TRIA distributor; 2 headlamps.

DIMENSIONS AND WEIGHT wheel base: 92.91 in, 236 cm; tracks: 53.15 in, 135 cm front, 53.94 in, 137 cm rear; length: 162.60 in, 413 cm; width: 62.99 in, 160 cm; height: 53.54 in, 136 cm; ground clearance: 59.06 in, 15 cm; weight: 1,872 lb, 849 kg; weight distribution: 51% front, 49% rear; turning circle: 36.7 ft, 11.2 m; fuel tank: 12.1 imp gal, 14.5 US gal, 55 l.

BODY saloon/sedan; 4 doors, 5 seats, separate front seats, reclining backrests.

PRACTICAL INSTRUCTIONS fuel: 93 oct petrol; oil: engine 6.2 imp pt, 7.4 US pt, 3.5 l, SAE 30 SE, change every 4,700 miles, 7,500 km - gearbox and final drive 3 imp pt, 3.6 US pt, 1.7 l, SAE 80, no change recommended; spark plug: NGK BP5ES; tappet clearances (cold): inlet 0.008 in, 0.20 mm, exhaust 0.016 in, 0.40 mm; valve timing: 5°18' 33°20' 45°21' 6°36'; tyre pressure: front 24 psi, 1.7 atm, rear 26 psi, 1.8 atm.

OPTIONALS 54 Ah battery; 55 A or 666 W alternator; 175/70 SR x 13 tyres; light alloy wheels; air-conditioning; tinted glass; iodine headlamps; heated rear window.

1500 M 1.8 W

PRICE EX WORKS: 113,800* pesos

ENGINE front, 4 stroke; 4 cylinders, vertical, in line; 109.7 cu in, 1,798 cc (3.39 x 3.04 in, 86.1 x 77.2 mm); compression ratio: 8.6:1; max power (DIN): 76 hp (56 kW) at 5,000 rpm; max torque (DIN): 96 lb ft, 13.2 kg m (129 Nm) at 3,200 rpm; max engine rpm: 5,800; 42.3 hp/l (31.1 kW/l); cast iron block and head; 5 crankshaft bearings; valves: overhead, in line, push-rods and rockers; camshafts: 1, side; lubrication: rotary pump, full flow filter, 7 imp pt, 8.5 US pt, 4 l; 1 Holley A-RX-7035A single barrel carburettor; fuel feed: mechanical pump; water-cooled, 13 imp pt, 15.6 US pt, 7.4 l.

TRANSMISSION driving wheels: rear; clutch: single dry plate (diaphragm); gearbox: mechanical; gears: 4, fully synchronized; ratios: I 3.317, II 2.029, III 1.366, IV 1, rev 3.450; lever: central; final drive: hypoid bevel; axle ratio: 3.540; width of rims: 4.5"; tyres: 155 SR x 13.

PERFORMANCE max speeds: (I) 31 mph, 50 km/h; (II) 47 mph, 75 km/h; (III) 78 mph, 125 km/h; (IV) 93 mph, 149 km/h; power-weight ratio: 27.8 lb/hp (37.7 lb/kW), 12.6 kg/hp (17.1 kg/kW); carrying capacity: 882 lb, 400 kg; acceleration: 0-50 mph (0-80 km/h) 9.5 sec; speed in direct drive at 1,000 rpm: 21.7 mph, 35 km/h; consumption: 31.4 m/imp gal, 26.1 m/US gal, 9 l x 100 km.

CHASSIS integral; front suspension: independent, by McPherson, lower trailing links, coil springs, anti-roll bar, telescopic dampers; rear: rigid axle, lower trailing radius arms, upper oblique torque arms, coil springs, telescopic dampers.

STEERING rack-and-pinion; turns lock to lock: 3.66.

BRAKES front disc, rear drum, servo, dual circuit; lining area: front 15.7 sq in, 101 sq cm, rear 53.5 sq in, 345 sq cm, total 69.2 sq in, 446 sq cm.

ELECTRICAL EQUIPMENT 12 V; 48 Ah battery; 38 A alternator; Chrysler-TRIA distributor; 2 iodine headlamps.

DIMENSIONS AND WEIGHT wheel base: 97.99 in, 249 cm; tracks: 50.98 in, 129 cm front, 51.26 in, 130 cm rear; length: 166.54 in, 423 cm; width: 62.52 in, 159 cm; height: 55.91 in, 142 cm; ground clearance: 5.59 in, 14 cm; weight: 2,117 lb, 960 kg; weight distribution: 54.2% front, 45.8% rear; turning circle: 31.8 ft, 9.7 m; fuel tank: 9.9 imp gal, 11.9 US gal, 45 l.

BODY saloon/sedan; 4 doors; 5 seats, separate front seats, reclining backrests with built-in headrests.

PRACTICAL INSTRUCTIONS fuel: 89-100 oct petrol; oil: engine 7 imp pt, 8.5 US pt, 4 l, change every 3,700 miles, 6,000 km - gearbox 3 imp pt, 3.6 US pt, 1.7 l - final drive 2.3 imp pt, 2.7 US pt, 1.3 l; greasing: 2 points; tyre pressure: front 24 psi, 1.7 atm, rear 26 psi, 1.8 atm.

OPTIONALS Borg-Warner 45 automatic transmission with 4 ratios (I 3, II 1.940, III 1.350, IV 1, rev 4.690); heated rear window; air-conditioning.

1500 M 1.8 Rural W

See 1500 M 1.8 W, except for:

PRICE EX WORKS: 122,400* pesos

PERFORMANCE power-weight ratio: 29.5 lb/hp (40.1 lb/kW), 13.4 kg/hp (18.2 kg/kW).

CHASSIS rear suspension: 4 swinging links.

DIMENSIONS AND WEIGHT length: 169.29 in, 430 cm; height: 55.51 in, 141 cm; weight: 2,250 lb, 1,021 kg; weight distribution: 45.8% front, 54.2% rear.

BODY estate car/st. wagon; 4+1 doors.

VOLKSWAGEN 1500 M 1.8 Rural W

CHEVROLET BRAZIL

Chevette Series

2-dr Sedan
4-dr Sedan
2+1-dr Hatchback Sedan
SL 2-dr Sedan
SL 4-dr Sedan
SL 2+1-dr Hatchback Sedan
Marajó 2+1-dr Caravan
Marajó SL 2+1-dr Caravan

Power team:	Standard for:	Optional for:
62 hp	all	—
70 hp	—	all
72 hp (alcohol)	—	all
73 hp	—	all

62 hp power team

ENGINE front, 4 stroke; 4 cylinders, in line; 85.3 cu in, 1,398 cc (3.23 x 2.61 in, 82 x 66.2 mm); compression ratio: 8.5:1; max power (SAE): 62 hp (46 kW) at 5,600 rpm; max torque (SAE): 76 lb ft, 10.5 kg m (103 Nm) at 3,200 rpm; max engine rpm: 6,500; 44.3 hp/l (32.9 kW/l); cast iron block and head; 5 crankshaft bearings; valves: overhead, rockers; camshafts: 1, overhead, cogged belt; lubrication: gear pump, full flow filter, 6.2 imp pt, 7.4 US pt, 3.5 l; 1 Solex or Wecarbras downdraught single barrel carburettor; fuel feed: mechanical pump; water-cooled, 12.3 imp pt, 14.8 US pt, 7 l.

62 HP POWER TEAM

TRANSMISSION driving wheels: rear; clutch: single dry plate (diaphragm); gearbox: mechanical; gears: 4, fully synchronized; ratios: I 3.746, II 2.157, III 1.378, IV 1, rev 3.815; lever: central; final drive: hypoid bevel; axle ratio: 4.100; width of rims: 5"; tyres: 165 x 13.

PERFORMANCE max speed: 88 mph, 140 km/h; power-weight ratio: 2-dr sedans 30.4 lb/hp (41 lb/kW), 13.8 kg/hp (18.6 kg/kW); carrying capacity: 915 lb, 415 kg; speed in direct drive at 1,000 rpm: 16 mph, 25.7 km/h; consumption: 39.3 m/imp gal, 32.7 m/US gal, 7.2 l x 100 km.

CHASSIS integral; front suspension: independent, wishbones, coil springs, anti-roll bar, telescopic dampers; rear: rigid axle, twin trailing radius arms, transverse linkage bar, coil springs, anti-roll bar, telescopic dampers.

STEERING rack-and-pinion; turns lock to lock: 3.50.

BRAKES front disc (diameter 9.21 in, 23.4 cm), rear drum, servo; swept area: total 248 sq in, 1,600 sq cm.

ELECTRICAL EQUIPMENT 12 V; 36 Ah battery; 28 A alternator; Arno Bosch distributor; 2 headlamps.

DIMENSIONS AND WEIGHT wheel base: 94.09 in, 239 cm; front and rear track: 51.18 in, 130 cm; length: Sedan and Marajó models 164.96 in, 419 cm - hatchback sedans 155.90 in, 396 cm; width: 61.81 in, 157 cm; height: 51.97 in, 132 cm - Marajó models 54.33 in, 138 cm; ground clearance: 5.51 in, 14 cm; weight: 2-dr sedans 1,883 lb, 854 kg - 4-dr sedans 1,932 lb, 876 kg - hatchback sedans 1,916 lb, 869 kg - Marajó models 1,987 lb, 901 kg; turning circle: 32.1 ft, 9.8 m; fuel tank: 9.9 imp gal, 11.9 US gal, 45 l - Marajó models 13.6 imp gal, 16.4 US gal, 62 l.

BODY saloon/sedan, 2, 2+1 or 4 doors - hatchback, 2+1 doors - estate car/st. wagon, 2+1 doors; 5 seats, separate front seats, reclining backrests, built-in headrests; luxury equipment; (for hatchback sedans only) folding rear seat.

PRACTICAL INSTRUCTIONS fuel: 73-82 oct petrol; oil: engine 6.2 imp pt, 7.4 US pt, 3.5 l, SAE 20 W-40, change every 4,600 miles, 7,500 km - gearbox 2.5 imp pt, 3 US pt, 1.4 l, SAE 90, change every 18,600 miles, 30,000 km - final drive 1.4 imp pt, 1.7 US pt, 0.8 l, SAE 90, change every 28,000 miles, 45,000 km; greasing: none; tappet clearances: inlet 0.010 in, 0.25 mm, exhaust 0.010 in, 0.25 mm; valve timing: 34° 86° 66° 54°; tyre pressure: front 17 psi, 1.2 atm, rear 21 psi, 1.5 atm - Marajó models front 19 psi, 1.3 atm, rear 23 psi, 1.6 atm.

OPTIONALS 5-speed fully synchronized mechanical gearbox; heated rear window; tinted glass; air-conditioning; 175/70 SR x 13 tyres; (for Marajó models only) rear window wiper-washer and metallic spray.

70 hp power team

See 62 hp power team, except for:

ENGINE 97.6 cu in, 1,599 cc (3.23 x 2.98 in, 82 x 75.7 mm); max power (SAE): 70 hp (52 kW) at 5,600 rpm; max torque (SAE): 86 lb ft, 11.8 kg m (116 Nm) at 3,200 rpm; 43.8 hp/l (32.5 kW/l).

TRANSMISSION gears: 5, fully synchronized; ratios: I 3.746, II 2.157, III 1.378, IV 1, V 0.840, rev 3.815; axle ratio: 3.900.

PERFORMANCE max speed: 90 mph, 145 km/h; power-weight ratio: 2-dr sedans 26.9 lb/hp (36.1 lb/kW), 12.2 kg/hp (16.4 kg/kW).

PRACTICAL INSTRUCTIONS tyre pressure: front 20 psi, 1.4 atm, rear 24 psi, 1.7 atm - Marajó models rear 26 psi, 1.8 atm.

72 hp (alcohol) power team

See 62 hp power team, except for:

ENGINE alcohol; 97.6 cu in, 1,599 cc (3.23 x 2.98 in, 82 x 75.7 mm); max power (SAE): 72 hp (53 kW) at 5,600 rpm; max torque (SAE): 89 lb ft, 12.3 kg m (121 Nm) at 3,200 rpm; 45 hp/l (33.1 kW/l).

TRANSMISSION gears: 5, fully synchronized; ratios: I 3.746, II 2.157, III 1.378, IV 1, V 0.840, rev 3.815; axle ratio: 3.900; width or rims: 5.5"; tyres: 175/70 SR x 13 (standard).

PERFORMANCE max speed: 90 mph, 145 km/h; power-weight ratio: 2-dr sedans 27.1 lb/hp (36.8 lb/kW), 12.3 kg/hp (16.7 kg/kW).

ELECTRICAL EQUIPMENT 32 A alternator.

DIMENSIONS AND WEIGHT length: 157 in, 399 cm; weight: 2-dr sedans 1,956 lb, 887 kg.

BODY rear spoiler.

PRACTICAL INSTRUCTIONS tyre pressure: front 20 psi, 1.4 atm, rear 24 psi, 1.7 atm - Marajó models rear 26 psi, 1.8 atm.

OPTIONALS heated rear window; tinted glass; folding rear seat; electromagnetic fan; aluminium wheels; rear window wiper-washer.

CHEVROLET Chevette Marajó SL Caravan

73 hp power team

See 62 hp power team, except for:

ENGINE 97.6 cu in, 1,599 cc (3.23 x 2.98 in, 82 x 75.7 mm); max power (SAE): 73 hp (54 kW) at 5,600 rpm; max torque (SAE): 90 lb ft, 12.4 kg m (122 Nm) at 3,200 rpm; 45.7 hp/l (33.8 kW/l); 1 downdraught twin barrel carburettor.

TRANSMISSION gears: 5, fully synchronized; ratios: I 3.746, II 2.157, III 1.378, IV 1, V 0.840, rev 3.815; axle ratio: 3.900.

PERFORMANCE max speed: 93 mph, 150 km/h; power-weight ratio: 2-dr sedans 26.9 lb/hp (36.2 lb/kW), 12.2 kg/hp (16.4 kg/kW).

DIMENSIONS AND WEIGHT weight: 2-dr sedans 1,956 lb, 887 kg.

PRACTICAL INSTRUCTIONS tyre pressure: front 20 psi, 1.4 atm, rear 24 psi, 1.7 atm - Marajó models rear 26 psi, 1.8 atm.

Monza Series

2-dr Notchback Sedan
2+1-dr Hatchback Coupé
4-dr Notchback Sedan
SL-E 2-dr Notchback Sedan

Power team:	Standard for:	Optional for:
73 hp	all	—
72 hp (alcohol)	—	all
84 hp	—	all

73 hp power team

ENGINE front, 4 stroke; 4 cylinders, transverse, in line; 97.5 cu in, 1,598 cc (3.14 x 3.12 in, 80 x 79.5 mm); compression ratio: 8:1; max power (SAE): 73 hp (54 kW) at 5,400 rpm; max torque (SAE): 89 lb ft, 12.3 kg m (121 Nm) at 3,000 rpm; max engine rpm: 7,000-7,500; 45.7 hp/l (33.8 kW/l); cast iron block, light alloy head; 5 crankshaft bearings; valves: overhead, rockers; camshafts: 1, overhead, cogged belt; lubrication: gear pump, full flow filter, 6.2 imp pt, 7.4 US pt, 3.5 l; 1 Solex or Wecarbras downdraught single barrel carburettor; fuel feed: mechanical pump; water-cooled, 12.3 imp pt, 14.8 US pt, 7 l.

TRANSMISSION driving wheels: front; clutch: single dry plate (diaphragm); gearbox: mechanical; gears: 4, fully synchronized; ratios: I 3.420, II 1.950, III 1.280, IV 0.890, rev 3.330; lever: central; final drive: spur gears; axle ratio: 4.190; width of rims: 5.5"; tyres: 185/70 SR x 13.

PERFORMANCE max speed: 94 mph, 151 km/h; power-weight ratio: 2-dr Notchback Sedan 30.4 lb/hp (41.2 lb/kW), 13.8 kg/hp (18.7 kg/kW); carrying capacity: 1,091 lb, 495 kg; acceleration: 0-50 mph (0-80 km/h) 10 sec; consumption: 40.9 m/imp gal, 34.1 m/US gal, 6.9 l x 100 km.

CHASSIS integral; front suspension: independent, by McPherson, coil springs, control arms, anti-roll bar, telescopic dampers; rear: rigid axle, transverse linkage bar, coil springs, telescopic dampers.

STEERING rack-and-pinion; turns lock to lock: 4.30.

BRAKES front disc, rear drum, servo; swept area: front 164.3 sq in, 1,060 sq cm, rear 87.6 sq in, 565 sq cm, total 251.9 sq in, 1,625 sq cm.

ELECTRICAL EQUIPMENT 12 V; 36 Ah battery; 35 A alternator; Arno-Bosch distributor; 2 headlamps.

DIMENSIONS AND WEIGHT wheel base: 101.18 in, 257 cm; front and rear track: 55.51 in, 141 cm; length: 167.72 in, 426 cm - 4-dr Notchback Sedan 172.05 in, 437 cm; width: 65.75 in, 167 cm; height: 53.15 in, 135 cm - 4-dr Notchback Sedan 53.45 in, 136 cm; ground clearance: 5.51 in, 14 cm; weight: 2-dr Notchback Sedan 2,227 lb, 1,010 kg - Hatchback Coupé 2,238 lb, 1,015 kg - 4-dr Notchback Sedan, 2,271 lb, 1,030 kg - SL-E Notchback Sedan 2,282 lb, 1,035 kg; weight distribution: 60% front, 40% rear; turning circle: 35.7 ft, 10.9 m; fuel tank: 13.4 imp gal, 16.1 US gal, 61 l.

BODY saloon/sedan, 2 or 4 doors - coupé, 2+1 doors; 5 seats, separate front seats.

PRACTICAL INSTRUCTIONS fuel: 73 oct petrol; oil: engine 6.2 imp pt, 7.4 US pt, 3.5 l, SAE 15W-50, change every 6,200 miles, 10,000 km - gearbox and final drive 3.5 imp pt, 4.2 US pt, 2 l, SAE 80, no change recommended; greasing:

CHEVROLET Monza SL-E Notchback Sedan

CHEVROLET Diplomata Coupé

none; valve timing: 29° 80° 68° 42°; tyre pressure: front 29 psi, 1.9 atm, rear 31 psi, 2.3 atm.

OPTIONALS 5-speed fully synchronized mechanical gearbox (I 3.420, II 1.950, III 1.280, IV 0.890, V 0.710, rev 3.330).

72 hp (alcohol) power team

See 73 hp power team, except for:

ENGINE alcohol; compression ratio: 12:1; max power (SAE): 72 hp (53 kW) at 5,200 rpm; max torque (SAE): 91 lb ft, 12.6 kg m (124 Nm) at 2,600 rpm; 45.1 hp/l (33.2 kW/l).

PERFORMANCE max speed: 93 mph, 150 km/h; power-weight ratio: 2-dr Notchback Sedan 30.9 lb/hp (42.1 lb/kW), 14 kg/hp (19.1 kg/kW); consumption: 34 m/imp gal, 28.3 m/US gal, 8.3 l x 100 km.

ELECTRICAL EQUIPMENT 42 A battery; 45 A alternator.

PRACTICAL INSTRUCTIONS fuel: 89 oct petrol; valve timing: 11° 71° 49° 33°.

84 hp power team

See 73 hp power team, except for:

ENGINE gas; 109.6 cu in, 1,796 cc (3.33 x 3.12 in, 84.8 x 79.5 mm); max power (SAE): 84 hp (62 kW) at 5,600 rpm; max torque (SAE): 100 lb ft, 13.8 kg m (135 Nm) at 3,200 rpm; 46.8 hp/l (34.5 kW/l).

PERFORMANCE max speed: 99 mph, 159 km/h; power-weight ratio: 2-dr Notchback Sedan 26.5 lb/hp (35.9 lb/kW), 12 kg/hp (16.3 kg/kW); consumption: 39.8 m/imp gal, 33.1 m/US gal, 7.1 l x 100 km.

Opala Series

4-dr Sedan
2-dr Coupé
2+1-dr Caravan

Power team:	Standard for:	Optional for:
80 hp	all	—
76 hp (alcohol)	—	all
116 hp	—	all

80 hp power team

ENGINE front, 4 stroke; 4 cylinders, in line; 151 cu in, 2,470 cc (4 x 3 in, 101.6 x 76.2 mm); compression ratio: 7.5:1; max power (SAE): 80 hp (59 kW) at 4,400 rpm; max torque (SAE): 120 lb ft, 16.6 kg m (163 Nm) at 2,400 rpm; max engine rpm: 6,500; 32.4 hp/l (23.9 kW/l); cast iron block and head; 5 crankshaft bearings; valves: overhead, push-rods and rockers, hydraulic tappets; camshafts: 1, side; lubrication: gear pump, full flow filter, 6.2 imp pt, 7.4 US pt, 3.5 l; 1 Wecarbras downdraught single barrel carburettor; fuel feed: mechanical pump; water-cooled, 15.1 imp pt, 18.2 US pt, 8.6 l, electromagnetic fan.

TRANSMISSION driving wheels: rear; clutch: single dry plate; gearbox: mechanical; gears: 4, fully synchronized; ratios: I 3.400, II 2.160, III 1.380, IV 1, rev 3.810; lever: steering column; final drive: hypoid bevel; axle ratio: 3.540; width of rims: 6"; tyres: 175 SR x 14.

PERFORMANCE max speed: 93 mph, 150 km/h - Caravan 87 mph, 140 km/h; power-weight ratio: Sedan 30.9 lb/hp (41.9 lb/kW), 14 kg/hp (19 kg/kW); carrying capacity: 1,091 lb, 495 kg; speed in direct drive at 1,000 rpm: 24.1 mph, 38.8 km/h; consumption: 22.6 m/imp gal, 18.8 m/US gal, 12.5 l x 100 km.

CHASSIS integral; front suspension: independent, wishbones, coil springs, anti-roll bar, telescopic dampers; rear: rigid axle, longitudinal torsion bars, transverse linkage bar, coil springs, anti-roll bar, telescopic dampers.

STEERING worm and roller; turns lock to lock: 3.75.

BRAKES front disc, internal radial fins, rear drum, servo.

ELECTRICAL EQUIPMENT 12 V; 45 Ah battery; 32 A alternator; Arno-Bosch distributor; 2 headlamps.

DIMENSIONS AND WEIGHT wheel base: 105.12 in, 267 cm; tracks: 56.30 in, 143 cm front, 55.51 in, 141 cm rear; length: 184.25 in, 468 cm - Caravan 183.07 in, 465 cm; width: 68.90 in, 175 cm; height: Sedan 54.72 in, 139 cm - Coupé 53.54 in, 136 cm - Caravan 54.72 in, 139 cm; ground clearance: 7.09 in, 18 cm; weight: Sedan 2,470 lb, 1,120 kg - Coupé 2,467 lb, 1,119 kg - Caravan 2,514 lb, 1,140 kg; turning circle: 37.1 ft, 11.3 m; fuel tank: 14.3 imp gal, 17.2 US gal, 65 l.

BODY saloon/sedan, 4 doors - coupé, 2 doors - estate car/st. wagon, 2+1 doors; 6 seats, bench front seats; (for Caravan only) folding rear seat.

PRACTICAL INSTRUCTIONS fuel: 73 oct petrol; oil: engine 6.2 imp pt, 7.4 US pt, 3.5 l, SAE 20W-40, change every 4,700 miles, 7,500 km - gearbox 2.1 imp pt, 2.5 US pt, 1.2 l, SAE 90, change every 18,600 miles, 30,000 km - final drive 1.3 imp pt, 2.1 US pt, 0.9 l, change every 28,000 miles, 45,000 km; greasing: none; valve timing: 33° 81° 76° 38°; tyre pressure: front 21 psi, 1.5 atm, rear 23 psi, 1.6 atm - Caravan rear 26 psi, 1.8 atm.

OPTIONALS 3- or 5-speed fully synchronized mechanical gearbox; power steering; separate front seats, reclining backrests; air-conditioning; tinted glass; metallic spray; heater; electric rear window; 195/70 SR x 14 tyres; rev counter; rear window wiper-washer.

76 hp (alcohol) power team

See 80 hp power team, except for:

ENGINE alcohol; compression ratio 10.5:1; max power (SAE): 76 hp (56 kW) at 4,000 rpm; max torque (SAE): 123 lb ft, 17 kg m (167 Nm) at 2,000 rpm; 30.8 hp/l (22.7 kW/l); 1 downdraught twin barrel carburettor.

116 hp power team

See 80 hp power team, except for:

ENGINE 6 cylinders, in line; 250 cu in, 4,093 cc (3.87 x 3.53 in, 98.4 x 89.7 mm); max power (SAE): 116 hp (85 kW) at 4,200 rpm; max torque (SAE): 192 lb ft, 26.5 kg m (260 Nm) at 2,200 rpm; max engine rpm: 6,000; 28.3 hp/l (20.8 kW/l); 7 crankshaft bearings; lubrication: 8.8 imp pt, 10.6 US pt, 5 l; 1 Wecarbras downdraught twin barrel carburettor; cooling: 18 imp pt, 21.6 US pt, 10.2 l.

TRANSMISSION gearbox ratios: I 3.070, II 2.020, III 1.390, IV 1, rev 3.570; axle ratio: 3.080.

PERFORMANCE max speed: about 106 mph, 170 km/h; power-weight ratio: Sedan 22.3 lb/hp (30.4 lb/kW), 10.1 kg/hp (13.8 kg/kW); speed in direct drive at 1,000 rpm: 21.4 mph, 34 km/h; consumption: 18.2 m/imp gal, 15.2 m/US gal, 15.5 l x 100 km.

DIMENSIONS AND WEIGHT weight: Sedan 2,580 lb, 1,170 kg - Coupé 2,578 lb, 1,169 kg - Caravan 2,624 lb, 1,190 kg.

PRACTICAL INSTRUCTIONS oil: engine 8.8 imp pt, 10.6 US pt, 5 l.

OPTIONALS 3-speed fully synchronized mechanical gearbox; "Automatic" automatic transmission, hydraulic torque converter and planetary gears with 3 ratios (I 2.310, II 1.460, III 1, rev 1.850), max ratio of converter at stall 2.10.

Diplomata Series

4-dr Sedan
2-dr Coupé

Power team:	Standard for:	Optional for:
84 hp	both	—
76 hp (alcohol)	—	both
116 hp	—	both

84 hp power team

ENGINE front, 4 stroke; 4 cylinders, in line; 151 cu in, 2,470 cc (4 x 3 in, 101.6 x 76.2 mm); compression ratio: 7.5:1; max power (SAE): 84 hp (62 kW) at 4,600 rpm; max torque (SAE): 120 lb ft, 16.6 kg m (163 Nm) at 2,400 rpm; max engine rpm: 6,500; 34 hp/l (25.1 kW/l); cast iron block and head; 5 crankshaft bearings; valves: overhead, push-rods and rockers, hydraulic tappets; camshafts: 1, side; lubrication: gear pump, full flow filter, 6.2 imp pt, 7.4 US pt, 3.5 l; 1 Wecarbras downdraught twin barrel carburettor; fuel feed: mechanical pump; water-cooled, 15.1 imp pt, 18.2 US pt, 8.6 l.

TRANSMISSION driving wheels: rear; clutch: single dry plate; gearbox: mechanical; gears: 4, fully synchronized; ratios: I 3.400, II 2.160, III 1.380, IV 1, rev 3.810; lever: central; final drive: hypoid bevel; axle ratio: 3.540; width of rims: 6"; tyres: 175 SR x 14.

PERFORMANCE max speed: 93 mph, 150 km/h; power-weight ratio: Sedan 31.3 lb/hp (42.3 lb/kW), 14.2 kg/hp (19.2 kg/kW); carrying capacity: 1,091 lb, 495 kg; speed in direct drive at 1,000 rpm: 25.7 mph, 41.3 km/h; consumption: 22.6 m/imp gal, 18.8 m/US gal, 12.5 l x 100 km.

CHASSIS integral; front suspension: independent, wishbones, coil springs, anti-roll bar, telescopic dampers; rear: rigid axle, longitudinal torsion bars, transverse linkage bar, coil springs, anti-roll bar, telescopic dampers.

STEERING worm and roller; turns lock to lock: 3.75.

BRAKES front disc, internal radial fins, rear drum, servo.

ELECTRICAL EQUIPMENT 12 V; 45 Ah battery; 55 A alternator; Arno-Bosch distributor; 2 headlamps.

DIMENSIONS AND WEIGHT wheel base: 105.12 in, 267 cm; tracks: 56.30 in, 143 cm front, 55.51 in, 141 cm rear, length: 186.61 in, 474 cm; width: 69.68 in, 177 cm; height: Sedan 54.72 in, 139 cm - Coupé 53.54 in, 136 cm; ground clearance: 7.09 in, 18 cm; weight: Sedan 2,631 lb, 1,193 kg - Coupé 2,613 lb, 1,185 kg; turning circle: 37.1 ft, 11.3 m; fuel tank: 14.3 imp gal, 17.2 US gal, 65 l.

BODY saloon/sedan, 4 doors - coupé, 2 doors; 5 seats, separate front seats, reclining backrests.

PRACTICAL INSTRUCTIONS fuel: 73 oct petrol; oil: engine 6.2 imp pt, 7.4 US pt, 3.5 l, SAE 20W-40, change every 4,700 miles, 7,500 km - gearbox 2.1 imp pt, 2.5 US pt, 1.2 l, SAE 90, change every 18,600 miles, 30,000 km - final drive 1.3 imp pt, 2.1 US pt, 0.9 l, change every 28,000 miles, 45,000 km; greasing: none; valve timing: 33° 81° 76° 38°; tyre pressure: front 23 psi, 1.6 atm, rear 26 psi, 1.8 atm.

OPTIONALS 3- and 5-speed fully synchronized mechanical gearbox; vinyl roof; 195/70 SR x 14 tyres; rev counter.

76 hp (alcohol) power team

See 84 hp power team, except for:

ENGINE alcohol; compression ratio: 10.5:1; max power (SAE): 76 hp (56 kW) at 4,000 rpm; max torque (SAE): 123 lb ft, 17 kg m (167 Nm) at 2,000 rpm; 30.8 hp/l (22.7 kW/l).

116 hp power team

See 84 hp power team, except for:

ENGINE 6 cylinders, in line; 250 cu in, 4,093 cc (3.87 x 3.53 in, 98.4 x 89.7 mm); max power (SAE): 116 hp (85 kW) at 4,200 rpm; max torque (SAE): 192 lb ft, 26.5 kg m (260 Nm) at 2,200 rpm; max engine rpm: 6,000; 28.3 hp/l (20.8 kW/l); 7 crankshaft bearings; lubrication: 8.8 imp pt, 10.6 US pt, 5 l; cooling: 18.5 imp pt, 22.2 US pt, 10.5 l.

TRANSMISSION gearbox ratios: I 3.070, II 2.020, III 1.390, IV 1, rev 3.570; axle ratio: 3.080; tyres: 195/70 SR x 14.

PERFORMANCE max speed: about 106 mph, 170 km/h; power-weight ratio: Sedan 23.6 lb/hp (32.2 lb/kW), 10.7 kg/hp (14.6 kg/kW); speed in direct drive at 1,000 rpm: 21.4 mph, 34 km/h; consumption: 18.2 m/imp gal, 15.2 m/US gal, 15.5 l x 100 km.

DIMENSIONS AND WEIGHT weight: Sedan 2,741 lb, 1,243 kg - Coupé 2,723 lb, 1,235 kg.

PRACTICAL INSTRUCTIONS oil: engine 8.8 imp pt, 10.6 US pt, 5 l.

116 HP POWER TEAM

OPTIONALS 3- and 5-speed fully synchronized mechanical gearbox; "Automatic" automatic transmission, hydraulic torque converter and planetary gears with 3 ratios (I 2.310, II 1.460, III 1, rev 1.850), max ratio of converter at stall 2.10.

Comodoro Series

4-dr Sedan
2-dr Coupé
2+1-dr Caravan

Power team:	Standard for:	Optional for:
80 hp	all	—
76 hp (alcohol)	—	all
116 hp	—	all

80 hp power team

ENGINE front, 4 stroke; 4 cylinders, in line; 151 cu in, 2,470 cc (4 x 3 in, 101.6 x 76.2 mm); compression ratio: 7.5:1; max power (SAE): 80 hp (59 kW) at 4,400 rpm; max torque (SAE): 120 lb ft, 16.6 kg m (163 Nm) at 2,400 rpm; max engine rpm: 6,500; 32.4 hp/l (23.9 kW/l); cast iron block and head; 5 crankshaft bearings; valves: overhead, in line, push-rods and rockers, hydraulic tappets; camshafts: 1, side; lubrication: gear pump, full flow filter, 6.3 imp pt, 7.6 US pt, 3.6 l; 1 Wecarbras downdraught single barrel carburettor; fuel feed: mechanical pump; water-cooled, 18 imp pt, 21.6 US pt, 10.2 l, electromagnetic fan.

TRANSMISSION driving wheels: rear; clutch: single dry plate; gearbox: mechanical; gears: 4, fully synchronized; ratios: I 3.400, II 2.160, III 1.38, IV 1, rev 3.810; lever: steering column; final drive: hypoid bevel; axle ratio: 3.540; width of rims: 6"; tyres: 175 SR x 14.

PERFORMANCE max speed: 96 mph, 154 km/h; power-weight ratio: Sedan 31.3 lb/hp (42.6 lb/kW), 14.2 kg/hp (19.3 kg/kW); carrying capacity: 1,091 lb, 495 kg; speed in direct drive at 1,000 rpm: 24.2 mph, 38.8 km/h; consumption: 22.6 m/imp gal, 18.8 m/US gal, 12.5 l x 100 km/h.

CHASSIS integral; front suspension: independent, wishbones, coil springs, anti-roll bar, telescopic dampers; rear: rigid axle, longitudinal torsion bars, transverse linkage bar, coil springs, anti-roll bar, telescopic dampers.

STEERING worm and roller.

BRAKES front disc, internal radial fins, rear drum, dual circuit, vacuum servo.

ELECTRICAL EQUIPMENT 12 V; 45 Ah battery; 32 A alternator; Arno distributor; 2 headlamps.

DIMENSIONS AND WEIGHT wheel base: 105.12 in, 267 cm; tracks: 56.30 in, 143 cm front, 55.51 in, 141 cm rear; length: 185.43 in, 471 cm - Caravan 184.25 in, 468 cm; width: 69.68 in, 177 cm; height: Sedan 54.72 in, 139 cm - Coupé 53.54 in, 136 cm - Caravan 54.72 in, 139 cm; ground clearance: 7.09 in, 18 cm; weight: Sedan 2,509 lb, 1,138 kg - Coupé 2,492 lb, 1,130 kg - Caravan 2,556 lb, 1,159 kg; turning circle: 37.1 ft, 11.3 m; fuel tank: 14.3 imp gal, 17.2 US gal, 65 l.

BODY saloon/sedan, 4 doors - coupé, 2 doors - estate car/st. wagon, 2+1 doors; 5 seats, separate front seats, reclining backrests; (for Caravan only) folding rear seat.

PRACTICAL INSTRUCTIONS fuel: 73 oct petrol; oil: engine 6.3 imp pt, 21.6 US pt, 3.6 l, SAE 20W-40, change every 4,700 miles, 7,500 km - gearbox 2.1 imp pt, 2.5 US pt, 1.2 l, SAE 90, change every 18,600 miles, 30,000 km - final drive 1.3 imp pt, 2.1 US pt, 0.9 l, change every 28,000 miles, 45,000 km; greasing: none; valve timing: 33° 81° 76° 38°; tyre pressure: front 23 psi, 1.6 atm, rear 26 psi, 1.8 atm - Caravan rear 30 psi, 2.1 atm.

OPTIONALS 3- and 5-speed fully synchronized mechanical gearbox; power steering; air-conditioning; tinted glass; metallic spray; vinyl roof; heater; electric rear window; 195/70 SR x 14 tyres; rev counter; rear window wiper-washer.

76 hp (alcohol) power team

See 80 hp power team, except for:

ENGINE alcohol; compression ratio: 10.5:1; max power (SAE) 76 hp (56 kW) at 4,000 rpm; max torque (SAE): 123 lb ft, 17 kg m (167 Nm) at 2,000 rpm; 30.8 hp/l (22.7 kW/l); 1 downdraught twin barrel carburettor.

116 hp power team

See 80 hp power team, except for:

ENGINE 6 cylinders, in line; 250 cu in, 4,093 cc (3.87 x 3.53 in, 98.4 x 89.7 mm); max power (SAE): 116 hp (85 kW) at 4,200 rpm; max torque (SAE): 192 lb ft, 26.5 kg m (260 Nm) at 2,200 rpm; max engine rpm: 6,000; 28.3 hp/l (20.8 kW/l); 7 crankshaft bearings; 1 Wecarbras downdraught twin barrel carburettor.

CHEVROLET Comodoro Caravan

TRANSMISSION gearbox ratios: I 3.070, II 2.020, III 1.390, IV 1, rev 3.570; axle ratio: 3.080.

PERFORMANCE max speed: about 106 mph, 170 km/h; power-weight ratio: Sedan 22.5 lb/hp (30.9 lb/kW), 10.2 kg/hp (14 kg/kW); speed in direct drive at 1,000 rpm: 21.4 mph, 34 km/h; consumption: 18.2 m/imp gal, 15.2 m/US gal, 15.5 l x 100 km.

DIMENSIONS AND WEIGHT weight: Sedan 2,620 lb, 1,188 kg - Coupé 2,602 lb, 1,180 kg - Caravan 2,666 lb, 1,209 kg.

OPTIONALS 3-speed fully synchronized mechanical gearbox; "Automatic" automatic transmission, hydraulic torque converter and planetary gears with 3 ratios (I 2.310, II 1.460, III 1, rev 1.850), max ratio of converter at stall 2.10.

Veraneio

4+1-dr Caravan
Luxo 4+1-dr Caravan
Super Luxo 4+1-dr Caravan

ENGINE front, 4 stroke; 6 cylinders, vertical, in line; 250 cu in, 4,093 cc (3.87 x 3.53 in, 98.4 x 89.7 mm); compression ratio: 7.5:1; max power (SAE): 130 hp (96 kW) at 4,400 rpm; max torque (SAE): 198 lb ft, 27.3 kg m (268 Nm) at 2,400 rpm; max engine rpm: 4,500; 31.8 hp/l (23.4 kW/l); cast iron block and head; 7 crankshaft bearings; valves: overhead, in line, push-rods and rockers; camshafts: 1, side; lubrication: gear pump, full flow filter, 8.8 imp pt, 10.6 US pt, 5 l; 1 Wecarbras-Solex downdraught twin barrel carburettor; fuel feed: mechanical pump; water-cooled, 18 imp pt, 21.6 US pt, 10.2 l.

TRANSMISSION driving wheels: rear; clutch: single dry plate (diaphragm); gearbox: mechanical; gears: 3, fully synchronized; ratios: I 3.617, II 1.753, III 1, rev 3.761; lever: steering column; final drive: hypoid bevel, limited slip; axle ratio: 3.900; width of rims: 5.5"; tyres: 7.10 x 15.

PERFORMANCE max speed: 90 mph, 145 km/h; power-weight ratio: 32.8 lb/hp (44.7 lb/kW), 14.9 kg/hp (20.3 kg/kW); carrying capacity: 1,191 lb, 540 kg; speed in direct drive at 1,000 rpm: 20.9 mph, 33.6 km/h; consumption: 17.7 m/imp gal, 14.7 m/US gal. 16 l x 100 km.

CHASSIS box-type ladder frame; front suspension: independent, wishbones, coil springs, telescopic dampers; rear: rigid axle, longitudinal trailing arms, coil springs, anti-roll bar, telescopic dampers.

STEERING worm and roller.

BRAKES drum; lining area: total 100.4 sq in, 648 sq cm.

ELECTRICAL EQUIPMENT 12 V; 45 Ah battery; 37 A alternator; Arno distributor; 2 headlamps.

DIMENSIONS AND WEIGHT wheel base: 114.96 in, 292 cm; tracks: 64.56 in, 164 cm front, 61.02 in, 155 cm rear; length: 203.15 in, 516 cm - Luxo 207.87 in, 528 cm; width: 77.95 in, 198 cm; height: 68.11 in, 173 cm; ground clearance: 7.87 in, 20 cm; weight: 4,344 lb, 1,970 kg; turning circle: 42.6 ft, 13 m; fuel tank: 19.4 imp gal, 22.9 US gal, 88 l.

BODY estate car/st. wagon; 4+1 doors; 6 seats, bench front seats; folding rear seat; (for Luxo only) luxury equipment.

PRACTICAL INSTRUCTIONS fuel: 73 oct petrol; oil: engine 8.8 imp pt, 10.6 US pt, 5 l, SAE 10W-50, change every 4,600 miles, 7,500 km - gearbox 2.1 imp pt, 2.5 US pt, 1.3 l, SAE 90, change every 15,500 miles, 25,000 km - final drive 3.5 imp pt, 4.2 US pt, 2 l, change every 31,000 miles, 50,000 km; greasing: none; valve timing: 11°30' 52°30' 51° 13°; tyre pressure: front 30 psi, 2.1 atm, rear 30 psi, 2.1 atm.

VARIATIONS

(alcohol engine)
ENGINE 10:1 compression ratio, max power (SAE) 130 hp (96 kW) at 4,000 rpm, max torque (SAE) 202 lb ft, 27.8 kg m (273 Nm) at 2,500 rpm.

OPTIONALS 4-speed fully synchronized mechanical gearbox (I 3.070, II 2.020, III 1.390, IV 1, rev 3.570); power steering; heater; 8.25 x 15 tyres; metallic spray; (for Super Luxo only) vinyl roof.

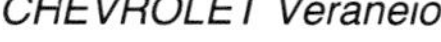

CHEVROLET Veraneio

ENVEMO 90 Super Coupé

ENVEMO BRAZIL

90 Super Coupé / Cabriolet

ENGINE rear, 4 stroke; 4 cylinders, horizontally opposed; 96.7 cu in, 1,584 cc (3.37 x 2.72 in, 85.5 x 69 mm); compression ratio: 7.2:1; max power (DIN): 65 hp (48 kW) at 4,600 rpm; max torque (DIN): 94 lb ft, 13 kg m (128 Nm) at 2,600 rpm; max engine rpm: 5,400; 41 hp/l (30.3 kW/l); light alloy block and head; 4 crankshaft bearings; valves: overhead, push-rods and rockers; camshafts: 1, central; lubrication: gear pump, 4.4 imp pt, 5.3 US pt, 2.5 l; 2 Solex 32 PDSIT downdraught twin barrel carburettors; fuel feed: mechanical pump; air-cooled.

TRANSMISSION driving wheels: rear; clutch: single dry plate; gearbox: mechanical; gears: 4, fully synchronized; ratios: I 3.800, II 2.060, III 1.320, IV 0.890, rev 3.700; lever: central; final drive: spiral bevel; axle ratio: 4.125; width of rims: 5.5"; tyres: 165 SR x 15.

PERFORMANCE max speed: 103 mph, 165 km/h; power-weight ratio: 29.2 lb/hp (39.7 lb/kW), 13.2 kg/hp (17.9 kg/kW); carrying capacity: 772 lb, 350 kg; speed in top at 1,000 rpm: 22 mph, 35 km/h; consumption: 32.5 m/imp gal, 27 m/US gal, 8.7 l x 100 km.

CHASSIS platform, reinforced side members; front suspension: independent, twin trailing links, anti-roll bar, transverse laminated torsion bars, telescopic dampers; rear: independent, swinging semi-axles, transverse laminated torsion bars, anti-roll bar, telescopic dampers.

STEERING worm and roller.

BRAKES front disc, rear drum; lining area: front 12.4 sq in, 80 sq cm, rear 69.8 sq in, 450 sq cm, total 82.2 sq in, 530 sq cm.

ELECTRICAL EQUIPMENT 12 V; 36 Ah battery; 25 A alternator; Bosch distributor; 4 headlamps.

DIMENSIONS AND WEIGHT wheel base: 82.68 in, 210 cm; tracks: 51.97 in, 132 cm front, 53.54 in, 136 cm rear; length: 157.87 in, 401 cm; width: 65.75 in, 167 cm; height: 52.36 in, 133 cm; ground clearance: 5.51 in, 14 cm; weight: 1,896 lb, 860 kg; turning circle: 36.1 ft, 11 m; fuel tank: 10.1 imp gal, 12.1 US gal, 46 l.

BODY coupé - convertible, in fiberglass material; 2 doors; 2+2 seats, separate front seats, reclining backrests, headrests.

PRACTICAL INSTRUCTIONS fuel: 82 oct petrol; oil: engine 4.4 imp pt, 5.3 US pt, 2.5 l, SAE 20W-40, change every 3,100 miles, 5,000 km; tyre pressure: front 26 psi, 1.8 atm, rear 28 psi, 2 atm.

OPTIONALS leather upholstery; fog lamps; tinted glass; heated rear window; electric windows; (for convertible only) detachable roof, hardtop and tonneau cover.

FARUS BRAZIL

ML 929

ENGINE Fiat, rear, 4 stroke; 4 cylinders, in line; 79.1 cu in, 1,297 cc (2.99 x 2.81 in, 76 x 71.5 mm); compression ratio: 7.5:1; max power (DIN): 63 hp (46 kW) at 5,500 rpm; max torque (DIN): 73 lb ft, 10.1 kg m (99 Nm) at 3,250 rpm; max engine rpm: 7,000; 48.6 hp/l (35.8 kW/l); cast iron block, light alloy head; 5 crankshaft bearings; valves: overhead, in line, push-rods and rockers; camshafts: 1, overhead; lubrication: gear pump, full flow filter, 7.9 imp pt, 9.5 US pt, 4.5 l; 1 Weber 32 DMTR 49/250 downdraught twin barrel carburettor; fuel feed: mechanical pump; water-cooled, 19.7 imp pt, 23.7 US pt, 11.2 l.

TRANSMISSION driving wheels: rear; clutch: single dry plate (diaphragm); gearbox: mechanical; gears: 4, fully synchronized; ratios: I 4.091, II 2.235, III 1.454, IV 0.959, rev 3.714; lever: central; final drive: helical cylindrical; axle ratio: 4.080; width of rims: 7"; tyres: 185/70 SR x 13.

PERFORMANCE max speeds: (I) 28 mph, 45 km/h; (II) 52 mph, 83 km/h; (III) 80 mph, 128 km/h; (IV) 106 mph, 170 km/h; power-weight ratio: 26.2 lb/hp (35.7 lb/kW), 11.9 kg/hp (16.2 kg/kW); carrying capacity: 750 lb, 340 kg; acceleration: standing ¼ mile 17.6 sec, 0-50 mph (0-80 km/h) 7.1 sec; speed in top at 1,000 rpm: 17 mph, 27 km/h; consumption: 46.3 m/imp gal, 38.6 m/US gal, 6.1 l x 100 km.

CHASSIS integral; front suspension: independent, by McPherson, coil springs, telescopic dampers; rear: independent, by McPherson, coil springs, telescopic dampers.

STEERING rack-and-pinion; turns lock to lock: 3.40.

BRAKES disc; swept area: front 150.7 sq in, 972 sq cm, rear 150.7 sq in, 972 sq cm, total 301.4 sq in, 1,944 sq cm.

ELECTRICAL EQUIPMENT 12 V; 36 Ah battery; 490 W alternator; Bosch distributor; 4 headlamps.

DIMENSIONS AND WEIGHT wheel base: 94.49 in, 240 cm; tracks: 56.30 in, 143 cm front, 57.48 in, 146 cm rear; length: 157.48 in, 400 cm; width: 66.14 in, 148 cm; height: 43.31 in, 110 cm; ground clearance: 5.90 in, 15 cm; weight: 1,654 lb, 750 kg; weight distribution: 42% front, 58% rear; turning circle: 33.5 ft, 10.2 m; fuel tank: 17.6 imp gal, 21.1 US gal, 80 l.

BODY coupé; 2 doors; 2+2 seats, separate front seats.

PRACTICAL INSTRUCTIONS fuel: 90 oct petrol; oil: engine 7.9 imp pt, 9.5 US pt, 4.5 l, SAE 20W-40, change every 6,200 miles, 10,000 km - gearbox and final drive 5.5 imp pt, 6.6 US pt, 3.1 l, SAE 90 EP, change every 18,600 miles, 30,000 km; greasing: none; spark plug: NGK BP 7 E; tappet clearances: inlet 0.016 in, 0.40 mm, exhaust 0.020 in, 0.50 mm; valve timing: 6° 46° 47° 7°; tyre pressure: front 26 psi, 1.8 atm, rear 28 psi, 2 atm.

OPTIONALS 4-speed mechanical gearbox with 4.417 axle ratio; light alloy wheels; air-conditioning; metallic spray; electric windows; velvet upholstery.

TS 1.6

See ML 929, except for:

ENGINE Volkswagen, rear, 4 stroke; 4 cylinders, in line; 96.9 cu in, 1,588 cc (3.13 x 3.15 in, 79.5 x 80 mm); compression ratio: 8.3:1; max power (DIN): 80 hp (59 kW) at 5,600 rpm; max torque (DIN): 87 lb ft, 12 kg m (118 Nm) at 3,000 rpm; 50.4 hp/l (37.1 kW/l); lubrication: 6.2 imp pt, 7.4 US pt, 3.5 l; 1 Solex 32/35 DIDTA downdraught twin barrel carburettor.

TRANSMISSION gearbox ratios: I 3.450, II 1.950, III 1.290, IV 0.910, rev 3.170; axle ratio: 4.110.

PERFORMANCE max speeds: (I) 34 mph, 54 km/h; (II) 60 mph, 96 km/h; (III) 89 mph, 143 km/h; (IV) 117 mph, 188 km/h; power-weight ratio: 20.7 lb/hp (28.1 lb/kW), 9.4 kg/hp (12.7 kg/kW); acceleration: standing ¼ mile 17.3 sec, 0-50 mph (0-80 km/h) 7.4 sec; speed in top at 1,000 rpm: 18 mph, 29 km/h; consumption: 38.7 m/imp gal, 32.2 m/US gal, 7.3 l x 100 km.

ELECTRICAL EQUIPMENT 770 W alternator.

PRACTICAL INSTRUCTIONS oil: engine 6.2 imp pt, 7.4 US pt, 3.5 l, SAE 20W-40, change every 4,300 miles, 7,000 km - gearbox and final drive 2.6 imp pt, 3.2 US pt, 1.5 l, SAE 80 EP, change every 24,900 miles, 40,000 km; tappet clearances: inlet 0.010 in, 0.25 mm, exhaust 0.018 in, 0.45 mm; valve timing: 4° 46° 44° 6°.

FARUS TS 1.6

FIAT Spazio CL Sedan

FIAT BRAZIL

147 / Spazio Series

PRICES EX WORKS:	cruzeiros
1 147 C 2+1-dr Sedan	**3,623,000**
2 Spazio CL 2+1-dr Sedan	**4,309,000**
3 147 C Panorama 2+1-dr St. Wagon	**4,190,000**
4 147 CL Panorama 2+1-dr St. Wagon	**4,682,000**
5 Spazio TR 2+1-dr Sedan	**5,252,000**

Power team:	Standard for:	Optional for:
51 hp	1 to 3	—
57 hp	4	—
70 hp	5	2

51 hp power team

ENGINE front, transverse, 4 stroke; 4 cylinders, in line; 64 cu in, 1,049 cc (2.99 x 2.23 in, 76 x 57.8 mm); compression ratio: 8:1; max power (DIN): 51 hp (38 kW) at 5,600 rpm; max torque (DIN): 55 lb ft, 7.6 kg m (75 Nm) at 3,000 rpm; max engine rpm: 6,000; 48.6 hp/l (35.8 kW/l); cast iron block, light alloy head; 5 crankshaft bearings; valves: overhead; camshafts: 1, overhead, cogged belt; lubrication: rotary pump, full flow filter (cartridge), 6.1 imp pt, 7.4 US pt, 3.5 l; 1 Solex-Brosol H 32 DIS-1 downdraught carburet-

51 HP POWER TEAM

tor; fuel feed: mechanical pump; water-cooled, 10.2 imp pt, 12.3 US pt, 5.8 l.

TRANSMISSION driving wheels: front; clutch: single dry plate (diaphragm); gearbox: mechanical; gears: 4, fully synchronized; ratios: I 4.091, II 2.235, III 1.461, IV 0.967, rev 3.714; lever: central; final drive: helical spur gears; axle ratio: 4.417; width of rims: 4"; tyres: 145 SR x 13.

PERFORMANCE max speeds: (I) 21 mph, 34 km/h; (II) 37 mph, 60 km/h; (III) 57 mph, 92 km/h; (IV) 84 mph, 135 km/h; power-weight ratio: 147 C Sedan 33.8 lb/hp (45.9 lb/kW), 15.3 kg/hp (20.8 kg/kW); carrying capacity: 882 lb, 400 kg; speed in top at 1,000 rpm: 15.6 mph, 25.6 km/h; consumption: 44.8 m/imp gal, 37.3 m/US gal, 6.3 l - 147 C Panorama 44.1 m/imp gal, 36.8 m/US gal, 6.4 l x 100 km.

CHASSIS integral; front suspension: independent, by McPherson, coil springs/telescopic damper struts, lower wishbones, anti-roll bar; rear: independent, single wide-based wishbones, transverse anti-roll leafspring, telescopic dampers.

STEERING rack-and-pinion; turns lock to lock: 3.80.

BRAKES front disc, rear drum; lining area: front 12 sq in, 77 sq cm, rear 16.7 sq in, 108 sq cm, total 28.7 sq in, 185 sq cm.

ELECTRICAL EQUIPMENT 12 V; 36 Ah battery; 420 W alternator; Bosch distributor; 2 headlamps.

DIMENSIONS AND WEIGHT wheel base: 87.40 in, 222 cm; tracks: 50.24 in, 128 cm front, 51.18 in, 130 cm rear; length: 146.06 in, 371 cm - Spazio CL 147.24 in, 374 cm - 147 C Panorama 154.33 in, 392 cm; width: 60.83 in, 154 cm - 147 C Panorama and Spazio CL 61.81 in, 157 cm; height: 53.15 in, 135 cm - 147 C Panorama 55.91 in, 142 cm; ground clearance: 5.10 in, 14 cm; weight: 147 C Sedan 1,720 lb, 780 kg - Spazio CL 1,742 lb, 790 kg - 147 C Panorama 1,797 lb, 815 kg; weight distribution: 49.6% front, 50.4% rear; turning circle: 31 ft, 9.6 m; fuel tank: 11.7 imp gal, 14 US gal, 53 l - 147 C Panorama 11.4 imp pt, 13.7 US pt, 52 l.

BODY saloon/sedan - estate car/st. wagon; 2+1 doors; 5 seats, separate front seats; (for Spazio CL only) reclining backrests.

PRACTICAL INSTRUCTIONS fuel: 80 oct petrol; oil: engine 6.1 imp pt, 7.4 US pt, 3.5 l, SAE 25W-40, change every 6,200 miles, 10,000 km - gearbox 5.2 imp pt, 6.6 US pt, 3.1 l, SAE 90, change every 18,600 miles, 30,000 km; greasing: none; spark plug: NGK-BP7E or Bosch W 175 T 30; tappet clearances: inlet 0.016 in, 0.40 mm, exhaust 0.020 in, 0.50 mm; valve timing: 6° 46° 47° 7°; tyre pressure: front 26 psi, 1.8 atm, rear 29 psi, 2 atm.

VARIATIONS

(alcohol engine)
ENGINE 79 cu in, 1,297 cc (2.99 x 2.81 in, 76 x 71.5 mm), 10.6:1 compression ratio, max power (DIN) 58 hp (43 kW) at 5,200 rpm, max torque (DIN) 71 lb ft, 9.8 kg m (96 Nm) at 2,600 rpm, 45.1 hp/l (33.2 kW/l), max speeds (I) 22 mph, 36 km/h, (II) 40 mph, 65 km/h, (III) 62 mph, 100 km/h, (IV) 87 mph, 140 km/h.

OPTIONALS servo brake; electronic ignition; metallic spray; reclining backrests (standard for Spazio CL); (for 147 C Panorama only) rear window wiper-washer; (for Spazio CL and 147 C Panorama only) heated rear window; (for Spazio CL only) 5-speed mechanical gearbox (I 4.091, II 2.235, III 1.461, IV 1.033, V 0.863, rev 3.714) and headrests.

57 hp power team

See 51 hp power team, except for:

ENGINE 79 cu in, 1,297 cc (2.99 x 2.81 in, 76 x 71.5 mm); max power (DIN): 57 hp (42 kW) at 5,200 rpm; max torque (DIN): 71 lb ft, 9.8 kg m (96 Nm) at 3,000 rpm; max engine rpm: 5,800; 43.9 hp/l (32.3 kW/l); lubrication: 7 imp pt, 8.5 US pt, 4 l; cooling: 12.3 imp pt, 14.8 US pt, 7 l.

TRANSMISSION axle ratio: 3.764.

PERFORMANCE max speeds: (I) 22 mph, 36 km/h; (II) 40 mph, 65 km/h; (III) 62 mph, 100 km/h; (IV) 87 mph, 140 km/h; power-weight ratio: 32.5 lb/hp (44.2 lb/kW), 14.7 kg/hp (20 kg/kW); speed in top at 1,000 rpm: 17 mph, 27 km/h.

DIMENSIONS AND WEIGHT length: 154.33 in, 392 cm; width: 61.81 in, 157 cm; height: 55.51 in, 141 cm; weight: 1,852 lb, 840 kg; fuel tank: 11.4 imp gal, 13.7 US gal, 52 l.

BODY estate car/st. wagon.

70 hp power team

See 51 hp power team, except for:

ENGINE 79 cu in, 1,297 cc (2.99 x 2.81 in, 76 x 71.5 mm); max power (DIN): 70 hp (52 kW) at 5,600 rpm; max torque

FIAT 147 CL Panorama Station Wagon

(DIN): 74 lb ft, 10.2 kg m (100 Nm) at 3,000 rpm; 54 hp/l (39.7 kW/l); lubrication: 7 imp pt, 8.5 US pt, 4 l; 1 Weber 34 DMTR 49/250 downdraught twin barrel carburettor; cooling: 12.3 imp pt, 14.8 US pt, 7 l.

TRANSMISSION axle ratio: 3.764.

PERFORMANCE max speeds: (I) 22 mph, 36 km/h; (II) 40 mph, 65 km/h; (III) 62 mph, 100 km/h; (IV) 96 mph, 154 km/h; power-weight ratio: 25.5 lb/hp (34.7 lb/kW), 11.6 kg/hp (15.7 kg/kW); acceleration: standing ¼ mile 18.8 sec, 0-50 mph, (0-80 km/h) 14 sec; speed in top at 1,000 rpm: 17 mph, 27 km/h.

DIMENSIONS AND WEIGHT length: 147.24 in, 374 cm; width: 61.81 in, 157 cm; weight: 1,786 lb, 810 kg.

BODY saloon/sedan.

Oggi CS

PRICE EX WORKS: 4,746,000 cruzeiros

ENGINE front, transverse, 4 stroke; 4 cylinders, in line; 79 cu in, 1,297 cc (2.99 x 2.81 in, 76 x 71.5 mm); compression ratio: 8:1; max power (DIN): 57 hp (42 kW) at 5,200 rpm; max torque (DIN): 71 lb ft, 9.8 kg m (96 Nm) at 3,000 rpm; max engine rpm: 5,800; 49.3 hp/l (32.3 kW/l); cast iron block, light alloy head; 5 crankshaft bearings; valves: overhead; camshafts: 1, overhead; lubrication: rotary pump, full flow filter, 7 imp pt, 8.5 US pt, 4 l; 1 Solex-Brosol H 32 DIS-3 downdraught carburettor; fuel feed: mechanical pump; water-cooled, 12.3 imp pt, 14.8 US pt, 7 l.

TRANSMISSION driving wheels: front; clutch: single dry plate; gearbox: mechanical; gears: 4, fully synchronized; ratios: I 4.091, II 2.235, III 1.461, IV 1.033, rev 3.714; lever: central; final drive: helical spur gears; axle ratio: 3.764; width of rims: 4"; tyres: 145 SR x 13.

PERFORMANCE max speeds: (I) 22 mph, 36 km/h; (II) 40 mph, 65 km/h; (III) 62 mph, 100 km/h; (IV) 88 mph, 141 km/h; power-weight ratio: 31.7 lb/hp (43.1 lb/kW), 14.4 kg/hp (19.6 kg/kW); carrying capacity: 882 lb, 400 kg; speed in top at 1,000 rpm: 17 mph, 27 km/h; consumption: 44.8 m/imp gal, 37.3 m/US gal, 6.3 l x 100 km.

FIAT Oggi CS

CHASSIS integral; front suspension: independent, by McPherson, coil springs/telescopic damper struts, anti-roll bar; rear: independent, single wide based wishbones, transverse anti-roll leafspring, telescopic dampers.

STEERING rack-and-pinion; turns lock to lock: 3.80.

BRAKES front disc, rear drum, servo; lining area: front 12 sq in, 77 sq cm, rear 16.7 sq in, 108 sq cm, total 28.7 sq in, 185 sq cm.

ELECTRICAL EQUIPMENT 12 V; 36 Ah battery; 420 W alternator; Bosch distributor; 2 headlamps.

DIMENSIONS AND WEIGHT wheel base: 87.40 in, 222 cm; tracks: 51.18 in, 130 cm front, 51.97 in, 132 cm rear; length: 156.30 in, 397 cm; width: 61.81 in, 157 cm; height: 52.76 in, 134 cm; ground clearance: 5.51 in, 14 cm; weight: 1,808 lb, 820 kg; weight distribution: 49.6% front, 50.4% rear; turning circle: 31 ft, 9.6 m; fuel tank: 11.4 imp gal, 13.7 US gal, 52 l.

BODY saloon/sedan; 2 doors; 5 seats, separate front seats, built-in headrests.

PRACTICAL INSTRUCTIONS fuel: 80 oct petrol; oil: engine 7 imp pt, 8.5 US pt, 4 l, SAE 25W-40, change every 6,200 miles, 10,000 km - gearbox 5.2 imp pt, 6.6 US pt, 3.1 l, SAE 90, change every 18,600 miles, 30,000 km; greasing: none; spark plug: NGK-BP7E or Bosch W 175 T 30; tappet clearances: inlet 0.016 in, 0.40 mm, exhaust 0.020 in, 0.50 mm; valve timing: 6° 46° 47° 7°; tyre pressure: front 26 psi, 1.8 atm, rear 29 psi, 2 atm.

VARIATIONS

(alcohol engine)
ENGINE 10.6:1 compression ratio, max power (DIN) 58 hp (43 kW) at 5,200 rpm, max torque (DIN) 71 lb ft, 9.8 kg m (96 Nm) at 2.600 rpm, 45.1 hp/l (33.2 kW/l).

OPTIONALS 5-speed fully synchronized mechanical gearbox (I 4.091, II 2.235, III 1.461, IV 1.033, V 0.863, rev 3.714); metallic spray; electronic ignition; heated rear window; rear window wiper-washer.

Alfa Romeo Ti-4

PRICE EX WORKS: 15,007,000 cruzeiros

ENGINE front, longitudinal, 4 stroke; 4 cylinders, vertical, in line; 141 cu in, 2,310 cc (3.46 x 3.74 in, 88 x 95 mm); compression ratio: 7.9:1; max power (DIN): 130 hp (96 kW) at 5,500 rpm; max torque (DIN): 138 lb ft, 19 kg m (186 Nm) at 4,000 rpm; max engine rpm: 5,600; 56.3 hp/l (41.4 kW/l); cast iron block, light alloy head; 5 crankshaft bearings; valves: overhead, Vee-slanted at 90°, thimble tappets; camshafts: 2, overhead; lubrication: gear pump, full flow filter, 12.3 imp pt, 14.8 US pt, 7 l; 2 Solex C-40 ADD HE-12 sidedraught twin barrel carburettor; fuel feed: mechanical pump; water-cooled, 16 imp pt, 19.2 US pt, 9.1 l, electric thermostatic fan.

TRANSMISSION driving wheels: rear; clutch: single dry plate (diaphragm), hydraulically controlled; gearbox: mechanical; gears: 5, fully synchronized; ratios: I 3.303, II 1.985, III 1.353, IV 1, V 0.790, rev 3.008; lever: central; final drive: hypoid bevel; axle ratio: 4.778; width of rims: 6"; tyres: 195/70 HR x 14.

PERFORMANCE max speeds: (I) 26 mph, 41 km/h; (II) 42 mph, 68 km/h; (III) 62 mph, 100 km/h; (IV) 84 mph, 135 km/h; (V) 109 mph, 175 km/h; power-weight ratio: 23.9 lb/hp (32.6 lb/kW), 10.9 kg/hp (14.8 kg/kW); carrying capacity: 882 lb, 400 kg; acceleration: 0-50 mph (0-80 km/h) 6.9 sec; speed in top at 1,000 rpm: 21.3 mph, 34 km/h; consumption: 27.4 m/imp gal, 22.8 m/US gal, 10.3 l x 100 km.

FIAT Alfa Romeo Ti-4

CHASSIS integral; front suspension: independent, wishbones (lower trailing links), coil springs, telescopic dampers; rear: rigid axle, trailing arms, coil springs, telescopic dampers.

STEERING worm and gear, servo; turns lock to lock: 3.60.

BRAKES disc (front diameter 11.02 in, 28 cm, rear 11.06 in, 28.1 cm), dual circuit, rear compensator, servo; swept area: front 207.1 sq in, 1,336 sq cm, rear 207.1 sq in, 1,336 sq cm, total 414.2 sq in, 2,672 sq cm.

ELECTRICAL EQUIPMENT 12 V; 65 Ah battery; 660 W alternator; Bosch electronic ignition; 4 iodine headlamps.

DIMENSIONS AND WEIGHT wheel base: 107.09 in, 272 cm; front and rear track: 55.12 in, 140 cm; length: 185.83 in, 472 cm; width: 66.54 in, 169 cm; height: 53.54 in, 136 cm; ground clearance: 5.90 in, 15 cm; weight: 3,113 lb, 1,412 kg; weight distribution: 47.6% front, 52.4% rear; turning circle: 41 ft, 12.6 m; fuel tank: 22 imp gal, 26.4 US gal, 100 l.

BODY saloon/sedan; 4 doors; 5 seats, separate front seats, built-in headrests on rear seats, reclining backrests.

PRACTICAL INSTRUCTIONS fuel: 80 oct petrol; oil: engine 12.3 imp pt, 14.8 US pt, 7 l, SAE 25W-40, change every 6,200 miles, 10,000 km - gearbox 3.2 imp pt, 3.9 US pt, 1.8 l, SAE 90W, change every 18,600 miles, 30,000 km - final drive 2.9 imp pt, 3.5 US pt, 1.6 l, SAE 90W, change every 18,600 miles, 30,000 km; greasing: 2 points, every 6,200 miles, 10,000 km; spark plug: NGK-BP7E; tappet clearances: inlet 0.016 in, 0.40 mm, exhaust 0.018 in, 0.45 mm; valve timing: 13°20' 48°28' 48°28' 13°20'; tyre pressure: front 24 psi, 1.7 atm, rear 26 psi, 1.8 atm.

VARIATIONS

(alcohol engine)
ENGINE 10.6:1 compression ratio, max power (DIN) 115 hp (85 kW) at 5,200 rpm, max torque (DIN) 134 lb ft, 18.5 kg m (181 Nm) at 3,600 rpm, 1 Solex-Brosol H34 SEIE downdraught twin barrel carburettor, max speed 108 mph, 173 km/h.

OPTIONALS air-conditioning; light alloy wheels; leather upholstery; tinted glass; metallic spray; heater; heated rear window; electric windows.

FORD BRAZIL

Corcel II Series

PRICES EX WORKS:	cruzeiros
L 2-dr Sedan	**5,556,000**
GL 2-dr Sedan	**6,082,000**
Belina L 2+1-dr St. Wagon	**5,836,000**
Belina GL 2+1-dr St. Wagon	**6,358,000**

Power team:	Standard for:	Optional for:
65 hp	all	—
63 hp (alcohol)	all	—

65 hp power team

ENGINE front, 4 stroke; 4 cylinders, vertical, in line; 94.9 cu in, 1,555 cc (3.03 x 3.29 in, 77 x 83.5 mm); compression ratio: 9:1; max power (SAE): 65 hp (48 kW) at 4,800 rpm; max torque (SAE): 78 lb ft, 10.8 kg m (106 Nm) at 2,400 rpm; max engine rpm: 5,800; 41.9 hp/l (30.8 kW/l); cast iron block, light alloy head; 5 crankshaft bearings; valves: overhead, push-rods and rockers; camshafts: 1, in crankcase; lubrication: gear pump, full flow filter, 5.3 imp pt, 6.3 US pt, 3 l; 1 Wecarbras DMTB 2V32 downdraught carburettor; fuel feed: mechanical pump; sealed circuit cooling, water, 7.9 imp pt, 9.5 US pt, 4.5 l.

TRANSMISSION driving wheels: front; clutch: single dry plate; gearbox: mechanical; gears: 4 - GL 5, fully synchronized; ratios: I 3.120, II 1.910, III 1.270, IV 0.950 - GL V 0.750, rev 3.620; lever: central; final drive: hypoid bevel; axle ratio: 3.840; width of rims: 5"; tyres: 180/70 SR x 13.

PERFORMANCE max speeds: (I) 27 mph, 44 km/h; (II) 43 mph, 69 km/h; (III) 66 mph, 107 km/h; (IV) 88 mph, 141 km/h - GL (V) 91 mph, 146 km/h; power-weight ratio: L 31.2 lb/hp (42.4 lb/kW), 14.2 kg/hp (19.2 kg/kW); carrying capacity: 882 lb, 400 kg; speed in top at 1,000 rpm: 17 mph, 27 km/h; consumption: 32.8 m/imp gal, 27.3 m/US gal, 8.6 l x 100 km.

CHASSIS integral; front suspension: independent, wishbones, upper trailing arms, coil springs, anti-roll bar, telescopic dampers; rear: rigid axle, upper and lower trailing arms, coil springs, telescopic dampers.

STEERING rack-and-pinion; turns lock to lock: 3.39.

BRAKES front disc, rear drum, servo; lining area: total 150 sq in, 968 sq cm.

ELECTRICAL EQUIPMENT 12 V; 36 Ah battery; 30 A alternator; Bosch distributor; 2 headlamps.

DIMENSIONS AND WEIGHT wheel base: 96.06 in, 244 cm; tracks: 53.50 in, 136 cm front, 53.14 in, 135 cm rear; length: 177.95 in, 452 cm - Belina L 176.77 in, 449 cm; width: 65.35 in, 166 cm; height: 53.14 in, 135 cm; ground clearance: 5.50 in, 14 cm; weight: L Sedan 2,033 lb, 922 kg - GL Sedan 2,115 lb, 959 kg - Belina L St. Wagon 1,987 lb, 901 kg - Belina GL St. Wagon 2,022 lb, 917 kg; weight distribution: 46% front, 54% rear; turning circle: 36.7 ft, 11.2 m; fuel tank: sedans 12.5 imp gal, 15.1 US gal, 57 l - st. wagons 13.8 imp gal, 16.6 US gal, 63 l.

BODY saloon/sedan; 2 doors - estate car/st. wagon, 2+1 doors; 5 seats, separate front seats.

OPTIONALS (for L only) 5-speed fully synchronized mechanical gearbox, 0.750 ratio in V; magnetic clutch fan.

63 hp (alcohol) power team

See 65 hp power team, except for:

ENGINE alcohol; 81.8 cu in, 1,341 cc (2.81 x 3.29 in, 71.5 x 83.5 mm); compression ratio: 12:1; max power (SAE): 63 hp (46 kW) at 5,000 rpm; max torque (SAE): 76 lb ft, 10.5 kg m (103 Nm) at 2,800 rpm; 47 hp/l (34.3 kW/l); 1 Wecarbras 1V downdraught carburettor.

PERFORMANCE power-weight ratio: L 32.2 lb/hp (44.1 lb/kW), 14.6 kg/hp (20 kg/kW).

Del Rey Series

PRICES EX WORKS:	cruzeiros
2-dr Sedan	**6,803,000**
4-dr Sedan	**6,970,000**
Ouro 2-dr Sedan	**8,570,000**
Ouro 4-dr Sedan	**8,714,000**
Ouro Scala 2+1-dr St. Wagon	**8,891,000**

Power team:	Standard for:	Optional for:
65 hp	all	—
73 hp (alcohol)	all	—

65 hp power team

ENGINE front, 4 stroke; 4 cylinders, vertical, in line; 94.9 cu in, 1,555 cc (3.03 x 3.29 in, 77 x 83.5 mm); compression ratio: 9:1; max power (SAE): 65 hp (48 kW) at 4,800 rpm; max torque (SAE): 78 lb ft, 10.8 kg m (106 Nm) at 2,400 rpm; max engine rpm: 5,800; 41.9 hp/l (30.8 kW/l); cast iron block, light alloy head; 5 crankshaft bearings; valves: overhead, push-rods and rockers; camshafts: 1, in crankcase; lubrication: gear pump, full flow filter, 5.3 imp pt, 6.3 US pt, 3 l; 1 Wecarbras DMTB 2V 32 downdraught carburettor; fuel feed: mechanical pump; sealed circuit cooling, water, 7.9 imp pt, 9.5 US pt, 4.5 l.

TRANSMISSION driving wheels: front; clutch: single dry plate; gearbox: mechanical; gears: 5, fully synchronized; ratios: I 3.120, II 1.910, III 1.270, IV 0.950, V 0.750, rev 3.620; lever: central; final drive: hypoid bevel; axle ratio: 3.840; width of rims: 5"; tyres: 180/70 SR x 13.

PERFORMANCE max speeds: (I) 27 mph, 44 km/h; (II) 43 mph, 69 km/h; (III) 66 mph, 107 km/h; (IV) 88 mph, 141 km/h; (V) 91 mph, 146 km/h; power-weight ratio: 2-dr Sedan 33 lb/hp (44.8 lb/kW), 14.9 kg/hp (20.3 kg/kW); carrying capacity: 882 lb, 400 kg; speed in top at 1,000 rpm: 17 mph, 27 km/h; consumption: 32.8 m/imp gal, 27.3 m/US gal, 8.6 l x 100 km.

CHASSIS integral; front suspension: independent, wishbones, upper trailing arms, coil springs, anti-roll bar, telescopic dampers; rear: rigid axle, upper and lower trailing arms, coil springs, telescopic dampers.

STEERING rack-and-pinion; turns lock to lock: 3.39.

BRAKES front disc, rear drum, servo; lining area: total 150 sq in, 968 sq cm.

ELECTRICAL EQUIPMENT 12 V; 36 Ah battery - Ouro models 42 Ah battery; 30 A alternator - Ouro models 40 A alternator; 2 headlamps.

DIMENSIONS AND WEIGHT wheel base: 96.06 in, 244 cm; tracks: 53.94 in, 137 cm front, 52.36 in, 133 cm rear; length: 177.17 in, 450 cm; width: 66.14 in, 168 cm; height: 53.14 in, 135 cm; ground clearance: 5.12 in, 13 cm; weight: 2-dr Sedan 2,145 lb, 973 kg - 4-dr Sedan 2,181 lb, 989 kg - Ouro 2-dr Sedan 2,154 lb, 977 kg - Ouro 4-dr Sedan 2,203 lb, 999 kg; weight distribution: 46% front, 54% rear; turning circle: 36.7 ft, 11.2 m; fuel tank: 12.5 imp gal, 15.1 US gal, 57 l.

BODY saloon/sedan, 2 or 4 doors - estate car/st. wagon, 2+1 doors; 5 seats, separate front seats; (for Ouro models only) light alloy wheels, headrests and electric windows; metallic spray.

OPTIONALS automatic transmission, hydraulic torque converter and planetary gears with 3 ratios (I 2.500, II 1.500, III 1, rev 2), 3.865 axle ratio; headlamps with wiper-washers; sunroof; air-conditioning; (except Ouro models) headrests.

FORD Corcel II GL Sedan

FORD Del Rey Ouro Sedan

FORD Escort Series

73 hp (alcohol) power team

See 65 hp power team, except for:

ENGINE alcohol; compression ratio: 12:1; max power (SAE): 73 hp (54 kW) at 5,200 rpm; max torque (SAE): 86 lb ft, 11.8 kg m (116 Nm) at 3,600 rpm; 46.9 hp/l (34.7 kW/l).

PERFORMANCE power-weight ratio: 2-dr Sedan 29.3 lb/hp (39.7 lb/kW), 13.3 kg/hp (18 kg/kW).

Escort Series

PRICES EX WORKS:	cruzeiros
1 2-dr Sedan	**5,011,000**
2 L 2-dr Sedan	**5,576,000**
3 GL 2-dr Sedan	**6,430,000**
4 Ghia 2-dr Sedan	**7,171,000**
5 4-dr Sedan	**5,228,000**
6 L 4-dr Sedan	**5,793,000**
7 GL 4-dr Sedan	**6,652,000**
8 Ghia 4-dr Sedan	**7,395,000**
9 XR-3 2-dr Sedan	**7,840,000**

Power team:	Standard for:	Optional for:
65 hp	1 to 8	—
63 hp (alcohol)	1 to 8	—
83 hp (alcohol)	9	—

65 hp power team

ENGINE front, 4 stroke; 4 cylinders, vertical, in line; 94.9 cu in, 1,555 cc (3.03 x 3.29 in, 77 x 83.5 mm); compression ratio: 9:1; max power (SAE): 65 hp (48 kW) at 4,800 rpm; max torque (SAE): 78 lb ft, 10.8 kg m (206 Nm) at 2,400 rpm; max engine rpm: 5,800; 41.9 hp/l (30.8 kW/l); cast iron block, light alloy head; 5 crankshaft bearings; valves: overhead, push-rods and rockers; camshafts: 1, in crankcase; lubrication: gear pump, full flow filter, 5.3 imp pt, 6.3 US pt, 3 l; 1 Wecarbras DMTB 2V 32 downdraught carburettor; fuel feed: mechanical pump; sealed circuit cooling, water, 7.9 imp pt, 9.5 US pt, 4.5 l.

TRANSMISSION driving wheels: front; clutch: single dry plate; gearbox: mechanical; gears: 5, fully synchronized; ratios: I 3.150, II 1.910, III 1.270, IV 0.950, V 0.750, rev 3.620; lever: central; final drive: hypoid bevel; axle ratio: 3.840; width of rims: 4.5" - GL and Ghia 5"; tyres: 165 SR x 13.

PERFORMANCE max speeds: (I) 29 mph, 47 km/h; (II) 45 mph, 72 km/h; (III) 68 mph, 109 km/h; (IV) 91 mph, 146 km/h; (V) 95 mph, 152 km/h; power-weight ratio: 2-dr Sedan 28.1 lb/hp (38.2 lb/kW), 12.7 kg/hp (17.3 kg/kW); carrying capacity: 1,144 lb, 519 kg; consumption: 36.7 m/imp gal, 30.6 m/US gal, 7.7 l x 100 km.

CHASSIS integral; front suspension: independent, wishbones, upper trailing arms, anti-roll bar, coil springs, telescopic dampers; rear: independent, wishbones, upper trailing arms, coil springs, telescopic dampers.

STEERING rack-and-pinion; turns lock to lock: 3.63 - GL and Ghia 4.

BRAKES front disc, rear drum, servo; swept area: total 487 sq in, 3,143 sq cm.

ELECTRICAL EQUIPMENT 12 V; 43 Ah battery; 45 A alternator; 2 headlamps.

DIMENSIONS AND WEIGHT wheel base: 94.48 in, 240 cm; tracks: 55.12 in, 140 cm front, 55.90 in, 142 cm rear; length: 136.61 in, 347 cm; width: 64.56 in, 164 cm; height: 54.33 in, 138 cm; ground clearance: 4.57 in, 11.6 cm; weight: 2-dr Sedan 1,830 lb, 830 kg; turning circle: 17.7 ft, 5.4 m; fuel tank: 10.5 imp gal, 12.7 US gal, 48 l.

BODY saloon/sedan; 2 or 4 doors; 5 seats, separate front seats.

OPTIONALS sunroof; metallic spray; air-conditioning.

63 hp (alcohol) power team

See 65 hp power team, except for:

ENGINE alcohol; 81.8 cu in, 1,341 cc (2.81 x 3.29 in, 71.5 x 83.5 mm); compression ratio: 12:1; max power (SAE): 63 hp (46 kW) at 5,000 rpm; max torque (SAE): 76 lb ft, 10.5 kg m (103 Nm) at 2,800 rpm; 47 hp/l (34.3 kW/l); 1 Wecarbras 1V downdraught carburettor.

PERFORMANCE power-weight ratio: 2-dr Sedan 29.1 lb/hp (39.7 lb/kW), 13.2 kg/hp (18 kg/kW).

83 hp (alcohol) power team

See 65 hp power team, except for:

ENGINE alcohol; compression ratio: 12:1; max power (SAE): 83 hp (61 kW) at 5,600 rpm; max torque (SAE): 92 lb ft, 12.8 kg m (125 Nm) at 4,000 rpm; 53.4 hp/l (39.2 kW/l).

TRANSMISSION axle ratio: 4.060; width of rims: 5.5"; tyres: 185/60 HR x 14.

PERFORMANCE max speed: 107 mph, 172 km/h; power-weight ratio: 24.1 lb/hp (32.7 lb/kW), 10.9 kg/hp (14.8 kg/kW); carrying capacity: 981 lb, 445 kg.

STEERING turns lock to lock: 3.63.

BRAKES front internal radial fins.

ELECTRICAL EQUIPMENT fog lamps.

DIMENSIONS AND WEIGHT weight: 1,996 lb, 905 kg.

BODY 2 doors.

GURGEL BRAZIL

X-12

PRICES EX WORKS:	cruzeiros
X-12 2-dr St. Wagon	**4,058,000**
X-12 TR 2-dr St. Wagon	**4,334,000**

ENGINE Volkswagen, rear, 4 stroke; 4 cylinders, horizontally opposed; 96.7 cu in, 1,584 cc (3.37 x 2.72 in, 85.5 x 69 mm); compression ratio: 7.2:1; max power (DIN): 50 hp (37 kW) at 4,200 rpm; max torque (DIN): 80 lb ft, 11 kg m (108 Nm) at 2,200 rpm; max engine rpm: 4,600; 31.6 hp/l (23.2 kW/l); block with cast iron liners and light alloy fins, light alloy head; 4 crankshaft bearings; valves: overhead, push-rods and rockers; camshafts: 1, central, lower; lubrication: gear pump, oil cooler, 4.4 imp pt, 5.3 US pt, 2.5 l; 1 Solex H 30 downdraught single barrel carburettor; fuel feed: mechanical pump; air-cooled.

TRANSMISSION driving wheels: rear; clutch: single dry plate; gearbox: mechanical; gears: 4, fully synchronized; ratios: I 3.800, II 2.060, III 1.320, IV 0.890, rev 3.880; lever: central; final drive: spiral bevel; axle ratio: 4.375; width of rims: 5.5"; tyres: 5.60 x 15.

PERFORMANCE max speeds: (I) 17 mph, 27 km/h; (II) 32 mph, 51 km/h; (III) 50 mph, 80 km/h; (IV) 73 mph, 118 km/h; power-weight ratio: X-12 TR 35.3 lb/hp (47.6 lb/kW), 16 kg/hp (21.6 kg/kW); carrying capacity: 882 lb, 400 kg; acceleration: 0-50 mph (0-80 km/h) 10.1 sec; speed in top at 1,000 rpm: 18.6 mph, 30 km/h; consumption: 28.2 m/imp gal, 23.5 m/US gal, 10 l x 100 km.

CHASSIS backbone platform; front suspension: independent, swinging semi-axles, swinging longitudinal trailing arms, transverse torsion bars, telescopic dampers; rear: independent, twin swinging longitudinal trailing arms, transverse laminated torsion bars, telescopic dampers.

STEERING worm and roller; turns lock to lock: 2.50.

BRAKES drum; lining area: front 20 sq in, 132 sq cm, rear 20.8 sq in, 134 sq cm, total 40.8 sq in, 266 sq cm.

PUMA GTC 1.6 E Convertible

ELECTRICAL EQUIPMENT 12 V; 36 Ah battery; 350 W dynamo; Bosch distributor; 2 headlamps.

DIMENSIONS AND WEIGHT wheel base: 90.31 in, 204 cm; tracks: 53.15 in, 135 cm front, 55.12 in, 140 cm rear; length: 51.57 in, 331 cm; width: 64.57 in, 164 cm; height: 61.02 in, 155 cm; ground clearance: 13.11 in, 33 cm; weight: X-12 TR 1,764 lb, 800 kg - X-12 L 1,632 lb, 740 kg; weight distribution: 60% front, 40% rear; turning circle: 36.1 ft, 11 m; fuel tank: 8.1 imp gal, 9.8 US gal, 37 l.

BODY estate car/st. wagon, in plastic material; 2 doors; 3 seats, separate adjustable front seats.

PRACTICAL INSTRUCTIONS fuel: 73 oct petrol; oil: engine 4.4 imp pt, 5.3 US pt, 2.5 l, SAE 20W-40, change every 3,100 miles, 5,000 km - gearbox 4.4 imp pt, 5.3 US pt, 2.5 l, SAE 90 EP, change every 9,300 miles, 15,000 km; greasing: every 6,200 miles, 10,000 km, 4 points; valve timing: 9°48' 35°02' 44°28' 4°04'; tyre pressure: front 16 psi, 1.1 atm, rear 20 psi, 1.4 atm.

OPTIONALS limited slip differential; anti-roll bar on front and rear suspension.

LAFER BRAZIL

MP

PRICES EX WORKS:	**cruzeiros**
2-dr Roadster	**7,541,000**
TI 2-dr Roadster	**8,090,000**

ENGINE Volkswagen, rear, 4 stroke; 4 cylinders, horizontally opposed; 96.7 cu in, 1,584 cc (3.37 x 2.72 in, 85.5 x 69 mm); compression ratio: 7.2:1; max power (SAE): 65 hp (48 kW) at 4,600 rpm; max torque (SAE): 87 lb ft, 12 kg m (118 Nm) at 3,200 rpm; max engine rpm: 4,800; 41 hp/l (30.2 kW/l); light alloy block and head; 4 crankshaft bearings; valves: overhead, in line, push-rods and rockers; camshafts: 1, central, lower; lubrication: gear pump, filter in sump, oil cooler, 4.4 imp pt, 5.3 US pt, 2.5 l; 2 Solex H 32 34PDSI.3 twin barrel carburettors; fuel feed: mechanical pump; air-cooled.

TRANSMISSION driving wheels: rear; clutch: single dry plate; gearbox: mechanical; gears: 4, fully synchronized; ratios: I 3.800, II 2.060, III 1.320, IV 0.890, rev 3.880; lever: central; final drive: spiral bevel; axle ratio: 4.125; width of rims: 4.5"; tyres: 5.60 x 15.

PERFORMANCE max speeds: (I) 25 mph, 41 km/h; (II) 48 mph, 77 km/h; (III) 71 mph, 115 km/h; (IV) 86 mph, 138 km/h; power-weight ratio: 25.8 lb/hp (35.1 lb/kW), 11.7 kg/hp (15.9 kg/kW); acceleration: standing ¼ mile 22.5 sec, 0-50 mph (0-80 km/h) 9.9 sec; speed in direct drive at 1,000 rpm: 19.6 mph, 31.6 km/h; consumption: 32.8 m/imp gal, 27.3 m/US gal, 8.6 l x 100 km.

CHASSIS backbone platform, rear auxiliary frame; front suspension: independent, twin swinging longitudinal trailing arms, transverse laminated torsion bars, anti-roll bar, telescopic dampers; rear: independent, semi-trailing arms, transverse compensating torsion bars, anti-roll bar, telescopic dampers.

STEERING worm and roller; turns lock to lock: 2.60.

BRAKES front disc (diameter 10.94 in, 27.8 cm), rear drum; lining area: front 11.7 sq in, 76 sq cm, rear 56.4 sq in, 364 sq cm, total 68.2 sq in, 440 sq cm.

ELECTRICAL EQUIPMENT 12 V; 36 Ah battery; 350 W alternator; Bosch distributor; 2 headlamps.

LAFER MP

DIMENSIONS AND WEIGHT wheel base: 94.49 in, 240 cm; tracks: 51.57 in, 131 cm front, 53.15 in, 135 cm rear; length: 153.94 in, 391 cm; width: 61.81 in, 157 cm; height: 53.15 in, 135 cm; ground clearance: 5.90 in, 15 cm; weight: 1,676 lb, 760 kg; weight distribution: 40% front, 60% rear; turning circle: 36.1 ft, 11 m; fuel tank: 10.1 imp gal, 12.1 US gal, 46 l.

BODY roadster; 2 doors; 2 separate seats; (for TI only) luxury equipment; electric windows.

PRACTICAL INSTRUCTIONS fuel: 70-75 oct petrol; oil: engine 4.4 imp pt, 5.3 US pt, 2.5 l, change every 3,100 miles, 5,000 km - gearbox 4.4 imp pt, 5.3 US pt, 2.5 l; greasing: every 6,200 miles, 10,000 km; spark plug: NGK B6H; tyre pressure: front 15 psi, 1.1 atm, rear 18 psi, 1.3 atm.

OPTIONALS 175 SR x 14 tyres with light alloy wheels; hardtop; 3 auxiliary halogen headlamps; leather upholstery; tinted glass.

PUMA BRAZIL

GTI 1.6 E / GTC 1.6 E

PRICES EX WORKS:	**cruzeiros**
GTI 1.6 E 2-dr Coupé	**3,719,000***
GTC 1.6 E 2-dr Convertible	**4,019,000***

ENGINE Volkswagen, rear, 4 stroke; 4 cylinders, horizontally opposed; 96.7 cu in, 1,584 cc (3.37 x 2.72 in, 85.5 x 69 mm); compression ratio: 9:1; max power (SAE): 90 hp (66 kW) at 5,800 rpm; max torque (SAE): 96 lb ft, 13.2 kg m (129 Nm) at 3,000 rpm; max engine rpm: 6,000; 56.8 hp/l (41.8 kW/l); block with cast iron liners and light alloy fins, light alloy head; 4 crankshaft bearings; valves: overhead, push-rods and rockers; camshafts: 1, central, lower; lubrication: gear pump, filter in sump, oil cooler, 4.4 imp pt, 5.3 US pt, 2.5 l; 2 Solex-Brosol H40 EIS downdraught single barrel carburettors; fuel feed: mechanical pump; air-cooled.

TRANSMISSION driving wheels: rear; clutch: single dry plate; gearbox: mechanical; gears: 4, fully synchronized; ratios: I 3.800, II 2.060, III 1.320, IV 0.890, rev 3.880; lever: central; final drive: spiral bevel; axle ratio: 4.125; width of rims: 6"; tyres: front 185/70 HR x 14, rear 195/70 HR x 14.

PERFORMANCE max speeds: (I) 26 mph, 42 km/h; (II) 47 mph, 76 km/h; (III) 75 mph, 120 km/h; (IV) 113 mph, 182 km/h; power-weight ratio: 18.4 lb/hp (25 lb/kW), 8.3 kg/hp (11.3 kg/kW); carrying capacity: 507 lb, 230 kg; acceleration: 0-50 mph (0-80 km/h) 12.5 sec; speed in top at 1,000 rpm: 19.9 mph, 32 km/h; consumption: 35.3 m/imp gal, 29.4 m/US gal, 8 l x 100 km.

CHASSIS backbone, rear auxiliary frame; front suspension: independent, twin swinging longitudinal trailing arms, transverse torsion bars, anti-roll bar, telescopic dampers; rear: independent, semi-trailing arms, transverse linkage by oblique swinging trailing arms, transverse torsion bars, telescopic dampers.

STEERING worm and roller; turns lock to lock: 2.70.

BRAKES front disc (diameter 10.94 in, 27.8 cm), rear drum; lining area: front 11.2 sq in, 72 sq cm, rear 52.6 sq in, 339 sq cm, total 63.8 sq in, 441 sq cm.

ELECTRICAL EQUIPMENT 12 V; 36 Ah battery; 350 W alternator; Bosch distributor; 2 iodine headlamps.

DIMENSIONS AND WEIGHT wheel base: 84.65 in, 215 cm; tracks: 54.64 in, 139 cm front, 55.11 in, 140 cm rear; length: 157.48 in, 400 cm; width: 65.55 in, 166 cm; height: 47.24 in, 120 cm; ground clearance: 5.98 in, 15.2 cm; weight: 1,654 lb, 750 kg; weight distribution: 40% front, 60% rear; turning circle: (right) 31.8 ft, 9.7 m, (left) 35.4 ft, 10.8 m; fuel tank: 8.8 imp gal, 10.6 US gal, 40 l.

BODY coupé - convertible, in reinforced fiberglass material; 2 doors; 2 seats, reclining backrests, built-in headrests; light alloy wheels; tinted glass.

VARIATIONS

ENGINE 103.7 cu in, 1,700 cc.
ENGINE 109.8 cu in, 1,800 cc.

OPTIONALS 4-speed fully synchronized mechanical gearbox (I 2.570, II 1.610, III 1.240, IV 0.960, rev 3.880), 4.375 axle ratio; 4-speed fully synchronized mechanical gearbox (I 1.740, II 1.320, III 1.120, IV 0.960, rev 3.880), 3.880 axle ratio; ZF limited slip differential; anti-roll bar on rear suspension; (for GTC Convertible only) hardtop.

GTB S2 Sport 2+2

PRICE EX WORKS: 6,968,000* cruzeiros

ENGINE front, 4 stroke; 6 cylinders, in line; 250 cu in, 4,097 cc (3.87 x 3.52 in, 98.4 x 89.5 mm); compression ratio: 7.8:1; max power (SAE): 171 hp (126 kW) at 4,800 rpm; max torque (SAE): 236 lb ft, 32.5 kg m (319 Nm) at 2,600 rpm; max engine rpm: 5,000; 41.7 hp/l (30.7 kW/l); cast iron block and head; 7 crankshaft bearings; valves: overhead, in line, push-rods and rockers, hydraulic tappets; camshafts: 1, side; lubrication: gear pump, full flow filter, 7 imp pt, 8.5 US pt, 4 l; 1 DFV or Solex-Brosol 40 downdraught single barrel carburettor; fuel feed: mechanical pump; water-cooled, 18 imp pt, 21.6 US pt, 10.2 l.

TRANSMISSION driving wheels: rear; clutch: single dry plate (diaphragm), hydraulically controlled; gearbox: mechanical; gears: 4, fully synchronized; ratios: I 3.070, II 2.020, III 1.390, IV 1, rev 3.570; lever: central; final drive: hypoid bevel; axle ratio: 3.080; width of rims: 7"; tyres: 225/60 SR x 14.

PERFORMANCE max speeds: (I) 40 mph, 64 km/h; (II) 61 mph, 98 km/h; (III) 88 mph, 142 km/h; (IV) 123 mph, 198 km/h; power-weight ratio: 12.6 lb/hp (17.2 lb/kW), 5.7 kg/hp (7.8 kg/kW); carrying capacity: 617 lb, 280 kg; speed in direct drive

GURGEL X-12 TR Station Wagon

LAFER MP

GTB S2 SPORT 2+2

at 1,000 rpm: 24.6 mph, 39.6 km/h; consumption: 21.4 m/imp gal, 17.8 m/US gal, 13.2 l x 100 km.

CHASSIS box-type perimeter frame with cross members; front suspension: independent, wishbones (lower trailing links), coil springs, telescopic dampers; rear: rigid axle, twin upper longitudinal leading arms, lower transverse arms, telescopic dampers.

STEERING worm and roller.

BRAKES front disc, rear drum, servo.

ELECTRICAL EQUIPMENT 12 V; 44 Ah battery; 32 A alternator; Bosch distributor; 2 iodine headlamps.

DIMENSIONS AND WEIGHT wheel base: 95.28 in, 242 cm; front and rear track: 55.51 in, 141 cm; length: 169.29 in, 429 cm; width: 72.44 in, 184 cm; height: 50.39 in, 128 cm; ground clearance: 5.91 in, 15 cm; weight: 2,161 lb, 980 kg; turning circle: 33.8 ft, 10.3 m; fuel tank: 15.4 imp gal, 18.5 US gal, 70 l.

BODY coupé, in reinforced fiberglass material; 2 doors; 2+2 seats, separate front seats, reclining backrests; light alloy wheels; tinted glass; air-conditioning; power steering.

Sta MATILDE SM 4.1

QT BRAZIL

Jeg TL 4 x 4

ENGINE Volkswagen, rear, 4 stroke; 4 cylinders, horizontally opposed; 96.7 cu in, 1,584 cc (3.37 x 2.72 in, 85.5 x 69 mm); compression ratio: 7.2:1; max power (DIN): 54 hp (40 kW) at 4,200 rpm; max torque (DIN): 78 lb ft, 10.8 kg m (106 Nm) at 3,000 rpm; max engine rpm: 4,600; 34.1 hp/l (25.1 kW/l); block with cast iron liners and light alloy fins, light alloy head; 4 crankshaft bearings; valves: overhead, push-rods and rockers; camshafts: 1, central, lower; lubrication: gear pump, full flow filter, 4.4 imp pt, 5.3 US pt, 2.5 l, oil cooler; 2 Solex H 32 PDSI downdraught carburettors; fuel feed: mechanical pump; air-cooled.

TRANSMISSION driving wheels: front and rear; clutch: single dry plate; gearbox: mechanical; gears: 4, fully synchronized; ratios: I 3.800, II 2.060, III 1.320, IV 0.880, rev 3.880; lever: central; final drive: hypoid bevel; axle ratio: 5.143; width of rims: 5"; tyres: 7.35 x 15.

PERFORMANCE max speed: 65 mph, 104 km/h; power-weight ratio: 39.9 lb/hp (54 lb/kW), 18.1 kg/hp (24.5 kg/kW); carrying capacity: 882 lb, 400 kg; consumption: 26.2 m/imp gal, 21.8 m/US gal, 10.8 l x 100 km at 50 mph, 80 km/h.

CHASSIS box-type ladder frame; front suspension: independent, two longitudinal radius arms, transverse torsion bar, anti-roll bar, telescopic dampers; rear: independent, longitudinal radius arms, coil springs, telescopic dampers.

STEERING worm-and-roller; turns lock to lock: 3.50.

BRAKES drum, 2 independent hydraulic circuits.

ELECTRICAL EQUIPMENT 12 V; 36 Ah battery; 35 A alternator; Delco or Wapsa distributor; 2 headlamps.

DIMENSIONS AND WEIGHT wheel base: 78.74 in, 200 cm; tracks: 54.48 in, 146 cm front, 59.06 in, 150 cm rear; length: 129.92 in, 330 cm; width: 64.96 in, 165 cm; height: 66.93 in, 170 cm; ground clearance: 9.84 in, 25 cm; weight: 2,161 lb, 980 kg; weight distribution: 44.9% front, 55.1% rear; turning circle: 39.4 ft, 12 m; fuel tank: 12.1 imp gal, 14.5 US gal, 55 l - extra tank 4.4 imp gal, 5.3 US gal, 20 l.

BODY estate car/st. wagon; 2+1 doors; 5 seats, separate front seats; canvas top.

PRACTICAL INSTRUCTIONS fuel: 73-75 oct petrol; oil: engine 4.4 imp pt, 5.3 US pt, 2.5 l - gearbox 4.4 imp pt, 5.3 US pt, 2.5 l - final drive 3.5 imp pt, 4.2 US pt, 2 l; tappet clearances: inlet 0.004 in, 0.10 mm, exhaust 0.004 in, 0.10 mm; tyre pressure: front 17 psi, 1.2 atm, rear 23 psi, 1.6 atm.

OPTIONALS hardtop.

Sta MATILDE BRAZIL

SM 4.1

PRICE EX WORKS: 14,105,000 cruzeiros

ENGINE GM, front, 4 stroke; 6 cylinders, in line; 249.8 cu in, 4,093 cc (3.87 x 3.53 in, 98.4 x 89.6 mm); compression ratio: 7.8:1; max power (SAE): 171 hp (126 kW) at 4,800 rpm; max torque (SAE): 236 lb ft, 32.5 kg m (319 Nm) at 2,600 rpm; max engine rpm: 5,300; 41.7 hp/l (30.7 kW/l); cast iron block and head; 7 crankshaft bearings; valves: overhead, hydraulic tappets; camshafts: 1, side, chain-driven; lubrication: gear pump, full flow filter, 8.8 imp pt, 10.6 US pt, 5 l; 1 DVF downdraught twin barrel carburettor; air cleaner; fuel feed: mechanical pump; water-cooled, 18 imp pt, 21.6 US pt, 20.2 l.

TRANSMISSION driving wheels: rear; clutch: single dry plate; gearbox: mechanical; gears: 4, fully synchronized; ratios: I 3.400, II 2.160, III 1.380, IV 1, rev 3.810; lever: central; final drive: hypoid bevel; axle ratio: 3.810; width of rims: 6"; tyres: 215/70 HR x 15.

PERFORMANCE max speeds: (I) 28 mph, 45 km/h; (II) 50 mph, 80 km/h; (III) 71 mph, 115 km/h; (IV) 124 mph, 200 km/h; power-weight ratio: 15.5 lb/hp (21 lb/kW), 7 kg/hp (9.5 kg/kW); carrying capacity: 1,103 lb, 500 kg; acceleration: 0-50 mph (0-80 km/h) 10 sec; speed in direct drive at 1,000 rpm: 25 mph, 40 km/h; consumption: 23.5 m/imp gal, 19.6 m/US gal, 12 l x 100 km.

CHASSIS integral; front suspension: independent, upper wishbones (lower central arms), longitudinal torsion bars, Panhard cross bar, anti-roll bar, coil springs, telescopic dampers; rear: rigid axle, swinging longitudinal leading arms, transverse leafsprings, telescopic dampers.

STEERING worm and roller, servo.

BRAKES disc, dual circuit, servo.

ELECTRICAL EQUIPMENT 12 V; 44 Ah battery; 51 A alternator; Bosch distributor; 4 headlamps.

DIMENSIONS AND WEIGHT wheel base: 93.31 in, 237 cm; front and rear track: 55.51 in, 141 cm; length: 64.57 in, 418 cm; width: 67.72 in, 172 cm; height: 51.97 in, 132 cm; ground clearance: 5.91 in, 15 cm; weight: 2,646 lb, 1,200 kg; turning circle: 34.4 ft, 10.5 m; fuel tank: 14.3 imp gal, 17.2 US gal, 65 l.

BODY coupé, in fiberglass material; 2 doors; 2+2 seats, separate front seats; light alloy wheels; tinted glass.

PRACTICAL INSTRUCTIONS fuel: 80 oct petrol; oil: engine 8.8 imp pt, 10.6 US pt, 5 l, SAE 20W-40, change every 3,100 miles, 5,000 km; greasing: none; spark plug: AC 46 N.

OPTIONALS alcohol engine, 10:1 compression ratio, max power (SAE) 122 hp (90 kW) at 4,000 rpm, 5,500 max engine rpm, 29.8 hp/l (22 kW/l); automatic transmission; air-conditioning.

VOLKSWAGEN BRAZIL

Fusca

PRICE EX WORKS: 2,552,000* cruzeiros

ENGINE rear, 4 stroke; 4 cylinders, horizontally opposed; 78.4 cu in, 1,285 cc (3.03 x 2.72 in, 77 x 69 mm); compression ratio: 6.8:1; max power (DIN): 38 hp (28 kW) at 4,000 rpm; max torque

QT Jeg TL 4 x 4

VOLKSWAGEN Gol LS Limousine

VOLKSWAGEN Voyage LS Limousine

(DIN): 62 lb ft, 8.5 kg m (83 Nm) at 2,200 rpm; max engine rpm: 4,600; 29.6 hp/l (21.8 kW/l); block with cast iron liners and light alloy fins, light alloy head; 4 crankshaft bearings; valves: overhead, push-rods and rockers; camshafts: 1, central, lower; lubrication: gear pump, filter in sump, oil cooler, 4.4 imp pt, 5.3 US pt, 2.5 l; 1 Solex H 30 PIC downdraught single barrel carburettor; fuel feed: mechanical pump; air-cooled.

TRANSMISSION driving wheels: rear; clutch: single dry plate; gearbox: mechanical; gears: 4, fully synchronized; ratios: I 3.800, II 2.060, III 1.320, IV 0.880, rev 3.880; lever: central; final drive: spiral bevel; axle ratio: 4.375; width of rims: 4.5"; tyres: 5.60 x 15.

PERFORMANCE max speeds: (I) 17 mph, 28 km/h; (II) 32 mph, 52 km/h; (III) 50 mph, 80 km/h; (IV) 75 mph, 120 km/h; power-weight ratio: 45.2 lb/hp (61.4 lb/kW), 20.5 kg/hp (27.8 kg/kW); carrying capacity: 838 lb, 380 kg; acceleration: 0-50 mph (0-80 km/h) 14.3 sec; speed in top at 1,000 rpm: 18.6 mph, 30 km/h; consumption: 39.8 m/imp gal, 33.1 m/US gal, 7.1 l x 100 km.

CHASSIS backbone platform; front suspension: independent, twin swinging longitudinal trailing arms, transverse laminated torsion bars, anti-roll bar, telescopic dampers; rear: independent, swinging semi-axles, swinging longitudinal trailing arms, transverse torsion bars, telescopic dampers.

STEERING worm and roller, telescopic dampers; turns lock to lock: 2.70.

BRAKES drum; lining area: front 56.43 sq in, 364 sq cm, rear 56.43 sq in, 364 sq cm, total 112.86 sq in, 728 sq cm.

ELECTRICAL EQUIPMENT 12 V; 36 Ah battery; 350 W dynamo; Bosch distributor; 2 headlamps.

DIMENSIONS AND WEIGHT wheel base: 94.49 in, 240 cm; tracks: 51.18 in, 130 cm front, 53.15 in, 135 cm rear; length: 158.66 in, 403 cm; width: 60.63 in, 154 cm; height: 59.06 in, 150 cm; ground clearance: 5.91 in, 15 cm; weight: 1,720 lb, 780 kg; turning circle: 36.1 ft, 11 m; fuel tank: 9 imp gal, 10.8 US gal, 41 l.

BODY saloon/sedan; 2 doors; 5 seats, separate front seats, adjustable headrests.

PRACTICAL INSTRUCTIONS fuel: 73 oct petrol; oil: engine 4.4 imp pt, 5.3 US pt, 2.5 l, SAE 10W-20 (winter) 20W-40 (summer), change every 4,600 miles, 7,500 km - gearbox and final drive 5.5 imp pt, 6.3 US pt, 3 l, SAE 90 EP, no chance recommended; greasing: every 6,200 miles, 10,000 km, 4 points; spark plug: 145°; tappet clearances: inlet 0.004 in, 0.10 mm, exhaust 0.004 in, 0.10 mm; valve timing: 9°48' 35°02' 44°28' 4°14'; tyre pressure: front 16 psi, 1.1 atm, rear 20 psi, 1.4 atm.

OPTIONALS alcohol engine; electronic ignition; heating; built-in headrests.

Gol

PRICES EX WORKS:	cruzeiros
S 2+1-dr Limousine	**3,434,000**
LS 2+1-dr Limousine	**3,710,000**

ENGINE front, 4 stroke; 4 cylinders, horizontally opposed; 96.7 cu in, 1,584 cc (3.37 x 2.72 in, 85.5 x 69 mm); compression ratio: 7.2:1; max power (DIN): 55 hp (40 kW) at 4,600 rpm; max torque (DIN): 80 lb ft, 11 kg m (110 Nm) at 3,000 rpm; max engine rpm: 4,600; 34.7 hp/l (25.3 kW/l); block with cast iron liners and light alloy fins, light alloy head; 4 crankshaft bearings; valves: overhead, push-rods and rockers; camshafts: 1, central, lower; lubrication: gear pump, filter in sump, oil cooler, 4.4 imp pt, 5.3 US pt, 2.5 l; 2 Solex 32 PDSI downdraught single barrel carburettors; fuel feed: mechanical pump; air-cooled.

TRANSMISSION driving wheels: front; clutch: single dry plate (diaphragm); gearbox: mechanical; gears: 4, fully synchronized; ratios: I 3.800, II 2.060, III 1.320, IV 0.880, rev 3.880; lever: central; final drive: spiral bevel; axle ratio: 3.875; width of rims: 4.5"; tyres: 155 SR x 13.

PERFORMANCE max speeds: (I) 22 mph, 36 km/h; (II) 41 mph, 66 km/h; (III) 64 mph, 103 km/h; (IV) 88 mph, 142 km/h; power-weight ratio: 31.3 lb/hp (43 lb/kW), 14.2 kg/hp (19.5 kg/kW); carrying capacity: 860 lb, 390 kg; acceleration: 0-50 mph (0-80 km/h) 10.3 sec; speed in top at 1,000 rpm: 19.2 mph, 30.9 km/h; consumption: 29.4 m/imp gal, 24.5 m/US gal, 9.6 l x 100 km.

CHASSIS integral, front auxiliary subframe; front suspension: independent, by McPherson, lower wishbones, anti-roll bar, coil springs/telescopic damper struts; rear: independent, swinging longitudinal trailing arms linked by T-section cross beam, coil springs/telescopic damper struts.

STEERING rack-and-pinion; turns lock to lock: 3.64.

BRAKES front disc, rear drum, dual circuit, servo.

ELECTRICAL EQUIPMENT 12 V; 36 Ah battery; 350 W alternator; Bosch distributor; 2 headlamps.

DIMENSIONS AND WEIGHT wheel base: 84.40 in, 236 cm; tracks: 48.30 in, 135 cm front, 48.90 in, 137 cm rear; length: 136 in, 379 cm; width: 57.30 in, 160 cm; height: 49.20 in, 137 cm; ground clearance: 5.12 in, 13 cm; weight: 1,720 lb, 780 kg; weight distribution: 49.5% front, 50.5% rear; turning circle: 31.4 ft, 9.7 m; fuel tank: 12.3 imp gal, 14.6 US gal, 55 l.

BODY saloon/sedan; 2+1 doors; 5 seats, separate front seats, reclining backrests, headrests; folding rear seat; (for LS only) luxury equipment.

PRACTICAL INSTRUCTIONS fuel: 73 oct petrol; oil: engine 4.4 imp pt, 5.3 US pt, 2.5 l, SAE 20W-40, change every 4,700 miles, 7,500 km - gearbox and final drive 4.4 imp pt, 5.3 US pt, 2.5 l, SAE 80, no change recommended; greasing: none; spark plug: Bosch W 125 T 30 or NGK BPSGS; tappet clearances: inlet 0.004 in, 0.10 mm, exhaust 0.004 in, 0.10 mm; tyre pressure: front 22 psi, 1.5 atm, rear 26 psi, 1.8 atm.

OPTIONALS alcohol engine; halogen headlamps; heated rear window; electronic ignition; tinted glass; metallic spray; 175/70 SR x 13 tyres; light alloy wheels.

Voyage Series

PRICES EX WORKS:	cruzeiros
S 2-dr Limousine	**4,161,000**
S 4-dr Limousine	**4,266,000**
LS 2-dr Limousine	**4,447,000**
LS 4-dr Limousine	**4,578,000**
GLS 2-dr Limousine	**4,841,000**
GLS 4-dr Limousine	**4,961,000**

Power team:	Standard for:	Optional for:
73 hp	all	—
82 hp (alcohol)	—	all

73 hp power team

ENGINE front, slanted 20° to right, 4 stroke; 4 cylinders, in line; 96.9 cu in, 1,588 cc (3.13 x 3.15 in, 79.5 x 80 mm); compression ratio: 8.3:1; max power (DIN): 73 hp (54 kW) at 5,200 rpm; max torque (DIN): 88 lb ft, 12.1 kg m (119 Nm) at 2,600 rpm; max engine rpm: 5,800; 45.9 hp/l (34 kW/l); cast iron block, light alloy head; 5 crankshaft bearings; valves: overhead, in line, thimble tappets; camshafts: 1, overhead, cogged belt; lubrication: gear pump, full flow filter, 6.2 imp pt, 7.4 US pt, 3.5 l; 1 Wecarbrás progressive downdraught carburettor; fuel feed: mechanical pump; water-cooled, 9 imp pt, 10.8 US pt, 5.1 l, electric thermostatic fan.

TRANSMISSION driving wheels: front; clutch: single dry plate (diaphragm); gearbox: mechanical; gears: 4, fully synchronized; ratios: I 3.454, II 1.940, III 1.290, IV 0.910, rev 3.170; lever: central; final drive: spiral bevel; axle ratio: 4.111; width of rims: S 4.5" - LS and GLS 5"; tyres: S 155 SR x 13 - LS and GLS 175/70 SR x 13.

PERFORMANCE max speeds: (I) 28 mph, 45 km/h; (II) 50 mph, 80 km/h; (III) 75 mph, 121 km/h; (IV) 97 mph, 156 km/h; power-weight ratio: 4-dr 25.4 lb/hp (34.3 lb/kW), 11.5 kg/hp (15.6 kg/kW); carrying capacity: 926 lb, 420 kg; acceleration: 0-50 mph (0-80 km/h) 8.3 sec; speed in top at 1,000 rpm: 16.7 mph, 26.9 km/h; consumption: 34.4 m/imp gal, 28.7 m/US gal, 8.2 l x 100 km.

CHASSIS integral, front auxiliary subframe; front suspension: independent, by McPherson, lower wishbones, anti-roll bar, coil springs/telescopic damper struts; rear: independent, swinging longitudinal trailing arms linked by a V-section cross beam, coil springs/telescopic damper struts.

STEERING rack-and-pinion; turns lock to lock: 3.40.

BRAKES front disc, rear drum, dual circuit, servo.

ELECTRICAL EQUIPMENT 12 V; 36 Ah battery; 490 W alternator; Bosch distributor; 2 headlamps.

DIMENSIONS AND WEIGHT wheel base: 84.40 in, 236 cm; tracks: 48.30 in, 135 cm front, 48.90 in, 137 cm rear; length: S 159.80 in, 406 cm - LS and GLS 160.75 in, 408 cm; width: 57.30 in, 160 cm; height: 53.54 in, 136 cm; ground clearance: 5.31 in, 13.5 cm; weight: 2-dr 1,808 lb, 820 kg - 4-dr 1,852 lb, 840 kg; weight distribution: 50% front, 50% rear; turning circle: 33.5 ft, 10.2 m; fuel tank: 12.1 imp gal, 14.5 US gal, 55 l.

BODY saloon/sedan; 2 or 4 doors; 5 seats, separate front seats, reclining backrests, headrests; (for LS and GLS models only) luxury equipment.

PRACTICAL INSTRUCTIONS fuel: 73 oct petrol; oil: engine 6.2 imp pt, 7.4 US pt, 3.5 l, SAE 20W-40, change every 4,700 miles, 7,500 km - gearbox and final drive 3 imp pt, 3.6 US pt, 1.7 l, SAE 80, no change recommended; greasing: none; spark plug: M 14 1.25; tappet clearances: inlet 0.008 in, 0.20 mm, exhaust 0.016 in, 0.40 mm; tyre pressure: front 24 psi, 1.7 atm, rear 25 psi, 1.8 atm.

OPTIONALS electronic ignition; halogen headlamps; heated rear window; tinted glass; metallic spray; heating light alloy wheels.

VOLKSWAGEN Parati GLS Station Wagon

82 hp (alcohol) power team

See 73 hp power team, except for:

ENGINE alcohol; compression ratio: 10.8:1; max power (DIN): 82 hp (60 kW) at 5,200 rpm; max torque (DIN): 88 lb ft, 12.1 kg m (119 Nm) at 4,000 rpm; 51.6 hp/l (37.8 kW/l).

PERFORMANCE max speed: 101 mph, 162 km/h; power-weight ratio: 4-dr 22.5 lb/hp (30.9 lb/kW), 10.2 kg/hp (14 kg/kW); acceleration: 0-50 mph (0-80 km/h) 7.3 sec; consumption: 24.6 m/imp gal, 20.5 m/US gal, 11.5 l x 100 km.

ELECTRICAL EQUIPMENT Bosch electronic ignition (standard).

OPTIONALS halogen headlamps; heated rear window; tinted glass; metallic spray; heating; light alloy wheels.

Parati Series

PRICES EX WORKS:	cruzeiros
S 2+1-dr St. Wagon	**3,964,000**
LS 2+1-dr St. Wagon	**4,472,000**
GLS 2+1-dr St. Wagon	**4,865,000**

Power team:	Standard for:	Optional for:
65 hp	all	—
82 hp (alcohol)	—	all

65 hp power team

ENGINE front, slanted 20° to right, 4 stroke; 4 cylinders, in line; 96.9 cu in, 1,588 cc (3.13 x 3.15 in, 79.5 x 80 mm); compression ratio: 8.3:1; max power (DIN): 65 hp (48 kW) at 5,600 rpm; max torque (DIN): 72 lb ft, 10 kg m (98 Nm) at 3,200 rpm; max engine rpm: 5,800; 40.9 hp/l (30.2 kW/l); cast iron block, light alloy head; 5 crankshaft bearings; valves: overhead, in line, thimble tappets; camshafts: 1, overhead, cogged belt; lubrication: gear pump, full flow filter, 6.2 imp pt, 7.4 US pt, 3.5 l; 1 Wecarbrás progressive downdraught carburettor; fuel feed: mechanical pump; water-cooled, 9 imp pt, 10.8 US pt, 5.1 l, electric thermostatic fan.

TRANSMISSION driving wheels: front; clutch: single dry plate (diaphragm); gearbox: mechanical; gears: 4, fully synchronized; ratios: I 3.454, II 1.940, III 1.290, IV 0.910, rev 3.170; lever: central; final drive: spiral bevel; axle ratio: 4.111; width of rims: 5"; tyres: 175/70 SR x 13.

PERFORMANCE max speeds: (I) 28 mph, 45 km/h; (II) 50 mph, 80 km/h; (III) 75 mph, 121 km/h; (IV) 98 mph, 158 km/h; power-weight ratio: 29.8 lb/hp (40.4 lb/kW), 13.5 kg/hp (18.3 kg/kW); carrying capacity: 1,102 lb, 500 kg; acceleration: 0-50 mph (0-80 km/h) 8.8 sec; speed in top at 1,000 rpm: 16.7 mph, 26.9 km/h; consumption: 34.4 m/imp gal, 28.7 m/US gal, 8.2 l x 100 km.

CHASSIS integral, front auxiliary subframe; front suspension: independent, by McPherson, lower wishbones, anti-roll bar, coil springs/telescopic damper struts; rear: independent, swinging longitudinal trailing arms linked by a V-section cross beam, coil springs/telescopic damper struts.

STEERING rack-and-pinion; turns lock to lock: 3.40.

BRAKES front disc, rear drum, dual circuit, servo.

ELECTRICAL EQUIPMENT 12 V; 36 Ah battery; 490 W alternator; Bosch distributor; 2 headlamps.

DIMENSIONS AND WEIGHT wheel base: 84.40 in, 236 cm; tracks: 48.30 in, 135 cm front, 48.90 in, 137 cm rear; length: S 160.24 in, 407 cm - LS and GLS 161.02 in, 409 cm; width: 63.78 in, 162 cm; height: 54.33 in, 138 cm; ground clearance: 5.91 in, 15 cm; weight: 1,940 lb, 880 kg; weight distribution: 49% front, 51% rear; turning circle: 33.5 ft, 10.2 m; fuel tank: 12.1 imp gal, 14.5 US gal, 55 l.

ALLARD J2X-2

BODY estate car/st. wagon; 2+1 doors; 5 seats, separate front seats, reclining backrests, headrests; folding rear seat; (for LS and GLS only) luxury equipment.

PRACTICAL INSTRUCTIONS fuel: 73 oct petrol; oil: engine 6.2 imp pt, 7.4 US pt, 3.5 l, SAE 20W-40, change every 4,700 miles, 7,500 km - gearbox and final drive 3 imp pt, 3.6 US pt, 1.7 l, SAE 80, no change recommended; greasing: none; spark plug: M 14 125; tappet clearances: inlet 0.008 in, 0.20 mm, exhaust 0.016 in, 0.40 mm; tyre pressure: front 24 psi, 1.7 atm, rear 28 psi, 2 atm.

OPTIONALS electronic ignition; halogen headlamps; heated rear window; tinted glass; metallic spray; heating; light alloy wheels; rear window wiper-washer.

82 hp (alcohol) power team

See 65 hp power team, except for:

ENGINE compression ratio: 10.8:1; max power (DIN): 82 hp (60 kW) at 5,200 rpm; max torque (DIN): 88 lb ft, 12.1 kg m (199 Nm) at 4,000 rpm; 51.6 hp/l (37.8 kW/l).

PERFORMANCE max speed: 102 mph, 164 km/h; power-weight ratio: 23.6 lb/hp (32.4 lb/kW), 10.7 kg/hp (14.7 kg/kW); acceleration: 0-50 mph (0-80 km/h) 8.5 sec; consumption: 24.6 m/imp gal, 20.5 m/US gal, 11.5 l x 100 km.

ELECTRICAL EQUIPMENT Bosch electronic ignition (standard).

OPTIONALS halogen headlamps; heated rear window; tinted glass; metalic spray; heating; light alloy wheels; rear window wiper-washer.

Passat Series

PRICES EX WORKS:	cruzeiros
Special 2-dr Limousine	**4,306,000**
LS 2-dr Limousine	**4,606,000**
LS 2+1-dr Limousine	**4,829,000**
LS 4-dr Limousine	**4,910,000**
GTS 2-dr Limousine	**5,917,000**
LSE 4-dr Limousine	**5,855,000**

VOLKSWAGEN Passat GTS Limousine

Power team:	Standard for:	Optional for:
73 hp	all	—
82 hp (alcohol)	—	all

73 hp power team

ENGINE front, slanted 20° to right, 4 stroke; 4 cylinders, in line; 96.9 cu in, 1,588 cc (3.13 x 3.15 in, 79.5 x 80 mm); compression ratio: 8.3:1; max power (DIN): 73 hp (54 kW) at 5,200 rpm; max torque (DIN): 88 lb ft, 12.1 kg m (119 Nm) at 2,600 rpm; max engine rpm: 5,800; 45.9 hp/l (34 kW/l); cast iron block, light alloy head;.5 crankshaft bearings; valves: overhead, in line, thimble tappets; camshafts: 1, overhead, cogged belt; lubrication: gear pump, full flow filter, 6.2 imp pt, 7.4 US pt, 3.5 l; 1 Wecarbras progressive downdraught carburettor; fuel feed: mechanical pump; water-cooled, 9 imp pt, 10.8 US pt, 5.1 l, electric thermostatic fan.

TRANSMISSION driving wheels: front; clutch: single dry plate (diaphragm); gearbox: mechanical; gears: 4, fully synchronized; ratios: I 3.454, II 1.940, III 1.290, IV 0.910, rev 3.170; lever: central; final drive: spiral bevel; axle ratio: 4.111; width of rims: 5"; tyres: 175/70 SR x 13.

PERFORMANCE max speeds: (I) 28 mph, 45 km/h; (II) 50 mph, 81 km/h; (III) 76 mph, 122 km/h; (IV) 97 mph, 154 km/h; power-weight ratio: 4-dr 27.6 lb/hp (37.4 lb/kW), 12.5 kg/hp (16.9 kg/kW); carrying capacity: 992 lb, 450 kg; acceleration: 0-50 mph (0-80 km/h) 8.7 sec; speed in top at 1,000 rpm: 16.7 mph, 26.8 km/h; consumption: 33.2 m/imp gal, 27.7 m/US gal, 8.5 l x 100 km.

CHASSIS integral, front auxiliary subframe; front suspension: independent, by McPherson, lower wishbones, anti-roll bar, coil springs/telescopic damper struts; rear: rigid axle, trailing radius arms, transverse linkage bar, coil springs, anti-roll bar, telescopic dampers.

STEERING rack-and-pinion; turns lock to lock: 3.94.

BRAKES front disc, rear drum, dual circuit, servo.

ELECTRICAL EQUIPMENT 12 V; 42 Ah battery; 490 W alternator; Bosch distributor; 2 halogen headlamps.

DIMENSIONS AND WEIGHT wheel base: 97.24 in, 247 cm; tracks: 52.76 in, 134 cm front, 52.83 in, 134 cm rear; length: 168.90 in, 429 cm; width: 62.99 in, 160 cm; height: 53.35 in, 135 cm; ground clearance: 5.12 in, 13 cm; weight: 2-dr 1,962 lb, 890 kg - 4-dr 2,018 lb, 915 kg; weight distribution: 50% front, 50% rear; turning circle: 33.8 ft, 10.3 m; fuel tank: 13.2 imp gal, 15.8 US gal, 60 l.

BODY saloon/sedan; 2, 2+1 or 4 doors; 5 seats, separate front seats, reclining backrests - (for GTS and LSE only) headrests; (for 2+1-dr only) folding rear seat.

PRACTICAL INSTRUCTIONS fuel: 73 oct petrol; oil: engine 6.2 imp pt, 7.4 US pt, 3.5 l, SAE 20W-40, change every 4,700 miles, 7,500 km - gearbox and final drive 3 imp pt, 3.6 US pt, 1.7 l, SAE 80, no change recommended; greasing: none; spark plug: Bosch W 145 T2 - NGK BP 6 G - M 14 125; tappet clearances: inlet 0.008 in, 0.20 mm, exhaust 0.016 in, 0.40 mm; tyre pressure: front 24 psi, 1.7 atm, rear 28 psi, 2 atm.

OPTIONALS electronic ignition; light alloy wheels; sunroof; heated rear window; tinted glass; air-conditioning; metallic spray; heating; Recaro seats.

82 hp (alcohol) power team

See 73 hp power team, except for:

ENGINE compression ratio: 12:1; max power (DIN): 82 hp (60 kW) at 5,200 rpm; max torque (DIN): 93 lb ft, 12.9 kg m (126 Nm) at 2,600 rpm; 51.6 hp/l (37.8 kW/l).

PERFORMANCE max speed: 99 mph, 160 km/h; power-weight ratio: 4-dr 24.7 lb/hp (33.5 lb/kW), 11.2 kg/hp (15.2 kg/kW);

acceleration: 0-50 mph (0-80 km/h) 7.9 sec; consumption: 24.6 m/imp gal, 20.5 m/US gal, 11.5 l x 100 km.

ELECTRICAL EQUIPMENT Bosch electronic ignition (standard).

OPTIONALS light alloy wheels; sunroof; heated rear window; tinted glass; air-conditioning; metallic spray; heating; Recaro seats.

ALLARD CANADA

J2X-2

PRICE EX WORKS: $ 41,200

ENGINE Chrysler, front, 4 stroke; 8 cylinders in Vee; 318 cu in, 5,211 cc (3.91 x 3.31 in, 99.2 x 84 mm); compression ratio: 8.5:1; max power (SAE net): 130 hp (97 kW) at 4,000 rpm; max torque (SAE net): 230 lb ft, 31.8 kg m (312 Nm) at 2,000 rpm; max engine rpm: 4,200; 24 hp/l (18.6 kW/l); 5 crankshaft bearings; valves: overhead, in line, push-rods and rockers, hydraulic tappets; camshafts: 1, at centre of Vee; lubrication: rotary pump, full flow filter, 10 imp pt, 12 US pt, 4.7 l; 1 Holley downdraught twin barrel carburettor; fuel feed: mechanical pump; water-cooled, 26.5 imp pt, 31.9 US pt, 15.1 l.

TRANSMISSION driving wheels: rear; clutch: single dry plate (diaphragm); gearbox: mechanical; gears: 4, fully synchronized; ratios: I 3.090, II 1.670, III 1, IV 0.730, rev 3; lever: central; final drive: hypoid bevel.

PERFORMANCE max speed: 140 mph, 224 km/h; power-weight ratio: 16.8 lb/hp (22.8 lb/kW), 7.6 kg/hp (10.3 kg/kW).

CHASSIS front suspension: independent, wishbones, coil springs, telescopic dampers; rear: rigid axle, adjustable coil springs, telescopic dampers, Watts linkage.

STEERING rack-and-pinion; turns lock to lock: 4.20.

BRAKES front disc, rear drum, servo.

ELECTRICAL EQUIPMENT 12 V; 325 Ah battery; 60 A alternator; Chrysler transistorized ignition; 2 headlamps.

DIMENSIONS AND WEIGHT wheel base: 100 in, 254 cm; tracks: 56 in, 142 cm front, 52 in, 132 cm rear; length: 163 in, 414 cm; width: 63 in, 160 cm; height: 46 in, 117 cm; ground clearance: 7.30 in, 18.5 cm; weight: 2,180 lb, 981 kg; weight distribution: 61% front, 39% rear; fuel tank: 19 imp gal, 23.8 US gal, 85 l.

BODY sports; 2 doors; 2 seats, bench front seats; leather upholstery.

OPTIONALS turbocharger; automatic transmission with 3 ratios (I 2.450, II 1.450, III 1, rev 2.200); aero screens; all weather equipment; second side-mounted spare tyre.

AURORA CANADA

Aurora Mk II

PRICE EX WORKS: Canadian $ 46,000

ENGINE Ford, front, 4 stroke; 8 cylinders in Vee; 302 cu in, 4,950 cc (4 x 3 in, 101.6 x 76.2 mm); compression ratio: 8.4:1; max power (SAE net): 206 hp (152 kW) at 4,500 rpm; max torque (SAE net): 250 lb ft, 34.5 kg m (338 Nm) at 2,800 rpm; max engine rpm: 5,000; 41.6 hp/l (30.6 kW/l); cast iron block and head; 5 crankshaft bearings; valves: overhead, in line, push-rods and rockers, hydraulic tappets; camshafts: 1, at centre of Vee; lubrication: rotary pump, full flow filter, 6.7 imp pt, 8 US pt, 3.8 l; 1 downdraught carburettor with Variable Venturi; air cleaner; exhaust system with catalytic converter; fuel feed: mechanical pump; water-cooled, 19.9 imp pt, 24 US pt, 11.3 l.

TRANSMISSION driving wheels: rear; clutch: single dry plate; gearbox: mechanical; gears: 5, fully synchronized; lever: steering column; final drive: hypoid bevel; axle ratio: 3.080; tyres: Michelin TRX 220 55R x 390.

PERFORMANCE max speed: 142 mph, 228 km/h; power-weight ratio: 10.6 lb/hp (14.1 lb/kW), 4.8 kg/hp (6.4 kg/kW); carrying capacity: 353 lb, 160 kg; acceleration: standing ¼ mile 13.8 sec; consumption: 31.4 m/imp gal, 26 m/US gal, 9 l x 100 km.

CHASSIS space frame; front suspension: independent, unequal length control arms, coil springs/telescopic dampers, anti-roll bar; rear: independent, equal length tubular control arms, coil springs/telescopic dampers, anti-roll bar.

STEERING rack-and-pinion; turns lock to lock: 2.80.

BRAKES disc, internal radial fins.

AURORA Aurora Mk II

ELECTRICAL EQUIPMENT 12 V; 36 Ah battery; 60 A alternator; Ford ignition; 2 headlamps.

DIMENSIONS AND WEIGHT wheel base: 90 in, 229 cm; tracks: 52 in, 132 cm front, 51 in, 129 cm rear; length: 162 in, 411 cm; width: 60.25 in, 153 cm; height: 46 in, 117 cm; ground clearance: 6 in, 15.2 cm; weight: 2,160 lb, 979 kg; weight distribution: 50% front, 50% rear; fuel tank: 12.5 imp gal, 15 US gal, 57 l.

BODY roadster, in fiberglass material; 2 doors; 2 separate seats; folding soft top; aluminium wheels; leather upholstery.

OPTIONALS wire wheels; air-conditioning.

CHEVROLET CANADA

Chevette Scooter Series

PRICES EX WORKS:	**Canadian $**
4+1-dr Hatchback Sedan	6,074
2+1-dr Hatchback Coupé	5,812

Power team:	**Standard for:**	**Optional for:**
65 hp	both	—
51 hp (diesel)	—	both

65 hp power team

ENGINE front, 4 stroke; 4 cylinders, vertical, in line; 97.6 cu in, 1,599 cc (3.23 x 2.98 in, 82 x 75.6 mm); compression ratio: 9:1; max power (SAE net): 65 hp (48 kW) at 5,200 rpm; max torque (SAE net): 80 lb ft, 11.1 kg m (109 Nm) at 3,200 rpm; max engine rpm: 5,600; 40.6 hp/l (29.9 kW/l); cast iron block and head; 5 crankshaft bearings; valves: overhead, hydraulic tappets; camshafts: 1, overhead, cogged belt; lubrication: gear pump, full flow filter, 6.7 imp pt, 8 US pt, 3.8 l; 1 Holley downdraught twin barrel carburettor; air cleaner; exhaust system with catalytic converter; fuel feed: mechanical pump; water-cooled, 15.3 imp pt, 18.4 US pt, 8.7 l.

TRANSMISSION driving wheels: rear; clutch: single dry plate (diaphragm); gearbox: mechanical; gears: 4, fully synchronized; ratios: I 3.750, II 2.160, III 1.380, VI 1, rev 3.820; lever: central; final drive: hypoid bevel; axle ratio: 3.360; width of rims: 5"; tyres: P 155/80 R x 13.

PERFORMANCE max speed: 90 mph, 145 km/h; power-weight ratio: Sedan 32 lb/hp (43.2 lb/kW), 14.5 kg/hp (19.6 kg/kW); speed in direct drive at 1,000 rpm: 17.9 mph, 28.8 km/h; consumption: 34.9 m/imp gal, 29 m/US gal, 8.1 l x 100 km.

CHASSIS integral with cross member reinforcements; front suspension: independent, wishbones, coil springs, anti-roll bar, telescopic dampers; rear: rigid axle (torque tube), longitudinal trailing radius arms, coil springs, transverse linkage bar, anti-roll bar, telescopic dampers.

STEERING rack-and-pinion; turns lock to lock: 3.60.

BRAKES front disc (diameter 9.68 in, 24.6 cm), rear drum; swept area: total 279.8 sq in, 1,084 sq cm.

ELECTRICAL EQUIPMENT 12 V; 2,500 W battery; 42 A alternator; Delco-Remy high energy ignition; 2 headlamps.

DIMENSIONS AND WEIGHT wheel base: Sedan 97.30 in, 247 cm - Coupé 94.30 in, 239 cm; front and rear track: 51.20 in, 130 cm; length: Sedan 164.90 in, 419 cm - Coupé 161.90 in, 410 cm; width: 61.80 in, 157 cm; height: 52.90 in, 134 cm; ground clearance: 5.30 in, 13.5 cm; weight: Sedan 2,079 lb, 943 kg - Coupé 2,031 lb, 921 kg; turning circle: 34.3 ft, 10.5 m; fuel tank: 10.3 imp gal, 12.5 US gal, 47 l.

BODY saloon/sedan; 4+1 doors - coupé, 2+1 doors; 4 seats, separate front seats, built-in headrests.

OPTIONALS 5-speed fully synchronized mechanical gearbox (I 3.760, II 2.180, III 1.360, IV 1, V 0.860, rev 3.760); Turbo-Hydramatic 180 automatic transmission, hydraulic torque converter and planetary gears with 3 ratios (I 2.400, II 1.480, III 1, rev 1.920), max ratio of converter at stall 2.25; possible manual selection, central lever, 3.620 axle ratio; heavy-duty battery; servo brake; vinyl roof; heavy-duty radiator; tilt of steering wheel; heated rear window; air-conditioning; de luxe equipment; Custom two-tone paint equipment.

CHEVROLET Chevette Scooter Hatchback Coupé

PONTIAC Acadian Hatchback Sedan

AYMESA Condor GT Sedan

51 hp (diesel) power team

See 65 hp power team, except for:

ENGINE diesel; 111 cu in, 1,819 cc (3.31 x 3.23 in, 84 x 82 mm); compression ratio: 22:1; max power (SAE net): 51 hp (38 kW) at 5,000 rpm; max torque (SAE net): 72 lb ft, 9.9 kg m (97 Nm) at 2,000 rpm; max engine rpm: 5,400; 28 hp/l (20.6 kW/l); valves: mechanical tappets; Bosch injection pump; cooling: 14.2 imp pt, 16.9 US pt, 8 l.

TRANSMISSION gears: 5, fully synchronized; ratios: I 3.790, II 2.180, III 1.420, IV 1, V 0.860, rev 3.760.

PERFORMANCE max speed: 84 mph, 135 km/h; power-weight ratio: Sedan 43.7 lb/hp (58.7 lb/kW), 19.8 kg/hp (26.6 kg/kW); consumption: 47 m/imp gal, 40 m/US gal, 5.9 l x 100 km.

ELECTRICAL EQUIPMENT 5,000 W battery.

DIMENSIONS AND WEIGHT weight: Sedan 2,228 lb, 1,010 kg - Coupé 2,122 lb, 962 kg.

OPTIONALS Turbo-Hydramatic 200 automatic transmission, hydraulic torque converter and planetary gears with 3 ratios (I 2.740, II 1.570, III 1, rev 2.070), max ratio of converter at stall 2.40, possible manual selection, 3.360 or 3.620 axle ratio.

FORD CANADA

For technical data, see Ford USA.

MERCURY CANADA

For technical data, see Mercury USA.

PONTIAC CANADA

Acadian Series

PRICES EX WORKS:	Canadian $
Scooter 4+1-dr Hatchback Sedan	**6,074**
Scooter 2+1-dr Hatchback Coupé	**5,812**
4+1-dr Hatchback Sedan	**6,583**
2+1-dr Hatchback Coupé	**6,400**

Power team:	Standard for:	Optional for:
65 hp	all	—
51 hp (diesel)	all	—

65 hp power team

ENGINE front, 4 stroke; 4 cylinders, vertical, in line; 97.6 cu in, 1,599 cc (3.23 x 2.98 in, 82 x 75.6 mm); compression ratio: 9:1; max power (SAE net): 65 hp (48 kW) at 5,200 rpm; max torque (SAE net): 80 lb ft, 11.1 kg m (109 Nm) at 3,200 rpm; max engine rpm: 5,600; 40.6 hp/l (29.9 kW/l); cast iron block and head; 5 crankshaft bearings; valves: overhead, hydraulic tappets; camshafts: 1, overhead, cogged belt; lubrication: gear pump, full flow filter, 6.7 imp pt, 8 US pt, 3.8 l; 1 Holley downdraught twin barrel carburettor; air cleaner; exhaust system with catalytic converter; fuel feed: mechanical pump; water-cooled, 15.3 imp pt, 18.4 US pt, 8.7 l.

TRANSMISSION driving wheels: rear; clutch: single dry plate (diaphragm); gearbox: mechanical; gears: 4, fully synchronized; ratios: I 3.750, II 2.160, III 1.380, IV 1, rev 3.820; lever: central; final drive: hypoid bevel; axle ratio: 3.360; width of rims: 5''; tyres: P 155/80 R x 13.

PERFORMANCE max speed: 90 mph, 145 km/h; power-weight ratio: Hatchback Sedan and Coupé 31.6 lb/hp (43 lb/kW), 14.4 kg/hp (19.5 kg/kW); speed in direct drive at 1,000 rpm: 17.9 mph, 28.8 km/h; consumption: 34.9 m/imp gal, 29 m/US gal, 8.1 l x 100 km.

CHASSIS integral with cross member reinforcements; front suspension: independent, wishbones, coil springs, anti-roll bar, telescopic dampers; rear: rigid axle (torque tube), longitudinal trailing radius arms, coil springs, transverse linkage bar, anti-roll bar, telescopic dampers.

STEERING rack-and-pinion; turns lock to lock: 3.60.

BRAKES front disc (diameter 9.68 in, 24.6 cm), rear drum; swept area: total 279.8 sq in, 1,804 sq cm.

ELECTRICAL EQUIPMENT 12 V; 2,500 W battery; 42 A alternator; Delco-Remy high energy ignition; 2 headlamps.

DIMENSIONS AND WEIGHT wheel base: 97.30 in, 247 cm - coupés 94.30 in, 239 cm; front and rear track: 51.20 in, 130 cm; length: 164.90 in, 419 cm - coupés 161.90 in, 410 cm; width: 61.80 in, 157 cm; height: 52.90 in, 134 cm; ground clearance: 5.30 in, 13.5 cm; weight: Scooter Hatchback Coupé 2,031 lb, 921 kg - Scooter Hatchback Sedan 2,079 lb, 943 kg - Hatchback Sedan and Hatchback Coupé 2,028 lb, 920 kg; turning circle: 34.3 ft, 10.5 m; fuel tank: 10.3 imp gal, 12.5 US gal, 47 l.

BODY saloon/sedan, 4+1 doors - coupé, 2+1 doors; 4 seats, separate front seats, built-in headrests.

OPTIONALS 5-speed fully synchronized mechanical gearbox (I 3.760, II 2.180, III 1.360, IV 1, V 0.860, rev 3.760); Turbo-Hydramatic 180 automatic transmission, hydraulic torque converter and planetary gears with 3 ratios (I 2.400, II 1.480, III 1, rev 1.920), max ratio of converter at stall 2.25, possible manual selection, central lever, 3.620 axle ratio; heavy-duty battery; servo brake; vinyl roof; heavy-duty radiator; tilt of steering wheel; heated rear window; air-conditioning; de luxe equipment; Custom two-tone paint equipment.

PONTIAC Acadian Scooter

51 hp (diesel) power team

See 65 hp power team, except for:

ENGINE diesel; 111 cu in, 1,819 cc (3.31 x 3.23 in, 84 x 82 mm); compression ratio: 22:1; max power (SAE net): 51 hp (38 kW) at 5,000 rpm; max torque (SAE net): 72 lb ft, 9.9 kg m (97 Nm) at 2,000 rpm; max engine rpm: 5,400; 28 hp/l (20.6 kW/l); valves: mechanical tappets; Bosch injection pump; cooling: 14.2 imp pt, 16.9 US pt, 8 l.

TRANSMISSION gears: 5, fully synchronized; ratios: I 3.790, II 2.180, III 1.420, IV 1, V 0.860, rev 3.760.

PERFORMANCE max speed: 84 mph, 135 km/h; power-weight ratio: Scooter Hatchback Sedan 40.8 lb/hp (55.4 lb/kW), 18.5 kg/hp (25.1 kg/kW); consumption: 47 m/imp gal, 40 m/US gal, 5.9 l x 100 km.

ELECTRICAL EQUIPMENT 5,000 W battery.

DIMENSIONS AND WEIGHT weight: Scooter Hatchback Coupé 2,122 lb, 962 kg - Hatchback Coupé 2,168 lb, 983 kg - sedans 2,228 lb, 1,010 kg.

OPTIONALS Turbo-Hydramatic 200 automatic transmission, hydraulic torque converter and planetary gears with 3 ratios (I 2.740, II 1.570, III 1, rev 2.070), max ratio of converter at stall 2.40, possible manual selection, 3.360 or 3.620 axle ratio.

TIMMIS CANADA

Ford V8 Roadster

PRICE EX WORKS: Canadian $ 50,000

ENGINE Ford, front, 4 stroke; 8 cylinders in Vee; 239.4 cu in, 3,923 cc (3.19 x 3.75 in, 80.9 x 95.2 mm); compression ratio: 8:1; max power (DIN): 125 hp (92 kW) at 3,800 rpm; max torque (DIN): 200 lb ft, 27.6 kg m (271 Nm) at 1,850 rpm; max engine rpm: 4,200; 31.9 hp/l (23.5 kW/l); cast iron block and head; 3 crankshaft bearings; valves: side; camshafts: 1, at centre of Vee; lubrication: gear pump, 8 imp pt, 9.5 US pt, 4.5 l; 1 Ford downdraught twin barrel carburettor; fuel feed: mechanical pump; water-cooled, 44 imp pt, 52.9 US pt, 25 l.

TRANSMISSION driving wheels: rear; clutch: single dry plate; gearbox: mechanical; gears: 3, II and III synchronized; lever: central; final drive: hypoid bevel; axle ratio: 3.300, 3.540 or 3.550; tyres: Firestone 6.00 x 16.

PERFORMANCE max speed: 100 mph, 161 km/h; power-weight ratio: 18.7 lb/hp (25.6 lb/kW), 8.5 kg/hp (11.6 kg/kW); carrying capacity: 700 lb, 317 kg; consumption: 20 m/imp gal, 16.7 m/US gal, 14.1 l x 100 km.

CHASSIS separate X frame; front suspension: independent, transverse leafsprings, anti-roll bar, telescopic dampers; rear: rigid axle, twin semi-elliptic leafsprings, telescopic dampers.

STEERING worm and roller; turns lock to lock: 5.

BRAKES drum; swept area: front 186 sq in, 1,200 sq cm, rear 186 sq in, 1,200 sq cm, total 372 sq in, 2,400 sq cm.

ELECTRICAL EQUIPMENT 6 V; 90 Ah battery; dynamo; Ford distributor; 2 headlamps.

DIMENSIONS AND WEIGHT wheel base: 112 in, 284 cm; tracks: 55.20 in, 140 cm front, 56.68 in, 144 cm rear; length: 175.90 in, 447 cm; width: 67.38 in, 171 cm; height: 65.50 in, 166 cm; ground clearance: 9 in, 22.9 cm; weight: 2,350 lb, 1,066 kg; weight distribution: 55% front, 45% rear; turning circle: 40 ft, 12.2 m; fuel tank: 11.7 imp gal, 14 US gal, 53 l.

BODY roadster, in fiberglass material; 2 doors; 2 seats, bench front seats; bucket seats; canvas top; wire wheels.

PRACTICAL INSTRUCTIONS fuel: 98 oct petrol; oil: engine 8 imp pt, 9.5 US pt, 4.5 l, SAE 30, change every 2,000 miles, 3,200 km - gearbox 2.1 imp pt, 2.5 US pt, 1.2 l, SAE 90, change every 6 months - final drive 1.6 imp pt, 2 US pt, 0.9 l, SAE 90, change every 6 months; greasing: every 2,000 miles, 3,200 km, 15 points; spark plug: Champion H-10; tappet clearances: inlet 0.012 in, 0.30 mm, exhaust 0.014 in, 0.35 mm; valve timing: 0° 44° 48° 6°; tyre pressure: front and rear 26 psi, 1.8 atm.

TIMMIS Ford V8 Roadster

AYMESA — ECUADOR

Gala / Condor GT

PRICES EX WORKS:	sucres
Gala 2+1-dr Sedan	**814,000**
Condor GT 2+1-dr Sedan	**553,000**

ENGINE front, 4 stroke; 4 cylinders, in line; 85.4 cu in, 1,400 cc (3.22 x 2.60 in, 81.9 x 66.2 mm); compression ratio: 8.5:1; max power (DIN): 71 hp (52 kW) at 6,000 rpm; max torque (DIN): 71 lb ft, 9.8 kg m (96 Nm) at 3,800 rpm; max engine rpm: 6,400; 50.7 hp/l (37.3 kW/l); cast iron or light alloy block, light alloy head; 4 crankshaft bearings; valves: overhead, push-rods and rockers; camshafts: 1, overhead; lubrication: mechanical pump, metal/paper filter, 6.2 imp pt, 7.4 US pt, 3.5 l; 1 Solex H 34 SEIE downdraught twin barrel carburettor; fuel feed: mechanical pump; water-cooled, 12.3 imp pt, 14.8 US pt, 7 l.

TRANSMISSION driving wheels: rear; clutch: single dry plate; gearbox: mechanical; gears: 4, fully synchronized; ratios: I 3.746, II 2.156, III 1.378, IV 1, rev 3.800; lever: central; final drive: hypoid bevel; width of rims: 6"; tyres: 165/70 SR x 14.

PERFORMANCE max speed: 99 mph, 160 km/h; power-weight ratio: 25.5 lb/hp (34.7 lb/kW), 11.6 kg/hp (15.7 kg/kW); consumption: 28.8 m/imp gal, 24 m/US gal, 9.8 l x 100 km.

CHASSIS integral; front suspension: independent, wishbones, coil springs, anti-roll bar, telescopic dampers; rear: rigid axle, coil springs, anti-roll bar, telescopic dampers.

STEERING rack-and-pinion.

BRAKES front disc, rear drum, servo.

ELECTRICAL EQUIPMENT 12 V; 38 Ah battery; 32-38 A alternator; Bosch distributor; 2 headlamps.

DIMENSIONS AND WEIGHT wheel base: Gala 94.09 in, 239 cm - Condor 92.13 in, 234 cm; front and rear track: 51.18 in, 130 cm; length: 165.35 in, 420 cm; width: 61.81 in, 157 cm; height: 51.97 in, 132 cm; ground clearance: 7.87 in, 20 cm; weight: 1,814 lb, 823 kg; fuel tank: 7.9 imp gal, 9.5 US gal, 36 l.

BODY saloon/sedan; 2+1 doors; 5 seats, separate front seats.

VOLKSWAGEN — MEXICO

1200 L

ENGINE rear, 4 stroke; 4 cylinders, horizontally opposed; 72.7 cu in, 1,192 cc (3.03 x 2.52 in, 77 x 64 mm); compression ratio: 7.3:1; max power (DIN): 34 hp (25 kW) at 3,800 rpm; max torque (DIN): 56 lb ft, 7.7 kg m (76 Nm) at 1,700 rpm; max engine rpm: 4,500; 28.5 hp/l (21 kW/l); block with cast iron liners and light alloy fins, light alloy head; 4 crankshaft bearings; valves: overhead, push-rods and rockers; camshafts: 1, central, lower; lubrication: gear pump, filter in sump, oil cooler, 4.4 imp pt, 5.3 US pt, 2.5 l; 1 Solex 30 PICT downdraught single barrel carburettor; fuel feed: mechanical pump; air-cooled.

TRANSMISSION driving wheels: rear; clutch: single dry plate; gearbox: mechanical; gears: 4, fully synchronized; ratios: I 3.780, II 2.060, III 1.260, IV 0.890, rev 4.010; lever: central; final drive: spiral bevel; axle ratio: 4.375; width of rims: 4.5"; tyres: 155 SR x 15.

PERFORMANCE max speeds: (I) 18 mph, 31 km/h; (II) 35 mph, 57 km/h; (III) 58 mph, 94 km/h; (IV) 71 mph, 115 km/h; power-weight ratio: 50.6 lb/hp (68.8 lb/kW), 22.9 kg/hp (31.2 kg/kW); carrying capacity: 882 lb, 400 kg; acceleration: standing ¼ mile 23 sec, 0-50 mph (0-80 km/h) 17 sec; speed in top at 1,000 rpm: 18.6 mph, 30 km/h; consumption: 42.2 m/imp gal, 35.1 m/US gal, 6.7 l x 100 km at 56 mph, 90 km/h.

CHASSIS backbone platform; front suspension: independent, twin swinging longitudinal trailing arms, transverse laminated torsion bars, anti-roll bar, telescopic dampers; rear: independent, swinging semi-axles, swinging longitudinal trailing arms, transverse torsion bars, telescopic dampers.

STEERING worm and roller, telescopic damper; turns lock to lock: 2.60.

BRAKES drum, dual circuit; lining area: total 111 sq in, 716 sq cm.

ELECTRICAL EQUIPMENT 12 V; 36 Ah battery; 30 A alternator; Bosch distributor; 2 headlamps.

DIMENSIONS AND WEIGHT wheel base: 94.49 in, 240 cm; tracks: 51.57 in, 131 cm front, 53.15 in, 135 cm rear; length: 159.84 in, 406 cm; width: 61.02 in, 155 cm; height: 59.06 in, 150 cm; ground clearance: 5.90 in, 15 cm; weight: 1,720 lb, 780 kg; weight distribution: 43% front, 57% rear; turning circle: 36.1 ft, 11 m; fuel tank: 8.8 imp gal, 10.6 US gal, 40 l.

BODY saloon/sedan; 2 doors; 5 seats, separate front seats, adjustable backrests.

PRACTICAL INSTRUCTIONS fuel: 87 oct petrol; oil: engine 4.4 imp pt, 5.3 US pt, 2.5 l, SAE 10W-20 (winter) 20W-30 (summer), change every 3,100 miles, 5,000 km - gearbox and final drive 5.3 imp pt, 6.3 US pt, 3 l, SAE 90, change every 31,000 miles, 50,000 km; greasing: every 6,200 miles, 10,000 km, 4 points; spark plug: 175°; tappet clearances: inlet 0.004 in, 0.10 mm, exhaust 0.004 in, 0.10 mm; valve timing: 6° 35°5' 42°5' 3°; tyre pressure: front 16 psi, 1.1 atm, rear 24 psi, 1.7 atm.

AMERICAN MOTORS — USA

Renault Alliance

PRICES EX WORKS:	$
2-dr Sedan	**5,959**
L 2-dr Sedan	**6,465**
L 4-dr Sedan	**6,715**
DL 2-dr Sedan	**7,065**
DL 4-dr Sedan	**7,365**
Limited 4-dr Sedan	**8,027**

ENGINE Renault, front, transverse, 4 stroke; 4 cylinders, in line; 85.2 cu in, 1,397 cc (2.99 x 3.03 in, 76 x 77 mm); compression ratio: 9:1; max power (DIN): 61 hp (45 kW) at 5,000 rpm; max torque (DIN): 75 lb ft, 10.3 kg m (101 Nm) at 2,500 rpm; max engine rpm; 5,500; 43.6 hp/l (32.1 kW/l);

VOLKSWAGEN 1200 L

AMERICAN MOTORS Renault Alliance DL Sedan

RENAULT ALLIANCE

cast iron block, light alloy head; 5 crankshaft bearings; valves: overhead, push-rods and rockers; camshafts: 1, side; lubrication: gear pump, full flow filter, 8.4 imp pt, 10.1 US pt, 4.8 l; Bendix injection; fuel feed: electric pump; sealed circuit cooling, liquid, expansion tank, 8.2 imp pt, 9.9 US pt, 4.7 l, electric thermostatic fan.

TRANSMISSION driving wheels: front; clutch: single dry plate (diaphragm); gearbox: mechanical; gears: 4 - DL and Limited sedans 5, fully synchronized; ratios: I 3.730, II 2.060, III 1.270, IV 0.900, rev 3.540 - DL and Limited sedans I 3.730, II 2.060, III 1.270, IV 0.900, V 0.730, rev 3.540; lever: central; final drive: spiral bevel; axle ratio: 3.300 - DL and Limited sedans 3.860; width of rims: 5"; tyres: 155/80 HR x 13 - DL and Limited sedans 175/80 HR x 13 (standard).

PERFORMANCE max speed: 93 mph, 150 km/h; power-weight ratio: 2-dr sedans 32.3 lb/hp (43.9 lb/kW), 14.6 kg/hp (19.8 kg/kW); consumption: 45.5 m/imp gal, 38 m/US gal, 6.2 l x 100 km - DL and Limited sedans 40.9 m/imp gal, 34 m/US gal, 6.9 l x 100 km.

CHASSIS integral; front suspension: independent, by McPherson, coil spring/telescopic damper struts, lower wishbones, anti-roll bar; rear: independent, swinging longitudinal trailing arms, transverse semi-torsion bars, telescopic dampers.

STEERING rack-and-pinion; turns lock to lock: 4.

BRAKES front disc (diameter 9.30 in, 23.8 cm), rear drum, dual circuit, rear compensator, servo; swept area: total 293.10 sq in, 1,891 sq cm.

ELECTRICAL EQUIPMENT 12 V; 58 Ah battery; 50 A alternator; 4 headlamps - Limited Sedan halogen headlamps.

DIMENSIONS AND WEIGHT wheel base: 97.80 in, 249 cm; tracks: 55.20 in, 140 cm front, 52.80 in, 134 cm rear; length: 163.80 in, 416 cm; width: 65 in, 165 cm; height: 51.30 in, 130 cm; ground clearance: 4.72 in, 12 cm; weight: 2-dr sedans 1,970 lb, 893 kg - 4-dr sedans 2,000 lb, 907 kg; weight distribution: 60% front, 40% rear; turning circle: 32.7 ft, 10 m; fuel tank: 10.3 imp gal, 12.4 US gal, 47 l.

BODY saloon/sedan; 2 or 4 doors; 5 seats, separate front seats, reclining backrests; rear window wiper-washer; (standard for DL and Limited sedans only) tinted glass.

VARIATIONS

(for California only)
ENGINE max power (DIN) 63 hp (46 kW) at 5,000 rpm, 45.1 hp/l (33.2 kW/l), Bosch electronic injection.
PERFORMANCE power-weight ratio 2-dr sedans 31.3 lb/hp (42.5 lb/kW), 14.1 kg/hp (19.2 kg/kW).

OPTIONALS automatic transmission, hydraulic torque converter and planetary gears with 3 ratios (I 2.500, II 1.500, III 1, rev 2), max ratio of converter at stall 2.19, possible manual selection, 3.560 axle ratio, consumption 33.6 m/imp gal, 28 m/US gal, 8.4 l x 100 km; 175/80 HR x 13 tyres (except DL and Limited sedans); light alloy wheels with 5.5" wide rims; tinted glass (except DL and Limited sedans); air-conditioning; metallic spray; heavy-duty battery.

Renault Encore

PRICES EX WORKS:	$
2+1-dr Hatchback Sedan	**5,755**
S 2+1-dr Hatchback Sedan	**6,365**
S 4+1-dr Hatchback Sedan	**6,615**
LS 2+1-dr Hatchback Sedan	**6,995**
LS 4+1-dr Hatchback Sedan	**7,197**
GS 2+1-dr Hatchback Sedan	**7,547**

ENGINE Renault, front, transverse, 4 stroke; 4 cylinders, in line; 85.2 cu in, 1,397 cc (2.99 x 3.03 in, 76 x 77 mm); compression ratio: 9:1; max power (DIN): 61 hp (45 kW) at 5,000 rpm; max torque (DIN): 75 lb ft, 10.3 kg m (101 Nm) at 2,500 rpm; max engine rpm: 5,500; 43.6 hp/l (32.1 kW/l); cast iron block, light alloy head; 5 crankshaft bearings; valves: overhead, push-rods and rockers; camshafts: 1, side; lubrication: gear pump, full flow filter, 6.6 imp pt, 8 US pt, 3.8 l; Bendix injection; fuel feed: electric pump; sealed circuit cooling, liquid, expansion tank, 8.2 imp pt, 9.9 US pt, 4.7 l, electric thermostatic fan.

TRANSMISSION driving wheels: front; clutch: single dry plate (diaphragm); gearbox: mechanical; gears: 4, fully synchronized; ratios: I 3.730, II 2.060, III 1.270, IV 0.900, rev 3.540; lever: central; final drive: spiral bevel; axle ratio: 3.300; width of rims: 5"; tyres: 155/80 HR x 13.

PERFORMANCE max speed: 93 mph, 150 km/h; power-weight ratio: 2+1-dr sedans 32.9 lb/hp (44.7 lb/kW), 14.9 kg/hp (20.3 kg/kW); consumption: 45.5 m/imp gal, 38 m/US gal, 6.2 l x 100 km.

CHASSIS integral; front suspension: independent, by McPherson, coil spring/telescopic damper struts, lower wishbones, anti-roll bar; rear: independent, swinging longitudinal trailing arms, transverse semi-torsion bars, telescopic dampers.

STEERING rack-and-pinion; turns lock to lock: 4.

AMERICAN MOTORS Renault Encore LS Hatchback Sedan

BRAKES front disc (diameter 9.30 in, 23.8 cm), rear drum, dual circuit, rear compensator, servo; swept area: total 293.10 sq in, 1,891 sq cm.

ELECTRICAL EQUIPMENT 12 V; 58 Ah battery; 50 A alternator; 4 headlamps.

DIMENSIONS AND WEIGHT wheel base: 97.80 in, 249 cm; tracks: 55.20 in, 140 cm front, 52.80 in, 134 cm rear; length: 160.60 in, 408 cm; width: 65 in, 165 cm; height: 51.30 in, 130 cm; ground clearance: 4.72 in, 12 cm; weight: 2+1-dr sedans 2,006 lb, 910 kg - 4+1-dr sedans 2,034 lb, 923 kg; weight distribution: 60% front, 40% rear; turning circle: 32.7 ft, 10 m; fuel tank: 10.3 imp gal, 12.4 US gal, 47 l.

BODY saloon/sedan, 2+1 or 4+1 doors; 5 seats, separate front seats, reclining backrests.

VARIATIONS

(for California only)
ENGINE max power (DIN) 63 hp (46 kW) at 5,000 rpm, 45.1 hp/l (33.2 kW/l), Bosch electronic injection.
PERFORMANCE power-weight ratio 2+1-dr sedans 31.9 lb/hp (43.3 lb/kW), 14.4 kg/hp (19.6 kg/kW).

OPTIONALS automatic transmission, hydraulic torque converter and planetary gears with 3 ratios (I 2.500, II 1.500, III 1, rev 2), max ratio of converter at stall 2.19, possible manual selection, 3.560 axle ratio, consumption 33.6 m/imp gal, 28 m/US gal, 8.4 l x 100 km; 5-speed mechanical gearbox (I 3.730, II 2.060, III 1.270, IV 0.900, V 0.730, rev 3.540), 3.860 axle ratio; 175/80 HR x 13 tyres; light alloy wheels with 5.5" wide rims; tinted glass; rear window wiper-washer; air-conditioning; metallic spray; heavy-duty battery.

Eagle Series

PRICES EX WORKS:	$
4-dr Sedan	**9,495**
4+1-dr St. Wagon	**10,225**
Limited 4+1-dr St. Wagon	**10,695**

Power team:	Standard for:	Optional for:
105 hp	all	—
120 hp	—	all

105 hp power team

ENGINE front, 4 stroke; 4 cylinders, in line; 150.5 cu in, 2,460 cc (3.88 x 3.19 in, 98.4 x 81 mm); compression ratio: 9.2:1; max power (SAE net): 105 hp (77 kW) at 5,000 rpm; max torque (SAE net): 132 lb ft, 18.2 kg m (179 Nm) at 3,000 rpm; max engine rpm: 5,500; 42.6 hp/l (31.4 kW/l); cast iron block and head; 5 crankshaft bearings; valves: overhead, in line, push-rods and rockers, hydraulic tappets; camshafts: 1, side; lubrication: gear pump, full flow filter, 4.9 imp pt, 5.9 US pt, 2.8 l; 1 Carter or Weber single barrel carburettor; air cleaner; exhaust system with catalytic converter; fuel feed: mechanical pump; water-cooled, 10.7 imp pt, 12.9 US pt, 6.1 l.

TRANSMISSION driving wheels: front and rear; clutch: single dry plate (diaphragm); gearbox: mechanical; gears: 4, fully synchronized; ratios: I 4.030, II 2.370, III 1.500, IV 1, rev 3.760; lever: central; final drive: hypoid bevel; axle ratio: 3.540; width of rims: 6"; tyres: P 195/75 R x 15.

PERFORMANCE max speed: 88 mph, 142 km/h; power-weight ratio: Coupé 28.9 lb/hp (39.4 lb/kW), 13.1 kg/hp (17.8 kg/kW); consumption: 28.8 m/imp gal, 24 m/US gal, 9.8 l x 100 km.

CHASSIS integral; front suspension: independent, wishbones, coil springs, anti-roll bar, telescopic dampers; rear: rigid axle, semi-elliptic leafsprings, telescopic dampers.

STEERING recirculating ball, servo; turns lock to lock: 3.

BRAKES front disc (diameter 11.02 in, 30 cm), front internal radial fins, rear drum, servo; swept area: total 329 sq in, 2,123 sq cm.

ELECTRICAL EQUIPMENT 12 V; 45 Ah battery; 42 A alternator; Delco-Remy ignition; 4 headlamps.

DIMENSIONS AND WEIGHT wheel base: 109.27 in, 278 cm; tracks: 59.60 in, 151 cm front, 57.56 in, 146 cm rear; length: 180.94 in, 459 cm; width: 72.34 in, 184 cm; height: 54.35 in, 138 cm; ground clearance: 6.85 in, 17.4 cm; weight: Sedan 3,280 lb, 1,487 kg - st. wagons 3,310 lb, 1,501 kg; turning circle: 39.4 ft, 12 m; fuel tank: 17.6 imp gal, 21 US gal, 80 l.

AMERICAN MOTORS Eagle Sedan

AMERICAN MOTORS Eagle Limited Station Wagon

BODY saloon/sedan, 4 doors - estate car/st. wagons, 4+1 doors; 5 or 6 seats, separate front seats.

OPTIONALS Torque-Command automatic transmission, hydraulic torque converter and planetary gears with 3 ratios (I 2.740, II 1.550, III 1, rev 2.200), max ratio of converter at stall 2.50, possible manual selection, consumption 25.2 m/imp gal, 21 m/US gal, 11.2 l x 100 km; 5-speed fully synchronized mechanical gearbox (I 4.030, II 2.370, III 1.500, IV 1, V 0.860, rev 3.760); P 215/65 R x 15 tyres; halogen headlamps; fog headlamps; air-conditioning; electric windows; electric door locks; digital clock; tinted glass; metallic spray; heavy-duty suspension; heavy-duty battery; (for st. wagons only) sunroof; (for st. wagons only) rear window wiper-washer.

120 hp power team

See 105 hp power team, except for:

ENGINE 6 cylinders, in line; 258 cu in, 4,228 cc (3.75 x 3.90 in, 95.2 x 99 mm); max power (SAE net): 120 hp (88 kW) at 3,600 rpm; max torque (SAE net): 210 lb ft, 28.9 kg m (284 Nm) at 1,800 rpm; max engine rpm: 4,100; 28.4 hp/l (20.8 kW/l); 7 crankshaft bearings; lubrication: 7 imp pt, 8.5 US pt, 4 l; 1 Carter BBD downdraught twin barrel carburettor; cooling: 23.2 imp pt, 27.9 US pt, 13.2 l.

TRANSMISSION axle ratio: 2.730.

PERFORMANCE max speed: 90 mph, 145 km/h; power-weight ratio: Coupé 25.3 lb/hp (34.4 lb/kW), 11.5 kg/hp (15.6 kg/kW); consumption: 24.1 m/imp gal, 20 m/US gal, 11.7 l x 100 km.

OPTIONALS 5-speed fully synchronized mechanical gearbox (I 4.030, II 2.370, III 1.500, IV 1, V 0.760, rev 3.760); (except Coupé) with automatic transmission consumption 22.7 m/imp gal, 19 m/US gal, 12.4 l x 100 km.

AVANTI USA

Avanti II

PRICE EX WORKS: $ 31,860

ENGINE Chevrolet, front, 4 stroke; 8 cylinders in Vee; 305 cu in, 4,999 cc (3.73 x 3.48 in, 94.8 x 88.4 mm); compression ratio: 9.5:1; max power (SAE net): 190 hp (140 kW) at 4,800 rpm; max torque (SAE net): 240 lb ft, 33.1 kg m (325 Nm) at 3,200 rpm; max engine rpm: 5,000; 38 hp/l (28 kW/l); cast iron block and head; 5 crankshaft bearings; valves: overhead, in line, push-rods and rockers, hydraulic tappets; camshafts: 1, at centre of Vee; lubrication: gear pump, full flow filter, 8.3 imp pt, 10 US pt, 4.7 l; 1 Rochester downdraught 4-barrel carburettor; thermostatic air cleaner; exhaust system with catalytic converter; fuel feed: mechanical pump; water-cooled, 25.4 imp pt, 30.5 US pt, 14.4 l.

TRANSMISSION driving wheels: rear; gearbox: Turbo-Hydramatic GM automatic transmission, hydraulic torque converter and planetary gears with 3 ratios and overdrive, max ratio of converter at stall 1.90, possible manual selection; ratios: I 3.060, II 1.630, III 1, overdrive 0.700, rev 2.070; lever: central; final drive: hypoid bevel, limited slip; axle ratio: 2.870; width of rims: 7"; tyres: P205/75R x 15.

PERFORMANCE power-weight ratio: 20.4 lb/hp (27.4 lb/kW), 8.8 kg/hp (11.9 kg/kW).

CHASSIS box-type ladder frame, X cross members; front suspension: independent, wishbones, coil springs, anti-roll bar, telescopic dampers; rear: rigid axle, semi-elliptic leafsprings, upper torque arms, anti-roll bar, telescopic dampers.

STEERING cam and lever, tilt of steering wheel, servo; turns lock to lock: 4.80.

BRAKES front disc, internal radial fins, rear drum, servo.

ELECTRICAL EQUIPMENT 12 V; 74 Ah battery; 63 A alternator; Delco-Remy high energy ignition; 2 headlamps.

DIMENSIONS AND WEIGHT wheel base: 109 in, 277 cm; tracks: 57.37 in, 146 cm front, 56.56 in, 144 cm rear; length: 193.10 in, 490 cm; width: 70.40 in, 179 cm; height: 54.40 in, 138 cm; ground clearance: 6.19 in, 15.7 cm; weight: 3,680 lb, 1,669 kg; turning circle: 37.5 ft, 11.4 m; fuel tank: 15.8 imp gal, 19 US gal, 72 l.

BODY coupé, in fiberglass material; 2 doors; 4 seats, separate front seats, built-in headrests; heated rear window; tinted glass; air-conditioning.

OPTIONALS electric moonroof; electric windows; electric door locks; cruise control; all leather interior fog lamps; automatic speed control; reclining front seats; genuine wood veneer dash and console panels; Recaro front seats; wire wheels; Magnum "500" wheels.

BUICK USA

Skyhawk Series

PRICES EX WORKS:	$
1 4-dr Sedan	**7,350**
2 2-dr Coupé	**7,140**
3 4+1-dr St. Wagon	**7,685**
4 Limited 4-dr Sedan	**7,845**
5 Limited 2-dr Coupé	**7,649**
6 Limited 4+1-dr St. Wagon	**8,135**
7 T-type 2-dr Coupé	**8,161**

Power team:	Standard for:	Optional for:
84 hp	7	1 to 6
86 hp	1 to 6	—
150 hp	—	7

84 hp power team

ENGINE front, 4 stroke; 4 cylinders, transverse, vertical, in line; 110 cu in, 1,800 cc (3.33 x 3.12 in, 84.8 x 79.5 mm); compression ratio: 9:1; max power (SAE net): 84 hp (62 kW) at 5,200 rpm; max torque (SAE net): 102 lb ft, 14 kg m (138 Nm) at 2,800 rpm; max engine rpm: 5,700; 45.7 hp/l (33.7 kW/l); cast iron block, light alloy head; 5 crankshaft bearings; valves: overhead, in line, rockers, hydraulic tappets; camshafts: 1, overhead; lubrication: gear pump, full flow filter, 6.7 imp pt, 8 US pt, 3.8 l; exhaust system with catalytic converter; throttle-body electronic fuel injection; fuel feed; electric pump; water-cooled, 13 imp pt, 15.6 US pt, 7.4 l.

TRANSMISSION driving wheels: front; clutch: single dry plate (diaphragm); gearbox: mechanical; gears: 5, fully synchronized; ratios: I 3.910, II 2.150, III 1.450, IV 1.030, V 0.740, rev 3.500; lever: central; final drive: helical spur gears; axle ratio: 3.450:; width of rims: 5"; tyres: P 195/70 R x 13.

PERFORMANCE max speed: 99 mph, 159 km/h; power-weight ratio: T-type 28.4 lb/hp (38.6 lb/kW), 12.9 kg/hp (17.5 kg/kW); carrying capacity: 880 lb, 400 kg; speed in top at 1,000 rpm: 19.6 mph, 31.6 km/h; consumption: 34.8 m/imp gal, 29 m/US gal, 8.1 l x 100 km.

CHASSIS integral; front suspension: independent, by McPherson, stamped lower control arms, anti-roll bar, coil springs/telescopic damper struts; rear: rigid axle, swinging longitudinal leading arms, coil springs, telescopic dampers.

STEERING rack-and-pinion; turns lock to lock: 4.04.

BRAKES front disc (diameter 9.72 in, 24.7 cm), internal radial fins, rear drum, servo; swept area: total 252 sq in, 1,624 sq cm.

ELECTRICAL EQUIPMENT 12 V; 500 A battery; 56 A alternator; Delco-Remy transistorized ignition; 4 headlamps.

DIMENSIONS AND WEIGHT wheel base: 101.20 in, 257 cm; tracks: 55.40 in, 141 cm front, 55.20 in, 140 cm rear; length: 171.30 in, 445 cm; width: 65 in, 165 cm; height: 53.60 in, 136 cm; ground clearance: 6.20 in, 15.7 cm; weight: 2,399 lb, 1,088 kg; weight distribution: 64% front, 36% rear; turning circle: 34.7 ft, 10.6 m; fuel tank: 11.2 imp gal, 13.6 US gal, 51 l.

BODY saloon/sedan, 4 doors - coupé, 2 doors - estate car/st. wagon, 4+1 doors; 5 seats, separate front seats, built-in headrests.

OPTIONALS Turbo-Hydramatic 125-C automatic transmission, hydraulic torque converter and planetary gears with 3 ratios (I 2.840, II 1.600, III 1, rev 2.070), max ratio of converter at stall 2.38, possible manual selection; 3.180 axle ratio; 5-speed fully synchronized mechanical gearbox (I 3.910, II 2.150, III 1.330, IV 0.920, V 0.740, rev 3.500); air-conditioning; power steering; heavy-duty battery; speed control; heated rear window; anti-roll bar on rear suspension; 465 A battery; 94 A alternator; electric door locks; electric windows; automatic air-conditioning; heavy-duty suspension; 6" wide rims; P 205/60 R x 14 tyres; fog lamps; rear window wiper-washer.

86 hp power team

See 84 hp power team, except for:

ENGINE 121 cu in, 1,983 cc (3.50 x 3.15 in, 89 x 80 mm); compression ratio: 9.3:1; max power (SAE net): 86 hp (63

AVANTI Avanti II

BUICK Skyhawk Limited Station Wagon

86 HP POWER TEAM

kW) at 4,900 rpm; max torque (SAE net): 100 lb ft, 13.8 kg m (135 Nm) at 2,800 rpm; max engine rpm: 5,400; 43.3 hp/l (31.9 kW/l); cast iron block and head; cooling: 16 imp pt, 19.2 US pt, 9.1 l.

TRANSMISSION gears: 4, fully synchronized; ratios: I 3.530, II 1.950, III 1.240, IV 0.810, rev 3.420; axle ratio: 4.100; tyres: P 175/80 R x 13.

PERFORMANCE max speed: 100 mph, 161 km/h; power-weight ratio: Sedan 28.7 lb/hp (39.2 lb/kW), 13 kg/hp (17.8 kg/kW); consumption: 33.6 m/imp gal, 28 m/US gal, 8.4 l x 100 km.

ELECTRICAL EQUIPMENT 390 A battery; 66 A alternator.

DIMENSIONS AND WEIGHT length: sedans and st. wagons 173.30 in, 451 cm; height: st. wagons 54.40 in, 138 cm; ground clearance: st. wagons 6.70 in, 17 cm; weight: Sedan 2,436 lb, 1,104 kg - Coupé 2,883 lb, 1,307 kg - St. Wagon 2,507 lb, 1,137 kg - Limited Sedan 2,471 lb, 1,120 kg - Limited Coupé 2,424 lb, 1,099 kg - Limited St. Wagon 2,536 lb, 1,150 kg.

OPTIONALS Turbo-Hydramatic automatic transmission, hydraulic torque converter and planetary gears with 3 ratios (I 2.840, II 1.600, III 1, rev 2.070), max ratio of converter at stall 2.70, possible manual selection, 3.180 or 3.430 axle ratio; 500 A battery; 85 A alternator.

150 hp power team

See 84 hp power team, except for:

ENGINE turbocharged; compression ratio: 8:1; max power (SAE net): 150 hp (110 kW) at 5,600 rpm; max torque (SAE net): 150 lb ft, 20.7 kg m (203 Nm) at 2,800 rpm; max engine rpm: 6,000; 83.3 hp/l (61.3 kW/l); Bosch Port electronic fuel injection.

TRANSMISSION gears: 4, fully synchronized; ratios: I 3.530, II 1.950, III 1.240, IV 0.810, rev 3.420; axle ratio: 3.650.

PERFORMANCE max speed: 106 mph, 170 km/h; power-weight ratio: 16 lb/hp (21.7 lb/kW), 7.2 kg/hp (9.9 kg/kW); consumption: not declared.

ELECTRICAL EQUIPMENT 78 A alternator.

BODY coupé; 2 doors.

OPTIONALS 3.330 axle ratio with automatic transmission; 465 A battery; 94 A alternator.

Skylark Series

PRICES EX WORKS:	**$**
1 Custom 4-dr Sedan	**7,716**
2 Custom 2-dr Coupé	**7,554**
3 Limited 4-dr Sedan	**8,292**
4 Limited 2-dr Coupé	**8,128**
5 T-type 2-dr Coupé	**9,568**

Power team:	**Standard for:**	**Optional for:**
92 hp	1 to 4	—
112 hp	—	1 to 4
135 hp	5	1 to 4

92 hp power team

ENGINE front, transverse, 4 stroke; 4 cylinders, in line; 151 cu in, 2,475 cc (4 x 3 in, 101.6 x 76.2 mm); compression ratio: 9:1; max power (SAE net): 92 hp (68 kW) at 4,400 rpm; max torque (SAE net): 132 lb ft, 18.2 kg m (179 Nm) at 2,800 rpm; max engine rpm: 4,800; 37.2 hp/l (27.3 kW/l); cast iron block and head; 5 crankshaft bearings; valves: overhead, in line, push-rods and rockers, hydraulic tappets; camshafts: 1, side; lubrication: gear pump, full flow filter, 4.9 imp pt, 5.9 US pt, 2.8 l; throttle-body electronic injection; air cleaner; exhaust system with catalytic converter; fuel feed: electric pump; water-cooled, 15.1 imp pt, 18.1 US pt, 8.6 l.

TRANSMISSION driving wheels: front; clutch: self-adjusting single dry plate (diaphragm); gearbox: mechanical; gears: 4, fully synchronized; ratios: I 3.530, II 1.950, III 1.240, IV 0.730, rev 3.920; lever: steering column; final drive: spiral bevel; axle ratio: 3.320:; width of rims: 5.5"; tyres: P185/80R x 13.

PERFORMANCE max speed: 95 mph, 153 km/h; power-weight ratio: Custom Sedan 27.9 lb/hp (37.8 lb/kW), 12.6 kg/hp (17.2 kg/kW); speed in top at 1,000 rpm: 19.8 mph, 31.8 km/h; consumption: 30 m/imp gal, 25 m/US gal, 9.4 l x 100 km.

CHASSIS integral; front suspension: independent, by McPherson, coil springs, stamped lower control arms, telescopic dampers; rear: rigid axle, lower trailing radius arms, upper oblique torque arms, coil springs, telescopic dampers.

STEERING rack-and-pinion, servo; turns lock to lock: 3.13.

BRAKES front disc (diameter 9.72 in, 24.7 cm), internal radial fins, rear drum; swept area: total 261.6 sq in, 1,687 sq cm.

ELECTRICAL EQUIPMENT 12 V; 390 A battery; 42 A alternator; Delco-Remy high energy ignition; 2 headlamps.

DIMENSIONS AND WEIGHT wheel base: 104.90 in, 266 cm; tracks: 58.70 in, 149 cm front, 57 in, 145 cm rear; length: 181 in, 460 cm; width: 69.10 in, 175 cm; ground clearance: 6.20 in, 15.7 cm; weight: Custom Sedan 2,562 lb, 1,162 kg - Custom Coupé 2,531 lb, 1,148 kg - Limited Sedan 2,588 lb, 1,174 kg - Limited Coupé 2,557 lb, 1,160 kg; weight distribution: 63% front, 37% rear; turning circle: 41 ft, 12.5 m; fuel tank: 12.1 imp gal, 14.6 US gal, 55 l.

BODY saloon/sedan, 4 doors - coupé, 2 doors; 5 seats, separate front seats, built-in headrests.

OPTIONALS Turbo-Hydramatic 125-C automatic transmission with 3 ratios (I 2.840, II 1.600, III 1, rev 2.070), max ratio of converter at stall 2.30, possible manual selection, steering column lever, 2.840 or 2.390 axle ratio; tilt of steering wheel; intermittent wiper; roof carrier; sunroof; reclining seats; custom interior; heated rear window; air-conditioning; servo brake; electric windows; electric door locks; P205/70R x 13 or P 215/60 R x 14 tyres; heavy-duty battery; 94 A alternator; 500 A battery; heavy-duty cooling; cruise speed control; halogen headlamps; heavy-duty suspension; vinyl roof.

112 hp power team

See 92 hp power team, except for:

ENGINE 6 cylinders, Vee-slanted at 60°; 173 cu in, 2,835 cc (3.50 x 3 in, 89 x 76.2 mm); compression ratio: 8.4:1; max power (SAE net): 112 hp (82 kW) at 5,100 rpm; max torque (SAE net): 148 lb ft, 20.4 kg m (200 Nm) at 2,400 rpm; max engine rpm: 5,500; 39.5 hp/l (29.1 kW/l); 4 crankshaft bearings; camshafts: 1, at centre of Vee; lubrication: 6.7 imp pt, 7.9 US pt, 3.8 l; 1 Rochester 17059761 downdraught twin barrel carburettor; cooling: 18.3 imp pt, 22 US pt, 10.4 l.

PERFORMANCE max speed: 106 mph, 170 km/h; power-weight ratio: Custom Sedan 22.8 lb/hp (31 lb/kW), 10.4 kg/hp (14.1 kg/kW); speed in top at 1,000 rpm: 23.1 mph, 37.3 km/h; consumption: 25.2 m/imp gal, 21 m/US gal, 11.2 l x 100 km.

DIMENSIONS AND WEIGHT weight: Custom Sedan 2,556 lb, 1,160 kg - Custom Coupé 2,514 lb, 1,141 kg - Limited Sedan 2,588 lb, 1,174 kg - Limited Coupé 2,557 lb, 1,160 kg.

OPTIONALS with automatic transmission 2.530 axle ratio.

135 hp power team

See 92 hp power team, except for:

ENGINE 6 cylinders, Vee-slanted at 60°; 173 cu in, 2,835 cc (3.50 x 3 in, 89 x 76.2 mm); compression ratio: 8.9:1; max power (SAE net): 135 hp (100 kW) at 5,400 rpm; max torque (SAE net): 145 lb ft, 20 kg m (196 Nm) at 2,400 rpm; max engine rpm: 6,000; 47.6 hp/l (35 kW/l); 4 crankshaft bearings; camshafts: 1, at centre of Vee; lubrication: 6.7 imp pt, 7.9 US pt, 3.8 l; 1 Rochester E2SE downdraught twin barrel carburettor; cooling: 18.3 imp pt, 22 US pt, 10.4 l.

TRANSMISSION axle ratio: 3.650.

PERFORMANCE max speed: 118 mph, 190 km/h; power-weight ratio: T-type Coupé 19.8 lb/hp (27 lb/kW), 9 kg/hp (12.2 kg/kW); consumption: 25.2 m/imp gal, 21 m/US gal, 11.2 l x 100 km.

DIMENSIONS AND WEIGHT weight: T-type Coupé 2,679 lb, 1,215 kg.

OPTIONALS with automatic transmission 3.330 axle ratio.

Century Series

PRICES EX WORKS:	**$**
1 Custom 4-dr Sedan	**9,283**
2 Custom 2-dr Coupé	**9,119**
3 Custom 4+1-dr St. Wagon	**9,669**
4 Limited 4-dr Sedan	**9,738**
5 Limited 2-dr Coupé	**9,571**
6 Limited 4+1-dr St. Wagon	**10,096**
7 T-type 4-dr Sedan	**10,684**
8 T-type 2-dr Coupé	**10,520**

BUICK Skylark T-type Coupé

BUICK Century Limited Sedan

Power team:	Standard for:	Optional for:
90 hp	3,6	—
92 hp	1 to 6	—
110 hp	—	1 to 6
125 hp	7,8	1 to 6
85 hp (diesel)	—	1 to 6

90 hp power team

ENGINE front, transverse, 4 stroke; 4 cylinders, in line; 151 cu in, 2,475 cc (4 x 3 in, 101.6 x 76.2 mm); compression ratio: 8.2:1; max power (SAE net): 90 hp (66 kW) at 4,000 rpm; max torque (SAE net): 134 lb ft, 18.4 kg m (181 Nm) at 2,400 rpm; max engine rpm: 4,400; 36.4 hp/l (26.8 kW/l); cast iron block and head; 5 crankshaft bearings; valves: overhead, in line, push-rods and rockers, hydraulic tappets; camshafts: 1, side; lubrication: gear pump, full flow filter, 4.9 imp pt, 5.9 US pt, 2.8 l; throttle-body electronic injection; air cleaner; exhaust system with catalytic converter; fuel feed: electric pump; water-cooled, 17.8 imp pt, 21.4 US pt, 10.1 l.

TRANSMISSION driving wheels: front; gearbox: Turbo-Hydramatic 125 C automatic transmission, hydraulic torque converter and planetary gears with 3 ratios, max ratio of converter at stall 2.35, possible manual selection; ratios: I 2.840, II 1.600, III 1, rev 2.070; lever: steering column; final drive: helical spur gears; axle ratio: 2.390; width of rims: 5.5"; tyres: P 185/75 R x 14.

PERFORMANCE max speed: 100 mph, 161 km/h; power-weight ratio: Custom St. Wagon 32.3 lb/hp (43.9 lb/kW), 14.6 kg/hp (19.9 kg/kW); carrying capacity: 920 lb, 420 kg; speed in direct drive at 1,000 rpm: 22.7 mph, 36.6 km/h; consumption: 29.5 m/imp gal, 25 m/US gal, 9.4 l x 100 km.

CHASSIS integral; front suspension: independent, by McPherson, lower wishbones, coil springs/telescopic damper struts; rear: rigid axle, trailing lower radius arms, coil springs, Panhard rod, telescopic dampers.

STEERING rack-and-pinion, servo; turns lock to lock: 3.13.

BRAKES front disc (diameter 9.72 in, 24.7 cm), rear drum, servo; swept area: total 288.3 sq in, 1,860 sq cm.

ELECTRICAL EQUIPMENT 12 V; 405 A battery; 85 A alternator; Delco-Remy high energy transistorized ignition; 4 headlamps.

DIMENSIONS AND WEIGHT wheel base: 104.90 in, 266 cm; tracks: 58.70 in, 149 cm front, 56.70 in, 144 cm rear; length: 190.90 in, 485 cm; width: 69.40 in, 176 cm; height: 54.20 in, 137 cm; ground clearance: 6.20 in, 15.8 cm; weight: Custom St. Wagon 2.906 lb, 1,318 kg - Limited St. Wagon 2,914 lb, 1,321 kg; weight distribution: 63% front, 37% rear; turning circle: 41 ft, 12.5 m; fuel tank: 13.3 imp gal, 15.7 US gal, 59 l.

BODY estate car/st. wagon, 4+1 doors; 6 seats, separate front seats, built-in headrests.

OPTIONALS air-conditioning; vinyl roof; electric windows; sunroof; P 195/75 R x 14 tyres.

92 hp power team

See 90 hp power team, except for:

ENGINE compression ratio: 9:1; max power (SAE net): 92 hp (68 kW) at 4,400 rpm; max torque (SAE net): 132 lb ft, 18.2 kg m (179 Nm) at 2,800 rpm; max engine rpm: 5,000; 37.2 hp/l (27.3 kW/l).

TRANSMISSION axle ratio: 2.390 - California 2.840.

DIMENSIONS AND WEIGHT length: 189.10 in, 480 cm; width: sedans 67.70 in, 172 cm - coupés 67.69 in, 171 cm; height: 53.70 in, 136 cm; weight: Custom Coupé 2,690 lb, 1,220 kg - Custom Sedan 2,738 lb, 1,242 kg - Limited Coupé 2,711 lb, 1,230 kg - Limited Sedan 2,759 lb, 1,251 kg.

BODY saloon/sedan, 4 doors - coupé, 2 doors - estate car/st. wagon, 4+1 doors; 5 seats, separate front seats.

110 hp power team

See 90 hp power team, except for:

ENGINE 6 cylinders, Vee-slanted at 90°; 181 cu in, 2,966 cc (3.80 x 2.66 in, 96.5 x 67.6 mm); compression ratio: 8.4:1; max power (SAE net): 110 hp (81 kW) at 4,800 rpm; max torque (SAE net): 145 lb ft, 20 kg m (196 Nm) at 2,600 rpm; max engine rpm: 5,200; 37.1 hp/l (27.3 kW/l); 4 crankshaft bearings; camshafts: 1, at centre of Vee; lubrication: 6.7 imp pt, 8 US pt, 3.8 l; 1 Rochester E2SE twin barrel carburettor; cooling: 21.3 imp pt, 25.6 US pt, 12.1 l.

TRANSMISSION gearbox: automatic transmission with max ratio of converter at stall 2.16; axle ratio: 2.530 - California 2.970.

PERFORMANCE max speed: 105 mph, 168 km/h; power-weight ratio: Custom Sedan 24.9 lb/hp (33.8 lb/kW), 11.3 kg/hp (15.3 kg/kW); speed in direct drive at 1,000 rpm: 20.9 mph, 33.6 km/h; consumption: 25 m/imp gal, 21 m/US gal, 11.2 l x 100 km.

BODY saloon/sedan, 4 doors - coupé, 2 doors - estate car/st. wagons, 4+1 doors; 5 seats, separate front seats.

OPTIONALS automatic transmission with 4 ratios, 3.060 - California 3.330 axle ratio.

125 hp power team

See 90 hp power team, except for:

ENGINE 6 cylinders, Vee-slanted at 90°; 231 cu in, 3,785 cc (3.80 x 3.40 in, 96.4 x 86.3 mm); compression ratio: 8:1; max power (SAE net): 125 hp (92 kW) at 4,400 rpm; max torque (SAE net): 195 lb ft, 26.9 kg m (264 Nm) at 2,000 rpm; max engine rpm: 5,100; 33 hp/l (24.3 kW/l); lubrication: 6.7 imp pt, 8 US pt, 3.8 l; Bosch Jetronic electronic fuel injection; cooling: 20 imp pt, 24 US pt, 11.4 l.

BUICK Century Series (3.8-litre engine)

TRANSMISSION gearbox: Turbo-Hydramatic THM 440-T4 automatic transmission, hydraulic torque converter and planetary gears with 3 ratios and overdrive, max ratio of converter at stall 1.68, possible manual selection; ratios: I 2.920, II 1.570, III 1, overdrive 0.700, rev 2.380; axle ratio: 2.840.

PERFORMANCE max speed: 99 mph, 161 km/h; power-weight ratio: T-type Sedan: 23.2 lb/hp (31.6 lb/kW), 10.5 kg/hp (14.3 kg/kW); consumption: 25 m/imp gal, 21 m/US gal, 11.2 l x 100 km.

ELECTRICAL EQUIPMENT 56 A alternator.

DIMENSIONS AND WEIGHT weight: T-type Sedan 2,903 lb, 1,316 kg - T-type Coupé 2,855 lb, 1,295 kg.

BODY saloon/sedan, 4 doors - coupé, 2 doors - estate car/st. wagons, 4+1 doors; 5 seats, separate front seats.

85 hp (diesel) power team

See 90 hp power team, except for:

ENGINE diesel; 6 cylinders, Vee-slanted at 90°; 262 cu in, 4,294 cc (4.06 x 3.38 in, 103 x 86 mm); compression ratio: 21.6:1; max power (SAE net): 85 hp (62 kW) at 3,600 rpm; max torque (SAE net): 165 lb ft, 22.7 kg m (223 Nm) at 1,600 rpm; max engine rpm: 4,100; 19.8 hp/l (14.6 kW/l); 4 crankshaft bearings; camshafts: 1, at centre of Vee; lubrication: 10.7 imp pt, 12.6 US pt, 6 l; Detroit diesel injection pump; fuel feed: mechanical pump.

TRANSMISSION gearbox: automatic transmission with max ratio of converter at stall 1.64; tyres: P 195/75 R x 14 (standard).

PERFORMANCE max speed: 96 mph, 155 km/h; consumption: 32 m/imp gal, 27 m/US gal, 8.7 l x 100 km.

BRAKES disc (diameter 10.24 in, 26 cm); swept area: total 285 sq in, 1,839 sq cm.

ELECTRICAL EQUIPMENT 750 A battery; 66 A alternator.

DIMENSIONS AND WEIGHT fuel tank: 13.6 imp gal, 16.4 US gal, 62 l.

BODY saloon/sedan, 4 doors - coupé, 2 doors - estate car/st. wagon, 4+1 doors; 5 seats, separate front seats.

Regal Series

PRICES EX WORKS:		$
1	4-dr Sedan	**9,681**
2	2-dr Coupé	**9,497**
3	Limited 4-dr Sedan	**10,273**
4	Limited 2-dr Coupé	**10,135**
5	T-type 2-dr Coupé	**12,130**

Power team:	Standard for:	Optional for:
110 hp	1 to 4	—
125 hp	—	1 to 4
200 hp	5	—
85 hp (diesel)	—	1 to 4

110 hp power team

ENGINE front, 4 stroke; 6 cylinders, Vee-slanted at 90°; 231 cu in, 3,785 cc (3.80 x 3.40 in, 96.4 x 86.3 mm); compression ratio: 8:1; max power (SAE net): 110 hp (81 kW) at 3,800 rpm; max torque (SAE net): 190 lb ft, 26.2 kg m (257 Nm) at 1,600 rpm; max engine rpm: 4,200; 29.1 hp/l (21.4 kW/l); cast iron block and head; 4 crankshaft bearings; valves: overhead, in line, push-rods and rockers, hydraulic tappets; camshafts: 1, at centre of Vee; lubrication: gear pump, full flow filter, 6.7 imp pt, 8 US pt, 3.8 l; 1 Rochester 2 ME downdraught twin barrel carburettor; thermostatic air cleaner; fuel feed: mechanical pump; water-cooled, 21.6 imp pt, 26 US pt, 12.3 l.

TRANSMISSION driving wheels: rear; gearbox: Turbo-Hydramatic THM 200-C automatic transmission, hydraulic torque converter and planetary gears with 3 ratios, max ratio of converter at stall 2.20, possible manual selection; ratios: I 2.740, II 1.570, III 1, rev 2.070; lever: steering column; final drive: hypoid bevel; axle ratio: 2.410 - California 3.230; width of rims: 6"; tyres: P 195/75 x 14.

PERFORMANCE max speed: 98 mph, 157 km/h; power-weight ratio: Sedan 29.3 lb/hp (39.8 lb/kW), 13.2 kg/hp (18 kg/kW); consumption: 25.3 m/imp gal, 21 m/US gal, 11.2 l x 100 km.

CHASSIS perimeter box-type frame; front suspension: independent, wishbones, coil springs, telescopic dampers; rear: rigid axle, coil springs, torque arms, transverse linkage bar, telescopic dampers.

STEERING recirculating ball, variable ratio servo; turns lock to lock: 3.64.

BRAKES disc (diameter 10.50 in, 22.7 cm), internal radial fins, servo; swept area: total 312.7 sq in, 2,017 sq cm.

ELECTRICAL EQUIPMENT 12 V; 315 A battery; 56 A alternator; Delco-Remy transistorized ignition; 4 headlamps.

110 HP POWER TEAM

DIMENSIONS AND WEIGHT wheel base: 108.10 in, 274 cm; tracks: 58.50 in, 149 cm front, 57.80 in, 146 cm rear; length: 200.30 in, 509 cm; width: 71.60 in, 182 cm; height: 54.60 in, 139 cm; ground clearance: 5.70 in, 14.5 cm; weight: Sedan 3,219 lb, 1,460 kg - Coupé 3,172 lb, 1,439 kg - Limited Sedan 3,247 lb, 1,473 kg - Limited Coupé 3,199 lb, 1,451 kg; turning circle: 41.5 ft, 12.6 m; fuel tank: 15 imp gal, 18.1 US gal, 68 l.

BODY saloon/sedan, 4 doors - coupé, 2 doors; 5 seats, separate front seats.

OPTIONALS 3.080 or 3.230 axle ratio; tilt of steering wheel; heavy-duty cooling; heavy-duty battery; heated rear window; reclining backrests; electric windows; air-conditioning; automatic air-conditioning; electric sunroof; P 205/75 x 14 tyres; 550 A battery; 85 A alternator; vinyl roof; limited slip differential; digital clock; sunroof; speed control.

125 hp power team

See 110 hp power team, except for:

ENGINE 252 cu in, 4,130 cc (3.96 x 3.40 in, 100.7 x 86.4 mm); max power (SAE net): 125 hp (92 kW) at 4,000 rpm; max torque (SAE net): 205 lb ft, 28.3 kg m (277 Nm) at 2,000 rpm; max engine rpm: 4,400; 40.3 hp/l (22.3 kW/l); 1 Rochester M4ME downdraught 4-barrel carburettor; cooling: 21.7 imp pt, 25.8 US pt, 12.4 l.

PERFORMANCE max speed: 100 mph, 161 km/h; power-weight ratio: Sedan 25.8 lb/hp (35 lb/kW), 11.7 kg/hp (15.9 kg/kW); consumption: 21.6 m/imp gal, 18 m/US gal, 13.1 l x 100 km.

200 hp power team

See 110 hp power team, except for:

ENGINE turbocharged; max power (SAE net): 200 hp (147 kW) at 4,000 rpm; max torque (SAE net): 300 lb ft, 41.4 kg m (406 Nm) at 2,400 rpm; max engine rpm: 4,500; 52.8 hp/l (38.9 kW/l); 1 Rochester M4ME downdraught 4-barrel carburettor; cooling: 21.7 imp pt, 25.8 US pt, 12.4 l.

TRANSMISSION gearbox: Turbo-Hydramatic THM 200-4R automatic transmission, hydraulic torque converter and planetary gears with 3 ratios and overdrive, max ratio of converter at stall 1.80, possible manual selection; ratios: I 2.740, II 1.570, III 1, overdrive 0.670, rev 2.070; axle ratio: 3.420; width of rims: 7''; tyres: P 215/70 R x 15.

PERFORMANCE max speed: 118 mph, 190 km/h; power-weight ratio: 16.7 lb/hp (22.7 lb/kW), 7.6 kg/hp (10.3 kg/kW); consumption: 23 m/imp gal, 19 m/US gal, 12.3 l x 100 km.

ELECTRICAL EQUIPMENT 500 A battery; 94 A alternator.

DIMENSIONS AND WEIGHT weight: 3,342 lb, 1,515 kg.

BODY coupé; 2 doors.

OPTIONALS P 215/75 R x 15 tyres; heavy-duty suspension.

85 hp (diesel) power team

See 110 hp power team, except for:

ENGINE diesel; 262 cu in, 4,294 cc (4.06 x 3.38 in, 103 x 86 mm); compression ratio: 21.6:1; max power (SAE net): 85 hp (62 kW) at 3,600 rpm; max torque (SAE net): 165 lb ft, 22.8 kg m (223 Nm) at 1,600 rpm; max engine rpm: 4,000; 19.8 hp/l (14.6 kW/l); lubrication: 10.7 imp pt, 12.6 US pt, 6 l; Detroit diesel injection pump; cooling: 22 imp pt, 26 US pt, 12.5 l.

TRANSMISSION gearbox: Turbo-Hydramatic THM 200-4R automatic transmission, hydraulic torque converter and planetary gears with 3 ratios and overdrive, max ratio of converter at stall 1.90, possible manual selection; ratios: I 2.740, II 1.570, III 1, overdrive 0.670, rev 2.070; axle ratio: 2.930.

PERFORMANCE max speed: 95 mph, 153 km/h; power-weight ratio: Sedan 38.6 lb/hp (52.5 lb/kW), 17.5 kg/hp (23.8 kg/kW); consumption: 30 m/imp gal, 25 m/US gal, 9.4 l x 100 km.

ELECTRICAL EQUIPMENT 500 A battery; 78 A alternator.

OPTIONALS 94 A alternator.

BUICK Regal T-type Coupé

Le Sabre Series

PRICES EX WORKS:	$
Custom 4-dr Sedan	**10,140**
Limited 4-dr Sedan	**10,951**
Limited 2-dr Coupé	**10,791**

Power team:	Standard for:	Optional for:
110 hp	all	—
125 hp	—	all
140 hp	—	all
105 hp (diesel)	—	all

110 hp power team

ENGINE front, 4 stroke; 6 cylinders, Vee-slanted at 90°; 231 cu in, 3,785 cc (3.80 x 3.40 in, 96.5 x 86.4 mm); compression ratio: 8:1; max power (SAE net): 110 hp (81 kW) at 3,800 rpm; max torque (SAE net): 190 lb ft, 26.2 kg m (257 Nm) at 1,600 rpm; max engine rpm: 4,200; 28.9 hp/l (21.3 kW/l); cast iron block and head; 4 crankshaft bearings; valves: overhead, in line, push-rods and rockers, hydraulic tappets; camshafts: 1, at centre of Vee; lubrication: gear pump, full flow filter, 6.7 imp gal, 8 US pt, 3.8 l; 1 Rochester 2 ME downdraught twin barrel carburettor; thermostatic air cleaner; catalytic converter; fuel feed: mechanical pump; water-cooled, 21.6 imp pt, 26 US pt, 12.3 l.

TRANSMISSION driving wheels: rear; gearbox: Turbo-Hydramatic THM 200-C automatic transmission, hydraulic torque converter and planetary gears with 3 ratios, max ratio of converter at stall 2.20, possible manual selection; ratios: I 2.740, II 1.570, III 1, rev 2.070; lever: steering column; final drive: hypoid bevel; axle ratio: 2.730; width of rims: 6''; tyres: P 205/75 x 15.

PERFORMANCE max speed: 110 mph, 177 km/h; power-weight ratio: Custom Sedan 32.9 lb/hp (44.8 lb/kW), 14.9 kg/hp (20.3 kg/kW); consumption: 22.9 m/imp gal, 19 m/US gal, 12.3 l x 100 km.

CHASSIS perimeter box-type frame; front suspension: independent, wishbones, coil springs, anti roll bar, telescopic dampers; rear: rigid axle, coil springs, control arms, transverse linkage bar, telescopic dampers.

STEERING recirculating ball, variable ratio servo; turns lock to lock: 3.37.

BRAKES front disc (diameter 9.5 in, 241 cm), internal radial fins, rear drum, servo; swept area: total 344 sq in, 2,219 sq cm.

ELECTRICAL EQUIPMENT 12 V; 390 A battery; 56 A alternator; Delco-Remy transistorized ignition; 4 headlamps.

DIMENSIONS AND WEIGHT wheel base: 116 in, 294 cm; tracks: 61.80 in, 157 cm front, 60.70 in, 154 cm rear; length: 218.40 in, 555 cm; width: 78 in, 198 cm; height: sedans 56.70 in, 144 cm - Coupé 56 in, 142 cm; weight: Custom Sedan 3,622 lb, 1,642 kg - Limited Sedan 3,668 lb, 1,663 kg - Limited Coupé 3,635 lb - 1,648 kg; turning circle: 43.3 ft, 13.2 m; fuel tank: 20.9 imp gal, 25 US gal, 95 l.

BODY saloon/sedan, 4 doors - coupé, 2 doors; 6 seats, separate front seats.

OPTIONALS heavy-duty battery; heavy-duty cooling; automatic levelling control; P 215/75 x 15 tyres; 6'' or 7'' wide rims; speed control; electric windows; reclining backrests; air-conditioning; automatic air-conditioning; 3.230 axle ratio; vinyl roof; limited slip differential; heavy duty suspension; sunroof; 94 A alternator.

BUICK Le Sabre Custom Sedan

125 hp power team

See 110 hp power team, except for:

ENGINE 252 cu in, 4,130 cc (3.96 x 3.40 in, 100.7 x 86.4 mm); max power (SAE net): 125 hp (92 kW) at 4,000 rpm; max torque (SAE net): 205 lb ft, 28.3 kg m (287 Nm) at 2,000 rpm; max engine rpm: 4,400; 30.3 hp/l (22.3 kW/l); 1 Rochester M4MC downdraught 4-barrel carburettor.

TRANSMISSION Turbo-Hydramatic THM 200-4R automatic transmission, hydraulic torque converter and planetary gears with 3 ratios and overdrive, max ratio of converter at stall 2.15, possible manual selection; ratios: I 2.740, II 1.570, III 1, overdrive 0.670, rev 2.070; axle ratio: 3.230.

PERFORMANCE max speed: 117 mph, 188 km/h; power-weight ratio: Custom Sedan 29.1 lb/hp (39.5 lb/kW), 13.2 kg/hp (17.9 kg/kW); consumption: 20.5 m/imp gal, 17 m/US gal, 13.8 l x 100 km.

OPTIONALS 3.730 axle ratio; 85 A alternator.

140 hp power team

See 110 hp power team, except for:

ENGINE 8 cylinders in Vee; 305 cu in, 4,999 cc (3.80 x 3.40 in, 96.5 x 86 mm); max power (SAE net): 140 hp (103 kW) at 3,600 rpm; max torque (SAE net): 240 lb ft, 33.1 kg m (336

Nm) at 1,600 rpm; max engine rpm: 4,000; 28 hp/l (20.6 kW/l); 1 Rochester M4ME downdraught 4-barrel carburettor; cooling: 26 imp pt, 31.3 US pt, 14.8 l.

TRANSMISSION gearbox: Turbo-Hydramatic THM 200-4R automatic transmission, hydraulic torque converter and planetary gears with 3 ratios and overdrive, max ratio of converter at stall 1.90, possible manual selection; ratios: I 2.740, II 1.570, III 1, overdrive 0.670, rev 2.070; axle ratio: 2.730 or 3.230; width of rims: 7"; tyres: P 225/75 x 15.

PERFORMANCE max speed: 118 mph, 190 km/h; power-weight ratio: Custom Sedan 25.9 lb/hp (35.1 lb/kW), 11.7 kg/hp (15.9 kg/kW); consumption: 20.5 m/imp gal, 17 m/US gal, 13.8 l x 100 km.

OPTIONALS 3.080 axle ratio.

105 hp (diesel) power team

See 110 hp power team, except for:

ENGINE diesel; 350 cu in, 5,736 cc (4.06 x 3.38 in, 103 x 86 mm); compression ratio: 21.6:1; max power (SAE net): 105 hp (78 kW) at 3,200 rpm; max torque (SAE net): 200 lb ft, 27.6 kg m (271 Nm) at 1,600 rpm; max engine rpm: 3,500; 18.4 hp/l (13.6 kW/l); 5 crankshaft bearings; lubrication: 12.4 imp pt, 14.8 US pt, 7.1 l; Detroit diesel injection pump; cooling: 30.4 imp pt, 36.6 US pt, 17.3 l.

TRANSMISSION gearbox: Turbo-Hydramatic THM 200-4R automatic transmission, hydraulic torque converter and planetary gears with 3 ratios and overdrive, max ratio of converter at stall 1.90, possible manual selection; ratios: I 2.740, II 1.570, III 1, overdrive 0.670, rev 2.070; axle ratio: 2.930.

PERFORMANCE max speed: 95 mph, 153 km/h; power-weight ratio: Custom Sedan 34.6 lb/hp (47.1 lb/kW), 15.7 kg/hp (21.3 kg/kW); consumption: 26 m/imp gal, 22 m/US gal, 10.7 l x 100 km.

ELECTRICAL EQUIPMENT 2 x 405 A batteries; 78 A alternator.

Electra Series

PRICES EX WORKS:	$
1 Limited 4-dr Sedan	**13,344**
2 Limited 2-dr Coupé	**13,167**
3 Park Avenue 4-dr Sedan	**15,056**
4 Park Avenue 2-dr Coupé	**14,900**
5 4+1-dr Estate Wagon	**14,495**

Power team:	Standard for:	Optional for:
125 hp	1 to 4	—
140 hp	5	1 to 4
105 hp (diesel)	—	all

125 hp power team

ENGINE front, 4 stroke; 6 cylinders, Vee-slanted at 90°; 252 cu in, 4,130 cc (4 x 3.40 in, 100.7 x 86.4 mm); compression ratio: 8:1; max power (SAE net): 125 hp (92 kW) at 4,000 rpm; max torque (SAE net): 205 lb ft, 28.3 kg m (287 Nm) at 2,000 rpm; max engine rpm: 4,400; 30.5 hp/l (22.4 kW/l); cast iron block and head; 4 crankshaft bearings; valves: overhead, in line, push-rods and rockers, hydraulic tappets; camshafts: 1, at centre of Vee; lubrication: gear pump, full flow filter, 6.7 imp pt, 8 US pt, 3.8 l; 1 Rochester M4ME downdraught 4-barrel carburettor; thermostatic air cleaner; fuel feed: mechanical pump; water-cooled, 21.6 imp pt, 26 US pt, 12.3 l.

BUICK Electra Estate Wagon

TRANSMISSION driving wheels: rear; gearbox: Turbo-Hydramatic 200-4R automatic transmission, hydraulic torque converter and planetary gears with 3 ratios and overdrive, max ratio of converter at stall 2.20, possible manual selection; ratios: I 2.740, II 1.570, III 1, overdrive 0.670, rev 2.070; lever: steering column; final drive: hypoid bevel; axle ratio: 3.230; width of rims: 6"; tyres: P 215/75 R x 15.

PERFORMANCE max speed: 110 mph, 177 km/h; power-weight ratio: Limited Sedan 30.8 lb/hp (41.9 lb/kW), 14 kg/hp (19 kg/kW); consumption: 20.4 m/imp gal, 17 m/US gal, 13.8 l x 100 km.

CHASSIS perimeter box-type frame; front suspension: independent, wishbones, coil springs, anti-roll bar, telescopic dampers; rear: independent, coil springs, control arms, transverse linkage bar, telescopic dampers.

STEERING recirculating ball, variable ratio servo; turns lock to lock: 3.37.

BRAKES front disc (diameter 11 in, 279 cm), front internal radial fins, rear drum, rear compensator, servo; swept area: total 396.6 sq in, 2,559 sq cm.

ELECTRICAL EQUIPMENT 12 V; 390 A battery; 56 A alternator; Delco-Remy transistorized ignition; 4 headlamps.

DIMENSIONS AND WEIGHT wheel base: 118.90 in, 302 cm; tracks: 61.80 in, 157 cm front, 61 in, 154 cm rear; length: 221.30 in, 562 cm; width: 76.20 in, 193 cm; height: sedans 56.90 in, 145 cm - coupés 56 in, 142 cm; ground clearance: sedans 7.51 in, 19 cm - coupés 8.30 in, 21 cm; weight: Limited Coupé 3,194 lb, 1,423 kg - Limited Sedan 3,854 lb, 1,748 kg - Park Avenue Coupé 3,838 lb, 1,741 kg - Park Avenue Sedan 3,904 lb, 1,771 kg; turning circle: 43.3-44.9 ft, 13.2-13.7 m; fuel tank: 20.9 imp gal, 25 US gal, 95 l.

BODY saloon/sedan, 4 doors - coupé, 2 doors; 6 seats, separate front seats.

OPTIONALS reclining backrests; heated rear window; electric windows; speed control; P 225/75 x 15 tyres; heavy-duty battery; antitheft; automatic air-conditioning; tilt and telescopic steering column; electric doors; reclining backrests; vinyl roof; limited slip differential; 7" wide rims; 3.730 axle ratio; sunroof; heavy-duty suspension; heavy-duty cooling; cruise control; 94 A alternator.

BUICK Riviera Convertible

140 hp power team

See 125 hp power team, except for:

ENGINE 8 cylinders in Vee; 305 cu in, 4,999 cc (3.80 x 3.40 in, 96.5 x 86 mm); compression ratio: 8.1:1; max power (SAE net): 140 hp (103 kW) at 3,600 rpm; max torque (SAE net): 240 lb ft, 33.1 kg m (336 Nm) at 1,600 rpm; 28 hp/l (20.6 kW/l); cooling: 26 imp pt, 31.3 US pt, 14.8 l.

TRANSMISSION axle ratio: 2.730 or 3.230; tyres: P 225/75 R x 15.

PERFORMANCE max speed: 115 mph, 185 km/h; power-weight ratio: Estate Wagon 31.1 lb/hp (42.2 lb/kW), 14.1 kg/hp (19.1 kg/kW).

DIMENSIONS AND WEIGHT height: 59.10 in, 150 cm; ground clearance: 8 in, 20.3 cm; weight: Estate Wagon 4,295 lb, 1,948 kg; turning circle: 43.4-45.1 ft, 13.2-13.7 m; fuel tank: 18.3 imp gal, 22 US gal, 83 l.

BODY saloon/sedan, 4 doors - coupés, 2 doors - estate car/st. wagon, 4+1 doors.

OPTIONALS 3.080 axle ratio (not available in California).

105 hp (diesel) power team

See 125 hp power team, except for:

ENGINE diesel; 8 cylinders in Vee; 350 cu in, 5,736 cc (4.06 x 3.38 in, 103 x 86 mm); compression ratio: 21.6:1; max power (SAE net): 105 hp (78 kW) at 3,200 rpm; max torque (SAE net): 200 lb ft, 27.6 kg m (271 Nm) at 1,600 rpm; max engine rpm: 3,500; 18.4 hp/l (13.6 kW/l); 5 crankshaft bearings; lubrication: 12.4 imp pt, 14.8 US pt, 7.1 l; Detroit diesel injection pump; cooling: 30.4 imp pt, 36.6 US pt, 17.3 l.

TRANSMISSION max ratio of converter at stall 1.90; axle ratio: 2.930.

PERFORMANCE max speed: 100 mph, 161 km/h; power-weight ratio: Limited Sedan 36.7 lb/hp (49.9 lb/kW), 16.6 kg/hp (22.6 kg/kW); consumption: 27.7 m/imp gal, 23 m/US gal, 10.2 l x 100 km.

ELECTRICAL EQUIPMENT 2 x 405 A batteries; 78 A alternator.

BODY saloon/sedan, 4 doors - coupés, 2 doors - estate car/st. wagon, 4+1 doors.

Riviera Series

PRICES EX WORKS:	$
1 2-dr Coupé	**15,979**
2 2-dr Convertible	**25,844**
3 T-type 2-dr Coupé	**17,062**

Power team:	Standard for:	Optional for:
125 hp	1,2	—
140 hp	—	1,2
190 hp	3	2
105 hp (diesel)	—	1

125 hp power team

ENGINE front, 4 stroke; 6 cylinders, Vee-slanted at 90°; 252 cu in, 4,130 cc (3.96 x 3.40 in, 100.7 x 86.4 mm); compression ratio: 8:1; max power (SAE net): 125 hp (92 kW) at 4,000 rpm; max torque (SAE net): 205 lb ft, 28.3 kg m (277 Nm) at 2,000 rpm; max engine rpm: 4,000; 30.3 hp/l (22.3 kW/l); cast iron block and head; 4 crankshaft bearings; valves: overhead, in line, push-rods and rockers,

125 HP POWER TEAM

hydraulic tappets; camshafts: 1, at centre of Vee; lubrication: gear pump, full flow filter, 6.7 imp pt, 7.9 US pt, 3.8 l; 1 Rochester M4ME downdraught 4-barrel carburettor; thermostatic air cleaner; exhaust system with catalytic converter; fuel feed: mechanical pump; water-cooled, 21.7 imp pt, 25.8 US pt, 12.4 l.

TRANSMISSION driving wheels: front; gearbox: Torque-Hydramatic 325-4L automatic transmission, hydraulic torque converter and planetary gears with 3 ratios and overdrive, max ratio of converter at stall 2.20, possible manual selection; ratios: I 2.740, II 1.570, III 1, overdrive 0.670, rev 2.070; lever: steering column; final drive: hypoid bevel; axle ratio: 3.150; width of rims: 6"; tyres: P 205/75 R x 15.

PERFORMANCE max speed: 100 mph, 161 km/h; power-weight ratio: Coupé 29.6 lb/hp (40.2 lb/kW), 13.4 kg/hp (18.2 kg/kW); speed in top at 1,000 rpm: 25.4 mph, 40.8 km/h; consumption: 19.2 m/imp gal, 16 m/US gal, 14.7 l x 100 km.

CHASSIS channel section perimeter type frame; front suspension: independent, wishbones, longitudinal torsion bars, anti-roll bar, telescopic dampers; rear: independent, swinging longitudinal trailing arms, coil springs, automatic levelling control, telescopic dampers.

STEERING recirculating ball, servo; turns lock to lock: 2.99.

BRAKES front disc (diameter 10.50 in, 26.7 cm), front internal radial fins, rear drum, rear compensator, servo; swept area: total 307.8 sq in, 1,985 sq cm.

ELECTRICAL EQUIPMENT 12 V; 390 A battery; 70 A alternator; Delco-Remy transistorized ignition; 4 headlamps.

DIMENSIONS AND WEIGHT wheel base: 114 in, 289 cm; tracks: 59.30 in, 151 cm front, 60 in, 152 cm rear; length: 206.60 in, 525 cm; width: 72.80 in, 185 cm; height: 54.20 in, 138 cm; ground clearance: 5.60 in, 14.2 cm; weight: Coupé 3,679 lb, 1,669 kg - Convertible 3,786 lb, 1,650 kg; turning circle: 44.2 ft, 13.5 m; fuel tank: 17.4 imp gal, 21.1 US gal, 88 l.

BODY coupé - convertible; 2 doors; 4 seats, separate front seats, built-in headrests; electric tinted windows; air-conditioning.

OPTIONALS heavy-duty cooling; heavy-duty battery; heavy-duty alternator; tilt of steering wheel; speed control; heated rear window; electric sunroof; heavy-duty suspension; reclining backrests; 3.360 axle ratio; rear disc brakes; 550 A battery; 108 A alternator; P 225/70 R x 15 tyres.

140 hp power team

See 125 hp power team, except for:

ENGINE 8 cylinders in Vee; 307 cu in, 5,032 cc (3.80 x 3.38 in, 96.5 x 86 mm); max power (SAE net): 140 hp (103 kW) at 3,600 rpm; max torque (SAE net): 240 lb ft, 33.1 kg m (324 Nm) at 1,600 rpm; 27.8 hp/l (20.5 kW/l); 5 crankshaft bearings; 1 Rochester M4MC downdraught 4-barrel carburettor; fuel feed: electric pump; cooling: 27.3 imp pt, 32.8 US pt, 15.5 l.

TRANSMISSION axle ratio: 2.730.

PERFORMANCE max speed: 107 mph, 172 km/h; power-weight ratio: Coupé 26.2 lb/hp (35.7 lb/kW), 11.9 kg/hp (16.2 kg/kW); speed in top at 1,000 rpm: 31.1 mph, 50 km/h; consumption: 20.1 m/imp gal, 17 m/US gal, 13.9 l x 100 km.

ELECTRICAL EQUIPMENT 78 A alternator.

DIMENSIONS AND WEIGHT fuel tank: 17.6 imp gal, 21 US gal, 80 l.

OPTIONALS 3.150 axle ratio; 94 A alternator.

190 hp power team

See 125 hp power team, except for:

ENGINE turbocharged; 231 cu in, 3,785 cc (3.80 x 3.40 in, 96.5 x 86.4 mm); max power (SAE net): 190 hp (140 kW) at 4,000 rpm; max torque (SAE net): 300 lb ft, 41.4 kg m (406 Nm) at 2,400 rpm; max engine rpm: 4,500; 50.2 hp/l (36.9 kW/l); lubrication: 8.3 imp pt, 9.9 Us pt, 4.7 l; electronic fuel injection; fuel feed: electric pump; cooling: 22.2 imp pt, 26.6 US pt, 12.6 l.

TRANSMISSION max ratio of converter at stall 1.80.

PERFORMANCE max speed: 117 mph, 189 km/h; power-weight ratio: T-type Coupé 19.3 lb/hp (26.2 lb/kW), 8.7 kg/hp (11.9 kg/kW); consumption: 19.2 m/imp gal, 16 m/US gal, 14.7 l x 100 km.

ELECTRICAL EQUIPMENT 500 A battery; 94 A alternator.

DIMENSIONS AND WEIGHT weight: T-type Coupé 3,666 lb, 1,663 kg.

OPTIONALS 630 A battery.

105 hp (diesel) power team

See 125 hp power team, except for:

ENGINE diesel; 350 cu in, 5,736 cc (4.06 x 3.38 in, 103.9 x 86 mm); compression ratio: 21.6:1; max power (SAE net): 105 hp (78 kW) at 3,200 rpm; max torque (SAE net): 200 lb ft, 27.6 kg m (271 Nm) at 1,600 rpm; max engine rpm: 3,500; 18.4 hp/l (13.6 kW/l); 5 crankshaft bearings; lubrication: 12.4 imp pt, 14.8 US pt, 7.1 l; Detroit diesel injection pump; cooling: 30.3 imp pt, 36.4 US pt, 17.2 l.

TRANSMISSION axle ratio: 2.930.

PERFORMANCE max speed: 100 mph, 161 km/h; power-weight ratio: 35.1 lb/hp (47.2 lb/kW), 15.9 kg/hp (21.4 kg/kW); speed in top at 1,000 rpm: 28.6 mph, 45.7 km/h; consumption: 27 m/imp gal, 23 m/US gal, 10.2 l x 100 km.

ELECTRICAL EQUIPMENT 2 x 405 A batteries; 94 A alternator.

BODY coupé; 2 doors.

OPTIONALS 2 x 550 A batteries.

CADILLAC Cimarron

CADILLAC USA

Cimarron

PRICE EX WORKS: $ 12,614

ENGINE front, 4 stroke; 4 cylinders, in line; 121 cu in, 1,989 cc (3.50 x 3.15 in, 89 x 80 mm); compression ratio: 9.3:1; max power (SAE net): 88 hp (66 kW) at 4,800 rpm; max torque (SAE net): 110 lb ft, 15.2 kg m (149 Nm) at 2,400 rpm; max engine rpm: 5,300; 47.9 hp/l (35.9 kW/l); cast iron block and head; 5 crankshaft bearings; valves: overhead, in line, push-rods and rockers, hydraulic tappets; camshafts: 1, side, chain-driven; lubrication: gear pump, full flow filter, 6.7 imp pt, 8 US pt, 3.8 l; throttle-body electronic fuel ignition; air cleaner; exhaust system with catalytic converter; fuel feed: electric pump; water-cooled, 14.4 imp pt, 17.2 US pt, 8.2 l.

TRANSMISSION driving wheels: front; clutch: single dry plate; gearbox: mechanical; gears: 5, fully synchronized; ratios: I 3.920, II 2.150, III 1.330, IV 0.920, V 0.740, rev 3.500; lever: central; final drive: helical spur gears; axle ratio: 3.830; width of rims: 5.5"; tyres: 195/70 R x 13.

PERFORMANCE max speed: 104 mph, 165 km/h; power-weight ratio: 29.4 lb/hp (39.2 lb/kW), 13.3 kg/hp (17.8 kg/kW); carrying capacity: 882 lb, 400 kg; speed in top at 1,000 rpm: 18.2 mph, 29.3 km/h; consumption: 32.4 m/imp gal, 27 m/US gal, 8.7 l x 100 km.

CHASSIS integral; front suspension: independent, by McPherson, lower wishbones, coil springs/telescopic damper struts, anti-roll bar; rear: rigid axle, swinging longitudinal leading arms, coil springs, anti-roll bar, telescopic dampers.

STEERING rack-and-pinion, servo; turns lock to lock: 2.50.

BRAKES front disc (diameter 9.70 in, 24.7 cm), internal radial fins, rear drum, servo; swept area: total 251 sq in, 1,624 sq cm.

ELECTRICAL EQUIPMENT 12 V; 75 Ah battery; 78 A alternator; Delco-Remy high energy ignition; 4 headlamps.

DIMENSIONS AND WEIGHT wheel base: 101.20 in, 257 cm; front and rear track: 55.40 in, 141 cm; length: 173 in, 440 cm; width: 66.30 in, 168 cm; height: 52 in, 132 cm; ground clearance: 6.80 in, 17 cm; weight: 2,582 lb, 1,171 kg; weight distribution: 65% front, 35% rear; turning circle: 38.2 ft, 11.6 m; fuel tank: 11.4 imp gal, 13.6 US gal, 52 l.

BODY saloon/sedan; 4 doors; 5 seats, separate front seats, built-in headrests; air-conditioning; leather upholstery.

OPTIONALS automatic transmission, hydraulic torque converter and planetary gears with 3 ratios (I 2.840, II 1.600, III 1, rev 2.070), max ratio of converter at stall 2.70, 3.180 axle ratio, 27.6 m/imp gal, 23 m/US gal, 10.2 l x 100 km; 3.430 axle ratio; heavy-duty cooling; heavy-duty battery; electric seats; electric windows; electric door locks; sunroof; speed control; tilt of steering wheel; cruise control; heavy-duty radiator.

De Ville / Fleetwood Series

PRICES EX WORKS:	$
1 De Ville 4-dr Sedan	**17,625**
2 De Ville 2-dr Coupé	**17,140**

CADILLAC De Ville Sedan

CADILLAC Fleetwood Brougham Coupé

Fleetwood Brougham 4-dr Sedan	**20,451**
Fleetwood Brougham 2-dr Coupé	**19,942**
Fleetwood 4-dr Limousine	**30,454**
Fleetwood Formal 4-dr Limousine	**31,512**

ower team:	Standard for:	Optional for:
35 hp	1 to 4	—
40 hp	5	—
50 hp	6	—
05 hp (diesel)	—	all

135 hp power team

:NGINE front, 4 stroke; 8 cylinders in Vee; 250 cu in, 4,097 cc 3.46 x 3.31 in, 88 x 84 mm); compression ratio: 8.5:1; max ower (SAE net): 135 hp (94 kW) at 4,400 rpm; max torque SAE net): 200 lb ft, 27.6 kg m (270 Nm) at 2,200 rpm; max ngine rpm: 4,500; 30.5 hp/l (22.9 kW/l); light alloy block, wet ners, cast iron head; 5 crankshaft bearings; valves: overhead, n line, push-rods and rockers, hydraulic tappets; camshafts: 1, t centre of Vee, chain-driven; lubrication: gear pump, full flow lter, 6.6 imp pt, 7.9 US pt, 3.8 l; digital fuel injection; air leaner; exhaust system with catalytic converter; fuel feed: lectric pump; water-cooler, 17.6 imp pt, 20.9 US pt, 10 l.

RANSMISSION driving wheels: rear; gearbox: Turbo-lydramatic 200 4R automatic transmission, hydraulic torque onverter and planetary gears with 4 ratios, max ratio of onverter at stall 2.35, possible manual selection; ratios: I .740, II 1.570, III 1, IV 0.667, rev 2.070; lever: steering olumn; final drive: hypoid bevel; axle ratio: 3.420 or 3.730; vidth of rims: 6"; tyres: 215/75 R x 15.

ERFORMANCE max speed: 102 mph, 165 km/h; power-weight atio: De Ville Sedan 29.5 lb/hp (40.2 lb/kW), 13.4 kg/hp (18.2 g/kW); carrying capacity: 1,058 lb, 480 kg; speed in top at ,000 rpm: 23.8 mph, 38.3 km/h; consumption: 20 m/imp gal, 17 n/US gal, 13.7 l x 100 km.

CHASSIS box-type ladder frame with cross members; front suspension: independent, wishbones, coil springs, anti-roll bar, elescopic dampers; rear: rigid axle, swinging longitudinal lead-ng arms, coil springs, telescopic dampers.

STEERING recirculating ball, servo; turns lock to lock: 3.20.

BRAKES front disc (diameter 11.70 in, 29.8 cm), internal radial fins, rear drum, servo; swept area: front 236.5 sq in, 1,528 sq cm, rear 138.2 sq in, 892 sq cm, total 374.7 sq in, 2,420 sq cm.

ELECTRICAL EQUIPMENT 12 V; 80 A alternator; Delco-Remy transistorized contactless ignition; 4 headlamps.

DIMENSIONS AND WEIGHT wheel base: 121.54 in, 308 cm; tracks: 61.85 in, 157 cm front, 60.68 in, 154 cm rear; length: 220.87 in, 561 cm; width: 76.38 in, 194 cm; height: De Ville Sedan 56.69 in, 144 cm - Fleetwood Brougham Sedan 55.51 in, 141 cm - coupés 54.72 in, 139 cm; ground clearance: 5.51 in, 14 cm; weight: De Ville Sedan 3,982 lb, 1,806 kg - De Ville Coupé 3,942 lb, 1,788 kg - Fleetwood Brougham Sedan 4,035 lb, 1,830 kg - Fleetwood Brougham Coupé 3,991 lb, 1,810 kg; weight distribution: 54% front, 46% rear; turning circle: 44.1 ft, 13.4 m; fuel tank: 20.9 imp gal, 25 US gal, 95 l.

BODY saloon/sedan, 4 doors - coupé, 2 doors; 6 seats, separate front seats, built-in headrests; electric windows; electric seats; electronic air-conditioning.

OPTIONALS electric door locks; sunroof; simulated convertible roof; heated rear window; speed control; automatic levelling control; electric lever center; cruise control; antitheft.

140 hp power team

See 135 hp power team, except for:

ENGINE 368 cu in, 6,033 cc (3.80 x 4.06 in, 96.5 x 103.1 mm); compression ratio: 8.2:1; max power (SAE net): 140 hp (105 kW) at 3,800 rpm; max torque (SAE net): 265 lb ft, 36.5 kg m (359 Nm) at 1,400 rpm; max engine rpm: 4,200; 23.2 hp/l (17.4 kW/l); cast iron block and head; digital fuel injection selecting 8, 6, or 4 cylinders; cooling: 35.7 imp pt, 42.9 US pt, 20.3 l.

TRANSMISSION gearbox: Turbo-Hydramatic 400 automatic transmission, hydraulic torque converter and planetary gears with 3 ratios, max ratio of converter at stall 2, possible manual selection; ratios: I 2.480, II 1.480, III 1, rev 2.070; axle ratio: 3.080; tyres: HR 78 x 15/D.

PERFORMANCE max speed: 92 mph, 148 km/h; power-weight ratio: 34 lb/hp (45.4 lb/kW), 15.4 kg/hp (20.6 kg/kW); carrying capacity: 1,230 lb, 560 kg; speed in direct drive at 1,000 rpm: 21.9 mph, 35.2 km/h; consumption: 12 m/imp gal, 10 m/US gal, 23.5 l x 100 km.

STEERING turns lock too lock: 3.90.

BRAKES swept area: front 236.8 sq in, 1,528 sq cm, rear 198.5 sq in, 1,216 sq cm, total 453.3 sq in, 2,744 sq cm.

DIMENSIONS AND WEIGHT wheel base: 144.50 in, 367 cm; length: 244.10 in, 620 cm; height: 56.90 in, 151 cm; ground clearance: 5.60 in, 15.1 cm; weight: 4,765 lb, 2.161 kg; weight distribution: 55% front, 45% rear; turning circle: 51.1 ft, 15.6 m.

BODY limousine; 4 doors; 8 seats, built-in headrests; electric windows; electronic air-conditioning.

150 hp power team

See 135 hp power team, except for:

ENGINE 368 cu in, 6,033 cc (3.80 x 4.06 in, 96.5 x 103.1 mm); compression ratio: 8.2:1; max power (SAE net): 150 hp (110 kW) at 3,800 rpm; max torque (SAE net): 265 lb ft, 36.6 kg m (359 Nm) at 1,600 rpm; max engine rpm: 4,200; 24.8 hp/l (18.3 kW/l); cast iron block and head; 1 downdraught 4-barrel carburettor; cooling: 35.7 imp pt, 42.9 US pt, 20.3 l.

TRANSMISSION tyres: HR 78 x 15/D.

PERFORMANCE max speed: 94 mph, 152 km/h; power-weight ratio: 32.4 lb/hp (44 lb/kW), 14.7 kg/hp (19.9 kg/kW); consumption: not declared.

STEERING turns lock to lock: 3.90.

BRAKES swept area: front 236.8 sq in, 1,528 sq cm, rear 198.5 sq in, 1,216 sq cm, total 453.3 sq in, 2,744 sq cm.

DIMENSIONS AND WEIGHT wheel base: 144.50 in, 367 cm; length: 244.10 in, 620 cm; height: 56.90 in, 151 cm; ground clearance: 5.60 in, 15.1 cm; weight: 4,855 lb, 2,202 kg; weight distribution: 55% front, 45% rear; turning circle: 51.1 ft, 15.6 m.

BODY limousine; 4 doors; 7 seats, built-in headrests; electric windows; automatic air-conditioning; glass partition.

105 hp (diesel) power team

See 135 hp power team, except for:

ENGINE diesel; 350 cu in, 5,740 cc (4.06 x 3.34 in, 103 x 86 mm); compression ratio: 22.7:1; max power (SAE net): 105 hp (79 kW) at 3,200 rpm; max torque (SAE net): 200 lb ft, 27.7 kg m (272 Nm) at 1,600 rpm; max engine rpm: 3,500; 18.3 hp/l (13.8 kW/l); cast iron block and head; lubrication: 11.6 imp pt, 13.9 US pt, 6.6 l; Stanadyne-Hartford injection pump; fuel feed: mechanical pump; cooling: 39.4 imp pt, 46.9 US pt, 22.4 l.

TRANSMISSION axle ratio: 2.930.

PERFORMANCE max speed: 93 mph, 155 km/h; power-weight ratio: De Ville Sedan 37.9 lb/hp (51.5 lb/kW), 17.2 kg/hp (23.4 kg/kW); consumption: 23.6 m/imp gal, 20 m/US gal, 11.7 l x 100 km.

ELECTRICAL EQUIPMENT 2 batteries.

DIMENSIONS AND WEIGHT fuel tank: 21.5 imp gal, 26 US gal, 98 l.

Eldorado / Seville Series

PRICES EX WORKS:	$
1 Eldorado 2-dr Coupé	**20,343**
2 Eldorado 2-dr Convertible	**31,286**
3 Seville 4-dr Sedan	**22,468**

Power team:	Standard for:	Optional for:
135 hp	all	—
105 hp (diesel)	—	1,3

135 hp power team

ENGINE front, 4 stroke; 8 cylinders in Vee; 250 cu in, 4,097 cc (3.46 x 3.31 in, 88 x 84 mm); compression ratio: 8.5:1; max power (SAE net): 135 hp (101 kW) at 4,400 rpm; max torque (SAE net): 200 lb ft, 27.6 kg m (271 Nm) at 2,200 rpm; max engine rpm: 4,400; 30.5 hp/l (22.9 kW/l); light alloy block, wet liners, cast iron head; 5 crankshaft bearings; valves: overhead, in line, push-rods and rockers, hydraulic tappets; camshafts: 1, at centre of Vee, chain-driven; lubrication: gear pump, full flow filter, 8.3 imp pt, 9.9 US pt, 4.7 l; digital fuel injection; air cleaner; exhaust system with catalytic converter; fuel feed: electric pump; water-cooled, 19.9 imp pt, 23.7 US pt, 11.3 l.

TRANSMISSION driving wheels: front; gearbox: Turbo-Hydramatic 325 4L automatic transmission, hydraulic torque converter and planetary gears with 4 ratios, max ratio of converter at stall 2.35, possible manual selection; ratios: I 2.740, II 1.570, III 1, IV 0.667, rev 2.070; lever: steering column; final drive: hypoid bevel; axle ratio: 3.150; width of rims: 6"; tyres: P 205/75 R x 15.

PERFORMANCE max speed: 102 mph, 165 km/h; power-weight ratio: Eldorado models 29.9 lb/hp (40.6 lb/kW), 13.6 kg/hp (18.4 kg/kW); carrying capacity: 882 lb, 400 kg; speed in top at 1,000 rpm: 23.8 mph, 38.3 km/h; consumption: 19.8 m/imp gal, 16.9 m/US gal, 13.7 l x 100 km.

CHASSIS box-type ladder frame with cross members; front suspension: independent, wishbones, longitudinal torsion bar, anti-roll bar, telescopic dampers; rear: independent, swinging

CADILLAC Eldorado Biarritz Convertible

135 HP POWER TEAM

longitudinal trailing arms, coil springs, automatic levelling control, anti-roll bar, telescopic dampers.

STEERING recirculating ball, servo; turns lock to lock: Eldorado models 2.90 - Seville 3.

BRAKES disc (diameter 10.40 in, 26.5 cm), internal radial fins, servo; swept area: front 198 sq in, 1,277 sq cm, rear 198 sq in, 1,277 sq cm, total 396 sq in, 2,554 sq cm.

ELECTRICAL EQUIPMENT 12 V; 80 A alternator; Delco-Remy transistorized contactless ignition; 4 headlamps.

DIMENSIONS AND WEIGHT wheel base: 114 in, 289 cm; tracks: 59.30 in, 151 cm front, 60.60 in, 154 cm rear; length: Eldorado models 204.50 in, 519 cm - Seville 204.80 in, 520 cm; width: 71.50 in, 182 cm; height: 54.30 in, 138 cm; ground clearance: 5.60 in, 14.1 cm; weight: Eldorado models 3,733 lb, 1,693 kg - Seville Sedan 3,803 lb, 1,725 kg; weight distribution: 55% front, 45% rear; turning circle: 42.2 ft, 12.8 m; fuel tank: 17.2 imp gal, 20.3 US gal, 77 l.

BODY saloon/sedan, 4 doors - coupé, 2 doors - convertible, 2 doors; 5 seats, separate front seats, built-in headrests; electric windows; electric seats; electronic air-conditioning.

OPTIONALS leather upholstery; heated rear window; sunroof; 100 A alternator; simulated convertible roof; speed control; heavy-duty suspension; Biarritz equipment; Touring equipment; Elegante equipment; cruise control; tilt of steering wheel; heavy-duty battery; (for Eldorado Touring Coupé only) P 225/70 R x 15 tyres; tinted glass; vinyl roof; 3.360 axle ratio.

105 hp (diesel) power team

See 135 hp power team, except for:

ENGINE diesel; 350 cu in, 5,740 cc (4.06 x 3.38 in, 103 x 86 mm); compression ratio: 22.7:1; max power (SAE net): 105 hp (79 kW) at 3,200 rpm; max torque (SAE net): 200 lb ft, 27.6 kg m (271 Nm) at 1,600 rpm; max engine rpm: 3,700; 18.3 hp/l (24.8 kW/l); cast iron block and head; lubrication: 11.6 imp pt, 13.9 US pt, 6.6 l; Stanadyne-Hartford injection pump; fuel feed: mechanical pump; cooling: 39.4 imp pt, 46.9 US pt, 22.4 l.

TRANSMISSION axle ratio: 2.930.

PERFORMANCE max speed: 93 mph, 155 km/h; power-weight ratio: Eldorado Coupé 39.2 lb/hp (53.3 lb/kW), 17.7 kg/hp (24.1 kg/kW); consumption: 26.6 m/imp gal, 22 m/US gal, 10.6 l x 100 km.

ELECTRICAL EQUIPMENT 2 batteries.

DIMENSIONS AND WEIGHT weight: Eldorado Coupé 4,114 lb, 1,866 kg - Seville Sedan 4,185 lb, 1,898 kg.

BODY saloon/sedan, 4 doors - coupé, 2 doors.

CHEVROLET USA

Chevette Series

PRICES EX WORKS:	$
4+1-dr Sedan	**5,333**
2+1-dr Coupé	**4,997**
CS 4+1-dr Sedan	**5,636**
CS 2+1-dr Coupé	**5,489**

Power team:	Standard for:	Optional for:
65 hp	all	—
51 hp (diesel)	—	all

65 hp power team

ENGINE front, 4 stroke; 4 cylinders, vertical, in line; 97.6 cu in, 1,599 cc (3.23 x 2.98 in, 82 x 75.6 mm); compression ratio: 9:1; max power (SAE net): 65 hp (48 kW) at 5,200 rpm; max torque (SAE net): 80 lb ft, 11 kg m (108 Nm) at 3,200 rpm; max engine rpm: 5,600; 40.7 hp/l (29.9 kW/l); cast iron block and head; 5 crankshaft bearings; valves: overhead, hydraulic tappets; camshafts: 1, overhead, cogged belt; lubrication: gear pump, full flow filter, 6.7 imp pt, 8 US pt, 3.8 l; 1 Holley 14004464 (14004472 for California only) downdraught twin barrel carburettor; air cleaner; exhaust system with catalytic converter; fuel feed: mechanical pump; water-cooled, 15 imp pt, 18 US pt, 8.5 l.

TRANSMISSION driving wheels: rear; clutch: single dry plate (diaphragm); gearbox: mechanical; gears: 4, fully synchronized; ratios: I 3.750, II 2.160, III 1.380, IV 1, rev 3.820; lever: central; final drive: hypoid bevel; axle ratio: 3.360 - 3.620 (for California only); width of rims: 5''; tyres: P155/80 R x 13.

PERFORMANCE max speed: 90 mph, 145 km/h; power-weight ratio: 4+1-dr Sedan 32.5 lb/hp (44.1 lb/kW), 14.7 kg/hp (20

CADILLAC Seville Sedan

kg/kW); speed in direct drive at 1,000 rpm: 17.9 mph, 28.8 km/h; consumption: 37.1 m/imp gal, 31 m/US gal, 7.6 l x 100 km.

CHASSIS integral with cross member reinforcement; front suspension: independent, wishbones, coil springs, anti-roll bar, telescopic dampers; rear: rigid axle (torque tube), longitudinal trailing radius arms, coil springs, transverse linkage bar, anti-roll bar, telescopic dampers.

STEERING rack-and-pinion; turns lock to lock: 3.60.

BRAKES front disc (diameter 9.68 in, 24.6 cm), rear drum; swept area: total 279.8 sq in, 1,804 sq cm.

ELECTRICAL EQUIPMENT 12 V; 2,500 W battery; 42 A alternator; Delco-Remy high energy ignition; 2 headlamps.

DIMENSIONS AND WEIGHT wheel base: coupés 94.30 in, 239 cm - sedans 97.30 in, 247 cm; front and rear track: 51.20 in, 130 cm; length: coupés 161.90 in, 411 cm - sedans 164.90 in, 419 cm; width: 61.80 in, 157 cm; height: 52.80 in, 134 cm; ground clearance: 5.30 in, 13.5 cm; weight: 2+1-dr Coupé 2,047 lb, 928 kg - CS 2+1-dr Coupé 2,090 lb, 948 kg - 4+1-dr Sedan 2,110 lb, 957 kg - CS 4+1-dr Sedan 2,149 lb, 975 kg.

BODY saloon/sedan, 4+1 doors - coupé, 2+1 doors; 4 seats, separate front seats, built-in headrests.

OPTIONALS (except California) 5-speed fully synchronized mechanical gearbox (I 3.760, II 2.180, III 1.360, IV 1, V 0.860, rev 3.760); Turbo-Hydramatic 180 automatic transmission, hydraulic torque converter and planetary gears with 3 ratios (I 2.400, II 1.480, III 1, rev 1.920), max ratio of converter at stall 2.20, possible manual selection, central lever, 3.620 axle ratio; heavy-duty battery; servo brake; vinyl roof; heavy-duty radiator; tilt of steering wheel; heated rear window; air-conditioning; de luxe equipment; Custom two-tone paint equipment; power steering.

51 hp (diesel) power team

See 65 hp power team, except for:

ENGINE Isuzu, diesel; 111 cu in, 1,819 cc (3.31 x 3.23 in, 84 x 82 mm); compression ratio: 22:1; max power (SAE net): 51 hp (38 kW) at 5,000 rpm; max torque (SAE net): 72 lb ft, 9.9 kg m (97 Nm) at 2,000 rpm; max engine rpm: 5,400; 28 hp/l (20.6 kW/l); valves: mechanical tappets; Bosch injection pump; cooling: 15 imp pt, 18 US pt, 8.5 l.

TRANSMISSION gears: 5, fully synchronized; ratios: I 3.790, II 2.180, III 1.420, IV 1, V 0.860, rev 3.760.

PERFORMANCE max speed: 84 mph, 135 km/h; power-weight ratio: sedans 43.7 lb/hp (59.4 lb/kW), 19.8 kg/hp (26.9 kg/kW); consumption: 47 m/imp gal, 40 m/US gal, 5.9 l x 100 km.

ELECTRICAL EQUIPMENT 5,000 W battery.

DIMENSIONS AND WEIGHT weight: 2+1-dr Coupé 2,122 lb, 962 kg - CS 2+1-dr Coupé 2,168 lb, 983 kg - sedans 2,228 lb, 1,010 kg.

OPTIONALS (except California) turbo-Hydramatic 200 C automatic transmission, hydraulic torque converter and planetary gears with 3 ratios (I 2.740, II 1.570, III 1, rev 2.070), max ratio of converter at stall 2.08, possible manual selection, 3.360 or 3.620 axle ratio.

Cavalier Series

PRICES EX WORKS:	$
4-dr Notchback Sedan	**6,222**
4+1-dr Liftgate Wagon	**6,375**
CS 4-dr Notchback Sedan	**6,666**
CS 4+1-dr Liftgate Wagon	**6,821**
Type 10 2-dr Notchback Coupé	**6,447**
Type 10 2+1-dr Hatchback Coupé	**6,654**
Type 10 2-dr Convertible	**11,299**

ENGINE front, 4 stroke; 4 cylinders, transverse, in line; 121 cu in, 1,989 cc (3.50 x 3.15 in, 89 x 80 mm); compression ratio: 9.3:1; max power (SAE net): 88 hp (66 kW) at 4,800 rpm; max torque (SAE net): 110 lb ft, 15.2 kg m (149 Nm) at 2,400 rpm; max engine rpm: 5,200; 47.8 hp/l (35.2 kW/l); cast iron block and head; 5 crankshaft bearings; valves: overhead, in line, push-rods and rockers, hydraulic tappets; camshafts: 1, side, chain-driven; lubrication: gear pump, full flow filter, 6.7 imp pt, 8 US pt, 3.8 l; throttle body electronic fuel injection; air cleaner; exhaust system with catalytic converter; fuel feed: electric pump; water-cooled, 15.8 imp pt, 19 US pt, 9 l.

TRANSMISSION driving wheels: front; clutch: single dry plate (diaphragm); gearbox: mechanical; gears: 4, fully synchronized;

CHEVROLET Chevette Sedan

CHEVROLET Cavalier Type 10 Notchback Coupé

CHEVROLET Citation Hatchback Coupé

ratios: I 3.530, II 1.950, III 1.240, IV 0.810, rev 3.420; lever: central; final drive: helical spur gears; axle ratio: 3.320; width of rims: 5"; tyres: P 175/80 R x 13.

PERFORMANCE max speed: 95 mph, 153 km/h; power-weight ratio: sedans 27.1 lb/hp (36.9 lb/kW), 12.3 kg/hp (16.7 kg/kW); carrying capacity: 700 lb, 320 kg; speed in top at 1,000 rpm: 18.6 mph, 30 km/h; consumption: 32.4 m/imp gal, 27 m/US gal, 8.7 l x 100 km.

CHASSIS integral; front suspension: independent, by McPherson, lower wishbones, coil springs/telescopic damper struts; rear: rigid axle, coil springs, telescopic dampers.

STEERING rack-and-pinion; turns lock to lock: 4.04.

BRAKES front disc (diameter 9.72 in, 24.7 cm), rear drum, servo; swept area: total 251.8 sq in, 1,624 sq cm.

ELECTRICAL EQUIPMENT 12 V; 405 Ah battery; 42 A alternator; Delco-Remy high energy transistorized ignition; 2 headlamps.

DIMENSIONS AND WEIGHT wheel base: 101.20 in, 257 cm; tracks: 55.40 in, 141 cm front, 55.20 in, 140 cm rear; length: sedans and coupés 172.40 in, 438 cm - st. wagons 173 in, 439 cm; width: 66 in, 168 cm; height: sedans 53.90 in, 137 cm - coupés 52 in, 132 cm - st. wagons 54.40 in, 138 cm; ground clearance: 6.80 in, 17.2 cm; weight: sedans 2,389 lb, 1,084 kg - Type 10 Hachback Coupé 2,418 lb, 1,097 kg - Type 10 Notchback Coupé 2,369 lb, 1,074 kg - Type 10 Convertible 2,584 lb, 1,172 kg - st. wagons 2,461 lb, 1,116 kg.

BODY saloon/sedan, 4 doors - coupé and convertible, 2 doors - hatchback coupé, 2+1 doors - estate car/st. wagon, 4+1 doors; 4 seats, separate front seats, built-in headrests, reclining backrests; heated rear window.

OPTIONALS 5-speed fully synchronized mechanical gearbox (I 3.910, II 2.150, III 1.330, IV 0.920, V 0.740, rev 3.500), 4.100 axle ratio; Turbo-Hydramatic 125 C automatic transmission, hydraulic torque converter and planetary gears with 3 ratio; 4.100 axle ratio; disc brakes with internal radial fins; tilt of steering wheel; power steering; air-conditioning; electric windows; electric front seats; detachable sunroof; rear window wiper-washer; speed control; P 195/70 R x 13 tyres; 7 wide rims.

Citation Series

PRICES EX WORKS:	$
4+1-dr Hatchback Sedan	**7,046**
2+1-dr Notchback Coupé	**6,445**
2+1-dr Hatchback Coupé	**6,900**

Power team:	Standard for:	Optional for:
92 hp	all	—
112 hp	—	all
135 hp	—	all

92 hp power team

ENGINE front, transverse, 4 stroke; 4 cylinders, in line; 151 cu in, 2,475 cc (4 x 3 in, 101.6 x 76.2 mm); compression ratio: 9:1; max power (SAE net): 92 hp (68 kW) at 4,000 rpm; max torque (SAE net): 134 lb ft, 18.4 kg m (181 Nm) at 2,800 rpm; max engine rpm: 4,400; 37.2 hp/l (27.3 kW/l); cast iron block and head; 5 crankshaft bearings; valves: overhead, in line, push-rods and rockers, hydraulic tappets; camshafts: 1, side; lubrication: gear pump, full flow filter, 4.9 imp pt, 5.9 US pt, 2.8 l; throttle body electronic fuel injection; air cleaner; exhaust system with catalytic converter; fuel feed: electric pump; water-cooled, 15.3 imp pt, 18.4 US pt, 8.7 l.

TRANSMISSION driving wheels: front; clutch: self-adjusting single dry plate (diaphragm); gearbox: mechanical; gears: 4, fully synchronized; ratios: I 3.530, II 1.950, III 1.240, IV 0.730, rev 3.420; lever: central; final drive: spiral bevel; axle ratio: 3.320 or 3.650; width of rims: 5.5"; tyres: P 185/80 R x 13.

PERFORMANCE max speed: 96 mph, 155 km/h; power-weight ratio: Sedan 27.1 lb/hp (36.9 lb/kW), 12.3 kg/hp (16.7 kg/kW); speed in top at 1,000 rpm: 19.8 mph, 31.8 km/h; consumption: 32.4 m/imp gal, 27 m/US gal, 8.7 l x 100 km.

CHASSIS integral; front suspension: independent, by McPherson, coil springs, lower control arms, telescopic dampers; rear: rigid axle, trailing arm, control arms, coil springs, telescopic dampers.

STEERING rack-and-pinion; turns lock to lock: 3.50.

BRAKES front disc (diameter 9.72 in, 24.7 cm), internal radial fins, rear drum; swept area: total 261.6 sq in, 1,687 sq cm.

ELECTRICAL EQUIPMENT 12 V; 3,200 W battery; 42 A alternator; Delco-Remy high energy ignition; 2 headlamps.

DIMENSIONS AND WEIGHT wheel base: 104.90 in, 266 cm; tracks: 58.70 in, 149 cm front, 57 in, 145 cm rear; length: 176.70 in, 449 cm; width: 68.30 in, 174 cm; height: 53.90 in, 137 cm; ground clearance: 5.60 in, 14.2 cm; weight: Sedan 2,507 lb, 1,138 kg - coupés 2,471 lb, 1,121 kg; weight distribution: 63% front, 37% rear; turning circle: 41 ft, 12.5 m; fuel tank: 12.1 imp gal, 14.5 US gal, 55 l.

BODY saloon/sedan, 4+1 doors - coupés, 2+1 doors; 5 seats, separate front seats, built-in headrests.

OPTIONALS automatic transmission with 3 ratios (I 2.840, II 1.600, III 1, rev 2.070), max ratio of converter at stall 1.90, possible manual selection, steering column lever, 2.840 or 2.390 axle ratio; tilt of steering wheel; sunroof; reclining seats; Custom upholstery; heated rear window; air-conditioning; servo brake; tilt of steering wheel; power steering; electric windows; electric door lock; de luxe equipment; sport equipment; P 205/70 R x 13 tyres; heavy-duty battery; 500 A battery; 78 A alternator; heavy-duty cooling.

112 hp power team

See 92 hp power team, except for:

ENGINE 6 cylinders, Vee-slanted at 60°; 173 cu in, 2,835 cc (3.50 x 3 in, 89 x 76.2 mm); compression ratio: 8.5:1; max power (SAE net): 112 hp (82 kW) at 4,800 rpm; max torque (SAE net): 145 lb ft, 20 kg m (196 Nm) at 2,100 rpm; max engine rpm: 5,300; 39.5 hp/l (29.1kW/l); 4 crankshaft bearings; camshafts: 1, at centre of Vee; lubrication: 6.7 imp pt, 7.9 US pt, 3.8 l; 1 Rochester E2SE downdraught twin barrel carburettor; fuel feed: mechanical pump; cooling: 17.8 imp pt, 21.4 US pt, 10.1 l.

TRANSMISSION gearbox ratios: I 3.530, II 1.950, III 1.240, IV 0.810, rev 3.420.

PERFORMANCE max speed: 106 mph, 170 km/h; power-weight ratio: Sedan 21.8 lb/hp (29.7 lb/kW), 9.9 kg/hp (13.4 kg/kW); speed in top at 1,000 rpm: 23.1 mph, 37.3 km/h.

DIMENSIONS AND WEIGHT weight: Sedan 2,571 lb, 1,166 kg - coupés 2,538 lb, 1,151 kg.

OPTIONALS automatic transmission with 2.530 axle ratio.

135 hp power team

See 92 hp power team, except for:

ENGINE 6 cylinders, Vee-slanted at 60°; 173 cu in, 2,835 cc (3.50 x 3 in, 89 x 76.2 mm); compression ratio: 8.9:1; max power (SAE net): 135 hp (99 kW) at 5,400 rpm; max torque (SAE net): 145 lb ft, 20.1 kg m (197 Nm) at 2,400 rpm; max engine rpm: 5,600; 47.6 hp/l (35.1 kW/l); 4 crankshaft bearings; camshafts: 1, at centre of Vee; lubrication: 6.7 imp pt, 7.9 US pt, 3.8 l; 1 Rochester E2SE downdraught twin barrel carburettor; fuel feed: mechanical pump; cooling: 17.8 imp pt, 21.4 US pt, 10.1 l.

TRANSMISSION gearbox ratios: I 3.310, II 1.950, III 1.240, IV 0.810, rev 3.420; axle ratio: 3.650.

PERFORMANCE max speed: 109 mph, 175 km/h; power-weight ratio: Sedan 18.8 lb/hp (25.5 lb/kW), 8.5 kg/hp (11.6 kg/kW); speed in top at 1,000 rpm: 23.1 mph, 37.3 km/h; consumption: 25.2 m/imp gal, 21 m/US gal, 11.2 l x 100 km.

DIMENSIONS AND WEIGHT weight: Sedan 2,571 lb, 1,661 kg - coupés 2,538 lb, 1,151 kg.

OPTIONALS automatic transmission with 3.330 axle ratio.

Camaro Series

PRICES EX WORKS:	$
1 2-dr Coupé	**7,995**
2 Berlinetta 2-dr Coupé	**10,895**
3 Z 28 2-dr Coupé	**10,620**

Power team:	Standard for:	Optional for:
92 hp	1	—
107 hp	2	1
150 hp	3	1,2
190 hp	—	3

92 hp power team

ENGINE front, 4 stroke; 4 cylinders, in line; 151 cu in, 2,475 cc (4 x 3 in, 101.6 x 76.2 mm); compression ratio: 9:1; max power (SAE net): 92 hp (68 kW) at 4,000 rpm; max torque (SAE net): 134 lb ft, 18.5 kg m (181 Nm) at 2,800 rpm; max engine rpm: 4,400; 37.2 hp/l (27.3 kW/l); cast iron block and head; 5 crankshaft bearings; valves: overhead, in line, push-rods and rockers, hydraulic tappets; camshafts: 1, side; lubrication: gear pump, full flow filter, 4.9 imp pt, 5.9 US pt, 2.8 l; throttle-body electronic fuel injection; air cleaner; exhaust system with catalytic converter; fuel feed: electric pump; water-cooled, 15.3 imp pt, 18.4 US pt, 8.7 l.

TRANSMISSION driving wheels: rear; clutch: single dry plate (diaphragm); gearbox: mechanical; gears: 4, fully synchronized; ratios: I 3.500, II 2.480, III 1.660, IV 1, rev 3.500; lever: central; final drive: hypoid bevel; axle ratio: 3.420; width of rims: 6"; tyres: P 195/75 R x 14.

PERFORMANCE max speed: 100 mph, 161 km/h; power-weight ratio: 31.4 lb/hp (42.7 lb/kW), 14.2 kg/hp (19.4 kg/kW); speed in direct drive at 1,000 rpm: 22.7 mph, 35.6 km/h; consumption: 29 m/imp gal, 24 m/US gal, 9.8 l x 100 km.

CHASSIS integral; front suspension: independent, by McPherson, wishbones, coil springs, anti-roll bar, telescopic dampers; rear: rigid axle, swinging longitudinal leading arms, anti-roll bar, coil springs, telescopic dampers.

STEERING recirculating ball, servo; turns lock to lock: 2.70.

BRAKES front disc (diameter 10.50 in, 26.7 cm), internal radial fins, rear drum, servo.

ELECTRICAL EQUIPMENT 12 V; 405 A battery; 42 A alternator; Delco-Remy light energy ignition; 4 headlamps.

DIMENSIONS AND WEIGHT wheel base: 101 in, 257 cm; tracks: 60.63 in, 154 cm front, 61.41 in, 156 cm rear; length: 187.80 in, 477 cm; width: 72.80 in, 185 cm; height: 50 in, 127 cm; ground clearance: 4.61 in, 11.7 cm; weight: 2,892 lb, 1,312 kg; weight distribution: 54% front, 46% rear; fuel tank: 13.5 imp gal, 16 US gal, 60 l.

BODY coupé; 2 doors; 4 seats, separate front seats, built-in headrests.

OPTIONALS 5-speed fully synchronized mechanical gearbox (I 3.760, II 2.180, III 1.420, IV 1, V 0.860, rev 3.760), 3.730 axle ratio; Turbo-Hydramatic 700R-4 automatic transmission, hydraulic torque converter and planetary gears with 4 ratios (I 3.060, II 1.630, III 1, IV 0.700, rev 2.290), 3.730 axle ratio; electric windows.

CHEVROLET Camaro Z 28 Coupé

CHEVROLET Celebrity Station Wagon

107 hp power team

See 92 hp power team, except for:

ENGINE 6 cylinders, Vee-slanted at 60°; 173 cu in, 2,835 cc (3.50 x 2.99 in, 89 x 76 mm); compression ratio: 8.5:1; max power (SAE net): 107 hp (78 kW) at 4,800 rpm; max torque (SAE net): 145 lb ft, 20 kg m (196 Nm) at 2,100 rpm; max engine rpm: 5,300; 37.7 hp/l (27.7 kW/l); 4 crankshaft bearings; camshafts: 1, at centre of Vee; lubrication: 6.7 imp pt, 7.9 US pt, 3.8 l; 1 Rochester E2SE downdraught twin barrel carburettor; fuel feed: mechanical pump.

TRANSMISSION (standard) gears: 5, fully synchronized; ratios: I 3.500, II 2.140, III 1.360, IV 1, V 0.780, rev 3.390; axle ratio: 3.420; width of rims: 7"; tyres: P 205/70 R x 14.

PERFORMANCE max speed: 105 mph, 169 km/h; power-weight ratio: 28 lb/hp (38.1 lb/kW), 12.7 kg/hp (17.3 kg/kW); consumption: 24.1 m/imp gal, 20 m/US gal, 11.7 l x 100 km.

ELECTRICAL EQUIPMENT 315 A battery; 66 A alternator.

DIMENSIONS AND WEIGHT weight: 2,999 lb, 1,360 kg.

OPTIONALS Turbo-Hydramatic 700 R-4 automatic transmission with 4 ratios (I 3.080, II 1.630, III 1, IV 0.700, rev 2.290), 3.230 axle ratio; electric windows.

150 hp power team

See 92 hp power team, except for:

ENGINE 8 cylinders in Vee; 305 cu in, 4,999 cc (3.74 x 3.48 in, 95 x 88.4 mm); compression ratio: 8.6:1; max power (SAE net): 150 hp (110 kW) at 4,000 rpm; max torque (SAE net): 240 lb ft, 33 kg m (324 Nm) at 2,400 rpm; max engine rpm: 4,500; 30.4 hp/l (22.4 kW/l); camshafts: 1, at centre of Vee; lubrication: 7.9 imp pt, 9.5 US pt, 4.5 l; 1 Rochester E4MC downdraught 4-barrel carburettor; dual exhaust system; fuel feed: mechanical pump; cooling: 25.2 imp pt, 30.2 US pt, 14.4 l.

TRANSMISSION gears: 5, fully synchronized; ratios: I 2.950, II 1.940, III 1.340, IV 1, V 0.730, rev 2.760; axle ratio: 3.230; tyres: P 215/65 HR x 15.

PERFORMANCE max speed: 125 mph, 201 km/h; power-weight ratio: 21.2 lb/hp (28.9 lb/kW), 9.6 kg/hp (13.1 kg/kW); consumption: 24 m/imp gal, 20 m/US gal, 11.8 l x 100 km.

ELECTRICAL EQUIPMENT 500 A battery; 94 A alternator.

DIMENSIONS AND WEIGHT weight: 3,186 lb, 1,445 kg.

OPTIONALS 3.080 or 3.730 axle ratio.

190 hp power team

See 92 hp power team, except for:

ENGINE 8 cylinders in Vee; 305 cu in, 4,999 cc (3.74 x 3.48 in, 95 x 88.4 mm); compression ratio: 9.5:1; max power (SAE net): 190 hp (139 kW) at 4,800 rpm; max torque (SAE net): 240 lb ft, 33.1 kg m (325 Nm) at 3,200 rpm; max engine rpm: 5,300; 38 hp/l (28 kW/l); 4 crankshaft bearings; camshafts: 1, at centre of Vee; lubrication: 8.3 imp pt, 9.9 US pt, 4.7 l; 1 Rochester E4 MC downdraught 4-barrel carburettor; dual exhaust system; cooling: 26.4 imp pt, 31.7 US pt, 15 l.

TRANSMISSION (standard) gears: 5, fully synchronized; ratios: I 2.950, II 1.940, III 1.340, IV 1, V 0.730, rev 2.760; axle ratio: 3.730; tyres: 215/65 HR x 15.

PERFORMANCE max speed: 128 mph, 205 km/h; power-weight ratio: 16.8 lb/hp (22.9 lb/kW), 7.6 kg/hp (10.3 kg/kW); consumption: 19.2 m/imp gal, 16 m/US gal, 14.7 l x 100 km.

ELECTRICAL EQUIPMENT 500 A battery; 94 A alternator.

DIMENSIONS AND WEIGHT weight: 3,197 lb, 1,450 kg.

OPTIONALS with automatic transmission 3.420 axle ratio.

Celebrity Series

PRICES EX WORKS:	$
4-dr Sedan	7,890
2-dr Coupé	7,711
4+1-dr 9-pass. St. Wagon	8,214

Power team:	Standard for:	Optional for:
92 hp	all	—
112 hp	—	all
130 hp	—	all
85 hp (diesel)	—	all

CHEVROLET Monte Carlo SS Coupé

92 hp power team

ENGINE front, transverse, 4 stroke; 4 cylinders, in line; 151 cu in, 2,475 cc (4 x 3 in, 101.6 x 76.2 mm); compression ratio: 9:1; max power (SAE net): 92 hp (68 kW) at 4,000 rpm; max torque (SAE net): 134 lb ft, 18.5 kg m (181 Nm) at 2,800 rpm; max engine rpm: 4,400; 37.2 hp/l (27.3 kW/l); cast iron block and head; 5 crankshaft bearings; valves: overhead, in line, push-rods and rockers, hydraulic tappets; camshafts: 1, side; lubrication: gear pump, full flow filter, 4.9 imp pt, 5.9 US pt, 2.8 l; throttle-body electronic fuel injection; air cleaner; exhaust system with catalytic converter; fuel feed: electric pump; water-cooled, 16.2 imp pt, 19.4 US pt, 9.2 l.

TRANSMISSION driving wheels: front; clutch: single dry plate (diaphragm); gearbox: mechanical; gears: 4, fully synchronized; ratios: I 3.530, II 1.950, III 1.240, IV 0.810, rev 3.420; lever: central; final drive: helical spur gears; axle ratio: 3.650; width of rims: 5.5"; tyres: P 185/80 R x 13.

PERFORMANCE max speed: 96 mph, 155 km/h; power-weight ratio: Sedan 29.4 lb/hp (40 lb/kW), 13.3 kg/hp (18.1 kg/kW); carrying capacity: 880 lb, 400 kg; speed in top at 1,000 rpm: 17.6 mph, 28.3 km/h; consumption: 30 m/imp gal, 25 m/US gal, 9.4 l x 100 km.

CHASSIS integral; front suspension: independent, by McPherson, coil springs/telescopic damper struts, lower control arms; rear: rigid axle, trailing arm, control arms, coil springs, telescopic dampers.

STEERING rack-and-pinion, servo; turns lock to lock: 3.05.

BRAKES front disc (diameter 9.72 in, 24.7 cm), internal radial fins, rear drum, servo; swept area: total 271 sq in, 1,746 sq cm.

ELECTRICAL EQUIPMENT 12 V; 405 A battery; 42 A alternator; Delco-Remy high energy ignition; 4 headlamps.

DIMENSIONS AND WEIGHT wheel base: 104.90 in, 266 cm; tracks: 58.70 in, 149 cm front, 57 in, 145 cm rear; length: 188.40 in, 478 cm - St. Wagon 190.80 in, 485 cm; width: 69.30 in, 176 cm; height: 54.10 in, 137 cm; ground clearance: 5.50 in, 14.1 cm; weight: Sedan 2,703 lb, 1,226 kg - Coupé 2,668 lb, 1,210 kg - St. Wagon 2,851 lb, 1,293 kg; weight distribution: Sedan 62% front, 38% rear; turning circle: 37 ft, 11.2 m; fuel tank: 13.2 imp gal, 15.7 US gal, 59 l.

BODY saloon/sedan, 4 doors - coupé, 2 doors - estate car/st. wagon, 4+1 doors; 6 or 9 seats, separate front seats, built-in headrests.

OPTIONALS Turbo-Hydramatic 125 C automatic transmission, hydraulic torque converter and planetary gears with 3 ratios (I 2.840, II 1.600, III 1, rev 2.070), 2.840 axle ratio; steering column lever; electric door locks; vinyl roof; air-conditioning; speed control; self-sealing tyres; electric windows; reclining backrests; 500 A battery.

112 hp power team

See 92 hp power team, except for:

ENGINE 6 cylinders, Vee-slanted at 60°; 173 cu in, 2,835 cc (3.50 x 3 in, 89 x 76.2 mm); compression ratio: 8.5:1; max power (SAE net): 112 hp (82 kW) at 4,800 rpm; max torque (SAE net): 145 lb ft, 20 kg m (196 Nm) at 2,100 rpm; max engine rpm: 5,300; 39.5 hp/l (29.1 kW/l); 4 crankshaft bearings; camshafts: 1, at centre of Vee; lubrication: 6.7 imp pt, 7.9 US pt, 3.8 l; 1 Rochester E2SE downdraught twin barrel carburettor; cooling: 20.8 imp pt, 24.9 US pt, 11.8 l.

TRANSMISSION (standard) gearbox: Turbo-Hydramatic 125 C automatic transmission, hydraulic torque converter and planetary gears with 3 ratios, max ratio of converter at stall 1.95, possible manual selection; ratios: I 2.840, II 1.600, III 1, rev 2.070; lever: central or steering column; axle ratio: 2.840.

PERFORMANCE max speed: 106 mph, 170 km/h; power-weight ratio: Sedan 24.1 lb/hp (32.8 lb/kW), 11.1 kg/hp (14.9 kg/kW).

ELECTRICAL EQUIPMENT 315 A battery; 66 A alternator.

DIMENSIONS AND WEIGHT weight: Sedan 2,730 lb, 1,238 kg - Coupé 2,710 lb, 1,229 kg - St. Wagon 2,862 lb, 1,298 kg.

OPTIONALS 440-T-4 automatic transmission with 4 ratios (I 2.920, II 1.570, III 1, IV 0.700, rev 2.380), 3.060 axle ratio.

130 hp power team

See 92 hp power team, except for:

ENGINE 6 cylinders, Vee-slanted at 60°; 173 cu in, 2,835 cc (3.50 x 3 in, 89 x 76.2 mm); compression ratio: 8.9:1; max power (SAE net): 130 hp (96 kW) at 5,400 rpm; max torque (SAE net): 145 lb ft, 20 kg m (196 Nm) at 2,400 rpm; max engine rpm: 6,000; 45.8 hp/l (33.7 kW/l); 4 crankshaft bearings; camshafts: 1, at centre of Vee; lubrication: 6.7 imp pt, 7.9 US pt, 3.8 l; 1 Rochester E2SE downdraught twin barrel carburettor; cooling: 20.8 imp pt, 24.9 US pt, 11.8 l.

TRANSMISSION (standard) gearbox: Turbo-Hydramatic 125 C automatic transmission, hydraulic torque converter and planetary gears with 3 ratios, max ratio of converter at stall 1.95, possible manual selection; ratios: I 2.840, II 1.600, III 1, rev 2.070; lever: central or steering column; axle ratio: 3.330.

PERFORMANCE max speed: 106 mph, 170 km/h; power-weight ratio: Sedan 21.1 lb/hp (28.7 lb/kW), 9.5 kg/hp (13 kg/kW).

DIMENSIONS AND WEIGHT weight: Sedan 2,745 lb, 1,245 kg - Coupé 2,723 lb, 1,235 kg - St. Wagon 2,870 lb, 1,302 kg.

85 hp (diesel) power team

See 92 hp power team, except for:

ENGINE diesel; 6 cylinders, Vee-slanted at 90°; 262 cu in, 4,294 cc (4.06 x 3.38 in, 103 x 86 mm); compression ratio: 22.8:1; max power (SAE net): 85 hp (63 kW) at 3,600 rpm; max torque (SAE net): 165 lb ft, 22.8 kg m (223 Nm) at 1,600 rpm; max engine rpm: 4,000; 19.8 hp/l (14.6 kW/l); cast iron block and head; 4 crankshaft bearings; camshafts: 1, at centre of Vee; lubrication: 10.1 imp pt, 12 US pt, 5.7 l; diesel fuel injection pump; fuel feed: electric pump; cooling: 23 imp pt, 19.1 US pt, 12.3 l.

TRANSMISSION axle ratio: 2.660.

PERFORMANCE max speed: 90 mph, 145 km/h; power-weight ratio: Sedan 32.1 lb/hp (43.6 lb/kW), 14.5 kg/hp (19.8 kg/kW).

ELECTRICAL EQUIPMENT 2 batteries; 770 A battery; 94 A alternator.

DIMENSIONS AND WEIGHT weight: Sedan 2,888 lb, 1,310 kg - Coupé 2,866 lb, 1,300 kg.

OPTIONALS 1,100 A battery; with 440 T-4 automatic transmission 2.840 - St. Wagon 3.060 axle ratio.

Monte Carlo Series

PRICES EX WORKS:	$
2-dr Coupé	**8,936**
SS 2-dr Coupé	**10,700**

Power team:	Standard for:	Optional for:
110 hp (3,753 cc)	both	—
110 hp (3,785 cc)	both	—
150 hp	—	both
180 hp	—	both
105 hp (diesel)	—	both

110 hp (3,753 cc) power team

(not available in California)

ENGINE front, 4 stroke; 6 cylinders in Vee; 229 cu in, 3,753 cc (3.73 x 3.48 in, 94.9 x 88.4 mm); compression ratio: 8.6:1; max power (SAE net): 110 hp (81 kW) at 4,000 rpm; max torque (SAE net): 190 lb ft, 26.1 kg m (256 Nm) at 1,600 rpm; max engine rpm: 4,500; 29.3 hp/l (21.5 kW/l); cast iron block and head; 4 crankshaft bearings; valves: overhead, in line, push-rods and rockers, hydraulic tappets; camshafts: 1, at centre of Vee; lubrication: gear pump, full flow filter, 7.4 imp pt, 8.4 US pt, 4 l; 1 Rochester downdraught twin barrel carburettor; thermostatic air cleaner; exhaust system with catalytic converter; fuel feed: mechanical pump; water-cooled, 25.2 imp pt, 30.2 US pt, 14.3 l.

TRANSMISSION driving wheels: rear; gearbox: Turbo-Hydramatic 250 automatic transmission, hydraulic torque converter and planetary gears with 3 ratios, max ratio of converter at stall 2, possible manual selection; ratios: I 2.520, II 1.520, III 1, rev 1.930; lever: steering column; final drive: hypoid bevel; axle ratio: 2.410; width of rims: 6"; tyres: P 195/75 R x 14.

PERFORMANCE max speed: 100 mph, 161 km/h; power-weight ratio: 29.3 lb/hp (39.9 lb/kW), 13.3 kg/hp (18.1 kg/kW); speed in direct drive at 1,000 rpm: 29.8 mph, 47.7 km/h; consumption: 23.7 m/imp gal, 20 m/US gal, 11.8 l x 100 km.

CHASSIS perimeter box-type with front and rear cross members; front suspension: independent, wishbones, coil springs, anti-roll bar, telescopic dampers; rear: rigid axle, lower trailing radius arms, upper oblique torque arms, coil springs, anti-roll bar, telescopic dampers.

CHEVROLET Impala Sedan

STEERING recirculating ball, servo; turns lock to lock: 3.30.

BRAKES front disc (diameter 10.50 in, 26.7 cm), front internal radial fins, rear drum, servo; swept area: total 307.8 sq in, 1,985 sq cm.

ELECTRICAL EQUIPMENT 12 V; 405 A battery; 37 A alternator; Delco-Remy high energy ignition; 4 headlamps.

DIMENSIONS AND WEIGHT wheel base: 108.10 in, 274 cm; tracks: 58.50 in, 149 cm front, 57.80 in, 147 cm rear; length: 200.40 in, 509 cm; width: 71.80 in, 183 cm; height: 54.30 in, 138 cm - SS 55 in, 140 cm; ground clearance: 8.20 in, 21 cm; weight: 3,177 lb, 1,441 kg; weight distribution: 57% front, 43% rear; turning circle: 40.5 ft, 12.4 m; fuel tank: 15.3 imp gal, 18.1 US gal, 68 l.

BODY coupé; 2 doors; 6 seats, bench front seats, built-in headrests.

OPTIONALS Turbo-Hydramatic 200 R-4 automatic transmission, hydraulic torque converter and planetary gears with 4 ratios (I 2.740, II 1.570, III 1, IV 0.670, rev 0.670); heavy-duty cooling; limited slip differential; heavy-duty battery; 2.730 axle ratio; 500 A battery; 90 A alternator; heavy-duty front and rear suspension; air-conditioning; heated rear window; electric windows; electric sunroof; removable glass roof panels; electric door lock; separate front seats.

110 hp (3,783 cc) power team

See 110 hp (3,753 cc) power team, except for:

ENGINE 231 cu in, 3,785 cc (3.80 x 3.40 in, 96.5 x 86.5 mm); compression ratio: 8:1; max power (SAE net): 110 hp (81 kW) at 3,800 rpm; max engine rpm: 4,300; 29 hp/l (21.3 kW/l); cooling: 20.6 imp pt, 24.7 US pt, 11.7 l.

ELECTRICAL EQUIPMENT 56 A alternator.

150 hp power team

(not available in California)

See 110 hp (3,753 cc) power team, except for:

ENGINE 8 cylinders in Vee; 305 cu in, 4,999 cc (3.74 x 3.48 in, 94.9 x 88.4 mm); max power (SAE net): 150 hp (110 kW) at 4,000 rpm; max torque (SAE net): 240 lb ft, 33.1 kg m (324 Nm) at 2,400 rpm; max engine rpm: 4,500; 30 hp/l (22 kW/l); 5 crankshaft bearings; lubrication: 7.9 imp pt, 9.5 US pt, 4.5 l; 1 Rochester downdraught 4-barrel carburettor; cooling: 27.3 imp pt, 32.8 US pt, 15.5 l.

TRANSMISSION axle ratio: 2.290.

PERFORMANCE max speed: 105 mph, 170 km/h; power-weight ratio: 21.3 lb//hp (29 lb/kW), 9.6 kg/hp (13.1 kg/kW); speed in direct drive at 1,000 rpm: 31.4 mph, 50.2 km/h; consumption: 21.6 m/imp gal, 18 m/US gal, 13.1 l x 100 km.

DIMENSIONS AND WEIGHT weight: 3,197 lb, 1,450 kg.

180 hp power team

See 110 hp (3,753 cc) power team, except for:

ENGINE 8 cylinders in Vee; 305 cu in, 4,999 cc (3.74 x 3.48 in, 94.9 x 88.4 mm); compression ratio: 9.5:1; max power (SAE net): 180 hp (132 kW) at 4,800 rpm; max torque (SAE net): 235 lb ft, 32.4 kg m (318 Nm) at 3,200 rpm; max engine rpm: 5,300; 36 hp/l (26.5 kW/l); 5 crankshaft bearings; 1 Rochester downdraught 4-barrel carburettor; cooling: 26.4 imp pt, 31.7 US pt, 15 l.

TRANSMISSION gearbox: Turbo-Hydramatic 350-C automatic transmission, hydraulic torque converter and planetary gears with 3 ratios and overdrive; ratios: I 2.740, II 1.570, III 1, overdrive 0.670, rev 2.070; axle ratio: 3.420.

PERFORMANCE max speed: 109 mph, 175 km/h; power-weight ratio: 17.9 lb/hp (24.3 lb/kW), 8.1 kg/hp (11 kg/kW); consumption: 21.6 m/imp gal, 18 m/US gal, 13.1 l x 100 km.

DIMENSIONS AND WEIGHT weight: 3,220 lb, 1,461 kg.

OPTIONALS (except California) with Turbo-Hydramatic 200 4-R automatic transmission 3.730 axle ratio.

105 hp (diesel) power team

(not available in California)

See 110 hp (3,753 cc) power team, except for:

ENGINE diesel; 8 cylinders in Vee; 350 cu in, 5,736 cc (4.06 x 3.38 in, 103.9 x 86 mm); compression ratio: 22.1:1; max power (SAE net): 105 hp (78 kW) at 3,200 rpm; max torque (SAE net): 200 lb ft, 27.6 kg m (270 Nm) at 1,600 rpm; max engine rpm: 3,600; 18.4 hp/l (13.6 kW/l); 5 crankshaft bearings; lubrication: 12.4 imp pt, 14.8 US pt, 7.1 l; Stanadyne diesel fuel injection; cooling: 30.8 imp pt, 37 US pt, 17.5 l.

TRANSMISSION gearbox: Turbo-Hydramatic 200 C automatic transmission, hydraulic torque converter and planetary gears with 3 ratios, max ratio of converter at stall 1.90, possible manual selection; ratios: I 2.740, II 1.570, III 1, rev 2.070; axle ratio: 2.290.

PERFORMANCE max speed: 100 mph, 161 km/h; power-weight ratio: 31.7 lb/hp (43.2 lb/kW), 14.4 kg/hp (19.4 kg/kW); consumption: 27 m/imp gal, 23 m/US gal, 10.2 l x 100 km.

ELECTRICAL EQUIPMENT 66 A alternator.

DIMENSIONS AND WEIGHT weight: 3,533 lb, 1,602 kg.

Impala / Caprice Classic Series

PRICES EX WORKS:	$
1 Impala 4-dr Sedan	**8,895**
2 Caprice Classic 4-dr Sedan	**9,399**
3 Caprice Classic 2-dr Coupé	**9,253**
4 Caprice Classic 4+1-dr 9-pass. St. Wagon	**10,210**

Power team:	Standard for:	Optional for:
110 hp (3,753 cc)	1 to 2	—
110 hp (3,785 cc)	1 to 2	—
150 hp	4	1 to 3
105 hp (diesel)	—	all

110 hp (3,753 cc) power team

(not available in California)

ENGINE front, 4 stroke; 6 cylinders, in Vee; 229 cu in, 3,753 cc (3.73 x 3.48 in, 94.9 x 88.4 mm); compression ratio: 8.6:1; max power (SAE net): 110 hp (81 kW) at 4,000 rpm; max torque (SAE net): 190 lb ft, 26.1 kg m (256 Nm) at 1,600 rpm; max engine rpm: 4,500; 29.3 hp/l (21.6 kW/l); cast iron block and head; 4 crankshaft bearings; valves: overhead, in line, push-rods and rockers, hydraulic tappets; camshafts: 1, at centre of Vee; lubrication: gear pump, full flow filter, 7.4 imp pt, 8.4 US pt, 4 l; 1 Rochester E2SE downdraught twin barrel carburettor; thermostatic air cleaner; exhaust system with catalytic converter; fuel feed: mechanical pump; water-cooled, 23.6 imp pt, 28.3 US pt, 13.4 l.

TRANSMISSION driving wheels: rear; gearbox: Turbo-Hydramatic 250 automatic transmission, hydraulic torque converter and planetary gears with 3 ratios, max ratio of converter at stall 2, possible manual selection; ratios: I 2.520, II 1.520, III

110 HP (3,753 cc) POWER TEAM

1, rev 1.930; lever: steering column; final drive: hypoid bevel; axle ratio: 2.730; width of rims: 6"; tyres: P 205/75 R x 15.

PERFORMANCE max speed: 99 mph, 159 km/h; power-weight ratio: Impala 31.7 lb/hp (43.1 lb/kW), 14.4 kg/hp (19.5 kg/kW); speed in direct drive at 1,000 rpm: 28.6 mph, 45.7 km/h; consumption: 22.9 m/imp gal, 19 m/US gal, 12.3 l x 100 km.

CHASSIS perimeter box-type with 2 cross members; front suspension: independent, wishbones, coil springs, anti-roll bar, telescopic dampers; rear: rigid axle, lower trailing radius arms, upper oblique torque arms, coil springs, anti-roll bar, telescopic dampers.

STEERING recirculating ball, servo; turns lock to lock: 3.20.

BRAKES front disc (diameter 11 in, 27.9 cm), front internal radial fins, rear drum, servo; swept area: total 329.8 sq in, 2,127 sq cm.

ELECTRICAL EQUIPMENT 12 V; 405 A battery; 37 A alternator; Delco-Remy high energy ignition; 4 headlamps.

DIMENSIONS AND WEIGHT wheel base: 116 in, 294 cm; tracks: 62 in, 157 cm front, 61 in, 154 cm rear; length: 212.10 in, 538 cm; width: 75.30 in, 191 cm; height: 56.40 in, 143 cm; ground clearance: 11.10 in, 28 cm; weight: Impala 3,486 lb, 1,582 kg - Caprice Classic 3,531 lb, 1,602 kg; weight distribution: 55% front, 45% rear; turning circle: 44.5 ft, 13.6 m; fuel tank: 20.9 imp gal, 25 US gal, 95 l.

BODY saloon/sedan, 4 doors - coupé, 2 doors; 6 seats, bench front seats, built-in headrests.

OPTIONALS central lever; limited slip differential; 3.230 axle ratio; electric windows; heavy-duty suspension; P 215/70 R x 15 or P 225/70 R x 15 tyres; automatic speed control; heated rear window; tilt of steering wheel; electric sunroof; vinyl roof; air-conditioning; heavy-duty cooling, 70 A alternator; 500 A battery.

110 hp (3,785 cc) power team

See 110 hp (3,753 cc) power team, except for:

ENGINE 231 cu in, 3,785 cc (3.80 x 3.40 in, 96.5 x 86.5 mm); compression ratio: 8:1; max power (SAE net): 110 hp (81 kW) at 3,800 rpm; max engine rpm: 4,300; 29.3 hp/l (21.5 kW/l); cooling: 19.5 imp pt, 23.5 US pt, 11.1 l.

TRANSMISSION gearbox: Turbo-Hydramatic 200 C automatic transmission, hydraulic torque converter and planetary gears with 3 ratios, max ratio of converter at stall 1.91, possible manual selection; ratios: I 2.740, II 1.570, III 1, rev 2.070.

STEERING turns lock to lock: 3.30.

ELECTRICAL EQUIPMENT 355 A battery; 56 A alternator.

150 hp power team

See 110 hp (3,753 cc) power team, except for:

ENGINE 8 cylinders in Vee; 305 cu in, 4,999 cc (3.74 x 3.48 in, 94.9 x 88.4 mm); max power (SAE net): 150 hp (110 kW) at 4,000 rpm; max torque (SAE net): 240 lb ft, 33.1 kg m (324 Nm) at 2,400 rpm; max engine rpm: 4,400; 30 hp/l (22 kW/l); 5 crankshaft bearings; 1 Rochester downdraught 4-barrel carburettor; cooling: 25.7 imp pt, 30.9 US pt, 14.6 l.

TRANSMISSION gearbox: Turbo-Hydramatic 700-4R automatic transmission, hydraulic torque converter and planetary gears with 4 ratios, max ratio of converter at stall 5.80; ratios: I 3.060, II 1.630, III 1, IV 0.700, rev 2.290; axle ratio: 2.730.

PERFORMANCE max speed: 108 mph, 173 km/h; power-weight ratio: Impala 23.1 lb/hp (31.4 lb/kW), 10.5 kg/hp (14.2 kg/kW); speed in top at 1,000 rpm: 32.4 mph, 51.8 km/h; consumption: 20.4 m/imp gal, 17 m/US gal, 13.8 l x 100 km.

STEERING turns lock to lock: 3.16 - St. Wagon 3.30.

ELECTRICAL EQUIPMENT 500 A battery; 56 A alternator.

DIMENSIONS AND WEIGHT tracks: St. Wagon 62 in, 157 cm front, 64 in, 162 cm rear; length: St. Wagon 215.10 in, 546 cm; width: St. Wagon 79.30 in, 201 cm; height: St. Wagon 58.10 in, 147 cm; weight: Impala 3,532 lb, 1,602 kg - Caprice Classic Sedan 3,594 lb, 1,630 kg - Caprice Classic Coupé 3,497 lb, 1,586 kg - Caprice Classic St. Wagon 4,069 lb, 1,845 kg.

BODY saloon/sedan, 4 doors - coupé, 2 doors - estate car/st. wagon, 4+1 doors.

OPTIONALS Turbo-Hydramatic 200-R4 automatic transmission, hydraulic torque converter and planetary gears with 4 ratios (I 2.740, II 1.570, III 1, IV 0.670, rev 2.070), 2.730 axle ratio; 3.080 axle ratio.

105 hp (diesel) power team

See 110 hp (3,753 cc) power team, except for:

ENGINE diesel; 8 cylinders in Vee; 350 cu in, 5,736 cc (4.06 x 3.38 in, 103.9 x 86 mm); compression ratio: 22.1:1; max power (SAE net): 105 hp (78 kW) at 3,200 rpm; max torque (SAE net): 200 lb ft, 27.6 kg m (270 Nm) at 1,600 rpm; max engine rpm: 3,700; 18.4 hp/l (13.6 kW/l); 5 crankshaft bearings; lubrication:

CHEVROLET Caprice Classic Series

12.4 imp pt, 14.8 US pt, 7.1 l; diesel fuel injection; cooling: 30.1 imp pt, 36.1 US pt, 17.1 l.

TRANSMISSION gearbox: Turbo-Hydramatic 200 C automatic transmission, hydraulic torque converter and planetary gears with 3 ratios, max ratio of converter at stall 1.90, possible manual selection; ratios: I 2.740, II 1.570, III 1, rev 2.070; axle ratio: 2.410 - Caprice Classic St. Wagon 2.930 (standard).

PERFORMANCE max speed: 85 mph, 136 km/h; power-weight ratio: Impala 39.5 lb/hp (53.1 lb/kW), 17.9 kg/hp (24.1 kg/kW); speed in direct drive at 1,000 rpm: 28.6 mph, 45.7 km/h; consumption: 27.6 m/imp gal, 23 m//US gal, 10.2 l x 100 km.

ELECTRICAL EQUIPMENT 2 batteries; 810 A battery; 66 A alternator.

DIMENSIONS AND WEIGHT weight: Impala 3,729 lb, 1,693 kg - Caprice Classic Sedan 3,782 lb, 1,717 kg - Caprice Classic Coupé 3,698 lb, 1,677 kg - Caprice Classic St. Wagon 4,208 lb, 1,910 kg.

BODY saloon/sedan, 4 doors - coupé, 2 doors - estate car/st. wagon, 4+1 doors.

OPTIONALS (except Caprice Classic St. Wagon) 2.930 axle ratio with 200-4R automatic transmission.

Corvette

PRICE EX WORKS: $ 23,360

ENGINE front, 4 stroke; 8 cylinders in Vee; 350 cu in, 5,736 cc (4 x 3.48 in, 101.6 x 88.4 mm); compression ratio: 9:1; max power (SAE net): 205 hp (151 kW) at 4,200 rpm; max torque (SAE net): 290 lb ft, 40 kg m (392 Nm) at 2,800 rpm; max engine rpm: 5,000; 34.9 hp/l (25.7 kW/l); cast iron block and head; 5 crankshaft bearings; valves: overhead, in line, push-rods and rockers, hydraulic tappets; camshafts: 1, at centre of Vee; lubrication: gear pump, full flow filter, 7.4 imp pt, 8.4 US pt, 4 l; throttle-body electronic fuel injection; thermostatic air cleaner; dual exhaust system with catalytic converter; fuel feed: 2 electric pumps; water-cooled, 34.5 imp pt, 41.4 US pt, 19.6 l, viscous coupling thermostatic fan.

TRANSMISSION driving wheels: rear; gearbox: Turbo-Hydramatic 700 R-4 automatic transmission, hydraulic torque converter and planetary gears with 4 ratios, max ratio of converter at stall 1.85, possible manual selection; ratios: I 3.060, II 1.630, III 1, IV 0.700, rev 2.290; lever: central; final drive: hypoid bevel, limited slip; axle ratio: 2.730; width of rims: 8"; tyres: P 255/50 VR x 16.

PERFORMANCE max speed: 124 mph, 198 km/h; power-weight ratio: 15.6 lb/hp (21.2 lb/kW), 7.1 kg/hp (9.6 kg/kW); speed in top at 1,000 rpm: 30.6 mph, 49.3 km/h; consumption: 19.2 m/imp gal, 16 m/US gal, 14.7 l x 100 km.

CHASSIS ladder frame with cross members; front suspension: independent, wishbones, coil springs, anti-roll bar, telescopic dampers; rear: independent, wishbones, semi-axle as upper arms, transverse single leaf reinforced fiberglass leaf spring, trailing radius arms, telescopic dampers.

STEERING rack-and-pinion, servo, tilt of steering wheel; turns lock to lock: 2.36.

BRAKES disc, internal radial fins, servo; swept area: total 329.9 sq in, 2,128 sq cm.

ELECTRICAL EQUIPMENT 12 V; 550 A battery; 97 A alternator; Delco-Remy high energy ignition; 4 retractable headlamps.

DIMENSIONS AND WEIGHT wheel base: 96 in, 244 cm; tracks: 59.60 in, 151 cm front, 60.40 in, 153 cm rear; length: 176.50 in, 448 cm; widht: 71 in, 180 cm; height: 46.70 in, 118 cm; ground clearance: 5 in, 12.6 cm; weight: 3,192 lb, 1,448 kg; fuel tank: 16.7 imp gal, 20.1 US gal, 76 l.

BODY coupé, in plastic material; 2+1 doors; 2 seats, built-in headrests; electric windows; air-conditioning.

OPTIONALS 4-speed and overdrive fully synchronized mechanical gearbox (I 2.880, II 1.910, III 1.330, IV 1, overdrive 0.670, rev 2.780), 3.070 or 3.310 axle ratio; Gymkhana suspension; heavy-duty battery; heated rear window; tinted glass; removable tinted glass roof panels; automatic speed control; aluminium wheels.

CHRYSLER USA

Le Baron Series

PRICES EX WORKS:	$
1 2-dr Sedan	**8,783**
2 4-dr Sedan	**9,067**
3 2-dr Convertible	**11,595**
4 Town and Country 4+1-dr St. Wagon	**9,856**

Power team:	Standard for:	Optional for:
96 hp	all	—
101 hp	—	all
140 hp	—	1 to 3

96 hp power team

ENGINE front, 4 stroke; 4 cylinders, transverse, in line; 135 cu in, 2,213 cc (3.44 x 3.62 in, 87.5 x 92 mm); compression ratio: 9:1; max power (SAE net): 96 hp (71 kW) at 5,200 rpm; max torque (SAE net): 119 lb ft, 16.4 kg m (161 Nm) at 3,200 rpm; max engine rpm: 5,700; 43.4 hp/l (31.9 kW/l); cast iron block, light alloy head; 5 crankshaft bearings; valves: overhead, in line, rockers, hydraulic tappets; camshafts: 1, overhead; lubrication: rotary pump, full flow filter, 6.8 imp pt, 8 US pt, 3.8 l; 1 Holley 6520 downdraught twin barrel carburettor; exhaust system with catalytic converter; fuel feed: mechanical pump; water-cooled, 14.6 imp pt, 17.2 US pt, 8.2 l.

CHEVROLET Corvette

CHRYSLER Le Baron Convertible

TRANSMISSION driving wheels: front; clutch: single dry plate; gearbox: mechanical; gears: 5, fully synchronized; ratios: I 3.290, II 2.080, III 1.450, IV 1.040, V 0.720, rev 3.140; lever: central; final drive: helical spur gears; axle ratio: 2.570; width of rims: 5.5"; tyres: 185/70 or 185/75 R x 14.

PERFORMANCE max speed: 96 mph, 155 km/h; power-weight ratio: 2-dr Sedan 25.8 lb/hp (35 lb/kW), 11.7 kg/hp (15.9 kg/kW); carrying capacity: 904 lb, 410 kg; speed in top at 1,000 rpm: 21 mph, 33.8 km/h; consumption: 32.4 m/imp gal, 27 m/US gal, 8.7 l x 100 km.

CHASSIS integral; front suspension: independent, wishbones, coil springs, telescopic damper struts, anti-roll bar; rear: rigid axle, lower trailing radius arms with track bar, coil springs, telescopic dampers.

STEERING rack-and-pinion, adjustable steering wheel, servo; turns lock to lock: 3.20.

BRAKES front disc, internal radial fins, rear drum, servo; swept area: total 253 sq in, 1,632 sq cm.

ELECTRICAL EQUIPMENT 12 V; 335 A battery; 60 A alternator; Essex or Prestolite transistorized ignition; 4 halogen headlamps.

DIMENSIONS AND WEIGHT wheel base: 100 in, 254 cm; tracks: 57.60 in, 146 cm front, 57 in, 145 cm rear; length: 179.70 in, 456 cm; width: 68.50 in, 174 cm; height: 52.70 in, 134 cm - Convertible 54.10 in, 137 cm; ground clearance: 4.70 in, 11.9 cm; weight: 2-dr Sedan 2,473 lb, 1,122 kg - 4-dr Sedan 2,560 lb, 1,161 kg - Convertible 2,594 lb, 1,176 kg - St. Wagon 2,676 lb, 1,214 kg; turning circle: 37.7 ft, 11.5 m; fuel tank: 11.6 imp gal, 14 US gal, 53 l.

BODY saloon/sedan, 2 or 4 doors - convertible, 2 doors - estate car/st. wagon 4+1 doors; 6 seats, separate front seats, built-in headrests.

OPTIONALS Torqueflite automatic transmission, hydraulic torque converter and planetary gears with 3 ratios (I 2.690, II 1.550, III 1, rev 2.100), 3.020 axle ratio; convertible roof; air-conditioning; 78 A alternator; 500 A battery; automatic speed control; adjustable tilt of steering wheel; electric windows; electric seats.

101 hp power team

See 96 hp power team, except for:

ENGINE 156 cu in, 2,555 cc (3.59 x 3.86 in, 91.1 x 98 mm); compression ratio: 8.7:1; max power (SAE net): 101 hp (74 kW) at 4,800 rpm; max torque (SAE net): 140 lb ft, 19.3 kg m (190 Nm) at 2,800 rpm; max engine rpm: 5,400; 39.5 hp/l (29.1 kW/l).

TRANSMISSION (standard) gearbox: Torqueflite automatic transmission, hydraulic torque conveter and planetary gears with 3 ratios, max ratio of converter at stall 2, possible manual selection; ratios: I 2.690, II 1.550, III 1, rev 2.100; axle ratio: 3.020.

PERFORMANCE max speed: 100 mph, 161 km/h; power-weight ratio: 2-dr Sedan 25.4 lb/hp (34.5 lb/kW), 11.5 kg/hp (15.6 kg/kW); consumption: 30 m/imp gal, 25 m/US gal, 9.4 l x 100 km.

ELECTRICAL EQUIPMENT 500 A battery (standard); 75 A alternator.

DIMENSIONS AND WEIGHT weight: 2-dr Sedan 2,560 lb, 1,161 kg - 4-dr Sedan 2,603 lb, 1,180 kg - Convertible 2,637 lb, 1,196 kg - St. Wagon 2,730 lb, 1,238 kg.

VARIATIONS

(for California only)
ENGINE max power (SAE net) 99 hp (73 kW) at 4,800 rpm, max torque (SAE net) 137 lb ft, 19 kg m (185 Nm) at 2,800 rpm, 38.7 hp/l (28.6 kW/l).

PERFORMANCE power-weight ratio 2-dr Sedan 25.8 lb/hp (35.1 lb/kW), 11.7 kg/hp (15.9 kg/kW).

OPTIONALS convertible roof; air-conditioning; 78 A alternator; automatic speed control; adjustable tilt of steering wheel; electric windows; electric seats.

140 hp power team

See 96 hp power team, except for:

ENGINE turbocharged; max power (SAE net): 140 hp (103 kW) at 5,600 rpm; max torque (SAE net): 160 lb ft, 22.1 kg m (217 Nm) at 3,600 rpm; max engine rpm: 6,100; 63.2 hp/l (46.5 kW/l); electronic fuel injection; turbocharger; fuel feed: electric pump.

TRANSMISSION (standard) gearbox: Torqueflite automatic transmission, hydraulic torque conveter and planetary gears with 3 ratios, max ratio of converter at stall 2, possible manual selection; ratios: I 2.690, II 1.550, III 1, rev 2.100; axle ratio: 3.020.

PERFORMANCE max speed: 106 mph, 170 km/h; power-weight ratio: Convertible 18.9 lb/hp (25.7 lb/kW), 8.6 kg/hp (11.7 kg/kW); consumption: 26.4 m/imp gal, 22 m/US gal, 10.7 l x 100 km.

ELECTRICAL EQUIPMENT 90 A alternator.

DIMENSIONS AND WEIGHT weight: 2-dr Sedan 2,566 lb, 1,164 kg - Convertible 2,653 lb, 1,203 kg.

BODY saloon/sedan, 2 or 4 doors - convertible, 2 doors.

OPTIONALS convertible roof; air-conditioning; 500 A battery; automatic speed control; adjustable tilt of steering wheel; electric windows; electric seats.

Laser Series

PRICES EX WORKS:	$
2-dr Hatchback Coupé	8,648
XE 2-dr Hatchback Coupé	10,546

Power team:	Standard for:	Optional for:
99 hp	both	—
142 hp	—	both

99 hp power team

ENGINE front, 4 stroke; 4 cylinders, transverse, in line; 135 cu in, 2,213 cc (3.44 x 3.62 in, 87.5 x 92 mm); compression ratio: 9:1; max power (SAE net): 99 hp (73 kW) at 5,600 rpm; max torque (SAE net): 121 lb ft, 16.7 kg m (164 Nm) at 3,200 rpm; max engine rpm: 6,100; 44.7 hp/l (32.9 kW/l); cast iron block, light alloy head; 5 crankshaft bearings; valves: overhead, in line, rockers, hydraulic tappets; camshafts: 1, overhead, lubrication: rotary pump, full flow filter, 6.8 imp pt, 8 US pt, 3.8 l; throttle-body electronic fuel injection; thermostatic air cleaner; exhaust gas recirculation with catalytic converter; fuel feed: electric pump; water-cooled, 14.6 imp pt, 17.2 US pt, 8.2 l.

TRANSMISSION driving wheels: front; clutch: single dry plate; gearbox: mechanical; gears: 5, fully synchronized; ratios: I 3.290, II 2.080, III 1.450, IV 1.040, V 0.720, rev 3.140; lever: central; final drive: helical spur gears; axle ratio: 2.570; width of rims: 5.5"; tyres: P 185/70 R x 14.

PERFORMANCE max speed: 99 mph, 159 km/h; power-weight ratio: Hatchback Coupé 25.8 lb/hp (35.1 lb/kW), 11.7 kg/hp (15.9 kg/kW); consumption: 28 m/imp gal, 24 m/US gal, 10.1 l x 100 km.

CHASSIS integral; front suspension: independent, wishbones (lower control arms), coil springs/telescopic damper struts, anti-roll bar; rear: rigid axle, lower trailing radius arms with track bar, coil springs, telescopic dampers.

STEERING rack-and-pinion, servo; turns lock to lock: 2.50.

BRAKES front disc, rear drum, servo; swept area: total 275 sq in, 1,776 sq cm.

ELECTRICAL EQUIPMENT 12 V; 370 A battery; 90 A alternator; 4 halogen headlamps.

DIMENSIONS AND WEIGHT wheel base: 97 in, 246 cm; tracks: 57.60 in, 146 cm front, 57.20 in, 145 cm rear; length: 175 in, 445 cm; width: 69.30 in, 176 cm; height: 50.30 in, 128 cm; ground clearance: 4.60 in, 11.6 cm; weight: Hatchback Coupé 2,550 lb, 1,159 kg - XE Hatchback Coupé 2,569 lb, 1,168 kg; turning circle: 33.5 ft, 10.2 m; fuel tank: 11.7 imp gal, 14 US gal, 53 l.

BODY coupé; 2 doors; 4 seats, separate front seats, reclining backrests, built-in headrests.

OPTIONALS Torqueflite automatic transmission, hydraulic torque converter and planetary gears with 3 ratios (I 2.690, II 1.550, III 1, rev 2.100), max ratio of converter at stall 2, possible manual selection, 3.220 axle ratio; sunroof; air-conditioning; wiper on rear window; electric windows; electric door locks; automatic speed control.

142 hp power team

See 99 hp power team, except for:

ENGINE turbocharged; max power (SAE net): 142 hp (105 kW) at 5,600 rpm; max torque (SAE net): 160 lb ft, 22.1 kg m (216 Nm) at 3,600 rpm; 64.2 hp/l (47.2 kW/l); turbocharger.

PERFORMANCE max speed: 100 mph, 160 km/h; power-weight ratio: XE Hatchback Coupé 18.6 lb/hp (25.2 lb/kW), 8.4 kg/hp (11.4 kg/kW); consumption: 26.4 m/imp gal, 22 m/US gal, 10.7 l x 100 km.

ELECTRICAL EQUIPMENT 500 A battery.

DIMENSIONS AND WEIGHT weight: Hatchback Coupé 2,613 lb, 1,188 kg - XE Hatchback Coupé 2,632 lb, 1,196 kg.

CHRYSLER Laser Hatchback Coupé

CHRYSLER New Yorker Sedan

E Class / New Yorker Series

PRICES EX WORKS: $

	$
E Class 4-dr Sedan	9,565
New Yorker 4-dr Sedan	12,179

Power team:	Standard for:	Optional for:
99 hp	both	—
101 hp	—	both
140 hp	—	both

99 hp power team

ENGINE front, 4 stroke; 4 cylinders, transverse, in line; 135 cu in, 2,213 cc (3.44 x 3.62 in, 87.5 x 92 mm); compression ratio: 9:1; max power (SAE net): 99 hp (73 kW) at 5,600 rpm; max torque (SAE net): 121 lb ft, 16.7 kg m (164 Nm) at 3,200 rpm; max engine rpm: 6,100; 44.7 hp/l (32.9 kW/l); cast iron block, light alloy head; 5 crankshaft bearings; valves: overhead, in line, rockers, hydraulic tappets; camshafts: 1, overhead, cogged belt; lubrication: rotary pump, full flow filter, 6.8 imp pt, 8 US pt, 3.8 l; throttle-body electronic fuel injection; exhaust system with catalytic converter; fuel feed: electric pump; water-cooled, 14.6 imp pt, 17.2 US pt, 8.2 l.

TRANSMISSION driving wheels: front; gearbox: Torqueflite automatic transmission, hydraulic torque converter and planetary gears with 3 ratios, max ratio of converter at stall 2, possible manual selection; ratios: I 2.690, II 1.550, III 1, rev 2.100; lever: steering column; final drive: helical spur gears; axle ratio: 3.020; width of rims: 5.5"; tyres: E-Class P 185/70 R x 14 - New Yorker P 185/75 R x 14.

PERFORMANCE max speed: 99 mph, 159 km/h; power-weight ratio: E-Class 12.8 lb/hp (35.7 lb/kW), 11.9 kg/hp (16.2 kg/kW); speed in direct drive at 1,000 rpm: 18.6 mph, 30 km/h; consumption: 30 m/imp gal, 25 m/US gal, 9.4 l x 100 km.

CHASSIS integral; front suspension: independent, wishbones, coil springs, anti-roll bar, telescopic dampers; rear: rigid axle, lower trailing radius arms with track bar, wishbones, coil springs, telescopic dampers.

STEERING rack-and-pinion, servo; turns lock to lock: 3.20.

BRAKES front disc, rear drum, servo; swept area: total 283 sq in, 1,825 sq cm.

ELECTRICAL EQUIPMENT 12 V; 370 A battery; 90 A alternator; 4 halogen headlamps.

DIMENSIONS AND WEIGHT wheel base: 103.10 in, 262 cm; tracks: 57.60 in, 146 cm front, 57 in, 145 cm rear; length: 185.60 in, 471 cm; width: 68.30 in, 173 cm; height: 52.90 in, 135 cm; ground clearance: 4.70 in, 11.9 cm; weight: E-Class 2,595 lb, 1,179 kg - New Yorker 2,738 lb, 1,244 kg; turning circle: 35.6 ft, 11 m; fuel tank: 11.7 imp gal, 14 US gal, 53 l.

BODY saloon/sedan, 4 doors; 6 seats, separate front seats, built-in headrests.

VARIATIONS

(for California only)
ENGINE max power (SAE net) 99 hp (73 kW) at 4,800 rpm, max torque (SAE net) 137 lb ft, 18.9 kg m (185 Nm) at 2,800 rpm, max engine rpm 5,300, 44.7 hp/l (33 kW/l).

OPTIONALS 500 A battery; air-conditioning; electric windows; electric door locks; automatic speed control; adjustable tilt of steering wheel; reclining backrests; electronic navigator.

101 hp power team

See 99 hp power team, except for:

ENGINE 155.9 cu in, 2,555 cc (3.59 x 3.86 in, 91.1 x 98 mm); compression ratio: 8.7:1; max power (SAE net): 101 hp (74 kW) at 4,800 rpm; max torque (SAE net): 140 lb ft, 19.3 kg m (189 Nm) at 2,800 rpm; max engine rpm: 5,300; 39.5 hp/l (29.1 kW/l); lubrication: 7.6 imp pt, 9.1 US pt, 4.3 l.

PERFORMANCE max speed: 92 mph, 148 km/h; power-weight ratio: E-Class 26.3 lb/hp (35.7 lb/kW), 11.9 kg/hp (16.2 kg/kW); consumption: 27.7 m/imp gal, 23 m/US gal, 10.2 l x 100 km.

ELECTRICAL EQUIPMENT (standard) 500 A battery; 75 A alternator.

DIMENSIONS AND WEIGHT weight: E-Class 2,659 lb, 1,209 kg - New Yorker 2,801 lb, 1,273 kg.

OPTIONALS air-conditioning; electric windows; electric door locks; automatic speed control; adjustable tilt of steering wheel; reclining backrests; electronic navigator.

140 hp power team

See 99 hp power team, except for:

ENGINE turbocharged; compression ratio: 8.1:1; max power (SAE net): 140 hp (103 kW) at 5,600 rpm; max torque (SAE net): 160 lb ft, 22.1 kg m (216 Nm) at 3,600 rpm; 63.2 hp/l (46.5 kW/l); turbocharger; air cleaner.

PERFORMANCE max speed: 100 mph, 160 km/h; power-weight ratio: E-Class 19 lb/hp (25.8 lb/kW), 8.6 kg/hp (11.7 kg/kW); consumption: 26.4 m/imp gal, 22 m/US gal, 10.7 l x 100 km.

ELECTRICAL EQUIPMENT (standard) 500 A battery.

DIMENSIONS AND WEIGHT weight: E-Class 2,651 lb, 1,205 kg - New Yorker 2,738 lb, 1,244 kg.

OPTIONALS air-conditioning; electric windows; electric door locks; automatic speed control; adjustable tilt of steering wheel; reclining backrests; electronic navigator.

Executive Series

PRICES EX WORKS:

		$
1	4-dr Sedan	18,966
2	4-dr Limousine	21,966

Power team:	Standard for:	Optional for:
101 hp	both	—
140 hp	—	1

101 hp power team

ENGINE front, 4 stroke; 4 cylinders, transverse, in line; 156 cu in, 2,555 cc (3.59 x 3.86 in, 91.1 x 98 mm); compression ratio: 8.7:1; max power (SAE net): 101 hp (74 kW) at 4,800 rpm; max torque (SAE net): 140 lb ft, 19.3 kg m (190 Nm) at 2,800 rpm; max engine rpm: 5,400; 39.5 hp/l (29.1 kW/l); cast iron block, light alloy head; 5 crankshaft bearings; valves: overhead, in line, rockers, hydraulic tappets; camshafts: 1, overhead; lubrication: rotary pump, full flow filter, 6.8 imp pt, 8 US pt, 3.8 l; 1 Holley 6520 downdraught twin barrel carburettor; exhaust system with catalytic converter; fuel feed: mechanical pump; water-cooled, 14.6 imp pt, 17.2 US pt, 8.2 l.

TRANSMISSION driving wheels: front; gearbox: Torqueflite automatic transmission, hydraulic torque converter and planetary gears with 3 ratios, max ratio of converter at stall 2, possible manual selection; ratios: I 2.690, II 1.550, III 1, rev 2.100; lever: central; final drive: hypoid spur gears; axle ratio: 3.020; width of rims: 5.5"; tyres: 185/70 or 185/75 R x 15.

PERFORMANCE max speed: 100 mph, 161 km/h; power-weight ratio: Sedan 29.8 lb/hp (40.5 lb/kW), 13.5 kg/hp (18.3 kg/kW); consumption: 25.2 m/imp gal, 21 m/US gal, 11.2 l x 100 km.

CHASSIS integral; front suspension: independent, wishbones, coil springs/telescopic damper struts, anti-roll bar; rear: rigid axle, lower trailing radius arms with track bar, coil springs, tescopic dampers.

STEERING rack-and-pinion, adjustable tilt, servo; turns lock to lock: 3.20.

BRAKES front disc, front internal radial fins, rear drum, servo; swept area: total 253 sq in, 1,632 sq cm.

ELECTRICAL EQUIPMENT 12 V; 500 A battery; 75 A alternator; Essex or Prestolite contactless transistorized ignition; 4 halogen headlamps.

DIMENSIONS AND WEIGHT wheel base: Sedan 315 in, 124 cm - Limousine 332 in, 131 cm; tracks: 57.60 in, 146 cm front, 57.20 in, 145 cm rear; length: Sedan 203.40 in, 516 cm - Limousine 210.40 in, 534 cm; width: 68.50 in, 174 cm; height: 53 in, 135 cm; ground clearance: 4.70 in, 11.9 cm; weight: Sedan 3,007 lb, 1,364 kg - Limousine 3,042 lb, 1,380 kg; turning circle: Sedan 41.2 ft, 12.5 m - Limousine 43.2 ft, 13.2 m; fuel tank: 11.6 imp gal, 14 US gal, 53 l.

BODY saloon/sedan; 4 doors; 5 seats, separate front seats, built-in headrests.

OPTIONALS air-conditioning; automatic speed control; **electric** windows; electric seats.

140 hp power team

See 101 hp power team, except for:

ENGINE turbocharged; 135 cu in, 2,213 cc (3.44 x 3.62 in, 87.5 x 92 mm); compression ratio: 8.1:1; max power (SAE net): 140 hp (103 kW) at 5,600 rpm; max torque (SAE net): 160 lb ft, 22.1 kg m (217 Nm) at 3,600 rpm; max engine rpm: 6,100; 64 hp/l (47 kW/l); electronic fuel injection; turbocharger; fuel feed: electric pump.

TRANSMISSION axle ratio: 3.220.

PERFORMANCE max speed: 106 mph, 170 km/h; power-weight ratio: 18.3 lb/hp (24.9 lb/kW), 8.3 kg/hp (11.3 kg/kW); consumption: 26.4 m/imp gal, 22 m/US gal, 10.7 l x 100 km.

ELECTRICAL EQUIPMENT 90 A alternator.

DIMENSIONS AND WEIGHT weight: 2,566 lb, 1,164 kg.

CHRYSLER Executive Limousine

CHRYSLER Fifth Avenue Sedan

DAYTONA Migi Roadster

Newport / Fifth Avenue

PRICES EX WORKS: $

Newport 4-dr Sedan —
Fifth Avenue 4-dr Sedan 13,990

ENGINE front, 4 stroke; 8 cylinders in Vee; 318 cu in, 5,211 cc (3.91 x 3.31 in, 99.2 x 84 mm); compression ratio: 8.5:1; max power (SAE net): 130 hp (97 kW) at 4,000 rpm; max torque (SAE net): 235 lb ft, 32.4 kg m (318 Nm) at 1,600 rpm; max engine rpm: 4,500; 24.9 hp/l (18.4 kW/l); 5 crankshaft bearings; valves: overhead, in line, push-rods and rockers, hydraulic tappets; camshafts: 1, at centre of Vee; lubrication: rotary pump, full flow filter, 6.8 imp pt, 8 US pt, 3.8 l; fuel feed: mechanical pump; 1 Carter C-BBD-8291 S downdraught twin barrel carburettor; water-cooled, 25 imp pt, 30 US pt, 14.2 l.

TRANSMISSION driving wheels: rear; gearbox: Torqueflite automatic transmission, hydraulic torque converter and planetary gears with 3 ratios, max ratio of converter at stall 2, possible manual selection; ratios: I 2.740, II 1.540, III 1, rev 2.220; lever: steering column; final drive: hypoid bevel; axle ratio: 2.940; width of rims: 7"; tyres: P 205/75 R x 15.

PERFORMANCE max speed: 96 mph, 155 km/h; power-weight ratio: Newport 27.9 lb/hp (37.9 lb/kW), 12.6 kg/hp (17.2 kg/kW); speed in direct drive at 1,000 rpm: 26 mph. 41.8 km/h; consumption: 20.4 m/imp gal, 17 m/US gal, 13.8 l x 100 km.

CHASSIS integral with isolated front cross members; front suspension: independent, wishbones, lower trailing links, longitudinal torsion bar, anti-roll bar, telescopic dampers; rear: rigid axle, semi-elliptic leafsprings, telescopic dampers.

STEERING recirculating ball, servo; turns lock to lock: 3.50.

BRAKES front disc, rear drum, servo; swept area: total 355 sq in, 2,292 sq cm.

ELECTRICAL EQUIPMENT 12 V; 430 A battery; 78 A alternator; Essex or Prestolite or Mopar transistorized ignition with electronic spark control; 4 headlamps.

DIMENSIONS AND WEIGHT wheel base: 112.70 in, 286 cm; tracks: 60 in, 152 cm front, 59.50 in, 151 cm rear; length: 206.70 in, 525 cm; width: 74.20 in, 189 cm; height: 55.30 in, 140 cm; ground clearance: 5.90 in, 15 cm; weight: Newport 3,620 lb, 1,642 kg - Fifth Avenue 3,747 lb, 1,700 kg; weight distribution: 55.5% front, 44.5% rear; turning circle: 43.6 ft, 13.3 m; fuel tank: 15.2 imp gal, 18 US gal, 68 l.

BODY saloon/sedan; 4 doors; 6 seats, separate front seats, built-in headrests.

OPTIONALS heavy-duty cooling; limited slip differential; light aloy wheels; heavy-duty suspension; adjustable tilt of steering wheel; automatic speed control; reclining backrests; electric windows; tinted glass; heated rear window; electric sunroof; vinyl roof; halogen headlamps; air-conditioning; light equipment; heavy-duty equipment.

DAYTONA USA

Migi / Moya

PRICES EX WORKS: $

Migi 2-dr Roadster 17,500
Moya 2-dr Roadster 11,500

ENGINE Volkswagen, rear, 4 stroke; 4 cylinders, horizontally opposed; 96.7 cu in, 1,584 cc (3.37 x 2.72 in, 85.5 x 69 mm); compression ratio: 7.2:1; max power (DIN): 56 hp (41 kW) at 4,200 rpm; max torque (DIN): 80 lb ft, 11 kg m (108 Nm) at 3,000 rpm; max engine rpm: 4,600; 35.4 hp/l (26 kW/l); block with cast iron liners and light alloy fins, light alloy head; 4 crankshaft bearings; valves: overhead, push-rods and rockers; camshafts: 1, central, lower; lubrication: gear pump, filter in sump, oil cooler, 4.4 imp pt, 5.3 US pt, 2.5 l; 2 Solex H 32 twin barrel carburettors; fuel feed: mechanical pump; air-cooled.

TRANSMISSION driving wheels: rear; clutch: single dry plate; gearbox: mechanical; gears: 4, fully synchronized; ratios: I 3.800, II 2.060, III 1.320, IV 0.880, rev 3.880; lever: central; final drive: spiral bevel; axle ratio: 4.125; width of rims: 5"; tyres: 5.60 x 15.

PERFORMANCE max speed: about 90 mph, 145 km/h; power-weight ratio: 24.6 lb/hp (33.4 lb/kW), 11.1 kg/hp (15.1 kg/kW); speed in top at 1,000 rpm: 21.2 mph, 34.2 km/h; consumption: 37.2 m/imp gal, 31 m/US gal, 7.6 l x 100 km.

CHASSIS backbone platform; front suspension: independent, twin swinging longitudinal trailing arms, transverse laminated torsion bars, anti-roll bar, telescopic dampers; rear: independent, swinging semi-axles, swinging longitudinal trailing arms, transverse torsion bars, telescopic dampers.

STEERING worm and roller; turns lock to lock: 2.60.

BRAKES front disc (diameter 10.94 in, 27.8 cm), rear drum; lining area: front 11.8 sq in, 76 sq cm, rear 56.4 sq in, 364 sq cm, total 68.2 sq in, 440 sq cm.

ELECTRICAL EQUIPMENT 12 V; 36 Ah battery; 350 W dynamo; Bosch distributor; 4 headlamps.

DIMENSIONS AND WEIGHT wheel base: 94.50 in, 240 cm; tracks: 51.50 in, 131 cm front, 53 in, 134 cm rear; length: 137 in, 348 cm; width: 60 in, 152 cm; ground clearance: 5.91 in, 15 cm; weight: 1,375 lb, 624 kg; turning circle: 36.1 ft, 11 m; fuel tank: 9 imp gal, 10.8 US gal, 41 l.

BODY roadster, in fiberglass material; 2 doors; 2 seats; tonneau cover.

OPTIONALS luxury interior; wire wheels; wooden steering wheel.

DE COURVILLE USA

Roadster

PRICE EX WORKS: $ 65,500

ENGINE front, 4 stroke; 8 cylinders in Vee; 302 cu in, 4,950 cc (4 x 3 in, 101.6 x 76.2 mm); compression ratio: 8.4:1; max power (SAE net): 139 hp (102 kW) at 3,600 rpm; max torque (SAE net): 250 lb ft, 34.5 kg m (338 Nm) at 1,600 rpm; max engine rpm: 4,000; 28.1 hp/l (20.6 kW/l); cast iron block and head; 5 crankshaft bearings; valves: overhead, in line, push-rods and rockers, hydraulic tappets; camshafts: 1, at centre of Vee; lubrication: rotary pump, full flow filter, 6.7 imp pt, 8 US pt, 3.8 l; electronic injection; air cleaner; exhaust system with catalytic converter; 1 downdraught twin barrel carburettor; fuel feed: electric pump; water-cooled, 22.5 imp pt, 27.2 US pt, 12.8 l.

TRANSMISSION driving wheels: rear; gearbox: automatic transmission, hydraulic torque converter and planetary gears with 4 ratios and overdrive, max ratio of converter at stall 2.29, possible manual selection; ratios: I 2.400, II 1.470, III 1, overdrive 0.670, rev 2; lever: steering column; final drive: hypoid bevel, limited slip; axle ratio: 3.080.

PERFORMANCE max speed: 110 mph, 177 km/h; power-weight ratio: 24.5 lb/hp (33.3 lb/kW), 11.1 kg/hp (15.1 kg/kW); consumption: 31.4 m/imp gal, 26 m/US gal, 9 l x 100 km - 21.6 m/imp gal, 18 m/US gal, 13.1 l x 100 km at town speed.

CHASSIS front suspension: independent, A arms, coil springs, anti-roll bar, telescopic dampers; rear: rigid axle, torque arms, coil springs, telescopic dampers.

STEERING recirculating ball, servo; turns lock to lock: 4.

BRAKES front disc, rear drum (diameter 11 in, 27.9 cm), servo.

ELECTRICAL EQUIPMENT 12 V; alternator; Delco ignition; 4 headlamps.

DE COURVILLE Roadster

ROADSTER

DIMENSIONS AND WEIGHT wheel base: 118.30 in, 300 cm; tracks: 62.20 in, 158 cm front, 62 in, 157 cm rear; length: 181.50 in, 461 cm; height: 53.50 in, 136 cm; ground clearance: 7 in, 17.8 cm; weight: 3,400 lb, 1,542 kg; weight distribution: 50% front, 50% rear; turning circle: 39.4 ft, 12 m; fuel tank: 16.7 imp gal, 20 US gal, 76 l.

BODY roadster, steel body; 2 doors; 2 separate bucket seats; leather upholstery.

DODGE USA

Omni / Charger Series

PRICES EX WORKS:

		$
1	Omni 4+1-dr Hatchback Sedan	**5,830**
2	Omni SE 4+1-dr Hatchback Sedan	**6,148**
3	Charger 2+1-dr Hatchback Coupé	**6,494**
4	Charger 2.2 2+1-dr Hatchback Coupé	**7,288**
5	Charger Shelby 2+1-dr Hatchback Coupé	**8,541**

Power team:	Standard for:	Optional for:
65 hp	1 to 3	—
96 hp	4	1,2,3,5
110 hp	5	1 to 4

65 hp power team

ENGINE front, transverse, 4 stroke; 4 cylinders, in line; 97.1 cu in, 1,591 cc (3.17 x 3.07 in, 80.5 x 78 mm); compression ratio: 8.8:1; max power (SAE net): 65 hp (48 kW) at 4,800 rpm; max torque (SAE net): 87 lb ft, 12 kg m (118 Nm) at 2,800 rpm; max engine rpm: 5,300; 40.8 hp/l (30 kW/l); cast iron block, light alloy head; 5 crankshaft bearings; valves: overhead, in line, thimble tappets; camshafts: 1, overhead, cogged belt; lubrication: gear pump, full flow filter, 5.8 imp pt, 7 US pt, 3.3 l; 1 Holley 65205220 downdraught twin barrel carburettor; air cleaner; exhaust system with catalytic converter; fuel feed: mechanical pump; water-cooled, 11.6 imp pt, 14 US pt, 6.6 l.

TRANSMISSION driving wheels: front; clutch: single dry plate; gearbox: mechanical; gears: 4 fully synchronized; ratios: I 3.290, II 1.890, III 1.210, IV 0.880, rev 3.140; lever: central; final drive: helical spur gears; axle ratio: 2.690; width of rims: 5"; tyres: 165/80 R x 13.

PERFORMANCE max speed: 91 mph, 146 km/h; power-weight ratio: Omni Hatchback Sedan 34.1 lb/hp (46.4 lb/kW), 28.6 kg/hp (21 kg/kW); consumption: 40.9 m/imp gal, 34 m/US gal, 6.8 l x 100 km.

CHASSIS integral; front suspension: independent, wishbones, anti-roll bar, coil springs, telescopic dampers; rear: independent, semi-trailing arms, coil springs, telescopic dampers.

STEERING rack-and-pinion; turns lock to lock: 3.60.

BRAKES front disc, front internal radial fins, rear drum; swept area: total 202 sq in, 1,303 sq cm.

ELECTRICAL EQUIPMENT 12 V; 335 A battery; 65 A alternator; Essex or Prestolite transistorized ignition with electronic spark control; 2 headlamps.

DODGE Omni Hatchback Sedan

DIMENSIONS AND WEIGHT wheel base: Coupé 96.60 in, 245 cm - sedans 99.10 in, 252 cm; tracks: 56.10 in, 143 cm front, 55.60 in, 141 cm rear; length: Coupé 173.30 in, 440 cm - sedans 164.80 in, 419 cm; width: Coupé 66.70 in, 169 cm - sedans 65.80 in, 167 cm; height: Coupé 50.80 in, 129 cm - sedans 53.10 in, 135 cm; ground clearance: 4.50 in, 11 cm; weight: Omni Hatchback Sedan 2,220 lb, 1,007 kg - Omni SE Hatchback Sedan 2,180 lb, 989 kg - Charger Hatchback Coupé 2,334 lb, 1,059 kg; weight distribution: 61% front, 39% rear; turning circle: 36.1 ft, 11 m; fuel tank: 10.8 imp gal, 12.9 US gal, 49 l.

BODY saloon/sedan, 4+1 doors - coupé, 2+1 doors; 5 seats, separate front seats, built-in headrests; heated rear window.

OPTIONALS Torqueflite automatic transmission, hydraulic torque converter and planetary gears with 3 ratios (I 2.690, II 1.550, III 1, rev 2.100), 3.020 axle ratio; power steering; 430 A battery; heavy-duty cooling; P 195/60 R x 14 tyres; 5.5" wide rims; servo brake; reclining backrests; rear window wiper-washer; sunroof; speed control; air-conditioning.

96 hp power team

See 65 hp power team, except for:

ENGINE 135 cu in, 2,213 cc (3.44 x 3.62 in, 87.5 x 92 mm); compression ratio: 9:1; max power (SAE net): 96 hp (71 kW) at 5,200 rpm; max torque (SAE net): 119 lb ft, 16.4 kg m (161 Nm) at 3,200 rpm; max engine rpm: 5,700; 43.4 hp/l (31.9 kW/l); cooling: 14.4 imp pt, 17.3 US pt, 8.2 l.

TRANSMISSION (for Shelby Charger Hatchback Coupé only) gears: 5, fully synchronized; ratios: I 3.290, II 2.080, III 1.450, IV 1.040, V 0.720, rev 3.140; axle ratio: 2.200.

PERFORMANCE max speed: 93 mph, 150 km/h; power-weight ratio: Charger 2.2 Hatchback Coupé 24.4 lb/hp (33.1 lb/kW), 11 kg/hp (15 kg/kW); consumption: 34.9 m/imp gal, 29 m/US gal, 8.1 l x 100 km.

DIMENSIONS AND WEIGHT weight: Charger Hatchback Coupé 2,339 lb, 1,061 kg.

OPTIONALS 5-speed fully synchronized mechanical gearbox (except Shelby Charger Hatchback Coupé); Torqueflite automatic transmission, hydraulic torque converter and planetary gears with 3 ratios (I 2.690, II 1.550, III 1, rev 2.100), max ratio of converter at stall 2, possible manual selection, 3.020 or 2.780 axle ratio.

110 hp power team

See 65 hp power team, except for:

ENGINE 135 cu in, 2,213 cc (3.44 x 3.62 in, 87.5 x 92 mm); compression ratio: 9.6:1; max power (SAE net): 110 hp (81 kW) at 5,600 rpm; max torque (SAE net): 129 lb ft, 17.7 kg m (173 Nm) at 3,600 rpm; max engine rpm: 6,000; 49.7 hp/l (36.6 kW/l); cooling: 14.4 imp pt, 17.3 US pt, 8.2 l.

TRANSMISSION gears: 5, fully synchronized; ratios: I 3.290, II 2.080, III 1.450, IV 1.040, V 0.720, rev 3.140; axle ratio: 2.780.

PERFORMANCE max speed: 100 mph, 161 km/h; power-weight ratio: Shelby Charger Hatchback Coupé 21.8 lb/hp (29.6 lb/kW), 9.9 kg/hp (13.4 kg/kW); consumption: 32.4 m/imp gal, 27 m/US gal, 8.7 l x 100 km.

DIMENSIONS AND WEIGHT weight: Shelby Charger Hatchback Coupé 2,392 lb, 1,085 kg.

OPTIONALS Torqueflite automatic transmission, hydraulic torque converter and planetary gears with 3 ratios (I 2.690, II 1.550, III 1, rev 2.100), max ratio of converter at stall 2, possible manual selection, 3.020 or 2.780 axle ratio.

Aries Series

PRICES EX WORKS:

		$
1	2-dr Sedan	**6,837**
2	4-dr Sedan	**6,949**
3	Custom 4+1-dr St. Wagon	**7,736**
4	SE 2-dr Sedan	**7,463**
5	SE 4-dr Sedan	**7,589**
6	SE 4+1-dr St. Wagon	**8,195**

Power team:	Standard for:	Optional for:
96 hp	all	—
101 hp	—	3,6

DODGE Shelby Charger Hatchback Coupé

DODGE Aries Sedan

DODGE Aries Custom Station Wagon

96 hp power team

ENGINE front, transverse, vertical, 4 stroke; 4 cylinders, in line; 135 cu in, 2,213 cc (3.44 x 3.62 in, 87.5 x 92 mm); compression ratio: 9:1; max power (SAE net): 96 hp (71 kW) at 5,200 rpm; max torque (SAE net): 119 lb ft, 16.4 kg m (161 Nm) at 3,200 rpm; max engine rpm: 5,700; 43.4 hp/l (31.9 kW/l); cast iron block, light alloy head; 5 crankshaft bearings; valves: overhead, in line, hydraulic tappets, rockers; camshafts: 1, overhead; lubrication: rotary pump, full flow filter, 6.7 imp pt, 8 US pt, 3.8 l; 1 Holley 6520 downdraught twin barrel carburettor; exhaust system with catalytic converter; fuel feed: mechanical pump; water-cooled, 14.4 imp pt, 17.3 US pt, 8.2 l.

TRANSMISSION driving wheels: front; clutch: single dry plate; gearbox: mechanical; gears: 4, fully synchronized; ratios: I 3.290, II 1.890, III 1.210, IV 0.880, rev 3.140; lever: central; final drive: helical spur gears; axle ratio: 2.690; width of rims: 5"; tyres: P 175/80 R x 13.

PERFORMANCE max speed: 90 mph, 145 km/h; power-weight ratio: 2-dr Sedan 24.5 lb/hp (33.3 lb/kW), 11.1 kg/hp (15.1 kg/kW); speed in top at 1,000 rpm: 24.9 mph, 40 km/h; consumption: 34.9 m/imp gal, 29 m/US gal, 9.1 l x 100 km.

CHASSIS integral; front suspension: independent, wishbones, coil springs, anti-roll bar, telescopic dampers; rear: rigid axle, coil springs, anti-roll bar, telescopic dampers.

STEERING rack-and-pinion; turns lock to lock: 4.

BRAKES front disc, front internal radial fins, rear drum; swept area: total 209.1 sq in, 1,349 sq cm.

ELECTRICAL EQUIPMENT 12V; 335 A battery; 60 A alternator; Essex or Prestolite transistorized ignition with combustion computer; 2 headlamps.

DIMENSIONS AND WEIGHT wheel base: 100.10 in, 254 cm; tracks: 57.60 in, 146 cm front, 57 in, 145 cm rear; length: sedans 176 in, 447 cm - st. wagons 176.20 in, 448 cm; width: 68.60 in, 174 cm; height: 2-dr sedans and st. wagons 52.30 in, 133 cm - 4-dr sedans 52.70 in, 134 cm; ground clearance: 4.50 in, 11 cm; weight: 2-dr Sedan 2,354 lb, 1,068 kg - 4-dr Sedan 2,361 lb, 1,071 kg - SE 2-dr Sedan 2,364 lb, 1,071 kg - SE 4-dr Sedan 2,394 lb, 1,086 kg - Custom St. Wagon 2,450 lb, 1,111 kg - SE St. Wagon 2,501 lb, 1,134 kg; weight distribution: 61% front, 39% rear; turning circle: 34.8 ft, 10.3 m; fuel tank: 11.7 imp gal, 14 US gal, 53 l.

BODY saloon/sedan, 2 or 4 doors - estate car/st. wagon, 4+1 doors; 6 seats, separate front seats, built-in headrests.

OPTIONALS 5-speed fully synchronized mechanical gearbox (I 3.290, II 2.080, III 1.450, IV 1.040, V 0.720, rev 3.140), 2.200 axle ratio; Torqueflite automatic transmission, hydraulic torque converter and planetary gears with 3 ratios (I 2.690, II 1.550, III 1, rev 2.100), max ratio of converter at stall 2, possible manual selection, 2.780 or 3.020 axle ratio, steering column or central lever; 500 A battery; 78 A alternator; servo brake; power steering; heavy-duty suspension; air-conditioning; automatic speed control; digital clock; tinted glass; electric windows; electric doors; tilt of steering wheel; P 185/70 R x 13 tyres; 5.5" wide rims.

101 hp power team

See 96 hp power team, except for:

ENGINE 155.9 cu in, 2,555 cc (3.59 x 3.86 in, 91.1 x 98 mm); compression ratio: 8.7:1; max power (SAE net): 101 hp (74 kW) at 4,800 rpm; max torque (SAE net): 140 lb ft, 19.3 kg m (189 Nm) at 2,800 rpm; max engine rpm: 5,300; 39.5 hp/l (29.1 kW/l); lubrication: 7.6 imp pt, 9.1 US pt, 4.3 l.

TRANSMISSION (standard) gearbox: Torqueflite automatic transmission, hydraulic torque converter and planetary gears with 3 ratios, max ratio of converter at stall 2, possible manual selection; ratios: I 2.690, II 1.550, III 1, rev 2.100; axle ratio: 3.020.

PERFORMANCE max speed: 92 mph, 148 km/h; power-weight ratio: Custom St. Wagon 25.2 lb/hp (34.2 lb/kW), 11.4 kg/hp (15.5 kg/kW); consumption: 27.7 m/imp gal, 23 m/US gal, 10.2 l x 100 km.

ELECTRICAL EQUIPMENT 75 A alternator; 500 A battery (standard).

DIMENSIONS AND WEIGHT weight: Custom St. Wagon 2,540 lb, 1,152 kg - SE St. Wagon 2,590 lb, 1,175 kg; weight distribution: 50.2% front, 49.8% rear.

BODY estate car/st. wagon; 4+1 doors.

OPTIONALS vinyl roof; rear window wiper-washer.

600 Series

PRICES EX WORKS:

		$
1	2-dr Sedan	**8,376**
2	4-dr Sedan	**8,903**
3	2-dr Convertible	**10,595**
4	ES 4-dr Sedan	**9,525**

Power team:	Standard for:	Optional for:
96 hp	1,3	—
99 hp	2,4	—
101 hp	—	all
142 hp	—	all

96 hp power team

ENGINE front, transverse, vertical, 4 stroke; 4 cylinders, in line; 135 cu in, 2,213 cc (3.44 x 3.62 in, 87.5 x 92 mm); compression ratio: 9:1; max power (SAE net): 96 hp (71 kW) at 5,200 rpm; max torque (SAE net): 119 lb ft, 16.4 kg m (161 Nm) at 3,200 rpm; max engine rpm: 5,700; 43.4 hp/l (31.9 kW/l); cast iron block, light alloy head; 5 crankshaft bearings; valves: overhead, in line, hydraulic tappets, rockers; camshafts: 1, overhead; lubrication: rotary pump, full flow filter, 6.7 imp pt, 8 US pt, 3.8 l; 1 Holley 6520 downdraught twin barrel carburettor; exhaust system with catalytic converter; fuel feed: mechanical pump; water-cooled, 14.4 imp pt, 17.3 US pt, 8.2 l.

DODGE 600 Convertible

TRANSMISSION driving wheels: front; clutch: single dry plate; gearbox: mechanical; gears: 5, fully synchronized; ratios: I 3.290, II 2.080, III 1.450, IV 1.040, V 0.720, rev 3.140; lever: central; final drive: helical spur gears; axle ratio: 2.570; width of rims: 5.5"; tyres: 185/70 R x 14.

PERFORMANCE max speed: 90 mph, 145 km/h; power-weight ratio: Sedan 25.8 lb/hp (35 lb/kW), 11.7 kg/hp (15.9 kg/kW); speed in top at 1,000 rpm: 24.9 mph, 40 km/h; consumption: 32.5 m/imp gal, 27 m/US gal, 8.7 l x 100 km.

CHASSIS integral; front suspension: independent, wishbones, coil springs, anti-roll bar, telescopic dampers; rear: rigid axle, coil springs, anti-roll bar, telescopic dampers.

STEERING rack-and-pinion, servo - Convertible tilt of steering wheel; turns lock to lock: 3.20.

BRAKES front disc (diameter 10.03 in, 25.5 cm), internal radial fins, rear drum, servo; swept area: total 253.1 sq in, 1,632 sq cm.

ELECTRICAL EQUIPMENT 12 V; 335 A battery; 60 A alternator; 4 headlamps.

DIMENSIONS AND WEIGHT wheel base: 100.10 in, 254 cm; tracks: 57.60 in, 146 cm front, 57 in, 145 cm rear; length: 179.50 in, 456 cm; width: 68.50 in, 174 cm; height: Sedan 52.60 in, 134 cm - Convertible 54.10 in, 137 cm; ground clearance: 4.70 in, 11.9 cm; weight: Sedan 2,474 lb, 1,122 kg - Convertible 2,595 lb, 1,177 kg.

BODY saloon/sedan - convertible; 2 doors; sedan, 6 seats - convertible, 2 seats, separate front seats, built-in headrests.

OPTIONALS Torqueflite automatic transmission, hydraulic torque converter and planetary gears with 3 ratios (I 2.690, II 1.550, III 1, rev 2.100), max ratio of converter at stall 2, possible manual selection, 3.020 axle ratio; air-conditioning; electric windows; 500 A battery; 78 A alternator; electric door locks; automatic speed control; electric front seats; electronic trip computer.

99 hp power team

See 96 hp power team, except for:

ENGINE max power (SAE net): 99 hp (73 kW) at 5,600 rpm; max torque (SAE net): 121 lb ft, 16.7 kg m (164 Nm) at 3,200 rpm; max engine rpm: 6,100; 44.7 hp/l (32.9 kW/l); Throttle-body electronic fuel injection; thermostatic air cleaner; exhaust gas recirculation with catalytic converter; fuel feed: electric pump.

TRANSMISSION (standard) gearbox: Torqueflite automatic transmission, hydraulic torque converter and planetary gears with 3 ratios, max ratio of converter at stall 2, possible manual selection; ratios: I 2.690, II 1.550, III 1, rev 2.100; lever: central; axle ratio: 3.020.

PERFORMANCE max speed: 99 mph, 159 km/h; power-weight ratio: Sedan 26.3 lb/hp (35.7 lb/kW), 11.9 kg/hp (16.2 kg/kW); consumption: 28.8 m/imp gal, 24 m/US gal, 9.8 l x 100 km.

ELECTRICAL EQUIPMENT 370 A battery; 90 A alternator.

DIMENSIONS AND WEIGHT weight: Sedan 2,593 lb, 1,179 kg - ES Sedan 2,553 lb, 1,160 kg.

BODY saloon/sedan; 4 doors; 6 seats, separate front seats, built-in headrests.

101 hp power team

See 96 hp power team, except for:

ENGINE 155.9 cu in, 2,555 cc (3.59 x 3.86 in, 91.1 x 98 mm); compression ratio: 8.7:1; max power (SAE net): 101 hp (74 kW) at 4,800 rpm; max torque (SAE net): 140 lb ft, 19.3 kg m (189 Nm) at 2,800 rpm; max engine rpm: 5,300; 39.5 hp/l (29.1 kW/l); lubrication: 7.6 imp pt, 9.1 US pt, 4.3 l.

TRANSMISSION (standard) gearbox: Torqueflite automatic transmission, hydraulic torque converter and planetary gears with 3 ratios, max ratio of converter at stall 2, possible manual selection - ES Sedan mechanical; gears: 5, fully synchronized; ratios: I 2.690, II 1.550, III 1, rev 2.100 - ES Sedan I 3.290, II 2.080, III 1.450, IV 1.040, V 0.720, rev 3.140; axle ratio: 3.020 - ES 2.570.

PERFORMANCE max speed: 92 mph, 148 km/h; power-weight ratio: 4-dr Sedan 26.3 lb/hp (35.8 lb/kW), 11.9 kg/hp (16.2 kg/kW); consumption: 27.6 m/imp gal, 23 m/US gal, 10.2 l x 100 km.

ELECTRICAL EQUIPMENT (standard) 500 A battery; 75 A alternator.

DIMENSIONS AND WEIGHT weight: 4-dr Sedan 2,655 lb, 1,207 kg - ES 4-dr Sedan 2,655 lb, 1,207 kg.

BODY saloon/sedan, 2 or 4 doors - convertible, 2 doors.

142 hp power team

See 96 hp power team, except for:

ENGINE turbocharged; max power (SAE net): 142 hp (104 kW) at 5,600 rpm; max torque (SAE net): 160 lb ft, 22.1 kg

DODGE 600 ES Sedan

142 HP POWER TEAM

m (216 Nm) at 3,600 rpm; 64.2 hp/l (47.2 kW/l); electronic fuel injection with turbocharger; air cleaner; exhaust gas recirculation with catalytic converter; fuel feed: electric pump.

TRANSMISSION (standard for sedans only) gearbox: Torqueflite automatic transmission, hydraulic torque converter and planetary gears with 3 ratios, max ratio of converter at stall 2, possible manual selection - ES Sedan mechanical; gears: 5, fully synchronized; ratios: I 2.690, II 1.550, III 1, rev 2.100 - ES Sedan I 3.290, II 2.080, III 1.450, IV 1.040, V 0.720, rev 3.140; axle ratio: 3.020 - ES Sedan 2.570.

PERFORMANCE max speed: 100 mph, 160 km/h; power-weight ratio: ES Sedan 18.4 lb/hp (25 lb/kW), 8.3 kg/hp (11.3 kg/kW); consumption: 26.4 m/imp gal, 22 m/US gal, 10.7 l x 100 km.

ELECTRICAL EQUIPMENT (standard) 500 A battery; 90 A alternator.

DIMENSIONS AND WEIGHT weight: 4-dr Sedan 2,656 lb, 1,204 kg - ES Sedan 2,611 lb, 1,186 kg.

BODY saloon/sedan, 2 or 4 doors - convertible, 2 doors.

OPTIONALS (for ES Sedan only) Torqueflite automatic transmission with 3 ratios.

Daytona Series

PRICES EX WORKS:	$
1 2+1-dr Hatchback Coupé	8,308
2 Turbo 2+1-dr Hatchback Coupé	10,227

Power team:	Standard for:	Optional for:
99 hp	1	—
142 hp	2	1

99 hp power team

ENGINE front, transverse, vertical, 4 stroke; 4 cylinders, in line; 135 cu in, 2,213 cc (3.44 x 3.62 in, 87.5 x 92 mm); compression ratio: 9:1; max power (SAE net): 99 hp (73 kW) at 5,600 rpm; max torque (SAE net): 121 lb ft, 16.7 kg m (164 Nm) at 3,200 rpm; max engine rpm: 6,100; 44.7 hp/l (32.9 kW/l); cast iron block, light alloy head; 5 crankshaft bearings; valves: overhead, in line, hydraulic tappets, rockers; camshafts: 1, overhead; lubrication: rotary pump, full flow filter, 6.7 imp pt, 8 US pt, 3.8 l; Throttle-body electronic fuel injection; thermostatic air cleaner; exhaust gas recirculation with catalytic converter; fuel feed: electric pump; water-cooled.

TRANSMISSION driving wheels: front; clutch: single dry plate; gearbox: mechanical; gears: 5, fully synchronized; ratios: I 3.290, II 2.080, III 1.450, IV 1.040, V 0.720, rev 3.140; lever: central; final drive: helical spur gears; axle ratio: 2.570; width of rims: 5.5"; tyres: P 185/70 R x 14.

PERFORMANCE max speed: 100 mph, 161 km/h; power-weight ratio: 25.8 lb/hp (35 lb/kW), 11.7 kg/hp (15.9 kg/kW); consumption: 27.7 m/imp gal, 23 m/US gal, 10.2 l x 100 km.

CHASSIS integral; front suspension: independent, wishbones, coil springs, anti-roll bar, telescopic dampers; rear: rigid axle, radius arms with track bar, coil springs, telescopic dampers.

STEERING rack-and-pinion, servo; turns lock to lock: 2.50.

BRAKES front disc (diameter 10.03 in, 25.5 cm), internal radial fins, rear drum, servo; swept area: total 275.4 sq in, 1,776 sq cm.

ELECTRICAL EQUIPMENT 12 V; 370 A battery; 90 A alternator; 4 headlamps.

DIMENSIONS AND WEIGHT wheel base: 97 in, 246 cm; tracks: 57.60 in, 146 cm front, 57.20 in, 145 cm rear; length: 175 in, 444 cm; width: 69.30 in, 176 cm; height: 50.30 in, 128 cm; ground clearance: 4.60 in, 11.6 cm; weight: 2,546 lb, 1,157 kg; fuel tank: 11.7 imp gal, 14 US gal, 53 l.

BODY coupé; 2+1 doors; 4 seats, separate front seats, reclining backrests, built-in headrests.

OPTIONALS Torqueflite automatic transmission, hydraulic torque converter and planetary gears with 3 ratios (I 2.690, II 1.550, III 1, rev 2.100), max ratio of converter at stall 2, possible manual selection, 3.220 axle ratio; tilt of steering wheel; air-conditioning; sunroof; wiper-washer on rear window; electric windows; electric door lock; automatic speed control; P 195/60 R x 15 tyres; 6" wide rims.

142 hp power team

See 99 hp power team, except for:

ENGINE turbocharged; max power (SAE net): 142 hp (104 kW) at 5,600 rpm; max torque (SAE net): 160 lb ft, 22.1 kg m (216 Nm) at 3,600 rpm; max engine rpm: 6,200; 64.2 hp/l (47.2 kW/l); electronic fuel injection with turbocharger; air-cleaner.

PERFORMANCE max speed: 100 mph, 160 km/h; power-weight ratio: Turbo Hatchback Coupé 18.7 lb/hp (25.5 lb/kW), 8.5 kg/hp (11.6 kg/kW); consumption: 26.4 m/imp gal, 22 m/US gal, 10.7 l x 100 km.

ELECTRICAL EQUIPMENT 500 A battery.

DIMENSIONS AND WEIGHT weight: Turbo Hatchback Coupé 2,655 lb, 1,207 kg - Hatchback Coupé 2,609 lb, 1,186 kg.

Diplomat Series

PRICES EX WORKS:	$
Salon 4-dr Sedan	9,180
SE 4-dr Sedan	10,165

Power team:	Standard for:	Optional for:
130 hp	all	—
165 hp	—	all

130 hp power team

ENGINE front, 4 stroke; 8 cylinders in Vee; 318 cu in, 5,211 cc (3.91 x 3.31 in, 99.2 x 84 mm); compression ratio: 8.5:1; max power (SAE net): 130 hp (97 kW) at 4,000 rpm; max torque (SAE net): 235 lb ft, 31.7 kg m (319 Nm) at 1,600 rpm; max engine rpm: 4,500; 24.9 hp/l (18.4 kW/l); cast iron block and head; 5 crankshaft bearings; valves: overhead, in line, hydraulic tappets, push-rods and rockers; camshafts: 1, at centre of Vee; lubrication: rotary pump, full flow filter, 6.7 imp pt, 8 US pt, 3.8 l; 1 Carter BBD-8291 S downdraught twin barrel carburettor; air cleaner; exhaust system with catalytic converter; fuel feed: mechanical pump; water-cooled, 25 imp pt, 30 US pt, 14.2 l.

TRANSMISSION driving wheels: rear; gearbox: Torqueflite automatic transmission, hydraulic torque converter and planetary gears with 3 ratios, max ratio of converter at stall 2, possible manual selection; ratios: I 2.740, II 1.540, III 1, rev 2.220; lever: steering column; axle ratio: 2.260 - (for California only) 2.940; width of rims: 7"; tyres P 205/75 R x 15.

PERFORMANCE max speed: 102 mph, 164 km/h; power-weight ratio: Salon 27.4 lb/hp (37.2 lb/kW), 12.4 kg/hp (16.9 kg/kW); speed in direct drive at 1,000 rpm: 25.5 mph, 41 km/h; consumption: 20.4 m/imp gal, 17 m/US gal, 13.8 l x 100 km.

CHASSIS integral with isolated front cross members; front suspension: independent, wishbones, transverse torsion bars, anti-roll bar, telescopic dampers; rear: rigid axle, semi-elliptic leafsprings, telescopic dampers.

STEERING recirculating ball, servo; turns lock to lock: 3.50.

BRAKES front disc (diameter 10.82 in, 27.5 cm), front internal radial fins, rear drum, rear compensator, servo; swept area: total 355.2 sq in, 2,292 sq cm.

ELECTRICAL EQUIPMENT 12 V; 430 A battery; 60 A alternator; Essex or Prestolite transistorized ignition with electronic spark control; 4 headlamps.

DIMENSIONS AND WEIGHT wheel base: 112.70 in, 286 cm; tracks: 60 in, 152 cm front, 59.50 in, 151 cm rear; length: 205.70 in, 522 cm; width: 74.20 in, 188 cm; height: 55.30 in, 140 cm; ground clearance: 5.90 in, 15 cm; weight: Salon 3,556 lb, 1,613 kg - SE 3,625 lb, 1,642 kg; turning circle: 43.6 ft, 13.3 m; fuel tank: 15 imp gal, 18 US gal, 68 l.

BODY saloon/sedan; 4 doors; 6 seats, separate front seats, built-in headrests.

OPTIONALS manual or automatic air-conditioning; 78 A alternator; 500 A battery; digital clock; tinted glass; halogen headlamps; electric door locks; tilt of steering wheel; cruise control; sunroof; vinyl roof; electric windows; electric front seats; speed control.

165 hp power team

See 130 hp power team, except for:

ENGINE max power (SAE net): 165 hp (123 kW) at 4,000 rpm; max torque (SAE net): 240 lb ft, 33.1 kg m (325 Nm) at 2,000 rpm; 31.7 hp/l (23.6 kW/l); valves: overhead, in line, hydraulic tappets; 1 Carter TQ-9295 downdraught 4-barrel carburettor.

TRANSMISSION axle ratio: 2.200.

PERFORMANCE max speed: 104 mph, 166 km/h; power-weight ratio: Salon 21.8 lb/hp (29.1 lb/kW), 9.9 kg/hp (13.2 kg/kW).

DIMENSIONS AND WEIGHT weight: Salon 3.584 lb, 1,626 kg; weight distribution: 57% front, 43% rear.

DODGE Daytona Turbo Hatchback Coupé

DODGE Diplomat Salon Sedan

DODGE Caravan

Caravan

PRICE EX WORKS: $ 8,669

101 hp power team

(standard)

ENGINE front, transverse, 4 stroke; 4 cylinders, in line; 135 cu in, 2,213 cc (3.13 x 3.40 in, 80 x 86 mm); compression ratio: 9:1; max power (SAE net): 101 hp (74 kW) at 5,600 rpm; max torque (SAE net): 121 lb ft, 16.7 kg m (164 Nm) at 3,600 rpm; max engine rpm: 6,100; 45.6 hp/l (33.6 kW/l); cast iron block, light alloy head; 5 crankshaft bearings; valves: overhead, in line, hydraulic tappets, rockers; camshafts: 1, overhead; lubrication: rotary pump, full flow filter, 7.6 imp pt, 9.1 US pt, 4.3 l; 1 Holley downdraught twin barrel carburettor; exhaust system with catalytic converter; fuel feed: mechanical pump; water-cooled.

TRANSMISSION driving wheels: rear; clutch: single dry plate; gearbox: mechanical; gears: 5, fully synchronized; ratios: I 3.290, II 1.890, III 1.210, IV 0.880, V 0.720, rev 3.140; lever: steering column; final drive: helical spur gears; axle ratio: 2.560; width of rims: 5.5"; tyres: P 185/75 R x 14.

PERFORMANCE max speed: 92 mph, 148 km/h; power-weight ratio: 28.8 lb/hp (39.2 lb/kW), 13.1 kg/hp (17.8 kg/kW); carrying capacity: 2,500 lb, 1,134 kg; consumption: 34.8 m/imp gal, 29 m/US gal, 8.1 l x 100 km.

CHASSIS integral; front suspension: independent, Iso strut, wishbones, coil springs, telescopic dampers; rear: independent, leaf springs, coil springs, telescopic dampers.

STEERING rack-and-pinion, servo.

BRAKES front disc, front internal radial fins, rear drum, servo; swept area: front 194.5 sq in, 1,254 sq cm, rear 139.9 sq in, 902.3 sq cm, total 334.4 sq in, 2,156 sq cm.

ELECTRICAL EQUIPMENT 12 V; 335 A battery; 60 A alternator; transistorized ignition; 4 headlamps.

DIMENSIONS AND WEIGHT wheel base: 112 in, 284 cm; tracks: 59.90 in, 152 cm front, 62.10 in, 158 cm rear; length: 175.90 in, 447 cm; width: 69.60 in, 177 cm; height: 64.60 in, 164 cm; ground clearance: 5.40 in, 13.7 cm; weight: 2,911 lb, 1,320 kg; turning circle: 41 ft, 12.5 m; fuel tank: 12.5 imp gal, 15 US gal, 57 l.

BODY estate car/st. wagon; 2+1 doors; 5 or 6 seats, separate front seats.

OPTIONALS Torqueflite automatic transmission, hydraulic torque converter and planetary gears with 3 ratios (I 2.690, II 1.550, III 1, rev 2.100), 3.220 axle ratio; P 195/75 R x 14 SBR or P 205/70 R x 14 SBR tyres; electric windows, electric locks, electric seats; 90 A alternator; 500 A battery; electric speed control; tinted glass; light alloy wheels; air-conditioning; heavy-duty battery; heavy-duty suspension; heated rear window.

99 hp power team

(optional)

See 101 hp power team, except for:

ENGINE 155.9 cu in, 2.555 cc (3.59 x 3.86 in, 91.1 x 98 mm); compression ratio: 8.7:1; max power (SAE net): 99 hp (73 kW) at 4,800 rpm; max torque (SAE net): 143 lb ft, 19.7 kg m (193 Nm) at 2,000 rpm; max engine rpm: 5,300; 38.7 hp/l (28.5 kW/l).

TRANSMISSION (standard) gearbox: Torqueflite automatic transmission, hydraulic torque converter and planetary gears with 3 ratios, max ratio of converter at stall 2, possible manual selection; ratios: I 2.690, II 1.550, III 1, rev 2.100; axle ratio: 3.220; tyres: P 205/70 R x 14 (standard).

PERFORMANCE power-weight ratio: 38.3 lb/hp (52.1 lb/kW), 17.3 kg/hp (23.6 kg/kW); consumption: 28.8 m/imp gal, 24 m/US gal, 9.8 l x 100 km.

ELECTRICAL EQUIPMENT (standard) 500 A battery; (standard) 90 A alternator; Mopor electric transistorized ingition.

DIMENSIONS AND WEIGHT weight: 3,790 lb, 1,719 kg; fuel tank: 16.7 imp gal, 20 US gal, 76 l.

ELEGANT MOTORS USA

856 Auburn Speedster

PRICE EX WORKS: $ 36,000

ENGINE Chevrolet Corvette, front, 4 stroke; 8 cylinders in Vee; 350 cu in, 5,736 cc (4 x 3 in, 101.6 x 88.4 mm); compression ratio: 8.9:1; max power (SAE net): 230 hp (169 kW) at 5,200 rpm; max torque (SAE net): 275 lb ft, 37.9 kg m (371 Nm) at 3,600 rpm; max engine rpm: 5,600; 40.1 hp/l (29.7 kW/l); cast iron block and head; 5 crankshaft bearings; valves: overhead, in line, push-rods and rockers, hydraulic tappets; camshafts: 1, at centre of Vee; lubrication: gear pump, full flow filter, 8.3 imp pt, 9.9 US pt, 4.7 l; 1 Rochester 17080228 downdraught 4-barrel carburettor; thermostatic air cleaner; dual exhaust system with catalytic converter; fuel feed: mechanical pump; water-cooled, 34.5 imp pt, 41.4 US pt, 19.6 l, viscous coupling thermostatic fan.

TRANSMISSION driving wheels: rear; clutch: single dry plate, semi-centrifugal; gearbox: mechanical; gears: 4, fully synchronized; ratios: I 2.880, II 1.910, III 1.330, IV 1, rev 2.780; lever: central; final drive: hypoid bevel, limited slip; axle ratio: 3.070; width of rims: 8"; tyres: P225/70R x 15.

PERFORMANCE max speed: 135 mph, 217 km/h; power-weight ratio: 13 lb/hp (17.6 lb/kW), 5.9 kg/hp (8 kg/kW).

CHASSIS ladder frame with cross members; front suspension: independent, wishbones, coil springs, anti-roll bar, telescopic dampers; rear: independent, wishbones, semi-axle as upper arms, transverse semi-elliptic leafspring, trailing radius arms, telescopic dampers.

STEERING recirculating ball, servo, tilt of steering wheel; turns lock to lock: 2.92.

BRAKES disc (diameter 11.75 in, 30 cm), internal radial fins, servo; swept area: total 498.30 sq in, 3,214 sq cm.

ELECTRICAL EQUIPMENT 12 V; 3,500 W battery; 63 A alternator; Delco-Remy high energy ignition; 4 headlamps.

DIMENSIONS AND WEIGHT wheel base: 128 in, 325 cm; tracks: 61.70 in, 157 cm front, 62.50 in, 159 cm rear; length: 203.94 in, 518 cm; height: 57.09 in, 145 cm; ground clearance: 8 in, 20.3 cm; weight: 3,000 lb, 1,360 kg; fuel tank: 20 imp gal, 24 US gal, 91 l.

BODY roadster, in fiberglass material; 2 doors; 2 seats.

OPTIONALS GM Turbo-Hydramatic automatic transmission.

898 Phaeton

See 856 Auburn Speedster, except for:

PRICE EX WORKS: $ 45,000

TRANSMISSION width of rims: front 7".

DIMENSIONS AND WEIGHT length: 207.13 in, 526 cm; width: 78 in, 198 cm; height: 56 in, 142 cm.

BODY phaeton, in fiberglass material; 2 doors; 4 seats, separate front seats.

898 Elegantè Phaeton Brougham

See 856 Auburn Speedster, except for:

PRICE EX WORKS: $ 60,000

BODY phaeton, in fiberglass material; 2 doors; 4 seats, separate front seats; electric windows; hardtop.

ELEGANT MOTORS 856 Auburn Speedster

ERA USA

427 SC Cobra Replica

PRICES EX WORKS: $ 34,900
$ 14,800 (kit form)

ENGINE Ford, front, 4 stroke; 8 cylinders in Vee; 427 cu in, 6,997 cc (4.23 x 3.78 in, 107.4 x 95.9 mm); compression ratio: 12:1; max power (DIN): 425 lb ft, 66.2 kg m (649 Nm) at 3,700 rpm; max torque (DIN): 480 lb ft, 66.2 kg m (649 Nm) at 3,700 rpm; max engine rpm: 6,600; 60.7 hp/l (44.7 kW/l); cast iron block and head; 5 crankshaft bearings; valves: overhead, push-rods and rockers; camshafts: 1, at centre of Vee; lubrication: rotary pump, 8.4 imp pt, 10 US pt, 4.8 l; 1 Holley downdraught 4-barrel carburettor; fuel feed: mechanical pump; water-cooled, 32.6 imp pt, 39 US pt, 18.5 l.

TRANSMISSION driving wheels: rear; clutch: single dry plate; gearbox: mechanical; gears: 4, fully synchronized; ratios: I 2.320, II 1.690, III 1.290, IV 1, rev 2.320.

PERFORMANCE max speed: 180 mph, 289 km/h; power-weight ratio: 6 lb/hp (8.2 lb/kW), 2.7 kg/hp (3.7 kg/kW); consumption: 14.4 m/imp gal, 12 m/US gal, 19.6 l x 100 km.

CHASSIS front suspension: independent, unequal length A arms, anti-roll bar, coil springs, telescopic dampers; rear: independent, lower trailing arm, side links, coil springs, telescopic dampers.

STEERING rack-and-pinion.

BRAKES disc.

ELECTRICAL EQUIPMENT 12 V; 46 Ah battery; alternator; 2 headlamps.

DIMENSIONS AND WEIGHT wheel base: 90 in, 229 cm; front and rear track: 56 in, 142 cm; length: 156 in, 396 cm; width: 68 in, 173 cm; height: 49 in, 124 cm; ground clearance: 5 in, 12.7 cm; weight: 2,550 lb, 1,156 kg; weight distribution: 50% front, 50% rear; fuel tank: 13.4 imp gal, 16 US gal, 61 l.

BODY roadster, in fiberglass material; 2 doors; 2 bucket seats.

OPTIONALS electric pump; side pipes; roll-bar.

ERA 427 SC Cobra Replica

EXCALIBUR USA

Series IV

PRICES EX WORKS:	$
2-dr Phaeton	**56,500**
2-dr Roadster	**59,000**

ENGINE Chevrolet, front, 4 stroke; 8 cylinders in Vee; 305 cu in, 4,999 cc (3.74 x 3.48 in, 94.9 x 88.4 mm); compression ratio: 8.5:1; max power (SAE net): 155 hp (113 kW) at 4,000 rpm; max torque (SAE net): 230 lb ft, 31.7 kg m (312 Nm) at 2,400 rpm; max engine rpm: 4,400; 32 hp/l (24 kW/l); 5 crankshaft bearings; valves: overhead, in line, push-rods and rockers, hydraulic tappets; camshafts: 1, at centre of Vee; lubrication: gear pump, full flow filter, 7.4 imp pt, 8.4 US pt, 4 l; 1 Rochester downdraught 4-barrel carburettor; air cleaner; exhaust system with catalytic converter; fuel feed: mechanical pump; water-cooled.

TRANSMISSION driving wheels: rear; gearbox: Turbo-Hydramatic 700-R-4 automatic transmission, hydraulic torque converter and planetary gears with 4 ratios, max ratio of converter at stall 1.90, possible manual selection; ratios: I 3.060, II 1.620, III 1, IV 0.700, rev 2.090; lever: central; final drive: hypoid bevel, limited slip; axle ratio: 3.070; width of rims: 8''; tyres: P235 R75 x 15.

PERFORMANCE max speed: 110 mph, 177 km/h; power-weight ratio: 28.4 lb/hp (38.9 lb/kW), 12.8 kg/hp (17.5 kg/kW); consumption: 21.5 m/imp gal, 18 m/US gal, 13.1 l x 100 km.

CHASSIS box-type ladder frame; front suspension: independent, wishbones, coil springs, anti-roll bar, telescopic dampers; rear: independent, semi-axle as upper pivoting arm and angular strut rod as lower pivoting arm, transverse semi-elliptic leafspring, trailing radius arms, anti-roll bar, telescopic dampers adjustable while running.

STEERING recirculating ball, variable ratio, tilt and telescopic, servo; turns lock to lock: 3.

BRAKES disc, internal radial fins, servo; swept area: total 461 sq in, 2,973 sq cm.

ELECTRICAL EQUIPMENT 12 V; 73 Ah battery; 85 A alternator; Delco-Remy high energy ignition; 4 headlamps.

DIMENSIONS AND WEIGHT wheel base: 125 in, 317 cm; front and rear track: 63 in, 160 cm; length: 207 in, 526 cm; width: 75 in, 190 cm; height: 59 in, 150 cm; ground clearance: 7 in, 18 cm; weight: 4,400 lb, 1,993 kg; weight distribution: 46% front, 54% rear; fuel tank: 20.8 imp gal, 25 US gal, 95 l.

BODY phaeton, 2 doors, 4 seats, separate front seats - roadster, 2 doors, 2+2 seats, rear rumble seats.

FORD USA

Escort Series

PRICES EX WORKS:	$
L 2+1-dr Hatchback Sedan	**6,193**
L 4+1-dr Hatchback Sedan	**6,407**
L 4+1-dr St. Wagon	**6,621**
GL 2+1-dr Hatchback Sedan	**6,690**
GL 4+1-dr Hatchback Sedan	**6,904**
GL 4+1-dr St. Wagon	**7,081**
LX 4+1-dr Hatchback Sedan	**8,156**
LX 4+1-dr St. Wagon	**8,247**
GT 2+1-dr Hatchback Sedan	**7,901**

Power team:	Standard for:	Optional for:
70 hp	all	—
80 hp	—	all
120 hp	—	all
52 hp (diesel)	—	all

70 hp power team

ENGINE front, transverse, 4 stroke; 4 cylinders, in line; 97.6 cu in, 1,599 cc (3.15 x 3.13 in, 80 x 79.5 mm); compression ratio: 9:1; max power (SAE net): 70 hp (51 kW) at 4,600 rpm; max torque (SAE net): 88 lb ft, 12.1 kg m (119 Nm) at 2,600 rpm; max engine rpm: 5,100; 43.7 hp/l (32.2 kW/l); cast iron block, light alloy head; 5 crankshaft bearings; valves: overhead, Vee-slanted, rockers, hydraulic tappets; camshafts: 1, overhead, cogged belt; lubrication: gear pump, full flow filter, 5.5 imp pt, 7.1 US pt, 3.3 l; 1 Holley ATX 304-C downdraught twin barrel carburettor; air cleaner; exhaust system with catalytic converter; fuel feed: mechanical pump; water-cooled, 11 imp pt, 13.3 US pt, 6.3 l.

TRANSMISSION driving wheels: front; clutch: single dry plate; gearbox: mechanical; gears: 4, fully synchronized; ratios: I 3.230, II 1.900, III 1.230, IV 0.810, rev 3.460; lever: central; final drive: hypoid bevel; axle ratio: 3.040; width of rims: 4.5''; tyres: P 165/80 R x 13.

EXCALIBUR Series IV Phaeton

FORD Escort GL Station Wagon

PERFORMANCE max speed: 90 mph, 145 km/h; power-weight ratio: L 2+1-dr Hatchback Sedan 29.7 lb/hp (40.3 lb/kW), 13.4 kg/hp (18.3 kg/kW); consumption: 44.8 m/imp gal, 37 m/US gal, 6.3 l x 100 km.

CHASSIS integral; front suspension: independent, by McPherson, coil springs, anti-roll bar, telescopic dampers; rear: independent, modified McPherson strut, coil springs, lower arm, telescopic dampers.

STEERING rack-and-pinion; turns lock to lock: 3.50.

BRAKES front disc (diameter 9.25 in, 23.5 cm), front internal radial fins, rear drum; swept area: front 147.4 sq in, 951 sq cm, rear 56.1 sq in, 362 sq cm, total 203.5 sq in, 1,313 sq cm.

ELECTRICAL EQUIPMENT 12 V; 310 A battery; 40 A alternator; Motorcraft transistorized ignition; 2 headlamps.

DIMENSIONS AND WEIGHT wheel base: 94.20 in, 239 cm; tracks: 54.70 in, 139 cm front, 56 in, 142 cm rear; length: 2+1-dr sedans 163.90 in, 416 cm - 4+1-dr models 165 in, 419 cm; width: 65.90 in, 167 cm; height: 53.30 in, 135 cm; ground clearance: 2+1-dr sedans 5 in, 12.6 cm - 4+1-dr sedans 5.10 in, 13 cm - St. wagons 4.70 in, 12 cm; weight: L 2+1-dr Hatchback Sedan 2,077 lb, 942 kg - GL 2+1-dr Hatchback Sedan 2,119 lb, 962 kg - L 4+1-dr Hatchback Sedan 2,130 lb, 966 kg - L 4+1-dr St. Wagon 2,162 lb, 979 kg - GL 4+1-dr Hatchback Sedan 2,172 lb, 984 kg - GL 4+1-dr St. Wagon 2,202 lb, 998 kg - LX 4+1-dr Hatchback Sedan 2,206 lb, 1,001 kg - LX 4+1-dr St. Wagon 2,235 lb, 1,012 kg; weight distribution: 62% front, 38% rear; turning circle: 35.7 ft, 10.9 m; fuel tank: 10.5 imp gal, 13 US gal, 49 l.

BODY saloon/sedan, 2+1 or 4+1 doors - estate car/st. wagon, 4+1 doors; 4 seats, separate front seats; folding rear seat.

OPTIONALS transaxle automatic transmission, hydraulic torque converter and planetary gears with 3 ratios (I 2.790, II 1.610, III 1, rev 1.970), max ratio of converter at stall 2.37, possible manual selection, 3.310 axle ratio; P 185/65 R 365 TRX tyre with 5" wide rims; 380 A battery; 60 A alternator; 3.590 axle ratio; sunroof; speed control; power steering; heavy-duty suspension; reclining backrests; light alloy wheels; servo brake; heavy-duty battery; tilt of steering wheel; digital clock; electric rear window; tinted glass; wiper-washer on rear window; electric door locks.

FORD Escort GT Hatchback Sedan

80 hp power team

See 70 hp power team, except for:

ENGINE max power (SAE net): 80 hp (60 kW) at 5,400 rpm; max torque (SAE net): 88 lb ft, 12.1 kg m (119 Nm) at 3,000 rpm; max engine rpm: 6,000; 50 hp/l (36.8 kW/l); 1 downdraught twin barrel carburettor or electronic fuel injection; fuel feed: mechanical or electric pump.

TRANSMISSION gears: 5, fully synchronized; ratios: I 3.600, II 2.120, III 1.390, IV 1.020, rev 3.620; final drive: 2, hypoid bevel; axle ratio: 2.730.

PERFORMANCE max speed: 94 mph, 152 km/h; power-weight ratio: L 2+1-dr Hatchback Sedan 26.8 lb/hp (36.4 lb/kW), 12.1 kg/hp (16.5 kg/kW); consumption 32.4 m/imp gal, 27 m/US gal, 8.7 l x 100 km.

STEERING servo; turns lock to lock: 3.04.

ELECTRICAL EQUIPMENT 380 A battery (standard).

DIMENSIONS AND WEIGHT weight: L 2+1-dr Hatchback Sedan 2,143 lb, 972 kg - GL 2+1-dr Hatchback Sedan 2,187 lb, 992 kg - L 4+1-dr Hatchback Sedan 2,196 lb, 996 kg - L 4+1-dr St. Wagon 2,224 lb, 1,009 kg - GL 4+1-dr Hatchback Sedan 2,235 lb, 1,014 kg - GL 4+1-dr St. Wagon 2,266 lb, 1,028 kg - LX 4+1-dr Hatchback Sedan 2,273 lb, 1,031 kg - LX 4+1-dr St. Wagon 2,297 lb, 1,042 kg.

120 hp power team

See 70 hp power team, except for:

ENGINE turbocharged; compression ratio: 8:1; max power (SAE net): 120 hp (88 kW) at 5,200 rpm; max torque (SAE net): 120 lb ft, 16.5 kg m (162 Nm) at 3,400 rpm; max engine rpm: 5,700; 75 hp/l (55.2 kW/l); electronic fuel injection; turbocharger.

TRANSMISSION gears: 5, fully synchronized; ratios: I 3.600, II 2.120, III 1.390, IV 1.020, V 1.020, rev 3.620; final drive: 2, hypoid bevel; axle ratio: 2.730.

PERFORMANCE max speed: 111 mph, 178 km/h; power-weight ratio: GT 2+1-dr Hatchback Sedan 18.1 lb/hp (24.5 lb/kW), 8.2 kg/hp (11.1 kg/kW); consumption: 33.6 m/imp gal, 28 m/US gal, 8.4 l x 100 km.

STEERING servo; turns lock to lock: 3.04.

ELECTRICAL EQUIPMENT 410 A battery; 65 A alternator.

DIMENSIONS AND WEIGHT weight: GT 2+1-dr Hatchback Sedan 2,167 lb, 983 kg.

52 hp (diesel) power team

See 70 hp power team, except for:

ENGINE diesel; 121 cu in, 1,999 cc (3.39 x 3.39 in, 86 x 86 mm); compression ratio: 22.5:1; max power (SAE net): 52 hp (38 kW) at 3,600 rpm; max torque (SAE net): 82 lb ft, 11.3 kg m (111 Nm) at 2,400 rpm; max engine rpm: 4,100; 26 hp/l (19.1 kW/l); lubrication: 8.8 imp pt, 10.5 US pt, 5 l; diesel fuel injection.

TRANSMISSION gears: 5, fully synchronized; ratios: I 3.930, II 2.120, III 1.390, IV 0.980, V 0.980, rev 3.620; final drive: 2, hypoid bevel; axle ratio: 3.250 or 2.610.

PERFORMANCE power-weight ratio: L 2+1-dr Hatchback Sedan 42.4 lb/hp (57.6 lb/kW), 19.2 kg/hp (26.1 kg/kW); consumption: 55.3 m/imp gal, 46 m/US gal, 5.1 l x 100 km.

ELECTRICAL EQUIPMENT 950 A x 2 batteries; 60 A alternator (standard).

DIMENSIONS AND WEIGHT weight: L 2+1-dr Hatchback Sedan 2,205 lb, 1,000 kg.

OPTIONALS 65 A alternator.

EXP Series

PRICES EX WORKS:	$
1 2+1-dr Coupé	7,860
2 Turbo 2+1-dr Coupé	10,260

Power team:	Standard for:	Optional for:
80 hp	1	—
120 hp	2	—

80 hp power team

ENGINE front, transverse, 4 stroke; 4 cylinders, in line; 97.6 cu in, 1,599 cc (3.15 x 3.13 in, 80 x 79.5 mm); compression ratio: 9:1; max power (SAE net): 80 hp (60 kW) at 5,400 rpm; max torque (SAE net): 88 lb ft, 12.1 kg m (119 Nm) at 3,000 rpm; max engine rpm: 5,900; 50 hp/l (36.8 kW/l); cast iron block, light alloy head; 5 crankshaft bearings; valves: overhead, Vee-slanted, rockers, hydraulic tappets; camshafts: 1, overhead, cogged belt; lubrication: gear pump, full flow filter, 5.5 imp pt, 7.1 US pt, 3.3 l; 1 Holley downdraught twin barrel carburettor; air cleaner; exhaust system with catalytic converter; fuel feed: mechanical pump; water-cooled, 11.1 imp pt, 13.3 US pt, 6.3 l.

TRANSMISSION driving wheels: front; clutch: single dry plate (diaphragm); gearbox; mechanical; gears: 5, fully synchronized; ratios: I 3.600, II 2.120, III 1.390, IV 1.020, V 1.020, rev 3.620; lever: central; final drive: 2, hypoid bevel; axle ratio: 3.730 or 2.730; width of rims: 5"; tyres: P 165/80 R x 13.

PERFORMANCE max speed: 96 mph, 155 km/h; power-weight ratio: Coupé 27.6 lb/hp (37.5 lb/kW), 12.5 kg/hp (17 kg/kW); consumption: 32.4 m/imp gal, 27 m/US gal, 8.7 l x 100 km.

CHASSIS integral; front suspension: independent, by McPherson, coil springs, anti-roll-bar, telescopic dampers; rear; independent, modified McPherson strut, coil springs, lower arm, telescopic dampers.

STEERING rack-and-pinion; turns lock to lock: 3.50.

BRAKES front disc (diameter 9.25 in, 23.5 cm), front internal radial fins, rear drum, servo; swept area: front 147.4 sq in, 951 sq cm, rear 67.2 sq in, 434 sq cm, total 214.6 sq in, 1,385 sq cm.

ELECTRICAL EQUIPMENT 12 V; 310 A battery; 40 A alternator; Motorcraft transistorized contactless ignition; 2 headlamps.

DIMENSIONS AND WEIGHT wheel base: 94.20 in, 239 cm; tracks: 54.70 in, 139 cm front, 56 in, 142 cm rear; length: 170.30 in, 433 cm; width: 65.90 in, 167 cm; heigh: 50.50 in, 128 cm; ground clearance: 5.30 in, 13.4 cm; weight: 2,212 lb, 1,002 kg; weight distribution: 63% front, 37% rear; turning circle: 35.7 ft, 10.9 m; fuel tank: 10.8 imp gal, 12.9 US gal, 49 l.

BODY coupé; 2+1 doors; 2 seats, separate seats, built-in headrests.

OPTIONALS Transaxle automatic transmission, hydraulic torque converter and planetary gears with 3 ratios (I 2.790, II 1.610, III 1, rev 1.970), max ratio of converter at stall 2.37, possible manual selection; 3.310 axle ratio; power steering; tilt of steering wheel; 380 or 410 A battery; 60 or 65 A alternator; air-conditioning; speed control; wiper-washer on rear window; steering column lever; electric door locks; heavy-duty battery; digital clock; 5.5" wide rims; P 185/65 R x 14 or P 165/70 R x 13 tyres; tinted glass.

FORD EXP Turbo Coupé

120 hp power team

See 80 hp power team, except for:

ENGINE turbocharged; compression ratio: 8.1:1; max power (SAE net): 120 hp (88 kW) at 5,200 rpm; max torque (SAE net): 120 lb ft, 16.6 kg m (163 Nm) at 3,400 rpm; max engine rpm: 5,700; 75 hp/l (55 kW/l); electronic fuel injection.

PERFORMANCE max speed: 99 mph, 159 km/h; power-weight ratio: 18.7 lb/hp (25.4 lb/kW), 8.4 kg/hp (11.5 kg/kW); consumption: 31.3 m/imp gal, 26 m/US gal, 9 l 100 km.

STEERING servo (standard).

ELECTRICAL EQUIPMENT 380 A battery (standard).

DIMENSIONS AND WEIGHT weight: 2,243 lb, 1,017 kg.

FORD Tempo L Sedan

Tempo Series

PRICES EX WORKS:	$
L 2-dr Sedan	**7,330**
L 4-dr Sedan	**7,330**
GL 2-dr Sedan	**7,550**
GL 4-dr Sedan	**7,550**
GLX 2-dr Sedan	**8,019**
GLX 4-dr Sedan	**8,019**

Power team:	Standard for:	Optional for:
84 hp	all	—
52 hp (diesel)	all	—

84 hp power team

ENGINE front, 4 stroke; 4 cylinders, in line; 140 cu in, 2,300 cc (3.70 x 3.30 in, 93.5 x 84 mm); compression ratio: 9:1; max power (SAE net): 84 hp (62 kW) at 4,600 rpm; max torque (SAE net): 118 lb ft, 16.3 kg m (160 Nm) at 2,600 rpm; max engine rpm: 5,100; 36.5 hp/l (26.9 kW/l); cast iron block and head; 5 crankshaft bearings; valves: overhead, Vee-slanted, rockers, hydraulic tappets; camshafts: 1, overhead, cogged belt; lubrication: rotary pump, full flow filter, 6.7 imp pt, 8 US pt, 3.8 l; 1 Holley 800 RPM downdraught single barrel carburettor; fuel feed: mechanical pump; water-cooled, 13.4 imp pt, 16 US pt, 7.6 l.

TRANSMISSION driving wheels: front; clutch: single dry plate; gearbox: mechanical; gears: 4, fully synchronized; ratios: I 3.230, II 1.920, III 1.230, IV 0.810, rev 3.460; lever: central; final drive: hypoid bevel; axle ratio: 3.040; width of rims: 5"; tyres: P 175/80 R x 13.

PERFORMANCE max speed: 96 mph, 154 km/h; power-weight ratio: L 2-dr Sedan 28.5 lb/hp (38.7 lb/kW), 12.9 kg/hp (17.6 kg/kW); consumption: 32.4 m/imp gal, 27 m/US gal, 8.7 l x 100 km.

CHASSIS integral; front suspension: independent, by McPherson, wishbones (lower control arms), coil springs/telescopic damper struts, anti-roll bar; rear: independent, by McPherson, lower trailing radius arms, upper oblique torque arms, coil springs, telescopic dampers.

STEERING rack-and-pinion; turns lock to lock: 3.52.

BRAKES front disc (diameter 9.30 in, 23.5 cm), front internal radial fins, rear compensator, rear drum; swept area: front 147.4 sq in, 951 sq cm, rear 54 sq in, 348 sq cm, total 201.4 sq in, 1,299 sq cm.

ELECTRICAL EQUIPMENT 12 V; 45 Ah battery; 40 A alternator; Motorcraft transistorized contactless ignition; 2 halogen headlamps.

DIMENSIONS AND WEIGHT wheel base: 99.90 in, 254 cm; tracks: 54.70 in, 139 cm front, 57.60 in, 146 cm rear; length: 176.20 in, 447 cm; width: 68.30 in, 173 cm; height: 52.70 in, 134 cm; ground clearance: 5 in, 12.8 cm; weight: L 2-dr Sedan 2,394 lb, 1,086 kg - L 4-dr Sedan 2,443 lb, 1,108 kg - GL 2-dr Sedan 2,418 lb, 1,097 kg - GL 4-dr Sedan 2,465 lb, 1,119 kg - GLX 2-dr Sedan 2,416 lb, 1,096 kg - GLX 4-dr Sedan 2,488 lb, 1,128 kg; turning circle: 38.7 ft, 11.8 m; fuel tank: 11.7 imp gal, 14 US gal, 53 l.

BODY saloon/sedan, 2 or 4 doors; 5 seats, separate front seats, built-in headrests.

OPTIONALS 5-speed fully synchronized mechanical gearbox (I 3.600, II 2.120, III 1.390, IV 1.020, V 1.020, rev 3.620), 3.330 axle ratio; automatic transmission, hydraulic torque converter and planetary gears with 3 ratios(I 2.790, II 1.610, III 1, rev 1.970), max ratio of converter at stall 2.10, possible manual selection; 3.230 axle ratio; P 185/65 R x 13 tyres; heavy-duty battery; vinyl roof; speed control; power steering; heavy-duty suspension; electric seats; electric windows; air-conditioning; tilt of steering wheel; cruise control; metallic spray; sunroof; tinted glass; servo brake.

52 hp (diesel) power team

See 84 hp power team, except for:

ENGINE diesel; 121 cu in, 1,999 cc (3.39 x 3.39 in, 86 x 86 mm); compression ratio: 22.5:1; max power (SAE net): 52 hp (38 kW) at 3,600 rpm; max torque (SAE net): 82 lb ft, 11.3 kg m (111 Nm) at 2,400 rpm; max engine rpm: 4,100; 26 hp/l (19.1 kW/l); cast iron block, light alloy head; lubrication: 8.8 imp pt, 10.6 US pt, 5 l; electronic fuel injection.

TRANSMISSION gears: 5, fully synchronized; ratios: I 3.930, II 2.120, III 1.390, IV 0.980, V 0.980, rev 3.620; final drive: 2, hypoid bevel; axle ratio: 3.730.

PERFORMANCE max speed: 96 mph, 155 km/h; power-weight ratio: L 2-dr Sedan 47.7 lb/hp (64.8 lb/kW), 21.6 kg/hp (29.4 kg/kW); consumption 30 m/imp gal, 25 m/US gal, 9.4 l x 100 km.

ELECTRICAL EQUIPMENT 105 Ah battery.

DIMENSIONS AND WEIGHT weight: L 2-dr Sedan 2,477 lb, 1,124 kg - L 4-dr Sedan 2,536 lb, 1,150 kg - GL 2-dr Sedan 2,501 lb, 1,134 kg - GL 4-dr Sedan 2,560 lb, 1,161 kg - GLX 2-dr Sedan 2,527 lb, 1,146 kg - GLX 4-dr Sedan 2,569 lb, 1,165 kg.

LTD Series

PRICES EX WORKS:	$
1 4-dr Sedan	**9,031**
2 4+1-dr St. Wagon	**10,406**

Power team:	Standard for:	Optional for:
88 hp	1	—
120 hp	both	—
165 hp	1	—

88 hp power team

ENGINE front, 4 stroke; 4 cylinders, in line; 140 cu in, 2,300 cc (3.78 x 3.13 in, 95.9 x 79.5 mm); compression ratio: 9:1; max power (SAE net): 88 hp (64 kW) at 4,000 rpm; max torque (SAE net): 122 lb ft, 16.8 kg m (165 Nm) at 2,400 rpm; max engine rpm: 4,600; 38.2 hp/l (28.1 kW/l); cast iron block and head; 5 crankshaft bearings; valves: overhead, Vee-slanted, rockers, hydraulic tappets; camshafts: 1, overhead, cogged belt; lubrication: rotary pump, full flow filter, 6.7 imp pt, 8 US pt, 3.8 l; 1 Carter downdraught single barrel carburettor; air cleaner; exhaust system with catalytic converter; fuel feed: mechanical pump; water-cooled, 14.4 imp pt, 17.3 US pt, 8.2 l.

TRANSMISSION driving wheels: rear; gearbox: Select-Shift automatic transmission, hydraulic torque converter and planetary gears with 3 ratios, max ratio of converter at stall 2.25, possible manual selection; ratios: I 2.460, II 1.460, III 1, rev 2.190; lever: steering column; final drive: hypoid bevel; axle ratio: 3.270; width of rims: 5"; tyres: P 185/75 R x 14.

PERFORMANCE max speed: 96 mph, 154 km/h; power-weight ratio: 33.9 lb/hp (46 lb/kW), 15.3 kg/hp (20.9 kg/kW); speed in direct drive at 1,000 rpm: 20.9 mph, 33.5 km/h; consumption: 27.6 m/imp gal, 23 m/US gal, 10.2 l x 100 km.

CHASSIS platform with front subframe; front suspension: independent, by McPherson, wishbones (lower control arms), coil springs/telescopic damper struts, anti-roll bar; rear: rigid axle, lower trailing radius arms, upper oblique torque arms, transverse linkage bar, coil springs, telescopic dampers.

STEERING rack-and-pinion, servo; turns lock to lock: 3.05.

BRAKES front disc (diameter 10.06 in, 25.5 cm), front internal radial fins, rear drum, servo; swept area: front 176.6 sq in, 1,140 sq cm, rear 99 sq in, 639 sq cm, total 275.6 sq in, 1,779 sq cm.

ELECTRICAL EQUIPMENT 12 V; 380 A battery; 40 A alternator; Motorcraft transistorized contactless ignition; 4 headlamps.

DIMENSIONS AND WEIGHT wheel base: 105.60 in, 268 cm; tracks: 56.60 in, 144 cm front, 57 in, 145 cm rear; length: 196.50 in, 499 cm; width: 71 in, 180 cm; height: 53.60 in, 136 cm; ground clearance: 4.90 in, 12.5 cm; weight: 2,981 lb, 1,352 kg; turning circle: 3.90 ft, 11.9 m; fuel tank: 13.2 imp gal, 16 US gal, 60 l.

BODY saloon/sedan; 4 doors; 4 seats, separate front seats, reclining backrests, built-in headrests.

OPTIONALS propane engine with 3.080 axle ratio; 3.450 axle ratio; limited slip differential; P 195/75 R x 14 or P 205/75 R x 14 tyres with 5.5" wide rims; central lever; electric windows; heavy-duty suspension; tinted glass; air-conditioning; heated rear window; sunroof; cruise control; metallic spray; two-tone paint.

FORD Tempo GLX Sedan

120 hp power team

See 88 hp power team, except for:

ENGINE 6 cylinders in Vee; 232 cu in, 3,785 cc (3.80 x 3.40 in, 96.8 x 86 mm); compression ratio: 8.6:1; max power (SAE net): 120 hp (88 kW) at 3,600 rpm; max torque (SAE net): 205 lb ft, 28.3 kg m (277 Nm) at 1,600 rpm; max engine rpm: 4,000; 31.7 hp/l (23.3 kW/l); cast iron block, light alloy head; 4 crankshaft bearings; lubrication: 8.2 imp pt, 9.9 US pt, 4.7 l; 1 4-K 700 DR (4-K 650 DR for California only) downdraught twin barrel carburettor or Throttle-body electronic fuel injection; fuel feed: electric pump; cooling: 17.7 imp pt, 21.3 US pt, 10.1 l.

PERFORMANCE max speed: 110 mph, 177 km/h; power-weight ratio: Sedan 25 lb/hp (34 lb/kW), 11.3 kg/hp (15.4 kg/kW); consumption: 24.1 m/imp gal, 20 m/US gal, 11.7 l x 100 km.

ELECTRICAL EQUIPMENT 60 A alternator.

DIMENSIONS AND WEIGHT height: St. Wagon 54.30 in, 13.8 cm; ground clearance: St. Wagon 5.20 in, 13.2 cm; weight: Sedan 3,001 lb, 1,361 kg - St. Wagon 3,123 lb, 1,417 kg.

BODY saloon/sedan, 4 doors - estate car/st. wagon, 4+1 doors.

OPTIONALS Overdrive automatic transmission, hydraulic torque converter and planetary gears with 3 ratios and overdrive (I 2.400, II 1.470, III 1, overdrive 0.670, rev 2), max ratio of converter at stall 2.53, possible manual selection, 3.270 or 3.450 axle ratio.

165 hp power team

See 88 hp power team, except for:

ENGINE 8 cylinders in Vee; 302 cu in, 4,950 cc (4 x 3 in, 101.6 x 76.2 mm); compression ratio: 8.3:1; max power (SAE net): 165 hp (121 kW) at 3,800 rpm; max torque (SAE net): 245 lb ft, 33.8 kg m (331 Nm) at 2,000 rpm; max engine rpm: 4,300; 33.3 hp/l (24.5 kW/l); camshafts: 1, central, lower; lubrication: 8.2 imp pt, 9.9 US pt, 4.7 l; central fuel injection; fuel feed: electric pump; cooling: 17.7 imp pt, 21.3 US pt, 10.1 l.

TRANSMISSION gearbox: Overdrive automatic transmission, hydraulic torque converter and planetary gears with 3 ratios and overdrive, max ratio of converter at stall 2.53, possible manual selection; ratios: I 2.400, II 1.470, III 1, overdrive 0.670, rev 2; axle ratio: 3.080.

PERFORMANCE max speed: 115 mph, 185 km/h; power-weight ratio: 23 lb/hp (31.3 lb/kW), 10.4 kg/hp (14.2 kg/kW); consumption: not declared.

ELECTRICAL EQUIPMENT 455 A battery; 100 A alternator.

DIMENSIONS AND WEIGHT weight: 3,798 lb, 1,723 kg.

Mustang Series

PRICES EX WORKS:	$
1 L 2-dr Hatchback Sedan	7,470
2 L 2+1-dr Hatchback Sedan	7,640
3 LX 2-dr Hatchback Sedan	7,660
4 LX 2+1-dr Hatchback Sedan	7,870
5 LX 2-dr Convertible	12,220
6 GT 2+1-dr Hatchback Sedan	9,950
7 GT 2-dr Convertible	13,420
8 SVO 2+1-dr Hatchback Sedan	15,970

Power team:	Standard for:	Optional for:
88 hp	1 to 4,8	—
120 hp	5	1 to 4
145 hp	7	—
165 hp	6	1 to 4,7
175 hp (2,300 cc)	8	—
175 hp (4,950 cc)	6	1 to 4,7

88 hp power team

ENGINE front, 4 stroke; 4 cylinders, in line; 140 cu in, 2,300 cc (3.78 x 3.12 in, 95.9 x 79.4 mm); compression ratio: 9:1; max power (SAE net): 88 hp (65 kW) at 4,000 rpm; max torque (SAE net): 122 lb ft, 16.8 kg m (165 Nm) at 2,400 rpm; max engine rpm: 4,500; 38.2 hp/l (28.1 kW/l); cast iron block and head; 5 crankshaft bearings; valves: overhead, Vee-slanted, rockers, hydraulic tappets; camshafts: 1, overhead; lubrication: rotary pump, full flow filter, 8.3 imp pt, 9.9 US pt, 4.7 l; 1 Carter downdraught single barrel carburettor; air cleaner; exhaust system with catalytic converter; fuel feed: mechanical pump; water-cooled, 17.1 imp pt, 20.5 US pt, 9.7 l.

TRANSMISSION driving wheels: rear; clutch: single dry plate; gearbox: mechanical; gears: 4, fully synchronized; ratios: I 3.980, II 2.140, III 1.490, IV 1, rev 3.990; lever: central; final drive: hypoid bevel; axle ratio: 3.270 or 3.450; width of rims: 5"; tyres: P 185/75 R x 14.

PERFORMANCE max speed: 96 mph, 154 km/h; power-weight ratio: L 2-dr Hatchback Sedan 43.4 lb/hp (31.9 lb/kW), 14.5 kg/hp (19.7 kg/kW); consumption: 28.8 m/imp gal, 24 m/US gal, 9.8 l x 100 km.

FORD Mustang GT Hatchback Sedan

CHASSIS platform with front subframe; front suspension: independent, by McPherson, wishbones (lower control arms), coil springs/telescopic damper struts, anti-roll bar; rear: rigid axle, lower trailing radius arms, upper oblique torque arms, anti-roll bar, coil springs, telescopic dampers.

STEERING rack-and-pinion; turns lock to lock: 4.08.

BRAKES front disc (diameter 10.06 in, 25.5 cm), front internal radial fins, rear compensator, rear drum; swept area: front 176.6 sq in, 1,140 sq cm, rear 99 sq in, 639 sq cm, total 275.6 sq in, 1,779 sq cm.

ELECTRICAL EQUIPMENT 12 V; 310 A battery; 40 A alternator; Motorcraft transistorized contactless ignition; 4 headlamps.

DIMENSIONS AND WEIGHT wheel base: 100.50 in, 255 cm; tracks: 56.60 in, 144 cm front, 57 in, 145 cm rear - SVO Hatchback Sedan 57.80 in, 147 cm front, 58.30 in, 148 cm rear; length: 179.10 in, 455 cm; width: 69.10 in, 175 cm; heigh: 51.90 in, 132 cm; ground clearance: 4.90 in, 12.5 cm; weight: L 2-dr Hatchback Sedan 2,601 lb, 1,180 kg - L and LX 2+1-dr Hatchback Sedans 2,665 lb, 1,208 kg - LX 2-dr Hatchback Sedan 2,710 lb, 1,229 kg - SVO Hatchback Sedan 2,822 lb, 1,280 kg; turning circle: 37.3 ft, 11.4 m; fuel tank: 12.7 imp gal, 15.4 US gal, 58 l.

BODY saloon/sedan; 2 or 2+1 doors; 4 seats, separate front seats, reclining backrests, built-in headrests.

OPTIONALS Select-Shift C-3 automatic transmission, hydraulic torque converter and planetary gears with 3 ratios (I 2.470, II 1.470, III 1, rev 2.110), max ratio of converter at stall 2.90, central or steering column lever; limited slip differential; P 195/75 R x 14 or P 205/70 R x 14 tyres; heavy-duty suspension; power steering; servo brake; tinted glass; light alloy wheels; air-conditioning; heated rear window; sunroof; T-bar roof; cruise control; metallic spray; two-tone paint.

120 hp power team

See 88 hp power team, except for:

ENGINE 6 cylinders in Vee; 232 cu in, 3,800 cc (3.80 x 3.40 in, 96.8 x 86 mm); compression ratio: 8.6:1; max power (SAE net): 120 hp (88 kW) at 3,600 rpm; max torque (SAE net): 205 lb ft, 28.3 kg m (277 Nm) at 1,600 rpm; max engine rpm: 4,100; 31.5 hp/l (23.2 kW/l); 1 downdraught twin barrel carburettor or Throttle-body electronic fuel injection; fuel feed: mechanical or electric pump; cooling: 20.4 imp pt, 24.5 US pt, 11.6 l.

TRANSMISSION gearbox: Overdrive automatic transmission, hydraulic torque converter and planetary gears with 3 ratios and overdrive; ratios: I 2.400, II 1.470, III 1, overdrive 0.670, rev 2; axle ratio: 3.080.

PERFORMANCE max speed: 98 mph, 157 km/h; power-weight ratio: 25.1 lb/hp (34.4 lb/kW), 11.4 kg/hp (15.6 kg/kW); consumption: 24.1 m/imp gal, 20 m/US gal, 11.7 l x 100 km.

ELECTRICAL EQUIPMENT 380 A battery.

DIMENSIONS AND WEIGHT weight: 3,020 lb, 1,370 kg.

BODY saloon/sedan, 2 or 2+1 doors - convertible, 2 doors.

OPTIONALS 3.450 axle ratio.

FORD Mustang SVO Hatchback Sedan

145 hp power team

See 88 hp power team, except for:

ENGINE turbocharged; compression ratio: 8:1; max power (SAE net): 145 hp (107 kW) at 4,600 rpm; max torque (SAE net): 180 lb ft, 24.8 kg m (244 Nm) at 3,600 rpm; max engine rpm: 5,100; 63 hp/l (46.4 kW/l); lubrication: 8.4 imp pt, 10.1 US pt, 4.8 l; electronic fuel injection; exhaust gas recirculation with catalytic converter; fuel feed: electric pump; cooling: 15.7 imp pt, 18.8 US pt, 8.9 l.

TRANSMISSION gears: 5, fully synchronized; ratios: I 4.030, II 2.370, III 1.500, IV 1, V 0.760, rev 3.760; axle ratio: 3.450.

PERFORMANCE max speed: 99 mph, 159 km/h; power-weight ratio: 20.6 lb/hp (28 lb/kW), 9.3 kg/hp (12.7 kg/kW); consumption: 25.2 m/imp gal, 21 m/US gal, 11.2 l x 100 km.

STEERING servo (standard); turns lock to lock: 3.05.

ELECTRICAL EQUIPMENT 450 A battery; Autolite transistorized contactless ignition.

DIMENSIONS AND WEIGHT weight: 2,987 lb, 1,354 kg.

BODY convertible; 2 doors.

OPTIONALS heavy-duty battery.

165 hp power team

See 88 hp power team, except for:

ENGINE 8 cylinders in Vee; 302 cu in, 4,950 cc (4 x 3 in, 109.7 x 76.2 mm); compression ratio: 8.3:1; max power (SAE net): 165 hp (121 kW) at 3,800 rpm; max torque (SAE net); 245 lb ft, 33.8 kg m (331 Nm) at 2,000 rpm; max engine rpm: 4,400; 33.3 hp/l (24.5 kW/l); electronic fuel injection; fuel feed: electronic pump; cooling: 21.8 imp pt, 26.2 US pt, 12.4 l.

TRANSMISSION Overdrive automatic transmission, hydraulic torque converter and planetary gears with 3 ratios and overdrive; ratios: 1 2.400, II 1.470, III 1, overdrive 0.670, rev 2; axle ratio: 3.270.

PERFORMANCE max speed: 114 mph, 183 km/h; power-weight ratio: GT Hatchback Sedan 17.6 lb/hp (24 lb/kW), 8 kg/hp (10.9 kg/kW); consumption: not declared.

ELECTRICAL EQUIPMENT 450 A battery; 60 A alternator; Autolite transistorized contactless ignition.

DIMENSIONS AND WEIGHT weight: GT Hatchback Sedan 2,910 lb, 1,320 kg.

BODY saloon/sedan, 2 or 2+1 doors - convertible, 2 doors.

175 hp (2,300 cc) power team

See 88 hp power team, except for:

ENGINE turbocharged; compression ratio: 8:1; max power (SAE net): 175 hp (129 kW) at 4,400 rpm; max torque (SAE net): 155 lb ft, 21.4 kg m (210 Nm) at 3,000 rpm; max engine rpm: 4,900; 76 hp/l (56 kW/l); lubrication: 8.4 imp pt, 10.1 US pt, 4.8 l; electronic fuel injection; exhaust gas recirculation with catalytic converter; fuel feed: electric pump; cooling: 15.7 imp pt, 18.8 US pt, 8.9 l.

TRANSMISSION gears: 5, fully synchronized; ratios: I 4.030, II 2.370, III 1.500, IV 1, V 0.760, rev 3.760; axle ratio: 3.450; width of rims: 7"; tyres: P 225/50 R x 16.

PERFORMANCE max speed: 110 mph, 177 km/h; power-weight ratio: 17.1 lb/hp (23.2 lb/kW), 7.7 kg/hp (10.5 kg/kW); acceleration: standing ¼ 15.2 sec, 0-50 mph (0-80 km/h) 5.3 sec; consumption: 25.2 m/imp gal, 21 m/US gal, 11.2 l x 100 km.

STEERING variable rack-and-pinion, servo (standard); turns lock to lock: 3.05.

ELECTRICAL EQUIPMENT 540 A battery; Autolite transistorized contactless ignition.

DIMENSIONS AND WEIGHT weight: 2,992 lb, 1,357 kg.

BODY 2+1 doors.

OPTIONALS heavy-duty battery.

175 hp (4,950 cc) power team

See 88 hp power team, except for:

ENGINE 8 cylinders in Vee; 302 cu in, 4,950 cc (4 x 3 in, 109.7 x 76.2 mm); compression ratio: 8.3:1; max power (SAE net): 175 hp (129 kW) at 4,000 rpm; max torque (SAE net): 245 lb ft, 33.8 kg m (331 Nm) at 2,200 rpm; 35.3 hp/l (26 kW/l); 1 Holley 4180 C downdraught 4-barrel carburettor; cooling: 21.8 imp pt, 26.2 US pt, 12.4 l.

TRANSMISSION gears: 5, fully synchronized; ratios: I 2.950, II 1.940, III 1.340, IV 1, V 0.730, rev 2.760; axle ratio: 3.080.

PERFORMANCE max speed: 117 mph, 188 km/h; power-weight ratio: GT Hatchback Sedan 17.2 lb/hp (23.3 lb/kW), 7.8 kg/hp (10.6 kg/kW); consumption: not declared.

ELECTRICAL EQUIPMENT 310 A battery; 60 A alternator.

DIMENSIONS AND WEIGHT weight: GT Hatchback Sedan 3,013 lb, 1,362 kg.

BODY saloon/sedan, 2 or 2+1 doors - convertible, 2 doors.

OPTIONALS 3.270 axle ratio.

Thunderbird Series

PRICES EX WORKS:	$
1 2-dr Coupé	**10,665**
2 Elan 2-dr Coupé	**13,093**
3 Fila 2-dr Coupé	**14,903**
4 Turbo 2-dr Coupé	**12,762**

Power team:	Standard for:	Optional for:
120 hp	all	—
140 hp	all	—
145 hp	4	—

120 hp power team

ENGINE front, 4 stroke; 6 cylinders in Vee; 231 cu in, 3,797 cc (3.80 x 3.40 in, 96.8 x 86 mm); compression ratio: 8.6:1; max power (SAE net): 120 hp (88 kW) at 3,600 rpm; max torque (SAE net): 205 lb ft, 28.3 kg m (277 Nm) at 1,600 rpm; max engine rpm: 4,100; 31.6 hp/l (23.2 kW/l); cast iron block, light alloy head; 4 crankshaft bearings; valves: overhead, push-rods and rockers; camshafts: 1, at centre of Vee; lubrication: rotary pump, full flow filter, 8.2 imp pt, 9.9 US pt, 4.7 l; 1 4-K 700 DR (4-K 650-DR for California only) downdraught twin barrel carburettor or central fuel injection; air cleaner; exhaust system with catalytic converter; fuel feed: mechanical pump; water-cooled, 20.4 imp pt, 24.5 US pt, 11.6 l.

TRANSMISSION driving wheels: rear; gearbox: Select-Shift automatic transmission, hydraulic torque converter and planetary gears with 3 ratios, max ratio of converter at stall 2.25, possible manual selection; ratios: I 2.460, II 1.460, III 1, rev 2.190; lever: steering column; final drive: hypoid bevel; axle ratio: 2.730; width of rims: 5"; tyres: P 195/75 R x 14.

PERFORMANCE max speed: 116 mph, 187 km/h; power-weight ratio: 25.6 lb/hp (34.7 lb/kW), 11.6 kg/hp (15.7 kg/kW); speed in direct drive at 1,000 rpm: 31.2 mph, 50.2 km/h; consumption: 24.1 m/imp gal, 20 m/US gal, 11.7 l x 100 km.

CHASSIS integral with two cross members; front suspension: independent, by McPherson, wishbones (lower control arm), anti-roll bar, coil springs, telescopic dampers; rear: rigid axle, lower trailing radius arms, upper oblique arms, coil springs, telescopic dampers.

FORD Thunderbird Coupé

STEERING rack-and-pinion, servo; turns lock to lock: 3.05.

BRAKES front disc (diameter 10.06 in, 25.5 cm), front internal radial fins, rear compensator, rear drum, servo; swept area: front 176.6 sq in, 1,140 sq cm, rear 99 sq in, 638 sq cm, total 275.6 sq in, 1,778 sq cm.

ELECTRICAL EQUIPMENT 12 V; 380 A battery; 40 A alternator; Motorcraft transistorized ignition; 4 headlamps.

DIMENSIONS AND WEIGHT wheel base: 103.80 in, 264 cm; tracks: 58.10 in, 148 cm front, 58.50 in, 149 cm rear; length: 197.60 in, 502 cm; width: 71.10 in, 181 cm; height: 53.20 in, 135 cm; ground clearance: 4.80 in, 12.2 cm; weight: Coupé 3,069 lb, 1,392 kg - Elan 3,163 lb, 1,434 kg; turning circle: 12.1 ft, 39.4 m; fuel tank: 17.4 imp gal, 21 US gal, 79 l.

BODY coupé; 2 doors; 5 seats, separate front seats, built-in headrests.

OPTIONALS Overdrive automatic transmission, hydraulic torque converter and planetary gears with 3 ratios and overdrive (I 2.400, II 1.470, III 1, overdrive 0.670, rev 2), steering column lever, 3.270 or 3.450 axle ratio; consumption 25.2 m/imp gal, 21 m/US gal, 11.2 l x 100 km; 3.080 axle ratio; central lever: P 205/70 R x 14 WSW - P 205/70 R x 14 BSW - P 20/55 R x 390 BSW tyres; 60 A alternator; heavy-duty battery; automatic air-conditioning; tilt of steering wheel; speed control; electric windows; electric defroster rear window; sunroof; heavy-duty suspension; vinyl roof; simulate convertible roof; tinted glass; limited slip differential; halogen headlamps; heavy-duty radiator.

140 hp power team

See 120 hp power team, except for:

ENGINE 8 cylinders in Vee; 302 cu in, 4,950 cc (4 x 3 in, 101.6 x 76.2 mm); compression ratio: 8.4:1; max power (SAE net): 140 hp (103 kW) at 3,200 rpm; max torque (SAE net): 250 lb ft, 34.5 kg m (338 Nm) at 1,600 rpm; max engine rpm: 3,700; 28.3 hp/l (20.8 kW/l); cast iron block and head; 5 crankshaft bearings; camshafts: 1, central, lower; lubrication: gear pump, full flow filter, oil cooler, 6.7 imp pt, 8 US pt, 3.8 l; throttle-body fuel injection; fuel feed: electric pump; cooling: 22.2 imp pt, 26.6 US pt, 12.6 l.

TRANSMISSION (standard) gearbox: Overdrive automatic transmission, hydraulic torque converter and planetary gears with 3 ratios and overdrive, max ratio of converter at stall 2.30, possible manual selection; ratios: I 2.400, II 1.470, III 1, overdrive 0.670, rev 2; lever: central; axle ratio: 3.080.

PERFORMANCE max speed: 102 mph, 164 km/h; power-weight ratio: Coupé 11.2 lb/hp (31.1 lb/kW), 10.3 kg/hp (14.1 kg/kW); consumption: 21.7 m/imp gal, 18 m/US gal, 13 l x 100 km.

ELECTRICAL EQUIPMENT 450 A battery; 60 A alternator (standard).

DIMENSIONS AND WEIGHT weight: Coupé 3,203 lb, 1,453 kg - Elan and Fila 3,247 lb, 1,473 kg.

145 hp power team

See 120 hp power team, except for:

ENGINE turbocharged; 4 cylinders, in line; 140 cu in, 2,300 cc (3.78 x 3.13 in, 95.9 x 79.5 mm); compression ratio: 8:1; max power (SAE net): 145 hp (107 kW) at 4,600 rpm; max torque (SAE net): 180 lb ft, 24.8 kg m (243 Nm) at 3,600 rpm; max engine rpm: 5,100; 63 hp/l (46.4 kW/l); cast iron block and head; 5 crankshaft bearings; lubrication: 7.6 imp pt, 9.1 US pt, 4.3 l; electronic fuel injection; turbocharger; cooling: 15.7 imp pt, 18.8 US pt, 8.9 l.

TRANSMISSION clutch: single dry plate; gearbox: mechanical; gears: 5, fully synchronized; ratios: I 4.030, II 2.370, III 1.490, IV 1, V 0.860, rev 3.760; lever: central; axle ratio: 3.450.

PERFORMANCE max speed: 113 mph, 183 km/h; power-weight ratio: 15.5 lb/hp (21.1 lb/kW), 9.6 kg/hp (13 kg/kW); consumption: 25.2 m/imp gal, 21 m/US gal, 11.2 l x 100 km.

ELECTRICAL EQUIPMENT 450 A battery; 60 A alternator (standard).

DIMENSIONS AND WEIGHT weight: 3,073 lb, 1,394 kg.

OPTIONALS Select-Shift automatic transmission, hydraulic torque converter and planetary gears with 3 ratios (I 2.470, II 1.470, III 1, rev 2.110), central lever, 3.450 axle ratio.

FORD Thunderbird Turbo Coupé

FORD LTD Crown Victoria Sedan

LTD Crown Victoria / Country Squire Series

PRICES EX WORKS:	$
Crown Victoria 2-dr Sedan	11,430
Crown Victoria 4-dr Sedan	11,430
Country Squire 4+1-dr St. Wagon	11,590

Power team:	Standard for:	Optional for:
140 hp	all	—
155 hp	all	—
180 hp	all	—

140 hp power team

ENGINE front, 4 stroke; 8 cylinders in Vee; 302 cu in, 4,950 cc (4 x 3 in, 101.6 x 76.2 mm); compression ratio: 8.4:1; max power (SAE net): 140 hp (103 kW) at 3,200 rpm; max torque (SAE net): 250 lb ft, 34.5 kg m (338 Nm) at 1,600 rpm; max engine rpm: 3,700; 28.3 hp/l (20.8 kW/l); cast iron block and head; 5 crankshaft bearings; valves: overhead, Vee-slanted, rockers, hydraulic tappets; camshafts: 1, overhead, cogged belt; lubrication: gear pump, full flow filter, 8.2 imp pt, 9.9 US pt, 4.7 l; throttle-body electronic fuel injection; exhaust system with catalytic converter; fuel feed: mechanical pump; water-cooled, 22.2 imp pt, 26.6 US pt, 12.6 l.

TRANSMISSION driving wheels: rear; gearbox: Overdrive automatic transmission, hydraulic torque converter and planetary gears with 3 ratios and overdrive, max ratio of converter at stall 2.28, possible manual selection; ratios: I 2.400, II 1.470, III 1, overdrive 0.670, rev 2; lever: steering column; final drive: hypoid bevel; axle ratio: 3.080; width of rims: 6.5"; tyres: P 215/75 R x 14.

PERFORMANCE max speed: 105 mph, 169 km/h; power-weight ratio: 2-dr Sedan 26.4 lb/hp (35.8 lb/kW), 11.9 kg/hp (16.3 kg/kW); consumption: 20.4 m/imp gal, 17 m/US gal, 13.8 l x 100 km.

CHASSIS platform with front subframe; front suspension: independent, wishbones (lower control arms), coil spring/telescopic damper struts, anti-roll bar; rear: rigid axle, lower trailing radius arms, upper oblique torque arms, transverse linkage bar, anti-roll bar, coil springs, telescopic dampers.

STEERING recirculating ball, servo; turns lock to lock: 3.40.

BRAKES front disc, front internal radial fins, rear compensator, rear drum, servo; swept area: front 228.7 sq in, 1,475 sq cm, rear 157.1 sq in, 1,013 sq cm, total 385.8 sq in, 2,488 sq cm - St. Wagon front 228.6 sq in, 1,474 sq cm, rear 155.9 sq in, 1,005 sq cm, total 384.5 sq in, 2,479 sq cm.

ELECTRICAL EQUIPMENT 12 V; 450 A battery; 60 A alternator; Motorcraft transistorized contactless ignition; 4 headlamps.

DIMENSIONS AND WEIGHT wheel base: 114.30 in, 290 cm; tracks: 62.20 in, 158 cm front, 62 in, 157 cm rear; length: 211 in, 536 cm - St. Wagon 215 in, 546 cm; width: 77.50 in, 197 cm - St. Wagon 79.30 in, 201 cm; height: 2-dr Sedan 55.30 in, 140 cm - 4-dr Sedan 55.20 in, 140 cm - St. Wagon 56.80 in, 144 cm; ground clearance: 5.20 in, 13.1 cm; weight: Crown Victoria 2-dr Sedan 3,689 lb, 1,674 kg - Crown Victoria 4-dr Sedan 3,730 lb, 1,692 kg - Crown Victoria St. Wagon 3,936 lb, 1,786 kg; fuel tank: 16.7 imp gal, 20 US gal, 76 l.

BODY saloon/sedan; 2 or 4 doors - estate car/st. wagon, 4+1 doors; 6 seats, separate front seats, built-in headrests.

OPTIONALS 3.550 axle ratio; tilt of steering wheel; electric windows; limited slip differential; 225/75 R x 14 or P 205/75 R x 15 tyres; (for sedans only) heavy-duty suspension; tinted glass; light alloy wheels; air-conditioning; heated rear window; sunroof; T-bar roof; cruise control; metallic spray; two-tone paint; speed control; heavy-duty radiator; (for St. Wagon only) luggage rack; 100 A alternator; digital clock.

155 hp power team

See 140 hp power team, except for:

ENGINE max power (SAE net): 155 hp (114 kW) at 3,600 rpm; max torque (SAE net): 265 lb ft, 36.6 kg m (359 Nm) at 2,000 rpm; max engine rpm: 4,200; 31.3 hp/l (23 kW/l); 1 downdraught twin barrel carburettor.

PERFORMANCE max speed: 106 mph, 171 km/h; power-weight ratio: 2-dr Sedan 24.1 lb/hp (32.8 lb/kW), 10.9 kg/hp (14.9 kg/kW); consumption: not declared.

DIMENSIONS AND WEIGHT weight: Crown Victoria 2-dr Sedan 3,735 lb, 1,695 kg - Crown Victoria 4-dr Sedan 3,776 lb, 1,713 kg - Country Squire St. Wagon 3,970 lb, 1,801 kg.

180 hp power team

See 140 hp power team, except for:

ENGINE 351 cu in, 5,753 cc (4 x 3.50 in, 101.6 x 88.9 mm); compression ratio: 8.3:1; max power (SAE net): 180 hp (132 kW) at 3,600 rpm; max torque (SAE net): 285 lb ft, 39.3 kg m (386 Nm) at 2,400 rpm; max engine rpm: 4,300; 31.4 hp/l (23 kW/l); 1 downdraught carburettor with Variable Venturi; cooling: 29.3 imp pt, 28.8 US pt, 13.6 l.

TRANSMISSION max ratio of converter at stall 1.95; axle ratio: 2.730.

PERFORMANCE max speed: 115 mph, 185 km/h; power-weight ratio: 2-dr Sedan 20.9 lb/hp (28.4 lb/kW), 9.4 kg/hp (12.9 kg/kW); consumption: not declared.

ELECTRICAL EQUIPMENT 475 A battery.

DIMENSIONS AND WEIGHT weight: Crown Victoria 2-dr Sedan 3,765 lb, 1,708 kg - Crown Victoria 4-dr Sedan 3,806 lb, 1,727 kg - Country Squire St. Wagon 4,012 lb, 1,820 kg.

ITD USA

Stiletto

PRICE EX WORKS: $ 29,500

ENGINE Chevrolet, front, 4 stroke; 8 cylinders in Vee; 305 cu in, 4,999 cc (3.74 x 3.48 in, 95 x 88.4 mm); compression ratio: 9:1; max power (DIN): 190 hp (140 kW) at 4,800 rpm; max torque (DIN): 240 lb ft, 33.1 kg m (325 Nm) at 3,200 rpm; max engine rpm: 5,200; 38 hp/l (28 kW/l); cast iron block and head; 5 crankshaft bearings; valves: overhead, in line, push-rods and rockers, hydraulic tappets; camshafts: 1, at centre of Vee; lubrication: mechanical pump, 10 imp pt, 12 US pt, 5.7 l; 1 Rochester Quadrajet downdraught 4-barrel carburettor; fuel feed: electric pump; water-cooled, 20 imp pt, 24 US pt, 11.3 l.

TRANSMISSION driving wheels: rear; gearbox: Turbo-Hydramatic automatic transmission, hydraulic torque converter and planetary gears with 3 ratios and overdrive, max ratio of converter at stall 1.90, possible manual selection; ratios: I 3.060, II 1.630, III 1, overdrive 0.790, rev 2.070; lever: central; axle ratio: 3.730; width of rims: 7"; tyres: P 215/65 R x 15.

PERFORMANCE max speed: 130 mph, 209 km/h; power-weight ratio: 18.4 lb/hp (25 lb/kW), 8.3 kg/hp (11.4 kg/kW); consumption: not declared.

CHASSIS integral; front suspension: independent, by McPherson, wishbones, anti-roll bar, coil springs/telescopic dampers struts; rear: torque tube, Panhard rod, coil springs, telescopic dampers.

STEERING recirculating ball, servo; turns lock to lock: 2.50.

BRAKES front disc, internal radial fins, rear drum, servo.

ELECTRICAL EQUIPMENT 12 V; Delco-Remy high energy ignition; 2 retractable headlamps.

FORD Ltd Country Squire Station Wagon

ITD Stiletto

STILETTO

DIMENSIONS AND WEIGHT wheel base: 112.50 in, 286 cm; tracks: 60.70 in, 154 cm front, 61.60 in, 156 cm rear; length: 203.50 in, 517 cm; width: 72.10 in, 183 cm; height: 48.50 in, 123 cm; ground clearance: 7 in, 18 cm; weight: 3,500 lb, 1,588 kg; weight distribution: 58.4% front, 41.6% rear; fuel tank: 16 imp gal, 19.2 US gal, 73 l.

BODY coupé; 2 doors; 4 seats, separate front seats, built-in headrests; tinted glass; heated rear window.

OPTIONALS 5-speed fully synchronized mechanical gearbox (I 2.950, II 1.940, III 1.340, IV 1, V 0.730); cruise control, electric windows; heavy-duty cooling.

JEEP CJ-7 Laredo Roadster

JEEP USA

CJ-7 Roadster

PRICE EX WORKS: $ 6,995

84 hp power team

(standard)

ENGINE front, 4 stroke; 4 cylinders, in line; 150.4 cu in, 2,466 cc (3.88 x 3.19 in, 98.4 x 81 mm); compression ratio: 9.2:1; max power (DIN): 84 hp (62 kW) at 3,600 rpm; max torque (DIN): 125 lb ft, 17.2 kg m (169 Nm) at 2,600 rpm; max engine rpm: 4,100; 34 hp/l (25.1 kW/l); cast iron block and head; 5 crankshaft bearings; valves: overhead, in line, push-rods and rockers, hydraulic tappets; camshafts: 1, side; lubrication: gear pump, full flow filter, 6.7 imp pt, 8 US pt, 3.8 l; 1 Holley 5210 downdraught twin barrel carburettor; air cleaner; exhaust system with catalytic converter; fuel feed: mechanical pump; water-cooled, 17.8 imp pt, 21.4 US pt, 10.1 l.

TRANSMISSION driving wheels: front (automatically-engaged with transfer box low ratio) and rear; clutch: single dry plate; gearbox: mechanical; gears: 4, fully synchronized; ratios: I 4.030, II 2.370, III 1.500, IV 1, rev 3.760; lever: central; final drive: hypoid bevel; axle ratio: 3.540; width of rims: 5.5''; tyres: P 255/75 D 15.

PERFORMANCE max speed: 78 mph, 125 km/h; power-weight ratio: 31.1 lb/hp (42.2 lb/kW), 14 kg/hp (19 kg/kW); speed in direct drive at 1,000 rpm: 15 mph, 25 km/h; consumption: 27.5 m/imp gal, 23 m/US gal, 10.2 l x 100 km.

CHASSIS perimeter box-type with cross members; front suspension: rigid axle, semi-elliptic leafsprings, anti-roll bar, telescopic dampers; rear: rigid axle, semi-elliptic leafsprings, telescopic dampers.

STEERING recirculating ball; turns lock to lock: 5.25.

BRAKES front disc (diameter 11.75 in, 29.8 cm), internal radial fins, rear drum, servo.

ELECTRICAL EQUIPMENT 12 V; 55 Ah battery; 42 A alternator; electronic ignition; 2 headlamps.

DIMENSIONS AND WEIGHT wheel base: 93.50 in, 237 cm; tracks: 51.50 in, 131 cm front, 50 in, 127 cm rear; length: 153.20 in, 389 cm; width: 68.60 in, 174 cm; height: 67.60 in, 172 cm; ground clearance: 6.90 in, 17.4 cm; weight: 2,603 lb, 1,183 kg; turning circle: 35.9 ft, 10.9 m; fuel tank: 12.5 imp gal, 15 US gal, 57 l.

BODY roadster; no doors; 4 seats, separate front seats.

OPTIONALS 5-speed fully synchronized mechanical gearbox (I 4.030, II 2.370, III 1.500, IV 1, V 0.860, rev 3.760); Turbo-Hydramatic automatic transmission, hydraulic torque converter and planetary gears with 3 ratios (I 2.710, II 1.550, III 1, rev 2.200), possible manual selection, 4.090 axle ratio; rear limited slip differential; sports steering wheel; power steering with 4 turns lock to lock; all or half metal top; Scrambler, Renegade, Laredo and Pick-up equipment with luxury interior; rear bench seats; heavy-duty suspension; light alloy wheels; racing style roll bar, heavy-duty cooling and L 78 x 15 tyres with 7'' wide rims; styled steel wheels; bench rear seats with H 78 x 15 G or 9 x 15 tyres and 2+1 doors; full plastic top; sunroof; heavy-duty battery.

110 hp power team

(optional)

See 84 hp power team, except for:

ENGINE 6 cylinders, in line; 258 cu in, 4,228 cc (3.75 x 3.90 in, 95.2 x 99 mm); max power (DIN): 110 hp (81 kW) at 3,000 rpm; max torque (DIN): 205 lb ft, 28.3 kg m (277 Nm) at 1,800 rpm; max engine rpm: 3,600; 26 hp/l (19.1 kW/l); 7 crankshaft bearings; lubrication: 10 imp pt, 12 US pt, 5.7 l; 1 downdraught twin barrel carburettor; cooling: 17.4 imp pt, 21 US pt, 9.9 l.

TRANSMISSION axle ratio: 2.730.

PERFORMANCE max speed: 80 mph, 128 km/h; power-weight ratio: 25 lb/hp (34 lb/kW), 11.3 kg/hp (15.4 kg/kW); speed in direct drive at 1,000 rpm: 23.6 mph, 38 km/h; consumption: 21.6 m/imp gal, 18 m/US gal, 13.1 l x 100 km.

DIMENSIONS AND WEIGHT weight: 2,750 lb, 1,250 kg.

OPTIONALS 3.310 axle ratio.

Cherokee / Wagoneer Series

PRICES EX WORKS:	$
Cherokee Sport 2+1-dr Wagon	**9,995**
Cherokee Sport 4+1-dr Wagon	**10,295**
Wagoneer Sport 4+1-dr Wagon	**12,444**
Wagoneer Sport Limited 4+1-dr Wagon	**17,076**

Power team:	Standard for:	Optional for:
105 hp	all	—
112 hp	all	—

105 hp power team

ENGINE front, 4 stroke; 4 cylinders, in line; 151 cu in, 2,475 cc (3.88 x 3.19 in, 98.4 x 81 mm); compression ratio: 9.2:1; max power (DIN): 105 hp (77 kW) at 5,000 rpm; max torque (DIN): 132 lb ft, 18.2 kg m (179 Nm) at 3,000 rpm; max engine rpm: 5,500; 42.4 hp/l (31.2 kW/l); cast iron block and head; 5 crankshaft bearings; valves: overhead, in line, push-rods and rockers, hydraulic tappets; camshafts: 1, side; lubrication: gear pump, full flow filter, 6.7 imp pt, 8 US pt, 3.8 l; 1 downdraught single barrel carburettor; air cleaner; exhaust system with catalytic converter; fuel feed: mechanical pump; water-cooled, 17.8 imp pt, 21.4 US pt, 10.1 l.

TRANSMISSION driving wheels: front and rear (Quadra-Trac system with central limited slip differential); clutch: single dry plate; gearbox: mechanical; gears: 4, fully synchronized; ratios: I 3.930, II 2.330, III 1.540, IV 1, rev 3.760; lever: central; final drive: hypoid bevel; axle ratio: 3.310; width of rims: 6''; tyres: P 195/75 R x 15.

PERFORMANCE max speed: 90 mph, 145 km/h; power-weight ratio: Cherokee Sport 2+1-dr Wagon 27.5 lb/hp (37.4 lb/kW), 12.5 kg/hp (16.9 kg/kW); consumption: 27.6 m/imp gal, 23 m/US gal, 10.2 l x 100 km.

CHASSIS perimeter box-type with cross members; front and rear suspension: rigid axle, semi-elliptic leafsprings, anti-roll bar, telescopic dampers.

STEERING recirculating ball, variable ratio, servo; turns lock to lock: 3.50.

BRAKES front disc, rear drum, servo.

ELECTRICAL EQUIPMENT 12 V; 58 Ah battery; 56 A alternator; electronic ignition; 2 headlamps.

DIMENSIONS AND WEIGHT wheel base: 101.40 in, 258 cm; front and rear track: 57 in, 145 cm; length: 165.30 in, 420 cm; width: 69.30 in, 176 cm; height: 64.10 in, 163 cm; ground clearance: 8.70 in, 22.2 cm; weight: Cherokee Sport 2+1-dr Wagon 2,886 lb, 1,310 kg; turning circle: 36.1 ft, 11 m; fuel tank: 11.2 imp gal, 13.5 US gal, 51 l.

BODY estate car/st. wagon; 2+1 or 4+1 doors; 5 seats, separate front seats.

OPTIONALS (standard for Wagoneer Sport Wagon) 5-speed fully synchronized mechanical gearbox, consumption 28.8 m/imp gal, 24 m/US gal, 9.8 l x 100 km; (standard for Wagoneer Sport Limited Wagon) Turbo-Hydramatic automatic transmission, hydraulic torque converter and planetary gearx with 3 ratios (I 2.740, II 1.550, III 1, rev 2.200), possible manual selection, 3.730 axle ratio, consumption 25.2 m/imp gal, 21 m/US gal, 11.2 l x 100 km; rear limited slip differential; light alloy wheels; sports steering wheel; tilt of steering wheel; De Luxe interior; heavy-duty cooling; heavy-duty suspension; tinted glass; heated rear window; air-conditioning; Pioneer, Chief, or Laredo equipment; electric sunroof; fuel tank 16.5 imp gal, 20 US gal, 75 l.

112 hp power team

See 105 hp power team, except for:

JEEP Grand Wagoneer

ENGINE 8 cylinders in Vee; 173 cu in, 2,837 cc (3.50 x 2.99 in, 88.9 x 76 mm); compression ratio: 8.5:1; max power (DIN): 112 hp (82 kW) at 4,800 rpm; max torque (DIN): 145 lb ft, 20 kg m (196 Nm) at 2,100 rpm; 39.5 hp/l (29 kW/l); 1 downdraught twin barrel carburettor.

PERFORMANCE max speed: 92 mph, 148 km/h; power-weight ratio: Cherokee Sport 2+1-dr Wagon 25.7 lb/hp (35 lb/kW), 11.7 kg/hp (15.9 kg/kW); consumption: 22.9 m/imp gal, 19 m/US gal, 12.3 l x 100 km.

Grand Wagoneer

PRICE EX WORKS: $ 19,306

110 hp power team

(standard)

ENGINE front, 4 stroke; 6 cylinders, in line; 258 cu in, 4,228 cc (3.75 x 3.90 in, 95.2 x 99 mm); compression ratio: 9.2:1; max power (DIN): 110 hp (82 kW) at 3,000 rpm; max torque (DIN): 205 lb ft, 28.3 kg m (277 Nm) at 1,800 rpm; max engine rpm: 4,000; 26 hp/l (19.1 kW/l); cast iron block and head; 7 crankshaft bearings; valves: overhead, in line, push-rods and rockers, hydraulic tappets; camshafts: 1, side; lubrication: gear pump, full flow filter, 10 imp pt, 12 US pt, 5.7 l; 1 Carter downdraught twin barrel carburettor; fuel feed: mechanical pump; water-cooled, 17.4 imp pt, 21 US pt, 9.9 l.

TRANSMISSION driving wheels: front and rear (Quadra-Trac system with central limited slip differential); gearbox: Turbo-Hydramatic automatic transmission, hydraulic torque converter and planetary gears with 3 ratios, max ratio of converter at stall 2.3, possible manual selection; ratios: I 2.450, II 1.550, III 1, rev 2.200; lever: central; final drive: hypoid bevel; axle ratio: 2.730; width of rims: 7"; tyres: P 225/75 R x 15.

PERFORMANCE max speed: 90 mph, 145 km/h; power-weight ratio: 38.5 lb/hp (52.3 lb/kW), 17.4 kg/hp (23.7 kg/kW); carrying capacity: 1,058 lb, 480 kg; speed in direct drive at 1,000 rpm: 22.5 mph, 36.2 km/h; consumption: 20.4 m/imp gal, 17 m/US gal, 13.8 l x 100 km.

CHASSIS perimeter box-type cross members; front suspension: rigid axle, semi-elliptic leafsprings, telescopic dampers; rear: rigid axle, semi-elliptic leafsprings, anti-roll bar, telescopic dampers.

STEERING recirculating ball, variable ratio, servo; turns lock to lock: 3.50.

BRAKES front disc (diameter 12 in, 30 cm), rear drum, servo.

ELECTRICAL EQUIPMENT 12 V; 55 Ah battery; 56 A alternator; electronic ignition; 2 headlamps.

DIMENSIONS AND WEIGHT wheel base: 108.70 in, 276 cm; tracks: 59.40 in, 151 cm front, 57.80 in, 147 cm rear; length: 186.40 in, 473 cm; width: 74.80 in, 190 cm; height: 66.70 in, 169 cm; ground clearance: 7.20 in, 18.3 cm; weight: 4,221 lb, 1,919 kg; turning circle: 37.7 ft, 11.5 m; fuel tank: 16.9 imp gal, 20.3 US gal, 77 l.

BODY estate car/st. wagon; 4+1 doors; 6 seats, bench front seats; folding rear seat; luxury equipment.

OPTIONALS 4- or 5-speed fully synchronized mechanical gearbox; 3.310 axle ratio; light alloy wheels; tilt of steering wheel; 70 Ah battery; heavy-duty cooling; heavy-duty suspension; tinted glass; heated rear window; air-conditioning; electric sunroof; heavy-duty battery.

JEEP Cherokee Sport Pioneer Wagon

KELMARK GT

144 hp power team

(optional)

See 110 hp power team, except for:

ENGINE 8 cylinders in Vee; 360 cu in, 5,899 cc (4.08 x 3.44 in, 103.6 x 87.3 mm); compression ratio: 8.2:1; max power (DIN): 144 hp (106 kW) at 3,200 rpm; max torque (DIN): 280 lb ft, 38.4 kg m (379 Nm) at 1,500 rpm; max engine rpm: 3,500; 24.4 hp/l (18 kW/l); 5 crankshaft bearings; camshafts: 1, at centre of Vee; lubrication: 8.3 imp pt, 9.9 US pt, 4.7 l; air cleaner; cooling: 21.6 imp pt, 26 US pt, 12.3 l.

PERFORMANCE max speed: 99 mph, 159 km/h; power-weight ratio: 31 lb/hp (42.1 lb/kW), 14 kg/hp (19.1 kg/kW); speed in direct drive at 1,000 rpm: 26.4 mph, 42.5 km/h.

KELMARK USA

GT

PRICE EX WORKS: $ 14,800

ENGINE Volkswagen, rear, 4 stroke; 4 cylinders, horizontally opposed; 102.4 cu in, 1,679 cc (3.54 x 2.60 in, 90 x 66 mm); compression ratio: 8.5:1; max power (DIN): 100 hp (74 kW) at 5,000 rpm; max torque (DIN): 110 lb ft, 13.8 kg m (135 Nm) at 3,500 rpm; max engine rpm: 5,500; 59.6 hp/l (43.8 kW/l); light alloy block and head, separate cylinders with Ferral chromium walls; 4 crankshaft bearings; valves: overhead, in line, push-rods and rockers; camshafts: 1, central, lower; lubrication: gear pump, filter in sump, oil cooler, 6.2 imp pt, 7.4 US pt, 3.5 l; 2 Weber downdraught carburettors; fuel feed: electric pump; air-cooled.

TRANSMISSION driving wheels: rear; clutch: single dry plate (diaphragm), hydraulically controlled; gearbox: mechanical; gears: 4, fully synchronized; ratios: I 3.560, II 2.060, III 1.250, IV 0.890; lever: central; final drive: hypoid bevel; width of rims: front 7", rear 8.5"; tyres: ER60 x 14 front, GR50 x 15 rear.

PERFORMANCE max speed: 125 mph, 201 km/h; power-weight ratio: 17 lb/hp (23.1 lb/kW), 7.7 kg/hp (10.5 kg/kW); speed in top at 1,000 rpm: 24.9 mph, 40 km/h; consumption: 42.2 m/imp gal, 35 m/US gal, 6.7 l x 100 km.

CHASSIS backbone platform; front suspension: independent, twin swinging longitudinal trailing arms, transverse laminated torsion bars, anti-roll bar, telescopic dampers; rear: independent, swinging semi-axles, swinging longitudinal trailing arms, transverse torsion bars, telescopic dampers.

STEERING rack-and-pinion.

BRAKES front disc, rear drum.

ELECTRICAL EQUIPMENT 12 V; 43 Ah battery; alternator; Bosch distributor; 2 headlamps.

DIMENSIONS AND WEIGHT wheel base: 95 in, 241 cm; tracks: 58 in, 147 cm front, 60 in, 152 cm rear; length: 174 in, 442 cm; width: 73 in, 185 cm; height: 45 in, 114 cm; ground clearance: 7 in, 17.8 cm; weight: 1,700 lb, 771 kg; weight distribution: 40% front, 60% rear; fuel tank: 8.4 imp gal, 10 US gal, 38 l.

BODY coupé, in plastic material; 2 doors; 2 seats.

OPTIONALS light alloy wheels; air-conditioning; sunroof; leather upholstery; fog lamps.

LINCOLN USA

Continental / Designer Series

PRICES EX WORKS:	$
Continental 4-dr Sedan	22,293
Designer Valentino 4-dr Sedan	24,741
Designer Givenchy 4-dr Sedan	24,766

Power team:	Standard for:	Optional for:
140 hp	all	—
115 hp (diesel)	—	all

140 hp power team

ENGINE front, 4 stroke; 8 cylinders in Vee; 302 cu in, 4,950 cc (4 x 3 in, 101.6 x 76.2 mm); compression ratio: 8.4:1; max power (SAE net): 140 hp (103 kW) at 3,200 rpm; max torque (SAE net): 250 lb ft, 34.5 kg m (338 Nm) at 1,600 rpm; max engine rpm: 3,700; 28.3 hp/l (20.8 kW/l); cast iron block and head; 5 crankshaft bearings; valves: overhead, in line, push-rods and rockers; camshafts: 1, central, lower; lubrication: gear pump, full flow filter, oil cooler, 8.3 imp pt, 9.9 US pt, 4.7 l; throttle-body electronic fuel injection; air cleaner; exhaust system with catalytic converter; fuel feed: electric pump; water-cooled, 22.2 imp pt, 26.6 US pt, 12.6 l.

TRANSMISSION driving wheels: rear; gearbox: automatic transmission, hydraulic torque converter and planetary gears with 3 ratios and overdrive, max ratio of converter at stall 2.28, possible manual selection; ratios: I 2.400, II 1.470, III 1, overdrive 0.670, rev 2; lever: steering column; final drive: hypoid bevel; axle ratio: 3.080 - California 3.270; width of rims: 5.5"; tyres: P 215/70 R x 15.

PERFORMANCE max speed: 100 mph, 161 km/h; power-weight ratio: Continental 26.8 lb/hp (36.4 lb/kW), 12.1 kg/hp (16.5 kg/kW); carrying capacity: 882 lb, 400 kg; speed in overdrive/top at 1,000 rpm: 24.5 mph, 38.9 km/h; consumption: 20.2 m/imp gal, 16.8 m/US gal, 14 l x 100 km.

CHASSIS integral box-type ladder frame; front suspension: independent, modified McPherson system, coil springs, anti-roll bar, lower trailing arms, telescopic dampers; rear: rigid axle, upper and lower trailing arms, coil springs, anti-roll bar, telescopic dampers.

STEERING rack-and-pinion, servo; turns lock to lock: 3.05.

BRAKES disc (front diameter 10.91 in, 27.7 cm, rear 11.20 in, 28.6 cm), internal radial fins, servo; swept area: front 221.6 sq in, 1,429 sq cm, rear 210.4 sq in, 1,357 sq cm, total 432 sq in, 2,786 sq cm.

ELECTRICAL EQUIPMENT 12 V; 71 Ah battery; 70 A alternator; Motorcraft contactless transistorized ignition; 4 headlamps.

DIMENSIONS AND WEIGHT wheel base: 108.60 in, 276 cm; tracks: 58.40 in, 148 cm front, 59 in, 150 cm rear; length: 200.70 in, 510 cm; width: 73.60 in, 187 cm; height: 55.50 in, 141 cm; ground clearance: 5.60 in, 14.3 cm; weight: Continental Sedan 3,750 lb, 1,701 kg - Designer sedans 3,782 lb, 1,716 kg; weight distribution: 54% front, 46% rear; fuel tank: 18.5 imp gal, 22.3 US gal, 84 l.

BODY saloon/sedan; 4 doors; 5 seats, separate front seats, built-in headrests; electric windows; electric front seats; air-conditioning; tinted glass.

OPTIONALS limited slip differential; heavy-duty battery; electric glass; sunroof; leather upholstery; light alloy wheels; halogen headlamps.

LINCOLN Continental Sedan

LINCOLN Mark VII Sedan

115 hp (diesel) power team

See 140 hp power team, except for:

ENGINE BMW, turbocharged, diesel; 6 cylinders, in line; 147 cu in, 2,400 cc (3.15 x 3.19 in, 80 x 81 mm); compression ratio: 23:1; max power (SAE net): 115 hp (85 kW) at 4,800 rpm; max torque (SAE net): 155 lb ft, 21.4 kg m (210 Nm) at 2,400 rpm; max engine rpm: 5,200; 47.9 hp/l (35.4 kW/l); cast iron block, light alloy head; 4 crankshaft bearings; camshafts: 1, at centre of Vee; lubrication: 8.8 imp pt, 10.5 US pt, 5 l; turbocharger; cooling: 19.5 imp pt, 23.4 US pt, 11.1 l.

TRANSMISSION max ratio of converter at stall 2.57; ratios: I 2.730, II 1.560, III 1, overdrive 0.730, rev 2.090; lever: central or steering column; axle ratio: 3.730.

PERFORMANCE max speed: 90 mph, 145 km/h; power-weight ratio: Continental 32.6 lb/hp (44.1 lb/kW), 14.9 kg/hp (20 kg/kW); consumption: 30 m/imp gal, 25 m/US gal, 9.4 l x 100 km.

Mark VII Series

PRICES EX WORKS:	$
2-dr Sedan	22,231
Bill Blass Designer 2-dr Sedan	25,331
Versace Designer 2-dr Sedan	24,930
LSC 2-dr Sedan	24,230

Power team:	Standard for:	Optional for:
140 hp	all	—
115 hp (diesel)	—	all

140 hp power team

ENGINE front, 4 stroke; 8 cylinders in Vee; 302 cu in, 4,950 cc (4 x 3 in, 101.6 x 76.2 mm); compression ratio: 8.4:1; max power (SAE net): 140 hp (103 kW) at 3,200 rpm; max torque (SAE net): 250 lb ft, 34.5 kg m (338 Nm) at 1,600 rpm; max engine rpm: 3,700; 28.3 hp/l (20.8 kW/l); cast iron block and head; 5 crankshaft bearings; valves: overhead, in line, push-rods and rockers; camshafts: 1, at centre of Vee; lubrication: gear pump, full flow filter, oil cooler, 8.3 imp pt, 9.9 US pt, 4.7 l; throttle-body electronic fuel injection; air cleaner; exhaust system with catalytic converter; fuel feed: electric pump; water-cooled, 22.2 imp pt, 26.6 US pt, 12.6 l.

TRANSMISSION driving wheels: rear; gearbox: automatic transmission, hydraulic torque converter and planetary gears with 3 ratios and overdrive, max ratio of converter at stall 2.28, possible manual selection; ratios: I 2.400, II 1.470, III 1, overdrive 0.670, rev 2; lever: steering column; final drive: hypoid bevel; axle ratio: 3.080 - California 3.270; width of rims: 5.5"; tyres: P 215/70 R x 15.

PERFORMANCE max speed: 100 mph, 161 km/h; power-weight ratio: Sedan 25.9 lb/hp (35.2 lb/kW), 11.7 kg/hp (15.9 kg/kW); carrying capacity: 882 lb, 400 kg; speed in overdrive/top at 1,000 rpm: 24.5 mph, 38.9 km/h; consumption: 20.2 m/imp gal, 16.8 m/US gal, 14 l x 100 km.

CHASSIS integral; front suspension: independent, modified McPherson system, coil springs, anti-roll bar, lower trailing arms, telescopic dampers; rear: rigid axle, upper and lower trailing arms, coil springs, anti-roll bar, telescopic dampers.

STEERINO recirculating ball, servo; turns lock to lock: 3.05.

BRAKES front disc, rear drum, internal radial fins, servo; swept area: front 228.7 sq in, 1,475 sq cm, rear 157.1 sq in, 1,013 sq cm, total 385.8 sq in, 2,488 sq cm.

ELECTRICAL EQUIPMENT 12 V; 71 Ah battery; 70 A alternator; 4 headlamps.

DIMENSIONS AND WEIGHT wheel base: 108.50 in, 276 cm; tracks: 58.40 in, 148 cm front, 59 in, 150 cm rear; length: 202.80 in, 515 cm; width: 70.90 in, 180 cm; height: 54.20 in, 137 cm; ground clearance: 5.60 in, 14.3 cm; weight: Sedan 3,625 lb, 1,644 kg - Designer sedans 3,691 lb, 1,800 kg - LSC Sedan 3,653 lb, 1,600 kg; weight distribution: 57% front, 43% rear; fuel tank: 15 imp gal, 18 US gal, 68 l.

BODY saloon/sedan; 2 doors; 6 seats, separate front seats, built-in headrests; tinted glass; electric windows; air-conditioning.

OPTIONALS electric glass moonroof; electric mirrors; P205/75R x 15 W/WSW tyres with 6.5" wide rims; digital instrument panel; electric seats; keyless entry system; sunroof; automatic garage door opening; (for California only) 3.080 axle ratio; (for LSC only) 3.270 axle ratio.

115 hp (diesel) power team

See 140 hp power team, except for:

ENGINE BMW, turbocharged, diesel; 6 cylinders, in line; 147 cu in, 2,400 cc (3.15 x 3.19 in, 80 x 81 mm); compression ratio: 23:1; max power (SAE net): 115 hp (85 kW) at 4,800 rpm; max torque (SAE net): 155 lb ft, 21.4 kg m (210 Nm) at 3,400 rpm; max engine rpm: 5,200; 47.9 hp/l (35.4 kW/l); cast iron block, light alloy head; 4 crankshaft bearings; camshafts: 1, central, lower; lubrication: 8.8 imp pt, 10.5 US pt, 5 l; turbocharger; cooling: 19.5 imp pt, 23.4 US pt, 11.1 l.

TRANSMISSION max ratio of converter at stall 2.57; ratios: I 2.730, II 1.560, III 1, overdrive 0.730, rev 2.090; lever: central or steering column; axle ratio: 3.730.

PERFORMANCE max speed: 90 mph, 145 km/h; power-weight ratio: Sedan 31.5 lb/hp (42.6 lb/kW), 14.3 kg/hp (19.3 kg/kW); consumption: 30 m/imp gal, 25 m/US gal, 9.4 l x 100 km.

Town Car / Signature / Designer Series

PRICES EX WORKS:	$
Town Car 4-dr Sedan	18,595
Signature 4-dr Sedan	20,564
Designer 4-dr Sedan	22,230

Power team:	Standard for:	Optional for:
140 hp	all	—
155 hp	all	—

140 hp power team

ENGINE front, 4 stroke; 8 cylinders in Vee; 302 cu in, 4,950 cc (4 x 3 in, 101.6 x 76.2 mm); compression ratio: 8.4:1; max power (SAE net): 140 hp (103 kW) at 3,200 rpm; max torque (SAE net): 250 lb ft, 34.5 kg m (338 Nm) at 1,600 rpm; max engine rpm: 3,700; 28.3 hp/l (20.8 kW/l); cast iron block and head; 5 crankshaft bearings; valves: overhead, in line, push-rods and rockers; camshafts: 1, central, lower; lubrication: gear pump, full flow filter, 8.3 imp pt, 9.9 US pt, 4.7 l; throttle-body fuel injection; air cleaner; exhaust system with catalytic converter; fuel feed: electric pump; water-cooled, 22.2 imp pt, 26.6 US pt, 12.6 l.

TRANSMISSION driving wheels: rear; gearbox: automatic transmission, hydraulic torque converter and planetary gears with 3 ratios and overdrive, max ratio of converter at stall 2.28, possible manual selection; ratios: I 2.400, II 1.470, III 1, overdrive 0.670, rev 2; lever: steering column; final drive: hypoid bevel; axle ratio: 3.080; width of rims: 6"; tyres: P 215/70 R x 15.

PERFORMANCE max speed: 100 mph, 161 km/h; power-weight ratio: Town Car 29 lb/hp (39.4 lb/kW), 13.1 kg/hp (17.9 kg/kW); carrying capacity: 882 lb, 400 kg; speed in overdrive top at 1,000 rpm: 22.5 mph, 38.9 km/h; consumption: 20.2 m/imp gal, 16.8 m/US gal, 14 l x 100 km.

CHASSIS integral; front suspension: independent, modified McPherson system, coil springs, anti-roll bar, lower trailing arms, anti-roll bar, telescopic dampers; rear: rigid axle,

LINCOLN Town Car Sedan

MERCURY Lynx L Hatchback Sedan

upper and lower trailing arms, coil springs, anti-roll bar, telescopic dampers.

STEERING recirculating ball, servo; turns lock to lock: 3.4.

BRAKES front disc, rear drum, internal radial fins, servo; swept area: front 228.7 sq in, 1,475 sq cm, rear 157.1 sq in, 1,013 sq cm, total 432 sq in, 2,786 sq cm.

ELECTRICAL EQUIPMENT 12 V; 71 Ah battery; 60 A alternator; 4 headlamps.

DIMENSIONS AND WEIGHT wheel base: 117.30 in, 298 cm; tracks: 62.20 in, 158 cm front, 62 in, 157 cm rear; length: 219 in, 556 cm; width: 78.10 in, 198 cm; height: 55.90 in, 142 cm; ground clearance: 14.1 in, 5.60 cm; weight: Town Car Sedan 4,062 lb, 1,843 kg - Designer Sedan 4,073 lb, 1,848 kg - Signature Sedan 4,104 lb, 1,862 kg; weight distribution: 54% front, 46% rear; turning circle: 40 ft, 12.2 m; fuel tank: 15 imp gal, 18 US gal, 68.1 l.

BODY saloon/sedan; 4 doors; 6 seats, separate front seats, built-in headrests; electric windows; electric front seats; air-conditioning; tinted glass.

OPTIONALS electric glass moonroof; electric mirrors; P205/75 x 15 W/WSW tyres with 6.5" wide rims; digital instrument panel; electric seats; tilt of steering wheel; electric door locks; keyless entry system; automatic garage door opening; Cartier equipment; 3.550 axle ratio.

155 hp power team

See 140 hp power team, except for:

ENGINE max power (SAE net): 155 hp (114 kW) at 3,600 rpm; max torque (SAE net): 265 lb ft, 36.5 kgm (358 Nm) at 2,000 rpm; max engine rpm: 4,100; 31.3 hp/l (23 kW/l); 1 downdraught twin barrel carburettor or throttle-body fuel injection; fuel feed: mechanical or electric pump.

PERFORMANCE max speed: 104 mph, 168 km/h; power-weight ratio: Town Car 26.5 lb/hp (36 lb/kW), 12 kg/hp (16.3 kg/kW); consumption: 19.2 m/imp gal, 16 m/US gal, 14.7 l x 100 km.

DIMENSIONS AND WEIGHT weight: Town Car Sedan 4,107 lb, 1,863 kg - Designer Sedan 4,119 lb, 1,868 kg - Signature Sedan 4,149 lb, 1,882 kg.

MERCURY USA

Lynx Series

PRICES EX WORKS:	$
L 2+1-dr Hatchback Sedan	6,066
L 4+1-dr Hatchback Sedan	6,541
L 4+1-dr St. Wagon	6,756
GS 2+1-dr Hatchback Sedan	6,803
GS 4+1-dr Hatchback Sedan	7,017
GS 4+1-dr St. Wagon	7,195
RS 2+1-dr Hatchback Sedan	7,949
LTS 4+1-dr Hatchback Sedan	8,187

Power team:	Standard for:	Optional for:
70 hp	all	—
80 hp	all	—
84 hp	all	—
120 hp	all	—
52 hp (diesel)	all	—

70 hp power team

ENGINE front, transverse, 4 stroke; 4 cylinders, in line; 97.6 cu in, 1,599 cc (3.15 x 3.13 in, 80 x 79.5 mm); compression ratio: 9:1; max power (SAE net): 70 hp (51 kW) at 4,600 rpm; max torque (SAE net): 88 lb ft, 12.1 kg m (119 Nm) at 2,600 rpm; max engine rpm: 5,100; 43.7 hp/l (32.2 kW/l); cast iron block, light alloy head; 5 crankshaft bearings; valves: overhead, Vee-slanted, rockers, hydraulic tappets; camshafts: 1, overhead, cogged belt; lubrication: gear pump, full flow filter, 5.8 imp pt, 7 US pt, 3.3 l; 1 Holley downdraught twin barrel carburettor; air cleaner; exhaust system with catalytic converter; fuel feed: mechanical pump; water-cooled, 11.1 imp pt, 13.3 US pt, 6.3 l.

TRANSMISSION driving wheels: front; clutch: single dry plate; gearbox: mechanical; gears: 4, fully synchronized; ratios: I 3.580, II 2.050, III 1.230, IV 0.810, rev 3.460 - (not available in California) I 3.230, II 1.900, III 1.230, IV 0.810, rev 3.460; lever: central; final drive: hypoid bevel; axle ratio: 3.590 - (not available in California) 3.040; width of rims: 4.5"; tyres: P 165/80 R x 13.

PERFORMANCE max speed: 90 mph, 145 km/h; power-weight ratio: L 2+1-dr Hatchback Sedan 29.8 lb/hp (40.5 lb/kW), 13.5 kg/hp (18.3 kg/kW); consumption: 32.4 m/imp gal, 27 m/US gal, 8.7 l x 100 km.

CHASSIS integral; front suspension: independent, by McPherson, coil springs, anti-roll bar, telescopic dampers; rear: independent, modified McPherson strut, coil springs, lower arm, telescopic dampers.

STEERING rack-and-pinion; turns lock to lock: 3.50.

BRAKES front disc (diameter 9.29 in, 23.6 cm), front internal radial fins, rear drum; swept area: front 147.4 sq in, 951 sq cm, rear 54 sq in, 348 sq cm, total 201.4 sq in, 1,299 sq cm.

ELECTRICAL EQUIPMENT 12 V; 310 Ah battery; 40 A alternator; Motorcraft transistorized contactless ignition; 2 headlamps.

DIMENSIONS AND WEIGHT wheel base: 94.20 in, 239 cm; tracks: 54.70 in, 139 cm front, 56 in, 142 cm rear; length: sedans 163.90 in, 416 cm - st. wagons 165 in, 419 cm; width: 65.90 in, 167 cm; height: 2+1-dr sedans 53.30 in, 135 cm - 4+1-dr sedans 53.40 in, 136 cm - st. wagons 53.30 in, 135 cm; ground clearance: 2+1-dr sedans 5 in, 12.6 cm - 4+1-dr sedans 5.10 in, 13 cm - st. wagons 4.70 in, 12 cm; weight: L 2+1-dr Hatchback Sedan 2,084 lb, 946 kg - L 4+1-dr Hatchback Sedan 2,136 lb, 969 kg - L St. Wagon 2,167 lb, 981 kg - GS 2+1-dr Hatchback Sedan 2,125 lb, 964 kg - GS 4+1-dr Hatchback Sedan 2,177 lb, 984 kg - GS St. Wagon 2,206 lb, 990 kg - RS Hatchback Sedan 2,174 lb, 987 kg - LTS Hatchback Sedan 2,172 lb, 985 kg; weight distribution: 62% front, 38% rear; fuel tank: 10.7 imp gal, 13 US gal, 49 l.

BODY saloon/sedan, 2+1 or 4+1 doors - estate car/st. wagon, 4+1 doors; 4 seats, separate front seats; folding rear seats.

OPTIONALS transaxle automatic transmission, hydraulic torque converter and planetary gears with 3 ratios (I 2.790, II 1.610, III 1, rev 1.970), max ratio of converter at stall 2.37, possible manual selection; 5 or 5.5" wide rims; P 185/65 R x 13; air-conditioning; heavy-duty radiator; sunroof; speed control; power steering; servo brake; heavy-duty suspension; wiper-washer on rear window; light alloy wheels; 45 A alternator; heavy-duty battery; heated rear window; tinted glass; electric door locks; digital clock; tilt of steering wheel.

MERCURY Lynx GS Station Wagon

80 hp power team

See 70 hp power team, except for:

ENGINE max power (SAE net): 80 hp (60 kW) at 5,400 rpm; max torque (SAE net): 88 lb ft, 12.1 kg m (119 Nm) at 3,000 rpm; max engine rpm: 6,000; 50 hp/l (36.8 kW/l).

TRANSMISSION gears: 5, fully synchronized; ratios: I 3.600, II 2.120, III 1.390, IV 1.020, V 1.020, rev 3.620; axle ratio: 3.730 or 2.730.

PERFORMANCE power-weight ratio: L 2+1-dr Hatchback Sedan 26.1 lb/hp (35.4 lb/kW), 11.8 kg/hp (16 kg/kW).

OPTIONALS 60 A alternator.

84 hp power team

See 70 hp power team, except for:

ENGINE max power (SAE net): 84 hp (62 kW) at 5,200 rpm; max torque (SAE net): 90 lb ft, 12.4 kg m (122 Nm) at 2,800 rpm; max engine rpm: 5,700; 52.5 hp/l (38.6 kW/l); electronic fuel injection; fuel feed: electric pump.

TRANSMISSION gears: 5, fully synchronized; ratios: I 3.600, II 2.120, III 1.390, IV 1.020, V 1.020, rev 3.620; axle ratio: 3.730 or 2.730.

PERFORMANCE power-weight ratio: L 2+1-dr Hatchback Sedan 24.8 lb/hp (33.7 lb/kW), 11.2 kg/hp (15.3 kg/kW).

OPTIONALS 60 A alternator.

120 hp power team

See 70 hp power team, except for:

ENGINE compression ratio: 8:1; max power (SAE net): 120 hp (88 kW) at 5,200 rpm; max torque (SAE net): 120 lb ft, 16.5 kg m (162 Nm) at 3,400 rpm; max engine rpm: 5,700; 75 hp/l (55 kW/l); electronic fuel injection; fuel feed: electric pump.

TRANSMISSION gears: 5, fully synchronized; ratios: I 3.600, II 2.120, III 1.390, IV 1.020, V 1.020, rev 3.620; axle ratio: 3.730 or 2.730.

PERFORMANCE max speed: 99 mph, 160 km/h; power-weight ratio: L 2+1-dr Hatchback Sedan 17.4 lb/hp (23.7 lb/kW), 7.9 kg/hp (10.7 kg/kW); consumption: 33.6 m/imp gal, 28 m/US gal, 8.4 l x 100 km.

ELECTRICAL EQUIPMENT 410 A battery; 60 A alternator.

OPTIONALS 65 A alternator.

52 hp (diesel) power team

See 70 hp power team, except for:

ENGINE diesel; 121.3 cu in, 1,989 cc (3.39 x 3.39 in, 86 x 86 mm); compression ratio: 22.5:1; max power (SAE net): 52 hp (38 kW)at 3,600 rpm; max torque (SAE net): 90 lb ft, 12.4 kg m (122 Nm) at 2,800 rpm; max engine rpm: 4,100; 26.1 hp/l (19.2 kW/l); lubrication: 8.8 imp pt, 10.5 US pt, 5 l; fuel injection.

TRANSMISSION gears: 5, fully synchronized; ratios: I 3.930, II 2.120, III 1.390, IV 0.980, V 0.980, rev 3.620; axle ratio: 3.520 or 2.610.

PERFORMANCE max speed: 85 mph, 136 km/h; power-weight ratio: L 2+1-dr Hatchback Sedan 40.1 lb/hp (54.5 lb/kW), 18.2 kg/hp (24.7 kg/kW); consumption: 55.3 m/imp gal, 46 m/US gal, 5.1 l x 100 km.

ELECTRICAL EQUIPMENT 950 A battery; 60 A alternator.

OPTIONALS 65 A alternator.

Topaz Series

PRICES EX WORKS:	$
GS 2-dr Sedan	7,875
GS 4-dr Sedan	7,875
LS 2-dr Sedan	8,278
LS 4-dr Sedan	8,278

Power team:	Standard for:	Optional for:
84 hp	all	—
52 hp (diesel)	all	—

84 hp power team

ENGINE front, 4 stroke; 4 cylinders, transverse, vertical, in line; 140 cu in, 2,300 cc (3.70 x 3.30 in, 93.5 x 84 mm); compression ratio: 9:1; max power (SAE net): 84 hp (62 kW) at 4,600 rpm; max torque (SAE net): 118 lb ft, 16.3 kg m (159 Nm) at 2,600 rpm; max engine rpm: 5,100; 36.5 hp/l (26.8 kW/l); cast iron block and head; 5 crankshaft bearings; valves: overhead, Vee-slanted, rockers; camshafts: 1, overhead, cogged belt; lubrication: gear pump, full flow filter, 6.7 imp pt, 8 US pt, 3.8 l; 1 Holley downdraught single barrel carburettor; fuel feed: mechanical pump; water-cooled, 13.9 imp pt, 16.4 US pt, 7.8 l.

TRANSMISSION driving wheels: front; clutch: single dry plate; gearbox: mechanical; gears: 4, fully synchronized; ratios: I 3.230, II 1.920, III 1.230, IV 0.810, rev 3.460; lever: central; final drive: helical spur gears; axle ratio: 3.040; width of rims: 5"; tyres: P 175/80 R x 13.

PERFORMANCE max speed: 100 mph, 161 km/h; power-weight ratio: GS 2-dr Sedan 29 lb/hp (39.5 lb/kW), 13.1 kg/hp (17.9 kg/kW); consumption: 32.4 m/imp gal, 27 m/US gal, 8.7 l x 100 km.

CHASSIS integral; front suspension: independent, by McPherson, lower wishbones (control arm), coil springs, anti-roll bar, telescopic dampers; rear: independent, by McPherson strut, lower arm, upper oblique torque arms, coil springs, telescopic dampers.

STEERING rack-and-pinion; turns lock to lock: 3.52.

BRAKES front disc, front internal radial fins, rear drum, servo; swept area: front 147.4 sq in, 951 sq cm, rear 54 sq in, 348 sq cm, total 201.4 sq in, 1,299 sq cm.

ELECTRICAL EQUIPMENT 12 V; 380 A battery; Motorcraft transistorized contactless ignition; 2 headlamps.

DIMENSIONS AND WEIGHT wheel base: 99.90 in, 254 cm; tracks: 54.70 in, 139 cm front, 57.60 in, 146 cm rear; length: 176.2 in, 447 cm; width: 68.30 in, 173 cm; height: 52.70 in, 134 cm; ground clearance: 5 in, 12.7 cm; weight: GS 2-dr Sedan 2,438 lb, 1,106 kg - GS 4-dr Sedan 2,522 lb, 1,142 kg - LS 2-dr Sedan 2,462 lb, 1,115 kg - LS 4-dr Sedan 2,543 lb, 1,147 kg; turning circle: 38.7 ft, 11.8 m; fuel tank: 11.6 imp gal, 14 US gal, 53 l.

BODY saloon/sedan; 2 or 4 doors; 5 seats, separate seats, built-in headrests.

OPTIONALS 5-speed fully synchronized mechanical gearbox (I 3.600, II 2.120, III 1.390, IV 1.020, V 1.020, rev 3.620), 3.330 axle ratio; transaxle automatic transmission, hydraulic torque converter and planetary gears with 3 ratios (I 2.790, II 1.610, III 1, rev 1.970), max ratio of converter at stall 2.10, possible manual selection, 3.230 axle ratio; P 185/65 R x 13; heavy-duty battery; sunroof; speed control; power steering; heavy-duty suspension; electric seats; electric windows; air-conditioning; servo brake; tilt of steering wheel.

52 hp (diesel) power team

See 84 hp power team, except for:

ENGINE 121 cu in, 1,985 cc (3.39 x 3.39 in, 86 x 86 mm); compression ratio: 22.5:1; max power (SAE net): 52 hp (38 kW)at 3,600 rpm; max torque (SAE net): 82 lb ft, 11.3 kg m (111 Nm) at 2,400 rpm; max engine rpm: 4,000; 26.2 hp/l (19.3 kW/l); cast iron block, light alloy head; lubrication: 8.8 imp pt, 10.5 US pt, 5 l; fuel injection.

MERCURY Topaz GS Sedan

TRANSMISSION (standard) gears: 5, fully synchronized; ratios: I 3.930, II 2.120, III 1.390, IV 0.980, V 0.980, rev 3.620; axle ratio: 3.730.

PERFORMANCE max speed: 87 mph, 140 km/h; power-weight ratio: GS 2-dr Sedan 46.9 lb/hp (63.7 lb/kW), 21.2 kg/hp (28.9 kg/kW); consumption: 49.5 m/imp gal, 41 m/US gal, 5.7 l x 100 km.

ELECTRICAL EQUIPMENT 105 Ah battery.

DIMENSIONS AND WEIGHT fuel tank: 12.7 imp gal, 15.3 US gal, 38 l.

Marquis Series

PRICES EX WORKS:	$
1 4-dr Sedan	9,153
2 4+1-dr St. Wagon	9,650

Power team:	Standard for:	Optional for:
88 hp	1	—
120 hp	both	—

88 hp power team

ENGINE front, 4 stroke; 4 cylinders, in line; 140 cu in, 2,300 cc (3.78 x 3.12 in, 96 x 79.4 mm); compression ratio: 9:1; max power (SAE net): 88 hp (65 kW) at 4,000 rpm; max torque (SAE net): 122 lb ft, 16.8 kg m (165 Nm) at 2,400 rpm; max engine rpm: 4,500; 38.2 hp/l (28.1 kW/l); cast iron block and head; 5 crankshaft bearings; valves: overhead, Vee-slanted, rockers; camshafts: 1, overhead, cogged belt; lubrication: rotary pump, full flow filter, 8.3 imp pt, 9.9 US pt, 4.7 l; 1 Carter downdraught single barrel carburettor; fuel feed: mechanical pump; water-cooled, 14.4 imp pt, 17.3 US pt, 8.2 l.

TRANSMISSION driving wheels: rear; gearbox: Select-Shift C-3 automatic transmission, hydraulic torque converter and planetary gears with 3 ratios, max ratio of converter at stall 2.90, possible manual selection; ratios: I 2.470, II 1.470, III 1, rev 2.110; lever: steering column; final drive: hypoid bevel; axle ratio: 3.270 or 3.450; width of rims: 5"; tyres: P 185/75 R x 14.

PERFORMANCE max speed: 96 mph, 154 km/h; power-weight ratio: Sedan 33.9 lb/hp (46.1 lb/kW), 15.4 kg/hp (20.9 kg/kW); consumption: 27.6 m/imp gal, 23 m/US gal, 10.2 l x 100 km.

CHASSIS integral; front suspension: independent, by McPherson, wishbones (lower control arms), coil springs/telescopic damper struts, anti-roll bar; rear: rigid axle, lower trailing radius arms, upper oblique torque arms, coil springs, telescopic dampers.

STEERING rack-and-pinion, servo; turns lock to lock: 3.05.

BRAKES front disc, front internal radial fins, rear drum, servo; swept area: front 176.6 sq in, 1,140 sq cm, rear 98.9 sq in, 638 sq cm, total 275.5 sq in, 1,778 sq cm.

ELECTRICAL EQUIPMENT 12 V; 380 A battery; 40 A alternator; Motorcraft transistorized contactless ignition; 4 headlamps.

DIMENSIONS AND WEIGHT wheel base: 105.60 in, 268 cm; tracks: 56.60 in, 144 cm front, 57 in, 145 cm rear; length: 196.50 in, 499 cm, width: 71 in, 180 cm; height: 53.60 in, 136 cm; ground clearance: 4.90 in, 12.5 cm; weight: 2,988 lb, 1,355 kg; turning circle: 39 ft, 11.9 m; fuel tank: 13.2 imp gal, 16 US gal, 60 l.

BODY saloon/sedan; 4 doors; 5 seats, separate front seats.

VARIATIONS

(propane engine)
TRANSMISSION 3.080 axle ratio.
ELECTRICAL EQUIPMENT 54 Ah battery.

OPTIONALS 70 A alternator; electric windows; electric seats; digital clock; speed control; electric door locks; P 195/75 R x 14 tyres; air-conditioning; rear window wiper-washer; electric clock; heated rear window; heavy-duty suspension; light alloy wheels; vinyl roof; tilt of steering wheel; trip computer; tinted glass; heavy-duty battery; metallic spray.

120 hp power team

See 88 hp power team, except for:

MERCURY Marquis Sedan

MERCURY Marquis Station Wagon

ENGINE 6 cylinders, slanted at Vee; 232 cu in, 3,797 cc (3.80 x 3.40 in, 96.8 x 86 mm); compression ratio: 8.6:1; max power (SAE net): 120 hp (88 kW) at 3,600 rpm; max torque (SAE net): 205 lb ft, 28.3 kg m (277 Nm) at 1,600 rpm; max engine rpm: 4,100; 31.6 hp/l (23.3 kW/l); cast iron block, light alloy head; 4 crankshaft bearings; valves: overhead, in line, push-rods and rockers; camshafts: 1, at centre of Vee, chain-driven, 1 495-4K 700 DR - (for California only) 4K 650 DR downdraught twin barrel carburettor or throttle-body fuel injection; air cleaner; exhaust system with catalytic converter; fuel feed: electric pump; cooling: 17.8 imp pt, 21.4 US pt, 10.1 l.

TRANSMISSION automatic transmission, hydraulic torque converter and planetary gears with 3 ratios, max ratio of converter at stall 2.25, possible manual selection; ratios: I 2.460, II 1.460, III 1, rev 2.190; axle ratio: 2.730 or 3.080; width of rims: (for St. Wagon only) 5.5".

PERFORMANCE max speed: 102 mph, 180 km/h; power-weight ratio: Sedan 24.9 lb/hp (33.9 lb/kW), 11.3 kg/hp (15.3 kg/kW); consumption: 24.1 m/imp gal, 20 m/US gal, 11.7 l x 100 km.

ELECTRICAL EQUIPMENT 60 A alternator.

DIMENSIONS AND WEIGHT weight: Sedan 3,005 lb, 1,363 kg - St. Wagon 3,128 lb, 1,419 kg.

BODY saloon/sedan, 4 doors - estate car/st. wagon, 4+1 doors.

OPTIONALS Overdrive automatic transmission, hydraulic torque converter and planetary gears with 3 ratios and overdrive, 3.270 or 3.450 axle ratio, central lever.

Capri Series

PRICES EX WORKS:	$
1 GS 2+1-dr Hatchback Coupé	8,132
2 RS 2+1-dr Hatchback Coupé	10,196

Power team:	Standard for:	Optional for:
88 hp	both	—
120 hp	both	—
165 hp	both	—
175 hp (2,300 cc)	2	—
175 hp (4,950 cc)	both	—

88 hp power team

ENGINE front, 4 stroke; 4 cylinders, in line; 140 cu in, 2,300 cc (3.78 x 3.12 in, 96 x 79.4 mm); compression ratio: 9:1; max power (SAE net): 88 hp (65 kW) at 4,000 rpm; max torque (SAE net): 122 lb ft, 16.8 kg m (165 Nm) at 2,400 rpm; max engine rpm: 4,500; 38.2 hp/h (28.1 kW/l); cast iron block and head; 5 crankshaft bearings; valves: overhead, Vee-slanted, rockers; camshafts: 1, overhead, cogged belt; lubrication: rotary pump, full flow filter, 8.3 imp pt, 9.9 US pt, 4.7 l; 1 downdraught single barrel carburettor; fuel feed: mechanical pump; water-cooled, 34.7 imp pt, 41.6 US pt, 9.7 l.

TRANSMISSION driving wheels: rear; clutch: single dry plate; gearbox: mechanical; gears: 4, fully synchronized; ratios: I 3.980, II 2.140, III 1.490, IV 1, rev 3.990; lever: central; final drive: hypoid bevel; axle ratio: 3.080; width of rims: 5"; tyres: P 185/75 R x 14.

PERFORMANCE max speed: 96 mph, 154 km/h; power-weight ratio: 31.7 lb/hp (43.1 lb/kW), 14.3 kg/hp (19.5 kg/kW); consumption: 28.8 m/imp gal, 24 m/US gal, 9.8 l x 100 km.

CHASSIS integral; front suspension: independent, by McPherson, wishbones (lower control arms), coil springs, anti-roll bar, telescopic dampers; rear: rigid axle, lower trailing radius arms, upper oblique torque arms, coil springs, telescopic dampers.

STEERING rack-and-pinion; turns lock to lock: 4.08.

BRAKES front disc (diameter 10.06 in, 25.6 cm), front internal radial fins, rear drum, servo; swept area: front 176.6 sq in, 1,140 sq cm, rear 99 sq in, 639 sq cm, total 275.6 sq in, 1,779 sq cm.

ELECTRICAL EQUIPMENT 12 V; 310 A battery; 40 A alternator; 4 headlamps.

DIMENSIONS AND WEIGHT wheel base: 100.50 in, 255 cm; tracks: 56.60 in, 414 cm front, 57 in, 145 cm rear; length: 179.10 in, 455 cm; width: 69.10 in, 175 cm; height: 51.90 in, 132 cm; ground clearance: 4.90 in, 12.5 cm; weight: GS 2,786 lb, 1,264 kg - RS 2,790 lb, 1,265 kg; turning circle: 37.4 ft, 11.4 m; fuel tank: 12.8 imp gal, 15.3 US gal, 58 l.

BODY coupé; 2+1 doors; 4 seats, separate front seats, reclining backrests, built-in headrests.

OPTIONALS Select-Shift automatic transmission, hydraulic torque converter and planetary gears with 3 ratios (I 2.470, II 1.470, III 1, rev 2.110), max ratio of converter at stall 2.90, possible manual selection, 3.270 axle ratio, consumption 27.6 m/imp gal, 23 m/US gal, 10.2 l x 100 km; 3.450 axle ratio; central or steering column lever; P 195/75 R x 14 - P 205/70 R x 14 - P 220/55 R - 390 BSW tyres with 5.5" wide rims; heavy-duty battery; 55 Ah battery; 60 A alternator, air-conditioning; power steering; tilt of steering wheel; speed control; electric windows; sunroof; heavy-duty suspension; tinted glass.

120 hp power team

See 88 hp power team, except for:

ENGINE 6 cylinders, slanted at Vee; 231 cu in, 3,797 cc (3.80 x 3.40 in, 96.8 x 86 mm); compression ratio: 8.6:1; max power (SAE net): 120 hp (88 kW) at 3,600 rpm; max torque (SAE net): 205 lb ft, 28.3 kg m (277 Nm) at 1,600 rpm; max engine rpm: 4,100; 31.6 hp/l (23.2 kW/l); cast iron block, light alloy head; 4 crankshaft bearings; valves: overhead, in line, push-rods and rockers; camshafts: 1, at centre of Vee, chain-driven; throttle-body fuel injection or 1 49S-4K 700 DR - (for California only) 4K 650 DR downdraught twin barrel carburettor; fuel feed: mechanical or electric pump; cooling: 17.8 imp pt, 21.4 US pt, 10.1 l.

TRANSMISSION (standard) gearbox: Select-Shift automatic transmission, hydraulic torque converter and planetary gears with 3 ratios, max ratio of converter at stall 2.90, possible manual selection; ratios I 2.470, II 1.470, III 1, rev 2.110; axle ratio: 2.730 - Automatic Overdrive automatic transmission, hydraulic torque converter and planetary gears with 3 ratios and overdrive, max ratio of converter at stall 2.530, possible manual selection; ratios: I 2.400, II 1.470, III 1, overdrive 0.670, rev 2; axle ratio: 3.080.

PERFORMANCE max speed: 100 mph, 161 km/h; power-weight ratio: GS 24.1 lb/hp (32.7 lb/kW), 10.9 kg/hp (14.8 kg/kW); consumption: 24.1 m/imp gal, 20 m/US gal, 11.7 l x 100 km.

ELECTRICAL EQUIPMENT 380 A battery.

DIMENSIONS AND WEIGHT weight: GS 2,887 lb, 1,310 kg - RS 2,894 lb, 1,313 kg.

175 hp power team

See 88 hp power team, except for:

ENGINE 8 cylinders in Vee; 302 cu in, 4,950 cc (4 x 3 in, 101.6 x 76.2 mm); compression ratio: 8.3:1; max power (SAE net): 165 hp (121 kW) at 3,800 rpm; max torque (SAE net): 245 lb ft, 33.8 kg m (332 Nm) at 2,000 rpm; max engine rpm: 4,300; 33.3 hp/l (24.5 kW/l); valves: overhead, in line, push-rods and rockers; electronic fuel injection; air cleaner; exhaust system with catalytic converter; cooling: 17.8 imp pt, 21.4 US pt, 10.1 l.

TRANSMISSION gearbox: Automatic Overdrive automatic transmission, hydraulic torque converter and planetary gears with 3 ratios and overdrive, max ratio of converter at stall 2.28, possible manual selection; ratios: I 2.400, II 1.470, III 1, overdrive 0.670, rev 2; axle ratio: 3.270.

PERFORMANCE max speed: 117 mph, 189 km/h; power-weight ratio: GS 18.1 lb/hp (24.5 lb/kW), 8.2 kg/hp (11.1 kg/kW);consumption: 21.7 m/imp gal, 18 m/US gal, 13 l x 100 km.

ELECTRICAL EQUIPMENT 450 A battery; 60 A alternator (standard).

DIMENSIONS AND WEIGHT weight: GS 2,976 lb, 1,350 kg - RS 2,983 lb, 1,353 kg.

175 hp (2,300 cc) power team

See 88 hp power team, except for:

ENGINE turbocharged; compression ratio: 8:1; max power (SAE net): 175 hp (129 kW) at 4,400 rpm; max torque (SAE net): 155 lb ft, 21.4 kg m (210 Nm) at 3,000 rpm; max engine rpm: 5,000; 76 hp/l (56 kW/l); lubrication: 8.4 imp pt, 10.1 US pt, 4.8 l; electronic fuel injection; air cleaner; exhaust system with catalytic converter; fuel feed: electric pump; cooling: 15.7 imp pt, 18.8 US pt, 8.9 l.

TRANSMISSION gears: 5, fully synchronized; ratios: I 4.030, II 2.370, III 1.500, IV 1, V 0.860, rev 3.760; axle ratio: 3.450.

PERFORMANCE max speed: 118 mph, 190 km/h; power-weight ratio: 16.5 lb/hp (22.5 lb/kW), 7.5 kg/hp (10.2 kg/kW); consumption: 25.2 m/imp gal, 21 m/US gal, 11.2 l x 100 km.

ELECTRICAL EQUIPMENT 450 A battery.

DIMENSIONS AND WEIGHT weight: 2,897 lb, 1,313 kg.

175 hp (4,930 cc) power team

See 88 hp power team, except for:

ENGINE 8 cylinders in Vee; 302 cu in, 4,950 cc (4 x 3 in, 101.6 x 76.2 mm); compression ratio: 8.3:1; max power (SAE net): 175 hp (129 kW) at 4,000 rpm; max torque (SAE net): 245 lb ft, 33.8 kg m (331 Nm) at 2,200 rpm; max engine rpm: 4,600; 35.3 hp/l (26 kW/l); valves: overhead, in line, push-rods and rockers; 1 Holley 4180C-4V downdraught 4-barrel carburettor; cooling: 17.8 imp pt, 21.4 US pt, 10.1 l.

MERCURY Capri RS Hatchback Coupé

175 HP (4,930 cc) POWER TEAM

TRANSMISSION gears: 5, fully synchronized; ratios: I 2.950, II 1.940, III 1.340, IV 1, V 0.730, rev 2.760; axle ratio: 3.080.

PERFORMANCE max speed: 120 mph, 193 km/h; power-weight ratio: GS 17.1 lb/hp (23.3 lb/kW), 7.7 kg/hp (10.5 kg/kW); consumption: not declared.

ELECTRICAL EQUIPMENT 60 A alternator (standard).

DIMENSIONS AND WEIGHT weight: GS 2,994 lb, 1,358 kg - RS 3,001 lb, 1,361 kg.

OPTIONALS 3.270 axle ratio.

Cougar Series

PRICES EX WORKS:	$
1 2-dr Coupé	**10,410**
2 LS 2-dr Coupé	**11,697**
3 XR-7 Turbo 2-dr Coupé	**13,497**

Power team:	Standard for:	Optional for:
120 hp	1,2	—
140 hp	1,2	—
145 hp	3	—

120 hp power team

ENGINE front, 4 stroke; 6 cylinders, slanted at Vee; 231 cu in, 3,797 cc (3.80 x 3.40 in, 96.8 x 86 mm); compression ratio: 8.6:1; max power (SAE net): 120 hp (88 kW) at 3,600 rpm; max torque (SAE net): 205 lb ft, 28.3 kg m (277 Nm) at 2,600 rpm; max engine rpm: 4,100; 31.6 hp/l (23.2 kW/l); cast iron block, light alloy head; 4 crankshaft bearings; valves: overhead, in line, push-rods and rockers; camshafts: 1, at centre of Vee, chain-driven; lubrication: gear pump, full flow filter, 8.2 imp pt, 9.9 US pt, 4.7 l; 1 downdraught twin barrel carburettor or throttle-body electronic fuel injection; fuel feed: mechanical or electric pump; water-cooled, 20.4 imp pt, 24.5 US pt, 11.6 l.

TRANSMISSION driving wheels: rear; gearbox: Select-Shift automatic transmission, hydraulic torque converter and planetary gears with 3 ratios, possible manual selection; ratios: I 2.460, II 1.460, III 1, rev 2.190; lever: steering column; final drive: hypoid bevel; axle ratio: 2.730; width of rims: 5"; tyres: P 195/75 R x 14.

PERFORMANCE max speed: 113 mph, 183 km/h; power-weight ratio: 2-dr 25.5 lb/hp (34.7 lb/kW), 11.6 kg/hp (15.7 kg/kW); speed in direct drive at 1,000 rpm: 31.2 mph, 50.2 km/h; consumption: 24.1 m/imp gal, 20 m/US gal, 11.7 l x 100 km.

CHASSIS integral; front suspension: independent, by McPherson, wishbones (lower control arm), coil springs, anti-roll bar, telescopic dampers; rear: rigid axle, lower trailing radius arms, upper oblique torque arms, coil springs, telescopic dampers.

STEERING rack-and-pinion, servo; turns lock to lock: 3.05.

BRAKES front disc (diameter 10.06 in, 25.5 cm), front internal radial fins, rear compensator, rear drum, servo; swept area: front 176.6 sq in, 1,140 sq cm, rear 99 sq in, 638 sq cm, total 275.5 sq in, 1,778 sq cm.

ELECTRICAL EQUIPMENT 12 V; 380 A battery; 40 A alternator; Motorcraft transistorized ignition; 4 headlamps.

DIMENSIONS AND WEIGHT wheel base: 103.80 in, 264 cm; tracks: 58.10 in, 148 cm front, 58.50 in, 149 cm rear; length: 197.60 in, 502 cm; width: 71.10 in, 181 cm; height: 53.40 in, 136 cm; ground clearance: 4.89 in, 122 cm; weight: 2-dr 3,065 lb, 1,390 kg - LS 3,094 lb, 1,403 kg; turning circle: 12.1 ft, 39.4 m; fuel tank: 17.4 imp gal, 21 US gal, 79 l.

BODY coupé; 2 doors; 4 seats, separate front seats, built-in headrests.

OPTIONALS Automatic Overdrive automatic transmission, hydraulic torque converter and planetary gears with 3 ratios and overdrive (I 2.400, II 1.470, III 1, overdrive 0.670, rev 2), max ratio of converter at stall 2.53, possible manual selection, 3.270 or 3.450 axle ratio, consumption 25.2 m/imp gal, 21 m/US gal, 11.2 l x 100 km; 3.080 axle ratio; central lever; 60 A alternator; 55 Ah battery; P 205/70 R x 14 or P 220/55 R-390 BSW tyres with 5.5" wide rims; heavy-duty battery; automatic air-conditioning; tilt of steering wheel; speed control; electric defroster on rear window; electric windows; sunroof; heavy-duty suspension; vinyl roof; halogen headlamps; tinted glass.

140 hp power team

See 120 hp power team, except for:

ENGINE 8 cylinders in Vee; 302 cu in, 4,950 cc (4 x 3 in, 101.6 x 76.2 mm); compression ratio: 8.4:1; max power (SAE net): 140 hp (103 kW) at 3,200 rpm; max torque (SAE net): 250 lb ft, 34.5 kg m (338 Nm) at 1,600 rpm; max engine rpm: 3,700; 28.3 hp/l (20.8 kW/l); cast iron block and head; 5 crankshaft bearings; valves: overhead, in line, hydraulic tappets; throttle-body fuel injection; fuel feed: electric pump; cooling: 23 imp pt, 28 US pt, 12.6 l.

TRANSMISSION (standard) gearbox: Automatic Overdrive automatic transmission, hydraulic torque converter and planetary gears with 3 ratios and overdrive, max ratio of converter at stall 2.30, possible manual selection; ratios: I 2.400, II 1.470, III 1, overdrive 0.670, rev 2; axle ratio: 3.080.

PERFORMANCE max speed: 115 mph, 185 km/h; power-weight ratio: 2-dr Coupé 21.9 lb/hp (29.7 lb/kW), 9.9 kg/hp (13.5 kg/kW); consumption: 21.7 m/imp gal, 18 m/US gal, 13 l x 100 km.

ELECTRICAL EQUIPMENT 450 A battery; (standard) 60 A alternator.

DIMENSIONS AND WEIGHT fuel tank: 17.1 imp gal, 20.6 US gal, 78 l.

145 hp power team

See 120 hp power team, except for:

ENGINE turbocharged; 140 cu in, 2,300 cc (3.78 x 3.12 in, 96 x 79.4 mm); compression ratio: 8:1; max power (SAE net): 145 hp (107 kW) at 4,600 rpm; max torque (SAE net): 180 lb ft, 24.8 kg m (244 Nm) at 3,600 rpm; max engine rpm: 5,100; 63 hp/l (46 kW/l); cast iron block and head; 5 crankshaft bearings; lubrication: rotary pump, full flow filter; electronic fuel injection; exhaust gas recirculation with catalytic converter; cooling: 15.6 imp pt, 18.8 US pt, 8.9 l.

TRANSMISSION clutch: single dry plate; gearbox: mechanical; gears: 5, fully synchronized; ratios: I 4.030, II 2.370, III 1.490, IV 1, V 0.860; axle ratio: 3.450; lever: central.

PERFORMANCE max speed: 115 mph, 185 km/h; power-weight ratio: 21 lb/hp (28.6 lb/kW), 9.5 kg/hp (13 kg/kW); consumption: not declared.

ELECTRICAL EQUIPMENT 450 A battery; 60 A alternator (standard).

DIMENSIONS AND WEIGHT weight: 3,053 lb, 1,384 kg.

MERCURY Cougar XR-7 Turbo Coupé

Grand Marquis Series

PRICES EX WORKS:	$
2-dr Sedan	**12,056**
4-dr Sedan	**12,120**
Brougham 4+1-dr St. Wagon	**12,296**

Power team:	Standard for:	Optional for:
140 hp	all	—
155 hp	all	—
180 hp	all	—

140 hp power team

ENGINE front, 4 stroke; 8 cylinders in Vee; 302 cu in, 4,950 cc (4 x 3 in, 101.6 x 76.2 mm); compression ratio: 8.4:1; max power (SAE net): 140 hp (103 kW) at 3,200 rpm; max torque (SAE net): 250 lb ft, 34.5 kg m (338 Nm) at 1,600 rpm; max engine rpm: 3,700; 28.3 hp/l (20.8 kW/l); cast iron block and head; 5 crankshaft bearings; valves: overhead, in line, push-rods and rockers, hydraulic tappets; camshafts: 1, at centre of Vee; lubrication: rotary pump, full flow filter, 8.2 imp pt, 9.9 US pt, 4.7 l; throttle-body fuel injection; air cleaner; exhaust system with catalytic converter; fuel feed: electric pump; water-cooled, 23 imp pt, 28 US pt, 12.6 l.

TRANSMISSION driving wheels: rear; gearbox: Automatic Overdrive automatic transmission, hydraulic torque converter and planetary gears with 3 ratios and overdrive, max ratio of converter at stall 2.28, possible manual selection; ratios: I 2.400, II 1.470, III 1, overdrive 0.670, rev 2; lever: steering column; final drive: hypoid bevel; axle ratio: 3.080 or 3.550; width of rims: 5"; tyres: P 215/75 R x 14.

PERFORMANCE max speed: 99 mph, 159 km/h; power-weight ratio: 2-dr Sedan 26.7 lb/hp (36.2 lb/kW), 12.1 kg/hp (16.4 kg/kW); speed in top at 1,000 rpm: 24.6 mph, 39.5 km/h; consumption: 20.4 m/imp gal, 17 m/US gal, 13.8 l x 100 km.

CHASSIS integral; front suspension: independent, coil springs, wishbones, anti-roll bar, telescopic dampers; rear: rigid axle, lower trailing radius arms, upper oblique torque arms, coil springs, telescopic dampers.

STEERING recirculating ball, servo; turns lock to lock: 3.40.

BRAKES front disc (diameter 11.08 in, 28.1 cm), internal radial fins, rear drum, servo; swept area: sedans front 228.7 sq in, 1,475 sq cm, rear 157.1 sq in, 1,013 sq cm, total 385.8 sq in, 2,488 sq cm - St. Wagon front 228.4 sq in, 1,473 sq cm, rear 155.9 sq in, 1,005 sq cm, total 384.3 sq in, 2,478 sq cm.

ELECTRICAL EQUIPMENT 12 V; 475 A battery; 60 A alternator; Motorcraft transistorized contactless ignition; 4 headlamps.

MERCURY Grand Marquis Sedan

DIMENSIONS AND WEIGHT wheel base: 114.30 in, 290 cm; tracks: 62.20 in, 158 cm front, 62 in, 157 cm rear; length: sedans 214 in, 544 cm - St. Wagon 218 in, 553 cm; width: sedans 77.50 in, 197 cm - St. Wagon 79.30 in, 201 cm; height: sedans 55.20 in, 140 cm - St. Wagon 56.80 in, 144 cm; ground clearance: 5.70 in, 13.1 cm; weight: 2-dr Sedan 3,734 lb, 1,694 kg - 4-dr Sedan 3,780 lb, 1,715 kg - Brougham St. Wagon 3,981 lb, 1,806 kg; turning circle: 39.2 ft, 11.9 m; fuel tank: 15 imp gal, 18 US gal, 68 l.

BODY saloon/sedan; 2 or 4 doors - estate car/st. wagon, 4+1 doors; 6 seats, separate front seats, built-in headrests.

OPTIONALS P 205/75 R x 14 BSW - P 205/75 R x 15 W/WSW and P 225/75 R x 14 WSW tyres with 6.5" wide rims; limited slip differential; light alloy wheels; electric windows; digital or electric clock; tilt of steering wheel; tinted glass; vinyl roof; sunroof; manual or automatic air-conditioning; automatic speed control; heavy-duty suspension; 100 A alternator; electric door locks; heavy-duty radiator.

155 hp power team

See 140 hp power team, except for:

ENGINE max power (SAE net): 155 hp (114 kW) at 3,600 rpm; max torque (SAE net): 265 lb ft, 36.5 kg m (358 Nm) at 2,000 rpm; max engine rpm: 4,100; 31.3 hp/l (23 kW/l); 1 downdraught twin barrel carburettor or electric fuel injection; fuel feed: mechanical or electric pump.

PERFORMANCE power-weight ratio: 2-dr Sedan 24.4 lb/hp (33.2 lb/kW), 11.1 kg/hp (15 kg/kW).

DIMENSIONS AND WEIGHT weight: 2-dr Sedan 3,780 lb, 1,715 kg - 4-dr Sedan 3,826 lb, 1,735 kg - Brougham St. Wagon 4,015 lb, 1,822 kg.

180 hp power team

See 140 hp power team, except for:

ENGINE 351 cu in, 5,753 cc (4 x 3.50 in, 101.6 x 88.9 mm); compression ratio: 8.3:1; max power (SAE net): 180 hp (132 kW) at 3,600 rpm; max torque (SAE net): 285 lb ft, 39.3 kg m (386 Nm) at 2,400 rpm; max engine rpm: 4,200; 31.3 hp/l (23 kW/l); 1 downdraught twin barrel carburettor; exhaust gas recirculation with 2 catalytic converters; cooling: 17.8 imp pt, 27.7 US pt, 13 l.

TRANSMISSION axle ratio: 2.730.

PERFORMANCE max speed: 105 mph, 170 km/h; power-weight ratio: 2-dr Sedan 21.2 lb/hp (28.8 lb/kW), 9.6 kg/hp (13 kg/kW); speed in top at 1,000 rpm: 24.4 mph, 39.3 km/h; consumption: not declared.

DIMENSIONS AND WEIGHT weight: 2-dr Sedan 3,810 lb, 1,729 kg - 4-dr Sedan 3,856 lb, 1,750 kg - Brougham St. Wagon 4,057 lb, 1,840 kg.

MERCURY Grand Marquis Brougham Station Wagon

OLDSMOBILE USA

Firenza Series

PRICES EX WORKS:	$
4-dr Sedan	**7,301**
S 2-dr Coupé	**7,214**
SX 2-dr Coupé	**7,957**
LX 4-dr Sedan	**7,853**
Cruiser 4+1-dr St. Wagon	**7,521**
Cruiser LX 4+1-dr St. Wagon	**8,073**

Power team:	Standard for:	Optional for:
82 hp	—	all
88 hp	all	—

82 hp power team

ENGINE front, 4 stroke; 4 cylinders, transverse, vertical, in line; 112 cu in, 1,836 cc (3.34 x 3.13 in, 84.8 x 79.5 mm); compression ratio: 9:1; max power (SAE net): 82 hp (61 kW) at 5,200 rpm; max torque (SAE net): 102 lb ft, 14 kg m (139 Nm) at 2,800 rpm; max engine rpm: 5,600; 44.6 hp/l (32.8 kW/l); cast iron block and head; 5 crankshaft bearings; valves: overhead, in line, push-rods and rockers, hydraulic tappets; camshafts: 1, side; lubrication: gear pump, full flow filter, 6.7 imp pt, 8 US pt, 3.8 l; injection pump; fuel feed: electric pump; water-cooled, 13.6 imp pt, 16.3 US pt, 7.5 l.

TRANSMISSION driving wheels: front; clutch: single dry plate (diaphragm); gearbox: mechanical; gears: 5, fully synchronized; ratios: I 3.910, II 2.150, III 1.450, IV 1.030, V 0.740, rev 3.500; lever: central; final drive: helical spur gears; axle ratio: 3.450; width of rims: 5"; tyres: 175/80 R x 13.

PERFORMANCE max speed: 99 mph, 159 km/h; power-weight ratio: Sedan 30 lb/hp (40.8 lb/kW), 13.6 kg/hp (18.5 kg/kW); consumption: 34.8 m/imp gal, 29 m/US gal, 8.1 l x 100 km.

CHASSIS integral; front suspension: independent, by McPherson, lower wishbones, anti-roll bar, coil springs/telescopic damper struts; rear: rigid axle, swinging longitudinal leading arms, coil springs, telescopic dampers.

STEERING rack-and-pinion; turns lock to lock: 4.04.

BRAKES front disc (diameter 9.72 in, 24.7 cm), internal radial fins, rear drum, servo; swept area: total 252 sq in, 1,624 sq cm.

ELECTRICAL EQUIPMENT 12 V; 390 A battery; 63 A alternator; Delco-Remy transistorized ignition; 4 headlamps.

DIMENSIONS AND WEIGHT wheel base: 101.20 in, 257 cm; tracks: 55.40 in, 141 cm front, 55.20 in, 140 cm rear; length: coupés 174.30 in, 442 cm - sedans and st. wagons 176.20 in, 447 cm; width: 65 in, 165 cm; height: coupés 51 in, 131 cm - sedans 53.70 in, 136 cm - st. wagons 55.20 in, 140 cm; ground clearance: 6.40 in, 16.3 cm - st. wagon 6.60 in, 16.9 cm; weight: Sedan 2,461 lb, 1,116 kg - LX Sedan 2,505 lb, 1,136 kg - S Coupé 2,457 lb, 1,115 kg - SX Coupé 2,504 lb, 1,136 kg - Cruiser St. Wagon 2,496 lb, 1,132 kg - Cruiser LX St. Wagon 2,520 lb, 1,143 kg; weight distribution: 64% front, 36% rear; turning circle: 34.4 ft, 10.5 m; fuel tank: 11.8 imp gal, 14 US gal, 53 l.

BODY saloon/sedan, 4 doors - coupé, 2 doors - estate car/st. wagon, 4+1 doors; 6 seats, separate front seats, built-in headrests.

OPTIONALS Turbo-Hydramatic automatic transmission, hydraulic torque converter and planetary gears with 3 ratios (I 2.840, II 1.600, III 1, rev 2.070), max ratio of converter at stall 2.70, possible manual selection, 3.180 axle ratio, consumption 32.4 m/imp gal, 27 m/US gal, 8.7 l x 100 km; 3.430 axle ratio; air-conditioning; power steering with 2.88 turns lock to lock; limited slip differential; heavy-duty battery; heavy-duty alternator; heavy-duty suspension; speed control; heated rear window; tilt of steering wheel; self-sealing tyres; side windows; electric seats; courtesy lamp; sunroof; vinyl roof; tinted glass; GT equipment.

88 hp power team

See 82 hp power team, except for:

ENGINE 121 cu in, 1,983 cc (3.50 x 3.15 in, 89 x 80 mm); max power (SAE net): 88 hp (66 kW) at 4,800 rpm; max torque (SAE net): 110 lb ft, 15.2 kg m (139 Nm) at 2,400 rpm; max engine rpm: 5,300; 44.4 hp/l (32.7 kW/l).

TRANSMISSION gears: 4, fully synchronized; ratios: I 3.530, II 1.950, III 1.240, IV 0.810, rev 3.420; axle ratio: 4.100; width of rims: 5.5"; tyres: P 175/80 R x 13.

PERFORMANCE max speed: 102 mph, 164 km/h; power-weight ratio: Sedan 28 lb/hp (38 lb/kW) 12.7 kg/hp (17.2 kg/kW); consumption: 33.6 m/imp gal, 28 m/US gal, 8.4 l x 100 km.

ELECTRICAL EQUIPMENT 500 A battery; 42 A alternator.

OPTIONALS 5-speed fully synchronized mechanical gearbox (I 3.910, II 2.150, III 1.450, IV 1.030, V 0.740, rev 3.500), 3.830 axle ratio; Turbo-Hydramatic 125 C automatic transmission, hydraulic torque converter and planetary gears with 3 ratios (I 2.840, II 1.600, III 1, rev 2.070), max ratio of converter at stall 2.70, possible manual selection, 3.180 axle ratio, consumption 32.4 m/imp gal, 27 m/US gal, 8.7 l x 100 km; 3.430 axle ratio.

Omega Series

PRICES EX WORKS:	$
4-dr Sedan	**7,832**
2-dr Coupé	**7,634**
Brougham 4-dr Sedan	**8,104**
Brougham 2-dr Coupé	**7,923**

Power team:	Standard for:	Optional for:
92 hp	all	—
112 hp	—	all
130 hp	—	all

OLDSMOBILE Firenza S Coupé

OLDSMOBILE Omega Sedan

92 hp power team

ENGINE front, transverse, 4 stroke; 4 cylinders, in line; 151 cu in, 2,475 cc (4 x 3 in, 101.6 x 76.2 mm); compression ratio: 8.2:1; max power (SAE net): 92 hp (69 kW) at 4,000 rpm; max torque (SAE net): 134 lb ft, 18.5 kg m (181 Nm) at 2,800 rpm; max engine rpm: 4,500; 37.2 hp/l (27.3 kW/l); cast iron block and head; 5 crankshaft bearings; valves: overhead, in line, push-rods and rockers, hydraulic tappets; camshafts: 1, side; lubrication: gear pump, full flow filter, 5.3 imp pt, 6.5 US pt, 3 l; throttle-body electronic fuel injection; air cleaner; exhaust system with catalytic converter; fuel feed: electric pump; water-cooled, 15.8 imp pt, 19 US pt, 9 l.

TRANSMISSION driving wheels: front; clutch: self-adjusting single dry plate (diaphragm); gearbox: mechanical; gears: 4, fully synchronized; ratios: I 3.530, II 1.950, III 1.240, IV 0.730, rev 3.420; lever: central; final drive: spiral bevel; axle ratio: 3.320; width of rims: 5.5"; tyres: P 185/80 R x 13.

PERFORMANCE max speed: 87 mph, 140 km/h; power-weight ratio: Sedan 27.5 lb/hp (37.4 lb/kW), 12.5 kg/hp (17 kg/kW); speed in top at 1,000 rpm: 19.8 mph, 31.8 km/h; consumption: 32.5 m/imp gal, 27 m/US gal, 8.7 l x 100 km.

CHASSIS integral; front suspension: independent, by McPherson, coil springs, stamped lower control arms, telescopic dampers; rear: rigid axle, trailing arm, stamped control arms, coil springs, telescopic dampers.

STEERING rack-and-pinion, servo; turns lock to lock: 3.15.

BRAKES front disc (diameter 9.72 in, 24.7 cm), internal radial fins, rear drum; swept area: total 272.7 sq in, 1,759 sq cm.

ELECTRICAL EQUIPMENT 12 V; 390 A battery; 42 A alternator; Delco-Remy high energy ignition; 2 headlamps.

DIMENSIONS AND WEIGHT wheel base: 105 in, 266 cm; tracks: 58.70 in, 149 cm front, 57 in, 145 cm rear; length: 182.80 in, 464 cm; width: 69.80 in, 177 cm; height: 53.70 in, 136 cm; ground clearance: 5.50 in, 13.8 cm; weight: Sedan 2,533 lb, 1,149 kg - Coupé 2,503 lb, 1,135 kg - Brougham Sedan 2,558 lb, 1,160 kg - Brougham Coupé 2,520 lb, 1,143 kg; weight distribution: 63% front, 37% rear; turning circle: 40.3 ft, 12.3 m; fuel tank: 12.1 imp gal, 14.5 US gal, 55 l.

BODY saloon/sedan, 4 doors - coupé, 2 doors; 5 seats, separate front seats, built-in headrests.

OPTIONALS Turbo-Hydramatic automatic transmission with 3 ratios (I 2.840, II 1.600, III 1, rev 2.070), max ratio of converter at stall 1.95, possible manual selection, steering column or central lever, 2.390 axle ratio, consumption 30 m/imp gal, 25 m/US gal, 9.4 l x 100 km; (for California only) 2.840 axle ratio; tilt of steering wheel; intermittent wiper-washer; sunroof; reclining seats; custom interior; heated rear window; air-conditioning; servo brake; power steering; electric windows; electric door locks; P 205/70 R x 13 tyres; heavy-duty battery; heavy-duty alternator; 63 or 70 A alternator; heavy-duty cooling; sunroof; vinyl roof; cruise control; speed control; courtesy lamp; tinted glass; heavy-duty radiator; ES equipment.

112 hp power team

See 92 hp power team, except for:

ENGINE 6 cylinders, Vee-slanted at 60°; 173 cu in, 2,835 cc (3.50 x 3 in, 89 x 76.2 mm); compression ratio: 8.5:1; max power (SAE net): 112 hp (84 kW) at 4,800 rpm; max torque (SAE net): 145 lb ft, 20 kg m (196 Nm) at 2,100 rpm; max engine rpm: 5,300; 39.5 hp/l (29.1 kW/l); 4 crankshaft bearings; camshafts: 1, at centre of Vee; lubrication: 6.7 imp pt, 7.9 US pt, 3.8 l; 1 Rochester 17081651 downdraught twin barrel carburettor; cooling: 16.9 imp pt, 20.2 US pt, 9.7 l.

PERFORMANCE max speed: 106 mph, 170 km/h; power-weight ratio: Sedan 22.6 lb/hp (30.7 lb/kW), 10.2 kg/hp (13.9 kg/kW); speed in top at 1,000 rpm: 23.1 mph, 37.3 km/h; consumption: 25.2 m/imp gal, 21 m/US gal, 11.2 l x 100 km.

DIMENSIONS AND WEIGHT weight: Sedan 2,588 lb, 1,174 kg - Coupé 2,546 lb, 1,155 kg - Brougham Sedan 2,612 lb, 1,185 kg - Brougham Coupé 2,579 lb, 1,170 kg.

OPTIONALS 2.530 axle ratio with automatic transmission.

130 hp power team

See 92 hp power team, except for:

ENGINE 6 cylinders, Vee-slanted at 60°; 173 cu in, 2,835 cc (3.50 x 3 in, 89 x 76.2 mm); compression ratio: 8.9:1; max power (SAE net): 130 hp (97 kW) at 5,400 rpm; max torque (SAE net): 145 lb ft, 20 kg m (196 Nm) at 2,400 rpm; max engine rpm: 5,900; 45.8 hp/l (33.7 kW/l); 4 crankshaft bearings; camshafts: 1, at centre of Vee; lubrication: 6.7 imp pt, 7.9 US pt, 3.8 l; 1 Rochester downdraught twin barrel carburettor; cooling: 16.9 imp pt, 20.2 US pt, 9.7 l.

TRANSMISSION axle ratio: 3.650.

PERFORMANCE max speed: 106 mph, 170 km/h; power-weight ratio: Sedan 19.5 lb/hp (26.5 lb/kW), 8.8 kg/hp (12 kg/kW); consumption: 25.2 m/imp gal, 21 m/US gal, 11.2 l x 100 km.

OPTIONALS 3.330 axle ratio with automatic transmission.

Cutlass Ciera Series

PRICES EX WORKS:	$
1 LS 4-dr Sedan	**9,203**
2 LS 2-dr Coupé	**9,014**
3 Brougham 4-dr Sedan	**9,721**
4 Brougham 2-dr Coupé	**9,519**
5 Cruiser 4+1-dr St. Wagon	**9,551**

Power team:	Standard for:	Optional for:
92 hp	all	—
110 hp	—	all
125 hp	—	1 to 4
85 hp (diesel)	—	all

92 hp power team

ENGINE front, transverse, 4 stroke; 4 cylinders, in line; 151 cu in, 2,475 cc (4 x 3 in, 101.6 x 76.2 mm); compression ratio: 8.2:1; max power (SAE net): 92 hp (69 kW) at 4,000 rpm; max torque (SAE net): 134 lb ft, 18.5 kg m (181 Nm) at 2,800 rpm; max engine rpm: 4,500; 37.1 hp/l (27.3 kW/l); cast iron block and head; 5 crankshaft bearings; valves: overhead, in line, push-rods and rockers, hydraulic tappets; camshafts: 1, side; lubrication: gear pump, full flow filter, 5.3 imp pt, 6.5 US pt, 3 l; throttle-body electronic fuel injection; air cleaner; exhaust system with catalytic converter; fuel feed: mechanical pump; water-cooled, 16 imp pt, 19.2 US pt, 9.1 l.

TRANSMISSION driving wheels: front; gearbox: Turbo-Hydramatic automatic transmission, hydraulic torque converter and planetary gears with 3 ratios, max ratio of converter at stall 1.85, possible manual selection; ratios: I 2.840, II 1.600, III 1, rev 2.070; lever: central or steering column; final drive: helical spur gears; axle ratio 2.390; width of rims: 5.5"; tyres: P 185/80 R x 13.

PERFORMANCE max speed: 87 mph, 140 km/h; power-weight ratio: Coupé 29.5 lb/hp (40.1 lb/kW), 13.3 kg/hp (18.2 kg/kW); speed in direct drive at 1,000 rpm: 19.8 mph, 31.8 km/h; consumption: 30 m/imp gal, 25 m/US gal, 9.4 l x 100 km.

CHASSIS integral; front suspension: independent, by McPherson, coil springs/telescopic damper struts; rear: rigid axle, swinging longitudinal leading arms, coil springs, telescopic dampers.

STEERING rack-and-pinion, servo; turns lock to lock: 3.15.

BRAKES front disc, internal radial fins, rear drum, servo; swept area: total 272.7 sq in, 1,759 sq cm.

ELECTRICAL EQUIPMENT 12 V; 3,200 W battery; 42 A alternator; Delco-Remy high energy ignition; 4 headlamps.

DIMENSIONS AND WEIGHT wheel base: 104.90 in, 266 cm; tracks: 58.70 in, 149 cm front, 57 in, 145 cm rear; length: 188.40 in, 478 cm - St. Wagon 191 in, 485 cm; width: 69.50 in, 177 cm; height: 54.10 in, 137 cm - St. Wagon 54.50 in, 138 cm; ground clearance: 5.70 in, 14.4 cm - St. Wagon 5.80 in, 14.7 cm; weight: LS Coupé 2,691 lb, 1,220 kg - Brougham Coupé 2,717 lb, 1,232 kg - LS Sedan 2,714 lb, 1,231 kg - Brougham Sedan 2,738 lb, 1,242 kg - Cruise St. Wagon 2,906 lb, 1,318 kg; weight distribution: sedans 62% front, 38% rear; turning circle: 38 ft, 11.6 m; fuel tank: 12.1 imp gal, 14.5 US gal, 55 l.

BODY saloon/sedan, 4 doors - coupé, 2 doors - estate car/st. wagon, 4+1 doors; 6 seats, separate front seats, built-in headrests.

OPTIONALS electric door locks; vinyl roof; air-conditioning; speed control; self-sealing tyres; 2.840 axle ratio; halogen headlamps; P 195/70 R x 14 or P 195/75 R x 14 tyres; electric door locks; electric windows; heavy-duty suspension; tilt of steering wheel.

110 hp power team

See 92 hp power team, except for:

ENGINE 6 cylinders in Vee; 181 cu in, 2,966 cc (3.80 x 2.66 in, 96.5 x 67.6 mm); compression ratio: 8.4:1; max power (SAE net): 110 hp (81 kW) at 4,800 rpm; max torque (SAE net): 145 lb ft, 20 kg m (196 Nm) at 2,600 rpm; max engine rpm: 5,200; 37.1 hp/l (27.3 kW/l); 4 crankshaft bearings; camshafts: 1, at centre of Vee; 1 Rochester E2SE twin barrel carburettor; cooling: 24.2 imp pt, 28.6 US pt, 13.7 l.

TRANSMISSION axle ratio: 2.530 - St. Wagon 2.970.

PERFORMANCE max speed: 105 mph, 168 km/h; power-

OLDSMOBILE Cutlass Ciera LS Sedan

OLDSMOBILE Cutlass Ciera Cruiser Station Wagon

weight ratio: LS Sedan 24.7 lb/hp (33.5 lb/kW), 11.2 kg/hp (15.2 kg/kW); speed in direct drive at 1,000 rpm: 20.9 mph, 33.6 km/h; consumption: 22.9 m/imp gal, 19 m/US gal, 12.3 l x 100 km.

DIMENSIONS AND WEIGHT weight: Brougham Coupé 2,752 lb, 1,248 kg - LS Coupé 2,769 lb, 1,256 kg - LS Sedan 2,791 lb, 1,266 kg - Brougham Sedan 2,815 lb, 1,277 kg - Cruiser St. Wagon 3,001 lb, 1,361 kg.

OPTIONALS Turbo-Hydramatic 440-T4 automatic transmission with 3 ratios and overdrive (I 2.920, II 1.570, III 1, overdrive 0.700, rev 2.380), steering column or central lever, 3.060 or 3.330 axle ratio.

125 hp power team

See 92 hp power team, except for:

ENGINE 6 cylinders in Vee; 231 cu in, 3,785 cc (3.80 x 3.40 in, 96.5 x 86.4 mm); compression ratio: 8:1; max power (SAE net): 125 hp (92 kW) at 4,000 rpm; max torque (SAE net): 205 lb ft, 28.3 kg m (277 Nm) at 2,000 rpm; 33 hp/l (24.3 kW/l); lubrication: 8.3 imp pt, 9.9 US pt, 4.7 l; fuel injection; fuel feed: electric pump; cooling: 24.2 imp pt, 28.6 US pt, 13.7 l.

TRANSMISSION gearbox: Turbo-Hydramatic 440-T4 automatic transmission, hydraulic torque converter and planetary gear with 3 ratios and overdrive; ratios: I 2.920, II 1.570, III 1, overdrive 0.700, rev 2.380; axle ratio: 2.840.

PERFORMANCE max speed: 107 mph, 172 km/h; power-weight ratio: LS Sedan 22.3 lb/hp (30.3 lb/kW), 10.1 kg/hp (13.5 kg/kW); consumption: 22.9 m/imp gal, 19 m/US gal, 12.3 l x 100 km.

DIMENSIONS AND WEIGHT weight: Brougham Coupé 2,752 lb, 1,248 kg - LS Coupé 2,769 lb, 1,256 kg - LS Sedan 2,791 lb, 1,266 kg - Brougham Sedan 2,815 lb, 1,277 kg.

BODY saloon/sedan, 4 doors - coupé, 2 doors.

85 hp (diesel) power team

See 92 hp power team, except for:

ENGINE diesel; 6 cylinders in Vee; 262 cu in, 4,294 cc (4.06 x 3.38 in, 103 x 86 mm); compression ratio: 22.8:1; max power (SAE net): 85 hp (63 kW) at 3,600 rpm; max torque (SAE net): 165 lb ft, 22.8 kg m (223 Nm) at 1,600 rpm; max engine rpm: 4,100; 19.8 hp/l (14.6 kW/l); 4 crankshaft bearings; camshafts: 1, at centre of Vee; lubrication: 10.1 imp pt, 12 US pt, 5.7 l; diesel fuel injection pump; fuel feed: electric pump; cooling: 15.6 imp pt, 18.8 US pt, 8.9 l.

TRANSMISSION clutch: single dry plate; gearbox: mechanical; gears: 4, fully synchronized; ratios: I 3.530, II 1.950, III 1.240, IV 0.810, rev 3.420; lever: central; axle ratio: 2.660 (not available in California).

PERFORMANCE power-weight ratio: LS Sedan 32 lb/hp (43.4 lb/kW), 14.5 kg/hp (19.7 kg/kW); consumption: 32.4 m/imp gal, 27 m/US gal, 8.7 l x 100 km.

ELECTRICAL EQUIPMENT 385 A x 2 batteries; 66 or 94 A alternator.

DIMENSIONS AND WEIGHT weight: Brougham Coupé 2,910 lb, 1,320 kg - LS Coupé 2,932 lb, 1,330 kg - LS Sedan 2,932 lb, 1,330 kg - Brougham Sedan 2,959 lb, 1,342 kg - Cruiser St. Wagon 3,001 lb, 1,361 kg.

OPTIONALS Turbo-Hydramatic 125-C automatic transmission, hydraulic torque converter and planetary gears with 3 ratios (I 2.840, II 1.600, III 1, rev 2.070), max ratio of converter at stall 1.85, possible manual selection, 2.390 axle ratio; (standard for California) Turbo-Hydramatic 440-T4 automatic transmission with 3 ratios and overdrive (I 2.920, II 1.570, III 1, overdrive 0.700, rev 2.380), 2.840 axle ratio - St. Wagon 3.060 axle ratio.

Cutlass Series

PRICES EX WORKS:	$
Supreme 4-dr Sedan	9,529
Supreme 2-dr Coupé	9,376
Supreme Brougham 4-dr Sedan	10,145
Supreme Brougham 2-dr Coupé	10,015
Calais 2-dr Coupé	10,274

OLDSMOBILE Cutlass Calais Coupé

Power team:	Standard for:	Optional for:
110 hp	all	—
140 hp	—	all
85 hp (diesel)	—	all
105 hp (diesel)	—	all

110 hp power team

ENGINE front, 4 stroke; 6 cylinders in Vee; 231 cu in, 3,785 cc (3.80 x 3.40 in, 96.5 x 86.4 mm); compres sion ratio: 8:1; max power (SAE net): 110 hp (81 kW) at 3,800 rpm; max torque (SAE net): 190 lb ft, 26.1 kg m (256 Nm) at 1,600 rpm; max engine rpm: 4,300; 29.3 hp/l (21.5 kW/l); cast iron block and head; 4 crankshaft bearings; valves: overhead, in line, push-rods and rockers, hydraulic tappets; camshafts: 1, at centre of Vee; lubrication: gear pump, full flow filter, 8.3 imp pt, 9.9 US pt, 4.7 l; 1 Rochester 2ME carburettor; fuel feed: mechanical pump; water-cooled, 22.9 imp pt, 27.5 US pt, 13 l.

TRANSMISSION driving wheels: rear; gearbox: Turbo-Hydramatic 200C or 250C automatic transmission, hydraulic torque converter and planetary gears with 3 ratios, max ratio of converter at stall 1.9 or 2.20, possible manual selection; ratios: I 2.740, II 1.570, III 1, rev 2.070 or I 2.520, II 1.520, III 1, rev 1.930; lever: central or steering column; final drive: hypoid bevel; axle ratio 2.410; width of rims: 6''; tyres: P 195/75 R x 14.

PERFORMANCE max speed: 99 mph, 159 km/h; power-weight ratio: Supreme Sedan 29.6 lb/hp (40.2 lb/kW), 13.4 kg/hp (18.2 kg/kW); speed in direct drive at 1,000 rpm: 24.2 mph, 38.9 km/h; consumption: 25 m/imp gal, 21 m/US gal, 11.2 l x 100 km.

CHASSIS channel section perimeter-type frame; front suspension: independent, wishbones, coil springs, anti-roll bar, telescopic dampers; rear: rigid axle, lower trailing radius arms, upper oblique torque arms, coil springs, telescopic dampers.

STEERING recirculating ball, servo; turns lock to lock: 4.13.

BRAKES front disc, front internal radial fins, rear drum, rear compensator, servo; swept area: total 312.7 sq in, 2,017 sq cm.

ELECTRICAL EQUIPMENT 12 V; 2,500 W battery; 42 A alternator; Delco-Remy transistorized ignition; 4 headlamps.

DIMENSIONS AND WEIGHT wheel base: 108.10 in, 274 cm; tracks: 58.50 in, 149 cm front, 57.80 in, 147 cm rear; length: sedans 200.40 in, 508 cm - coupés 200 in, 507 cm; width: sedans 71.90 in, 183 cm - coupés 71.60 in, 181 cm; height: sedans 55.90 in, 143 cm - coupés 54.90 in, 139 cm; ground clearance: 5.20 in, 13.1 cm; weight: Supreme Sedan 3,256 lb, 1,476 kg - Supreme Coupé 3,204 lb, 1,453 kg - Supreme Brougham Sedan 3,286 lb, 1,490 kg - Supreme Brougham Coupé 3,280 lb, 1,488 kg; turning circle: coupés 38.2 ft, 11.6 m - sedans 37.3 ft, 11.3 m; fuel tank: 15.2 imp gal, 18.2 US gal, 69 l.

BODY saloon/sedan, 4 doors - coupé, 2 doors; 5 seats, separate front seats, built-in headrests.

OPTIONALS 3.080 or 3.230 axle ratio; limited slip differential; P 205/75 R x 14 tyres; automatic levelling control; heavy-duty suspension; heavy-duty cooling; heavy-duty battery; power steering; tilt of steering wheel; heavy-duty alternator; heated rear window; electric windows; automatic speed control; electric sunroof; air-conditioning; electric door locks; vinyl roof; self-sealing tyres.

140 hp power team

See 110 hp power team, except for:

ENGINE 8 cylinders in Vee; 305 cu in, 4,999 cc (3.80 x 3.38 in, 96.5 x 85.9 mm); max power (SAE net): 140 hp (103 kW) at 3,600 rpm; max torque (SAE net): 240 lb ft, 33.1 kg m (324 Nm) at 1,600 rpm; max engine rpm: 4,000; 28 hp/l (20.6 kW/l); 1 Rochester M4 downdraught 4-barrel carburettor; cooling: 27.6 imp pt, 32.8 US pt, 15.7 l.

TRANSMISSION gearbox: Turbo-Hydramatic 200 C automatic transmission, hydraulic torque converter and planetary gears with 3 ratios, max ratio of converter at stall 2.20, possible manual selection; ratios: I 2.740, II 1.570, III 1, rev 2.070; lever: steering column or central; axle ratio: 2.140.

PERFORMANCE max speed: 105 mph, 170 km/h; power-weight ratio: Supreme Sedan 23.5 lb/hp (31.9 lb/kW), 10.6 kg/hp (14.5 kg/kW); consumption: 21.7 m/imp gal, 18 m/US gal, 13 l x 100 km.

OPTIONALS Turbo-Hydramatic 200-4R automatic transmission with 4 ratios (I 2.740, II 1.570, III 1, IV 0.670, rev 2.070), 2.560 axle ratio.

85 hp (diesel) power team

See 110 hp power team, except for:

ENGINE diesel; 262 cu in, 4,294 cc (4.06 x 3.38 in, 103 x 86 mm); compression ratio: 22.8:1; max power (SAE net): 85 hp (63 kW) at 3,600 rpm; max torque (SAE net): 165 lb ft, 22.8 kg m (223 Nm) at 1,600 rpm; max engine rpm: 4,000; 19.8 hp/l (14.6 kW/l); lubrication: 10.1 imp pt, 12 US pt, 5.7 l; diesel injection pump; fuel feed: electric pump; cooling: 23.9 imp pt, 28.8 US pt, 13.6 l.

85 HP (DIESEL) POWER TEAM

PERFORMANCE max speed: 87 mph, 140 km/h; power-weight ratio: Supreme Sedan 38.7 lb/hp (52.6 lb/kW), 17.5 kg/hp (23.9 kg/kW); consumption: 31.3 m/imp gal, 26 m/US gal, 9 l x 100 km.

ELECTRICAL EQUIPMENT 385 A x 2 batteries.

OPTIONALS Turbo-Hydramatic 200-4 R automatic transmission with 4 ratios (I 2.740, II 1.570, III 1, IV 0.670, rev 2.070), 2.930 axle ratio; 63 or 78 A alternator.

105 hp (diesel) power team

See 110 hp power team, except for:

ENGINE diesel; 8 cylinders in Vee; 350 cu in, 5,736 cc (4.06 x 3.38 in, 103.9 x 86 mm); compression ratio: 22.7:1; max power (SAE net): 105 hp (78 kW) at 3,200 rpm; max torque (SAE net): 200 lb ft, 27.6 kg m (271 Nm) at 1,600 rpm; max engine rpm: 3,500; 18.4 hp/l (13.6 kW/l); lubrication: 12.4 imp pt, 14.8 US pt, 7.1 l; Detroit-Diesel injection pump; cooling: 28.7 imp pt, 33.9 US pt, 16.4 l.

TRANSMISSION axle ratio: 2.290 or 2.730.

PERFORMANCE max speed: 94 mph, 151 km/h; power-weight ratio: Supreme Sedan 31.3 lb/hp (42.1 lb/kW), 14.2 kg/hp (19.1 kg/kW); speed in direct drive at 1,000 rpm: 28.6 mph, 45.7 km/h; consumption: 27.6 m/imp gal, 23 m/US gal, 10.2 l x 100 km.

ELECTRICAL EQUIPMENT 405 A battery; 63 A alternator.

OPTIONALS Turbo-Hydramatic 200-4 R automatic transmission with 4 ratios (I 2.740, II 1.570, III 1, IV 0.670, rev. 2.070), 2.730 axle ratio; 78 A alternator.

Delta 88 / Ninety-Eight / Custom Cruiser Series

PRICES EX WORKS:		$
1	Delta 88 Royale 4-dr Sedan	**10,051**
2	Delta 88 Royale 2-dr Coupé	**9,939**
3	Delta 88 Royale Brougham 4-dr Sedan	**10,499**
4	Delta 88 Royale Brougham 2-dr Coupé	**10,408**
5	Ninety-Eight Regency 4-dr Sedan	**14,151**
6	Ninety-Eight Regency 2-dr Coupé	**13,974**
7	Ninety-Eight Regency Brougham 4-dr Sedan	**15,201**
8	Custom Cruiser 4+1-dr St. Wagon	**10,839**

Power team:	Standard for:	Optional for:
110 hp	1 to 7	—
140 hp	8	1 to 7
105 hp (diesel)	—	all

110 hp power team

ENGINE front, 4 stroke; 6 cylinders in Vee; 231 cu in, 3,785 cc (3.80 x 3.40 in, 96.5 x 86.5 mm); compression ratio: 8:1; max power (SAE net): 110 hp (81 kW) at 3,800 rpm; max torque (SAE net): 190 lb ft, 26.1 kg m (256 Nm) at 1,600 rpm; max engine rpm: 4,200; 29.3 hp/l (21.5 kW/l); cast iron block and head; 4 crankshaft bearings; valves: overhead, in line, push-rods and rockers, hydraulic tappets; camshafts: 1, at centre of Vee; lubrication: gear pump, full flow filter, 7.4 imp pt, 8.4 US pt, 4 l; 1 Rochester 17080490 downdraught twin barrel carburettor; fuel feed: mechanical pump; water-cooled, 22.9 imp pt, 27.5 US pt, 13 l.

TRANSMISSION driving wheels: rear; gearbox: Turbo-Hydramatic 250 automatic transmission, hydraulic torque converter and planetary gears with 3 ratios, max ratio of converter at stall 1.90, possible manual selection; ratios: I 2.740, II 1.570, III 1, rev 2.070; lever: steering column; final drive: hypoid bevel; axle ratio: 2.730; width of rims: 6"; tyres: P 205/75 R x 15.

PERFORMANCE max speed: 95 mph, 153 km/h; power-weight ratio: Delta 88 Royale Sedan 32 lb/hp (43.5 lb/kW), 14.5 kg/hp (19.7 kg/kW); speed in direct drive at 1,000 rpm: 29.8 mph, 47.7 km/h; consumption: 22.8 m/imp gal, 19 m/US gal, 12.4 l x 100 km.

CHASSIS perimeter box-type with front and rear cross members; front suspension: independent, wishbones, coil springs, anti-roll bar, telescopic dampers; rear: rigid axle, lower trailing radius arms, upper oblique torque arms, coil springs, telescopic dampers.

STEERING recirculating ball, servo; turns lock to lock: 4.10.

BRAKES front disc, front internal radial fins, rear drum, servo; swept area: total 384.2 sq in, 2,478 sq cm.

ELECTRICAL EQUIPMENT 12 V; 2,500 W battery; 42 A alternator; Delco-Remy transistorized ignition; 4 headlamps.

DIMENSIONS AND WEIGHT wheel base: 116 in, 294 cm; tracks: 61.70 in, 157 cm front, 60.70 in, 154 cm rear; length: 218 in, 555 cm; width: 76.30 in, 194 cm; height: sedans 56.70 in, 144 cm - coupés 56 in, 142 cm; ground clearance: 6.30 in, 16 cm; weight: Delta 88 Royale Sedan 3,530 lb, 1,601 kg - Delta 88 Royale Coupé 3,492 lb, 1,584 kg - Delta 88 Royale Brougham Coupé 3,525 lb, 1,559 kg; turning circle: 42.8 ft, 13 m; fuel tank: 20.9 imp gal, 25 US gal, 95 l.

OLDSMOBILE Delta 88 Royale Brougham Sedan

BODY saloon/sedan, 4 doors - coupé, 2 doors; 6 seats, separate front seats, built-in headrests.

OPTIONALS 3.230 axle ratio; limited slip differential; heavy-duty cooling; heavy-duty suspension; heavy-duty battery; halogen headlamps; heated rear window; trip computer; anti-theft; electric sunroof; electric backrests; tilt and telescopic steering wheel; P 215/75 R x 15 tyres; tinted glass.

140 hp power team

See 110 hp power team, except for:

ENGINE 8 cylinders in Vee; 307 cu in, 5,032 cc (3.80 x 3.38 in 96.5 x 86 mm); max power (SAE net): 140 hp (103 kW) at 3,600 rpm; max torque (SAE net): 240 lb ft, 33.1 kg m (324 Nm) at 1,600 rpm; max engine rpm: 4,000; 27.8 hp/l (20.5 kW/l); 5 crankshaft bearings; lubrication: 6.6 imp pt, 7.8 US pt, 3.8 l; 1 Rochester M4MC downdraught 4-barrel carburettor; cooling: 23.4 imp pt, 30 US pt, 14.5 l.

TRANSMISSION (except Delta 88 models) Turbo-Hydramatic 200-4 R automatic transmission, hydraulic torque converter and planetary gears with 4 ratios, max ratio of converter at stall 1.90, possible manual selection; ratios: I 2.740, II 1.570, III 1, IV 0.670, rev 2.070; lever: central or steering column; axle ratio: 2.730 - (not available in California) 2.930 - (for Delta 88 models only) 2.410.

PERFORMANCE max speed: 107 mph, 172 km/h; power-weight ratio: St. Wagon 29.5 lb/hp (40.1 lb/kW), 13.4 kg/hp (18.2 kg/kW); speed in direct drive at 1,000 rpm: 31.1 mph, 50 km/h; consumption: 20.1 m/imp gal, 17 m/US gal, 13.9 l x 100 km.

STEERING turns lock to lock: St. Wagon 3.50 - other models 4.

BRAKES swept area: total 396.6 sq in, 2,559 sq cm.

DIMENSIONS AND WEIGHT (for Ninety-Eight models and St. Wagon only) wheel base: 119 in, 302 cm - St. Wagon 116 in, 294 cm; tracks: 61.70 in, 157 cm front, 60.70 in, 154 cm rear - St. Wagon 62.10 in, 158 cm front, 64.10 in, 163 cm rear; length: 221.40 in, 562 cm - St. Wagon 220 in, 560 cm; width: 76.30 in, 194 cm - St. Wagon 79.80 in, 203 cm; height: 57.20 in, 145 cm - St. Wagon 58.50 in, 148 cm; ground clearance: 12.2 in, 31 cm; weight: Custom Cruiser St. Wagon 4,127 lb, 1,872 kg; turning circle: 43.5 ft, 13.2 m - St. Wagon 42.8 ft, 13 m; fuel tank: St. Wagon 18.6 imp gal, 22 US gal, 83 l.

BODY saloon/sedan, 4 doors - coupé, 2 doors - estate car/st. wagon, 4+1 doors; 6 seats - St. Wagon 9 seats, separate front seats, built-in headrests.

OPTIONALS (for Delta 88 models only) Turbo-Hydramatic 200-4 R automatic transmission with 2.730 axle ratio; 3.080 or 3.230 axle ratio (except for California).

105 hp (diesel) power team

See 110 hp power team, except for:

ENGINE diesel; 8 cylinders in Vee; 350 cu in, 5,736 cc (4.06 x 3.38 in, 103.9 x 86 mm); compression ratio: 22.7:1; max power (SAE net): 105 hp (78 kW) at 3,200 rpm; max torque (SAE net): 200 lb ft, 27.6 kg m (271 Nm) at 1,600 rpm; max engine rpm: 3,500; 18.4 hp/l (13.6 kW/l); 5 crankshaft bearings; lubrication: 12.4 imp pt, 14.8 US pt, 7.1 l; Detroit-Diesel injection pump; cooling: 30.4 imp pt, 36.5 US pt, 17.3 l.

TRANSMISSION gearbox: Turbo-Hydramatic 200-4 R automatic transmission, hydraulic torque converter and planetary gears with 3 ratios and overdrive, max ratio of converter at stall 2.20, possible manual selection; ratios: I 2.740, II 1.570, III 1, overdrive 0.670, rev 2.070; axle ratio: 2.930.

PERFORMANCE max speed: 85 mph, 136 km/h; power-weight ratio: Delta 88 Royale Sedan 33.6 lb/hp (45.7 lb/kW), 15.2 kg/hp (20.7 kg/kW); speed in top at 1,000 rpm: 28.6 mph, 45.7 km/h; consumption: 27 m/imp gal, 23 m/US gal, 10.2 l x 100 km.

ELECTRICAL EQUIPMENT 405 A x 2 batteries; 78 A alternator.

BODY saloon/sedan, 4 doors - coupé, 2 doors - estate car/st. wagon, 4+1 doors; 6 seats - st. wagon 9 seats, separate front seats, built-in headrests.

OLDSMOBILE Ninety-Eight Regency Sedan

OPTIONALS Turbo-Hydramatic 200 C automatic transmission, hydraulic torque converter and planetary gears with 3 ratios (I 2.740, II 1.570, III 1, rev 2.070), 2.410 axle ratio.

Toronado

PRICE EX WORKS: $ 16,107

125 hp power team

(standard)

ENGINE front, 4 stroke; 6 cylinders in Vee; 252 cu in, 4,130 cc (3.96 x 3.40 in, 100.7 x 86.4 mm); compression ratio: 8:1; max power (SAE net): 125 hp (92 kW) at 4,000 rpm; max torque (SAE net): 205 lb ft, 28.3 kg m (277 Nm) at 2,000 rpm; max engine rpm: 4,300; 30.3 hp/l (22.3 kW/l); cast iron block and head; 4 crankshaft bearings; valves: overhead, in line, push-rods and rockers; hydraulic tappets; camshafts: 1, at centre of Vee; lubrication: gear pump, full flow filter, 6.7 imp pt, 7.9 US pt, 3.8 l; 1 Rochester M4ME downdraught 4-barrel carburettor; thermostatic air cleaner; exhaust system with catalytic converter; fuel feed: mechanical pump; water-cooled, 23.1 imp pt, 27.7 US pt, 13.1 l.

TRANSMISSION driving wheels: front; gearbox: Turbo-Hydramatic 200-4R automatic transmission, hydraulic torque converter and planetary gears with 4 ratios, max ratio of converter at stall 2, possible manual selection; ratios: I 2.740, II 1.570, III 1, IV 0.670, rev 2.070; lever: steering column; final drive: hypoid bevel; axle ratio: 3.150; width of rims: 6"; tyres: 205/75 R x 15.

PERFORMANCE max speed: 100 mph, 161 km/h; power-weight ratio: 29.5 lb/hp (40.1 lb/kW), 13.4 kg/hp (18.2 kg/kW); speed in top at 1,000 rpm: 25.4 mph, 40.8 km/h; consumption: 19.2 m/imp gal, 16 m/US gal, 14.7 l x 100 km.

CHASSIS channel section perimeter-type frame; front suspension: independent, wishbones, longitudinal torsion bars, anti-roll bar, telescopic dampers; rear: independent, swinging longitudinal trailing arms, coil springs, automatic levelling control, telescopic dampers.

STEERING recirculating ball, servo; turns lock to lock: 3.

BRAKES front disc, front internal radial fins, rear drum, rear compensator, servo; swept area: total 307.8 sq in, 1,985 sq cm.

ELECTRICAL EQUIPMENT 12 V; 80 Ah battery; 70 A alternator; Delco-Remy transistorized ignition; 4 headlamps.

DIMENSIONS AND WEIGHT wheel base: 114 in, 289 cm; tracks: 59.30 in, 151 cm front, 60 in, 152 cm rear; length: 206 in, 523 cm; width: 71 in, 180 cm; height: 54.60 in, 138 cm; ground clearance: 5.80 in, 15 cm; weight: 3,704 lb, 1,680 kg; turning circle: 39.9 ft, 12.1 m; fuel tank: 17.6 imp gal, 21 US gal, 80 l.

BODY coupé; 2 doors; 5 or 6 seats, separate front seats, built-in headrests; electric tinted windows; air-conditioning.

OPTIONALS heavy-duty cooling; heavy-duty battery; heavy-duty alternator; tilt of steering wheel; rear disc brakes; speed control; heated rear window; electric sunroof; heavy-duty suspension; reclining backrests; P 225/70 R x 15 tyres; vinyl roof.

140 hp power team

(optional)

See 125 hp power team, except for:

ENGINE 8 cylinders in Vee; 307 cu in, 5,032 cc (3.80 x 3.38 in, 96.5 x 86 mm); max power (SAE net): 140 hp (103 kW) at 3,600 rpm; max torque (SAE net): 240 lb ft, 33.1 kg m (324 Nm) at 1,600 rpm; max engine rpm: 4,000; 27.8 hp/l (20.5 kW/l); 5 crankshaft bearings; 1 Rochester M4MC downdraught 4-barrel carburettor; cooling: 27.3 imp pt, 32.8 US pt, 15.5 l.

TRANSMISSION axle ratio: 2.730.

PERFORMANCE max speed: 107 mph, 172 km/h; power-weight ratio: 26.7 lb/hp (36.4 lb/kW), 12.1 kg/hp (16.5 kg/kW); speed in top at 1,000 rpm: 31.1 mph, 50 km/h; consumption: 20.4 m/imp gal, 17 m/US gal, 13.8 l x 100 km.

DIMENSIONS AND WEIGHT weight: 3,733 lb, 1,693 kg.

105 hp (diesel) power team

(optional)

See 125 hp power team, except for:

ENGINE diesel; 8 cylinders in Vee; 350 cu in, 5,736 cc (4.06 x 3.38 in, 103.9 x 86 mm); compression ratio: 22.7:1; max power (SAE net): 105 hp (78 kW) at 3,200 rpm; max torque (SAE net): 200 lb ft, 27.6 kg m (271 Nm) at 1,600 rpm; max engine rpm: 3,500; 18.4 hp/l (13.6 kW/l); 5 crankshaft bearings; lubrication: 11.6 imp pt, 14 US pt, 6.6 l; Detroit-Diesel injection pump; cooling: 30.3 imp pt, 36.4 US pt, 17.2 l.

TRANSMISSION axle ratio: 2.930 (not available in California).

PERFORMANCE max speed: 94 mph, 151 km/h; power-weight ratio: 35.6 lb/hp (48.4 lb/kW), 16.1 kg/hp (21.9 kg/kW); speed in top at 1,000 rpm: 28.6 mph, 45.7 km/h; consumption: 26.4 m/imp gal, 22 m/US gal, 10.7 l x 100 km.

ELECTRICAL EQUIPMENT 2 batteries.

DIMENSIONS AND WEIGHT weight: 3,746 lb, 1,699 kg.

PHILLIPS USA

Berlina I / S.E.

PRICES EX WORKS:	$
Berlina I 2-dr Coupé	**59,500**
Berlina S.E. 2-dr Coupé	**64,500**

ENGINE Chevrolet Corvette, front, 4 stroke; 8 cylinders in Vee; 350 cu in, 5,736 cc (4 x 3.48 in, 101.6 x 88.4 mm); compression ratio: 9:1; max power (SAE net): 200 hp (147 kW) at 4,200 rpm; max torque (SAE net): 285 lb ft, 39.3 kg m (385 Nm) at 2,800 rpm; max engine rpm: 5,000; 34.9 hp/l (25.7 kW/l); cast iron block and head; 5 crankshaft bearings; valves: overhead, in line, push-rods and rockers, hydraulic tappets; camshafts: 1, at centre of Vee; lubrication: gear pump, full flow filter, 8.3 imp pt, 9.9 US pt, 4.7 l; throttle-body electronic full injection; thermostatic air cleaner; dual exhaust system with catalytic converter; fuel feed: 2 electric pumps; water-cooled, 34.5 imp pt, 41.4 US pt, 19.6 l, viscous coupling thermostatic fan.

TRANSMISSION driving wheels: rear; gearbox: 700-R4 automatic transmission, hydraulic torque converter and planetary gears with 4 ratios, max ratio of converter at stall 2, possible manual selection; ratios: I 3.060, II 1.630, III 1, IV 0.700, rev 2.290; lever: central; final drive: hypoid bevel, limited slip; axle ratio: 2.720; width of rims: 8"; tyres: 225/70 R x 15.

PERFORMANCE max speed: 124 mph, 198 km/h; power-weight ratio: 16 lb/hp (21.8 lb/kW), 7.3 kg/hp (9.9 kg/kW); speed in top at 1,000 rpm: 30.6 mph, 49.3 km/h; consumption: 19.2 m/imp gal, 16 m/US gal, 14.7 l x 100 km.

CHASSIS ladder frame with cross members; front suspension: independent, wishbones, coil springs, anti-roll bar, telescopic dampers; rear: independent, wishbones, semi-axle as upper arms, transverse single leaf reinforced fiberglass leafspring, trailing radius arms, telescopic dampers.

STEERING recirculating ball, servo, tilt of steering wheel; turns lock to lock: 2.58.

BRAKES disc (diameter 11.75 in, 30 cm), internal radial fins, servo; swept area: total 498.3 sq in, 3,214 sq cm.

ELECTRICAL EQUIPMENT 12 V; 3,500 W battery; 63 A alternator; Delco-Remy high energy ignition; 4 headlamps.

DIMENSIONS AND WEIGHT wheel base: 120.08 in, 305 cm; tracks: 58.66 in, 149 cm front, 59.45 in, 151 cm rear; length: 185.04 in, 470 cm; width: 69 in, 175 cm; height: 48 in, 122 cm; ground clearance: 4.30 in, 10.9 cm; weight: 3,205 lb, 1,454 kg; weight distribution: 46% front, 54% rear; turning circle: 38.6 ft, 11.8 m; fuel tank: 20 imp gal, 24 US gal, 91 l.

BODY coupé; 2 doors; 2 seats.

OPTIONALS tinted glass; (for Berlina S.E. Coupé only) trip computer.

PLYMOUTH USA

Horizon / Turismo Series

PRICES EX WORKS:		$
1	Horizon 4+1-dr Hatchback Sedan	**5,830**
2	Horizon SE 4+1-dr Hatchback Sedan	**6,148**
3	Turismo 2+1-dr Hatchback Coupé	**6,594**
4	Turismo 2.2 2+1-dr Hatchback Coupé	**7,288**

Power team:	Standard for:	Optional for:
64 hp	1 to 3	—
96 hp	—	1 to 3
101 hp	4	—
110 hp	—	all

64 hp power team

ENGINE front, transverse, 4 stroke; 4 cylinders, in line; 97.1 cu in, 1,591 cc (3.17 x 3.07 in, 80.6 x 78 mm); compression ratio: 8.8:1; max power (SAE net): 64 hp (47 kW) at 4,800 rpm; max torque (SAE net): 87 lb ft, 12 kg m (118 Nm) at 2,800 rpm; max engine rpm: 5,300; 40.2 hp/l (29.6 kW/l); cast iron block, light alloy head; 5 crankshaft bearings; valves: overhead, in line, thimble tappets; camshafts: 1, overhead, cogged belt; lubrication: gear pump, full flow filter, 5.8 imp pt, 7 US pt, 3.3 l; 1 Holley 6520 downdraught twin barrel carburettor; air cleaner; exhaust system with catalytic converter; fuel feed: mechanical pump; water-cooled, 11.6 imp pt, 14 US pt, 6.6 l.

TRANSMISSION driving wheels: front; clutch: single dry plate (diaphragm); gearbox: mechanical; gears: 4, fully synchronized; ratios: I 3.290, II 1.890, III 1.210, IV 0.880, rev 3.140; lever: central; final drive: spiral bevel; axle ratio: 2.690 (not available in California); width of rims: 5"; tyres: 165/80 R x 13.

OLDSMOBILE Toronado

PHILLIPS Berlina S.E. Coupé

64 HP POWER TEAM

PERFORMANCE max speed: 90 mph, 145 km/h; power-weight ratio: Horizon Hatchback Sedan 33.6 lb/hp (45.7 lb/kW), 15.2 kg/hp (20.7 kg/kW); carrying capacity: 706 lb, 320 kg; speed in top at 1,000 rpm: 16.5 mph, 26.4 km/h; consumption: 40.9 m/imp gal, 34 m/US gal, 6.9 l x 100 km.

CHASSIS integral; front suspension: independent, lower wishbones, anti-roll bar, coil springs/telescopic damper struts; rear: independent, semi-trailing arms, coil springs, telescopic dampers.

STEERING rack-and-pinion; turns lock to lock: 3.60.

BRAKES front disc, front internal radial fins, rear drum; swept area: total 201.9 sq in, 1,302 sq cm.

ELECTRICAL EQUIPMENT 12 V; 335 A battery; 65 A alternator; Essex or Prestolite transistorized ignition with electronic spark control; 2 headlamps.

DIMENSIONS AND WEIGHT wheel base: sedans 99.10 in, 251 cm - Coupé 96.60 in, 245 cm; tracks: 56.10 in, 143 cm front, 55.60 in, 141 cm rear; length: sedans 164.80 in, 419 cm - Coupé 173.70 in, 441 cm; width: sedans 65.80 in, 167 cm - Coupé 66.70 in, 169 cm; height: sedans 53.10 in, 135 cm - Coupé 50.80 in, 129 cm; ground clearance: sedans 4.90 in, 12.4 cm - Coupé 4.50 in, 11.4 cm; weight: Horizon Hatchback Sedan 2,151 lb, 976 kg - Horizon SE Hatchback Sedan 2,100 lb, 989 kg - Turismo Hatchback Coupé 2,220 lb, 1,007 kg; turning circle: 36.1 ft, 11 m; fuel tank: 10.8 imp gal, 13 US gal, 49 l.

BODY saloon/sedan, 4+1 doors - coupé, 2+1 doors; 4 seats, separate front seats, built-in headrests; heated rear window.

OPTIONALS Torqueflite automatic transmission, hydraulic torque converter and planetary gears with 3 ratios (I 2.690, II 1.550, III 1, rev 2.100), max ratio of converter at stall 2, possible manual selection; (except California) 3.020 axle ratio; power steering, 2.88 turns lock to lock; servo brake; heavy-duty cooling; tinted glass; sunroof.

96 hp power team

See 64 hp power team, except for:

ENGINE 135 cu in, 2,213 cc (3.44 x 3.62 in, 87.5 x 92 mm); compression ratio: 9:1; max power (SAE net): 96 hp (71 kW) at 5,200 rpm; max torque (SAE net): 119 lb ft, 16.4 kg m (161 Nm) at 3,200 rpm; max engine rpm: 5,700; 43.4 hp/l (31.9 kW/l); lubrication: 6.7 imp pt, 8 US pt, 3.8 l; cooling: 14.4 imp pt, 17.3 US pt, 8.2 l.

PERFORMANCE max speed: 99 mph, 159 km/h; power-weight ratio: Turismo Hatchback Coupé 23.6 lb/hp (32.1 lb/kW), 10.7 kg/hp (14.6 kg/kW); consumption: 34.9 m/imp gal, 29 m/US gal, 8.1 l x 100 km.

ELECTRICAL EQUIPMENT 60 A alternator.

DIMENSIONS AND WEIGHT weight: Horizon Hatchback Sedan 2,197 lb, 997 kg - Horizon SE Hatchback Sedan 2,226 lb, 1,010 kg - Turismo Hatchback Coupé 2,266 lb, 1,028 kg.

OPTIONALS 5-speed fully synchronized mechanical gearbox (I 3.290, II 2.080, III 1.450, IV 1.040, V 0.720, rev 3.140), 2.200 axle ratio; 2.780 axle ratio with automatic transmission; air-conditioning; 430 A battery.

101 hp power team

See 64 hp power team, except for:

ENGINE 135 cu in, 2,213 cc (3.44 x 3.62 in, 87.5 x 92 mm); compression ratio: 9:1; max power (SAE net): 101 hp (74 kW) at 5,200 rpm; max torque (SAE net): 124 lb ft, 17.1 kg m (168 Nm) at 3,200 rpm; max engine rpm: 5,700; 45.6 hp/l (33.6 kW/l); lubrication: 6.7 imp pt, 8 US pt, 3.8 l; cooling: 14.4 imp pt, 17.3 US pt, 8.2 l.

PERFORMANCE max speed: 100 mph, 161 km/h; power-weight ratio: 23 lb/hp (31.3 lb/kW), 10.4 kg/hp (14.2 kg/kW); consumption: 33.6 m/imp gal, 28 m/US gal, 8.4 l x 100 km.

ELECTRICAL EQUIPMENT 60 A alternator.

DIMENSIONS AND WEIGHT weight: 2,327 lb, 1,056 kg.

BODY coupé; 2+1 doors.

OPTIONALS 5-speed fully synchronized mechanical gearbox (I 3.290, II 2.080, III 1.450, IV 1.040, V 0.720, rev 3.140), 2.570 axle ratio; 2.780 or 3.020 axle ratio with automatic transmission.

110 hp power team

See 64 hp power team, except for:

ENGINE 135 cu in, 2,213 cc (3.44 x 3.62 in, 87.5 x 92 mm); compression ratio: 9.6:1; max power (SAE net): 110 hp (81 kW) at 5,600 rpm; max torque (SAE net): 129 lb ft, 17.8 kg m (175 Nm) at 3,600 rpm; max engine rpm: 6,100; 49.7 hp/l (36.6 kW/l); lubrication: 6.7 imp pt, 8 US pt, 3.8 l; cooling: 14.4 imp pt, 17.3 US pt, 8.2 l.

PLYMOUTH Horizon Hatchback Sedan

PERFORMANCE max speed: 100 mph, 161 km/h; power-weight ratio: Horizon SE Hatchback Sedan 20.3 lb/hp (27.6 lb/kW), 9.2 kg/hp (12.5 kg/kW); consumption: 33.6 m/imp gal, 28 m/US gal, 8.4 l x 100 km.

ELECTRICAL EQUIPMENT 430 A battery; 60 A alternator.

DIMENSIONS AND WEIGHT weight: Horizon Hatchback Sedan 2,206 lb, 1,001 kg - Horizon SE Hatchback Sedan 2,235 lb, 1,014 kg - Turismo Hatchback Coupé 2,275 lb, 1,032 kg - Turismo 2.2 Hatchback Coupé 2,332 lb, 1,058 kg.

OPTIONALS 5-speed fully synchronized mechanical gearbox (I 3.290, II 2.080, III 1.450, IV 1.040, V 0.720, rev 3.140), 2.780 axle ratio; speed control; power steering.

Reliant Series

PRICES EX WORKS:		$
1	2-dr Sedan	**6,837**
2	4-dr Sedan	**6,949**
3	Custom 4+1-dr St. Wagon	**7,736**
4	SE 2-dr Sedan	**7,463**
5	SE 4-dr Sedan	**7,589**
6	SE 4+1-dr St. Wagon	**8,195**

Power team:	Standard for:	Optional for:
96 hp	all	—
101 hp	—	3,6

96 hp power team

ENGINE front, transverse, vertical, 4 stroke; 4 cylinders, in line; 135 cu in, 2,213 cc (3.44 x 3.62 in, 87.5 x 92 mm); compression ratio: 9:1; max power (SAE net): 96 hp (71 kW) at 5,200 rpm; max torque (SAE net): 119 lb ft, 16.4 kg m (161 Nm) at 3,200 rpm; max engine rpm: 5,700; 43.4 hp/l (31.9 kW/l); cast iron block, light alloy head; 5 crankshaft bearings; valves: overhead, in line, hydraulic tappets, rockers; camshafts: 1, overhead; lubrication: rotary pump, full flow filter, 6.7 imp pt, 8 US pt, 3.8 l; 1 Holley 6520 downdraught twin barrel carburettor; exhaust system with catalytic converter; fuel feed: mechanical pump; water-cooled, 14.4 imp pt, 17.3 US pt, 8.2 l.

TRANSMISSION driving wheels: front; clutch: single dry plate; gearbox: mechanical; gear: 4, fully synchronized; ratios: I 3.290, II 1.890, III 1.210, IV 0.880, rev 3.140; lever: central; final drive: helical spur gears; axle ratio: 2.690; width of rims: 5"; tyres: P 175/80 R x 13.

PERFORMANCE max speed: 94 mph, 152 km/h; power-weight ratio: 2-dr Sedan 24.5 lb/hp (33.4 lb/kW), 11.1 kg/hp (15.1 kg/kW); speed in top at 1,000 rpm: 16.5 mph, 26.4 km/h; consumption: 34.9 m/imp gal, 29 m/US gal, 8.1 l x 100 km.

CHASSIS integral; front suspension: independent, coil springs, telescopic damper struts, anti-roll bar; rear: independent, trailing radius arms, coil springs, anti-roll bar, telescopic dampers.

STEERING rack-and-pinion; turns lock to lock: 4.

BRAKES front disc (diameter 9.28 in, 23.6 cm), front internal radial fins, rear drum; swept area: total 209.1 sq in, 1,349 sq cm.

ELECTRICAL EQUIPMENT 12 V; 335 A battery; 60 A alternator; Essex or Prestolite transistorized ignition with combustion computer; 2 headlamps.

DIMENSIONS AND WEIGHT wheel base: 100.10 in, 254 cm; tracks: 57.60 in, 146 cm front, 57 in, 145 cm rear; length: sedans 176 in, 447 cm - st. wagons 176.20 in, 447 cm; width: 68.60 in, 174 cm; height: 2-dr sedans 52.30 in, 133 cm - 4-dr sedans 52.70 in, 134 cm - st. wagons 52.40 in, 133 cm; ground clearance: 4.50 in, 11.4 cm; weight: 2-dr Sedan 2,354 lb, 1,068 kg - 4-dr Sedan 2,361 lb, 1,071 kg - SE 2-dr Sedan 2,364 lb, 1,072 kg - SE 4-dr Sedan 2,394 lb, 1,085 kg - Custom St. Wagon 2,450 lb, 1,111 kg - SE St. Wagon 2,501 lb, 1,134 kg; turning circle: 37.2 ft, 11 m; fuel tank: 11.7 imp gal, 14 US pt, 53 l.

BODY saloon/sedan, 2 or 4 doors - estate car/st. wagon, 4+1 doors; 6 seats, separate front seats, built-in headrests.

OPTIONALS 5-speed fully synchronized mechanical gearbox (I 3.290, II 2.080, III 1.450, IV 1.040, V 0.720, rev 3.140), 2.200 axle ratio; Torqueflite automatic transmission, hydraulic torque converter and planetary gears with 3 ratios (I 2.690, II 1.550, III 1, rev 2.100), max ratio of converter at stall 2, possible manual selection, central lever, 2.780 axle ratio; power steering; servo brake; air-conditioning; digital clock; rear window wiper-washer.

PLYMOUTH Reliant Sedan

PLYMOUTH Gran Fury

101 hp power team

See 96 hp power team, except for:

ENGINE 155.9 cu in, 2,555 cc (3.59 x 3.86 in, 91.1 x 98 mm); compression ratio: 8.7:1; max power (SAE net): 101 hp (74 kW) at 4,800 rpm; max torque (SAE net): 140 lb ft, 19.3 kg m (189 Nm) at 2,800 rpm; max engine rpm: 5,300; 39.5 hp/l (29.1 kW/l); lubrication: 7.6 imp pt, 9.1 US pt, 4.3 l.

TRANSMISSION (standard) gearbox: Torqueflite automatic transmission, hydraulic torque converter and planetary gears with 3 ratios, max ratio of converter at stall 2, possible manual selection; ratios: I 2.690, II 1.550, III 1, rev 2.100; axle ratio: 3.020.

PERFORMANCE max speed: 98 mph, 158 km/h; power-weight ratio: Custom St. Wagon 25.1 lb/hp (34.4 lb/kW), 11.4 kg/hp (15.6 kg/kW); consumption: 27.7 m/imp gal, 23 m/US gal, 10.2 l x 100 km.

ELECTRICAL EQUIPMENT 500 A battery; 75 A alternator.

DIMENSIONS AND WEIGHT weight: Custom St. Wagon 2,540 lb, 1,152 kg - SE St. Wagon 2,590 lb, 1,175 kg.

BODY estate car/st. wagon; 4+1 doors.

OPTIONALS power steering; servo brake; air-conditioning; digital clock; rear window wiper-washer.

Gran Fury

PRICE EX WORKS: $ 9,180

130 hp power team

(standard)

ENGINE 8 cylinders in Vee; 318 cu in, 5,211 cc (3.91 x 3.31 in, 99.2 x 84 mm); compression ratio: 8.7:1; max power (SAE net): 130 hp (97 kW) at 4,000 rpm; max torque (SAE net): 235 lb ft, 32.4 kg m (318 Nm) at 1,600 rpm; max engine rpm: 4,600; 24.9 hp/l (18.4 kW/l); cast iron block and head; 5 crankshaft bearings; valves: overhead, in line, hydraulic tappets; camshafts: 1, at centre of Vee; lubrication: rotary pump, full flow filter, 6.7 imp pt, 8 US pt, 3.8 l; 1 Carter BBD-8291S downdraught twin barrel carburettor; fuel feed: mechanical pump; water-cooled, 25 imp pt, 30 US pt, 14.2 l.

TRANSMISSION driving wheels: rear; gearbox: Torqueflite automatic transmission, hydraulic torque converter and planetary gears with 3 ratios, max ratio of converter at stall 2, possible manual selection; ratios: I 2.740, II 1.540, III 1, rev 2.220; lever: steering column; final drive: hypoid bevel; axle ratio: 2.260 - 2.940 (for California only); width of rims: 7"; tyres: P 205/75 R x 15.

PERFORMANCE max speed: 102 mph, 164 km/h; power-weight ratio: 27.4 lb/hp (37.2 lb/kW), 12.4 kg/hp (16.9 kg/kW); speed in direct drive at 1,000 rpm: 34.2 mph, 57.5 km/h; consumption: 20 m/imp gal, 17 m/US gal, 13.8 l x 100 km.

CHASSIS integral with isolated front cross members; front suspension: independent, wishbones, longitudinal torsion bars, anti-roll bar, telescopic dampers; rear: rigid axle, semi-elliptic leafspring, telescopic dampers.

STEERING recirculating ball, servo; turns lock to lock: 3.50.

BRAKES front disc, front internal radial fins, rear drum, rear compensator, servo.

ELECTRICAL EQUIPMENT 12 V; 430 A battery; 60 A alternator; Essex or Prestolite or Mopar transistorized ignition with electronic spark control; 4 headlamps.

DIMENSIONS AND WEIGHT wheel base: 112.70 in, 286 cm; tracks: 60 in, 152 cm front, 59.50 in, 151 cm rear; length: 205.70 in, 522 cm; width: 74.20 in, 188 cm; height: 55.30 in, 140 cm; ground clearance: 5.90 in, 15 cm; weight: 3,558 lb, 1,614 kg; turning circle: 43.6 ft, 13.3 m; fuel tank: 15.2 imp gal, 18 US gal, 68 l.

BODY saloon/sedan; 4 doors; 6 seats, bench front seats, bench front seats, built-in headrests.

OPTIONALS heavy-duty cooling; limited slip differential; P 225/70 R x 15 tyres; heavy-duty suspension; tilt of steering wheel; heavy-duty battery; halogen headlamps; heated rear window with 100 A alternator; electric windows; electric sunroof; speed control device; reclining backrests; Landau vinyl roof; air-conditioning; heavy-duty equipment.

PLYMOUTH Voyager

165 hp power team

(optional)

See 130 hp power team, except for:

ENGINE max power (SAE net): 165 hp (123 kW) at 4,400 rpm; max torque (SAE net): 240 lb ft, 33.1 kg m (325 Nm) at 1,600 rpm; max engine rpm: 5,000; 31.6 hp/l (23.6 kW/l); 1 Carter downdraught 4-barrel carburettor; cooling: 25.9 imp pt, 31.1 US pt, 14.7 l.

PERFORMANCE max speed: 106 mph, 170 km/h; power-weight ratio: 21.7 lb/hp (29.5 lb/kW), 9.8 kg/hp (13.4 kg/kW); speed in direct drive at 1,000 rpm: 31.2 mph, 52.4 km/h.

DIMENSIONS AND WEIGHT weight: 3,576 lb, 1,622 kg.

Voyager

PRICE EX WORKS: $ 8,669

101 hp power team

(standard)

ENGINE front, transverse, 4 stroke; 4 cylinders, in line; 135 cu in, 2,213 cc (3.13 x 3.40 in, 80 x 86 mm); compression ratio: 9:1; max power (SAE net): 101 hp (74 kW) at 5,600 rpm; max torque (SAE net): 121 lb ft, 16.7 kg m (164 Nm) at 3,600 rpm; max engine rpm: 6,100; 45.6 hp/l (33.6 kW/l); cast iron block, light alloy head; 5 crankshaft bearings; valves: overhead, in line, hydraulic tappets, rockers; camshafts: 1, overhead; lubrication: rotary pump, full flow filter, 7.6 imp pt, 9.1 US pt, 4.3 l; 1 Holley downdraught twin barrel carburettor; exhaust system with catalytic converter; fuel feed: mechanical pump; water-cooled.

TRANSMISSION driving wheels: rear; clutch: single dry plate; gearbox: mechanical; gear: 5, fully synchronized; ratios: I 3.290, II 1.890, III 1.210, IV 0.880, V 0.720, rev 3.140; lever: steering column; final drive: helical spur gears; axle ratio: 2.560; width of rims: 5.5"; tyres: P 185/75 R x 14 SBR.

PERFORMANCE max speed: 92 mph, 148 km/h; power-weight ratio: 28.8 lb/hp (39.2 lb/kW), 13.1 kg/hp (17.8 kg/kW); carrying capacity: 2,500 lb, 1,134 kg; consumption: 34.8 m/imp gal, 29 m/US gal, 8.1 l x 100 km.

CHASSIS integral; front suspension: independent, Iso strut, wishbones, coil springs, telescopic dampers; rear: independent, leafsprings, coil springs, telescopic dampers.

STEERING rack-and-pinion, servo.

BRAKES front disc, front internal radial fins, rear drum, servo; swept area: front 194.54 sq in, 1,254 sq cm, rear 139.94 sq in, 902.3 sq cm, total 334.4 sq in, 2,156 sq cm.

ELECTRICAL EQUIPMENT 12 V; 335 A battery; 60 A alternator; transistorized ignition; 4 headlamps.

DIMENSIONS AND WEIGHT wheel base: 112 in, 284 cm; tracks: 59.90 in, 152 cm front, 62.10 in, 158 cm rear; length: 175.90 in, 447 cm; width: 69.60 in, 177 cm; height: 64.60 in, 164 cm; ground clearance: 5.40 in, 13.7 cm; weight: 2,911 lb, 1,320 kg; turning circle: 41 ft, 12.5 m; fuel tank: 12.5 imp gal, 15 US pt, 57 l.

BODY estate car/st. wagon; 2+1 doors; 5 or 6 seats, separate front seats.

OPTIONALS Torqueflite automatic transmission, hydraulic torque converter and planetary gars with 3 ratios (I 2.690, II 1.550, III 1, rev 2.100), 3.220 axle ratio; P 195/75 R x 14 SBR or P 205/70 R x 14 SBR tyres; electric windows; electric loocks; electric seats; 90 A alternator; 500 A battery; automatic speed control; tinted glass; light alloy wheels; air-conditioning; heavy-duty battery; heavy-duty suspension; rear window wiper-washer; SE equipment.

99 hp power team

(optional)

See 101 hp power team, except for:

ENGINE 155.9 cu in, 2,555 cc (3.59 x 3.86 in, 91.1 x 98 mm); compression ratio: 8.7:1; max power (SAE net): 99 hp (73 kW) at 4,800 rpm; max torque (SAE net): 143 lb ft, 19.7 kg m (193 Nm) at 2,000 rpm; max engine rpm: 5,300; 38.7 hp/l (28.5 kW/l).

TRANSMISSION (standard) gearbox: Torqueflite automatic transmission, hydraulic torque converter and planetary gears with 3 ratios, max ratio of converter at stall 2, possible manual selection; ratios: I 2.690, II 1.550, III 1, rev 2.100; axle ratio: 3.220; tyres: P 205/70 R x 14 (standard).

PERFORMANCE power-weight ratio: 38.3 lb/hp (52.1 lb/kW), 17.3 kg/hp (23.6 kg/kW); consumption: 28.8 m/imp gal, 24 m/US gal, 9.8 l x 100 km.

ELECTRICAL EQUIPMENT (standard) 500 A battery; (standard) 90 A alternator; Mopor electric transistorized ignition.

DIMENSIONS AND WEIGHT weight: 3,790 lb, 1,719 kg; fuel tank: 16.7 imp gal, 20 US gal, 76 l.

PONTIAC USA

1000 Series

PRICES EX WORKS:	$
4+1-dr Hatchback Sedan	5,824
2+1-dr Hatchback Coupé	5,621

Power team:	Standard for:	Optional for:
65 hp	both	—
51 hp (diesel)	—	both

65 hp power team

ENGINE front, 4 stroke; 4 cylinders, vertical, in line; 97.6 cu in, 1,599 cc (3.23 x 2.98 in, 82 x 75.6 mm); compression ratio: 9:1; max power (SAE net): 65 hp (48 kW) at 5,200 rpm; max torque (SAE net): 80 lb ft, 11.1 kg m (109 Nm) at 3,200 rpm; max engine rpm: 5,600; 40.6 hp/l (29.9 kW/l); cast iron block and head; 5 crankshaft bearings; valves: overhead, hydraulic tappets; camshafts: 1, overhead, cogged belt; lubrication: gear pump, full flow filter, 6.7 imp pt, 8 US pt, 3.8 l; 1 Holley downdraught twin barrel carburettor; air cleaner; exhaust system with catalytic converter; fuel feed: mechanical pump; water-cooled, 15.3 imp pt, 18.4 US pt, 8.7 l.

TRANSMISSION driving wheels: rear; clutch: single dry plate (diaphragm); gearbox: mechanical; gears: 4, fully synchronized; ratios: I 3.750, II 2.160, III 1.380, IV 1, rev 3.820; lever: central; final drive: hypoid bevel; axle ratio: 3.360 (3.620 for California only); width of rims: 5"; tyres: P 155/80 R x 13.

PERFORMANCE max speed: 90 mph, 145 km/h; power-weight ratio: Sedan 32.9 lb/hp (44.7 lb/kW), 14.9 kg/hp (20.3 kg/kW); speed in direct drive at 1,000 rpm: 17.9 mph, 28.8 km/h; consumption: 37.2 m/imp gal, 31 m/US gal, 7.6 l x 100 km.

CHASSIS integral with cross member reinforcements; front suspension: independent, wishbones, coil springs, anti-roll bar, telescopic dampers; rear: rigid axle (torque tube), longitudinal trailing radius arms, coil springs, transverse linkage bar, anti-roll bar, telescopic dampers.

STEERING rack-and-pinion; turns lock to lock: 3.60.

BRAKES front disc (diameter 9.68 in, 24.6 cm), rear drum; swept area: total 279.8 sq in, 1,804 sq cm.

ELECTRICAL EQUIPMENT 12 V; 310 A battery; 42 A alternator; Delco-Remy high energy ignition; 2 headlamps.

DIMENSIONS AND WEIGHT wheel base: Coupé 94.30 in, 239 cm - Sedan 97.30 in, 247 cm; front and rear track: 51.20 in, 130 cm; length: Sedan 164.90 in, 419 cm - Coupé 161.90 in, 411 cm; width: 61.80 in, 157 cm; height: 52.80 in, 134 cm; ground clearance: 5.30 in, 13.5 cm; weight: Coupé 2,079 lb, 943 kg - Sedan 2,138 lb, 970 kg; turning circle: Coupé 34.3 ft, 10.5 m - Sedan 34.9 lb, 10.6 kg; fuel tank: 10.3 imp gal, 12.5 US gal, 47 l.

BODY saloon/sedan, 4+1 doors - coupé, 2+1 doors; 4 seats, separate front seats, built-in headrests.

OPTIONALS 5-speed fully synchronized mechanical gearbox (I 3.760, II 2.180, III 1.360, IV 1, V 0.860, rev 3.760); Turbo-Hydramatic 180 automatic transmission, hydraulic torque converter and planetary gears with 3 ratios (I 2.420, II 1.480, III 1, rev 1.960), max ratio of converter at stall 2.25, possible manual selection, central lever, 3.360 or 3.620 axle ratio, power steering, consumption 36.2 m/imp gal, 30 m/US gal, 7.8 l x 100 km; heavy-duty battery; servo brake; vinyl roof; heavy-duty radiator; tilt of steering wheel; heated rear window; air-conditioning; De Luxe equipment; Custom two-tone paint equipment; sunroof; rear window wiper-washer; sport suspension; P 175/70 R x 13 SBR tyres; halogen headlamps; light alloy wheels.

51 hp (diesel) power team

See 65 hp power team, except for:

ENGINE diesel; 111 cu in, 1,818 cc (3.31 x 3.23 in, 84 x 82 mm); compression ratio: 22:1; max power (SAE net): 51 hp (38 kW) at 5,000 rpm; max torque (SAE net): 72 lb ft, 9.9 kg m (97 Nm) at 2,000 rpm; max engine rpm: 5,500; 28 hp/l (20.6 kW/l); valves: mechanical tappets; Bosch injection pump; cooling: 14.7 imp pt, 17.7 US pt, 8.4 l.

TRANSMISSION gears: 5, fully synchronized; ratios: I 3.760, II 2.170, III 1.410, IV 1, V 0.860, rev 3.750; axle ratio: 3.360.

PERFORMANCE max speed: 84 mph, 135 km/h; power-weight ratio: Sedan 45 lb/hp (61.1 lb/kW), 20.4 kg/hp (27.7 kg/kW); consumption: 52.2 m/imp gal, 43 m/US gal, 5.4 l x 100 km.

ELECTRICAL EQUIPMENT 550 A battery; 50 A alternator.

DIMENSIONS AND WEIGHT weight: Sedan 2,293 lb, 1,040 kg - Coupé 2,233 lb, 1,013 kg.

PONTIAC 1000 Hatchback Coupé

2000 Sunbird Series

PRICES EX WORKS:		$
1	4-dr Notchback Sedan	6,799
2	2+1-dr Hatchback Coupé	6,995
3	2-dr Notchback Coupé	6,675
4	4+1-dr St. Wagon	7,115
5	LE 4-dr Notchback Sedan	7,499
6	LE 2-dr Notchback Coupé	7,333
7	LE 2-dr Convertible	11,749
8	LE 4+1-dr St. Wagon	7,819
9	SE 4-dr Notchback Sedan	9,185
10	SE 2+1-dr Hatchback Coupé	9,489
11	SE 2-dr Notchback Coupé	9,019

Power team:	Standard for:	Optional for:
84 hp	1 to 8	—
88 hp	—	1 to 6,8
150 hp	9 to 11	1 to 3,5 to 7

84 hp power team

ENGINE front, transverse; 4 cylinders, in line; 109 cu in, 1,796 cc (3.34 x 3.13 in, 84.8 x 79.5 mm); compression ratio: 9:1; max power (SAE net): 84 hp (62 kW) at 5,200 rpm; max torque (SAE net): 102 lb ft, 14 kg m (138 Nm) at 2,800 rpm; max engine rpm: 5,500; 46.7 hp/l (34.4 kW/l); light alloy head, cast iron block; 5 crankshaft bearings; valves: overhead, in line, rockers; camshafts: 1, overhead, cogged belt; lubrication: gear pump, full flow filter, 6.6 imp pt, 8 US pt, 3.8 l; throttle-body electronic fuel injection; exhaust system with catalytic converter; air cleaner; fuel feed: electric pump; water-cooled, 13.2 imp pt, 15.6 US pt, 7.4 l.

TRANSMISSION driving wheels: front; clutch: single dry plate (diaphragm); gearbox: mechanical; gears: 5, fully synchronized; ratios: I 3.910, II 2.150, III 1.450, IV 1.030, V 0.740, rev 3.500; lever: central; final drive: helical spur gears; axle ratio: 3.450; width of rims: 5"; tyres: P 175/80 R x 13.

PERFORMANCE max speed: 94 mph, 152 km/h; power-weight ratio: Notchback Sedan 28.7 lb/hp (39 lb/kW), 13 kg/hp (17.7 kg/kW); carrying capacity: 700 lb, 320 kg; speed in top at 1,000 rpm: 21.6 mph, 34.8 km/h; consumption: 34.8 m/imp gal, 29 m/US gal, 8.1 l x 100 km.

CHASSIS integral; front suspension: independent, by McPherson, lower wishbones, coil springs/telescopic damper struts; rear: rigid axle, coil springs, telescopic dampers.

STEERING rack-and-pinion - Convertible servo; turns lock to lock: 4.04 - Convertible 2.88.

BRAKES front disc (diameter 9.72 in, 24.7 cm), rear drum, servo; swept area: total 251.8 sq in, 1,624 sq cm.

ELECTRICAL EQUIPMENT 12 V; 500 A battery; 56 A alternator; Delco-Remy high energy transistorized ignition; 4 headlamps.

DIMENSIONS AND WEIGHT wheel base: 101.18 in, 257 cm; tracks: 55.35 in, 141 cm front, 55.16 in, 140 cm rear; length: 175.71 in, 446 cm - st. wagons 176.37 in, 448 cm; width: 66.22 in, 168 cm - Hatchback Coupé 66.53 in, 169 cm; height: coupés 51.57 in, 131 cm - Convertible 52.75 in, 134 cm - sedans and st. wagons 53.93 in, 137 cm; ground clearance: 5.90 in, 15 cm; weight: Notchback Sedan 2,412 lb, 1,094 kg - St. Wagon 2,487 lb, 1,128 kg - Notchback Coupé 2,347 lb, 1,065 kg - Hatchback Coupé 2,424 lb, 1,099 kg - LE Notchback Sedan 2,436 lb, 1,105 kg - LE Notchback Coupé 2,384 lb, 1,082 kg - LE Convertible 2,514 lb, 1,140 kg - LE St. Wagon 2,502 lb, 1,135 kg; weight distribution: sedans 65% front, 35% rear; fuel tank: 12.3 imp gal, 14.7 US gal, 52 l.

BODY saloon/sedan, 4 doors - coupé, 2 or 2+1 doors - convertible, 2 doors - estate car/st. wagon 4+1 doors; 5 seats, separate front seats, built-in headrests.

OPTIONALS 5-speed fully synchronized mechanical gearbox (I 3.910, II 2.150, III 1.330, IV 0.920, V 0.740, rev 3.500); Turbo-Hydramatic automatic transmission with 3 ratios (I 2.840, II 1.600, III 1, rev 2.070), 3.190 axle ratio; 3.430 axle ratio, consumption 32.4 m/imp gal, 27 m/US gal, 8.7 l x 100 km; air-conditioning; adjustable steering; heavy-duty battery; electric windows; speed control; heated rear window; two-tone paint; (standard for Convertible) power steering; 94 A alternator; halogen headlamps; electric door locks; electric seats; heavy-duty radiator; rear window wiper-washer; tilt of steering wheels; sunroof; 195/70 R x 13 or 205/60 R x 14 tyres.

PONTIAC 2000 Sunbird SE Hatchback Coupé

PONTIAC Fiero SE Coupé

PONTIAC Phoenix LE Hatchback Sedan

88 hp power team

See 84 hp power team, except for:

ENGINE 122 cu in, 2,000 cc (3.50 x 3.15 in, 89 x 80 mm); compression ratio: 9.3:1; max power (SAE net): 88 hp (63 kW) at 4,800 rpm; max torque (SAE net): 110 lb ft, 15.1 kg m (148 Nm) at 2,400 rpm; max engine rpm: 5,300; 47.9 hp/l (35.2 kW/l); cast iron block and head; valves: overhead, in line, push-rods and rockers, hydraulic tappets; camshafts: 1, side, chain-driven; fuel feed: mechanical pump; cooling: 16 imp pt, 19.2 US pt, 9.1 l.

TRANSMISSION gears: 4, fully synchronized; ratios: I 3.530, II 1.950, III 1.240, IV 0.810, rev 3.420; axle ratio: 4.100.

PERFORMANCE max speed: 96 mph, 154 km/h; power-weight ratio: Notchback Coupé 26.7 lb/hp (36.3 lb/kW), 12.1 kg/hp (16.5 kg/kW); speed in top at 1,000 rpm: 18.6 mph, 30 km/h; consumption: 33.6 m/imp gal, 28 m/US gal, 8.4 l x 100 km.

BODY saloon/sedan, 4 doors - coupé, 2 or 2+1 doors - estate car/st. wagon, 4+1 doors.

150 hp power team

See 84 hp power team, except for:

ENGINE turbocharged; compression ratio: 8:1; max power (SAE net): 150 hp (110 kW) at 5,600 rpm; max torque (SAE net): 150 lb ft, 20.7 kg m (203 Nm) at 2,800 rpm; max engine rpm: 6,100; 83.5 hp/l (61.4 kW/l); turbocharger.

TRANSMISSION gears: 4, fully synchronized; ratios: I 3.530, II 1.950, III 1.240, IV 0.810, rev 3.420; axle ratio: 3.650.

PERFORMANCE max speed: 100 mph, 161 km/h; power-weight ratio: SE Notchback Sedan 16.8 lb/hp (22.9 lb/kW), 7.6 kg/hp (10.4 kg/kW).

ELECTRICAL EQUIPMENT 465 A battery; 66 A alternator.

DIMENSIONS AND WEIGHT weight: SE Notchback coupé 2,469 lb, 1,120 kg - SE Hatchback Coupé 2,477 lb, 1,124 kg - SE Notchback Sedan 2,528 lb, 1,147 kg.

BODY saloon/sedan, 4 doors - coupé, 2 or 2+1 doors - convertible, 2 doors.

OPTIONALS with automatic transmission 3.330 axle ratio.

Fiero

PRICES EX WORKS:	$
2-dr Coupé	**8,499**
SE 2-dr Coupé	**8,599**

ENGINE front, transverse, 4 stroke; 4 cylinders, in line; 151 cu in, 2,475 cc (4 x 3 in, 101.6 x 76.2 mm); compression ratio: 9:1; max power (SAE net): 92 hp (68 kW) at 4,000 rpm; max torque (SAE net): 134 lb ft, 18.5 kg m (181 Nm) at 2,800 rpm; max engine rpm: 4,500; 37.2 hp/l (27.3 kW/l); cast iron block and head; 5 crankshaft bearings; valves: overhead, inline, push-rods and rockers, hydraulic tappets; camshafts: 1, side; lubrication: gear pump, full flow filter, 4.9 imp pt, 5.9 US pt, 2.8 l; throttle-body electronic fuel injection; air cleaner; exhaust system with catalytic converter; fuel feed: electric pump; water-cooled, 22.9 imp pt, 27.5 US pt, 13 l.

TRANSMISSION driving wheels: rear; clutch: single dry plate; gearbox: mechanical; gears: 4, fully synchronized; ratios: I 3.530, II 1.950, III 1.240, IV 0.810, rev 3.420; lever: central; final drive: spiral bevel; axle ratio: 4.100; width of rims: 5.5" - SE 6"; tyres: P 185/80 R x 13 - SE P 215/60 R x 14.

PERFORMANCE max speed: 97 mph, 156 km/h; power-weight ratio: 26.7 lb/hp (36.4 lb/kW), 12.1 kg/hp (16.5 kg/kW); consumption: 31.3 m/imp gal, 26 m/US gal, 9 l x 100 km.

CHASSIS space-frame with non-structured Enduroflex panels; front suspension: independent, wishbones, coil springs, anti-roll bar, telescopic dampers; rear: independent, by McPherson, lower control radius arms, coil springs, telescopic dampers.

STEERING rack-and-pinion.

BRAKES disc, servo.

ELECTRICAL EQUIPMENT 12 V; 405 A battery; 66 A alternator; Delco-Remy ignition; 2 headlamps.

DIMENSIONS AND WEIGHT wheel base: 93.40 in, 237 cm; tracks: 57.80 in, 147 cm front, 58.70 in, 149 cm rear; length: 160.70 in, 408 cm; width: 68.90 in, 175 cm; height: 46.90 in, 119 cm; ground clearance: 5.40 in, 13.8 cm; weight: 2,459 lb, 1,116 kg; turning circle: 39.7 ft, 12.1 m; fuel tank: 8.3 imp gal, 10 US gal, 38 l.

BODY coupé; 2 doors; 2 separate seats, built-in headrests.

OPTIONALS 4-speed fully synchronized mechanical gearbox (I 3.530, II 1.950, III 1.240, IV 0.730, rev 3.420), 3.320 or 2.420 axle ratio; Turbo-Hydramatic automatic transmission, hydraulic torque converter and planetary gears with 3 ratios (I 2.840, II 1.600, III 1, rev 2.070), max ratio of converter at stall 2.35, possible manual selection, 3.180 axle ratio; power steering; air-conditioning; heavy-duty battery; electric windows; electric door locks; tilt of steering wheel.

Phoenix Series

PRICES EX WORKS:	$
1 4+1-dr Hatchback Sedan	**7,165**
2 2-dr Notchback Coupé	**7,090**
3 LE 4+1-dr Hatchback Sedan	**7,816**
4 LE 2-dr Notchback Coupé	**7,683**
5 SE 2-dr Notchback Coupé	**9,071**

Power team:	Standard for:	Optional for:
92 hp	1 to 4	—
112 hp	—	1 to 4
130 hp	5	1 to 4

92 hp power team

ENGINE front, transverse, 4 stroke; 4 cylinders, in line; 151 cu in, 2,475 cc (4 x 3 in, 101.6 x 76.2 mm); compression ratio: 9:1; max power (SAE net): 92 hp (68 kW) at 4,400 rpm; max torque (SAE net): 132 lb ft, 18.2 kg m (179 Nm) at 2,800 rpm; max engine rpm: 4,800; 37.2 hp/l (27.3 kW/l); cast iron block and head; 5 crankshaft bearings; valves: overhead, in line, push-rods and rockers, hydraulic tappets; camshafts: 1, side; lubrication: gear pump, full flow filter, 4.9 imp pt, 5.9 US pt, 2.8 l; throttle-body electronic fuel injection; air cleaner; exhaust system with catalytic converter; fuel feed: electric pump; water-cooled, 17.9 imp pt, 14.9 US pt, 8.5 l.

TRANSMISSION driving wheels: front; clutch: self-adjusting single dry plate (diaphragm); gearbox: mechanical; gears: 4, fully synchronized; ratios: I 3.530, II 1.950, III 1.240, IV 0.730, rev 3.420; lever: central; final drive: spiral bevel; axle ratio: 3.320; width of rims: 5.5"; tyres: P185/80 R x 13 - LE models P205/70 R x 13.

PERFORMANCE max speed: 97 mph, 156 km/h; power-weight ratio: Hatchback Sedan 27.8 lb/hp (37.7 lb/kW), 12.6 kg/hp (17.1 kg/kw); speed in top at 1,000 rpm: 19.8 mph, 31.8 km/h; consumption: 32.5 m/imp gal, 27 m/US gal, 8.7 l x 100 km.

CHASSIS integral; front suspension: independent, by McPherson, coil springs, stamped lower control arms, telescopic dampers; rear: rigid axle, trailing arm, stamped control arms, coil springs, telescopic dampers.

STEERING rack-and-pinion; turns lock to lock: 3.50.

BRAKES front disc (diameter 9.72 in, 24.7 cm), internal radial fins, rear drum; swept area: total 261.6 sq in, 1,687 sq cm.

ELECTRICAL EQUIPMENT 12 V; 405 A battery; 42 A alternator; Delco-Remy high energy ignition; 2 headlamps.

DIMENSIONS AND WEIGHT wheel base: 104.90 in, 266 cm; tracks: 58.70 in, 149 cm front, 57 in, 145 cm rear; length: sedans 183.07 in, 465 cm - coupés 182 in, 463 cm; width: 68.11 in, 175 cm; weight: Hatchback Sedan 2,554 lb, 1,159 kg - Notchback Coupé 2,463 lb, 1,117 kg - LE Hatchback Sedan 2,573 lb, 1,167 kg - LE Notchback Coupé 2,545 lb, 1,154 kg; weight distribution: 63% front, 37% rear; turning circle: 41 ft, 12.5 m; fuel tank: 12.4 imp gal, 14.7 US gal, 55 l.

BODY saloon/sedan, 4+1 doors - coupé, 2 doors; 5 seats, separate front seats, built-in headrests.

OPTIONALS automatic transmission with 3 ratios (I 2.840, II 1.600, III 1, rev 2.070), max ratio of converter at stall 1.98, possible manual selection, steering column lever, 2.390 or 2.840 axle ratio, consumption 30 m/imp gal, 27 m/US gal, 9.4 l x 100 km; 3.650 axle ratio; tilt of steering wheel; intermittent wiper; roof carrier; sunroof; reclining seats; custom interior; heated rear window; air-conditioning; servo brake; power steering; electric windows; electric door locks; P205/70 R x 13 tyres (except LE models); heavy-duty battery; 70 or 94 A alternator; heavy-duty cooling; anti-roll bar on rear suspension; cruise control; electric seats; light alloy wheels.

112 hp power team

See 92 hp power team, except for:

ENGINE 6 cylinders, Vee-slanted at 60°; 171 cu in, 2,803 cc (3.50 x 2.99 in, 88.8 x 76 mm); compression ratio: 8.5:1; max power (SAE net): 112 hp (84 kW) at 4,800 rpm; max torque (SAE net): 145 lb ft, 20 kg m (196 Nm) at 2,100 rpm; max engine rpm: 5,300; 40 hp/l (30 kW/l); 4 crankshaft bearings;

PONTIAC Fiero SE Coupé

112 HP POWER TEAM

camshafts: 1, at centre of Vee; lubrication: 6.7 imp pt, 7.9 US pt, 3.8 l; 1 Rochester E2SE downdraught twin barrel carburettor; cooling: 25.2 imp pt, 21 US pt, 11.2 l.

PERFORMANCE max speed: 106 mph, 170 km/h; power-weight ratio: Hatchback Sedan 23.4 lb/hp (31.8 lb/kW), 10.6 kg/hp (14.4 kg/kW); speed in top at 1,000 rpm: 23.1 mph, 37.3 km/h; consumption: 26.4 m/imp gal, 22 m/US gal, 10.7 l x 100 km.

DIMENSIONS AND WEIGHT weight: Hatchback Sedan 2,623 lb, 1,190 kg - Notchback Coupé 2,579 lb, 1,170 kg - LE Hatchback Sedan 2,628 lb, 1,192 kg - LE Notchback Coupé 2,568 lb, 1,165 kg.

OPTIONALS 2.530 axle ratio with automatic transmission.

130 hp power team

See 92 hp power team, except for:

ENGINE 6 cylinders, Vee-slanted at 60°; 171 cu in, 2,803 cc (3.50 x 2.99 in, 88.9 x 76 mm); compression ratio: 8.9:1; max power (SAE net): 130 hp (96 kW) at 5,400 rpm; max torque (SAE net): 145 lb ft, 20.1 kg m (197 Nm) at 2,400 rpm; max engine rpm: 5,600; 46.4 hp/l (34.2 kW/l); 4 crankshaft bearings; camshafts: 1, at centre of Vee; lubrication: 6.7 imp pt, 7.9 US pt, 3.8 l; 1 Rochester E2SE downdraught twin barrel carburettor; cooling: 17.6 imp pt, 21.1 US pt, 10 l.

TRANSMISSION axle ratio: 3.650.

PERFORMANCE max speed: 106 mph, 170 km/h; power-weight ratio: SE Notchback Coupé 20.6 lb/hp (28 lb/kW), 9.4 kg/hp (12.7 kg/kW); speed in top at 1,000 rpm: 23.1 mph, 37.3 km/h; consumption: 26.4 m/imp gal, 22 m/US gal, 10.7 l x 100 km.

DIMENSIONS AND WEIGHT weight: SE Notchback Coupé 2,681 lb, 1,216 kg.

OPTIONALS 3.330 or 3.060 axle ratio with automatic transmission.

6000 Series

PRICES EX WORKS:	$
1 4-dr Notchback Sedan	**8,873**
2 2-dr Notchback Coupé	**8,699**
3 4+1-dr St. Wagon	**9,221**
4 LE 4-dr Notchback Sedan	**9,292**
5 LE 2-dr Notchback Coupé	**9,142**
6 LE 4+1-dr St. Wagon	**9,612**
7 STE 4-dr Notchback Sedan	**14,437**

Power team:	Standard for:	Optional for:
92 hp	1 to 6	—
112 hp	—	1 to 6
130 hp	7	—
85 hp (diesel)	—	1 to 6

92 hp power team

ENGINE front, transverse, 4 stroke; 4 cylinders, in line; 151 cu in, 2,475 cc (4 x 3 in, 101.6 x 76.2 mm); compression ratio: 9:1; max power (SAE net): 92 hp (68 kW) at 4,400 rpm; max torque (SAE net): 132 lb ft, 18.2 kg m (179 Nm) at 2,800 rpm; max engine rpm: 4,900; 37.1 hp/l (27.3 kW/l); cast iron block and head; 5 crankshaft bearings; valves: overhead, in line, push-rods and rockers, hydraulic tappets; camshafts: 1, side; lubrication: gear pump, full flow filter, 4.9 imp pt, 5.9 US pt, 2.8 l; throttle-body electronic fuel injection; air cleaner; exhaust system with catalytic converter; fuel feed: electric pump; water-cooled, 14.9 imp pt, 17.9 US pt, 8.5 l.

PONTIAC 6000 STE Notchback Sedan

TRANSMISSION driving wheels: front; gearbox: automatic transmission, hydraulic torque converter and planetary gears with 3 ratios, max ratio of converter at stall 1.90, possible manual selection; ratios: I 2.840, II 1.600, III 1, rev 2.070; lever: central or steering column; final drive: helical spur gears; axle ratio: 2.390 - LE models and St. Wagon 2.840; width of rims: 5.5''; tyres: P 185/75 R x 14 BW.

PERFORMANCE max speed: 87 mph, 140 km/h; power-weight ratio: Notchback Sedan 29.9 lb/hp (40.6 lb/kW), 13.5 kg/hp (18.4 kg/kW); carrying capacity: 882 lb, 400 kg; acceleration: speed in direct drive at 1,000 rpm: 19.8 mph, 31.8 km/h; consumption: 30 m/imp gal, 25 m/US gal, 9.4 l x 100 km.

CHASSIS integral; front suspension: independent, by McPherson, stamped lower control arms, coil springs/telescopic damper struts; rear: rigid axle, swinging longitudinal leading arms, coil springs, telescopic dampers.

STEERING rack-and-pinion, servo; turns lock to lock: 3.05.

BRAKES front disc (diameter 9.72 in, 24.7 cm), internal radial fins, rear drum, servo; swept area: total 270.60 sq in, 1,746 sq cm.

ELECTRICAL EQUIPMENT 12 V; 405 A battery; 42 A alternator; Delco-Remy high energy ignition; 4 headlamps.

DIMENSIONS AND WEIGHT wheel base: 104.90 in, 266 cm; tracks: 58.70 in, 149 cm front, 57 in, 145 cm rear; length: 188.80 in, 479 cm; width: 72 in, 183 cm; height: 53.30 in, 136 cm - st. wagons 60 in, 137 cm; ground clearance: 7.10 in, 18.1 cm; weight: Notchback Coupé 2,707 lb, 1,228 kg - Notchback Sedan 2,748 lb, 1,246 kg - St. Wagon 2,909 lb, 1,320 kg - LE Notchback Coupé 2,731 lb, 1,239 kg - LE Notchback Sedan 2,772 lb, 1,257 kg - LE St. Wagon 2.924 lb, 1,326 kg; weight distribution: Notchback Sedan 62% front, 38% rear; turning circle: 41 ft, 12.5 m; fuel tank: 13.2 imp gal, 15.7 US gal, 59 l.

BODY saloon/sedan, 4 doors - coupé, 2 doors - estate car/st. wagon, 4+1 doors; 5 seats, separate front seats, built-in headrests.

OPTIONALS (for Notchback Coupé and Sedan) 2.840 axle ratio; (for LE Notchback Coupé and Sedan) 2.390 axle ratio; electric door locks; vinyl roof; air-conditioning; self-sealing tyres; 185/80 R x 14 or 195/75 R x 14 tyres; electric windows; 66, 78 and 94 A alternator; electronic speed control; halogen headlamps; tilt of steering wheel; sunroof.

112 hp power team

See 92 hp power team, except for:

ENGINE 6 cylinders, Vee-slanted at 60°; 171 cu in, 2,803 cc (3.50 x 2.99 in, 88.8 x 76 mm); compression ratio: 8.5:1; max power (SAE net): 112 hp (84 kW) at 4,800 rpm; max torque (SAE net): 145 lb ft, 20 kg m (196 Nm) at 2,100 rpm; max engine rpm: 5,300; 40 hp/l (29.4 kW/l); 4 crankshaft bearings; camshafts: 1, at centre of Vee; lubrication: 6.7 imp pt, 7.9 US pt, 3.8 l; 1 Rochester E2SE downdraught twin barrel carburettor; cooling: 20.8 imp pt, 24.9 US pt, 11.8 l.

TRANSMISSION axle ratio 2.840.

PERFORMANCE max speed: 106 mph, 170 km/h; power-weight ratio: Notchback Sedan 24.5 lb/hp (33.3 lb/kW), 11.1 kg/hp (15.1 kg/kW); consumption: 24.1 m/imp gal, 20 m/US gal, 11.7 l x 100 km.

ELECTRICAL EQUIPMENT 315 A battery; (standard) 66 A alternator).

DIMENSIONS AND WEIGHT weight: Notchback Coupé 2,793 lb, 1,267 kg - Notchback Sedan 2,833 lb, 1,285 kg - St. Wagon 2,996 lb, 1,359 kg - LE Notchback Coupé 2,817 lb, 1,278 kg - LE Notchback Sedan 2,857 lb, 1,296 kg - LE St. Wagon 3,009 lb, 1,365 kg.

OPTIONALS 440-T4 automatic transmission, hydraulic torque converter and planetary gears with 4 ratios (I 2.920, II 1.570, III 1, IV 0.700, rev 2.380), max ratio of converter at stall 1.90, possible manual selection, 3.060 axle ratio.

130 hp power team

See 92 hp power team, except for:

ENGINE 6 cylinders, Vee-slanted at 60°; 171 cu in, 2,803 cc (3.50 x 2.99 in, 88.8 x 76 mm); compression ratio: 8.9:1; max power (SAE net): 130 hp (96 kW) at 5,400 rpm; max torque (SAE net): 145 lb ft, 20.1 kg m (197 Nm) at 2,400 rpm; max engine rpm: 5,900; 46.4 hp/l (34.1 kW/l); 4 crankshaft bearings; camshafts: 1, at centre of Vee; lubrication: 6.7 imp pt, 7.9 US pt, 3.8 l; 1 Rochester E2SE downdraught twin barrel carburettor; cooling: 20.8 imp pt, 24.9 US pt, 11.8 l.

TRANSMISSION axle ratio 3.330.

PERFORMANCE max speed: 108 mph, 175 km/h; power-weight ratio: 23 lb/hp (31.3 lb/kW), 10.4 kg/hp (14.2 kg/kW); consumption: 24 m/imp gal, 20 m/US gal, 11.7 l x 100 km.

ELECTRICAL EQUIPMENT 54 Ah battery; 97 A alternator.

DIMENSIONS AND WEIGHT weight: 2,990 lb, 1,356 kg.

BODY saloon/sedan; 4 doors.

OPTIONALS 3.330 axle ratio.

85 hp (diesel) power team

See 92 hp power team, except for:

ENGINE diesel; 6 cylinders, Vee-slanted at 90°; 262 cu in, 4,294 cc (4.05 x 3.38 in, 103 x 86 mm); compression ratio: 21.6:1; max power (SAE net): 85 hp (63 kW) at 3,600 rpm; max torque (SAE net): 165 lb ft, 22.8 kg m (223 Nm) at 1,600 rpm; max engine rpm: 4,100; 19.8 hp/l (14.6 kW/l); 4 crankshaft bearings; camshafts: 1, at centre of Vee; lubrication: 10.1 imp pt, 12 US pt, 5.7 l; diesel injection pump; fuel feed: electric pump; cooling: 21.5 imp pt, 25.8 US pt, 12.2 l.

PERFORMANCE max speed: 90 mph, 145 km/h; power-weight ratio: Notchback Sedan 34.4 lb/hp (46.7 lb/kW), 15.5 kg/hp (21.2 kg/kW); consumption: 32.4 m/imp gal, 27 m/US gal, 8.7 l x 100 km.

ELECTRICAL EQUIPMENT 770 A battery; 94 A alternator (standard).

DIMENSIONS AND WEIGHT weight: Notchback Sedan 2,919 lb, 1,324 kg - Notchback Coupé 2,899 lb, 1,315 kg - St. Wagon 3.064 lb, 1,390 kg - LE Notchback Coupé 2,906 lb, 1,318 kg - LE Notchback Sedan 2,926 lb, 1,327 kg - LE St. Wagon 3,078 lb, 1,396 kg.

OPTIONALS 440-T4 automatic transmission, hydraulic torque converter and planetary gears with 4 ratios (I 2.920, II 1.570, III 1, IV 0.700, rev 2.380), max ratio of converter at stall 1.90, possible manual selection, 2.840 - st. wagons 3.060 axle ratio.

PONTIAC 6000 LE Station Wagon

Firebird Series

PRICES EX WORKS:	$
1 2-dr Hatchback Coupé	**8,349**
2 SE 2-dr Hatchback Coupé	**10,649**
3 Trans Am 2-dr Hatchback Coupé	**10,699**

PONTIAC Firebird SE Hatchback Coupé

Power team:	Standard for:	Optional for:
92 hp	1	—
107 hp	—	1,2
125 hp	2	—
150 hp	3	1,2
190 hp	—	3

92 hp power team

ENGINE front, transverse, 4 stroke; 4 cylinders, in line; 151 cu in, 2,475 cc (4 x 3 in, 101.6 x 76.2 mm); compression ratio: 9:1; max power (SAE net): 92 hp (68 kW) at 4,400 rpm; max torque (SAE net): 132 lb ft, 18.2 kg m (179 Nm) at 2,800 rpm; max engine rpm: 4,900; 37.2 hp/l (27.3 kW/l); cast iron block and head; 5 crankshaft bearings; valves: overhead, in line, push-rods and rockers, hydraulic tappets; camshafts: 1, side; lubrication: gear pump, full flow filter, 4.9 imp pt, 5.9 US pt, 2.8 l; throttle-body electronic fuel injection; air cleaner; exhaust system with catalytic converter; fuel feed: electric pump; water-cooled, 15.3 imp pt, 18.4 US pt, 8.7 l.

TRANSMISSION driving wheels: front; clutch: self-adjusting single dy plate (diaphragm); gearbox: mechanical; gears: 4, fully synchronized; ratios: I 3.760, II 2.180, III 1.420, IV 1, rev 3.760; lever: central; final drive: spiral bevel; axle ratio: 3.420; width of rims: 6"; tyres: P 195/75 R x 14.

PERFORMANCE max speed: 100 mph, 161 km/h; power-weight ratio: 31.1 lb/hp (42.3 lb/kW), 14.1 kg/hp (19.2 kg/kW); speed in direct drive at 1,000 rpm: 22.7 mph, 35.6 km/h; consumption: 28.8 m/imp gal, 24 m/US gal, 9.8 l x 100 km.

CHASSIS integral; front suspension: independent, wishbones, coil springs, anti-roll bar, telescopic dampers; rear: rigid axle, swinging longitudinal leading arms, anti-roll bar, coil springs, telescopic dampers.

STEERING recirculating ball, servo; turns lock to lock: 2.70.

BRAKES front disc (diameter 10.50 in, 26.7 cm), internal radial fins, rear drum, servo.

ELECTRICAL EQUIPMENT 12 V; 500 A battery; 42 A alternator; Delco-Remy transistorized ignition; 4 headlamps.

PONTIAC Firebird Trans Am Hatchback Coupé

DIMENSIONS AND WEIGHT wheel base: 101 in, 257 cm; tracks: 60.63 in, 154 cm front, 61.41 in, 156 cm rear; length: 189.90 in, 482 cm; width: 72.44 in, 184 cm; height: 49.61 in, 126 cm; ground clearance: 4.40 in, 11.3 cm; weight: 2,859 lb, 1,297 kg; weight distribution: 54% front, 46% rear; fuel tank: 13.5 imp gal, 16 US gal, 60 l.

BODY coupé; 2 doors; 4 seats, separate front seats, built-in headrests.

OPTIONALS Turbo-Hydramatic 700 4-R automatic transmission, hydraulic torque converter and planetary gears with 3 ratios and overdrive (I 3.060, II 1.630, III 1, overdrive 0.700, rev 2.290), max ratio of converter at stall 2.48, possible manual selection, 3.730 axle ratio; 5-speed fully synchronized mechanical gearbox (I 3.760, II 2.180, III 1.420, IV 1, V 0.720, rev 3.760), 3.730 axle ratio, consumption 30 m/imp gal, 25 m/US gal, 9.4 l x 100 km; electric windows, tilt of steering wheel; tinted glass; electric seats; air-conditioning; electric door locks; P 205/70 R x 14 tyres with 7" wide rims; 78 A alternator.

107 hp power team

See 92 hp power team, except for:

ENGINE 6 cylinders, Vee-slanted at 60°; 173 cu in, 2,835 cc (3.50 x 2.99 in, 88.8 x 76 mm); compression ratio: 8.5:1; max power (SAE net): 107 hp (79 kW) at 4,800 rpm; max torque (SAE net): 145 lb ft, 20 kg m (196 Nm) at 2,100 rpm; max engine rpm: 5,300; 37.7 hp/l (27.8 kW/l); 4 crankshaft bearings; camshafts: 1, at centre of Vee; lubrication: 6.7 imp pt, 7.9 US pt, 3.8 l; 1 Rochester E2SE downdraught twin barrel carburettor.

TRANSMISSION (standard) gears: 5, fully synchronized; ratios: I 3.500, II 2.140, III 1.360, IV 1, V 0.780, rev 3.390; axle ratio: SE 3.730; width of rims: 7" (standard); tyres: P 205/70 R x 14 (standard).

PERFORMANCE max speed: 105 mph, 169 km/h; power-weight ratio: SE 27.1 lb/hp (36.8 lb/kW), 12.3 kg/hp (16.7 kg/kW); consumption: 30 m/imp gal, 25 m/US gal, 9.4 l x 100 km.

ELECTRICAL EQUIPMENT 66 A alternator; 4 retractable headlamps.

DIMENSIONS AND WEIGHT weight: SE Coupé 2,915 lb, 1,322 kg.

125 hp power team

(not available in California)

See 92 hp power team, except for:

ENGINE 6 cylinders, Vee-slanted at 60°; 173 cu in, 2,835 cc (3.50 x 2.99 in, 88.8 x 76 mm); compression ratio: 8.9:1; max power (SAE net): 125 hp (92 kW) at 5,400 rpm; max torque (SAE net): 145 lb ft, 20 kg m (196 Nm) at 2,400 rpm; max engine rpm: 6,000; 44.1 hp/l (32.4 kW/l); 4 crankshaft bearings; camshafts: 1, at centre of Vee; lubrication: 6.7 imp pt, 7.9 US pt, 3.8 l; 1 Rochester E2SE downdraught twin barrel carburettor.

TRANSMISSION (standard) gears: 5, fully synchronized; ratios: I 3.500, II 2.140, III 1.360, IV 1, V 0.780, rev 3.390; axle ratio: 3.230; width of rims: 7" (standard); tyres: P 205/70 R x 14 (standard).

PERFORMANCE max speed: 108 mph, 175 km/h; power-weight ratio: 23.3 lb/hp (31.7 lb/kW), 10.5 kg/hp (14.4 kg/kW); consumption: 24.1 m/imp gal, 20 m/US gal, 11.7 l x 100 km.

ELECTRICAL EQUIPMENT 66 A alternator; 4 retractable headlamps.

DIMENSIONS AND WEIGHT weight: 2,915 lb, 1,322 kg.

OPTIONALS Turbo-Hydramatic 700 4-R automatic transmission, hydraulic torque converter and planetary gears with 3 ratios and overdrive (I 3.060, II 1.630, III 1, overdrive 0.700, rev 2.290), max ratio of converter at stall 2.48, possible manual selection; 3.730 axle ratio.

150 hp power team

See 92 hp power team, except for:

ENGINE 8 cylinders in Vee; 305 cu in, 4,999 cc (3.74 x 3.48 in, 95 x 88.4 mm); compression ratio: 8.6:1; max power (SAE net): 150 hp (110 kW) at 4,000 rpm; max torque (SAE net): 240 lb ft, 33 kg m (324 Nm) at 2,400 rpm; max engine rpm: 4,600; 30.4 hp/l (22.4 kW/l); camshafts: 1, at centre of Vee; lubrication: 8.1 imp pt, 9.7 US pt, 4.5 l; 1 Rochester E4MC downdraught 4-barrel carburettor; dual exhaust system; cooling: 25.3 imp pt, 30.4 US pt, 14.4 l.

TRANSMISSION gears: 5, fully synchronized; ratios: I 2.950, II 1.940, III 1.340, IV 1, V 0.730, rev 2.760; axle ratio: Trans Am 3.730 - other models 3.230; width of rims: 7" (standard); tyres: Trans Am P 205/70 HR x 14 (standard).

PERFORMANCE max speed: 125 mph, 201 km/h; power-weight ratio: Trans Am 21.3 lb/hp (28.9 lb/kW), 9.6 kg/hp (13.1 kg/kW); consumption: 19.2 m/imp gal, 16 m/US gal, 14.7 l x 100 km.

DIMENSIONS AND WEIGHT weight: Trans Am Coupé 3,191 lb, 1,447 kg.

OPTIONALS Turbo-Hydramatic 700 4-R automatic transmission, hydraulic torque converter and planetary gears with 3 ratios and overdrive (I 3.060, II 1.630, III 1, overdrive 0.700, rev 2.290), max ratio of converter at stall 2.34, possible manual selection, Trans Am 3.230 - other models 3.080 axle ratio, consumption 21.7 m/imp gal, 18 m/US gal, 13 l x 100 km.

190 hp power team

See 92 hp power team, except for:

ENGINE 8 cylinders in Vee; 305 cu in, 4,999 cc (3.74 x 3.48 in, 95 x 88.4 mm); compression ratio: 9.5:1; max power (SAE net): 190 hp (140 kW) at 4,800 rpm; max torque (SAE net): 240 lb ft, 33.1 kg m (325 Nm) at 3,200 rpm; max engine rpm: 5,300; 38 hp/l (27.9 kW/l); camshafts: 1, at centre of Vee; lubrication: 8.1 imp pt, 9.7 US pt, 4.5 l; 1 Rochester downdraught 4-barrel carburettor; cooling: 26.5 imp pt, 31.5 US pt, 15.6 l.

TRANSMISSION gears: 5, fully synchronized; ratios: I 2.950, II 1.940, III 1.340, IV 1, V 0.730, rev 2.760; axle ratio: 3.730; width of rims: 7" (standard); tyres: P 215/65 R x 15.

PERFORMANCE max speed: 127 mph, 205 km/h; power-weight ratio: 17 lb/hp (23.1 lb/kW), 7.7 kg/hp (10.4 kg/kW).

DIMENSIONS AND WEIGHT weight: 3,232 lb, 1,466 kg.

OPTIONALS Turbo-Hydramatic 700 4-R automatic transmission, hydraulic torque converter and planetary gears with 3 ratios and overdrive (I 3.060, II 1.630, III 1, overdrive 0.700, rev 2.290), max ratio of converter at stall 2.34, possible manual selection, 3.420 axle ratio.

Grand Prix Series

PRICES EX WORKS:	$
2-dr Notchback Coupé	**9,145**
LE 2-dr Notchback Coupé	**9,624**
Brougham 2-dr Notchback Coupé	**10,299**

Power team:	Standard for:	Optional for:
110 hp	all	—
150 hp	—	all
105 hp (diesel)	—	all

110 hp power team

ENGINE front, 4 stroke; 6 cylinders, Vee-slanted at 90°; 231 cu in, 3,785 cc (3.80 x 3.40 in, 96.5 x 86.4 mm); compression ratio: 8:1; max power (SAE net): 110 hp (82 kW) at 3,800 rpm; max torque (SAE net): 190 lb ft, 26.2 kg m (257 Nm) at 1,600 rpm; max engine rpm: 4,400; 29.1 hp/l (21.4 kW/l); cast iron block and head; 4 crankshaft bearings; valves: overhead, in line, push-rods and rockers, hydraulic tappets; camshafts: 1, at centre of Vee; lubrication: gear pump, full flow filter, 6.7 imp pt, 8 US pt, 3.8 l; 1 Rochester E2SE downdraught twin barrel electronic carburettor; thermostatic air cleaner; exhaust system with catalytic converter; fuel feed: mechanical pump; water-cooled, 20.6 imp pt, 24.7 US pt, 11.7 l.

TRANSMISSION driving wheels: rear; gearbox: Turbo-Hydramatic 200-C automatic transmission, hydraulic torque converter and planetary gears with 3 ratios, max ratio of converter at stall 2, possible manual selection; ratios: I 2.520, II 1.520, III 1, rev 1.930; lever: steering column; final drive: hypoid bevel; axle ratio: 2.410; width of rims: 6"; tyres: P 195/75 R x 14.

110 HP POWER TEAM

PERFORMANCE max speed: about 96 mph, 154 km/h; power-weight ratio: Notchback Coupé 29.2 lb/hp (39.6 lb/kW), 13.2 kg/hp (17.9 kg/kW); speed in direct drive at 1,000 rpm: 28.3 mph, 45.6 km/h; consumption: 25.2 m/imp gal, 21 m/US gal, 11.2 l x 100 km.

CHASSIS perimeter frame; front suspension: independent, wishbones, coil springs, anti-roll bar, telescopic dampers; rear: rigid axle, lower trailing radius arms, upper torque arms, coil springs, telescopic dampers.

STEERING recirculating ball; turns lock to lock: 3.30.

BRAKES front disc (diameter 10.50 in, 26.7 cm), front internal radial fins, rear drum, rear compensator.

ELECTRICAL EQUIPMENT 12 V; 315 A battery; 56 A alternator; Delco-Remy transistorized ignition; 4 headlamps.

DIMENSIONS AND WEIGHT wheel base: 108.10 in, 275 cm; tracks: 58.50 in, 149 cm front, 57.80 in, 147 cm rear; length: 201.90 in, 513 cm; width: 72.30 in, 184 cm; height: 54.72 in, 139 cm; ground clearance: 6.30 in, 16.1 cm; weight: Notchback Coupé 3,207 lb, 1,455 kg - LE Notchback Coupé 3,227 lb, 1,464 kg - Brougham Notchback Coupé 3,265 lb, 1,481 kg; fuel tank: 15.2 imp gal, 18.2 US gal, 69 l.

BODY coupé; 2 doors; 6 seats, separate front seats, built-in headrests.

OPTIONALS Turbo-Hydramatic 250-C automatic transmission, hydraulic torque converter and planetary gears with 3 ratios (I 2.740, II 1.570, III 1, rev 2.070), 3.230 axle ratio; 3.080 axle ratio; limited slip differential; P 205/70 R x 14 or P 205/75 R x 14 tyres; power steering; tilt of steering wheel; servo brake; heavy-duty battery; heavy-duty alternator; heavy-duty radiator; electric windows; automatic levelling and speed controls; heated rear window; electric sunroof; reclining backrests; air-conditioning; leather upholstery; 78, 85 or 94 A alternator.

150 hp power team

See 110 hp power team, except for:

ENGINE 8 cylinders in Vee; 305 cu in, 4,999 cc (3.74 x 3.48 in, 95 x 84.4 mm); compression ratio: 8.6:1; max power (SAE net): 150 hp (110 kW) at 4,000 rpm; max torque (SAE net): 240 lb ft, 33 kg m (324 Nm) at 2,400 rpm; max engine rpm: 4,600; 30.4 hp/l (22.4 kW/l); camshafts: 1, at centre of Vee; lubrication: 8.1 imp pt, 9.7 US pt, 4.5 l; 1 Rochester E4MC downdraught 4-barrel carburettor; dual exhaust system; cooling: 27.3 imp pt, 32.8 US pt, 15.5 l.

TRANSMISSION (standard) Turbo-Hydramatic 250-C automatic transmission, hydraulic torque converter and planetary gears with 3 ratios, possible manual selection; ratios: I 2.740, II 1.570, III 1, rev 2.070; axle ratio: 2.290.

PERFORMANCE max speed: 125 mph, 201 km/h; power-weight ratio; Notchback Coupé 21.7 lb/hp (29.5 lb/kW), 9.8 kg/hp (13.4 kg/kW); consumption: 20.4 m/imp gal, 17 m/US gal, 13.8 l x 100 km.

BRAKES servo (standard).

DIMENSIONS AND WEIGHT weight: Notchback Coupé 3,254 lb, 1,476 kg - LE Notchback Coupé 3,462 lb, 1,570 kg - Brougham Notchback Coupé 3,384 lb, 1,535 kg.

OPTIONALS 2.730 axle ratio; Turbo-Hydramatic 200 4-R automatic transmission, hydraulic torque converter and planetary gears with 3 ratios and overdrive (I 2.740, II 1.570, III 1, overdrive 0.670, rev 2.070), consumption 21.4 m/imp gal, 18 m/US gal, 13.1 l x 100 km.

PONTIAC Grand Prix Brougham Notchback Coupé

105 hp (diesel) power team

See 110 hp power team, except for:

ENGINE diesel; 8 cylinders in Vee; 350 cu in, 5,736 cc (4.06 x 3.38 in, 103 x 86 mm); compression ratio: 22.5:1; max power (SAE net): 105 hp (78 kW) at 3,200 rpm; max torque (SAE net): 200 lb ft, 27.6 kg m (271 Nm) at 1,600 rpm; max engine rpm: 3,500; 18.3 hp/l (13.6 kW/l); 5 crankshaft bearings; lubrication: 12.5 imp pt, 15 US pt, 7.1 l; diesel injection pump; air cleaner; cooling: 30.6 imp pt, 36.8 US pt, 17.4 l.

TRANSMISSION axle ratio: 2.290.

PERFORMANCE power-weight ratio: Notchback Coupé 31.6 lb/hp (43 lb/kW), 14.3 kg/hp (19.5 kg/kW); consumption: 27.6 m/imp gal, 23 m/US gal, 10.2 l x 100 km.

ELECTRICAL EQUIPMENT 2 batteries; 63 A alternator.

OPTIONALS Turbo-Hydramatic 200 4-R automatic transmission, hydraulic torque converter and planetary gears with 3 ratios and overdrive (I 2.740, II 1.570, III 1, overdrive 0.670, rev 2.070), 2.730 axle ratio.

Bonneville Series

PRICES EX WORKS:	**$**
4-dr Notchback Sedan	**9,131**
LE 4-dr Notchback Sedan	**9,358**
Brougham 4-dr Notchback Sedan	**9,835**

Power team:	**Standard for:**	**Optional for:**
110 hp	all	—
150 hp	—	all
105 hp (diesel)	—	all

110 hp power team

ENGINE front, 4 stroke; 6 cylinders, Vee-slanted at 90°; 231 cu in, 3,785 cc (3.80 x 3.40 in, 96.5 x 86.4 mm); compression ratio: 8:1; max power (SAE net): 110 hp (82 kW) at 3,800 rpm; max torque (SAE net): 190 lb ft, 26.2 kg m (257 Nm) at 1,600 rpm; max engine rpm: 4,400; 29.1 hp/l (21.4 kW/l); cast iron block and head; 4 crankshaft bearings; valves: overhead, in line, push-rods and rockers, hydraulic tappets; camshafts: 1, at centre of Vee; lubrication: gear pump, full flow filter, 6.7 imp pt, 8 US pt, 3.8 l; 1 Rochester E2SE downdraught twin barrel electronic carburettor; air cleaner; exhaust system with catalytic converter; fuel feed: mechanical pump; water-cooled, 20.6 imp pt, 24.7 US pt, 11.7 l.

TRANSMISSION driving wheels: rear; gearbox: Turbo-Hydramatic 200-C automatic transmission, hydraulic torque converter and planetary gears with 3 ratios, max ratio of converter at stall 2, possible manual selection; ratios: I 2.520, II 1.520, III 1, rev 1.940; lever: steering column; final drive: hypoid bevel; axle ratio: 2.410 (2.730 for California only); width of rims: 6"; tyres: P 205/75 R x 15.

PERFORMANCE max speed: 93 mph, 149 km/h; power-weight ratio: Notchback Sedan 28.7 lb/hp (39 lb/kW), 13 kg/hp (17.7 kg/kW); speed in direct drive at 1,000 rpm: 23.3 mph, 37.5 km/h; consumption: 25.2 m/imp gal, 21 m/US gal, 11.2 l x 100 km.

CHASSIS perimeter frame; front suspension: independent, wishbones, coil springs, anti-roll bar, telescopic dampers; rear: rigid axle, lower trailing radius arms, upper oblique torque arms, coil springs, telescopic dampers.

STEERING recirculating ball, variable ratio servo; turns lock to lock: 3.30.

BRAKES front disc (diameter 11 in, 27.9 cm), front internal radial fins, rear drum, servo; swept area: total 337.3 sq in, 2,176 sq cm.

ELECTRICAL EQUIPMENT 12 V; 315 A battery; 56 A alternator; Delco-Remy transistorized ignition; 4 headlamps.

DIMENSIONS AND WEIGHT wheel base: 108.10 in, 275 cm; tracks: 61.70 in, 157 cm front, 57.70 in, 147 cm rear; length: 200.20 in, 508 cm; width: 71.25 in, 181 cm; height: 55.90 in, 141 cm; ground clearance: 6.70 in, 12.9 cm; weight: Notchback Sedan 3,155 lb, 1,431 kg - LE Notchback Sedan 3,164 lb, 1,435 kg - Brougham Notchback Sedan 3,176 lb, 1,441 kg; turning circle: 41.6 ft, 12.7 m; fuel tank: 15.2 imp gal, 18.2 US gal, 69 l.

BODY saloon/sedan; 4 doors; 5 seats, separate front seats, built-in headrests.

OPTIONALS limited slip differential; 3.230 axle ratio; GR78 x 15 or HR78 x 15 tyres; GR70 x 15 tyres with 7" wide rims; tilt of steering wheel; automatic levelling control; electric windows; reclining backrests; speed control; heated rear window; heavy-duty battery; heavy-duty alternator; air-conditioning; 78, 85 or 94 A alternator.

PONTIAC Bonneville LE Notchback Sedan

150 hp power team

See 110 hp power team, except for:

ENGINE 8 cylinders in Vee; 305 cu in, 4,999 cc (3.74 x 3.48 in, 95 x 84.4 mm); compression ratio: 8.6:1; max power (SAE net): 150 hp (110 kW) at 4,000 rpm; max torque (SAE net): 240 lb ft, 33 kg m (324 Nm) at 2,400 rpm; max engine rpm: 4,600; 30.4 hp/l (22.4 kW/l); camshafts: 1, at centre of Vee; lubrication: 8.1 imp pt, 9.7 US pt, 4.5 l; 1 Rochester E4MC downdraught 4-barrel carburettor; dual exhaust system; cooling: 27.3 imp pt, 32.8 US pt, 15.5 l.

TRANSMISSION Turbo-Hydramatic 250-C automatic transmission, hydraulic torque converter and planetary gears with 3 ratios, possible manual selection; ratios: I 2.740, II 1.570, III 1, rev 2.070; axle ratio: 2.290.

PERFORMANCE max speed: 125 mph, 201 km/h; power-weight ratio: Notchback Sedan 22.1 lb/hp (30.1 lb/kW), 10 kg/hp (13.6 kg/kW); consumption: 20.4 m/imp gal, 17 m/US gal, 13.8 l x 100 km.

PONTIAC Bonneville LE Notchback Sedan

PONTIAC Parisienne Brougham Sedan

DIMENSIONS AND WEIGHT weight: Notchback Sedan 3,199 lb, 1,451 kg - LE Notchback Sedan 3,230 lb, 1,465 kg - Brougham Notchback Sedan 3,155 lb, 1,471 kg.

OPTIONALS leather upholstery; 2.730 axle ratio; Turbo-Hydramatic 200 4-R automatic transmission, hydraulic torque converter and planetary gears with 3 ratios and overdrive (I 2.740, II 1.570, III 1, overdrive 0.670, rev 2.070), consumption 21.4 m/imp gal, 18 m/US gal, 13.1 l x 100 km.

105 hp (diesel) power team

See 110 hp power team, except for:

ENGINE diesel; 8 cylinders in Vee; 350 cu in, 5,736 cc (4.06 x 3.38 in, 103 x 86 mm); compression ratio: 22.5:1; max power (SAE net): 105 hp (77 kW) at 3,200 rpm; max torque (SAE net): 200 lb ft, 27.6 kg m (271 Nm) at 1,600 rpm; max engine rpm: 3,500; 18.3 hp/l (13.5 kW/l); 5 crankshaft bearings; lubrication: 12.5 imp pt, 15 US pt, 7.1 l; diesel injection pump; cooling: 29.9 imp pt, 36 US pt, 17 l.

TRANSMISSION axle ratio: 2.290.

PERFORMANCE power-weight ratio: Notchback Sedan 33.2 lb/hp (45 lb/kW), 15 kg/hp (20.4 kg/kW); speed in direct drive at 1,000 rpm: 26.4 mph, 42.4 km/h; consumption: 27.6 m/imp gal, 23 m/US gal, 10.2 l x 100 km.

ELECTRICAL EQUIPMENT 2 batteries.

DIMENSIONS AND WEIGHT weight: Notchback Sedan 3,486 lb, 1,581 kg - LE Notchback Sedan 3,494 lb, 1,585 kg - Brougham Notchback Sedan 3,508 lb, 1,591 kg.

OPTIONALS Turbo-Hydramatic 200 4-R automatic transmission, hydraulic torque converter and planetary gears with 3 ratios and overdrive (I 2.740, II 1.570, III 1, overdrive 0.670, rev. 2.070), 2.730 axle ratio.

Parisienne Series

PRICES EX WORKS:	$
1 4-dr Sedan	**9,881**
2 4+1-dr St. Wagon	**10,394**
3 Brougham 4-dr Sedan	**10,281**

Power team:	Standard for:	Optional for:
110 hp	1,3	—
150 hp	2	1,3
105 hp (diesel)	—	all

110 hp power team

ENGINE front, 4 stroke; 6 cylinders, Vee-slanted at 90°; 231 cu in, 3,785 cc (3.80 x 3.40 in, 96.5 x 86.4 mm); compression ratio: 8:1; max power (SAE net): 110 hp (82 kW) at 3,800 rpm; max torque (SAE net): 190 lb ft, 26.2 kg m (257 Nm) at 1,600 rpm; max engine rpm: 4,400; 29.1 hp/l (21.4 kW/l); cast iron block and head; 4 crankshaft bearings; valves: overhead, in line, push-rods and rockers, hydraulic tappets; camshafts: 1, at centre of Vee; lubrication: gear pump, full flow filter, 6.7 imp pt, 8 US pt, 3.8 l; 1 Rochester E2SE downdraught twin barrel electronic carburettor; thermostatic air cleaner; exhaust system with catalytic converter; fuel feed: mechanical pump; water-cooled, 20.6 imp pt, 24.7 US pt, 11.7 l.

TRANSMISSION driving wheels: rear; gearbox: Turbo-Hydramatic 200-C automatic transmission, hydraulic torque converter and planetary gears with 3 ratios, max ratio of converter at stall 2.38, possible manual selection; ratios: I 2.740, II 1.570, III 1, rev 2.070; lever: steering column; final drive: hypoid bevel; axle ratio: 2.730; width of rims: 6"; tyres: P 205/75 R x 15.

PERFORMANCE max speed: 96 mph, 154 km/h; power-weight ratio: Sedan 31.7 lb/hp (43 lb/kW), 14.3 kg/hp (19.5 kg/kW); consumption: 22.7 m/imp gal, 19 m/US gal, 12.4 l x 100 km.

CHASSIS perimeter frame; front suspension: independent, wishbones, coil springs, anti-roll bar, telescopic dampers; rear: rigid axle, lower trailing radius arms, upper oblique torque arms, coil springs, anti-roll bar, telescopic dampers.

STEERING recirculating ball, servo; turns lock to lock: 3.13.

BRAKES front disc, rear drum, servo; swept area: total 329.8 sq in, 2,127 sq cm.

ELECTRICAL EQUIPMENT 12 V; 355 A battery; 42 A alternator; Delco-Remy transistorized ignition; 4 headlamps.

DIMENSIONS AND WEIGHT wheel base: 116 in, 295 cm; tracks: 61.80 in, 157 cm front, 60.80 in, 154 cm rear; length: 212.20 in, 539 cm; width: 75.30 in, 191 cm; height: 56.40 in, 143 cm; ground clearance: 6.40 in, 16.2 cm; weight: Sedan 3,484 lb, 1,580 kg - Brougham Sedan 3,531 lb, 1,601 kg; turning circle: 44.6 ft, 13.6 m; fuel tank: 20.9 imp gal, 25.1 US gal, 95 l.

BODY saloon/sedan; 4 doors; 5 seats, separate front seats, built-in headrests.

OPTIONALS 78, 85 or 94 A alternator; 3.230 axle ratio; air-conditioning; electric door locks; vinyl roof; electric windows; sport suspension; limited slip differential; heavy-duty battery; speed control; cornering lamps; halogen headlamps; heavy-duty cooling; sunroof; heated rear window; heavy-duty suspension; P 225/70 R x 15 tyres with 7" wide rims; tilt of steering wheel.

150 hp power team

See 110 hp power team, except for:

ENGINE 8 cylinders in Vee; 305 cu in, 4,999 cc (3.74 x 3.48 in, 95 x 84.4 mm); compression ratio: 8.6:1; max power (SAE net): 150 hp (110 kW) at 4,000 rpm; max torque (SAE net): 240 lb ft, 33 kg m (324 Nm) at 2,400 rpm; max engine rpm: 4,600; 30.4 hp/l (22.4 kW/l); lubrication: 8.1 imp pt, 9.7 US pt, 4.5 l; 1 Rochester E4MC downdraught 4-barrel carburettor; dual exhaust system; cooling: 27.3 imp pt, 32.8 US pt, 15.5 l.

TRANSMISSION gearbox: Turbo-Hydramatic 700 4-R automatic transmission, hydraulic torque converter and planetary gears with 3 ratios and overdrive, max ratio of converter at stall 2.15, possible manual selection; ratios: I 3.060, II 1.630, III 1, overdrive 0.700, rev 2.290; width of rims: (standard) 7"; tyres (standard): P 225/70 R x 15.

PERFORMANCE max speed: 125 mph, 201 km/h; power-weight ratio: St. Wagon 27.1 lb/hp (37 lb/kW), 12.3 kg/hp (16.8 kg/kW); consumption: 20.4 m/imp gal, 17 m/US gal, 13.8 l x 100 km.

ELECTRICAL EQUIPMENT 55 A alternator.

DIMENSIONS AND WEIGHT tracks: 62.20 in, 158 cm front, 64.10 in, 163 cm rear; length: 215.10 in, 546 cm; width: 79.30 in, 201 cm; height: 58.10 in, 148 cm; ground clearance: 6.70 in, 17 cm; weight: St. Wagon 4,080 lb, 1,850 kg; turning circle: 45.3 ft, 13.8 m.

BODY saloon/sedan, 4 doors - estate car/st. wagon, 4+1 doors.

OPTIONALS (except California) 3.080 axle ratio.

105 hp (diesel) power team

See 110 hp power team, except for:

ENGINE diesel; 8 cylinders in Vee; 350 cu in, 5,736 cc (4.06 x 3.38 in, 103 x 86 mm); compression ratio: 22.5:1; max power (SAE net): 105 hp (78 kW) at 3,200 rpm; max torque (SAE net): 200 lb ft, 27.6 kg m (271 Nm) at 1,600 rpm; max engine rpm: 3,500; 18.3 hp/l (13.6 kW/l); 5 crankshaft bearings; lubrication: 12.5 imp pt, 15 US pt, 7.1 l; diesel injection pump; air cleaner; cooling: 30.6 imp pt, 36.8 US pt, 17.4 l.

PONTIAC Parisienne Station Wagon

STUTZ Victoria

STUTZ Victoria

105 HP (DIESEL) POWER TEAM

TRANSMISSION (for St. Wagon only) gearbox: Turbo-Hydramatic 200 4-R automatic transmission, hydraulic torque converter and planetary gears with 3 ratios and overdrive, max ratio of converter at stall 1.90, possible manual selection; ratios: I 2.740, II 1.570, III 1, overdrive 0.670, rev 2.070; axle ratio: 2.930.

PERFORMANCE power-weight ratio: Sedan 33.2 lb/hp (45.1 lb/kW), 15 kg/hp (20.4 kg/kW); consumption: 27.6 m/imp gal, 23 m/US gal, 10.2 l x 100 km.

ELECTRICAL EQUIPMENT 250 A x 2 batteries; 63 A alternator.

BODY saloon/sedan, 4 doors - estate car/st. wagon, 4+1 doors.

OPTIONALS (except St. Wagon) Turbo-Hydramatic 200 4-R automatic transmission, hydraulic torque converter and planetary gears with 4 ratios (I 2.740, II 1.570, III 1, IV 0.670, rev 2.070), 2.930 axle ratio.

STUTZ USA

Victoria

PRICE EX WORKS: $ 125,000

ENGINE GM, front, 4 stroke; 8 cylinders in Vee; 350 cu in, 5,736 cc (4.06 x 3.38 in, 103.8 x 86 mm); compression ratio: 7.9:1; max power (DIN): 160 hp (118 kW) at 3,600 rpm; max torque (DIN): 270 lb ft, 37.2 kg m (365 Nm) at 2,000 rpm; max engine rpm: 4,000; 27.9 hp/l (20.5 kW/l); cast iron block and head; 5 crankshaft bearings; valves: overhead, in line, push-rods and rockers, hydraulic tappets; camshafts: 1, at centre of Vee; lubrication: gear pump, full flow filter, 10 imp pt, 12 US pt, 5.7 l; 1 Rochester M4MC downdraught 4-barrel carburettor; fuel feed: mechanical pump; water-cooled, 25.2 imp pt, 30.2 US pt, 14.4 l.

TRANSMISSION driving wheels: rear; gearbox: Turbo-Hydramatic 350 automatic transmission, hydraulic torque converter and planetary gears with 3 ratios, max ratio of converter at stall 2, possible manual selection; ratios: I 2.520, II 1.520, III 1, rev 1.930; final drive: hypoid bevel.

PERFORMANCE max speed: 106 mph, 170 km/h; power-weight ratio: 28.1 lb/hp (38.2 lb/kW), 12.7 kg/hp (17.3 kg/kW); consumption: 16.5 m/imp gal, 14 m/US gal, 16.9 l x 100 km.

CHASSIS box-perimeter frame; front suspension: independent, wishbones, coil springs, anti-roll bar, adjustable telescopic dampers; rear: rigid axle, lower trailing radius arms, upper oblique torque arms, coil springs, anti-roll bar, automatic telescopic dampers.

STEERING recirculating ball, variable ratio servo, tilt of steering wheel; turns lock to lock: 3.30.

BRAKES front disc (diameter 11 in, 27.9 cm), front internal radial fins, rear drum, servo; swept area: total 337.3 sq in, 2,175 sq cm.

ELECTRICAL EQUIPMENT 12 V; 3,200 W battery; alternator; Delco-Remy transistorized ignition; 2 headlamps.

DIMENSIONS AND WEIGHT wheel base: 126 in, 320 cm; tracks: 61.70 in, 157 cm front, 60.70 in, 154 cm rear; length: 234 in, 594 cm; width: 79 in, 201 cm; height: 54 in, 137 cm; ground clearance: 5.60 in, 14.2 cm; weight: 4,500 lb, 2,041 kg; fuel tank: 17.2 imp gal, 20.6 US gal, 78 l.

BODY saloon/sedan; 4 doors; 5-6 seats, bench front seats, built-in headrests; on-board computer; tinted glass; electric windows; electric seats; air-conditioning; leather or velour upholstery; beverage consolle.

OPTIONALS electric sunroof.

STUTZ Blackhawk VII Coupé

Blackhawk VII / Bearcat

PRICES EX WORKS:	$
Blackhawk VII 2-dr Coupé	**84,500**
Bearcat 2-dr Convertible	**129,500**

ENGINE GM, front, 4 stroke; 8 cylinders in Vee; 350 cu in, 5,736 cc (4.06 x 3.38 in, 103.8 x 86 mm); compression ratio: 7.9:1; max power (DIN): 160 hp (118 kW) at 3,600 rpm; max torque (DIN): 270 lb ft, 37.2 kg m (265 Nm) at 2,000 rpm; max engine rpm: 4,000; 27.9 hp/l (20.5 kW/l); cast iron block and head; 5 crankshaft bearings; valves: overhead, in line, push-rods and rockers, hydraulic tappets; camshafts: 1, at centre of Vee; lubrication: gear pump, full flow filter, 10 imp pt, 12 US pt, 5.7 l; 1 Rochester M4MC downdraught 4-barrel carburettor; fuel feed: mechanical pump; water-cooled, 25.2 imp pt, 30.2 US pt, 14.4 l.

TRANSMISSION driving wheels: rear; gearbox: Turbo-Hydramatic 350 automatic transmission, hydraulic torque converter and planetary gears with 3 ratios, max ratio of converter at stall 2, possible manual selection; ratios: I 2.520, II 1.520, III 1, rev 1.930; final drive: hypoid bevel.

PERFORMANCE max speed: 106 mph, 170 km/h; power-weight ratio: Coupé 27.8 lb/hp (37.7 lb/kW), 12.6 kg/hp (17.1 kg/kW) - Convertible 28.4 lb/hp (38.6 lb/kW), 12.9 kg/hp (17.5 kg/kW); consumption: 16.5 m/imp gal, 14 m/US gal, 16.9 l x 100 km.

CHASSIS box-perimeter frame; front suspension: independent, wishbones, coil springs, anti-roll bar, adjustable telescopic dampers; rear: rigid axle, lower trailing radius arms, upper oblique torque arms, coil springs, anti-roll bar, automatic telescopic dampers.

STEERING recirculating ball, variable ratio servo, tilt of steering wheel; turns lock to lock: 3.30.

BRAKES front disc (diameter 11 in, 27.9 cm), front internal radial fins, rear drum, servo; swept area: total 337.3 sq in, 2,175 sq cm.

ELECTRICAL EQUIPMENT 12 V; 3,200 W battery; alternator; Delco-Remy transistorized ignition; 2 headlamps.

DIMENSIONS AND WEIGHT wheel base: 116 in, 295 cm; tracks: 61.60 in, 156 cm front, 61.10 in, 155 cm rear; length: 227 in, 577 cm; width: 79 in, 201 cm; height: 54 in, 137 cm; weight: Coupé 4,450 lb, 2,018 kg - Convertible 4,550 lb, 2,063 kg; fuel tank: 20.9 imp gal, 25 US gal, 95 l.

BODY coupé - convertible; 2 doors; 5-6 seats, bench front seats, built-in headrests; on-board computer; tinted glass; electric windows; electric seats; air-conditioning; leather or velour upholstery.

OPTIONALS electric sunroof.

Royale Limousine

PRICE EX WORKS: $ 285,000

ENGINE GM, front, 4 stroke; 8 cylinders in Vee; 425 cu in, 6,964 cc (4.08 x 4.06 in, 104 x 103 mm); compression ratio: 8.2:1; max power (DIN): 180 hp (132 kW) at 4,000 rpm; max torque (DIN): 320 lb ft, 44.2 kg m (433 Nm) at 2,000 rpm; max engine rpm: 4,500; 25.7 hp/l (18.9 kW/l); cast iron block and head; 5 crankshaft bearings; valves: overhead, in line, push-rods and rockers, hydraulic tappets; camshafts: 1, at centre of Vee; lubrication: gear pump, full flow filter, 8.3 imp pt, 9.9 US pt, 4.7 l; 1 Rochester M4ME downdraught 4-barrel carburettor; fuel feed: mechanical pump; water-cooled, 34.7 imp pt, 41.6 US pt, 19.8 l.

TRANSMISSION driving wheels: rear; gearbox: Turbo-Hydramatic 400 automatic transmission, hydraulic torque converter and planetary gears with 3 ratios, max ratio of converter at stall 2, possible manual selection; ratios: I

STUTZ Bearcat Convertible

STUTZ Bearcat Convertible

2.480, II 1.480, III 1, rev 2.070; lever: steering column; final drive: hypoid bevel.

PERFORMANCE max speed: 112 mph, 180 km/h.

CHASSIS ladder frame with cross members; front suspension: independent, wishbones, coil springs, anti-roll bar, telescopic dampers; rear: rigid axle, lower trailing radius arms, upper oblique torque arms, coil springs, automatic telescopic dampers.

STEERING recirculating ball, variable ratio servo, tilt of steering wheel; turns lock to lock: 3.50.

BRAKES front disc (diameter 11.74 in, 29.8 cm), front internal radial fins, rear drum, servo; swept area: total 425.3 sq in, 2,743 sq cm.

ELECTRICAL EQUIPMENT 12 V; 365 A battery; alternator; Delco-Remy transistorized ignition; 2 headlamps.

DIMENSIONS AND WEIGHT wheel base: 171.86 in, 436 cm; tracks: 61.70 in, 157 cm front, 60.70 in, 154 cm rear; length: 295.27 in, 750 cm; width: 80 in, 203 cm; height: 56 in, 142 cm; ground clearance: 6.10 in, 15.6 cm; fuel tank: 20.9 imp gal, 25 US gal, 95 l.

BODY limousine; 4 doors; 7 seats, separate front seats, built-in headrests.

OPTIONALS electric sunroof at centre of car; throne seat for 2 hydraulically raised above roof line; 136.81 in, 347 cm or 144.50 in, 367 cm wheel base.

TOTAL REPLICA USA

Hi Boy

PRICE EX WORKS: $ 20,000

ENGINE Chevrolet, front, 4 stroke; 8 cylinders in Vee; 350 cu in, 5,736 cc (4 x 3.48 in, 101.6 x 88.3 mm); compression ratio: 8:1; max power (DIN): 250 hp (184 kW); 43.6 hp/l (32.1 kW/l); cast iron block and head; 5 crankshaft bearings; valves: overhead, in line, push-rods and rockers, hydraulic tappets; camshafts: 1, at centre of Vee; lubrication: gear pump, full flow filter, 8.3 imp pt, 10 US pt, 4.7 l; 1 Holley 450 CFM 4-barrel carburettor; fuel feed: mechanical pump; water-cooled, 19.9 imp pt, 24 US pt, 11.3 l.

TRANSMISSION driving wheels: rear; gearbox: Turbo-Hydramatic automatic transmission, hydraulic torque converter and planetary gears with 3 ratios; lever: central; final drive: hypoid bevel.

PERFORMANCE max speed: about 100 mph, 161 km/h; power-weight ratio: 11.5 lb/hp (15.4 lb/kW), 5.2 kg/hp (7 kg/kW); consumption: 23.9 m/imp gal, 20 m/US gal, 11.8 l x 100 km.

CHASSIS perimeter box-type with front and rear cross members; front suspension: rigid axle, semi-elliptic leafsprings, telescopic dampers; rear: rigid axle, lower trailing radius arms, upper oblique torque arms, coil springs, telescopic dampers.

STEERING recirculating ball.

BRAKES front disc, rear drum, twin master cylinder.

ELECTRICAL EQUIPMENT 12 V; alternator; Delco-Remy high energy ignition; 2 headlamps.

DIMENSIONS AND WEIGHT wheel base: 106 in, 269 cm; length: 186 in, 472 cm; width: 68 in, 173 cm; height: 64.50 in, 164 cm; ground clearance: 5.50 in, 14 cm; weight: 2,850 lb, 1,292 kg; fuel tank: 9.9 imp gal, 12 US gal, 45 l.

BODY roadster, in fiberglass material; 2 doors; 2+2 seats, in rumble seat, bench front seats; chrome windshield frame with tinted glass and stainless posts; heater; luggage rack with matching chrome bumpers; wire wheels; sunroof.

OPTIONALS rear-mounted spare tyre without luggage rack; side curtains.

Ford "B"

PRICES EX WORKS:	$
4-dr Phaeton	**30,000**
2-dr Roadster	**25,000**

ENGINE Chevrolet, front, 4 stroke; 8 cylinders in Vee; 350 cu in, 5,736 cc (4 x 3.48 in, 101.6 x 88.3 mm); compression ratio: 8:1; max power (DIN): 250 hp (184 kW); 43.6 hp/l (32.1 kW/l); cast iron block and head; 5 crankshaft bearings; valves: overhead, in line, push-rods and rockers, hydraulic tappets; camshafts: 1, at centre of Vee; lubrication: gear pump, full flow filter, 8.3 imp pt, 10 US pt, 4.7 l; 1 Holley 450 CFM 4-barrel carburettor; fuel feed: mechanical pump; water-cooled, 19.9 imp pt, 24 US pt, 11.3 l.

TRANSMISSION driving wheels: rear; gearbox: Turbo-Hydramatic automatic transmission, hydraulic torque converter and planetary gears with 3 ratios; lever: central; final drive: hypoid bevel.

PERFORMANCE max speed: about 100 mph, 161 km/h; power-weight ratio: 11.5 lb/hp (15.4 lb/kW), 5.2 kg/hp (7 kg/kW); consumption: 23.9 m/imp gal, 20 m/US gal, 11.8 l x 100 km.

CHASSIS perimeter box-type with front and rear cross members; front suspension: rigid axle, semi-elliptic leafsprings, telescopic dampers; rear: rigid axle, lower trailing radius arms, upper oblique torque arms, coil springs, telescopic dampers.

STEERING recirculating ball.

BRAKES front disc, rear drum, twin master cylinder.

ELECTRICAL EQUIPMENT 12 V; alternator; Delco-Remy high energy ignition; 2 headlamps.

DIMENSIONS AND WEIGHT wheel base: 106 in, 269 cm; length: 186 in, 472 cm; width: 68 in, 173 cm; height: 64.50 in, 164 cm; ground clearance: 5.50 in, 14 cm; weight: 2,850 lb, 1,292 kg; fuel tank: 9.9 imp gal, 12 US gal, 45 l.

BODY phaeton, 4 doors - roadster, 2 doors, in fiberglass material; Phaeton 4 seats, bench front seats - Roadster 2+2 seats, in rumble seat; chrome windshield frame with tinted glass and stainless posts; heater; luggage rack with matching chrome bumpers; wire wheels.

OPTIONALS side mounted spare tyre without luggage rack; side curtains.

VOLKSWAGEN USA

Rabbit Series

PRICES EX WORKS:		$
1	L 2+1-dr Hatchback Sedan	**6,390**
2	L 4+1-dr Hatchback Sedan	**6,600**
3	GL 4+1-dr Hatchback Sedan	**7,130**
4	GTI 2+1-dr Hatchback Sedan	**8,350**
5	L Diesel 2+1-dr Hatchback Sedan	**6,390**
6	L Diesel 4+1-dr Hatchback Sedan	**7,040**

TOTAL REPLICA Ford "B" Phaeton

TOTAL REPLICA Ford "B" Roadster

VOLKSWAGEN Rabbit L Hatchback Sedan

RABBIT SERIES

Power team:	Standard for:	Optional for:
65 hp	1 to 3	—
74 hp	—	1 to 3
90 hp	4	—
52 hp (diesel)	5,6	—

65 hp power team

ENGINE front, transverse, 4 stroke; 4 cylinders, vertical, in line; 105 cu in 1,715 cc (3.13 x 3.40 in, 79.5 x 86.4 mm); compression ratio: 8.2:1; max power (SAE net): 65 hp (51 kW) at 5,000 rpm; max torque (SAE net): 88 lb ft, 12.1 kg m (119 Nm) at 2,800 rpm; max engine rpm: 5,500; 36.1 hp/l (26.5 kW/l); cast iron block, light alloy head; 5 crankshaft bearings; valves: overhead, in line, thimble tappets; camshafts: 1, overhead, cogged belt; lubrication: gear pump, full flow filter, 7 imp pt, 8.4 US pt, 4 l; 1 downdraught single barrel carburettor; fuel feed: mechanical pump; water-cooled, expansion tank, 10.9 imp pt, 13.1 US pt, 6.2 l, electric thermostatic fan.

TRANSMISSION driving wheels: front; clutch: single dry plate; gearbox: mechanical; gears: 4, fully synchronized; ratios: I 3.450, II 1.750, III 1.060, IV 0.700, rev 3.170; lever: central; final drive: spiral bevel; axle ratio: 3.890; width of rims: 4.5" - GL 5"; tyres: P 155/80 R x 13 - GL P 175/70 R x 13.

PERFORMANCE max speed: 92 mph, 148 km/h; power-weight ratio: L 2+1-dr 29.2 lb/hp (39.6 lb/kW), 13.2 kg/hp (17.9 kg/kW); consumption: 37 m/imp gal, 31 m/US gal, 7.6 l x 100 km.

CHASSIS integral; front suspension: independent, by McPherson, lower wishbones, coil springs, telescopic dampers; rear: independent, torsional beam axle, trailing arms, coil springs, telescopic dampers.

STEERING rack-and-pinion; turns lock to lock: 3.90.

BRAKES front disc (diameter 9.40 in, 23.9 cm), rear drum, servo.

ELECTRICAL EQUIPMENT 12 V; 54 Ah battery; 65 A alternator; electronic ignition; 2 headlamps.

DIMENSIONS AND WEIGHT wheel base: 94.50 in, 240 cm; tracks: 54.70 in, 139 cm front, 53.50 in, 136 cm rear; length: 154.30 in, 398 cm; width: 63.40 in, 161 cm - GL 64.20 in, 163 cm; height: L 2+1-dr 53.20 in, 135 cm - L 4+1-dr 52.90 in, 134 cm; ground clearance: 4.60 in, 11.7 cm; weight: L 2+1-dr 1,894 lb, 859 kg - L 4+1-dr 1,938 lb, 879 kg - GL 2,004 lb, 909 kg; turning circle: 31.2 ft, 9.5 m; fuel tank: 8.8 imp gal, 10.6 US gal, 40 l.

BODY saloon/sedan; 2+1 or 4+1 doors; 5 seats, separate front seats, built-in headrests; folding rear seat; heated rear window.

OPTIONALS 5-speed mechanical gearbox (I 3.450, II 1.940, III 1.290, IV 0.910, V 0.710, rev 3.170), 3.890 axle ratio; automatic transmission, hydraulic torque converter and planetary gears with 3 ratios, possible manual selection (I 2.710, II 1.500, III 1, rev 2.460), 3.570 axle ratio, consumption 30 m/imp gal, 25 m/US gal, 9.4 l x 100 km.

74 hp power team

See 65 hp power team, except for:

ENGINE max power (SAE net): 74 hp (54 kW) at 5,000 rpm; max torque (SAE net): 90 lb ft, 12.4 kg m (122 Nm) at 3,000 rpm; 43.1 hp/l (31.5 kW/l); electronic fuel injection; fuel feed: electric pump.

PERFORMANCE power-weight ratio: L 2+1-dr 26.2 lb/hp (35.6 lb/kW), 11.8 kg/hp (16.1 kg/kW).

DIMENSIONS AND WEIGHT weight: L 2+1-dr 1,936 lb, 878 kg - L 4+1-dr 1,980 lb, 898 kg - GL 2,092 lb, 949 kg.

90 hp power team

See 65 hp power team, except for:

ENGINE 109 cu in, 1,786 cc (3.19 x 3.40 in, 81 x 86.4 mm); compression ratio: 8.5:1; max power (SAE net): 90 hp (66 kW) at 5,500 rpm; max torque (SAE net): 100 lb ft, 13.8 kg m (135 Nm) at 3,000 rpm; electronic fuel injection; fuel feed: electric pump.

TRANSMISSION (standard) gears: 5, fully synchronized; ratios: I 3.450, II 1.940, III 1.290, IV 0.980, V 0.710, rev 3.170; axle ratio: 3.940; width of rims: 6"; tyres: 185/60 x 14.

PERFORMANCE max speed: 107 mph, 172 km/h; power-weight ratio: 22.3 lb/hp (30.4 lb/kW), 10.1 kg/hp (13.8 kg/kW); consumption: 31.4 m/imp gal, 26 m/US gal, 9 l x 100 km.

DIMENSIONS AND WEIGHT weight: 2,010 lb, 912 kg.

BODY 2+1 doors.

52 hp (diesel) power team

See 65 hp power team, except for:

ENGINE diesel; 97 cu in, 1,588 cc (3.01 x 3.40 in, 76.5 x 86.4 mm); compression ratio: 23:1; max power (SAE net): 52 hp (38 kW) at 4,800 rpm; max torque (SAE net): 71 lb ft, 9.8 kg m (96 Nm) at 2,000 rpm; max engine rpm: 5,200; 32.7 hp/l (23.9 kW/l); Bosch injection pump.

PERFORMANCE max speed: 96 mph, 155 km/h; power-weight ratio: L Diesel 2+1-dr 37.4 lb/hp (50.8 lb/kW), 16.9 kg/hp (23.1 kg/kW); consumption: 50.4 m/imp gal, 42 m/US gal, 5.6 l x 100 km.

ELECTRICAL EQUIPMENT 63 Ah battery.

DIMENSIONS AND WEIGHT weight: L Diesel 2+1-dr 1,962 lb, 890 kg - L Diesel 4+1-dr 2,006 lb, 910 kg.

VOLKSWAGEN Rabbit L Hatchback Sedan

VOLKSWAGEN Rabbit GTI Hatchback Sedan

Middle East
Africa
Asia
Australasia

Models now in production

Illustrations and technical information

OTOSAN TURKEY

Anadol 16

PRICE EX WORKS: 1,075,000 liras

ENGINE front, 4 stroke; 4 cylinders, in line; 97.2 cu in, 1,593 cc (3.45 x 2.60 in, 87.6 x 66 mm); compression ratio: 8.2:1; max power (DIN): 70 hp (52 kW) at 5,300 rpm; max torque (DIN): 83 lb ft, 11.5 kg m (113 Nm) at 2,700 rpm; max engine rpm: 5,800; 43.9 hp/l (32.6 kW/l); 5 crankshaft bearings; valves: overhead, in line, rockers; camshafts: 1, overhead; lubrication: rotary pump, full flow filter, 6.2 imp pt, 7.4 US pt, 3.5 l; 1 variable Venturi downdraught single barrel carburettor; fuel feed: mechanical pump; water-cooled, 14.4 imp pt, 17.3 US pt, 8.2 l.

TRANSMISSION driving wheels: rear; clutch: single dry plate (diaphragm); gearbox: mechanical; gears: 4, fully synchronized; ratios: I 3.580, II 2.010, III 1.397, IV 1, rev 3.324; lever: central; final drive: hypoid bevel; axle ratio: 4.125; width of rims: 5"; tyres: 165 SR x 13.

PERFORMANCE max speed: 90 mph, 145 km/h; power-weight ratio: 29.8 lb/hp (39.9 lb/kW), 13.5 kg/hp (18.1 kg/kW); carrying capacity: 1,279 lb, 580 kg; speed in direct drive at 1,000 rpm: 15.8 mph, 25.5 km/h; consumption: 29.1 m/imp gal, 24.2 m/US gal, 9.7 l x 100 km.

CHASSIS box-type perimeter frame with cross members; front suspension: independent, wishbones, coil springs, anti-roll bar, telescopic dampers; rear: rigid axle, semi-elliptic leafsprings, telescopic dampers.

STEERING rack-and-pinion; turns lock to lock: 4.

BRAKES front disc, rear drum, servo; lining area: front 15.8 sq in, 102 sq cm, rear 75.8 sq in, 489 sq cm, total 91.6 sq in, 591 sq cm.

ELECTRICAL EQUIPMENT 12 V; 45 Ah battery; 540 W alternator; Motorcraft distributor; 2 headlamps.

DIMENSIONS AND WEIGHT wheel base: 100.79 in, 256 cm; tracks: 51.97 in, 132 cm front, 50.39 in, 128 cm rear; length: 177.56 in, 451 cm; width: 64.57 in, 164 cm; height: 55.51 in, 141 cm; ground clearance: 6.69 in, 17 cm; weight: 2,084 lb, 945 kg; weight distribution: 40% front, 60% rear; turning circle: 35.1 ft, 10.7 m; fuel tank: 8.6 imp gal, 10.3 US gal, 39 l.

BODY saloon/sedan, in plastic material; 4 doors; 5 seats, separate front seats.

PRACTICAL INSTRUCTIONS fuel: 87 oct petrol; oil: engine, 6.2 imp pt, 7.4 US pt, 3.5 l - gearbox and final drive 1.8 imp pt, 2.1 US pt, 1 l, SAE 80-90 EP, no change recommended; greasing: none; tappet clearances: inlet 0.009 in, 0.22 mm, exhaust 0.017 in, 0.43 mm; spark plug: Motorcraft AGR 22; valve timing: 23° 53° 53° 23°; tyre pressure: front 24-26 psi, 1.7-1.8 atm, rear 24-36 psi, 1.7-2.5 atm.

OPTIONALS 3.890 axle ratio; 4.5" wide rims.

OTOSAN Anadol 16

TOFAS TURKEY

Murat 131

ENGINE Fiat, front, 4 stroke; 4 cylinders, vertical, in line; 79.1 cu in, 1,297 cc (2.99 x 2.81 in, 76 x 71.5 mm); compression ratio: 7.8:1; max power (SAE): 70 hp (52 kW) at 5,250 rpm; max torque (SAE): 72 lb ft, 10 kg m (98 Nm) at 3,400 rpm; max engine rpm: 5,750; 54 hp/l (39.7 kW/l); cast iron block, light alloy head; 5 crankshaft bearings; valves: overhead, in line, slanted at 10°, push-rods and rockers; camshafts: 1, side, in crankcase, cogged belt; lubrication: gear pump, full flow filter (cartridge), 7.4 imp pt, 8.9 US pt, 4.2 l; 1 Solex 32 TEIE 42 downdraught twin barrel carburettor; fuel feed: mechanical pump; water-cooled, 13.4 imp pt, 16.1 US pt, 7.6 l, electric thermostatic fan.

TRANSMISSION driving wheels: rear; clutch: single dry plate (diaphragm); gearbox: mechanical; gears: 4, fully synchronized; ratios: I 3.667, II 2.100, III 1.361, IV 1, rev 3.526; lever: central; final drive: hypoid bevel; axle ratio: 4.100; width of rims: 4.5"; tyres: 165 SR x 13.

PERFORMANCE max speed: 93 mph, 150 km/h; power-weight ratio: 31.1 lb/hp (41.7 lb/kW), 14.1 kg/hp (18.9 kg/kW); carrying capacity: 882 lb, 400 kg; acceleration: standing ¼ mile 19.2 sec; speed in direct drive at 1,000 rpm: 15.7 mph, 25.3 km/h; consumption: 31.7 m/imp gal, 26.4 m/US gal, 8.9 l x 100 km.

CHASSIS integral; front suspension: independent, by McPherson, coil springs/telescopic damper struts, lower wishbones, anti-roll bar; rear: rigid axle, twin trailing lower radius arms, transverse linkage bar, coil springs, telescopic dampers.

STEERING rack-and-pinion; turns lock to lock: 3.40.

BRAKES front disc (diameter 8.94 in, 22.7 cm), rear drum, rear compensator, servo; lining area: front 19.2 sq in, 124 sq cm, rear 36.9 sq in, 238 sq cm, total 56.1 sq in, 362 sq cm.

ELECTRICAL EQUIPMENT 12 V; 45 Ah battery; 44 A alternator; Marelli distributor; 2 headlamps.

DIMENSIONS AND WEIGHT wheel base: 98.03 in, 249 cm; tracks: 53.94 in, 137 cm front, 51.57 in, 131 cm rear; length: 166.93 in, 424 cm; width: 64.17 in, 163 cm; height: 55.12 in, 140 cm; ground clearance: 5.51 in, 14 cm; weight: 2,172 lb, 985 kg; weight distribution: 53% front, 47% rear; turning circle: 34.8 ft, 10.6 m; fuel tank: 11 imp gal, 13.2 US gal, 50 l.

BODY saloon/sedan; 4 doors; 5 seats, separate front seats.

EL NASR EGYPT

Nasr 127 CL

ENGINE front, transverse, 4 stroke; 4 cylinders, vertical, in line; 55.1 cu in, 903 cc (2.56 x 2.68 in, 65 x 68 mm); compression ratio: 8.7:1; max power (DIN): 43 hp (32 kW) at 5,600 rpm; max torque (DIN): 47 lb ft, 6.5 kg m (64 Nm) at 3,000 rpm; max engine rpm: 6,400; 47.7 hp/l (35.1 kW/l); cast iron block, light alloy head; 3 crankshaft bearings; valves: overhead, in line, push-rods and rockers; camshafts: 1, side; lubrication: gear pump, full flow filter, 6.3 imp pt, 7.6 US pt, 3.6 l; 1 Bressel 30 IBA 22/350 or Solex C 30 31-40 downdraught single barrel carburettor; fuel feed: mechanical pump; water-cooled, 8.8 imp pt, 10.6 US pt, 5 l, electric thermostatic fan.

TRANSMISSION driving wheels: front; clutch: single dry plate; gearbox: mechanical; gears: 4, fully synchronized; ratios: I 3.583, II 2.235, III 1.454, IV 1.042, rev 3.714; lever: central; final drive: hypoid bevel; axle ratio: 4.152; width of rims: 5"; tyres: 135 SR x 13.

PERFORMANCE max speeds: (I) 25 mph, 40 km/h; (II) 40 mph, 65 km/h; (III) 62 mph, 100 km/h; (IV) 83 mph, 133 km/h; power-weight ratio: 57.7 lb/hp (78.5 lb/kW), 26.2 kg/hp (35.7 kg/kW); carrying capacity: 882 lb, 400 kg; acceleration: standing ¼ mile 20.9 sec; speed in top at 1,000 rpm: 15.8 mph, 25.4 km/h; consumption: 43.4 m/imp gal, 36.2 m/US gal, 6.5 l x 100 km.

CHASSIS integral; front suspension: independent, by McPherson, coil springs/telescopic damper struts, lower wishbones, anti-roll bar; rear: independent, swinging arms, transverse anti-roll leafsprings, coil springs, telescopic dampers.

STEERING rack-and-pinion; turns lock to lock: 3.50.

BRAKES front disc (diameter 8.94 in, 22.7 cm), rear drum, dual circuit, rear compensator; lining area: front 19.2 sq in, 124 sq cm, rear 33.3 sq in, 215 sq cm, total 52.5 sq in, 339 sq cm.

ELECTRICAL EQUIPMENT 12 V; 34 Ah battery; 43 A alternator; 2 headlamps.

DIMENSIONS AND WEIGHT wheel base: 87.40 in, 222 cm; tracks: 50.79 in, 129 cm front, 51.18 in, 130 cm rear; length: 146.46 in, 372 cm; width: 61.02 in, 155 cm; height: 50.39 in, 128 cm; ground clearance: 5.12 in, 13 cm; weight: 2,492 lb, 1,130 kg; turning circle: 31.5 ft, 9.6 m; fuel tank: 6.6 imp gal, 7.9 US gal, 30 l.

BODY saloon/sedan; 4+1 doors; 5 seats, separate front seats, folding rear seat.

PRACTICAL INSTRUCTIONS fuel: 90 oct petrol; oil: engine 6.3 imp pt, 7.6 US pt, 3.6 l, SAE 15W-40, change every 6,200 miles, 10,000 km - gearbox and final drive 4.2 imp pt, 5.1 US pt, 2.4 l, SAE 80W/90, change every 18,600 miles, 30,000 km; greasing: none; spark plug: Champion RN 9Y, Bosch WR 7D or Marelli CW 7 LPR; tappet clearances: inlet 0.006 in, 0.15 mm, exhaust 0.008 in, 0.20 mm; valve timing: 17° 43° 57° 3°; tyre pressure: front 24 psi, 1.7 atm, rear 27 psi, 1.9 atm.

Nasr 128 CL

ENGINE front, transverse, slanted 20° to front, 4 stroke; 4 cylinders, vertical, in line; 68.1 cu in, 1,116 cc (3.15 x 2.19 in, 80 x 55.5 mm); compression ratio: 9.2:1; max power (DIN): 55 hp (40 kW) at 6,000 rpm; max torque (DIN): 57 lb ft, 7.9 kg m (77 Nm) at 3,000 rpm; max engine rpm: 6,000; 49.3 hp/l (36.2 kW/l); cast iron block, light alloy head; 5 crankshaft bearings; valves: overhead, thimble tappets; camshafts: 1, overhead, cogged belt; lubrication: gear pump, full flow filter, 7.4 imp pt, 8.9 US pt, 4.2 l; 1 Weber 32 ICEV or Solex C 32 DISA 41 downdraught single barrel carburettor; fuel feed: mechanical pump; water-cooled, expansion tank, 11.4 imp pt, 13.7 US pt, 6.5 l, electric thermostatic fan.

TOFAS Murat 131

EL NASR Nasr Ritmo 65 CL

TRANSMISSION driving wheels: front; clutch: single dry plate (diaphragm); gearbox: mechanical; gears: 4, fully synchronized; ratios: I 3.583, II 2.235, III 1.454, IV 1.042, rev 3.714; lever: central; final drive: cylindrical gears; axle ratio: 3.765; width of rims: 4.5"; tyres: 145 SR x 13.

PERFORMANCE max speeds: (I) 30 mph, 48 km/h; (II) 50 mph, 80 km/h; (III) 75 mph, 120 km/h; (IV) 87 mph, 140 km/h; power-weight ratio: 32.3 lb/hp (44.4 lb/kW), 14.6 kg/hp (20.1 kg/kW); carrying capacity: 882 lb, 400 kg; acceleration: standing ¼ mile 19.7 sec, 0-50 mph (0-80 km/h) 15.8 sec; speed in top at 1,000 rpm: 13.7 mph, 22.1 km/h; consumption: 35.3 m/imp gal, 29.4 m/US gal, 8 l x 100 km.

CHASSIS integral; front suspension: independent, by McPherson, coil springs/telescopic damper struts, lower wishbones, anti-roll bar; rear: independent, single wide-based wishbones, transverse leafsprings, telescopic dampers.

STEERING rack-and-pinion; turns lock to lock: 3.50.

BRAKES front disc (diameter 8.94 in, 22.7 cm), rear drum, rear compensator, servo; lining area: front 19.2 sq in, 124 sq cm, rear 33.5 sq in, 216 sq cm, total 52.7 sq in, 340 sq cm.

ELECTRICAL EQUIPMENT 12 V; 34 Ah battery; 33 A alternator; Marelli distributor; 2 headlamps.

DIMENSIONS AND WEIGHT wheel base: 136.22 in, 345 cm; tracks: 51.57 in, 131 cm front, 51.77 in, 131 cm rear; length: 151.18 in, 384 cm; width: 62.60 in, 159 cm; height: 55.91 in, 142 cm; ground clearance: 5.71 in, 14.5 cm; weight: 1,775 lb, 805 kg; weight distribution: 61.5% front, 38.5% rear; turning circle: 35.8 ft, 10.9 m; fuel tank: 8.4 imp gal, 10 US gal, 38 l.

BODY saloon/sedan; 4 doors; 5 seats, separate front seats.

PRACTICAL INSTRUCTIONS fuel: 85 oct petrol; oil: engine 7.4 imp pt, 8.9 US pt, 4.2 l, SAE 20W-30, change every 6,200 miles, 10,000 km - gearbox and final drive 5.5 imp pt, 6.6 US pt, 3.1 l, SAE 90, change every 18,600 miles, 30,000 km; greasing: every 18,600 miles, 30,000 km; spark plug: Marelli; tappet clearances: inlet 0.016 in, 0.40 mm, exhaust 0.020 in, 0.50 mm; valve timing: 12° 52° 52° 12°; tyre pressure: front 26 psi, 1.8 atm, rear 24 psi, 1.7 atm.

Nasr Ritmo 65 CL

ENGINE front, 4 stroke; 4 cylinders, in line; 79.4 cu in, 1,301 cc (3.40 x 2.18 in, 86.4 x 55.5 mm); compression ratio: 9.1:1; max power (DIN): 65 hp (48 kW) at 5,800 rpm; max torque (DIN): 71 lb ft, 9.8 kg m (96 Nm) at 3,500 rpm; 49.9 hp/l (36.7 kW/l); cast iron block, light alloy head; 5 crankshaft bearings; valves: overhead, thimble tappets; camshafts: 1, overhead, cogged belt; lubrication: gear pump, cartridge filter, 8.3 imp pt, 9.9 US pt, 4.7 l; 1 Weber 32 ICEV 22 or Solex CB2 DISA/2 downdraught twin barrel carburettor; fuel feed: mechanical pump; water-cooled, expansion tank, 13.9 imp pt, 16.7 US pt, 7.9 l.

TRANSMISSION driving wheels: front; clutch: single dry plate; gearbox: mechanical; gears: 5, fully synchronized; ratios: I 3.583, II 2.235, III 1.454, IV 1.042, V 0.863, rev 3.714; lever: central; final drive: cylindrical gears; axle ratio: 3.765; width of rims: 4.5"; tyres: 145 SR x 13.

PERFORMANCE max speeds: (I) 31 mph, 50 km/h; (II) 43 mph, 75 km/h; (III) 75 mph, 120 km/h; (IV) and (V) 93 mph, 150 km/h; power-weight ratio: 30 lb/hp (40 lb/kW), 13.8 kg/hp (18.4 kg/kW); carrying capacity: 882 lb, 400 kg; speed in top at 1,000 rpm: 16.3 mph, 26.2 km/h; consumption: 35.3 m/imp gal, 29.4 m/US gal, 8 l x 100 km.

CHASSIS integral; front suspension: independent, by McPherson, lower wishbones, trailing links, coil springs/telescopic damper struts; rear: independent, by McPherson, lower wishbones, transverse semi-elliptic leafsprings, telescopic dampers.

STEERING rack-and-pinion; turns lock to lock: 3.50.

BRAKES front disc (diameter 8.94 in, 22.7 cm), rear drum, dual circuit, rear compensator; lining area: front 19.2 sq in, 124 sq cm, rear 33.3 sq in, 215 sq cm, total 52.5 sq in, 339 sq cm.

ELECTRICAL EQUIPMENT 12 V; 45 Ah battery; 45 A alternator; Marelli distributor; 2 headlamps.

DIMENSIONS AND WEIGHT wheel base: 96.38 in, 245 cm; tracks: 55.12 in, 140 cm front, 55.31 in, 140 cm rear; length: 155.12 in, 394 cm; width: 65 in, 165 cm; height: 55.12 in, 140 cm; weight: 1,895 lb, 895 kg; weight distribution: 62.5% front, 37.5% rear; turning circle: 33.8 ft, 10.3 m; fuel tank: 11.2 imp gal, 13.5 US gal, 51 l.

BODY saloon/sedan; 4+1 doors; 5 seats, separate front seats, folding rear seats.

PRACTICAL INSTRUCTIONS fuel: 85 oct petrol; oil: engine 7.7 imp pt, 9.3 US pt, 4.4 l, SAE 10W-40, change every 6,200 miles, 10,000 km - gearbox and final drive 5.3 imp pt, 6.3 US pt, 3 l, SAE 80W-90, change every 18,600 miles, 30,000 km; spark plug: Fiat 11.4 JR; valve timing: 12° 52° 52° 12°; tyre pressure: front 27 psi, 1.9 atm, rear 31 psi, 2.2 atm.

Nasr Polonez

ENGINE front, 4 stroke; 4 cylinders, in line; 90.4 cu in, 1,481 cc (3.03 x 3.13 in, 77 x 79.5 mm); compression ratio: 9.2:1; max power (DIN): 82 hp (60 kW) at 5,200 rpm; max torque (DIN): 84 lb ft, 11.6 kg m (114 Nm) at 3,400 rpm; max engine rpm: 6,000; 55.4 hp/l (40.5 kW/l); cast iron block, light alloy head; 3 crankshaft bearings; valves: overhead, push-rods and rockers; camshafts: 1, side, chain-driven; lubrication: gear pump, cartridge filter, 7 imp pt, 8.5 US pt, 4 l; 1 Weber 34 DC MP 2/25 vertical twin barrel carburettor; air cleaner; fuel feed: mechanical pump; water-cooled, 13.2 imp pt, 15.8 US pt, 7.5 l, electric thermostatic fan.

TRANSMISSION driving wheels: rear; clutch: single dry plate (diaphragm), hydraulically controlled; gearbox: mechanical; gears: 4, fully synchronized; ratios: I 3.753, II 2.132, III 1.378, IV 1, rev 3.867; lever: central; final drive: hypoid bevel; axle ratio: 4.100; width of rims: 5"; tyres: 175 SR x 13.

PERFORMANCE max speeds: (I) 25 mph, 40 km/h; (II) 44 mph, 71 km/h; (III) 69 mph, 111 km/h; (IV) 90 mph, 145 km/h; power-weight ratio: 30.6 lb/hp (41.9 lb/kW), 13.9 kg/hp (19 kg/kW); carrying capacity: 882 lb, 400 kg; acceleration: standing ¼ mile 11 sec; speed in direct drive at 1,000 rpm: 16.8 mph, 27 km/h; consumption: 29.4 m/imp gal, 24.5 m/US gal, 9.6 l x 100 km.

CHASSIS integral; front suspension: independent, wishbones, coil springs, anti-roll bar acting as lower trailing arms, telescopic dampers; rear: rigid axle, 3 semi-elliptic leafsprings, telescopic dampers.

STEERING worm and roller; turns lock to lock: 3.

BRAKES disc, servo; lining area: front 19.2 sq in, 124 sq cm, rear 19.2 sq in, 124 sq cm, total 38.4 sq in, 248 sq cm.

ELECTRICAL EQUIPMENT 12 V; 45 Ah battery; 528 W alternator; ZEM distributor; 4 headlamps, 2 halogen fog lamps.

DIMENSIONS AND WEIGHT wheel base: 98.78 in, 251 cm; tracks: 51.57 in, 131 cm front, 50.79 in, 129 cm rear; length: 168.20 in, 427 cm; width: 64.96 in, 165 cm; height: 57.87 in, 147 cm; ground clearance: 5.12 in, 13 cm; weight: 2,514 lb, 1,140 kg; weight distribution: 45% front, 55% rear; turning circle: 35.4 ft, 10.8 m; fuel tank: 9.9 imp gal, 11.9 US gal, 45 l.

BODY saloon/sedan; 4+1 doors; 5 seats, separate front seats, reclining backrests, adjustable headrests; heated rear window; rear window wiper-washer.

PRACTICAL INSTRUCTIONS fuel: 90 oct petrol; oil: engine 7 imp pt, 8.5 US pt, 4 l, SAE 10W-30/20W-40, change every 6,200 miles, 10,000 km - gearbox 2.6 imp pt, 3.2 US pt, 1.5 l, SAE 90 EP, change every 18,600 miles, 30,000 km - final drive 2.1 imp pt, 2.5 US pt, 1.2 l, SAE 90 EP, change every 18,600 miles, 30,000 km; spark plug: Champion N 9 Y; tappet clearances: inlet 0.008 in, 0.20 mm, exhaust 0.010 in, 0.25 mm; valve timing: 6° 44° 48° 2°; tyre pressure: front 26 psi, 1.8 atm, rear 27 psi, 1.9 atm.

OPTIONALS folding rear seats.

Nasr 131 CL

ENGINE front, 4 stroke; 4 cylinders, vertical, in line; 96.7 cu in, 1,585 cc (3.31 x 2.81 in, 84 x 71.5 mm); compression ratio: 9.1:1; max power (DIN): 85 hp (62 kW) at 5,600 rpm; max torque (DIN): 92 lb ft, 12.7 kg m (125 Nm) at 3,000 rpm; max engine rpm: 5,300; 63.1 hp/l (46.4 kW/l); cast iron block, light alloy head; 5 crankshaft bearings; valves: overhead, in line, slanted at 10°, push-rods and rockers; camshafts: 1, overhead, cogged belt; lubrication: gear pump, full flow filter (cartridge), 6.9 imp pt, 8.2 US pt, 3.9 l; 1 Weber 32 ADF/50 downdraught twin barrel carburettor; fuel feed: mechanical pump; water-cooled, 13 imp pt, 13.5 US pt, 7.4 l, electric thermostatic fan.

TRANSMISSION driving wheels: rear; clutch: single dry plate (diaphragm); gearbox: mechanical; gears: 4, fully synchronized; ratios: I 3.612, II 2.045, III 1.357, IV 1, rev 3.244; lever: central; final drive: hypoid bevel; axle ratio: 3.900; width of rims: 5"; tyres: 165 SR x 13.

PERFORMANCE max speeds: (I) 28 mph, 45 km/h; (II) 50 mph, 80 km/h; (III) 75 mph, 120 km/h; (IV) 99 mph, 160 km/h; power-weight ratio: 37.1 lb/hp (50.3 lb/kW), 16.8 kg/hp (22.8 kg/kW); carrying capacity: 992 lb, 450 kg; consumption: 38.7 m/imp gal, 32.7 m/US gal, 7.3 l x 100 km at 56 mph, 90 km/h.

CHASSIS integral; front suspension: independent, by McPherson, coil springs/telescopic damper struts, lower wishbones, anti-roll bar; rear: independent, transverse linkage bar, coil springs, telescopic dampers.

STEERING rack-and-pinion; turns lock to lock: 3.50.

BRAKES front disc (diameter 8.94 in, 22.7 cm), rear drum, dual circuit, rear compensator, servo; lining area: front 19.2 sq in, 124 sq cm, rear 41.9 sq in, 270 sq cm, total 61.1 sq in, 394 sq cm.

ELECTRICAL EQUIPMENT 12 V; 45 Ah battery; 45 A alternator; 2 headlamps.

DIMENSIONS AND WEIGHT wheel base: 98.03 in, 249 cm; tracks: 54.72 in, 139 cm front, 52.36 in, 133 cm rear; length: 167.72 in, 426 cm; width: 64.57 in, 164 cm; height: 55.55 in, 141 cm; ground clearance: 4.72 in, 12 cm; weight: 3,142 lb, 1,425 kg; turning circle: 35 ft, 10.6 m; fuel tank: 12.1 imp gal, 14.5 US gal, 55 l.

EL NASR Polonez

NASR 131 CL

BODY saloon/sedan; 4 doors; 5 seats, separate front seats, reclining backrests.

PRACTICAL INSTRUCTIONS fuel: 85 oct petrol; oil: engine 6.9 imp pt, 8.2 US pt, 3.9 l, SAE 15W/40, change every 6,200 miles, 10,000 km - gearbox 3.2 imp pt, 3.8 US pt, 1.8 l, SAE 90 EP, change every 18,600 miles, 30,000 km; spark plug: Bosch W 70 or Fiat CL 4 J; tappet clearances: inlet 0.009 in, 0.30 mm, exhaust 0.011 in, 0.40 mm; valve timing: 2° 42° 42° 2°; tyre pressure: front 26 psi, 1.8 atm, rear 27 psi, 1.9 atm.

EL NASR Nasr 131 CL

PEUGEOT NIGERIA

504 GR

ENGINE front, slanted at 45° to right, 4 stroke; 4 cylinders, in line; 109.6 cu in, 1,796 cc (3.31 x 3.19 in, 84 x 81 mm); compression ratio: 7.5:1; max power (DIN): 73 hp (54 kW) at 5,500 rpm; max torque (DIN): 101 lb ft, 14 kg m (137 Nm) at 2,500 rpm; max engine rpm: 6,000; 40.6 hp/l (29.9 kW/l); cast iron block, wet liners, light alloy head, hemispherical combustion chambers; 5 crankshaft bearings; valves: overhead, Vee-slanted, push-rods and rockers; camshafts: 1, side; lubrication: gear pump, metal gauze filter, 7 imp pt, 8.5 US pt, 4 l; 1 Solex 34 BICSA 3 downdraught single barrel carburettor; fuel feed: mechanical pump; water-cooled, 13.7 imp pt, 16.5 US pt, 7.8 l, electromagnetic thermostatic fan.

TRANSMISSION driving wheels: rear; clutch: single dry plate (diaphragm), hydraulically controlled; gearbox: mechanical; gears: 4, fully synchronized; ratios: I 3.704, II 2.153, III 1.410, IV 1, rev 3.747; lever: central; final drive: hypoid bevel; axle ratio: 3.700; width of rims: 5"; tyres: 165 SR x 14.

PERFORMANCE max speed: 94 mph, 152 km/h; power-weight ratio: 34.1 lb/hp (46.4 lb/kW), 15.4 kg/hp (21 kg/kW); carrying capacity: 1,169 lb, 530 kg; consumption: 30.1 m/imp gal, 25 m/US gal, 9.4 l x 100 km at 75 mph, 120 km/h.

CHASSIS integral; front suspension: independent, by McPherson, coil springs/telescopic damper struts, lower wishbones, anti-roll bar; rear: rigid axle, trailing lower radius arms, upper oblique torque arms, coil springs, anti-roll bar, telescopic dampers.

STEERING rack-and-pinion; turns lock to lock: 4.50.

BRAKES front disc (diameter 10.75 in, 27.3 cm), rear drum, dual circuit, rear compensator, servo; swept area: total 400.5 sq in, 2,583 sq cm.

ELECTRICAL EQUIPMENT 12 V; 45 Ah battery; 500 W alternator; Ducellier distributor; 2 headlamps.

DIMENSIONS AND WEIGHT wheel base: 107.87 in, 274 cm; tracks: 55.91 in, 142 cm front, 52.36 in, 133 cm rear; length: 176.77 in, 449 cm; width: 66.54 in, 169 cm; height: 57.48 in, 146 cm; ground clearance: 6.30 in, 16 cm; weight: 2,492 lb, 1,130 kg; turning circle: 35.8 ft, 10.9 m; fuel tank: 12.3 imp gal, 14.8 US gal, 56 l.

BODY saloon/sedan; 4 doors; 5 seats, separate front seats, reclining backrests; heated rear window; electric windows; tinted glass.

PRACTICAL INSTRUCTIONS fuel: 95 oct petrol; oil: engine 7 imp pt, 8.5 US pt, 4 l, SAE 20W-40, change every 3,100 miles, 5,000 km - gearbox 1.9 imp pt, 2.3 US pt, 1.1 l, SAE 20W-40, change every 6,200 miles, 10,000 km - final drive 2.8 imp pt, 3.4 US pt, 1.6 l, GP 90, change every 6,200 miles, 10,000 km; greasing: every 3,100 miles, 5,000 km, 6 points; tappet clearances: inlet 0.004 in, 0.10 mm, exhaust 0.010 in, 0.25 mm; tyre pressure: front 21 psi, 1.5 atm, rear 26 psi, 1.8 atm.

OPTIONALS air-conditioning.

504 SR

See 504 GR, except for:

BODY air-conditioning (standard).

504 Station Wagon

ENGINE front, slanted at 45° to right, 4 stroke; 4 cylinders, in line; 109.6 cu in, 1,796 cc (3.31 x 3.19 in, 84 x 81 mm); compression ratio: 7.5:1; max power (DIN): 73 hp (54 kW) at 5,500 rpm; max torque (DIN): 101 lb ft, 14 kg m (137 Nm) at 2,500 rpm; max engine rpm: 6,000; 40.6 hp/l (29.9 kW/l); cast iron block, wet liners, light alloy head, hemispherical combustion chambers; 5 crankshaft bearings; valves: overhead, Vee-slanted, push-rods and rockers; camshafts: 1, side; lubrication: gear pump, metal gauze filter, 7 imp pt, 8.5 US pt, 4 l; 1 Solex 34 BICSA 3 downdraught single barrel carburettor; fuel feed: mechanical pump; water-cooled, 13.7 imp pt, 16.5 US pt, 7.8 l, electromagnetic thermostatic fan.

TRANSMISSION driving wheels: rear; clutch: single dry plate (diaphragm), hydraulically controlled; gearbox: mechanical; gears: 4, fully synchronized; ratios: I 3.704, II 2.153, III 1.410, IV 1, rev 3.747; lever: steering column; final drive: hypoid bevel; axle ratio: 4.222; width of rims: 5"; tyres: 185 SR x 14.

PERFORMANCE max speed: 88 mph, 142 km/h; power-weight ratio: 38.5 lb/hp (52.4 lb/kW), 17.5 kg/hp (23.7 kg/kW); carrying capacity: 1,477 lb, 670 kg; consumption: 26.9 m/imp gal, 22.4 m/US gal, 10.5 l x 100 km at 75 mph, 120 km/h.

CHASSIS integral; front suspension: independent, by McPherson, coil springs/telescopic damper struts, lower wishbones, anti-roll bar; rear: rigid axle, trailing lower radius arms, upper oblique torque arms, 4 coil springs, anti-roll bar, telescopic dampers.

STEERING rack-and-pinion; turns lock to lock: 4.50.

BRAKES front disc (diameter 10.75 in, 27.3 cm), rear drum, dual circuit, rear compensator, servo; swept area: total 400.5 sq in, 2,583 sq cm.

ELECTRICAL EQUIPMENT 12 V; 55 Ah battery; 500 W alternator; Ducellier distributor; 2 headlamps.

DIMENSIONS AND WEIGHT wheel base: 114.17 in, 290 cm; tracks: 55.91 in, 142 cm front, 53.54 in, 136 cm rear; length: 118.98 in, 480 cm; width: 66.54 in, 169 cm; height: 61.02 in, 155 cm; ground clearance: 6.50 in, 16.5 cm; weight: 2,811 lb, 1,275 kg; turning circle: 37.4 ft, 11.4 m; fuel tank: 13.2 imp gal, 15.8 US gal, 60 l.

BODY estate car/st. wagon; 4+1 doors; 5 seats, separate front seats, reclining backrests; heated rear window; folding rear seat.

PRACTICAL INSTRUCTIONS fuel: 95 oct petrol; oil: engine 7 imp pt, 8.5 US pt, 4 l, SAE 20W-40, change every 3,100 miles, 5,000 km - gearbox 1.9 imp pt, 2.3 US pt, 1.1 l, SAE 20W-40, change every 6,200 miles, 10,000 km - final drive 2.8 imp pt, 3.4 US pt, 1.6 l, GP 90, change every 6,200 miles, 10,000 km; greasing: every 3,100 miles, 5,000 km, 6 points; tappet clearances: inlet 0.004 in, 0.10 mm, exhaust 0.010 in, 0.25 mm; tyre pressure: front 21 psi, 1.5 atm, rear 26 psi, 1.8 atm.

OPTIONALS air-conditoning.

PEUGEOT 504 Station Wagon

505 GL

ENGINE front, slanted at 45° to right, 4 stroke; 4 cylinders, in line; 109.6 cu in, 1,796 cc (3.31 x 3.19 in, 84 x 81 mm); compression ratio: 7.5:1; max power (DIN): 73 hp (54 kW) at 5,500 rpm; max torque (DIN): 101 lb ft, 14 kg m (137 Nm) at 2,500 rpm; max engine rpm: 6,000; 40.6 hp/l (29.9 kW/l); cast iron block, wet liners, light alloy head, hemispherical combustion chambers; 5 crankshaft bearings; valves: overhead, Vee-slanted, push-rods and rockers; camshafts: 1, side; lubrication: gear pump, metal gauze filter, 7 imp pt, 8.5 US pt, 4 l; 1 Solex 34 BICSA 3 downdraught twin barrel carburettor; fuel feed: mechanical pump; water-cooled, 13.7 imp pt, 16.5 US pt, 7.8 l, electromagnetic thermostatic fan.

TRANSMISSION driving wheels: rear; clutch: single dry plate (diaphragm), hydraulically controlled; gearbox: mechanical; gears: 4, fully synchronized; ratios: I 3.704, II 2.153, III 1.410, IV 1, rev 3.747; lever: central; final drive: hypoid bevel; axle ratio: 3.580; width of rims: 5"; tyres: 175 SR x 14.

PERFORMANCE max speed: 99 mph, 160 km/h; power-weight ratio: 36.8 lb/hp (48.5 lb/kW), 16.7 kg/hp (22.2 kg/kW); carrying capacity: 1,058 lb, 480 kg; consumption: 31 m/imp gal, 25.8 m/US gal, 9.1 l x 100 km at 75 mph, 120 km/h.

CHASSIS integral; front suspension: independent, by McPherson, coil springs/telescopic damper struts, lower wishbones, anti-roll bar; rear: independent, oblique semi-trailing arms, coil springs, anti-roll-bar, telescopic dampers.

STEERING rack-and-pinion; turns lock to lock: 4.50.

BRAKES front disc (diameter 10.75 in, 27.3 cm), rear drum, dual circuit, rear compensator, servo; swept area: total 400.5 sq in, 2,583 sq cm.

ELECTRICAL EQUIPMENT 12 V; 45 Ah battery; 500 W alternator; Ducellier distributor; 2 halogen headlamps.

DIMENSIONS AND WEIGHT wheel base: 107.87 in, 274 cm; tracks: 57.48 in, 146 cm front, 56.30 in, 143 cm rear;

PEUGEOT 505 SL

length: 180.31 in, 458 cm; width: 67.72 in, 172 cm; height: 57.09 in, 145 cm; ground clearance: 4.72 in, 12 cm; weight: 2,646 lb, 1,200 kg; weight distribution: 53% front, 47% rear; turning circle: 36.7 ft, 11.2 m; fuel tank: 12.3 imp gal, 14.8 US gal, 56 l.

BODY saloon/sedan; 4 doors; 5 seats, separate front seats, reclining backrests; heated rear window; air-conditioning; tinted glass; leather upholstery.

PRACTICAL INSTRUCTIONS fuel: 87 oct petrol; oil: engine 7 imp pt, 8.5 US pt, 4 l, SAE 20W-40, change every 3,100 miles, 5,000 km - gearbox 1.9 imp pt, 2.3 US pt, 1.1 l, SAE 20W-40, change every 6,200 miles, 10,000 km - final drive 2.8 imp pt, 3.4 US pt, 1.6 l, GP 90, change every 6,200 miles, 10,000 km; greasing: every 3,100 miles, 5,000 km, 6 points; tappet clearances: inlet 0.004 in, 0.10 mm, exhaust 0.010 in, 0.25 mm; tyre pressure: front 23 psi, 1.6 atm, rear 27 psi, 1.9 atm.

505 SL

See 505 GL, except for:

ENGINE 120.3 cu in, 1,971 cc (3.46 x 3.19 in, 88 x 81 mm); compression ratio: 8:1; max power (DIN): 88 hp (65 kW) at 4,800 rpm; max torque (DIN): 116 lb ft, 16 kg m (157 Nm) at 3,000 rpm; max engine rpm: 5,500; 44.6 hp/l (32.9 kW/l); 1 Zenith 35-40 INAT or Solex 32-35 TMIMA downdraught twin barrel carburettor; cooling: 12.5 imp pt, 15 US pt, 7.1 l.

TRANSMISSION gears: 5, fully synchronized; ratios: I 3.592, II 2.088, III 1.368, IV 1, V 0.823, rev 3.634; axle ratio: 3.890; width of rims: 5.5"; tyres: 185/70 T x 14.

PERFORMANCE power-weight ratio: 30.1 lb/hp (40.9 lb/kW), 13.6 kg/hp (18.5 kg/kW).

STEERING servo.

BODY electric windows.

VOLKSWAGEN NIGERIA

Golf / Jetta

Golf CL 4+1-dr Limousine
Jetta C 4-dr Limousine
Jetta CL 4-dr Limousine

ENGINE front, transverse, slanted at 15° to front, 4 stroke; 4 cylinders, vertical, in line; 104.6 cu in, 1,715 cc (3.13 x 3.40 in, 79.5 x 86.4 mm); compression ratio: 8.2:1; max power (DIN): 75 hp (55 kW) at 5,000 rpm; max torque (DIN): 100 lb ft, 13.8 kg m (135 Nm) at 2,800 rpm; max engine rpm: 5,500; 43.7 hp/l (32.1 kW/l); cast iron block, light alloy head; 5 crankshaft bearings; valves: overhead, in line, thimble tappets; camshafts: 1, overhead, cogged belt; lubrication: gear pump, full flow filter, 7.9 imp pt, 9.5 US pt, 4.5 l; 1 Solex 34 PICT downdraught single barrel carburettor; fuel feed: mechanical pump; liquid-cooled, expansion tank, 7.9 imp pt, 9.5 US pt, 4.5 l, electric thermostatic fan.

TRANSMISSION driving wheels: front; clutch: single dry plate, hydraulically controlled; gearbox: mechanical; gears: 4, fully synchronized; ratios: I 3.450, II 1.940, III 1.290, IV 0.969, rev 3.170; lever: central; final drive: spiral bevel; axle ratio: 3.890; width of rims: 5; tyres: 165 SR x 13.

PERFORMANCE max speed: 98 mph, 158 km/h - Jetta models 97 mph, 156 km/h; power-weight ratio: Golf 24.3 lb/hp (33.1 lb/kW), 11 kg/hp (15 kg/kW); carrying capacity: 1,003 lb, 455 kg; speed in top at 1,000 rpm: 19.6 mph, 31.6 km/h; consumption: not declared.

CHASSIS integral; front suspension: independent, by McPherson, lower wishbones, coil springs/telescopic damper struts; rear: independent, swinging longitudinal trailing arms linked by a T-section cross-beam, coil springs/telescopic damper struts.

STEERING rack-and-pinion.

BRAKES front disc, rear drum, 2 x circuits, servo.

ELECTRICAL EQUIPMENT 12 V; 63 Ah battery; 65 A alternator; Bosch distributor; 2 headlamps - Jetta models 4 headlamps.

DIMENSIONS AND WEIGHT wheel base: 94.49 in, 240 cm; tracks: 54.72 in, 139 cm front, 53.46 in, 136 cm rear; length: 150.20 in, 381 cm - Jetta models 164.98 in, 419 cm; width: 63.39 in, 161 cm; height: 55.51 in, 141 cm; ground clearance: 4.92 in, 12.5 cm; weight: Golf 1,819 lb, 825 kg - Jetta sedans 1,918 lb, 870 kg; turning circle: 34.4 ft, 10.5 m; fuel tank: 8.8 imp gal, 10.6 US gal, 40 l.

BODY saloon/sedan; 4 or 4+1 doors; 5 seats, separate front seats, headrests; heated rear window.

PRACTICAL INSTRUCTIONS fuel: 91 oct petrol; oil: engine 7.9 imp pt, 9.5 US pt, 4.5 l, SAE 10W-50, change every 4,700 miles, 7,500 km - gearbox and final drive 2.5 imp pt, 3 US pt, 1.4 l, SAE 80, no change recommended; greasing: none; spark plug: Bosch W9D; tappet clearances: inlet 0.009 in, 0.25 mm, exhaust 0.016 in, 0.40 mm; tyre pressure: front 26 psi, 1.8 atm, rear 26 psi, 1.8 atm.

Beetle 1500

PRICE EX WORKS: 5,295 naira

ENGINE rear, 4 stroke; 4 cylinders, horizontally opposed; 81.1 cu in, 1,493 cc (3.27 x 2.72 in, 83 x 69 mm); compression ratio: 6.8:1; max power (SAE): 42 hp (31 kW) at 4,000 rpm; max torque (SAE): 78 lb ft, 10.8 kg m (106 Nm) at 2,600 rpm; max engine rpm: 4,200; 28.1 hp/l (20.8 kW/l); cast iron block, light alloy head; crankshaft bearings: 4; valves: 2 per cylinder, overhead, push-rods and rockers; camshafts: 1, central, lower; lubrication: gear pump, filter in sump, oil cooler; lubrication: 4.4 imp pt, 5.3 US pt, 2.5 l; 1 Solex H30 PIC downdraught twin barrel carburettor; fuel feed: mechanical pump; air-cooled.

TRANSMISSION driving wheels: rear; clutch: single dry plate; gearbox: mechanical; gears: 4, fully synchronized; ratios: I 3.800, II 2.060, III 1.320, IV 0.880, rev 3.880; lever: central; final drive: spiral bevel; axle ratio: 4.125; width of rims: 4.5; tyres: 5.60 x 15.

PERFORMANCE max speeds: (I) 18 mph, 29 km/h; (II) 34 mph, 54 km/h; (III) 55 mph, 89 km/h; (IV) 79 mph, 127 km/h; power-weight ratio: 42 lb/hp (56.9 lb/kW), 19 kg/hp (25.8 kg/kW); carrying capacity: 838 lb, 380 kg; acceleration: 0-50 mph (0-80 km/h) 13 sec; speed in top at 1,000 rpm: 18.6 mph, 30 km/h; consumption: 32.1 m/imp gal, 26.7 m/US gal, 8.8 l x 100 km.

CHASSIS backbone platform; front suspension: independent, twin swinging longitudinal trailing arms, transverse laminated torsion bars, anti-roll bar, telescopic dampers; rear: independent, swinging semi-axles, swinging longitudinal trailing arms, transverse torsion bars, telescopic dampers.

STEERING worm and roller, telescopic dampers; turns lock to lock: 2.70.

BRAKES drum; lining area: front 56.43 sq in, 364 sq cm, rear 56.43 sq in, 364 sq cm, total 112.86 sq in, 728 sq cm.

ELECTRICAL EQUIPMENT 12 V; 36 Ah battery; 45 A alternator; Bosch distributor; 2 headlamps.

DIMENSIONS AND WEIGHT wheel base: 94.49 in, 240 cm; tracks: 51.57 in, 131 cm front, 53.15 in, 135 cm rear; length: 159.45 in, 405 cm; width: 60.63 in, 154 cm; height: 59.06 in, 150 cm; ground clearance: 5.91 in, 15 cm; weight: 1,764 lb, 800 kg; turning circle: 36.1 ft, 11 m; fuel tank: 9 imp gal, 10.8 US gal, 41 l.

BODY saloon/sedan; 2 doors; 5 seats, separate front seats, adjustable backrests.

PRACTICAL INSTRUCTIONS fuel: 85 oct petrol; oil: engine 4.4 imp pt, 5.3 US pt, 2.5 l, SAE 20W-30, change every 3,100 miles, 5,000 km - gearbox and final drive 5.3 imp pt, 6.3 US pt, 3 l, SAE 90, change every 31,000 miles, 50,000 km; greasing: every 6,200 miles, 10,000 km, 4 points; spark plug: Bosch W145T1.1; tappet clearances: inlet 0.004 in, 0.10 mm, exhaust 0.004 in, 0.10 mm; valve timing: 7°30' 37° 44°30' 4°; tyre pressure: front 16 psi, 1.1 atm, rear 24 psi, 1.7 atm.

Passat TS

PRICE EX WORKS: 8,595 naira

ENGINE front, slanted at 20° to right, 4 stroke; 4 cylinders, in line; 96.9 cu in, 1,588 cc (3.13 x 3.15 in, 79.5 x 80 mm); compression ratio: 8.2:1; max power (DIN): 75 hp (55 kW) at 5,600 rpm; max torque (DIN): 89 lb ft, 12.3 kg m (121 Nm) at 3,200 rpm; max engine rpm: 6,000; 47.2 hp/l (34.8 kW/l); cast iron block, light alloy head; 5 crankshaft bearings; valves: overhead, thimble tappets; camshafts: 1, overhead, cogged belt; lubrication: gear pump, full flow filter, 6.2 imp pt, 7.4 US pt, 3.5 l; 1 Solex 1B3 downdraught single barrel carburettor; fuel feed: mechanical pump; liquid-cooled, expansion tank, 7.9 imp pt, 9.5 Us pt, 4.5 l, electric thermostatic fan.

TRANSMISSION driving wheels: front; clutch: single dry plate (diaphragm); gearbox: mechanical; gears: 4, fully synchronized; ratios: I 3.450, II 1.950, III 1.290, IV 1.090, rev 3.170; lever: central; final drive: spiral bevel; axle ratio: 4.110; width of rims: 5; tyres: 175/70 SR x 13.

PERFORMANCE max speed: 99 mph, 160 km/h; power-weight ratio: 26.9 lb/hp (36.7 lb/kW), 12.2 kg/hp (16.6 kg/kW); carrying capacity: 937 lb, 425 kg; speed in top at 1,000 rpm: 17.7 mph, 28.6 km/h; consumption: 31.4 m/imp gal, 26.1 m/US gal, 9 l x 100 km at 75 mph, 120 km/h.

CHASSIS integral, front auxiliary subframe; front suspension: independent, by McPherson, lower wishbones, anti-roll bar, coil springs, telescopic damper struts; rear: rigid axle, trailing radius arms, transverse linkage bar, coil springs, anti-roll bar, telescopic dampers.

VOLKSWAGEN Golf CL Limousine

VOLKSWAGEN Jetta CL Limousine

PASSAT TS

STEERING rack-and-pinion, damper.

BRAKES front disc (diameter 9.41 in, 23.9 cm), rear drum, 2 x circuits, servo.

ELECTRICAL EQUIPMENT 12 V; 54 Ah battery; 55 A alternator; Bosch distributor; 4 halogen headlamps.

DIMENSIONS AND WEIGHT wheel base: 97.24 in, 247 cm; tracks: 52.76 in, 134 cm front, 53.15 in, 135 cm rear; length: 168.90 in, 429 cm; width: 62.99 in, 160 cm; height: 54.25 in, 138 cm; ground clearance: 6.02 in, 15.3 cm; weight: 2,018 lb, 915 kg; turning circle: 35.1 ft, 10.7 m; fuel tank: 13.2 imp gal, 15.8 US gal, 60 l.

BODY saloon/sedan; 4 doors; 5 seats, separate front seats, reclining backrests, headrests; heated rear window; laminated windscreen; air-conditioning.

PRACTICAL INSTRUCTIONS fuel: 91 oct petrol; oil: engine 6.2 imp pt, 7.4 US pt, 3.5 l, SAE 10W-50, change every 4,700 miles, 7,500 km - gearbox and final drive 3.2 imp pt, 3.8 US pt, 1.8 l, SAE 80, no change recommended; greasing: none; spark plug: Bosch W7D; tappet clearances: inlet 0.009 in, 0.25 mm, exhaust 0.016 in, 0.45 mm; tyre pressure: front 26 psi, 1.8 atm, rear 26 psi, 1.8 atm.

Santana

PRICES EX WORKS:	naira
LX 4-dr Limousine	10,995
GX 4-dr Limousine	11,870

ENGINE front, slanted at 20° to right, 4 stroke; 4 cylinders, in line; 108.7 cu in, 1,781 cc (3.19 x 3.40 in, 81 x 86.4 mm); compression ratio: 8.5:1; max power (DIN): 90 hp (66 kW) at 5,000 rpm; max torque (DIN): 107 lb ft, 14.8 kg m (145 Nm) at 3,300 rpm; max engine rpm: 6,000; 50.5 hp/l (37.1 kW/l); cast iron block, light alloy head; 5 crankshaft bearings; valves: overhead, thimble tappets; camshafts: 1, overhead, cogged belt; lubrication: gear pump, full flow filter, 6.2 imp pt, 7.4 US pt, 3.5 l; 1 Keihin downdraught carburettor; fuel feed: mechanical pump; liquid-cooled, expansion tank, 7.9 imp pt, 9.5 Us pt, 4.5 l, electric thermostatic fan.

TRANSMISSION driving wheels: front; clutch: single dry plate (diaphragm); gearbox: mechanical; gears: 4, fully synchronized; ratios: I 3.455, II 1.789, III 1.133, IV 0.829, rev 3.167; lever: central; final drive: spiral bevel; axle ratio: 4.111; width of rims: 5.5"; tyres: 185/70 SR x 13.

PERFORMANCE max speed: 106 mph, 170 km/h; power-weight ratio: 24.1 lb/hp (32.9 lb/kW), 10.9 kg/hp (14.9 kg/kW); carrying capacity: 1,047 lb, 475 kg; acceleration: 0-50 mph (0-80 km/h) 7.4 sec; speed in top at 1,000 rpm: 20.2 mph, 32.5 km/h; consumption: 34 m/imp gal, 28.3 m/US gal, 8.3 l x 100 km at 75 mph, 120 km/h.

CHASSIS integral, front auxiliary subframe; front suspension: independent, by McPherson, lower wishbones, anti-roll bar, coil springs, telescopic damper struts; rear: rigid axle, trailing radius arms, transverse linkage bar, coil springs, anti-roll bar, telescopic dampers.

STEERING rack-and-pinion, damper.

BRAKES front disc (diameter 9.41 in, 23.9 cm), rear drum, 2 x circuits, rear compensator, servo.

ELECTRICAL EQUIPMENT 12 V; 63 Ah battery; 65 A alternator; Bosch distributor; 2 halogen headlamps.

DIMENSIONS AND WEIGHT wheel base: 100.39 in, 255 cm; tracks: 55.67 in, 141 cm front, 55.98 in, 142 cm rear; length: 178.94 in, 454 cm; width: 66.73 in, 169 cm; height: 55.43 in, 140 cm; ground clearance: 5.71 in, 14.5 cm; weight: 2,172 lb, 985 kg; turning circle: 35.1 ft, 10.7 m; fuel tank: 13.2 imp gal, 15.8 US gal, 60 l.

BODY saloon/sedan; 4 doors; 5 seats, separate front seats, reclining backrests, headrests; heated rear window; laminated windscreen; air-conditioning.

PRACTICAL INSTRUCTIONS fuel: 91 oct petrol; oil: engine 6.2 imp pt, 7.4 US pt, 3.5 l, SAE 10W-50, change every 4,700 miles, 7,500 km - gearbox and final drive 3.2 imp pt, 3.8 US pt, 1.8 l, SAE 80, no change recommended; greasing: none; spark plug: Bosch W; tappet clearances: inlet 0.009 in, 0.25 mm, exhaust 0.016 in, 0.45 mm; tyre pressure: front 26 psi, 1.8 atm, rear 26 psi, 1.8 atm.

BMW — SOUTH AFRICA

318i

PRICE EX WORKS: 12,530 rand

ENGINE front, 4 stroke; 4 cylinders, in line; 107.7 cu in, 1,776 cc (3.50 x 2.30 in, 89 x 71 mm); compression ratio: 9.5:1; max power (DIN): 105 hp (77 kW) at 5,800 rpm; max torque (DIN): 107 lb ft, 14.8 kg m (145 Nm) at 4,500 rpm; max engine rpm: 6,200; 59.1 hp/l (43.5 kW/l); cast iron block, light alloy head, hemispherical combustion chambers; 5 crankshaft bearings; valves: overhead, rockers; camshafts: 1, overhead; lubrication: rotary pump, full flow filter, 7 imp pt, 8.5 US pt, 4 l; Bosch L-Jetronic injection; fuel feed: electric pump; water-cooled, 12.3 imp pt, 14.8 US pt, 7 l.

TRANSMISSION driving wheels: rear; clutch: single dry plate; gearbox: mechanical; gears: 5, fully synchronized; ratios: I 3.720, II 2.020, III 1.320, IV 1, V 0.810, rev 3.450; lever: central; final drive: hypoid bevel; axle ratio: 3.910; width of rims: 5.5"; tyres: 175/70 HR x 14.

PERFORMANCE max speed: 112 mph, 179 km/h; power-weight ratio: 21.6 lb/hp (29.4 lb/kW), 9.8 kg/hp (13.9 kg/kW); carrying capacity: 1,014 lb, 460 kg; consumption: 40.8 m/imp gal, 34 m/US gal, 6.9 l x 100 km at 56 mph, 90 km/h.

CHASSIS integral; front suspension: independent, coil springs/telescopic damper struts, anti-roll bar; rear: independent, semi-trailing arms, coil springs, telescopic dampers.

STEERING rack-and-pinion; turns lock to lock: 4.09.

BRAKES front disc, rear drum, vacuum servo.

ELECTRICAL EQUIPMENT 12 V; 50 Ah battery; 80 A alternator; 4 halogen headlamps.

DIMENSIONS AND WEIGHT wheel base: 101.18 in, 257 cm; tracks: 55.52 in, 141 cm front, 55.91 in, 142 cm rear; length: 170 in, 433 cm; width: 64.97 in, 165 cm; height: 54.33 in, 138 cm; ground clearance: 4.84 in, 12.3 cm; weight: 2,271 lb, 1,030 kg; turning circle: 34.4 ft, 10.5 m; fuel tank: 16.5 imp gal, 19.8 US gal, 75 l.

BODY saloon/sedan; 2 doors; 4 seats, separate front seats, reclining backrests, adjustable built-in headrests; heated rear window; tinted glass.

PRACTICAL INSTRUCTIONS fuel: 98 oct petrol; oil: engine 6.6 imp pt, 8 US pt, 3.7 l, SAE 20W-50; greasing: none; spark plug: Bosch W 145 T 30 or Champion N 9 YC; tappet clearances: inlet 0.008 in, 0.20 mm, exhaust 0.008 in, 0.20 mm; valve timing: 18° 66° 66° 18°; tyre pressure: front 26 psi, 1.8 atm, rear 28 psi, 2 atm.

OPTIONALS ZF 3 HP 22 automatic transmission, hydraulic torque converter and planetary gears with 3 ratios (I 2.480, II 1.480, III 1, rev 2.090), 3.640 axle ratio, consumption 40.2 m/imp gal, 33.5 m/US gal, 7 l x 100 km at 56 mph, 90 km/h; electric sunroof; air-conditioning; metallic spray; leather upholstery; electric windows; light alloy rims.

320i

See 318i, except for:

PRICE EX WORKS: 14,860 rand

ENGINE 6 cylinders, in line; 121.4 cu in, 1,990 cc (3.15 x 2.60 in, 80 x 66 mm); compression ratio: 9.8:1; max power (DIN): 125 hp (92 kW) at 5,800 rpm; max torque (DIN): 126 lb ft, 17.3 kg m (170 Nm) at 4,000 rpm; max engine rpm: 6,400; 62.8 hp/l (46.2 kW/l); 7 crankshaft bearings; lubrication: gear pump, full flow filter, 7.6 imp pt, 9.1 US pt, 4.3 l; cooling: 18.5 imp pt, 22.2 US pt, 10.5 l.

TRANSMISSION axle ratio: 3.640.

PERFORMANCE max speed: 118 mph, 189 km/h; power-weight ratio: 19.3 lb/hp (26.2 lb/kW), 8.8 kg/hp (11.9 kg/kW); consumption: 42.6 m/imp gal, 35.4 m/US gal, 6.6 l x 100 km at 56 mph, 90 km/h.

STEERING servo; turns lock to lock: 4.12.

ELECTRICAL EQUIPMENT 63 Ab battery.

DIMENSIONS AND WEIGHT weight: 2,414 lb, 1,095 kg.

PRACTICAL INSTRUCTIONS valve timing: 22° 50° 62° 10°; tyre pressure: front 28 psi, 2 atm, rear 31 psi, 2.2 atm.

OPTIONALS with 3-speed automatic transmission, max speed 117 mph, 187 km/h and consumption 36.5 m/imp gal, 30.4 m/US gal, 7.7 l x 100 km at 56 mph, 90 km/h; electric sunroof; electric windows; metallic spray; air-conditioning; leather upholstery.

VOLKSWAGEN Passat TS

323i

See 318i, except for:

PRICE EX WORKS: 16,270 rand

ENGINE 6 cylinders, in line; 141.2 cu in, 2,316 cc (3.15 x 3.02 in, 80 x 76.8 mm); compression ratio: 9.8:1; max power (DIN): 150 hp (110 kW) at 6,000 rpm; max torque (DIN): 151 lb ft, 20.9 kg m (205 Nm) at 4,000 rpm; 64.8 hp/l (47.5 kW/l); 7 crankshaft bearings; lubrication: gear pump, full flow filter, 7.6 imp pt, 9.1 US pt, 4.3 l; cooling: 18.5 imp pt, 22.2 US pt, 10.5 l.

TRANSMISSION gearbox ratios: I 3.830, II 2.200, III 1.400, IV 1, V 0.810, rev 3.460; axle ratio: 3.640; final drive: limited slip (25%).

PERFORMANCE max speed: 127 mph, 203 km/h; power-weight ratio: 15.6 lb/hp (21.2 lb/kW), 7.7 kg/hp (10.5 kg/kW); consumption: 42 m/imp gal, 34.9 m/US gal, 6.7 l x 100 km at 56 mph, 90 km/h.

STEERING servo; turns lock to lock: 4.12.

BRAKES disc.

ELECTRICAL EQUIPMENT 63 Ah battery; fog lamps; automatically adjustable height of headlamps.

DIMENSIONS AND WEIGHT weight: 2,536 lb, 1,150 kg.

PRACTICAL INSTRUCTIONS valve timing: 22° 50° 62° 10°; tyre pressure: front 28 psi, 2 atm, rear 31 psi, 2.2 atm.

OPTIONALS with ZF 3 HP 22 automatic transmission, 3.460 axle ratio and consumption 36.1 m/imp gal, 30 m/US gal, 7.8 l x 100 km at 56 mph, 90 km/h.

518i

PRICE EX WORKS: 14,550 rand

ENGINE front, 4 stroke; 4 cylinders, in line; 107.7 cu in, 1,776 cc (3.50 x 2.30 in, 89 x 71 mm); compression ratio: 10:1; max power (DIN): 105 hp (77 kW) at 5,800 rpm; max torque (DIN): 107 lb ft, 14.8 kg m (145 Nm) at 4,500 rpm; max engine rpm: 6,400; 59.1 hp/l (43.5 kW/l); cast iron block, light alloy head, hemispherical combustion chambers; 5 crankshaft bearings; valves: overhead, rockers; camshafts: 1, overhead; lubrication: rotary pump, full flow filter (cartridge), 7 imp pt, 8.5 US pt, 4 l; Bosch K-Jetronic injection; fuel feed: electric pump; water-cooled, 12.7 imp pt, 15.2 US pt, 7.2 l.

TRANSMISSION driving wheels: rear; clutch: single dry plate; gearbox: mechanical; gears: 5, fully synchronized; ratios: I 3.717, II 2.019, III 1.316, IV 1, V 0.805, rev 3.440; lever: central; final drive: hypoid bevel; axle ratio: 4.270; width of rims: 6"; tyres: 175 HR x 14.

PERFORMANCE max speed: 105 mph, 169 km/h; power-weight ratio: 26.1 lb/hp (35.4 lb/kW), 11.8 kg/hp (16.1 kg/kW); carrying capacity: 1,014 lb, 460 kg; consumption: 41.5 m/imp gal, 34.6 m/US gal, 6.8 l x 100 km at 56 mph, 90 km/h.

CHASSIS integral; front suspension: independent, by McPherson, coil springs/telescopic damper struts, anti-roll bar; rear: independent, semi-trailing arms, coil springs, telescopic dampers.

STEERING ZF, worm and roller; turns lock to lock: 4.36.

BRAKES front disc, rear drum, vacuum servo.

ELECTRICAL EQUIPMENT 12 V; 55 Ah battery; 65 A alternator; electronic ignition; 4 halogen headlamps.

DIMENSIONS AND WEIGHT wheel base: 103.94 in, 264 cm; tracks: 55.91 in, 142 cm front, 57.87 in, 147 cm rear; length: 181.89 in, 462 cm; width: 66.54 in, 169 cm; height: 55.91 in, 142 cm; ground clearance: 5.47 in, 13.9 cm; weight: 2,734 lb, 1,240 kg; turning circle: 34.4 ft, 10.5 m; fuel tank: 15.4 imp gal, 18.5 US gal, 70 l.

BODY saloon/sedan; 4 doors; 5 seats, separate front seats, reclining backrests, adjustable built-in headrests; laminated windscreen; tinted glass; heated rear window; air-conditioning.

PRACTICAL INSTRUCTIONS fuel: 98 oct petrol; oil: engine 7 imp pt, 8.5 US pt, 4 l, SAE 20W-50 - gearbox 2.8 imp pt, 3.4 US pt, 1.6 l, SAE 80, change every 18,600 miles, 30,000 km - final drive 2.8 imp pt, 3.4 US pt, 1.6 l, hypoid 90; greasing: none; spark plug: Bosch W 145 T 30 or Champion N10 Y; tappet clearances: inlet 0.006-0.008 in, 0.15-0.20 mm, exhaust 0.006-0.008 in, 0.15-0.20 mm; valve timing: 4° 52° 52° 4°; tyre pressure: front 27 psi, 1.9 atm, rear 27 psi, 1.9 atm.

OPTIONALS ZF 3 HP 22 automatic transmission, hydraulic torque converter and planetary gears with 3 ratios (I 2.478, II 1.478, III 1, rev 2.090), max speed 103 mph, 165 km/h, consumption 35.8 m/imp gal, 29.8 m/US gal, 7.9 l x 100 km at steady 56 mph, 90 km/h; leather upholstery; electric sunroof; metallic spray; automatic speed control; electric windows; fog lamps; light alloy wheels.

520i

See 518i, except for:

PRICE EX WORKS: 17,590 rand

ENGINE 6 cylinders, in line; 121.4 cu in, 1,990 cc (3.15 x 2.60 in, 80 x 66 mm); compression ratio: 9.8:1; max power (DIN): 125 hp (92 kW) at 5,800 rpm; max torque (DIN): 125 lb ft, 17.3 kg m (170 Nm) at 4,000 rpm; 62.8 hp/l (46.2 kW/l); 7 crankshaft bearings; lubrication: gear pump, full flow filter (cartridge), 7.4 imp pt, 8.9 US pt, 4.2 l; Bosch K-Jetronic injection; water-cooled, 21.1 imp pt, 25.4 US pt, 12 l.

PERFORMANCE max speed: 113 mph, 182 km/h; power-weight ratio: 22.4 lb/hp (30.4 lb/kW), 10.2 kg/hp (13.7 kg/kW); consumption: 40.4 m/imp gal, 33.6 m/US gal, 7 l x 100 km at steady 56 mph, 90 km/h.

STEERING servo; turns lock to lock: 3.96.

DIMENSIONS AND WEIGHT weight: 2,800 lb, 1,270 kg.

BODY saloon/sedan; 4 doors; 5 seats, separate front seats, reclining backrests, adjustable built-in headrests; tinted glass; heated rear window.

PRACTICAL INSTRUCTIONS valve timing: 11° 47° 51° 7°; tyre pressure: front 30 psi, 2.1 atm, rear 30 psi, 2.1 atm.

OPTIONALS with 3-speed ZF 3HP 22 automatic transmission max speed 108 mph, 175 km/h and consumption 32.8 m/imp gal, 27.3 m/US gal, 8.6 l x 100 km at steady 56 mph, 90 km/h; electric sunroof; leather upholstery; metallic spray; automatic speed control.

BMW 318i

BMW 318i - 320i - 323i

528i

See 518i, except for:

PRICE EX WORKS: 22,790 rand

ENGINE 6 cylinders, in line; 170.1 cu in, 2,788 cc (3.39 x 3.15 in, 86 x 80 mm); max power (DIN): 184 hp (135 kW) at 5,800 rpm; max torque (DIN): 177 lb ft, 24.5 kg m (240 Nm) at 4,200 rpm; 66 hp/l (48.4 kW/l); 7 crankshaft bearings; lubrication: 10.1 imp pt, 12.1 US pt, 5.7 l; Bosch L-Jetronic injection; cooling: 21.1 imp pt, 25.4 US pt, 12 l.

TRANSMISSION gearbox ratios: I 3.822, II 2.202, III 1.398, IV 1, V 0.812, rev 3.705; axle ratio: 3.450; tyres: 195/70 HR x 14.

PERFORMANCE max speed: 129 mph, 207 km/h; power-weight ratio: 17 lb/hp (22.9 lb/kW), 7.7 kg/hp (10.4 kg/kW); consumption: 39.8 m/imp gal, 33.1 m/US gal, 7.1 l x 100 km at steady 56 mph, 90 km/h.

STEERING ZF worm and roller, servo; turns lock to lock: 4.62.

BRAKES disc, vacuum servo.

ELECTRICAL EQUIPMENT 65 Ah battery; 70 A alternator.

DIMENSIONS AND WEIGHT weight: 3,153 lb, 1,430 kg.

BODY saloon/sedan; 4 doors; 5 seats, separate front seats, reclining backrests, adjustable front and rear built-in headrests; tinted glass; heated rear window.

PRACTICAL INSTRUCTIONS oil: engine 8.8 imp pt, 10.6 US pt, 5 l; tappet clearances: inlet 0.010-0.012 in, 0.25-0.30 mm, exhaust 0.010-0.012 in, 0.25-0.30 mm; valve timing: 14° 54° 54° 14°; tyre pressure: front 30 psi, 2.1 atm, rear 30 psi, 2.1 atm.

OPTIONALS with 3-speed ZF 3 HP 22 automatic transmission, max speed 124 mph, 200 km/h and consumption 31 m/imp gal, 25.8 m/US gal, 9.1 l x 100 km at steady 56 mph, 90 km/h; electric sunroof; leather upholstery; metallic spray.

535i

See 518i, except for:

PRICE EX WORKS: 30,400 rand

ENGINE 6 cylinders, in line; 210.7 cu in, 3,453 cc (3.68 x 3.30 in, 93.4 x 84 mm); max power (DIN): 218 hp (160 kW) at 5,200 rpm; max torque (DIN): 229 lb ft, 31 kg m (310 Nm) at 4,000 rpm; 63.1 hp/l (46.4 kW/l); 7 crankshaft bearings; valves: overhead, Vee slanted at 50°; camshafts: 1, overhead, chain-driven; lubrication: 10.1 imp pt, 12.1 US pt, 5.7 l; Bosch L-Jetronic injection; cooling: 20.6 imp pt, 25.4 US pt, 12 l.

TRANSMISSION gearbox ratios: I 3.822, II 2.202, III 1.398, IV 1, V 0.812, rev 3.705; axle ratio: 3.070; final drive: hypoid bevel, limited slip; width of rims: 7"; tyres: 200/60 VR x 14.

PERFORMANCE max speed: 138 mph, 222 km/h; power-weight ratio: 14.9 lb/hp (20.3 lb/kW), 6.7 kg/hp (9.1 kg/kW);

BMW 323i

535i

consumption: 37.2 m/imp gal, 30.9 m/US gal, 7.6 l x 100 km at 56 mph, 90 km/h.

CHASSIS rear suspension: anti-roll bar.

STEERING servo; turns lock to lock: 4.60.

BRAKES disc.

ELECTRICAL EQUIPMENT 65 Ah battery; 70 A alternator.

DIMENSIONS AND WEIGHT weight: 3,241 lb, 1,470 kg.

BODY saloon/sedan; 4 doors; 5 seats, separate front seats, reclining backrests, adjustable built-in headrests; light alloy wheels (standard); air-conditioning; tinted glass; heated rear window.

OPTIONALS 5-speed fully synchronized mechanical gearbox (I 3.717, II 2.403, III 1.766, IV 1.236, V 1, rev 4.233); sunroof.

728i

PRICE EX WORKS: 27,900 rand

ENGINE front, 4 stroke; 6 cylinders, in line; 170.1 cu in, 2,788 cc (3.39 x 3.15 in, 86 x 80 mm); compression ratio: 9.3:1; max power (DIN): 184 hp (135 kW) at 5,800 rpm; max torque (DIN): 181 lb ft, 25 kg m (240 Nm) at 4,200 rpm; max engine rpm: 6,200; 63 hp/l (46.7 kW/l); cast iron block, light alloy head; 7 crankshaft bearings; valves: overhead, rockers; camshafts: 1, overhead; lubrication: rotary pump, full flow filter, 10 imp pt, 12 US pt, 5.7 l; Bosch L-Jetronic injection; fuel feed: electronic pump; water-cooled, 21.1 imp pt, 25.4 US pt, 12 l.

TRANSMISSION driving wheels: rear; clutch: single dry plate; gearbox: mechanical; gears: 5, fully synchronized; ratios: I 3.830, II 2.200, III 1.400, IV 1, V 0.810, rev 3.460; lever: central; final drive: hypoid bevel; axle ratio: 3.640; width of rims: 6"; tyres: 195/70 HR x 14.

PERFORMANCE max speed: 125 mph, 201 km/h; power-weight ratio: 17.7 lb/hp (24.2 lb/kW), 8 kg/hp (11 kg/kW); carrying capacity: 1,058 lb, 480 kg; speed in top at 1,000 rpm: 19.7 mph, 31.7 km/h; consumption: 35.8 m/imp gal, 30 m/US gal, 7.9 l x 100 km at steady 56 mph, 90 km/h.

CHASSIS integral; front suspension: independent, by McPherson, coil springs/telescopic damper struts, anti-roll bar; rear: independent, semi-trailing arms, coil springs, telescopic dampers.

STEERING ZF worm and roller, servo, adjustable height of steering wheel; turns lock to lock: 3.80.

BRAKES disc.

ELECTRICAL EQUIPMENT 12 V; 55 Ah battery; 1,120 W alternator; Bosch distributor; 4 halogen headlamps.

DIMENSIONS AND WEIGHT wheel base: 110.24 in, 280 cm; tracks: 59.45 in, 151 cm front, 59.84 in, 152 cm rear; length: 191.30 in, 486 cm; width: 70.90 in, 180 cm; height: 56.30 in, 143 cm; ground clearance: 4.88 in, 12.4 cm; weight: 3,263 lb, 1,480 kg; turning circle: 38 ft, 11.6 m; fuel tank: 22 imp gal, 26.4 US gal, 100 l.

BODY saloon/sedan; 4 doors; 5 seats, separate front seats, reclining backrests, adjustable built-in headrests; heated rear window; tinted glass; electric windows.

PRACTICAL INSTRUCTIONS fuel: 98 oct petrol; oil: engine 10 imp pt, 12 US pt, 5.7 l, SAE 20W-50 - gearbox 2.8 imp pt, 3.4 US pt, 1.6 l, SAE 80 - final drive 3.3 imp pt, 4 US pt, 1.9 l, SAE 90; greasing: none; spark plug: Bosch W 175 T 30 or Champion N 10 Y; tappet clearances: inlet 0.010-0.012 in, 0.25-0.30 mm, exhaust 0.010-0.012 in, 0.25-0.30 mm; valve timing: 14° 54° 54° 14°; tyre pressure: front 33 psi, 2.3 atm, rear 33 psi, 2.3 atm.

OPTIONALS ZF 4 HP 22 automatic transmission, hydraulic torque converter and planetary gears with 4 ratios (I 2.478, II 1.478, III 1, IV 0.728, rev 2.090), max ratio of converter at stall 2, possible manual selection, max speed 122 mph, 195 km/h, consumption 36.1 m/imp gal, 30.3 m/US gal, 7.8 l x 100 km at 56 mph, 90 km/h; leather upholstery; electric sunroof; light alloy wheels; rear headrests; air-conditioning; self-levelling rear suspension.

733i

See 728i, except for:

PRICE EX WORKS: 37,200 rand

ENGINE 195.8 cu in, 3,210 cc (3.50 x 3.39 in, 89 x 86 mm); max power (DIN): 197 hp (145 kW) at 5,500 rpm; max torque (DIN): 211 lb ft, 29.1 kg m (285 Nm) at 4,300 rpm; 61.4 hp/l (45.2 kW/l).

TRANSMISSION final drive: hypoid bevel, limited slip; axle ratio: 3.450; width of rims: 6.5"; tyres: 205/70 VR x 14.

PERFORMANCE max speed: 130 mph, 208 km/h; power-weight ratio: 16.9 lb/hp (23 lb/kW), 7.8 kg/hp (10.6 kg/kW); consumption: 33.5 m/imp gal, 27.9 m/US gal, 8.4 l x 100 km at steady 56 mph, 90 km/h.

ELECTRICAL EQUIPMENT 66 Ah battery; electronic ignition.

BMW 728i

DIMENSIONS AND WEIGHT front track: 59.06 in, 150 cm; ground clearance: 5.20 in, 13.2 cm; weight: 3,329 lb, 1,510 kg.

BODY saloon/sedan; 4 doors; 5 seats, separate front seats, reclining backrests, adjustable front and rear built-in headrests; heated rear window; tinted glass; light alloy wheels (standard); electric windows; fog headlamps; air-conditioning (standard).

PRACTICAL INSTRUCTIONS tyre pressure: front 31 psi, 2.2 atm, rear 31 psi, 2.2 atm.

OPTIONALS with 4-speed ZF 4 HP 22 automatic transmission max speed 126 mph, 202 km/h and consumption 36.1 m/imp gal, 29.9 m/US gal, 7.8 l x 100 km at steady 56 mph, 90 km/h; electric sunroof; leather upholstery; self levelling rear suspension.

735i

See 728i, except for:

PRICE EX WORKS: 45,000 rand

ENGINE 209.2 cu in, 3,430 cc (3.62 x 3.39 in, 92 x 86 mm); max power (DIN): 218 hp (160 kW) at 5,200 rpm; max torque (DIN): 229 lb ft, 31.6 kg m (310 Nm) at 4,000 rpm; max engine rpm: 6,100; 63.6 hp/l (46.8 kW/l)

TRANSMISSION axle ratio: 3.450; width of rims: 6.5"; tyres: 220/55 VR x 14.

PERFORMANCE max speed: 136 mph, 217 km/h; power-weight ratio: 15.4 lb/hp (21 lb/kW), 7 kg/hp (9.6 kg/kW); consumption: 34.7 m/imp gal, 28.8 m/US gal, 8.1 l x 100 km at 56 mph, 90 km/h.

ELECTRICAL EQUIPMENT 66 Ah battery; 66 A alternator.

DIMENSIONS AND WEIGHT weight: 3,351 lb, 1,520 kg.

BODY saloon/sedan; 4 doors; 5 seats, separate front seats, electrically adjustable height, reclining backrests, adjustable front and rear built-in headrests; heated rear window; fog lamps; tinted glass; electric windows; light alloy wheels (standard) .

OPTIONALS with 4-speed ZF 4 HP 22 automatic transmission max speed 132 mph, 211 km/h and consumption 35.6 m/imp gal, 29.5 m/US gal, 7.9 l x 100 km at steady 56 mph, 90 km/h; self-levelling rear suspension; active check control on board computer; electric sunroof; leather upholstery.

BMW 520i

745i

See 728i, except for:

PRICE EX WORKS: 65,000 rand

ENGINE 210.7 cu in, 3,453 cc (3.68 x 3.31 in, 93.4 x 84 mm); max power (DIN): 290 hp (213 kW) at 6,500 rpm; max torque (DIN): 251 lb ft, 34.7 kg m (340 Nm) at 4,500 rpm; max engine rpm: 5,900; 84 hp/l (61.8 kW/l)

TRANSMISSION gearbox ratios: I 3.717, II 2.403, III 1.766, IV 1.236, V 1, rev 4.233; axle ratio: 3.450; tyres: 205/55 x 16 front, 225/50 x 16 rear.

PERFORMANCE max speed: 151 mph, 241 km/h; power-weight ratio: 13.1 lb/hp (17.8 lb/kW), 5.9 kg/hp (8.1 kg/kW).

ELECTRICAL EQUIPMENT 66 Ah battery; digital electronic system.

DIMENSIONS AND WEIGHT weight: 3,788 lb, 1,718 kg.

BODY electrically adjustable front and rear seats, adjustable front and rear built-in headrests; self levelling rear suspension.

OPTIONALS with 4-speed ZF 4 HP 22 automatic transmission, max speed 144 mph, 231 km/h; electric sunroof.

FORD SOUTH AFRICA

Escort Series

PRICES EX WORKS:	rand
1 1300 GL 4+1-dr Sedan	**7,335**
2 1600 GLE 4+1-dr Sedan	**8,995**
3 XR3 2+1-dr Sedan	**9,255**

Power team:	Standard for:	Optional for:
67 hp	1	—
86 hp	2	—
96 hp	3	—

67 hp power team

ENGINE front, overhead, 4 stroke; 4 cylinders, in line; 79.1 cu in, 1,297 cc (3.19 x 2.48 in, 81 x 63 mm); compression ratio: 9.2:1; max power (DIN): 67 hp (49 kW) at 5,600 rpm; max torque (DIN): 68 lb ft, 9.4 kg m (92 Nm) at 3,250 rpm; max engine rpm: 6,000; 51.7 hp/l (37.8 kW/l); cast iron block, and head; 5 crankshaft bearings; valves: overhead, push-rod and rockers; camshafts: 1, overhead; lubrication: gear pump, full flow filter, 6.2 imp pt, 7.4 US pt, 3.5 l; 1 Weber Venturi twin barrel carburettor; fuel feed: mechanical pump; water-cooled, 11.1 imp pt, 13.3 US pt, 6.3 l.

TRANSMISSION driving wheels: front; clutch: single dry plate (diaphragm); gearbox: mechanical; gears: 4, fully synchronized; ratios: I 3.580, II 2.050, III 1.350, IV 0.951, rev 3.770; lever: central; final drive: hypoid bevel; axle ratio: 4.056; width of rims: 5"; tyres: 155 SR x 15.

BMW 735i

FORD Escort 1600 GLE Sedan

PERFORMANCE max speeds: (I) 25 mph, 40 km/h; (II) 43 mph, 70 km/h; (III) 66 mph, 106 km/h; (IV) 96 mph, 155 km/h; power-weight ratio: 30.2 lb/hp (41.4 lb/kW), 13.7 kg/hp (18.8 kg/kW); carrying capacity: 889 lb, 403 kg; acceleration: 0-50 mph (0-80 km/h) 9.6 sec; speed in top at 1,000 rpm: 16.7 mph, 26.8 km/h; consumption: 48.7 m/imp gal, 40.6 m/US gal, 5.8 l x 100 km at 50 mph, 80 km/h.

CHASSIS integral; front suspension: independent, by McPherson, coil springs, anti-roll bar, double acting telescopic dampers; rear: independent, modified McPherson struts, coil spring, swinging arms, longitudinal bars, telescopic dampers.

STEERING rack-and-pinion; turns lock to lock: 3.69.

BRAKES front disc, rear drum, servo; swept area: front 55.7 sq in, 359 sq cm, rear 152.7 sq in, 985 sq cm, total 108.4 sq in, 1,344 sq cm.

ELECTRICAL EQUIPMENT 12 V; 40 Ah battery; 45 A alternator; 2 headlamps.

DIMENSIONS AND WEIGHT wheel base: 94.49 in, 240 cm; tracks: 54.33 in, 138 cm front, 56.30 in, 143 cm rear; length: 156.30 in, 397 cm; width: 64.57 in, 164 cm; height: 54.72 in, 139 cm; ground clearance: 6.89 in, 17.5 cm; weight: 2,029 lb, 920 kg; weight distribution: 57.8% front, 42.2% rear; turning circle: 32.8 ft, 10 m; fuel tank: 11 imp gal, 13.2 US gal, 50 l.

BODY saloon/sedan; 4+1 doors; 5 seats, separate adjustable front seats, reclining backrests; folding rear seats.

PRACTICAL INSTRUCTIONS fuel: 98 oct petrol; oil: engine 5.6 imp pt, 6.8 US pt, 3.2 l, SAE 20W-50, change every 6,200 miles, 10,000 km - gearbox and final drive 4.9 imp pt, 5.9 US pt, 2.8 l, SAE 80; spark plug: Motorcraft Super AGPR 12 C; tappet clearances: inlet 0.008 in, 0.20 mm, exhaust 0.022 in, 0.55 mm; tyre pressure: front 26-28 psi, 1.8-2 atm, rear 28-34 psi, 2-2.4 atm.

OPTIONALS metallic spray; tinted glass; heated rear window.

86 hp power team

See 67 hp power team, except for:

ENGINE 97.4 cu in, 1,597 cc (3.15 x 3.13 in, 79.6 x 79.5 mm); compression ratio: 9.5:1; max power (DIN): 86 hp (63 kW) at 6,000 rpm; max torque (DIN): 95 lb ft, 13.1 kg m (128 Nm) at 3,400 rpm; max engine rpm: 6,700; 53.8 hp/l (39.6 kW/l); cast iron block, light alloy head; valves: overhead, hydraulic tappets; lubrication: 6.5 imp pt, 7.8 US pt, 3.7 l; cooling: 12.1 imp pt, 14.8 US pt, 6.9 l.

TRANSMISSION gears: 5, fully synchronized; ratios: I 3.154, II 1.905, III 1.276, IV 0.951, V 0.760, rev 3.615; axle ratio: 3.840; tyres: 165 SR x 13.

PERFORMANCE max speeds: (I) 35 mph, 57 km/h; (II) 58 mph, 94 km/h; (III) 81 mph, 131 km/h; (IV) 102 mph, 164 km/h; (V) 103 mph, 165 km/h; power-weight ratio: 24.2 lb/hp (32.9 lb/kW), 10.9 kg/hp (14.9 kg/kW); carrying capacity: 878 lb, 400 kg; acceleration: standing ¼ mile 18.9 sec, 0-50 mph (0-80 km/h) 8.6 sec; speed in top at 1,000 rpm: 18.5 mph, 29.7 km/h; consumption: 43.3 m/imp gal, 36.2 m/US gal, 6.5 l x 100 km.

ELECTRICAL EQUIPMENT 2 halogen headlamps.

DIMENSIONS AND WEIGHT wheel base: 94.37 in, 239 cm; front track: 54.72 in, 139 cm; length: 159.80 in, 406 cm; width: 62.80 in, 159 cm; height: 52.68 in, 134 cm; ground clearance: 7.05 in, 17.9 cm; weight: 2,179 lb, 944 kg; weight distribution: 58.9% front, 41.1% rear.

BODY reclining backrests with built-in headrests.

PRACTICAL INSTRUCTIONS oil: engine 6.5 imp pt, 7.8 US pt, 3.7 l, SAE 20W-50; valve timing: 18° 50° 61° 7°.

OPTIONALS air-conditioning.

96 hp power team

See 67 hp power team, except for:

ENGINE 97.4 cu in, 1,597 cc (3.15 x 3.13 in, 79.6 x 79.5 mm); compression ratio: 9.5:1; max power (DIN): 96 hp (71 kW) at 6,000 rpm; max torque (DIN): 98 lb ft, 13.5 kg m (132 Nm) at 4,000 rpm; max engine rpm: 6,700; 60.1 hp/l (44.2 kW/l); cast iron block, light alloy head; valves: overhead, hydraulic tappets; lubrication: 6.5 imp pt, 7.8 US pt, 3.7 l; cooling: 12.1 imp pt, 14.8 US pt, 6.9 l.

TRANSMISSION gears: 5, fully synchronized; ratios: I 3.154, II 1.905, III 1.276, IV 0.951, V 0.760, rev 3.615; axle ratio: 4.059; width of rims: 5.5''; tyres: 175/70 SR x 13.

PERFORMANCE max speeds: (I) 34 mph, 55 km/h; (II) 57 mph, 91 km/h; (III) 82 mph, 132 km/h; (IV) and (V) 109 mph, 176 km/h; power-weight ratio: 21.5 lb/hp (29.2 lb/kW), 9.7 kg/hp (13.2 kg/kW); carrying capacity: 878 lb, 400 kg; acceleration: standing ¼ mile 17.7 sec, 0-50 mph (0-80 km/h) 7.3 sec; speed in top at 1,000 rpm: 16.3 mph, 26.3 km/h; consumption: 44.8 m/imp gal, 37.3 m/US gal, 6.3 l x 100 km.

ELECTRICAL EQUIPMENT 2 halogen headlamps.

DIMENSIONS AND WEIGHT wheel base: 94.37 in, 239 cm; front track: 54.72 in, 139 cm; length: 159.60 in, 405 cm; height: 53.55 in, 137 cm; ground clearance: 6.20 in, 15.8 cm; weight: 2,062 lb, 935 kg; weight distribution: 58.9% front, 41.1% rear.

BODY 2+1 doors; reclining backrests with built-in headrests.

PRACTICAL INSTRUCTIONS oil: engine 6.5 imp pt, 7.8 US pt, 3.7 l, SAE 20W-50; valve timing: 20° 56° 60° 14°.

OPTIONALS air-conditioning.

Sierra Series

PRICES EX WORKS:	rand
1 1600 GL 4+1-dr Sedan	**9,990**
2 2000 GL 4+1-dr Sedan	**10,970**
3 2000 GL Automatic 4+1-dr Sedan	**11,405**
4 2300 GLE 4+1-dr Sedan	**12,485**
5 2300 GLE Automatic 4+1-dr Sedan	**12,970**

Power team:	Standard for:	Optional for:
80 hp	1	—
105 hp	2,3	—
114 hp	4,5	—

80 hp power team

ENGINE front, 4 stroke; 4 cylinders, vertical, in line; 97.4 cu in, 1,597 cc (3.15 x 3.13 in, 81 x 77.6 mm); compression ratio: 9.2:1; max power (DIN): 80 hp (59 kW) at 5,500 rpm; max torque (DIN): 89 lb ft, 12.2 kg m (120 Nm) at 2,800 rpm; max engine rpm: 6,300; 50.1 hp/l (36.8 kW/l); cast iron block and head; 5 crankshaft bearings; valves: overhead, push-rods and rockers; camshafts: 1, in block; lubrication: gear pump, full flow filter, 7.4 imp pt, 8.9 US pt, 4.2 l; 1 Weber Venturi twin barrel carburettor; fuel feed: mechanical pump; water cooled, 14.1 imp pt, 16.9 US pt, 8 l.

TRANSMISSION driving wheels: rear; clutch: single dry plate (diaphragm); gearbox: mechanical; gears: 4, fully synchronized; ratios: I 3.650, II 1.970, III 1.370, IV 1, rev 3.660; lever: central; final drive: hypoid bevel; axle ratio: 3.700; width of rims: 5.5''; tyres: 165 SR x 13.

PERFORMANCE max speeds: (I) 31 mph, 50 km/h; (II) 57 mph, 92 km/h; (III) 82 mph, 132 km/h; (IV) 112 mph, 180 km/h; power-weight ratio: 29.6 lb/hp (40.3 lb/kW), 13.4 kg/hp (18.3 kg/kW); carrying capacity: 1,114 lb, 505 kg; acceleration: 0-50 mph (0-80 km/h) 8 sec; speed in direct drive at 1,000 rpm: 18.2 mph, 29.3 km/h; consumption: 39.8 m/imp gal, 33.1 m/US gal, 7.1 l x 100 km.

CHASSIS integral; front suspension: independent, by McPherson, lower wishbones, coil springs/telescopic damper struts, anti-roll bar; rear: independent, lower wish-

FORD Sierra 2300 GLE Sedan

80 HP POWER TEAM

bones, trailing radius arms, coil springs, anti-roll bar, telescopic dampers.

STEERING rack-and-pinion; turns lock to lock: 4.15.

BRAKES front disc, rear drum, servo; swept area: front 160.8 sq in, 1,037 sq cm, rear 71.2 sq in, 459 sq cm, total 232 sq in, 1,496 sq cm.

ELECTRICAL EQUIPMENT 12 V; 45 Ah battery; 45 A alternator; Ford breakerless electronic ignition; 2 halogen headlamps.

DIMENSIONS AND WEIGHT wheel base: 102.68 in, 261 cm; tracks: 57.12 in, 145 cm front, 57.80 in, 147 cm rear; length: 172.99 in, 439 cm; width: 67.05 in, 170 cm; height: 55.43 in, 141 cm; ground clearance: 5.87 in, 15 cm; weight: 2,373 lb, 1,076 kg; weight distribution: 51.2% front, 48.8% rear; turning circle: 34.8 ft, 10.6 m; fuel tank: 13.2 imp gal, 15.8 US gal, 60 l.

BODY saloon/sedan; 4+1 doors; 5 seats, separate front seats, reclining backrests, headrests.

PRACTICAL INSTRUCTIONS fuel: 98 oct petrol; oil: engine 7.4 imp pt, 8.9 US pt, 4.2 l, SAE 20-W50, change every 6,200 miles, 10,000 km - gearbox 2.8 imp pt, 3.4 US pt, 1.5 l, SAE 80 EP - final drive 1.4 imp pt, 1.7 US pt, 0.8 l; greasing: none; spark plug: AG 152 C; tappet clearances: inlet 0.012 in, 0.30 mm, exhaust 0.022 in, 0.55 mm; valve timing: 27° 65° 65° 27°; tyre pressure: front 24 psi, 1.7 atm, rear 26 psi, 1.8 atm.

OPTIONALS metallic spray; tinted glass.

105 hp power team

See 80 hp power team, except for:

ENGINE 121.6 cu in, 1,993 cc (3.89 x 3.03 in, 90.8 x 76.9 mm); max power (DIN): 105 hp (77 kW) at 5,200 rpm; max torque (DIN): 116 lb ft, 16 kg m (157 Nm) at 4,000 rpm; max engine rpm: 6,200; 52.7 hp/l (38.6 kW/l); camshafts: 1, overhead; lubrication: 6.5 imp pt, 7.8 US pt, 3.7 l.

TRANSMISSION gearbox: GL mechanical - GL Automatic Ford C3 automatic transmission, hydraulic torque converter and planetary gears with 3 ratios, possible manual selection; gears: GL 5, fully synchronized; ratios: GL I 3.650, II 1.970, III 1.370, IV 1, V 0.820, rev 3.660 - GL Automatic I 2.474, II 1.474, III 1, rev 2.111.

PERFORMANCE max speeds: (I) 25 mph, 41 km/h; (II) 48 mph, 77 km/h; (III) 69 mph, 111 km/h; (IV) 94 mph, 152 km/h; (V) 116 mph, 187 km/h; power-weight ratio: 33.4 lb/hp (45.4 lb/kW), 15.1 kg/hp (20.6 kg/kW); carrying capacity: 1,147 lb, 520 kg; speed in top at 1,000 rpm: 22.4 mph, 36.1 km/h.

DIMENSIONS AND WEIGHT weight: 3,506 lb, 1,590 kg.

PRACTICAL INSTRUCTIONS oil: engine 6.5 imp pt, 7,8 US pt, 3.7 l.

OPTIONALS speed control.

114 hp power team

See 80 hp power team, except for:

ENGINE 6 cylinders, Vee-slanted at 60°; 139.9 cu in, 2,294 cc (3.54 x 2.37 in, 90 x 60.1 mm); max power (DIN): 114 hp (84 kW) at 5,300 rpm; max torque (DIN): 130 lb ft, 18 kg m (176 Nm) at 3,000 rpm; max engine rpm: 6,000; 49.6 hp/l (37 kW/l); 4 crankshaft bearings; camshafts: 1, at centre of Vee; lubrication: 7.8 imp pt, 9.2 US pt, 4.7 l; 1 Solex 35/35 EEIT downdraught twin barrel carburettor; cooling: 20.1 imp pt, 24.1 US pt, 11.4 l.

TRANSMISSION gearbox: GLE mechanical - GLE Automatic Ford C3 automatic transmission, hydraulic torque converter and planetary gears with 3 ratios, possible manual selection; gears: GLE, 5, fully synchronized; ratios: GLE I 3.650, II 1.970, III 1.370, IV 1, V 0.820, rev 3.660 - GLE Automatic I 2.474, II 1.474, III 1, rev 2.111; axle ratio: 3.660; tyres: 175 SR x 13.

PERFORMANCE max speeds: (I) 33 mph, 53 km/h; (II) 62 mph, 99 km/h; (III) 89 mph, 143 km/h; (IV) and (V) 115 mph, 185 km/h; power-weight ratio: 23 lb/hp (31.3 lb/kW), 10.4 kg/hp (14.2 kg/kW); carrying capacity: 1,114 lb, 503 kg; acceleration: standing ¼ mile 17.7 sec, 0-50 mph (0-80 km/h) 7.5 sec; speed in top at 1,000 rpm: 20.3 mph, 32.7 km/h; consumption: 37.5 m/imp gal, 31.4 m/US gal, 7.5 l x 100 km.

STEERING servo; turns lock to lock: 3.58.

ELECTRICAL EQUIPMENT 55 A alternator; 4 halogen headlamps.

DIMENSIONS AND WEIGHT length: 174.21 in, 442 cm; width: 67.72 in, 172 cm; weight: 2,648 lb, 1,191 kg; weight distribution: 52.9% front, 47.1% rear.

PRACTICAL INSTRUCTIONS oil: engine 7.8 imp pt, 9.2 US pt, 4.7 l; spark plug: AGR 22 C; tappet clearances: inlet 0.010 in, 0.35 mm, exhaust 0.018 in, 0.40 mm; valve timing: 20° 56° 62° 14°.

OPTIONALS sunroof; speed control; ari-conditioning.

FORD Granada 3000 Ghia Sedan

Granada Series

PRICES EX WORKS:	rand
1 2000 GLE 4-dr Sedan	**14,745**
2 3000 GLE 4-dr Sedan	**16,535**
3 3000 GLE Automatic 4-dr Sedan	**17,350**
4 3000 Ghia 4-dr Sedan	**22,525**

Power team:	Standard for:	Optional for:
105 hp	1	—
140 hp	2	—
159 hp	3,4	—

105 hp power team

ENGINE front, 4 stroke; 4 cylinders, in line; 121.6 cu in, 1,993 cc (3.57 x 3.03 in, 90.8 x 76.9 mm); compression ratio: 9.2:1; max power (DIN): 105 hp (77 kW) at 5,500 rpm; max torque (DIN): 116 lb ft, 16 kg m (158 Nm) at 4,000 rpm; max engine rpm: 6,600; 52.7 hp/l (38.6 kW/l); cast iron block and head; 5 crankshaft bearings; valves: overhead, Vee-slanted, rockers; camshafts: 1, overhead, cogged belt; lubrication: rotary pump, full flow filter, 6.6 imp pt, 7.8 US pt, 3.7 l; 1 Weber downdraught carburettor; fuel feed: mechanical pump; water-cooled, 12.3 imp pt, 14.8 US pt, 7 l.

TRANSMISSION driving wheels: rear; clutch: single dry plate; gearbox: mechanical; gears: 4, fully synchronized; ratios: I 3.650, II 1.970, III 1.370, IV 1, rev 3.666; lever: central; final drive: hypoid bevel; axle ratio: 3.500; width of rims: 5.5"; tyres: 175 SR x 14.

PERFORMANCE max speed: 102 mph, 164 km/h; power-weight ratio: 27.7 lb/hp (37.7 lb/kW), 12.6 kg/hp (17.1 kg/kW); carrying capacity: 992 lb, 450 kg; acceleration: 0-50 mph (0-80 km/h) 8.8 sec; speed in direct drive at 1,000 rpm: 17.9 mph, 28.8 km/h; consumption: 36.2 m/imp gal, 30.1 m/US gal, 7.8 l x 100 km at 50 mph, 80 km/h.

CHASSIS integral; front suspension: independent, wishbones (lower trailing links), coil springs, anti-roll bar, telescopic dampers; rear: independent, semi-trailing arms, coil springs, telescopic dampers.

STEERING rack-and-pinion; turns lock to lock: 4.40.

BRAKES front disc (diameter 10.31 in, 26.2 cm), rear drum, servo; swept area: total 334.3 sq in, 2,156 sq cm.

ELECTRICAL EQUIPMENT 12 V; 40 Ah battery; 45 A alternator; 2 halogen headlamps.

DIMENSIONS AND WEIGHT wheel base: 109.01 in, 277 cm; tracks: 59.64 in, 151 cm front, 60.31 in, 153 cm rear; length: 183.07 in, 465 cm; width: 70.51 in, 179 cm; height: 56.10 in, 142 cm; ground clearance: 6.49 in, 16.5 cm; weight: 2,911 lb, 1,320 kg; weight distribution: 48.9% front, 51.1% rear; turning circle: 33.8 ft, 10.3 m; fuel tank: 22 imp gal, 26 US gal, 100 l.

BODY saloon/sedan; 4 doors; 5 seats, separate front seats, reclining backrests

OPTIONALS metallic spray; tinted glass; laminated windscreen.

140 hp power team

See 105 hp power team, except for:

ENGINE 6 cylinders, Vee-slanted at 60°; 182.7 cu in, 2,994 cc (3.69 x 2.85 in, 93.7 x 72.4 mm); compression ratio: 9:1; max power (DIN): 140 hp (103 kW) at 5,000 rpm; max torque (DIN): 174 lb ft, 24.1 kg m (237 Nm) at 3,000 rpm; max engine rpm: 6,000; 46.7 hp/l (34.4 kW/l); 4 crankshaft bearings; valves: overhead, push-rods and rockers; lubrication: gear pump, full flow filter, 9.9 imp pt, 11.8 US pt, 5.6 l; 1 Weber Venturi downdraught twin barrel carburettor; cooling: 17.4 imp pt, 21.4 US pt, 11 l.

TRANSMISSION ratios: I 3.160, II 1.950, III 1.410, IV 1, rev 3.350.

PERFORMANCE max speeds: (I) 37 mph, 60 km/h; (II) 59 mph, 95 km/h; (III) 81 mph, 130 km/h; (IV) 112 mph, 181 km/h; power-weight ratio: 22.8 lb/hp (31 lb/kW), 10.3 kg/hp (14 kg/kW); carrying capacity: 1,180 lb, 535 kg; acceleration: standing ¼ mile 17.6 sec, 0-50 mph (0-80 km/h) 7.2 sec; speed in direct drive at 1,000 rpm: 20.4 mph, 32.9 km/h; consumption: 28.2 m/imp gal, 23.5 m/US gal, 10 l x 100 km at 75 mph, 120 km/h.

CHASSIS front and rear suspension: double acting telescopic dampers.

OPEL Kadett GLS Sedan

OPEL Kadett Voyage Station Wagon

STEERING servo; turns lock to lock: 3.50.

ELECTRICAL EQUIPMENT 55 Ah battery; 55 A alternator;

DIMENSIONS AND WEIGHT wheel base: 109.05 in, 277 cm; front and rear track: 60.24 in, 153 cm; length: 183.86 in, 466 cm; weight: 3,188 lb, 1,446 kg; weight distribution: 51.9% front, 48.1% rear; turning circle: 34.8 ft, 10.6 m.

BODY adjustable headrests.

OPTIONALS speed control; air-conditioning.

159 hp power team

See 105 hp power team, except for:

ENGINE 6 cylinders, Vee-slanted at 60°; 182.7 cu in, 2,994 cc (3.69 x 2.85 in, 93.7 x 72.4 mm); compression ratio: 8.9:1; max power (DIN): 159 hp (117 kW) at 5,200 rpm; max torque (DIN): 191 lb ft, 26.4 kg m (267 Nm) at 3,000 rpm; max engine rpm: 5,500; 53.1 hp/l (39 kW/l); 4 crankshaft bearings; valves: overhead, push-rods and rockers; camshafts: 1, at centre of Vee; lubrication: 9.9 imp pt, 11.8 US pt, 5.6 l; 1 Weber 38/38 EGAS downdraught twin barrel carburettor; cooling: 20.1 imp pt, 24.1 US pt, 11.4 l.

TRANSMISSION gearbox: Ford C3 automatic transmission, hydraulic torque converter and planetary gears with 3 ratios, possible manual selection; ratios: I 2.470, II 1.470, III 1, rev 2.111; width of rims: Ghia 6"; tyres: Ghia 185 SR x 14.

PERFORMANCE max speed: GLE about 114 mph, 183 km/h - Ghia 110 mph, 177 km/h; power-weight ratio: GLE 18 lb/hp (26.7 lb/kW), 8.2 kg/hp (12.1 kg/kW); acceleration: Ghia 0-50 mph (0-80 km/h) 8.4 sec; speed in direct drive at 1,000 rpm: GLE 20.8 mph, 33.4 km/h - Ghia 20.2 mph, 32.5 km/h; consumption: GLE 24 m/imp gal, 20.1 m/US gal, 11.7 l x 100 km - Ghia 27.7 m/imp gal, 23.1 m/US gal, 10.2 l x 100 km.

STEERING servo; turns lock to lock: 3.50.

BRAKES front internal radial fins.

ELECTRICAL EQUIPMENT 45 Ah battery; 55 A alternator;

DIMENSIONS AND WEIGHT tracks: Ghia 62.13 in, 158 cm front, 60.83 in, 154 cm rear; length: Ghia 183.54 in, 466 cm; weight: GLE 3,120 lb, 1,415 kg - Ghia 3,355 lb, 1,525 kg.

BODY saloon/sedan; 4 doors; 5 seats, separate front seats, reclining backrests; (for Ghia only) adjustable built-in headrests, luxury equipment, tinted glass (standard) and air-conditioning.

OPTIONALS metallic spray; automatic cruise control; laminated windscreen; (for GLE only) tinted glass and air-conditioning.

OPEL SOUTH AFRICA

Kadett Series

PRICES EX WORKS:	rand
1 1.2 4+1-dr Sedan	7,455*
2 GL 1.3 4+1-dr Sedan	8,150*
3 Voyage 1.3 4+1-dr St. Wagon	8,925*
4 GLS 1.6 4+1-dr Sedan	9,140*
5 SR 1.6 4+1-dr Sedan	9,360*
6 Berlina 1.6 4+1-dr Sedan	9,645*
7 Voyage 1.6 4+1-dr St. Wagon	9,395*

Power team:	Standard for:	Optional for:
60 hp	1	—
75 hp	2,3	—
90 hp	4 to 7	—

60 hp power team

ENGINE front, transverse, 4 stroke; 4 cylinders, in line; 73 cu in, 1,196 cc (3.11 x 2.40 in, 79 x 61 mm); compression ratio: 9:1; max power (DIN): 60 hp (44 kW) at 5,800 rpm; max torque (DIN): 65 lb ft, 9 kg m (88 Nm) at 3,000-3,600 rpm; 46.3 hp/l (33.9 kW/l); cast iron block and head; 3 crankshaft bearings; valves: overhead, push-rods and rockers; camshafts: 1, side, chain-driven; lubrication: gear pump, full flow filter, 4.8 imp pt, 5.7 US pt, 2.7 l; 1 Solex 35 PDSI downdraught single barrel carburettor; fuel feed: mechanical pump; water-cooled, 8.1 imp pt, 9.7 US pt, 4.6 l, electric thermostatic fan.

TRANSMISSION driving wheels: front; clutch: single dry plate (diaphragm); gearbox: mechanical; gears: 4, fully synchronized; ratios: I 3.545, II 1.957, III 1.303, IV 0.892, rev 3.182; lever: central; final drive: helical spur gears; axle ratio: 4.290; width of rims: 5"; tyres: 155 SR x 13.

PERFORMANCE max speed: 93 mph, 150 km/h; power-weight ratio: 32.2 lb/hp (43.9 lb/kW), 14.6 kg/hp (19.9 kg/kW); carrying capacity: 882 lb, 400 kg; speed in top at 1,000 rpm: 15.9 mph, 25.3 km/h; consumption: 48 m/imp gal, 41 m/US gal, 5.8 l x 100 km at 53 mph, 85 km/h.

CHASSIS integral; front suspension: independent, by McPherson, coil springs/telescopic damper struts, heavy-duty rubber bearings, direction-stabilizing swivelling radius arm; rear: crank compound, progressively acting coil springs, auxiliary rubber springs, telescopic dampers.

STEERING rack-and-pinion; turns lock to lock: 3.90.

BRAKES front disc, rear drum, dual circuit; lining area: total 66.03 sq in, 426 sq cm.

ELECTRICAL EQUIPMENT 12 V; 36 Ah battery; 45 A alternator; Bosch distributor; 2 headlamps.

DIMENSIONS AND WEIGHT wheel base: 98.98 in, 251 cm; tracks: 55.12 in, 140 cm front, 55.35 in, 141 cm rear; length: 157.40 in, 399 cm; width: 64.40 in, 164 cm; height: 54.30 in, 138 cm; ground clearance: 5.12 in, 13 cm; weight: 1,929 lb, 875 kg; fuel tank: 12 imp gal, 15 US gal, 55 l.

BODY saloon/sedan; 4+1 doors; 5 seats, separate front seats; rear window wiper-washer.

OPTIONALS anti-roll bar on front and rear suspension; servo brake; 44 or 55 Ah battery; sunroof; metallic spray.

75 hp power team

See 60 hp power team, except for:

ENGINE 79.1 cu in, 1,297 cc (2.95 x 2.89 in, 75 x 73.4 mm); compression ratio: 9.2:1; max power (DIN): 75 hp (55 kW) at 5,800 rpm; max torque (DIN): 75 lb ft, 10.3 kg m (101 Nm) at 3,800-4,600 rpm; 57.8 hp/l (42.4 kW/l); light alloy head; 5 crankshaft bearings; valves: overhead, in line, rockers, hydraulic tappets; camshafts: 1, overhead, cogged belt; 1 GMF Varajet II downdraught twin barrel carburettor; cooling: 14.4 imp pt, 17.3 US pt, 8.2 l.

PERFORMANCE max speed: 98 mph, 158 km/h; power-weight ratio: GL 26.7 lb/hp (36.4 lb/kW), 12.1 kg/hp (16.5 kg/kW); consumption: 47 m/imp gal, 40 m/US gal, 6 l x 100 km at 53 mph, 85 km/h.

CHASSIS front and rear suspension: anti-roll bar (standard).

BRAKES servo (standard).

DIMENSIONS AND WEIGHT length: Voyage 166 in, 421 cm; height: Voyage 53 in, 134 cm; ground clearance: Voyage 5.30 in, 13.4 cm; weight: GL Sedan 2,000 lb, 907 kg - Voyage St. Wagon 2,024 lb, 918 kg.

BODY saloon/sedan - estate car/st. wagon.

90 hp power team

See 60 hp power team, except for:

ENGINE 97.5 cu in, 1,598 cc (3.15 x 3.13 in, 80 x 79.5 mm); compression ratio: 9.2:1; max power (DIN): 90 hp (66 kW) at 5,800 rpm; max torque (DIN): 93 lb ft, 12.8 kg m (126 Nm) at 3,800-4,200 rpm; 56.3 hp/l (41.4 kW/l); cast iron block, light alloy head; valves: overhead, push-rods and rockers, hydraulic tappets; camshafts: 1, overhead; lubrication: 5.6 imp pt, 6.8 US pt, 3.2 l; 1 GMF Varajet II downdraught twin barrel carburettor; cooling: 14.9 imp pt, 17.9 US pt, 8.5 l.

TRANSMISSION gearbox ratios: I 3.417, II 1.952, III 1.276, IV 0.707, rev 3.330; final drive: hypoid bevel; axle ratio: 3.940; width of rims: 5.5"; tyres: 175/70 SR x 13.

PERFORMANCE max speeds: (I) 28 mph, 45 km/h; (II) 48 mph, 78 km/h; (III) 75 mph, 120 km/h; (IV) 109 mph, 175 km/h; power-weight ratio: sedans 23.1 lb/hp (31.5 lb/kW), 10.5 kg/hp (14.3 kg/kW); carrying capacity: 1,136 lb, 515 kg; acceleration: standing ¼ mile 18 sec, 0-50 mph (0-80 km/h) 7.5 sec; speed in top at 1,000 rpm: 19.9 mph, 31.8 km/h; consumption: 34 m/imp gal, 28.3 m/US gal, 8.3 l x 100 km at 75 mph, 120 km/h.

CHASSIS front and rear suspension: anti-roll bar (standard).

BRAKES servo (standard).

DIMENSIONS AND WEIGHT weight: sedans, 2,084 lb, 945 kg; fuel tank: sedans 11 imp gal, 13.2 US gal, 50 l - St. Wagon 12 imp gal, 15 US gal, 55 l.

BODY saloon/sedan - estate car/st. wagon.

OPTIONALS automatic transmission, hydraulic torque converter and planetary gears with 3 ratios (I 2.840, II 1.600, III 1, rev 2.070), 3.330 axle ratio.

OPEL Ascona GLS Sedan

Ascona

PRICES EX WORKS:	rand
GL 4-dr Sedan	**9,850***
GLS 4-dr Sedan	**10,570***

ENGINE front, transverse, 4 stroke; 4 cylinders, in line; 97.5 cu in, 1,598 cc (3.15 x 3.13 in, 80 x 79.5 mm); compression ratio: 9.2:1; max power (DIN): 90 hp (66 kW) at 5,800 rpm; max torque (DIN): 93 lb ft, 12.8 kg m (126 Nm) at 3,800-4,200 rpm; max engine rpm: 6,600; 56.3 hp/l (41.3 kW/l); cast iron block, light alloy head; 5 crankshaft bearings; valves: overhead, in line, rockers, hydraulic tappets; camshafts: 1, overhead, cogged belt; lubrication: gear pump, full flow filter, 5.6 imp pt, 6.8 US pt, 3.2 l; 1 GMF Varajet downdraught twin barrel carburettor; fuel feed: mechanical pump; anti-freeze liquid cooled, 15.1 imp pt, 18.1 US pt, 8.6 l, electric thermostatic fan.

TRANSMISSION driving wheels: front; clutch: single dry plate (diaphragm); gearbox: mechanical; gears: 4, fully synchronized; ratios: I 3.417, II 1.952, III 1.276, IV 0.892, rev 3.330; lever: central; final drive: hypoid bevel; axle ratio: 3.940; width of rims: 5"; tyres: GL 165 SR x 13 - GLS 185/70 SR x 13.

PERFORMANCE max speeds: (I) 28 mph, 45 km/h; (II) 48 mph, 78 km/h; (III) 75 mph, 120 km/h; (IV) 109 mph, 175 km/h; power-weight ratio: 25.1 lb/hp (34.4 lb/kW), 11.4 kg/hp (15.6 kg/kW); carrying capacity: 1,102 lb, 500 kg; acceleration: standing ¼ mile 18 sec, 0-50 mph (0-80 km/h) 7.5 sec; speed in top at 1,000 rpm: 18.1 mph, 29.2 km/h; consumption: 34 m/imp gal, 28.3 m/US gal, 8.3 l x 100 km at 75 mph, 120 km/h.

CHASSIS integral; front suspension: independent, by McPherson, coil springs/telescopic damper struts, anti-roll bar, heavy-duty rubber bearings, direction stabilizing radius arm; rear: crank compound, progressively acting coil springs, auxiliary rubber springs, anti-roll bar, telescopic dampers.

STEERING rack-and-pinion; turns lock to lock: 4.

BRAKES front disc, rear drum, dual circuit, servo; lining area: total 70.08 sq in, 452 sq cm.

ELECTRICAL EQUIPMENT 12 V; 36 Ah battery; 45 A alternator; Bosch distributor; 2 headlamps.

DIMENSIONS AND WEIGHT wheel base: 101.34 in, 257 cm; tracks: 55.12 in, 140 cm front, 55.35 in, 141 cm rear; length: 171.89 in, 437 cm; width: 65.67 in, 167 cm; height: 54.92 in, 139 cm; ground clearance: 5.12 in, 13 cm; weight: 2,183 lb, 990 kg; turning circle: 33.1 ft, 10.1 m; fuel tank: 13.4 imp gal, 16.1 US gal, 61 l.

BODY saloon/sedan; 4 doors; 5 seats, separate front seats.

OPTIONALS automatic transmission, hydraulic torque converter and planetary gears with 3 ratios (I 2.840, II 1.600, III 1, rev 2.070), 3.740 axle ratio; 5 speed fully synchronized mechanical gearbox (I 3.417, II 1.952, III 1.276, IV 0.892, V 0.707, rev 3.330).

Rekord Series

PRICES EX WORKS:	rand
1 L 2.0 4-dr Sedan	**10,660***
2 GL 2.0 4-dr Sedan	**11,140***
3 Berlina S 2.0 4-dr Sedan	**12,555***
4 S 2.0 4-dr St. Wagon	**11,375***

Power team:	Standard for:	Optional for:
100 hp	1,2	—
110 hp	3,4	—

100 hp power team

ENGINE front, 4 stroke; 4 cylinders, vertical, in line; 120.8 cu in, 1,979 cc (3.74 x 2.75 in, 95 x 69.8 mm); compression ratio: 9:1; max power (DIN): 100 hp (74 kW) at 5,200 rpm; max torque (DIN): 117 lb ft, 16.1 kg m (158 Nm) at 3,800 rpm; max engine rpm: 5,500; 50.5 hp/l (37.2 kW/l); cast iron block and head; 5 crankshaft bearings; valves: overhead, in line, rockers, hydraulic tappets; camshafts: 1, overhead; lubrication: gear pump, full flow filter, 6.7 imp pt, 8 US pt, 3.8 l; 1 Varajet downdraught twin barrel carburettor; fuel feed: mechanical pump; anti-freeze liquid-cooled, 16 imp pt, 19.2 US pt, 9.1 l.

TRANSMISSION driving wheels: rear; clutch: single dry plate (diaphragm); gearbox: mechanical; gears: 5, fully synchronized; ratios: I 3.717, II 2.019, III 1.316, IV 1, V 0.805, rev 3.317; lever: central; final drive: hypoid bevel; axle ratio: 3.700; width of rims: 5.5"; tyres: 175 SR x 14.

PERFORMANCE max speed: 107 mph, 173 km/h; power-weight ratio: 24.6 lb/hp (33.3 lb/kW), 11.1 kg/hp (15.1 kg/kW); carrying capacity: 882 lb, 400 kg; speed in direct drive at 1,000 rpm: 20.7 mph, 33.3 km/h; consumption: 27.7 m/imp gal, 23.1 m/US gal, 10.2 l x 100 km.

CHASSIS integral: front suspension: independent, wishbones, lower trailing links, coil springs, anti-roll bar, telescopic dampers; rear: rigid axle, trailing lower radius arms, upper torque arms, transverse linkage bar, coil springs, anti-roll bar, telescopic dampers.

OPEL Commodore GL Sedan

STEERING recirculating ball; turns lock to lock: 4.

BRAKES front disc (diameter 9.37 in, 23.8 cm), rear drum, servo; lining area: total 85.7 sq in, 553 sq cm.

ELECTRICAL EQUIPMENT 12 V; 32 Ah battery; 37 A alternator; 2 headlamps.

DIMENSIONS AND WEIGHT wheel base: 105.40 in, 267 cm; tracks: 56.34 in, 143 cm front, 55.59 in, 141 cm rear; length: 108.75 in, 459 cm; width: 68.03 in, 173 cm; height: 55.71 in, 141 cm; ground clearance: 5.12 in, 13 cm; weight: 2,459 lb, 1,115 kg; turning circle: 32.6 ft, 9.9 m; fuel tank: 15.4 imp gal, 18.5 US gal, 70 l.

BODY saloon/sedan; 4 doors; 5 seats, separate front seats, reclining backrests, headrests.

OPTIONALS automatic transmission with 3 ratios (I 2.400, II 1.480, III 1, rev 1.920), max ratio of converter at stall 2.50, possible manual selection, max speed 99 mph, 160 km/h, consumption 23.2 m/imp gal, 19.3 m/US gal, 12.2 l x 100 km.

110 hp power team

See 100 hp power team, except for:

ENGINE compression ratio: 9.4:1; max power (DIN): 110 hp (81 kW) at 5,400 rpm; max torque (DIN): 120 lb ft, 16.5 kg m (162 Nm) at 3,000 rpm; 55.6 hp/l (40.9 kW/l); lubrication: 7.2 imp pt, 8.7 US pt, 4.1 l; Bosch LE-Jetronic injection; fuel feed: electric pump; cooling: 17 imp pt, 20.3 US pt, 9.7 l.

PERFORMANCE power-weight ratio: 22.3 lb/hp (30.4 lb/kW), 10.1 kg/hp (13.8 kg/kW).

DIMENSIONS AND WEIGHT height: 54.58 in, 139 cm.

BODY saloon/sedan - estate car/st. wagon.

Commodore

PRICES EX WORKS:	rand
L Automatic 4-dr Sedan	**12,765***
GL 4-dr Sedan	**15,245***
GL Automatic 4-dr Sedan	**15,495***

ENGINE front, 4 stroke; 6 cylinders, in line; 169.9 cu in, 2,784 cc (3.62 x 2.75 in, 92 x 69.8 mm); compression ratio: 9:1; max power (DIN): 140 hp (103 kW) at 5,200 rpm; max torque (DIN): 161 lb ft, 22.2 kg m (218 Nm) at 3,400 rpm; max engine rpm: 6,150; 50.3 hp/l (37 kW/l); cast iron block and head; 7 crankshaft bearings; valves: overhead, push-rods and rockers; camshafts: 1, overhead; lubrication: gear pump, full flow filter, 7.6 imp pt, 9.1 US pt, 4.3 l; 1 Solex 4 A 1 downdraught twin barrel carburettor; fuel feed: mechanical pump; water-cooled, 18.4 imp pt, 22.1 US pt, 10.5 l.

TRANSMISSION driving wheels: rear; clutch: single dry plate (diaphragm); gearbox: mechanical - GL sedans automatic transmission, hydraulic torque converter and planetary gears with 3 ratios (I 2.400, II 1.480, III 1, rev 1.920), possible manual selection; gears: 5, fully synchronized; ratios: I 3.820, II 2.190, III 1.390, IV 1, V 0.810, rev 3.700; lever: central; final drive: hypoid bevel; axle ratio: 3.500; width of rims: 6"; tyres: 175 HR x 14.

PERFORMANCE max speed: 127 mph, 205 km/h; power-weight ratio: 19.2 lb/hp (26.1 lb/kW), 8.7 kg/hp (11.8 kg/kW).

CHASSIS integral; front suspension: independent, wishbones, lower trailing links, coil springs, anti-roll bar, telescopic dampers; rear: rigid axle, trailing lower radius arms, upper torque arms, transverse linkage bar, coil springs, anti-roll bar, telescopic dampers.

STEERING recirculating ball, servo; turns lock to lock: 4.

BRAKES front disc (diameter 9.37 in, 23.8 cm), rear drum, servo; lining area: total 85.7 sq in, 553 sq cm.

ELECTRICAL EQUIPMENT 12 V; 32 Ah battery; 37 A alternator; electronic ignition; 2 headlamps.

DIMENSIONS AND WEIGHT wheel base: 105.40 in, 267 cm; tracks: 56.34 in, 143 cm front, 55.59 in, 141 cm rear; length: 187.79 in, 477 cm; width: 68.03 in, 173 cm; height: 56.69 in, 144 cm; ground clearance: 5.12 in, 13 cm; weight: 2,683 lb, 1,217 kg; turning circle: 32.6 ft, 9.9 m; fuel tank: 15.4 imp gal, 18.5 US gal, 70 l.

BODY saloon/sedan; 4 doors; 5 seats, separate front seats, reclining backrests, headrests.

OPTIONALS metallic spray; tinted glass.

OPEL Senator

Senator

PRICE EX WORKS: 25,500* rand

ENGINE front, 4 stroke; 6 cylinders, in line; 181.1 cu in, 2,968 cc (3.74 x 2.75 in, 95 x 69.8 mm); compression ratio: 9.4:1; max power (DIN): 180 hp (132 kW) at 5,800 rpm; max torque (DIN): 183 lb ft, 25.3 kg m (248 Nm) at 4,200 rpm; max engine rpm: 6,450; 60.6 hp/l (44.6 kW/l); cast iron block and head; 7 crankshaft bearings; valves: overhead, rockers, hydraulic tappets; camshafts: 1, overhead; lubrication: gear pump, full flow filter, 10.6 imp pt, 12.7 US pt, 6 l; Bosch L-Jetronic injection; fuel feed: electric pump; water-cooled, 18 imp pt, 21.6 US pt, 10.2 l.

TRANSMISSION driving wheels: rear; gearbox: automatic transmission, hydraulic torque converter and planetary gears with 3 ratios, possible manual selection; ratios: I 2.400, II 1.480, III 1, rev 1.920; lever: central; final drive: hypoid bevel; axle ratio: 3.500; width of rims: 6"; tyres: 195/70 HR x 14.

PERFORMANCE max speed: 127 mph, 205 km/h; power-weight ratio: 16.8 lb/hp (22.8 lb/kW), 7.6 kg/hp (10.3 kg/kW); carrying capacity: 1,224 lb, 555 kg; acceleration: standing ¼ mile 17.5 sec, 0-50 mph (0-80 km/h) 8 sec; speed in direct drive at 1,000 rpm: 23.2 mph, 37.4 km/h.

CHASSIS integral; front suspension: independent, by McPherson, wishbones, lower trailing links, coil springs, anti-roll bar, telescopic dampers; rear: independent, semi-trailing arms, coil springs, anti-roll bar, telescopic dampers.

STEERING recirculating ball, servo; turns lock to lock: 4.

BRAKES disc; swept area: front 23.2 sq in, 150 sq cm, rear 17.4 sq in, 112 sq cm, total 40.6 sq in, 262 sq cm.

ELECTRICAL EQUIPMENT 12 V; 55 Ah battery; 55 A alternator; Delco distributor; 2 halogen headlamps.

DIMENSIONS AND WEIGHT wheel base: 105.51 in, 268 cm; tracks: 56.85 in, 144 cm front, 57.48 in, 146 cm rear; length: 189.58 in, 481 cm; width: 68.11 in, 173 cm; height: 53.54 in, 136 cm; ground clearance: 5.12 in, 13 cm; weight: 3,021 lb, 1,370 kg; weight distribution: 51% front, 49% rear; turning circle: 32.6 ft, 9.9 m; fuel tank: 16.5 imp gal, 19.8 US gal, 75 l.

BODY saloon/sedan; 4 doors; 5 seats, separate front seats, reclining backrests, headrests.

PAYKAN — IRAN

Low Line / High Line

ENGINE British Talbot, front, longitudinal, 4 stroke; 4 cylinders, in line; 97.5 cu in, 1,598 cc (3.43 x 2.63 in, 87.3 x 66.7 mm); compression ratio: 8.8:1; max power (DIN): 65 hp (48 kW) at 4,600 rpm; max torque (DIN): 89 lb ft, 12.3 kg m (121 Nm) at 2,800 rpm; max engine rpm: 5,200; 40.1 hp/l (29.9 kW/l); cast iron block and head; 5 crankshaft bearings; valves: overhead, push-rods and rockers; camshafts: 1, side, chain-driven; lubrication: rotary pump, full flow filter, 7 imp pt, 8.5 US pt, 4 l; 1 Zenith-Stromberg 150 CDS downdraught single barrel carburettor; fuel feed: mechanical pump; water-cooled, 12.3 imp pt, 14.8 US pt, 7 l.

TRANSMISSION driving wheels: rear; clutch: single dry plate (diaphragm); gearbox: mechanical; gears: 4, fully synchronized; ratios: I 3.353, II 2.140, III 1.392, IV 1, rev 3.569; lever: central; final drive: hypoid bevel; axle ratio: 3.890; width of rims: 4.5"; tyres: 155 HR x 13.

PERFORMANCE max speeds: (I) 28 mph, 45 km/h; (II) 45 mph, 72 km/h; (III) 70 mph, 113 km/h; (IV) 85 mph, 134 km/h; power-weight ratio: 31.2 lb/hp (42.4 lb/kW), 14.1 kg/hp (19.2 kg/kW); carrying capacity: 904 lb, 410 kg; acceleration: standing ¼ mile 20.8 sec, 0-50 mph (0-80 km/h) 11.4 sec; speed in direct drive at 1,000 rpm: 17.5 mph, 28.1 km/h; consumption: 30 m/imp gal, 25 m/US gal, 9.4 l x 100 km.

CHASSIS integral; front suspension: independent, by McPherson, coil springs, telescopic dampers; rear: independent, semi-elliptic leafsprings, telescopic dampers.

STEERING recirculating ball; turns lock to lock: 3.36.

BRAKES front disc, rear drum, servo; swept area: front 175.2 sq in, 1,130 sq cm, rear 97.4 sq in, 628 sq cm, total 272.6 sq in, 1,758 sq cm.

ELECTRICAL EQUIPMENT 12 V; 40 Ah battery; 16 ACR alternator; Lucas distributor; 2 headlamps.

DIMENSIONS AND WEIGHT wheel base: 80.71 in, 205 cm; front and rear track: 51.97 in, 132 cm; length: 170.87 in, 434 cm; width: 63.39 in, 161 cm; height: 55.91 in, 142 cm; ground clearance: 5.71 in, 14.5 cm; weight: 2,029 lb, 920 kg; weight distribution: 58% front, 42% rear; turning circle: 36.7 ft, 11.2 m; fuel tank: 9.9 imp gal, 11.9 US gal, 45 l.

BODY saloon/sedan; 4 doors; 4-5 seats, separate front seats, reclining backrests; (for High Line only) luxury equipment.

PAYKAN High Line

HINDUSTAN — INDIA

Contessa

ENGINE front, 4 stroke; 4 cylinders, in line; 90.9 cu in, 1,489 cc (2.87 x 3.50 in, 73 x 88.9 mm); compression ratio: 7.2:1; max power (SAE): 49 hp (36 kW) at 4,200 rpm; max torque (SAE): 74 lb ft, 10.2 kg m (104 Nm) at 3,000 rpm; max engine rpm: 4,800; 32.9 hp/l (24.2 kW/l); cast iron block and head; 3 crankshaft bearings; valves: overhead, in line, push-rods and rockers; camshafts: 1, side; lubrication: gear pump, full flow filter, 8 imp pt, 9.6 US pt, 4.5 l; 1 Solex M32 PBIC downdraught carburettor; fuel feed: mechanical pump; water-cooled, 15 imp pt, 18 US pt, 8.5 l.

TRANSMISSION driving wheels: rear; clutch: single dry plate; gearbox: mechanical; gears: 4, II, III and IV synchronized; ratios: I 3.807, II 2.253, III 1.506, IV 1, rev 3.807; lever: central; final drive: hypoid bevel; axle ratio: 4.555; width of rims: 5"; tyres: 6.40 x 13.

PERFORMANCE max speeds: (I) 20 mph, 32 km/h; (II) 33 mph, 53 km/h; (III) 50 mph, 80 km/h; (IV) 75 mph, 120 km/h; power-weight ratio: 50 lb/hp (68.1 lb/kW), 22.7 kg/hp (30.9 kg/kW); carrying capacity: 807 lb, 366 kg; speed in direct drive at 1,000 rpm: 15.6 mph, 25 km/h.

CHASSIS front suspension: independent, wishbones, upper and lower arms, coil springs, anti-roll bar, telescopic dampers; rear: rigid axle, trailing arms (Panhard rod), coil springs, anti-roll bar, telescopic dampers.

STEERING rack-and-pinion; turns lock to lock: 4.

BRAKES drum: swept area: front 141.4 sq in, 912 sq cm, rear 98.9 sq in, 638.6 sq cm, total 240.3 sq in, 1,550 sq cm.

ELECTRICAL EQUIPMENT 12 V; 60 Ah battery; 270 W dynamo; Lucas-TVS 25 D4 distributor; 2 headlamps.

DIMENSIONS AND WEIGHT wheel base: 105.12 in, 267 cm; tracks: 56.30 in, 143 cm front, 55.51 in, 141 cm rear; length: 179.92 in, 457 cm; width: 66.93 in, 170 cm; height: 53.94 in, 137 cm; ground clearance: 6.30 in, 16 cm; weight: 2,452 lb, 1,112 kg; weight distribution: 45.5% front, 54.5% rear; turning circle: 37.4 ft, 11.4 m; fuel tank: 14.3 imp gal, 17.2 US gal, 65 l.

BODY saloon/sedan; 4 doors; 5 seats, separate front seats.

PRACTICAL INSTRUCTIONS fuel: 83 oct petrol; oil: engine 8 imp pt, 9.6 US pt, 4.5 l, change every 3,000 miles, 4,800 km - gearbox 1.9 imp pt, 2.3 US pt, 1.1 l, SAE 90, change every 6,000 miles, 9,600 km - final drive 2.5 imp pt, 3 US pt, 1.4 l, change every 6,000 miles, 9,600 km; tappet clearances: inlet 0.015 in, 0.38 mm, exhaust 0.015 in, 0.38 mm; valve timing: 5° 45° 40° 10°; tyre pressure: front 26 psi, 1.8 atm, rear 28 psi, 2 atm.

Ambassador Mk 4

PRICE EX WORKS: 48,587 rupees

For diesel engine add 15,570 rupees.

49 hp power team

(standard)

ENGINE front, 4 stroke; 4 cylinders, in line; 90.9 cu in, 1,489 cc (2.87 x 3.50 in, 73 x 88.9 mm); compression ratio: 7.2:1; max power (SAE): 49 hp (36 kW) at 4,200 rpm; max torque (SAE): 74 lb ft, 10.2 kg m (104 Nm) at 3,000 rpm; max engine rpm: 4,800; 32.9 hp/l (24.2 kW/l); cast iron block and head; 3 crankshaft bearings; valves: overhead, in line, push-rods and rockers; camshafts: 1, side; lubrication: gear pump, full flow filter, 8 imp pt, 9.6 US pt, 4.5 l; 1 SU type HS 2 semi-downdraught or Solex M32 PBIC downdraught carburettor; fuel feed: mechanical pump; water-cooled, 14.1 imp pt, 16.9 US pt, 8 l.

TRANSMISSION driving wheels: rear; clutch: single dry plate; gearbox: mechanical; gears: 4, II, III and IV synchronized; ratios: I 3.807, II 2.253, III 1.506, IV 1, rev 3.807; lever: steering column; final drive: hypoid bevel; axle ratio: 4.555; width of rims: 4"; tyres: 5.90 x 15.

PERFORMANCE max speeds: (I) 21 mph, 33 km/h; (II) 35 mph, 56 km/h; (III) 52 mph, 84 km/h; (IV) 75 mph, 121 km/h; power-weight ratio: 50 lb/hp (68.1 lb/kW), 22.7 kg/hp (30.9 kg/kW); carrying capacity: 850 lb, 386 kg; acceleration: standing ¼ mile 27 sec, 0-50 mph (0-80 km/h) 24.8 sec; speed in direct drive at 1,000 rpm: 16.5 mph, 26.4 km/h; consumption: 44.1 m/imp gal, 36.8 m/US gal, 6.4 l x 100 km.

HINDUSTAN Contessa

HINDUSTAN Ambassador Mk 4

HINDUSTAN Trekker

49 HP POWER TEAM

CHASSIS integral; front suspension: independent, wishbones, longitudinal torsion bars, telescopic dampers; rear: rigid axle, semi-elliptic leafsprings, telescopic dampers.

STEERING rack-and-pinion; turns lock to lock: 3.72.

BRAKES drum (diameter 8 in, 20.3 cm), rear compensator; lining area: front 48.1 sq in, 310 sq cm, rear 48.1 sq in, 310 sq cm, total 96.2 sq in, 620 sq cm.

ELECTRICAL EQUIPMENT 12 V; 60 Ah battery; 270 W dynamo; Lucas Prestolite distributor; 2 headlamps.

DIMENSIONS AND WEIGHT wheel base: 97 in, 246 cm; tracks: 53.80 in, 137 cm front, 53 in, 135 cm rear; length: 169.80 in, 431 cm; width: 66.14 in, 168 cm; height: 63 in, 160 cm; ground clearance: 6.25 in, 15.9 cm; weight: 2,456 lb, 1,114 kg; weight distribution: 55% front axle, 45% rear axle; turning circle: 35.5 ft, 10.8 m; fuel tank: 12 imp gal, 14.4 US gal, 55 l.

BODY saloon/sedan; 4 doors; 5 seats, bench front seats.

PRACTICAL INSTRUCTIONS fuel: 83 oct petrol; oil: engine 8 imp pt, 9.6 US pt, 4.5 l, SAE 30W-40, change every 3,000 miles, 4,800 km - gearbox 1.9 imp pt, 2.3 US pt, 1.1 l, change every 6,000 miles, 9,600 km - final drive 2.5 imp pt, 3 US pt, 1.4 l, change every 6,000 miles, 9,600 km; tappet clearances (hot): inlet 0.015 in, 0.37 mm, exhaust 0.015 in, 0.37 mm; valve timing: 5° 45° 40° 10°; tyre pressure: front 24 psi, 1.7 atm, rear 28 psi, 2 atm.

OPTIONALS servo brake; central gear lever; De Luxe equipment.

59 hp power team

(optional)

See 49 hp power team, except for:

ENGINE 107.4 cu in, 1,760 cc (3.13 x 3.50 in, 79.4 x 88.9 mm); compression ratio: 7.6:1; max power (SAE): 59 hp (43 kW) at 4,400 rpm; max torque (SAE): 86 lb ft, 11.8 kg m (116 Nm) at 3,000 rpm; max engine rpm: 5,000; 33.5 hp/l (24.4 kW/l).

PERFORMANCE max speeds: (I) 21 mph, 33 km/h; (II) 34 mph, 54 km/h; (III) 51 mph, 82 km/h; (IV) 77 mph, 124 km/h; power-weight ratio: 41.7 lb/hp (57.1 lb/kW), 18.9 kg/hp (25.9 kg/kW).

40 hp (diesel) power team

(optional)

See 49 hp power team, except for:

ENGINE diesel; compression ratio: 23:1; max power (SAE): 40 hp (29 kW) at 4,000 rpm; max torque (SAE): 62 lb ft, 8.5 kg m (83 Nm) at 2,000 rpm; max engine rpm: 4,000; 26.9 hp/l (19.5 kW/l).

TRANSMISSION axle ratio: 4.875.

PERFORMANCE max speeds: (I) 17 mph, 27 km/h; (II) 28 mph, 45 km/h; (III) 41 mph, 66 km/h; (IV) 62 mph, 99 km/h; power-weight ratio: 63.7 lb/hp (88 lb/kW), 28.9 kg/hp (39.9 kg/kW); carrying capacity: 805 lb, 365 kg; acceleration: standing ¼ mile 29 sec, 0-50 mph (0-80 km/h) 46.8 sec; speed in direct drive at 1,000 rpm: 15.5 mph, 24.9 km/h; consumption: 56.5 m/imp gal, 47 m/US gal, 5 l x 100 km.

ELECTRICAL EQUIPMENT 75 Ah battery.

DIMENSIONS AND WEIGHT width: 63 in, 160 cm; weight: 2,553 lb, 1,158 kg; weight distribution: 57.3% front axle, 42.7% rear axle.

PRACTICAL INSTRUCTIONS fuel: diesel; valve timing: 5° 45° 40° 10°.

Trekker

PRICE EX WORKS: 61,585 rupees

40 hp (diesel) power team

(standard)

ENGINE diesel; front, 4 stroke; 4 cylinders, in line; 90.9 cu in, 1,489 cc (2.87 x 3.50 in, 73 x 88.9 mm); compression ratio: 23:1; max power (SAE): 40 hp (29 kW) at 4,000 rpm; max torque (SAE): 62 lb ft, 8.5 kg m (83 Nm) at 2,000 rpm; max engine rpm: 4,000; 26.9 hp/l (19.5 kW/l); cast iron block and head; 3 crankshaft bearings; valves: overhead, in line, push-rods and rockers; camshafts: 1, side; lubrication: gear pump, full flow filter, 8 imp pt, 9.6 US pt, 4.5 l; 1 SU type HS 2 semi-downdraught or Solex M32 PBIC downdraught carburettor; fuel feed: mechanical pump; water-cooled, 14.1 imp pt, 16.9 US pt, 8 l.

TRANSMISSION driving wheels: rear; clutch: single dry plate; gearbox: mechanical; gears: 4, II, III and IV synchronized; ratios: I 3.807, II 2.253, III 1.506, IV 1, rev 3.807; lever: central; final drive: hypoid bevel; axle ratio: 4.875; width of rims: 4.5"; tyres: 6.40 x 15.

PERFORMANCE max speeds: (I) 17 mph, 27 km/h; (II) 28 mph, 45 km/h; (III) 41 mph, 66 km/h; (IV) 60 mph, 96 km/h; power-weight ratio: 64.4 lb/hp (88.9 lb/kW), 29.2 kg/hp (40.3 kg/kW); carrying capacity: 1,433 lb, 650 kg; acceleration: standing ¼ mile 29 sec, 0-50 mph (0-80 km/h) 68 sec; speed in direct drive at 1,000 rpm: 15.9 mph, 25.6 km/h; consumption: 42.2 m/imp gal, 35.1 m/US gal, 6.7 l x 100 km.

CHASSIS tubular frame; front suspension: independent, wishbones, longitudinal torsion bars, telescopic dampers; rear: rigid axle, semi-elliptic leafsprings, telescopic dampers.

STEERING rack-and-pinion; turns lock to lock: 3.72.

BRAKES drum (diameter 8 in, 20.3 cm), rear compensator; lining area: front 81.7 sq in, 527 sq cm, rear 68.7 sq in, 443 sq cm, total 150.4 sq in, 970 sq cm.

ELECTRICAL EQUIPMENT 12 V; 75 Ah battery; 270 W dynamo; 2 headlamps.

DIMENSIONS AND WEIGHT wheel base: 91 in, 231 cm; tracks: 55.50 in, 140 cm front, 53.50 in, 136 cm rear; length: 151 in, 383 cm; width: 65 in, 165 cm; height: 70.87 in, 180 cm; ground clearance: 7.80 in, 19.8 cm; weight: 2,578 lb, 1,169 kg; weight distribution: 56% front, 44% rear; turning circle: 34.8 ft, 10.6 m; fuel tank: 10.1 imp gal, 12.1 US gal, 46 l.

BODY open; no doors; 9 seats, bench front and rear seats.

PRACTICAL INSTRUCTIONS fuel: diesel; oil: engine 8 imp pt, 9.6 US pt, 4.5 l, SAE 20W-30, change every 3,000 miles, 4,800 km - gearbox 1.9 imp pt, 2.3 US pt, 1.1 l, change every 6,000 miles, 9,700 km - final drive 2.5 imp pt, 3 US pt, 1.4 l, change every 6,000 miles, 9,700 km; tappet clearances (hot): inlet 0.015 in, 0.37 mm, exhaust 0.015 in, 0.37 mm; valve timing: 5° 45° 40° 10°; tyre pressure: front 26 psi, 1.8 atm, rear 30 psi, 2.1 atm.

OPTIONALS servo brake.

49 hp power team

(optional)

See 40 hp (diesel) power team, except for:

ENGINE petrol; compression ratio: 7.2:1; max power (SAE): 49 hp (36 kW) at 4,200 rpm; max torque (SAE): 74 lb ft, 10.2 kg m (104 Nm) at 3,000 rpm; max engine rpm: 4,800; 32.9 hp/l (24.2 kW/l).

PERFORMANCE max speeds: (I) 20 mph, 32 km/h; (II) 33 mph, 53 km/h; (III) 49 mph, 79 km/h; (IV) 72 mph, 116 km/h; power-weight ratio: 52.7 lb/hp (71.7 lb/kW), 23.9 kg/hp (32.5 kg/kW).

ELECTRICAL EQUIPMENT 60 Ah battery.

PRACTICAL INSTRUCTIONS fuel: 83 oct petrol; valve timing: 5° 45° 40° 10°.

59 hp power team

(optional)

See 40 hp (diesel) power team, except for:

ENGINE petrol; 107.4 cu in, 1,760 cc (3.13 x 3.50 in, 79.4 x 88.9 mm); compression ratio: 7.6:1; max power (SAE): 59 hp (43 kW) at 4,400 rpm; max torque (SAE): 86 lb ft, 11.8 kg m (116 Nm) at 3,000 rpm; max engine rpm: 5,000; 33.5 hp/l (24.4 kW/l).

PERFORMANCE max speeds: (I) 21 mph, 33 km/h; (II) 34 mph, 54 km/h; (III) 51 mph, 82 km/h; (IV) 75 mph, 121 km/h; power-weight ratio: 43.7 lb/hp (60 lb/kW), 19.8 kg/hp (27.2 kg/kW).

ELECTRICAL EQUIPMENT 60 Ah battery.

PRACTICAL INSTRUCTIONS fuel: 83 oct petrol; valve timing: 5° 45° 40° 10°.

PREMIER INDIA

Padmini

PRICE EX WORKS: 58,474 rupees

ENGINE front, 4 stroke; 4 cylinders, vertical, in line; 66.5 cu in, 1,089 cc (2.68 x 2.95 in, 68 x 75 mm); compression ratio: 7.3:1; max power (SAE): 40 hp (29 kW) at 4,800 rpm; max torque (SAE): 57 lb ft, 7.9 kg m (77 Nm) at 2,400 rpm; max engine rpm: 4,800; 36.7 hp/l (26.4 kW/l); cast iron block, light alloy head; 3 crankshaft bearings; valves: overhead, in line, push-rods and rockers; camshafts: 1, side; lubrication: rotary pump, by-pass filter, 5.3 imp pt, 6.3 US pt, 3 l; 1 32 BIC type IBX downdraught single barrel carburettor; fuel feed: mechanical pump; water-cooled, 7.9 imp pt, 9.5 US pt, 4.5 l.

TRANSMISSION driving wheels: rear; clutch: single dry plate; gearbox: mechanical; gears: 4, II, III and IV synchronized; ratios: I 3.860, II 2.380, III 1.570, IV 1, rev 3.860; lever: steering column; final drive: hypoid bevel; axle ratio: 4.300; width of rims: 3.5"; tyres: 5.20 x 14.

PERFORMANCE max speeds: (I) 19 mph, 30 km/h; (II) 31 mph, 50 km/h; (III) 47 mph, 75 km/h; (IV) 75 mph, 120 km/h; power-weight ratio: 49.3 lb/hp (68 lb/kW), 22.4 kg/hp (30.9 kg/kW); carrying capacity: 882 lb, 400 kg; acceleration:

SIPANI Dolphin Hatchback Sedan

BEIJING BJ 750

standing ¼ mile 26.9 sec, 0-50 mph (0-80 km/h) 20.3 sec; speed in direct drive at 1,000 rpm: 15.6 mph, 25 km/h; consumption: 42.2 m/imp gal, 35.1 m/US gal, 6.7 l x 100 km.

CHASSIS integral; front suspension: independent, wishbones, anti-roll bar, coil springs, telescopic dampers; rear: rigid axle, anti-roll bar, semi-elliptic leafsprings, telescopic dampers.

STEERING worm and roller; turns lock to lock: 4.80.

BRAKES drum; lining area: front 76.9 sq in, 496 sq cm, rear 76.9 sq in, 496 sq cm, total 153.8 sq in, 992 sq cm.

ELECTRICAL EQUIPMENT 12 V; 45 Ah battery; 264 W dynamo; Lucas distributor; 2 headlamps.

DIMENSIONS AND WEIGHT wheel base: 92.13 in, 234 cm; tracks: 48.50 in, 123 cm front, 47.83 in, 121 cm rear; length: 155.12 in, 394 cm; width: 57.50 in, 146 cm; height: 57.75 in, 147 cm; ground clearance: 5.04 in, 12.8 cm; weight: 1,973 lb, 895 kg; weight distribution: 45.6% front axle, 54.4% rear axle; turning circle: 34.7 ft, 10.9 m; fuel tank: 8.4 imp gal, 10 US gal, 38 l.

BODY saloon/sedan; 4 doors; 5 seats, bench front seats.

PRACTICAL INSTRUCTIONS fuel: 83 oct petrol; oil: engine 5.3 imp pt, 6.3 US pt, 3 l, SAE 30-50, change every 5,600 miles, 9,000 km - gearbox 1.9 imp pt, 2.3 US pt, 1.1 l, SAE 90 EP, change every 18,600 miles, 30,000 km - final drive 1.1 imp pt, 1.3 US pt, 0.6 l, SAE 90 EP, change every 18,600 miles, 30,000 km; spark plug: MICO HB-W-175 Z 1; tappet clearances: inlet 0.004 in, 0.10 mm, exhaust 0.004 in, 0.10 mm; valve timing: 16° 56° 56° 16°; tyre pressure: front 22 psi, 1.5 atm, rear 28 psi, 2 atm.

Padmini De Luxe

See Padmini, except for:

PRICE EX WORKS: 66,943 rupees

ENGINE compression ratio: 8:1; max power (SAE): 47 hp (35 kW) at 5,000 rpm; max torque (SAE): 58 lb ft, 8 kg m (78 Nm) at 3,000 rpm; max engine rpm: 5,000; 43.6 hp/l (31.8 kW/l); 1 32 PBIC type IBX downdraught single barrel carburettor.

TRANSMISSION lever: central.

PERFORMANCE max speeds: (I) 21 mph, 33 km/h; (II) 34 mph, 54 km/h; (III) 51 mph, 81 km/h; (IV) 80 mph, 128 km/h; power-weight ratio: 42 lb/hp (56.4 lb/kW), 19 kg/hp (25.6 kg/kW); consumption: 35.3 m/imp gal, 29.4 m/US gal, 8 l x 100 km.

BODY separate front seats; safety belts.

PRACTICAL INSTRUCTIONS fuel: 93 oct petrol.

SIPANI INDIA

Dolphin

PRICES EX WORKS:	**rupees**
2-dr Hatchback Sedan	**58,500**
2+1-dr St. Wagon	—

ENGINE Reliant, front, 4 stroke; 4 cylinders, vertical, in line; 51.7 cu in, 848 cc (2.46 x 2.72 in, 62.5 x 69.1 mm); compression ratio: 8.5:1; max power (DIN): 38 hp (28 kW) at 5,500 rpm; max torque (DIN): 46 lb ft, 6.3 kg m (62 Nm) at 3,500 rpm; max engine rpm: 5,500; 44.8 hp/l (33 kW/l); light alloy block and head, wet liners; 3 crankshaft bearings; valves: overhead, in line, push-rods and rockers; camshafts: 1, side; lubrication: rotary pump, full flow filter, 5.5 imp pt, 6.6 US pt, 3.1 l; 1 SU HS2 1¼ semi-downdraught single barrel carburettor; fuel feed: mechanical pump; water-cooled, 6.5 imp pt, 7.8 US pt, 3.7 l.

TRANSMISSION driving wheels: rear; clutch: single dry plate (diaphragm); gearbox: mechanical; gears: 4, fully synchronized; ratios: I 3.876, II 2.046, III 1.319, IV 1, rev 3.250; lever: central; final drive: spiral bevel; axle ratio: 3.545; width of rims: 3.5"; tyres: 145 x 10.

PERFORMANCE max speeds: (I) 24 mph, 39 km/h; (II) 45 mph, 73 km/h; (III) 71 mph, 114 km/h; (IV) 80 mph, 128 km/h; power-weight ratio: 30.6 lb/hp (41.7 lb/kW), 13.9 kg/hp (18.9 kg/kW); carrying capacity: 700 lb, 317 kg; acceleration: standing ¼ mile 20.4 sec, 0-50 mph (0-80 km/h) 11.8 sec; speed in direct drive at 1,000 rpm: 17 mph, 27.3 km/h; consumption: 56.5 m/imp gal, 47 m/US gal, 5 l x 100 km.

CHASSIS box section side members and channel section diagonal reinforcements; front suspension: independent, wishbones, anti-roll bar, coil springs/telescopic damper units; rear: rigid axle, semi-elliptic leafsprings, telescopic dampers.

STEERING rack-and-pinion; turns lock to lock: 3.50.

BRAKES drum (diameter 7 in, 17.8 cm); swept area: front 66 sq in, 426 sq cm, rear 55 sq in, 355 sq cm, total 121 sq in, 781 sq cm.

ELECTRICAL EQUIPMENT 12 V; 30 Ah battery; 28 A alternator; Lucas distributor; 2 headlamps.

DIMENSIONS AND WEIGHT wheel base: 84.50 in, 215 cm; tracks: 48.50 in, 123 cm front, 49 in, 124 cm rear; length: 131 in, 333 cm - St. Wagon 131.75 in, 335 cm; width: 56 in, 142 cm; height: 55 in, 140 cm; ground clearance: 5 in, 12.7 cm; weight: 1,170 lb, 530 kg; turning circle: 24 ft, 7.3 m; fuel tank: 6 imp gal, 7.1 US gal, 27 l.

BODY saloon/sedan, 2 doors - estate car/st. wagon, 2+1 doors, in g.r.p. material; 4 seats, separate front seats, reclining backrests; heated rear window; folding rear seat.

PRACTICAL INSTRUCTIONS fuel: 93 oct petrol; oil: engine 5.5 imp pt, 6.6 US pt, 3.1 l, SAE 20W-40, change every 6,000 miles, 9,700 km - gearbox 1.1 imp pt, 1.3 US pt, 0.6 l, SAE 80 EP, change every 12,000 miles, 19,400 km - final drive 2.2 imp pt, 2.5 US pt, 1.2 l, SAE 90 EP, change every 6,000 miles, 9,700 km; greasing: every 6,000 miles, 9,700 km, 7 points; tappet clearances: inlet 0.010 in, 0.25 mm, exhaust 0.010 in, 0.25 mm; valve timing: 13° 72° 54° 29°; tyre pressure: front 20 psi, 1.4 atm, rear 22 psi, 1.6 atm.

OPTIONALS 5" wide rims; light alloy wheels; metallic spray.

PREMIER Padmini De Luxe

BEIJING CHINA (People's Republic)

BJ 750

ENGINE front, 4 stroke; 4 cylinders, vertical, in line; 149.2 cu in, 2,445 cc (3.62 x 3.62 in, 92 x 92 mm); compression ratio: 8.5:1; max power (DIN): 100 hp (74 kW) at 4,500 rpm; max torque (DIN): 141 lb ft, 19.5 kg m (191 Nm) at 2,800-3,200 rpm; max engine rpm: 5,000; 40.9 hp/l (30.1 kW/l); light alloy block and head; 5 crankshaft bearings; valves: overhead, Vee-slanted, push-rods and rockers; camshafts: 1, side; lubrication: gear pump, full flow filter, 10.9 imp pt, 13.1 US pt, 6.2 l; 1 downdraught twin barrel carburettor; fuel feed: mechanical pump; water-cooled, 18.5 imp pt, 22.2 US pt, 10.5 l.

TRANSMISSION driving wheels: rear; clutch: single dry plate; gearbox: mechanical; gears: 4, fully synchronized; ratios: I 3.874, II 2.289, III 1.350, IV 1, rev 3.874; lever: central; final drive: hypoid bevel; axle ratio: 3.909; width of rims: 7"; tyres: 6.94 x 14.

PERFORMANCE max speed: 87 mph, 140 km/h; power-weight ratio: 32 lb/hp (43.5 lb/kW), 14.5 kg/hp (19.7 kg/kW); carrying capacity: 717 lb, 325 kg; acceleration: standing ¼ mile 22 sec; consumption: 31.4 m/imp gal, 26.1 m/US gal, 9 l x 100 km.

CHASSIS box-type ladder frame; front suspension: independent, torsion bar, coil springs, telescopic dampers; rear: independent, coil springs, telescopic dampers.

BJ 750

STEERING recirculating ball; turns lock to lock: 5.50.

BRAKES front disc, rear drum, servo.

ELECTRICAL EQUIPMENT 12 V; 54 Ah battery; 350 W alternator; 2 headlamps.

DIMENSIONS AND WEIGHT wheel base: 109.84 in, 279 cm; tracks: 56.69 in, 144 cm front, 57.36 in, 146 cm rear; length: 189.05 in, 480 cm; width: 70.08 in, 178 cm; height: 56.30 in, 143 cm; ground clearance: 6.30 in, 16 cm; weight: 3,208 lb, 1,455 kg; weight distribution: 51.1% front, 48.9% rear; turning circle: 38.4 ft, 11 m; fuel tank: 13.2 imp gal, 15.8 US gal, 60 l.

BODY saloon/sedan; 4 doors; 5 seats, separate front seats.

BJ 212

ENGINE front, 4 stroke; 4 cylinders, vertical, in line; 149.2 cu in, 2,445 cc (3.62 x 3.62 in, 92 x 92 mm); compression ratio: 6.6:1; max power (SAE): 75 hp (55 kW) at 3,500-4,000 rpm; max torque (SAE): 127 lb ft, 17.5 kg m (172 Nm) at 2,000-2,500 rpm; max engine rpm: 4,000; 30.7 hp/l (22.6 kW/l); cast iron block, light alloy head; 5 crankshaft bearings; valves: overhead, Vee-slanted, push-rods and rockers; camshafts: 1, side; lubrication: gear pump, full flow filter, 10.9 imp pt, 13.1 US pt, 6.2 l; 1 type K-22D downdraught single barrel carburettor; fuel feed: mechanical pump; water-cooled, 18.5 imp pt, 22.2 US pt, 10.5 l.

TRANSMISSION driving wheels: front (automatically engaged with transfer box low ratio) and rear; clutch: single dry plate, hydraulically controlled; gearbox: mechanical; gears: 3, II and III synchronized; ratios: I 3.115, II 1.772, III 1, rev 3.738; transfer box ratios: high 1.200, low 2.648; lever: central; final drive: spiral bevel; axle ratio: 4.550; width of rims: 4.5"; tyres: 6.50 x 16.

PERFORMANCE max speeds: (I) 20 mph, 32 km/h; (II) 35 mph, 56 km/h; (III) 61 mph, 98 km/h; power-weight ratio: 45 lb/hp (61.3 lb/kW), 20.4 kg/hp (27.8 kg/kW); carrying capacity: 882 lb, 400 kg; consumption: 16.6 m/imp gal, 13.8 m/US gal, 17 l x 100 km.

CHASSIS box-type ladder frame; front and rear suspension: rigid axle, semi-elliptic leafsprings, telescopic dampers.

STEERING worm and double roller.

BRAKES drum; lining area: total 153.5 sq in, 990 sq cm.

ELECTRICAL EQUIPMENT 12 V; 54 Ah battery; 250 W dynamo; 2 headlamps.

DIMENSIONS AND WEIGHT wheel base: 90.55 in, 230 cm; front and rear track: 56.69 in, 144 cm; length: 153.54 in, 390 cm; width: 68.90 in, 175 cm; height: 73.62 in, 187 cm; ground clearance: 8.66 in, 22 cm; weight: 3,374 lb, 1,530 kg; weight distribution: 52% front, 48% rear; turning circle: 39.4 ft, 12 m; fuel tank: 13.2 imp gal, 15.8 US gal, 60 l - (separate tank) 5.5 imp gal, 6.6 US gal, 25 l.

BODY open; 4 doors; 5 seats, separate front seats; canvas roof.

BJ 212 E

See BJ 212, except for:

ENGINE compression ratio: 7.2:1; max power (SAE): 70 hp (51 kW) at 4,000 rpm; max torque (SAE): 123 lb ft, 17 kg m (167 Nm) at 2,200 rpm; 28.6 hp/l (21.1 kW/l); light alloy block and head; 1 type 231/A16 downdraught single barrel carburettor.

TRANSMISSION final drive: hypoid bevel; axle ratio: 5.375.

PERFORMANCE power-weight ratio: 47.9 lb/hp (65.1 lb/kW), 21.7 kg/hp (29.5 kg/kW); carrying capacity: 1,323 lb, 600 kg; consumption: 18.8 m/imp gal, 15.7 m/US gal, 15 l x 100 km.

STEERING recirculating ball.

ELECTRICAL EQUIPMENT 56 Ah battery.

DIMENSIONS AND WEIGHT length: 151.97 in, 386 cm; height: 75.39 in, 191 cm; ground clearance: 7.87 in, 20 cm; weight: 3,352 lb, 1,520 kg.

BODY hardtop; 8 seats.

HONG QI CA-770 B

HONG QI CHINA (People's Republic)

CA-770 B

ENGINE front, 4 stroke; 8 cylinders in Vee; 344.9 cu in, 5,652 cc (3.94 x 3.54 in, 100 x 90 mm); compression ratio: 8.5:1; max power (SAE): 220 hp (162 kW) at 4,400 rpm; max torque (SAE): 304 lb ft, 42 kg m (412 Nm) at 2,800-3,000 rpm; max engine rpm: 4,400; 38.9 hp/l (28.6 kW/l); cast iron block and head; 5 crankshaft bearings; valves: overhead, in line, push-rods and rockers; camshafts: 1, at centre of Vee; lubrication: gear pump, full flow filter, 9.7 imp pt, 11.6 US pt, 5.5 l; 1 type 241 downdraught 4-barrel carburettor; fuel feed: mechanical pump; water-cooled, 9-pass. 52.8 imp pt, 63.4 US pt, 30 l - 6-pass. 44 imp pt, 52.9 US pt, 25 l.

TRANSMISSION driving wheels: rear; gearbox: automatic transmission, hydraulic torque converter and planetary gears with 2 ratios, max ratio of converter at stall 2.50; ratios: I 1.720, II 1, rev 2.390; lever: steering column; final drive: hypoid bevel; axle ratio: 9-pass. 3.900 - 6-pass. 3.540; width of rims: 6"; tyres: 9-pass. 8.90 x 15 - 6-pass. 8.20 x 15.

PERFORMANCE max speed: 9-pass. 99 mph, 160 km/h - 6-pass. 112 mph, 180 km/h; power-weight ratios: 9-pass. 27.3 lb/hp (37.3 lb/kW), 12.4 kg/hp (16.9 kg/kW) - 6-pass. 22.7 lb/hp (30.9 lb/kW), 10.3 kg/hp (14 kg/kW); carrying capacity: 9-pass. 1,588 lb, 720 kg - 6-pass. 1,058 lb, 480 kg; consumption: 9-pass. 14.1 m/imp gal, 11.8 m/US gal, 20 l x 100 km - 6-pass. 15.7 m/imp gal, 13.1 m/US gal, 18 l x 100 km.

CHASSIS box-type ladder frame; front suspension: independent, wishbones. coil springs, horizontal torsion bars, telescopic dampers; rear: rigid axle, semi-elliptic leafsprings, telescopic dampers.

STEERING recirculating ball, servo.

BRAKES drum, dual circuit.

ELECTRICAL EQUIPMENT 12 V; 68 Ah battery - (for 9-pass. only) 2 x 68 Ah batteries; 36 A dynamo; 2 headlamps.

DIMENSIONS AND WEIGHT wheel base: 9-pass. 146.46 in, 372 cm - 6-pass. 120.87 in, 307 cm; tracks: 62.20 in, 158 cm front, 61.02 in, 155 cm rear; length: 9-pass. 235.43 in, 598 cm - 6-pass. 209.84 in, 533 cm; width: 78.35 in, 199 cm; height: 64.57 in, 164 cm; ground clearance: 7.09 in, 18 cm; weight: 9-pass. 6,020 lb, 2,730 kg - 6-pass. 5,005 lb, 2,270 kg; weight distribution: 9-pass. 52.2% front, 47.8% rear - 6-pass. 54% front, 46% rear; turning circle: 9-pass. 49.2 ft, 15 m - 6-pass. 42 ft, 12.8 m; fuel tank: 17.6 imp gal, 21.1 US gal, 80 l.

BODY limousine; 4 doors; 9 seats in three rows or 6 seats, bench front seats; electric rear seat; electric windows; air-conditioning.

SHANGHAI 760 A

SHANGHAI CHINA (People's Republic)

Santana Shanghai

ENGINE Volkswagen, front, slanted 20° to right, 4 stroke; 4 cylinders, in line; 96.9 cu in, 1,588 cc (3.13 x 3.15 in, 79.5 x 80 mm); compression ratio: 8.2:1; max power (DIN): 85 hp (63 kW) at 5,600 rpm; max torque (DIN): 93 lb ft, 12.9 kg m (127 Nm) at 3,200 rpm; max engine rpm: 6,100; 53.5 hp/l (39.4 kW/l); cast iron block, light alloy head; 5 crankshaft bearings; valves: overhead, in line, thimble tappets; camshafts: 1, overhead, cogged belt; lubrication: gear pump, full flow filter, 5.3 imp pt, 6.3 US pt, 3 l; 1 Solex 2B5 downdraught twin barrel carburettor; fuel feed: mechanical pump; liquid cooled, expansion tank, 8.1 imp pt, 9.7 US pt, 4.6 l, electric thermostatic fan.

TRANSMISSION driving wheels: front; clutch: single dry plate (diaphragm); gearbox: mechanical; gears: 4, fully synchronized; ratios: I 3.450, II 1.940, III 1.290, IV 0.910, rev 3.170; lever: central; final drive: spiral bevel; axle ratio: 4.111; width of rims: 5"; tyres: 165 SR x 13.

PERFORMANCE max speed: 103 mph, 166 km/h; power-weight ratio: 25.6 lb/hp (34.5 lb/kW), 11.6 kg/hp (15.6 kg/kW); carrying capacity: 1,047 lb, 475 kg; acceleration: 0-50 mph (0-80 km/h) 8.8 sec; speed in top at 1,000 rpm: 16.3 mph, 26.3 km/h; consumption: 32.5 m/imp gal, 27 m/US gal, 8.7 l x 100 km at 75 mph, 120 km/h.

CHASSIS integral, front auxiliary subframe; front suspension: independent, by McPherson, lower wishbones, anti-roll bar, coil springs/telescopic damper struts; rear: rigid axle, trailing radius arms, transverse linkage bar, coil springs, anti-roll bar, telescopic dampers.

STEERING rack-and-pinion, damper.

BRAKES front disc (diameter 9.41 in, 23.9 cm), rear drum, 2 x circuits, rear compensator, servo.

ELECTRICAL EQUIPMENT 12 V; 36 Ah battery; 45 A alternator; transistorized ignition; 2 headlamps.

DIMENSIONS AND WEIGHT wheel base: 100.39 in, 255 cm; tracks: 55.12 in, 140 cm front, 55.43 in, 141 cm rear; length:

SHANGHAI Santana Shanghai

DAEWOO Maepsy-Na

178.94 in, 454 cm; width: 66.73 in, 169 cm; height: 55.43 in, 140 cm; weight: 2,172 lb, 985 kg; turning circle: 35.4 ft, 10.8 m; fuel tank: 13.2 imp gal, 15.8 US gal, 60 l.

BODY saloon/sedan; 4 doors; 5 seats, separate front seats, reclining backrests with headrests; heated rear window.

PRACTICAL INSTRUCTIONS fuel: 86 oct petrol; oil: engine 5.3 imp pt, 6.3 US pt, 3 l, SAE 20W-30, change every 9,000 miles, 15,000 km - gearbox and final drive 3.2 imp pt, 3.8 US pt, 1.8 l, SAE 80, no change recommended; greasing: none; spark plug: 175°; tappet clearances: inlet 0.008-0.012 in, 0.20-0.30 mm, exhaust 0.016-0.020 in, 0.40-0.50 mm; tyre pressure: front 24 psi, 1.7 atm, rear 24 psi, 1.7 atm.

OPTIONALS automatic transmission hydraulic torque converter and planetary gears with 3 ratios (I 2.710, II 1.500, III 1, rev 2.430), 3.730 axle ratio, max speed 100 mph, 161 km/h, acceleration 0-50 mph (0-80 km/h) 10.2 sec, consumption 29.4 m/imp gal, 24.5 m/US gal, 9.6 l x 100 km at 75 mph, 120 km/h; 4+E 5-speed fully synchronized mechanical gearbox (I 3.450, II 1.940, III 1.290, IV 0.910, V 0.730, rev 3.170), consumption 36.2 m/imp gal, 30.2 m/US gal, 7.8 l x 100 km at 75 mph, 120 km/h; power steering; 185/70 SR x 13 tyres; sunroof; electric windows; air-conditioning; halogen headlamps; metallic spray.

760 A

ENGINE front, 4 stroke; 6 cylinders, in line; 136.2 cu in, 2,232 cc (3.15 x 2.91 in, 80 x 74 mm); compression ratio: 7.7:1; max power (SAE): 90 hp (73 kW) at 4,800 rpm; max torque (SAE): 109 lb ft, 15 kg m (147 Nm) at 3,500 rpm; max engine rpm: 5,000; 40.3 hp/l (73.8 kW/l); cast iron block, light alloy head; 4 crankshaft bearings; valves: overhead, in line; camshafts: 1, side; lubrication: gear pump, full flow filter, 10.8 imp pt, 12.7 US pt, 6 l; 1 Shangfu 593 downdraught twin barrel carburettor; fuel feed: mechanical pump; water-cooled, 19.4 imp pt, 23.3 US pt, 11 l.

TRANSMISSION driving wheels: rear; clutch: single dry plate; gearbox: mechanical; gears: 4, fully synchronized; ratios: I 3.520, II 2.320, III 1.520, IV 1, rev 3.290; lever: steering column; final drive: hypoid bevel; axle ratio: 4.110; width of rims: 5"; tyres: 6.70 x 13.

PERFORMANCE max speed: 81 mph, 130 km/h; power-weight ratio: 35.7 lb/hp (44.1 lb/kW), 16.2 kg/hp (20 kg/kW); carrying capacity: 882 lb, 400 kg; consumption: 23.5 m/imp gal, 19.6 m/US gal, 12 l x 100 km.

CHASSIS integral; front and rear suspension: independent, coil springs, telescopic dampers.

STEERING recirculating ball.

BRAKES drum, servo.

ELECTRICAL EQUIPMENT 12 V; 54 Ah battery; 220 W dynamo; 2 headlamps.

DIMENSIONS AND WEIGHT wheel base: 111.02 in, 282 cm; tracks: 56.69 in, 144 cm front, 58.27 in, 148 cm rear; length: 191.34 in, 486 cm; width: 69.68 in, 177 cm; height: 62.20 in, 158 cm; ground clearance: 5.51 in, 14 cm; weight: 3,219 lb, 1,460 kg; weight distribution: 59% front, 41% rear; turning circle: 36.7 ft, 11.2 m; fuel tank: 14.1 imp gal, 16.9 US gal, 64 l.

BODY saloon/sedan; 4 doors; 5 seats, bench front seats.

PRACTICAL INSTRUCTIONS tappet clearances: inlet 0.004 in, 0.10 mm, exhaust 0.008 in, 0.20 mm; valve timing: 12° 44° 51° 15°; tyre pressure: front 30 psi, 2.1 atm, rear 31 psi, 2.2 atm.

DAEWOO KOREA

Maepsy-Na

ENGINE front, 4 stroke; 4 cylinders; 91 cu in, 1,492 cc (3.25 x 2.75 in, 82.5 x 69.8 mm); compression ratio: 8.6:1; max power (DIN): 60 hp (44 kW) at 5,000 rpm; max torque (DIN): 74 lb ft, 10.2 kg m (100 Nm) at 3,000 rpm; max engine rpm: 5,400; 40.2 hp/l (29.6 kW/l); cast iron block and head; 5 crankshaft bearings; valves: overhead; camshafts: 1, overhead; lubrication: gear pump, full flow filter, 6.2 imp pt, 7.4 US pt, 3.5 l; 1 Nikki Stromberg 2-BBL downdraught carburettor; fuel feed: mechanical pump; water-cooled, 12.3 imp pt, 14.8 US pt, 7 l.

DAEWOO Maepsy-Na

TRANSMISSION driving wheels: rear; clutch: single dry plate; gearbox: mechanical; gears: 4, fully synchronized; ratios: I 3.640, II 2.120, III 1.336, IV 1, rev 3.522; lever: central; final drive: hypoid bevel; axle ratio: 3.700; width of rims: 4.5"; tyres: 6.15 x 13.

PERFORMANCE max speeds: (I) 25 mph, 41 km/h; (II) 44 mph, 71 km/h; (III) 70 mph, 113 km/h; (IV) 93 mph, 150 km/h; power-weight ratio: 33.8 lb/hp (46 lb/kW), 15.3 kg/hp (20.8 kg/kW); speed in direct drive at 1,000 rpm: 17 mph, 28 km/h; consumption: 52.3 m/imp gal, 43.5 m/US gal, 5.4 l x 100 km at 37 mph, 60 km/h.

CHASSIS integral; front suspension: independent, wishbones, coil springs, telescopic damper struts; rear: semi-floating arms, coil springs, telescopic dampers.

STEERING rack-and-pinion; turns lock to lock: 4.70.

BRAKES front disc, rear drum, servo; lining area: front 4.5 sq in, 29 sq cm, rear 12.3 sq in, 79.4 sq cm, total 16.8 sq in, 108.4 sq cm.

ELECTRICAL EQUIPMENT 12 V; 40 Ah battery; 480 W alternator; Bosch distributor; 2 halogen headlamps.

DIMENSIONS AND WEIGHT wheel base: 94.68 in, 240 cm; tracks: 51.18 in, 130 cm front, 51.38 in, 131 cm rear; length: 167.79 in, 426 cm; width: 63.46 in, 161 cm; height: 53.74 in, 136 cm; ground clearance: 6.38 in, 16 cm; weight: 2,029 lb, 920 kg; weight distribution: 50.2% front, 49.8% rear; turning circle: 15.1 ft, 4.6 m; fuel tank: 11.4 imp gal, 13.7 US gal, 52 l.

BODY saloon/sedan; 4 doors; 5 seats, separate front seats, built-in headrests; heated rear window.

PRACTICAL INSTRUCTIONS fuel: 86 oct petrol; oil: engine 6.2 imp pt, 7.4 US pt, 3.5 l, SAE 10W-30 - gearbox 1.9 imp pt, 2.3 US pt, 1.1 l, GL5-80W - final drive 2.5 imp pt, 3 US pt, 1.4 l, GL5-90W; greasing: none; spark plug: BP6HS; tappet clearances: inlet 0.012 in, 0.30 mm, exhaust 0.012 in, 0.30 mm; valve timing: 34° 76° 70° 28°; tyre pressure: front 24 psi, 1.7 atm, rear 24 psi, 1.7 atm.

Royale Series

1 XQ 4-dr Sedan
2 Prince 4-dr Sedan
3 Salon 4-dr Sedan

Power team:	Standard for:	Optional for:
60 hp	1	—
85 hp	2	—
101 hp	3	—

60 hp power team

ENGINE front, 4 stroke; 4 cylinders; 91 cu in, 1,492 cc (3.25 x 2.75 in, 82.5 x 69.8 mm); compression ratio: 8.6:1; max power (DIN): 60 hp (44 kW) at 5,000 rpm; max torque (DIN): 74 lb ft, 10.2 kg m (100 Nm) at 3,000 rpm; max engine rpm: 5,400; 40.2 hp/l (29.6 kW/l); cast iron block and head; 5 crankshaft bearings; valves: overhead; camshafts: 1, overhead; lubrication: gear pump, full flow filter, 6.2 imp pt, 7.4 US pt, 3.5 l; 1 Nikki-Stromberg downdraught twin barrel carburettor; fuel feed: mechanical pump; water-cooled, 10.9 imp pt, 13.1 US pt, 6.2 l.

TRANSMISSION driving wheels: rear; clutch: single dry plate; gearbox: mechanical; gears: 4, fully synchronized; ratios: I 4.017, II 2.147, III 1.318, IV 1, rev 3.765; lever: central; final drive: hypoid bevel; axle ratio: 4.620; width of rims: 5"; tyres: 175 SR x 14.

PERFORMANCE max speeds: (I) 23 mph, 37 km/h; (II) 39 mph, 63 km/h; (III) 63 mph, 102 km/h; (IV) 84 mph, 135 km/h; power-weight ratio: 41.2 lb/hp (56 lb/kW), 18.6 kg/hp (25.4 kg/kW); speed in direct drive at 1,000 rpm: 16 mph, 25 km/h; consumption: 45.5 m/imp gal, 37.9 m/US gal, 6.2 l x 100 km at 37 mph, 60 km/h.

60 HP POWER TEAM

CHASSIS integral; front suspension: independent, by McPherson, coil springs/telescopic damper struts; rear: rigid axle, trailing arms, coil springs, telescopic dampers.

STEERING recirculating ball; turns lock to lock: 4.

BRAKES front disc, rear drum, servo; lining area: front 22.5 sq in, 145 sq cm, rear 62.8 sq in, 405 sq cm, total 85.3 sq in, 550 sq cm.

ELECTRICAL EQUIPMENT 12 V; 40 Ah battery; 540 W alternator; Bosch distributor; 2 halogen headlamps.

DIMENSIONS AND WEIGHT wheel base: 105.04 in, 267 cm; tracks: 56.50 in, 143 cm front, 55.59 in, 141 cm rear; length: 181.77 in, 462 cm; width: 67.95 in, 173 cm; height: 55.90 in, 142 cm; ground clearance: 7.09 in, 18 cm; weight: 2,470 lb, 1,120 kg; weight distribution: 49.1% front, 50.9% rear; turning circle: 15.7 ft, 4.8 m; fuel tank: 14.3 imp gal, 17.2 US gal, 65 l.

BODY saloon/sedan; 4 doors; 5 seats, separate front seats, built-in headrests; heated rear window; fog lamps.

PRACTICAL INSTRUCTIONS fuel: 86 oct petrol; oil: engine 6.2 imp pt, 7.4 US pt, 3.5 l, SAE 10W-30 - gearbox 1.9 imp pt, 2.3 US pt, 1.1 l, GL5-80 W - final drive 2.5 imp pt, 3 US pt, 1.4 l, GL5-90W; greasing: none; spark plug: BP6HS; tappet clearances: inlet 0.012 in, 0.30 mm, exhaust 0.012 in, 0.30 mm; valve timing: 34° 76° 70° 28°; tyre pressure: front 26 psi, 1.8 atm, rear 26 psi, 1.8 atm.

85 hp power team

See 60 hp power team, except for:

ENGINE 115.7 cu in, 1,897 cc (3.66 x 2.75 in, 93 x 69.8 mm); max power (DIN): 85 hp (63 kW) at 5,000 rpm; max torque (DIN): 105 lb ft, 14.5 kg m (142 Nm) at 3,100 rpm; 44.8 hp/l (33 kW/l).

TRANSMISSION axle ratio: 3.700.

PERFORMANCE max speeds: (I) 26 mph, 42 km/h; (II) 48 mph, 78 km/h; (III) 78 mph, 126 km/h; (IV) 104 mph, 168 km/h; power-weight ratio: 29.3 lb/hp (39.9 lb/kW), 13.3 kg/hp (18.1 kg/kW); speed in direct drive at 1,000 rpm: 19 mph, 31 km/h; consumption: 45.2 m/imp gal, 37.6 m/US gal, 6.3 l x 100 km at 37 mph, 60 km/h.

DIMENSIONS AND WEIGHT length: 182.48 in, 463 cm; width: 68.50 in, 174 cm; weight: 2,492 lb, 1,130 kg.

101 hp power team

See 60 hp power team, except for:

ENGINE 120.8 cu in, 1,979 cc (3.74 x 2.75 in, 95 x 69.8 mm); compression ratio: 9:1; max power (DIN): 101 hp (74 kW) at 5,200 rpm; max torque (DIN): 115 lb ft, 15.9 kg m (156 Nm) at 3,800 rpm; max engine rpm: 6,000; 51 hp/l (37.6 kW/l).

TRANSMISSION gearbox: automatic transmission, hydraulic torque converter and planetary gears with 3 ratios, possible manual selection; ratios: I 2.400, II 1.480, III 1, rev 1.920; axle ratio: 3.700.

PERFORMANCE max speeds: (I) 44 mph, 71 km/h; (II) 71 mph, 115 km/h; (III) 106 mph, 170 km/h; power-weight ratio: 27.5 lb/hp (37.4 lb/kW), 12.5 kg/hp (17 kg/kW); consumption: 38.7 m/imp gal, 32.2 m/US gal, 7.3 l x 100 km at 37 mph, 60 km/h.

STEERING servo.

ELECTRICAL EQUIPMENT 55 Ah battery; 600 W alternator.

DAEWOO Royale XQ Sedan

DIMENSIONS AND WEIGHT length: 185.08 in, 470 cm; width: 68.70 in, 174 cm; weight: 2,778 lb, 1,260 kg; weight distribution: 52.8% front, 47.2% rear.

BODY vinyl roof.

PRACTICAL INSTRUCTIONS fuel: 95 oct petrol; oil: engine: 6.2 imp pt, 7.4 US pt, 3.5 l, SAE 10W-20; valve timing: 32° 90° 72° 50°.

HYUNDAI KOREA

Pony Series

PRICES IN GB AND EX WORKS:	£	won
L 4+1-dr Hatchback Sedan	4,099*	3,604,000
GL 4+1-dr Hatchback Sedan	4,348*	4,153,000
GLS 4+1-dr Hatchback Sedan	4,497*	4,324,000

Power team:	Standard for:	Optional for:
80 hp	all	—
92 hp	—	all

80 hp power team

ENGINE Mitsubishi, front, 4 stroke; 4 cylinders, vertical, in line; 75.5 cu in, 1,238 cc (2.87 x 2.91 in, 73 x 74 mm); compression ratio: 9:1; max power (JIS): 80 hp (59 kW) at 6,300 rpm; max torque (JIS): 78 lb ft, 10.8 kg m (106 Nm) at 4,000 rpm; max engine rpm: 6,500; 64.6 hp/l (47.7 kW/l); hemispherical combustion chambers; 5 crankshaft bearings; valves: overhead, rockers; camshafts: 1, overhead; lubrication: trochoid pump (cartridge), 7 imp pt, 8.4 US pt, 4 l; 1 Mikuni Kogyo (Stromberg type) downdraught twin barrel carburettor; fuel feed: mechanical pump; water-cooled, 10.5 imp pt, 12.7 US pt, 6 l.

TRANSMISSION driving wheels: rear; clutch: single dry plate (diaphragm); gearbox: mechanical; gears: 4, fully synchronized; ratios: I 3.525, II 2.193, III 1.442, IV 1, rev 3.867; lever: central; final drive: hypoid bevel; axle ratio: 4.222; width of rims: 4.5"; tyres: 6.15 x 13.

PERFORMANCE max speeds: (I) 28 mph, 45 km/h; (II) 45 mph, 73 km/h; (III) 69 mph, 111 km/h; (IV) 96 mph, 155 km/h; power-weight ratio: 24.4 lb/hp (33.2 lb/kW), 11.1 kg/hp (15.1 kg/kW); carrying capacity: 714 lb, 324 kg; speed in direct drive at 1,000 rpm: 15.8 mph, 25.4 km/h; consumption: 37.4 m/imp gal, 31.2 m/US gal, 7.5 l x 100 km.

CHASSIS integral; front suspension: independent, by McPherson, coil springs/telescopic damper struts, lower wishbones (trailing links), anti-roll bar; rear: rigid axle, semi-elliptic leafsprings, telescopic dampers.

STEERING recirculating ball; turns lock to lock: 4.20.

BRAKES front disc (diameter 8 in, 20.2 cm), rear drum - GL and GLS disc, servo; lining area: front 9.6 sq in, 62 sq cm, rear 19.2 sq in, 124 sq cm, total 28.8 sq in, 186 sq cm.

ELECTRICAL EQUIPMENT 12 V; 40 Ah battery; 480 W alternator; Mitsubishi distributor; 4 halogen headlamps.

DIMENSIONS AND WEIGHT wheel base: 92.13 in, 234 cm; tracks: 51.18 in, 130 cm front, 50.79 in, 129 cm rear; length: 158.66 in, 403 cm; width: 61.42 in, 156 cm; height: 53.54 in, 136 cm; ground clearance: 6.50 in, 16.5 cm; weight: 2,007 lb, 910 kg; weight distribution: 53% front, 47% rear; turning circle: 29.5 ft, 9 m; fuel tank: 9.9 imp gal, 11.9 US gal, 45 l.

BODY saloon/sedan; 4+1 doors; 5 seats, separate front seats, reclining backrests, headrests; (standard for GLS) air-conditioning and heated rear window.

PRACTICAL INSTRUCTIONS fuel: 88 oct petrol; oil: engine 7 imp pt, 8.4 US pt, 4 l, SAE 10W-30, change every 3,100 miles, 5,000 km - gearbox 3 imp pt, 3.6 US pt, 1.7 l, SAE 80, change every 24,900 miles, 40,000 km - final drive 1.9 imp pt, 2.3 US pt, 1.1 l, SAE 80-90, change every 24,900 miles, 40,000 km; greasing: none; tappet clearances: inlet 0.006 in, 0.15 mm, exhaust 0.010 in, 0.25 mm; valve timing: 18° 50° 48° 20°; tyre pressure: front 24 psi, 1.7 atm, rear 24 psi, 1.7 atm.

OPTIONALS automatic transmission, hydraulic torque converter and planetary gears with 3 ratios (I 2.450, II 1.450, III 1, rev 2.220), possible manual selection; (except GLS) air-conditioning and heated rear window; 155 SR x 13 tyres; radial tyres; laminated windscreen; metallic spray; rear window wiper-washer.

HYUNDAI Pony GLS Hatchback Sedan

92 hp power team

See 80 hp power team, except for:

ENGINE 87.8 cu in, 1,439 cc (2.87 x 3.38 in, 73 x 86 mm); max power (JIS): 92 hp (68 kW) at 6,300 rpm; max torque (JIS): 91 lb ft, 12.5 kg m (123 Nm) at 4,000 rpm; 63.9 hp/l (47.3 kW/l).

TRANSMISSION axle ratio: 3.909.

PERFORMANCE max speeds: (I) 30 mph, 49 km/h; (II) 49 mph, 79 km/h; (III) 75 mph, 120 km/h; (IV) 99 mph, 160 km/h; power-weight ratio: 21.8 lb/hp (29.5 lb/kW), 9.9 kg/hp (13.4 kg/kW); carrying capacity: 772 lb, 350 kg; speed in direct drive at 1,000 rpm: 17.1 mph, 27.5 km/h.

DIMENSIONS AND WEIGHT length: 156.69 in, 398 cm; weight distribution: 51% front, 49% rear.

OPTIONALS automatic transmission, hydraulic torque converter and planetary gears with 3 ratios (I 2.450, II 1.450, III 1, rev 2.220), possible manual selection; 155 SR x 13 tyres; radial tyres; laminated windscreen; air-conditioning; metallic spray; heated rear window.

Stellar Series

PRICES EX WORKS:	won
1 1400 L 4-dr Sedan	**4,244,000**
2 1400 SL 4-dr Sedan	**4,859,000**
3 1600 L 4-dr Sedan	**4,315,000**
4 1600 SL 4-dr Sedan	**4,931,000**
5 1600 GSL 4-dr Sedan	**5,825,000**

Power team:	Standard for:	Optional for:
92 hp	1,2	—
100 hp	3 to 5	—

92 hp power team

ENGINE Mitsubishi, front, 4 stroke; 4 cylinders, in line; 87.8 cu in, 1,439 cc (2.87 x 3.39 in, 73 x 86 mm); compression ratio: 9:1; max power (JIS): 92 hp (68 kW) at 6,300 rpm; max torque (JIS): 91 lb ft, 12.5 kg m (122 Nm) at 4,000 rpm; max engine rpm: 6,800; 63.9 hp/l (47 kW/l); cast iron block, light alloy head; 5 crankshaft bearings; valves: overhead, Vee-slanted, rockers; camshafts: 1, overhead; lubrication: gear pump, full flow filter, 6.2 imp pt, 7.4 US pt, 3.5 l; 1 Stromberg 26-30 DIDTA-11 downdraught twin barrel carburettor; fuel feed: mechanical pump; water-cooled, 8.8 imp pt, 10.6 US pt, 5 l.

TRANSMISSION driving wheels: rear; clutch: single dry plate (diaphragm); gearbox: mechanical; gears: 4, fully synchronized; ratios: I 3.525, II 2.193, III 1.442, IV 1, rev 3.867; lever: central; final drive: hypoid bevel; axle ratio: 3.909; width of rims: 4.5"; tyres: 165 SR x 13.

PERFORMANCE max speed: 99 mph, 160 km/h; power-weight ratio: 24 lb/hp (32.5 lb/kW), 10.9 kg/hp (14.8 kg/kW); consumption: 44.1 m/imp gal, 36.8 m/US gal, 6.4 l x 100 km at 56 mph, 75 km/h.

CHASSIS integral; front suspension: independent, by McPherson, coil springs/telescopic damper struts, lower wishbones (trailing links), anti-roll bar; rear: rigid axle, lower trailing arms, diagonal renforcing links, upper diagonal torque rods, coil springs, telescopic dampers.

STEERING rack-and-pinion, collapsible steering wheel; turns lock to lock: 3.71.

BRAKES front disc, rear drum, dual circuit, servo.

ELECTRICAL EQUIPMENT 12 V; 45 Ah battery; 45 A alternator; Mitsubishi distributor; 2 headlamps.

DIMENSIONS AND WEIGHT wheel base: 101.87 in, 258 cm; tracks: 56.69 in, 144 cm front, 55.91 in, 142 cm rear; length: 174.02 in, 442 cm; width: 67.32 in, 172 cm; height: 53.94 in, 137 cm; ground clearance: 6.83 in, 17.4 cm; weight: 2,205 lb, 1,000 kg; weight distribution: 53.4% front, 46.6% rear; turning circle: 29.5 ft, 9.1 m; fuel tank: 11 imp gal, 13.2 US gal, 50 l.

BODY saloon/sedan; 4 doors; 5 seats, separate front seats, reclining backrests, adjustable headrests; laminated windscreen.

OPTIONALS 5-speed fully synchronized mechanical gearbox (I 3.444, II 2, III 1.316, IV 1, V 0.853, rev 3.667); automatic transmission, hydraulic torque converter and planetary gears with 3 ratios (I 2.450, II 1.450, III 1, rev 2.220); heated rear window; air-conditioning; metallic spray; halogen headlamps; luxury interior; 185/70 HR x 13 tyres with 5" wide rims.

100 hp power team

See 92 hp power team, except for:

ENGINE 97.4 cu in, 1,597 cc (3.03 x 3.39 in, 76.9 x 86 mm); compression ratio: 8.5:1; max power (JIS): 100 hp (74 kW) at 6,300 rpm; max torque (JIS): 108 lb ft, 14.4 kg m (141 Nm) at 4,000 rpm; 62.6 hp/l (46.3 kW/l).

HYUNDAI Stellar 1600 GSL Sedan

TRANSMISSION gears: 5, fully synchronized; ratios: I 3.444, II 2, III 1.316, IV 1, V 0.853, rev 3.667; axle ratio: 3.470; width of rims: 5" (standard); tyres: 185 HR x 13.

PERFORMANCE power-weight ratio: 22.1 lb/hp (30 lb/kW), 10 kg/hp (13.6 kg/kW).

ELECTRICAL EQUIPMENT 2 halogen headlamps (standard).

BODY heated rear window (standard).

OPTIONALS automatic transmission, hydraulic torque converter and planetary gears with 3 ratios (I 2.450, II 1.450, III 1, rev 2.220).

YLN TAIWAN

721

SD 4-dr Sedan
HB 4+1-dr Hatchback Sedan

ENGINE Nissan, front, 4 stroke; 4 cylinders, vertical, in line; 97.5 cu in, 1,598 cc (3.07 x 3.29 in, 78 x 83.6 mm); compression ratio: 9:1; max power (JIS): 81 hp (60 kW) at 5,200 rpm; max torque (JIS): 96 lb ft, 13.3 kg m (130 Nm) at 3,200 rpm; max engine rpm: 5,600; 50.7 hp/l (37.3 kW/l); cast iron block, light alloy head; 5 crankshaft bearings; valves: overhead, push-rods and rockers; camshafts: 1, overhead; lubrication: trochoid pump, by cartridge, 7.6 imp pt, 9.1 US pt, 4.3 l; 1 Kikaki 21 E 304-071 downdraught twin barrel carburettor; fuel feed: mechanical pump; water-cooled, 11.1 imp pt, 13.3 US pt, 6.3 l.

TRANSMISSION driving wheels: front; clutch: single dry plate (diaphragm); gearbox: mechanical; gears: 5, fully synchronized; ratios: I 3.333, II 1.955, III 1.286, IV 0.902, V 0.733, rev 3.417; lever: central; final drive: helical spur gears; axle ratio: 3.650; width of rims: 5"; tyres: 165 SR x 13.

PERFORMANCE max speeds: (I) 30 mph, 48 km/h; (II) 48 mph, 78 km/h; (III) 65 mph, 105 km/h; (IV) 99 mph, 160 km/h; (V) 92 mph, 148 km/h; power-weight ratio: 25 lb/hp (34.1 lb/kW), 11.3 kg/hp (15.4 kg/kW); consumption: 52.3 m/imp gal, 43.6 m/US gal, 5.4 l x 100 km.

CHASSIS integral; front suspension: independent, by McPherson, coil springs, telescopic dampers; rear: independent, by McPherson, 4 links, coil springs, telescopic dampers.

STEERING rack-and-pinion; turns lock to lock: 2.80.

BRAKES front disc, rear drum; lining area: front 24.1 sq in, 156 sq cm, rear 42.3 sq in, 273 sq cm, total 66.5 sq in, 429 sq cm.

ELECTRICAL EQUIPMENT 12 V; 60 Ah battery; 720 W alternator; Shihlin HP5-13E10 distributor; 2 headlamps.

DIMENSIONS AND WEIGHT wheel base: 97.24 in, 247 cm; tracks: 56.30 in, 143 cm front, 55.51 in, 141 cm rear; length: 174.80 in, 444 cm; width: 64.96 in, 165 cm; height: 54.72 in, 139 cm; ground clearance: 6.50 in, 16.5 cm; weight: 2,029 lb, 920 kg; weight distribution: 65% front, 35% rear; turning circle: 34.1 ft, 10.4 m; fuel tank: 12.1 imp gal, 14.5 US gal, 55 l.

BODY saloon/sedan; 4 or 4+1 doors; 5 seats, separate front seats.

PRACTICAL INSTRUCTIONS fuel: 92 oct petrol; oil: engine 7.6 imp pt, 9.1 US pt, 4.3 l, SAE W30, change every 6,200 miles, 10,000 km - gearbox and final drive 4.8 imp pt, 5.7 US pt, 2.7 l, SAE 90 EP, change every 24,900 miles, 40,000 km; greasing: every 24,900 miles, 40,000 km, 10 points; spark plug: BP5ES; tappet clearances: inlet 0.010 in, 0.25 mm, exhaust 0.012 in, 0.30 mm; valve timing: 12° 44° 46° 14°; tyre pressure: front 28 psi, 2 atm, rear 28 psi, 2 atm.

807 GX

See 721, except for:

ENGINE 6 cylinders, in line; 146 cu in, 2,393 cc (3.27 x 2.90 in, 83 x 73.7 mm); compression ratio: 8.6:1; max power (JIS): 135 hp (99 kW) at 5,600 rpm; max torque (JIS): 129 lb ft, 17.8 kg m (174 Nm) at 3,600 rpm; 56.4 hp/l (41.5 kW/l); 7 crankshaft bearings; lubrication: 7.2 imp pt, 8.7 US pt, 4.1 l; 1 Hitachi DAF 432-14C downdraught twin barrel carburettor; fuel feed: electric pump; cooling: 16.7 imp pt, 20.1 US pt, 9.5 l.

TRANSMISSION driving wheels: rear; gearbox: automatic transmission, hydraulic torque converter and planetary gears with 3 ratios, possible manual selection; ratios: I 2.458, II 1.458, III 1, rev 2.182; final drive: hypoid bevel; axle ratio: 4.100; width of rims: 5.5"; tyres: 195/70 HR x 14.

PERFORMANCE max speeds: (I) 34 mph, 55 km/h; (II) 59 mph, 95 km/h; (III) 96 mph, 155 km/h; power-weight ratio: 22.2 lb/hp (30.2 lb/kW), 10 kg/hp (13.7 kg/kW); consumption: 25.4 m/imp gal, 21.2 m/US gal, 11.1 l x 100 km.

CHASSIS rear suspension: 5 links.

STEERING servo; turns lock to lock: 3.80.

BRAKES lining area: front 22.3 sq in, 144 sq cm, rear 76.9 sq in, 496 sq cm, total 99.2 sq in, 640 sq cm.

ELECTRICAL EQUIPMENT Shihlin D609-56A distributor.

DIMENSIONS AND WEIGHT wheel base: 105.91 in, 269 cm; tracks: 55.12 in, 140 cm front, 54.72 in, 139 cm rear; length: 189.37 in, 481 cm; width: 67.32 in, 171 cm; height: 56.30 in, 143 cm; weight: 2,999 lb, 1,360 kg; weight distribution: 58% front, 42% rear; fuel tank: 15.8 imp gal, 19 US gal, 72 l.

PRACTICAL INSTRUCTIONS oil: engine 7.2 imp, pt, 8.7 US pt, 4.1 l - gearbox 2.8 imp pt, 3.4 US pt, 1.6 l; final drive 1.6 imp pt, 1.9 US pt, 0.9 l; greasing: 10 points; spark plug: BP6ES or L45PW; tappet clearances: inlet 0.008 in, 0.20 mm, exhaust 0.010 in, 0.25 mm; valve timing: 8° 52° 50° 10°.

YLN 807 GX

311 SD

ENGINE Nissan, front, 4 stroke; 4 cylinders, in line; 90.7 cu in, 1,487 cc (2.99 x 3.23 in, 76 x 82 mm); compression ratio: 9:1; max power (JIS): 70 hp (52 kW) at 5,200 rpm; max torque (JIS): 85 lb ft, 11.7 kg m (115 Nm) at 3,200 rpm; max engine rpm: 5,600; 47.1 hp/l (34.6 kW/l); cast iron block, light alloy head; 5 crankshaft bearings; valves: overhead, Vee-slanted, rockers; camshafts: 1, overhead; lubrication: trochoid pump, full flow filter, 6.3 imp pt, 7.6 US pt, 3.6 l; 1 Hitachi DCX 306-6 downdraught twin-barrel carburettor; fuel feed: mechanical pump; water-cooled, 8.3 imp pt, 9.9 US pt, 4.7 l.

TRANSMISSION driving wheels: front; clutch: single dry plate (diaphragm); gearbox: mechanical; gears: 5, fully synchronized; ratios: I 3.333, II 1.955, III 1.286, IV 0.902, V 0.733; lever: central; final drive: helical spur gears; axle ratio: 3.789; width of rims: 4.5"; tyres: 155 HR x 13.

PERFORMANCE max speeds: (I) 28 mph, 45 km/h; (II) 47 mph, 75 km/h; (III) 65 mph, 105 km/h; (IV) 96 mph, 155 km/h; (V) 99 mph, 160 km/h; power-weight ratio: 25.7 lb/hp (34.9 lb/kW), 11.6 kg/hp (15.8 kg/kW); consumption: 49.5 m/imp gal, 41.3 m/US gal, 5.7 l x 100 km.

CHASSIS integral; front suspension: independent, by McPherson, coil springs/telescopic damper struts, lower wishbones; rear: independent, trailing arms, coil springs, telescopic dampers.

STEERING rack-and-pinion; turns lock to lock: 4.

BRAKES front disc, rear drum; lining area: front 20.5 sq in, 132 sq cm, rear 35.8 sq in, 231 sq cm, total 56.3 sq in, 363 sq cm.

ELECTRICAL EQUIPMENT 12 V; 60 Ah battery; 600 W alternator; 2 headlamps.

DIMENSIONS AND WEIGHT wheel base: 94.49 in, 240 cm; tracks: 54.92 in, 139 cm front, 54.13 in, 137 cm rear; length: 162.79 in, 413 cm; width: 63.77 in, 162 cm; height: 54.72 in, 139 cm; ground clearance: 6.69 in, 17 cm; weight: 1,797 lb, 815 kg; weight distribution: 62.5% front, 37.5% rear; turning circle: 29.5 ft, 9 m; fuel tank: 11 imp gal, 13.2 US gal, 50 l.

BODY saloon/sedan; 4 doors; 5 seats, separate front seats, reclining backrests.

PRACTICAL INSTRUCTIONS oil: engine 5.9 imp, pt, 7.1 US pt, 3.4 l, change every 6,200 miles, 10,000 km - gearbox 4.7 imp pt, 5.7 US pt, 2.7 l, change every 24,900 miles, 40,000 km; greasing: none; tappet clearances: inlet 0.011 in, 0.28 mm, exhaust 0.011 in, 0.28 mm; valve timing: 11° 41° 46° 6°; tyre pressure: front and rear 26 psi, 1.8 atm.

YLN 311 SD

DAIHATSU JAPAN

Mira / Cuore Series

PRICES EX WORKS: yen

		yen
1	Mira A 2+1-dr Sedan	**488,000**
2	Mira B 2+1-dr Sedan	**512,000**
3	Mira C 2+1-dr Sedan	**597,000**
4	Mira S 2+1-dr Sedan	**635,000**
5	Mira A 4WD 2+1-dr Sedan	**642,000**
6	Mira B 4WD 2+1-dr Sedan	**719,000**
7	Cuore MO 2+1-dr Sedan	**590,000**
8	Cuore MGF 2+1-dr Sedan	**680,000**
9	Cuore MGX 2+1-dr Sedan	**762,000**
10	Cuore MG 4-dr Sedan	**682,000**
11	Cuore MGE 4-dr Sedan	**720,000**
12	Cuore MGL 4-dr Sedan	**754,000**
13	Mira Turbo T 2+1-dr Sedan	**642,000**
14	Mira Turbo R 2+1-dr Sedan	**725,000**

For GB prices, see price index.

Power team:	Standard for:	Optional for:
30 hp	1 to 4	—
30 hp (4WD)	5,6	—
31 hp	7 to 12	—
41 hp	13,14	—

30 hp power team

ENGINE front, transverse, 4 stroke; 2 cylinders, in line; 33.4 cu in, 547 cc (2.82 x 2.68 in, 71.6 x 68 mm); compression ratio: 9.2:1; max power (JIS): 30 hp (22 kW) at 6,000 rpm; max torque (JIS): 30 lb ft, 4.2 kg m (41 Nm) at 3,500 rpm; max engine rpm: 7,800; 54.8 hp/l (40.4 kW/l); cast iron block, light alloy head; 3 crankshaft bearings; valves: overhead, rockers; camshafts: 1 overhead, cogged belt; lubrication: rotary pump, full flow filter, 5.1 imp pt, 6.1 US pt, 2.9 l; 1 Aisan downdraught twin barrel carburettor; fuel feed: mechanical pump; exhaust emission control by ignition timing retardation and carburettor adjustment; water-cooled, 3.5 imp pt, 4.2 US pt, 2 l.

TRANSMISSION driving wheels: front; clutch: single dry plate (diaphragm); gearbox: mechanical; gears: 4, fully synchronized; ratios: I 3.666, II 2.100, III 1.464, IV 0.971, rev 3.529; lever: central; final drive: hypoid bevel; axle ratio: 5.470; width of rims: 3.5"; tyres: 5.00 x 10 - S 145 SR x 10.

PERFORMANCE max speeds: (I) 18 mph, 29 km/h; (II) 29 mph, 47 km/h; (III) 43 mph, 70 km/h; (IV) 68 mph, 110 km/h; power-weight ratio: 39.4 lb/hp (53.5 lb/kW), 17.8 kg/hp (24.2 kg/kW); carrying capacity: 706 lb, 320 kg; consumption: 74.3 m/imp gal, 61.9 m/US gal, 3.8 l x 100 km at 37 mph, 60 km/h.

CHASSIS integral; front suspension: independent, by McPherson, coil springs/telescopic damper struts, lower wishbones (trailing links); rear: rigid axle, semi-elliptic leafsprings, telescopic dampers.

STEERING rack-and-pinion; turns lock to lock: 3.30.

BRAKES drum, single circuit - S front disc, rear drum, servo; lining area: front 18.6 sq in, 120 sq cm, rear 18.6 sq in, 120 sq cm, total 37.2 sq in, 240 sq cm.

ELECTRICAL EQUIPMENT 12 V; 26 Ah battery; 35 A alternator; 2 headlamps.

DIMENSIONS AND WEIGHT wheel base: 84.65 in, 215 cm; tracks: 47.44 in, 120 cm front, 47.64 in, 121 cm rear; length: 126.84 in, 319 cm; width: 54.92 in, 139 cm; height: 54.13 in, 137 cm; weight: 1,180 lb, 535 kg; weight distribution: 62% front, 38% rear; turning circle: 31.5 ft, 9.6 m; fuel tank: 5.7 imp gal, 6.9 US gal, 26 l.

BODY saloon/sedan; 2+1 doors; 2 or 4 seats, separate front seats.

OPTIONALS 5-speed fully synchronized mechanical gearbox (I 3.666, II 2.100, III 1.464, IV 0.971, V 0.795, rev 3.529); automatic transmission, hydraulic torque converter and planetary gears with 2 ratios (I 1.821, II 1, rev 1.821), 5.081 axle ratio.

30 hp (4WD) power team

See 30 hp power team, except for:

TRANSMISSION driving wheels: front or front and rear; gears: 4, fully synchronized, auxiliary transfer box; ratios: I 3.666, II 2.100, III 1.464, IV 0.971, rev 4.313; transfer box ratios: high 1.282, low 5.222; final drive: front helical spur gears, rear hypoid bevel; axle ratios: front 5.917, rear 4.625; tyres: 145 SR x 12.

PERFORMANCE max speed: 65 mph, 105 km/h.

STEERING turns lock to lock: 3.20.

DIMENSIONS AND WEIGHT height: 57.08 in, 145 cm; ground clearance: 6.29 in, 16 cm; weight: 1,378 lb, 625 kg; turning circle: 32.1 ft, 9.8 m.

31 hp power team

See 30 hp power team, except for:

ENGINE max power (JIS): 31 hp (23 kW) at 6,000 rpm; 51.2 hp/l (37.7 kW/l); emission control by secondary induction, catalytic converter and exhaust gas recirculation.

TRANSMISSION axle ratio: 5.294; tyres: 5.20 x 10.

PERFORMANCE power-weight ratio: 2+1-dr sedans 38.1 lb/hp (51.3 lb/kW), 17.3 kg/hp (23.3 kg/kW); consumption: 83.1 m/imp gal, 69.2 m/US gal, 3.4 l x 100 km at 37 mph, 60 km/h.

CHASSIS rear suspension: independent, semi-trailing arms, coil springs, telescopic dampers.

BRAKES MGX front disc, rear drum, servo.

DIMENSIONS AND WEIGHT weight: 2+1-dr sedans 1,180 lb, 535 kg - 4-dr sedans 1,235 lb, 560 kg.

BODY saloon/sedan; 2+1 or 4 doors; 2 or 4 seats, separate front seats.

41 hp power team

See 30 hp power team, except for:

ENGINE turbocharged; compression ratio: 8.2:1; max power (JIS): 41 hp (30 kW) at 6,000 rpm; max torque (JIS): 41 lb ft, 5.7 kg m (56 Nm) at 2,500 rpm; 74.9 hp/l (55.2 kW/l); turbocharger with wastegate.

DAIHATSU Cuore MGL Sedan

TRANSMISSION gears: 5, fully synchronized; ratios: I 3.666, II 2.100, III 1.646, IV 0.971, V 0.795, rev 4.313; axle ratio: 4.938; tyres: 145 SR x 10.

PERFORMANCE max speed: 68 mph, 110 km/h; power-weight ratio: 29.6 lb/hp (40.2 lb/kW), 13.4 kg/hp (18.2 kg/kW).

BRAKES front disc, rear drum, servo.

DIMENSIONS AND WEIGHT weight: 1,213 lb, 550 kg.

Charade Series

PRICES EX WORKS:	yen
1 TD 2+1-dr Sedan	**635,000**
2 TG 2+1-dr Sedan	**688,000**
3 TL 2+1-dr Sedan	**770,000**
4 CG 4+1-dr Sedan	**713,000**
5 CF 4+1-dr Sedan	**833,000**
6 TS 4+1-dr Sedan	**844,000**
7 TX 2+1-dr Sedan	**944,000**
8 CX 4+1-dr Sedan	**904,000**
9 Turbo 2+1-dr Sedan	**954,000**
10 Turbo 4+1-dr Sedan	**985,000**
11 TG Diesel 2+1-dr Sedan	**788,000**
12 TS Diesel 2+1-dr Sedan	**919,000**
13 TX Diesel 2+1-dr Sedan	**1,019,000**
14 CG Diesel 4+1-dr Sedan	**813,000**
15 CF Diesel 4+1-dr Sedan	**933,000**
16 CX Diesel 4+1-dr Sedan	**979,000**

For GB prices, see price index.

Power team:	Standard for:	Optional for:
55 hp	1 to 5	—
60 hp	6 to 8	—
80 hp	9,10	—
38 hp (diesel)	11 to 16	—

55 hp power team

ENGINE front, transverse, 4 stroke; 3 cylinders, in line; 60.6 cu in, 993 cc (2.99 x 2.87 in, 76 x 73 mm); compression ratio: 9.5:1; max power (JIS): 55 hp (40 kW) at 5,500 rpm; max torque (JIS): 57 lb ft, 7.8 kg m (76 Nm) at 2,800 rpm; max engine rpm: 6,000; 55.4 hp/l (40.8 kW/l); cast iron block, light alloy head; 4 crankshaft bearings; valves: overhead, push-rods and rockers, Vee-slanted; camshafts: 1, overhead, cogged belt; lubrication: trochoid pump, full flow filter, 5.9 imp pt, 6.1 US pt, 2.9 l; 1 Aisan-Stromberg downdraught twin barrel carburettor; fuel feed: mechanical pump; emission control by catalytic converter, secondary air induction and exhaust gas recirculation; water-cooled, 5.3 imp pt, 6.3 US pt, 3 l, electric thermostatic fan.

TRANSMISSION driving wheels: front; clutch: single dry plate (diaphragm); gearbox: mechanical; gears: 4, fully synchronized; ratios: I 3.090, II 1.842, III 1.230, IV 0.864, rev 3.142; lever: central; final drive: helical spur gears; axle ratio: 4.500; width of rims: 5"; tyres: 6.00 x 12.

PERFORMANCE max speeds: (I) 29 mph, 47 km/h; (II) 48 mph, 77 km/h; (III) 73 mph, 117 km/h; (IV) 84 mph, 135 km/h; power-weight ratio: TD 25.7 lb/hp (34.9 lb/kW), 11.6 kg/hp (15.8 kg/kW); carrying capacity: 882 lb, 400 kg; consumption: 56.5 m/imp gal, 47 m/US gal, 5 l x 100 km on Japanese emission test cycle.

CHASSIS integral; front suspension: independent, by McPherson, coil springs/telescopic damper struts, transverse I arms, anti-roll bar; rear: rigid axle, lower trailing links, upper torque rods, Panhard rod, coil springs, telescopic dampers.

STEERING rack-and-pinion; turns lock to lock: 3.70.

BRAKES front disc (diameter 6.46 in, 14.6 cm), rear drum, (diameter 7.08 in, 18 cm), dual circuit, servo.

ELECTRICAL EQUIPMENT 12 V; 30 Ah battery; 45 A alternator; 2 headlamps.

DIMENSIONS AND WEIGHT wheel base: 91.34 in, 232 cm; tracks: 52.76 in, 134 cm front, 51.57 in, 131 cm rear; length: 139.76 in, 355 cm; width: 61.02 in, 155 cm; height: 55.12 in, 140 cm; ground clearance: 7.09 in, 18 cm; weight: TD and TG sedans 1,411 lb, 640 kg - TL Sedan 1,455 lb, 660 kg - CG Sedan 1,444 lb, 655 kg; turning circle: 31.5 ft, 9.6 m; fuel tank: 7.7 imp gal, 9.2 US gal, 35 l.

BODY saloon/sedan; 2+1 or 4+1 doors; 5 seats, separate front seats, reclining backrests, headrests.

VARIATIONS

ENGINE carburettor with air fuel ratio adjustment, emission control by 3-way catalytic converter.
TRANSMISSION 5-speed fully synchronized mechanical gearbox (I 3.090, II 1.842, III 1.230, IV 0.864, V 0.707), 4.235 axle ratio, 4.5" wide rims, 145 SR x 13 tyres.
PERFORMANCE power-weight ratio 26.9 lb/hp (36.5 lb/kW), 12.2 kg/hp (16.6 kg/kW), consumption 62.7 m/imp gal, 52.3 m/US gal, 4.5 l x 100 km on Japanese emission test cycle.
DIMENSIONS AND WEIGHT weight 1,477 lb, 670 kg.
BODY 4+1 doors.

OPTIONALS automatic transmission, hydraulic torque converter and planetary gears with 2 ratios (I 1.821, II 1, rev 1.821), 4.210 axle ratio.

DAIHATSU Mira S Sedan

60 hp power team

See 55 hp power team, except for:

ENGINE compression ratio: 9.1:1; max power (JIS): 60 hp (44 kW) at 5,600 rpm; max torque (JIS): 60 lb ft, 8.3 kg m (81 Nm) at 3,200 rpm; max engine rpm: 6,200; 60.4 hp/l (44 kW/l); non-turbulence generating pot cylinder head; oxidizing catalyst, secondary air induction and exhaust gas recirculation.

TRANSMISSION gears: 5, fully synchronized; ratios: I 3.090, II 1.842, III 1.230, IV 0.861, V 0.707, rev 3.142; axle ratio: 4.933; width of rims: 4.5"; tyres: 145 SR x 13 - TX 155 SR x 13.

PERFORMANCE max speed: 87 mph, 140 km/h; power-weight ratio: TS 24.2 lb/hp (33 lb/kW), 11 kg/hp (15 kg/kW); consumption: 51.3 m/imp gal, 42.8 m/US gal, 5.5 l x 100 km on Japanese emission test cycle.

CHASSIS TX rear suspension: anti-roll bar.

DIMENSIONS AND WEIGHT weight: TS 1,455 lb, 660 kg - TX 1,510 lb, 685 kg - CX 1,499 lb, 680 kg.

OPTIONALS sunroof (for TX and CX sedans only).

80 hp power team

See 55 hp power team, except for:

ENGINE turbocharged; compression ratio: 8:1; max power (JIS): 80 hp (59 kW) at 5,500 rpm; max torque (JIS): 87 lb ft, 12 kg m (118 Nm) at 3,500 rpm; 80.6 hp/l (59.3 kW/l); turbocharger with wastegate.

TRANSMISSION gears: 5, fully synchronized; ratios: I 3.090, II 1.842, III 1.230, IV 0.864, V 0.707, rev 3.142; axle ratio: 4.642; width of rims: 4.5"; tyres: 165/70 HR x 13.

PERFORMANCE max speeds: (I) 28 mph, 45 km/h; (II) 47 mph, 75 km/h; (III) 74 mph, 120 km/h; (IV) 97 mph, 156 km/h; (V) 99 mph, 160 km/h; power-weight ratio: 19.2 lb/hp (26.1 lb/kW), 8.7 kg/hp (11.8 kg/kW); consumption: 53.3 m/imp gal, 44.4 m/US gal, 5.3 l x 100 km on Japanese emission test cycle.

CHASSIS rear suspension: anti-roll bar.

DIMENSIONS AND WEIGHT weight: 1,532 lb, 695 kg.

BODY 2+1 doors.

38 hp (diesel) power team

See 55 hp power team, except for:

ENGINE diesel; compression ratio: 21.5:1; max power (JIS): 38 hp (28 kW) at 4,800 rpm; max torque (JIS): 46 lb ft, 6.3 kg m (62 Nm) at 3,500 rpm; max engine rpm: 5,000; 38.3 hp/l (28.2 kW/l); valves: in line, thimble tappets; lubrication: rotary pump, 5.6 imp pt, 6.8 US pt, 3.2 l; Bosch VE injection; swirl chamber type.

TRANSMISSION gears: 5, fully synchronized; ratios: I 3.090, II 1.842, III 1.230, IV 0.867, V 0.707, rev 3.142; axle ratio: TG and CG sedans 4.500 - TS, TX, CF and CX sedans 4.933; tyres: TS, CF and CX sedans 145 SR x 13 - TX 155 SR x 13.

PERFORMANCE max speed: 74 mph, 120 km/h; power-weight ratio: TG 39.2 lb/hp (53.3 lb/kW), 17.8 kg/hp (24.2 kg/kW); consumption: 104.5 m/imp gal, 87.1 m/US gal, 2.7 l x 100 km at 37 mph, 60 km/h.

CHASSIS TX rear suspension: anti-roll bar.

DIMENSIONS AND WEIGHT weight: TG Sedan 1,488 lb, 675 kg - TS Sedan 1,543 lb, 700 kg - TX Sedan 1,588 lb, 720 kg - CG Sedan 1,521 lb, 690 kg - CF Sedan 1,554 lb, 705 kg - CX Sedan 1,577 lb, 715 kg.

OPTIONALS sunroof (for TX only).

Charmant Series

PRICES EX WORKS:	yen
1 1300 LC 4-dr Sedan	**1,006,000**
2 1300 LE 4-dr Sedan	**1,092,000**
3 1500 LGX 4-dr Sedan	**1,176,000**
4 1500 Altair G 4-dr Sedan	**1,258,000**
5 1500 Altair L 4-dr Sedan	**1,358,000**

For GB prices, see price index.

Power team:	Standard for:	Optional for:
74 hp	1,2	—
83 hp	3 to 5	—

74 hp power team

ENGINE front, 4 stroke; 4 cylinders, in line; 78.7 cu in, 1,290 cc (2.95 x 2.87 in, 75 x 73 mm); compression ratio: 9.5:1; max power (JIS): 74 hp (54 kW) at 5,600 rpm; max torque (JIS): 78 lb ft, 10.7 kg m (105 Nm) at 3,600 rpm; max engine rpm: 6,000; 57.4 hp/l (42.2 kW/l); cast iron block, light alloy head; 5 crankshaft bearings; valves: overhead, push-rods and rockers; camshafts: 1, side; lubrication: trochoid pump, full flow filter, 6.2 imp pt, 7.4 US pt, 3.5 l; 1 Aisan 4 K-U downdraught twin barrel carburettor; emission control by secondary air induction, catalytic converter and exhaust gas recirculation; fuel feed: mechanical pump; water-cooled, 10.8 imp pt, 12.7 US pt, 6 l.

TRANSMISSION driving wheels: rear; clutch: single dry plate (diaphragm); gearbox: mechanical; gears: 4, fully synchronized; ratios: I 3.789, II 2.220, III 1.435, IV 1, rev 4.317; lever: central; final drive: hypoid bevel; axle ratio: 3.727; width of rims: 4.5"; tyres: 6.15 x 13.

PERFORMANCE max speeds: (I) 28 mph, 45 km/h; (II) 48 mph, 77 km/h; (III) 73 mph, 117 km/h; (IV) 96 mph, 155 km/h; power-weight ratio: LC 24.7 lb/hp (33.6 lb/kW), 11.2 kg/hp (15.2 kg/kW); carrying capacity: 882 lb, 400 kg; consumption: 40.7 m/imp gal, 34.2 m/US gal, 6.9 l x 100 km.

CHASSIS integral; front suspension: independent, by McPherson, coil springs/telescopic damper struts, lower transverse

DAIHATSU Charade TX Sedan

74 HP POWER TEAM

arms, trailing locating rods, anti-roll bar; rear: rigid axle, lower trailing links, Panhard rod, coil springs, telescopic dampers.

STEERING rack-and-pinion; turns lock to lock: 3.30.

BRAKES front disc, rear drum, dual circuit, servo; lining area: front 22.9 sq in, 148 sq cm, rear 41.6 sq in, 268 sq cm, total 64.5 sq in, 416 sq cm.

ELECTRICAL EQUIPMENT 12 V; 30 Ah battery; 50 A alternator; contactless fully transistorized distributor; 2 headlamps.

DIMENSIONS AND WEIGHT wheel base: 94.49 in, 240 cm; tracks: 51.97 in, 132 cm front, 52.36 in, 133 cm rear; length: LC 163.39 in, 415 cm - LE 165.35 in, 420 cm; width: 64.17 in, 163 cm; height: 54.33 in, 138 cm; ground clearance: 6.69 in, 17 cm; weight: LC 1,830 lb, 830 kg - LE 1,874 lb, 850 kg; weight distribution: 55% front, 45% rear; turning circle: 33.8 ft, 10.6 m; fuel tank: 11 imp gal, 13.2 US gal, 50 l.

BODY saloon/sedan; 4 doors; 5 seats, separate front seats.

OPTIONALS 5-speed fully synchronized mechanical gearbox, V 0.865; automatic transmission with 3 ratios (I 2.666, II 1.450, III 1, rev 2.703), 3.909 axle ratio; air-conditioning.

DAIHATSU Charmant 1500 Altair G Sedan

83 hp power team

See 74 hp power team, except for:

ENGINE 88.6 cu in, 1,452 cc (3.05 x 3.03 in, 77.5 x 77 mm); compression ratio: 9:1; max power (JIS): 83 hp (61 kW) at 5,600 rpm; max torque (JIS): 86 lb ft, 11.8 kg m (116 Nm) at 3,600 rpm; 57.2 hp/l (42.1 kW/l); camshafts: 1, overhead, cogged belt; lubrication: 6.9 imp pt, 8.2 US pt, 3.9 l; 1 Aisin 34-U downdraught twin barrel carburettor; cooling: 10.4 imp pt, 12.9 US pt, 5.9 l.

TRANSMISSION gears: 5, fully synchronized; ratios: I 3.789, II 2.220, III 1.435, IV 1, V 0.865, rev 4.317; width of rims: 5"; tyres: 155 SR x 13.

PERFORMANCE max speed: 99 mph, 160 km/h; power-weight ratio: LGX 23.1 lb/hp (31.4 lb/kW), 10.5 kg/hp (14.2 kg/kW).

STEERING Altair sedans servo.

DIMENSIONS AND WEIGHT weight: LGX 1,918 lb, 870 kg - Altair sedans 1,951 lb, 885 kg.

Delta

PRICES (Tokyo):	yen
SD Middle-roof 4+1-dr Wagon	**1,180,000**
SE Hi-roof 4+1-dr Wagon	**1,492,000**
SG Sunroof 4+1-dr Wagon	**1,543,000**
SQ Sunroof 4+1-dr Wagon	**1,945,000**

ENGINE front, under the front seat, 4 stroke; 4 cylinders, in line; 110 cu in, 1,812 cc (3.38 x 3.07 in, 86 x 78 mm); compression ratio: 8.8:1; max power (JIS): 95 hp (70 kW) at 5,200 rpm; max torque (JIS): 112 lb ft, 15.5 kg m (152 Nm) at 3,400 rpm; max engine rpm: 5,400; 52.4 hp/l (38.6 kW/l); 5 crankshaft bearings; valves: 2 per cylinder, overhead, push-rods and rockers; camshafts: 1, side; lubrication: rotary pump, full flow filter, 7.4 imp pt, 8.9 US pt, 4.2 l; 1 downdraught twin barrel carburettor; fuel feed: mechanical pump; water-cooled.

TRANSMISSION driving wheels: rear; clutch: single dry plate (diaphragm); gearbox: mechanical; gears: 5, fully synchronized; ratios: I 3.704, II 2.020, III 1.368, IV 1, V 0.802, rev 4.472; lever: steering column; final drive: hypoid bevel; axle ratio: 4.100; tyres: 175 SR x 13 - SQ 185/70 SR x 13.

PERFORMANCE power-weight ratio: SD 27.4 lb/hp (37.2 lb/kW) 12.4 kg/hp (16.9 kg/kW); consumption: 49.6 m/imp gal, 41.3 m/US gal, 5.7 l x 100 km at 37 mph, 60 km/h.

CHASSIS integral; front suspension: independent, double wishbones, coil springs, anti-roll bar, telescopic dampers; rear: rigid axle, lower trailing links, Panhard rod, coil springs, anti-roll bar, telescopic dampers.

STEERING recirculating ball - SE and SQ servo.

BRAKES front disc, rear drum, servo.

ELECTRICAL EQUIPMENT 12 V; 33 Ah battery; 40 A alternator; Denso distributor; 2 headlamps.

DIMENSIONS AND WEIGHT wheel base: 87.79 in, 223 cm; tracks: 55.90 in, 142 cm front, 54.33 in, 138 cm rear; length: 168.50 in, 428 cm - SQ 175.19 in, 445 cm; width: 65.74 in, 167 cm; height: SD 71.65 in, 182 cm - SE 76.37 in, 194 cm - SG and SQ 76.77 in, 195 cm; ground clearance: 6.30 in, 16 cm; weight: SD Middle-roof Wagon 2,601 lb, 1,180 kg - SG and SQ Sunroof st. wagons 2,701 lb, 1,225 kg - SE Hi-roof Wagon 2,767 lb, 1,255 kg; turning circle: 41.7 ft, 10.6 m.

BODY estate car/st. wagon; 4+1 doors; 7 or 9 seats, separate front seats.

OPTIONALS automatic transmission, hydraulic torque converter and planetary gears with 4 ratios (I 2.450, II 1.450, III 1, IV 0.689, rev 2.222), 4.100 axle ratio; electronic digital instruments.

Taft

PRICES (Tokyo):	yen
STD (soft top) 2-dr Open	**1,367,000**
DX (soft top, steel doors) 2-dr Open	**1,520,000**
Deluxe (steel body) 2-dr Hardtop	**1,604,000**
Deluxe (resin top) 2-dr Hardtop	**1,734,000**

For GB prices, see price index.

ENGINE diesel, front, 4 stroke; 4 cylinders, in line; 168.7 cu in, 2,765 cc (3.62 x 4.94 in, 92 x 104 mm); compression ratio: 21.5:1; max power (JIS): 77 hp (56 kW) at 3,600 rpm; max torque (JIS): 129 lb ft, 17.8 kg m (174 Nm) at 2,200 rpm; max engine rpm: 3,800; 27.8 hp/l (20.5 kW/l); cast iron block and head; 3 crankshaft bearings; valves: overhead, push-rods and rockers; camshafts: 1, side; lubrication: trochoid pump, full flow filter, 9.7 imp pt, 11.6 US pt, 5.5 l; Denso plunger type mechanical injection pump; water-cooled, 17.6 imp pt, 21.1 US pt, 10 l.

TRANSMISSION driving wheels: rear or front and rear; clutch: single dry plate (diaphragm); gearbox: mechanical; gears: 4, fully synchronized - Deluxe (resin top) 5; ratios: I 3.717, II 2.504, III 1.408, IV 1, rev 4.434 - Deluxe (resin top) I 3.717, II 2.177, III 1.408, IV 1, V 0.876, rev 4.434; transfer box ratios: high 1.300, low 2.407; lever: central; final drive: hypoid bevel; front and rear axle ratio: 3.363; width of rims: 4.5"; tyres: 6.00 x 16.

PERFORMANCE max speeds: (I) 19 mph, 30 km/h; (II) 31 mph, 50 km/h; (III) 47 mph, 76 km/h; (IV) and (V) 65 mph, 105 km/h; power-weight ratio: STD 20.1 lb/hp (27.2 lb/kW), 9.1 kg/hp (12.3 kg/kW); consumption: 47.1 m/imp gal, 39.2 m/US gal, 6 l x 100 km at 37 mph, 60 km/h.

CHASSIS box-section ladder frame; front and rear suspension: rigid axle, semi-elliptic leafsprings, telescopic dampers.

STEERING recirculating ball; turns lock to lock: 2.70.

BRAKES front disc, rear drum, servo.

ELECTRICAL EQUIPMENT 12 V; 100 Ah battery; 40 A alternator; 2 headlamps.

DIMENSIONS AND WEIGHT wheel base: 79.53 in, 202 cm; front and rear track: 47.24 in, 120 cm; length: 138.58 in, 352 cm; width: 57.48 in, 146 cm; height: STD and DX 73.03 in, 185 cm - Deluxe hardtops 73.62 in, 187 cm; ground clearance: 8.46 in, 21.5 cm; weight: STD Open 1,543 lb, 700 kg - DX Open 1,565 lb, 710 kg - Deluxe hardtops 1,576 lb, 715 kg; weight distribution: 56% front, 44% rear; turning circle: 35.4 ft, 10.8 m; fuel tank: 10.3 imp gal, 12.7 US gal, 48 l.

BODY open or hardtop; 2 doors; 2 or 4 seats, separate front seats; canvas top.

OPTIONALS power take-off.

DAIHATSU Delta SQ Sunroof Wagon

FORD JAPAN

Laser Series

PRICES (Tokyo):		yen
1	1500 L 2+1-dr Hatchback Sedan	**879,000**
2	1500 L 4-dr Sedan	**933,000**
3	1500 L 4+1-dr Hatchback Sedan	**915,000**
4	1500 ES 2+1-dr Hatchback Sedan	**1,126,000**
5	1500 Ghia 4-dr Sedan	**1,121,000**
6	1500 Ghia 4+1-dr Hatchback Sedan	**1,107,000**
7	1500 EGI 2+1-dr Hatchback Sedan	**1,232,000**
8	1500 Turbo 2+1-dr Hatchback Sedan	**1,372,000**

Power team:	Standard for:	Optional for:
85 hp	1 to 6	—
95 hp	7	—
115 hp	8	—

85 hp power team

ENGINE front, transverse, 4 stroke; 4 cylinders, in line; 231 cu in, 1,490 cc (3.03 x 3.14 in, 77 x 80 mm); compression ratio: 9:1; max power (JIS): 85 hp (62 kW) at 5,500 rpm; max torque (JIS): 89 lb ft, 12.3 kg m (120 Nm) at 3,500 rpm; max engine rpm: 6,000; 57 hp/l (42 kW/l); cast iron block, light alloy head; 5 crankshaft bearings; valves: overhead, rockers; camshafts: 1 overhead, chain-driven; lubrication: rotary pump, full flow filter, 6.5 imp pt, 7.8 US pt, 3.7 l; 1

DAIHATSU Taft STD (soft top) Open

downdraught twin barrel carburettor; fuel feed: electric pump; water-cooled, 10.6 imp pt, 12.7 US pt, 6 l.

TRANSMISSION driving wheels: front; clutch: single dry plate (diaphragm); gearbox: mechanical; gears: 5, fully synchronized; ratios: I 3.416, II 1.842, III 1.290, IV 0.918, V 0.775, rev 3.214; lever: central; final drive: helical spur gears; axle ratio: 3.850; width of rims: L and Ghia sedans 4.5" - ES Sedan 5"; tyres: L and Ghia sedans 155 SR x 13 - ES Sedan 175/70 SR x 13.

PERFORMANCE max speed: 99 mph, 160 km/h; power-weight ratio: L 2+1-dr Hatchback Sedan 20.5 lb/hp (27.8 lb/kW), 9.3 kg/hp (12.6 kg/kW); consumption: 47.1 m/imp gal, 39.2 m/US gal, 6 l x 100 km on Japanese emission test cycle.

CHASSIS front suspension: independent, by McPherson, coil springs/telescopic damper struts, lower arm - ES anti-roll bar; rear: independent, trailing arms, twin transverse links, coil springs, anti-roll bar, telescopic dampers.

STEERING rack-and-pinion; turns lock to lock: 3.60.

BRAKES front disc, rear drum, servo; lining area: front 27.9 sq in, 180 sq cm, rear 74.1 sq in, 478 sq cm, total 102 sq in, 658 sq cm.

ELECTRICAL EQUIPMENT 12 V; 30 or 45 Ah battery; 50 A alternator; contactless fully electronic ignition; 2 headlamps.

DIMENSIONS AND WEIGHT wheel base: 93.31 in, 237 cm; front and rear track: 54.72 in, 139 cm; length: 2+1 and 4+1-dr hatchback sedans 155.30 in, 395 cm - 4-dr sedans 163.50 in, 415 cm; width: 64.17 in, 163 cm; height: 53.93 in, 137 cm; ground clearance: 5.91 in, 15 cm; weight: L and ES 2+1-dr hatchback sedans 1,741 lb, 790 kg - L 4+1-dr Hatchback Sedan 1,775 lb, 805 kg - L 4-dr Sedan 1,786 lb, 810 kg - ES Hatchback Sedan 1,808 lb, 820 kg - Ghia 4-dr Sedan 1,830 lb, 830 kg - Ghia 4+1-dr Hatchback Sedan 1,841 lb, 835 kg; turning circle: 30.2 ft, 9.2 m; fuel tank: 9.2 imp gal, 11.1 US gal, 42 l.

BODY saloon/sedan; 2+1, 4 or 4+1 doors; 4 seats, separate front seats, built-in headrests.

OPTIONALS JATCO automatic transmission, hydraulic torque converter and planetary gears with 3 ratios (I 2.841, II 1.541, III 1, rev 2.400), 3.631 axle ratio.

95 hp power team

See 85 hp power team, except for:

ENGINE max power (JIS): 95 hp (70 kW) at 5,800 rpm; max torque (JIS): 91 lb ft, 12.6 kg m (123 Nm) at 4,000 rpm; 63.8 hp/l (47 kW/l); electronic fuel injection.

TRANSMISSION gearbox ratios: I 3.153, II 1.842, III 1.290, IV 0.918, V 0.775, rev 4.105; width of rims: 5"; tyres: 175/70 SR x 13.

PERFORMANCE power-weight ratio: 18.3 lb/hp (24.9 lb/kW), 8.3 kg/hp (11.3 kg/kW); consumption: 43.5 m/imp gal, 36.2 m/US gal, 6.5 l x 100 km on Japanese emission test cycle.

CHASSIS front suspension: anti-roll bar.

BODY 2+1 doors.

115 hp power team

See 85 hp power team, except for:

ENGINE turbocharged; compression ratio: 8.2:1; max power (JIS): 115 hp (85 kW) at 5,800 rpm; max torque (JIS): 120 lb ft, 16.5 kg m (162 Nm) at 3,500 rpm; max engine rpm: 6,300; 77.2 hp/l (56.8 kW/l); electronic fuel injection, turbocharger with wastegate.

TRANSMISSION gearbox ratio: I 3.307, II 1.833, III 1.233, IV 0.970, V 0.795, rev 3.133; width of rims: 5"; tyres: 185/60 HR x 14.

PERFORMANCE max speed: 112 mph, 180 km/h; power-weight ratio: 17.2 lb/hp (23.3 lb/kW), 7.8 kg/hp (10.6 kg/kW); consumption: 43.5 m/imp gal, 36.2 m/US gal, 6.5 l x 100 km on Japanese emission test cycle.

CHASSIS front suspension: anti-roll bar.

DIMENSIONS AND WEIGHT weight: 1.973 lb, 895 kg.

BODY 2+1 doors.

OPTIONALS automatic transmission not available.

FORD Laser 1500 Turbo Hatchback Sedan

Telstar Series

PRICES (Tokyo):	yen
1 1600 GL 4-dr Sedan	1,203,000
2 1800 GL 4-dr Sedan	1,243,000
3 1800 GL TX5 4-dr Hatchback Sedan	1,268,000
4 1800 Ghia 4-dr Sedan	1,429,000
5 1800 Ghia TX5 4-dr Sedan	1,480,000
6 2000 MEGI Ghia 4-dr Sedan	1,640,000
7 2000 MEGI S-TX5 4+1-dr Hatchback Sedan	1,723,000
8 2000 MEGI Ghia S-TX5 4+1-dr Hatchback Sedan	1,756,000
9 2000 MEGI Ghia Turbo TX5 4+1-dr Hatchback Sedan	—
10 2000 Ghia Diesel 4-dr Sedan	—

Power team:	Standard for:	Optional for:
90 hp	1	—
100 hp	2 to 5	—
120 hp	6 to 8	—
145 hp	9	—
72 hp (diesel)	10	—

90 hp power team

ENGINE front, transverse, 4 stroke; 4 cylinders, in line; 96.9 cu in, 1,587 cc (3.18 x 3.37 in, 81 x 77 mm); compression ratio: 8.6:1; max power (JIS): 90 hp (66 kW) at 5,700 rpm; max torque (JIS): 94 lb ft, 13 kg m (127 Nm) at 3,500 rpm; max engine rpm: 6,000; 56.7 hp/l (41.7 kW/l); cast iron block, light alloy head; 5 crankshaft bearings; valves: overhead, rockers; camshafts: 1, overhead, cogged belt; lubrication: gear pump, full flow filter, 7.9 imp pt, 9.5 US pt, 4.5 l; 1 downdraught twin barrel carburettor; air cleaner; exhaust system with control, twin spark plug, gas recirculation, secondary air induction and catalytic converter; fuel feed: electric pump; water-cooled, 12.3 imp pt, 14.8 US pt, 7 l, electric thermostatic fan.

TRANSMISSION driving wheels: front; clutch: single dry plate (diaphragm); gearbox: mechanical; gears: 5, fully synchronized; ratios: I 3.307, III 1.833, III 1.233, IV 0.970, V 0.795, rev 3.133; lever: central; final drive: helical spur gears; axle ratio: 3.850; width of rims: 4.5"; tyres: 165 SR x 13.

PERFORMANCE max speeds: (I) 29 mph, 47 km/h; (II) 54 mph, 87 km/h; (III) 81 mph, 130 km/h; (IV) and (V) 99 mph, 160 km/h; power-weight ratio: 23.6 lb/hp (32.1 lb/kW), 10.7 kg/hp (14.6 kg/kW); consumption: 39.6 m/imp gal, 33.6 m/US gal, 7 l x 100 km on Japanese emission test cycle.

CHASSIS integral; front suspension: independent, by McPherson, lower arms, coil springs/telescopic damper struts, anti-roll bar; rear: independent, twin transverse linkage bars, trailing radius arm, coil springs/telescopic damper struts, anti-roll bar.

STEERING rack-and-pinion; turns lock to lock: 3.80.

BRAKES front disc (diameter 7 in, 17.8 cm), rear drum, servo; lining area: front 29.7 sq in, 192 sq cm, rear 29.7 sq in, 192 sq cm, total 59.5 sq in, 384 sq cm.

ELECTRICAL EQUIPMENT 12 V; 33 or 45 Ah battery; 60 A alternator; contactless transistorized ignition; 2 headlamps.

DIMENSIONS AND WEIGHT wheel base: 99.18 in, 251 cm; tracks: 56.30 in, 143 cm front, 55.54 in, 142 cm rear; length: 17.24 in, 438 cm; width: 66.50 in, 169 cm; height: 54.72 in, 139 cm; ground clearance: 5.90 in, 15 cm; weight: 2,127 lb, 965 kg; weight distribution: 62% front, 38% rear; turning circle: 33.3 ft, 10.8 m; fuel tank: 13.2 imp gal, 15.8 US gal, 60 l.

BODY saloon/sedan; 4 doors; 5 seats, separate front seats, built-in headrests.

OPTIONALS JATCO automatic transmission, hydraulic torque converter and planetary gears with 3 ratios (I 2.841, II 1.541, III 1, rev 2.400), 3.631 axle ratio; air-conditioning.

100 hp power team

See 90 hp power team, except for:

ENGINE 109.7 cu in, 1,789 cc (3.38 x 3.03 in, 86 x 77 mm); max power (JIS): 100 hp (74 kW) at 5,700 rpm; max torque (JIS): 110 lb ft, 15.2 kg m (149 Nm) at 3,500 rpm; 55.9 hp/l (41.1 kW/l).

TRANSMISSION gearbox ratios: I 3.307, II 1.833, III 1.233, IV 0.970, V 0.755, rev 3.133.

PERFORMANCE max speeds: (I) 29 mph, 47 km/h; (II) 54 mph, 87 km/h; (III) 81 mph, 130 km/h; (IV) and (V) 106 mph, 170 km/h; power-weight ratio: GL Sedan 21.3 lb/hp (28.9 lb/kW), 9.6 kg/hp (13.1 kg/kW); consumption: 37.7 m/imp gal, 31.4 m/US gal, 7.5 l x 100 km on Japanese emission test cycle.

STEERING Ghia sedans servo; turns lock to lock: 3.

DIMENSIONS AND WEIGHT height: 55 in, 139 cm - GL TX5 and Ghia TX5 sedans 54.33 in, 135 cm; weight: GL Sedan 2,127 lb, 965 kg - GL TX5 Hatchback Sedan 2,138 lb, 970 kg - Ghia Sedan 2,182 lb, 990 kg - Ghia TX5 Sedan 2,205 lb, 1,000 kg.

120 hp power team

See 90 hp power team, except for:

ENGINE 122 cu in, 1,998 cc (3.38 x 3.38 in, 86 x 86 mm); max power (JIS): 120 hp (88 kW) at 5,500 rpm; max torque (JIS): 123 lb ft, 17 kg m (166 Nm) at 3,000 rpm; 60.1 hp/l (44 kW/l); electronic fuel injection.

TRANSMISSION width of rims: Ghia Sedan 5" - S-TX5 and Ghia S-TX5 hatchback sedans 5.5"; tyres: Ghia Sedan 165 SR x 14 - S-TX5 and Ghia S-TX5 hatchback sedans 185/70 SR x 14.

PERFORMANCE max speeds: (I) 30 mph, 50 km/h; (II) 54 mph, 87 km/h; (III) 83 mph, 133 km/h; (IV) and (V) 112 mph, 180 km/h; power-weight ratio: Ghia Sedan 18.7 lb/hp (25.5 lb/kW), 8.5 kg/hp (11.5 kg/kW); consumption: 35.3 m/imp gal, 29.4 m/US gal, 8 l x 100 km on Japanese emission test cycle.

CHASSIS S-TX5 and Ghia S-TX5 hatchback sedans electronic variable dampers.

STEERING servo; turns lock to lock: 3.

BRAKES disc, servo; lining area: total 48.3 sq in, 312 sq cm.

DIMENSIONS AND WEIGHT height: Ghia Sedan 55.60 in, 141 cm - S-TX5 and Ghia S-TX5 hatchback sedans 53.50 in, 136 cm; weight: Ghia Sedan 2,249 lb, 1,020 kg - S-TX5 and Ghia S-TX5 hatchback sedans 2,293 lb, 1,040 kg.

BODY 4 or 4+1 doors.

OPTIONALS with JATCO automatic transmission, 3.450 axle ratio; air-conditioning.

145 hp power team

See 90 hp power team, except for:

ENGINE turbocharged; 122 cu in, 1,998 cc (3.38 x 3.38 in, 86 x 86 mm); compression ratio: 7.8:1; max power (JIS): 145 hp (107 kW) at 5,000 rpm; max torque (JIS): 159 lb ft, 22 kg m (216 Nm) at 3,000 rpm; max engine rpm: 5,500; 72.6 hp/l (53.4 kW/l); electronic fuel injection; turbocharger with wastegate.

TRANSMISSION gearbox ratios: I 3.307, II 1.833, III 1.233, IV 0.914, V 0.755, rev 3.133; width of rims: 5.5"; tyres: 185/70 HR x 14.

PERFORMANCE max speed: 112 mph, 180 km/h; power-weight ratio: 16.3 lb/hp (22.1 lb/kW), 7.4 kg/hp (10 kg/kW); consumption: 34.8 m/imp gal, 29 m/US gal, 8.1 l x 100 km on Japanese emission test cycle.

STEERING servo.

BRAKES disc.

DIMENSIONS AND WEIGHT height: 53.74 in, 136 cm; weight: 2,359 lb, 1,070 kg.

BODY 4+1 doors.

OPTIONALS air-conditioning.

72 hp power team

See 90 hp power team, except for:

ENGINE diesel; 122 cu in, 1,998 cc (3.38 x 3.38 in, 86 x 86 mm); compression ratio: 22.7:1; max power (JIS): 72 hp (53 kW) at 4,650 rpm; max torque (JIS): 100 lb ft, 13.8 kg m (135 Nm) at 2,750 rpm; max engine rpm: 5,100; 36 hp/l (26.5 kW/l); valves: in line, rockers, thimble tappets; lubrication: 10.6 imp pt, 12.7 US pt, 6 l; Bosch VE injection pump; Ricardo Comet swirl combustion chamber; cooling: 15.8 imp pt, 19 US pt, 9 l.

TRANSMISSION gearbox ratios: I 3.307, II 1.833, III 1.233, IV 0.914, V 0.755, rev 3.133.

PERFORMANCE power-weight ratio: 32.5 lb/hp (44.1 lb/kW), 14.7 kg/hp (20 kg/kW); consumption: 76.3 m/imp gal, 63.6 m/US gal, 3.7 l x 100 km at 37 mph, 60 km/h.

STEERING servo.

DIMENSIONS AND WEIGHT weight: 2,337 lb, 1,060 kg.

OPTIONALS JATCO automatic transmission, hydraulic torque converter and planetary gears with 3 ratios (I 2.841, II 1.541, III 1, rev 2.400), 3.450 axle ratio.

FORD Telstar 2000 Ghia Diesel Sedan

HONDA JAPAN

City Series

PRICES (Tokyo):	yen
1 PRO 1200 T 2+1-dr Hatchback Sedan	**598,000**
2 PRO 1200 F 2+1-dr Hatchback Sedan	**668,000**
3 1200 E 2+1-dr Hatchback Sedan	**770,000**
4 1200 E1 2+1-dr Hatchback Sedan	**770,000**
5 1200 R 2+1-dr Hatchback Sedan	**780,000**
6 1200 RH high-roof 2+1-dr Hatchback Sedan	**810,000**
7 1200 Turbo 2+1-dr Hatchback Sedan	**1,090,000**
8 1200 Turbo II 2+1-dr Hatchback Sedan	**1,230,000**

Power team:	Standard for:	Optional for:
61 hp	1,2	—
63 hp	3,4	—
67 hp	5,6	—
100 hp	7	—
110 hp	8	—

61 hp power team

ENGINE front, transverse, 4 stroke, CVCC-II charge stratification with new tunnel shaped combustion chambers; 4 cylinders, vertical, in line; 75.1 cu in, 1,231 cc (2.60 x 3.54 in, 66 x 90 mm); compression ratio: 9:1; max power (JIS): 61 hp (45 kW) at 5,000 rpm; max torque (JIS): 71 lb ft, 9.8 kg m (96 Nm) at 3,000 rpm; max engine rpm: 6,000; 49.6 hp/l (36.6 kW/l); light alloy block and head, wet liners; 5 crankshaft bearings; valves: 3 per cylinder, overhead, Vee-slanted, rockers; camshafts: 1, overhead, cogged belt; lubrication: rotary pump, full flow filter, 7 imp pt, 8.5 US pt, 4 l; 1 Keihin-Honda CVCC downdraught 3-barrel carburettor; fuel feed: electric pump; emission control by CVCC-II charge stratification, oxidizing catalytic converter in exhaust manifold and exhaust gas recirculation; water-cooled, 8.8 imp pt, 10.6 US pt, 5 l.

TRANSMISSION driving wheels: front; clutch: single dry plate (diaphragm); gearbox: mechanical; gears: 4, fully synchronized; ratios: I 3.181, II 1.823, III 1.181, IV 0.846, rev 2.916; lever: central; final drive: helical spur gears; axle ratio: 3.875; width of rims: 4"; tyres: 145 SR x 12.

PERFORMANCE max speed: 90 mph, 145 km/h; power-weight ratio: PRO 1200 T 22.9 lb/hp (31.1 lb/kW), 10.4 kg/hp (14.1 kg/kW); carrying capacity: 706 lb, 320 kg; consumption: not declared.

CHASSIS integral, front longitudinal subframe; front suspension: independent, by McPherson, coil springs/telescopic damper struts, lower transverse arms, trailing diagonal links; rear: independent, transverse arms, trailing links, coil springs, telescopic dampers.

STEERING rack-and-pinion; turns lock to lock: 3.60.

BRAKES front disc (diameter 8.39 in, 21.3 cm), rear drum, dual circuit.

ELECTRICAL EQUIPMENT 12 V; 30 Ah battery; 45 A alternator; Mitsubishi distributor; 2 headlamps.

DIMENSIONS AND WEIGHT wheel base: 87.40 in, 222 cm; front and rear track: 53.94 in, 137 cm; length: 133.07 in, 338 cm; width: 61.81 in, 157 cm; height: 57.87 in, 147 cm; weight: PRO 1200 T 1,400 lb, 635 kg - PRO 1200 F 1,433 lb, 650 kg; weight distribution: 64% front, 36% rear; turning circle: 32.1 ft, 9.8 m; fuel tank: 9 imp gal, 10.8 US gal, 41 l.

BODY saloon/sedan; 2+1 doors; PRO 1200 T 2 seats - PRO 1200 F 4 seats, separate front seats.

OPTIONALS Hondamatic semi-automatic transmission with 3 ratios (I 2.047, II 1.285, III 0.911), 3.105 axle ratio; air-conditioning.

63 hp power team

See 61 hp power team, except for:

ENGINE compression ratio: 10:1; max power (JIS): 63 hp (46 kW) at 5,000 rpm; max torque (JIS): 72 lb ft, 10 kg m (98 Nm) at 3,000 rpm; 51.2 hp/l (37.4 kW/l).

TRANSMISSION gears: 5, fully synchronized; ratios: I 2.916, II 1.764, III 1.181, IV 0.846, V 0.714, rev 2.916.

PERFORMANCE power-weight ratio: 23.3 lb/hp (31.9 lb/kW), 10.6 kg/hp (14.5 kg/kW); consumption: 53.3 m/imp gal, 44.4 m/US gal, 5.3 l x 100 km - 1200 E1 58.8 m/imp gal, 49 m/US gal, 4.8 l x 100 km on Japanese emission test cycle.

BRAKES servo.

DIMENSIONS AND WEIGHT weight: 1,466 lb, 665 kg.

BODY 4 seats.

67 hp power team

See 61 hp power team, except for:

ENGINE compression ratio: 10:1; max power (JIS): 67 hp (49 kW) at 5,500 rpm; max torque (JIS): 72 lb ft, 10 kg m (98 Nm) at 3,500 rpm; max engine rpm: 6,500; 54.4 hp/l (39.8 kW/l).

TRANSMISSION gears: 5, fully synchronized; ratios: I 2.916, II 1.764, III 1.181, IV 0.846, V 0.714, rev 2.916; axle ratio: 4.428; tyres: 165/70 SR x 12.

PERFORMANCE max speed: not declared; power-weight ratio: R 21.9 lb/hp (29.9 lb/kW), 9.9 kg/hp (13.6 kg/kW).

CHASSIS rear suspension: anti-roll bar.

BRAKES servo.

DIMENSIONS AND WEIGHT height: RH high-roof 61.81 in, 157 cm; weight: R Hatchback Sedan 1,466 lb, 665 kg - RH high-roof Hatchback Sedan 1,488 lb, 675 kg.

BODY 4 seats.

100 hp power team

See 61 hp power team, except for:

ENGINE turbocharged; compression ratio: 7.5:1; max power (JIS): 100 hp (74 kW) at 5,500 rpm; max torque (JIS): 109 lb ft, 15 kg m (147 Nm) at 3,000 rpm; 81.2 hp/l (60.1 kW/l); Honda digital computer programmed injection; turbocharger.

TRANSMISSION gears: 5, fully synchronized; ratios: I 2.916, II 1.764, III 1.181, IV 0.846, V 0.655, rev 2.916; axle ratio: 4.066; width of rims: 4.5"; tyres: 165/70 HR x 12.

PERFORMANCE max speed: 112 mph, 180 km/h; power-weight ratio: 15.2 lb/hp (20.6 lb/kW), 6.9 kg/hp (9.3 kg/kW); consumption: 52.3 m/imp gal, 43.6 m/US gal, 5.4 l x 10 km on Japanese emission test cycle.

CHASSIS front and rear suspension: anti-roll bar.

STEERING turns lock to lock: 3.40.

DIMENSIONS AND WEIGHT weight: 1,521 lb, 690 kg.

110 hp power team

See 61 hp power team, except for:

ENGINE turbocharged; compression ratio: 7.6:1; max power (JIS): 110 hp (81 kW) at 5,500 rpm; max torque (JIS): 118 lb ft, 16.3 kg m (160 Nm) at 3,000 rpm; 89.4 hp/l (65.8 kW/l); Honda programmed injection by digital computer; turbocharger with intercooler and computer controlled wastegate.

TRANSMISSION gears: 5, fully synchronized; ratios: I 2.916, II 1.764, III 1.181, IV 0.846, V 0.655, rev 2.916; axle ratio: 4.066; tyres: 185/60 HR x 13.

PERFORMANCE max speed: 112 mph, 180 km/h; power-weight ratio: 14.7 lb/hp (20 lb/kW), 6.7 kg/hp (9.1 kg/kW); consumption: 49.6 m/imp gal, 41.3 m/US gal, 5.7 l x 100 km on Japanese emission test cycle.

HONDA City 1200 R Hatchback Sedan

CHASSIS front and rear suspension: anti-roll bar.

DIMENSIONS AND WEIGHT tracks: 55.12 in, 140 cm front, 54.72 in, 139 cm rear; length: 134.65 in, 342 cm; width: 63.98 in, 162 cm; weight: 1,621 lb, 735 kg.

OPTIONALS sunroof.

Civic Series

PRICES (Tokyo):	yen
1 1300 23U 2+1-dr Hatchback Sedan	**798,000**
2 1300 23E 2+1-dr Hatchback Sedan	**880,000**
3 1300 23L 2+1-dr Hatchback Sedan	**910,000**
4 1300 33U 4-dr Sedan	**875,000**
5 1300 33L 4-dr Sedan	**975,000**
6 1300 53U Shuttle 4+1-dr Sedan	**957,000**
7 1500 25M 2+1-dr Hatchback Sedan	**998,000**
8 1500 25R 2+1-dr Hatchback Sedan	**1,028,000**
9 1500 35M 4-dr Sedan	**1,048,000**
10 1500 35G 4-dr Sedan	**1,160,000**
11 1500 55M Shuttle 4+1-dr Sedan	**1,078,000**
12 1500 55J Shuttle 4+1-dr Sedan	**1,162,000**
13 1500 55G Shuttle 4+1-dr Sedan	**1,200,000**
14 1500 25i 2+1-dr Hatchback Sedan	**1,189,000**
15 1500 35i 4-dr Sedan	**1,260,000**
16 1500 55i Shuttle 4+1-dr Sedan	**1,300,000**

For GB and USA prices, see price index.

Power team:	Standard for:	Optional for:
80 hp	1 to 6	—
90 hp	7 to 13	—
100 hp	14 to 16	—

80 hp power team

ENGINE front, transverse, 4 stroke, stratified charge; 4 cylinders, vertical, in line; 81.9 cu in, 1,342 cc (2.91 x 3.07 in, 74 x 78 mm); compression ratio: 10:1; max power (JIS): 80 hp (59 kW) at 6,000 rpm; max torque (JIS): 82 lb ft, 11.3 kg m (111 Nm) at 3,500 rpm; max engine rpm: 6,500; 59.6 hp/l (44 kW/l); light alloy block with cast iron liners, light alloy head; 5 crankshaft bearings; valves: 3 per cylinder (two intake and one exhaust) plus 1 CVCC auxiliary intake chamber valve per cylinder, overhead, Vee-slanted, rockers; camshafts: 1, overhead, cogged belt; lubrication: rotary pump, full flow filter, 7 imp pt, 8.5 US pt, 4 l; 1 Keihin-Honda CVCC downdraught 3-barrel carburettor; fuel feed: mechanical pump; emission control by CVCC stratified charge combustion, catalytic converter and exhaust gas recirculation; water-cooled, 8.8 imp pt, 10.6 US pt, 5 l, electric thermostatic fan.

TRANSMISSION driving wheels: front; clutch: single dry plate (diaphragm); gearbox: mechanical; gears: 4, fully synchronized - 23E, 23L and 33L sedans 5, fully synchronized; ratios: I 3.272, II 1.666, III 1.041, IV 0.777, rev 2.916 - 23E, 23L and 33L sedans I 3.272, II 1.666, III 1.041, IV 0.777, V 0.655, rev 2.916; lever: central; final drive: helical spur gears; axle ratio: 4.066 - 23E 3.722 - 53U Sedan 4.266; width of rims: 4.5" - 23E, 23L and 33L sedans 5"; tyres: 155 SR x 13 - 23E 165/70 SR x 13.

PERFORMANCE max speeds: (I) 31 mph, 50 km/h; (II) 62 mph, 100 km/h; (III) 90 mph, 145 km/h; (IV) 93 mph, 150 km/h - 23E, 23L and 33L sedans (I) 35 mph, 56 km/h; (II) 68 mph, 110 km/h; (III) 93 mph, 150 km/h; (IV) and (V) 93 mph, 150 km/h; power-weight ratio: 23U 20.4 lb/hp (27.7 lb/kW), 9.2 kg/hp (12.5 kg/kW); carrying capacity: 882 lb, 400 kg; consumption: 51.4 m/imp gal, 42.8 m/US gal, 5.5 l x 100 km on Japanese emission test cycle - 23E, 23L and 33L sedans 56.5 m/imp gal, 47 m/US gal, 5 l x 100 km on Japanese emission test cycle.

CHASSIS integral; front suspension: independent, by McPherson, coil springs/telescopic damper struts, longitudinal torsion bars, lower transverse arms, leading locating links - 23E, 23L and 33L sedans anti-roll bar; rear: rigid tubular beam axle with sway-bearings, trailing arms, Panhard rod, coil springs, telescopic dampers.

STEERING rack-and-pinion; turns lock to lock: 4.10.

BRAKES front disc (diameter 9.09 in, 23.1 cm), rear drum, dual circuit, servo.

ELECTRICAL EQUIPMENT 12 V; 30 Ah battery; 55 A alternator; transistorized ignition; 2 headlamps.

DIMENSIONS AND WEIGHT wheel base: hatchback sedans 93.70 in, 238 cm - sedans 96.46 in, 245 cm; tracks: 55.12 in, 140 cm front, 55.71 in, 141 cm rear; length: hatchback sedans 150 in, 381 cm - sedans 163.20 in, 414 cm - 53U Shuttle Sedan 157.09 in, 399 cm; width: 64.17 in, 163 cm; height: hatchback sedans 52.76 in, 134 cm - sedans 54.53 in, 138 cm - 53U Shuttle Sedans 58.66 in, 149 cm; ground clearance: 6.30 in, 16 cm; weight: 23U Hatchback Sedan 1,632 lb, 740 kg - 23E Hatchback Sedan 1,665 lb, 755 kg - 23L Hatchback Sedan 1,676 lb, 760 kg - 33U Sedan 1,742 lb, 790 kg - 33L Sedan 1,764 lb, 800 kg - 53U Shuttle Sedan 1,808 lb, 820 kg; turning circle: 30.8 ft, 9.4 m; fuel tank: 9.9 imp gal, 11.9 US gal, 45 l.

BODY saloon/sedan; 2+1, 4 or 4+1 doors; 5 seats, separate front seats.

OPTIONALS Hondamatic semi-automatic transmission with 3 ratios (I 1.782, II 1.206, III 0.828, rev 1.954), 3.588 axle ratio.

HONDA Civic 1500 35G Sedan

90 hp power team

See 80 hp power team, except for:

ENGINE 90.8 cu in, 1,488 cc (2.91 x 3.41 in, 74 x 86.5 mm); compression ratio: 9.2:1; max power (JIS): 90 hp (66 kW) at 6,000 rpm; max torque (JIS): 93 lb ft, 12.8 kg m (126 Nm) at 3,500 rpm; 60.5 hp/l (44.4 kW/l).

TRANSMISSION gears: 5, fully synchronized; ratios: I 2.916, II 1.764, III 1.181, IV 0.846, V 0.714, rev 2.916 - 25M, 35M and 55M sedans I 3.272, II 1.666, III 1.041, IV 0.777, V 0.655, rev 2.916; axle ratio: 4.266 - 25M and 35M sedans 3.722 - 55M Shuttle Sedan 3.875; width of rims: 5"; tyres: 165/70 SR x 13 - 25M and 35M sedans 155 SR x 13.

PERFORMANCE power-weight ratio: 25M 18.9 lb/hp (25.7 lb/kW), 8.6 kg/hp (11.7 kg/kW); consumption: 25M 50.4 m/imp gal, 42 m/US gal, 5.6 l x 100 km on Japanese emission test cycle - 55G 41.5 m/imp gal, 34.6 m/US gal, 6.8 l x 100 km on Japanese emission test cycle.

CHASSIS front suspension: anti-roll bar; rear: 25R and 55J sedans anti-roll bar.

STEERING 35G and 55G sedans servo.

DIMENSIONS AND WEIGHT weight: 25M Hatchback Sedan 1,698 lb, 770 kg - 25R Hatchback Sedan 1,764 lb, 800 kg - 35M Sedan 1,786 lb, 810 kg - 35G Sedan 1,830 lb, 830 kg - 55M Shuttle Sedan 1,808 lb, 820 kg - 55J Shuttle Sedan 1,918 lb, 870 kg - 55G Shuttle Sedan 1,907 lb, 865 kg.

OPTIONALS (for 25R only) sunroof.

100 hp power team

See 80 hp power team, except for:

ENGINE 90.8 cu in, 1,488 cc (2.91 x 3.41 in, 74 x 86.5 mm); compression ratio: 8.7:1; max power (JIS): 100 hp (74 kW) at 5,800 rpm; max torque (JIS): 96 lb ft, 13.2 kg m (130 Nm) at 4,000 rpm; 67.2 hp/l (49.7 kW/l); Honda programmed electronic injection: CVCC charge stratification and 3-way catalytic converter system for emission control; fuel feed: electric pump.

TRANSMISSION gears: 5, fully synchronized; ratios: I 2.916, II 1.764, III 1.181, IV 0.846, V 0.714, rev 2.916; axle ratio: 25i 4.466 - 35i 3.875 - 55i 4.428; width of rims: 5"; tyres: 175/70 SR x 13.

PERFORMANCE max speeds: 25i (I) 35 mph, 56 km/h; (II) 56 mph, 90 km/h; (III) 78 mph, 126 km/h; (IV) and (V) 112 mph, 180 km/h; power-weight ratio: 25i 18 lb/hp (24.3 lb/kW), 8.1 kg/hp (11 kg/kW); consumption: 35i 44.1 m/imp gal, 36.8 m/US gal, 6.4 l x 100 km on Japanese emission test cycle.

CHASSIS front and rear suspension: anti-roll bar.

BRAKES front disc, internal radial fins.

DIMENSIONS AND WEIGHT weight: 25i Hatchback Sedan 1,797 lb, 815 kg - 35i Sedan 1,852 lb, 840 kg - 55i Shuttle Sedan 1,940 lb, 880 kg.

OPTIONALS Hondamatic semi-automatic transmission with 3 ratios (I 2.380, II 1.560, III 1, rev 1.954); sunroof.

Ballade Series

PRICES (Tokyo):	yen
1 1300 CR-U 4-dr Sedan	**885,000**
2 1300 CR-B 4-dr Sedan	**945,000**
3 1300 CR-L 4-dr Sedan	**1,020,000**
4 1500 CR-M 4-dr Sedan	**1,068,000**
5 1500 CR-Extra 4-dr Sedan	**1,180,000**
6 1500 CR-i 4-dr Sedan	**1,280,000**

Power team:	Standard for:	Optional for:
80 hp	1 to 3	—
90 hp	4,5	—
100 hp	6	—

80 hp power team

ENGINE front, transverse, 4 stroke, stratified charge; 4 cylinders, vertical, in line; 81.9 cu in, 1,342 cc (2.91 x 3.07 in, 74 x 78 mm); compression ratio: 10:1; max power (JIS):

80 HP POWER TEAM

80 hp (59 kW) at 6,000 rpm; max torque (JIS): 82 lb ft, 11.3 kg m (111 Nm) at 3,500 rpm; max engine rpm: 6,500; 59.6 hp/l (44 kW/l); light alloy block with cast iron liners, light alloy head; 5 crankshaft bearings; valves: 3 per cylinder (two intake and one exhaust) plus 1 CVCC auxiliary intake chamber valve per cylinder, overhead, Vee-slanted, rockers; camshafts: 1, overhead, cogged belt; lubrication: rotary pump, full flow filter, 7 imp pt, 8.5 US pt, 4 l; 1 Keihin-Honda CVCC downdraught 3-barrel carburettor; fuel feed: mechanical pump; emission control by CVCC stratified charge combustion, catalytic converter and exhaust gas recirculation; water-cooled, 8.8 imp pt, 10.6 US pt, 5 l, electric thermostatic fan.

TRANSMISSION driving wheels: front; clutch: single dry plate (diaphragm); gearbox: mechanical; gears: 4, fully synchronized - CR-B and CR-L sedans 5, fully synchronized; ratios: I 3.272, II 1.666, III 1.041, IV 0.777, rev 2.916 - CR-B and CR-L sedans I 3.272, I 1.666, III 1.041, IV 0.777, V 0.655, rev 2.916; lever: central; final drive: helical spur gears; axle ratio: 4.066; width of rims: 4.5" - CR-B and CR-L sedans 5"; tyres: 6.15 x 13 - CR-B and CR-L sedans 155 SR x 13.

PERFORMANCE max speeds: (I) 31 mph, 50 km/h; (II) 62 mph, 100 km/h; (III) 90 mph, 145 km/h; (IV) 93 mph, 150 km/h; power-weight ratio: CR-U 21.8 lb/hp (29.5 lb/kW), 9.9 kg/hp (13.4 kg/kW); carrying capacity: 882 lb, 400 kg; consumption: 51.4 m/imp gal, 42.8 m/US gal, 5.5 l x 100 km on Japanese emission test cycle.

CHASSIS integral; front suspension: independent, by McPherson, coil springs/telescopic damper struts, longitudinal torsion bars, lower transverse arms, leading locating links, anti-roll bar; rear: rigid tubular beam axle with sway-bearing, trailing arms, Panhard rod, coil springs telescopic dampers.

STEERING rack-and-pinion; turns lock to lock: 4.10.

BRAKES front disc (diameter 9.09 in, 23.1 cm), rear drum, dual circuit, servo.

ELECTRICAL EQUIPMENT 12 V; 30 Ah battery; 55 A alternator; transistorized ignition; 2 headlamps.

DIMENSIONS AND WEIGHT wheel base: 96.46 in, 245 cm; tracks: 55.12 in, 140 cm front, 55.71 in, 141 cm rear; length: 163.78 in, 416 cm; width: 64.17 in, 163 cm; height: 54.53 in, 138 cm; ground clearance: 6.30 in, 16 cm; weight: CR-U Sedan 1,742 lb, 790 kg - CR-B Sedan 1,753 lb, 795 kg - CR-L Sedan 1,786 lb, 810 kg; turning circle: 32.8 ft, 10 m; fuel tank: 10.1 imp gal, 12.1 US gal, 46 l.

BODY saloon/sedan; 4 doors; 5 seats, separate front seats.

OPTIONALS Hondamatic semi-automatic transmission with 3 ratios (I 1.782, II 1.206, III 0.828, rev 1.954), 3.588 axle ratio.

90 hp power team

See 80 hp power team, except for:

ENGINE 90.8 cu in, 1,488 cc (2.91 x 3.41 in, 74 x 86.5 mm); compression ratio: 9.2:1; max power (JIS): 90 hp (66 kW) at 6,000 rpm; max torque (JIS): 93 lb ft, 12.8 kg m (126 Nm) at 3,500 rpm; 60.5 hp/l (44.4 kW/l).

TRANSMISSION gears: 5, fully synchronized; ratios: I 3.272, II 1.666, III 1.041, IV 0.777, V 0.655, rev 2.916; axle ratio: 3.727; width of rims: 5"; tyres: 155 SR x 13 - CR-M 165/70 SR x 13.

PERFORMANCE power-weight ratio: CR-M 19.8 lb/hp (27.1 lb/kW), 9 kg/hp (12.3 kg/kW).

STEERING CR-M servo.

DIMENSIONS AND WEIGHT weight: CR-M Sedan 1,786 lb, 810 kg - CR-Extra Sedan 1,808 lb, 820 kg.

100 hp power team

See 80 hp power team, except for:

ENGINE 90.8 cu in, 1,488 cc (2.91 x 3.41 in, 74 x 86.5 mm); compression ratio: 8.7:1; max power (JIS): 100 hp (74 kW) at 5,800 rpm; max torque (JIS): 96 lb ft, 13.2 kg m (130 Nm) at 4,000 rpm; 67.2 hp/l (49.7 kW/l); Honda programmed electronic injection; CVCC charge stratification and 3-way catalytic converter system for emission control: fuel feed: electric pump.

TRANSMISSION gears: 5, fully synchronized; ratios: I 2.916, II 1.764, III 1.181, IV 0.846, V 0.714, rev 2.916; axle ratio: 4.428; width of rims: 5"; tyres: 175/70 SR x 13.

PERFORMANCE max speeds: (I) 35 mph, 56 km/h; (II) 56 mph, 90 km/h; (III) 78 mph, 126 km/h; (IV) and (V) 112 mph, 180 km/h; power-weight ratio: 18.5 lb/hp (25 lb/kW), 8.4 kg/hp (11.4 kg/kW); consumption: 39.8 m/imp gal, 33.1 m/US gal, 7.1 l x 100 km on Japanese emission test cycle.

CHASSIS rear suspension: anti-roll bar.

BRAKES front disc, internal radial fins.

DIMENSIONS AND WEIGHT weight: 1,852 lb, 840 kg.

OPTIONALS Hondamatic semi-automatic transmission with 3 ratios (I 2.380, II 1.560, III 1, rev 1.954), 3.875 axle ratio; sunroof.

HONDA Ballade 1500 CR-i Sedan

Ballade Sports Series

PRICES (Tokyo):	yen
1 1.3 CR-X 2+1-dr Coupé	**993,000**
2 1.5i CR-X 2+1-dr Coupé	**1,270,000**

Power team:	Standard for:	Optional for:
80 hp	1	—
110 hp	2	—

80 hp power team

ENGINE front, transverse, 4 stroke, stratified charge; 4 cylinders, vertical, in line; 81.9 cu in, 1,342 cc (2.91 x 3.07 in, 74 x 78 mm); compression ratio: 10:1; max power (JIS): 80 hp (59 kW) at 6,000 rpm; max torque (JIS): 82 lb ft, 11.3 kg m (111 Nm) at 3,500 rpm; max engine rpm: 6,500; 59.6 hp/l (44 kW/l); light alloy block with cast iron liners, light alloy head; 5 crankshaft bearings; valves: 3 per cylinder (two intake and one exhaust) plus 1 CVCC auxiliary intake chamber valve per cylinder, overhead, Vee-slanted, rockers; camshafts: 1, overhead, cogged belt; lubrication: rotary pump, full flow filter, 7 imp pt, 8.5 US pt, 4 l; 1 Keihin-Honda CVCC downdraught 3-barrel carburettor; fuel feed: mechanical pump; emission control by CVCC stratified charge combustion, catalytic converter and exhaust gas recirculation; water-cooled, 8.8 imp pt, 10.6 US pt, 5 l, electric thermostatic fan.

TRANSMISSION driving wheels: front; clutch: single dry plate (diaphragm); gearbox: mechanical; gears: 5, fully synchronized; ratios: I 3.272, II 1.666, III 1.041, IV 0.777, V 0.655, rev 2.916; lever: central; final drive: helical spur gears; axle ratio: 3.727; width of rims: 5"; tyres: 165/70 x 13.

PERFORMANCE max speeds: (I) 34 mph, 54 km/h; (II) 55 mph, 88 km/h; (III) 81 mph, 130 km/h; (IV) and (V) 99 mph, 160 km/h; power-weight ratio: 22 lb/hp (29.9 lb/kW), 10 kg/hp (13.6 kg/kW); carrying capacity: 706 lb, 320 kg; consumption: 56.5 m/imp gal, 47 m/US gal, 5 l x 100 km on Japanese emission test cycle.

CHASSIS integral; front suspension: independent, by McPherson, coil springs/telescopic damper struts, longitudinal torsion bars, lower transverse ams; leading locating links, anti-roll bar; rear: rigid tubular beam axle with sway-bearing, trailing arms, Panhard rod, coil springs, telescopic dampers.

STEERING rack-and-pinion; turns lock to lock: 4.10.

BRAKES front disc (diameter 9.09 in, 23.1 cm), rear drum, dual circuit, servo.

ELECTRICAL EQUIPMENT 12 V; 30 Ah battery; 55 A alternator; transistorized ignition; 2 headlamps.

DIMENSIONS AND WEIGHT wheel base: 86.61 in, 220 cm; tracks: 55.12 in, 140 cm front, 55.71 in, 141 cm rear; length: 144.68 in, 367 cm; width: 63.98 in, 162 cm; height: 50.98 in, 129 cm; ground clearance: 6.30 in, 16 cm; weight: 1,764 lb, 800 kg; weight distribution: 63% front, 37% rear; turning circle: 30.8 ft, 9.4 m; fuel tank: 9 imp gal, 10.8 US gal, 41 l.

BODY coupé; 2+1 doors; 2+2 seats, separate front seats.

OPTIONALS Hondamatic semi-automatic transmission with 3 ratios (I 1.782, II 1.206, III 0.828, rev 1.954), 3.588 axle ratio.

110 hp power team

See 80 hp power team, except for:

ENGINE 90.8 cu in, 1,488 cc (2.91 x 3.41 in, 74 x 86.5 mm); compression ratio: 8.7:1; max power (JIS): 110 hp (81 kW) at 5,800 rpm; max torque (JIS): 100 lb ft, 13.8 kg m (135 Nm) at 4,000 rpm; 73.9 hp/l (54.4 kW/l); Honda programmed electronic injection; CVCC charge stratification and 3-way catalytic converter system for emission control; fuel feed: electric pump.

TRANSMISSION gearbox ratios: I 2.916, II 1.764, III 1.181, IV 0.846, V 0.714, rev 2.916; axle ratio: 4.428.

PERFORMANCE max speeds: (I) 34 mph, 55 km/h; (II) 67 mph, 108 km/h; (III) 106 mph, 170 km/h; (IV) and (V) 112 mph, 180 km/h; power-weight ratio: 16 lb/hp (21.8 lb/kW), 7.3 kg/hp (9.9 kg/kW); consumption: 47.1 m/imp gal, 39.2 m/US gal, 6 l x 100 km on Japanese emission test cycle.

HONDA Ballade Sports 1.5i CR-X Coupé

HONDA Accord 1800 RXT Hatchback Coupé

CHASSIS rear suspension: anti-roll bar.

BRAKES front disc, internal radial fins.

OPTIONALS Hondamatic semi-automatic transmission with 3 ratios (I 2.380, II 1.560, III 1, rev 1.954), 3.588 axle ratio; 175/70 SR x 13 or 185/60 HR x 14 tyres; light alloy wheels.

Accord Series

PRICES (Tokyo)	yen
1 1600 RL 2+1-dr Hatchback Sedan	**1,205,000**
2 1600 RX 2+1-dr Hatchback Coupé	**1,305,000**
3 1600 GC 4-dr Sedan	**1,081,000**
4 1600 GL 4-dr Sedan	**1,196,000**
5 1600 GX 4-dr Sedan	**1,308,000**
6 1800 RU 2+1-dr Hatchback Coupé	**1,300,000**
7 1800 RX 2+1-dr Hatchback Coupé	**1,360,000**
8 1800 RXT 2+1-dr Hatchback Coupé	**1,497,000**
9 1800 GL 4-dr Sedan	**1,265,000**
10 1800 GX 4-dr Sedan	**1,363,000**
11 1800 GXR 4-dr Sedan	**1,543,000**

For GB and USA prices, see price index.

Power team:	Standard for:	Optional for:
94 hp	1 to 5	—
110 hp	6 to 11	—

94 hp power team

ENGINE front, transverse, 4 stroke, stratified charge; 4 cylinders, in line; 97.5 cu in, 1,598 cc (3.15 x 3.13 in, 80 x 79.5 mm); compression ratio: 9:1; max power (JIS): 94 hp (69 kW) at 5,800 rpm; max torque (JIS): 99 lb ft, 13.6 kg m (133 Nm) at 3,500 rpm; max engine rpm: 6,500; 58.8 hp/l (43.2 kW/l); cast iron block, light alloy head; 5 crankshaft bearings; valves: 3 per cylinder (two intake and one exhaust) plus 1 CVCC auxiliary intake chamber valve per cylinder, overhead, rockers; camshafts: 1, overhead, cogged belt; lubrication: rotary pump, full flow filter, 7 imp pt, 8.5 US pt, 4 l; 1 Keihin-Honda CVCC downdraught 3-barrel carburettor; fuel feed: electric pump; emission control by CVCC charge stratification, secondary air induction, exhaust gas recirculation and oxidizing catalytic converter; water-cooled, 12.3 imp pt, 14.8 US pt, 7 l.

TRANSMISSION driving wheels: front; clutch: single dry plate (diaphragm), hydraulically controlled; gearbox: mechanical; gears: 5, fully synchronized; ratios: I 3.181, II 1.842, III 1.200, IV 0.870, V 0.676, rev 3; lever: central; final drive: helical spur gears; axle ratio: 3.866 - GC and RL models 3.705; width of rims: 5''; tyres: 165 SR x 13.

PERFORMANCE max speeds: (I) 35 mph, 57 km/h; (II) 61 mph, 98 km/h; (III) 95 mph, 153 km/h; (IV) and (V) 106 mph, 170 km/h; power-weight ratio: RL 21.8 lb/hp (29.7 lb/kW), 9.9 kg/hp (13.5 kg/kW); consumption: 42.2 m/imp gal, 35.1 m/US gal, 6.7 l x 100 km on Japanese emission test cycle.

CHASSIS integral, front auxiliary sub-frame; front suspension: independent, by McPherson, coil springs/telescopic damper struts, lower transverse arms, trailing locating links, anti-roll bar; rear: independent, by McPherson, coil springs/telescopic damper struts, lower transverse arms, trailing links hatchback coupés anti-roll bar.

STEERING rack-and-pinion - RX, GL and GX models servo; turns lock to lock: 3.50 - RX, GL and GX models 2.70.

BRAKES front disc (diameter 9.09 in, 23.1 cm), rear drum, dual circuit, rear compensator, servo.

ELECTRICAL EQUIPMENT 12 V; 33 Ah battery; 60 A alternator; contactless transistorized ignition; 2 headlamps.

DIMENSIONS AND WEIGHT wheel base: 96.46 in, 245 cm; tracks: 56.89 in, 144 cm front, 55.91 in, 142 cm rear; length: hatchback coupés 167.52 in, 425 cm - sedans 175.39 in, 445 cm; width: 65.55 in, 166 cm; height: hatchback coupés 53.35 in, 135 cm - sedans 54.13 in, 137 cm; ground clearance: 6.50 in, 16 cm; weight: RL Hatchback Coupé 2,051 lb, 930 kg - RX Hatchback Coupé 2,073 lb, 940 kg - GC Sedan 2,062 lb, 935 kg - GL Sedan 2,095 lb, 950 kg - GX Sedan 2,106 lb, 955 kg; turning circle: 36.7 ft, 11.2 m; fuel tank: 13.2 imp gal, 15.8 US gal, 60 l.

BODY coupé, 2+1 doors - saloon/sedan, 4 doors; 5 seats, separate front seats.

OPTIONALS Hondamatic semi-automatic transmission with 4 ratios (I 2.380, II 1.561, III 1.032, IV 0.729, rev 1.954), 3.875 axle ratio.

HONDA Vigor 1800 VXR Sedan

110 hp power team

See 94 hp power team, except for:

ENGINE 111.6 cu in, 1,829 cc (3.15 x 3.58 in, 80 x 91 mm); max power (JIS): 110 hp (81 kW) at 5,800 rpm; max torque (JIS): 110 lb ft, 15.2 kg m (149 Nm) at 3,500 rpm; 60.1 hp/l (44.3 kW/l).

TRANSMISSION axle ratio: 4.071 - RU 3.866; tyres: RX and RXT hatchback coupés 185/70 SR x 13.

PERFORMANCE max speeds: (I) 34 mph, 55 km/h; (II) 59 mph, 95 km/h; (III) 90 mph, 145 km/h; (IV) and (V) 111 mph, 178 km/h; power-weight ratio: RU 18.8 lb/hp (25.6 lb/kW), 8.5 kg/hp (11.6 kg/kW); consumption: 38.2 m/imp gal, 31.8 m/US gal, 7.4 l x 100 km on Japanese emission test cycle.

STEERING servo (except RU).

DIMENSIONS AND WEIGHT weight: RU Hatchback Coupé 2,073 lb, 940 kg - RX Hatchback Coupé 2,095 lb, 950 kg - GX Sedan 2,117 lb, 940 kg - GXR Sedan 2,150 lb, 975 kg.

OPTIONALS with semi-automatic transmission 3.785 axle ratio; automatic levelling control on rear suspension; electric sunroof; cruise control; navigation/information system; digital/graphic instrument display (for GXR and RXT models only).

Quint - Quintet

PRICES (Tokyo):	yen
TL 4+1-dr Sedan	**972,000**
TS 4+1-dr Sedan	**1,110,000**
TE 4+1-dr Sedan	**1,217,000**
TER 4+1-dr Sedan	**1,328,000**
XE 4+1-dr Sedan	**1,317,000**
XER 4+1-dr Sedan	**1,428,000**

For GB prices, see price index.

ENGINE front, transverse, 4 stroke, stratified charge; 4 cylinders, in line; 97.7 cu in, 1,601 cc (3.03 x 3.39 in, 77 x 86 mm); compression ratio: 8.8:1; max power (JIS): 90 hp (65 kW) at 5,500 rpm; max torque (JIS): 96 lb ft, 13.2 kg m (130 Nm) at 3,500 rpm; max engine rpm: 6,000; 56.2 hp/l (40.6 kW/l); cast iron block, light alloy head; 5 crankshaft bearings; valves: 3 per cylinder (one intake and one exhaust in main combustion chamber, one intake in auxiliary chamber), overhead, rockers; camshafts: 1, overhead, cogged belt; lubrication: trochoid pump, full flow filter, 7 imp pt, 8.5 US pt, 4 l; 1 Keihin CVCC downdraught 3-barrel carburettor; fuel feed: electric pump; water-cooled, 10.6 imp pt, 12.7 US pt, 6 l.

TRANSMISSION driving wheels: front; clutch: single dry plate (diaphragm); gearbox: mechanical; gears: 5, fully synchronized; ratios: I 3.181, II 1.944, III 1.291, IV 0.928, V 0.774, rev 3; lever: central; final drive: helical spur gears; axle ratio: 4.071; width of rims: 4.5''; tyres: TL 6.15 x 13 - other models 155 SR x 13.

PERFORMANCE max speeds: (I) 29 mph, 47 km/h; (II) 48 mph, 78 km/h; (III) 73 mph, 117 km/h; (IV) and (V) 93 mph, 150 km/h; power-weight ratio: TL 21.2 lb/hp (29.3 lb/kW), 9.6 kg/hp (13.3 kg/kW); carrying capacity: 882 lb, 400 kg; consumption: 40.9 m/imp gal, 34.1 m/US gal, 6.9 l x 100 km on Japanese emission test cycle.

CHASSIS integral, front auxiliary frame; front suspension: independent, by McPherson, coil springs/telescopic damper struts, lower transverse arms, diagonal links, anti-roll bar; rear: independent, by McPherson, coil springs/telescopic damper struts, lower transverse arms, radius rods - TE, XE, TER and XER sedans anti-roll bar.

STEERING rack-and-pinion - TE, XE, TER and XER sedans servo.

BRAKES front disc, rear drum, servo.

ELECTRICAL EQUIPMENT 12 V; 40 Ah battery; 50 A alternator; contactless fully electronic ignition; 2 headlamps.

DIMENSIONS AND WEIGHT wheel base: 92.91 in, 236 cm; tracks: 53.54 in, 136 cm front, 54.33 in, 138 cm rear; length: 161.61 in, 410 cm; width: 63.78 in, 162 cm; height: 53.35 in, 135 cm; ground clearance: 6.30 in, 16 cm; weight: TL Sedan 1,907 lb, 865 kg - TS Sedan 1,940 lb, 880 kg - TE Sedan 1,973 lb, 895 kg - XE Sedan 2,018 lb, 915 kg - TER Sedan 1,996 lb, 905 kg - XER Sedan 2,040 lb, 925 kg; turning circle: 36.1 ft, 11 m; fuel tank: 11 imp gal, 13.2 US gal, 50 l.

BODY saloon/sedan; 4+1 doors; 5 seats, separate front seats.

OPTIONALS Hondamatic semi-automatic transmission with 3 ratios (I 2.047, II 1.370, III 0.969, rev 1.954), 3.105 axle ratio; air-conditioning.

Vigor

PRICES (Tokyo):	yen
1800 TU 2+1-dr Hatchback Coupé	**1,320,000**
1800 TX 2+1-dr Hatchback Coupé	**1,380,000**
1800 TXL 2+1-dr Hatchback Coupé	**1,662,000**
1800 VL 4-dr Sedan	**1,255,000**
1800 VX 4-dr Sedan	**1,383,000**
1800 VXR 4-dr Sedan	**1,553,000**

VIGOR

ENGINE front, transverse, 4 stroke, stratified charge; 4 cylinders, in line; 111.6 cu in, 1,829 cc (3.15 x 3.58 in, 80 x 91 mm); compression ratio: 9:1; max power (JIS): 110 hp (81 kW) at 5,800 rpm; max torque (JIS): 110 lb ft, 15.2 kg m (149 Nm) at 3,500 rpm; max engine rpm: 6,000; 60.1 hp/l (44.3 kW/l); cast iron block, light alloy head; 5 crankshaft bearings; valves: 3 per cylinder (two intake and one exhaust) plus 1 CVCC auxiliary intake chamber valve per cylinder, overhead, rockers; camshafts: 1, overhead, cogged belt; lubrication: rotary pump, full flow filter, 7 imp pt, 8.5 US pt, 4 l; 1 Keihin-Honda CVCC downdraught 3-barrel carburettor; fuel feed: electric pump; emission control by CVCC charge stratification, secondary air induction, exhaust gas recirculation and oxidizing catalytic converter; water-cooled, 12.3 imp pt, 14.8 US pt, 7 l.

TRANSMISSION driving wheels: front; clutch: single dry plate (diaphragm), hydraulically controlled; gearbox: mechanical; gears: 5, fully synchronized; ratios: I 3.181, II 1.842, III 1.200, IV 0.870, V 0.676, rev 3; lever: central; final drive: helical spur gears; axle ratio: 4.071 - TU 3.866; width of rims: 5"; tyres: 165 SR x 13 - TXL 185/70 SR x 13.

PERFORMANCE max speeds: (I) 34 mph, 55 km/h; (II) 59 mph, 95 km/h; (III) 90 mph, 145 km/h; (IV and (V) 111 mph, 178 km/h; power-weight ratio: TU 18.8 lb/hp (25.6 lb/kW), 8.5 kg/hp (11.6 kg/kW); consumption: 38.2 m/imp gal, 31.8 m/US gal, 7.4 l x 100 km on Japanese emission test cycle.

CHASSIS integral, front auxiliary sub-frame; front suspension: independent, by McPherson, coil springs/telescopic damper struts, lower transverse arms, trailing locating links, anti-roll bar; rear: independent, by McPherson, coil springs/telescopic damper struts, lower transverse arms, trailing links - hatchback coupés anti-roll bar.

STEERING rack-and-pinion, servo (except TU); turns lock to lock: 2.70.

BRAKES front disc (diameter 9.09 in, 23.1 cm), rear drum, dual circuit, rear compensator, servo.

ELECTRICAL EQUIPMENT 12 V; 47 Ah battery; 65 A alternator; contactless transistorized ignition; 4 headlamps.

DIMENSIONS AND WEIGHT wheel base: 96.46 in, 245 cm; tracks: 56.89 in, 144 cm front, 55.91 in, 142 cm rear; length: hatchback coupés 167.52 in, 425 cm - sedans 175.39 in, 445 cm; width: 65.55 in, 166 cm; height: hatchback coupés 53.35 in, 135 cm - sedans 54.13 in, 137 cm; ground clearance: 6.50 in, 16 cm; weight: TU Hatchback Coupé 2,073 lb, 940 kg - TX Hatchback Coupé 2,095 lb, 950 kg - TXL Hatchback Coupé 2,161 lb, 980 kg - VL Sedan 2,106 lb, 955 kg - VX Sedan 2,117 lb, 960 kg - VXR Sedan 2,183 lb, 990 kg; turning circle: 36.7 ft, 11.2 m; fuel tank: 13.2 imp gal, 15.8 US gal, 60 l.

BODY coupé, 2+1 doors - saloon/sedan, 4 doors; 5 seats, separate front seats.

OPTIONALS Hondamatic automatic transmission with 4 ratios (I 2.380, II 1.561, III 1.032, IV 0.729, rev 1.954), 3.875 axle ratio; automatic levelling control on rear suspension; electric sunroof; anti-brake-locking system with rear disc brakes (for RXL and VXR models only); cruise control; navigation/information system; digital/graphic instrument display (for TXL and VXR models only).

Prelude

PRICES (Tokyo):	yen
XC 2-dr Coupé	**1,360,000**
XZ 2-dr Coupé	**1,524,000**
XX 2-dr Coupé	**1,718,000**

For GB and USA prices, see price index.

ENGINE front, transverse, 4 stroke, CVCC charge stratification with auxiliary combustion chambers; 4 cylinders, in line; 112 cu in, 1,829 cc (3.15 x 3.58 in, 80 x 91 mm); compression ratio: 9.4:1; max power (JIS): 125 hp (91 kW) at 5,800 rpm; max torque (JIS): 113 lb ft, 15.6 kg m (153 Nm) at 4,000 rpm; max engine rpm: 6,000; 68.3 hp/l (49.7 kW/l); 5 crankshaft bearings; valves: 3 per cylinder (2 intake, 1 exhaust), in main combustion chamber, overhead, Vee-slanted, rockers; camshafts: 1, overhead, cogged belt; lubrication: trochoid pump, full flow filter, 7 imp pt, 8.5 US pt, 4 l; 2 CV variable Venturi horizontal carburettors for main chambers and 1 CVCC horizontal carburettor for auxiliary chambers; fuel feed: electric pump; emission control by CVCC charge stratification, oxidizing catalytic converter and exhaust gas recirculation; water-cooled, 12.3 imp pt, 14.8 US pt, 7 l, electric thermostatic fan.

TRANSMISSION driving wheels: front; clutch: single dry plate (diaphragm); gearbox: mechanical; gears: 5, fully synchronized; ratios: I 3.181, II 1.944, III 1.250, IV 0.933, V 0.727, rev 3; lever: central; final drive: helical spur gears; axle ratio: 4.071; width of rims: 5"; tyres: XC 165 SR x 13 - XZ 185/70 HR x 13 - XX 185/70 SR x 13.

PERFORMANCE max speeds: (I) 34 mph, 54 km/h; (II) 53 mph, 85 km/h; (III) 83 mph, 133 km/h; (IV) and (V) 112 mph, 180 km/h; power-weight ratio: XC 16.8 lb/hp (23.1 lb/kW), 7.6 kg/hp (10.5 kg/kW); consumption: 65.7 m/imp gal, 54.7 m/US gal, 4.3 l x 100 km at 37 mph, 60 km/h on Japanese emission test cycle.

HONDA Prelude XX Coupé

CHASSIS integral, H-shaped front sub-frame; front suspension: independent, double wishbones, lower forged I-arms, trailing diagonal links, pressed short twisted upper arms, coil springs, anti-roll bar, telescopic dampers; rear: independent, by McPherson, coil springs/telescopic damper struts, transverse arms, trailing links, anti-roll bar.

STEERING rack-and-pinion - XX servo.

BRAKES XC front disc (diameter 7.48 in, 19 cm), rear drum - XZ and XX disc, front internal radial fins, dual circuit, servo.

ELECTRICAL EQUIPMENT 12 V; 33 Ah battery; 60 A alternator; transistorized ignition; 2 retractable headlamps.

DIMENSIONS AND WEIGHT wheel base: 96.46 in, 245 cm; front and rear track: 57.87 in, 147 cm; length: 169.09 in, 429 cm; width: 66.54 in, 169 cm; height: 47.24 in, 120 cm; ground clearance: 6.30 m, 16 cm; weight: XC Coupé 2,106 lb, 955 kg - XZ Coupé 2,128 lb, 965 kg - XX Coupé 2,161 lb, 980 kg; weight distribution: 62% front, 38% rear; turning circle: 36.1 ft, 11 m; fuel tank: 13.2 imp gal, 15.8 US gal, 60 l.

BODY coupé; 2 doors; 4 seats, separate front seats, headrests, reclining backrests; electric sunroof.

OPTIONALS Hondamatic automatic transmission, hydraulic torque converter and constant mesh with 4 ratios (I 2.380, II 1.560, III 1.032, IV 0.777, rev 1.954); electronically controlled 4-wheel anti-skid brakes with 120 hp engine and 3.875 axle ratio; LCD electronic instrument with digital speedometer.

ISUZU JAPAN

Gemini Series

	PRICES (Tokyo):	yen
1	1600 LD 4-dr Sedan	**954,000**
2	1600 LT 4-dr Sedan	**1,048,000**
3	1600 LS 4-dr Sedan	**1,124,000**
4	1600 LS 2-dr Coupé	**1,154,000**
5	1800 LT 4-dr Sedan	**1,077,000**
6	1800 Minx 4-dr Sedan	**1,151,000**
7	1800 Minx 2-dr Coupé	**1,181,000**
8	1800 LJ 4-dr Sedan	**1,334,000**
9	1800 LS 4-dr Sedan	**1,184,000**
10	1800 LS 2-dr Coupé	**1,179,000**
11	1800 LG 4-dr Sedan	**1,199,000**
12	1800 LG 2-dr Coupé	**1,299,000**
13	ZZR 4-dr Sedan	**1,557,000**
14	ZZR 2-dr Coupé	**1,587,000**
15	ZZT 4-dr Sedan	**1,680,000**
16	ZZT 2-dr Coupé	**1,720,000**
17	LD Special 4-dr Sedan	**996,000**
18	LD 4-dr Sedan	**1,081,000**
19	LT 4-dr Sedan	**1,190,000**
20	LT 2-dr Coupé	**1,220,000**
21	Minx 4-dr Sedan	**1,260,000**
22	Minx 2-dr Coupé	**1,295,000**
23	LJ 4-dr Sedan	**1,430,000**
24	LS 4-dr Sedan	**1,246,000**
25	LS 2-dr Coupé	**1,276,000**
26	Electro-diesel LT/E 4-dr Sedan	**1,290,000**
27	Electro-diesel LJ/E 4-dr Sedan	**1,545,000**
28	Diesel Turbo Special 4-dr Sedan	**1,149,000**
29	Diesel Turbo LG 4-dr Sedan	**1,384,000**

Power team:	Standard for:	Optional for:
100 hp	1 to 4	—
110 hp	5 to 12	—
130 hp	13 to 16	—
61 hp (diesel)	17 to 25	—
66 hp (diesel)	26,27	—
73 hp (diesel)	28,29	—

100 hp power team

ENGINE front, 4 stroke; 4 cylinders, in line; 97.6 cu in, 1,584 cc (3.23 x 2.95 in, 82 x 75 mm); compression ratio: 8.7:1; max power (JIS): 100 hp (74 kW) at 6,000 rpm; max torque (JIS): 101 lb ft, 14 kg m (136 Nm) at 4,000 rpm; max engine rpm: 6,500; 63.1 hp/l (46.4 kW/l); cast iron block, light alloy head; 5 crankshaft bearings; valves: overhead, rockers; camshafts: 1, overhead; lubrication: rotary pump, full flow filter, 8.8 imp pt, 10.6 US pt, 5 l; 1 Nikki-Stromberg downdraught twin barrel carburettor, emission control by 3-way catalytic converter with oxygen sensor and exhaust gas recirculation; fuel feed: electric pump; water-cooled, 10.8 imp pt, 12.7 US pt, 6 l.

TRANSMISSION driving wheels: rear; clutch: single dry plate (diaphragm); gearbox: mechanical; gears: LD Sedan 4 - LT and LS models 5, fully synchronized; ratios: LD Sedan I 3.507, II 2.175, III 1.418, IV 1, rev 3.826 - LT and LS models I 3.507, II 2.175, III 1.418, IV 1, V 0.855, rev 3.759; lever: central; final drive: hypoid bevel; axle ratio: 3.583; width of rims: 5"; tyres: LD and LT sedans 6.15 x 13 - LS models 155 SR x 13.

PERFORMANCE max speeds: (I) 29 mph, 47 km/h; (II) 48 mph, 78 km/h; (III) 73 mph, 117 km/h; (IV) and (V) 103 mph, 165 km/h; power-weight ratio: LD 20.3 lb/hp (27.6 lb/kW), 9.2 kg/hp (12.5 kg/kW); carrying capacity: 882 lb, 400 kg; speed in direct drive at 1,000 rpm: 16.2 mph, 26.1 km/h; consumption: 38.2 m/imp gal, 31.8 m/US gal, 7.4 l x 100 km.

CHASSIS integral; front suspension: independent, wishbones, coil springs, anti-roll bar, telescopic dampers; rear: rigid axle, lower radius arms, torque tube, Panhard rod, coil springs, telescopic dampers.

STEERING rack-and-pinion; turns lock to lock: 4.20.

BRAKES front disc, rear drum, servo; lining area: front 17.4 sq in, 112 sq cm, rear 49 sq in, 316 sq cm, total 66.4 sq in, 428 sq cm.

HONDA Prelude XX Coupé

ISUZU Gemini ZZR Coupé

ISUZU Florian Aska 2000 Diesel LX Sedan

ELECTRICAL EQUIPMENT 12 V; 35 Ah battery; alternator; Hitachi distributor; 2 headlamps.

DIMENSIONS AND WEIGHT wheel base: 94.49 in, 240 cm; tracks: 51.18 in, 130 cm front, 51.38 in, 130 cm rear; length: 166.54 in, 423 cm; width: 61.81 in, 157 cm; height: sedans 53.54 in, 136 cm - Coupé 52.76 in, 134 cm; ground clearance: 6.30 in, 16 cm; weight: LD Sedan 2,040 lb, 925 kg - LT Sedan 2,076 lb, 940 kg - LS Sedan 2,086 lb, 945 kg - LS Coupé 2,040 lb, 925 kg; weight distribution: 55% front, 45% rear; turning circle: 32.8 ft, 10 m; fuel tank: 11.4 imp gal, 13.7 US gal, 52 l.

BODY saloon/sedan, 4 doors - coupé, 2 doors; 4 seats, separate front seats.

OPTIONALS air-conditioning.

110 hp power team

See 100 hp power team, except for:

ENGINE 110.9 cu in, 1,817 cc (3.31 x 2.23 in, 84 x 82 mm); compression ratio: 8.5:1; max power (JIS): 110 hp (81 kW) at 5,600 rpm; max torque (JIS): 112 lb ft, 15.5 kg m (152 Nm) at 4,000 rpm; 60.5 hp/l (44.5 kW/l).

TRANSMISSION gears: 5, fully synchronized; ratios: I 3.467, II 1.989, III 1.356, IV 1, V 0.782, rev 3.438; tyres: LT and Minx models 6.15 x 13 - LJ and LS models 155 SR x 13 - LG models 175/70 SR x 13.

PERFORMANCE max speed: 106 mph, 170 km/h; power-weight ratio: LT 19 lb/hp (25.9 lb/kW), 8.6 kg/hp (11.7 kg/kW).

DIMENSIONS AND WEIGHT weight: LT and Minx sedans 2,095 lb, 950 kg - LJ Sedan 2,150 lb, 975 kg - LS and LG sedans 2,106 lb, 955 kg - Minx Coupé 2,051 lb, 930 kg - LS and LG coupés 2,062 lb, 935 kg.

OPTIONALS Aishin-Warner automatic transmission, hydraulic torque converter and planetary gears with 3 ratios (I 2.450, II 1.450, III 1, rev 2.222).

130 hp power team

See 100 hp power team, except for:

ENGINE 110.9 cu in, 1,817 cc (3.31 x 3.23 in, 84 x 82 mm); compression ratio: 9:1; max power (JIS): 130 hp (96 kW) at 6,400 rpm; max torque (JIS): 120 lb ft, 16.5 kg m (162 Nm) at 5,000 rpm; max engine rpm: 6,800; 71.5 hp/l (52.7 kW/l); valves: overhead, thimble tappets; camshafts: 2, overhead, cogged belt; electronic injection; 3-way catalytic converter with oxygen sensor.

TRANSMISSION gears: 5, fully synchronized; ratios: I 3.207, II 1.989, III 1.356, IV 1, V 0.855, rev 3.438; width of rims: ZZT models 5" - ZZR models 5.5"; tyres: 175 HR x 13.

PERFORMANCE max speeds: (I) 35 mph, 56 km/h; (II) 57 mph, 92 km/h; (III) 91 mph, 146 km/h; (IV) and (V) 112 mph, 180 km/h; power-weight ratio: ZZR Sedan 16.9 lb/hp (22.9 lb/kW), 7.6 kg/hp (10.4 kg/kW); speed in direct drive at 1,000 rpm: 16.5 mph, 26.5 km/h; consumption: 31 m/imp gal, 26 m/US gal, 9.1 l x 100 km.

CHASSIS rear suspension: anti-roll bar.

BRAKES disc, servo; lining area: front 17.4 sq in, 112 sq cm, rear 17.4 sq in, 112 sq cm, total 34.8 sq in, 224 sq cm.

ELECTRICAL EQUIPMENT 50 A alternator; electronic ignition.

DIMENSIONS AND WEIGHT tracks: 51.57 in, 131 cm front, 51.97 in, 132 cm rear; weight: ZZR Sedan 2,172 lb, 985 kg - ZZT Sedan 2,196 lb, 995 kg - ZZR Coupé 2,128 lb, 965 kg - ZZT Coupé 2,161 lb, 980 kg; weight distribution: 57% front, 43% rear.

OPTIONALS limited slip differential.

61 hp (diesel) power team

See 100 hp power team, except for:

ENGINE diesel; 110.9 cu in, 1,817 cc (3.31 x 3.23 in, 84 x 82 mm); compression ratio: 21:1; max power (JIS): 61 hp (46 kW) at 5,000 rpm; max torque (JIS): 81 lb ft, 11.2 kg m (110 Nm) at 2,000 rpm; max engine rpm: 5,200; 33.5 hp/l (25 kW/l); cast iron block and head; lubrication: 9.7 imp pt, 11.7 US pt, 5.5 l; Bosch VE diesel injection; cooling: 12.2 imp pt, 14.4 US pt, 7 l.

TRANSMISSION gears: 4 - LT and Minx models 5, fully synchronized; ratios: I 3.467, II 1.989, III 1.356, IV 1, rev 3.500 - LT and Minx models V 0.782; tyres: 6.15 x 13 - LT and Minx models 155 SR x 13.

PERFORMANCE max speeds: (I) 26 mph, 42 km/h; (II) 46 mph, 74 km/h; (III) 68 mph, 110 km/h; (IV) and (V) 90 mph, 145 km/h; power-weight ratio: LD Special Sedan 35.5 lb/hp (47 lb/kW), 16.1 kg/hp (21.3 kg/kW); speed in direct drive at 1,000 rpm: 17.4 mph, 27.9 km/h; consumption: 80 m/imp gal, 67 m/US gal, 3.4 l x 100 km at 37 mph, 60 km/h.

ELECTRICAL EQUIPMENT 65 Ah battery; 50 A alternator.

DIMENSIONS AND WEIGHT weight: LD and LD Special sedans 2,161 lb, 980 kg - LT and Minx sedans 2,194 lb, 995 kg - LT and Minx coupés 2,150, 975 kg - LJ Sedan 2,249 lb, 1,020 kg - LS Sedan 2,205 lb, 1,000 kg - LS Coupé 2,161 lb, 980 kg; weight distribution: 58% front, 42% rear.

OPTIONALS automatic transmission (except LD and LD Special sedans).

66 hp (diesel) power team

See 100 hp power team, except for:

ENGINE diesel; 110.9 cu in, 1,817 cc (3.31 x 3.23 in, 84 x 82 mm); compression ratio: 21:1; max power (JIS): 66 hp (49 kW) at 5,000 rpm; max torque (JIS): 81 lb ft, 11.2 kg m (110 Nm) at 2,000 rpm; max engine rpm: 5,200; 36.3 hp/l (26.7 kW/l); cast iron block and head; lubrication: trochoid pump, full flow filter, 9.7 imp pt, 11.7 US pt, 5.5 l; Bosch VE electronic injection; cooling: 12.2 imp pt, 14.4 US pt, 7 l.

TRANSMISSION gears: 5, fully synchronized; ratios: I 3.736, II 1.963, III 1.364, IV 1, V 0.775, rev 3.402; axle ratio: 3.583; tyres: 155 SR x 13.

PERFORMANCE max speed: 93 mph, 150 km/h; power-weight ratio: LT/E 33.4 lb/hp (45.4 lb/kW), 15.1 kg/hp (20.6 kg/kW); consumption: 88.3 m/imp gal, 73.5 m/US gal, 3.2 l x 100 km at 37 mph, 60 km/h.

ELECTRICAL EQUIPMENT 65 Ah battery; 50 A alternator.

DIMENSIONS AND WEIGHT length: 166.77 in, 423 cm; weight: LT/E Sedan 2,205 lb, 1,000 kg - LJ/E Sedan 2,481 lb, 1,025 kg.

BODY saloon/sedan; 4 doors.

73 hp (diesel) power team

See 100 hp power team, except for:

ENGINE diesel, turbocharged; 110.9 cu in, 1,817 cc (3.31 x 3.23 in, 84 x 82 mm); compression ratio: 21:1; max power (JIS): 73 hp (54 kW) at 5,000 rpm; max torque (JIS): 116 lb ft, 16 kg m (157 Nm) at 2,000 rpm; max engine rpm: 5,200; 40.2 hp/l (29.6 kW/l); cast iron block and head; lubrication: trochoid pump, full flow filter, 9.7 imp pt, 11.7 US pt, 5.5 l; Bosch VE electronic injection; turbocharger; cooling: 12.2 imp pt, 14.4 US pt, 7 l.

TRANSMISSION gears: 5, fully synchronized; ratios: I 3.736, II 1.963, III 1.364, IV 1, V 0.775, rev 3.402; tyres: 155 SR x 13.

PERFORMANCE max speeds: (I) 25 mph, 40 km/h; (II) 48 mph, 77 km/h; (III) 70 mph, 112 km/h; (IV) 93 mph, 153 km/h; (V) 99 mph, 160 km/h; power-weight ratio: Special 30.2 lb/hp (41.1 lb/kW), 13.7 kg/hp (18.6 kg/kW); consumption: 85.6 m/imp gal, 71.3 m/US gal, 3.3 l x 100 km at 37 mph, 60 km/h.

CHASSIS rear suspension: anti-roll bar.

DIMENSIONS AND WEIGHT weight: Special Sedan 2,205 lb, 1,000 kg - LG Sedan 2,238 lb, 1,015 kg.

BODY saloon/sedan; 4 doors.

OPTIONALS Aishin-Warner automatic transmission, hydraulic torque converter and planetary gears with 3 ratios (I 2.450, II 1.450, III 1, rev 2.222).

Florian Aska Series

PRICES (Tokyo):		yen
1	1800 LD 4-dr Sedan	**1,137,000**
2	1800 LT 4-dr Sedan	**1,202,000**
3	1800 LF 4-dr Sedan	**1,334,000**
4	2000 LT 4-dr Sedan	**1,252,000**
5	2000 LF 4-dr Sedan	**1,441,000**
6	2000 LS 4-dr Sedan	**1,407,000**
7	2000 LJ 4-dr Sedan	**1,547,000**
8	2000 LX 4-dr Sedan	**1,687,000**
9	2000 LX-E 4-dr Sedan	**1,859,000**
10	2000 Turbo LT 4-dr Sedan	**1,490,000**
11	2000 Turbo LS 4-dr Sedan	**1,640,000**
12	2000 Turbo LJ 4-dr Sedan	**1,805,000**
13	2000 Diesel LD 4-dr Sedan	**1,272,000**
14	2000 Diesel LT 4-dr Sedan	**1,322,000**
15	2000 Diesel LF 4-dr Sedan	**1,511,000**
16	2000 Diesel LJ 4-dr Sedan	**1,627,000**
17	2000 Diesel LX 4-dr Sedan	**1,757,000**
18	2000 Diesel Turbo LT 4-dr Sedan	**1,490,000**
19	2000 Diesel Turbo LS 4-dr Sedan	**1,650,000**
20	2000 Diesel Turbo LJ 4-dr Sedan	**1,815,000**

Power team:	Standard for:	Optional for:
105 hp	1 to 3	—
110 hp	4 to 8	—
115 hp	9	—
150 hp	10 to 12	—
66 hp (diesel)	13 to 17	—
89 hp (diesel)	18 to 20	—

105 hp power team

ENGINE front, 4 stroke; 4 cylinders, vertical, in line; 110.9 cu in, 1,817 cc (3.31 x 3.23 in, 84 x 82 mm); compression ratio: 9:1; max power (JIS): 105 hp (77 kW) at 5,600 rpm; max torque (JIS): 112 lb ft, 15.5 kg m (152 Nm) at 3,600 rpm; max engine rpm: 6,000; 57.8 hp/l (42.5 kW/l); cast iron block, light alloy head; 5 crankshaft bearings; valves: overhead, Vee-slanted, rockers; camshafts: 1, overhead, cogged belt; lubrication: trochoid pump, full flow filter, 7.9 imp pt, 9.5 US pt, 4.5 l; 1 Stromberg 21 E304-24 downdraught twin barrel carburettor; emission control by catalytic converter, exhaust gas recirculation and secondary air induction; fuel feed: electric pump; water-cooled, 14.1 imp pt, 16.9 US pt, 8 l, electric thermostatic fan.

TRANSMISSION driving wheels: front; clutch: single dry plate (diaphragm); gearbox: mechanical; gears: 5, fully synchronized; ratios: I 3.909, II 2.150, III 1.333, IV 0.923, V 0.744, rev 3.500; lever: central; final drive: helical spur gears; axle ratio: 3.450; width of rims: 5"; tyres: LD 6.45 x 13 - LT and LF 165 SR x 13.

PERFORMANCE max speeds: (I) 29 mph, 47 km/h; (II) 52 mph, 84 km/h; (III) 85 mph, 137 km/h; (IV) and (V) 109 mph, 175 km/h; power-weight ratio: LD 20.3 lb/hp (27.6 lb/kW), 9.2 kg/hp (12.5 kg/kW); consumption: 40.9 m/imp gal, 34.1 m/US gal, 6.9 l x 100 km on Japanese emission test cycle.

105 HP POWER TEAM

CHASSIS integral; front suspension: independent, by McPherson, coil springs, telescopic dampers struts, lower A-arms; rear: rigid axle, coil springs, telescopic dampers.

STEERING rack-and-pinion - LF servo; turns lock to lock: 4.40 - LF 3.20.

BRAKES front disc (diameter 7.40 in, 18.8 cm), rear drum (diameter 7.99 in, 20.3 cm), dual circuit, servo.

ELECTRICAL EQUIPMENT 12 V; 30 Ah battery; 60 A alternator; fully transistorized ignition; 2 headlamps.

DIMENSIONS AND WEIGHT wheel base: 101.57 in, 258 cm; tracks: 55.31 in, 140 cm front, 55.51 in, 141 cm rear; length: LD 174.41 in, 443 cm - LT and LF 174.80 in, 444 cm; width: 65.75 in, 167 cm; height: 54.13 in, 137 cm; ground clearance: 6.10 in, 15 cm; weight: LD Sedan 2,139 lb, 970 kg - LT Sedan 2,150 lb, 975 kg - LF Sedan 2,172 lb, 985 kg; weight distribution: 65% front, 35% rear; turning circle: 36.4 ft, 11.1 m; fuel tank: 12.3 imp gal, 14.8 US gal, 56 l.

BODY saloon/sedan; 4 doors; 5 seats, separate front seats.

110 hp power team

See 105 hp power team, except for:

ENGINE 121.7 cu in, 1,994 cc (3.46 x 3.23 in, 88 x 82 mm); compression ratio: 8.8:1; max power (JIS): 110 hp (81 kW) at 5,400 rpm; max torque (JIS): 123 lb ft, 17 kg m (167 Nm) at 3,400 rpm; max engine rpm: 5,800; 55.2 hp/l (40.6 kW/l).

TRANSMISSION gearbox ratios: I 3.727, II 2.043, III 1.448, IV 1.027, V 0.829, rev 3.500; axle ratio: 3.500; tyres: 165 SR x 13 - LS nad LX 185/70 SR x 13.

PERFORMANCE max speeds: (I) 30 mph, 48 km/h; (II) 57 mph, 92 km/h; (III) 82 mph, 132 km/h; (IV and (V) 109 mph, 175 km/h; power-weight ratio: LT 19.6 lb/hp (26.7 lb/kW), 8.9 kg/hp (12.1 kg/kW); consumption: 37.6 m/imp gal, 31.3 m/US gal, 7.5 l x 100 km on Japanese emission test cycle.

CHASSIS front suspension: anti-roll bar.

STEERING variable ratio servo.

DIMENSIONS AND WEIGHT length: 174.80 in, 444 cm; weight: LT Sedan 2,161 lb, 980 kg - LF Sedan 2,183 lb, 990 kg - LS Sedan 2,227 lb, 1,010 kg - LJ Sedan 2,260 lb, 1,025 kg - LX Sedan 2,304 lb, 1,045 kg.

OPTIONALS automatic transmission, hydraulic torque converter and planetary gears with 3 ratios (I 2.840, II 1.600, III 1, rev 2.070), 3.333 axle ratio.

115 hp power team

See 105 hp power team, except for:

ENGINE 121.7 cu in, 1,994 cc (3.46 x 3.23 in, 88 x 82 mm); max power (JIS): 115 hp (85 kW) at 5,400 rpm; max torque (JIS): 127 lb ft, 17.5 kg m (172 Nm) at 3,400 rpm; max engine rpm: 5,800; 57.7 hp/l (42.4 kW/l); carburettor with automatic air-fuel ratio adjustment.

TRANSMISSION gearbox ratios: I 3.727, II 2.043, III 1.448, IV 1.027, V 0.829, rev 3.500; axle ratio: 3.500; tyres: 185/70 SR x 13.

PERFORMANCE max speed: 109 mph, 175 km/h; power-weight ratio: 20.2 lb/hp (27.4 lb/kW), 9.1 kg/hp (12.4 kg/kW); consumption: 37.1 m/imp gal, 30.9 m/US gal, 7.6 l x 100 km on Japanese emission test cycle.

STEERING variable ratio servo.

DIMENSIONS AND WEIGHT length: 174.80 in, 444 cm; weight: 2,315 lb, 1,050 kg.

150 hp power team

See 105 hp power team, except for:

ENGINE turbocharged; 121.7 cu in, 1,994 cc (3.46 x 3.23 in, 88 x 82 mm); compression ratio: 8.2:1; max power (JIS): 150 hp (110 kW) at 5,400 rpm; max torque (JIS): 167 lb ft, 23 kg m (226 Nm) at 3,000 rpm; max engine rpm: 5,800; 75.2 hp/l (55.4 kW/l); electronic fuel injection; turbocharger with wastegate.

TRANSMISSION gearbox ratios: I 3.909, II 2.150, III 1.333, IV 0.923, V 0.744, rev 3.500; axle ratio: 3.190; tyres: 185/70 SR x 13.

PERFORMANCE max speeds: (I) 30 mph, 48 km/h; (II) 57 mph, 92 km/h; (III) 92 mph, 148 km/h; (IV) and (V) 112 mph, 180 km/h; power-weight ratio: LT 14.9 lb/hp (20.2 lb/kW), 6.7 kg/hp (9.2 kg/kW); consumption: 35.7 m/imp gal, 29.8 m/US gal, 7.9 l x 100 km on Japanese emission test cycle.

CHASSIS front suspension: anti-roll bar; rear: LS anti-roll bar.

STEERING variable ratio servo.

DIMENSIONS AND WEIGHT length: 174.80 in, 444 cm; weight: LT Sedan 2,227 lb, 1,010 kg - LS Sedan 2,249 lb, 1,020 kg - LJ Sedan 2,304 lb, 1,045 kg.

OPTIONALS 5.5" or 6" wide rims; 195/60 R x 14 tyres.

ISUZU Piazza XL Coupé

66 hp (diesel) power team

See 105 hp power team, except for:

ENGINE diesel; 121.7 cu in, 1,995 cc (3.31 x 3.54 in, 84 x 90 mm); compression ratio: 21:1; max power (JIS): 66 hp (49 kW) at 4,500 rpm; max torque (JIS): 92 lb ft, 12.7 kg m (124 Nm) at 2,500 rpm; lubrication: 9.7 imp pt, 11.7 US pt, 5.5 l; Bosch VE electronic injection; Ricardo Comet swirl combustion chamber.

TRANSMISSION gearbox ratios: I 3.909, II 2.150, III 1.448, IV 1.027, V 0.744, rev 3.500; axle ratio: 3.578; tyres: 165 SR x 17 - LJ and LX 185/70 SR x 13.

PERFORMANCE max speed: 90 mph, 145 km/h; power-weight ratio: LD 35.1 lb/hp (47.7 lb/kW), 15.9 kg/hp (21.6 kg/kW); consumption: 88.3 m/imp gal, 73.5 m/US gal, 3.2 l x 100 km at 37 mph, 60 km/h.

STEERING variable ratio servo.

DIMENSIONS AND WEIGHT weight: LD Sedan 2,315 lb, 1,050 kg - LT Sedan 2,326 lb, 1,055 kg - LJ Sedan 2,414 lb, 1,095 kg - LX Sedan 2,448 lb, 1,110 kg.

OPTIONALS automatic transmission, hydraulic torque converter and planetary gears with 3 ratios (I 2.840, II 1.600, III 1, rev 2.070).

89 hp (diesel) power team

See 105 hp power team, except for:

ENGINE diesel, turbocharged; 121.7 cu in, 1,995 cc (3.31 x 3.54 in, 84 x 90 mm); compression ratio: 21:1; max power (JIS): 89 hp (65 kW) at 4,500 rpm; max torque (JIS): 138 lb ft, 19 kg m (186 Nm) at 2,500 rpm; max engine rpm: 4,900; 44.6 hp/l (32.8 kW/l); lubrication: 9.7 imp pt, 11.7 US pt, 5.5 l; Bosch VE electronic injection; Ricardo Comet swirl combustion chamber; turbocharger.

TRANSMISSION gearbox ratios: I 3.909, II 2.150, III 1.448, IV 1.027, V 0.744, rev 3.500; tyres: 185/70 SR x 13.

PERFORMANCE max speed: 109 mph, 175 km/h; power-weight ratio: LT 26.7 lb/hp (36.2 lb/kW), 12.1 kg/hp (16.4 kg/kW); consumption: 88.3 m/imp gal, 73.5 m/US gal, 3.2 l x 100 km at 37 mph, 60 km/h.

STEERING variable ratio servo.

DIMENSIONS AND WEIGHT length: 174.80 in, 444 cm; weight: LT Sedan 2,370 lb, 1,075 kg - LS Sedan 2,392 lb, 1,085 kg - LJ Sedan 2,580 lb, 1,170 kg.

Piazza Series

PRICES (Tokyo):	yen
1 XJ 2+1-dr Coupé	**1,670,000**
2 Bella 2+1-dr Coupé	**1,723,000**
3 XL 2+1-dr Coupé	**1,867,000**
4 XG 2+1-dr Coupé	**2,019,000**
5 XE 2+1-dr Coupé	**2,529,000**

For USA prices, see price index.

Power team:	Standard for:	Optional for:
120 hp	1 to 3	—
135 hp	4,5	—

120 hp power team

ENGINE front, 4 stroke; 4 cylinders, in line; 118.9 cu in, 1,949 cc (3.43 x 3.23 in, 87 x 82 mm); compression ratio: 8.8:1; max power (JIS): 120 hp (88 kW) at 5,800 rpm; max torque (JIS): 120 lb ft, 16.5 kg m (162 Nm) at 4,000 rpm; max engine rpm: 6,500; 61.8 hp/l (45.3 kW/l); cast iron block, light alloy head; 5 crankshaft bearings; valves: overhead, push-rods and rockers; camshafts: 1, overhead; lubrication: trochoid pump, full flow filter, 8.8 imp pt, 10.6 US pt, 5 l; electronic injection; fuel feed: electric pump; emission control by 3-way catalytic converter; water-cooled, 10.6 imp pt, 12.7 US pt, 6 l.

TRANSMISSION driving wheels: rear; clutch: single dry plate (diaphragm); gearbox: mechanical; gears: 5, fully synchronized; ratios: I 3.312, II 2.054, III 1.400, IV 1, V 0.840, rev 3.550; lever: central; final drive: hypoid bevel; axle ratio: 3.583; width of rims: 5.5"; tyres: 165 SR x 13 - XL 185/70 HR x 13.

PERFORMANCE max speeds: (I) 35 mph, 56 km/h; (II) 57 mph, 92 km/h; (III) 85 mph, 137 km/h; (IV) and (V) 112 mph, 180

ISUZU Rodeo 4WD

km/h; power-weight ratio: XJ 20.5 lb/hp (27.7 lb/kW), 9.3 kg/hp (12.6 kg/kW); consumption: 32.5 m/imp gal, 27 m/US gal, 8.7 l x 100 km.

CHASSIS integral; front suspension: independent, wishbones, coil springs, anti-roll bar, telescopic dampers; rear: rigid axle, lower trailing links, torque tube, Panhard rod, coil springs, anti-roll bar, telescopic dampers.

STEERING rack-and-pinion - XL servo; turns lock to lock: 4.50 - XL 3.20.

BRAKES disc, front internal radial fins, servo; lining area: front 24.2 sq in, 156 sq cm, rear 17.4 sq in, 112 sq cm, total 41.6 sq in, 268 sq cm.

ELECTRICAL EQUIPMENT 12 V; 45 Ah battery; 50 A alternator; Hitachi pointless electronic ignition; 2 headlamps.

DIMENSIONS AND WEIGHT wheel base: 96.06 in, 244 cm; tracks: 52.76 in, 134 cm front, 53.12 in, 135 cm rear; length: 169.68 in, 431 cm; width: 64.96 in, 165 cm; height: 51.18 in, 130 cm; ground clearance: 6.10 in, 15.5 cm; weight: XJ and Bella coupés 2,459 lb, 1,115 kg - XL Coupé 2,481 lb, 1,125 kg; weight distribution: 58% front, 42% rear; turning circle: 34.8 ft, 10.6 m; fuel tank: 12.8 imp gal, 15.3 US gal, 58 l.

BODY coupé; 2+1 doors; 5 seats, separate front seats.

OPTIONALS limited slip differential; air-conditioning.

135 hp power team

See 120 hp power team, except for:

ENGINE compression ratio: 9:1; max power (JIS): 135 hp (99 kW) at 6,200 rpm; max torque (JIS): 123 lb ft, 17 kg m (167 Nm) at 5,000 rpm; max engine rpm: 6,800; 69.3 hp/l (50.8 kW/l); valves: overhead, thimble tappets; camshafts: 2, overhead, chain-driven.

TRANSMISSION axle ratio: 3.909; tyres: XE 185/70 HR x 13 - XG 195/60 HR x 14.

PERFORMANCE power-weight ratio: XG Coupé 18.9 lb/hp (25.7 lb/kW), 8.5 kg/hp (11.6 kg/kW).

STEERING servo; turns lock to lock: 3.20.

DIMENSIONS AND WEIGHT weight: XG Coupé 2,547 lb, 1,155 kg - XE Coupé 2,624 lb, 1,190 kg.

OPTIONALS Aishin automatic transmission, hydraulic torque converter and planetary gears with 4 ratios (I 2.450, II 1.450, III 1, IV 0.689, rev 2.222).

Rodeo 4WD

PRICES (Tokyo):	yen
LD Short Wheelbase (steel body)	1,628,000
LT Short Wheelbase (steel body)	1,808,000
LT Short Wheelbase (soft top)	—
LD Long Wheelbase (steel body)	1,730,000
LT Long Wheelbase (steel body)	1,910,000

ENGINE diesel, front, 4 stroke; 4 cylinders, vertical, in line; 136.6 cu in, 2,239 cc (3.46 x 3.62 in, 88 x 92 mm); compression ratio: 21:1; max power (JIS): 73 hp (54 kW) at 4,000 rpm; max torque (JIS): 103 lb ft, 14.2 kg m (139 Nm) at 2,400 rpm; max engine rpm: 4,700; 32.6 hp/l (24 kW/l); cast iron block, light alloy head; 5 crankshaft bearings; valves: overhead, push-rods and rockers; camshafts: 1, side; Ricardo Comet swirl combustion chambers; lubrication: rotary pump, full flow filter, 11.4 imp pt, 13.4 US pt, 6.5 l; Bosch injection pump; fuel feed: mechanical pump; emission control by secondary air induction, catalytic converter and exhaust gas recirculation; water-cooled, 14.1 imp pt, 16.9 US pt, 8 l.

TRANSMISSION driving wheels: rear or front and rear; clutch: single dry plate (diaphragm); gearbox: mechanical; gears: 4, fully synchronized, auxiliary transfer box; ratios: I 4.128, II 2.798, III 1.482, IV 1, rev 3.725; transfer box ratios: high 1, low 1.870; lever: central; final drive: hypoid bevel; axle ratio: 4.555; width of rims: LD models 4.5" - LT models 6"; tyres: LD models 6.00 x 16 - LT models H78 x 15.

PERFORMANCE max speeds (high ratio): (I) 19 mph, 30 km/h; (II) 28 mph, 45 km/h; (III) 52 mph, 84 km/h; (IV) 78 mph, 125 km/h; power-weight ratio: LD Short Wheelbase 42 lb/hp (57.1 lb/kW), 19 kg/hp (25.9 kg/kW); carrying capacity: 882 lb, 400 kg; consumption: 47.1 m/imp gal, 31.9 m/US gal, 6.2 l x 100 km at 37 mph, 60 km/h.

CHASSIS ladder frame; front suspension: independent, wishbones, torsion bars, anti-roll bar, telescopic dampers; rear: rigid axle, semi-elliptic leafsprings, telescopic dampers.

STEERING recirculating ball - LT steel body models servo; turns lock to lock: 4.40 - LT steel body models 3.60.

BRAKES front disc, rear drum, dual circuit, servo; lining area: front 27.9 sq in, 180 sq cm, rear 68.2 sq in, 440 sq cm, total 96.1 sq in, 620 sq cm.

ELECTRICAL EQUIPMENT 12 V; 80 Ah battery; 50 A alternator; 2 headlamps.

DIMENSIONS AND WEIGHT wheel base: 90.55 in, 230 cm short wheelbase models - 104.33 in, 265 cm long wheelbase models; length: 160.24 in, 407 cm short wheelbase models - 174.02 in, 442 cm long wheelbase models; width: 64.96 in, 165 cm; height: 70.87 in, 180 cm; ground clearance: 8.85 in, 22.5 cm; weight: LD Short Wheelbase (steel body) 3,065 lb, 1,390 kg - LT Short Wheelbase (steel body) 3,142 lb, 1,425 kg - LT Short Wheelbase (soft top) 2,977 lb, 1,350 kg - LD Long Wheelbase (steel body) 3,153 lb, 1,430 kg - LT Long Wheelbase (steel body) 3,230 lb, 1,465 kg; fuel tank: 11 imp gal, 13.2 US gal, 50 l.

BODY open, 2+1 doors - estate car/st. wagon, 2+1 doors; 5 seats, separate front seats.

MAZDA JAPAN

Familia Series

	PRICES (Tokyo):	yen
1	1300 XC 2+1-dr Hatchback Sedan	760,000
2	1300 XC 4+1-dr Hatchback Sedan	798,000
3	1300 XC 4-dr Sedan	818,000
4	1300 XT 2+1-dr Hatchback Sedan	845,000
5	1300 XT 4+1-dr Hatchback Sedan	881,000
6	1300 XT 4-dr Sedan	896,000
7	1300 XL 2+1-dr Hatchback Sedan	900,000
8	1300 XL 4+1-dr Hatchback Sedan	936,000
9	1300 XL 4-dr Sedan	951,000
10	1500 XT 2+1-dr Hatchback Sedan	881,000
11	1500 XT 4+1-dr Hatchback Sedan	917,000
12	1500 XT 4-dr Sedan	932,000
13	1500 XL 2+1-dr Hatchback Sedan	1,013,000
14	1500 XL 4+1-dr Hatchback Sedan	1,028,000
15	1500 XL 4-dr Sedan	1,042,000
16	1500 XE 4+1-dr Hatchback Sedan	1,078,000
17	1500 XE 4-dr Sedan	1,092,000
18	1500 XG 2+1-dr Hatchback Sedan	1,084,000
19	1500 XG 4-dr Sedan	1,112,000
20	1500 XG 2+1-dr Hatchback Sedan	1,169,000
21	1500 XGi 4-dr Sedan	1,197,000
22	1500 Turbo XG 2+1-dr Hatchback Sedan	1,250,000
23	1500 Turbo XG 4-dr Sedan	1,283,000

For GB prices, see price index.

Power team:	Standard for:	Optional for:
74 hp	1 to 9	—
85 hp	10 to 19	—
95 hp	20,21	—
115 hp	22,23	—

74 hp power team

ENGINE front, transverse, 4 stroke; 4 cylinders, in line; 79.1 cu in, 1,296 cc (3.03 x 2.74 in, 77 x 69.6 mm); compression ratio: 9.2:1; max power (JIS): 74 hp (53 kW) at 5,500 rpm; max torque (JIS): 76 lb ft, 10.5 kg m (103 Nm) at 3,500 rpm; max engine rpm: 6,000; 57.1 hp/l (40.9 kW/l); cast iron block, light alloy head; 5 crankshaft bearings; valves: overhead, rockers; camshafts: 1, overhead; lubrication: rotary pump, full flow filter, 6.5 imp pt, 7.8 US pt, 3.7 l; 1 downdraught twin barrel carburettor; fuel feed: electric pump; Mazda stabilized combustion system with 3-way catalytic converter, secondary air induction and exhaust gas recirculation; water-cooled, 10.6 imp pt, 12.7 US pt, 6 l, electric thermostatic fan.

TRANSMISSION driving wheels: front; clutch: single dry plate (diaphragm); gearbox: mechanical; gears: 4, fully synchronized; ratios: I 3.416, II 1.947, III 1.290, IV 0.918, rev 3.214; lever: central; final drive: helical spur gears; axle ratio: 3.850; width of rims: 4.5"; tyres: 6.15 x 13 - XT and XL sedans 155 SR x 13.

PERFORMANCE max speeds: (I) 28 mph, 45 km/h; (II) 52 mph, 83 km/h; (III) 78 mph, 125 km/h; (IV) 93 mph, 150 km/h; power-weight ratio: XC 2+1-dr 22.8 lb/hp (31.8 lb/kW), 10.3 kg/hp (14.4 kg/kW); carrying capacity: 882 lb, 400 kg; consumption: 47.8 m/imp gal, 40.5 m/US gal, 5.8 l x 100 km on Japanese emission test cycle.

CHASSIS integral; front suspension: independent, by McPherson, coil springs/telescopic damper struts, lower wishbones, anti-roll bar; rear: independent, twin transverse link, trailing link, coil springs/telescopic dampers.

STEERING rack-and-pinion; turns lock to lock: 3.60.

BRAKES front disc, rear drum, servo; lining area: front 27.9 sq in, 180 sq cm, rear 74.1 sq in, 478 sq cm, total 102 sq in, 658 sq cm.

ELECTRICAL EQUIPMENT 12 V; 30 or 45 Ah battery; 50 A alternator; contactless fully electronic ignition; 2 headlamps.

DIMENSIONS AND WEIGHT wheel base: 93.11 in, 236 cm; tracks: 54.72 in, 139 cm front, 54.92 in, 139 cm rear; length: hatchback sedans 155.71 in, 395 cm - sedans 163.58 in, 415 cm; width: 64.17 in, 163 cm; height: 54.13 in, 137 cm; ground clearance: 5.91 in, 15 cm; weight: XC 2+1-dr 1,687 lb, 765 kg - XT 2+1-dr 1,709 lb, 775 kg - XL 2+1-dr 1,720 lb, 780 kg - XC 4+1-dr 1,720 lb, 780 kg - XT 4+1-dr 1,742 lb, 790 kg - XL 4+1-dr 1,753 lb, 795 kg - XC 4-dr 1,742 lb, 790 kg - XT 4-dr 1,753 lb, 795 kg - XL 4-dr 1,764 lb, 800 kg; weight distribution: 65% front, 35% rear; turning circle: 30.2 ft, 9.2 m; fuel tank: 9.2 imp gal, 11.1 US gal, 42 l.

BODY saloon/sedan; 2+1, 4+1 or 4 doors; 5 seats, separate front seats, built-in headrests.

85 hp power team

See 74 hp power team, except for:

ENGINE 90.9 cu in, 1,490 cc (3.03 x 3.15 in, 77 x 80 mm); compression ratio: 9:1; max power (JIS): 85 hp (61 kW) at 5,500 rpm; max torque (JIS): 89 lb ft, 12.3 kg m (121 Nm) at 3,500 rpm; 57 hp/l (40.9 kW/l).

TRANSMISSION gears: 5, fully synchronized; ratios: I 3.416, II 1.947, III 1.290, IV 0.918, V 0.775, rev 3.214; width of rims: XG sedans 5"; tyres: XT sedans 6.15 x 13 - XL and XE sedans 155 SR x 13 - XG sedans 175/70 SR x 13.

ISUZU Rodeo 4WD

MAZDA Familia 1500 XE Sedan

85 HP POWER TEAM

PERFORMANCE max speed: 99 mph, 160 km/h; power-weight ratio: XT 2+1-dr 20.2 lb/hp (28.2 lb/kW), 9.2 kg/hp (12.8 kg/kW); consumption: 46.3 m/imp gal, 38.6 m/US gal, 6.1 l x 100 km on Japanese emission test cycle.

CHASSIS front suspension: anti-roll bar (for XG sedans only); rear: anti-roll bar.

DIMENSIONS AND WEIGHT weight: XT 2+1-dr 1,720 lb, 780 kg - XL 2+1-dr 1,742 lb, 790 kg - XG 2+1-dr and XT 4-dr 1,808 lb, 820 kg - XL and XT 4+1-dr and XE 4-dr 1,797 lb, 815 kg - XL 4-dr 1,786 lb, 810 kg.

OPTIONALS JATCO 3-speed automatic transmission (except XG sedans); sunroof.

95 hp power team

See 74 hp power team, except for:

ENGINE 90.9 cu in, 1,490 cc (3.03 x 3.15 in, 77 x 80 mm); compression ratio: 9:1; max power (JIS): 95 hp (70 kW) at 5,800 rpm; max torque (JIS): 91 lb ft, 12.6 kg m (124 Nm) at 5,800 rpm; 64 hp/l (46.9 kW/l); electronic fuel injection.

TRANSMISSION gears: 5, fully synchronized; ratios: I 3.153, II 1.842, III 1.290, IV 0.918, V 0.775, rev 3.214; axle ratio: 4.105; width of rims: 5"; tyres: 175/70 HR x 13.

PERFORMANCE max speeds: (I) 34 mph, 55 km/h; (II) 51 mph, 82 km/h; (III) 76 mph, 122 km/h; (IV) and (V) 112 mph, 180 km/h; power- weight ratio: XGi 2+1-dr 19.2 lb/hp (26.2 lb/kW), 8.7 kg/hp (11.9 kg/kW); consumption: 43.4 m/imp gal, 36.2 m/US gal, 6.5 l x 100 km on Japanese emission test cycle.

CHASSIS front and rear suspension: anti-roll bar.

DIMENSIONS AND WEIGHT weight: XGi 2+1-dr 1,830 lb, 830 kg - XGi 4-dr 1,874 lb, 850 kg.

BODY 2+1 or 4 doors.

115 hp power team

See 74 hp power team, except for:

ENGINE turbocharged; 90.9 cu in, 1,490 cc (3.03 x 3.15 in, 77 x 80 mm); compression ratio: 8.2:1; max power (JIS): 115 hp (85 kW) at 5,800 rpm; max torque (JIS): 119 lb ft, 16.5 kg m (162 Nm) at 3,500 rpm; 77 hp/l (56.8 kW/l); electronic fuel injection; turbocharger with wastegate.

TRANSMISSION gears: 5, fully synchronized; ratios: I 3.307, II 1.833, III 1.223, IV 0.970, V 0.795, rev 3.133; axle ratio: 3.850; width of rims: 5"; tyres: 175/70 HR x 13.

PERFORMANCE max speeds: (I) 31 mph, 50 km/h; (II) 51 mph, 82 km/h; (III) 81 mph, 130 km/h; (IV) 99 mph, 160 km/h; (V) 112 mph, 180 km/h; power-weight ratio: XG 2+1-dr 16.4 lb/hp (22.3 lb/kW), 7.4 kg/hp (10.1 kg/kW); consumption: 43.4 m/imp gal, 36.2 m/US gal, 6.5 l x 100 km on Japanese emission test cycle.

CHASSIS front and rear suspension: anti-roll bar.

DIMENSIONS AND WEIGHT weight: XG Turbo 2+1-dr 1,885 lb, 855 kg - XG Turbo 4-dr 1,940 lb, 880 kg.

BODY 2+1 or 4 doors.

Familia (USA)

PRICES IN USA:	$
GLC 2+1-dr Hatchback Sedan	**14,995***
GLC De Luxe 2+1-dr Hatchback Sedan	**15,895***
GLC De Luxe 4-dr Sedan	**16,445***
GLC Luxury 2+1-dr Hatchback Sedan	**16,495***
GLC Luxury 4-dr St. Wagon	**17,095***

ENGINE front, transverse, 4 stroke; 4 cylinders, in line; 90.9 cu in, 1,490 cc (3.03 x 3.15 in, 77 x 80 mm); compression ratio: 9:1; max power (SAE net): 68 hp (49 kW) at 5,500 rpm; max torque (SAE net): 82 lb ft, 11.3 kg m (111 Nm) at 3,500 rpm; max engine rpm: 6,000; 45.6 hp/l (32.9 kW/l); cast iron block, light alloy head; 5 crankshaft bearings; valves: overhead, rockers; camshafts: 1, overhead; lubrication: rotary pump, full flow filter, 6.5 imp pt, 7.8 US pt, 3.7 l; 1 downdraught twin barrel carburettor; fuel feed: electric pump; Mazda stabilized combustion system with 3-way catalytic converter, secondary air induction and exhaust gas recirculation; water-cooled, 10.6 imp pt, 12.7 US pt, 6 l, electric thermostatic fan.

TRANSMISSION driving wheels: front; clutch: single dry plate (diaphragm); gearbox: mechanical; gears: 4, fully synchronized; ratios: I 3.416, II 1.947, III 1.290, IV 0.918, rev 3.214; lever: central; final drive: helical spur gears; axle ratio: 3.850; width of rims: 4.5"; tyres: 6.15 x 13 or 155 SR x 13.

PERFORMANCE max speeds: (I) 28 mph, 45 km/h; (II) 52 mph, 83 km/h; (III) 78 mph, 125 km/h; (IV) 93 mph, 150 km/h; power-weight ratio: 2+1-dr hatchback sedans 27.5 lb/hp (38.2 lb/kW), 12.5 kg/hp (17.3 kg/kW); carrying capacity: 882 lb, 400 kg; consumption: 47.1 m/imp gal, 39.2 m/US gal, 6 l x 100 km (EPA).

CHASSIS integral; front suspension: independent, by McPherson, coil springs/telescopic damper struts, lower wishbones, anti-roll bar; rear: independent, twin transverse links, trailing links, coil springs/telescopic dampers.

MAZDA Capella 2000 Turbo GT-X Sedan

STEERING rack-and-pinion; turns lock to lock: 3.60.

BRAKES front disc, rear drum, servo; lining area: front 27.9 sq in, 180 sq cm, rear 74.1 sq in, 478 sq cm, total 102 sq in, 658 sq cm.

ELECTRICAL EQUIPMENT 12 V; 30 or 45 Ah battery; 50 A alternator; contactless fully electronic ignition; 2 headlamps.

DIMENSIONS AND WEIGHT wheel base: 93.11 in, 236 cm; tracks: 54.72 in, 139 cm front, 54.92 in, 139 cm rear; length: 159.05 in, 404 cm; width: 64.17 in, 163 cm; height: 54.13 in, 137 cm; ground clearance: 5.91 in, 15 cm; weight: 2+1-dr hatchback sedans 1,870 lb, 848 kg - 4-dr models 1,916 lb, 869 kg; weight distribution: 65% front, 35% rear; turning circle: 30.2 ft, 9.2 m; fuel tank: 9.2 imp gal, 11.1 US gal, 42 l.

BODY saloon/sedan, 2+1 or 4 doors - estate car/st. wagon, 4 doors; 5 seats, separate front seats, built-in headrests.

OPTIONALS JATCO automatic transmission with 3 ratios (I 2.841, II 1.541, III 1, rev 2.400), 3.631 axle ratio, consumption 38.7 m/imp gal, 32.2 m/US gal, 7.3 l x 100 km (EPA).

Capella Series

	PRICES (Tokyo):	yen
1	1600 SG 4-dr Sedan	**987,000**
2	1600 SG-L 4-dr Sedan	**1,082,000**
3	1600 SG-L 2-dr Coupé	**1,150,000**
4	1600 SG-S 4-dr Sedan	**1,177,000**
5	1600 SG-S 2-dr Coupé	**1,220,000**
6	1800 SG-L 4-dr Sedan	**1,217,000**
7	1800 SG-S 2-dr Coupé	**1,260,000**
8	1800 SG-X 4-dr Sedan	**1,367,000**
9	1800 GT-S 4-dr Sedan	**1,327,000**
10	1800 GT-S 2-dr Coupé	**1,375,000**
11	2000 GT-X 4-dr Sedan	**1,587,000**
12	2000 GT-X 2-dr Coupé	**1,745,000**
13	2000 Limited 4-dr Sedan	**1,627,000**
14	2000 Turbo GT 4-dr Sedan	**1,534,000**
15	2000 Turbo GT-S 4-dr Sedan	**1,651,000**
16	2000 Turbo GT-S 2-dr Coupé	**1,699,000**
17	2000 Turbo GT-X 4-dr Sedan	**1,776,000**
18	2000 Turbo GT-X 2-dr Coupé	**1,869,000**
19	2000 SG-L 4-dr Sedan	**1,282,000**
20	2000 SG-X 4-dr Sedan	**1,482,000**

For GB prices, see price index.

Power team:	Standard for:	Optional for:
90 hp	1 to 5	—
100 hp	6 to 10	—
120 hp	11 to 13	—
145 hp	14 to 18	—
72 hp (diesel)	19,20	—

90 hp power team

ENGINE front, 4 stroke; 4 cylinders, in line; 96.8 cu in, 1,586 cc (3.18 x 3.03 in, 81 x 77 mm); compression ratio: 8.6:1; max power (JIS): 90 hp (66 kW) at 5,700 rpm; max torque (JIS): 94 lb ft, 13 kg m (127 Nm) at 3,500 rpm; max engine rpm: 6,000; 56.7 hp/l (41.7 kW/l); cast iron block, light alloy head; 5 crankshaft bearings; valves: overhead, rockers; camshafts: 1, overhead; lubrication: gear pump, full flow filter, 7.9 imp pt, 9.5 US pt, 4.5 l; 1 Nikki 242302 downdraught twin barrel carburettor with automatic air-fuel ratio adjustment; Mazda stabilized combustion system with 3-way catalytic converter, secondary air induction and exhaust gas recirculation; fuel feed: electric pump; water-cooled, 12.3 imp pt, 14.8 US pt, 7 l.

TRANSMISSION driving wheels: front; clutch: single dry plate (diaphragm); gearbox: mechanical; gears: 4, fully synchronized - SG-S models 5; ratios: I 3.307, II 1.833, III 1.233, IV 0.970 (SG-S models V 0.795), rev 3.133; lever: central; final drive: hypoid bevel; axle ratio: 3.850; width of rims: 4.5"; tyres: 6.45 x 13.

PERFORMANCE max speeds: (I) 30 mph, 48 km/h; (II) 54 mph, 87 km/h; (III) 81 mph, 130 km/h; (IV) and (V) 99 mph, 160 km/h; power-weight ratio: SG-S Sedan 23.8 lb/hp (32.6 lb/kW), 10.8 kg/hp (14.8 kg/kW); consumption: 40.4 m/imp gal, 33.6 m/US gal, 7 l x 100 km on Japanese emission test cycle.

CHASSIS integral; front suspension: independent, by McPherson, coil springs/telescopic damper struts, transverse arms, trailing locating rods, anti-roll bar; rear: independent, by Mazda TTL, lower trailing arms, upper torque rods, coil springs, telescopic dampers - SG-L and SG-S models anti-roll bar.

STEERING rack-and-pinion; turns lock to lock: 3.80.

BRAKES front disc, rear drum, dual circuit, servo; lining area: front 22.9 sq in, 148 sq cm, rear 39.7 sq in, 256 sq cm, total 62.6 sq in, 404 sq cm.

ELECTRICAL EQUIPMENT 12 V; 33 Ah battery; 60 A alternator; IC high energy ignition; 4 headlamps.

DIMENSIONS AND WEIGHT wheel base: 98.82 in, 251 cm; tracks: 56.29 in, 143 cm front, 55.90 in, 142 cm rear; length: 174.40 in, 443 cm; width: 65.53 in, 169 cm; height: sedans 54.72 in, 139 cm - coupés 53.35 in, 135 cm; ground clearance: 6.10 in, 15.5 cm; weight: SG Sedan and SG-L Coupé 2,083 lb, 945 kg - SG-S Coupé 2,094 lb, 950 kg - SG-L Sedan 2,105 lb, 955 kg - SG-S Sedan 2,138 lb, 970 kg; weight distribution: 62% front, 38% rear; turning circle: 33.4 ft, 10.2 m; fuel tank: 13.2 imp gal, 15.8 US gal, 60 l.

BODY saloon/sedan, 4 doors - coupé, 2 doors; 5 seats, separate front seats.

OPTIONALS JATCO automatic transmission, hydraulic torque converter and planetary gears with 3 ratios (I 2.841, II 1.541, III 1, rev 2.400), 3.631 axle ratio; power steering; air-conditioning.

100 hp power team

See 90 hp power team, except for:

ENGINE 109.1 cu in, 1,789 cc (3.38 x 3.03 in, 86 x 77 mm); max power (JIS): 100 hp (74 kW) at 5,700 rpm; max torque (JIS): 100 lb ft, 15.2 kg m (149 Nm) at 3,500 rpm; 55.9 hp/l (41.1 kW/l).

MAZDA Capella 2000 Turbo GT-X Sedan

MAZDA Luce RE 13 B Limited Hardtop

TRANSMISSION gears: 5, fully synchronized; ratios: I 3.307, II 1.833, III 1.233, IV 0.970, V 0.755, rev 3.133; width of rims: GT-S models 5"; tyres: GT-S models 185/70 SR x 13.

PERFORMANCE max speed: 105 mph, 170 km/h; power-weight ratio: SG-X Sedan 21.9 lb/hp (29.7 lb/kW), 9.9 kg/hp (13.4 kg/kW); consumption: 37.7 m/imp gal, 31.4 m/US gal, 7.5 l x 100 km on Japanese emission test cycle.

CHASSIS rear suspension: anti-roll bar (except SG-L Sedan).

DIMENSIONS AND WEIGHT height: sedans 54.72 in, 139 cm - coupés 53.14 in, 135 cm; weight: SG-S Coupé 2,105 lb, 955 kg - SG-L Sedan and GT-S Coupé 2,127 lb, 965 kg - GT-S Sedan 2,138 lb, 970 kg - SG-X Sedan 2,160 lb 980 kg.

120 hp power team

See 90 hp power team, except for:

ENGINE 121.9 cu in, 1,998 cc (3.38 x 3.38 in, 86 x 86 mm); max power (JIS): 120 hp (88 kW) at 5,500 rpm; max torque (JIS): 124 lb ft, 17 kg m (167 Nm) at 3,000 rpm; max engine rpm: 5,800; 60 hp/l (44.2 kW/l); electronic fuel injection with single point injector.

TRANSMISSION gears: 5, fully synchronized; ratios: I 3.307, II 1.833, III 1.233, IV 0.970, V 0.795, rev 3.133; width of rims: Limited 5" - GT-X models 5.5"; tyres: Limited 165 SR x 14 - GT-X models 185/70 SR x 14.

PERFORMANCE max speeds: (I) 31 mph, 50 km/h; (II) 54 mph, 87 km/h; (III) 83 mph, 133 km/h; (IV) 105 mph, 170 km/h; (V) 112 mph, 180 km/h; power-weight ratio: Limited 19.1 lb/hp (26 lb/kW), 8.6 kg/hp (11.8 kg/kW); consumption: 35.3 m/imp gal, 29.4 m/US gal, 8 l x 100 km on Japanese emission test cycle.

STEERING servo (standard); turns lock to lock: 3.

BRAKES disc, servo; lining area: front 31.3 sq in, 202 sq cm, rear 18.6 sq in, 120 sq cm, total 49.9 sq in, 322 sq cm.

DIMENSIONS AND WEIGHT length: 177.75 in, 451 cm; height: sedans 55.51 in, 141 cm - Coupé 53.54 in, 136 cm; weight: GT-X Coupé 2,271 lb, 1,030 kg - GT-X Sedan 2,282 lb, 1,035 kg - Limited Sedan 2,293 lb, 1,040 kg.

OPTIONALS with JATCO automatic transmission 3.450 axle ratio; air-conditioning; 195/60 R x 15 tyres.

145 hp power team

See 90 hp power team, except for:

ENGINE turbocharged; 121.9 cu in, 1,998 cc (3.38 x 3.38 in, 86 x 86 mm); compression ratio: 7.8:1; max power (JIS): 145 hp (107 kW) at 5,000 rpm; max torque (JIS): 159 lb ft, 22 kg m (216 Nm) at 3,000 rpm; 73 hp/l (53.4 kW/l); electronic fuel injection with single point injector; turbocharger with wastegate.

TRANSMISSION gears: 5, fully synchronized; ratios: I 3.307, II 1.883, III 1.233, IV 0.914, V 0.755, rev 3.133; width of rims: 5.5"; tyres: 185/70 HR x 14.

PERFORMANCE max speed: 112 mph, 180 km/h; power-weight ratio: GT 4-dr 16.2 lb/hp (22 lb/kW), 7.3 kg/hp (9.9 kg/kW); consumption: 34.8 m/imp gal, 29 m/US gal, 8.1 l x 100 km on Japanese emission test cycle.

DIMENSIONS AND WEIGHT weight: GT, GT-S and GT-X 4-dr 2,348 lb, 1,065 kg - GT-S and GT-X 2-dr 2,304 lb, 1,045 kg.

OPTIONALS 195/60 R x 15 H tyres.

72 hp (diesel) power team

See 90 hp power team, except for:

ENGINE diesel; 121.9 cu in, 1,998 cc (3.38 x 3.38 in, 86 x 86 mm); compression ratio: 22.7:1; max power (JIS): 72 hp (53 kW) at 4,650 rpm; max torque (JIS): 100 lb ft, 13.8 kg m (135 Nm) at 2,750 rpm; 36 hp/l (26.5 kW/l); valves: in line, rockers, thimble tappets; camshafts: 1, overhead, cogged belt; Ricardo Comet swirl combustion chambers; lubrication: 10.6 imp pt, 12.7 US pt, 6 l; Bosch VE injection pump; cooling: 15.8 imp pt, 19 US pt, 9 l.

TRANSMISSION gears: 5, fully synchronized; ratios: I 3.307, II 1.833, III 1.233, IV 0.914, V 0.755, rev 3.133; tyres: 165 SR x 13.

PERFORMANCE power-weight ratio: SG-L 31.7 lb/hp (43.1 lb/kW), 14.4 kg/hp (19.5 kg/kW); consumption: 76.3 m/imp gal, 63.5 m/US gal, 3.7 l x 100 km at 37 mph, 60 km/h.

DIMENSIONS AND WEIGHT weight: SG-L 2,282 lb, 1,035 kg - SG-X 2,304 lb, 1,045 kg.

BODY saloon/sedan; 4 doors.

OPTIONALS JATCO automatic transmission, hydraulic torque converter and planetary gears with 3 ratios (I 2.841, II 1.541, III 1, rev 2.400), 3.450 axle ratio.

Luce Series

PRICES (Tokyo):		yen
1	2000 SG-L 4-dr Sedan	1,337,000
2	2000 SG-S 4-dr Sedan	1,431,000
3	2000 SG-X 4-dr Sedan	1,553,000
4	2000 SG-X 4-dr Hardtop	1,639,000
5	2000 EGI SG-X 4-dr Sedan	1,690,000
6	2000 EGI SG-X 4-dr Hardtop	1,796,000
7	RE 12 A GS-X 4-dr Sedan	1,560,000
8	RE 12 A GS-X 4-dr Hardtop	1,673,000
9	RE 12 A Turbo Limited 4-dr Sedan	2,356,000
10	RE 12 A Turbo Limited 4-dr Hardtop	2,437,000
11	RE 12 A Turbo GT 4-dr Sedan	1,894,000
12	RE 12 A Turbo GT 4-dr Hardtop	1,976,000
13	RE 13 B Limited 4-dr Sedan	2,388,000
14	RE 13 B Limited 4-dr Hardtop	2,469,000
15	DE SG-L 4-dr Sedan	1,462,000
16	DE SG-X 4-dr Sedan	1,708,000

Power team:	Standard for:	Optional for:
110 hp	1 to 4	—
120 hp	5,6	—
130 hp	7,8	—
160 hp	13,14	—
165 hp	9 to 12	—
70 hp (diesel)	15,16	—

110 hp power team

ENGINE front, 4 stroke; 4 cylinders, in line; 121.9 cu in, 1,998 cc (3.38 x 3.38 in, 86 x 86 mm); compression ratio: 8.6:1; max power (JIS): 110 hp (81 kW) at 5,500 rpm; max torque (JIS): 123 lb ft, 17 kg m (167 Nm) at 3,000 rpm; max engine rpm: 6,000; 55 hp/l (40.5 kW/l); cast iron block, light alloy head; 5 crankshaft bearings; valves: overhead, Vee-slanted, rockers; camshafts: 1, overhead, cogged belt; lubrication: gear pump, full flow filter, 7.6 imp pt, 9.1 US pt, 4.3 l; 1 Nikki downdraught twin barrel carburettor; Mazda stabilized combustion system with 3-way catalytic converter, secondary air induction and exhaust gas recirculation; fuel feed: electric pump; water-cooled, 12.3 imp pt, 14.8 US pt, 7 l.

TRANSMISSION driving wheels: rear; clutch: single dry plate (diaphragm); gearbox: mechanical; gears: 4, fully synchronized; ratios: I 3.489, II 1.888, III 1.330, IV 1, V 0.851, rev 3.758; lever: central; final drive: hypoid bevel; axle ratio: 3.727; width of rims: 5.5"; tyres: SG-L 6.45 x 14 - SG-X models 175 SR x 14.

PERFORMANCE power-weight ratio: SG-L 21.4 lb/hp (29.1 lb/kW), 9.7 kg/hp (13.2 kg/kW); consumption: 34.4 m/imp gal, 28.7 m/US gal, 8.2 l x 100 km on Japanese emission test cycle.

CHASSIS integral; front suspension: independent, by McPherson, coil springs/telescopic damper struts, lower transverse arms, trailing links, anti-roll bar; rear: rigid axle, trailing arms, upper torque rods, Panhard rod, coil springs, telescopic dampers.

STEERING rack-and-pinion, servo; turns lock to lock: 4.50.

BRAKES front disc, rear drum, dual circuit, servo; lining area: front 26.6 sq in, 172 sq cm, rear 59.5 sq in, 384 sq cm, total 86.1 sq in, 556 sq cm.

ELECTRICAL EQUIPMENT 12 V; 33 Ah battery; 60 A alternator; fully transistorized ignition; 4 headlamps.

DIMENSIONS AND WEIGHT wheel base: 102.76 in, 261 cm; tracks: 56.30 in, 143 cm front, 55.12 in, 140 cm rear; length: sedans 184.64 in, 469 cm - Hardtop 183.66 in, 466 cm; width: 66.54 in, 169 cm; height: sedans 55.71 in, 141 cm - Hardtop 53.54 in, 136 cm; weight: SG-L 2,359 lb, 1,070 kg - SG-S 2,392 lb, 1,085 kg - SG-X Sedan 2,403 lb, 1,090 kg - SG-X Hardtop 2,436 lb, 1,105 kg.

BODY saloon/sedan - hardtop; 4 doors; 5 seats, separate front seats.

OPTIONALS JATCO automatic transmission, hydraulic torque converter and planetary gears with 3 ratios (I 2.841, II 1.541, III 1, rev 2.400), 3.909 axle ratio.

120 hp power team

See 110 hp power team, except for:

ENGINE max power (JIS): 120 hp (86 kW) at 5,500 rpm; max torque (JIS): 123 lb ft, 17 kg m (167 Nm) at 3,300 rpm; 60.9 hp/l (43.7 kW/l); Denso-Bosch L-Jetronic electronic injection; 3-way catalyst with oxygen sensor.

TRANSMISSION axle ratio: 3.909; tyres: Sedan 175 SR x 14 - Hardtop 195/70 SR x 14.

PERFORMANCE consumption: 32.8 m/imp gal, 27.3 m/US gal, 8.6 l x 100 km on Japanese emission test cycle.

CHASSIS rear suspension: independent, semi-trailing arms, coil springs, anti-roll bar, telescopic dampers.

BRAKES disc.

DIMENSIONS AND WEIGHT rear track: 55.90 in, 142 cm; weight: Sedan 2,491 lb, 1,130 kg - Hardtop 2,536 lb, 1,150 kg.

OPTIONALS JATCO automatic transmission, hydraulic torque converter and planetary gears with 4 ratios (I 2.841, II 1.541, III 1, IV 0.720, rev 2.400).

130 hp power team

See 110 hp power team, except for:

ENGINE front, 4 stroke, Wankel rotary type with Mazda emission control system (oxidizing partially 3-way catalytic converter and secondary air injection); 2 co-axial 3-lobe rotors; 35 x 2 cu in, 573 x 2 cc; max power (JIS): 130 hp (96 kW) at 7,000 rpm; max torque (JIS): 120 lb ft, 16.5 kg m (162 Nm) at 4,000 rpm; lubrication: trochoid pump, full flow filter, forced lubrication/cooling of rotors, 9.2 imp pt, 11.2 US pt, 5.2 l; 1 downdraught 4-barrel carburettor; water-cooled housings, 15.8 imp pt, 19 US pt, 9 l, oil-cooled rotors.

TRANSMISSION gearbox: mechanical with hydraulic fluid coupling; gearbox ratios: I 3.622, II 2.186, III 1.419, IV 1, V 0.858, rev 3.493; axle ratio: 4.100; width of rims: 5.5"; tyres: 175 SR x 14.

PERFORMANCE max speed: 112 mph, 180 km/h; power-weight ratio: Sedan 19 lb/hp (25.9 lb/kW), 8.6 kg/hp (11.8 kg/kW); consumption: 28.2 m/imp gal, 23.5 m/US gal, 10 l x 100 km on Japanese emission test cycle.

MAZDA Luce RE 13 B Limited Hardtop

130 HP POWER TEAM

CHASSIS rear suspension: independent, semi-trailing arms, anti-roll bar.

STEERING servo; turns lock to lock: 3.50.

BRAKES disc, front internal radial fins, servo.

DIMENSIONS AND WEIGHT rear track: 55.90 in, 142 cm; weight: Sedan 2,481 lb, 1,125 kg - Hardtop 2,513 lb, 1,140 kg.

OPTIONALS JATCO automatic transmission, hydraulic torque converter and planetary gears with 4 ratios (I 2.841, II 1.541, III 1, IV 0.720, rev 2.400).

160 hp power team

See 110 hp power team, except for:

ENGINE front, 4 stroke, Wankel rotary type with Mazda emission control system (partially oxidizing 3-way catalytic converter and secondary air injection); 2 co-axial 3-lobe rotors; 40 x 2 cu in, 654 x 2 cc; max power (JIS): 160 hp (118 kW) at 6,000 rpm; max torque (JIS): 149 lb ft, 20.5 kg m (201 Nm) at 3,000 rpm; electronic fuel injection with one injector per bank; 6 petrol injectors induction system with positively controlled power, secondary ports and resonance charge, plenum chamber-induction tracts; lubrication: 9.1 imp pt, 11 US pt, 5.2 l; water-cooled housings, 15.8 imp pt, 19 US pt, 9 l, oil-cooled rotors.

TRANSMISSION gearbox: JATCO automatic transmission hydraulic torque converter and planetary gears with 4 ratios; ratios: I 2.841, II 1.541, III 1, IV 0.791, rev 2.400; axle ratio: 4.100; tyres: 195/70 SR x 14.

PERFORMANCE power-weight ratio: Limited Sedan 16.8 lb/hp (22.8 lb/kW), 7.6 kg/hp (10.3 kg/kW); consumption: 22 m/imp gal, 18.7 m/US gal, 12.6 l x 100 km on Japanese emission test cycle.

CHASSIS rear suspension: independent, semi-trailing arms, coil springs, anti-roll bar, electronically controlled dampers automatic or manual levelling control.

BRAKES disc, internal radial fins.

DIMENSIONS AND WEIGHT rear track: 55.90 in, 142 cm; weight: Limited Sedan 2,679 lb, 1,215 kg - Limited Hardtop 2,723 lb, 1,235 kg.

165 hp power team

See 110 hp power team, except for:

ENGINE turbocharged, front, 4 stroke; Wankel rotary type with Mazda emission control system (oxidizing partially 3-way catalytic converter and secondary air injection); 2 co-axial 3-lobe rotors; 35 x 2 cu in, 573 x 2 cc; max power (JIS): 165 hp (121 kW) at 6,500 rpm; max torque (JIS): 166 lb ft, 23 kg m (225 Nm) at 4,000 rpm; max engine rpm: 7,000; lubrication: trochoid pump, full flow filter, forced lubrication/cooling of rotors, 9.2 imp pt, 11.2 US pt, 5.2 l; electronic injection; fuel feed: electric pump; turbocharger; water-cooled housings, 14.1 imp pt, 17 US pt, 8 l, oil-cooled rotors.

TRANSMISSION gearbox ratios: I 3.622, II 2.186, III 1.419, IV 1, V 0.791, rev 3.493; axle ratio: 3.909; tyres: 195/70 SR x 14.

PERFORMANCE max speed: 132 mph, 213 km/h; power-weight ratio: Limited Sedan 16 lb/hp (21.8 lb/kW), 7.3 kg/hp (9.9 kg/kW); consumption: 27.7 m/imp gal, 23.1 m/US gal, 10.2 l x 100 km on Japanese emission test cycle.

CHASSIS front suspension: anti-roll bar; rear: independent, semi-trailing arms, coil springs, anti-roll bar, telescopic dampers.

MAZDA Cosmo 2000 XG-X Sedan

STEERING servo.

BRAKES disc, internal radial fins, servo.

DIMENSIONS AND WEIGHT tracks: 56.30 in, 143 cm front, 55.90 in, 142 cm rear; length: sedans 183.86 in, 467 cm - hardtops 182.68 in, 464 cm; weight: Limited Sedan 2,646 lb, 1,200 kg - Limited Hardtop 2,679 lb, 1,215 kg - GT Sedan 2,547 lb, 1,155 kg - GT Hardtop 2,569 lb, 1,165 kg.

OPTIONALS electric sunroof; trip computer; JATCO automatic transmission, hydraulic torque converter with 4 ratios (I 2.841, II 1.541, III 1, IV 0.720, rev 2.400).

70 hp (diesel) power team

See 110 hp power team, except for:

ENGINE diesel; 134.2 cu in, 2,200 cc; compression ratio: 21:1; max power (JIS): 70 hp (50 kW) at 4,000 rpm; max torque (JIS): 105 lb ft, 14.5 kg m (142 Nm) at 2,400 rpm; 31.8 hp/l (22.7 kW/l); cast iron block and head; valves: overhead, in line, push-rods and rockers; camshafts: 1, side; swirl chamber type; Bosch VE injection; cooling: 17.6 imp pt, 21.1 US pt, 10 l.

TRANSMISSION gearbox ratios: I 3.622, II 2.186, III 1.419, IV 1, V 0.791, rev 3.493; tyres: 175 SR x 14.

PERFORMANCE max speed: 87 mph, 140 km/h; power-weight ratio: DE SG-L 36.8 lb/hp (50.1 lb/kW), 16.7 kg/hp (22.7 kg/kW); consumption: 62.8 m/imp gal, 52.3 m/US gal, 4.5 l x 100 km at 37 mph, 60 km/h.

DIMENSIONS AND WEIGHT weight: DE SG-L 2,580 lb, 1,170 kg - DE SG-X 2,668 lb, 1,210 kg.

Cosmo Series

PRICES (Tokyo):		yen
1	2000 XG-L 4-dr Sedan	**1,337,000**
2	2000 XG-S 4-dr Sedan	**1,431,000**
3	2000 XG-X 4-dr Sedan	**1,553,000**
4	2000 XG-X 4-dr Hardtop	**1,639,000**
5	2000 XG-X 2-dr Coupé	**1,656,000**
6	2000 EGI XG-X 4-dr Sedan	**1,690,000**
7	2000 EGI XG-X 4-dr Hardtop	**1,796,000**
8	2000 EGI XG-X 2-dr Coupé	**1,798,000**
9	RE 12 A GS-X 4-dr Sedan	**1,560,000**
10	RE 12 A GS-X 4-dr Hardtop	**1,673,000**
11	RE 12 A GS-X 2-dr Coupé	**1,667,000**
12	RE 12 A Turbo Limited 4-dr Sedan	**2,356,000**
13	RE 12 A Turbo Limited 4-dr Hardtop	**2,437,000**
14	RE 12 A Turbo Limited 2-dr Coupé	**2,485,000**
15	RE 12 A Turbo GT 4-dr Sedan	**1,894,000**
16	RE 12 A Turbo GT 4-dr Hardtop	**1,976,000**
17	RE 12 A Turbo GT 2-dr Coupé	**1,963,000**
18	RE 13 B Limited 4-dr Sedan	**2,388,000**
19	RE 13 B Limited 4-dr Hardtop	**2,469,000**
20	DE 2200 XG-L 4-dr Sedan	**1,462,000**
21	DE 2200 XG-X 4-dr Sedan	**1,708,000**

Power team:	Standard for:	Optional for:
110 hp	1 to 5	—
120 hp	6 to 8	—
130 hp	9 to 11	—
160 hp	18,19	—
165 hp	12 to 17	—
70 hp (diesel)	20,21	—

110 hp power team

ENGINE front, 4 stroke, 4 cylinders, in line; 121.9 cu in, 1,998 cc (3.38 x 3.38 in, 86 x 86 mm); compression ratio: 8.6:1; max power (JIS): 110 hp (81 kW) at 5,500 rpm; max torque (JIS): 123 lb ft, 17 kg m (167 Nm) at 3,000 rpm; max engine rpm: 6,000; 55 hp/l (40.5 kW/l); cast iron block, light alloy head; 5 crankshaft bearings; valves: overhead, Vee-slanted, rockers; camshafts: 1, overhead, cogged belt; lubrication: gear pump, full flow filter, 7.6 imp pt, 9.1 US pt, 4.3 l; 1 Nikki downdraught twin barrel carburettor; Mazda stabilized combustion system with 3-way catalytic converter, secondary air induction and exhaust gas recirculation; fuel feed: electric pump; water-cooled, 12.3 imp pt, 14.8 US pt, 7 l.

TRANSMISSION driving wheels: rear; clutch: single dry plate (diaphragm); gearbox: mechanical; gears: 5, fully synchronized; ratios: I 3.489, II 1.888, III 1.330, IV 1, V 0.851, rev 3.758; lever: central; final drive: hypoid bevel; axle ratio: 3.727; width of rims: 5.5"; tyres: XG-L 6.45 x 14 - XG-S 175 SR x 14.

PERFORMANCE power-weight ratio: XG-L 21.4 lb/hp (29.1 lb/kW), 9.7 kg/hp (13.2 kg/kW); consumption: 34.4 m/imp gal, 28.7 m/US gal, 8.2 l x 100 km on Japanese emission test cycle.

CHASSIS integral; front suspension: independent, by McPherson, coil springs/telescopic damper struts, lower transverse arms, trailing links, anti-roll bar; rear: rigid axle, trailing arms, upper torque rods, Panhard rod, coil springs, telescopic dampers.

STEERING rack-and-pinion, servo; turns lock to lock: 4.50.

BRAKES front disc, rear drum, dual circuit, servo; lining area: front 26.6 sq in, 172 sq cm, rear 59.5 sq in, 384 sq cm, total 86.1 sq in, 556 sq cm.

ELECTRICAL EQUIPMENT 12 V; 33 Ah battery; 60 A alternator; transistorized ignition; 2 headlamps.

DIMENSIONS AND WEIGHT wheel base: 102.76 in, 261 cm; tracks: 53.30 in, 143 cm front, 55.12 in, 140 cm rear; length: sedans 184.64 in, 469 cm - Hardtop and Coupé 183.66 in, 466 cm; width: 66.54 in, 169 cm; height: sedans 55.71 in, 141 cm - Hardtop 53.54 in, 136 cm - Coupé 52.75 in, 134 cm; weight: XG-L 2,359 lb, 1,070 kg - XG-S 2,392 lb, 1,085 kg - XG-X Sedan 2,403 lb, 1,090 kg - XG-X Hardtop 2,436 lb, 1,105 kg - XG-X Coupé 2,469 lb, 1,120 kg.

BODY saloon/sedan, 4 doors - hardtop, 4 doors - coupé, 2 doors; 5 seats, separate front seats.

OPTIONALS JATCO automatic transmission, hydraulic torque converter and planetary gears with 3 ratios (I 2.841, II 1.541, III 1, rev 2.400), 3.909 axle ratio.

MAZDA Cosmo RE 13 B Limited Sedan

120 hp power team

See 110 hp power team, except for:

ENGINE max power (JIS): 120 hp (86 kW) at 5,500 rpm; max torque (JIS): 123 lb ft, 17 kg m (167 Nm) at 3,500 rpm; 60.1 hp/l (44.2 kW/l); Denso-Bosch L-Jetronic electronic injection; 3-way catalyst with oxygen sensor.

TRANSMISSION axle ratio: 3.909; tyres: Sedan 175 SR x 14 - XG-X hardtop and coupé 195/70 SR x 14.

PERFORMANCE power-weight ratio: XG-X sedan 20.8 lb/hp (28.2 lb/kW), 9.4 kg/hp (12.8 kg/kW); consumption: 32.4 m/imp gal, 27 m/US gal, 8.6 l x 100 km on Japanese emission test cycle.

CHASSIS rear suspension: independent, semi-trailing arms, coil springs/telescopic dampers, anti-roll bar.

BRAKES disc, front internal radial fins.

DIMENSIONS AND WEIGHT rear track: 55.90 in, 142 cm; height: coupé 52.75 in, 134 cm; weight: XG-X 2,492 lb, 1,130 kg - XG-X hardtop 2,536 lb, 1,150 kg - coupé 2,503 lb, 1,135 kg.

OPTIONALS JATCO automatic transmission, hydraulic torque converter with top gear lack up and 4 ratios (I 2.841, II 1.541, III 1, IV 0.720, rev 2.400).

130 hp power team

See 110 hp power team, except for:

ENGINE front, 4 stroke, Wankel rotary type with Mazda emission control system (oxidizing partially 3-way catalytic converter and secondary air injection); 2 co-axial 3-lobe rotors; 35 x 2 cu in, 573 x 2 cc; max power (JIS): 130 hp (96 kW) at 7,000 rpm; max torque (JIS): 120 lb ft, 16.5 kg m (162 Nm) at 4,000 rpm; lubrication: trochoid pump, full flow filter, forced lubrication/cooling of rotors, 9.2 imp pt, 11.2 US pt, 5.2 l; 1 downdraught 4-barrel carburettor; water-cooled housings, 15.8 imp pt, 19 US pt, 9 l.

TRANSMISSION gearbox: mechanical with hydraulic fluid coupling; gears: 5, fully synchronized; ratios: I 3.622, II 2.186, III 1.419, IV 1, V 0.858, rev 3.493; axle ratio: 4.100; tyres: 195/70 SR x 14.

PERFORMANCE max speed: 112 mph, 180 km/h; power-weight ratio: GS-X sedan 19.2 lb/hp (26 lb/kW), 8.7 kg/hp (11.8 kg/kW); consumption: 28.2 m/imp gal, 23.5 m/US gal, 10 l x 100 km on Japanese emission test cycle.

CHASSIS rear suspension: independent, semi-trailing arms, coil springs/telescopic dampers, anti-roll bar.

STEERING servo; turns lock to lock: 3.50.

BRAKES disc, front internal radial fins, servo.

DIMENSIONS AND WEIGHT rear track: 55.90 in, 142 cm; weight: GS-X sedan 2,492 lb, 1,130 kg - GS-X hardtop 2,536 lb, 1,150 kg - GS-X coupé 2,503 lb, 1,135 kg.

OPTIONALS JATCO automatic transmission, hydraulic torque converter with top gear lockup and 4 ratios (I 2.841, II 1.541, III 1, IV 0.720, rev 2.400).

160 hp power team

See 110 hp power team, except for:

ENGINE front, 4 stroke, Wankel rotary type with Mazda emission control system (partially oxidizing 3-way catalytic converter and secondary air injection); 2 co-axial 3-lobe rotors; 40 x 2 cu in, 654 x 2 cc; max power (JIS): 160 hp (118 kW) at 6,000 rpm; max torque (JIS): 149 lb ft, 20.5 kg m (201 Nm) at 3,000 rpm; electronic fuel injection with one injector per bank; 6 petrol injectors induction system with positively controlled power, secondary ports and resonance charge, plenum chamber-induction tracts; lubrication: 9.1 imp pt, 11 US pt, 5.2 l; water-cooled housings, 15.8 imp pt, 19 US pt, 9 l, oil-cooled rotors.

MAZDA Cosmo RE 13 B Limited Hardtop

TRANSMISSION gearbox: JATCO automatic transmission, hydraulic torque converter and planetary gears with 4 ratios; ratios: I 2.841, II 1.541, III 1, IV 0.791, rev 2.400; axle ratio: 4.100; tyres: 195/70 SR x 14.

PERFORMANCE power-weight ratio: Limited Sedan 16.8 lb/hp (22.8 lb/kW), 7.6 kg/hp (10.3 kg/kW); consumption: 22 m/imp gal, 18.7 m/US gal, 12.6 l x 100 km on Japanese emission test cycle.

CHASSIS rear suspension: independent, semi-trailing arms, coil springs, anti-roll bar, electronically controlled dampers automatic or manual levelling control.

BRAKES disc, internal radial fins.

ELECTRICAL EQUIPMENT 4 headlamps.

DIMENSIONS AND WEIGHT rear track: 55.90 in, 142 cm; weight: Limited Sedan 2,679 lb, 1,215 kg - Limited Hardtop 2,723 lb, 1,235 kg.

BODY saloon/sedan - hardtop; 4 doors.

165 hp power team

See 110 hp power team, except for:

ENGINE turbocharged; front, 4 stroke, Wankel rotary type with Mazda emission control system (oxidizing partially 3-way catalytic converter and secondary air injection); 2 co-axial 3-lobe rotors; 35 x 2 cu in, 573 x 2 cc; max power (JIS): 165 hp (121 kW) at 6,500 rpm; max torque (JIS): 166 lb ft, 23 kg m (225 Nm) at 4,000 rpm; max engine rpm: 7,000; lubrication: trochoid pump, full flow filter, forced lubrication/cooling of rotors, 9.2 imp pt, 11.2 US pt, 5.2 l; electronic injection; fuel feed: electric pump; turbocharger; water-cooled housings, 14.1 imp pt, 17 US pt, 8 l, oil-cooled rotors.

TRANSMISSION gearbox: mechanical; gearbox ratios: I 3.622, II 2.186, III 1.419, IV 1, V 0.791, rev 3.493; axle ratio: 3.909; tyres: 195/70 SR x 14.

PERFORMANCE max speed: 132 mph, 213 km/h; power-weight ratio: Limited Sedan 16.1 lb/hp (21.8 lb/kW), 7.2 kg/hp (9.9 kg/kW); consumption: 27.7 m/imp gal, 23.1 m/US gal, 10.2 l x 100 km on Japanese emission test cycle.

CHASSIS front suspension: anti-roll bar; rear: independent, semi-trailing arms, coil springs, anti-roll bar, telescopic dampers - Limited models electronically adjustable dampers.

BRAKES disc, internal radial fins, servo.

DIMENSIONS AND WEIGHT rear track: 55.90 in, 142 cm; weight: Limited Sedan 2,646 lb, 1,200 kg - Limited Hardtop 2,679 lb, 1,215 kg - Limited Coupé 2,657 lb, 1,205 kg - GT Sedan 2,536 lb, 1,150 kg - GT Hardtop 2,569 lb, 1,165 kg - GT Coupé 2,547 lb, 1,155 kg.

OPTIONALS JATCO automatic transmission hydraulic torque converter and planetary gears with 4 ratios; ratios: I 2.841, II 1.541, III 1, IV 0.720, rev 2.400); electric sunroof; trip computer.

70 hp (diesel) power team

See 110 hp power team, except for:

ENGINE diesel; 134.2 cu in, 2,200 cc; compression ratio: 21:1; max power (JIS): 70 hp (50 kW) at 4,000 rpm; max torque (JIS): 105 lb ft, 14.5 kg m (142 Nm) at 2,400 rpm; 31.8 hp/l (22.7 kW/l); cast iron block and head; valves: overhead, in line, push-rods and rockers; camshafts: 1, side; swirl chambers type; Bosch VE injection; cooling: 17.6 imp pt, 21.1 US pt, 10 l.

TRANSMISSION gearbox ratios: I 3.622, II 2.186, III 1.419, IV 1, V 0.791, rev 3.493; tyres: 175 SR x 14.

PERFORMANCE max speed: 87 mph, 140 km/h; power-weight ratio: XG-L 36.9 lb/hp (50.1 lb/kW), 16.7 kg/hp (22.7 kg/kW); consumption: 62.8 m/imp gal, 52.3 m/US gal, 4.5 l x 100 km at 37 mph, 60 km/h.

DIMENSIONS AND WEIGHT weight: XG-L Sedan 2,580 lb, 1,170 kg - XG-X Sedan 2,668 lb, 1,210 kg.

BODY saloon/sedan; 4 doors.

626

PRICES IN USA:	$
De Luxe 4-dr Sedan	7,895*
De Luxe 2-dr Coupé	8,295*
Luxury 4-dr Sedan	9,445*
Luxury 2-dr Coupé	9,845*
Luxury 4+1-dr Hatchback Sedan	10,395*

ENGINE front, 4 stroke; 4 cylinders, in line: 121.9 cu in, 1,998 cc (3.38 x 3.38 in, 86 x 86 mm); compression ratio: 8.6:1; max power (SAE net): 83 hp (61 kW) at 4,800 rpm; max torque (SAE net): 105 lb ft, 14.5 kg m (142 Nm) at 2,500 rpm; 41.5 hp/l (30.5 kW/l); cast iron block, light alloy head; 5 crankshaft bearings; valves: overhead, rockers; camshafts: 1, overhead; lubrication: gear pump, full flow filter, 7.7 imp pt, 9.3 US pt, 4.4 l; 1 Nikki 242302 downdraught twin barrel carburettor with automatic air-fuel ratio adjustment; Mazda stabilized combustion system with 3-way catalytic converter, secondary air induction and exhaust gas recirculation; fuel feed: electric pump; water-cooled, 12.5 imp pt, 15 US pt, 7.1 l.

TRANSMISSION driving wheels: front; clutch: single dry plate (diaphragm); gearbox: mechanical; gears: 5, fully synchronized; ratios: I 3.307, II 1.833, III 1.233, IV 0.970, V 0.795, rev 3.133; lever: central; final drive: hypoid bevel; axle ratio: 3.850; width of rims: 5"; tyres: 165 SR x 14.

PERFORMANCE max speed: 106 mph, 170 km/h; power-weight ratio: De Luxe Sedan 29.1 lb/hp (39.5 lb/kW), 13.1 kg/hp (17.9 kg/kW); consumption: 37.7 m/imp gal, 31.4 m/US gal, 7.5 l x 100 km (EPA).

CHASSIS integral; front suspension: independent, by McPherson, coil springs/telescopic damper struts, transverse arms, trailing locating rods, anti-roll bar; rear: independent, lower trailing arms, upper torque rods, Panhard rod, coil springs, anti-roll bar, telescopic dampers.

STEERING rack-and-pinion; turns lock to lock: 3.80.

BRAKES front disc, rear drum, dual circuit, servo; lining area: front 22.9 sq in, 148 sq cm, rear 39.7 sq in, 256 sq cm, total 62.6 sq in, 404 sq cm.

ELECTRICAL EQUIPMENT 12 V; 50-60 Ah battery; 60 A alternator; IC high energy ignition; 4 headlamps.

DIMENSIONS AND WEIGHT wheel base: 98.82 in, 251 cm; tracks: 56.29 in, 143 cm front, 55.90 in, 142 cm rear; length: 177.75 in, 451 cm; width: 66.53 in, 169 cm; height: De Luxe and Luxury sedans 55.51 in, 141 cm - De Luxe and Luxury coupés and Luxury Hatchback Sedan 53.74 in, 136 cm; ground clearance: 6.30 in, 15 cm; weight: De Luxe and Luxury sedans 2,412 lb, 1,094 kg - De Luxe and Luxury coupés 2,385 lb, 1,082 kg - Luxury Hatchback Sedan 2,425 lb, 1,100 kg; turning circle: 33.5 ft, 10.2 m; fuel tank: 13.2 imp gal, 15.3 US gal, 60 l.

BODY saloon/sedan, 4 or 4+1 doors - coupé, 2 doors; 5 seats, separate front seats, reclining backrests, built-in headrests.

OPTIONALS JATCO automatic transmission, hydraulic torque converter and planetary gears with 3 ratios (I 2.841, II 1.541, III 1, rev 2.400); light alloy wheels with 5.5" wide rims; 185/70 SR x 13 tyres; power steering; air-conditioning.

MAZDA 626 Luxury Hatchback Sedan

Savanna RX 7 Series

PRICES (Tokyo):	yen
1 GT 2+1-dr Coupé	**1,623,000**
2 GT-X 2+1-dr Coupé	**1,878,000**
3 SE Limited 2+1-dr Coupé	**2,274,000**
4 Turbo GT 2+1-dr Coupé	**1,847,000**
5 Turbo GT-X 2+1-dr Coupé	**2,152,000**
6 Turbo SE Limited 2+1-dr Coupé	**2,568,000**

For GB prices, see price index.

Power team:	Standard for:	Optional for:
130 hp	1 to 3	—
165 hp	4 to 6	—

130 hp power team

ENGINE front, 4 stroke, Wankel rotary type with Mazda REAPS emission control system (catalytic converter and secondary air injection); 2 co-axial 3-lobe rotors; 35 x 2 cu in, 573 x 2 cc; compression ratio: 9.4:1; max power (JIS): 130 hp (96 kW) at 7,000 rpm; max torque (JIS): 120 lb ft, 16.5 kg m (162 Nm) at 4,000 rpm; max engine rpm: 7,000; cast iron side housings, light alloy trochoid housings, cast iron rotors; 2 crankshaft bearings; lubrication: trochoid pump, full flow filter, forced lubrication/cooling of rotors, 8.1 imp pt, 9.7 US pt, 4.6 l; 1 Nikki downdraught 4-barrel carburettor; fuel feed: electric pump; water-cooled housings, 16.7 imp pt, 20 US pt, 9.5 l, oil-cooled rotors.

TRANSMISSION driving wheels: rear; clutch: single dry plate (diaphragm), hydraulically controlled; gearbox: mechanical; gears: 5, fully synchronized; ratios: I 3.622, II 2.186, III 1.419, IV 1, V 0.858, rev 3.493; lever: central; final drive: hypoid bevel; axle ratio: 3.933; width of rims: 5"; tyres: 185/70 HR x 13.

PERFORMANCE max speeds: (I) 32 mph, 52 km/h; (II) 54 mph, 87 km/h; (III) 82 mph, 132 km/h; (IV) and (V) 112 mph, 180 km/h; power-weight ratio: GT 17 lb/hp (23 lb/kW), 7.7 kg/hp (10.5 kg/kW); acceleration: standing ¼ mile 15.8 sec; consumption: 25.9 m/imp gal, 21.6 m/US gal, 10.9 l x 100 km on Japanese emission test cycle.

CHASSIS integral; front suspension: independent, by McPherson, coil springs/telescopic damper struts, transverse arms, trailing locating rods, anti-roll bar; rear: rigid axle, lower trailing links, upper torque rods, Watts linkage, coil springs, telescopic dampers.

STEERING recirculating ball; turns lock to lock: 3.70.

BRAKES front disc, internal radial fins, rear drum - SE Limited rear disc, dual circuit, servo; lining area: front 24.8 sq in, 160 sq cm, rear 39.7 sq in, 256 sq cm, total 64.5 sq in, 416 sq cm.

ELECTRICAL EQUIPMENT 12 V; 35 Ah battery; 63 A alternator; 2 retractable headlamps.

DIMENSIONS AND WEIGHT wheel base: 95.30 in, 242 cm; tracks: 55.90 in, 142 cm front, 55.12 in, 140 cm rear; length: 170.08 in, 432 cm; width: 65.94 in, 167 cm; height: 49.60 in, 126 cm; ground clearance: 6.10 in, 15.5 cm; weight: GT 2,194 lb, 995 kg - GT-X and SE Limited 2,205 lb, 1,000 kg; weight distribution: 54% front, 46% rear; turning circle: 34.8 ft, 10.6 m; fuel tank: 12.1 imp gal, 14.5 US gal, 55 l.

BODY coupé; 2+1 doors; 2+2 seats, separate front seats; detachable sunroof (for SE Limited only).

OPTIONALS JATCO automatic transmission, hydraulic torque converter and planetary gears with 4 ratios (I 2.458, II 1.458, III 1, IV 0.720, rev 2.181), acceleration standing ¼ mile 17.4 sec; air-conditioning.

165 hp power team

See 130 hp power team, except for:

ENGINE turbocharged; max power (JIS): 165 hp (121 Nm) at 6,500 rpm; max torque (JIS): 166 lb ft, 23 kg m (225 Nm) at 4,000 rpm; lubrication: 9.2 imp pt, 11 US pt, 5.2 l; electronic fuel injection with one injector per bank; turbocharger with wastegate control; water-cooled housing, 15.3 imp pt, 18.4 US pt, 8.7 l.

TRANSMISSION axle ratio: 3.909; width of rims: 5.5"; tyres: 205/60 R x 14 H.

PERFORMANCE max speed: 143 mph, 230 km/h; power-weight ratio: Turbo GT 13.6 lb/hp (18.5 lb/kW), 6.2 kg/hp (8.4 kg/kW); consumption: 28.2 m/imp gal, 23.5 m/US gal, 10 l x 100 km on Japanese emission test cycle.

CHASSIS front and rear suspension: manually adjustable dampers.

STEERING Turbo GT-X and Turbo SE Limited servo.

BRAKES disc, internal radial fins.

DIMENSIONS AND WEIGHT weight: Turbo GT 2,249 lb, 1,020 kg - Turbo GT-X and Turbo SE Limited 2,282 lb, 1,035 kg.

OPTIONALS sunroof.

MAZDA Savanna RX 7 Turbo SE Limited Coupé

MITSUBISHI JAPAN

Minica Series

PRICES (Tokyo):	yen
1 Econo S 2+1-dr Sedan	**478,000**
2 Econo S II 2+1-dr Sedan	**498,000**
3 Econo L 2+1-dr Sedan	**623,000**
4 Ami TL 2+1-dr Sedan	**578,000**
5 Ami GL 2+1-dr Sedan	**676,000**
6 Ami XL 2+1-dr Sedan	**713,000**
7 Ami LX 2+1-dr Sedan	**755,000**
8 Econo Turbo 2+1-dr Sedan	**615,000**
9 Ami L Turbo 2+1-dr Sedan	**785,000**

Power team:	Standard for:	Optional for:
29 hp	1 to 3	—
31 hp	4 to 7	—
39 hp	8,9	—

29 hp power team

ENGINE front, 4 stroke; 2 cylinders, in line; 33.3 cu in, 546 cc (2.75 x 2.79 in, 70 x 71 mm); compression ratio: 9:1; max power (JIS): 29 hp (21 kW) at 5,500 rpm; max torque (JIS): 30 lb ft, 4.2 kg m (40 Nm) at 3,000 rpm; max engine rpm: 5,800; 53.1 hp/l (39.1 kW/l); cast iron block, light alloy head; 3 crankshaft bearings; valves: overhead, 3 per cylinder (one intake, one exhaust in main combustion chamber, one jet air valve), rockers; camshafts: 1, overhead; lubrication: rotary pump, full flow filter, 5.1 imp pt, 6.1 US pt, 2.9 l; 1 Mikuni 24-30 DIDS downdraught twin barrel carburettor; fuel feed: electric pump; emission control by secondary air induction, catalytic converter and exhaust gas recirculation; water-cooled, 5.3 imp pt, 6.3 US pt, 3 l.

TRANSMISSION driving wheels: rear; clutch: single dry plate (diaphragm); gearbox: mechanical; gears: 4, fully synchronized; ratios: I 3.882, II 1.681, III 1.473, IV 1, rev 4.271; lever: central; final drive: hypoid bevel; axle ratio: 5.428; width of rims: 3.5"; tyres: 5.00 x 10.

MITSUBISHI Minica Ami L Turbo Sedan

PERFORMANCE max speeds: (I) 20 mph, 32 km/h; (II) 34 mph, 55 km/h; (III) 53 mph, 85 km/h; (IV) 68 mph, 110 km/h; power-weight ratio: 42 lb/hp (57 lb/kW), 19 kg/hp (25.8 kg/kW); consumption: 58.8 m/imp gal, 49 m/US gal, 4.8 l x 100 km on Japanese emission test cycle.

CHASSIS integral; front suspension: independent, by McPherson, coil springs/telescopic damper struts, anti-roll bar, lower wishbones (trailing links); rear: rigid axle, lower trailing arms, upper torque rods, Panhard rod, coil springs, telescopic dampers.

STEERING recirculating ball; turns lock to lock: 3.10.

BRAKES drum, dual circuit; lining area: total 67 sq in, 432 sq cm.

ELECTRICAL EQUIPMENT 12 V; 24 Ah battery; 25 A alternator; Mitsubishi distributor; 2 headlamps.

DIMENSIONS AND WEIGHT wheel base: 80.71 in, 205 cm; tracks: 48.03 in, 122 cm front, 46.85 in, 119 cm rear; length: 125.59 in, 319 cm; width: 55.12 in, 140 cm; height: 53.96 in, 137 cm; ground clearance: 5.51 in, 14 cm; weight: 1,213 lb, 550 kg; fuel tank: 5.9 imp gal, 7.1 US gal, 27 l.

BODY saloon/sedan; 2+1 doors; 2 or 4 seats, separate front seats, reclining backrests, built-in headrests; folding rear seat.

OPTIONALS automatic transmission, hydraulic torque converter and planetary gears with 2 ratios (I 1.681, II 1, rev 1.733), 5.428 axle ratio.

31 hp power team

See 29 hp power team, except for:

ENGINE max power (JIS): 31 hp (23 kW) at 5,500 rpm; 56.7 hp/l (41.7 kW/l).

TRANSMISSION axle ratio: 4.625; tyres: 5.20 x 10.

PERFORMANCE power-weight ratio: TL 39.4 lb/hp (53.7 lb/kW), 17.9 kg/hp (24.3 kg/kW).

DIMENSIONS AND WEIGHT height: 52.76 in, 134 cm; weight: Ami TL and GL sedans 1,224 lb, 555 kg - Ami XL Sedan 1,235 lb, 560 kg.

39 hp power team

See 29 hp power team, except for:

ENGINE turbocharged; max power (JIS): 39 hp (29 kW) at 5,500 rpm; max torque (JIS): 40 lb ft, 5.5 kg m (54 Nm) at 3,500 rpm; 71.4 hp/l (52.6 kW/l); turbocharger with wastegate.

TRANSMISSION gearbox ratios: I 3.882, II 2.265, III 1.473, IV 1, rev 4.271; axle ratio: 4.625; tyres: 145 SR x 10.

PERFORMANCE power-weight ratio: 32.3 lb/hp (43.8 lb/kW), 14.6 kg/hp (19.9 kg/kW); consumption: 60.1 m/imp gal, 50 m/US gal, 4.7 l x 100 km on Japanese emission test cycle.

DIMENSIONS AND WEIGHT weight: 1,257 lb, 570 kg.

Lancer EX Series

PRICES (Tokyo):	yen
1 1200 Custom-Business 4-dr Sedan	**772,000**
2 1200 Custom 4-dr Sedan	**816,000**
3 1200 GL 4-dr Sedan	**890,000**
4 1400 GL 4-dr Sedan	**953,000**
5 1400 XL 4-dr Sedan	**983,000**
6 1400 SL 4-dr Sedan	**1,018,000**
7 1600 XL 4-dr Sedan	**1,066,000**
8 1600 XL Super 4-dr Sedan	**1,219,000**
9 1600 GT 4-dr Sedan	**1,106,000**

10	1800 GSL Turbo 4-dr Sedan	**1,598,000**
11	1800 GT Turbo Intercooler 4-dr Sedan	**1,485,000**
12	1800 GSR Turbo Intercooler 4-dr Sedan	**1,640,000**

Power team:	**Standard for:**	**Optional for:**
70 hp	1 to 3	—
80 hp	4 to 6	—
86 hp	7 to 9	—
135 hp	10	—
160 hp	11,12	—

70 hp power team

ENGINE front, 4 stroke; 4 cylinders, vertical, in line; 75.9 cu in, 1,244 cc (2.74 x 3.23 in, 69.5 x 82 mm); compression ratio: 9:1; max power (JIS): 70 hp (51 kW) at 5,500 rpm; max torque (JIS): 78 lb ft, 10.7 kg m (105 Nm) at 3,000 rpm; max engine rpm: 6,000; 56.3 hp/l (41.4 kW/l); cast iron block, light alloy head; 5 crankshaft bearings; valves: overhead, Vee-slanted, 3 per cylinder, two inlet, (one for high swirl effect), rockers; camshafts: 1, overhead; lubrication: rotary pump, full flow filter, 7 imp pt, 8.4 US pt, 4 l; 1 Stromberg 26-30 DIDTA 11 downdraught twin barrel carburettor; fuel feed: mechanical pump; water-cooled, 10.6 imp pt, 12.7 US pt, 6 l.

TRANSMISSION driving wheels: rear; clutch: single dry plate (diaphragm); gearbox: mechanical; gears: 4, fully synchronized - GL 5; ratios: I 3.525, II 2.112, III 1.442, IV 1, rev 3.867 - GL I 3.444, II 2, III 1.316, IV 1, V 0.853, rev 3.667; lever: central; final drive: hypoid bevel; axle ratio: 3.909 - GL 4.222; width of rims: 4"; tyres: 6.15 x 13 - GL 155 SR x 13.

PERFORMANCE max speeds: (I) 28 mph, 45 km/h; (II) 47 mph, 76 km/h; (III) 68 mph, 110 km/h; (IV) 93 mph, 150 km/h; power-weight ratio: Custom 28.1 lb/hp (38.3 lb/kW), 12.8 kg/hp (17.4 kg/kW); consumption: 39.8 m/imp gal, 33.1 m/US gal, 7.1 l x 100 km on Japanese emission test cycle.

CHASSIS integral; front suspension: independent, by McPherson, coil springs/telescopic damper struts, lower wishbones (trailing links), anti-roll bar; rear: rigid axle, lower trailing arms with diagonal reinforcing links, upper diagonal torque rods, coil springs, telescopic dampers.

STEERING recirculating ball, variable ratio; turns lock to lock: 3.80.

BRAKES front disc, rear drum; lining area: front 24.8 sq in, 160 sq cm, rear 47.8 sq in, 308 sq cm, total 72.6 sq in, 468 sq cm.

ELECTRICAL EQUIPMENT 12 V; 60 Ah battery; 40 A alternator; Mitsubishi distributor; 2 headlamps.

DIMENSIONS AND WEIGHT wheel base: 96.06 in, 244 cm; tracks: 52.56 in, 133 cm front, 52.17 in, 132 cm rear; length: 166.34 in, 422 cm; width: 63.78 in, 162 cm; height: 54.33 in, 138 cm; ground clearance: 6.30 in, 16 cm; weight: Custom Sedan 1,973 lb, 895 kg - GL Sedan 1,985 lb, 900 kg; weight distribution: 53% front, 47% rear; turning circle: 34.1 ft, 10.4 m; fuel tank: 11 imp gal, 13.2 US gal, 50 l.

BODY saloon/sedan; 4 doors; 5 seats, separate front seats, reclining backrests, built-in headrests.

OPTIONALS automatic transmission with 3 ratios (I 2.452, II 1.452, III 1, rev 2.214).

80 hp power team

See 70 hp power team, except for:

ENGINE 86 cu in, 1,410 cc (2.91 x 3.23 in, 74 x 82 mm); max power (JIS): 80 hp (59 kW) at 5,500 rpm; max torque (JIS): 88 lb ft, 12.1 kg m (119 Nm) at 3,500 rpm; 58.1 hp/l (42.8 kW/l); 1 Stromberg 28-32 DIDSA downdraught twin barrel carburettor.

TRANSMISSION gears: 4, fully synchronized - SL 5; axle ratio: 3.909 - SL 4.222; tyres: 6.15 x 13 - SL 155 SR x 13.

PERFORMANCE power-weight ratio: GL 24.7 lb/hp (33.5 lb/kW), 11.2 kg/hp (15.2 kg/kW).

DIMENSIONS AND WEIGHT weight: GL Sedan 1,973 lb, 895 kg - XL Sedan 1,985 lb, 900 kg - SL Sedan 2,007 lb, 910 kg.

86 hp power team

See 70 hp power team, except for:

ENGINE 97.4 cu in, 1,597 cc (3.03 x 3.39 in, 76.9 x 86 mm); compression ratio: 8.5:1; max power (JIS): 86 hp (63 kW) at 5,000 rpm; max torque (JIS): 98 lb ft, 13.5 kg m (132 Nm) at 3,000 rpm; 53.8 hp/l (39.6 kW/l); twin silent-shaft, contra-rotating balancers; 1 Stromberg 28-72 DIDTA downdraught twin barrel carburettor.

TRANSMISSION gears: 5, fully synchronized; axle ratio: 3.909; width of rims: 5"; tyres: 6.45 x 13 - GT 165 SR x 13.

PERFORMANCE max speed: 96 mph, 155 km/h; power-weight ratio: XL 23.8 lb/hp (32.6 lb/kW), 10.8 kg/hp (14.8 kg/kW); consumption: 38.2 m/imp gal, 31.8 m/US gal, 7.4 l x 100 km on Japanese emission test cycle.

BRAKES GT disc.

DIMENSIONS AND WEIGHT height: 54.92 in, 139 cm - GT 54.72 in, 139 cm; weight: XL Sedan 2,051 lb, 930 kg - XL Super Sedan 2,073 lb, 940 kg - GT Sedan 2,106 lb, 955 kg.

OPTIONALS (for XL sedans only) automatic transmission with 3 ratios (I 2.452, II 1.452, III 1, rev 2.222).

135 hp power team

See 70 hp power team, except for:

ENGINE turbocharged; 109.5 cu in, 1,795 cc (3.17 x 3.46 in, 81 x 88 mm); compression ratio: 8:1; max power (JIS): 135 hp (99 kW) at 5,800 rpm; max torque (JIS): 145 lb ft, 20 kg m (196 Nm) at 3,500 rpm; max engine rpm: 6,300; 75.2 hp/l (55.3 kW/l); lubrication: oil cooler, 7.6 imp pt, 9.1 US pt, 4.3 l; Mitsubishi ECI twin injector electronic injection; Mitsubishi turbocharger with exhaust wastegate; emission control by MCA-Jet third valve air injection combustion system, exhaust gas recirculation and catalytic converter; fuel feed: electric pump.

TRANSMISSION gears: 5, fully synchronized; ratios: I 3.740, II 2.136, III 1.360, IV 1, V 0.856, rev 3.578; axle ratio: 3.909; width of rims: 5"; tyres: 185/70 HR x 13.

PERFORMANCE max speeds: (I) 27 mph, 43 km/h; (II) 47 mph, 76 km/h; (III) 69 mph, 114 km/h; (IV) 95 mph, 155 km/h; (V) 112 mph, 180 km/h; power-weight ratio: 16.8 lb/hp (22.9 lb/kW), 7.6 kg/hp (10.4 kg/kW); consumption: 35.3 m/imp gal, 29.4 m/US gal, 8 l x 100 km on Japanese emission test cycle.

STEERING turns lock to lock: 4.20.

BRAKES disc.

DIMENSIONS AND WEIGHT tracks: 53.54 in, 136 cm front, 52.76 in, 134 cm rear; ground clearance: 5.91 in, 15 cm; weight: 2,260 lb, 1,025 kg.

160 hp power team

See 70 hp power team, except for:

ENGINE turbocharged; 109.5 cu in, 1,795 cc (3.17 x 3.46 in, 80.6 x 88 mm); compression ratio: 7.5:1; max power (JIS): 160 hp (118 kW) at 5,800 rpm; max torque (JIS): 159 lb ft, 22 kg m (216 Nm) at 3,500 rpm; max engine rpm: 6,300; 89.1 hp/l (65.6 kW/l); lubrication: oil cooler, 7.6 imp pt, 9.1 US pt, 4.3 l; Mitsubishi ECI twin injector electronic injection; turbocharger with exhaust wastegate; emission control by MCA-Jet recirculation and catalytic converter; fuel feed: electric pump; air-cooled.

TRANSMISSION gears: 5, fully synchronized; ratios: I 3.740, II 2.136, III 1.360, IV 1, V 0.856, rev 3.578; axle ratio: 3.909; tyres: GT 175/70 HR x 14 - GSR 195/60 HR x 14.

PERFORMANCE max speed: 112 mph, 180 km/h; power-weight ratio: GT 14.4 lb/hp (19.6 lb/kW), 6.5 kg/hp (8.9 kg/kW); consumption: 32.8 m/imp gal, 27.3 m/US gal, 8.6 l x 100 km on Japanese emission test cycle.

CHASSIS rear suspension: anti-roll bar.

STEERING GSR servo.

BRAKES disc, front and rear internal radial fins.

DIMENSIONS AND WEIGHT tracks: 53.74 in, 136 cm front, 52.76 in, 134 cm rear; width: GT 63.39 in, 161 cm - GSR 63.78 in, 162 cm; height: GT 54.72 in 139 mm - GSR 54.53 in, 138 cm; weight: GT Turbo Intercooler Sedan 2,304 lb, 1,045 kg - GSR Turbo Intercooler Sedan 2,392 lb, 1,085 kg.

OPTIONALS automatic transmission not available.

Lancer Fiore Series

PRICES (Tokyo):		**yen**
1	1300 CE 4-dr Sedan	**815,000**
2	1300 CG 4-dr Sedan	**960,000**
3	1500 CG-F 4-dr Sedan	**998,000**
4	1500 CX 4-dr Sedan	**1,120,000**
5	1500 CX Extra 4-dr Sedan	**1,250,000**
6	1600 Turbo GSR-T 4-dr Sedan	**1,360,000**
7	1800 Diesel CG 4-dr Sedan	**1,145,000**
8	1800 Diesel CX 4-dr Sedan	**1,235,000**

Power team:	**Standard for:**	**Optional for:**
77 hp	1,2	—
87 hp	3 to 5	—
120 hp	6	—
65 hp (diesel)	7,8	—

77 hp power team

ENGINE front, transverse, 4 stroke; 4 cylinders, in line; 79.2 cu in, 1,298 cc (2.79 x 3.23 in, 71 x 82 mm); compression ratio: 9.7:1; max power (JIS): 77 hp (57 kW) at 5,500 rpm; max torque (JIS): 80 lb ft, 11 kg m (108 Nm) at 3,500 rpm; max engine rpm: 5,800; 59.3 hp/l (43.7 kW/l); cast iron block, light alloy head; 5 crankshaft bearings; valves: overhead, Vee-slanted, push-rods and rockers; camshafts: 1, overhead, cogged belt; lubrication: gear pump, full flow filter, 6.2 imp pt, 7.4 US pt, 3.5 l; 1 Stromberg downdraught twin barrel carburettor; Mitsubishi MCA-Jet super lean-burn, low emission engine with third air inlet valve, exhaust gas recirculation and catalytic converter; fuel feed: mechanical pump; water-cooled, 8.8 imp pt, 10.6 US pt, 5 l, electric thermostatic fan.

TRANSMISSION driving wheels: front; clutch: single dry plate (diaphragm); gearbox: mechanical; gears: CE 4, fully synchronized - CG 4 and Super-Shift 2-speed transfer box; ratios: CE I 3.619, II 1.888, III 1.121, IV 0.856, rev 3.358 - CG I 2.800, II 1.576, III 0.973, IV 0.744, rev 2.916; primary reduction ratio: (economy) 1.151, (power) 1.535; lever: CE central - GT two levers; final drive: helical spur gears; axle ratio: CE 3.666 - CG 3.421; width of rims: 4.5"; tyres: CE 145 SR x 13 - CG 155 SR x 13.

PERFORMANCE max speeds: (I) 27 mph, 43 km/h; (II) 52 mph, 83 km/h; (III) 86 mph, 139 km/h; (IV) 93 mph, 150 km/h; power-weight ratio: CE 22.9 lb/hp (31.2 lb/kW), 10.4 kg/hp (14.1 kg/kW); consumption: CE 47.1 m/imp gal, 39.2 m/US gal, 6 l - CG 53.3 m/imp gal, 44.4 m/US gal, 5.3 l x 100 km on Japanese emission test cycle.

CHASSIS integral; front suspension: independent, by McPherson, lower A arms, coil springs/telescopic damper struts; rear: independent, trailing arms, coil springs, telescopic dampers.

MITSUBISHI Minica Ami L Turbo Sedan

MITSUBISHI Lancer EX 1800 GSR Turbo Intercooler Sedan

77 HP POWER TEAM

STEERING rack-and pinion; turns lock to lock: 4.80.

BRAKES front disc (diameter 7.79 in, 198 cm), rear drum (diameter 7.09 in, 18 cm), dual circuit, servo.

ELECTRICAL EQUIPMENT 12 V; 40 Ah battery; 50 A alternator; transistorized ignition; pointless distributor; 2 headlamps.

DIMENSIONS AND WEIGHT wheel base: 93.70 in, 238 cm; tracks: 54.72 in, 139 cm front, 52.76 in, 134 cm rear; length: 162.40 in, 412 cm; width: CE 63.78 in, 162 cm - CG 64.37 in, 163 cm; height: 53.54 in, 136 cm; ground clearance: 5.91 in, 15 cm; weight: CE Sedan 1,764 lb, 800 kg - CG Sedan 1,775 lb, 805 kg; weight distribution: 64% front, 36% rear; turning circle: 32.1 ft, 9.8 m; fuel tank: 9.9 imp gal, 11.9 US gal, 45 l.

BODY saloon/sedan; 4 doors; 5 seats, separate front seats, built-in headrests.

OPTIONALS (for CE Sedan only) automatic transmission, hydraulic torque converter and planetary gears with 3 ratios (I 2.846, II 1.581, III 1, rev 2.176), 3.943 axle ratio, 155 SR x 13 tyres, anti-roll bar front suspension.

87 hp power team

See 77 hp power team, except for:

ENGINE CX Mitsubishi MD electronically-controlled variable displacement engine; 89.6 cu in, 1,468 cc (2.97 x 3.23 in, 75.5 x 82 mm); compression ratio: 9.4:1 - CX 9.5:1; max power (JIS): 87 hp (64 kW)at 5,500 rpm; max torque (JIS): 91 lb ft, 12.5 kg m (123 Nm) at 5,500 rpm; 59.3 hp/l (43.6 kW/l).

TRANSMISSION gears: CG-F 4, fully synchronized - CX 4 and Super-Shift 2-speed transfer box; ratios: CG-F I 3.643, II 1.926, III 1.136, IV 0.855, rev 3.446 - CX I 2.769, II 1.550, III 0.961, IV 0.724, rev 3.446; primary reduction ratio: (economy) 1.181, (power) 1.526; lever: CG-F central - CX two levers; axle ratio: CG-F 3.446 - CX 3.470; tyres: 155 SR x 13 (standard).

PERFORMANCE max speed: 99 mph, 160 km/h; power-weight ratio: CG-F 20.8 lb/hp (28.3 lb/kW), 9.4 kg/hp (12.8 kg/kW); consumption: CG-F 45.5 m/imp gal, 37.9 m/US gal, 6.2 l - CX 57.6 m/imp gal, 48 m/US gal, 4.9 l x 100 km on Japanese emission test cycle.

CHASSIS front suspension: anti-roll bar (standard).

STEERING servo; turns lock to lock: 3.

DIMENSIONS AND WEIGHT width: 64.37 in, 163 cm; weight: CG-F Sedan 1,808 lb, 820 kg - CX Sedan 1,841 lb, 835 kg - CX Extra Sedan 1,896 lb, 860 kg.

OPTIONALS (for CG-F only) automatic transmission, 3.598 axle ratio.

120 hp power team

See 77 hp power team, except for:

ENGINE turbocharged; 97.4 cu in, 1,597 cc (3.03 x 3.39 in, 76.9 x 86 mm); compression ratio: 7.6:1; max power (JIS): 120 hp (88 kW) at 5,500 rpm; max torque (JIS): 127 lb ft, 17.5 kg m (172 Nm) at 3,000 rpm; 75.1 hp/l (55.3 kW/l); lubrication: 7 imp pt, 8.5 US pt, 4 l; electronic injection; fuel feed: electric pump; turbocharger with exhaust wastegate.

TRANSMISSION gears: 5, fully synchronized; ratios: I 4.226, II 2.365, III 1.467, IV 1.105, V 0.855, rev 4.109; axle ratio: 3.466; width of rims: 5"; tyres: 175/70 SR x 13.

PERFORMANCE max speeds: (I) 24 mph, 39 km/h; (II) 43 mph, 70 km/h; (III) 71 mph, 114 km/h; (IV) 95 mph, 153 km/h; (V) 112 mph, 180 km/h; power-weight ratio: 16.3 lb/hp (22.1 lb/kW), 7.4 kg/hp (10 kg/kW); consumption: 39.6 m/imp gal, 32.7 m/US gal, 7.2 l x 100 km on Japanese emission test cycle.

MITSUBISHI Mirage 1500 CX-S Hatchback Sedan

MITSUBISHI Lancer Fiore 1500 CX Sedan

CHASSIS front and rear suspension: anti-roll bar.

BRAKES front internal radial fins.

DIMENSIONS AND WEIGHT weight: 1,951 lb, 885 kg.

OPTIONALS automatic transmission, hydraulic torque converter and planetary gears with 3 ratios (I 2.551, II 1.488, III 1, rev 2.176), 3.641 axle ratio.

65 hp (diesel) power team

See 77 hp power team, except for:

ENGINE diesel; 109.5 cu in, 1,795 cc (3.17 x 3.46 in, 80.6 x 88 mm); compression ratio: 21.5:1; max power (JIS): 65 hp (48 kW) at 4,500 rpm; max torque (JIS): 83 lb ft, 11.5 kg m (113 Nm) at 2,500 rpm; 36.2 hp/l (26.7 kW/l); lubrication: 10 imp pt, 12 US pt, 5.7 l; Bosch VE injection; swirl combustion chamber; cooling: 10.6 imp pt, 12.7 US pt, 6 l.

TRANSMISSION gears: 5, fully synchronized; ratios: I 4.226, II 2.365, III 1.467, IV 1.105, V 0.855, rev 4.109; axle ratio: 3.166; tyres: 155 SR x 13 (standard).

PERFORMANCE max speed: 90 mph, 145 km/h; power-weight ratio: CG 30.9 lb/hp (42 lb/kW), 14 kg/hp (19 kg/kW); consumption: 91.1 m/imp gal, 75.9 m/US gal, 3.1 l x 100 km at 37 mph, 60 km/h on Japanese emission test cycle.

CHASSIS front and rear suspension: anti-roll bar.

STEERING servo.

DIMENSIONS AND WEIGHT weight: Diesel CG Sedan 2,007 lb, 910 kg - Diesel CX Sedan 2,040 lb, 925 kg.

OPTIONALS automatic transmission not available.

Mirage Series

	PRICES (Tokyo):	**yen**
1	1300 CE 2+1-dr Hatchback Sedan	**755,000**
2	1300 CE 4-dr Sedan	**815,000**
3	1300 CG 4-dr Sedan	**960,000**
4	1300 CG 4+1-dr Hatchback Sedan	**945,000**
5	1300 CG-L 2+1-dr Hatchback Sedan	**885,000**
6	1300 CS 4+1-dr Hatchback Sedan	**845,000**
7	1500 CG-F 4-dr Sedan	**998,000**
8	1500 CG-F 4+1-dr Hatchback Sedan	**988,000**
9	1500 CX 4-dr Sedan	**1,120,000**
10	1500 CG 2+1-dr Hatchback Sedan	**980,000**
11	1500 CG 4+1-dr Hatchback Sedan	**1,040,000**
12	1500 CX-S 2+1-dr Hatchback Sedan	**1,045,000**
13	1500 CX Super 4+1-dr Hatchback Sedan	**1,160,000**
14	1600 GSR Turbo 4+1-dr Hatchback Sedan	**1,345,000**
15	1600 GSR-T Turbo 2+1-dr Hatchback Sedan	**1,360,000**
16	1800 Diesel CG 4-dr Sedan	**1,145,000**
17	1800 Diesel CG 4+1-dr Hatchback Sedan	**1,130,000**
18	1800 Diesel CX 4-dr Sedan	**1,235,000**
19	1800 Diesel CX 4+1-dr Hatchback Sedan	**1,220,000**

For GB prices, see price index.

Power team:	Standard for:	Optional for:
77 hp	1 to 6	—
87 hp	7 to 13	—
120 hp	14,15	—
65 hp (diesel)	16 to 19	—

77 hp power team

ENGINE front, transverse, 4 stroke; 4 cylinders, in line; 79.2 cu in, 1,298 cc (2.79 x 3.23 in, 71 x 82 mm); compression ratio: 9.7:1; max power (JIS): 77 hp (57 kW) at 5,500 rpm; max torque (JIS): 80 lb ft, 11 kg m (108 Nm) at 3,500 rpm; max engine rpm: 5,800; 59.3 hp/l (43.7 kW/l); cast iron block, light alloy head; 5 crankshaft bearings; valves: overhead, Vee-slanted, push-rods and rockers; camshafts: 1, overhead, cogged belt; lubrication: gear pump, full flow filter, 6.2 imp pt, 7.4 US pt, 3.5 l; 1 Stromberg downdraught twin barrel carburettor - CG air fuel ratio adjustement; Mitsubishi MCA-Jet super lean-burn low emission engine with third air inlet valve, exhaust gas recirculation and catalytic converter; fuel feed: mechanical pump; water-cooled, 8.8 imp pt, 10.6 US pt, 5 l, electric thermostatic fan.

TRANSMISSION driving wheels: front; clutch: single dry plate (diaphragm); gearbox: mechanical; gears: 4, fully synchronized - CG 4 and Super-Shift 2-speed transfer box; ratios: I 3.619, II 1.888, III 1.121, IV 0.856, rev 3.358 - CG I 2.800, II 1.576, III 0.973, IV 0.744, rev 2.916; primary reduction ratio: (economy) 1.151, (power) 1.535; lever: central - CG two levers; final drive: helical spur gears; axle ratio: 3.666 - CG 3.421; width of rims: 4.5"; tyres: 145 SR x 13 - CG 155 SR x 13 (standard).

PERFORMANCE max speeds: (I) 27 mph, 43 km/h; (II) 52 mph, 83 km/h; (III) 86 mph, 139 km/h; (IV) 93 mph, 150 km/h; power-weight ratio: CE 4-dr Sedan 22.9 lb/hp (31.2 lb/kW), 10.4 kg/hp (14.1 kg/kW); consumption: 43.1 m/imp gal, 39.2 m/US gal, 6 l - CG 53.3 m/imp gal, 44.4 m/US gal, 5.3 l x 100 km on Japanese emission test cycle.

CHASSIS integral; front suspension: independent, by McPherson, lower A arms, coil springs/telescopic damper struts; rear: independent, trailing arms, coil springs, telescopic dampers.

STEERING rack-and-pinion; turns lock to lock: 4.80.

BRAKES front disc (diameter 7.79 in, 19.8 cm), rear drum (diameter 7.09 in, 18 cm), dual circuit, servo.

ELECTRICAL EQUIPMENT 12 V; 40 Ah battery; 50 A alternator; transistorized ignition; pointless distributor; 2 headlamps.

DIMENSIONS AND WEIGHT wheel base: 93.70 in, 238 cm; tracks: 54.72 in, 139 cm front, 52.76 in, 134 cm rear; length: CE and CG 162.40 in, 412 cm - CG-L and CS 152.36 in, 387 cm; width: CE 63.78 in, 162 cm - other models 64.37 in, 163 cm; height: 53.54 in, 136 cm; weight: CG-L and CE hatchback sedans 1,709 lb, 775 kg - CE Sedan and CS Hatchback Sedan 1,764 lb, 800 kg - CG sedans 1,775 lb, 805 kg; ground clearance: 5.90 in, 15 cm; weight distribution: 64% front, 36% rear; turning circle: 32 ft, 9.8 m; fuel tank: 9.9 imp gal, 11.9 US gal, 45 l.

BODY saloon/sedan; 2+1, 4 or 4+1 doors; 5 seats, separate front seats, built-in headrests.

OPTIONALS automatic transmission, hydraulic torque converter and planetary gears with 3 ratios (I 2.846, II 1.581, III I, rev 2.176), 3.943 axle ratio; 155 SR x 13 tyres; anti-roll bar on front suspension.

87 hp power team

See 77 hp power team, except for:

ENGINE CG-F Mitsubishi MD electronically-controlled variable displacement engine; 89.6 cu in, 1,468 cc (2.97 x 3.23 in, 75.5 x 82 mm); compression ratio: 9.4:1 - CG-F 9.5:1; max power (JIS): 87 hp (64 kW) at 5,500 rpm; max torque (JIS): 91 lb ft, 12.5 kg m (123 Nm) at 5,500 rpm; 59.3 hp/l (43.6 kW/l).

TRANSMISSION gears: CG-F Hatchback Sedan 4, fully synchronized - other models 4 with Super-Shift 2 speed transfer box; ratios: I 2.769, II 1.550, III 0.961, IV 0.724, rev 2.692; primary reduction ratio: (economy) 1.181 (power) 1.526; axle ratio: 3.687 - CX Super 3.470; tyres: 155 SR x 13 (standard).

PERFORMANCE max speed: 99 mph, 160 km/h; power-weight ratio: CG-F Sedan 20.8 lb/hp (28.3 lb/kW), 9.4 kg/hp (12.8 kg/kW); consumption: CG-F Hatchback Sedan 45.5 m/imp gal, 37.9 m/US gal, 6.2 l - other models 57.6 m/imp gal, 48 m/US gal, 4.9 l x 100 km on Japanese emission test cycle.

CHASSIS front suspension: anti-roll bar (standard).

STEERING CX servo; turns lock to lock: 3.

DIMENSIONS AND WEIGHT width: 64.37 in, 163 cm; weight: CG 2+1-dr Hatchback Sedan 1,775 lb, 805 kg - CG-F 4-dr Sedan and CG-F 4+1-dr Hatchback Sedan 1,808 lb, 820 kg - CX 4-dr Sedan and CX-S 2+1-dr Hatchback Sedan 1,841 lb, 835 kg - CX Super 4+1-dr Hatchback Sedan 1,852 lb, 840 kg.

OPTIONALS automatic transmission, 3.598 axle ratio.

120 hp power team

See 77 hp power team, except for:

ENGINE turbocharged; 97.4 cu in, 1,597 cc (3.03 x 3.39 in, 76.9 x 86 mm); compression ratio: 7.6:1; max power (JIS): 120 hp (88 KW) at 5,500 rpm; max torque (JIS): 127 lb ft, 17.5 kg m (172 Nm) at 5,000 rpm; 75.1 hp/l (55.3 kW/l); lubrication: 7 imp pt, 8.5 US pt, 4 l; electronic injection; fuel feed: electric pump; turbocharger with exhaust wastegate.

TRANSMISSION gears: 5, fully synchronized; ratios: I 4.226, II 2.365, III 1.467, IV 1.105, V 0.855, rev 4.109; axle ratio: 3.466; width of rims: 5"; tyres: 175/70 SR x 13.

PERFORMANCE max speeds: (I) 24 mph, 39 km/h; (II) 43 mph, 70 km/h; (III) 71 mph, 114 km/h; (IV) 95 mph, 153 km/h; (V) 112 mph, 180 km/h; power-weight ratio: 16.2 lb/hp (22 lb/kW), 7.3 kg/hp (10 kg/kW); consumption: 39.6 m/imp gal, 32.7 m/US gal, 7.2 l x 100 km on Japanese emission test cycle.

CHASSIS front and rear suspension: anti-roll bar.

BRAKES front internal radial fins.

DIMENSIONS AND WEIGHT weight: 1,940 lb, 880 kg.

BODY 2+1 or 4+1 doors.

OPTIONALS automatic transmission, hydraulic torque converter and planetary gears with 3 ratios (I 2.551, II 1.488, III 1, rev 2.176), 3.641 axle ratio (for GSR Turbo only).

65 hp (diesel) power team

See 77 hp power team, except for:

ENGINE diesel; 109.5 cu in, 1,795 cc (3.17 x 3.46 in, 80.6 x 88 mm); compression ratio: 21.5:1; max power (JIS): 65 hp (48 KW) at 4,500 rpm; max torque (JIS): 83 lb ft, 11.5 kg m (113 Nm) at 2,500 rpm; 36.2 hp/l (26.7 kW/l); lubrication: 10 imp pt, 12 US pt, 5.7 l; Bosch VE injection; swirl combustion chamber; cooling: 10.6 imp pt, 12.7 US pt, 6 l.

TRANSMISSION gears: 5, fully synchronized; ratios: I 4.226, II 2.365, III 1.467, IV 1.105, V 0.855, rev 4.109; axle ratio: 3.166; tyres: 155 SR x 13 (standard).

PERFORMANCE max speed: 90 mph, 145 km/h; power-weight ratio: CG 4-dr Sedan 30.9 lb/hp (42 lb/kW), 14 kg/hp (19 kg/kW); consumption: 91.1 m/imp gal, 75.9 m/US gal, 3.1 l x 100 km at 37 mph, 60 km/h on Japanese emission test cycle.

CHASSIS front and rear suspension: anti-roll bar.

STEERING servo.

DIMENSIONS AND WEIGHT weight: Diesel CG sedans 2,007 lb, 910 kg - Diesel CX 4+1-dr Hatchback Sedan 2,029 lb, 920 kg - Diesel CX 4-dr Sedan 2,040 lb, 925 kg.

BODY 4 or 4+1 doors.

OPTIONALS automatic transmission not available.

Tredia Series

PRICES (Tokyo):	yen
1 1400 GL 4-dr Sedan	998,000
2 1400 GF 4-dr Sedan	1,130,000
3 1400 GX 4-dr Sedan	1,060,000
4 1600 SE 4-dr Sedan	1,175,000
5 1600 Super Saloon 4-dr Sedan	1,295,000
6 1800 Super Saloon 4-dr Sedan	1,405,000
7 1800 Turbo GT-X 4-dr Sedan	1,445,000
8 1800 Turbo Super Saloon 4-dr Sedan	1,535,000

For GB prices, see price index.

Power team:	Standard for:	Optional for:
82 hp	1 to 3	—
88 hp	4,5	—
100 hp	6	—
135 hp	7,8	—

82 hp power team

ENGINE front, transverse, 4 stroke; 4 cylinders, vertical, in line; 86 cu in, 1,410 cc (2.91 x 3.23 in, 74 x 82 mm); compression ratio: 9:1; max power (JIS): 82 hp (60 kW) at 5,500 rpm; max torque (JIS): 88 lb ft, 12.1 kg m (119 Nm) at 3,000 rpm; max engine rpm: 6,000; 58.1 hp/l (42.8 kW/l); cast iron block, light alloy head; 5 crankshaft bearings; valves: 3 per cylinder, overhead, Vee-slanted; camshafts: 1, overhead; lubrication: gear pump, full flow filter, 6.2 imp pt, 7.4 US pt, 3.5 l; 1 Mikuni downdraught twin barrel carburettor; Mitsubishi MCA-Jet super lean-burn low emission engine with third air inlet valve, exhaust gas recirculation and oxidizing catalyst; fuel feed: mechanical pump; water-cooled, 10.6 imp pt, 12.7 US pt, 6 l.

MITSUBISHI Tredia 1600 Super Saloon Sedan

TRANSMISSION driving wheels: front; clutch: single dry plate (diaphragm); gearbox: mechanical; gears: 4, fully synchronized and Super-Shift 2-speed transfer box; ratios: I 2.769, II 1.550, III 0.961, IV 0.724, rev 2.692; primary reduction ratios: (economy) 1.181, (power) 1.526; lever: central; final drive: helical spur gears; axle ratio: 3.470; width of rims: 4.5"; tyres: GL 6.15 x 13 - GX and GF 155 SR x 13.

PERFORMANCE max speeds: (I) 31 mph, 50 km/h; (II) 55 mph, 88 km/h; (III) 84 mph, 135 km/h; (IV) 96 mph, 155 km/h; power-weight ratio: GL 23.1 lb/hp (31.4 lb/kW), 10.4 kg/hp (14.2 kg/kW); consumption: 45.6 m/imp gal, 37.9 m/US gal, 6.2 l x 100 km on Japanese emission test cycle.

CHASSIS integral; front suspension: independent, by McPherson, coil springs/telescopic damper struts, lower arms (trailing links), anti-roll bar; rear: independent, coil springs, telescopic dampers, trailing radius arms, anti-roll bar.

STEERING rack-and-pinion; turns lock to lock: 4.20 or 3.60.

BRAKES front disc, rear drum, servo; lining area: front 24.8 sq in, 160 sq cm, rear 33.4 sq in, 216 sq cm, total 58.3 sq in, 376 sq cm.

ELECTRICAL EQUIPMENT 12 V; 45 Ah battery; 45 A alternator; Mitsubishi distributor; 2 headlamps.

DIMENSIONS AND WEIGHT wheel base: 96.06 in, 244 cm; tracks: 55.50 in, 141 cm front, 53.94 in, 137 cm rear; length: 169.10 in, 428 cm - GF 172.44 in, 438 cm; width: GL 64.96 in, 165 cm - GX and GF 65.35 in, 166 cm; height: 53.54 in, 136 cm; ground clearance: 5.90 in, 15 cm; weight: GL Sedan 1,896 lb, 860 kg - GX Sedan 1,907 lb, 865 kg - GF Sedan 2,007 lb, 910 kg; turning circle: 35.4 ft, 10.8 m; fuel tank: 11 imp gal, 13.2 US gal, 50 l.

BODY saloon/sedan; 4 doors; 5 seats, separate front seats.

OPTIONALS automatic transmission with 3 ratios (I 2.846, II 1.581, III 1, rev 2.176), 3.943 axle ratio.

88 hp power team

See 82 hp power team, except for:

ENGINE 97.4 cu in, 1,597 cc (3.03 x 3.39 in, 76.9 x 86 mm); compression ratio: 8.5:1; max power (JIS): 88 hp (65 kW) at 5,000 rpm; max torque (JIS): 98 lb ft, 13.5 kg m (132 Nm) at 3,000 rpm; 55.1 hp/l (40.6 kW/l); lubrication: trochoid pump, full flow filter, 7 imp pt, 8.5 US pt, 4 l.

MITSUBISHI Tredia 1600 Super Saloon Sedan

TRANSMISSION tyres: 155 SR x 13.

PERFORMANCE max speeds: (I) 30 mph, 48 km/h; (II) 53 mph, 85 km/h; (III) 84 mph, 135 km/h; (IV) 96 mph, 155 km/h; power-weight ratio: SE 23.6 lb/hp (32 lb/kW), 10.7 kg/hp (14.5 kg/kW); consumption: 40.9 m/imp gal, 34.1 m/US gal, 6.9 l x 100 km on Japanese emission test cycle.

DIMENSIONS AND WEIGHT length: 172.44 in, 438 cm; width: 65.35 in, 166 cm; ground clearance: 61.02 in, 15 cm; weight: SE Sedan 2,073 lb, 940 kg - Super Saloon Sedan 2,095 lb, 950 kg.

OPTIONALS automatic transmission with 3 ratios (I 2.846, II 1.581, III 1, rev 2.176), 3.597 axle ratio, consumption 36.7 m/imp gal, 30.5 m/US gal, 7.7 l x 100 km on Japanese emission test cycle.

100 hp power team

See 82 hp power team, except for:

ENGINE 109.5 cu in, 1,795 cc (3.17 x 3.46 in, 80.6 x 88 mm); compression ratio: 8.5:1; max power (JIS): 100 hp (74 kW) at 5,500 rpm; max torque (JIS): 109 lb ft, 15 kg m (147 Nm) at 3,500 rpm; 55.7 hp/l (40.1 kW/l); lubrication: 7 imp pt, 8.5 US pt, 4 l; twin silent-shaft, contra rotating balancers.

TRANSMISSION tyres: 165 SR x 13.

PERFORMANCE max speed: 105 mph, 170 km/h; power-weight ratio: 21.7 lb/hp (29.5 lb/kW), 9.8 kg/hp (13.4 kg/kW); consumption: 36.7 m/imp gal, 30.5 m/US gal, 7.7 l x 100 km on Japanese emission test cycle.

STEERING servo; turns lock to lock: 2.90.

DIMENSIONS AND WEIGHT length: 172.44 in, 438 cm; widht: 65.35 in, 166 cm; height: 53.93 in, 137 cm; weight: 2,172 lb, 985 kg.

OPTIONALS automatic transmission with 3 ratios (I 2.846, II 1.581, III 1, rev 2.176), 3.597 axle ratio.

135 hp power team

See 82 hp power team, except for:

ENGINE turbocharged; 109.5 cu in, 1,795 cc (3.17 x 3.46 in, 80.6 x 88 mm); compression ratio: 7.5:1; max power (JIS): 135 hp (99 kW) at 5,800 rpm; max torque (JIS): 145 lb ft, 20 kg m (196 Nm) at 3,500 rpm; 75.2 hp/l (55.3 kW/l); lubrication: 7 imp pt, 8.5 US pt, 4 l; Mitsubishi electronic injection; fuel feed: electric pump; twin silent-shaft, contra-rotating balancers.

TRANSMISSION gears: 5, fully synchronized; ratios: I 4.226, II 2.365, III 1.467, IV 1.105, V 0.855, rev 4.109; axle ratio: 3.466; tyres: 165 SR x 13.

PERFORMANCE max speed: 112 mph, 180 km/h; power-weight ratio: GT-X 17.1 lb/hp (23.2 lb/kW), 7.7 kg/hp (10.5 kg/kW); consumption: 36.7 m/imp gal, 30.5 m/US gal, 7.7 l x 100 km on Japanese emission test cycle.

STEERING servo.

BRAKES front internal radial fins.

DIMENSIONS AND WEIGHT length: 172.44 in, 438 cm; weight: Turbo Super Saloon Sedan 2,282 lb, 1,035 kg - Turbo GT-X Sedan 2,304 lb, 1,045 kg.

OPTIONALS electronic automatic transmission, hydraulic torque converter and planetary gears with 3 ratios (I 2.846, II 1.581, III 1, rev 2.176), 3.665 axle ratio.

Cordia Series

PRICES (Tokyo):		yen
1	1600 SR 2+1-dr Coupé	**1,037,000**
2	1600 SL 2+1-dr Coupé	**1,090,000**
3	1600 SE 2+1-dr Coupé	**1,240,000**
4	1800 SE 2+1-dr Coupé	**1,455,000**
5	1800 Turbo GT 2+1-dr Coupé	**1,598,000**
6	1800 Turbo GSR 2+1-dr Coupé	**1,598,000**
7	1800 Turbo GSR-S 2+1-dr Coupé	**1,765,000**

For GB prices, see price index.

Power team:	Standard for:	Optional for:
88 hp	1 to 3	—
100 hp	4	—
135 hp	5 to 7	—

88 hp power team

ENGINE front, transverse, 4 stroke; 4 cylinders, vertical, in line; 97.4 cu in, 1,597 cc (3.03 x 3.39 in, 76.9 x 86 mm); compression ratio: 8.5:1; max power (JIS): 88 hp (65 kW) at 5,000 rpm; max torque (JIS): 98 lb ft, 13.5 kg m (132 Nm) at 3,000 rpm; max engine rpm: 6,000; 55.1 hp/l (40.6 kW/l); cast iron block, light alloy head; 5 crankshaft bearings; valves: overhead, Vee-slanted, rockers; camshafts: 1, overhead; lubrication: trochoid pump, full flow filter, 7 imp pt, 8.3 US pt, 4 l; 1 Mikuni downdraught twin barrel carburettor; Mitsubishi MCA-Jet super lean-burn low emission engine with third air inlet valve, exhaust gas recirculation and oxidizing catalyst; fuel feed: mechanical pump; water-cooled, 10.6 imp pt, 12.7 US pt, 6 l.

TRANSMISSION driving wheels: front; clutch: single dry plate (diaphragm); gearbox: mechanical; gears: 4 with Super-Shift 2-speed transfer box; ratios: I 2.769, II 1.550, III 0.961, IV 0.724, rev 2.692; primary reduction ratios: (economy) 1.181, (power) 1.526; lever: central; final drive: helical spur gears; axle ratio: 3.470; width of rims: 4.5"; tyres: SR 155 SR x 13 - SL and ST 165 SR x 13.

PERFORMANCE max speeds: (I) 30 mph, 48 km/h; (II) 53 mph, 85 km/h; (III) 84 mph, 135 km/h; (IV) 96 mph, 155 km/h; power-weight ratio: SR 22.7 lb/hp (30.8 lb/kW), 10.3 kg/hp (14 kg/kW); consumption: 41.5 m/imp gal, 34.6 m/US gal, 6.8 l x 100 km on Japanese emission test cycle.

CHASSIS integral; front suspension: independent, by McPherson, coil springs/telescopic damper struts, lower arms (trailing links), anti-roll bar; rear: independent, coil springs, telescopic dampers, trailing radius arms, anti-roll bar.

STEERING rack-and-pinion; turns lock to lock: 4.20.

BRAKES front disc, rear drum, servo; lining area: front 24.8 sq in, 160 sq cm, rear 33.4 sq in, 216 sq cm, total 58.2 sq in, 376 sq cm.

ELECTRICAL EQUIPMENT 12 V; 45 Ah battery; 45 A alternator; Mitsubishi distributor; 2 headlamps.

DIMENSIONS AND WEIGHT wheel base: 96.06 in, 244 cm; tracks: 55.50 in, 141 cm front, 53.94 in, 137 cm rear; length: 173.03 in, 439 cm; width: SR 64.96 in, 165 cm - SL and SE 65.35 in, 166 cm; height: SR 51.57 in, 131 cm - SL and SE 51.96 in, 132 cm; ground clearance: SR 5.90 in, 15 cm - SL and SE 6.10 in, 15.5 cm; weight: SR Coupé 1,996 lb, 905 kg - SL Coupé 2,018 lb, 815 kg - SE Coupé 2,051 lb, 930 kg; weight distribution: 62% front, 38% rear; turning circle: 35.4 ft, 10.8 m; fuel tank: 11 imp gal, 13.2 US gal, 50 l.

BODY coupé; 2+1 doors; 5 seats, separate front seats.

OPTIONALS (for SE only) automatic transmission with 3 ratios (I 2.846, II 1.581, III 1, rev 2.176), 3.597 axle ratio, consumption 37.2 m/imp gal, 30.9 m/US gal, 7.6 l x 100 km on Japanese emission test cycle.

100 hp power team

See 88 hp power team, except for:

ENGINE 109.5 cu in, 1,795 cc (3.17 x 3.46 in, 80.6 x 88 mm); max power (JIS): 100 hp (74 kW) at 5,500 rpm; max torque (JIS): 109 lb ft, 15 kg m (147 Nm) at 3,500 rpm; 55.7 hp/l (41 kW/l); lubrication: gear pump; cooling: 12.3 imp pt, 14.8 US pt, 7 l.

TRANSMISSION tyres: 165 SR x 13.

PERFORMANCE max speed: 105 mph, 170 km/h; power-weight ratio: 21.5 lb/hp (29.2 lb/kW), 9.7 kg/hp (13.3 kg/kW); consumption: 36.7 m/imp gal, 30.5 m/US gal, 7.7 l x 100 km on Japanese emission test cycle.

STEERING servo; turns lock to lock: 2.90.

DIMENSIONS AND WEIGHT width: 65.35 in, 166 cm; height: 51.96 in, 132 cm; weight: 2,150 lb, 975 kg.

OPTIONALS automatic transmission with 3 ratios (I 2.846, II 1.581, III 1, rev 2.176), 3.597 axle ratio.

135 hp power team

See 88 hp power team, except for:

ENGINE turbocharged; 109.5 cu in, 1,795 cc (3.17 x 3.46 in, 80.6 x 88 mm); compression ratio: 7.5:1; max power (JIS): 135 hp (99 kW) at 5,800 rpm; max torque (JIS): 145 lb ft, 20 kg m (196 Nm) at 3,500 rpm; 75.2 hp/l (55.3 kW/l); lubrication: gear pump; fuel feed: electric pump; Mitsubishi electronic injection; twin silent-shaft, contra rotating balancers.

MITSUBISHI Cordia 1800 Turbo GSR Coupé

TRANSMISSION gears: 5, fully synchronized; ratios: I 4.226, II 2.365, III 1.467, IV 1.105, V 0.855, rev 4.109; axle ratio: 3.466; tyres: GT and GSR 165 SR x 13 - GSR-S 185/70 SR x 13.

PERFORMANCE max speed: 112 mph, 180 km/h; power-weight ratio: GT 16.6 lb/hp (22.5 lb/kW), 7.5 kg/hp (10.2 kg/kW); consumption: 31.7 m/imp gal, 26.4 m/US gal, 8.9 l x 100 km on Japanese emission test cycle.

STEERING GSR and GSR-S servo.

BRAKES front internal radial fins.

DIMENSIONS AND WEIGHT width: 65.55 in, 166 cm; weight: Turbo GT Coupé 2,238 lb, 1,015 kg - Turbo GSR Coupé 2,271 lb, 1,030 kg - Turbo GSR-S Coupé 2,282 lb, 1,035 kg.

OPTIONALS electronic automatic transmission, hydraulic torque converter and planetary gears with 3 ratios (I 2.846, II 1.581, III 1, rev 2.176), 3.665 axle ratio.

Chariot Series

PRICES (Tokyo):		yen
1	1600 ME 4+1-dr St. Wagon	**1,152,000**
2	1600 MF 4+1-dr St. Wagon	**1,298,000**
3	1800 MT 4+1-dr St. Wagon	**1,464,000**
4	1800 MX 4+1-dr St. Wagon	**1,590,000**
5	1800 Turbo MR 4+1-dr St. Wagon	**1,703,000**

Power team:	Standard for:	Optional for:
88 hp	1,2	—
100 hp	3,4	—
135 hp	5	—

88 hp power team

ENGINE front, transverse, 4 stroke; 4 cylinders, vertical, in line; 97.4 cu in, 1,597 cc (3.03 x 3.39 in, 76.9 x 86 mm); compression ratio: 8.5:1; max power (JIS): 88 hp (65 kW) at 5,000 rpm; max torque (JIS): 98 lb ft, 13.5 kg m (132 Nm) at 3,000 rpm; max engine rpm: 6,000; 55.1 hp/l (40.6 kW/l); cast iron block, light alloy head; 5 crankshaft bearings; valves: overhead, push-rods and rockers; camshafts: 1, overhead, cogged belt; lubrication: trochoid pump, full flow filter, 7 imp pt, 8.3 US pt, 4 l; 1 Stromberg 28-32 DIDTA downdraught twin barrel carburettor; Mitsubishi MCA-Jet super lean-burn low emission engine with third air inlet valve, exhaust gas recirculation and secondary air induction; fuel feed: mechanical pump; water-cooled, 10.6 imp pt, 12.7 US pt, 6 l, electric thermostatic fan.

TRANSMISSION driving wheels: front; clutch: single dry plate (diaphragm); gearbox: mechanical; gears: ME 5, fully synchronized - MF 4 and Super-Shift 2-speed transfer box; ratios: ME I 4.226, II 2.365, III 1.467, IV 1.105, V 0.855, rev 4.109 - MF I 2.769, II 1.550, III 0,961, IV 0.724, rev 2.692; primaty reduction ratios: (economy) 1.181, (power) 1.526; lever: central; final drive: helical spur gears; axle ratio: 3.470; width of rims: 4.5"; tyres: 165 SR x 13.

PERFORMANCE max speeds: (I) 23 mph, 37 km/h; (II) 40 mph, 64 km/h; (III) 66 mph, 107 km/h; (IV) and (V) 93 mph, 150 km/h; power-weight ratio: ME 24.6 lb/hp (33.4 lb/kW), 11.1 kg/hp (15.1 kg/kW); consumption: 35.2 m/imp gal, 29 m/US gal, 8.1 l x 100 km on Japanese emission test cycle.

CHASSIS integral; front suspension: independent, by McPherson, coil springs/telescopic damper struts, anti-roll bar; rear: independent, trailing arms, coil springs, anti-roll bar, adjustable dampers.

STEERING rack-and-pinion - MF servo; turns lock to lock: 4.20 - MF 3.

BRAKES front disc (diameter 7.80 in, 198 cm), rear drum (diameter 7.09 in, 18 cm), dual circuit, servo.

ELECTRICAL EQUIPMENT 12 V; 33 Ah battery; 50 A alternator; Mitsubishi distributor; 2 headlamps.

DIMENSIONS AND WEIGHT wheel base: 103.35 in, 262 cm; tracks: 55.51 in, 141 cm front, 54.13 in, 137 cm rear; lenght: 169.09 in, 429 cm; width: 65.57 in, 164 cm; height: 60.04 in, 152 cm; ground clearance: 5.91 in, 15 cm; weight: ME St. Wagon 2,161 lb, 980 kg - ME St. Wagon 2,183 lb, 990 kg; weight distribution: 60% front, 40% rear; turning circle: 37.4 ft, 11.4 m; fuel tank: 11 imp gal, 13.2 US gal, 50 l.

BODY estate car/st. wagon; 4+1 doors; 7 seats, separate front seats.

MITSUBISHI Chariot 1800 Turbo MR Station Wagon

MITSUBISHI Galant Sigma 2000 Royal Sedan

100 hp power team

See 88 hp power team, except for:

ENGINE 109.5 cu in, 1,795 cc (3.17 x 3.46 in, 80.6 x 88 mm); max power (JIS): 100 hp (74 kW) at 5,500 rpm; max torque (JIS): 109 lb ft, 15 kg m (147 Nm) at 3,500 rpm; 55.7 hp/l (41 kW/l); 1 Stromberg 32-35 DIDTA downdraught twin barrel carburettor; twin silent-shaft, contra-rotating balancers.

TRANSMISSION tyres: MT 185/70 SR x 13.

PERFORMANCE max speed: 99 mph, 160 km/h; power-weight ratio: MT 23.2 lb/hp (31.5 lb/kW), 10.5 kg/hp (14.3 kg/kW); consumption: 31.7 m/imp gal, 26.4 m/US gal, 8.9 l x 100 km on Japanese emission test cycle.

STEERING servo; turns lock to lock: 3.

DIMENSIONS AND WEIGHT weight: MT St. Wagon 2,315 lb, 1,050 kg - MX St. Wagon 2,370 lb, 1,075 kg.

OPTIONALS electronic automatic transmission, hydraulic torque converter and planetary gears with 3 ratios (I 2.846, II 1.581, III 1, rev 2.176), 3.597 axle ratio.

135 hp power team

See 88 hp power team, except for:

ENGINE turbocharged; 109.5 cu in, 1,795 cc (3.17 x 3.46 in, 80.6 x 88 mm); compression ratio: 7.5:1; max power (JIS): 135 hp (99 kW) at 5,800 rpm; max torque (JIS): 145 lb ft, 20 kg m (196 Nm) at 3,500 rpm; lubrication: gear pump; Mitsubishi electronic injection; fuel feed: electric pump; twin silent-shaft, contra-rotating balancers.

TRANSMISSION gears: 5, fully synchronized; ratios: I 4.226, II 2.365, III 1.467, IV 1.105, V 0.855, rev 4.109; axle ratio: 3.466; tyres: 185/70 SR x 13.

PERFORMANCE max speeds: (I) 26 mph, 42 km/h; (II) 48 mph, 77 km/h; (III) 76 mph, 123 km/h; (IV) 102 mph, 164 km/h; (V) 109 mph, 175 km/h; power-weight ratio: 18.1 lb/hp (24.7 lb/kW), 8.2 kg/hp (11.2 kg/kW); consumption: 31.7 m/imp gal, 26.4 m/US gal, 8.9 l x 100 km on Japanese emission test cycle.

MITSUBISHI Galant Sigma 1800 (turbo engine)

STEERING servo.

BRAKES front internal radial fins.

DIMENSIONS AND WEIGHT length: 175 in, 444 cm; weight: 2,448 lb, 1,110 kg.

OPTIONALS electronic automatic transmission, hydraulic torque converter and planetary gears with 3 ratios (I 2.846, II 1.581, III 1, rev 2.176), 3.665 axle ratio.

Galant / Eterna Series

PRICES (Tokyo):

		yen
1	Galant Sigma 1800 LS 4-dr Sedan	1,070,000
2	Galant Sigma 1800 LG 4-dr Sedan	1,165,000
3	Galant Sigma 1800 L Touring 4-dr Sedan	1,323,000
4	Galant Sigma 1800 Super Touring 4-dr Sedan	1,440,000
5	Galant Sigma 1800 Super Touring E 4-dr Sedan	1,640,000
6	Eterna Sigma 1800 LX Touring 4-dr Sedan	1,313,000
7	Eterna Sigma 1800 Super Touring 4-dr Sedan	1,440,000
8	Galant Sigma 1800 Turbo Super Touring 4-dr Sedan	1,699,000
9	Eterna Sigma 1800 Turbo Super Touring 4-dr Sedan	1,699,000
10	Galant Sigma 2000 Super Saloon 4-dr Sedan	1,748,000
11	Galant Sigma 2000 Royal 4-dr Sedan	2,320,000
12	Eterna Sigma 2000 Super Saloon 4-dr Sedan	1,748,000
13	Eterna Sigma 2000 Royal 4-dr Sedan	2,320,000
14	Galant Sigma 2000 Turbo GSR-X 4-dr Sedan	1,955,000
15	Eterna Sigma 2000 Turbo GSR-X 4-dr Sedan	1,955,000

For GB prices, see price index.

Power team:	Standard for:	Optional for:
105 hp	1 to 7	—
110 hp	10 to 13	—
135 hp	8,9	—
145 hp	14,15	—

105 hp power team

ENGINE front, transverse, 4 stroke; 4 cylinders, vertical, in line; 107.1 cu in, 1,755 cc (3.17 x 3.39 in, 80.6 x 86 mm); compression ratio: 9:1; max power (JIS): 105 hp (77 kW) at 5,500 rpm; max torque (JIS): 109 lb ft, 15 kg m (147 Nm) at 3,500 rpm; max engine rpm: 6,000; 59.8 hp/l (44 kW/l); cast iron block, light alloy head; twin silent-shaft, contra rotating balancers; 5 crankshaft bearings; valves: overhead, Vee-slanted, push-rods and rockers; camshafts: 1, overhead, cogged belt; lubrication: gear pump, full flow filter, 7 imp pt, 8.5 US pt, 4 l; 1 Stromberg 32-35 DIDTA downdraught twin barrel carburettor with air-fuel ratio adjustement; emission control by MCA-Jet, 3-way catalytic converter and exhaust gas recirculation; fuel feed: mechanical pump; water-cooled, 8.8 imp pt, 10.6 US pt, 5 l, electric thermostatic fan.

TRANSMISSION driving wheels: front; clutch: single dry plate (diaphragm); gearbox: mechanical; gears: 4, fully synchronized - LX Touring and Super Touring 5; ratios: I 4.226, II 2.365, III 1.467, IV 1.105 - LX Touring and Super Touring V 0.855, rev 4.109; lever: central; final drive: helical spur gears; axle ratio: 3.166; width of rims: 4.5"; tyres: LS 6.45 x 13 - other models 165 SR x 13.

PERFORMANCE max speeds: (I) 27 mph, 44 km/h; (II) 51 mph, 82 km/h; (III) 81 mph, 130 km/h; (IV) and (V) 106 mph, 170 155 km/h; power-weight ratio: LS 20.8 lb/hp (28.3 lb/kW), 9.4 kg/hp (12.8 kg/kW); consumption: 39.2 m/imp gal, 32.6 m/US gal, 7.2 l x 100 km on Japanese emission test cycle.

CHASSIS integral; front suspension: independent, by McPherson, coil springs/telescopic damper struts, lower A arms, anti-roll bar; rear: U-shaped swinging semi-axles, trailing arms, Panhard rod, coil springs, anti-roll bar, telescopic dampers.

STEERING rack-and-pinion - LX Touring and Super Touring servo; turns lock to lock: 4.30 - LX Touring and Super Touring 3.

BRAKES front disc, internal radial fins (diameter 7.56 in, 19.2), rear drum (diameter 7.99 in, 20.3 cm), dual circuit, servo.

ELECTRICAL EQUIPMENT 12 V; 40 Ah battery; 55 A alternator; pointless distributor; 4 headlamps.

DIMENSIONS AND WEIGHT wheel base: 102.36 in, 260 cm; tracks: 56.89 in, 144 cm front, 55.31 in, 140 cm rear; lenght: 179.53 in, 456 cm; width: 66.73 in, 169 cm; height: 54.53 in, 138 cm; ground clearance: 6.10 in, 15 cm; weight: Galant Sigma LS and LG sedans 2,183 lb, 990 kg - Eterna Sigma LX Touring Sedan 2,216 lb, 1,005 kg - Galant Sigma and Eterna Sigma Super Touring sedans 2,282 lb, 1,035 kg - Galant Sigma Super Touring E Sedan 2,348 lb, 1,065 kg; weight distribution: 66% front, 35% rear; turning circle: 36.7 ft, 11.2 m; fuel tank: 13.2 imp gal, 15.8 US gal, 60 l.

BODY saloon/sedan; 4 doors; 5 seats, separate front seats.

OPTIONALS (for LX Touring only) 4-speed 4 and Super-Shift mechanical gearbox with transfer box (I 2.769, II 1.550, III 0.961, IV 0.724, rev 2.692 - primary reduction ratios (economy) 1.181, (power) 1.526), 3.466 axle ratio; automatic transmission, hydraulic torque converter and planetary gears with 3 ratios (I 2.864, II 1.581, III 1, rev 2.176), 3.597 axle ratio.

110 hp power team

See 105 hp power team, except for:

ENGINE 121.9 cu in, 1,997 cc (3.35 x 3.46 in, 85 x 88 mm); compression ratio: 8.5:1; max power (JIS): 110 hp (79 kW) at 5,500 rpm; max torque (JIS): 121 lb ft, 16.7 kg m (164 Nm) at 3,500 rpm; 55.1 hp/l (39.6 kW/l); valves: 3 per cylinder (one intake and one exhaust in main combustion chamber, one intake in auxiliary chamber), hydraulic tappets; cooling: 12.3 imp pt, 14.8 US pt, 7 l.

TRANSMISSION gearbox: Super Saloon mechanical - Royal (standard) automatic transmission, hydraulic torque converter and planetary gears with 4 ratios; gears: Super Saloon 5, fully synchronized - Royal 4; ratios: Super Saloon I 4.226, II 2.365, III 1.467, IV 1.105, V 0.855, rev 4.109 - Royal I 2.846, II 1.581, III 1, IV 0.685, rev 2.176; axle ratio: Super Saloon 3.187 - Royal 3.665; width of rims: 5"; tyres: 185/70 SR x 13.

PERFORMANCE max speed: Super Saloon 109 mph, 175 km/h - Royal 106 mph, 170 km/h; power-weight ratio: Super Saloon 22 lb/hp (29.8 lb/kW), 9.9 kg/hp (13.5 kg/kW); consumption: Super Saloon 33.2 m/imp gal, 27.7 m/US gal, 8.5 l - Royal 30 m/imp gal, 25 m/US gal, 9.4 l x 100 km on Japanese emission test cycle.

CHASSIS Royal electronic levelling control dampers.

STEERING servo.

DIMENSIONS AND WEIGHT weight: Galant Sigma and Eterna Sigma Super Saloon sedans 2,414 lb, 1,095 kg - Galant Sigma and Eterna Sigma Royal sedans 2,558 lb, 1,160 kg.

OPTIONALS (for Super Saloon only) automatic transmission, hydraulic torque converter and planetary gears with 4 ratios (I 2.846, II 1.581, III 1, IV 0.685, rev 2.176).

135 hp power team

See 105 hp power team, except for:

ENGINE turbocharged; compression ratio: 7.5:1; max power (JIS): 135 hp (99 kW) at 5,800 rpm; max torque (JIS): 145 lb ft, 20 kg m (196 Nm) at 3,500 rpm; 76.9 hp/l (56.6 kW/l); Mitsubishi electronic injection; fuel feed: electric pump; turbocharger; cooling: 12.3 imp pt, 14.8 US pt, 7 l.

TRANSMISSION gears: 5, fully synchronized; ratios: I 4.226, II 2.365, III 1.467, IV 1.105, V 0.855, rev 4.109; axle ratio: 3.466; width of rims: 5"; tyres: 185/70 HR x 14.

PERFORMANCE max speed: 112 mph, 180 km/h; power-weight ratio: 17.8 lb/hp (24.2 lb/kW), 8.1 kg/hp (11 kg/kW); consumption: 32.1 m/imp gal, 26.4 m/US gal, 8.9 l x 100 km on Japanese emission test cycle.

STEERING servo.

DIMENSIONS AND WEIGHT weight: 2,403 lb, 1,090 kg.

OPTIONALS automatic transmission, hydraulic torque converter and planetary gears with 3 ratios (I 2.846, II 1.581, III 1, rev 2.176), 3.665 axle ratio.

145 hp power team

See 105 hp power team, except for:

ENGINE turbocharged; 121.9 cu in, 1,997 cc (3.35 x 3.46 in, 85 x 88 mm); compression ratio: 7.5:1; max power (JIS): 145 hp (104 kW) at 5,500 rpm; max torque (JIS): 159 lb ft, 22 kg m (216 Nm) at 3,000 rpm; 72.6 hp/l (52.1 kW/l);

145 HP POWER TEAM

lubrication: oil cooler, 7.6 imp pt, 9.1 US pt, 4.3 l; Mitsubishi electronic injection; fuel feed: electric pump; Mitsubishi turbocharger; cooling: 12.3 imp pt, 14.8 US pt, 7 l.

TRANSMISSION gears: 5, fully synchronized; ratios: I 4.070, II 2.244, III 1.467, IV 1.105, V 0.855, rev 4.109; axle ratio: 3.187; width of rims: 5.5"; tyres: 195/60 SR x 14.

PERFORMANCE max speed: 112 mph, 180 km/h; power-weight ratio: 17 lb/hp (23.2 lb/kW), 7.7 kg/hp (10.5 kg/kW); consumption: 34 m/imp gal, 28.3 m/US gal, 8.3 l x 100 km on Japanese emission test cycle.

STEERING servo; turns lock to lock: 3.

DIMENSIONS AND WEIGHT weight: 2,470 lb, 1,120 kg.

OPTIONALS automatic transmission, hydraulic torque converter and planetary gearbox with 4 ratios (I 2.846, II 1.581, III 1, IV 0.685, rev 2.176), 3.665 axle ratio.

Galant Lambda Series

PRICES (Tokyo):	yen
1 1800 Super Touring 2-dr Coupé	**1,511,000**
2 2000 Turbo GE 2-dr Coupé	**1,577,000**
3 2000 Turbo GT 2-dr Coupé	**1,690,000**
4 2000 Turbo GSR 2-dr Coupé	**1,960,000**
5 2300 Turbo Diesel 2-dr Coupé	**1,735,000**

For GB prices, see price index.

Power team:	Standard for:	Optional for:
100 hp	1	—
145 hp	2 to 4	—
95 hp (diesel)	5	—

100 hp power team

ENGINE front, 4 stroke; 4 cylinders, in line; 109.5 cu in, 1,795 cc (3.17 x 3.46 in, 81 x 88 mm); compression ratio: 8.5:1; max power (JIS): 100 hp (74 kW) at 5,500 rpm; max torque (JIS): 109 lb ft, 15 kg m (147 Nm) at 3,500 rpm; max engine rpm: 6,000; 55.7 hp/l (41.2 kW/l); 5 crankshaft bearings; twin silent-shaft, contra-rotating balancers; valves: overhead, with third air inlet valve, rockers; camshafts: 1, overhead, cogged belt; lubrication: gear pump, full flow filter, 7 imp pt, 8.5 US pt, 4 l; 1 downdraught twin barrel carburettor; fuel feed: mechanical pump; water-cooled, 12.3 imp pt, 14.8 US pt, 7 l.

TRANSMISSION driving wheels: rear; clutch: single dry plate (diaphragm); gearbox: mechanical; gears: 5, fully synchronized; ratios: I 3.444, II 2, III 1.316, IV 1, V 0.853, rev 3.667; lever: central; final drive: hypoid bevel; axle ratio: 3.909; width of rims: 5"; tyres: 185/70 HR x 13.

PERFORMANCE max speeds: (I) 33 mph, 53 km/h; (II) 53 mph, 86 km/h; (III) 80 mph, 128 km/h; (IV) and (V) 106 mph, 170 km/h; power-weight ratio: 24.6 lb/hp (33.4 lb/kW), 11.1 kg/hp (15.2 kg/kW); carrying capacity: 882 lb, 400 kg; consumption: 32.5 m/imp gal, 27 m/US gal, 8.7 l x 100 km on Japanese emission test cycle.

CHASSIS integral; front suspension: independent, by McPherson, coil springs/telescopic damper struts, lower wishbones (trailing links), anti-roll bar; rear: rigid axle, lower trailing links with diagonal locating members, upper diagonal torque rods, coil springs, telescopic dampers.

STEERING recirculating ball, variable ratio, servo; turns lock to lock: 3.60.

BRAKES disc, servo; lining area: front 19.2 sq in, 124 sq cm, rear 47.8 sq in, 308 sq cm, total 67 sq in, 432 sq cm.

ELECTRICAL EQUIPMENT 12 V; 35 Ah battery; 40 A alternator; Mitsubishi distributor; 2 or 4 headlamps.

DIMENSIONS AND WEIGHT wheel base: 99.61 in, 253 cm; tracks: 54.53 in, 138 cm front, 53.74 in, 136 cm rear; length: 179.92 in, 457 cm; width: 65.94 in, 167 cm; height: 53.35 in, 135 cm; ground clearance: 6.30 in, 16 cm; weight: 2,459 lb, 1,115 kg; weight distribution: 54% front, 46% rear; turning circle: 36.1 ft, 11 m; fuel tank: 13.2 imp gal, 15.8 US gal, 60 l.

BODY coupé; 2 doors; 5 seats, separate front seats.

145 hp power team

See 100 hp power team, except for:

ENGINE turbocharged; 121.9 cu in, 1,997 cc (3.35 x 3.46 in, 85 x 88 mm); compression ratio: 8:1; max power (JIS): 145 hp (104 kW) at 5,500 rpm; max torque (JIS): 159 lb ft, 22 kg m (216 Nm) at 3,000 rpm; 72.6 hp/l (52.1 kW/l); Mitsubishi ECI digital electronic injection; fuel feed: electric pump; Mitsubishi turbocharger.

TRANSMISSION gearbox ratios: I 3.740, II 2.136, III 1.360, IV 1, V 0.856, rev 3.578; axle ratio: 3.545; tyres: GT 185/70 HR x 14 - GE and GSR 195/70 HR x 14.

PERFORMANCE max speed: 112 mph, 180 km/h; power-weight ratio: GE 18.3 lb/hp (25.4 lb/kW), 8.3 kg/hp (11.5 kg/kW); consumption: 35.3 m/imp gal, 29.4 m/US gal, 8 l x 100 km on Japanese emission test cycle.

MITSUBISHI Galant Lambda 2000 Turbo GSR Coupé

CHASSIS rear suspension: independent, lower trailing arms, transverse arms, torque tube, coil springs, telescopic dampers.

DIMENSIONS AND WEIGHT front and rear track: 54.33 in, 138 cm; weight: Turbo GE and GT coupés 2,646 lb, 1,200 kg - Turbo GSR Coupé 2,756 lb, 1,250 kg.

OPTIONALS (for GSR only) automatic transmission with 4 ratios (I 2.452, II 1.452, III 1, IV 0.688, rev 2.212).

95 hp (diesel) power team

See 100 hp power team, except for:

ENGINE diesel, turbocharged; 143.2 cu in, 2,346 cc (3.59 x 3.54 in, 91 x 90 mm); compression ratio: 21:1; max power (JIS): 95 hp (68 kW) at 4,200 rpm; max torque (JIS): 134 lb ft, 18.5 kg m (182 Nm) at 3,000 rpm; max engine rpm: 4,400; 40.5 hp/l (28.9 kW/l); lubrication: 8.9 imp pt, 10.8 US pt, 5.1 l; Bosch VE injection pump; Mitsubishi swirl chamber; Mitsubishi exhaust driven turbocharger.

TRANSMISSION gearbox ratios: I 3.740, II 2.136, III 1.360, IV 1, V 0.856, rev 3.635; axle ratio: 3.545; tyres: 165 SR x 14.

PERFORMANCE max speed: 93 mph, 150 km/h; power-weight ratio: 28.1 lb/hp (38.2 lb/kW), 12.7 kg/hp (17.3 kg/kW); consumption: 65.7 m/imp gal, 54.7 m/US gal, 4.3 l x 100 km at 37 mph, 60 km/h on Japanese emission test cycle.

DIMENSIONS AND WEIGHT tracks: 53.94 in, 137 cm front, 53.35 in, 135 cm rear; weight: 2,668 lb, 1,210 kg.

Starion Series

PRICES (Tokyo):	yen
1 2000 Turbo GSR-I 2+1-dr Coupé	**1,815,000**
2 2000 Turbo GSR-II Automatic 2+1-dr Coupé	**2,090,000**
3 2000 Turbo GSR-III Automatic 2+1-dr Coupé	**2,320,000**
4 2000 Turbo GSR-X 2+1-dr Coupé	**2,745,000**
5 2000 Turbo GSR-II Intercooler 2+1-dr Coupé	**2,134,000**
6 2000 Turbo GSR-III Intercooler 2+1-dr Coupé	**2,320,000**

For GB prices, see price index.

Power team:	Standard for:	Optional for:
145 hp	1 to 4	—
175 hp	5,6	—

145 hp power team

ENGINE turbocharged; front, 4 stroke; 4 cylinders, vertical, in line; 121.9 cu in, 1,997 cc (3.35 x 3.46 in, 85 x 88 mm); compression ratio: 8:1; max power (JIS): 145 hp (107 kW) at 5,500 rpm; max torque (JIS): 159 lb ft, 22 kg m (216 Nm) at 3,500 rpm; max engine rpm: 6,000; 72.6 hp/l (53.4 kW/l); twin silent-shaft, contra-rotating balancers; 5 crankshaft bearings; valves: overhead, Vee-slanted, rockers; camshafts: 1, overhead; lubrication: gear pump, full flow filter, 7 imp pt, 8.5 US pt, 4 l; Mitsubishi MCA-Jet super lean-burn low emission engine with third air inlet valve, exhaust gas recirculation and oxidizing catalyst; fuel feed: electric pump; water-cooled, 14.1 imp pt, 16.9 US pt, 8 l.

TRANSMISSION driving wheels: rear; clutch: single dry plate (diaphragm); gearbox: mechanical; gears: 5, fully synchronized; ratios: I 3.740, II 2.136, III 1.360, IV 1, V 0.856, rev 3.578; final drive: hypoid bevel; lever: central; axle ratio: 3.909; width of rims: 5.5" or 6"; tyres: 195/70 HR x 14.

PERFORMANCE max speeds: (I) 30 mph, 48 km/h; (II) 53 mph, 85 km/h; (III) 84 mph, 135 km/h; (IV) and (V) 112 mph, 180 km/h; power-weight ratio: GSR-I 18 lb/hp (24.5 lb/kW), 8.2 kg/hp (11.1 kg/kW); consumption: 32.8 m/imp gal, 27 m/US gal, 8.7 l x 100 km on Japanese emission test cycle.

CHASSIS integral; front suspension: independent, by McPherson, coil springs/telescopic damper struts, lower transverse I arms, trailing links, anti-roll bar; rear: independent, by McPherson, lower wishbones, coil springs/telescopic damper struts, anti-roll bar.

STEERING recirculating ball, servo (except GSR-I); turns lock to lock: 3.50 - GSR-I 4.

BRAKES disc, internal radial fins; lining area: front 28.5 sq in, 184 sq cm, rear 19.8 sq in, 128 sq cm, total 48.3 sq in, 312 sq cm.

ELECTRICAL EQUIPMENT 12 V; 33 Ah battery; 55 A alternator; 2 retractable headlamps.

DIMENSIONS AND WEIGHT wheel base: 95.67 in, 243 cm; front and rear track: 54.72 in, 139 cm; length: 173.23 in, 440 cm; width: 66.73 in, 169 cm; height: 51.96 in, 132 cm; ground clearance: 6.20 in, 16 cm; weight: GSR-I 2.613 lb, 1,185 kg - GSR-X 2,734 lb, 1,240 kg.

BODY coupé; 2+1 doors; 4 seats, separate front seats.

OPTIONALS automatic transmission, hydraulic torque converter and planetary gears with 4 ratios (I 2.452, II 1.452, III 1, IV 0.688, rev 2.212).

175 hp power team

See 145 hp power team, except for:

ENGINE compression ratio: 7.5:1; max power (JIS): 175 hp (129 kW) at 5,500 rpm; max torque (JIS): 181 lb ft, 25 kg m (245 Nm) at 3,500 rpm; 87.6 hp/l (64.5 kW/l); turbocharger with exhaust wastegate; air-cooled.

TRANSMISSION gearbox ratios: I 3.369, II 2.035, III 1.360, IV 1, V 0.856, rev 3.578; tyres: 215/60 HR x 15.

PERFORMANCE power-weight ratio: GSR-II 15.3 lb/hp (20.8 lb/kW), 6.9 kg/hp (9.4 kg/kW); consumption: 32.1 m/imp gal, 26.4 m/US gal, 8.9 l x 100 km on Japanese emission test cycle.

CHASSIS rear suspension: semi-trailing arms.

STEERING rack-and-pinion.

DIMENSIONS AND WEIGHT weight: Turbo GSR-II Intercooler Coupé 2,481 lb, 1,125 kg - Turbo GSR-III Intercooler Coupé 2,701 lb, 1,225 kg.

Debonair

PRICES (Tokyo):	yen
Super De Luxe 4-dr Sedan	**2,491,000**
Executive SE 4-dr Sedan	**2,553,000**

ENGINE front, 4 stroke; 4 cylinders, in line; 155.9 cu in, 2,555 cc (3.59 x 3.86 in, 91.1 x 98 mm); compression ratio: 8.2:1; max power (JIS): 120 hp (88 kW) at 5,000 rpm; max torque (JIS): 152 lb ft, 21 kg m (206 Nm) at 3,000 rpm; max engine rpm: 5,500; 47 hp/l (34.6 kW/l); cast iron block, light alloy head; Mitsubishi twin contra-rotating balancing shafts; 5 crankshaft bearings; valves: overhead, rockers; camshafts: 1, overhead; lubrication: rotary pump, full flow filter, 8.8 imp pt, 10.6 US pt, 5 l; 1 Stromberg 30-32 DIDTA downdraught twin barrel carburettor; emission control with thermal reactor and exhaust gas recirculation; fuel feed: mechanical pump; water-cooled, 13.2 imp pt, 15.9 US pt, 7.5 l.

TRANSMISSION driving wheels: rear; gearbox: automatic transmission, hydraulic torque converter and planetary gears with 3 ratios, possible manual selection; ratios: I

2.680, II 1.508, III 1, rev 2.310; lever: steering column; final drive: hypoid bevel; axle ratio: 3.889; tyres: 175 SR x 14.

PERFORMANCE max speeds: (I) 35 mph, 57 km/h; (II) 65 mph, 105 km/h; (III) 96 mph, 155 km/h; power-weight ratio: 25.4 lb/hp (34.6 lb/kW), 11.5 kg/hp (15.7 kg/kW); consumption: 22.6 m/imp gal, 18.8 m/US gal, 12.5 l x 100 km on Japanese emission test cycle.

CHASSIS integral; front suspension: independent, double wishbones, coil springs/telescopic damper struts, anti-roll bar; rear: rigid axle, semi-elliptic leafsprings, telescopic dampers.

STEERING recirculating ball, servo.

BRAKES front disc, rear drum, servo.

ELECTRICAL EQUIPMENT 12 V; 60 Ah battery; 55 A alternator; Mitsubishi distributor; 4 headlamps.

DIMENSIONS AND WEIGHT wheel base: 105.91 in, 269 cm; front and rear track: 54.72 in, 139 cm; length: 183.86 in, 467 cm; width: 66.54 in, 169 cm; height: 57.48 in, 146 cm; ground clearance: 6.69 in, 17 cm; weight: 3,043 lb, 1,380 kg; weight distribution: 56% front, 44% rear; fuel tank: 15.4 imp gal, 18.5 US gal, 70 l.

BODY saloon/sedan; 4 doors; 5 seats, separate front seats.

Pajero Series

PRICES (Tokyo):	yen
1 DX 2000 (soft top) Wagon	**1,356,000**
2 DX 2000 (steel body) Wagon	**1,464,000**
3 XL 2000 Turbo (steel body) 2+1-dr Wagon	**2,200,000**
4 DX 2300 Diesel (soft top) Wagon	**1,496,000**
5 DX 2300 Diesel (steel body) Wagon	**1,611,000**
6 DX 2300 Turbo Diesel (soft top) Wagon	**1,695,000**
7 DX 2300 Turbo Diesel (steel body) Wagon	**1,915,000**

For GB prices, see price index.

Power team:	Standard for:	Optional for:
110 hp	1,2	—
145 hp	3	—
75 hp (diesel)	4,5	—
95 hp (diesel)	6,7	—

110 hp power team

ENGINE front, 4 stroke; 4 cylinders, in line; 121.9 cu in, 1,997 cc (3.34 x 3.46 in, 85 x 88 mm); compression ratio: 8.5:1; max power (JIS): 110 hp (81 kW) at 5,500 rpm; max torque (JIS): 121 lb ft, 16.7 kg m (164 Nm) at 3,500 rpm; max engine rpm: 6,000; 55.1 hp/l (40.5 kW/l); cast iron block, light alloy head; 5 crankshaft bearings; valves: overhead, Vee-slanted, push-rods and rockers; camshafts: 1, overhead; lubrication: gear pump, full flow filter, 8.8 imp pt, 10.6 US pt, 5 l; 1 30-32 DIDTA downdraught twin barrel carburettor; fuel feed: mechanical pump; water-cooled, 12.3 imp pt, 14.8 US pt, 7 l.

TRANSMISSION driving wheels: front or front and rear; clutch: single dry plate (diaphragm); gearbox: mechanical; gears: 5, fully synchronized and 2-ratio transfer box; ratios: I 3.740, II 2.136, III 1.360, IV 1, V 0.856, rev 3.578; transfer box ratios: low 1.944, high 1; lever: central; final drive: hypoid bevel; axle ratio: 4.875; width of rims: 5.5" or 6"; tyres: 7.60 x 15.

PERFORMANCE max speeds: (I) 25 mph, 40 km/h; (II) 43 mph, 70 km/h; (III) 68 mph, 110 km/h; (IV) and (V) 84 mph, 135 km/h; power-weight ratio: (soft top) 25.8 lb/hp (35 lb/kW), 11.7 kg/hp (15.9 kg/kW); consumption: 38.7 m/imp gal, 32.2 m/US gal, 7.3 l x 100 km at 37 mph, 60 km/h on Japanese emission test cycle.

CHASSIS box-type ladder frame; front suspension: independent, double wishbones, coil springs, telescopic dampers; rear: rigid axle, semi-elliptic leafsprings, telescopic dampers.

STEERING recirculating ball; turns lock to lock: 5.10.

BRAKES front disc, rear drum, servo; lining area: front 32.8 sq in, 212 sq cm, rear 80.6 sq in, 520 sq cm, total 113.4 sq in, 732 sq cm.

ELECTRICAL EQUIPMENT 12 V; 33 Ah battery; 45 A alternator; Mitsubishi distributor; 2 headlamps.

DIMENSIONS AND WEIGHT wheel base: 92.51 in, 235 cm; tracks: 55.11 in, 140 cm front, 53.93 in, 137 cm rear; length: 152.36 in, 387 cm; width: 66.14 in, 168 cm; height: (soft top) 72.83 in, 185 cm - (steel body) 73.62 in, 187 cm; ground clearance: 9 in, 23 cm; weight: DX 2000 (soft top) Wagon 2,833 lb, 1,285 kg - DX 2000 (steel body) Wagon 2,899 lb, 1,315 kg; weight distribution: 51% front, 49% rear; turning circle: 36.7 ft, 11.2 m; fuel tank: 13.2 imp gal, 15.3 US gal, 60 l.

BODY estate car/st. wagon; 4+1 doors; 5 seats, separate front seats.

OPTIONALS limited slip differential; mechanical winch; front wheel free-wheeling; steering damper kit.

145 hp power team

See 110 hp power team, except for:

ENGINE turbocharged; compression ratio: 8:1; max power (JIS): 145 hp (107 kW) at 5,500 rpm; max torque (JIS): 159 lb ft, 22 kg m (216 Nm) at 3,000 rpm; 72.6 hp/l (53.4 kW/l); Mitsubishi electronic injection; fuel feed: electric pump; turbocharger with exhaust wastegate.

TRANSMISSION axle ratio: 4.625; tyres: 215 SR x 15.

PERFORMANCE power-weight ratio: 21.5 lb/hp (29.2 lb/kW), 9.7 km/hp (13.2 kg/kW); consumption: 26.9 m/imp gal, 22.4 m/US gal, 10.5 l x 100 km on Japanese emission test cycle.

CHASSIS front and rear suspension: anti-roll bar.

STEERING servo.

DIMENSIONS AND WEIGHT length: 154.72 in, 393 cm; height: 72.23 in, 186 cm; weight: 3,109 lb, 1,410 kg.

BODY 2+1 doors.

75 hp (diesel) power team

See 110 hp power team, except for:

ENGINE diesel; 4 cylinders, vertical, in line; 143 cu in, 2,346 cc (3.58 x 3.54 in, 91 x 90 mm); compression ratio: 21:1; max power (JIS): 75 hp (55 kW) at 4,200 rpm; max torque (JIS): 108 lb ft, 15 kg m (147 Nm) at 2,500 rpm; max engine rpm: 4,400; 32 hp/l (23 kW/l); lubrication: 9.5 imp pt, 11.4 US pt, 5.4 l; vane-type mechanical injection pump; Mitsubishi swirl chambers; cooling: 14.1 imp pt, 16.9 US pt, 8 l.

TRANSMISSION gears: 4, fully synchronized and 2-ratio transfer box; ratios: I 4.330, II 2.355, III 1.574, IV 1, rev 4.142; transfer box ratios: low 1.944, high 1.

PERFORMANCE max speeds: (I) 15 mph, 25 km/h; (II) 29 mph, 47 km/h; (III) 47 mph, 75 km/h; (IV) 71 mph, 115 km/h; power-weight ratio: (soft top) 40.2 lb/hp (54.5 lb/kW), 18.2 km/hp (24.7 kg/kW); consumption: 45.6 m/imp gal, 37.9 m/US gal, 6.2 l x 100 km at 37 mph, 60 km/h on Japanese emission test cycle.

ELECTRICAL EQUIPMENT 70 Ah battery.

DIMENSIONS AND WEIGHT weight: DX 2300 Diesel (soft top) Wagon 4,090 lb, 1,855 kg - DX 2300 Diesel (steel body) Wagon 4,134 lb, 1,875 kg.

95 hp (diesel) power team

See 110 hp power team, except for:

ENGINE diesel, turbocharged; 4 cylinders, vertical, in line; 143 cu in, 2,346 cc (3.58 x 3.54 in, 91 x 90 mm); compression ratio: 18.5:1; max power (JIS): 95 hp (70 kW) at 4,200 rpm; max torque (JIS): 134 lb ft, 18.5 kg m (181 Nm) at 3,000 rpm; max engine rpm: 4,400; 40.5 hp/l (29.8 kW/l); lubrication: 9.5 imp pt, 11.4 US pt, 5.4 l; vane-type mechanical injection pump; Mitsubishi swirl chambers; turbocharger; cooling: 14.1 imp pt, 16.9 US pt, 8 l.

TRANSMISSION tyres: H 78 x 15.

PERFORMANCE max speeds: (I) 17 mph, 28 km/h; (II) 33 mph, 53 km/h; (III) 53 mph, 85 km/h; (IV) 71 mph, 115 km/h; (V) 78 mph, 125 km/h; power-weight ratio: (soft top) 32.6 lb/hp (44.3 lb/kW), 14.8 kg/hp (20.1 kg/kW); consumption: 47.9 m/imp gal, 39.9 m/US gal, 5.9 l x 100 km at 37 mph, 60 km/h on Japanese emission test cycle.

ELECTRICAL EQUIPMENT 70 Ah battery.

DIMENSIONS AND WEIGHT length: 154.72 in, 393 cm; height: (soft top) 72.63 in, 184 cm - (steel body) 73.22 in, 186 cm; weight: DX 2300 Turbo Diesel (soft top) Wagon 3,098 lb, 1,405 kg - DX 2300 Turbo Diesel (steel body) Wagon 3,197 lb, 1,450 kg.

Jeep Series

PRICES (Tokyo):	yen
1 L-J59 (soft top) 2+1-dr Wagon	**1,350,000**
2 L-J57 (soft top) 2+1-dr Wagon	**1,385,000**
3 L-J37 4+1-dr Wagon	**1,718,000**
4 K-J54 (soft top) 4+1-dr Wagon	**1,525,000**
5 K-J36 4+1-dr Wagon	**1,881,000**
6 K-J44 (soft top) 4+1-dr Wagon	**1,588,000**

Power team:	Standard for:	Optional for:
100 hp	1	—
120 hp	2,3	—
80 hp (diesel)	4 to 6	—

100 hp power team

ENGINE front, 4 stroke; 4 cylinders, vertical, in line; 121.7 cu in, 1,995 cc (3.31 x 3.54 in, 84 x 90 mm); compression ratio: 8.5:1; max power (JIS): 100 hp (74 kW) at 5,000 rpm; max torque (JIS): 123 lb ft, 17 kg m (167 Nm) at 3,000 rpm; max engine rpm: 5,400; 50.1 hp/l (36.9 kW/l; cast iron block, light alloy head; 5 crankshaft bearings; valves: overhead, Vee-slanted, rockers; camshafts: 1, overhead; lubrication: rotary pump, full flow filter, 7.6 imp pt, 9.1 US pt, 4.3 l; 1 Stromberg 30-32 DIDTA downdraught twin barrel carburettor; Mitsubishi MCA-Jet third air inlet valve lean-burn system; fuel feed: mechanical pump; water-cooled, 14 imp pt, 17 US pt, 8 l.

TRANSMISSION driving wheels: front (automatically engaged with transfer box) and rear; clutch: single dry plate (diaphragm), hydraulically controlled; gearbox: mechanical; gears: 4, fully synchronized; ratios: I 3.300, II 1.795, III 1.354, IV 1, rev 3.157; transfer box: low 2.306, high 0.093; lever: central; final drive: hypoid bevel; axle ratio: 5.375; width of rims: 4.5"; tyres: 7.60 x 15.

PERFORMANCE max speeds: (I) 25 mph, 40 km/h; (II) 45 mph, 73 km/h; (III) 60 mph, 97 km/h; (IV) 75 mph, 120 km/h; power-weight ratio: 25.4 lb/hp (34.3 lb/kW), 11.5 kg/hp

MITSUBISHI Starion 2000 Turbo GSR-II Intercooler Coupé

MITSUBISHI Pajero XL 2000 Turbo (steel body) Wagon

MITSUBISHI Jeep K-J44 (soft top) Wagon

100 HP POWER TEAM

(15.5 kg/kW); carrying capacity: 551 lb, 250 kg; speed in direct drive at 1,000 rpm: 13.8 mph, 22.2 km/h; consumption: 32.5 m/imp gal, 27 m/US gal, 8.7 l x 100 km at 37 mph, 60 km/h on Japanese emission test cycle.

CHASSIS box-type ladder frame; front and rear suspension: rigid axle, semi-elliptic leafsprings, telescopic dampers.

STEERING recirculating ball.

BRAKES drum.

ELECTRICAL EQUIPMENT 12 V; 35 Ah battery; 35 A alternator; Mitsubishi distributor; 2 headlamps.

DIMENSIONS AND WEIGHT wheel base: 79.92 in, 203 cm; front and rear track: 51.18 in, 130 cm; length: 137.40 in, 349 cm; width: 65.55 in, 166 cm; height: 75.60 in, 192 cm; ground clearance: 8.27 in, 21 cm; weight: 2,536 lb, 1,150 kg; weight distribution: 55% front, 45% rear; turning circle: 40 ft, 12.2 m; fuel tank: 9.7 imp gal, 11.6 US gal, 44 l.

BODY open; 2+1 detachable doors; 4 seats, separate front seats.

120 hp power team

See 100 hp power team, except for:

ENGINE 155.9 cu in, 2,555 cc (3.58 x 3.86 in, 91 x 98 mm); max power (JIS): 120 hp (88 kW) at 5,000 rpm; max torque (JIS): 154 lb ft, 21.3 kg m (209 Nm) at 3,000 rpm; 47 hp/l (34.6 kW/l).

TRANSMISSION lever: steering column.

PERFORMANCE power-weight ratio: L-J57 21.3 lb/hp (29 lb/kW), 9.7 kg/hp (13.1 kg/kW); consumption: 30.4 m/imp gal, 25.3 m/US gal, 9.3 l x 100 km at 37 mph, 60 km/h on Japanese emission test cycle.

ELECTRICAL EQUIPMENT 50 Ah battery.

DIMENSIONS AND WEIGHT wheel base: L-J37 103.94 in, 264 cm; length: L-J57 137.40 in, 349 cm - L-J37 168.90 in, 429 cm; width: L-J57 75.59 in, 192 cm - L-J37 63.78 in, 162 cm; height: L-J57 75.60 in, 192 cm - L-J37 74.41 in, 189 cm; weight: L-J57 (soft top) Wagon 2,558 lb, 1,160 kg - L-J37 Wagon 3,330 lb, 1,510 kg.

BODY open with detachable canvas doors or metal doors and metal or soft top - estate car/st. wagon; 4+1 doors; 4 or 9 seats, separate front seats.

80 hp (diesel) power team

See 100 hp power team, except for:

ENGINE diesel; 162.3 cu in, 2,659 cc (3.62 x 3.94 in, 92 x 100 mm); compression ratio: 20:1; max power (JIS): 80 hp (59 kW) at 3,700 rpm; max torque (JIS): 130 lb ft, 18 kg m (177 Nm) at 2,200 rpm; 30.1 hp/l (22.2 kW/l).

TRANSMISSION lever: steering column.

PERFORMANCE max speed: 62 mph, 100 km/h; power-weight ratio: K-J54 35.6 lb/hp (48.5 lb/kW), 16.2 kg/hp (22 kg/kW); consumption: 35.3 m/imp gal, 29.4 m/US gal, 8 l x 100 km at 37 mph, 60 km/h on Japanese emission test cycle.

ELECTRICAL EQUIPMENT 24 V; 70 Ah x 2 batteries.

DIMENSIONS AND WEIGHT wheel base: K-J54 79.92 in, 203 cm - K-J44 and K-J36 103.94 in, 264 cm; length: K-J54 137.40 in, 349 cm - K-J36 168.90 in, 429 cm; width: K-J44 65.75 in, 167 cm - K-J36 63.78 in, 162 cm; height: K-J54 75.20 in, 191 cm - K-J44 76.77 in, 195 cm - K-J36 74.41 in, 189 cm; weight: K-J54 (soft top) Wagon 2,855 lb, 1,255 kg - K-J44 (soft top) Wagon 3,285 lb, 1,490 kg - K-J36 Wagon 3,638 lb, 1,650 kg.

BODY open with detachable canvas doors or metal doors and metal or soft top - estate car/st. wagon; 4+1 doors; 4 or 9 seats, separate front seats.

NISSAN JAPAN

March

PRICES (Tokyo):	yen
E 2+1-dr Sedan	**635,000**
L 2+1-dr Sedan	**685,000**
S 2+1-dr Sedan	**760,000**
G 2+1-dr Sedan	**798,000**
FC 4+1-dr Hatchback Sedan	**750,000**
FT 4+1-dr Hatchback Sedan	**835,000**

For GB prices, see price index.

ENGINE front, transverse, 4 stroke; 4 cylinders, vertical, in line; 60.2 cu in, 987 cc (2.68 x 2.68 in, 68 x 68 mm); compression ratio: 9.5:1; max power (JIS): 57 hp (42 kW) at 6,000 rpm; max torque (JIS): 58 lb ft, 8 kg m (78 Nm) at 3,600 rpm; max engine rpm: 6,500; 57.7 hp/l (42.5 kW/l; light alloy block and head; 5 crankshaft bearings; valves: overhead, rockers; camshafts: 1, overhead; lubrication: trochoid pump, full flow filter, 5.3 imp pt, 6.2 US pt, 3 l; 1 Hitachi DCCU 306/53A twin barrel downdraught carburettor; exhaust gas recirculation, secondary air induction, oxidizing catalytic converter; fuel feed: mechanical pump; water-cooled, 7.9 imp pt, 8.5 US pt, 4 l, electric fan.

TRANSMISSION driving wheels: front; clutch: single dry plate (diaphragm); gearbox: mechanical; gears: 4, fully synchronized; ratios: I 3.412, II 1.958, III 1.258, IV 0.921, rev 3.385; lever: central; final drive: helical spur gears; axle ratio: 4.050; with of rims: 4''; tyres: E and L 5.95 x 12 - other models 145 SR x 12.

PERFORMANCE max speeds: (I) 29 mph, 47 km/h; (II) 56 mph, 90 km/h; (III) and (IV) 87 mph, 140 km/h; power-weight ratio: E 23.6 lb/hp (31.8 lb/kW), 10.7 kg/hp (14.5 kg/kW); consumption: 53.3 m/imp gal, 44.4 m/US gal, 5.3 l x 100 km on Japanese emission test cycle.

CHASSIS integral; front suspension: independent, by McPherson, lower A-type arms, coil springs, telescopic dampers; rear: rigid axle, lower links, upper diagonal torque rods, coil springs, telescopic dampers.

STEERING rack-and-pinion; turns lock to lock: 3.48.

BRAKES front disc, rear drum, servo.

ELECTRICAL EQUIPMENT 12 V; 30 Ah battery; 40 A alternator; 2 headlamps.

DIMENSIONS AND WEIGHT wheel base: 90.55 in, 230 cm; tracks: 52.76 in, 134 cm front, 52.36 in, 133 cm rear; length: 143.31 in, 364 cm; width: 61.42 in, 156 cm; height: 54.72 in, 139 cm; ground clearance: 6.49 in, 16.5 cm; weight: E Sedan 1,345 lb, 610 kg - FC Sedan 1,378 lb, 625 kg; weight distribution: 63% front, 37% rear; turning circle: 32.1 ft, 9.8 m; fuel tank: 8.8 imp gal, 10.6 US gal, 40 l.

BODY saloon/sedan; 2+1 or 4+1 doors; 5 seats, separate front seats.

VARIATIONS

(for L only)
ENGINE electronically controlled feedback carburettor; exhaust oxygen sensor, 3-way catalytic converter.
TRANSMISSION 5-speed fully synchronized mechanical gearbox (I 3.412, II 1.731, III 1.121, IV 0.850, V 0.721, rev 3.385), 3.810 axle ratio, 155 SR x 12 tyres.
PERFORMANCE consumption 58.8 m/imp pt, 49 m/US pt, 4.8 l x 100 km on Japanese emission test cycle.

OPTIONALS (except L) 5-speed fully synchronized mechanical gearbox (I 3.412, II 1.731, III 1.121, IV 0.850, V 0.721, rev 3.385); automatic transmission, hydraulic torque converter and planetary gears with 3 ratios (I 2.826, II 1.542, III 1, rev 2.364), 4.050 axle ratio; power steering.

Pulsar Series

	PRICES (Tokyo):	yen
1	1300 T 2+1-dr Hatchback Sedan	**756,000**
2	1300 TC 2+1-dr Hatchback Sedan	**810,000**
3	1300 TC 4+1-dr Hatchback Sedan	**820,000**
4	1300 TS 2+1-dr Hatchback Sedan	**869,000**
5	1300 TS 4+1-dr Hatchback Sedan	**879,000**
6	1300 TS-L 4+1-dr Hatchback Sedan	**938,000**
7	1500 TS-L 2+1-dr Hatchback Sedan	**983,000**
8	1500 TS-L 4+1-dr Hatchback Sedan	**1,003,000**
9	1500 TS-G 2+1-dr Hatchback Sedan	**1,053,000**
10	1500 TS-G 4+1-dr Hatchback Sedan	**1,095,000**
11	1500 TS-GE 2+1-dr Hatchback Sedan	**1,185,000**
12	1500 TS-GE 4-dr Hatchback Sedan	**1,175,000**
13	1500 TS-L 4-dr Sedan	**1,035,000**
14	1500 TS-G 4-dr Sedan	**1,127,000**
15	1500 TS-GE 4-dr Sedan	**1,222,000**
16	1500 EXA 2-dr Coupé	**1,175,000**
17	1500 EXA-E 2-dr Coupé	**1,285,000**
18	1500 Turbo 2+1-dr Hatchback Sedan	**1,360,000**
19	1500 Turbo 4+1-dr Hatchback Sedan	**1,350,000**
20	1500 Turbo 4-dr Sedan	**1,397,000**
21	1500 Turbo EXA 2-dr Coupé	**1,460,000**
22	Diesel 4-dr Sedan	**1,156,000**
23	Diesel 4+1-dr Hatchback Sedan	**1,124,000**

NISSAN March E Sedan

NISSAN Pulsar 1500 EXA Coupé

For GB and USA prices, see price index.

Power team:	Standard for:	Optional for:
75 hp	1 to 6	—
85 hp	7-10,13-15	—
95 hp	11,12,16,17	—
115 hp	18 to 21	—
61 hp (diesel)	22,23	—

75 hp power team

ENGINE front, transverse, 4 stroke; 4 cylinders, in line; 77.5 cu in, 1,270 cc (2.99 x 2.75 in, 76 x 70 mm); compression ratio: 9:1; max power (JIS): 75 hp (55 kW) at 6,000 rpm; max torque (JIS): 78 lb ft, 10.7 kg m (105 Nm) at 3,600 rpm; max engine rpm: 6,500; 59.1 hp/l (43.5 kW/l; cast iron block, light alloy head; 5 crankshaft bearings; valves: overhead, rockers; camshafts: 1, overhead, cogged belt; lubrication: trochoid pump, full flow filter, 6 imp pt, 7.1 US pt, 3.4 l; 1 Nikki 217260-011 twin barrel carburettor; exhaust system with secondary air induction, gas recirculation and catalytic converter; fuel feed: mechanical pump; water-cooled, 7.4 imp pt, 8.9 US pt, 4.2 l, electric thermostatic fan.

TRANSMISSION driving wheels: front; clutch: single dry plate (diaphragm); gearbox: mechanical; gears: 4, fully synchronized; ratios: I 3.333, II 1.955, III 1.286, IV 0.902, rev 3.417; lever: central; final drive: helical spur gears; axle ratio: 3.895; width of rims: 4.5"; tyres: 6.15 x 13.

PERFORMANCE max speed: 99 mph, 160 km/h; power-weight ratio: TC 2+1-dr 21.9 lb/hp (30 lb/kW), 18.4 kg/hp (13.5 kg/kW); carrying capacity: 882 lb, 400 kg; consumption: 47.1 m/imp gal, 39.2 m/US gal, 6 l x 100 km on Japanese emission test cycle.

CHASSIS integral; front suspension: independent, by McPherson, coil springs/telescopic damper struts, lower wishbones; rear: independent, trailing arms, coil springs, telescopic dampers.

STEERING rack-and-pinion; turns lock to lock: 3.90.

BRAKES front disc, rear drum, servo; lining area: front 14.3 sq in, 92 sq cm, rear 42.2 sq in, 272 sq cm, total 56.5 sq in, 364 sq cm.

NISSAN Sunny Turbo Le Prix Hatchback Sedan

ELECTRICAL EQUIPMENT 12 V; 30 Ah battery; 50 A alternator; Mitsubishi distributor; 2 retractable headlamps.

DIMENSIONS AND WEIGHT wheel base: 94.88 in, 241 cm; tracks: 54.72 in, 139 cm front, 53.93 in, 137 cm rear; length: 156 in, 396 cm; width: 64 in, 162 cm; height: 54.72 in, 139 cm; ground clearance: 6.69 in, 17 cm; weight: TC and T 2+1-dr hatchback sedans 1,641 lb, 745 kg - TS 2+1-dr Hatchback Sedan 1,653 lb, 750 kg - TS 4+1-dr Hatchback Sedan 1,663 lb, 755 kg - TS-L Hatchback Sedan 1,674 lb, 760 kg; weight distribution: 63% front, 37% rear; turning circle: 33.4 ft, 10.2 m; fuel tank: 11 imp gal, 13.2 US gal, 50 l.

BODY saloon/sedan; 2+1 or 4+1 doors; 5 seats, separate front seats.

OPTIONALS 5-speed fully synchronized mechanical gearbox (V ratio 0.733); automatic transmission, hydraulic torque converter and planetary gears with 3 ratios (I 2.826, II 1.543, III 1, rev 2.364), 3.600 axle ratio.

85 hp power team

See 75 hp power team, except for:

ENGINE 90.7 cu in, 1,487 cc (2.99 x 3.23 in, 76 x 82 mm); max power (JIS): 85 hp (63 kW) at 5,600 rpm; max torque (JIS): 90 lb ft, 12.3 kg m (121 Nm) at 3,600 rpm; max engine rpm: 6,000; 57.2 hp/l (42.1 kW/l); 1 Hitachi DCY 306-1 downdraught twin barrel carburettor.

TRANSMISSION axle ratio: 3.789; tyres: 155 SR x 13.

PERFORMANCE max speed: 102 mph, 165 km/h; power-weight ratio: TS-L 2+1-dr 20.4 lb/hp (27.7 lb/kW), 9.2 kg/hp (12.5 kg/kW).

DIMENSIONS AND WEIGHT height: 55 in, 139 cm; weight: TS-L and TS-G 2+1-dr hatchback sedans 1,719 lb, 780 kg - TS-X 2+1-dr Hatchback Sedan 1,730 lb, 785 kg - TS-L 4+1-dr Hatchback Sedan 1,741 lb, 790 kg - TS-G 4+1-dr Hatchback Sedan 1,786 lb, 810 kg.

BODY 2+1, 4 or 4+1 doors.

VARIATIONS

ENGINE 9.3:1 compression ratio, max torque (JIS) 92 lb ft, 12.5 kg m (123 Nm) at 3,600 rpm, knock sensor and ignition retard system.
TRANSMISSION (standard) 5-speed fully synchronized mechanical gearbox (I 3.063, II 1.708, III 1.133, IV 0.814, V 0.681, rev 3.417), 3.550 axle ratio.
PERFORMANCE consumption 49.6 m/imp gal, 41.3 m/US gal, 5.7 l x 100 km on Japanese emission test cycle.

OPTIONALS 5-speed fully synchronized mechanical gearbox (V ratio 0.733); automatic transmission, hydraulic torque converter and planetary gears with 3 ratios (I 2.826, II 1.543, III 1, rev 2.364), 3.364 axle ratio; power steering.

95 hp power team

See 75 hp power team, except for:

ENGINE 90.7 cu in, 1,487 cc (2.99 x 3.23 in, 76 x 82 mm); max power (JIS): 95 hp (70 kW) at 6,000 rpm; max torque (JIS): 92 lb ft, 12.5 kg m (123 Nm) at 3,600 rpm; 63.9 hp/l (47 kW/l); Nissan EGI electronic fuel injection; fuel feed: electric pump; cooling: 10 imp pt, 12.7 US pt, 6 l.

TRANSMISSION (standard) gears: 5, fully synchronized; ratios: I 3.063, II 1.826, III 1.207, IV 0.902, V 0.733, rev 3.417; axle ratio: 4.167; tyres: 165/70 SR x 13.

PERFORMANCE max speed: 106 mph, 170 km/h; power-weight ratio: 19.2 lb/hp (26.1 lb/kW), 8.7 kg/hp (11.9 kg/kW); consumption: 42.8 m/imp gal, 35.6 m/US gal, 6.6 l x 100 km on Japanese emission test cycle.

CHASSIS EXA and EXA-E front suspension: anti-roll bar.

DIMENSIONS AND WEIGHT tracks: 54.13 in, 138 cm front, 52.95 in, 134 cm rear; length: 155 in, 396 cm - EXA and EXA-E 162 in, 412 cm; height: 55 in, 139 cm - EXA and EXA-E 53 in, 135 cm; weight: 1,808 lb, 820 kg.

BODY saloon/sedan, 2+1 or 4+1 doors - coupé, 2 doors.

OPTIONALS automatic transmission, hydraulic torque converter and planetary gears with 3 ratios (I 2.826, II 1.543, III 1, rev 2.364), 3.364 axle ratio.

115 hp power team

See 75 hp power team, except for:

ENGINE turbocharged; 90.7 cu in, 1,487 cc (2.99 x 3.27 in, 76 x 83 mm); compression ratio: 8:1; max power (JIS): 115 hp (85 kW) at 5,600 rpm; max torque (JIS): 123 lb ft, 17 kg m (167 Nm) at 3,200 rpm; max engine rpm: 6,000; 77.3 hp/l (57.2 kW/l); AiResearch T2 turbocharger with wastegate; electronic injection; emission control by 3-way catalytic converter and exhaust gas recirculation; fuel feed: electric pump; cooling: 10.8 imp pt, 12.7 US pt, 6 l.

TRANSMISSION (standard) gearbox ratios: I 3.333, II 1.955, III 1.286, IV 0.902, V 0.733, rev 3.417; axle ratio: 3.789; width of rims: 5"; tyres: 175/70 SR x 13.

PERFORMANCE max speed: 112 mph, 180 km/h; power-weight ratio: Turbo hatchback sedans 17 lb/hp (22.9 lb/kW), 7.7 kg/hp (10.4 kg/kW); consumption: 41.5 m/imp gal, 34.6 m/US gal, 6.8 l x 100 km on Japanese emission test cycle.

CHASSIS front suspension: anti-roll bar.

BRAKES disc.

ELECTRICAL EQUIPMENT 45 Ah battery.

DIMENSIONS AND WEIGHT weight: Turbo hatchback sedans and Turbo Sedan 1,940 lb, 880 kg - Turbo EXA Coupé 1,951 lb, 885 kg.

OPTIONALS automatic transmission, hydraulic torque converter and planetary gears with 3 ratios (I 2.826, II 1.543, III 1, rev 2.364), 3.167 axle ratio, oil cooler.

61 hp (diesel) power team

See 75 hp power team, except for:

ENGINE diesel; 102.5 cu in, 1,680 cc (3.15 x 3.29 in, 80 x 83.6 mm); compression ratio: 22.2:1; max power (JIS): 61 hp (45 kW) at 5,000 rpm; max torque (JIS): 77 lb ft, 10.6 kg m (59 Nm) at 2,800 rpm; 36.3 hp/l (26.8 kW/l); valves: overhead, thimble tappets; lubrication: gear pump, full flow filter, 7 imp pt, 8.5 US pt, 4 l; Ricardo Comet swirl combustion chambers; Bosch VE injection pump; cooling: 12.3 imp pt, 14.8 US pt, 7 l.

TRANSMISSION (standard) gearbox ratios: I 3.333, II 1.955, III 1.286, IV 0.902, V 0.733, rev 3.417; axle ratio: 3.789; tyres: 155 SR x 13.

PERFORMANCE max speed: 90 mph, 145 km/h; power-weight ratio: Sedan 32.2 lb/hp (43.7 lb/kW), 14.6 kg/hp (19.8 kg/kW); consumption: 91.1 m/imp gal, 75.9 m/US gal, 3.1 l x 100 km at 37 mph, 60 km/h on Japanese emission test cycle.

STEERING turns lock to lock: 3.70.

DIMENSIONS AND WEIGHT weight: Diesel Sedan 1,962 lb, 890 kg - Diesel Hatchback Sedan 1,940 lb, 880 kg.

OPTIONALS automatic transmission, hydraulic torque converter and planetary gears with 3 ratios (I 2.826, II 1.543, III 1, rev 2.364), 3.167 axle ratio, oil cooler.

Sunny Series

PRICES (Tokyo):		yen
1	1300 CT 4-dr Sedan	**805,000**
2	1300 DX 4-dr Sedan	**844,000**
3	1300 GL 4-dr Sedan	**899,000**
4	1300 SGL 4-dr Sedan	**1,013,000**
5	1300 California DL 4+1-dr Hatchback Sedan	**943,000**
6	1300 California GL-L 4+1-dr Hatchback Sedan	**1,028,000**
7	1500 GX-L 2+1-dr Hatchback Sedan	**995,000**
8	1500 GX-S 2+1-dr Hatchback Sedan	**1,065,000**
9	1500 GX-X 2+1-dr Hatchback Sedan	**1,025,000**
10	1500 GX-R 2+1-dr Hatchback Sedan	**1,099,000**
11	1500 GL 4-dr Sedan	**965,000**
12	1500 SGL 4-dr Sedan	**1,063,000**
13	1500 SGX 4-dr Sedan	**1,117,000**
14	1500 California GL-L 4+1-dr Hatchback Sedan	**1,076,000**
15	1500 California SGL 4+1-dr Hatchback Sedan	**1,153,000**
16	1500 California SGX 4+1-dr Hatchback Sedan	**1,207,000**
17	1500 SGX-E 4-dr Sedan	**1,214,000**
18	Turbo Le Prix 2+1-dr Hatchback Sedan	**1,378,000**
19	Turbo Le Prix 4-dr Sedan	**1,384,000**
20	1700 Diesel GL 4-dr Sedan	**1,086,000**
21	1700 Diesel SGL 4-dr Sedan	**1,184,000**
22	1700 Diesel California GL-L 4+1-dr Hatchback Sedan	**1,197,000**

SUNNY SERIES

For GB and USA prices, see price index.

Power team:	Standard for:	Optional for:
75 hp	1 to 6	—
85 hp	7 to 16	—
95 hp	17	—
115 hp	18,19	—
61 hp (diesel)	20 to 22	—

75 hp power team

ENGINE front, 4 stroke; 4 cylinders, transverse, in line; 75.5 cu in, 1,270 cc (2.99 x 2.76 in, 76 x 70 mm); compression ratio: 9:1; max power (JIS): 75 hp (55 kW) at 6,000 rpm; max torque (JIS): 78 lb ft, 10.7 kg m (105 Nm) at 3,600 rpm; max engine rpm: 6,500; 59.1 hp/l (43.5 kW/l); cast iron block, light alloy head; 5 crankshaft bearings; valves: overhead, Vee-slanted, rockers; camshafts: 1, overhead, cogged belt; lubrication: trochoid pump, full flow filter, 6 imp pt, 7.2 US pt, 3.3 l; 1 Nikki 217260-21 downdraught twin barrel carburettor; exhaust system with secondary air induction, gas recirculation and catalytic converter; fuel feed: mechanical pump; water-cooled, 7.4 imp pt, 8.8 US pt, 4.2 l, electric thermostatic fan.

TRANSMISSION driving wheels: front; clutch: single dry plate (diaphragm); gearbox: mechanical; gears: 4, fully synchronized; ratios: I 3.333, II 1.955, III 1.286, IV 0.902, rev 3.417; lever: central; final drive: helical spur gears; axle ratio: 3.895; width of rims: 4"; tyres: 6.15 x 13 - SGL and GL-L 145 SR x 13.

PERFORMANCE max speed: 99 mph, 160 km/h; power-weight ratio: GL 22.2 lb/hp (30.1 lb/kW), 10 kg/hp (13.7 kg/kW); carrying capacity: 882 lb, 400 kg; speed in top at 1,000 rpm: 19.6 mph, 26.7 km/h; consumption: 45 m/imp gal, 37.9 m/US gal, 6.2 l x 100 km on Japanese emission test cycle.

CHASSIS integral; front suspension: independent, by McPherson, lower wishbones, coil springs, telescopic damper struts; rear: independent, trailing arms, coil springs, telescopic dampers.

STEERING rack-and-pinion; turns lock to lock: 3.90.

BRAKES front disc (diameter 8.19 in, 20.8 cm), rear drum, servo.

ELECTRICAL EQUIPMENT 12 V; 40 Ah battery; 50 A alternator; Hitachi electronic ignition; 2 headlamps.

DIMENSIONS AND WEIGHT wheel base: 94.49 in, 240 cm; tracks: 54.72 in, 139 cm front, 54.50 in, 138 cm rear; length: 159.45 in, 405 cm; width: 63.78 in, 162 cm; height: 63.78 in, 162 cm; ground clearance: 6.69 in, 17 cm; weight: GL Sedan and California GL-L Hatchback Sedan 1,663 lb, 755 kg - SGL Sedan 1,685 lb, 765 kg - CT Sedan 1,674 lb, 760 kg - California DL Hatchback Sedan 1,797 lb, 815 kg; weight distribution: 62% front, 38% rear; turning circle: 30.8 ft, 10 m; fuel tank: 11 imp gal, 13.2 US gal, 50 l.

BODY saloon/sedan; 4 or 4+1 doors; 5 seats, separate front seats, built-in headrests.

OPTIONALS automatic transmission, hydraulic torque converter and planetary gears with 3 ratios (I 2.826, II 1.543, III 1, rev 2.364), 3.600 axle ratio.

85 hp power team

See 75 hp power team, except for:

ENGINE 90.7 cu in, 1,487 cc (2.99 x 3.23 in, 76 x 82 mm); max power (JIS): 85 hp (63 kW) at 5,600 rpm; max torque (JIS): 90 lb ft, 12.3 kg m (121 Nm) at 3,600 rpm; max engine rpm: 6,000; 57.2 hp/l (42.1 kW/l); 1 Hitachi DCR 306-11-A twin barrel carburettor; cooling: 8.4 imp pt, 10 US pt, 4.7 l.

TRANSMISSION axle ratio: 3.789; width of rims: 4.5"; tyres: GL 145 SR x 13 - SGL, California GL-L and California SGL 155 SR x 13 - SGX, GX-R and California SGX 165/70 SR x 13.

PERFORMANCE max speed: 103 mph, 165 km/h; power-weight ratio: GL 21.5 lb/hp (29.3 lb/kW), 9.8 kg/hp (13.3 kg/kW); consumption: 44.4 m/imp gal, 37.3 m/US gal, 6.3 l x 100 km on Japanese emission test cycle.

DIMENSIONS AND WEIGHT tracks: 55 in, 139 cm front, 54 in, 137 cm rear; weight: GX-L, GX-S, GX-X and GX-R hatchback sedans 1,830 lb, 830 kg - GL Sedan 1,740 lb, 790 kg - SGL and SGX sedans 1,764 lb, 800 kg - California GL-L Hatchback Sedan 1,830 lb, 830 kg - California SGL and California SGX hatchback sedans 1,863 lb, 845 kg.

BODY 2+1, 4 or 4+1 doors.

VARIATIONS

ENGINE 9.3:1 compression ratio, max torque (JIS) 92 lb ft, 12.5 kg m (123 Nm) at 3,600 rpm, electronic carburettor, knock sensor with retard adjustment system.
TRANSMISSION 5-speed mechanical gearbox (I 3.063, II 1.708, III 1.133, IV 0.816, V 0.681, rev 3.417), 3.550 axle ratio, 145 SR x 13 tyres.
PERFORMANCE consumption 49 m/imp gal, 41.3 m/US gal, 5.7 l x 100 km on Japanese emission test cycle.

OPTIONALS 3.364 axle ratio with automatic transmission; 5-

NISSAN Sunny (1.5-litre turbo engine)

speed fully synchronized mechanical gearbox (I 3.333, II 1.955, III 1.286, IV 0.902, V 0.733, rev 3.417); power steering.

95 hp power team

See 75 hp power team, except for:

ENGINE 90.7 cu in, 1,487 cc (2.99 x 3.23 in, 76 x 82 mm); max power (JIS): 95 hp (70 kW) at 6,000 rpm; max torque (JIS): 92 lb ft, 12.5 kg m (123 Nm) at 3,600 rpm; max engine rpm: 6,400; 63.9 hp/l (47 kW/l); Nissan EGI electronic fuel injection; fuel feed: electric pump; cooling: 8.4 imp pt, 10 US pt, 4.7 l.

TRANSMISSION gears: 5, fully synchronized; ratios: I 3.063, II 1.826, III 1.207, IV 0.902, V 0.733, rev 3.417; axle ratio: 4.167; tyres: 165/70 HR x 13.

PERFORMANCE max speed: 105 mph, 170 km/h; power-weight ratio: 18.8 lb/hp (25.5 lb/kW), 8.6 kg/hp (11.6 kg/kW); consumption: 42.2 m/imp gal, 35.1 m/US gal, 6.7 l x 100 km on Japanese emission test cycle.

DIMENSIONS AND WEIGHT weight: 1,808 lb, 820 kg.

BODY 4 doors.

115 hp power team

See 75 hp power team, except for:

ENGINE turbocharged; 90.7 cu in, 1,487 cc (2.99 x 3.23 in, 76 x 82 mm); compression ratio: 8:1; max power (JIS): 115 hp (85 kW) at 5,600 rpm; max torque (JIS): 123 lb ft, 17 kg m (167 Nm) at 3,200 rpm; 77.3 hp/l (56.9 kW/l); EGI electronic fuel injection; turbocharger; exhaust system closed-loop type with oxygen sensor feedback, 3-way catalyst and exhaust gas recirculation; fuel feed: electric pump; cooling: 10.6 imp pt, 12.7 US pt, 6 l.

TRANSMISSION gears: 5, fully synchronized; ratios: I 3.333, II 1.955, III 1.286, IV 0.902, V 0.733, rev 3.417; axle ratio: 3.789; width of rims: 4.5"; tyres: 175/70 SR x 13.

PERFORMANCE max speed: 112 mph, 180 km/h; power-weight ratio: Sedan 16.5 lb/hp (22.3 lb/kW), 7.5 kg/hp (10.1 kg/kW); consumption: 41.5 m/imp gal, 34.6 m/US gal, 16.8 l x 100 km on Japanese emission test cycle.

CHASSIS front suspension: anti-roll bar.

STEERING turns lock to lock: 3.70.

BRAKES disc, servo.

DIMENSIONS AND WEIGHT weight: Le Prix Sedan 1,896 lb, 860 kg.

BODY 2+1 or 4 doors.

61 hp (diesel) power team

See 75 hp power team, except for:

ENGINE diesel; 102.5 cu in, 1,680 cc (3.15 x 3.39 in, 80 x 86 mm); compression ratio: 22.2:1; max power (JIS): 61 hp (45 kW) at 5,000 rpm; max torque (JIS): 77 lb ft, 10.6 kg m (104 Nm) at 2,800 rpm; max engine rpm: 6,000; 36.3 hp/l (26.7 kW/l); lubrication: 7 imp pt, 8.2 US pt, 4 l; Bosch VE fuel injection; cooling: 12.3 imp pt, 14.8 US pt, 7 l.

TRANSMISSION gears: 5, fully synchronized; ratios: I 3.333, II 1.955, III 1.286, IV 0.901, V 0.733, rev 3.417; axle ratio: 3.780; tyres: 155 SR x 13.

PERFORMANCE max speed: 90 mph, 145 km/h; power-weight ratio: GL 31.5 lb/hp (42.6 lb/kW), 14.3 kg/hp (19.3 kg/kW); consumption: 91.1 m/imp gal, 75.9 m/US gal, 3.1 l x 100 km on Japanese emission test cycle.

ELECTRICAL EQUIPMENT 70 Ah battery.

DIMENSIONS AND WEIGHT weight: Diesel GL Sedan 1,918 lb, 870 kg - Diesel SGL Sedan 1,940 lb, 880 kg - Diesel California GL-L Hatchback Sedan 2,029 lb, 920 kg.

Langley Series

PRICES (Tokyo):		yen
1	D 2+1-dr Hatchback Sedan	937,000
2	D 4+1-dr Hatchback Sedan	1,023,000
3	L 2+1-dr Hatchback Sedan	1,105,000
4	L 4+1-dr Hatchback Sedan	957,000
5	X 2+1-dr Hatchback Sedan	1,043,000
6	X 4+1-dr Hatchback Sedan	1,140,000
7	GT 2+1-dr Hatchback Sedan	1,237,000
8	GT 4+1-dr Hatchback Sedan	1,227,000
9	Turbo GT 2+1-dr Hatchback Sedan	1,407,000
10	Turbo GT 4+1-dr Hatchback Sedan	1,397,000
11	Diesel L-D 4+1-dr Hatchback Sedan	1,164,000

Power team:	Standard for:	Optional for:
85 hp	1 to 6	—
95 hp	7,8	—
115 hp	9,10	—
61 hp (diesel)	11	—

85 hp power team

ENGINE front, transverse, 4 stroke; 4 cylinders, in line; 90.7 cu in, 1,487 cc (2.99 x 3.23 in, 76 x 82 mm); compression ratio: 9:1; max power (JIS): 85 hp (63 kW) at 5,600 rpm; max torque (JIS): 90 lb ft, 12.3 kg m (121 Nm) at 3,600 rpm; max engine rpm: 6,000; 57.2 hp/l (42.1 kW/l); cast iron block, light alloy head; 5 crankshaft bearings; valves: overhead, Vee-slanted, rockers; camshafts: 1, overhead, cogged belt; lubrication: trochoid pump, full flow filter, 6 imp pt, 7.1 US pt, 3.4 l; 1 Hitachi DCY 306-11 twin barrel carburettor; fuel feed: mechanical pump; exhaust system with secondary air induction, gas recirculation and catalytic converter; water-cooled, 8.3 imp pt, 9.9 US pt, 4.7 l, electric termostatic fan.

TRANSMISSION driving wheels: front; clutch: single dry plate

NISSAN Sunny Turbo Le Prix Hatchback Sedan

(diaphragm); gearbox: mechanical; gears: 4, fully synchronized; ratios: I 3.333, II 1.955, III 1.286, IV 0.902, rev 3.417; lever: central; final drive: helical spur gears; axle ratio: 3.789; width of rims: 4.5"; tyres: 155 SR x 13.

PERFORMANCE max speed: 102 mph, 165 km/h; power-weight ratio: D 2+1-dr 20 lb/hp (27.1 lb/kW), 9.1 kg/hp (12.3 kg/kW); consumption: 45.6 m/imp gal, 37.9 m/US gal, 6.2 l x 100 km on Japanese emission test cycle.

CHASSIS integral; front suspension: independent, by McPherson, lower A-shape arms, coil springs, telescopic dampers; rear: independent, trailing arms, coil springs, telescopic dampers.

STEERING rack-and-pinion; turns lock to lock: 3.90.

BRAKES front disc, rear drum, servo.

ELECTRICAL EQUIPMENT 12 V; 30 Ah battery; 50 A alternator; Hitachi ignition distributor; 4 headlamps.

DIMENSIONS AND WEIGHT wheel base: 95 in, 241 cm; tracks: 55 in, 139 cm front, 54 in, 137 cm rear; length: 156 in, 396 cm; width: 64 in, 162 cm; height: 55 in, 139 cm; ground clearance: 6.69 in, 17 cm; weight: D 2+1-dr Hatchback Sedan 1,697 lb, 770 kg - D 4+1-dr Hatchback Sedan 1,719 lb, 780 kg - L 2+1-dr Hatchback Sedan 1,720 lb, 781 kg - X 2+1-dr Hatchback Sedan 1,730 lb, 785 kg - L 4+1-dr Hatchback Sedan 1,741 lb, 790 kg - X 4+1-dr Hatchback Sedan 1,752 lb, 795 kg; weight distribution: 62% front, 38% rear; turning circle: 33.4 ft, 10.2 m; fuel tank: 11.2 imp gal, 13.2 US gal, 50 l.

BODY saloon/sedan; 2+1 or 4+1 doors; 5 seats, separate front seats.

VARIATIONS

ENGINE 9.3:1 compression ratio, max torque (JIS) 90 lb ft, 12.5 kg m (122 Nm) at 3,600 rpm, knock sensor and ignition retard system emission control by electronically-controlled carburettor, 3-way catalytic converter and exhaust recirculation.
TRANSMISSION 5-speed fully synchronized mechanical gearbox (I 3.063, II 1.708, III 1.133, IV 0.814, V 0.681, rev 3.417), 3.550 axle ratio.
PERFORMANCE consumption 49.6 m/imp gal, 41.3 m/US gal, 5.7 l x 100 km on Japanese emission test cycle.
DIMENSIONS AND WEIGHT weight D 2+1-dr Hatchback Sedan 1,697 lb, 770 kg.

OPTIONALS 5-speed fully synchronized mechanical gearbox (V ratio 0.733) (for L and X 4+1-dr hatchback sedans only); power steering (for L and X hatchback sedans only).

95 hp power team

See 85 hp power team, except for:

ENGINE max power (JIS): 95 hp (70 kW) at 6,000 rpm; max torque (JIS): 91 lb ft, 12.5 kg m (123 Nm) at 3,600 rpm; max engine rpm: 6,500; 63.9 hp/l (47 kW/l); Nissan EGI electronic injection; fuel feed: electric pump.

TRANSMISSION (standard) gears: 5, fully synchronized; ratios: I 3.063, II 1.826, III 1.207, IV 0.902, V 0.733, rev 3.417; axle ratio: 4.167; width of rims: 5"; tyres: 165/70 SR x 13.

PERFORMANCE max speed: 105 mph, 170 km/h; power-weight ratio: GT 4+1-dr 19.2 lb/hp (26.1 lb/kW), 8.7 kg/hp (11.9 kg/kW); consumption: 42.8 m/imp gal, 35.6 m/US gal, 6.6 l x 100 km on Japanese emission test cycle.

DIMENSIONS AND WEIGHT weight: GT 4+1-dr Hatchback Sedan 1,828 lb, 830 kg.

OPTIONALS automatic transmission, hydraulic torque converter and planetary gears with 3 ratios (I 2.826, II 1.543, III 1, rev 2.364), 3.364 axle ratio.

115 hp power team

See 85 hp power team, except for:

ENGINE turbocharged; 90.7 cu in, 1,487 cc (2.99 x 3.23 in, 76 x 82 mm); compression ratio: 8:1; max power (JIS): 115 hp (85 kW) at 5,600 rpm; max torque (JIS): 123 lb ft, 17 kg m (167 Nm) at 3,200 rpm; 77.4 hp/l (56.9 kW/l); AiResearch T2 turbocharger; electronic fuel injection, emission control by 3-way catalytic converter and exhaust gas recirculation; fuel feed: electric pump; cooling: 10 imp pt, 12.7 US pt, 6 l.

TRANSMISSION (standard) gears: 5, fully synchronized; ratios: I 3.333, II 1.955, III 1.286, IV 0.902, V 0.733, rev 3.417; width of rims: 5"; tyres: 175/70 SR x 13.

PERFORMANCE max speed: 112 mph, 180 km/h; power-weight ratio: GT 2+1-dr 16.9 lb/hp (22.9 lb/kW), 7.6 kg/hp (10.4 kg/kW); consumption: 41.5 m/imp gal, 34.6 m/US gal, 6.8 l x 100 km on Japanese emission test cycle.

CHASSIS front suspension: anti-roll bar.

BRAKES disc, servo.

ELECTRICAL EQUIPMENT 45 Ah battery.

DIMENSIONS AND WEIGHT weight: Turbo GT 2+1-dr Hatchback Sedan 1,940 lb, 880 kg - Turbo GT 4+1-dr Hatchback Sedan 1,962 lb, 890 kg.

OPTIONALS automatic transmission, hydraulic torque converter and planetary gears with 3 ratios (I 2.826, II 1.543, III 1, rev 2.364), 3.167 axle ratio, oil cooler.

NISSAN Langley Turbo GT Hatchback Sedan

61 hp (diesel) power team

See 85 hp power team, except for:

ENGINE diesel; 102.5 cu in, 1,680 cc (3.15 x 3.29 in, 80 x 83.6 mm); compression ratio: 22.2:1; max power (JIS): 61 hp (45 kW) at 5,000 rpm; max torque (JIS): 77 lb ft, 10.6 kg m (104 Nm) at 2,800 rpm; 36.3 hp/l (26.7 kW/l); valves: overhead, thimble tappets; lubrication: ger pump, full flow filter, 7 imp pt, 8.5 US pt, 4 l; Ricardo Comet swirl combustion chambers; fuel feed: electric pump; cooling: 10 imp pt, 12.7 US pt, 7 l.

TRANSMISSION (standard) gears: 5, fully synchronized; ratios: I 3.333, II 1.955, III 1.286, IV 0.902, V 0.733, rev 3.417.

PERFORMANCE max speed: 90 mph, 145 km/h; power-weight ratio: 31.9 lb/hp (43.3 lb/kW), 14.5 kg/hp (19.6 kg/kW); consumption: 91.1 m/imp gal, 75.9 m/US gal, 3.1 l x 100 km on Japanese emission test cycle.

STEERING turbs lock to lock: 3.70.

DIMENSIONS AND WEIGHT weight: 1,962 lb, 890 kg.

BODY 4+1 doors.

OPTIONALS automatic transmission, hydraulic tòrque converter and planetary gears with 3 ratios (I 2.826, II 1.543, III 1, rev 2.364), 3.167 axle ratio, oil cooler.

Prairie Series

PRICES (Tokyo):		yen
1	1500 JW 4+1-dr St. Wagon	**1,190,000**
2	1800 JW-L 4+1-dr St. Wagon	**1,293,000**
3	1800 JW-G 4+1-dr St. Wagon	**1,410,000**
4	1800 RV 4+1-dr St. Wagon	**1,265,000**
5	1800 RV-S 4+1-dr St. Wagon	**1,345,000**
6	1800 SS-G 4+1-dr St. Wagon	**1,385,000**

For GB prices, see price index.

Power team:	Standard for:	Optional for:
85 hp	1	—
100 hp	2 to 6	—

85 hp power team

ENGINE front, transverse, 4 stroke; 4 cylinders, vertical, in line; 90.7 cu in, 1,487 cc (2.99 x 3.23 in, 76 x 82 mm); compression ratio: 9:1; max power (JIS): 85 hp (63 kW) at 5,600 rpm; max torque (JIS): 91 lb ft, 12.3 kg m (121 Nm) at 3,600 rpm; max engine rpm: 6,000; 57.2 hp/l (42.1 kW/l); cast iron block, light alloy head; 5 crankshaft bearings; valves: overhead, Veeslanted, rockers; camshafts: 1, overhead, cogged belt; lubrication: trochoid pump, full flow filter, 6 imp pt, 7.1 US pt, 3.4 l; 1 Hitachi DCY 306-1 downdraught twin barrel carburettor; fuel feed: mechanical pump; exhaust system with secondary air induction, oxidizing catalyst, gas recirculation and catalytic converter; water-cooled, 8.9 imp pt, 10.5 US pt, 5 l, electric termostatic fan.

TRANSMISSION drivihg wheels: front; clutch: single dry plate (diaphragm); gearbox: mechanical; gears: 4, fully synchronized; ratios: I 3.333, II 1.956, III 1.286, IV 0.902, rev 3.417; lever: central; final drive: helical spur gears; axle ratio: 3.895; width of rims: 4.5"; tyres: 155 SR x 13.

PERFORMANCE max speeds: (I) 27 mph, 44 km/h; (II) 47 mph, 76 km/h; (III) 70 mph, 113 km/h; (IV) 93 mph, 150 km/h; power-weight ratio: 25.3 lb/hp (34.4 lb/kW), 11.5 kg/hp (15.6 kg/kW); consumption: 42 m/imp gal, 36 m/US gal, 6.7 l x 100 km on Japanese emission test cycle.

CHASSIS integral; front suspension: independent, by McPherson, lower arms, coil springs, telescopic dampers; rear: independent, trailing arms, torsion bars, telescopic dampers.

STEERING rack-and-pinion; turns lock to lock: 3.70.

BRAKES front disc, rear drum, servo.

ELECTRICAL EQUIPMENT 12 V; 30 Ah battery; 50 A alternator; Hitachi distributor; 2 headlamps.

DIMENSIONS AND WEIGHT wheel base: 98.82 in, 251 cm; tracks: 56.30 in, 143 cm front, 54.72 in, 139 cm rear; length: 161.02 in, 409 cm; width: 64.96 in, 165 cm; height: 62.99 in, 160 cm; ground clearance: 7.08 in, 18 cm; weight: 2,150 lb, 975 kg; weight distribution: 57% front, 43% rear; turning circle: 36.8 ft, 11 m; fuel tank: 11 imp gal, 13.2 US gal, 50 l.

BODY estate car/st. wagon; 4+1 doors; 8 seats, bench front seats.

NISSAN Prairie 1800 JW-G Station Wagon

100 hp power team

See 85 hp power team, except for:

ENGINE 110 cu in, 1,809 cc (3.27 x 3.29 in, 83 x 83.6 mm); compression ratio: 8.8:1; max power (JIS): 100 hp (74 kW) at 5,600 rpm; max torque (JIS): 110 lb ft, 15.2 kg m (149 Nm) at 2,800 rpm; 55.3 hp/l (40.7 kW/l); 1 Hitachi DCR 340-30 downdraught twin barrel carburettor; cooling: 10.6 imp pt, 12.7 US pt, 6 l.

TRANSMISSION gearbox ratios: I 3.063, II 1.826, III 1.207, IV 0.902, rev 3.417; axle ratio: 3.650; tyres: 165 SR x 13.

PERFORMANCE max speed: 99 mph, 160 km/h; power-weight ratio: JW-L 22.5 lb/hp (30.6 lb/kW), 10.2 kg/hp (13.9 kg/kW); consumption: 39.2 m/imp gal, 32.7 m/US gal, 7.2 l x 100 km on Japanese emission test cycle.

ELECTRICAL EQUIPMENT 33 Ah battery.

DIMENSIONS AND WEIGHT weight: JW-L St. Wagon 2,205 lb, 1,000 kg.

BODY (for RV and SS-G only) 5 seats, separate front seats.

OPTIONALS automatic transmission, hydraulic torque converter and planetary gears with 3 ratios (I 2.286, II 1.543, III 1, rev 2.364), 3.650 axle ratio; power steering; light alloy wheels with 5" wide rims.

NISSAN Liberta Villa 1500 SSS Turbo Sedan

Liberta Villa Series

PRICES (Tokyo):	yen
1 1500 FC 4-dr Sedan	**958,000**
2 1500 FL 4-dr Sedan	**1,055,000**
3 1500 GF 4-dr Sedan	**1,147,000**
4 1500 GF-E 4-dr Sedan	**1,239,000**
5 1500 SSS Turbo 4-dr Sedan	**1,409,000**
6 1700 Diesel FL-D 4-dr Sedan	**1,176,000**

Power team:	Standard for:	Optional for:
85 hp	1 to 3	—
95 hp	4	—
115 hp	5	—
61 hp (diesel)	6	—

85 hp power team

ENGINE front, transverse, 4 stroke; 4 cylinders, vertical, in line; 90.7 cu in, 1,487 cc (2.99 x 3.23 in, 76 x 82 mm); compression ratio: 9:1; max power (JIS): 85 hp (63 kW) at 5,600 rpm; max torque (JIS): 90 lb ft, 12.3 kg m (121 Nm) at 3,600 rpm; max engine rpm: 6,000; 57.2 hp/l (42.1 kW/l); cast iron block, light alloy head; 5 crankshaft bearings; valves: overhead, Veeslanted, rockers; camshafts: 1, overhead, cogged belt; lubrication: trochoid pump, full flow filter, 6 imp pt, 7.2 US pt, 3.3 l; 1 Hitachi DCV 306-1 downdraught twin barrel carburettor; fuel feed: mechanical pump; water-cooled, 8.4 imp pt, 10 US pt, 4.7 l.

TRANSMISSION driving wheels: front; clutch: single dry plate (diaphragm); gearbox: mechanical; gears: 4, fully synchronized - GF 5; ratios: I 3.333, II 1.955, III 1.286, IV 0.902 - GF V 0.733, rev 3.417; lever: central; final drive: helical spur gears; axle ratio: 3.789; width of rims: 4.5"; tyres: 155 SR x 13.

PERFORMANCE max speed: 102 mph, 165 km/h; power-weight ratio: 20.2 lb/hp (27.1 lb/kW), 9.2 kg/hp (12.5 kg/kW); consumption: 45.6 m/imp gal, 37.9 m/US gal, 6.2 l x 100 km on Japanese emission test cycle.

CHASSIS integral; front suspension: independent, by McPherson, lower arms, coil springs, telescopic dampers; rear: independent, trailing arms, coil springs, telescopic dampers.

STEERING rack-and-pinion; turns lock to lock: 3.90.

BRAKES front disc, rear drum.

ELECTRICAL EQUIPMENT 12 V; 30 Ah battery; 50 A alternator; Hitachi distributor; 4 headlamps.

DIMENSIONS AND WEIGHT wheel base: 94.88 in, 241 cm; tracks: 54.72 in, 139 cm front, 53.94 in, 137 cm rear; length: 162.20 in, 412 cm; width: 63.78 in, 162 cm; height: 54.72 in, 139 cm; ground clearance: 6.69 in, 17 cm; weight: 1,720 lb, 780 kg; weight distribution: 62% front, 38% rear; turning circle: 33.5 ft, 10.2 m; fuel tank: 11 imp gal, 13.2 US gal, 50 l.

BODY saloon/sedan; 4 doors; 5 seats, separate front seats.

VARIATIONS

ENGINE 9.3:1 compression ratio, max torque (JIS) 92 lb ft, 12.5 kg m (123 Nm) at 3,600 rpm, electronic carburettor, knock sensor with retard adjustment system.
TRANSMISSION 5-speed fully synchronized mechanical gearbox (I 3.063, II 1.708, III 1.133, IV 0.814, V 0.681, rev 3.417), 3.550 axle ratio.
PERFORMANCE consumption 49 m/imp gal, 41.3 m/US gal, 5.7 l x 100 km on Japanese emission test cycle.

OPTIONALS automatic transmission, hydraulic torque converter and planetary gears with 3 ratios (I 2.826, II 1.543, III 1, rev 2.364), 3.364 axle ratio; power steering.

95 hp power team

See 85 hp power team, except for:

ENGINE max power (JIS): 95 hp (70 kW) at 6,000 rpm; max torque (JIS): 92 lb ft, 12.5 kg m (123 Nm) at 3,600 rpm; max engine rpm: 6,400; 63.9 hp/l (47 kW/l); Nissan EGI electronic fuel injection; fuel feed: electric pump.

TRANSMISSION gears: 5, fully synchronized; ratios: I 3.063, II 1.826, III 1.207, IV 0.902, V 0.733, rev 3.417; axle ratio: 4.167; tyres: 165/70 SR x 13.

PERFORMANCE max speed: 105 mph, 170 km/h; power-weight ratio: 18.8 lb/hp (25.5 lb/kW), 8.6 kg/hp (11.6 kg/kW); consumption: 40.6 m/imp gal, 34 m/US gal, 6.9 l x 100 km on Japanese emission test cycle.

DIMENSIONS AND WEIGHT weight: 1,784 lb, 820 kg.

115 hp power team

See 85 hp power team, except for:

ENGINE turbocharged; 90.7 cu in, 1,487 cc (2.99 x 3.23 in, 76 x 82 mm); compression ratio: 8:1; max power (JIS): 115 hp (85 kW) at 5,600 rpm; max torque (JIS): 123 lb ft, 17 kg m (167 Nm) at 3,200 rpm; 77.4 hp/l (56.9 kW/l); AiResearch T2 turbocharger, electronic fuel injection; emission control by 3-way catalytic converter and exhaust gas recirculation; fuel feed: electric pump; cooling: 10 imp pt, 12.7 US pt, 6 l.

TRANSMISSION gears: 5, fully synchronized; ratios: I 3.333, II 1.955, III 1.286, IV 0.902, V 0.733, rev 3.417; width or rims: 5"; tyres: 175/70 SR x 13.

PERFORMANCE max speed: 112 mph, 180 km/h; power-weight ratio: 16.9 lb/hp (22.9 lb/kW), 7.6 kg/hp (10.4 kg/kW); consumption: 41.5 m/imp gal, 34.6 m/US gal, 6.8 l x 100 km on Japanese emission test cycle.

BRAKES disc.

ELECTRICAL EQUIPMENT 45 Ah battery.

DIMENSIONS AND WEIGHT weight: 1,940 lb, 880 kg.

OPTIONALS automatic transmission, hydraulic torque converter and planetary gears with 3 ratios (I 2.826, II 1.543, III 1, rev 2.364), 3.167 axle ratio, oil cooler.

61 hp (diesel) power team

See 85 hp power team, except for:

ENGINE diesel; 102.5 cu in, 1,680 cc (3.15 x 3.29 in, 80 x 83.6 mm); compression ratio: 22.2:1; max power (JIS): 61 hp (45 kW) at 5,000 rpm; max torque (JIS): 77 lb ft, 10.6 kg m (104 Nm) at 2,800 rpm; 36.3 hp/l (26.7 kW/l); valves: overhead, thimble tappets; lubrication: gear pump, full flow filter, 7 imp pt, 8.5 US pt, 4 l; Ricardo Comet swirl combustion chambers; fuel feed: electric pump; cooling: 10 imp pt, 12.7 US pt, 7 l.

TRANSMISSION gears: 5, fully synchronized; ratios: I 3.333, II 1.955, III 1.286, IV 0.902, V 0.733, rev 3.417.

PERFORMANCE max speed: 90 mph, 145 km/h; power-weight ratio: 31.9 lb/hp (43.3 lb/kW), 14.5 kg/hp (19.6 kg/kW); consumption: 91.1 m/imp gal, 75.9 m/US gal, 3.1 l x 100 km on Japanese emission test cycle.

STEERING turns lock to lock: 3.70.

DIMENSIONS AND WEIGHT weight: 1,962 lb, 890 kg.

OPTIONALS automatic transmission, hydraulic torque converter and planetary gears with 3 ratios (I 2.826, II 1.543, III 1, rev 2.364), 3.167 axle ratio, oil cooler.

Laurel Spirit Series

PRICES (Tokyo):	yen
1 1500 LT 4-dr Sedan	**991,000**
2 1500 LT-G 4-dr Sedan	**1,024,000**
3 1500 LF 4-dr Sedan	**1,099,000**
4 1500 XJ 4-dr Sedan	**1,189,000**
5 1500 XJ-E 4-dr Sedan	**1,247,000**
6 1500 Turbo XJ 4-dr Sedan	**1,407,000**

Power team:	Standard for:	Optional for:
85 hp	1 to 4	—
95 hp	5	—
115 hp	6	—

NISSAN Laurel Spirit 1500 Turbo XJ Sedan

85 hp power team

ENGINE front, transverse, 4 stroke; 4 cylinders, vertical, in line; 90.7 cu in, 1,487 cc (2.99 x 3.23 in, 76 x 82 mm); compression ratio: 9:1; max power (JIS): 85 hp (63 kW) at 5,600 rpm; max torque (JIS): 90 lb ft, 12.3 kg m (121 Nm) at 3,600 rpm; max engine rpm: 6,000; 57.2 hp/l (42.1 kW/l); cast iron block, light alloy head; 5 crankshaft bearings; valves: overhead, Vee-slanted, rockers; camshafts: 1, overhead, cogged belt; lubrication: trochoid pump, full flow filter, 6 imp pt, 7.2 US pt, 3.3 l; 1 Hitachi DCY 306-1 downdraught twin barrel carburettor; fuel feed: mechanical pump; water-cooled, 8.4 imp pt, 10 US pt, 4.7 l.

TRANSMISSION driving wheels: front; clutch: single dry plate (diaphragm); gearbox: mechanical; gears: 4, fully synchronized - XJ 5; ratios: I 3.333, II 1.955, III 1.286, IV 0.902 - XJ V 0.733, rev 3.417; lever: central; final drive: helical spur gears; axle ratio: 3.789; width of rims: 4.5''; tyres: 145 SR x 13 - LF and XJ 155 SR x 13.

PERFORMANCE max speed: 102 mph, 165 km/h; power-weight ratio: 20.2 lb/hp (27.1 lb/kW), 9.2 kg/hp (12.5 kg/kW); consumption: 45.6 m/imp gal, 37.9 m/US gal, 6.2 l x 100 km on Japanese emission test cycle.

CHASSIS integral; front suspension: independent, by McPherson, lower arms, coil springs, telescopic dampers; rear: independent, trailing arms, coil springs, telescopic dampers.

STEERING rack-and-pinion; turns lock to lock: 3.90.

BRAKES front disc, rear drum.

ELECTRICAL EQUIPMENT 12 V; 30 Ah battery; 50 A alternator; Hitachi distributor; 2 headlamps.

DIMENSIONS AND WEIGHT wheel base: 94.88 in, 240 cm; tracks: 54.72 in, 139 cm front, 53.94 in, 137 cm rear; length: 159.15 in, 405 cm; width: 63.78 in, 162 cm; height: 54.72 in, 139 cm; ground clearance: 6.69 in, 17 cm; weight: 1,720 lb, 780 kg; weight distribution: 62% front, 38% rear; turning circle: 32.8 ft, 10 m; fuel tank: 11 imp gal, 13.2 US gal, 50 l.

BODY saloon/sedan; 4 doors; 5 seats, separate front seats.

VARIATIONS

ENGINE 9.3:1 compression ratio, max torque (JIS) 92 lb ft, 12.5 kg m (123 Nm) at 3,600 rpm, electronic carburettor, knock sensor with retard adjustment system.
TRANSMISSION 5-speed fully synchronized mechanical gearbox (I 3.063, II 1.708, III 1.133, IV 0.814, V 0.681, rev 3.417), 3.550 axle ratio.
PERFORMANCE consumption 49 m/imp gal, 41.3 m/US gal, 5.7 l x 100 km on Japanese emission test cycle.

OPTIONALS (for LF only) 5-speed fully synchronized mechanical gearbox (I 3.333, II 1.955, III 1.286, IV 0.902, V 0.733, rev 3.417); automatic transmission, hydraulic torque converter and planetary gears with 3 ratios (I 2.826, II 1.543, III 1, rev 2.364), 3.364 axle ratio; power steering.

95 hp power team

See 85 hp power team, except for:

ENGINE max power (JIS): 95 hp (70 kW) at 6,000 rpm; max torque (JIS): 92 lb ft, 12.5 kg m (123 Nm) at 3,600 rpm; 63.9 hp/l (47 kW/l); Nissan EGI electronic fuel injection; fuel feed: electric pump.

TRANSMISSION gears: 5, fully synchronized; ratios: I 3.063, II 1.826, III 1.207, IV 0 902, V 0.733, rev 3.417; axle ratio: 4.167; tyres: 165/70 SR x 13.

PERFORMANCE max speed: 105 mph, 170 km/h; power-weight ratio: 18.8 lb/hp (25.5 lb/kW), 8.6 kg/hp (11.6 kg/kW); consumption: 40.6 m/imp gal, 34 m/US gal, 6.9 l x 100 km on Japanese emission test cycle.

DIMENSIONS AND WEIGHT weight: 1,784 lb, 820 kg.

115 hp power team

See 85 hp power team, except for:

ENGINE turbocharged; 90.7 cu in, 1,487 cc (2.99 x 3.23 in, 76 x 82 mm); compression ratio: 8:1; max power (JIS): 115 hp (85 kW) at 5,600 rpm; max torque (JIS): 123 lb ft, 17 kg m (167 Nm) at 3,200 rpm; 77.4 hp/l (56.9 kW/l); AiResearch T2 turbocharger, electronic fuel injection; emission control by 3-way catalytic converter and exhaust gas recirculation; fuel feed: electric pump; cooling: 10 imp pt, 12.7 US pt, 6 l.

TRANSMISSION gears: 5, fully synchronized; ratios: I 3.333, II 1.955, III 1.286, IV 0.955, V 0.733, rev 3.417; width of rims: 5''; tyres: 175/70 SR x 13.

PERFORMANCE max speed: 112 mph, 180 km/h; power-weight ratio: 16.5 lb/hp (22.4 lb/kW), 7.5 kg/hp (10.2 kg/kW); consumption: 41.5 m/imp gal, 34.6 m/US gal, 6.8 l x 100 km on Japanese emission test cycle.

BRAKES disc.

ELECTRICAL EQUIPMENT 45 Ah battery.

DIMENSIONS AND WEIGHT weight: 1,896 lb, 860 kg.

NISSAN Stanza 1800 RX Sedan

OPTIONALS automatic transmission, hydraulic torque converter and planetary gears with 3 ratios (I 2.826, II 1.543, III 1, rev 2.364), 3.167 axle ratio, oil cooler.

Stanza / Auster Series

PRICES (Tokyo):

		yen
1	Stanza 1600 LE 4-dr Sedan	**1,017,000**
2	Stanza 1600 LX 4-dr Sedan	**1,073,000**
3	Stanza 1600 LX-G 4-dr Sedan	**1,231,000**
4	Auster 1600 LE 4-dr Sedan	**1,028,000**
5	Auster 1600 GS 4-dr Sedan	**1,089,000**
6	Auster 1600 GS-X 4-dr Sedan	**1,240,000**
7	Stanza 1600 LX-G 2+1-dr Hatchback Sedan	**1,275,000**
8	Auster 1600 GS-X 2+1-dr Hatchback Sedan	**1,279,000**
9	Stanza 1800 LX 4-dr Sedan	**1,168,000**
10	Stanza 1800 SGX 4-dr Sedan	**1,346,000**
11	Auster 1800 GS-L 4-dr Sedan	**1,198,000**
12	Auster 1800 GS-X 2+1-dr Hatchback Sedan	**1,390,000**
13	Auster 1800 GS-X 4-dr Sedan	**1,350,000**
14	Stanza 1800 RX 2+1-dr Hatchback Sedan	**1,345,000**
15	Stanza 1800 RX 4-dr Sedan	**1,303,000**
16	Stanza 1800 Z-EX 4-dr Sedan	**1,571,000**
17	Auster 1800 GT-EX 2+1-dr Hatchback Sedan	**1,616,000**
18	Auster 1800 GT-EX 4-dr Sedan	**1,571,000**

For GB and USA prices, see price index.

Power team:	Standard for:	Optional for:
90 hp	1 to 8	—
100 hp	9 to 13	—
110 hp	14 to 18	—

90 hp power team

ENGINE front, transverse, 4 stroke; 4 cylinders, in line; 97.5 cu in, 1,598 cc (3.07 x 3.29 in, 78 x 83.6 mm); compression ratio: 9:1; max power (JIS): 90 hp (66 kW) at 5,600 rpm; max torque (JIS): 98 lb ft, 13.6 kg m (133 Nm) at 2,800 rpm; max engine rpm: 6,000; 56.3 hp/l (41.5 kW/l); cast iron block, light alloy head; 5 crankshaft bearings; valves: overhead, Vee-slanted, rockers; camshafts: 1, overhead, cogged belt; lubrication: gear pump, full flow filter, 6.9 imp pt, 8.1 US pt, 3.9 l; 1 Nikki 21 E 304-04 downdraught twin barrel carburettor; air cleaner; exhaust system with NAPS-Z control, twin spark plug, gas recirculation, secondary air induction and catalytic converter; fuel feed: mechanical pump; water-cooled, 10.7 imp pt, 12.7 US pt, 6 l, electric thermostatic fan.

TRANSMISSION driving wheels: front; clutch: single dry plate (diaphragm); gearbox: mechanical; gears: 4, fully synchronized; ratios: I 3.333, II 1.955, III 1.286, IV 0.902, rev 3.417; lever: central; final drive: helical spur gears; axle ratio: 3.650; width of rims: 5''; tyres: 6.45 x 13 - hatchback sedans 165 SR x 13.

PERFORMANCE max speed: 95 mph, 155 km/h; power-weight ratio: Stanza LE 21.6 lb/hp (29.3 lb/kW), 9.8 kg/hp (13.3 kg/kW); carrying capacity: 882 lb, 400 kg; speed in top at 1,000 rpm: 17.2 mph, 27.7 km/h; consumption: 40.9 m/imp gal, 34.1 m/US gal, 6.9 l x 100 km on Japanese emission test cycle.

CHASSIS integral; front suspension: independent, by McPherson, lower wishbones, coil springs/telescopic damper struts; rear: independent, by McPherson, twin transverse linkage bars, trailing radius arm, coil springs/telescopic damper struts.

STEERING rack-and-pinion; turns lock to lock: 3.60.

BRAKES front disc (diameter 7.28 in, 18.5 cm), rear drum, servo.

ELECTRICAL EQUIPMENT 12 V; 33 Ah battery; 50 A alternator; Hitachi or Mitsubishi contactless transistorized ignition; 2 headlamps.

DIMENSIONS AND WEIGHT wheel base: 97.24 in, 247 cm; tracks: 56.30 in, 143 cm front, 55.51 in, 141 cm rear; length: 169.29 in, 430 cm - hatchback sedans 166.14 in, 422 cm; width: 64.96 in, 165 cm - hatchbac sedans 65.35 in, 166 cm; height: 55.33 in, 138 cm - hatchback sedans 53.54 in, 136 cm; ground clearance: 6.69 in, 17 cm; weight: Stanza and Auster LE sedans 1,894 lb, 880 kg - Stanza LX and Auster GS sedans 1,973 lb, 895 kg - Stanza LX-G and Auster GS-X sedans 2,026 lb, 920 kg - Stanza LX-G and Auster GS-X hatchback sedans 2,040 lb, 925 kg; weight distribution: 65% front, 35% rear; turning circle: 33.3 ft, 10.8 m; fuel tank: 12 imp gal, 14 US gal, 54 l.

BODY saloon/sedan; 2+1 or 4 doors; 5 seats, separate front seats, built-in headrests.

OPTIONALS 5-speed fully synchronized mechanical gearbox (V ratio 0.733); automatic transmission, hydraulic torque converter and planetary gears with 3 ratios (I 2.826, II 1.543, III 1, rev 2.364), 3.476 axle ratio; power steering.

100 hp power team

See 90 hp power team, except for:

ENGINE 110 cu in, 1,809 cc (3.27 x 3.29 in, 83 x 83.6 mm); compression ratio: 8.8:1; max power (JIS): 100 hp (74 kW) at 5,600 rpm; max torque (JIS): 110 lb ft, 15.2 kg m (149 Nm) at 2,800 rpm; 55.3 hp/l (40.7 kW/l); 1 Hitachi DCR 340-30 downdraught twin barrel carburettor.

TRANSMISSION tyres: 165 SR x 13.

PERFORMANCE max speed: 103 mph, 165 km/h; power-weight ratio: Stanza LX 20.7 lb/hp (28.1 lb/kW), 9.4 kg/hp (12.8 kg/kW); consumption: 37.8 m/imp gal, 31.8 m/US gal, 7.4 l x 100 km on Japanese emission test cycle.

STEERING (standard) servo; turns lock to lock: 2.80.

DIMENSIONS AND WEIGHT weight: Stanza LX and Auster GS-L sedans 2,043 lb, 940 kg - Stanza SGX and Auster GS-X sedans 2,095 lb, 950 kg - Auster GS-X Hatchback Sedan 2,106 lb, 955 kg.

NISSAN Stanza-Auster Series (110 hp engine)

110 hp power team

See 90 hp power team, except for:

ENGINE 110 cu in, 1,809 cc (3.27 x 3.29 in, 83 x 83.6 mm); compression ratio: 8.8:1; max power (JIS): 110 hp (81 kW) at 5,600 rpm; max torque (JIS): 120 lb ft, 16.5 kg m (162 Nm) at 3,600 rpm; 60.8 hp/l (44.8 kW/l); Nissan EGI electronic fuel injection; fuel feed: electric pump.

TRANSMISSION (standard) gears: 5, fully synchronized; ratios: I 3.333, II 1.955, III 1.286, IV 0.902, V 0.733, rev 3.417; tyres: 185/70 SR x 13.

PERFORMANCE max speed: 106 mph, 170 km/h; power-weight ratio: Stanza RX 19 lb/hp (25.8 lb/kW), 8.6 kg/hp (11.7 kg/kW); consumption: 36.4 m/imp gal, 30.6 m/US gal, 7.7 l x 100 km on Japanese emission test cycle.

STEERING servo (standard).

BRAKES front internal radial fins.

DIMENSIONS AND WEIGHT length: 173 in, 440 cm; weight: Stanza Z-EX and Auster GT-EX sedans 2,147 lb, 975 kg - Stanza RX Sedan 2,095 lb, 950 kg - Austero GT-EX Hatchback Sedan 2,161 lb, 980 kg - Stanza RX Hatchback Sedan 2,106 lb, 955 kg.

Bluebird Series

	PRICES (Tokyo):	yen
1	1600 L 4-dr Sedan	**1,040,000**
2	1600 LX 4-dr Sedan	**1,136,000**
3	1600 LX-L 4-dr Sedan	**1,232,000**
4	1800 LX 4-dr Sedan	**1,201,000**
5	1800 SLX 4-dr Sedan	**1,352,000**
6	1800 SSS 4-dr Sedan	**1,360,000**
7	1800 SLX-G 4-dr Hardtop	**1,466,000**
8	1800 SSS 4-dr Hardtop	**1,425,000**
9	1800 LX 4+1-dr St. Wagon	**1,318,000**
10	1800 SSS-E 4-dr Sedan	**1,470,000**
11	1800 SSS-EX 4-dr Sedan	**1,696,000**
12	1800 Turbo SSS 4-dr Sedan	**1,628,000**
13	1800 Turbo SSS-S 4-dr Sedan	**1,716,000**
14	1800 Turbo SSS-X 4-dr Sedan	**1,871,000**
15	1800 Turbo SSS 4-dr Hardtop	**1,693,000**
16	1800 Turbo SSS-S 4-dr Hardtop	**1,781,000**
17	1800 Turbo SSS-X 4-dr Hardtop	**1,936,000**
18	1800 Turbo SSS-XG 4-dr Hardtop	**2,186,000**
19	1800 Turbo SSS 4+1-dr St. Wagon	**1,688,000**
20	2000 SLX-G 4-dr Sedan	**1,718,000**
21	2000 SLX-G 4-dr Hardtop	**1,783,000**
22	2000 Diesel LX 4-dr Sedan	**1,368,000**

For GB prices, see price index.

Power team:	Standard for:	Optional for:
90 hp	1 to 3	—
100 hp	4 to 9	—
110 hp	20,21	—
115 hp	10,11	—
135 hp	12 to 19	—
67 hp (diesel)	22	—

90 hp power team

ENGINE front, transverse, 4 stroke; 4 cylinders, in line; 97.5 cu in, 1,598 cc (3.07 x 3.29 in, 78 x 83.6 mm); compression ratio: 9:1; max power (JIS): 90 hp (66 kW) at 5,600 rpm; max torque (JIS): 99 lb ft, 13.6 kg m (133 Nm) at 2,800 rpm; max engine rpm: 6,000; 56.3 hp/l (41.4 kW/l); cast iron block, light alloy head; 5 crankshaft bearings; valves: overhead, Vee-slanted; camshafts: 1, overhead, cogged belt; lubrication: gear pump, full flow filter, 6.2 imp pt, 7.4 US pt, 3.5 l; 1 Nikki 21 E 304-36 downdraught twin barrel carburettor; NAPS fast-burn system with two spark plugs per cylinder, exhaust gas recirculation, secondary air induction and oxidizing catalytic converter; fuel feed: mechanical pump; water-cooled, 12.3 imp pt, 14.8 US pt, 7 l.

TRANSMISSION driving wheels: rear; clutch: single dry plate (diaphragm); gearbox: mechanical; gears: 4, fully synchronized; ratios: I 3.333, II 1.955, III 1.286, IV 0.902, rev 3.417; lever: central; final drive: hypoid bevel; axle ratio: 3.895; width of rims: 4.5''; tyres: 165 SR x 13.

PERFORMANCE max speeds: (I) 28 mph, 45 km/h; (II) 47 mph, 75 km/h; (III) 75 mph, 120 km/h; (IV) 103 mph, 165 km/h; power-weight ratio: 23.5 lb/hp (32 lb/kW), 10.7 kg/hp (14.5 kg/kW); consumption: 41.5 m/imp gal, 34.6 m/US gal, 6.8 l x 100 km on Japanese emission test cycle.

CHASSIS integral; front suspension: independent, by McPherson, lower arms, trailing links, coil springs, anti-roll bar, telescopic dampers; rear: independent, by McPherson, lower transverse links, trailing links, anti-roll bar, coil springs, telescopic dampers.

STEERING rack-and-pinion; turns lock to lock: 4.40.

BRAKES front disc, rear drum, servo.

ELECTRICAL EQUIPMENT 12 V; 33 Ah battery; 60 A alternator; Hitachi distributor; 2 headlamps.

DIMENSIONS AND WEIGHT wheel base: 99.21 in, 252 cm; tracks: 53.94 in, 137 cm front, 53.54 in, 136 cm rear; length: 172.83 in, 432 cm; width: 64.57 in, 164 cm; height:

NISSAN Bluebird 1800 Turbo SSS-S Hardtop

54.83 in, 138 cm; ground clearance: 6.29 in, 16 cm; weight: 2,117 lb, 960 kg; weight distribution: 53% front, 47% rear; turning circle: 36.1 ft, 11 m; fuel tank: 13.6 imp gal, 16.4 US gal, 62 l.

BODY saloon/sedan; 4 doors; 5 seats, separate front seats.

OPTIONALS (for LX and LX-L only) automatic transmission, hydraulic torque converter and planetary gears with 3 ratios (I 2.826, II 1.543, III 1, rev 2.364), 3.476 axle ratio.

100 hp power team

See 90 hp power team, except for:

ENGINE 110.4 cu in, 1,809 cc (3.27 x 3.29 in, 83 x 83.6 mm); compression ratio: 8.8:1; max power (JIS): 100 hp (74 kW) at 5,600 rpm; max torque (JIS): 110 lb ft, 15.2 kg m (149 Nm) at 2,800 rpm; 55.3 hp/l, (40.7 kW/l).

TRANSMISSION SSS gears: 5, fully synchronized; ratios: I 3.063, II 1.826 III 1.207, IV 0.920, V 0.733, rev 3.417; axle ratio: 4.056; tyres: LX, SLX and SLX-G 165 SR x 13 - SSS 185/70 SR x 13.

PERFORMANCE max speed: 106 mph, 170 km/h; power-weight ratio: LX Sedan 21.2 lb/hp (28.8 lb/kW), 9.6 kg/hp (13 kg/kW).

STEERING turs lock to lock: 4.60.

DIMENSIONS AND WEIGHT: length: sedans 171.65 in, 436 cm - hardtops 177.17 in, 450 cm - St. Wagon 173.23 in, 440 cm; height: sedans 54.72 in, 139 cm - hardtops 53.94 in, 137 cm - St. Wagon 55.91 in, 142 cm; weight: LX Sedan 2,128 lb, 965 kg - SLX Sedan 2,150 lb, 975 kg - SSS Sedan 2,205 lb, 1,000 kg - SLX-G Hardtop 2,249 lb, 1,020 kg - SSS Hardtop 2,282 lb, 1,035 kg - LX St. Wagon 2,249 lb, 1,020 kg.

BODY saloon/sedan, 4 doors - hardtop, 4 doors - estate car/st. wagon, 4+1 doors.

110 hp power team

See 90 hp power team, except for:

ENGINE 120.4 cu in, 1,973 cc (3.33 x 3.46 in, 84.5 x 88 mm); compression ratio: 8.5:1; max power (JIS): 110 hp (81 kW) at 5,600 rpm; max torque (JIS): 123 lb ft, 17 kg m (167 Nm)) at 3,600 rpm; 55.7 hp/l, (41 kW/l).

TRANSMISSION gears: 5, fully synchronized; ratios: I 3.063, II 1.826, III 1.207, IV 0.902, V 0.733, rev 3.417; axle ratio: 3.789; width of rims: 5''; tyres: 185/70 SR x 13.

PERFORMANCE max speed: 112 mph, 180 km/h; power-weight ratio: SLX-G Sedan 21.1 lb/hp (28.8 lb/kW), 9.6 kg/hp (13 kg/kW); consumption: 34.4 m/imp gal, 28.7 m/US gal, 8.2 l x 100 km on Japanese emission test cycle.

STEERING servo.

DIMENSIONS AND WEIGHT weight: SLX-G Sedan 2,326 lb, 1,055 kg - SLX-G Hardtop 2,370 lb, 1,075 kg.

BODY saloon/sedan - hardtop; 4 doors.

OPTIONALS automatic transmission, hydraulic torque converter and planetary gears with 4 ratios (I 2.785, II 1.545, III 1, IV 0.694, rev 2.272), 3.642 axle ratio; electronic power steering.

115 hp power team

See 90 hp power team, except for:

ENGINE 110.4 cu in, 1,809 cc (3.27 x 3.29 in, 83 x 83.6 mm); compression ratio: 8.8:1; max power (JIS): 115 hp (85 kW) at 6,000 rpm; max torque (JIS): 120 lb ft, 16.5 kg m (162 Nm) at 3,600 rpm; 63.6 hp/l (46.8 kW/l); Nissan EGI electronic injection, emission control by 3-way catalytic converter and exhaust gas recirculation; fuel feed: electric pump.

TRANSMISSION gears: 5, fully synchronized; ratios: I 3.063, II 1.826, III 1.207, IV 0.902, V 0.733, rev 3.417; axle ratio: 4.036; width of rims: 5''; tyres: 185/70 SR x 14.

PERFORMANCE max speeds: (I) 35 mph, 56 km/h; (II) 55 mph, 88 km/h; (III) 81 mph, 130 km/h; (IV) and (V) 112 mph, 180 km/h; power-weight ratio: SSS-E 20.1 lb/hp (27.4 lb/kW), 9.1 kg/hp (12.4 kg/kW); consumption: 37.7 m/imp gal, 31.4 m/US gal, 7.5 l x 100 km on Japanese emission test cycle.

STEERING SSS-EX servo.

NISSAN Bluebird 1800 Turbo SSS Station Wagon

BRAKES disc, servo.

DIMENSIONS AND WEIGHT weight: SSS-E Sedan 2,315 lb, 1,050 kg - SSS-EX Sedan 2,437 lb, 1,105 kg.

OPTIONALS automatic transmission, hydraulic torque converter and planetary gears with 3 ratios (I 2.826, II 1.543, III 1, rev 2.364), 3.737 axle ratio.

135 hp power team

See 90 hp power team, except for:

ENGINE turbocharged; 110.4 cu in, 1,809 cc (3.27 x 3.29 in, 83 x 83.6 mm); compression ratio: 8.8:1; max power (JIS): 135 hp (99 kW) at 6,000 rpm; max torque (JIS): 145 lb ft, 20 kg m (196 Nm) at 3,600 rpm; 74.6 hp/l (54.9 kW/l); Nissan EGI electronic injection; turbocharger with wastegate; emission control by 3-way catalytic converter and exhaust gas recirculation; fuel feed: electric pump; cooling: 13.7 imp pt, 16.5 US pt, 7.8 l.

TRANSMISSION gears: 5, fully synchronized; ratios: I 3.400, II 1.955, III 1.272, IV 0.911, V 0.740, rev 3.428; width of rims: 5"; tyres: 185/70 SR x 14.

PERFORMANCE max speeds: (I) 34 mph, 54 km/h; (II) 54 mph, 87 km/h; (III) 85 mph, 136 km/h; (IV) and (V) 112 mph, 180 km/h; power-weight ratio: SSS Sedan 17.5 lb/hp (23.8 lb/kW), 7.9 kg/hp (10.8 kg/kW); consumption: 38.2 m/imp gal, 31.8 m/US gal, 7.4 l x 100 km on Japanese emission test cycle.

STEERING SSS-X servo - SSS-XG electronic servo.

BRAKES disc, servo.

DIMENSIONS AND WEIGHT tracks: 57.48 in, 146 cm front, 57.09 in, 145 cm rear; length: sedans and hardtops 177.17 in, 450 cm - St. Wagon 173.23 in, 440 cm; weight: Turbo SSS Sedan 2,359 lb, 1,070 kg - Turbo SSS-S Sedan 2,403 lb, 1,090 kg - Turbo SSS-X Sedan 2,481 lb, 1,125 kg - Turbo SSS Hardtop 2,437 lb, 1,105 kg - Turbo SSS-S Hardtop 2,481 lb, 1,125 kg - Turbo SSS-X Hardtop 2,558 lb, 1,160 kg - Turbo SSS-XG Hardtop 2,580 lb, 1,170 kg - Turbo SSS St. Wagon 2,448 lb, 1,110 kg.

BODY saloon/sedan, 4 doors - hardtop, 4 doors - estate car/st. wagon, 4+1 doors.

OPTIONALS automatic transmission, hydraulic torque converter and planetary gears with 4 ratios (I 2.785, II 1.545, III 1, IV 0.694, rev 2.272), 3.642 axle ratio.

67 hp (diesel) power team

See 90 hp power team, except for:

ENGINE diesel; 119 cu in, 1,952 cc (3.34 x 3.38 in, 85 x 86 mm); compression ratio: 22.2:1; max power (JIS): 67 hp (49 kW) at 4,600 rpm; max torque (JIS): 90 lb ft, 12.5 kg m (122 Nm) at 2,400 rpm; max engine rpm: 4,800; 34.3 hp/l (25.3 kW/l); cast iron block and head; valves: overhead, in line, rockers; Ricardo Comet swirl chamber; lubrication: 7.1 imp pt, 8.5 US pt, 4 l, oil cooler; Bosch VE injection pump.

TRANSMISSION gears: 5, fully synchronized; ratios: I 3.400, II 1.955, III 1.272, IV 0.911, V 0.740, rev 3.428.

PERFORMANCE max speed: 90 mph, 145 km/h; power-weight ratio: 35.9 lb/hp (48.8 lb/kW), 16.3 kg/hp (22.1 kg/kW); consumption: 74.3 m/imp gal, 71.9 m/US gal, 3.8 l x 100 km at steady 37 mph, 60 km/h on Japanese emission test cycle.

ELECTRICAL EQUIPMENT 60 Ah battery.

DIMENSIONS AND WEIGHT weight: 2,403 lb, 1,090 kg.

OPTIONALS automatic transmission, hydraulic torque converter and planetary gears with 4 ratios (I 2.785, II 1.545, III 1, IV 0.694, rev 2.272), 3.876 axle ratio.

Leopard Series

PRICES (Tokyo):		yen
1	180 GX 4-dr Hardtop	**1,484,000**
2	180 SGX 4-dr Hardtop	**1,656,000**
3	200X GX 4-dr Hardtop	**1,689,000**
4	200X SGX 4-dr Hardtop	**1,896,000**
5	200X ZGX 2-dr Hardtop	**2,347,000**
6	200X ZGX 4-dr Hardtop	**2,347,000**
7	Turbo GX 2-dr Hardtop	**1,845,000**
8	Turbo GX 4-dr Hardtop	**1,845,000**
9	Turbo SGX 2-dr Hardtop	**2,077,000**
10	Turbo SGX 4-dr Hardtop	**2,077,000**
11	Turbo ZGX 2-dr Hardtop	**2,535,000**
12	Turbo ZGX 4-dr Hardtop	**2,535,000**
13	Turbo ZGX Super Edition 2-dr Hardtop	**2,759,000**
14	Turbo ZGX Super Edition 4-dr Hardtop	**2,759,000**

Power team:	Standard for:	Optional for:
105 hp	1,2	—
125 hp	3 to 6	—
145 hp	7 to 14	—

105 hp power team

ENGINE front, 4 stroke; 4 cylinders, in line; 108 cu in, 1,770 cc (3.35 x 3.07 in, 85 x 78 mm); compression ratio: 8.8:1; max power (JIS): 105 hp (77 kW) at 6,000 rpm; max torque (JIS): 109 lb ft, 15 kg m (147 Nm) at 3,600 rpm; max engine rpm: 6,500; 59.3 hp/l (43.7 kW/l); cast iron block, light alloy head; 5 crankshaft bearings; valves: overhead, Vee-slanted, rockers; camshafts: 1, overhead; lubrication: rotary pump, full flow filter, 7.7 imp pt, 9.2 US pt, 4.4 l; 1 Hitachi downdraught twin barrel carburettor; fuel feed: mechanical pump; Nissan NAPS-Z emission control with 2 spark plugs per cylinder and catalytic converter; water-cooled, 15.8 imp pt, 18.8 US pt, 9 l.

NISSAN Leopard Turbo ZGX Hardtop

TRANSMISSION driving wheels: rear; clutch: single dry plate (diaphragm); gearbox: mechanical; gears: 5, fully synchronized; ratios: I 3.321, II 2.077, III 1.308, IV 1, V 0.833, rev 3.382; lever: central; final drive: hypoid bevel; axle ratio: 4.111; width of rims: 5"; tyres: 175 SR x 14.

PERFORMANCE max speeds: (I) 32 mph, 52 km/h; (II) 50 mph, 80 km/h; (III) 79 mph, 127 km/h; (IV) and (V) 106 mph, 170 km/h; power-weight ratio: GX 23.2 lb/hp (31.5 lb/kW), 10.5 kg/hp (14.3 kg/kW); carrying capacity: 882 lb, 400 kg; speed in direct drive at 1,000 rpm: 18.2 mph, 29.2 km/h; consumption: 33.6 m/imp gal, 28.5 m/US gal, 8.3 l x 100 km on Japanese emission test cycle.

CHASSIS integral; front suspension: independent, by McPherson, lower transverse arms, trailing rods, anti-roll bar, coil springs, telescopic damper struts; rear: rigid axle, lower trailing arms, upper linkage bars, anti-roll bar, coil springs, telescopic dampers.

STEERING rack-and-pinion; turns lock to lock: 3.70.

BRAKES front disc, rear drum, servo.

ELECTRICAL EQUIPMENT 12 V; 33 Ah battery; 60 A alternator; Hitachi or Mitsubishi distributor; 4 headlamps.

DIMENSIONS AND WEIGHT wheel base: 103 in, 262 cm; tracks: 55 in, 140 cm front, 54 in, 138 cm rear; length: 182 in, 463 cm; width: 67 in, 169 cm; height: 53 in, 135 cm; ground clearance: 6.30 in, 16 cm; weight: GX Hardtop 2,436 lb, 1,105 kg - SGX Hardtop 2,469 lb, 1,120 kg; weight distribution: 52% front, 48% rear; turning circle: 37.5 ft, 11.6 m; fuel tank: 13.9 imp gal, 16.4 US gal, 62 l.

BODY hardtop; 4 doors; 5 seats, separate front seats, front and rear built-in headrests.

OPTIONALS automatic transmission, hydraulic torque converter and planetary gears with 3 ratios (I 2.458, II 1.458, III 1, rev 2.182), possible manual selection; TRX equipment.

125 hp power team

See 105 hp power team, except for:

ENGINE 6 cylinders, in line; 122 cu in, 1,998 cc (3.07 x 2.74 in, 78 x 69.7 mm); compression ratio: 9.1:1; max power (JIS): 125 hp (92 kW) at 6,000 rpm; max torque (JIS): 124 lb ft, 17 kg m (167 Nm) at 4,400 rpm; 62.5 hp/l (46 kW/l); 7 crankshaft bearings; valves: overhead, in line, rockers; lubrication: 8.8 imp pt, 10.5 US pt, 5 l; Nissan ECCS electronic injection with digital engine control; fuel feed: electric pump; cooling: 16.9 imp pt, 20.1 US pt, 9.6 l.

TRANSMISSION gearbox ratios: I 3.592, II 2.246, III 1.415, IV 1, V 0.813, rev 3.657; width of rims: 5.5"; tyres: 185/70 SR x 14.

PERFORMANCE max speeds: (I) 30 mph, 48 km/h; (II) 47 mph, 75 km/h; (III) 72 mph, 115 km/h; (IV) and (V) 112 mph, 180 km/h; power-weight ratio: GX 21 lb/hp (28.5 lb/kW), 9.5 kg/hp (12.9 kg/kW); consumption: 28 m/imp gal, 23.5 m/US gal, 10 l x 100 km on Japanese emission test cycle.

CHASSIS rear suspension: independent, semi-trailing arms, coil springs, anti-roll bar, telescopic dampers.

STEERING servo.

BRAKES disc, internal radial fins, servo.

ELECTRICAL EQUIPMENT electronic ignition.

DIMENSIONS AND WEIGHT rear track: 54.70 in, 139 cm; height: 4-dr hardtops 53 in, 135 cm - 2-dr Hardtop 52.70 in, 134 cm; ground clearance: 6.10 in, 15.5 cm; weight: GX Hardtop 2,623 lb, 1,190 kg - SGX Hardtop 2,668 lb, 1,210 kg - ZGX 2-dr Hardtop 2,645 lb, 1,200 kg - ZGX 4-dr Hardtop 2,789 lb, 1,265 kg; weight distribution: 54% front, 46% rear.

BODY 2 or 4 doors.

OPTIONALS automatic transmission, hydraulic torque converter and planetary gears with 4 ratios (I 2.842, II 1.542, III 1, IV 0.686, rev 2.400), 3.900 axle ratio.

145 hp power team

See 105 hp power team, except for:

ENGINE turbocharged; 6 cylinders, in line; 122 cu in, 1,998 cc (3.07 x 2.74 in, 78 x 69.7 mm); max power (JIS): 145 hp (107 kW) at 5,600 rpm; max torque (JIS): 153 lb ft, 21 kg m (206 Nm) at 3,200 rpm; max engine rpm: 6,000; 72.6 hp/l (53.4 kW/l); 7 crankshaft bearings; valves: overhead, in line, rockers; camshafts: 1, overhead, chain-driven; lubrication: 8.9 imp pt, 10.6 US pt, 5 l; Nissan ECCS digital electronic fuel injection; AiResearch T03 exhaust turbocharger with wastegate; fuel feed: electric pump; cooling: 17.8 imp pt, 21 US pt, 10 l.

TRANSMISSION gearbox ratios: I 3.592, II 2.246, III 1.415, IV 1, V 0.813, rev 3.657; axle ratio: 3.900; width of rims: 5.5"; tyres: 195/70 SR x 14 - ZGX 195/70 HR x 14.

PERFORMANCE max speeds: (I) 29 mph, 47 km/h; (II) 47 mph, 76 km/h; (III) 75 mph, 120 km/h; (IV) and (V) 112 mph, 180 km/h; power-weight ratio: GX 4-dr 18.3 lb/hp (24.9 lb/kW), 8.3 kg/hp (11.3 kg/kW); speed in top at 1,000 rpm: 22.4 mph, 36 km/h; consumption: 29 m/imp gal, 25 m/US gal, 9.5 l x 100 km on Japanese emission test cycle.

CHASSIS rear suspension: independent, semi-trailing arms, coil springs, anti-roll bar, telescopic dampers - ZGX automatic levelling control.

STEERING SGX and ZGX servo.

NISSAN Leopard Turbo ZGX Hardtop

145 HP POWER TEAM

BRAKES disc, servo.

DIMENSIONS AND WEIGHT weight: Turbo GX 4-dr Hardtop 2,654 lb, 1,205 kg - Turbo SGX 4-dr Hardtop 2,698 lb, 1,225 kg - Turbo ZGX 4-dr Hardtop 2,819 lb, 1,280 kg - Turbo GX 2-dr Hardtop 2,632 lb, 1,195 kg - Turbo SGX 2-dr Hardtop 2,676 lb, 1,215 kg - Turbo ZGX 2-dr Hardtop 2,797 lb, 1,270 kg.

BODY 2 or 4 doors.

OPTIONALS automatic transmission, hydraulic torque converter and planetary gears with 4 ratios (I 2.842, II 1.542, III 1, IV 0.686, rev 2.400).

Silvia / Gazelle Series

	PRICES (Tokyo):	**yen**
1	Silvia 1800 R-L 2-dr Coupé	**1,330,000**
2	Silvia 1800 R-X 2-dr Coupé	**1,420,000**
3	Gazelle 1800 R-X 2-dr Coupé	**1,420,000**
4	Silvia 1800 R-X 2+1-dr Hatchback Coupé	**1,500,000**
5	Gazelle 1800 R-X 2+1-dr Hatchback Coupé	**1,500,000**
6	Silvia 1800 R-XE 2-dr Coupé	**1,611,000**
7	Gazelle 1800 R-XE 2-dr Coupé	**1,611,000**
8	Silvia 1800 R-XE 2+1-dr Hatchback Coupé	**1,690,000**
9	Gazelle 1800 R-XE 2+1-dr Hatchback Coupé	**1,690,000**
10	Silvia 1800 Turbo R-L 2-dr Coupé	**1,690,000**
11	Silvia 1800 Turbo R-X 2-dr Coupé	**1,890,000**
12	Silvia 1800 Turbo R-XG 2-dr Coupé	**2,140,000**
13	Gazelle 1800 Turbo R-X 2-dr Coupé	**1,890,000**
14	Gazelle 1800 Turbo R-XG 2-dr Coupé	**2,360,000**
15	Silvia 1800 Turbo R-L 2+1-dr Hatchback Coupé	**1,770,000**
16	Silvia 1800 Turbo R-X 2+1-dr Hatchback Coupé	**1,970,000**
17	Silvia 1800 Turbo R-XG 2+1-dr Hatchback Coupé	**2,100,000**
18	Gazelle 1800 Turbo R-X 2+1-dr Hatchback Coupé	**1,970,000**
19	Gazelle 1800 Turbo R-XG 2+1-dr Hatchback Coupé	**2,320,000**
20	Silvia 2000 RS-X 2-dr Coupé	**2,240,000**
21	Silvia 2000 RS-X 2+1-dr Hatchback Coupé	**2,323,000**
22	Silvia 2000 Turbo RS-X 2-dr Coupé	**2,540,000**
23	Gazelle 2000 Turbo RS-X 2-dr Coupé	**2,540,000**
24	Silvia 2000 Turbo RS-X 2+1-dr Hatchback Coupé	**2,520,000**
25	Gazelle 2000 Turbo RS-X 2+1-dr Hatchback Coupé	**2,520,000**

Power team:	**Standard for:**	**Optional for:**
100 hp	1 to 5	—
115 hp	6 to 9	—
135 hp	10 to 19	—
150 hp	20,21	—
190 hp	22 to 25	—

100 hp power team

ENGINE front, 4 stroke; 110.4 cu in, 1,809 cc (3.27 x 3.29 in, 83 x 83.6 mm); compression ratio: 8.8:1; max power (JIS): 100 hp (74 kW) at 5,600 rpm; max torque (JIS): 110 lb ft, 15.2 kg m (149 Nm) at 2,800 rpm; max engine rpm: 6,000; 55.3 hp/l (40.7 kW/l); cast iron block, light alloy head; 5 crankshaft bearings; valves: overhead, Vee-slanted, rockers; camshafts: 1, overhead, cogged belt; lubrication: gear pump, full flow filter, 6.2 imp pt, 7.4 US pt, 3.5 l; 1 Hitachi DCR 340-35 downdraught twin barrel carburettor; emission control by 3-way catalytic converter, exhaust gas recirculation and secondary air induction; fuel feed: mechanical pump; water-cooled, 12.3 imp pt, 14.8 US pt, 7 l.

TRANSMISSION driving wheels: rear; clutch: single dry plate (diaphragm); gearbox: mechanical; gears: 5, fully synchronized; ratios: I 3.321, II 1.902, III 1.308, IV 1, V 0.833, rev 3.382; lever: central; final drive: hypoid bevel; axle ratio: 3.700; width of rims: 5"; tyres: 165 SR x 14.

PERFORMANCE max speeds: (I) 31 mph, 50 km/h; (II) 56 mph, 90 km/h; (III) 81 mph, 130 km/h; (IV) and (V) 109 mph, 175 km/h; power-weight ratio: Silvia R-L 21.2 lb/hp (28.8 lb/kW), 9.6 kg/hp (13.1 kg/kW); consumption: 39.8 m/imp gal, 33.1 m/US gal, 7.1 l x 100 km on Japanese emission test cycle.

CHASSIS integral; front suspension: independent by McPherson, coil springs/telescopic damper struts, lower arms, trailing links, anti-roll bar; rear: rigid axle, coil springs, upper diagonal torque rods, telescopic dampers.

STEERING rack-and-pinion; turns lock to lock: 4.10.

BRAKES front disc, rear drum, front internal radial fins, dual circuit, servo.

ELECTRICAL EQUIPMENT 12 V; 33 Ah battery; 60 A alternator; Hitachi or Mitsubishi distributor; 2 retractable headlamps.

DIMENSIONS AND WEIGHT wheel base: 95.28 in, 242 cm; tracks: 54.33 in, 138 cm front, 53.54 in, 136 cm rear; length: 171.26 in, 435 cm; width: 65.35 in, 166 cm; height: 52.36 in, 136 cm; ground clearance: 5.90 in, 15 cm; weight: Silvia R-L Coupé 2,117 lb, 960 kg - Silvia and Gazelle R-X coupés 2,161 lb, 980 kg - Silvia and Gazelle R-X hatchback coupés 2,205 lb, 1,000 kg; weight distribution: 55% front, 45% rear; turning circle: 33.4 ft, 10.8 m; fuel tank: 11.7 imp gal, 14 US gal, 53 l.

NISSAN Silvia 1800 Turbo R-X Coupé

BODY coupé; 2 or 2+1 doors; 2+2 seats, separate front seats.

OPTIONALS automatic transmission, hydraulic torque converter and planetary gears with 3 ratios (I 2.842, II 1.543, III 1, rev 2.400); power steering, 2.90 turns lock to lock.

115 hp power team

See 100 hp power team, except for:

ENGINE max power (JIS): 115 hp (85 kW) at 6,000 rpm; max torque (JIS): 120 lb ft, 16.5 kg m (162 Nm) at 3,600 rpm; max engine rpm: 6,500; 63.6 hp/l (46.8 kW/l); Bosch L-Jetronic injection; fuel feed: electric pump.

TRANSMISSION tyres: 185/70 SR x 14.

PERFORMANCE max speed: 112 mph, 180 km/h; power-weight ratio: Silvia R-XE Coupé 19.2 lb/hp (26 lb/kW), 8.7 kg/hp (11.8 kg/kW); consumption: 38.2 m/imp gal, 31.9 m/US gal, 7.4 l x 100 km on Japanese emission test cycle.

DIMENSIONS AND WEIGHT weight: Silvia and Gazelle R-XE coupés 2,205 lb, 1,000 kg - Silvia and Gazelle R-XE hatchback coupés 2,249 lb, 1,020 kg.

135 hp power team

See 100 hp power team, except for:

ENGINE turbocharged; compression ratio: 8.3:1; max power (JIS): 135 hp (100 kW) at 6,000 rpm; max torque (JIS): 145 lb ft, 20 kg m (196 Nm) at 3,600 rpm; max engine rpm: 6,400; 76.3 hp/l (56.1 kW/l); Nissan ECCS electronic fuel injection; AiResearch T2 turbocharger with wastegate knock sensor and ignition retard system.

TRANSMISSION gearbox ratios: I 3.592, II 2.057, III 1.361, IV 1, V 0.813; axle ratio: 3.657; width of rims: 5.5"; tyres: 185/70 SR x 14.

PERFORMANCE max speed: 112 mph, 180 km/h; power-weight ratio: Silvia Turbo R-L Coupé 17.6 lb/hp (23.6 lb/kW), 8 kg/hp (10.7 kg/kW); consumption: 39.2 m/imp gal, 32.7 m/US gal, 7.2 l x 100 km on Japanese emission test cycle.

CHASSIS rear suspension: independent, semi-trailing arms, coil springs, anti-roll bar, telescopic dampers.

BRAKES disc, servo.

DIMENSIONS AND WEIGHT rear track: 54.35 in, 141 cm; ground clearance: 6.50 in, 16.5 cm; weight: Silvia Turbo R-L Coupé 2,368 lb, 1,075 kg - Silvia Turbo R-XG Coupé 2,467 lb, 1,120 kg - Silvia Turbo R-X Hatchback Coupé 2,445 lb, 1,110 kg - Silvia Turbo R-XG Hatchback Coupé 2,533 lb, 1,150 kg.

OPTIONALS automatic transmission, hydraulic torque converter and planetary gears with 4 ratios (I 2.842, II 1.542, III 1, V 0.686, rev 2.400); light alloy wheels with 6" wide rims; 195/60 HR x 15 tyres; electric sunroof.

150 hp power team

See 100 hp power team, except for:

ENGINE 121.4 cu in, 1,990 cc (3.50 x 3.54 in, 89 x 90 mm); compression ratio: 9.1:1; max power (JIS): 150 hp (110 kW) at 6,000 rpm; max torque (JIS): 134 lb ft, 18.5 kg m (181 Nm) at 4,800 rpm; max engine rpm: 6,400; 75.4 hp/l (55.5 kW/l); valves: overhead, Vee-slanted, thimble tappets; camshafts: 2, overhead, chain-driven; Nissan ECCS electronic fuel injection.

TRANSMISSION final drive: hypoid bevel, limited slip; axle ratio: 4.111; width of rims: 5.5"; tyres: 185/70 HR x 14.

PERFORMANCE max speed: 112 mph, 180 km/h; power-weight ratio: 15.9 lb/hp (21.7 lb/kW), 7.2 kg/hp (9.8 kg/kW); consumption: 47.9 m/imp gal, 39.9 m/US gal, 5.9 l x 100 km at steady 37 mph, 60 km/h on Japanese emission test cycle.

STEERING (standard) servo; turns lock to lock: 2.90.

BRAKES disc, servo.

DIMENSIONS AND WEIGHT weight: 2,392 lb, 1,085 kg.

190 hp power team

See 100 hp power team, except for:

ENGINE turbocharged; 121.4 cu in, 1,990 cc (3.50 x 3.54 in, 89 x 90 mm); compression ratio: 8:1; max power (JIS): 190 hp (140 kW) at 6,400 rpm; max torque (JIS): 167 lb ft, 23 kg m (226 Nm) at 4,800 rpm; max engine rpm: 7,000; 95.5 hp/l (70.3 kW/l); valves: overhead, Vee-slanted, thimble tappets; camshafts: 2, overhead, chain-driven; lubrication: 7 imp pt, 8.5 US pt, 4 l; Nissan ECCS electronic injection; turbocharger with wastegate; emission control by 3-way catalytic converter; fuel feed: electric pump, cooling: 14.1 imp tp, 16.9 US pt, 8 l, electric thermostatic fan.

TRANSMISSION axle ratio: 3.900; final drive: hypoid bevel, limited slip; width of rims: 6"; tyres: 195/60 HR x 15.

PERFORMANCE max speeds: (I) 34 mph, 54 km/h; (II) 60 mph, 97 km/h; (III) 87 mph, 140 km/h; (IV) and (V) 112 mph, 180 km/h; power-weight ratio: 13.6 lb/hp (18.5 lb/kW), 6.1 kg/hp (8.4 kg/kW); consumption: 28.8 m/imp gal, 24 m/US gal, 9.8 l x 100 km on Japanese emission test cycle.

CHASSIS rear suspension: independent, semi-trailing arms, coil springs, anti-roll bar, telescopic dampers.

STEERING (standard) servo; turns lock to lock: 2.90.

BRAKES disc, servo.

DIMENSIONS AND WEIGHT tracks: 55.12 in, 140 cm front, 55.91 in, 142 cm rear; length: 174.41 in, 443 cm; weight: 2,580 lb, 1,170 kg.

Skyline Series

	PRICES (Tokyo):	**yen**
1	1800 TL 4-dr Sedan	**1,161,000**
2	1800 TI-L 2-dr Sedan	**1,284,000**
3	1800 TI-L Extra 4-dr Sedan	**1,361,000**
4	1800 TI-L Extra 4+1-dr Hatchback Sedan	**1,449,000**
5	1800 TI-EL 4-dr Sedan	**1,448,000**
6	1800 TI-EX 4-dr Sedan	**1,546,000**
7	2000 GT-EL 4-dr Sedan	**1,555,000**
8	2000 GT-EX 2-dr Hardtop	**1,771,000**
9	2000 GT-EX 4-dr Sedan	**1,716,000**
10	2000 GT-EX 4+1-dr Hatchback Sedan	**1,826,000**
11	2000 Turbo GT-E 4-dr Sedan	**1,685,000**
12	2000 Turbo GT-EL 2-dr Hardtop	**1,806,000**
13	2000 Turbo GT-EX 4-dr Sedan	**1,751,000**
14	2000 Turbo GT-EX 2-dr Hardtop	**1,952,000**
15	2000 Turbo GT-EX 4+1-dr Hatchback Sedan	**1,897,000**
16	2000 RS 2-dr Hardtop	**2,176,000**
17	2000 RS 4-dr Sedan	**2,121,000**
18	2000 Turbo RS 2-dr Hardtop	**2,426,000**
19	2000 Turbo RS-X 2-dr Hardtop	**2,691,000**
20	2000 Turbo RS 4-dr Sedan	**2,371,000**
21	2000 Turbo RS-X 4-dr Sedan	**2,636,000**
22	280 D GT-L Diesel 4-dr Sedan	**1,640,000**
23	280 D GT-X Diesel 4-dr Sedan	**1,802,000**

NISSAN Gazelle 2000 Turbo RS-X Coupé

NISSAN Skyline 2000 RS Hardtop

Power team:	Standard for:	Optional for:
100 hp	1 to 4	—
110 hp	5,6	—
125 hp	7 to 10	—
145 hp	11 to 15	—
150 hp	16,17	—
190 hp	18 to 21	—
91 hp (diesel)	22,23	—

100 hp power team

ENGINE front, transverse, 4 stroke; 4 cylinders, vertical, in line; 110.4 cu in, 1,809 cc (3.27 x 3.29 in, 83 x 83.6 mm); compression ratio: 8.8:1; max power (JIS): 100 hp (74 kW) at 5,600 rpm; max torque (JIS): 110 lb ft, 15.2 kg m (149 Nm) at 2,800 rpm; max engine rpm: 6,000; 55.3 hp/l (40.7 kW/l); cast iron block, light alloy head; 5 crankshaft bearings; valves: overhead, rockers; camshafts: 1, overhead, cogged belt; lubrication: gear pump, full flow filter, 6.2 imp pt, 7.4 US pt, 3.5 l; 1 Hitachi DCR 340-32 twin barrel carburettor; NAPS fast-burn system with two spark plugs per cylinder, exhaust gas recirculation, secondary air induction and oxidizing catalytic converter; fuel feed: mechanical pump; water-cooled, 13.6 imp pt, 16.3 US pt, 7.7 l.

TRANSMISSION driving wheels: rear; clutch: single dry plate (diaphragm); gearbox: mechanical; gears: 4, fully synchronized; ratios: I 3.321, II 1.902, III 1.308, IV 1, rev 3.382; lever: central; final drive: hypoid bevel; axle ratio: 3.700; width of rims: 4.5"; tyres: TL 6.45 x 14 - other models 165 SR x 14.

PERFORMANCE max speeds: (I) 43 mph, 70 km/h; (II) 56 mph, 90 km/h; (III) 81 mph, 130 km/h; (IV) 106 mph, 170 km/h; power-weight ratio: TL 23.2 lb/hp (31.3 lb/kW), 10.5 kg/hp (14.2 kg/kW); consumption: 37.7 m/imp gal, 31.4 m/US gal, 7.5 l x 100 km on Japanese emission test cycle.

CHASSIS integral; front suspension: independent, by McPherson, coil springs/telescopic damper struts, lower wishbones (trailing links), anti-roll bar; rear: rigid axle, lower trailing links, upper torque rods, coil springs, telescopic dampers.

STEERING recirculating ball; turns lock to lock: 4.30.

NISSAN Skyline 2000 RS Hardtop

BRAKES front disc, rear drum, servo; lining area: front 15.5 sq in, 100 sq cm, rear 54 sq in, 348 sq cm, total 69.5 sq in, 448 sq cm.

ELECTRICAL EQUIPMENT 12 V; 40 Ah battery; 60 A alternator; Hitachi distributor; 2 headlamps.

DIMENSIONS AND WEIGHT wheel base: 102.76 in, 261 cm; tracks: 55.51 in, 141 cm front, 54.72 in, 139 cm rear; length: 181.89 in, 462 cm; width: 63.35 in, 166 cm; height: 65.35 in, 166 cm; ground clearance: 6.69 in, 17 cm; weight: TL Sedan 2,315 lb, 1,050 kg - TI-L Sedan 2,328 lb, 1,055 kg - TI-L Extra Sedan 2,337 lb, 1,060 kg - TI-L Hatchback Sedan 2,381 lb, 1,080 kg; weight distribution: 54% front, 46% rear; turning circle: 31.4 ft, 10.2 m; fuel tank: 14.5 imp gal, 17.2 US gal, 65 l.

BODY saloon/sedan; 4 or 4+1 doors; 5 seats, separate front seats.

OPTIONALS automatic transmission, hydraulic torque converter and planetary gears with 3 ratios (I 2.458, II 1.458, III 1, rev 2.182).

110 hp power team

See 100 hp power team, except for:

ENGINE max power (JIS): 110 hp (81 kW) at 5,600 rpm; max torque (JIS): 123 lb ft, 16.5 kg m (164 Nm) at 3,600 rpm; 60.8 hp/l (44.7 kW/l); Nissan EGI electronic injection.

TRANSMISSION gears: 5, fully synchronized; ratios: I 3.321, II 2.077, III 1.308, IV 1, V 0.833, rev 3.382; tyres: TI-EL 165 SR x 14 - TI-EX 185/70 HR x 14.

PERFORMANCE max speed: 112 mph, 180 km/h; power-weight ratio: TI-EL 21.7 lb/hp (29.5 lb/kW), 9.9 kg/hp (13.4 kg/kW); consumption: 36.2 m/imp gal, 30.2 m/US gal, 7.8 l x 100 km on Japanese emission test cycle.

DIMENSIONS AND WEIGHT weight: TI-EL Sedan 2,390 lb, 1,085 kg - TI-EX Sedan 2,445 lb, 1,110 kg.

BODY 4 doors.

OPTIONALS power steering.

125 hp power team

See 100 hp power team, except for:

ENGINE 6 cylinders, in line; 121.9 cu in, 1,998 cc (3.07 x 2.74 in, 78 x 69.7 mm); compression ratio: 8.6:1; max power (JIS): 125 hp (92 kW) at 6,000 rpm; max torque (JIS): 123 lb ft, 17 kg m (167 Nm) at 4,000 rpm; 62.6 hp/l (46 kW/l); 7 crankshaft bearings; lubrication: 10 imp pt, 12 US pt, 5.7 l; Nissan ECCS electronic injection; emission control with 3-way catalytic converter and exhaust gas recirculation; fuel feed: electric pump; cooling: 15.8 imp pt, 19 US pt, 9 l.

TRANSMISSION gears: 5, fully synchronized; ratios: I 3.592, II 2.246, III 1.415, IV 1, V 0.813, rev 3.675; axle ratio: 4.111; width of rims: 5.5"; tyres: 185/70 HR x 14.

PERFORMANCE max speeds: (I) 28 mph, 45 km/h; (II) 47 mph, 76 km/h; (III) 71 mph, 115 km/h; (IV) and (V) 112 mph, 180 km/h; power-weight ratio: GT-EL 20.3 lb/hp (27.6 lb/kW), 9.2 kg/hp (12.5 kg/kW); consumption: 27.7 m/imp gal, 23.1 m/US gal, 10.2 l x 100 km on Japanese emission test cycle.

CHASSIS rear suspension: independent, semi-trailing arms, coil springs, telescopic dampers.

STEERING recirculating ball, variable ratio; turns lock to lock: 3.40.

DIMENSIONS AND WEIGHT tracks: 55.51 in, 141 cm front, 55.12 in, 140 cm rear; width: GT-EX 64.37 in, 163 cm; weight: GT-EL Sedan 2,536 lb, 1,150 kg - GT-EX Sedan 2,602 lb, 1,180 kg - GT-EX Hardtop 2,624 lb, 1,190 kg - GT-EX Hatchback Sedan 2,646 lb, 1,200 kg; turning circle: 38 ft, 11.6 m.

BODY saloon/sedan, 4 or 4+1 doors - hardtop, 2 doors.

OPTIONALS automatic transmission, hydraulic torque converter and planetary gears with 4 ratios (I 2.842, II 1.542, III 1, IV 0.686, rev 2.400), max speed 106 mph, 170 km/h; light alloy wheels.

145 hp power team

See 100 hp power team, except for:

ENGINE turbocharged; 6 cylinders, in line; 121.9 cu in, 1,998 cc (3.07 x 2.74 in, 78 x 69.7 mm); compression ratio: 7.6:1; max power (JIS): 145 hp (107 kW) at 5,600 rpm; max torque (JIS): 153 lb ft, 21 kg m (206 Nm) at 3,200 rpm; 72.5 hp/l (53.4 kW/l); 7 crankshaft bearings; lubrication: 10 imp pt, 12 US pt, 5.7 l; AiResearch TO3 exhaust turbocharger; Nissan ECCS electronic injection; fuel feed: electric pump; cooling: 15.8 imp pt, 19 US pt, 9 l.

TRANSMISSION gears: 5, fully synchronized; ratios: I 3.592, II 2.246, III 1.415, IV 1, V 0.813, rev 3.657; axle ratio: 3.900; tyres: GT-E 195/60 HR x 15 - other models 185/70 SR x 14.

PERFORMANCE max speed: 112 mph, 180 km/h; power-weight ratio: GT-E 18.1 lb/hp (24.5 lb/kW), 8.2 kg/hp (11.1 kg/kW); consumption: 27.4 m/imp gal, 23 m/US gal, 10.2 l x 100 km on Japanese emission test cycle.

CHASSIS rear suspension: independent, semi-trailing arms, coil springs, telescopic dampers - GT-E models anti-roll bar and adjustable dampers.

STEERING GT-EX servo.

BRAKES front internal radial fins, rear disc.

DIMENSIONS AND WEIGHT tracks: 55.51 in, 141 cm front, 55.11 in, 140 cm rear; width: 65.75 in, 167 cm; height: sedans 58.35 in, 138 cm - hardtops 53.54 in, 136 cm; ground clearance 5.09 in, 15 cm; weight: Turbo GT-E Sedan 2,624 lb, 1,190 kg - Turbo GT-EX Sedan 2,646 lb, 1,200 kg - Turbo GT-EX Hardtop 2,668 lb, 1,210 kg - Turbo GT-EL Sedan 2,690 lb, 1,220 kg - Turbo GT-EX Hatchback Sedan 2,734 lb, 1,240 kg.

BODY saloon/sedan, 4 doors - hardtop, 2 doors.

OPTIONALS automatic transmission, hydraulic torque converter and planetary gears with 4 ratios (I 2.482, II 1.542, III 1, IV 0.686, rev 2.400).

150 hp power team

See 100 hp power team, except for:

ENGINE 121.4 cu in, 1,990 cc (3.50 x 3.54 in, 89 x 90 mm); max power (JIS): 150 hp (110 kW) at 6,000 rpm; max torque (JIS): 135 lb ft, 18.5 kg m (181 Nm) at 4,800 rpm; 75.4 hp/l (55.5 kW/l); valves: overhead, Vee-slanted, thimble tappets; camshafts: 2, overhead; lubrication: 8.9 imp pt, 10.6 US pt, 5 l; Nissan ECCS digital electronic injection; fuel feed: electric pump; cooling: 14.2 imp pt, 16.9 US pt, 8 l.

TRANSMISSION gears: 5, fully synchronized; ratios: I 3.321, II 1.902, III 1.308, IV 1, V 0.833, rev 3.382; axle ratio: 4.111; width of rims: 5.5"; tyres: 195/70 HR x 14.

PERFORMANCE max speeds: (I) 30 mph, 48 km/h; (II) 53 mph, 86 km/h; (III) 80 mph, 128 km/h; (IV) and (V) 112 mph, 180 km/h; power-weight ratio: Sedan 16.7 lb/hp (22.8 lb/kW), 7.6 kg/hp (10.3 kg/kW); speed in top at 1,000 rpm: 22.4 mph, 36 km/h; consumption: 28 m/imp gal, 23.6 m/US gal, 10 l x 100 km on Japanese emission test cycle.

150 HP POWER TEAM

CHASSIS rear suspension: independent, semi-trailing arms, coil springs, anti roll bar, two-position adjustable telescopic dampers.

BRAKES front internal radial fins, rear disc, pressure control valve.

DIMENSIONS AND WEIGHT tracks: 55.51 in, 141 cm front, 55.11 in, 140 cm rear; width: 65.75 in, 167 cm; height: Sedan 54.33 in, 138 cm - Hardtop 53.33 in, 136 cm; ground clearance: 6.10 in, 15.5 cm; weight: RS Sedan 2,514 lb, 1,140 kg - RS Hardtop 2,536 lb, 1,150 kg.

BODY saloon/sedan, 4 doors - hardtop, 2 doors.

OPTIONALS limited slip differential; power steering.

190 hp power team

See 100 hp power team, except for:

ENGINE turbocharged; 121.4 cu in, 1,990 cc (3.50 x 3.54 in, 89 x 90 mm); compression ratio: 8:1; max power (JIS): 190 hp (140 kW) at 6,400 rpm; max torque (JIS): 167 lb ft, 23 kg m (226 Nm) at 4,800 rpm; max engine rpm: 7,000; 95.5 hp/l (70.3 kW/l); valves: overhead Vee-slanted, thimble tappets; camshafts: 2, overhead, chain-driven; lubrication: 7 imp pt, 8.9 US pt, 4 l; Nissan ECCS fuel injection; turbocharger with wastegate.

TRANSMISSION gears: 5, fully synchronized; ratios: I 3.321, II 1.902, III 1.308, IV 1, V 0.838, rev 3.382; axle ratio: 3.900; final drive: limited slip; width of rims: 6''; tyres: 205/60 HR x 15.

PERFORMANCE max speed: 112 mph, 180 km/h; power-weight ratio: RS Sedan 13.7 lb/hp (18.7 lb/kW), 6.2 kg/hp (8.5 kg/kW); consumption: 28.8 m/imp gal, 24 m/US gal, 9.8 l x 100 km on Japanese emission test cycle.

CHASSIS rear suspension: independent, semi-trailing arms, coil springs, anti-roll bar, telescopic dampers.

BRAKES disc, servo.

DIMENSIONS AND WEIGHT tracks: 55.91 in, 142 cm front, 55.51 in, 141 cm rear; height: sedans 54.72 in, 139 cm - hardtops 53.54 in, 130 cm; weight: Turbo RS Sedan 2,613 lb, 1,185 kg - Turbo RS-X Sedan 2,767 lb, 1,255 kg - Turbo RS Hardtop 2,635 lb, 1,195 kg - Turbo RS-X Hardtop 2,723 lb, 1,235 kg.

BODY saloon/sedan, 4 doors - hardtop, 2 doors.

OPTIONALS (for RS-X only) automatic transmission, hydraulic torque converter and planetary gears with 4 ratios (I 2.482, II 1.542, III 1, IV 0.686, rev 2.400); power steering.

91 hp (diesel) power team

See 100 hp power team, except for:

ENGINE diesel; 6 cylinders, in line; 170 cu in, 2,792 cc (3.33 x 3.27 in, 84.5 x 83 mm); compression ratio: 22:1; max power (JIS): 91 hp (67 kW) at 4,600 rpm; max torque (JIS): 126 lb ft, 17.3 kg m (170 Nm) at 2,400 rpm; max engine rpm: 4,800; 32.5 hp/l (23.9 kW/l); cast iron block and head; 7 crankshaft bearings; valves: overhead, in line, rockers; Ricardo Comet swirl chamber; lubrication: rotary pump, 7.1 imp pt, 8.5 US pt, 4 l; Bosch injection pump; cooling: 19.6 imp pt, 23.3 US pt, 11 l.

TRANSMISSION gears: 5, fully synchronized; ratios: I 3.321, II 2.077, III 1.308, IV 1, V 0.752, rev 3.382; axle ratio: 3.900; tyres: 185/70 SR x 14.

PERFORMANCE max speed: 96 mph, 155 km/h; power-weight ratio: GT-L 28.9 lb/hp (39.3 lb/kW), 13.1 kg/hp (17.8 kg/kW); consumption: 58.8 m/imp gal, 49.8 m/US gal, 4.7 l x 100 km at steady 37 mph, 60 km/h on Japanese emission test cycle.

ELECTRICAL EQUIPMENT 70 Ah battery.

DIMENSIONS AND WEIGHT weight: GT-L Diesel Sedan 2,632 lb, 1,195 kg - GT-X Diesel Sedan 2,698 lb, 1,225 kg.

BODY 4 doors.

OPTIONALS automatic transmission, hydraulic torque converter and planetary gears with 3 ratios (I 2.458, II 1.458, III 1, rev 2.182), 3.700 axle ratio.

Laurel Series

NISSAN Laurel 2000 Turbo Medalist Sedan

PRICES (Tokyo):		yen
1	1800 STD 4-dr Sedan	**1,151,000**
2	1800 GL 4-dr Sedan	**1,276,000**
3	1800 GL 4-dr Hardtop	**1,363,000**
4	1800 SGL 4-dr Sedan	**1,442,000**
5	1800 SGL 4-dr Hardtop	**1,517,000**
6	2000 GL 4-dr Sedan	**1,341,000**
7	2000 GL 4-dr Hardtop	**1,409,000**
8	2000 SGL 4-dr Sedan	**1,479,000**
9	2000 SGL 4-dr Hardtop	**1,547,000**
10	2000 GL 4-dr Sedan	**1,564,000**
11	2000 GL 4-dr Hardtop	**1,681,000**
12	2000 SGL 4-dr Sedan	**1,689,000**
13	2000 SGL 4-dr Hardtop	**1,796,000**
14	2000 Medalist 4-dr Sedan	**2,048,000**
15	2000 Medalist 4-dr Hardtop	**2,180,000**
16	2000 Turbo GX 4-dr Sedan	**1,785,000**
17	2000 Turbo GX 4-dr Hardtop	**1,861,000**
18	2000 Turbo SGX 4-dr Sedan	**1,895,000**
19	2000 Turbo SGX 4-dr Hardtop	**1,974,000**
20	2000 Turbo Medalist 4-dr Sedan	**2,285,000**
21	2000 Turbo Medalist 4-dr Hardtop	**2,360,000**
22	2000 Diesel STD 4-dr Sedan	**1,256,000**
23	2000 Diesel GL 4-dr Sedan	**1,418,000**
24	2800 Diesel VL-6 4-dr Sedan	**1,633,000**
25	2800 Diesel VL-6 4-dr Hardtop	**1,709,000**
26	2800 Diesel VX-6 4-dr Sedan	**1,756,000**
27	2800 Diesel VX-6 4-dr Hardtop	**1,833,000**

For GB prices, see price index.

Power team:	Standard for:	Optional for:
100 hp	1 to 5	—
110 hp	6 to 9	—
125 hp	10 to 15	—
145 hp	16 to 21	—
65 hp (diesel)	22,23	—
91 hp (diesel)	24 to 27	—

100 hp power team

ENGINE front, 4 stroke; 4 cylinders, in line; 110.4 cu in, 1,809 cc (3.27 x 3.29 in, 83 x 83.6 mm); compression ratio: 8.8:1; max power (JIS): 100 hp (74 kW) at 5,600 rpm; max torque (JIS): 110 lb ft, 15.2 kg m (149 Nm) at 2,800 rpm; max engine rpm: 6,000; 55.3 hp/l (40.7 kW/l); cast iron block, light alloy head; 5 crankshaft bearings; valves: overhead, Vee-slanted, rockers; camshafts: 1, overhead; lubrication: rotary pump, full flow filter, 6.2 imp pt, 7.4 US pt, 3.5 l; Nissan NAPS-Z fast-burn engine with 2 spark plugs per cylinder; 1 Hitachi DCR 340-1 downdraught twin barrel carburettor; emission control with catalytic converter, secondary air induction and exhaust gas recirculation; fuel feed: mechanical pump; water-cooled, 13.6 imp pt, 16.3 US pt, 7.7 l.

TRANSMISSION driving wheels: rear; clutch: single dry plate (diaphragm); gearbox: mechanical; gears: 4, fully synchronized; ratios: I 3.382, II 2.013, III 1.312, IV 1, rev 3.365; lever: central; final drive: hypoid bevel; axle ratio: 3.889; width of rims: 4.5''; tyres: 6.45 x 14.

PERFORMANCE max speeds: (I) 30 mph, 48 km/h; (II) 52 mph, 83 km/h; (III) 77 mph, 124 km/h; (IV) 99 mph, 160 km/h; power-weight ratio: GL Sedan 23 lb/hp (31.3 lb/kW), 10.4 kg/hp (14.2 kg/kW); consumption: 37.7 m/imp gal, 31.4 m/US gal, 7.5 l x 100 km on Japanese emission test cycle.

CHASSIS integral; front suspension: independent, by McPherson, coil springs/telescopic damper struts, lower wishbones (trailing links), anti-roll bar; rear: rigid axle, lower trailing links, upper torque rods, coil springs, telescopic dampers.

STEERING recirculating ball - SGL servo; turns lock to lock: 4 - SGL 3.20.

BRAKES front disc, rear drum, servo; lining area: front 22.3 sq in, 144 sq cm, rear 54 sq in, 348 sq cm, total 76.3 sq in, 492 sq cm.

ELECTRICAL EQUIPMENT 12 V; 35 Ah battery; 50 A alternator; Hitachi distributor; 2 headlamps.

DIMENSIONS AND WEIGHT wheel base: 105.12 in, 267 cm; tracks: 55.50 in, 141 cm front, 54.70 in, 139 cm rear; length: 182 in, 463 cm; width: 66.53 in, 169 cm; height: sedans 55.31 in, 140 cm - hardtops 54.30 in, 138 cm; ground clearance: 6.69 in, 17 cm; weight: STD Sedan 2,304 lb, 1,045 kg - GL Sedan 2,337 lb, 1,060 kg - GL Hardtop 2,392 lb, 1,085 kg; turning circle: 38 ft, 11.6 m; fuel tank: 14.6 imp gal, 17.2 US gal, 65 l.

BODY saloon/sedan or hardtop; 4 doors; 5 seats, separate front seats.

OPTIONALS automatic transmission, hydraulic torque converter and planetary gears with 3 ratios (I 2.458, II 1.458, III 1, rev 2.182), central lever; 5.5'' wide rims light alloy wheels with 185/70 HR x 14 tyres.

110 hp power team

See 100 hp power team, except for:

ENGINE 119 cu in, 1,952 cc (3.35 x 3.38 in, 85 x 86 mm); max power (JIS): 110 hp (81 kW) at 5,600 rpm; max torque

NISSAN Laurel 2000 Turbo Medalist Hardtop

NISSAN Cedric 3000 V30 Brougham Hardtop

(JIS): 120 lb ft, 16.5 kg m (162 Nm) at 3,600 rpm; 56.4 hp/l (41.3 kW/l).

TRANSMISSION gearbox ratios: I 3.592, II 2.246, III 1.415, IV 1, rev 3.657.

PERFORMANCE power-weight ratio: GL Sedan 21.6 lb/hp (29.3 lb/kW), 9.8 kg/hp (13.3 kg/kW); consumption: 27 m/imp gal, 22.5 m/US gal, 10.5 l x 100 km on Japanese emission test cycle.

DIMENSIONS AND WEIGHT weight: GL Sedan 2,370 lb, 1,075 kg - SGL Sedan 2,458 lb, 1,115 kg - GL Hardtop 2,425 lb, 1,100 kg - SGL Hardtop 2,513 lb, 1,140 kg.

125 hp power team

See 100 hp power team, except for:

ENGINE 6 cylinders, in line; 121.9 cu in, 1,998 cc (3.07 x 2.74 in, 78 x 69.7 mm); max power (JIS): 125 hp (92 kW) at 6,000 rpm; max torque (JIS): 126 lb ft, 17 kg m (167 Nm) at 4,000 rpm; 62.5 hp/l (46 kW/l); 7 crankshaft bearings; lubrication: 10 imp pt, 12 US pt, 5.7 l; Bosch electronic fuel injection; Nissan ECCS digital engine control; emission control with 3-way catalytic converter; fuel feed: electric pump; cooling: 15.8 imp pt, 19 US pt, 9 l.

TRANSMISSION gears: 5, fully synchronized; ratios: I 3.592, II 2.246, III 1.415, IV 1, V 0.813, rev 3.657; axle ratio: 4.111; tyres: 185/70 HR x 14.

PERFORMANCE max speed: 109 mph, 175 km/h; power-weight ratio: sedans 20.3 lb/hp (27.6 lb/kW), 9.2 kg/hp (12.5 kg/kW); consumption: 25.7 m/imp gal, 21.8 m/US gal, 10.9 l x 100 km on Japanese emission test cycle.

CHASSIS (for hardtops only) rear suspension: independent, semi-trailing arms, coil springs, telescopic dampers.

STEERING servo; turns lock to lock: 3.20.

BRAKES rear compensator - hardtops rear disc.

DIMENSIONS AND WEIGHT rear track: hardtops 55.30 in, 140 cm; length: 182.09 in, 426 cm; weight: sedans 2,535 lb, 1,150 kg - hardtops 2,745 lb, 1,245 kg.

OPTIONALS automatic transmission, hydraulic torque conveter and planetary gears with 4 ratios (I 2.842, II 1.542, III 1, IV 0.686, rev 2.400), 3.900 axle ratio; 5.5'' wide rims light alloy wheels.

145 hp power team

See 100 hp power team, except for:

ENGINE turbocharged; 6 cylinders, in line; 122 cu in, 1,998 cc (3.07 x 2.74 in, 78 x 69.7 mm); compression ratio: 7.6:1; max power (JIS): 145 hp (107 kW) at 5,600 rpm; max torque (JIS): 153 lb ft, 21 kg m (206 Nm) at 3,200 rpm; 72.5 hp/l (53.4 kW/l); 7 crankshaft bearings; lubrication: 10 imp pt, 12 US pt, 5.7 l; AiResearch TO3 exhaust turbocharger; Nissan electronic injection with digital engine control; cooling: 15.8 imp pt, 19 US pt, 9 l.

TRANSMISSION gears: 5, fully synchronized; ratios: I 3.592, II 2.246, III 1.415, IV 1, V 0.813, rev 3.657; axle ratio: 3.900; tyres: 185/70 SR x 14.

PERFORMANCE max speed: 112 mph, 180 km/h; power-weight ratio: sedans 18.1 lb/hp (24.7 lb/kW), 8.2 kg/hp (11.2 kg/kW); consumption: 25 m/imp gal, 21.3 m/US gal, 11.1 l x 100 km on Japanese emission test cycle.

CHASSIS rear suspension; independent, semi-trailing arms, coil springs, anti-roll bar, telescopic dampers.

STEERING servo.

BRAKES hardtops rear disc.

DIMENSIONS AND WEIGHT height: hardtops 54.30 in, 138 cm - sedans 55.10 in, 140 cm; weight: sedans 2,634 lb, 1,195 kg - hardtops 2,689 lb, 1,220 kg.

OPTIONALS automatic transmission, hydraulic torque converter and planetary gears with 4 ratios (I 2.842, II 1.542, III 1, IV 0.686, rev 2.400).

65 hp (diesel) power team

See 100 hp power team, except for:

ENGINE diesel; 119.1 cu in, 1,952 cc (3.35 x 3.39 in, 85 x 86 mm); compression ratio: 22.2:1; max power (JIS): 65 hp (48 kW) at 4,600 rpm; max torque (JIS): 91 lb ft, 12.5 kg m (123 Nm) at 2,400 rpm; max engine rpm: 4,800; 33.3 hp/l (24.5 kW/l); cast iron block and head; valves: overhead, in line, rockers; Bosch VE electronic injection, Ricardo Comet swirl combustion chambers.

TRANSMISSION gears: 5, fully synchronized; ratios: I 3.592, II 2.057, III 1.361, IV 1, V 0.813, rev 3.657; axle ratio: 4.111; tyres: 6.45 x 14.

PERFORMANCE power-weight ratio: STD 37.8 lb/hp (51.4 lb/kW), 17.1 kg/hp (23.3 kg/kW); consumption: 60.1 m/imp gal, 50 m/US gal, 4.7 l x 100 km on Japanese emission test cycle.

DIMENSIONS AND WEIGHT weight: Diesel STD Sedan 2,459 lb, 1,115 kg - Diesel GL Sedan 2,481 lb, 1,125 kg.

BODY saloon/sedan.

91 hp (diesel) power team

See 100 hp power team, except for:

ENGINE diesel; 6 cylinders, in line; 170 cu in, 2,792 cc (3.33 x 3.27 in, 84.5 x 83 mm); compression ratio: 22:1; max power (JIS): 91 hp (67 kW) at 4,600 rpm; max torque (JIS): 126 lb ft, 17.3 kg m (170 Nm) at 2,400 rpm; max engine rpm: 4,800; 32.5 hp/l (23.9 kW/l); cast iron block and head; 7 crankshaft bearings; Ricardo Comet swirl chamber; lubrication: 7.1 imp pt, 8.5 US pt, 4 l; Bosch injection pump; cooling: 19.6 imp pt, 23.3 US pt, 11 l.

NISSAN Gloria 2800 Diesel 28D-6 Custom S Hardtop

TRANSMISSION gears: 5, fully synchronized; ratios: I 3.321, II 2.077, III 1.308, IV 1, V 0.752, rev 3.382; tyres: 185/70 SR x 14.

PERFORMANCE max speed: 96 mph, 155 km/h; power-weight ratio: VL-6 28.7 lb/hp (39 lb/kW), 13 kg/hp (17.7 kg/kW); consumption: 48.7 m/imp gal, 41.3 m/US gal, 5.7 l x 100 km at steady 37 mph, 60 km/h on Japanese emission test cycle.

STEERING servo.

ELECTRICAL EQUIPMENT 70 Ah battery; 60 A alternator.

DIMENSIONS AND WEIGHT weight: Diesel VL-6 models 2,612 lb, 1,185 kg - Diesel VX-6 models 2,667 lb, 1,210 kg.

Cedric / Gloria Series

PRICES (Tokyo):		yen
1	Cedric 2000 STD 4-dr Sedan	**1,312,000**
2	Cedric 2000 De Luxe 4-dr Sedan	**1,438,000**
3	Cedric 2000 V20E Custom De Luxe 4-dr Sedan	**1,769,000**
4	Cedric 2000 V20E GL 4-dr Sedan	**2,027,000**
5	Cedric 2000 V20E SGL 4-dr Sedan	**2,506,000**
6	Cedric 2000 V20E Custom S 4-dr Hardtop	**1,941,000**
7	Cedric 2000 V20E GL 4-dr Hardtop	**2,391,000**
8	Cedric 2000 V20E SGL 4-dr Hardtop	**2,684,000**
9	Cedric 2000 V20E De Luxe 4+1-dr St. Wagon	**1,822,000**
10	Cedric 2000 V20E GL 4+1-dr St. Wagon	**2,098,000**
11	Cedric 2000 V20 Turbo SGL 4-dr Sedan	**2,850,000**
12	Cedric 2000 V20 Turbo Brougham 4-dr Sedan	**3,080,000**
13	Cedric 2000 V20 Turbo S 4-dr Hardtop	**2,516,000**
14	Cedric 2000 V20 Turbo SGL 4-dr Hardtop	**2,894,000**
15	Cedric 2000 V20 Turbo F 4-dr Hardtop	**3,018,000**
16	Cedric 2000 V20 Turbo Brougham 4-dr Hardtop	**3,242,000**
17	Cedric 3000 V30 Brougham 4-dr Sedan	**3,263,000**
18	Cedric 3000 V30 Brougham 4-dr Hardtop	**3,415,000**
19	Gloria 2800 Diesel 28D-6 STD 4-dr Sedan	**1,447,000**
20	Gloria 2800 Diesel 28D-6 De Luxe 4-dr Sedan	**1,674,000**
21	Gloria 2800 Diesel 28D-6 GL 4-dr Sedan	**2,059,000**
22	Gloria 2800 Diesel 28D-6 SGL 4-dr Sedan	**2,722,000**
23	Gloria 2800 Diesel 28D-6 Custom S 4-dr Hardtop	**1,938,000**
24	Gloria 2800 Diesel 28D-6 GL 4-dr Hardtop	**2,221,000**
25	Gloria 2800 Diesel 28D-6 SGL 4-dr Hardtop	**2,895,000**
26	Gloria 2800 Diesel 28D-6 Custom De Luxe 4+1-dr St. Wagon	**2,026,000**

For GB prices, see price index.

Power team:	Standard for:	Optional for:
110 hp	1,2	—
130 hp	3 to 10	—
170 hp	11 to 16	—
180 hp	17,18	—
91 hp (diesel)	19 to 26	—

110 hp power team

ENGINE front, 4 stroke; 4 cylinders, vertical, in line; 120.4 cu in, 1,973 cc (3.33 x 3.46 in, 84.5 x 88 mm); compression ratio: 8.5:1; max power (JIS): 110 hp (81 kW) at 5,600 rpm; max torque (JIS): 123 lb ft, 17 kg m (167 Nm) at 3,600 rpm; max engine rpm: 6,000; 55.7 hp/l (41 kW/l); cast iron block, light alloy head; 5 crankshaft bearings; valves: overhead, Vee-slanted, rockers; camshafts: 1, overhead, cogged belt; lubrication: gear pump, full flow filter, 6.2 imp pt, 7.4 US pt, 3.5 l; 1 Hitachi DFP 3423 downdraught twin barrel carburettor; emission control by 3-way catalytic converter, exhaust gas recirculation and secondary air induction; fuel feed: mechanical pump; water-cooled, 10.6 imp pt, 12.7 US pt, 6 l.

TRANSMISSION driving wheels: rear; clutch: single dry plate (diaphragm); gearbox: mechanical; gears: 5, fully synchronized; ratios: I 3.592, II 2.057, III 1.361, IV 1, V 0.813, rev 3.657; lever: central; final drive: hypoid bevel; axle ratio: 4.375; width of rims: 5''; tyres: 6.95 x 14.

PERFORMANCE max speed: 106 mph, 170 km/h; power-weight ratio: STD 25.6 lb/hp (34.7 lb/kW), 11.6 kg/hp (15.8 kg/kW); consumption: 29.4 m/imp gal, 24.5 m/US gal, 9.6 l x 100 km on Japanese emission test cycle.

CHASSIS integral; front suspension: independent, by McPherson, coil springs/telescopic damper struts, lower transverse arms, trailing links, anti-roll bar; rear: rigid axle, lower trailing arms, upper torque rod, Panhard rod, coil springs, anti-roll bar, telescopic dampers.

STEERING recirculating ball; turns lock to lock: 4.80.

BRAKES front disc (diameter 10.5 in, 26 cm), rear drum, dual circuit, servo.

ELECTRICAL EQUIPMENT 12 V; 33 Ah battery; 60 A alternator; Hitachi or Mitsubishi distributor; STD 4 headlamps - De Luxe 2 headlamps.

DIMENSIONS AND WEIGHT wheel base: 93.31 in, 273 cm; tracks: 56.30 in, 143 cm front, 55.12 in, 140 cm rear; length: 184.65 in, 469 cm; width: 66.54 in, 169 cm; height: 56.30 in, 143 cm; ground clearance: 6.70 in, 17 cm; weight:

110 HP POWER TEAM

Cedric STD Sedan 2,811 lb, 1,275 kg - Cedric De Luxe Sedan 2,844 lb, 1,290 kg; weight distribution: 53% front, 47% rear; turning circle: 40 ft, 12.2 m; fuel tank: 15.8 imp gal, 19 US gal, 72 l.

BODY saloon/sedan; 4 doors; 5 seats, separate front seats - 6 seats, bench front seats.

OPTIONALS 4-speed fully synchronized mechanical gearbox (I 3.352, II 1.641, III 1, IV 0.784, rev 3.657), steering column, 185 SR x 14 tyres.

130 hp power team

See 110 hp power team, except for:

ENGINE 6 cylinders in Vee; 121.9 cu in, 1,998 cc (3.07 x 2.74 in, 78 x 69.7 mm); compression ratio: 9.5:1; max power (JIS): 130 hp (96 kW) at 6,000 rpm; max torque (JIS): 127 lb ft, 17.5 kg m (172 Nm) at 4,400 rpm; max engine rpm: 6,400; 65.1 hp/l (47.9 kW/l); 4 crankshaft bearings; valves: overhead, hydraulic tappets; camshafts: 2, overhead, cogged belt; lubrication: 7 imp pt, 8.5 US pt, 4 l; Nissan ECCS electronic injection; fuel feed: electric pump; cooling: 14.1 imp pt, 16.9 US pt, 8 l.

TRANSMISSION axle ratio: 4.625; tyres: 185 SR x 14.

PERFORMANCE max speed: 112 mph, 180 km/h; power-weight ratio: Custom De Luxe 21.6 lb/hp (29.4 lb/kW), 9.8 kg/hp (13.4 kg/kW); consumption: 25.2 m/imp gal, 21 m/US gal, 11.2 l x 100 km on Japanese emission test cycle.

STEERING GL and SGL servo; turns lock to lock: 3.70.

BRAKES disc, front internal radial fins.

ELECTRICAL EQUIPMENT hardtops 70 A alternator; 2 headlamps.

DIMENSIONS AND WEIGHT height: st. wagons 59.06 in, 150 cm; weight: Cedric V20E Custom De Luxe Sedan 2,811 lb, 1,275 kg - Cedric V20E SGL Sedan 2,977 lb, 1,350 kg - Cedric V20E GL Sedan 2,867 lb, 1,300 kg - Cedric V20E Custom S Hardtop 2,889 lb, 1,310 kg - Cedric V20E SGL Hardtop 3,065 lb, 1,390 kg - Cedric V20E De Luxe St. Wagon 2,922 lb, 1,325 kg - Cedric V20E GL St. Wagon 2,988 lb, 1,355 kg; fuel tank: st. wagons 13.2 imp gal, 15.8 US gal, 60 l.

BODY saloon/sedan, 4 doors - hardtop, 4 doors - estate car/st. wagon, 4+1 doors.

OPTIONALS 4-speed electronically-controlled automatic transmission (I 2.842, II 1.542, III 1, IV 0.686, rev 2.400).

170 hp power team

See 110 hp power team, except for:

ENGINE turbocharged; 6 cylinders in Vee; 121.9 cu in, 1,998 cc (3.07 x 2.74 in, 78 x 69.7 mm); compression ratio: 8:1; max power (JIS): 170 hp (125 kW) at 6,000 rpm; max torque (JIS): 159 lb ft, 22 kg m (216 Nm) at 4,000 rpm; max engine rpm: 6,400; 85.1 hp/l (62.6 kW/l); 4 crankshaft bearings; valves: overhead, hydraulic tappets; camshafts: 2, overhead, cogged belt; lubrication: 7 imp pt, 8.5 US pt, 4 l; Nissan ECCS electronic injection; turbocharger with wastegate; fuel feed: electric pump; cooling: 14.1 imp pt, 16.9 Us pt, 8 l.

TRANSMISSION width of rims: 5.5"; tyres: 185 SR x 14 - Turbo S 195/70 HR x 14.

PERFORMANCE max speed: 112 mph, 180 km/h; power-weight ratio: Turbo SGL Sedan 18.3 lb/hp (24.7 lb/kW), 8.3 kg/hp (11.2 kg/kW); consumption: 28.2 m/imp gal, 23.5 m/US gal, 10 l x 100 km on Japanese emission test cycle.

STEERING servo; turns lock to lock: 3.70.

BRAKES disc, front internal radial fins.

ELECTRICAL EQUIPMENT Brougham 45 Ah battery; 70 A alternator.

DIMENSIONS AND WEIGHT weight: Cedric V20 Turbo SGL Sedan 3,098 lb, 1,405 kg - Cedric V20 Turbo Brougham Sedan 3,153 lb, 1,430 kg - Cedric V20 Turbo S Hardtop 2,988 lb, 1,355 kg - Cedric V20 Turbo SGL Hardtop 3,109 lb, 1,410 kg - Cedric V20 Turbo Brougham Hardtop 3,241 lb, 1,470 kg.

BODY saloon/sedan, 4 doors - hardtop, 4 doors; 5 seats, separate front seats.

OPTIONALS 4-speed electronically-controlled automatic transmission (I 2.842, II 1.542, III 1, IV 0.686, rev 2.400).

NISSAN Fairlady 3000 300 ZX 2-seater Coupé

180 hp power team

See 110 hp power team, except for:

ENGINE 6 cylinders in Vee; 180.6 cu in, 2,960 cc (3.47 x 3.27 in, 87 x 83 mm); compression ratio: 9:1; max power (JIS): 180 hp (133 kW) at 5,200 rpm; max torque (JIS): 192 lb ft, 26.5 kg m (260 Nm) at 4,000 rpm; 60.8 hp/l (44.7 kW/l); 4 crankshaft bearings; valves: overhead, hydraulic tappets; camshafts: 2, overhead, cogged belt; lubrication: 7 imp pt, 8.5 US pt, 4 l; Nissan ECCS electronic injection; fuel feed: electric pump; cooling: 15.8 imp pt, 19 US pt, 9 l.

TRANSMISSION gearbox: automatic transmission, hydraulic torque converter with electronically-controlled lock-up on all forward ratios, planetary gears with 4 ratios and electronically-controlled dual shift modes; ratios: I 2.458, II 1.458, III 1, IV 0.686, rev 2.182; axle ratio: 3.889; tyres: 185 SR x 14.

PERFORMANCE max speed: 112 mph, 180 km/h; power-weight ratio: Sedan 17.9 lb/hp (24.3 lb/kW), 8.1 kg/hp (11.3 kg/kW); consumption: 23.2 m/imp gal, 19.2 m/US gal, 12.2 l x 100 km on Japanese emission test cycle.

STEERING servo; turns lock to lock: 3.70.

BRAKES disc, front internal radial fins.

ELECTRICAL EQUIPMENT 45 Ah battery; 70 A alternator; 2 headlamps.

DIMENSIONS AND WEIGHT length: 191.34 in, 486 cm; width: 67.72 in, 172 cm; height: Sedan 53.30 in, 143 cm - Hardtop 55.91 in, 142 cm; weight: Cedric V30 Brougham Sedan 3,131 lb, 1,460 kg - Cedric V30 Brougham Hardtop 3,252 lb, 1,475 kg.

BODY saloon/sedan or hardtop.

OPTIONALS (for Brougham Sedan only) electronic power steering.

91 hp (diesel) power team

See 110 hp power team, except for:

ENGINE diesel; 6 cylinders in Vee; 170.3 cu in, 2,792 cc (3.33 x 3.27 in, 84.5 x 83 mm); compression ratio: 22:1; max power (JIS): 91 hp (67 kW) at 4,600 rpm; max torque (JIS): 126 lb ft, 17.3 kg m (170 Nm) at 2,400 rpm; max engine rpm: 4,800; 32.5 hp/l (23.9 kW/l); lubrication: 10 imp pt, 11.8 US pt, 5.7 l; Bosch diesel injection pump; Ricardo Comet swirl chamber; cooling: 17.5 imp pt, 20.6 US pt, 10 l.

TRANSMISSION axle ratio: 4.111; tyres: 185 SR x 14.

PERFORMANCE max speed: 96 mph, 155 km/h; power-weight ratio: STD 33.7 lb/hp (45.6 lb/kW), 15.3 kg/hp (20.7 kg/kW); consumption: 41.8 m/imp gal, 35.1 m/US gal, 6.7 l x 100 km at 37 mph, 60 km/h on Japanese emission test cycle.

STEERING servo; turns lock to lock: 3.20.

BRAKES disc, front internal radial fins.

ELECTRICAL EQUIPMENT 70 Ah battery.

DIMENSIONS AND WEIGHT weight: Gloria Diesel 28D-6 STD Sedan 3,064 lb, 1,390 kg - Gloria Diesel 28D-6 GL Sedan 3,141 lb, 1,425 kg - Gloria Diesel 28D-6 Custom S Hardtop 3,130 lb, 1,420 kg - Gloria Diesel 28D-6 GL Hardtop 3,197 lb, 1,450 kg - Gloria Diesel 28D-6 SGL Hardtop 3,318 lb, 1,505 kg.

BODY saloon/sedan, 4 doors - hardtop, 4 doors - estate car/st. wagon 4+1 doors.

OPTIONALS 4-speed electronically-controlled automatic transmission (I 2.458, II 1.548, III 1, IV 0.686, rev 2.182), 3.889 axle ratio.

NISSAN President Sovereign Sedan

Fairlady Series

PRICES (Tokyo):		yen
1	2000 Z 2-seater 2+1-dr Coupé	**1,950,000**
2	2000 ZS 2-seater 2+1-dr Coupé	**2,186,000**
3	2000 ZG 2-seater 2+1-dr Coupé	**2,375,000**
4	2000 Z 2+2-seater 2+1-dr Coupé	**2,030,000**
5	2000 ZS 2+2-seater 2+1-dr Coupé	**2,266,000**
6	2000 ZG 2+2-seater 2+1-dr Coupé	**2,455,000**
7	3000 300 ZX 2-seater 2+1-dr Coupé	**3,200,000**
8	3000 300 ZX 2+2-seater 2+1-dr Coupé	**3,270,000**

For GB and USA prices, see price index.

Power team:	Standard for:	Optional for:
170 hp	1 to 6	—
230 hp	7,8	—

170 hp power team

ENGINE turbocharged, front, 4 stroke; 6 cylinders, in Vee; 121.9 cu in, 1,998 cc (3.07 x 2.74 in, 78 x 69.7 mm); compression ratio: 8:1; max power (JIS): 170 hp (125 kW) at 6,000 rpm; max torque (JIS): 159 lb ft, 22 kg m (216 Nm) at 4,000 rpm; max engine rpm: 6,400; 85.1 hp/l (62.6 kW/l); cast iron block, light alloy head; 4 crankshaft bearings; valves: overhead, rockers, hydraulic tappets; camshafts: 2, overhead, cogged belt; lubrication: gear pump, full flow filter, 7.6 imp pt, 9.1 US pt, 4.3 l; Nissan ECCS electronic injection; turbocharger with wastegate; emissin control by 3-way catalytic converter and exhaust gas recirculation; fuel feed: electric pump; water-cooled, 18.5 imp pt, 22.2 US pt, 10.5 l.

TRANSMISSION driving wheels: rear; clutch: single dry plate (diaphragm); gearbox: mechanical; gears: 5, fully synchronized; ratios: I 3.592, II 2.057, III 1.361, IV 1, V 0.813, rev 3.657; lever: central; final drive: hypoid bevel; axle ratio: 4.111; width of rims: 5.5" - ZG 6.5"; tyres: 195/70 HR x 14 - ZG 205/60 HR x 15.

PERFORMANCE max speeds: (I) 29 mph, 47 km/h; (II) 50 mph, 80 km/h; (III) 76 mph, 123 km/h; (IV) and (V) 112 mph, 180 km/h; power-weight ratio: Z 2-seater 15 lb/hp (20.5 lb/kW), 6.8 kg/hp (9.3 kg/kW); acceleration: standing ¼ mile 15.7 sec; consumption: 29.4 m/imp gal, 24.5 m/US gal, 9.6 l x 100 km on Japanese emission test cycle.

CHASSIS integral; front suspension: independent, by McPherson, coil springs/telescopic damper struts, lower transverse arms, trailing links, anti-roll bar; rear: independent, semi-trailing arms, coil springs, anti-roll bar, telescopic dampers.

STEERING rack-and-pinion - ZS and ZG servo; turns lock to lock: 3.60 - ZS and ZG 2.80.

BRAKES disc, front internal radial fins, dual circuit, servo.

ELECTRICAL EQUIPMENT 12 V; 33 Ah battery; 70 A alternator; Hitachi or Mitsubishi distributor; 2 semi-retractable headlamps.

DIMENSIONS AND WEIGHT wheel base: 2-seater coupés 91.34 in, 232 cm - 2+2-seater coupés 99.21 in, 252 cm; tracks: 55.51 in, 141 cm front, 56.30 in, 143 cm rear; length: 2-seater coupés 170.47 in, 433 cm - 2+2-seater coupés 178.25 in, 455 cm; width: 66.54 in, 169 cm; height: 50.79 in, 129 cm; ground clearance: 5.90 in, 15 cm; weight: Z 2-seater Coupé 2,558 lb, 1,160 kg - ZS 2-seater Coupé 2,668 lb, 1,210 kg - ZG 2-seater Coupé 2,679 lb, 1,215 kg - Z 2+2-seater Coupé 2,668 lb, 1,210 kg - ZS and ZG 2+2-seater coupés 2,756 lb, 1,250 kg.

BODY coupé; 2+1 doors; 2 or 2+2 seats, separate front seats, headrests.

OPTIONALS (for ZS and ZG 2+2-seater only) 4-speed electronically-controlled automatic transmission (I 2.842, II 1.542, III 1, IV 0.686, rev 2.400).

230 hp power team

See 170 hp power team, except for:

ENGINE turbocharged; 180.6 cu in, 2,960 cc (3.47 x 3.27 in, 87 x 83 mm); compression ratio: 7.8:1; max power (JIS): 230 hp (169 kW) at 5,200 rpm; max torque (JIS): 246 lb ft, 34 kg m (334 Nm) at 3,600 rpm; max engine rpm: 5,600; 77.7 hp/l (57.2 kW/l); cooling: 19.4 imp pt, 23 US pt, 11 l.

TRANSMISSION gearbox ratios: I 3.350, II 2.056, III 1.376, IV 1, V 0.770, rev 3.151; width of rims: 6.5"; tyres: 215/60 HR x 15.

PERFORMANCE max speed: 112 mph, 180 km/h; power-weight ratio: ZX 2-seater 12.8 lb/hp (17.2 lb/kW), 5.8 kg/hp (7.8 kg/kW).

STEERING servo.

DIMENSIONS AND WEIGHT width: 67.72 in, 172 cm; weight: 300 ZX 2-seater Coupé 2,922 lb, 1,325 kg - 300 ZX 2+2-seater Coupé 3,010 lb, 1,365 kg.

OPTIONALS automatic transmission, hydraulic torque converter and planetary gears with 4 ratios (I 2.458, II 1.458, III 1, IV 0.686, rev 2.182).

President

PRICES (Tokyo):	yen
C 4-dr Sedan	**4,513,000**
D 4-dr Sedan	**5,072,000**
Sovereign 4-dr Sedan	**5,743,000**

ENGINE front, 4 stroke; 8 cylinders in Vee; 269.3 cu in, 4,414 cc (3.62 x 3.27 in, 92 x 83 mm); compression ratio: 8.6:1; max power (JIS): 200 hp (147 kW) at 4,800 rpm; max torque (JIS): 250 lb ft, 34.5 kg m (338 Nm) at 3,200 rpm; max engine rpm: 5,200; 45.1 hp/l (33.2 kW/l); cast iron block, light alloy head; 5 crankshaft bearings; valves: overhead, Vee-slanted, push-rods and rockers, hydraulic tappets; camshafts: 1, at centre of Vee; lubrication: gear pump, full flow filter, 8.3 imp pt, 9.9 US pt, 4.7 l; Bosch L-Jetronic injection; emission control with 2 catalytic converters and exhaust gas recirculation; fuel feed: electric pump; water-cooled, 28.2 imp pt, 33.8 US pt, 16 l.

TRANSMISSION driving wheels: rear; gearbox: automatic transmission, hydraulic torque converter and planetary gears with 3 ratios, possible manual selection; ratios: I 2.458, II 1.458, III 1, rev 2.182; lever: steering column; final drive: hypoid bevel; axle ratio: 3.364; width of rims: 6"; tyres: 205 SR x 14.

PERFORMANCE max speeds: (I) 42 mph, 68 km/h; (II) 65 mph, 115 km/h; (III) 112 mph, 180 km/h; power-weight ratio: C 21 lb/hp (28.6 lb/kW), 9.5 kg/hp (12.9 kg/kW); consumption: 15.5 m/imp gal, 12.9 m/US gal, 18.2 l x 100 km on Japanese emission test cycle.

CHASSIS integral; front suspension: independent, wishbones, coil springs, anti-roll bar, telescopic dampers; rear: rigid axle, lower trailing arms, upper torque rod, coil springs, telescopic dampers.

STEERING recirculating ball, servo; turns lock to lock: 4.10.

BRAKES front disc, rear drum, servo; lining area: front 26.7 sq in, 172 sq cm, rear 71.9 sq in, 464 sq cm, total 98.6 sq in, 636 sq cm.

ELECTRICAL EQUIPMENT 12 V; 60 Ah battery; 600 W alternator; Hitachi distributor; 4 headlamps.

DIMENSIONS AND WEIGHT wheel base: 112.20 in, 285 cm; tracks: 59.84 in, 152 cm front, 59.06 in, 150 cm rear; length: C 206.69 in, 525 cm - D and Sovereign 207.87 in, 528 cm; width: 72.05 in, 183 cm; height: 58.27 in, 148 cm; ground clearance: 7.28 in, 18 cm; weight: C Sedan 4,021 lb, 1,905 kg - D Sedan 4,289 lb, 1,945 kg - Sovereign Sedan 4,366 lb, 1,980 kg; weight distribution: 54% front, 46% rear; turning circle: 42 ft, 12.8 m; fuel tank: 20.9 imp gal, 25.1 US gal, 95 l.

BODY saloon/sedan; 4 doors; 6 seats, bench front seats, reclining backrests, built-in headrests; electric windows.

OPTIONALS air-conditioning; separate front seats.

Safari Series

PRICES (Tokyo):		yen
1	Standard roof 2+1-dr St. Wagon	**1,684,000**
2	Standard roof AD 2+1-dr St. Wagon	**2,175,000**
3	High roof AD 2+1-dr St. Wagon	**2,121,000**
4	Long Van DX 4+1-dr St. Wagon	**2,068,000**
5	Long Van AD 4+1-dr St. Wagon	**2,302,000**
6	Long Van High roof AD 4+1-dr St. Wagon	**2,348,000**
7	Standard roof Turbo AD 2+1-dr St. Wagon	**2,265,000**
8	Long Van Turbo AD 4+1-dr St. Wagon	**2,516,000**

For GB prices, see price index.

Power team:	Standard for:	Optional for:
95 hp (diesel)	1 to 6	—
120 hp (diesel)	7,8	—

95 hp (diesel) power team

ENGINE diesel, front, 4 stroke; 6 cylinders, in line; 198 cu in, 3,246 cc (3.27 x 3.94 in, 83 x 100 mm); compression ratio: 20.8:1; max power (JIS): 95 hp (70 kW) at 3,600 rpm; max torque (JIS): 160 lb ft, 22 kg m (216 Nm) at 1,800 rpm; max engine rpm: 4,000; 29.3 hp/l (21.5 kW/l); cast iron block and head; 4 crankshaft bearings; valves: overhead, in line, push-rods and rockers; camshafts: 1, side; lubrication: gear pump, full flow filter, 13.3 imp pt, 15.8 US pt, 7.5 l; Bosch injection pump; fuel feed: mechanical pump; water-cooled, 22.7 imp pt, 27 US pt, 12.9 l.

TRANSMISSION driving wheels: rear or front and rear; clutch: single dry plate (diaphragm); gearbox: mechanical; gears: 5, fully synchronized with 2-ratio transfer box; ratios: I 3.897, II 2.370, III 1.440, IV 1, V 0.825, rev 4.267; transfer box ratios: high 1, low 2.220; levers: 2, central; final drive: hypoid bevel; axle ratio: 4.375; width of rims: 5.5"; tyres: 6.50 x 16.

PERFORMANCE max speed: 75 mph, 120 km/h; power-weight ratio: 38.8 lb/hp (52.7 lb/kW), 17.6 kg/hp (23.9 kg/kW); consumption: 42.8 m/imp gal, 35.6 m/US gal, 6.6 l x 100 km on Japanese emission test cycle.

CHASSIS box-type ladder frame; front suspension: rigid axle, semi-elliptic leafsprings, anti-roll bar, telescopic dampers; rear: rigid axle, semi-elliptic leafsprings, telescopic dampers.

STEERING recirculating ball - AD servo; turns lock to lock: 4.50.

BRAKES front disc, rear drum, front internal radial fins, servo.

ELECTRICAL EQUIPMENT 24 V; 80 Ah battery; 25 A alternator; 2 headlamps.

DIMENSIONS AND WEIGHT wheel base: 92.50 in, 235 cm; tracks: 55.30 in, 140 cm front, 55.50 in, 141 cm rear; length: 160 in, 407 cm; width: 66.50 in, 169 cm; height: 72.60 in, 184 cm; ground clearance: 9 in, 23 cm; weight: 3,682 lb, 1,670 kg; weight distribution: 52% front, 48% rear; turning circle: 38.2 ft, 11.8 m; fuel tank: 18.2 imp gal, 21.7 US gal, 82 l.

BODY estate car/st. wagon, in fiberglass material; 2+1 or 4+1 doors; 5 seats, separate front seats.

OPTIONALS power winch; headlamps with wiper-washer.

120 hp (diesel) power team

See 95 hp (diesel) power team, except for:

ENGINE diesel, turbocharged; max power (JIS): 120 hp (88 kW) at 4,000 rpm; max torque (JIS): 196 lb ft, 27 kg m (265 Nm) at 2,000 rpm; turbocharger with wastegate.

TRANSMISSION tyres: 205/80 HR x 16.

STEERING servo.

DIMENSIONS AND WEIGHT wheel base: Standard roof 92.52 in, 235 cm - Long van 116.93 in, 297 in; length: Standard roof 166.54 in, 423 cm - Long van 184.65 in, 469 cm; height: 77.95 in, 198 cm; ground clearance: 7.90 in, 20 cm; weight: Standard roof Turbo AD St. Wagon 4,046 lb, 1,835 kg - Long van Turbo AD St. Wagon 4,333 lb, 1,965 kg.

NISSAN Safari Long Van DX Station Wagon

SUBARU JAPAN

Rex Series

PRICES EX WORKS:		yen
1	Combi F 2+1-dr Sedan	**514,000**
2	Combi FR 2+1-dr Sedan	**516,000**
3	Combi FL 2+1-dr Sedan	**570,000**
4	Combi XL 2+1-dr Sedan	**634,000**
5	S 2+1-dr Sedan	**585,000**
6	S 4+1-dr Sedan	**600,000**
7	SE 2+1-dr Sedan	**701,000**
8	SG 2+1-dr Sedan	**732,000**
9	SR 4+1-dr Sedan	**625,000**
10	SL 4+1-dr Sedan	**719,000**
11	SX 4+1-dr Sedan	**782,000**
12	Combi TL 4WD 2+1-dr Sedan	—
13	Combi TX 4WD 2+1-dr Sedan	—
14	Combi Turbo 2+1-dr Sedan	**698,000**

Power team:	Standard for:	Optional for:
31 hp (544 cc)	1 to 11	—
31 hp (544 cc, 4WD)	12,13	—
41 hp	14	—

31 hp (544 cc) power team

ENGINE front, transverse, 4 stroke; 2 cylinders, in line; 33.2 cu in, 544 cc (2.99 x 2.36 in, 76 x 60 mm); compression ratio:

31 HP (544 cc) POWER TEAM

9.5:1; max power (JIS): 31 hp (23 kW) at 6,000 rpm; max torque (JIS): 32 lb ft, 4.4 kg m (43 Nm) at 3,500 rpm; max engine rpm: 6,500; 56.9 hp/l (41.9 kW/l); cast iron block, light alloy head; 3 crankshaft bearings; valves: overhead, Vee-slanted, rockers; camshafts: 1, overhead; lubrication: trochoid pump, full flow filter, 4.9 imp pt, 5.9 US pt, 2.8 l; 1 Hitachi DCG306 downdraught twin barrel carburettor; fuel feed: mechanical pump; water-cooled, 5.3 imp pt, 6.3 US pt, 3 l.

TRANSMISSION driving wheels: front; clutch: single dry plate (diaphragm); gearbox: mechanical; gears: 4, fully synchronized; ratios: I 4.083, II 2.437, III 1.666, IV 1.115, rev 4; lever: central; final drive: helical spur gears; axle ratio: 4.352 - Combi 4.529; width of rims: 3.5''; tyres: 5.20 x 10 - Combi 5.00 x 10.

PERFORMANCE max speed: 68 mph, 110 km/h - Combi 62 mph, 100 km/h; power-weight ratio: Combi F 39.5 lb/hp (53.7 lb/kW), 17.9 kg/hp (24.3 kg/kW); carrying capacity: 706 lb, 320 kg; consumption: 58.8 m/imp gal, 48 m/US gal, 4.8 l x 100 km.

CHASSIS integral; front and rear suspension: independent, by McPherson, semi-trailing arms, torsion bars, telescopic dampers.

STEERING rack-and-pinion; turns lock to lock: 3.60.

BRAKES drum; lining area: front 37.2 sq in, 240 sq cm, rear 33.5 sq in, 216 sq cm, total 70.7 sq in, 456 sq cm.

ELECTRICAL EQUIPMENT 12 V; 26 Ah battery; 255 A alternator; Hitachi distributor; 2 headlamps.

DIMENSIONS AND WEIGHT wheel base: 100.39 in, 255 cm; front and rear track: 48.02 in, 122 cm; length: 125.79 in, 319 cm; width: 54.72 in, 139 cm; height: 53.15 in, 135 cm - Combi 53.94 in, 137 cm; weight: Combi FL and S 2+1-dr sedans 1,213 lb, 550 kg - Combi F, XL and SE sedans 1,224 lb, 555 kg - SG Sedan 1,235 lb, 560 kg - S 4+1-dr and SL sedans 1,246 lb, 565 kg - S 4+1-dr and SL sedans 1,246 lb, 565 kg - SR Sedan 1,257 lb, 570 kg - SX Sedan 1,768 lb, 575 kg; weight distribution: 62% front, 38% rear; turning circle: 30.2 ft, 9.2 m; fuel tank: 6.8 imp gal, 8.2 US gal, 31 l.

BODY saloon/sedan; 2+1 or 4+1 doors; 4 seats, separate front seats.

OPTIONALS magnetic clutch.

31 hp (544 cc, 4WD) power team

See 31 hp (544 cc) power team, except for:

TRANSMISSION driving wheels: front or front and rear; gears: 5, fully synchronized; ratios: I 4.181, II 2.444, III 1.520, IV 1.032, V 0.823, rev 4.090; axle ratio: 6.166; tyres: 135 SR x 12.

PERFORMANCE power-weight ratio: Combi TL 45.6 lb/hp (61.9 lb/kW), 20.6 kg/hp (28.1 kg/kW.

BRAKES front disc, rear drum, servo.

DIMENSIONS AND WEIGHT height: 54.53 in, 138 cm; ground clearance: 7.28 in, 18 cm; weight: Combi TX, 4WD Sedan 1,411 lb, 610 kg - Combi TX 4WD Sedan 1,422 lb, 645 kg.

BODY 2+1 doors.

OPTIONALS magnetic clutch not available.

41 hp power team

See 31 hp (544 cc) power team, except for:

ENGINE turbocharged; compression ratio: 8.5:1; max power (JIS): 41 hp (30 kW) at 6,000 rpm; max torque (JIS): 43 lb ft, 5.9 kg m (58 Nm) at 3,500 rpm; turbocharger with exhaust wastegate.

TRANSMISSION gears: 5, fully synchronized; ratios: I 3.833, II 2.263, III 1.520, IV 1.032, V 0.878, rev 3.461; axle ratio: 4.937; tyres: 135 SR x 12.

SUBARU Rex Combi XL Sedan

PERFORMANCE power-weight ratio: 45.8 lb/hp (62.2 lb/kW), 20.7 kg/hp (28.2 kg/kW).

BRAKES front disc, rear drum, servo.

DIMENSIONS AND WEIGHT weight: 1,874 lb, 850 kg.

BODY 2+1 doors.

OPTIONALS magnetic clutch not available.

Domingo Series

PRICES EX WORKS:		yen
1	CF 4+1-dr Wagon	**898,000**
2	CS 4+1-dr Wagon	**1,035,000**
3	CS-S 4+1-dr Wagon	**1,115,000**
4	GF 4WD 4+1-dr Wagon	**1,048,000**
5	GS 4WD 4+1-dr Wagon	**1,185,000**
6	GS-S 4WD 4+1-dr Wagon	**1,265,000**

Power team:	Standard for:	Optional for:
56 hp (997 cc)	1 to 3	—
56 hp (997 cc, 4WD)	4 to 6	—

56 hp (997 cc) power team

ENGINE rear, transverse, 4 stroke, Vee-slanted; 3 cylinders, in line with contra-rotating balancers; 60.8 cu in, 997 cc (3.07 x 2.74 in, 78 x 69.6 mm); compression ratio: 9.5:1; max power (JIS): 56 hp (41 kW) at 5,400 rpm; max torque (JIS): 62 lb ft, 8.5 kg m (83 Nm) at 3,200 rpm; max engine rpm: 5,800; 56.2 hp/l (41.3 kW/l); cast iron block, light alloy head; 4 crankshaft bearings; valves: overhead, Vee-slanted, rockers; camshafts: 1, overhead, cogged belt; lubrication: trochoid pump, full flow filter, 4.9 imp pt, 5.9 US pt, 2.8 l; 1 Hitachi HCK 34 sidedraught carburettor; fuel feed: electric pump; emission control by secondary air induction, catalytic converter and exhaust gas recirculation; water-cooled, 11.4 imp pt, 13.7 US pt, 6.5 l, electric thermostatic fan.

TRANSMISSION driving wheels: rear; clutch: single dry plate (diaphragm); gearbox: mechanical; gears: 5, fully synchronized; ratios: I 3.166, II 1.950, III 1.269, IV 0.843, V 0.685, rev 3.583; lever: central; final drive: helical spur gears; axle ratio: 4.928; width of rims: 4''; tyres: 155 SR x 12.

PERFORMANCE max speeds: (I) 23 mph, 37 km/h; (II) 37 mph, 60 km/h; (III) 55 mph, 88 km/h; (IV) and (V) 75 mph, 120 km/h; power-weight ratio: CF 31.7 lb/hp (43.1 lb/kW), 14.4 kg/hp (19.5 kg/kW); consumption: 42.1 m/imp gal, 35.1 m/US gal, 6.7 l x 100 km on Japanese emission test cycle.

CHASSIS box-type ladder frame; front suspension: independent, by McPherson, coil springs/telescopic damper struts, transverse I arms, anti-roll bar; rear: independent, semi-trailing arms; coil springs/telescopic dampers.

STEERING rack-and-pinion; turns lock to lock: 3.90.

BRAKES front disc, rear drum, dual circuit, servo; lining area: front 19.8 sq in, 128 sq cm, rear 31.6 sq in, 204 sq cm, total 51.4 sq in, 332 sq cm.

ELECTRICAL EQUIPMENT 12 V; 33 Ah battery; 45 A alternator; pointless distributor; 4 headlamps.

DIMENSIONS AND WEIGHT wheel base: 71.06 in, 180 cm; front and rear track: 47.64 in, 121 cm; length: 134.25 in, 341 cm; width: 56.30 in, 143 cm; height: 73.62 in, 187 cm; ground clearance: 8.07 in, 20 cm; weight: CF Wagon 1,775 lb, 805 kg - CS Wagon 1,819 lb, 825 kg - CS-S Wagon 1,863 lb, 845 kg; fuel tank: 8.8 imp gal, 10.6 US gal, 40 l.

BODY estate car/st. wagon; 4+1 doors; 7 seats, separate front seats.

56 hp (997 cc, 4WD) power team

See 56 hp (997 cc) power team, except for:

TRANSMISSION driving wheels: front or front and rear; gearbox ratios: I 3.454, II 1.950, III 1.269, IV 0.843, V 0.685, rev 3.583; final drive: front hypoid bevel, rear helical spur gears; axle ratio: front 5.833, rear 3.888.

PERFORMANCE power-weight ratio: GF 33.9 lb/hp (46 lb/kW), 15.4 kg/hp (20.9 kg/kW); consumption: 36.7 m/imp gal, 30.5 m/US gal, 7.7 l x 100 km on Japanese emission test cycle.

DIMENSIONS AND WEIGHT weight: GF 4WD Wagon 1,896 lb, 860 kg - GS 4WD Wagon 1,940 lb, 880 kg - GS-S 4WD Wagon 1,984 lb, 900 kg.

SUBARU Domingo GS-S 4WD Wagon

Leone Series

PRICES EX WORKS:		yen
1	1300 2+1-dr Swingback Sedan	**757,000**
2	1300 LG 2+1-dr Swingback Sedan	**862,000**
3	1300 L 4-dr Sedan	**907,000**
4	1600 LG 4-dr Sedan	**972,000**
5	1600 GLF 4-dr Sedan	**1,030,000**
6	1600 GLT 4-dr Sedan	**1,173,000**
7	1600 GLS 2+1-dr Swingback Sedan	**1,065,000**
8	1600 4WD E 2+1-dr Swingback Sedan	**1,230,000**
9	1800 GTL 4-dr Sedan	**1,220,000**
10	1800 GTS 4-dr Sedan	**1,380,000**
11	1800 GTX 2-dr Hardtop	**1,395,000**
12	1800 4WD 4-dr Sedan	**1,482,000**
13	1800 4WD 2+1-dr Swingback Sedan	**1,372,000**
14	1800 4WD 4+1-dr Touring Wagon	**1,395,000**
15	1800 4WD RX 2-dr Hardtop	**1,507,000**
16	1800 4WD Turbo 4-dr Sedan	**1,840,000**
17	1800 4WD Turbo 4+1-dr Touring Wagon	**1,895,000**

For GB and USA prices, see prices index.

Power team:	Standard for:	Optional for:
72 hp	1,2	—
87 hp (1,595 cc)	3 to 7	—

SUBARU Leone 1800 4WD Turbo Touring Wagon

SUBARU Leone 1800 4WD Turbo Sedan

87 hp (1,595 cc, 4WD)	8	—
100 hp (1,781 cc)	9 to 11	—
100 hp (1,781 cc, 4WD)	12 to 14	—
100 hp	15	—
120 hp	16,17	—

72 hp power team

ENGINE front, SEEC-T low emission system with secondary air induction, exhaust gas recirculation and 3-way catalytic converter (open loop system), 4 stroke; 4 cylinders, horizontally opposed; 79.2 cu in, 1,298 cc (3.27 x 2.36 in, 83 x 60 mm); compression ratio: 9:1; max power (JIS): 72 hp (53 kW) at 5,600 rpm; max torque (JIS): 76 lb ft, 10 kg m (98 Nm) at 3,600 rpm; max engine rpm: 6,000; 55.4 hp/l (40.7 kW/l); light alloy block with cast iron liners, light alloy head; 3 crankshaft bearings; valves: overhead, push-rods and rockers; camshafts: 1, under crankshaft; lubrication: rotary pump, full flow filter, 6.1 imp pt, 7.2 US pt, 3.5 l; 1 Hitachi-Zenith DCG 306 twin barrel carburettor; fuel feed: electric pump; water-cooled, 8.9 imp pt, 10.5 US pt, 5 l, electric fan.

TRANSMISSION driving wheels: front; clutch: single dry plate (diaphragm); gearbox: mechanical; gears: 4, fully synchronized; ratios: I 3.666, II 2.157, III 1.379, IV 0.971, rev 4.100; lever: central; final drive: hypoid bevel; axle ratio: 3.889; width of rims: 4.5"; tyres: 6.15 x 13.

PERFORMANCE max speeds: (I) 27 mph, 44 km/h; (II) 46 mph, 75 km/h; (III) 71 mph, 115 km/h; (IV) 93 mph, 150 km/h; power-weight ratio: 25.1 lb/hp (34.1 lb/kW), 11.4 kg/hp (15.5 kg/kW); carrying capacity: 882 lb, 400 kg; speed in top at 1,000 rpm: 15.5 mph, 25 km/h; consumption: 42.2 m/imp gal, 35.1 m/US gal, 6.7 l x 100 km on Japanese emission test cycle.

CHASSIS integral; front suspension: independent, by McPherson, coil springs/telescopic damper struts, lower wishbones (trailing links), anti-roll bar; rear: independent, semi-trailing arms, torsion bars, telescopic dampers.

STEERING rack-and-pinion; turns lock to lock: 3.80.

BRAKES front disc, rear drum.

ELECTRICAL EQUIPMENT 12 V; 35 Ah battery; 50 A alternator; Hitachi distributor; 4 headlamps.

DIMENSIONS AND WEIGHT wheel base: 93.70 in, 238 cm; tracks: 52.80 in, 134 cm front, 53.54 in, 136 cm rear; length: 152.76 in, 388 cm; width: 63.39 in, 161 cm; height: 53.54 in, 136 cm; ground clearance: 6.89 in, 17.5 cm; weight: 1,810 lb, 820 kg; weight distribution: 62% front, 38% rear; turning circle: 34.2 ft, 10.4 m; fuel tank: 15.7 imp gal, 13.2 US gal, 50 l.

BODY saloon/sedan; 2+1 doors; 5 seats, separate front seats, built-in headrests.

87 hp (1,595 cc) power team

See 72 hp power team, except for:

ENGINE 97.3 cu in, 1,595 cc (3.62 x 2.36 in, 92 x 60 mm); max power (JIS): 87 hp (64 kW) at 5,600 rpm; max torque (JIS): 89 lb ft, 12.3 kg m (120 Nm) at 3,600 rpm; 54.5 hp/l (40.1 kW/l); 1 Hitachi-Zenith-Stromberg DCG 306 downdraught twin barrel carburettor.

TRANSMISSION gears: 4 - GLS and GLT 5, fully synchronized; ratios: I 3.307, II 1.944, III 1.344, IV 0.942 - GLS and GLT V 0.725, rev 4.100; lever: central.

PERFORMANCE max speeds: (I) 30 mph, 48 km/h; (II) 51 mph, 82 km/h; (III) 74 mph, 120 km/h; (IV) and (V) 99 mph, 160 km/h; power-weight ratio: L 22 lb/hp (30 lb/kW), 10 kg/hp (13.6 kg/kW); speed in top at 1,000 rpm: 16.6 mph, 26.7 km/h; consumption: 39.8 m/imp gal, 33.1 m/US gal, 7.1 l x 100 km on Japanese emission test cycle.

BRAKES disc, servo; lining area: front 24.2 sq in, 156 sq cm, rear 26.1 sq in, 168 sq cm, total 50.3 sq in, 324 sq cm.

DIMENSIONS AND WEIGHT wheel base: 96.85 in, 246 cm - GLS 93.70 in, 238 cm; tracks: 52.36 in, 133 cm front, 52.76 in, 134 cm rear; length: 164.76 in, 418 cm - GLS 154.13 in, 391 cm; width: 63.79 in, 162 cm - L and GLF 63.39 in, 161 cm; height: 53.54 in, 136 cm; weight: GLS Swingback Sedan 1,885 lb, 855 kg - L Sedan 1,907 lb, 865 kg - LG Sedan 1,929 lb, 875 kg - GLF Sedan 1,951 lb, 885 kg - GLT Sedan 1,973 lb, 895 kg.

BODY 2+1 or 4 doors.

OPTIONALS 3-speed automatic transmission.

87 hp (1,595 cc, 4WD) power team

See 72 hp power team, except for:

ENGINE 97.3 cu in, 1,595 cc (3.62 x 2.36 in, 92 x 60 mm); max power (JIS): 87 hp (64 kW) at 5,600 rpm; max torque (JIS): 89 lb ft, 12.3 kg m (120 Nm) at 3,600 rpm; 54.5 hp/l (40.1 kW/l); 1 Hitachi-Zenith-Stromberg DCG 306 downdraught twin barrel carburettor.

TRANSMISSION driving wheels: front or front and rear; gearbox: mechanical and transfer box; ratios: I 4.090, II 2.157, III 1.379, IV 0.971, rev 4.100; lever: central with auxiliary transfer lever; axle ratio: 3.889 front, 3.900 rear; tyres: 155 SR x 13.

PERFORMANCE max speeds: (I) 25 mph, 40 km/h; (II) 47 mph, 72 km/h; (III) 71 mph, 115 km/h; (IV) 90 mph, 145 km/h; power-weight ratio: 23 lb/hp (31.6 lb/kW), 10.5 kg/hp (14.3 kg/kW); speed in top at 1,000 rpm: 15 mph, 24.2 km/h; consumption: 36 m/imp gal, 30 m/US gal, 7.7 l x 100 km on Japanese emission test cycle.

BRAKES front disc, rear drum, servo; lining area: front 24.2 sq in, 156 sq cm, rear 26.1 sq in, 168 sq cm, total 50.3 sq in, 324 sq cm.

DIMENSIONS AND WEIGHT wheel base: 93.40 in, 237 cm; tracks: 51.81 in, 131 cm front, 52.99 in, 134 cm rear; length: 156.81 in, 398 cm; width: 63.83 in, 162 cm; height: 55.75 in, 141 cm; ground clearance: 8.07 in, 20.5 cm; weight: 2,020 lb, 915 kg; weight distribution: 60% front, 40% rear.

100 hp (1,781 cc) power team

See 72 hp power team, except for:

ENGINE 108.7 cu in, 1,781 cc (3.62 x 2.64 in, 92 x 67 mm); compression ratio: 8.7:1; max power (JIS): 100 hp (74 kW) at 5,600 rpm; max torque (JIS): 109 lb ft, 15 kg m (147 Nm) at 3,600 rpm; 56.1 hp/l (41.3 kW/l); lubrication: 7 imp pt, 8.3 US pt, 4 l; 1 Hitachi DCM 306 downdraught twin barrel carburettor.

TRANSMISSION gears: 5, fully synchronized; ratios: I 3.307, II 1.950, III 1.344, IV 0.942, V 0.725, rev 3.583; axle ratio: 3.700; tyres: 155 SR x 13 - GTS 175/70 HR x 13.

PERFORMANCE max speeds: (I) 31 mph, 50 km/h; (II) 54 mph, 87 km/h; (III) 79 mph, 128 km/h; (IV) and (V) 106 mph, 170 km/h; power-weight ratio: GTL 19.6 lb/hp (26.7 lb/kW), 8.9 kg/hp (12.1 kg/kW); speed in top at 1,000 rpm: 17.6 mph, 28.3 km/h; consumption: 37 m/imp gal, 30 m/US gal, 7.7 l x 100 km on Japanese emission test cycle.

CHASSIS rear suspension: GTS anti-roll bar.

BRAKES front disc, rear drum - GTS disc, servo; lining area: front 24.2 sq in, 156 sq cm, rear 26.1 sq in, 168 sq cm, total 50.3 sq in, 324 sq cm.

DIMENSIONS AND WEIGHT length: GTL 163.58 in, 415 cm - GTS 168 in, 427 cm; weight: GTL Sedan 2,084 lb, 945 kg - GTS Sedan 2,106 lb, 955 kg - GTX Hardtop 2,095 lb, 950 kg.

BODY saloon/sedan, 4 doors - hardtop, 2 doors.

OPTIONALS automatic transmission, hydraulic torque converter and planetary gears with 3 ratios (I 2.600, II 1.505, III 1, rev 2.167), 3.604 axle ratio.

100 hp (1,781 cc, 4WD) power team

See 72 hp power team, except for:

ENGINE 108.7 cu in, 1,781 cc (3.62 x 2.64 in, 92 x 67 mm); compression ratio: 8.7:1; max power (JIS): 100 hp (74 kW) at 5,600 rpm; max torque (JIS): 109 lb ft, 15 kg m (147 Nm) at 3,600 rpm; 56.1 hp/l (41.3 kW/l); lubrication: 7 imp pt, 8.3 US pt, 4 l; 1 Hitachi DCM 306 downdraught twin barrel carburettor.

TRANSMISSION driving wheels: front or front and rear; gears: 4, fully synchronized and 2-ratio transfer box; ratios: I 3.636, II 2.157, III 1.266, IV 0.885, rev 3.583; transfer box ratios: high 1, low 1.462; axle ratio: 3.889 front, 3.900 rear; tyres: 155 SR x 13.

PERFORMANCE max speeds: (I) 28 mph, 45 km/h; (II) 47 mph, 76 km/h; (III) 81 mph, 130 km/h; (IV) 90 mph, 145 km/h; power-weight ratio: Sedan 21.8 lb/hp (29.7 lb/kW), 9.9 kg/hp (13.5 kg/kW); consumption: 34 m/imp gal, 28 m/US gal, 8.3 l x 100 km on Japanese emission test cycle.

DIMENSIONS AND WEIGHT wheel base: Sedan and Touring Wagon 96.46 in, 245 cm - Swingback Sedan 93.30 in, 237 cm; tracks: 51.77 in, 131 cm front, 52.76 in, 134 cm rear; length: Sedan 167.32 in, 425 cm - Swingback Sedan 156.69 in, 298 cm - Touring Wagon 168.31 in, 427 cm; width: 63.78 in, 162 cm; height: Sedan 57.87 in, 147 cm - Swingback Sedan 55.91 in, 142 cm - Touring Wagon 57.87 in, 147 cm; weight: 4WD Sedan 2,183 lb, 990 kg - 4WD Swingback Sedan 2,018 lb, 915 kg - 4WD Touring Wagon 2,282 lb, 1,035 kg.

BODY saloon/sedan, 2+1 or 4 doors - estate car/st. wagon, 4+1 doors.

OPTIONALS automatic transmission with 3 ratios (I 2.600, II 1.505, III 1, rev 2.167), 3.796 axle ratio.

110 hp power team

See 72 hp power team, except for:

ENGINE 108.7 cu in, 1,781 cc (3.62 x 2.64 in, 92 x 67 mm); compression ratio: 9.5:1; max power (JIS): 110 hp (81 kW) at 6,000 rpm; max torque (JIS): 109 lb ft, 15 kg m (147 Nm) at 4,000 rpm; max engine rpm: 6,500; 61.8 hp/l (45.4 kW/l); lubrication: 7 imp pt, 8.3 US pt, 4 l; 2 Hitachi-Stromberg downdraught twin barrel carburettors.

TRANSMISSION driving wheels: front and rear; gears: 4, fully synchronized and 2-ratio transfer box; ratios: I 3.636, II 1.950, III 1.344, IV 0.942, rev 3.583; transfer box ratios: high 1, low 1.203; axle ratio: 3.700; tyres: 175/70 SR x 13.

PERFORMANCE max speed: 112 mph, 180 km/h; power-weight ratio: 19.6 lb/hp (26.7 lb/kW), 8.9 kg/hp (12.1 kg/kW); consumption: 25.7 m/imp gal, 21.4 m/US gal, 11 l x 100 km on Japanese emission test cycle.

CHASSIS rear suspension: anti-roll bar.

STEERING servo; turns lock to lock: 3.50.

BRAKES front internal radial fins.

DIMENSIONS AND WEIGHT wheel base: 96.46 in, 245 cm; tracks: 52.76 in, 134 cm front, 53.94 in, 137 cm rear; length: 164.76 in, 418 cm; width: 63.78 in, 162 cm; height: 54.33 in, 138 cm; weight: 2,161 lb, 980 kg.

BODY hardtop; 2 doors.

120 hp power team

See 72 hp power team, except for:

ENGINE turbocharged; 108.7 cu in, 1,781 cc (3.62 x 2.64 in, 92 x 62 mm); compression ratio: 7.7:1; max power (JIS): 120 hp (88 kW) at 5,200 rpm; max torque (JIS): 138 lb ft, 19 kg m (186

120 HP POWER TEAM

Nm) at 2,400 rpm; max engine rpm: 5,800; 67.3 hp/l (49.6 kW/l); lubrication: 7 imp pt, 8.3 US pt, 4 l; turbocharger.

TRANSMISSION driving wheels: front and rear; gearbox: automatic transmission, hydraulic torque converter and planetary gears with 3 ratios, possible manual selection; ratios: I 2.600, II 1.505, III 1, rev 2.167; axle ratio: 3.452; tyres: 175/70 SR x 13.

PERFORMANCE max speeds: (I) 40 mph, 65 km/h; (II) 70 mph, 112 km/h; (III) 103 mph, 165 km/h; power-weight ratio: Sedan 19.2 lb/hp (26.1 lb/kW), 8.7 kg/hp (11.8 kg/kW); consumption: 27.7 m/imp gal, 23.1 m/US gal, 10.2 l x 100 km on Japanese emission test cycle.

CHASSIS rear suspension: anti-roll bar.

STEERING servo.

DIMENSIONS AND WEIGHT wheel base: 96.46 in, 245 cm; tracks: 51.97 in, 132 cm front, 53.15 in, 135 cm rear; length: Sedan 167.91 in, 426 cm - Touring Wagon 168.70 in, 428 cm; height: Sedan 54.72 in, 139 cm - Touring Wagon 57.09 in, 145 cm; weight: 4WD Turbo Sedan 2,304 lb, 1,045 kg - 4WD Turbo Touring Wagon 2,414 lb, 1,095 kg.

BODY saloon/sedan, 4 doors - estate car/st. wagon, 4+1 doors.

SUZUKI Fronte FSA Sedan

SUZUKI JAPAN

Fronte Series

PRICES (Tokyo):	yen
1 FSA 4+1-dr Sedan	**605,000**
2 FSC 4+1-dr Sedan	**685,000**
3 FSG 4+1-dr Sedan	**725,000**
4 SS 80 F 4+1-dr Hatchback Sedan	—
5 SS 80 G 2+1-dr Hatchback Sedan	—

Power team:	Standard for:	Optional for:
29 hp	1 to 3	—
40 hp	4,5	—

29 hp power team

ENGINE front, transverse, 4 stroke; 3 cylinders, in line; 33.1 cu in, 543 cc (2.36 x 2.44 in, 60 x 62 mm); compression ratio: 9.5:1; max power (JIS): 29 hp (21 kW) at 6,000 rpm; max torque (JIS): 30 lb ft, 4.2 kg m (41 Nm) at 4,000 rpm; max engine rpm: 7,000; 53.4 hp/l (39.3 kW/l); cast iron block, light alloy head; 4 crankshaft bearings; valves: overhead, in line, rockers; camshafts: 1, overhead; lubrication: gear pump, full flow filter, 5.1 imp pt, 6 US pt, 2.9 l; 1 Mikuni-Solex downdraught twin barrel carburettor; fuel feed: mechanical pump; water-cooled, 6.1 imp pt, 7.2 US pt, 3.5 l, electric fan.

TRANSMISSION driving wheels: front; clutch: single dry plate (diaphragm); gearbox: mechanical; gears: 4, fully synchronized; ratios: I 3.384, II 2.055, III 1.280, IV 0.892, rev 2.833; lever: central; final drive: helical spur gears; axle ratio: 5.687; width of rims: 3.5"; tyres: 5.20 x 10.

PERFORMANCE max speeds: (I) 19 mph, 30 km/h; (II) 31 mph, 50 km/h; (III) 47 mph, 75 km/h; (IV) 68 mph, 110 km/h; power-weight ratio: FSA 42.2 lb/hp (57.4 lb/kW), 19.1 kg/hp (26 kg/kW); speed in top at 1,000 rpm: 9.8 mph, 15.7 km/h; consumption: 56 m/imp gal, 47 m/US gal, 5 l x 100 km on Japanese emission test cycle.

CHASSIS integral; front suspension: independent, by McPherson, lower transverse arms, coil springs/telescopic damper struts; rear: rigid axle, semi-elliptic leafsprings, telescopic dampers.

STEERING rack-and-pinion; turns lock to lock: 2.75.

BRAKES drum; lining area: front 31.6 sq in, 204 sq cm, rear 31.6 sq in, 204 sq cm, total 63.2 sq in, 408 sq cm.

ELECTRICAL EQUIPMENT 12 V; 24 Ah battery; 35 A alternator; 2 headlamps.

DIMENSIONS AND WEIGHT wheel base: 84.65 in, 215 cm; tracks: 47.64 in, 121 cm front, 46.06 in, 117 cm rear; length: 125.59 in, 319 cm; width: 54.70 in, 139 cm; height: 52.36 in, 133 cm; ground clearance: 6.69 in, 17 cm; weight: FSA Sedan 1,225 lb, 555 kg - FSC and FSG sedans 1,236 lb, 560 kg; weight distribution: 63% front, 37% rear; turning circle: 28.9 ft, 8.8 m; fuel tank: 6 imp gal, 7.1 US gal, 27 l.

BODY saloon/sedan; 4+1 doors; 4 seats, separate front seats.

OPTIONALS automatic transmission, hydraulic torque converter and planetary gears with 2 ratios (I 1.821, II 1, rev 1.821, primary reduction 1.137), 4.684 axle ratio.

40 hp power team

See 29 hp power team, except for:

ENGINE 48.6 cu in, 796 cc (2.70 x 2.83 in, 68.5 x 72 mm); compression ratio: 8.2:1; max power (JIS): 40 hp (29 kW) at 5,500 rpm; max torque (JIS): 43 lb ft, 6 kg m (59 Nm) at 3,000 rpm; 50.3 hp/l (36.4 kW/l).

TRANSMISSION tyres: 145/70 SR x 12.

PERFORMANCE power-weight ratio: 34.6 lb/hp (47.8 lb/kW), 15.7 kg/hp (21.7 kg/kW).

BRAKES front disc, rear drum.

DIMENSIONS AND WEIGHT length: 129.53 in, 329 cm; width: 55.12 in, 140 cm; weight: 1,389 lb, 630 kg.

BODY 2+1 or 4+1 doors.

SUZUKI Alto 4WD C Sedan

Cervo

PRICES (Tokyo):	yen
CS 2+1-dr Hatchback Coupé	**580,000**
CSL 2+1-dr Hatchback Coupé	**687,000**

ENGINE front, transverse, 4 stroke; 3 cylinders, in line; 33.1 cu in, 543 cc (2.44 x 2.36 in, 62 x 60 mm); compression ratio: 9.5:1; max power (JIS): 29 hp (21 kW) at 6,000 rpm; max torque (JIS): 30 lb ft, 4.2 kg m (41 Nm) at 4,000 rpm; max engine rpm: 7,000; 53.4 hp/l (39.3 kW/l); cast iron block, light alloy head; 4 crankshaft bearings; valves: overhead, push-rods and rockers; camshafts: 1, overhead; lubrication: gear pump, full flow filter, 5.1 imp pt, 6.1 US pt, 2.9 l; 1 Mikuni-Solex twin barrel downdraught carburettor; emission control by secondary air induction, exhaust gas recirculation and oxidizing catalyst; fuel feed: mechanical pump; water-cooled, 6.2 imp pt, 7.4 US pt, 3.5 l, electric fan.

TRANSMISSION driving wheels: front; clutch: single dry plate (diaphragm); gearbox: mechanical; gears: 4, fully synchronized - CSL 5; ratios: I 3.384, II 2.055, III 1.280, IV 0.892 - CSL V 0.774, rev 2.916; lever: central; final drive: helical spur gears; axle ratio: 5.294; width of rims: 3.5"; tyres: 5.20 x 10.

PERFORMANCE max speeds: (I) 22 mph, 35 km/h; (II) 35 mph, 57 km/h; (III) 56 mph, 90 km/h; (IV) 68 mph, 110 km/h; power-weight ratio: 40.3 lb/hp (54.8 lb/kW), 18.3 kg/hp (24.8 kg/kW); consumption: 58.8 m/imp gal, 49 m/US gal, 4.8 l x 100 km on Japanese emission test cycle.

CHASSIS integral; front suspension: independent, by McPherson, lower transverse arms, coil springs, telescopic dampers, anti-roll bar; rear: rigid axle, semi-elliptic leafsprings, telescopic dampers.

STEERING rack-and-pinion; turns lock to lock: 2.75.

BRAKES drum; lining area: front 31.6 sq in, 204 sq cm, rear 31.6 sq in, 204 sq cm, total 63.2 sq in, 408 sq cm.

ELECTRICAL EQUIPMENT 12 V; 24 Ah battery; 35 A alternator; 2 headlamps.

DIMENSIONS AND WEIGHT wheel base: 84.65 in, 215 cm; tracks: 48.03 in, 122 cm front, 46.06 in, 117 cm rear; length: 125.79 in, 319 cm; width: 54.92 in, 139 cm; height: 50.79 in, 129 cm; ground clearance: 6.29 in, 16 cm; weight: CS Hatchback Coupé 1,169 lb, 530 kg; weight distribution: 64% front, 36% rear; turning circle: 28.9 ft, 8.8 m; fuel tank: 5.9 imp gal, 7.1 US gal, 27 l.

BODY coupé; 2+1 doors; 4 seats, separate front seats.

OPTIONALS automatic transmission, hydraulic torque converter and planetary gears with 2 ratios (I 1.821, II 1, rev 1.821), 4.684 axle ratio.

Alto Hatchback

PRICES (Tokyo):	yen
MS-B 2-seater 2+1-dr Sedan	**470,000**
MS-C 2+2-seater 2+1-dr Sedan	**498,000**
MS-CL 2+2-seater 2+1-dr Sedan	**558,000**
MS-CG 2+2-seater 2+1-dr Sedan	**628,000**

For GB prices, see price index.

ENGINE front, transverse, 4 stroke; 3 cylinders, in line; 33.1 cu in, 543 cc (2.44 x 2.36 in, 62 x 60 mm); compression ratio: 9.5:1; max power (JIS): 28 hp (21 kW) at 6,000 rpm; max torque (JIS): 30 lb ft, 4.2 kg m (41 Nm) at 4,000 rpm; max engine rpm: 7,000; 51.6 hp/l (37.9 kW/l); cast iron block, light alloy head; 4 crankshaft bearings; valves: overhead, push-rods and rockers; camshafts: 1, overhead; lubrication: gear pump, full flow filter, 5.1 imp pt, 6.1 US pt, 2.9 l; 1 Mikuni-Solex single barrel downdraught carburettor; fuel feed: mechanical pump; water-cooled, 6.2 imp pt, 7.4 US pt, 3.5 l, electric fan.

TRANSMISSION driving wheels: front; clutch: single dry plate (diaphragm); gearbox: mechanical; gears: 4, fully synchronized; ratios: I 3.384, II 2.055, III 1.280, IV 0.892, rev 2.918; lever: central; final drive: helical spur gears; axle ratio: 5.588; width of rims: 3.5"; tyres: 5.00 x 10.

PERFORMANCE max speeds: (I) 20 mph, 32 km/h; (II) 32 mph, 52 km/h; (III) 52 mph, 83 km/h; (IV) 58 mph, 110 km/h; power-weight ratio: MS-B 42.1 lb/hp (57.3 lb/kW), 19.1 kg/hp (26 kg/kW); consumption: 83.1 m/imp gal, 69.2 m/US gal, 3.4 l x 100 km at 37 mph, 60 km/h.

CHASSIS integral; front suspension: independent, by McPherson, lower transverse arms, coil springs, anti-roll bar, telescopic dampers; rear: rigid axle, semi-elliptic leafsprings, telescopic dampers.

STEERING rack-and-pinion; turns lock to lock: 2.75.

BRAKES drum; lining area: front 31.6 sq in, 204 sq cm, rear 31.6 sq in, 204 sq cm, total 63.2 sq in, 408 sq cm.

ELECTRICAL EQUIPMENT 12 V; 24 Ah battery; 35 A alternator; 2 headlamps.

DIMENSIONS AND WEIGHT wheel base: 84.65 in, 215 cm; tracks: 48.02 in, 121 cm front, 46.06 in, 117 cm rear; length: 125.79 in, 319 cm; width: 54.92 in, 139 cm; height: 52.36 in, 133 cm; ground clearance: 6.29 in, 16 cm; weight: MS-B 2-seater Sedan 1,180 lb, 535 kg; weight distribution: 64% front, 36% rear; turning circle: 28.9 ft, 8.8 m; fuel tank: 5.9 imp gal, 7.1 US gal, 27 l.

BODY saloon/sedan; 2+1 doors; 2 or 2+2 seats, separate front seats.

OPTIONALS automatic transmission, hydraulic torque converter and planetary gears with 2 ratios (I 1.821, II 1, rev 1.831), 4.684 axle ratio.

Alto 4WD

See Alto Hatchback, except for:

PRICES (Tokyo):	yen
C 2+1-dr Sedan	**618,000**
G 2+1-dr Sedan	**718,000**

TRANSMISSION driving wheels: front or front and rear; gearbox: mechanical and transfer box; ratios: I 4.100, II 2.166, III 1.375, IV 0.933, rev 3.363; lever: central with auxiliary transfer lever; axle ratio: 5.733 front, 3.272 rear; width of rims: 3.5"; tyres: 4.50/12 ULT.

PERFORMANCE power-weight ratio: 47.6 lb/hp (64.8 lb/kW), 21.6 kg/hp (29.4 kg/kW).

DIMENSIONS AND WEIGHT tracks: 48.03 in, 122 cm front, 46.46 in, 118 cm rear; height: 53.94 in, 137 cm; ground clearance: 6.50 in, 16.5 cm; weight: 1,334 lb, 605 kg; fuel tank: 5.7 imp gal, 7.9 US gal, 26 l.

Jimny Series

PRICES (Tokyo):	yen
1 SJ 30 F 2-dr Wagon	**770,000**
2 SJ 30 FK 2-dr Wagon	**780,000**
3 SJ 30 FM 2-dr Wagon	**820,000**
4 SJ 30 VM 2-dr Wagon	**858,000**
5 1100 S40 FK (soft top) 2-dr Wagon	**985,000**
6 1000 SJ40 VC 2-dr Wagon	**1,085,000**

Power team:	Standard for:	Optional for:
28 hp (2-stroke)	1 to 4	—
52 hp (4-stroke)	5,6	—

28 hp power team

(2-stroke engine)

ENGINE front, 2 stroke; 3 cylinders, in line; 32.8 cu in, 539 cc (2.40 x 2.42 in, 61 x 61.5 mm); compression ratio: 6.5:1; max power (JIS): 28 hp (21 kW) at 4,500 rpm; max torque (JIS): 38 lb ft, 5.3 kg m (52 Nm) at 3,000 rpm; max engine rpm: 6,000; 51.9 hp/l (39 kW/l); cast iron block, light alloy head; 4 crankshaft bearings, on ball bearings; lubrication: mechanical pump, injection to cylinders and crankshaft bearings, total loss system, 8.8 imp pt, 10.6 US pt, 5 l; 1 Solex downdraught carburettor; fuel feed: mechanical pump; water-cooled, 7.2 imp pt, 8.7 US pt, 4.1 l.

TRANSMISSION driving wheels: rear or front and rear; clutch: single dry plate (diaphragm); gearbox: mechanical; gears: 4, fully synchronized and 2-ratio transfer box; ratios: I 3.834, II 2.358, III 1.542, IV 1, rev 4.026; transfer box ratios: I 3.052, II 1.741; levers: central; final drive: hypoid bevel; axle ratio: 4.777; width of rims: 4.5"; tyres: 6.00 x 16.

PERFORMANCE max speeds: (I) 15 mph, 24 km/h; (II) 20 mph, 38 km/h; (III) 37 mph, 60 km/h; (IV) 56 mph, 90 km/h; power-weight: SJ 30 F 54.3 lb/hp (73.8 lb/kW), 24.6 kg/hp (33.5 kg/kW); carrying capacity: 551 lb, 250 kg; consumption: 45.6 m/imp gal, 37.9 m/US gal, 6.2 l x 100 km at 37 mph, 60 km/h.

CHASSIS box-type ladder frame; front and rear suspension: rigid axle, semi-elliptic leafsprings, telescopic dampers.

STEERING recirculating ball; turns lock to lock: 3.20.

BRAKES drum.

ELECTRICAL EQUIPMENT 12 V; 24 Ah battery; 35 A alternator; Nihon Denso distributor; 2 headlamps.

DIMENSIONS AND WEIGHT wheel base: 79.92 in, 203 cm; tracks: 46.85 in, 119 cm front, 44.09 in, 112 cm rear; length: 125.59 in, 319 cm; width: 54.72 in, 139 cm; height: SJ 30 FK and FM 66.94 in, 169 cm - SJ 30 F 67.32 in, 171 cm - SJ 30 VM 66.93 in, 170 cm; weight: SJ 30 F Wagon 1,521 lb, 690 kg - SJ 30 FK Wagon 1,555 lb, 705 kg - SJ 30 FM Wagon 1,588 lb, 720 kg - SJ 30 VM Wagon 1,643 lb, 745 kg; turning circle: 28.9 ft, 8.8 m; fuel tank: 8.8 imp gal, 10.6 US gal, 40 l.

BODY estate car/st. wagon; 2 doors; canvas top; steel body.

52 hp power team

(4-stroke engine)

See 28 hp power team, except for:

ENGINE front, 4 stroke; 4 cylinders, in line; 97.2 cu in, 970 cc (2.58 x 2.83 in, 65.5 x 72 mm); max power (JIS): 52 hp (38 kW) at 5,000 rpm; max torque (JIS): 59 lb ft, 8.2 kg m (80 Nm) at 3,500 rpm; 53.6 hp/l (39.4 kW/l); valves: overhead, rocker arms; camshafts: 1, overhead; lubrication: gear pump, full flow filter, 5.3 imp pt, 6.2 US pt, 3 l; 1 Mikuni-Solex sidedraught carburettor; cooling: 7 imp pt, 8.5 US pt, 4 l.

TRANSMISSION gearbox ratios: I 3.163, II 1.945, III 1.421, IV 1, rev 3.321; transfer box ratios: high 1.589, low 2.557; axle ratio: 4.111; tyres: 195 SR x 15.

PERFORMANCE max speed: 58 mph, 110 km/h; power-weight ratio: S40 FK 34.1 lb/hp (46.4 lb/kW), 15.5 kg/hp (21 kg/kW); consumption: 43.5 m/imp gal, 36.2 m/US gal, 6.5 l x 100 km at 37 mph, 60 km/h.

DIMENSIONS AND WEIGHT tracks: 47.64 in, 121 cm front, 48.03 in, 122 cm rear; length: 131.89 in, 335 cm; width: 57.48 in, 146 cm; height S40 FK 64.14 in, 168 cm - SJ 40 VC 66.54 in, 169 cm; weight: S40 FK (soft top) Wagon 1,775 lb, 805 kg - SJ 40 VC Wagon 1,852 lb, 840 kg.

VARIATIONS

(for export only)
ENGINE max power (SAE net) 45 hp (33 kW) at 5,500 rpm, max torque (SAE net) 54 lb ft, 7.5 kg m (73 Nm) at 3,000 rpm, 46.4 hp/l (34.1 kW/l).
PERFORMANCE power-weight ratio 39.7 lb/hp (54 lb/kW), 18 kg/hp (24.5 kg/kW).
DIMENSIONS AND WEIGHT length 134.25 in, 341 cm, weight 1,786 lb, 810 kg.

Cultus

PRICES (Tokyo):	yen
GU 2+1-dr Sedan	**635,000**
GA 2+1-dr Sedan	**698,000**
GL 2+1-dr Sedan	**798,000**
GE 2+1-dr Sedan	**828,000**
GC 2+1-dr Sedan	**848,000**
GS 2+1-dr Sedan	**980,000**

ENGINE front, transverse, 4 stroke; 3 cylinders, in line; 60.6 cu in, 993 cc (2.91 x 2.99 in, 74 x 77 mm); compression ratio: 9.5:1; max power (JIS): 60 hp (44 kW) at 5,500 rpm; max torque (JIS): 62 lb ft, 8.5 kg m (83 Nm) at 3,500 rpm; max engine rpm: 6,000; 60.4 hp/l (44.5 kW/l); light alloy block and head, cast iron liners; 4 crankshaft bearings; valves: overhead, Vee-slanted, rockers; camshafts: 1, overhead, cogged belt; lubrication: gear pump, full flow filter, 5.3 imp pt, 6.3 US pt, 3 l; 1 Hitachi downdraught twin barrel carburettor with air-fuel ratio adjustment; emission control with 3-way catalytic converter and exhaust gas recirculation; fuel feed: mechanical pump; water-cooled, 7.6 imp pt, 9.1 US pt, 4.3 l, electric thermostatic fan.

TRANSMISSION driving wheels: front; clutch: single dry plate (diaphragm); gearbox: mechanical; gears: GU and GA 4, fully synchronized - other models 5; ratios: GU and GA I 3.416, II 1.894, III 1.280, IV 0.914 - other models V 0.757, rev 2.916; lever: central; final drive: helical spur gears; axle ratio: 4.105 - GE 3.789; width of rims: 4"; tyres: GU, GA and GL 5.95 x 12 - GE, GC and GS 145 SR x 12.

PERFORMANCE max speeds: (I) 25 mph, 40 km/h; (II) 47 mph, 75 km/h; (III) 58 mph, 110 km/h; (IV) and (V) 90 mph, 145 km/h; power-weight ratio: GU 22.8 lb/hp (31 lb/kW), 10.3 kg/hp (14 kg/kW); consumption: 61.4 m/imp gal, 51.1 m/US gal, 4.6 l x 100 km on Japanese emission test cycle.

CHASSIS integral; front suspension: independent, by McPherson, coil springs/telescopic damper struts, lower transverse arms, trailing links, anti-roll bar; rear: rigid axle, semi-elliptic leafsprings, telescopic dampers.

STEERING rack-and-pinion; turns lock to lock: 3.50.

BRAKES front disc (diameter 7.09 in, 18 cm), rear drum, dual circuit - GL, GE, GC and GS servo.

ELECTRICAL EQUIPMENT 12 V; 45 Ah battery; 45 A alternator; Hitachi electronic ignition; 2 headlamps.

DIMENSIONS AND WEIGHT wheel base: 88.14 in, 224 cm; tracks: 52.36 in, 133 cm front, 51.18 in, 130 cm rear; length: 140.94 in, 358 cm; width: 60.24 in, 153 cm; height: 53.15 in, 135 cm; ground clearance: 7.09 in, 18 cm; weight: GU and GA sedans 1,367 lb, 620 kg; weight distribution: 63% front, 37% rear; turning circle: 30.2 ft, 9.2 m; fuel tank: 6.8 imp gal, 8.2 US gal, 31 l.

BODY saloon/sedan; 2+1 doors; 5 seats, separate front seats.

SUZUKI Jimny 1000 SJ40 VC Wagon

SUZUKI Cultus GU Sedan

TOYOTA Starlet Si EFI Sedan

TOYOTA — JAPAN

Starlet Series

PRICES (Tokyo):

		yen
1	Standard 2+1-dr Sedan	**687,000**
2	DX 2+1-dr Sedan	**762,000**
3	DX-A 2+1-dr Sedan	**717,000**
4	DX-A 4+1-dr Sedan	**788,000**
5	XL 2+1-dr Sedan	**845,000**
6	XL 4+1-dr Sedan	**871,000**
7	XL EFI 2+1-dr Sedan	**941,000**
8	XL Lisse 2+1-dr Sedan	**898,000**
9	XL Lisse 4+1-dr Sedan	**924,000**
10	S 2+1-dr Sedan	**951,000**
11	S 4+1-dr Sedan	**977,000**
12	SE 4+1-dr Sedan	**965,000**
13	SE EFI 4+1-dr Sedan	**1,061,000**
14	Si EFI 2+1-dr Sedan	**996,000**

For GB and USA prices, see price index.

Power team:	Standard for:	Optional for:
74 hp	1 to 6, 8 to 12	—
79 hp	7,13,14	—

74 hp power team

ENGINE front, 4 stroke; 4 cylinders, in line; 78.7 cu in, 1,290 cc (2.95 x 2.87 in, 75 x 73 mm); max power (JIS): 74 hp (54 kW) at 5,600 rpm; max torque (JIS): 78 lb ft, 10.7 kg m (105 Nm) at 3,600 rpm; max engine rpm: 6,000; 57.4 hp/l, (42.2 kW/l); cast iron block, light alloy head; 5 crankshaft bearings; valves: overhead, push-rods and rockers; camshafts: 1, side; lubrication: rotary pump, full flow filter, 6.2 imp pt, 7.4 US pt, 3.5 l; 1 Aisan 4K-U downdraught twin barrel carburettor; emission control with 3-way catalyst, secondary air induction and exhaust gas recirculation; fuel feed: mechanical pump; water-cooled, 8.8 imp pt, 10.6 US pt, 5 l.

TRANSMISSION driving wheels: rear; clutch: single dry plate (diaphragm); gearbox: mechanical; gears: 4, fully synchronized - S models 5; ratios: I 3.789, II 2.220, III 1.435, IV 1 - S V 0.865, rev 4.316; lever: central; final drive: hypoid bevel; axle ratio: Standard and DX-A 3.154 - XL - DX and SE 3.308 - S 3.583; width of rims: 4.5''; tyres: 145 SR x 13.

PERFORMANCE max speeds: (I) 31 mph, 50 km/h; (II) 53 mph, 86 km/h; (III) 87 mph, 140 km/h; (IV) 102 mph, 165 km/h; power-weight ratio: Standard 20.7 lb/hp (28.2 lb/kW), 9.4 kg/hp (12.8 kg/kW); carrying capacity: 882 lb, 400 kg; consumption: 52.3 m/imp gal, 43.6 m/US gal, 5.4 l x 100 km on Japanese emission test cycle.

CHASSIS integral; front suspension: independent, by McPherson, coil springs/telescopic dampers, lower wishbones, anti-roll bar; rear: rigid axle, coil springs/telescopic dampers, trailing lower radius arms, upper torque arms.

STEERING rack-and-pinion; turns lock to lock: 3.10.

BRAKES front disc, rear drum, servo; lining area: front 19.8 sq in, 128 sq cm, rear 31.6 sq in, 204 sq cm, total 51.4 sq in, 332 sq cm.

ELECTRICAL EQUIPMENT 12 V; 32 Ah battery; 45 A alternator; Denso distributor; 2 headlamps.

DIMENSIONS AND WEIGHT wheel base: 90.55 in, 230 cm; tracks: 50.79 in, 129 cm front, 50.19 in, 127 cm rear; length: 148 in, 375 cm; width: 60.04 in, 152 cm; height: 53.94 in, 137 cm - S 53.54 in, 136 cm; ground clearance: 6.50 in, 16.5 cm - S 6.30 in, 16 cm; weight: Standard and DX-A 2+1-dr sedans 1,543 lb, 700 kg - DX 2+1-dr Sedan 1,554 lb, 705 kg - XL 2+1-dr and DX-A 4+1-dr sedans 1,587 lb, 720 kg - XL 4+1-dr Sedan 1,620 lb, 735 kg - S and SE 4+1-dr sedans 1,654 lb, 750 kg; weight distribution: 55% front, 45% rear; turning circle: 32.1 ft, 9.8 m; fuel tank: 8.8 imp gal, 10.6 US gal, 40 l.

BODY saloon/sedan; 2+1 or 4+1 doors; 5 seats, separate front seats.

OPTIONALS (except S) 5-speed mechanical gearbox (V ratio 0.865), max speed 103 mph, 165 km/h; Toyoglide automatic transmission, hydraulic torque converter and planetary gears with 3 ratios (I 2.666, II 1.450, III 1, rev 2.703), 3.417 axle ratio; 155/SR x 13 tyres (for S only).

79 hp power team

See 74 hp power team, except for:

ENGINE max power (JIS): 79 hp (58 kW) at 5,000 rpm; max torque (JIS): 85 lb ft, 11.7 kg m (115 Nm) at 4,200 rpm; 61.2 hp/l (45 kW/l); electronic fuel injection.

TRANSMISSION (standard) gears: 5, fully synchronized; ratios: I 3.789, II 2.123, III 1.323, IV 1, V 0.865, rev 4.316; axle ratio: 3.154 - Si and SE EFI I 3.789, II 2.220, III 1.435, IV 1, V 0.865, rev 4.316; axle ratio 3.583.

PERFORMANCE max speeds: (I) 28 mph, 45 km/h; (II) 50 mph, 80 km/h; (III) 74 mph, 120 km/h; (IV) and (V) 106 mph, 170 km/h; consumption: 54.3 m/imp gal, 45.2 m/US gal, 5.2 l x 100 km on Japanese emission test cycle.

DIMENSIONS AND WEIGHT weight XL EFI Sedan 1,620 lb, 735 kg - Si EFI Sedan 1,642 lb, 745 kg - SE EFI Sedan 1,686 lb, 765 kg.

OPTIONALS 155 SR x 13 tyres.

Corolla FWD Series

PRICES (Tokyo):

		yen
1	1300 Custom DX 4-dr Sedan	**832,000**
2	1300 DX 4-dr Sedan	**863,000**
3	1300 GL 4-dr Sedan	**944,000**
4	1500 DX 4-dr Sedan	**924,000**
5	1500 GL 4-dr Sedan	**998,000**
6	1500 SE 4-dr Sedan	**1,088,000**
7	1500 SX 4+1-dr Hatchback Sedan	**1,113,000**
8	1500 ZX 4+1-dr Hatchback Sedan	**1,204,000**
9	1600 SR 4-dr Sedan	**1,193,000**
10	1600 SX 4+1-dr Hatchback Sedan	**1,236,000**
11	1600 ZX 4+1-dr Hatchback Sedan	**1,320,000**
12	1800 DX 4-dr Sedan	**1,035,000**
13	1800 GL 4-dr Sedan	**1,135,000**
14	1800 SE 4-dr Sedan	**1,201,000**
15	1800 SX 4+1-dr Hatchback Sedan	**1,223,000**

For GB and USA prices, see price index.

Power team:	Standard for:	Optional for:
75 hp	1 to 3	—
83 hp	4 to 8	—
100 hp	9 to 11	—
65 hp (diesel)	12 to 15	—

75 hp power team

ENGINE front, 4 stroke; 4 cylinders, in line; 79 cu in, 1,295 cc (2.99 x 2.79 in, 76 x 71 mm); compression ratio: 9.3:1; max power (JIS): 75 hp (55 kW) at 6,000 rpm; max torque (JIS): 79 lb ft, 10.9 kg m (107 Nm) at 3,600 rpm; max engine rpm: 6,400; 57.9 hp/l (42.6 kW/l); cast iron block, light alloy head; 5 crankshaft bearings; valves: overhead, push-rods and rockers; camshafts: 1, overhead; lubrication: gear pump, full flow filter, 6.5 imp pt, 7.8 US pt, 3.7 l; 1 Aisan 4 K-U downdraught twin barrel carburettor; emission control with 3-way catalytic converter, secondary air induction and exhaust gas recirculation; fuel feed: mechanical pump; water-cooled, 8.8 imp pt, 10.6 US pt, 5 l.

TRANSMISSION driving wheels: front; clutch: single dry plate (diaphragm); gearbox: mechanical; gears: 4, fully synchronized; ratios: I 3.545, II 1.904, III 1.310, IV 0.969, rev 4.316; lever: central; final drive: helical spur gears; axle ratio: 3.722; width of rims: 4.5''; tyres: 145 SR x 13.

PERFORMANCE max speeds: (I) 31 mph, 50 km/h; (II) 57 mph, 92 km/h; (III) 83 mph, 134 km/h; (IV) 99 mph, 160 km/h; power-weight ratio: Custom DX 24.7 lb/hp (33.6 lb/kW), 11.2 kg/hp (15.2 kg/kW); consumption: 46.8 m/imp gal, 37.3 m/US gal, 6.3 l x 100 km on Japanese emission test cycle.

CHASSIS integral; front suspension: independent, by McPherson, coil springs/telescopic damper struts, lower A-arms; rear: independent, by McPherson, lower trailing links, twin transverse arms, coil springs, telescopic dampers.

STEERING rack-and-pinion; turns lock to lock: 4.07.

BRAKES front disc, rear drum, servo; lining area: front 19.8 sq in, 128 sq cm, rear 41.6 sq in, 268 sq cm, total 61.4 sq in, 396 sq cm.

ELECTRICAL EQUIPMENT 12 V; 30 Ah battery; 50 A alternator; Nihon-Denso distributor; 2 headlamps.

DIMENSIONS AND WEIGHT wheel base: 95.66 in, 243 cm; tracks: 56.30 in, 143 cm front, 55.51 in, 141 cm rear; length: 162.99 in, 414 cm; width: 63.38 in, 161 cm; height: 54.53 in, 138 cm; weight: Custom DX and DX sedans 1,852 lb, 840 kg - GL Sedan 1,863 lb, 845 kg; turning circle: 33.4 ft, 10.2 m; fuel tank: 11 imp gal, 13.2 US gal, 50 l.

BODY saloon/sedan; 4 doors; 5 seats, separate front seats, reclining backrests, built-in headrests.

OPTIONALS Toyoglide automatic transmission with 3 ratios (I 2.810, II 1.549, III 1, rev 2.296), 3.330 axle ratio; 155 SR x 13 tyres.

83 hp power team

See 75 hp power team, except for:

ENGINE 89 cu in, 1,452 cc (3.05 x 3.03 in, 77.5 x 77 mm); max power (JIS): 83 hp (61 kW) at 5,600 rpm; max torque (JIS): 87 lb ft, 12 kg m (118 Nm) at 3,600 rpm; max engine rpm: 6,000; 57.2 hp/l (42.1 kW/l); valves: overhead, rockers; camshafts: 1, overhead, cogged belt; 1 Aisan 3A-U downdraught twin barrel carburettor; secondary air induction, 3-way catalytic converter and exhaust gas recirculation; cooling: 10.5 imp pt, 12.7 US pt, 6 l.

TRANSMISSION GL, SE, SX and ZX gears: 5, fully synchronized; ratios: I 3.545, II 2.041, III 1.310, IV 0.945, V 0.731, rev 3.153; width of rims: SE, SX and ZX 5''; tyres: GL, SE, SX and ZX 155 SR x 13.

PERFORMANCE max speeds: (I) 30 mph, 48 km/h; (II) 56 mph, 90 km/h; (III) 80 mph, 128 km/h; (IV) and (V) 103 mph, 165 km/h; power-weight ratio: DX 21.8 lb/hp (29.5 lb/kW), 9.9 kg/hp (13.4 kg/kW); consumption: 42.7 m/imp gal, 35.6 m/US gal, 6.6 l x 100 km on Japanese emission test cycle.

CHASSIS rear suspension: SX and ZX anti-roll bar.

DIMENSIONS AND WEIGHT weight: DX Sedan 1,808 lb, 820 kg - GL Sedan 1,863 lb, 845 kg - SE Sedan 1,907 lb, 865 kg - SX Sedan 1,929 lb, 875 kg - ZX Sedan 1,973 lb, 895 kg.

BODY 4 or 4+1 doors.

OPTIONALS Toyoglide automatic transmission with 3 ratios, 3.333 axle ratio; power steering.

TOYOTA Starlet Si EFI Sedan

100 hp power team

See 75 hp power team, except for:

ENGINE 96.9 cu in, 1,588 cc (3.18 x 3.03 in, 81 x 77 mm); max power (JIS): 100 hp (74 kW) at 5,600 rpm; max torque (JIS): 101 lb ft, 14 kg m (137 Nm) at 4,000 rpm; max engine rpm: 6,000; 62.9 hp/l (46.3 kW/l); TCCA electronic fuel injection; fuel feed: electric pump; emission control by 3-way catalytic converter; cooling: 10.6 imp pt, 12.7 US pt, 6 l.

TRANSMISSION gears: 5, fully synchronized; ratios: I 3.166, II 1.904, III 1.310, IV 0.969, V 0.815, rev 3.250; axle ratio: 3.941; width of rims: 5''; tyres: 175/70 HR x 13.

PERFORMANCE max speeds: (I) 31 mph, 50 km/h; (II) 53 mph, 86 km/h; (III) 78 mph, 125 km/h; (IV) 102 mph, 165 km/h; (V) 112 mph, 180 km/h; power-weight ratio: SR 19.2 lb/hp (26 lb/kW), 8.7 kg/hp (11.8 kg/kW); consumption: 40.3 m/imp gal, 33.6 m/US gal, 7 l x 100 km on Japanese emission test cycle.

CHASSIS front and rear suspension: anti-roll bar.

STEERING servo.

DIMENSIONS AND WEIGHT weight: SR Sedan 1,929 lb, 875 kg - SX Hatchback Sedan 1,973 lb, 895 kg - ZX Hatchback Sedan 2,017 lb, 915 kg.

BODY 4 or 4+1 doors.

OPTIONALS automatic transmission, hydraulic torque converter and planetary gears with 4 ratios (I 3.643, II 2.008, III 1.296, IV 0.892, rev 2.977), 2.821 axle ratio.

TOYOTA Corolla FWD 1600 ZX Hatchback Sedan

65 hp (diesel) power team

See 75 hp power team, except for:

ENGINE diesel; 112 cu in, 1,839 cc (3.26 x 3.34 in, 83 x 85 mm); compression ratio: 22.5:1; max power (JIS): 65 hp (48 kW) at 4,500 rpm; max torque (JIS): 83 lb ft, 11.5 kg m (113 Nm) at 3,000 rpm; max engine rpm: 4,800; 35.3 hp/l (26 kW/l); valves: 2 per cylinder, overhead, thimble tappets; camshafts: 1, overhead, cogged belt; lubrication: trochoid pump, full flow filter; Bosch VE electronic fuel injection.

TRANSMISSION gears: 5, fully synchronized; ratios: I 3.538, II 2.041, III 1.322, IV 0.945, V 0.731, rev 3.153; axle ratio: 3.735; width or fims: 5''; tyres: 155 SR x 13.

PERFORMANCE max speeds: (I) 23 mph, 37 km/h; (II) 40 mph, 64 km/h; (III) 62 mph, 100 km/h; (IV) 87 mph, 140 km/h; (V) 93 mph, 150 km/h; power-weight ratio: DX 31.2 lb/hp (42.4 lb/kW), 14.1 kg/hp (19.2 kg/kW); consumption: 88.3 m/imp gal, 73.5 m/US gal, 3.2 l x 100 km at 37 mph, 60 km/h on Japanese emission test cycle.

DIMENSIONS AND WEIGHT weight: DX and GL sedans 2,028 lb, 920 kg - SE Sedan 2,072 lb, 940 kg - SX Sedan 2,083 lb, 945 kg.

BODY 4 or 4+1 doors.

OPTIONALS with 3-speed automatic transmission, 3.356 axle ratio.

Sprinter FWD Series

	PRICES (Tokyo):	yen
1	1300 Special DX 4-dr Sedan	**854,000**
2	1300 DX 4-dr Sedan	**885,000**
3	1300 XL 4-dr Sedan	**966,000**
4	1500 DX 4-dr Sedan	**946,000**
5	1500 XL 4-dr Sedan	**1,020,000**
6	1500 SE 4-dr Sedan	**1,110,000**
7	1500 SX 4+1-dr Hatchback Sedan	**1,135,000**
8	1500 ZX 4+1-dr Hatchback Sedan	**1,226,000**
9	1600 SR 4-dr Sedan	**1,215,000**
10	1600 SX 4+1-dr Hatchback Sedan	**1,258,000**
11	1600 ZX 4+1-dr Hatchback Sedan	**1,342,000**
12	1800 DX 4-dr Sedan	**1,057,000**
13	1800 XL 4-dr Sedan	**1,157,000**
14	1800 SE 4-dr Sedan	**1,223,000**
15	1800 SX 4+1-dr Hatchback Sedan	**1,245,000**

Power team:	Standard for:	Optional for:
75 hp	1 to 3	—
83 hp	4 to 8	—
100 hp	9 to 11	—
65 hp (diesel)	12 to 15	—

75 hp power team

ENGINE front, 4 stroke; 4 cylinders, in line; 79 cu in, 1,295 cc (2.99 x 2.79 in, 76 x 71 mm); compression ratio: 9.3:1; max power (JIS): 75 hp (55 kW) at 6,000 rpm; max torque (JIS): 79 lb ft, 10.9 kg m (107 Nm) at 3,600 rpm; max engine rpm: 6,400; 57.9 hp/l (42.6 kW/l); cast iron block, light alloy head; 5 crankshaft bearings; valves: overhead, push-rods and rockers; camshafts: 1, overhead, cogged belt; lubrication: gear pump, full flow filter, 6.5 imp pt, 7.8 US pt, 3.7 l; 1 Aisan 2A downdraught twin barrel carburettor; emission control with 3-way catalytic converter, secondary air induction and exhaust gas recirculation; fuel feed: mechanical pump; water-cooled, 8.8 imp pt, 10.6 US pt, 5 l, electric fan.

TRANSMISSION driving wheels: front; clutch: single dry plate (diaphragm); gearbox: mechanical; gears: 4, fully synchronized; ratios: I 3.545, II 1.904, III 1.310, IV 0.969, rev 4.316; final drive: helical spur gears; axle ratio: 3.722; width of rims: 4.5''; tyres: 145 SR x 13.

PERFORMANCE max speeds: (I) 31 mph, 50 km/h; (II) 57 mph, 92 km/h; (III) 83 mph, 134 km/h; (IV) 99 mph, 160 km/h; power-weight ratio: Special DX 24.8 lb/hp (33.7 lb/kW), 11.2 kg/hp (15.3 kg/kW); consumption: 46.8 m/imp gal, 37.3 m/US gal, 6.3 l x 100 km on Japanese emission test cycle.

CHASSIS integral; front suspension: independent, by McPherson, coil springs/telescopic damper struts, lower A-arms; rear: independent, by McPherson, lower trailing links, twin transverse arms, coil springs, telescopic dampers.

STEERING rack-and-pinion; turns lock to lock: 4.07.

BRAKES front disc, rear drum, servo; lining area: front 26.7 sq in, 172 sq cm, rear 36 sq in, 232 sq cm, total 62.7 sq in, 404 sq cm.

ELECTRICAL EQUIPMENT 12 V; 30 Ah battery; 50 A alternator; transistorized ignition; 2 headlamps.

DIMENSIONS AND WEIGHT wheel base: 95.66 in, 243 cm; tracks: 56.30 in, 143 cm front, 55.51 in, 141 cm rear; length: 166.78 in, 416 cm; width: 64.56 in, 164 cm; height: 54.53 in, 138 cm; ground clearance: 6.30 in, 16 cm; weight: DX Sedan 1,852 lb, 840 kg - Special DX and XL sedans 1,863 lb, 845 kg; turning circle: 33.4 ft, 10.2 m; fuel tank: 11 imp gal, 13.2 US gal, 50 l.

BODY saloon/sedan; 4 doors; 5 seats, separate front seats.

OPTIONALS automatic transmission, hydraulic torque converter and planetary gears with 3 ratios (I 2.810, II 1.549, III 1, rev 2.296), 3.333 axle ratio; 155 SR x 13 tyres.

83 hp power team

See 75 hp power team, except for:

ENGINE 89 cu in, 1,452 cc (3.05 x 3.03 in, 77.5 x 77 mm); max power (JIS): 83 hp (61 kW) at 5,600 rpm; max torque (JIS): 87 lb ft, 12 kg m (118 Nm) at 3,600 rpm; max engine rpm: 6,000; 57.2 hp/l (42.1 kW/l); 1 Aisan 3A-U downdraught twin barrel carburettor; cooling: 10.5 imp pt, 12.7 US pt, 6 l.

TRANSMISSION XL, SE, SX and ZX gears: 5, fully synchronized; ratios: I 3.545, II 2.041, III 1.310, IV 0.945, V 0.731, rev 3.153; width of rims: SE, XL and ZX 5''; tyres: DX 145 SR x 13 - ather models 155 SR x 13.

PERFORMANCE max speeds: (I) 30 mph, 48 km/h; (II) 56 mph, 90 km/h; (III) 80 mph, 128 km/h; (IV) and (V) 103 mph, 165 km/h; power-weight ratio: DX 21.9 lb/hp (29.8 lb/kW), 9.9 kg/hp (13.5 kg/kW); consumption: 42.7 m/imp gal, 35.6 m/US gal, 6.6 l x 100 km on Japanese emission test cycle.

CHASSIS SX and ZX rear suspension: anti-roll bar.

DIMENSIONS AND WEIGHT weight: DX Sedan 1,819 lb, 825 kg - XL Sedan 1,874 lb, 850 kg - SE Sedan 1,918 lb, 870 kg - SX Hatchback Sedan 1,929 lb, 875 kg - ZX Hatchback Sedan 1,973 lb, 895 kg.

BODY 4 or 4+1 doors.

OPTIONALS automatic transmission, hydraulic torque converter and planetary gears with 3 ratios (I 2.810, II 1.549, III 1, rev 2.296); 3.333 axle ratio; power steering.

100 hp power team

See 75 hp power team, except for:

ENGINE 96.9 cu in, 1,588 cc (3.18 x 3.03 in, 81 x 77 mm); max power (JIS): 100 hp (74 kW) at 5,600 rpm; max torque (JIS): 101 lb ft, 14 kg m (137 Nm) at 4,000 rpm; max engine rpm: 6,000; 62.9 hp/l (46.3 kW/l); TCCA electronic fuel injection; fuel feed: electric pump; emission control by 3-way catalytic converter; cooling: 10.6 imp pt, 12.7 US pt, 6 l.

TRANSMISSION gears: 5, fully synchronized; ratios: I 3.166, II 1.904, III 1.310, IV 0.969, V 0.815, rev 3.250; axle ratio: 3.941; width of rims: 5''; tyres: 175/70 SR x 13.

PERFORMANCE max speeds: (I) 31 mph, 50 km/h; (II) 53 mph, 86 km/h; (III) 78 mph, 125 km/h; (IV) 102 mph, 165 km/h; (V) 112 mph, 180 km/h; power-weight ratio: SR 19.2 lb/hp (26 lb/kW), 8.7 kg/hp (11.8 kg/kW); consumption: 40.3 m/imp gal, 33.6 m/US gal, 7 l x 100 km on Japanese emission test cycle.

CHASSIS front and rear suspension: anti-roll bar.

TOYOTA Sprinter FWD 1500 SE Sedan

100 HP POWER TEAM

STEERING servo.

DIMENSIONS AND WEIGHT weight: SR Sedan 1,929 lb, 875 kg - SX Hatchback Sedan 1,973 lb, 895 kg - ZX Hatchback Sedan 2,017 lb, 915 kg.

BODY 4 or 4+1 doors.

OPTIONALS automatic transmission, hydraulic torque converter and planetary gears with 4 ratios (I 3.643, II 2.008, III 1.296, IV 0.892, rev 2.977), 2.821 axle ratio.

65 hp (diesel) power team

See 75 hp power team, except for:

ENGINE diesel; 112 cu in, 1,839 cc (3.26 x 3.34 in, 83 x 85 mm); compression ratio: 22.5:1; max power (JIS): 65 hp (48 kW) at 4,500 rpm; max torque (JIS): 83 lb ft, 11.5 kg m (113 Nm) at 3,000 rpm; max engine rpm: 4,800; 35.3 hp/l (26 kW/l); valves: overhead, thimble tappets; lubrication: trochoid pump, full flow filter; Bosch VE electronic fuel injection; cooling: 7.5 imp pt, 9.1 US pt, 4.3 l.

TRANSMISSION gears: 5, fully synchronized; ratios: I 3.538, II 2.041, III 1.322, IV 0.945, V 0.731, rev 3.153; axle ratio: 3.735; width of rims: 5''; tyres: 155 SR x 13 (standard).

PERFORMANCE max speeds: (I) 23 mph, 37 km/h; (II) 40 mph, 64 km/h; (III) 62 mph, 100 km/h; (IV) 87 mph, 140 km/h; (V) 93 mph, 150 km/h; power-weight ratio: DX 31.2 lb/hp (42.4 lb/kW), 14.1 kg/hp (19.2 kg/kW); consumption: 88.3 m/imp gal, 73.5 m/US gal, 3.2 l x 100 km at 37 mph, 60 km/h on Japanese emission test cycle.

CHASSIS rear suspension: anti-roll bar.

DIMENSIONS AND WEIGHT weight: DX and XL sedans 2,028 lb, 920 kg - SE Sedan 2,072 lb, 940 kg - SX Hatchback Sedan 2,083 lb, 945 kg.

BODY 4 or 4+1 doors.

OPTIONALS automatic transmission, hydraulic torque converter and planetary gears with 3 ratios (I 2.810, II 1.549, III 1, rev 2.296), 3.356 axle ratio.

Corolla II / Corsa / Tercel Series

	PRICES (Tokyo):	yen
1	Tercel 1300 VC 4-dr Sedan	**842,000**
2	Tercel 1300 VC 4+1-dr Hatchback Sedan	**833,000**
3	Tercel 1300 VL 4-dr Sedan	**891,000**
4	Tercel 1300 VL 4+1-dr Hatchback Sedan	**885,000**
5	Tercel 1300 SE 4-dr Sedan	**1,088,000**
6	Corsa 1300 DX 4-dr Sedan	**842,000**
7	Corsa 1300 DX 4+1-dr Hatchback Sedan	**833,000**
8	Corsa 1300 GX 4-dr Sedan	**891,000**
9	Corsa 1300 GX 4+1-dr Hatchback Sedan	**885,000**
10	Corsa 1300 GX Sophia 4+1-dr Hatchback Sedan	**915,000**
11	Corolla II 1300 CD 2+1-dr Hatchback Sedan	**769,000**
12	Corolla II 1300 DX 2+1-dr Hatchback Sedan	**799,000**
13	Corolla II 1300 DX 4+1-dr Hatchback Sedan	**833,000**
14	Corolla II 1300 GL 2+1-dr Hatchback Sedan	**851,000**
15	Corolla II 1300 GL 4+1-dr Hatchback Sedan	**885,000**
16	Corolla II 1300 GL Lime 2+1-dr Hatchback Sedan	**871,000**
17	Tercel 1500 VC 4+1-dr Hatchback Sedan	**888,000**
18	Tercel 1500 VL 4-dr Sedan	**969,000**
19	Tercel 1500 VL 4+1-dr Hatchback Sedan	**962,000**
20	Tercel 1500 VE 4-dr Sedan	**1,099,000**
21	Tercel 1500 VE 4+1-dr Hatchback Sedan	**1,119,000**
22	Corsa 1500 DX 4+1-dr Hatchback Sedan	**888,000**
23	Corsa 1500 GX 4+1-dr Sedan	**969,000**
24	Corsa 1500 GX 4+1-dr Hatchback Sedan	**962,000**
25	Corsa 1500 GX Sophia 4+1-dr Hatchback Sedan	**1,027,000**
26	Corsa 1500 EX 4-dr Sedan	**1,124,000**
27	Corsa 1500 EX 4+1-dr Hatchback Sedan	**1,099,000**
28	Corolla II 1500 DX 4+1-dr Hatchback Sedan	**888,000**
29	Corolla II 1500 GL 4+1-dr Hatchback Sedan	**962,000**
30	Corolla II 1500 GL Lime 4+1-dr Hatchback Sedan	**1,027,000**
31	Corolla II 1500 SE 2+1-dr Hatchback Sedan	**1,053,000**
32	Corolla II 1500 SE 4+1-dr Hatchback Sedan	**1,089,000**
33	Tercel 1500 VS 4-dr Sedan	**1,072,000**
34	Tercel 1500 VS 4+1-dr Hatchback Sedan	**1,049,000**
35	Corsa 1500 SX 4-dr Sedan	**1,072,000**
36	Corsa 1500 SX 4+1-dr Hatchback Sedan	**1,049,000**
37	Corolla II 1500 SR 2+1-dr Hatchback Sedan	**1,013,000**
38	Corolla II 1500 SR 4+1-dr Hatchback Sedan	**1,049,000**

For GB and USA prices, see price index.

Power team:	Standard for:	Optional for:
75 hp	1 to 16	—
83 hp	17 to 32	—
86 hp	33 to 38	—

75 hp power team

ENGINE front, 4 stroke; 4 cylinders, in line; 79 cu in, 1,295 cc (3 x 2.80 in, 76.2 x 71.4 mm); compression ratio: 9.3:1;

TOYOTA Corolla II 1500 SR Hatchback Sedan

max power (JIS): 75 hp (55 kW) at 6,000 rpm; max torque (JIS): 79 lb ft, 10.9 kg m (107 Nm) at 3,600 rpm; max engine rpm: 6,300; 57.9 hp/l (42.6 kW/l); cast iron block, light alloy head; 5 crankshaft bearings; valves: overhead, rockers; camshafts: 1, overhead; lubrication: gear pump, full flow filter, 6.5 imp pt, 7.8 US pt, 3.7 l; 1 Aisan 2A-U twin barrel downdraught carburettor; emission control with catalytic converter, secondary air induction and exhaust gas recirculation; fuel feed: mechanical pump; water-cooled, 8.8 imp pt, 10.6 US pt, 5 l.

TRANSMISSION driving wheels: front; clutch: single dry plate (diaphragm); gearbox: mechanical; gears: 4, fully synchronized; ratios: I 3.666, II 2.070, III 1.376, IV 1, rev 3.410; lever: central; final drive: hypoid bevel; axle ratio: 3.583; tyres: 145 SR x 13.

PERFORMANCE max speeds: (I) 29 mph, 46 km/h; (II) 49 mph, 79 km/h; (III) 74 mph, 120 km/h; (IV) 99 mph, 160 km/h; power-weight ratio: Tercel VC 4-dr Sedan 24.1 lb/hp (32.8 lb/kW), 10.9 kg/hp (14.8 kg/kW); consumption: 46.2 m/imp gal, 39.2 m/US gal, 6.1 l x 100 km on Japanese emission test cycle.

CHASSIS integral; front suspension: independent, by McPherson, coil springs/telescopic damper struts, transverse trailing arms, trailing links, anti-roll bar; rear: independent, coil springs, trailing arms, anti-roll bar, telescopic dampers.

STEERING rack-and-pinion; turns lock to lock: 3.70.

BRAKES front disc, rear drum, servo; lining area: front 19.8 sq in, 128 sq cm, rear 31.6 sq in, 204 sq cm, total 51.4 sq in, 332 sq cm.

ELECTRICAL EQUIPMENT 12 V; 33 Ah battery; 40 A alternator; Denso distributor; 2 headlamps.

DIMENSIONS AND WEIGHT wheel base: 95.66 in, 243 cm; tracks: 54.52 in, 138 cm front, 53.94 in, 137 cm rear; length: Corolla II 152.75 in, 388 cm - Tercel and Corsa hatchback sedans 153.93 in, 391 cm - Tercel and Corsa sedans 160.62 in, 408 cm; width: 63.58 in, 161 cm; height: 54.33 in, 138 cm; weight: Corolla II CD Hatchback Sedan 1,719 lb, 780 kg - Corolla II DX 2+1-dr Hatchback Sedan 1,730 lb, 785 kg - Corolla II GL 2+1-dr Hatchback Sedan 1,764 lb, 800 kg - Tercel VC, Corsa DX and Corolla II DX 4+1-dr hatchback sedans 1,808 lb, 820 kg - Corsa DX and Tercel VC sedans 1,830 lb, 830 kg - Tercel VL, Corsa GX and Corolla II GL 4+1-dr hatchback sedans 1,841 lb, 835 kg; weight distribution: 61% front, 39% rear; turning circle: 34.8 ft, 10.6 m; fuel tank: 9.9 imp gal, 11.9 US gal, 45 l.

BODY saloon/sedan; 2+1, 4 or 4+1 doors; 5 seats, separate front seats.

OPTIONALS automatic transmission, hydraulic torque converter and planetary gears with 3 ratios (I 2.773, II 1.451, III 0.962, rev 2.603); 4-speed mechanical gearbox (I 3.885, II 2.070, III 1.202, IV 1, rev 3.154), 3.154 axle ratio.

83 hp power team

See 75 hp power team, except for:

ENGINE 88.6 cu in, 1,452 cc (3.05 x 3.03 in, 77.5 x 77 mm); max power (JIS): 83 hp (61 kW) at 6,000 rpm; max torque (JIS): 87 lb ft, 12 kg m (118 Nm) at 3,600 rpm; 57.2 hp/l (42 kW/l); 1 Aisan 3A-U downdraught twin barrel carburettor.

PERFORMANCE power-weight ratio: Tercel VC 21.8 lb/hp (29.5 lb/kW), 9.9 kg/hp (13.4 kg/kW); consumption: 43.5 m/imp gal, 36.2 m/US gal, 6.5 l x 100 km on Japanese emission test cycle.

DIMENSIONS AND WEIGHT weight: Corolla II SE 2+1-dr, Corolla II DX, Corsa DX and Tercel VC hatchback sedans 1,808 lb, 820 kg - Corsa GX and Tercel VL sedans 1,841 lb, 835 kg - Corsa GX and Tercel VL hatchback sedans 1,852 lb 840 kg - Corsa EX and Tercel VE sedans 1,863 lb, 845 kg - Corolla II SE 4+1-dr and Tercel VE hatchback sedans 1,874 lb, 850 kg.

OPTIONALS 5-speed mechanical gearbox (V ratio 0.825); automatic transmission, hydraulic torque converter and planetary gear with 3 ratios (I 2.773, II 1.451, III 0.962, rev 2.603); power steering.

86 hp power team

See 75 hp power team, except for:

ENGINE 89 cu in, 1,452 cc (3.05 x 3.03 in, 77.5 x 77 mm); max power (JIS): 86 hp (63 kW) at 6,000 rpm; max torque

TOYOTA Tercel 1500 VE Sedan

TOYOTA Sprinter Trueno RWD 1600 GT Apex Liftback Coupé

(JIS): 89 lb ft, 12.3 kg m (121 Nm) at 4,000 rpm; max engine rpm: 6,400; 59.2 hp/l (43.5 kW/l); knock sensor and ignition retard system; 1 V-type Variable Venturi downdraught carburettor.

TRANSMISSION gears: 5, fully synchronized; ratios: I 3.666, II 2.070, III 1.376, IV 1, V 0.825, rev 3.418; axle ratio: 3.727; tyres: 165/70 SR x 13.

PERFORMANCE max speed: 102 mph, 165 km/h; power-weight ratio: Corolla II SR 2+1-dr 21.3 lb/hp (28.9 lb/kW), 9.6 kg/hp (13.1 kg/kW); consumption: 41.5 m/imp gal, 34.6 m/US gal, 6.8 l x 100 km on Japanese emission test cycle.

DIMENSIONS AND WEIGHT weight: Corolla II SR 2+1-dr Hatchback Sedan 1,830 lb, 830 kg - Corsa SX and Tercel VS sedans 1,885 lb, 855 kg - Corolla II SR 4+1-dr, Corsa SX and Tercel VS hatchback sedans 1,896 lb, 860 kg.

OPTIONALS automatic transmission, hydraulic torque converter and planetary gears with 3 ratios (I 2.773, II 1.451, III 0.962, rev 2.600).

Corolla Levin RWD Series

PRICES (Tokyo):		**yen**
1	GL 2-dr Coupé	**1,060,000**
2	SE 2-dr Coupé	**1,122,000**
3	SR 2+1-dr Hatchback Coupé	**1,133,000**
4	GT 2-dr Coupé	**1,322,000**
5	GT Apex 2-dr Coupé	**1,523,000**
6	GT Apex 2+1-dr Hatchback Coupé	**1,548,000**
7	GTV 2+1-dr Hatchback Coupé	**1,368,000**

Power team:	**Standard for:**	**Optional for:**
83 hp	1 to 3	—
130 hp	4 to 7	—

83 hp power team

ENGINE front, 4 stroke; 4 cylinders, in line; 88.6 cu in, 1,452 cc (3.05 x 3.03 in, 77.5 x 77 mm); compression ratio: 9:1; max power (JIS): 83 hp (61 kW) at 5,600 rpm; max torque (JIS): 87 lb ft, 12 kg m (118 Nm) at 3,600 rpm; max engine rpm: 6,000; 57.1 hp/l (42.1 kW/l); cast iron block, light alloy head; 5 crankshaft bearings; valves: overhead, push-rods and rockers; camshafts: 1, overhead, cogged belt; lubrication: gear pump, full flow filter, 6.5 imp pt, 7.8 US pt, 3.7 l; 1 Aisan 3A-U downdraught twin barrel carburettor; emission control with 3-way catalytic converter, secondary air induction and exhaust gas recirculation; fuel feed: mechanical pump; water-cooled, 8.8 imp pt, 10.6 US pt, 5 l.

TRANSMISSION driving wheels: rear; clutch: single dry plate (diaphragm); gearbox: mechanical; gears: 5, fully synchronized; ratios: I 3.789, II 2.220, III 1.435, IV 1, V 0.865, rev 4.316; lever: central; final drive: hypoid bevel; axle ratio: 3.727; width of rims: 5"; tyres: 155 SR x 13.

PERFORMANCE max speeds: (I) 28 mph, 45 km/h; (II) 48 mph, 77 km/h; (III) 73 mph, 117 km/h; (IV) and (V) 105 mph, 170 km/h; power-weight ratio: GL 22.7 lb/hp (30.9 lb/kW), 10.3 kg/hp (14 kg/kW); consumption: 42.1 m/imp gal, 35.1 m/US gal, 6.7 l x 100 km on Japanese emission test cycle.

CHASSIS integral; front suspension: independent, by McPherson, coil springs/telescopic damper struts, lower wishbones (trailing links), anti-roll bar; rear: rigid axle, lower trailing radius arms, upper oblique torque arms, Panhard rod, coil springs, anti-roll bar, telescopic dampers.

STEERING rack-and-pinion - SE servo; turns lock to lock: 3.50.

BRAKES front disc, rear drum, servo; lining area: front 22.9 sq in, 148 sq cm, rear 41.5 sq in, 268 sq cm, total 64.4 sq in, 416 sq cm.

ELECTRICAL EQUIPMENT 12 V; 33 Ah battery; 55 A alternator; transistorized ignition; 2 headlamps.

DIMENSIONS AND WEIGHT wheel base: 94.48 in, 240 cm; tracks: 53.54 in, 136 cm front, 53.14 in, 135 cm rear; length: 164.56 in, 418 cm; width: 64.17 in, 163 cm; height: 52.75 in, 134 cm; ground clearance: 6.10 in, 15.5 cm; weight: GL Coupé 1,885 lb, 855 kg - SE Coupé 1,907 lb, 865 kg - SR Hatchback Coupé 1,940 lb, 880 kg; turning circle: 34.1 ft, 10.4 m; fuel tank: 11 imp gal, 13.2 US gal, 50 l.

BODY coupé, 2 or 2+1 doors; 5 seats, separate front seats.

OPTIONALS automatic transmission, hydraulic torque converter and planetary gears with 4 ratios (I 2.450, II 1.450, III 1, IV 0.688, rev 2.222), 3.909 axle ratio.

130 hp power team

See 83 hp power team, except for:

ENGINE 96.8 cu in, 1,587 cc (3.19 x 3.03 in, 81 x 77 mm); compression ratio: 9.4:1; max power (JIS): 130 hp (96 kW) at 6,600 rpm; max torque (JIS): 110 lb ft, 15.2 kg m (149 Nm) at 5,200 rpm; max engine rpm: 7,000; 81.9 hp/l (60.3 kW/l); valves: overhead, Vee-slanted, thimble tappets; camshafts: 2, overhead, cogged belt; electronic fuel injection; Toyota variable induction system with dual induction passages and butterfly control valve; emission control by 3-way catalytic converter; cooling: 9.8 imp pt, 11.8 US pt, 5.6 l.

TRANSMISSION gearbox ratios: I 3.587, II 2.022, III 1.384, IV 1, V 0.861, rev 3.484; axle ratio: 4.300; tyres: 185/70 HR x 13 - GTV 185/60 R 14 H.

PERFORMANCE max speeds: (I) 31 mph, 50 km/h; (II) 56 mph, 90 km/h; (III) 80 mph, 128 km/h; (IV) 109 mph, 175 km/h; (V) 112 mph, 180 km/h; power-weight ratio: GT Coupé 33.5 lb/hp (45.6 lb/kW), 15.2 kg/hp (20.6 kg/kW); consumption: 36.6 m/imp gal, 30.5 m/US gal, 7.7 l x 100 km on Japanese emission test cycle.

STEERING GT Apex Coupé servo; turns lock to lock: 3.

BRAKES rear disc.

DIMENSIONS AND WEIGHT weight: GT Coupé 1,984 lb, 900 kg - GT Apex Coupé 2,039 lb, 925 kg - GT Apex Atchback Coupé 2,072 lb, 940 kg - GTV Hatchback Coupé 2,061 lb, 935 kg.

OPTIONALS 4-speed automatic transmission not available; 4.100 axle ratio; power steering (except GT Apex Coupé).

Sprinter Trueno RWD Series

PRICES (Tokyo):		**yen**
1	1500 XL 2-dr Coupé	**1,092,000**
2	1500 SE 2-dr Coupé	**1,154,000**
3	1500 SR 2+1-dr Liftback Coupé	**1,165,000**
4	1600 GT 2-dr Coupé	**1,354,000**
5	1600 GT Apex 2-dr Coupé	**1,538,000**
6	1600 GT Apex 2+1-dr Liftback Coupé	**1,563,000**
7	1600 GTV 2+1-dr Liftback Coupé	**1,400,000**

Power team:	**Standard for:**	**Optional for:**
83 hp	1 to 3	—
130 hp	4 to 7	—

83 hp power team

ENGINE front, 4 stroke; 4 cylinders, in line; 88.6 cu in, 1,452 cc (3.05 x 3.03 in, 77.5 x 77 mm); compression ratio: 9:1; max power (JIS): 83 hp (61 kW) at 5,600 rpm; max torque (JIS): 87 lb ft, 12 kg m (118 Nm) at 3,600 rpm; max engine rpm: 6,000; 52.7 hp/l (42.1 kW/l); cast iron block, light alloy head; 5 crankshaft bearings; valves: overhead, push-rods and rockers; camshafts: 1, overhead, cogged belt, chain-driven; lubrication: gear pump, full flow filter, 6.5 imp pt, 7.8 US pt, 3.7 l; 1 Aisan 3A-U downdraught twin barrel carburettor; emission control by 3-way catalytic converter, secondary air induction and exhaust gas recirculation; fuel feed: mechanical pump; water-cooled, 8.8 imp pt, 10.6 US pt, 5 l.

TRANSMISSION driving wheels: rear; clutch: single dry plate (diaphragm); gearbox: mechanical; gears: 5, fully synchronized; ratios: I 3.789, II 2.220, III 1.435, IV 1, V 0.865, rev 4.316; final drive: hypoid bevel; axle ratio: 3.727; width of rims: 5"; tyres: 155 SR x 13.

PERFORMANCE max speeds: (I) 28 mph, 45 km/h; (II) 48 mph, 77 km/h; (III) 73 mph, 117 km/h; (IV) and (V) 106 mph, 170 km/h; power-weight ratio: XL 22.8 lb/hp (31.1 lb/kW), 10.3 kg/hp (14.1 kg/kW); consumption: 42.1 m/imp gal, 35.1 m/US gal, 6.7 l x 100 km on Japanese emission test cycle.

CHASSIS integral; front suspension: independent, by McPherson, lower transverse arms, trailing diagonal locating links, coil springs, anti-roll bar, telescopic dampers; rear: rigid axle, lower trailing links, upper torque rods, Panhard rod, coil springs, anti-roll bar, telescopic dampers.

STEERING rack-and-pinion - SE servo; turns lock to lock: 3.50.

BRAKES front disc, rear drum, servo; lining area: front 22.9 sq in, 148 sq cm, rear 41.5 sq in, 268 sq cm, total 64.4 sq in, 416 sq cm.

ELECTRICAL EQUIPMENT 12 V; 33 Ah battery; 55 A alternator; transistorized ignition; 2 headlamps.

DIMENSIONS AND WEIGHT wheel base: 94.48 in, 240 cm; tracks: 53.54 in, 136 cm front, 53.14 in, 135 cm rear; length: 165.74 in, 421 cm; width: 64.17 in, 163 cm; height: 52.75 in, 134 cm; ground clearance: 6.10 in, 15.5 cm; weight: XL Coupé 1,896 lb, 860 kg - SE Coupé 1,918 lb, 870 kg - SR Liftback Coupé 1,951 lb, 885 kg; turning circle: 34.1 ft, 10.4 m; fuel tank: 11 imp gal, 13.2 US gal, 50 l.

BODY coupé, 2 or 2+1 doors; 5 seats, separate front seats.

OPTIONALS automatic transmission, hydraulic torque converter and planetary gears with 4 ratios (I 2.450, II 1.450, III 1, IV 0.688, rev 2.222), 3.909 axle ratio.

130 hp power team

See 83 hp power team, except for:

ENGINE 96.8 cu in, 1,587 cc (3.19 x 3.03 in, 81 x 77 mm); compression ratio: 9.4:1; max power (JIS): 130 hp (96 kW) at 6,600 rpm; max torque (JIS): 110 lb ft, 15.2 kg m (149 Nm) at 5,200 rpm; max engine rpm: 7,000; 81.9 hp/l (60.3 kW/l); valves: overhead, Vee-slanted, thimble tappets; camshafts: 2, overhead, cogged belt, chain-driven; electronic fuel injection; Toyota variable induction system with dual induction passages and bytterfly control valve; emission control by 3-way catalytic converter; cooling: 9.8 imp pt, 11.8 US pt, 5.6 l.

TRANSMISSION gearbox ratios: I 3.587, II 2.022, III 1.384, IV 1, V 0.861, rev 3.484; axle ratio: 4.300; tyres: 185/70 HR x 13 - GTV 185/60 R x 14 H.

PERFORMANCE max speeds: (I) 31 mph, 50 km/h; (II) 56 mph, 90 km/h; (III) 80 mph, 128 km/h; (IV) 109 mph, 175 km/h; (V) 112 mph, 180 km/h; power-weight ratio: GT Coupé 15.3 lb/hp (20.8 lb/kW), 6.9 kg/hp (9.4 kg/kW); consumption: 36.6 m/imp gal, 30.5 m/US gal, 7.7 l x 100 km on Japanese emission test cycle.

STEERING GT Apex coupés servo; turns lock to lock: 3.

BRAKES rear disc.

ELECTRICAL EQUIPMENT 2 retractable headlamps.

DIMENSIONS AND WEIGHT weight: GT Coupé 1,995 lb, 905 kg - GT Apex Coupé 2,039 lb, 925 kg - GT Apex and GTV liftback coupés 2.072 lb, 940 kg.

OPTIONALS 4-speed automatic transmission not available; power steering (except GT Apex coupés).

TOYOTA Corolla Levin RWD GT Apex Coupé

TOYOTA Carina 1800 twin cam Turbo GT-TR Coupé

Carina Series

PRICES (Tokyo):		yen
1	1500 Standard 4-dr Sedan	**945,000**
2	1500 DX 4-dr Sedan	**1,008,000**
3	1500 SG 4-dr Sedan	**1,051,000**
4	1500 SG 2-dr Coupé	**1,102,000**
5	1500 SE 4-dr Sedan	**1,264,000**
6	1500 SE 2-dr Coupé	**1,304,000**
7	1500 ST 4-dr Sedan	**1,142,000**
8	1600 ST 2-dr Coupé	**1,195,000**
9	1600 twin cam GT 4-dr Sedan	**1,489,000**
10	1600 twin cam GT 2-dr Coupé	**1,537,000**
11	1600 twin cam GT-R 4-dr Sedan	**1,672,000**
12	1600 twin cam GT-R 2-dr Coupé	**1,739,000**
13	1800 SG 4-dr Sedan	**1,168,000**
14	1800 SE 4-dr Sedan	**1,429,000**
15	1800 SE 2-dr Coupé	**1,467,000**
16	1800 ST 4-dr Sedan	**1,258,000**
17	1800 ST 2-dr Coupé	**1,311,000**
18	1800 4+1-dr St. Wagon	**1,350,000**
19	1800 twin cam Turbo GT-T 4-dr Sedan	**1,696,000**
20	1800 twin cam Turbo GT-T 2-dr Coupé	**1,768,000**
21	1800 twin cam Turbo GT-TR 4-dr Sedan	**1,908,000**
22	1800 twin cam Turbo GT-TR 2-dr Coupé	**1,952,000**
23	1800 Diesel SG 4-dr Sedan	**1,258,000**
24	1800 Diesel SE 4-dr Sedan	**1,473,000**

For GB prices, see price index.

Power team:	Standard for:	Optional for:
83 hp	1 to 8	—
100 hp	13 to 18	—
130 hp	9 to 12	—
160 hp	19 to 22	—
65 hp (diesel)	23,24	—

83 hp power team

ENGINE front, 4 stroke; 4 cylinders, in line; 88.6 cu in, 1,452 cc (3.05 x 3.03 in, 77.5 x 77 mm); compression ratio: 9:1; max power (JIS): 83 hp (61 kW) at 5,600 rpm; max torque (JIS): 87 lb ft, 12 kg m (118 Nm) at 3,600 rpm; max engine rpm: 6,000; 57.2 hp/l (42.1 kW/l); cast iron block, light alloy head; 5 crankshaft bearings; valves: overhead, rockers; camshafts: 1, overhead, cogged belt; lubrication: gear pump, full flow filter, 6.9 imp pt, 8.2 US pt, 3.9 l; 1 3A-U downdraught twin barrel carburettor; fuel feed: mechanical pump; emission control by 3-way catalytic converter, secondary air induction and exhaust gas recirculation; water-cooled, 8.8 imp pt, 10.6 US pt, 5 l.

TRANSMISSION driving wheels: front; clutch: single dry plate (diaphragm); gearbox: mechanical; gears: 4 - ST Coupé 5, fully synchronized; ratios: I 3.587, II 2.022, III 1.384, IV 1, rev 3.484 - ST Coupé I 3.587, II 2.022, III 1.384, IV 1, V 0.861, rev 3.484; lever: central; final drive: hypoid bevel; axle ratio: 3.909; width of rims: 4.5"; tyres: 165 SR x 13.

PERFORMANCE max speeds: (I) 27 mph, 45 km/h; (II) 50 mph, 80 km/h; (III) 73 mph, 118 km/h; (IV) 99 mph, 160 km/h; power-weight ratio: Standard 28.3 lb/hp (38.5 lb/kW), 11.3 kg/hp (15.4 kg/kW); consumption: 39.8 m/imp gal, 33.1 m/US gal, 7.1 l x 100 km on Japanese emission test cycle.

CHASSIS integral; front suspension: independent, by McPherson, trailing links, transverse arms, coil springs/telescopic damper struts, anti-roll bar; rear: rigid axle, lower trailing links, upper torque rods, Panhard rod, coil springs, telescopic damper struts.

STEERING rack-and-pinion; turns lock to lock: 3.50.

BRAKES front disc, rear drum, dual circuit, servo.

ELECTRICAL EQUIPMENT 12 V; 40 Ah battery; 55 A alternator; Nihon-Denso pointless distributor; sedans 4 headlamps - coupés 2 headlamps.

DIMENSIONS AND WEIGHT wheel base: 98.43 in, 250 cm; tracks: 53.94 in, 137 cm front, 53.15 in, 135 cm rear; length: 140.08 in, 432 cm - ST Coupé 172.83 in, 439 cm; width: 64.96 in, 165 cm; height: sedans 54.72 in, 139 cm - coupés 53.15 in, 135 cm; weight: Standard Sedan 2,105 lb, 955 kg - DX Sedan 2,127 lb, 965 kg - SG Coupé and ST Sedan 2,160 lb, 980 kg - SG Sedan and ST Coupé 2,193 lb, 995 kg - SE Sedan 2,205 lb, 1,000 kg - SE Coupé 2,216 lb, 1,005 kg; weight distribution: 52% front, 48% rear; turning circle: 36.1 ft, 11 m; fuel tank: 13.4 imp gal, 16.1 US gal, 61 l.

BODY saloon/sedan, 4 doors - coupé, 2 doors; 5 seats, separate front seats.

OPTIONALS (standard for ST Coupé) 5-speed fully synchronized mechanical gearbox (V ratio 0.861); automatic transmission, hydraulic torque converter and planetary gears with 3 ratios (I 2.666, II 1.450, III 1, rev 2.703), 4.100 axle ratio.

100 hp power team

See 83 hp power team, except for:

ENGINE 111.8 cu in, 1,832 cc (3.17 x 3.54 in, 80.5 x 90 mm); max power (JIS): 100 hp (74 kW) at 5,400 rpm; max torque (JIS): 112 lb ft, 15.5 kg m (152 Nm) at 3,400 rpm; 54.6 hp/l (40.2 kW/l); valves: overhead, hydraulic tappets and rockers; lubrication: trochoid pump, full flow filter, 7 imp pt, 8.5 US pt, 4 l; 1 1S-U secondary air induction, 3-way catalytic converter with oxygen sensor and exhaust gas recirculation; cooling: 10.6 imp pt, 12.7 US pt, 6 l.

TRANSMISSION gears: SE Sedan 5, fully synchronized; ratios: I 3.587, II 2.022, III 1.384, IV 1, V 0.861, rev 3.484; axle ratio: 3.583.

PERFORMANCE max speeds: (I) 30 mph, 48 km/h; (II) 56 mph, 90 km/h; (III) 80 mph, 128 km/h; (IV) and (V) 99 mph, 160 km/h; power-weight ratio: ST Sedan 22.3 lb/hp (30 lb/kW), 10.1 kg/hp (13.6 kg/kW); consumption: 38.2 m/imp gal, 31.8 m/US gal, 7.4 l x 100 km on Japanese emission test cycle.

CHASSIS SG rear suspension: anti-roll bar.

DIMENSIONS AND WEIGHT length: SE Sedan 172.83 in, 439 cm - St. Wagon 175.98 in, 447 cm; height: St. Wagon 55.12 in, 140 cm; weight: ST Sedan 2,227 lb, 1,010 kg - ST Coupé 2,250 lb, 1,025 kg - SE Sedan 2,282 lb, 1,035 kg - SE Coupé 2,293 lb, 1,040 kg - St. Wagon 2,304 lb, 1,045 kg.

BODY saloon/sedan, 4 doors - coupé, 2 doors - estate car/st. wagon, 4+1 doors.

OPTIONALS automatic transmission, hydraulic torque converter and planetary gears with 4 ratios (I 2.450, II 1.450, III 1, IV 0.689, rev 2.222), 3.909 axle ratio; power steering.

130 hp power team

See 83 hp power team, except for:

ENGINE 96.8 cu in, 1,587 cc (3.19 x 3.03 in, 81 x 77 mm); compression ratio: 9.4:1; max power (JIS): 130 hp (96 kW) at 6,600 rpm; max torque (JIS): 110 lb ft, 15.2 kg m (149 Nm) at 5,200 rpm; max engine rpm: 7,000; 81.9 hp/l (60.3 kW/l); valves: overhead, Vee-slanted, thimble tappets; camshafts: 2, overhead, cogged belt; lubrication: 6.5 imp pt, 7.8 US pt, 3.7 l; electronic fuel injection; Toyota variable induction system with dual induction passages and butterfly control valve; emission control by 3-way catalytic converter; cooling: 9.8 imp pt, 11.8 US pt, 5.6 l.

TRANSMISSION (standard) gears: 5, fully synchronized; ratios: I 3.587, II 2.022, III 1.384, IV 1, V 0.861, rev 3.484; axle ratio: 4.300; width of rims: 5"; tyres: 185/70 SR x 14.

PERFORMANCE max speed: 112 mph, 180 km/h; power-weight ratio: GT Sedan 18.4 lb/hp (25 lb/kW), 8.3 kg/hp (11.3 kg/kW); consumption: 35.7 m/imp gal, 29.8 m/US gal, 7.9 l x 100 km on Japanese emission test cycle.

CHASSIS rear suspension: independent, semi-trailing arms, anti-roll bar, coil springs, telescopic dampers.

BRAKES rear disc.

DIMENSIONS AND WEIGHT weight: GT Sedan 2,392 lb, 1,085 kg - GT-R Sedan 2,414 lb, 1,095 kg - GT Coupé 2,425 lb, 1,100 kg - GT-R Coupé 2,447 lb, 1,110 kg.

OPTIONALS 3-speed automatic transmission not available.

TOYOTA Carina 1800 twin cam Turbo GT-TR Coupé

160 hp power team

See 83 hp power team, except for:

ENGINE turbocharged; 108 cu in, 1,770 cc (3.35 x 3.07 in, 85 x 78 mm); compression ratio: 7.8:1; max power (JIS): 160 hp (118 kW) at 6,000 rpm; max torque (JIS): 152 lb ft, 21 kg m (206 Nm) at 4,800 rpm; max engine rpm: 6,500; 90.4 hp/l (66.5 kW/l); valves: overhead, thimble tappets; camshafts: 2, overhead, chain-driven; lubrication: trochoid pump, full flow filter, 7.4 imp pt, 8.9 US pt, 4.2 l; exhaust turbocharger, 3-way catalytic converter with oxygen sensor; fuel feed: electric pump; water-cooled, 13.4 imp pt, 16.1 US pt, 7.6 l.

TRANSMISSION (standard) gears: 5, fully synchronized; ratios: I 3.566, II 2.056, III 1.384, IV 1, V 0.850, rev 4.091; axle ratio: 4.100; width of rims: 5.5"; tyres: 185/70 RX x 14.

PERFORMANCE max speeds: (I) 28 mph, 46 km/h; (II) 50 mph, 80 km/h; (III) 74 mph, 120 km/h; (IV) 101 mph, 162 km/h; (V) 112 mph, 180 km/h; power-weight ratio: GT-T Sedan 15.8 lb/hp (21.4 lb/kW), 7.1 kg/hp (9.7 kg/kW); consumption: 31.7 m/imp gal, 26.4 m/US gal, 8.9 l x 100 km on Japanese emission test cycle.

CHASSIS rear suspension: independent, semi-trailing arms, anti-roll bar, telescopic dampers.

DIMENSIONS AND WEIGHT tracks: 54.92 in, 139 cm front, 54.52 in, 138 cm rear; length: 172.83 in, 439 cm; height: sedans 55.10 in, 140 cm - coupés 53.74 in, 136 cm; ground clearance: 6.10 in, 15.5 cm; weight: GT-T and GT-TR sedans 2,491 lb, 1,130 kg - GT-T and GT-TR coupés 2,524 lb, 1,145 kg.

OPTIONALS automatic transmission, hydraulic torque converter and planetary gears with 4 ratios (I 2.450, II 1.450, III 1, IV 0.689, rev 2.222); power steering, 3.10 turns lock to lock of steering wheel; limited slip differential.

65 hp (diesel) power team

See 83 hp power team, except for:

ENGINE diesel; 112 cu in, 1,839 cc (3.26 x 3.34 in, 83 x 85 mm); compression ratio: 22.5:1; max power (JIS): 65 hp (48 kW) at 4,500 rpm; max torque (JIS): 83 lb ft, 11.5 kg m (113 Nm) at 3,000 rpm; max engine rpm: 4,200; 35.3 hp/l (26 kW/l); valves: overhead, thimble tappets; lubrication: trochoid pump; Bosch VE electronic fuel injection.

TRANSMISSION (standard) gears: 5, fully synchronized; ratios: I 3.625, II 2.043, III 1.394, IV 1, V 0.802, rev 4.039.

PERFORMANCE power-weight ratio: SG 35.4 lb/hp (48.2 lb/kW), 16 kg/hp (21.8 kg/kW); consumption: 80.7 m/imp gal, 67.2 m/US gal, 3.5 l x 100 km at 37 mph, 60 km/h on Japanese emission test cycle.

DIMENSIONS AND WEIGHT length: SG 170.27 in, 432 cm - SE 172.83 in, 439 cm; weight: SG Sedan 2,304 lb, 1,045 kg - SE Sedan 2,381 lb, 1,080 kg.

BODY saloon/sedan; 4 doors.

OPTIONALS automatic transmission, hydraulic torque converter and planetary gears with 4 ratios (I 2.450, II 1.450, III 1, IV 0.689, rev 2.222), 4.100 axle ratio.

TOYOTA Corona FWD 1800 EX Sedan

TOYOTA Corona RWD 1800 twin cam Turbo GT-TR Hardtop

Corona FWD Series

PRICES (Tokyo):	yen
1 1500 Standard 4-dr Sedan	978,000
2 1500 DX 4-dr Sedan	1,055,000
3 1500 GX 4-dr Sedan	1,094,000
4 1500 GX 4+1-dr Sedan	1,192,000
5 1500 EX 4-dr Sedan	1,320,000
6 1500 EX 4+1-dr Sedan	1,397,000
7 1800 GX 4-dr Sedan	1,243,000
8 1800 GX 4+1-dr Sedan	1,314,000
9 1800 EX 4-dr Sedan	1,444,000
10 1800 EX 4+1-dr Sedan	1,490,000
11 1800 EFI EX 4-dr Sedan	1,611,000
12 1800 EFI EX 4+1-dr Sedan	1,659,000
13 1800 EFI EX 4-dr Sedan	1,387,000
14 1800 EFI SX 4+1-dr Sedan	1,659,000
15 2000 Diesel GX 4-dr Sedan	1,338,000
16 2000 Diesel EX 4-dr Sedan	1,539,000

Power team:	Standard for:	Optional for:
83 hp	1 to 6	—
105 hp	7 to 10	—
115 hp	11 to 14	—
72 hp (diesel)	15,16	—

83 hp power team

ENGINE front, 4 stroke; 4 cylinders, in line; 88.6 cu in, 1,452 cc (3.05 x 3.03 in, 77.5 x 77 mm); compression ratio: 9.3:1; max power (JIS): 83 hp (61 kW) at 5,600 rpm; max torque (JIS): 87 lb ft, 12 kg m (118 Nm) at 3,600 rpm; max engine rpm: 6,000; 57.1 hp/l (42.1 kW/l); cast iron block, light alloy head; 5 crankshaft bearings; valves: overhead, in line, push-rods and rockers; camshafts: 1, overhead, cogged belt; lubrication: gear pump, full flow filter, 6.5 imp pt, 7.8 US pt, 3.7 l; 1 downdraught twin barrel carburettor; emission control with catalytic converter, secondary air induction and exhaust gas recirculation; fuel feed: mechanical pump; water-cooled, 10.5 imp pt, 12.6 US pt, 6 l, electric fan.

TRANSMISSION driving wheels: front; clutch: single dry plate (diaphragm); gearbox: mechanical; gears: 4, fully synchronized - GX 5; ratios: I 3.545, II 1.904, III 1.310, IV 0.969 - GX V 0.815, rev 3.520; final drive: helical spur gears; axle ratio: 3.722; width of rims: 5"; tyres: 165 SR x 13.

PERFORMANCE max speeds: (I) 29 mph, 47 km/h; (II) 54 mph, 87 km/h; (III) 82 mph, 132 km/h; (IV) and (V) 102 mph, 165 km/h; power-weight ratio: Standard 24.7 lb/hp (33.6 lb/kW), 11.2 kg/hp (15.2 kg/kW); consumption: 43.4 m/imp gal, 36.2 m/US gal, 6.5 l x 100 km on Japanese emission test cycle.

CHASSIS integral; front suspension: independent, by McPherson, lower A-arms, coil springs/telescopic damper struts; rear: independent, by McPherson, trailing links, twin transverse arms, coil springs/telescopic damper struts.

STEERING rack-and-pinion; turns lock to lock: 4.07.

BRAKES front disc, rear drum, servo; lining area: front 26.7 sq in, 172 sq cm, rear 41.5 sq in, 268 sq cm, total 68.2 sq in, 440 sq cm.

ELECTRICAL EQUIPMENT 12 V; 40 Ah battery; 50 Ah alternator; transistorized ignition; 2 headlamps.

DIMENSIONS AND WEIGHT wheel base: 99.21 in, 252 cm; tracks: 56.29 in, 143 cm front, 56.69 in, 144 cm rear; length: EX 4-dr Sedan 172.04 in, 437 cm - 4-dr sedans 171.25 in, 435 cm - 4+1-dr sedans 170.47 in, 433 cm; width: 65.74 in, 167 cm; height: 53.54 in, 136 cm; ground clearance: 6.30 in, 16 cm; weight: Standard and DX sedans 2,050 lb, 930 kg - GX 4-dr Sedan 2,061 lb, 935 kg - EX 4-dr and GX 4+1-dr sedans 2,116 lb, 960 kg - EX 4+1-dr Sedan 2,150 lb, 980 kg; weight distribution: 61% front, 39% rear; turning circle: 36.1 ft, 11 m; fuel tank: 12.1 imp gal, 14.5 US gal, 55 l.

BODY saloon/sedan; 4 or 4+1 doors; 5 seats, separate front seats.

OPTIONALS automatic transmission, hydraulic torque converter and planetary gears with 3 ratios (I 2.810, II 1.549, III 1, rev 2.296), 3.519 axle ratio.

105 hp power team

See 83 hp power team, except for:

ENGINE 111.7 cu in, 1,832 cc (3.16 x 3.54 in, 80.5 x 90 mm); compression ratio: 9:1; max power (JIS): 105 hp (77 kW) at 5,400 rpm; max torque (JIS): 116 lb ft, 16 kg m (157 Nm) at 3,000 rpm; 57.3 hp/l (42.2 kW/l); valves: overhead, hydraulic tappets, push-rods and rockers; lubrication: trochoid pump; electronic fuel injection; fuel feed: electric pump; cooling: 11.9 imp pt, 14.4 US pt, 6.8 l.

TRANSMISSION gears: 5, fully synchronized; ratios: I 2.041, II 1.322, III 0.945, IV 0.731, V 0.815, rev 3.153; axle ratio: 3.736.

PERFORMANCE max speeds: (I) 31 mph, 50 km/h; (II) 53 mph, 85 km/h; (III) 82 mph, 132 km/h; (IV) and (V) 109 mph, 175 km/h; power-weight ratio: GX 4-dr Sedan 20.2 lb/hp (27.4 lb/kW), 9.1 kg/hp (12.4 kg/kW); consumption: 42.1 m/imp gal, 35.1 m/US gal, 6.7 l x 100 km on Japanese emission test cycle.

CHASSIS front suspension: anti-roll bar.

STEERING servo.

DIMENSIONS AND WEIGHT weight: GX 4-dr Sedans 2,116 lb, 960 kg - EX 4-dr and GX 4+1-dr sedans 2,182 lb, 990 kg - EX 4+1-dr Sedan 2,227 lb, 1,010 kg.

OPTIONALS automatic transmission, hydraulic torque converter and planetary gears with 4 ratios (I 3.643, II 2.008, III 1.296, IV 0.892, rev 2.977), 2.724 axle ratio.

115 hp power team

See 83 hp power team, except for:

ENGINE 111.7 cu in, 1,832 cc (3.16 x 3.54 in, 80.5 x 90 mm); compression ratio: 9:1; max power (JIS): 115 hp (85 kW) at 5,400 rpm; max torque (JIS): 121 lb ft, 16.7 kg m (164 Nm) at 4,000 rpm; 62.7 hp/l (46.2 kW/l); valves: overhead, hydraulic tappets, push-rods and rockers; lubrication: trochoid pump; Toyota D-jetro electronic fuel injection; emission control by 3-way catalytic converter; fuel feed: electric pump; cooling: 11.9 imp pt, 14.4 US pt, 6.8 l.

TRANSMISSION gears: 5, fully synchronized; ratios: I 2.041, II 1.322, III 0.945, IV 0.731, rev 3.153; axle ratio: 3.944; tyres: 175/70 SR x 13.

PERFORMANCE max speeds: (I) 30 mph, 48 km/h; (II) 47 mph, 75 km/h; (III) 73 mph, 118 km/h; (IV) 104 mph, 168 km/h; (V) 112 mph, 180 km/h; power-weight ratio: EX 4-dr Sedan 19.1 lb/hp (25.9 lb/kW), 8.6 kg/hp (11.7 kg/kW); consumption: 35.2 m/imp gal, 29.4 m/US gal, 8 l x 100 km on Japanese emission test cycle.

CHASSIS front and rear suspension: anti-roll bar.

STEERING servo.

DIMENSIONS AND WEIGHT weight: SX 4-dr Sedan 2,193 lb, 995 kg - EX 4-dr Sedan 2,216 lb, 1,005 kg - SX 4+1-dr Sedan 2,249 lb, 1,020 kg - EX 4+1-dr Sedan 2,260 lb, 1,025 kg.

OPTIONALS automatic transmission, hydraulic torque converter and planetary gears with 4 ratios (I 3.643, II 2.008, III 1.296, IV 0.892, rev 2.977), 2.892 axle ratio.

72 hp (diesel) power team

See 83 hp power team, except for:

ENGINE diesel; 120.4 cu in, 1,974 cc (3.38 x 3.34 in, 86 x 85 mm); compression ratio: 22.5:1; max power (JIS): 72 hp (53 kW) at 4,500 rpm; max torque (JIS): 93 lb ft, 12.8 kg m (125 Nm) at 3,000 rpm; max engine rpm: 4,800; 36.4 hp/l (26.8 kW/l); valves: overhead, in line, thimble tappets; lubrication: trochoid pump, full flow filter, 6.6 imp pt, 8 US pt, 3.8 l; Ricardo Comet swirl chamber; Bosch VE electronic injection.

TRANSMISSION gears: 5, fully synchronized; ratios: I 2.041, II 1.322, III 0.945, IV 0.984, V 0.731, rev 3.153; axle ratio: 3.736.

PERFORMANCE max speed: 96 mph, 155 km/h; power-weight ratio: GX 30.6 lb/hp (41.6 lb/kW), 13.8 kg/hp (18.9 kg/kW); consumption: 88.2 m/imp gal, 73.5 m/US gal, 3.2 l x 100 km at 37 mph, 60 km/h on Japanese emission test cycle.

STEERING servo.

DIMENSIONS AND WEIGHT weight: GX Sedan 2,205 lb, 1,000 kg - EX Sedan 2,271 lb, 1,030 kg.

BODY 4 doors.

OPTIONALS automatic transmission, hydraulic torque converter and planetary gears with 4 ratios (I 3.643, II 2.008, III 1.296, IV 0.892, rev 2.977), 2.892 axle ratio.

Corona RWD Series

PRICES (Tokyo):	yen
1 1500 Standard 4-dr Sedan	978,000
2 1500 DX 4-dr Sedan	1,055,000
3 1500 GX 4-dr Sedan	1,094,000
4 1600 twin cam GT 4-dr Sedan	1,540,000
5 1600 twin cam GT 4-dr Hardtop	1,592,000
6 1600 twin cam GT Sport 4-dr Sedan	1,711,000
7 1600 twin cam GT Sport 4-dr Hardtop	1,763,000
8 1800 GX 4-dr Sedan	1,243,000
9 1800 GX 4-dr Hardtop	1,335,000
10 1800 EX 4-dr Hardtop	1,512,000
11 1800 twin cam Turbo GT-T 4-dr Sedan	1,735,000
12 1800 twin cam Turbo GT-T 4-dr Hardtop	1,787,000
13 1800 twin cam Turbo GT-TR 4-dr Sedan	1,947,000
14 1800 twin cam Turbo GT-TR 4-dr Hardtop	2,003,000

Power team:	Standard for:	Optional for:
83 hp	1 to 3	—
100 hp	8 to 10	—
130 hp	4 to 7	—
160 hp	11 to 14	—

83 hp power team

ENGINE front, 4 stroke; 4 cylinders, in line; 88.6 cu in, 1,452 cc (3.05 x 3.03 in, 77.5 x 77 mm); compression ratio: 9:1; max power (JIS): 83 hp (61 kW) at 5,600 rpm; max torque (JIS): 87 lb ft, 12 kg m (118 Nm) at 3,600 rpm; max engine rpm: 6,000; 57.1 hp/l (42.1 kW/l); cast iron block, light alloy head; 5 crankshaft bearings; valves: overhead, push-rods and rockers; camshafts: 1, overhead, cogged belt, chain-driven; lubrication: gear pump, full flow filter, 6.9 imp pt, 8.2 US pt, 3.9 l; 1 Aisan 3A-U downdraught twin barrel carburettor; emission control with catalytic converter, secondary air induction and exhaust gas recirculation; fuel feed: mechanical pump; water-cooled, 8.8 imp pt, 10.6 US pt, 5 l.

TRANSMISSION driving wheels: rear; clutch: single dry plate (diaphragm); gearbox: mechanical; gears: 4, fully syn-

83 HP POWER TEAM

chronized; ratios: I 3.587, II 2.022, III 1.384, IV 1, rev 3.484; final drive: hypoid bevel; axle ratio: 3.727; tyres: 165 SR x 13.

PERFORMANCE max speed: 99 mph, 160 km/h; power-weight ratio: Standard 25.6 lb/hp (34.9 lb/kW), 11.6 kg/hp (15.8 kg/kW); consumption: 40.3 m/imp gal, 33.6 m/US gal, 7 l x 100 km on Japanese emission test cycle.

CHASSIS integral; front suspension: independent, by McPherson, coil springs, telescopic damper struts, lower wishbones (trailing links), anti-roll bar; rear: rigid axle, twin trailing radius arms, Panhard rod, coil springs, telescopic dampers.

STEERING rack-and-pinion.

BRAKES front disc, rear drum, servo.

ELECTRICAL EQUIPMENT 12 V; 40 Ah battery; 55 Ah alternator; Denso distributor; 2 headlamps.

DIMENSIONS AND WEIGHT wheel base: 98.43 in, 250 cm; tracks: 54.13 in, 137 cm front, 53.14 in, 135 cm rear; length: 176.96 in, 449 cm; width: 65.35 in, 166 cm; height: 54.52 in, 138 cm; ground clearance: 6.10 in, 15.5 cm; weight: Standard Sedan 2,127 lb, 965 kg - DX Sedan 2,138 lb, 970 kg - GX Sedan 2,150 lb, 975 kg; weight distribution: 52% front, 48% rear; turning circle: 36 ft, 11 m; fuel tank: 13.4 imp gal, 16.1 US gal, 61 l.

BODY saloon/sedan; 4 doors; 5 seats, separate front seats.

OPTIONALS automatic transmission, hydraulic torque converter and planetary gears with 3 ratios (I 2.666, II 1.450, III 1, rev 2.703), 4.100 axle ratio.

100 hp power team

See 83 hp power team, except for:

ENGINE 111.7 cu in, 1,832 cc (3.16 x 3.54 in, 80.5 x 90 mm); max power (JIS): 100 hp (74 kW) at 5,400 rpm; max torque (JIS): 112 lb ft, 15.5 kg m (152 Nm) at 3,400 rpm; 54.6 hp/l (40.2 kW/l); valves: overhead, hydraulic tappets, rockers; lubrication: trochoid pump, full flow filter, 7 imp pt, 8.5 US pt, 4 l; 1 N-type downdraught twin barrel carburettor; cooling: 10.8 imp pt, 12.7 US pt, 6 l.

TRANSMISSION axle ratio: 3.583.

PERFORMANCE max speed: 105 mph, 170 km/h; power-weight ratio: GX Sedan 22.2 lb/hp (30.1 lb/kW), 10 kg/hp (13.7 kg/kW); consumption: 38.2 m/imp gal, 31.8 m/US gal, 7.4 l x 100 km on Japanese emission test cycle.

STEERING EX servo.

DIMENSIONS AND WEIGHT length: GX Sedan 176.96 in, 449 cm - hardtops 177.36 in, 450 cm; width: GX Sedan 65.35 in, 166 cm - hardtops 65.74 in, 167 cm; height: hardtops 51.77 in, 131 cm - GX Sedan 54.92 in, 139 cm; weight: GX Sedan 2,216 lb, 1,005 kg - GX Hardtop 2,282 lb, 1,035 kg - EX Hardtop 2,337 lb, 1,060 kg; ground clearance: 6.10 in, 15.5 cm.

BODY saloon/sedan, 4 doors - hardtop, 2 doors.

OPTIONALS automatic transmission, hydraulic torque converter and planetary gears with 4 ratios (I 2.450, II 1.452, III 1, IV 0.689, rev 2.222), 3.909 axle ratio.

130 hp power team

See 83 hp power team, except for:

ENGINE 96.8 cu in, 1,587 cc (3.19 x 3.03 in, 81 x 77 mm); compression ratio: 9.4:1; max power (JIS): 130 hp (96 kW) at 6,600 rpm; max torque (JIS): 110 lb ft, 15.2 kg m (149 Nm) at 5,200 rpm; max engine rpm: 7,000; 81.9 hp/l (60.3 kW/l); valves: overhead, Vee-slanted, thimble tappets; camshafts: 2, overhead, cogged belt; lubrication: 6.5 imp pt, 7.8 US pt, 3.7 l; electronic fuel injection; Toyota variable induction system with dual induction passages and butterfly control valve; emission control by 3-way catalytic converter; cooling: 9.8 imp pt, 11.8 US pt, 5.6 l.

TRANSMISSION gears: 5, fully synchronized; ratios: I 3.587, II 2.022, III 1.384, IV 1, V 0.861, rev 3.484; axle ratio: 4.300; width of rims: 5"; tyres: 185/70 SR x 14 - GT Sport models 205/60 R x 15 H.

PERFORMANCE max speed: 112 mph, 180 km/h; power-weight ratio: sedans 18.5 lb/hp (25.1 lb/kW), 8.4 kg/hp (11.4 kg/kW); consumption: 35.7 m/imp gal, 29.8 m/US gal, 7.9 l x 100 km on Japanese emission test cycle.

CHASSIS rear suspension: independent, semi-trailing arms, coil springs, anti-roll bar, telescopic dampers.

BRAKES rear disc.

DIMENSIONS AND WEIGHT weight: GT and GT Sport sedans 2,403 lb, 1,090 kg - GT and GT Sport hardtops 2,425 lb, 1,100 kg.

BODY saloon/sedan, 4 doors - hardtop, 2 doors.

160 hp power team

See 83 hp power team, except for:

ENGINE turbocharged; 108 cu in, 1,770 cc (3.35 x 3.07 in, 85 x 78 mm); compression ratio: 7.8:1; max power (JIS): 160 hp (118 kW) at 6,000 rpm; max torque (JIS): 152 lb ft, 21 kg m (206 Nm) at 4,800 rpm; max engine rpm: 6,500; 90.4 hp/l (66.3 kW/l); valves: overhead, thimble tappets; camshafts: 2, overhead, chain-driven; lubrication: trochoid pump, full flow filter, 7.4 imp pt, 8.9 US pt, 4.2 l; electronic fuel injection; turbocharger; emission control with 3-way catalytic converter; cooling: 13.4 imp pt, 16.1 US pt, 7.6 l.

TRANSMISSION gears: 5, fully synchronized; ratios: I 3.566, II 2.056, III 1.384, IV 1, V 0.850, rev 4.091; axle ratio: 4.100; width of rims: 5.5"; tyres: 185/70 SR x 14.

PERFORMANCE max speeds: (I) 28 mph, 46 km/h; (II) 50 mph, 80 km/h; (III) 74 mph, 120 km/h; (IV) 101 mph, 162 km/h; (V) 112 mph, 180 km/h; power-weight ratio: GT-T Sedan 15.8 lb/hp (21.4 lb/kW), 7.1 kg/hp (9.7 kg/kW); consumption: 31.7 m/imp gal, 26.4 m/US gal, 8.9 l x 100 km on Japanese emission test cycle.

CHASSIS rear suspension: independent, semi-trailing arms, coil springs, anti-roll bar, telescopic dampers.

DIMENSIONS AND WEIGHT tracks: 54.92 in, 139 cm front, 54.33 in, 138 cm rear; length: sedans 179.92 in, 457 cm - hardtops 177.16 in, 450 cm; height: sedans 54.72 in, 139 cm, hardtops 51.96 in, 132 cm; ground clearance: 6.10 in, 15.5 cm; weight: GT-T Sedan 2,524 lb, 1,145 kg - GT-T Hardtop 2,546 lb, 1,155 kg - GT-TR Sedan 2,557 lb, 1,160 kg - GT-TR Hardtop 2,579 lb, 1,170 kg.

BODY saloon/sedan, 4 doors - hardtop, 2 doors.

OPTIONALS automatic transmission, hydraulic torque converter and planetary gears with 4 ratios (I 2.452, II 1.452, III 1, IV 0.689, rev 2.212); power steering, 3.10 turns lock to lock of steering wheel; limited slip differential.

TOYOTA Sprinter Carib AV-II Station Wagon

Sprinter Carib

PRICES (Tokyo):	yen
AV-I 4+1-dr St. Wagon	**1,288,000**
AV-II 4+1-dr St. Wagon	**1,488,000**

ENGINE front, 4 stroke; 4 cylinders, in line; 88.6 cu in, 1,452 cc (3.05 x 3.03 in, 77.5 x 77 mm); compression ratio: 9:1; max power (JIS): 83 hp (61 kW) at 5,600 rpm; max torque (JIS): 87 lb ft, 12 kg m (118 Nm) at 3,600 rpm; max engine rpm: 6,000; 57.1 hp/l (42.1 kW/l); cast iron block, light alloy head; 5 crankshaft bearings; valves: overhead, rockers; camshafts: 1, overhead, cogged belt; lubrication: gear pump, full flow filter, 6.5 imp pt, 7.8 US pt, 3.7 l; 1 Aisan 3A-U downdraught twin barrel carburettor; emission control with 3-way catalytic converter, secondary air induction and exhaust gas recirculation; fuel feed: mechanical pump; water-cooled, 8.8 imp pt, 10.6 US pt, 5 l.

TRANSMISSION driving wheels: front or front and rear; clutch: single dry plate (diaphragm); gearbox: mechanical; gears: 6, fully synchronized; ratios: I 4.714, II 3.660, III 2.070, IV 1.376, V 1, VI 0.825, rev 3.418; final drive: hypoid bevel; axle ratio: 3.727; tyres: AV-I 155 SR x 13 - AV-II 175/70 SR x 13.

PERFORMANCE max speeds: (I) 22 mph, 35 km/h; (II) 30 mph, 48 km/h; (III) 50 mph, 80 km/h; (IV) 78 mph, 125 km/h; (V) and (VI) 99 mph, 160 km/h; power-weight ratio: AV-I 25.8 lb/hp (35 lb/kW), 11.7 kg/hp (15.9 kg/kW); consumption: 39.8 m/imp gal, 33.1 m/US gal, 7.1 l x 100 km on Japanese emission test cycle.

CHASSIS integral; front suspension: independent, by McPherson, lower arms, coil springs/telescopic damper struts, anti-roll bar; rear: rigid axle, lower radius links, upper torque rods, Panhard rod, coil springs, anti-roll bar, telescopic dampers.

STEERING rack-and-pinion - AV-II servo; turns lock to lock: 3.60 - AV-II 3.37.

BRAKES front disc, rear drum, servo.

ELECTRICAL EQUIPMENT 12 V; 33 Ah battery; 40 Ah alternator; Nihon-Denso distributor; 2 headlamps.

DIMENSIONS AND WEIGHT wheel base: 95.67 in, 243 cm; tracks: 54.33 in, 138 cm front, 53.14 in, 135 cm rear; length: AV-I 164.17 in, 417 cm - AV-II 169.68 in, 431 cm; width: 63.58 in, 161 cm; height: 59.05 in, 150 cm; ground clearance: 6.70 in, 17 cm; weight: AV-I St. Wagon 2,138 lb, 970 kg - AV-II St. Wagon 2,238 lb, 1,015 kg; weight distribution: 54% front, 46% rear; turning circle: 33.4 ft, 10.2 m; fuel tank: 11 imp gal, 13.2 US gal, 50 l.

BODY estate car/st. wagon; 4+1 doors; 5 seats, separate front seats.

Celica Series

	PRICES (Tokyo):	yen
1	1600 twin cam GT 2-dr Coupé	**1,523,000**
2	1600 twin cam GT 2+1-dr Liftback Coupé	**1,610,000**
3	1600 twin cam GT-R 2-dr Coupé	**1,738,000**
4	1600 twin cam GT-R 2+1-dr Liftback Coupé	**1,814,000**
5	1800 SV 2-dr Coupé	**1,140,000**
6	1800 SV 2+1-dr Liftback Coupé	**1,212,000**
7	1800 ST 2-dr Coupé	**1,251,000**
8	1800 ST 2+1-dr Liftback Coupé	**1,318,000**
9	1800 SX 2-dr Coupé	**1,455,000**
10	1800 SX 2+1-dr Liftback Coupé	**1,533,000**
11	1800 twin cam Turbo GT-T 2-dr Coupé	**1,748,000**
12	1800 twin cam Turbo GT-T 2+1-dr Liftback Coupé	**1,835,000**
13	1800 twin cam Turbo GT-TR 2-dr Coupé	**1,958,000**
14	1800 twin cam Turbo GT-TR 2+1-dr Liftback Coupé	**2,035,000**

Power team:	Standard for:	Optional for:
100 hp	5 to 10	—
130 hp	1 to 4	—
160 hp	11 to 14	—

100 hp power team

ENGINE front, 4 stroke; 4 cylinders, in line; 111.8 cu in, 1,832 cc (3.17 x 3.54 in, 80.5 x 90 mm); compression ratio: 9:1; max power (JIS): 100 hp (74 kW) at 5,400 rpm; max torque (JIS): 112 lb ft, 15.5 kg m (152 Nm) at 3,400 rpm; max engine rpm: 6,000; 54.6 hp/l (40.2 kW/l); cast iron block, light alloy head; 5 crankshaft bearings; valves: overhead, rockers and hydraulic tappets; camshafts: 1, overhead, cogged belt; lubrication: gear pump, full flow filter, 7 imp pt, 8.5 US pt, 4 l; 1 1S-U downdraught twin barrel carburettor; fuel feed: mechanical pump; emission control by secondary air induction, 3-way catalytic converter with oxygen sensor and exhaust gas recirculation; water-cooled, 10.6 imp pt, 12.7 US pt, 6 l.

TRANSMISSION driving wheels: rear; clutch: single dry plate (diaphragm); gearbox: mechanical; gears: 4 - ST 5, fully synchronized; ratios: I 3.587, II 2.022, III 1.384, IV 1, rev 3.484 - ST I 3.587, II 2.022, III 1.384, IV 1, V 0.861, rev 3.484; lever: central; final drive: hypoid bevel; axle ratio: 3.727; width of rims: 4.5"; tyres: 165 SR x 13.

PERFORMANCE max speeds: (I) 28 mph, 45 km/h; (II) 52 mph, 84 km/h; (III) 75 mph, 120 km/h; (IV) 103 mph, 165 km/h - ST (V) 109 mph, 175 km/h; power-weight ratio: SV Coupé 22.2 lb/hp (30.1 lb/kW), 10 kg/hp (13.7 kg/kW); consumption: 36.5 m/imp gal, 30.5 m/US gal, 7.7 l x 100 km on Japanese emission test cycle.

CHASSIS integral; front suspension: independent, by McPherson, trailing links, transverse arms, coil springs/tele-

TOYOTA Celica Series (1600 twin cam engine)

scopic damper struts, anti-roll bar; rear: rigid axle, trailing links, upper torque rods, Panhard rod, coil springs/telescopic damper struts, anti-roll bar.

STEERING rack-and-pinion; turns lock to lock: 3.50.

BRAKES front disc, rear drum, dual circuit, servo.

ELECTRICAL EQUIPMENT 12 V; 40 Ah battery; 55 A alternator; Nihon-Denso pointless distributor; 2 headlamps.

DIMENSIONS AND WEIGHT wheel base: 98.43 in, 250 cm; tracks: 53.94 in, 137 cm front, 53.15 in, 135 cm rear; length: coupés 174.41 in, 443 cm - liftback coupés 176.77 in, 449 cm; width: 65.35 in, 166 cm; height: 51.57 in, 131 cm; ground clearance: coupés 6.10 in, 15.5 cm - liftback coupés 6.30 in, 16 cm; weight: SV Coupé 2,238 lb, 1,015 kg - ST Coupé 2,249 lb, 1,020 kg - SX and ST Liftback coupés 2,271 lb, 1,030 kg - SV Liftback Coupé 2,260 lb, 1,025 kg - SX Liftback Coupé 2,293 lb, 1,040 kg; turning circle: 36.7 ft, 11.2 m; fuel tank: 13.4 imp gal, 16.1 US gal, 61 l.

BODY coupé; 2 or 2+1 doors; 5 seats, separate front seats.

OPTIONALS automatic transmission, hydraulic torque converter and planetary gears with 4 ratios (I 2.450, II 1.450, III 1, IV 0.689, rev 2.222), 3.909 axle ratio; (for ST coupés only) power steering, 3.10 turns lock to lock of steering wheel.

130 hp power team

See 100 hp power team, except for:

ENGINE 96.8 cu in, 1,587 cc (3.19 x 3.03 in, 81 x 77 mm); compression ratio: 9.4:1; max power (JIS): 130 hp (96 kW) at 6,600 rpm; max torque (JIS): 110 lb ft, 15.2 kg m (149 Nm) at 5,200 rpm; max engine rpm: 7,000; 81.9 hp/l (60.3 kW/l); valves: overhead, Vee-slanted, thimble tappets; camshafts: 2, overhead, cogged belt; lubrication: 6.5 imp pt, 7.8 US pt, 3.7 l; electronic fuel injection; Toyota variable induction system with dual induction passages and butterfly control valve; emission control by 3-way catalytic converter; cooling: 9.8 imp pt, 11.8 US pt, 5.6 l.

TRANSMISSION gears: 5, fully synchronized; ratios: I 3.587, II 2.022, III 1.384, IV 1, V 0.861, rev 3.484; axle ratio: 4.556; width of rims: GT 5.5" - GT-R 6"; tyres: GT 185/70 SR x 14 - GT-R 195/60 R x 15 H.

PERFORMANCE max speed: 112 mph, 180 km/h; power-weight ratio: GT Coupé 18.6 lb/hp (25.2 lb/kW), 8.4 kg/hp (11.4 kg/kW); consumption: 34.8 m/imp gal, 29 m/US gal, 8.1 l x 100 km on Japanese emission test cycle.

CHASSIS rear suspension: independent, semi-trailing arms, anti-roll bar, coil springs, telescopic dampers.

BRAKES rear disc.

DIMENSIONS AND WEIGHT tracks: 55.11 in, 140 cm front, 54.72 in, 139 cm rear; weight: GT and GT-R coupés 2,414 lb, 1,095 kg - GT and GT-R liftback coupés 2,436 lb, 1,105 kg.

OPTIONALS automatic transmission not available.

160 hp power team

See 100 hp power team, except for:

ENGINE turbocharged; 108 cu in, 1,770 cc (3.35 x 3.07 in, 85 x 78 mm); compression ratio: 7.8:1; max power (JIS): 160 hp (118 kW) at 6,000 rpm; max torque (JIS): 152 lb ft, 21 kg m (206 Nm) at 4,800 rpm; max engine rpm: 6,500; 90.4 hp/l (66.5 kW/l); valves: overhead, thimble tappets; camshafts: 2, overhead, chain-driven; lubrication: trochoid pump, full flow filter, 7.4 imp pt, 8.9 US pt, 4.2 l; exhaust turbocharger; 3-way catalytic converter with oxygen sensor; fuel feed: electric pump; water-cooled, 13.4 imp pt, 16.1 US pt, 7.6 l.

TRANSMISSION gears: 5, fully synchronized; ratios: I 3.566, II 2.056, III 1.384, IV 1, V 0.850, rev 4.091; axle ratio: 4.100; width of rims: 5.5"; tyres: 185/70 SR x 14.

PERFORMANCE max speeds: (I) 28 mph, 46 km/h; (II) 50 mph, 80 km/h; (III) 74 mph, 120 km/h; (IV) 101 mph, 162 km/h; (V) 112 mph, 180 km/h; power-weight ratio: GT-T Coupé 15.8 lb/hp (21.4 lb/kW), 7.1 kg/hp (9.7 kg/kW); consumption: 31.7 m/imp gal, 26.4 m/US gal, 8.9 l x 100 km on Japanese emission test cycle.

CHASSIS rear suspension: independent, semi-trailing arms, coil springs, anti-roll bar, telescopic dampers.

BRAKES disc, front internal radial fins, servo.

DIMENSIONS AND WEIGHT tracks: 54.92 in, 139 cm front, 54.52 in, 138 cm rear; length: coupés 174.60 in, 443 cm - liftback coupés 175.20 in, 445 cm; height: 51.97 in, 132 cm; ground clearance: 6.10 in, 15.5 cm; weight: GT-T and GT-TR coupés 2,546 lb, 1,155 kg - GT-T and GT-TR liftback coupés 2,568 lb, 1,165 kg.

OPTIONALS automatic transmission, hydraulic torque converter and planetary gears with 4 ratios (I 2.450, II 1.450, III 1, IV 0.689, rev 2.222); power steering, 3.10 turns lock to lock of steering wheel; limited slip differential.

Vista / Camry Series

	PRICES (Tokyo):	**yen**
1	Vista 1800 VL 4-dr Sedan	**1,260,000**
2	Vista 1800 VL 4-dr Liftback Coupé	**1,313,000**
3	Vista 1800 VE 4-dr Sedan	**1,430,000**
4	Vista 1800 VE 4+1-dr Liftback Coupé	**1,477,000**
5	Vista 1800 VX 4-dr Sedan	**1,657,000**
6	Vista 1800 VX 4+1-dr Liftback Coupé	**1,699,000**
7	Camry 1800 XT 4-dr Sedan	**1,260,000**
8	Camry 1800 SE 4-dr Sedan	**1,430,000**
9	Camry 1800 ZX 4-dr Sedan	**1,657,000**
10	Vista 2000 VL 4-dr Sedan	**1,330,000**
11	Vista 2000 VL 4+1-dr Liftback Coupé	**1,383,000**
12	Vista 2000 VE 4-dr Sedan	**1,500,000**
13	Vista 2000 VE 4+1-dr Liftback Coupé	**1,547,000**
14	Vista 2000 VX 4-dr Sedan	**1,727,000**
15	Vista 2000 VX 4+1-dr Liftback Coupé	**1,769,000**
16	Camry 2000 XT 4-dr Sedan	**1,330,000**
17	Camry 2000 SE 4-dr Sedan	**1,500,000**
18	Camry 2000 ZX 4-dr Sedan	**1,727,000**
19	Vista 1800 Turbo Diesel VL 4-dr Sedan	**1,423,000**
20	Vista 1800 Turbo Diesel VE 4-dr Sedan	**1,608,000**
21	Vista 1800 Turbo Diesel VE 4+1-dr Liftback Coupé	**1,655,000**
22	Camry 1800 Turbo Diesel XT 4-dr Sedan	**1,423,000**
23	Camry 1800 Turbo Diesel SE 4-dr Sedan	**1,608,000**

For GB and USA prices, see price index.

Power team:	**Standard for:**	**Optional for:**
100 hp	1 to 9	—
120 hp	10 to 18	—
80 hp (diesel)	19 to 23	—

100 hp power team

ENGINE front, transverse, 4 stroke; 4 cylinders, in line; 111.7 cu in, 1,832 cc (3.16 x 3.54 in, 80.5 x 90 mm); compression ratio: 9:1; max power (JIS): 100 hp (74 kW) at 5,400 rpm; max torque (JIS): 112 lb ft, 15.5 kg m (152 Nm) at 3,400 rpm; max engine rpm: 6,000; 54.6 hp/l (40.2 kW/l); cast iron block, light alloy head; 5 crankshaft bearings; valves: overhead, hydraulic tappets, rockers; camshafts: 1, overhead, cogged belt; lubrication: trochoid pump, full flow filter; 1 N-type downdraught twin barrel carburettor; emission control with catalytic converter, secondary air induction and exhaust gas recirculation; fuel feed: mechanical pump; water-cooled.

TRANSMISSION driving wheels: front; clutch: single dry plate (diaphragm); gearbox: mechanical; gears: 5, fully synchronized; ratios: I 3.538, II 1.960, III 1.250, IV 0.945, V 0.731, rev 3.153; lever: central; final drive: helical spur gears; axle ratio: 3.550; width of rims: 5"; tyres: 165 SR x 13 - VX and ZX models 185/70 SR x 13.

PERFORMANCE max speeds: (I) 30 mph, 48 km/h; (II) 53 mph, 86 km/h; (III) 86 mph, 138 km/h; (IV) and (V) 106 mph, 170 km/h; power-weight ratio: Vista VL Sedan 22 lb/hp (30 lb/kW), 10 kg/hp (13.6 kg/kW); consumption: 39.8 m/imp gal, 33.1 m/US gal, 7.1 l x 100 km on Japanese emission test cycle.

CHASSIS integral; front suspension: independent, by McPherson, coil springs/telescopic damper struts, lower wishbones (trailing links), anti-roll bar; rear: independent, transverse linkage bar, coil springs, telescopic dampers - VX and ZX models anti-roll bar.

STEERING rack-and-pinion; servo.

BRAKES front disc, rear drum, servo.

ELECTRICAL EQUIPMENT 12 V; 35 Ah battery; 55 A alternator; Denso distributor; 2 headlamps.

DIMENSIONS AND WEIGHT wheel base: 102.36 in, 260 cm; front and rear track: 57.67 in, 146 cm; length: 55.90 in, 142 cm; width: Vista models 173.81 in, 441 cm - Camry models 173.22 in, 440 cm; height: sedans 54.92 in, 139 cm - liftback coupés 53.93 in, 137 cm; ground clearance: 6.29 in, 16 cm; weight: Vista VL and Camry XT sedans 2,216 lb, 1,005 kg - Vista VE and Camry SE sedans 2,249 lb, 1,020 kg - Vista VL Liftback Coupé 2,260 lb, 1,025 kg - Vista VX and Camry ZX sedans and Vista VE Liftback Coupé 2,293 lb, 1,040 kg - Vista VX Liftback Coupé 2,337 lb, 1,060 kg; weight distribution: 63% front, 37% rear; turning circle: 38 ft, 11.6 m; fuel tank: 12.1 imp gal, 14.5 US gal, 55 l.

BODY saloon/sedan, 4 doors - coupé, 4+1 doors; 5 seats, separate front seats.

OPTIONALS automatic transmission, hydraulic torque converter and planetary gears with 4 ratios (I 2.810, II 1.549, III 1, IV 0.706, rev 2.296), 3.533 axle ratio; electric sunroof.

TOYOTA Celica 1600 twin cam GT-R Coupé

TOYOTA Vista 2000 VX Liftback Coupé

120 hp power team

See 100 hp power team, except for:

ENGINE 121.8 cu in, 1,995 cc (3.30 x 3.54 in, 84 x 90 mm); compression ratio: 8.7:1; max power (JIS): 120 hp (88 kW) at 5,400 rpm; max torque (JIS): 127 lb ft, 17.6 kg m (172 Nm) at 4,000 rpm; 60.1 hp/l (44.3 kW/l); TCCS electronic fuel injection; fuel feed: electric pump.

TRANSMISSION tyres: VL, VE, XT and SE models 165 SR x 13 - VX and ZX models 185/70 SR x 13.

PERFORMANCE max speed: 112 mph, 180 km/h; power-weight ratio: Vista VL Sedan 18.6 lb/hp (25.2 lb/kW), 8.4 kg/hp (11.4 kg/kW); consumption: 36.7 m/imp gal, 30.5 m/US gal, 7.7 l x 100 km on Japanese emission test cycle.

CHASSIS rear suspension: VX and ZX models anti-roll bar.

STEERING rack-and-pinion, servo.

DIMENSIONS AND WEIGHT weight: Vista VL Sedan 2,227 lb, 1,010 kg - Vista VE and Camry SE sedans 2,260 lb, 1,025 kg - Vista VL Liftback Coupé 2,271 lb, 1,030 kg - Vista VX and Camry ZX sedans and Vista VE Liftback Coupé 2,304 lb, 1,045 kg - Vista VX Liftback Coupé 2,348 lb, 1,065 kg.

80 hp (diesel) power team

See 100 hp power team, except for:

ENGINE turbocharged, diesel; 112.2 cu in, 1,839 cc (3.26 x 3.34 in, 83 x 85 mm); compression ratio: 22.5:1; max power (JIS): 80 hp (59 kW) at 4,500 rpm; max torque (JIS): 112 lb ft, 15.5 kg m (152 Nm) at 2,400 rpm; max engine rpm: 5,000; 43.5 hp/l (32 kW/l); valves: overhead, thimble tappets; Bosch VE fuel injection; turbocharger.

TRANSMISSION axle ratio: 3.944; tyres: 165 SR x 13.

PERFORMANCE power-weight ratio: Vista Turbo Diesel VL 29.4 lb/hp (39.9 lb/kW), 13.3 kg/hp (18.1 kg/kW); consumption: 88.2 m/imp gal, 73.5 m/US gal, 3.2 l x 100 km at 37 mph, 60 km/h on Japanese emission test cycle.

CHASSIS rear suspension: anti-roll bar.

DIMENSIONS AND WEIGHT weight: Vista Turbo Diesel VL and Camry XT sedans 2,348 lb, 1,065 kg - Vista Turbo Diesel VE and Camry SE sedans 2,381 lb, 1,080 kg - Vista Turbo Diesel VE Liftback Coupé 2,425 lb, 1,100 kg.

OPTIONALS automatic transmission, hydraulic torque converter and planetary gears with 4 ratios (I 2.810, II 1.549, III 1, IV 0.706, rev 2.296), 3.729 axle ratio.

Mark II / Chaser Series

	PRICES (Tokyo):	yen
1	Mark II 1800 STD 4-dr Sedan	1,084,000
2	Mark II 1800 DX 4-dr Sedan	1,161,000
3	Mark II 1800 GL 4-dr Sedan	1,223,000
4	Mark II 1800 GL 4-dr Hardtop	1,280,000
5	Mark II 1800 GR 4-dr Sedan	1,372,000
6	Mark II 1800 GR 4-dr Hardtop	1,427,000
7	Chaser 1800 STD 4-dr Sedan	1,099,000
8	Chaser 1800 DX 4-dr Sedan	1,178,000
9	Chaser 1800 XL 4-dr Sedan	1,242,000
10	Chaser 1800 XL 4-dr Hardtop	1,293,000
11	Chaser 1800 XG 4-dr Sedan	1,379,000
12	Chaser 1800 XG 4-dr Hardtop	1,540,000
13	Mark II 2000 LE 4-dr Sedan	1,472,000
14	Mark II 2000 LE 4-dr Hardtop	1,530,000
15	Mark II 2000 LG 4-dr Sedan	1,647,000
16	Mark II 2000 LG 4-dr Hardtop	1,704,000
17	Mark II 2000 Grande 4-dr Sedan	2,025,000
18	Mark II 2000 Grande 4-dr Hardtop	2,073,000
19	Mark II 2000 LE 4+1-dr St. Wagon	1,540,000
20	Chaser 2000 SXL 4-dr Sedan	1,557,000
21	Chaser 2000 SXL 4-dr Hardtop	1,608,000
22	Chaser 2000 Avante 4-dr Sedan	1,994,000
23	Chaser 2000 Avante 4-dr Hardtop	2,064,000
24	Mark II 2000 Grande twin cam 24 4-dr Sedan	2,310,000
25	Mark II 2000 Grande twin cam 24 4-dr Hardtop	2,358,000
26	Chaser 2000 Avante twin cam 24 4-dr Sedan	2,304,000
27	Chaser 2000 Avante twin cam 24 4-dr Hardtop	2,349,000
28	Mark II 2000 Turbo LG Touring 4-dr Sedan	1,780,000
29	Mark II 2000 Turbo LG Touring 4-dr Hardtop	1,831,000
30	Mark II 2000 Turbo Grande 4-dr Sedan	2,294,000
31	Mark II 2000 Turbo Grande 4-dr Hardtop	2,342,000
32	Chaser 2000 Turbo SG Touring 4-dr Sedan	1,772,000
33	Chaser 2000 Turbo SG Touring 4-dr Hardtop	1,833,000
34	Chaser 2000 Turbo Avante 4-dr Sedan	2,263,000
35	Chaser 2000 Turbo Avante 4-dr Hardtop	2,333,000
36	Mark II 2200 Diesel DX 4-dr Sedan	1,337,000
37	Mark II 2200 Diesel GL 4-dr Sedan	1,398,000
38	Chaser 2200 Diesel DX 4-dr Sedan	1,344,000
39	Chaser 2200 Diesel XL 4-dr Sedan	1,407,000
40	Mark II 2400 Turbo Diesel LE 4-dr Sedan	1,761,000
41	Chaser 2400 Turbo Diesel SXL 4-dr Sedan	1,772,000

TOYOTA Mark II 2000 Grande Sedan

For USA prices, see price index.

Power team:	Standard for:	Optional for:
100 hp	1 to 12	—
125 hp	13 to 23	—
145 hp	28 to 35	—
160 hp	24 to 27	—
72 hp (diesel)	36 to 39	—
96 hp (diesel)	40,41	—

100 hp power team

ENGINE front, transverse, 4 stroke; 4 cylinders, in line; 111.7 cu in, 1,832 cc (3.16 x 3.54 in, 80.5 x 90 mm); compression ratio: 9:1; max power (JIS): 100 hp (74 kW) at 5,400 rpm; max torque (JIS): 112 lb ft, 15.5 kg m (152 Nm) at 3,400 rpm; max engine rpm: 6,000; 54.6 hp/l (40.2 kW/l); cast iron block, light alloy head; 5 crankshaft bearings; valves: overhead, hydraulic tappets, rockers; camshafts: 1, overhead, cogged belt, chain-driven; lubrication: trochoid pump, full flow filter; 1 N-type downdraught twin barrel carburettor; emission control with catalytic converter, secondary air induction and exhaust gas recirculation; fuel feed: mechanical pump; water-cooled.

TRANSMISSION driving wheels: rear; clutch: single dry plate (diaphragm); gearbox: mechanical; gears: 5, fully synchronized; ratios: I 3.566, II 2.056, III 1.384, IV 1, V 0.850, rev 4.091; lever: central; final drive: hypoid bevel; axle ratio: 3.727; width of rims: 5''; tyres: STD, DX, GL and XL models 6.45 x 14 - XG and GR models 175 SR x 14.

PERFORMANCE power-weight ratio: Mark II STD 23.2 lb/hp (31.6 lb/kW), 10.5 kg/hp (14.3 kg/kW); carrying capacity: 882 lb, 400 kg; consumption: 34.4 m/imp gal, 28.7 m/US gal, 8.2 l x 100 km on Japanese emission test cycle.

CHASSIS integral; front suspension: independent, by McPherson, lower transverse arms, diagonal trailing locating rods, coil springs/telescopic damper struts, anti-roll bar; rear: rigid axle, lower trailing links, upper torque rods, coil springs, Panhard rod, telescopic dampers.

STEERING recirculating ball, variable ratio - GR and XG models servo; turns lock to lock: 4.30.

BRAKES front disc, rear drum, servo; lining area: front 25.4 sq in, 164 sq cm, rear 53.9 sq in, 348 sq cm, total 79.3 sq in, 512 sq cm.

ELECTRICAL EQUIPMENT 12 V; 33 Ah battery; 55 A alternator; Nihon Denso distributor; 4 headlamps.

DIMENSIONS AND WEIGHT wheel base: 104.13 in, 261 cm; front and rear track: 53.93 in, 137 cm; length: Mark II STD, DX and GL models 178.54 in, 453 cm - other models 183.85 in, 467 cm; width: Mark II STD and DX sedans 65.74 in, 167 cm - GL sedans 66.14 in, 168 cm - other models 66.53 in, 169 cm; height: sedans 56.10 in, 142 cm - hardtops 54.72 in, 139 cm; weight: Mark II STD and DX sedans 2,326 lb, 1,055 kg - Mark II GL and Chaser STD and DX sedans 2,359 lb, 1,070 kg - Chaser XL Sedan 2,392 lb, 1,085 kg - Mark II GL and Chaser XL hardtops 2,403 lb, 1,090 kg - Mark II GR Sedan 2,458 lb, 1,115 kg - Mark II GR Hardtop 2,469 lb, 1,120 kg - Chaser XG Sedan 2,491 lb, 1,130 kg - Chaser XG Hardtop 2,502 lb, 1,135 kg; ground clearance: 6.69 in, 17 cm; turning circle: 38 ft, 11.6 m; fuel tank: 14.3 imp gal, 17.2 US gal, 65 l.

BODY saloon/sedan - hardtop; 4 doors; 5 seats, separate front seats.

OPTIONALS automatic transmission, hydraulic torque converter and planetary gears with 4 ratios (I 2.452, II 1.452, III 1, IV 0.688, rev 2.212), 4.100 axle ratio.

125 hp power team

See 100 hp power team, except for:

ENGINE 6 cylinders, in line; 121.3 cu in, 1,988 cc (2.95 x 2.95 in, 75 x 75 mm); compression ratio: 8.8:1; max power (JIS): 125 hp (92 kW) at 5,400 rpm; max torque (JIS): 126 lb ft, 17.5 kg m (172 Nm) at 4,400 rpm; 62.9 hp/l (46.2 kW/l); 7 crankshaft bearings; camshafts: 1, overhead, cogged belt; lubrication: 9.4 imp pt, 11.2 US pt, 5.3 l; Denso-Bosch L-Jetronic injection; 3-way catalytic converter with oxygen sensor; fuel feed: electric pump.

TRANSMISSION tyres: LE, LG and SXL models 175 SR x 14 - other models 185/70 HR x 14.

PERFORMANCE max speeds: (I) 32 mph, 52 km/h; (II) 54 mph, 87 km/h; (III) 81 mph, 130 km/h; (IV) and (V) 109 mph, 175 km/h; power-weight ratio: Mark II LE models 19.6 lb/hp (26.7 lb/kW), 8.9 kg/hp (12.1 kg/kW); speed in top at 1,000 rpm: 28 mph, 45 km/h; consumption: 28.2 m/imp gal, 23.5 m/US gal, 10 l x 100 km on Japanese emission test cycle.

CHASSIS rear suspension: LE, LG and SXL models rigid axle, lower trailing arms, upper torque rods, Panhard rods, coil springs, telescopic dampers - other models independent, semi-trailing arms, coil springs, anti-roll bar, telescopic dampers.

STEERING LG and Avante models servo; turns lock to lock: 3.30.

ELECTRICAL EQUIPMENT 60 Ah battery; 60 A alternator; electronic contactless ignition.

DIMENSIONS AND WEIGHT length: 183 in, 464 cm; width: 66.50 in, 169 cm; weight: Mark II LE models 2,458 lb, 1,115 kg - Mark II LG models 2,525 lb, 1,145 kg - Mark II Grande models 2,700 lb, 1,225 kg - Chaser SXL models 2,491 lb, 1,130 kg - Chaser Avante models 2,689 lb, 1,220 kg; weight distribution: 53% front, 47% rear.

BODY saloon/sedan, 4 doors - hardtop, 4 doors - estate car/st. wagon, 4+1 doors.

OPTIONALS automatic transmission, hydraulic torque converter and planetary gears with 4 ratios (I 2.452, II 1.452, III 1, IV 0.688, rev 2.212).

145 hp power team

See 100 hp power team, except for:

ENGINE turbocharged; 6 cylinders, in line; 121.3 cu in, 1,988 cc (2.95 x 2.95 in, 75 x 75 mm); compression ratio:

TOYOTA Mark II 2000 Grande Sedan

TOYOTA Chaser 2000 Avante Hardtop

7.6:1; max power (JIS): 145 hp (107 kW) at 5,600 rpm; max torque (JIS): 156 lb ft, 21.5 kgm (211 Nm) at 3,000 rpm; 72.9 hp/l (53.7 kW/l); 7 crankshaft bearings; valves: overhead, Vee-slanted, rockers; camshafts: 1, overhead, chain-driven; lubrication: gear pump, full flow filter, 10.9 imp pt, 13.1 US pt, 6.2 l; Toyota EFI electronic injection; turbocharger with exhaust wastegate and twin knock sensor; 3-way catalytic converter with oxygen sensor; fuel feed: electric pump; cooling: 19.4 imp pt, 23.3 US pt, 11 l.

TRANSMISSION (standard) gearbox: automatic transmission, hydraulic torque converter and planetary gears with 4 ratios, possible manual selection; ratios: I 2.452, II 1.452, III 1, IV 0.688, rev 2.212; axle ratio: 4.100; tyres: 185/70 HR x 14.

PERFORMANCE max speed: 112 mph, 180 km/h; power-weight ratio: Mark II Turbo LG Touring Sedan 18.8 lb/hp (25.6 lb/kW), 8.5 kg/hp (11.6 kg/kW); consumption: 23.9 m/imp gal, 19.9 m/US gal, 11.8 l x 100 km on Japanese emission test cycle.

CHASSIS rear suspension: independent, semi-trailing arms, coil springs, anti-roll bar, telescopic dampers.

STEERING servo; turns lock to lock: 3.30.

BRAKES disc, front internal radial fins.

DIMENSIONS AND WEIGHT front and rear track: 54.72 in, 139 cm; weight: Mark II Turbo LG Touring and Chaser Turbo SG Touring sedans 2,734 lb, 1,240 kg - Mark II Turbo Grande and Chaser Turbo Avante sedans 2,789 lb, 1,265 kg - Mark II Turbo LG Touring and Chaser Turbo SG Touring hardtops 2,745 lb, 1,245 kg - Mark II Turbo Grande and Chaser Turbo Avante hardtops 2,789 lb, 1,265 kg.

160 hp power team

See 100 hp power team, except for:

ENGINE 6 cylinders, in line; 121.3 cu in, 1,988 cc (2.95 x 2.95 in, 75 x 75 mm); compression ratio: 9.1:1; max power (JIS): 160 hp (118 kW) at 6,400 rpm; max torque (JIS): 134 lb ft, 18.5 kgm (181 Nm) at 5,200 rpm; max engine rpm: 6,800; 80.5 hp/l (59.2 kW/l); 7 crankshaft bearings; valves: overhead, thimble tappets; camshafts: 2, overhead, cogged belt, chain-driven; lubrication: 9.3 imp pt, 11.2 US pt, 5.3 l; electronic fuel injection; fuel feed: electric pump; emission by 3-way catalytic converter with oxygen sensor; cooling: 12.3 imp pt, 14.8 US pt, 7 l.

TRANSMISSION axle ratio: 4.100; width of rims: 5.5"; tyres: 185/70 SR x 14.

PERFORMANCE max speed: 112 mph, 180 km/h; power-weight ratio: Mark II Grande twin cam 24 Sedan 17.2 lb/hp (23.3 lb/kW), 7.8 kg/hp (10.6 kg/kW); consumption: 31.4 m/imp gal, 26.1 m/US gal, 9.1 l x 100 km on Japanese emission test cycle.

CHASSIS rear suspension: independent, semi-trailing arms, coil springs, telescopic dampers, anti-roll bar.

STEERING servo; turns lock to lock: 3.10.

BRAKES disc, internal radial fins, servo.

ELECTRICAL EQUIPMENT 50 Ah battery; 70 Ah alternator.

DIMENSIONS AND WEIGHT front and rear track: 54.72 in, 139 cm; length: 183.85 in, 467 cm; weight: Chaser Avante twin cam 24 Sedan 2,734 lb, 1,240 kg - Mark II Grande twin cam 24 models and Chaser Avante twin cam 24 Hardtop 2,745 lb, 1,245 kg.

72 hp (diesel) power team

See 100 hp power team, except for:

ENGINE diesel; 134 cu in, 2,188 cc (3.50 x 3.40 in, 90 x 86 mm); compression ratio: 21.5:1; max power (JIS): 72 hp (53 kW) at 4,200 rpm; max torque (JIS): 105 lb ft, 14.5 kg m (142 Nm) at 2,400 rpm; max engine rpm: 4,500; 32.9 hp/l (24.2 kW/l); lubrication: gear pump, 11.4 imp pt, 13.7 US pt, 6.5 l; Bosch injection pump; Ricardo Comet swirl combustion chambers; cooling: 17.6 imp pt, 21.1 US pt, 10 l.

PERFORMANCE max speeds: (I) 24 mph, 38 km/h; (II) 39 mph, 63 km/h; (III) 58 mph, 93 km/h; (IV) 81 mph, 130 km/h; (V) 87 mph, 140 km/h; power-weight ratio: DX sedans 35.1 lb/hp (47.6 lb/kW), 15.9 kg/hp (21.6 kg/kW); consumption: 62.8 m/imp gal, 52.3 m/US gal, 4.5 l x 100 km at 37 mph, 60 km/h on Japanese emission test cycle.

CHASSIS rear suspension: rigid axle, lower trailing arms, upper torque arms, upper torque rods, Panhard rod, coil springs, telescopic dampers.

STEERING GL servo.

ELECTRICAL EQUIPMENT 60 Ah battery.

DIMENSIONS AND WEIGHT length: 182.50 in, 464 cm; width: 67.50 in, 169 cm; weight: Chaser Diesel DX and Mark II Diesel DX sedans 2,524 lb, 1,145 kg - Mark II Diesel GL Sedan 2,579 lb, 1,170 kg.

BODY saloon/sedan.

OPTIONALS 5-speed fully synchronized mechanical gearbox (I 3.287, II 2.043, III 1.394, IV 1, V 0.853); automatic transmission, hydraulic torque converter and planetary gears with 4 ratios (I 2.452, II 1.452, III 1, IV 0.688, rev 2.212), 4.100 axle ratio.

96 hp (diesel) power team

See 100 hp power team, except for:

ENGINE turbocharged, diesel; 149.2 cu in, 2,446 cc (3.62 x 3.62 in, 92 x 92 mm); compression ratio: 20:1; max power (JIS): 96 hp (71 kW) at 4,000 rpm; max torque (JIS): 141 lb ft, 19.5 kg m (191 Nm) at 2,400 rpm; max engine rpm: 4,400; 39.2 hp/l (28.9 kW/l); cast iron block and head; lubrication: 11.4 imp pt, 13.7 US pt, 6.5 l; electronic injection; modified Ricardo Comet swirl chambers; exhaust turbocharger with wastegate; cooling: 17.6 imp pt, 21.1 US pt, 10 l.

TRANSMISSION (standard) automatic transmission, hydraulic torque converter and planetary gears with 4 ratios; ratios: I 2.452, II 1.452, III 1, IV 0.688, rev 2.212; axle ratio: 3.909; tyres: 175 SR x 14.

PERFORMANCE power-weight ratio: Mark II LE 29.2 lb/hp (39.7 lb/kW), 13.2 kg/hp (18 kg/kW); consumption: 56.5 m/imp gal, 47 m/US gal, 5 l x 100 km at 37 mph, 60 km/h on Japanese emission test cycle.

CHASSIS rear suspension: independent, semi-trailing arms, coil springs, telescopic dampers.

DIMENSIONS AND WEIGHT length: 183.85 in, 467 cm; width: 66.53 in, 169 cm; height: 55.90 in, 142 cm; weight: Mark II Turbo Diesel LE and Chaser Turbo Diesel SXL sedans 2,800 lb, 1,270 kg.

BODY saloon/sedan.

OPTIONALS power steering.

Cresta Series

	PRICES (Tokyo):	yen
1	1800 Custom 4-dr Hardtop	**1,271,000**
2	1800 Super Custom 4-dr Hardtop	**1,402,000**
3	2000 Super De Luxe 4-dr Hardtop	**1,582,000**
4	2000 Super Lucent 4-dr Hardtop	**2,030,000**
5	2000 Super Lucent twin cam 24 4-dr Hardtop	**2,315,000**
6	2000 Turbo Super Touring 4-dr Hardtop	**1,820,000**
7	2000 Turbo Super Lucent 4-dr Hardtop	**2,299,000**
8	2200 Diesel Custom 4-dr Hardtop	**1,427,000**
9	2200 Diesel Super Custom 4-dr Hardtop	**1,613,000**

Power team:	Standard for:	Optional for:
100 hp	1,2	—
125 hp	3,4	—
145 hp	6,7	—
160 hp	5	—
72 hp (diesel)	8,9	—

100 hp power team

ENGINE front, transverse, 4 stroke; 4 cylinders, in line; 111.7 cu in, 1,832 cc (3.16 x 3.54 in, 80.5 x 90 mm); compression ratio: 9:1; max power (JIS): 100 hp (74 kW) at 5,400 rpm; max torque (JIS): 112 lb ft, 15.5 kg m (152 Nm) at 3,400 rpm; max engine rpm: 6,000; 54.6 hp/l (40.2 kW/l); cast iron block, light alloy head; 5 crankshaft bearings; valves: overhead, hydraulic tappets, rockers; camshafts: 1, overhead, cogged belt, chain-driven; lubrication: trochoid pump, full flow filter; 1 N-Type downdraught twin barrel carburettor; emission control with catalytic converter, secondary air induction and exhaust gas recirculation; fuel feed: mechanical pump; water-cooled.

TRANSMISSION driving wheels: rear; clutch: single dry plate (diaphragm); gearbox: mechanical; gears: 5, fully synchronized; ratios: I 3.566, II 2.056, III 1.384, IV 1, V 0.850, rev 4.091; lever: central; final drive: hypoid bevel; axle ratio: 3.727; width of rims: 5"; tyres: Custom 6.45 x 14 - Super Custom 175 SR x 14.

PERFORMANCE power-weight ratio: Custom 24 lb/hp (32.7 lb/kW), 10.9 kg/hp (14.8 kg/kW); consumption: 34.4 m/imp gal, 28.7 m/US gal, 8.2 l x 100 km on Japanese emission test cycle.

CHASSIS integral; front suspension: independent, by McPherson, lower transverse arms, diagonal locating links, anti-roll bar, telescopic dampers; rear: rigid axle, lower trailing arms, upper torque rods, Panhard rod, coil springs, telescopic dampers.

STEERING recirculating ball - Super Custom servo; turns lock to lock: 4.20 - Super Custom 3.30.

TOYOTA Cresta 2000 Super Lucent Hardtop

100 HP POWER TEAM

BRAKES front disc, rear drum, servo; lining area: front 25.4 sq in, 164 sq cm, rear 53.9 sq in, 348 sq cm, total 79.3 sq in, 512 sq cm.

ELECTRICAL EQUIPMENT 12 V; 35 Ah battery; 55 A alternator; contactless transistorized ignition; 4 headlamps.

DIMENSIONS AND WEIGHT wheel base: 104.13 in, 264 cm; front and rear track: 53.93 in, 137 cm; length: 183.85 in, 467 cm; width: 66.53 in, 169 cm; height: 54.72 in, 139 cm; weight: Custom Hardtop 2,403 lb, 1,090 kg - Super Custom Hardtop 2,469 lb, 1,120 kg; ground clearance: 6.70 in, 17 cm; turning circle: 38 ft, 11.6 m; fuel tank: 14.3 imp gal, 17.2 US gal, 65 l.

BODY hardtop; 4 doors; 5 seats, separate front seats.

OPTIONALS automatic transmission, hydraulic torque converter and planetary gears with 4 ratios (I 2.452, II 1.452, III 1, IV 0.688, rev 2.212), 4.100 axle ratio.

125 hp power team

See 100 hp power team, except for:

ENGINE 6 cylinders, in line; 121 cu in, 1,988 cc (2.95 x 2.95 in, 75 x 75 mm); compression ratio: 8.8:1; max power (JIS): 125 hp (92 kW) at 5,400 rpm; max torque (JIS): 126 lb ft, 17.5 kg m (172 Nm) at 4,400 rpm; 62.9 hp/l (46.2 kW/l); 7 crankshaft bearings; camshafts: 1, overhead, cogged belt; lubrication: 9.4 imp pt, 11.2 US pt, 5.3 l; Denso-Bosch L-Jetronic injection; 3-way catalytic converter with oxygen sensor; fuel feed: electric pump; cooling: 12.5 imp pt, 14.8 US pt, 7 l.

TRANSMISSION width of rims: 5.5"; tyres: Super De Luxe 175 SR x 14 - Super Lucent 185/70 HR x 14.

PERFORMANCE max speeds: (I) 33 mph, 53 km/h; (II) 57 mph, 92 km/h; (III) 78 mph, 126 km/h; (IV) and (V) 109 mph, 175 km/h; power-weight ratio: Super De Luxe 19.8 lb/hp (26.8 lb/kW), 9 kg/hp (12.2 kg/kW); speed in top at 1,000 rpm: 18.1 mph, 29.2 km/h; consumption: 27.5 m/imp gal, 23.3 m/US gal, 10.2 l x 100 km on Japanese emission test cycle.

CHASSIS Super Lucent rear suspension: independent, semi-trailing arms, coil springs, anti-roll bar, telescopic dampers.

STEERING servo; turns lock to lock: 3.30.

BRAKES Super Lucent rear disc.

ELECTRICAL EQUIPMENT 60 Ah battery.

DIMENSIONS AND WEIGHT weight: Super De Luxe Hardtop 2,469 lb, 1,120 kg - Super Lucent Hardtop 2,657 lb, 1,205 kg; weight distribution: 52% front, 48% rear.

145 hp power team

See 100 hp power team, except for:

ENGINE turbocharged; 6 cylinders, in line; 121 cu in, 1,988 cc (2.95 x 2.95 in, 75 x 75 mm); compression ratio: 7.6:1; max power (JIS): 145 hp (107 kW) at 5,600 rpm; max torque (JIS): 149 lb ft, 21.5 kg m (211 Nm) at 3,000 rpm; 72.9 hp/l (53.7 kW/l); 7 crankshaft bearings; camshafts: 1, overhead, chain-driven; lubrication: gear pump, full flow filter, 10.9 imp pt, 13.1 US pt, 6.2 l; Toyota EFI electronic injection; turbocharger with exhaust wastegate and twin knock sensor; cooling: 19.4 imp pt, 23.3 US pt, 11 l.

TRANSMISSION (standard) gearbox: automatic transmission, hydraulic torque converter and planetary gears with 4 ratios, possible manual selection; ratios: I 2.452, II 1.452, III 1, IV 0.688, rev 2.212; axle ratio: 4.100; tyres: 185/70 HR x 14.

TOYOTA Cresta 2000 Super Lucent Hardtop

PERFORMANCE max speed: 112 mph, 180 km/h; power-weight ratio: 19.2 lb/hp (26.2 lb/kW), 8.7 kg/hp (12.4 kg/kW); consumption: 23.8 m/imp gal, 19.9 m/US gal, 11.8 l x 100 km on Japanese emission test cycle.

CHASSIS rear suspension: independent, semi-trailing arms, anti-roll bar, telescopic dampers.

STEERING servo.

BRAKES disc, front internal radial fins.

DIMENSIONS AND WEIGHT front and rear track: 54.77 in, 139 cm; weight: 2,789 lb, 1,265 kg.

160 hp power team

See 100 hp power team, except for:

ENGINE 6 cylinders, in line; 121.3 cu in, 1,988 cc (2.95 x 2.95 in, 75 x 75 mm); max power (JIS): 160 hp (118 kW) at 6,400 rpm; max torque (JIS): 134 lb ft, 18.5 kg m (181 Nm) at 5,200 rpm; max engine rpm: 6,800; 80.5 hp/l (59.2 kW/l); 7 crankshaft bearings; valves: overhead, thimble tappets; camshafts: 2, overhead, cogged belt, chain-driven; lubrication: 9.3 imp pt, 11.2 US pt, 5.3 l; electronic fuel injection; fuel feed: electric pump; emission by 3-way catalytic converter with oxygen sensor; cooling: 12.3 imp pt, 14.8 US pt, 7 l.

TRANSMISSION axle ratio: 4.100; width of rims: 5.5"; tyres: 185/70 SR x 14.

PERFORMANCE max speed: 112 mph, 180 km/h; power-weight ratio: 17.2 lb/hp (23.3 lb/kW), 7.8 kg/hp (10.6 kg/kW); consumption: 31.4 m/imp gal, 26.1 m/US gal, 9.1 l x 100 km on Japanese emission test cycle.

CHASSIS rear suspension: independent, semi-trailing arms, coil springs, anti-roll bar, telescopic dampers.

STEERING servo; turns lock to lock: 3.10.

ELECTRICAL EQUIPMENT 50 Ah battery; 70 Ah alternator.

DIMENSIONS AND WEIGHT front and rear track: 54.72 in, 139 cm; weight: 2,745 lb, 1,245 kg.

TOYOTA Soarer 2800 GT Limited Coupé

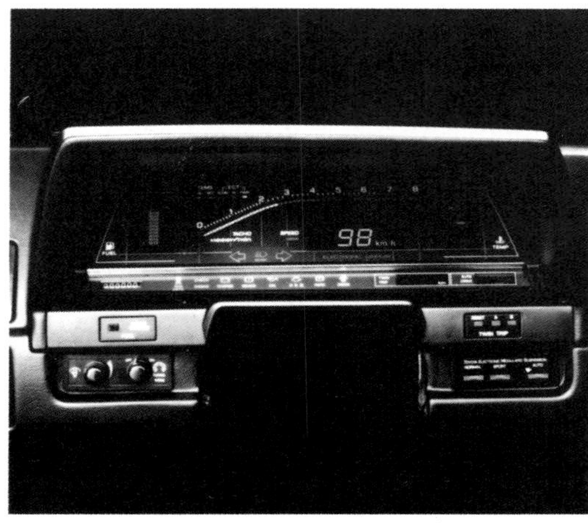

TOYOTA Soarer 2800 GT Limited Coupé

72 hp (diesel) power team

See 100 hp power team, except for:

ENGINE diesel; 134 cu in, 2,188 cc (3.50 x 3.40 in, 90 x 86 mm); compression ratio: 21.5:1; max power (JIS): 72 hp (53 kW) at 4,200 rpm; max torque (JIS): 105 lb ft, 14.5 kg m (142 Nm) at 2,400 rpm; max engine rpm: 4,500; 54.6 hp/l (44.2 kW/l); lubrication: gear pump, full flow filter, 11.4 imp pt, 13.7 US pt, 6.5 l; Bosch VE injection pump; Ricardo Comet swirl combustion chambers; cooling: 17.6 imp pt, 21.1 US pt, 10 l.

TRANSMISSION axle ratio: 3.909.

PERFORMANCE max speeds: (I) 24 mph, 38 km/h; (II) 29 mph, 63 km/h; (III) 58 mph, 93 km/h; (IV) 81 mph, 130 km/h; (V) 87 mph, 140 km/h; power-weight ratio: Custom 36.7 lb/hp (49.9 lb/kW), 16.6 kg/hp (22.6 kg/kW); consumption: 62.8 m/imp gal, 52.3 m/US gal, 4.5 l x 100 km at 37 mph, 60 km/h on Japanese emission test cycle.

STEERING servo.

DIMENSIONS AND WEIGHT weight: Diesel Custom Hardtop 2,646 lb, 1,200 kg - Diesel Super Custom Hardtop 2,712 lb, 1,230 kg.

OPTIONALS automatic transmission, hydraulic torque converter and planetary gears with 4 ratios (I 2.452, II 1.452, III 1, IV 0.688, rev 2.212), 4.100 axle ratio.

Soarer Series

PRICES (Tokyo):	yen
1 2000 VII 2-dr Coupé	**1,919,000**
2 2000 VR 2-dr Coupé	**2,052,000**
3 2000 VX 2-dr Coupé	**2,343,000**
4 2000 Turbo 2-dr Coupé	**2,453,000**
5 2000 GT 2-dr Coupé	**2,708,000**
6 2800 GT 2-dr Coupé	**2,911,000**
7 2800 GT Limited 2-dr Coupé	**3,422,000**

Power team:	Standard for:	Optional for:
125 hp	1 to 3	—
160 hp (1,988 cc)	5	—
160 hp (1,988 cc, turbocharged)	4	—
170 hp	6,7	—

125 hp power team

ENGINE front, 4 stroke; 6 cylinders, in line; 121.3 cu in, 1,988 cc (2.95 x 2.95 in, 75 x 75 mm); compression ratio: 8.8:1; max power (JIS): 125 hp (92 kW) at 5,400 rpm; max torque (JIS): 127 lb ft, 17.5 kg m (172 Nm) at 4,400 rpm; max engine rpm: 6,000; 62.9 hp/l (46.2 kW/l); cast iron block, light alloy head; 7 crankshaft bearings; valves: overhead, rockers, hydraulic tappets; camshafts: 1, overhead, cogged belt; lubrication: gear pump, full flow filter, 9.2 imp pt, 11.1 US pt, 5.3 l; Toyota EFI electronic injection; fuel feed: electric pump; emission by 3-way catalytic converter; water-cooled, 12.3 imp pt, 14.8 US pt, 7 l.

TRANSMISSION driving wheels: front; clutch: single dry plate (diaphragm); gearbox: mechanical; gears: 5, fully synchronized; ratios: I 3.285, II 1.894, III 1.275, IV 1, V 0.860, rev 3.768; lever: central; final drive: hypoid bevel; axle ratio: 3.909; width of rims: 5.5"; tyres: 185/70 HR x 14 - VR 195/70 HR x 14.

PERFORMANCE max speeds: (I) 31 mph, 50 km/h; (II) 55 mph, 88 km/h; (III) 82 mph, 132 km/h; (IV) and (V) 112 mph, 180 km/h; power-weight ratio: VII 20.5 lb/hp (27.9 lb/kW), 9.3 kg/hp (12.7 kg/kW); consumption: 30 m/imp gal, 25 m/US gal, 9.4 l x 100 km on Japanese emission test cycle.

CHASSIS integral; front suspension: independent, by McPherson, transverse arms, trailing links, coil springs/telescopic damper struts, anti-roll bar; rear: independent, semi-trailing arms, coil springs/telescopic damper struts, anti-roll bar.

STEERING rack-and-pinion, servo; turns lock to lock: 3.50.

BRAKES disc, dual circuit, servo.

ELECTRICAL EQUIPMENT 12 V; 60 Ah battery; 60 A alternator; electronic ignition; 4 headlamps.

DIMENSIONS AND WEIGHT wheel base: 104.72 in, 266 cm; tracks: 55.91 in, 142 cm front, 56.30 in, 143 cm rear; length: 183.07 in, 465 cm; width: 66.54 in, 169 cm; height: 53.54 in, 136 cm; ground clearance: 6.50 in, 16.5 cm; weight: VII Coupé 2,602 lb, 1,180 kg - VR Coupé 2,613 lb, 1,185 kg - VX Coupé 2,690 lb, 1,220 kg; weight distribution: 52% front, 48% rear; turning circle: 39.4 ft, 12 m; fuel tank: 11.2 imp gal, 13.4 US gal, 61 l.

BODY coupé; 2 doors; 5 seats, separate front seats.

OPTIONALS automatic transmission, hydraulic torque converter and planetary gears with 4 ratios (I 2.452, II 1.452, III 1, IV 0.688, rev 2.212), 4.100 axle ratio, max speed 109 mph, 175 km/h, consumption 23.9 m/imp gal, 19.9 m/US gal, 11.8 l x 100 km on Japanese emission test cycle.

160 hp (1,988 cc) power team

See 125 hp power team, except for:

ENGINE compression ratio: 9.1:1; max power (JIS): 160 hp (118 kW) at 6,400 rpm; max torque (JIS): 134 lb ft, 18.5 kg m (181 Nm) at 5,200 rpm; max engine rpm: 6,800; 80.5 hp/l (59.2 kW/l); valves: overhead, Vee-slanted, thimble tappets; camshafts: 2, overhead, cogged belt, chain-driven; lubrication: trochoid pump; TCCS electronic fuel injection; emission by 3-way catalytic converter with oxygen sensor.

TRANSMISSION gearbox ratios: I 3.566, II 2.056, III 1.384, IV 1, V 0.850, rev 4.091; axle ratio: 4.100; tyres: 205/60 R x 15 H.

PERFORMANCE max speeds: (I) 33 moh, 54 km/h; (II) 58 mph, 93 km/h; (III) 86 mph, 138 km/h; (IV) and (V) 112 mph, 180 km/h; power-weight ratio: 16.9 lb/hp (23 lb/kW), 7.7 kg/hp (10.4 kg/kW); consumption: 31 m/imp gal, 25.8 m/US gal, 9.1 l x 100 km on Japanese emission test cycle.

BRAKES rear internal radial fins.

DIMENSIONS AND WEIGHT weight: 2,712 lb, 1,230 kg.

OPTIONALS automatic transmission, hydraulic torque converter and planetary gears with 4 ratios (I 2.452, II 1.452, III 1, IV 0.688, rev 2.212).

160 hp (1,988 cc, turbocharged) power team

See 125 hp power team, except for:

ENGINE turbocharged; compression ratio: 8:1; max power (JIS): 160 hp (118 kW) at 6,400 rpm; max torque (JIS): 134 lb ft, 18.5 kg m (181 Nm) at 5,200 rpm; valves: overhead, Vee-slanted, rockers; camshafts: 1, overhead, chain-driven; lubrication: 10.9 imp pt, 13.1 US pt, 6.2 l; turbocharger with exhaust wastegate and twin knock sensor; cooling: 19.4 imp pt, 23.3 US pt, 11 l.

TRANSMISSION (standard) gearbox: automatic transmission, hydraulic torque converter and planetary gears with 4 ratios, possible manual selection; ratios: I 2.452, II 1.452, III 1, IV 0.688, rev 2.212; axle ratio: 4.300; tyres: 205/60 R x 15 H.

PERFORMANCE power-weight ratio: 17.3 lb/hp (23.5 lb/kW), 7.8 kg/hp (10.6 kg/kW); consumption: 31 m/imp gal, 25.8 m/US gal, 9.1 l x 100 km on Japanese emission test cycle.

BRAKES internal radial fins.

DIMENSIONS AND WEIGHT tracks: 56.69 in, 144 cm front, 57.09 in, 145 cm rear; weight: 2,767 lb, 1,255 kg.

OPTIONALS auomatic transmission not available.

170 hp power team

See 125 hp power team, except for:

ENGINE 168.4 cu in, 2,759 cc (3.23 x 3.35 in, 83 x 85 mm); max power (JIS): 170 hp (125 kW) at 5,600 rpm; max torque (JIS): 174 lb ft, 24 kg m (235 Nm) at 4,400 rpm; 61.6 hp/l (45.3 kW/l); camshafts: 2, overhead; lubrication: 10 imp pt, 12 US pt, 5.7 l; emission control by 3-way catalytic converter and exhaust gas recirculation; cooling: 14.1 imp pt, 16.9 US pt, 8 l.

TRANSMISSION axle ratio: 3.727; tyres: 205/60 R x 15 H.

PERFORMANCE max speeds: (I) 35 mph, 56 km/h; (II) 60 mph, 97 km/h; (III) 89 mph, 144 km/h; (IV) and (V) 112 mph, 180 km/h; power-weight ratio: GT Coupé 17 lb/hp (22.9 lb/kW), 7.7 kg/hp (10.4 kg/kW); consumption: 25.2 m/imp gal, 21 m/US gal, 11.2 l x 100 km on Japanese emission test cycle.

BRAKES internal radial fins.

TOYOTA Supra 2800 GT Liftback Coupé

DIMENSIONS AND WEIGHT tracks: 56.69 in, 144 cm front, 57.09 in, 145 cm rear; weight: GT Coupé 2,877 lb, 1,305 kg.

OPTIONALS automatic transmission, hydraulic torque converter and planetary gears with 4 ratios (I 2.452, II 1.452, III 1, IV 0.688, rev 2.212).

Celica XX / Supra Series

PRICES (Tokyo):	yen
1 XX 2000 S 2+1-dr Liftback Coupé	**1,747,000**
2 XX 2000 G 2+1-dr Liftback Coupé	**1,908,000**
3 XX 2000 S Turbo 2+1-dr Liftback Coupé	**2,047,000**
4 XX 2000 G Turbo 2+1-dr Liftback Coupé	**2,229,000**
5 XX 2000 GT twin cam 2+1-dr Liftback Coupé	**2,167,000**
6 Supra 2800 GT 2+1-dr Liftback Coupé	**2,339,000**

For GB and USA prices, see price index.

Power team:	Standard for:	Optional for:
125 hp	1,2	—
160 hp (1,988 cc)	5	—
160 hp (1,988 cc turbocharged)	3,4	—
170 hp	6	—

125 hp power team

ENGINE front, 4 stroke; 6 cylinders, in line; 121.3 cu in, 1,988 cc (2.95 x 2.95 in, 75 x 75 mm); compression ratio: 8.8:1; max power (JIS): 125 hp (92 kW) at 6,000 rpm; max torque (JIS): 127 lb ft, 17.5 kg m (172 Nm) at 4,400 rpm; max engine rpm: 6,400; 62.9 hp/l (46.2 kW/l); cast iron block, light alloy head; 7 crankshaft bearings; valves: overhead, rockers, hydraulic tappets; camshafts: 1, overhead, cogged belt; lubrication: gear pump, full flow filter, 9.2 imp pt, 11.1 US pt, 5.3 l; Toyota-Denso electronic fuel injection; fuel feed: electric pump; emission control by secondary air induction, 3-way catalytic converter with oxygen sensor and exhaust gas recirculation; water-cooled, 12.7 imp pt, 14.8 US pt, 7 l.

TRANSMISSION driving wheels: rear; clutch: single dry plate (diaphragm); gearbox: mechanical; gears: 5, fully synchronized; ratios: I 3.285, II 1.894, III 1.275, IV 1, V 0.860, rev 3.768; lever: central; final drive: hypoid bevel; axle ratio: 3.909; width of rims: 5"; tyres: S 185/70 SR x 14 - G 195/70 SR x 14.

PERFORMANCE max speeds: (I) 33 mph, 54 km/h; (II) 54 mph, 87 km/h; (III) 85 mph, 137 km/h; (IV) and (V) 112 mph, 180 km/h; power-weight ratio: S 20.8 lb/hp (28.3 lb/kW), 9.4 kg/hp (12.8 kg/kW); consumption: 26.2 m/imp gal, 21.9 m/US gal, 10 l x 100 km on Japanese emission test cycle.

CHASSIS integral; front suspension: independent, by McPherson, trailing links, transverse arms, coil springs/telescopic damper struts, anti-roll bar; rear: independent, semi-trailing arms, upper torque rods, Panhard rod, coil springs/telescopic damper struts, anti-roll bar.

STEERING rack-and-pinion, servo; turns lock to lock: 3.10.

BRAKES front disc, internal radial fins, rear drum, servo.

ELECTRICAL EQUIPMENT 12 V; 40 Ah battery; 55 A alternator; Nihon-Denso pointless distributor; 2 headlamps.

DIMENSIONS AND WEIGHT wheel base: 102.76 in, 261 cm; tracks: 55.91 in, 142 cm front, 54.33 in, 138 cm rear; length: 183.46 in, 466 cm; width: 66.14 in, 168 cm; height: 51.57 in, 131 cm; ground clearance: 6.10 in, 15.5 cm; weight: XX S Liftback Coupé 2,602 lb, 1,180 kg - XX G Liftback Coupé 2,604 lb, 1,181 kg; weight distribution: 52% front, 48% rear; turning circle: 38.7 ft, 11.8 m; fuel tank: 13.4 imp gal, 16.1 US gal, 61 l.

BODY coupé; 2+1 doors; 4 seats, separate front seats.

OPTIONALS automatic transmission, hydraulic torque converter and planetary gears with 4 ratios (I 2.452, II 1.452, III 1, IV 0.688, rev 2.212), 4.300 axle ratio.

160 hp (1,988 cc) power team

See 125 hp power team, except for:

ENGINE compression ratio: 9.1:1; max power (JIS): 160 hp (118 kW) at 6,400 rpm; max torque (JIS): 134 lb ft, 18.5 kg m (181 Nm) at 5,200 rpm; max engine rpm: 6,800; 80.5 hp/l (59.2 kW/l); 7 crankshaft bearings; valves: overhead, thimble tappets; camshafts: 2, overhead, cogged belt, chain-driven; lubrication: trochoid pump, full flow filter, 9.3 imp pt, 11.2 US pt, 5.3 l; electronic fuel injection; emission by 3-way catalytic converter with oxygen sensor; cooling: 12.3 imp pt, 14.8 US pt, 7 l.

TRANSMISSION gearbox ratios: I 3.566, II 2.056, III 1.384, IV 1, V 0.850, rev 4.091; axle ratio: 4.300; width of rims: 5.5"; tyres: 195/70 SR x 14.

PERFORMANCE power-weight ratio: 16.7 lb/hp (22.6 lb/kW), 7.5 kg/hp (10.2 kg/kW); consumption: 31.4 m/imp gal, 26.1 m/US gal, 9 l x 100 km on Japanese emission test cycle.

DIMENSIONS AND WEIGHT weight: 2,668 lb, 1,210 kg.

OPTIONALS automatic transmission, hydraulic torque converter and planetary gears with 4 ratios (I 2.452, II 1.452, III 1, IV 0.688, rev 2.212).

160 hp (1,988 cc, turbocharged) power team

See 125 hp power team, except for:

ENGINE turbocharged; compression ratio: 8:1; max power (JIS): 160 hp (118 kW) at 5,400 rpm; max torque (JIS): 170 lb ft, 23.5 kg m (230 Nm) at 3,000 rpm; max engine rpm: 6,000; 80.4 hp/l (59.2 kW/l); 7 crankshaft bearings; valves: overhead, rockers; camshafts: 1, overhead, chain-driven; lubrication: 10.9 imp pt, 13.1 US pt, 6.2 l; turbocharger with

TOYOTA Supra 2800 GT Liftback Coupé

160 HP POWER TEAM

exhaust wastegate and twin knock sensor; cooling: 19.4 imp pt, 23.3 US pt, 11 l.

TRANSMISSION (standard) gearbox: automatic transmission, hydraulic torque converter and planetary geas with 4 ratios, possible manual selection; ; ratios: I 2.452, II 1.452, III 1, IV 0.688, rev 2.212; axle ratio: 4.300; width of rims: 5.5"; tyres: XXS 185/70 SR x 14 - XXG 195/70 SR x 14.

PERFORMANCE power-weight ratio: S 17.3 lb/hp (23.5 lb/kW), 7.8 kg/hp (10.6 kg/kW); consumption: 24.1 m/imp gal, 20.1 m/US gal, 11.7 l x 100 km on Japanese emission test cycle.

DIMENSIONS AND WEIGHT weight: XX/S Turbo Liftback Coupé 2,767 lb, 1,255 kg - XX G Turbo Liftback Coupé 2,778 lb, 1,260 kg.

OPTIONALS automatic transmission not available.

170 hp power team

See 125 hp power team, except for:

ENGINE 168.4 cu in, 2,759 cc (3.27 x 3.35 in, 83 x 85 mm); max power (JIS): 170 hp (125 kW) at 5,600 rpm; max torque (JIS): 174 lb ft, 24 kg m (235 Nm) at 4,400 rpm; 61.6 hp/l (45.3 kW/l); valves: overhead, Vee-slanted, rockers, hydraulic tappets; camshafts: 2, overhead, cogged belt; lubrication: 10 imp pt, 12 US pt, 5.7 l; Toyota EFI electronic injection; emission control by 3-way catalytic converter and exhaust gas recirculation; cooling: 14.1 imp pt, 16.9 US pt, 8 l.

TRANSMISSION gearbox ratios: I 3.255, II 1.894, III 1.275, IV 1, V 0.783, rev 3.768; tyres: 195/70 HR x 14.

PERFORMANCE max speeds: (I) 35 mph, 56 km/h; (II) 60 mph, 97 km/h; (III) 89 mph, 144 km/h; (IV) and (V) 112 mph, 180 km/h; power-weight ratio: 16 lb/hp (21.8 lb/kW), 7.2 kg/hp (39.5 kg/kW); consumption: 25.4 m/imp gal, 21.2 m/US gal, 11.1 l x 100 km on Japanese emission test cycle.

DIMENSIONS AND WEIGHT weight: 2,723 lb, 1,235 kg.

OPTIONALS automatic transmission, hydraulic torque converter and planetary gearbox with 4 ratios (I 2.452, II 1.452, III 1, IV 0.688, rev 2.212).

Crown Series

	PRICES (Tokyo):	yen
1	2000 EFI Standard 4-dr Sedan	1,462,000
2	2000 EFI De Luxe 4-dr Sedan	1,719,000
3	2000 EFI Super De Luxe 4-dr Sedan	2,003,000
4	2000 EFI Super De Luxe 4+1-dr St. Wagon	2,065,000
5	2000 EFI Super Saloon 4-dr Sedan	2,250,000
6	2000 EFI Super Saloon 4-dr Hardtop	2,361,000
7	2000 EFI Super Saloon 4+1-dr St. Wagon	2,365,000
8	2000 EFI Super Edition 4-dr Hardtop	2,118,000
9	2000 EFI Turbo Super Saloon 4-dr Sedan	2,619,000
10	2000 EFI Turbo Super Saloon 4-dr Hardtop	2,722,000
11	2000 EFI Turbo Super Edition 4-dr Hardtop	2,427,000
12	2000 EFI twin cam Royal Saloon 4-dr Sedan	3,047,000
13	2000 EFI twin cam Royal Saloon 4-dr Hardtop	3,027,000
14	2800 EFI twin cam Royal Saloon 4-dr Sedan	3,245,000
15	2800 EFI twin cam Royal Saloon 4-dr Hardtop	3,412,000
16	2400 Diesel Standard 4-dr Sedan	1,509,000
17	2400 Diesel De Luxe 4-dr Sedan	1,775,000
18	2400 Turbo Diesel Super De Luxe 4-dr Sedan	2,152,000
19	2400 Turbo Diesel Super De Luxe 4+1-dr St. Wagon	2,267,000
20	2400 Turbo Diesel Super Saloon 4-dr Sedan	2,632,000
21	2400 Turbo Diesel Super Saloon 4-dr Hardtop	2,597,000
22	2400 Turbo Diesel Super Saloon 4+1-dr St. Wagon	2,603,000
23	2400 Turbo Diesel Super Edition 4-dr Hardtop	2,232,000

For GB prices, see price index.

Power team:	Standard for:	Optional for:
125 hp	1 to 8	—
145 hp	9 to 11	—
160 hp	12,13	—
170 hp	14,15	—
83 hp (diesel)	16,17	—
96 hp (diesel)	18 to 23	—

125 hp power team

ENGINE front, 4 stroke; 6 cylinders, vertical, in line; 121.3 cu in, 1,988 cc (2.95 x 2.95 in, 75 x 75 mm); compression ratio: 8.8:1; max power (JIS): 125 hp (92 kW) at 5,400 rpm; max torque (JIS): 127 lb ft, 17.5 kg m (172 Nm) at 4,400 rpm; max engine rpm: 5,800; 62.8 hp/l (46.3 kW/l); cast iron block and head; 7 crankshaft bearings; valves: overhead, push-rods and rockers, hydraulic tappets; camshafts: 1, overhead, cogged belt, chain-driven; lubrication: gear pump, full flow filter, 9.3 imp pt, 11.2 US pt, 5.3 l; Toyota TCCS electronic fuel injection; emission control with catalytic converter, secondary air induction and exhaust gas recirculation; fuel feed: electric pump; water-cooled, 12.3 imp pt, 14.8 US pt, 7 l.

TOYOTA Crown 2800 EFI twin cam Royal Saloon Sedan

TRANSMISSION driving wheels: rear; clutch: single dry plate (diaphragm); gearbox: mechanical; gears: 4, fully synchronized - Super De Luxe, Super Saloon and Super Edition models 5; ratios: I 3.352, II 1.627, III 1, IV 0.802 - Super De Luxe, Super Saloon and Super Edition models V 0.850, rev 4.091; final drive: hypoid bevel; axle ratio: 4.556; width of rims: 5.5"; tyres: 185 SR x 14.

PERFORMANCE max speeds: (I) 27 mph, 43 km/h; (II) 45 mph, 73 km/h; (III) 67 mph, 108 km/h; (IV) 94 mph, 152 km/h; (V) 106 mph, 170 km/h; power-weight ratio: EFI Standard 22.1 lb/hp (30.1 lb/kW), 10 kg/hp (13.6 kg/kW); consumption: 27.6 m/imp gal, 23 m/US gal, 10.2 l x 100 km on Japanese emission test cycle.

CHASSIS box-type perimeter frame; front suspension: independent, double wishbones, coil springs, anti-roll bar, telescopic dampers; rear: rigid axle, lower trailing arms, upper torque rods, Panhard rod, coil springs, telescopic dampers.

STEERING recirculating ball, servo; turns lock to lock: 2.90.

BRAKES front disc, rear drum - (Super Saloon models rear disc), servo; lining area: front 28.5 sq in, 184 sq cm, rear 75.6 sq in, 488 sq cm - Super Saloon models 22.3 sq in, 144 sq cm, total 104.1 sq in, 672 sq cm - Super Saloon models 50.8 sq in, 328 sq cm.

ELECTRICAL EQUIPMENT 12 V; 45 Ah battery; 60 A alternator; transistorized ignition; 2 headlamps.

DIMENSIONS AND WEIGHT wheel base: 107.08 in, 272 cm; tracks: 56.69 in, 144 cm front, 55.18 in, 140 cm rear; length: 184.64 in, 469 cm; width: 66.53 in, 169 cm; height: sedans 56.69 in, 144 cm - hardtops 55.51 in, 141 cm - st. wagons 59.44 in, 151 cm; ground clearance: 6.70 in, 17 cm; weight: EFI Standard Sedan 2,767 lb, 1,255 kg - EFI De Luxe Sedan 2,800 lb, 1,270 kg - EFI Super De Luxe Sedan 2,888 lb, 1,310 kg - EFI Super Edition Hardtop 2,910 lb, 1,320 kg - EFI Super Saloon Sedan and EFI Super De Luxe St. Wagon 2,954 lb, 1,340 kg - EFI Super Saloon Hardtop 2,987 lb, 1,355 kg - Super Saloon St. Wagon 3,075 lb, 1,395 kg; weight distribution: 55% front, 45% rear; turning circle: 39.3 ft, 12 m; fuel tank: sedans and hardtops 15.8 imp gal, 19 US gal, 72 l - st. wagons 14.1 imp gal, 16.9 US gal, 64 l.

BODY saloon/sedan; 4 doors - hardtop, 4 doors - estate car/st. wagon, 4+1 doors; 5 or 6 seats, separate front seats.

OPTIONALS automatic transmission, hydraulic torque converter and planetary gears with 4 ratios (I 2.452, II 1.452, III 1, IV 0.688, rev 2.212), 4.778 axle ratio.

145 hp power team

See 125 hp power team, except for:

ENGINE turbocharged; compression ratio: 8:1; max power (JIS): 145 hp (107 kW) at 5,600 rpm; max torque (JIS): 156 lb ft, 21.5 kg m (211 Nm) at 3,000 rpm; 72.9 hp/l (53.7 kW/l); valves: overhead, Vee-slanted, rockers; AiResearch TO3 exhaust turbocharger with twin knock sensors; emission control by 3-way catalytic converter with oxygen sensor.

TRANSMISSION (standard) gearbox: automatic transmission, hydraulic torque converter and planetary gears with 4 ratios, possible manual selection; ratios: I 2.826, II 1.493, III 1, IV 0.688, rev 2.703.

PERFORMANCE max speed: 112 mph, 180 km/h; power-weight ratio: Super Saloon Sedan 21.4 lb/hp (29.1 lb/kW), 9.7 kg/hp (13.2 kg/kW); consumption: 23.9 m/imp gal, 19.9 m/US gal, 11.8 l x 100 km on Japanese emission test cycle.

CHASSIS rear suspension: anti-roll bar.

BRAKES rear disc.

DIMENSIONS AND WEIGHT weight: EFI Turbo Super Saloon Sedan 3,180 lb, 1,410 kg - EFI Turbo Super Edition Hardtop 3,075 lb, 1,395 kg - EFI Turbo Super Saloon Hardtop 3,141 lb, 1,425 kg.

BODY saloon/sedan - hardtop; 4 doors.

160 hp power team

See 125 hp power team, except for:

ENGINE compression ratio: 9:1; max power (JIS): 160 hp (118 kW) at 6,400 rpm; max torque (JIS): 134 lb ft, 18.5 kg m (181 Nm) at 5,200 rpm; max engine rpm: 6,800; valves: overhead, Vee-slanted, thimble tappets; camshafts: 2, overhead, cogged belt, chain-driven; lubrication: trochoid pump, full flow filter, 8.2 imp pt, 9.9 US pt, 4.7 l; emission control by 3-way catalytic converter.

TRANSMISSION gears: 5, fully synchronized; ratios: I 3.566, II 2.056, III 1.384, IV 1, V 0.850, rev 4.091.

PERFORMANCE max speed: 112 mph, 180 km/h; power-weight ratio: Royal Saloon Sedan 19.7 lb/hp (26.8 lb/kW), 8.9 kg/hp (12.1 kg/kW); consumption: 28.8 m/imp gal, 24 m/US gal, 9.8 l x 100 km on Japanese emission test cycle.

CHASSIS rear suspension: independent, semi-trailing arms, coil springs, anti-roll bar, telescopic dampers.

BRAKES rear disc.

DIMENSIONS AND WEIGHT rear track: 56.69 in, 144 cm; weight: EFI twin cam Royal Saloon Sedan 3,153 lb, 1,430 kg - EFI twin cam Royal Saloon Hardtop 3,142 lb, 1,425 kg.

BODY saloon/sedan - hardtop: 4 doors.

OPTIONALS self-levelling rear suspension; (for Royal Saloon Hardtop only) electronic instrument display.

170 hp power team

See 125 hp power team, except for:

ENGINE 169 cu in, 2,759 cc (3.27 x 3.35 in, 83 x 85 mm); max power (JIS): 170 hp (125 kW) at 5,400 rpm; max torque

TOYOTA Crown 2800 EFI twin cam Royal Saloon Sedan

TOYOTA Century E Sedan

(JIS): 174 lb ft, 24 kg m (235 Nm) at 4,400 rpm; max engine rpm: 6,000; 61.6 hp/l (45.3 kW/l); valves: overhead, rockers, hydraulic tappets; camshafts: 2, overhead, cogged belt; lubrication: 9.7 imp pt, 11.6 US pt, 5.5 l; Toyota-TCCS digital engine management system with electronic injection; emission control by 3-way catalytic converter and exhaust gas recirculation; cooling: 14.1 imp pt, 16.9 US pt, 8 l.

TRANSMISSION (standard) gearbox: automatic transmission, hydraulic torque converter and planetary gears with 4 ratios, possible manual selection; ratios: I 2.452, II 1.452, III 1, IV 0.688, rev 2.212; axle ratio: 4.100; tyres: 195/70 SR x 14.

PERFORMANCE max speed: 112 mph, 180 km/h; power-weight ratio: Royal Saloon Sedan 19.2 lb/hp (26.1 lb/kW), 8.7 kg/hp (11.8 kg/kW); consumption: 23 m/imp gal, 19.1 m/US gal, 12.3 l x 100 km on Japanese emission test cycle.

CHASSIS rear suspension: independent, semi-trailing arms, anti-roll bar, coil springs, telescopic dampers.

BRAKES rear disc, front internal radial fins.

DIMENSIONS AND WEIGHT rear track: 56.29 in, 143 cm; weight: EFI twin cam Royal Saloon Sedan 3,263 lb, 1,480 kg - EFI twin cam Royal Saloon Hardtop 3,285 lb, 1,490 kg.

BODY saloon/sedan - hardtop; 4 doors.

OPTIONALS self-levelling rear suspension.

83 hp (diesel) power team

See 125 hp power team, except for:

ENGINE diesel; 4 cylinders, in line; 149.2 cu in, 2,446 cc (3.62 x 3.62 in, 92 x 92 mm); compression ratio: 22.3:1; max power (JIS): 83 hp (61 kW) at 4,000 rpm; max torque (JIS): 123 lb ft, 17 kg m (167 Nm) at 2,400 rpm; max engine rpm: 4,600; 33.9 hp/l (25 kW/l); 5 crankshaft bearings; lubrication: 11.4 imp pt, 13.7 US pt, 6.5 l; Bosch VE electronic fuel injection; cooling: 15.8 imp pt, 19 US pt, 9 l.

TRANSMISSION gears: 5, fully synchronized; ratios: I 3.566, II 2.056, III 1.384, IV 1, V 0.850, rev 4.091; axle ratio: 4.100.

PERFORMANCE max speed: 90 mph, 145 km/h; power-weight ratio: Standard 35.5 lb/hp (48.2 lb/kW), 16.1 kg/hp (21.8 kg/kW); consumption: 62.7 m/imp gal, 52.3 m/US gal, 4.5 l x 100 km at 37 mph, 60 km/h on Japanese emission test cycle.

DIMENSIONS AND WEIGHT weight: Diesel Standard Sedan 2,943 lb, 1,335 kg - Diesel De Luxe Sedan 2,987 lb, 1,355 kg.

BODY saloon/sedan; 4 doors.

OPTIONALS automatic transmission, hydraulic torque converter and planetary gears with 4 ratios (I 2.452, II 1.452, III 1, IV 0.688, rev 2.212), 4.300 axle ratio.

96 hp (diesel) power team

See 125 hp power team, except for:

ENGINE turbocharged, diesel; 149.2 cu in, 2,446 cc (3.62 x 3.62 in, 92 x 92 mm); compression ratio: 20:1; max power (JIS): 96 hp (71 kW) at 4,000 rpm; max torque (JIS): 141 lb ft, 19.5 kg m (191 Nm) at 2,400 rpm; max engine rpm: 4,400; 39.2 hp/l (28.9 kW/l); 5 crankshaft bearings; lubrication: 11.4 imp pt, 13.7 US pt, 6.5 l; Bosch VE injection pump; turbocharger with wastegate; cooling: 17.6 imp pt, 21.1 US pt, 10 l.

TRANSMISSION gears: 5, fully synchronized; ratios: I 3.556, II 2.056, III 1.384, IV 1, V 0.850, rev 4.091; axle ratio: 3.909.

PERFORMANCE max speed: 96 mph, 155 km/h; power-weight ratio: Super De Luxe Sedan 32.4 lb/hp (44.1 lb/kW), 14.7 kg/hp (20 kg/kW); consumption: 58.8 m/imp gal, 49 m/US gal, 4.8 l x 100 km at 37 mph, 60 km/h on Japanese emission test cycle.

DIMENSIONS AND WEIGHT weight: Turbo Diesel Super De Luxe Sedan 3,109 lb, 1,410 kg - Turbo Diesel Super Saloon Sedan 3,186 lb, 1,445 kg - Turbo Diesel Super Edition Hardtop 3,120 lb, 1,415 kg - Turbo Diesel Super Saloon Hardtop 3,175 lb, 1,440 kg - Turbo Diesel Super De Luxe St. Wagon 3,164 lb, 1,435 kg - Turbo Diesel Super Saloon St. Wagon 3,252 lb, 1,475 kg.

OPTIONALS electronically controlled fuel injection engine; automatic transmission, hydraulic torque converter and planetary gears with 4 ratios (I 2.452, II 1.452, III 1, IV 0.688, rev 2.212), 4.300 axle ratio.

Century

PRICES (Tokyo):	yen
D 4-dr Sedan	**4,950,000**
E 4-dr Sedan	**5,600,000**

ENGINE front, 4 stroke; 8 cylinders in Vee; 243.7 cu in, 3,994 cc (3.42 x 3.30 in, 87 x 84 mm); compression ratio: 8.5:1; max power (JIS): 190 hp (140 kW) at 4,800 rpm; max torque (JIS): 239 lb ft, 33 kg m (323 Nm) at 3,600 rpm; max engine rpm: 5,400; 47.5 hp/l (35 kW/l); light alloy block and head; 5 crankshaft bearings; valves: overhead, push-rods and rockers; camshafts: 1, at centre of Vee; lubrication: trochoid pump, full flow filter, 9.2 imp pt, 12 US pt, 5.2 l; Bosch-Denso L-Jetronic electronic injection; emission control by 3-way catalytic converter with oxygen sensor, secondary air induction and exhaust gas recirculation; fuel feed: electric pump; water-cooled, 23.6 imp pt, 28.3 US pt, 13.4 l.

TRANSMISSION driving wheels: rear; gearbox: automatic transmission, hydraulic torque converter and planetary gears with 3 ratios, max ratio of converter at stall 2; ratios: I 2.452, II 1.452, III 1, rev 2.212; lever: steering column; final drive: hypoid bevel; axle ratio: 3.154; tyres: 195 SR x 14 or 205/70 SR x 14.

PERFORMANCE max speed: 112 mph, 180 km/h; power-weight ratio: D 23.6 lb/hp (32 lb/kW), 10.6 kg/hp (14.5 kg/kW); carrying capacity: 1,058 lb, 480 kg; consumption: 17.5 m/imp gal, 14.6 m/US gal, 16.1 l x 100 km on Japanese emission test cycle.

CHASSIS integral; front suspension: independent, by McPherson, lower transverse arms, trailing links, anti-roll bar, coil springs, telescopic dampers; rear: rigid axle, lower radius arms, upper torque arm, Panhard rod, coil springs, anti-roll bar, telescopic dampers.

STEERING recirculating ball, servo; turns lock to lock: 3.70.

BRAKES disc, servo; swept area: front 92.7 sq in, 598 sq cm, rear 75 sq in, 484 sq cm, total 167.7 sq in, 1,082 sq cm.

ELECTRICAL EQUIPMENT 12 V; 60 Ah battery; 80 A alternator; Nihon-Denso distributor; 2 iodine headlamps.

DIMENSIONS AND WEIGHT wheel base: 112.60 in, 286 cm; front and rear track: 61.02 in, 155 cm; length: 201.57 in, 512 cm; width: 74.41 in, 189 cm; height: 57.08 in, 145 cm; ground clearance: 6.10 in, 15.5 cm; weight: D Sedan 4,476 lb, 2,030 kg - E Sedan 4,531 lb, 2,055 kg; weight distribution: 51% front, 49% rear; turning circle: 41.3 ft, 12.6 m; fuel tank: 20.9 imp gal, 25.1 US gal, 95 l.

BODY saloon/sedan; 4 doors; 5 or 6 seats, bench or separate front seats.

OPTIONALS limited slip differential; leather seats (for E only).

Blizzard

PRICES (Tokyo):	yen
Standard (soft top)	**1,281,000**
De Luxe (soft top)	**1,319,000**
De Luxe (soft top, steel doors)	**1,347,000**
FRP De Luxe	**1,682,000**
De Luxe Wagon	**1,511,000**

ENGINE diesel; front, 4 stroke; 4 cylinders, in line; 133.5 cu in, 2,188 cc (3.54 x 3.38 in, 90 x 86 mm); compression ratio: 21.5:1; max power (JIS): 72 hp (53 kW) at 4,200 rpm; max torque (JIS): 105 lb ft, 14.5 kg m (142 Nm) at 2,400 rpm; max engine rpm: 4,500; 32.9 hp/l (24.2 kW/l); cast iron block and head; 5 crankshaft bearings; valves: overhead, rockers; camshafts: 1, overhead; lubrication: 11.4 imp pt, 13.7 US pt, 6.5 l; Bosch VE electronic injection; Ricardo Comet swirl chambers; fuel feed: mechanical pump; water-cooled, 15.8 imp pt, 19 US pt, 9 l.

TRANSMISSION driving wheels: rear or front and rear; clutch: single dry plate (diaphragm); gearbox: mechanical; gears: 4, fully synchronized and 2-speed transfer box - FRP 5; ratios: I 3.717, II 2.504, III 1.513, IV 1, rev 4.434 - FRP I 3.717, II 2.177, III 1.513, IV 1, V 0.876, rev 4.434; transfer box ratios: low 2.407, high 1.300; lever: central, two lever control; final drive: hypoid bevel; axle ratio: 3.909; tyres: 6.00 x 15 - FRP H78 x 15.

PERFORMANCE max speed: 68 mph, 110 km/h; power-weight ratio: Standard 37.1 lb/hp (50.4 lb/kW), 16.8 kg/hp (22.8 kg/kW); consumption: 45.6 m/imp gal, 37.9 m/US gal, 6.2 l x 100 km at 37 mph, 60 km/h on Japanese emission test cycle.

CHASSIS box-type ladder frame; front and rear suspension: rigid axle, semi-elliptic leafsprings, telescopic dampers.

STEERING recirculating ball.

BRAKES front disc, rear drum, servo.

ELECTRICAL EQUIPMENT 12 V; 100 Ah battery; 12-40 A alternator; 2 headlamps.

DIMENSIONS AND WEIGHT wheel base: 79.52 in, 202 cm; front and rear track: 47.24 in, 120 cm; length: 138.58 in, 352 cm; width: 57.48 in, 146 cm; height: soft top models

TOYOTA Blizzard FRP De Luxe

TOYOTA Landcruiser 60 Wagon

TOYOTA Landcruiser 60 Wagon

BLIZZARD

73.03 in, 185 cm - other models 73.62 in, 187 cm; ground clearance: 8.50 in, 21.5 cm; weight: Standard and De Luxe (soft top) models 2,668 lb, 1,210 kg - De Luxe (soft top, steel doors) 2,778 lb, 1,260 kg - FRP De Luxe 2,888 lb, 1,310 kg; weight distribution: 56% front, 44% rear; turning circle: 35.4 ft, 10.8 m; fuel tank: 10.5 imp gal, 12.7 US gal, 48 l.

BODY open - canvas top - canvas top and steel doors - FRP top with steel doors; 2 doors; 2 or 4 seats, separate front seats.

OPTIONALS power winch.

Landcruiser Series

PRICES (Tokyo):	yen
1 60 4+1-dr Wagon	1,827,000
2 42 Diesel 4+1-dr Wagon	1,777,000
3 42 Diesel (soft top) 4+1-dr Wagon	1,556,000
4 46 Diesel 4+1-dr Wagon	1,865,000
5 46 Diesel (soft top) 4+1-dr Wagon	1,605,000
6 60 Diesel 4+1-dr Wagon (98 hp)	1,930,000
7 60 Diesel 4+1-dr Wagon (115 hp)	2,276,000

For GB and USA prices, see price index.

Power team:	Standard for:	Optional for:
140 hp	1	—
98 hp (diesel)	2 to 6	—
115 hp (diesel)	7	—

140 hp power team

ENGINE front, 4 stroke; 6 cylinders, in line; 258 cu in, 4,230 cc (3.70 x 4 in, 94 x 101.6 mm); compression ratio: 7.8:1; max power (JIS): 140 hp (103 kW) at 3,600 rpm; max torque (JIS): 218 lb ft, 30 kg m (294 Nm) at 1,800 rpm; max engine rpm: 4,000; 33.1 hp/l (24.4 kW/l); cast iron block and head; 7 crankshaft bearings; valves: overhead, in line, push-rods and rockers; camshafts: 1, side; lubrication: gear pump, full flow filter, 14.2 imp pt, 16.9 US pt, 8 l; 1 Aisan 2 F downdraught twin barrel carburettor; fuel feed: mechanical pump; water-cooled, 28.5 imp pt, 34 US pt, 16 l.

TRANSMISSION driving wheels: rear or front and rear; clutch: single dry plate (diaphragm); gearbox: mechanical; gears: 4, fully synchronized and 2-ratio transfer box; ratios: I 4.843, II 2.618, III 1.516, IV 1, rev 4.843; transfer box ratios: low 1.960, high 1; levers: 2, central; final drive: hypoid bevel; axle ratio: 3.700; width of rims: 5.5''; tyres: 7.00 x 15.

PERFORMANCE max speeds: (I) 17 mph, 28 km/h; (II) 35 mph, 56 km/h; (III) 60 mph, 96 km/h; (IV) 87 mph, 140 km/h; power-weight ratio: 29.8 lb/hp (40.5 lb/kW), 13.5 kg/hp (18.4 kg/kW); carrying capacity: 882 lb, 400 kg; speed in direct drive at 1,000 rpm: 21.7 mph, 35 km/h; consumption: 23.7 m/imp gal, 20.1 m/US gal, 11.8 l x 100 km at 37 mph, 60 km/h on Japanese emission test cycle.

CHASSIS box type ladder frame; front and rear suspension: rigid axle, semi-elliptic leafsprings, telescopic dampers.

STEERING recirculating ball, variable ratio; turns lock to lock: 4.

BRAKES front disc, rear drum, servo; lining area: front 27.9 sq in, 180 sq cm, rear 72.5 sq in, 468 sq cm, total 100.4 sq in, 648 sq cm.

ELECTRICAL EQUIPMENT 12 V; 50 Ah battery; 40 A alternator; Denso ignition; 2 headlamps.

DIMENSIONS AND WEIGHT wheel base: 107 in, 273 cm; tracks: 58 in, 147 cm front, 57.50 in, 146 cm rear; length: 187 in, 475 cm; width: 71 in, 180 cm; height: 71.50 in, 181 cm; ground clearance: 8.30 in, 21 cm; weight: 4,178 lb, 1,895 kg; weight distribution: 52% front, 48% rear; turning circle: 43.4 ft, 13.4 m; fuel tank: 20 imp gal, 23.8 US gal, 90 l.

BODY open or estate car/st. wagon; 4+1 doors; 5 seats, separate front seats.

OPTIONALS power steering.

98 hp (diesel) power team

See 140 hp power team, except for:

ENGINE diesel; 4 cylinders, in line; 209 cu in, 3,431 cc (4.02 x 4.13 in, 102 x 105 mm); compression ratio: 20:1; max power (JIS): 98 hp (72 kW) at 3,500 rpm; max torque (JIS): 167 lb ft, 23 kg m (225 Nm) at 2,200 rpm; max engine rpm: 3,600; 28.6 hp/l (21 kW/l); 5 crankshaft bearings; valves: overhead, push-rods and rockers; lubrication: 13 imp pt, 15.5 US pt, 7.3 l; Bosch injection pump; cooling: 23 imp pt, 27 US pt, 13 l.

TRANSMISSION axle ratio: 4.111.

PERFORMANCE max speeds: (I) 16 mph, 26 km/h; (II) 29 mph, 47 km/h; (III) 52 mph, 83 km/h; (IV) 71 mph, 115 km/h; power-weight ratio: 42 Diesel Wagon 38.8 lb/hp (52.7 lb/kW), 17.6 kg/hp (23.9 kg/kW); speed in direct drive at 1,000 rpm: 20.7 mph, 33.3 km/h; consumption: 38 m/imp gal, 32 m/US gal, 7.4 l x 100 km at 37 mph, 60 km/h on Japanese emission test cycle.

ELECTRICAL EQUIPMENT 24 V; 2 x 60 Ah batteries; 25 A alternator.

DIMENSIONS AND WEIGHT wheel base: 42 models 89.96 in, 228 cm - 46 models 95.67 in, 243 cm - 60 107.48 in, 273 cm; tracks: 42 and 46 models 55.70 in, 141 cm front, 55.12 in, 140 cm rear - 60 58.07 in, 147 cm front, 57.48 in, 146 cm rear; length: 42 models 154.13 in, 391 cm - 46 models 168.30 in, 427 cm - 60 187 in, 475 cm; width: 42 and 46 models 66.53 in, 169 cm - 60 70.87 in, 180 cm; height: 42 models 76.38 in, 194 cm - 46 models 75.98 in, 193 cm - 60 71.26 in, 181 cm; ground clearance: 8.20 in, 21 cm; weight: 42 Diesel (soft top) Wagon 3,715 lb, 1,685 kg - 42 Diesel Wagon 3,792 lb, 1,720 kg - 46 Diesel (soft top) Wagon 3,902 lb, 1,770 kg - 60 Diesel Wagon 4,255 lb, 1,930 kg; turning circle: 37.4 ft, 11.4 m; fuel tank: 42 and 46 models 18.7 imp gal, 22.4 US gal, 85 l - 60 20 imp gal, 23.8 US gal, 90 l.

BODY steel body or soft top.

OPTIONALS 5-speed fully synchronized mechanical gearbox (I 4.843, II 2.618, III 1.516, IV 1, V 0.845, rev 4.843); power steering; power take-off/winch; 215 SR x 15 tyres.

115 hp (diesel) power team

See 140 hp power team, except for:

ENGINE diesel; 242.8 cu in, 3,980 cc (3.58 x 4 in, 91 x 102 mm); compression ratio: 19.7:1; max power (JIS): 115 hp (85 kW) at 3,500 rpm; max torque (JIS): 188 lb ft, 26 kg m (255 Nm) at 2,400 rpm; max engine rpm: 3,800; 28.9 hp/l (21.3 kW/l); valves: overhead, push-rods and rockers; plunger type injection pump.

TRANSMISSION gears: 5, fully synchronized; ratios: I 4.843, II 2.618, III 1.516, IV 1, V 0.845, rev 4.843; tyres: 215 SR x 15.

PERFORMANCE power-weight ratio: 38.8 lb/hp (53.8 lb/kW), 17.6 kg/hp (24.3 kg/kW); consumption: 40.9 m/imp gal, 34.1 m/US gal, 6.9 l x 100 km at 37 mph, 60 km/h on Japanese emission test cycle.

STEERING (standard) servo.

DIMENSIONS AND WEIGHT tracks: 58.46 in, 148 cm front, 57.87 in, 147 cm rear; length: 187 in, 473 cm; width: 70.86 in, 180 cm; height: 74.40 in, 189 cm; weight: 4,465 lb, 2,025 kg; ground clearance: 7.20 in, 18.5 cm.

BODY steel body; high roof.

FORD AUSTRALIA

Laser Series

PRICES EX WORKS:	Australian $
1 L 4+1-dr Hatchback Sedan	7,652
2 GL 2+1-dr Hatchback Sedan	7,796
3 GL 4+1-dr Hatchback Sedan	7,987
4 Ghia 4+1-dr Hatchback Sedan	9,427
5 Sport 2+1-dr Hatchback Sedan	9,741

Power team:	Standard for:	Optional for:
65 hp	1 to 3	—
73 hp	4	3
80 hp	5	—

65 hp power team

ENGINE front, transverse, 4 stroke; 4 cylinders, in line; 79.1 cu in, 1,296 cc (3.03 x 2.74 in, 77 x 69.6 mm); compression ratio: 9.2:1; max power (DIN): 65 hp (48 kW) at 6,000 rpm; max torque (DIN): 69 lb ft, 9.5 kg m (93 Nm) at 3,500 rpm; max engine rpm: 6,300; 50.1 hp/l (36.9 kW/l); cast iron block, light alloy head; 5 crankshaft bearings; valves: overhead; camshafts: 1, overhead; lubrication: mechanical pump, full flow filter, 6.5 imp pt, 7.8 US pt, 3.7 l; 1 downdraught twin barrel carburettor; fuel feed: mechanical pump; water-cooled, 9.7 imp pt, 11.6 US pt, 5.5 l.

TRANSMISSION driving wheels: front; clutch: single dry plate; gearbox: mechanical; gears: 4, fully synchronized; ratios: I 3.416, II 1.842, III 1.290, IV 0.918, rev 3.214; lever: central; final drive: hypoid bevel; axle ratio: 4.105; width of rims: 5''; tyres: 155/70 SR x 13.

PERFORMANCE max speed: about 96 mph, 154 km/h; power-weight ratio: 26.2 lb/hp (35.5 lb/kW), 11.9 kg/hp (16.1 kg/kW); carrying capacity: 706 lb, 320 kg; consumption: 45.6 m/imp gal, 37.9 m/US gal, 6.2 l x 100 km.

CHASSIS front suspension: independent, by McPherson, coil springs/telescopic damper struts; rear: independent, trailing arms, twin side links, coil springs, anti-roll bar, telescopic dampers.

STEERING rack-and-pinion; turns lock to lock: 3.60.

BRAKES front disc, rear drum, servo.

ELECTRICAL EQUIPMENT 12 V; 33 Ah battery; alternator; 2 headlamps.

DIMENSIONS AND WEIGHT wheel base: 93.31 in, 236 cm; front and rear track: 54.72 in, 139 cm; length: 156.30 in, 397 cm; width: 64.17 in, 163 cm; height: 52.36 in, 133 cm; ground clearance: 5.91 in, 15 cm; weight: 1,896 lb, 860 kg; turning circle: 30.2 ft, 9.2 m; fuel tank: 9.2 imp gal, 11.1 US gal, 42 l.

BODY saloon/sedan; 2+1 or 4+1 doors; 4 seats, separate front seats.

OPTIONALS 5-speed mechanical gearbox, V gear ratio 0.775.

73 hp power team

See 65 hp power team, except for:

ENGINE 90.9 cu in, 1,490 cc (3.03 x 3.15 in, 77 x 80 mm); max power (DIN): 73 hp (53 kW) at 5,500 rpm; max torque (DIN): 81 lb ft, 11.2 kg m (110 Nm) at 3,000 rpm; 49 hp/l (36.1 kW/l).

PERFORMANCE power-weight ratio: 26 lb/hp (35.3 lb/kW), 11.8 kg/hp (16.1 kg/kW).

DIMENSIONS AND WEIGHT weight: 1,863 lb, 845 kg.

BODY 4+1 doors.

OPTIONALS (standard for Ghia only) 5-speed mechanical gearbox, V ratio 0.775; 3-speed automatic transmission (I 2.841, II 1.541, III 1, rev 2.400), 3.631 axle ratio; 175/70 SR x 13 tyres (standard for Ghia).

80 hp power team

See 65 hp power team, except for:

ENGINE 90.9 cu in, 1,490 cc (3.03 x 3.15 in, 77 x 80 mm); max power (DIN): 80 hp (58 kW) at 5,500 rpm; max torque (DIN): 85 lb ft, 11.7 kg m (115 Nm) at 3,500 rpm; 53.7 hp/l (39.5 kW/l).

TRANSMISSION 3.850 axle ratio; tyres: 175/70 SR x 13 (standard).

PERFORMANCE power-weight ratio: 23.3 lb/hp (31.7 lb/kW), 10.6 kg/hp (14.4 kg/kW); consumption: 48.7 m/imp gal, 40.6 m/US gal, 5.8 l x 100 km.

BODY 2+1-dr doors.

OPTIONALS 3-speed automatic transmission (I 2.841, II 1.541, III 1, rev 2.400), 3.631 axle ratio.

Meteor GL

PRICE EX WORKS: Australian $ 8,660

ENGINE front, 4 stroke; 4 cylinders, in line; 90.9 cu in, 1,490 cc (3.03 x 3.15 in, 77 x 80 mm); compression ratio: 9:1; max power (DIN): 73 hp (54 kW) at 5,500 rpm; max torque (DIN): 81 lb ft, 11.2 kg m (110 Nm) at 3,000 rpm; max engine rpm: 6,000; 49 hp/l (36 kW/l); cast iron block, light alloy head; 5 crankshaft bearings; valves: overhead, rockers; camshafts: 1, overhead; lubrication: gear pump, full flow filter, 6.5 imp pt, 7.8 US pt, 3.7 l; 1 downdraught single barrel carburettor; fuel feed: mechanical pump; water-cooled, 9.7 imp pt, 11.7 US pt, 5.5 l.

TRANSMISSION driving wheels: front; clutch: single dry plate (diaphragm); gearbox: mechanical; gears: 5, fully synchronized; ratios: I 3.416, II 1.947, III 1.290, IV 0.918, V 0.775, rev 3.214; lever: central; final drive: hypoid bevel; axle ratio: 3.850; width of rims: 5"; tyres: 78 S ZR x 13.

PERFORMANCE power-weight ratio: 26.7 lb/hp (36.3 lb/kW), 12.1 kg/hp (16.4 kg/kW); consumption: 35.3 m/imp gal, 29.4 m/US gal, 8 l x 100 km.

CHASSIS integral; front suspension: independent, by McPherson, coil springs, telescopic damper strut; rear: independent, trailing arms, trailing links, coil springs, anti-roll bar, telescopic dampers.

STEERING rack-and-pinion; turns lock to lock: 3.60.

BRAKES front disc, rear drum, servo.

ELECTRICAL EQUIPMENT 12 V; 40 Ah battery; 50 A alternator; 2 headlamps.

DIMENSIONS AND WEIGHT wheel base: 92.91 in, 236 cm; front and rear track: 54.72 in, 139 cm; length: 163.39 in, 415 cm; width: 64.17 in, 163 cm; height: 53.94 in, 137 cm; ground clearance: 5.90 in, 15 cm; weight: 1,947 lb, 883 kg; turning circle: 30.2 ft, 9.2 m; fuel tank: 9.2 imp gal, 11.1 US gal, 42 l.

BODY saloon/sedan; 4 doors; 5 seats, separate front seats.

Telstar

PRICES EX WORKS:	Australian $
GL 4-dr Sedan	10,195
Ghia 4-dr Sedan	11,480
TX5 GL 4+1-dr Hatchback Sedan	11,743
TX5 Ghia 4+1-dr Hatchback Sedan	12,966

ENGINE front, 4 stroke; 4 cylinders, in line; 121.3 cu in, 1,998 cc (3.39 x 3.39 in, 86 x 86 mm); compression ratio: 8.6:1; max power (DIN): 94 hp (69 kW) at 5,000 rpm; max torque (DIN): 116 lb ft, 16 kg m (157 Nm) at 3,500 rpm; max engine rpm: 6,000; 47 hp/l (34.6 kW/l); cast iron block, light alloy head; 5 crankshaft bearings; valves: overhead, slanted, push-rods and rockers; camshafts: 1, overhead; lubrication: rotary pump, full flow filter, 5.6 imp pt, 6.8 US pt, 3.2 l; 1 Venturi downdraught twin barrel carburettor; fuel feed: mechanical pump; water-cooled, 12.3 imp pt, 14.8 US pt, 7 l.

TRANSMISSION driving wheels: front; clutch: single dry plate (diaphragm); gearbox: mechanical; gears: 4, fully synchronized; ratios: I 3.307, II 1.833, III 1.233, IV 0.970, rev 3.133; lever: central; final drive: helical spur gears; axle ratio: 3.850; width of rims: 5"; tyres: 155/70 SR x 13.

PERFORMANCE max speeds: (I) 33 mph, 53 km/h; (II) 59 mph, 95 km/h; (III) 88 mph, 142 km/h; (IV) 108 mph, 174 km/h; power-weight ratio: 24.2 lb/hp (32.8 lb/kW), 10.9 kg/hp (14.9 kg/kW); carrying capacity: 1,014 lb, 460 kg; acceleration: standing ¼ mile 18 sec, 0-50 mph (0-80 km/h) 8.7 sec; consumption: 26.9 m/imp gal, 22.4 m/US gal, 10.5 l x 100 km at 75 mph, 120 km/h.

CHASSIS integral; front suspension: independent, by McPherson, radius arms, coil springs, anti-roll bar, telescopic dampers; rear: independent, by McPherson, coil springs, anti-roll bar, telescopic dampers.

STEERING rack-and-pinion; turns lock to lock: 3.60.

BRAKES front disc, rear drum, servo; swept area: front 178 sq in, 1,148 sq cm, rear 49.6 sq in, 320 sq cm, total 227.6 sq in, 1,468 sq cm.

ELECTRICAL EQUIPMENT 12 V; 60 Ah battery; 60 A alternator; Mitsubishi breakerless distributor; 2 headlamps.

DIMENSIONS AND WEIGHT wheel base: 98.84 in, 251 cm; tracks: 56.30 in, 143 cm front, 56.10 in, 14 cm rear; length: 172.44 in, 438 cm; width: 66.54 in, 169 cm; height: 55.51 in, 141 cm; ground clearance: 5.90 in, 15 cm; weight: 2,271 lb, 1,030 kg; weight distribution: 59% front, 41% rear; turning circle: 33.5 ft, 10.2 m; fuel tank: 13.2 imp gal, 15.8 US gal, 60 l.

BODY saloon/sedan; 4 or 4+1 doors; 5 seats, separate front seats.

OPTIONALS 5-speed mechanical gearbox, V gear ratio 0.795; 3-speed automatic transmission (I 2.841, II 1.541, III 1, rev 2.400 ratios), 3.450 axle ratio.

Falcon / Fairmont Series

PRICES EX WORKS:		Australian $
1	Falcon GL 4-dr Sedan	11,648
2	Falcon GL 4+1-dr St. Wagon	12,443
3	Fairmont 4-dr Sedan	14,399
4	Fairmont 4+1-dr St. Wagon	15,349
5	Fairmont Ghia 4-dr Sedan	18,773

FORD Laser GL Hatchback Sedan

Power team:	Standard for:	Optional for:
122 hp	1,2	—
133 hp	3 to 5	1,2
150 hp	—	all

122 hp power team

ENGINE front, 4 stroke; 6 cylinders, vertical, in line; 199.7 cu in, 3,272 cc (3.68 x 3.13 in, 93.5 x 79.5 mm); compression ratio: 9.1:1; max power (DIN): 122 hp (90 kW) at 4,000 rpm; max torque (DIN): 178 lb ft, 24.5 kg m (240 Nm) at 2,300 rpm; max engine rpm: 4,800; 37.3 hp/l (27.4 kW/l); cast iron block, light alloy head; 7 crankshaft bearings; valves: overhead, push-rods and rockers, hydraulic tappets; camshafts: 1, side; lubrication: gear pump, full flow filter, 7 imp pt, 8.5 US pt, 4 l; 1 Weber downdraught single barrel carburettor; fuel feed: mechanical pump; water-cooled, 15.5 imp pt, 18.6 US pt, 8.8 l.

TRANSMISSION driving wheels: rear; clutch: single dry plate (diaphragm), hydraulically controlled; gearbox: mechanical; gears: 3, fully synchronized; ratios: I 2.950, II 1.690, III 1, rev 3.670; lever: steering column; final drive: hypoid bevel; axle ratio: 2.920; width of rims: 5.5"; tyres: ER78S x 14.

PERFORMANCE max speed: about 102 mph, 164 km/h; power-weight ratio: Sedan 24.7 lb/hp (33.6 lb/kW), 11.2 kg/hp (15.2 kg/kW); carrying capacity: 882 lb, 400 kg; speed in direct drive at 1,000 rpm: 20.5 mph, 33 km/h; consumption: 18 m/imp gal, 15.1 m/US gal, 15.7 l x 100 km.

CHASSIS integral; front suspension: independent, wishbones, lower trailing links, coil springs, anti-roll bar, telescopic dampers; rear: rigid axle, telescopic dampers - St. Wagon semi-elliptic leafsprings - Sedan trailing arms with longitudinal Watts linkage and anti-roll bar.

STEERING recirculating ball; turns lock to lock: 5.

BRAKES front disc (diameter 11.25 in, 28.6 cm), rear drum; swept area: total 297.2 sq in, 1,917 sq cm.

ELECTRICAL EQUIPMENT 12 V; 45 Ah battery; 38 A alternator; Autolite distributor; 2 headlamps.

DIMENSIONS AND WEIGHT wheel base: Sedan 110 in, 279 cm - St. Wagon 116 in, 295 cm; tracks: 61.40 in, 154 cm

FORD Meteor GL

FORD Telstar TX5 GL Hatchback Sedan

FORD Fairlane ZK Sedan

FORD LTD FD

122 HP POWER TEAM

front, 60 in, 152 cm rear; length: Sedan 186.50 in, 474 cm - St. Wagon 196.10 in, 498 cm; width: 73.20 in, 186 cm; height: Sedan 54 in, 137 cm - St. Wagon 55 in, 139 cm; ground clearance: Sedan 5.40 in, 13.7 cm - St. Wagon 6.40 in, 16.2 cm; weight: Sedan 3,014 lb, 1,367 kg - St. Wagon 3,314 lb, 1,503 kg; turning circle: Sedan 37.7 ft, 11.5 m - St. Wagon 40.7 ft, 12.4 m; fuel tank: Sedan 17 imp gal, 20.1 US gal, 76 l - St. Wagon 15.9 imp gal, 19.2 US gal, 73 l.

BODY saloon/sedan, 4 doors - estate car/st. wagon, 4+1 doors; 5 seats, separate front seats.

OPTIONALS Borg-Warner 35 automatic transmission, hydraulic torque converter and planetary gears with 3 ratios (I 2.390, II 1.450, III 1, rev 2.090), max ratio of converter at stall 2, possible manual selection; ER70H x 14 tyres; power steering; rear disc brakes; tinted glass; vinyl roof; GS Rally equipment; reclining backrests; sunroof (for Sedan only).

133 hp power team

See 122 hp power team, except for:

ENGINE 249.7 cu in, 4,092 cc (3.68 x 3.91 in, 93.5 x 99.3 mm); compression ratio: 9.3:1; max power (DIN): 133 hp (98 kW) at 3,600 rpm; max torque (DIN): 225 lb ft, 31 kg m (304 Nm) at 2,000 rpm; max engine rpm: 4,600; 32.5 hp/l (23.9 kW/l).

PERFORMANCE power-weight ratio: sedans 22.6 lb/hp (30.8 lb/kW), 10.3 kg/hp (14 kg/kW); speed in direct drive at 1,000 rpm: 22 mph, 35.4 km/h; consumption: 17.5 m/imp gal, 14.7 m/US gal, 16.1 l x 100 km.

BRAKES front disc, internal radial fins, rear drum, servo.

OPTIONALS Borg-Warner 35 automatic transmission, steering column or central lever, 2.920 axle ratio; 4-speed fully synchronized mechanical gearbox (I 3.060, II 1.840, III 1.320, IV 1, rev 3.040), central lever, 3.230 axle ratio; air-conditioning; electric windows.

150 hp power team

See 122 hp power team, except for:

ENGINE 249.7 cu in, 4,092 cc (3.68 x 3.91 in, 93.5 x 99.3 mm); compression ratio: 9.3:1; max power (DIN): 150 hp (111 kW) at 3,800 rpm; max torque (DIN): 240 lb ft, 33.1 kg m (325 Nm) at 2,800 rpm; max engine rpm: 4,800; 36.6 hp/l (27 kW/l); Bosch LE II Jetronic fuel injection; fuel feed: electric pump.

PERFORMANCE max speed: 116 mph, 186 km/h; power-weight ratio: sedans 20.1 lb/hp (27.3 lb/kW), 9.1 kg/hp (12.4 kg/kW); consumption: 17.5 m/imp gal, 14.7 m/US gal, 16.1 l x 100 km.

BRAKES front disc, internal radial fins, rear drum, servo.

OPTIONALS Borg-Warner 35 automatic transmission, steering column or central lever, 2.92 axle ratio; 4-speed fully synchronized mechanical gearbox (I 3.060, II 1.840, III 1.320, IV 1, rev 3.040), central lever, 3.230 axle ratio; air-conditioning; electric windows.

Fairlane ZK Sedan

PRICE EX WORKS: Australian $ 19,646

133 hp power team

(standard)

ENGINE front, 4 stroke; 6 cylinders, vertical, in line; 249.7 cu in, 4,092 cc (3.68 x 3.91 in, 93.5 x 99.3 mm); compression ratio: 9.3:1; max power (DIN): 133 hp (98 kW) at 3,600 rpm; max torque (DIN): 225 lb ft, 31 kg m (304 Nm) at 2,000 rpm; max engine rpm: 4,900; 32.5 hp/l (23.9 kW/l); cast iron block, light alloy head; 7 crankshaft bearings; valves: overhead, push-rods and rockers, hydraulic tappets; camshafts: 1, side; lubrication: gear pump, full flow filter, 7 imp pt, 8.5 US pt, 4 l; 1 Weber downdraught twin barrel carburettor; fuel feed: mechanical pump; water-cooled, 15.5 imp pt, 18.6 US pt, 8.8 l.

TRANSMISSION driving wheels: rear; gearbox: Borg-Warner 35 automatic transmission, hydraulic torque converter and planetary gears with 3 ratios: I 2.400, II 1.470, III 1; lever: central; final drive: hypoid bevel; axle ratio: 2.770; width of rims: 6''; tyres: ER70H x 14.

PERFORMANCE max speed: 102 mph, 164 km/h; power-weight ratio: 27 lb/hp (36.7 lb/kW), 12.2 kg/hp (16.6 kg/kW); carrying capacity: 882 lb, 400 kg; acceleration: standing ¼ mile 17 sec, 0-50 mph (0-80 km/h) 8.6 sec; speed in direct drive at 1,000 rpm: 22 mph, 35.4 km/h; consumption: 17.5 m/imp gal, 14.7 m/US gal, 16.1 l x 100 km.

CHASSIS integral; front suspension: independent, wishbones, lower trailing links, coil springs, anti-roll bar, telescopic dampers; rear: rigid axle, trailing arms with longitudinal Watts linkage, anti-roll bar, telescopic dampers.

STEERING recirculating ball, servo; turns lock to lock: 2.60.

BRAKES disc, servo.

ELECTRICAL EQUIPMENT 12 V; 45 Ah battery; 40 A alternator; Autolite distributor; 4 headlamps.

DIMENSIONS AND WEIGHT wheel base: 116.14 in, 295 cm; tracks: 61.40 in, 156 cm front, 61.10 in, 153 cm rear; length: 197.80 in, 502 cm; width: 73.50 in, 187 cm; height: 54.90 in, 139 cm; weight: 3,592 lb, 1,629 kg; turning circle: 41.7 ft, 12.7 m; fuel tank: 17.6 imp gal, 21 US gal, 80 l.

BODY saloon/sedan; 4 doors; 5 seats, separate front seats.

OPTIONALS sunroof; air-conditioning.

150 hp power team

(optional)

See 133 hp power team, except for:

ENGINE max power (DIN): 150 hp (111 kW) at 3,800 rpm; max torque (DIN): 240 lb ft, 33.1 kg m (325 Nm) at 2,800 rpm; max engine rpm: 4,800; 36.6 hp/l (27 kW/l); Bosch LE II Jetronic fuel injection; fuel feed: electric pump.

PERFORMANCE max speed: 116 mph, 186 km/h; power-weight ratio: 23.9 lb/hp (32.6 lb/kW), 10.9 kg/hp (14.8 kg/kW).

LTD FD

PRICE EX WORKS: Australian $ 29,226

ENGINE front, 4 stroke; 6 cylinders, vertical, in line; 249.7 cu in, 4,092 cc (3.68 x 3.91 in, 93.5 x 99.3 mm); compression ratio: 9.1:1; max power (DIN): 150 hp (111 kW) at 3,800 rpm; max torque (DIN): 240 lb ft, 33.1 kg m (325 Nm) at 3,800 rpm; max engine rpm: 4,800; 36.6 hp/l (27 kW/l); cast iron block, light alloy head; 7 crankshaft bearings; valves: overhead, push-rods and rockers, hydraulic tappets; camshafts: 1, side; lubrication: gear pump, full flow filter, 7 imp pt, 8.5 US pt, 4 l; Bosch LE II Jetronic fuel injection; fuel feed: electric pump; water-cooled, 15.5 imp pt, 18.6 US pt, 8.8 l.

TRANSMISSION driving wheels: rear; clutch: single dry plate (diaphragm), hydraulically controlled; gearbox: mechanical; gears: 3, fully synchronized; ratios: I 2.950, II 1.690, III 1, rev 3.670; lever: steering column; final drive: hypoid bevel; axle ratio: 2.920; width of rims: 5.5''; tyres: ER 78 S x 14.

PERFORMANCE max speed: 116 mph, 186 km/h; power-weight ratio: 20.1 lb/hp (27.3 lb/kW), 9.1 kg/hp (12.4 kg/kW); carrying capacity: 882 lb, 400 kg; speed in direct drive at 1,000 rpm: 20.5 mph, 33 km/h; consumption: 17.5 m/imp gal, 14.7 m/US gal, 16.1 l x 100 km.

CHASSIS integral; front suspension: independent, wishbones, lower trailing links, coil springs, anti-roll bar, telescopic dampers; rear: rigid axle, trailing arms with longitudinal Watts linkage, anti-roll bar, telescopic dampers.

STEERING recirculating ball; turns lock to lock: 5.

BRAKES front disc (diameter 11.25 in, 28.6 cm), front internal radial fins, rear drum, servo; swept area: total 296.9 sq in, 1,191 sq cm.

ELECTRICAL EQUIPMENT 12 V; 45 Ah battery; 40 A alternator; Autolite distributor; 4 headlamps.

DIMENSIONS AND WEIGHT wheel base: 116 in, 294 cm; tracks: 61.40 in, 156 cm front, 60.10 in, 153 cm rear; length: 197.80 in, 502 cm; width: 73.50 in, 187 cm; height: 54.90 in, 139 cm; weight: 3,966 lb, 1,799 kg; fuel tank: 17.6 imp gal, 21 US gal, 80 l.

BODY saloon/sedan; 4 doors; 5 seats, separate front seats.

OPTIONALS Borg-Warner 35 automatic transmission, steering column or central lever; 4-speed fully synchronized mechanical gearbox (I 3.060, II 1.840, III 1.320, IV 1, rev 3.040), central lever, 3.230 axle ratio; air-conditioning; electric windows; sunroof.

HOLDEN AUSTRALIA

Gemini TF Series

PRICES EX WORKS:	Australian $
1 4-dr Sedan	7,054
2 SL 4-dr Sedan	7,565
3 SLX 4-dr Sedan	8,185
4 ZZ/Z 4-dr Sedan	8,915
5 SLX Diesel 4-dr Sedan	9,537

Power team:	Standard for:	Optional for:
67 hp	1 to 4	—
54 hp (diesel)	5	—

67 hp power team

ENGINE front, 4 stroke; 4 cylinders, in line; 97.6 cu in, 1,584 cc (3.23 x 2.95 in, 82 x 75 mm); compression ratio: 8.3:1; max power (DIN): 67 hp (49 kW) at 4,800 rpm; max torque (DIN): 78 lb ft, 10.8 kg m (106 Nm) at 3,600 rpm; max engine rpm: 6,500;

42.3 hp/l (31.3 kW/l); cast iron block, light alloy head; 5 crankshaft bearings; valves: overhead, rockers; camshafts: 1, overhead; lubrication: rotary pump, full flow filter, 8.8 imp pt, 10.6 US pt, 5 l; 1 Nikki-Stromberg downdraught twin barrel carburettor; fuel feed: electric pump; water-cooled, 10.8 imp pt, 12.7 US pt, 6 l.

TRANSMISSION driving wheels: rear; clutch: single dry plate (diaphragm); gearbox: mechanical; gears: 4, fully synchronized; ratios: I 3.790, II 2.175, III 1.417, IV 1, rev 3.826; lever: central; final drive: hypoid bevel; axle ratio: 3.900; width of rims: 5"; tyres: YR78S x 13.

PERFORMANCE max speeds: (I) 31 mph, 50 km/h; (II) 50 mph, 81 km/h; (III) 76 mph, 123 km/h; (IV) 96 mph, 154 km/h; power-weight ratio: 31 lb/hp (42.2 lb/kW), 14.1 kg/hp (19.1 kg/kW); carrying capacity: 882 lb, 400 kg; acceleration: standing ¼ mile 19.4 sec; speed in direct drive at 1,000 rpm: 16.2 mph, 26.1 km/h; consumption: 30.1 m/imp gal, 25 m/US gal, 9.4 l x 100 km.

CHASSIS integral; front suspension: independent, wishbones, coil springs, anti-roll bar, telescopic dampers; rear: rigid axle, lower radius arms, torque tube, Panhard rod, coil springs, anti-roll bar, telescopic dampers.

STEERING rack-and-pinion; turns lock to lock: 3.80.

BRAKES front disc (diameter 9.41 in, 23.9 cm), rear drum; swept area: total 266.5 sq in, 1,719 sq cm.

ELECTRICAL EQUIPMENT 12 V; 40 Ah battery; 50 A alternator; Nippon Denso distributor; 2 headlamps.

DIMENSIONS AND WEIGHT wheel base: 94.49 in, 240 cm; front and rear track: 51.18 in, 130 cm; length: 166.50 in, 423 cm; width: 61.81 in, 157 cm; height: 52.40 in, 133 cm; ground clearance: 5.71 in, 14.5 cm; weight: 2,079 lb, 943 kg; turning circle: 31.1 ft, 9.5 m; fuel tank: 11.4 imp gal, 13.7 US gal, 52 l.

BODY saloon/sedan; 4 doors; 5 seats, separate front seats.

OPTIONALS 5-speed fully synchronized mechanical gearbox (V 0.855 ratio); Trimatic automatic transmission, hydraulic torque converter and planetary gears with 3 ratios (I 2.310, II 1.460, III 1), central lever; air-conditioning.

54 hp (diesel) power team

See 67 hp power team, except for:

ENGINE diesel; 110.9 cu in, 1,817 cc (3.31 x 3.23 in, 84 x 82 mm); compression ratio: 21:1; max power (DIN): 54 hp (40 kW) at 5,000 rpm; max torque (DIN): 78 lb ft, 10.8 kg m (105 Nm) at 2,000 rpm; max engine rpm: 5,200; 29.7 hp/l (21.9 kW/l); cast iron block and head; lubrication: 9.7 imp pt, 11.7 US pt, 5.5 l; Bosch VE diesel injection; cooling: 12.2 imp pt, 14.4 US pt, 7 l.

PERFORMANCE max speeds: (I) 26 mph, 42 km/h; (II) 46 mph, 74 km/h; (III) 68 mph, 110 km/h; (IV) 90 mph, 145 km/h; power-weight ratio: 42.9 lb/hp (58.4 lb/kW), 19.5 kg/hp (26.5 kg/kW); speed in direct drive at 1,000 rpm: 17.4 mph, 27.9 km/h; consumption: 80 m/imp gal, 67 m/US gal, 3.4 l x 100 km at 37 mph, 60 km/h.

ELECTRICAL EQUIPMENT 65 Ah battery.

DIMENSIONS AND WEIGHT weight: 2,320 lb, 1,052 kg; weight distribution: 58% front, 42% rear.

Camira JB

PRICES EX WORKS:	Australian $
SL 4-dr Sedan	**9,296**
SL 4+1-dr St. Wagon	**9,821**
SJ 4-dr Sedan	**10,046**
SLX 4-dr Sedan	**9,938**
SLX 4+1-dr St. Wagon	**10,513**
SLE 4-dr Sedan	**11,133**
SLE 4+1-dr St. Wagon	**11,823**

HOLDEN Gemini ZZ/Z Sedan

ENGINE front, transverse, 4 stroke; 4 cylinders; 97.5 cu in, 1,598 cc (3.15 x 3.13 in, 80 x 79.5 mm); compression ratio: 9.2:1; max power (DIN): 84 hp (62 kW) at 4,800 rpm; max torque (DIN): 93 lb ft, 12.8 kg m (126 Nm) at 3,600 rpm; max engine rpm: 6,500; 52.6 hp/l (38.7 kW/l); light alloy block and head; 5 crankshaft bearings; valves: overhead, in line; camshafts: 1, overhead; lubrication: gear pump, full flow filter, 6.5 imp pt, 7.8 US pt, 3.7 l; 1 Varajet II downdraught twin barrel carburettor; fuel feed: mechanical pump; water-cooled, 14.1 imp pt, 16.9 US pt, 8 l.

TRANSMISSION driving wheels: front; clutch: single dry plate; gearbox: mechanical; gears: 5, fully synchronized; ratios: I 3.420, II 1.950, III 1.280, IV 0.890, V 0.710, rev 3.330; lever: central; final drive: hypoid bevel; axle ratio: 4.070; width of rims: 5.5"; tyres: 195/60 HR x 14.

PERFORMANCE power-weight ratio: 26.6 lb/hp (36.2 lb/kW), 12.1 kg/hp (16.4 kg/kW); carrying capacity: 904 lb, 410 kg; speed in top at 1,000 rpm: 16.4 mph, 26.4 km/h; consumption: 45.6 m/imp gal, 37.9 m/US gal, 6.2 l x 100 km.

CHASSIS integral; front suspension: independent, by McPherson, rubber elements, trailing radius arms, telescopic damper strut; rear: U-shaped tubular rigid axle (swept-back ends), rubber elements, coil springs, anti-roll bar, telescopic dampers.

STEERING rack-and-pinion, variable ratio; turns lock to lock: 4.72.

BRAKES front disc, rear drum; swept area: front 148.5 sq in, 958 sq cm, rear 111 sq in, 716 sq cm, total 259.5 sq in, 1,674 sq cm.

ELECTRICAL EQUIPMENT 12 V; 50 Ah battery; 45 A alternator; Bosch electronic ignition; 2 headlamps.

DIMENSIONS AND WEIGHT wheel base: 101.18 in, 257 cm; front and rear track: 55.51 in, 141 cm; length: 170.87 in, 434 cm; width: 65.35 in, 166 cm; height: 53.15 in, 135 cm; ground clearance: 5.91 in, 15 cm; weight: 2,238 lb, 1,015 kg; turning circle: 35.4 ft, 10.8 m; fuel tank: 13.2 imp gal, 15.8 US gal, 60 l.

BODY saloon/sedan; 4 doors - estate car/st. wagon, 4+1 doors; 5 seats, separate front seats, reclining backrests.

OPTIONALS 3-speed Turbo-Hydramatic automatic transmission; 5-speed fully synchronized mechanical gearbox (I 3.420, II 1.950, III 1.280, IV 0.890, V 0.710, rev 3.330), 3.940 axle ratio.

HOLDEN Camira JB SLE Sedan

HOLDEN Camira JB SLE Sedan

Commodore Series

PRICES EX WORKS:		Australian $
1	4 VH-SL 4-dr Sedan	—
2	4 VH SL 4+1-dr St. Wagon	—
3	6 VH SL 4-dr Sedan	**11,227**
4	6 VH SL 4+1-dr St. Wagon	**11,917**
5	6 VH SL-E 4-dr Sedan	**18,667**
6	6 VH SL 4-dr Sedan	**14,014**
7	6 VH SL-X 4+1-dr St. Wagon	**15,090**

Power team:	Standard for:	Optional for:
79 hp	1,2	—
103 hp	3,4	—
113 hp	5 to 7	3,4
136 hp	—	3 to 7
171 hp	—	3 to 7

79 hp power team

(for export only)

ENGINE front, 4 stroke; 4 cylinders, in line; 115.4 cu in, 1,892 cc (3.50 x 3 in, 88.9 x 76.2 mm); compression ratio: 8.7:1; max power (DIN): 79 hp (58 kW) at 4,600 rpm; max torque (DIN): 104 lb ft, 14.3 kg m (140 Nm) at 2,400 rpm; max engine rpm: 6,000; 41.8 hp/l (30.7 kW/l); cast iron block and head; 5 crankshaft bearings; valves: overhead, hydraulic tappets; camshafts: 1, side; lubrication: gear pump, full flow filter, 7.5 imp pt, 8.9 US pt, 4.2 l; 1 GM Strasbourg Varajet downdraught twin barrel carburettor; fuel feed: mechanical pump; water-cooled, 14 imp pt, 16.7 US pt, 7.9 l.

TRANSMISSION driving wheels: rear; clutch: single dry plate; gearbox: mechanical; gears: 4, fully synchronized; ratios: I 3.510, II 2.020, III 1.410, IV 1, rev 3.570; lever: central; final drive: hypoid bevel; axle ratio: 3.900; width of rims: 5.5"; tyres: BR78S x 13.

PERFORMANCE max speeds: (I) 29 mph, 47 km/h; (II) 51 mph, 82 km/h; (III) 73 mph, 118 km/h; (IV) 91 mph, 146 km/h; power-weight ratio: 32.4 lb/hp (44.1 lb/kW), 14.7 kg/hp (20 kg/kW); carrying capacity: 882 lb, 400 kg; acceleration: standing ¼ mile 20 sec, 0-50 mph (0-80 km/h) 11.5 sec; consumption: 23.5 m/imp gal, 19.6 m/US gal, 12 l x 100 km at town speed.

CHASSIS front suspension: independent, by McPherson, coil springs, anti-roll bar, telescopic dampers; rear: rigid axle, 4 trailing arms, Panhard rod, coil springs, telescopic dampers.

STEERING rack-and-pinion, servo; turns lock to lock: 4.10.

BRAKES front disc, rear drum, servo.

ELECTRICAL EQUIPMENT 12 V; 48 Ah battery; 40 A alternator; 2 headlamps.

DIMENSIONS AND WEIGHT wheel base: 105.12 in, 267 cm; tracks: 58.27 in, 148 cm front, 56.69 in, 144 cm rear; length: 185.43 in, 471 cm; width: 67.72 in, 172 cm; height: 53.54 in, 136 cm; weight: 2,553 lb, 1,158 kg; turning circle: 33.5 ft, 10.2 m; fuel tank: 13.9 imp gal, 16.6 US gal, 63 l.

BODY saloon/sedan, 4 doors - estate car/st. wagon, 4+1 doors; 4 seats, separate front seats.

103 hp power team

See 79 hp power team, except for:

ENGINE 6 cylinders, in line; 173.9 cu in, 2,850 cc; compression ratio: 9:1; max power (DIN): 103 hp (76 kW) at 4,400 rpm; max torque (DIN): 142 lb ft, 19.6 kg m (192 Nm) at 2,800 rpm; 36.1 hp/l (26.7 kW/l); 1 Varajet II downdraught twin barrel carburettor.

HOLDEN Camira JB SLE Station Wagon

HOLDEN Commodore 6 VH SL-E Sedan

103 HP POWER TEAM

TRANSMISSION gearbox ratios: I 3.050, II 2.190, III 1.510, IV 1, rev 3.050; axle ratio: 3.550; width of rims: 6"; tyres: CR78S x 14.

PERFORMANCE max speed: 101 mph, 163 km/h; power-weight ratio: 26 lb/hp (35.3 lb/kW), 11.8 kg/hp (16 kg/kW); acceleration: standing ¼ mile 18.7 sec, 0-50 mph (0-80 km/h) 9 sec; consumption: 19.5 m/imp gal, 16.2 m/US gal, 14.5 l x 100 km at town speed.

CHASSIS rear suspension: anti-roll bar.

BRAKES swept area: total 287.1 sq in, 1,852 sq cm.

DIMENSIONS AND WEIGHT tracks: 57.09 in, 145 cm front, 55.91 in, 142 cm rear; height: 54.33 in, 138 cm; weight: 2,686 lb, 1,218 kg.

113 hp power team

See 79 hp power team, except for:

ENGINE 6 cylinders, in line; 201.2 cu in, 3,298 cc (3.63 x 3.25 in, 92.1 x 82.5 mm); max power (DIN): 113 hp (83 kW) at 4,000 rpm; max torque (DIN): 171 lb ft, 23.6 kg m (231 Nm) at 2,400 rpm; 34.3 hp/l (25.2 kW/l); cooling: 15 imp pt, 18 US pt, 8.5 l.

TRANSMISSION gearbox: Trimatic automatic transmission, hydraulic torque converter and planetary gears with 3 ratios, possible manual selection; ratios: I 2.480, II 1.480, III 1, rev 2.080; axle ratio: 3.080; width of rims: 6"; tyres: 205/60 HR x 15.

PERFORMANCE max speed: about 106 mph, 170 km/h; power-weight ratio: 24.5 lb/hp (33.3 lb/kW), 11.1 kg/hp (15.1 kg/kW); consumption: 20.2 m/imp gal, 16.8 m/US gal, 14 l x 100 km at town speed.

STEERING turns lock to lock: 3.30.

BRAKES disc, servo; swept area: total 319.5 sq in, 2,061 sq cm.

DIMENSIONS AND WEIGHT weight: 2,769 lb, 1,256 kg.

BODY reclining backrests.

136 hp power team

See 79 hp power team, except for:

ENGINE 8 cylinders in Vee; 252.7 cu in, 4,142 cc (3.63 x 3.06 in, 92.1 x 77.8 mm); compression ratio: 9:1; max power (DIN): 136 hp (100 kW) at 4,200 rpm; max torque (DIN): 199 lb ft, 27.4 kg m (269 Nm) at 2,000 rpm; 32.8 hp/l (24.1 kW/l); camshafts: 1, at centre of Vee; lubrication: 8.4 imp pt, 10.1 US pt, 4.8 l; 1 Quadrajet downdraught 4-barrel carburettor.

TRANSMISSION gearbox ratios: I 3.050, II 2.190, III 1.510, IV 1, rev 3.050; axle ratio: 3.080.

PERFORMANCE max speeds: (I) 49 mph, 79 km/h; (II) 68 mph, 110 km/h; (III) 91 mph, 146 km/h; (IV) 124 mph, 200 km/h; power-weight ratio: 21.8 lb/hp (29.8 lb/kW), 9.9 kg/hp (13.5 kg/kW); consumption: 14.9 m/imp gal, 12.4 m/US gal, 19 l x 100 km at town speed.

BRAKES disc, servo; swept area: total 319.5 sq in, 2,061 sq cm.

DIMENSIONS AND WEIGHT tracks: 57.09 in, 145 cm front, 55.91 in, 142 cm rear; length: 186.22 in, 473 cm; height: 53.94 in, 137 cm; weight: 2,972 lb, 1,348 kg.

OPTIONALS Cruise control automatic transmission; rear headrests; electric windows.

171 hp power team

See 79 hp power team, except for:

ENGINE 8 cylinders in Vee; 305.1 cu in, 5,044 cc (4 x 3.06 in, 101.5 x 77.7 mm); compression ratio: 9.2:1; max power (DIN): 171 hp (125 kW) at 4,400 rpm; max torque (DIN): 267 lb ft, 36.8 kg m (361 Nm) at 2,800 rpm; max engine rpm: 5,400; 34.2 hp/l (25.2 kW/l); valves: overhead, push-rods and rockers; camshafts: 1, at centre of Vee; lubrication: rotary pump, full flow filter, 8.4 imp pt, 10.1 US pt, 4.8 l; 1 Rochester downdraught 4-barrel carburettor; cooling: 19.9 imp pt, 23.9 US pt, 11.3 l.

PERFORMANCE power-weight ratio: 15 lb/hp (20.4 lb/kW), 6.8 kg/hp (9.2 kg/kW).

Commodore SS VH

PRICE EX WORKS: Australian $ 14,619

ENGINE front, 4 stroke; 8 cylinders in Vee; 252.7 cu in, 4,142 cc (3.63 x 3.06 in, 92.1 x 77.8 mm); compression ratio: 9:1; max power (DIN): 136 hp (100 kW) at 4,200 rpm; max torque (DIN): 199 lb ft, 27.4 kg m (269 Nm) at 2,000 rpm; max engine rpm: 5,000; 32.8 hp/l (24.1 kW/l); cast iron block and head; 5 crankshaft bearings; valves: overhead, push-rods and rockers; camshafts: 1, at centre of Vee; lubrication: gear pump, full flow filter, 8.4 imp pt, 10.1 US pt, 4.8 l; 1 Quadrajet downdraught 4-barrel carburettor; fuel feed: mechanical pump; water-cooled, 19.9 imp pt, 23.9 US pt, 11.3 l.

TRANSMISSION driving wheels: rear; clutch: single dry plate (diaphragm); gearbox: mechanical; gears, 4, fully synchronized; ratios: I 2.540, II 1.830, III 1.380, IV 1, rev 2.540; lever: central; final drive: hypoid bevel; axle ratio: 3.080; width of rims: 7"; tyres: ER 6O HR x 15.

PERFORMANCE max speed: 119 mph, 192 km/h; power-weight ratio: 22.2 lb/hp (30.2 lb/kW), 10.1 kg/hp (13.7 kg/kW); consumption: 16.6 m/imp gal, 13.8 m/US gal, 17 l x 100 km.

CHASSIS integral; front suspension: independent, by McPherson, coil springs, anti-roll bar, telescopic dampers; rear: rigid axle, upper and lower trailing arms, Panhard rod, anti-roll bar, telescopic dampers.

STEERING rack-and-pinion, servo; turns lock to lock: 3.30.

BRAKES disc, servo.

ELECTRICAL EQUIPMENT 12 V; 66 Ah battery; 65 A alternator; 2 headlamps.

DIMENSIONS AND WEIGHT wheel base: 105.04 in, 267 cm; tracks: 57.09 in, 145 cm front, 55.91 in, 142 cm rear; length: 185.04 in, 470 cm; width: 68.11 in, 173 cm; height: 53.94 in, 137 cm; ground clearance: 5.27 in, 13.4 cm; weight: 3,021 lb, 1,370 kg; turning circle: 33.5 ft, 10.2 m; fuel tank: 13.9 imp gal, 16.6 US gal, 63 l.

BODY saloon/sedan; 4 doors; 5 seats, separate front seats.

OPTIONALS 5-litre engine.

Statesman Series II

PRICES EX WORKS:	Australian $
De Ville 4-dr Sedan	**19,772**
Caprice 4-dr Sedan	**29,299**

ENGINE front, 4 stroke; 8 cylinders in Vee; 305.1 cu in, 5,044 cc (4 x 3.06 in, 101.6 x 77.8 mm); compression ratio: 9.2:1; max power (DIN): 171 hp (126 kW) at 4,400 rpm; max torque (DIN): 267 lb ft, 36.8 kg m (361 Nm) at 2,800 rpm; max engine rpm: 5,400; 34.2 hp/l (25.2 kW/l); cast iron block and head; 5 crankshaft bearings; valves: overhead, push-rods and rockers; camshafts: 1, at centre of Vee; lubrication: rotary pump, full flow filter, 8.4 imp pt, 10.1 US pt, 4.8 l; 1 Rochester downdraught 4-barrel carburettor; fuel feed: mechanical pump; water-cooled, 19.9 imp pt, 23.9 US pt, 11.3 l.

TRANSMISSION driving wheels: rear; gearbox: automatic transmission, hydraulic torque converter and planetary gears with 3 ratios, possible manual selection; ratios: I 2.480, II 1.480, III 1, rev 2.080; lever: central; final drive: hypoid bevel; axle ratio: 2.600; width of rims: 7"; tyres: ER 60 HR x 15.

PERFORMANCE max speeds: (I) 36 mph, 58 km/h; (II) 69 mph, 111 km/h; (III) 114 mph, 184 km/h; power-weight ratio: 22.3 lb/hp (30 lb/kW), 10.1 kg/hp (13.6 kg/kW); carrying capacity: 882 lb, 400 kg; acceleration: standing ¼ mile 17.1 sec, 0-50

HOLDEN Commodore SS VH

mph (0-80 km/h) 7.2 sec; consumption: 14.9 m/imp gal, 12.4 m/US gal, 19 l x 100 km at town speed.

CHASSIS integral; front suspension: independent, unequal arms, coil springs, anti-roll bar, telescopic dampers; rear: rigid axle, coil springs, anti-roll bar, telescopic dampers.

STEERING recirculating ball, servo; turns lock to lock: 5.20.

BRAKES disc, servo; swept area: front 211.6 sq in, 1,365 sq cm, rear 224.5 sq in, 1,448 sq cm, total 436.1 sq in, 2,813 sq cm.

ELECTRICAL EQUIPMENT 12 V; 62 Ah battery; 55 A alternator; 4 headlamps.

DIMENSIONS AND WEIGHT wheel base: 113.78 in, 289 cm; tracks: 59.84 in, 152 cm front, 60.24 in, 153 cm rear; length: 202.76 in, 515 cm; width: 74.41 in, 189 cm; height: 54.72 in, 139 cm; ground clearance: 5 in, 12.7 cm; weight: 3,790 lb, 1,719 kg; turning circle: 40.3 ft, 12.3 m; fuel tank: 20 imp gal, 24 US gal, 91 l.

BODY saloon/sedan; 4 doors; 5 seats, separate front seats, reclining backrests.

HOLDEN Statesman Series II De Ville Sedan

PERFORMANCE power-weight ratio: 26.3 lb/hp (35.8 lb/kW), 11.9 kg/hp (16.3 kg/kW).

OPTIONALS automatic transmission, hydraulic torque converter and planetary gears with 3 ratios (I 2.846, II 1.581, III 1, rev 2.176), 2.800 axle ratio.

MITSUBISHI AUSTRALIA

Colt Series

PRICES EX WORKS:	Australian $
1 XL 4+1-dr Hatchback Sedan	**7,366**
2 GL 4+1-dr Hatchback Sedan	**7,786**
3 SE 4+1-dr Hatchback Sedan	**8,721**
2 GSR 4+1-dr Hatchback Sedan	**8,881**

Power team:	Standard for:	Optional for:
70 hp	1,2	—
75 hp	3,4	—

70 hp power team

ENGINE front, 4 stroke; 4 cylinders, in line; 87.8 cu in, 1,439 cc (2.87 x 3.39 in, 73 x 86 mm); compression ratio: 9:1; max power (DIN): 70 hp (52 kW) at 5,600 rpm; max torque (DIN): 75 lb ft, 10.4 kg m (102 Nm) at 4,400 rpm; max engine rpm: 6,000; 48.6 hp/l (35.8 kW/l); cast iron block, light alloy head; 5 crankshaft bearings; valves: overhead, rockers; camshafts: 1, overhead; lubrication: gear pump, full flow filter, 6.2 imp pt, 7.4 US pt, 3.5 l; 1 downdraught twin barrel carburettor; fuel feed: mechanical pump; water-cooled, 8.8 imp pt, 10.6 US pt, 5 l.

TRANSMISSION driving wheels: front; clutch: single dry plate (diaphragm); gearbox: mechanical; gears: 4, fully synchronized and Super-Shift with 2 transfer box; ratios: I 3.272, II 1.831, III 1.136, IV 0.855, rev 3.181; lever: central; final drive: hypoid bevel; axle ratio: 3.470; width of rims: 4.5"; tyres: 78 ZR x 13.

PERFORMANCE power-weight ratio: 28.2 lb/hp (38.3 lb/kW), 12.8 kg/hp (17.4 kg/kW); consumption: 33.7 m/imp gal, 31.4 m/US gal, 7.5 l x 100 km.

CHASSIS integral; front suspension: independent, by McPherson, coil springs, telescopic dampers; rear: independent, trailing arms, coil springs, anti-roll bar, telescopic dampers.

STEERING rack-and-pinion; turns lock to lock: 3.90.

BRAKES front disc, rear drum, servo.

ELECTRICAL EQUIPMENT 12 V; 45 Ah battery; 40 A alternator; 2 headlamps.

DIMENSIONS AND WEIGHT wheel base: 93.70 in, 238 cm; tracks: 53.94 in, 137 cm front, 52.76 in, 134 cm rear; length: 153.94 in, 391 cm; width: 62.60 in, 159 cm; height: 53.15 in, 135 cm; ground clearance: 6.77 in, 17.2 cm; weight: 1,973 lb, 895 kg; turning circle: 33 ft, 10 m; fuel tank: 8.8 imp gal, 10.6 US gal, 40 l.

BODY saloon/sedan; 4+1 doors; 5 seats, separate front seats.

75 hp power team

See 70 hp power team, except for:

ENGINE 97.4 cu in, 1,597 cc (3.03 x 3.39 in, 76.9 x 86 mm); compression ratio: 8.5:1; max power (DIN): 75 hp (54 kW) at 5,200 rpm; max torque (DIN): 83 lb ft, 11.4 kg m (112 Nm) at 4,000 rpm; 46.9 hp/l (34.6 kW/l).

Sigma GH Series

PRICES IN GB AND EX WORKS:	£	Australian $
1 XL 4-dr Sedan	5,699*	8,602
2 XL 4+1-dr St. Wagon	6,099*	9,052
3 GL 4-dr Sedan	—	9,434
4 GL 4+1-dr St. Wagon	—	9,884
5 SE 4-dr Sedan	6,599*	10,609
6 SE 4+1-dr St. Wagon	6,999*	11,059
7 GSR 4-dr Sedan	7,600*	10,725

Power team:	Standard for:	Optional for:
81 hp	1,2	—
94 hp	3 to 6	—
102 hp	7	3 to 6

81 hp power team

ENGINE front, 4 stroke; 4 cylinders, in line; 97.5 cu in, 1,597 cc (3.03 x 3.39 in, 76.9 x 86 mm); compression ratio: 8.5:1; max power (DIN): 81 hp (60 kW) at 5,600 rpm; max torque (DIN): 83 lb ft, 11.5 kg m (117 Nm) at 3,200 rpm; max engine rpm: 6,000; 50.7 hp/l (37.5 kW/l); cast iron block, light alloy head; 5 crankshaft bearings; valves: overhead, Vee-slanted, rockers; camshafts: 1, overhead; lubrication: rotary pump, full flow filter, 7 imp pt, 8.5 US pt, 4 l; 1 Stromberg downdraught twin barrel carburettor; air cleaner; fuel feed: mechanical pump; water-cooled, 10.6 imp pt, 12.7 US pt, 6 l.

TRANSMISSION driving wheels: rear; clutch: single dry plate (diaphragm); gearbox: mechanical; gears: 4, fully synchronized; ratios: I 3.525, II 2.193, III 1.492, IV 1, rev 3.867; lever: central; final drive: hypoid bevel; axle ratio: 3.890; width of rims: 5"; tyres: 185 SR x 14.

PERFORMANCE max speeds: (I) 30 mph, 48 km/h; (II) 48 mph, 78 km/h; (III) 71 mph, 115 km/h; (IV) 96 mph, 155 km/h; power-weight ratio: Sedan 28.4 lb/hp (38.5 lb/kW), 12.8 kg/hp (17.5 kg/kW); carrying capacity: 838 lb, 380 kg; acceleration: standing ¼ mile 19.2 sec, 0-50 mph (0-80 km/h) 9.8 sec; speed in direct drive at 1,000 rpm: 16 mph, 26 km/h; consumption: 26.2 m/imp gal, 21.8 m/US gal, 10.8 l x 100 km at 75 mph, 120 km/h.

CHASSIS integral; front suspension: independent, by McPherson, coil springs/telescopic damper struts, lower wishbones (trailing links), anti-roll bar; rear: rigid axle, semi-elliptic leafsprings, telescopic dampers.

STEERING recirculating ball.

BRAKES front disc (diameter 9.02 in, 22.9 cm), front internal radial fins, rear drum, servo; lining area: total 67 sq in, 432 sq cm.

ELECTRICAL EQUIPMENT 12 V; 40 Ah battery; 40 A alternator; Mitsubishi distributor; 4 headlamps.

DIMENSIONS AND WEIGHT wheel base: 99.21 in, 252 cm; tracks: 53.94 in, 137 cm front, 52.80 in, 134 cm rear; length: 175.98 in, 447 cm; width: 65.35 in, 166 cm; height: 53.94 in, 137 cm; ground clearance: 5.50 in, 14 cm; weight: Sedan 2,295 lb, 1,041 kg - St. Wagon 2,525 lb, 1,145 kg; turning circle: 36.1 ft, 11 m; fuel tank: 13.2 imp gal, 15.8 US gal, 60 l.

BODY saloon/sedan, 4 doors - estate car/st. wagon, 4+1 doors; 5 seats, separate front seats.

OPTIONALS 5-speed mechanical gearbox (I 3.369, II 2.035, III 1.360, IV 1, V 0.856, rev 3.635); automatic transmission, hydraulic torque converter and planetary gears with 3 ratios (I 2.393, II 1.450, III 1, rev 2.090), 3.545 axle ratio; 5.5" wide rims; AR78S x 14 tyres; light alloy wheels; laminated windscreen; heated rear window; halogen headlamps; adjustable height of steering wheel; central door locking; metallic spray.

94 hp power team

See 81 hp power team, except for:

ENGINE 121.7 cu in, 1,995 cc (3.31 x 3.54 in, 84 x 90 mm); compression ratio: 9.5:1; max power (DIN): 94 hp (70 kW) at 5,600 rpm; max torque (DIN): 112 lb ft, 15.5 kg m (152 Nm) at 2,400 rpm; 47.1 hp/l (34.9 kW/l); lubrication: gear pump, full

MITSUBISHI Colt XL Hatchback Sedan

94 HP POWER TEAM

flow filter, 7.6 imp pt, 9.1 US pt, 4.3 l; 1 Stromberg 30-32 DIDTA downdraught twin barrel carburettor; water-cooled, 13.6 imp pt, 16.3 US pt, 7.7 l.

TRANSMISSION (standard) gears: 5, fully synchronized; ratios: I 3.369, II 2.035, III 1.360, IV 1, V 0.856, rev 3.635; axle ratio: 3.700.

PERFORMANCE max speed: 99 mph, 160 km/h; power-weight ratio: GL Sedan 26.5 lb/hp (31.1 lb/kW), 12 kg/hp (14.1 kg/kW); consumption: 23.9 m/imp gal, 19.9 m/US gal, 11.8 l x 100 km at 75 mph, 120 km/h.

BRAKES disc.

ELECTRICAL EQUIPMENT electronic ignition.

102 hp power team

See 81 hp power team, except for:

ENGINE 156 cu in, 2,555 cc (3.62 x 3.36 in, 91.9 x 98 mm); max power (DIN): 102 hp (76 kW) at 4,800 rpm; max torque (DIN): 142 lb ft, 19.6 kg m (192 Nm) at 2,500 rpm; 39.9 hp/l (29.4 kW/l); lubrication: gear pump, full flow filter, 7.6 imp pt, 9.1 US pt, 4.3 l; cooling: 14 imp pt, 16.7 US pt, 8 l.

TRANSMISSION gearbox (standard) automatic transmission, hydraulic torque converter and planetary gears with 3 ratios, possible manual selection; ratios: I 2.393, II 1.450, III 1, rev 2.090; axle ratio: 3.420.

PERFORMANCE max speed: 104 mph, 167 km/h; power-weight ratio: 22.3 lb/hp (30.3 lb/kW), 10.1 kg/hp (13.8 kg/kW); consumption: 25 m/imp gal, 20.8 m/US gal, 11.3 l x 100 km at 75 mph, 120 km/h.

BODY saloon/sedan; 4 doors.

MITSUBISHI Sigma GH XL Sedan

NISSAN AUSTRALIA

Pulsar Series

PRICES EX WORKS:	Australian $
1 GL 4+1-dr Hatchback Sedan	**8,270**
2 GL 4-dr Sedan	**8,470**
3 GX 4+1-dr Hatchback Sedan	**8,900**
4 GX 4-dr Sedan	**9,100**

Power team:	Standard for:	Optional for:
60 hp	1,2	—
70 hp	3,4	—

60 hp power team

ENGINE front, 4 stroke; 4 cylinders, in line; 77.5 cu in, 1,270 cc (2.99 x 2.76 in, 76 x 70 mm); compression ratio: 9:1; max power (DIN): 60 hp (44 kW) at 5,600 rpm; max torque (DIN): 71 lb ft, 9.8 kg m (96 Nm) at 3,600 rpm; max engine rpm: 6,000; 47.2 hp/l (34.8 kW/l); cast iron block, light alloy head; 5 crankshaft bearings; valves: overhead, rockers; camshafts: 1, overhead; lubrication: gear pump, full flow filter, 6 imp pt, 7.2 US pt, 3.4 l; 1 Nikki downdraught twin barrel carburettor; fuel feed: mechanical pump; water-cooled, 8.8 imp pt, 10.2 US pt, 5 l.

TRANSMISSION driving wheels: front; clutch: single dry plate (diaphragm); gearbox: mechanical; gears: 5, fully synchronized; ratios: I 3.333, II 1.955, III 1.286, IV 0.902, V 0.733, rev 3.417; lever: central; final drive: hypoid bevel; axle ratio: 3.895; width of rims: 4.5"; tyres: 155 SR x 13.

PERFORMANCE power-weight ratio: 29.6 lb/hp (40.2 lb/kW), 13.4 kg/hp (18.3 kg/kW); consumption: 37.7 m/imp gal, 31.4 m/US gal, 7.5 l x 100 km.

CHASSIS integral; front suspension: independent, by McPherson, coil springs, anti-roll bar, telescopic dampers; rear: independent, trailing arms, coil springs, telescopic dampers.

STEERING rack-and-pinion; turns lock to lock: 4.

BRAKES front disc, rear drum, servo.

ELECTRICAL EQUIPMENT 12 V; 40 Ah battery; 40 A alternator; 2 headlamps.

DIMENSIONS AND WEIGHT wheel base: 94.88 in, 241 cm; tracks: 54.72 in, 139 cm front, 53.94 in, 137 cm rear; length: 155.91 in, 396 cm; width: 64.96 in, 162 cm; height: 54.72 in, 139 cm; ground clearance: 6.50 in, 16.5 cm; weight: 1,775 lb, 805 kg; turning circle: 33.5 ft, 10.2 m; fuel tank: 11 imp gal, 13.2 US gal, 50 l.

BODY saloon/sedan; 4 or 4+1 doors; 5 seats, separate front seats.

OPTIONALS automatic transmission, hydraulic torque converter and planetary gears with 3 ratios (I 2.826, II 1.543, III 1, rev 2.364), 3.364 axle ratio; tinted laminated windscreen.

70 hp power team

See 60 hp power team, except for:

ENGINE 90.8 cu in, 1,488 cc (2.99 x 3.23 in, 76 x 82 mm); max power (DIN): 70 hp (51 kW) at 5,200 rpm; max torque (DIN): 85 lb ft, 11.7 kg m (115 Nm) at 3,200 rpm; max engine rpm: 5,800; 47 hp/l (34.6 kW/l); 7 crankshaft bearings.

TRANSMISSION axle ratio: 3.789.

PERFORMANCE power-weight ratio: 25.3 lb/hp (34.5 lb/kW), 11.5 kg/hp (15.6 kg/kW).

Bluebird

PRICES EX WORKS:	Australian $
GL 4-dr Sedan	**9,210**
GL 4+1-dr St. Wagon	**9,660**
GX 4-dr Sedan	**9,740**
GX 4+1-dr St. Wagon	**10,300**
LX 4-dr Sedan	**11,070**
LX 4+1-dr St. Wagon	**11,450**
TRX 4-dr Sedan	**10,650**

ENGINE front, 4 stroke; 4 cylinders, in line; 119.1 cu in, 1,952 cc (3.35 x 3.36 in, 85 x 86 mm); compression ratio: 8.5:1; max power (DIN): 98 hp (72 kW) at 5,200 rpm; max torque (DIN): 114 lb ft, 15.8 kg m (155 Nm) at 3,600 rpm; max engine rpm: 6,000; 50.2 hp/l (36.9 kW/l); cast iron block, light alloy head; 5 crankshaft bearings; valves: overhead; camshafts: 1, overhead; lubrication: gear pump, full flow filter, 7.6 imp pt, 9.1 US pt, 4.3 l; 1 Nikki downdraught twin barrel carburettor; fuel feed: mechanical pump; water-cooled, 13.2 imp pt, 15.9 US pt, 7.5 l.

TRANSMISSION driving wheels: rear; clutch: single dry plate (diaphragm); gearbox: mechanical; gears: 4, fully synchronized; ratios: I 3.650, II 1.970, III 1.370, IV 1, rev 3.650; lever: central; final drive: hypoid bevel; axle ratio: 3.700; width of rims: 5"; tyres: BR 70 x 14.

PERFORMANCE max speeds: (I) 30 mph, 49 km/h; (II) 57 mph, 91 km/h; (III) 81 mph, 131 km/h; (IV) 101 mph, 162 km/h; power-weight ratio: 25.4 lb/hp (34.6 lb/kW), 11.5 kg/hp (15.7 kg/kW); acceleration: standing ¼ mile 19 sec, 0-50 mph (0-80 km/h) 9.2 sec; consumption: 24.4 m/imp gal, 20.3 m/US gal, 11.6 l x 100 km.

CHASSIS integral; front suspension: independent, by McPherson, coil springs, anti-roll bar, telescopic dampers; rear: rigid axle, coil springs, telescopic dampers.

STEERING rack-and-pinion; turns lock to lock: 3.30.

BRAKES disc, servo.

ELECTRICAL EQUIPMENT 12 V; 48 Ah battery; 45 A alternator; 2 headlamps.

NISSAN Pulsar GX Sedan

NISSAN Pulsar GX Hatchback Sedan

NISSAN Bluebird LX Sedan

TOYOTA Corona CS-X Sedan

DIMENSIONS AND WEIGHT wheel base: 99.21 in, 252 cm; tracks: 54.33 in, 138 cm front, 53.54 in, 136 cm rear; length: 174.02 in, 442 cm; width: 64.96 in, 165 cm; height: 54.72 in, 139 cm; ground clearance: 6.96 in, 17.5 cm; weight: 2,492 lb, 1,130 kg; turning circle: 36.1 ft, 11 m; fuel tank: 13.6 imp gal, 16.4 US gal, 62 l.

BODY saloon/sedan, 4 doors - estate car/st. wagon, 4+1 doors; 5 seats, separate front seats.

TOYOTA AUSTRALIA

Corolla Series

PRICES EX WORKS:	Australian $
1 S 4-dr Sedan	7,640
2 S 4+1-dr St. Wagon	8,370
3 CS 4-dr Sedan	8,160
4 CS 4+1-dr St. Wagon	8,810
5 CSX 4-dr Sedan	8,875

Power team:	Standard for:	Optional for:
64 hp	1,2	—
78 hp	3 to 5	—

64 hp power team

ENGINE front, 4 stroke; 4 cylinders, in line; 78.7 cu in, 1,290 cc (2.95 x 2.87 in, 75 x 73 mm); compression ratio: 9:1; max power (DIN): 64 hp (47 kW) at 5,400 rpm; max torque (DIN): 72 lb ft, 10 kg m (98 Nm) at 3,800 rpm; max engine rpm: 6,000; 49.6 hp/l (36.5 kW/l); cast iron block, light alloy head; 5 crankshaft bearings; valves: overhead, push-rods and rockers; camshafts: 1, in crankcase; lubrication: rotary pump, full flow filter, 6.2 imp pt, 7.4 US pt, 3.5 l; 1 downdraught twin barrel carburettor; fuel feed: mechanical pump; water-cooled, 9.2 imp pt, 11 US pt, 5.2 l.

TRANSMISSION driving wheels: rear; clutch: single dry plate (diaphragm); gearbox: mechanical; gears: 4, fully synchronized; ratios: I 3.789, II 2.220, III 1.435, IV 1, rev 4.316; lever: central; final drive: hypoid bevel; axle ratio: 3.889; width of rims: 4''; tyres: ZR 78 S x 13.

PERFORMANCE max speeds: (I) 25 mph, 40 km/h; (II) 45 mph, 72 km/h; (III) 67 mph, 108 km/h; (IV) 96 mph, 155 km/h; power-weight ratio: 30.8 lb/hp (41.9 lb/kW), 14 kg/hp (19 kg/kW); consumption: 40.4 m/imp gal, 33.6 m/US gal, 7 l x 100 km.

CHASSIS integral; front suspension: independent, by McPherson, anti-roll bar, coil springs, telescopic dampers; rear: rigid axle, semi-elliptic leafsprings, anti-roll bar, telescopic dampers.

STEERING rack-and-pinion; turns lock to lock: 3.30.

BRAKES front disc, rear drum, servo.

ELECTRICAL EQUIPMENT 12 V; 40 Ah battery; 40 A alternator; 2 headlamps.

DIMENSIONS AND WEIGHT wheel base: 94.49 in, 240 cm; tracks: 51.97 in, 132 cm front, 52.36 in, 133 cm rear; length: 164.87 in, 418 cm; width: 63.39 in, 161 cm; height: 54.72 in, 139 cm; weight: 1,973 lb, 895 kg; turning circle: 30.8 ft, 9.4 m; fuel tank: 11 imp gal, 13.2 US gal, 50 l.

BODY saloon/sedan, 4 doors - estate car/st. wagon, 4+1 doors; 5 seats, separate front seats.

OPTIONALS 3 speed automatic transmission (I 2.390, II 1.450, III 1, rev 2.390).

78 hp power team

See 64 hp power team, except for:

ENGINE 96.8 cu in, 1,587 cc (3.53 x 2.76 in, 85 x 70 mm); max power (DIN): 78 hp (57 kW) at 5,600 rpm; max torque (DIN): 94 lb ft, 13 kg m (128 Nm) at 2,400 rpm; 49.1 hp/l (36.2 kW/l); cooling: 9.9 imp pt, 11.8 US pt, 5.6 l.

TRANSMISSION gears: CSX Sedan 5, fully synchronized; ratios: I 3.587, II 2.022, III 1.384, IV 1, V 0.861, rev 3.484; axle ratio: 3.909.

PERFORMANCE max speeds: (I) 24 mph, 39 km/h; (II) 47 mph, 76 km/h; (III) 66 mph, 107 km/h; (IV) and (V) 99 mph, 160 km/h; power-weight ratio: 25.3 lb/hp (34.4 lb/kW), 11.5 kg/hp (15.6 kg/kW); consumption: 39.7 m/imp gal, 32.2 m/US gal, 7.3 l x 100 km.

ELECTRICAL EQUIPMENT 33 Ah battery; Nippon-Denso distributor.

OPTIONALS (standard for CSX Sedan) 5-speed mechanical gearbox (I 3.587, II 2.022, III 1.384, IV 1, V 0.861, rev 3.484); 3-speed automatic transmission (I 2.390, II 1.450, III 1, rev 2.390).

TOYOTA Corolla CS Sedan

Corona

PRICES EX WORKS:	Australian $
S 4-dr Sedan	9,170
S 4+1-dr St. Wagon	9,820
CS 4-dr Sedan	9,910
CS 4+1-dr St. Wagon	10,560
CS-X 4-dr Sedan	11,425

ENGINE front, 4 stroke; 4 cylinders, in line; 121.7 cu in, 1,995 cc (3.31 x 3.54 in, 84 x 90 mm); compression ratio: 8.7:1; max power (DIN): 98 hp (72 kW) at 5,200 rpm; max torque (DIN): 116 lb ft, 16.1 kg m (158 Nm) at 3,200 rpm; max engine rpm: 6,000; 49.1 hp/l (36.1 kW/l); cast iron block, light alloy head; 5 crankshaft bearings; valves: overhead, in line, push-rods and rochers; camshafts: 1, overhead; lubrication: trochoid pump, full flow filter, 8.1 imp pt, 9.7 US pt, 4.6 l; 1 downdraught twin barrel carburettor; fuel feed: mechanical pump; water-cooled, 13.2 imp pt, 15.9 US pt, 7.5 l.

TRANSMISSION driving wheels: rear; clutch: single dry plate (diaphragm); gearbox: mechanical; gears: 4, fully synchronized; ratios: I 3.650, II 2.140, III 1.370, IV 1, rev 3.660; lever: central; final drive: hypoid bevel; axle ratio: 3.890; width of rims: 5''; tyres: BR 78 x 14.

PERFORMANCE max speeds: (I) 33 mph, 53 km/h; (II) 51 mph, 82 km/h; (III) 80 mph, 128 km/h; (IV) and (V) 106 mph, 170 km/h; power-weight ratio: 24.1 lb/hp (32.6 lb/kW), 10.8 kg/hp (14.8 kg/kW); acceleration: standing ¼ mile 18.2 sec, 0-50 mph (0-80 km/h) 8.2 sec; consumption: 35.3 m/imp gal, 29.4 m/US gal, 8 l x 100 km.

CHASSIS integral; front suspension: independent, by McPherson, coil springs, anti-roll bar, telescopic dampers; rear: rigid axle, upper torque rod, coil springs, anti-roll bar, telescopic dampers.

STEERING rack-and-pinion; turns lock to lock: 3.70.

BRAKES front disc, rear drum, servo.

ELECTRICAL EQUIPMENT 12 V; 33 Ah battery; 55 A alternator; Nippon-Denso electronic ignition; 4 headlamps.

DIMENSIONS AND WEIGHT wheel base: 98.43 in, 250 cm; tracks: 53.94 in, 137 cm front, 53.15 in, 135 cm rear; length: 176.77 in, 449 cm; width: 63.35 in, 166 cm; height: 54.35 in, 138 cm; ground clearance: 6.30 in, 16 cm; weight: 2,337 lb, 1,060 kg; weight distribution: 53% front, 47% rear; turning circle: 32.8 ft, 10 m; fuel tank: 13.4 imp gal, 16.1 US gal, 61 l.

BODY saloon/sedan, 4 doors - estate car/st. wagon, 4+1 doors; 5 seats, separate front seats.

OPTIONALS 5-speed mechanical gearbox (I 3.650, II 2.140, III 1.370, IV 1, V 0.850, rev 3.384); 3-speed automatic transmission (I 2.390, II 1.450, III 1, rev 2.390).

CAR MANUFACTURERS AND COACHBUILDERS

An outline of their history, structure and activities

CAR MANUFACTURERS

A.C. CARS Ltd **Great Britain**

Founded in 1900 by Portwine & Weller, assumed title Autocarriers (A.C.) Ltd in 1907, moved from London to Thames Ditton in 1911. Present title since 1930. Chairman: W.D. Hurlock. Works Director: W.A Hurlock. Secretary/Financial Director: A. Wilson. Head office, press office and works: Summer Rd, Thames Ditton, Surrey KT7 0RD. 100 employees. About 120 cars produced in 1982. Models: ACE Bristol 2 l Le Mans (1959); ACE Cobra Le Mans (1963). Entries and wins in numerous competitions (Monte Carlo Rally, Le Mans, etc.).

ADAM OPEL AG **Germany (Federal Republic)**

Founded in 1862. Owned by General Motors Corp. USA since 1929. Chairman: F. Beickler, H.W. Gäb, F.W. Lohr. Directors: W. Schlotfeldt, K. Kartzke, D.D. Campbell, F. Schwenger, J.E. Rhame, I.G. Bagshaw. Head office and press office: 6090 Rüsselsheim/Main. Works: Bochum, Kaiserslautern, Rüsselsheim, Berlin. 59,688 employees. 96,094 cars produced 1982. Car production begun in 1898. Most important models: 10/18 (1908); 4/8 (1909); 6/16 (1910); 8/25 (1920); 4/12 (1924); 4/14 (1925-29); Olympia (1935); Super Six, Admiral (1938); Kapitän (1939); Rekord (1961); Kadett (1962); Admiral, Diplomat (1964), Commodore (1968); GT (1969); Ascona, Manta (1970); Senator, Monza (1978).

ASSEMBLY IN OTHER COUNTRIES — **Belgium:** GM Continental S.A. (associated company), Noorderlaan 75, Antwerp (assem. Kadett, Ascona, Manta). **Indonesia:** P.T. Garmak Motors Ltd, Djakarta (assem. Rekord). **Korea:** Saehan Motor Company, Hanshin Bldg, 62-10, 2GA Chung Mu-Ro, Jung-Gu, Seoul (assem. Rekord). **Morocco:** Société Marocaine de Mécanique Industrielle et Automobile, Blvd. Moulay Ismael 22, Casablanca (assem. Rekord). **Philippines:** GM Philipinas Inc., Barrio Almanza, Las Pinas, Metro Manila (assem. Ascona, Manta, Rekord). **Portugal:** GM de Portugal Ltda, (associated company), Av. Marechal Gomes da Costa 33, Lisbon (assem. Kadett, Rekord). **South Africa:** GM South African, Kempston Rd, P.O.B. 1137, Port Elizabeth (assem. Kadett, Ascona, Rekord, Senator). **Spain:** GM España, S.A., Poligano de Entrerrios Figueruelas, Zaragoza (manuf, and assem. Opel Corsa). **Thailand:** Asoke Motors, 211-213 Asoke Rd, Sukhumwit, Bangkok 11 (assem. Rekord). **Uruguay:** GM Uruguay S.A. (associated company), Casilla de Correo 234, Montevideo (assem. Ascona, Rekord). **Zaire:** GM Zaire S.A.R.L. (associated company), Blvd Patrice Lumumba, Masina 1, Kinshasa (assem. Ascona).

ALFA ROMEO S.p.A. **Italy**

Founded in 1910 as Anonima Lombarda Fabbrica Automobili, became Accomandita Semplice Ing. Nicola Romeo in 1915, Società Anonima Italiana Ing. Nicola Romeo & C. in 1918, S.A. Alfa Romeo in 1930. Became part of IRI group in 1933 and assumed name of S.A. Alfa Romeo Milano-Napoli in 1939. Present title since 1946. For volume of production it holds second place in Italian motor industry. President: E. Massacesi. Vice-President and Managing Director: C. Innocenti. Managing Director and General Manager: A. Lingiardi. Head office and press office: Arese (Milan), Works: Arese (Milan), Pomigliano d'Arco (Naples). 42,300 employees. 188,800 vehicles produced in 1982. Most important models: 24 hp (1910); 40-60 hp (1913); RL Targa Florio (1923); P2 (1924); 6C-1500 (1926); 6C-1750 (1929); 8C-2300 (1930); P3 (1932); 8C-2600 (1933); 8C-2900 (1935); 158 (1938); 6C-2500 SS (1939); 2500 Freccia d'Oro (1947); 1900 (1950); Giulietta Sprint (1954); Giulietta Berlina (1955); Giulietta Spider (1956); Giulietta TI (1957); 2000 (1958); Giulia TI, Giulia Sprint, Giulia Spider, 2600 (1962); Giulia Sprint GT, Giulia TZ (1963); Giulia 1300, Giulia Spider Veloce (1964); Giulia 1300 TI, Giulia Super, GTA (1965); Junior (1966); 1750, 1300 Spider Junior, GTA, 1300 Junior, "33" Coupé (1968); Giulia 1600 S, 1300 Junior Z (1969); Giulia 1300 Super, Montreal (1970); 2000 Berlina, 2000 GT Veloce, 2000 Spider Veloce (1970); 2000 Berlina, 2000 GT Veloce, 2000 Spider Veloce (1971); 2000 Spider Veloce (1971); Alfasud (1972); Alfetta (1973), Giulietta (1977); Alfa 6 2.5 (1979), Alfetta GTV 6 2.5 (1980), Alfetta 2.0 Turbodiesel (1980), Giulietta 2.0 Turbodiesel (1983), Alfetta 2.4 Turbodiesel (1983), Alfa 33 (1983), Arna L, Arna SL (1983), Alfa 6 2.5 Turbodiesel (1983), Alfa 6 2.0 (1983), Alfa 33 1.3 4x4 (1983). Entries and wins in numerous competitions. European Mountain Championship and European Touring Challenge Cup in 1967, in 1968 the 33/2 l was classified first at Daytona, in Targa Florio and Nürburgring 1000 km. In 1969 Alfa Romeo won European Touring Challenge Cup, National Championship for Makes in Brazil, three American National Drivers Championships and numerous national championships. In 1970, first place in European Championship for Touring Cars and many national championships. In 1971, in Makers' International Championship, a 33-3 was placed outright first in Brands Hatch 1000 km, in Targa Florio and Watkins Glen 6 Hour. It won European Touring Car Makers' Championship, coming first and second in final classification. In 1971 it also won a series of international championships, including Austrian Mountain Championship and Belgian Touring Drivers' Championship, Dutch Touring Championship for Touring Cars up to 1300 cc, Italian Absolute Championship for Special Touring Cars, American National Championship for SCCA Drivers, class C Sedan and Class C Sports Racing, and finally Venezuelan National Championship outright. In 1973 2000 GTV won Coupe du Roi and in 1974 2000 GTV won Coupe du Roi and 33 TT 12 finished 1, 2 and 3 in Monza 1000 km. 1975 holders of World Championship for Makes and 1977 of World Sports Car Championship.

ASSEMBLY IN OTHER COUNTRIES - **Malaysia:** City Motors Sdn Bhd (concessionaire), Foo yet Kai Bldg 270, Hugh how St, Ipoh Perak (assem. Alfasud 1.3, 1.5, Alfetta 1.8, 2.0); Swedish Motor Assemblies (concessionaire), Kuala Lumpur (assem. Alfasud 1.3, 1.5, Alfetta 1.8, 2.0). **South Africa:** Alfa Romeo South Africa (Pty) Ltd (associated company), P.O.B. 78439, Wynberg-Sandton (assem. Alfasud 1.3, 1.5, Alfasud Sprint Veloce 1.3, 1.5, Giulietta 1.8, Alfetta 1.8, 2.0, Alfetta GTV 2.0, Alfetta GTV 6 2.5). **Thailand:** Siam Europe Motors (concessionaire), 404 Phayatha Rd, Bangkok (assem. Alfasud 1.3, Giulietta 1.6, Alfetta 2.0). **Zimbabwe:** Willowvale Motors (concessionaire), Dagenham Rd, Harare (assem. Alfasud 1.5). 8,000 vehicles produced outside Italy in 1982.

ALLARD MOTOR COMPANY Ltd **Canada**

Originally incorporated in Great Britain in 1946, the company is now registered in Canada. Allard cars won many races and rallies in both Europe and Americas including 1952 Monte Carlo and 1947 Lisbon rallies. A J2X and JR Allard came first and second in vintage racing in Laguna, California in 1981. Car production had ceased in 1959 until resumed with J2X-2 in 1979. Chairman: M.A. Stein. President: M.A. Stein. Directors: M.A. Stein, M.V. Kellermann, H.R. Nathan. Head office, press office and works: 5305 Maingate Drive, Mississauga, Ontario. 12 employees. 26 cars produced in 1982.

ALPINE RENAULT - see RÉGIE NATIONALE DES USINES RENAULT

AMERICAN MOTORS CORPORATION **USA**

(Makes: Renault Alliance and Encore, Eagle, Jeep vehicles)

Established in 1954 as result of merger between Nash-Kelvinator Corp. and Hudson Motor Car Co; acquired Jeep Corp., Feb. 1970. Regie Renault of France signed manufacturing, distributing and financing agreements with AMC in 1979 and acquired 46.4% equity ownership in 1980. Chairman: W.P. Tippett. President: J.J. Dedeurwaerder. Central office and press office: American Center Building, 27777 Franklin Rd, Southfield, Mich. 48034. Technical Center: 14250 Plymouth Rd., Detroit, Mich. 48232. Passenger car works: 5626, 25th Ave, Kenosha, Wisc. 53140; 3880 N. Richards, Milwaukee, Wisc. 53201, Jeep plant: Toledo, Ohio. Plastics operations: Windsor Plastics, Inc., 601 N. Congress Ave, Evansville, Ind., 47711; Mercury Plastics Co., Inc., 34501 Harper, Mt Clemens, Mich. 48043; Evart Products Co., Evart, Mich. 49631 (subsidiaries-injection moulding); AM General Corp., 32500 Van Born Rd, Wayne, Mich. 48184 (subsidiary). Works: 701 W. Chippewa Ave, South Bend, Ind., 46623; 13200 E. McKinley Hwy, Mishawaka, Ind., 46544; 1428 West Henry St. Indianapolis, Ind. 46221 (military trucks, post-office delivery trucks and transit buses). 20,800 employees. 131,724 cars and 85,472 Jeep vehicles produced in 1982.

MANUFACTURE AND ASSEMBLY IN OTHER COUNTRIES — **Australia:** Australian Motor Industries Ltd (associated company), G.P. O.B. 2006S, 155 Bertie St, Port Melbourne (Cherokee). **Bangladesh:** Pragoti Industries Ltd, 96 Agrabad Commercial Area, Chittagong (assem. Jeep CJ Series). **Canada:** American Motors (Canada) Ltd (subsidiary), Brampton, Ont. (Eagle). **Egypt:** Arab American Vehicle Co., P.O.B. 2419, Cairo (assem. Jeep CJ-7, CJ-8, CJ-20 and Wagoneer). **India:** Mahindra & Mahindra Ltd, Gateway Bldg, Apollo Bunder, Bombay (assem. Jeep CJ). **Indonesia:** N.V. Indonesian Service Co. Ltd, P.O.B. 121, Djakarta-Kota (assem. Jeep CJ and J-10). **Israel:** Matmar Industries Ltd, P.O.B. 1007, Haifa (assem. Jeep CJ-5 and pickups). **Japan:** Mitsubishi Heavy Industries Ltd, No. 10, 2-chome, Marunouchi, Chiyoda-ku, Tokyo (manuf. Jeep CJ-5). **Kenya:** Jeep Africa Lft, P.O.B. 30567, Nairobi (assem. Jeep CJ and Cherokee). **Korea:** Shinjin Jeep Co., 62-7 Ika Choong Mu-Ro Choong Ku, Seoul (assem. Jeep CJ-5). **Mexico:** Vehiculos Automotores Mexicanos S.A., Poniente 150, num. 837, Industrial Vallejo, Mexico City 16, D.F. (assem. American, Gremlin, J-20, Jeep CJ-5 and Wagoneer). **Morocco:** S.I.D.A. 84 Av. Lalla Yaquote, Casablanca (assem. Jeep CJ Series). **Pakistan:** Naya Daur Motors Ltd., State Life Bldg, Dr. Ziauddin Ahmed Rd, Karachi 3 (assem. Jeep trucks, Jeep station wagons and CJ-5). **Philippines:** Jeep Philippines, Guevent Bldg, 49 Libertad St, Mandaluyong, Rizal (assem. Jeep CJ-5, CJ-6). **Portugal:** C. Santos Commercio Industria Lda., Ave. de Liberdad 35-10, Lisboa (assem. Jeep CJ Series). **Spain:** Construcciones y Auxiliar de Ferrocarriles S.A., V.I.A.S.A. Division, Apdo 279, Zaragoza (manuf. Jeep CJ-5). **Sri Lanka:** Government of Sri Lanka, 100 Hyde Park Corner, Colombo (assem. Jeep CJ Series). **Taiwan:** Yue Loong Motor Co. Ltd, 150 Nanking East Rd, Sec. II, Taipei (assem. Jeep CJ-5). **Thailand:**

● *The information given in these discriptions refers specifically to cars and therefore does not cover the activities in which any of the car manufacturers are engaged in other fields of industry.*

Thai Yarnyon Co. Ltd, 388/3 Petchburi Rd, Bangkok (assem. Jeep CJ-5). **Venezuela:** Constructora Venezolana de Vehiculos C.A., P.O.B. 61033, Caracas (assem. Jeep CJ Series); Jeep de Venezuela S.A., Apdo 41-42, Tejerias, Edo Uragua (assem. Jeep J-10 and Wagoneer), 8,834 passengers cars and 23,083 Jeep vehicles produced outside USA in 1982.

AMI - TOYOTA — Australia

Toyota cars introduced to Australia through Australian Motor Industries Ltd in 1962 and assembly for Toyotas commenced in 1963. Toyota purchased 10% of AMI in 1968 and a further 40% in 1971. In 1976 Toyota elected to become an Australian manufacturer. Toyota Manufacturing Australia Ltd established 1977 to build engines and panels. Along with Thiess-Toyota (light trucks) AMI-Toyota held third place in vehicle sales in 1982. Chairman: Sir Gordon Allard. Deputy Chairman: H. Tamura. Managing Director: N. Itaya. Directors: J.M. Hambleton, H. Hanai, S. Toyoda. Head office and press office: 155 Bertie St, Port Melbourne, Victoria. Works: Port Melbourne and Altona, Victoria. 2,108 employees. 42,986 cars produced in 1982.

APAL - see AUTOMOBILE APAL S.A.

ARGYLL TURBO CARS Ltd — Great Britain

Founded in 1977. Directors: R.M. Henderson, R. Gray-Stevens, A. Smith, H. Crow, T.H. Hopkins. Head office and works: Minnow House, Lochgilphaed, Argyll, Scotland.

ARKLEY - see JOHN BRITTEN GARAGES Ltd

ARO - see INTREPRINDEREA MECANICA MUSCEL

ASTON MARTIN LAGONDA Ltd — Great Britain

Founded in 1913 as Bamford & Martin, it is one of the greatest names in the world of touring and competition cars. The name "Aston Martin" recalls the many successes in the Aston Clinton Hill Climb. In 1947, when it was taken over by David Brown, the title was changed to Aston Martin Lagonda Ltd. In 1975 the company went into voluntary liquidation and was then taken over by a consortium, Aston Martin (1975) Ltd. In 1980 C.H. Industrials and Pace Petroleum acquired control of Aston Martin. In 1983 Automotive Investments, the company's US Distributor, acquired a majority shareholding. Executive Chairman: V. Gauntlett. Joint Chairman: N.F. Papanicolaou. Managing Director: W.H. Archer. Directors: W.R. Bannard, M.H.L. Bowler, P.J. Livanos, J.P. Papanicolaou, J.A. Wall. Works: Tickford St, Newport Pagnell, Bucks. MK 16 9AN. 325 employees. 175 cars produced in 1982. Most important models: Lionel Martin series (1921-25); first 1.5 l series (1927-32); second 1.5 l series (1932-34); third 1.5 l series (1934-36); 2 l series with single overhead camshaft (1936-40); 2 l DB1 series (1948-50); 2.6 l DB2 series (1950-1953); 2.6 and 2.9 l DB3 series (1952-1953); 2.6 and 2.9 l DB2/4 series (1953-55); 2.9 l DB3S series (1955-56); 2.9 l DB2/4 Mk II series (1955-57); 2.6 l, 2.9 l Lagonda Saloon, Convertible (1949-1956); 2.9 l DB Mk III series (1957-59); 3.7 l DB4 series (1959-63); 3.7 l DB4 GT series (1959-63); 4 l Lagonda Rapide (1961-63); 4 l DB5 series (1963-65); 4 l DB6 Saloon and Volante Convertible (1965-69); DB6 Mk 2 Saloon with electronic fuel injection or carburettor induction (1969-70); DBS 4 l Saloon (1967); DBS V8 Saloon 5.35 l 4 O.H.C. fuel injection engine (1969); V8 (1973); Lagonda 4-door (1974); Lagonda 4-door (1976); V8 Vantage (1977); Volante (1978). Entries in numerous competitions (Le Mans, Spa, Tourist Trophy, Nürburgring, Aintree). Won Le Mans and World Sports Car Championship in 1959.

ATELIERS DE CONSTRUCTIONS AUTOMOBILES — Switzerland

Founded in 1968. Proprietor: F. Sbarro. Head office and press office: ACA Atelier, 1411 Les Tuileries-de-Grandson. Works: as above, Grandson. 15 employees. 98 cars produced in 1982.

ATLANTIS MOTOR COMPANY Ltd — Great Britain

Company founded in 1980 to design and produce vintage replica type cars; the A1 is the first model. Production has began in 1983. Chairman and Managing Director: M. Booth. Secretary: Q.M.A. Booth. Head office, press office and works: Little London, Northwold, Thetford, Norfolk. 4 esployees.

AUDI NSU AUTO UNION AG — Germany (Federal Republic)

Established in 1969 as result of merger between Auto Union GmbH (founded in Zwickau in 1932 and transferred to Ingolstadt in 1949 when Zwickau company was nationalized) and NSU Motorenwerke AG (founded in 1873 at Riedlingen, moved to Neckarsulm in 1880; changed its name to Neckarsulmer Fahrzeugwerke AG in 1919 and became NSU Motorenwerke AG in 1960). Board of Directors: W. Habbel, F. Piëch, G. Kurrle, R. Gerich, M. Posth, H. Stübig. Head office and press office: Postfach 220, D-8070 Ingolstadt. Works: as above, Neckarsulm. 30,627 employees. 308,092 cars produced in 1982. Most important models: NSU Ro 80 (1967); Audi 100 and 100 LS (1969); Audi 100 Coupé S (1970); Audi 100 GL (1971); Audi 80, 80 L. 80 S, 80 LS, 80 GL (1972); Audi 100 (1976); Audi 100 5E (1977); Audi 80 (1978), Audi 200 5T (1980); Audi 100 (1982); Audi 200 Turbo (1983).

ASSEMBLY IN OTHER COUNTRIES — **South Africa:** VW of South Africa Ltd (associated company), P.O.B. 80, Uitenhage (assem. Audi 100 range).

AURORA CARS Ltd — Canada

Founded in 1977. President: D. Hatch. Vice-President: B. Hobson. Chairman of the Board: J. Plaxton. Head office and works: 36 Shelley Rd, Richmond Hill, Ontario L4C 5G3. 30 employees. 102 cars produced in 1982.

AUSTIN - see BL P.l.c.

AUTOBIANCHI — Italy

Created in 1955 in collaboration between Edoardo Bianchi firm and Fiat and Pirelli. Incorporated into Fiat in 1968 as Autobianchi, retaining, however, own maker's marks but incorporating sales organisation and maintenance services into Lancia. Office: Lancia, v. V. Lancia 27, 10141 Turin. 78,047 cars produced in 1982. See FIAT Auto S.p.A.

AUTOKRAFT Ltd — Great Britain

Managing Director: B.A. Angliss. Director: C.R. Angliss. Head office, press office and works: Unit 815, Brooklands Industrial Park, Weybridge, Surrey. 40 employees.

AUTOMOBILE APAL S.A. — Belgium

Chairman: E. Pery. Head office, press office and works: rue de la Fontaine 25, B-4570 Blegny. 30 employees, 80 cars produced in 1982.

AUTOMOBILES CITROËN — France

Founded in 1919 by André Citroën, became S.A. André Citroën in 1924, Citroën S.A. in 1968 and S.A. Automobiles Citroën in 1975. Present title since 1980. December 1974 38.2% of stock acquired by Automobiles Peugeot S.A. Since May 1976 Citroën S.A. is owned by the Peugeot S.A. group (to which Automobiles Peugeot S.A. belongs also). The first car launched since the merger of the two firms is the Citroën LN, presented in the summer of 1976. Board of Directors: J. Lombard, X. Karcher, R. Ravenel. Head office and press office: 62 Blvd Victor Hugo, Neuilly sur Seine 92208 Cedex. Works: as above; Levallois, Aulnay, Clichy, Saint-Ouen, Asnières, Nanterre, Rennes-La-Barre-Thomas, Rennes-La-Janais, Caen, Meudon, Saint-Etienne, Mulhouse, Reims, Metz, Tremery, Charleville. About 43,000 employees. 552,263 cars produced in 1982. Most important models: Torpedo A Type (1919); B2 10 CV (1921); 5 CV (1922); B12 10 CV (1925); B14 (1926); C6 (1928); 7A, 7 and 11 CV (1934); 15 Six (1938); 2 CV (1948); 2 CV 425 cc (1954); DS 19 (1955); ID 19 (1957); 2 CV 4 x 4 (1958); Ami 6 3 CV (1961); Ami 6 Break DS Pallas (1964); DS 21 (1965); Dyane (1967); Mehari (1968); SM and GS (1970); CX (1974); LN (1976); Visa, LNA (1978); Mehari 4 x 4 (1978); GSA (1979); CX Automotique (1980); Visa II (1981); BX (1982). Entries and first places in numerous competitions: World Distance and Speed Record at Montlhéry (1932-33), 28th Monte Carlo Rally and Constructors' Cup (1959), Liège-Sofia-Liège Road Marathon (1961), Norwegian Snow and Ice Winter Rally, Lyon Charbonnière-Solitude, Alpine Trophy, Thousand Lakes Rally, Constructors' Cup, Trophy of Nations (1962), Finnish Snow Rally, Northern Roads, Lyon-Charbonnière-Solitude, Norwegian Winter Rally, International Alpine Criterium, Constructors' Cup in Monte Carlo Rally and Liège-Sofia-Liège Marathon, Tour of Corsica (1963), Spa-Sofia-Liège Marathon (1964), Rallye Neige et Giace, Mobil Economy Run, Coupe des Alpes, Monte Carlo (1966), Constructors' Cup in Morocco Rally 1969-1977); Morocco Rally, TAP Portugal (1969); Chamonix Winter Run (1970); Morocco Rally (1970-71); World Cup Wembley-Munich (1974); Senegal Car Tour and Constructors' Cup London-Sydney (1977), Morocco Rally (1969, 1970 and 1971), Senegal Rally (1978, 1979).

MANUFACTURE AND ASSEMBLY IN OTHER COUNTRIES — **Indonesia:** P.T. Alun, Jalan Prof. Dr. Supamo SH 233 (subsidiary), P.O.B. 1326 Djakarta (assem. GSA). **Portugal:** Sociedad Citroën Lusitania SARL (subsidiary), Estrada de Nelas, Beira Alto, Mangualde (Dyane, GS, CX, Visa, MH, FAF). **Spain:** Citroën Hispania (subsidiary), free zone of Vigo (manuf. 2CV, Dyane, GSA, CX). **Tunisia:** Société Tunisienne d'Industrie Automobile (LNA).

AUTOMOBILES DANGEL S.A. — Frnace

Founded in 1980. President and Managing Director: H. Dangel. Head office, press office and works: 5 rue du Canal, 68780 Sentheim. 45 employees. 600 cars produced in 1983.

AUTOMOBILES MONTEVERDI Ltd — Switzerland

Founded in 1967. Chairman and Managing Director: P. Monteverdi. Vice-Chairman: P. Berger. Head office, press office and works: Oberwilerstr. 14-20, 4102 Binningen/Basel. 170 employees. 350 cars produced in 1981. Most important models: 2-seater (1968); High Speed 375 L 2+2 (1969); Hai 450 SS (1970); High Speed 375/4 Limousine (1971); Berlinetta (1972); Hai 450 GTS (1973); Palm Beach (1975); Sierra (1977).

AUTOMOBILES PEUGEOT — France

Founded in 1890 under the title "Les Fils de Peugeot Frères". Present title since 1966. Controlled since 1965 by Peugeot S.A. Merger with Automobiles Talbot on 1 January 1980. Board of Directors: J. Calvet (Chairman and Managing Director), J. Boillot (Vice-Chairman and Managing Director), L. Collaine (General Manager). Head office and press office: 75 Av. de la Grande Armée, Paris 75016. Works: Dijon, Lille, Mulhouse, Saint-Etienne, Sochaux, Vesoul, Bondy, La Rochelle, Sept Fons, Sully-Loire, Valancienne. About 60,000 employees. 552,263 vehicles produced in 1982. Most important models: Bébé Peugeot (1911); 201, 202 (1938); 301, 302, 402, 203 (1948); 403 (1955); 404 (1960); 204 (1965); 504 (1968); 304 (1969); 604 (1975); 305 (1978); 505 (1979); 205 (1983).

MANUFACTURE AND ASSEMBLY IN OTHER COUNTRIES — **Chile:** AFCH, Santiago (assem. 305,504). **Malaysia:** Asia Automobiles Industries, Petaling-Jaya (assem. 304, 504). **Nigeria:** Peugeot Automobiles Nigeria, Turakí Ali House, 3 Kanta Rd, Kaduna (assem. 504, 505). **Paraguay:** Automotores y Maquinaria, C.C. 1160, Asuncion (assem. 404, 504). **Portugal:** Movauto, Setubal (assem. 104, 304, 404, 504). **South Africa:** SIGMA (subsidiary), Johannesburg (assem. 305, 504, 505).

AUTOMOBILES STIMULA S.a.r.l. — France

Manufacturer of replicars in small series. Managing Director: X. de la Chapelle. Head office, press office and works: Chemin de Sacuny, 69530 Brignais. Production of Bugatti 55 began in 1978.

AUTOMOVILES TALBOT S.A. — Spain

Founded in 1951 as Barreiros Diesel S.A., 40% of shares were bought in 1963 by Chrysler Motor Corporation which became majority shareholder in 1967 eventually owing 99% of shares. Became Chrysler España in 1970. In 1978 a controlling interest was acquired by PSA Peugeot-Citroën. Present title since 1979. President: E. Chaves Viciana. Managing Director: G. Roy. Head office and press office: Apdo 140, Madrid 21. Works: Villaverde, Madrid. 14,500 employees. About 53,000 cars produced in 1982.

AUTOS y MÁQUINAS del ECUADOR S.A. — Ecuador

(Make: Aymesa)

Founded in 1968. General Manager: P. Acosta Espinosa. Assistant General Manager: R.J. Edmeades. Finance Manager: S.F. Dickson. Production Manager: F. Arteaga Valdiveso. Head office, press office and works: Casilla 370-A, Quito, Ecuador. 410 employees. 1,680 cars produced in 1982. Most important models: Condor (1970); Gala (1983). Condor winner Rally a Nariño (1982), has run in Caminos del Inca (Peru) and placed among the first 10 in all rallies held in Ecuador.

AVANTI MOTOR CORPORATION — USA

Founded in 1965, the corporation has been under new ownership since 1982. Chairman and CEO: S.H. Blake. President: S.H. Blake. Vice-President: J.S. Auten. Secretary and Treasurer: R.L. Bubick. Head office and works: P.O. 1916, South Bend, Ind. 46634. 150 employees, 200 cars produced in 1982.

AYMESA - see AUTOS y MÁQUINAS del ECUADOR S.A.

AZLK - AVTOMOBILNY ZAVOD IMENI LENINSKOGO KOMSOLA — USSR

(Make: Moskvich)

Press office: Avtoexport, Ul. Volkhonka 14, Moscow 119902. Works: Moscow, Izhevsk. 27,000 employees. About 200,000 cars produced in 1982.

BAYERISCHE MOTOREN WERKE AG **Germany (Federal Republic)**

Established in 1916 as Bayerische Flugzeugwerke AG. Present title since 1918. Chairman: E. von Kuenheim. Members of the Board: H. Hagen, F. Köhne, E.C. Sarfert. Head office and press office: P.O.B. 400240, 8 Munich 40. Works: Munich, Landshut, Dingolfing. 39,777 employees. 378,769 cars produced in 1982. Most important models: 3/15 hp Saloon (1928); 326, 327, 328 (1936); 501 6 cyl. (1951); V8 (1954); 503 and 507 Sport (1955); 700 (1959); 1500 (1962); 1800 (1963); 2000 (1966); 2002, 2500, 2800 (1968); 3,0, CS (1971); 520, 520 i (1972); 2002 Turbo (1973); 518 (1974); 320 (1975); 633 CSi (1976); 323i; 728, 730, 733i; (1977); 635 CSi (1978); 728i, 732i, 735i, 745i, M1 (1979). Entries and wins in numerous competitions (Mille Miglia, Monza 12 hour, Hockenheim, Nürburgring, Friburg Mountain Record, Brands Hatch, European Mountain Championship, Salzburgring, Rally TAP; winner 1968, 1969, 1973, 1976, 1978 and 1979 European Touring Cars Championship; 1973, 1974, 1975, 1978 and 1979 European F2 Championship; 1977, 1978 World Championship for Makes (under 2000 cc).

ASSEMBLY IN OTHER COUNTRIES — **South Africa:** BMW (South Africa) (Pty) Ltd, 6 Frans Du Toit St, Rosslyn, Pretoria (assem. 318i, 320i, 323i, 518i, 520i, 528i, 535, 728i, 733i, 735i, 745i). About 16,000 cars assembled outside Federal Republic in 1982.

BEIJING AUTOMOBILE WORKS **China (People's Republic)**

Founded in 1938, it assumed the name Beijing Automobile Repair Works in 1949 and then changed to Beijing Automobile Accessories Works. Engaged at first in repairing motor vehicles, in 1958 it began to produce passenger cars, the trade marks being JingGangShan, Beijing and DongFangHong. In the same year the title was changed to Beijing Automobile Works. In 1963 it began to manufacture light-duty cross-country vehicles. From 1966 to 1974 it was called the Dong Fang Hong Automobile Works but in 1975 changed back to Beijing Automobile Works. Director: Zhao Nai Lin. Head office, press office and works: Chuihangliu, Chaoyangqu, Beijing. 10,117 employees. 17,000 units produced in 1981. Present models are BJ-212, BJ-212A, and BJ-212E, and its trade marks are JingGangShan, Beijing and DongFangHong.

BENTLEY MOTORS Limited **Great Britain**

Founded in 1920, taken over by Rolls-Royce Ltd in 1931, specializing in high-class vehicles. Works and press office: Crewe, Ches. CWl, 3 Pl. Most important models: first Bentley 3.5 l manufactured by Rolls-Royce (1933); 4.5 l (1936); 4.5 l MK VI (1946); Continental (1951); "R" Type (1952); S1 (1955); S2 (1959); S3 (1962) "T" series (1965); Corniche (1971); T2 (1977), Mulsanne (1980), Mulsanne Turbo (1982).

BERTONE (Carrozzeria) S.p.A. **Italy**

Founded in 1912. Produces small and medium series of car bodies: bespoke production for car manufacturing firms and construction of prototypes. President and Managing Director: N. Bertone. Head office: c.so Peschiera 223, Turin. Press office and works: c.so Canonico Allamano 40-46, 10095 Grugliasco, Turin.

BITTER-AUTOMOBILE GmbH & Co. KG **Germany (Federal Republic)**

Head office and press office: Berliner Str. 57, 5830 Schwelm. 25 employees, 130 cars produced in 1982.

BL P.l.c. **Great Britain**

(Makes: Austin, Morris, MG, Rover, Triumph, Jaguar, Daimler, Land Rover).

BL P.l.c., 99% of whose shares are now held by British Government, is Britain's largest producer of motor vehicles. Formed in May 1968, following merger between British Motor Holdings (BMC and Jaguar) and Leyland Motor Corporation (Leyland Motors, Rover and Triumph), it employs more than 100,000 throughout the world. Worldwide sales of Austin Morris, MG, Rover and Triumph cars are responsibility of Austin Rover Group Ltd, Canley, Coventry. Worldwide sales of Jaguar and Daimler cars are responsibility of Jaguar Cars Ltd, Browns Lane, Coventry, and sales of Land Rover and Range Rover are handled by Land Rover Ltd, Lode Lane, Solihull. Head office: BL P.l.c., 35/38 Portman Square, London W1H OHQ. Chairman: Sir Austin Bide. 425,741 cars produced in 1982.

MANUFACTURE AND ASSEMBLY IN OTHER COUNTRIES — The Company sells its vehicles in 175 countries. Major manufacturing and assembly plants are in Madras in India (commercial vehicles), Sydney in Australia (commercial vehicles), and Cape Town and Hong Kong. For specific details apply to BL P.l.c., 35-38 Portman Square, London W1H OHQ.

BMW (South Africa) (Pty) Ltd **South Africa**

A privatly owned company began assembly of BMW 1800 and 2000 models with Glas bodywork in 1968. In 1973 the Munich-based parent company, Bayerische Motoren Werke, took control over the South African operation. South Africa has the only BMW production plant in the world outside Germany. In 1974 the 5-series was launched with the 7-series following in 1978 and the 3-series in 1983. These models are continuously updated as technology advances. BMW South Africa is actively involved in motorsport in various classes and categories. Chairman: E. von Kuenheim. Managing Director: E. von Koeber. Directors: D.F. Balfour, V.H. Doolan, G.J.J.F. Steyn, H.K. Zwiefelhofer, B. Pischetsrieder, B.M. Gilfillan, N.E. Wiehahn. Head office and press office: André Greyvenstein Rd, Isando 1600. Works: 6 Frans Du Toit St, Rosslyn, Pretoria. 2,600 employees. About 16,000 cars produced in 1982.

BRISTOL CARS Ltd **Great Britain**

Established in 1946 as Car Division of Bristol Aeroplane Co., became affiliated company of Bristol Aeroplane Co. in 1955, and subsidiary of Bristol Siddeley Engines In 1959. Became privately owned company in 1960 and owned by partnership from 1966. Chairman and Managing Director: T.A.D. Crook. Head office, press office: 368-370 Kensington High St, London. Works: Filton, Bristol BS 997AR. 104 cars produced in 1982. Most important models: 400 (1947); 401 and 402 (1949); 403 and 404 (1953-55); 405 (1954-58); 406 (1958); 407 (1961); 408 (1963); 409 (1965); 410 (1967); 411 (1969); 412 (1975); 603 (1976); 412/S2, Beaufighter (1980); Brigand, Britannia, Beaufighter (1983). Entries and first places in numerous competitions with Bristol cars or Bristol-engined cars (Monte Carlo Rally, Targa Florio, Mille Miglia) with F1 and F2 (British GP, GP of Europe, Sebring, Reims, Montlhéry, Le Mans, etc.), from 1946 until 1955.

BUICK - see GENERAL MOTORS CORPORATION

CADILLAC - see GENERAL MOTORS CORPORATION

CATERHAM CAR Sales Ltd **Great Britain**

In 1973 took over manufacture of Lotus Seven introduced by Lotus Cars Ltd in 1957. Directors: G.B. Nearn, D.S. Wakefield, M.J. Nearn. Head office, press office and works: Seven House, Town End, Caterham Hill, Surrey CR3 5UG. 18 employees. About 200 cars produced in 1982. Models: Super Seven Series III powered by Lotus big valve twin cam engine; Ford 1600 GT OHV; Ford/Sprint 1600.

CHANGCHUN AUTOMOBILE PLANT **China (People's Republic)**

(Make: Hong Qi)

Changchun No. 1 Automobile Plant was founded in 1953. The Limousine Division was founded in 1963 and expanded in 1972. Director: Huang Zhao Luan. Head office, press office and works: Dongfeng Dajie, Chaoyangqu, Changahun, Ji Lin Province. 1,900 employees. About 300 units produced in 1981. Most important models: Hong Qi CA 770A (1963), CA 770B.

CHEVROLET - see GENERAL MOTORS CORPORATION, GENERAL MOTORS DO BRASIL, GENERAL MOTORS OF CANADA Ltd

CHRYSLER CORPORATION **USA**

(Makes: Chrysler, Dodge, Plymouth)

Founded in 1925 as successor to Maxwell Motors Corp. It holds third place in U.S. motor industry. Chrysler Corp. American operations are made up of a U.S. Automotive Sales selling Chrysler, Dodge, Plymouth cars and trucks. Chairman and CEO: L.A. Iacocca. Vice-Chairman: G. Greenwald. President and N. American Automotive Operations: H.K. Sperlich. Head office and press office Chrysler Corp.: 12000 Lynn Townsend Dr., Highland Park Mich. Mailing address: Chrysler Corp., Chrysler Center, P.O. Box 1919, Detroit, Mich. 48288. Works: 5 vehicle assembly plants (U.S.), 1 (Canada) and 18 supporting manufacturing plants throughout the U.S. and Canada. 73,300 employees in U.S., 11,258 in Canada. 600,502 (U.S.), 149,442 (Canada) cars produced in 1982. Most important models: Chrysler (1924); Plymouth and Dodge (1928).

MANUFACTURE IN OTHER COUNTRIES — **Mexico:** Chrysler de Mexico, S.A. (subsidiary), P.O. Box 53-951, Mexico 17, D.F. Mexico (manuf. Dodge Dart, Volare). 76,342 cars produced outside USA and Canada in 1982.

CITROËN - see AUTOMOBILES CITROËN

CITROËN (Portugal) - see AUTOMOBILES CITROËN

CLASSIC-CAR JANSSEN **Germany (Federal Republic)**

Manufacturer of replicars in small series. Head office, press office and works: Am Raffelberg 4, D-5880 Lüdenscheid.

CLASSIC-CAR-OLDTIMERBAU **Germany (Federal Republic)**

Manufacturer of replicars in small series. Head office, press office and works: Otto-Lilienthal-Str. 14, D-64000 Fulda.

COMPANHIA INDUSTRIAL SANTA MATILDE Inc. Co. **Brazil**

Chairman: H.J. Pimentel Duarte da Fonseca. Vice-Chairman: L.C.Amaro da Silveira. Directors: A.L. Pimentel Duarte da Fonseca, J.C. Pimentel Duarte da Fonseca, S. Torres Meurer, Z. Paraquett Marques. Head office and press office: Rua Buenos Aires 100, Rio de Janeiro 20070. Works: Rua Isaltino Silveira 768, Tres Rios 25800, Rio de Janeiro. 50 cars produced in 1982.

CUSTOCA **Austria**

Proprietor: G. Höller. Head office and works: 8714 Kraubath/Mur 55. 12 employees. 250 cars produced in 1980.

DACIA - see INTREPRINDEREA DE AUTOTURISME PITESTI

DAEWOO MOTOR COMPANY Ltd **Korea**

Formerly Saehan Motor Company. Present title since 1981. President: M.G. Choi. Head office and works: 199 Cheong-Cheon-Dong, Bug-gu, Incheon. Press Office: Daewoo Center Bldg, 12th F1 541, 5-GA, Namdaemun-ro, Jung-gu, Seoul.

DAIHATSU KOGYO COMPANY Ltd **Japan**

Established in 1907 as Hatsudoki Seizo Kabushiki Kaisha, present title since 1951. Now belong to Toyota Group of companies. Chairman: E. Ohhara. President: T. Eguchi. Executive Vice-Presidents: J. Ono, H. Yasumura. Senior Managing Directors: J. Takahashi, J. Ohsuga. Managing Directors: Y. Izumi, E. Asuke. Head office and works: 1-1 Daihatsu-cho, Ikeda-shi, Osaka, Ohyamasaki-machi, Otokuni-gun, Kyoto-fu. Press office: Daihatsu Motor Sales Co. Ltd, 2-7 Ninonbashi-Honcho, Chuoku, Tokyo. 10,700 employees. 265,629 (including 4WD Tafts) vehicles produced in 1982. Production of 4-wheeled vehicles begun in 1958. Most important models: Compagno Station Wagon (1963); Compagno 800 Sedan (1964); Compagno Spider and Sedan (1965); Fellow 360 (1966); Consorte Berlina (1969); Fellow Max (1970); Charmant (1974); Charade (1977); Charade Runabout (1978); Mira (1980); Cuore (1980); Charade (1982).

MANUFACTURE IN OTHER COUNTRIES — **Costa Rica:** Ensembladora Automotriz, P.O.B. 41.12, San José. **Greece:** Automeccanica S.A., Ilissou 47, Athens. **Indonesia:** P.T. Gaya Motor, VL Sulawasi 2 Pandiung Priok, Djakarta. **Malaysia:** Borneo Toyota Assembly Sdn. Bdh, P.O.B. 814, Kuala Lumpur. **New Zealand:** General Motors New Zealand Ltd, Alexander Rd, Trentham, Upperhutt, Wellington. **Thailand:** Bangchan General Assembly Co., Ltd, 99 Moo 4 Sukhapibal Rd, Tambol Kannayao Amphur, Bankgkapi. **South Africa:** Alfa Romeo South Africa (Pty) Ltd, Pretoria, 750 Main Rd, Wunberg Sandton. **Taiwan:** Yue Tyan Machinery MFG Co. Ltd, Taipei. 9,380 cars produced outside Japan in 1982.

DAIMLER - see BL P.l.c.

DAIMLER-BENZ AG **Germany (Federal Republic)**

(Make: Mercedes-Benz)

Established in 1926 as a result of merger between Daimler-Motorengesellschaft and Benz & Cie; it is the best-known German manufacturer of highclass cars. Board of Directors: W. Breitschwerdt (Chairman); W. Ulsamer, W. Niefer, R. Osswald, H.C. Hoppe, E. Reuter (members). Head office and press office: Mercedes-Strasse 136, 7 Stuttgart. Works: as above; Sindelfingen, Mannheim, Gaggenau, Berlin-Marienfelde, Düsseldorf, Bad Homburg, Wörth/Rhein. 149,118 employees. 458,345 cars produced in 1982. Most important models: Stuttgart 200, Mannheim (1926); Stuttgart 260, Mannheim 350 and Sport-Wagen SSK (1928); Grosser Mercedes (1930); Nürburg 500 (1931); 170 V (1935); 260 D, first Diesel car (1935); Grosser Mercedes (1938); 170 V (1946); 300 SL (1954); 190 SL (1955); 180 b/Db and 220 Sb (1959); 190 c/Dc and 300 SE (1961); 230 SL and 600 (1963); 250 (1966); 200, 220, 230, 250, 280 S, 280 SE, 300 SEL 6.3, 250 C, 250 SE (1968); 280 SE 3.5, 300 SEL 3.5 (1969); 350 SL, 450 SL (1971); 280 SE, 350 SE, 450 SE (1972); 240 D, 230/4 (1973); 240 D 3.0 (1974); 450 SEL 6.9 (1975); 200 D, 280 E (1976); 230-280 C, 280 CE (1977); 300 SD, 450 SLC, 240 - 300 TD, 230-250 T, 280 TE

(1978); 380 SE, 380 SEL, 500 SE, 500 SEL (1979); 200, 200 T, 230 E, 230 LE, 230 TE, 380 SL, 380 SLC, 500 SL, 500 SLC, 300 TD (1980). First places in numerous international competitions (1894-1955; 1978-1980).

DANGEL - see AUTOMOBILES DANGEL S.A.

DAYTONA AUTOMOTIVE FIBERGLASS Inc. **USA**

Established in 1976. President: LaVerne Martincic. Vice-President: M. Zimmerman. Production Manager and Secretary: E. Kuhel. Head office, press office and works: 819 Carswell Ave, Holly Hill, Fla. 32017.

De COURVILLE **USA**

Formerly de Courville Group Inc. and now independent. President: N. de Courville. Head office and press office: 999 North Doheny Drive, Los Angeles, Ca. 90069. Works: Gatsby Coachworks, P.O. Box 23099, San Josè, Ca. 95153.

DESANDE - see GRAND PRIX METALCRAFT

DE TOMASO MODENA S.p.A. AUTOMOBILI **Italy**

Founded in 1959. President: A. de Tomaso. Managing Director and General Manager: A. Bertocchi. Head office, press office and works: v. Emilia Ovest 1250, Modena. 60 employees. About 100 cars produced in 1982. Most important models: Berlinetta Vallelunga with Ford Cortina 1500 engine (two-seater); Sport Prototype 5-litre (1965); Mangusta with V8 4700 engine (1966); Pantera with V8 5700 engine, 310 hp (1970); Deauville 4-door with 5700 engine (1971); Longchamp 2+2 with V8 5700 engine (1973); Longchamp Spider (1982); Pantera GT 5 (1982).

DODGE - see CHRYSLER CORPORATION

DONKERVOORT **Holland**

Established in 1978. Proprietor: J. Donkervoort. Head office and works: Laan van Niftarlake 10, 3612 BS Tienhoven (Utr.). 4 employees. 30 cars produced in 1982.

Dr. Ing. h.c. F. PORSCHE A.G. **Germany (Federal Republic)**

Founded in 1948. Owned by Porsche Holding Co. Chairman: F. Porsche. Managing Director: P.W. Schutz. Directors: H. Branitzki, H. Bott, H. Lange. Head office and press office: Porschestr. 42, 7 Stuttgart-Zuffenhausen. Works: Schwieberdingerstr., 7 Stuttgart-Zuffenhausen. 5,558 employees. 36,329 cars produced in 1982. Most important models: type 356/1100, 1300, 1300 S, 1500 S (1950-1955); 356 A/1300, 1300 S, 1600, 1600 S, Carrera (1955-1959); 356 B/1600, 1600 S, 1600 S-90, Carrera (1959-1963); 356 C/1600 C, 1600 SC (1963-1965); 911, 912 (1965-1966); 911, 911 S, 912 (1967); 911 T, S, 912 (1968); 911 T, E, S, Carrera (1969-1976); 924, Turbo (1976); 928 (1977). First places in numerous international competitions: Le Mans 24 hours with 1100 Coupé (1951), Sebring (1958-59), European Mountain Championship (1960-68), Targa Florio and Nürburgring (1959-1967-68-69-70-73), Constructors' Cup for F2 cars (1960), European Rally Championship with Carrera (1961), GT World Championship up to 2000 cc (1962-63-64-65), World Cup for speed and endurance, European Touring Car Trophy, 32 national championships. Overall wins in Le Mans 24 hours (1970-71-76-77-79-81-82), Rallye Monte Carlo winners (1968-69-70-78), International Rallye Championship (1968-69-70), Grand Touring Car Championship and International Manufacturers Championship (1969-70-71-76-77-78-79).

DUTTON CARS Ltd **Great Britain**

First Dutton built in 1968. Chairman and Managing Director: T. Dutton-Wooley. Head office and works: 53 Broadwater St, Worthing, W. Sussex BN14 9BY.

ELEGANT MOTORS Inc. **USA**

Founded in 1971. Owner: D.O. Amy. Head office, press office and works: Box 30188. Indianapolis, In 46230. 8 employees. 140 cars produced in 1982.

EL-NASR AUTOMOTIVE MANUFACTURING Co. **Egypt**

Founded in 1959. Chairman: A. I. Gazarin. Vice-Chairman: O. M. Amin. Head office, press office and works: Wadi-Hof, Helwan.

ENVEMO - ENGENHARIA DE VEICULOS E MOTORES **Brazil**

Founded in 1965. Manufacturer of cars, off-road vehicles, and racing accessories. Specializing in engineering and developing high output engines for road and race, and also in restoration of classic cars. Directors: L.F. Gonçalves, A.M. Gonçalves, J.G. Whitaker Ribeiro. Head office, press office and works: Rua Olimpiadas, 237 Vila Olimpia, SP. 150 employees. About 100 cars produced in 1982.

ERA REPLICA AUTOMOBILES Inc. **USA**

A division of International Automobile Enterprises Inc. Established in 1967 as International Automobile Enterprises. Incorporated 1972. Production started October 1980. President: P.R. Gaudette. Vice-President: T.J. Portante. General Manager: P.E. Portante. Secretary and Treasurer: R. Putnam. Head office and works: 608-612 East Main St, New Britain, Conn. 04051. Press office: JVS Enterprises, 19 Cook Close, Ridge Field, Conn. 12 employees. 42 cars produced in 1982.

EXCALIBUR AUTOMOBILE CORPORATION **USA**

Founded in 1964 as SS Automobiles Inc. Present title since 1976. President: D.B. Stevens. Executive Vice-President: W.C. Stevens. Head office and works: 1735 South 106th St, Milwaukee, Wisc. 53214. 125 employees. 212 cars produced in 1982. Models: Roadster, Phaeton.

FABRYKA SAMOCHÓDOW MALOLITRAZOWYCH **Poland**

(Makes: 126, Syrena)

Founded in 1972. State-owned company. Director: J. Jelonek. Head office and press office: ul. Sarni Stok 93, 43-300 Bielsko-Biala. Works: Bielsko-Biala. About 175,000 126 P and 10,000 Syrena cars produced in 1981.

FABRYKA SAMOCHÓDOW OSOBOWYCH **Poland**

Founded in 1949. State-owned Company. Chairman: J. Bielecki. Vice-Presidents: M. Karwas, S. Tyminski, J. Burchard, Z. Chorazy, J. Salamokczyk. Head office, press office and works: ul. Stalingradzka 50, Warsaw. 25,000 employees. About 82,000 cars produced in 1981. Most important models: Warzawa 223, 224 (1964-1973); Syrena 104 (1958-1973); Polski-Fiat 125 P (1968); Polonez (1978). Entries in rallies (Monte Carlo, Acropolis, 1000 Lakes, etc.).

FARUS Ltda INDUSTRIA DE VEÍCULOS ESPORTIVOS **Brazil**

Chairman: A. Russo. Vice-Chairman: G. Russo. Financial Director: P. Russo Santiago De Resende. General Manager: A. Zinoviev. Head office, press office and works: Rua Divisa Nova, 30-A, Salgado Filho, Belo Horizonte, Minas Gerais. 130 employees. About 130 cars produced in 1981.

FASA-RENAULT **Spain**

Founded in 1951. President: M. Guasch Molins. Vice-President: C. Weets. Managing Director: M. Bougler. Head office: Arco de Ladrillo 58, Valladolid. Press office: Avda de Burgos 89, Aptdo 262, Madrid 34. Works: Valladolid, Palencia, Sevilla. 21,813 employees. 325,754 cars produced in 1982.

FERRARI Società per azioni Esercizio Fabbriche Automobili e Corse **Italy**

Founded in 1929 as Scuderia Ferrari, became Società Auto-Avio Costruzioni Ferrari in 1940 and Ferrari S.p.A.-SEFAC in 1960. Since 1-7-1969, Fiat has been associated on joint venture basis and company has used its present title. Its name is bound up with superb technical achievements in field of racing and GT cars. Hon. President: E. Ferrari. President: V. Ghidella. Managing Director: G. Sguazzini. Head office: vl. Trento Trieste 31, 41100 Modena. Press office and works: v. Abetone Inferiore 4, 41053 Maranello (Modena). 1,599 employees (including Scaglietti, Modena). 2,209 cars produced in 1982. Most important GT models: 125 (1947); 166 Inter (1949); 340 America (1952); 250 GT, V12 250 GT, Superfast (1961); 275 GTB 4 Berlinetta (1963); Dino 206 GT Berlinetta, 365 Coupé GT 2+2 (1967): 365 GTB 4 Berlinetta, 246 GT Dino (1969); 308 GTB (1975). Entries and wins in various world competitions and championships. 25 times world champion.

FIAT AUTO S.p.A. **Italy**

Founded in July 1899 as Società Anonima Fabbrica Italiana di Automobili Torino, in October that year it adopted the title F.I.A.T. for engines and vehicles, which from 1918 on is written FIAT either with capital or small letters. In 1968, FIAT incorporated Autobianchi which is still produced as separate make. In 1969 it took over Lancia and acquired 50% of Ferrari shares and in 1971 took over Abarth, incorporated in 1981. In 1976, reorganisation of Fiat Group was practically completed. The new Fiat Holding is a structure in which all sectors are now organized with their own design, production and marketing responsibilities, some as individual legal entities and others with Fiat S.p.A. but with similar management autonomy. Among these is Fiat Auto S.p.A. (incorporating Lancia-Autobianchi and Abarth). Head office: corso Agnelli 200, Turin. Press office: corso Marconi 10, 10100 Turin. Works: Turin Mirafiori, Turin S. Paolo, Rivalta, Chivasso, Verrone, Villar Perosa, Vado Ligure, Desio, Florence, Sulmona, Termoli, Cassino, Termini Imerese. President: U. Agnelli. Managing Director: V. Ghidella. 116,086 employees. 1,212,300 vehicles produced in 1982 (including Abarth, Autobianchi and Lancia). Most important models: Fiat 3½ HP (1899-1900); 6 HP and 8 HP, 12 HP, 24-32 HP (1900-04); 16-24 HP (1903-04); Brevetti and 60 HP (1905-09); 18-24 (1908); Fiacre mod. 1 (1908-10); Fiat 1,2,3,4,5 (1910-18); Zero and 3 ter (1912-15); 2B and 3A (1912-21); 70 (1915-20); 501 (1919-26); 505 and 510 (1919-25); Superfiat (1921-22); 519 (1922-24); 502 (1923-26); 509 (1925-27); 503 and 507 (1926-27); 512 (1926-28); 520 (1927-29); 521 (1928-31); 525 (1928-29); 525 S (1929-31); 514 and 514 MM (1929-32); 515, 522 C and 524 C (1931-34); 508 Balilla and 508 S Balilla Sport (1932-37); 518 Ardita (1933-38); 527 Ardita 2500 (1934-36); 1500 (1935-48); 500 (1936-48); 508 C Balilla 1100 (1937-39); 2800 (1938-44); 1100 (1939-48); 500 B and Giardiniera (1948-49); 1100 B and 1500 D (1948-49); 1500 E (1949-50); 1100 E (1949-53); 500 C (1949-54); 500 C Giardiniera (1949-52); 1100 ES (1950-51); 1400, 1400 A and 1400 B (1950-58); 500 C Belvedere (1951-55); 1900 A and 1900 B (1952-58); 8V (1952-54); Nuova 1100 and Nuova 1100 Familiare (1953-56); 1100 TV (1953-56); 600 (1955-60); 1100/103 E (1956-57); Nuova 500 Trasformabile (1957-60); 1100/103 D (1957-60); Nuova 500 Sport (1958-60); 1200 Gran Luce (1957-60); 1200 Trasformabile (1958-59); 1100/103 H (1959-60); 1800 and 1800 Familiare (1959-61); 1100 Special (1960-62); 500 D (1960-65); 600 D Multipla, 500 Giardiniera (1960-68); 1300, 1500, 1300 Familiare, 2300 Coupé, 2300 S Coupé (1961-68); 1600 S Cabriolet (1962-66); 850 (1964-71); 124 and 124 Sport Spider (1966); Dino Spider (1966); 125, Dino Coupé, 124 Sport Coupé,850, 850 Idroconvert (1967); 850 Special Sport Coupé, Sport Spider, 500 L, 124 Special, 125 Special (1968); 128, 128 Familiare, 124 Sport Coupé 1600, 124 Sport Spider 1600, Dino Coupé 2400, Dino Spider 2400, 130 (1969); 124 Special T (1970); 127, 128 Rally, 128 Coupé, 130 3200, 130 Coupé (1971); 126, 127 3 Porte, X 1/9, 124 Spider Rally, 124 Coupé and Spider 1600 and 1800, 132 (1972); 126 Tetto Apribile, 132 GLS, 128 Special, 127 Special, 131 Mirafiori (1974); 128 3P (1975); 126 Personal (1976); 132 1600-2000, 127 900-1050 CL (1972). It has been entering competitions since 1900, when true racing car was not yet born. First national wins, followed by many others. In Automobile Tour of Italy with 6-8 HP, a car with two horizontal rear cylinders. Since 1904 numerous first places in international field. In 1927 officially retired from motor racing. Since 1970 works competition in rallies. In 1977, 1978, and 1980 World Rally Championship with Fiat 131 Abarth. In 1972, 1974, 1975, 1976 and 1983 world Rally championship with Lancia Rally.

MANUFACTURE AND ASSEMBLY IN OTHER COUNTRIES — **Argentina:** Sevel S.A. (associated company), Calle Umberto I 1,001, 1,682 Villa Bosch (manuf. Fiat 147, 128; Peugeot 504, 505). **Brazil:** Fiat Automoveis Co. (affiliated company), Rodovia Fernaõo Dias, km 9, Betim, Minas Gerais (manuf. Alfa Romeo, 147). **Chile:** Fiat Chile S.A. (affiliated company), Carmen 8, Santiago (assem. 600, 125). **Colombia:** Compania Colombiana Automotriz S.A. (associated company), Calle 13 n. 38-54, Bogotà (assem. 128, 125). **Egypt:** El-Nasr Automotive Mfg Co. Ltd (licensee company), Wadi-Hof, Helwan, Cairo (assem. 127, Ritmo, 131, Polonez). **Indonesia:** Daha Motors (licensee company), Medan Merkeda Selatan 2, Djakarta (assem. 131, 127, 132 S). **Malaysia:** Sharikat Fiat Distributors (licensee company), Tanglin Rd 99/101, Singapore (assem. 127, 128, 131, 132). **Morocco:** Somaca (associated company), km 12 Autoroute de Rabat, Casablanca (assem. 127, 131, 132). **Poland:** FSO (licensee company), Stalingradzka 23, Warszawa (manuf. 125 P; FSM (licensee company), Bialsko-Biala (manuf. 126). **Portugal:** Somave Sarl (licensee company), Av. Eng. Duarte Pacheco 15, Lisbon (assem. 131). **Thailand:** Karnasuta General Assembly Co. (licensee company), P.O.B. 1421, Bangkok (assem. 128, 131, 132 S). **Turkey:** Tofas (associated company), Zincirlikuyu, Buynkdere Caddesi 145, Kat 4,5 Levent, Istanbul (manuf. 131). **Venezuela:** Fiav (associated company), Urbanizacion Industrial Soco, La Victoria, E. do Aragna (assem. 131, 132). **Yugoslavia:** Zavodi Crvena Zastava (licensee company), Span, Boraca 2, Kragujevac (manuf. Zastava 750, 128, 1300, 1500, 125 PZ, 126 P, 132 GLS). **Zambia:** Livingstone Motor Assemblers Ltd (associated company), P.O.B. 2718, Lusaka (assem. 127, 128, 131, 132 S).

FIAT AUTOMOVEIS S.A. **Brazil**

(Makes: Alfa Romeo, Fiat)

Founded in March 1973, started production in June 1976. Chairman: M.A. Gonçalves De Souza. Vice-Chairman: A. De Vito. Manging Director: S. Valentino. Head office, press office and works: Rodovia Fernaõ Dias, km 429, 32500 Betim, Minas Gerais. 9,000 employees. 130,883 cars produced in 1982.

Models: 147 L (1976); 147 L (1977); 147, 147 L, 147 GL, 147 GLS, 147 Rallye, Alfa Romeo B, Alfa romeo TI (1979); 147, 147 L, 147 GL, 147 GLS, 147 Rallye, Panorama C, Alfa Romeo SL, Alfa Romeo TI-4 (1980); 147, 147 L, 147 GL, 147 GLS, 147 Rallye, Panorama C, Alfa Romeo SL, Alfa Romeo TI-4, Panorama CL, (1981), 147 C, 147 CL, 147 TOP, 147 Racing, Panorama C, Panorama CL, Alfa Romeo TI-4, Alfa Romeo Alcool TI (1982). Entries in numerous Brazilian rallies.

FORD BRASIL S.A. **Brazil**

Established in 1919. Ford-Willys merge in 1967. President: R.M. Gerrity. Vice-President: T.A. Turner. Directors: T.J. Drake, W.R. Kyle, J.M. Branco Ribeiro, J.P. Dias, L.H. De Ferran. Head office and press office: Av. Rudge Ramos 1501, São Paulo. Works; Av. Henry Ford 1787, São Paulo; Av. do Taboão 899, São Bernardo do Campo; Parque das Industrias, Taubaté, SP; Av. Henry Ford 17, Osasco, SP. 21,000 employees. 112,000 cars produced in 1982. Most important models: Ford T (1924); Willys Jeep (1954); Rural CJ-5 (1958); Renault Dauphine (1959); Aero Willys (1960); Itamaraty (1965); Ford Galaxie 500 (1967); Corcel Sedan and Ford LTD Landau (1968); Corcel Coupé (1969); Corcel Sedan and Ford LTD Landau (1968); Corcel Coupé (1969); Corcel Belina Station Wagon (1970); Maverick (1973); Corcel II, Corcel II Belina (1977); Del Rey (1981); Escort (1983). Entries in numerous competitions from 1962 to 1968. Brazilian Makers Championship in 1972-73 with Corcel. Brazilian Touring Car Championship (Group 1) in 1973-74 with Maverick. Brazilian Makers Championship with Avallone-Ford in 1974 and with Hollywood-Berta-Ford in 1975. Formula Ford-Corcel promoter in 1971-1983. Promoter of group one Fia Corcel II Brazilian Tournament, started in 1979, discontinued 1983. Debut of Ford Escort in the Brazilian Championship of Makes, 1983.

FORD MOTOR ARGENTINA S.A. **Argentina**

Incorporated 1959. President: J.M. Courard. Directors: J.H. Nogueira, G.F.J. Alfonso Correas, T.R. Landajo, E.J. Lorenzo, P.W. Muller, D.R.C. Towers. Head office and press office: cc Central 696, Buenos Aires. Works: Pacheco. 7,300 employees. 35,138 cars produced in 1982.

FORD MOTOR COMPANY **USA**

(Makes: Ford, Lincoln, Mercury)

Founded in 1903, is the second largest of the American motor manufacturers. Chairman and Chief Executive Officer: P. Caldwell. Vice-Chairman of the Board and Chairman of the Executive Committee: W.C. Ford. President and Chief Operating Officer: D.E. Peterson. Executive Vice-President International Automotive Operations: R.A. Lutz. Executive Vice-President North American Automotive Operations: H.A. Poling. Components include Ford Division (300 Renaissance Center, P.O.B. 43303, Detroit, Mich. 48423. Vice-President and General Manager L.E. Lataif) and Lincoln-Mercury Division (300 Renaissance Center, P.O.B. 43322, Detroit, Mich. 48243. Vice-President and General Manager G.B. MacKenzie). World headquarters: The American Rd, Dearborn, Mich. Car and truck assembly plants: Atlanta, Ga.; Chicago, Ill.; Dearborn, Wayne (2) and Wixom, Mich.; Kansas City and St. Louis, Mo.; Lorain and Avon Lake, Ohio; Louisville, Ky. (2); Metuchen, N.J.; Norfolk, Va.; Twin Cities, Minn. 155,900 employees. 1,104,074 cars produced in 1982.

MANUFACTURE AND ASSEMBLY IN OTHER COUNTRIES (excluding models of Ford Motor Company Ltd, Great Britain, of Ford Motor Company of Canada Ltd, Canada, Ford Werke AG, Germany, of Ford Brasil S.A., Brazil and of Ford Motor Company of Australia Ltd, (Australia) — **Argentina:** Ford Motor Argentina S.A. (subsidiary), C.C. Central 696, Buenos Aires (manuf. and assem. Fairlane, Falcon, Taunus). **Ireland:** Henry Ford & Sons Ltd (subsidiary). Cork (assem. Sierra). **Malaysia:** Sdn. Bhd. P.O.B. 2612 Kuala Lumpur (assem. Laser, Telstar). **Mexico:** Ford Motor Co. S.A. (subsidiary), Mexico City (manuf. and assem. Fairmont, Grand Marquis, Mustang). **New Zealand:** Ford Motor Co. of New Zealand Ltd (subsidiary), P.O.B. 30012, Lower Hutt (assem. Falcon, Laser, Testar, Fairlane). **Philippines:** Herautility Vehicle, P.O.B. 415, Makati Metro, 3117 Manila (assem. Telstar, Laser, Granada). **Spain:** Ford España S.A. (subsidiary), Edificio Cuzco III/P. Castellana 135, Madrid 15 (manuf. and assem. Fiesta, Escort). **South Africa:** Ford Motor Co. of South Africa (Pty) Ltd (subsidiary), P.O.B. 788, Port Elizabeth (assem. Granada, Sierra, Escort). **Taiwan:** Ford Lio Ho Motor Co. Ltd (subsidiary), Taipel (assem. Laser, Telstar, Granada). **Uruguay:** Ford (Uruguay) S.A. (subsidiary), C.C. 296, Montevideo (assem. Falcon). **Venezuela:** Ford Motor de Venezuela S.A. (subsidiary), Apdo Postal 354 Valencia (assem. Corcel II, Del Rey, Conquistador, Cougar). 2,305,950 cars and trucks produced outside USA in 1982.

FORD MOTOR COMPANY Ltd **Great Britain**

From 1903-1909, Ford sales in Britain were handed by agencies, but following the world launch of the Model T Ford in London in October 1908, opportunity was taken to form an English branch company, incorporated in 1909. Manufacture began in October 1911 in Trafford Park, Manchester, the first European car factory to incorporate a moving production line (from 1913). In 1931, having built well over 300,000 cars, Trafford Park was succeeded by the vast new Dagenham factory, then Europe's biggest car plant, built beside the River Thames near London. From here, Ford has produced millions of significant cars, including the 8 hp Model Y (1932), the Prefect (1939) and Anglia (1940), the V8 Pilot (1947), Consul and Zephyr Mk I (1950), Anglia 105E (1959) and Mk I Cortina (1962). A second car plant was opened at Halewood, Merseyside in the 1960s. Today, Dagenham, now Britain's most highly-robotised car plant, is still at the heart of Ford's British making cars, trucks, tractors and components. 60,000 employees. In 1982, Ford's British factories built 307,640 Fiestas, Escorts, Cortinas and Sierras. Head Office and Public Affairs: Eagle Way, Warley, Brentwood, Essex CM13 3BW.

ASSEMBLY IN OTHER COUNTRIES — The Company's KD Operations are responsible for the export of cars and trucks in component form for assembly overseas at 16 overseas assembly plants in 14 countries around the world. Vehicles are supplied in KD form, as opposed to built-up, to comply with import regulations designed to create local employment by setting up a vehicle assembly and components supply industry. Total KD volume for all products in 1982 was around 160,000 units of which 60% were Cortinas.

FORD MOTOR COMPANY (JAPAN) Ltd **Japan**

Wholly-owned subsidiary of Ford Motor Company, U.S.A. Founded in 1925 to assemble and market American Ford cars. Ceased operation in 1935 due to a change in Japanese industrial policy. Re-established in 1975 as importer and distributor of Ford automobiles, and later exporter as a new Ford marque to Australia and New Zealand of Toyo Kogyo produced automobiles. In 1982 started marketing the new marque in Japan but not the U.S.A. President and Representative Director: J.T. Eby. Head and press office: Toranomon 37 Mori Bldg, 5-1 Toranomon 3-chome, Minato-ku, Tokyo. Important models: Laser, Telstar.

FORD MOTOR COMPANY OF AUSTRALIA Ltd **Australia**

Founded in 1925 as an arm of Ford of Canada. Produced world's first car-based utility-type vehicle 1934. Underwent major expansion in late Fifties and Sixties with Falcon as main product line. Agreement with Tokyo Kogyo resulted in TK-based Laser in local production in 1980 and TK-based Telstar in 1983. Won market leadership from GM-Holden's in 1982. Chairman: Sir Brian Inglis. Managing Director: W.L. Dix. Directors: J.R. Marshall, M.F. Grandsen, K.W. Harrigan, G.S. Stallos, E.A. Witts, D.C. Jacobi. Head office and press office: Private Bag 6, Campbellfield, Victoria. Works: Campbellfield, Geelong, Victoria; Homebush, New South Wales; Eagle Farm, Queensland. 12,983 employees. About 130,000 cars produced in 1982.

FORD MOTOR COMPANY OF CANADA Ltd **Canada**

(Makes: Ford, Mercury)

Founded in 1904 in Windsor, Ont. Has always built a large percentage of all cars and trucks produced by Canadian automotive industry. President and Chief Executive Officer: K.W. Harrigan. Executive Vice-President: W. Mitchell. Vice-President, Industrial Relations: S. J. Surma. Vice-President, General Sales: K.A. Wright. Vice-President, General Parts and Service: W.G. Wilson. Treasurer: D. Rehor. Head office and press office: The Canadian Road, Oakville, Ont. L16J 5E4. Works: Oakville, St. Thomas, Windsor, Niagara Falls, Ont. 14,300 employees. 282,954 cars produced in 1982.

FORD MOTOR COMPANY OF SOUTH AFRICA **South Africa**

Established in 1923. Now among the leaders in South African motor industry. Managing Director: D.B. Pitt. Directors: K. Berning, N.G. Cohen, J.C. Dill, F.H. Ferreira, B.S. Rayner, D.M. Morris, K.O. Butler Wheelhouse. Head office and press office: 55 Albany Rd, Port Elizabeth, 6001. Works: Neave Township, Struandale, Deal Party (Port Elizabeth). 6,902 employees. 40,400 cars produced in 1982. Company competes in rallying and the "works" Escorts were champions in 1977, 1978, 1979, 1980, 1981 and won the 1982 South African Rally Championship Series. 1983 season used for development work on 1,200 RST Turbo Rally car. Competes in full championships in 1984.

FORD WERKE AG **Germany (Federal Republic)**

Founded in 1925. Owned by Ford Motor Company USA. Chairman and Managing Director; D. Goeudevert. Directors: R. Leite, H.J. Lehmann, W. Inden, G. Hartwig, V. Leichsering, E. Jokisch, G. Toepfer, A. Caspers. Head office and press office: Ottoplaz 2, Köln-Deutz. Works: Henry Ford-Strasse 1, Köln-Niehl, Saarlouis. 49,100 employees. 795,896 vehicles produced in 1982. Most important models: Köln 1 l, Rheinland 3 l (1933); Eifel 1.2 l (1935); Taunus (1938); Taunus (since 1948); 12M (1952); 15M (1955); 17M (1960); 12M (1962); 17M and 20M (1964); 12M and 15M (1966); 17M, 20M and 20M and 20M 2.3 l (1967); Escort (1968); Capri (1969); Taunus (1970); Consul, Granada (1972); Capri II (1974); Escort (1975); Fiesta (1976); Granada (1978); Sierra (1982); Orion (1983). Winner of East African Safari in 1969. European Saloon Car Championship 1971, 1972, 1974.

MANUFACTURE AND ASSEMBLY IN OTHER COUNTRIES — **Belgium:** Ford Werke AG Fabrieken (subsidiary), Genk, **South Africa:** Ford Motor Co. of South Africa (associated company), P.O.B. 788, Port Elizabeth (assem. Granada). **Taiwan:** Ford Lio Ho Motors Co. Ltd, Taipel (assem. Granada). 231,282 cars produced outside Federal Republic in 1982.

FSO - see FABRYKA SAMOCHODOW MALOLITRAZOWYCH and FABRIKA SAMOCHODOV OSOBOWYCH

FUJI HEAVY INDUSTRIES Ltd **Japan**

(Make: Subaru)

A part of former Nakajima Aircraft Co. Reorganized after the end of World War II and named Fuji Sangyo Co. In August 1945. Disbanded and divided into 12 smaller companies by order of occupying Allied Forces in 1950. Five of smaller companies reunited as Fuji Heavy Industries Ltd in 1953. Manufacturer of cars and commercial vehicles, aircraft and industrial power units. Joined Nissan Group in 1968. Member of Nissan Group. Chairman: E. Ohhara. President: S. Sasaki. Executive Vice-Presidents: S. Irie, T. Tajima. Senior Managing Directors: K. Kawabata, Z. Suzuki, H. Yamamoto, K. Kumada. Head office and press office: 1-7-2 Subaru Bldg, Nishi-Shinjuku, Shinjukuku, Tokyo. Works: Gumma, 10-1 Higashi Hon-cho, Ohta City; Mitaka, 3-9-6 Oshawa, Mitakashi. 14,000 employees. 413,653 cars produced in 1982. Most important models: 360 Sedan (1958); 1000 (1966); 1000 Sport (1967); 1300 G, R2 (1970); Leone (1971).

MANUFACTURE AND ASSEMBLY IN OTHER COUNTRIES – **Malaysia:** Wira Wearne, (Malaysia) Sdn. Bldg. **New Zealand:** Motor Holdings Ltd. **Thailand:** Universal Commercial Co., Ltd. 2,502 cars produced outside Japan in 1982.

GAZ - GORKOVSKI AVTOMOBILNY ZAVOD **USSR**

Press office: Avtoexport, Ul. Volkhonka 14, Moscow 119902. Works: Gorki. About 145,000 cars produced in 1982.

GENERAL MOTORS CORPORATION **USA**

(Makes: Buick, Cadillac, Chevrolet, Oldsmobile, Pontiac)

Founded in 1908, is largest car company in world with production range extending from the most economical and popular cars to the most costly. Chairman: R.B. Smith. Vice-Chairman: H.H. Kehrl. President: F.J. McDonald. Executive Vice-Presidents: R.R. Jensen, F.A. Smith. Head office: 3044 West Grand Blvd, Detroit, Mich. 48202. GM has five passenger-car divisions: Buick Motor Division (902 East Hamilton Ave, Flint, Mich. 48550), General Manager L.E. Reuss, 17,034 employees, 751,332 cars produced in 1982; Cadillac Motor Division (2860 Clark Ave, Detroit, Mich. 48202), General Manager R.D. Burger, 9,500 employees, 246,602 cars produced in 1982; Chevrolet Motor Division (30007 Van Dyke, Warren, Mich. 48090). General Manager R. Stempel. 46,500 employees, 1,099,115 cars produced in 1982; Oldsmobile Division (920 Townsend St, Lansing, Mich. 48921); General Manager J. Sanchez, 18,350 employees, 799,585 cars produced in 1982; Pontiac Motor Division (One Pontiac Plaza, Pontiac, Mich. 48053), General Manager W.E. Hoglund, 12,394 employees, 560,129 cars produced in 1982. 480,544 employees in U.S., 657,000 employees worldwide. 3,173,144 produced in U.S. in 1982, 6,241,458 cars and trucks worldwide. GM also owns General Motors - Holden's Pty Ltd (Australia), Adam Opel AG (Germany) and Vauxhall Motors Ltd (Great Britain).

MANUFACTURE AND ASSEMBLY IN OTHER COUNTRIES (excluding: non-American GM makes) — **Belgium:** GM Continental (subsidiary), 75 Norderlaan, Antwerp (assem. imported vehicles). **Brazil:** GM do Brasil S.A. (subsidiary), P.O.B. 8200 01000 Sao Paulo (manuf. passengers cars and commercial vehicles). **Chile:** GM Chile S.A. (subsidiary), Piloto Lazo 99, P.O.B. 14370, Santiago (assem. imported vehicles). **Colombia:** Fabrica Colombiana de Automotores S.A. (subsidiary), Apdo Aereo 7329 Bogota 1 (assem. imported vehicles). **Ecuador:** Autos y Maquinos del Ecuador S.A. (associated company), P.O.B. 370/A Quito (assem. imported vehicles). **Egypt:** GM Egypt, S.A.E. (associated company) Nile Hilton Hotel, Executive Business Center c/o General Morots Box 32, Cairo (assem. imported vehicles). **Greece:** GM Hellas, A.B.E.E. (subsidiary), P.O.B. 20 Amaroussion, Attica (assem. imported vehicles). **Japan:** Isuzu Motors Ltd (associated company) 22-01 Minami-01 6-chome Shinaguwaku 140, Tokyo (manuf. passengers cars and commercial vehicles). **Kenya:** GM Kenya Ltd (associated company), P.O.B. 30527, Nairobi (assem. imported vehicles). **Mexico:** G.M. de Mexico S.A. de C.V. (subsidiary), Apdo Postal

107/bis 1 Mexico (assem. passengers cars and commercial vehicles). **New Zealand:** GM New Zealand Ltd, (subsidiary), Trentham Assembly Plant,Alexander Rd, Upper Hutt (assem. imported vehicles). **Philippines:** GM Pilipinas, Inc. (associated company) P.O. Box 1478 MCC, Makati, Rizal 3117 (assem. imported vehicles). **Portugal:** GM de Portugal Ltda (subsidiary), P.O.B. 8115, 1802 Lisbon Codex (assem. imported vehicles). **South Africa:** GM South African (Pty) Ltd (subsidiary), Kempston Rd, P.O.B. 1137,Port Elizabeth (manuf. Opel, assem. imported vehicles). **Uruguay:** GM Uruguaya S.A. (subsidiary), Av. Sayago 1385, Montevideo (assem. imported vehicles). **Venezuela:** GM de Venezuela C.A. (subsidiary), Apdo 666 1100 Caracas (assem. imported vehicles). **Zaire:** GM Zaire S.E.R.L. (subsidiary), B.P. 11199 1 Kinshasa (assem. imported vehicles).

GENERAL MOTORS DO BRASIL **Brazil**

(Make: Chevrolet)

Subsidiary of GM Corporation. Managing Director: C.J. Vaughan. Head office, press office and works: Av. Goiás 1805, São Caetano do Sul, São Paulo. 20,600 employees. 151,587 cars produced in 1982.

GENERAL MOTORS - HOLDEN'S Pty Ltd **Australia**

Established in 1931 following merger between General Motors (Australia) Pty Ltd, and Holden Motor Body Builders Ltd. The Holden, Australia's first locally manufactured car, launched in 1948. Australian market leader from 1953-1981. Second place in vehicle market in 1982. Division of GM Corp. USA. Managing Director: C.S. Chapman. Directors: J.M. Butler, I.A. Deveson, E.A. Ellison, J.W.M. Watson, J.F. Bremner, E.E. Leathley, J.S. Loveridge, J.E. Whitesell, B.D. Dundas. Head office and press office: 241 Salmon St, Fishermens Bend, Melbourne, Victoria. Works: Fishermens Bend, Dandenong, Victoria; Woodville, Elizabeth, S. Australia; Acacia Ridge, Queensland. 18,913 employees. 141,300 cars produced in 1982.

GENERAL MOTORS OF CANADA Ltd **Canada**

(Makes: Chevrolet, Pontiac)

Established in 1918 as result of merger between McLaughlin Motor Car Company and Chevrolet Motor Car Company. It is a wholly owned subsidiary of General Motors Corp. President and General Manager: D.E. Hackworth. Vice-President and General Manufacturing Manager: A.G. Warner. Vice-President and General Sales Manager: R.M. Colcomb. Vice-President and Finance Manager: G.A. Peapples. Vice-President and General Manager, Diesel Division: J.C. Larmond. Head office and press office: 215 William St, E. Oshawa, Ontario L1G IK7. Works: as above; Ste. Therese, P.Q., St. Catharines, London, Windsor and Scarborough. 36,500 employees. 374,571 cars produced in 1982.

GENERAL MOTORS SOUTH AFRICAN (Pty) Ltd **South Africa**

(Make: Opel)

Founded in 1926. Managing Director: L.H. Wilking. Directors: D.B. Sneesby, J.P. McCormack, H.D. Carr, H.G. Carpenter, R.J. Ironside, A.R. Tregenza, O.R. Maas, I.D.J. van der Linde. Head office and press office: Kempston Rd, Port Elizabeth. Works: as above; Aloes (Engine Plant), nr. Port Elizabeth, 4,271 employees. 22,819 cars produced in 1982.

GIANNINI AUTOMOBILI S.p.A. **Italy**

Founded in 1920 as F.lli Giannini A. & D., it later became Giannini Automobili S.p.A. President and Managing Director: V. Polverelli. Head office, press office and works: v. Idrovore della Magliana 57, Rome. 47 employees. About 800 cars produced in 1982. Most important models: 750 Berlinetta San Remo (1949); Fiat 750 TV and 850 GT (1963); 850 Coupé Gazzella, Fiat 500 TV and 850 GT (1963); 850 Coupé Gazzella, Fiat 500 TV and TVS, 590 GT and GTS (1964); Fiat Berlina 850 S, 850 SL and 950, Fiat Coupé 850 and 1000, Fiat 1300 Super and 1500 GL, Fiat 500 TVS Montecarlo (1965); Fiat 128 NPS (1970); 650 NPL, 650 NP Modena, 128 NP-S, 128 NP Rally (1971). It is engaged above all in producing variations of Fiat cars. Entries in various competitions and first places in category in various Italian championships.

GINETTA CARS Ltd **Great Britain**

Founded in 1958. Chairman and Managing Director: K.R. Walklett. Directors: T.G. Walklett, D.J. Walklett, I.A. Walklett. Head office, press office and works: West End Works, Witham, Essex, GMB 1BE. 22 employees. 30 cars produced in 1982. Most important model: G.25.

G.P. VEHICLES **Great Britain**

Founded in 1968 as G.P. Speed Shop. Present title since 1975. Managing Director: J. Jobber. General Manager: P.D. Allnutt. Head office and press office: Unit 7, Worton Hall, Worton Rd, Isleworth, Middlesex TW7 6ER. Works: Unit 56 Padgate Lane, Moons Moat, South Redditch, Worcs. 38 employees. 300 cars produced in 1982.

GRAND PRIX METALCRAFT Ltd **Great Britain**

(Make: Desande)

Founded in 1968 as Sheetmetal Fabricators and Panel Beaters to the Motor Industry, the company produces Deetype Replica and Desande Roadster. Directors: P.C. Hingerton, R.W. Hingerton, A. Goodenough. Head office, press office and works: 2-3 Thane Works, Thane Villas, London, N. 7. 10 employees. 12 cars produced in 1982.

GROUP LOTUS CARS COMPANIES P.l.c. **Great Britain**

Founded in 1952. Chairman: D. Wickins. Group Board: D.A. Wickins, F.R. Bushell, P.R. Kirwan-Taylor, M.J. Kimberley, A.G. Curtis, K. Matsumoto. Managing Director: M.J. Kimberley. Head office, press office and works: Norwich, NR14 8EZ. 500 employees. 800 cars produced in 1982. Most important models: Mk Six (1952); Mk Eight, Mk Nine, Mk Ten, Elite (1957); Eleven (1960); Elan (1962); Cortina (1963); Elan + 2 (1967); Europa (1968); Elan Sprint, Elan + 2 'S' 130, Europa Twin Cam (1971); Europa Special (1972). Entries and first places in numerous international competitions with F1, F2, F3, F5 cars; seven F1 World Champion Constructors victories in last 10 years (Indianapolis, Le Mans, Monte Carlo GP, Pacific GP at Laguna Seca, etc.). May 1975 Elite design won European Don Safety Trophy.

GURGEL S.A.
INDÚSTRIA E COMÉRCIO DE VEÍCULOS **Brazil**

Chairman and President Director: J.A.C. do Amaral Gurgel. Head office and works: Rod. Washington Luiz, km 171, 13500 Rio Claro, S.P. Press office: Avda do Cursino 2400 Jardim de Saude, 04132 São Paulo. 300 employees. 580 cars produced in 1982.

HINDUSTAN MOTORS Ltd **India**

Founded in 1942. Chairman: G.P. Birla. Vice-Chairman: N.L. Hingorani. Directors: R.N. Mafatlal, B.P. Khaitan, G.D. Kothari, R.D. Thapar, C.K. Birla, R. Bajaj, M.V. Arunchalam. Head office and press office: Birla Bldg, 9/1 R.N. Mukherjee Rd, Calcutta 1. Works: P.O. Hindmotor, Hooghly, West Bengal. Car production begun in 1951. About 16,000 employees. 25,019 cars and trekkers produced in 1982. Most important models: Hindustan 10, Hindustan 14, Baby Hindustan, Landmaster (1954); Ambassador (1957); Ambassador Mk II (1963); Ambassador Mark III (1975); Trekker (1977); Ambassador Diesel (1978); Ambassador MK IV (1979).

HOLDEN - see GENERAL MOTORS - HOLDEN'S Pty Ltd

HONDA MOTOR COMPANY Ltd **Japan**

Founded in 1949 as Honda Gijitsu Kenkunjo. Present title since 1948. Manufacturer and exporter of motorcycles from 50 to 750 cc, automobiles, trucks, portable generators, general-purpose engines, power tillers, water pumps and outboard motors. Chairman: H. Sugiura. President: T. Kume, Executive Vice-Presidents: S. Schinomiya, N. Okamura, S. Ohkubo. Senior Managing Directors: K. Yoshizawa, F. Ishikawa. Directors and Advisors: S. Honda, T. Fujisawa, K. Kawashima. Head office and press office: 6-27-8 Jingumae, Shibuyaku, Tokyo, Japan 150. Works: Saitama, 8-1 Honcho, Wako-shi, Saitama-ken; Suzuka, 1907 Mirata-cho, Suzuka-shi, Mie-ken; Hamamatsu, 34 Oi-machi, Hamamatsushi, Shizuoka-ken; Sayama, 1-10 Shinsayama, Sayama-shi, Saltama-ken. 30,110 employees. 873,779 vehicles produced in 1982. Models: Sports 500 (1962); Sports 600 (1964); L 700, L 800 (1966); N360, LN360 (1967); N600 (1968); 1300 (1969); 1300 Coupé, NIII Sedan, Z Coupé (1970); Life (1971); Civic (1972); Civic CVCC 4-dr. Sedan (1973); Accord (1976); Prelude (1978); Quint, Ballade (1980); City (1981). Wins in F1 racings: Mexican GP (1965), Italian GP (1967). French GP and USA GP (1968) and entries in F1, F2, GP racings.

MANUFACTURE AND ASSEMBLY IN OTHER COUNTRIES — **Indonesia:** P.T. Prospect Motor (associated company), Jl Jos Sudarso, P.O.B. 31/TPK, Djakarta. **Malaysia:** Oriental Assemblers Sdn. Bhd Batu 2 Jl Tampoi P.O.B. 204, Johore Bahru. **New Zealand:** New Zealand Motor Corp. (associated company), Manners Plaza, 5765 Manners St, Wellington. **South Africa:** UCDD (PTY) Ltd, 29 Choeman St, P.O.B. 1717, Pretoria 0001. **Taiwan:** San Yang Industry Co. Ltd (joint venture), No. 124 Hsin-Ming Rd, Nelhu, Taipei. **U.S.A.:** Honda of America Mfg (incorporated) Marysville, Ohio. 104,460 cars produced outside Japan in 1982.

HONG QI - see CHANGCHUN AUTOMOBILE PLANT

HYUNDAI MOTOR COMPANY **Korea**

Founded in 1967. President: Chung, Se Yung. Vice-President: Lee, Yang Sup. Managing Director: Chon Song Won. Director: Lee Yoo il. Head office and press office: 140-2, Ke-Dong, Chongro-Ku, Seoul. Works: 700, Yangjung-Dong Ulsan. 12,000 employees. 91,000 cars produced in 1982. Most important models: Pony Sedan (1976); New Pony Sedan (1982); Stellar Sedan (1983).

INTREPRINDEREA DE AUTOTURISME PITESTI **Romania**

(Make: Dacia)

Head office and works: Pitesti 0300, Colibasi, Jud. Arges. Press office: Auto Dacia, 42 Mircea Voda St, Pitesti 0300. About 85,000 cars produced in 1982.

INTREPRINDEREA MECANICA MUSCEL **Romania**

(Make: Aro)

Head office and works: Cimpulung Muscel, Jud. Arges. Press office: Auto Dacia, 42 Mircea Voda St, Pitesti 0300.

ISUZU MOTORS Ltd **Japan**

Established in 1937 as result of merger between Ishikawajima motor manufacturing factory, which held Wolseley manufacturing licence from 1918 to 1927, and Tokyo Gas & Electric, which began the manufacture of military trucks in 1916. Present title since 1949. In 1971, it became a joint venture company with G.M. Corp. with capital participation of 34.2% by the latter. President: T. Okamoto. Executive Vice-Presidents: Y. Shimizu, H.V. Leonard, N. Ohishi, S. Hirose, K. Sano, J. Mizusawa, K. Tobiyama, K. Okumura. Head office and press office: 22-10 Minami-oi, 6-chome, Shinagawa-ku, Tokyo. Works: Kawasaki, 25-1 Tonomachi 3-chome, Kawasaki City; Fujisawa, 8 Tsuchitana, Fujisawa City. 15,935 employees. 138,151 cars (including 4WD vehicles) produced in 1982. Most important models: Bellett (1962); Bellett, Bellett Standard (1963); Florian (1967); 117 Coupé (1968); Bellett Gemini (1974); Piazza (1981).

MANUFACTURE AND ASSEMBLY IN OTHER COUNTRIES — **Philippines:** General Motors Pilipinas, Inc. Almasa, Las Pinas, Rizol. 46,200 cars produced outside Japan in 1982.

ITD - INTERNATIONAL TEAM OF DESIGNERS **USA**

Established in 1978 as Roaring 20's Motor Car Company. Changed to present name with introduction of the "Stiletto". President: M.A. Beal. Secretary and Treasurer: Elizabeth A. Roe, Head office, press office and works: 1332 Fayette St, El Cajon, Ca. 92020. 35 employees. 45 cars produced in 1982.

JAGUAR - see BL P.l.c.

JEEP - see AMERICAN MOTORS CORPORATION

JOHN BRITTEN GARAGES Ltd **Great Britain**

(Make: Arkley)

Founded in 1971. Proprietor: J. Britten. Head office, press office and works: Barnet Rd, Arkley, Barnet, Herts. 8 employees. 62 cars produced in 1982.

KELMARK ENGINEERING Inc. **USA**

Established in 1969. General Manager: J. Morrison. Head office: 2382 Jarco Drive, Holt, Mich. 48842. Press office: Kelmark Promotions, P.O.B. K, Okemos, Mich. 48864. Works: Holt, Mich. 22 employees. 130 cars produced in 1982. First GT produced in 1974.

KOUGAR CARS Ltd **Great Britain**

Founded in 1976 as Storcourt Wells Ltd. Present title since 1979. Managing Director: R. Stevens. Head office, press office and works: Overlook, Budletts, Uckfield, Sussex TN22 2EA. 5 employees. 21 cars produced in 1982.

LAFER S.A. INDUSTRIA E COMERCIO **Brazil**

Lafer S.A. Industria e Comercio is a Brazilian corporation controlled by the Lafer family. It is one of the greatest furniture manufactures in Brazil. In October 1972 entered the replicar field with the classic 1952 MG TD. A prototype appeared at the 1972 Brazilian Auto Show. Since then 3,500 cars were sold worldwide. Head office and press office: Rua Lavapés 6, 01519

São Paulo. Works: Rua Garcia Lorca 301, Vila Paulicéia, 09700 - São Bernardo do Campo, São Paulo. 900 employees. 252 cars produced in 1982.

LAMBORGHINI - see NUOVA AUTOMOBILI FERRUCCIO LAMBORGHINI S.p.A.

LANCIA **Italy**

Founded in 1906, noted for production of extremely well-finished prestige cars. In 1969 taken over by the Fiat Group and in 1978 incorporated into Fiat Auto S.p.A. Head office and press office: v. Vincenzo Lancia 27, Turin. Works: as above; v. Caluso 50, Chivasso (Turin); Strada comunale, Verrone (Vercelli). 68,263 cars produced in 1982. Most important models: Alfa, Dialfa (1908); Beta (1909); Gamma (1910); Delta, Didelta, Epsilon, Eta (1911); Theta (1913); Kappa (1919); Dikappa (1921); Trikappa (1922); Lambda (1923); Dilambda (1928); Artena, Astura (1931); Augusta (1933); Aprilia (1937); Ardea (1939); Aurelia (1950); Aurelia B20 (1951); Appia (1953); Flaminia (1957); Flavia (1960); Flavia Coupé and Convertible (1962); Flavia Sport, Fulvia (1963); Fulvia Coupé, Fulvia Sport (1965); Fulvia Coupé 1.3 HF (1966); Flavia 819 (1967); Fulvia Coupé 1.6 HF (1968); Flavia 2000 (1970); 2000 Berlina, 2000 Coupé (1971); Beta Berlina (1972); Beta Coupé (1973); Stratos (1974); Beta Spider, Beta HPE, Beta Monte Carlo (1975); Gamma Berlina, Gamma Coupé (1976); Delta (1979); Trevi (1980); Rally, Prisma (1982). Won World Rally Championship with Lancia Rally in 1983. See Fiat Auto S.p.A.

LAWIL S.p.A. **Italy**
Costruzioni Meccaniche Automobilistiche

Founded in 1969. President: C. Lavezzari. Director: M. Calvi. Head office, press office and works: v. Maretti 29, Varzi (Pavia). 45 employees. About 700 cars produced in 1982.

LEDL GmbH **Austria**

Founded in 1973. Proprietor: G. Ledl. Head office, press office and works: Pottendorfer Str. 73, A-2523 Tattendorf. 36 employees. 26 cars produced in 1981. Most important models: Europa 2001 (1974); Tanga (1978).

LENHAM MOTOR COMPANY **Great Britain**

Founded in 1962. Incorporating Lenham Sports Car Ltd and The Vintage & Sports Cars Ltd. Directors: J.K. Booty, P.J. Rix, G. Allfrey. Head office, press office and works: 47 West St, Harrietsham, Kent ME17 1HX. 15 employees. 5 cars produced in 1982. Championship 1600 cc GT cars in 1968.

LINCOLN - see FORD MOTOR COMPANY

LOTUS - see GROUP LOTUS CARS COMPANIES Ltd

(THE) LYNX COMPANY **Great Britain**

It is a company formed to produce prototypes and low volume specialist performance cars. It offers a unique service since it has a direct involvment in all aspects of motor car design and development by working alongside its associated company. Lynx Engineering, which specializes in the restoration and development of performance cars concentrating mainly on Jaguars. Head office, press office, sales and works: Lynx Engineering, Unit 8, Castleham Rd, Castleham Industrial Estate, St. Leonards-on-Sea, East Sussex TN 38 9NR. 35 employees. 38 cars produced in 1983.

MARCOS **Great Britain**

Founded in 1959, activities were interrupted from 1971 to 1981 when production of an improved version of the earlier model began. Sole proprietor: J. Marsh. Head office, press office and works: 153 West Wilts Trading Estate, Westbury, Wilts. 10 employees. 51 cars produced in 1981. Won Classic Sports Car Championship in 1978 and 1981.

MASERATI - see OFFICINE ALFIERI MASERATI S.p.A.

MAZDA - see TOYO KOGYO COMPANY Ltd

MERCEDES-BENZ - see DAIMLER-BENZ AG

MERCURY - see FORD MOTOR COMPANY and FORD MOTOR COMPANY OF CANADA Ltd

MIDAS CARS Ltd **Great Britain**

Formed in 1975, as D&H Fibreglass Techniques, the company acquired the Mini Marcos and expanded production. The Midas was developed between 1976 and 1979, entering production in 1979. Present title since 1982. Mini Marcos production phased out in June 1981. Directors: H.J.R. Dermott, B.A.R. Dermott, R.A. Oakes, S. Roberts. Head office, press office and works: St. Lukes Rd, Corby, Northants, NNI8 8AJ. 18 employees. About 60 cars produced in 1982.

MG - see BL P.l.c.

MINI - see BL P.l.c.

MITSUBISHI MOTORS AUSTRALIA Ltd **Australia**

Founded as Chrysler Australia Ltd in 1951. Absorbed Rootes Group in 1965. Began assembling Mitsubishi cars in 1971. Mitsubishi Motor Corporation bought Chrysler Australia Ltd in 1980. Held fifth place in Australian vehicle sales in 1982. Chairman: Y. Shimamura. Managing Director: G.G. Spurling. Deputy Managing Directors: D.B. Coleman, G.J. Longbottom. Head office and press office: 1284 South Rd, Clovelly Park, S. Australia. Works: Clovelly Park, Lonsdale, S. Australia. 3,794 employees. About 46,320 cars produced in 1982.

MITSUBISHI MOTORS CORPORATION **Japan**

Established in October 1917 as Mitsubishi Shipbuilding & Engineering Co. Ltd, later changed its name to Mitsubishi Heavy Industries Ltd. After the Second World War it split into three companies under Enterprise Reorganization Law, but these again reunited in June 1964 as Mitsubishi Heavy Industries Ltd. Products include ships and other vessels, railway vehicles, aircraft, space equipment, missiles, atomic equipment, heavy machinery. The Automobile Division became an independent company in June 1970 under name of Mitsubishi Motor Corp. In May 1971 it became a joint venture company with Chrysler Corp. (USA), with Mitsubishi Heavy Industries holding 85% and Chrysler 15% of shares. Chairman: T. Tojo. Vice-Chairman: T. Tomabechi. President: T. Tate. Executive Vice Presidents: Y. Okano, A. Okuda, T. Fukuda, S. Seki. Head office and press office: No. 33-8 Shiba 5-chome, Minatoku, Tokyo. Works: Mizushima, No. 1, 1-chome, Mizushima, Kalgandori, Kurashiki, Okoyama-Pref.; Nagaya, No. 2, Oyecho, Minato-ku, Nagoya. 24,000 employees. 600,170 cars produced in 1982.

MANUFACTURE AND ASSEMBLY IN OTHER COUNTRIES — **Australia:** Mitsubishi Motors Australia Ltd, 1284 South Rd, Clovelly Park, S.A. 5042. **Indonesia:** P.T. Kwama Yudha Kresuma Motors, Jaman Sepamyang, Surabaja. **Malaysia:** Kelang Perbana Kerre Sdn Bhd, 64 Jalan Langkasuka, Johore Baharu. **New Zealand:** Todd Motors Ltd, Todd Park Heriot Drive, Parirua. **Philippines:** Canlubung Automotive Resources Corp., Ortigas Ave., Cainta, Rizal Metro-Manila. **South Africa:** Sigma Motor Corp. Pty Ltd, Sigma park, Silverton. **Thailand:** United Development Motor Industries Co., Ltd Lamplatiew Khet, Lardkrabang, Bangkok. **Trinidad Tobago:** Amalgamated Industries Ltd, Tumpuna Rd, Arima. **Zimbabwe:** Leyland Zimbabwe Ltd, 17 Messetter Rd, Umatali. 51,264 cars produced outside Japan in 1982.

MONTEVERDI - see AUTOMOBILES MONTEVERDI Ltd

MORGAN MOTOR COMPANY Ltd **Great Britain**

Founded in 1910. Managing Director: P.H.G. Morgan. Head office, press office and works: Pickersleigh Rd, Malvern Link, Worcs. WR14 2LL. Production of 4-wheeled vehicles begun in 1936. 115 employees. 408 cars produced in 1982. Most important models: Morgan 4/4, Morgan Plus 8. Entries and wins in numerous competitions since 1911.

MORRIS - see BL P.l.c.

NISSAN MOTOR COMPANY Ltd **Japan**

Founded in 1933 under the name of Jidosha Seizo Co. Ltd. Present title since 1934. In 1966 it took over Prince Motors Ltd. Chairman: K. Kawamata. President: T. Ishihara. Executive Vice-Presidents: Y. Uchigawa, Y. Kume, K. Kanao, Y. Yokoyama. Senior Managing Directors: T. Hara, Y. Uno, T. Kohno, I. Kawai, Z. Sonoda, S. Tuakajiama. Head office and press office: Ginza, Chuo-ku, Tokyo. Works: Mitaka, 8-1, 5-chome, Shimo-Renjaku, Mitaka, Tokyo; Murayama, 6000 Nakafuji, Musashi-Murayama, Kitatama-gun, Tokyo; Agikubo, 5-1, 3-chome, Momoi, Suginami-ku, Tokyo; Oppama, 1, Natsushima-Cho, Yokosuka; Tochigi, 2500, Kaminokawa, Tochigi-ken; Yokohama 2, Takara-cho, Kanagawaku, Yokohama; Yoshiwara, 1-1, Takara-cho, Yoshiwara Fuji, Shizuoka-ken; Zama, 5070, Nagakubo, Zama, Kanagawa-Ken. 58,962 employees. 1,910,803 cars (including Safari 4WD vehicles) produced in 1981. Most important models: Cedric (1960); Sunny, Gloria (1962); President (1965); Datsun, Nissan Prince Royal (1966); Datsun Bluebird 510 (1967); Laurel (1968); Datsun 240-Z, Nissan Skyline (1969); Cherry (1970); Datsun Bluebird U (1972); Violet Auster, Stanza, Pulsar, Fairlady (1977); Liberta Villa, Prairie (1982). First places in Round Australia Rally (1958); East African Safari Rally and Kenya Rally (1966); Shell 4000 Canada Rally (1967-68); South Africa's Moonlight Rally and Beira Rally (1967); Zacateca Race, Malaysian Race, Aussie Race, Southern Cross Rally (1968); South African Castrol 2000 Rally, East African Safari Rally (1969-71).

MANUFACTURE AND ASSEMBLY IN OTHER COUNTRIES — **Australia:** Nissan Motor Manufacturing Co. Australia Ltd (subsidiary), Center Rd 3168, Clayton, Victoria. **Costa Rica:** Agencia Datsun SA, Apdo 3219, 1000 San Jose. **Ghana:** Japan Motors Trading Co., Ltd (associated company), P.O.B. 5216, Accra. **Greece:** N.J. Theocarakis S.R.A. 169 Leoforos Athinon Aigaleo, Athens. **Indonesia:** P.T. Wahana Wirawan Gedung Perkantoran Artamas, Jend. A. Yanni 2, Jakarta. **Ireland:** Datsun Ltd (associated company), Datsun House, P.O.B. 910, Naas Rd, Dublin 12. **Italy:** Alfa Romeo e Nissan autoveicoli S.p.A., Piano D'Ardine, Pratole Serra, Avellino. **Malaysia:** Tan Chong Motor Assemblies Sdn Bhd, 249 Jalan Segambut, Kuala Lumpur. **Mexico:** Nissan Mexicana S.A. de C.V. (joint venture), Avda. Insurgentes Sur No. 1457, Piso del 1° al 7°, Mexico City 19. **New Zealand:** Nissan Motor Distributors (N.Z.) 1975 Ltd (joint venture), P.O.B. 61133, Otara, Auckland. **Peru:** Nissan Motor del Peru S.A. (joint venture), P.O.B. 4265, Lima. **Philippines:** Universal Motor Corp. (associated company) 2232-34, Pasong Tamo Ave., Makati, Rizal. **South-Africa:** Datsun-Nissan Co. (PTY) Ltd, P.O.B. 10, Rosslyn, Pretoria, Transvaal. **Taiwan:** Yue Loong Motor Co. Ltd (associated company), 9th floor, 150 Nanking East Rd, Section 2, Taipei. **Thailand:** Prince Motors Ltd 86 Mu 1, T. Naiklong, Bang-Plakod Auphur Muang, Samputrakarn. **Trinidad Tobago:** Neal & Massy Ltd (associated company), P.O.B. 1298, Port-of-Spain. **Zimbabwe:** Inter Afric Holding Ltd, P.O.B. 1810 Harare. 196,775 vehicles produced outside Japan in 1982.

NISSAN AUSTRALIA Pty Ltd **Australia**

First Datsun imported into Australia in 1960. Nissan Motor Co. (Australia) Pty Ltd formed 1966. Nissan purchased Volkswagen manufacturing plant in 1976 and formed Nissan Motor Manufacturing Co Ltd Nissan Motor Co. (Australia) and Nissan Motor Manufacturing Co. merged in 1983 into Nissan Australia. Fourth place in vehicle sales in 1982. Managing Director: H. Rai. Directors: J. Wrigley, K. Yabuta, D. Lord, P. Keen. Head office and press office: 250 Frankston Rd, Dandenong, victoria. Works: Clayton, Dandenong, victoria. 2500 employees. About 42,673 cars produced in 1982.

NOVA SPORTS CARS Ltd **Great Britain**

Original company founded in 1971, assumed present title in 1977. Directors: C. Elam, C. Elam. Head office and works: Bridge Garage, Huddersfield Rd, Mirfield Yorks. 34 employees. 340 cars produced in 1982.

NUOVA AUTOMOBILI FERRUCCIO LAMBORGHINI S.p.A. **Italy**

Founded in 1962 as Automobili Ferruccio Lamborghini Sas. Present title since September 1980. President: P. Mimran. Head office, press office and works: v. Modena 1b, 40019 S. Agata Bolognese (Bologna). About 180 Employees. 98 cars produced in 1982. Models: 350 GT (1963); 400 GT (1966); Miura (1967); Espada, Islero (1968); Jarama (1970); Urraco (1971); Countach (1974); Countach S (1978), Jalpa (1982).

NUOVA INNOCENTI S.p.A. **Italy**

Founded in 1933 as Società Anonima Fratelli Innocenti became Innocenti Anonima per Applicazioni Tubolari Acciaio and Innocenti Società Generale per l'Industria Metallurgica e Meccanica S.p.A. and Innocenti S.p.A. in 1961. Taken over by BLMC in 1972 and in 1976 by GEPI and de Tomaso assuming present title. BL P.l.c. holds 5% of Nuova Innocenti. Production begun in May 1976. President: G. Bigazzi. Managing Director: A. de Tomaso. General Manager: A. Bertocchi. Head office and press office: v. Rubattino 37, Milan. Works: v. Pitteri 84, Milan. 2,280 employees. 22,578 cars produced in 1982. Most important models: Innocenti Austin A40 (1960); Innocenti Morris IM-3S (1963); Innocenti Austin J4 (1964); Innocenti Mini Minor (1965); Innocenti S. Spider (1966); Innocenti Mini Cooper Mk 2 (1968); Innocenti Mini Minor Mk 3, Mini Cooper Mk 3 and J5 (1970); Innocenti Mini 1000, Mini Cooper 1300 Mk 3, Austin J5 (1972); Innocenti Mini 90, Mini 120 and Regent (1974); Innocenti Mini De Tomaso (1977); Innocenti Mille (1980); Mini 90 LS II (1981); Mini 90 SL (1982).

OB & D - DESIGN ASSOCIATES Ltd **Great Britain**

Directors: B. Kurpil, R. Chudzij. Head office and press office: 67 Woodside, Ashby de la Zouch, Leics, LE6 5NU. Works: The

Annexe, Burton Rd, Ashby de la Zouch, Leics LE6 5LJ. 27 employees. 5 cars produced in 1982.

OFFICINE ALFIERI MASERATI S.p.A. **Italy**

Founded in 1926, it is famous for its GT and racing cars. Managing Director: A. de Tomaso. Head office, press office and works: v. Ciro Menotti 322, Modena. About 380 employees. About 2,300 cars produced in 1982. Most important models: A 6/1500 (1948); A6G/2000 (1954); 3500 GT (1956); 5000 GT (1958); 3500 GTI, 5000 GTI (1960); Mistral, Quattroporte (1964); Mexico, Ghibli (1966); Indy (1969); Bora (1971); Merak (1972); Khamsin (1974); Merak SS (1975); Kyalami, Merak 2000, Quattroporte (1976); Biturbo (1982). Victories up to 1957 in all types of motor racing: Targa Florio (1926), Indianapolis 500 Miles (1939-40), European Mountain Championship (1956-57), World Drivers' Championship with J.M. Fangio.

OLDSMOBILE - see GENERAL MOTORS CORPORATION

OLTCIT **Romania**

Founded in 1977 as the result of an agreement between Citroën and the Romanian government to produce the new Citroën Oltcit for marketing in Romania and COMECON countries. Production begun in 1982 with a goal of 130,000 vehicles per year. Head office and works: Oltcit S.A., Craiova. Press office: Auto Dacia, Foreign Trade Company, 42 Mircea Vodà St, 0300 Pitesti. 1,800 employees. About 7,000 cars produced in 1982.

OPEL - see ADAM OPEL AG

OTOSAN A.S. **Turkey**

Founded in 1959. It is part of Koç Group-Koç Holding and produces cars with fibreglass bodywork and Ford engines. General Manager: E. Gönül. Head office, press office and works: P.K. 102, Kadikoy, Istanbul. 1,861 employees. 407 cars produced in 1982.

PAYKAN **Iran**

Head office, press office and works: Iran National Manufacturing Co., Service Dept., P.O. Box 2118 Teheran. 70,634 cars produced in 1981.

PANTHER CAR COMPANY Ltd **Great Britain**

Founded in 1971 as Panther Westwinds Ltd, the firm was bought by Jindo Industries of South Korea in 1982. Present title since January 1981. Managing Director: Y.C. Kim. Company Secretary: S. Brain. Head office, press office and works: Canada Rd, Byfleet, Surrey. Most important models: J 72 4.2-litre (1972); Lazer, FF (1973); De Ville Saloon (1974); Rio (1975); Lima, De Ville Convertible (1976); Turbo Lima (1978); Kallista 1.6, Kallista V6 2.8 (1982). 110 employees. 350 cars produced in 1982.

PEUGEOT - see AUTOMOBILES PEUGEOT S.A

PEUGEOT S.A. **France**

Holding Company controlling interests of Automobiles Peugeot (Peugeot and Talbot cars) and Automobiles Citroën. P.S.A. acquired 38.2% of Citroën stock in December 1974 and overall control of that company in May 1976. In 1978 P.S.A. gained control of 3 Chrysler Europe production centres, in Great Britain, France and Spain and on 1 January 1979 it acquired whole of Chrysler interests in Europe. Chairman: J.P. Parayre. Vice-Chairman: J. Calvet. General Managers: J. Baratte, P. Peugeot. Head office and press office: 75 Av. de la Grande Armée, Paris 75116. See Automobiles Citroën, Automobiles Peugeot and Talbot et Cie.

PEUGEOT AUTOMOBILES NIGERIA **Nigeria**

Chairman: A.A. Abubakar. Managing Director: D. Lange. Head office, press office and works: Turaki Ali House 3, Kanta Rd, Kaduna. 4,200 employees. 56,001 cars produced in 1982.

PHILLIPS MOTOR CAR CORPORATION **USA**

President: C.W. Phillips. Secretary Treasurer: M.A. Phillips. Executive Vice-President: S.A. Clay. Head office, press office and works: 5201 N.W. 15 St, Margate, Florida 33063. 30 employees. 80 cars produced in 1982.

PININFARINA (Industrie) S.p.A. **Italy**

Founded in 1930. Produces special and de luxe bodies. President: S. Pininfarina. Managing Director: R. Carli. Member of Board: E. Carbonato. Head office: c. Stati Uniti 61, Turin. Works: v. Lesna 78-80. 10095 Grugliasco, Turin.

PLYMOUTH - see CHRYSLER CORPORATION

PONTIAC - see GENERAL MOTORS CORPORATION and GENERAL MOTORS OF CANADA Ltd

PORSCHE - see Dr. Ing. h.c. F. PORSCHE A.G.

PORTARO - see SEMAL - SOCIEDADE ELECTRO MECANICA DE AUTOMOVEIS Ltda

(THE) PREMIER AUTOMOBILES Ltd **India**

Founded in 1944. Chairman: V.L. Doshi. Vice-Chairman and Managing Director: P.N. Vencatesan. Head office and press office: 92/93, Maker Towers "F" 9th floor, Cuffe Parade, Colaba, Bombay - 400005. Works: L.B. Shastri Marg, Kurla, Bombay - 400 070. 9,978 employees. 20,711 cars produced in 1982.

PUMA INDUSTRIA DE VEICULOS S.A. **Brazil**

Founded in 1964 under name of Sociedade de Automòvels Luminari Ltda. Present title since 1975. President: R.A. Alves da Costa. Directors: L.C. Alves da Costa, M. Mastenguin, J.M. Hellmeister. Head office, press office and works: Av. Presidente Wilson 4385, C.P. 42649, São Paulo. 630 employees. About 450 cars produced in 1982. Models: Malzoni GT with DKW engine (1964-65); Puma GT with DKW engine (1966-67); Puma 1500 GT with VW engine (1968-69); Puma 1600 GTE with VW engine (1970); Puma 1600 GTE and GTS with VW engine (1971); Puma GTB 4100 with GM engine (1974); Puma GTE, GTS (1978).

QT - ENGENHARIA E EQUIPAMENTOS Ltda **Brazil**

Head office, press office and works: Rua das Orquídeas 451, Vila Marchi, São Bernardo do Campo, São Paulo.

RÉGIE NATIONALE DES USINES RENAULT **France**

Founded in 1898 under the name of Société Anonyme des Usines Renault. Present title since 1945 when it was nationalized. Acquired Automobiles Alpine S.A. in 1977. It is today the largest and most important motor manufacturer in France. President and General Manager: B. Hanon. Head office and press office: 34 quai du Point du Jour, Boulogne Billancourt 92109. Works: Pierre-Lefaucheux, Flins; Usine de Cléon, Cléon: Usine du Mans, Pierre-Piffault; Usine de Choisy, Choisy-le-Roy; Usine d'Orléans, St. Jean-de-la- Ruelle; Usine du Havre, Sandouville; Usine de Dreux, Dreux; Usine de Douai, Douai. 111,878 employees. 1,966,709 cars produced in 1982. Most important models: 1.75 CV (1898); 2 cylinder (1904); 35 CV (1912); Marne Taxi, Type AG, Type TT (1923); 45 hp (1923-27); Celtaquatre (1934); Viva Grand Sport (1938); 4 CV (1947); Fregate (1951); Dauphine (1957); Floride (1959); Floride S, Caravelle, 8 (1962); Caravelle 1100 (1963); 8 Major (1964); 16 (1965); 4 Parisienne (1966); 16 TE, 6 (1968); 12 (1969); R 5, R 15, R 17 (1971); R 16 TX (1973); R 30, R 20 (1975); R 14 (1976); R 18 (1978); Fuego, 5 Turbo, 20 Diesel, 18 Turbo, 18 Diesel (1980), 5 Alpine Turbo, 30 Turbo Diesel, Renault 9 (1981). Entries and wins in numerous competitions (Monte Carlo Rally, Alpine Rally, Tour de Corse, Liège-Rome-Liège, Sebring, Reims, Nürburgring, Mobil Economy Run, 24 hours of Le Mans 1978, French G.P. 1979, Brazilian G.P., South African G.P., Austrian G.P. (1980), French G.P., Dutch G.P., Italian G.P. (1981).

MANUFACTURE AND ASSEMBLY IN OTHER COUNTRIES — **Argentina:** Renault Argentina S.A. (subsidiary), Camino a Pajas Blancas, km 4, Cordoba (manuf. 4, 6, 12, 18, Fuego). **Australia:** Renault Australia Pty Ltd (subsidiary), Dougharty Rd, P.O. Box 60, West Heidelberg, Victoria (assem. 18, 20, 30). **Belgium:** Rnur (subsidiary), 499 Schaarbeeklei, Vilvoorde 1 (assem. 4, 5, 14). **Chile:** Automotores Franco Chilena (subsidiary), Casilla 10173, Los Andes (assem. 4); Corme Canica (concessionaire), Casilla 10173, Los Andes (assem. 18). **Colombia:** Sofasa (associated company), Apartado Aereo 4529, Medellin (assem. 4, 6, 12, 18); Socofam (associated company), Duitama, Boyaca (assem. 4, 6). **Eire:** Smith Engineering Ltd (subsidiary), Trinity St, Wexford (assem. 4, 4 light van). **Greece:** Soheca (concessionaire), Athens 126. **Indonesia:** Gaya Motors (concessionaire), Jalan'c Aphd, P.O Box 2126 DKT, Djakarta Fair, Djakarta. **Iran:** Saipa (concessionaire), 553 av. Eisenhower, Teheran. **Ivory Coast:** Safar (subsidiary), B.P. 2764, Abidjan (assem. 4, 5, 18). **Madagascar:** Somacoa (associated company), Route de Majunga, B.P. 796, Tananarive (assem. 4, 12). **Malaysia:** Champion Motors Sdn Bhd, Jalan Usaha, Shah Alam Selangor, P.O Box 814, Kuala Lumpur. **Mexico:** Diesel Association (concessionaire), Ciudad Sahagun, Hidalgo (assem. 4, 5, 12, 18). **Morocco:** Somaca, km 12 Autoroute de Rabat, Casablanca (assem. 5, 12, 18). **Philippines:** Renault Philippines (subsidiary), P.O. Box 1011, Makati, Rizal (assem. 20). **Portugal:** Industrias Lusitanas Renault (associated company), Fabrica de Guarda, Guarda Gare (assem. 4, 5, 12). **Singapore:** Associated Motor Industries (concessionaire), Taman Jurong, P.O.B. 19, Singapore 22. **South Africa:** Motors Assemblies Ltd (associated company), P.O. Box 12030, Jacobs, Durban (assem. 4, 5). **Spain:** Fasa-Renault S.A. (subsidiary), Apdo 262, Autopista de Francia, Madrid (assem. 4, 5, 6, 7, 9, 11, 12, 14, 18). **Trinidad:** Amalgamated Industries Ltd, Tumpuna Rd, Arima Trinidad, Port of Spain (assem. 10, 12). **Tunisia:** Stia (associated company), Route de Monastir, Sousse (assem. 4). **Turkey:** Oyak Renault (associated company), Zone Industrielle, P.K. 255, Bursa (assem. 12). **Uruguay:** Automotores, Cerro Largo 888, Santa Rosa, Montevideo (assem. 12). **Venezuela:** Cvvca (associated company), Edo Carabobo, Mariara (assem. 12, 18, 20, 30). **Yugoslavia:** Industrija Motornih Vozil (concessionaire), B.P. 60, Novo Mesto (assem. 4, 18). 285,011 vehicles produced outside Frandce in 1981.

RELIANT MOTOR P.l.c. **Great Britain**

Founded in 1934 under the name of Reliant Engineering Co. (Tamworth) Ltd. Present title since 1962. Acquired Bond Cars Ltd in 1969. Chairman: J.F. Nash. Managing Director: R.L. Spencer. Directors: C. Burton, E. Osmond, M.J. Bennett. Head office and works: Two Gates, Tamworth, Staffs. 600 employees. 7,460 vehicles produced in 1981. Most important models: First sports car Sabre (1960); Sabre 6 (1961); Regal 3/25 (1962); Scimitar GT, Rebel 700 (1964); Rebel 700 Estate (1967); Scimitar GTE (1968); Scimitar GTE Automatic, Kitten Saloon/ Estate (1975); New Scimitar GTE Overdrive/Automatic (1976), Bond Bug (1970); Robin Saloon/Estate and Van (1973); Rialto 2 and 3 doors, Fox (1982), all with glass fibre bodywork. Entries from 1962-64 in numerous competitions (Tulip Rally, RAC Rally of Great Britain, Monte Carlo Rally, Circuit of Ireland, Alpine Rally, Spa-Sofia-Liége Rally; winners of class in Total Economy Run in 1976 and 1977 with 55.5 mpg and 57.5 mpg respectively.

MANUFACTURE AND ASSEMBLY IN OTHER COUNTRIES — **India:** Sipani Automobiles, Bangalore, (assem. Dolphin). **Turkey:** Otosan A.S., P.O.B. 102, Kadikoy, Istanbul (manuf. Anadol).

RENAULT (France) - see RÉGIE NATIONALE DES USINES RENAULT

RENAULT ARGENTINA S.A. **Argentina**

Founded in 1955 under the name of Industrias Kaiser Argentina assumed title of Ika-Renault in 1968. Present title since 1975. Chairman: P. Gras. Vice-Chairmen: J. Ramondou, A.S. Selvetti. Managing Directors: J.M. Fangio, M. Lozada Echenique, F. Seneca, P. Lamirault, M. Van La Beck, F.J. Jaureguiberry. Head office and press office: Sarmiento 1230, Buenos Aires. Works: Camino a Pajas Blancas, km 4, Cordoba. 5,476 employees. 34,278 cars produced in 1982. Most important models: R4 (1963); Torino (1966); R6 (1970); R12 (1971); Torino GR, Torino ZX (1979).

ROLLS-ROYCE MOTORS Limited **Great Britain**

Rolls-Royce Motors Ltd was formed in April 1971 to take over the assets of the original Rolls-Royce Ltd in the automotive field. Merged with Vickers Ltd in 1980 but continues to manufacture Rolls-Royce and Bentley cars as Rolls-Royce Motors, the Motor Car Group of the new Company. The first Rolls-Royce car ran in 1904 and they have always specialised in the production of high class cars of great quality. Managing Director: R.W. Perry. Directors: R. Ashley, P.T. Ward, P.A. Hill, P.N. Jones, A.J. Romer, M.R.D. Dunn. Works: Crewe, Ches CWI 3 PL. 4,500 employees. 2,400 cars produced in 1982. Most important models: first Rolls-Royce in 1904; Silver Ghost (1906-25); Twenty (1911); Phantom I (1925-29); Phantom II (1929-36); Phantom III (1936); Silver Wraith (1946); Phantom IV (1950); Silver Cloud I (1955); Silver Cloud II, Phantom V (1959); Silver Cloud III (1962); Silver Shadow (1965); Phantom VI (1968); Corniche (1971); Camargue (1975); Silver Shadow II, Silver Wraith II (1977); Silver Spirit, Silver Spur (1980).

ROVER - see BL P.l.c.

RUSKA AUTOMOBILES B.V. **Holland**

Directors: A. Ruska sr, A. Ruska jr, Mrs Ruska-Spruyt. Head office and works: 115-127 Lauriergracht, 101b RK Amsterdam. Press office: 119 Lauriergracht, 101 RK Amsterdam. 12 employees. 420 cars produced in 1982.

SAAB-SCANIA AB **Sweden**

The first Saab car was made in 1950 by the former Svenska Aeroplan Aktiebolaget. Saab cars are currently manufactured by the Saab Car Division of Saab-Scania AB which was formed in 1969 through the merger of Saab Aktiebolag and Scania-Vabis. Other Saab-Scania products include Scania commercial vehicles, Saab military aircraft and commercial airliners, missiles, avionics, electronic equipment, electromedical equipment, industrial valves, measuring systems, etc. Chairman: S. Gustafsson. President: G. Karnsund. Chief Executive Saab Car Division: S. Wennlo. Group head office: S-581 88 Linköping. Head office and press office: Saab Car Division: S-611 81 Nyköping. Works: Trollhättan, Nyköping, Kristineham, Arlöv. 14,000 employees. 83,557 cars produced in 1982. Most important models: 92, 93 (1950-60); 95 Estate (1959-78); 96 (1960-1980); 96 V4 (1966); 99 (1968); Sonett III (1969); 99 Combi Coupé (1973), 900 (1979); 900 Sedan (1981); 900 CD (1982). Numerous wins in international rallies including Monte Carlo (twice), RAC (5 times), Tulip Rally, Baja 1000, Swedish KAK, Arctic and 1000 Lakes in Finland, etc.

MANUFACTURE IN OTHER COUNTRIES — **Finland:** Oy Saab-Valmet Ab Uusikaupunki (manuf. 99, 900). About 24,000 cars produced outside Sweden in 1982.

SBARRO - see ATELIERS DE CONSTRUCTION AUTOMOBILES

SEAT - SOCIEDAD ESPAÑOLA DE AUTOMOVILES DE TURISMO S.A. **Spain**

Founded in 1950. President: A.D. Alvarez. Vice-President: T. Galán. Managing Director: J. Pañella. Head office and press office: P. Castellana 278, Madrid 16. Works: Zona Franca, Martorell, Prat de Llobregat (Barcellona) Landaben (Pamplona). 25,235 employees. 246,408 cars produced in 1982. Most important models: 600 (1957); 1500 (1963); 850 (1956); 124 (1968); 1430 (1969); 127 (1971); 132 (1973); 133 (1974); 131 (1975); 1200 Sport (1976); 128 3P (1977); 132 Mercedes Diesel (1978); Ritmo, Lancia Beta Coupé, HPE (1979); Panda (1980); Fura (1981); Ronda (1982).

SEMAL - SOCIEDADE ELECTRO MECANICA DE AUTOMOVEIS Ltda **Portugal**

(Make: Portaro)

Founded in 1944. Director: H.M. Pires. Head office and press office: Rua Nova de S. Mamede, 7-2°, DT°, 1296 Lisboa. Works: E.N. 249/4, km 4,6 Trajouce-Oeiras. 460 employees. 700 cars produced in 1981. Production of Portaro began in 1974.

SEVEL ARGENTINA S.A. **Argentina**

(Makes: Fiat, Peugeot)

Created as the result of a merger between SAFRAR Sociedad Anónima Franco Argentina de Automotores CIF (manufacturing Peugeot vehicles in Argentina) and FIAT Autómoviles S.A. Argentina, beginning joint operations on 1 December 1980. In September 1981, Peugeot withdraw. President: V. Ghidella. Vice-Presidents: R. Zinn, R.A. Sanches. Directors: P.M. Sabatini, A. Amasanti, A. d'Emilio, A. De Vito, S. Corona. Head office and press office: Juramento 750, (1428) Capital Federal, Buenos Aires. Works: Fabrica Humberto 1° no. 1001, (1682) Villa Bosch, Buenos Aires: Fabrica Ruta 2 km. 37.5, (1884) Barazategui, Buenos Aires; Fabrica Ruta 9 km. 695, (5000) Cordoba, Cordoba. 4,700 employees. About 20,000 cars produced in 1982. Production includes Fiat 600, 128, 125 and Peugeot 504 and 505.

SHANGHAI AUTOMOBILE WORKS **China (People's Republic)**

Founded in 1920 as small repair shop. In 1949, it was changed from a private enterprise into a national one producing lightduty cross-country vehicles. It has the present title since 1958 when it begun to manufacture three-wheel motor vehicles. The Works began to produce passenger cars in 1959. The original trade mark, Phenix, was changed to Shanghai in 1962. Head office, press office and works: Luo Pu Rd, An Ting Town, Jiading County, Shanghai. Director: Xie Yian Hong. 2,696 employees. 5,100 cars produced in 1982.

ŠKODA - AUTOMOBILOVÉ ZÁVODY NÁRODNI PODNIK **Czechoslovakia**

Founded in 1894 by Laurin and Klement for the construction of velocipedes, assumed title of Laurin Klement Co. Ltd in 1907, Škoda in 1925, and in 1945 became national corporation (AZNP). Director: J. Banýr. Commercial Deputy Director: I. Sedlák. Head office, press office and works: Trida Rudé armady, Mladá Boleslav. 16,000 employees. 170,000 cars produced in 1982. Car production begun in 1905 (2-cylinder cars). Most important models: Laurin Klement (1905); E 4-cyl. (1907); "S"Type (1911); 100, 105, 110, 120 Type (1923); 4R, 6R (1924); 420, 422 (1934); Popular, Rapid (1935-39); 1101, 1102 (1945-53); 440 (1954); Octavia, Felicia (1955-59); Octavia Combi, 1202 (1962); 1000 MB (1964); 100 L, 110 L, 1203 (1969); 110 R Coupé (1970), 105, 120 GLS (1976); S-Rapid (1982).

SIPANI AUTOMOBILES Ltd **India**

Founded in 1974. Chairman: S.M.D. Shivananjappa IAS. Managing Director: S.R.K. Sipani. Technical Director: S.C. Arunachaiam. Head office, press office and works: 25/26 Industrial Suburb, Second Stage, Tumkur Rd, P.O.B. 2224, Bangalore 560022. 236 employees.

Sta. MATILDE - see COMPANHIA INDUSTRIAL SANTA MATILDE Inc. Co.

STIMULA - see AUTOMOBILES STIMULA S.a.r.l.

STUTZ MOTOR CAR OF AMERICA Inc. **USA**

Established in 1968. President and Chairman: J.D. O'Donnell. Secretary Treasurer and Director: R.L. Curotto. Head office and press office: 230 West 55th St, New York, N.Y. 10019. Works: Torino, Italy. 50 employees. 50 cars produced in 1982.

SUBARU - see FUJI HEAVY INDUSTRIES Ltd

SUZUKI MOTOR COMPANY Ltd **Japan**

Founded in 1909 under the name of Suzuki Shokkuki Selkakusho. Present title since 1954. Entered a capital partecipation with General Motors and its affiliate, Isuan Motor Co. President: O. Suzuki. Senior Managing Directors: S. Inagawa, K. Kume. Managing Directors: K. Nakamura, T. MAsuyama, H. Uchiyama. Head office and press office: 300 Kamimura, Hamagun, Shizouka-ken. Works: Kosai, Shirasuka 4520, Kosaishi, Suzuokaken; Iwata, Iwai 500; Iwata-shi, Shizouka-ken; Ohsuka, Ombuchi 6333, Omsuka-cho, Ogasagun, Shizouka-ken. 12,042 employees. 374,973 cars (including Jimny 4WD vehicles) produced in 1982. Most important models: Suzulight 360 (1955); Suzuki Fronte 360 LC10 (1967); Fronte 500 (1968); Fronte Coupé (1971); alto (1979); SS 80 (1980); Yimny/SY410 (1981).

SYRENA - see FABRYKA SAMOCHODÓW MALOLITRAZOWYCH

TALBOT et Cie. **France**

Established in 1934 under the title SIMCA (Société Industrielle de Mécanique et de Carrosserie Automobile), it passed under control of Chrysler Corp. in 1971 and then Peugeot S.A. in 1978. Merged with Automobiles Peugeot in January 1981. Managing Director: L. Collaine. General Manager: M. Pecqueux. Head office: 46 Av. de la Grande Armée, Paris 75016. Press office: 75 Av. de la Grande Armée, Paris 75016. Works: Poissy, About 25,000 employees. 242,032 cars produced in 1982. Most important models: Simca 5 (1936); Simca 6 (1948); Aronde (1952); Vedette (1955); Ariane (1957); Simca 1100 (1967); Simca 1000 Rallye (1970); Chrysler 160 and 180 (1971); Chrysler 2-litre (1973); 1307 and 1308 (1975); Horizon (1978); Solara and 1510 (1979); Tagora (1981); Samba (1981). In association with Matra: Bagheera (1973), Rancho (1977) and Murena (1980).

TALBOT MOTOR COMPANY Ltd **Great Britain**

Founded in 1917 as Rootes Motors Ltd. In 1967 became a member of Chrysler Group but in 1978 a controlling interest was acquired by PSA Peugeot-Citroën. Present title since January 1980. Chairman and Managing Director: G. Turnbull. International House P.O.B. 712, Bickenhill Lane, Birmingham. Works: Ryton On Dunsmore and Stoke, Coventry. 8,400 employees. 56,229 cars (including KD kits) produced in 1982.

MANUFACTURE AND ASSEMBLY IN OTHER COUNTRIES — **Iran:** I.N.I.M., P.O.B. 14/1637, km 18, Industrial Manufacturing Co. Ltd, Karadj Rd, Teheran (manuf. and assem. Paykan). 40,000 cars produced outside Great Britain in 1982.

TATRA NÁRODNI PODNIK **Czechoslovakia**

Tatra is one of oldest European motor manufacturers. In second half of 19th century de luxe coaches were being built in Nesselsdorf. Production of railway carriages was begun in 1882 and first motor-car, called the "President", was produced in 1897. General Manager: E. Lindovsky. Head office and press office: Koprivnice. Works: Tatra Koprivnice okres Novy Jičin. 400 cars produced in 1981. Most important models: President (1897); B Type (1902); E Type 12 hp (1905); K Type (1906); T 14/15 (1914); Tatra 4/12, Tatra 11 (1923); 17/31 (1926-30); Tatra 30 (1927-29); Tatra 24/30 (1930-34); Tatra 52 (1930-38); Tatra 57 (1932); Tatra 75 (1933-37); Tatra 77 (1934); Tatra 87 (1936-38); Tatraplan (1949); Tatra 603 (1957); Tatra 2-603 (1964); Tatra 613 (1975); T 613 Special (1980). Has been entering competitions since 1900 (Targa Florio, Leningrad-Moscow-Tbilisi-Moscow, Alpine Rally, Polsky Rally, Vltava Rally, Marathon de la Route, etc.).

TIMMIS MOTOR COMPANY Ltd **Canada**

Founded in 1968. Producing current model since that time. Only Canadian-owned assembly operation and only car plant in Western Canada. One of first companies in North America to build replicas. President: A.J. Timmis. Head office: 4351 Blenkinsop Rd, Victoria B.C. V8X2C3. Press office and works: 409 Swift St, Victoria. 6 employees. 10 cars produced in 1981.

TMC - THOMPSON MANUFACTURING Co. (Wexford) Ltd **Ireland**

Specializes in engineering design and development, manufacturing and consulting services. Directors: V. Thompson, P. Thompson, S. Thompson, F.A. Costin, A. Thompson. Head office, press office and works: Castlebridge, Wexford. 12 employees. Won its debut race at Mondello Park Racing Circuit in Ireland on 10 September 1983.

TOFAS - see FIAT AUTO S.p.A.

TOTAL PERFORMANCE Inc. **USA**

Established in 1971. President: M.V. Lauria. Vice-President: G.C. Gallicchio. Head office, press office and works: 406 S. Orchard St, Rt, 5, Wallingford, CT 06492. 15 employees. 25 cars produced in 1982.

TOYO KOGYO COMPANY Ltd **Japan**

(Make: Mazda)

Founded in 1920 under the name of Toyo Cork Kogyo Co. Ltd. Present title since 1927. Chairman: M. Iwasawa. President: Y. Yamasaki. Senior Managing Directors: K. Hoshino, T. Wakabayashi, Y. Wada, T. Mitsunari, G.B. Riggs, K. Yamamoto, M. Watanabe, H. Nakashima, A. Fujii, M. Ohhara. Head office and press office: 3-1 Shinchi, Fuchuco, Aki-gun, Hiroshima. Works: as above; Hofu Factory, 888 Nishiura, Hofu-City. 27,736 employees. 847,295 cars produced in 1982. Car production begun in 1930 with Mazda (3-speed). Most important models: R360 Coupé (1960); 360 and 600 (1962); 800 Sedan (1964); 1000 (1965); 1500 Sedan (1966); 1500 SS, 110 S (1967); R110 Coupé, R100 Coupé, 1800 Sedan (1968). RX-2, 616 Coupé and Sedan (1970); RX3 (1971); Cosmo RX5 (1975); 323/GLC (1977); RX7, 626 (1978). Entries in numerous competitions: Singapore GP (1966); Macao GP (1966-67); 84 hour Marathon (1968); Singapore GP, Francorchamps (1969); Francorchamps and Shell Springbok Series (1970).

MANUFACTURE AND ASSEMBLY IN OTHER COUNTRIES — **Columbia:** Companies Colombiana Automotriz SA, Calle 13, 38-54 Bogota. **Indonesia:** P.T. National Motors Co., JL Raya Bekasi KM18 Jakarta. **Ireland:** Ireland Motor Distributors Ltd, Long Mile Rd, Dublin 12. **Malaysia:** Asia Automobile Industries Sdn, Berhad, 11, Jalan Federal Highway, Petaling Jaya, Selangor. **New Zealand:** Mazda Motors of New Zealand Ltd, Otahuhu, Auckland, P.O. Box 22-472. **Portugal:** Sociedade Comercial Tasso de Sousa Lda., Rua de Sá da Bandeira, 557, Oporto. **South Africa:** Sigma Motor Corporation (Pty) Ltd, P.O. Box 411, Pretoria. **Thailand:** Sukosol and Mazda Motor Industry Co., Ltd, P.O.B. 24-100, Klongchan Post Office, Bangkok. **Trinidad Tobago:** Southern Sales & Service Co., Ltd, Cross Crossing, S. Fernando. **Zimbabwe:** Bob's Motor Ltd, 12th Ave, File St, P.O.B. 509 Bulawayo. 129,360 cars produced outside Japan in 1882.

TOYOTA (Australia) - see AMI-TOYOTA

TOYOTA MOTOR CORPORATION Ltd **Japan**

Founded in 1937. Merged with Toyota Motor Sales Company Ltd in June 1982 and changed title from Toyota Motor Company Ltd to Toyota Motor Corporation. Chairman: E. Toyoda. Vice-Chairman: S. Yamamuto. President: S. Toyoda. Executive Vice-Presidents: M. Morita, H. Ono, G. Tsuji. Senior Managing Directors: K. Matsumoto, K. Kusunoki, S. Aoki, M. Iwasaki, T. Ohshima, H. Kamio, I. Makino, A. Inoki. Head office and press office: 1, Toyota-cho, Toyota City. Works: Housha, 1, Toyota-cho, Toyota City; Motomachi, 1 Motomachi, Toyota City; Tokaoka, 1 Honda, Toyota City; Tsutsumi, 1 Tsutsumi-cho, Toyota City; Hiyoshi, 1 Miyoshimachi, Nishikamo-gun. 58,000 employees. 2,400,535 cars produced in 1982. Most important models: Toyo Ace (1954); Toyopet Crown (1955); Toyopet Corona (1957); Toyopet Crown Deluxe (1958); Toyopet Crown Diesel (1959); Toyopet New Corona and Publica (1960); Toyopet New Crown (1962); Crown Eight (1963); Toyota Corolla 1100 (1966); Toyota Century (1967); Toyota Corona Mk II, Toyota 1000 (1968); Celica, Carina (1970); Sprinter (1971); Corsa/Tercel (1978).

MANUFACTURE AND ASSEMBLY IN OTHER COUNTRIES — **Australia:** Australian Motor Industries Ltd, 155 Bertie St, Port Melbourne, Victoria 3207; Toyota Manufacturing Australia Ltd, cnr Grieve Parade and Dohertijs Rd, Altana North, Victoria 3025. **Indonesia:** P.T. Multi-Astra Motor, Jalan Jenderal Sudirman 5, Djakarta. **Ireland:** Toyota (Ireland) Ltd, Toyota House, Naas Rd, Clondalkin, Dublin. **Kenia:** Associated Vehicle Assemblers Ltd, Koinange St, Nairobi. **Malaysia:** Borneo Motors (Malaysia) Sdn Bhd, 76 Jalan Ampang, Kuala Lumpur. **New Zealand:** Consolidated Motor Distributors Ltd, 125-137 Johnsonville Rd, Wellington. **Peru:** Toyota Del Perù S.A., Las Begonias 441, 11 Piso San Isdro, Lima. **Philippines:** Delta Motor Corp., 7785 Pasong Tamo, Makati, Metro Manila. **South Africa:** Toyota Marketing Co. (Pty) Ltd, Stand 1, Wesco Park Sandton, Johannesburg. **Thailand:** Toyota Motor Thailand Co. Ltd, 180 Suriwongse Rd, Bangkok. **Trinidad Tobago:** Amar Auto Supplies Ltd, 177 Tragarete Rd, Port of Spain. 130,360 cars produced outside Japan in 1982 (KD).

TRABANT - see VEB SACHSENRING AUTOMOBILWERKE ZWICKAU

TRIUMPH - see BL P.l.c.

TVR ENGINEERING Ltd — **Great Britain**

Established in 1954 as Grantura Engineering Ltd. Present title since 1966. Chairman: P. Wheeler. Managing Director: S. Halstead. Head office, press office and works: Bristol Ave, Blackpool, Lancs. 98 employees. About 450 cars produced in 1982. Most important models: Mk I (1954-60); Mk II (1960); Mk II A (1962); Mk III (1963-64); Mk III 1800 (1963); Griffith series 200 (1964); Griffith 400 (1965); 200 V8 (1966); Tuscan SE, Vixen 1600 (1967); Vixen S2 (1968); Tuscan V6 (1969); 1600 M (1972-73); 2500 (1970-73); 2500 M, 3000 M (1972); Turbo (1975); Taimar (1976); Convertible (1978); Tasmin Coupé (1980); Tasmin Convertible (1981); Tasmin Plus 2 (1981); Tasmin 2 (1082); Tasmin 350 (1983). Entries and wins in numerous competitions. Outright winners of 1970, 1971 and 1972 Modsports Championships. 1976 win in class B production sports cars.

UAZ - ULIANOVSKY AVTOMOBILNY ZAVOD — **USSR**

Press office: Avtoexport, Ul. Volkhonka 14. Moscow 119902 Works: Ullanovsk.

VAUXHALL MOTORS Ltd — **Great Britain**

First Vauxhall car produced in 1903. Transferred from Vauxhall district of London to Luton in 1905. Present title since 1907. Taken over by General Motors Corp. in 1925. Chairman and Managing Director: J.M. Fleming. Directors: J.T. Battenberg III, I.A.K. McEwan, E.P. Naegel, W.E. Werner, W.R. DeLong, E.D. Fountain, G.E. Moore, C.B.E., R.H.A. Rogers, D. Savage, D. Valiance, D.T. Young, D. Wallis. Head office, press office: Kimpton Rd, Luton, Beds. Works: as above, Ellesmere Port, Cheshire. 11,600 employees. 194,847 cars produced in 1982. Most important models: 30/98 (1913); Kadett (1930); Velox (1948); Cresta Victor (1957); Viva (1963); Chevette (1975); Cavalier (1975); Carlton, Royale (1978); Astra, Viceroy (1980); Cavalier (1981); Nova (1983). Numerous successes on track and hill-climbs (1909 to 1924).

VAZ - VOLZHSKY AVTOMOBILNY ZAVOD — **USSR**

(Make: Lada)

Press office: Avtoexport, Ul. Volkhonka 14, Moscow 119902. Works: Togliatti. 78,000 employees. 780,000 cars produced in 1982.

VEB AUTOMOBILWERK EISENACH — **German Democratic Republic**

(Make: Wartburg)

Press office: Rennbahn 8, 59 Eisenach. About 60,000 cars produced in 1982.

VEB SACHSENRING AUTOMOBILWERKE ZWICKAU — **German Democratic Republic**

(Make: Trabant)

Founded in 1904 under the name of A. Horch Motorwagenwerke AG Zwickau, became Audi-Mobilwagenwerke AG Zwickau in 1909, merged with Auto Union in 1932, nationalized in 1946. Present title since 1958. Head office and press office: W. Rathenau Strasse, 95 Zwickau. 9,000 employees. About 120,000 cars produced in 1982. Most important models: world record 500 hp 16-cyl-rear-engined car (1937-38); DKW 3.5-5 I, F2, F3, F4, F5, F6, F7, F8, (two-stroke front drive engine up to 1945); F8 (1949-52); P70, S 240 (1955-59); Trabant P50 (1958-62); 600 (1962-63); 601 (1964). Entries in numerous competitions (Munich-Vienna-Budapest, Semperit, Thousand Lakes, Tulip, Monte Carlo, Vlatava, Pneumat (D.D.R.) Akropolis Rallies, Tour de Belgique).

VOLKSWAGEN (Mexico) - see VOLKSWAGENWERK AG

VOLKSWAGEN ARGENTINA S.A. — **Argentina**

Founded in 1959 as Fevre y Basset, changed to Chrysler Fevre in 1962 and to VW Argentina in 1980. Chairman: C. Mandry. Managing Director: H. Arndt. Head office and press office: Florencio Varela 1903, San Justo, Provincia Buenos Aires. Works: as above; Charcas 4200 Monte Chingolo, Buenos Aires. 3,250 employees. 14,287 cars produced in 1982.

VOLKSWAGEN DO BRASIL S.A. — **Brazil**

Founded in 1953. Chairman: W.F.J. Sauer. Head office, press office and works: v. Anchieta km 23.5, São Bernardo do Campo, São Paulo. CEP 09700. 33,176 employees. 324,133 cars produced in 1982.

VOLKSWAGEN OF AMERICA Inc. — **USA**

Volkswagen Manufacturing Corporation of America merged with Volkswagen of America on July 31, 1978. Volkswagen of America, Inc. (VWoA) was founded in 1955. Chairman: C.H. Hahn. President: N. Phillips. Head office: 888 W Big Beaver Rd, P.O.B. 3951 Troy, Mich. 48099. Works: VW Westmoreland, East Huntingdon Township, Pennsylvania. 7,000 employees. 84,027 Rabbits and 8,130 pickup trucks assembled in 1982. Assembly of VW Rabbit begun in 1978.

VOLKSWAGEN OF NIGERIA Ltd — **Nigeria**

Chairman: H. Babs. Akerele. Managing Director: W. Nadebusch. Directors: H. Bauer, H. Denfeld, M.D. Galadima, G. Hartwich. Head office, press office and works: km 17, Badagry Highway, Lagos.

VOLKSWAGENWERK AG — **Germany (Federal Republic)**

Founded in 1937 under name of Gesellschaft zur Vorbereitung des Deutschen Volkswagen mbH, became Volkswagenwerk GmbH in 1938. Present title since 1960. For volume of production is foremost German motor manufacturer. Board of Directors: C.H. Hahn (Chairman), H. Münzner (Deputy Chairman), K.H. Briam, G. Hartwich, F. Thomée, P. Frerk, E. Fiala, W.P. Schmidt. Head office and press office: D-3180 Wolfsburg. Works: as above; Braunschweig, Emden, Hannover, Kassel, Salzgitter. 239,116 employees. 2,130,075 cars produced in 1982. Most important models: Limousine 1200 (1945); 1200 Convertible (1959); 1200 Karmann-Ghia Coupé (1955); 1200 Karmann-Ghia Convertible (1957); 1500 and 1500 Karmann-Ghia Coupé (1961); 1500 N Limousine, 1500 S Limousine, 1500 S Karmann-Ghia Coupé (1963); 1600 TL (1965); 411 (1968); 411 E, 411 LE (1969); 1302, 1302 S, K 70 (1970)); 1303 (1972). Passat, Passat Variant (1973); Golf, Scirocco (1974); Polo (1975); Derby (1977); Golf Cabriolet, Jetta (1979).

MANUFACTURE AND ASSEMBLY IN OTHER COUNTRIES — **Argentina:** Volkswagen Argentina, S.A., Buenos Aires (assem. VW 1500). **Belgium:** Volkswagen Bruxelles, S.A., Brussels (Golf, Passat). **Brazil:** Volkswagen do Brazil S.A., São Bernardo do Campo (São Paulo), (manuf. 1200, Gol, Voyage, Passat). **Mexico:** Volkswagen de México S.A. de C.V. (associated company), Mexico City (1200, Caribe, Golf, Atlantic, Jetta). **Nigeria:** Volkswagen of Nigeria (associated company), Lagos-Badagry Highway, km 18, Lagos (manuf. 1200, Passat). **South Africa:** Volkswagen of South Africa Ltd (associated company). Uitenhage (assem. Passat, Golf, 1200, Audi 100). **USA:** Volkswagen of America Inc., Westmoreland, (assem. Rabbit). **Yugoslavia:** TAS Tvornica Automobila Sarajevo, Sarajevo (Jetta, Golf). 799,000 cars produced outside Federal Republic in 1981.

VOLVO CAR B.V. — **Holland**

Founded in 1928 by Hub and Wim van Doorne, assumed title Van Doorne's Automobielfabrieken in 1958. In 1975 A.B. Volvo obtained a controlling interest of 75% in Van Doorne's Automobielfabrieken B.V. which became Volvo Car B.V. a member of the Volvo Group. The Company designes and manufactures the compact medium-sized cars of the Volvo Car product range since 1975. 30% of the shares are held by Volvo Car Corporation and 70% of the shares are in Dutch hands. Managing Directors: A.H.C. Deleye, F. Sevenstern, G.P. Wright. Head office and press office: Steenovenweg 1, Helmond. Works: Born, Oss. About 5,650 employees. 90,829 cars produced in 1982.

VOLVO CAR CORPORATION — **Sweden**

Founded in 1926. President and General Manager: H. Frisinger. Head office, press office and works: S-405 08, Göteborg. 20,000 employees. 227,700 cars produced in 1982. Most important models: P4 (1927); 53-56 (1939); PV 50 (1944); PV 444 (1947); P 1900 (1954-57); 122S Amazon (1956); P 544 (1958-62); P 1800 (1961); 144 (1966); 164 (1968); 240 (1975); 343 (1976).

ASSEMBLY IN OTHER COUNTRIES — **Australia:** Volvo Australia Pty Ltd, Melbourne (Liverpool). **Belgium:** Volvo Europa N.V. (subsidiary), P.B. 237, Ghent. **Canada:** Volvo (Canada) Ltd, Willowdale. **Holland:** Volvo Car B.V. Steenonvenweg, Helmond. **Malaysia:** Swedish Motor Assemblies Sdn Bhd (subsidiary), Batu Tiga, Industrial Estate, Selangor. 61,000 cars produced outside Sweden in 1982.

WARTBURG - see VEB AUTOMOBILWERK EISENACH

YLN - YUE LOONG MOTOR COMPANY Ltd — **Taiwan**

Founded in 1953 as Yue Loong Engineering Co. Ltd. Present title since 1960. Chairman and President: Vivian W. Yen. Special Assistant to Chairman and President: C.C. Yen. Managing Director: V.Z. Faung. Head office and press office: 150 Nanking East Rd, Sec II, Taipei. Works: Hsin Tien Taipei; San Yi, Miao Li. 3,400 employees. 57,487 cars produced in 1982. Under licence of Nissan Motor Co. manufactures various types of sedans and light trucks. Most important models: 303 DX, 303 GX, 303 W, 311 SD, 712 H2, 721 SD, 721 HB, 912 GD, 807 GX.

ZAZ - ZAPOROZHSKY AVTOMOBILNY ZAVOD — **USSR**

Press office: Avtoexport, Ul. Volkhonka 14, Moscow 119902 Works: Zaporozhje. About 145,000 cars produced in 1982.

ZCZ - ZAVODI CRVENA ZASTAVA — **Yugoslavia**

Board of Directors: R. Micić, K. Sretenović, R. Andonović, B. Lugomirski, M. Vasiljević, S. Smiljanić. Head office, press office and works: Španskih boraca 4, 34000 Kragujevac. About 48,261 employees. 150,432 cars produced in 1982.

ZIL — **USSR**

Press office: Avtoexport, Ul. Volkhonka 14, Moscow 119902. Works: Moscow. About 500 cars produced in 1981.

COACHBUILDERS

ARAGONA MOTOR VEHICLES Inc. — **USA**

Founded in 1983. President and Chief Executive Offier: J. E. Aragona. Head office and press office: 36 Bates St, Mendon, Mass. 01756. Works: Besson-Gobbi S.A., Porto Alegre, Brazil.

ASTON MARTIN TICKFORD — **Great Britain**

Managing Director: S. Rawlinson. Head office and works: 58 Tanners Drive, Blakelands North, Milton Keynes MK14 5BW. PR. Consultants: Media Men Ltd, 3 Salisbury House, Union St, Bedford, Beds.

AVON COACHWORK Ltd — **Gread Britain**

Chairman and Managing Director: L. G. Hudson. Head office and press office: Ladbroke House, Millers Rd. Warwoik CV34 5AP.

(KAROSSERIE) BAUR GmbH — **Germany (Federal Republic)**

Directors: K. Baur, H. Baur. Head office, press office and works: Poststr. 40-62, 7 Stuttgart 1 - Berg.

BEAUJARDIN — **Canada**

Founded 1972 by B. Beaujardin. Automotive stylist and constructor of prototypes of motor cars, parts and accessories.

Head office and press office: 235 West Sherbrooke, Suite 1104, Montreal, P.Q., H2X 1X8.

BERTONE (Carrozzeria) S.p.A. — **Italy**

Founded in 1912. Produces small and medium series of car bodies; bespoke production for car manufacturing firms and construction of prototypes. President and Managing Director: N. Bertone. Head office: c.so Peschiera 223, Turin. Press office and works: c.so Canonico Allamano 40-46, 10095 Grugliasco, Turin.

BITTER-AUTOMOBILE GmbH & Co. KG — **Germany (Federal Republic)**

Head office and press office: Berliner Str. 57, 5830 Schwelm.

CLANCY — **Australia**

Office: Dr. M. Clancy, 210 Kooyong Rd, Toorak, Victoria.

COLEMAN-MILNE P.l.c. — **Great Britain**

Founded in 1953. Specialist in the manufacture of Grosvenor, Dorchester and Minster limousines. Chairman and Managing Director: R.S.C. Milne. Head office: Colmil Works, Wigan Rd, Hart Common, Westhoughton, Bolton, BL5 2EE.

CRAYFORD ENGINEERING GROUP — **Great Britain**

Founded in 1960, specialising in convertibles, estate cars and cross country vehicles. Managing Directors: D. McMullan, J.J. Smith. Head office: High Street, Westerham, Kent.

CUMBERFORD CORPORATION — **USA**

Head office: 6004 Techni-Center Drive, Austin, Texas 78721.

GATSBY COACHWORKS Ltd — **USA**

Established in 1979. President: W. «Sky» Clausen. Vice-President: L.D. Munson. Secretary and Treasurer: Susan L. Munson. Head office: 1718 Stone Ave, San José, Ca. 95125; P.O.B. 23099, San José, Ca. 95153.

GHIA S.p.A. — **Italy**

Founded in 1915. Produces car bodies. Managing Director: P. Sapino. Head office: v. A. da Montefeltro 5, 10134 Turin.

GLENFROME ENGINEERING Ltd — **Great Britan**

Founded in 1977 by K. Evans. Directors: K. Evans, M. Evans, J. Evans. Head office, press office and works: Imperial works Hudds Vale Rd, St. George, Bristol BSS 7 HY. 64 employees 137 cars produced in 1982.

GUANCI AUTOMOBILES Inc. — **USA**

Founded in 1978. President: J.J. Guanci, Jr. Head office and works: 220 North Madison St, Woodstock, Ill. 60098.

ITAL DESIGN SIRP S.p.A. — **Italy**

Founded in 1968. Styling and design of cars in small, medium and large series; construction of models and prototypes. Directors: L. Bosio, G. Giugiaro, A. Mantovani. Head office and press office: v. A. Grandi 11, 10024 Moncalieri, Turin.

JEHLE - AR-STUDIO XAVER JEHLE — **Liechtenstein**

Head office and works: Specki 14, 9494 Schaan.

LOGICAR AS — **Denmark**

Founded in 1982. Designer J. Jensen. First prototype shown at 1983 Frankfurt Motor Show. Directors: I. Langmach, J. Jensen, J. Pdersen, N. Lauridsen. Head office and works: Hjulmagervej 5, DK 8800 Viborg. Press office: Otto Werk Design, Bymarkasvej 4, Stevnstrop, DK 8870 Langaa. 18 employees.

(THE) LYNX COMPANY — **Great Britain**

Head office, press office, sales and works: Lynx Engineering, Unit 8, Castleham Rd, Castleham Industrial Estate, St. Leonards-on-Sea, East Sussex TN38 9NR.

MARAUDER COMPANY Inc — **USA**

Established 1970. President: R. Berry. Chief Executive Officer: C. Bloomfield. Head office, press office and works: R.R.2, Box 102, Potomac, Ill. 61865.

MICHELOTTI - Studio Tecnica Design Carrozzeria — **Italy**

Coachbuilding engineering studio for custom-made cars. Proprietor: Edgardo Michelotti. Head office, press office and works: strada dei Boschi 8, 10092 Beinasco, Turin.

MUGEN COMPANY Ltd — **Japan**

President: H. Honda. Head office: 2-15-11 Hazaore machi, Asaka shi. Saitama ken, 351 Japan.

OGLE DESIGN Ltd — **Great Britain**

Founded in 1954. Design and development of motor vehicles. Prototypes and models. Design include Reliant Scimitar GTE, Bond Bug, Aston Martin Sotheby Special and the Ogle Metro. Managing Director: Tom Karen. Head office, press office and works: Birds Hill, Letchworth, Hertfordshire, SG6 IJA.

PININFARINA (Industrie) S.p.A. — **Italy**

Founded in 1930. Produces special and de luxe bodies. President: S. Pininfarina, Managing Director: R. Carli, Member of Board: E. Carbonato. Head office: c. Stati Uniti 61, Turin. Works: v. Lesna 78-80, 10095 Grugliasco, Turin.

QUINCY-LYNN ENTERPRISES Inc. — **USA**

Established in 1974 as research and development firm. Incorporated March 1977. Company has developed several prototype urban cars, both gasoline and electric versions. President: R.Q. Riley. Secretary and Treasurer: D.L. Carey. Head office and press office: 11028 Nort 22nd Ave., Phoenix, Arizona 85029.

RVIA - SUNRISE AUTO CORPORATION — **USA**

President: R. Vick. Secretary/Treasurer: C. Vick. Head office and press office: P.O. Box 98944, Des Moines, Washington. Works: Marine View Drive, Des Moines, Washington. 3 employees. 24 cars produced to 1983.

SBARRO - ATELIERS DE CONSTRUCTIONS AUTOMOBILES — **Switzerland**

Founded in 1973. Proprietor: F. Sbarro. Head office, press office and works: ACA Atelier, 1411 Les Tuileries-de-Grandson. 98 cars produced in 1982.

SCARLATTI CARS — **South Africa**

Head office and works: 21 Koper St, Farramere, Benoni 1500.

(AUTOMOBILES) STIMULA Sarl — **France**

Manufacture of replicars in small series. Managing Director: X. de la Chapelle. Head office, press office and works: Chemin de Sacuny, 69530 Brignais.

VEHICLE DESIGN FORCE / VECTOR CARS — **USA**

Founded in 1976. President: G. Wiegert. Head office and press office: 1101 West Washington Blvd, Venice, Ca. 90291.

ZAGATO CAR s.r.l. — **Italy**

Founded in 1919. Produces car bodies. President: E. Zagato. Managing Director: G. Zagato. Press office and works: v. Arese, 20017 Terrazzano di Rho, Milan.

ELECTRIC CAR BUILDERS

BRIGGS & STRATTON CORPORATION — **USA**

Address: P.O.B. 702 Milwaukee, Wisconsin 53201.

C.E.D.R.E. - SEVE — **France**

Address: 31310, Montesquieu Volvestre.

DAIHATSU KOGYO COMPANY Ltd — **Japan**

Address: 1-1 Daihatsu-cho, Ikeda-City, Osaka 563.

ENFIELD — **Grand Britain**

Address: Electricity Council, Millbank, London SW1P 4 RD.

FAIRCLOUGH ELECTRIC VEHICLES Ltd — **Great Britain**

Address: Unit 3, Opportunities Centre, Halesfield 14, Telford, Shropshire.

GE - GENERAL ELECTRIC — **USA**

Address: Research and Development Center, P.O. Box 8, Schenectady, New York 12301.

GLOBE BATTERY DIVISION JOHNSON CONTROLS Inc. — **USA**

Address: 5757 North Green Bay Ave, Milwaukee, Wisconsin 53201.

LUCAS CHLORIDE EV SYSTEM Ltd — **Great Britan**

Address: Evelyn Rd, Birmingham B11 3JR.

MAZDA - TOYO KOGYO COMPANY Ltd — **Japan**

Address: 3-1 Fuchu-machi, Aki-gun, Hiroshima-ken.

MITSUBISHI MOTOR COPORATION — **Japan**

Address: No. 33-8 Shiba 5-chome, Minatoku, Tokyo.

NISSAN MOTOR COMPANY Ltd — **Japan**

Address: Ginza, Chuo-ku, Tokyo.

PGE - PROGETTI GESTIONI ECOLOGICHE — **Italy**

Address: via Rosellini 1, 20124 Milan.

QUINCY-LYNN ENTERPRISES Inc. — **USA**

Address: 11028 North 22nd Ave, Phoenix, Arizona 85029.

SUZUKI MOTOR COMPANY — **Japan**

Address: 300 Takatsuka, Kami-mura, Hamana-gun, Shizuoka-ken.

TEILHOL VOITURE ELECTRIQUE — **France**

Address; Zone Industrielle La Masse, 63600 Ambert.

TOYOTA MOTOR CORPORATION Ltd — **Japan**

Address: 1, Toyota-Cho, Toyota City.

UNIQUE MOBILITY Inc. — **USA**

Address: 3700 South Jason St, Englewood, Colorado 80110.

VESSA — **Switzerland**

Address: Société d'Electricité Romande, Rue du Lac 18, 1815 Clarens.

ZAGATO CAR s.r.l. — **Italy**

Address: Via Arese, 20017 Terrazzano di Rho, Milan.

Indexes

Name of car

Maximum speed

Makes, models and prices

NAME OF CAR

Cars called by names (in alphabetical order)

Model	Make
ACADIAN	PONTIAC (CDN)
ACCLAIM	TRIUMPH
ACCORD	HONDA
ALFA	ALFA ROMEO
ALFA ROMEO	FIAT (BR)
ALFASUD	ALFA ROMEO
ALFETTA	ALFA ROMEO
ALPINE	TALBOT (GB)
ALTO	SUZUKI
AMBASSADOR	HINDUSTAN
ANADOL	OTOSAN
ARGENTA	FIAT (I)
ARIES	DODGE
ARNA	ALFA ROMEO
ASCONA	OPEL (D, ZA)
ASTRA	VAUXHALL
AUSTER	NISSAN (J)
AUSTIN-HEALEY	LENHAM
BALLADE	HONDA
BEARCAT	STUTZ
BEAUFIGHTER	BRISTOL
BEETLE	VOLKSWAGEN (WAN)
BERLINA	PHILLIPS
BETA	LANCIA
BITURBO	MASERATI
BLACKHAWK	STUTZ
BLIZZARD	TOYOTA (J)
BLUEBIRD	NISSAN (AUS, J)
BONNEVILLE	PONTIAC (USA)
BRIGAND	BRISTOL
BRITANNIA	BRISTOL
BUGATTI	CLASSIC-CAR-OLDTIMERBAU, STIMULA
CABRIO	BERTONE
CAMARGUE	ROLLS-ROYCE
CAMARO	CHEVROLET (USA)
CAMIRA	HOLDEN
CAMPAGNOLA	FIAT (I)
CAMRY	TOYOTA (J)
CAPELLA	MAZDA
CAPRI	FORD (D, GB), MERCURY (CDN, USA)
CAPRICE	CHEVROLET (USA)
CARAVAN	DODGE
CARINA	TOYOTA (J)
CARLTON	VAUXHALL
CAVALIER	CHEVROLET (USA), VAUXHALL
CEDRIC	NISSAN (J)
CELEBRITY	CHEVROLET (USA)
CELICA	TOYOTA (J)
CENTURY	BUICK, TOYOTA (J)
CERVO	SUZUKI
CHAIKA	GAZ
CHARADE	DAIHATSU
CHARGER	DODGE
CHARIOT	MITSUBISHI (J)
CHARMANT	DAIHATSU
CHASER	TOYOTA (J)
CHEROKEE	JEEP
CHEVETTE	CHEVROLET (BR, CDN, USA), VAUXHALL
CIMARRON	CADILLAC
CITATION	CHEVROLET (USA)
CITY	HONDA, MINI
CIVIC	HONDA
CLUB	OLTCIT
COLT	MITSUBISHI (AUS)
COMMODORE	HOLDEN, OPEL (ZA)
COMODORO	CHEVROLET (BR)
CONDOR	AYMESA
CONTESSA	HINDUSTAN
CONTINENTAL	LINCOLN
CORCEL	FORD (BR)
CORDIA	MITSUBISHI (J)
CORNICHE	BENTLEY, ROLLS-ROYCE
COROLLA	TOYOTA (AUS, J)
CORONA	TOYOTA (AUS, J)
CORSA	OPEL (D), TOYOTA (J)
CORVETTE	CHEVROLET (USA)
COSMO	MAZDA
COSTIN	TMC

Model	Make
COUGAR	MERCURY (CDN, USA)
COUNTACH	LAMBORGHINI
CRESTA	TOYOTA (J)
CROWN	TOYOTA (J)
CULTUS	SUZUKI
CUORE	DAIHATSU
CUSTOM CRUISER	OLDSMOBILE
CUTLASS	OLDSMOBILE
DAYTONA	DODGE
DEAUVILLE	DE TOMASO
DEBONAIR	MITSUBISHI (J)
DEL REY	FORD (BR)
DELTA	DAIHATSU, LANCIA, OLDSMOBILE
DESIGNER	LINCOLN
DE VILLE	CADILLAC
DIPLOMAT	DODGE
DIPLOMATA	CHEVROLET (BR)
DOLPHIN	SIPANI
DOMINGO	SUBARU
DOUBLE-SIX	DAIMLER
EAGLE	AMERICAN MOTORS
ELDORADO	CADILLAC
ELECTRA	BUICK
ESCORT	FORD (BR, CDN, D, GB, USA, ZA)
ESPRIT	LOTUS
ETERNA	MITSUBISHI (J)
EXCEL	LOTUS
EXECUTIVE	CHRYSLER
FAIRLADY	NISSAN (J)
FAIRLANE	FORD (AUS, RA)
FAIRMONT	FORD (AUS)
FALCON	FORD (AUS, RA)
FAMILIA	MAZDA
FIERO	PONTIAC (USA)
FIESTA	FORD (D, GB)
FIFTH AVENUE	CHRYSLER
FIREBIRD	PONTIAC (USA)
FIRENZA	OLDSMOBILE
FLEETWOOD	CADILLAC
FLORIAN	ISUZU
FORD «B»	TOTAL REPLICA
FORD V8	TIMMIS
FOX	RELIANT
FRONTE	SUZUKI
FUEGO	RENAULT (F, RA)
FURA	SEAT
FUSCA	VOLKSWAGEN (BR)
GACEL	VOLKSWAGEN (RA)
GALA	AYMESA
GALANT	MITSUBISHI (J)
GAMMA	LANCIA
GAZELLE	NISSAN (J)
GEMINI	HOLDEN, ISUZU
GEPARD	CLASSIC-CAR JANSSEN
GLORIA	NISSAN (J)
GOL	VOLKSWAGEN (BR)
GOLD	MIDAS
GOLF	VOLKSWAGEN (D, WAN)
GRANADA	FORD (D, GB, ZA)
GRAND MARQUIS	MERCURY (CDN, USA)
GRAND PRIX	PONTIAC (USA)
GRAND WAGONEER	JEEP
GRAN FURY	PLYMOUTH
HI BOY	TOTAL REPLICA
HIGH LINE	PAYKAN
HORIZON	PLYMOUTH, TALBOT (E, F, GB)
HURRYCANE	CUSTOCA
IMPALA	CHEVROLET (USA)
ITAL	MORRIS
JALPA	LAMBORGHINI
JEEP	MITSUBISHI (J)
JEG	QT
JETTA	VOLKSWAGEN (D, WAN)
JIMNY	SUZUKI
KADETT	OPEL (D, ZA)
KALLISTA	PANTHER

Model	Make
LADA	VAZ
LAGONDA	ASTON MARTIN
LANCER	MITSUBISHI (J)
LANDAU	FORD (BR)
LANDCRUISER	TOYOTA (J)
LANGLEY	NISSAN (J)
LASER	CHRYSLER, FORD (AUS, J)
LAUREL	NISSAN (J)
LE BARON	CHRYSLER
LEONE	SUBARU
LEOPARD	NISSAN (J)
LE SABRE	BUICK
LIBERTA	NISSAN (J)
LIMOUSINE	DAIMLER
LONGCHAMP	DE TOMASO
LOW LINE	PAYKAN
LUCE	MAZDA
LYNX	MERCURY (CDN, USA)
MADISON	GP, OB & D
MAEPSY-NA	DAEWOO
MAESTRO	AUSTIN, MG
MANTA	OPEL (D)
MANTULA	MARCOS
MARCH	NISSAN (J)
MARK	LINCOLN, TOYOTA (J)
MARQUIS	MERCURY (CDN, USA)
MATRA	TALBOT (F)
MAYFAIR	MINI
MEHARI	CITROËN (F)
METEOR	FORD (AUS)
METRO	AUSTIN, MG
MIGI	DAYTONA
MINICA	MITSUBISHI (J)
MIRA	DAIHATSU
MIRAGE	MITSUBISHI (J)
MOKE	DUTTON
MONDIAL	FERRARI
MONTECARLO	CHEVROLET (USA), LANCIA
MONZA	CHEVROLET (BR), KOUGAR, OPEL (D)
MOSKVICH	AZLK
MOYA	DAYTONA
MULSANNE	BENTLEY
MURAT	TOFAS
MUSTANG	FORD (CDN, USA)
NASR	EL NASR
NEWPORT	CHRYSLER
NEW YORKER	CHRYSLER
NINETY-EIGHT	OLDSMOBILE
NOVA	VAUXHALL
NUOVA GIULIETTA	ALFA ROMEO
OGGI	FIAT (BR)
OMEGA	OLDSMOBILE
OMNI	DODGE
OPALA	CHEVROLET (BR)
ORION	FORD (D, GB)
PADMINI	PREMIER
PAJERO	MITSUBISHI (J)
PALINURO	BERTONE
PANDA	FIAT (I), GIANNINI, SEAT
PANTERA	DE TOMASO
PARATI	VOLKSWAGEN (BR)
PARISIENNE	PONTIAC (USA)
PASSAT	VOLKSWAGEN (D, BR, WAN)
PHANTOM	ROLLS-ROYCE
PHOENIX	PONTIAC (USA)
PIAZZA	ISUZU
POLO	VOLKSWAGEN (D)
POLONEZ	FSO
PONY	HYUNDAI
PRAIRIE	NISSAN (J)
PRELUDE	HONDA
PRESIDENT	NISSAN (J)
PRISMA	LANCIA
PULSAR	NISSAN (AUS, J)
QUATTROPORTE	MASERATI
QUINT-QUINTET	HONDA
RABBIT	VOLKSWAGEN (USA)
RALLY	LANCIA
RAPID	ŠKODA
REGAL	BUICK

Model	Make
REGATA	FIAT (I)
REGINA	RUSKA
REKORD	OPEL (D, ZA)
RELIANT	PLYMOUTH
RENAULT ALLIANCE	AMERICAN MOTORS
RENAULT ENCORE	AMERICAN MOTORS
REPLICA	SBARRO
REX	SUBARU
RIALTO	RELIANT
RITMO	FIAT (I), GIANNINI
RIVIERA	BUICK
ROADSTER	DE COURVILLE, DESANDE
RODEO	ISUZU, RENAULT (F)
RONDA	SEAT
ROYALE	DAEWOO, SBARRO, STUTZ
SAFARI	NISSAN (J)
SAGITTA	RUSKA
SAMBA	TALBOT (E, F)
SANTANA	SHANGHAI, VOLKSWAGEN (D, WAN)
SAVANNA	MAZDA
SCIMITAR	RELIANT
SCIROCCO	VOLKSWAGEN (D)
SENATOR	OPEL (D, ZA)
SERIES IV	EXCALIBUR
SEVILLE	CADILLAC
SIERRA	FORD (D, GB, ZA)
SIGMA	MITSUBISHI (AUS)
SIGNATURE	LINCOLN
SILVER	ROLLS-ROYCE
SILVIA	NISSAN (J)
SKYHAWK	BUICK
SKYLARK	BUICK
SKYLINE	NISSAN (J)
SOARER	TOYOTA (J)
SOLARA	TALBOT (E, F, GB)
SOVEREIGN	JAGUAR
SPAZIO	FIAT (BR)
SPECIAL	OLTCIT
SPEEDSTER	APAL
SPIDER	ALFA ROMEO
SPIDEREUROPA	PININFARINA
SPORTS	KOUGAR, NOVA
SPRINT	ALFA ROMEO
SPRINTER	TOYOTA (J)
SPYDER	GP
STANZA	NISSAN (J)
STARION	MITSUBISHI (J)
STARLET	TOYOTA (J)
STASH	SBARRO
STATESMAN	HOLDEN
STELLAR	HYUNDAI
STILETTO	ITD
STRATO	CUSTOCA
SUNNY	NISSAN (J)
SUPER	CATERHAM CARS, DONKERVOORT
SUPER EUROPA	SEVEL
TAFT	DAIHATSU
TAIFUN	CUSTOCA
TALON	GP
TASMIN	TVR
TAUNUS	FORD (RA)
TELSTAR	FORD (J)
TEMPO	FORD (CDN, USA)
TERCEL	TOYOTA (J)
THUNDERBIRD	FORD (CDN, USA)
TIARA	MONTEVERDI
TOPAZ	MERCURY (CDN, USA)
TORONADO	OLDSMOBILE
TOWN CAR	LINCOLN
TREDIA	MITSUBISHI (J)
TREKKER	HINDUSTAN
TREVI	LANCIA
TURBO	ARGYLL, LOTUS, NUOVA INNOCENTI
TURISMO	PLYMOUTH
UNO	FIAT (I)
VANDEN PLAS	ROVER
VERANEIO	CHEVROLET (BR)
VICTORIA	STUTZ
VIGOR	HONDA
VISA	CITROËN (F)
VISTA	TOYOTA (J)
VITESSE	ROVER
VOLGA	GAZ
VOYAGE	VOLKSWAGEN (BR)
VOYAGER	PLYMOUTH
WAGONEER	JEEP
WINDHOUND	SBARRO
ZASTAVA	ZCZ

Cars called by letters (in alphabetical order)

Model	Make
A.1.	ATLANTIS
A4 CITY	LAWIL
A 112	AUTOBIANCHI
A 310 V6	ALPINE RENAULT
AC	AUTOKRAFT
AS	LEDL
BB	FERRARI
BJ	BEIJING
BX	CITROËN (F)
CA-770	HONG QI
CJ	JEEP
CX	CITROËN (F)
D TYPE	LYNX
E CLASS	CHRYSLER
EXP	FORD (CDN, USA)
FAF	CITROËN (P)
G25	GINETTA
GSA	CITROËN (F)
GT	KELMARK
GTB	PUMA
GTC	PUMA
GTI	PUMA
GTV	ALFA ROMEO
H.P.	LANCIA
J2X-2	ALLARD
LM	LAMBORGHINI
LNA	CITROËN (F)
LTD	FORD (AUS, CDN, USA)
M 635	BMW (D)
ML	FARUS
MP	LAFER
PLUS 8	MORGAN
S3 VARZINA	LAWIL
SC	BITTER AUTOMOBILE
SM	Sta MATILDE
SS	ARKLEY
T 613-2	TATRA
TS	FARUS
V8	ASTON MARTIN
X1/9	BERTONE
X-12	GURGEL
XJ	JAGUAR

Cars called by numbers (in numerical order)

Model	Make
2 CV 6	CITROËN (F)
3 CILINDRI	NUOVA INNOCENTI
3-LITRE	MARCOS
4	FASA-RENAULT, RENAULT (F, RA)
4.2	DAIMLER
4/4 1600	MORGAN
5	FASA-RENAULT, RENAULT (F)
6	FASA-RENAULT, RENAULT (RA)
7	FASA-RENAULT
9	FASA-RENAULT, RENAULT (F)
10.0	ARO
10.1	ARO
10.3	ARO
10.4	ARO
11	FASA-RENAULT, RENAULT (F)
12	FASA-RENAULT, RENAULT (RA)
14	FASA-RENAULT, RENAULT (F)
18	FASA-RENAULT, RENAULT (F, RA)
25	RENAULT (F)
90	ENVEMO
99	SAAB
104	PEUGEOT (F)
105	ŠKODA, SYRENA
114	ZIL
117	ZIL
120	ŠKODA
125	FSO
126	FIAT (I), FSO, GIANNINI
127	FIAT (I)
131	FIAT (I), SEAT
147	FIAT (BR), SEVEL
150	TALBOT (E)
190	MERCEDES-BENZ
200	MERCEDES-BENZ
205	PEUGEOT (F)
208	FERRARI
230	MERCEDES-BENZ
240	ARO, MERCEDES-BENZ, VOLVO (S)
241	ARO
243	ARO
244	ARO
250	MERCEDES-BENZ
260	PORTARO
280	MERCEDES-BENZ
300	MERCEDES-BENZ
305	PEUGEOT (F)
308	FERRARI
315	BMW (D)
316	BMW (D)
318	BMW (D, ZA)
320	BMW (D, ZA)
323	BMW (D, ZA)
340	VOLVO (NL)
353	WARTBURG
360	VOLVO (NL)
380	MERCEDES-BENZ
400	FERRARI
427	ERA
469 B	UAZ
500	MERCEDES-BENZ
504	DANGEL, PEUGEOT (WAN), SEVEL
505	PEUGEOT (F, WAN), SEVEL
518	BMW (D, ZA)
520	BMW (D, ZA)
524	BMW (D)
525	BMW (D)
528	BMW (D, ZA)
535	BMW (ZA)
600	DODGE
601	TRABANT
604	PEUGEOT (F)
626	MAZDA
628	BMW (D)
635	BMW (D)
728	BMW (D, ZA)
732	BMW (D)
733	BMW (ZA)
735	BMW (D, ZA)
745	BMW (D, ZA)
760	SHANGHAI, VOLVO (S)
856	ELEGANT MOTORS
898	ELEGANT MOTORS
900	SAAB
911	PORSCHE
924	PORSCHE
928	PORSCHE
944	PORSCHE
968 M	ZAZ
969-A	ZAZ
1000	PONTIAC (USA)
1200	VOLKSWAGEN (D, MEX)
1310	DACIA
1500	VOLKSWAGEN (RA)
2000	MASERATI, PONTIAC (USA), ROVER
2300	ROVER
2400	ROVER
2600	ROVER
3000	AC
3500	ROVER
4104	ZIL
6000	PONTIAC (USA)

MAXIMUM SPEED

Up to 65 mph

	mph
LAWIL S3 Varzina Spider / A4 City Berlina	39
SUZUKI Jimny Series (28 hp)	56
ZAZ 969-A 4 x 4	56
SUZUKI Alto Hatchback / Alto 4WD / Jimny Series (52 hp)	58
HINDUSTAN Trekker (40 hp, diesel)	60
BEIJING BJ 212 / BJ 212 E	61
HINDUSTAN Ambassador Mk 4 (40 hp, diesel)	62
MITSUBISHI (J) Jeep Series (80 hp, diesel)	62
TRABANT 601 Limousine / 601 Tramp / 601 Universal / 601 S De Luxe	62
DAIHATSU Taft	65
FIAT (I) 126	65
FSO 126 P / 650	65
QT Jeg TL 4 x 4	65

From 66 mph to 100 mph

	mph
LAND ROVER 88" Short Wheelbase / 109" Long Wheelbase	66
DAIHATSU Mira Series (30 hp and 41 hp) / Cuore Series (30 hp and 41 hp)	68
FIAT (I) Campagnola Diesel Lunga	68
LAND ROVER One Ten 2¼ P	68
MITSUBISHI (J) Minica Series (29 hp and 39 hp)	68
RENAULT (F) Rodeo 5	68
SUBARU Rex Series (34 hp, 544 cc and 41 hp)	68
SUZUKI Fronte Series (29 hp) / Cervo	68
TOYOTA (J) Blizzard	68
ZCZ Zastava 750 LE	68
PORTARO 260	70
ARO 10.0 / 10.1 / 10.3 / 10.4 (54 hp) / 240-242 (70 hp, diesel)	71
FIAT (I) Panda 30 / Panda 30 Super / Campagnola Lunga / Campagnola Diesel	71
MERCEDES-BENZ 240 GD	71
MITSUBISHI (J) Pajero Series (75 hp, diesel)	71
TOYOTA (J) Landcruiser Series (98 hp, diesel)	71
UAZ 469 B	71
VOLKSWAGEN (D, MEX) 1200 L	71
HINDUSTAN Trekker (49 hp)	72
ARO 241-244 (70 hp, diesel)	73
CITROËN (F) 2 CV 6	73
CITROËN (P) Faf	73
FASA-RENAULT 4 TL	73
GURGEL X-12	73
LAND ROVER 109" V8 Long Wheelbase	73
DAIHATSU Charade Series (38 hp, diesel)	74
ARO 10.0-10.1-10.3-10.4 (62 hp)	75
AZLK Moskvich 2138 / Moskvich 2136	75
CITROËN (F) Mehari	75
FIAT (I) Campagnola	75
GIANNINI Fiat Giannini 126 Series (30 hp)	75
HINDUSTAN Contessa / Ambassador Mk 4 (49 hp) / Trekker (59 hp)	75
MITSUBISHI (J) Jeep Series (100 hp and 120 hp)	75
NISSAN (J) Safari Series (95 hp, diesel)	75
OLTCIT Special	75
PREMIER Padmini	75
RENAULT (F, RA) 4 Series	75
SUBARU Domingo Series (56 hp, 997 cc)	75
SYRENA 105	75
VOLKSWAGEN (BR) Fusca	75
ARO 240-243 (83 hp)	76
ZAZ 968 M	76
DANGEL 504 4 x 4 Series (70 hp, diesel)	77
HINDUSTAN Ambassador Mk 4 (59 hp)	77
ARO 241-244 (83 hp)	78
CITROËN (F) LNA / Visa	78
ISUZU Rodeo 4WD	78
JEEP CJ-7 Roadster (84 hp)	78
MITSUBISHI (J) Pajero Series (95 hp, diesel)	78
RENAULT (F) 5 Series (37 hp)	78
RENAULT (RA) 6 GTL	78
RUSKA Regina	78
WARTBURG 353 W Tourist / 353 W De Luxe	78
ZCZ Zastava 850	78
VOLKSWAGEN (WAN) Beetle 1500	79
PREMIER Padmini De Luxe	80
RELIANT Rialto	80
SIPANI Dolphin	80
AUTOBIANCHI A 112 Junior	81
DUTTON Moke Californian	81
FIAT (I) 127 Series (45 hp, diesel)	81
GIANNINI Fiat Giannini Panda Series (36 hp)	81
MERCEDES-BENZ 300 GD	81
MINI City E / Mayfair	81
PORTARO 260 Celta Turbo	81
SEAT Panda Series (42 hp)	81
SHANGHAI 760 A	81
ŠKODA 105 S / 105 L	81
WARTBURG 353 W	81
CLASSIC-CAR JANSSEN Gepard SS 100	82
SEAT Fura	82
VAZ Lada Niva 2121 4 x 4	82
EL NASR Nasr 127 CL	83
FASA-RENAULT 6 GTL / 7 GTL	83
PEUGEOT (F) 205 Series (45 hp)	83
RUSKA Regina Royal / Sagitta	83
CHEVROLET (CDN) Chevette Scooter Series (51 hp, diesel)	84
CHEVROLET (USA) Chevette Series (51 hp, diesel)	84
CLASSIC-CAR-OLDTIMERBAU Bugatti 35 B / Bugatti 55	84
DAEWOO Royale Series (60 hp)	84
DAIHATSU Charade Series (55 hp)	84
FASA-RENAULT 5 Series (45 hp)	84
FIAT (BR) 147 Series (51 hp) / Spazio Series (51 hp)	84
FIAT (I) Panda 4 x 4 / 127 Series (50 hp)	84
FORD (D, GB) Fiesta Series (45 hp)	84
GAZ Volga Indenor Diesel	84
MERCEDES-BENZ 200 Series (60 hp, diesel)	84
MITSUBISHI (J) Pajero Series (110 hp)	84
PONTIAC (CDN) Acadian Series (51 hp, diesel)	84
PONTIAC (USA) 1000 Series (51 hp, diesel)	84
SEVEL Fiat 147 Series (53 hp)	84
VOLKSWAGEN (D) Polo Limousine Series (40 hp) / Polo Classic Series (40 hp)	84
ZCZ Zastava Jugo 45 / Zastava 128 CL 1100 / Zastava 101 Series (55 hp)	84
AUTOBIANCHI A 112 Elite / A 112 LX	85
CHEVROLET (USA) Impala Series (105 hp, diesel) / Caprice Classic Series (105 hp, diesel)	85
GP Talon / Madison Roadster	85
MERCEDES-BENZ 230 G	85
MERCURY (CDN, USA) Lynx Series (52 hp, diesel)	85
PAYKAN Low Line / High Line	85
FASA-RENAULT 9 Series (48 hp) / 11 Series (48 hp)	86
FORD (GB) Granada 2500 Diesel Estate (69 hp, diesel)	86
LAFER MP	86
MORRIS Ital Series (61 hp)	86
PEUGEOT (F) 104 Series (50 hp)	86
RENAULT (F) 9 Series (48 hp) 11 Series (48 hp)	86
AUSTIN Metro Series (44 hp)	87
AZLK Moskvich 2140 / Moskvich 2140 IZh / Moskvich 2137 / Moskvich 2140 Combi IZh	87
BEIJING BJ 750	87
CITROËN (F) LNA 11 / Visa 11	87
DACIA 1310	87
EL NASR Nasr 128 CL	87
FASA-RENAULT 12 GTL Familiar / 14 Series (70 hp)	87
FIAT (I) Panda 45 / Panda 45 Super / Uno Series (45 hp and 45 hp, diesel) / 131 Series (60 hp, diesel)	87
GIANNINI Fiat Giannini 126 Series (37 hp)	87
LAND ROVER One Ten 3½ P	87
MAZDA Luce / Cosmo Series (70 hp, diesel)	87
MERCURY (CDN, USA) Topaz Series (52 hp, diesel)	87
NISSAN (J) March	87
OPEL (D) Corsa Series (45 hp)	87
PONTIAC (USA) 6000 Series (92 hp)	87
RENAULT (RA) 12 TL	87
SEAT Panda Series (45 hp) / Ronda Series (55 hp, diesel)	87
ŠKODA 120 L	87
TOYOTA (J) Mark II Series (72 hp, diesel) / Chaser Series (72 hp, diesel) / Cresta Series (72 hp, diesel) / Landcruiser Series (140 hp)	87
VAUXHALL Nova Series (45 hp)	87
VAZ Lada Series (62 hp)	87
VOLKSWAGEN (D) Santana Series (54 hp, diesel)	87
ZCZ Zastava 101 Series (65 hp)	87
AMERICAN MOTORS Eagle Series (110 hp)	88
CHEVROLET (BR) Chevette Series (62 hp)	88
FIAT (BR) Oggi CS	88
FORD (BR) Corcel II Series (65 hp)	88
FORD (GB) Fiesta - Escort Series (50 hp)	88
MERCEDES-BENZ 230 GE	88
NUOVA INNOCENTI 3 Cilindri	88
PEUGEOT (WAN) 504 St. Wagon	88
VOLKSWAGEN (BR) Gol	88
VOLKSWAGEN (D) Jetta Diesel	88
AUDI Audi 80 Diesel Series (54 hp)	89
FORD (D) Escort Series (50 hp)	89
MERCEDES-BENZ 240 D	89
OPEL (D) Kadett - Ascona Series (54 hp, diesel)	89
TALBOT (F) Samba Series (50 hp)	89
VAUXHALL Astra - Cavalier Series (54 hp, diesel)	89
VOLKSWAGEN (D) Passat Diesel	89
AMERICAN MOTORS Eagle Series (120 hp)	90
CHEVROLET (BR) Veraneio	90
CHEVROLET (CDN) Chevette Scooter Series (65 hp)	90
CHEVROLET (USA) Chevette Series (65 hp) / Celebrity Series (85 hp, diesel)	90
CITROËN (F) CX 25 Diesel Break	90
DAYTONA Migi / Moya	90
DODGE Aries Series (96 hp) / 600 Series (96 hp)	90
EL NASR Nasr Polonez	90
FASA-RENAULT 14 Series (59 hp)	90
FIAT (I) Ritmo Series (55 hp)	90
FORD (CDN, USA) Escort Series (70 hp and 52 hp, diesel)	90
FORD (D) Granada Series (69 hp, diesel)	90
FORD (GB) Granada 2500 Diesel Saloon (69 hp, diesel)	90
FSO 125 P / 1300	90
HOLDEN Gemini TF Series (54 hp, diesel)	90
HONDA City Series (61 hp)	90
ISUZU Gemini Series (61 hp, diesel) / Florian Aska Series (66 hp, diesel)	90
JEEP Cherokee Series (105 hp) / Wagoneer Series (105 hp) / Grand Wagoneer (110 hp)	90
LINCOLN Continental Series (115 hp, diesel) / Designer Series (115 hp, diesel) / Mark VII Series (115 hp, diesel)	90
MERCURY (CDN, USA) Lynx Series (70 hp)	90
MITSUBISHI (J) Lancer Fiore Series (65 hp, diesel) / Mirage Series (65 hp, diesel)	90
NISSAN (J) Pulsar - Sunny - Langley - Liberta Villa Series (61 hp, diesel) / Bluebird Series (67 hp, diesel)	90
OTOSAN Anadol 16	90
PLYMOUTH Horizon - Turismo Series (64 hp)	90
PONTIAC (CDN) Acadian Series (65 hp)	90
PONTIAC (USA) 1000 Series (65 hp) / 6000 Series (85 hp, diesel)	90
SEVEL Fiat 147 Series (61 hp) / Fiat Super Europa Series (60 hp)	90
SUZUKI Cultus	90
TALBOT (F) Matra Rancho	90
TOYOTA (J) Crown Series (83 hp, diesel)	90
VOLKSWAGEN (RA) 1500 W	90
ZCZ Zastava Jugo 55 / Zastava 128 CL 1300	90
CITROËN (F) CX 25 Diesel Berline	91
DANGEL 504 4 x 4 Series (96 hp)	91
DODGE Omni Series (65 hp) / Charger Series (65 hp)	91
FASA-RENAULT 9 Series (55 hp, diesel)	91

	mph
FIAT (I) Ritmo Series (58 hp, diesel)	**91**
FORD (BR) Corcel II GL Sedan (65 hp) / Del Rey Series (65 hp)	**91**
FORD (D) Fiesta - Escort Series (54 hp, diesel)	**91**
HOLDEN Commodore Series (79 hp)	**91**
PEUGEOT (F) 505 Break-Familial Series (76 hp, diesel)	**91**
RENAULT (F) 9 Series (55 hp, diesel)	**91**
TALBOT (F) Horizon Series (59 hp)	**91**
TALBOT (GB) Horizon Series (58 hp)	**91**
VAUXHALL Chevette	**91**
VOLKSWAGEN (D) Jetta Series (60 hp)	**91**
DODGE Aries Series (101 hp) / Caravan (101 hp)	**92**
JEEP Cherokee - Wagoneer Series (112 hp)	**92**
PLYMOUTH Voyager (101 hp)	**92**
RENAULT (F)18 GTD 4 x 4 Break (66 hp, diesel)	**92**
VOLKSWAGEN (D) Golf Diesel / Passat Variant Series (60 hp) / Santana Series (60 hp)	**92**
VOLKSWAGEN (USA) Rabbit Series (65 hp)	**92**
YLN 721	**92**
ALFA ROMEO Arna	**93**
AMERICAN MOTORS Renault Alliance / Renault Encore	**93**
AUDI Audi 80 Series (60 hp)	**93**
CADILLAC De Ville - Fleetwood - Eldorado - Seville Series (105 hp, diesel)	**93**
CHEVROLET (BR) Chevette Series (73 hp) / Opala Series (80 hp) / Diplomata Series (84 hp)	**93**
DAEWOO Maepsy-Na	**93**
EL NASR Nasr Ritmo 65 CL	**93**
FIAT (I) Regata Series (58 hp, diesel) / 131 Series (70 hp) / 131 Series (72 hp, diesel) / Argenta Diesel	**93**
FORD (D) Orion Series (54 hp, diesel)	**93**
FSO 125 P / 1500 Estate / Polonez LE	**93**
GAZ Volga 3102 Sedan / Volga 3102 St. Wagon	**93**
HONDA Civic - Ballade Series (80 hp) / Quint-Quintet	**93**
MAZDA Familia Series (74 hp) / Familia (USA)	**93**
MITSUBISHI (J) Lancer EX Series (70 hp) / Lancer Fiore - Mirage Series (77 hp) / Chariot Series (88 hp) / Galant Lambda Series (95 hp, diesel)	**93**
NISSAN (J) Prairie Series (85 hp)	**93**
OLTCIT Club	**93**
OPEL (D) Kadett Series (60 hp, 1,196 cc) / Ascona Series (60 hp)	**93**
OPEL (ZA) Kadett Series (60 hp)	**93**
PEUGEOT (F) 505 Series (76 hp, diesel)	**93**
PONTIAC (USA) Bonneville Series (110 hp and 105 hp, diesel)	**93**
SEAT Ronda Series (65 hp) / 131 Series (72 hp, diesel)	**93**
ŠKODA 120 LS / 120 GLS	**93**
SUBARU Leone Series (72 hp)	**93**
TALBOT (E) Horizon LD Berlina (65 hp, diesel)	**93**
TALBOT (F) Horizon Series (65 hp, diesel)	**93**
TALBOT (GB) Horizon Series (64 hp, diesel)	**93**
TOFAS Murat 131	**93**
TOYOTA (J) Corolla FWD Series (65 hp, diesel) / Sprinter FWD Series (65 hp, diesel)	**93**
VAUXHALL Astra Series (60 hp)	**93**
VOLKSWAGEN (RA) 1500 M 1.8 W / 1500 M 1.8 Rural W	**93**
VOLVO (NL) 340 Series (64 hp)	**93**
VOLVO (S) 240 Diesel	**93**
CADILLAC De Ville - Fleetwood Series (150 hp)	**94**
CHEVROLET (BR) Monza Series (73 hp)	**94**
CITROËN (F) CX 25 Diesel Familiale	**94**
FORD (GB) Sierra Series (60 hp)	**94**
OLDSMOBILE Cutlass Series (105 hp, diesel) / Toronado (105 hp, diesel)	**94**
PEUGEOT (F) 305 Berline Series (65 hp) / 305 Berline - 305 Break Series (65 hp, diesel)	**94**
PEUGEOT (WAN) 504 GR / 504 SR	**94**
PLYMOUTH Reliant Series (96 hp)	**94**
PONTIAC (USA) 2000 Sunbird Series (84 hp)	**94**
TALBOT (E) Samba Series (55 hp) / Horizon Series (59 hp)	**94**
VOLKSWAGEN (D) Golf Limousine Series (55 hp) / Passat Limousine Series (60 hp) / Passat Turbo-Diesel Variant	**94**
FASA-RENAULT 18 GTD Familiar (66 hp, diesel)	**95**
FORD (BR) Escort Series (65 hp)	**95**
FORD (RA) Taunus L 2000 / Falcon 2.3 Standard Sedan / Falcon 2.3 De Luxe Sedan / Falcon 3.0 Standard Sedan / Falcon 3.0 De Luxe Sedan / Falcon 3.0 Standard St. Wagon / Falcon 3.0 De Luxe St. Wagon	**95**
MORRIS Ital Series (77 hp)	**95**
NISSAN (J) Stanza - Auster Series (90 hp)	**95**
OLDSMOBILE Delta 88 Series (110 hp) / Ninety-Eight Series (110 hp) / Custom Cruiser Series (110 hp)	**95**
OPEL (D) Rekord Caravan Series (70 hp, diesel)	**95**
ŠKODA Rapid	**95**
TALBOT (GB) Alpine - Solara Series (67 hp)	**95**
VOLKSWAGEN (D) Polo Limousine - Polo Classic - Polo Coupé Series (55 hp) / Jetta Turbo-Diesel	**95**
ALFA ROMEO Nuova Giulietta 2.0 TD L / Alfetta 2.0 TD	**96**
APAL Speedster	**96**
AUDI Audi 100 - Audi 100 Avant Series (70 hp, diesel)	**96**
AUTOBIANCHI A 112 Abarth	**96**
BMW (D) 315	**96**
BUICK Century Series (85 hp, diesel)	**96**
CHEVROLET (BR) Comodoro Series (80 hp)	**96**
CITROËN (F) BX	**96**
CUSTOCA Hurrycane / Strato 80 ES / Taifun	**96**
DAIHATSU Charmant Series (74 hp)	**96**
FIAT (BR) 147 Series (70 hp) / Spazio Series (70 hp)	**96**
FIAT (I) Regata Series (68 hp) / Argenta 100	**96**
FORD (AUS) Laser Series (65 hp)	**96**
FORD (CDN, USA) EXP Series (80 hp) / Tempo Series (84 hp and 52 hp, diesel) / LTD Series (88 hp) / Mustang Series (88 hp)	**96**
FORD (D, GB) Sierra Series (67 hp, diesel)	**96**
FORD (RA) Fairlane 3600 LTD	**96**
FORD (ZA) Escort Series (67 hp)	**96**
FSO 125 P / 1500 Sedan	**96**
GIANNINI Fiat Giannini Panda Series (58 hp)	**96**
HOLDEN Gemini TF Series (67 hp)	**96**
HYUNDAI Pony Series (80 hp)	**96**
MERCEDES-BENZ 300 D Series (88 hp, diesel) / 280 GE	**96**
MERCURY (CDN, USA) Marquis - Capri Series (88 hp)	**96**
MITSUBISHI (AUS) Sigma GH Series (81 hp)	**96**
MITSUBISHI (J) Tredia Series (82 hp) / Cordia Series (88 hp) / Debonair	**96**
NISSAN (J) Skyline - Laurel - Cedric - Gloria Series (91 hp, diesel)	**96**
OPEL (D) Rekord Caravan Series (75 hp)	**96**
PEUGEOT (F) 205 Series (60 hp, diesel)	**96**
RENAULT (F) 25 Series (64 hp, diesel)	**96**
RENAULT (RA) 12 TS Break	**96**
TOYOTA (AUS) Corolla Series (64 hp)	**96**
TOYOTA (J) Corona FWD Series (72 hp, diesel) / Crown Series (96 hp, diesel)	**96**
TRIUMPH Acclaim	**96**
VAZ Lada Series (78 hp)	**96**
VOLKSWAGEN (D) Golf Cabriolet Series (75 hp) / Santana Series (70 hp, diesel)	**96**
VOLKSWAGEN (USA) Rabbit Series (52 hp, diesel)	**96**
YLN 807 GX	**96**
AUSTIN Maestro Series (68 hp)	**97**
CITROËN (F) CX 25 Diesel Pallas	**97**
FASA-RENAULT 18 GTD Berlina (66 hp, diesel)	**97**
FORD (RA) Falcon 3.6 Ghia Sedan	**97**
PONTIAC (USA) Fiero / Phoenix Series (92 hp)	**97**
RENAULT (F) 18 Series (64 hp) / 18 GTD Break (66 hp, diesel)	**97**
TALBOT (E) Horizon Series (65 hp, diesel) / 150 Series (73 hp) / Solara Series (73 hp)	**97**
VOLKSWAGEN (BR) Voyage - Passat Series (73 hp)	**97**
VOLKSWAGEN (D) Passat Turbo-Diesel Limousine	**97**
VOLKSWAGEN (RA) Gacel GL	**97**
VOLKSWAGEN (WAN) Jetta	**97**
AUDI Audi 80 Diesel Series (70 hp)	**98**
AUSTIN Maestro 1.6 Automatic Saloon (81 hp)	**98**
BUICK Regal Series (110 hp)	**98**
CITROËN (F) GSA Break	**98**
FORD (D, GB) Orion Series (69 hp)	**98**
GP Spyder	**98**
LAND ROVER Range Rover	**98**
PEUGEOT (F) 305 Break Series (74 hp)	**98**
PLYMOUTH Reliant Series (101 hp)	**98**
RENAULT (RA) 18 GTL Sedan	**98**
TALBOT (F) Solara Series (70 hp)	**98**
VOLKSWAGEN (BR) Parati Series (65 hp)	**98**
VOLKSWAGEN (WAN) Golf	**98**
AYMESA Gala - Condor GT	**99**
BERTONE Cabrio / Palinuro	**99**
BUICK Skyhawk Series (84 hp) / Century Series (125 hp)	**99**
CHEVROLET (BR) Monza Series (84 hp)	**99**
CHEVROLET (USA) Impala Series (110 hp, 3,785 cc) / Caprice Classic Series (110 hp, 3,753 cc)	**99**
CHRYSLER Laser - E Class - New Yorker Series (99 hp)	**99**
CITROËN (F) GSA Berline	**99**
DAIHATSU Charade Series (80 hp) / Charmant Series (83 hp)	**99**
EL NASR Nasr 131 CL	**99**
FIAT (I) Uno Series (70 hp) / Argenta Turbo Diesel	**99**
FORD (CDN, USA) EXP Series (120 hp)	**99**
FORD (D) Granada Series (90 hp)	**99**
FORD (J) Laser Series (85 hp) / Telstar Series (90 hp and 72 hp, diesel)	**99**
GIANNINI Fiat Giannini Ritmo Veloce 60 R	**99**
HONDA Ballade Sports Series (80 hp)	**99**
HONG QI CA-770 B 9-pass.	**99**
HYUNDAI Pony - Stellar Series (92 hp)	**99**
ISUZU Gemini Series (73 hp, diesel)	**99**
JEEP Grand Wagoneer Series (144 hp)	**99**
LANCIA Delta Berlina 1300 / Delta Berlina 1500 Automatica / Prisma Berlina 1300	**99**
MAZDA Capella Series (90 hp and 72 hp, diesel)	**99**
MERCEDES-BENZ 190 Series (72 hp, diesel)	**99**
MERCURY (CDN, USA) Lynx Series (120 hp) / Grand Marquis Series (140 hp)	**99**
NISSAN (J) Pulsar Series (75 hp) / Sunny Series (75 hp) / Prairie Series (100 hp) / Laurel Series (100 hp)	**99**
OLDSMOBILE Firenza Series (82 hp) / Cutlass Series (110 hp)	**99**
OPEL (D) Rekord Limousine Series (75 hp and 70 hp, diesel)	**99**
PEUGEOT (WAN) 505 GL / 505 SL	**99**
RENAULT (F) 18 GTD Berline (66 hp, diesel) / Fuego Series (64 hp)	**99**
SAAB 99 / 900 Series (100 hp)	**99**
TOYOTA (AUS) Corolla Series (78 hp)	**99**
TOYOTA (J) Corolla FWD - Sprinter FWD - Corolla II - Corsa - Tercel Series (75 hp) / Carina Series (83 hp and 65 hp, diesel) / Corona RWD Series (83 hp) / Sprinter Carib	**99**
VAUXHALL Cavalier Series (75 hp) / Carlton Series (71 hp, diesel)	**99**
VOLKSWAGEN (BR) Passat Series (82 hp, alcohol)	**99**
VOLKSWAGEN (D) Golf Turbo-Diesel	**99**
VOLKSWAGEN (WAN) Passat TS	**99**
VOLVO (NL) 340 Series (72 hp)	**99**
YLN 311 SD	**99**
CATERHAM CARS Super 7 1600 GT	**100**
CHEVROLET (USA) Camaro Series (92 hp) / Monte Carlo Series (110 hp, 3,753 cc) / Monte Carlo Series (105 hp, diesel)	**100**
CHRYSLER Laser Series (142 hp) / E Class - New Yorker Series (140 hp) / Executive Series (101 hp)	**100**
DODGE Omni - Charger Series (110 hp) / 600 Series (142 hp) / Daytona Series (99 hp and 142 hp)	**100**
FORD (GB) Granada st. wagons Series (105 hp)	**100**
LINCOLN Continental - Designer - Mark VII - Town Car - Signature Series (140 hp) / Designer (140 hp)	**100**
MERCURY (CDN, USA) Topaz Series (84 hp)	**100**
OLDSMOBILE Toronado (125 hp)	**100**
PANTHER Kallista 1.6	**100**
PONTIAC (USA) 2000 Sunbird Series (150 hp) / 100 Firebird Series (92 hp)	**100**
TIMMIS Ford V8 Roadster	**100**
TOTAL REPLICA Hi Boy / Ford "B"	**100**

From 101 mph to 120 mph

	mph
AUDI Audi 100 Avant Series (75 hp)	101
AUSTIN Metro Series (73 hp) / Maestro Series (81 hp)	101
CITROËN (F) BX 14	101
FASA-RENAULT 9 Series (72 hp) / 18 Series (79 hp)	101
MG Metro 1300	101
NISSAN (AUS) Bluebird	101
OPEL (D) Corsa Series (70 hp) / Kadett 1.3 SR	101
PEUGEOT (F) 505 Break-Familial Series (96 hp)	101
RENAULT (F) 9 Series (72 hp)	101
VAUXHALL Nova Series (70 hp)	101
VOLKSWAGEN (BR) Voyage Series (82 hp, alcohol)	101
ALFA ROMEO Alfasud TI 1.3 / Sprint 1.3 / Alfa 33 1.3 / Alfa 33 1.5 4 x 4 / Alfetta 2.4 TD	102
AUDI Audi 100 Series (75 hp)	102
BMW (D) 518	102
CITROËN (F) CX 20 Familiale	102
DODGE Diplomat Series (130 hp)	102
FIAT (I) Ritmo Series (82 hp)	102
FORD (AUS) Falcon - Fairmont Series (122 hp) / Fairlane ZK Sedan (133 hp)	102
FORD (D) Sierra Series (75 hp)	102
FORD (GB) Capri Series (73 hp)	102
FORD (ZA) Granada Series (105 hp)	102
LANCIA Prisma Berlina 1500 / Prisma Berlina 1500 Automatica	102
NISSAN (J) Langley Series (85 hp) / Liberta Villa Series (85 hp) / Laurel Spirit Series (85 hp)	102
OLDSMOBILE Firenza Series (88 hp)	102
OPEL (D) Manta Series (75 hp)	102
PEUGEOT (F) 104 Series (80 hp) / 604 Series (95 hp, diesel)	102
ROVER 2400 SD Turbo	102
SEVEL Fiat Super Europa Series (82 hp)	102
TALBOT (E) 150 Series (90 hp)	102
TALBOT (GB) Horizon Series (82 hp)	102
TOYOTA (J) Starlet Series (74 hp) / Corolla II - Corsa - Tercel Series (86 hp) / Corona FWD Series (83 hp)	102
VOLKSWAGEN (BR) Parati Series (82 hp, alcohol)	102
CITROËN (F) BX 19	103
ENVEMO 90 Super Coupé / 90 Super Cabriolet	103
GIANNINI Fiat Giannini Ritmo Turbo Diesel R	103
ISUZU Gemini Series (100 hp)	103
MERCEDES-BENZ 300 D Series (125 hp, diesel)	103
NISSAN (J) Bluebird Series (90 hp)	103
NUOVA INNOCENTI Turbo De Tomaso	103
OPEL (D) Corsa SR Limousine (70 hp)	103
SEAT 131 Series (95 hp)	103
SHANGHAI Santana Shanghai	103
SUBARU Leone Series (120 hp)	103
TOYOTA (J) Celica Series (100 hp)	103
VOLKSWAGEN (D) Jetta Series (85 hp)	103
VOLVO (NL) 360 Series (92 hp)	103
VOLVO (S) 240 Series (106 hp)	103
CITROËN (F) Visa GT / CX 20 Break	104
FORD (GB) Granada sedans Series (105 hp)	104
LANCIA Beta Coupé 1300	104
MERCEDES-BENZ 200 Series (109 hp)	104
MITSUBISHI (AUS) Sigma GH Series (102 hp)	104
PEUGEOT (F) 505 Series (100 hp)	104
ROVER 2000	104
SEVEL Peugeot 504 GR II / Peugeot 505 SR II	104
TALBOT (E, F) Solara Series (90 hp)	104
TALBOT (GB) Alpine - Solara Series (89 hp)	104
VOLKSWAGEN (D) Scirocco Series (75 hp)	104
ALFA ROMEO Nuova Giulietta 1.6 L	105
BMW (ZA) 518i	105
FORD (CDN, USA) LTD Crown Victoria Series (140 hp) / LTD Country 105 Squire Series (140 hp)	105
MERCURY (CDN, USA) Grand Marquis Series (180 hp)	105
OLDSMOBILE Cutlass Series (140 hp)	105
TOYOTA (J) Corolla Levin RWD Series (83 hp)	105
ALFA ROMEO Alfa 33 Quadrifoglio Oro / Alfetta 1.6 / Alfa 6 2.5 TD	106
AUDI Audi Coupé Series (90 hp) / Audi 100 Avant Series (87 hp, diesel)	106
BUICK Skyhawk Series (150 hp)	106
CATERHAM CARS Super 7 1600 GT Sprint	106
CHEVROLET (BR) Opala Series (116 hp) / Diplomata Series (116 hp) / Comodoro Series (116 hp)	106
CHEVROLET (USA) Celebrity Series (130 hp)	106
CHRYSLER Le Baron - Executive Series (140 hp)	106
CITROËN (F) CX 25 Diesel Turbo Break	106
DAEWOO Royale Series (101 hp)	106
FARUS ML 929	106
FASA-RENAULT 11 Series (80 hp)	106
FORD (RA) Taunus Ghia 2300 / Taunus Ghia 2300 S / Taunus GT / Taunus SP	106
HONDA Accord Series (94 hp)	106
LANCIA Trevi Berlina 1600	106
MAZDA 626	106
MITSUBISHI (J) Galant Series (105 hp) / Eterna Series (105 hp) / Galant Lambda Series (110 hp)	106
NISSAN (J) Stanza - Auster - Cedric - Gloria Series (110 hp) / Leopard Series (105 hp) / Skyline Series (100 hp)	106
OLDSMOBILE Omega Series (130 hp)	106
OPEL (D) Kadett Series (90 hp) / Kadett 1.6 SR	106
PEUGEOT (F) 305 Berline Series (94 hp) / 505 Series (95 hp, diesel)	106
PLYMOUTH Gran Fury (165 hp)	106
PONTIAC (USA) Phoenix Series (130 hp)	106
RENAULT (F) 11 Series (80 hp)	106
RENAULT (RA) 18 GTX Sedan / 18 GTX Break	106
STUTZ Victoria / Blackhawk VII / Bearcat	106
TOYOTA (AUS) Corona	106
TOYOTA (J) Starlet Series (79 hp) / Sprinter Trueno RWD Series (83 hp) / Vista - Camry Series (100 hp and 80 hp, diesel) / Crown Series (125 hp)	106
VAUXHALL Astra Series (90 hp)	106
VOLKSWAGEN (D) Polo Coupé Series (75 hp)	106
VOLKSWAGEN (WAN) Santana	106
VOLVO (S) 760 Turbo Diesel	106
AUDI Audi 100 Series (87 hp, diesel)	107
FORD (BR) Escort Series (83 hp, alcohol)	107
LANCIA H.P. Executive 1600	107
OPEL (ZA) Rekord Series (100 hp and 110 hp)	107
RENAULT (F) 25 Series (85 hp, diesel)	107
VAUXHALL Carlton Series (90 hp)	107
VOLKSWAGEN (D) Golf Cabriolet Series (112 hp)	107
VOLKSWAGEN (USA) Rabbit Series (90 hp)	107
CHEVROLET (USA) Impala Series (150 hp) / Caprice Classic Series (150 hp)	108
CITROËN (F) CX 25 Diesel Turbo Berline	108
FORD (AUS) Telstar	108
PONTIAC (USA) 6000 Series (130 hp)	108
ALFA ROMEO Alfetta 1.8	109
BMW (D) 316	109
CITROËN (F) BX 16 / CX 20 Berline	109
DESANDE Roadster	109
FIAT (BR) Alfa Romeo Ti-4	109
FIAT (I) 131 Series (113 hp) / Argenta 120 IE	109
FORD (RA) Fairlane V8 Elite	109
FORD (ZA) Escort Series (96 hp)	109
ISUZU Florian Aska Series (105 hp and 89 hp, diesel)	109
LANCIA Beta Coupé 1600	109
LEDL AS 130	109
MERCEDES-BENZ 190 Series (90 hp)	109
MG Maestro 1600	109
MITSUBISHI (J) Chariot Series (135 hp)	109
NISSAN (J) Silvia - Gazelle Series (100 hp)	109
OPEL (ZA) Kadett Series (90 hp) / Ascona	109
RENAULT (F) Fuego Series (88 hp, diesel)	109
SEAT Ronda Series (95 hp)	109
TALBOT (E, F) Samba - Horizon Series (90 hp)	109
TOYOTA (J) Celica ST (100 hp) / Mark II Series (125 hp) / Chaser Series (125 hp) / Cresta Series (125 hp)	109
ARKLEY SS	110
BUICK Le Sabre Series (110 hp) / Electra Series (125 hp)	110
DE COURVILLE Roadster	110
EXCALIBUR Series IV Phaeton / Series IV Roadster	110
FORD (ZA) Granada 3000 Ghia (159 hp)	110
MIDAS Gold 1.3 S Coupé	110
NOVA Sports	110
OB & D Madison Special	110
PANTHER Kallista 2.8	110
ALFA ROMEO Nuova Giulietta 1.8 L	111
FORD (CDN, USA) Escort Series (120 hp)	111
FORD (D) Fiesta Series (96 hp) / Capri Series (101 hp)	111
HONDA Accord Series (110 hp) / Vigor	111
LANCIA Prisma Berlina 1600	111
ALFA ROMEO Alfasud TI Quadrifoglio Verde / Sprint Quadrifoglio verde / Spider 1.6 / Alfa 6 2.0	112
BERTONE X1/9	112
BMW (D) 524 td	112
BMW (ZA) 318i	112
CATERHAM CARS Super 7	112
FIAT (I) Ritmo 105 TC / Regata Series (100 hp)	112
FORD (J) Laser Series (115 hp) / Telstar Series (145 hp)	112
FORD (RA) Falcon Ghia SP	112
FORD (ZA) Sierra Series (80 hp)	112
GAZ Chaika	112
HONDA City Series (110 hp) / Civic - Ballade Series (100 hp) / Ballade Sports Series (110 hp) / Prelude	112
HONG QI CA-770 B 6-pass.	112
ISUZU Gemini Series (130 hp) / Florian Aska Series (150 hp) / Piazza Series (120 hp and 135 hp)	112
LANCIA Delta Berlina 1600 GT / Trevi Berlina 2000 IE / Gamma Berlina 2000 / Gamma Coupé 2000	112
MAZDA Familia Series (115 hp) / Capella Series (145 hp) / Luce - Cosmo - Savanna RX 7 Series (130 hp)	112
MERCEDES-BENZ 230 E	112
MERCURY (CDN, USA) Marquis Series (120 hp)	112
MG Metro Turbo	112
MITSUBISHI (J) Lancer EX Series (160 hp) / Lancer Fiore - Mirage Series (120 hp) / Tredia - Cordia Series (135 hp) / Galant - Eterna - Galant Lambda - Starion Series (145 hp)	112
NISSAN (J) Pulsar - Sunny - Langley - Liberta Villa - Laurel Spirit Series (115 hp) / Bluebird Series (135 hp) / Silvia - Gazelle - Skyline Series (190 hp) / Laurel - Leopard Series (145 hp) / Cedric - Gloria Series (180 hp) / Fairlady Series (170 hp and 230 hp) / President	112
OPEL (D) Rekord Caravan Series (110 hp) / Senator Series (115 hp)	112
PININFARINA Spydereuropa	112
ROLLS-ROYCE Phantom VI	112
ROVER 2300	112
SBARRO Replica BMW 328 Standard / Replica BMW 328 Spéciale / Royale / Windhound 4 x 4	112
SEAT 131 Series (113 hp)	112
STIMULA Bugatti 55 Série II	112
STUTZ Royale Limousine	112
TMC Costin	112
TOYOTA (J) Corolla FWD - Sprinter FWD Series (100 hp) / Corolla Levin RWD - Sprinter Trueno RWD Series (130 hp) / Corona FWD Series (115 hp) / Vista-Camry Series (120 hp) / Carina - Corona RWD - Celica - Mark II - Chaser - Cresta Series (160 hp) / Soarer - Celica XX - Supra Series (125 hp and 170 hp) / Crown Series (170 hp) / Century	112
VOLVO (NL) 360 Series (115 hp)	112
BMW (ZA) 520i	113
FORD (CDN, USA) Thunderbird Series (145 hp)	113
MERCURY (CDN, USA) Cougar Series (120 hp)	113
PUMA GTI 1.6 E / GTC 1.6 E	113
RENAULT (F) 25 Series (103 hp)	113
VOLKSWAGEN (D) Passat Variant Series (115 hp) / Passat Variant Tetra	113
ALFA ROMEO Alfetta 2.0 / Alfetta Quadrifoglio Injection	114
AUDI Audi 80 - Audi 80 Quattro Series (115 hp)	114
BMW (D) 318i	114
FORD (GB) Granada st. wagons Series (150 hp)	114
FORD (ZA) Granada 3000 GLE Automatic (159 hp)	114
HOLDEN Statesman Series II	114
RENAULT (F) 18 Series (110 hp)	114
VOLKSWAGEN (D) Santana Series (115 hp)	114
ALFA ROMEO Nuova Giulietta 2.0 L	115
ATLANTIS A.1.	115
BMW (D) 525e / 520i	115

	mph
BUICK Electra Series (140 hp)	115
DAIMLER Limousine	115
FASA-RENAULT 18 Series (125 hp)	115
FORD (CDN, USA) LTD Series (165 hp) / LTD Crown Victoria - LTD Country Squire Series (180 hp)	115
FORD (ZA) Sierra Series (114 hp)	115
LANCIA Beta Coupé 2000 IE / H.P. Executive 2000 IE	115
MERCEDES-BENZ 250	115
MERCURY (CDN, USA) Cougar Series (145 hp)	115
MORGAN 4/4 1600	115
OPEL (D) Monza Series (115 hp)	115
RENAULT (RA) Fuego GTX	115
TVR Tasmin 200	115
FASA-RENAULT 5 Series (110 hp)	116
FORD (AUS) Falcon Series (150 hp) / Fairmont Series (150 hp) / Fairlane ZK Sedan (150 hp) / LTD FD	116
FORD (CDN, USA) Thunderbird Series (120 hp)	116
FORD (D, GB) Escort - Orion Series (105 hp)	116
OPEL (D) Kadett GTE / Ascona Series (115 hp) / Rekord Limousine Series (110 hp)	116
RENAULT (F) 5 Series (110 hp)	116
ROVER 2600	116
VAUXHALL Astra 1800i GTE / Cavalier Series (115 hp) / Carlton Series (110 hp)	116
BUICK Riviera Series (190 hp)	117
FARUS TS 1.6	117
FORD (CDN, USA) Mustang Series (175 hp, 4,950 cc)	117
JAGUAR XJ6 3.4	117
LAMBORGHINI LM-002	117
MORGAN 4/4 1600 TC	117
VOLKSWAGEN (D) Passat Limousine Series (115 hp)	117
ALFA ROMEO GTV 2.0 / Spider 2.0	118
BENTLEY Mulsanne / Corniche	118
BMW (ZA) 320i	118
BUICK Skylark Series (135 hp) / Regal Series (200 hp) / Le Sabre Series (140 hp)	118
FIAT (I) Ritmo Abarth 130 TC	118
FORD (D) Granada Series (150 hp)	118
FORD (GB) Granada sedans Series (150 hp)	118
LANCIA Trevi Berlina Volumex VX	118
PEUGEOT (F) 205 Series (105 hp) / 604 Series (155 hp)	118
PININFARINA Spidereuropa Volumex	118
RENAULT (F) 18 Turbo Break	118
ROLLS-ROYCE Silver Spirit / Silver Spur / Silver Spur with division / Corniche / Camargue	118
TATRA T 613-2 / T 613-2 Special	118
VOLVO (S) 240 Series (155 hp) / 760 GLE	118
HOLDEN Commodore SS VH	119
OPEL (D) Manta Series (110 hp)	119
VOLKSWAGEN (D) Golf Limousine Series (112 hp) / Scirocco Series (112 hp)	119
AUDI Audi 80 Quattro Series (136 hp)	120
GINETTA G25	120
LENHAM Austin-Healey 3000	120
MERCURY (CDN, USA) Capri Series (175 hp, 4,950 cc)	120
RELIANT Scimitar	120

Over 120 mph

	mph
ALFA ROMEO Alfa 6 2.5 Quadrifoglio Oro	121
CITROËN (F) CX 25 TRI Break	121
DONKERVOORT Super Eight	121
LANCIA Delta Berlina 1600 HF Turbo / Montecarlo / Gamma Berlina 2500 IE / Gamma Coupé 2500 IE	121
RENAULT (F) 18 Turbo Berline	121
AUDI Audi 100 Avant Series (136 hp)	122
BMW (D) 320i / 525i	122
PANTHER Kallista 2.8 Injection	123
PUMA GTB S2 Sport 2+2	123
AUDI Audi 100 - Audi 200 Series (136 hp)	124
CHEVROLET (USA) Corvette	124
CITROËN (F) CX 25 Pallas IE / CX 25 Prestige	124
HOLDEN Commodore Series (136 hp)	124
LANCIA Beta Coupé Volumex VX / H.P. Executive Volumex VX	124
MERCEDS-BENZ 280 E - 280-380-500 S Series (156 hp) / 280-380-500 SL Series (185 hp)	124
PHILLIPS Berlina I / Berlina S.E.	124
RENAULT (F) Fuego Series (132 hp)	124
Sta MATILDE SM 4.1	124
VOLVO (S) 760 Turbo	124
ZIL 114 Limousine / 117 Limousine / 4104 Limousine	124
AC 3000 ME	125
BITTER AUTOMOBILE SC Coupé	125
BMW (D, ZA) 728i	125
CITROËN (F) CX 25 GTI	125
KELMARK GT	125
KOUGAR Sports	125
RENAULT (F) 25 Series (144 hp)	125
ROVER 3500 SE / Vanden Plas	126
ALFA ROMEO GTV 6 2.5	127
BMW (D, ZA) 323i	127
DAIMLER 4.2	127
JAGUAR Sovereign 4.2	127
OPEL (D) Senator CD Automatic Limousine (180 hp)	127
OPEL (ZA) Commodore / Senator	127
PEUGEOT (F) 505 Series (160 hp)	127
PONTIAC (USA) Firebird Series (190 hp)	127
PORSCHE 924	127
ALFA ROMEO Nuova Giulietta 2.0 Turbodelta	128
CHEVROLET (USA) Camaro Series (190 hp)	128
LAMBORGHINI LM-004 / 7000	128
BMW (D) 732i	129
BMW (ZA) 528i	129
LEDL AS 160	129
ASTON MARTIN V8 Volante	130
BMW (ZA) 733i	130
FORD (D, GB) Sierra Series (150 hp) / Capri Series (160 hp)	130
ITD Stiletto	130
JAGUAR XJ6 4.2	130
KOUGAR Monza	130
MARCOS 3-litre Coupé	130
MERCEDES-BENZ 380-500 SEC Series (204 hp)	130
MORGAN Plus 8	130
OPEL (D) Senator Series (180 hp) / Monza GSE Hatchback Coupé (180 hp)	130
PORSCHE 944 (USA)	130
RENAULT (F) 5 Turbo 2	130
SAAB 900 Series (175 hp)	130
TALBOT (F) Matra Murena S	130
VOLKSWAGEN (D) Scirocco 16V Coupé	130
BMW (D) 528i / 735 CSi	132
MAZDA Luce - Cosmo Series (165 hp)	132
SBARRO Replica BMW 328 America	132
TVR Tasmin 280i	133
LOTUS Excel	134
MASERATI 2000 Biturbo / Biturbo 425	134
MONTEVERDI Tiara 3.8-5.0 (204 hp)	134
OPEL (D) Monza Series (180 hp)	134
BENTLEY Mulsanne Turbo	135
BMW (D) 735i	135
ELEGANT MOTORS 856 Auburn Speedster / 898 Phaeton / 898 Eleganté Phaeton Brougham	135
ROVER Vitesse	135
BMW (ZA) 735i	136
LANCIA Rally	137
MERCEDES-BENZ 280-380-500 SL Series (231 hp)	137
PORSCHE 944	137
BMW (ZA) 535i	138
LOTUS Esprit Series 3	138
ALLARD J2X-2	140
ALPINE RENAULT A 310 V6	140
ASTON MARTIN Lagonda	140
BRISTOL Britannia	140
MERCEDES-BENZ 280-380-500 S Series (231 hp) / 380-500 SEC Series (231 hp)	140
BMW (D) 745i Automatic	141
AURORA Aurora Mk II	142
AUTOKRAFT AC Mark IV	142
BMW (D) 635 CSi	142
JAGUAR XJSC 3.6 Convertible	142
AUDI Audi 200 Series (182 hp)	143
DE TOMASO Deauville	143
MASERATI Quattroporte	143
MAZDA Savanna RX 7 Series (165 hp)	143
MERCEDES-BENZ 190 Series (185 hp)	143
JAGUAR XJS 3.6 Coupé	145
FERRARI 400 Automatic i	146
MONTEVERDI Tiara 3.8-5.0 (231 hp)	146
PORSCHE 911 SC Coupé (USA) / 928 S (USA)	146
DE TOMASO Longchamp 2+2 / Longchamp G5S	149
FERRARI Mondial quattrovalvole	149
SBARRO Stash	149
ARGYLL Turbo GT	150
BRISTOL Brigand / Beaufighter	150
DAIMLER Double-Six	150
FERRARI 208 Turbo	150
JAGUAR Sovereign HE / XJS HE	150
LYNX D Type	150
BMW (ZA) 745i	151
LOTUS Turbo Esprit	152
PORSCHE 911 Carrera Coupé / 911 Carrera Targa / 911 Carrera Cabriolet	152
TVR Tasmin 350i Convertible	153
LAMBORGHINI Jalpa P 350	154
AUDI Audi Coupé Series (300 hp)	155
MARCOS Mantula	155
BMW (D) M 635 CSi	158
DE TOMASO Pantera L	158
PORSCHE 928 S	158
ASTON MARTIN V8	160
DE TOMASO Pantera GT5	162
PORSCHE 911 Turbo	162
ASTON MARTIN V8 Vantage	170
DE TOMASO Pantera GTS	174
FERRARI BB 512i	176
ERA 427 SC Cobra Replica	180
LAMBORGHINI Countach LP 500 S	180

ABBREVIATIONS FOR COUNTRIES

ARGENTINA	**RA**	GREAT BRITAIN AND IRELAND	**GB**	NIGERIA	**WAN**
AUSTRALIA	**AUS**	HOLLAND	**NL**	PORTUGAL	**P**
BRAZIL	**BR**	ITALY	**I**	SPAIN	**E**
CANADA	**CDN**	JAPAN	**J**	SOUTH AFRICA	**ZA**
FRANCE	**F**	MEXICO	**MEX**	SWEDEN	**S**
GERMANY FR	**D**			USA	**USA**

MAKES, MODELS AND PRICES

Page	MAKE AND MODEL	Price in GB £	Price in USA $	Price ex Works
	AC (Great Britain)			
150	3000 ME			12,658*
	ALFA ROMEO (Italy)			
192	Arna 1.2 L 2+1-dr Berlina	—		9,500,000*
192	Arna 1.2 SL 4+1-dr Berlina	4,185*		10,250,000*
192	Alfasud TI 1.3	5,995*		11,412,000*
192	Alfasud TI Quadrifoglio Verde	6,395*		12,498,000*
192	Sprint 1.3	6,495*		13,194,000*
193	Sprint Quadrifoglio Verde	7,145*		15,108,000*
193	Alfa 33 1.3	5,690*		12,204,000*
193	Alfa 33 Quadrifoglio Oro	6,590*		13,464,000*
193	Alfa 33 1.5 4x4	6,000*		—
194	Nuova Giulietta 1.6 L	6,695*		15,000,000*
194	Nuova Giulietta 1.8 L	7,550*		16,410,000*
194	Nuova Giulietta 2.0 L	7,860*		—
194	Nuova Giulietta 2.0 Turbodelta	—		26,400,000*
195	Nuova Giulietta 2.0 TD L	—		17,250,000*
195	Alfetta 1.6	—		16,392,000*
195	Alfetta 1.8	—		17,130,000*
195	Alfetta 2.0	8,750*		18,426,000*
195	Alfetta Quadrifoglio Injection	—		20,736,000*
196	Alfetta 2.0 TD	—		19,038,000*
196	Alfetta 2.4 TD	—		20,076,000*
196	GTV 2.0	8,800*		19,038,000*
196	GTV 6 2.5	10,950*	18,995*	28,663,000*
196	Spider 1.6	—		17,340,000*
197	Spider 2.0	—	16,000*	18,390,000*
197	Alfa 6 2.0	12,800*		22,200,000*
197	Alfa 6 2.5 Quadrifoglio Oro	—		31,050,000*
198	Alfa 6 2.5 TD	—		24,600,000*
	ALLARD (Canada)			
265	J2X-2			41,200
	ALPINE RENAULT (France)			
76	A 310 V6			140,860◊
	AMERICAN MOTORS (USA)			
267	Renault Alliance 2-dr Sedan			5,959
267	Renault Alliance L 2-dr Sedan			6,465
267	Renault Alliance L 4-dr Sedan			6,715
267	Renault Alliance DL 2-dr Sedan			7,065
267	Renault Alliance DL 4-dr Sedan			7,365
267	Renault Alliance Limited 4-dr Sedan			8,027
268	Renault Encore 2+1-dr Hatchback Sedan			5,755
268	Renault Encore S 2+1-dr Hatchback Sedan			6,365
268	Renault Encore S 4+1-dr Hatchback Sedan			6,615
268	Renault Encore LS 2+1-dr Hatchback Sedan			6,995
268	Renault Encore LS 4+1-dr Hatchback Sedan			7,197
268	Renault Encore GS 2+1-dr Hatchback Sedan			7,547
268	Eagle 4-dr Sedan			9,495
268	Eagle 4+1-dr St. Wagon			10,225
268	Eagle Limited 4+1-dr St. Wagon			10,695
	APAL (Belgium)			
74	Speedster			—
	ARGYLL (Great Britain)			
150	Turbo GT			23,750*
	ARKLEY (Great Britain)			
151	SS			8,750*

Page	MAKE AND MODEL	Price in GB £	Price in USA $	Price ex Works
	ARO (Romania)			
225	10.0			—
225	10.1			—
225	10.3			—
225	10.4			—
225	240			—
225	241			—
225	243			—
225	244			—
	ASTON MARTIN (Great Britain)			
151	V8		96,000*	39,999*
152	V8 Vantage		120,000*	45,000*
152	V8 Volante		115,000*	49,999*
152	Lagonda		150,000*	59,500*
	ATLANTIS (Great Britain)			
152	A.1.			33,150*
	AUDI (Germany FR)			
105	Audi 80 C 1.3 2-dr Limousine			16,345*
105	Audi 80 C 1.3 4-dr Limousine			17,075*
105	Audi 80 CL 1.3 2-dr Limousine			17,475*
105	Audi 80 CL 1.3 4-dr Limousine			18,205*
105	Audi 80 CL 1.6 2-dr Limousine			18,175*
105	Audi 80 CL 1.6 4-dr Limousine	6,551*		18,905*
105	Audi 80 GL 1.6 2-dr Limousine			19,515*
105	Audi 80 GL 1.6 4-dr Limousine			20,245*
105	Audi 80 CL 1.8 2-dr Limousine			18,815*
105	Audi 80 CL 1.8 4-dr Limousine			19,545*
105	Audi 80 GL 1.8 2-dr Limousine		12,390*	20,155*
105	Audi 80 GL 1.8 4-dr Limousine	7,321*	12,980*	20,885*
105	Audi 80 GTE 1.8 2-dr Limousine			22,265*
105	Audi 80 GTE 1.8 4-dr Limousine			22,995*
105	Audi 80 CD 2.0 4-dr Limousine	9,032*		25,455*
107	Audi 80 Diesel C 2-dr Limousine			18,250*
107	Audi 80 Diesel C 4-dr Limousine			18,980*
107	Audi 80 Diesel CL 2-dr Limousine			19,380*
107	Audi 80 Diesel CL 4-dr Limousine			20,110*
107	Audi 80 Diesel GL 2-dr Limousine			20,720*
107	Audi 80 Diesel GL 4-dr Limousine			21,450*
107	Audi 80 Diesel C Turbo 4-dr Limousine			21,175*
107	Audi 80 Diesel CL Turbo 4-dr Limousine	8,107*		22,305*
107	Audi 80 Diesel GL Turbo 4-dr Limousine			23,645*
107	Audi 80 Diesel CD Turbo 4-dr Limousine			25,545*
107	Audi 80 Quattro 2-dr Limousine			27,890*
107	Audi 80 Quattro 4-dr Limousine (115 hp)			28,620*
107	Audi 80 Quattro 4-dr Limousine (136 hp)	11,474*	16,500*	33,758*
108	Audi GL 1.8 2-dr Coupé			22,440*
108	Audi GT 2.0 2-dr Coupé	9,219*		27,085*
108	Audi GT 2.2 2-dr Coupé	9,808*	14,500*	29,190*
108	Audi Quattro 2.2 2-dr Coupé	17,722*	35,000*	66,685*
108	Audi Quattro Sport 2.2 2-dr Coupé			200,000*
109	Audi 100 1.8 (75 hp) 4-dr Limousine	8,772*		22,915*
109	Audi 100 CC 1.8 (75 hp) 4-dr Limousine			24,295*
109	Audi 100 1.8 (90 hp) 4-dr Limousine			23,825*
109	Audi 100 CC 1.8 (90 hp) 4-dr Limousine			25,205*
109	Audi 100 CS 1.8 4-dr Limousine			28,255*
109	Audi 100 CD 1.8 4-dr Limousine			30,285*
109	Audi 100 1.9 4-dr Limousine			25,045*
109	Audi 100 CC 1.9 4-dr Limousine	8,895*		26,425*
109	Audi 100 CS 1.9 4-dr Limousine			29,475*
109	Audi 100 CD 1.9 4-dr Limousine			31,505*
109	Audi 100 2.2 4-dr Limousine		16,480*	27,865*
109	Audi 100 CC 2.2 4-dr Limousine			29,245*
109	Audi 100 CS 2.2 4-dr Limousine	9,989*		32,295*
109	Audi 100 CD 2.2 4-dr Limousine	10,825*		33,635*
109	Audi 100 Diesel 4-dr Limousine			27,725*
109	Audi 100 CC Diesel 4-dr Limousine			29,105*
109	Audi 100 Turbo-Diesel 4-dr Limousine	11,245*		30,945*

The prices refer to all models listed in the volume. The first column shows the prices of cars imported into the United Kingdom; the second, the prices of cars imported into the United States of America; and the third, the prices of cars in the country of origin. Prices in the USA do not include US transportation fees, state and local taxes.

* *Prices including VAT and its equivalent in European countries and also SCT in Great Britain; prices of cars imported into the United States (East Coast) including ocean freight, US excise tax and import duty.*

◊ *Prices ex-showroom in European countries.*

 Due to the international monetary situation, all the prices shown are subject to confirmation.

Page	MAKE AND MODEL	Price in GB £	Price in USA $	Price ex Works
109	Audi 100 CC Turbo-Diesel 4-dr Limousine			32,325*
109	Audi 100 CS Turbo-Diesel 4-dr Limousine			35,375*
109	Audi 100 CD Turbo-Diesel 4-dr Limousine			36,715*
111	Audi 100 Avant 1.8 (75 hp) 4+1-dr Limousine			25,365*
111	Audi 100 Avant CC 1.8 (75 hp) 4+1-dr Limousine	9,319*		26,745*
111	Audi 100 Avant 1.8 (90 hp) 4+1-dr Limousine			26,275*
111	Audi 100 Avant CC 1.8 (90 hp) 4+1-dr Limousine			27,655*
111	Audi 100 Avant CS 1.8 4+1-dr Limousine			30,705*
111	Audi 100 Avant CD 1.8 4+1-dr Limousine			32,735*
111	Audi 100 Avant 2.2 4+1-dr Limousine		17,480*	30,315*
111	Audi 100 Avant CC 2.2 4+1-dr Limousine			31,695*
111	Audi 100 Avant CS 2.2 4+1-dr Limousine			34,745*
111	Audi 100 Avant CD 2.2 4+1-dr Limousine	12,714*		36,085*
111	Audi 100 Avant Diesel 4+1-dr Limousine			30,175*
111	Audi 100 Avant CC Diesel 4+1-dr Limousine			31,555*
111	Audi 100 Avant Turbo-Diesel 4+1-dr Limousine			33,395*
111	Audi 100 Avant CC Turbo-Diesel 4+1-dr Limousine			34,775*
111	Audi 100 Avant CS Turbo-Diesel 4+1-dr Limousine			37,825*
111	Audi 100 Avant CD Turbo-Diesel 4+1-dr Limousine			39,165*
112	Audi 200 4-dr Limousine			39,950*
112	Audi 200 Turbo 4-dr Limousine		22,250*	44,950*
	AURORA (Canada)			
265	Aurora Mk II			46,000
	AUSTIN (Great Britain)			
153	Metro City 2+1-dr Saloon			3,548*
153	Metro Standard 2+1-dr Saloon			3,899*
153	Metro L 2+1-dr Saloon			4,269*
153	Metro HLE 2+1-dr Saloon			4,600*
153	Metro 1.3 L 2+1-dr Saloon			4,499*
153	Metro 1.3 HLE 2+1-dr Saloon			4,829*
153	Metro 1.3 Automatic 2+1-dr Saloon			5,275*
153	Metro Vanden Plas 2+1-dr Saloon			5,249*
154	Maestro 1.3 4+1-dr Saloon			4,749*
154	Maestro 1.3 L 4+1-dr Saloon			5,199*
154	Maestro 1.3 HLE 4+1-dr Saloon			5,599*
154	Maestro 1.6 L 4+1-dr Saloon			5,499*
154	Maestro 1.6 HLS 4+1-dr Saloon			5,870*
154	Maestro 1.6 Automatic 4+1-dr Saloon			6,290*
154	Maestro 1.6 Vanden Plas 4+1-dr Saloon			6,775*
	AUTOBIANCHI (Italy)			
198	A 112 Junior			6,997,000◊
198	A 112 Elite			7,812,000◊
198	A 112 LX			8,628,000◊
198	A 112 Abarth			8,784,000◊
	AUTOKRAFT (Great Britain)			
154	AC Mark IV			25,000
	AVANTI (USA)			
269	Avanti II			31,860
	AYMESA (Ecuador)			
267	Gala 2+1-dr Sedan			814,000
267	Condor GT 2+1-dr Sedan			553,000
	AZLK (USSR)			
240	Moskvich 2138			—
241	Moskvich 2136			—
241	Moskvich 2140			—
241	Moskvich 2140 IZh			—
241	Moskvich 2137			—
241	Moskvich 2140 Combi IZh			—
	BEIJING (China People's Republic)			
331	BJ 750			—
332	BJ 212			—
332	BJ 212 E			—

Page	MAKE AND MODEL	Price in GB £	Price in USA $	Price ex Works
	BENTLEY (Great Britain)			
155	Mulsanne		97,950*	55,240*
155	Mulsanne Turbo		—	61,744*
155	Corniche		155,470*	73,168*
	BERTONE (Italy)			
199	2-dr Cabrio	7,198*	—	15,025,000◊
199	2-dr Palinuro	—	—	15,625,000◊
199	X 1/9	6,590*	12,990*	14,500,000◊
	BITTER AUTOMOBILE (Germany FR)			
112	SC Coupé			70,200*
	BMW (Germany FR)			
113	315	—		18,350*
113	316 2-dr Limousine	6,995*		21,100*
113	316 4-dr Limousine	7,345*		21,980*
114	318i 2-dr Limousine	7,950*		23,350*
114	318i 4-dr Limousine	8,300*		24,230*
114	320i 2-dr Limousine	8,845*		26,750*
114	320i 4-dr Limousine	9,195*		27,630*
114	323i 2-dr Limousine	9,935*		29,800*
114	323i 4-dr Limousine	10,285*		30,680*
114	518	8,455*		24,900*
114	520i	10,195*		29,400*
115	525e	—		31,350*
115	524td	—		32,650*
115	525i	12,135*		34,600*
115	528i	13,575*	24,565*	37,900*
115	728i	14,545*		42,200*
116	732i	16,360*		47,350*
116	735i	18,830*		53,850*
116	745i Automatic	—		65,700*
116	628 CSi	18,710*		57,250*
117	635 CSi	23,995*		67,750*
117	M 635 CSi	—		89,500*
	BMW (South Africa)			
322	318i			12,530
322	320i			14,860
323	323i			16,270
323	518i			14,550
323	520i			17,590
323	528i			22,790
323	535i			30,400
324	728i			27,900
324	733i			37,200
324	735i			45,000
324	745i			65,000
	BRISTOL (Great Britain)			
156	Britannia			47,778*
156	Brigand			49,827*
156	Beaufighter			45,847*
	BUICK (USA)			
269	Skyhawk 4-dr Sedan			7,350
269	Skyhawk 2-dr Coupé			7,140
269	Skyhawk 4+1-dr St. Wagon			7,685
269	Skyhawk Limited 4-dr Sedan			7,845
269	Skyhawk Limited 2-dr Coupé			7,649
269	Skyhawk Limited 4+1-dr St. Wagon			8,135
269	Skyhawk T-type 2-dr Coupé			8,161
270	Skylark Custom 4-dr Sedan			7,716
270	Skylark Custom 2-dr Coupé			7,554
270	Skylark Limited 4-dr Sedan			8,292
270	Skylark Limited 2-dr Coupé			8,128
270	Slylark T-type 2-dr Coupé			9,568
270	Century Custom 4-dr Sedan			9,283
270	Century Custom 2-dr Coupé			9,119
270	Century Custom 4+1-dr St. Wagon			9,669
270	Century Limited 4-dr Sedan			9,738
270	Century Limited 2-dr Coupé			9,571
270	Century Limited 4+1-dr St. Wagon			10,096
270	Century T-type 4-dr Sedan			10,684
270	Century T-type 2-dr Coupé			10,520
271	Regal 4-dr Sedan			9,681

Page	MAKE AND MODEL	Price in GB £	Price in USA $	Price ex Works
271	Regal 2-dr Coupé			9,497
271	Regal Limited 4-dr Sedan			10,273
271	Regal Limited 2-dr Coupé			10,135
271	Regal T-type 2-dr Coupé			12,130
272	Le Sabre Custom 4-dr Sedan			10,140
272	Le Sabre Limited 4-dr Sedan			10,951
272	Le Sabre Limited 2-dr Coupé			10,791
273	Electra Limited 4-dr Sedan			13,344
273	Electra Limited 2-dr Coupé			13,167
273	Electra Park Avenue 4-dr Sedan			15,056
273	Electra Park Avenue 2-dr Coupé			14,900
273	Electra 4+1-dr Estate Wagon			14,495
273	Riviera 2-dr Coupé			15,979
273	Riviera 2-dr Convertible			25,844
273	Riviera T-type 2-dr Coupé			17,062
	CADILLAC (USA)			
274	Cimarron 4-dr Sedan			12,614
274	De Ville 4-dr Sedan			17,625
274	De Ville 2-dr Coupé			17,140
275	Fleetwod Brougham 4-dr Sedan			20,451
275	Fleetwod Brougham 2-dr Coupé			19,942
275	Fleetwod 4-dr Limousine			30,454
275	Fleetwod Formal 4-dr Limousine			31,512
275	Eldorado 2-dr Coupé			20,343
275	Eldorado 2-dr Convertible			31,286
275	Seville 4-dr Sedan			22,468
	CATERHAM CARS (Great Britain)			
156	Super 7			7,834*
156	Super 7 1600 GT Roadster			6,267*
156	Super 7 1600 L-C Roadster			6,452*
156	Super 7 1600 GT Sprint			6,742*
	CHEVROLET (Brazil)			
253	Chevette 2-dr Sedan			—
253	Chevette 4-dr Sedan			—
253	Chevette 2+1-dr Hatchback Sedan			—
253	Chevette SL 2-dr Sedan			—
253	Chevette SL 4-dr Sedan			—
253	Chevette SL 2+1-dr Hatchback Sedan			—
253	Chevette Marajó 2+1-dr Caravan			—
253	Chevette Marajó SL 2+1-dr Caravan			—
254	Monza 2-dr Notchback Sedan			—
254	Monza 2-dr Hatchback Coupé			—
254	Monza 4-dr Notchback Sedan			—
254	Monza SL-E 2+1-dr Hatchback Coupé			—
255	Opala 4-dr Sedan			—
255	Opala 2-dr Coupé			—
255	Opala 2+1-dr Caravan			—
255	Diplomata 4-dr Sedan			—
255	Diplomata 2-dr Coupé			—
256	Comodoro 4-dr Sedan			—
256	Comodoro 2-dr Coupé			—
256	Comodoro 2+1-dr Caravan			—
256	Veraneio 4+1-dr Caravan			—
256	Veraneio Luxo 4+1-dr Caravan			—
256	Veraneio Super Luxo 4+1-dr Caravan			—
	CHEVROLET (Canada)			
265	Chevette Scooter 4+1-dr Hatchback Sedan			6,074
265	Chevette Scooter 2+1-dr Hatchback Coupé			5,812
	CHEVROLET (USA)			
276	Chevette 4+1-dr Sedan			5,333
276	Chevette 2+1-dr Coupé			4,997
276	Chevette CS 4+1-dr Sedan			5,636
276	Chevette CS 2+1-dr Coupé			5,489
276	Cavalier 4-dr Notchback Sedan			6,222
276	Cavalier 4+1-dr Liftgate Wagon			6,375
276	Cavalier CS 4-dr Notchback Sedan			6,666
276	Cavalier CS 4+1-dr Liftgate Wagon			6,821
276	Cavalier Type 10 2-dr Notchback Coupé			6,447
276	Cavalier Type 10 2+1-dr Hatchback Coupé			6,654
276	Cavalier Type 10 2-dr Convertible			11,299
277	Citation 4+1-dr Hatchback Sedan			7,046
277	Citation 2+1-dr Notchback Coupé			6,445
277	Citation 2+1-dr Hatchback Coupé			6,900
277	Camaro 2-dr Coupé			7,995
277	Camaro Berlinetta 2-dr Coupé			10,895

Page	MAKE AND MODEL	Price in GB £	Price in USA $	Price ex Works
277	Camaro Z 28 2-dr Coupé			10,620
278	Celebrity 4-dr Sedan			7,890
278	Celebrity 2-dr Coupé			7,711
278	Celebrity 4+1-dr 9-pass. St. Wagon			8,214
279	Monte Carlo 2-dr Coupé			8,936
279	Monte Carlo SS 2-dr Coupé			10,700
279	Impala 4-dr Sedan			8,895
279	Caprice Classic 4-dr Sedan			9,399
279	Caprice Classic 2-dr Coupé			9,253
279	Caprice Classic 4+1-dr 9 pass. St. Wagon			10,210
280	Corvette			23,360
	CHRYSLER (USA)			
280	Le Baron 2-dr Sedan			8,783
280	Le Baron 4-dr Sedan			9,067
280	Le Baron 2-dr Convertible			11,595
280	Le Baron Town and Country 4+1-dr St. Wagon			9,856
281	Laser 2-dr Hatchback Coupé			8,648
281	Laser XE 2-dr Hatchback Coupé			10,546
282	E Class 4-dr Sedan			9,565
282	New Yorker 4-dr Sedan			12,179
282	Executive 4-dr Sedan			18,966
282	Executive 4-dr Limousine			21,966
283	Newport 4-dr Sedan			—
283	Fifth Avenue 4-dr Sedan			13,990
	CITROËN (France)			
77	2 CV 6 Spécial 4-dr Berline	2,499*		28,280◊
77	2 CV 6 Club 4-dr Berline	2,798*		32,000◊
77	2 CV 6 Charleston 4-dr Berline	2,949*		32,880◊
77	Mehari	—		39,200◊
77	LNA	—		34,900◊
78	LNA 11 E 2+1-dr Coupé	3,140*		36,200◊
78	LNA 11 RE 2+1-dr Coupé	3,538*		39,760◊
78	Visa 4+1-dr Berline	3,189*		38,260◊
78	Visa Club 4+1-dr Berline	4,795*		41,200◊
78	Visa 11 E 4+1-dr Berline	3,725*		41,900◊
78	Visa 11 RE 4+1-dr Berline	3,995*		44,300◊
78	Visa 11 RE 4-dr Décapotable	5,550*		58,460◊
79	Visa GT	4,795*		53,700◊
79	GSA Spécial 4+1-dr Berline	4,535*		48,000◊
79	GSA Pallas 4+1-dr Berline	5,429*		55,560◊
79	GSA X 1 4+1-dr Berline	5,429*		52,400◊
79	GSA X 3 4+1-dr Berline	—		55,560◊
79	GSA Special 4+1-dr Break	4,962*		50,000◊
79	GSA Club 4+1-dr Break	—		53,600◊
80	BX	4,790*		54,000◊
80	BX 14 E 4-dr Berline	4,990*		57,900◊
80	BX 14 RE 4+1-dr Berline	5,451*		60,200◊
80	BX 16 RS 4+1-dr Berline	5,600*		63,980◊
80	BX 16 TRS 4+1-dr Berline	6,100*		68,300◊
80	BX 19 D 4-dr Berline	—		65,900◊
80	BX 19 TRD 4-dr Berline	—		72,200◊
81	CX 20 4-dr Berline	6,750*		75,700◊
81	CX 20 TRE 4-dr Berine	—		83,300◊
81	CX 20 4+1 Break	7,450*		86,000◊
81	CX 20 4+1-dr Familiale	7,714*		90,900◊
81	CX 25 Pallas IE	10,345*		104,000◊
82	CX 25 GTI	10,598*		106,600◊
82	CX 25 Prestige	14,914*		135,000◊
82	CX 25 TRI Break	10,671*		112,500◊
82	CX 25 Diesel 4-dr Berline	9,116*		87,000◊
82	CX 25 Diesel Pallas 4-dr Berline	9,352*		97,000◊
82	CX 25 Diesel 4+1-dr Break	9,188*		98,400◊
82	CX 25 Diesel 4+1-dr Familiale	9,452*		103,100◊
83	CX 25 Diesel Turbo RD 4-dr Berline	—		101,700◊
83	CX 25 Diesel Turbo TRD 4-dr Berline	10,862*		108,200◊
83	CX 25 Diesel Turbo 4-dr Limousine	—		118,200◊
83	CX 25 Diesel Turbo TRD 4+1-dr Break	11,362*		117,900◊
	CITROËN (Portugal)			
224	FAF			—
	CLASSIC-CAR JANSSEN (Germany FR)			
117	Gepard SS 100			43,000*
	CLASSIC-CAR-OLDTIMERBAU (Germany FR)			
117	Bugatti 35 B			17,000*
117	Bugatti 55			17,900*

Page	MAKE AND MODEL	Price in GB £	Price in USA $	Price ex Works
	CUSTOCA (Austria)			
74	Hurrycane			170,000
74	Strato 80 ES 2-dr Coupé			180,000
74	Taifun 2-dr Coupé			180,000
	DACIA (Romania)			
226	1310 Standard 4-dr Sedan	3,190*		—
226	1310 L 4-dr Sedan	3,490*		—
226	1310 L 4+1-dr Break	3,900*		—
226	1310 GL 4-dr Sedan	3,900*		—
226	1310 GL 4+1-dr Break	4,295*		—
226	1310 GLX 4-dr Sedan	4,295*		—
	DAEWOO (Korea)			
333	Maepsy-Na			—
333	Royale XQ 4-dr Sedan			—
333	Royale Prince 4-dr Sedan			—
333	Royale Salon 4-dr Sedan			—
	DAIHATSU (Japan)			
336	Mira A 2+1-dr Sedan			488,000
336	Mira B 2+1-dr Sedan			512,000
336	Mira C 2+1-dr Sedan			597,000
336	Mira S 2+1-dr Sedan	3,099*		635,000
336	Mira A 2+1-dr Sedan			642,000
336	Mira B 2+1-dr Sedan			719,000
336	Cuore MO 2+1-dr Sedan			590,000
336	Cuore MGF 2+1-dr Sedan			680,000
336	Cuore MGX 2+1-dr Sedan			762,000
336	Cuore MG 4-dr Sedan			682,000
336	Cuore MGE 4-dr Sedan			720,000
336	Cuore MGL 4-dr Sedan			754,000
336	Mira Turbo T 2+1-dr Sedan			642,000
336	Mira Turbo R 2+1-dr Sedan			725,000
337	Charade TD 2+1-dr Sedan	3,779*		635,000
337	Charade TG 2+1-dr Sedan			688,000
337	Charade TL 2+1-dr Sedan			770,000
337	Charade CG 4+1-dr Sedan	4,079*		713,000
337	Charade CF 4+1-dr Sedan			833,000
337	Charade TS 2+1-dr Sedan			844,000
337	Charade TX 2+1-dr Sedan			944,000
337	Charade CX 4+1-dr Sedan	4,329*		904,000
337	Charade Turbo 2+1-dr Sedan			954,000
337	Charade Turbo 4+1-dr Sedan			985,000
337	Charade TG Diesel 2+1-dr Sedan			788,000
337	Charade TS Diesel 2+1-dr Sedan			919,000
337	Charade TX Diesel 2+1-dr Sedan			1,019,000
337	Charade CG Diesel 4+1-dr Sedan	4,499*		813,000
337	Charade CF Diesel 4+1-dr Sedan			933,000
337	Charade CX Diesel 4+1-dr Sedan			979,000
337	Charmant 1300 LC 4-dr Sedan	4,649*		1,006,000
337	Charmant 1300 LE 4-dr Sedan	4,999*		1,092,000
337	Charmant 1500 LGX 4-dr Sedan	5,399*		1,176,000
337	Charmant 1500 Altair G 4-dr Sedan			1,258,000
337	Charmant 1500 Altair L 4-dr Sedan			1,358,000
338	Delta SD Middle-roof 4+1-dr Wagon			1,180,000
338	Delta SE Hi-roof 4+1-dr Wagon			1,492,000
338	Delta SG Sunroof 4+1-dr Wagon			1,543,000
338	Delta SQ Sunroof 4+1-dr Wagon			1,945,000
338	Taft STD (soft top) 2-dr Open			1,367,000
338	Taft DX (soft top, steel doors) 2-dr Open			1,520,000
338	Taft Deluxe (steel body) 2-dr Hardtop			1,604,000
338	Taft Deluxe (resin top) 2-dr Hardtop	8,493*		1,734,000
	DAIMLER (Great Britain)			
157	4.2			21,952*
157	Double-Six			24,991*
158	Limousine			25,994*
	DANGEL (France)			
83	Peugeot 504 4x4 GR 4+1-dr Break			109,931*
83	Peugeot 504 4x4 GRD 4+1-dr Break			117,130*
	DAYTONA (USA)			
283	Migi 2-dr Roadster			17,500
283	Moya 2-dr Roadster			11,500

Page	MAKE AND MODEL	Price in GB £	Price in USA $	Price ex Works
	DE COURVILLE (USA)			
283	Roadster			65,500
	DESANDE (Great Britain)			
158	Roadster			47,800
	DE TOMASO (Italy)			
199	Pantera L	—		49,800,000◊
200	Pantera GTS	22,730*		55,900,000◊
200	Pantera GT5	28,528*		62,900,000◊
200	Deauville	31,800*		64,000,000◊
200	Longchamp 2+2 2-dr Coupé	29,058*		60,850,000◊
200	Longchamp 2+2 2-dr Spyder	—		89,600,000◊
200	Longchamp GTS	—		64,800,000◊
	DODGE (USA)			
284	Omni 4+1-dr Hatchback Sedan			5,830
284	Omni SE 4+1-dr Hatchback Sedan			6,148
284	Charger 2+1-dr Hatchback Coupé			6,494
284	Charger 2.2 2+1-dr Hatchback Coupé			7,288
284	Shelby Charger 2+1-dr Hatchback Coupé			8,541
284	Aries 2-dr Sedan			6,837
284	Aries 4-dr Sedan			26,949
284	Aries Custom 4+1-dr St. Wagon			7,736
284	Aries SE 2-dr Sedan			7,463
284	Aries SE 4-dr Sedan			7,589
284	Aries SE 4+1-dr St. Wagon			8,195
285	600 2-dr Sedan			8,376
285	600 4-dr Sedan			8,903
285	600 2-dr Convertible			10,595
285	600 ES 4-dr Sedan			9,525
286	Daytona 2+1-dr Hatchback Coupé			8,308
286	Daytona Turbo 2+1-dr Hatchback Coupé			10,227
286	Diplomat Salon 4-dr Sedan			9,180
286	Diplomat SE 4-dr Sedan			10,165
287	Caravan			8,669
	DONKERVOORT (Holland)			
189	Super Eight			34,500
	DUTTON (Great Britain)			
158	Moke Californian			4,100*
	ELEGANT MOTORS (USA)			
287	856 Auburn Speedster			36,000
287	898 Phaeton			45,000
287	898 Elegante Phaeton Brougham			60,000
	EL NASR (Egypt)			
318	Nasr 127 CL			—
318	Nasr 128 CL			—
319	Nasr Ritmo 65 CL			—
319	Nasr Polonez			—
319	Nasr 131 CL			—
	ENVEMO (Brazil)			
257	90 Super Coupé			—
257	90 Super Cabriolet			—
	ERA (USA)			
288	427 SC Cobra Replica			34,900
	EXCALIBUR (USA)			
288	Series IV 2-dr Phaeton			56,500
288	Series IV 2-dr Roadster			59,000
	FARUS (Brazil)			
257	ML 929			—
257	TS 1.6			—
	FASA-RENAULT (Spain)			
227	4 TL			519,100◊
227	5 TL 2+1-dr Berlina			622,600◊

Page	MAKE AND MODEL	Price in GB £	Price in USA $	Price ex Works
227	5 TL 4+1-dr Berlina			649,600◊
227	5 GTL 2+1-dr Berlina			693,400◊
227	5 GTL 4+1-dr Berlina			720,700◊
227	5 TX 2+1-dr Berlina			827,500◊
227	5 Copa Turbo 2+1-dr Berlina			1,114,300◊
228	6 GTL			659,300◊
228	7 GTL			674,700◊
228	9 GTL 4-dr Berlina			845,300◊
228	9 TSE 4-dr Berlina			941,800◊
228	9 GTD 4-dr Berlina			980,500◊
228	11 GTL 4+1-dr Berlina			886,000◊
228	11 TSE 4+1-dr Berlina			968,800◊
229	12 GTL 4+1-dr Familiar			908,900◊
229	14 GTL 4+1-dr Berlina			812,600◊
229	14 GTS 4+1-dr Berlina			922,600◊
229	18 GTS 4-dr Berlina			1,092,500◊
229	18 GTS 4+1-dr Familiar			1,148,200◊
229	18 Turbo 4-dr Berlina			1,303,200◊
229	18 GTD 4-dr Berlina			1,257,200◊
229	18 GTD 4+1-dr Familiar			1,314,400◊
	FERRARI (Italy)			
201	208 Turbo GTB 2-dr Coupé	—	—	60,000,000*
201	208 Turbo GTS 2-dr Spider	—	—	61,600,000*
201	308 quattrovalvole GTB 2-dr Coupé	26,181*	52,900*	69,000,000*
201	308 quattrovalvole GTS 2-dr Spider	27,303*	61,175*	70,932,000*
202	Mondial quattrovalvole 2-dr Coupé	29,732*	59,500*	78,246,000*
202	Mondial quattrovalvole 2-dr Cabriolet	—	66,675*	89,700,000*
202	400 Automatic i	43,561*	—	111,504,000*
202	BB 512i	47,298*	—	121,992,000*
	FIAT (Brazil)			
257	147 C 2+1-dr Sedan			3,623,000
257	Spazio CL 2+1-dr Sedan			4,309,000
257	147 C Panorama 2+1-dr St. Wagon			4,190,000
257	147 CL Panorama 2+1-dr St. Wagon			4,682,000
257	Spazio TR 2+1-dr Sedan			5,252,000
258	Oggi CS			4,746,000
258	Alfa Romeo Ti-4			15,007,000
	FIAT (Italy)			
203	126	2,098*		4,770,000*
203	Panda 30			6,420,000*
204	Panda 30 Super			6,882,000*
204	Panda 45	3,030*		7,158,000*
204	Panda 45 Super	3,260*		7,878,000*
204	Panda 4x4			10,512,000*
204	Uno 45 2+1-dr Berlina	3,377*		8,124,000*
204	Uno 45 Super 2+1-dr Berlina			8,940,000*
204	Uno ES 2+1-dr Berlina	4,070*		9,444,000*
204	Uno 55 4+1-dr Berlina	3,776*		9,204,000*
204	Uno 55 Super 2+1-dr Berlina	3,980*		9,702,000*
204	Uno 55 Super 4+1-dr Berlina	4,160*		10,020,000*
204	Uno 70 Super 2+1-dr Berlina	4,420*		10,104,000*
204	Uno DS 2+1-dr Berlina			10,110,000*
204	Uno DS Super 4+1-dr Berlina			10,866,000*
205	127 1050 2+1-dr Berlina			7,188,000*
205	127 1050 2+1-dr Panorama			8,352,000*
205	127 Diesel 2+1-dr Berlina			9,420,000*
205	127 Diesel 2+1-dr Panorama			10,038,000*
206	Ritmo 60 2+1-dr Berlina	4,061*		8,898,000*
206	Ritmo 60 4+1-dr Berlina			9,966,000*
206	Ritmo ES 4+1-dr Berlina	4,476*		10,752,000*
206	Ritmo 70 Automatica 4+1-dr Berlina			11,010,000*
206	Ritmo Super 70 4+1-dr Berlina	4,752*		11,406,000*
206	Ritmo Super 85 4+1-dr Berlina	5,272*		12,498,000*
206	Ritmo Diesel 4+1-dr Berlina			12,180,000*
206	Ritmo Diesel L 4+1-dr Berlina			10,962,000*
207	Ritmo 105 TC	5,930*		12,756,000*
207	Ritmo Abarth 130 TC			15,468,000*
208	Regata 70 4-dr Berlina			11,304,000*
208	Regata 70 Super 4-dr Berlina			12,840,000*
208	Regata ES 4-dr Berlina			11,928,000*
208	Regata 85 Super 4-dr Berlina			13,170,000*
208	Regata 100 Super 4-dr Berlina			14,100,000*
208	Regata DS 4-dr Berlina			13,260,000*
209	131 CL 1300 4+1-dr Panorama			11,526,000*
209	131 Super 2000 4+1-dr Panorama			14,166,000*
209	131 Diesel CL 2000 4+1-dr Panorama			13,620,000*
209	131 Diesel Super 2500 4+1-dr Panorama			15,540,000*

Page	MAKE AND MODEL	Price in GB £	Price in USA $	Price ex Works
209	Argenta 100			13,854,000*
210	Argenta 120 IE	6,810*		16,836,000*
210	Argenta Diesel			16,356,000*
210	Argenta Turbo Diesel			18,942,000*
210	Campagnola			21,402,000*
211	Campagnola Lunga			21,972,000*
211	Campagnola Diesel			25,368,000*
211	Campagnola Diesel Lunga			25,998,000*
	FORD (Argentina)			
248	Taunus L 2000			97,465
248	Taunus Ghia 2300 4-dr Sedan			112,157
248	Taunus Ghia 2300 S 4-dr Sedan			144,269
248	Taunus GT 2-dr Coupé			118,099
248	Taunus SP 2-dr Coupé			138,534
248	Fairlane 3600 LTD			107,469
248	Fairlane V8 Elite			114,350
248	Falcon 2.3 Standard 4-dr Sedan			91,032
248	Falcon 2.3 De Luxe 4-dr Sedan			97,022
249	Falcon 3.0 Standard 4-dr Sedan			95,483
249	Falcon 3.0 De Luxe 4-dr Sedan			103,429
249	Falcon 3.0 Standard 4+1-dr St. Wagon			102,185
249	Falcon 3.0 De Luxe 4+1-dr St. Wagon			—
249	Falcon 3.6 Ghia Sedan			120,340
249	Falcon Ghia SP			122,218
	FORD (Australia)			
392	Laser L 4+1-dr Hatchback Sedan			7,652
392	Laser GL 2+1-dr Hatchback Sedan			7,796
392	Laser GL 4+1-dr Hatchback Sedan			7,987
392	Laser Ghia 4+1-dr Hatchback Sedan			9,427
392	Laser Sport 2+1-dr Hatchback Sedan			9,741
393	Meteor GL			8,660
393	Telstar GL 4-dr Sedan			10,195
393	Telstar Ghia 4-dr Sedan			11,480
393	Telstar TX5 GL 4+1-dr Hatchback Sedan			11,743
393	Telstar TX5 Ghia 4+1-dr Hatchback Sedan			12,966
393	Falcon GL 4-dr Sedan			11,648
393	Falcon GL 4+1-dr St. Wagon			12,443
393	Fairmont 4-dr Sedan			14,399
393	Fairmont 4+1-dr St. Wagon			15,349
393	Fairmont Ghia 4-dr Sedan			18,773
394	Fairlane ZK Sedan			19,646
394	LTD FD			29,226
	FORD (Brazil)			
259	Corcel II L 2-dr Sedan			5,556,000
259	Corcel II GL 2-dr Sedan			6,082,000
259	Corcel II Belina L 2+1-dr St. Wagon			5,836,000
259	Corcel II Belina GL 2+1-dr St. Wagon			6,358,000
259	Del Rey 2-dr Sedan			6,803,000
259	Del Rey 4-dr Sedan			6,970,000
259	Del Rey Ouro 2-dr Sedan			8,570,000
259	Del Rey Ouro 4-dr Sedan			8,714,000
259	Del Rey Ouro Scala 2+1-dr St. Wagon			8,891,000
260	Escort 2-dr Sedan			5,011,000
260	Escort L 2-dr Sedan			5,576,000
260	Escort GL 2-dr Sedan			6,430,000
260	Escort Ghia 2-dr Sedan			7,171,000
260	Escort 4-dr Sedan			5,228,000
260	Escort L 4-dr Sedan			5,793,000
260	Escort GL 4-dr Sedan			6,652,000
260	Escort Ghia 4-dr Sedan			7,395,000
260	Escort XR-3 2-dr Sedan			7,840,000
	FORD (Germany FR)			
118	Fiesta 2+1-dr Limousine			11,985*
118	Fiesta L 2+1-dr Limousine			12,995*
118	Fiesta S 2+1-dr Limousine			13,285*
118	Fiesta Ghia 2+1-dr Limousine			14,517*
118	Fiesta XR2 2+1-dr Limousine			—
119	Escort 2+1-dr Limousine			13,110*
119	Escort 4+1-dr Limousine			13,811*
119	Escort 2+1-dr Turnier			14,285*
119	Escort 4+1-dr Turnier			14,986*
119	Escort L 2+1-dr Limousine			14,114*
119	Escort L 4+1-dr Limousine			14,815*
119	Escort L 2+1-dr Turnier			15,108*
119	Escort L 4+1-dr Turnier			15,809*

Page	MAKE AND MODEL	Price in GB £	Price in USA $	Price ex Works
119	Escort GL 2+1-dr Limousine			15,960*
119	Escort GL 4+1-dr Limousine			16,061*
119	Escort GL 2+1-dr Turnier			17,703*
119	Escort GL 2+1-dr Turnier			17,655*
119	Escort Ghia 4+1-dr Limousine			17,761*
119	Escort 2-dr Cabriolet	7,278*		—
120	Escort XR3 i 2+1-dr Limousine			20,328*
120	Orion 1.3 GL 4-dr Limousine			17,085*
120	Orion 1.6 GL 4-dr Limousine			17,835*
120	Orion 1.6 Injection 4-dr Limousine			21,125*
120	Orion 1.6 Diesel 4-dr Limousine			19,015*
120	Sierra 2+1-dr Limousine			15,995*
120	Sierra 4+1-dr Limousine			17,350*
120	Sierra 4+1-dr Turnier			18,250*
120	Sierra L 2+1-dr Limousine			17,275*
120	Sierra L 4+1-dr Limousine			18,630*
120	Sierra L 4+1-dr Tournier			19,530*
120	Sierra GL 4+1-dr Limousine			19,965*
120	Sierra GL 4+1-dr Tournier			20,865*
120	Sierra Ghia 4+1-dr Limousine			22,600*
120	Sierra Ghia 4+1-dr Tournier			24,130*
120	Sierra XR4 i 2+1-dr Limousine			28,601*
122	Capri GT 2+1-dr Coupé			16,732*
122	Capri S 2+1-dr Coupé			19,637*
122	Capri 2.8 Injection 2+1-dr Coupé			28,601*
122	Granada L 4-dr Limousine			20,995*
122	Granada L 4+1-dr Turnier			22,245*
122	Granada GL 4-dr Limousine			23,970*
122	Granada GL 4+1-dr Turnier			25,525*
122	Granada Ghia 4-dr Limousine			30,055*
123	Granada Ghia 4+1-dr Turnier			31,855*
123	Granada 2.8 Injection 4-dr Limousine			31,380*
123	Granada 2.8 Injection 4+1-dr Turnier			33,721*
	FORD (Great Britain)			
158	Fiesta 950 Popular 2+1-dr Saloon			3,560*
158	Fiesta 950 Popular Plus 2+1-dr Saloon			3,950*
158	Fiesta 950 L 2+1-dr Saloon			4,320*
158	Fiesta 1100 Popular Plus 2+1-dr Saloon			4,155*
158	Fiesta 1100 L 2+1-dr Saloon			4,525*
158	Fiesta 1100 Ghia 2+1-dr Saloon			5,100*
159	Escort 1100 2+1-dr Saloon			4,188*
159	Escort 1100 4+1-dr Saloon			4,370*
159	Escort 1100 2+1-dr Estate			4,638*
159	Escort 1100 4+1-dr Estate			4,821*
159	Escort 1100 L 2+1-dr Saloon			4,652*
159	Escort 1100 L 4+1-dr Saloon			4,835*
159	Escort 1300 2+1-dr Saloon			4,568*
159	Escort 1300 4+1-dr Saloon			4,750*
159	Escort 1300 2+1-dr Estate			4,943*
159	Escort 1300 4+1-dr Estate			5,126*
159	Escort 1300 L 2+1-dr Saloon			5,032*
159	Escort 1300 L 4+1-dr Saloon			5,215*
159	Escort 1300 L 2+1-dr Saloon			5,408*
159	Escort 1300 L 4+1-dr Estate			5,590*
159	Escort 1300 GL 2+1-dr Saloon			5,307*
159	Escort 1300 GL 4+1-dr Saloon			5,490*
159	Escort 1300 GL 2+1-dr Estate			5,682*
159	Escort 1300 GL 4+1-dr Estate			5,865*
159	Escort 1300 Ghia 4+1-dr Saloon			6,017*
159	Escort 1600 L 2+1-dr Saloon			5,325*
159	Escort 1600 L 4+1-dr Saloon			5,507*
159	Escort 1600 L 2+1-dr Estate			5,700*
159	Escort 1600 L 4+1-dr Estate			5,883*
159	Escort 1600 GL 2+1-dr Saloon			5,599*
159	Escort 1600 GL 4+1-dr Saloon			5,782*
159	Escort 1600 GL 4+1-dr Estate			6,157*
159	Escort 1600 Ghia 4+1-dr Saloon			6,309*
159	Escort 1600 XR3i 2+1-dr Saloon			6,520*
160	Orion 1300 GL 4-dr Saloon			5,905*
160	Orion 1600 GL 4-dr Saloon			6,200*
160	Orion 1600 Ghia 4-dr Saloon			7,235*
160	Orion 1600 Injection Ghia 4-dr Saloon			7,435*
161	Sierra 1300 2+1-dr Saloon			5,000*
161	Sierra 1300 4+1-dr Saloon			5,183*
161	Sierra 1300 L 4+1-dr Saloon			5,672*
161	Sierra 1600 2+1-dr Saloon			5,312*
161	Sierra 1600 4+1-dr Saloon			5,495*
161	Sierra 1600 4+1-dr Estate			6,012*
161	Sierra 1600 L 2+1-dr Saloon			5,802*
161	Sierra 1600 L 4+1-dr Saloon			5,984*
161	Sierra 1600 L 4+1-dr Estate			6,510*
161	Sierra 1600 GL 4+1-dr Saloon			6,748*
161	Sierra 1600 GL 4+1-dr Estate			7,274*
161	Sierra 1600 Ghia 4+1-dr Saloon			8,042*
161	Sierra 2000 GL 4+1-dr Saloon			7,168*
161	Sierra 2000 GL 4+1-dr Estate			7,694*
161	Sierra 2000 Ghia 4+1-dr Saloon			8,462*
161	Sierra 2000 Ghia 4+1-dr Estate			8,972*
161	Sierra 2300 GL V6 Automatic 4+1-dr Saloon			8,061*
161	Sierra 2300 GL V6 Automatic 4+1-dr Estate			8,587*
161	Sierra 2300 Ghia V6 Automatic 4+1-dr Saloon			9,355*
161	Sierra 2300 Ghia V6 Automatic 4+1-dr Estate			9,865*
161	Sierra 2800 XR4i 2+1-dr Saloon			9,656*
161	Sierra 2300 Diesel 2+1-dr Saloon			5,749*
161	Sierra 2300 Diesel 4+1-dr Saloon			5,932*
161	Sierra 2300 Diesel 4+1-dr Estate			6,449*
161	Sierra 2300 L Diesel 2+1-dr Saloon			6,238*
161	Sierra 2300 L Diesel 4+1-dr Saloon			6,421*
161	Sierra 2300 L Diesel 4+1-dr Estate			6,947*
161	Sierra 2300 GL Diesel 4+1-dr Saloon			7,185*
161	Sierra 2300 GL 4+1-dr Estate			7,711*
162	Capri 1600 LS 2+1-dr Coupé			5,320*
162	Capri 2000 S 2+1-dr Coupé			6,385*
162	Capri 2.8 Injection 2+1-dr Coupé			8,653*
163	Granada 2000 L 4-dr Saloon			7,545*
163	Granada 2000 L 4+1-dr Estate			7,826*
163	Granada 2000 GL 4-dr Saloon			9,226*
163	Granada 2000 GL 4+1-dr Estate			9,453*
163	Granada 2300 L 4-dr Saloon			8,362*
163	Granada 2300 L 4+1-dr Estate			8,643*
163	Granada 2300 GL 4-dr Saloon			9,834*
163	Granada 2300 GL 4+1-dr Estate			10,061*
163	Granada 2300 Ghia X 4-dr Saloon			11,854*
163	Granada 2800 GL Automatic 4-dr Saloon			10,527*
163	Granada 2800 GL Automatic 4+1-dr Estate			10,754*
163	Granada 2800 Ghia Automatic 4-dr Saloon			10,919*
163	Granada 2800 Ghia Automatic 4+1-dr Estate			11,097*
163	Granada 2800 Ghia X Automatic 4-dr Saloon			12,547*
163	Granada 2800 Ghia X Automatic 4+1-dr Estate			12,710*
163	Granada 2800 Injection 4-dr Saloon			11,734*
163	Granada 2800 Injection 4+1-dr Estate			11,960*
163	Granada 2800i Ghia X Automatic 4-dr Saloon			13,099*
163	Granada 2800i Ghia X Automatic 4+1-dr Estate			13,262*
163	Granada 2500 Diesel 4-dr Saloon			8,579*
163	Granada 2500 Diesel 4+1-dr Estate			8,860*
	FORD (Japan)			
338	Laser 1500 L 2+1-dr Hatchback Sedan			879,000
338	Laser 1500 L 4-dr Sedan			933,000
338	Laser 1500 L 4+1-dr Hatchback Sedan			915,000
338	Laser 1500 ES 2+1-dr Hatchback Sedan			1,126,000
338	Laser 1500 Ghia 4-dr Sedan			1,121,000
338	Laser 1500 Ghia 4+1-dr Hatchback Sedan			1,107,000
338	Laser 1500 EGI 2+1-dr Hatchback Sedan			1,232,000
338	Laser 1500 Turbo 2+1-dr Hatchback Sedan			1,372,000
339	Telstar 1600 GL 4-dr Sedan			1,203,000
339	Telstar 1800 GL 4-dr Sedan			1,243,000
339	Telstar 1800 GL TX5 4-dr Hatchback Sedan			1,268,000
339	Telstar 1800 Ghia 4-dr Sedan			1,429,000
339	Telstar 1800 Ghia TX5 4-dr Sedan			1,480,000
339	Telstar 2000 MEGI Ghia 4-dr Sedan			1,640,000
339	Telstar 2000 MEGI S-TX5 4+1-dr Hatchback Sedan			1,723,000
339	Telstar 2000 MEGI Ghia S-TX5 4+1-dr Hatchback Sedan			1,756,000
339	Telstar 2000 MEGI Ghia Turbo S-TX5 4+1-dr Hatchback Sedan			—
339	Telstar 2000 Ghia Diesel 4-dr Sedan			—
	FORD (South Africa)			
324	Escort 1300 GL 4+1-dr Sedan			7,335
324	Escort 1600 GLE 4+1-dr Sedan			8,995
324	Escort XR3 2+1-dr Sedan			9,255
325	Sierra 1600 GL 4+1-dr Sedan			9,990

Page	MAKE AND MODEL	Price in GB £	Price in USA $	Price ex Works
325	Sierra 2000 GL 4+1-dr Sedan			10,970
325	Sierra 2000 GL Automatic 4+1-dr Sedan			11,405
325	Sierra 2300 GLE 4+1-dr Sedan			12,485
325	Sierra 2300 GLE Automatic 4+1-dr Sedan			12,970
326	Granada 2000 GLE 4-dr Sedan			14,745
326	Granada 3000 GLE 4-dr Sedan			16,535
326	Granada 3000 GLE Automatic 4-dr Sedan			17,350
326	Granada 3000 Ghia 4-dr Sedan			22,525
	FORD (USA)			
288	Escort L 2+1-dr Hatchback Sedan			6,193
288	Escort L 4+1-dr Hatchback Sedan			6,407
288	Escort L 4+1-dr St. Wagon			6,621
288	Escort GL 2+1-dr Hatchback Sedan			6,690
288	Escort GL 4+1-dr Hatchback Sedan			6,904
288	Escort GL 4+1-dr St. Wagon			7,081
288	Escort LX 4+1-dr Hatchback Sedan			8,156
288	Escort LX 4+1-dr St. Wagon			8,247
288	Escort GT 2+1-dr Hatchback Sedan			7,901
289	EXP 2+1-dr Coupé			7,860
289	EXP Turbo 2+1-dr Coupé			10,260
290	Tempo L 2-dr Sedan			7,330
290	Tempo L 4-dr Sedan			7,330
290	Tempo GL 2-dr Sedan			7,550
290	Tempo GL 4-dr Sedan			7,550
290	Tempo GLX 2-dr Sedan			8,019
290	Tempo GLX 4-dr Sedan			8,019
290	LTD 4-dr Sedan			9,031
290	LTD 4+1-dr St. Wagon			10,405
291	Mustang L 2-dr Hatchback Sedan			7,470
291	Mustang L 2+1-dr Hatchback Sedan			7,640
291	Mustang LX 2-dr Hatchback Sedan			7,660
291	Mustang LX 2+1-dr Hatchback Sedan			7,870
291	Mustang LX 2-dr Convertible			12,220
291	Mustang GT 2+1-dr Hatchback Sedan			9,950
291	Mustang GT 2-dr Convertible			13,420
291	Mustang SVO 2+1-dr Hatchback Sedan			15,970
292	Thunderbird 2-dr Coupé			10,065
292	Thunderbird Elan 2-dr Coupé			13,093
292	Thunderbird Fila 2-dr Coupé			14,903
292	Thunderbird Turbo 2-dr Coupé			12,762
293	LTD Crown Victoria 2-dr Sedan			11,430
293	LTD Crown Victoria 4-dr Sedan			11,430
293	LTD Country Squire 4+1-dr St. Wagon			11,590
	FSO (Poland)			
222	126 P / 650	—		—
223	125 P / 1300	2,599*		—
223	125 P / 1500 Populare II 4-dr Sedan	—		—
223	125 P / 1500 4-dr Sedan	2,899*		—
223	125 P / 1500 Estate	3,299*		—
223	Polonez LE Populare II 4+1-dr Hatchback Sedan	—		—
223	Polonez LE X 4+1-dr Hatchback Sedan	3,899*		—
	GAZ (USSR)			
241	Volga 3102			—
241	Volga 3102 Station Wagon			—
242	Volga Indenor Diesel			—
242	Chaika			—
	GIANNINI (Italy)			
211	Fiat Giannini 126 GP Base 2-dr Berlina			5,280,000*
211	Fiat Giannini 126 GP Personal 2-dr Berlina			5,680,000*
211	Fiat Giannini 126 GPS Base 2-dr Berlina			5,670,000*
211	Fiat Giannini 126 GPS Personal 2-dr Berlina			6,010,000*
212	Fiat Giannini Panda GT 30 2+1-dr Berlina			6,990,000*
212	Fiat Giannini Panda GT Super 2+1-dr Berlina			7,470,000*
212	Fiat Giannini Panda GTS 30 2+1-dr Berlina			7,430,000*
212	Fiat Giannini Panda GTS Super 2+1-dr Berlina			7,890,000*
212	Fiat Giannini Panda GT 45 2+1-dr Berlina			7,890,000*
212	Fiat Giannini Ritmo Veloce 60 R 2+1-dr Berlina			9,730,000*
212	Fiat Giannini Ritmo Veloce 60 R 4+1-dr Berlina			10,690,000*
213	Fiat Giannini Ritmo Turbo Diesel R			14,850,000*

Page	MAKE AND MODEL	Price in GB £	Price in USA $	Price ex Works
	GINETTA (Great Britain)			
164	G25			7,500*
	GP (Great Britain)			
164	Talon			6,500*
165	Spyder			6,300*
165	Madison Roadster			5,500*
165	Madison Coupé			6,000*
	GURGEL (Brazil)			
260	X-12 L 2-dr St. Wagon			4,058,000
260	X-12 TR 2-dr St. Wagon			4,334,000
	HINDUSTAN (India)			
329	Contessa			—
329	Ambassador Mk 4			48,587
330	Trekker			61,585
	HOLDEN (Australia)			
394	Gemini TF 4-dr Sedan			7,054
394	Gemini TF SL 4-dr Sedan			7,565
394	Gemini TF SLX 4-dr Sedan			8,185
394	Gemini TF ZZ/Z 4-dr Sedan			8,915
394	Gemini TF SLX Diesel 4-dr Sedan			9,537
395	Camira JB SL 4-dr Sedan			9,296
395	Camira JB SL 4+1-dr St. Wagon			9,821
395	Camira JB SJ 4-dr Sedan			10,046
395	Camira JB SLX 4-dr Sedan			9,938
395	Camira JB SLX 4+1-dr St. Wagon			10,513
395	Camira JB SLE 4-dr Sedan			11,133
395	Camira JB SLE 4+1-dr St. Wagon			11,823
395	Commodore 4 VH SL 4-dr Sedan			—
395	Commodore 4 VH SL 4+1-dr St. Wagon			—
395	Commodore 6 VH SL 4-dr Sedan			11,227
395	Commodore 6 VH SL 4+1-dr St. Wagon			11,917
395	Commodore 6 VH SL-E 4-dr Sedan			18,667
395	Commodore 6 VH SL-X 4-dr Sedan			14,014
395	Commodore 6 VH SL-X 4+1-dr St. Wagon			15,090
396	Commodore SS VH			14,619
396	Statesman Series II De Ville 4-dr Sedan			19,772
396	Statesman Series II Caprice 4-dr Sedan			29,299
	HONDA (Japan)			
340	City PRO 1200 T 2+1-dr Hatchback Sedan			598,000
340	City PRO 1200 F 2+1-dr Hatchback Sedan			668,000
340	City 1200 E 2+1-dr Hatchback Sedan			770,000
340	City 1200 E1 2+1-dr Hatchback Sedan			770,000
340	City 1200 R 2+1-dr Hatchback Sedan			780,000
340	City 1200 RH high-roof 2+1-dr Hatchback Sedan			810,000
340	City 1200 Turbo 2+1-dr Hatchback Sedan			1,090,000
340	City 1200 Turbo II 2+1-dr Hatchback Sedan			1,230,000
341	Civic 1300 23U 2+1-dr Hatchback Sedan			798,000
341	Civic 1300 23U 2+1-dr Hatchback Sedan		5,249*	880,000
341	Civic 1300 23L 2+1-dr Hatchback Sedan	4,275*	6,199*	910,000
341	Civic 1300 33U 4-dr Sedan			875,000
341	Civic 1300 33L 4-dr Sedan			975,000
341	Civic 1300 53U Shuttle 4+1-dr Sedan	4,515*		957,000
341	Civic 1500 25M 2+1-dr Hatchback Sedan		6,299*	998,000
341	Civic 1500 25R 2+1-dr Hatchback Sedan		6,599*	1,028,000
341	Civic 1500 35M 4-dr Sedan			1,048,000
341	Civic 1500 35G 4-dr Sedan			1,160,000
341	Civic 1500 55M Shuttle 4+1-dr Sedan		6,849*	1,078,000
341	Civic 1500 55J Shuttle 4+1-dr Sedan			1,162,000
341	Civic 1500 55G Shuttle 4+1-dr Sedan			1,200,000
341	Civic 1500 25i 2+1-dr Hatchback Sedan			1,189,000
341	Civic 1500 35i 4-dr Sedan		7,099*	1,260,000
341	Civic 1500 55i Shuttle 4+1-dr Sedan			1,300,000
341	Ballade 1300 CR-U 4-dr Sedan			885,000
341	Ballade 1300 CR-B 4-dr Sedan			945,000
341	Ballade 1300 CR-L 4-dr Sedan			1,020,000
341	Ballade 1500 CR-M 4-dr Sedan			1,068,000
341	Ballade 1500 CR-Extra 4-dr Sedan			1,180,000
341	Ballade 1500 CR-i 4-dr Sedan			1,280,000
342	Ballade Sports 1.3 CR-X 2+1-dr Coupé			993,000
342	Ballade Sports 1.5i CR-X 2+1-dr Coupé			1,270,000
343	Accord 1600 RL 2+1-dr Hatchback Coupé	5,370*		1,205,000
343	Accord 1600 RX 2+1-dr Hatchback Coupé	6,190*		1,305,000

Page	MAKE AND MODEL	Price in GB £	Price in USA $	Price ex Works
343	Accord 1600 GC 4-dr Sedan	5,720*		1,081,000
343	Accord 1600 GL 4-dr Sedan			1,196,000
343	Accord 1600 GX 4-dr Sedan	6,890*		1,308,000
343	Accord 1800 RU 2+1-dr Hatchback Coupé			1,300,000
343	Accord 1800 RX 2+1-dr Hatchback Coupé			1,360,000
343	Accord 1800 RXT 2+1-dr Hatchback Coupé			1,497,000
343	Accord 1800 GL 4-dr Sedan		8,549*	1,265,000
343	Accord 1800 GX 4-dr Sedan		9,949*	1,363,000
343	Accord 1800 GXR 4-dr Sedan			1,543,000
343	Quint-Quintet TL 4+1-dr Sedan	5,470*		972,000
343	Quint-Quintet TS 4+1-dr Sedan			1,110,000
343	Quint-Quintet TE 4+1-dr Sedan			1,217,000
343	Quint-Quintet TER 4+1-dr Sedan			1,328,000
343	Quint-Quintet XE 4+1-dr Sedan			1,317,000
343	Quint-Quintet XER 4+1-dr Sedan			1,428,000
343	Vigor 1800 TU 2+1-dr Hatchback Coupé			1,320,000
343	Vigor 1800 TX 2+1-dr Hatchback Coupé			1,380,000
343	Vigor 1800 TXL 2+1-dr Hatchback Coupé			1,662,000
343	Vigor 1800 VL 4-dr Sedan			1,255,000
343	Vigor 1800 VX 4-dr Sedan			1,383,000
343	Vigor 1800 VXR 4-dr Sedan			1,553,000
344	Prelude XC 2-dr Coupé	6,450*	9,995*	1,360,000
344	Prelude XZ 2-dr Coupé			1,524,000
344	Prelude XX 2-dr Coupé	7,645*		1,718,000
	HONG QI (China People's Republic)			
332	CA-770 B			—
	HYUNDAI (Korea)			
334	Pony T 4+1-dr Hatchback Sedan	4,099*		3,604,000
334	Pony GL 4+1-dr Hatchback Sedan	4,348*		4,153,000
334	Pony GLS 4+1-dr Hatchback Sedan	4,497*		4,324,000
335	Stellar 1400 L 4-dr Sedan			4,244,000
335	Stellar 1400 SL 4-dr Sedan			4,859,000
335	Stellar 1600 L 4-dr Sedan			4,315,000
335	Stellar 1600 SL 4-dr Sedan			4,931,000
335	Stellar 1600 GSL 4-dr Sedan			5,825,000
	ISUZU (Japan)			
344	Gemini 1600 LD 4-dr Sedan			954,000
344	Gemini 1600 LT 4-dr Sedan			1,048,000
344	Gemini 1600 LS 4-dr Sedan			1,124,000
344	Gemini 1600 LS 2-dr Coupé			1,154,000
344	Gemini 1800 LT 4-dr Sedan			1,077,000
344	Gemini 1800 Minx 4-dr Sedan			1,151,000
344	Gemini 1800 Minx 2-dr Coupé			1,181,000
344	Gemini 1800 LJ 4-dr Sedan			1,334,000
344	Gemini 1800 LS 4-dr Sedan			1,184,000
344	Gemini 1800 LS 2-dr Coupé			1,179,000
344	Gemini 1800 LG 4-dr Sedan			1,199,000
344	Gemini 1800 LG 2-dr Coupé			1,299,000
344	Gemini ZZR 4-dr Sedan			1,557,000
344	Gemini ZZR 2-dr Coupé			1,587,000
344	Gemini ZZT 4-dr Sedan			1,680,000
344	Gemini ZZT 2-dr Coupé			1,720,000
344	Gemini LD Special 4-dr Sedan			996,000
344	Gemini LD 4-dr Sedan			1,081,000
344	Gemini LT 4-dr Sedan			1,190,000
344	Gemini LT 2-dr Coupé			1,220,000
344	Gemini Minx 4-dr Sedan			1,260,000
344	Gemini Minx 2-dr Coupé			1,295,000
344	Gemini LJ 4-dr Sedan			1,430,000
344	Gemini LS 4-dr Sedan			1,246,000
344	Gemini LS 2-dr Coupé			1,276,000
344	Gemini Electro-diesel LT/E 4-dr Sedan			1,290,000
344	Gemini Electro-diesel LJ/E 4-dr Sedan			1,545,000
344	Gemini Diesel Turbo Special 4-dr Sedan			1,149,000
344	Gemini Diesel Turbo LG 4-dr Sedan			1,384,000
345	Florian Aska 1800 LD 4-dr Sedan			1,137,000
345	Florian Aska 1800 LT 4-dr Sedan			1,202,000
345	Florian Aska 1800 LF 4-dr Sedan			1,334,000
345	Florian Aska 2000 LT 4-dr Sedan			1,252,000
345	Florian Aska 2000 LF 4-dr Sedan			1,441,000
345	Florian Aska 2000 LS 4-dr Sedan			1,407,000
345	Florian Aska 2000 LJ 4-dr Sedan			1,547,000
345	Florian Aska 2000 LX 4-dr Sedan			1,687,000
345	Florian Aska 2000 LX-E 4-dr Sedan			1,859,000
345	Florian Aska 2000 Turbo LT 4-dr Sedan			1,490,000
345	Florian Aska 2000 Turbo LS 4-dr Sedan			1,640,000
345	Florian Aska 2000 Turbo LJ 4-dr Sedan			1,805,000
345	Florian Aska 2000 Diesel LD 4-dr Sedan			1,272,000
345	Florian Aska 2000 Diesel LT 4-dr Sedan			1,322,000
345	Florian Aska 2000 Diesel LF 4-dr Sedan			1,511,000
345	Florian Aska 2000 Diesel LJ 4-dr Sedan			1,627,000
345	Florian Aska 2000 Diesel LX 4-dr Sedan			1,757,000
345	Florian Aska 2000 Diesel Turbo LT 4-dr Sedan			1,490,000
345	Florian Aska 2000 Diesel Turbo LS 4-dr Sedan			1,650,000
345	Florian Aska 2000 Diesel Turbo LJ 4-dr Sedan			1,815,000
346	Piazza XJ 2+1-dr Coupé			1,670,000
346	Piazza Bella 2+1-dr Coupé			1,723,000
346	Piazza XL 2+1-dr Coupé			1,867,000
346	Piazza XG 2+1-dr Coupé			2,019,000
346	Piazza XE 2+1-dr Coupé		10,498*	2,529,000
347	Rodeo 4WD LD Short Wheelbase (steel body)			1,628,000
347	Rodeo 4WD LT Short Wheelbase (steel body)			1,808,000
347	Rodeo 4WD LT Short Wheelbase (soft top)			—
347	Rodeo 4WD LD Long Wheelbase (steel body)			1,730,000
347	Rodeo 4WD LT Long Wheelbase (steel body)			1,910,000
	ITD (USA)			
293	Stiletto			29,500*
	JAGUAR (Great Britain)			
166	XJ6 3.4			13,991*
166	XJS 3.6 2-dr Coupé			19,248*
166	XJSC 3.6 2-dr Convertible			20,756*
166	XJ6 4.2		31,100*	15,997*
167	Sovereign 4.2			18,494*
167	Sovereign HE			20,955*
167	XJS HE		34,700*	21,752*
	JEEP (USA)			
294	CJ-7 Roadster			6,995
294	Cherokee Sport 2+1-dr Wagon			9,995
294	Cherokee Sport 4+1-dr Wagon			10,295
294	Wagoneer Sport 4+1-dr Wagon			12,444
294	Wagoneer Sport Limited 4+1-dr Wagon			17,076
295	Grand Wagoneer			19,306
	KELMARK (USA)			
295	GT			14,800
	KOUGAR (Great Britain)			
168	Monza			10,000*
168	Sports			12,500*
	LAFER (Brazil)			
261	MP 2-dr Roadster			7,541,000
261	MP TI 2-dr Roadster			8,090,000
	LAMBORGHINI (Italy)			
213	Jalpa P 350	26,001*		65,500,000*
213	Countach LP 500 S	54,000*		125,500,000*
214	LM-002	—		—
214	LM-004/7000	—		—
	LANCIA (Italy)			
214	Delta Berlina 1300	4,950*		12,684,000◊
215	Delta Berlina 1500 Automatica	5,868*		14,892,000◊
215	Delta Berlina 1600 GT	5,990*		14,316,000◊
215	Delta Berlina 1600 HF Turbo	—		17,346,000◊
215	Prisma Berlina 1300	—		13,686,000◊
216	Prisma Berlina 1500	5,550*		13,998,000◊
216	Prisma Berlina 1500 Automatica	5,989*		15,270,000◊
216	Prisma Berlina 1600	6,150*		15,636,000◊
216	Beta Coupé 1300	—		14,682,000◊
216	Beta Coupé 1600	—		16,212,000◊
217	Beta Coupé 2000 IE	7,276*		17,946,000◊
217	Beta Coupé Volumex VX	7,995*		19,080,000◊

Page	MAKE AND MODEL	Price in GB £	Price in USA $	Price ex Works
217	Trevi Berlina 1600	6,620*		15,930,000◊
217	Trevi Berlina 2000 IE	7,192*		18,336,000◊
217	Trevi Berlina Volumex VX	—		19,608,000◊
218	H.P. Executive 1600	6,990*		16,002,000◊
218	H.P. Executive 2000 IE	7,975*		17,742,000◊
218	H.P. Executive Volumex VX	8,500*		18,690,000◊
218	Montecarlo	8,990*		19,746,000◊
219	Rally	—		47,544,000◊
219	Gamma Berlina 2000	—		21,918,000◊
219	Gamma Coupé 2000	—		28,206,000◊
219	Gamma Berlina 2500 IE	9,650*		28,228,000◊
220	Gamma Coupé 2500 IE	12,200*		34,182,000◊
	LAND ROVER (Great Britain)			
168	88" Short Wheelbase 2-dr Soft Top			6,729*
168	88" Short Wheelbase 2+1-dr St. Wagon			8,534*
168	88" Short Wheelbase County 2+1-dr St. Wagon			8,979*
169	109" Long Wheelbase 2-dr Soft Top			7,936*
169	109" Long Wheelbase 4+1-dr St. Wagon			9,121*
169	109" Long Wheelbase County 4+1-dr St. Wagon			9,537*
169	109" V8 Long Wheelbase 2-dr Soft Top			8,707*
169	109" V8 Long Wheelbase 4+1-dr St. Wagon			9,824*
169	109" V8 Long Wheelbase County 4+1-dr St. Wagon			10,241*
169	One Ten 2¼ P 2-dr Soft Top			8,009*
169	One Ten 2¼ P 4+1-dr St. Wagon			9,300*
169	One Ten 2¼ P County 4+1-dr St. Wagon			9,730*
169	One Ten 3½ P 2-dr Soft Top			8,939*
169	One Ten 3½ P 4+1-dr St. Wagon			10,251*
169	One Ten 3½ P County 4+1-dr St. Wagon			10,680*
170	Range Rover 2+1-dr Fleet Line 2			13,530*
170	Range Rover 2+1-dr St. Wagon			14,483*
170	Range Rover 4+1-dr St. Wagon			15,374*
	LAWIL (Italy)			
220	S3 Varzina Spider			5,004,000◊
220	A4 City Berlina			5,079,000◊
	LEDL (Austria)			
74	AS 130			214,634*
74	AS 160			235,647*
	LENHAM (Great Britain)			
170	Austin-Healey 3000			11,000
	LINCOLN (USA)			
295	Continental 4-dr Sedan			22,293
295	Designer Valentino 4-dr Sedan			24,741
295	Designer Givenchy 4-dr Sedan			24,766
296	Mark VII 2-dr Sedan			22,231
296	Mark VII Bill Blass Designer 2-dr Sedan			25,331
296	Mark VII Versace Designer 2-dr Sedan			24,930
296	Mark VII LSC 2-dr Sedan			24,230
296	Town Car 4-dr Sedan			18,595
296	Signature 4-dr Sedan			20,564
296	Designer 4-dr Sedan			22,230
	LOTUS (Great Britain)			
170	Excel			14,735*
171	Esprit Series 3			15,985*
171	Turbo Exprit			19,490*
	LYNX (Great Britain)			
171	D Type			24,800*
	MARCOS (Great Britain)			
172	3-litre Coupé			8,500*
172	Mantula			11,200*

Page	MAKE AND MODEL	Price in GB £	Price in USA $	Price ex Works
	MASERATI (Italy)			
220	2000 Biturbo		25,945*	22,503,000◊
220	Biturbo 425		—	28,441,000◊
221	Quattroporte		66,210*	55,522,000◊
	MAZDA (Japan)			
347	Familia 1300 XC 2+1-dr Hatchback Sedan	4,599*		760,000
347	Familia 1300 XC 4+1-dr Hatchback Sedan	4,769*		798,000
347	Familia 1300 XC 4-dr Sedan	4,849*		818,000
347	Familia 1300 XT 2+1-dr Hatchback Sedan			845,000
347	Familia 1300 XT 4+1-dr Hatchback Sedan			881,000
347	Familia 1300 XT 4-dr Sedan			896,000
347	Familia 1300 XL 2+1-dr Hatchback Sedan			900,000
347	Familia 1300 XL 4+1-dr Hatchback Sedan			936,000
347	Familia 1300 XL 4-dr Sedan			951,000
347	Familia 1500 XT 2+1-dr Hatchback Sedan			881,000
347	Familia 1500 XT 4+1-dr Hatchback Sedan	5,319*		917,000
347	Familia 1500 XT 4-dr Sedan			932,000
347	Familia 1500 XL 2+1-dr Hatchback Sedan			1,013,000
347	Familia 1500 XL 4+1-dr Hatchback Sedan			1,028,000
347	Familia 1500 XL 4-dr Sedan			1,042,000
347	Familia 1500 XE 4+1-dr Hatchback Sedan			1,078,000
347	Familia 1500 XE 4-dr Sedan			1,092,000
347	Familia 1500 XG 2+1-dr Hatchback Sedan	5,399*		1,084,000
347	Familia 1500 XG 4-dr Sedan	5,599*		1,112,000
347	Familia 1500 XG 2+1-dr Hatchback Sedan			1,169,000
347	Familia 1500 XGi 4-dr Sedan			1,197,000
347	Familia 1500 Turbo XG 2+1-dr Hatchback Sedan			1,250,000
347	Familia 1500 Turbo XG 4-dr Sedan			1,283,000
348	Familia (USA) GLC 2+1-dr Hatchback Sedan		4,995*	—
348	Familia (USA) GLC De Luxe 2+1-dr Hatchback Sedan		5,895*	—
348	Familia (USA) GLC De Luxe 4-dr Sedan		6,445*	—
348	Familia (USA) GLC Luxury 2+1-dr Hatchback Sedan		6,495*	—
348	Familia (USA) GLC Luxury 4-dr St. Wagon		7,095*	—
348	Capella 1600 SG 4-dr Sedan	5,499*		987,000
348	Capella 1600 SG-L 4-dr Sedan			1,082,000
348	Capella 1600 SG-L 2-dr Coupé			1,150,000
348	Capella 1600 SG-S 4-dr Sedan			1,177,000
348	Capella 1600 SG-S 2-dr Coupé			1,220,000
348	Capella 1800 SG-L 4-dr Sedan			1,217,000
348	Capella 1800 SG-S 2-dr Coupé			1,260,000
348	Capella 1800 SG-X 4-dr Sedan			1,367,000
348	Capella 1800 GT-S 4-dr Sedan			1,327,000
348	Capella 1800 GT-S 2-dr Coupé			1,375,000
348	Capella 2000 GT-X 4-dr Sedan	6,299*		1,587,000
348	Capella 2000 GT-X 2-dr Coupé	6,899*		1,745,000
348	Capella 2000 Limited 4-dr Sedan			1,627,000
348	Capella 2000 Turbo GT 4-dr Sedan			1,534,000
348	Capella 2000 Turbo GT-S 4-dr Sedan			1,651,000
348	Capella 2000 Turbo GT-S 2-dr Coupé			1,699,000
348	Capella 2000 Turbo GT-X 4-dr Sedan			1,776,000
348	Capella 2000 Turbo GT-X 2-dr Coupé			1,869,000
348	Capella 2000 SG-L 4-dr Sedan			1,282,000
348	Capella 2000 SG-X 4-dr Sedan			1,482,000
349	Luce 2000 SG-L 4-dr Sedan			1,337,000
349	Luce 2000 SG-S 4-dr Sedan			1,431,000
349	Luce 2000 SG-X 4-dr Sedan			1,553,000
349	Luce 2000 SG-X 4-dr Hardtop			1,639,000
349	Luce 2000 EGI SG-X 4-dr Sedan			1,690,000
349	Luce 2000 EGI SG-X 4-dr Hardtop			1,796,000
349	Luce RE 12A GS-X 4-dr Sedan			1,560,000
349	Luce RE 12A GS-X 4-dr Hardtop			1,673,000
349	Luce RE 12A Turbo Limited 4-dr Sedan			2,356,000
349	Luce RE 12A Turbo Limited 4-dr Hardtop			2,437,000
349	Luce RE 12A Turbo GT 4-dr Sedan			1,894,000
349	Luce RE 12A Turbo GT 4-dr Hardtop			1,976,000
349	Luce RE 13B Limited 4-dr Sedan			2,388,000
349	Luce RE 13B Limited 4-dr Hardtop			2,469,000
349	Luce DE SG-L 4-dr Sedan			1,462,000
349	Luce DE SG-X 4-dr Sedan			1,708,000
350	Cosmo 2000 XG-L 4-dr Sedan			1,337,000
350	Cosmo 2000 XG-S 4-dr Sedan			1,431,000
350	Cosmo 2000 XG-X 4-dr Sedan			1,553,000
350	Cosmo 2000 XG-X 4-dr Hardtop			1,639,000
350	Cosmo 2000 XG-X 2-dr Coupé			1,656,000
350	Cosmo 2000 EGI XG-X 4-dr Sedan			1,690,000
350	Cosmo 2000 EGI XG-X 4-dr Hardtop			1,796,000

Page	MAKE AND MODEL	Price in GB £	Price in USA $	Price ex Works
350	Cosmo 2000 EGI XG-X 2-dr Coupé			1,798,000
350	Cosmo RE 12A GS-X 4-dr Sedan			1,560,000
350	Cosmo RE 12A GS-X 4-dr Hardtop			1,673,000
350	Cosmo RE 12A GS-X 2-dr Coupé			1,667,000
350	Cosmo RE 12A Turbo Limited 4-dr Sedan			2,356,000
350	Cosmo RE 12A Turbo Limited 4-dr Hardtop			2,437,000
350	Cosmo RE 12A Turbo Limited 2-dr Coupé			2,486,000
350	Cosmo RE 12A Turbo GT 4-dr Sedan			1,894,000
350	Cosmo RE 12A Turbo GT 4-dr Hardtop			1,976,000
350	Cosmo RE 12A Turbo GT 2-dr Coupé			1,963,000
350	Cosmo RE 13B Limited 4-dr Sedan			2,388,000
350	Cosmo RE 13B Limited 4-dr Hardtop			2,469,000
350	Cosmo DE 2200 XG-L 4-dr Sedan			1,462,000
350	Cosmo DE 2200 XG-X 4-dr Sedan			1,708,000
351	626 De Luxe 4-dr Sedan		7,895*	—
351	626 De Luxe 2-dr Coupé		8,295*	—
351	626 Luxury 4-dr Sedan		9,445*	—
351	626 Luxury 2-dr Coupé		9,845*	—
351	626 Luxury 4+1-dr Hatchback Sedan		10,395*	—
352	Savanna RX 7 GT 2+1-dr Coupé	9,599*		1,623,000
352	Savanna RX 7 GT-X 2+1-dr Coupé			1,878,000
352	Savanna RX 7 SE Limited 2+1-dr Coupé			2,274,000
352	Savanna RX 7 Turbo GT 2+1-dr Coupé			1,847,000
352	Savanna RX 7 Turbo GT-X 2+1-dr Coupé			2,152,000
352	Savanna RX 7 Turbo SE Limited 2+1-dr Coupé			2,568,000
	MERCEDES-BENZ (Germany FR)			
124	190 4-dr Limousine	9,685*		26,471*
124	190 E 4-dr Limousine	10,640*		29,378*
124	190 E 2.3-16 4-dr Limousine	—	22,850*	49,590*
124	190 D 4-dr Limousine	—	22,930*	27,497*
125	200 4-dr Limousine	9,965*		27,508*
125	200 T 4+1-dr Limousine	10,750*		31,726*
125	200 D 4-dr Limousine	—		28,055*
125	230 E 4-dr Limousine	10,957*		30,860*
125	230 CE 2-dr Coupé	12,900*		36,822*
125	230 TE 4+1-dr Limousine	12,775*		35,078*
126	250 4-dr Limousine	12,320*		32,319*
126	250 Long Wheelbase 4-dr Limousine	18,500*		48,051*
126	240 D 4-dr Limousine	10,660*		29,925*
126	240 D Long Wheelbase 4-dr Limousine	—		45,714*
126	240 TD 4+1-dr Limousine	12,025*		34,143*
127	300 D 4-dr Limousine	12,280*	31,940*	32,433*
127	300 D Long Wheelbase 4-dr Limousine	18,500*		48,222*
127	300 TD 4+1-dr Limousine	13,055*	35,310*	36,651*
127	300 TD Turbodiesel 4+1-dr Limousine	—		43,548*
127	280 E 4-dr Limousine	14,280*		38,760*
127	280 CE 2-dr Coupé	16,200*		43,605*
127	280 TE 4+1-dr Limousine	15,810*		42,921*
128	280 S 4-dr Limousine	—		45,030*
128	280 SE 4-dr Limousine	16,990*		48,849*
128	280 SEL 4-dr Limousine	—		51,756*
128	380 SE 4-dr Limousine	20,435*	42,730*	59,052*
128	380 SEL 4-dr Limousine	22,855*		61,959*
128	500 SE 4-dr Limousine	24,675*		64,296*
128	500 SEL 4-dr Limousine	27,770*	51,200*	70,566*
129	380 SEC 2-dr Coupé	28,560*		80,142*
129	500 SEC 2-dr Coupé	31,890*	56,800*	85,386*
129	280 SL 2-dr Roadster	18,480*		55,404*
129	380 SL 2-dr Roadster	21,760*	43,820*	66,063*
129	500 SL 2-dr Roadster	23,990*		75,468*
130	230 G 2-dr Open	—		—
130	230 G 2+1-dr St. Wagon	—		—
130	230 G 4+1-dr Long Wheelbase St. Wagon	—		—
131	230 GE 2-dr Open	—		42,978*
131	230 GE 2+1-dr St. Wagon	14,195*		47,310*
131	230 GE 4+1-dr Long Wheelbase St. Wagon	—		52,896*
131	280 GE 2-dr Open	—		48,906*
131	280 GE 2+1-dr St. Wagon	15,795*		53,238*
131	280 GE 4+1-dr Long Wheelbase St. Wagon	16,645*		58,824*
131	240 GD 2-dr Open	—		40,584*
131	240 GD 2+1-dr St. Wagon	—		44,916*
131	240 GD 4+1-dr Long Wheelbase St. Wagon	—		50,502*
131	300 GD 2-dr Open	—		44,859*
131	300 GD 2+1-dr St. Wagon	15,015*		49,191*
131	300 GD 4+1-dr Long Wheelbase St. Wagon	15,935*		54,777*

Page	MAKE AND MODEL	Price in GB £	Price in USA $	Price ex Works
	MERCURY (USA)			
297	Lynx L 2+1-dr Hatchback Sedan			6,066
297	Lynx L 4+1-dr Hatchback Sedan			6,541
297	Lynx L 4+1-dr St. Wagon			6,756
297	Lynx GS 2+1-dr Hatchback Sedan			6,803
297	Lynx GS 4+1-dr Hatchback Sedan			7,017
297	Lynx GS 4+1-dr St. Wagon			7,195
297	Lynx RS 2+1-dr Hatchback Sedan			7,949
297	Lynx LTS 4+1-dr Hatchback Sedan			8,187
298	Topaz GS 2-dr Sedan			7,875
298	Topaz GS 4-dr Sedan			7,875
298	Topaz LS 2-dr Sedan			8,278
298	Topaz LS 4-dr Sedan			8,278
298	Marquis 4-dr Sedan			9,153
298	Marquis 4+1-dr St. Wagon			9,650
299	Capri GS 2+1-dr Hatchback Coupé			8,132
299	Capri RS 2+1-dr Hatchback Coupé			10,196
300	Cougar 2-dr Coupé			10,410
300	Cougar LS 2-dr Coupé			11,697
300	Cougar XR-7 Turbo 2-dr Coupé			13,497
300	Grand Marquis 2-dr Sedan			12,056
300	Grand Marquis 4-dr Sedan			12,120
300	Grand Marquis Brougham 4+1-dr St. Wagon			12,296
	MG (Great Britain)			
173	Metro 1300			5,249*
173	Metro Turbo			5,899*
173	Maestro 1600			6,554*
	MIDAS (Great Britain)			
173	Gold 1.3 S Coupé			5,150*
	MINI (Great Britain)			
174	City E 2-dr Saloon			3,098*
174	Mayfair 2-dr Saloon			3,630*
	MITSUBISHI (Australia)			
397	Colt XL 4+1-dr Hatchback Sedan	—		7,366
397	Colt GL 4+1-dr Hatchback Sedan	—		7,786
397	Colt SE 4+1-dr Hatchback Sedan	—		8,721
397	Colt GSR 4+1-dr Hatchback Sedan	—		8,881
397	Sigma GH XL 4-dr Sedan	5,699*		8,602
397	Sigma GH XL 4+1-dr St. Wagon	6,099*		9,052
397	Sigma GH GL 4-dr Sedan	—		9,434
397	Sigma GH GL 4+1-dr St. Wagon	—		9,884
397	Sigma GH SE 4-dr Sedan	6,599*		10,609
397	Sigma GH SE 4+1-dr St. Wagon	6,999*		11,059
397	Sigma GH GSR 4-dr Sedan	7,600*		10,725
	MITSUBISHI (Japan)			
352	Minica Econo S 2+1-dr Sedan			478,000
352	Minica Econo S II 2+1-dr Sedan			498,000
352	Minica Econo L II 2+1-dr Sedan			623,000
352	Minica Ami TL 2+1-dr Sedan			578,000
352	Minica Ami GL 2+1-dr Sedan			676,000
352	Minica Ami XL 2+1-dr Sedan			713,000
352	Minica Ami CX 2+1-dr Sedan			755,000
352	Minica Econo Turbo 2+1-dr Sedan			615,000
352	Minica Ami L Turbo 2+1-dr Sedan			785,000
352	Lancer EX 1200 Custom-Business 4-dr Sedan			772,000
352	Lancer EX 1200 Custom 4-dr Sedan			816,000
352	Lancer EX 1200 GL 4-dr Sedan			890,000
352	Lancer EX 1400 GL 4-dr Sedan			953,000
352	Lancer EX 1400 XL 4-dr Sedan			983,000
352	Lancer EX 1400 SL 4-dr Sedan			1,018,000
352	Lancer EX 1600 XL 4-dr Sedan			1,066,000
352	Lancer EX 1600 XL Super 4-dr Sedan			1,219,000
352	Lancer EX 1600 GT 4-dr Sedan			1,106,000
353	Lancer EX 1800 GSL Turbo 4-dr Sedan			1,598,000
353	Lancer EX 1800 GT Turbo Intercooler 4-dr Sedan			1,485,000
353	Lancer EX 1800 GSR Turbo Intercooler 4-dr Sedan			1,640,000
353	Lancer Fiore 1300 CE 4-dr Sedan			815,000
353	Lancer Fiore 1300 CG 4-dr Sedan			960,000

Page	MAKE AND MODEL	Price in GB £	Price in USA $	Price ex Works
353	Lancer Fiore 1300 CG-F 4-dr Sedan			998,000
353	Lancer Fiore 1500 CX 4-dr Sedan			1,120,000
353	Lancer Fiore 1500 CX Extra 4-dr Sedan			1,250,000
353	Lancer Fiore 1600 Turbo GSR-I 4-dr Sedan			1,360,000
353	Lancer Fiore 1800 Diesel CG 4-dr Sedan			1,145,000
353	Lancer Fiore 1800 Diesel CX 4-dr Sedan			1,235,000
354	Mirage 1300 CE 2+1-dr Hatchback Sedan	4,100*		755,000
354	Mirage 1300 CE 4-dr Sedan			815,000
354	Mirage 1300 CG 4-dr Sedan			960,000
354	Mirage 1300 CG 4+1-dr Hatchback Sedan			945,000
354	Mirage 1300 CG-L 2+1-dr Hatchback Sedan	4,725*		885,000
354	Mirage 1300 CS 4+1-dr Hatchback Sedan			845,000
354	Mirage 1500 CG-F 4-dr Sedan			998,000
354	Mirage 1500 CG-F 4+1-dr Hatchback Sedan			988,000
354	Mirage 1500 CX 4-dr Sedan			1,120,000
354	Mirage 1500 CG 2+1-dr Hatchback Sedan	5,250*		980,000
354	Mirage 1500 CG 4+1-dr Hatchback Sedan	5,775*		1,040,000
354	Mirage 1500 CX-S 2+1-dr Hatchback Sedan			1,045,000
354	Mirage 1500 CX Super 4+1-dr Hatchback Sedan	5,999*		1,160,000
354	Mirage 1600 GSR Turbo 4+1-dr Hatchback Sedan			1,345,000
354	Mirage 1600 GSR-T Turbo 2+1-dr Hatchback Sedan			1,360,000
354	Mirage 1800 Diesel CG 4-dr Sedan			1,145,000
354	Mirage 1800 Diesel CG 4+1-dr Hatchback Sedan			1,130,000
354	Mirage 1800 Diesel CX 4-dr Sedan			1,235,000
354	Mirage 1800 Diesel CX 4+1-dr Hatchback Sedan			1,220,000
355	Tredia 1400 GL 4-dr Sedan			998,000
355	Tredia 1400 GF 4-dr Sedan			1,130,000
355	Tredia 1400 GX 4-dr Sedan	6,029*		1,060,000
355	Tredia 1600 SE 4-dr Sedan			1,175,000
355	Tredia 1600 Super Saloon 4-dr Sedan	6,825*		1,295,000
355	Tredia 1800 Super Saloon 4-dr Sedan			1,405,000
355	Tredia 1800 Turbo GT-X 4-dr Sedan	8,199*		1,445,000
355	Tredia 1800 Turbo Super Saloon 4-dr Sedan			1,535,000
356	Cordia 1600 SR 2+1-dr Coupé			1,037,000
356	Cordia 1600 SL 2+1-dr Coupé			1,090,000
356	Cordia 1600 SE 2+1-dr Coupé	7,150*		1,240,000
356	Cordia 1800 SE 2+1-dr Coupé			1,455,000
356	Cordia 1800 Turbo GT 2+1-dr Coupé			1,598,000
356	Cordia 1800 Turbo GSR 2+1-dr Coupé			1,598,000
356	Cordia 1800 Turbo GSR-S 2+1-dr Coupé	8,399*		1,765,000
356	Chariot 1600 ME 4+1-dr St. Wagon			1,152,000
356	Chariot 1600 MF 4+1-dr St. Wagon			1,298,000
356	Chariot 1800 MT 4+1-dr St. Wagon			1,464,000
356	Chariot 1800 MX 4+1-dr St. Wagon			1,590,000
356	Chariot 1800 Turbo MR 4+1-dr St. Wagon			1,703,000
357	Galant Sigma 1800 LS 4-dr Sedan			1,070,000
357	Galant Sigma 1800 LG 4-dr Sedan			1,165,000
357	Galant Sigma 1800 L Touring 4-dr Sedan			1,323,000
357	Galant Sigma 1800 Super Touring 4-dr Sedan			1,140,000
357	Galant Sigma 1800 Super Touring E 4-dr Sedan			1,640,000
357	Eterna Sigma 1800 LX Touring 4-dr Sedan			1,313,000
357	Eterna Sigma 1800 Super Touring 4-dr Sedan			1,440,000
357	Galant Sigma 1800 Turbo Super Touring 4-dr Sedan			1,699,000
357	Eterna Sigma 1800 Turbo Super Touring 4-dr Sedan			1,699,000
357	Galant Sigma 2000 Super Saloon 4-dr Sedan	7,769*		1,748,000
357	Galant Sigma 2000 Royal 4-dr Sedan			2,320,000
357	Eterna Sigma 2000 Super Saloon 4-dr Sedan			1,748,000
357	Eterna Sigma 2000 Royal 4-dr Sedan			2,320,000
357	Galant Sigma 2000 Turbo GSR-X 4-dr Sedan	9,979*		1,955,000
357	Eterna Sigma 2000 Turbo GSR-X 4-dr Sedan			1,955,000

Page	MAKE AND MODEL	Price in GB £	Price in USA $	Price ex Works
358	Galant Lambda 1800 Super Touring 2-dr Coupé			1,514,000
358	Galant Lambda 2000 Turbo GE 2-dr Coupé			1,577,000
358	Galant Lambda 2000 Turbo GT 2-dr Coupé			1,690,000
358	Galant Lambda 2000 Turbo GSR 2-dr Coupé	11,100*		1,960,000
358	Galant Lambda 2300 Turbo Diesel 2-dr Coupé			1,735,000
358	Starion 2000 Turbo GSR-I 2+1-dr Coupé			1,815,000
358	Starion 2000 Turbo GSR-II Automatic 2+1-dr Coupé			2,090,000
358	Starion 2000 Turbo GSR-III Automatic 2+1-dr Coupé			2,320,000
358	Starion 2000 Turbo GSR-X 2+1-dr Coupé			2,745,000
358	Starion 2000 Turbo GSR-II Intercooler 2+1-dr Coupé			2,134,000
358	Starion 2000 Turbo GSR-III Intercooler 2+1-dr Coupé	12,499*		2,320,000
358	Debonair Super De Luxe 4-dr Sedan			2,491,000
358	Debonair Executive SE 4-dr Sedan			2,553,000
359	Pajero DX 2000 (soft top) Wagon	8,749*		1,356,000
359	Pajero DX 2000 (steel body) Wagon	9,449*		1,464,000
359	Pajero XL 2000 Turbo (steel body) 2+1-dr Wagon			2,200,000
359	Pajero DX 2300 Diesel (soft top) Wagon			1,496,000
359	Pajero DX 2300 Diesel (steel body) Wagon			1,611,000
359	Pajero DX 2300 Turbo Diesel (soft top) Wagon			1,695,000
359	Pajero DX 2300 Turbo Diesel (steel body) Wagon			1,915,000
359	Jeep L-J59 (soft top) 2+1-dr Wagon			1,350,000
359	Jeep L-J57 (soft top) 4+1-dr Wagon			1,385,000
359	Jeep L-J37 4+1-dr Wagon			1,718,000
359	Jeep K-J54 (soft top) 4+1-dr Wagon			1,525,000
359	Jeep K-J36 4+1-dr Wagon			1,881,000
359	Jeep K-J44 (soft top) 4+1-dr Wagon			1,588,000
	MONTEVERDI (Switzerland)			
239	Tiara 3.8 Luxus 4-dr Limousine			187,000*
239	Tiara 5.0 Luxus 4-dr Limousine			—
	MORGAN (Great Britain)			
174	4/4 1600 2-seater			8,569*
174	4/4 1600 4-seater			9,431*
175	4/4 1600 TC 2-seater			8,766*
175	4/4 1600 TC 4-seater			9,628*
175	Plus 8			11,651*
	MORRIS (Great Britain)			
175	Ital 1.3 SL 4-dr Saloon			4,354*
175	Ital 1.3 SL 4+1-dr Estate			5,168*
175	Ital 1.3 SLX 4-dr Saloon			4,897*
175	Ital 1.7 SL 4+1-dr Estate			5,388*
175	Ital 1.7 SLX 4-dr Saloon			5,115*
175	Ital 1.7 SLX 4+1-dr Estate			5,651*
	NISSAN (Australia)			
398	Pulsar GL 4+1-dr Hatchback Sedan			8,270
398	Pulsar GL 4-dr Sedan			8,470
398	Pulsar GX 4+1-dr Hatchback Sedan			8,900
398	Pulsar GX 4-dr Sedan			9,100
398	Bluebird GL 4-dr Sedan			9,210
398	Bluebird GL 4+1-dr St. Wagon			9,660
398	Bluebird GX 4-dr Sedan			9,740
398	Bluebird GX 4+1-dr St. Wagon			10,300
398	Bluebird LX 4-dr Sedan			11,070
398	Bluebird LX 4+1-dr St. Wagon			11,450
398	Bluebird TRX 4-dr Sedan			10,650
	NISSAN (Japan)			
360	March E 2+1-dr Sedan	3,750*		635,000
360	March L 2+1-dr Sedan	4,250*		685,000
360	March S 2+1-dr Sedan			760,000
360	March G 2+1-dr Sedan			798,000
360	March FC 4+1-dr Hatchback Sedan			750,000
360	March FT 4+1-dr Hatchback Sedan			835,000
360	Pulsar 1300 T 2+1-dr Hatchback Sedan			756,000

Page	MAKE AND MODEL	Price in GB £	Price in USA $	Price ex Works
360	Pulsar 1300 TC 2+1-dr Hatchback Sedan	4,484*		810,000
360	Pulsar 1300 TC 4+1-dr Hatchback Sedan	4,715*		820,000
360	Pulsar 1300 TS 2+1-dr Hatchback Sedan	4,711*		869,000
360	Pulsar 1300 TS 4+1-dr Hatchback Sedan	4,941*		879,000
360	Pulsar 1300 TS-L 4+1-dr Hatchback Sedan			938,000
360	Pulsar 1500 TS-L 2+1-dr Hatchback Sedan	5,350*		983,000
360	Pulsar 1500 TS-L 4+1-dr Hatchback Sedan			1,003,000
360	Pulsar 1500 TS-G 2+1-dr Hatchback Sedan			1,053,000
360	Pulsar 1500 TS-G 4+1-dr Hatchback Sedan			1,095,000
360	Pulsar 1500 TS-GE 2+1-dr Hatchback Sedan			1,185,000
360	Pulsar 1500 TS-GE 4+1-dr Hatchback Sedan			1,175,000
360	Pulsar 1500 TS-L 4-dr Sedan			1,035,000
360	Pulsar 1500 TS-G 4-dr Sedan			1,127,000
360	Pulsar 1500 TS-GE 4-dr Sedan			1,222,000
360	Pulsar 1500 EXA 2-dr Coupé		7,749*	1,175,000
360	Pulsar 1500 EXA-E 2-dr Coupé			1,285,000
360	Pulsar 1500 Turbo 2+1-dr Hatchback Sedan			1,360,000
360	Pulsar 1500 Turbo 4+1-dr Hatchback Sedan	6,400*		1,350,000
360	Pulsar 1500 Turbo 4-dr Sedan			1,397,000
360	Pulsar 1500 Turbo EXA 2-dr Coupé			1,460,000
360	Pulsar Diesel 4-dr Sedan			1,156,000
360	Pulsar Diesel 4+1-dr Hatchback Sedan			1,124,000
361	Sunny 1300 CT 4-dr Sedan	4,161*	5,199*	805,000
361	Sunny 1300 DX 4-dr Sedan	4,658*	6,349*	844,000
361	Sunny 1300 GL 4-dr Sedan	4,765*	6,549*	899,000
361	Sunny 1300 GLL 4-dr Sedan		7,049*	1,013,000
361	Sunny 1300 California DL 4+1-dr Hatchback Sedan		7,449*	943,000
361	Sunny 1300 California GL 4+1-dr Hatchback Sedan			1,028,000
361	Sunny 1500 GX-L 2+1-dr Hatchback Sedan	5,099*		995,000
361	Sunny 1500 GX-S 2+1-dr Hatchback Sedan	5,416*		1,065,000
361	Sunny 1500 GX-X 2+1-dr Hatchback Sedan	5,144*		1,025,000
361	Sunny 1500 GX-R 2+1-dr Hatchback Sedan	5,330*		1,099,000
361	Sunny 1500 GL 4-dr Sedan	5,519*	7,149*	965,000
361	Sunny 1500 SGL 4-dr Sedan			1,063,000
361	Sunny 1500 SGX 4-dr Sedan			1,117,000
361	Sunny 1500 California GL-L 4+1-dr Hatchback Sedan			1,076,000
361	Sunny 1500 California SGL 4+1-dr Hatchback Sedan			1,153,000
361	Sunny 1500 California SGX 4+1-dr Hatchback Sedan			1,207,000
361	Sunny 1500 SGX-E 4-dr Sedan			1,214,000
361	Sunny Turbo Le Prix 2+1-dr Hatchback Sedan			1,378,000
361	Sunny Turbo Le Prix 4-dr Sedan			1,384,000
361	Sunny 1700 Diesel GL 4-dr Sedan		6,749*	1,086,000
361	Sunny 1700 Diesel SGL 4-dr Sedan			1,184,000
361	Sunny 1700 Diesel California GL-L 4+1-dr Hatchback Sedan			1,197,000
362	Langley D 2+1-dr Hatchback Sedan			937,000
362	Langley D 4+1-dr Hatchback Sedan			1,023,000
362	Langley L 2+1-dr Hatchback Sedan			1,105,000
362	Langley L 4+1-dr Hatchback Sedan			957,000
362	Langley X 2+1-dr Hatchback Sedan			1,043,000
362	Langley X 4+1-dr Hatchback Sedan			1,140,000
362	Langley GT 2+1-dr Hatchback Sedan			1,237,000
362	Langley GT 4+1-dr Hatchback Sedan			1,227,000
362	Langley Turbo GT 2+1-dr Hatchback Sedan			1,407,000
362	Langley Turbo GT 4+1-dr Hatchback Sedan			1,397,000
362	Langley Diesel L-D 4+1-dr Hatchback Sedan			1,164,000
363	Prairie 1500 JW 4+1-dr St. Wagon	6,000*		1,190,000
363	Prairie 1800 JW 4+1-dr St. Wagon			1,293,000
363	Prairie 1800 JW-G 4+1-dr St. Wagon			1,410,000
363	Prairie 1800 RV 4+1-dr St. Wagon			1,265,000
363	Prairie 1800 RV-S 4+1-dr St. Wagon			1,345,000
363	Prairie 1800 SS-G 4+1-dr St. Wagon			1,385,000
364	Liberta Villa 1500 FC 4-dr Sedan			958,000
364	Liberta Villa 1500 FL 4-dr Sedan			1,055,000
364	Liberta Villa 1500 GF 4-dr Sedan			1,147,000
364	Liberta Villa 1500 GF-E 4-dr Sedan			1,239,000
364	Liberta Villa 1500 SSS Turbo 4-dr Sedan			1,409,000
364	Liberta Villa 1700 Diesel FL-D 4-dr Sedan			1,176,000

Page	MAKE AND MODEL	Price in GB £	Price in USA $	Price ex Works
364	Laurel Spirit 1500 LT 4-dr Sedan			991,000
364	Laurel Spirit 1500 LT-G 4-dr Sedan			1,024,000
364	Laurel Spirit 1500 LF 4-dr Sedan			1,099,000
364	Laurel Spirit 1500 XJ 4-dr Sedan			1,189,000
364	Laurel Spirit 1500 XJ-E 4-dr Sedan			1,247,000
364	Laurel Spirit 1500 Turbo XJ 4-dr Sedan			1,407,000
365	Stanza 1600 LE 4-dr Sedan	5,829*		1,017,000
365	Stanza 1600 LX 4-dr Sedan			1,073,000
365	Stanza 1600 LX-G 4-dr Sedan	5,995*		1,231,000
365	Auster 1600 LE 4-dr Sedan			1,028,000
365	Auster 1600 GS 4-dr Sedan			1,089,000
365	Auster 1600 GS-X 4-dr Sedan			1,240,000
365	Stanza 1600 LX-G 2+1-dr Hatchback Sedan	5,819*	8,299*	1,275,000
365	Auster 1600 GS-X 2+1-dr Hatchback Sedan	6,191*		1,279,000
365	Stanza 1800 LX 4-dr Sedan	6,695*		1,168,000
365	Stanza 1800 SGX 4-dr Sedan		8,499*	1,346,000
365	Auster 1800 GS-L 4-dr Sedan			1,198,000
365	Auster 1800 GS-X 2+1-dr Hatchback Sedan			1,390,000
365	Auster 1800 GS-X 4-dr Sedan			1,350,000
365	Stanza 1800 RX 2+1-dr Hatchback Sedan			1,345,000
365	Stanza 1800 RX 4-dr Sedan		9,099*	1,303,000
365	Stanza 1800 Z-EX 4-dr Sedan			1,571,000
365	Auster 1800 GF-EX 2+1-dr Hatchback Sedan			1,616,000
365	Auster 1800 GT-EX 4-dr Sedan			1,571,000
366	Bluebird 1600 L 4-dr Sedan			1,040,000
366	Bluebird 1600 LX 4-dr Sedan			1,136,000
366	Bluebird 1600 LX-L 4-dr Sedan			1,232,000
366	Bluebird 1800 LX 4-dr Sedan	5,991*		1,201,000
366	Bluebird 1800 SLX 4-dr Sedan			1,352,000
366	Bluebird 1800 SSS 4-dr Sedan			1,360,000
366	Bluebird 1800 SLX-G 4-dr Hardtop			1,466,000
366	Bluebird 1800 SSS 4-dr Hardtop			1,425,000
366	Bluebird 1800 LX 4+1-dr St. Wagon	6,395*		1,318,000
366	Bluebird 1800 SSS-E 4-dr Sedan			1,470,000
366	Bluebird 1800 SSS-EX 4-dr Sedan			1,696,000
366	Bluebird 1800 Turbo SSS 4-dr Sedan			1,628,000
366	Bluebird 1800 Turbo SSS-S 4-dr Sedan			1,716,000
366	Bluebird 1800 Turbo SSS-X 4-dr Sedan			1,871,000
366	Bluebird 1800 Turbo SSS 4-dr Hardtop			1,693,000
366	Bluebird 1800 Turbo SSS-S 4-dr Hardtop			1,781,000
366	Bluebird 1800 Turbo SSS-X 4-dr Hardtop			1,936,000
366	Bluebird 1800 Turbo SSS-XG 4-dr Hardtop			2,186,000
366	Bluebird 1800 Turbo SSS 4+1-dr St. Wagon			1,688,000
366	Bluebird 2000 SLX-G 4-dr Sedan			1,718,000
366	Bluebird 2000 SLX-G 4-dr Hardtop			1,783,000
366	Bluebird 2000 Diesel LX 4-dr Sedan			1,368,000
367	Leopard 1800 GX 4-dr Hardtop			1,484,000
367	Leopard 1800 SGX 4-dr Hardtop			1,656,000
367	Leopard 2000 XGX 4-dr Hardtop			1,689,000
367	Leopard 2000 XSGX 4-dr Hardtop			1,896,000
367	Leopard 2000 XZGX 2-dr Hardtop			2,347,000
367	Leopard 2000 XZGX 4-dr Hardtop			2,347,000
367	Leopard Turbo GX 2-dr Hardtop			1,845,000
367	Leopard Turbo GX 4-dr Hardtop			1,845,000
367	Leopard Turbo SGX 2-dr Hardtop			2,077,000
367	Leopard Turbo SGX 4-dr Hardtop			2,077,000
367	Leopard Turbo ZGX 2-dr Hardtop			2,535,000
367	Leopard Turbo ZGX 4-dr Hardtop			2,535,000
367	Leopard Turbo ZGX Super Edition 2-dr Hardtop			2,759,000
367	Leopard Turbo ZGX Super Edition 4-dr Hardtop			2,759,000
368	Silvia 1800 R-L 2-dr Coupé			1,330,000
368	Silvia 1800 R-X 2-dr Coupé			1,420,000
368	Gazelle 1800 R-X 2-dr Coupé			1,420,000
368	Silvia 1800 R-X 2-dr Hatchback Coupé			1,500,000
368	Gazelle 1800 R-X 2+1-dr Hatchback Coupé			1,500,000
368	Silvia 1800 R-XE 2-dr Coupé			1,611,000
368	Gazelle 1800 R-XE 2-dr Coupé			1,611,000
368	Silvia 1800 R-XE 2+1-dr Hatchback Coupé			1,690,000
368	Gazelle 1800 R-XE 2+1-dr Hatchback Coupé			1,690,000
368	Silvia 1800 Turbo R-L 2-dr Coupé			1,690,000
368	Silvia 1800 Turbo R-X 2-dr Coupé			1,890,000
368	Silvia 1800 Turbo R-XG 2-dr Coupé			2,140,000
368	Gazelle 1800 Turbo R-X 2-dr Coupé			1,890,000

Page	MAKE AND MODEL	Price in GB £	Price in USA $	Price ex Works
368	Gazelle 1800 Turbo R-XG 2-dr Coupé			2,360,000
368	Silvia 1800 Turbo R-L 2+1-dr Hatchback Coupé			1,770,000
368	Silvia 1800 Turbo R-X 2+1-dr Hatchback Coupé			1,970,000
368	Silvia 1800 Turbo R-XG 2+1-dr Hatchback Coupé			2,100,000
368	Gazelle 1800 Turbo R-X 2+1-dr Hatchback Coupé			1,970,000
368	Gazelle 1800 Turbo R-XG 2+1-dr Hatchback Coupé			2,320,000
368	Silvia 2000 RS-X 2-dr Coupé			2,240,000
368	Silvia 2000 RS-X 2+1-dr Hatchback Coupé			2,323,000
368	Silvia 2000 Turbo RS-X 2-dr Coupé			2,540,000
361	Gazelle 2000 Turbo RS-X 2-dr Coupé			2,540,000
368	Silvia 2000 Turbo RS-X 2+1-dr Hatchback Coupé			2,520,000
368	Gazelle 2000 Turbo RS-X 2+1-dr Hatchback Coupé			2,520,000
368	Skyline 1800 TL 4-dr Sedan			1,161,000
368	Skyline 1800 TI-L 2-dr Sedan			1,284,000
368	Skyline 1800 TI-L Extra 4-dr Sedan			1,361,000
368	Skyline 1800 TI-L Extra 4+1-dr Hatchback Sedan			1,449,000
368	Skyline 1800 TI-EL 4-dr Sedan			1,448,000
368	Skyline 1800 TI-EX 4-dr Sedan			1,546,000
368	Skyline 2000 GT-EL 4-dr Sedan			1,555,000
368	Skyline 2000 GT-EX 2-dr Hardtop			1,771,000
368	Skyline 2000 GT-EX 4-dr Sedan			1,716,000
368	Skyline 2000 GT-EX 4+1-dr Hatchback Sedan			1,826,000
368	Skyline 2000 Turbo GT-E 4-dr Sedan			1,685,000
368	Skyline 2000 Turbo GT-EL 2-dr Hardtop			1,806,000
368	Skyline 2000 Turbo GT-EX 4-dr Sedan			1,751,000
368	Skyline 2000 Turbo GT-EX 2-dr Hardtop			1,952,000
368	Skyline 2000 Turbo GT-EX 2-dr Sedan			1,897,000
368	Skyline 2000 RS4 2-dr Hardtop			2,176,000
368	Skyline 2000 RS 4-dr Sedan			2,121,000
368	Skyline 2000 Turbo RS 2-dr Hardtop			2,426,000
368	Skyline 2000 Turbo RS-X 2-dr Hardtop			2,691,000
368	Skyline 2000 Turbo RS 4-dr Sedan			2,371,000
368	Skyline 2000 Turbo RS-X 4-dr Sedan			2,636,000
368	Skyline 280 D GT-L Diesel 4-dr Sedan			1,640,000
368	Skyline 280 D GT-X Diesel 4-dr Sedan			1,802,000
370	Laurel 1800 STD 4-dr Sedan			1,151,000
370	Laurel 1800 GL 4-dr Sedan			1,276,000
370	Laurel 1800 GL 4-dr Hardtop			1,363,000
370	Laurel 1800 SGL 4-dr Sedan			1,442,000
370	Laurel 1800 SGL 4-dr Hardtop			1,517,000
370	Laurel 2000 GL 4-dr Sedan	6,990*		1,341,000
370	Laurel 2000 GL 4-dr Hardtop	6,394*		1,409,000
370	Laurel 2000 SGL 4-dr Sedan			1,479,000
370	Laurel 2000 SGL 4-dr Hardtop			1,547,000
370	Laurel 2000 GL 4-dr Sedan			1,564,000
370	Laurel 2000 GL 4-dr Hardtop			1,681,000
370	Laurel 2000 SGL 4-dr Sedan			1,689,000
370	Laurel 2000 SGL 4-dr Hardtop			1,796,000
370	Laurel 2000 Medalist 4-dr Sedan			2,048,000
370	Laurel 2000 Medalist 4-dr Hardtop			2,180,000
370	Laurel 2000 Turbo GX 4-dr Sedan			1,785,000
370	Laurel 2000 Turbo GX 4-dr Hardtop			1,861,000
370	Laurel 2000 Turbo SGX 4-dr Sedan			1,895,000
370	Laurel 2000 Turbo SGX 4-dr Hardtop			1,974,000
370	Laurel 2000 Turbo Medalist 4-dr Sedan			2,285,000
370	Laurel 2000 Turbo Medalist 4-dr Hardtop			2,360,000
370	Laurel 2000 Diesel STD 4-dr Sedan			1,256,000
370	Laurel 2000 Diesel GL 4-dr Sedan			1,418,000
370	Laurel 2800 Diesel VL-6 4-dr Sedan			1,633,000
370	Laurel 2800 Diesel VL-6 4-dr Hardtop			1,709,000
370	Laurel 2800 Diesel VX-6 4-dr Sedan			1,756,000
370	Laurel 2800 Diesel VX-6 4-dr Hardtop			1,833,000
371	Cedric 2000 STD 4-dr Sedan			1,312,000
371	Cedric 2000 De Luxe 4-dr Sedan			1,438,000
371	Cedric 2000 V20E Custom De Luxe 4-dr Sedan			1,769,000
371	Cedric 2000 V20E GL 4-dr Sedan			2,027,000
371	Cedric 2000 V20E SGL 4-dr Sedan			2,506,000
371	Cedric 2000 V20E Custom 4-dr Hardtop			1,941,000
371	Cedric 2000 V20E GL 4-dr Hardtop			2,391,000
371	Cedric 2000 V20E SGL 4-dr Hardtop			2,684,000
371	Cedric 2000 V20E De Luxe 4+1-dr St. Wagon			1,822,000
371	Cedric 2000 V20E GL 4+1-dr St. Wagon			2,098,000
371	Cedric 2000 V20 Turbo SGL 4-dr Sedan			2,850,000
371	Cedric 2000 V20 Turbo Brougham 4-dr Sedan			3,080,000
371	Cedric 2000 V20 Turbo S 4-dr Sedan			2,516,000
371	Cedric 2000 V20 Turbo SGL 4-dr Sedan			2,894,000
371	Cedric 2000 V20 Turbo F 4-dr Sedan			3,018,000
371	Cedric 2000 V20 Turbo Brougham 4-dr Hardtop			3,242,000
371	Cedric 3000 V30 Brougham 4-dr Sedan			3,263,000
371	Cedric 3000 V30 Brougham 4-dr Hardtop			3,415,000
371	Gloria 2800 Diesel 28 D-6 4-dr Sedan	9,721*		1,447,000
371	Gloria 2800 Diesel 28 D-6 De Luxe 4-dr Sedan			1,674,000
371	Gloria 2800 Diesel 28 D-6 GL 4-dr Sedan			2,059,000
371	Gloria 2800 Diesel 28 D-6 SGL 4-dr Sedan			2,722,000
371	Gloria 2800 Diesel 28 D-6 Custom S 4-dr Hardtop			1,938,000
371	Gloria 2800 Diesel 28 D-6 GL 4-dr Hardtop			2,221,000
371	Gloria 2800 Diesel 28 D-6 SGL 4-dr Hardtop			2,895,000
371	Gloria 2800 Diesel 28 D-6 Custom De Luxe 4+1-dr St. Wagon	9,361*		2,026,000
372	Fairlady 2000 Z 2-seater 2+1-dr Coupé		15,799*	1,950,000
372	Fairlady 2000 Z S 2-seater 2+1-dr Coupé			2,186,000
372	Fairlady 2000 ZG 2-seater 2+1-dr Coupé			2,375,000
372	Fairlady 2000 Z 2+2-seater 2+1-dr Coupé	11,617*	16,999*	2,030,000
372	Fairlady 2000 ZS 2+2-seater 2+1-dr Coupé			2,266,000
372	Fairlady 2000 ZG 2+2-seater 2+1-dr Coupé			2,455,000
372	Fairlady 3000 ZX 2-seater 2+1-dr Coupé		18,199*	3,200,000
372	Fairlady 3000 ZX 2+2-seater 2+1-dr Coupé			3,270,000
373	President C 4-dr Sedan			4,513,000
373	President D 4-dr Sedan			5,072,000
373	President Sovereign 4-dr Sedan			5,743,000
373	Safari Standard roof 2+1-dr St. Wagon	8,515*		1,684,000
373	Safari Standard roof AD 2+1-dr St. Wagon			2,175,000
373	Safari High roof AD 2+1-dr St. Wagon	9,315*		2,121,000
373	Safari Long Van DX 2+1-dr St. Wagon	9,627*		2,068,000
373	Safari Long Van AD 2+1-dr St. Wagon	10,368*		2,302,000
373	Safari Long Van High roof AD 2+1-dr St. Wagon			2,348,000
373	Safari Standard roof Turbo AD 2+1-dr St. Wagon			2,265,000
373	Safari Long Van Turbo AD 2+1-dr St. Wagon			2,516,000
	NOVA (Great Britain)			
176	Sports			4,300
	NUOVA INNOCENTI (Italy)			
221	3 Cilindri S 2+1-dr Berlina			7,069,000◊
221	3 Cilindri SL 2+1-dr Berlina			7,629,000◊
221	3 Cilindri SE 2+1-dr Berlina			8,261,000◊
222	Turbo De Tomaso			10,200,000◊
	OB & D (Great Britain)			
176	Madison Special			8,951*
	OLDSMOBILE (USA)			
301	Firenza 4-dr Sedan			7,301
301	Firenza S 2-dr Coupé			7,214
301	Firenza SX 2-dr Coupé			7,957
301	Firenza LX 4-dr Sedan			7,853
301	Firenza Cruiser 4+1-dr St. Wagon			7,521
301	Firenza Cruiser LX 4+1-dr St. Wagon			8,073
301	Omega 4-dr Sedan			7,832
301	Omega 2-dr Coupé			7,634
301	Omega Brougham 4-dr Sedan			8,104
301	Omega Brougham 2-dr Coupé			7,923
302	Cutlass Ciera LS 4-dr Sedan			9,203
302	Cutlass Ciera LS 2-dr Coupé			9,014
302	Cutlass Ciera Brougham 4-dr Sedan			9,721
302	Cutlass Ciera Brougham 2-dr Coupé			9,519
302	Cutlass Ciera Cruiser 4+1-dr St. Wagon			9,551
303	Cutlass Supreme 4-dr Sedan			9,529

Page	MAKE AND MODEL	Price in GB £	Price in USA $	Price ex Works
303	Cutlass Supreme 2-dr Coupé			9,376
303	Cutlass Supreme Brougham 4-dr Sedan			10,145
303	Cutlass Supreme Brougham 2-dr Coupé			10,015
303	Cutlass Calais 2-dr Coupé			10,274
304	Delta 88 Royale 4-dr Sedan			10,051
304	Delta 88 Royale 2-dr Coupé			9,939
304	Delta 88 Royale Brougham 4-dr Sedan			10,499
304	Delta 88 Royale Brougham 2-dr Coupé			10,408
304	Ninety-Eight Regency 4-dr Sedan			14,151
304	Ninety-Eight Regency 2-dr Coupé			13,974
304	Ninety-Eight Regency Brougham 4-dr Sedan			15,201
304	Custom Cruiser 4+1-dr St. Wagon			10,839
305	Toronado			16,107
	OLTCIT (Romania)			
226	Special			—
227	Club			—
	OPEL (Germany FR)			
131	Corsa 2+1-dr Limousine			11,975*
131	Corsa TR 2-dr Limousine			12,595*
131	Corsa Luxus 2+1-dr Limousine			13,140*
131	Corsa TR Luxus 2-dr Limousine			13,760*
131	Corsa Berlina 2+1-dr Limousine			14,135*
131	Corsa TR Berlina 2-dr Limousine			14,595*
131	Corsa SR 2+1-dr Limousine			15,290*
132	Kadett 2+1-dr Limousine			13,550*
132	Kadett 4+1-dr Limousine			14,260*
132	Kadett Luxus 2+1-dr Limousine			14,630*
132	Kadett Luxus 4+1-dr Limousine			15,340*
132	Kadett Berlina 2+1-dr Limousine			15,890*
132	Kadett Berlina 4+1-dr Limousine			16,600*
132	Kadett 2+1-dr Caravan			14,745*
132	Kadett 4+1-dr Caravan			15,455*
132	Kadett Luxus 2+1-dr Caravan			15,705*
132	Kadett Luxus 4+1-dr Caravan			16,415*
132	Kadett Voyage 2+1-dr Caravan			16,835*
132	Kadett Voyage 4+1-dr Caravan			17,545*
132	Kadett Voyage Berlina 4+1-dr Caravan			18,550*
133	Kadett 1.3 SR 2+1-dr Limousine			17,290*
133	Kadett 1.3 SR 4+1-dr Limousine			18,000*
134	Kadett 1.6 SR 2+1-dr Limousine			18,015*
134	Kadett 1.6 SR 4+1-dr Limousine			18,725*
134	Kadett GTE 2+1-dr Limousine			20,825*
134	Kadett GTE 4+1-dr Limousine			21,535*
134	Ascona 2-dr Limousine			15,725*
134	Ascona 4-dr Limousine			16,430*
134	Ascona 4+1-dr Limousine			16,985*
134	Ascona Luxus 2-dr Limousine			16,710*
134	Ascona Luxus 4-dr Limousine			17,415*
134	Ascona Luxus 4+1-dr Limousine			17,970*
134	Ascona Berlina 2-dr Limousine			18,060*
134	Ascona Berlina 4-dr Limousine			18,595*
134	Ascona Berlina 4+1-dr Limousine			19,660*
134	Ascona SR 2-dr Limousine			20,265*
134	Ascona SR 4-dr Limousine			20,970*
134	Ascona SR 4+1-dr Limousine			21,720*
134	Ascona SR/E 2-dr Limousine			21,680*
134	Ascona SR/E 4-dr Limousine			22,385*
134	Ascona SR/E 4+1-dr Limousine			23,135*
134	Ascona CD 4-dr Limousine			23,720*
134	Ascona CD 4+1-dr Limousine			24,770*
136	Manta GT 2-dr Coupé			17,765*
136	Manta CC GT 2+1-dr Hatchback Coupé			18,225*
136	Manta GT/E 2-dr Coupé	6,794*		21,370*
136	Manta CC GT/E 2+1-dr Hatchback Coupé	7,005*		21,985*
136	Rekord 4-dr Limousine			19,740*
136	Rekord Luxus 4-dr Limousine			20,595*
136	Rekord Berlina 4-dr Limousine			21,725*
136	Rekord CD 4-dr Limousine			26,135*
136	Rekord 2+1-dr Caravan			20,050*
136	Rekord 4+1-dr Caravan			20,810*
136	Rekord Luxus 4+1-dr Caravan			21,665*
136	Rekord Berlina 4+1-dr Caravan			23,530*
136	Rekord CD 4+1-dr Caravan			27,597*
138	Senator 4-dr Limousine			28,250*
138	Senator C 4-dr Limousine			31,025*
138	Senator CD Automatic 4-dr Limousine	13,994*		49,465*
138	Monza 2+1-dr Hatchback Coupé			29,770*

Page	MAKE AND MODEL	Price in GB £	Price in USA $	Price ex Works
138	Monza C 2+1-dr Hatchback Coupé			32,930*
138	Monza GSE 2+1-dr Hatchback Coupé	13,501*		43,440*
	OPEL (South Africa)			
327	Kadett 1.2 4-dr Sedan			7,455*
327	Kadett GL 1.3 4+1-dr Sedan			8,150*
327	Kadett Voyage 1.3 4+1-dr St. Wagon			8,925*
327	Kadett GLS 1.6 4+1-dr Sedan			9,140*
327	Kadett SR 1.6 4+1-dr Sedan			9,360*
327	Kadett Berlina 1.6 4+1-dr Sedan			9,645*
327	Kadett Voyage 1.6 4+1-dr St. Wagon			9,395*
328	Ascona GL 4-dr Sedan			9,850*
328	Ascona GLS 4-dr Sedan			10,570*
328	Rekord L 2.0 4-dr Sedan			10,660*
328	Rekord GL 2.0 4-dr Sedan			11,140*
328	Rekord Berlina S 2.0 4-dr Sedan			12,555*
328	Rekord S 2.0 4-dr St. Wagon			11,375*
328	Commodore L Automatic 4-dr Sedan			12,765*
328	Commodore GL 4-dr Sedan			15,245*
328	Commodore GL Automatic 4-dr Sedan			15,495*
329	Senator			25,500*
	OTOSAN (Turkey)			
318	Anadol 16			1,075,000
	PANTHER (Great Britain)			
176	Kallista 1.6			6,945*
177	Kallista 2.8			7,485*
177	Kallista 2.8 Injection			8,985*
	PAYKAN (Iran)			
329	Low Line			—
329	High Line			—
	PEUGEOT (France)			
84	104 GL 4+1-dr Berline	3,795*	—	39,759◊
84	104 Z 2+1-dr Coupé	3,845*	—	35,850◊
84	104 ZS 80 CV 2+1-dr Coupé	—	—	49,850◊
84	205 Standard 4+1-dr Berline	3,895*	—	39,800◊
84	205 GL 4+1-dr Berline (954 cc)	—	—	42,700◊
84	205 GL 4+1-dr Berline (1,124 cc)	4,395*	—	44,600◊
84	205 GR 4+1-dr Berline (1,124 cc)	—	—	47,300◊
84	205 GR 4+1-dr Berline (1,360 cc)	4,995*	—	49,500◊
84	205 SR 4+1-dr Berline	—	—	51,700◊
84	205 GT 4+1-dr Berline	5,395*	—	54,800◊
84	205 GTI 2+1-dr Berline	—	—	—
84	205 GTI 4+1-dr Berline	—	—	—
84	205 GLD 4+1-dr Berline	4,745*	—	51,500◊
84	205 GRD 4+1-dr Berline	5,345*	—	56,400◊
84	205 SRD 4+1-dr Berline	—	—	59,800◊
85	305 Standard 4-dr Berline	—	—	46,600◊
85	305 GL 4-dr Berline	5,095*	—	52,700◊
85	305 GR 4-dr Berline	5,445*	—	55,900◊
85	305 SR 4-dr Berline	5,695*	—	58,200◊
85	305 GT 4-dr Berline	6,145*	—	63,100◊
85	305 GLD 4-dr Berline	5,495*	—	61,800◊
85	305 SRD 4-dr Berline	—	—	68,000◊
87	305 GL 4+1-dr Break	5,495*	—	55,800◊
87	305 SR 4+1-dr Break	6,245*	—	63,800◊
87	305 GLD 4+1-dr Break	5,895*	—	64,800◊
87	305 SRD 4+1-dr Break	—	—	73,500◊
87	505 GL 4-dr Berline	6,995*	11,300*	63,400◊
87	505 GR 4-dr Berline	7,995*	—	69,400◊
87	505 SR 4-dr Berline	8,095*	14,845*	77,500◊
87	505 GTI 4-dr Berline	9,595*	15,800*	86,800◊
87	505 Turbo Injection (150 hp) 4-dr Berline	—	—	104,100◊
87	505 Turbo Injectio (160 hp) 4-dr Berline	—	—	—
87	505 GLD 4-dr Berline	7,745*	12,800*	72,700◊
87	505 GRD Turbo 4-dr Berline	9,095*	—	78,700◊
87	505 SRD Turbo 4-dr Berline	9,295*	16,345*	92,500◊
87	505 GTD Turbo 4-dr Berline	—	17,300*	97,600◊
89	505 GL 4+1-dr Break	7,745*	11,990*	68,200◊
89	505 GR 4+1-dr Break	8,795*	—	74,100◊
89	505 SR 4+1-dr Break	—	16,095*	83,600◊
89	505 GR 4+1-dr Familial	8,995*	—	82,500◊
89	505 SR 4+1-dr Familial	—	—	91,400◊
89	505 GLD 4+1-dr Break	8,495*	13,860*	77,500◊
89	505 GRD 4+1-dr Break	9,335*	—	84,800◊

Page	MAKE AND MODEL	Price in GB £	Price in USA $	Price ex Works
89	505 SRD 4+1-dr Break	—	17,965*	92,900◊
89	505 GRD 4+1-dr Familial	9,795*	—	93,200◊
89	505 SRD 4+1-dr Familial	—	—	100,700◊
90	604 GTI 4-dr Berline	12,395*	—	111,000◊
90	604 GTD Turbo 4-dr Berline	11,395*	21,285*	117,800◊
	PEUGEOT (Nigeria)			
320	504 GR			—
320	504 SR			—
320	504 Station Wagon			—
320	505 GL			—
321	505 SL			—
	PHILLIPS (USA)			
305	Berlina I 2-dr Coupé			59,500*
305	Berline S.E. 2-dr Coupé			64,500*
	PININFARINA (Italy)			
222	Spidereuropa		16,000*	16,300,000◊
222	Spidereuropa Volumex		—	22,000,000◊
	PLYMOUTH (USA)			
305	Horizon 4+1-dr Hatchback Sedan			5,830
305	Horizon SE 4+1-dr Hatchback Sedan			6,148
305	Turismo 2+1-dr Hatchback Coupé			6,594
305	Turismo 2.2 2+1-dr Hatchback Coupé			7,288
306	Reliant 2-dr Sedan			6,837
306	Reliant 4-dr Sedan			6,949
306	Reliant Custom 4+1-dr St. Wagon			7,736
306	Reliant SE 2-dr Sedan			7,463
306	Reliant SE 4-dr Sedan			7,589
306	Reliant SE 4+1-dr St. Wagon			8,195
307	Gran Fury			9,180
307	Voyager			8,669
	PONTIAC (Canada)			
266	Acadian Scooter 4+1-dr Hatchback Sedan			6,074
266	Acadian Scooter 2+1-dr Hatchback Coupé			5,812
266	Acadian 4+1-dr Hatchback Sedan			6,583
266	Acadian 2+1-dr Hatchback Coupé			6,400
	PONTIAC (USA)			
308	1000 4+1-dr Hatchback Sedan			5,824
308	1000 2+1-dr Hatchback Coupé			5,621
308	2000 Sunbird 4-dr Notchback Sedan			6,799
308	2000 Sunbird 2+1-dr Hatchback Coupé			6,995
308	2000 Sunbird 2-dr Notchback Coupé			6,675
308	2000 Sunbird 4+1-dr St. Wagon			7,115
308	2000 Sunbird LE 4-dr Notchback Sedan			7,499
308	2000 Sunbird LE 2-dr Notchback Coupé			7,333
308	2000 Sunbird LE 2-dr Convertible			11,749
308	2000 Sunbird LE 4+1-dr St. Wagon			7,819
308	2000 Sunbird SE 4-dr Notchback Sedan			9,185
308	2000 Sunbird SE 2+1-dr Hatchback Coupé			9,489
308	2000 Sunbird 2-dr Notchback Coupé			9,019
309	Fiero 2-dr Coupé			8,499
309	Fiero SE 2-dr Coupé			8,599
309	Phoenix 4+1-dr Hatchback Sedan			7,165
309	Phoenix 2-dr Notchback Coupé			7,090
309	Phoenix LE 4+1-dr Hatchback Sedan			7,816
309	Phoenix LE 2-dr Notchback Coupé			7,683
309	Phoenix SE 2-dr Notchback Coupé			9,071
310	6000 4-dr Notchback Sedan			8,873
310	6000 2-dr Notchback Coupé			8,699
310	6000 4+1-dr St. Wagon			9,221
310	6000 LE 4-dr Notchback Sedan			9,292
310	6000 LE 2-dr Notchback Coupé			9,142
310	6000 LE 4+1-dr St. Wagon			9,612
310	6000 STE 4-dr Notchback Sedan			14,437
310	Firebird 2-dr Hatchback Coupé			8,349
310	Firebird SE 2-dr Hatchback Coupé			10,649
310	Firebird Trans Am 2-dr Hatchback Coupé			10,699
311	Grand Prix 2-dr Notchback Coupé			9,145
311	Grand Prix LE 2-dr Notchback Coupé			9,624
311	Grand Prix Brougham 2-dr Notchback Coupé			10,299
312	Bonneville 4-dr Notchback Sedan			9,131

Page	MAKE AND MODEL	Price in GB £	Price in USA $	Price ex Works
312	Bonneville LE 4-dr Notchback Sedan			9,358
312	Bonneville Brougham 4-dr Notchback Sedan			9,835
313	Parisienne 4-dr Sedan			9,881
313	Parisienne 4+1-dr St. Wagon			10,394
313	Parisienne Brougham 4-dr Sedan			10,281
	PORSCHE (Germany FR)			
139	924	10,880*	—	33,250*
139	944	15,309*	—	43,950*
140	944 (USA)	—	21,440*	—
140	911 Carrera Coupé	21,464*	—	63,950*
140	911 SC Coupé (USA)	—	31,950*	—
140	911 Carrera Targa	21,464*	33,450*	67,050*
140	911 Carrera Cabriolet	24,340*	36,450*	71,200*
140	911 Turbo	33,878*	—	105,300*
141	928 S	30,679*	—	87,650*
141	928 S (USA)	—	44,000*	—
	PORTARO (Portugal)			
225	260 DCM 2+1-dr St. Wagon			827,900
225	260 Celta 2+1-dr St. Wagon			969,600
225	260 Celta Turbo			1,050,900
	PREMIER (India)			
330	Padmini			58,474
331	Padmini De Luxe			66,943
	PUMA (Brazil)			
261	GTI 1.6 E 2-dr Coupé			3,719,000*
261	GTC 1.6 E 2-dr Convertible			4,019,000*
261	GTB S2 Sport 2+2			6,968,000*
	QT (Brazil)			
262	Jeg TL 4x4			—
	RELIANT (Great Britain)			
177	Rialto 2-dr Saloon			3,335*
177	Rialto 2+1-dr Saloon			3,535*
177	Rialto GLS 2-dr Saloon			3,635*
177	Rialto GLS 2+1-dr Saloon			3,835*
177	Fox			3,250*
178	Scimitar GTC 2-dr Convertible			11,990*
178	Scimitar GTE 2+1-dr Estate Car			11,990*
	RENAULT (Argentina)			
249	4			—
249	6 GTL			—
250	12 TL			—
250	12 TS Break			—
250	18 GTL Sedan			—
250	18 GTX Sedan			—
250	18 GTX Break			—
250	Fuego GTX			—
	RENAULT (France)			
91	4 4+1-dr Break	—		30,088◊
91	4 TL 4+1-dr Break	—		33,188◊
91	4 GTL 4+1-dr Break	3,425*		36,288◊
91	5 2+1-dr Berline	3,290*		35,088◊
91	5 4+1-dr Berline	—		36,988◊
91	5 TL 2+1-dr Berline	3,995*		40,188◊
91	5 TL 4+1-dr Berline	—		42,088◊
91	5 GTL 2+1-dr Berline	4,350*		45,188◊
91	5 GTL 4+1-dr Berline	4,510*		47,088◊
91	5 Automatic 2+1-dr Berline	4,950*		48,860◊
91	5 Automatic 4+1-dr Berline	—		50,760◊
91	5 TS 2+1-dr Berline	—		47,892◊
91	5 TX 2+1-dr Berline	5,250*		55,092◊
91	5 TX Automatic 2+1-dr Berline	—		57,060◊
91	5 Alpine Turbo 2+1-dr Berline	5,950*		64,524◊
93	Rodeo 5	—		39,197◊
93	5 Turbo 2	—		102,492◊
93	9 C 4-dr Berline	—		45,460◊
93	9 TC 4-dr Berline	4,495*		48,060◊

Page	MAKE AND MODEL	Price in GB £	Price in USA $	Price ex Works
93	9 TL 4-dr Berline	—		49,524◊
93	9 GTL 4-dr Berline	4,995*		52,924◊
93	9 Automatic 4-dr Berline	5,595*		57,692◊
93	9 GTS 4-dr Berline	—		57,524◊
93	9 TSE 4-dr Berline	5,565*		59,624◊
93	9 TD 4-dr Berline	5,195*		54,860◊
93	9 GTD 4-dr Berline	—		59,060◊
93	9 TDE 4-dr Berline	—		64,760◊
94	11 TC 2+1-dr Berline	4,350*		47,060◊
94	11 GTC 4+1-dr Berline	—		52,660◊
94	11 TL 4+1-dr Berline	—		51,024◊
94	11 GTL 2+1-dr Berline	4,900*		55,024◊
94	11 GTL 4+1-dr Berline	5,070*		—
94	11 Automatic 4+1-dr Berline	5,870*		60,392◊
94	11 Automatic Electronic 4+1-dr Berline	—		71,292◊
94	11 GTS 4+1-dr Berline	—		56,824◊
94	11 TSE 4+1-dr Berline	5,975*		63,024◊
94	11 TSE Electronic 4+1-dr Berline	—		68,924◊
94	11 GTX 2+1-dr Berline	—		—
94	11 TXE 2+1-dr Berline	5,900*		—
94	11 TXE Electronic 2+1-dr Berline	—		—
96	18 4-dr Berline	—		47,024◊
96	18 4+1-dr Break	—		51,492◊
96	18 TL 4-dr Berline	4,870*		52,892◊
96	18 TL 4+1-dr Break	5,550*		57,392◊
96	18 GTL 4-dr Berline	5,700*		57,024◊
96	18 GTL 4+1-dr Break	6,100*		61,524◊
96	18 GTL 4x4 4+1-dr Break	—		76,000◊
96	18 GTX 4-dr Berline	6,890*		66,500◊
96	18 GTX 4+1-dr Break	7,390*		71,200◊
96	18 Automatic 4-dr Berline	6,010*		67,620◊
96	18 TD 4-dr Berline	5,575*		62,424◊
96	18 TD 4+1-dr Break	6,470*		66,924◊
96	18 GTD 4-dr Berline	—		68,392◊
96	18 GTD 4+1-dr Break	—		72,892◊
96	18 GTD 4x4 4+1-dr Break	—		87,400◊
97	18 Turbo 4-dr Berline	7,750*		78,324◊
97	18 Turbo 4+1-dr Break	—		83,024◊
97	Fuego TL 2+1-dr Coupé	5,350*		56,892◊
97	Fuego GTL 2+1-dr Coupé	—		66,924◊
97	Fuego GTS 2+1-dr Coupé	6,550*		69,756◊
97	Fuego Turbo 2+1-dr Coupé	8,700*		—
97	Fuego Turbo D 2+1-dr Coupé	—		93,992◊
98	25 TS 4+1-dr Berline	—		—
98	25 GTS 4+1-dr Berline	—		—
98	25 GTX 4+1-dr Berline	—		—
98	25 V6 Injection 4+1-dr Berline	—		—
98	25 TD 4+1-dr Berline	—		—
98	25 GTD 4+1-dr Berline	—		—
98	25 Turbo D 4+1-dr Berline	—		—
98	25 Turbo DX 4+1-dr Berline	—		—
	ROLLS-ROYCE (Great Britain)			
178	Silver Spirit		98,500*	55,240*
179	Silver Spur		109,000*	62,778*
179	Silver Spur with division		—	68,278*
179	Corniche		156,000*	73,168*
179	Camargue		150,600*	83,122*
180	Phantom VI		—	—
	ROVER (Great Britain)			
180	3500 SE 4+1-dr Saloon			12,747*
180	Vanden Plas 4+1-dr Saloon			14,179*
180	2000			8,098*
181	2300 4+1-dr Saloon			8,697*
181	2300 S 4+1-dr Saloon			9,965*
181	2600 S 4+1-dr Saloon			10,520*
181	2600 SE 4+1-dr Saloon			11,449*
181	Vitesse			15,249*
181	2400 SD Turbo			10,899*
	RUSKA (Holland)			
189	Regina			18,000
190	Regina Royal 2-dr Roadster			19,500
190	Sagitta 2-dr Roadster			19,500
	SAAB (Sweden)			
235	99 GL 4 gears 2-dr Sedan	—		—
235	99 GL 5 gears 2-dr Sedan	6,450*		—
235	99 GL 5 gears 4-dr Sedan	6,760*		—
235	900 GL 2+1-dr Hatchback Sedan	—	11,110*	—
235	900 GL 4-dr Sedan	7,320*	11,420*	—
235	900 GL 4+1-dr Hatchback Sedan	—		—
235	900 GLS 2+1-dr Hatchback Sedan	7,740*		—
235	900 GLS 4-dr Sedan	7,990*	14,310*	—
235	900 GLS 4+1-dr Hatchback Sedan	8,390*		—
235	900 I 2-dr Sedan	—		—
235	900 GLI 2+1-dr Hatchback Sedan	—		—
235	900 GLI 4-dr Sedan	8,690*		—
235	900 GLI 4+1-dr Hatchback Sedan	9,090*		—
235	900 GLE 4-dr Sedan	9,990*		—
235	900 Turbo 2+1-dr Hatchback Sedan	11,550*	16,940*	—
235	900 Turbo 4-dr Sedan	11,890*	17,400*	—
235	900 Turbo 4+1-dr Hatchback Sedan	12,450*		—
235	900 Turbo De Luxe 2+1-dr Hatchback Sedan	13,390*		—
235	900 Turbo De Luxe 4-dr Sedan	—		—
235	900 Turbo De Luxe 4+1-dr Hatchback Sedan	—		—
235	900 CD 4-dr Sedan	15,750*		—
235	900 Turbo 16 2+1-dr Hatchback Sedan	—		—
235	900 Turbo 16 4-dr Sedan	—		—
235	900 Turbo 16 4+1-dr Hatchback Sedan	—		—
235	900 Turbo 16 S 2+1-dr Hatchback Sedan	—		—
	SBARRO (Switzerland)			
239	Replica BMW 328 Standard 2-dr Roadster			50,000
239	Replica BMW 328 Spéciale 2-dr Roadster			60,000
239	Replica BMW 328 America			60,000
240	Stash 2-dr Coupé			120,000
240	Stash 2-dr Cabriolet			120,000
240	Stash HS 2-dr Cabriolet			140,000
240	Royale			250,000
240	Windhound 4 x 4			85,000
	SEAT (Spain)			
230	Panda 40 2+1-dr Berlina			385,000
230	Panda 40 Terra 2-dr Familiar			430,000
230	Panda Marbella 2+1-dr Berlina			469,500
231	Fura L 2+1-dr Berlina			451,000
231	Fura CL 2+1-dr Berlina			500,600
231	Fura CL 4+1-dr Berlina			524,600
231	Ronda 65 CL 4+1-dr Berlina			629,100
231	Ronda 75 CL 4+1-dr Berlina			650,000
231	Ronda 75 CLX STAR 4+1-dr Berlina			720,000
231	Ronda Crono 4+1-dr Berlina			780,000
231	Ronda Diesel L 4+1-dr Berlina			725,000
231	Ronda Diesel CL 4+1-dr Berlina			750,000
231	Ronda Diesel CLX 4+1-dr Berlina			805,000
231	131 Mirafiori 1600 CL 4-dr Berlina			719,300
231	131 Supermirafiori 1600 4-dr Berlina			765,600
231	131 Panorama Super 1600 4+1-dr Familiar			833,900
231	131 Supermirafiori 2000 4-dr Berlina			832,000
231	131 Diplomatic 4-dr Berlina			975,200
231	131 Mirafiori Diesel CL 2500 4-dr Berlina			919,600
231	131 Supermirafiori Diesel 2500 4-dr Berlina			991,700
231	131 Panorama Super Diesel 2500 4+1-dr Familiar			1,030,200
	SEVEL (Argentina)			
251	Fiat 147 1100 CL 5 2+1-dr Sedan			—
251	Fiat 147 1300 TR5 2+1-dr Sedan			—
251	Fiat Super Europa 1300 4-dr Sedan			—
251	Fiat Super Europa 1500 4-dr Sedan			—
251	Fiat Super Europa 1500 4+1-dr Familiar			—
251	Peugeot 504 GR II			—
251	Peugeot 505 SR II			—
	SHANGHAI (China People's Republic)			
332	Santana Shanghai			—
333	760 A			—

Page	MAKE AND MODEL	Price in GB £	Price in USA $	Price ex Works
	SIPANI (India)			
331	Dolphin 2-dr Hatchback Sedan			58,500
331	Dolphin 2+1-dr St. Wagon			—
	ŠKODA (Czechoslovakia)			
75	105 S	2,378*		—
75	105 L	—		—
75	120 L	2,509*		—
75	120 LS	2,869*		—
75	120 GLS	3,148*		—
76	Rapid	3,389*		—
	Sta MATILDE (Brazil)			
262	SM 4.1			14,105,000
	STIMULA (France)			
100	Bugatti 55 Série II			186,000*
	STUTZ (USA)			
314	Victoria			125,000
314	Blackhawk VII 2-dr Coupé			84,500
314	Bearcat 2-dr Convertible			129,500
314	Royale Limousine			285,000
	SUBARU (Japan)			
373	Rex Combi F 2+1-dr Sedan			514,000
373	Rex Combi FR 2+1-dr Sedan			516,000
373	Rex Combi FL 2+1-dr Sedan			570,000
373	Rex Combi XL 2+1-dr Sedan			634,000
373	Rex S 2+1-dr Sedan			585,000
373	Rex SE 2+1-dr Sedan			701,000
373	Rex SG 2+1-dr Sedan			732,000
373	Rex S 4+1-dr Sedan			600,000
373	Rex SR 4+1-dr Sedan			625,000
373	Rex SL 4+1-dr Sedan			719,000
373	Rex SX 4+1-dr Sedan			782,000
373	Rex Combi TL 4WD 2+1-dr Sedan			—
373	Rex Combi TX 4WD 2+1-dr Sedan			—
373	Rex Combi Turbo 2+1-dr Sedan			698,000
374	Domingo CF 4+1-dr Wagon			898,000
374	Domingo CS 4+1-dr Wagon			1,035,000
374	Domingo CS-S 4+1-dr Wagon			1,115,000
374	Domingo GF 4WD 4+1-dr Wagon			1,048,000
374	Domingo GS 4WD 4+1-dr Wagon			1,185,000
374	Domingo GS-S 4WD 4+1-dr Wagon			1,265,000
374	Leone 1300 2+1-dr Swingback Sedan			757,000
374	Leone 1300 LG 2+1-dr Swingback Sedan			862,000
374	Leone 1600 L 4-dr Sedan			907,000
374	Leone 1600 LG 4-dr Sedan			972,000
374	Leone 1600 GLF 4-dr Sedan			1,030,000
374	Leone 1600 GLT 4-dr Sedan	5,232*	6,600*	1,173,000
374	Leone 1600 GLS 2+1-dr Swingback Sedan			1,065,000
374	Leone 1600 4WD E 2+1-dr Swingback Sedan			1,230,000
374	Leone 1800 GTL 4-dr Sedan			1,220,000
374	Leone 1800 GTS 4-dr Sedan	5,300*	7,259*	1,380,000
374	Leone 1800 GTX 2-dr Hardtop		7,452*	1,395,000
374	Leone 1800 4WD 4-dr Sedan	5,995*		1,482,000
374	Leone 1800 4WD 2+1-dr Swingback Sedan			1,372,000
374	Leone 1800 4WD 4+1-dr Touring Wagon	6,997*	7,448*	1,395,000
374	Leone 1800 4WD RX 2-dr Hardtop			1,507,000
374	Leone 1800 4WD Turbo 4-dr Sedan		10,108*	1,840,000
374	Leone 1800 4WD Turbo 4+1-dr Touring Wagon		10,303*	1,895,000
	SUZUKI (Japan)			
376	Fronte FSA 4+1-dr Sedan			605,000
376	Fronte FSC 4+1-dr Sedan			685,000
376	Fronte FSG 4+1-dr Sedan			725,000
376	Fronte SS 80 F 4+1-dr Hatchback Sedan			—
376	Fronte SS 80 G 2+1-dr Hatchback Sedan			—
376	Cervo CS 2+1-dr Hatchback Coupé			580,000
376	Cervo CSL 2+1-dr Hatchback Coupé			687,000
376	Alto Hatchback MS-B 2-seater 2+1-dr Sedan	2,999*		470,000
376	Alto Hatchback MS-C 2-seater 2+1-dr Sedan			498,000
376	Alto Hatchback MS-CL 2+2-seater 2+1-dr Sedan			558,000
376	Alto Hatchback MS-CG 2+2-seater 2+1-dr Sedan			628,000
377	Alto 4WD C 2+1-dr Sedan			618,000
377	Alto 4WD G 2+1-dr Sedan			718,000
377	Jimny SJ 30 2-dr Wagon			770,000
377	Jimny SJ 30 FK 2-dr Wagon			780,000
377	Jimny SJ 30 FM 2-dr Wagon			820,000
377	Jimny SJ 30 VM 2-dr Wagon			858,000
377	Jimny 1100 S40 FK (soft top) 2-dr Wagon			985,000
377	Jimny 1100 SJ 40 VC 4-dr Wagon	4,599*		1,085,000
377	Cultus GU 2+1-dr Sedan			635,000
377	Cultus GA 2+1-dr Sedan			698,000
377	Cultus GL 2+1-dr Sedan			798,000
377	Cultus GE 2+1-dr Sedan			828,000
377	Cultus GC 2+1-dr Sedan			848,000
377	Cultus GS 2+1-dr Sedan			980,000
	SYRENA (Poland)			
224	105			—
	TALBOT (France)			
101	Samba LS 2+1-dr Berline	3,695*		38,950◊
101	Samba GL 2+1-dr Berline	4,345*		42,950◊
101	Samba 72 CV 2-dr Cabriolet	6,595*		62,850◊
101	Samba GLS 2+1-dr Berline	4,990*		50,950◊
101	Samba 80 CV 2-dr Cabriolet			69,200◊
101	Samba Rallye 2+1-dr Berline			49,900◊
102	Horizon LS 4+1-dr Berline			44,400◊
102	Horizon GL 4+1-dr Berline			51,400◊
102	Horizon EX 4+1-dr Berline			54,600◊
102	Horizon GLS 4+1-dr Berline			55,900◊
102	Horizon Premium 4+1-dr Berline			60,600◊
102	Horizon LD 4+1-dr Berline			53,600◊
102	Horizon EXD 4+1-dr Berline			63,700◊
103	Solara LS 4-dr Berline			52,500◊
103	Solara GL 4-dr Berline			59,300◊
103	Solara GLS 4-dr Berline			62,400◊
103	Solara SX 4-dr Berline			68,100◊
103	Matra Rancho 2+1-dr Break	7,245*		72,100◊
103	Matra Rancho X 2+1-dr Break			78,800◊
104	Matra Murena S			103,900◊
	TALBOT (Great Britain)			
181	Horizon 1.1 LE 4+1-dr Saloon			4,145*
181	Horizon 1.1 LS 4+1-dr Saloon			4,645*
181	Horizon 1.3 LS 4+1-dr Saloon			4,895*
181	Horizon 1.5 GL 4+1-dr Saloon			5,495*
181	Horizon 1.5 GLS 4+1-dr Saloon			5,850*
181	Horizon 1.9 LD 4+1-dr Saloon			5,420*
182	Alpine 1.3 LE 4+1-dr Saloon			4,895*
182	Alpine 1.3 LS 4+1-dr Saloon			5,345*
182	Alpine 1.3 GL 4+1-dr Saloon			5,995*
182	Alpine 1.6 LE 4+1-dr Saloon			5,145*
182	Alpine 1.6 LS 4+1-dr Saloon			5,595*
182	Alpine 1.6 GL 4+1-dr Saloon			6,245*
182	Alpine 1.6 GLS 4+1-dr Saloon			7,095*
183	Solara 1.3 LE 4-dr Saloon			4,795*
183	Solara 1.3 LS 4-dr Saloon			5,195*
183	Solara 1.3 GL 4-dr Saloon			5,845*
183	Solara 1.6 LE 4-dr Saloon			5,045*
183	Solara 1.6 LS 4-dr Saloon			5,445*
183	Solara 1.6 GL 4-dr Saloon			6,095*
183	Solara 1.6 GLS 4-dr Saloon			6,945*
	TALBOT (Spain)			
232	Samba LE 2+1-dr Berlina			581,900
232	Samba LS 2+1-dr Berlina			619,500
232	Samba GL 2+1-dr Berlina			681,500
232	Samba GL Confort 2+1-dr Berlina			722,700
232	Samba S 2+1-dr Berlina			806,800
232	Samba S 2-dr Cabriolet			1,707,100
232	Samba Rallye 2+1-dr Berlina			800,600
233	Horizon LS 4+1-dr Berlina			811,400
233	Horizon GL 4+1-dr Berlina			854,900
233	Horizon GL Automatic 4+1-dr Berlina			966,300
233	Horizon GLS 4+1-dr Berlina			956,300
233	Horizon S-2 4+1-dr Berlina			950,100
233	Horizon GT 4+1-dr Berlina			1,043,400

Page	MAKE AND MODEL	Price in GB £	Price in USA $	Price ex Works
233	Horizon LD 4+1-dr Berlina			997,600
233	Horizon GLD 4+1-dr Berlina			1,047,400
233	Horizon EXD 4+1-dr Berlina			1,127,300
234	150 GL 4+1-dr Berlina			1,038,900
234	150 LS 4+1-dr Berlina			999,700
234	150 LS Confort 4+1-dr Berlina			1,030,700
234	150 GT-2 4+1-dr Berlina			1,114,000
234	Solara GL 4-dr Berlina			1,045,500
234	Solara LS 4-dr Berlina			1,006,300
234	Solara Pullman 4-dr Berlina			1,028,100
234	Solara GLS 4-dr Berlina			1,095,400
234	Solara SX 4-dr Berlina			1,178,500
234	Solara SX Automatico 4-dr Berlina			1,265,000
	TATRA (Czechoslovakia)			
76	T 613-2			—
76	T 613-2 Special			—
	TIMMIS (Canada)			
266	Ford V8 Roadster			50,000
	TMC (Ireland)			
191	Costin			7,417*
	TOFAS (Turkey)			
318	Murat 131			—
	TOTAL REPLICA (USA)			
315	Hi Boy			20,000
315	Ford "B" 4-dr Phaeton			30,000
315	Ford "B" 2-dr Roadster			25,000
	TOYOTA (Australia)			
399	Corolla S 4-dr Sedan			7,640
399	Corolla S 4+1-dr St. Wagon			8,370
399	Corolla CS 4-dr Sedan			8,160
399	Corolla CS 4+1-dr St. Wagon			8,810
399	Corolla CSX 4-dr Sedan			8,875
399	Corona S 4-dr Sedan			9,170
399	Corona S 4+1-dr St. Wagon			9,820
399	Corona CS 4-dr Sedan			9,910
399	Corona CS 4+1-dr St. Wagon			10,560
399	Corona CS-X 4-dr Sedan			11,425
	TOYOTA (Japan)			
378	Starlet Standard 2+1-dr Sedan	4,144*	5,898*	687,000
378	Starlet DX 2+1-dr Sedan			762,000
378	Starlet DX-A 2+1-dr Sedan			717,000
378	Starlet DX-A 4+1-dr Sedan			788,000
378	Starlet XL 2+1-dr Sedan			845,000
378	Starlet XL 4+1-dr Sedan			871,000
378	Starlet XL EFI 2+1-dr Sedan			941,000
378	Starlet XL Lisse 2+1-dr Sedan			898,000
378	Starlet XL Lisse 4+1-dr Sedan			924,000
378	Starlet S 2+1-dr Sedan		5,948*	951,000
378	Starlet S 4+1-dr Sedan			977,000
378	Starlet SE 4+1-dr Sedan			965,000
378	Starlet SE EFI 4+1-dr Sedan			1,061,000
378	Starlet Si EFI 2+1-dr Sedan			996,000
378	Corolla FWD 1300 Custom DX 4-dr Sedan			832,000
378	Corolla FWD 1300 DX 4-dr Sedan		6,498*	863,000
378	Corolla FWD 1300 GL 4-dr Sedan	5,133*		944,000
378	Corolla FWD 1500 DX 4-dr Sedan			924,000
378	Corolla FWD 1500 GL 4-dr Sedan			998,000
378	Corolla FWD 1500 SE 4-dr Sedan			1,088,000
378	Corolla FWD 1500 SX 4+1-dr Hatchback Sedan			1,113,000
378	Corolla FWD 1500 ZX 4+1-dr Hatchback Sedan			1,204,000
378	Corolla FWD 1600 SR 4-dr Sedan			1,193,000
378	Corolla FWD 1600 SX 4+1-dr Hatchback Sedan			1,236,000
378	Corolla FWD 1600 ZX 4+1-dr Hatchback Sedan			1,320,000
378	Corolla FWD 1800 DX 4-dr Sedan		7,398*	1,035,000
378	Corolla FWD 1800 GL 4-dr Sedan			1,135,000
378	Corolla FWD 1800 SE 4-dr Sedan			1,201,000
378	Corolla FWD 1800 SX 4+1-dr Hatchback Sedan		7,298*	1,223,000

Page	MAKE AND MODEL	Price in GB £	Price in USA $	Price ex Works
379	Sprinter FWD 1300 Special DX 4-dr Sedan			854,000
379	Sprinter FWD 1300 DX 4-dr Sedan			885,000
379	Sprinter FWD 1300 XL 4-dr Sedan			966,000
379	Sprinter FWD 1500 DX 4-dr Sedan			946,000
379	Sprinter FWD 1500 XL 4-dr Sedan			1,020,000
379	Sprinter FWD 1500 SE 4-dr Sedan			1,110,000
379	Sprinter FWD 1500 SX 4+1-dr Hatchback Sedan			1,135,000
379	Sprinter FWD 1500 ZX 4+1-dr Hatchback Sedan			1,226,000
379	Sprinter FWD 1600 SR 4-dr Sedan			1,215,000
379	Sprinter FWD 1600 SX 4+1-dr Hatchback Sedan			1,258,000
379	Sprinter FWD 1600 ZX 4+1-dr Hatchback Sedan			1,342,000
379	Sprinter FWD 1800 DX 4-dr Sedan			1,057,000
379	Sprinter FWD 1800 XL 4-dr Sedan			1,157,000
379	Sprinter FWD 1800 SE 4-dr Sedan			1,223,000
379	Sprinter FWD 1800 SX 4+1-dr Hatchback Sedan			1,245,000
380	Tercel 1300 VC 4-dr Sedan			842,000
380	Tercel 1300 VC 4+1-dr Hatchback Sedan			833,000
380	Tercel 1300 VL 4-dr Sedan			891,000
380	Tercel 1300 VL 4+1-dr Hatchback Sedan	5,058*		885,000
380	Tercel 1300 SE 4-dr Sedan			1,088,000
380	Corsa 1300 DX 4-dr Sedan			842,000
380	Corsa 1300 DX 4+1-dr Hatchback Sedan			833,000
380	Corsa 1300 GX 4-dr Sedan			891,000
380	Corsa 1300 GX 4+1-dr Hatchback Sedan			885,000
380	Corsa 1300 GX Sophia 4+1-dr Hatchback Sedan			915,000
380	Corolla II 1300 CD 2+1-dr Hatchback Sedan			769,000
380	Corolla II 1300 DX 2+1-dr Hatchback Sedan			799,000
380	Corolla II 1300 DX 4+1-dr Hatchback Sedan			833,000
380	Corolla II 1300 GL 2+1-dr Hatchback Sedan			851,000
380	Corolla II 1300 GL 4+1-dr Hatchback Sedan			885,000
380	Corolla II 1300 GL Lime 2+1-dr Hatchback Sedan			871,000
380	Tercel 1500 VC 4+1-dr Hatchback Sedan		6,188*	888,000
380	Tercel 1500 VL 4-dr Sedan			969,000
376	Tercel 1500 VL 4+1-dr Hatchback Sedan			962,000
380	Tercel 1500 VE 4-dr Sedan			1,099,000
380	Tercel 1500 VE 4+1-dr Hatchback Sedan			1,119,000
380	Corsa 1500 DX 4+1-dr Hatchback Sedan			888,000
380	Corsa 1500 GX 4+1-dr Sedan			969,000
380	Corsa 1500 GX 4+1-dr Hatchback Sedan			962,000
380	Corsa 1500 GX Sophia 4+1-dr Hatchback Sedan			1,027,000
380	Corsa 1500 EX 4-dr Sedan			1,124,000
380	Corsa 1500 EX 4+1-dr Hatchback Sedan			1,099,000
380	Corolla II 1500 DX 4+1-dr Hatchback Sedan			888,000
380	Corolla II 1500 GL 4+1-dr Hatchback Sedan			962,000
380	Corolla II 1500 GL Lime 4+1-dr Hatchback Sedan			1,027,000
380	Corolla II 1500 SE 2+1-dr Hatchback Sedan		7,598*	1,053,000
380	Corolla II 1500 SE 4+1-dr Hatchback Sedan		7,778*	1,089,000
380	Tercel 1500 VS 4-dr Sedan			1,072,000
380	Tercel 1500 VS 4+1-dr Hatchback Sedan			1,049,000
380	Corsa 1500 SX 4-dr Sedan			1,072,000
380	Corsa 1500 SX 4+1-dr Hatchback Sedan			1,049,000
380	Corolla II 1500 SR 2+1-dr Hatchback Sedan			1,013,000
380	Corolla II 1500 SR 4+1-dr Hatchback Sedan			1,049,000
381	Corolla Levin RWD GL 2-dr Coupé			1,060,000
381	Corolla Levin RWD SE 2-dr Coupé			1,122,000
381	Corolla Levin RWD SE 2+1-dr Hatchback Coupé			1,133,000
381	Corolla Levin RWD GT 2-dr Coupé			1,322,000
381	Corolla Levin RWD GT Apex 2-dr Coupé			1,523,000
381	Corolla Levin RWD GT Apex 2+1-dr Hatchback Coupé			1,548,000
381	Corolla Levin RWD GTV 2+1-dr Hatchback Coupé			1,368,000

Page	MAKE AND MODEL	Price in GB £	Price in USA $	Price ex Works
381	Sprinter Trueno RWD 1500 XL 2-dr Coupé			1,092,000
381	Sprinter Trueno RWD 1500 SE 2-dr Coupé			1,154,000
381	Sprinter Trueno RWD 1500 SR 2+1-dr Liftback Coupé			1,165,000
381	Sprinter Trueno RWD 1600 GT 2-dr Coupé			1,354,000
381	Sprinter Trueno RWD 1600 GT Apex 2-dr Coupé			1,538,000
381	Sprinter Trueno RWD 1600 GT Apex 2+1-dr Liftback Coupé			1,563,000
381	Sprinter Trueno RWD 1600 GTV 2+1-dr Liftback Coupé			1,400,000
382	Carina 1500 Standard 4-dr Sedan			945,000
382	Carina 1500 DX 4-dr Sedan			1,008,000
382	Carina 1500 SG 4-dr Sedan			1,051,000
382	Carina 1500 SG 2-dr Coupé			1,102,000
382	Carina 1500 SE 4-dr Sedan			1,264,000
382	Carina 1500 SE 2-dr Coupé			1,304,000
382	Carina 1500 ST 4-dr Sedan			1,142,000
382	Carina 1500 ST 2-dr Coupé			1,195,000
382	Carina 1600 twin cam GT 4-dr Sedan	5,690*		1,489,000
382	Carina 1600 twin cam GT 2-dr Coupé			1,537,000
382	Carina 1600 twin cam GT-R 4-dr Sedan			1,672,000
382	Carina 1600 twin cam GT-R 2-dr Coupé			1,739,000
382	Carina 1800 SG 4-dr Sedan			1,168,000
382	Carina 1800 SE 4-dr Sedan			1,429,000
382	Carina 1800 SE 2-dr Coupé			1,467,000
382	Carina 1800 ST 4-dr Sedan			1,258,000
382	Carina 1800 ST 2-dr Coupé			1,311,000
382	Carina 1800 4+1-dr St. Wagon			1,350,000
382	Carina 1800 twin cam Turbo GT-T 4-dr Sedan			1,696,000
382	Carina 1800 twin cam Turbo GT-T 2-dr Coupé			1,768,000
382	Carina 1800 twin cam Turbo GT-TR 4-dr Sedan			1,908,000
382	Carina 1800 twin cam Turbo GT-TR 2-dr Coupé			1,952,000
382	Carina 1800 Diesel SG 4-dr Sedan			1,258,000
382	Carina 1800 Diesel SE 4-dr Sedan			1,473,000
383	Corona FWD 1500 Standard 4-dr Sedan			978,000
383	Corona FWD 1500 DX 4-dr Sedan			1,055,000
383	Corona FWD 1500 GX 4-dr Sedan			1,094,000
383	Corona FWD 1500 GX 4+1-dr Sedan			1,192,000
383	Corona FWD 1500 EX 4-dr Sedan			1,320,000
383	Corona FWD 1500 EX 4+1-dr Sedan			1,397,000
383	Corona FWD 1800 GX 4-dr Sedan			1,243,000
383	Corona FWD 1800 GX 4+1-dr Sedan			1,314,000
383	Corona FWD 1800 EX 4-dr Sedan			1,444,000
383	Corona FWD 1800 EX 4+1-dr Sedan			1,490,000
383	Corona FWD 1800 EFI EX 4-dr Sedan			1,611,000
383	Corona FWD 1800 EFI EX 4+1-dr Sedan			1,659,000
383	Corona FWD 1800 EFI SX 4-dr Sedan			1,387,000
383	Corona FWD 1800 EFI SX 4+1-dr Sedan			1,659,000
383	Corona FWD 2000 Diesel GX 4-dr Sedan			1,338,000
383	Corona FWD 2000 Diesel EX 4-dr Sedan			1,339,000
383	Corona RWD 1500 Standard 4-dr Sedan			978,000
383	Corona RWD 1500 DX 4-dr Sedan			1,055,000
383	Corona RWD 1500 GX 4-dr Sedan			1,094,000
383	Corona RWD 1600 twin cam GT 4-dr Sedan			1,540,000
383	Corona RWD 1600 twin cam GT 4-dr Hardtop			1,592,000
383	Corona RWD 1600 twin cam GT Sport 4-dr Sedan			1,711,000
383	Corona RWD 1600 twin cam GT Sport 4-dr Hardtop			1,763,000
383	Corona RWD 1800 GX 4-dr Sedan			1,243,000
383	Corona RWD 1800 GX 4-dr Hardtop			1,335,000
383	Corona RWD 1800 EX 4-dr Hardtop			1,512,000
383	Corona RWD 1800 twin cam Turbo GT-T 4-dr Sedan			1,735,000
383	Corona RWD 1800 twin cam Turbo GT-T 4-dr Hardtop			1,787,000
383	Corona RWD 1800 twin cam Turbo GT-TR 4-dr Sedan			1,947,000
383	Corona RWD 1800 twin cam Turbo GT-TR 4-dr Hardtop			2,003,000
384	Sprinter Carib AV-I 4+1-dr St. Wagon			1,288,000
384	Sprinter Carib AV-II 4+1-dr St. Wagon			1,488,000
384	Celica 1600 twin cam GT 2-dr Coupé			1,523,000
384	Celica 1600 twin cam GT 2+1-dr Liftback Coupé			1,610,000
384	Celica 1600 twin cam GT-R 2-dr Coupé			1,738,000

Page	MAKE AND MODEL	Price in GB £	Price in USA $	Price ex Works
384	Celica 1600 twin cam GT-R 2+1-dr Liftback Coupé			1,814,000
384	Celica 1800 SV 2-dr Coupé			1,140,000
384	Celica 1800 SV 2+1-dr Liftback Coupé			1,212,000
384	Celica 1800 ST 2-dr Coupé			1,251,000
384	Celica 1800 ST 2+1-dr Liftback Coupé			1,318,000
384	Celica 1800 SX 2-dr Coupé			1,455,000
384	Celica 1800 SX 2+1-dr Liftback Coupé			1,533,000
384	Celica 1800 twin cam Turbo GT-T 2-dr Coupé			1,748,000
384	Celica 1800 twin cam Turbo GT-T 2+1-dr Liftback Coupé			1,835,000
384	Celica 1800 twin cam Turbo GT-TR 2-dr Coupé			1,958,000
384	Celica 1800 twin cam Turbo GT-TR 2+1-dr Liftback Coupé			2,035,000
385	Vista 1800 VL 4-dr Sedan			1,260,000
385	Vista 1800 VL 4+1-dr Liftback Coupé			1,313,000
385	Vista 1800 VE 4-dr Sedan			1,430,000
385	Vista 1800 VE 4+1-dr Liftback Coupé			1,477,000
385	Vista 1800 VX 4-dr Sedan			1,657,000
385	Vista 1800 VX 4+1-dr Liftback Coupé			1,699,000
385	Camry 1800 XT 4-dr Sedan	6,070*		1,260,000
385	Camry 1800 SE 4-dr Sedan			1,430,000
385	Camry 1800 ZX 4-dr Sedan			1,657,000
385	Vista 2000 VL 4-dr Sedan			1,330,000
385	Vista 2000 VL 4+1-dr Liftback Coupé			1,383,000
385	Vista 2000 VE 4-dr Sedan			1,500,000
385	Vista 2000 VE 4+1-dr Liftback Coupé			1,547,000
385	Vista 2000 VX 4-dr Sedan			1,727,000
385	Vista 2000 VX 4+1-dr Liftback Coupé			1,769,000
385	Camry 2000 XT 4-dr Sedan		8,148*	1,330,000
385	Camry 2000 SE 4-dr Sedan		10,098*	1,500,000
385	Camry 2000 ZX 4-dr Sedan			1,727,000
385	Vista 1800 Turbo Diesel VL 4-dr Sedan			1,423,000
385	Vista 1800 Turbo Diesel VE 4-dr Sedan			1,608,000
385	Vista 1800 Turbo Diesel VE 4+1-dr Liftback Coupé			1,655,000
385	Camry 1800 Turbo Diesel XT 4-dr Sedan		9,248*	1,423,000
385	Camry 1800 Turbo Diesel SE 4-dr Sedan			1,608,000
386	Mark II 1800 STD 4-dr Sedan		13,795*	1,084,000
386	Mark II 1800 DX 4-dr Sedan			1,161,000
386	Mark II 1800 GL 4-dr Sedan			1,223,000
386	Mark II 1800 GL 4-dr Hardtop			1,280,000
386	Mark II 1800 GR 4-dr Sedan			1,372,000
386	Mark II 1800 GR 4-dr Hardtop			1,427,000
386	Chaser 1800 STD 4-dr Sedan			1,099,000
386	Chaser 1800 DX 4-dr Sedan			1,178,000
386	Chaser 1800 XL 4-dr Sedan			1,242,000
386	Chaser 1800 XL 4-dr Hardtop			1,293,000
386	Chaser 1800 XG 4-dr Sedan			1,379,000
386	Chaser 1800 XG 4-dr Hardtop			1,540,000
386	Mark II 2000 LE 4-dr Sedan			1,472,000
386	Mark II 2000 LE 4-dr Hardtop			1,530,000
386	Mark II 2000 LG 4-dr Sedan			1,647,000
386	Mark II 2000 LG 4-dr Hardtop			1,704,000
386	Mark II 2000 Grande 4-dr Sedan			2,025,000
386	Mark II 2000 Grande 4-dr Hardtop			2,073,000
386	Mark 2000 LE 4+1-dr St. Wagon		14,355*	1,540,000
386	Chaser 2000 SXL 4-dr Sedan			1,557,000
386	Chaser 2000 SXL 4-dr Hardtop			1,608,000
386	Chaser 2000 Avante 4-dr Sedan			1,994,000
386	Chaser 2000 Avante 4-dr Hardtop			2,064,000
386	Mark II 2000 Grande twin cam 24 4-dr Sedan			2,310,000
386	Mark II 2000 Grande twin cam 24 4-dr Hardtop			2,358,000
386	Chaser 2000 Avante twin cam 24 4-dr Sedan			2,304,000
386	Chaser 2000 Avante twin cam 24 4-dr Hardtop			2,349,000
386	Mark II 2000 Turbo LG Touring 4-dr Sedan			1,780,000
386	Mark II 2000 Turbo LG Touring 4-dr Hardtop			1,831,000
386	Mark II 2000 Turbo Grande 4-dr Sedan			2,294,000
386	Mark II 2000 Turbo Grande 4-dr Hardtop			2,342,000
386	Chaser 2000 Turbo SG Touring 4-dr Sedan			1,772,000

Page	MAKE AND MODEL	Price in GB £	Price in USA $	Price ex Works
386	Chaser 2000 Turbo SG Touring 4-dr Hardtop			1,833,000
386	Chaser 2000 Turbo Avante 4-dr Sedan			2,263,000
386	Chaser 2000 Turbo Avante 4-dr Hardtop			2,333,000
386	Mark II 2200 Diesel DX 4-dr Sedan			1,337,000
386	Mark II 2200 Diesel GL 4-dr Sedan			1,398,000
386	Chaser 2200 Diesel DX 4-dr Sedan			1,344,000
386	Chaser 2200 Diesel XL 4-dr Sedan			1,407,000
386	Mark II 2400 Turbo Diesel LE 4-dr Sedan			1,761,000
386	Chaser 2400 Turbo Diesel SXL 4-dr Sedan			1,772,000
387	Cresta 1800 Custom 4-dr Hardtop			1,271,000
387	Cresta 1800 Super Custom 4-dr Hardtop			1,402,000
387	Cresta 2000 Super De Luxe 4-dr Hardtop			1,582,000
387	Cresta 2000 Super Lucent 4-dr Hardtop			2,030,000
387	Cresta 2000 Super Lucent twin cam 24 4-dr Hardtop			2,315,000
387	Cresta 2000 Turbo Super Touring 4-dr Hardtop			1,820,000
387	Cresta 2000 Turbo Super Lucent 4-dr Hardtop			2,299,000
387	Cresta 2200 Diesel Custom 4-dr Hardtop			1,427,000
387	Cresta 2200 Diesel Super Custom 4-dr Hardtop			1,613,000
388	Soarer 2000 VII 2-dr Coupé			1,919,000
388	Soarer 2000 VR 2-dr Coupé			2,052,000
388	Soarer 2000 VX 2-dr Coupé			2,343,000
388	Soarer 2000 Turbo 2-dr Coupé			2,453,000
388	Soarer 2000 GT 2-dr Coupé			2,708,000
388	Soarer 2800 GT 2-dr Coupé			2,911,000
388	Soarer 2800 GT Limited 2-dr Coupé			3,422,000
389	Celica XX 2000 SI 2+1-dr Liftback Coupé			1,747,000
389	Celica XX 2000 G 2+1-dr Liftback Coupé			1,908,000
389	Celica XX 2000 S Turbo 2+1-dr Liftback Coupé			2,047,000
389	Celica XX 2000 G Turbo 2+1-dr Liftback Coupé			2,229,000
389	Celica XX 2000 GT twin cam 2+1-dr Liftback Coupé	7,846*	9,149*	2,167,000
389	Celica Supra 2000 GT 2+1-dr Liftback Coupé	10,593*	15,724*	2,339,000
390	Crown 2000 EFI Standard 4-dr Sedan			1,462,000
390	Crown 2000 EFI De Luxe 4-dr Sedan			1,719,000
390	Crown 2000 EFI Super De Luxe 4-dr Sedan			2,003,000
390	Crown 2000 EFI Super De Luxe 4+1-dr St. Wagon			2,065,000
390	Crown 2000 EFI Super Saloon 4-dr Sedan			2,250,000
390	Crown 2000 EFI Super Saloon 4-dr Hardtop			2,361,000
390	Crown 2000 EFI Super Saloon 4+1-dr St. Wagon			2,365,000
390	Crown 2000 EFI Super Edition 4-dr Hardtop			2,118,000
390	Crown 2000 EFI Turbo Super Saloon 4-dr Sedan			2,619,000
390	Crown 2000 EFI Turbo Super Saloon 4-dr Hardtop			2,722,000
390	Crown 2000 EFI Turbo Super Edition 4-dr Hardtop			2,427,000
390	Crown 2000 EFI twin cam Royal Saloon 4-dr Sedan			3,047,000
390	Crown 2000 EFI twin cam Royal Saloon 4-dr Hardtop			3,027,000
390	Crown 2800 EFI twin cam Royal Saloon 4-dr Sedan	11,721*		3,245,000
390	Crown 2800 EFI twin cam Royal Saloon 4-dr Hardtop			3,412,000
390	Crown 2400 Diesel Standard 4-dr Sedan			1,509,000
390	Crown 2400 Diesel De Luxe 4-dr Sedan			1,775,000
390	Crown 2400 Diesel Super De Luxe 4-dr Sedan			2,152,000
390	Crown 2400 Turbo Diesel Super De Luxe 4-dr St. Wagon			2,267,000
390	Crown 2400 Turbo Diesel Super Saloon 4-dr Sedan			2,632,000
390	Crown 2400 Turbo Diesel Super Saloon 4-dr Hardtop			2,597,000
390	Crown 2400 Turbo Diesel Super Saloon 4+1-dr St. Wagon			2,603,000
390	Crown 2400 Turbo Diesel Super Edition 4-dr Hardtop			2,232,000
391	Century D 4-dr Sedan			4,950,000

Page	MAKE AND MODEL	Price in GB £	Price in USA $	Price ex Works
391	Century E 4-dr Sedan			5,600,000
391	Blizzard Standard (soft top)			1,281,000
391	Blizzard De Luxe (soft top)			1,319,000
391	Blizzard De Luxe (soft top, steel doors)			1,347,000
391	Blizzard FRP De Luxe			1,682,000
391	Blizzard De Luxe Wagon			1,511,000
392	Landcruiser 60 4+1-dr Wagon			1,827,000
392	Landcruiser 42 Diesel 4+1-dr Wagon			1,777,000
392	Landcruiser 42 Diesel (soft top) 4+1-dr Wagon			1,556,000
392	Landcruiser 46 Diesel 4+1-dr Wagon			1,865,000
392	Landcruiser 46 Diesel (soft top) 4+1-dr Wagon			1,605,000
392	Landcruiser 60 Diesel 4+1-dr Wagon (98 hp)			1,930,000
392	Landcruiser 60 Diesel 4+1-dr Wagon (115 hp)	12,400*	13,768*	2,276,000
	TRABANT (Germany DR)			
104	601 Standard 2-dr Limousine			—
104	601 S 2-dr Limousine			—
105	601 Universal			—
105	601 S De Luxe			—
	TRIUMPH (Great Britain)			
183	Acclaim L 4-dr Saloon			4,998*
183	Acclaim HL 4-dr Saloon			5,249*
183	Acclaim HLS 4-dr Saloon			5,620*
183	Acclaim CD 4-dr Saloon			5,999*
	TVR (Great Britain)			
184	Tasmin 200 2-dr Coupé			10,384*
184	Tasmin 200 2-dr Convertible			10,280*
184	Tasmin 280i 2-dr Coupé			14,377*
184	Tasmin 280i +2 2-dr Coupé			15,500*
184	Tasmin 280i 2-dr Convertible			13,254*
184	Tasmin 350i Convertible			14,800*
	UAZ (USSR)			
242	469 B			—
	VAUXHALL (Great Britain)			
185	Nova 1.0 2-dr Saloon			3,653*
185	Nova 1.0 2+1-dr Hatchback Saloon			3,799*
185	Nova 1.0 L 2-dr Saloon			4,175*
185	Nova 1.0 L 2+1-dr Hatchback Saloon			4,372*
185	Nova 1.2 L 2-dr Saloon			3,789*
185	Nova 1.2 2+1-dr Hatchback Saloon			3,935*
185	Nova 1.2 L 2-dr Saloon			4,311*
185	Nova 1.2 L 2+1-dr Hatchback Saloon			4,507*
185	Nova 1.3 SR 2+1-dr Hatchback Saloon			5,199*
185	Astra 1200S 2+1-dr Hatchback Saloon			4,494*
185	Astra 1200S 4+1-dr Hatchback Saloon			4,669*
185	Astra 1200S L 2+1-dr Hatchback Saloon			4,932*
185	Astra 1200S L 4+1-dr Hatchback Saloon			5,108*
185	Astra 1300S 2+1-dr Estate Car			5,026*
185	Astra 1300S L 2+1-dr Hatchback Saloon			5,110*
185	Astra 1300S L 4+1-dr Hatchback Saloon			5,286*
185	Astra 1300S L 2+1-dr Estate Car			5,520*
185	Astra 1300S L 4+1-dr Estate Car			5,697*
185	Astra 1300S GL 4+1-dr Hatchback Saloon			5,697*
185	Astra 1600S L 4+1-dr Hatchback Saloon			5,499*
185	Astra 1600S L 4+1-dr Estate Car			5,910*
185	Astra 1600S GL 4+1-dr Hatchback Saloon			5,910*
186	Astra 1600S GL 4+1-dr Estate Car			6,321*
186	Astra 1600S SR 4+1-dr Hatchback Saloon			6,029*
186	Astra 1600D L 2+1-dr Hatchback Saloon			5,910*
186	Astra 1600D L 4+1-dr Estate Car			6,320*
186	Astra 1800i GTE			6,739*
187	Chevette L 4-dr Saloon			4,024*
187	Chevette L 2+1-dr Hatchback Saloon			3,939*
187	Chevette L 2+1-dr Estate Car			4,451*
187	Cavalier 1300S 4-dr Saloon			5,239*
187	Cavalier 1300S 4+1-dr Hatchback Saloon			5,371*
187	Cavalier 1300S L 4-dr Saloon			5,570*
187	Cavalier 1300S L 4+1-dr Hatchback Saloon			5,702*
187	Cavalier 1300S GL 4-dr Saloon			6,324*

Page	MAKE AND MODEL	Price in GB £	Price in USA $	Price ex Works
187	Cavalier 1300S GL 4+1-dr Hatchback Saloon			6,559*
187	Cavalier 1600S 4-dr Saloon			5,550*
187	Cavalier 1600S 4+1-dr Hatchback Saloon			5,682*
187	Cavalier 1600S 4+1-dr Estate Car			6,143*
187	Cavalier 1600S L 4-dr Saloon			5,882*
187	Cavalier 1600S L 4+1-dr Hatchback Saloon			6,014*
187	Cavalier 1600S L 4+1-dr Estate Car			6,562*
187	Cavalier 1600S GL 4-dr Saloon			6,634*
187	Cavalier 1600S GL 4+1-dr Hatchback Saloon			6,871*
187	Cavalier 1600S GL 4+1-dr Estate Car			7,475*
187	Cavalier 1600S GLS 4-dr Saloon			7,301*
187	Cavalier 1600S GLS 4+1-dr Hatchback Saloon			7,537*
187	Cavalier 1800i SRi 4-dr Saloon			7,127*
187	Cavalier 1800i SRi 4+1-dr Hatchback Saloon			7,364*
187	Cavalier 1800i CD 4-dr Saloon			8,459*
187	Cavalier 1800i CD 4+1-dr Hatchback Saloon			8,696*
187	Cavalier 1600D L 4-dr Saloon			6,314*
187	Cavalier 1600D L 4+1-dr Hatchback Saloon			6,446*
188	Carlton 1800 L 4-dr Saloon			7,094*
188	Carlton 1800 L 4+1-dr Estate Car			7,784*
188	Carlton 1800 GL 4-dr Saloon			7,553*
188	Carlton 1800 GL 4+1-dr Estate Car			8,385*
188	Carlton 2000 4-dr Saloon			7,429*
188	Carlton 2000 L 4+1-dr Estate Car			8,119*
188	Carlton 2000 GL 4-dr Saloon			7,889*
188	Carlton 2000 GL 4+1-dr Estate Car			8,718*
188	Carlton 2300i CD 4-dr Saloon			9,039*
188	Carlton 2300D L 4-dr Saloon			7,707*
188	Carlton 2300D L 4+1-dr Estate Car			8,397*
	VAZ (USSR)			
242	Lada 1200 4-dr Sedan	2,549*		—
242	Lada 1200 4+1-dr St. Wagon	2,844*		—
242	Lada 1300 4-dr Sedan	3,075*		—
242	Lada 1300 4+1-dr St. Wagon	—		—
242	Lada 1500 4-dr Sedan	—		—
242	Lada 1500 DL 4+1-dr St. Wagon	3,292*		—
242	Lada 1600 2107 4-dr Sedan	3,330*		—
243	Lada Niva 2121 4 x 4	5,204*		—
	VOLKSWAGEN (Argentina)			
252	1500 W			99,000*
253	Gacel GL			125,400*
253	1500 M 1.8 W			113,800*
253	1500 M 1.8 Rural W			122,400*
	VOLKSWAGEN (Brazil)			
262	Fusca			2,552,000*
263	Gol S 2+1-dr Limousine			3,434,000*
263	Gol LS 2+1-dr Limousine			3,710,000*
263	Voyage S 2-dr Limousine			4,161,000*
263	Voyage S 4-dr Limousine			4,266,000*
263	Voyage LS 2-dr Limousine			4,447,000*
263	Voyage LS 4-dr Limousine			4,578,000*
263	Voyage GLS 2-dr Limousine			4,841,000*
263	Voyage GLS 4-dr Limousine			4,961,000*
264	Parati S 2+1-dr St. Wagon			3,964,000*
264	Parati LS 2+1-dr St. Wagon			4,472,000*
264	Parati GLS 2+1-dr St. Wagon			4,865,000*
264	Passat Special 2-dr Limousine			4,306,000*
264	Passat LS 2-dr Limousine			4,606,000*
264	Passat LS 2+1-dr Limousine			4,829,000*
264	Passat LS 4-dr Limousine			4,910,000*
264	Passat GTS 2-dr Limousine			5,917,000*
264	Passat LSE 4-dr Limousine			5,855,000*
	VOLKSWAGEN (Germany FR)			
141	Polo C 1.0 2+1-dr Limousine	3,998*		12,465*
141	Polo CL 1.0 2+1-dr Limousine			13,400*
141	Polo GL 1.0 2+1-dr Limousine			14,395*
141	Polo C 1.3 2+1-dr Limousine			13,125*

Page	MAKE AND MODEL	Price in GB £	Price in USA $	Price ex Works
141	Polo CL 1.3 2+1-dr Limousine	4,537*		14,060*
141	Polo GL 1.3 2+1-dr Limousine	4,929*		15,055*
142	Polo Classic C 1.0 2-dr Limousine	3,998*		12,935*
142	Polo Classic CL 1.0 2-dr Limousine	4,583*		13,920*
142	Polo Classic GL 1.0 2-dr Limousine			14,525*
142	Polo Classic C 1.3 2-dr Limousine			13,595*
142	Polo Classic CL 1.3 2-dr Limousine			14,580*
142	Polo Classic GL 1.3 2-dr Limousine	4,929*		15,185*
142	Polo 1.3 2+1-dr Coupé			15,035*
142	Polo GT 1.3 2+1-dr Coupé			16,360*
142	1200 L			9,660*
143	Jetta C 1.3 2-dr Limousine	5,158*		14,320*
143	Jetta C 1.3 4-dr Limousine			15,035*
143	Jetta CL 1.3 2-dr Limousine			15,390*
143	Jetta CL 1.3 4-dr Limousine			16,105*
143	Jetta GL 1.3 2-dr Limousine			16,725*
143	Jetta GL 1.3 4-dr Limousine			17,440*
143	Jetta C 1.5 2-dr Limousine	4,926*		15,190*
143	Jetta C 1.5 4-dr Limousine			15,905*
143	Jetta CL 1.5 2-dr Limousine			16,260*
143	Jetta CL 1.5 4-dr Limousine			16,975*
143	Jetta GL 1.5 2-dr Limousine	6,402*		17,959*
143	Jetta GL 1.5 4-dr Limousine			18,310*
143	Jetta CL 1.6 2-dr Limousine			16,620*
143	Jetta CL 1.6 4-dr Limousine			17,335*
143	Jetta GL 1.6 2-dr Limousine	6,182*		17,955*
143	Jetta GL 1.6 2-dr Limousine		8,210*	18,670*
143	Jetta Diesel C 1.6 2-dr Limousine	5,840*		16,135*
143	Jetta Diesel C 1.6 4-dr Limousine			16,850*
143	Jetta Diesel CL 1.6 2-dr Limousine		7,390*	17,205*
143	Jetta Diesel CL 1.6 4-dr Limousine		7,610*	17,920*
143	Jetta Diesel GL 1.6 2-dr Limousine			18,540*
143	Jetta Diesel GL 1.6 4-dr Limousine			19,255*
144	Jetta Turbo-Diesel C 1.6 2-dr Limousine			18,405*
144	Jetta Turbo-Diesel C 1.6 4-dr Limousine			19,120*
144	Jetta Turbo-Diesel CL 1.6 2-dr Limousine			19,475*
144	Jetta Turbo-Diesel CL 1.6 4-dr Limousine			20,190*
144	Jetta Turbo-Diesel GL 1.6 2-dr Limousine			20,810*
144	Jetta Turbo-Diesel GL 1.6 4-dr Limousine		9,210*	21,525*
144	Golf C 1.3 2+1-dr Limousine			13,750*
144	Golf C 1.3 4+1-dr Limousine			14,465*
144	Golf CL 1.3 2+1-dr Limousine			14,765*
144	Golf CL 1.3 4+1-dr Limousine			15,480*
144	Golf GL 1.3 2+1-dr Limousine			16,325*
144	Golf GL 1.3 4+1-dr Limousine			17,040*
144	Golf C 1.6 2+1-dr Limousine			14,905*
144	Golf C 1.6 4+1-dr Limousine			15,620*
144	Golf CL 1.6 2+1-dr Limousine		6,530*	15,920*
144	Golf CL 1.6 4+1-dr Limousine		6,740*	16,635*
144	Golf GL 1.6 2+1-dr Limousine			17,480*
144	Golf GL 1.6 4+1-dr Limousine		7,130*	18,195*
144	Golf Carat 1.8 (90 hp) 4+1-dr Limousine			22,595*
144	Golf GTI 1.8 (112 hp) 2+1-dr Limousine	7,156*	8,350*	21,525*
144	Golf GTI 1.8 (112 hp) 4+1-dr Limousine			22,240*
145	Golf Diesel C 1.6 2+1-dr Limousine			15,565*
145	Golf Diesel C 1.6 4+1-dr Limousine			16,280*
145	Golf Diesel CL 1.6 2+1-dr Limousine		6,600*	16,580*
145	Golf Diesel CL 1.6 4+1-dr Limousine		6,810*	17,295*
145	Golf Diesel GL 1.6 2+1-dr Limousine			18,140*
145	Golf Diesel GL 1.6 4+1-dr Limousine			18,855*
145	Golf Turbo-Diesel C 1.6 2+1-dr Limousine			17,835*
145	Golf Turbo-Diesel C 1.6 4+1-dr Limousine			18,550*
145	Golf Turbo-Diesel CL 1.6 2+1-dr Limousine			18,850*
145	Golf Turbo-Diesel CL 1.6 4+1-dr Limousine			19,565*
145	Golf Turbo-Diesel GL 1.6 2+1-dr Limousine			20,410*
145	Golf Turbo-Diesel GL 1.6 4+1-dr Limousine			21,125*
145	Golf Turbo-Diesel GTD 1.6 2+1-dr Limousine			19,780*
145	Golf Turbo-Diesel GTD 1.6 4+1-dr Limousine			20,495*
145	Golf GL 1.6 2-dr Cabriolet	7,886*		22,830*
145	Golf GLI 1.8 2-dr Cabriolet	8,692*	10,980*	26,450*
146	Passat C 1.3 2+1-dr Limousine			16,455*
146	Passat C 1.3 4+1-dr Limousine			17,180*
146	Passat C 1.3 4+1-dr Variant			17,725*
146	Passat CL 1.3 2+1-dr Limousine			17,530*
146	Passat CL 1.3 4+1-dr Limousine			18,255*
146	Passat CL 1.3 4+1-dr Variant			18,830*
146	Passat C 1.6 2+1-dr Limousine			17,155*
146	Passat C 1.6 4+1-dr Limousine			17,880*
146	Passat C 1.6 4+1-dr Variant			18,425*
146	Passat CL 1.6 2+1-dr Limousine	5,833*		18,230*

Page	MAKE AND MODEL	Price in GB £	Price in USA $	Price ex Works
146	Passat CL 1.6 4+1-dr Limousine			18,955*
146	Passat CL 1.6 4+1-dr Variant	5,992*		19,530*
146	Passat GL 1.6 2+1-dr Limousine			19,910*
146	Passat GL 1.6 4+1-dr Limousine			20,635*
146	Passat GL 1.6 4+1-dr Variant			21,420*
146	Passat C 1.8 2+1-dr Limousine			17,790*
146	Passat C 1.8 4+1-dr Limousine			18,515*
146	Passat C 1.8 4+1-dr Variant			19,060*
146	Passat CL 1.8 2+1-dr Limousine	6,739*		18,865*
146	Passat CL 1.8 4+1-dr Limousine			19,590*
146	Passat CL 1.8 4+1-dr Variant	6,899*		20,165*
146	Passat GL 1.8 2+1-dr Limousine			20,545*
146	Passat GL 1.8 4+1-dr Limousine			21,270*
146	Passat GL 1.8 4+1-dr Variant			22,055*
146	Passat CL 2.0 4+1-dr Limousine			22,575*
146	Passat CL 2.0 4+1-dr Variant			23,150*
146	Passat GL 2.0 4+1-dr Limousine		12,980*	24,255*
146	Passat GL 2.0 4+1-dr Variant		13,780*	25,040*
147	Passat Diesel C 1.6 2+1-dr Limousine			18,355*
147	Passat Diesel C 1.6 4+1-dr Limousine			19,080*
147	Passat Diesel C 1.6 4+1-dr Variant			19,625*
147	Passat Diesel CL 1.6 2+1-dr Limousine			19,430*
147	Passat Diesel CL 1.6 4+1-dr Limousine			20,155*
147	Passat Diesel CL 1.6 4+1-dr Variant			20,730*
147	Passat Diesel GL 1.6 2+1-dr Limousine			21,110*
147	Passat Diesel GL 1.6 4+1-dr Limousine			21,835*
147	Passat Diesel GL 1.6 4+1-dr Variant			22,620*
147	Passat Turbo-Diesel C 1.6 4+1-dr Limousine			21,280*
147	Passat Turbo-Diesel C 1.6 4+1-dr Variant			21,825*
147	Passat Turbo-Diesel CL 1.6 4+1-dr Limousine			22,355*
147	Passat Turbo-Diesel CL 1.6 4+1-dr Variant			22,930*
147	Passat Turbo-Diesel GL 1.6 4+1-dr Limousine			24,035*
147	Passat Turbo-Diesel GL 1.6 4+1-dr Variant		14,330*	24,820*
148	Passat Variant Tetra			—
148	Santana CX 1.3 4-dr Limousine			18,040*
148	Santana CX 1.6 4-dr Limousine	5,883*		18,740*
148	Santana LX 1.6 4-dr Limousine			19,685*
148	Santana GX 1.6 4-dr Limousine			22,620*
148	Santana CX 1.8 4-dr Limousine			19,375*
148	Santana LX 1.8 4-dr Limousine	6,789*		20,320*
148	Santana GX 1.8 4-dr Limousine			23,255*
148	Santana LX5 2.0 4-dr Limousine			23,305*
148	Santana GX5 2.0 4-dr Limousine	8,358*		26,240*
148	Santana LX 1.6 Diesel 4-dr Limousine			20,885*
148	Santana GX 1.6 Diesel 4-dr Limousine			23,820*
148	Santana LX 1.6 Turbo-Diesel 4-dr Limousine			23,085*
148	Santana GX 1.6 Turbo-Diesel 4-dr Limousine			26,020*
149	Scirocco CL 1.6 2+1-dr Coupé			19,295*
149	Scirocco GL 1.6 2+1-dr Coupé			21,430*
149	Scirocco GT 1.6 2+1-dr Coupé			21,730*
149	Scirocco CL 1.8 (90 hp) 2+1-dr Coupé			20,370*
149	Scirocco GL 1.8 (90 hp) 2+1-dr Coupé		10,870*	22,505*
149	Scirocco GT 1.8 (90 hp) 2+1-dr Coupé			22,805*
149	Scirocco GTS 1.8 (90 hp) 2+1-dr Coupé			21,105*
149	Scirocco GTX 1.8 (90 hp) 2+1-dr Coupé			22,485*
149	Scirocco GLI 1.8 (112 hp) 2+1-dr Coupé			24,980*
149	Scirocco GTI 1.8 (112 hp) 2+1-dr Coupé			25,280*
149	Scirocco GTS 1.8 (112 hp) 2+1-dr Coupé			23,520*
149	Scirocco GTX 1.8 (112 hp) 2+1-dr Coupé			24,960*
150	Scirocco 16 V Coupé			—
	VOLKSWAGEN (Mexico)			
267	1200 L			—
	VOLKSWAGEN (Nigeria)			
321	Golf CL 4+1-dr Limousine			—
321	Jetta C 4-dr Limousine			—
321	Jetta CL 4-dr Limousine			—
321	Beetle 1500			5,295
321	Passat TS			8,595
322	Santana LX 4-dr Limousine			10,995
322	Santana GX 4-dr Limousine			11,870
	VOLKSWAGEN (USA)			
315	Rabbit L 2+1-dr Hatchback Sedan			6,390

Page	MAKE AND MODEL	Price in GB £	Price in USA $	Price ex Works
315	Rabbit L 4+1-dr Hatchback Sedan			6,600
315	Rabbit GL 4+1-dr Hatchback Sedan			7,130
315	Rabbit GTI 2+1-dr Hatchback Sedan			8,350
315	Rabbit L Diesel 2+1-dr Hatchback Sedan			6,390
315	Rabbit L Diesel 4+1-dr Hatchback Sedan			7,040
	VOLVO (Holland)			
190	340 Winner 2+1-dr Hatchback Sedan	—		17,490*
190	340 Luxe 2+1-dr Hatchback Sedan	—		18,390*
190	340 DL 2+1-dr Hatchback Sedan	4,892*		19,990*
190	340 DL 4+1-dr Hatchback Sedan	5,246*		21,550*
190	340 GL 2+1-dr Hatchback Sedan	5,190*		21,990*
190	340 GL 4+1-dr Hatchback Sedan	5,541*		23,350*
190	340 GL 4-dr Sedan	—		—
191	360 2+1-dr Hatchback Sedan	—		22,990*
191	360 4+1-dr Hatchback Sedan	—		24,350*
191	360 GLS 2+1-dr Hatchback Sedan	5,930*		24,990*
191	360 GLS 4+1-dr Hatchback Sedan	6,298*		26,350*
191	360 GLS 4-dr Sedan	—		—
191	360 GLT 2+1-dr Hatchback Sedan	6,577*		29,790*
191	360 GLT 4+1-dr Hatchback Sedan	6,946*		—
191	360 GLE 4-dr Sedan	6,699*		31,750*
	VOLVO (Sweden)			
237	240 4-dr Sedan	7,720*	—	67,600*
237	240 4+1-dr St. Wagon	8,250*	—	71,400*
237	240 GL 4-dr Sedan	8,351*	14,995*	73,300*
237	240 GL 4+1-dr St. Wagon	8,880*	15,550*	76,900*
237	240 GLE 4-dr Sedan	9,831*	—	83,800*
237	240 GLE 4+1-dr St. Wagon	9,780*	—	88,900*
237	240 GLT 4-dr Sedan	11,070*	—	90,400*
237	240 GLT 4+1-dr St. Wagon	10,560*	—	90,800*
237	240 Turbo 4-dr Sedan	—	—	95,900*
237	240 Turbo 4+1-dr St. Wagon	—	—	98,600*
238	240 Diesel 4-dr Sedan	—	15,480*	90,500*
238	240 Diesel 4+1-dr St. Wagon	—	16,035*	94,800*
238	760 GLE	12,693*	21,225*	—
238	760 Turbo	13,249*	—	131,800*
238	760 Turbo Diesel	13,649*	22,035*	—
	WARTBURG (Germany DR)			
105	353 W			—
105	353 W Tourist			—
105	353 W De Luxe			—
	YLN (Taiwan)			
335	721			—
335	807 GX			—
336	311 SD			—
	ZAZ (USSR)			
243	968 M			—
244	969-A 4 x 4			—
	ZCZ (Yugoslavia)			
244	Zastava 750 LE	—		129,000
245	Zastava 850	—		131,400
245	Zastava Jugo 45	2,749*		197,500
245	Zastava Jugo 55	—		—
245	Zastava 128 CL 1100	—		260,000
246	Zastava 128 CL 1300	—		286,000
246	Zastava 101 GT 55 2+1-dr Sedan	2,699*		215,000
246	Zastava 101 GT 55 4+1-dr Sedan	2,849*		225,000
246	Zastava 101 GTL 55 2+1-dr Sedan	3,199*		235,000
246	Zastava 101 GTL 55 4+1-dr Sedan	3,549*		245,000
246	Zastava 101 GT 65 2+1-dr Sedan	2,799*		220,000
246	Zastava 101 GT 65 4+1-dr Sedan	2,999*		230,000
246	Zastava 101 GTL 65 2+1-dr Sedan	3,299*		240,000
246	Zastava 101 GTL 65 4+1-dr Sedan	—		250,000
	ZIL (USSR)			
244	114 Limousine			—
244	117 Limousine			—
244	4104 Limousine			—